INDIAN TREES

AN ACCOUNT OF TREES, SHRUBS, WOODY CLIMBERS, BAMBOOS AND PALMS INDIGENOUS OR COMMONLY CULTIVATED IN THE

BRITISH INDIAN EMPIRE

INDIAN TREES

AN ACCOUNT OF TREES, SHRUBS, WOODY CLIMBERS, BAMBOOS AND PALMS INDIGENOUS OR COMMONLY CULTIVATED IN THE

BRITISH INDIAN EMPIRE

BY

DIETRICH BRANDIS, K.C.I.E.
Ph.D (Bonn), LL.D. (Edin.), F.R.S., F.L.S., F.R.G.S., and Hon. Member of the Royal Scottish Arboricultural Society, of the Society of American Foresters, and of the Pharmaceutical Society of Great Britain

ASSISTED BY INDIAN FORESTERS

GYAN

Published by

Gyan Publishing House
5, Ansari Road
Daryaganj, New Delhi-110002
Phone: 011-47034999, 9811692060
E-mail: books@gyanbooks.com

Distribution Network
gyanbooks.com
India, USA, Canada, UK, Australia, France

ISBN : 978-81-212-2245-7 (HB)
First Published, 1906

2nd Impression 2021

Printed at: Gyan Press, Delhi.

Indian Trees
Author: Dietrich Brandis

INDIAN TREES

AN ACCOUNT OF TREES, SHRUBS, WOODY CLIMBERS, BAMBOOS AND PALMS INDIGENOUS OR COMMONLY CULTIVATED IN THE

BRITISH INDIAN EMPIRE

BY

DIETRICH BRANDIS, K.C.I.E

Ph.D. (Bonn), LL.D. (Edin.), F.R.S., F.L.S., F.R.G.S., and Hon. Member of the Royal Scottish Arboricultural Society, of the Society of American Foresters, and of the Pharmaceutical Society of Great Britain

ASSISTED BY INDIAN FORESTERS

LONDON

ARCHIBALD CONSTABLE & CO LTD

16 JAMES STREET HAYMARKET S.W

1906

TABLE OF CONTENTS

up into trees.* What becomes of the permanent undershrubs here described, when the area is protected against fire, is not known; probably they are smothered by the surrounding vegetation. That some of these undershrubs were cultivated long ago in the Calcutta Botanic Garden is evident from Roxburgh's *Flora Indica*, but no record exists whether they had changed their habit when no longer exposed to the régime of annual fires.

In the old *Forest Flora of North-West and Central India* I drew attention to a number of these remarkable undershrubs, and wrote regarding them on a later occasion (*Ind. For.* XXVI. 10). It has given me great pleasure to find that Mr. Duthie, in his excellent *Flora of the Upper Gangetic Plain*, has fully recognized the importance of these interesting species, and it is satisfactory that in the Park of the Dehra Dun Forest School Kanjilal has at my suggestion commenced to cultivate a number (particularly *Grewia sapida*) in order to see whether they will change their habits when no longer exposed to the annual fires. It is possible, though not proved, that trees or large shrubs may, by the continuous action of the annual fires, gradually have been converted into undershrubs. Against this idea, however, stands the fact that *Careya herbacea, Erythrina resupinata* and most other species adverted to, differ from the arborescent species of the same genus by very definite characters in leaves, flowers and fruit. As far as known at present, *Premna* is the only genus which forms an exception in this respect. No less than 5 undershrubs are known in this genus, and 3 of these can hardly be separated by characters other than habit from species which are trees or large shrubs (cf. *P. pinguis, P. amplectens* and *P. macrophylla*, p. 511). Similar undershrubs are known from tropical Africa, and there are species in the Arctic regions (*Cornus suecica, C. canadensis, Rubus arcticus*), the shoots of which are killed annually by the frost of winter, the underground rootstock remaining alive.

I am fully aware that in speaking of these undershrubs and in describing them in this book I lay myself open to the charge of inconsistency. At the outset I said that the object of this book was entirely practical. I admit that no forest revenue can be made out of these undershrubs, and that they are not likely ever to play an important part in the system of forest management. But foresters who may cultivate these remarkable species will thereby be induced more completely to study the laws which govern the habits of plants and the conditions which may under certain circumstances cause the development and mutation of species. Indeed, I go further, and would venture to suggest that some of these remarkable undershrubs be cultivated in Indian Forest Gardens, although they are not likely immediately to increase the forest revenue. Their study may quite unexpectedly throw light upon some important forest questions. At the present day this may be pronounced fanciful by my young friends in India, and they may regret that their old friend has indulged in such fancies. They will I hope relent when they find practical suggestions of other kinds in this book, which I trust will be of real use to them in their work.

It now remains to express my deep gratitude to all those who have assisted me in this arduous work. During the progress of it I have had the great privilege of discussing many important points with Sir William Thiselton-Dyer, with Dr. Dukinfield H. Scott, Mr. W. B. Hemsley, Dr. Otto Stapf, Mr. C. B. Clarke, and with Dr. Augustine Henry. Mr. James Ramsay Drummond has kindly given me much valuable information regarding trees and shrubs of the Punjab. To Mr. C. H. Wright, of the Herbarium, Kew, I am indebted for the care which he has devoted to the index and for the assistance he has given me in preparing the manuscript for the press and in correcting the proofs. Mr. Martin Cole has been most useful in preparing excellent microscopic slides whenever I required them. Several Indian officers, while

* *Grewia scabrophylla* at times is an undershrub, when exposed to the annual fires; in other places it grows into a tall shrub. Other shrubs probably behave in the same manner.

on furlough at home, have assisted me materially in the work. Colonel A. A. Barrett has helped me to work up *Rosaceæ*, and otherwise assisted me greatly. Mr. H. H. Haines has most generously devoted considerable time, while at home on furlough, in assisting me in *Celastraceæ*, *Rhamnaceæ* and *Ampelideæ*. Mr. A. F. Broun, late Conservator of Forests in Ceylon and now Director of Woods and Forests in the Sudan, together with Mrs. Broun, have enabled me by their careful dissections and sketches to understand the species of *Strychnos* and other difficult genera. Mr. C. B. Smales has devoted a great part of his furlough from Burma to working up with me oaks and chesnuts, Ficus, palms and bamboos. His intimate practical knowledge of the bamboos of Upper Burma, their appearance and mode of growth, has been invaluable, and without his help I could never have mastered this difficult order. In connection with bamboos I wish to state that Dr. Otto Stapf has communicated to me the result of his as yet unpublished researches, which establish two great divisions of bamboos, one with, the other without endosperm in the ripe seed. Mr. T. F. Bourdillon has from the beginning been most useful in regard to the forest vegetation of Travancore. As already mentioned, Mr. Gilbert Rogers has given me most valuable information about palms and bamboos of the Andamans. Mr. A. E. Wild, late Conservator of Forests, Bengal, has helped me steadily from the beginning in examining the specimens at the Museum of the Royal Botanic Gardens, Kew.

I tender my thanks to His Majesty's Secretary of State for India for having purchased 300 copies of this book. Mr. C. B. Clarke has been a true friend in this matter; without his intervention the book would probably never have been published. The publishers have placed me under obligations by not losing patience with the long delay and the great bulk of the work, neither of which I anticipated when I commenced it.

I am keenly alive to the many imperfections of this work, and I know that numerous errors and omissions will be discovered in it. With the overwhelming mass of detail that had to be mastered, this, at my time of life, was perhaps unavoidable. In spite of these imperfections, the book will I hope in some respects facilitate the progress of good forest management in India. Not that the knowledge of species means good forest management. But it is the first step towards the study of matters which are of real importance in forestry; the habits, mode and rate of growth of trees, their ability to appropriate certain mineral substances from the soil, the capacity of their leaves and other green parts to take up carbon dioxide and to form timber, a capacity which varies in different species of trees to a degree not yet sufficiently recognized by botanists, and finally their habits of flowering and seeding, as well as their ability to reproduce themselves from coppice shoots or root-suckers. The study of the sylvicultural requirements of the different species is the foundation of a successful system of treatment, leading up to the greatest annual production of timber and other forest produce per acre. Foresters in India should always bear in mind that botany is not forestry, but that the knowledge of species is indispensable. With the enormous number of genera and species in India the acquisition of this knowledge is difficult. I hope I may have succeeded in smoothing the way a little, and in this hope I wish all my young friends, whether they have learnt their profession in Europe or at the Imperial Forest School in India, an honourable and prosperous career in the Indian forests. Should any one look down upon them because their work makes no show and does not bear fruit immediately, like that of the engineer and other public officers, they will console themselves with the proud consciousness that they are the guardians of the future and permanent interests of the 300 millions who inhabit the great British Indian Empire, and that they are contributing materially to ensure the comfort and welfare of future generations.

SYNOPSIS OF NATURAL ORDERS

The distinguishing characters are selected with special reference to the trees and shrubs described in this work.

First Class. ANGIOSPERMS.

Flowers bisexual or unisexual, as a rule with perianth, consisting of one or several whorls of leaves, free or connate (calyx and corolla). Ovules enclosed in an ovary, fertilized by the pollen-tube growing towards them through the tissue of stigma and style. Seeds enclosed in the fruit, embryo straight or curved, with or without endosperm.

First Sub-Class. DICOTYLEDONS.

The stem consists of pith, wood, bast and bark, which form concentric cylinders, wood and bast being separated in the growing stem by a continuous layer of long soft cells (cambium), which are transformed into new wood on the outside of the wood cylinder, and into new bast on the inside of the hollow bast cylinder. The wood consists of wood-fibres, vessels, wood-parenchyma and medullary rays. Many climbers have anomalous structure, also the erect woody species of *Plumbaginaceæ*, *Nyctaginaceæ*, *Amarantaceæ* and *Chenopodiaceæ* and a few trees of other orders: *Cocculus laurifolius*, *Dalbergia paniculata*, most *Combretaceæ*, *Strychnos*, and the non-Indian *Drimys*. Leaves net-veined. Parts of perianth, calyx or corolla usually in fours or fives. Embryo with two cotyledons which, when the seed germinates, are as a rule raised above ground (in *Garcinia*, *Ochrocarpus* and *Mesua* the embryo consists of a homogeneous fleshy mass).

I. POLYPETALÆ.

Flowers in the majority of species bisexual, as a rule with both calyx and corolla, the corolla consisting of distinct petals.

A. THALAMIFLORÆ (including *Disciflorœ*).

Sepals in the majority of cases distinct, petals and stamens hypogynous, ovary free. A well-developed disk in Orders 13 *Tamaricaceæ*, 25 *Rutaceæ*, 26 *Simarubaceæ*, 43 *Moringaceæ*, in Orders 28–32, 34–41 and in a few genera of 7 *Capparidaceæ*, 10 *Bixaceæ* and 21 *Tiliaceæ*.

1. ***Ranunculaceæ***, p. 1. Sepals deciduous, often petaloid. Stamens ∞, anthers adnate, longitudinally dehiscent. Carpels numerous, free, 1-celled.
2. ***Dilleniaceæ***, p. 3. L. alternate, simple, penninerved, petioles sheathing. Fl. large, white or yellow. Sepals 5, imbricate, persistent, petals 5, caducous. Carpels one or many, more or less cohering, styles free.
3. ***Magnoliaceæ***, p. 5. L. alternate, simple, most genera with convolute deciduous stipules. Sepals and petals alike, in whorls of three, imbricate, deciduous. Stamens 8, anthers basifixed. Carpels numerous, usually distinct, generally on an elongated torus. Embryo minute, endosperm uniform.

4. *Anonaceæ*, p. 9. L. alternate, simple, stipules none. Sepals 3, petals in one or two trimerous whorls. Stamens usually ∞, filaments short or none, anther-cells adnate to a broad connective. Carpels distinct in fruit (confluent in *Anona*). Seeds large, embryo small, endosperm ruminated.

5. *Menispermaceæ*, p. 22. Usually climbers with broad medullary rays and otherwise anomalous wood structure. L. alternate, simple, mostly palminerved, often peltate, stipules 0. Fl. small, unisexual, trimerous, sepals usually free. Stamens opposite to petals, usually 6, carpels free, as a rule 3. Embryo curved, with or without endosperm.

6. *Berberidaceæ*, p. 27. L. alternate, glabrous. Sepals and petals alike, usually trimerous, caducous. Stamens opposite to petals, anthers adnate, as a rule opening by valves. Carpels distinct, often one only. Endosperm fleshy.

7. *Capparidaceæ*, p. 31. L. as a rule alternate, stipules often present and spinescent. Fl. usually bisexual, often zygomorphic. As a rule sepals 4, petals 4. Stamens generally numerous, filaments filiform. Carpels connate into a 1-celled ovary with 2–4 parietal placentas, often on an elongated gynophore. Embryo curved, endosperm 0 or scanty.

8. *Resedaceæ*, p. 37. L. alternate, stipules minute or 0. Fl. in spikes or racemes, often zygomorphic, calyx 4–7-lobed. Stamens usually numerous, seated on a hypogynous disk. Carpels connate into a 1-celled ovary with 2–6 parietal placentas. Seeds numerous, reniform, endosperm 0.

9. *Violaceæ*, p. 37. L. as a rule alternate, stipules small or leafy. Fl. regular or zygomorphic, sepals 5, imbricate, persistent, petals 5. Stamens 5, filaments short or 0, connective broad and often produced above, anthers connivent or connate round the ovary. Carpels connate into a one-celled ovary with usually 3 parietal placentas. Seeds small, embryo straight in a fleshy endosperm.

10. *Bixaceæ*, p. 38. L. alternate, simple, mostly dentate, stipules small or 0. Fl. regular, 4- or 5-merous, stamens usually numerous. Ovary 1-celled, seeds few, arillate or with pulpy testa.

11. *Pittosporaceæ*, p. 42. L. alternate, simple, entire, stipules 0. Fl. regular, pentamerous and pentandrous, sepals free, as well as petals imbricate, anthers versatile. Embryo small, in copious endosperm.

12. *Polygalaceæ*, p. 43. L. alternate, simple, quite entire, stipules 0. Fl. bisexual, zygomorphic, sepals 5, the 2 inner larger, petaloid, petals 5 or 3. Stamens as a rule 8, filaments usually connate in a cleft sheath, anthers mostly opening by terminal pores.

13. *Tamaricaceæ*, p. 45. L. alternate, small, generally scale-like. Fl. regular, in spikes, racemes or panicles, sepals and petals usually free, pentamerous, sometimes tetramerous. Stamens as many as petals or twice their number. Capsule 3–5-valved, seeds tufted or winged.

14. *Hypericaceæ*, p. 47. L. opposite, often gland-dotted, stipules 0. Fl. regular, bisexual, sepals 5, imbricate, petals 5, contorted in bud. Stamens numerous, filaments usually connate into 3 or 5 bundles, anthers versatile. Endosperm 0.

15. *Guttiferæ*, p. 48. Juice resinous, yellow or greenish. L. opposite, simple, entire, usually coriaceous, stipules 0. Fl. regular, unisexual or polygamous, sepals 2–6, mostly in decussate pairs, petals as a rule 2–6, imbricate or contorted. Fr. usually indehiscent, seeds large, endosperm 0.

16. *Ternstrœmiaceæ*, p. 56. L. alternate, simple, generally coriaceous, stipules 0. Fl. regular, as a rule bisexual, sepals and petals usually pentamerous and imbricate. Stamens generally numerous, ovary 3–5-celled.

17. *Dipterocarpaceæ*, p. 63. Resinous trees. L. alternate, usually coriaceous, simple, penninerved, stipules large, enclosing the bud. Fl. bisexual, regular, calyx-segments 5, some or all as a rule much enlarged in fr. Petals 5, contorted, stamens 5, 10, or more, anthers adnate to filaments. Fruit indehiscent, 1-seeded.

18. *Ancistrocladaceæ*, p. 73. Glabrous, woody climbers, not resinous. L. entire, stipules minute, caducous. Fl. bisexual, regular, pentamerous, calyx adnate to the 1-celled ovary, segments much enlarged in fr.

19. *Malvaceæ*, p. 74. Wood soft and light. L. alternate, mostly stipulate, generally palminerved, hairs usually stellate. Fl. as a rule bisexual, regular, supported by 3 or more bracteoles. Sepals 5, valvate, more or less connate, petals 5, base adnate to staminal-column, contorted in bud. Stamens numerous, filaments variously connate, anthers 1-celled.

20. *Sterculiaceæ*, p. 79. L. alternate, mostly stipulate, hairs often stellate. Sepals 5, valvate, more or less connate, petals 5 or none. Stamens commonly monadelphous, anthers 2-celled. Fr. a dehiscent capsule or a whorl of distinct carpels.

21. *Tiliaceæ*, p. 93. L. alternate, simple, stipules deciduous. Fl. regular, almost always bisexual. Sepals 5, usually connate, valvate in bud. Stamens numerous, anthers 2-celled. Ovary 2–10-celled.

22. *Lineæ*, p. 106. L. alternate, simple, entire. Fl. bisexual, regular, sepals and petals pentamerous, sometimes tetramerous. Stamens 8 or 10, half the number often

sterile, filaments united at base, anthers versatile. Ovary 3–5-celled. Capsule dehiscing septicidally.

23. *Malpighiaceæ*, p. 108. L. usually opposite, simple, entire, stipules small or 0. Fl. often zygomorphic, calyx 5-lobed, petals 5, often fimbriate. Stamens 10, sometimes unequal. Fr. usually of one or more winged samaras.

24. *Geraniaceæ* (*Averrhoa*), p. 110. L. alternate, imparipinnate, stipules 0. Fl. bisexual, sepals 5, petals 5, stamens 10. Fr. oblong, fleshy, 5-ribbed.

25. *Rutaceæ*, p. 111. L. aromatic, dotted with translucent glands, stipules 0. Fl. regular, sepals and petals 4 or 5, stamens 4–5 or 8–10, filaments inserted on the outside of the disk.

26. *Simarubaceæ*, p. 124. Bark bitter, l. alternate, stipules deciduous or 0. Fl. regular, small, often unisexual, sepals 3–5, usually connate, petals 3–5. Stamens as many as petals or double their number, inserted outside the disk.

27. *Ochnaceæ*, p. 128. L. alternate, simple, glabrous, stipulate. Fl. regular, bisexual. Sepals 4 or 5, free, imbricate, persisting, petals 5 or more, deciduous, stamens 10 or ∞, anthers basifixed. Fr. of 3–10 one- or few-seeded drupes.

28. *Burseraceæ*, p. 129. Resinous. L. alternate, imparipinnate, sometimes 1-foliolate. Fl. small, regular, calyx 3–5-lobed, petals 3–5. Stamens as many as petals or twice their number, inserted on the disk or outside at its base. Ovary 2–5-celled, ovules 2 in each cell.

29. *Meliaceæ*, p.134. L. alternate, generally pinnate, stipules 0. Fl. regular, in cymose panicles, calyx small, 4–5-cleft, petals 4–5, stamens twice the number of petals, filaments generally united into a tube, disk between stamens and ovary, often tubular.

30. *Chailletiaceæ*, p. 146. L. alternate, entire, simple, stipules deciduous. Fl. 1-sexual or polygamous, petals 5, notched or bifid, stamens 5, disk of 5 glands, alternating with stamens. Ovary pubescent 2–3-celled, ovules 2, collateral in each cell. Endosperm 0, cotyledons thick.

31. *Olacaceæ*, p. 147. L. alternate, stipules 0. Fl. small, as a rule bisexual, calyx small or wanting, stamens opposite to petals or ∞. Ovary at base often 2–5-celled, ovules pendulous from a free axile placenta. Drupe 1-seeded. In Engler u. Prantl, Natürl. Pflanzenfam. III. 1. 231 placed near *Loranthaceæ* and *Santalaceæ*.

32. *Icacinaceæ*, p. 150. L. generally alternate, stipules 0. Fl. small, 1-sexual or polygamous, calyx small or wanting, stamens alternating with petals. Ovary 1-celled. Drupe 1-seeded.

33. *Ilicineæ*, p. 154. L. alternate, simple, usually coriaceous and evergreen, stipules minute. Fl. regular, usually 1-sexual, calyx 4–5-lobed, petals 4–5, connate at base. Stamens 4–5, alternating with petals, disk 0. Fr. a drupe, supported by the persistent calyx, stones 1-seeded, 2 or more.

34. *Celastraceæ*, p. 157. L. simple, as a rule opposite, stipules minute or none. Fl. regular, small, bisexual or polygamous, calyx small, 4- or 5-lobed, persistent. Disk large, surrounding the base of the 3–5-celled ovary or partially enclosing it, stamens 3–5, rarely 10, inserted on the disk.

35. *Rhamnaceæ*, p. 167. Branchlets or stipules often spinescent, l. simple. Fl. small, regular, calyx 4–5-cleft, lobes triangular, valvate in bud. disk lining or filling the calyx-tube, petals inserted at the mouth of calyx-tube. Stamens opposite to petals, often enclosed by them.

36. *Ampelideæ*, p. 175. Climbers, l. alternate, often compound. Fl. regular, calyx small, entire or 4–5-dentate, petals 4–5, valvate in bud. Stamens opposite to petals, inserted outside or between the lobes of the disk. Fr. a berry.

37. *Staphyleaceæ*, p. 180. L. opposite, stipulate, compound, leaflets stipellate. Fl. regular, bisexual, pentamerous, stamens 5, inserted outside the disk. Ovary 3-celled.

38. *Aceraceæ*, p. 181. L. opposite, stipules 0. Fl. regular, polygamous, calyx 5–12-parted, deciduous. Stamens generally 8, inserted outside or upon (rarely inside) the disk. Fruiting carpels winged.

39. *Sapindaceæ*, p. 184. L. alternate (opposite in *Æsculus*), stipules 0. Fl. sometimes zygomorphic, mostly polygamous. Stamens inserted between disk and ovary, filaments usually hairy, disk frequently unilateral. Ovary 3-celled, often 3-lobed.

40. *Sabiaceæ*, p. 193. L. alternate, stipules 0. Fl. small, calyx 4–5-partite, stamens 4–5, opposite to petals, anther-cells distinct, usually adnate to a large connective.

41. *Anacardiaceæ*, p. 195. L. in most genera alternate, stipules 0. Fl. regular, calyx 3–5-cleft (spathaceous in *Gluta*). petals 3–5, rarely 0. Stamens alternating with petals, inserted under, rarely on the disk. Ovary in 2 genera inferior, drupe 2–5-seeded.

42. *Coriariaceæ*, p. 209. L. opposite, simple, stipules 0. Fl. regular, bisexual, pentamerous, stamens 10. Fruiting carpels 5, distinct, 1-seeded, enclosed in the persistent succulent petals.

43. *Moringaceæ*, p. 209. Wood soft, l. deciduous, alternate, bi- or tri-pinnate, pinnæ and leaflets opposite, glands at base of petioles and pinnæ. Fl. large, bisexual, pentamerous, petals unequal. Fertile stamens 5, opposite to petals, alternating with sterile stamens. Fr. a long 1-celled 3-valved pod.

B. CALYCIFLORÆ.

Calyx gamosepalous, often adnate to ovary. Petals inserted on calyx, or on disk lining calyx-tube.

44. *Connaraceæ*, p. 210. L. alternate, imparipinnate or 1-foliolate, leaflets entire, coriaceous, stipules 0. Fl. usually bisexual and regular, pentamerous, petals linear-oblong, stamens 10, the epipetalous stamens generally shorter and often sterile. Carpels 5, free, mostly hairy, ovules 2, collateral. Fruiting carpel one, 2-valved.

45. *Leguminosæ*, p. 214. L. stipulate, as a rule alternate and compound. Fl. bisexual, petals 5, in the majority of genera zygomorphic, stamens 10 or ∞. Carpel one, free, ovules usually numerous, attached to the inner suture. Fr. a 1-celled pod, endosperm generally 0.

46. *Rosaceæ*, p. 277. L. stipulate, usually alternate. Fl. pentamerous, as a rule regular and bisexual, stamens usually numerous. Carpels mostly distinct, often adnate to and enclosed in the calyx-tube. Albumen 0 or scanty.

47. *Saxifragaceæ*, p. 296. L. simple. Fl. regular, 4- or 5-merous, calyx free or adnate to ovary, stamens free, as many as petals, twice the number or numerous. Carpels 2 or numerous, usually connate, ovules numerous. Seeds small, embryo minute, in copious albumen.

48. *Hamamelidaceæ*, p. 300. L. alternate, stipules usually deciduous. Fl. in compact heads or spikes, usually bracteate, calyx-tube more or less adnate to ovary, ovary 2-celled, styles 2, usually persistent. Testa shining.

49. *Rhizophoraceæ*, p. 302. L. opposite, usually coriaceous and entire, scars of petioles mostly prominent, stipules interpetiolar, deciduous. Fl. regular, generally bisexual, calyx more or less adnate to ovary, limb 4–14-lobed, lobes as a rule persistent, petals as many as sepals, stamens usually twice the number of petals. Fr. coriaceous, usually 1-seeded.

50. *Combretaceæ*, p. 306. L. simple, entire, stipules 0. Fl. usually bisexual and regular, calyx-tube adnate to ovary and produced beyond it, segments 4–5, valvate, petals often wanting. Stamens as many as calyx-segments or twice their number, perigynous. Fr. generally angled or winged.

51. *Myrtaceæ*, p. 316. L. simple, generally quite entire, either opposite with translucent glands or alternate without glands. Stipules 0. Fl. regular, generally bisexual. Ovary enclosed in and generally adnate to calyx-tube. Stamens ∞, inserted with the petals in the mouth of calyx-tube.

52. *Melastomaceæ*, p. 332. L. opposite, entire or nearly so, usually with 3–7 basal nerves, no translucent glands, stipules 0. Fl. regular, bisexual, calyx-tube entirely or partially adnate to ovary, segments 4 or 5, deciduous. Stamens twice the number of calyx-segments, inserted with petals on the edge of calyx-tube, connective often large.

53. *Lythraceæ*, p. 337. L. generally opposite, simple, entire. Calyx cup-shaped, persistent, segments valvate, often with intermediate teeth, petals when present imbricate and crumpled in bud. Ovary as a rule superior.

54. *Samydaceæ*, p. 342. L. alternate, distichous, stipules small. Fl. regular, inconspicuous, generally bisexual. Calyx persistent, tube short. Capsule 2–4-valved, seeds numerous.

55. *Passifloraceæ*, p. 345. L. alternate, usually lobed. Fl. regular, unisexual in *Papaya*, bisexual in *Passiflora*.

56. *Datiscaceæ*, p. 346. (*Tetrameles.*) L. deciduous, petiolate, broadly ovate. Fl. diœcious, ♂ calyx deeply 4-lobed, petals 0, stamens 4. Capsule crowned by the persistent calyx-segments, the valves terminating in the persistent styles.

57. *Cactaceæ*, p. 346. (*Opuntia.*) Stems and branches succulent, prickly. Fl. regular, bisexual, solitary, calyx-tube adnate to ovary, petals numerous, imbricate, stamens ∞. Fr. fleshy, seeds numerous.

58. *Araliaceæ*, p. 347. L. alternate, simple or compound. Fl. regular, usually pentamerous and umbellate. Calyx adnate to ovary, usually entire, petals caducous. Stamens inserted outside the epigynous disk, anthers didymous.

59. *Cornaceæ*, p. 354. L. entire, stipules 0. Fl. regular, calyx-tube adnate to ovary, limb persistent, segments small, petals 4 or 5, inserted with stamens round an epigynous disk. Fr. drupaceous.

II. GAMOPETALÆ.

Flowers in the majority of species bisexual, as a rule with both calyx and corolla, corolla gamopetalous.

60. *Caprifoliaceæ*, p. 357. L. opposite, stipules usually 0. Fl. bisexual, calyx-tube adnate to ovary, limb 3-5-toothed, corolla often zygomorphic, lobes 5. Stamens inserted on the corolla-tube.

61. *Rubiaceæ*, p. 364. L. opposite, sometimes whorled, stipules as a rule interpetiolar. Fl. as a rule bisexual and regular, calyx-tube adnate to ovary, corolla inserted round the epigynous disk, stamens inserted on the corolla-tube, alternating with its lobes. Ovary as a rule 2-celled.

62. *Compositæ*, p. 398. L. as a rule alternate, stipules 0. Inflorescence a dense head of many small fl., sessile on a broad receptacle and enclosed in an involucre of whorled or imbricate bracts. Calyx usually a pappus of hairs on the top of the ovary, stamens on the corolla-tube, anthers usually connate, connective produced upwards.

63. *Goodeniaceæ*, p. 403. (*Scævola.*) L. alternate, simple, stipules 0. Fl. bisexual, in short axillary cymes, calyx adnate to ovary, lobes 5. Corolla oblique, split on the back, stamens 5, inserted at the base of the corolla. Fr. a drupe, crowned by the enlarged calyx-segments.

64. *Ericaceæ*, p. 403. L. alternate, simple, stipules 0. Fl. bisexual, 4- or 5-merous, stamens as a rule twice the number of corolla-lobes, anther-cells opening at the top by pores or short slits. Ovary inferior or superior, 4-, 5- or many-celled, ovules numerous on an axile placenta.

65. *Epacridaceæ*, p. 412. (*Leucopogon.*) L. alternate, coriaceous, longitudinally nerved. Fl. 5-merous, anthers 1-celled, opening by a single longitudinal slit.

66. *Plumbaginaceæ*, p. 413. L. alternate, entire. Fl. regular, bisexual, pentamerous, sheathed by bracts, calyx 5-ribbed, ovary 1-celled, ovule 1.

67. *Myrsinaceæ*, p. 413. L. alternate, simple, generally gland-dotted, stipules 0. Calyx persistent, often enlarged in fr. Corolla-tube short or none, stamens opposite the corolla-segments. Ovary 1-celled, ovules on a free central placenta.

68. *Sapotaceæ*, p. 421. L. entire, usually alternate and coriaceous. Fl. bisexual, calyx persistent, segments 4–8, almost distinct, corolla-tube short, lobes 4–24. Fr. a 1–8-seeded berry, seeds oily, with a crustaceous shining testa.

69. *Ebenaceæ*, p. 428. L. entire, as a rule alternate, stipules 0. Fl. regular, usually diœcious, calyx gamosepalous, persistent and generally enlarged in fr., segments 3–6, corolla-segments 3–6, stamens usually twice the number of corolla-lobes, filaments variously connate at base, often in pairs, anthers basifixed. Rind of fr. coriaceous, seeds embedded in soft or viscid pulp.

70. *Styraceæ*, p. 437. L. alternate, stip. 0. Fl. bisexual, regular, 4–5-merous, calyx superior or inferior, limb persistent, petals free or connate, stamens 10 or numerous. Ovary 2–5-celled, ovules 1 or few on the inner angle.

71. *Oleaceæ*, p. 442. L. as a rule opposite, stip. 0. Fl. regular, as a rule bisexual, in trichotomous panicles, calyx small, often truncate. Stamens 2, filaments usually short, ovary free, 2-celled, ovules 1 or 2 in each cell.

72. *Salvadoraceæ*, p. 453. Glabrous, l. opposite, entire, stipules minute. Fl. small, tetramerous, calyx small, corolla membranous. Ovary free, 1–2-celled.

73. *Apocynaceæ*, p. 454. L. entire, as a rule opposite or whorled, stipules 0 or small, sometimes intrapetiolar. Fl. regular, bisexual, usually pentamerous. Calyx free, corolla-lobes spreading, mostly contorted in bud, stamens 5, inserted in the corolla-tube. Carpels 2, usually distinct. Seeds often with a tuft of hairs. Endosperm scanty.

74. *Asclepiadaceæ*, p. 465. L. entire, as a rule opposite, stipules 0. Fl. regular, bisexual, pentamerous. Calyx inferior, sepals imbricate in bud. Stamens 5, inserted on the base of the corolla, anthers cohering or connate, enclosing the stigma, pollen-grains as a rule united into waxy masses. Corona corolline or staminal. Carpels 2, distinct. Seeds usually winged and surmounted by a dense brush of hairs. Embryo large, in copious endosperm.

75. *Loganiaceæ*, p. 473. L. opposite, simple, generally connected by interpetiolar stipules or by a raised line. Fl. regular, usually bisexual, ovary free, 2-celled. Embryo straight, in copious endosperm.

76. *Boraginaceæ*, p. 478. L. as a rule alternate and simple, stipules 0. Fl. bisexual, as a rule regular and pentamerous, in unilateral spikes or racemes, calyx free, persistent, lobes valvate in bud. Ovary superior, cells 2, each with 2 ovules, or 4, each with one ovule. Fr. a drupe or consisting of 4 nutlets.

77. *Convolvulaceæ*, p. 483. L. alternate, stipules 0. Fl. large, bisexual, regular, pentamerous, sepals distinct, persistent. Fr. a berry or capsule, seeds 2–4.

78. *Solanaceæ*, p. 489. L. as a rule alternate, stipules 0. Fl. regular, pentamerous, calyx usually gamosepalous, ovary free. Fr. a berry or capsule, seeds numerous.

79. *Scrophulariaceæ*, p. 491. (*Wightia*, *Brandisia.*) L. usually opposite, stip. 0. Fl. usually bisexual, corolla bilabiate, stamens 4, didynamous. Fr. a capsule, seeds numerous.

80. *Bignoniaceæ*, p. 491. L. usually opposite, compound, leaflets opposite, stip. 0. Fl. bisexual, generally zygomorphic, calyx gamosepalous, truncate, split or toothed. Ovary free, supported by an annular disk. Fr. often elongated, generally dehiscent, the two valves separating from the dissepiment, to which numerous seeds are attached.

81. *Acanthaceæ*, p. 496. L. opposite, stip. 0. Fl. bisexual, mostly irregular. Ovary free, 2-celled, style filiform, bifid, one branch often obsolete. Capsule loculicidal, seeds seated on hard curved acute supports.

82. *Verbenaceæ*, p. 502. L. usually opposite or whorled, stip. 0. Fl. bisexual or by abortion polygamous, usually zygomorphic. Calyx as a rule gamosepalous and persistent, lobes imbricate, stamens usually 4, ovary 2- or 4-celled, 1 ovule in each cell.

83. *Labiatæ*, p. 515. Mostly aromatic, branches usually 4-sided, l. opposite or whorled, stip. 0. Fl. zygomorphic, calyx persistent, corolla usually 2-lipped, lobes imbricate in bud. Stamens didynamous, the 2 upper sometimes imperfect or wanting. Ovary free, usually 4-lobed, supported by the annular disk. Fr. of 4 one-seeded nutlets.

III. MONOCHLAMYDEÆ.

Fl. frequently unisexual, perianth as a rule simple, rarely a distinct calyx and corolla.

84. *Nyctaginaceæ*, p. 517. (*Pisonia.*) L. as a rule entire and opposite, stip. 0. Fl. usually bisexual, often involucrate, perianth small, petaloid. Ovary free, 1-celled, ovule 1. Fr. indehiscent, enclosed in the persistent perianth-tube.

85. *Amarantaceæ*, p. 517. Stip. 0. Fl. usually bisexual, perianth of 5 persistent sepals, imbricate in bud. Stamens opposite the sepals, ovary free, 1-celled. Seed one, embryo horseshoe-shaped or annular, surrounding a mealy endosperm.

86. *Chenopodiaceæ*, p. 518. L. alternate, rarely opposite, simple, stip. 0. Fl. small, perianth of 3–5 sepals, stamens opposite the sepals. Fr. generally enclosed in the perianth, seed one, embryo curved, annular or spiral.

87. *Polygonaceæ*, p. 519. L. alternate, simple, stipules scarious or membranous, usually sheathing. Fl. small, usually bisexual, perianth of 4–6 persistent segments, imbricate in bud, stamens opposite the segments. Ovary free, 1-celled, compressed or trigonous. Fr. a small hard nut, seed one.

88. *Aristolochiaceæ*, p. 521. L. alternate, stip. 0. Fl. bisexual, perianth campanulate or tubular, 3-lobed or 2-lipped, ovary inferior, placentas parietal, ovules numerous.

89. *Piperaceæ*, p. 522. (*Piper.*) L. alternate, entire, basal nerves 3 or more, stipules membranous, enclosing the buds. Fl. usually diœcious or polygamous, in catkin-like spikes, perianth 0, stamens 1–4, hypogynous. Berry 1-seeded, seed globose.

90. *Myristicaceæ*, p. 523. Aromatic, l. entire, penninerved, stip. 0. Fl. 1-sexual, perianth as a rule 3-lobed, valvate in bud, anthers 6–30, usually sessile, ovary free, ovule 1, erect. Seed arillate, endosperm oily, ruminate. In Engler u. Prantl, Natürl. Pflanzenfam. III. 2. 40 justly placed near *Anonaceæ*.

91. *Lauraceæ*, p. 526. Aromatic, l. as a rule entire and evergreen, stip. 0. Perianth regular, deeply 6-cleft, segments biseriate, tube often enlarged in fr., stamens perigynous, normally 12 in 4 circles, those of the innermost circle often wanting, those of the two outermost circles opposite to perianth-segments, anther-cells 2 or 4, opening by valves. Ovary free, 1-celled. Fr. a berry or drupe, seed one, cotyledons thick, oily. In Engler u. Prantl. Natürl. Pflanzenfam. III. 2. 106 placed in the vicinity of *Berberidaceæ* and *Menispermaceæ*.

92. *Hernandiaceæ*, p. 542. L. alternate, stip. 0. Perianth of 4–10 segments, stamens 3–5, anther-cells 2, opening by valves.

93. *Proteaceæ*, p. 543. L. hard, mostly alternate, stip. 0. Fl. bisexual, perianth of 4 segments, in bud valvately cohering into a cylindrical tube, tips free, recurved. Stamens 4, filaments inserted on perianth-segments. Ovary free, 1-celled. Seeds few.

94. *Thymelæaceæ*, p. 544. L. simple, quite entire. Fl. usually bisexual, perianth tubular or campanulate, lobes 4 or 5, imbricate in bud. Stamens inserted on the perianth, usually twice the number of lobes. Ovary free, usually 1-celled.

95. *Elæagnaceæ*, p. 546. Often spinescent, with silvery or brown stellate scales or hairs. L. alternate, quite entire, stip. 0. Fr. indehiscent, entirely enclosed within the lower fleshy part of perianth, seed 1, radicle inferior.

96. *Loranthaceæ*, p. 547. Parasitic on stems and branches. L. entire, usually opposite, sometimes wanting. Fl. regular, perianth simple or double, stamens equal to and opposite the petals or perianth-lobes. Ovary inferior, 1-celled, ovule 1, adnate all round to the ovary walls. Fr. usually viscid.

97. *Santalaceæ*, p. 553. Mostly root-parasites. L. entire, stip. 0. Perianth usually adnate to ovary, 5–8-lobed, stamens opposite to lobes, ovary 1-celled, ovules several. Drupe or nut 1-seeded.

98. *Euphorbiaceæ*, p. 555. L. in most genera alternate, undivided and stipulate. Fl. as a rule unisexual. Perianth calycine, several genera with petals. Ovary superior, as a rule of 3 carpels, more or less united, styles 3, ovules 1 or 2 in each cell, pendulous from the inner angle.

99. *Ulmaceæ*, p. 593. L. distichous, undivided, stipulate. Perianth 4–9-lobed or of 4–5 sepals, stamens opposite to perianth-segments, rarely twice their number. Ovary of 2 carpels, usually 1-celled, ovule 1, pendulous.

100. *Moraceæ*, p. 597. L. usually alternate, stipules large, often amplexicaul. Fl. unisexual, crowded on receptacles, which are globose, cylindric or hollow. ♀ perianth of 4 sepals or segments, often fleshy in fr. Ovary 1-celled, ovule 1, usually pendulous.

101. *Urticaceæ*, p. 616. L. alternate, stipulate, as a rule dentate, basal n. 3. Fl. unisexual, sessile, usually in compact heads or clusters, stamens 4 or 5, opposite to perianth-segments, filaments inflexed in bud. Ovule erect, orthotropous.

102. *Platanaceæ*, p. 619. L. alternate, palminerved, lobed, stipules large. Fl. monœcious, in unisexual globose heads on long axillary peduncles, sepals and petals minute, anthers linear, almost sessile, ovaries hairy at base, as many as sepals. In Engler u. Prantl, Natürl. Pflanzenfam. III. 2*a*. 137, placed near *Hamamelidaceæ* and *Rosaceæ*.

103. *Juglandaceæ*, p. 619. L. alternate, pinnate, stip. 0. Fl. monœcious, ♂ in lateral pendulous catkins. ♀ in few- or many-fld. spikes, perianth adnate to the 1-celled ovary, ovule 1, erect. Cotyledons oily, endosperm 0.

104. *Myricaceæ*, p. 620. Aromatic, l. alternate, coriaceous, stipules 0. Fl. unisexual, in catkins, stamens 8–6 in the axils of broad bracts. Fr. fleshy, endocarp bony, seed 1, endosperm 0.

105 *Casuarinaceæ*, p. 620. Branchlets slender, deciduous, ribbed, jointed, membranous dentate sheaths at the joints, the teeth alternating with the ribs of the next joint above. Fl. unisexual, ♂ monandrous, ♀ in small ovoid spikes at the ends of lateral branchlets. Fr. a woody globose cone.

106. *Betulaceæ*, p. 621. L. alternate, undivided, as a rule serrate, stipules deciduous. Fl. early in spring, ♂ in drooping catkins, anther-cells as a rule distinct, ♀ in spikes, ovary 2-celled, 1 pendulous ovule in each cell, styles 2, long, filiform, perianth 0 or adnate to ovary.

107. *Fagaceæ*, p. 624. L. alternate, simple, penninerved, stip. deciduous, Fl. monœcious, ♂ in drooping catkins or in erect spikes, anther-cells not distinct. ♀ in spikes, each fl. or group of fl. enclosed in an involucre of numerous bracts, coalescing in fr., perianth adnate to ovary. Ovary 2–6-celled, 2 pendulous ovules in each cell.

108. *Salicaceæ*, p. 636. L. deciduous, alternate, simple, stipulate. Fl. diœcious, in catkins similar in both sexes, 1 fl. in the axil of each bract, a disk at the base of stamens and ovary, perianth 0. Ovary 1-celled, ovules ∞ on 2–4 parietal placentas. Seeds ∞, minute, enclosed by long silky, deciduous hairs.

Second Sub-Class. MONOCOTYLEDONS.

Fibro-vascular bundles scattered in the cellular tissue of the stem, closely packed near the circumference and more sparse near the centre. Pith, wood and bark not distinct, no continuous cambium layer and no regular increase in thickness by the formation of concentric layers of new wood and bark. (*Dracæna* and *Cordyline* abnormal.) Leaves on sheaths or broad-based petioles, the blade usually with longitudinal nerves and undivided transverse veins. Perianth, when present, stamens and usually carpels, in threes or multiples of 3. Embryo small, usually in copious endosperm, cotyledon one, remaining enclosed in the germinating seed.

109. *Liliaceæ*, p. 640. Perianth in 2 series, imbricate in bud, stamens mostly 6. Ovary 3-celled, style 1, ovules attached to the inner angle of cells.

110. *Palmæ*, p. 642. Stem solid, usually unbranched, in most genera with a terminal crown of pinnately or palmately divided l., petiole broad-based, pinnæ or segments usually folded longitudinally. Inflorescence with large sheathing bracts, fl. unisexual or polygamous, calyx and corolla of 3 segments each. Carpels 3, usually united in a 3-celled ovary. Endosperm horny or oily.

111. *Pandanaceæ*, p. 658. Stem solid, dividing into dichotomous branches, each branch with a tuft of linear sheathing l. in tristichous spirals, edges and midrib usually spinous. Inflorescence clothed with leafy spathes, fl. diœcious, small, crowded, perianth 0. Fr. a syncarpium of numerous more or less obconical fruits, endosperm oily.

112. *Gramineæ* (*Bambuseæ*), p. 660. Stems above ground hollow, jointed, branches usually fascicled at the nodes. L. linear or oblong, on long split sheaths. Fl. usually bisexual, in distichous spikelets, each fl. in the axil of a bract (glume) with an inner usually 2-nerved bract (palea). Stamens 3 or 6, in a few species ∞, usually supported by thin scales (lodicules). Seed 1, embryo with a large fleshy scutellum, and in most genera with a farinaceous endosperm.

Second Class. GYMNOSPERMS.

Fl. unisexual, perianth none or incomplete. Ovules free, not enclosed in an ovary, fertilized by the pollen-tube entering the micropyle or a tube formed by the integument. Seeds naked, embryo straight with copious endosperm.

113. *Gnetaceæ*, p. 685. Stem and branches jointed at the nodes. L. opposite or reduced to a short sometimes 3–4-dentate sheath. Fl. unisexual, ♀ one erect ovule, integument single, prolonged into a tube. Ovule enclosed in a perianth, which usually becomes fleshy in fr.

114. *Coniferæ*, p. 688. Branches often whorled, l. alternate, usually acicular, often tufted. Fl. unisexual, without perianth, ♂: deciduous catkins, with antheriferous scales. Seeds at the base of carpellary scales, often forming a cone. Endosperm mostly oily, cotyledons 2 or more.

115. *Cycadaceæ*, p. 697 (*Cycas*). Trunk cylindric, sometimes branched, with terminal tufts of rigid, pinnate leaves, pith and bark large. Fl. diœcious, at the apex of trunk among the leaves, ♂ in erect cones with numerous thick scales, bearing on the under-surface ∞ globose anther-cells. ♀: carpophylls densely woolly in crowded whorls around the top of trunk, each with 1–5 pairs of ovules on its edge.

ERRATA

Page xxii line 7, for *Coco* read *Cocoa*
,, 2 ,, 19, for **Buchananiana** read **Buchanananiana**
,, 3 ,, 17, for *Saurania* read *Saurauja*
,, 6 ,, 12 from below, for *Vaung* read *Yaung*
,, 9 ,, 8, for *T.* read *I.*
,, ,, ,, 10, for *T.* read *I.*
,, 11 ,, 6, *for* South *read* Sonth.
,, 12 ,, 8 from below, *for* 36C *read* 76
,, 14 ,, 13, and 8 from below, *for* Circass, *read* Circars
,, 25 ,, 13 from below, *for* petals *read* pet.
,, 27 ,, 23 from below, *for* Sikkim, Himalaya *read* Sikkim Himalaya
,, 30 lines 27–28, *for* leaf, bearing *read* leaf-bearing
,, 34 line 19 from below, for longispina read *longispina*
,, 35 ,, 4, *for* Yemetthen *read* Yemethen
,, 39 ,, 21 from below, *for* bark *read* back
,, 46 ,, 10 from below, *for* Lahaue *read* Lahaul
,, 47 bottom line, *for* Cratoxylum *read* Cratoxylon
,, 48 line 17, for *Sathange hnauk* read *Sathange ohnauk*
,, 55 ,, 31, *for* 5 *read* 2
,, ,, ,, 13 from below, for *Nagesar* read *Nageshwar*
,, ,, ,, 11 from below, for *Gangau* read *Gangaw*
,, 59 ,, 13, for *Ensynaxis* read *Eusynaxis*
,, 63 ,, 18, for **manrotricha** read **macrotricha**
,, 87 ,, 9, *for* 3 *read* 11
,, ,, ,, 21 from below, *for* many flowered, subtended *read* many, fl. subtended
,, 98 ,, 22, for *Tagaw* read *Tayaw*
,, 100 ,, 21 from below, *for* orary *read* ovary
,, 103 ,, 23, *for* flower *read* inflorescence
,, 113 ,, 7, for *Metimè* read *Metme*
,, ,, ,, 13 from below, *for* $\frac{1}{2}$ in. across, *read* 1 in. long
,, 128 ,, 2 from below, for *A.* read *O.*
,, 129 ,, 9, *for* Anbl. *read* Aubl.
,, ,, ,, 13, *for* Hanbd. *read* Handb.
,, 136 ,, 14 from below, before W. insert 2
,, 138 ,, 4, from below, *for* Katha *read* Kathò
,, 140 ,, 17, *for* 3–4 *read* $\frac{3}{4}$
,, 143 ,, 6, *for* Cocos *read* Coco
,, 151 ,, 26, *for* 388 *read* 588
,, 159 ,, 13 from below, *for* Cocos *read* Coco
,, 160 ,, 15 from below, *for* Thankyeghat *read* Thaukyeghat
,, 163 ,, 5, *for* Duphla *read* Daphla
,, ,, ,, 11 from below, *dele* R.
,, 174 ,, 7, *for* pal *read* pale
,, 176 ,, 32, for *C.* read *V.*
,, 180 ,, 4 from below, *for* L. *read* Leaflets
,, 184 ,, 2 from below, *dele* lobed
,, 190 ,, 3 from below, *for* ♂ and ♂ *read* ♂ and ☿
,, 193 ,, 7, for *Kyobo* read *Gyobo*
,, ,, ,, 8, strike out *piscidia*
,, 196 ,, 10 and 13, *read* 204 *for* 205
,, ,, ,, 28, *for* ovules *read* ovule
,, 197 ,, 23, *for* Bucki-amelæ *read* Bucki-amela
,, 200 ,, 24, for *Ihingan* read *Jhingan*
,, 203 ,, 2, *for* hill *read* hills
,, 204 ,, 20, *for* Lepoha *read* Lepcha

Page 204 line 8 from below, for *Thi hon* read *Thiho*
,, 205 ,, 12 from below, for 6 *read* 7
,, ,, ,, 5 from below, *for* 7 *read* 8
,, 206 ,, 21, add Thayet, Burm.
,, 231 ,, 10, *for* ercet *read* erect
,, ,, ,, 26 from below, for *Seluppya* read *Seleippya*
,, 232 ,, 25 from below, for *Erythrna* read *Erythrina*
,, 241 ,, 15, for *Ngayamin* read *Ngayanin*
,, 251 ,, 9, for **zollingeriana** read **Zollingeriana**
,, ,, ,, 23 from below, for *Jntsia* read *Intsia*
,, 273 ,, 26 from below, for *Jnga* read *Inga*
,, ,, ,, 4 from below, for *Jnga* read *Inga*
,, 287 ,, 26, *for* Hayara *read* Hazara
,, 288 ,, 21, *for* Harial *read* Hariab
,, 296 ,, 10, *for* 2 *read* 20
,, 300 ,, 15, *for* Geneva *read* Genera
,, ,, ,, 13 from below, *read* Kun. *for* Kan.
,, 312 lines 15–16, *for* l. petiolate, opposite in some species, whorled, *read* l. petiolate, opposite, in some species whorled
,, 312 line 27, for *Thamaka-nwè* Burm. read *Thamaka-nwè*, Burm.
,, 334 ,, 28, *for* Anamalai hills, Ceylon, *read* Anamalay hills.—Ceylon
,, 340 ,, 27, for *Mehudi* read *Mehndi*
,, 341 ,, 12 from below, for *Henslovia* read *Henslowia*
,, 345 ,, 25, *for* Singhbhum-Mahendragiri *read* Singhbhum. Mahendragiri
,, 346 ,, 19, *for* 5 *read* 4
,, 376 ,, 25 from below, *for* Cochinchina, stems *read* Cochinchina. Stems
,, 379 ,, 20, for *Kurmuri* read *Karmari*
,, 395 ,, 16 from below, for **formicarium** read **formicarum**
,, 411 ,, 7 from below, *for* Moolejit *read* Mooleyit
,, 414 ,, 22, *for* 6 *read* 1
,, 417 ,, 19, *for* javadies *read* Javadies
,, ,, ,, 23, for *R* read *E*
,, 424 ,, 14, for *Perottetiana* read *Perrottetiana*
,, 432 ,, 3 from below, for *Timburui* read *Timburni*
,, 435 ,, 23 from below, *for* 2–3½ *read* 2–5
,, ,, ,, 18 from below, *strike out* slightly
,, 444 ,, 19, for *ghaut* read *ghant*
,, 450 ,, 25, for *Chameli* read *Chambeli*
,, 454 ,, 36 from below, *for* edges *read* wedges
,, 457 ,, 24, for A read R, and for *verticellata* read *verticillatu*
,, 459 ,, 3, for *Satuin* read *Satvin*
,, 460 ,, 21, for *Zulat* read *Zalat*
,, 465 ,, 9, for **ovalifolius** read **ovatifolius**
,, 487 ,, 20, *for* 4 B. *read* 4. P.
,, 494 ,, 20, *for* Thabet *read* Thabeit
,, 511 ,, 4, *for* H *read* P.
,, ,, ,, 11 from below, *for* 9 *read* 7
,, 517 ,, 11 from below, for *T* read *P*
,, 527 head line, read LAURACEAE for LAVRACEAE
,, 533 line 30, for *Culitlaban* read *Culitlawan*.
,, 536 ,, 26, *for* Ceylon II *read* Ceylon III
,, 541 ,, 15 from below, *for* E *read* L
,, ,, ,, 2 from below, for **Daphniphyllum** read **Daphnidium**
,, 545 ,, 3 from below, *for* S *read* L.
,, 549 ,, 7 from below, *strike out* (solitary in *L. Stocksii*)
,, 554 ,, 3, for XXXIX read XXIX
,, 564 bottom line, *for* ♂ fl. *read* ♀ fl.
,, 575 line 24 from below, for *Perottetianum* read *Perrottetianum*
,, 593 ,, 16, *for* 8 *read* ∞
,, 620 ,, 3 from below, *for* long *read* bony
,, 632 ,, 10 from below, *for* 107 *read* 197
,, 633 ,, 6, for *xylocarpus* read *xylocarpa*
,, 634 ,, 23, *for* 8 *read* 84
,, 640 ,, 13, *for* T *read* P.
,, 653 ,, 9 from below, for *Garuba* read *Guruba*
,, 654 ,, 13 from below, *for* flabellum *read* flagellum
,, 657 ,, 16, *for* P *read* T
,, 691 ,, 28, *for* P. *read* Pinus

INDIAN TREES

ORDER I. RANUNCULACEÆ. Gen. Pl. i. 1.

Tribe **Clematideæ**. Erect or climbing shrubs. Leaves opposite, usually compound, stipules 0, petioles often woody, twisted round supports. Sepals petaloid, valvate. Stamens ∞, carpels ∞, each with one pendulous ovule. Fruit, a head of sessile or stalked achenes.

Petals none . . . . 1. CLEMATIS.
Petals 6–12 . . . . 2. NARAVELIA.

1. CLEMATIS, Linn.; Fl. Brit. Ind. i. 2.

Woody climbers. Sepals usually 4, petals 0, achenes usually with long feathery styles. Species 100, a few in tropical, mostly in temperate climates. Of the 20 Indian species only the larger and more common kinds are mentioned here.

A. Pedicels 1-flowered, in axillary fascicles, leaves trifoliolate.

1. **C. montana**, Ham.; Wall. Pl. As. Rar. t. 217. Vern. *Garol*, Pangi; *Kāuni*, N.W.

Leaves fascicled on arrested branchlets, leaflets ovate or ovate-lanceolate, coarsely toothed, 1½–2½ in. long. Fl. white, 2–3 in. diam., pedicels longer than leaves. Stamens glabrous.

Himalaya from the Indus eastwards, generally 7,000–9,000, ascending to 12,000 ft. Khasi hills. Fl. April–June. 2. **C. barbellata**, Edgew. North-West Himalaya, 8,000–10,000 ft. Fl. dull purple, sepals acuminate, pubescent on both surfaces, anthers bearded.

B. Fl. in axillary panicles, sepals spreading, filaments glabrous.

3. **C. smilacifolia**, Wall.—Syn. *C. subpeltata*, Wall. Pl. As. Rar. t. 20. Syn. *C. Munroana*, Wight Ill. t. 1.

Branches furrowed, leaves usually 1-foliolate, at times 3-foliolate, petioles twisted woody; leaflets coriaceous, glabrous, 4–10 in. long, ovate, base rounded or deeply cordate, entire or remotely serrate. Panicles 6–12 in., fl. 1–1½ in. diam., sepals 4–5, coriaceous, oblong, at length reflexed, outside dull brown tomentose, inside purple. Feathery styles in fruit 2 in. long.

Sikkim, Khasi hills, Burma hills, Western Coast from North Kanara southwards, in evergreen forests. Fl. C. S.—Ceylon, lower montane zone. Malay Archipelago. 4. **C. grata**, Wall. Pl. As. Rar. t. 98. North-West Himalaya 2,000–8,000 ft., Upper Burma, China, leaves pinnate, leaflets 5, broadly ovate, acuminate, inciso-serrate or 3-lobed, pubescent or tomentose beneath. Fl. white, ¾ in. diam.

5. **C. Gouriana,** Roxb.; Wight Ic. 933–4. Vern *Belkûm*, *Belkangu*, N.W.

Leaves pinnate, often bipinnate, leaflets ovate or ovate-lanceolate, acuminate, entire or irregularly serrate, 2–3 in. long, 3–5 basal nerves, upper part of petiole often without leaflets, woody, twisted round supports. Fl. greenish-white ½ in. diam.

Sub-himalayan tract, ascending to 4,000 ft.; Burma, upper and lower; Western Peninsula. Fl. R. S.—Ceylon, Malay Peninsula and Archipelago.

C. Fl. in axillary panicles, sepals spreading, filaments hairy.

6. **C. Wightiana,** Wall.; Wight Ic. t. 935.

Soft-tomentose, leaves pinnate, leaflets usually 5, broadly cordate or ovate, 3–5 lobed, densely villous beneath. Fl. 1–2 in. diam. Sepals tawny-tomentose outside, filaments with long white silk.

Western Ghats, from Mahableshwar southwards, common on the Nilgiris. Fl. Jan.–Feb. 7. **C. orientalis,** Linn. Dry valleys of the inner N.W. Himalaya, glabrous, glaucous, leaves pinnate or bipinnate, leaflets lobed, varying from linear-lanceolate to broad-ovate; fl. 1½ in. across, yellow, mottled with purple, sepals 4.

D. Fl. in axillary panicles, sepals erect with recurved tips.

10. **C. Buchaniana,** DC.; Collett Simla Fl. fig. 1. Vern. *Kāuni*, *Bāli*, Jauns.

A large woody climber, greyish tomentose, leaves pinnate, leaflets 5–7, broadly ovate, coarsely serrate or 3–5 lobed. Fl. campanulate, cream coloured, sepals ribbed, filaments linear, densely hairy.

Himalaya, from the Punjab eastwards, 5,000–10,000 ft., Khasi hills. Fl. Aug.–Dec.

11. **C. connata,** DC. Himalaya, from Kashmir eastwards, closely allied to 10, but nearly glabrous, fl. smaller and petioles generally connate into a flat coriaceous or woody expansion. 12. **C. grewiæflora,** DC. Himalaya, from Kumaon eastwards, ascending to 5,000 ft. Manipur, Shan hills, Upper Burma, densely and softly tawny or rusty tomentose, leaves pinnate, leaflets 3–5, cordate or broadly ovate. Fl. 1½ in. long, tawny tomentose outside, filaments filiform above. 13. **C. acuminata,** DC. Himalaya, from Kedar Kanta eastwards, Khasi hills to Patkoy range, leaves trifoliolate glabrous, leaflets ovate or ovate-lanceolate, entire or distantly toothed, fl. yellow sepals slightly pubescent outside.

2. NARAVELIA, DC.; Fl. Brit. Ind. i. 6.

Climbing shrubs, leaves pinnate, leaflets 2 opposite, common petiole prolonged into a tendril. Fl. in large axillary panicles. Sepals 4, petals 6–12, linear-spathulate, achenes with long hairy styles. Species 2.

1. **N. zeylanica,** DC.—Syn. *Atragene zeylanica*, Linn.; Roxb. Cor. Pl. t. 188. Vern. *Sat-gyo-yit*, Burm.; *Nara-wel*, Singhal.

Branchlets, petioles and inflorescence pubescent, leaflets broad-ovate, acuminate, 3–4 in. long, entire or with a few large teeth, softly tomentose beneath, with 5–7 prominent basal nerves, tendril deflexed at right angles to the petiole. Fl. yellowish green, panicles lax, usually longer than leaves. Sepals ¼–⅓ in., tomentose outside, soon deciduous, petals as long as sepals, linear spreading, achenes hairy, with hairy style 2 in. long.

Sub-himalayan tract, from Nepal eastwards, ascending to 3,000 ft., Burma, Western Peninsula. Fl. at different times between June and Dec. Ceylon, Malay Archipelago, South China. 2. **N. laurifolia,** Wall. Martaban and Tenasserim, Malay Peninsula and Archipelago, to the Philippines. Glabrous, fl. cream coloured, petals broader at the end, more or less spathulate.

ORDER II. DILLENIACEÆ. Gen. Pl. i. 10.

Trees or shrubs, rarely herbs, not aromatic, with simple alternate penniveined leaves and dilated petioles, often winged and sheathing at base. Flowers large, bisexual, regular, white or yellow, single or in cymose fascicles. Sepals usually 5, persistent, imbricate in bud. Petals generally 5, deciduous. Stamens mostly ∞, hypogynous, free. Anthers basifixed, or laterally adnate to the connective. Ovary free, consisting of one or several more or less distinct carpels, styles always distinct. Seeds with an arillus, albuminous, embryo minute.

Remarkable anatomical characters: Hairs never glandular, always one-celled, sometimes stellate, and surface of leaves often rough, the roughness being caused in some species by short thick-walled hairs; in others (species of the American genus *Curatella*, which are used to polish wood and even metals) by siliceous concretions in the epidermis, and in some by sacs filled with raphides protruding above the surface. Medullary rays in the wood very broad; hence on a radial section the remarkably mottled appearance of the wood. The wood fibres always have bordered pits.

The genera *Saurania* and *Actinidia*, placed by Baillon and Gilg (Engler u. Prantl. iii. 6, p. 125, 126) in this order, are here included under *Ternstroemiaceæ*.

Trees, flowers solitary or fasciculate, connective not broader than filament, carpels connate . . . . 1. DILLENIA.

Shrubs or climbers, fl. in axillary or terminal panicles, connective broad
- Carpels 3–5, free, ovules ∞ in 2 series . . . . . 2. TETRACERA.
- Carpel 1, ovules 2–3 . . . . 3. DELIMA.

1. DILLENIA, Linn.; Fl. Brit. Ind. i. 36.

Trees with large dentate or crenate leaves, crowded at the ends of thick branchlets. Secondary nerves numerous, parallel, nearly straight, very prominent. Flowers scented, anthers opening by small terminal slits or pores, carpels 5–20, cohering with the axis, ovules indefinite, styles spreading. Fruit enclosed by the enlarged coriaceous or fleshy sepals. Species 25, Indo-Malayan region.

A. Evergreen. Fl. white.

1. **D. indica**, Linn.—Syn. *D. speciosa*, Thunb.; Wight Ic. t. 823; Bedd. Fl. Sylv. t. 103. Vern. *Chalta*, Beng. Hind.; *Motha Karmal*, Mar.; *Kanagala*, Kan.; *Thabyu*, Burm.; *Masang*, Kachin.

A middle-sized tree, trunk short, erect, branches spreading, leaves lanceolate, coriaceous, pubescent beneath, hard when old. Secondary nerves 30–40 pair, ending in the points of serratures. Petiole hairy 1–2, blade 10–14 in. long. Carpels 20, styles linear recurved. Fruit 3–5 in. diam., hard outside, fleshy within; seeds reniform, numerous, hairy along the edges, embedded in pellucid glutinous pulp.

Sub-himalayan tract, from Nepal eastwards. Moister regions of both peninsulas, chiefly along streams. Frequently planted. Fl. R. S.—Ceylon.

2. **D. bracteata**, Wight Ic. t. 358.

Branchlets and petioles grey-silky. Leaves coriaceous, broadly elliptic, obtuse or emarginate, slightly crenate, on both sides glabrous, petiole ½, blade 3–5 in. long. Secondary nerves 12–20 pair. Fl. in few fld. racemes, 2–3 in. diam., sepals silky, carpels 5.

Veligondas and other hills on the east side of the peninsula.

B. Deciduous, fl. appearing before the leaves, yellow, solitary.

3. **D. aurea,** Smith.—Kurz, F. Fl. i. 20. Syn. *D. ornata*, Wall. Pl. As. Rar. t. 23. Vern. *Aggāi*, Oudh; *Kallĕi*, Gond, Satpuras; *Korkotta*, Kol. *Byu*, Burm.

Youngest shoots grey—or tawny-silky. Leaves coriaceous, obovate, narrowed into a channelled and sheathing petiole. Secondary nerves 20–30 pair, tertiary prominent, parallel, often branching and anastomosing, petiole $1\frac{1}{4}$–2 in., blade 6–12 in. long. Fl. solitary, 2–3 in. diam., peduncles 1–$1\frac{1}{2}$ in. long, carpels 8–10.

Sal forests of Oudh and Central Provinces (Banjar Valley). Mandevi (D.B. Feb., 1870), Burma, hills between Sitang and Salween rivers, 2,000–4,000 ft. Sheds leaves Feb., Mar. Fl. before young leaves appear, April, May.

4. **D. pulcherrima,** Kurz, F. Fl. i. 19. Vern. *Byu*, Lower, *Linshaw*, Upper Burma.

Supposed to differ from *D. aurea* by larger elliptic leaves with a rounded base, softly and grey-pubescent while young. Secondary nerves further apart, tertiary nerves not more prominent than the minute reticulate veins. Fl. 3–4 in. diam., peduncles $1\frac{3}{4}$–3 in. long, carpels 12. Foresters in Burma will eventually determine whether these two species are really distinct. Pierre, Fl. For. Cochinch. t. 11, 12, 13, unites them.

Upper and Lower Burma, chiefly in Eng forest. Fl. H. S.

C. Deciduous, fl. appearing before the leaves, yellow, fasciculate.

5. **D. pentagyna,** Roxb. Cor. Pl. t. 20; Bedd. Fl. Sylv. t. 104. Vern. *Aggai*, Oudh; *Telea Sāg*, Mandevi; *Sūa*, Gond, Satpuras; *Rai*, Kol; *Kari*, *Karmal*, Mar.; *Kangal*, *Kanagola*, Kan.; *Nay teku*, Tam.; *Koda punna*, Mal.; *Zinbyun*, Burm.

Bark grey or pale brown, with shallow depressions of irregular shape, caused by the exfoliation of the outer layers. Leaves silky, pubescent when young, 12–36 in., narrowed into short winged sheathing petioles, secondary nerves 30–40 pair, excurrent (as well as some branch nerves) into fine silky teeth. Fl. 1 in. diam., 5–10, fasciculate on tuberosities along 2–3 year-old branchlets marked by the scars of the sheathing petioles, pedicels slender, 1–3 in. long. Carpels 5, fruit with the enlarged fleshy sepals, $\frac{1}{2}$–$\frac{3}{4}$ in. diam.

Sal forests in the sub-himalayan tract, from Oudh eastwards. Deciduous forests in both peninsulas. Sheds its leaves in H.S., comes into fl. soon afterwards. *D. pilosa*, Roxb., is described by Kurz F. Fl. i. 20, with large solitary fl. In Fl. Brit. Ind. i. 38 it is identified with *D. pentagyna*.

6. **D. scabrella,** Roxb.; Wall. Pl. As. Rar. t. 22.

Young shoots with long silky hairs. Leaves narrow-lanceolate or oblanceolate, membranous, upperside rough, underside roughish-tomentose, teeth minute, petiole 1–$1\frac{1}{2}$, blade 6–12 in. long, secondary nerves 30–40, almost at right angles to midrib. Fl. $1\frac{1}{2}$ in. diam., 3–7 fasciculate on slender bracteate pedicels, 1–2 in. long. Sepals nearly glabrous, carpels 5–7.

Assam, Khasi hills, Chittagong, Andamans. Fl. H.S. with the fresh leaves or before the leaves are out. 7. **D. parviflora,** Griff. Lower Burma, differs by rigidly coriaceous leaves, softly tomentose beneath, longer petioles, calyx and pedicels densely tomentose.

2. TETRACERA, Linn.; Fl. Brit. Ind. i. 31.

Woody climbers rarely trees or shrubs, with entire, coriaceous, erect, generally harsh leaves. Fl. in terminal cymose panicles. Sepals 4–6, petals as many, stamens ∞, anther cells distinct, attached to a broad connective, which gradually narrows into the filament. Carpels 3–5, free, coriaceous, dehiscent when ripe. Species 24, in the tropics of both hemispheres.

1. **T. laevis,** Vahl.—Syn. *T. Rheedii,* DC.; Wight Ic. t. 70.
A glabrous climber. Leaves elliptic-oblong, entire or distantly dentate, 3–5 in. long, secondary nerves 6–8 pair. Fl. white, 1 in. diam.

Malabar and Travancore, Ceylon. Fl. March. 2. **T. Assa,** DC. (Chittagong, Lower Burma, Malay Peninsula and Archipelago) is similar, but has hairy branchlets.

3. DELIMA, Linn.; Fl. Brit. Ind. i. 31.

(Included under *Tetracera* by Gilg in Engler u. Prantl, iii. 6, 112.)

Characters of *Tetracera*, but leaves crenate-serrate and carpel solitary, with 2–3 ovules. Seed solitary, with a cup-shaped, toothed arillus in a coriaceous follicle. Species 2, one in South America.

D. sarmentosa, Linn.; Kurz, F. Fl. i. 22.
An evergreen, large climber, with rough reddish-brown branches. Leaves elliptic, blade 3–6, petiole ¾ in. long, secondary nerves 10–20 pair, prominent beneath, very rough from minute, adpressed scattered stiff hairs. Fl. small white, in large axillary and terminal panicles.

Assam, Cachar, Chittagong, Burma. Fl. R. S.—Malay Peninsula and Archipelago

ORDER III. MAGNOLIACEÆ. Gen. Pl. i. 16.

Trees or shrubs, sometimes climbing, often aromatic. Leaves alternate, in most genera with amplexicaul convolute deciduous stipules. Flowers solitary, generally large and bisexual. Sepals and petals similar, arranged as a rule in trimerous whorls. Stamens free, numerous, anther cells adnate to filaments. Ovaries numerous, generally spirally arranged on the elongated torus. Ovules attached to the ventral suture. Embryo minute, in an abundant oily albumen.

Important anatomical characters: Sacs containing resin in the parenchyma of leaves, often visible as transparent dots; wood fibres with bordered pits, the wood of *Drimys* (South America, Australia, Borneo) consisting entirely of such fibres with bordered pits, without vessels, resembling the wood of Conifers.

A. Shrubs or trees, stipules convolute, embracing the leafbuds. Fl. bisexual, carpels in fruit on an elongated axis.
  a. Carpels dehiscing dorsally, not separating from the axis.
  Ovaries immediately over the stamens, or only separated from them by a short interval; carpels in fruit closely packed.
    Ovules 2, fruit cylindric . . . . 1. MAGNOLIA.
    Ovules 6 or more, fruit ovoid . . . . . . 2. MANGLIETIA.
  Ovaries separated by a distinct internode from stamens, carpels in fruit more or less distant . . . . . 3. MICHELIA.
  b. Carpels dehiscing ventrally or indehiscent, separating from the axis . . . . 4. TALAUMA.

B. Shrubs, stipules 0. Fl. bisexual, carpels in one whorl . ILLICIUM (p. 9).

C. Climbing shrubs, stipules 0. Fl. unisexual.
  Fruiting carpels in an elongated spike . . . . . 5. SCHIZANDRA.
  Fruiting carpels in a globose head . . . . . . KADSURA (p. 9).

1. MAGNOLIA, Linn.; Fl. Brit. Ind. i, 41.

Trees, rarely shrubs, leafbuds enveloped in the convolute stipules. Sepals 3, petals 6–12, in whorls of 3. No interval, or only a short interval between ovaries and stamens. Each ovary with 2 collateral ovules. Fruit a dense spike of dorsally dehiscing carpels, which are more or less connate. Outer layers of testa fleshy. Species 18, North America and Mexico, China and Japan, mountains of India.

1. **M. pterocarpa,** Roxb. Corom. Pl. t. 266; Ann. Bot. Gard. Calc. iii. t. 53.—Syn. *M. sphenocarpa*, Wall.; Fl. B. Ind. i. 41.

A large evergreen tree, the youngest parts tawny-pilose. Leaves coriaceous, quite glabrous when full grown, 8–16 in. long, secondary nerves 12–18 pair. Flowers fragrant, terminal, campanulate, 2–3½ in. across, on a stout peduncle, 1½–2 in. long. Sepals coriaceous, green outside, petals fleshy, white. Fruiting spike 5–7 by 1½–2½ in. Carpels ½–¾ in. long, narrowed into long lanceolate spreading coriaceous beaks. Seeds orange.

Subhimalayan tract from Nepal eastwards, Assam, Khasi and Chittagong hills. Pegu (Kurz).

2. **M. Campbellii,** Hook. fil. & Thoms.; Ann. Bot. G. Calc. iii. t. 51, 52 Vern. *Lal Champ*, Nepal.

A large deciduous tree, wood white, not heavy. Leaves 4–12 in. long, underside pale, silky tomentose when young, nearly glabrous when full grown, secondary nerves 12–16 pair. Flowers terminal, 6–10 in. across, appearing when the tree is leafless, scented, rose-coloured, occasionally white. Sepals and petals similar, 12–15. Fruiting spike cylindric, 6–8 in. by 1 in. Seeds red.

Himalaya, 7,000–10,000 ft., from Nepal eastwards. Manipur, 8,000 ft. Fl. April.

The other species may be classified as follows:—

No interval between ovaries and stamens: 3. **M. globosa,** Hook. f. & Thoms.; Ann. Bot. G. Calc. iii. t. 50. Sikkim, 9,000–10,000 feet. A small tree, leaves membranous, ovate, 5–8 in., rusty tomentose beneath, chiefly along nerves 4. **M. Gustavi,** King, l. c. t. 61. Makúm forest, Assam. Leaves lanceolate, entirely glabrous, 5–7 in.

A short interval between ovaries and stamens: 5. **M. Griffithii,** Hook. f. & Thoms.; Ann. B. G. C. iii. t. 48, 49. Assam. Leaves elliptic or elliptic-oblong, pale and hairy beneath, 9–13 in. 6. **M. Pealiana,** King, l. c. t. 59. Makúm Forest, Assam. Leaves from a rounded base, elliptic-oblong, 6–9 in.

2. MANGLIETIA, Blume; Fl. Brit. Ind. 42 (included under *Magnolia* by Prantl in Engler u. Prantl, iii. 2, p. 16).

Differs from *Magnolia* by the large number, 6 or more, of ovules in the ovary. Species 5, mountains of tropical Asia.

1. **M. insignis,** Blume; Ann. Bot. Gard. Calc. iii. t. 55.—Syn. *Magnolia insignis*, Wall. Pl. As. Rar. t. 182. Vern. *Vaung saga* Burm.

A large evergreen tree, youngest branches petioles and pedicels pubescent, otherwise glabrous. Leaves thinly coriaceous, lanceolate, 5–10 in. long; secondary nerves not much more conspicuous than the shorter intermediate ones, which are joined by prominent polygonal venation. Fl. scented, 4–5 in. across. Sepals 3, dull red, with greenish veins; petals 9, pure white or whitish yellow, tinged with pink. Fruiting spike narrowly ovoid, 3–5 in. long.

Sikkim (rare), Nepal, Assam, Khasi hills, 3,000–6,000ft., Naga hills. Ruby mines district, Upper Burma, 6,500 ft. 2. **M. Caveana,** Hook. fil. & Thoms.; Ann Bot. Gard. Calc. iii. t. 57, 57 bis. Khasi hills 2,000-3,000 ft., Makúm Forest, Assam. Leaves elliptic or elliptic-oblong, 8–10 in.

3. **MICHELIA**, Linn.; Fl. Brit. Ind. i. 42.

Trees, mostly evergreen, buds enveloped in the convolute stipules. Leaves thinly coriaceous, tertiary nerves prominently reticulate. Sepals and petals similar, 9–15, in whorls of 3. Filaments flat, anthers introrse. Ovaries separated from the stamens by a distinct internode, style generally much shorter than ovary. Fruit a lax, rarely dense spike of woody or coriaceous dorsally dehiscing carpels. Species 16, Indo-Malayan region, mostly on the mountains.

A. Leaves small, 3–6 in. long, fl. white.

1. **M. Cathcartii,** Hook. f. & Th.; Ann. Bot. Gard. Calc. iii. t. 60. Vern. *Titi Champ*, Nep.

A large evergreen tree, heartwood dark olive-brown, young branches densely silky. Leaves pale beneath, acuminate, midrib hairy on both surfaces, chiefly on the upper. Fl. terminal, 3–4 in. diam., white, turning red in drying, perianth leaves 9, inner gradually smaller. Stamens more than 1 in. long, overtopping the ovaries, which are sessile and densely imbricate.

Sikkim Himalaya 5,000–7,000 ft. Naga hills. Fl. May, June.

2. **M. nilagirica,** Zenker; Wight Ic. t. 938; Bedd. Fl. Sylv. t. 62; Ann. Bot. Gard. Calc. t. 65.—Syn. *M. pulneyensis*, Wight Ill. t. 5.

A moderate sized tree, buds silky. Leaves shortly and bluntly acuminate. Fl. 1½–2 in. across, on short generally leafless axillary branchlets. Perianth leaves usually 12, the inner narrower. Stamens shorter than gynæcium. Ovaries silky, with 2–4 ovules. Fruiting spike interrupted, 2–3 in. long, carpels warty, apiculate, mixed with many abortive carpels. Seeds bright scarlet.

Nilgiris, Palnis and other hills in the peninsula, Ceylon. Fl. H. S.

B. Leaves moderate sized or large, 4–12 in. long.

3. **M. oblonga,** Wall.; Ann. Bot. Gard. Calc. iii. t. 67. Vern. *Bor Soppa*, Ass.

A very tall tree, entirely glabrous. Leaves thinly coriaceous, 4–6 in. long. Secondary nerves 7–9 pair, somewhat prominent beneath. Fl. yellowish white, 3–4 in. across. Fruiting spike lax, 6–7 in. long. Carpels sessile, woody, lenticellate, blunt.

Assam, Silhet. Fl. C. S. Nearly allied are the following, which are all entirely glabrous: 4. **M. Mannii,** King; Ann. iii. t. 70. Assam, Silhet. Leaves rigidly coriaceous, fl. smaller, ripe carpels distant, oblong, slightly apiculate. 5. **M. punduana,** Hook. f. & Thoms.; Ann. iii. t. 66. Assam, Khasi hills. Leaves thinly coriaceous. Secondary nerves not much more conspicuous than the shorter intermediate and the reticulate tertiary nerves. Fl. 1½ in. across. Ripe carpels distant, compressed, not beaked. 6. **M. Kisopa,** DC.; Ann. iii. t. 58 B. Kumaon and Nepal 5,000–7,000 ft., rare in Sikkim. Leaves coriaceous. Fl. 1–1½ in. across. Carpels small, ¼ in. diam., compressed, shortly apiculate.

7. **M. lanuginosa,** Wall.; Ann. Bot. Gard. Calc. iii. t. 62. Vern. *Gogay Champ*, Nepal.

A large deciduous tree, branchlets and underside of full grown leaves densely pale-grey tomentose. Leaves lanceolate. Fl. axillary, yellowish white, 2½–3 in. across. Perianth leaves 12–18, oblanceolate. Ovaries densely lanate, style glabrous. Fruiting spike lax, 4–5 in. long. Carpels compressed, shortly stalked, woody, warty, ½–1 in. Seeds orange.

Eastern Himalaya, from Nepal eastwards, 5,000–7,000 ft. Khasi hills. Fl. R. S.

8. **M. excelsa,** Blume; Ann. Bot. Gard. Calc. iii. t. 63. Vern. *Bara Champ, Safed Champ*, Nepal.

A large deciduous tree, heartwood olive-brown, buds clothed with brown, dark red or ferruginous tomentum, full grown leaves nearly glabrous. Fl. axillary, white, scented, 4 in. across. Perianth leaves 12, obovate and spathulate. Fruiting spike lax, 4–8 in. long. Carpels ½ in., shortly beaked. Seeds red.

Himalaya from Nepal eastwards, 5,000–8,000 ft. Khasi and Naga hills. Fl. March.

9. **M. Champaca,** Linn.; Brandis F. Fl. t. 1.—Syn. *M. aurantiaca*, Wall.; Pl. As. Rar. t. 147. Vern. *Champ*, *Champa*, Hind.; *Sampighi*, Kan.; *Champakam*, Tel.; *Shembuga*, Tam.; *Saga*, Burm.

A large evergreen tree, heartwood light brown, young shoots silky. Leaves nearly glabrous when full grown, blade 8–10, petiole slender, ¾–1 in. Fl. yellow or orange, strongly scented, shortly pedunculate, 2 in. across. Perianth leaves 15. Fruiting spike compact, 3–6 in. long. Carpels ovoid, blunt, lenticellate. Seeds brown.

Wild on the Western Ghats in the southern portion of the peninsula (Beddome), in Sikkim (up to 3,000 ft.) and in Lower Burma (Kurz). Cultivated in the moister parts of India and Burma. Fl. H. and R. S. 10. **M. manipurensis,** Watt MSS. Khongui hill, Manipur, April, 1882, G. Watt. A remarkable species resembling *M. Champaca*. Leaves puberulous beneath, with very minute hairs, style as long as ovary, which is clothed with ferruginous hairs. Fruit unknown. 11. **M. montana,** Blume; Ann. Bot. G. Calc. iii. t. 68. Sikkim, Assam, Silhet, Java. An anomalous species with only 1 or 2 carpels, which are 1–2 in. long, 1 in. broad, woody. Leaves 3–8 in., elliptic. Secondary nerves 8–12 pair, prominent beneath.

4. TALAUMA, Juss.; Fl. Brit. Ind. i. 40.

Differs from *Magnolia* by the structure of the fruiting spike. Carpels woody, and dehiscing by the ventral suture, or spongy and indehiscent, but finally separating from the axis. Species 20, in the tropical and subtropical regions of Eastern Asia and South America.

A. Carpels woody, dehiscing by the ventral suture, leaves glabrous beneath or nearly so.

1. **T. Hodgsoni,** Hook. fil. & Thoms.: Ann. Bot. Gard. Calc. iii. tab. 47. *Balukhat*, Nepal.

A moderate sized tree, quite glabrous, except the puberulous young carpels. Leaves coriaceous, 8–20 in. long, nerves 15–25 pair, reticulate veins raised, prominent. Petiole 1½–2½ in., slender, base thickened. Fl. white, terminal, campanulate, 3 in. long, sepals and petals similar, fleshy. Fruit ovoid, 4–6 in. long, consisting of numerous imbricating woody carpels, separating from a woody deeply pitted axis.

Sikkim, ascending to 6,000 ft. Assam, Khasi hills, Cachar, *Taungmè*, Upper Burma. 2. **T. andamanica,** King; Ann. Bot. Gard. Calc. iii. t. 43. Andamans. A shrub or small tree. Leaves oblanceolate, blade 7–10 in., petiole ½–1 in.; fl. globose, 1½ in. diam. 3. **T. Rabaniana,** Hook. fil. & Thoms.; Ann. Bot. Gard. Calc. iii. t. 46. Khasi hills, Mergui (Kurz). Leaves lanceolate; blade 8–12 in.; petiole 1¼–2 in. long; fl. 2–2½ in. 4. **T. mutabilis,** Blume; Ann. Bot. G. Calc. iii. t. 44.—Syn. *T. Candollei*, Kurz; F. Fl. i. 24. Tenasserim. A shrub, fl. ovoid, 2½ in. long.

FIG. 1.—Talauma Hodgsoni. Hook. f. & Thoms. ½.

B. Carpels spongy or corky, indehiscent, confluent, separating when ripe from the central woody axis, leaves pubescent beneath.

5. **T. spongocarpa,** King, Ann. iii. tab. 47 (bis). Upper Burma. Secondary nerves 7–9 pair, prominent beneath, as well as the shorter intermediate ones. 6. **T. phellocarpa,** King, Ann. iii. t. 47 (ter). Sib-sagar district and Mikir hills, Assam. Secondary nerves 12–16 pair, not much more distinct than the reticulate veins between them.

Illicium, Linn., comprises several evergreen aromatic shrubs with coriaceous leaves, readily known by the arrangement of the one-seeded carpels in one radiating whorl. When ripe they are woody and split at the upturned ventral suture, so that the seed becomes visible. Of the Indian species *T. Griffithii*, Hook. f. & Thoms.; Ann. Bot. Gard. Calc. iii. 40A, Bhutan, Khasi hills, with 10–15 ovaries, is the most notable. *T. anisatum*, Loureiro, of China, yields the well known Star-anise.

5. SCHIZANDRA, Michaux; Fl. Brit. Ind. i. 44.

Climbing shrubs with exstipulate, glabrous, mostly membranous leaves. Fl. unisexual. Sepals and petals similar, 9 or 12, in trimerous whorls. ♂: 5–30 stamens, filaments often fleshy and confluent, anthers free or more or less immersed in the fleshy mass of confluent filaments. ♀: Ovaries numerous, densely imbricate round a conical torus, which elongates considerably when the carpels ripen. Species 6, mountains of India, China, Java and North America.

A. Filaments connate below, free above.

1. **S. grandiflora,** Hook. fil. & Thoms.; Ann. iii. t. 69A; Collett, Simla Fl. fig. 6. Vern. *Rodl*, Paternalla; *Ballon*, Jaunsar; *Singoto*, Nepal.

Leaves membranous, approximate at the ends of branchlets, 3–4 in. long, with distant minute obtuse teeth, petioles slender, ¾–1 in. long. Fl. white, fragrant, solitary, nodding, more than 1 in. across, on slender peduncles 1½ in. long. Fruit with a cylindrical fleshy axis, 6–9 in. long, bearing numerous scarlet fleshy 2-seeded carpels.

Himalaya, from the Sutlej eastwards, 6,000–10,000 ft. Fl. May, June. Extends to Western China. 2. **S. elongata,** Hook. f. & Thoms.; Ann. Bot. G. Calc. iii. t. 69 B. Himalaya, from Nepal eastwards, 5,000–8,000 ft., China, a powerful climber, leaves broader, petioles longer. Fl. yellowish, smaller, less than 1 in. across. Fruiting spike 3–4 in. long.

B. Filaments connate into a fleshy mass.

3. **S. propinqua,** Hook. f. & Thoms.; Ann. iii. t. 41A. Sub-himalayan tract, from Garhwal eastwards, ascending to 5,000 ft., China. Leaves ovate-lanceolate, petiole ⅓–½ in. Fl. yellow or orange, ¼ in. diam., on short pedicels. Fruiting spike fleshy, 6 in. long. 4. **S. axillaris,** Hook. f. & Thoms.; Ann. iii. t. 74A. Khasi hills, Shan States, Upper Burma, 4,000 ft. Differs by narrower lanceolate, thinly coriaceous leaves. Fl. small, scarlet. Fruiting spike 1–2 in. long.

Kadsura, Kaempfer, comprises several large glabrous woody climbers, the leaves without stipules, fl. unisexual, the fruit a globose head of indehiscent fleshy 1-seeded carpels. 1. **K. Roxburghiana,** Arnott; Ann. iii. t. 73A. Foot of Eastern Himalaya to 5,000 ft., Assam. Structure of wood normal, vessels large. Leaves ovate-lanceolate, inner filaments connate, fruit 1–2 in diam., carpels shortly beaked. 2. **K. Wightiana,** Arn.: Ann. iii. t. 74B. Malabar. Leaves broadly ovate, denticulate in the upper half, filaments all free, carpels truncate.

ORDER IV. ANONACEÆ. Gen. Pl. i. 20.

Trees or shrubs, erect or climbing, bark of branchlets marked by numerous longitudinal anastomosing narrow ridges. Leaves alternate, simple, entire, exstipulate. Flowers bisexual, rarely unisexual. Sepals 3, free or connate, usually valvate. Petals 6, hypogynous, biseriate, the 3 inner sometimes wanting. Stamens usually numerous, filaments short or none, the 2 anther cells adnate on the outside of the broad connective. Ovaries 1-celled, as a rule hairy and numerous, with the stamens on a convex or conical, rarely flat or concave torus. Fruit usually consisting of numerous 1- or many-seeded carpels, dry or succulent, on stalks, often long, which lengthen as the fruit ripens, rarely dehiscent or united in one fleshy fruit. Seeds large, embryo small, albumen ruminate, often separable into 2 halves marked by a longitudinal furrow on the testa.

Remarkable anatomical characters:—Spherical or lenticular cells containing resin in the parenchyma of leaves, often visible as pellucid dots. On a transverse section the timber of all species shows numerous fine transverse bars, at right angles to the medullary rays, consisting of wood parenchyma. Hairs, when present, 1-celled or few-celled, stellate in some genera.

A. Ripe carpels indehiscent, distinct, mostly stalked.
 I.—The 3 outer petals small, similar to sepals.
  Ovules 6 or more, inner petals always saccate at base . 1. SACCOPETALUM.
  Ovules 1–2, inner petals mostly thin, flat.
   Connective acute, stamens few or numerous . 2. MILIUSA.
   Connective broad, obtuse, stamens always numerous . . . . 3. PHÆANTHUS.
 II.—Petals uniform in shape and texture, fl. globose or campanulate.
  Petals imbricate in bud, ovules 6–12 . . . . 4. SAGERÆA.
  Petals valvate in bud, ovules 1–2 . . . . . 5. POPOWIA.
 III.—Petals uniform, erect or spreading, the inner wanting in 2 species of Unona. Ripe carpels numerous.
  Petals valvate in bud.
   Ovules 1–2, ripe carpels 1-seeded . . . . 6. POLYALTHIA.
   Ovules 2–8, 1-seriate, ripe carpels constricted between seeds . . . . 7. UNONA.
   Ovules many 2-seriate, connective lanceolate . CANANGIUM (p. 16).
  Petals imbricate in bud, ovules many, 2-seriate, connective obtuse . . . . 8. UVARIA.
 IV.—Petals uniform, erect or spreading, ripe carpels 1–6, few seeded . . . . 9. ALPHONSEA.
 V.—All petals, or the inner only, connivent, closing over stamens and ovaries.
  1. Inner petals dissimilar, generally smaller, conniving over stamens and ovaries, the blades cohering by their edges.
   a. Inner petals narrowed into a linear claw.
  Stamens 6–12, ovoid, anther cells contiguous . 10. OROPHEA.
  Stamens ∞, cuneate, connective broad, truncate or triangular . . . . 11. MITREPHORA.
   b. Inner petals not narrowed into a linear claw.
  Style oblong or clavate . . . . OXYMITRA (p. 19).
  Style cylindrical, generally bifid . . . . . 12. GONIOTHALAMUS.
  2. Petals nearly equal, similar in shape (the inner sometimes smaller), all or the inner only with a concave base.
  Ovaries many, petals thick, fleshy, connivent, the inner smaller . . . . 13. MELODORUM.
  Ovaries 1 or more, petals narrow linear, from a concave base . . . . XYLOPIA (p. 20).
  Ovaries 2 or more, ovules 2, petals flat from a concave base, fl. on woody, hooked peduncles . . 14. ARTABOTRYS.
  Ovary 1, ovules numerous, calyx cup-shaped, truncate, or deeply 3-cleft . . . . . CYATHOCALYX (p. 21).
B. Ripe carpels dehiscent, distinct . . . . . . ANAXAGOREA (p. 21).
C. Carpels united into a large fleshy fruit . . . . . 15. ANONA.

1. SACCOPETALUM, Bennett; Fl. Brit. Ind. i. 88.

Deciduous trees, fl. bisexual. Inner petals saccate at base, much larger than sepals and the three outer petals. Stamens indefinite, connective prolonged into a conspicuous appendage. Ovaries indefinite, ovules 6 or more. Species 5, 1 Australian, the others of Eastern Asia.

1. **S. tomentosum,** Hook. f. & Thoms.; Bedd. Fl. Sylv. t. 39; Ic. Pl. Ind. Or. t. 49; Ann. iv. t. 207.—Syn. *Uvaria tomentosa*, Roxb. Cor. Pl. t. 35. Vern. *Kari, Um, Umbi, Hūm,* Hindi, Mar.; *Omē,* South; *Gonda palaso,* Uriya; *Chilka-dūdu,* Tel.; *Hessare,* Kan.

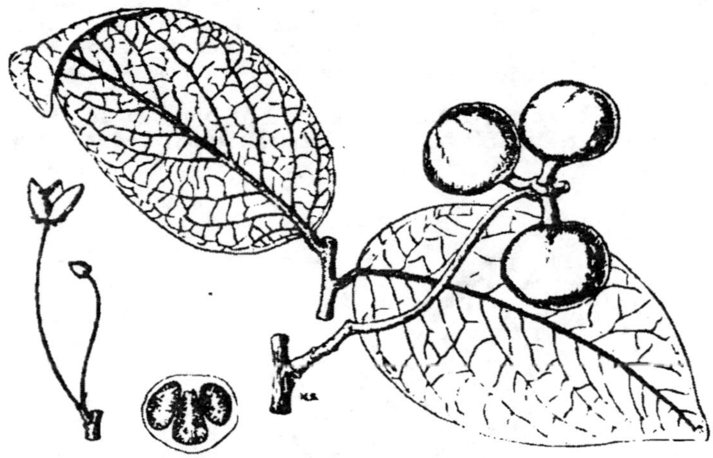

Fig. 2.—Saccopetalum tomentosum, Hook. f. & Thoms. Leaf, fr.; section of fruit, fl. ½.

A large tree, branchlets tomentose. Full grown leaves glabrous, excepting midrib, 3–6 in. long, ovate oblong. Fl. solitary or in pairs, pedicels hairy, very slender, 2–3 in. long; minute bracteoles at the base. Sepals and outer petals lanceolate, spreading; inner petals ½–¾ in. long, ovate-lanceolate. Ripe carpels tomentose, dark purple, with a pungent smell, 1 in. diam., 3–4 seeded, on stalks ⅓–½ in. long.

Oudh and Gorakhpur forests, Aravalli hills, Satpura range, Behar, Orissa, Northern Circars (not uncommon in Sāl forests), Western Ghats and throughout the Peninsula. Fl. H.S.

2. **S. longiflorum**, Hook. fil.; Ann. iv. 208, inner petals 1⅓ in. long, is cultivated in the Botan. Garden, Calcutta, said to have been brought from Chittagong. 3. **S. sclerocarpum,** Hook. f. & Thoms.; Ann. iv. t. 208 bis.—Syn. *Miliusa sclerocarpa*, Kurz F. Fl. i. 48, Martaban and Tenasserim, is imperfectly known.

2. MILIUSA, Leschenault; Fl. Brit. Ind. i. 86.

Deciduous trees, fl. usually bisexual, in one species polygamous. Sepals 3, small, petals 6 in 2 series, the outer similar to sepals, the inner thin, flat and much larger. Stamens definite or indefinite, connective more or less apiculate. Ovaries indefinite, linear-oblong, ovules 1–2. Species 24. Indo-Malayan.

1. **M. velutina,** H. f. & Thoms.; Bedd. Fl. Sylv. t. 37; Ic. Pl. Ind. Or. t. 87; Brand., Forest Fl. t. 2; Ann. Bot. Gard. Calc. iv. t. 206; Vern. *Dom sāl,* N. W. India: *Barhi, kāri, Kajrauta, Ler,* Oudh, Central Provinces; *Omē, Ombē,* Singbhūm; *Kāna Kaitha,* Mal.; *Thabut gyi,* Burm.

A middle-sized tree, branchlets, leaves and flowers densely silky tomentose. Leaves 3–9 in. long, from a rounded or slightly cordate base ovate-oblong, petioles short. Fl. on slender 2–3 in. long pedicels, in short racemes at the ends of short branchlets, generally with a few leaves at the base. Sepals and outer petals lanceolate or ovate, inner petals 3 times their length, triangular or ovate, silky tomentose outside, dark purple and glabrous inside. Ovaries pubescent, ovules 2. Ripe carpels ½ in. diam., 2-seeded, on stalks ¼–⅓ in. long, forming a round head.

Sub-himalayan tract from the Ganges eastwards, ascending to 1,500 ft., Central India, Chota Nagpore, Northern Circars, Burma. Fl. H. S. The young leaves appear in April or May.

Other species with bisexual fl. are: 2. **M. macrocarpa,** Hook. f. & Thoms.; Ann. iv,

t. 202A, a small glabrous tree of Sikkim, 2,500–6000 ft., Assam and the Khasi hills, leaves lanceolate acuminate 5–7 in., ripe carpels cylindric ⅜ in. long. 3. **M. Wightiana,** Hook. f. & Thoms.; Bedd. Ic. Pl. Ind. Or. t. 86; Ann. iv. t. 202B, a small glabrous tree of the Tinnevelli and Travancore hills, leaves 2–4 in., ripe carpels ⅓ in. long. Two glabrous shrubs: 4. **M. nilagirica,** Bedd. l.c. t. 88; Ann. iv. t. 203A, of the Nilgiris. Leaves 2–4 in. long. 5. **M. indica,** Lesch.; Bedd. l.c. t. 85; Ann. iv. t. 205. Evergreen forests from Kanara to Malabar, leaves 2 in., ripe carpels ½ in. long, purple.

6. **M. Roxburghiana,** Hook. f. & Thoms.; Ann. iv. t. 189B.

A tree, attains 50 ft., branchlets softly pubescent. Leaves lanceolate, long-

FIG. 8.—Miliusa Roxburghiana, Hook. f. & Thoms. Leaf, fl., fruit. ½.

acuminate, 3–6 in. Fl. diœcious or polygamous, sepals and 3 outer petals green, lanceolate or linear, reflexed, inner petals obtuse, fleshy, ½ in. long, dark greenish-red. Ripe carpels nearly globose, ¼ in. diam. on slender stalks. Seed 1, rarely 2.

Subhimalayan tract in Sikkim, ascending to 2,000 ft., Assam, Chittagong hills, Burma. Fl. H.S. *M. tristis*, Kurz F. Fl. i. 47, possibly a variety with larger leaves and flowers.

3. PHÆANTHUS, Hook. fil. & Thoms.; Fl. Brit. Ind. i. 72.

Trees or shrubs, often climbing, the outer petals small like the sepals, the inner large, flat, coriaceous, ovate-triangular from a broad base. Stamens numerous, anther cells distant, connective broad, obtuse, often produced beyond anthers. Ovaries numerous, style cylindric or clavate, ovules 1–2. Ripe carpels stalked, 1-seeded.

1. **P. andamanicus,** King, Ann. iv. t. 201A, Andamans. Leaves thin, elliptic-lanceolate acuminate, glabrous, 5–7 in., secondary nerves slender, nearly at right angles to midrib, not much more prominent than tertiary nerves and intra-marginal veins.

2. **P. malabaricus,** Bedd. Ic. Pl. Ind. Or. t. 86C. Ann. t. 201B. South Wainad, 2,000 ft. Outer petals twice as large as sepals, inner red, thick and fleshy, twice the size of the outer.

4. SAGERÆA, Dalz.; Gen. Pl. i. 22.

Glabrous evergreen trees or shrubs, leaves shining coriaceous, second. nerves not much more prominent than intermediate and tertiary nerves. Fl. globose, bisexual or unisexual, fasciculate on woody tubercles, often on the old wood. Sepals small, connate at base or free and slightly imbricate. Petals imbricate, concave, the 3 outer a little larger than the 3 inner. Stamens on a flat torus, 9–24, short, broad and fleshy, anthers cells contiguous or distant, on a broad truncate connective. Ovaries 3–6, style short, ovules 6–8. Ripe carpels globose or ovoid, shortly stalked. Species 6, in tropical Asia. I follow King (Ann. iv. 6) in re-establishing *Sageræa*, united with *Bocagea* in Fl. Brit. India i. 92.

A. Fl. bisexual.

1. **S. laurina**, Dalzell; Ann. iv. t. 35B.—Syn. *Bocagea Dalzellii*, Hook. f. & Thoms. Fl. Brit. Ind. i. 92. Vern. *Sageri*, *Har-kinjal*, Mar.

A middle-sized tree, leaves 4–7 in., fl. white, $\frac{1}{4}$–$\frac{1}{3}$ in. diam., pedicels short. Sepals distinct, slightly imbricate, outer petals larger, but not twice the size of inner; stamens 12–18, anther cells contiguous. Ripe carpels nearly sessile, 1 in. diam.

Evergreen forests of the Konkan (north as far as Matheran) and North Kanara. Fl. Oct., Nov. 2. **S. Dalzellii**, Bedd. Ic. t. 42. Anamallays, in dense moist woods. Travancore, evergreen forest, 2,000 ft.; leaves 10–14 in. Fl. bright yellow, $\frac{1}{2}$ in. diam., pedicels 1–1$\frac{1}{2}$ in. long, sepals connate at base, ciliate, anthers 12–24. United with *S. laurina* by King, Ann. iv. p. 8.

B. Fl. unisexual.

3. **S. Listeri**, King l.c. t. 35A, Chittagong hill tracts, branchlets slender, round, leaves 4–5 in., ripe carpels broadly ovoid. 4. **S. elliptica**, Hook. f. & Thoms.; Ann. iv. t. 34 (*Bocagea elliptica*, Fl. Brit. Ind. i. 92) Tenasserim, leaves 8–14 in., ripe carpels globose.

5. POPOWIA, Endl.; Fl. Brit. Ind. i. 68.

Evergreen shrubs or trees, generally small. Fl. small, often polygamous, solitary or a few together, sessile or shortly pedunculate, campanulate or subglobose, opening but slightly. Petals valvate in bud, outer spreading, inner thick, concave, connivent. Ovaries few, not more than 8, ovules 1–2. Ripe carpels generally on short stalks. Species 33, Asiatic, Australian, one African.

1. **P. Hookeri**, King, Ann. iv. t. 165A.—Syn. *Polyalthia argentea*, Hook. fil. & Thoms. Fl. Brit. Ind. i. 67.

A shrub, nearly glabrous, leaves 3-7 in. long, silvery beneath, ripe carpels oblong, granulate, glabrous, $\frac{3}{4}$ in. long.

Assam, Khasi and Naga hills. Fl. R. S.

2. **P. Kurzii**, King, Ann. iv. t. 163B.—Syn. *Polyalthia macrophylla*, Hook. f. & Thoms. Fl. Brit. Ind. i. 66; *P. dubia*, Kurz, F. Fl. i. 38.

A shrub or small tree, branchlets and underside of younger leaves tawny-woolly. Leaves 6–10 in., secondary nerves 10–14 p. prominent beneath, arching, joined by intramarginal veins. Fl. sessile, tomentose, campanulate, polygamous, solitary or in pairs. Fruit unknown.

Andamans, Tenasserim. Fl. R.S.

The remaining species have small leaves. 3. **P. Beddomeana**, Hook. fil. & Thoms. Fl. Br. Ind. i. 68; Ann. iv. t. 160B.—Syn. *P. ramosissima*, Bedd. Ic. Pl. Or. t. 75, hills between Tinnevelli and Travancore, branchlets tomentose, leaves 2 in. long. 4. **P. nitida**, King, Ann. iv. t. 165B. Andamans, Nicobars. Leaves thinly coriaceous, 2-4 in. long, shining, carpels ovoid, $\frac{1}{3}$ in. long, seeds 1–3. 5. **P. Helferi**, Hook. fil. & Thoms.; Ann. iv. t. 160A. Andamans, Tenasserim. Leaves membranous, long acuminate, 3–5 in. long.

6. POLYALTHIA, Blume; Fl. Brit. Ind. i. 62.

Trees or shrubs, mostly evergreen. Fl. usually bisexual, sepals 3, petals 6, longer than sepals, as a rule equal, stamens ∞, short, closely packed on a convex torus, anther cells concealed by the overlapping connective. Ovaries numerous, style globose, cylindric or clavate, ovules 1 or 2. Fr. a cluster of numerous carpels generally on long stalks. Species 50, 3 African, 2 Australian, the rest of tropical Asia.

A. Ovule 1, fl. solitary.

1. **P. suberosa,** Benth. & Hook. f.; Bedd. Ic. Pl. Or. t. 56; Ann. iv. t. 77c.—Syn. *Uvaria suberosa*, Roxb. Cor. Pl. t. 34. Vern. *Kuradia*, Uriya.

A small tree, bark corky, branchlets pubescent. Leaves distichous, elliptic-oblong, sometimes broader at apex, glabrous when full grown, 2–4 in. Fl. small, on slender extra-axillary peduncles, shorter than leaf, bracts near base small, linear. Sepals less than half the length of petals, petals oval, reddish-brown, silky outside. Ripe carpels black, ¼ in. diam. Stalks slender, longer than carpels, but not more than twice their length.

Oudh forests, Behar, Northern Circass., east side of the peninsula, Tenasserim. Fl. H.S. Ceylon, China.

2. **P. cerasoides,** Benth. & Hook. fil.; Bedd. Fl. Sylv. t. 1; Ann. iv. t. 86B. —Syn. *Uvaria cerasoides*, Roxb. Cor. Pl. t. 33. Vern. *Sandi Ome*, Kol; *Gutti*, Tel; *Thabut-thein*, Burm.

A middle-sized deciduous tree, branchlets tomentose. Leaves distichous,

Fig. 4.—Polyalthia cerasoides, Benth. & Hook. fil. Leaf, fl., fruit. ½.

membranous, oblong-lanceolate, acuminate, glabrous above, pale and more or less tomentose beneath. Fl. ⅓ in. diam., green, on tomentose pedicels, shorter than leaf, bracts 1 or 2, small or large, ovate. Sepals ovate, membranous, petals ¼ in. long, equal. Ripe carpels numerous, red, ¼ in. diam., on slender stalks twice their length or longer.

Behar, Chota Nagpore, Northern Circass., Western Ghats from Nasik southwards, throughout the peninsula. Burma, often in Eng. forests. Fl. February to May. 3. **P. coffeoides,** Benth. & Hook. f.; Bedd. Ic. Pl. Ind. Or. t. 53; Ann. iv. t. 91. Wainād and Anamalai hills. A glabrous tree. Sepals short, petals 1½ in. Carpels oblong, 1 in., narrowed into a shorter stalk. 4. **P. andamanica,** Kurz; Ann. iv. t. 90. Andamans. A shrub, branchlets tomentose, carpels oblong. 5. **P. Jenkinsii,** Benth. & Hook. f.; Ann. iv. t. 96. Assam, Silhet, Malay peninsula. A tree, fl. 2 in. diam.

B. Ovule 1, fl. fasciculate, umbellate or corymbose.

6. **P. longifolia,** Benth. & Hook. fil.; Bedd. Fl. Sylv. t. 38; Ann. iv. t. 99. —Syn. *Guatteria longifolia,* Wall.; Wight Ic. t. i. Vern. *Asok, Devidari,* Hind.; *Putrajivi,* Kan.; *Aranei,* Mal.

A tall tree, entirely glabrous. Leaves lanceolate, long-acuminate, undulate, pellucid-dotted, 5–8 in. Fl. yellowish green, on long slender pedicels, in sessile or shortly pedunculate umbels. Petals from a broad base lanceolate, long-acuminate, spreading. Sepals broad, short. Ripe carpels ovoid, ¾ in., stalk ½ in. long.

Indigenous in Ceylon, largely planted in avenues in most parts of India, as far north as Hushiarpur. Fl. February, May.

7. **P. fragrans,** Benth. & Hook. f.; Bedd. Ic. Pl. Ind. Or. t. 54; Ann. iv. t. 100A. Vern. *Nedunār,* Mal.

A large tree, branchlets minutely but densely tawny-tomentose. Leaves elliptic or ovate, shining above, dull, often puberulous beneath, 6–8 in. long. Secondary nerves 12-15 pair, prominent beneath. Fl. in tomentose shortly pedunculate corymbs, petals linear 1½ in., sepals small, orbicular Carpels ovoid, 1–1½ in. long.

Evergreen forests of the Western Ghats, from the Ratnagiri district southwards. Fl. November. 8. **P. simiarum,** Benth. & Hook. f.; Ann. iv. t. 101. Assam, Chittagong, Burma, and the Andamans, Siam, Cochin China. A large tree. Leaves 5–11 in. secondary nerves 12–16 pair, prominent. Fl. in sessile fascicles, petals linear, spreading. 1½ in. long. Carpels 1½ in. long, orange to bluish black when riper.

C. Ovules 2 or 3, superposed. Fl. solitary.

9. **P. Korinti,** Benth. & Hook. fil.; Ann. iv. t. 110A.—Syn. *Guatteria Korinti,* Dunal; Wight. Ic. t. 398.

A spreading shrub, branchlets pubescent. Leaves nearly glabrous, elliptic, narrowed to both ends, 3–6 in. Secondary nerves not much more prominent than the reticulate veins. Fl. bright green, ½–¾ in. diam., on slender pedicels, petals spreading. Carpels numerous, ovoid, ⅓ in. long, red when ripe, stalks short.

Western Peninsula, Ceylon. Fl. September. 10. **P. obliqua,** Hook. f. & Thoms.: Ann. iv. t. 100B. Chittagong hills, Malacca, Sumatra. A tree or shrub. Leaves from an oblique base, oblong-lanceolate. Secondary nerves 6–8 pair, arching, joined by intramarginal veins at a distance from margin.

7. UNONA, Linn.; Fl. Brit. Ind. i. 58.

Trees or shrubs, erect or climbing. Petals long, the 3 inner often a little smaller, wanting in two species. Stamens crowded cuneate, anther cells linear, extrorse, concealed by the subglobose or truncate, rarely conical, apex of connective. Ovaries numerous, ovules 2–8, 1-serrate on the ventral suture. Ripe carpels elongate, generally much constricted between seeds. Species 50, tropical Asia and Africa.

A. Petals 6, in 2 rows.

1. **U. Desmos,** Dunal; Ann. iv. t. 73.

A spreading evergreen shrub, often climbing, branchlets rufous-pubescent. Leaves thinly coriaceous, glabrous above, sparingly pubescent beneath. Secondary nerves 8–12 pair, slender but prominent. Fl. solitary, nodding, on slender extra-axillary peduncles, 2–6 in. long. Petals coriaceous, ovate-lanceolate, 1–2 in. long. Ripe carpels numerous, stalked, glabrous, constricted between the 2 or 3 ovoid joints, ½–¾ in. long.

Assam, Chittagong, Lower Burma, Malay Peninsula. Fl. June.

2. **U. discolor,** Vahl; Bedd. Ic.Pl. Ind. Or. t. 51.; Ann. iv. t. 74.—Syn. *U. undulata*, Wall. Pl. As. Rar. t. 265.

An evergreen, often climbing shrub, youngest shoots pubescent. Leaves membranous, oblong-lanceolate, 3–7 in. Fl. solitary, on slender extra-axillary often leaf-opposed peduncles, 1–2 in. long. Petals greenish-yellow, narrowly lanceolate, 1–3 in. long. Ripe carpels numerous, purple, stalked, ¾ to 1½ in. long, joints 2–5, the constrictions between the joints often slender and pubescent.

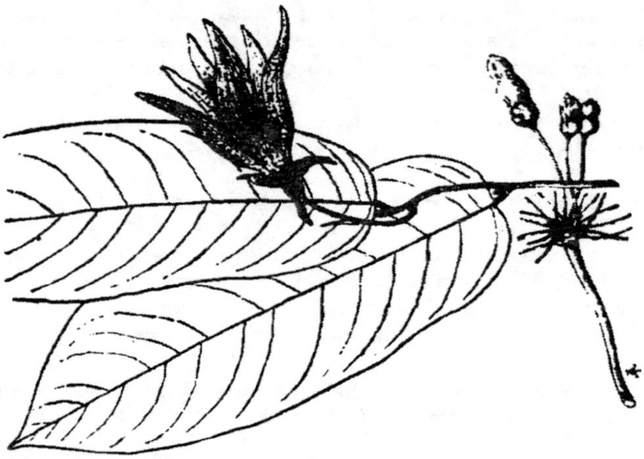

FIG. 5.—Unona discolor, Vahl. Leaf, fl., fr. ½.

Base of eastern Himalaya, Assam, Chittagong, Upper and Lower Burma, Western Peninsula. Fl. May–July. 3. **U. pannosa,** Dalz.; Bedd. Ic. Pl. Ind. Or. t. 52; Ann. iv. t. 72. A small tree of the Western Ghats from the Konkan southwards. Leaves membranous, 2–8 in. Fl. straw-coloured, petals 1½ in., densely clothed with brown silky hairs. Carpels sessile, ovoid, 1–3 seeded. 4. **U. viridiflora,** Bedd. Ic. Pl. Ind. Or. t. 158; Ann. iv. t. 75. A gigantic climber. Travancore Ghats. Leaves ovate-lanceolate, acuminate. Petals lanceolate, silky, 1–2½ in. long. 5. **U. dumosa,** Roxb.; Ann. iv. t. 76. Silhet, Assam, Malay Peninsula. Branchlets and underside of leaves softly tomentose. 6. **U. Lawii,** Hook. fil. & Thoms.; Bedd. l.c. t. 73; Ann. iv. 77A. An erect or climbing shrub on the Western Ghats from the Konkan southwards. Leaves 2–4 in., petals linear, 1–2 in., carpels of 1–2 ovoid joints. 7. **U. latifolia,** Hook. fil. & Thoms.; Ann. iv. t. 78. (*U. Brandisana*, Pierre Fl. For. Coch. t. 19). A large deciduous tree on the Salween river south of the Karenni country. Cochinchina, Malay Peninsula. Branchlets and underside of leaves grey-tomentose. Leaves ovate or orbicular. Fl. scented, petals veined, 2 in. long.

B. Petals 3, sometimes 2 only, those of the inner row wanting.

8. **U. Dasymaschala,** Blume; Ann. t. iv. 81.

An evergreen scrambling shrub, shoots softly pubescent. Leaves thinly coriaceous, oblong-lanceolate, 4½–8½ in. long. Fl. solitary, nodding, 1½–3 in. long, on peduncles 1¼–1¾ in. Petals fleshy, lanceolate, 3 in. long. Ripe carpels numerous, on short stalks, joints 3–7, oblong.

Lower Burma, Andamans. Fl. June. Malay Peninsula and Sumatra. 9. **U. longiflora,** Roxb.; Ann. iv. t. 80. Glabrous evergreen shrub of Assam, the Khasi hills and Chittagong, also Perak. Fl. crimson, petals 5 in. long.

Canangium odoratum, Baillon; Ann. iv. t. 67.—Syn. *Cananga odorata*, Hook. f. & Thoms.; Fl. Brit. Ind. i. 56. Vern. *Kadatnyan*, Burm., is an evergreen tree, 30–60 ft. Leaves 4–8 in., often oblique. Fl. pale yellow, fragrant, drooping, on long pedicels in 2–6 fld., shortly pedunculate racemes. Petals 6, lanceolate, equal, 3 in. long, connective produced beyond anthers into a short lanceolate process. Ripe carpels 10–12, stalked, ¾ in. long, nearly black when ripe, with 6–12 flat seeds. Indigenous in Martaban and Tenasserim, the Malay Peninsula and Archipelago; elsewhere cultivated.

7. UVARIA, Linn.; Fl. Brit. Ind. i. 47.

Climbing or scrambling shrubs, generally with stellate pubescence. Fl. yellow, purple or brown, usually large and showy. Sepals, 3 often connate at base. Petals 6, imbricate, nearly equal, spreading. Stamens indefinite, connective ovoid or truncate, obtuse, anther cells lateral. Ovaries numerous, ovules as a rule many, in two rows on the ventral suture. Torus (apex of pedicel) generally much enlarged in fruit. About 110 species, a few African, Australian, the rest in tropical and subtropical Asia.

A. Full grown leaves densely tomentose beneath.

1. **U. macrophylla,** Roxb.; Wall. Pl. As. Rar. t. 122; Bedd. Ic. Pl. Ind. Or. t. 81; Ann. 4. t. 10. Vern. *Thabwot-nwe*, Burm.

A large climber, branchlets and petioles rusty tomentose. Leaves coriaceous, elliptic-oblong, sometimes broader towards the apex, base rounded or slightly cordate, upper surface glabrous, except the tomentose midrib and nerves, lower lax rusty-tomentose, 5–12 in. long. Secondary nerves 10–15 pair, prominent as well as tertiary nerves and intramarginal veins. Fl. 1½ in. across, dark purple, in short axillary racemes, sometimes solitary, sepals rusty-tomentose. Ripe carpels glabrous, oblong, blunt at the ends, 1–1½ in., stalks ½–1 in. long, on the woody enlarged torus. Seeds numerous.

Silhet, Chittagong, Burma. Fl. H.S. Also Malay Peninsula, Ceylon, Java.

2. **U. purpurea,** Blume; Ann. Bot. G. Calc. iv. t. 12.—Syn. *U. grandiflora*, Roxb.; Wall. Pl. As. Rar. t. 121 (*Thabwot*, Burm.). Burma and Malay Archipelago, South China. Fl. solitary, crimson or dark purple, 2–3 in. diam., on a thick pedicel ½–2 in. long, with 2 or 3 large ovate or rounded bracts. Ripe carpels cylindric, tomentose, 1½–2½ in. long, pulp sweet, edible. 3. **U. Hamiltoni,** Hook. fil. & Thoms.; Ann. iv. t. 6. Subhimalayan tract from Sikkim eastwards, Assam, Khasi hills, Chota Nagpore (in ravines), Eastern Bengal, Upper Burma, Andamans. A powerful climber with brick red fl., solitary or fasciculate, 1½–2½ in. across, pedicels 1 in. long, with a tomentose rounded bract. Ripe carpels ovoid, 1½ in. long, scarlet. 4. **U. hirsuta,** Jack; Ann. iv. t. 14. Burma and Malay Archipelago. Branchlets, buds, and ripe carpels densely clothed with long hairs and dark rusty wool. Ripe carpels cylindric, 1½–2 in. long. 5. **U. ferruginea,** Ham.; Ann. iv. t. 15.—Syn. *Ellipeia ferruginea*, Hook. fil. Fl. Brit. Ind. i. 52. Eng forests of the Irrawaddi valley and Tenasserim. A low deciduous shrub, fl. 1 in. diam., ripe carpels almost sessile, ½ in. long, red, glabrous.

B. Full grown leaves entirely glabrous or pubescent along nerves only.

6. **U. Narum,** Wall.; Ann. iv. t. 21; Talbot List 3. Vern. *Naram panal*, Mar.

A large climber, all parts except inflorescence glabrous. Leaves pale brown beneath, oblong-lanceolate, 6–9 in. long. Secondary nerves slender, not prominent. Fl. 1–1½ in. diam., yellow, solitary, on slender peduncles 1¾–2 in. long. Petals connate at base, sometimes more than 6. Fruiting carpels numerous, glabrous, scarlet, cylindric or ovoid. Stalks 1½–2 in. long.

Evergreen forests of the Western Ghats from the Konkan southwards. Fl. C. S. Ceylon. King, Ann. iv. p. 28 tab. 22; and Cooke, Fl. Bombay i. 9, separate from this *U. Hookeri* (*U. Narum*, Wight Ill. t. 6) with ovoid carpels, tapering to both ends, on thick stalks, and larger fl.

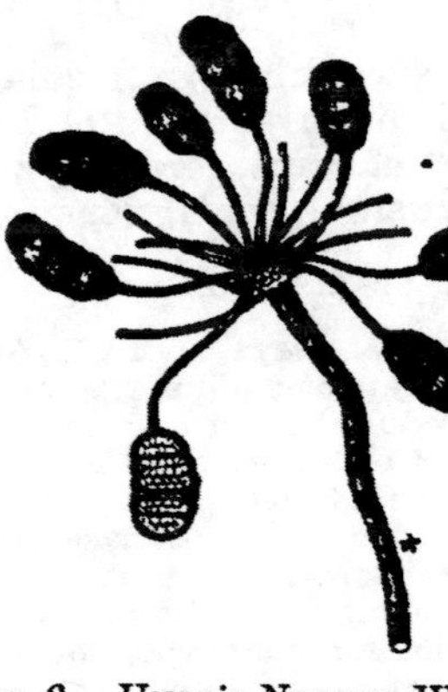

FIG. 6.—Uvaria Narum, Wall. Fr. and section. ½.

The other species of this section may be classified as follows:—

a. *Leaves perfectly glabrous, small*, 2–5 *in.*

7. **U. micrantha,** Hook. f. & Thoms.; Ann. iv. t. 18. Lower Burma, Andamans, Malay Peninsula and Archipelago. Fl. ½ in. diam., ripe carpels stalked, ovoid, ½ in. 2–4 seeded. Leaves resemble *Popowia nitida*, King.
8. **U. zeylanica,** Linn.; Ann. iv. t. 19. Malabar and Travancore, Ceylon. Fl. ¾ in. diam., carpels nearly sessile, ovoid, ½ in. long.

b. *Leaves perfectly glabrous*, 4–8 *in. long.*

9. **U. lurida,** Hook. f. & Thoms.; Ann. iv. t. 23. Sikkim, Khasi hills, Russelkonda

hills, Ganjam district. Leaves coriaceous, secondary nerves 10–12 pair, slender but prominent beneath, numerous shorter intermediate nerves. Fl. on short pedicels, ripe carpels 1–1⅓ in. long, torulose, stalks 4–6 in.

c. *Leaves hairy along nerves beneath, 4–8 in. long; branchlets hairy.*

10. **U. ptychocalyx,** Miq.; Ann. iv. t. 28. Lower Burma, Sumatra, Borneo. Leaves broad, shortly acuminate. Secondary nerves prominent beneath, 14–18 pair, pubescent as well as midrib on the upper side. Carpels globose, ½ in. diam., tubercled and hairy, stalk 1 in. long. 11. **U. bracteata**, Roxb.; Ann. iv. t. 7. Silhet, Tenasserim. Calyx pubescent, ripe carpels ovoid or cylindric, 2 in. long.

9. ALPHONSEA, H. f. & Th.; Fl. B. Ind. i. 88.

Evergreen trees or shrubs. Leaves generally glabrous, secondary nerves as a rule not more prominent than the reticulate veins between them. Fl. buds generally conical, sepals 3, small, petals 6, erect or spreading, often saccate at base, larger than sepals. Torus cylindric or hemispheric. Stamens ∞. Ovaries 1–12, ovules 4–10 in 2 rows. Ripe carpels 1–6, few seeded. Species 13, of tropical and sub-tropical Asia.

1. **A. lutea,** Hook. f. & Thoms.; Bedd. Ic. Pl. Or. t. 91; Ann. iv. t. 209.—Syn. *Uvaria lutea*, Roxb. Cor. Pl. t. 36. Vern. *Nwa-la-byut*, Upper Burma.

A large tree, shoots minutely rufous-strigose. Leaves glabrous above, strigose along nerves beneath, 3–6 in. long. Fl. ½ in. diam., fasciculate, on short woody bracteolate peduncles. Pedicels 1 in., with 2 small bracteoles in the middle. Ripe carpels 4–6, broadly ovoid, pointed, 1¼–1½ in. long, on short thick stalks. Seeds 3–6.

Silhet, Orissa, Burma, Ceylon. Fl. H.S.

2. **A. ventricosa,** Hook. f. & Thoms.; Ann. iv. t. 210. Assam, Chittagong, Andamans. A tall tree. Leaves rigidly coriaceous, shining, 6–9 in., secondary nerves slender, 12–18 pair. Fl. clustered in short racemes. Ripe carpels 4–6, 1½ in. long. 3. **A. madraspatana,** Bedd. Ic. Pl. Or. t. 92, Fl. Sylv. t. 76; Ann. iv. t. 214A. Common along streams in the Cuddapah and North Arcot hills. A shady tree, glabrous except fl. and fruit. Leaves elliptic or elliptic-lanceolate 3–4 in. long, obtuse at the apex. Fl. bright yellow, ovaries 3–4. 4. **A. zeylanica,** Hook. f. & Thoms.; Bedd. Ic. Pl. Ind. Or. t. 90; Ann. iv. t. 214B. Travancore and Tinnevelli hills. Ceylon. A tree, young shoots pubescent, otherwise glabrous. Leaves lanceolate acuminate, 2–4 in.

10. OROPHEA, Blume; Fl. Brit. Ind. i. 90.

Trees or shrubs, fl. small, sometimes unisexual, axillary. Sepals 3, valvate, petals 6, valvate, outer ovate, inner clawed, generally longer and cohering by their margins, forming a mitriform cap. Stamens 6–12, ovoid, fleshy; anther cells dorsal, contiguous. Ovaries 3–15, ovules 4. Species 25, Eastern Asia.

A. Stamens 6.

1. **O. polycarpa,** A. DC.; Ann. iv. p. 101, t. 151A. Andamans, Martaban, Tenasserim. Leaves elliptic-oblong, acuminate, 3–4 in. long. Fl. several on slender flexuose branching peduncles with bracts at the bends. Inner petals spreading, oblong, narrowed into a short claw. Carpels globose, ⅓ in. diam. This species is anomalous: all the following have the inner petals cohering by their tips or margins. 2. **O. hexandra,** Blume; Ann. iv. t. 147B. Tenasserim, Andamans. Leaves 4–6 in. Carpels oblong, 1½ in., seed generally solitary, narrowly cylindric. 3. **O. Brandisii,** Hook. f. & Th.; Ann. iv. t. 147A. Martaban, Tenasserim. A small tree. Leaves 6–10 in., peduncles 1–2 fld., inner petals ⅗ in. long, blade trapeziform, shorter than claw. Ripe carpels sessile, oblong, 1 in. long. 4. **O. zeylanica,** Hook. fil. & Thoms.; Ann. iv. 146B. North Kanara, Ceylon. Leaves 2–4 in., carpels globose, ⅓ in. diam.

B. Stamens 12.

5. **O. uniflora,** Hook. fil. & Thoms.; Bedd. Ic. Pl. Ind. Or. t. 69; Ann. iv. t. 144A. Western Ghats, from Coorg to Travancore. A middle-sized tree, wood hard, very tough. Leaves 2–4 in., fl. solitary, drooping, cream coloured. Ripe carpels globose, ⅓ in. diam. 6. **O. Thomsoni,** Bedd. l.c. t. 67; Ann. iv. t. 144B. Leaves 2–3 in., peduncles short,

2–3 fld. Carpels globose. 7. **O. erythrocarpa,** Bedd. l.c. t. 68; Ann. iv. t. 145A. Anamallay hills. Leaves 3–4 in., peduncles 3–4 fld., tomentose, fl. ½ in. diam. Ripe carpels red, oblong, 1 in. long.

11. MITREPHORA, Blume; Fl. Brit. Ind. i. 76.

Evergreen trees, fl. sometimes unisexual, petals 6, the 3 outer spreading, veined, the 3 inner narrowed into a flat claw, blades concave, cohering at the edges and vaulted over the stamens. Stamens ∞, cuneate, connective broad, truncate or triangular. Ovaries numerous, ovules 24 or more, biseriate. Species 10, tropical Asia.

1. **M. Maingayi,** Hook. f. & Thoms.; Ann. iv. t. 154.—Syn. *M. vandæflora*, Kurz, F. Fl. i. 45. Vern. *Thabut-net*, Upper Burma.

A large tree, branchlets softly rusty-tomentose. Leaves elliptic or ovate, 3–7 in. long, secondary nerves 6–12 pair, prominent beneath. Fl. showy, on slender pedicels, generally 2–5 on short leafless woody branchlets, closely set with the scars of tomentose bracts. Sepals densely silky outside, as long as broad. Petals yellow, mottled with red, the outer undulate 1½ × ¾ in., the inner on linear claws, blades cohering by their hairy edges. Ripe carpels 1 in. long, broadly ovoid, densely tomentose, seeds 4, stalks stout, ¾ in.

Burma. Fl. February–April. Malay Peninsula, Java.

2. **M. grandiflora,** Bedd. Ic. Pl. Ind. Or. t. 101; Fl. Sylv. t. 75; Ann. iv. t. 155. South Kanara Ghats at 2,000 ft. Branchlets minutely pubescent, fl. 2–3 in. diam., turning from pure white to yellow. Ripe carpels sessile, ovoid, ¾–1 in., seed 1. 3. **M. tomentosa,** Hook. fil. & Thoms.; Ann. iv. t. 153. Assam, Chittagong, Pegu. Branchlets and underside of leaves softly tomentose. Leaves 6–9 in., secondary nerves prominent, 10–15 pair. 4. **M. Heyneana,** Thw.; Bedd. Ic. Pl. Ind. Or. t. 77; Ann. iv. t. 152B. Palni and Tinnevelli hills. Ceylon. Leaves glabrous, ovate-lanceolate, 2–4 in. 5. **M. reticulata,** Hook. f. & Thoms.; Ann. iv. 156A. Tenasserim, Malay Peninsula. Leaves glabrous, excepting midrib, 5–7 in. Secondary nerves 12–15 pair, prominent beneath. Ripe carpels ovoid, ¾ in. long. 6. **M. Prainii,** King; Ann. iv. 158. Andamans. Shoots grey-pubescent. Leaves 6–9 in., glabrous excepting midrib, secondary nerves prominent, 12–15 pair.

Oxymitra, Blume. Shrubs, erect or climbing. Petals 6, the 3 outer large, the inner much smaller, not clawed, conniving over stamens and ovaries. Stamens numerous. Style oblong or clavate, recurved, ovules 1–2. Ripe carpels 1 seeded, stalks short. 1. **O. fornicata,** Hook. fil. & Thoms.; Ann. iv. t. 156B. Silhet, Assam, Chittagong hills, Tenasserim, Andamans. Scandent, leaves membranous, glaucous beneath, tertiary nerves parallel, prominent. Fl. rusty-pubescent, sepals membranous, ovate-lanceolate, ⅜ in. long. Outer petals thin, yellow, 2 in. long. Ripe carpels cylindric, subsessile. 2. **O. Maclellandii,** Hook. f. & Thoms.; Ann. iv. t. 169. Martaban, Tenasserim. Erect, leaves thinly coriaceous, 7–10 in., purplish brown beneath, secondary nerves 12–18 pair, prominent beneath; tertiary nerves parallel. Sepals short, petals coriaceous, the outer 1½ in. long.

12. GONIOTHALAMUS, Blume; Fl. Brit. Ind. i. 72.

Shrubs or small trees. Secondary nerves joined by more or less distinct intramarginal loops. Distichous scaly bracts on peduncles. Petals 6, inner smaller, clavate, cohering, so as to form a vaulted cap over stamens and ovaries. Stamens numerous, connective produced beyond anther cells into a variously shaped process. Ovaries many, style cylindric or subulate, simple or 2 fid. Ripe carpels 1 seeded, often supported by the persistent bracts or sepals. Species 47, eastern tropical Asia.

1. **G. cardiopetalus,** Hook. fil. & Thoms.; Ann. iv. p. 93, t. 129; Bedd. Ic. Pl. Ind. Or. t. 62.

A shrub or small tree, branchlets minutely pubescent. Leaves thinly coriaceous, entirely glabrous, 6–9 in. long, margin undulate. Fl. ¾ in. diam. on short peduncles. Style cylindric, stigma 2-cleft. Ripe carpels oblong, sessile, ¾ in. long.

Evergreen forests of the Western Ghats, from North Kanara to Malabar. Fl. March.

2. **G. sesquipedalis,** Hook. fil. & Thoms.; Ann. iv. t. 139.—Syn. *Guatteria sesquipedalis,* Wall. Ic. Pl. As. Rar. t. 266.

A glabrous shrub. Leaves rigidly coriaceous, oblong-lanceolate, 6–14 in., both surfaces shining, the lower paler, secondary nerves 12–18 pair, prominent beneath, as well as the intramarginal loops. Fl. greenish-yellow, sweet-scented, axillary or supra-axillary, solitary or in pairs, on short stout pedicels. Ripe carpels few, nearly sessile, ovoid, apiculate, ¾–1 in. long, orange red when ripe, supported by the persistent veined broadly ovate sepals.

Foot of Sikkim Himalaya, ascending to 5,000 ft., Assam, Burma. 3. **G. Wightii,** Hook. fil. & Thoms.; Bedd. Ic. Pl. Ind. Or. t. 63; Ann. t. 122B, hills between Tinnevelli and Travancore, a small tree, outer petals ⅓–½ in., leaves lanceolate, 3–4 in. 4. **G. wynadensis,** Bedd. l.c. t. 61; Ann. iv. t. 128A, Wainad, a large shrub. Leaves 8–11 in., secondary nerves prominent beneath. 5. **G. Simonsii,** Hook. fil. & Thoms.; Ann. iv. t. 137, Khasi hills, branchlets and underside of leaves along nerves brown tomentose. Leaves 9–14 in., secondary nerves 14–18, prominent beneath. 6. **G. Griffithii,** Hook. fil. & Thoms.; Ann. iv. t. 136, Tenasserim. Sepals broadly ovate, outer petals lanceolate acuminate 2 in. long.

13. MELODORUM, Dunal; Fl. Brit. Ind. i. 78.

Shrubs, mostly climbing. Leaves large, elliptic- or lanceolate-oblong, secondary nerves numerous, prominent. Fl. buds pyramidal or conical. Sepals 3 small, connate at base, petals thick, fleshy, connivent, the 3 inner generally smaller, triquetrous above, hollowed below on the inner face. Ovaries many, style cylindric, generally short, ovules 2 or more. Species 35, tropical Asia.

A. Leaves rusty tomentose or pubescent beneath.

1. **M. rubiginosum,** Hook. fil. & Thoms.; Ann. iv. t. 183.

Branchlets rusty tomentose. Leaves 3–9 in., carpels velvety, ovoid obtuse, 1 in. long, stalk tomentose, as long as carpels.

Assam, Chittagong, Martaban, Tenasserim. Fl. C. S. 2. **M. bicolor,** Hook. fil. & Thoms.; Ann. iv. t. 175B, Sikkim, Assam, Burma. Leaves roughly tomentose beneath, 3–7 in. Fl. woolly outside, carpels globose 1 in. diam., stalks short. 3. **M. verrucosum,** Hook. fil. & Thoms.; Ann. iv. t. 177A, Khasi hills, Yunan. Leaves lanceolate, 2–5 in. Carpels globose, densely tuberculate, 1½–2 in. diam., narrowed into a stalk 4–8 in.

B. Leaves glabrous beneath.

4. **M. Wallichii,** Hook. fil. & Thoms.; Ann. iv. t. 175A, Assam, Khasi hills. Leaves oblong-lanceolate, 3–8 in. long, secondary nerves 10–12 pair, carpels ovoid ½ in. diam., stalks 1⅓ in. 5. **M. polyanthum,** Hook. fil. & Thoms.; Ann. iv. t. 172A, Assam, Khasi hills, Chittagong hill tract. Leaves lanceolate, 5–8 in. Fl. small in bracteate sessile or shortly pedunculate umbels. 6. **M. macranthum,** Kurz; Ann. iv. t. 186, Andamans, a tree, leaves elliptic-oblong, 6–8 in., secondary nerves slender, outer petals 3–5 in., ripe carpels oblong, 1¼–1½ in., does not perhaps belong to this genus.

Xylopia parvifolia, Hook. fil. & Thoms.; Bedd. Ic. Pl. Ind. Or. t. 43, Fl. Sylv. t. 172; Ann. iv. t. 190A (*Sánthu,* Mal.) is a lofty tree with huge buttresses, in the evergreen forests of Travancore, also in Ceylon. Leaves coriaceous, 2½–3½ in. long, secondary nerves indistinct, reticulate veins visible on both sides. Fl. buds linear, fl. ⅜ in. long, yellow, in axillary few fld. subsessile fascicles. Petals nearly equal, from a broad base narrow-linear, silky pubescent outside, the 3 inner with a concave base. Ovaries 5, oblong, pubescent, style as long as ovary, glabrous, stigma longer than style, hairy. Ripe carpels blunt, tapering to the base, pubescent, 1–1½ in. long. The representative in India of a large genus (60–70 species) in the tropics of both hemispheres.

14. ARTABOTRYS, R. Brown; Fl. Brit. Ind. i. 53.

Evergreen, scrambling or climbing shrubs. Peduncles extra-axillary, hooked, recurved, generally thick and woody, often grappling supports, bearing single fl. or fascicles of fl. Petals 6, nearly equal; base of all concave, closing over stamens and ovaries, limb spreading. Ovaries few or numerous, ovules 2, erect, collateral. Species 32, tropical Africa and Eastern Asia.

A. Petals lanceolate or elliptic.

1. **A. zeylanicus,** Hook. fil. & Thoms.; Bedd. Ic. Pl. Ind. Or. t. 48: Ann. iv. p. 43 t. 53.

An enormous climber. Leaves coriaceous, quite glabrous, shining, 3–6 in. long. Peduncles flat, bearing 1–4 fl. Petals coriaceous, brownish, lanceolate, densely tomentose, the outer 1¼ in. long, the inner a little smaller. Ripe carpels sessile, ribbed, mucronate.

Evergreen forests of the Western Ghats, from Kanara southwards. Fl. November. Ceylon.

FIG. 7.—Artabotrys zeylanicus, Hook. fil. & Thoms. Leaf, fl., fr.

2. **A. odoratissimus,** R. Brown; Ann. iv. t. 55.

A large scrambling glabrous shrub. Leaves thinly coriaceous, oblong-lanceolate, 4–6 in. long. Fl. solitary or in pairs, greenish yellow, exceedingly fragrant, petals acute, minutely sericeous, 1¼–1½ in. long. Ovaries glabrous. Ripe carpels 8–15, pyriform, apiculate, narrowed into a short stalk, 1¼–1½ in. long, yellow.

Indigenous in Tenasserim (Kurz, F. Fl. i. 31) and Ceylon, cultivated throughout India. Fl. H. and R. S. 3. **A. Kurzii,** Hook. fil. & Thoms.: Ann. iv. t. 47, a straggling or climbing deciduous shrub in the Eng forests of the Irawaddi valley (*Nyané*, Upper Burma) Branchlets, petioles, and nerves on the underside of leaves pubescent, petals velvety obtuse ¾ in. 4. **A. crassifolius,** Hook. fil. & Thoms.; Ann. iv. t. 51; Kurz, F. Fl. i. 30, an evergreen woody climber in Tenasserim.

B. Petals fleshy, cylindric clavate or triquetrous.

5. **A. suaveolens,** Blume; Kurz, F. Fl. i. 32; Ann. iv. t. 61.

A large climber. Leaves shining, acuminate, 2–4 in. long. Fl. fasciculate, on recurved flat woody peduncles, which sometimes lengthen out to 5 inches. Petals fleshy, tomentose, ⅓–½ in., blade cylindric to clavate. Ripe carpels few, ellipsoid, glabrous, ½ in. long.

Silhet, Chittagong, Burma, Malay Peninsula. Fl. R. S. 6. **A. burmanicus,** A. D. C.; Ann. iv. t. 62, Manipur, Burma. Leaves 4–7 in., rusty pubescent beneath, secondary nerves 8–10 pair, prominent, joined by distinct intramarginal veins, petals narrow-linear 1 in. long. 7. **A. speciosus,** Kurz; Ann. iv. t. 57, Andamans, with yellow fl. 1½ in. long.

Cyathocalyx zeylanicus, Champion; Bedd. Ic. Pl. Ind. Or. t. 47; Ann. iv. t. 42, is a tree common in the evergreen forests of the Western Ghats, from South Kanara southwards, glabrous, calyx an obscurely 3-toothed truncate cup. Petals 6, nearly equal, base concave, closing over stamens and ovaries. Ovary solitary, glabrous, with numerous ovules. Ripe carpel irregularly ovoid, 1½–3 in. long, subsessile. 2. **C. martabanicus,** Hook. fil. & Thoms.; Ann. iv. t. 43, a middle-sized tree of Martaban and Tenasserim, similar, but with a deeply 3-cleft calyx.

Anaxagorea luzoniensis, A. Gray; Ann. t. 118A.—Syn. *A. zeylanica*, Hook. fil. & Thoms.; Bedd. Ic. Pl. Ind. Or. t. 46, Burma, Andamans, Ceylon, Malay Peninsula and Archipelago, is a small evergreen shrub, entirely glabrous. Leaves membranous, with pellucid dots. Fl. white, ½ in. diam., solitary on short pedicels, ovaries few, glabrous. Ripe carpels clavate, narrowed into a thick stalk, 1–2 seeded, dehiscing, 2 valved.

15. ANONA, Linn.; Fl. Brit. Ind. i. 78.

Trees or shrubs with bisexual fl. Sepals small, petals 6 or 3. Stamens indefinite, crowded round a hemispherical torus, connective overlapping the anthers. Carpels united into a large fleshy fruit, seeds numerous, embedded in a soft pulp.

A. squamosa, Linn. *Custard apple.* Vern. *Sitaphal, Saripha,* Hind. Wholly glabrous, leaves oblong-lanceolate, 2–3 in. long, pellucid dotted, with a peculiar smell. Fl. greenish, single or in pairs, on pedicels as long as flower. Exterior petals lanceolate, triquetrous, thick and fleshy, 1 in. long, 3 interior minute or wanting. Fruit 2–4 in. diam., seeds oblong, brownish black.

Indigenous in the West Indies, completely domesticated over a great part of India, cultivated as far north as Gurdaspur in the Punjab. Fl. H. S.

Other species cultivated in India: 2. **A. muricata**, Linn.; *Sour-sop.* 3. **A. reticulata**, Linn.; *Bullock's heart.* Vern. *Ramphal.*

ORDER V. MENISPERMACEÆ. Gen. Pl. i. 30.

Climbing or twining, rarely erect shrubs. Leaves alternate, usually palminerved, often peltate, stipules 0. Fl. small, diœcious or polygamous. Sepals usually 6, the outer 3 often minute. Petals usually 6, sometimes wanting. ♂: Stamens commonly 6, free, opposite to petals, or anthers on a staminal column. ♀: Carpels distinct, 3, sometimes more, or 1 only, ovule 1 (2 in *Fibraurea*). Fruit generally drupaceous, the seed enclosed in a woody or coriaceous endocarp, usually curved or horseshoe shaped, scar of style often near the base of carpel.

Remarkable anatomical characters.—The wood of all species has broad medullary rays, alternating with broad wedges of wood, and as a rule very large vessels. Many species have concentric bands of bast (phloëm) in the wood. This is the case in *Cissampelos Pareira, Cyclea Burmanni, Cocculus macrocarpus, villosus* and *Leæba*, and also in *Cocculus laurifolius*, one of the few trees in this order. These bands of bast in the wood have been called concentric, frequently however they are partial, alternating masses of wood and bast occupying portions only of the circumference.

The following species, and probably many others besides, have no bands of bast in the wood: *Lophophyllum bicristatum, Tinospora cordifolia, Coscinium fenestratum* and *Hæmatocarpus Thomsoni.*

A. Ovary 1, style scar basal, leaves generally peltate.
- Sepals 6–10, free, petals 3–5, free . . . . . 1. STEPHANIA.
- Sepals 4, free, petals of male 4, connate . . . . CISSAMPELOS (p. 23).
- Sepals 4–8, connate, petals of male 4–8 connate . . 2. CYCLEA.
- Sepals 4–8, connate, petals of male 0, leaves cordate. LOPHOPHYLLUM (p. 24).

B. Ovaries 3, style scar terminal.
- Filaments distinct . . . . 3. TINOSPORA.
- Anthers on a staminal column, sepals 12 . . . . 4. ASPIDOCARYA.
- Anthers on a staminal column, sepals 6 . . . . PARABÆNA (p. 24).

C. Ovaries 3, sometimes more, style scar basal or ventral, filaments distinct, leaves generally not peltate.
- Seed albuminous, globose . . . . 5. ANAMIRTA.
- Seed albuminous, horseshoe shaped, sepals 6.
  - Petals 3, ovaries 3–6 . . . . COSCINIUM (p. 25).
  - Petals 6, ovaries 3–12 . . . . 6. TILIACORA.
  - Petals 6, ovaries 3–6, style subulate . . . . . 7. COCCULUS.
  - Petals 6, ovaries 3, style bifid . . . . . PERICAMPYLUS (p. 26).
  - Petals 5–8, ovaries 3 . . . . 8. LIMACIA.
- Seed exalbuminous
  - Sepals, petals, stamens 6 . . . . . . PACHYGONE (p. 27).
  - Sepals and petals 6, stamens 9 . . . . . PYCNARHENA (p. 27).
  - Sepals 9–12, petals 6, stamens 6 . . . . . HÆMATOCARPUS (p. 27).
  - Sepals 8, petals 2, stamens 8 . . . . . ANTITAXIS (p. 27).

1. STEPHANIA, Lour. ; Fl. Brit. Ind. i. 102.

Slender but widely spreading perennial glabrous climbers, hardly woody. Leaves peltate, membranous, basal nerves numerous. Fl. umbellate, in compound pedunculate umbels. ♂ : Sepals 6–10, ovate or obovate, petals 3–5, obovate, fleshy, anthers 6, connate round the top of the staminal column. ♀ : Sepals 1–5, petals of male, no staminodes. Ovary 1, style 3–6 partite. Endocarp horseshoe shaped, tubercled. Seed almost annular. About 8 species, from tropical Africa to Polynesia and Australia.

1. **S. hernandifolia**, Walp.—Syn. *Clypea hernandifolia*, W. & A. ; Wight Ic. t. 939.

Leaves ovate, pale beneath, blade 2–4, petiole 1–2 in. Umbels capitate, ripe carpels ⅙ in. diam., fasciculate (one only in each flower).

Subhimalayan tract, from Nepal eastwards, Assam, Khasi hills, Bengal, Burma, Western Ghats and coast, Ceylon. Fl. March–August. Malay Peninsula and Archipelago, Cochinchina, Southern China, Polynesia and Australia. 2. **S. rotunda**, Lour. ; Vern. *Parha*, Dūn. Subhimalayan tract from the Jumna eastwards, ascending to 6,000 ft. Assam to Burma, Western Ghats and coast. A large bulbous-rooted climber ; leaves round, often sinuate-lobed, 3–7 in. diam. ; fl. yellow, on slender pedicels. 3. **S. elegans**, Hook. fil. & Thoms. Subhimalayan tract from Garhwal eastwards, ascending to 6,000 ft. Khasi hills. A wiry climber ; leaves elongate-deltoid, acuminate, 2–4 in. ; metallic lustre underneath. Peduncles filiform, longer than petioles. Berries small, red, transparent.

Cissampelos Pareira, Linn. ; Brandis, F. Fl. 10 ; Collett Simla Fl. fig. 7.—Vern. *Katori*, *pataki*, *tikri*, Pb. ; *Parhe*, Dūn, is a climber with herbaceous or slender woody branches, on a short stout stem ; branches more or less grey tomentose ; leaves generally peltate ; male fl. tetramerous, in small lax cymose clusters, at the end of short slender axillary peduncles ; female fl. in elongate simple or compound racemes, with numerous broad alternate foliaceous bracts, ovary 1. Ripe carpels ⅙ in. diam., style scar basal, endocarp transversely ridged and tuberculate, seed horseshoe shaped. Subhimalayan tract, from the Indus eastwards, ascending to 4,000 ft. Chota Nagpore. Common in both peninsulas, not in the arid region. Fl. March–October. Cosmopolitan in tropical and subtropical countries.

2. CYCLEA, Arnott ; Fl. Brit. Ind. i. 104.

Climbing shrubs, branchlets longitudinally ribbed, leaves peltate, fl. in axillary panicles. Male : Calyx 4–8 lobed, petals 4–8, more or less connate. Anthers 4–6, on the top of the staminal column, connate, bursting transversely. Female : Sepal 1 oblong, petal 1 orbicular. Ovary 1, style short, 3–5 lobed. Drupe pisiform, style scar near base, endocarp tubercled, seed horseshoe shaped. Species 6. Madagascar, India, China.

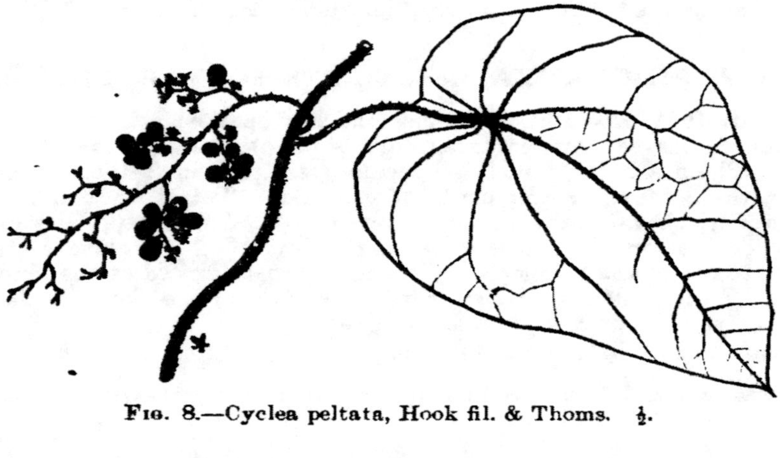

Fig. 8.—Cyclea peltata, Hook fil. & Thoms. ½.

1. **C. peltata,** Hook. fil. & Thoms. Vern. *Paryel*, Mar.

Leaves deltoid, entire, branchlets petioles and underside of leaves hairy, ♂ : Calyx campanulate, 4–lobed, corolla an irregularly 4–lobed cup. Drupe pilose.

Sikkim, Assam, Khasi hills, Burma, Western coast of the Peninsula, from the Konkan southwards. Fl. R. S. Malay Peninsula and Archipelago. Nearly allied and very similar: 2. **C. Burmanni** Miers, Western Ghats and coast from the Konkan southwards, Ceylon. Leaves elongate, deltoid, acuminate, slightly undulate or sinuate, corolla urceolate, nearly entire, drupes pearly white, the dense masses of fruit like miniature bunches of white grapes.

Lophophyllum bicristatum, Griff.; Fl. Brit. Ind. i. 105, is a tall woody climber of the lower hills of Sikkim (to 2,000 ft.), Bhutan, the Khasi hills and Manipur. Branchlets, petioles and underside of leaves hairy; leaves cordate, not peltate; tertiary nerves prominently reticulate, ♂ without petals, ♀ with 2 fleshy sepals. One circle only of wood wedges, which bifurcate near the bark.

3. TINOSPORA, Miers; Fl. Brit. Ind. i. 96.

Deciduous climbers, stems succulent, corky; leaves membranous, not peltate, with 5–7 basal nerves. Fl., when the plant is leafless, in axillary or terminal racemes or panicles. Sepals 6, the 3 inner larger; petals 6, smaller than the inner sepals. ♂ : Stamens 6, free, filaments thick, often adnate to petals, anther cells bursting obliquely. ♀ : Staminodes 6, clavate, ovaries 3, stigma broad. Drupes 1–3, style scar terminal, seed generally curved round the intruded endocarp. Species 9, tropics of Asia, Australia and Africa.

1. **T. cordifolia,** Miers.—Syn. *Cocculus cordifolius*, DC.; Wight Ic. t. 485, 486. Vern. *Batindu*, Pb.; *Gūlel*, *guloh*, *gurach*, Hind.; *Gulwail*, Mar.

A glabrous climber. Leaves cordate, blade 1–2½ in., petiole 1–2 in. long. Fl. yellow, in slender racemes or racemose panicles, drupes 1–3, red, succulent, ⅓ in. diam., endocarp smooth.

Subhimalayan tract, from the Jumna eastwards, Central India and Western Peninsula, Chittagong, Andamans. Fl. February–April. Nearly allied: 2. **T. nudiflora,** Kurz, F. Fl. i. 52. *Sindōn manwé*, Burm. Lower Burma. Shoots densely whitish-tomentose. Leaves ovate, softly pubescent, pale beneath, drupes juicy, 1 in. diam., orange-yellow.

3. **T. malabarica,** Miers; Trimen Handbook Ceylon, i. 38.

Stems ½ in. diam., smooth and shining, bark papery, shoots pubescent, leaves cordate, pubescent above, whitish-tomentose beneath, blade 4–5 in. Ripe carpels crimson, ½ in. diam., endocarp tubercled.

Western Peninsula, Sikkim, Khasi hills and Chittagong. Fl. February–May. Following Trimen I unite with this: *T. tomentosa*, Miers; Fl. Brit. Ind. i. 96. Nearly allied: 4. **T. crispa,** Miers. Assam to Burma, Malay Peninsula. Leaves glabrous, blade 2–6 in., petiole 1–3 in. long, drupe 1 in. long, ovoid.

4. ASPIDOCARYA, Hook. fil. & Thoms.; Fl. Brit. Ind. i. 95.

1. **A. uvifera,** Hook. fil. & Thoms. (the only species).

A climber, leaves ovate-cordate, slightly peltate, basal nerves 3–5, petioles 2–3 in. Fl. in slender panicles. Sepals green, 12, in 2–4 rows, the 6 outer narrow, the 6 inner broadly-ovate or orbicular. Petals 6, smaller than the inner sepals, obovate, the edges incurved. ♂ : Anthers 6, bursting transversely, on the top of a slender staminal column. ♀ : 6 clavate staminodia opposite to petals and enveloped by them, 3 carpels, united at the top by a 3 fid stigma. Fruit a fleshy edible drupe, consisting of one flat 1-seeded carpel, ¾ in. long, rarely 2 or 3, style scar terminal.

Sikkim, ascending to 5,000 ft. Fl. H. S.

Parabæna sagittata' Miers. Subhimalayan tract from Nepal eastwards, ascending to

8,000 ft., Khasi hills, Chittagong, Burma. Leaves cordate or sagittate, often sinuate toothed, fl. in pedunculate dichotomous cymes, sepals 6, drupes ovoid tuberculate ⅛ in. long.

5. ANAMIRTA, Colebrooke; Fl. Brit. Ind. i. 98.

Species 2 or perhaps more, India, Malay Archipelago.

A. paniculata, Colebr.; Trimen Handb. Ceylon, i. 40.—Syn. *A. Cocculus*, Wight et Arn. Vern. *Kakmari*, Hind.

A powerful glabrous climber, stems woody, 4 in. diam., twisting round supports and sending out numerous rootlets, bark thick, spongy, deeply cracked. Leaves thinly coriaceous, cordate or broadly ovate, blade 4–8, petiole 2–6 in. long, basal nerves 3–5. Fl. green, scented, in long pendulous panicles, sepals 6, petals 0. ♂ : Numerous 2-celled anthers, round the top of a short thick central column. ♀ : 4–5 carpels, style lateral. Drupes usually 2, black, ½ in. diam., on short thick stalks, in ample panicles.

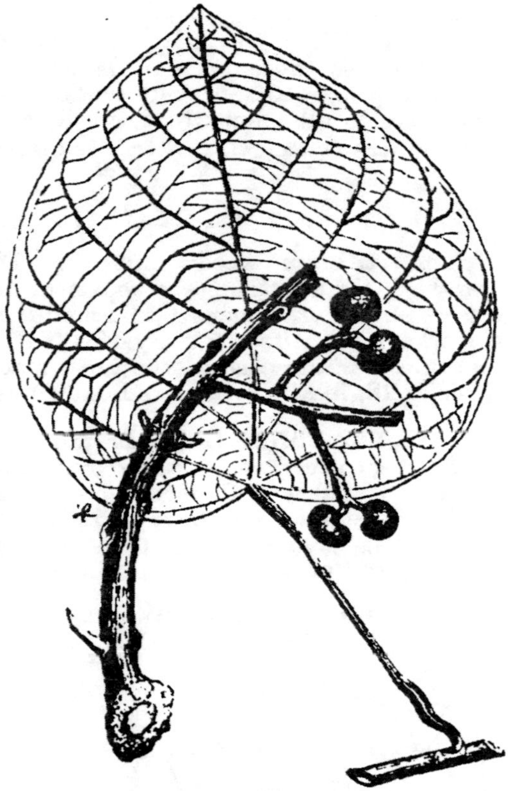

Fig. 9.—Anamirta paniculata, Colebr. Leaf, fruit. ½.

Assam, Khasi hills, both Peninsulas. Ceylon. Fl. February in Burma, May, June in Ceylon. Also Malay Archipelago. The dry fruit (*Cocculus indicus*) an article of trade. Seeds extremely bitter, used to adulterate beer and in India to intoxicate fish. Contain Picrotoxin, a poisonous substance.

Coscinium fenestratum, Colebrooke. Ceylon, probably also in the Peninsula. A woody climber, young shoots and underside of leaves yellow-tomentose, leaves broadly ovate or cordate, in young plants peltate, blade 4–8, petals 3–4 in., fl. diœcious, in dense globose heads; sepals 6, petals 3, stamens 6, the 3 inner cohering half way up. Drupes 1–3, ½ in. diam. Cotyledons orbicular, thin, laciniate.

Fig. 10.—Tiliacora racemosa, Colebr. ½. Section of carpel ⅟.

6. TILIACORA, Colebrooke; Fl. Brit. Ind. i. 99.

T. racemosa, Colebr. (the only species). Vern. *Karwant*, Oudh, *Tiliakoru*, Beng.

A large evergreen climber, perfectly glabrous, leaves ovate, blade 3–5 in., petiole 1 in. long, 3 basal nerves, the lowest pair of secondary nerves from near the base, reticulate veins conspicuous. Fl. yellow, supported by small bracts, in axillary panicles. Sepals 6, in 2 series, the inner much larger; petals 6, minute, stamens 6, ovaries 3–12. Ripe carpels 1–10, on short stalks, blunt, ½ in. long, endocarp wrinkled, seed bent double, albumen oily, cotyledons linear.

Oudh forests, Bengal, Western Peninsula. Fl. R. S. but also at other times. Ceylon.

7. COCCULUS, DC.; Fl. Brit. Ind. i. 101.

Small trees or woody climbers. Fl. panicled, sepals 6, the inner larger, petals 6, shorter than the sepals of the inner circle, concave, embracing the stamens. ♂ : Stamens 6, filaments free, anthers terminal, the cells opening by transverse slits. ♀ : Ovaries 3–6. Drupes generally 3, compressed, scar of style near the base on the inner side, endocarp tuberculate, horseshoe shaped. Species 18, in all tropical and subtropical countries.

1. **C. laurifolius**, DC.; Brandis F. Fl. 9. Vern. *Tilphara*, N.W.

An erect evergreen shrub or moderate sized tree, leaves lanceolate, 3-nerved, shining, the 2 lateral nerves prominent, extending beyond the middle of the leaf. Fl. small, in axillary panicles.

N.W. Himalaya from Chamba to Nepal, ascending to 5,000 ft. Anamalai hills. Shan hills, Upper Burma, at 4,000 ft. Fl. H. S. Java, China, Japan.

2. **C. macrocarpus**, Wight et Arn.—Syn. *C. glaucescens*, Kurz, F. Fl. B. B. i. 55. Vern. *Vatoli*, *Vat-yel*, Mar.

FIG. 11.—Cocculus macrocarpus, Wight et Arn. ½.

A gigantic glabrous woody climber, stem as thick as a man's leg, bark smooth, branchlets with numerous slender ribs, leaves round, pale beneath, blade 2–4 in. diam., often broader than long, petiole 2–4 in. long, 3–5 basal nerves. Fl. numerous, pale yellow, in pendulous panicles, 1–2 ft. long, mostly from the old wood. Ripe carpels 1–2, obliquely obovoid, nearly 1 in. long, tapering into a short neck, endocarp with transverse ridges.

West side of the Peninsula, from Matheran southwards. Khasi hills, Chittagong, Lower Burma. Fl. February–March. Ceylon, moist low country, Sumatra, Celebes, South China.

Two small woody climbers, common in hedges: 3. **C. villosus**, DC.; Vern. *Paukh*, Oudh, common in the plains and lower hills of both Peninsulas. Branchlets, leaves and inflorescence grey-tomentose, leaves ovate or ovate-oblong, obtuse, often mucronate, 1–3 in. long; 4. **C. Leaeba**, DC., dry and arid regions of Western India, Punjab, Sind, Baluchistan (—hanging down over the perpendicular stony sides of dry watercourses--), Western Rajputana, Deccan—Afghanistan, Arabia, tropical and subtropical Africa. Branches and young leaves pubescent, leaves oblong or trapezoid, obtuse, often lobed, ½–1½ in. long.

Pericampylus incanus, Miers. Sikkim, Assam, Khasi hills, Burma, Malay Peninsula and Archipelago, is a tomentose climbing shrub, leaves membranous, from a straight or cordate, sometimes slightly peltate base, broadly ovate or nearly orbicular, pale beneath, 5 basal nerves. Fl. in axillary cymose panicles, petals 6, ovaries 3, style 2 fid, segments subulate. Drupes red, the size of a pea, endocarp horseshoe shaped, crested and echinate.

8. LIMACIA, Loureiro; Fl. Brit. Ind. i. 100.

Woody climbers, leaves coriaceous, triplinerved or with 3 basal nerves. Fl. in panicles, sepals 6–10, petals 5-8, embracing the stamens, smaller than the sepals of the inner circle. ♂: Stamens 3–9, sometimes more, anthers adnate, bursting vertically. ♀: Staminodes 6, ovaries 3. Drupes obovoid or reniform, style scar near the base, seed long cylindrical, curved round the intruded endocarp. Species 8–10, Eastern tropical Asia, Solomon Islands, North Australia.

1. **L. cuspidata,** Hook. fil. & Thoms.; Trimen Handb. Ceylon i. 42.

Evergreen, young shoots pubescent, leaves 2–3 in. long, longer on vigorous shoots, stamens 8–12. Drupes nearly globose, $\frac{1}{3}$–$\frac{1}{2}$ in. long, dull reddish purple.

Assam, Silhet, Tenasserim, Ceylon, Cochinchina, China. Fl. R. S. 2. **L. triandra,** Miers. Lower Burma, Malay Peninsula. Leaves triplinerved, 2–4 in. long, sepals 9, thick, stamens 3. 3. **L. velutina,** Miers. Mergui, Malay Peninsula. Branches velvety, leaves tomentose, 2–6 in., basal and secondary nerves prominent beneath.

Pachygone ovata, Miers; Fl. Brit. Ind. i. 105.—Syn. *P. odorifera*, Miers; Kurz, F. Fl. i. 56; *Cissampelos Plukenetii*, DC.; Wight Ic. t. 824, 825. Vern. *Ngu pyu*, Burm., Coromandel coast (Sriharikota), but also inland; common in the swamp forests of the plains of Lower Burma, also on limestone rocks. A large evergreen spreading shrub with long drooping and climbing branches, branchlets and petioles hairy, leaves ovate, coriaceous, glabrous, shining, basal nerves 3–5, fl. white, with a strong honey scent, pedicellate, generally panicled in the axils of linear hairy bracts, in slender axillary racemes, sepals 6, the 3 outer smaller, petals 6, small, embracing the filaments. Ovaries 3; ripe carpels reniform, glabrous, $\frac{1}{3}$ in. long, style scar basal. 2. **P. dasycarpa,** Kurz, F. Fl. i. 56. Tenasserim, the drupes densely tomentose, is closely allied.

Pycnarrhena pleniflora, Miers; Fl. Brit. Ind. i. 106. Assam, Silhet, is a large, erect or scrambling shrub, shoots often tomentose, branchlets ribbed, leaves oblong-lanceolate, acuminate, thinly coriaceous, secondary nerves 6–8 pair, impressed above, very prominent beneath, joined at a distance from the edge by conspicuous intramarginal veins, fl. in axillary capitate clusters. Sepals 6, the inner larger, petals 6, stamens 9, filaments short. Drupe $\frac{1}{2}$ in. long, style scar lateral.

Another climber with exalbuminous seeds is **Hæmatocarpus Thomsoni,** Miers; Fl. Brit. Ind. i. 106. Sikkim, Himalaya and Khasi hills. Perfectly glabrous, leaves rigidly coriaceous, elliptic lanceolate, the 3 basal nerves running along the edge nearly to the apex; secondary nerves conspicuous, almost at right angles to midrib.

Antitaxis calocarpa, Kurz, F. Fl. i. 57, Chittagong, Andamans and Nicobars, is a large evergreen woody diœcious climber, leaves oblong-lanceolate, penninerved, secondary nerves not much more conspicuous than the finely reticulate veins, pedicels numerous, paniculate, filiform, $\frac{1}{4}$–$\frac{1}{2}$ in. long. Sepals 8, in decussate pairs, the inner larger, petals 2 small, stamens 8. Drupes 1–3, glabrous, shining, scarlet, $\frac{3}{4}$ in. long, style scar ventral, endocarp brittle, seed nearly globular, concave ventrally, albumen none, cotyledons fleshy, half round, incurved.

ORDER VI. BERBERIDACEÆ. Gen. Pl. i. 40.

(*Berberideæ.*)

(*Lardizabalaceæ* and *Berberidaceæ*, Engler und Prantl, iii. 2, pp. 67, 70.)

Glabrous shrubs, sometimes climbing. Leaves alternate, simple or compound. Sepals and petals free, usually trimerous. Stamens 4–6, opposite to petals, anthers adnate. Carpels 1–3, ovules few or numerous. Seeds with copious albumen.

A. Lardizabaleæ. Flowers unisexual or polygamous, anthers opening by slits, carpels 3.
- Climbers, leaves 3–9 foliolate, stamens free . . . . 1. HOLBŒLLIA.
- Climbers, leaves 3 foliolate, stamens monadelphous . . PARVATIA (p. 28).
- Erect shrubs, leaves pinnate . . . . DECAISNEA (p. 28).

B. Berbereæ. Erect shrubs or herbs, fl. bisexual, anthers opening by valves, carpel 1.
- Shrubs, generally spiny, fl. yellow, ovules few basal . 2. BERBERIS.

1. HOLBŒLLIA, Wall.; Fl. Brit. Ind. i. 108.

Species two, 1 Chinese.

1. **H. latifolia**, Wall.; Brandis, F. Fl. 13. Vern. *Gophla*, N.W.

A large climber, the ends of branches often transformed into tendrils. Outer bark corky, deeply cleft vertically. Wedges of wood with large vessels, separated by very broad medullary rays, no rings of bast in the wood. Leaves 3–9-foliolate, leaflets acuminate, ovate-lanceolate, blade 3–6, petiole ½ in. Fl. monœcious, purplish-green, sweet-scented. Sepals 6, petals 6, minute, stamens 6, ovaries 3. Fruit consisting of 2–3 fleshy edible oblong carpels, 2–4 in. long, seeds numerous, in several vertical rows, immersed in pulp.

Himalaya 4,000–9,000 ft., from Kashmir eastwards. Assam, Khasi hills, Manipur. Fl. April, May.

Parvatia Brunoniana, Decaisne; Fl. Brit. Ind. i. 108, Assam, Khasi hills, Taëpo mountain, S.E. of Toungoo, 5,000 ft. A large climbing shrub with trifoliolate leaves. Fl. monœcious, greenish yellow, in axillary fascicled racemes. Ripe carpels 1–1½ in. long, ovoid, many-seeded.

Decaisnea insignis, Hook. fil. & Thoms., Fl. Brit. Ind. i. 107, in humid forests of the inner valleys of Sikkim and Bhutan (7,000–9,000 ft.) is a small tree 10 ft. high, stem simple or with a few branches, each bearing a tuft of large imparipinnate leaves, 2–3 ft. long, leaflets opposite, glaucous beneath, common petiole constricted above insertion of leaflets. Fl. green, monœcious, in long racemes. Sepals 6, acuminate, in 2 rows, petals 0, stamens 6, monadelphous, ovaries 3, with many 2-seriate ovules. Fruit consisting of three yellow, fleshy, edible, spreading follicles, seeds many. Wood normal, medullary rays narrow, pith large.

2. BERBERIS, Linn.; Fl. Brit. Ind. i. 108.

Spiny shrubs with yellow wood. Leaves spinous-toothed, simple or imparipinnate. Fl. yellow, sepals 6, imbricate in two series, with a few appressed bracts, petals 6, imbricate, stamens 6, anther cells opening by recurved valves. Ovary 1, stigma peltate, sessile or on a short style, ovules usually few, basal. Fr. a berry. Upwards of 100 species, many variable, closely allied, and difficult to keep apart. Temperate and subtropical regions of the northern hemisphere and temperate South America.

Section I.—Mahonia. Leaves imparipinnate, leaflets opposite.

1. **B. nepalensis**, Spreng.—Syn. *B. Leschenaultii*, Wall.; Wight Ic. t. 940. Vern. *Kandlu*, *Sharor*, Chamba; *Khoru*, Jauns, *Maranthu*, Trav.

An evergreen shrub. Leaflets 6–12 pair, ovate-lanceolate, 1–5 in. long, the lowest pair often near the base, much smaller and nearly orbicular, common petiole articulate at the insertion of leaflets, frequently two small subulate stipules on its broad, nearly sheathing base. Upper leaves often reduced to sheathing bracts. Racemes long, compact, several at the ends of branches. Berry blue-glaucous, ovoid (globose on the Nilgiris).

Outer Himalaya, 6,000–8,000 ft., from the Ravi eastwards. Khasi hills, Manipur, Burma hills, Nilgiris. Fl. October–April.

Section II.—Berberis proper. Branches ribbed; leaves simple, gradually narrowed into a short petiole, those on elongated shoots generally reduced to simple or 3–7 forked spines, in the axils of which are arrested branchlets, bearing tufts of leaves. The shoots with elongated internodes generally grow from the terminal bud of a short arrested branch.

A. Fl. in racemes, corymbs or umbels.

2. **B. vulgaris**, Linn.; Hooker's Stud. Fl. 3rd ed. 15.—Barberry. Vern. *Chochar*, *Chamchūr*, Hattu.

Deciduous, bark grey, branchlets red. Leaves membranous or thinly coriaceous, glaucous beneath, serrate with equal spinulose teeth, crowded on arrested branchlets in the axils of 3-fid, rarely 5-fid or simple spines. Racemes pedunculate, stigma broad, sessile. Berry ovoid or cylindric, as long as or shorter than pedicel, usually red when ripe.

North-West Himalaya, mostly in shady forest of Silver Fir, Spruce and Oak, 8,000-12,000 ft. Fl. March–June. Tibet, Northern Asia, Japan and China, Afghanistan, Europe. A form with thinly coriaceous leaves in Baluchistan.

3. **B. aristata**, DC.; Brand. F. Fl. 12; Collett Simla Fl. fig. 8.—Syn. *B. tinctoria*, Leschenault; Wight Ill. t. 8. Vern. *Kashmal*, *Kaumul*, *Kammûl*, Simla; *Bagi Sutrum*, Kan; *Kingora*, Garhwal.

Branches shining, reddish-brown, slightly drooping. Leaves coriaceous, more or less persistent, obovate or oblanceolate, green beneath, entire or with few large distant spinescent teeth. Fl. golden yellow, in long drooping compound racemes, much longer than leaves, peduncles and pedicels slender. Berries spindle-shaped, tapering into a short style, stigma small subglobose.

Outer Himalaya, Indus to Bhutan, 4,000–10,000 ft., Nilgiris, Ceylon. Fl. March–June. On high exposed ridges a stunted shrub with smaller leaves and short racemes.

4. **B. Lycium**, Royle; Brandis F. Fl. 12. Vern. *Kashmal*, *Chochar*, *Chotra*, Simla.

An erect shrub, bark grey or whitish, branches rigid. Leaves narrow, lanceolate or oblanceolate, coriaceous, mucronate, generally entire, bright green above, glaucous beneath. Fl. small, pale yellow, in corymbose, at times compound racemes, which generally are as long as or a little longer than leaves. Pedicels slender, longer than the blue ovoid berries, style distinct, stigma capitate.

Outer North-West Himalaya on clearances, along the roadside, often gregarious, from Kashmir to Garhwal, 3,000–8,000 ft. Fl. March, April, a fortnight earlier than *B. aristata*.

5. **B. asiatica**, Roxb.; Brandis F. Fl. 12.

Bark pale, the arrested leaf-bearing shoots often on the top of stout woody tuberculate branchlets of previous years. Leaves rigidly coriaceous, white beneath, obovate, sometimes nearly orbicular, nerves and veins strongly reticulate, lacunose between the veins. Seedlings have broadly-ovate leaves, petiole slender, more than twice the length of blade. The juvenile state of other species (*B. Wallichiana*, *B. concinna*) is similar. Fl. in short corymbose racemes. Berries large, ovoid, often nearly globose, red or black, stigma capitate on a distinct style.

Outer Himalaya, from Kumaun eastward, ascending to 7,500 ft. Párasnáth in Behar. Fl. H. S.

FIG. 12.—Berberis asiatica, Roxb. Seedling and fruiting branch. ½.

6. **B. coriaria,** Royle; Bot. Register vol. xxvii. (1841) t. 46. Vern. *Tharmala*, *Chochar*, *Kambra*, Narkanda, Bagi.

A tall shrub, branches grey, rigid, spines generally trifid, ½ in. long, from a broad base. Leaves thickly coriaceous, 1–3 in. long, upper side dark green, with prominent whitish reticulate veins, under side pale green, shining, lacunose when dry, oblanceolate or obovate, narrowed into a short petiole, the upper half serrate, teeth large, spinescent. Racemes stiff, simple, sessile, longer than leaves, pedicels in the axils of persistent, lanceolate, often serrate bracts, with 2 minute lateral bracteoles. Berry ovoid, covered with thick white bloom, purple when ripe. Stigma broad, flat, on a distinct style.

North-West Himalaya, from Kulu to Kumaun, 8,000–10,000 ft., extending into the inner dry valleys. Abundant on the great ridge which separates the Sutlej and Tons valleys, from Narkanda to Sungri. Fl. March–May. I call this remarkable species *B. coriaria* out of deference to the authorities at Kew. The figure quoted has red berries, stated to be without bloom, and it is very doubtful whether *B. coriaria*, Royle, is this species.

7. **B. umbellata,** Wall.; Fl. Brit. Ind. i. 110.

Leaves more or less deciduous, obovate or oblanceolate, glaucous beneath, sparingly serrulate. Fl. in umbelliform corymbs on a long naked peduncle, berries ovoid-oblong, stigma flat, sessile.

Himalaya 9,000–11,000 ft., from Kashmir eastwards. Fl. May–June. 8. **B. virescens,** Hook. fil., Bot. Mag. t. 7116, Kashmir, Sikkim (9,000 ft.), Bhutan. Leaves small ⅜–1¼ in., fl. pale yellow or greenish-yellow, fasciculate or in few fld. racemes. Berry oblong, scarlet, stigma nearly sessile.

B. Peduncles fascicled, 1 flowered.

9. **B. Wallichiana,** DC.; Wall. Pl. As. Rar. t. 243.

Evergreen. Leaves rigidly coriaceous, lanceolate, tufted, the arrested leaf, bearing shoots often on the top of stout woody tuberculate branchlets up to 1 in. long, spines 3–7 fid. Fascicles generally many-flowered, pedicels slender. Berries ovoid, purple.

Himalaya, from Nepal eastwards, 8,000–10,000 ft., Khasi hills, Manipur, Upper Burma, Ruby Mines, and Southern Shan States at 4,000 ft. Fl. April, May. 10. **B. ulicina,** Hook. fil. & Thoms.; Ladak, Western Tibet, a small densely spiny shrub, 1–2 ft. high. Fl. on short peduncles, crowded.

The following three species have solitary peduncles: 11. **B. angulosa,** Wall.; Kashmir, Nepal, Sikkim (11,000–13,000 ft.). Leaves 1–1½ in., usually quite entire, peduncle longer than leaf, stout, curved, berry globose or broadly oblong, red, ⅓–½ in. long. 12. **B. macrosepala,** Hook. fil., Inner Sikkim Himalaya, 12,000–13,000 ft. Leaves obovate, spinulose-toothed, ¾–1½ in., berries ½–¾ in., red, 6–10 seeded. 13. **B. concinna,** Hook. fil., Garhwal, Kumaon, 9,000–13,000 ft. Interior valleys of Sikkim, 12,000–13,000 ft., a small much branched shrub, forming dense tufts or cushions. Leaves ½–¾ in., obovate, spinous-toothed, white beneath, peduncles slender, exceeding the leaves. Fl. bright orange, berries ⅓–¾ in.

14. **B. insignis,** Hook. fil. & Thoms.; Gamble List 5.

A large shrub, resembling holly, differs from all Indian species of this section by the leaves not being crowded on short arrested branchlets, but separated by well developed internodes. Leaves lanceolate, rigidly coriaceous, shining on both surfaces, with long spinescent teeth, 3–6 in. long; secondary nerves numerous, prominent beneath, copiously branching towards the edge. Fl. golden-yellow, 3–20 in a fascicle, berries ⅓ in., black.

Sikkim, 8,000–10,000 ft., Bhutan, China. Fl. spring and autumn.

ORDER VII. CAPPARIDACEÆ. Gen. Pl. i. 103.

(*Capparideæ.*)

Herbs, shrubs, or trees, sometimes climbing. Leaves simple or 3–9 foliolate, stipules mostly spinescent, in some genera wanting. Fl. usually bisexual, often zygomorphic. Sepals 4, free or connate, petals 4, sometimes 2 or none, imbricate or open in bud. Stamens exserted, generally numerous. Ovary 1, consisting of 2 or more carpels, generally 1-celled, as a rule raised on an elongated gynophore, ovules ∞ on 2 or more parietal placentas. Seeds without albumen, embryo incurved.

Remarkable anatomical characters.—In species of *Maerua*, *Cadaba*, and *Roydsia* the wood is interrupted by concentric bands of bast (phloëm).

Calyx tube lined by the disk.
- Leaves 3–5 foliolate, petals 0, fruit ovoid . . . . 1. NIEBUHRIA.
- Leaves simple, petals 4, fruit moniliform . . . . 2. MAERUA.
- Leaves simple, petals 0, fruit globose . . . . . BOSCIA (p. 32).

Sepals 4, open in bud, leaves 3-foliolate . . . . . 3. CRATÆVA.

Sepals 4, imbricate or outer valvate, leaves simple.
- Stamens 4–6, inserted high up on the gynophore . 4. CADABA.
- Stamens numerous, inserted at the base of gynophore 5. CAPPARIS.

Sepals 6, ovary 3-celled . . . . 6. ROYDSIA.

1. NIEBUHRIA, DC.; Fl. Brit. Ind. i. 171.

Species about 8, most in South Africa.

N. linearis, DC.; Wight Ic. t. 174.—Syn. *Maerua linearis*, Pax in Engler u. Prantl, iii. 2. 234.

A small tree with pale grey bark and 3–5 foliolate leaves, leaflets lanceolate, 1–3 in. long, midrib distinct, second. nerves scarcely visible. Racemes terminal, few fld. Calyx tube ovoid, limb 4-cleft, valvate, petals 0. Stamens ∞ inserted on the gynophore considerably above its base. Ovules numerous on 2 parietal placentas. Berry ovoid, 1-seeded, cotyledons fleshy, involute.

Hills on the east side of the Western Peninsula.

FIG. 18.—Maerua arenaria, Hook. fil. & Thoms. ½.

2. MAERUA, Forskahl Fl. Brit. Ind. i. 171.

Species about 20, some in Arabia, most in tropical Africa.

M. arenaria, Hook. fil. & Thoms.; Trimen Ceylon i. 58. Syn. *M. ovalifolia*, Camb.; Cooke, Fl. Bomb. i. 41. Vern. *Vika*, Guzerat.

A large woody climber, bark light grey, leaves

elliptic or elliptic-lanceolate, ½–3 in. Fl. greenish-white, scented, in terminal or lateral corymbs, calyx tube lined by a disk, on the edge of which the 4 short petals are inserted. Stamens ∞, inserted on the gynophore above its base. Ovary short, ovules numerous on 2 parietal placentas. Fruit yellow, 1–3 in. long, fleshy, moniliform, many seeded, each seed portion forming almost a separate berry. Cotyledons fleshy, involute.

Drier parts of North-West India, the Peninsula and Ceylon. Fl. C. S.

Boscia variabilis, Coll. et Hemsl.; Journ. Linn. Soc. xxviii. t. 1.—Syn. *Niebuhria variabilis*, Kurz, F. Fl. i. 59, Meiktila and elsewhere in Upper Burma. A small tree, shoots puberulous, leaves simple, 1–2½ in., narrowly oblong, calyx tube very short, lined by a fleshy annular disk, petals 0, ovary with a small number of ovules on two placentas.

3. CRATÆVA, Linn.; Fl. Brit. Ind. i. 172.

Deciduous trees with trifoliolate leaves. Fl. large, sometimes unisexual, corymbose. Sepals 4, deciduous, petals long-clawed, open in bud, both inserted on a fleshy often lobed disk. Stamens numerous on a short column at the base of a filiform gynophore. Placentas 2 with numerous ovules. Species 10, in the tropics of both hemispheres.

1. **C. religiosa**, Forst.; Bedd. Fl. Sylv. t. 116.—Syn. *C. Roxburghii*, R. Br.; Kurz, F. Fl. i. 66; Trimen Handb. i. 59. Vern. *Bărna*, *biliana*, *varvunna*, Hind.; *Nirvala*, Mar.; *Narăve*, Kan.; *Maralingam*, Tam.; *Kadat*, Burm.

A moderate-sized tree, large white lenticels on branches, bark with grey horizontal wrinkles, wood yellowish-white, even- close- and smooth-grained. Leaves clustered at the ends of branchlets, common petiole 2–4 in. long, leaflets ovate-lanceolate, acuminate, the lateral from an oblique basis, petiolules articulate. Fl. 2 in. diam., cream-coloured. Fr. ovoid or globose, 2–3 in. diam.; rind hard, rough, with numerous white specks; seeds ¼ in. long, numerous, reniform, in a yellow pulp.

Subhimalayan tract, from the Ravi eastwards, ascending to 2,000 ft. Both Peninsulas, in low and shady places, chiefly near banks of streams. Often planted. Fl. H. S., with and after the young leaves. Dry country of Ceylon (fl. Dec.). Tonkin, China, Formosa, Malay Archipelago, Polynesia, Tropical Africa. 2. **C. hygrophila**, Kurz, F. Fl. i. 67 (*Yekadat*, Burm.). Swamp forest of the Irawaddi valley, a shrub or small tree, fruit cylindric, 4–5 in. long. 3. **C. lophosperma**, Kurz. Assam, Shan hills, Upper Burma; fl. smaller, fruit globose, 2-celled, seeds tuberculate.

4. CADABA, Forskahl; Fl. Brit. Ind. i. 172.

Unarmed shrubs. Leaves simple or 3-foliolate. Sepals free. Petals clawed, 4 or 2, rarely 0. Disk trumpet-shaped or spathulate; stamens 4–6, inserted high up on the gynophore. Ovules ∞, on 2–4 parietal placentas. Fruit slender, fleshy, sometimes dehiscent. Cotyledons convolute. Species 14, dry regions of Western Asia and Tropical Africa, one in the Malay Archipelago and North-West Australia.

1. **C. indica**, Lamk. Vern. *Shegurti*, Kan.

A straggling tree or shrub. Leaves simple, 1–1½ in. Fl. yellowish-white; petals 4, limb oblong. Disk process ¾ in., curved, pink. Fruit cylindric, irregularly torulose, 1–2 in. long.

Central Provinces, Berar, Gujarat, Deccan, dry country of Ceylon. Fl. October–March.

Two species with simple leaves: 2. **C. farinosa**, Forsk.; Engler und Prantl, iii. 2, fig. 141. Sind, Arabia, Abyssinia. A straggling, much branching shrub. Leaves ½ in., oblong; petals spathulate. 3. **C. heterotricha**, Stocks; Sind. A small rigid tree. Leaves broad-ovate or orbicular, glaucous-grey, often with minute stellate and glandular hairs.

One species with trifoliolate leaves. 4. **C. trifoliata**, Wight et Arn.; Nellore, Tinnevelli, dry region of Ceylon. Leaflets lanceolate, 2 in. long, secondary nerves distinct, sepals ovate, the outer larger, veined, petals pale yellow or white, claw long, slender, limb nearly orbicular. Disk process ¾ in. long, hollow, dilated at the end, orange-yellow.

5. CAPPARIS, Linn.; Fl. Brit. Ind. i. 173.

Trees or shrubs, often climbing, as a rule with stipulary thorns. Leaves simple, often variable in shape and size. Fl. generally regular, often large; sepals 4, free, mostly imbricate in bud; petals 4, sessile, imbricate; stamens ∞, inserted on a small disk, filaments longer than petals. Ovary on a slender gynophore, mostly 1-celled; ovules ∞ on 2–6 parietal placentas. Fruit fleshy, seeds many, embedded in pulp, cotyledons convolute. Species 125, in all warm regions, not in North America.

A. Fl. solitary, axillary, nearly all western species.

1. **C. spinosa**, Linn.; Brand. F. Fl. 14.—Syn. *C. Murrayana*, Graham; Wight Ic. t. 379; *C. leucophylla*, DC.; Collett Simla Fl. 38. *Caper plant.* Vern. *Kabbar*, Arab.; *Kakri, kander*, Pb.; *Bussar*, Kunāwar; *Kalvari*, Sind.

A trailing shrub, with long green branches, young shoots frequently downy with soft hairs. Leaves broad-ovate or obovate, thick, mostly glabrous when full grown; stout, generally recurved, stipular spines at the base of petiole. Fl. 1–3 in. across, pedicel equal to or longer than leaf. Petals at first pure white, pink and purplish red as they fade. Stamens longer than petals, filaments slender, purple. Fruit 1–3 in. long, on a strong gynophore, bent downwards when ripe, opening irregularly by 3–4 valves, crimson inside.

Punjab, Sind, Guzerat (Powergarh), Western Ghats as far south as Mahabaleshwar (here on the western moist face of the Ghats). Inner dry valleys of North-West Himalaya, ascending to 12,000 ft., Western Tibet and Yarkand. Fl. according to locality between January and October. Western Asia, North Africa, and South Europe. The flower buds (pickled) are the capers of Europe. In Ladakh the young leaves eaten as vegetable.

2. **C. divaricata**, Lamk.; Wight Ic. t. 889.—Syn. *C. stylosa*, DC.; Bedd. Manual 13 t. 2. Vern. *Wagāti*, Mar.

A large shrub or small tree, shoots glabrous or pubescent. Leaves linear or elliptic, stipular spines straight. Fl. green, 2½ in. diam., pedicels ½–1 in. Fruit ribbed, tubercled, nearly globose, 2–3 in. diam.

Common all over the Deccan, on stony ground and on black soil in Babul forests.

Nearly allied: 3. **C. hastigera**, Hance, a Chinese shrub, also found in Upper Burma, young shoots with minute caducous stellate hairs; leaves with two obtuse lobes at the base, sometimes lanceolate, entire, the only Eastern species as yet known in this section. 4. **C. grandiflora**, Wall.—Syn. *C. pyrifolia*, Wight et Arn.; Wight Ic. t. 1,047. Southern portion of the western peninsula. Branchlets tomentose. Leaves ovate, acute, mucronate, pubescent beneath. Fl. 3 in. diam., pedicels ¼–½ in. 5. **C. zeylanica**, Linn.—Syn. *C. brevispina*, DC.; Hook. Ic. t. 126; Vern. *Wagutti*, Mar. Coast scrub forests, Ganjam. Western Deccan, dry country of Ceylon, glabrous. Leaves ovate-lanceolate, pale beneath, 1½–4 in., secondary and reticulate tertiary nerves prominent. Fl. sometimes in pairs, 1½–2 in. diam. white, petals with a basal blotch of yellow, which turns purple. Fruit 1½ in. bright scarlet. 6. **C. Heyneana**, Wall. Evergreen forests of the Western Ghats from the Konkan southwards, young shoots floccose, stipulary spines minute or wanting. Leaves 3–6 in., coriaceous, shining above, ovate or lanceolate; secondary nerves prominent, joined by distinct intramarginal loops. Fl. pale blue, 4–5 in. diam., sometimes in pairs.

B. Fl. in corymbs or umbels, western species.

7. **C. aphylla**, Roth; Brand. F. Fl. 14, t. 3. Vern. *Karīl, Kari, Kair, Karil*, North-West India; *Kiral*, Sind; *Ker, Kera Guj*, Mar.

A glabrous, almost leafless shrub, at times a small tree, rarely 20 ft. high;

trunk short, erect, often 4–5 ft. girth, branches numerous, green, divaricating, forming a dense rounded crown, wood close-grained, tough, roots immense, spreading deep and wide. Leaves on young shoots only, caducous, linear, $\frac{1}{8}$ in., occasionally larger spathulate, to $\frac{1}{2}$ in. long, stipular thorns yellowish, straight. Fl. 1 in. diam., red or scarlet, rarely yellow, in corymbs on short lateral branchlets. Fruit 2 in. long, $\frac{1}{2}$–$\frac{2}{3}$ in. diam., red, on a gynophore 1 in. long.

Arid and dry regions of the Western Peninsula, from the Punjab and Sind to Tuticorin. Fl. October–June.

8. **C. Roxburghii,** DC.; Wight Ic. t. 1,048. Vern. *Poorwi*, Mar

A large woody climber, branchlets finely tomentose. Leaves 2–3 in., glabrous, elliptic, petioles $\frac{1}{2}$ in., stipular thorns sometimes wanting. Fl. white, $1\frac{1}{2}$ in. diam. in corymbs of 4–10 at the ends of branches. Fruit globose, $1\frac{1}{2}$–2 in. diam., on a woody stalk $2\frac{1}{2}$ in. long.

Evergreen forests on the Western Ghats from North Kanara southwards, also on the east side of the peninsula (Sriharikota), Fl. H. S. Nearly allied, but quite distinct, is 9. **C. Moonii,** Wight; Trimen Handb. Ceylon i. 62, Western Ghats, from Khandala southwards, Ceylon. A very ornamental shrub, branchlets brown, glabrous, shining. Leaves elliptic-oblong, 3–4 in. Fl. white 4–5 in. diam., in many fld. corymbs at the ends of branches, peduncles stout 2–3 in. long. Fruit globose, 2–4 in. diam., on a woody stalk.

10. **C. grandis,** Linn. fil. Vern. *Pachunda, Katarni*, Mar.

A small tree, generally unarmed, trunk thick, short, branchlets and leaves softly tomentose beneath. Leaves 2–3 in., rhomboid-ovate or obovate; secondary nerves 8–10 pair, distinct, as well as the reticulate tertiary nerves between. Fl. white, $\frac{3}{4}$ in. diam., in many fld. corymbs at the ends of branches, pedicels thick, tomentose. Fruit purple, size of a nutmeg.

Chanda, Deccan, and east side of the peninsula. Fl. March to October, Ceylon. Kurz, F. Fl. i. 64, states that it is frequent in the dry forests of the Prome district. A specimen marked by him *C. grandis*, L., and *auricans*, Kurz, is different; the flowers are smaller and they are on very slender pedicels.

11. **C. parviflora,** Hook. fil. & Thoms.; southernmost parts of the Western Peninsula, a large spreading shrub, unarmed. Leaves 2–5 in. elliptic-lanceolate, acuminate. Fl. less than $\frac{1}{2}$ in. diam. on slender pedicels, in 3–10 fld. shortly pedunculate umbels. Fruit pisiform. 12. **C. pedunculosa,** Wall. Western Ghats, from Matheran southwards, also on the east side of the peninsula. A spreading shrub with stipulary thorns, varying in length, leaves broadly ovate, 1 in. long. Fl. $\frac{1}{2}$ in. across on slender pedicels 1–$1\frac{1}{2}$ in. long. Fruit globose. Not specifically distinct is **C. longispina,** Hook. fil. & Thoms., with straight divaricate long stipular spines. 13. **C. diversifolia,** Wight et Arn. Southern part of the Western Peninsula. A glabrous shrub with flexuose branches. Leaves on some branches linear, 1–2 in. long, on others ovate-lanceolate, stipulary thorns sharp, recurved. Fl. purple, $1\frac{1}{2}$ in. diam. in few fld. terminal corymbs. Fruit ovoid, $1\frac{1}{2}$ in. long.

C. **Fl. in umbels or corymbs. Eastern species and species common to both regions.**

14. **C. sepiaria,** Linn.; Brand. F. Fl. 15; Kurz, F. Fl. i. 66. Vern. *Katān, Katāran*, Merwara.

A thorny shrub or small tree. Branchlets pubescent. Leaves 1–3 in. elliptic or elliptic-lanceolate, downy beneath. Fl. white, $\frac{1}{3}$ in. diam., in many fld. terminal or axillary umbels, pedicels filiform. Fruit globose, black when ripe, $\frac{1}{2}$ in. diam.

Punjab and north-west, not common, Merwara hills. Common in the drier districts of both Peninsulas, Eng forest of Burma. Fl. February–May—Ceylon, Malay Peninsula and Archipelago. 15. **C. orbiculata,** Wall., Upper Burma, is a rigid spreading shrub. Leaves $\frac{3}{4}$–1 in. long, from a slightly cordate base broadly obovate, or nearly orbicular, stipular thorns sharp recurved, from a thick downy base. Fl. small, in pedunculate umbels, pedicels filiform, peduncles slender. Kurz, F. Fl. i. 64, is disposed to identify this species with *C. grandis*, which however is unarmed. 16. **C. glauca**, Wall.; Linn. Soc. Journ. xxviii. 19. Meiktila, dry region of Upper Burma. An erect shrub. Leaves either obovate ¾ in., or linear 1–2 in. long. Fl. small, glabrous, on filiform pedicels in many fld. umbels. 17. **C. flavicans**, Wall. Yemetthen, dry region of Upper Burma. Leaves obovate, ½–1 in. Fl. unisexual, small, petals densely woolly outside. 18. **C. versicolor**, Griff.; Mergui. Climbing. Leaves lanceolate glabrous, shining above, pale beneath. Fl. glabrous, 2 in. diam., white, afterwards rose, in terminal corymbs. 19. **C. trinervia**, Hook. fil. & Thoms.; Tenasserim, Siam. Branches brown-tomentose. Leaves 2–4 in., secondary nerves 3 pair, distinct, the lowest pair from near the base. Fl. 1½–2 in. diam., on stout rusty-tomentose pedicels from the axils of the uppermost leaves and in terminal, many fld. corymbs.

D. Fl. in terminal racemes or panicles, mostly Eastern species.

20. **C. floribunda**, Wight Ill. t. 14.

A large woody climber. Branches glabrous, thorns few. Leaves coriaceous, glabrous. Fl. ½ in. diam., white, on slender pedicels, in pedunculate umbels, which are arranged in large terminal panicles. Stamens about 8. Fruit 1 in. diam., globose.

Both sides of the Western Peninsula, from Vizagapatam southwards. Tenasserim, Ceylon. 21. **C. pumila**, Champion; Khasi hills, Sikkim to 8,000 ft., China. A large scrambling shrub. Branchlets pubescent. Leaves glabrous, lanceolate, acuminate. Fl. ½ in. diam., white, in large terminal panicles. 22. **C. assamica**, Hook. fil. & Thoms.; Assam. Branchlets glabrous. Leaves lanceolate, 4–6 in., secondary nerves 8–10 pair, prominent beneath, thorns minute. Fl. very small, in terminal many fld. racemes. 23. **C. burmanica**, Coll. et Hemsl., Journ. Linn. Soc. xxviii. 19 t. 2. Dry plains of Upper Burma. An unarmed shrub. Branchlets finely greyish-pubescent. Leaves coriaceous 1 in., elliptic or almost orbicular. Fl. ⅜ in. diam., in large terminal panicles. 24. **C. andamanica**, King, Ann. Garden Calcutta, vol. v. 119 t. 137. Beach of South Andaman island. A glabrous climber, unarmed. Leaves coriaceous 3–4 in. Fl. small, in many fld. crowded umbels arranged in large terminal panicles. 25. **C. ambigua**, Kurz, F. Fl. i. 65; Ann. Garden, Calcutta, vol. v. 120 t. 138. Andamans, a thorny climber. Branchlets puberulous. Leaves 4–5 in. Berry 1½ in. Seed 1.

E. Fl. axillary and supra-axillary, in vertical lines on the branches.

26. **C. horrida**, Linn. fil.; Wight Ic. t. 173. Vern. *Hins*, *Kalhins*, N.W.; *Waghati*, Mar.; *Karalwa*, Oudh; *Atanday*, Tam.; *Namani-thanlyet*, Burm.

A scrambling shrub, at times climbing over tall trees. Shoots and young leaves covered with dense rusty, caducous pubescence. Leaves 2–4 in., ovate, elliptic, at times obovate and even lanceolate, obtuse, more often mucronate, second. nerves 4–8 pair, stipulary thorns, stout, recurved. Pedicels supra-axillary, 2–4 in., a vertical line, the uppermost flower opening first. Fl. 1–2 in. diam., at first white, turning pink afterwards, often so numerous that the bush looks like a mass of white and

FIG. 14.—Capparis horrida, Linn. fil. ½.

pink, filaments purple. Fruit obovoid or globose, 1–1½ in. diam., reddish brown.

Plains and lower hills in most parts of India and Burma. Fl. December to April. Also Ceylon, Malay Peninsula and Archipelago. *C. acuminata*, Willd., Fl. Brit. Ind. i. 178, may possibly only be a form of *C. horrida*.

A scrambling, thorny shrub, common on the Aravalli hills in Merwara (*Gitōran*), branchlets and l. softly tomentose, l. broadly elliptic, 2–3 in., second. n. 10–15 pair, fr. 1 in. diam., glabrous shining, gynophore stout, has not yet been named.

27. **C. tenera,** Dalz.; Vern. *Sun let thè*, Burm.

A straggling glabrous armed climber. Leaves membranous or thinly coriaceous, 1½–3 in. Fl. white, ⅓–½ in. across, 2–4 in a vertical series, pedicels filiform, ¾–1½ in. long, petals tomentose outside. Fruit small, few-seeded.

Evergreen forests of the Western Ghats, Konkan and North Kanara. Assam, Manipur (cultivated as a hedge plant), Andamans, Lower and Upper Burma. Fl. H.S.—Ceylon. To this probably belongs *C. disticha*, Kurz, F. Fl. i. 62.

The following species of this section all belong to the Eastern region: 28. **C. multiflora.** Hook. fil. & Thoms., Sikkim, up to 5,000 ft., Manipur, Upper Burma. A large unarmed shrub or small tree with long branches. Leaves 6–12 in., membranous, secondary nerves 8–12 pair, with shorter intermediate, as well as intramarginal nerves, prominent beneath. Fl. small, on slender pedicels, in long rows along branches, forming elongated many fld. racemes, generally with a few leaves at the top. 29. **C. olacifolia,** Hook. fil. & Thoms. Subhimalayan tract from Nepal eastwards, in Sikkim under Khair and Sissoo along river banks. Assam, Shan States, Upper Burma. A large shrub. Branchlets pubescent. Leaves 3–5 in., glabrous, ovate-lanceolate, acuminate. Fl. 1⅓ in. across, white, anthers blue. Fruit ¾ in. diam., red or black, shining. 30. **C. viminea,** Hook. fil. & Thoms.—Syn. *C. membranifolia*, Kurz, F. Fl. i. 61. Sikkim (to 4,000 ft.), Assam, Bhutan, Upper and Lower Burma. A large glabrous shrub, thorns wanting or minute. Leaves membranous, 3–6 in. long, elliptic, abruptly acuminate. Fl. 1 in. across, white, 2–5 in a vertical row. Fruit purple, ½ in. diam. 31. **C. sabiaefolia,** Hook. fil. & Thoms. Khasi and Naga hills, Yunan. A large unarmed glabrous shrub. Differs from 30 by ovate-lanceolate leaves 2–3 in., and smaller pisiform 1–2-seeded fruit. 32. **C. micracantha,** DC. Pegu, Tenasserim, Malay Peninsula. A large shrub or small tree, glabrous, thorns minute. Leaves 4–8 in., coriaceous, shining, secondary nerves 6–8 pair, prominent beneath. Fl. white with a blue centre, 1⅓ in. across, 2–4 in a vertical series, pedicels ½ in. or less. Fruit ovoid, 2–3 in. 33. **C. xanthophylla,** Coll. et Hemsl., Journ. Linn. Soc. xxviii. 20. Dry region of the middle Irawaddi, Yemethen. Thorns minute. Leaves coriaceous, 2–3 in., narrowed into petiole ½ in. long. Buds and flowers rusty-tomentose.

6. ROYDSIA, Roxb.; Fl. Brit. Ind. i. 180.

Unarmed woody climbers. Branches often lenticellate. Leaves simple. Fl. in racemes or panicles. Calyx deeply 6 partite, segments biseriate; petals 0. Stamens ∞ inserted at the base of the cylindric gynophore. Ovary 3-celled, ovules biseriate in the angles of the cells. Fruit fleshy, endocarp woody or crustaceous, 3-valved, 1-celled. Seed 1, cotyledons fleshy, unequal, the larger embracing the smaller. Species 6, eastern tropical Asia.

A. Styles 3, ovules many.

1. **R. suaveolens,** Roxb. Cor. Pl. t. 289. Vern. *Khegra*, Ass.; *Ngan nwe*, Burm.

A large climber. Branches with raised white dots. Leaves 6–12 in., acute or abruptly acuminate, glabrous. Fl. ⅔ in. diam., sweet-scented, anthers bright yellow. Drupe 1½ in., orange-coloured, covered with a thin brittle rind, endocarp smooth.

Sikkim, ascending to 3,000 ft., Assam, Bhutan, Khasi hills, Manipur. Upper Burma. Fl. Febr.-May. 2. **R. obtusifolia,** Hook. fil. & Thoms.; Lower Burma, plains of the delta and valleys. Leaves 4–5 in., glabrous, oblong, obtuse at both ends, endocarp muricate with long soft prickles.

B. Style 1 with 3 minute stigmas, ovules few.

3. **R. parviflora**, Griff.; Fl. Brit. Ind. i. 409.

Leaves glabrous, 4–7 in. Fl. ¼ in. across, inodorous, densely tomentose, in large axillary or terminal panicles, ovules about 4 in each cell.

Pegu, Upper Burma, Malay Peninsula. 4. **R. fasciculata**, King, Ann. Gard. Calc. v. 121, t. 140A. Banks of Yoonzaleen river, Burma. Young branches, under side of leaves and inflorescence softly puberulous. Leaves 3–4½ in. long. Fl. ¼ in. across, in short fasciculate racemes.

Fig. 15.—Roydsia suaveolens, Roxb. ½.

Order VIII.—**Resedaceæ.** *Ochradenus baccatus*, Delile; Fl. Brit. Ind. i. 182, Sind, Baluchistan, desert regions of Western Asia and North-eastern Africa, is a densely ramified strong smelling shrub, attaining 10–12 ft., with long wiry green branches. Leaves ½–1½in., fleshy, linear-spathulate. Fl. minute, yellowish, often unisexual, on short pedicels in long rigid racemes. Calyx flat, rotate, 5-toothed, petals 0, disk unilateral, stamens 10–12. Ovary closed, not open at the top, 3-beaked, ovules many on 3 parietal placentas. Fruit a white few-seeded berry.

Order IX. VIOLACEÆ. Gen. Pl. i. 114.

(*Violarieæ.*)

Herbs or shrubs, leaves alternate, stipulate. Fl. regular or zygomorphic, pentamerous, filaments short, connective produced beyond the anther cells. Ovary 1-celled, ovules many, on 3 parietal placentas. Fruit a 3-valved capsule, albumen fleshy.

1. ALSODEIA, Thouars; Fl. Brit. Ind. i. 186.

Shrubs, rarely trees. Leaves simple, tertiary nerves distinct, parallel, stipules rigid. Fl. small, regular, sepals 5, rigid, petals 5, peduncles with many bracts. Stamens 5, inserted on the edge of an annular disk or inside of it, connective produced into a broad membranous appendage. Style straight, stigma terminal, seeds few. Species 50, in the tropics of both hemispheres.

1. **A. bengalensis**, Wall.; Kurz, F. Fl. i. 70.

An evergreen shrub, at times a small tree attaining 25 ft., entirely glabrous. Leaves 3–5 in., serrulate, stipules narrow. Fl. ⅙ in. diam., glabrous, fasciculate in the axils of leaves or of fallen leaves, disk thick, 5-lobed, stamens included, anthers free, ovary and style glabrous.

Sikkim, Silhet, East Bengal, Andamans, Lower Burma. Fl. H. S.

2. **A. zeylanica,** Thwaites; Bedd. Fl. Sylv. t. 229.
Differs by puberulous branchlets, the leaves obscurely serrulate, stipules broadly subulate and conspicuously ribbed.

Evergreen forests, Malabar, Travancore, Ceylon. Fl. C. S. 3. **A. Roxburghii,** Wall. Silhet, Andamans, Siam. Leaves 1–1½ in. stamens exserted, anthers cohering in a cone. 4. **A. racemosa,** Hook. fil. & Thoms. (*A. longiracemosa*, Kurz, F. Fl. i. 70). Assam, Lower Burma. A small tree. Leaves 3–4 in. serrate, pale beneath, racemes slender, solitary, 3–5 in. long, bracts conspicuous, lanceolate, ribbed, anthers free, bearded at base. 5. **A. mollis,** Hook. fil. & Thoms. Tenasserim. A shrub. Shoots, young leaves and fl. densely tomentose. Leaves 6–10 in., capsule densely pubescent.

ORDER X. BIXACEÆ. Gen. Pl. i. 122.

(*Bixaceæ*, Warburg in Engler und Prantl, iii. 6. 307, and a portion of *Flacourtiaceæ*, ibid. iii. 6a. p. 1.)

Trees or shrubs, with alternate simple leaves. Stipules 0, minute or early deciduous. Fl. regular, often 1-sexual, tetramerous or pentamerous. Anthers 2-celled, bursting by slits or pores. Disk thickened, often glandular. Ovary one, generally 1-celled, ovules on several parietal placentas. Seeds frequently with an arillus or a pulpy testa, embryo enclosed in a fleshy, generally oily albumen, cotyledons foliaceous.

The 2 first genera, *Cochlospermum* (*Maximilianea*, Mart. et Schrank) and *Bixa*, in Engler and Prantl stand under *Bixaceæ*, the rest under *Flacourtiaceæ*.

A. Fl. bisexual, petals 4–6.	
Leaves palmately lobed or divided	1. COCHLOSPERMUM.
Leaves entire, fl. large, petals 5, contorted in bud	BIXA (p. 39).
Leaves entire, fl. small, petals 4–6, imbricate in bud	2. SCOLOPIA.
B. Fl. as a rule diœcious, petals 0.	
Ovary 2–6 celled	3. FLACOURTIA.
Ovary 1-celled	4. XYLOSMA.
C. Fl. diœcious, petals with a scale or a flat pubescent gland at the base.	
Sepals connate, filaments free ∞	5. GYNOCARDIA.
Sepals connate, filaments united in a column, anthers 5	RYPAROSA (p. 41).
Sepals free 5, petals 5, stamens 15, free, filaments glabrous	6. HYDNOCARPUS.
Sepals free 4, petals 8, stamens 20–32, filaments free, hairy	TARAKTOGENOS (p. 42).

1. COCHLOSPERMUM, Kunth; Fl. Brit. Ind. i. 189.

Trees or shrubs. Leaves palmately lobed or divided. Fl. bisexual; sepals 5, deciduous, petals 5, contorted in bud. Stamens indefinite, inserted on a disk without glands, anther cells opening with a short slit at the top. Ovules numerous on 3–5 parietal placentas, style 1, filiform. Capsule 3–5 valved, seeds numerous, reniform, with long woolly hairs. Albumen oily. Species 13, 1 in India, 3 in Africa, 3 in Australia, the remainder in tropical America.

1. **C. Gossypium,** DC.; Bedd. Fl. Sylv. t. 171; Kurz, F. Fl. i. 72. Vern. *Kūmbi*, *Gabdi*, Hind.; *Gejra*, Sahar.; *Hupu*, Kol.; *Ganiār*, Gond.; *Ganēri*, Bhil.; *Gongal*, *Gunglay*, *Gulgul*, Mar.; *Kongillam*, Tam.; *Buruga*, Kan.
A soft-wooded deciduous tree, with few thick short branches. Leaves near the ends of branches, palmately 5-lobed, 4–9 in. diam., lobes shortly acuminate, entire, grey-tomentose beneath, petioles 4–6 in. Fl. 4–5 in. diam., golden-yellow, sepals silky, capsules pear-shaped, 3–4 in. long.

Subhimalayan tract, from the Sutlej to the Sarda river, Behar, Bandelkhand, Central Provinces, Deccan and east side of the Peninsula. Fl. February–April. Dry region of the Irawaddi valley.—Ceylon, Malay Peninsula, Cambodia. Yields a colourless gum.

Bixa orellana, Linn.; Wight Ill. t. 17; Bedd. Fl. Sylv. t. 79, *Arnotto.* Vern. *Thidin,* Burm.; a native of America, but long cultivated and naturalized in India, is a small tree with few branches, leaves cordate, acuminate. Fl. large, 1–2 in. diam., white or pink, capsule reddish-brown, clothed with soft prickles. Seeds covered with a red pulp (originally fleshy papillæ on the testa), which yields the well known dye, albumen farinaceous. Fl. R. S.

2. SCOLOPIA, Schreber; Fl. Brit. Ind. i. 190.

Trees, often with axillary spines. Leaves coriaceous, the lowest pair or pairs of secondary nerves from the base. Fl. 2-sexual, small, in axillary racemes. Sepals 4–6, petals similar to sepals, imbricate in bud. Stamens numerous, anthers opening by slits, connective produced beyond anthers. Ovules few, on 3–4 parietal placentas. Berry 2–4 seeded. Species 16, 1 in Australia, the rest in tropical Asia and Africa.

1. **S. crenata,** Clos; Bedd. Fl. Sylv. t. 78.—Syn. *S. acuminata,* Clos; Trimen Handb. Ceylon i. 70.

A middle-sized tree, thorny while young, glabrous except inflorescence, wood red, close grained. Leaves ovate or ovate-lanceolate, 3–6 in., more or less distinctly crenate. Fl. in axillary racemes, pedicels 1–3 fld., connective of anthers glabrous. Berry green, globose, ¾ in. diam.

Common in the forests of the Western Ghats, from North Kanara southwards, Nilgiris, Shevaroys, Malnād of Mysore. Fl. H. S. Ceylon, Borneo, Philippines.

2. **S. Roxburghii,** Clos; Kurz, F. Fl. i. 73. Mergui, Malay Peninsula. Branches armed with long, strong, straight and compound spines. Fl. yellow, solitary, connective ciliate, fruit olive-shaped.

3. FLACOURTIA, Commers.; Fl. Brit. Ind. i. 191.

Trees or shrubs, mostly armed with spinescent branchlets, young shoots and leaves often red. Leaves toothed or crenate, the lowest or the two lowest pairs of secondary nerves proceeding from the base. Fl. small, diœcious in most species, sepals 4–5 imbricate, petals 0. *Male:* Stamens numerous, anthers attached by the bark, opening by slits. *Female:* Ovary 2–6 celled, the parietal placentas meeting in the centre, disk annular, lobed, or of distinct glands. Styles 2–10, short, free, or connate. Fruit a drupe with a number of 1-seeded stones. Cotyledons orbicular. Species 15, difficult to distinguish, tropical Africa and Asia.

A. Leaves elliptic or lanceolate, length of blade more than twice its greatest width.

1. **F. cataphracta,** Roxb.; Kurz, F. Fl. i. 74. Vern. *Na-ywè,* Burm.

A middle-sized deciduous tree, wood reddish, close-grained, stem armed with compound spines, young shoots slightly pubescent. Leaves glabrous, lanceolate or ovate-lanceolate, 2–4 in. Sepals hairy within, edges ciliate. Ovary narrowed into a short, cylindrical or conical style. Stigmas 4–6, capitate. Fruit globose, ¾ in. diam., stones 10–14.

Subhimalayan tract, from Nepal eastwards, Burma. Fl. C. S.

The following 3 species have the secondary nerves very prominent beneath: 2. **F. montana,** Graham. Konkan, north and south Kanara. A very thorny tree, branchlets softly tomentose. Leaves 4–8 in., glabrous above, except the hairy midrib, slightly pubescent beneath. Fl. diœcious in fascicled, densely pubescent racemes. 3. **F. mollis,** Hook. fil. & Thoms. Tenasserim, Kachin hills of Upper Burma. Branchlets and underside of leaves densely and softly tomentose. Leaves 5–7 in., elliptic-lanceolate. Fl. diœcious, in short axillary racemes. 4. **F. inermis,** Roxb.; Cor. Pl. t. 222. A native of

the Malay Archipelago, cultivated in India on account of its acid edible fruit. An unarmed evergreen tree, leaves glabrous, 4–8 in., fl. bisexual, fruit red, seeds 8–10.

B. Leaves ovate or obovate, length of blade not more than twice its greatest width.

5. **F. sepiaria,** Roxb. Cor. pl. t. 68. Vern. *Tambat*, Mar.; *Miridi*, Kan.

A much-branched shrub or small tree, the branchlets as a rule terminating in sharp rigid spines, which bear leaves and flowers. Leaves 1–2 in., glabrous, obovate from a cuneate base. Fl. yellowish, diœcious, styles 3–4, distinct. Drupe purple, ¼ in. diam.

Bengal, Sundarbans, Chittagong, Burma. Scrub on the Coromandel coast, Deccan, Kanara, Kurg, Nilgiris, Travancore. Fl. C.S. Ceylon, Java.

6. **F. Ramontchi,** L'Héritier; Brand. F. Fl. 18; Wight Ic. t. 85.—Syn. *F. sapida*, Roxb. Cor. Pl. t. 69. Vern. *Katāi*, Hind.; *Kakein*, C. P.; *Gargóti*, Berar; *Mehrlo*, Kol.; *Kaikún*, Merwara; *Kānker*, Bauswara; *Pakèr*, *Kaker*, *Bhekal*, *Tamlat*, Mar.; *Gapra*, Coorg.

Fig. 16.—Flacourtia. Ramontchi, L'Hérit. ½.

A large shrub, under favourable conditions a moderate-sized tree, with a short trunk and thorny branches, wood tough, close-grained. Leaves deciduous, 1–5 in., variable in shape from ovate to obovate, glabrous above, more or less pubescent beneath. Fl. yellow, diœcious, in short, simple or compound racemes, generally pubescent. Styles 5–11. Drupe ½ in., dark-red or black, edible, stones superposed in two tiers.

Subhimalayan tract, from the Punjab eastwards, Rajputana, Behar, Central India, the Deccan and the Peninsula, mostly in dry open places and on rocky hills. Manipur. Dry and Eng forests of the Irawaddi valley (Kurz, F. Fl. i. 75). The leaves fall in January–February, the new foliage appears April and May. Fl. November–March. Also in Ceylon and the Malay Archipelago.

4. XYLOSMA, Forster; Fl. Brit. Ind. i. 194.

Characters of *Flacourtia*, but ovary 1-celled, placentas 2, rarely more, parietal, ovules few. Style 1, short. Fruit a small 2–8 seeded berry. Species 30, tropical and subtropical regions of both hemispheres.

1. **X. longifolium,** Clos; Brand. F. Fl. t. 4. Vern. *Cherinda*, *Chirunda*, Pb.; *Katpatia*, *Katari*, Hind.

A moderate-sized tree, glabrous, often armed with strong straight axillary spines. Leaves 4–9 in., coriaceous, shining, lanceolate, or oblong-lanceolate. Secondary nerves 8–10 pair, arching. Fl. small, diœcious, in short axillary glomerate panicles. Stigma indistinctly lobed, berry ¼ in. diam.

Subhimalayan tract and outer hills, ascending to 5,000 ft., from the Punjab eastwards, Manipur. Fl. January–May. China. 2. **X. controversum,** Clos. Nepal, Khasi hills, Assam, China. Nearly allied, differs by broader leaves, 3–6 in. long, secondary nerves 6–8 pair. 3. **X. latifolium,** Hook. f. & Thoms. Bababuden hills, Mysore. A large thorny tree, branchlets, petioles and inflorescence finely pubescent, panicles slender. Berry ⅛ in. diam.

5. GYNOCARDIA, R. Br.; Fl. Brit. Ind. i. 195.

G. odorata, R. Br. in Roxb. Cor. Pl. t. 299 (the only species). Vern. *Chaulmugra*, Beng.

A large evergreen tree, perfectly glabrous, wood hard, red or brown. Leaves coriaceous, oblong, abruptly acuminate, quite entire, 6–10 in. long. Secondary nerves 4–6 pair, prominent beneath. Fl. scented, pale yellow, fragrant, in large fascicles on the trunk or a few in the leaf axils, diœcious. Calyx cup-shaped, 5–toothed, petals 5, with a ciliate scale at the base of each. ♂ : Stamens ∞, anthers basifixed, linear. ♀ : Larger, staminodes 10–15, villous, ovary 1-celled, styles 5, stigma large cordate, ovules ∞ on 5 parietal placentas. Fruit globose, 3–5 in. diam., rind thick, hard, rough. Seed obovoid, 1 in. long, immersed in pulp. Cotyledons flat in oily albumen.

Subhimalayan tract, ascending to 4,000 ft., from Sikkim eastwards, Khasi hills, Chittagong, Burma. Fl. H. S. Pulp of fruit used to poison fish. The Chaulmugra oil of commerce is supposed to be made of the seeds. This, however, is doubtful, and it is supposed that they are the produce of *Taraktogenos Kurzii*, King.

Ryparosa Kurzii, King, in Journ. As. Soc. Beng. vol. 59 (1891), 125; Ann. Gard. Calc. v. 2 t. 154 (*Ryparia cæsia*, Kurz, F. Fl. i. 78). Andamans, Nicobars. A small evergreen tree. Leaves 8–12 in., elliptic. Secondary nerves 6–8 pair, prominent beneath, intermediate and tertiary nerves conspicuously reticulate. Fl. small, diœcious, in axillary tawny-pubescent racemes, the male attaining 12 in. Calyx globose in bud, 3–5 cleft, Petals 5, imbricate, each with a large sericeous scale at the base. Filaments united in a column, anthers 5, ovate, ovary with 1–3 biovulate parietal placentas. Fruit globose, 2-seeded.

6. HYDNOCARPUS, Gaertner; Fl. Brit. Ind. i. 196.

Trees, leaves serrate or entire, stipules deciduous. Fl. few together or solitary, or fasciculate on short thick woody branchlets in the axils of fallen leaves. Sepals 5, imbricate in bud. Petals 5, with scales at the base. ♂ : Stamens 5–8, filaments free, glabrous, anther cells often separate on a broad connective. ♀ : Stamens similar, but anthers without pollen. Ovary 1–celled, ovules many, on 3–6 parietal placentas. Stigmas 3–5 sessile, spreading, lobed. Berry globose, crowned with the persistent stigma, rind hard. Seeds many, embedded in pulp, albumen oily. Species 12, tropical Asia.

Fig. 17.—Hydnocarpus Wightiana, Blume ♀. ½.

1. **H. Wightiana,** Blume.—Syn. *H. inebrians,* Wall.; Wight Ill. t. 16. Vern. *Kastel, Kantel,* Mar.; *Toratti,* Kan.; *Maravetti,* Tam.

A tall tree, branchlets and racemes slightly pubescent. Leaves 4–9 in., membranous or thinly coriaceous, elliptic- or oblong-lanceolate, acuminate, often deeply serrate. Secondary nerves arching, prominent, tertiary nerves not conspicuous, transverse, parallel. Fl. white, ½–1 in. diam, petals ciliate, twice as long as the ovate fimbriate scales. Fruit tomentose, 2–4 in. diam.

Common along the Western Ghats from the Konkan southwards, ascending to 2,000 ft., also below the Ghats in Malabar and Kanara. Fl. H. S. Fruit used to intoxicate fish, the oil of the seeds medicinally in cutaneous diseases. 2. **H. alpina,** Wight Ic. t. 942; Bedd. Fl. Sylv. t. 77. Nilgiris to 6,000 ft., Ceylon (low country). Young shoots nearly glabrous. Leaves 4–6 in., quite entire, veins finely reticulate. Petals oblong-lanceolate, glabrous, equal to the linear scales. 3. **H. castanea,** Hook. fil. & Thoms. Andamans, Tenasserim and Mergui Archipelago. A middle-sized tree, perfectly glabrous. Leaves thickly coriaceous, 8–14 in. Fruit size of an orange, rugose.

Taraktogenos Kurzii, King, in Journ. As. Soc. Beng. vol. 59 (1891), p. 123 (*Hydnocarpus heterophyllus,* Kurz, F. Fl. i. 77). Vern. *Kalawso,* Burm. Eastern and southern slopes of the Pegu Yoma, very frequent in Martaban. An evergreen tree, 40–50 ft. Shoots, young leaves and inflorescence tawny pubescent. Leaves thinly coriaceous, entire, 7–10 in., lanceolate or oblong-lanceolate. Secondary nerves very prominent beneath, tertiary numerous, transverse, and parallel. Sepals 4, petals 8 broadly ovate, ciliate, each with a flat fleshy pubescent gland at the base. Stamens 24, free, filaments hairy. Fruit size of an orange, tawny-velvety. Seeds numerous, embedded in pulp.

ORDER XI. PITTOSPORACEÆ. Gen. Pl. i. 130.

(*Pittosporeæ.*)

Trees or shrubs. Leaves alternate, simple, entire, often crowded at the ends of branches, almost verticillate, stipules 0. Fl. pentamerous, usually bisexual, sepals and petals imbricate. Stamens 5, opposite to sepals, anthers versatile. Ovary 1, of 2 rarely 3–5 carpels, 1-celled or 2–5-celled by the projection of the parietal placentas. Style 1, stigma often lobed. Ovules many. Fruit capsular, sometimes an indehiscent berry. A small embryo in copious albumen.

PITTOSPORUM, Banks; Fl. Brit. Ind. i. 198.

Erect trees or shrubs. Sepals often connate at base, petals erect, claws often connate. Ovary incompletely 2–3-celled. Capsule 2- rarely 3-valved, the placenta in the middle of each valve. Seeds embedded in a viscid pulp.

A. Branchlets glabrous, young shoots sometimes puberulous, leaves glabrous.

1. **P. tetraspermum,** Wight et Arn.; Wight Ic. t. 971; Bedd. Manual t. 2. A large shrub or small tree. Leaves 2–3 in., reticulate veins between secondary nerves. Fl. ⅓ in., greenish yellow, few, in small terminal, nearly sessile umbels. Capsule rough, glabrous, globose, apiculate, 4-seeded, ⅓ in. diam., valves hard, almost woody.

Western Ghats from the Konkan southwards, Nilgiris. Fl. February–March. Ceylon.

2. **P. floribundum,** Wight et Arn.; Brand. F. Fl. 19. Vern. *Yekadi,* Mar.

A small tree. Leaves 4–6 in., pale beneath, margin waved. Fl. yellowish, ¼ in. long, in short compact terminal panicles, consisting of numerous many-flowered dense corymbs. Capsule glabrous, ¼ in. diam., valves coriaceous. Seeds 1–4, occasionally 8.

Subhimalayan tract and outer ranges, from the Jumna eastwards, in Sikkim 5,000–8,000 ft. Khasi hills, Shan hills, Upper Burma, Western Ghats from the Konkan to the Nilgiris. Fl. January–June.

3. **P. nilghirense,** Wight et Arn.; Wight Ill. t. 70. Nilgiris, Sigur, Bolampatty valley, Palni hills. A shrub or small tree. Fl. ⅓ in. long, in slender glabrous 3–8 fld. corymbs, often several from one leaf axil. Capsule somewhat compressed, ⅓ in. long, seeds 6. 4. **P. humile,** Hook. fil. & Thoms. Khasi hills. A small much-branched shrub. Leaves narrowly lanceolate, 2 by ½ in. Fl. ⅙ in. long, in short, fasciculate, few fld. racemes. 5. **P. glabratum,** Lindl. Khasi hills, Manipur, China. A small tree. Leaves linear-lanceolate, 2–4 in., pale beneath. Fl. ½–⅝ in., pale yellow, in lax terminal corymbs. Capsule 1 in. long, ovoid-oblong, 3-valved.

B. Branchlets tomentose, leaves hairy beneath.

6. **P. eriocarpum,** Royle; Brand. F. Fl. 19. Vern. *Meda tūmri*, North-West Provinces.

A small tree with spreading branches. Branchlets, leaves and inflorescence yellowish-tomentose. Leaves 3–8 in., secondary nerves 8–16 pair. Fl. ⅓ in., pale yellow, in short compact terminal panicles. Sepals lanceolate, densely tomentose. Capsule tomentose, ½ in. diam., valves thick, woody, broad-ovate.

Outer North-West Himalaya, Jumna to Sarda, 3,000–6,500 ft. Fl. March, April.

7. **P. dasycaulon,** Miquel. *Gapsundi*, Mar. Evergreen Ghat forests from the Konkan to Travancore. Leaves 3–5 in., glabrous when full grown, except along midrib, secondary nerves not conspicuous. Fl. ⅓ in., in dense terminal panicles, sepals ovate, ciliate. Capsule ⅔ in. diam. 8. **P. ferrugineum,** Ait.; Kurz, F. Fl. i. 78. Tenasserim, Malabar, Malay Peninsula. A spreading, much-branched tree. Branchlets, young leaves and inflorescence rusty-pubescent. Fl. ¼ in., in lax pedunculate compound corymbs, sepals narrow acuminate.

ORDER XII. POLYGALACEÆ. Gen. Pl. i. 134.

(*Polygaleæ.*)

Herbs, rarely trees or shrubs, erect or scandent. Leaves alternate, simple, quite entire. Stipules 0. Fl. zygomorphic, bisexual, 3-bracteate. Sepals 5, as a rule free, the 2 inner larger, petaloid (wings). Petals 3–5, unequal, the lowest concave, generally keel-shaped. Stamens 4–8, filaments usually united into a sheath, anthers mostly opening by terminal pores. Ovary 1–3-celled, style generally curved.

Herbs or erect shrubs, capsule 2-valved	1. POLYGALA.
Trees or erect shrubs, fruit indehiscent, not winged .	2. XANTHOPHYLLUM.
Climbers, fruit indehiscent, winged	3. SECURIDACA.

1. POLYGALA, Linn.; Fl. Brit. Ind. i. 200.

Mostly herbs, a few shrubs. Sepals often persistent, the 2 inner petaloid. Petals 3, united at the base with the staminal sheath, the lowest keel-shaped and generally crested. Stamens 8, filaments united in their lower half into a split sheath. Ovary 2-celled, one ovule in each cell. Capsule 2-valved, 2-seeded. Species 450, in both hemispheres, chiefly in warmer regions.

1. **P. arillata,** Hamilton; Wall. Pl. As. Rar. t. 100; Wight Ic. t. 946.—Syn. *Chamæbuxus arillata*, Hassk.; Kurz, F. Fl. i. 79.

A large shrub, attaining 12 ft., young shoots pubescent. Leaves membranous, elliptic-lanceolate, 4–6 in., petiole ¼–½ in. Fl. ½–¾ in., yellow and purple. Capsule coriaceous, ½ in. diam., rugose when dry. Seeds globose, nearly covered with a fleshy orange-coloured arillus, exalbuminous, cotyledons fleshy.

Outer Himalaya from Nepal eastwards, 2,000–7,000 ft. Khasi hills, Upper Burma, Hills of the western coast. Fl. June–August. Ceylon, Malay Archipelago, China.

2. **P. Karensium**, Kurz (*Chamæbuxus Karensium*, Kurz, F. Fl. i. 79), is a small glabrous shrub, frequent on the hills east of Toungoo, 4,000–6,000 ft. Leaves lanceolate, pale beneath, narrowed into a petiole ½–1 in. long. Fl. white, with pale lilac tips, in short unilateral racemes. Capsule ⅓ in. diam., membranous. Seeds obovate, silky.

2. XANTHOPHYLLUM, Roxb.; Fl. Brit. Ind. i. 208.

Trees or shrubs, leaves turning yellow in drying. Sepals 5, nearly equal. Petals 4 or 5, unequal, zygomorphic, the lowest keeled. Stamens 8, distinct, partly attached to base of petals. Disk annular, often lobed, hypogynous. Ovary 1-celled. Fruit indehiscent, 1-celled. Seed without albumen, arillus none. Species 40, from India to New Guinea and tropical Australia.

A. Flowers more than ⅓ in. long, ovules 4–14.

1. **X. flavescens**, Roxb. Cor. Pl. t. 284; Kurz, F. Fl. i. 81.—Syn. *X. Arnottianum*, Wight; Bedd. Manual t. 3. Vern. *Muttei*, Tam.; *Thitpyu*, Burm.

A large glabrous evergreen tree. Leaves coriaceous, 4–7 in. Secondary nerves 5–7 pair, finely and conspicuously reticulate veins between them. Fl. ⅓–½ in. long, yellow, in axillary or terminal panicles. Sepals finely tomentose. Ovary densely strigose, with pluricellular hairs. The number of ovules varies from 4–12 (the forms *X. angustifolium*, Wight Ill. 50 t. 23, and *X. virens*, Roxb. Cor. Pl. t. 284; Kurz, F. Fl. i. 81, have only 4 ovules). Fruit globose, ⅔ in. diam., olive green, walls very thick.

West side of the peninsula, from the Nilgiris southwards, Silhet, Chittagong hills, Lower and Upper Burma. Fl. February–May. Also Ceylon, Java, Sumatra. 2. **X. affine**, Korth.; Kurz, F. Fl. i. 82. Tenasserim, Malay Peninsula. A shrub or tree. Leaves thinly coriaceous, sepals tomentose, ovary glabrous, ovules 8–14.

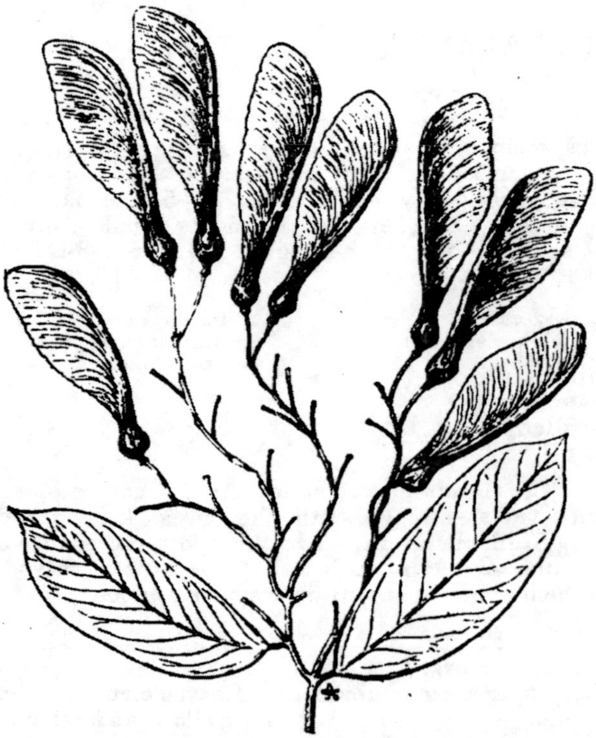

FIG. 18.—Securidaca tavoyana, Wall. ½.

B. Flowers less than ⅓ in. long, ovules 4.

3. **X. glaucum**, Wall.; Kurz, F. Fl. i. 81. Vern. *Thitpyu*, Lower, *Thit Kayin*, Upper Burma.

A glabrous evergreen tree. Leaves chartaceous, glaucous and opaque beneath, reticulate veins distinct. Fl. white, ¼–⅓ in. long, in large lax, slightly pubescent panicles, ovary with 1-celled hairs. Fruit glabrous, verrucose, ⅓–½ in. diam.

Upper and Lower Burma, in moist places, often forming strips of pure shady forest. Fl. March, April. Malay Peninsula.

4. **X. andamanicum**, King, Ann. Bot. Gard. Calc. vol. v. t. 161. Andamans. A small tree. Leaves thinly coriace-

ous, ovary glabrous, fruit smooth, shining. 5. **X. Griffithii**, Hook. fil. Mergui, Malacca and Perak. A tree attaining 50 ft., leaves coriaceous, ovary tomentose. Fruit (unripe) tawny tomentose.

3. SECURIDACA, Linn.; Fl. Brit. Ind. i. 207.

Species 30, tropics of both hemispheres.

S. tavoyana, Wall.—Syn. *S. inappendiculata*, Hassk.; Kurz, F. Fl. i. 80. A large woody climber, wood anomalous, numerous masses of xylem separated by tangential and radial bands of bast (phloëm). Fl. red, in racemes forming a lax terminal panicle. Sepals deciduous, petals 3, the 2 lateral minute, adnate to the staminal sheath, the third concave and hooded. Fruit 1-seeded, indehiscent, a long coriaceous wing at the upper end.

Assam, Silhet, Chittagong, Burma. Fl. August. China.

ORDER XIII. TAMARICACEÆ. Gen. Pl. i. 159.

(*Tamariscineæ*.)

Undershrubs, shrubs, rarely trees or perennial herbs. Leaves alternate, small, generally scale-like, sessile with a broad base, imbricating. Fl. regular, usually bisexual, in spikes, racemes or panicles, in some genera solitary. Sepals and petals pentamerous, sometimes tetramerous, generally free. Stamens 5, 10, or numerous, inserted on an annular glandular disk, anthers versatile, dehiscing longitudinally. Ovary syncarpous, of 3–5 carpels, ovules numerous, on 3–5 placentas, which sometimes are enlarged, so as to divide the ovary into cells. Capsule 3–5 valved. Albumen small or wanting, embryo straight.

Stamens 5 or 10, free, styles 3 or 4, short, each with a large capitate stigma . . . . 1. TAMARIX.
Stamens 10, filaments united into a short tube, ovary tapering into a short style with 3 sessile stigmas . 2. MYRICARIA.

1. TAMARIX, Linn.; Fl. Brit. Ind. i. 248.

Shrubs or small trees, medullary rays broad, very prominent on radial section. Leaves minute, scale-like. In the juvenile state the leaves are longer, lanceolate from a broad base, up to ¼ in. long. Fl. white or pink, in spikes or dense racemes. Sepals and petals free. Stamens 5–10, inserted on an annular disk. Ovary 1-celled, placentas at the bottom of the ovary, styles 3 or 4, short. Seeds small, with a long coma, consisting of a setiform axis studded with long hairs. Species 65, Europe, Asia, and Africa.

Several species, in India, chiefly *T. gallica* and *T. dioica*, are gregarious, covering extensive areas on river banks. On the Indus the seeds of these species, and of other trees, which are borne down by the river, are deposited on the new formations of alluvial land, which are submerged during the floods. When the floods have subsided, the seeds germinate, and in early spring these lands are covered with a dense forest of *Tamarix*, with a sprinkling of other trees, chiefly of *Populus euphratica*.

A. Stamens 5.

1. **T. gallica**, Linn.; Wight Ill. t. 24; Brand. F. Fl. t. 5.—Syn. *T. indica*, Roxb. Vern. *Ghazlei*, Baluch.; *Ghaz*, Pusht.; *Pilchi*, Pb.; *Lei*, *Lai*, *Jhau*, Sind; *Jhau*, Beng.

A glaucous gregarious shrub or small tree, wood reddish. Leaves minute, not sheathing, apex acute, patent or loosely appressed. Fl. mostly bisexual, pentamerous, white or pink, crowded in long slender spikes collected in dense panicles at the ends of branches and forming large irregular masses of flower. Bracts shorter than fl. Disk slightly 5- or 10-crenate, filaments not dilated at base, styles short, stigma often almost sessile. Capsule $\frac{3}{16}$ in. long, more than twice the length of the withered sepals supporting it.

From western Tibet, where it ascends to 11,000 ft., following the Indus and its main tributaries through the Punjab and Sind. Western Peninsula in sandy river beds and on the sea coast. Fl. Aug.–Feb. Ceylon, on the coast in the drier districts. Widely distributed in the countries round the Mediterranean, through western and northern Asia, to China and Japan. Kurz, F. Fl. i. 83, gives this species from Pegu. I have not seen specimens. Roxburgh's species *T. indica* may have to be restored. See Niedenzu de genere Tamarice, Braunsberg, 1895. 2. **T. salina**, Dyer, Salt range, Punjab, differs by broader leaves, and filaments dilated at base.

3. **T. dioica**, Roxb.; Brand. F. Fl. t. 6. Vern. *Lei*, *Pilchi*, Pb.; *Jhau*, Oudh; *Byaung-chedauk*, Upper Burma.

A glaucous gregarious shrub. Leaves sheathing, sheath tubular, apex acuminate, closely appressed, with a broad white margin. Fl. diœcious, pentamerous, purple or light pink, in stiff compact cylindrical pedunculate spikes often forming loose panicles at the ends of branches. Bracts as long as, or nearly as long as, flowers. ♂: Stamens alternating with the 5 lobes of the fleshy disk, anthers distinctly apiculate. ♀: 5 thin linear staminodia, styles filiform, thickened at the end, longer than ovary. Capsule $\frac{3}{16}$ in. long, about twice the length of the withered sepals and petals at its base.

Throughout northern India, ascending to 2,500 ft. in the outer Himalaya. Sind, Western Peninsula, Bengal, Assam. Burma, dry region of the Irawaddi valley, chiefly on sandbanks in river beds. Fl. May–October.

4. **T. articulata**, Vahl; Brand. F. Fl. t. 7.—Syn. *T. orientalis*, Forsk. Vern. *Farash*, Pb.; *Asrelei*, Sind.

A middle-sized tree with an erect trunk, frequently 6–7 ft. in girth, wood white, branchlets articulate at base of sheath, often grey with saline efflorescence. Leaves sheathing, sheath $\frac{1}{10}$ in. long, obliquely truncate, apex triangular, acute, appressed. Sheath and apex with impressed glands. Fl. bisexual or monœcious, loosely scattered on long slender spikes, which are generally collected at the ends of branches in loose panicles. Bracts shorter than fl. Disk entire or indistinctly 5-lobed. Capsule $\frac{1}{6}$ in. long.

Punjab, ascending to 1,200 ft., extending east to the Jumna. Upper and Middle Sind. Grows well on saline soils. The extremities of branchlets and the leaves on older branchlets are shed during the cold season, new shoots and leaves come out about May. Fl. May to September. A variety in the Punjab with upright branches. Afghanistan, western Asia, Egypt, and Somaliland.

B. Stamens 10.

5. **T. ericoides**, Rottl.—Syn. *Trichaurus ericoides*, Wight et Arn.; Wight Ill. t. 24, B. Ic. 22. Vern. *Jhaura*, Merwara; *Jao*, *sarub*, *sarata*, Mar.; *Shushar*, Pangi, Lahaue.

A beautiful shrub or small tree. Leaves amplexicaul, hardly sheathing, ovate-lanceolate, acuminate. Fl. larger than any of the others, $\frac{3}{16}$ in. long, heath-like, pale pink, at times white, on short pedicels, in crowded terminal spike-like racemes. Disk 10-lobed, alternate stamens shorter. Capsule $\frac{1}{2}$ in. long.

Western Peninsula in the beds of rivers, extending north to the western foot of the Aravalli hills, to Behar and Bengal. Fl. Sept.–Dec. 6. **T. stricta**, Boiss. Sind, covered with greyish-white dry and tasteless powder. Leaves sheathing, almost truncate, covered with round white elevated dots.

2. MYRICARIA, Desv.; Fl. Brit. Ind. i. 249.

Fl. bisexual, pink or white, in long racemes. Stamens more or less united in a tube. Species 10, Europe, Central Asia, China.

1. **M. germanica**, Desv.; Brand. F. Fl. t. 8.—Syn. *M. bracteata*, Royle Ill. t. 44. Vern. *Hombu*, *Umbu*, North-West Himalaya.

A gregarious shrub. Leaves sessile, linear-lanceolate, generally crowded, less than ⅛ in. long. Fl. pink, on short pedicels, in dense cylindrical racemes often 12 in. long. Bracts longer than pedicels, ovate-lanceolate, with broad membranous lacerate margins, caducous.

Abundant in the inner arid regions of the Himalaya from Iskardo to Sikkim, between 5,000 and 10,000 ft., occasionally to 15,000 ft. Chiefly in sandy stream beds, where it often covers large areas. Fl. July, Aug. Also in Tibet, Afghanistan, western and northern Asia, and on the mountains of Europe. 2. **M. elegans**, Royle; Kunawar, Spiti, Lahaul, Ladak and Zanskar, often associated with *M. germanica*. Leaves larger, oblanceolate, fl. white.

ORDER XIV. HYPERICACEÆ. Gen. Pl. i. 163.

(*Hypericineæ*.)

(Included under *Guttiferæ*, Engler u. Prantl, iii 6. 205.)

Herbs or shrubs, rarely trees. Leaves opposite, often punctate, entire in the species here described, stipules 0. Fl. bisexual, regular, cymose or solitary, sepals and petals each 5, sepals imbricate, petals contorted in bud. Stamens ∞ in 3 or 5 bundles, anthers versatile. Ovary of 3–5 carpels, 1- or 3–5-celled, styles filiform, free or united, ovules on parietal or axile placentas. Seeds without albumen.

Capsule opening loculicidally, seeds winged . . . . 1. CRATOXYLON.
Capsule opening septicidally or at the junction of carpels, seeds not winged . . . . HYPERICUM (p. 48).

1. CRATOXYLON, Blume; Fl. Brit. Ind. i. 257.

Fl. in axillary or terminal cymose panicles, sepals persistent. Fleshy hypogynous glands alternating with the staminal bundles. Ovary 3-celled styles 3, distinct. Capsule dehiscing loculicidally, seeds winged at the upper end. Species 12 in tropical Asia.

1. **C. polyanthum**, Korth.; Kurz, F. Fl. i. 84.

A middle-sized glabrous tree thorny, (Pierre, Fl. For. Cochin. t. 50). Leafless in H. S., stem fluted, heartwood dark-coloured. Leaves elliptic-lanceolate, glaucous beneath, reticulate veins distinct. Fl. pink or bright red, in 3' fld. axillary cymes, often solitary, petals persistent some time after flowering, hypogynous glands large, nearly half the length of petals. Capsule oblong, considerably longer than sepals, nearly twice their length.

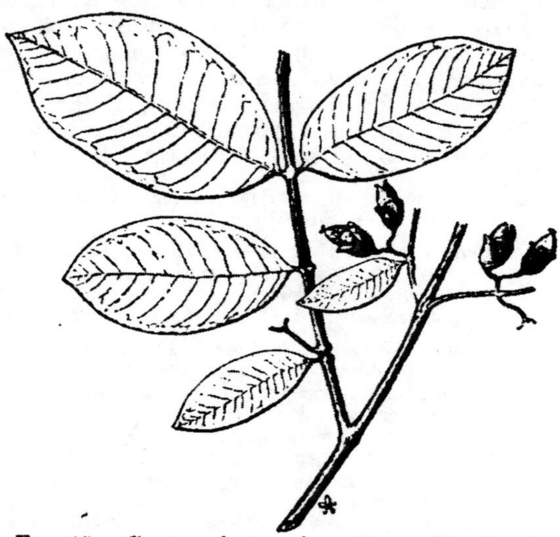

FIG. 19.—Cratoxylum polyanthum, Korth. ½.

Martaban and Tenasserim, Andamans. Fl. March, April. Also in Cochinchina, Cambodia, Borneo, China.

2. **C. neriifolium**, Kurz. Vern. *Bèbya*, Burm.

Differs by narrower lanceolate leaves. Fl. in few fld. cymes, forming lax terminal panicles, capsules ovoid, slightly longer than sepals.

Chittagong, dry country of Irawaddi valley, common, yields good fuel, Pegu, Tenasserim. Fl. H. S. Cambodia. 3. **C. arborescens**, Blume; Malay Peninsula and Archipelago, reported from Moulmein, evergreen. Leaves coriaceous, fl. scarlet, in large terminal panicles.

The following species are leafless in the H. S., and have very delicate caducous petals: 4. **C. formosum**, Benth. & Hook. fil.; Kurz, F. Fl. i. 84. Andamans, Siam, Malay Peninsula and Archipelago. A glabrous tree, generally small, but at times attaining 80 ft. Leaves broadly elliptic, thinly coriaceous when mature. Fl. ½ in., pure white, with a slight red tinge, capsule ¾ in., three times the length of calyx. 5. **C. prunifolium**, Dyer; Pierre, Fl. Cochinch. t. 52 (*C. pruniflorum*, Kurz, F. Fl. i. 84). A small pubescent deciduous shrub or tree, usually armed with sharp spinescent branchlets, in the Eng forests of Burma and in Cochinchina. (*Sathange hnauk*, Upper Burma.) Leaves obovate to linear oblong, grey-velvety beneath. Fl. ¼–⅓ in. lilac or pink.

Of **Hypericum**, Linn., Fl. Brit. Ind. i. 253, with large yellow flowers, seeds not winged, 19 species are known in India, mostly perennial, a few annual herbs. Some are shrubs up to 6 ft. high, of which may be mentioned :—

A. *Styles longer than ovary.* 1. **H. mysorense**, Heyne; Wight Ic. t. 56. Western Ghats, from the Konkan southwards, Nilgiris, Palnis, Ceylon. Leaves oblong-lanceolate approximate. Fl. 2–2½ in. diam. 2. **H. cernuum**, Roxb.; *Piuli*, N.W. North-West Himalaya, Indus to Nepal, Kuram valley, Afghanistan. Leaves elliptic-lanceolate, glaucous beneath. Fl. 2 in. diam.

B. *Styles not longer than ovary.* 3. **H. Hookerianum**, Wight et Arn.; Wight Ic. 959. Himalaya 6,000–11,000 ft. from Kumaon eastwards, Khasi hills, Upper Burma, Nilgiris, Java. Branches terete. Leaves 1–4 in., ovate-lanceolate, obtuse Fl. 2 in. diam. 4. **H. patulum**, Thunb. (*H. oblongifolium*, Wall. Pl. As. Rar. t. 244.) Himalaya, from Kashmir eastwards, Khasi hills, Manipur. Branches 2-edged, leaves 1–2 in., elliptic-lanceolate. Fl. 1 in. diam.

ORDER XV. **GUTTIFERÆ.** Gen. Pl. i. 167.

(Vesque in DC. Monogr. Phan. vol. viii., 1893.)

Trees, rarely shrubs, as a rule evergreen and entirely glabrous. Leaves opposite, generally without stipules. Fl. regular, generally polygamous, sometimes bisexual. Sepals 2–6, often in decussate pairs, petals 2–6, imbricate or contorted, in some cases 0. (In this order the sepals are arranged in pairs in the same way as leaves, while petals have a spiral arrangement.) Stamens as a rule indefinite, hypogynous, filaments often connate in bundles. Ovary generally 1–5 celled. Fruit usually indehiscent, seeds without albumen.

Resin-canals and -cavities in leaves, pith and bark. Transverse bars of wood parenchyma between medullary rays.

A. Ovary 2–12 celled, cells with one, rarely two ovules, stigma peltate, sessile, rarely on a short style. Embryo a homogeneous fleshy mass.

Calyx of 4 or 5 sepals	1. GARCINIA.
Calyx closed in bud, bursting into 2 valves . . .	2. OCHROCARPUS.

B. Ovary 1–2 celled, ovules 1–4 in each cell, style slender, or 2 styles. Embryo of two fleshy cotyledons, sometimes consolidated.

Secondary nerves ∞, close, conspicuous, style 1, stigma generally peltate	3. CALOPHYLLUM.
Secondary nerves many, joined by transverse veins, styles 2, stigma minute	4. POECILONEURON.
Secondary nerves very close but indistinct, stigma peltate	5. MESUA.
Secondary nerves distant, not conspicuous, stigma 4 fid.	6. KAYEA.

1. GARCINIA, Linn.; Fl. Brit. Ind. i. 259.

Trees, rarely shrubs, as a rule entirely glabrous, in most species with a yellow rarely white, resinous juice in the bark, pith and endocarp, perhaps also in the wood. Leaves evergreen, rarely stipulate. Fl. cymose or solitary, polygamous. Sepals 4 or 5, petals 4 or 5, imbricate. *Male*: Stamens numerous, collected in a ring or in several bundles, which surround a rudimentary ovary, more often on a central often 4-cornered mass, rarely free. *Female* or *bisexual*: A 2–12 celled ovary crowned by a large peltate stigma, which is usually sessile, ovules solitary in each cell attached to the inner angle. Stamens or staminodes generally surrounding the ovary. Fruit with a coriaceous rind, seeds embedded in pulp. The embryo consists of a large homogeneous fleshy mass, the cells of which are filled with oil. Species 180, tropics of the old world.

A. Fl. pentamerous, occasionally on the same tree tetramerous. *Male*: Stamens in 5 bundles surrounding a distinct rudimentary ovary.

1. **G. Xanthochymus**, Hook. fil.—Syn. *Xanthochymus pictorius*, Roxb. Cor. Pl. t. 196; Bedd. Fl. Sylv. t. 88. Vern. *Jharambi*, Mar.; *Deva garige*, *Janagi*, Kan.; *Nela mawu*, Coorg; *Madaw*, Burm.

A moderate-sized tree with dense dark green shining foliage, branchlets quadrangular, dilated below the nodes. Leaves thickly coriaceous, oblong or elliptic-oblong, acute, blade 8–14, petiole ¾–1 in., thick, channelled on the upper side, secondary nerves numerous, parallel, alternating with shorter intermediate nerves. Fl. fasciculate on thick uneven axillary protuberances, pedicels 1 in., petals ⅓ in., orbicular, spreading, thin. *Male*: Stamens in 5 broad bundles of 3–5, on a fleshy lobed disk. *Bisexual*: ovary 5-celled, stigma 5-lobed. Fruit dark yellow 2–3 in. diam.

Sikkim, ascending to 3,000 ft., Assam, Khasi and Chittagong hills, Burma, Andamans. Western Peninsula, in the Circars, but chiefly in the evergreen forests along the Western Ghats, from North Kanara southwards. Fl. H. S. Fr. C. S. Also in Penang.

2. **G. spicata**, Hook. fil.; Trimen Handb. Ceyl. i. 98.—Syn. *G. ovalifolia*, Fl. Brit. Ind. i. 269 (*G. spicata* is the older name and *G. ovalifolia*, Oliver, is an African species). Vern. *Haldi*, Mar.

A moderate-sized tree, with wide-spreading branches, branchlets angular. Leaves broadly elliptic, obtuse, secondary nerves numerous, blade 3–6, petiole ¼–½ in. Fl. on short pedicels, fasciculate on axillary protuberances (undeveloped branchlets), which frequently lengthen out and form spiciform racemes up to 6 in. long. Ovary 3–4 celled, stigma 3–5 lobed. Fruit green, the size of a walnut.

Western Ghats, from Matheran southwards. On the east side near the Pulicat lake. Fl. H. S. Also in Ceylon. A var. with larger l. and fl. on the ghats of the Konkan and of Kanara, Fl. C. S. (Cooke, Fl. Bombay i. 79). 3. **G. andamanica**, King. Andamans (*G. dulcis*, Kurz, F. Fl. i. 92). Branchlets thick, angular, pubescent. Leaves 8–11 in., from a broad base elongate-ovate, secondary nerves 14–16 pair, prominent beneath. Fruit bright yellow 1–1½ in. crowned by the persistent 5-lobed stigma.

B. Fl. tetramerous. *Male*: Stamens surrounding a rudimentary ovary. *Female*: ovary 5–12 celled.

4. **G. Mangostana**, Linn. *The Mangosteen.* Vern. *Mingut*, Burm.

An evergreen glabrous middle-sized tree, attaining under favourable circumstances 60 ft. and more. Leaves thickly coriaceous, 6–10 in., elliptic-oblong, secondary nerves numerous, parallel, alternating with shorter intermediate nerves, joined by distinct intramarginal veins. Fl. as a rule bisexual, solitary or in pairs at the ends of branchlets, 2 in. diam. Stamens many, filaments slender, flat at base and sometimes connate, anthers ovate-oblong, 2-celled. Ovary 5–8 celled, stigma sessile, thick, 5–8 lobed. (Male fl. described by Rox-

burgh: stamens ∞ on the 4 lobes of a large fleshy receptacle.) Fruit globose, dark purple, rind thick, full of yellow resinous juice, seeds embedded in snow-white delicious pulp.

Home unknown, cultivated in the moister regions of tropical Asia. Fl. November-February., Fr. May, June. The distribution of sexes in *Garcinia* merits careful study. Pierre has examined more than 1,500 Mangosteen trees, without finding a single male fl. But he adds that several species produce male fl. while young, and female fl. at a later age. Pierre, Fl. For. Cochinch. t. 54.

Nearly allied: 5. **G. pedunculata,** Roxb.; Wight Ic. t. 114, 115. Rangpur (Bengal), Assam. Cultivated on account of the pleasantly acid fruit. Leaves 6–12 in., narrowed into petiole 1–1½ in. long, secondary nerves distant, 10–14 pair. Male fl. large, in 8–12-fld. panicles. Fruit yellow, size of a small melon. 6. **G. travancorica,** Bedd. Fl. Sylv. i. 178. Tinnevelli and Travancore Ghats, in the southernmost portion of the Peninsula, gregarious in places. A middle-sized tree, very ornamental. Leaves 2–4 in., linear-oblong, secondary nerves numerous, parallel, almost at right angles to midrib, distinct but not prominent, alternating regularly with shorter intermediate nerves. Ovary 4-celled. Fruit 1¼–1¾ in., ovoid to globose, seeds 1–2.

7. **G. speciosa,** Wall. Pl. As. Rar. t. 258; Kurz, F. Fl. i. 88. Vern. *Parawa*, Burm.

A large evergreen tree. Leaves coriaceous, elliptic-lanceolate, secondary nerves parallel, numerous, alternating with faint shorter intermediate nerves. Fl. sweet-scented; ♂: 1–1½ in. diam., on slender peduncles ¾ in., in fascicles of 4–5 at the ends of branchlets, anthers ∞ ovate, nearly sessile on the fleshy 4-lobed mass round the short thick abortive ovary, which is crowned by a large yellow convex orbicular stigma. ♀: Solitary, stigma entire or indistinctly 4-lobed. Fruit globose, 2 in. diam., bright red when ripe, pulp very acid.

Tenasserim and Andamans. Fl. February–April.

Nearly allied are the following eastern species: 8. **G. moulmeinensis,** Pierre; Vesque Guttiferæ in DC. Monogr. Phan. viii. 394, Burma, probably *G. cornea*, Kurz, F. Fl. i. 88. 9. **G. Kurzii,** Pierre; Vesque l.c. 408, and 10. **G. Kingii,** Pierre; Vesque, l.c. 407, both from the Andamans. 11. **G. affinis,** Wall. (under *G. cornea*, L., in Fl. Brit. Ind. i. 260, *G. cornea*, L.; Vesque l.c. 397 is a native of Amboina), Silhet. 12. **G. atroviridis,** Griff., Fl. Brit. Ind. i. 266. Assam, Malay Peninsula.

C. Fl. tetramerous. ♂: Stamens surrounding a rudimentary ovary. ♀: Ovary 2-celled.

13. **G. stipulata,** T. And.; Fl. Brit. Ind. i. 267; Gamble List, 7.

A middle-sized, sometimes a large tree. Leaves 6–12 in., thickly coriaceous, elliptic-oblong or elliptic-lanceolate, secondary nerves 10–16 pair, prominent beneath, with shorter intermediate nerves, tertiary nerves parallel, obliquely transverse, stipules small, early deciduous. Fl. ♂: In shortly pedunculate 3–7-fld. cymes, axillary, or above the scars of fallen leaves, pedicels ½–¾ in., bracteolate above their base and in the axils of acute or rounded bracts. Stamens many, in an annular mass enclosing the rudimentary pistil. ♀: Singly or in pairs. Fruit yellow, oblong, 2-celled and 2-seeded.

Subhimalayan tract, from Sikkim eastwards, ascending to 5,000 ft. Common in the valleys of the Tista and its affluents. Fl. August, September.

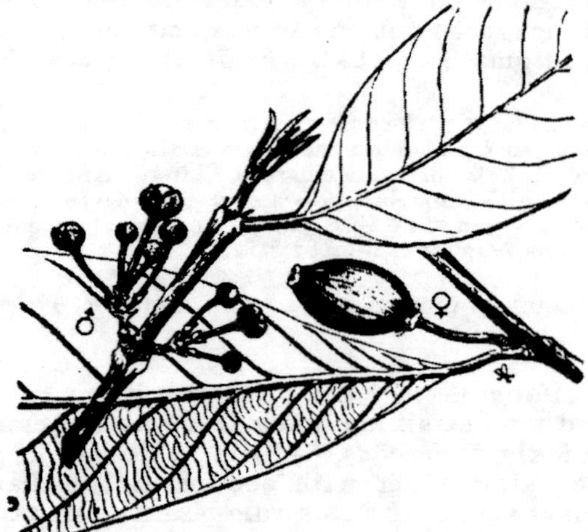

FIG. 20. Garcinia stipulata, T. And. ½.

Nearly allied: 14. **G. anomala**, Planch. et Triana. Khasi hills. A small erect tree, branches often whorled. Leaves coriaceous, turning yellow in drying, secondary nerves numerous, parallel, stipules 0. Fl. greenish-yellow, inodorous, cymes 3-fld., pedicels supported by foliaceous bracts ⅜ in. long, petals ½ in. long. Fr. 1½ in. diam., pericarp thin. 15. **G. merguensis**, Wight Ic. t. 116; Kurz, F. Fl. i. 89. Malay Peninsula from Mergui southwards, a middle-sized tree. Leaves 3–4 in., turning brown in drying, secondary nerves indistinct. Fl. small, ♂ in many-fld. cymes, anthers numerous, on 4 distinct thick fleshy bundles surrounding a large rudimentary pistil.

D. Fl. tetramerous. *Male*: a central round or 4-sided mass with numerous 2-celled anthers.

16. **G. paniculata**, Roxb.; Wight Ic. t. 112. Vern. *Bubi Kowa*, Silhet.

A middle-sized tree. Leaves 6–9 in., membranous, elliptic-lanceolate, narrowed into petiole ¾–1 in. long, secondary nerves distant, 8–10 pair, tertiary transverse, faint, numerous. Sepals green, smaller than petals, the inner obtuse, larger than the outer, petals white, imbricate. ♂: in pyramidal panicles with decussate branches, often longer than leaves, anthers numerous, imbricate on a large globose central mass. ♀: in pedunculate sometimes branching spikes, stigma hemispherical, entire, tubercled. A few staminodia surrounding the ovary. Fruit yellow, 1 in. diam., the seeds immersed in pulp, similar in taste to that of a mangosteen.

Bhutan, Assam, Khasi hills, Silhet. Fl. November, December. Fr. July.

17. **G. echinocarpa**, Thw.; Trimen Handb. Ceylon, i. 96.

A tree attaining 50 ft., trunk thick, throwing out long aërial roots. Leaves 3–5 in., coriaceous, ovate or obovate, tapering into the ½–¾ in. long petiole,

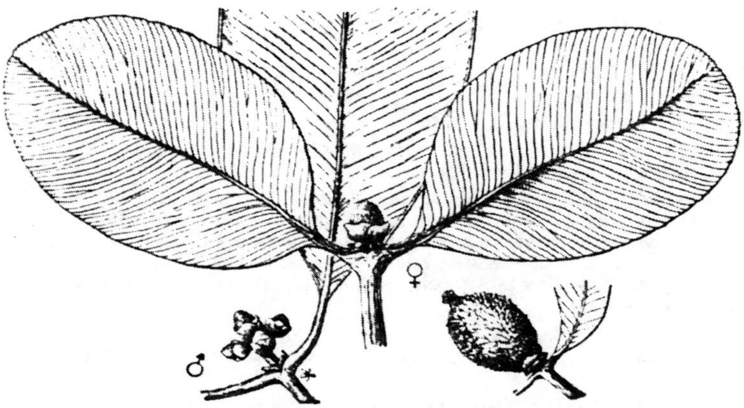

FIG. 21.—Garcinia echinocarpa, Thw. ½.

secondary nerves numerous, parallel. Fl. greenish, sessile. ♂: in clusters, stamens numerous on a thick 4-sided central mass, anther cells 2, adnate to a thick connective. ♀: Ovary 4-celled, covered with numerous imbricate fleshy scales. Fr. 1–1½ in. long, covered with sharp tubercles, seeds 1–3.

In evergreen forests, abundant on the Tinnevelli hills, in Travancore above 3,000 ft., Fl. April. Ceylon.

18. **G. Cambogia**, Desrouss.; Roxb. Cor. Pl. t. 298; Bedd. Fl. Sylv. t. 85. To this species probably belong: *G. conicarpa*, Wight Ic. t. 121, and *G. papilla*, Wight, Spic. Nilg. t. 28, 29, Ic. t. 960. Vern. *Upagi mara*, Kan.; *Manthulli*, Coorg; *Gorakkapulli*, Trav.

A middle-sized tree. Leaves 4–6 in., broadly lanceolate, blade 4–6 in., narrowed into petiole ½ in. long, secondary nerves 8–12 pair, with shorter intermediate ones. Fl. yellow, or orange. ♂ : Numerous 2-celled anthers on short filaments upon a short thick central receptacle. Bisexual or ♀ : Stamens 6–20, often sterile, free or connate in bundles, surrounding the ovary, which is 6–10 celled, stigma 6–10 lobed. Fruit varying in shape, 2½–3 in diam., yellow or reddish, with 6–10 deep furrows which are continued nearly to the apex.

Evergreen forests along the Western Ghats from Kanara southwards. Fl. C. and H. S. Fr. R. S.

19. **G. indica,** Choisy; Pierre, Fl. For. Coch. t. 80.—Syn. *G. purpurea*, Roxb.; Bedd. Ic. Pl. Ind. Or. t. 270. Vern. *Kokum*, Hind.; *Murgal*, Kan.; *Ratamba*, Mar.

Fig. 22.—Garcinia indica, Choisy. ½.

A slender tree with drooping branches, branchlets black. Leaves red when young, 2–4 in., thickly membranous, lanceolate, occasionally oblanceolate, nearly sessile, secondary nerves slender, 6–10 pair, a few shorter very slender intermediate nerves between. Fl. small — ♂ : In terminal 3–7-flowered often pedunculate cymes, pedicels ¼ in. long, anthers ∞, 2-celled on short filaments crowded on a central hemispherical receptacle. ⚥ : Solitary, stamens 10–18 in 4 bundles alternating with petals. Ovary 5–7 celled, stigma 6–7 radiate, each ray with 2 lines of tubercles. Fruit globose, 1½ in. diam., not grooved, purple, seeds embedded in a red acid pulp.

Western coast and Western Ghats from Matheran southwards. Often planted. Fl. November–February. Fr. April, May.

Closely allied are: 20. **G. microstigma,** Kurz, F. Fl. i. 91. A single-stemmed or meagre shrub, not unfrequent on South Andaman. Leaves similar to but larger than those of *G. indica*. 21. **G. lanceæfolia,** Roxb.; Wight Ic. t. 168, Assam, Khasi hills, Silhet, Chittagong hills. A slender bush. Leaves 2–4 in., thickly membranous, lanceolate, acuminate, calyx yellowish-green, petals bright red. Fr. orange yellow, obovoid, 1 in. diam., seeds 6–8.

E. Fl. tetramerous. ♂ : a central 4-sided mass with 4-celled anthers.

22. **G. Cowa,** Roxb.—Syn. *G. Kydia*, Roxb.; Wight Ic. t. 113; Kurz, F. Fl. i. 90. Vern. *Taungthale*, Burm.

A large tree with drooping branches. Leaves 4–5 in., membranous, broadly lanceolate, secondary nerves faint, very oblique, 6–10 pair. Fl. yellow or reddish yellow, ½ in. diam. ♂ : In 3–8-fld. umbels, stamens numerous, densely covering a fleshy almost 4-cornered central mass; rudimentary pistil 0, anthers 4-celled, the cells at the 4 angles of a thick connective. ♀ : Ovary globose 6–8 celled, style grooved, stigma broad, granular. Fruit the size of a small orange, yellow or dark purple, 6–8 grooved, terminated by a nipple-shaped protuberance.

Assam, Silhet, Chittagong, Chota Nagpore, Nilgiris and elsewhere in the Peninsula. Lower Burma, Andamans. Fl. February–May. Fr. May, June.

Nearly allied is 23. **G. succifolia,** Kurz (1872); F. Fl. i. 91 (*G. loniceroides*, T. And., Fl. Brit. Ind. i. 264 (1874). Upper Burma, Sittang and Irawaddi valleys in Lower Burma. Leaves lanceolate, 2–4 in. long.

F. Fl. tetramerous. ♂ : Anthers on a central mass, 1-celled, dehiscing transversely.

24. **G. Morella,** Desrouss.; Bedd. Fl. Sylv. t. 86. Syn. *Hebradendron cambogioides*, Graham; Wight Ill. t. 44.

A middle-sized tree, branchlets quadrangular. Leaves 3–5 in., thinly coriaceous, broadly lanceolate. Fl. greenish-white, sessile in the axils of fallen leaves. ♂ : 2–3 together, anthers 1-celled dehiscing transversely, filaments short, on a central thick 4-sided column. ♀ : Staminodes 12, connate at base in a ring round the globular 4-celled ovary, stigma peltate, irregularly lobed and tubercled. Fruit ¾ in. diam., seeds 4.

North Kanara, evergreen forests (Talbot); South Kanara, moist forests of the plains and ghats to 2,000 ft. (Bedd.). Fl. November. Fr. February, March. Common in Ceylon, moist low country to 2,000.

Closely allied are the following species: 25. **G. pictoria,** Roxb.; Wight Ic. t. 102; Bedd. Fl. Sylv. t. 87. A common tree in the forests on the west side of the peninsula up to 8,500 ft. (Bedd.). Staminodia in the female flower in 3–4 fleshy bundles, each having 2–7 sterile clavate anthers. 26. **G. elliptica,** Wall.; Vesque Guttiferæ, 478. Khasi hills, Silhet. The horizontal anthers of the male flower often bent down at the ends.

The pigment obtained from *G. Morella* and *pictoria* is equal to the gamboge of commerce, which is yielded by a Siamese species, *G. Hanburyi*, Hook. fil.; Pierre, Fl. Forest. t. 73, 74. It exudes from incisions made in the bark.

27. **G. Choisyana,** Wall., and 28. **G. heterandra,** Wall., of the Eastern Peninsula, have broadly ovate leaves, the former membranous, the latter thickly coriaceous. 29. **G. Wightii,** T. And., from the Western Peninsula, has linear-lanceolate leaves.

2. OCHROCARPUS, Thouars; Fl. Brit. Ind. i. 270.

Differs from *Garcinia* chiefly by the calyx, which is entirely closed at first, and afterwards splits into 2, sometimes 3 valves or sepals. Petals 4, stamens numerous, filaments slender, filiform, entirely free or only connate at base. Ovary 2-celled, 2 ovules in each cell, or 4-celled, one ovule only in each cell.

Species 12, 7 in Madagascar, 1 in tropical Africa, the rest in India and the Indian Archipelago, eastwards to New Guinea and Fiji. Not in Ceylon.

1. **O. longifolius,** Benth. & Hook. fil.; Bedd. Fl. Sylv. t. 89.—Syn. *Calysaccion longifolium*, Wight Ic. t. 1999. Vern. *Wundy, Punay, Suringi*, Kan.

A large tree. Leaves 5–9 in., rigidly coriaceous, oblong and oblong-lanceolate, generally acute, secondary nerves indistinct, veins in dry leaves distinctly and minutely reticulate. Fl. male and bisexual, ⅜ in. diam., white, streaked with red, in dense fascicles, with numerous bracts at base, in the axils of fallen leaves or on the old wood, sepals reflexed during flowering, petals acute. Fr. obliquely ovoid, pointed, 1 in. long.

Western Ghats from Khandala to Malabar. Fl. March, often cultivated. The globose flower buds are used for dying silk.

Closely allied is 2. **O. siamensis,** T. And. (including **O. nervosus,** Kurz, F. Fl. i. 94). Lower and Upper Burma, Siam, Cambodia, sometimes in Eng forests. Leaves smaller, obtuse or emarginate. Fl. solitary or in few-fld. lax fascicles, on long slender pedicels.

3. CALOPHYLLUM, Linn.; Fl. Brit. Ind. i. 271.

Trees with shining coriaceous leaves, secondary nerves ∞, straight, closely and evenly parallel, nearly at right angles to midrib, buds as a rule puberulous with minute rusty hairs. Wood reddish, medullary rays distinct on a radial less distinct on a transverse section, being similar in colour to the intervening tissue. Fl. ♂ and ♀ in axillary or terminal panicles, sepals 4, petals none, or 4–8, the 2 inner or all sepals petaloid. Stamens ∞, filaments filiform, free or connate at base. Ovary 1-celled, style slender, stigma generally peltate, ovules few, mostly one only. Drupe with a crustaceous endocarp, cotyledons thick, fleshy, the cells filled with oil. Species 60, tropics of both hemispheres.

A. Petals 4.

1. **C. Inophyllum,** Linn.; Wight Ic. t. 77. *Alexandrian laurel, Punna,* Malyal.

A middle-sized ornamental tree or shrub, glabrous, buds only with minute

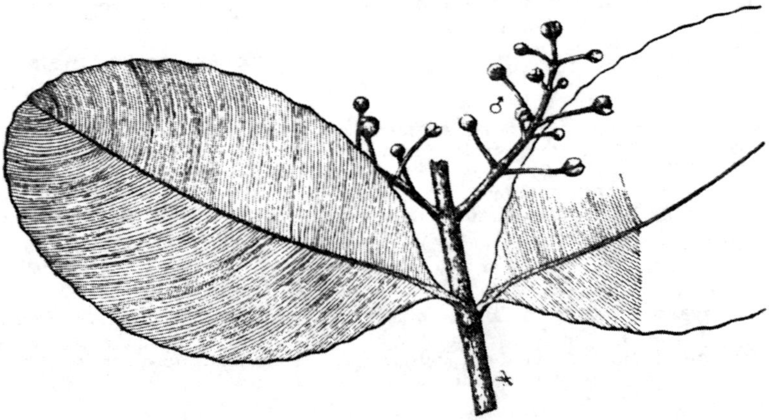

Fig. 28.—Calophyllum Inophyllum, Linn. ½.

rusty hairs. Leaves elliptic, elliptic-lanceolate or obovate, blade 4–8, narrowed into petiole ½–1 in. long. Fl. scented, white, 1 in. diam., in axillary racemes. Fr. yellow, 1 in. diam.

A littoral species, on the west coast from Bombay, on the east coast from Orissa southwards. Andamans and Tenasserim. Fl. C. S. On the sea coast, within the tropics, from Madagascar to Australia and the Pacific. Often cultivated. The seeds yield oil.

2. **C. elatum,** Bedd. Fl. Sylv. t. 2. This and *C. tomentosum* are known as the *Poon spar tree.*

A tall tree, wood light red, shining, branchlets and petioles glabrous. Leaves elliptic-lanceolate, blade 3–5, petiole ½–1 in. long. Fl. in ample terminal pubescent panicles, sepals hairy, the 2 outer small, the 2 inner petaloid, and as large as petals. Fr. ovoid, apiculate, 1¼ in. long.

Evergreen forests of the Western Ghats, and adjoining hills, from South Kanara to the Palnis. Fl. January–Febuary. 3. **C. tomentosum,** Wight Ic. t. 110. Evergreen forests of North Kanara, branchlets and petioles rusty-tomentose. Fl. in axillary racemes, the 4 sepals of nearly equal size. 4. **C. polyanthum,** Wall. Sikkim to 5,000 ft., Khasi hills, hills east of Toungoo (Kurz, F. Fl. i. 95). A large tree, almost entirely glabrous. Leaves lanceolate, blade 4–7, petiole marginate, ½–1 in. Fl. white, ⅓ in. diam., in axillary racemes and terminal panicles. Fr. globose, ⅝ in. diam. 5. **C. trapezifolium,** Thwaites. Travancore evergreen forest, 4,000 ft.—Ceylon. A large tree, leaves obovate, 1–1½ in., narrowed into short petiole. Fl. nearly 1 in. diam., in few-fld. axillary racemes near the ends of branches. Fr. ovoid, apiculate, ⅝ in. long.

B. Petals none or early deciduous.

6. **C. Wightianum,** Wall.—Syn. *C. decipiens,* Wight Ic. t. 106. The *Poon spar* of Travancore. Vern. *Bobbi,* Mar.; *Iria, Irai,* Kan.; *Katta punna,* Travancore.

A tree, lofty in Travancore, middle-sized elsewhere, almost entirely glabrous, bark yellow (Talbot), branchlets angular. Leaves rigidly coriaceous, obovate, obtuse. Fl. ⅓ in. diam. on axillary racemes, shorter than leaves, petals sometimes present in the bud. Fr. 1 by ¾ in.

On the banks of rivers and in evergreen forest, Western Ghats ascending to 4,500 ft., from North Kanara southwards. Fl. December–April. A remarkable variety, possibly a distinct species, with elliptic acute leaves, fr. small, ½ in. long, oil made from the seed, fl. Oct., Nov., occurs along river banks in Travancore and possibly further north (*Cheru punna, Atta punna, Pora punna*, Travancore). To this may belong Bedd., Fl. Sylv. t. 90. 7. **C. amœnum**, Wall.; Kurz, F. Fl. i. 95; Vesque in Monogr. Phan. viii. 576 (*C. retusum*, Wall., Fl. Brit. Ind. i. 272, in part). Tenasserim and Andamans, young shoots, petioles and inflorescence with minute rusty pubescence. Leaves elliptic, rigidly coriaceous, blade 2–4 in., narrowed into petiole ½–1 in. long. Fr. globose ⅓ in. diam. 8. **C. spectabile**, Willd. Tenasserim, Andamans and Nicobar. *Pantaga*, Burm. A large tree. Leaves 7–10 in. long, woolly beneath along midrib. Fl. ⅜ in. diam., on pedicels ¾ in. long, in short umbelliform axillary cymes, sepals all petaloid. Fr. globose, ¾ in. diam.

4. PŒCILONEURON, Bedd.; Fl. Brit. Ind. i. 278.

Trees, branchlets and petioles clothed with minute hairs. Leaves coriaceous, secondary nerves ∞, close, joined at right angles by numberless transverse veins. Fl. bisexual; (♂ fl. not yet found ?). Calyx of 4 or 5 sepals, imbricate in bud, petals 5 or 6, contorted or imbricate. Stamens 16–20, filaments free, slightly united at base, anthers basifixed. Ovary 2-celled, 2 ovules in each cell. Styles 2, filiform. Species 2.

1. **P. indicum**, Bedd. Fl. Sylv. t. 3. Vern. *Kirbally, Balagi*, Kan. *Puthan kolli*, Trav.

A large tree. Leaves 4–9 in., acuminate, secondary nerves very close and equidistant. Fl. yellowish-white, in terminal panicles, sepals 5, petals 5, contorted, anthers tuberculate, each cell consisting of numerous superposed compartments.

Evergreen forests of the Western Ghats from South Kanara southwards, ascending to 4,000 ft. Fl. C. and H. S. 5. **P. pauciflorum**, Bedd., Fl. Sylv. t. 98. Banks of rivers on the South Tinnevelli and Travancore mountains (Vern. *Pudangalli*), secondary nerves less close and regular. Fl. solitary or in pairs, sepals 4 unequal, petals 6 imbricate, anthers smooth. Fruit globose, pointed, ¾ in. diam., dehiscent, valves 2, coriaceous, seed 1.

5. MESUA, Linn.; Fl. Brit. Ind. i. 277.

Three species in Fl. Brit. Ind., one transferred by Vesque to *Kayea*, the third (*M. Thwaitesii* of Ceylon) united by him with *M. ferrea*.

M. ferrea, Linn.; Wight Ic. t. 118; Vesque, Guttiferæ in DC. Monogr. Phan. 630.—Syn. *M. coromandeliana*, Wight; Bedd. Fl. Sylv. t. 64; *M. pedunculata*, Wight Ic. t. 119. *M. speciosa*, Chois.; Wight Ic. t. 961, Spicilegium Neilg. t. 30, 31. Vern. *Nagesar*, Beng.; *Nahor*, Assam; *Naga-kesara*, Tel.; *Nagchampa*, Mar.; *Nága sampige*, Kan.; *Irupu mara*, Coorg; *Nāngul*, Tam.; *Gangau*, Burm.

A large evergreen tree, heartwood dark red, extremely hard, medullary rays extremely fine. The young shoots at first brilliant red, then pink, gradually passing into dark green. Leaves 2–6 in., coriaceous, lanceolate, upper side shining, under side covered with a white waxlike powder, secondary nerves very close, but indistinct. Fl. 3–4 in. diam., solitary, nearly sessile, bisexual. Sepals 4 in 2 rows, petals 4, imbricate, stamens ∞, anthers linear, basifixed. Ovary 2-celled, 2 ovules in each cell, style filiform, stigma peltate. Fruit pointed, 1–1½ in., 2-valved, valves tough, supported by the enlarged sepals, seeds 1–4, testa hard, shining, embryo a fleshy homogeneous mass.

Western Duars and Assam, Khasi hills, Chittagong. Upper Burma, Tenasserim,

Andaman Islands, western coast from North Kanara southwards. Generally in evergreen forests. Commonly cultivated. Fl. February–April. Also in Ceylon and the Malay Peninsula.

6. KAYEA, Wall.; Fl. Brit. Ind. i. 276.

Trees glabrous, secondary nerves distant, not prominent. Sepals 4, petals 4, imbricate, stamens ∞ distinct, ovary 1-celled, ovules 4, rarely 8, erect, style long, filiform, stigma 4-fid. Fruit indehiscent, in most species enclosed in the greatly enlarged calyx, pericarp coriaceous, seeds 1–4, cotyledons large, fleshy. Species 20, eastern peninsula and Indian Archipelago.

1. **K. floribunda**, Wall. Pl. As. Rar. t. 210.

A large tree. Leaves 5–9 in., coriaceous, oblong-lanceolate. Fl. in large terminal panicles, sepals green, nearly orbicular, petals white with pink edges, anthers golden-yellow. Fruit 1-seeded, enclosed by the thick wrinkled yellow much enlarged calyx.

Sikkim to 3,000 ft., Assam, Khasi hills, Burma hills, east of Toungoo. 2. **K. nervosa**, T. Anders.; Kurz, F. Fl. i. 96. Tenasserim. Leaves chartaceous, 2–4 in., elliptic-lanceolate. Fl. 1¾ in. diam., solitary or 2–3 together, terminal or axillary, petals obovate. Fruit supported by but not enclosed in the enlarged calyx. 3. **K. Manii**, King, Ann. Gard. Calc. v. 2, 144. Andamans. Leaves coriaceous, 5–7 in. Fl. ⅓–½ in. diam. on slender pedicels in fasciculate racemes.

ORDER XVI. TERNSTRŒMIACEÆ. Gen. Pl. i. 177.

(*Theaceæ*, Engler und Prantl iii. 6. 175, with the exception of *Saurauja* and *Actinidia*, placed under *Dilleniaceæ* [l.c. 125, 126] and *Stachyurus*, which constitutes Gilg's Order *Stachyuraceæ* [l.c. 192].)

Shrubs or trees, rarely climbing. Leaves alternate, simple, often serrate, stipules 0. Fl. usually showy and bisexual, regular, generally pentamerous, sepals and petals in a few cases more numerous. Stamens generally numerous. Ovary free (half inferior in *Anneslea*), cells 3–5, numerous in *Actinidia*, styles as many as cells.

A. Peduncles 1-flowered, anthers basifixed, embryo curved.
- Ovary free, fl. bisexual as a rule, anthers glabrous . 1. TERNSTRŒMIA.
- Ovary free, fl. bisexual, anthers pilose.
  - Ovary 3–5 celled, seeds numerous . . . . . . 2. ADINANDRA.
  - Ovary 2–4 celled, seeds few . . . . . . 3. CLEYERA.
- Ovary free, fl. diœcious . . . . 4. EURYA.
- Ovary half inferior . . . . 5. ANNESLEA.

B. Peduncles 1-flowered, anthers versatile, embryo straight.
- Fruit indehiscent . . . . 6. PYRENARIA.
- Fruit dehiscent.
  - Seeds winged, radicle inferior . . . . . . 7. SCHIMA.
  - Seeds winged, radicle superior . . . . . . 8. GORDONIA.
  - Seeds wingless . . . . 9. CAMELLIA.

C. Fl. in cymes or panicles, anthers versatile, fruit pulpy, embryo straight in copious albumen.
- Fl. pentamerous, stamens many.
  - Styles numerous . . . . 10. ACTINIDIA.
  - Styles 3–5 . . . . 11. SAURAUJA.
- Fl. tetramerous, stamens few . . . . STACHYURUS (p. 63).

1. TERNSTRŒMIA, Linn. fil.; Fl. Brit. Ind. i. 280.

Glabrous trees or shrubs. Leaves coriaceous, entire or dentate. Fl. solitary, calyx supported by 2 bracteoles. Sepals 5, petals 5, both imbricate and connate at base. Stamens many, free, filaments generally short, anthers basifixed, glabrous, obtuse or shortly apiculate. Ovary 2–3 celled, ovules 2, rarely 1 or more than 2 in each cell, pendulous from the apex. Seeds 2–4, testa bony, albumen 0, embryo horseshoe-shaped. Species 30, tropical Asia and America.

1. **T. japonica**, Thunb.—Syn. *T. gymnanthera*, Bedd. Fl. Sylv. t. 91; *Cleyera gymnanthera*, W. et A.; Wight Ic. t. 47. Vern. *Kaymone*, *Kamoni*, Nilgiris.

A large tree, stunted at high elevations. Leaves crowded at the ends of branches, entire, 2–3 in. long, gradually narrowed into a petiole ½–1 in. long, secondary nerves indistinct. Peduncles ½–1 in., axillary, or more often above the scars of fallen leaves. Fl. pale yellow, corolla spreading ½–⅔ in. diam. Fruit ¾ in. diam., tipped with persistent style, and supported by bracteoles and sepals. Seeds 3–4, red.

Sikkim 7,000–8,000 ft., Khasi hills, Upper and Lower Burma, Nilgiris. Fl. December to June. Also Ceylon, China, Japan. 2. **T. penangiana**, Choisy; Kurz, F. Fl. i. 99. Andamans and Tenasserim, Malay Peninsula, Cochinchina. Leaves 4–8 in., obovate. Fl. diœcious, nearly 1 in. across, anthers not apiculate. Fr. 1½ in. diam., seeds 4, covered by a reddish pulp, resembling that of *Bixa orellana*.

FIG. 24.—Ternstrœmia japonica, Thunb. Seed cut open. ½.

2. ADINANDRA, Jack.; Fl. Brit. Ind. i. 281.

Species 12, one African, one in China and Formosa, the rest in the Malay Peninsula and Indian Archipelago.

1. **A. villosa**, Choisy; Kurz, F. Fl. i. 100.

A middle-sized tree, young branches, leafbuds, petioles, under side of leaves as well as back of sepals and petals clothed with long silky hairs. Leaves 4–5 in., coriaceous, shortly acuminate. Fl. axillary, mostly bisexual, on short pedicels, bracteoles caducous, some distance below the flower. Stamens 20–30 free, slightly attached to base of petals, silky, apiculate. Ovary 5-celled, hairy, style cylindric, glabrous, stigma minute, ovules numerous, pendulous from the apex. Fruit ½ in. diam., silky, seeds numerous, reniform, embryo horseshoe-shaped, albumen 0.

Lower Burma, chiefly in Eng forest. Fl. H. S. Also in Perak. Pierre, Fl. For. t. 125, unites this with *A. integerrima*, T. And. King, Journ. As. Soc. Bengal, vol. 59 (1891), 190, keeps them separate. 2. **A. Griffithii**, Dyer, a small tree, Khasi hills, has glabrous buds, leaves and flowers, the stamens sparingly hairy, and the style deeply 5-fid.

3. CLEYERA, DC.; Fl. Brit. Ind. i. 283.

(Included under *Eurya* in Engler u. Prantl iii. 6. 189.)

Species 6, India, China, Japan, Central America and the West Indies.

1. **C. ochnacea**, DC.

A small tree. Leaves 3–5 in. Fl. yellow, axillary, fascicled, peduncles ¾–1 in. long, thickened towards the apex, bracteoles minute. Stamens numerous, anthers pilose, shorter than filaments. Ovary generally 4-celled, style filiform, stigma 2–3- partite.

Nepal, Khasi hills, Ruby Mines district, Upper Burma. Fl. R. S. Also China, Japan. *C. japonica*, Sieb. & Zucc. (not Thunb.), with which this species is identified in the enumeration of Chinese plants, Journ. Linn. Soc. xxiii. 76, has white petals, otherwise there is no difference. *C. grandiflora*, Hook. fil. & Thoms. Khasi hills, with larger leaves and usually solitary flowers is perhaps not specifically distinct.

4. **EURYA,** Thunb.; Fl. Brit. Ind. i. 284.

Shrubs or small trees. Leaves mostly serrate. Fl. diœcious, sepals and petals imbricate, petals united at base, stamens 12–15, attached to the base of the corolla, anthers adnate. Ovary mostly 3-celled, styles 3, distinct or partially united. Fruit indehiscent, seeds numerous, small, angular, albumen copious, oily.

1. **E. japonica,** Thunb.; Kurz, F. Fl. i. 101.; Bedd. Fl. Sylv. t. 92.—Syn. *E. Wightiana*, Wight Ill. t. 38. Vern. *Jhingni*, Nep.; *Huluni*, Nilgiris; *Taung lapet*, *Taw lapet* (*wild tea*), Burm.

A shrub or a small tree; prominent raised lines on branchlets descending on both sides from the insertion of leaves. Leaves 2–5 in., lanceolate or ovate-lanceolate, obtusely serrate, glabrous, rarely pubescent while young. Fl. small, white, on short nodding pedicels, 2 or 3 together, rarely solitary, in the axils of leaves, sepals quite glabrous, style deeply 3- rarely 4–5-cleft, berries numerous, the size of a peppercorn, mucronate.

Outer Himalaya, from Sikkim eastwards, 3,000–6,000 ft., Western Ghats and hills adjoining them, from Kanara southwards. Hills of Upper and Lower Burma. Fl. throughout the year, chiefly R. S. Also Ceylon, from 4,000 ft. upwards, Malay Archipelago, China, Japan, Korea, Fiji Islands.

2. **E. acuminata,** DC.; Royle Ill. t. 25. Vern. *Sanu jhingni*, Nep.

Supposed to differ from E. *japonica* by young shoots being hairy, by more narrowly lanceolate leaves, often hairy beneath, and by the flowers in dense fascicles of 5 or more. In the F. Fl. of North-West and Central India, p. 24, I united them; Kurz, Trimen and the Flora of Brit. Ind. keep them separate.

Outer Himalaya, from the Jumna eastwards, 3,000–9,000 ft., Khasi hills, Chittagong. Burma hills, often in *Pinus kasya* forests. Malay Peninsula and Archipelago. 3. **E. symplocina,** Blume, Sikkim 5,000–7,000 ft., Bhutan, Assam, Khasi, and Naga hills, Manipur, Burma, is a middle-sized tree. Leaves 3–5 in., secondary nerves 8–12 pair, fairly distinct, peduncles silky, sepals silky outside, styles united. 4. **E. trichocarpa,** Korth. Khasi hills, Bhutan, Amboina. Pubescent, ovary densely silky, styles united to ⅔ of their length.

5. **ANNESLEA,** Wall.; Fl. Brit. Ind. i. 280.

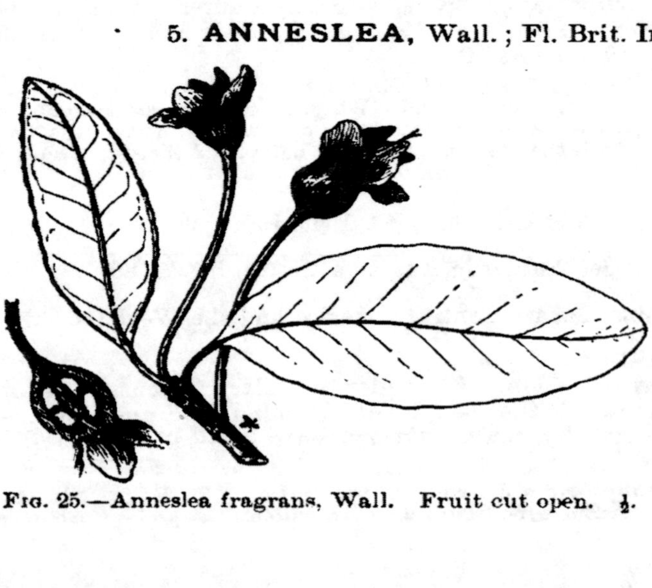

FIG. 25.—Anneslea fragrans, Wall. Fruit cut open. ½.

A. fragrans, Wall.; Pl. As. Rar. t. 5, the only species; Pierre, Fl. For. t. 127.

A moderate-sized tree. Leaves crowded at the ends of branches, 3–5 in., narrowed into petiole 1 in. long, secondary nerves indistinct. Fl. white, peduncles 2–3 in. Stamens ∞, glabrous, anthers long-apiculate, torus enlarged, cup-shaped, passing into a calyx tube adnate to the 3-celled ovary, ovules many in each cell, pendulous. Fruit 1 in. diam., crowned by the large persistent sepals, seed cylindric, testa woody, inner integument thin but tough, embryo horseshoe-shaped, albumen 0.

Manipur. Common in the Eng forests of the plains and hills in Upper and Lower Burma. Fl. January–April. Also Malay Peninsula, Cochinchina, and the Philippines. I follow **Pierre** in regarding *A. monticola*, Kurz, F. Fl. i. 98, as belonging to this species.

6. PYRENARIA, Blume ; Fl. Brit. Ind. i. 289.

Leaves thinly coriaceous, styles 5, free, or partially united. Ovary 5-celled, ovules 2 in each cell. Fruit indehiscent, fleshy-coriaceous, seeds oblong, stout, without a wing, testa woody, albumen 0. Species 7, Malay Peninsula and Indian Archipelago.

1. P. barringtoniæfolia, Seem.—Syn. *Ensynaxis barringtonifolia*, Griffith, Notulæ iv. 560, Ic. Pl. As. t. 603 iii.

A scrambling shrub. Leaves 8–10 in., glabrous, obovate from a cuneate base, abruptly acuminate, strongly serrate, secondary nerves 8–10 pairs, joined at a distance from the edge by intramarginal veins. Fl. yellowish white, 1½ in. diam., almost sessile, supported by coriaceous erose-crenate bracts, which gradually pass into sepals, bracts and sepals tomentose outside. Styles distinct.

Garo hills. Upper Assam. Fl. H. S. 2. **P. camelliæflora,** Kurz, hills of Lower Burma. Branchlets pubescent. Leaves 5–7 in., yellowish green when dry. Drupe obovoid, 1 in., seeds 2. 3. **P. diospyricarpa,** Kurz, F. Fl. i. 104. Branchlets pubescent. Leaves 4–5 in. Drupes obovoid, the size of a small pear, 4–5 ribbed, waxy yellow.

7. SCHIMA, Reinw. ; Fl. Brit. Ind. i. 288.

Evergreen trees. Leaves entire or crenate. Fl. showy, solitary on axillary peduncles, two deciduous bracteoles under calyx. Sepals 5, nearly equal, petals 5, slightly connate at the base, the outermost concave, often hood-like. Stamens many, filaments adnate to base of petals, attached to the back of anthers above their base. Ovary 5-celled, style simple or lobed at the apex with broad spreading stigmas, ovules 2–6 in each cell, attached laterally. Capsule globose, woody, loculicidal, with a persistent axis. Seeds flat, kidney-shaped, winged on the back, albumen thin, cotyledons foliaceous, radicle inferior, curved upwards. Species 3 or 4, eastern Asia, tropical and subtropical.

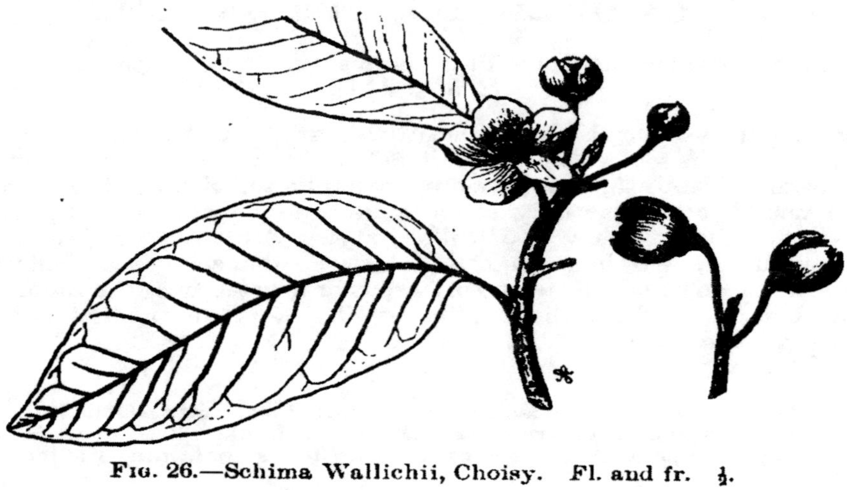

FIG. 26.—Schima Wallichii, Choisy. Fl. and fr. ½.

1. **S. Wallichii,** Choisy (1854). Vern. *Chilauni*, Nepal, Sikkim, Duars; *Samching*, Bhutia; *Dingan*, Khasi; *Mukria Sāl*, Assam; *Laukya*, Upper Burma.

A tall tree, bark dark grey, rugged, wood red, moderately hard, durable, but shrinks and warps (42–50 lb. per cub. ft.). Coppices readily. Buds, branchlets, petioles and under side of leaves pubescent, sometimes tomentose. Leaves 4–6 in., chartaceous, entire or slightly crenate. Fl. 1½–2 in. diam., white, fragrant, stamens yellow, peduncles ¾–2 in.

Subhimalayan tract, from Nepal eastwards, ascending to 5,000 ft., Khasi hills, Manipur, Chittagong hills, Upper Burma, Yunan. Fl. April–June. Fr. C. S. 2. **S. Noronhæ**, Blume (1825); King, Journ. As. Soc. Beng. vol. 59 (1891) 201.—Syn. *S. crenata*, Korthals; Fl. Brit. Ind. i. 289. Upper Burma, Ruby Mines, 6,000 ft. (*Thityabyu*), Martaban, Tenasserim, Malay Peninsula, Cochinchina, Indian Archipelago, China. Supposed to differ by leaves more distinctly crenate and larger fr., but is probably only a form of *S. Wallichii*, which, when this view is adopted, will be known by the older name *S. Noronhæ*. 3. **S. Khasiana**, Dyer. Khasi hills. Glabrous, except the silky buds, sepals and petals. Leaves strongly serrate, veins distinctly reticulate between tertiary nerves, peduncles stout, ¾ in. Fl. 2½ in. diam. Of *S. monticola*, Kurz, I have seen no specimens, and none from Burma of *S. bancana*, Miq.

8. GORDONIA, Ellis; Fl. Brit. Ind. i. 290.

Differs from *Schima* in the following points: bracteoles, sepals and petals passing by a regular gradation from bracteoles to petals, filaments often connate at base into a fleshy cup or 5 thick fleshy bundles. Capsule oblong, woody. Seeds prolonged upwards into an oblong wing, albumen 0, embryo straight, radicle superior. Species 10, eastern tropical and subtropical Asia, Southern Atlantic States of North America.

1. **G. obtusa,** Wall.; Bedd. Fl. Sylv. t. 83. Wight, Spicil. Neilg. t. 20. Vern. *Nagetta*, Nilgiris.

A middle-sized tree, buds and flowers silky. Leaves 2–4 in., glabrous, crenate, obtuse, the cuneate base narrowed into a short petiole. Fl. white, 1½ in. across, capsule 1 in., 5-angled.

Western Ghats, from the Konkan southwards, Nilgiris, Palnis. Fl. June–Sept. 2 **G. excelsa**, Blume; Sikkim 4,000–6,000 ft., Bhutan, Khasi hills, Malay Peninsula and Archipelago, has lanceolate acuminate leaves, 4–10 in., capsule 1–1½ in. long.

9. CAMELLIA, Linn.; Fl. Brit. Ind. i. 292.

(*Thea*, Linn.; Baillon, Histoire des Plantes iv. 252; Engler und Prantl iii. 6. 182.)[1]

Evergreen trees or shrubs, leaves mostly serrate. Fl. showy, axillary, bracteolate, solitary or a few together. Sepals 5–6, imbricate, similar to bracteoles, the inner larger. Petals 5, rarely more, strongly imbricate. Stamens ∞, the outer filaments often partially connate into a ring or tube, the inner free, anthers versatile. Ovary 3–5 celled, styles 3–5, free or partly connate, ovules pendulous, 4–5 in each cell. Capsule dehiscing loculicidally, seeds mostly solitary in each cell, testa coriaceous or crustaceous, the inner coat thin and membranous, radicle short, albumen 0. Cotyledons oily. Species 16, India, China, and Japan.

[1] Linnæus, and after him Seemann (*Camellia* and *Thea*, Transactions Linn. Soc. xxii. 337), kept the two genera separate. Bentham and Hooker in Genera Plant. i. 187, united them, giving preference to the name *Camellia*, as containing the larger number of species.

A. Flowers nodding, capsule supported by the persistent sepals.

1. **C. Thea,** Link; Brand. F. Fl. 25.—Syn. *C. Bohea,* Griffith, the China plant, and *C. theifera,* Griffith, the indigenous Assam plant; *C. theifera,* Fl. Brit. Ind. i. 292; *Thea sinensis* (not *chinensis*), Linn. Sp. Plant. *The Tea plant.* Vern. *Letpet,* Burm.

A shrub or small tree, glabrous or slightly pubescent. Fl. solitary, peduncles with a few distinct bracts, sometimes a second flower in the axil of one of them. Sepals round, very obtuse. Petals white, obovate, obtuse, glabrous or pubescent on the back. Stamens glabrous, ovary villous, styles 3 glabrous, connate beyond the middle. Capsule depressed, 3-cornered, 3-seeded. Testa hard, shining.

Indigenous in Upper Assam (discovered 1834) and in the hilly country to the east of it (the Assam plant has larger more acuminate leaves, and has a more arborescent habit than the shrub cultivated in China). Also indigenous in Upper Burma, Katha district, 2,000 ft., Ruby Mines district, 7,000 ft., and the northern Shan States. Cultivated ages ago in China and Japan. Since 1840 cultivated extensively in Assam, Cachar, Sikkim, the N.W. Himalaya and the Nilgiris. Grown in Ceylon on a large scale. Fl. C. S.

2. **C. caudata,** Wall.; Kurz, F. Fl. i. 108.

A small tree with a spreading crown, branchlets, petioles and under side of leaves hairy. Leaves 3–4 in., lanceolate, long-acuminate. Fl. ¾–1 in. diam., white, 2–3 together, peduncles short, covered with imbricating bracts, sepals and petals silky outside. Stamens clothed with long hairs, ovary and styles hairy. Capsule ¾ in. diam., 1-celled, 1-seeded.

Bhutan, Khasi hills, Burma, hills east of Toungoo. Fl. November–March.

B. Flowers erect, sepals deciduous.

3. **C. drupifera,** Lour.—Syn. *C. Kissi,* Wall., As. Researches xiii. 430, and Pl. As. Rar. t. 256. Vern. *Hingua,* Nep.; *Letpet,* Burm.

A large shrub or small tree, branches spreading, branchlets and petioles more or less hairy. Leaves elliptic-lanceolate, acuminate, serrulate in the upper half, 3–4 in. long, secondary nerves 6–8 pair, faint. Fl. white, erect, on short peduncles, bearing broad silky imbricating bracts, solitary or 2–3. Petals obovate, ¾–1 in. long, falling soon after flowering. Stamens 70–80, glabrous, ⅓ in. long, filaments free, dilated below. Ovary hairy, style glabrous, in the upper half 2–3-fid, ovary and style ½ in. long. Capsule nearly 1 in. diam., depressed-globose, peduncle marked by the scars of bracts and sepals.

Himalaya, from Nepal eastwards, 4,000–7,000 ft., Assam, Khasi hills. Burma, hills east of Toungoo, 2,000 ft., Ruby Mines hills, 6,000 ft. Fl. C. S.

Closely allied is 4. **C. caduca,** C. B. Clarke MSS., Khasi hills, above the Bishop's falls in large quantity in the river bed on rocks and sand submerged during floods. Bhutan, Sikkim. Leaves narrower, on both sides minutely wrinkled, secondary nerves quite obscure. Fl. much smaller, petals ½ in., cuneate, emarginate, very early caducous. Stamens ¼–⅓ in., outer series 30, filaments in their lower half united into a tube, inner series 5–10, free. Capsule pyriform, pointed, ⅓ in. 5. **C. lutescens,** Dyer, Mishmi hills, a shrub. Leaves 2–3½ in., caudate-acuminate, closely serrate, secondary nerves 6–8 pair, distinct. Fl. fragrant, white, turning yellow. Stamens 20–30, filaments broad, the outer combined into a short irregular fleshy tube. Ovary globose, densely silky, styles short, recurved.

10. ACTINIDIA, Lindl.; Fl. Brit. Ind. i. 285.

Climbing shrubs, structure of wood normal, vessels very large. Leaves membranous. Fl. polygamous or diœcious, in axillary cymes. Sepals 5, petals 5, imbricate. Stamens ∞, free, anthers versatile. Ovary cells numerous, styles as many as cells, divergent, elongated after flowering. Fruit fleshy, embryo straight in copious albumen. Species 10, China, Japan, and eastern Himalaya.

1. **A. callosa**, Lindl. Vern. *Tikiphal*, Nep.

A large climber, stems attaining 4 in. diam., bark corky, brown, rough. Leaves elliptic, 4–6 in., shortly acuminate, glabrous, sepals oblong obtuse, tomentose, styles clavate. Fruit ¾ in., ovoid, pleasantly acid, edible.

Himalaya, from Garhwal eastwards, 3,000–8,000 ft., Khasi hills, Manipur, Shan hills, at 5,000 ft. Fl. May, June. Also in China and Japan. 2. **A. strigosa**, Hook. fil. & Thoms., Sikkim 6,000–8,000 ft., common about Darjeeling. Branchlets, petioles, and under side of leaves hispid with long hairs. Fl. ¾ in. diam., white or light pink, sepals slightly pubescent. Fruit 1¼ in., edible.

11. **SAURAUJA**, Willd.; Fl. Brit. Ind. i. 286. (*Saurauia*, Gilg in Engler u. Prantl iii. 6. 127.)

Trees or shrubs, shoots more or less strigose or scaly. Leaves approximate at the ends of branches, usually serrate, secondary nerves prominent, parallel. Fl. usually bisexual, in cymose panicles, axillary or from the old wood. Sepals 5, strongly imbricate, petals 5, connate at base, imbricate, often forming a cup-shaped corolla. Stamens numerous, anthers opening at the top by a pore or short slit. Ovary 3–5 celled, ovules numerous, styles 3–5 distinct or united. Fruit indehiscent, generally somewhat fleshy. Seeds small, with copious albumen. Species 60, tropical and subtropical Asia and America.

A. Flowers in axillary pedunculate cymose panicles, bracts deciduous.

1. **S. napaulensis**, DC.; Wall. Pl. As. Rar. t. 178; Brandis, F. Fl. 25. Vern. *Gogea*, *Gogina*, *Goganda*, Hind.; *Ratendu*, Jaunsar.

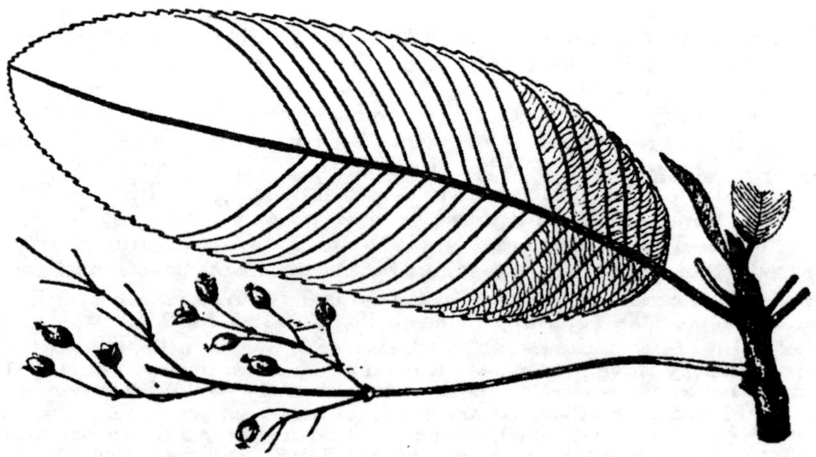

FIG. 27.—Saurauja napaulensis, DC. ½.

Small tree or large shrub, wood soft, spongy, boughs ending in tufts of leaves, among which are the flower panicles. Young shoots, petioles and under side of leaves covered with scurfy tomentum, mixed with brown deciduous acuminate scales. Leaves 10–15 in., strongly serrate, secondary nerves 25–30 pair. Fl. pink, in pedunculate panicles, styles 4 or 5 distinct, conspicuous.

Outer Himalaya, 2,500–7,000 ft, from the Jumna eastwards. Khasi hills, Manipur. Fl. H. S., R. S. Fruit viscid, eaten. 2. **S. Griffithii**, Dyer. Sikkim, Terai, and outer valleys, to 6,000 ft. Branchlets, petioles and inflorescence densely clothed with soft woolly ferruginous tomentum. Leaves bright green above, brown, softly tomentose beneath, 8–12 by 4–6 in., with sharp spinulose teeth, petiole 2–3 in. Panicle on peduncle 6–8 in. long.

B. Flowers mostly on the old wood, in trichotomous cymes, bracts in pairs at all the ramifications.

3. **S. Roxburghii,** Wall.; Kurz, F. Fl. 103. Vern. *Auli gogen*, Nep.; *Thit ngayan*, Burma.

A middle-sized evergreen tree, the young parts covered with a mealy scurf, intermixed with minute scales. Leaves 8–12 in. Cymes hairy, many-flowered, bracts deltoid, acute. Fl. ¼ in. diam., stamens ∞, styles 3–5.

Sikkim, Terai and outer valleys, ascending to 4,000 ft., Assam, Khasi hills, Manipur, Chittagong, hills east of Toungoo, 2,000–6,000 ft. Upper Burma, 1,500–3,000 ft. Fl. C. S., H. S.

4. **S. fasciculata,** Wall. Pl. As. Rar. t. 148. *Saré gogen*, Nep. Nepal, Sikkim, 2,000–5,000 ft. A small tree. Leaves ferrugineo-tomentose beneath. Fl. ⅓ in. diam., white, afterwards pink. 5. **S. punduana,** Wall. Sikkim, Terai, and outer valleys, ascending to 6,000 ft., Upper Assam, Khasi hills, Manipur, Burma. Cymes many-flowered, ramifications densely covered with acute scales, bracts broad-ovate. Fl. ⅔ in. diam. 6. **S. tristyla,** DC.; Malay Peninsula, said to extend north into Tenasserim. Leaves spinulose-serrate, 7–10 in. Fl. unisexual, ½ in. diam., on slender pedicels, in fascicles of 2–6 mostly on the old wood, petals white, stamens 20, styles 3, rarely 4. 7. **S. macrotricha,** Kurz, F. Fl. i. 106. Assam, Khasi hills, Upper Burma. Branchlets, petioles and under side of leaves densely clothed with long stiff hairs. Leaves narrow-lanceolate, serratures setose, secondary nerves 12–15 pair, arcuate. Fl. red. 8. **S. cerea,** Griff. (*S. arcuata*, Kurz, F. Fl. i. 108). Bhutan, Upper Burma. Young parts covered with appressed hard sharp scales. Leaves obovate, blade 8–10 in., petiole ¼–½ in. Fl. 1 in. diam., petals waxy, white, base blood-red.

Stachyurus himalaicus, Hook. fil. & Thoms., Himalaya, from Nepal eastwards, 5,000–8,000 ft., Manipur, China, is a small tree or extensively scrambling shrub, glabrous, fl. tetramerous, in short lateral spikes on long pendulous branches. Stamens 8, ovary 4-celled, style simple, stigma capitate-peltate, ovules many. Berries ⅕ in. diam.

ORDER XVII. DIPTEROCARPACEÆ. Gen. Pl. i. 189.

(*Dipterocarpeæ.*)

(Brandis in Journal Linnean Society, vol. xxxi. (1895) p. 1.)

Resinous trees, rarely shrubs, mostly evergreen. Leaves alternate, stipulate, simple, penniveined, generally coriaceous, petioles mostly thickened below the blade. Young shoots and inflorescence, calyx and outside of petals in most species pubescent, hairs 1-celled, generally stellate or fasciculate. Fl. bisexual, regular, pentamerous, in spikes or racemes, these often unilateral and mostly paniculate. Receptacle fleshy, broad, flat or obconical, often concave, bearing on its outer edge the calyx, the segments of which as a rule are much enlarged in fruit. Petals contorted, stamens 5, 10, or more, anthers introrse, adnate to filaments, which are mostly short, the connective being often prolonged beyond the anthers. Ovary 3-celled, often prolonged into a fleshy stylopodium, in some cases immersed in the hollow receptacle. Two collateral ovules in each cell, attached to the inner angle. Fruit 1-seeded, pericarp coriaceous, indehiscent. Seed with or without albumen, cotyledons fleshy, bifid, often stipitate, in most species filled with starch, in others with oil, while some contain both.

Remarkable anatomical characters.—Resin ducts are found in the pith of the young stem and branches, in the pith of all vascular bundles, in the petiole, midrib, nerves and veins of leaves as well as of those bundles which run through the bark. The walls of these ducts are lined by a stratum of thin-walled secreting cells. In many species similar ducts are also found in the wood. They contain an essential oil, known as wood-oil in the case of *Dipterocarpus*, as camphor-oil in the case of *Dryobalanops*. Exposed to the air, outside or in cavities of the trunk, these essential oils are transformed into resin or camphor.

Cortical leaf traces.—Some distance below the node the leaf traces separate from the central cylinder and run through the bark before they enter the petiole. There are generally three leaf traces, one apical, two lateral, all consisting of a vascular bundle with one or several resin ducts in the pith. In some cases these traces run in the bark through an entire internode.

Structure of petiole.—The 3 vascular bundles, which enter the petiole, forming its central cylinder, remain distinct in rare cases. As a rule they ramify and coalesce, forming at the base of the petiole an intricate mass of xylem and phloëm with a number of resin ducts, and in most species the internal structure of the petiole changes in its progress from the base to the blade. For systematic purposes it is convenient to examine the petiole immediately below the base of the blade. At this point we frequently find a semicircle of vascular bundles, more or less united, each with its resin duct, and inside this semicircle one or several vascular bundles with or without resin ducts.

Structure of wood.—Vessels moderate-sized, often in groups, enclosed in a narrow white ring consisting of wood parenchyma. Medullary rays fine and moderately broad, generally equidistant, the horizontal cells of these in many cases very long, 3 mm. in *Dipterocarpus alatus*. These longitudinal cells, as well as the resin ducts in the younger wood, are filled with essential oil. Many species have a distinct dark-coloured heartwood. Resin ducts, vessels, fissures and other cavities in the *old wood* are filled with resin.

Biological features.—As a rule large trees, with tall, regularly shaped trunks. With few exceptions they do not bear flowers and seed until they have attained a considerable age. As a rule they seed annually, though the quantity of seed produced varies from year to year. In the Malay Peninsula and in Ceylon, however, there are species which flower periodically, some every sixth year. The seed germinates soon after ripening, in some cases before it falls to the ground. Several species (Sâl, Eng) are gregarious and form forests of considerable extent, in which they prevail over their companions.

Geographical distribution.—The Order is limited to the Indo-Malayan region, from the Seychelles to New Guinea. Of the 325 species (in 16 genera) at present known, 80 are here described. Of species found elsewhere may be mentioned: (1) *Dryobalanops aromatica*, Gaertn. f., Johore, Sumatra, Borneo, and probably on the Philippine Islands, yields the Borneo camphor, which is deposited in cavities in the wood in the shape of beautiful colourless or light yellow crystals. (2) *Shorea selanica*, Blume, Amboina, produces large quantities of transparent amber-like resin, hanging down from the branches in conical or cylindrical masses, often as thick as a man's leg. (3) Several species, the seeds of which contain fat resembling tallow (*Tang kawang*), which is an important article of trade in the Malay Archipelago. The chief of these are: *Shorea stenoptera*, Burck; *S. aptera*, Burck; *S. gysbertiana*, Burck; and *S. pinanga*, Scheffer, all in Borneo; *Isoptera borneensis*, Scheffer, Malay Peninsula, Bangka, Borneo.

The Order divides itself naturally into 5 tribes and 16 genera. One tribe (*Dryobalanopseæ*) and 7 genera of the other tribes are not represented in the British Indian Empire.

I. *Dipterocarpeæ.*—Calyx tube enclosing the fruit; 2 lobes expanding into long wings. Stamens more than 20; connective prolonged into a long point. Ovary with a large fleshy stylopodium.

Stipules large, amplexicaul, calyx tube free, stamens ∞, style filiform . . . . 1. DIPTEROCARPUS.

Stipules small, deciduous, calyx tube adnate to fruit, stamens 20-35, style short . . . . 2. ANISOPTERA.

II. *Shoreæ.*—Calyx as a rule imbricate in bud, in most cases the 2 or 3 outer segments accrescent in fruit, forming long wings. Stamens mostly 15, rarely more (*Shorea*, section *Eushorea*), in a few cases 10. Connective usually awned.

Wings 2; appendix of connective long, pointed, as a rule a large stylopodium . . . . 3. HOPEA.

Wings 3; anthers with 5 pointed appendages . . . 4. PENTACME.

Wings 3; appendix of connective as a rule long, pointed 5. SHOREA.

Wings 5; calyx in bud nearly valvate; anthers with 3 short appendages . . . . 6. PARASHOREA.

Lobes of fruiting calyx slightly and evenly enlarged, thick, sometimes woody, appendage of connective long, pointed. Stylopodium generally distinct . . . . 7. BALANOCARPUS.

III. *Vaticeæ.*—Calyx valvate in bud. Stamens 15, anthers short, oval. Appendix of connective short, obtuse, no stylopodium . . . . 8. VATICA.

IV. *Vaterieæ.*—Calyx imbricate in bud. Lobes of fruiting calyx equal and shorter than fruit. Stamens ∞. Anthers linear-oblong with 1 or 2 appendages . . 9. VATERIA.

1. DIPTEROCARPUS, Gaertn. f.; Fl. Brit. Ind. i. 295.

Tall, regularly shaped trunks, no heartwood. Leaves are renewed at the end of the hot season, when the old leaves fall. Secondary nerves prominent, straight, joined by parallel tertiary nerves. In bud the two halves of the leaf are folded upon each other and the sections between two secondary nerves are also folded in half. Fl. large, pink, in short few-fld. axillary panicles. Receptacle concave, continued into a campanulate or obconical calyx tube with 5 segments, 2 of which are larger. Stamens ∞, connective prolonged into a long point, anther cells mostly equal. Ovary generally hairy, continued into a conical fleshy stylopodium, style filiform, stigma minute. Tube of fruiting calyx enclosing fruit, but not adnate to it, globose or ovoid, smooth or with 5 ribs or wings, alternating with calyx segments, two of which develop into large longitudinally veined wings. Pericarp thin at the base, thick and fibrous in the upper portion. The cotyledons of the germinating seed remain enclosed in the pericarp and fruiting calyx, being attached to the radicle by long petioles. Species 64.

Numerous (up to 100) resin ducts in a leaf-bearing internode near the circumference of the pith. The lateral leaf traces enter the bark at varying levels, generally in the upper half of the internode. Numerous stipular traces in the bark below the node. Frequently large mucilage cavities in pith and cortex.

A. Tube of fruiting calyx smooth.

1. **D. turbinatus**, Gaertn. f.—Syn. *D. lævis*, Ham.; Roxb. Cor. Pl. t. 213; Kurz, F. Fl. i. 114. Vern. *Gurjun*, Chittagong; *Kanyin-ni*, Burm.

Leaves ovate or ovate-lanceolate, blade 5–12 in., petiole rarely more than ⅕ the length of blade, secondary nerves 14–18 pair. Varies greatly in regard to the pubescence of young shoots, leaves and inflorescence. Kurz calls the form with glabrous and glossy leaves *D. lævis*, that with hoary leaves *D. turbinatus*.

Cachar, Tipperah, Chittagong hills, Burma, Andamans, Malay Peninsula. Fl. April. Fruit May. As a rule not gregarious, but scattered in mixed forest, generally taller than the trees associated with it. North of Bhamo *D. lævis* is reported to grow gregarious in patches. Yields wood oil. Heartwood reddish-grey, not durable. Closely allied is 2. **D. indicus**, Bedd. Fl. Sylv. t. 94 (*D. turbinatus*, Cooke, Bombay Fl. i. 84). *Yennemara*, Coorg; *Ennai*, Tam.; *Velayani*, Mal. Evergreen forest of the Western Ghats from North Kanara southwards. Fl. January–March. Petioles longer, ⅓ to ¼ the length of blade, and secondary nerves less numerous, 10–15 pair.

3. **D. obtusifolius**, Teysm.; Kurz, F. Fl. i. 115.

Young shoots, petioles and inflorescence densely clothed with long pale tawny hair. Leaves broadly ovate, obtuse, to 9 in. long, pubescent above, softly tomentose beneath, secondary nerves 12–14 pair. Fl. showy, pink, shortly pedicellate on short axillary racemes. Fruit 1¼ in. diam.

Throughout the Eastern Peninsula, 20° N. Lat. its northern limit. In Cochinchina and Cambodia very common and gregarious. Ascends to 3,000 ft. in Pegu and Martaban; at higher elevations gregarious, forming forests similar to those of *D. tuberculatus*. *D. vestitus*, Wall., Tavoy, very similar and probably not specifically distinct.

4. **D. pilosus**, Roxb.; Kurz F. Fl. i. 115.—Syn. *D. Baudii*, Korthals.

Young shoots, stipules and petioles densely clothed with tawny fascicled hairs. Leaves elliptic-oblong, shortly acuminate, 8–18 in. long, ciliate at the edges, hairy beneath, secondary nerves 20–25 pair. Fruiting calyx glabrous, ovoid, 2 in. long, wings to 9 in. Fruit densely pubescent.

Damp forests in the upper part of the Assam valley, Chittagong hills, Aracan, Lower Burma. Andamans (?). Fruit April. Sumatra (gregarious, Korthals), Bangka. Yields a semifluid resin.

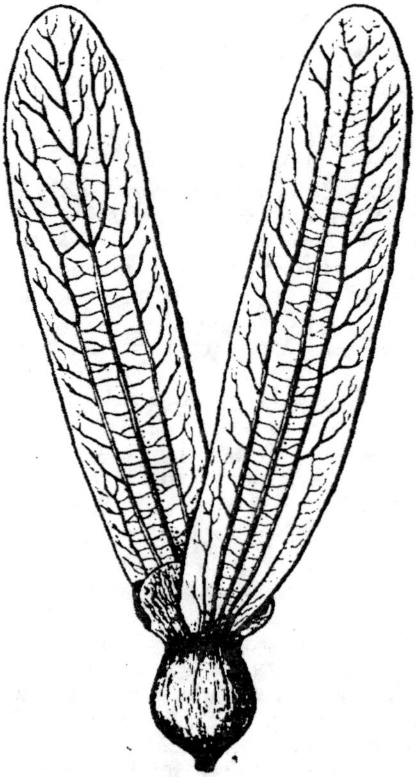

FIG. 28.—Dipterocarpus pilosus, Roxb. ½.

B. Tube of fruiting calyx with 5 protuberances near its mouth.

5. **D. tuberculatus,** Roxb.; Kurz, F. Fl. i. 113. Vern. *Eng* (*In*), Burm.

Stipules 4–5 in. long, greyish-tomentose. Leaves up to 18 in. long and 14 in. broad, cordate or broadly-ovate, apex rounded, glossy above, glabrous or slightly pubescent beneath, secondary nerves 10–15 pair, arching. Fl. large, petals 1¼ in. long, tomentose outside. Fruiting calyx tube obovate, velvety when young, glabrous when mature, between the segments produced into 5 sharp knobs. Nuts tomentose.

Throughout the Eastern Peninsula from Pegu to Cambodia, northern limit at 25° N. Lat. Eminently gregarious, forming extensive forests on laterite at the foot of the hills of Lower and Upper Burma, accompanied by subordinate species, *Terminalia*, *Eugenia*, *Dillenia*, *Symplocos* and others. Yields wood oil and resin. Fl. April. Fr. May. Heartwood red, moderately durable.

C. Tube of fruiting calyx with 5 longitudinal wings.

6. **D. alatus,** Roxb.; Kurz, F. Fl. i. 116. Vern. *Kanyinbyu*, Burm.

Shoots and stipules pubescent. Leaves ovate or elliptic, acute, pubescent beneath, margin ciliate, secondary nerves 12–15 pair, blade 4–6 in., petiole (softly hairy) 1–1½ in. long. Wings on fruiting calyx tube broad, half the diameter of tube or more.

Pegu, Tenasserim, Siam, Cambodia. Fl. April, fruit May. Not gregarious, but scattered in mixed forests, generally taller than the trees associated with it. Heartwood greyish-red, not durable. The medullary rays consist of two classes of cells, long and short; the long cells (up to 0·12 inch long) are filled with wood oil.

Closely allied and possibly not distinct is 7. **D. costatus,** Gaertn. f., Lower Burma, South Tipperah, near the coast (Hamilton), wings on calyx tube narrow. 8. **D. incanus,** Roxb. Pegu, South Andaman (common), Chittagong (doubtful), Tongkah in Siam on the east coast of the Malay Peninsula at its north extremity. Branchlets, young shoots and petioles softly hairy. Leaves ovate, thinly pubescent on both surfaces, margin ciliate. 9. **D. Bourdilloni,** Brandis in Hook. Ic. Plant. t. 2403 (*Kar angili*, Mal.). Carcoor Ghat (Malabar), Travancore, evergreen forest in the low country. A lofty tree, young shoots, branchlets and petiole softly velvety. Leaves elliptic, shortly acuminate, tomentose beneath, 6–10 in. long, secondary nerves 12–18 pair, tube of fruiting calyx glabrous, 1½ in. long, wings on tube ¼ in. wide. Similar to *D. insignis*, Thwaites, of Ceylon, but distinct.

2. ANISOPTERA, Korthals; Fl. Brit. Ind. i. 300.

Stipules small, early deciduous. Stamens 20–35, anther cells unequal, connective prolonged into a long awn. Stylopodium thick, fleshy, bearing 3, sometimes 4–6, short styles. Fruiting calyx adnate to fruit, globose or campanulate, 2 segments much larger than the others, with 3 prominent longitudinal nerves and numerous transverse veins. Species 15.

In the circumference of the pith 18–24 resin ducts. The lateral leaf traces enter the bark at varying levels, in some species at the base of the internode. In the petiole a complete circle of 7-13 vascular bundles, with a resin duct in each, and a central mass of vascular bundles, without resin ducts.

1. **A. glabra,** Kurz, F. Fl. i. 112. Vern. *Thin kadu*, Burm.

Evergreen, glabrous, except the pubescent inflorescence, wood hard, dark olive-green. Leaves coriaceous, elliptic-oblong. Fruiting calyx-tube much constricted at the mouth. the 2 larger segments oblanceolate, with 3 prominent longitudinal nerves, joined at right angles by conspicuous transverse veins.

Pegu, Martaban, Cambodia and Cochinchina. Fl. April, May. 2. **A. oblonga,** Dyer (*Shorea nervosa*, Kurz). Tenasserim. Young shoots and leaves on the nerves beneath with scattered tufts of minute stellate hairs.

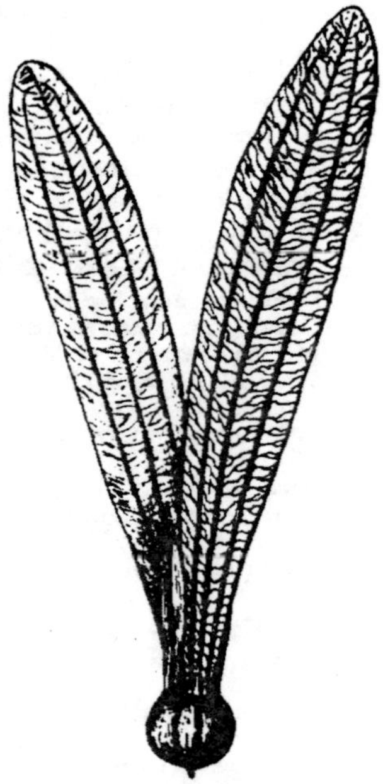

Fig. 29.—Anisoptera glabra, Kurz. ½.

3. HOPEA, Roxb.; Fl. Brit. Ind. i. 308.

Stipules small or minute, early deciduous. Fl. in unilateral spikes or racemes, arranged in ample racemose panicles, calyx often glabrous, petals always hairy outside. Calyx segments imbricate, the two outer growing out into thin membranous wings as the fruit ripens. Stamens 15, of which 10 in 5 pairs are episepalous, in a few species 10, anther cells equal, connective prolonged into a long awn. Stylopodium generally large. Seeds without albumen, cotyledons thick, fleshy, concave, one enclosing the other, both bifid to the base. Radicle and petioles of cotyledons embedded in a groove between the lobes of the outer cotyledon, while the lignified placenta with the remains of dissepiments intrudes between the lobes of the inner, they are filled with starch and oil, the former generally prevailing. Species 46, one in New Guinea.

Resin ducts in the pith 8–12 at the base of a leaf-bearing internode. The 2 lateral leaf traces run a short distance only through the bark.

Sect. I.—Euhopea. Secondary nerves not more than 20 pair, not approximate.

A. Calyx grey-tomentose.

1. **H. odorata,** Roxb., Cor. Pl. t. 210. Vern. *Thingan*, Burm.

Evergreen, wood yellowish-brown, close- and even-grained, very durable. Glabrous, except inflorescence. Leaves ovate-lanceolate, secondary nerves 12 pair. Fl. fragrant, in axillary grey-tomentose panicles, petals ciliate at margin, anthers oblong. Ovary gradually narrowed into conical stylopodium and long cylindrical style. Ovary and stylopodium puberulous.

Moist forests in the southern portion of the Eastern Peninsula, from Pegu and Tenasserim to Cochinchina. Andamans. Also reported from Chittagong. Not gregarious, but scattered in mixed forests. Fl. March, April. Fruit May, June.

2. **H. parviflora,** Beddome, Fl. Sylv. t. 7. The *Ironwood* of Malabar. Vern. *Bovumara*, Kan.; *Nirkongu*, Tinnevelli.

Differs from 1 by petals not ciliate, anthers small orbicular, ovary and stylopodium glabrous, stigma 3-fid, stylopodium ovoid, constricted at base.

Moist forests of the Western Ghats, from South Kanara southwards. Fl. March. 3. **H. oblongifolia,** Dyer. Mergui. Secondary nerves 10 pair, between them a multitude of fine veins, closely reticulate, stylopodium cylindric. 4. **H. Helferi,** Brandis (*Vatica Helferi*, Dyer). Mergui, 60 miles inland, branchlets tomentose. Leaves from a cordate unequal-sided base, oblong. Fl. pedicelled in terminal panicles, ovary glabrous.

B. Calyx glabrous.

5. H. Wightiana, Wall.; Wight Ill. t. 37. Vern. *Karsi*, Mar.; *Haiga*, Kan.; *Ila pongu*, Tam.

Youngest branchlets and petioles softly pubescent, otherwise glabrous. Leaves coriaceous, oblong, 6–8 in. long, petiole short. Fl. in axillary fascicled panicles, shorter than the leaves, petals pubescent outside. Upper portion of ovary puberulous, stylopodium glabrous, slightly verrucose, style short. Round echinate galls frequent in the axils of leaves.

Evergreen forests at the foot of the Western Ghats, from North Kanara southwards. Often gregarious, covering large tracts in the low country of South Kanara. Fl. March–June. 6. **H. glabra,** Wight et Arn.—(*H. Wightiana* var. *glabra*, Bedd. Fl. Sylv. t. 96). Ghats of Tinnevelli and Travancore. Leaves lanceolate, 3–4 in. long, secondary nerves 8 pair. Ovary, stylopodium and outside of petals slightly puberulous. 7. **H. racophlœa,** Dyer.—Syn. *H. malabarica*, Bedd. Ic. Pl. Ind. Or. t. 185 (*Karung Kongu*, Tam.; *Veduvali Kongu*, Mal.), Travancore. A large glabrous tree, bark dark, peeling off in long recurved strips, which hang all round the trunk. Leaves ovate, caudate-acuminate, blade 2–4½, petiole slender, ½ in. long. Panicles 2–4 in one leaf axil. Stylopodium cylindric, slightly narrowed at base. Larger segments of fruiting calyx spathulate, obtuse, with 7–11 longitudinal nerves.

Sect. II.—Dryobalanoides. Secondary nerves numerous, approximate, often obscure.

8. **H. Griffithii,** Kurz. Mergui, Malay Peninsula. Main secondary nerves 14–24 pair, with numerous shorter intermediate nerves, joined by very closely reticulate veins. Panicles glabrous, axillary, much shorter than leaf. Stylopodium broad, constricted at base, glabrous.

4. PENTACME, A. DC.; Brandis in Journ. Linn. Soc. vol. 31 (1895) 72.

Species 3, Eastern Peninsula and Philippines.

P. suavis, A. DC.—Syn. *P. siamensis*, Kurz, F. Fl. i. 119; *Shorea siamensis*, Miq.; Fl. Brit. Ind. i. 304. Vern. *Engyin*, Burm.

A large tree, heartwood brown, hard and durable, on dry ridges a shrub. Leafless during part of the hot season, when the tree is covered with large panicles of showy flowers. Leaves ovate, whitish-tomentose beneath while quite young. Fl. ¾ in. across, petals orbicular, at flowering time forming a hollow globe, open at the top, enclosing stamens and ovary. Stamens 15, anthers oblong, cells equal, the valves of each cell, as well as the connective, prolonged into a short awn, so that each anther has 5 subulate appendages. Ovary glabrous, prolonged into a conical stylopodium, style filiform, glabrous. All calyx segments enlarged in fruit, but the three outer much larger than the others, all narrowed into a stalk, which expands into a broad base, appressed to the base of fruit, but not enclosing it. Cotyledons thick, fleshy, stipitate, concave, enclosing each other, filled with fat and oil, radicle short, plumula conspicuous.

Throughout the Eastern Peninsula, extending to 25° N. Lat. Gregarious in Upper Burma and Cochinchina, scattered in the Eng forest of Lower Burma. Fl. H. S.

5. SHOREA, Roxb.; Fl. Brit. Ind. i. 303.

Stipules in a few species large and persistent, in most small and early deciduous. Leaves coriaceous, secondary nerves prominent, tertiary mostly parallel. Flowers as a rule in unilateral spikes or racemes, which are distichous and regularly alternating on the branches of large axillary and terminal panicles. Each flower subtended by 2 bracteoles, mostly deciduous, in a few species persistent and conspicuous. Sepals strongly imbricate, hairy. Petals hairy outside. Anther cells generally equal; connective as a rule prolonged into a pointed appendage. Segments of fruiting calyx with their broad bases tightly enclosing the fruit, the 3 outer ones larger and much longer than fruit. Cotyledons fleshy, filled with starch or fat oil, concave, one embracing the other, and the lignified placenta with remains of dissepiments enclosed by them. Species 89, of which 7 are here described.

In the circumference of the pith at the base of internode from 3 to 30 resin ducts. Three leaf traces enter petiole, the 2 lateral enter the bark at different levels. The petiole below insertion of blade as a rule has a semicircle of 7 or 9 half-moon shaped vascular bundles, distinct or confluent, each with a resin duct. The central mass of vascular bundles consists of several curved bands, with or without resin ducts.

A. Stamens 20–60, appendage of connective ciliate, stylopodium large, hairy, as well as ovary; style short, glabrous, stigma minute. The species of this section have young shoots and inflorescence grey stellately pubescent.

1. **S. robusta,** Gaertn. f.; Roxb. Cor. Pl. t. 212; Bedd. Pl. Sylv. t. 4. Brandis F. Fl. 26 t. 9. *The Sāl tree.* Vern. *Sāl, sakhu,* Hind; *Koroh,* Oudh; *Sarei, rinjal,* C. P.; *Sarjom,* Kol; *Salwa, soringhi,* Uriya; *Gugal,* Tel.

A large gregarious tree, heartwood dark brown, coarse- and cross-grained, hard, heavy, strong and tough. Leaves when full grown glabrous and shining, 4–10 in. long, from a rounded or cordate base broad-ovate, more or less acuminate, ending in an obtuse point, secondary nerves 10–12 pair, stipules caducous, petiole ⅛ the length of blade. Fl. yellowish on short pedicels, in unilateral racemes arranged in large compound axillary and terminal panicles. Calyx and petals softly grey tomentose outside, calyx lobes short, triangular. Petals 4 times the length of calyx, orange inside. Wings of fruiting calyx obtuse, oblong or spathulate, the larger 2–3 in. long, with 10–15 parallel longitudinal nerves and distinct straight or oblique transverse veins.

The area occupied by the Sāl tree forms two irregular but fairly defined belts, separated by the Gangetic plain. The northern or subhimalayan belt extends from the Kangra valley in the Punjab to the Darrang and Nowgong districts in Assam. Further to the north-west the cold is too severe, while further east in the Brahmaputra valley the climate is too moist throughout the year. The southern or Central India belt extends from the Coromandel coast west to the Pachmarhi sandstone hills, and south to the Godavari river. Never quite leafless, the young foliage appears in March with the flowers. The seed ripens in June and germinates immediately, often before falling to the ground.

2. **S. Tumbuggaia,** Roxb.; Bedd. Fl. Sylv. t. 5.—Syn. *Vatica Tumbuggaia,* Wight et Arn.; Wight Ic. t. 27. Vern. *Tamba, Jalari,* Tel. Hills of Cuddapah and North Arcot. A large tree, differs chiefly by smaller leaves, secondary nerves 8–10 pair, petiole ⅓–½ length of blade.

3. **S. obtusa,** Wall.; Kurz, F. Fl. i. 118; Pierre, Fl. For. Cochinch. t. 234. Vern. *Thitya,* Burm.

A large tree, heartwood similar to that of Sāl, but more even-grained. Leaves 4–6 in., oblong, obtuse, narrowed into petiole ⅛–⅙ length of blade, secondary nerves 10–14 pair.

Eastern Peninsula, not known north of 20° N. Lat., generally associated with *Dipterocarpus tuberculatus*; in Cambodia, according to Pierre, forming pure forests by itself.

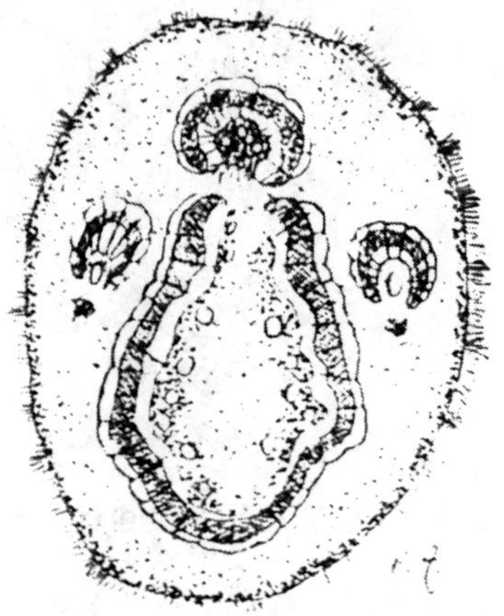

FIG. 30.—Shorea obtusa, Wall. Transverse section of internode below insertion of petiole, magnified 17 times. Three leaf traces in the bark, the apical with 3 resin ducts, each of the two lateral with one.

B. Stamens 15–20, rarely more, anthers oblong, connective terminating in a long filiform naked appendage. Ovary mostly glabrous, no stylopodium, style longer than ovary, stigma generally 3-dentate.

4. **S. Talura**, Roxb.—Syn. *S. laccifera*, Heyne; Bedd. Fl. Sylv. t. 6; *Vatica laccifera*, Wight Ic. t. 164. Vern. *Talūra, talāri*, Tam; *Jalāri*, Tel.; *Jhalli*, Kan.

A large tree, perfectly glabrous, only petals pubescent on the outside, and sepals ciliate on edges, wood very hard, heartwood small. Leaves 3–4 in., from a more or less rounded base, elliptic-oblong, obtuse, petiole $\frac{1}{3}$–$\frac{1}{4}$ length of blade. Fl. light pink, $\frac{1}{2}$ in. long, in drooping axillary panicles, ramifications slender, almost filiform. Stamens 15, in 3 rows. Anthers of the 5 interior stamens longer than the others, appendage of connective equal to anther, scabrous at the end. Larger wings of fruiting calyx 3 in. long, narrowed above the broad base, which completely encloses the fruit.

Hills of the southern Deccan, also on the west side, in evergreen forests, from North Kanara southwards. Fl. C. S. Closely allied and perhaps not specifically distinct is 5. **S. floribunda,** Kurz, F. Fl. i. 119, Tenasserim; base of leaves acute.

6. **S. assamica**, Dyer. Vern. *Makai*, Assam.

A tall tree, shoots, stipules and young leaves softly tomentose, stipules $\frac{2}{3}$ in., lanceolate, nearly falcate. Fl. $\frac{1}{2}$ in. on very short pedicels, sepals and petals hairy outside. Stamens 15, appendage long, glabrous. Ovary and base of style hairy, style filiform, longer than ovary. Fruiting calyx glabrous, wings coriaceous, the longer 3–5 in., the shorter more than half as long.

Upper Assam, forests at the foot of the Naga hills, in Sibsagar and Lakhimpur districts. Fl. September. 7. **S. gratissima,** Dyer. Tenasserim, Singapore. Glabrous except branches of inflorescence outside, of calyx and petals. Fl. $\frac{1}{3}$ in., in unilateral paniculate racemes, stamens 20–25, top of ovary and base of style slightly puberulous. Wings of fruiting calyx thin, membranous.

6. PARASHOREA, Kurz, F. Fl. i. 117.

Species 4, 1 in Sumatra, 2 in the Philippine Islands.

1. **P. stellata**, Kurz; Pierre, Fl. For. Cochinch. t. 224.—Syn. *Shorea stellata*, Dyer, Fl. Brit. Ind. i. 304. Vern. *Kaunghmu*, Burm.

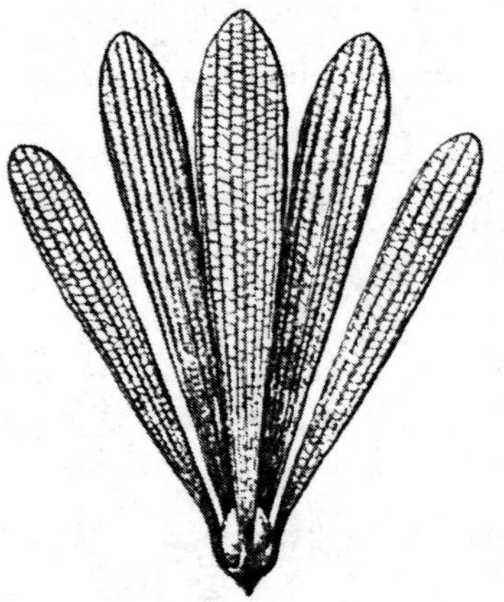

Fig. 31.—Parashorea stellata, Kurz. $\frac{1}{2}$.

A tall evergreen tree, attaining 150 ft. Leaves pale beneath, blade 4–6, petiole $\frac{1}{2}$–1 in. long, secondary nerves 8–10 pair, tertiary nerves numerous, parallel, not more conspicuous than the reticulate veins between them. Fl. small, cream-coloured, in large axillary and terminal panicles. Sepals almost valvate in bud, like the petals grey-velvety outside. Stamens 15, anthers hirsute, linear, on short filaments, prolongation of connective short, obtuse. Ovary hairy, globose, prolonged into a cylindric furrowed style, no stylopodium. Segments of fruiting calyx nearly equal, tube not enlarged, the ovoid acuminate velvety fruit free and exposed.

Martaban and Tenasserim, also Malay Peninsula. Scarce in the southern portion of the Pegu Yoma. Fl. March, April.

7. BALANOCARPUS, Beddome, Foresters' Manual, 237.

Trees, glabrous except inflorescence, stipules minute, deciduous. Fl. supported by 2 bracteoles, in unilateral racemes, arranged in compound panicles. Calyx on a flat torus, distinctly imbricate. Stamens 15, in some species 10, filaments much dilated at base, anthers short, ovate, connective prolonged into a straight apical awn, longer than anther. Segments of fruiting calyx enlarged and thickened, not much longer than fruit, enclosing its base. Fruit oblong or globose, apiculate, often with numerous raised lines. Species 14, 1 in Ceylon, 7 in the Malay Peninsula, 4 in Borneo, 2 Indian.

1. **B. utilis**, Bedd., Fl. Sylv. t. 330.—Syn. *Hopea longifolia*, Dyer, Fl. Brit. Ind. i. 309. Vern. *Kong*, *Kara kong*, Tinnevelli.

A lofty tree, young shoots and inflorescence hoary. Leaves lanceolate, obtuse, secondary nerves 10–12 pair, tertiary parallel, visible on both sides of leaf. Fl. $\frac{1}{6}$–$\frac{1}{8}$ in. long, stamens 15, awn twice or three times the length of anther. Fruit globose, $\frac{1}{2}$ in. diam., veined, not ribbed.

Tinnevelli hills, south of Courtallam, 1,000–3,000 ft. 2. **B. erosa**, Bedd. Fl. Sylv. t. 329. Tinnevelli hills 2,000–3,000 ft. Leaves oblong from a cordate, often unequal-sided base, tertiary nerves reticulate. Fruit ovoid, 1 in. long, with numerous longitudinal lines.

8. VATICA, Linn.; Fl. Brit. Ind. i. 301.

Brandis, Journ. Linn. Soc. vol. 31, 116 (*Synaptea* and *Vatica*, Trimen Handb. Ceylon i. 126, 127; *Vatica* and *Retinodendron*, King, Journ. As. Soc. Beng. vol. 62, 100, 127).

Trees, sometimes shrubs. Leaves mostly coriaceous, tertiary nerves reticulate. Fl. in spikes or racemes, not unilateral, arranged in terminal and axillary panicles. Calyx segments valvate, petals as a rule much longer than broad, erect, not spreading when expanded. Stamens 15, of which 10 (in 5 pairs) stand opposite to the sepals. Filaments of the 10 outer stamens very short, those of the 5 inner much longer. In a few species 10 stamens. Anthers short, glabrous, cells very unequal, diverging at the base, appendix of connective obtuse. Ovary either free or half immersed in the obconical receptacle, generally hairy, often pitted, style usually shorter than ovary, often ribbed and furrowed, stigma capitate or conical. Segments of fruiting calyx either equal, or two segments growing out into long wings. Species 45, Eastern Peninsula and Indian Archipelago.

A. (Subgenus Retinodendron.) Ovary free, segments of fruiting calyx equal, shorter than fruit, spreading or reflexed.

1. **V. Roxburghiana**, Blume; Bedd. Fl. Sylv. t. 95; Trimen Handb. Ceylon i. 128.—Syn. *V. chinensis*, Linn.; Brandis in Journ. Linn. Soc. vol. 31, p. 119 (the older name, but the tree does not grow in China, and Blume's name is better known). Vern. *Vella payin*, Mal.

A moderate-sized tree, young shoots and inflorescence slightly pubescent. Leaves from a rounded base elliptic-lanceolate, blade 4–9, petiole $1\frac{1}{2}$–2 in. long. Fl. $\frac{2}{3}$ in. in axillary panicles, shorter than leaves, pedicels as long as calyx, 5-ribbed. Fruit nearly globose, $1\frac{1}{2}$ in. diam., densely pubescent, indehiscent but marked with 3 vertical grooves supported at base by the enlarged thinly coriaceous sepals, pericarp very thick, fibrous, woody.

Western Ghats, South Kanara to Travancore. Fl. H. S. Also Ceylon, moist low country.

2. **V. lanceæfolia**, Blume; Kurz, F. Fl. i. 122. Vern. *Morhal*, *Makrai*, Assam.

A large shrub, sometimes a tree, youngest shoots and inflorescence mealy-puberulous. Leaves from an acute base oblong-lanceolate, chartaceous, pale beneath, blade 5–8, petiole $\frac{1}{3}$ in. long. Fl. yellowish-white, fragrant, $\frac{3}{4}$ in. long, anthers ovate-oblong, the cells with a blunt beak at the base, appendage of connective cylindric, as long as anthers. Fruit ovoid, 1 in. long.

Fig. 32.—Vatica lanceæfolia, Blume. Fl. and fr. ½.

Assam, in the valley as well as on the hills surrounding it, Cachar, Chittagong hills. Upper Burma on the Irawaddi above Bhamo. Fl. April, May. 3. **V. Griffithii**, Brandis. Mogaung, Upper Burma. A tree. Leaves rigidly coriaceous, blade 4–9, petiole ½ in. long. Fl. yellow, scented, in much ramified axillary panicles.

B. (Subgenus Synaptea). Ovary as a rule entirely or partially immersed in receptacle, 2 segments of fruiting calyx expanding into long wings.

4. **V. grandiflora,** Dyer.—Syn. *Anisoptera odorata,* Kurz, F. Fl. i. 112.

A middle-sized deciduous tree, young shoots and inflorescence clothed with ferruginous stellate tomentum. Leaves coriaceous, elliptic, blade 5–7, petiole ¾–1 in. long. Fl. ¾ in., ovary slightly immersed in the receptacle, densely clothed with stellate hairs. Wings of fruiting calyx oblanceolate, the larger 2½ in. long with stellate deciduous pubescence, the smaller one-third their length.

Martaban, Tenasserim, Singapore. 5. **V. faginea,** Dyer, Tenasserim, Perak, Cochin-china, is very similar and perhaps not specifically distinct. Leaves and flowers smaller, blade 4–5, petiole ⅓–½ in. long. Fl. ½ in.

6. **V. Scaphula,** Dyer; Fl. Brit. Ind. i. 301. Vern. *Boil shora,* Mugh (Roxb. Fl. Ind. ii. 611).

A large tree. Leaves elliptic-oblong, blade 5–8 in., petiole much thickened in the upper half, 1 in. long, midrib and 14–16 pair secondary nerves very prominent beneath, tertiary nerves parallel and reticulate. Fl. ½ in. diam., in ample terminal panicles, ramifications and calyx grey tomentose with long stellate hairs, petals white, nearly glabrous, broadly ovate, spreading. Stamens 10.

Maskhal Island, Chittagong district, canoes made of it. Fl. C. S. The anatomy of this anomalous species merits further study.

9. **VATERIA,** Linn.; Fl. Brit. Ind. i. 313.

Species 3, one in Ceylon, another on the Seychelles.

1. **V. indica,** Linn.; Roxb. Cor. pl. t. 288; Wight Ill. t. 36.—Syn. *V. malabarica,* Blume; Bedd. Fl. Sylv. t. 84. The *Piney Varnish Tree.* Vern. *Dhupada, Gugli,* Kan.; *Bili dupa,* Coorg; *Vellei Kuntrikam,* Tam.; *Payin.* Mal.

A large handsome evergreen tree, young shoots and inflorescence clothed with scurfy stellate tomentum. Leaves coriaceous, glabrous, elliptic-oblong, blade 4–10, petiole 1–1½ in. long, secondary nerves 14–16 pair, prominent beneath as well as midrib. Fl. ½ in. across, in large terminal panicles, pedicels longer than calyx segments. Petals spreading, slightly pubescent outside. Stamens 40–50, filaments short, anthers linear, hairy at base, cells unequal, the outer much longer, appendix of connective as long as anther. Ovary tomentose, style filiform, stigma minute. Fruit ovoid, 2–2½ in. long, splitting open into 3 valves, fruiting calyx small, segments reflexed. Cotyledons filled with fat (Piney tallow).

Evergreen forests along the Western Ghats, ascending to 4,000 ft. Planted largely as an avenue tree below and above ghat in the moister western districts of Mysore. Fl. H. S.

ORDER XVIII. ANCISTROCLADACEÆ. Planchon; Gilg in Engler u. Prantl, Nat. Pflanzenfam. iii. 6. p. 274.

Only Genus: **ANCISTROCLADUS**, Wall.; Fl. Brit. Ind. i. 299.

Evergreen, glabrous, woody climbers, numerous strong hooked tendrils terminating the principal branches, the leaf- and flower-bearing branchlets being axillary. Leaves entire, sessile, lanceolate, usually in tufts at the ends of branchlets, stipules minute, caducous. Fl. bisexual, calyx adnate to ovary, lobes 5, imbricate, petals 5, slightly contorted. Stamens 5 or 10, filaments broad, short, connate at base. Ovary 1-celled, ovule solitary. Fruiting calyx much enlarged. No resin ducts. Species 8, one in tropical Africa, the others in eastern tropical Asia.

A. Leaves broad, width more than 4 times their length.

1. **A. extensus**, Wall.; King, Journ. As. Soc. Beng. vol. 62 ii. (1893) 137.

A strong climber. Leaves coriaceous, obovate or broadly oblanceolate, secondary nerves distinct, joined by intramarginal veins. Panicle repeatedly dichotomous. Lobes of fruiting calyx unequal, the larger 1½–1¾ in. long.

Lower Burma, Andamans. Fl. C. S. 2. **A. Heyneanus**, Wall.; Wight Ic. t. 1987–88 (*Kardor*, *Kardal*, Mar.). Western Ghats, from the Thana district southwards, in evergreen forest. Leaves elliptic-lanceolate, secondary nerves not more conspicuous than the reticulate veins between, panicle twice dichotomous. Lobes of fruiting calyx narrow, unequal, with distinct parallel nerves.

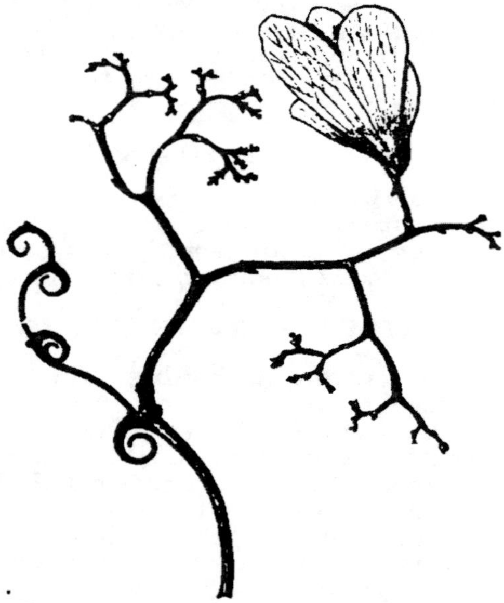

FIG. 33.—Ancistrocladus extensus, Wall. ½.

B. Leaves narrow, width less than 4 times their length.

3. **A. Wallichii**, Planchon; Kurz, F. Fl i. 111.

A large woody climber with dark-brown twisted stems, numerous strong black hooked tendrils on the branchlets. Leaves lanceolate and oblanceolate, 1–2 ft. long, midrib stout. Fl.

purplish, in dichotomous loose panicles, shorter than leaves. Fruiting calyx lobes nearly equal, about ½ in. long.

Silhet, Cachar, Chittagong, Pegu, Tenasserim. Fl. C. S. 4. **A. Griffithii,** Planch. (*Pan ben nwè*) Burm.) Lower Burma. Swamp forests and muddy river banks. Leaves 5–10 in., panicles repeatedly dichotomous, ramifications slender flexuose. Fl. pale lilac or pink. 5. **A. attenuatus,** Dyer, Tenasserim and Andamans. Leaves 12–15 in., linear cuneate, midrib prominent, ramifications of panicles stout, bracts triangular, acute, lobes of fruiting calyx unequal, 2 lobes larger, ⅜ in. long.

ORDER XIX. MALVACEÆ. Gen. Pl. i. 195.

(*Malvaceæ* and *Bombacaceæ*, Engler und Prantl iii. 6. pp. 30, 53.)

Herbs, rarely arborescent, younger parts as a rule clothed with stellate hairs, wood light, soft. Leaves alternate, mostly stipulate, generally palminerved. Fl. large, regular, as a rule bisexual. Sepals generally 5, more or less connate, valvate in bud. Petals 5, hypogynous, usually adnate to the base of staminal column, in bud twisted or imbricate. Stamens usually ∞, monadelphous. Anthers 1-celled, bursting lengthwise. Ovary syncarpous, carpels numerous, usually in a whorl round a conical torus. Fruit a number of distinct carpels or a capsule, opening loculicidally. Seeds generally without albumen.

A. Staminal tube truncate or 5-toothed, bearing short filaments on the outside.
- Bracteoles 5, persistent, as long as calyx or half its length . . . . 1. HIBISCUS.
- Bracteoles minute, deciduous . . . . . . 2. THESPESIA.

B. Staminal tube short, divided into filaments, calyx leathery, leaves digitate.
- Stamens 5, capsule 5-valved, filled with silky wool . 3. ERIODENDRON.
- Stamens numerous, capsule 5-valved, filled with silky wool . . . . 4. BOMBAX.
- Stamens numerous, fruit woody, indehiscent, filled with mealy pulp . . . . ADANSONIA (p. 78).

C. Staminal tube divided into numerous filaments, leaves simple, penniveined . . . . DURIO (p. 78).

D. Staminal tube divided into 5 antheriferous segments.
- Leaves penniveined, oblong-lanceolate, entire . . 5. CULLENIA.
- Leaves with 5–7 basal nerves, orbicular or nearly so . 6. KYDIA.

1. HIBISCUS, Linn.; Fl. Brit. Ind. i. 334.

Herbs, shrubs or trees. Leaves often lobed. Calyx supported by a whorl of 5 or more bracteoles. Staminal tube bearing on the outside short filaments along its entire length, and sometimes also at the apex, summit truncate or 5-toothed, anthers reniform. Ovary 5-celled, the cells alternating with petals. Styles 5, spreading, connate below. Capsule 5-valved, sometimes 10-celled. Species 150, chiefly in the tropics of both hemispheres.

1. **H. macrophyllus,** Roxb.; Wall. Pl. As. Rar. t. 51. Vern. *Yetwùn*, Burm.

A middle-sized tree. Branchlets, petioles and inflorescence densely clothed. with soft tomentum mixed with long tawny fasciculate hairs, ¼–⅓ in. long or longer. Leaves entire, cordate, softly tomentose on both sides, blade 6–12 in. diam., petiole 6–10 in. long. Stipules oblong, convolute, hispid-tomentose, 2 in. long, deciduous. Fl. in axillary pedunculate cymes, each flower enclosed in bud by two large ovate deciduous bracts. Bracteoles 10–12, linear-lanceolate, as long as calyx. Corolla 2–3 in. diam., yellow, with a dark purple eye, turning purple. Capsule pointed, hispid. Seeds reniform, on the edge with long tawny hairs.

Assam, Chittagong, Burma, Malay Peninsula, frequent on deserted Toungyas and in secondary forest. Fl. March, April. 2. **H. collinus**, Roxb. Western Peninsula and Ceylon. A large shrub or small tree. Leaves nearly glabrous, 3-lobed, lobes acuminate. Fl. axillary, solitary. Bracteoles 7–10, a little shorter than calyx. Capsule depressed, globose, densely hispid.

3. **H. tiliaceus**, Linn.; Bedd. Manual 29 t. iv. f. 1.—Syn. *Paritium tiliaceum*, Wight et Arn.; Wight Ic. t. 7. Vern. *Nirparutti*, Mal.; *Thinban*, Burm.

A small much-branched tree, young shoots and inflorescence pubescent. Leaves entire, from a cordate base nearly orbicular, shortly grey-pubescent beneath, blade 3–8 in. diam., petiole 1–5 in. long. Stipules broad, early deciduous Fl. in axillary or terminal few-fld. racemes. Bracteoles 10, connate, half the length of calyx. Corolla 2-3 in. diam., pale yellow, with a crimson centre, red in the evening. Capsule 10-celled, seeds slightly pilose.

FIG. 34.—Hibiscus tiliaceus, Linn. fr. ½.

Beach and tidal forests on the coasts of both peninsulas and Ceylon, ascending the river as far as the tide. Gregarious. Fl. December–March. Sea coasts in the tropics of both hemispheres.

Three species from China and Japan commonly grown in gardens:—4. **H. Rosa sinensis**, Linn. Leaves nearly glabrous, ovate, entire at the base, coarsely toothed at apex. Fl. solitary, axillary. Bracteoles 6 or 7, linear, half the length of calyx. 5. **H. mutabilis**, Linn. Leaves velvety, with 3–5 shallow lobes. Bracteoles 10, linear, shorter than calyx. Fl. pure white at first, delicate pink before fading. 6. **H. syriacus**, Linn. Leaves nearly glabrous, 3-lobed, coarsely dentate, base cuneate. Fl. solitary on short peduncles. Bracteoles 6 or 7, linear, shorter than calyx.

2. THESPESIA, Correa; Fl. Brit. Ind. i. 345.

Trees or shrubs. Bracteoles few, deciduous, sometimes wanting. Calyx truncate or minutely toothed. Staminal tube 5-toothed at the apex. Style club-shaped, 5-furrowed, entire or 5-toothed. Species 6, Madagascar, tropical Asia and Australia.

1. **T. populnea**, Correa; Wight Ic. t. 8: Bedd. Fl. Sylv. t. 63. *The Tulip* or *Portia* tree. Vern. *Parash*, Beng.; *Dumbla*, Sundarb.; *Bhendy*, Mar.; *Hurarasi*, Kan.; *Portia, pursa, pursang*, Tam.

A middle-sized evergreen tree of rapid growth, heartwood small, dark-coloured. Leaves cordate, acuminate, entire, on both sides with minute peltate scales, blade 3–5, petiole 1–4 in. Fl. axillary, solitary or 2 together. Bracteoles none, or early deciduous. Calyx cup-shaped, truncate. Corolla yellow, passing into purplish pink when withering, 2 in. diam. Capsule dehiscent or indehiscent, seeds silky.

Beach and tidal forests along the western coast from the Konkan southwards, coasts of Chittagong, Burma and the Andamans. Fl. throughout the year. Littoral throughout the tropics. In the Western Peninsula largely planted as an avenue tree.

FIG. 35.—Thespesia populnea, Correa. ½.

2. **T. Lampas**, Dalz. et Gibs.—*T. macrophylla*, Blume; T. Cooke, Fl. Bombay i. 114. *Hibiscus Lampas*, Cav.; Wight Ic. t. 5. Vern. *Ban kapās*, *Kakhi*, Hind. A large shrub. Common in deciduous forests of both peninsulas. Young shoots and leaves beneath shortly stellate tomentose. Leaves more or less lobed, bracteoles minute. Calyx nearly truncate, with 5 small distant subulate lobes. Corolla 3½ in. across, bright yellow with a crimson centre. Seeds small, club-shaped, black and glossy.

3. ERIODENDRON, DC.; Fl. Brit. Ind. i. 349. (*Ceiba*, Gaertner; Schumann in Engler u. Prantl iii. 6. 62.)

Species 9, mostly American.

E. anfractuosum, DC.; Wight Ic. t. 400; Bedd. Manual t. iv. fig. 2.—Syn. *E. orientale*, Kurz, F. Fl. i. 131; *Ceiba pentandra*, Gaertner.

A large deciduous glabrous tree, branches horizontal in whorls, stems armed with woody conical prickles. Leaves digitate, leaflets 5–8, glaucescent beneath. Fl. creamy white, 1–1½ in. long, in numerous axillary fascicles on short stout tubercles near the ends of branches, appearing with or before the young leaves. Calyx campanulate, with 5 obtuse teeth, persistent. Petals twice to three times the length of calyx. Stamens 5, connate at base into a fleshy tube. Capsule 3–5 in., tardily dehiscent, 5-celled, cells lined with long white silky wool. Seeds glabrous, bearing a few dense tufts of silky hair.

Indigenous on the Andamans, the Malay Peninsula and Archipelago, and in tropical America. Often planted in Burma and India. Fl. January–March.

4. BOMBAX, Linn.; Fl. Brit. Ind. i. 349.

Deciduous trees with digitate glabrous leaves. Peduncles axillary, 1-flowered, congregated at the ends of branchlets. Calyx leathery, cup-shaped, splitting irregularly. Staminal tube short, divided into numerous filaments, longer than tube, each bearing a 1-celled anther. Ovary 5-celled, ovules numerous. Capsule loculicidal, 5-valved, inside thickly clothed with long silky hairs, in which the seeds are embedded in dense wool. Cotyledons much folded, enclosing the radicle, albumen thin. Species 40–50, chiefly in Central and South America, a few in Africa.

FIG. 36.—Eriodendron anfractuosum, DC. ½.

1. **B. malabaricum**, DC.; Wight Ill. t. 29; Bedd. Fl. Sylv. t. 82.—Syn. *B. heptaphyllum*, Cav.; Roxb. Cor. pl. t. 247. *The Cotton tree.* Vern. *Simal, shembal*, Hind.; *Idel*, Kol; *Sayar*, Mar.; *Burla, sauri*, Kan.; *Burgha, buraga*, Tel.; *Illavū*, Tam. Mal.; *Letpan*, Burm.

A very large tree, stem generally with large buttresses at the base, wood white, very soft, turning dark on exposure. Branches in whorls of 5–7, spreading nearly horizontally, the stem of young trees covered with sharp conical prickles. Leaflets 5 or 7, lanceolate, 4–8 in. long, common petiole as long as or longer than leaflets. Fl. appearing before the leaves, large, scarlet, occasionally white, calyx inside silky tomentose. Petals 2–3 in. long, stellate-tomentose on both faces. Filaments about 70, much longer than staminal column, the 5 inner stout, forked at the top, each branch bearing an anther, some intermediate ones simple, the numerous outer ones at the base united in 5 clusters. Anthers long, afterwards twisted. Capsule oblong, hard, woody, 4–5 in. long. Seeds glabrous, embedded in silky wool.

Subhimalayan tract, from the Indus eastward, ascending to 3,500 ft. Common in both peninsulas and often cultivated. Leafless from December until April. Fl. February, March. Fruit April, May. Also in Ceylon, Java, Sumatra, Queensland and North Australia.

2. **B. insigne**, Wall. Pl. As. Rar. t. 79, 80. Burma, Andamans, Malay Peninsula, Western Ghats, Kanara. Trunk without prickles, branches armed with prickles or un-

armed. Fl. scarlet or white, petals 5–6 in. long. Stamens 400 to 600. Capsule glabrous, 7–10 in. long. 3. **B. anceps**, Pierre, Fl. For. Cochinch. t. 175. Pegu (*Didu Letpan, Kokyè*). Shan hills, Upper Burma, Cochinchina. Fl. white, petals 3 in. long, pubescent on both faces. Stamens about 350, staminal tube ½ in. long. Style glabrous. *B. cambodiense*, Pierre l.c. t. 174, has a hairy style.

Adansonia digitata, Linn., the *Baobab* or *Monkey bread* tree, indigenous in tropical Africa, and often cultivated, is a large tree with a disproportionately thick trunk, rapidly tapering upward and divided into large limbs. Leaves digitate, leaflets 5 or 7, lanceolate, downy beneath. Fl. large, white, staminal tube thick, longer than the free portion of filaments. Anthers linear, contorted. Fruit pendulous, oblong-obovoid, 8–12 in. long, filled with tough fibres and a mealy slightly acid pulp, in which the kidney-shaped brown hard shining seeds are immersed.

Durio zibethinus, Linn., the *Doorian* (*Duyin*, Burm.), indigenous in the Malay Archipelago, is cultivated in Tenasserim. Leaves entire, penninerved, elliptic-oblong, both surfaces shining, the upper glabrous, the lower clothed with orbicular scales. Fl. 2 in. long, on pendulous dichotomous panicles, mostly from the old wood, on stem and branches. Inflorescence, involucre and calyx clothed with shining orbicular scales. Bracteoles more or less connate, calyx leathery, 5 lobes on a short tube. Petals 5, spathulate. Staminal tube divided into 4–5 bundles, filaments numerous, each bearing several anther cells on a globose fleshy connective. Fruit ovoid-oblong, 8–12 in. long, densely covered with large smooth pyramidal prickles. Seeds pale yellow, embedded in a thick cream-coloured pulp (the confluent arilli) of delicious taste but offensive smell.

5. CULLENIA, Wight; Fl. Brit. Ind. i. 350.

C. excelsa, Wight Ic. t. 1761, 62. The only species. Bedd. Manual t. iv. fig. 3. Vern. *Veduplā*, Tam.; *Kārayani*, Mal.

A tall tree, wood moderately soft, not durable. Young shoots covered with peltate scales. Leaves oblong-lanceolate, entire, penninerved, caudate-acuminate, glabrous above, covered beneath with silvery or orange-coloured peltate scales. Stipules 0. Fl. reddish-brown, in large clusters on the old wood. Bracteoles connate into a tube splitting irregularly into 3–5 lobes. Calyx tubular, obscurely 5-lobed, as well as bracteolar tube completely covered with large peltate scales, petals 0. Staminal tube exserted, divided into 5 filiform segments, each segment bearing along its length numerous minute anthers in globose clusters. Ovary 5-celled, ovules 2 in each cell. Style hairy, longer than stamens, stigma globose. Fruit 4–5 in. long, densely covered with long prickles, valves 3–5. Seeds few, 1⅓ in. long, testa hard, shining, brown, nearly covered by a large fleshy white arillus. Cotyledons fleshy, no albumen.

Western Ghats up to 4,000 ft., from Coorg southwards. Fl. H. S. Ceylon, moist region, 2,000–5,000 ft. Common.

6. KYDIA, Roxb.; Fl. Brit. Ind. i. 348.

Fl. numerous, male and bisexual, in large terminal panicles. Bracteoles 4–6, leafy, connate at the base, in fruit accrescent and spreading. Calyx campanulate, 5-lobed. Petals 5, longer than calyx, attached by their claws to the base of staminal column. Staminal tube divided into 5 linear segments, 3–8 sessile anthers at the end of each segment, style 3-cleft. Capsule globose, 3-celled, opening loculicidally, 3-seeded. Species 2, Indian.

1. **K. calycina**, Roxb. Cor. Pl. t. 215 (the bisexual plant); Wight Ic. t. 879, 880.—Syn. *K. fraterna*, Roxb. l.c. t. 216 (the male plant); *K. Roxburghiana*, Wight Ic. t. 881. Vern. *Pula, puli, patha*, Hind.; *Bargah, Baranga*, Centr. Prov. (N. C.); *Kopāsia*, Uriya; *Warung, Iliya*, Mar.; *Bellakā, Bendi*, Kan.; *Potri, pandiki*, Tel.; *Tabo, Dwalôk, Myethlwa*, Burm.

A large shrub or small tree, wood greyish-white, soft, no heartwood, medullary rays joined by white transverse bars of parenchyma, resembling wood of Anonaceæ. Young shoots, inflorescence and under side of leaves grey- or tawny-tomentose. Leaves nearly orbicular, angled or slightly lobed, blade 3–5, petiole 1–2½ in. long. Bracteoles slightly pubescent, in the bisexual flower longer than calyx, when the seed ripens, 3 or 4 times the length of calyx. Capsule tomentose, seeds reniform.

Subhimalayan tract from the Indus eastward, common in the deciduous forests of both peninsulas. The old leaves are shed in February, the new foliage appears in April and May. Fl. July–October. Fruit ripens C. S., and hangs on the tree for months.

2. **K. glabrescens,** Masters. Bhutan, Assam, Malacca. Leaves obovate or orbicular, nearly glabrous. Bracteoles spathulate, glabrous, shining.

ORDER XX. **STERCULIACEÆ.** Gen. Pl. i. 214.

Trees, shrubs, climbers or herbs, frequently tomentose with stellate hairs. Leaves alternate, mostly stipulate. Fl. regular, rarely zygomorphic, bisexual or unisexual. Calyx more or less deeply divided into 5, rarely less, valvate lobes or segments. Petals 5 or none. Stamens commonly monadelphous, with 5, 10 or 15 2–celled anthers. Fruit carpels either distinct or united into a loculicidally dehiscent capsule.

A. Fl. unisexual or polygamous, petals none.
- Anthers 5–25, fruit carpels dehiscent . . . . . 1. STERCULIA.
- Anthers 5, carpels woody, indehiscent . . . . . 2. HERITIERA.

B. Fl. bisexual, erect shrubs or trees, leaves palmately lobed or angled.
- Capsule ovoid, woody or coriaceous . . . . . 3. ERIOLÆNA.
- Capsule cylindrical, coriaceous, hairy . . . . 4. HELICTERES.
- Capsule turbinate, membranous . . . . . ABROMA (p. 89).

C. Fl. bisexual, climbing shrubs, capsule globose, covered with prickles or bristles . . . . 5. BUETTNERIA.

D. Fl. bisexual, trees, rarely shrubs, staminal column short, divided into 20 filaments, 15 with, 5 without anthers, capsule tomentose or hoary, mostly cylindrical . . 6. PTEROSPERMUM.

E. Fl. bisexual, trees, rarely shrubs, leaves not lobed or angled.
- (*a*) Leaves oblong- or ovate-lanceolate.
  - Fl. in axillary fascicles, petals short, orbicular, concave, hairy . . . . LEPTONYCHIA (p. 92).
  - Fl. in terminal corymbose panicles, petals clawed . 7. REEVESIA.
- (*b*) Leaves ovate-oblong, from an unequal-sided base claw of petals concave, blade bifid, segments linear . . . . GUAZUMA (p. 92).
- (*c*) Leaves broad-ovate, base often cordate.
  - Petals equal, spathulate, marcescent, capsule coriaceous, ovoid . . . . MELOCHIA (p. 92).
  - Petals unequal, capsule membranous, inflated, pyriform . . . . KLEINHOVIA (p. 92).

Theobroma Cacao, Linn. A native of the West Indies and adjoining parts of South America cultivated on the Nilgiris and elsewhere. The seeds yield cocoa.

1. **STERCULIA,** Linn.; Fl. Brit. Ind. i. 354 (*Sterculia, Brachychiton, Pterygota, Firmiana*, Schumann in Engl. u. Prantl iii. 6. 96, 97).

Trees, wood soft light, often spongy, vessels large, medullary rays prominent, bast very tough, Hairs stellate. Leaves entire, lobed or digitate. Fl. unisexual or polygamous. Calyx more or less deeply 5- rarely 4-cleft, usually coloured. Petals none. Anthers 5, 10, 12, in some species 20 or 25, on a staminal column, which in the female and bisexual flower is adnate to a long or short gynophore. Ovary of 5 distinct carpels, 2 or more ovules in each. Fruit carpels (follicles), spreading, woody, coriaceous, or thin foliaceous, opening along the inner edge. Cotyledons of some species flat, thin, albumen adhering to them, of others thick and fleshy, without albumen. Species 100–120, chiefly in tropical Asia, one section (*Brachychiton*) in Australia.

A. Follicles woody or coriaceous, opening when the seeds ripen.

(*a*) Leaves digitate.

1. **S. fœtida**, Linn.; Wight Ic. t. 181, 364. Vern. *Jangal Badām*, Hind.; *Pinari*, Tam.; *Letkŏk*, *Shawbyu*, Burm.

A large deciduous tree. Leaflets 7–9, elliptic-lanceolate, when full grown coriaceous and glabrous beneath, petiole 8 in. long, stipules ensiform, caducous. Fl. red and yellow or dull purple, smell most offensive, in racemiform panicles, 6–12 in. long. Calyx deeply 5-cleft, the lobes ½ in. long, oblong or lanceolate, spreading gynophore as long as or longer than calyx tube. Ovary villous. Follicles woody, scarlet, almost glabrous outside, fibrous inside. Seeds black, 10–15 in each. Cotyledons thick, fleshy, albumen 0.

Western coast, from the Konkan southwards, Burma. Fl. April, May. Fr. C. S., the seeds roasted and eaten. A widely spread tree, from eastern tropical Africa to North Australia. 2. **S. versicolor**, Wall. Pl. As. Rar. t. 59. Upper Burma. A small tree, leaflets grey beneath, fl. small, in panicles 8–12 in. long, fragrant, first yellow, afterwards deep orange. Calyx lobes ¼ in., inflexed, and connivent at the top.

(*b*) Leaves simple, palmately lobed.

3. **S. urens**, Roxb., Cor. Pl. t. 24; Brandis F. Fl. 33. Vern. *Gular*, Hind.; *Kulu*, *Karhar*, Central Provinces; *Tele*, Kol; *Karai*, *Kandol*, Mar.; *Kalauri*, Panch Mahals.

A large deciduous tree, bark smooth, white or greenish-grey, exfoliating in large thin irregular plates. Leaves crowded at the ends of branches, tomentose beneath, nearly glabrous above, cordate, shallowly 5-lobed, lobes entire, acuminate, blade 8–12 in., petioles 6–10 in. long. Fl. in crowded, erect, more or less pyramidal panicles, clothed with a dense sticky tomentum of glandular stellate hairs, a few bisexual, mixed with a large number of male flowers. ♂: Staminal column short, anthers about 20. ⚥: Gynophore short, thick. Fruit of 4–5 sessile, radiating, ovoid, thickly coriaceous carpels, 3 in. long, red when ripe, covered outside with stiff stinging bristles. Seeds 3–6 in each carpel, oblong, dark brown.

Subhimalayan tract, from the Ganges eastward. Common in dry deciduous forests, often associated with *Boswellia*, throughout the Peninsula and on the hills of Rajputana, Central India and Behar. Dry forests of Burma. Fl. C. S. Fr. H. S. Also in Ceylon.

4. **S. villosa**, Roxb.; Brand. F. Fl. 32. t. 10. Vern. *Udal*, *udār*, Hind.; *Godgodālo*, *Gūlkandar*, Pb.; *Sisi*, Kol; *Sarda*, *Kuthada*, Mar.; *Savaya*, Kan.; *Murutthan*, Tam.; *Vakka*, Mal.; *Shawni*, Burm.

A moderate-sized deciduous tree, bast very tough, young shoots, petioles and inflorescence tawny-tomentose. Leaves crowded at the ends of branches, densely tomentose beneath, deeply 5–7 lobed, lobes oblong or ovate-oblong, toothed or lobed, blade 12–18 in. across, petiole as long as blade. Stipules large, broadly-lanceolate, deciduous. Fl. yellow, on slender pedicels, loosely arranged in long drooping panicles, 5–8 panicles at the end of thick leafless branches, marked with the scars of fallen leaves. Male and bisexual flowers mixed, the former more numerous. Calyx campanulate, outside clothed with stellate hairs. ⚥: Gynophore as long as calyx tube, ovary globose, surrounded at its base by a membranous ring, adnate to the gynophore and bearing on its edge 10 anthers. Follicles 2–5, sessile, coriaceous, bright red when ripe, 1½–3 in. long, clothed inside and outside with stiff stellate hairs, seeds several in each follicle.

Subhimalayan tract and outer hills from the Indus eastward, ascending to 3,500 ft., Punjab salt range, Oudh forests. Central India and Western Peninsula. Sikkim,

Assam, Khasi hills, Andamans, Burma. Valued and in many places exterminated on account of the bast, of which ropes for dragging timber are made. Fl. March, April. Fr. June, July. Coppices readily.

FIG. 37.—Sterculia villosa, Roxb. ½.

5. **S. ornata,** Wall.; Kurz, F. Fl. i. 136; King in Journ. As. Soc. Beng., 60, ii. (1892) 62.—Syn. *S. armata*, Mast. in part. Vern. *Shaw wa*, Burm.

A middle-sized deciduous tree, young shoots tomentose with soft crimson (brown when dry) often glandular hairs. Leaves from a deeply cordate base almost reniform, more or less deeply divided into 5 or 7 acuminate lobes, underside densely tomentose, upper side sprinkled with minute fascicled hairs. Panicles softly tomentose, several at the ends of the thick branches, 8–15 in. long, many-flowered. Fl. large, calyx widely campanulate, ¾ in. diam., pale ochre coloured with a reddish base. Follicles 3–4 in. long, first densely

clothed with pungent fragile hairs, glabrescent afterwards, brilliant orange-scarlet when ripe.

Lower Burma, probably also on the Andamans. The ropes made of the bast as good as those of *S. villosa.* Fl. Febr. Closely allied: 6. **S. hypochra,** Pierre, Fl. Cochinch. t. 185. Lower Burma, T. H. Aplin, April, 1888. ♂ fl. smaller, ⅓ in. across, calyx segments half the length of tube or less, panicles 12 in. long, ample, drooping, ramifications slender, pedicels filiform.

(c) Leaves simple, entire.

7. **S. guttata,** Roxb.; Wight Ic. t. 487; Bedd. Fl. Sylv. t. 105. Vern. *Kūkāri*, Thāna; *Kukar, goldār*, Mar.; *Happu-savaga*, Kan.; *Kawili, Thondi*, Tam.; *Kāvalam*, Mal.

A large or middle-sized tree. Leaves from a rounded or slightly cordate base

Fig. 38.—Sterculia guttata, Roxb. ½.

ovate, shortly acuminate, entire, under side as well as petioles tomentose, blade 5–10, petiole 1–3 in. long, secondary nerves 8–12 pair, the lowest pair basal. Fl. white or pale yellow, with an offensive smell, in racemiform, rusty or tawny tomentose panicles at the ends of branches. Calyx divided to near the base into

5 thick segments, outside rusty tomentose, inside dark purple with long hairs, staminal column $\frac{1}{3}$ in. long, slender, glabrous, anthers 10–12. Follicles 3 in. long, red, with large black seeds, which are roasted and eaten.

On the west side of the Peninsula from the Thal Ghat southwards, frequent in evergreen forest (Andamans, Burma doubtful), Ceylon. 8. **S. Roxburghii,** Wall. Sikkim, up to 6,000 ft., Assam, Khasi hills. A small tree. Differs by glabrous elliptic-oblong leaves, blade 4–5, petiole 1–2 in. long, short racemes with slender peduncles and filiform pedicels. Follicles 3–4 in. pink. 9. **S. striatiflora,** Mast. Amber Mines, Upper Burma. A shrub. Leaves glabrous, membranous, oblanceolate, blade 8–18, petiole 1 in., midrib and secondary nerves prominent, panicle shorter than leaves, calyx funnel-shaped, striated.

10. **S. alata,** Roxb. Cor. Pl. t. 287.—Syn. *S. Haynii*, Bedd. Fl. Sylv. t. 230. Vern. *Anei thondi*, Tam.; *Letkôk*, Burm.

A large deciduous tree. Leaves from a cordate base broadly-ovate, entire, both surfaces glabrous, blade 4–12, petiole 2–4 in. long, basal nerves 5 or 7, prominent beneath, the middle one with 4 pair of secondary nerves. Fl. in short rusty-tomentose racemes, calyx $\frac{3}{4}$ in. long, campanulate, divided halfway into 5 or 6 thick lanceolate segments, which are rusty stellate-tomentose outside and red-veined within. Follicles stalked, woody, nearly globose, 5 in. diam. Seeds oblong, with a large obovate thick spongy terminal wing, $2\frac{1}{2}$ in. long and $1\frac{1}{4}$ in. broad.

Tista valley, Sikkim, not common, Silhet, Chittagong. North Kanara, Tinnevelli and Travancore. Lower Burma, Andamans. Fl. Febr., March. Malay Peninsula.

11. **S. coccinea,** Roxb.; Kurz, F. Fl. i. 137.

An evergreen shrub or small tree. Leaves glabrous, oblong-lanceolate, entire,

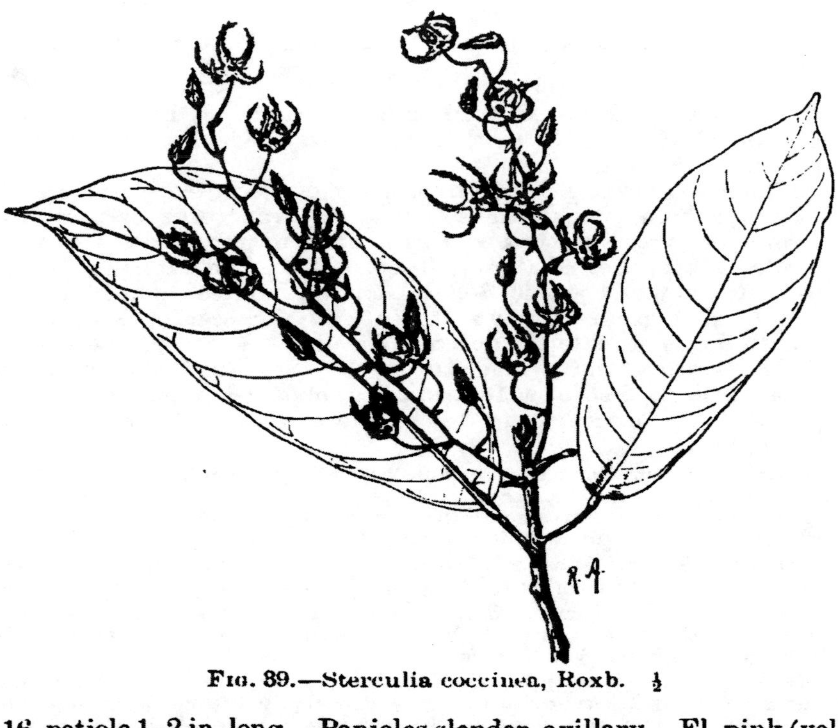

Fig. 39.—Sterculia coccinea, Roxb. $\frac{1}{2}$

blade 6–16, petiole 1–2 in. long. Panicles slender, axillary. Fl. pink (yellowish, Duars) on capillary pedicels, $\frac{1}{2}$ in. long, buds narrow-conical, calyx 5-lobed nearly to the base, lobes linear, $\frac{1}{3}$–$\frac{1}{2}$ in., often cohering at the tip, long spreading hairs on them. Follicles coriaceous, lanceolate, crimson, 3–4 by $\frac{3}{4}$ in.

Sikkim, ascending to 8,000 ft., Bhutan, Assam, Khasi hills, Burma. Fl. August–October, in Burma March (Kurz). Nearly allied: 12. **S. lævis**, Wall. Pegu and Tenasserim, Malay Peninsula. Petioles 1–2 in., panicles shorter, follicles narrower. 13. **S. nobilis**, Rob. Brown. A native of China, sometimes cultivated in India, has elliptic leaves, blade 5–9, petiole 1–2 in., large drooping panicles and fragrant flowers. A very remarkable species of this group is 14. **S. cognata**, Prain. Kachin hills, Upper Burma. Leaves glabrous, narrow-oblanceolate, blade 9 by 1¼ in. gradually narrowed into short hirsute petiole, secondary nerves numerous, joined by prominent intramarginal veins, panicles short, ramifications filiform, calyx segments ½ in. slightly pilose.

15. **S. Balanghas**, Linn.; Wight Ill. t. 30; Trimen Handb. i. 165.

Youngest shoots, petioles and inflorescence clothed with tawny stellate pubescence. Leaves ovate or elongate-elliptic, blade 5–15, petiole 1–2 in. long. Panicles 4–5 in. long. Fl. scented, greenish purple, follicles 3–4 by 1 in., shortly stalked, minutely pubescent, brilliant orange-scarlet, seeds ⅞ in., ovoid, jet, black, shining.

Travancore and ghats of Tinnevelli, Ceylon, low country common. Fl. R. S.

The following 4 species are closely allied to each other, and with *S. Balanghas*, with which some day perhaps they may be united. 16. **S. rubiginosa**, Ventenat; King, in Journ. As. Soc. Bengal, vol. 60 (1892) p. 69. Tenasserim, Malay Peninsula. A tree 20–50 ft., rusty-tomentose. 17. **S. ensifolia**, Masters; King, l.c. p. 70. Mergui, Malay Peninsula. A shrub or small tree. Leaves lanceolate or oblanceolate, caudate-acuminate, rusty-tomentose beneath. 18. **S. angustifolia**, Roxb.; King, l.c. 68, Martaban, Perak. A small tree, velvety rusty-tomentose. 19. **S. parviflora**, Roxb.; King, l.c. 66. Silhet, Andamans, Nicobar, Tenasserim, Malay Peninsula. A tree 20–50 ft., the youngest shoots ferruginous-tomentose. Fl. smaller than of the preceding.

20. **S. populifolia**, Roxb.; Wall. Pl. As. Rar. t. 3; Pierre, Fl. For. Cochinch. t. 197. Hills of the Coromandel coast and throughout French Indo-China. A small tree. Leaves deeply cordate, blade 3–4, petiole 2–6 in. long, basal nerves 7–9, calyx ½ in., follicles stalked, terminated by a membranous oblique strongly veined obtuse wing.

B. Follicles membranous, opening soon after fertilization, long before the seeds ripen.

21. **S. colorata**, Roxb. Cor. Pl. t. 25; Brandis F. Fl. 34. Vern. *Bodula walena, samari*, Hind.; *Mutruk*, Ajmere; *Sisi*, Kol, Sonth.; *Khowsey*, Mar. *Karaka*, Tel.; *Wetshaw*, Burm.

A middle-sized, often a large tree, stem often fluted, wood grey, very soft medullary rays broad, conspicuous, joined by transverse bars of wood parenchyma, youngest shoots clothed with grey stellate pubescence. Leaves crowded at the ends of branches, shallowly 3- or 5-lobed, lobes triangular acuminate, blade 6–12 in. across, petiole 3–8 in. long. Panicles numerous, erect, from bright coral-red to greyish-brown, the entire inflorescence, as well as the calyx covered with dense stellate tomentum. Calyx ⅝–1½ in. long, persistent, funnel-shaped, the mouth with 5 triangular teeth. Staminal column as long as, or longer than calyx. Follicles 1–5, stalked, oblong-lanceolate, obtuse, membranous, pink outside, opening long before the seeds ripen, and bearing 2 seeds near the base.

Subhimalayan tract from the Jumna eastward, ascending to 4,000 ft. Central Provinces, the Peninsula, Lower and Upper Burma. Leafless during winter. Fl. March, April, the young leaves generally appear after the flowers. Fr. June, July.

According to some botanists, this consists of three distinct species:

(*a*) *S. colorata*, Roxb. Western Peninsula. Adult leaves on both sides perfectly glabrous, panicles bright coral red. Calyx in fl. ⅝–¾ in. long, ¼–⅓ in. across at mouth.

(*a*) *S. fulgens*, Wall. Burma, Malay Peninsula, Sumatra, Java. Full grown leaves harsh beneath with dense minute stellate pubescence. Panicles orange or dull yellow, calyx in fl. 1¼–1½ in. long, ½ in. across.

(*c*) *S. pallens*, Wall. (*Khardala*, N. W.). Subhimalayan tract. Branchlets, petioles and under side of adult leaves more or less densely velvety, upper side pubescent or glabrous. Panicles and calyx greyish brown, calyx in fl. ⅝–¾ in. long and ⅓–½ across at mouth.

22. **S. scaphigera**, Wall.; Kurz, F. Fl. i. 140. Burma, Cochinchina, Malay Archipelago, Sumatra. A tall deciduous glabrous tree. Leaves ovate, blade 5-10, petiole 2-5

in. long. Follicles 1–5, on stout pubescent stalks, opening long before maturity, 6–8 in. long, membranous, conspicuously veined, boat-shaped. Seed 1 (rarely 2) attached to the very base of the follicle. 23. **S. campanulata,** Wall.; Kurz, F. Fl. i. 189. Marta-

Fig. 40.—Sterculia colorata, Roxb. Fl. fr. ½.

ban, eastern slopes of the Pegu Yoma, Nicobars, Malay Peninsula, Cochinchina, Malay Archipelago. A large deciduous tree. Leaves broadly ovate from a cordate base, blade 4–6, petiole 2–5 in. Calyx campanulate, as a rule persistent in fruit. Follicles 3–6, 2–3 in. long, membranous, veined, saccate, ending in an oblong-lanceolate wing, purple outside, yellowish-brown inside. Seed at the base of the follicle, generally one only.

2. HERITIERA, Aiton; Fl. Brit. Ind. i. 362.

Evergreen trees. Leaves simple, coriaceous, quite entire, silver-scaly beneath. Fl. small, unisexual, in axillary panicles. Calyx 4–5, sometimes 6–7 cleft. Petals 0. ♂ : Staminal column slender, bearing a ring of 4–5 2-celled anthers at the top. ♀ : Ovary of 5 nearly distinct carpels with 1 or 2 ovules. Ripe carpels woody, indehiscent, keeled or winged. Cotyledons thick, albumen none. Species 6 or 7, tropics of the old world and of Australia.

A. Littoral species.

1. **H. littoralis,** Dryander; Bedd. Manual t. 11, fig. 6. Vern. *Sunder, Sundri*, Beng. *Pinlè kanazo*, Burm.

A middle-sized gregarious tree, heartwood dark red, very hard, medullary rays reddish, intervening tissue dark red. Leaves elliptic-oblong from a rounded or slightly cordate base, blade 5–10, petiole ½–¾ in. Panicles shorter than leaves, fl. pale greenish-pink, calyx ⅛ in. long. Ripe carpels 1–3, 1½–3 in., glabrous, shining, with a strong sharp keel.

FIG. 41.—Heritiera littoralis, Dryander. ½.

Coast of Burma and the Andamans, coasts of the Peninsula and Ceylon. Fl. R. S. Seashore within the tropics of the old world and Australia. 2. **H. Fomes,** Buch. (*H. minor*, Roxb.; Kurz, F. Fl. i. 141). Sundriban, sea coast of Burma and the Malay Peninsula. Leaves narrowed towards the base, blade 4–6, petiole ½ in., ripe carpels obliquely compressed, slightly keeled.

B. Inland species.

3. **H. macrophylla,** Wall.; Kurz, F. Fl. i. 141; Bot. Mag. t. 7192.

A large tree. Leaves elliptic-oblong, acuminate, bright silvery beneath, blade 7–14, petiole 2–4 in. Panicles large, half the length of leaves. Fl. pink. Fr. globose, rough, with an abrupt, flat beak.

Khasi hills, Cachar, Manipur, Upper Tenasserim (Pierre, Fl. For. Cochinch. t. 204 reports it from the Delta of the Mekong river). 4. **H. acuminata,** Wall. Khasi hills Leaves lanceolate, long acuminate, blade 3–5, petiole ½–¾ in. Fl. white, ripe carpels globose ¾ in., wing coriaceous, 1½ in. long.

5. **H. Papilio,** Bedd. Fl. Sylv. t. 218.

A lofty tree, wood red, very hard, young shoots and inflorescence clothed with golden stellate tomentum. Leaves lanceolate, shining above, silvery beneath, blade 4–5, petiole ¾ in. long. Panicles twice or three times the length of petiole, ripe carpels with a broad oblique membranous wing, 2–3 times the length of carpel, veined with numerous strong parallel nerves.

Common in the evergreen forests of the Tinnevelli and Travancore Ghats at 3,000 ft. and upwards. Fl. R. S. Prain, Ann. Gard. Calc. ix., 9, unites 4 and 5. 6. **H. dubia,** Wall.; Prain in Ann. Gard. Calc. ix. t. 3. Khasi hills, l. ovate, glabrous above, densely silvery-lepidote beneath, ripe carpels 1½ in. long, compressed, cuneate-oblong, a narrow thick wing on one side. Nearly allied to *H. littoralis.*

3. ERIOLÆNA, DC.; Fl. Brit. Ind. i. 370.

Deciduous trees or large shrubs with stellate pubescence, heartwood close-grained. Leaves cordate toothed, with 5–9 basal nerves, stipules deciduous. Peduncles axillary, 1–many-flowered. Fl. bisexual, buds supported by an involucre of 3–5 bracteoles, generally laciniate and early caducous, calyx deeply 5-cleft, rarely 4-cleft, segments hairy on both sides. Petals usually 5, sometimes 4, on thick and broad claws, tomentose inside. Filaments connate at base into a short tube, anthers linear, 2-celled, cells parallel. Ovary tomentose, 5–10-celled, style erect, stigmas 5–10, spreading. Capsule woody, 5–10-celled, dehiscing loculicidally, dissepiments attached to the valves. Seeds numerous, winged above. Species 7–8, Asiatic.

A. Bracteoles laciniate, petals 5.

1. **E. Wallichii,** DC., Mém. Mus. Paris x. 1823 t. 5; Gamble list 12.

A tree, wood red-brown, hard, close grained. Young shoots, petioles and under side of leaves clothed with dense soft greyish tomentum, stipules lanceolate, as a rule deeply laciniate. Fl. large, solitary on axillary pedicels, 3–4 in. long, subtended by 5 broad deeply-cut bracteoles. Calyx segments on both sides densely tawny-woolly, 1½ in. long, style and stigma with long hairs.

Oudh forests, Sikkim. Fl. H. S.

2. **E. Hookeriana,** Wight et Arn.; Bedd. Manual, 35, t. v.; Brandis, F. Fl. 36. Vern. *Bundun,* Kol; *Guagoli,* Sonth.

A small tree, young shoots, petioles and under side of leaves clothed with soft brown or tawny tomentum. Peduncles axillary many flowered, subtended by pinnatisect bracteoles. Calyx segments ¾–1 in. long, style hairy. Capsule 1 in. long, sharply bent down, valves tubercled, not keeled.

Common in the deciduous forests of the Satpuras, in Berar and in the Western Peninsula. Chota Nagpore, probably also in Behar. Fl. R. S., C. S. Closely allied and perhaps not specifically distinct is 3. **E. Stocksii,** Hook. fil. & Thoms.; west side of the Peninsula, from the Aravalli hills (*Giali, dhaula Giala*) the Panch Mehals (*Jehali*) to the Konkan. Under side of leaves grey or tawny-tomentose, peduncles 1–3 fld., bracteoles deeply laciniate, so as to appear mossy.

4. **E. Candollei,** Wall., Pl. As. Rar. t. 64; Kurz, F. Fl. i. 148. Vern. *Doani,* Burm.

A large tree, heartwood brick red, beautifully mottled, young shoots, petioles and under side of leaves thinly tawny pubescent. Fl. yellow, generally in terminal panicles, bracteoles 3 under each flower, deeply cut, style glabrous. Capsule 2 in. long, valves obtusely keeled, not tuberculate.

Bhutan. Burma, not uncommon in deciduous forests. Ruby Mines district. To this possibly belong specimens collected by me, Nov. 1863, in fruit on the banks of the Choti Gandak, Gorakhpur district. (Vern. *Bim.*)

5. **E. quinquelocularis,** Wight Ic. t. 882 (*Microchlæna* under the plate; Bedd. Fl. Sylv. Manual t. 5.

A small tree, young shoots, and under side of leaves clothed with short but dense silvery or tawny pubescence. Fl. in large terminal panicles, bracteoles at a distance from the flowers, minute, dentate, early deciduous. Sepals 1 in.,

FIG. 42.—Eriolæna quinquelocularis, Wight. Fl., fr. ½.

style hairy, capsule ovoid, 1 in. long, valves slightly tubercled, at times quite smooth.

Western Peninsula, chiefly on the west side, from Bombay southwards. Fl. July, August.

B. Bracteoles entire or nearly so, petals usually 4.

6. **E. spectabilis**, Planchon.—Syn. *Wallichia spectabilis*, DC. in Mém. Mus. Paris. x. (1823) t. 6.

A small tree, young shoots and under side of leaves with short grey or tawny pubescence. Fl. in large terminal panicles, involucre of 2–4 linear rarely dentate bracteoles ⅛ in. below flower. Sepals 1¼ in., as a rule 4, petals 4, stamens 40–50, style hairy below, glabrous above. Capsule 1½ in. long.

Nepal, Manipur, abundant in oak forests at 3,500 ft., Mogok in Upper Burma 4,500 ft., on open exposed slopes with *Kydia calycina*. Fl. April, May.

4. HELICTERES, Linn.; Fl. Brit. Ind. i. 365.

Shrubs, rarely trees. Fl. bisexual. Calyx tubular, more or less equally 5-cleft. Petals 5, clawed, usually zygomorphic. Staminal column adnate to gynophore, bearing 5 or 10 anthers. Ovary 5-lobed, 5-celled, several ovules in each cell. Fruit carpels 5, opening along their inner edge, straight or spirally twisted. Albumen scanty, cotyledons folded round the radicle. Species 40, tropics of both hemispheres.

A. Fruit spirally twisted.

1. **H. Isora**, Linn.; Wight Ic. t. 180. Vern. *Maror-phal*, *Kapāsi*, Hind.;

Petchmura, Sonth.; *Kaval*, *Orla*, Uriya; *Kevani*, *Muradsing*, Mar.; *Kavargi*, *Kauri*, Kan.; *Kaiva*, Tam.; *Thungé che*, Burm.

A large roughly tomentose shrub. Leaves from a more or less cordate—often oblique—base, broadly obovate or orbicular, shortly acuminate, irregularly toothed, sometimes slightly lobed, blade 4–5, petiole ½ in., basal nerves 4–7, stipules linear, deciduous. Fl. brick-red, in axillary, sometimes extra-axillary fascicles, pedicels shorter than calyx. Calyx ½ in., petals twice as long, the 2 larger spathulate, the 3 others with two teeth at the end of claw. Fruit 1–2 in. long, on a gynophore nearly as long, cylindrical, hairy, twisted.

Subhimalayan tract, from the Jhelum eastward, throughout Central India, the Western Peninsula, and probably Burma. Fl. April to December, fresh foliage in April. Ceylon, Malay Peninsula, and Archipelago. Australia.

B. Fruit straight, not twisted.

2. **H. hirsuta**, Lour.; Kurz, F. Fl. i. 143; King, Journ. As. Soc. Beng. lx. (1892) 82.—Syn. *H. spicata*, Colebr.; Fl. Brit. Ind. i. 366.

A shrub, softly tomentose. Leaves ovate or ovate-lanceolate, basal nerves 3–5. Fl. purple or deep blue, tinged with pink, in short axillary racemes. Fruit 1–1¼ in., cylindric, acuminate, densely clothed with long stellate wool and soft prickles (var. *lanigera* very densely woolly).

Tenasserim. Fl. March, Malay Peninsula. 3. **H. angustifolia**, Linn. (*H. obtusa*, Wall.; Kurz, F. Fl. i. 144). Tenasserim, Malay Peninsula, China. Leaves lanceolate, grey-tomentose beneath, 3 basal nerves, calyx ¼ in., petals a little longer. Fruit cylindric, ½–¾ in. long, densely covered with soft villous prickles. 4. **H. elongata**, Wall. Sikkim, Assam, Burma, Yunan. Leaves obliquely ovate-lanceolate, thinly stellate-pubescent. Fl. in axillary or terminal elongate racemes, as long as or longer than leaf. Fruit 1–1½ in. long, cylindric, beaked. 5. **H. glabriuscula**, Wall. Upper Burma. Leaves oblong-lanceolate, 1–1½ in., softly pubescent, peduncles axillary 2–3 fld. Fl. less than ½ in. Fruit ½ in., stellate-pubescent, valves beaked.

Abroma augusta, Linn.; Bedd. Fl. Sylv. Manual t. 5, is a small tree, indigenous in the Malay Archipelago, perhaps also in the Peninsula, naturalized in many parts of India. Branchlets, under side of leaves and inflorescence soft-pubescent. Leaves ovate from a cordate base, often lobed or angled, basal nerves 5–7. Peduncles extra-axillary with 2–3 large purple bisexual fl. Sepals 1 in., persistent, petals contorted in bud, claw concave. Staminal tube short, 5 petaloid staminodes alternating with 5 sessile anthers. Capsule turbinate, membranous, 5-angled, 5-winged.

5. BUETTNERIA, Linn.; Fl. Brit. Ind. i. 376.

Large woody climbers, flowers minute, in axillary much branched cymes. Fl. bisexual, petals 5, a narrow fleshy blade, with 2 small lateral lobes on a concave claw. Staminal tube with 5 broad truncate or emarginate teeth, and between them 5 extrorse anthers. Capsule globose, echinate, 5-celled, 5-valved, the cells 1-seeded. Species 50, a few in tropical and subtropical Asia and Africa, the rest in America.

1. **B. pilosa**, Roxb.; Kurz, F. Fl. i. 151. Vern. *Tattaya-nwè*, Burm.

A large climber, the stem as thick as a man's thigh. Leaves cordate serrulate, shortly 3–5 lobed, lobes acuminate, blade 5–6, petiole 4–5 in. Capsules globose, ¾ in. diam., densely covered with long brown rigid but flexible bristles.

Sikkim up to 4,000 ft., Assam, Khasi hills, Manipur, Chittagong, Burma. Fl. May–July.

2. **B. aspera**, Colebr.; Kurz, F. Fl. i. 151.

A powerful woody climber, often with a tree-like stem. Leaves cordate, entire, glabrous and shining above, blade 5–8, petiole 2–5 in. Capsule globose, 1½–2 in. diam., armed with many long sharp spines.

Sikkim, ascending to 4,000 ft., Khasi hills, Andamans, Burma. Fl. May, June. Cochinchina, China. 3. **B. crenulata,** Wall. Pegu, Tenasserim. Leaves ovate-acuminate, blade 3–4, petiole 1–3 in. long, capsule ¾–1 in. diam., prickles ¼ in. long. 4. **B. andamanensis,** Kurz. Andamans, Tenasserim (Thaungyeen, March, 1859 D.B.). Leaves 3–5 lobed, capsules ¾–1 in. diam., prickles on a conical base, unequal in length.

6. PTEROSPERMUM, Schreber ; Fl. Brit. Ind. i. 366.

Trees, rarely shrubs, hairs stellate. Fl. bisexual, bracteolate, calyx deeply 5-cleft, deciduous. Staminal column short, adnate to the gynophore, divided into 20 filaments, 15 with linear anthers, 5 without anthers (staminodia). Ovary 5-celled, stigma club-shaped and furrowed. Capsule woody or coriaceous, opening loculicidally in 5 valves. Seeds winged at the end, albumen none or scanty, cotyledons wrinkled or folded. Species 18, tropical Asia.

A. Western species.

1. **P. suberifolium,** Lam. ; Trimen Handb. Ceylon i. 169. Vern. *Bayalo*, Uriya ; *Tada, Narudu*, Tel.

A middle-sized tree, branchlets and inflorescence densely clothed with fine ferruginous or tawny stellate hairs. Leaves distichous, 2–4 in., from a rounded base obovate-oblong, acuminate, often irregularly lobed in the upper part, upper side glabrous, under side white or yellowish, felted with fine stellate hairs. Fl. yellowish-white, sweet scented, peduncles short, axillary, sometimes bearing 2–3 flowers, bracteoles deciduous, linear. Calyx 1 in., capsule 2–3 in. long, ¾ in. diam., attenuate into a stalk ½–¾ in. long, tapering at the apex to a point, white-velvety.

Fig. 43.—Pterospermum suberifolium, Lam. Fl. fr. ½.

Western Peninsula on the east side, along the coast and inland on the hills, ascending to 3,000 ft.

2. **P. Heyneanum,** Wall. ; Wight Ic. 489. Vern. *Tada*, Tel.

A middle-sized tree, branchlets, petioles and inflorescence rusty-tomentose. Leaves greyish-brown, tomentose beneath, variable in shape, ordinarily oblong, coarsely toothed or lobed, blade 4–6, petiole ⅓ in. long, those on coppice shoots palmately lobed, on petioles 2–3 in. long. Peduncles axillary, a little longer than petiole, 1–3 fld., bracteoles palmatifid, calyx 2 in. long, petals obliquely spathulate. Capsule brown-velvety, 2–2½ in. long.

Western Peninsula on the east side, along the coast and inland on the hills. Fl. C. S.

Nearly allied : 3. **P. reticulatum,** Wight et Arn. (*Polavu*, Tam.) West side of the Peninsula, from North Kanara southwards. Fl. 2–3 together, nearly sessile, supported by numerous imbricate deeply laciniate bracts almost mossy, segments filiform. Calyx 1–1½ in. 4. **P. obtusifolium,** Wight. Tinnevelli Ghats. Leaves cuneate or obovate, obtuse, coarsely toothed. Fl. small, calyx ¾ in., capsule 2–3 in. long, verrucose when young. 5. **P. glabrescens**, Wight et Arn. (*Vatta Polavu*, Tam.) Tinnevelli Ghats. Leaves entire, obovate, shortly acuminate, blade 5–8, petiole ½–1 in., calyx 4 in. long, capsule 4–5 in., with 5 sharp raised ridges.

6. **P. rubiginosum**, Heyne; Bedd. Fl. Sylv. t. 106. Vern. *Chinna polavu*, Tam.; *Malavuram*, *Thodali*, Mal.

A tall tree, branchlets, under side of leaves and inflorescence red-brown or tawny pubescent. Leaves 1–3 in., very oblique, the upper half much larger, rounded at base. Fl. solitary, axillary, sepals linear, 2 in. long. Capsule cylindric pentagonal, 2 in. long.

FIG. 44.—Pterospermum Heyneanum, Wall. Fl. branch and coppice shoot. ½.

West side of the Peninsula, in evergreen forests, from Malabar southwards, ascending to 3,000 ft. Fl. September–January.

B. Eastern species.

7. **P. acerifolium**, Willd.; Wight Ic. t. 631; Brandis, F. Fl. t. 11. Vern. *Hati paila*, Nep.; *Taung petwūn*, Burm.

A tall evergreen tree, bark smooth grey, thin, heartwood red. Branchlets and inflorescence clothed with ferruginous tomentum. Leaves large from obovate to orbicular, often peltate, sinuately lobed, glabrous above, grey-tomentose beneath, blade 6–15, petiole 4–12 in. Calyx segments linear, up to 5 in. long, petals pure white. Capsule brown-tomentose, pentagonal, 2–6 in. long. Seeds numerous, with large brown membranous wings. The capsule is believed to take more than 12 months to ripen.

Foot of Himalaya, from the Jumna eastward, in Sikkim ascending to 4,000 ft. Khasi hills, Manipur, Chittagong, Burma. Fl. H. S. 8. **P. aceroides**, Wall. Tenasserim and Andamans. Fl. December–February. Leaves oblong or obovate-oblong, not lobed, petiole ½ in. Fl. solitary or in 3–4 fld. axillary cymes, sepals 2–3 in. long.

9. **P. semisagittatum**, Ham.; Kurz, F. Fl. i. 146. Vern. *Nagyi*, Burm.

A middle-sized deciduous tree, trunk longitudinally channeled, branchlets, under side of leaves and inflorescence softly tawny-tomentose. Leaves 3–9 in., from an unequal base oblong-lanceolate, almost sessile, one basal lobe rounded, the other longer, triangular, often long-acuminate, stipules deeply pinnatifid, segments filiform. Fl. large, white, on short axillary peduncles, solitary or a few together, supported by a woolly involucre of large pinnatifid bracteoles, segments filiform. Petals broad-obovate. Capsule woody, 3 in. long, cylindrical, rusty-tomentose.

Chittagong hill tracts, Upper and Lower Burma. Fl. H. S.

10. **P. lanceæfolium**, Roxb.; Brandis, F. Fl. 35.

A large tree, young shoots and under side of leaves with short tawny, sometimes grey tomentum. Leaves lanceolate from a rounded, nearly equal-sided base. Fl. fragrant, axillary, on peduncles longer than calyx, bracteoles few, bifid or trifid, segments subulate. Calyx 1¼ in., petals white. Capsules lanceolate, hairy, 2–3 in. by ¾–1 in.

Khasi hills, Manipur, Chittagong. Fl. H. S. (specimens from Ceylon and the Konkan are doubtful). 11. **P. Blumeanum**, Korth.; King, in Journ. As. Soc. Bengal 60 (1892) 84. (*P. cinnamomeum*, Kurz, and *javanicum*, Jungh.; Kurz, F. Fl. i. 147.) Assam, Martaban and Tenasserim, Malay Peninsula and Archipelago. Leaves very unequal sided, blade 3–5, petiole ¼ in., calyx 2 in., capsule woody, cylindric, 3–4 in. long.

Leptonychia glabra, Turcz.; Kurz, F. Fl. i. 150, is a small tree in the evergreen forests of the Western Ghats, from the Carcoor Ghat southwards; in Tenasserim, the Andamans, the Malay Peninsula and Archipelago. Leaves oblong-lanceolate, acuminate, quite entire. Fl. bisexual, in axillary fascicles, petals 5, valvate, short, orbicular, concave, hairy. Staminal tube short, bearing an inner series of 5 short fleshy subulate, an outer series of 5–10 ligulate staminodes, and between these two series a third of 10 stamens. Capsule coriaceous, ½ in. long, rugose, seed 1, oblong, black. (*L. moacurroides*, Bedd., Fl. Sylv. t. 114; *L. heteroclita*, Kurz, supposed to differ by 10 staminodes in the outer series, probably is the same species.)

7. REEVESIA, Lindl.; Fl. Brit. Ind. i. 363.

Shrubs or trees. Leaves simple, entire, penniveined, the lowest pair of lateral nerves basal. Fl. bisexual, in terminal corymbose panicles, calyx campanulate, 5-dentate, petals clawed. Staminal column adnate to gynophore, much longer than petals, bearing a globose head of 2-celled anthers. Ovary 5-celled, 5-lobed, 2 ovules in each cell. Capsule woody, septicidally 5-valved. Seeds winged downwards, cotyledons flat, foliaceous, in a fleshy albumen. Species 3, from the eastern Himalaya to China.

1. **R. Wallichii**, Brown; Khasi hills, China, a middle-sized tree. Leaves glabrous, ovate from a rounded or acute base. Fl. white, capsule obtuse, 1½–2 in. long, the valves separating in two along the dorsal suture. 2. **R. pubescens**, Masters, Sikkim 3,000–5,000 ft., differs by pubescent leaves with a broad often nearly cordate base, larger pink flowers.

Guazuma tomentosa, H. B. & Kunth; Wight Ill. t. 31; Bedd. Fl. Sylv. t. 107. A tree indigenous in tropical America, but often planted in India. Leaves from an unequal-sided base ovate-oblong, acuminate. Fl. bisexual, small, yellow and purple, in axillary many fld. cymes. Petals: claw concave, lamina of 2 linear segments. On the staminal tube 5 petaloid staminodes, alternating with 5 filaments, each bearing several anthers. Capsule ovoid, woody, tubercled, resembling a mulberry.

Melochia velutina, Bedd. Fl. Sylv. Manual t. 5 (*Visenia umbellata*, Wight Ic. t. 509), is a small soft-wooded, ornamental tree, indigenous in the Malay Archipelago (in Lower Burma, Kurz), cultivated frequently throughout India. Branchlets, petioles, under side of leaves and inflorescence velvety-tomentose. Leaves broad-ovate from a cordate or rounded base, serrate, basal nerves 5–7, blade 4–9, petiole 1–4 in. long. Fl. bisexual, pale pink, sometimes white, in large corymbose axillary and terminal panicles, calyx cup-shaped, cleft half way into 5 triangular segments, petals 5, spathulate, equal, marcescent. Stamens 5, filaments at base connate into a short tube. Ovary 5-celled, 2 ovules in each cell, styles 5, free. Capsule loculicidally 5-valved.

Kleinhovia Hospita, Linn.; Bedd. Man. t. 4. A showy tree, indigenous in the delta of the Mekong river, on the seashore of the Malay Archipelago, but also inland in tropical East Africa and Australia, cultivated in the Western Peninsula. Leaves 5–7 nerved, broadly ovate, often with a cordate base. Fl. rose-coloured, 2-sexual, in large terminal panicles. Sepals 5, distinct, equal, petals unequal, zygomorphic. Staminal tube adnate to gynophore, enlarged into a 5-fid cup, each segment bearing 3 2-celled anthers, cells divergent. Five small acute staminodes between segments. Capsule inflated pyriform, membranous, loculicidally 5-valved. Seeds 1–2 in each cell, tubercled, cotyledons convolute.

ORDER XXI. TILIACEÆ. Gen. Pl. i. 228.

(*Elæocarpaceæ* and *Tiliaceæ*, Schumann in Engler u. Prantl iii. 6. pp. 1, 8.)

Trees or shrubs, some genera herbaceous. Leaves alternate, simple, stipules deciduous. Fl. regular, generally bisexual and pentamerous. Sepals free or connate, valvate. Stamens numerous, free, sometimes in bundles. Anthers 2-celled. Ovary free, 2–10-celled, ovules attached to axile placentas. Stamens and ovary as a rule on an elevated androgynophore, sepals and petals at its base. Seeds with or without albumen.

Sacs containing mucilage in pith, bark and the leaf parenchyma. These mucilage sacs are wanting in *Elæocarpus* and *Echinocarpus*. This is one reason for separating *Elæocarpaceæ*.

A. Sepals connate into a cup, staminodes 5.
  Carpels distinct, 2-valved, 1-seeded . . . . . 1. BROWNLOWIA.
  Fruit indehiscent, 1-seeded, winged . . . . . 2. PENTACE.
B. Sepals connate, no staminodes . . . . 3. BERRYA.
C. Sepals free, petals as a rule with a thickened or glandular claw.
  Fruit a drupe with several stones . . . . . 4. GREWIA.
  Capsule winged, separating into 3–5 1-seeded carpels COLUMBIA (p. 101).
  Fruit woody, triquetrous, slightly winged, 1-seeded . ERINOCARPUS (p. 101).
D. Sepals free, petals not clawed.
  Fruit covered with prickles or bristles . . . . . 5. ECHINOCARPUS.
  Fruit a fleshy drupe, with 1 stone, 1 or more seeded . 6. ELÆOCARPUS.

Plagiopteron suaveolens, Griff.; Calc. Journ. Nat. Hist. iv. (1844) t. 13; Kurz, F. Fl. i. 172, is a scandent shrub of Mergui. Leaves opposite, elliptic-oblong, acuminate, 4–5 in. Fl. small, greenish, very fragrant, in dense axillary panicles, ramifications opposite, sepals minute, petals linear-oblong, revolute. Ovary entire, 3-celled, 2 ovules in each cell, style subulate. Fruit dry, with 3 wings ¾ in. long. Kurz classes this species under *Malpighiaceæ*.

1. BROWNLOWIA, Roxb.; Fl. Brit. Ind. i. 381.

Trees, with scaly or stellate pubescence. Leaves with 3–9 basal nerves. Fl. numerous, in large terminal panicles. Calyx campanulate, irregularly 3–5 cleft. Stamens many, filaments free on a raised torus. Anthers broad, sometimes nearly globose. Inside the stamens, surrounding the ovary, 5 petaloid staminodes, opposite the petals. Carpels 5, more or less cohering, each with 2 ovules ultimately free, 2-valved, 1-seeded. Albumen none, cotyledons thick fleshy. Species 10–15, tropical Asia.

1. **B. elata**, Roxb., Cor. Pl. t. 265; Kurz, F. Fl. i. 153.

A lofty evergreen tree, young shoots rusty- or tawny-puberulous. Leaves cordate, petiole 2–4, blade 4–12 in. long, coriaceous, glossy above, glaucescent and puberulous beneath. Fl. yellow, ½–¾ in. diam. Calyx ¼ in. long, scurfy-tomentose. Carpels woody, usually 2–3, 1–1½ in. diam., ash-grey, minutely puberulous, suture prominent.

Tidal forests of Chittagong and Tenasserim. Fl. H. S. 2. **B. lanceolata**, Benth. An evergreen shrub or tree of the tidal and Mangrove forests of the Sundriban and the Burma coast. Leaves lanceolate or oblong-lanceolate, pale beneath. Fl. small, carpels globose, ½ in. diam. 3. **B. peltata**, Benth.; Kurz, F. Fl. i. 153 (*B. Helferiana*, Pierre, F. Fl. Cochinch. under t. 130). A small tree of Tenasserim; has round peltate leaves, petiole 7–8 in. long, blade with 9 basal nerves, 8–10 in. long, calyx velvety outside.

2. **PENTACE,** Hassk.; Fl. Brit. Ind. i. 381.

Trees with leathery leaves and numerous small flowers in terminal panicles. Calyx campanulate, 5-fid. Stamens numerous, filaments usually in 5 bundles. Staminodes 5, short. Ovary 5-celled. Fruit dry, indehiscent, 1-celled, 1-seeded, with 3–10 large membranous wings. Embryo large, in a thin albumen. Species 15, Burma and the Eastern Peninsula.

FIG. 45.—Pentace burmanica, Kurz. ½.

1. **P. burmanica,** Kurz, F. Fl. i. 154. Vern. *Thitka*, Burm.

A large evergreen tree, wood red (white when fresh cut), shining, not hard, even grained, medullary rays prominent on radial section, young shoots pubescent. Leaves ovate- or obovate-oblong, acuminate, more or less sinuate-lobed, glossy above, pale and pubescent beneath. Secondary nerves 5–7 pair, the lowest pair basal. Inflorescence tawny-tomentose. Stamens in 5 bundles of 4–7 each, the bundles alternating with long linear staminodes. Capsule with 5 broad membranous wings, 1–1½ in. long.

Evergreen and semi-evergreen forests on the hills of Burma. Fl. February, March. Also on the hills of Cambodia. 2. **P. Griffithii,** King, in Journ. As. Soc. Beng., vol. 60, ii. 104, of Tavoy, has leaves with 5 basal nerves, the 2 outer close to the margin, the 3 inner very prominent, large flowers (¼ in. diam.) and a capsule with 10 wings.

3. **BERRYA,** Roxb.; Fl. Brit. Ind. i. 383.

B. Ammonilla, Roxb., Cor. Pl. 264. The only species. Wight Ill. t. 34; Bedd. Fl. Sylv. t. 58. Vern. Petwūn, Burm.

A tall tree with smooth pale bark, heartwood dark red, very hard. Leaves cordate, acute, bright green, with 5–7 basal nerves, margin undulating, glabrous above, glabrous or slightly pubescent beneath. Petiole 2–4, blade 5–8 in. long. Stipules ½ in. long, linear-setaceous. Fl. white, numerous, ½ in. diam., in lax terminal panicles. Stamens ∞, free, no staminodes. Ovary 3–4-celled. Capsule supported by the persistent calyx, globose, pubescent, with 6 horizontally spreading, blunt, papery wings 1 in. long. Seeds 1–4 in each cell.

Malabar, Travancore, Ceylon, Andamans, Burma. Fl. C. S. Pierre, Fl. For. Cochinch. t. 188, regards the tree of the Eastern Peninsula, leaves softly tomentose beneath, as a distinct species—*B. mollis*, Wall.

4. **GREWIA,** Linn.; Fl. Brit. Ind. i. 383.

Trees or shrubs, mostly deciduous, at times scrambling or climbing. Branchlets, leaves and sepals mostly clothed with stellate hairs. Simple hairs on petals, androgynophore and ovary. Leaves more or less distinctly dentate, rarely lobed, base generally oblique, with 3, rarely 4 or 5 basal nerves. Fl. in pedunculate, generally umbelliform cymes. Sepals valvate, often coloured on the inside, deciduous. Petals shorter than sepals, in most species with a thick base (claw), bearing on the inside an area, generally papillose, surrounded by a densely villous, semicircular or circular rim. Stamens as a rule ∞, free, together with the ovary on a raised more or less costate torus (androgynophore or gonophore), the ridges of which alternate with the petals, the lower part glabrous, the upper hairy or tomentose. Ovary 2 or 4-celled, in most species tomentose, style 1, ovules as a rule 8. Stigma generally broad, more or less distinctly 5-lobed. Fruit a drupe, often deeply lobed, with 1–4 pyrenes, which are 1- or few-seeded, the endocarp often osseous, surrounded by a fibrous mesocarp. Over 100 species, tropical and sub-tropical, from Africa to Queensland.

A. Fl. bisexual, petals with a distinct claw.

(*a*) Peduncles mostly solitary, leaf opposed, rarely terminal or axillary, blade of petals twice the length of claw.

1. **G. oppositifolia,** Roxb.; Wight Ic. t. 82; Brandis, F. Fl. t. 12. Vern. *Katār*, Pusht.; *Dhaman*, *Pharan*, *Bhimal*, *Biùl*, *Behùl*, North-West Himalaya.

A middle-sized tree, wood white, with small irregularly shaped heartwood. Leaves 2–4 in., ovate, acuminate. Peduncles single, leaf opposed, $\frac{1}{3}$–1 in. long. Pedicels 1–8, supported by linear deciduous bracts. Sepals $\frac{1}{2}$–1 in. Petals shorter than sepals, yellowish red, blade linear, twice the length of claw. Drupe deeply 2–4 lobed, fleshy. Fruit olive-green, then black, with scattered hairs.

Suleiman range, Baluchistan (3,500 ft.), Salt range. Himalaya, extending eastward to Nepal and ascending to 6,000 ft. The leaves are shed in March, the new leaves come out in April and May. Fl. March, June.

2. **G. populifolia,** Vahl; Trimen Handb. Ceylon t. 18. Vern. *Gango*, *Gangerūn*, Rajputana.

A shrub with stiff divaricate branches, bark white, wood yellowish-white, tough. Branchlets and leaves slightly rough with short stellate hairs. Leaves broadly ovate, sometimes obovate, coarsely dentate, blade $\frac{1}{2}$–2 in., petioles slender, $\frac{1}{4}$–$\frac{1}{2}$ in. long. Peduncles slender, generally leaf opposed and solitary, with 1–3 large white flowers. Sepals $\frac{3}{4}$ in., blade attached to back of claw. Gonophore glabrous, with 5 densely villous teeth. Ovary glabrous as a rule. Drupe shining, orange, of 2–4 distinct globular lobes, each with a 2-celled stone.

Dry and arid regions of North-West India, Sind and the Deccan. Salt range, foot of North-West Himalaya, ascending to 2,000 ft. Fl. July-December. Dry country of Ceylon, western Asia, Egypt, tropical Africa.

FIG. 46.—Grewia populifolia, Vahl. $\frac{1}{2}$.

(*b*) Peduncles mostly solitary and axillary, leaves with 3 basal nerves. Western species.

3. **G. columnaris,** Smith; Wight Ic. t. 44. Vern. *Tegali,* Tel.

A scrambling, at times almost climbing shrub, rough with short stellate hairs. Leaves 2–3 in., ovate-lanceolate. Peduncles mostly solitary, axillary, extra-axillary or terminal, $\frac{1}{4}$–$\frac{1}{2}$ in., with 3–5 yellowish-white flowers on short bracteate pedicels. Sepals $\frac{1}{2}$, petals $\frac{1}{3}$ in., blade triangular, narrower than, and nearly as long as, claw. Gonophore 5-ridged, the tomentose part with 5 villous teeth, stigma radiate, 5-lobed. Drupes pyriform, indistinctly 4-lobed.

Both sides of the Western Peninsula. Fl. May–November. Ceylon, dry country. Closely allied is 4. **G. emarginata,** Wight et Arn., a shrub on the Nilgiris Palnis and Tinnevelli hills. Leaves woolly beneath, flowers larger, white, peduncles longer and drupes deeply 2–4 lobed.

5. **G. orientalis,** Linn.; Trimen Handb. Ceylon i. 176. Vern. *Tegali,* Tel.

A scrambling often climbing shrub. Leaves 3–4 in., nearly glabrous, ovate-lanceolate. Peduncles solitary, terminal, axillary or extra-axillary. Fl. large, white. Sepals $\frac{3}{4}$–1 in., petals $\frac{1}{6}$ in. Blade triangular, as long as claw and attached at its back. Gonophore as in 3. Drupes globose, scarcely lobed, $\frac{2}{3}$ in. diam.

Moister districts on both sides of the Western Peninsula, from Kanara southwards. Fl. R. S. Closely allied and perhaps not specifically distinct is 6. **G. bracteata,** Roth. Hills of the Karnatic. Drupes indistinctly 2–4 lobed, hairy.

7. **G. umbellifera,** Bedd.—Syn. *G. Ritchiei,* Mast.; Fl. Brit. Ind. i. 389.

A lofty scandent shrub, at times a tree, the stem at the base often covered with blunt woody protuberances. Branchlets, petioles and inflorescence with rusty stellate pubescence. Leaves 3–5 in. long, elliptic-oblong, shortly acuminate, 3-nerved, the 2 lateral basal nerves extending to the middle of the blade or beyond it. Peduncles $\frac{1}{2}$–$1\frac{1}{2}$ in. long, generally 1, sometimes 2, mostly axillary, bearing 5–15 large flowers. Sepals $\frac{1}{3}$–$\frac{2}{3}$, petals $\frac{1}{4}$–$\frac{1}{3}$ in., blade as long as or longer than claw. Gonophore long, cylindric, tomentose, the lower glabrous portion very short. Fruit of 4 distinct drupes, $\frac{1}{4}$–$\frac{1}{3}$ in. diam.

Western Ghats from the Concan southwards. Nearly allied is 8. **G. heterotricha,** Masters, in evergreen forests on the Western Ghats from North Kanara southwards. A lofty climber, branchlets, petioles and under side of leaves rusty-tomentose. Peduncles 1–$1\frac{1}{2}$ in. long, axillary or leaf opposed. Fruit unknown. *G. umbellata,* Roxb.; King, in As. Soc. Bengal, vol. 60 (1892) 110, is a Malayan species, not found in the Western Peninsula.

(*c*) Peduncles mostly solitary and axillary, leaves with 3 basal nerves. Eastern species and species of both peninsulas.

9. **G. scabrida,** Wall.; Kurz, F. Fl. i. 158.

An evergreen shrub. Branchlets, petioles and inflorescence shortly rusty-tomentose. Leaves 5–6 in., ovate-lanceolate, serrate, chartaceous, rough with short stellate hairs, especially beneath, the tertiary nerves parallel and prominent beneath. Peduncles axillary, short, bearing 2–5 flowers. Sepals $\frac{1}{2}$–$\frac{2}{3}$, petals $\frac{1}{4}$ in., blade as long as or longer than claw. Gonophore $\frac{1}{6}$ in. long, the glabrous part very short, the tomentose portion 5-ribbed. Drupe $\frac{3}{4}$ in. diam., slightly 2–4 lobed.

Assam, Tenasserim. Fl. September. Nearly allied: 10. **G. nagensium,** Prain, Journ. As. Soc. Bengal, vol. 69 ii. (1900) 168. Assam. Leaves tomentose. Fruit of 2 distinct verrucose drupes.

11. **G. lævigata,** Vahl. Vern. *Phiran, Dūn, Udapai,* Tam.; *Kwe-tayaw,* Upper, *Kyet-tayaw,* Lower Burma.

A small or middle-sized tree, wood white, soft. Leaves 4–7 in., oblong-lanceolate, acuminate, membranous, nearly glabrous, under side with a few scattered hairs. Secondary nerves 4–6 pair, the lowest pair from the base. Peduncles axillary, slender, often 2–3 together, bearing umbelliform bracteate cymes of 3–5 flowers. Sepals $\frac{1}{2}$–1 in., 3-nerved, petals $\frac{1}{7}$–$\frac{1}{5}$ in., blade triangular, shorter, rarely longer than claw. Tomentose part of gonophore shorter than glabrous portion, at times reduced to a narrow villous band. Drupes 1–3, rarely 4, nearly distinct.

Fig. 47.—Grewia lævigata, Vahl. $\frac{1}{2}$.

Outer Himalaya, from the Jumna eastward, ascending to 3,000 ft. Both Peninsulas. Fl. June–October. Leaves renewed in April. Nearly allied, united with it by Pierre, Fl. For. Cochinch. t. 161 : 12. **G. multiflora**, Juss. (*G. sepiaria*, Roxb.). Sikkim. Assam, Khasi hills, a shrub, leaves and flowers smaller. Gonophore glabrous, with a fringe of hairs at top. Fruit didymous, 4-seeded.

(*d*) Peduncles fasciculate, axillary, gonophore glabrous with a fringe of hairs at top.

a. Leaves narrow, with 3, rarely 4 or 5 basal nerves.

13. **G. salvifolia**, Heyne ; Brandis For. Fl. 43. Vern. *Saras, siris*, Merwara ; *Bursu*, Kol ; *Vulipi*, Kan.

A shrub or small tree, heartwood dark brown, hard, branchlets, inflorescence and under side of leaves white or grey, with short pubescence. Leaves 2–3 in., lanceolate or oblong-lanceolate, edge entire, undulate or serrulate. Peduncles slender, with 2–3 conspicuous yellow flowers. Sepals $\frac{1}{3}$ in., on both sides silky, petals $\frac{1}{8}$ in., the blade longer than claw, back of claw hairy. Fruit generally of two distinct round drupes.

Dry and arid regions of North-West India and the Deccan. Fl. April–September. Nearly allied, and perhaps not specifically distinct, is 14. **G. excelsa**, Vahl. Singbhum, Behar, Bundelkhand and Coromandel coast. An erect tree. Leaves 3–6 in., with oblique base and sometimes 4 or 5 basal nerves. Under side of leaves white or green. Fl. May.

15. **G. pilosa**, Lam. ; Brandis F. Fl. 39. Vern. *Pasangan, pisangan*, Rajputana ; *Tegali*, Tel.

A large straggling shrub, branchlets, petioles, under side of leaves and inflorescence rough with fine light-brown stellate hairs. Leaves 2–4 in., oblong or lanceolate-oblong, serrate. Secondary nerves 4–5 pair, the lowest pair from the base. Peduncles short, about $\frac{1}{4}$ in. long, buds hirsute, constricted in the middle. Sepals $\frac{1}{2}$–$\frac{2}{3}$, petals $\frac{1}{5}$ in. long. Blade 3 times the length of claw, bifid, with numerous longitudinal nerves, back of blade hirsute with stiff hairs. Gonophore glabrous, cup-shaped, edge ciliate. Anthers hairy, style hairy in the lower part, stigma 2-dentate, ovules numerous. Rind of fruit crustaceous, with short stellate hairs.

Oudh, Behar, Aravalli hills, and throughout the Western Peninsula. Fl. July–September. A species remarkable by the shape of gonophore, hairy anthers and stigma. Whether this is the plant described by Lamarck as *G. pilosa* is doubtful. *G. carpinifolia*, Juss.; Fl. Brit. Ind. i. 387, anthers glabrous, ovules 8, grows in tropical Africa, and is not known from India.

β. Leaves broad, with 5, sometimes only with 4, basal nerves.

16. **G. rotundifolia**, Juss., Ann. Mus. Hist. Nat. Paris iv. (1804) t. 50 f. 3; Wight Ic. t. 45.

Leaves 1–1$\frac{1}{2}$ in., grey-tomentose, chiefly beneath, obovate or orbicular Peduncles slender, $\frac{1}{2}$–$\frac{3}{4}$ in., pedicels longer than flowers. Buds distinctly ribbed, cylindric. Sepals $\frac{1}{3}$, petals $\frac{1}{5}$–$\frac{1}{4}$ in., blade twice the length of claw. Gonophore $\frac{1}{12}$ in., glabrous, ribbed, 5 obtuse hairy teeth at top.

Coromandel coast, Nilgiris (united with *G. orbiculata* in Fl. Brit. Ind. i. 386; this however, has 3-nerved leaves and petals without claws).

17. **G. asiatica**, Linn. Vern. *Pharsa*, *Phalsa*, *Dhamin*, *Karra*, Hind.; *Sial posra*, Nep.; *Gonyia*, Kol; *Jana*, *Tadasāl*, Kan.; *Unu*, Tam.; *Chadicha*. Mal.; *Tagaw*, *Pintayaw*, Burm.

A middle-sized tree, bark greyish-white or greyish-brown, sapwood whitish, heartwood small, irregularly shaped, dark brown. Branchlets and under side of leaves varying from glabrous to densely and softly tomentose. Leaves varying from broad-cordate to obliquely ovate. Stipules varying from linear to foliaceous and broadly falcate. Peduncles axillary, in fascicles of 2–10, varying in length from $\frac{1}{2}$–2 in., each bearing 3–5 flowers. Sepals $\frac{1}{4}$–$\frac{1}{2}$, petals $\frac{1}{8}$–$\frac{1}{4}$ in., yellow or red and yellow, blade as long as or longer than claw. Fruit globose, with pleasantly acid pulp, indistinctly lobed.

Common in both Peninsulas, largely grown in gardens on account of the fruit. Fl. January–May. This extremely variable tree was described under three species by me, F. Fl. 40, and by Kurz, F. Fl. i. 160. My subsequent experience in India has convinced me that these forms cannot be maintained as species, their distinguishing characters not being constant. Their characters are ordinarily defined as follows:—

1. **G. asiatica,** Linn. The cultivated form. Leaves broad-cordate, more or less tomentose beneath, stipules linear, buds cylindrical or clavate, flowers large, fruit large. 2. **G. vestita,** Wall. (*G. elastica*, Royle). Chiefly in the subhimalayan tract from the Indus to Sikkim. Leaves small, ovate, usually much longer than broad, under side with thick greyish-yellow tomentum. Stipules linear, buds obovoid. 3. **G. tiliaefolia,** Vahl. Chiefly in the Peninsula and Ceylon, also in North-West India. Leaves large, very oblique, nearly glabrous, or hoary beneath. Stipules leafy, falcate, auriculate. Masters, in Fl. Brit. Ind. i. 386, unites *G. vestita* and *G. asiatica*.

18. **G. sapida,** Roxb., is a remarkable undershrub, common in grass lands of the Dūns and subhimalayan tract, ascending to 3,000 ft., also in Upper Burma, with a short woody underground stem, throwing up annually, after the fires have passed over the ground, a number of herbaceous shoots 1–2 ft. high. Flowers yellow, in umbels of 2–4, sepals $\frac{1}{3}$–$\frac{1}{2}$, petals $\frac{1}{8}$–$\frac{1}{4}$ in., blade linear, twice the length of claw. Fruit slightly lobed, stones enclosed in sweetish pulp.

19. **G. villosa,** Willd.; Brandis, F. Fl. 39. Vern. *Dhokelan*, Merwara.

A shrub, often gregarious, branches, leaves and inflorescence densely silky with long stellate hairs. Leaves nearly orbicular from a cordate base, 1–4 in. diam., rugose, transverse veins numerous, prominent and parallel, tufts of silky hairs on the serratures. Fl. dull yellow, peduncles very short in compact axillary clusters. Sepals linear, membranous, $\frac{1}{3}$ in. long, clothed on both sides with short stellate, outside also with long simple hairs, the tips often with a long branched and stellate process. Blade of petal thin, twice the length of claw. Fruit globose, a distinct crustaceous brown rind, with tufts of long stellate hairs, pulp pleasant.

Dry region of North-West India and the Deccan. Fl. June–September. Tropical Africa.

20. **G. abutilifolia,** Juss.; Kurz, F. Fl. i. 161. Vern. *Pet-ok, Tayaw-a,* Upper Burma.

A shrub (deciduous, Smales), sometimes only 2 ft. high, branchlets, leaves and inflorescence roughly stellate-tomentose. Leaves 4–8 in. long, broadly ovate, almost orbicular, often slightly lobed, tertiary nerves distinct beneath. Peduncles very short, in compact axillary clusters. Sepals $\frac{1}{3}$–$\frac{1}{2}$, petals $\frac{1}{8}$ in., blade shorter than or as long as claw. Gonophore glabrous, edge villous, small tufts of hair at base between petals. Drupe slightly 2–4-lobed, $\frac{1}{3}$–$\frac{1}{2}$ in. diam., edible.

Sikkim, Assam, Manipur, Chittagong, Burma, chiefly in Eng forest, but also on Taungya clearings. Chanda district. Peninsula, chiefly on the west side. Fl. R. S. Cochinchina.

21. **G. scabrophylla,** Roxb.—Syn. *G. sclerophylla,* Roxb. Hort. Beng. 42; Wight Ic. t. 89; Brandis F. Fl. 39. Vern. *Petshat,* Burm.

A shrub, branchlets, under side of leaves and inflorescence clothed with soft tawny tomentum. Leaves 4–9 in. long, ovate or obovate, tertiary nerves distinct beneath. Peduncles short. Fl. large, blade of petals obovate, longer than, often twice the length of claw. Gonophore glabrous, edge villous, 5 small tufts of hair at base between petals. Fruit globose, not lobed, $\frac{1}{2}$–$\frac{3}{4}$ in. diam., rind crustaceous, hairy, stones 4, 1–2 seeded in sweet gelatinous pulp.

Subhimalayan tract and outer valleys, from the Jumna eastward. Oudh forests, northern Circars, Assam, Pegu, Upper Burma. In Engdain and grass lands a small shrub 3 ft. high, burnt down every year (Smales). A similar habit in the grass lands of the Duars (Haines). Fl. April – September. *G. sclerophylla* is the older name, but *G. scabrophylla* is supported by full description in Roxb., Fl. Ind. ii. 584.

FIG. 48.—Grewia scabrophylla, Roxb. Stamens and ovary, petal, sepal, three times magnified.

(*c*) **Inflorescence a large terminal panicle. Fl. nearly sessile, in 3-fld. heads, supported by lanceolate often laciniate bracts, stigma minutely 2–4-dentate.**

22. **G. Microcos,** Linn.; Wight Ill. t. 33.—Syn. *G. ulmifolia,* Roxb. Vern. *Myat-ya,* Burm.

A middle-sized tree, at times only a shrub, young shoots and petioles slightly pubescent. Leaves ovate- or oblong-lanceolate, acuminate, 4–8 in. long, secondary nerves 5–8 pair, the lowest pair basal, stipules lanceolate. Fl. yellowish-white, sepals $\frac{1}{4}$, petals $\frac{1}{16}$ in., blade equal to claw, often bifid. Gonophore glabrous, with a woolly fringe at top, ovary glabrous. Fruit globose, $\frac{1}{3}$ in. diam., not lobed.

Evergreen forests of the Western Ghats, from Satara southwards, Khasi hills, Chittagong, Burma. The best covering leaf for Burmese cigars. Fl. March–July. Ceylon, Cochinchina, Java, Sumatra.

23. **G. calophylla,** Kurz, F. Fl. i. 157. Andamans and Nicobars. A middle-sized evergreen tree. Leaves glabrous, coriaceous, 8 in. long. Sepals $\frac{3}{8}$, petals $\frac{1}{4}$–$\frac{1}{3}$ in., blade

linear, twice the length of claw or longer. Gonophore $\frac{1}{8}$ in., upper portion velvety, equal to the lower glabrous and ribbed portion. Ovary and style slightly puberulous. Fruit obovoid, $1\frac{1}{3}$ in. long.

24. **G. sinuata,** Wall. Swamp forests of the alluvial plains, Lower Burma. A large shrub. Leaves 1–2 in. long, sinuately lobed, hairy beneath. Fl. small, in short panicles at the ends of branches. Sepals $\frac{1}{4}$, petals $\frac{1}{8}$ in., blade equal to claw, claw hairy on back. Gonophore glabrous, 5 villous teeth at the edge. Ovary glabrous. Fruit pyriform, $\frac{1}{3}$–$\frac{1}{2}$ in. long.

B. Fl. bisexual, petals without a distinct claw.

25. **G. orbiculata,** Rottler; Fl. Brit. Ind. i. 386.

Branchlets, leaves and inflorescence hoary. Leaves elliptic, 1–$1\frac{1}{2}$ in. long, dentate, 3- sometimes 5-nerved, softly grey-pubescent beneath. Peduncles slender, $\frac{3}{4}$ in., bearing umbels of 3–5 flowers. Pedicels as long as or longer than sepals. Buds ovoid or globose, tomentose, indistinctly ribbed. Sepals $\frac{1}{4}$ in., petals thin, veined, $\frac{1}{6}$ in., oblanceolate, glabrous with only a few hairs on the slightly thickened base.

Deccan and east side of Peninsula. Similar in appearance to *G. rotundifolia*, Juss.

26. **G. leptopetala,** sp. nov.—Syn. *G. tiliæfolia*, Bedd. Fl. Sylv. t. 108.

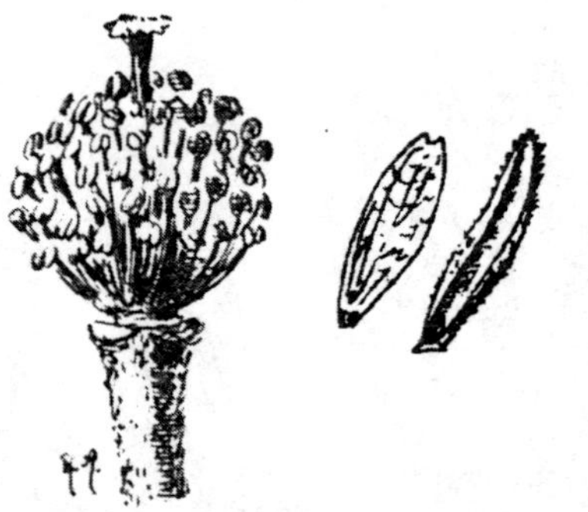

Fig. 49.—Grewia leptopetala, Brandis. Stamens and ovary, petal, sepal, three times magnified.

Branchlets and under side of leaves varying from glabrous to densely and softly tomentose, leaves from broad-cordate to obliquely ovate, stipules varying from linear to foliaceous and broadly falcate. Peduncles axillary, slender, in fascicles of 2–6, short, not as a rule exceeding $\frac{1}{2}$ in., each bearing 2–5 flowers. Petals thin, veined, lanceolate or linear, often 2-fid at tip, perfectly glabrous, excepting a few hairs on the slightly thickened base. Drupes generally 2-lobed, $\frac{1}{3}$ in. diam.

North-West Provinces, Chittagong, Western Peninsula, south as far as Travancore. Not known from Burma. Fl. January–April. This species exhibits a variation as to pubescence and shape of leaves almost parallel to that of *G. asiatica*. The glabrous form is chiefly in the Peninsula, the hoary form chiefly on the west side of the Peninsula, while the tomentose is mostly found in Northern India. 27. **G. elatostemoides,** Coll. et Hemsl.: Journ. Linn. Soc. vol. 28. p. 27. Fort Stedman, Shan hills, 8,000 ft. A small tree. Leaves 8 in. obliquely ovate, 4-nerved, under side with white short pubescence. Peduncles axillary, short. Sepals $\frac{1}{4}$, petals $\frac{1}{6}$ in., glabrous, veined, lanceolate.

To this group also belongs *G. eriocarpa*, Juss.; Pierre, Fl. For. t. 158, of Cochin China and Java, as well as species from Borneo and Africa.

C. Fl. polygamous, generally male and bisexual.

28. **G. polygama,** Roxb.; Brandis, F. Fl. 42.

A shrub or small tree, heartwood pale brown. Branches bifarious, spreading, branchlets, petioles, under side of leaves velvety, inflorescence strigose with long stellate hairs. Leaves lanceolate, 2–5 in., sharply serrate. Peduncles short, slender, axillary, generally fasciculate. Sepals $\frac{1}{4}$, petals $\frac{1}{8}$ in., blade equal to claw, which is hairy on back. Stamens as a rule 10–12, but sometimes more numerous. Stigma 5-lobed, lobes spreading, deeply cut into numerous segments. Fruit $\frac{1}{3}$ in. diam., more or less 2–4-lobed, hairy.

Subhimalayan tract and outer valleys, ascending to 4,000 ft., Salt range, Behar Assam. The Konkan. Burma. Fl. R. S. Ceylon.

29. **G. hirsuta,** Vahl; Kurz, F. Fl. i. 159. Vern. *Kyettayaw*, Burm.

A small shrub. Branchlets, petioles and underside of leaves hirsute or tomentose. Buds ovoid, densely pilose. Sepals $\frac{1}{4}$–$\frac{1}{3}$, petals $\frac{1}{9}$–$\frac{1}{10}$ in., blade rounded, as long as claw. Anthers glabrous. In some specimens the hairs at the top of gynophore as long as filaments. Stigma bifid, branches penicillate, ovules 8. Rind of fr. crustaceous, with long hairs.

Western Peninsula, both in the dry and moist districts. Burma. Fl. H. R. S. Pierre, Fl. For. Cochinch. t. 167, suggests the union of 28 and 29. Closely allied are: 30. **G. microstemma,** Wall.; Kurz, F. Fl. i. 160. Burma. With broader oblique leaves, often 4-nerved. 31. **G. humilis,** Wall. Bengal, Burma. Leaves small, 1–2 in.

5. **COLUMBIA,** Pers.; Fl. Brit. Ind. i. 393. Species 7, tropical Asia.

1. **C. floribunda,** Wall.; Kurz, F. Fl. i. 156, is a shrub of Burma, the Naga hills and Manipur, also found in Tonkin and Yunan. Leaves rough on both sides with stellate hairs, from a cordate sometimes rounded base, obovate-oblong, usually lobed at the tip, petioles 1–2 in. long. Fl. small, pentamerous, in few-fld. involucrate heads on terminal panicles, petals nearly as long as sepals, yellow with scarlet dots. Capsule $\frac{3}{4}$ in. diam., stellate-hairy, winged, separating when ripe into 3 or 4 indehiscent 1-seeded 2-winged carpels. 2. **C. flagrocarpa,** C. B. Clarke, MSS. Chittagong hill tracts. A tree 40 ft. high, branchlets and under side of leaves softly tomentose, leaves ovate-lanceolate from an oblique base, capsule 3–5-winged, 1 in. across, seed portion clothed with stellate bristles. 3. **C. merguensis,** Planch. Mergui. Leaves lanceolate, stellate-pubescent beneath. Fruit 3-winged, 1 in. across.

Erinocarpus Nimmoanus, Graham; Bedd. Fl. Sylv. t. 110. Vern. *Chira*, Mar.; *Kadubendi*, Kan., is a small tree common in deciduous forests of North Kanara, the Belgaum district and the Konkan, with large cordate, slightly 3–5-lobed leaves, palmately 7–9-nerved, 8 in. diam., petiole 3–5 in. Fl. yellow, 1–2 in. across, in terminal panicles. Fruit 1$\frac{1}{2}$–2 in. long, woody, triquetrous, slightly winged, covered with large broad-based prickles. Seed 1, albuminous.

6. **ECHINOCARPUS,** Blume; Fl. Brit. Ind. i. 399 (Included under *Sloanea*, Linn., by Schumann in Engler u. Prantl iii. 6. 5).

Trees with penniveined leaves. Peduncles axillary, 1-flowered. Sepals 4–5, imbricate. Petals 4–5, variously cut. Stamens numerous, free, on a thick disk. Anthers linear, opening by a terminal pore. Capsule woody or coriaceous, loculicidal, covered with prickles or bristles, 3–6- or by abortion 1-celled. Seeds albuminous. Species 12, Indo-Malayan and Australian.

1. **E. sterculiaceus,** Benth.; Fl. Brit. Ind. i. 400. Vern. *Banj*, Nep.

A large tree, young shoots puberulous. Leaves minutely serrulate, 8–10 in. long, petiole 2 in., glabrous above, softly tomentose beneath. Secondary nerves and veins prominent. Capsule pendulous, red, globose, 2 in. diam., 5–6-celled, densely covered with straight sharp subulate minutely hispid spines $\frac{1}{2}$–$\frac{3}{4}$ in. long.

Sikkim, Bhutan, hills of Martaban and Tenasserim, 3,000–5,000 ft.

2. **E. Sigun,** Blume; Kurz, F. Fl. i. 162; Pierre, Fl. For. Cochinch. t. 169. —Syn. *E. Murex*, Benth., Fl. Brit. Ind. i. 399.

A large tree, nearly glabrous. Leaves oblong lanceolate, entire. Capsule ovoid, woody, 1–1$\frac{1}{2}$ in. long, 3–4-valved. Valves covered with rigid prickles $\frac{1}{2}$ in. long, blunt from a conical base.

Khasi hills, 3,000–5,000 ft., Tenasserim. Fl. April. Cambodia, Java.

3. **E. assamicus,** Benth. Vern. *Phul Hingri*, Assam.

A middle-sized tree. Leaves 9–12 in. long, elliptic, abruptly acuminate, nearly glabrous, petiole 1–2 in. Fruit 2 in. long, densely studded with slender spines 1 in. long.

Sikkim, Assam, Charduar, Nambar and Makūm forest.

4. **E. dasycarpus,** Benth.; Fl. Brit. Ind. i. 400. Vern. *Gobria*, Nep.

A large tree, wood soft, grey. Leaves coriaceous, elliptic-lanceolate, entire or serrulate, glabrous, secondary nerves prominent beneath. Blade 4–6, petiole 1 in. Peduncles crowded near ends of branches, often fasciculate. Fl. 1 in. across. Capsule globose, 1 in. diam., 4–5-valved, the valves covered with a dense felt of short deciduous bristles.

Sikkim, 3,000–8,000 ft., Bhutan. Fl. November. China. 5. **E. tomentosus,** Benth. Sikkim, Bhutan, Manipur, Yunan. Capsule larger, similarly covered. Leaves densely and softly tomentose beneath.

6. ELÆOCARPUS, Linn.; Fl. Brit. Ind. i. 400.

Evergreen trees, with penniveined leaves, old leaves often red before falling. Fl. in the species here described bisexual, racemose, in the axils of early deciduous bracts. Petals fringed or lobed, rarely entire, inserted at the base of a thick glandular disk or torus, induplicate-valvate in bud. Stamens numerous, inserted inside the disk. Anthers linear, opening at the top by two confluent short slits. Ovary 2–5-celled, style 1, subulate. A drupe, stone 1-celled or 2–5-celled, 1 seed in each cell. Albumen fleshy, cotyledons flat, broad. 123 species known, most in the two Peninsulas and the Malay Archipelago. Outside this area from Madagascar and Socotra to China and Japan and the Pacific Islands.

A. Ovary 5- sometimes 4-celled. Fl. small and middle-sized, sepals $\frac{1}{5}$–$\frac{1}{3}$ in. long.

1. **E. Ganitrus,** Roxb.—Syn. *Ganitrus sphærica*, Gaertn.; Wight Ic. t. 66. Vern. *Rudrak*, *Rudraksch*.

Attains 60 ft. Leaves membranous, lanceolate, obscurely serrulate, nearly glabrous, 3–6 in., petiole $\frac{1}{4}$–$\frac{1}{2}$ in. long. Secondary nerves 10–15 pair. Fl. white, in compact drooping racemes, shorter than leaves, from the axils of fallen leaves. Sepals $\frac{1}{4}$–$\frac{1}{3}$ in. long, petals a little longer, obovate, laciniate beyond the middle, pedicels longer than sepals. Torus short, fleshy, wrinkled, pubescent. Anthers nearly sessile, 25–35, the longer valve with 1 or 2 white bristles. Fruit globose, bluish-purple, $\frac{3}{4}$–1 in. diam. Stone elegantly tubercled, marked with 5 vertical grooves, 4–5-celled, often only 1-seeded.

Nepal, Assam, Chittagong. Fl. C. S. Malay Peninsula, Java and Celebes. 2. **E. stipularis,** Bl.; Kurz, F. Fl. i. 170. A large tree in the evergreen forests of the Martaban and Tenasserim hills. Branchlets, petioles, under side of leaves and inflorescence soft-tomentose. Leaves elliptic or elliptic-oblong, blade 3–7, petiole 1 in. long. Stipules broad, palmately lobed, 3–5-nerved. Fl. small, sepals $\frac{1}{8}$ in., pedicels longer than sepals, torus of 5 distinct globose truncate 2-grooved fleshy glands. Stamens 20–25, filaments half the length of anthers. Stone 1-seeded, in thin pulp.

B. Ovary 3-celled, each cell with 2 collateral ovules. Fl. small, sepals not over $\frac{1}{4}$, rarely $\frac{1}{3}$ in., petals cuneate, deeply laciniate. Longer anther valve ciliate.

3. **E. serratus,** Linn.; Trimen Handb. Ceylon i. 184 t. 20.—Syn. *E. cuneatus*, Wight; Fl. Brit. Ind. i. 402 (with 3-celled stone). Vern. *Ulang Kārei*, Tam.

Leaves thickly chartaceous, from an acute base elliptic or elliptic-obovate, crenate, glabrous above, with a few thin hairs beneath. Fl. white, racemes mostly axillary, sepals $\frac{1}{4}$ in., pedicels as long as sepals, petals 3-fid to the middle, segments laciniate. Disk of 5 distinct tomentose glands. Stamens 25–30, filaments much shorter than glands, the longer anther valve ciliate. Drupe ovoid, more or less acuminate at both ends, 1–1$\frac{1}{4}$ in. Stone strongly tubercled in a copious pulp, often 1-celled, 1-seeded.

Evergreen forests of the Western Ghats, from North Kanara southwards. Fl. C. S., R. S. Ceylon moist region. 4. **E. floribundus,** Blume; King, in Journ. As. Soc. Bengal, vol. 60 ii. (1892) 128; vern. *Jalpai*, of Sikkim, Assam and Burma, is supposed to be different. Petiole usually longer and blade generally thinner, stone almost smooth with 3 vertical grooves. I am disposed to refer all Indian specimens to *E. serratus*, Linn., which Gamble, List 18, gives from Sikkim. *E. floribundus* of Cochinchina and Java has smaller flowers, sepals $\frac{1}{5}$–$\frac{1}{6}$ in., and may be different. 5. **E. lacunosus,** Wall.; Kurz, F. Fl. i. 168; Pierre, Fl. For. Cochinch. t. 144. Vern. *Butalet*, Burm. Evergreen forests of Lower Burma. Young shoots and racemes silky-hairy, sepals $\frac{1}{6}$ in. Leaves cuneate or obovate, obtuse, narrowed into short petiole, racemes lax, stone with rounded tubercles. This possibly is *E. longifolius*, Wall.

6. **E. robustus,** Roxb.; Kurz, F. Fl. i. 169.

Leaves ovate from a rounded base, acuminate, pubescent and pale beneath, blade 6–9, petiole $\frac{3}{4}$–$1\frac{1}{2}$ in., thickened and geniculate at the insertion of blade. Secondary nerves 8–12 pair. Sepals $\frac{1}{3}$ in., petals broad-cuneate, much larger than sepals. Disk fleshy, consisting of 5 distinct tomentose lobes. Stamens 30–40, anthers on short filaments, one valve ciliate. Style thickened at the base, articulate with the ovary. Drupe ovoid, 1–$1\frac{1}{4}$ in. long. Stone rugose, slightly 3-grooved, 3-celled.

Sikkim, Western Duars, Assam, Cachar, Chittagong, Burma, Malay Peninsula. Fl H. S. To this probably belongs *E. Helferi*, Kurz, Fl. Brit. Ind. i. 402. 7. **E. sikkimensis**, Masters. Evergreen forests at the foot of the Sikkim and Bhutan Himalaya, ascending to 5,000 ft. Young shoots and inflorescence grey-pubescent, the pedicels more than twice the length of calyx, sepals $\frac{1}{4}$ in. long. 8. **E. Wallichii,** Kurz, F. Fl. i. 169. Eng forests of Lower Burma. Branchlets, petioles and under side of leaves tawny-tomentose.

9. **E. lanceæfolius,** Roxb.; Wight Ic. t. 65. Vern. *Bhadras*, Nep.

A large tree, perfectly glabrous, excepting the flower. Wood soft, light-coloured. Leaves lanceolate, thinly coriaceous, narrowed into a short petiole. Secondary nerves 6–12 pair, joined by conspicuous intramarginal veins. Racemes mostly infra-axillary, stiff, shorter than leaves. Sepals nearly glabrous, $\frac{1}{4}$ in. long, disk consisting of 5 distinct hairy glands. Anthers on filaments half their length, shortly ciliate at tip. Drupe oblong, $1\frac{1}{2}$ in. long, stone 1-seeded, slightly tubercled.

Common about Darjeeling, 6,000–8,000 ft., Khasi hills; 4,000–5,000 ft., Manipur. Fl. R. S. According to Kurz, F. Fl. i. 168, in Tenasserim.

Species 3–9 are closely allied. In course of time Indian foresters will be able to say whether mode of growth and other biological characters justify the classification here attempted, which is based upon characters, which in this genus are variable.

C. Ovary 3-celled, each cell with 2 collateral ovules. Fl. small, sepals not over $\frac{1}{4}$ in., petals cuneate, deeply laciniate. Anthers not ciliate.

10. **E. oblongus,** Gaertn. Fruct. i. 202 t. 43; Wight Ic. t. 46. Vern. *Hanal tadi*, Kan.; *Bike mara*, Nilgiris; *Khatta Karei*, Tam.

Young shoots puberulous. Leaves coriaceous, as a rule glabrous, underside sometimes minutely hairy, broadly elliptic, petiole glandular-thickened at apex, about 1 in., blade 4–6 in. long. Secondary nerves arcuate, branching, prominent, tertiary reticulate. Racemes shorter than leaves, bracts caducous, longer than buds, dentate. Sepals red, $\frac{1}{5}$ in. long. Petals cut not quite to the middle. Filaments bent, as long as anthers or longer. Style pilose at the base, not articulate with ovary. Drupe ovoid, more or less acuminate at both ends, 1-seeded.

Evergreen forest on the Western Ghats from the Konkan southwards. Bababúden hills, Nilgiris, Anamalais. Fl. April–June. Gaertner's specimen was from the Leiden Museum, and probably is not this species at all, the fruit is obtuse at both ends. The name therefore may eventually have to be changed. *E. leptostachya*, Wall., and *E. lucidus*, Roxb., Fl. Brit. Ind. i. 403, are doubtful. 11. **E. hygrophilus,** Kurz, F. Fl. i. 168. Common in the plains of Lower Burma. Leaves coriaceous, obovate, narrowed into a short petiole. Racemes lax, sepals $\frac{1}{6}$ in. Fruit lanceolate, acuminate at both ends. Nearly allied to *E. decipiens*, Hemsley, from China, and *E. photiniæfolius*, Hook. et Arn. from Japan. 12. **E. Braceanus,** Watt, Naga hills 5,000 ft., Manipur 6,000–7,000, Kachin hills in Upper Burma, is a very remarkable tree. Branchlets, inflorescence, under side of leaves along nerves rusty- or dark grey-tomentose. Leaves oblong, serrate, midrib and nerves very prominent. Fl. on short pedicels, supported by round, serrate or laciniate, tomentose bracteoles. Petals laciniate nearly to the base.

D. Ovary 2- rarely 3-celled, each cell with 2 rows of superposed ovules. Fl. middle-sized, sepals $\frac{1}{3}$–$\frac{2}{3}$ in., petals cuneate, deeply cut, anthers terminated by a long awn or bristle.

13. **E. aristatus,** Roxb.; Wight Ic. t. 63.—Vern. *Garali,* Assam.

Leaves obovate or oblanceolate, blade 5–12 in., gradually narrowed into a petiole 1–2 in., which is thickened and geniculate at the insertion of blade, upper side glabrous, underside with a few hairs on nerves. Secondary nerves 10–20 pair, prominent beneath. Racemes pubescent, 10–15 fld., pedicels nearly as long as sepals, sepals $\frac{1}{2}$–$\frac{2}{3}$ in., densely pubescent outside. Petals yellow (Roxb. Fl. Ind. ii. 600, white in Icones Roxburghianæ), with long soft hairs at the back. Stamens 45–50, awn equal or nearly equal to anther. Ovary tomentose. Stone rugose with two raised ridges (deeply tuberculate in a specimen from Sikkim).

Subhimalayan tract from Sikkim eastward. Dwars (a large tree), Khasi hills, Chittagong, Burma, Andamans. Fl. April, May. This probably is *E. simplex*, Kurz, F. Fl. i. 165.

14. **E. tuberculatus,** Roxb.; Bedd. Fl. Sylv. t. 113.—Syn. *Monocera tuberculata,* Wight et Arn.; Wight Ic. t. 62, Ill. t. 35.

Similar to 13, but leaves pubescent beneath, inflorescence rusty-tomentose. Stamens more numerous, up to 80. Fl. white, stone compressed, deeply tuberculate.

Common in the evergreen forests of the Western Ghats and adjoining hill ranges, from Mahableshwar southwards. Fl. C. S. I am disposed to think that 13 and 14 are one species. Glabrous specimens (called *E. aristatus*) have been collected in the Konkan, while tomentose specimens (called *E. tuberculatus*) are known from Burma. The other characters are not more reliable than the pubescence of leaves. 15. **E. rugosus,** Roxb.; Wight Ic. t. 61. Chittagong, Makûm forest, Assam (D. B., April, 1879). Leaves approximate near the ends of branches, glabrous, obovate-spathulate, lower part narrow, with a rounded base, widening gradually into a broad apex. Blade 6–12 in., petiole 0, or very short and broad, inflorescence rusty-tomentose. Sepals $\frac{2}{3}$ in., pedicels longer than sepals. Petals pale yellow (Icones Roxburghianæ), silky on both sides. Stamens 45, ovary grooved, tomentose. Stone rugose. *E. grandifolius*, Kurz, F. Fl. 165, with larger leaves, gradually narrowed into petiole, and pubescent beneath, may possibly belong to this.

16. **E. ferrugineus,** Bedd. Fl. Sylv. t. 112.—Syn. *Monocera ferruginea,* Wight Ic. t. 205.

Branchlets, petioles, under side of leaves and inflorescence densely rusty-tomentose. Leaves coriaceous, elliptic, the two halves bent back so as to be boat-shaped. Blade 4–5, petiole $\frac{3}{4}$–1 in. long. Racemes 6–12-flowered, pedicels as long as or shorter than sepals. Sepals $\frac{1}{3}$ in. long, silky outside, glabrous inside, petals silky on both sides. Petals oblong-cuneate, upper edge with 10–12 villous teeth. Stamens 20, awns not half as long as anthers. Ovary tomentose, 3-celled, ovules numerous, superposed. Drupe ovoid, $\frac{3}{4}$ in. long.

Nilgiris. Palni and Anamalai hills. Fl. April. 17. **E. Munroii,** Mast. Evergreen forests of the Western Ghats from the Konkan southwards. Leaves perfectly glabrous, ovate-lanceolate, chartaceous, crenate. Blade 2–4, petiole 1–1$\frac{1}{2}$ in. Racemes short, with 8–10 flowers. Sepals $\frac{1}{3}$ in. long, slightly pubescent outside. Stamens 20, awn shorter than anther. Ovary 2-celled, tomentose. 18. **E. acuminatus,** Wall.; Fl. B. Ind. i. 406. Assam and Khasi hills. Leaves glabrous, lanceolate, narrowed into short petiole. Racemes short, pedicels twice the length of sepals, which are $\frac{1}{4}$–$\frac{1}{3}$ in., midrib prominent on inside. Petals cuneate, hairy on both faces, teeth 10–15, lanceolate, glabrous. Stamens 30–40, filaments glabrous, as long as anthers, thickened at the base. Awn short, hairy like anther. Ovary 2-celled, glabrous.

E. Ovary 2-celled, each cell with two rows of superposed ovules. Fl. large, sepals $\frac{2}{3}$ in. and longer. Petals cuneate, deeply cut. Anthers terminated by a long awn or bristle, rarely mucronate.

19. **E. obtusus,** Blume; King in Journ. As. Soc. Beng. vol. 60 ii. 134,

where it is explained why the older name, *E. Monoceras*, Cav., Fl. Brit. Ind. i. 405, has not been used by him for the Indian tree.

Leaves perfectly glabrous, oblanceolate, narrowed gradually into a slender petiole. Blade 3–7, petiole 1–1½ in. Secondary nerves 5–10 pair. Racemes corymbose, shorter than leaves, with 4–8 large flowers. Peduncles and pedicels slender, the latter longer than sepals; sepals ¾ in. long, narrowly linear-lanceolate. Petals oblong-cuneate, divided into 2–3 laciniate segments, silky outside

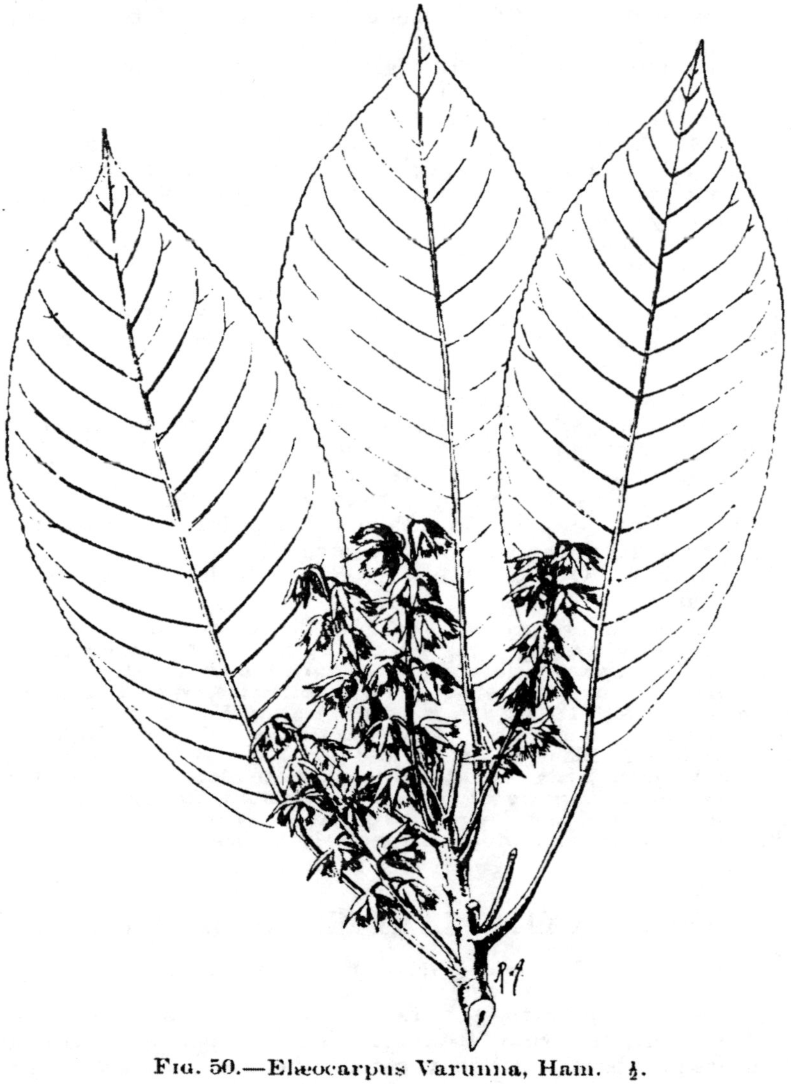

FIG. 50.—Elæocarpus Varunna, Ham. ½.

with appressed hairs, base thickened and hairy inside. Torus annular, tomentose, 20-costate. Stamens up to 70, filaments hairy, awn as long as anther, ovary tomentose. Drupe ovoid, obtuse, 1½ in. long. Stone strongly tuberculate, 1-seeded.

Western Dwars, Tondu forest (Haines), Assam, Burma. Fl. May. Mekông delta, Malay Peninsula. This probably is *E. littoralis*, Kurz (not T. et B.) F. Fl. i. 167. 20. **E. venustus**, Bedd. Fl. Sylv. t. 174, Travancore Ghats at 4,500 ft., with large snow-white fragrant flowers, is similar, but differs in less numerous stamens, up to 40, in the anthers, which are mucronate, not awned, glabrous filaments and ovary. 21. **E. bracteatus,** Kurz, F. Fl. i. 165, is a large tree. Upper Assam (D. B.), Thounggeen and Yonzaleen (D. B.), Shan hills (Collett). Leaves perfectly glabrous, elliptic, obovate, crenate, narrowed into a petiole $\frac{1}{2}$–1 in. long, which is thickened and geniculate at apex. Secondary nerves 8–10 pair. Racemes short, corymbose. Pedicels 3 times the length of sepals, in the axils of oblong-obovate, often serrate bracts. Sepals $\frac{3}{8}$ in. long. Awn nearly as long as anther, ovary 2-celled, tomentose, stone wrinkled.

22. **E. grandiflorus,** Smith; Kurz, F. Fl. i. 166; Pierre, Fl. For. Coch. t. 142.—Syn. *Monocera grandiflora*, Hooker, Bot. Mag. t. 4680. Vern. *Ye Saga*, Burm.

A large shrub or small tree, entirely glabrous, except flowers. Leaves lanceolate, more or less crenate. Petiole $\frac{1}{4}$ in., not thickened at apex. Racemes 3–6 fld., shorter than leaves, flowers scented, pedicels long, slender, in the axils of oblong bracts. Sepals red, $\frac{3}{4}$–1 in. long, glabrous outside, silky inside. Petals white or cream-coloured, silky outside. Disk cylindric, tomentose, sulcate. Awn about the length of anther. Ovary pubescent, 2-celled. Stone covered with woody reflexed spines.

Thaukyeghat near Toungoo (Kurz), Upper Burma (Prager, Smales). Fl. April, May. Cochinchina, Java.

F. Ovary 2- or 3-celled, ovules superposed in two rows. Fl. small and middle-sized, sepals $\frac{1}{5}$–$\frac{1}{3}$ in. Petals broader at base. Anthers with short awns.

23. **E. Varunna,** Ham.; Kurz, F. Fl. i. 165.

Young shoots grey, silky. Leaves perfectly glabrous, elliptic-lanceolate, serrate. Petiole thickened and geniculate at the top. Blade 4–8, petiole 1–3 in. long. Secondary nerves 10–14 pair, prominent. Racemes axillary, numerous, 10–12 fld., pedicels a little longer than sepals. Buds and flowers outside grey with silky hairs. Sepals $\frac{1}{5}$ in. Petals oblong, broader at the base, hairy on both sides, with 7–10 linear teeth. Stamens 25–40, on a 10-lobed torus, awn shorter than anther. Ovary ribbed, hairy, 3-celled. Drupe $\frac{1}{2}$ in. long, stone smooth, 1-seeded.

Subhimalayan tract in evergreen forests, from Nepal eastward, ascending in Sikkim to 4,000 ft. Assam, Chittagong. Fl. March, April. 24. **E. prunifolius,** Wall., Khasi hills, Manipur, is similar, but leaves almost entire, and smaller. Blade 2–4, petiole 1–1½ in. Sepals $\frac{1}{4}$ in., awn very short. 25. **E. petiolatus**, Wall.; King, in Journ. As. Soc. Beng. vol. 60 ii. (1892) 130 (*E. integer*, Masters, not Wall.). Silhet, Cachar, Burma, Malay Peninsula and Archipelago. Leaves coriaceous, shining, elliptic, entire, acute or shortly acuminate. Blade 4–6, petals 1–3 in. Racemes shorter than leaves, sepals $\frac{1}{4}$ in. Petals oblong, the apex cut into 10–14 subulate glabrous teeth. Ovary 2-celled. Drupe $\frac{1}{2}$ in diam., stone slightly rugose. 26. **E. Griffithii,** Masters. Tenasserim, Malay Peninsula. Racemes axillary, longer than leaves, as well as flowers whitish-silky. Sepals $\frac{1}{3}$ in. Petals ovate, acuminate, irregularly fimbriate.

ORDER XXII. LINEÆ. Gen. Pl. i. 241.

Linaceæ and *Erythroxylaceæ*, Engler u. Prantl iii. 4. 27, 37.

Herbs, shrubs or small trees. Leaves alternate, simple, generally quite entire. Fl. regular, as a rule bisexual. Sepals 5, petals 5. Stamens 5 or 10, filaments united at base, anthers versatile 2-celled. Ovary 3–5-celled, styles 3–5, free, or more or less connate. Several species of *Linum*, *Reinwardtia*, and probably also of other genera are remarkable on account of their dimorphic and polymorphic flowers with varying relative length of styles and stamens.

Stamens 10, fruit a drupe, seeds several, woody hooks on branchlets	1. HUGONIA.
Stamens 5, staminodes 5, fruit a capsule	REINWARDTIA (p. 107).
Stamens 10, fruit a capsule	IXONANTHES (p. 107).
Stamens 10, fruit a 1-seeded drupe	2. ERYTHROXYLON.

1. HUGONIA, Linn.; Fl. Brit. Ind. i. 413.

Species 11, tropical Africa, Asia, Australia.

H. Mystax, Linn.; Wight Ill. t. 32. Vern. *Kaki Bira*, Tel.

A scrambling shrub, branches spreading, set with numerous short stiff yellow tomentose branchlets, leafless below, bearing in the axils of the lowest leaves a pair of woody, reflexed, circinate tomentose spines (modified peduncles, occasionally bearing flowers), above them tufts of leaves and axillary flowers. Leaves alternate, stipules subulate. Fl. yellow, 1 in. across, sepals 5, unequal, imbricate, petals 5, contorted. Stamens 10, filaments connate at base. Ovary 5-celled, styles 5 distinct. Drupe red or yellow, ½ in. long, endocarp bony, grooved, seeds 2–3.

Western Peninsula, from the Konkan on the west, the Northern Circars on the east side southwards. Fl. May–October. Ceylon.

Fig. 51.—Hugonia Mystax, Linn. ½.

Reinwardtia trigyna, Planchon, common in northern India and the Peninsula. Shan hills, Upper Burma, is a small shrub, leaves elliptic-lanceolate, entire or nearly so, with large bright yellow flowers, sepals and petals 5, stamens 10, styles 3, sometimes 4 or 5, remarkable on account of the great variation in the relative length of styles and stamens. Not specifically distinct is *R. tetragyna*, Planchon, Sikkim, Khasi hills, Behar, Chota Nagpore, Peninsula. Leaves larger, dentate, styles 3–5, generally 4.

Ixonanthes khasiana, Hook. fil., Khasi hills, is a small tree with elliptic-lanceolate membranous leaves, 3–4½ in. Fl. ⅓ in. long, in dense fld. cymes on slender peduncles, shorter than leaves.

2. ERYTHROXYLON, Linn.; Fl. Brit. Ind. i. 414.

Shrubs or small trees, glabrous, leaves alternate, quite entire, stipules intrapetiolar. Fl. bisexual, pentamerous, petals with a scale, generally bifid, at the top of the claw, stamens 10, filaments united into a short tube. Ovary 3-celled, styles 3, often connate below. Drupe 1-seeded, generally supported by the persistent calyx and staminal tube. Species 90, tropical, mostly American. *E. Coca*, Lam., the leaves of which are extensively used as a powerful stimulant in South America, and which yield the valuable anæsthetic Cocaine, might be grown on the Nilgiris and elsewhere.

A. Western species.

1. **E. monogynum,** Roxb. Cor. Pl. t. 88.—Syn. *E. indicum*, Bedd. Fl. Sylv. t. 81; *Sethia indica*, DC.; Wight Ill. t. 48. Vern. *Dēvadāru*, Tel., Kan.; *Semlichan*, Tam.

A shrub or small tree. Heartwood very hard, dark-brown. Leaves cuneate, 1–2 in. long, dull, not shining, glaucous-brown beneath when dry, stipules triangular, long, acuminate. Fl. axillary, generally in fascicles of 1–4, style trifid at top. Drupe oblong, apiculate, bright scarlet, supported by the persistent sepals and stamens.

Western Peninsula, from the Godavari southwards. Fl. August–November. Ceylon, common in the dry country. 2. **E. lanceolatum,** Wight, Courtallum, Ceylon. Differs by larger lanceolate shining leaves, 2–4 in. long, stipules early deciduous, and solitary flowers.

B. Eastern species.

3. **E. Kunthianum,** Wall.; Kurz, F. Fl. i. 171. Khasi hills, hills east of Toungoo, Thaungyeen. Fl. March–May. A stunted deciduous tree. Leaves elliptic-lanceolate, opaque above, pale glaucous-brown beneath. Fl. sometimes unisexual, styles distinct. 4. **E. burmanicum,** Griff., Tenasserim, Malay Peninsula, differs by obovate obtuse leaves, glossy above and styles connate to the middle.

ORDER XXIII. MALPIGHIACEÆ. Gen. Pl. i. 247.

Climbing shrubs, rarely erect. Leaves opposite, simple, stipules 0 or inconspicuous. Fl. regular or zygomorphic, bisexual, pentamerous. Calyx deeply divided, petals free, disk obscure. Stamens 10. Ovary free, 3-celled, 3-lobed, ovules solitary. Fruit carpels 1–3, usually winged.

Fl. zygomorphic, petals clawed, unequal, 1 stamen longer than the rest, style 1 . . . . . . 1. HIPTAGE.
Fl. regular, petals sessile, equal, stamens equal, styles 3 2. ASPIDOPTERYS.

1. HIPTAGE, Gaertner; Fl. Brit. Ind. i. 418.

Fl. generally white, zygomorphic, the 5th petal larger and coloured. Large glands adnate to the pedicel below the calyx. Stamens 10, all antheriferous, one much longer than the rest. Fruit of 1–3 samaras, connate at the base, each terminating in three long wings. Species 8, south-eastern Asia.

1. **H. Madablota,** Gaertn.; Wight Ill. t. 50.—Syn. *Gaertnera racemosa*, Roxb. Cor. Pl. t. 18. Vern. *Madho-lota*, *Madh-malti*, Hind.; *Boro mali*, Uriya; *Halad wail*, Mar.; *Bi nwè*, Upper Burma.

A tall spreading and climbing shrub, the trunk stout, erect. Branchlets, young leaves and inflorescence hoary or appressed tomentose, full grown leaves glabrous. Leaves elliptic-lanceolate, acute or shortly acuminate, 4–6 in. long, secondary nerves 4–6 pair. Fl. ¾–1 in. diam., very fragrant, petals fimbriate, the 5th petal dashed with yellow. Wings coriaceous, the middle one lanceolate or oblanceolate, 1–2 in. long, the two lateral half as long, linear-oblong.

Subhimalayan tract, from the Indus eastward, ascending to 3,000 ft. Common, chiefly near watercourses and in moist places, throughout Central India, the Western Peninsula and Burma. Fl. January–March. Malay Peninsula and Archipelago, South China. 2. **H. obtusifolia,** DC.; Kurz, F. Fl. i. 173. Pegu Yoma in deep ravines. China. A woody evergreen climber, the trunk cable-like, up to 100 ft. long. Leaves coriaceous, glossy and dark green above, petals with a villous fringe. 3. **H. acuminata,** Wall.; Khasi hills, Manipur. A bushy dense shrub. Leaves coriaceous, glabrous, lanceolate; tertiary nerves parallel and reticulate, prominent; racemes short, dense, clothed with thick brown tomentum. 4. **H. parvifolia,** Wight et Arn. Peninsula from the Nilgiris southwards, Ceylon. Leaves lanceolate, glabrous, shining above, wings membranous, all linear-lanceolate; the middle one 1 in. long, bifid at the apex.

5. **H. candicans,** Hook. fil.; Kurz, F. Fl. i. 174. Vern. *Taung-thaw-ga*, Lower; *Bein-thein*, Upper Burma.

A small deciduous tree or shrub. Branchlets, inflorescence and under side of leaves whitish or yellowish-grey tomentose. Leaves ovate or elliptic 2-4 in. Fl. scented, white or lilac, 5th petal with a bright yellow blotch near the base, wings pink, middle one lanceolate, 1½-2 in., the two lateral broad, obtuse, ⅓ in. long.

Dry and Eng forest in the Irawaddi valley, from Prome upwards, Manipur, Shan hills. Fl. March. Cochinchina. 6. **H. sericea,** Hook. fil. Tenasserim, Malay Peninsula. A woody climber, branchlets and inflorescence clothed with soft brown hairs, racemes slender, 3-6 in. long. Fl. ⅓-½ in. diam. Wings of fruit linear-lanceolate, the middle one 1½-2 in. long, the lateral ones shorter.

2. ASPIDOPTERYS, A. Juss.; Fl. Brit. Ind. i. 419.

Fl. small, regular, yellow or white, in axillary or terminal panicles, no glands on pedicel, petals quite entire, not clawed. Stamens 10, equal. Ovary 3-lobed, styles 3, glabrous, stigmas capitate. Fruit of 3 elongated nuts, which separate when mature, each surrounded by an orbicular or oblong membranous wing. Species 14, tropical Asia.

A. Leaves glabrous beneath, or nearly so.

1. **A. Roxburghiana,** A. Juss.—Syn. *Triopteris indica*, Roxb. Cor. Pl. t. 160.

A woody climber, inflorescence, rusty-tomentose, branchlets, petioles and midrib beneath often rusty-pubescent. Leaves elliptic-ovate, blade 3-4, petiole ⅓ in. long. Petals ⅛ in. long. Wings of fruit oblong, 1½ in. long.

Sikkim, Assam, Khasi and Naga hills. Western Peninsula. Fl. August-October. 2. **A. Helferiana,** Kurz. Tenasserim and Andamans, Shan hills. A large climber. Leaves broadly elliptic, glaucous, often slightly hairy beneath. Fl. on slender pedicels, umbellate, umbels arranged in axillary, slender, rusty-tomentose, panicles. Wings of fruit ovate, thinly membranous, 1 in. long.

The following two species have a small dorsal wing or crest on the nucleus: 3. **A. canarensis,** Dalz. (probably *A. glomerata*, Wight Ic. t. 1986.) Evergreen forests of the Kanara and Malabar Ghats, glabrous. Leaves thinly coriaceous, elliptic-lanceolate, blade 3-5, petiole ½ in. Fl. crowded in axillary fascicles. Wings of fruit nearly orbicular, 1 in. diam., shining, thinly membranous. 4. **A. concava,** A. Juss. Tenasserim, Malay Peninsula. Glabrous. Wings of fruit orbicular, thinly hyaline, with raised veins.

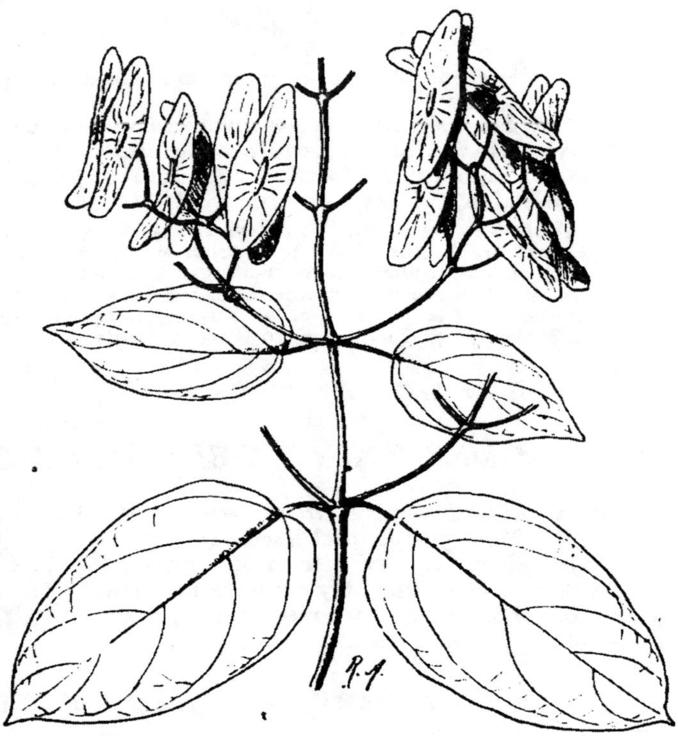

FIG. 52.—Aspidopterys Roxburghiana, A. Juss. ½.

B. Leaves tomentose or pubescent beneath.

5. **A. nutans,** Hook. fil.; Kurz, F. Fl. i. 175.

A woody climber, young shoots and inflorescence pubescent. Leaves broadly

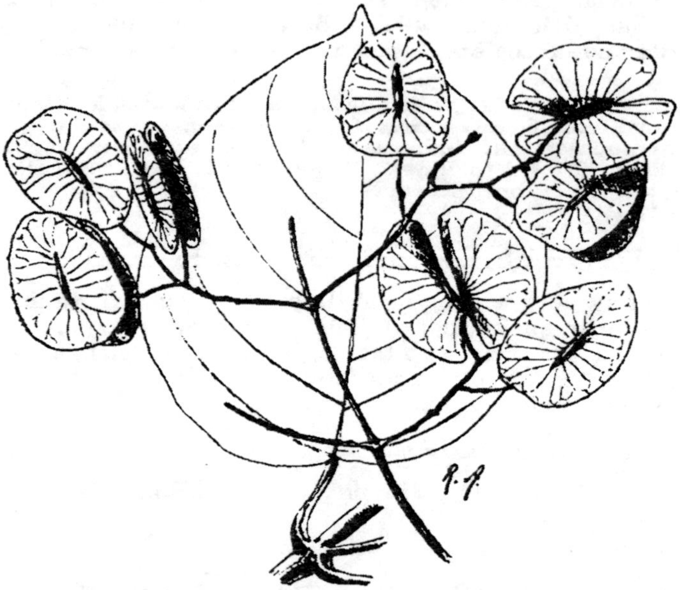

Fig. 53.—Aspidopterys nutans, Hook fil. ½.

ovate, shortly acuminate, silky beneath, blade 4–10, petiole 1–2 in. Wings of fruit broad-ovate, 1–1½ in. long.

Sikkim, ascending to 3,900 ft., Assam, Manipur, Upper Burma. Fl. July–December. 6. **A. hirsuta,** A. Juss. (*Hiræa hirsuta*, Wall. Pl. As. Rar. t. 13). Irawaddi valley, from Prome upwards. Branchlets and inflorescence hirsute with long tawny hairs, leaves obovate, on both sides clothed with long soft hairs, flowers white, petals nearly ¼ in. long, wings of fruit oblong 1½ by ½ in.

7. **A. Wallichii,** Hook. fil. — Syn. *A. lanuginosa*, A. Juss.; Brandis, F. Fl. 44.

A large climber. Young shoots, under side of leaves and inflorescence clothed with soft white or grey tomentum. Leaves ovate from a cordate or rounded base, acuminate, blade 4–5, petiole ¾ in. Panicle graceful, lax, pendulous, petals ⅛ in., ovary clothed with long white hairs. Wings of fruit oval, 1½ in. long.

Subhimalayan tract, from Dehra Dún to Nepal, ascending to 4,000 ft. Fl. R. S. 8. **A. cordata,** A. Juss. Western coast and Western Ghats, from Bombay southwards. Young shoots, under side of leaves and inflorescence clothed with whitish appressed hairs. Leaves cordate, acuminate, blade 3–7, petiole 1–2 in. Wings of fruit nearly orbicular. Of *A. tomentosa*, A. Juss., a native of Java, given by Kurz (F. Fl. i. 175) from Martaban, I have seen no Burma specimens.

ORDER XXIV. GERANIACEÆ. Gen. Pl. i. 269.

Tribe *Oxalideæ* (*Oxalidaceæ*, a distinct order in Engler u. Prantl iii. 4. 15). Mostly perennial herbs, rarely trees or shrubs. Leaves alternate, generally compound. Fl. bisexual, regular, sepals 5, imbricate in bud, persistent, petals 5, free or slightly connate at base. Stamens 10, the 5 outer opposite to petals, shorter and at times sterile, filaments slightly connate at base. Ovary 5-celled, styles 5 distinct.

AVERRHOA, Linn.; Fl. Brit. Ind. i. 439.

Trees. Leaves imparipinnate, sensitive, leaflets nearly opposite, stipules 0. Fl. in cymose panicles, ovules numerous in each cell. Fr. oblong, fleshy, indehiscent. Embryo straight, with thin foliaceous cotyledons in a fleshy albumen. Species 2, cultivated in the tropics of the old and new world, native country unknown.

1. **A. Carambola,** Linn. Sans. *Karmara.* Vern. *Kamrak, Kamaranga*, Hind.; *Pulichi*, Mal.; *Saung gya*, Burm.

Leaflets ovate, acuminate, 2–5 pair. Fl. small, variegated white and purple, panicles axillary, sometimes on the old wood. Calyx glabrous, the shorter stamens usually minute and sterile. Fruit yellow, ellipsoid, 3 in. long, with 5 prominent ridges. Funicle of seed dilated into a fleshy bilabiate, irregularly cut arillus.

Cultivated on account of its fruit for ages in India and Burma, as far north as Lahore. Fl. Febr.-Aug. Fr. C. S. 2. **A. Bilimbi,** Linn.; Bedd. Fl. Sylv. t. 117. Vern. *Bilimbi*, Hind. Cultivated and run wild in tropical India. Leaflets oblong, acuminate, 6–14 pair. Fl. dark brownish purple, ½ in. long, in panicles on the old wood of stem and branches, inflorescence and calyx rusty pubescent. Fruit yellow, oblong, slightly furrowed, seeds without arillus.

ORDER XXV. RUTACEÆ. Gen. Pl. i. 278.

Shrubs or trees, a few genera herbaceous, as a rule strongly aromatic. Leaves alternate (except *Evodia* and *Melicope*), compound or simple, dotted with translucent glands, stipules none. Fl. regular, 4–5-merous, rarely 3-merous, sepals free or connate. Stamens as a rule 4–5 or 8–10, filaments usually free, inserted on the outside of an annular or cylindrical disk. Carpels 4–5, mostly connate.

Cavities containing ethereal oil in the tissue of leaves, flowers and fruit as well as in the bark, are an important character of this order, separating it from *Meliaceæ* and other allied orders. The ethereal oils secreted into these cavities from the surrounding tissue cause the aromatic smell of most *Rutaceæ*; in most cases they can readily be seen as translucent glands.

A. Unarmed, leaves opposite, leaflets entire, flowers polygamous.
  Stamens 4–5 . . . . 1. EVODIA.
  Stamens 8 . . . . MELICOPE (p. 112).

B. Unarmed, leaves imparipinnate.
  Styles short, persistent, leaflets 1–5, rarely 7 . . 2. GLYCOSMIS.
  Styles deciduous, ovary linear, 2-celled . . . . 3. MURRAYA.
  Style deciduous, ovary 4–5-celled.
    Stamens 10, filaments subulate . . . . . 4. MICROMELUM.
    Stamens 8 or 10, filaments dilated below the subulate tip . . . . 5. CLAUSENA.

C. Unarmed, leaves 1-foliolate, flowers polygamous.
  Fl. 4-merous, stamens 8 . . . . 6. ACRONYCHIA.
  Fl. 5-merous, stamens 5 . . . . 7. SKIMMIA.

D. Mostly armed, leaves 3-foliolate or imparipinnate, petiole often winged.
  Ovules 1–2 in each cell.
    Stamens 3–8, flowers often unisexual . . . 8. ZANTHOXYLUM.
    Stamens 8–10, flowers bisexual . . . . . 9. LIMONIA.
  Ovules numerous in each cell.
    Leaves imparipinnate . . . . 10. FERONIA.
    Leaves trifoliolate . . . . 11. ÆGLE.

E. Mostly armed, leaves 3-foliolate.
  Fl. unisexual . . . . 12. TODDALIA.
  Fl. bisexual.
    Fl. 3-merous, stamens 6, leaflets crenate . . TRIPHASIA (p. 120).
    Fl. 4–5-merous, leaflets coriaceous, entire . . 13. LUVUNGA.

F. Mostly armed, leaves 1-foliolate.
  Ovules 1–2 in each cell.
    Erect, fl. in racemes or corymbs, anthers oblong or ovate . . . . 14. ATALANTIA.
    Often scandent, fl. solitary or fascicled . . 15. PARAMIGNYA.
  Ovules numerous in each cell . . . . . . 16. CITRUS.

1. EVODIA, Forst.; Fl. Brit. Ind. i. 487.

Evergreen, mostly aromatic shrubs or trees. L. opposite, simple or compound, leaflets quite entire. Fl. small, polygamous, 4–5-merous, in panicled axillary cymes. Stamens 4–5, filaments subulate, anthers oblong. Ovary deeply 4-lobed, 4-celled, ovules 2 in each cell, stigma 4-lobed. Carpels separating in fruit, 2-valved, 1–2 seeds in each. Species 45, from Madagascar through India and the Malay Archipelago to Australia and Polynesia.

A. Leaves 3-foliolate, rarely 1-foliolate.

2. **E. Roxburghiana**, Benth.—Syn. *E. triphylla*, Bedd. Fl. Sylv. Manual t. 6, f. 2; *Zanthoxylon triphyllum*, Wight Ic. t. 204.

A small tree with opposite branches, young shoots puberulous. L. 3-foliolate, petiole 1–4 in. long, panicles divaricate, as long as or longer than petioles. Ripe carpels 2–4, wrinkled, $\frac{1}{8}$ in. long, seeds black, shining.

Western Ghats, from the Konkan southwards, Nilgiris, Palnis. Hills of Upper and Lower Burma. Fl. R. S., Fr. C. S.—Ceylon, Malay Peninsula and Archipelago. 2. **E. triphylla**, DC., common on the hills of Martaban and Tenasserim, and in Upper Burma. A slender shrub, differs very slightly by the more prominent secondary nerves and intramarginal veins, and the panicles much shorter than petioles. 3. **E. glabra**, Blume. Andamans. A tree attaining 70 ft., perfectly glabrous, leaflets thinly coriaceous, obovate, shortly and abruptly acuminate, 4–10 in. long; secondary nerves 10–15 pair, prominent beneath. 4. **E. viticina**, Wall. Tenasserim. A shrub. Internodes with 4 decurrent lines. Leaves often 1-foliolate, leaflets lanceolate, pale beneath, 2–4 in. long, panicles contracted, shorter than petiole.

B. Leaves imparipinnate.

5. **E. fraxinifolia**, Hook. fil.; Vern. *Kanukpa*, Nep.

A moderate-sized, strongly aromatic tree. L. perfectly glabrous, leaflets 3–6 pair, 4–9 in. long, oblong-lanceolate, acuminate, sometimes slightly crenulate, base often oblique. Fl. greenish-white, sepals small, obtuse, petals much longer, linear, hairy above. ♂: Filaments hairy, longer than petals, four rudimentary acuminate ovaries. ♀: Fr. red, $\frac{1}{2}$ in. diam.

Outer Himalaya, 4,000–7,000 ft., from Nepal eastward. Khasi hills. Fl. May. Closely allied are: 6. **E. melisæfolia**, Benth. Assam, Cachar, China. Glabrous. Leaflets 3–4 in., base very oblique, panicle loose, terminal, ramifications slender. 7. **E. rutæcarpa**, Hook. fil. & Thoms. Inner valleys of the Sikkim Himalaya, 7,000–10,000 ft., China, Japan. A small tree with dense foliage, not aromatic, branchlets, leaves, and inflorescence clothed with soft velvety pubescence, panicles 3–4 in. diam., ramifications stout.

Melicope indica, Wight Ic. t. 1051, Bedd. Manual t. 6, f. 1, is a glabrous shrub or small tree, common on the higher ranges of the Nilgiris near the western and south-western edge. Leaves opposite, 1-foliolate, elliptic or obovate, entire, blade 3–4, petiole 1 in. long. Fl. 3–5 on long axillary peduncles, 4-merous, stamens 8. Carpels 4, nearly distinct, styles united in the capitate 4-lobed stigma. Ovules 2 in each carpel. Ripe carpels 2–4, free, coriaceous, dehiscing on the inner face, seed black, shining, cotyledons large, flat, in oily albumen. The genus comprises 15 species, mostly Polynesian.

2. GLYCOSMIS, Correa; Fl. Brit. Ind. i. 499.

Species 6 in the Indo-Malayan region.

G. pentaphylla, Correa; Bedd. Fl. Sylv. Manual, t. vi. fig. 6; Brandis, F. Fl. 49.—Syn. *Limonia pentaphylla*, Roxb. Cor. Pl. t. 84; *L. arborea*, Roxb. ib. t. 85. Vern. *Ban Nimbu*, Hind.; *Kirmira*, Mar.; *Gonji*, *Gunji*, Tel.; *Pānal*, Mal.; *Taw shauk*, Lower; *Obok*, Upper Burma.

Evergreen, unarmed, a shrub or small tree. Leaves imparipinnate, leaflets generally alternate 1, 3, 5, rarely 7. Fl. in axillary pedunculate panicles, 2–4 in. long, pentamerous, bisexual, stamens 10, filaments flat. Ovary 2–5-celled, 1 ovule in each cell, style thick, fleshy, short, not jointed with ovary. Berry irregularly globose, white, pink or blue, $\frac{1}{3}$ in. diam.

Dehra Dūn, undergrowth in moist forests. Gangetic plain, often as underwood in Mangoe groves, Oudh forests. Sikkim, ascending to 4,000 ft., Assam. Both Peninsulas. Fl. and fr. throughout the year. Ceylon, Malay Peninsula and Archipelago, Australia.

A most variable species, the forms of which are described in Fl. Brit. Ind. i. 500. In Trimen Journ. of Botany, 1876, p. 33, S. Kurz divides *G. pentaphylla* into 10 species, 7 of which are found in British India. 2. **G. montana**, Pierre, a small tree in Cochinchina, may possibly be found in Upper Burma, panicles very short, stamens unequal, 5 shorter, anthers not apiculate, style fleshy, as long as ovary. A species, probably new, is a small tree 20 ft. high in evergreen forest, Pudaw, Upper Burma (Smales Febr. 1901, *Metimè*, Burm.), leaflets 7–9, panicle terminal, large, spreading, petals rusty-pilose outside, filaments thick, short, the epipetalous anthers almost sessile.

3. MURRAYA, Linn.; Fl. Brit. Ind. i. 502.

Shrubs or small trees. L. imparipinnate, leaflets alternate. Fl. bisexual, pentamerous, petals imbricate, stamens 10. Ovary on a more or less elongated disk, linear, 2-celled, style deciduous. Fr. a 1–2-seeded berry, albumen 0, cotyledons plano-convex. Species 4, of the Indo-Malayan region.

1. **M. exotica**, Linn.; Wight Ic. t. 96; Bedd. Fl. Sylv. Manual t. vii. p. 2; Brandis, F. Fl. 48. Vern. *Marchula*, North-West; *Bilgar*, Dūn.; *Otali*, Kol; *Karepaku*, Tel.; *Konji*, Tam.; *Thanatka*, Burm.; *Moksongayok*, Pyinmana (Troup.).

Fig. 54.—Murraya exotica, Linn. ½.

A large shrub or small tree, evergreen, youngest parts pubescent. Bark ash-grey, wood white, close-grained, resembling boxwood. Leaflets usually 5–7, quite glabrous, shining, 1–3 in. long. Fl. campanulate, ½ in. across, white, fragrant, in short axillary and terminal corymbs. Ovary linear, 2-celled, style filiform, stigma capitate. Berries ½ in. long, red, acuminate at both ends, 2-seeded.

Outer Himalaya, from the Jumna eastward, ascending to 4,500 ft. Assam. Burma Upper and Lower, Satpura range. Hills of the Peninsula. Fl. March–September. The bark used as a cosmetic by Burmese ladies. 2. **M. elongata**, Alph. DC.; Fl. Brit. Ind. i. 503. Upper Burma (Wallich). Leaflets 4–5 in. Berry ⅜ in. long. May possibly only be a variety.

3. **M. Koenigii**, Spreng.—Syn. *Bergera Koenigii*, Linn.; Roxb. Cor. Pl. t. 112; Wight Ic. t. 13. Vern. *Gandhla, Gandhela, Kāthnim*, Hind.; *Kari-Bevu*, Kan.; *Kare paku*, Tel.

A small pubescent tree with a short trunk and a close shady crown, leafless during a short time in the hot season, all parts with a powerful peculiar smell.

Leaflets 11–25, from an oblique base ovate-lanceolate, 1 in. long. Fl. white, in terminal corymbose panicles. Ovary 2-celled, style short, cylindrical. Fr. $\frac{1}{3}$ in. diam., black, rugose.

Outer Himalaya, from the Ravi eastward, ascending to 5,000 ft., Assam, Chittagong, Burma Upper and Lower. Evergreen and deciduous forests of the Peninsula, often as underwood. Fl. H. S.

4. MICROMELUM, Blume; Fl. Brit. Ind. i. 501.

Species 6, Indo-Malayan region.

1. **M. pubescens,** Blume; Bedd. Fl. Sylv. Manual t. vii., f. 1. Engler u Prantl iii. 4, 186 fig. 107. Vern. *Tanyinbo*, Burm.

A small evergreen tree, the younger parts pubescent. L. alternate, imparipinnate, leaflets 7–15, alternate or nearly opposite, 4–6 in. long, from an oblique base ovate-lanceolate, entire. Fl. strongly scented, $\frac{1}{3}$–$\frac{1}{2}$ in. diam., in large hoary terminal corymbose compound cymes, calyx cupshaped, entire or 5-toothed, petals 5, tomentose outside, thick, valvate, or slightly imbricate in bud, $\frac{1}{4}$ in. long, stamens 10. Ovary hairy, 5-celled, style articulate with ovary, stigma capitate. Berry dry, glabrous, 1–2-seeded. Albumen 0, cotyledons folded and crumpled.

Nepal, Sikkim, ascending to 3,000 ft., Assam, Khasi and Naga hills, Bengal. Gúmsúr hills, Ganjam (Bedd.) Chittagong. Upper and Lower Burma. Fl. December–February. Ceylon, Malay Peninsula and Archipelago, China. 2. **M. hirsutum,** Oliver; Kurz, F. Fl. i. 187. Burma Upper and Lower. A low shrub, densely tomentose, leaflets smaller, repand-serrate. Ovary densely hirsute. Unripe berries pubescent. Possibly only a variety of *M. pubescens.*

5. CLAUSENA, Burm.; Fl. Brit. Ind. i. 503.

Shrubs or trees with imparipinnate, mostly deciduous leaves, leaflets membranous. Fl. small, 4–5-merous, petals imbricate, stamens 8 or 10, the alternate shorter, filaments dilated below the subulate tip. Ovary stipitate, 4–5-celled, ovules 2 in each cell, style deciduous immediately after flowering or later. Albumen 0, cotyledons plano-convex. Species 14, chiefly Indo-Malayan, a few in China, Africa and Australia.

A. Ovary hairy.

1. **C. pentaphylla,** DC.; Brandis, F. Fl. 49. Vern. *Ratanjote*, *Teyrar*, Hind.

A strongly aromatic shrub, young shoots and inflorescence silky-tomentose, full-grown leaves pubescent. Leaflets 5 or 7, nearly opposite, 4–6 in. long, secondary nerves prominent beneath. Fl. yellowish, in terminal panicles. Berry verrucose, pale orange, $\frac{1}{3}$–$\frac{1}{2}$ in. long.

Subhimalayan tract, Garhwal to Sikkim, Oudh forests. Fl. H. S.

2. **C. excavata,** Burm.; Kurz, F. Fl. i. 188. Vern. *Ote Armu*, Kol; *Seitnan*, Burm.

A shrub or small tree (an undershrub in Sal and Eng forest) strongly and unpleasantly aromatic, young shoots and inflorescence pubescent or tomentose, leaflets 15–30, alternate, pubescent beneath. Fl. greenish-yellow, tetramerous, in lax terminal cymose panicles. Berry $\frac{3}{4}$ in. broadly oblong.

Subhimalayan tract, from Nepal eastward, Chota Nagpore, Chittagong, Burma. Often in Sal and Eng forest. Fl. H. S. Malay Peninsula and Archipelago. 3. **C. Wampi,** Blanco, a small nearly glabrous, pleasantly aromatic tree, a native of China, is grown in gardens; berry edible, size and shape of a gooseberry.

B. Ovary glabrous.

4. **C. indica,** Oliver; Trimen Handbook Ceylon, i. 221. Vern. *Vepillei*, Tam

A shrub or small tree, leaflets 7–13, chartaceous, alternate, 1½–3 in. long, base very oblique, edge wavy, shining, glabrous on both sides. Fl. 5-merous, greenish-white, laxly arranged in a terminal corymbose panicle, petals glabrous, thin, ⅛ in long. Ovary 2–5-celled, glabrous, tuberculate. Somewhat resembles *Micromelum pubescens*.

Evergreen forests of the Western Ghats, from North Kanara southwards. Fl. H. S.

5. **C. Willdenowii,** W. et A. Prodr.; Trimen Handb. Ceylon, i. 222. Vern. *Kat Vepillei*, Tam.; *Potti*, Mal.

A shrub or small tree, young shoots pubescent, leaflets 7–15, membranous,

FIG. 55.—Clausena Willdenowii, W. et A. ½.

1½–2½ in. long. Fl. 4–5-merous, white, in slender simple axillary racemes, shorter than leaves. Ovary on a short narrow gynophore, slightly 4–5-lobed at tip, 4–5-celled, fruit globose, ⅓–½ in. diam.

Evergreen forests of the Western Ghats from Sattara southwards, Sikkim, Naga hills, Burma, Ceylon. Fl. H. S. Bedd. Fl. Sylv. Manual t. vii. p. 8, represents the ovary as hairy. The following Eastern species with alternate leaflets belong to this section—*a. Fl. in terminal panicles*: 6. **C. heptaphylla,** W. et A. Lower Bengal Khasi hills, Chittagong, Burma. Glabrous, leaflets 5–11, equal or slightly oblique at base, 2–6 in. long. 7. **C. macrophylla,** Hook. fil. Tenasserim. Softly villous, leaflets equal or slightly oblique at base, 5–7 in. long. 8. **C. Wallichii,** Oliver. Burma. Leaflets 13–17, glabrous, rhomboid, crenulate, 2–3 in. long. *b. Fl. in axillary racemes*: 9. **C. suffruticosa,** W. et A., Chittagong, Khasi hills, China. A low undershrub, softly tomentose, leaflets 5–17, oblique, 3–4 in. long.

6. ACRONYCHIA Forst.; Fl. Brit. Ind. i. 498.

Species 17, tropical Asia, China, Japan, Australia, and Polynesia.

A. laurifolia, Blume.—Syn. *A. pedunculata*, Miq.; Bedd. Fl. Sylv. Manual t. vi. f. 4.; *Cyminosma pedunculata*, DC.; Wight Ill. t. 65 (fl. figured as 5-merous).

A large evergreen shrub or moderate-sized tree, very variable. Leaves opposite, glabrous, 1-foliolate, quite entire. Fl. polygamous, 4-merous, white or yellowish green, fragrant, in axillary pedunculate trichotomous cymes. Petals linear, more or less villous within. Stamens 8, filaments subulate, hairy at base, inserted outside a thick 8-grooved tomentose disk, those alternating with petals longer. Ovary tomentose 4-celled, ovules 2 in each cell, superposed. Fruit globose, often grooved at top, $\frac{1}{3}$–$\frac{1}{2}$ in. diam., 3–5-seeded. Albumen copious, cotyledons oblong, flat.

Eastern Dūn, rare (Kanjilal F. Fl., 50). Sikkim to 4,000 ft., Assam, Chittagong, Pegu, Tenasserim, Andamans. Western Ghats, from North Kanara southwards, Palni and Anamalai hills. Fl. June–December. Ceylon, Malay Peninsula and Archipelago. Cochinchina.

7. SKIMMIA, Thunb.; Fl. Brit. Ind. i. 499.

Species 3, Himalaya, China, and Japan.

S. Laureola, Sieb. and Zucc.; Brandis F. Fl. 50.—Syn. *Limonia Laureola*, Wall. Pl. As. Rar. t. 245. Vern. *Ner, Nehār, Gurlpata*, N.W. Him.; *Patrang*, Kunawar; *Chumlāni*, Nep.

A gregarious, evergreen, wholly glabrous, strongly aromatic shrub, small in the N.W., often a small tree in Sikkim, wood white, close-grained. L. alternate, simple, quite entire, midrib prominent. Fl. bright yellow (greenish-yellow or white in Sikkim), pentamerous, polygamous, in short crowded terminal panicles. Stamens 5, alternating with petals. Fr. ellipsoid, red (black in Sikkim), $\frac{1}{2}$–$\frac{3}{4}$ in. long, fleshy, with 1–3 cartilaginous 1-seeded kernels. Albumen fleshy, cotyledons flat.

Himalaya, from the Indus eastward, 5,000–11,000 ft. Fl. April, May. Fr. Oct., Nov. Afghanistan. The Japanese species, *S. japonica*, Thunb., united with this in Engler u. Prantl iii. 4. 181, has 4-merous flowers.

8. ZANTHOXYLUM, Linn.; Fl. Brit. Ind. i. 492. (*Xanthoxylum* and *Fagara*, Engler u. Prantl iii. 4. 115.)

Shrubs or trees, nearly always armed, prickles on stems and branches generally on a corky conical base. L. alternate, 3-foliolate or imparipinnate. Fl. small, generally unisexual, and 4–5-merous. Either (*Fagara*) with sepals and petals, the former smaller, or (*Zanthoxylum*) a perigonium of 5–8 leaves. Stamens in all cases alternate with petals or perigonium leaves. Ovary of 1–5 distinct oblique 1-celled carpels, styles sometimes connate at the apex. Ripe carpels 1–5, globose, generally coriaceous, dehiscing ventrally. Seeds shining, blue or black. Embryo in a fleshy albumen, radicle short, cotyledons flat. Species 140 in tropical and subtropical regions.

A. Common petiole winged, perigonium of 5–8 leaves. Leaves imparipinnate.

1. **Z. alatum,** Roxb.; Brandis F. Fl. 47. Vern. *Tezbal*, Hind.; *Timbar, Timru*, Bashahr, Jaunsar; *Timūr*, Nep.

A shrub, at times a small tree, almost entirely glabrous, wood white, close-grained, prickles shining, strong, broad and flat on branchlets petioles and midrib, those on older branches often on a conical corky base. Leaflets opposite, 2–4 pair, sessile, lanceolate, sec. n. indistinct. Fl. yellow, diœcious, in lax sparingly branched axillary panicles. Ripe carpels rugose, red, solitary, rarely 2–3.

Outer Himalaya, from the Indus eastward, ascending to 7,000 ft., Khasi and Naga

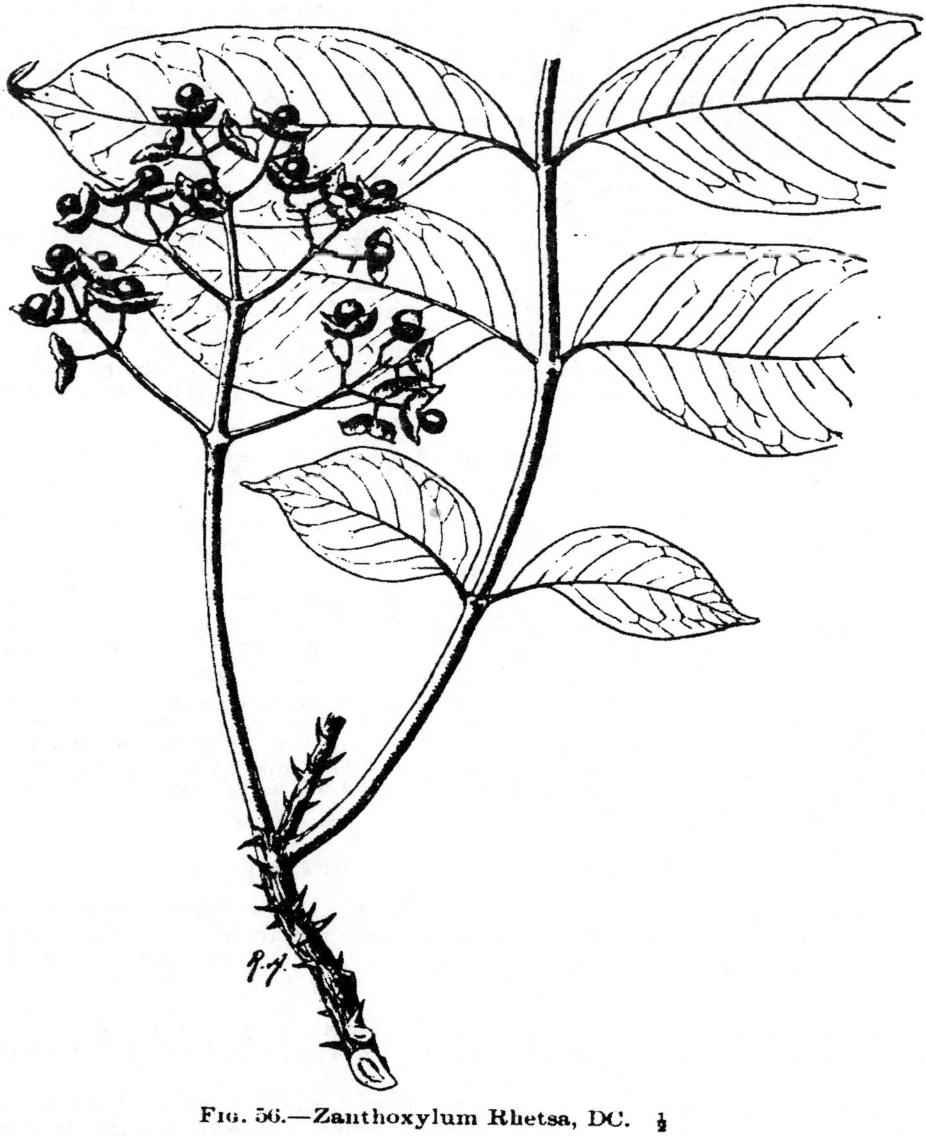

FIG. 56.—Zanthoxylum Rhetsa, DC. ½

hills, hills of Vizagapatam and Ganjam. Fl. Oct., Nov. Bark used for intoxicating fish. 2. **Z. Acanthopodium,** DC. Outer Himalaya, Kumaon to Sikkim, Khasi hills, differs by distinct sec. n. Sometimes pubescent. Fl. in round, compact clusters, ripe carpels 2–4. Both species have a strong pungent smell.

B. Common petiole not winged, sepals 4–5, petals as many. Panicles or clusters of flowers mostly axillary, ramifications alternate.

3. **Z. ovalifolium**, Wight; Bedd. Fl. Sylv. Manual t. 6. f. 3.

A large shrub or small tree, quite glabrous, often unarmed. L. trifoliolate, leaflets 3–4 in., coriaceous, crenulate, sec. n. numerous, slender, parallel.

Sikkim Terai and outer valleys, ascending to 3,000 ft., Assam, Khasi hills. Western Ghats from Kanara southwards. Fl. March, April. 4. **Z. Hamiltonianum**, Wall. Sikkim, Assam, Upper Burma, a large scrambling shrub, thorns on stem and branches on a large corky conical base, branchlets and petioles pubescent or velvety, leaflets 2–8 pair, opposite, entire, 4–7 in., glossy on both surfaces, sec. n. and intramarginal veins prominent. Fl. green, in short axillary panicles. 5. **Z. tetraspermum**, W. et A. Western Ghats from Coorg southwards, Nilgiris, Anamalais, Ceylon, a large climber with long rope-like stems, set with woody conical spine-tipped prickles, branchlets and petioles armed with numerous small deflexed spines, leaflets opposite, 3–4 pair, very glossy, coarsely serrate, sec. n. slender, numerous. Fl. yellowish-pink, in terminal and axillary panicles.

6. **Z. oxyphyllum**, Edgew. Vern. *Siritakdangji*, Lepcha.

A glabrous shrub, often climbing over tall forest trees, prickles usually recurved. Leaflets lanceolate, 3–10 pair, alternate and opposite. Fl. tetramerous, large, lilac, $\frac{1}{4}$–$\frac{1}{3}$ in. diam.

Outer Himalaya, from Garhwal eastward, 4,000–9,000 ft. Khasi hills, Manipur. Fl. H. S., R. S. 7. **Z. tomentellum**, Hook. fil., Sikkim and Bhutan to 5,000 ft., a small tree with horizontal branches, sparingly prickly, branchlets, petioles, under side of leaflets and inflorescence velvety, leaflets alternate, entire, 6–8 pair. 8. **Z. Khasianum**, Hook. fil., Khasi hills, a scandent shrub, very fragrant, sparingly prickly, leaflets 8–10 pair, alternate, rarely opposite, lanceolate, caudate-acuminate, 1–2 in., panicles axillary, pubescent.

C. Common petiole not winged, sepals 4, petals as many. Panicles terminal, ramifications opposite, pith large, septate.

9. **Z. Rhetsa**, DC. Vern. *Rhetsa Maun*, Tel. (the *Assembly tree*, Roxb. Fl. Ind. i. 417); *Tirphal*, Mar.; *Jummina*, Kan.; *Mulillam*, *Katta Murakku*, Mal.

A large tree, prickles numerous on trunk, branches and petioles, those on the old wood with a solid conical base. The prickly stem resembles that of *Bombax*. Leaflets opposite, 8–20 pair, glabrous, very oblique, entire, the terminal often wanting. Fl. yellow, in large terminal panicles.

Western Ghats and coast, from the Konkan southwards, chiefly in moist evergreen forests, also on the seashore. Northern Circars. Fl. July–November. 10. **Z. Budrunga**, Wall. (*Maya-nin*, Burm.). Assam, Khasi hills, Dacca, Chittagong, Lower Burma (Kurz). An evergreen aromatic tree, trunk spinous, prickles on branches few, incurved, leaflets 5–10 pairs, shallowly crenate, sinus glandular, base oblique. Pierre, Fl. For. Cochinch. t. 290, unites this with **Z. Rhetsa**.

9. LIMONIA, Linn.; Fl. Brit. Ind. i. 507.

Shrubs or small trees, often spiny. Leaves 3-foliolate or imparipinnate, common petiole winged. Fl. 4–5-merous, petals imbricate in bud. Stamens 8–10, filaments subulate. Ovary 4–5-celled, style deciduous, ovules 1–2 in each cell. Berry globose, 1–4 seeded. Species 2–3, tropical Asia.

1. **L. acidissima**, Linn.; Brandis F. Fl. 47.—Syn. *L. crenulata*, Roxb. Cor. Pl. t. 86. Vern. *Beli*, Hind.; *Bhenta*, Uriya; *Nayi bel*, Kan.; *Thanatka*, Burm.

A glabrous shrub, sometimes a small tree, branches rigid, flexuose, thorns straight, $\frac{1}{2}$–1 in. long. L. imparipinnate, leaflets opposite, wings between insertion of leaflets oblong or obovate, wings and leaflets crenate. Fl. tetramerous, white, fragrant, in short axillary racemes, often with 1 or 2 leaves. Petals pellucid-punctate. Ovary 4-celled, 1 ovule in each cell. Berry black when ripe, $\frac{1}{3}$–$\frac{1}{2}$ in. diam.

Outer Himalaya, Sutlej to Garhwal, ascending to 4,000 ft. Assam, Yunan, Western Peninsula. Fl. H. S. A pubescent form, found by J. W. Oliver in the Pakokku district of Upper Burma, may possibly be *L. pubescens*, Wall. 2. **L. alternans**, Wall., Pegu,

Tenasserim. Unarmed, common petiole narrowly winged, leaflets alternate, fl. 5-merous.
3. **L. alata,** W. et A.; Wight Ill t. 41. Bedd. Fl. Sylv. Manual t. 7, p. 4. Western Peninsula (*Munukudu*, Nellore). A small glabrous spinescent tree. L. trifoliolate, leaflets obovate, quite entire, the lateral smaller. Fl. 4–5-merous, in short hoary panicles. Ovules 2 in each cell. Berry globose, 1 in. diam.

10. FERONIA, Gaertn.; Fl. Brit. Ind. i. 516.

F. Elephantum, Correa (the only species); Roxb. Cor. Pl. t. 141; Wight Ic. t. 15. Bedd. Fl. Sylv. t. 121.—*Elephant- or Wood-Apple.* Vern. *Bilin, Kaitha, Kāt bel,* Hind.; *Kawith,* Mar.; *Velaga,* Tel.; *Byala,* Kan.; *Vilva,* Tam.; *Thibin,* Burma.

A middle-sized glabrous, deciduous tree, armed with strong straight axillary thorns. L. alternate, imparipinnate, leaflets opposite, 1–4 pair, cuneate or obovate, crenate at the tip, common petiole often narrow-winged. Fl. dull red, generally unisexual, in lax panicles, male and bisexual flowers frequently on the same inflorescence. Stamens 10–12, filaments short, subulate, from a broad villous base. Fr. globose, grey, rough, 2–3 in. diam., rind hard, woody, seeds numerous, oblong, embedded in fleshy edible pulp.

Generally cultivated in both Peninsulas; indigenous in South India and Ceylon, Fl. Feb.–April.

11. ÆGLE, Correa; Fl. Brit. Ind. i. 516.

Species: 2 in the Indo-Malayan region, 1 in Japan, and 1 in tropical West Africa.

A. Marmelos, Correa; Roxb. Cor. Pl. t. 143; Wight Ic. t. 16; Bedd. Fl. Sylv. t. 161. *The Bael tree.* Vern. *Bēl, Bili,* Hind.; *Lohagasi,* Kol; *Mahika,* Gond; *Bila patri,* Kan.; *Maredu,* Tel.; *Vilva,* Tam.; *Kovalam,* Mal.; *Okshit,* Burma.

A small or middle-sized tree, armed with axillary, straight, sharp spines, wood yellowish-white, close-grained, strongly aromatic when fresh cut, no heartwood. L. alternate, trifoliolate, leaflets sometimes 5, ovate-lanceolate, crenate. Fl. bisexual, 4–5-merous, greenish-white, in short lateral panicles with a fine honey scent. Calyx flat, teeth small, petals imbricate, stamens numerous, filaments short, anthers linear. Fr. 4–6 in. diam., rind smooth, grey or yellow. Seeds numerous, oblong, flat, testa densely clothed with thick fibrous hairs, in a thick orange-coloured sweet aromatic pulp.

Wild in the subhimalayan tract and outer hills, from the Jhelum eastward, also in South India and Burma. Cultivated throughout India on account of its fruit. Fl. H. S

12. TODDALIA, Juss.; Fl. Brit. Ind. i. 497.

Shrubs or trees, with strong pungent smell. L. alternate, 3-foliolate. Fl. unisexual, 2–3- or 5-merous, stamens alternating with petals. Ovary entire, 2–5-celled, 2 ovules in each cell. Seeds reniform, testa coriaceous, albumen fleshy, embryo curved.

1. **T. aculeata,** Pers.; Wight Ill. t. 66.—Syn. *Xanthoxylum floribundum,* Wall. Pl. As. Rar. t. 232. Vern. *Kānj,* Hind.; *Tunda para,* Uriya; *Merapu gandra,* Tel.; *Kyanza, Tsuhūn,* Burm.

A large scandent shrub, prickles on branchlets sharp, recurved, stems and branches armed with numerous large woody conical tubercles, terminated by short curved spines, young shoots rusty-tomentose, leaflets crenulate, greatly varying in length, in the semi-evergreen scrub near Madras 1½–2 in., elsewhere often 4 in. long (called *T. floribunda*). Fl. small, yellowish-green,

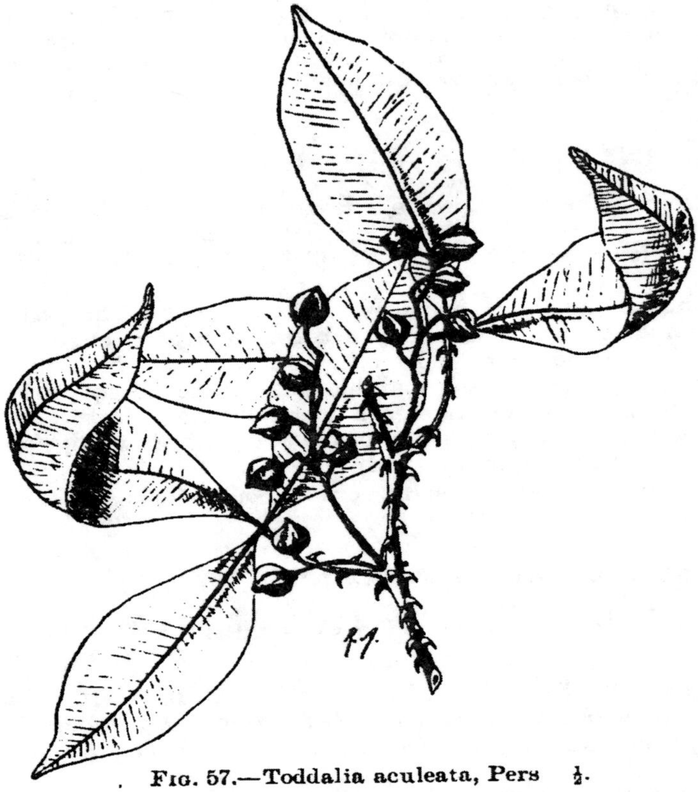

FIG. 57.—Toddalia aculeata, Pers ½.

in axillary panicles longer than petiole. Fr. globose, ¼ in. diam., orange-coloured, 3–5-celled.

Outer Himalaya, from Kumaon eastward, ascending to 5,000 ft. Khasi hills. Burma. Western Peninsula. Fl. October–January.—Ceylon, China. 2. **T. bilocularis**, W. et A.; Bedd. Ic. Ind. Or. t. 167. Western Ghats, Anamalais, Tinnevelli hills, Travancore, a tree, with dense dark green foliage, unarmed, leaflets (always 3, not 6–10, Fl. Brit. Ind.) quite entire, shining, 6–10 in. long. Fl. 2–3-merous.

Triphasia trifoliata, DC., is a small glabrous spiny shrub, the original home uncertain, frequently grown in gardens, often runs wild. L. trifoliolate, leaflets crenulate, the lateral smaller, oblique. Fl. white, fragrant, ½ in. long, axillary, solitary, or in few-fld. cymes. Calyx 3-lobed, petals 3 imbricate, stamens 6. Berry ovoid, ½ in. long, seeds 1–3.

13. LUVUNGA, Hamilton; Fl. Brit. Ind. i. 508.

Glabrous, climbing shrubs, usually armed with strong axillary spines. L. 3-foliolate, leaflets coriaceous, quite entire. Calyx cup-shaped, entire or irregularly 4–6-lobed. Petals 4–5, thick, imbricate. Stamens 8 or 10, inserted around a cupular fleshy disk, filaments subulate. Ovary 2–4-celled, style stout, deciduous, ovules 2, superposed in each cell. Berry large, rind thick, very resinous, seeds 2–3, cotyledons fleshy, albumen 0. Species 4, tropical Asia.

1. **L. eleutherandra**, Dalz.; Trimen Handb. Ceylon i. 224.

Branches long flexuose, set with stout, sharp, woody, often deflexed thorns 1 in. long, bark yellowish-white. Leaflets 3–8 in., elliptic or elliptic-oblong. Fl. white, fragrant, in glabrous axillary fasciculate racemes, fl. just before opening ⅓–½ in., filaments free. Berry globose, ¾ in. diam.

Western Ghats, evergreen forest, from the Konkan southwards. Fl. H. S. Ceylon, Malay Peninsula. Closely allied, and perhaps not specifically distinct: 2. **L. scandens**, Ham. Assam, Silhet, Burma, Cochinchina, Malay Peninsula and Archipelago, leaflets 5–12 in., elliptic-lanceolate, filaments more or less connate.

14. ATALANTIA, Correa; Fl. Brit. Ind. i. 511.

Evergreen shrubs or trees, mostly spinescent. L. 1-foliolate, coriaceous. Fl. in racemes or corymbs, calyx 3–5-lobed, petals imbricate, free or adnate to stamens. Stamens 6–10, rarely more, filaments free or connate, anthers oblong. Ovary 2–5-celled, style deciduous. Berry large, 1–5-seeded, rind thick, cotyledons fleshy, plano-convex, albumen 0. Species 13, Indo-Malayan region.

A. Filaments connate into a tube.

1. **A. monophylla,** Correa; Bedd. Fl. Sylv. Manual t. vii. f. 5.—Syn. *A. floribunda*, Wight Ic. t. 1611; *Limonia monophylla*, Linn.; Roxb. Cor. Pl. t. 83. Vern. *Rān Limbu*, *Makur Limbu*, Mar.; *Kata Narunga*, Uriya; *Katta naragam*, Tam.; *Adivi nimma*, *Yerra monu kudu*, Tel.

A glabrous shrub or small tree, wood yellow, hard, and close-grained, branches numerous, rigid, the older armed with short spines. L. 1–3 in., obtuse, generally notched at the tip. Fl. white, $\frac{1}{3}$–$\frac{1}{2}$ in. long, in axillary corymbs, pedicels slender, $\frac{1}{4}$–$\frac{1}{2}$ in. long. Calyx rupturing irregularly, petals 4, anthers 8, elliptic, inserted on the triangular teeth of the staminal tube, style long, cylindrical. Ovary on a short annular disk. Fr. 1 in. diam., 1-seeded.

FIG. 58.—Atalantia monophylla, Correa. $\frac{1}{2}$.

Kanara. Western districts of Mysore, Nilgiris. Hills of the northern Circars, the Ceded districts and the Karnatik. Sriharikota. Khasi hills, Andamans, Burma. Fl. Oct.–Dec. Ceylon, Malay Peninsula. *A. macrophylla*, Kurz, is a variety with larger leaves and fruits. 2. **A. racemosa,** W. et A. (*Sclerostylis atalantioides*, Wight Ic. t. 71). Tam., evergreen forests of the Western Ghats, from Khandala southwards, differs by short pedicels, fl. in racemes up to 8 in. long, calyx regularly 3–4-lobed, anther-cells divergent at base, disk inconspicuous. Possibly not specifically distinct.

B. Filaments free.

3. **A. missionis,** Oliver.—Syn. *Limonia missionis*, Wight Ic. t. 175.

A small thorny glabrous tree. L. ovate, apex obtuse or rounded. Fl. numerous, $\frac{1}{2}$ in. long, 4–5-merous, in erect panicles 1–3 in. long, stamens 8 or 10, filaments slender, quite distinct, anthers linear-oblong, ovary 4–5-celled, narrowed into a short stalk, 2 collateral ovules in each cell. Fr. globose, 1 in. diam., seeds numerous, globose, embedded in glutinous mucilage.

Evergreen forests of the Western Ghats, from North Kanara southwards. Hills of the Karnatik. Fl. Dec.–April.—Ceylon. 4. **A. ceylanica,** Oliver; Nilgiris, Anamalais, Ceylon. Fl. in short racemes, calyx 4-lobed, ovary 2-celled. 5. **A. caudata,** Hook. fil., Khasi hills, a glabrous, unarmed shrub, branches slender. L. elliptic-lanceolate, caudate acuminate, tip broad, 2-lobed. Fl. $\frac{1}{4}$–$\frac{1}{3}$ in. diam., white, fragrant, in short slender racemes.

15. PARAMIGNYA, Wight; Fl. Brit. Ind. i. 509.

Erect or climbing evergreen shrubs, often with axillary spines. L. 1-foliolate, quite entire. Fl. axillary, solitary or fascicled. Petals 4–5. Stamens 8–10, inserted at the base of a columnar disk (gynophore), filaments free, anthers linear. Berry ovoid, often contracted at base, rind thick, seeds 1–5. Species 6, tropical and subtropical Asia.

1. **P. monophylla,** Wight Ill. t. 42. Vern. *Kurwa wagutti*, Mar.

A large climbing thorny shrub, spines sharp, recurved. L. coriaceous, elliptic or elliptic-lanceolate, acuminate, 4–6 in. long. Petals ¾ in. long, calyx and outside of petals woolly pubescent, calyx lobes 5, short, rounded, filaments slightly hairy. Berry pyriform, 1 in. long or more.

Sikkim, Bhutan, Khasi hills, Tenasserim. Western Ghats, in evergreen forest. Fl. Sept.–March. Ceylon, Philippines. 2. **P. grandiflora,** Oliver; Tenasserim; erect, spines ½ in., calyx campanulate, lobes rounded, petals ¾ in., ovary pilose. 3. **P. armata,** Oliver; Bedd. Ic. t. 275. Western Ghats, Andamans, Ceylon, scandent, leaves

Fig. 59.—Paramignya monophylla, Wight. ½.

caudate-acuminate, calyx-segments broadly triangular, petals ½ in., lower ⅔ of filaments thick, woolly. The following species have smaller flowers: 4. **P. longispina,** Hook. fil. (*P. angulata*, Kurz), erect, spines in pairs below petioles, ½–1½ in. long, petals ⅛ in., berries 3–5-lobed, angular. 5. **P. Griffithii,** Hook. fil.; Assam, Burma, Malay Peninsula; scandent, spines ¼ in., calyx small, cup-shaped, with 5 sharp teeth, ovary tomentose. 6. **P. citrifolia,** Hook. fil.; Chittagong, Andamans; scandent, petals ⅓ in.

16. CITRUS, Linn.; Fl. Brit. Ind. i. 514.

Evergreen shrubs or trees, generally armed with axillary thorns, wood close- and even-grained. L. coriaceous, simple, petiole often winged. Fl. white, or tinged with red, scented, sometimes unisexual. Calyx cup-shaped, 4–5-cleft. Petals 4–5, rarely more, thick, gland-dotted, imbricate in bud. Stamens 20–60, filaments more or less connate in bundles. Ovary on a large annular or cup-shaped disk, cells numerous, ovules axile, biseriate, 4–8 in each cell. Fr. globose or oblong, rind full of glands filled with aromatic essential oil, pulp divided by thin membranous dissepiments into 9–15 cells, which are filled with numerous transverse vesicles containing sweet or acid juice. Seeds few in each cell, testa leathery, albumen none, embryo straight with a short radicle and thick oily cotyledons, which in the germinating seed remain enclosed in the testa. Often 2 or 3 embryos in one seed.

1. **C. medica**, Linn.; Brandis F. Fl. 51. The *Citron*, *Lemon*, *Sweet* and *acid Lime*. Vern. *Nimbu*.

Young shoots glabrous, purple. L. glabrous, 3–6 in., elliptic-oblong, ovate or ovate-lanceolate, petioles naked or winged. Fl. white, often pink outside, unisexual, stamens 25–55. Generally bears flowers and fruit at all or at most seasons of the year.

Found by myself apparently wild (1) in the outer valleys of Kumaon (1875, 81), (l. broadly elliptic); (2) on the Pachmarhi hills, Centr. Prov. (1869, 77), (l. obtuse, elliptic or obovate-oblong); (3) in the outer valleys of Sikkim (1879), (l. like 2); (4) Damra hât, Garo hills (1879), a tree 6 ft. girth, 40 ft. high (l. elliptic); (5) Upper Yunzalin valley above Lomatee in swamps and near streams (1880) (l. elliptic-oblong, acute). Reported as wild in the eastern Dūn, on the Satpura hills and the Western Ghats in the Bombay Presidency (Talbot) in Chittagong, and on the Khasi hills (Hooker & Thomson).

Of the more important cultivated forms may be mentioned: *a*. The *Citron*. Fr. large, oblong, obovoid or irregularly shaped, and often lobed or fingered, rind thick, very aromatic. *b*. The *Lemon* (*Zitrone*, German). Fr. ovoid, pale yellow, knobbed, rind thin, pulp abundant, very acid. *c*. The *acid Lime* of India. *d*. The *sweet Lime* of India; fl. often pure white; fr. globose, smooth, skin thin, adhering to the pulp, juice sweet, not aromatic.

2. **C. Aurantium**, Linn.; The *bitter* and *sweet Orange*. Vern. *Narengi*.

Young shoots glabrous, greenish-white. L. glabrous, 3–6 in., elliptic or ovate, acuminate, petioles naked or winged, wings often obovate, as large as the blade or nearly so. Fl. pure white, bisexual, stamens 15–30. Fr. globose, often depressed. Bears flowers and fruit generally at one season of the year only.

Found wild or apparently wild in Garhwal (Thomson), Kumaon (Strachey), Sikkim and the Khasi hills (Hooker), Manipur (Watt), mountain forests in the Peninsula (Beddome).

Of the more commonly cultivated forms may be mentioned: *a*. The *loose-skinned Orange*, grown at many places in India and Burma, on a large scale in the valley above Chela, below Cherra Punji, and at other places on the south face of the Khasi hills, where they ripen in autumn. Also at Nagpore, where they yield two crops in the year, the first crop from November to January, and the second in March and April. *b*. *The common sweet Orange*, the skin tightly adhering to the pulp. The *bitter* or *Seville* Orange is rarely cultivated in India.

The excellent account of the Oranges and Lemons cultivated on the island of Madeira in Lowe, Manual Flora of Madeira, 1868. p. 71, restricts *C. medica* to 1 (*a*) and calls 1(*b*, *c*, *d*) *C. Limonium*, while he regards 2 (*a*) as a separate species, *C. nobilis*, Lour. Engler, in Engler u. Prantl iii. 4. 200, maintains *C. nobilis* and classes 1 (*c*) as a separate species, *C. hystrix*, DC.

3. **C. decumana**, Linn., the *Shaddock* or *Pumelo*, young shoots pubescent, rind thick, vesicles of pulp distinct, is also cultivated in gardens.

ORDER XXVI. SIMARUBACEÆ. Gen. Pl. i. 306.

(In Engler u. Prantl iii. 4. 355 *Balanites* is placed under *Zygophyllaceæ*).

Shrubs or trees with bitter bark, l. alternate, simple or compound, not gland-dotted, stipules none, sometimes stipular prickles, hairs almost always 1-celled. Fl. regular, often unisexual, sepals 3–5, usually connate, petals 3–5, mostly imbricate in bud. Stamens as many as petals, or double the number, inserted outside the disk, which is annular, cupular, sometimes elongate into a gynophore, filaments free. Ovary of 1–5 usually more or less distinct carpels, generally 1 ovule in each. Fr. carpels 1-seeded.

A. L. simple, entire.
  L. 7–10 in. long, elliptic-oblong coriaceous, shining . 1. SAMADERA.
  L. 1 in. long, linear spathulate, silky velvety . . SURIANA (p. 124).

B. L. 2-foliate, fl. 2-sexual, 5-merous, stamens 10 . . . 2. BALANITES.

C. L. imparipinnate or 3-foliolate.
  Fl. bisexual, 4–6-merous, stamens 8–12 . . . . . 3. HARRISONIA.
  Fl. polygamous, fr. winged . . . . 4. AILANTHUS.
  Fl. polygamous or unisexual, fr. not winged.
    Leaflets 15–20 pair, coriaceous, fl. 5-merous, stamens 5 EURYCOMA (p. 127).
    Leaflets 1–6 pair, fl. 4–5-merous, stamens 4–5, drupes 2–4.
      Drupes supported by persistent calyx and petals . 5. PICRASMA.
      Calyx and petals deciduous . . . . . . 6. BRUCEA.

1. SAMADERA, Gaertn.; Fl. Brit. Ind. i. 518.

Species 7, from Madagascar to Polynesia.

S. indica, Gaertn.; Wight Ill. t. 68. Vern. *Karinghota*, Mal.; *Kathè*, Burm. A small glabrous tree, wood soft, bark transversely cracked. L. simple, coriaceous, shining, elliptic-oblong, quite entire, 7–10 in. long. Fl. bisexual, 4-merous, pinkish-yellow, in pedunculate umbels, petals oblong, ¾–1 in. long, stamens 8, filaments with a small hairy scale at base, ovary on a gynophore, deeply 4-lobed. Fruit of one carpel, thickly coriaceous, shining, compressed, keeled, 2 by 1½ in.

South Konkan and Malabar on banks of streams, Mergui. Fl. March.—Ceylon, Indian Archipelago. Bark (*niepa*) used as a febrifuge. Oil made of the seeds. *S. lucida*, Wall. Pl. As. Rar. t. 168; Tenasserim, Andaman islands, umbels on short peduncles, fr. smaller strongly reticulate, probably is only a variety.

Suriana maritima, Linn., is a small shrub common on the sea coast throughout the tropics. On the Andamans, may be found on the coast of Burma, rare in Ceylon. Leaves simple entire, linear-spathulate, 1 in. long, silky velvety. Fl. yellow on short axillary racemes, petals ⅓ in. long.

2. BALANITES, Delile; Fl. Brit. Ind. i. 522.

Shrubs or small trees, usually armed with axillary or supra-axillary spines, leaves 2-foliate, leaflets entire. Fl. bisexual, 5-merous, stamens 10, inserted at the base of the fleshy cup-shaped 10-furrowed disk. Ovary pilose, 5-celled, 1 ovule in each cell. Fr. a drupe, endocarp bony or crustaceous, seed 1. Cotyledons thick, plane-convex, albumen 0. Species 2 or 3, in the dry regions of North Africa, Abyssinia, Arabia and Syria.

B. Roxburghii, Planchon; Brandis, F. Fl. 59.—Syn. *B. ægyptiaca*, Wight, Ic. t. 274. Vern. *Hingu, Hingan, Hingōta*, Hind.; *Thit-palwe*, Burm. A scraggy shrub, in favourable situations a small tree 30 ft. high, wood yellowish white, moderately hard; medullary rays short, white, conspicuous in the darker tissue; bark yellow or cinereous; the roots spread far and throw up rootsuckers at a considerable distance from the trunk, thorns sharp, often leaf and fl. bearing. Branchlets, young leaves and inflorescence pubescent, in dry localities hoary-tomentose. Fl. white or green, fragrant, in lateral racemes or fascicles. Drupe ovoid, 1½–2 in. long, 5-grooved, pulp bitter with an offensive greasy smell, stone hard, tubercled.

Chiefly in the drier parts of India and Burma, as far north as Delhi, common in the open country, particularly on stiff clay soil. New leaves in March, fl. H.S. This species is united with *B. ægyptiaca*, Delile, in Engler u. Prantl iii 4. 355.

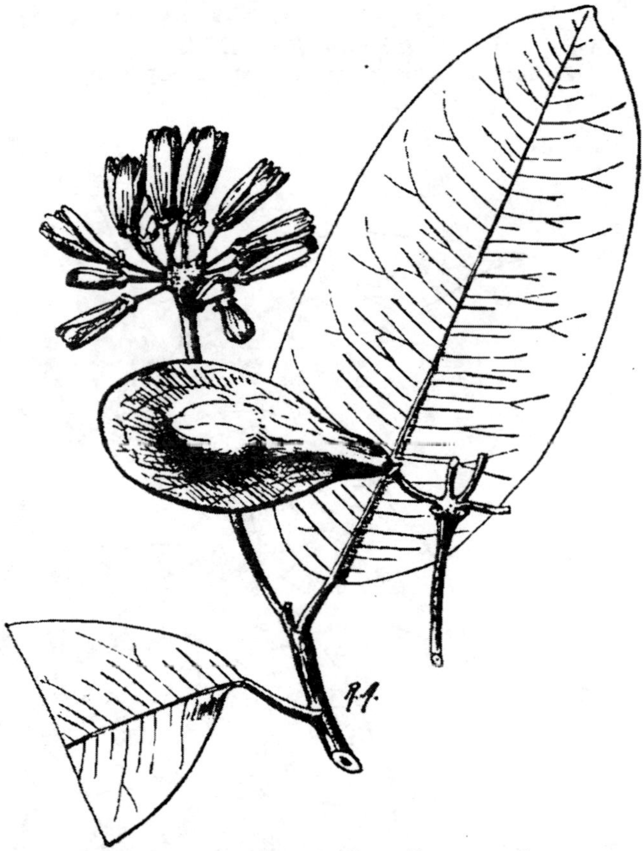

FIG. 60.—Samadera indica, Gaertn. ½.

3. HARRISONIA, R. Brown; Fl. Brit. Ind. i. 519

Spiny shrubs, leaves imparipinnate or 3-foliolate. Fl. 4–6-merous, bisexual, in corymbose racemes. Stamens 8–12, hairy scales at the base of filaments. Ovary globose 4–5-celled. Species 4, tropical Africa, Asia and Australia.

1. **H. Bennetii**, Hook. fil.; Kurz, F. Fl. i. 203. Vern. *Tabu*, Burm.

A small deciduous tree, armed with short straight stipular prickles, young shoots puberulous. Leaves imparipinnate, the common petiole narrowly winged, leaflets opposite, obliquely ovate, 1 in. long, fl. white, pentamerous, corymbs at the ends of branches. Fruit globose, 2–5-celled, ⅓ in. diam.

Dry forests of Upper and Lower Burma, fl. April. Malay Archipelago, South China. A variety, possibly a distinct species, in Upper Burma, branchlets and leaves grey-pubescent, fl. 5–7-merous, scales half the length of filaments. 2. **H. Brownii**, A. Juss., Andamans, Philippines, North Australia, has 3-foliolate leaves, leaflets coarsely serrate, the terminal largest, fl. 4-merous.

4. AILANTHUS, Desf.; Fl. Brit. Ind. i. 518.

Large trees, wood soft, white, leaves pinnate, approximate at the ends of branches. Fl. polygamous, in large axillary panicles, calyx small, 5-cleft, petals 5, spreading, valvate, the edges bent inwards. ♂ : Stamens 10. ⚥ : Stamens 2–3. ♀ : Stamens 0. Carpels 1–5 more or less distinct. Fruit of 1–5 flat membranous linear-oblong carpels, the seed in the middle. Species 7, India, Malaya, China, Australia.

1. **A. excelsa**, Roxb. Cor. Pl. t. 23; Wight, Ill. t. 67; Brandis, F. Fl. 58.

Vern. *Arua*, Rajputana; *Maharukh*, Hind., Mar.; *Maha nim*, Uriya; *Pedda manu*, Tel.; *Matti Pongilyam*, Mal.

Deciduous, bark grey, leaves tomentose, up to 3 ft. long, leaflets 8–14 pair,

FIG. 61.—Ailanthus malabarica, DC. ½.

nearly opposite, from an unequal-sided base broadly falcate-lanceolate, deeply serrate, often lobed. Panicles ample, shorter than leaves, fl. yellowish, petals glabrous, filaments glabrous, shorter than anthers, ripe carpels 2 in.

Indigenous in the Peninsula, commonly planted throughout India, as far north as

Saharanpur. Leafless in the early part of C.S. New leaves in March, April. Fl. April, May. 2. **A. glandulosa**, Desf. Japan, China, cultivated in Northern India, leaves pubescent or nearly glabrous, leaflets with a few glandular teeth near the base, otherwise entire, petals woolly-tomentose inside, filaments larger than anthers, hispid at base, ripe carpels 1–2 in.

3. **A. malabarica**, DC.; Wight, Ic. t. 1604; Bedd. Fl. Sylv. t. 122. Vern. *Dhup, Guggul dhup*, Kan.; *Peru*, Tam.

A lofty tree, bark thick, rough, often with bright reddish grains of resin, leaflets 5–10 pair, glabrous, entire, lanceolate, filaments glabrous, much longer than anthers, ripe carpels oblong rounded at both ends 3–5 by ¾ in.

Evergreen forests along the Western Ghats from the Konkan southwards, from the coast to 3,000 ft. Pegu Yoma, eastern slopes, Kurz, F. Fl. i. 201. Fl. February, March. The resin (*matti pal*) used in medicine and as incense. Ceylon, Malay Peninsula, China.

Eurycoma longifolia, Jack, Tenasserim, Malay Peninsula and Archipelago, is an evergreen shrub or small tree, leaves imparipinnate, leaflets 15–20 pair, coriaceous, oblong-lanceolate, entire, shining above, pale beneath, panicles axillary, rusty-glandular, at the ends of branches, shorter than leaves, fl. brownish-red, polygamous, pentamerous, stamens 5, alternating with petals, 5 two-lobed scales (staminodia) opposite to petals. Drupes 3–5, stipitate, hard, ovoid ½–⅝ in. long.

5. PICRASMA, Bl.; Fl. Brit. Ind. i. 520.

All parts very bitter, leaves imparipinnate, fl. unisexual, 4–5-merous, in corymbose panicles. Stamens 4–5, carpels 3–5, distinct on a thick disk, styles free at base and top, connate in the middle. Fr. of 1–3 fleshy or coriaceous drupes, supported by the persistent calyx and petals. A straight embryo in fleshy albumen. Species 6, tropical and subtropical countries of both hemispheres.

1. **P. quassioides**, Bennett; Brandis, F. Fl. 39. Vern. *Tutāi, Tithāi*, Trita, Pb., N.W.

A tall, scrambling shrub. L. and inflorescence pubescent. Leaflets opposite, nearly sessile, 4–6 pair, serrate. Fl. small, greenish, generally pentamerous. Drupes black, ¼ in. diam.

Outer Himalaya, Kashmir to Nepal, ascending occasionally to 8,000 ft. Bhutan. Fl. April–June. China.

2. **P. javanica**, Blume; King in Journ. As. Soc. Beng. vol. 62. ii. (1893) 228 (includes *P. nepalensis*, Benn., and *P. andamanica*, Kurz).

An evergreen glabrous tree, leaflets 1–3 pair, entire, acuminate. Fl. tetramerous, greenish-white, drupes 2–4, white, ½ in. diam.

Nepal, Sikkim, Khasi hills, Andamans, Lower Burma. Fl. March. China, Cochinchina, Java.

6. BRUCEA, Miller; Fl. Brit. Ind. i. 520.

All parts very bitter, leaves imparipinnate, fl. polygamous, minute, tetramerous, in axillary panicles. Stamens 4, inserted beneath the 4-lobed disk. Ovary deeply 4-lobed. Drupes 4, ovoid, somewhat fleshy. Albumen 0. Species 6, tropical, from Africa to Australia.

1. **B. sumatrana**, Roxb.; Kurz, F. Fl. i. 202.

A large evergreen shrub, branchlets, leaves and inflorescence tawny pubescent, leaflets opposite, 4–6 pair, ovate-lanceolate, coarsely serrate. Fl. purple, in small distant racemiform panicles, often as long as leaves. Drupes black, ovoid, ¼ in. long.

Assam, Tenasserim. Fl. March. Malay Peninsula and Archipelago, South China. 2. **B. mollis**, Wall. Sikkim, Khasi hills, Bhutan, Manipur, Burma (Thoungyeen, D.B., March 1862) leaflets nearly glabrous, lanceolate, entire, drupes ½ in. long.

ORDER XXVII. OCHNACEÆ. Gen. Pl. i. 316.

Shrubs or trees. L. alternate, simple, glabrous, stipulate. Fl. yellow or orange, on jointed pedicels. Sepals 5, free, imbricate, petals 5 or more. Stamens 10 or indefinite, anthers linear. Ovary deeply 3–10-lobed and -celled, cells 1 ovulate, style 1 slender. Fr. of 3–10 drupes, sessile upon the enlarged torus or disk. Albumen none.

Stamens ∞ . . . . 1. OCHNA.
Stamens 10 . . . . 2. GOMPHIA.

1. OCHNA, Schreber; Fl. Brit. Ind. i. 523.

Deciduous. L. serrate, stipules distinct, almost intrapetiolar. Fl. yellow, sepals coloured, persistent, petals 5–12, stamens ∞, shorter than petals, anthers generally opening by terminal pores, filaments often persistent. Species 25–30, tropical Asia and Africa.

A. Filaments shorter than anthers.

1. **O. squarrosa**, Roxb. Cor. Pl. t. 89; Wight, Ill. t. 69. Vern. *Koniari*, Uriya.

A shrub or small tree. L. elliptic or elliptic-lanceolate, acute, narrowed into a short petiole, 3–5 in. long, finely serrulate, sec. n. numerous, slender, parallel. Fl. while in leaf, fragrant, in corymbose racemes, mostly at the ends of short leafless woody branchlets, pedicels 1–1½ in., petals 5–12, as long as sepals, anthers many times longer than the short filaments. Drupes ⅓ in. long, fruiting sepals generally erect.

Assam, Burma, Western Peninsula. Fl. Febr., March. Ceylon. To this possibly belongs *O. brevipes*, Planchon, Pegu. 2. **O. fruticulosa**, Kurz, F. Fl. i. 206, hills east of Toungoo, ascending to 5,000 ft. (Gallatly, 1877) also in the Eng forest of Upper Burma (Smales, *Indaing-seni*, Burm.), a low shrub 2–3 ft., stems perennial slender, grey, fl. 1–1½ in. across, appearing before the leaves in few-fld. umbels, at the end of short branchlets, petals 5. 3. **O. pumila**, Ham.; Brandis, F. Fl. 60. Subhimalayan tract, chiefly in Sal forests, from the Dehra Dūn to Sikkim, Eastern Satpura hills, a low undershrub with a perennial rootstock, throwing up annually (after the jungle fires of the hot season) a number of short subherbaceous stems, bearing leaves and flowers, leaves oblanceolate, serrate with cuspidate teeth. Fl. appear with the leaves, 1½–2 in. across, in 2–4-fld. bracteate umbels on peduncles 2–3 in. long, petals 5.

4. **O. Gamblei**, King mss.; *Kukka movi*, Tel.

A large shrub or small tree, branches stiff erect. L. coriaceous, glaucous, often whitish, broadly elliptic, obtuse, sometimes obovate, sessile, often with cordate base, 3–5 × 2–3 in. Fl. ¾–1 in. across, on slender pedicels, 1½–2 in. long, in dense many-fld. corymbs at the ends of short woody leafless branchlets, sepals 4–5, petals 6–8, filaments ¼–½ length of anthers.

Western Peninsula, from Chanda to Travancore, common on the dry rocky hills of Anantapur, Cuddapah, and on the Veligondas. Kambakum hill (D.B. 1881). Fl. H. S.

B. Filaments as long as anthers or longer.

5. **O. Wallichii**, Planchon; Kurz, F. Fl. i. 205.—Syn. *O. andamanica*, Kurz. Vern. *Yodaya*, Lower, *Indaing seni*, Upper Burma.

A tree, attaining 50 ft. L. 4–8 in. long, inflorescence similar to *A. squarrosa*, fl. appearing with or before the leaves, petals 5, much longer than sepals, anthers shorter than filaments, drupes $\frac{1}{3}$–$\frac{1}{2}$ in. long on a large hemispherical disk.

Silhet, Andamans, Nicobars, Lower and Upper Burma. Fl. Febr.–April. Malay Peninsula.

6. **O. Wightiana,** Wall.; Wight, Ic. t. 223; Trimen Handb. Ceylon i. 233.
A shrub or small tree, glabrous. L. $1\frac{1}{2}$–2 in. Fl. after the leaves, solitary or 2–3 together, $\frac{1}{2}$ in. across, anthers as long as stamens.

Southern part of Western Peninsula, fl. May, June. Ceylon.

2. GOMPHIA, Schreber; Fl. Brit. Ind. i. 525 (*Ouratea*, Aubl.; Engl. u. Prantl iii. 6. 140).

Species 80–100, tropical, more than half in America, a number in Africa and a few in Asia.

1. **G. angustifolia,** Vahl; Trimen Hanbd. Ceylon i. 235.
A small, much-branched tree, glabrous. L. 3–7 in., coriaceous, lanceolate, secondary nerves ∞, parallel, joined by distinct intramarginal veins. Fl. $\frac{1}{2}$ in. across, in pyramidal, terminal and axillary panicles, petals twice as long as sepals, obovate, narrowed into a linear claw, stamens 10, anthers nearly sessile, opening by terminal pores. Ripe carpels quite distinct, on the sides of a large convex disk.

West side of the Peninsula, chiefly in evergreen forests, from the South Konkan southwards. Fl. R. S. 2. **G. sumatrana,** Jack, closely allied, differs by larger petals and more diffuse panicles, and is given by Kurz, F. Fl. i. 206, for Tenasserim on the sea coast

ORDER XXVIII. BURSERACEÆ. Gen. Pl. i. 321.

Resinous trees or shrubs. L. generally alternate, imparipinnate, 3-foliolate, in some cases 1-foliolate, stipules generally 0. Fl. mostly small, bisexual or polygamous. Calyx 3–5-cleft, petals 3–5. Stamens as many as petals or twice their number, inserted on the edge or outside at the base of disk, anthers 2-celled, dehiscent longitudinally. Ovary free, 2–5-celled, ovules generally two in each cell, hanging side by side from the top of the central angle. Fruit drupaceous, either indehiscent with a 3–6-celled hard stone, or valvately dehiscent with several separate stones. Albumen 0, cotyledons often lobed, generally twisted or crumpled.

Resin canals in the bast (phloëm), in some species also in the pith.
- Fr. dehiscent, 3-valved . . . . 1. BOSWELLIA.
- Fr. an indehiscent drupe.
  - Calyx 3-fid, valvate, drupe usually trigonous . . . 2. CANARIUM.
  - Calyx 4–6-toothed or lobed.
    - Calyx campanulate 10-ribbed, 5-cleft, lined by a thin crenate disk . . . . 3. GARUGA.
    - Calyx 4–6-lobed, disk annular . . . . . . 4. BURSERA.
    - Calyx 4–6-toothed, small, fl. paniculate . . . . 5. PROTIUM.
    - Calyx 4-toothed, fl. few, fasciculate . . . . . 6. BALSAMODENDRON.

Filicium, Thwaites, is classed under *Sapindaceæ*.

1. BOSWELLIA, Roxb.; Fl. Brit. Ind. i. 527.

Species 10. North-Eastern tropical Africa, excepting *B. serrata*.

B. serrata, Roxb.—Syn. *B. glabra*, Roxb. Cor. Pl. t. 207; Bedd. Fl. Sylv. t. 124; *B. thurifera*, Colebrooke; Brandis, F. Fl. 61. Vern. *Salai*, *Saler*, Hind.; *Salga*, Sonth.; *Andaka*, Tel.; *Maddi*, Kan.; *Kundrikam*, Tam.

A deciduous, middle-sized tree with a spreading flat crown. Bark nearly ½ in. thick, greenish ash-coloured, peeling off in thin smooth flakes. Young shoots and leaves pubescent, with simple hairs. L. imparipinnate, crowded at the ends of branches, leaflets 8–15 pair, opposite or nearly opposite, sessile, lanceolate, more or less deeply crenate, apex generally obtuse. Fl. bisexual, calyx small 5–7-cleft, petals 5–7. Stamens 10–12, inserted at the base of the red annular, fleshy disk. Ovary 3-celled, half immersed in the disk, 2 collateral ovules in each cell. Fr. 3-valved, the valves separating from the dissepiments, which remain attached to the axis. Seeds 3, enclosed in heart-shaped stones attached to the inner angle. Cotyledons trifid, lobes laciniate, radicle superior.

Subhimalayan tract, from the Sutlej eastwards and throughout the drier parts of the Western Peninsula to within 10–20 miles of the Western Ghats. Always in deciduous forests, and often gregarious, forming open forests, associated with *Sterculia urens*. The leaves fall about March and April, the fresh foliage comes out in June. Fl. when the tree is leafless, sometimes before the old leaves fall or after the fresh leaves have appeared. Coppices well and grows readily from cuttings.

2. CANARIUM, Linn.; Fl. Brit. Ind. i. 531.

Evergreen, balsamiferous trees. L. imparipinnate, sometimes stipulate, leaflets coriaceous. Fl. polygamous, the male in long, the female (with rudimentary stamens) in short panicles, usually trimerous, calyx cup-shaped or campanulate. Stamens 6, filaments connate into a tube, or free and inserted on the edge of or outside an annular disk, ovary 2–3-celled, ovules 2 in each cell. Drupe more or less distinctly trigonous, stone 1–3-celled, cotyledons contortuplicate. Species 30–50, tropics of the Old World.

A. Filaments connate into a tube.

1. **C. strictum**, Roxb.; Bedd. Fl. Sylv. t. 128; King in Journ. As. Soc. Beng. vol. 62 (1893), t. 11. *Black dammer tree.* Vern. *Manda dhup, Ral dhup*, Kan.; *Kundri Kam*, Tam.; *Thelli*, Mal.

A very large tree, the young foliage brilliant crimson, branchlets, petiole, midrib and nerves beneath densely clothed with soft reddish-brown tomentum, leaflets 3–4 pair, serrate or crenulate while young, 3–6 in. long, sec. n. prominent beneath. ♂: Fl. ⅓ in. long, in a narrow racemiform panicle 6–9 in. long, calyx tubular with 3 shallow broad teeth, petals coriaceous, oblong, rudimentary ovary depressed, lobed, hispid. ♀: Fl. ½ in. long, in short few-fld. racemes. Drupe 1½ in. long.

Evergreen forests along the Western Ghats to 4,500 ft., from the Konkan southwards. Fl. H. S. Fr. C. S. A black dammar exudes from incisions in the trunk, and is an article of local trade. 2. **C. bengalense**, Roxb.; King l.c. t. 10. Assam and Silhet, (Vern. *Nerebi*, Sibsagar). A tall glabrous tree, leaflets 5–10 pair, entire, 3–7 in. long, calyx campanulate, 3 broad shallow teeth, drupe 1½ in. A clear amber-like resin exudes from wounds in the bark. 3. **C. euphyllum**, Kurz. North Arakan and South Andaman, branchlets very stout, youngest shoots puberulous. L. glabrous when full grown, 2–3 ft. long, leaflets with an unequal-sided base, rounded or subcordate, calyx cut half-way down into 3 broad teeth, drupe ovoid, not trigonous, 1¾ in. long.

4. **C. sikkimense**, King, l.c. t. 12. Vern. *Gogul dhup*, Nepal.

A very tall tree, wood white, open grained, soft, light, branchlets, petioles and under side of leaves rusty-tomentose. Leaflets 5 pair, broadly ovate or elliptic, minutely crenate-serrate, upper surface glabrous, shining. Calyx campanulate, cut to ⅓ its length into 3 broad obtuse teeth. Drupe narrowly cylindric or obovoid, 1¾ in. long.

Sikkim, outer valleys to 3,000 ft. Resin used as incense. 5. **C. resiniferum**, Brace, Assam and Khasi hills, King l.c. t. 13 (*Dhuna* or *Dhua*, Assam), leaflets almost glabrous, resin used to make torches.

B. Filaments free, flat, inserted on the edge of or outside the disk.

5. **C. coccineo-bracteatum**, Kurz, South Andaman, shoots minutely pubescent, leaves 10–18 in. long, stipules large, pectinately lobed, bracts longer than buds, tomentose outside, scarlet. 7. **C. Manii**, King, South Andaman, branchlets slender, scurfy-puberulous, leaflets 2–3 pair, entire, quite glabrous, thinly coriaceous, bracts oblong obtuse, tomentose, longer than buds. Drupes ovoid-ellipsoid, not trigonous, 1–1½ in. long, calyx persistent.

3. GARUGA, Roxb.; Fl. Brit. Ind. i. 528.

Species 3, Indo-Malayan.

G. pinnata, Roxb. Cor. Pl. t. 208; Bedd. Fl. Sylv. t. 118; Brandis, F. Fl. t. 13. Vern. *Kharpat*, *Kaikar*, Hind.; *Dabdabi*, Nep.; *Armu*, Kol; *Karur*,

FIG. 62.—Bursera serrata, Colebr. ½.

Sonth.; *Gharri*, Gond; *Kudak*, Mar. *Godda*, Kan.; *Garuga*, *gargu*, Tel.; *Chinyôk*, Burm.

A large deciduous tree, young shoots and inflorescence grey-pubescent. L. imparipinnate, crowded near the ends of branches, leaflets 6–9 pair, opposite or nearly so, lanceolate or ovate-lanceolate, crenate. Fl. yellow, in axillary panicles, several at the ends of branches. Calyx campanulate, 10-ribbed, 5-cleft, lined by a thin disk with a crenate margin, on the edge of which the 5 petals and 10 stamens are inserted. Ovary 4–5-celled, 2 collateral ovules in each cell. Fr. a globose fleshy drupe, enclosing 2, rarely more, bony, 1-seeded, tuberculated stones.

Subhimalayan tract and outer valleys, ascending to 3,500 ft. from the Jumna eastwards, often in Sāl forest. Deciduous forests in the greater part of the Western Peninsula and Burma. Leafless during the greater part of the dry season. Fresh foliage, April or May, with the fl. or after them. Grows readily from cuttings. Fr. eaten raw and pickled.

4. BURSERA, Linn.; Fl. Brit. Ind. i. 530.

As here accepted, 40 species, mostly of tropical America.

B. serrata, Colebr.; Kurz, F. Fl. i. 208.—Syn. *Protium serratum*, Engler. Vern. *Najor*, Assam; *Kandior*, Kol; *Suru potri moi*, Uriya; *Thadi*, Lower, *Yit padi*, Upper Burma.

A large evergreen tree. L. imparipinnate, pubescent or nearly glabrous, leaflets opposite, elliptic-oblong, acuminate, serrate or nearly entire, blade 3–4, petals ½ in., tertiary nerves conspicuously reticulate. Panicles axillary, lax, shorter than leaves. Fl. green, pentamerous, calyx small, lobes rounded, petals valvate in bud, stamens 10, nearly equal, ovary hairy, surrounded by a broad crenate disk. Drupes on thick peduncles, globose, often 2–3-furrowed, red, ¾ in. diam., containing 1–3 one-seeded nuts.

Assam, Cachar, Chittagong, Chota Nagpur, Orissa, Northern Circars. Burma, Upper and Lower. Fl. March, April.

5. PROTIUM, W. et A.; Fl. Brit. Ind. i. 530.

Aromatic trees. L. 3-foliolate or imparipinnate. Fl. polygamous, small, in much-branched panicles, 4–6-merous, disk lining the bottom of the calyx tube, stamens 8–12, unequal, on the free edge of the disk. Ovary 2–4-celled, ovules 3 in each cell. The only real difference between this and *Balsamodendron* is in the inflorescence. Engler unites the 2 genera under *Commiphora* and Trimen includes *P. caudatum* under *Balsamodendron*. As here defined, *Protium* includes 3–4 species.

1. **P. caudatum,** W. et A.; Bedd. Fl. Sylv. t. 125. Vern. *Kanda ragi*, *Konda mamidi*, Tel.; *Kiluvai*, Tam.; *Konda mavu*, Kan.

A middle-sized deciduous tree, bark smooth, flakes off in large pieces. L. imparipinnate, leaflets opposite, 1–5 pair, 2 in. long, broad ovate-lanceolate, as a rule long-acuminate. Panicles dichotomous, lax; linear bracts at the base of ramifications. Ovary 2-celled. Fr. a fleshy drupe, ½ in. diam., stone 1-seeded.

Western Peninsula, the young leaves appear with the flowers in March. Ceylon. 2. **P. pubescens,** W. et A., Anamalai hills, closely allied, leaflets pubescent, obtusely acuminate, panicle dense, ramifications not dichotomous.

6. BALSAMODENDRON, Kunth; Fl. Brit. Ind. i. 529.

Small trees or shrubs, yielding aromatic resin; branches often thorny. L. crowded at the ends of short branchlets, imparipinnate or 1–3-foliolate. Fl. polygamous, fasciculate on arrested branchlets, calyx campanulate or urceolate 3–4-cleft, petals 3–4, stamens 6–8, on the edge of an erect cupular disk. Ovary 4-celled, surrounded by the disk, 2 collateral ovules in each cell. Fr. a drupe, the rind splitting more or less irregularly into 2–4 valves, leaving the pulp exposed, which encloses the nuts, which are bony, 1-seeded and partially connate. Embryo straight, the radicle pointing upwards, cotyledons thin, crumpled and plaited. Species 10, India, Arabia, tropical and southern Africa.

1. **B. Berryi**, Arn.; Bedd. Fl. Sylv. t. 126; Brandis, F. Fl. 65.

A small fragrant, very thorny tree, branchlets spinescent, at right angles to

FIG. 63.—Balsamodendron Berryi, Arn. ½.

branches. L. 3-foliolate, petioles slender, leaflets sessile, obovate, glabrous, generally entire, the terminal larger than the lateral ones. Fl. subsessile, fascicled, disk small, bearing 6–8 stamens, alternately smaller, the longer ones opposite to petals, in the male flower stamens longer than calyx. Drupe oblong, apiculate.

Dry forests in the southern Deccan, cultivated as a hedge plant all over South India. Fl. February, March. Dry parts of Ceylon. 2. **B. pubescens**, Stocks, Hook. Journ. Bot. i. (1849) t. 9 (*Commiphora Stocksiana*, Engler) (*Baya*, *Bai*, Baluch.) Baluchistan and hills of South-Western Sind, as far south as Karachi, an unarmed pubescent shrub or small tree,leaves trifoliolate, generally crowded on short arrested branchlets, distant on vigorous shoots and then often imparipinnate. Fl. 4-merous, stamens 8, equal. Drupe red, pulp orange-coloured.

3. **B. Mukul**, Hook.; Stocks in Hook. Journ. Bot. i. (1849) t. 8. Brandis, F. Fl. 64. Vern. *Gūgal*, Sind, Rajputana.

A stunted shrub or dwarfed tree, branches thick, spreading, branchlets often spinescent. Trunk knotty, the outer bark coming off in rough flakes, leaving exposed an inner layer, which is bright, shining, and peels off in rolls like thin paper. L. generally approximate at the ends of thick short arrested branchlets, obovate, almost sessile, the tapering base entire, the upper part toothed. On luxuriant shoots the leaves are distant, trifoliolate, the lateral leaflets small. Fl. unisexual, subsessile, 2 or 3 together, petals 4–5, strap-shaped, stamens 8–10, alternately longer. Drupe red when ripe.

4. **B. Roxburghii**, Arn. (*Commiphora Agallocha*, Engler), Assam, Silhet, East Bengal, spinescent. L. on slender petioles, at the ends of which are often 2 minute leaflets, fl. red.

Sind, Baluchistan, Kattiawar, Rajputana, Khandeish, Bellary. Fl. Aug.–October.

ORDER XXIX. MELIACEÆ. Gen. Pl. i. 327.

Trees or shrubs. L. alternate, generally pinnate, leaflets in most genera quite entire, stipules 0. Fl. regular, mostly bisexual, cymose, cymes generally panicled. Calyx small, mostly 4–5-cleft. Petals free, rarely connate. Stamens as a rule double the number of petals, filaments generally united into a tube, anthers 2-celled. Disk, when present, between stamens and ovary, often forming a tube, enclosing the ovary partly or entirely. Ovary 3–5-celled, style 1 or stigma sessile; ovules, either 1–2 in each cell or numerous. Fr. a capsule or indehiscent, mostly with coriaceous pericarp, seeds with or without albumen.

Engler in Engler u. Prantl iii. 4. 171 places *Chloroxylon* under *Rutaceæ* chiefly on account of the translucent glands in the leaves, which form one of the distinguishing characters of that order.

A. Ovules 1 or 2 in each cell, seeds not winged.

I. Staminal tube half the length of stamens or less, or stamens free. Leaflets always entire.

- L. imparipinnate, leaflets 9. Panicles axillary, corymbose, long pedunculate, tube half the length of stamens, capsule 2-valved . . . . 1. HEYNEA.
- L. imparipinnate, 3-foliolate or 1-foliolate. Panicles terminal or axillary, stamens free or connate, fr. tomentose . . . . 2. WALSURA.
- Leaflets often serrate, stamens connate only at base, fr. scarlet . . . . CIPADESSA (p. 137).

II. Staminal tube complete, oblong or linear.

- L. simple . . . . 3. TURRÆA.
- L. trifoliolate . . . . 4. SANDORICUM.
- L. pinnate, leaflets entire.
  - Fl. bisexual, oblong, anthers short, ovules 2 . . 5. DYSOXYLUM.
  - Fl. polygamous, linear, anthers linear, ovule 1 . 6. CHISOCHETON.
- L. pinnate, leaflets mostly serrate.
  - Petals cohering half way, disk tubular, fl. 1–$1\frac{1}{2}$ in. MUNRONIA (p. 139).
  - Petals free, disk inconspicuous, fl. $\frac{1}{2}$ in. . . 7. AZADIRACHTA
- L. bi- or tri-pinnate . . . . 8. MELIA.

III. Staminal tube complete, globose, fl. bisexual.

- Littoral trees, leaflets 3–7, anthers 8 . . . . . 9. CARAPA.
- Shrubs or small trees on the Ghats, leaflets 1 or 3, anthers 5 or 6 . . . . BEDDOMEA (p. 141).

IV. Staminal tube complete, globose, fl. polygamous.

- Petals 3 or 4, ovary 3-celled, anthers 3–10, capsule dehiscent . . . . 10. AMOORA.
- Fl. 5-merous, anthers 5, fr. dry, indehiscent . . . 11. AGLAIA.
- Fl. 5-merous, anthers 10, fr. fleshy . . . . 12. LANSIUM.

B. Ovules numerous, seeds winged, staminal tube complete.

- Seeds winged at both ends . . . . 13. SOYMIDA.
- Seeds winged at one end
  - Petals $\frac{1}{3}$–$\frac{1}{2}$ in., capsule 3–6 in. . . . . . SWIETENIA (p. 144)
  - Petals $\frac{1}{2}$ in., capsule $1\frac{1}{2}$ in. . . . . . . 14. CHUKRASIA.

C. Ovules 8–12 in each cell, seeds winged, stamens distinct.

- Stamens 4–6, ovary 5-celled . . . . . . 15. CEDRELA.
- Stamens 10, ovary 3-celled, translucent glands in leaves 16. CHLOROXYLON.

8. HEYNEA, Roxb.; Fl. Brit. Ind. i. 565.

United with *Walsura* by Kurz and others. Species 3, Indo-Malayan region.

H. trijuga, Roxb. Cor. Pl. t. 260.—Syn. *H. affinis*, A. Juss.; Bedd. Fl. Sylv. t. 134; *Walsura trijuga* and *pubescens*, Kurz, F. Fl. i. 225. Vern. *Gundira*, Mar.; *Kora*, Kan.; *Kora hadi*, Mal.

A tree, sometimes shrubby. L. imparipinnate, leaflets opposite 4 pair, 2–6 in., pale and often softly pubescent beneath. Fl. white, in axillary corymbose panicles, peduncle nearly as long as leaf. Calyx campanulate, 4–5 cleft, petals valvate in bud, staminal tube 8–10-fid., segments 2-dentate, anthers between the subulate teeth of segments. Capsule $\frac{1}{2}$–$\frac{2}{3}$ in. diam., valves 2, broad, obtuse. Seed enclosed in a thin white arillus, testa orange, brown afterwards.

FIG. 64.—Heynea trijuga, Roxb. Fr fl. $\frac{1}{2}$.

Subhimalayan tract, from Kumaun eastward, ascending in Sikkim to 4,000 ft., Khasi hills, Manipur, Singbhum, Rumpa hills, Godavery district. Western Ghats from Poona southward, Nilgiris. In Burma on the hills between Sitang and Salween. Fl. February–June. L. renewed H. S., never quite leafless. Yunan, Tonkin, Cambodia.

2. WALSURA, Roxb.; Fl. Brit. Ind. i. 563.

Trees with imparipinnate, 3-foliolate or unifoliolate leaves, leaflets opposite, quite entire, often pale and glaucous beneath. Fl. small, bisexual, in axillary or terminal panicles. Calyx 5-fid, petals 5, ovate-oblong, spreading, slightly imbricated or nearly valvate. Filaments 8 or 10, free or partly connate. Disk annular, fleshy. Ovary 2-3-celled, embedded in the disk, ovules 2 collateral in each cell. Fr. a shortly tomentose berry, 1- rarely 2-seeded, seed without albumen, enclosed in a fleshy arillus. Species 12, Indo-Malayan.

1. **W. piscidia**, Roxb.; Wight, Ill. t. 55. Vern. *Yerra Valudu*, Tel.; *Valsura*, Tam.

A glabrous, generally middle-sized, at times a large tree, with ash-coloured bark and hard reddish-brown wood, tough, made into combs. L. trifoliolate, leaflets 2–3 in. long. Filaments broad, flat, hairy inside, slightly connate

FIG. 65.—Walsura piscidia, Roxb. Fr. fl. ½.

at base. Fr. ovoid, bright-yellow. Seed 1, completely enveloped in a white juicy arillus.

Western Peninsula, on both sides, south of the Godavery river. Fl. November, December. Ceylon. **W. ternata**, Roxb. Northern Circars and Godavery forests. A small tree, leaves trifoliolate, leaflets coriaceous, shining, whitish beneath, lanceolate, fl. milk-white, in axillary panicles shorter than leaves.

3. **W. villosa**, Wall.; Kurz, F. Fl. i. 223. Vern. *Gyobo*, Burm.

A moderate-sized tree, leafless in the hot season, branchlets, petioles and inflorescence densely pubescent. Leaflets 2 pair, 2–4 in. long, slightly pubescent beneath. Filaments flat, connate ⅓ of their length, hairy.

Common in Lower and Upper Burma, often stunted in Eng forest on poor soil. Fl., March, April. Cochinchina. 4. **W. hypoleuca**, Kurz (probably identical with *W. oxycarpa*, Kurz). Lower Burma and Andamans, leaflets 6–8 in., quite glabrous, filaments only connate at base, is united with (3) by Pierre, Fl. For. Cochin. t. 354. 5. **W. Candollei**, King. Andamans, leaflets 5, glabrous, pale beneath, 2–4 in., filaments connate ⅓ of their length. 6. **W. multijuga**, King. Upper Burma (King), Malay Peninsula and Archipelago. Leaflets 3–4 pair, coriaceous, glabrous, dull beneath, 2–5 in., sec. n.

prominent beneath. 7. **W. tubulata,** Hiern, Sikkim, Khasi hills, leaflets 3, quite glabrous, shining above, glaucous beneath, fl. ¼ in. diam., staminal tube 10-lobed at apex, lobes bifid, anthers between the segments.

8. **W. robusta,** Roxb.; Vern. *Gyobo*, Burm.

An evergreen tree, attains 60 ft. Leaflets 1–2 pair, glabrous, shining above, dull beneath, sec. n. 6–7, more or less prominent. Filaments quite free, subulate, pubescent. Fr. ¾ in. diam., 2-celled, seed 1.

Assam, Khasi hills, Lower Burma, Andamans. Fl. May.

Cipadessa fruticosa, Blume (*Mallea Rothii*, A. Juss.; Bedd. Fl. Sylv. Man. t. 8). Vern. *Ranabili*, Uriya; *Chitundi*, Kan.; *Pulipan*, Tam. Chota Nagpore, Orissa, Western Peninsula, Upper Burma, Ceylon, Java, Philippines. A shrub or small tree. L. imparipinnate, leaflets 3–5 pair, entire or coarsely serrate. Fl. white, in axillary pedunculate panicles, petals 5, ⅛ in. long, valvate in bud, filaments broad, connate at base into a short tube, bifid at the apex, anthers inserted between the teeth, ovary 5-celled. Fr. scarlet, 5-furrowed, ⅛–¼ diam.

3. TURRÆA, Linn.; Fl. Brit. Ind. i. 541.

L. simple. Calyx campanulate, 4–5-fid, petals 4–5 elongate, linear or spathulate, imbricate in bud. Staminal tube long, anthers 8–10 inserted within the mouth, alternating with the teeth of tube. Ovary 5- or more-celled, 2 superposed ovules in each cell, stigma capitate. Capsule loculicidal, valves woody or coriaceous, separating from the winged axis. Albumen fleshy, embryo foliaceous. Species 40, tropical, chiefly in Africa and Madagascar, a smaller number in Asia and Australia.

T. villosa, Benn.; Wight Ic. t. 1593.

A large shrub or small tree, deciduous, more or less pubescent with short hairs. Fl. appearing before the leaves, white, sweet-scented, 1–1½ in. long, in axillary clusters, anthers longer than the short teeth of staminal tube. Capsule globose, ½ in. diam.

Western Ghats, from Mahabaleshwar southwards, also reported from Guzerat. Fl. April, May. 2. **T. virens,** Linn.; a glabrous shrub with shining coriaceous leaves, slightly emarginate at the tip, anthers shorter than the subulate teeth of staminal tube, capsule ⅓ in. long, hairy; doubtful whether a native of the Peninsula.

4. SANDORICUM, Cav.; Fl. Brit. Ind. i. 553.

Evergreen trees with trifoliolate coriaceous leaves, the lateral shortly, the terminal long-petiolulate. Fl. 5-merous, in axillary panicles. Disk enclosing ovary and base of style. Ovary 5-celled, on the enlarged torus, 2 collateral ovules in each cell. Fr. globose, fleshy, 3–5-celled, 1 seed in each cell, cotyledons thick, fleshy, no albumen. Species 6, all Indo-Malayan.

S. indicum, Cav.; Roxb. Cor. Pl. t. 261; Bedd. Fl. Sylv. t. 319. Vern. *Thitto*, Burm.

Attains 60 ft., wood close-grained, moderately hard, med. rays conspicuous on radial section. Branchlets, inflorescence and leaves velvety. Fl. yellow, in narrow axillary panicles. Staminal tube 10-dentate, style articulate at base, clavate above, ending in a thickened ring, bearing 5 obtuse stigmatic lobes. Fr. globose, 3 in. diam., yellow and velvety when ripe, exocarp a fleshy and edible pulp, endocarp lining the cells, horny, covered with a densely felted mass of long pluricellular hairs, over ⅛ in. long. Cotyledons filled with starch and oil.

Evergreen forests of Pegu and Tenasserim, largely cultivated in Burma. Fl. C.; Fr. H. S.

5. DYSOXYLUM, Blume; Fl. Brit. Ind. i. 546.

Evergreen trees, leaves pari-, rarely impari-pinnate, leaflets entire, base oblique. Fl. bisexual, 4–5-merous, calyx deciduous, petals slightly imbricate or valvate, anthers short, inserted inside the staminal tube below its edge. Disk tubular, as long as or longer than ovary. Ovary usually hairy, 3–5-celled, ovules 2 in each cell. Capsule coriaceous, 4–5-valved, loculicidal. Seeds without albumen, cotyledons thick, fleshy, plumule often hairy. Species 100, Indo-Malayan.

A. Fl. in ample pyramidal panicles.

1. **D. procerum**, Hiern; Kurz, F. Fl. i. 214. Vern. *Lasuni*, Nep.

Wood bright red, moderately hard, medull. rays the colour of the intervening tissue, young shoots slightly pubescent. Leaflets 7–12, opposite or alternate, 6–14 in. long, fl. white on short bracteolate pedicels, in ample panicles about as long as leaves. Disk woolly inside, twice the length of the hairy 3–4-celled ovary. Fr. 2 in. diam.

Sikkim, Khasi hills, Assam, Manipur, Pegu and Tenasserim. Fl. C. S. Malacca. 2. **D. Hamiltonii**, Hiern, Sikkim, Assam, Silhet, leaflets 10–18, opposite or nearly so, hairy beneath, very oblique, fl. smell strong of garlic. 3. **D. thyrsoideum**, Griff., South Andaman, Malay Peninsula, leaflets 6–8, glabrous, shining, 4–10 in., disk densely hairy at mouth. 4. **D. grande**, Hiern, Silhet, leaflets 12, alternate, 5–9 in. long, disk glabrous outside. 5. **D. arborescens**, Miq., South Andaman, Malay Peninsula and Archipelago, small tree, leaflets opposite, 2–3 pair, panicles lax, 2–4 in.

B. Panicles contracted, racemiform, sparingly branched.

6. **D. binectariferum**, Hook. fil.—Syn. *D. macrocarpum*, Thwaites (not of Blume); Bedd. Fl. Sylv. t. 150. Vern. *Kadu gadda*, Kan.

A large tree, wood close-grained, young shoots and inflorescence minutely puberulous. Leaflets alternate, 6–8, obliquely ovate-lanceolate, 4–6 in. long, tertiary nerves indistinct. Fl. white, tetramerous, ⅓ in. long, calyx cup-shaped truncate obscurely toothed, disk glabrous inside, 8-dentate, closely surrounding the hairy ovary. Fr. 2½ in. long, red, 4-celled, 4-seeded, seeds polished, dark purple.

Sikkim, Khasi hills, Chittagong, Western Ghats from Khandala southwards. Fl. R. S. Ceylon, Cochinchina. 7. **D. reticulatum**, King, Journ. As. Soc. Beng. vol. 65, ii. (1897) 114. Sikkim, Cachar, leaflets mostly alternate, tertiary nerves prominently reticulate, fl. ¼ in., disk fleshy, glandular-pubescent. Capsule pyriform, 3 in. long.

8. **D. malabaricum**, Bedd.—Syn. *D. glandulosum*, Talbot List 39. Vern. *Vellei agil*, Mal.

A large tree. L. 12 in. long, young shoots grey-pubescent with minute hairs, petiole sharply angled, leaflets 6–10, nearly opposite, 4–9 in. long, sec. n. conspicuous beneath. Panicles contracted, with few branches, shorter than leaves. Fl. 4-merous, ⅓ in. long, calyx deeply 4-lobed, disk truncate, hairy inside. Fr. 2 in. long, nearly globose, bright yellow and verrucose when ripe. Seeds 3–4, angular, dark brown.

Evergreen forests of the Western Ghats, North Kanara, Coorg, Anamalais, Travancore. Fl. February. Yields the white cedar wood of Travancore. Nearly allied: 9. **D. Beddomei**, Hiern (*Adanthei*, Tam.). South Travancore, evergreen forest. A very large tree, wood pale yellow and scented, petioles terete, leaflets alternate. Fr. purple, smooth, globose, 2–3 in. diam. 10. **D. pallens**, Hiern, Sikkim, Khasi hills, Upper Assam, leaflets 6–10, alternate, 4–10 in. long, sec. n. prominent, calyx deeply 4-cleft, disk glabrous on both sides. Fr. 1⅓ by 1 in.

The only species with glabrous ovary is 11. **D. Oliveri**, n. spec., a large tree in the evergreen forest above Katha 6,000 ft., Ruby Mines district (J. W. Oliver, May, 1890), nearly allied to the Malayan *D. costulatum*, Miq. (*D. brevipes*, Hiern), leaves glabrous, paripinnate, common petiole angular, leaflets opposite, 6–24 in. long, sec. n. 14–16 pair, prominent beneath, panicles ample, as long as leaves; fl. ⅓ in., sweet scented, calyx glabrous, shallow-cupular indistinctly 5-dentate, petals linear, glabrous, staminal tube glabrous, entire at mouth, anthers 10 glabrous, included, disk tubular, longer than ovary, ciliate at mouth, fruit green when ripe, 3 in. diam., smooth, seeds glossy, scarlet.

6. CHISOCHETON, Bl.; Fl. Brit. Ind. i. 550 (*Schizochiton*, Kurz, F. Fl. i. 215).

Evergreen trees or shrubs. L. mostly paripinnate, petiole produced beyond the last pair, bearing abortive leaflets. Leaflets entire, opposite or nearly opposite, more or less oblique. Fl. polygamous, as a rule in divaricately branched, generally supra-axillary, panicles. Anthers linear. Disk generally short and fleshy. Ovary 2–4-celled, ovules 1 in each cell, style long, filiform. Species 22, Indo-Malayan.

1. **C. paniculatus**, Hiern.—Syn. *Guarea paniculata*, Roxb.; Wight, Ic. t. 146. *Bauri phal*, Nep.; *Dingari*, Mechi.

A large tree, younger leaves and inflorescence hairy. L. up to 3 ft. long, leaflets 5–12 pair, 4–10 in. long, pale beneath. Panicles usually longer than leaves. Fl. linear, $\frac{1}{2}$–$\frac{2}{3}$ in. Capsule globose, 1–2 in. diam., orange-red. Seeds 3–4, aril white, fleshy, with crenate margin.

Sikkim, Assam, Khasi hills. Tavoy, Fr. C. S.

2. **C. grandiflorus**, Kurz, F. Fl. i. 216.

Attains 50 ft. Common petiole and underside of leaves densely and softly pubescent, leaflets 6–8 in. long, 4–6 pair, sometimes with an odd one. Fl. $\frac{1}{2}$ in. long, nearly sessile, silky-tomentose, panicles slender, on long peduncles. Capsule yellow, pear-shaped, 3-valved and 3-lobed, $1\frac{1}{2}$ in. long, pericarp thick coriaceous, seeds enclosed in an orange-coloured arillus.

Martaban and Tenasserim, Andamans. Fr. March, April. 3. **C. dysoxylifolius**, Kurz; Thoungyeen forests, entirely glabrous except the pubescent panicles, leaflets 5–7 pair, 4–10 in. long, sec. n. prominent beneath. Fl. $\frac{1}{2}$ in. long, hexamerous, staminal tube densely hairy outside, 6-cleft at the summit, anthers alternating with the lobes. 4. **C. divergens**, Blume (*C. fragrans*, Hiern); Malay Peninsula, reported by Wallich from Burma, is nearly glabrous, leaflets 4–12 pair, membranous, 2–6 in., fl. $\frac{1}{4}$ in., polygamous, fr. pear-shaped, minutely tomentose, $1\frac{1}{2}$ in. diam., 2-celled. 5. **C. costatus**, Hiern; Cachar, fl. unknown, hence the genus uncertain, leaflets 10–11, alternate, pale olive and velvety beneath, sec. n. prominent, fr. 2–3-lobed and celled, orange, 1–$1\frac{1}{2}$ in. long.

Munronia Wallichii, Wight (*M. neilgherrica*, Wight Ill. t. 54; *Turræa pinnata*, Wall. Pl. As. Rar. t. 119); Sikkim to 3,000 ft., Khasi hills, Nilgiris, a shrub with imparipinnate leaves, leaflets opposite, 3–4 pair, lanceolate, 1–5 in., fl. 1–$1\frac{1}{4}$ in. long, white or pink, hairy outside, crowded at the ends of branches, staminal tube with 10 anthers alternating with subulate teeth. Disk membranous, tubular, sheathing ovary and base of style. Ovary 5-celled, ovules 2 in each cell, superposed. Capsule 5-lobed, hairy.

7. AZADIRACHTA, Adr. Juss.; Trimen Handb. Ceylon i. 244.

A. indica, A. Juss. (the only species).—Syn. *Melia Azadirachta*, Linn.; Bedd. Fl. Sylv. t. 14; *M. indica*, Brandis F. Fl. 67. The *Neem* or *Margoza tree*. Vern. *Nim*, Hind.; *Tama*, *Tamaka*, Burm.; *Vepa*, Tel.; *Olle-bevu*, Kan.

A large glabrous evergreen tree, heartwood red, hard. Leaflets 7–9 pair, often alternate, obliquely falcate-lanceolate, serrate, the odd one often wanting. Fl. white, strongly honey-scented, pentamerous, in axillary panicles shorter than leaf. Staminal tube 10-dentate, anthers inserted within the tube opposite its teeth. Drupe the size of an olive, yellow, afterwards purple, kernel cartilaginous, 1-celled 1-seeded, cotyledons plane-convex, fleshy, notched at base, albumen 0.

Wild in the dry region of the Irawadi valley from Prome upwards. Cultivated and naturalized throughout India, in the Punjab to the Jhelum, rare west of the Sutlej. Fl. H. S.

8. MELIA, Linn.; Fl. Brit. Ind. i. 543.

Trees with bipinnate or tripinnate leaves, calyx segments 5–6, short. Petals 5–6, linear-spathulate. Stamens 10–12, monadelphous; anthers inserted on the edge of the tube between the teeth. Ovary 3–6-celled, 2 superposed ovules in each cell. Fr. a dry or fleshy drupe, the stone 5-celled, each cell with one pendulous seed, cotyledons foliaceous, albumen thin. Species 12, Indo-Malayan.

1. **M. Azedarach,** Linn.; Wight Ic. t. 160; Bedd. Fl. Sylv. t. 13. *Persian Lilac.* Vern. *Drek.* Pb.; *Bakain*, Hind.; *Dek*, Dūn; *Yerri vepa, Turaka vepa*, Tel.; *Hutchu bevu*, Kan.; *Vembu*, Tam., Mal.

A middle-sized deciduous tree, young shoots and inflorescence sparsely clothed with deciduous stellate hairs, heartwood light red, annual rings marked by a belt of large vessels. Pinnæ 3–4 pair, more or less opposite. Leaflets 3–12, ovate-lanceolate, more or less deeply serrate, sometimes lobed. Fl. lilac, with a strong honey-scent. Staminal tube purple, ⅓ in. long, teeth 20–30, linear, anthers glabrous, shorter than or as long as teeth. Stigma clavate 5-toothed. Drupe yellow when ripe, 3–4 in. long.

Cultivated and naturalized throughout India and Burma. Stands more cold than the *Neem*, grows at 9,000 feet in Bashahr (Chini). Supposed to be indigenous in Baluchistan and the Jhelum valley in Kashmir. Fl. H. S.

2. **M. composita,** Willd.; Bedd. Fl. Sylv. t. 12; King in Journ. As. Soc. Bengal, vol. 64 (1895) 18. Syn. *M. robusta*, Roxb. Fl. Ind. ii. 397; *M. dubia*, Fl. Brit. Ind. i. 545 (not Cav.). Vern. *Labshi*, Nep.; *Maha limbu*, Uriya; *Heb-bevu*, Kan.; *Malei Vembu*, Tam., Mal.

A tall tree of rapid growth, heartwood reddish. Young shoots and inflorescence clothed with mealy stellate hairs. L. bipinnate, leaflets opposite, ovate-lanceolate, sometimes serrulate. Fl. white, staminal tube ⅓ in. long, hairy, mouth woolly, divided into 10 more or less laciniate teeth, anthers longer than teeth and inserted between them. Stigma 5-toothed. Drupe ovoid 1–1½ in.

Sikkim, ascending to 6,000 ft. (Gamble List 16), Nambar Forest, Assam (D.B. March, 1879) Gumsur hills, Northern Circars. Western Ghats from Bombay southwards. Fl. Jan.–March. Ceylon, Malay Peninsula, Cochinchina, Java, China, Australia. Specimens from the Khasi hills and Manipur, the staminal tube ⅓ in. long, drupe nearly globose, ¾ in. long, have been referred to M. *Toosendan*, Sieb. et Zucc. of Japan. Hardly different is *M. birmanica*, Kurz, F. Fl. i. 213 (*Taw thamaka*, Burm.), Pegu, Bhamo, supposed by King to be identical with *M. superba*, Roxb.

9. CARAPA, Aublet; Fl. Brit. Ind. i. 566.

Evergreen glabrous trees. L. paripinnate, leaflets opposite, quite entire. Fl. bisexual, in axillary panicles. Calyx short, in the Indian species dentate, petals 4, edges slightly overlapping, contorted in bud. Staminal tube urceolate or globose, mouth 8-dentate, anthers inserted between the teeth, nearly included. Ovary glabrous, 4-celled, the base immersed in the thick fleshy disk, cells with 2–8 ovules, style short, stigma broad discoid. Fr. globose, large, pericarp fleshy, dehiscing by 4 valves. Seeds large angular without albumen, cotyledons contain starch and oil. Species 6, tropical, mostly littoral.

1. **C. obovata,** Blume; Kurz, F. Fl. i. 226.—Syn. *C. moluccensis*, Bedd. Fl. Sylv. t. 136 (not of Lamk.); *Xylocarpus obovatus*, A. Juss.; Harms in Engler u. Prantl iii. 4. 278. Vern. *Pinlè ôn*, Burm.; *Karambola, Dhundol*, Sund.

A small tree, heartwood reddish-brown, hard, leaves 3–6 in. long, leaflets 1–2 pair, coriaceous, obovate, apex broad, obtuse, base narrowed. Panicles 1½–2½ in. long, stout, few-flowered. Fruit 7–10 in. diam.

Seashore and Mangrove swamps along the western coast from the Konkan southwards, Sundriban, Chittagong, Burma, Andamans, Ceylon. Fl. R. S. Malay Archipelago, Fiji islands, Africa, Australia. The leaves of young plants are elliptic-lanceolate, acute. 2. **C. moluccensis**, Lamk. (*Xylocarpus Granatum*, Willd., *Pussur*, Sund.). Sundriban, Andamans, Malay Peninsula and Archipelago. Tropical Africa, Australia. A middle-sized tree, l. 4–10 in. long, leaflets usually 2 sometimes 3 pair, thinly coriaceous, ovate from a broad base, acute. Panicles 3–5 in. long, slender with lax few-flowered branches, fl. pinkish yellow. Fr. 3–5 in. diam., 4-grooved, brown, valves woody. Kurz describes the flower as pentamerous.

Beddomea differs from *Carapa* by petals 4–6 strongly imbricate in bud, anthers 5–6, cells narrow, on a thick connective, ovary hairy, 3–5-celled, cells with 2 ovules.
1. **B. indica**, Hook. f. Western Ghats from Coorg to Cape Comorin. A large shrub, young shoots lepidote, leaflets 3, 3–7 in. long, fruit 1–1½ in. long, rough with close set rusty scales. 2. **B. simplicifolia**, Bedd. Fl. Sylv. t. 135, Western Ghats common, from South Kanara to Travancore. A small tree, leaflets solitary, 3–6 in. long, fruit oblong, size of a pigeon's egg, acute at both ends, densely rusty-tomentose.

Fig. 66.—Carapa obovata, Blume. ½.

10. AMOORA, Roxb.; Fl. Brit. Ind. i. 559.

Evergreen trees, leaves imparipinnate, leaflets oblique. Fl. polygamous, male fl. usually paniculate, fertile fl. often racemose or spicate. Calyx 3–5-partite. Petals 3 (4 in 2 species) thick, concave, strongly imbricated. Staminal tube nearly globose, anthers 3–10, included, in one row. Disk inconspicuous. Ovary 3-celled, cells 1–2-ovuled, stigma sessile. Capsule 3-valved or indehiscent, seeds 1–3, enclosed in a fleshy arillus.—Species 25, one Australian, the rest Indian and Malayan.

A. Leaflets opposite.

1. **A. Rohituka**, W. & A.; Bedd. Fl. Sylv. t. 132. Vern. *Sohaga*, Oudh; *Bandriphal*, Nep.; *Sikaroro*, Kol; *Thitni*, Burm.

A middle-sized tree, with a heavy crown, in Burma attains 60 ft., wood pale red, youngest shoots pubescent. Leaflets 5–7 pair, 3–9 in. long, secondary nerves prominent beneath, 10–15 pair. Fl. sessile, ♂ in panicled spikes, ♀ in solitary spikes much shorter than leaves. Anthers 6, attached to the tube at its base. Fruit globose, yellow when ripe, 1–1½ in. diam., pericarp coriaceous 3-valved. Seed one, oblong with a scarlet arillus.

Subhimalayan tract, from the Rapti river eastwards, in Sikkim to 6,000 ft., Assam, Burma, Chota Nagpore, Western Ghats and adjoining hill ranges, from the Satara district southwards. Fl. R. S. Ceylon, Malay Peninsula.

2. **A. cucullata,** Roxb. Corom. Pl. t. 258. Vern. *Amur*, *Latmi*, Sundrib.; *Thitni*, Burm.

A glabrous, middle-sized, at times a large tree, heartwood red. Leaflets 2–4 pair, falcate, very oblique at the base, 3–5 in. long; secondary nerves indistinct. Fl. pedicellate, ♂ in panicles, ♂ in short few fld. supra-axillary racemes. Anthers 6. Fruit globose, 2½ in. diam., pericarp leathery, 3-valved. Seeds 3 with an orange-coloured arillus.

Khasi hills, Sundriban, Burma. Fl. R. S. C. S. 3. **A. Wallichii,** King.—Syn. *A. spectabilis*, Fl. B. Ind. i. 561; Kurz, F. Fl. i. 221, Assam, Burma and Andamans, has male and female flowers on the same panicles, 10 anthers, leaflets 5–6 pair, pale beneath. 4. **A. canarana,** Benth. et Hook., Western Ghats from the Konkan southwards. Leaflets 2–3 pair, sometimes alternate, calyx cup-shaped, 4–5-toothed, petals 3, sometimes 4, anthers 6, at times 7.

B. Leaflets alternate.

5. **A. Lawii,** Bedd. Fl. Sylv. t. 133 (*Buramb*, Mar.), evergreen forests on the west side of the Peninsula from the Konkan southwards. Leaflets 3–5, fl. generally tetramerous, ovary 3-celled. 6. **A. chittagonga,** Hiern, Bhutan, Upper Assam, Chittagong, Pegu. Leaflets 3–7, calyx cup-shaped, 3-toothed, anthers 6, ovary 2-celled. King in As. Soc. Beng. vol. 64 (1895) 51 states, that this is an *Aglaia*. 6. **A. Manii,** King MSS., South Andaman. Leaflets 11–15, fertile fl. in long axillary panicles.

11. AGLAIA, Lour.; Fl. Brit. Ind. i. 554.

Evergreen trees, leaves imparipinnate. Fl. polygamous, small, globose, paniculate, as a rule pentamerous, petals imbricate, staminal tube more or less globose, anthers usually 5, rarely more, included or half exserted. Disk inconspicuous, stigma sessile or nearly so. Fr. indehiscent, 1–2-celled, seeds 1 or 2, testa often with a fleshy outer layer, resembling an arillus. Species 7, Indo-Malayan region, China, Polynesia.

A. Shoots and inflorescence scaly, adult leaves glabrous, leaflets 1–4 pair.

1. **A. odoratissima,** Blume; King, Journ. As. Soc. Beng. vol. 64 (1895) 67. Syn. *A. Roxburghiana*, Miq.; Bedd. Fl. Sylv. t. 130; *Milnea Roxburghii*, Wight, Ic. t. 166. Vern. *Yewa Aduga*, Kan., Tel.; *Chokala*, Tam.

A large tree (near the coast in Kanara a shrub), wood bright red, hard, very tough, youngest shoots and inflorescence clothed with round peltate scales. Leaflets glabrous, opposite, 1–3 pair, 2–5 in. long, pale beneath, naked part of common petiole as long as the upper portion. Fr. buff-coloured, velvety, ¾ in. diam. Seeds ovoid, surrounded with a white thick slightly acid edible pulp, embryo green.

Western Peninsula, the northern limit Mount Aboo on the west and Midnapore on the east side. Fl. R.S., C.S. Ceylon, Malay Peninsula, Sumatra, Java. 2. **A. oligophylla,** Miq. Tenasserim, Malay Peninsula, Sumatra. Leaflets 1–2 pair. Fr. globose, supported by the remains of persistent calyx. 3. **A. fusca,** King. South Andaman. Leaflets 2–3 pair. Fl. tetramerous. 4. **A. glaucescens,** King. South Andaman. Leaflets 2–4 pair. Panicles as long as leaves. Fl. 4- or 5-merous. 5. **A. Khasiana,** Hiern. Khasi hills. Leaflets 1–2 pair, panicles much shorter than leaves, ferrugineous. Fl. ⅛–¼ in. 6. **A. Wallichii,** Hiern. Silhet. Leaflets opposite 3–4 pair, elliptic-lanceolate, 2–4 in. long. Fl. small in short panicles. 7. **A. paniculata,** Kurz, F. Fl. i. 219, Pegu Yoma. Leaflets alternate, 2 pair, 4–9 in. long. Fl. minute in ample rusty scaly tomentose panicles.

B. Shoots and inflorescence scaly, leaves glabrous, leaflets 4 pair or more.

8. **A. crassinervia,** Kurz. Tenasserim. Leaflets 6–10 in. long, secondary nerves prominent beneath. 9. **A. Ganggo,** Miq. South Andaman, Nicobars, Sumatra. Leaflets 5–7 pair, 4–5 in. long, fl. crowded in ample panicles as long as leaves, the lower branches distant. 10. **A. andamanica,** Hiern. (*Amoora dysoxyloides*, Kurz). Tenasserim, Andamans, Great Cocos island. Leaflets alternate, 4–6 in. long, fl. crowded in short panicles, 2–3 in. long. 11. **A. perviridis,** Hiern. Sikkim, Khasi hills, Assam. A small tree, leaves and buds deep green, leaflets opposite, 5–6 pair, 2–5 in. long, fl. minute in ample panicles, nearly as long as leaves. 12. **A. argentea,** Blume. Pegu Yoma

FIG. 67.—Aglaia odoratissima, Bl. ½.

Nicobars, Malay Peninsula and Archipelago. A small slender tree, young shoots, inflorescence and underside of leaves densely covered with round silvery or pale brown scales, intermixed with stellate hairs, leaflets 3–5 pair, 5–12 in. long, the terminal longest, secondary nerves prominent.

C. Shoots and inflorescence with scales and stellate hairs, underside of leaves pubescent or tomentose.

13. **A. edulis,** A. Gray (identified by King with *A. trichostemon* C.DC.). Sikkim (Gamble list 16), Assam, Silhet, Malay Peninsula. Leaflets 4–6 pair, 4–8 in. long, upper surface glabrous, the lower sparsely pubescent. Fr. subglobose, densely rusty-tomentose. 14. **A. Griffithii,** Kurz, F. Fl. i. 129. Mergui, Malay Peninsula. Leaflets 6–9 pair, oblong-lanceolate, 3–5 in. long, upper surface glabrous, except tomentose midrib nerves

on lower surface rusty-tomentose, fl. very minute, depressed-globose, broader than long, calyx half the length of petals. Fr. pyriform 1¾ in. long. 15. **A. minutiflora**, Bedd. Ic. Pl. Ind. Or. t. 193, Anamalai, Tinnevelli and Travancore Ghats, above 2,000 ft. Leaflets 4–6 pair, lower surface densely rusty-tomentose, fl. globose, $\frac{1}{12}$ in. diam., calyx, ¼ the length of petals.

Some of these 15 species will probably be united, when they are studied in the forests and not from herbarium specimens only.

12. LANSIUM, Rumphius; Fl. Brit. Ind. i. 557.

Differs from *Aglaia* by having 10 anthers in 2 rows, the shorter ones included, the longer partly exserted.

1. **L. anamalayanum,** Bedd. Fl. Sylv. t. 131. Vern. *Santhana viri*, Tam. Leaflets alternate, 3–5, 3–4½ in. long, obtusely acuminate. Fr. oblong, ⅔ in. diam., 2-seeded, seeds covered with a fleshy integument.

Evergreen forests of the Western Ghats from Kanara southwards. Fl. April, May. 2. **L. decandrum,** King l. c. 51 (*Amoora decandra*, Hiern; Fl. B. Ind. i. 562), outer Himalaya from Nepal eastwards, ascending in Sikkim to 6,000 ft., has opposite leaflets, 3–6 pair, fl. red, 4- or 5-merous, ♂ in ample panicles, ♀ in axillary spikes, fr. globose-obovoid, 4–5-celled, 1½ in. diam., with 4–5 seeds. 3. **L. domesticum,** Jack. Malay Peninsula and Archipelago. Cultivated on account of its fruit in tropical India. Leaflets 5–9, alternate, coriaceous, broadly elliptic, spikes of bisexual fl. from the trunk and larger branches, fr. 1–2 in. diam., seeds 2, embedded in much transparent pulp.

13. SOYMIDA, Adr. Juss.; Fl. Brit. Ind. i. 567.

One Indian species, and one or two from East Africa.

S. febrifuga, Adr. Juss., the only species; Bedd. Fl. Sylv. t. 8; Brandis F. Fl. 71.—Syn. *Swietenia febrifuga*, Roxb. Cor. Pl. t. 17. Vern. *Rohan*, Hind.; *Sumi*, Tel.; *Sohan*, Uriya; *Soymida*, Palkonda hills; *Some-mara*, *Sumbi*, Kan.

A large tree, trunk tall, straight, symmetrical, bark bitter, heartwood distinct, bright red when fresh cut, dark reddish-brown when dry, very hard and very durable. Leaves paripinnate, petiole with a thickened base, leaflets opposite, 3–6 pair, 2–4 in. long. Secondary nerves 10–14 pair, alternating with shorter intermediate ones, tertiary nerves prominently reticulate. Fl. bisexual, pentamerous, greenish-white, in large terminal panicles, with triangular bracts. Petals obovate, narrowed into a claw, contorted in bud. Staminal tube cup-shaped, 10-cleft, each segment with 2 short fleshy teeth, the anthers between them on a short filament. Capsule 1–2 in. long, 5-celled, the 5 valves separating from the dissepiments, which remain attached to the thick spongy axis. Seeds numerous in each cell, flat, imbricated, winged at both ends.

Western Peninsula and Central India, extending to the hills south of Mirzapur in the east, and to Merwara in the west. Doubtful in Burma. The young foliage issues in April and May, while part of the old leaves are still on the tree. Fl. April, May.

Swietenia Mahagoni, Linn., the *Mahogany* tree of Central America and the West Indies, differs by an urceolate 10-dentate staminal tube and seeds winged at the upper end only. *S. macrophylla*, King, is a remarkable variety or species, raised at the Calcutta Bot. Gardens from Honduras seed in 1872. Leaves, capsules (6×8 in.) and seeds much larger, growth more rapid. Seeds more freely at Calcutta.

14. CHUKRASIA, Adr. Jussieu, Mém. Mus. Hist. Natur. xix. (1830) p. 251. Wight and Arnott altered the original name into *Chickrassia*; Fl. Brit. Ind. i. 567.

C. tabularis, A. Juss., the only species; Wight. Ill. t. 56; Bedd. Fl. Sylv. t. 9.—*Chittagong wood*. Vern. *Chikrasi*, Beng.; *Pabba*, Mar.; *Kul hathuri*, Kan.; *Dal mara*, Coorg; *Yimma*, Burm.

A tall tree, usually deciduous, heartwood brown with a satin lustre. Leaves pinnate, leaflets 10–24, as a rule alternate, unequal-sided, 2–5 in. long, upper surface glabrous, lower pubescent. Fl. white, ½ in. long. Petals oblong, erect, imbricate in bud. Staminal tube cylindric, with 10 short teeth, anthers on the edge of the tube. Ovary cylindric, usually 3-celled, with numerous biseriate ovules in each cell. Capsule ovoid, 1½ in. long, valves usually 3, woody, separating entirely from the broad axis. Seeds numerous, flat, closely packed, broadly winged.

Sikkim, Chittagong, Andamans, Burma. Western Peninsula, along the Western Ghats, also on the Sandúr hills of the Deccan. Fl. H. S. and R. S. Ceylon, Malay Peninsula, Cochinchina, Borneo, China.—2. **C. velutina,** Roemer; Kurz, F. Fl. i. 227. Burma, Cochinchina. Branchlets, leaves and inflorescence velvety, capsules black, shining, apiculate, is a distinct species or very marked variety.

15. CEDRELA, Linn.; Fl. Brit. Ind. i. 568.

Trees with pinnate leaves and paniculate bisexual fl. Wood light, soft, red, no heartwood, vessels large, conspicuous on a vertical section. Petals 5, erect. Disk thick, fleshy, 5-lobed or cylindrical. Filaments 4–6, inserted on the edge of the disk, subulate, anthers oblong, versatile. Ovary 5-celled, narrowed into a style, stigma broad, often 5-lobed, ovules pendulous, biseriate, 8–12 in each cell. Capsule opening by 5 valves, the valves separating from the dissepiments, which remain attached to the axis, forming a pentagonal column of soft white pith. Seeds numerous, imbricate, flat, winged. Albumen scanty, embryo straight with foliaceous cotyledons, the radicle pointing upwards. Species 16, tropical Asia, America and Australia.

Cedrela odorata, L., and other species furnish the West Indian Cedar wood. The American species have a cylindrical disk and wings at base of seed only. The Asiatic and Australian species with short disk and seeds winged at the top or at both ends have been placed in a separate genus, *Toona*, by Pierre Fl. For. Coch. t. 358; Harms, Engler u. Prantl iii. 4. 269 and others.

1. **C. Toona,** Roxb. Cor. Pl. t. 238; Wight Ic. t. 161; Bedd. Fl. Sylv. t. 10: Brandis F. Fl. t. 14. *The Toon tree.* Vern. *Tūn, Tūni, Tunni, Maha nīm*, Hind.; *Katangai*, Kol; *Todu*, Mar.; *Tundu, Devdari*, Kan.; *Noga*, Coorg; *Thēvatharam*, Tam.; *Mathagiri vembu*, Mal.; *Thitkado*, Lower, *Tautama*, Upper Burma.

A large, rapidly growing tree, nearly evergreen. Wood red, not hard, shining, does not split or warp, annual rings marked by wider vessels. L. glabrous, paripinnate, leaflets opposite or nearly so, 5–10 pair, lanceolate or ovate-lanceolate, acuminate, often unequal-sided and falcate, entire or undulate, blade 3–5, petiolule ¼–¾ in. Panicles terminal, cymose, generally shorter than leaves, the last ramifications pubescent. Fl. white, honey-scented, ⅙–¼ in. long. Sepals 5, ciliate, obtuse, petals ciliate on the edges, otherwise glabrous, on the inside thickened. Stamens 5, inserted on 5 fleshy orange-coloured hairy lobes of the disk. Filaments glabrous, ovary hairy, capsule smooth, ¾–1 in. long. Seeds with membranous wings at both ends.

Subhimalayan tract, from the Indus eastwards, ascending to 5,000 ft. Evergreen forests of the Western Ghats and other hills of the Western Peninsula (not in Ceylon), Khasi hills, Manipur, Upper and Lower Burma. Cultivated extensively; while young requires shelter against frost in the plains of the Punjab, but grows freely afterwards. The old leaves are shed gradually during the cold season, the young foliage comes out February–April with the fl., seed ripens May-July, the empty capsules remaining on the tree for months.

2. **C. serrata,** Royle Ill. t. 25; Brandis F. Fl. 73. Collett, Simla Fl. fig. 26. Vern. *Drawi, Dal, Dalra, Dauri, Krishing*, N. W. Himalaya.

Differs from *Toona* by leaves generally imparipinnate, leaflets mostly serrate, green above, glaucous beneath. Panicles longer than leaves, drooping. Fl.

occasionally hexamerous. Sepals and petals often not ciliate, petals at the base on the inside prominently keeled, 5 filiform staminodes alternating with stamens. Ovary glabrous, seeds winged at the top only.

Outer Himalaya from the Indus to the Nepal, ascending to 8,000 ft. Manipur, Upper Burma (*C. longifolia*, Wall.). Fl. May, June. 3. **C. microcarpa,** C.DC. Outer Himalayan ranges, Kumaon to Sikkim, ascending to 6,000 ft., Assam, Upper Burma (*Taw tama*), leaflets mostly alternate, shining above, unequal sided, almost falcate, one side rounded at base, blade 3–6, petiolule $\frac{1}{4}$–$\frac{3}{4}$ in. Fl. $\frac{1}{8}$–$\frac{1}{4}$ in., sometimes 4-merous, filaments hairy, ovary hirsute, capsule 1–1$\frac{1}{2}$ in. long, warty, upper wing of seed smaller than lower. 4. **C. multijuga,** Kurz, Pegu Yoma, eastern slopes, Salween 2,500–3,000 ft. Young shoots and common petiole tawny pubescent, leaflets nearly opposite, requires further study. *C. hirsuta*, King MSS., Sikkim, may possibly be the same. 5. **C. febrifuga,** C.DC. (*Toona febrifuga*, Pierre, Fl. For. Cochin. t. 358), common in Cochinchina, leaflets alternate, petals hairy inside, ovary and filaments hairy, seeds winged at both ends, will probably be found in Upper Burma. I am disposed to refer to it specimens collected by J. W. Oliver along streams in Upper Burma (*Petsut Ye tama*), as well as specimens coll. by Troup in the hill forests east of the Meiktila district (*Yedama*, *Shinshit*).

16. CHLOROXYLON, DC.; Fl. Brit. Ind. i. 569.

C. Swietenia, DC., the only species. Wight Ill. t. 56 bis; Bedd. Fl. Sylv. t. 11. Syn. *Swietenia Chloroxylon*, Roxb. Cor. pl. t. 64. *Satinwood*. Vern. *Bhera*, Hind.; *Bhira*, Gond; *Sengel-sali*, Kol; *Billa*, Tel.; *Hurgalu*, Kan.

A middle-sized tree, wood yellow, hard, heavy, with a beautiful satin lustre, inner wood darker, but no distinct heartwood. Young parts, petioles and inflorescence clothed with short grey pubescence. L. paripinnate, leaflets 10–20 pair, gland-dotted, unequal-sided, obtuse, 1 in. long. Fl. bisexual, cream-coloured, in small terminal and axillary panicles. Petals 5-clawed, spreading, imbricate in bud. Disk fleshy, 10-lobed. Stamens 10, inserted outside the disk at its base, anthers cordate, apiculate, versatile. Ovary immersed in the disk, 3-celled, ovules 8 in each cell. Capsule oblong, coriaceous, 3-celled, loculicidally 3-valved, the dissepiments remaining attached to the valves. Seeds imbricate, oblong, winged.

Common in the deciduous forests of the Western Peninsula, its limit being the northern edge of the Satpura range. Fl. March–April, the leaves are renewed in May. Dry region of Ceylon.

ORDER XXX. CHAILLETIACEÆ. Gen. Pl. i. 340.

(*Dichapetalaceæ*, Engler u. Prantl iii. 4. 345.)

Trees or shrubs. L. alternate, quite entire, stipules deciduous. Fl. small, mostly polygamous, sepals 5, more or less united, petals 5, free, notched or bifid, stamens 5, alternate with and sometimes adnate to base of petals. Disk of 5 glands, alternating with stamens, ovary pubescent or villous, 2–3-celled, ovules in pairs, pendulous from the top of each cell. Drupe pubescent or hispid, often didymous, embryo large, radicle small superior, cotyledons thick, albumen 0.

CHAILLETIA, DC.; Fl. Brit. Ind. i. 570.

(*Dichapetalum*, Du Petit Thouars; Engler u. Prantl iii. 4. 348.)

1. **C. gelonioides,** Hook. fil.; Bedd. Fl. Sylv. Manual t. 9.—Syn. *C. sumatrana*, Miq.; Trimen Handb. i. 254; *Moacurra gelonioides*, Roxb.

A small tree or shrub, twigs slender, young shoots pubescent. L. ovate-lanceolate, acuminate, reticulate veins distinct, blade 3–5, petiole $\frac{1}{8}$ in. long,

stipules small, setaceous, pubescent, unequal. Fl. pale-green, in axillary or extra-axillary compact cymes, sepals concave, pubescent, petals bifid, connective dilated, styles 2 very short. Fr. ½–⅔ in. diam., compressed, orbicular didymous, dehiscent, mesocarp bright red.

Western Ghats from the Konkan southwards, Anamalais, Khasi hills, Silhet, Cachar, Chittagong. Fl. March–June. Ceylon, Malay Peninsula. 2. **C. andamanica,** King, South Andaman island. L. elliptic-obovate or oblanceolate; fl. in pedunculate cymes. 3. **C. Helferiana,** Kurz, Tenasserim, Malay Peninsula. Scandent. L. elliptic-oblong, midrib strigose beneath, reticulate veins faint, drupe broader than long. 4. **C. longipetala,** Turcz. (*macropetala*, Kurz), Tenasserim, a shrub or tree, leaves silky beneath; cymes densely tomentose, sepals greyish pubescent, petals longer than sepals.

ORDER XXXI. OLACACEÆ. Engler in Engler u. Prantl iii. 1. 231.

(*Olacineæ*, tribes i. *Olaceæ*, ii. *Opilieæ*. Gen. Pl. i. 343.)

Trees or shrubs, often climbing. L. almost always alternate, stipules 0. Fl. small, as a rule bisexual, calyx small or wanting, petals (or segments of perianth) free or connate, stamens as many as petals and opposite to them, or more numerous. Ovary at base often 2–5-celled, ovules 1 or few, pendulous from a free axile placenta. Drupe 1-seeded, embryo minute, in the apex of the fleshy albumen.

A. Stamens or stamens and staminodes more numerous than petals.
- Petals 3 not bearded, stamens 3, staminodes 5, calyx enlarged in fruit . . . . 1. OLAX.
- Petals bearded, stamens 8–10 . . . . . . XIMENIA (p. 148).

B. Stamens as many as petals, calyx and corolla present. Fl. usually pentamerous.
- Calyx tube adnate to ovary, enlarged in fr. . . ERYTHROPALUM (p. 148
- Calyx cup-shaped, petals free, hairy within . . 2. STROMBOSIA.
- Calyx truncate, supported by an involucre, corolla funnel-shaped . . . . SCHOEPFIA (p. 149).
- Fl. 5–7-merous, petals free, thick concave at base . 3. ANACOLOSA.

C. Stamens as many as petals or segments of perianth, no calyx.
- Fl. 4–5-merous, bracts small, perianth campanulate, hairy . . . . 4. CANSJERA.
- Fl. 4-merous, bracts large, perianth urceolate . . LEPIONURUS (p. 150).
- Fl. 5-merous, in bud covered by large imbricating bracts, segments of perianth free . . . . OPILIA (p. 150).

1. OLAX, Linn.; Fl. Brit. Ind. i. 574.

Shrubs, small trees, or climbers. L. entire, petioles short. Calyx cup-shaped, enlarged after flowering, petals 5–6, fertile stamens 3–5, and 5 bifid linear staminodes, ovary free 1-celled or with 3 imperfect cells. Drupe more or less enclosed by the accrescent calyx. Embryo small, near the apex of the fleshy albumen. Species 25–30, tropics of the Old World.

1. O. scandens, Roxb. Cor. Pl. t. 102; Brandis F. Fl. 75. Vern. *Rimilbiri*, Kol; *Ehir*, Sonth.; *Boderia*, Uriya; *Harduli*, Mar.

A powerful climber, structure of wood normal, vessels large. A few stout thorns on the older branches. Branchlets, petioles and midrib pubescent. L. distichous, ovate-oblong, 2–3 in. long. Fl. white, in short axillary racemes, pedicels erect, less than half the length of fl., petals more or less cohering; anthers 3. Drupe yellow, three-fourths enclosed in the enlarged calyx.

Subhimalayan tract of Kumaon. Oudh forests. Behar, Western Peninsula. Burma.

Fl. C. S. Ceylon, China. 2. **O. Wightiana,** Wall. Erect or climbing, evergreen forests on the west side of the Peninsula, from North Kanara southwards. L. glabrous, shining, 3–4 in., base often rounded. Fl. cream-coloured in axillary often compound corymbs, pedicels spreading, longer than half the flower, drupe nearly covered by the calyx. Closely allied is 3. **O. imbricata,** Roxb. Chittagong, Tenasserim, Andamans, Indian Archipelago; an unarmed climber, branchlets terete. L. 3–6 in., racemes distichous, the rather large bracts imbricating in bud. *O. merguensis*, Planchon, Tenasserim, Malaya, is not specifically different. 4. **O. acuminata,** Wall., Assam, Bhutan, Khasi hills, Silhet, Dacca, branchlets angled. L. lanceolate or ovate-lanceolate, racemes few fld., shorter than or as long as petioles, drupe red, fleshy. 5. **O. nana,** Wall., is a small undershrub in grass lands of the Subhimalayan tract and Bengal, with a large woody rootstock, which sends up shoots annually after the jungle fires, with subsessile lanceolate leaves and solitary axillary flowers on slender peduncles.

FIG. 68.—Olax scandens, Roxb. ½.

Ximenia americana, Linn. (*Pinlè Kayin, Pinlè Zi*, Burma). A glabrous straggling shrub armed with short straight spines, on the coast of Tenasserim and the Andamans. Inland on dry stony ground in the Deccan; littoral in the tropics of both hemispheres. L. blunt, entire, 1½–2 in. long, turning black in drying. Fl. whitish, generally bisexual, ⅓ in. long, calyx cup-shaped, 4–5-toothed, petals revolute, on the upper surface densely bearded, stamens 8–10. Drupe ovoid, 1 in. long, orange red when ripe, pulp edible, stone hard, 1-seeded.

Erythropalum scandens, Blume, Sikkim, Khasi hills, Manipur, Chittagong, Burma, Cochinchina, Malay Peninsula and Archipelago, is a powerful woody climber, with axillary tendrils. L. membranous, ovate, with three basal nerves, blade 4–6, petiole ¾–2 in. Fl. minute, pentamerous, bisexual, in slender, long peduncled, dichotomous cymes, calyx tube adnate to ovary and much enlarged in fruit. Petals short, broad, slightly coherent at base, inserted outside the large cupular, fleshy, 5-lobed disk, stamens 5, opposite to petals. Fr. oblong, ¾–1 in., yellowish, crowned by the scars of the calyx lobes, embryo minute, near the apex of the large fleshy albumen. Two other species closely allied and probably not distinct: 2. **E. populifolium,** Masters; Western Ghats from North Kanara southwards. L. subcoriaceous, triangular-cordate. 3. **E. vagum,** Masters; Sikkim, Assam, Khasi hills, Cachar. L. subcoriaceous, ovate-oblong, blade 4–9 in., basal nerves 3–5.

2. STROMBOSIA, Bl.; Fl. Brit. Ind. i. 579.

Evergreen trees. Fl. bisexual, pentamerous, in short axillary cymose fascicles. Calyx cup-shaped, free or adnate to base of ovary, petals free, hairy within, stamens 5, opposite to petals. Drupe crowned by the remains of calyx, embryo minute, in a fleshy albumen. Species 6, Indo-Malayan region.

1. S. ceylanica, Gardner; Bedd. Fl. Sylv. t. 137.

Trunk erect, branches drooping, wood soft, shining, pale yellowish-brown. L. coriaceous, glabrous, shining, elliptic-oblong, blade 4–6, petiole ½ in. Fl. pale greenish-white. Fr. ¾–1 in.

Evergreen forests of the Western Ghats from the Konkan southwards. Fl. C. S.

Ceylon. 2. **S. javanica,** Blume. Tenasserim, Malay Peninsula. A middle-sized tree. L. oblong-lanceolate, blade 4–7, petiole ½–1 in.

Schoepfia fragrans, Wall., Nepal, Assam, Khasi hills, is a middle-sized tree, bark corky, whitish. L. lanceolate, blade 2–4, petiole ¼ in. Fl. golden-yellow, very fragrant, ⅙ in. long, in axillary racemes, pedicels slender, nearly as long as flower. Involucre immediately below the calyx, of 3 bracts, connate into a cup. Calyx truncate, adherent to ovary. Corolla twice the length of calyx, funnel-shaped, lobes 5, lanceolate, stamens 5, adnate to the corolla, and opposite to its lobes, a tuft of hair above their insertion. Drupe supported by the persistent involucre, stone thin, striated, embryo minute in the apex of the fleshy albumen. Closely allied and perhaps not specifically distinct is: 2. **S. acuminata,** Wall. Khasi hills. L. broader. Fl. ⅓ in., pedicels much shorter than flower. 3. **S. Griffithiana,** Valeton, Bhutan, is imperfectly known.

3. ANACOLOSA, Blume; Fl. Brit. Ind. i. 580.

Evergreen trees or shrubs. Fl. 5–7-merous, in axillary cymose fascicles. Calyx generally glabrous, cup-shaped, indistinctly toothed, not accrescent. Petals free, thick and concave at base, stamens opposite to petals and concealed in the cavity, filaments short, flat. Drupe surrounded by the accrescent disk, stone crustaceous, embryo minute at the apex of the fleshy albumen. Species 5 or 6, Indo-Malayan region.

1. **A. densiflora,** Bedd. Fl. Sylv. t. 138. Vern. *Katta vekkali, Kalmanikam*, Mal.

A lofty tree, wood brittle. L. oblong-lanceolate, base rounded, 4–5 in., petioles short. Fl. in dense axillary clusters, pale-yellowish, very fragrant. Petals densely hairy on the upper surface.

Evergreen forests of the Anamalai hills and Travancore, ascending to 2,000 ft. Fl, Sept.–Dec. "The boughs a perfect mass of very fragrant flower," Bedd. 2. **A. ilicoides.** Mast.; Khasi hills. A small spreading tree. L. oblong-lanceolate, base acute. Fl. few, in lax cymes. 3. **A. Griffithii,** Mast. Tenasserim and Andamans. L. ovate-lanceolate, blade 2–4, petiole ⅓–½ in., cymes few fld., petals hairy at the apex of the concave portion, otherwise glabrous, anthers hairy. 4. **A. puberula,** Kurz. Andamans and Nicobars. L. ovate-lanceolate, blade 3–6, petiole ¼–⅓ in. long. Pedicels and outside of calyx rusty-pubescent, petals glabrous, excepting a tuft of long hairs at the apex of the cavity, anthers hairy.

4. CANSJERA, Juss.; Fl. Brit. Ind. i. 582.

Climbing shrubs. Fl. small, bisexual, 4–5-merous, in short axillary spikes, bracts small. Calyx 0, corolla campanulate, hairy. Stamens 4–5, adnate to corolla and opposite to lobes, hypogynous scales alternating with stamens, filaments filiform. Ovary fleshy, 1-celled, ovule 1, pendulous. Drupe supported by the marcescent corolla, embryo straight in the axis of the fleshy albumen, cotyledons sometimes 3, long, plane-convex. Species 3–4, tropical Asia, China, Australia.

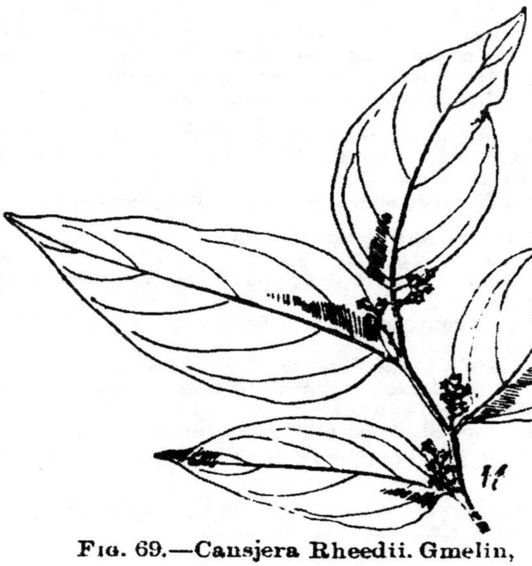

Fig. 69.—Cansjera Rheedii. Gmelin, ½.

1. **C. Rheedii,** Gmelin; Wight Ic. t. 1861; Bedd.

Fl. Sylv. Manual t. 26; Brandis F. Fl. 75. Syn. *C. scandens*, Roxb. Cor. Pl. t. 103.

A large evergreen climber, armed with scattered stout spines, branchlets, petioles and inflorescence pubescent. L. ovate-lanceolate, glabrous or slightly pubescent, 1½–4 in. long. Fl. yellow, perianth hairy outside. Fr. orange-red, ½ in. long.

Oudh forests. Behar. Western Peninsula, generally in evergreen moist forest. Tenasserim, Andamans. Fl. Sept.–Mar. Fr. H. S. Ceylon, Malay Peninsula and Archipelago. Nearly allied and probably not specifically distinct: 2. **C. parvifolia,** Kurz. Tenasserim. L. small, pubescent. 3. **C. zizyphifolia,** Griff., and 4. **C. Helferiana,** Valeton. Tenasserim.

Lepionurus sylvestris, Blume; King in Journ. As. Soc. Bengal, vol. 64 (1896) 105 (*L. oblongifolius*, Mast.). Sikkim, Assam, Khasi and Naga hills, Tenasserim, Malay Peninsula and Archipelago. A glabrous shrub or small tree, branches pale when dry. L. 4–7 in. Fl. tetramerous, bisexual, in axillary spikes ½–1¼ in. long, at first enveloped by the large ovate acute membranous deciduous bracts. Calyx 0, perianth urceolate, lined by the disk. Stamens exserted, filaments broad. Fr. ⅓–½ in. long.

Opilia amentacea, Roxb. Cor. Pl. t. 158; Wight Ill. t. 40; Bedd. Fl. Sylv. Manual t. 9. Western Peninsula, Burma, Upper and Lower, Ceylon dry country, Malay Peninsula and Archipelago, New Guinea, Australia, tropical Africa. A weak, scrambling shrub, branchlets finely pubescent. L. glabrous 2–3 in. Fl. minute, yellow, bisexual. Clusters of 2–4 flowers, in short erect axillary spikes, covered before expansion by round acute ciliate bracts, overlapping the buds. Calyx 0, petals 5 free. Stamens 5, opposite to petals, alternating with short fleshy staminodes, style short, truncate.

ORDER XXXII. ICACINACEÆ. Engler in Engler u. Prantl iii. 5. 233.

(*Olacineæ*, tribes iii. *Icacineæ*, iv. *Phytocreneae*. Gen. Pl. i. 344.)

Shrubs, trees or large climbers. L. generally alternate, stipules 0. Fl. small, mostly polygamous or diœcious, calyx small or wanting, petals or segments of perianth free or connate, stamens alternating with petals or perianth segments. Ovary mostly 1-celled, ovules pendulous from the apex of the cavity. Drupe 1-seeded.

A. L. alternate; fl. bisexual, rarely polygamous; shrubs or trees.
- Corolla campanulate, midrib of lobes prominent . . . 1. GOMPHANDRA.
- Petals free, hairy above, style terminal . . . . . 2. MAPPIA.
- Petals free, glabrous, style lateral . . . . . . 3. APODYTES.

B. L. alternate; fl. polygamous; shrubs or trees.
- Calyx 5-lobed, petals 5, fleshy, more or less cohering, apex inflexed . . . . PHLEBOCALYMNA (p. 152).
- Sepals 5, corolla tubular, teeth 5, spreading . . . GONOCARYUM (p. 152).

C. L. alternate, fl. diœcious, climbers.
- Calyx 0, perianth 4–5-lobed.
  - L. broad, ♂ ∞ in long panicles, ♀ in solitary globose heads . . . . 4. PHYTOCRENE.
  - L. glabrous, lanceolate or ovate, fl. in long pedunculate heads . . . . 5. MIQUELIA.
  - L. harsh, lanceolate, with shallow distant teeth, ♂ in lax filiform axillary spikes, ♀ in small heads on filiform peduncles . . . . PYRENACANTHA (p.153).
- Calyx 4–5-lobed, petals free, albumen 0 . . . . . 6. SARCOSTIGMA.
- Sepals 5, petals 5, cotyledons orbicular, in a fleshy albumen . . . . NATSIATUM (p. 154).

D. L. opposite; fl. diœcious: calyx cup-shaped, 5-toothed, corolla 3–5-lobed, hairy outside . . . . . 7. IODES.

1. GOMPHANDRA, Wall.; Fl. Brit. Ind. i. 585 (*Stemonurus*, Blume; Engl. u. Prantl iii. 5. 247).

Trees or shrubs, Fl. bisexual or polygamous, 4-5- sometimes 6-merous. Calyx cup-shaped, teeth short. Corolla campanulate, lobes acuminate, inflexed, midrib prominent on the inside. Stamens 5, hypogynous, alternating with corolla lobes, filaments flat, as long as or longer than corolla, often papillose or hairy, anther cells distinct, pendulous from the filiform apex of the filament. Drupe surmounted by the remains of the disk, endocarp crustaceous. Embryo minute, albumen fleshy bipartite. Species 8–10, tropical Asia.

1. **G. polymorpha**, Wight Ic. t. 953.—Syn. *G. coriacea*, Wight; Bedd. Fl. Sylv. Manual t. 9.

A shrub, glabrous except inflorescence, which is more or less papillose or puberulous. L. thinly coriaceous, most variable in shape, cymes terminal or leaf-opposed, pedunculate, much longer than petiole. Fl. sometimes 6-merous, polygamous.

Western Ghats from North Kanara southwards, often forming the underwood in evergreen forests. Fl. March–Sept. Ceylon. 2. Closely allied is **G. axillaris**, Wall. Khasi hills (not in the Western Peninsula). L. membranous, cymes axillary, as long as or shorter than petiole. 3. **G. comosa**, King, South Andaman. Fl. 4-merous, connective and upper part of filaments densely covered with long white glandular-pointed hairs. 4. **G. penangiana**, Wall. (*Stemonurus penangianus*, Miers; Kurz F. Fl. i. 238.) Tenasserim, Malay Peninsula. Fl. 4-merous, filaments with a few white hairs at the back. 5. **G. andamanica**, King (*Apodytes andamanica*, Kurz). Andaman and Nicobar Islands. An evergreen tree, branchlets tawny-puberulous. L. 5–8 in., filaments quite glabrous. Fr. 1 in. long.

2. MAPPIA, Jacq.; Fl. Brit. Ind. i. 388.

Species 4, tropical Asia and America.

1. **M. fœtida**, Miers, in Ann. & Mag. Nat. Hist. ii. vol. 9 (1852) p. 395, and Contributions to Botany, vol. i. p. 64 (simultaneous publications). Bedd. Fl. Sylv. t. 141. Vern., *Kala gaura*, *Kalgur*, *Ganera*, Mar.; *Arali*, Tam.

A small tree or large shrub, with strong smell, particularly the flowers. Medull. rays broad, prominent on a radial section. Young shoots and underside of leaves thinly pubescent. L. ovate, acuminate, base often unequal-sided, blade 2–8 in., petiole 1–2 in. Fl. yellow in terminal corymbose panicles, generally bisexual. Calyx hairy, 5-lobed. Petals free, hairy above. Stamens 5, hypogynous, alternating with petals, inserted outside the cup-shaped disk. Ovary hairy, style terminal. Drupe oblong, obtuse, red, $\frac{3}{4}$ in. long.

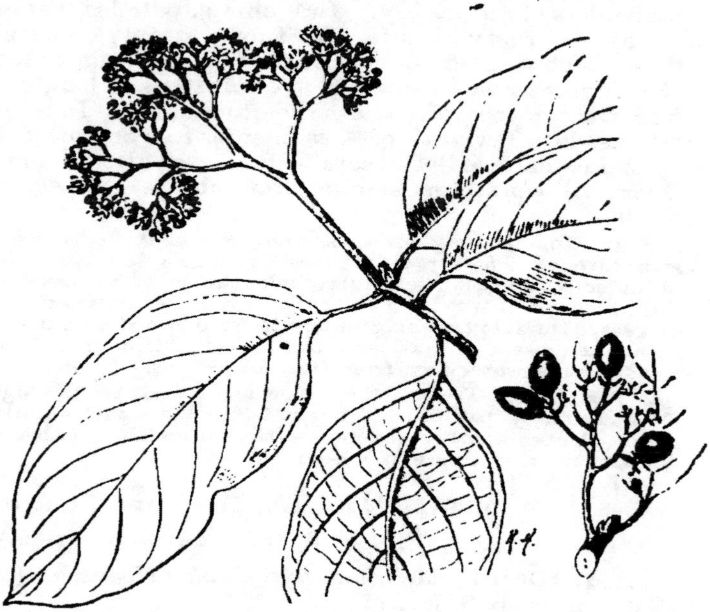

FIG. 70.—Mappia fœtida, Miers. Fl., fr. $\frac{1}{2}$.

Western Ghats from

the Konkan southwards, generally in evergreen forests. Nilgiris, Anamalais, Palnis. Fl. March–Aug. No difference between this and *M. ovata*, Miers, and *oblonga*, Miers. *M. tomentosa*, Miers (*Stemonurus* (?) *fœtidus*, Wight Ic. t. 955) Nilgiris, inflorescence and under side of leaves tomentose, is a remarkable form of this most variable species.

3. APODYTES, E. Meyer ; Fl. Brit. Ind. i. 587.

(Species 7, tropical Asia and Africa.)

1. **A. Benthamiana,** Wight Ic. t. 1153 ; Bedd. Fl. Sylv. t. 140.

A middle-sized tree. L. coriaceous, turning black in drying, obtuse elliptic-ovate. Fl. bisexual, pentamerous, white, ¼ in. long, in short rigid terminal panicles, calyx minute, cup-shaped, petals free, valvate. Stamens 5, alternating with petals, anthers oblong, sagittate, longer than filaments. Ovary hairy, obliquely gibbous, style lateral. Drupe reniform, scar of style lateral, embryo small, in the apex of fleshy albumen.

Nilgiris, Anamalais, Travancore and Tinnevelli hills, 5–7,000 ft. Fl. Feb. Ceylon. 2. **A. Beddomei,** Masters. North Kanara 2,000 ft., South Kanara, Nilgiris. Tinnevelli hills at 3,000 ft. A handsome tree. L. ovate acuminate, membranous, panicles ample. Fl. ⅛ in.. Ovary glabrous.

Phlebocalymna Griffithiana, Mast. (*Gonocaryum Griffithianum*, Kurz F. Fl. i. 241) is a middle-sized glabrous evergreen tree, frequent in swamp forests of Tenasserim and Southern Pegu. L. coriaceous, shining above, 3–6 in. long. Fl. minute, polygamous, pentamerous, the male in small globose heads, the bisexual flowers in short axillary spikes, sepals broad-ovate, acute, thick, petals more or less cohering. Stamens alternating with petals. Fr. 2 in. long, pericarp woody, oblong. *P. Lobbiana*, Mast., is probably the same.

Gonocaryum gracile, Miquel ; Kurz F. Fl. i. 240, Tenasserim, Sumatra. An evergreen shrub or tree, has a 2-celled ovary, the fruit is dry, spongy, 4-gonous, 1-seeded, the second cell small and empty.

4. PHYTOCRENE, Wall. ; Fl. B. Ind. i. 591.

(Species 7, Indo-Malayan region.)

1. **P. gigantea,** Wall. Pl. As. Rar. t. 216.

A gigantic woody climber, the trunk often 12 in. thick, irregularly tubercled, branchlets often prickly. Branchlets, petioles, nerves and underside of leaves tawny- or rusty-hirsute. L. from a deeply cordate base broadly ovate, sometimes 3-lobed, blade 6–10, petiole 2–3 in. long, basal nerves 3. Fl. diœcious, ♂ : Innumerable in small globose clusters on long compact racemiform panicles, from the old wood, often near the ground. ♀ : In large solitary globose pedunculate heads. Perianth of 4 segments, free or united below, in the ♂ supported by an involucre of 3–5 bracts. Stamens 4, alternating with segments of perianth. Ovary villous, stigma sessile, often lobed. Drupes numerous, packed in large heads.

Pegu Yoma, along streams, more frequent in Tenasserim. Fl. Feb.–March. The structure of *Phytocrene* is most remarkable. Outside a continuous but narrow cylinder of wood, which surrounds the pith, are seen on a transverse section 5–17 radial masses of wood with very wide vessels, alternating with narrower radial masses of bast. Outside this original cylinder of wood and bast, older stems show numerous detached masses of wood and bast, arranged more or less in concentric zones. Large quantities of water flow from fresh cut stems.

2. **P. bracteata,** Wall. Malay Peninsula and Archipelago, supposed to grow in South Tenasserim. ♂ panicles cylindric, 4–8 in. long, with subulate, curved hispid bracts, ½ in. long. Drupes densely covered with yellowish bristles, crowded in dense pendulous clusters, as large as a man's head.

5. MIQUELIA, Meissner : Fl. Brit Ind. i. 593.

(Species 5, Indo-Malayan region.)

1. **M. Kleinii,** Meissn.—Syn *Jenkinsia assamica*, Griff., Calc. Journ. Nat. Hist. vol. iv. p. 321 t. 12.

A climbing shrub. L. lanceolate, entire, blade 4–6, petiole 1 in. long. Fl. diœcious, capitate, male heads on long slender peduncles. Perianth 4–5-lobed supported by an involucre of 4–5 bracts, which in the male is separated by a long pedicel from the perianth. Stamens alternating with the segments of perianth, filaments short. Stigma nearly sessile, 4-lobed. Drupe $\frac{3}{4}$ in. long, yellowish, obliquely ovoid, endocarp crustaceous, rugose outside.

Upper Assam, Khasi hills. Fl. H. S. 2. **M. dentata**, Bedd., Anamalais. L. ovate, remotely and coarsely toothed, base truncate or cordate.

Pyrenacantha volubilis, Hook. Tinnevelli, foot of Ghats. Ceylon, dry country. A slender climber with milky juice, young shoots pubescent. L. lanceolate, base narrow truncate, with shallow distant teeth, harsh beneath from short stiff hairs. Sec. n. joined by intramarginal veins, conspicuous beneath. Fl. minute, diœcious. Calyx 0, perianth deeply 4–5-fid, ♂ in lax filiform axillary spikes 2 in. long, ♀ in small heads on filiform axillary peduncles. Drupe red, stone thin

FIG. 71.—Sarcostigma Kleinii, W. et A. $\frac{1}{2}$.

6. SARCOSTIGMA, W. et A.; Fl. Brit. Ind. i. 594.

(Species 3 or 4, tropical Asia.)

1. S. Kleinii, W. et A.; Wight Ic. t. 1854.

A climbing shrub. L. elliptic-oblong, coriaceous, glabrous, venation prominently reticulate, blade 4–10, petiole $\frac{1}{4}$–$\frac{3}{4}$ in. long. Fl. minute, diœcious, in sessile clusters along a long slender rachis. Calyx small 4–5-lobed, petals 5, nearly free. Stamens 5, alternating with petals, filaments flat, glabrous. Ovary hairy, stigma sessile, conical. Fr. 1–1½ in., bright orange-red, albumen 0, cotyledons fleshy, wrapping round the short superior radicle.

Western Ghats, in evergreen forests, from the Konkan southwards. Fl. Nov. Closely allied is: 2. **S. Wallichii,** Baillon. (*S. edule*, Kurz.) L. downy beneath, spikes rusty tomentose. Drupe clothed with orange-coloured down, pulp edible.

Natsiatum herpeticum, Ham. Sikkim Terai and outer valleys. Assam, Khasi hills, Chittagong, Pegu Yoma. A large climber, with thin wiry branches; branchlets, petioles, leaves and inflorescence rough with short stiff hairs. L. cordate, basal nerves 5–7, blade 4–6 in., petiole 2–5 in. long. Fl. diœcious, pentamerous, in long slender bracteate spiciform hirsute racemes. Sepals and petals hairy, linear-lanceolate, fertile stamens alternating with staminodes, which are opposite to petals, filaments very short, anthers sagittate. Drupe ¾ in., black, cotyledons fleshy, orbicular, in a fleshy albumen.

7. **IODES,** Blume; Fl. Brit. Ind. i. 505.

Shrubs climbing by means of woody axillary or extra-axillary tendrils L. opposite. Fl. diœcious, small, in short cymes on thick pedicels or in ample cymose axillary or extra-axillary panicles. Calyx small, cup-shaped, 5-toothed, corolla 3–5 lobed, outside densely clothed with long hairs. Stamens alternating with segments of corolla. Stigma sessile, 5–lobed. Drupe supported by the persistent calyx, cotyledons flat leafy, radicle superior, in fleshy albumen. Species about 8. Tropical Africa and Indo-Malayan region.

1. **I. Hookeriana,** Baillon; Kurz F. Fl. i. 244.
Branchlets and underside of leaves tawny-strigose. L. elliptic-oblong, base acute or slightly cordate, 4–8 in., petioles ¼–¾ in. long, venation conspicuously reticulate beneath. Cymes short few fld. Drupe 1–1¼ in., yellowish-red.

Assam, Khasi hills, Chittagong. Fl. C. S. Closely allied and perhaps not specifically distinct is 2: **I. Thomsoniana,** Baillon, Chittagong, an immense climber, l. obovate acuminate, narrowed into a cordate base. 3. **I. ovalis,** Blume (*I. tomentella*, Kurz F, Fl. i. 248). Tenasserim, Malay Peninsula. L. ovate acuminate, panicles ample, drooping. much longer than leaves. *I. Brandisii*, Kurz, Thoungyeen, is probably not distinct.

ORDER XXXIII. **ILICINEÆ.** Gen. Pl. i. 355.

(*Aquifoliaceæ*, Engler u. Prantl iii. 5. 183.)

ILEX, Linn.; Fl. Brit. Ind. i. 598.

Shrubs or trees, wood white, close-grained. L. alternate, simple, usually coriaceous and (in Indian species, with few exceptions) evergreen, stipules minute. At the base of the current year's internode are frequently imperfect bract-like leaves which had enveloped the leafbuds. Fl. usually diœcious, sometimes bisexual, in axillary cymes. Calyx 4–5 lobed, corolla rotate, petals free or connate at the base, deciduous, imbricate. Stamens 4–5, alternating with petals, adhering to the base of corolla, the imperfect stamens in the ♀ sometimes hypogynous. Ovary 2–12-celled. Stigmas 2–12 sessile or nearly sessile, free or confluent. Drupe globose, supported by the persistent calyx, stones 2–16, 1-seeded, embryo minute in a fleshy albumen. Species over 200, cosmopolitan, the majority tropical.

A. Fl. 4-merous, in dense short axillary, frequently branched cymes.

(*a.*) L. generally spinescent.

1. **I. dipyrena,** Wall. Pl. As. Rar. t. 292; Brandis, F. Fl. 76 t. 15.

Collett, Simla Fl. Fig. 27. *Himalayan Holly.* Vern. *Kanderu*, *Kalucho*, North-West Himalaya.

A middle sized tree, nearly glabrous. L. shining, elliptic-lanceolate, generally with large strong spinescent teeth, some quite entire. Fl. bisexual, white, 4-merous, ¼ in. diam., in axillary subglobose clusters, pedicels very short, stout, bracts small. Ovary 2- rarely 3–4-celled. Drupe ½ in. diam., stones usually 2.

Himalaya, from the Indus eastward 5,000–9,500 ft. Fl. April–June. 2. **I. Pernyi**, Franch. (China) var. *manipurensis*, Loes., Manipur (Watt), Loesener, Monographia Aquifoliacearum, i. 279. 3. **I. insignis**, Hook. f. (*Lisu*, Nep.). Sikkim 6–8,000 ft. A small tree, branchlets stout. L. spinous-toothed or obscurely serrate, second. n., intramarginal veins and tertiary nerves prominent beneath, blade 6–9, petiole ½–1 in. Drupes bright red, subsessile, stone 1–3-seeded.

(*b.*) L. serrate or entire, not spinescent.

4. **I. odorata**, Ham.; Brandis, F. Fl. 77.

A small tree. L. elliptic-oblong, minutely serrate, blade 5–9, petiole ⅓–⅔ in. Fl. white, ⅛ in. diam., unisexual, ♂ in short panicled cymes, ♀ in globose sessile clusters. Drupes black, ¼ in. diam. on slender pedicels as long as drupes.

Outer ranges of North-West Himalaya, Simla to Nepal, ascending to 6,000 ft. Fl. April. 5. **I. sikkimensis**, King, Journ. As. Soc. Bengal, 55 (1887), p. 265, t. 13. Sikkim, 6–10,000 ft., Manipur at 8,000 ft., attains 50 ft., leaf buds covered by numerous large imbricated broadly-ovate, blunt puberulous bracts (the lowest bract leaf-like). L. minutely serrate, blade 5–7, petiole ⅔–1 in. long. Fl. diœcious, in short rounded corymbs at the ends of short woody branchlets. Drupes yellow, ⅛ in. diam. on pedicels longer than drupe. 6. **I. Hookeri**, King l. c. 266. t. 14, Tongloo, Chumbi valley, Sikkim, 9–10,000 ft. A small deciduous tree. L. lanceolate, serrate, blade 3–5, petiole ⅓–1 in. Fl. polygamous, in dense sessile clusters, covered when in bud by imbricate ovate orbicular bracts. Fr. ⅛ in. diam. on short pedicels, in small clusters of 2 or 3. Two species found by Watt in Manipur with coriaceous almost entire leaves and 1-seeded fruit are: 7. **I. Clarkei**, Loesener Monographia Aquifoliacearum i. 274, and 8. **I. monopyrena**, Watt; Loes. ib. 275.

B. Fl. ♂ in panicled cymes, sometimes solitary or fasciculate, ♀ solitary or fascicled.

(*a.*) L. quite entire, or nearly so.

9. **I. malabarica**, Bedd. Fl. Sylv. t. 143.

A small tree, quite glabrous. L. lanceolate, blade 3–4, petiole ⅛–¼ in. Fl. $\frac{1}{10}$ in. diam., ♂ in shortly panicled umbels, pedicels slender, ♀ solitary or fascicled. Calyx-lobes usually 6, broad, ciliate, petals 4–6, ciliolate, style stout, cylindric. Drupe ⅛ in., crowned by persistent style, pedicel longer than drupe.

Western Ghats, from the Konkan southwards, in evergreen forests and on the banks of streams, Nilgiris, Anamalais. Fl. Feb.–March. 10. **I. Walkeri**, Wight & Gard., Palni hills, Ceylon. A small much branched tree. L. ¾–1½ in. Loesener calls the Palni plant *I. Thwaitesii*.

(*b.*) L. toothed or serrate.

11. **I. denticulata**, Wall.; Wight Ill. t. 149; Bedd. Sylv. t. 142.

A very large tree. L. rigidly coriaceous, serrate, narrowed into a broad marginate petiole, blade 2–3, petiole ¼–½ in. Fl. 4-merous, ♂ in short, subsessile cymes, ♀ fascicled. Drupe ⅓ in. diam., stones 4, trigonous, woody, pedicels stout, as long as drupe.

Nilgiris and Anamalais, 6–8,000 ft. Fl. Jan.–Feb. Ceylon, upper mountain zone. Closely allied is 12. **I. theæfolia**, Wall. (*I. gaultheriæfolia*, Kurz), Khasi, Mishmi hills. Tenasserim (Kurz). L. caudate-acuminate. Fl. 5-merous. Drupe ¼ in. diam. 13. **I. Griffithii**, Hook. f. (referred by Loesener to *I. triflora*, Blume, from Java), Assam, Khasi hills, Malay Peninsula. A shrub or small tree, branchlets more or less pubescent. L. obtusely serrulate, blade 2–3, petiole ¼ in. Drupe ¼ in. diam., generally solitary, pedicel longer than drupe. 14. **I. embelioides**, Hook. f., Khasi hills. A small tree, glabrous. L. elliptic-lanceolate, caudate-acuminate, with small scattered spinulose teeth along the margin, blade $1\frac{1}{2}$–2, petiole $\frac{1}{4}$ in. Fl. 4-merous in axillary clusters. Drupe $\frac{1}{8}$ in, stones 4, pedicel as long as drupe. 15. **I. Thomsoni,** Hook. f. (*I. crenata,* Thunb. var. *Thomsonii,* Loesener, Monographia Aquifoliacearum, i. 202), Bhutan, Khasi hills. A small bright green shrub, branchlets puberulous. L. $\frac{1}{2}$–1 in., oblanceolate or obovate. Fl. 4-merous, ♂ in few fld. cymes or solitary. Drupe $\frac{1}{4}$ in. diam., stones 4. 16. **I. intricata,** Hook. f., Sikkim and East Nepal, 10–11,000 ft. A rigid shrub, forming matted masses with interlaced woody branches. L. $\frac{1}{8}$–$\frac{1}{2}$ in., obovate. Sec. n. 4–5 pair, conspicuous beneath. Fl. solitary, ♀ sessile. Drupes red, $\frac{1}{4}$ in. diam., stones 4. 17. **I. fragilis,** Hook. f., Sikkim and Bhutan, 7–10,000 ft. A small deciduous, wholly glabrous tree, with brittle branches. L. membranous, elliptic or ovate, acuminate. Fl. 5-merous, $\frac{1}{8}$ in. diam., both ♂ and ♀ fasciculate. Drupes red, $\frac{1}{3}$ in. diam., pedicels short, stout.

C. Fl. umbellate, umbels often paniculate. L. entire.

18. **I. Wightiana,** Wall.; Wight Ic. t. 1216; Bedd. Fl. Sylv. t. 142.

A very large tree, often attaining a great girth. L. elliptic, blade $1\frac{1}{2}$–3 in., petiole $\frac{1}{4}$–$\frac{1}{3}$ in. Fl. 5–6-merous, ♂ and ♀ in peduncled puberulous umbels. Drupe red, $\frac{1}{4}$ in. diam.

Nilgiris 6–8,000 ft. Fl. March, April. 19. **I. Gardneriana,** Wight Ic. t. 1217, Nilgiris (west side). A shrub or small tree. L. ovate-lanceolate, caudate-acuminate, blade 3–4, petiole $\frac{1}{2}$–$\frac{3}{4}$ in. Fl. 5-merous.

20. **I. Godajam,** Colebr.; Fl. Brit. Ind. i. 604.

A large deciduous tree, young shoots and inflorescence pubescent. L. membranous, elliptic, pale beneath, blade 2–4, petiole $\frac{1}{4}$–$\frac{1}{3}$ in. Fl. fragrant, often appearing before the leaves, 4–5-merous, polygamous, ♂ in long pedunculate umbels, these often in lateral panicles, pedicels as long as flower. Fr. ovoid, $\frac{1}{8}$–$\frac{1}{6}$ in., sulcate, stones 4–6.

FIG. 72.—Ilex Godajam, Colebr. $\frac{1}{2}$.

Sikkim Terai, West Duars, Assam, Silhet. Fl. Feb.–April. Closely allied 21. **I. sulcata,** Wall. (*I. umbellulata,* Loesener), Silhet, Chittagong, Pegu, Tenasserim. A tree or shrub, l. larger, umbels not in panicles, but on the low naked part of leaf-bearing branchlets. Drupes ovoid, $\frac{1}{4}$ in. long, deeply 8-furrowed, stones numerous, generally 8. This probably is the tree described as *I. Godajam,* by Kurz, F. Fl. i. 245. 22. **I. venulosa,** Hook. f., Khasi and Naga hills. L. coriaceous shining, elliptic-oblong caudate-acuminate, blade 5–7, petiole 1 in. long. Sec. n. 12–18 pair conspicuous, as well as the intramarginal veins and the shorter intermediate nerves. Fl. polygamous, 4–6-merous, arranged in dense round axillary panicles. Drupes red, $\frac{1}{8}$ in. diam.

23. **I. excelsa,** Wall. (*I. exsulca,* Brandis F. Fl. 76.) Vern. *Kanial,* Gadugad.

A large evergreen, glabrous tree. L. chartaceous, elliptic, acuminate, blade 2–4, petiole $\frac{1}{2}$–1 in. Fl. 4–5-merous, 8–12, in shortly pedunculate umbels,

axillary or below the leaves, peduncles pubescent, stout, compressed, ¼–½ in. Drupe globose, ⅛ in. diam., stones 5.

Tehri-Garhwal. Kumaon. Nepal. Khasi hills. Fl. May. A variety with the leaves pubescent beneath, is called *I. hypotricha*, Loesener. Two Malayan species reported from Mergui: 24. **I. macrophylla,** Wall. L. elliptic-oblong, blade 4–6, petiole ⅓ in. Fl. in dense pedunculate umbels, peduncles often dichotomous. 25. **I. cymosa,** Blume. L. 3–5 petiole ¼–⅓ in. Fl. in lax umbels, arranged in ample dichotomous panicles.

ORDER XXXIV. CELASTRACEÆ. Gen. Pl. i. 357.

(*Celastrineæ.*)

Loesener (Engler u. Prantl iii. 5. p. 189, 222) adopts two orders, *Celastraceæ*, stamens 4–5, rarely 10, albumen as a rule fleshy, and *Hippocrateaceæ* (*Hippocratea, Salacia*), stamens as a rule 3, albumen wanting.

Trees or shrubs. L. in the majority of species opposite, stipules minute, early deciduous, or none. Inflorescence generally cymose. Calyx small, 4–5-cleft, imbricate. Petals 4–5, spreading, not clawed, imbricate. Stamens 3, 4 or 5, rarely 10, inserted on the disk and, if isomerous, alternating with petals. Disk large, surrounding the base of the 3–5-celled ovary or partially enclosing it. Embryo straight, radicle inferior, in a few cases lateral.

In *Celastraceæ*, as far as known, the wood, even of climbing species, has a normal structure, the medullary rays are generally broad, and the vessels large. In *Hippocratea* and *Salacia* matters are different, and the wood of all Indian species of these two genera, climbing as well as erect, merits careful study. The repeated concentric bands of bast (phloëm) are frequently interrupted and are often joined by radial bands, so that on a transverse section numerous masses of xylem appear separated by tangential and radial bands of bast, similar to the structure mentioned under *Securidaca*. Several American species of these two genera have been well described and figured in Schenck, Anatomie der Lianen, 1893, p. 131, tab. vii.

A. Fr. follicular or a dehiscent capsule.
  L. opposite, seeds not winged.
    Petals free, disk fleshy, capsule 3–5-celled.
      Cymes axillary, ovules 2 in each cell . . . . 1. EUONYMUS.
      Cymes mostly supra-axillary, ovules solitary . 2. GLYPTOPETALUM.
    Petals connate at base, capsule 1-celled, 1-seeded . 3. MICROTROPIS.
  L. generally opposite, seeds winged.
    Seeds winged at the lower end, carpels distinct in fruit 4. HIPPOCRATEA.
    Seeds winged at the upper end, capsule 3-valved . KOKOONA (p. 161).
    Seeds winged nearly all round, capsule 3-valved . 5. LOPHOPETALUM.
  L. alternate.
    L. serrate. Fl. in panicled cymes, stamens on edge of disk . . . . 6. CELASTRUS.
    L. serrate. Fl. in dichotomous cymes, stamens under the disk . . . . 7. GYMNOSPORIA.
    L. entire . . . . 8. KURRIMIA.

B. Fr. indehiscent.
  Stamens 5, inserted under the edge of disk.
    A tree. Fl. in pendunculate dichotomous cymes . 9. ELÆODENDRON.
    A shrub. Fl. in small subsessile cymes . . . PLEUROSTYLIA (p. 165).
    A tree. Ovary half adnate to calyx tube . . . SIPHONODON (p. 165).
  Stamens 3, inserted on the disk or apparently on the ovary. . . . . 10. SALACIA.

1. EUONYMUS, Linn.; Fl. Brit. Ind. i. 607.

Trees or shrubs, the Indian species mostly evergreen, wood white, even-grained, vessels very small, medull. rays extremely fine. L. generally coriaceous, opposite, stipules deciduous. Fl. bisexual, in axillary cymes. Calyx flat, 4–6-cleft. Stamens alternating with petals, both inserted on a broad fleshy

4–6-lobed disk. Ovary 3–5-celled, immersed in disk. Ovules 2 superposed in each cell, style short. Capsule 3-5-lobed, angled or winged, dehiscence loculicidal, cells 1–2-seeded, seeds with a fleshy arillus, embryo straight in oily albumen. Species 60–80, most in the Indo-Malayan region, some in Europe, North and Central America and Australia.

A. Species of the Western Peninsula.

1. **E. indicus,** Heyne.—Syn. *E. Goughii*, Wight Ic. t. 215.

A middle-sized tree. L. elliptic, generally entire, blade 3–4, petiole ¼ in. Peduncles axillary 1–3-fld., solitary. Fl. 5-merous, petals reddish, ciliate, orbicular. Fr. 5-lobed, longer than broad, angles acute.

Western Ghats in evergreen forests. Nilgiris. Fl. Dec.–May. 2. **E. crenulatus,** Wall.; Wight Ic. t. 973; Bedd. Fl. Sylv. t. 144. Palnis and Nilgiris. A small tree, peduncles solitary, 1–7-fld. Fr. as long as broad, ½ in. long, angles obtuse. 3. **E. dichotomus,** Heyne, southern part of Western Ghats. A small tree, l. lanceolate, entire. Fr. 5-lobed at top. 4. **E. paniculatus,** Wight. Syn. *E. crenulatus*, Wight Ic. t. 214. Shivagherry hills. L. crenate, peduncles fascicled, bearing compound dichotomous cymes. 5. **E. serratifolius,** Bedd. Ic. Pl. Or. t. 171. Nilgiris, Carcoor Ghat, 3,000 ft. A shrub, l. prominently serrate. Fr. nearly globose, with 5 rounded lobes. 6. **E. angulatus,** Wight Ic. t. 1053. Nilgiris, Coorg. A small tree, branchlets sharply quadrangular, l. shining above, sec. n. indistinct. Fl. ¼ in. across, 5–6-merous, dull red. Fr. turbinate, obtusely angled.

B. Himalayan and Eastern species.

(*a*) Fr. echinate.

7 **E. echinatus,** Wall.; Royle Ill. t. 31. Vern. *Laduli*, Garhw.

A large shrub, often epiphytic, branchlets with 4 raised lines. L. crenate or serrate, blade 1½–2½, petiole ⅙–¼ in. Sec. n. spreading, 7–8 pair. Fl. 4-merous, ⅕ in. across. Fr. nearly globose, ¼–⅜ in. diam.

Himalaya, Kashmir to Sikkim, 7,000–12,000 ft. Fl. March, April. 8. **E. cinereus,** Lawson, Mishmi, Assam. Scandent. L. obovate, blade 3, petiole ¼–⅓ in. Sec. n. 3–5 pairs. Fr. depressed-globose, echinate, ½ in. diam.

(*b*) Fr. not echinate. Fl. usually pentamerous.

9. **E. tingens,** Wall.; Brandis F. Fl. 79. Collett, Simla Fl. fig. 28. Vern. *Skiosh*, Bussahir; *Bhambeli*, Jauns.

A small tree. L. crenate or serrate, blade 1½–2½, petiole ¼ in. Cymes fascicled. Fl. ½ in. across. Fr. ½ in. long, angles acute.

Himalaya, Sutlej to Nepal, 6,500–10,000 ft. Fl. April–June. 10. **E. javanicus,** Blume, Tenasserim, Malay Peninsula. A small tree. L. entire or slightly serrate, blade 4–6, petiole ⅓–½ in. Peduncles 1-fld., fascicled, petals oblong, fimbriate. Fr. ⅜ in. long, angles sharp. 11. **E. glaber,** Roxb., Bhutan, Manipur, Upper and Lower Burma. L. chartaceous, blade 4–7, petiole ½ in. Cymes solitary, axillary, 2–3 in. long. Fl. ¼–⅓ in. across. *E. timorensis*, Zipp. Pegu and Tenasserim, is probably not distinct. 12. **E. attenuatus,** Wall. Khasi hills, Cachar. L. entire, blade 3–6, petiole ½ in. Cymes solitary or 2 in one axil, 1–2 in. Fr. 5-lobed, a little broader than long. 13. **E. macrocarpus,** Gamble. Khumpung, Bhutan 7,500 ft. A large climber, l. crenate-serrate, cymes fasciculate on arrested woody branchlets. Fl. ¼–⅓ in diam. Fr. 1½ in. long 5-angular, valves acuminate.

(*c*.) Fr. not echinate. Fl. mostly tetramerous.

14. **E. lacerus,** Ham.; Brandis, F. Fl. 78.—Syn. *E. fimbriatus*, Wall. *Lichhoi*, *Angao*, Jauns.

A small deciduous tree. L. membranous, red in autumn before falling, blade 1–3½ by 1–2, petiole ¼–⅓ in. Cymes fasciculate at the base of the new shoot, fl. ⅕ in. across. Fr. ¼–⅓ in. long, with 4 spreading tapering wings, nearly ½ in. long.

Kuram valley, Trans-Indus 8–10,000 ft., Himalaya 6–11,000 ft., Indus to Sikkim. Fl. March–June. 15. **E. grandiflorus,** Wall. Pl. As. Rar. t. 254. Kumaon, Nepal, Khasi hills. Shan hills, Upper Burma, 4,000 ft. L. serrulate, cymes solitary, 3–5-fld., peduncles as long as leaves. Fl. ½ in. across. Fr. nearly globose, 4-angled, calyx persistent, prominent. 16. **E. bullatus**, Wall. Sikkim, Assam, Khasia, Manipur to 4,000 ft. A small tree. l. ovate-lanceolate nearly entire, blade 4–10, petiole ½ in. sec. n. 7–10 pair very prominent beneath. Fr. ⅓–½ in. diam., as long as broad.

17. **E. pendulus**, Wall.; Brandis, F. Fl. 79. *Tulli*, Hazara; *Bhambela*, Jauns.

A middle-sized tree, young shoots reddish-brown, shining. L. sharply serrate, blade 2–5, petiole ¼–⅓ in. sec. n. slender. Cymes frequently from the axils of bracts below the leaves, peduncle long, branches short. Fl. ⅓ in. Fr. broader than long, 3–4-lobed, angles often winged.

Locally (nowhere common) in the Himalaya, from Hazara to Assam, not known from Sikkim. Fl. April, May. 18. **E. frigidus**, Wall. Sikkim 7-12,000 ft. A straggling shrub. L. exceedingly variable, from narrow-linear to elliptic-lanceolate, serrate, blade 3–7, petiole ⅙–⅛ in. Fr. as broad as long, winged or not. A remarkable variety (Bhutan, Griffith; Khasi hills, C. B. Clarke) with 4 wings ⅓ in. long is *E. Lawsonii*, C. B. Clarke. 19. **E. Griffithii**, Kurz, Martaban hills, not unfrequent. A shrub (scandent, Griff.). Branches 4-angular, almost winged. L. sessile, slightly toothed, cymes short, branches filiform, divaricating. 20. **E. theæfolius**, Wall. Nepal, Assam, Khasi hills, Manipur. A shrub, branches with raised lines, l. sinuate-toothed, blade 2–3½, petiole ¼ in. Fr. nearly globose, obtusely 4-angled, ⅓ in. diam.

21. **E. Hamiltonianus**, Wall.; Brandis, F. Fl. t. 16. Vern. *Tritu*, Chamba; *Papar*, Pangi; *Batal*, Punjab; *Dadūl*, Jauns.

A small deciduous tree, bark often corky. L. membranous, serrulate, blade 3–6, petiole ⅓–½ in. Cymes axillary, or below the leaves, often on arrested branchlets, peduncles short. Fl. ¼–⅓ in. across, numerous. Fr. deeply 4-lobed, angles obtuse.

Outer Himalaya, 3,800–8,500 ft., common in places. Khasi hills, Manipur. Fl. March-June. China (wood used for carving and engraving). 22. **E. vagans**, Wall. Nepal, Sikkim. A climbing shrub, l. serrate, blade 2–3, petiole ⅙ in., cymes 1–2 in. long. Fr. nearly globose, ⅓ in. diam.

2. GLYPTOPETALUM, Thwaites; Fl. Brit. Ind. i. 612.

Differs from *Euonymus* by cymes generally supra-axillary, ovules solitary and pendulous from the top of the cell. Species 7, Indo-Malayan region.

1. **G. zeylanicum**, Thwaites; Trimen Handb. Ceylon i. 268.

A small tree. L. elliptic or elliptic-lanceolate, serrate or nearly entire, blade 3–6, petiole ¼ in. Cymes supra-axillary, shorter than leaves. Fl. ½ in. across, ovary conical, conspicuous, petals spreading or reflexed, with 2 oval shallow pits on the upper surface. Fr. green, depressed globose, 1–4-lobed.

Anamalais. Tinnevelli Ghats. Travancore. Fl. Feb. Ceylon. 2. **G. grandiflorum**, Bedd. Ic. Pl. Ind. Or. t. 102. Wainad, 2–3,000 ft. A large shrub. L. 4–7 in. Cymes supra-axillary, peduncles slender, 4–6 in. long, 3-flowered. Fl. bright yellow, ¾–1 in., petals without pits. 3. **G. calocarpum**, Prain (*Euonymus calocarpus*, Kurz), Tenasserim, North Andaman, Nicobars, Cocos Islands. A shrub or small tree, similar to *G. zeylanicum*, differs by entire leaves, cymes axillary or not, and smaller flowers. 4. **G. Griffithii**, Prain. Mishmi. Very similar, supposed to differ by very short cymes, peduncle shorter than petiole and pedicels. 5. **G. sclerocarpum**, Kurz (*Euonymus sclerocarpus*, Kurz, F. Fl. i. 250), Kambalu hill, Pegu Yoma. A tree. L. 6–12 in., entire or faintly serrate. Fr. nearly globose, ½ in. diam., rough.

3. MICROTROPIS, Wall.; Fl. Brit. Ind. i. 613.

Glabrous evergreen trees or shrubs. L. opposite, coriaceous, stipules 0. Fl. sometimes unisexual, usually pentamerous. Calyx more or less campanulate, disk lining the calyx tube or none, petals mostly connate at the base. Stamens often inserted on the base of petals. Ovary free, 2–3-celled, 2 collateral ovules in each cell. Capsule coriaceous, 2-valved, 1-celled, 1-seeded, supported by the persistent calyx.

1. **M. discolor**, Wall.; Kurz F. Fl. i. 251.

A shrub or small tree. L. thinly coriaceous, caudate-acuminate, blade 3–7 in., narrowed into a short petiole. Cymes bracteolate, dense, axillary or supra-axillary. Fl. ⅛ in. across, whitish. Fr. ovoid, 2-valved, ½–¾ in. long, seed 1, shining scarlet.

Kumaon, Sikkim, from the foot of the hills ascending to 7,000 ft., Khasi hills Manipur, Martaban and Tenasserim. Fl. Nov.–March. 2. **M. latifolia**, Wight. Western Ghats from the Konkan southwards, Nilgiris. A small tree. L. very coriaceous, margin thickened, blade 4–5 in., narrowed into a short petiole, cymes dense, sessile. Fr. ½ in., oblong. 3. **M. ramiflora**, Wight Ic. t. 977. Nilgiris, Anamalais, Palnis at high elevations. A middle-sized tree. L. very coriaceous, obtuse, broadly elliptic or obovate, margin thickened, blade 2½–4 in., petiole ¼ in., cymes dense, sessile, mostly on the previous year's wood below the leaves. Fr. ½ in. 4. **M. densiflora**, Wight Ic. t. 1052. Higher ranges of the Nilgiris and Palnis. L. resembling 3, cymes axillary, peduncle ⅛ in. Fr. cylindric, ¾ in. 5. **M. microcarpa**, Wight Ic. t. 975. Western Ghats from the Konkan southwards. A shrub, l. elliptic, obtuse, blade 1–3, petiole ¼ in., cymes axillary, lax, often clustered towards the ends of branches, peduncle ½–1 in., petals obovate-cuneate. Fr. ⅓ in., seed brown. 6. **M. ovalifolia**, Wight Ic. 976. Higher ranges of Nilgiris and Palnis. A shrub or small tree. L. similar to 5, cymes axillary and below the leaves, peduncle ¾–1 in. Fl. numerous, petals orbicular. Fr. cylindric, ½ in., apiculate, seed crimson. 5 and 6 are possibly not specifically distinct. 7. **M. bivalvis**, Wall., Tenasserim, Malay Peninsula and Archipelago. A small tree. L. elliptic acuminate, 3–4 in., narrowed into a petiole ¼–⅓ in. Cymes extra-axillary, very lax, peduncles slender, 1–2 in. long. Fr. ovoid, apiculate ½ in. long. Beddome (Fl. Sylv. Manual, 65) states that *M. Wallichiana*, Wight, a Ceylon tree, is found in the western forests of the Peninsula.

4. HIPPOCRATEA, Linn.; Fl. Brit. Ind. i. 623.

Climbing shrubs or small trees. L. coriaceous, opposite, entire or serrate. Fl. bisexual. Calyx small, 5-parted, petals 5, spreading. Stamens 3, filaments flat, recurved. Ovary 3-celled, style short, ovules in each cell 2–10, 2-seriate on the inner angle. Fr. separating into 3 distinct flat coriaceous usually dehiscent 2- or more-seeded carpels, seeds compressed, winged, attached to the base of carpel. Cotyledons greenish-yellow, fleshy. Species 70–90, tropics of both hemispheres.

A. Fl. minute, $\frac{1}{10}$ in. across or less.

1. **H. indica**, Willd.; Roxb. Cor. Pl. t. 130.

A glabrous climbing shrub. L. ovate, more or less serrate, blade 2–3½, petiole ⅓ in. Fl. rusty yellow, in axillary pedunculate cymes. Fr. carpels oblong, striated 1–1½ in. long, ⅓ in. broad.

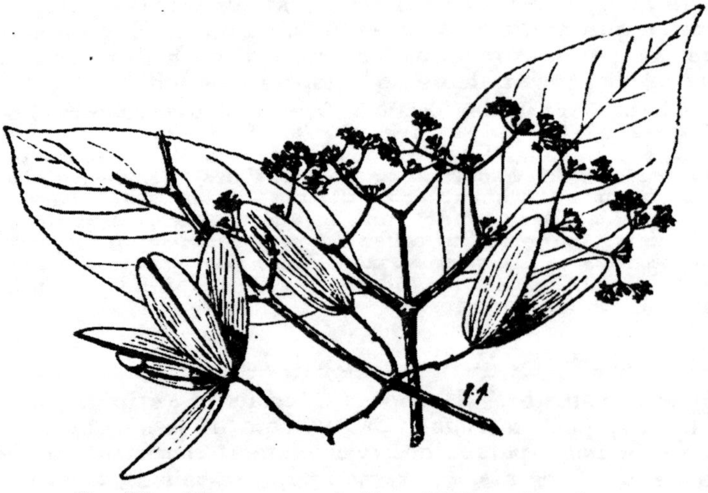

FIG. 73.—Hippocratea indica, Willd. Fr., fl. ½.

Western Peninsula, on the west side, from the Konkan southwards. Burma. Thankyeghat forest. Malay Peninsula. Fl. Jan.-April. 2. **H. arborea**, Roxb. Cor. Pl. t. 205 (*Metehkar*, Oudh). Oudh, Bhutan, Khasi hills. A large climber, ascending the largest forest trees, often enveloping them with its thick heavy foliage. L. serrulate, 5–6 in. long. Carpel 3 by 1½ in. Probably only a large form of *H. indica*.

B. Fl. small, $\frac{1}{8}$ in. and more across. Western species.

3. H. Grahami, Wight Ic. t. 380.

L. coriaceous, shining, entire or nearly so, blade 3–8, petiole $\frac{1}{2}$ in. Cymes generally much longer than leaf. Fl. $\frac{1}{6}$–$\frac{1}{8}$ in. across. Fr. $3\frac{1}{2}$ by 1 in., obtuse or emarginate, striated.

Ghats of the Konkan and North Kanara. . Fl. H. S.

4 H. obtusifolia, Roxb.; Wight Ic. 963.

L. variable in size and shape, 2–6 in. long, more or less crenate, veins finely reticulate. Cymes shorter than leaves, often forming terminal panicles. Fl. $\frac{1}{4}$–$\frac{1}{3}$ in. Fr. 2 in. long, seeds 4.

Western Peninsula on both sides, from the Konkan southwards. Fl. C. and H. S. 5. **H. Arnottiana,** Wight. West coast of Western Peninsula, from South Kanara southwards, Ceylon. L. coriaceous, shining, in the upper part faintly serrate, veins distinctly reticulate. Fl. $\frac{1}{8}$ in. across. Fr. $2\frac{1}{2}$ in. long.

C. Fl. small, $\frac{1}{8}$ in. and more. Eastern species.

6. **H. macrantha,** Korthals. Chittagong, Duffla hills, Tenasserim, Malay Peninsula. L. coriaceous, shining, more or less crenate, blade 4–7, petiole $\frac{1}{4}$ in. Fl. $\frac{1}{3}$ inch across, pale yellow or white, cymes short, $1-1\frac{1}{2}$ in. long. Ripe carpels 2, 3–4 in. long. 7. **H. Lobbii,** Lawson. Maulmein. L. broadly elliptic, blade 3–4, petiole $1-1\frac{1}{4}$ in. Cymes shorter than leaf. Fl. $\frac{1}{8}$ in. diam. 8. **H. andamanica,** King. Andamans. L. entire. Cymes often in ample terminal panicles. Fl. $\frac{1}{6}$ in. across. 9. **H. nicobarica,** Kurz. Nicobars. L. more or less serrate.

Kokoona littoralis, Lawson (*Lophopetalum littorale*, Kurz, *Môndaing*, Burm.) Pegu and Tenasserim, on low lands inundated during the rains. A large evergreen tree, wood grey, med. rays extremely fine and numerous. L. coriaceous, entire, opposite, 3–5 in. long. Fl. whitish, in axillary and terminal panicles. Capsules $2\frac{1}{2}$–3 in. long, coriaceous, 3-angled, seeds winged at the apex, with the wing $1\frac{1}{2}$–2 in. long, seeds oily, albumen 0.

5. LOPHOPETALUM, Wight; Fl. Brit. Ind. i. 614.

Glabrous trees and shrubs, wood light-coloured, med. rays extremely fine and numerous. L. opposite or alternate, entire, usually coriaceous. Stipules 0. Fl. bisexual, in cymose panicles. Calyx obtusely 5-lobed, disk large, flat, petals either confluent with it at the base, or inserted under its margin, sometimes crested or papillose on their upper surface. Stamens 5, inserted on the surface of the disk. Ovary triquetrous, 3-celled, ovules 7–12 in each cell. Capsule coriaceous, 3-valved, seeds imbricate, winged nearly all round, radicle lateral, cotyledons flat, albumen probably none. Species about 10, Indo-Malayan region.

1. L. Wightianum, Arn.; Wight Ic. t. 162; Bedd. Fl. Sylv. t. 145. Vern. *Balpale*, Kan.; *Venkotta*, Mal.

A large tree, wood close-grained. L. usually opposite, blade 3–6, petiole $\frac{1}{3}$–$\frac{1}{2}$ in. Fl. $\frac{3}{4}$ in. across, dull reddish, in ample axillary and terminal panicled cymes, petals with a corrugated crest. Capsule sharply triangular, 3–4 in. long.

West coast of the Peninsula, ascending on the Ghats to 3,000 ft., from the Konkan southwards. Fl. March–April. 2. **L. fimbriatum,** Wight. Sukna, Sikkim Terai (Gamble). Silhet, Chittagong, Martaban, Tenasserim. A tree, petiole $\frac{1}{2}$–1 in. fl. $\frac{1}{3}$–$\frac{1}{2}$ in. across, yellow to red, petals with a fimbriate crest. 3. **L. floribundum,** Wight, Mergui. A tree, inflorescence sometimes rusty-pubescent. Fl. $\frac{1}{6}$–$\frac{1}{8}$ in. across, petals not crested.

4. L. Wallichii, Kurz, F. Fl. i. 255; Pierre, Fl. Forest. Cochinch. t. 306. Vern. *Katbo*, Upper; *Môndaing*, Upper and Lower Burma.

A large glabrous deciduous tree, bark smooth, wood grey, moderately hard, concentric bands of wood-parenchyma. L. opposite or nearly so, elliptic or ovate, blade 3–6, petiole 1–1½ in. Fl. creamy white, ⅓ in. across, in ample terminal or axillary panicles, petals more or less papillose or crested on the upper surface, disk papillose, not confluent with petals, ovary purple. Capsule 3½ in. long, nearly woody, seeds flat, cotyledons 1 × ⅓ in.

Upper and Lower Burma in Eng or dry deciduous forest, on sandstone or alluvium. Fl. C. S., leafless H. S. Cambodia, Laos. 5. **L. celastroides,** Lawson. Rangoon, Maulmein. Supposed to differ by smaller leaves. 6. **L. filiforme,** Lawson. Mergui. Branches slender, l. elliptic-oblong, long-acuminate, blade 3 × 1¼, petiole ⅓ in. Branches of cymes filiform, petals not crested.

6. CELASTRUS, Linn.; Fl. Brit. Ind. i. 617.

Scandent shrubs. L. alternate, serrate. Fl. polygamous in panicled cymes. Calyx 5-cleft, petals 5, disk broad concave. Stamens 5 on the edge of disk. Ovary 2–4-celled, ovules 2 in each cell, stigma 3-lobed. Capsule 1–3-valved, seeds enclosed in a fleshy, coloured arillus, albumen copious.

A. Branches lenticelled.

1. **C. paniculata,** Willd.; Wight Ill. t. 72; Ic. t. 158. Vern. *Malkagni,* Hind.; *Kakundan,* Oudh; *Kujri,* Kol, Sonth.; *Kangondi,* Kan.; *Myinkaukhnayaung,* Burm.; *Wina,* Chindwin.

A large climbing shrub, deciduous (Smales), wood yellowish, med. rays

FIG. 74.—Celastrus paniculata, Willd. Fl., fr. ½.

broad. L. serrate, acuminate, blade 2½–5, petiole ¼–½ in. Fl. ⅛ in. diam., green, in large terminal drooping panicles. Stigma 3-lobed. Capsule 3-valved, seeds 3–6, completely enclosed in a red arillus.

Subhimalayan tract from the Jhelam eastward, ascending to 6,000 ft., Central India, Western Peninsula, Pegu, Upper Burma. Fl. Mar.–July. Fr. C. S. 2. **C. stylosa,** Wall. Nepal, Sikkim 6–8,000 ft., Khasi hills. A large climbing shrub, cymes short, axillary, or forming short terminal racemes. Fl. ⅙–¼ in.

B. Branches not lenticelled.

3. **C. monosperma,** Roxb. Sikkim 3–6,000, Assam, Khasi hills, Cachar. A climbing shrub. L. elliptic-lanceolate, blade 3–6, petiole $\frac{1}{8}$–$\frac{1}{2}$ in. Cymes arranged in elongated axillary and terminal panicles. Capsule $\frac{1}{3}$–$\frac{1}{4}$ in. long, 3-valved, seed 1. 4. **C. venulosa,** Wall. Sikkim Terai, Silhet, Duphla hills. A climber. Cymes in racemiform panicles 3–5 in. long.

7. GYMNOSPORIA, W. et A.; Fl. Brit. Ind. i. 618.

Shrubs or small trees, differing from *Celastrus* by fl. in dichotomous cymes and stamens inserted under the disk.

A. Armed, spines often bearing leaves and flowers.

1. **G. montana,** Lawson; Fl. Brit. Ind. i. 621.—Syn. *Celastrus montana*, Roxb.; Wight Ic. t. 382; *C. senegalensis*, Lamarck; Brandis F. Fl. p. 81. Vern. *Vingar*, Baluch.; *Baikal*, Hind.; *Kakra*, Ajm.; *Bharati*, Mar.; *Danti*, Tel.; *Tandrasi*, Kan.

FIG. 75.—Gymnosporia montana, Lawson. Fl. fr. $\frac{1}{2}$

A tall shrub, under favourable circumstances a small tree, trunk short, crooked. L. grey, coriaceous, exceedingly variable in shape and size, obovate, oblanceolate to linear-spathulate, narrowed into the petiole. The specimens from Sind and Rajputana, including the drier parts of the Punjab, have narrow, those from the Peninsula have broad leaves. Fl. small, pale greenish white, cymes axillary or fasciculate on short branchlets, often forming terminal elongate panicles. Capsule $\frac{1}{5}$ in., usually 2-valved, seeds 1, 2, rarely 3, with or without an arillus.

Common in the Punjab, Sind, Rajputana, the Central Provinces, Behar and the drier districts of the Peninsula. Fl. at various times throughout the year. Afghanistan, Western Asia, tropical Africa. 2. **G. Wallichiana,** Sprengel. Western Peninsula. Sec. n. not much more prominent than the reticulate tertiary nerves. Fr. $\frac{1}{3}$ in. diam. 3. **G. emarginata,** Roth (*Chinta*, Tel.). Western Peninsula, Ceylon. Fl. on long slender pedicels, $\frac{1}{2}$ in. Fr. $\frac{1}{4}$ in. diam.

B. Armed, spines usually naked.

4. **G. Royleana,** Wall.—Syn. *Celastrus spinosa*, Royle; Brandis F. Fl. p. 80; *Dzaral*, Trans. Ind.; *Pataki*, *Kander*, Pb.

A stiff dense shrub 8–12 ft. high. L. obovate, acute, greyish, spines axillary, slender. Cymes mostly axillary, petals reddish with white edges. Fr. $\frac{1}{3}$ in. diam.

Punjab. Subhimalayan tract, east to R. Kumaon, Fl. and Fr. almost throughout the year.. 5. **G. rufa,** Wall. Subhimalayan tract, Kumaon to Bhutan ascending to 6,000 ft., Khasi hills. A tree, l. lanceolate, blade 2–5, petiole $\frac{1}{4}$–$\frac{1}{3}$ in. Cymes axillary or below the leaves, fascicled, peduncles and pedicels filiform. Fl. white. Capsule $\frac{1}{4}$ in. diam. 6. **G. Falconeri,** Lawson. North-West India. L. pubescent beneath. Capsules $\frac{1}{4}$ in. diam. 7. **G. rugulosa,** Lawson. Mishmi. L. slightly serrate, nearly entire, blade 4–6, petiole $\frac{1}{2}$ in. Capsules slightly rugose, $\frac{1}{2}$ in. diam. 8. **G. pallida,** Collett et Hemsley. Southern Shan hills 3–4,000 ft. A shrub, spines few, l. 3–5 in. Cymes 1–1$\frac{1}{2}$ in. long. Fr. $\frac{1}{2}$ in. diam. 9. **G. Heyneana,** W. et A. Palni hills. L. broadly elliptic, blade 3–5, petiole $\frac{1}{3}$ in. Cymes axillary near the ends of branches, when in fruit 2–3 in. long. Fl. $\frac{1}{4}$–$\frac{1}{3}$ in. Fr. $\frac{1}{2}$ in. diam.

C. Unarmed. Western species.

10. **G. ovata,** Wall. Nilgiris, Malabar, Palni hills. L. 2–3 in., cymes much branched, axillary and terminal, 1 in. long. Fl. 1/8 in. across. Capsules 1/2 in. diam. Specimens collected by Sir Henry Collett on the southern Shan hills have been referred to this species. 11. **G. Rothiana,** W. et A., Konkan and North Kanara. A small tree. L. obovate, narrowed into petiole 3 in. long. Cymes dense, nearly sessile, mostly below the leaves. Fr. obovoid, 1/2–3/4 in. long. According to Dr. Ritchie this species is sometimes armed. 12. **G. puberula,** Lawson, Konkan. Inflorescence and underside of leaves slightly pubescent. L. membranous, obovate, acute, 2–3 in. long, narrowed into short petiole. Cymes lax, few-fld., peduncles and pedicels filiform.

D. Unarmed. Eastern species.

13. **G. acuminata,** Hook. f.

A large shrub or small tree. L. lanceolate, crenate-serrate, 3–7 in., narrowed into the short petiole. Cymes solitary or fascicled, axillary or on short lateral tubercles, peduncles and pedicels filiform. Capsule 1/3 in. long, mostly 2-valved, 2-seeded, the lower half of seed enclosed in a laciniate arillus.

Sikkim 4–7,000, Assam, Bhutan, Khasi hills, Upper Burma. Fl. April–June. 14. **G. neglecta,** Lawson. Khasi hills. A shrub. L. elliptic, serrate, blade 4–6, petiole 1/3–1/2 in. Fr. globose, 1/3 in. long, 3-valved, seeds 1–3. 15. **G. oblanceolata,** Lawson. Irawadi above Bhamo. L. oblanceolate, serrate in the upper half, 3–4 × 3/4 in., tapering into the short petiole. Sec. n. 5-6 pair very oblique. 16. **G. salicifolia,** Lawson. Assam. L. narrowly lanceolate, serrate, 3–4 × 1/2 in. Sec. n. faint.

8. KURRIMIA, Wall.; Fl. Brit. Ind. i. 621.

Glabrous trees. L. alternate, coriaceous, entire, congregated towards the ends of branches. Calyx 5-fid, petals 5, spreading or recurved, stamens inserted with petals under the margin of the disk. Ovary 2-celled, ovules 2 from the base of each cell. Capsule dehiscing by 2 valves, 1–2-seeded. Seeds more or less covered by a fleshy arillus, embryo oblong, albumen fleshy. Species 7–8, Indo-Malayan region.

1. **K. pulcherrima,** Wall.—Syn. *K. robusta*, Kurz. Vern. *Gwedauk*, Burm.

A large evergreen tree, quite glabrous. L. oblong-lanceolate, blade 4–6, petiole 3/4–1 in. Sec. n. prominent beneath, about 12 pair. Fl. in slender axillary, often fascicled racemes, shorter than leaves. Capsules ovoid-oblong, 1–1½ in. long, seeds generally 2, shining, arillus bright yellow, afterwards orange.

Western Duars, Assam, Silhet, Chittagong, Burma, Siam, Cochinchina, Tonkin. Fl. April–Aug. 2. **K. bipartita,** Lawson. Shevagherry hills. A handsome tree, l. thickly coriaceous, shining, elliptic, sec. n. very conspicuous beneath. Capsule deeply 2-lobed, lobes oblong, 1–1½ in. long, 1-seeded, at length dehiscing. To this species should be referred *Trochisandra indica*, Bedd. Fl. Sylv. t. 120. Anamalai hills, 3–6,000 ft., quoted by Lawson under *K. paniculata*, Wall., a Malayan species.

9. ELÆODENDRON, Jacq. fil.; Fl. Brit. Ind. i. 623.

(Included in *Cassine*, Linn., by Loesener in Engler u. Prantl iii. 5. 214.)

Species about 30, tropical Asia, America and Australia. South Africa.

1. **E. glaucum,** Pers.—Syn. *E. Roxburghii*, Wight Ill. t. 71; Bedd. Fl. Sylv. t. 148; Brandis F. Fl. 82. Vern. *Morindu*, Pb.; *Jamrassi*, Hind.; *Dhebri, paniala*, Dūn; *Chauri, Metkar*, Oudh; *Miri*, Kol; *Neowri*, Sonth.; *Tamruj, Aran*, Mar.; *Neradi*, Tel.; *Mukarti*, Kan.; *Karuvāli*, Tam.

A deciduous tree, middle-sized in dry localities, very large in moist evergreen forests, wood whitish, close-grained. L. glabrous, generally opposite, coriaceous, elliptic, crenate, stipules small, deciduous. Cymes axillary, dichotomous, lax, as long as or shorter than leaf, peduncle longer than petiole, branches divaricating. Fl. 4–5-merous, disk fleshy, angled. Stamens inserted under the edge of the disk, filaments recurved, anther cells attached to a broad connective, diverging at base. Drupe ovoid ½ in. long, yellowish-green when ripe, endocarp crustaceous, 1–2-celled, 1–2-seeded.

Subhimalayan tract and outer valleys, ascending to 6,000 ft., Ravi to Sikkim. Bandelkhand, Behar, Central provinces. Peninsula. Fl. Febr.-June. 2. **E. subrotundum,** King. Andamans, Malay Peninsula. A small tree. L. entire, almost orbicular. Fl. always tetramerous, disk not lobed.

Pleurostylia Wightii, W. et A.; Wight Ic. t. 155 (*Pairi*, Tel.). Western Ghats from the Konkan southwards. A shrub or small tree, med. rays extremely fine, combs made of the wood. L. opposite, oblanceolate, entire, 1–2 in. long, narrowed into short petiole. Fl. small, in small subsessile cymes, axillary and below the leaves, calyx 4-lobed, petals 5. Fr. coriaceous, indehiscent, ⅛–¼ in., seeds 1, rarely 2.

Siphonodon celastrineus, Griff.; Kurz, F. Fl. i. 254 (*Myauk-okshit*, Burm.). Martaban, eastern slopes of Pegu Yoma. An evergreen glabrous tree, med. rays of two classes, fine and very broad. L. alternate, elliptic oblong, crenate-serrate, blade 4–7, petiole ¼ in. long. Fl. pentamerous, yellowish, ¼–⅓ in. across, axillary, solitary, or 2–4 on a short thick peduncle, pedicels thick, ⅙–¼ in. Ovary half adnate to the calyx tube, cells numerous, irregularly placed in different planes, 1 ovule in each. Fr. a hard fleshy berry, 1–1½ in. diam., with numerous woody 1-seeded pyrenes.

10. SALACIA, Linn.; Fl. Brit. Ind. i. 625.

Scrambling or climbing shrubs, glabrous, branches sometimes circinately twisted at the base. L. opposite, stipules 0. Fl. fascicled or cymose. Calyx 5-parted, petals 5. Stamens 3, sometimes 4, inserted on the disk, often between its upper margin and the ovary, disk sometimes with a free lower margin, upper margin free or appressed to the ovary, filaments flat, ultimately recurved, anther cells oblique or transverse, rarely parallel. Ovary conical, more or less immersed in and confluent with the disk, mostly 3-gonous, 3-celled, ovules 3–8 on the inner angle of each cell, style undivided or none.

A. Fl. fasciculate on tubercles, ovary free, or not enveloped by the disk more than half-way up.

1. **S. flavescens,** Kurz, F. Fl. i. 260.
A large climber. L. entire or serrate, acuminate, blade 3–8, petiole ⅓–½ in. Fl. ⅛ in., pedicels slender, ¼–⅓ in., disk with a prominent free upper margin, stamens inserted within it. Fr. 1½–2 in.

Tenasserim. Fl. R. S.

2. **S. Smaliana,** spec. n. Vern. *Nwè-ngan*, Burm.
An evergreen climber. L. entire, elliptic or obovate, obtuse, blade 5–9, petiole ¾ in. Fl. few, yellow, ⅓–½ in., inodorous, pedicels thick, ⅓–¼ in., upper margin of disk conspicuous, lower margin undulating, stamens inserted between the trigonous ovary and the upper margin, anther cells distinct, style long.

On low ground and edges of swamps with *Eugenia*; Gaungbyu forest, Upper Burma. Fl. April. 3. **S. multiflora,** Wight, Tenasserim, differs from 2 by acute leaves. Fl. numerous, ⅛ in. across, on filiform pedicels ½–¾ in., disk annular, surrounding the ovary, anther cells terminal, transverse.

B. Fl. fasciculate on tubercles, ovary enveloped by the disk more than half-way up, stamens appearing as if inserted on the ovary.

(*a*) Fl. large.

4. **S. latifolia,** Wall.; King in Journ. As. Soc. Beng. vol. 65 (1897), p. 366.
A scandent shrub. L. entire or nearly so, blade 3–6, petiole ½–¾ in. Fl.

$\frac{1}{3}$–$\frac{1}{2}$ in., pedicels obovate, disk large, fleshy, stamens inserted on its upper edge, filaments long. Fr. 1 in. diam.

Andamans, Nicobars, Malay Peninsula. 5. **S. grandiflora**, Kurz. Tenasserim. L. entire, blade 8–12 in., petiole $\frac{1}{3}$–$\frac{3}{4}$ in. Fl. $\frac{1}{3}$–$\frac{1}{2}$ in., pedicels $\frac{1}{8}$–$\frac{1}{4}$ in., filaments very short. To this King (l. c. 366) refers *S. longifolia*, Hook. fil.

(*b*) Fl. small.

6. **S. Roxburghii**, Wall.; Kurz F. Fl. i. 259.

A lofty climber. L. entire, elliptic-oblong, acuminate, blade 3–4, petiole $\frac{1}{4}$ in. Fl. $\frac{1}{8}$ in., on short stiff pedicels, $\frac{1}{10}$–$\frac{1}{8}$ in. Disk with a ring at base, filaments very short, anther cells terminal, transverse.

Assam, Khasi hills (Chittagong, Lower Burma, Kurz). Fl. March. 7. **S. verrucosa**, Wight. Martaban and Tenasserim, Java. L. entire or slightly serrate, blade 4–7 in., narrowed into petiole $\frac{1}{4}$–$\frac{1}{3}$ in. Fl. numerous, $\frac{1}{8}$ in. across, pedicels slender, $\frac{1}{3}$–$\frac{1}{2}$ in. 8. **S. macrosperma**, Wight Ic. t. 962, West side of the Peninsula, from the Konkan southwards. A scandent shrub. L. entire, elliptic-oblong, blade $2\frac{1}{2}$–5, petiole $\frac{1}{4}$–$\frac{1}{3}$ in. Fl. $\frac{1}{8}$ in., very numerous in dense fascicles, pedicels $\frac{1}{8}$–$\frac{1}{4}$ in. Lower margin of disk thick like a ring, anthers nearly sessile. Fr. orange, irregularly obovoid, 1–2 in. long.

9. **S. prinoides**, DC.; Kurz, F. Fl. i. 260. Vern. *Dimal*, *Modhuphal*, Sundrib.

A straggling shrub or small tree, sometimes climbing. L. elliptic-lanceolate, slightly crenate, blade 2–$3\frac{1}{2}$, petiole $\frac{1}{4}$ in. Fl. $\frac{1}{4}$ in. across, 3–6 on minute bracteate axillary tubercles, pedicels $\frac{1}{4}$–$\frac{1}{3}$ in., filaments long. Fr. red, globose, $\frac{1}{2}$ in. diam.

FIG. 76.—Salacia prinoides, DC. Fl. fr. $\frac{1}{2}$.

Sundriban, both sides of the Western Peninsula, Khasi hills, Silhet, Cachar, Andamans. Burma, in the tidal forests, also inland. Fl. C. S., also at other times. Ceylon, Malay Peninsula and Archipelago. 10. **S. reticulata**, Wight. Quilon. A large woody climber, l. entire or faintly crenate, blade 2–$4\frac{1}{2}$, petiole $\frac{1}{4}$–$\frac{1}{2}$ in. Fl. $\frac{1}{4}$ in., pedicels $\frac{1}{4}$–$\frac{1}{3}$ in. Fr. pinkish orange, $\frac{3}{4}$–$1\frac{1}{2}$ in. 11. **S. membranacea**, Lawson. Sikkim, Khasi hills. Scandent, branchlets frequently circinnate and thickened. L. thinly chartaceous, entire, narrow-elliptic, blade $3\frac{1}{2}$–5, petiole $\frac{1}{4}$–$\frac{1}{3}$ in. Fl. few on short, stiff, erect pedicels, anthers subsessile. Fr. $1\frac{1}{3}$ in. diam. 12. **S. viminea**, Wall. Mergui. A spreading shrub, l. chartaceous, entire or slightly serrate, blade 3–6, petiole $\frac{1}{4}$ in. Fl. few, pedicels $\frac{1}{3}$ in. Ovary almost entirely enclosed by the disk, anthers subsessile on the top, anther cells terminal, transverse. The Tenasserim specimens have all opposite leaves, while what is supposed to be *S. viminea* from the Malay Peninsula has alternate leaves.

C. Fl. in axillary heads or pedunculate cymes.

13. **S. oblonga**, Wall.; Wight Ill. t. 47 B, Ic. t. 97; Bedd. Fl. Sylv. Manual t. 10. f. 4.

A climbing shrub. L. elliptic-oblong, more or less crenate-serrate, blade 2–5, petiole $\frac{1}{3}$–$\frac{1}{2}$ in. Fl. yellow, $\frac{1}{4}$ in. across, sessile, 3–6, in very shortly peduncled axillary heads. Ovary enveloped beyond the middle by the disk, anther cells parallel. Fr. $\frac{3}{4}$–$1\frac{1}{4}$ in., bright orange-red.

Western Ghats from the Konkan southwards. Fl. C. S., H. S. 14. **S. fruticosa**,

Heyne. Western Ghats from South Kanara southwards. Climbing. L. entire, long-acuminate, blade 3–4, petiole $\frac{1}{8}$–$\frac{1}{3}$ in. Fl. $\frac{1}{8}$ in. Ovary half enclosed in the disk, anther cells oblique. 15. **S. floribunda,** Wight (*S. longifolia*, Kurz F. Fl. i. 258). Assam, Khasi hills, Mergui. Branchlets frequently circinate at the base. L. elliptic-oblong, acuminate, serrate, blade 3–6, petiole $\frac{1}{8}$–$\frac{1}{2}$ in. Fl. $\frac{1}{8}$ in. across, cymes as long as or longer than petiole, peduncles $\frac{1}{4}$–$\frac{1}{2}$ in., disk with a free lower margin, slightly raised, stigma sessile. Fr. 1 in. diam. 16. **S. Griffithii,** Lawson, habitat unknown. Cymes dichotomous, lax, 2 in. across, on long peduncles. Fl. $\frac{1}{4}$ in., anthers sessile on the disk which nearly envelopes the ovary, style long.

ORDER XXXV. RHAMNACEÆ. Gen. Pl. i. 371.

(*Rhamneæ.*)

Trees or shrubs, not rarely climbing, often armed with spinescent branches or stipular spines. L. simple, alternate or opposite. Fl. small, green or yellow, often unisexual. Inflorescence generally cymose. Calyx 4–5 cleft, lobes triangular, valvate in bud. Petals inserted at the mouth of calyx-tube, or on the edge of the disk. Stamens opposite the petals and often enclosed by them. Disk lining or filling the calyx-tube. Ovary free, or more or less adhering to calyx-tube, 2- or 3-, rarely 4-celled, 1 erect ovule in each cell. Seeds 1–3

Structure of wood, even in the climbing species, normal as far as known.

A. Fr. dry, winged, 1-seeded, indehiscent	1. VENTILAGO.
B. Fr. a berry, sec. nerves numerous, parallel	2. BERCHEMIA.
C. Fr. a drupe, with a 1–3-celled stone, 3–5 basal nerves .	3. ZIZYPHUS.
D. Fr. a drupe with 2–4, mostly 3, distinct kernels (pyrenes), supported by the persistent but not enlarged calyx tube.	
L. mostly alternate, disk thin, lining calyx tube .	4. RHAMNUS.
L. mostly opposite, disk fleshy, filling calyx tube .	5. SAGERETIA.
E. Fr. indehiscent, nearly dry, 2–4-celled, 2–4-seeded.	
Armed. L. coriaceous, often opposite	6. SCUTIA.
Unarmed. L. membranous, alternate, ramifications of inflorescence fleshy in fruit	HOVENIA (p. 174).
F. Fr. dehiscent, pericarp generally coriaceous.	
Fr. superior, base supported by the persistent calyx tube	7. COLUBRINA.
Fr. flat, lower part enclosed in persistent calyx tube.	SMYTHEA (p. 175).
Fr. inferior, crowned by the persistent calyx limb.	
Fr. 3-winged or 3-angled. Fl. racemose . . .	8. GOUANIA.
Fr. obovoid-globose, not winged. Fl. umbellate .	HELINUS (p. 175).

1. VENTILAGO, Gaertn.; Fl. Brit. Ind. i. 630.

Shrubs or trees, unarmed, generally climbing. L. alternate. Fl. small, pentamerous, bisexual, fasciculate, fascicles axillary or in terminal panicles, calyx cup-shaped, lobes deciduous, keeled inside, petals enveloping the stamens, hooded or spathulate. Ovary 2-celled, styles 2. Fr. a subglobose indehiscent nut, seated on or partly enclosed by the persistent calyx tube, and prolonged into a linear coriaceous wing. Seed 1, cotyledons thick, fleshy, radicle inferior short, albumen 0.

1. **V. madraspatana,** Gaertn.; Roxb. Cor. Pl. t. 76; Wight Ic. t. 163; Brandis F. Fl. 96. Vern. *Kali bel*, Dūn; *Bonga-sarjom*, Kol; *Papri, Surabi*, Tel.: *Popli*, Kan.

A powerful climber, tendrils woody, branchlets, petioles and younger leaves pubescent. L. ovate or elliptic from a slightly oblique base, acuminate, entire or irregularly dentate, sec. n. 6–10 pair, arching, blade 3–4, petiole ⅛–¼ in. Fl. numerous, greenish, with a strong offensive smell, crowded on the branches of large terminal leafless panicles. Nut ¼ in. diam., pubescent.

Subhimalayan tract from the Jumna eastward. Oudh forests, Nepal, Behar, Central India and the Peninsula. Silhet, Assam, Burma. Fl. Nov.–March. I follow King, Journ. As. Soc. Bengal, vol. 65 (1897), 379, in uniting with this *V. calyculata*, Tulasne; Brandis F. Fl. 96, supposed to be recognized by broader leaves rounded at the base, a pubescent disk, and half the fruit enclosed in the cup-shaped calyx. 2. **V. bom-**

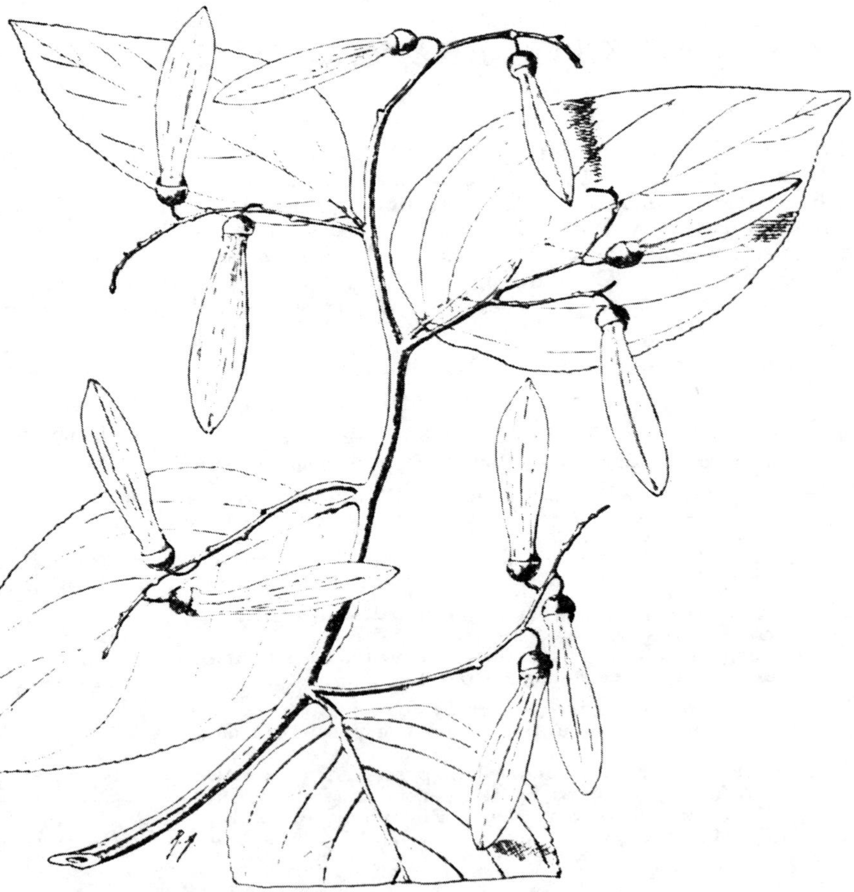

FIG. 77.—Ventilago madraspatana, Gaertn. var. calyculata. ½.

baiensis, Dalz. Ghats of Belgaum and North Kanara. Branchlets, petioles and inflorescence rusty-tomentose. L. shining above, hairy glands in the axils of nerves, sec. n. 2–4 pair, veins freely reticulate, blade 3–4, petiole ⅓ in. Fl. in dense axillary fascicles, not paniculate. Beddome (Index Ic. Pl. Or p. III.) quotes as synonym *Zizyphus wynadensis*, Bedd. Ic. Pl. Or. t. 114, a lofty tree, in dense forests of the Wainad. Two Malayan species with glabrous fruit are reported from Mergui. 3. **V. Maingayi,** Lawson, l. oblong-lanceolate, sec. n. 8–11 pair, wing 3–3½ in. long. 4. **V. leiocarpa,** Benth., also in China. L. ovate, edges more or less minutely serrate, sec. n. 6 or 7 pair, wing 2–2½ in. long.

Apteron lanceolatum, Kurz F. Fl. i. 263. Yainway forest on the eastern slopes of the Pegu Yoma, probably is a diseased state of *Ventilago madraspatana.*

2. BERCHEMIA, Necker; Fl. Brit. Ind. i. 637.

Unarmed shrubs or woody climbers, stipules foliaceous, often intra-axillary. L. alternate, sec. n. numerous, parallel, oblique. Fl. small, pentamerous, calyx lobes linear or triangular, deciduous. Style simple, often short, stigma capitate, lobed. Fr. a 2-celled berry on the persistent calyx. Species: Eastern Asia, 8; tropical Africa and North America 1 each.

A. Fl. in terminal or axillary panicles, calyx tube only persistent.

1. **B. floribunda**, Wall.; Brandis F. Fl. 91. Vern. *Kaulai*, Jauns. *Amili*, Garhw.; *Chiaduk*, Nep.

A large shrub or small tree, erect or climbing. L. ovate, acute or acuminate, blade 2–3, petiole $\frac{1}{2}$–$\frac{3}{4}$ in. Fl. clustered in large terminal panicles, pedicels shorter than calyx. Berry cylindrical, $\frac{1}{3}$–$\frac{1}{2}$ in. long.

Himalaya, Jhelum to Sikkim, ascending to 6,000 feet, Khasi hills. Fl. June, July (North-West), December (Sikkim). 2. **B. flavescens**, Wall. Sikkim, Upper Burma. Very similar. Fl. in short terminal axillary panicles, pedicels longer than flower.

B. Fl. in small clusters. Fr. supported by entire calyx.

3. **B. lineata**, DC.; Brandis F. Fl. 91. Vern. *Torbutei*, Pusht.; *Angari*, Jauns.

A small shrub, stipules small. L. $\frac{1}{2}$–$1\frac{1}{2}$ in. long. Fl. 2–4 together, either axillary or at the ends of branches. Berry blue, $\frac{1}{4}$ in. long.

Trans-Indus and in the Himalaya to Bhutan, ascending to 10,000 ft. Fl. May–July. 4. **B. Edgeworthii**, Lawson. Deoban, Western Nepal. Very similar, supposed to differ by longer stipules and less conspicuous secondary nerves, but probably not really different.

3. ZIZYPHUS, Juss.; Fl. Brit. Ind. i. 632.

Shrubs or trees. Medullary rays numerous, very fine. Generally armed with stipular spines, which as a rule are unequal, one straight, the other curved. L. alternate, more or less distichous, with 3, rarely 4 or 5, basal nerves. Fl. small, pentamerous, mostly bisexual, generally in axillary cymes. Calyx cup-shaped or broad-obconical, lobes keeled inside, petals sometimes wanting, disk lining the calyx tube, edge free, pentagonous or 5–10-lobed. Ovary immersed in disk, and more or less confluent with it, 2-celled, rarely 3- or 4-celled, styles 2–3, free or partly connate. Drupe as a rule fleshy, stone rugose or tuberculate, 1–3-celled, 1 seed in each cell, embryo in thin albumen, cotyledons thick, flat or convex, radicle short, inferior. Species 40, mostly Indo-Malayan, a few in Africa, America and Australia.

A. Cymes axillary, sessile or shortly pedunculate.

1. **Z. Jujuba**, Lam.; Wight Ic. t. 22; Bedd. Fl. Sylv. t. 149; Brandis F. Fl. t. 17. Vern. *Bēr*, Hind.; *Bor*, Mar.; *Janumjan*, Kol; *Yelandai*, Tam.; *Ringa*, Gond; *Regu*, Tel.; *Jelachi*, Kan.; *Ziben*, Burm.

A middle-sized tree. Branches drooping, armed with stipular spines, equal, or one straight, the other bent, rarely entirely unarmed. Branchlets, petioles, underside of leaves and inflorescence densely clothed with bright tawny or nearly white tomentum. L. variable, from ovate-oblong to nearly orbicular, obtuse or acute, entire or serrulate, blade $\frac{3}{4}$–$2\frac{1}{2}$, petiole $\frac{1}{10}$–$\frac{2}{5}$ in. long. Fl. greenish-yellow in short axillary nearly sessile cymes, petals unguiculate, lamina oblong, concave or hooded, disk fleshy, 10-lobed, styles 2, thick, connate to middle. Drupes varying in size and shape, generally $\frac{1}{2}$–$\frac{3}{4}$ in. long, orange or red when ripe, stalk half the length of drupe, stone tuberculate, bony, irregularly furrowed, mostly 2-celled.

Indigenous and naturalized throughout India and Burma, ascending in the outer

Fig. 78.—Zizyphus nummularia, W. & A. ½.

Himalaya to 4,500 ft. Grown in gardens for its fruit. The young foliage appears in March, April, while the old leaves are shedding, sometimes a second flush in July and August. Fl. usually April–Sept. Fr. Dec.–March. A remarkable form is Edgeworth's var. *hysudrica*, commonly cultivated in the Punjab. L. obtuse, often orbicular, glabrous or slightly pubescent beneath, the branches not drooping, but erect or spreading.

A shrubby form of this species, not gregarious, l. 1–2 by ¾–1½ in., fr. globose, yellow or reddish ⅓ in diam., is found in Singhboom (Haines).

2. **Z. nummularia,** W. et A., Prodr. i. 162 (1834); * Brandis F. Fl. 88.

Vern. *Jangra*, Sind: *Karkan*, Trans. Indus; *Bal*, *Malla*, *Kokan ber*, Pb.; *Bhor*, *Jhal Bhor*, Ajmere; *Paragi*, Kan.

A thorny shrub. Branches flexuose, divaricate at right angles, young shoots, underside of leaves and inflorescence grey-pubescent, spines slender, pilose when young, unequal, one slender ⅓–⅔ in, the other much shorter, hooked, bent downwards. L. elliptic or orbicular, ⅓–1 in. long. Cymes sessile. Drupes globose, edible, ⅓ in. diam., stone rugose, shell hard, bony.

Sind and Baluchistan. Dry region of North-Western India and the Deccan, south to the dry country near Cape Comorin. Gregarious, often covering extensive tracts with irregular rounded thorny masses of shrub. The old leaves shed early in the hot weather, and the fresh leaves appear immediately afterwards. Fl. March–June. Fr. Nov.–Jan.

3. **Z. Oenoplia,** Mill.; Brandis F. Fl. 86.—Syn. *Z. Napeca*, Roxb. Vern. *Makoh*, Sahar.; *Makai*, Oudh; *Makōr*, Mar.; *Yeruni*, Chanda; *Kontai Koli*, Uriya; *Paraki*, Tel.

A scrambling often climbing shrub, prickles short, sharp, often solitary. Branchlets, underside of leaves and inflorescence clothed with dense ferrugineous tomentum. L. oblique, ovate or ovate-lanceolate, minutely denticulate or almost entire, in the larger half of leaf often two basal nerves, making 4 altogether. Transverse nerves numerous, parallel, ascending. Fl. in short axillary sessile cymes. Drupe ¼ in. long, black, edible, stone tuberculate.

Subhimalayan tract from the Sutlej eastward, plains of Northern India, Chota Nagpore. Both Peninsulas. Fl. H. S. Fr. R. S., eaten. A common hedge plant in the Peninsula. A remarkable variety, possibly a species, is *Z. Brunoniana*, C. B. Clarke MSS., Silhet, Comilla, Chittagong, Pegu. Basal nerves always 3. Transverse nerves at right angles to midrib.

Fig. 79.—Zizyphus Oenoplia, Mill. ½.

4. **Z. incurva,** Roxb. Flora Indica i. 614.

A very large shrub, generally un-

* It is possible, though by no means certain, that *Z. rotundifolia*, Lamarck Encycl. Méth. Bot. iii. 319 (1813), may be intended for this plant. The name adopted by Wight et Arn. has been applied to the shrub for over sixty-five years and should be maintained.

armed, stipules sometimes spinescent. Young shoots, petioles and main nerves strigose. L. turning black when dry, coriaceous, ovate, acuminate, crenate, blade 2–4, petiole $\frac{1}{4}$–$\frac{1}{3}$ in. Basal nerves 3, sec. n. faint, veins reticulate. Cymes dichotomous, as well as outside of sepals rusty-tomentose, bracts ovate, buds obtuse not conical. Fl. $\frac{1}{8}$ in. diam., anther cells diverging. Drupe ellipsoid, blunt, $\frac{1}{3}$ in. long, putamen thick, hard, 2- celled.

Upper Burma and Shan States to 5,000 ft., common; Bhutan, Manipur, Nepal. Fl. May. Nilgiris (?) Roxburgh describes *Z. incurva* from Nepal as a well-armed shrub.

5. **Z. trinervia**, Roxb. (1813).—Syn. *Z. glabrata*, Heyne (1821); Wight Ic. t. 282. *Kurka tura*, Tam.

A small unarmed tree, youngest shoots and inflorescence pubescent. L. glabrous, obtuse, minutely serrate. Basal nerves prominent, continued to the apex, sec. n. faint, veins minutely reticulate, blade 1–3, petiole $\frac{1}{4}$ in. long. Cymes nearly sessile. Fl. $\frac{1}{4}$ in. diam., greenish-yellow, anther cells parallel, not diverging at base. Drupe $\frac{1}{2}$–$\frac{3}{4}$ in. long, often apiculate.

Nilgiris. A western species, while *Z. incurva* probably is limited to the eastern region. Western Ghats. Fl. April–Aug. 6. **Z. glabra,** Roxb.; Kurz F. Fl. 267; King Journ. As. Soc. Bengal, vol. 65 (1897), 375. Chittagong, Tenasserim, Andamans. A glabrous, lofty scandent shrub, armed with short, curved, sharp, usually solitary prickles. L. acuminate, tertiary (transverse) nerves ∞, parallel, joined by finely reticulate veins. Inflorescence hairy. Fl. $\frac{1}{8}$ in. diam. Fr. $\frac{1}{2}$ in. 7. **Z. Horsfieldii,** Miq.; King l. c. 376, Nicobars, Malay Peninsula, with a few distinct secondary nerves on the outside of the outer basal nerves, is probably not distinct. 8. **Z. vulgaris,** Lam.; *Anab*, Pushtu; *Sinjli*, Pb., cultivated in the Punjab, wild and cultivated in the North-West Himalaya, ascending to 6,500 ft. A hedge plant in Hazara. Indigenous and cultivated in Japan and China, Western Asia, North Africa and South Europe. A small thorny glabrous tree, heartwood brown, branches flexuose, branchlets frequently fasciculate, thorns unequal, one straight to $1\frac{1}{2}$ in. long, the other straight when young, afterwards hooked and bent down. L. obliquely ovate-lanceolate, mostly obtuse, bluntly serrate. Drupes dark red or black, ovoid or oblong, obtuse at both ends, $\frac{1}{2}$–$\frac{3}{4}$ in. long, stones tuberculate, strung up as beads. 9. **Z. oxyphylla,** Edgew.; Collett Fl. Simla, fig. 29; *Ghargurei*, Pushtu. Eastern flank of the Sulaimán range. Outer North-West Himalaya, 2,000–6,000 ft., east to the Ganges. A small tree. A few scattered hairs on young parts, otherwise glabrous, spines slender, purple, slightly unequal. L. from an oblique base ovate-lanceolate, blade $1\frac{1}{2}$–3, petiole $\frac{1}{8}$ in., cymes sessile. Drupe bright orange, ovoid, $\frac{1}{3}$ in. long. Combs made of the wood.

10. **Z. Xylopyrus**, Willd.; Brandis F. Fl. 90. Vern. *Kathber*, *Bhander*, N. W.; *Goti*, Hind. Mar. Tel.; *Chitena*, Oudh; *Ghattol*, *Ghat bor*, C. P.; *Karkata*, Sonth.; *Kottai*, Tam.

A large straggling shrub or small tree. Branchlets, inflorescence and underside of leaves pubescent or tomentose, on good soil often unarmed. L. broad-ovate or orbicular, finely serrulate, base often cordate. Basal nerves 3, sometimes 4 or 5, the midrib with 1–2 pair of sec. n., the lateral basal nerves with 3–5 sec. n. on the outside, blade $1\frac{1}{2}$–3, petiole $\frac{1}{4}$–$\frac{1}{3}$ in. Drupe globose, grey-tomentose, almost dry, $\frac{1}{2}$–1 in. diam., stone furrowed, 3-celled, 3-seeded.

Foot of the North-West Himalaya, Central India and the Western Peninsula. Fl. April, May. Conspicuous during the greater part of the year for its hard globose fruit. 11. **Z. horrida,** Roth. Bellary. Spines numerous from a stout conical base, shining, very sharp. L. $\frac{1}{2}$–1 in. long, cymes dense, peduncle $\frac{1}{4}$–$\frac{1}{3}$ in. Drupe globose, $\frac{1}{2}$ in. diam., 3-celled, 3-seeded. A remarkable species found by Dr. Watt (in leaf only) at Mao, Manipur, 6,000 ft. (No. 7429), spines numerous, on leaf-bearing branches straight, stout, $\frac{3}{4}$ in. long; on trunk and larger branches in pairs on an irregularly conical base, 1 in. diam. 12. **Z. apetala,** Hook. f. Sikkim 2–5,000 ft. Branchlets and inflorescence silky with ferrugineous hairs. L. obliquely ovate, acuminate, 3–4 in., cymes pedunculate, petals 0.

B. Cymes pedunculate, arranged in terminal or lateral panicles.

13. **Z. rugosa**, Lamk.; Wight Ic. t. 339; Brandis F. Fl. 89. Vern. *Suran*, *Churna*, Hind.; *Dhaura*, Oudh; *Sekra*, Sonth.; *Tūran*. *Churna*, Mar.; *Todali*, Mal.; *Myauksi*, Lower, *Tabu*, *Mintha tabu*, Upper Burma.

A straggling deciduous shrub, often climbing, occasionally a small tree, trunk often 2–3 ft. girth, armed with short recurved, often solitary spines, bark dark brown or black, exfoliating with rectangular scales. Branchlets, inflorescence, young spines and underside of leaves densely clothed with ferruginous or grey tomentum. L. ovate or elliptic, from an oblique often cordate base, blade 2–5, petiole ¼ in., basal nerves 3, rarely 4 or 5, prominent, as well as the sec. n. along midrib, and on the outside of the lateral nerves. Cymes large, pedunculate, axillary and terminal, forming a long compound generally drooping panicle. Petals none. Drupe ⅓ in. long, stone crustaceous, 1-celled, 1-seeded.

Subhimalayan tract from the Ganges eastward, ascending to 2,000 ft. Behar, Central India, Western Peninsula. Burma, (Shan Hills to 4,000 ft.). Fl. Nov.–March. Ceylon. 14. **Z. funiculosa,** Ham. Assam, Cachar, Khasi hills, Upper Burma (Griffith). Glabrous. L. shining elliptic, acuminate, blade 3, petiole ¼ in. long, transverse (tertiary) nerves parallel, very numerous; a few faint sec. n. on the outside of the outer basal nerves. Fl. ⅛ in. across.

4. RHAMNUS, Linn.; Fl. Brit Ind. i. 638.

Shrubs or trees. L. serrate, alternate, in some species subopposite, stipules small, mostly deciduous. Fl. often unisexual, calyx segments inside keeled, or with a prominent line, petals sometimes wanting, disk thin, clothing the calyx tube, petals and stamens inserted on its edge. Ovary free, 3–4-celled, narrowed into a 3–4-cleft style, stigma papillose, obtuse. Drupe on the persistent but not enlarged base of calyx, pyrenes 2–4, 1-seeded. Cotyledons flat, or with recurved margins, often green, radicle short. Species 60–70, mostly in the northern temperate zone, some on hills within the tropics.

A. Spinescent. Fl. 4-merous, petals minute.

1. **R. virgatus,*** Roxb.; Brandis F. Fl. 92.—Syn. *R. dahuricus*, Fl. Brit. Ind. i. 639; *R. hirsutus*, W. et A.; Wight Ic. t. 978; *Chakra*, *Sita pajja*, Pb.; *Chaulda*, *Thanthar*, Jauns.

A large shrub or small tree, heartwood brown, hard, pores in wavy radial belts, branchlets often spinescent, young shoots pubescent. L. membranous, almost opposite, glabrous, frequently fascicled on arrested branchlets, lanceolate or ovate-lanceolate, blade 1–4, petiole ¼–⅓ in. long. Fl. greenish, on slender pedicels, in axillary clusters, petals minute, linear or spathulate. Seed grooved, groove narrow, nearly closed.

Trans-Indus, Himalaya, 2,400–7,000 ft., from the Indus eastward. Manipur. Shan hills, Upper Burma, 4,000 ft. Fl. April–June, also at other times. 2. **R. persicus,** Boissier. Trans-Indus, Salt range, North-West Himalaya 2–5,000 ft. (*Nikki Kander*, Pb.; *Chirla*, Dūn). A tall shrub with stiff divaricate branches. L. ¼–1½ in., minutely tomentose beneath. Seeds with a wide open groove, the edges thickened.

FIG. 80.—Rhamnus Wightii, W. et A. ½.

B. Unarmed. Fl. 5-merous, petals 5.

3. **R. Wightii,** W. et A.; Wight Ic. t. 159.

A large shrub. L. subcoriaceous, turning black in drying, mostly alternate, closely and re-

* *Rhamnus* is masc. acc. to Linnæus, Bentham and Fl. Brit. Ind.

gularly serrate, the serratures tipped with incurved hard points, secondary and tertiary nerves conspicuous beneath, blade 3–4, petiole $\frac{1}{3}$–$\frac{1}{2}$ in. Fl. yellowish-green, ♂ clustered on axillary racemes, ♀ in axillary fascicles or on short racemes.

Western Ghats, from Mahabaleshwar southwards, Nilgiris, Palni hills. Fl. R. S. Ceylon.

4. **R. triqueter,** Wall.; Brandis F. Fl. 92.

A small tree, branchlets and leaves with dense short tomentum. L. ovate- or elliptic-oblong, sec. n. 6–10 pair, prominent, blade 2–5, petiole $\frac{1}{2}$–$\frac{3}{4}$ in. long. Fl. clustered on axillary racemes attaining 3 in., style 3–4-cleft, the branches cohering nearly to the apex. Seed with a broad open groove.

Salt range and North-West Himalaya, Jhelum to Sarda, 3–6,000 ft. Fl. May–Aug. 5. **R. nepalensis,** Wall. Nepal, Sikkim, to 3,000 ft. *Achal*, Nep. Bengal, Assam, Khasi hills, Upper Burma. A large shrub. L glabrous, sec. n. 5–7 pair, blade 3–6, petiole $\frac{1}{3}$–$\frac{1}{2}$ in. Fl. often unisexual in long often branching and leafy racemes, style 3–4-cleft at the apex, berries red.

C. Unarmed. Fl. 5-merous, petals none.

6. **R. purpureus,** Edgew.; Brandis F. Fl. 91, t. 18. Vern. *Rangrek*, Pb.; *Luhish*, Jauns.

A middle-sized tree, young shoots minutely pubescent, the previous year's branchlets purple. L. alternate, ovate-lanceolate, acuminate, sec. n. 6–10 pair, prominent, blade 3–4, petiole $\frac{1}{4}$ in. Fl. mostly bisexual, in axillary clusters or cymes, style short, 3-cleft nearly to the base. Drupe $\frac{1}{4}$ in. long, pear-shaped, bitter.

Outer North-West Himalaya, Indus to Sarda river, 4,500–10,000 ft. Fl. May, June. 7. **R. procumbens,** Edgew. Simla, Jaunsar, Kumaon, 7–8,000 ft. A small prostrate shrub. L. 1–1$\frac{1}{2}$ in., stipules persistent, subulate, as long as petiole. Fl. solitary, axillary, on long slender pedicels.

5. SAGERETIA, Brongn.; Fl. Brit. Ind. i. 641.

Unarmed or spinescent shrubs. Branches angular. L. generally opposite, the upper sometimes alternate, stipules small, deciduous. Fl. bisexual, pentamerous, sessile, in small clusters, supported by bracts, arranged in terminal or lateral panicles. Calyx a shallow cup, segments keeled inside, persistent. Disk thick, fleshy, filling the calyx tube, upper part free. Ovary 3-celled, narrowed into 3 short coherent styles. Drupe with 3 coriaceous indehiscent pyrenes. Cotyledons foliaceous, in thin fleshy albumen. Species 10, Central and Eastern Asia, Mexico and Florida.

1. **S. oppositifolia,** Brongn.; Brandis F. Fl. 95. Vern. *Gonta*, Dūn; *Manchi*, *Surābi*, Cuddapah.

A large shrub or small tree. Branchlets and underside of young leaves woolly-tomentose, branchlets often spinescent. L. shining above, acuminate, serrate, sec. n. 3–6 pair, arching, blade 2–4, petiole $\frac{1}{4}$ in. Spikes axillary and in terminal racemes. Drupe sweetish, edible, $\frac{1}{4}$ in. long.

Himalaya, Indus to Bhutan, 2–6,000 ft., Khasi hills. Konkan Ghats. Hills of the Ceded Districts and Northern Circars. Fl. spring to autumn. 2. **S. hamosa,** Brongn. Nepal, Nilgiris, Palni hills, China. Unarmed, or with stout short deflexed spines. L. glabrous, sec. n. arching, 6–10 pair, blade 4–5, petiole $\frac{1}{4}$–$\frac{1}{3}$ in.

3. **S. Brandrethiana,** Aitchison; Brandis F. Fl. 95. Vern. *Mangri*, Bal.; *Mumanāi*, Pushtu; *Gangēr*, Pb.

A shrub, at most 10–12 ft. high. Branches stiff, divergent, the younger decussate and frequently spinescent. Often only one of the two opposite buds develops, and at times the branchlets are whorled. Branchlets, inflorescence and underside of leaves clothed with white tomentum. L. entire or slightly dentate, ½–1 in. long, sec. n. 2–4 pair. Fl. panicles terminal and axillary. Fr. black when ripe, sweet, sold in bazaars.

Sind, Sulaiman range. Salt range. North-West Himalaya, Indus to Jhelum, ascending to 5,000 ft. Fl. and Fr. January–May. Afghanistan, Baluchistan, Persia, Arabia. Closely allied is 4. **S. theezans,** Brongn.; Collett Fl. Simla, fig. 80. North-West Himalaya, Upper Burma, China, Tonkin (*Hankalu*, Pangi; *Zartum*, Busshir). L. larger, ¾–1½ in. long, perfectly glabrous, both surfaces shining, lower pal. Specimens of *S. Brandrethiana*, with small but perfectly glabrous leaves, are known from Sind, Baluchistan, Muscat and Arabia. Possibly this species should be united with *S. theezans*.

6. SCUTIA, Comm.; Fl. Brit. Ind. i. 640.

Species about 8, tropics of both hemispheres.

S. indica, Brongn.; Wight Ill. t. 73.—Syn. *S. Rheediana*, Wight Ic. t. 1071. Vern. *Chimat*, Mar.

A straggling, glabrous shrub, armed with small sharp, curved spines. L. coriaceous, shining, pale beneath, opposite or alternate, elliptic, ovate or obovate, entire or faintly crenate. Fl. yellowish-green, in axillary few-fld. umbels on short peduncles. Drupe nearly dry, ⅓ in. long, supported by the persistent concave calyx tube.

Western Peninsula, both on dry hills in the Deccan, and along the Ghats of the Konkan, in Coorg and on the Nilgiris. Fl. Oct.–April. Ceylon, dry country.

Hovenia dulcis, Thunb. (*Chamun*, Chamba); Brandis F. Fl. 94. A tree, unarmed, indigenous in China, cultivated in Kumaon, Nepal, Sikkim, Bhutan and Japan. L. alternate, deciduous, ovate, from an unequal-sided base, serrate, acuminate, 3 prominent basal nerves. The ramifications of the inflorescence swell into an irregularly and unevenly oblong fleshy mass, variously bent, which is sweet and aromatic, the fruit 3-celled, 3-seeded, coriaceous, supported by the obconical calyx tube.

7. COLUBRINA, Rich.; Fl. Brit. Ind. i. 642.

Scandent or erect shrubs. L. alternate, penninerved, the lowest pair of nerves basal. Calyx tube hemispherical, filled with the thick annular lobed disk. Ovary immersed in the disk and confluent with it, 3-celled, style 3-cleft. Fr. dry, 3-celled, tardily dehiscent, globose, base supported by the persistent calyx tube. Species 15, the majority in tropical and subtropical America.

1. **C. asiatica,** Brongn.; Wight Ill. t. 74. Vern. *Guti*, Mar.

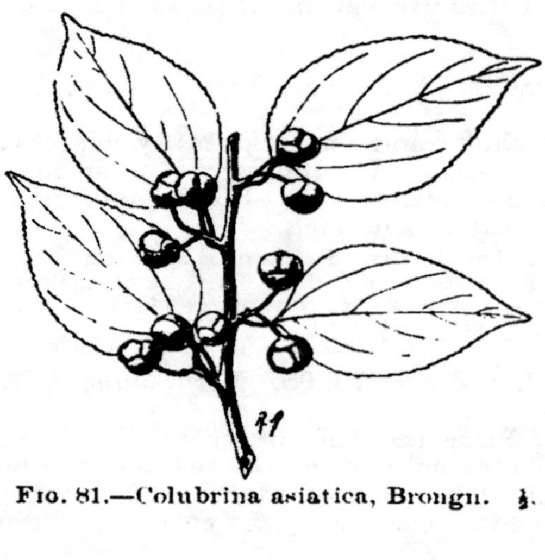

FIG. 81.—Colubrina asiatica, Brongn. ½.

A large unarmed spreading often scandent shrub or small tree, entirely glabrous. L. ovate from a rounded base, acuminate, crenate, blade 1½–2½ in., petiole ¼–⅓ in. Cymes axillary, few-fld., on short peduncles. Drupes pale brown, ⅓ in. long.

Western Ghats from the Konkan southward, also on the coast. Sea-coast of Lower Burma, Andamans, Nicobars. Fl. February. Ceylon, Malay Peninsula and Archipelago, China, New Guinea, Australia. 2. **C. travancorica,** Bedd. Ic. Pl. Ind. Or. t. 188. Travancore, Cochin. A large shrub, branchlets, petioles and young leaves with rust-coloured pubescence. L. ovate-oblong, 4–6 in. long. 3. **C. pubescens,** Kurz, Pegu, Martaban and Tenasserim. Branchlets and leaves tawny-pubescent. L. membranous, ovate-lanceolate, blade 1½–2½, petiole ⅓–½ in.

Smythea calpicarpa, Kurz, Tenasserim and Andamans. A scandent shrub, branchlets, petioles and inflorescence tawny-pubescent. L. lanceolate, remotely crenate-serrate, fine hairs on nerves, blade 2–4 in., petiole ⅛ in. Fl. bisexual, pentamerous, in clusters along narrow spiciform terminal racemes, petals cucullate, filaments incurved, anthers didymous. Ovary half inferior, 2-celled, styles 2 recurved. Fr. 3-celled, coriaceous, flat, dehiscent vertically into two valves, the lower part enclosed in the persistent calyx tube.

8. GOUANIA, Linn.; Fl. Brit. Ind. i. 643.

Unarmed shrubs, mostly climbing by means of terminal tendrils. L. alternate. Fl. polygamous in sessile clusters on axillary or terminal spikes. Ovary inferior, sunk in the disk, which fills the calyx tube. Fr. a dehiscent coriaceous capsule crowned by the persistent calyx-limb, 3-angled or 3-winged. Species 30–40 in all tropical countries.

1. **G. leptostachya,** DC.—Syn. *G. tiliaefolia*, Roxb. Cor. Pl. t. 98; *G. nepalensis*, Wall. Vern. *Batwasi*, Nep.

A large scandent shrub, wood normal, med. rays long and broad. L. broad-ovate, acuminate, base rounded or slightly cordate, base entire, upper part serrate or crenate, blade 3–4, petiole ¾–1 in. long. Spikes slender, 6–12 in. long. Fr. ½ in. diam.

Subhimalayan tract and outer hills, from the Jumna eastward, ascending to 6,000 ft. in Sikkim. Khasi hills, Lower Burma, Andamans. Fl. Aug., Sept. Tonkin, Cochinchina, Malay Peninsula and Archipelago. 2. **G. microcarpa,** DC. Western Ghats from the Konkan southwards, often in evergreen forest, Nilgiris, Ceylon, Malay Archipelago, differs by smaller quite entire leaves, spikes, calyx and young leaves densely pubescent. Fr. ⅓ in. diam. 3. **G. Brandisii,** Hassk. Martaban and Tenasserim. Branchlets, inflorescence and young leaves densely tawny- or rusty-tomentose. L. cordate-ovate, quite entire. Wings of fruit rounded. 4. **G. andamanica,** King; Journ. As. Soc. Bengal, vol. 65 (1897), 382. Common on middle Andaman island. Branchlets rusty-pubescent. Fr. rusty-tomentose, triquetrous, not winged.

Helinus lanceolatus, Brandis F. Fl. 574. Subhimalayan tract, ascending to 4,000 ft. Plains of Northern India, Behar, Pachmarhis, Godavery. A slender climbing shrub. L. entire, lanceolate, 1–3 in. long. Branchlets ending in simple tendrils. Fl. umbellate. Fr. coriaceous, obovoid-globose, not winged, 3-celled, tardily dehiscent.

ORDER XXXVI. AMPELIDEÆ. Gen. Pl. i. 386.

(*Vitaceæ*, Engler u. Prantl iii. 5. 427.)

Herbs or shrubs, erect or climbing. L. alternate. Fl. regular, inflorescence cymose, generally leaf-opposed. Calyx small, 4–5-dentate or entire, petals 4–5, valvate in bud. Stamens as many as and opposite to petals, inserted outside and often between the lobes of a hypogynous disk. Ovary 2–6-celled, ovules 2 (rarely 1) in each cell, style simple, stigma often sessile. Fr. a berry, seeds with a stony or crustaceous testa, embryo small, in a copious generally hard albumen.

Woody or herbaceous climbers, rarely erect, filaments free, ovary 2-celled . . . . 1. VITIS.
Erect shrubs or large herbs, filaments united into a tube, ovary 3–6-celled . . . . 2. LEEA.

1. VITIS, Linn.; Fl. Brit. Ind. i. 645.

Climbing, rarely erect shrubs or herbs. Tendrils generally leaf-opposed, often bearing the inflorescence. Stipules membranous, deciduous. Petals often cohering at the apex, when the entire corolla, lifted up by the stamens,

separates from the base and falls away. Ovary 2-celled, its base surrounded by the fleshy often 4–5-lobed disk. Fr. 1–4-seeded. Species about 400, cosmopolitan.

Planchon in DC. Monogr. Phan., vol. 5, divides *Vitis* into a number of genera; the species here noticed belong to the following: 1. **Vitis**, petals 5, united at apex. 2. **Ampelocissus**, petals 4, mostly 5, free. 3. **Cissus**, petals 4, style long. 4. **Tetrastigma**, petals 4, stigma nearly sessile, 4-lobed, inflorescence axillary. Fl. unisexual.

The wood, as a rule, is not interrupted by concentric rings of bast (phloëm). The rays are high and very broad, widening towards the circumference, the vessels are extremely wide (sometimes over 0·5 mm. diam.) mixed with smaller vessels. The flat-stemmed species have a peculiar structure. On two opposite sides of a central cylinder numerous alternating zones are formed, each consisting of wood inside and bast (phloëm) outside.

A. L. simple. Fl. bisexual, as a rule tetramerous. Cymes arranged in corymbs, often umbellate.

1. **V. adnata,** Wall.; Brandis F. Fl. 100.—Syn. *Cissus adnata*, Roxb.; Wight Ic. t. 144.

Trailing, young shoots more or less rusty-tomentose. L. cordate, rarely lobed, often longer than broad, bristle-serrate, more or less tomentose beneath, blade 3–4½, petiole 1–2½ in., stipules more or less adnate, consisting of a round shining centre, surrounded by a free scarious margin. Cymes short, compact, opposite to fully developed leaves, fl. greenish yellow. Fr. black, obovoid, ⅓ in. long, seed one. Fruiting pedicels recurved.

Oudh forests, Sikkim Terai, ascending to 3,000 ft., Assam, Khasi hills, Lower Bengal, Burma. West side of the Peninsula. Fl. February, while the plant is in full leaf. Ceylon, Malay Peninsula and Archipelago, Madagascar, New Guinea. 2. **V. repanda,** W. et A., *Pani lara*, Nep. Subhimalayan tract from Dehra Dún eastward, Assam, Bengal, Upper Burma, in Engdain and dry deciduous forest (*Hlèza*, Burm.), Western Peninsula. A very large deciduous climber with corky bark, branches woolly when young L. as broad as long, stipules oblong, free, cymes lax, appearing in May with the young leaves or before the leaves, fruiting pedicels rarely reflexed. *V. rosea*, Royle Ill. t. 26, fig. 1, with large leaves and pink flowers, is quoted as a synonym of *C. repanda* in Fl. Brit. Ind. i. 648. Species 1 and 2 are closely allied. 3. **V. tomentosa,** Heyne; Wight Ill. t. 57. Western Deccan from Dharwar southwards, the whole plant covered with a thick woolly persistent tomentum, l. more or less deeply lobed, lobes sometimes petiolate. Cymes compact on stout peduncles. Fl. pentamerous, scarlet, conspicuous in the white woolly tomentum. 4. **V. pallida,** W. et A., *Kondagu mara*, Kan. Western Peninsula, chiefly in the Deccan. An erect shrub, bark corky, stem thick, fleshy, hollow. L. cordate, repand serrate, blade 3–6, petiole 2–3 in., tendrils short or wanting, peduncle 1–2 in. thick, fleshy. Cyme compact, bracts and bracteoles large glabrous. Nearly allied is 5. **V. Woodrowii,** Stapf, common in the Deccan (*Girnal*, Mar.) Stems woody, attaining 3 in. diam., structure peculiar. L. larger, up to 9 in., petiole 6–10 in. long. 6. **V. glauca,** W. et A. Western Peninsula, distinguished by slender peduncles 2–3 in. long, bracts and bracteoles small, deciduous.

7. **V. Linnaei,** Wall.; Fl. Brit. Ind. i. 649, not of Kurz.—Syn. *Cissus vitigenea*, Linn.; King Journ. As. Soc. vol. 65 (1896) p. 110.

A climbing shrub in hedges, and ascending to the top of large trees, the whole plant softly and densely pubescent. L. variable in shape, from round, pentagonal to deeply 5-lobed, blade 2, petiole ½–1 in. Cymes bifurcate, as long as leaves. Fr. obovoid, ¼–⅓ in. long, fruiting pedicels recurved, seed one.

Central Provinces. Western Peninsula. Fl. June–Sept. Ceylon.

8. **V. discolor,** Dalz. Vern. *Sanu pureni*, Nep.; *Telit sayel*, Mar.

L. green above, variegated with white and purple beneath, glabrous, ovate-lanceolate, base cordate, bristly serrate, blade 3–8, petiole ½–3 in. Cymes short, peduncle ½–¾ in. Calyx purple, corolla yellow, seed one, rugose.

Sikkim 1–4,000 ft., Khasi hills, Manipur, Chittagong, Upper and Lower Burma, Andamans. West side of the Peninsula from the Konkan southwards. Fl. Aug., Sept. Malay Peninsula and Archipelago.

9. **V. repens,** W. et A.; Kurz F. Fl. i. 275.

A large climber. Branches often white, mealy. L. glabrous, ovate from a cordate base, acuminate, not lobed, with distant hairy teeth, blade 2–4, petiole 1–2½ in. Cymes large, half the length of leaf, peduncle 1–2½ in., seed usually one.

Sikkim, Khasi hills, Assam, Chittagong, Burma. West side of the Peninsula. Fl. June–Sept. (Khasi) March (Kanara). Malay Peninsula and Archipelago.

10. **V. quadrangularis,** Wall.; Wight Ic. t. 51; Brandis F. Fl. 100. Vern. *Harsankar*, Bomb.; *Nalleru*, Tel.

A perennial climber. Branches dichotomous, succulent, quadrangular, constricted at the nodes, angles winged. L. fleshy, entire, broad-ovate to 3–5-lobed, blade ¾–2, petiole ¼–½ in. Berry red, 1-seeded.

North-West India, Western Peninsula. Fl. R. S. Eastern tropical Africa, Arabia, Malay Archipelago.

B. L. simple. Fl. pentamerous. Cymes arranged in panicles (spikes in *V. indica*), inflorescence usually on the tendril.

11. **V. vinifera,** Linn.; Brandis F. Fl. 98. *The Grape Vine. Dākh*, Hind.

A large woody climber, tendrils long, bifid. L. glabrous above, clothed beneath with grey floccose deciduous tomentum, from a cordate base nearly orbicular, more or less deeply 5-lobed, edge cut into large unequal acute teeth; basal nerves 5, the midrib with 4–5 pair of prominent sec. n., petiole generally shorter than leaf, but longer than half its length. Fl. green, fragrant, petals cohering at the top. Fr. 3–5-seeded.

Indigenous in Armenia, the Caucasus and other parts of Western Asia, probably also in Greece. Apparently wild in the North-West Himalaya. Cultivated in Kashmir, Kunawar (the vineyards mostly destroyed by vine-disease between 1855 and 1860), the plains of North-West India and the Deccan.

12. **V. lanata,** Roxb. (King Journ. As. Soc. Beng. vol. 65 (1897), p. 111); Jacquem. Voy. Bot. t. 36. *Chakcha*, Bussahir; *Jarila lara*, Nep.; *Goele-lota*, Sundrib.

A powerful woody climber. Branches, petioles and inflorescence more or less woolly. L. from a flat or cordate base, ovate, acuminate, dentate, angled or indistinctly lobed, more or less clothed beneath with soft rusty tomentum. Cymes arranged in large compound panicles, one of the lower branches often terminating in a tendril or developed into a second panicle, giving the appearance of a bifurcate inflorescence, petals cohering at the apex. Seed 1.

Subhimalayan tract, ascending to 5,000 ft., from Hazara eastward. Assam, Khasi hills, Manipur, East Bengal, Chittagong, Burma. Fl. April, May. This species varies considerably in regard to the tomentum. A form, which is almost glabrous, is known from Kumaon, the Khasi hills, and Burma. These glabrous specimens are very similar to 13. **V. parvifolia,** Roxb., a species of Kashmir, Kumaon and Nepal, with acuminate l. 2–3 in. long, 1–2 in. broad. Fl. in short racemiform panicles 1–2 in. long. 14. **V. rugosa,** Wall. Kumaon, Burma, with edible grapes, has larger leaves 6–12 in. long, with dense reddish-brown tomentum beneath. Fl. deep red, the petals not cohering. In these (11–14) and other species with paniculate inflorescence, it often happens that the lowest branch of the panicle bears a second panicle, giving the appearance of a bifurcate inflorescence.

15. **V. latifolia,** Roxb.; Brandis F. Fl. 99. *Panibel*, Hind.; *Musal Murie*, Ajm. Plains of North India. Rajputana, Behar, Bengal, Assam. Peninsula. L. densely pubescent beneath, nearly orbicular from a cordate base, angled or 5-lobed, lobes dentate, tendrils long, bifid. Cymes on the tendrils in pyramidal often bifurcate panicles. 16. **V. barbata,** Wall. Assam, Khasi hills, plains of Bengal, Burma. Branches, petioles and inflorescence clothed with soft woolly hair and long thin brown bristles. L. clothed beneath with floccose pubescence, cordate, with large rounded basal lobes, 4–10 in. long. Cymes in large pyramidal panicles, hairs ⅛ in. long. 17. **V. indica,** Lawson. Fl. Brit. Ind. i. 658 (*Nardel*, Mar.) West side of the Peninsula, from the Konkan southwards. Branches, inflorescence, petioles and

underside of leaves densely clothed with soft rusty tomentum. L. hard, firm, cordate, 3–6 in. long, not lobed, the nerves terminating in hard glandular teeth. Cymes sessile along the rachis of a short compact cylindrical raceme. As pointed out by King (Journ. As. Soc. Beng. vol. 65 (1897), p. 112), *V. indica*, Linn., is a Ceylon species (*V. erioclada*, W. et A.). The correct name of the Indian species with cylindric racemes has still to be determined.

C. L. trifoliolate. Cymes umbellate, or arranged in corymbs.

18. **V. semicordata,** Wall.; King in Journ. As. Soc. Beng. vol. 65 (1897), pp. 113, 397.—Syn. *V. himalayana*, Brandis F. Fl. 100. Collett, Pl. Simla fig. 31; *V. neilgherrensis*, Wight Ic. t. 965. Vern. *Munderi*, Theog, near Simla; *Sever dakhan*, Bussahir; *Kandār*, Jauns.; *Chacheri*, Nep.

A large, soft-wooded climber, stem 5–6 in. diam., glabrous, or youngest shoots slightly pubescent, tendrils distichous, at times wanting. L. trifoliolate, the terminal leaflet ovate or obovate, the two lateral unequal-sided, falcate or semicordate, all sharp-serrate with cuspidate teeth, stipules oblong, early deciduous. Fl. yellowish-green, pentamerous, rarely tetramerous, in compound trichotomous cymes, peduncle as long as or shorter than petiole of the opposite leaf, petals ending in a conical hood, which encloses the anther before opening, reflexed after the flower has opened. Ovary slightly 5-lobed, narrowed into a short obtuse style.

Himalaya from Kashmir eastwards 3–9,000 ft., in Sikkim to 11,000 ft., Khasi hills, Palni hills. Burma. Fl. April–June. In autumn the leaves turn red. Varies with leaves from glabrous to hispid on the nerves beneath. 19. **V. carnosa,** Wall.; Brandis F. Fl. 101. *Karik, gidar dakh*, Pb.; *Katamba*, Ajm. Common in most parts of India and Burma. A large climber with herbaceous flattened stems, young parts softly pubescent. L. rough, trifoliolate, leaflets ovate or elliptic, the two lateral nearly sessile. Fl. tetramerous, greenish-white, in trichotomous compound cymes, peduncle longer than petiole of opposite leaf, petals separate, berries black, 2–4-seeded. This species King identifies with *V. trifolia*, Linn. Linnaeus' genus *Vitis* however was pentamerous.

D. L. digitately 5-foliolate, stems more or less flat.

20. **V. planicaulis,** Hook. f. Sikkim outer hills, to 4,000 ft., Assam, Khasi and Cachar hills. A vast climber, ascending to the top of the tallest trees, sending down from its branches long thin leafless bands, stems flat, to 18 in. wide and 1 in. thick, leaflets thinly coriaceous, with a rounded base, petiolule $\frac{3}{4}$–$1\frac{1}{4}$ in. long. Fl. 4-merous. Fr. round, $\frac{1}{2}$–$\frac{3}{4}$ in. diam., 1–2-seeded. 21. **V. elongata,** Wall. Sikkim Terai and valleys, to 4,000 ft., Silhet, Dacca, Konkan, North Kanara (on the coast). A large, glabrous climber, stems rather flattened. Fl. 4-merous. Fr. ellipsoid, 1-seeded, $\frac{1}{2}$–$\frac{3}{4}$ in. long.

E. L. pedately 5–11-foliolate. Cymes mostly axillary. Fl. unisexual (bisexual in *V. pedata*).

22. **V. lanceolaria,** Wall.; Brandis F. Fl. 101: Wight Ic. t. 177 ♂ and t. 28 ♀.—Syn. *V. muricata*, W. et A.: Wight Ic. t. 740. Vern. *Kajolit sayel*, Mar.; *Kyi-ni-nwé*, Burm.

A large woody evergreen glabrous climber, stems, branches and petioles often corky-tubercled, tendrils simple, glabrous. L. pedately 5-foliolate, those of coppice shoots often 3-foliolate, leaflets lanceolate or ovate-lanceolate, distantly serrate, 3–5 in. long. Fl. unisexual, pale yellow, tetramerous, stigma 4-lobed. Cymes axillary, dichotomously compound, peduncles short, the female cymes smaller, petals distinct. Fr. $\frac{1}{2}$ in. diam.

Kumaon, Nepal. Oudh forests. Sikkim (to 4,000 ft.). Silhet, Manipur. Western Ghats, from North Kanara southwards. Andamans, Lower Burma. Fl. Febr.–April. Ceylon. Closely allied is 23. **V. Hookeri,** Lawson. Sikkim, Assam, Bhutan, Khasia, Chittagong. Leaflets larger and fr. 1 in. diam. 24. **V. capreolata,** D. Don; *pani lahra*, Nep. Himalaya from Simla eastward. 3–7,000 ft., Khasi hills. Stems slender, leaflets $1\frac{1}{2}$–3 in. 25. **V. rumicisperma,** Lawson; *chacheri*, Nep. Sikkim, 5–7,000 ft., Khasi hills, Manipur. A large glabrous climber. Branches covered with corky tubercles, cymes compound-trichotomous, ample, longer than common petiole. Fr. edible, seed broadly triangular-obcordate, keeled.

26. **V. pedata,** Vahl; Kurz F. Fl. i. 273.

A woody climber, more or less softly pubescent. L. 7–11-foliolate, leaflets membranous, 4–8 in. long. Cymes sometimes axillary, compound-dichotomous. Fl. white or greenish-yellow, bisexual. Fr. $\frac{1}{3}$ in. diam., 3–4-seeded.

Assam, Khasi and Naga hills. Burma. West side of the Peninsula from the Konkan southwards. Fl. H. S., R. S. A remarkable species with pinnate leaves is 27. **V. rubifolia,** Wall. Assam and Khasi hills.

2. LEEA, Linn.; Fl. Brit. Ind. i. 664.

Large herbs or erect shrubs, stems and branches generally furrowed. L. imparipinnate, or tripinnate, rarely simple, leaflets opposite, petioles with broad sheathing base. Fl. pentamerous, in compound corymbose cymes, peduncles leaf-opposed, no tendrils, petals more or less cohering at the base and adhering to the staminal tube. Stamens 5, filaments short, inserted on the entire or 5-cleft staminal tube. Ovary 3–6-celled, one ovule in each cell, style short. Fr. a berry, seeds 3–6. Species 45, tropical Asia, a few in Africa and Australia.

A. Petals red.

1. **L. alata,** Edgew.; Brandis F. Fl. 102. Vern. *Lal galeni*, Nep.

A shrub 2–5 ft. Branches stiff, not succulent. L. pinnate, glabrous, leaflets 2–4 pair, sessile, oblong, sharply serrate, 6–10 in., rachis often narrowly winged. Fl. in dense rusty corymbs. Fr. red, $\frac{1}{4}$–$\frac{1}{3}$ in. diam.

Subhimalayan tract, from the Jumna eastward. Maimensingh. Fl. July, Aug.

2. **L. acuminata,** Wall.; Clarke in Trimen's Journal of Botany, vol. 10 (1881), p. 102. Vern. *Lal galeni*, Nep.

A large herbaceous shrub. L. bipinnate, leaflets ovate-lanceolate, acuminate, crenate-serrate, blade 3–6, petiole $\frac{1}{4}$–$\frac{1}{2}$ in. Corymbs coral-red. Fr. orange-yellow.

Sikkim, ascending to 5,000 ft., Assam, Manipur, Andamans. Fl. May–July. 3. **L. Wightii,** C.B.Clarke (*L. Staphylea*, Wight Ill. t. 58, not of Roxb.) Malabar Courtallum. L. bipinnate, leaflets ovate-lanceolate, sec. n. 8–12 pair, arching, conspicuous beneath.

B. Petals greenish-white.

4. **L. sambucina,** Willd.; Kurz F. Fl. i. 279.—Syn. *L. Staphylea*, Roxb. Wight Ic. t. 78. Vern. *Dino*, Mar.

A large shrub, glabrous. L. 2–3-pinnate, leaflets elliptic-oblong, coarsely serrate, blade 3–8, petiolule $\frac{1}{4}$–$\frac{3}{4}$ in. Corymbs spreading, 3–6 in. diam. Fr. black or dark blue.

Sikkim, ascending to 4,000 ft., Lower Bengal. West side of the Peninsula, from the Konkan southwards, Andamans, Burma. Fl. May–Aug. Malay Peninsula, Ceylon. In moist districts numerous short aërial roots descend from the branches. Closely allied and perhaps not specifically distinct are: 5. **L. gigantea,** Griff. Tenasserim, Malay Peninsula. A small tree with a single stem. 6. **L. umbraculifera,** C. B. Clarke. Sikkim, chiefly in valleys, ascending to 3,000 ft. A tree, attaining 50 ft., trunk as thick as a man's body.

7. **L. aequata,** Linn.; Kurz F. Fl. i. 281.—Syn. *L. hirta*, Roxb.; Fl. Brit. Ind. i. 668.

A large shrub, branchlets, petioles and underside of leaves hirsute. L. 2–3-pinnate, leaflets serrate oblong-lanceolate, 5–10 in. long, on the underside with numerous flat glandular disks, petioles short. Fr. black, $\frac{1}{4}$ in. diam.

Sikkim, ascending to 2,000 ft., Assam, Khasi hills, Sundriban, Chittagong, Lower Burma, Andamans. Evergreen forests near Karwar, Talbot, List 57. Fl. R. S. 8. **L. robusta,** Roxb. Sikkim, to 4,000 ft., Singhboom, Chanda district C.P., Mira hill, Kolaba district. Andamans. Lower Burma. Differs from 7 by the absence of the disks on the underside of leaflets. Fr. blue. 9. **L. bracteata,** C. B. Clarke. Oudh forests. Sikkim, to 8,000 ft., Khasi and Naga hills. A large shrub, sometimes a small tree. Branchlets, petioles and underside of leaves along nerves pubescent. L. pinnate and bipinnate, leaflets oblong-lanceolate, shallow-serrate, sec. n. prominent beneath, arching, terminating in intramarginal veins, tertiary nerves numerous, fine, parallel, inflorescence with numerous long linear bracts. Fr. orange-yellow.

10. **L. aspera,** Edgew.; Brandis F. Fl. 102. Vern. *Kawd okhdr*, Jaunsar. A stout, spreading shrub, pubescent. L. pinnate, rarely bipinnate, leaflets ovate-oblong, acuminate, upper surface often scabrous, the bifurcations of sec. n. running into the teeth, blade 4–8, petiole ½–1 in. long. Fr. ⅓ in., black when ripe.

Foot of North-West Himalaya, ascending to 6,000 ft., Bias to Nepal. Chota Nagpore, Western Peninsula. Fl. R. S. Closely allied is 11. **L. herbacea,** Ham. (*L. aspera*, Kurz F. Fl. i. 280). Vern. *Phekri galeni*, Nep.; *Ban chalita*, W. Duars; *Maham*, Kol. A shrub, stems numerous, bending over in all directions. L. mostly bipinnate. 12. **L. crispa,** Linn.; Kurz F. Fl. 280. Sikkim Terai, Assam, Khasi hills, Dacca, Chittagong, Lower Burma, Konkan, North Kanara (Talbot, List 57). A stiff shrub. L. pinnate, stems, branches and petioles generally with 6–8 narrow crisped wings, nearly glabrous, leaflets usually 5, oblong, 4–12 in. long, deeply and regularly serrate, sec. n. numerous, prominent beneath, straight, parallel, one to each serrature, tertiary nerves ∞, parallel. 13. **L. macrophylla,** Hornemann; Brandis F. Fl. 102 (*Hat Kul*, Sonth.; *Dinda*, Mar.). Subhimalayan tract from the Ganges eastward, Assam, Behar, Lower Burma. Western Ghats from the Konkan southwards. A large herbaceous shrub. L. simple, cordate, mealy-white beneath, blade 8–24 in., petiole 2–5 in.

ORDER XXXVII. STAPHYLEACEÆ. Pax in Engl. u. Prantl iii. 5. 258.

Shrubs or trees. L. opposite, stipulate, trifoliolate or imparipinnate, leaflets stipellate. Fl. regular, bisexual, pentamerous, stamens 5, inserted outside the disk. Ovary 3-celled, ovules 2 or more in each cell. Embryo straight, in fleshy albumen.

Fr. indehiscent, fleshy. Fl. small . . . . . . 1. TURPINIA.
Fr. a membranous inflated capsule. Fl. ½ in. long . . STAPHYLEA (p. 181).

1. TURPINIA, Vent.; Fl. Brit. Ind. i. 698.

Species 10, Indo-Malayan region, China, North and Central America.

T. pomifera, DC.—Syn. *T. nepalensis*, Bedd. Fl. Sylv. t. 159. Vern. *Thali*, Nep.; *Nila*, Nilgiris; *Taukshama*, *Daukyama*, Lower; *Sat-tamanè*, *taw-petsut*, Upper Burma.

A middle-sized, at times a large, evergreen tree, quite glabrous. L. imparipinnate, leaflets coriaceous, opposite, 1–4 pair, elliptic-oblong, acuminate, serrate, 3–7 in. long, stipules interpetiolar, triangular, caducous, as well as the lanceolate stipels. Fl. regular, bisexual, pentamerous in terminal and axillary panicles. Stamens 5, inserted outside the crenulate raised disk, ovary 3-celled, 3-lobed, styles 3, more or less connate, ovules 2–3 in each cell. Fr. green, yellow or purplish, 1–2 in. diam. Seeds angular, shining, albumen fleshy.

Nepal, Sikkim, Assam, Khasi hills, Chittagong, Burma, Upper and Lower. Western Ghats from the Konkan southwards, chiefly in evergreen forests. Nilgiris, Palnis. Fl. Jan.–June. Malay Peninsula, Ceylon, Yunan, Hongkong. Kurz F. Fl. i. 292 and Gamble, list 23, distinguish 2 species. *T. pomifera*, DC., in Sikkim from the Terai to 8,000 ft., in the tropical forests of Pegu and Martaban. L. 5–7 in. Fl. ¼ in. across. Fr. 1–2 in. diam. *T. nepalensis*, Wall. The high level form, in Sikkim at 4–7,000 ft., hill forests of Martaban, chiefly in the dry woods 3–7,200 ft., is a smaller tree. L. 3–4 in., caudate acuminate. Fl. ⅛ in. across. Fr. under 1 in. diam.

Staphylea Emodi, Wall. Vern. *Mārchob (snake stick), Nāgdaun, Chitra,* Pb. Trans Indus. North-West Himalaya, Indus to the Sarda river, descends to 2,500 and ascends to 9,000 ft. Usually scattered singly in mixed and coniferous forests. A shrub or small nearly glabrous tree, bark marked with conspicuous raised white longitudinal stripes. L. trifoliolate, common petiole as long as or longer than leaflets. Leaflets serrate, pale beneath, 3–6 in. long, the terminal petiolulate, the lateral sessile. Stipules linear, stipels setaceous, both early deciduous. Fl. bisexual, regular, pentamerous, in terminal short compact erect or drooping panicles, with numerous deciduous membranous bracts. Petals as long as calyx segments, both white, stamens 5, inserted outside the disk below its edge, anthers versatile. Fr. a membranous inflated capsule, 3-celled, dehiscent at the apex. Seeds few, compressed, bright brownish-grey, embryo straight, in the axis of a fleshy albumen, cotyledons thin, flat. Closely allied to, and may be regarded as a local form of, the North American *S. trifolia*, Linn.

ORDER XXXVIII. ACERACEÆ. Pax in Engl. u. Prantl iii. 5. 263.

Shrubs or trees. L. opposite, stipules 0. Fl. regular, polygamous, disk generally annular. Stamens inserted outside or upon, rarely inside, the disk, filaments free, as a rule glabrous. Ovary of 2 carpels, 2-celled, 2-lobed. Fruiting carpels winged, albumen 0.

ACER, Tournef.; Fl. Brit. Ind. i. 692.

Trees, mostly deciduous, buds covered with scales, the outer short, coriaceous, the inner developing when the buds open, oblong, membranous. Fl. male and bisexual, usually on different trees. Calyx generally 5-, sometimes 4–12-parted, deciduous. Disk thick, annular or cup-shaped. Stamens 4–12, generally 8, inserted on the disk, inside it or outside, filaments shorter in the bisexual, longer in the male flower. Petals none, or as many as calyx lobes, similar to them in colour and substance. Ovary of 2 carpels (2 ovules in each) which develop into 2 one-seeded samaras, the back produced into a large membranous reticulate wing, the lower edge of which is thickened. Albumen 0. Cotyledons irregularly folded, radicle generally long. Species 100, Europe, Asia and North America.

A. L. undivided.

1. **A. oblongum,** Wall.; Brandis F. Fl. 110. Vern. *Pangoi, Paranga,* Jauns.; *Kirmoli*, N. W.

A middle-sized tree. L. lanceolate-oblong, acuminate, entire, pale beneath, blade 3–5, petiole 1–2 in. Fl. pentamerous, in terminal corymbs, ramifications, pedicels and calyx hairy. Nuts unevenly gibbous, wings 1–$1\frac{1}{4}$ in. long.

Sivalik tract and outer Himalaya, Jhelum to Bhutan, ascending to 6,000 ft. Assam, Manipur. Never leafless, the young shoots of a beautiful brown colour. Fl. Feb.–April. 2 **A. lævigatum,** Wall. Pl. As. Rar. t. 104. Outer Himalaya, Garhwal to Sikkim, 5–9,000 ft., Khasi hills. *Putli*, Nep. A large tree, differs from 1 by short petioles $\frac{1}{2}$ in. long. L. not glaucous beneath, reticulate veins conspicuous. Fl. in lax terminal glabrous panicles, pedicels and calyx glabrous, nuts smooth. 3. **A. niveum,** Blume, Assam, hills of Martaban and Tenasserim. A very large tree, glabrous. L. ovate-lanceolate, entire, white beneath. Fl. in racemose glabrous corymbs. Wings of fruit 1–2 in. long. 4. **A. Hookeri,** Miq.; *Lal Kabashi*, Nep. Sikkim, Bhutan, 7–10,000 ft. A middle-sized tree, often grows from seed deposited in the fork of other trees. L. glabrous, ovate, caudate-acuminate, base frequently cordate, sometimes slightly lobed, closely serrate, basal nerves 5, blade 4–6, petiole $1\frac{1}{2}$–$3\frac{1}{3}$ in. Fl. in lax pendulous racemes, pedicels filiform $\frac{1}{4}$ in. Ripe carpels $\frac{3}{4}$ in. 5. **A. sikkimense,** Miq. Sikkim, Bhutan, 7–9,000 ft. A middle-sized tree. L. glabrous, shining, bright green on both sides, ovate, acuminate, entire or faintly serrate, base frequently cordate, basal nerves 5, blade 4–5, petiole $\frac{3}{8}$–1 in. Fl. nearly sessile in pendulous spikes. Ripe carpels $\frac{3}{8}$ in. 6. **A. stachyophyllum,** Hiern. Sikkim. L. velvety beneath, ovate, caudate-acuminate, serrate. Ripe carpels $1\frac{3}{4}$–2 in. long.

B. L. 3–7-lobed.

7. **A. pentapomicum**, J. L. Stewart; Brandis F. Fl. 111. Vern. *Teon*, Buss.

A middle-sized or small tree. L. broader than long, generally 3- sometimes 5-lobed, lobes spreading, obtusely dentate, basal nerves 3, blade 3, petiole 3 in. long. Carpels 1 in., wings erect or diverging.

FIG. 82.—Acer villosum, Wall. ½.

Kashmir to Kunawur, 2,800–7,000 ft., common locally and at times almost gregarious. Fl. Feb.-March. 8. **A. isolobum**, Kurz F. Fl. i. 289. Hill forests of Martaban, 5–7,000 ft. L. palmately 3-lobed, rounded at the 3-nerved base.

9. **A. villosum**, Wall.; Brandis F. Fl. 111. Vern. *Rangteon*, Kun.; *Kainju*, Jauns.

A large tree, young shoots and inflorescence clothed with long silky hairs. L. glabrous above when full grown, green and often pubescent beneath, cordate, 5-lobed, the two outer lobes very small, irregularly and remotely dentate, blade 5–7, petiole 4–6 in., basal nerves 5, the three inner penniveined. Fl. before the leaves, in pendulous racemiform panicles, at the ends of short lateral branchlets. Stamens 8 in the ♂ flower, much longer than calyx. Ripe carpels 1½–2½ in. long, wings erect or divergent. Nuts large, more or less pubescent, the 2 together forming a semicircle ½–¾ in across.

North-West Himalaya, 7–9,000 ft., from Kashmir to Kumaon. Fl. Feb.–March. 10. **A. Thomsoni,** Miq. Sikkim. Bhutan, Manipur, Burma. Closely allied, differs by l. 3-lobed, lateral lobes generally small. Fruit carpels red, 2½–3½ in. long, wing narrowed at the base.

11. **A. cæsium,** Wall.; Brandis F. Fl. tab. 31. Vern. *Mandar*, *Trekhan*, *Bodal*, Punj.; *Kainju*, N. W.

A large deciduous tree, trunk tall, straight, buds glabrous, the inner longer bud scales densely silky outside, petioles red. L. pale beneath, cordate, 5-lobed, lobes broadly triangular, the two outer lobes smaller, serratures large obtuse, basal nerves 5, numerous secondary nerves on the 3 inner nerves, blade 4–8, petiole 3–4 in. Fl. appearing soon after the leaves, in terminal corymbose panicles. Nuts unevenly gibbous, wings slightly divergent.

North-West Himalaya, Indus to Nepal 4-10,000 ft. Fl. April, May.

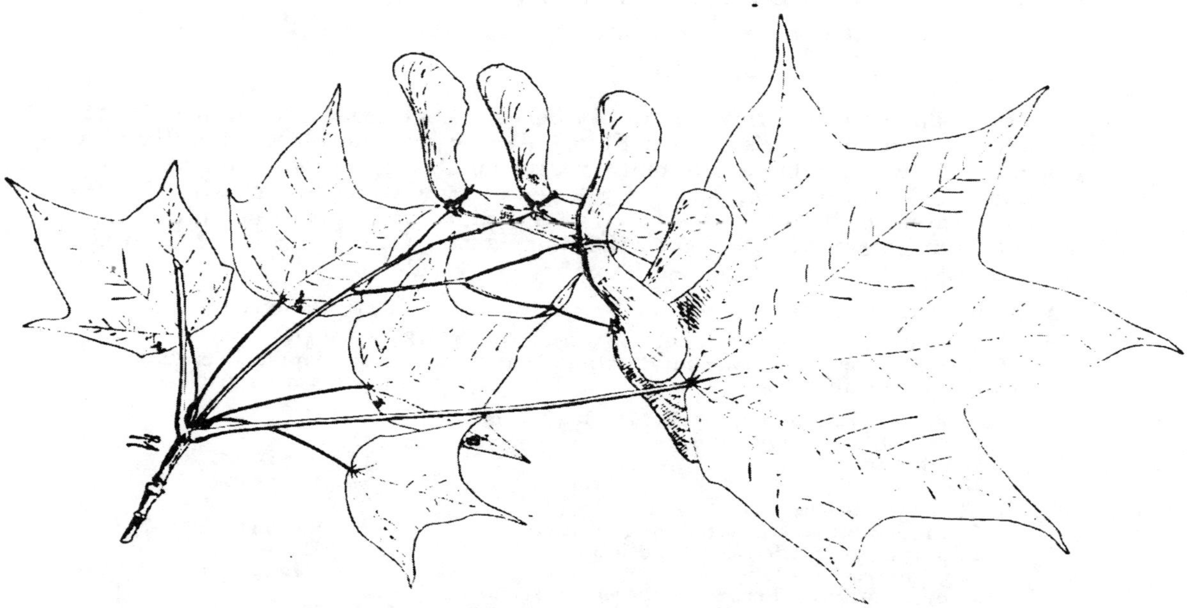

FIG. 83.—Acer pictum, Thunb. ½.

12. **A. caudatum,** Wall. Pl. As. Rar. t. 132; Collett Simla Fl. fig. 32. Vern. *Jarīma*, Mahasu; *Kainjli*, Jauns.; *Kabashi*, Nep.

A large deciduous tree. L. 5-lobed, lobes long-acuminate, the two outer small, blade 3–4, petiole 2–4 in. long. Fl. in lateral and terminal short glabrous corymbs or racemes. Fruiting racemes long, pendulous, carpels 1–1½ in., bright red, wings divergent or divaricate.

North-West Himalaya, Kashmir to Nepal, 8–11,000 ft. Fl. March, April. Sikkim, and the Chumbi valley adjoining it, 8–11,000 ft. The Sikkim tree often has divaricate wings. This is *A. pectinatum*, Wall. Pax in Engl. Jahrb. vii. 249. 13. **A. Papilio,** King, Journ. As. Soc. vol. 65 (1897), 115; Annals Bot. Garden Calc. IX. tab. 24. Sikkim, 11–12,500 ft. A small tree. L. similar to *A. caudatum*, inflorescence a long erect racemiform panicle. Carpels 1–1¼ in. long, wing obliquely and broadly rhomboid-triangular.

14. **A. pictum,** Thunb.; Brandis F. Fl. 112.—Syn. *A. cultratum*, Wall.; Collett Simla Fl. 99. *Wān*, Kashm.; *Kanzal*, Buss: *Kainchli*, *Kakāsi*, N. W.

A large, glabrous, deciduous tree, inner bud-scales oblong, bright brown-silky outside. L. broader than long, 5–7-lobed, base truncate or subcordate, lobes long-acuminate, separated by rounded sinus, margin entire, basal nerves 5–7, petiole longer than blade. Fl. appearing before or with the leaves, in sessile or shortly pedunculate corymbs, pedicels filiform, male and bisexual flowers on the same branch. Carpels $1\frac{1}{2}$ in. long, wings red, divaricate, almost in a line.

North-West Himalaya, Indus to Sarda, 4–9,000 ft., common in mixed forests above 7,000 ft. Bhutan (Griffith). Fl. April, May. L. turn yellow and red in autumn before they are shed. Pax (Engl. Jahrb. vii. 236) limits *A. pictum* to the tree of Japan and Mandshuria; the Himalayan and West Asiatic tree he refers to *A. Lobelii*, Ten. (*A. lætum*, C. A. Meyer). 15. **A. Campbellii**, Hook. fil. et Thoms. Sikkim, very common, 7–10,000 ft. A tall tree, wood even grained, works well, foliage bright light-green. L. deeply 5–7-lobed, serrulate, lobes caudate-acuminate, basal nerves conspicuously penninerved, petioles red. Fl. in elongate narrow panicles, carpels divaricate, 1 in. long, wings broad and rounded at apex.

ORDER XXXIX. SAPINDACEÆ. Gen. Pl. i. 388 (partly) *Hippocastaneaceæ*, Pax, and *Sapindaceæ*, Radlkofer in Engl. u. Prantl iii. 5. 273, 277.

Trees or shrubs, often climbing, rarely herbs. L. alternate, simple or pinnate, with the exception of *Æsculus*. Fl. regular or zygomorphic, generally polygamous. Sepals 5, imbricate in bud, or calyx small, cup-shaped (campanulate or tubular in *Æsculus*). Petals usually 4, generally with scales or tufts of hairs. Stamens inserted between disk and ovary, filaments as a rule hairy. Disk frequently unilateral, in *Dodonæa* inconspicuous. Ovary usually of 3 carpels, 3-celled, often 3-lobed. Albumen 0, embryo as a rule curved.

A. L. opposite, digitate	1. ÆSCULUS.
B. L. alternate, pinnate, trifoliolate or unifoliolate, leaflets serrate.	
L. pinnate, the basal pair small, stipuliform . .	POMETIA (p. 185).
L. tri- or uni-foliolate	2. ALLOPHYLUS.
C. L. alternate, pinnate or unifoliolate, leaflets entire.	
I. Fr. a dehiscent winged capsule.	
L. pinnate	3. GUIOA.
L. simple	4. DODONÆA.
II. Fr. a dehiscent capsule, not winged.	
L. simple, capsule inflated, membranous . . .	STOCKSIA (p. 187).
L. pinnate, capsule inflated, 2-lobed	5. HARPULLIA.
L. pinnate, capsule muricate, 3-valved . . .	PARANEPHELIUM (p. 187).
L. pinnate, capsule coriaceous, not muricate.	
Fl. 4-merous, sepals lanceolate, longer than petals	LEPIDOPETALUM (p. 187).
Calyx minute, cup-shaped	
Reticulate veins conspicuous, capsule pyriform	6. MISCHOCARPUS.
Reticulate veins obscure, capsule 2–3 lobed .	ARYTERA (p. 188).
III. Fr. indehiscent, entire, winged	ZOLLINGERIA (p. 188).
IV. Fr. indehiscent, entire, not winged.	
Common petiole broadly winged	7. FILICIUM.
Common petiole not winged.	
Petals 4–5, filaments hairy	8. LEPISANTHES.
Petals none	9. SCHLEICHERA.
V. Fr. indehiscent, lobed, sepals broadly imbricate.	
Fr. muricate. Fl. tetramerous	XEROSPERMUM (p. 190).
Fr. not muricate, ripe carpels quite distinct .	10. SAPINDUS.
Fr. not muricate, ripe carpels united at base.	
Fl. regular, disk complete.	
Petals not unguiculate, pericarp succulent	11. APHANIA.
Petals unguiculate, pericarp crustaceous . .	THRAULOCOCCUS (p. 192).
Fl. zygomorphic, disk unilateral	12. ERIOGLOSSUM.
VI. Fr. indehiscent, lobed, generally echinate or tubercled, calyx cup-shaped, segments valvate	13. NEPHELIUM.

1. ÆSCULUS, Linn.; Fl. Brit. Ind. i. 675.

Deciduous trees, with large scaly buds and opposite digitate leaves, stipules 0. Fl. showy, zygomorphic, in an ample upright terminal panicle, polygamous, the fertile flower generally near the base of the branches of the panicle, pedicels articulate, bracts deciduous. Calyx campanulate, 5-lobed, the lobes more or less unequal. Petals 5, often only 4, from the abortion of the 5th. Stamens 5–8, free, inserted inside of a lobed disk. Ovary 3-celled, 2 ovules in each cell. Fr. a large leathery capsule, loculicidally 2–3 valved, seeds 1–3, large, testa coriaceous, shining. Cotyledons thick, fleshy, incumbent on the short conical radicle, albumen 0. Species 14. Asia and North America.

1. **A. indica**, Colebr.; Brandis F. Fl. t. 19.—Syn. *Pavia indica*, Wall.; Jacquemont Voy. Bot. t. 35, *The Indian Horse Chestnut*. Vern. *Torjaga*, Trans Indus; *Kakra*, Kashm.; *Bankhor*, *Khanor*, Pb.; *Pu*, Kun.; *Pangār*, *Kandār*, Jauns.

A large deciduous tree, trunk short, attaining a large girth, wood white, soft, close-grained, med. rays very fine, very numerous. Outer scales of buds coriaceous, resinous, shining, inner membranous, slightly puberulous, oblong, 2 in. long, the leaves immediately above them with a broad membranous petiole. Leaflets 5–9, sharply serrate, blade 6–9, petiolules ½–1 in. long. Panicle 12–15 in. long, bearing numerous short-pedunculate scorpioid cymes. Calyx ⅓ in. long, irregularly lobed, often splitting so as to appear 2-lipped. Petals 4, white, red and yellow, 2 narrower than the rest. Stamens 7 or 8, filaments longer than petals. Disk unilateral. Capsule brown when ripe, rough, not echinate, irregularly ovoid. Seeds 1–2 in. diam.

Trans Indus in Kafiristan, 7–8,000 ft. North-West Himalaya, 4,000–9,000 ft. Indus to Nepal, chiefly in moist and shady valleys. Fl. April, May. Closely allied is 2. **A. punduana**, Wall. (*Cherimugri*, *Dingri*, Nep.) Sikkim (Hooker) Western Duars, Khasi hills, Upper Burma, Tenasserim, Siam, Tonkin. L. thinly coriaceous, leaflets nearly sessile, up to 15 in. long, obtusely serrulate. Panicle of scorpioid cymes on long peduncles, branches of panicle (peduncle and cyme) up to 4 in. long. Calyx ¼ in., 4 small and 1 broad obcordate segment. Seeds 1 in. diam.

Pometia pinnata, Forst.; King in Journ. As. Soc. Beng. vol. 65, 441.—Syn. *P. tomentosa*, Kurz F. Fl. i. 295; *P. eximia*, Bedd. Fl. Sylv. t. 157. Andamans, very common. Ceylon, Malay Peninsula. A middle-sized tree. L. paripinnate, leaflets 4–9 pair, serrate, the upper 4–12 in. long, the lowest pair small, round, resembling stipules, deciduous. Fl. minute, polygamous, in long cylindrical paniculate racemes. Calyx cup-shaped, pubescent, teeth 4–5, triangular, petals 4 or 5, small, without scales. Disk complete, glabrous. Stamens 5 or 6, anthers small, filaments hairy, long exserted. One, rarely two, oblong drupes, ½–1¼ in. long.

2. ALLOPHYLUS, Linn.; Fl. Brit. Ind. i. 673.

Shrubs or small trees. L. simple or trifoliolate, stipules 0. Fl. minute, polygamous, slightly zygomorphic, in spiciform racemes. Sepals 4, in pairs, the outer smaller. Petals 4, with a large hairy scale at the base. Disk one-sided, consisting of 4 rounded glands. Stamens 8, inserted inside the disk. Ovary 2-lobed, 2-celled, 1 ovule in each cell. Fr. indehiscent, of 2 distinct carpels. Cotyledons plicate, no endosperm. Species 80–90, in the tropics of all countries.

1. **A. Cobbe**, Blume; Kurz F. Fl. i. 299 (including *A. serratus*, DC. and *A. aporeticus*, Kz.).—Syn. *Schmidelia Cobbe*, DC.: Wight Ic. t. 964 (2); *S. villosa*, Wight Ic. t. 401; *S. Rheedii*, Wight Ic. t. 964; *Ornitrophe serrata*, Roxb. Cor. Pl. t. 61. Vern. *Tipani*, Mar.; *Guaguti*, Tel.

A tall, much branched scrambling shrub, or small tree, young shoots densely tomentose. L. trifoliolate, petiole 3–4 in., leaflets more or less serrate, softly pubescent on both sides, paler beneath. Fl. short, white or pale-yellow, on short pedicels in small fascicles on narrow spiciform axillary racemes, often paniculate, generally strigose. Sepals and petals nearly glabrous outside. Ripe carpels usually solitary, ¼ in. diam., ovoid, red.

FIG. 84.—Allophylus cobbe, Blume. ½.

Common throughout the Western Peninsula. Assam, Khasi hills, Chittagong, Burma. Fl. May–July. An exceedingly variable plant. 2. **A. concanicus**, Radlkofer. Konkan, Mira hill near Bombay. Scandent. Leaflets 3, entirely glabrous, shining, entire, broadly elliptic, tertiary nerves reticulate, conspicuous. Fl. in ample terminal panicles. 3. **A. zeylanicus** Linn. Sikkim Terai and outer hills, ascending to 3,000 ft. Assam, Cachar, Malay Peninsula and Ceylon. L. unifoliolate sinuate serrate, sec. n. excurrent into the serratures, blade 10–15, petiole 1–4 in. Fr. red. ⅓ in. diam.

3. GUIOA, Cav.: King in Journ. As. Soc. vol. 65 (1897), 443.

Erect shrubs or trees. L. alternate, pinnate, stipules 0, leaflets lanceolate, entire, coriaceous. Fl. pentamerous, nearly globose in bud, in simple or branched racemes. Sepals round, thick, concave, pubescent at the edges, imbricate. Petals with 2 pectinate scales. Disk generally incomplete. Stamens 8. Ovary 3-celled, 3-angled, ovule one in each cell. Fr. a dehiscent 3-winged capsule. Cotyledons fleshy and oily, folded. Species 33, IndoMalayan region, Australia, Oceania.

1. **G. fuscidula,** Radlk. *Cupania fuscidula*, Kurz; Fl. Brit Ind. i. 677. Tenasserim, a small evergreen tree. Branchlets, leaves and inflorescence pubescent. Leaflets 3–4 pair, 2–3 in. long. Fr. ½ in. diam. 2. **G. squamosa,** Radlk. (*Cupania glabrata*, Hiern, not of Kurz). Tenasserim, Malay Peninsula. A slender tree. Branchlets slightly rusty puberulous, leaflets glabrous, 2–4 in. long, 4–8 pair. Fr. 1 in. diam.

4. DODONÆA, Linn.; Fl. Brit. Ind. i. 697.

Species 46, mostly Australian.

D. viscosa, Linn.; Brandis F. Fl. 113.—Syn. *D. Burmanniana*, DC. Wight Ill. t. 52 Vern. *Ghisanni*, Baluch; *Sanatta*, *Mendru*, Pb.; *Kharata*, C.P.; *Bandari*, *Bundurgi*, Kan.

A gregarious shrub or small tree, attaining at times 20 ft., heartwood dark brown, extremely hard, med. rays fine. Branchlets angular, young shoots more or less viscid with bright yellow resin. L. varying from lanceolate to linear-cuneate, coriaceous, glabrous, shining, tapering into a short marginate petiole, midrib prominent, sec. n. numerous. Fl. regular, polygamous, in short terminal panicles. Sepals 5, petals 0. Stamens usually 8, as long as sepals in ♂, shorter than sepals in ☿ fl., filaments much shorter than anthers. Disk inconspicuous. Ovary 3- or 4-celled, 2 ovules in each cell, style cylindric, 2-lobed at top. Fr. a membranous capsule with 2–4 broad wings from base to style, ½ in. long and ¾ in. across including the wings, separating septicidally into as many valves as cells, each valve winged on its back. Seeds opaque, dark brown or black, with a thickened funicle.

Trans Indus, Afghanistan and Baluchistan. Common locally, often covering extensive tracts in the drier regions of North-West and Central India as well as in the Deccan. Also on the sea coast. Fl. R. S. Fr. C. S. Ceylon, Malay Peninsula and Archipelago. Tropics of most countries. A most interesting genus, which may possibly not belong to *Sapindaceæ*.

Stocksia brahuica, Benth., Baluchistan 6,000 ft., Afghanistan, Eastern Persia. A stiff thorny shrub 6–12 ft. high. L. linear, grey, generally fasciculate. Fl. yellow, in axillary fascicles. Sepals 5, ciliate, petals 4, oblong on a hairy claw. Disk oblique. Stamens 8, filaments hairy below, capsule membranous, inflated, obtusely trigonous, loculicidal, of a brilliant yellowish-red colour.

5. HARPULLIA, Roxb.; Fl. Brit. Ind. i. 691.

Species 6, Madagascar, Northern Australia, tropical Asia.

H. cupanioides, Roxb.—Syn. *H. imbricata*, Thw.; Bedd. Fl. Sylv. t. 158. Vern. *Harpulli*, Chitt.

A tall tree, l. pari-pinnate. Leaflets opposite or alternate, 3–6 pair, glabrous, 3–8 in. long. Fl. regular, 5-merous, polygamous, ½ in. long, in cymose panicles. Sepals erect, equal, imbricate, minutely pubescent outside, petals clawed, longer than sepals. Stamens 5, glabrous, inserted inside the small puberulous disk. Ovary 2-celled, ovules 2 in each cell, style filiform, stigma more or less twisted. Fr. an inflated 2-lobed capsule, brilliant orange, each lobe opening by 2 valves. Seeds black, usually one in each lobe.

Common in the evergreen forests of the Western Ghats from the Konkan southwards. Chittagong, Andamans. Fl. C. S. Fr. H. S. "A beautiful sight when covered with its brilliant orange fruit" (Bedd.). Ceylon, Malay Peninsula and Archipelago, Yunan. Trimen, Handbook Ceylon i. 312, regards the plant of Ceylon and the Western Peninsula (*H. imbricata*, Thw.) as different from the eastern tree.

Paranephelium xestophyllum, Miq.; Kurz F. Fl. i. 286 (*Scyphopetalum ramiflorum*, Hiern). Hookhoom Valley, Upper Burma. Tenasserim (Kurz). Sumatra. A small evergreen tree. L. coriaceous, shining, imparipinnate, leaflets opposite, 2–4 pair, entire, sec. n. 10–14 pair, blade 4–8, petiole ¼–½ in. Fl. minute, pink, in rusty-tomentose panicles, generally on the old wood. Petals 5, each forming a turbinate cup, glabrous outside, villous inside. Fr. a dehiscent 3-valved capsule, muricate.

Lepidopetalum Jackianum, Radlk.; Ann. Bot. Gard. Calc. ix. t. 28. (*Cupania Jackiana*, Hiern). Nicobar Islands. A small tree. L. pinnate, leaflets chartaceous, shining on both faces, 2–5 pair, alternate or nearly opposite. Sec. n. 8–10 pair, arching, prominent beneath, veins finely reticulate. Fl. tetramerous in short axillary racemes. Sepals lanceolate, petals much shorter than sepals, each with a large scale adnate to its edge. Stamens 8, short, filaments glabrous, anthers hirsute. Capsule coriaceous, compressed, obovate, 1¼ in. long, reddish-brown when ripe, dehiscent, 2-valved. Seed 1, black, arillus pale pink or white.

6. MISCHOCARPUS, Blume; King Journ. As. Soc. Bengal, vol. 65 (1897), p. 447.

Trees. L. alternate, paripinnate, stipules 0, leaflets entire, reticulate veins conspicuous. Fl. pentamerous, in axillary simple or branched racemes. Calyx minute, cup-shaped. Petals in some species wanting. Disk entire, annular. Stamens 8 or fewer. Capsule pyriform, blunt, 3-celled, seed enveloped in a thin arillus. Species 12. Indo-Malayan and Australasian.

1. **M. fuscescens**, Blume.—Syn. *Cupania Helferi*, Hiern; Kurz F. Fl. i. 285.

A large glabrous tree, only inflorescence puberulous. Leaflets 4–6, shining

and finely reticulate on both surfaces, 6–15 in. long. Stamens 8, long exserted. Disk hairy. Ovary hairy, style 2–3-fid. Fr. obovoid, with the stalk ½ in. long.

Manipur, among the oaks at 4,000 ft., Chittagong hill tract, Pegu, Tenasserim, Cochinchina, Malay Peninsula and Archipelago. Fl. Jan.–May. 2. **M. sundaicus,** Blume (*Cupania Lessertiana*, Camb.). South Andaman, Mergui, Malaya. Closely allied. Fr. truncately pyriform, ½ in. diam., while young sharply 3-angled. 3. **M. pentapetalus,** Radlk. (*Cupania sumatrana*, Miq.). Silhet, Khasi hills. Closely allied. Petals 5. Disk and stamens hairy.

Arytera littoralis, Blume (*Cupania adenophylla*, Planch.; Kurz F. Fl. i. 285). Tenasserim, from Maulmein to Mergui, Malay Peninsula and Archipelago. A small evergreen tree. Branchlets thinly rusty-puberulous. L. paripinnate, leaflets 2–3 pair, coriaceous, glabrous, sec. n. conspicuous beneath, reticulate veins obscure. Fl. pentamerous. Calyx minute, cup-shaped, petals broadly cuneate, emarginate or bifid, pubescent above, filaments long-exserted, hairy. Capsule coriaceous, 2-lobed, the lobes oblong, blunt.

Zollingeria macrocarpa, Kurz F. Fl. i 288. Dry forests of the Prome district (*Wetkyut*, Burm.). A large deciduous tree, young shoots tawny-pubescent. L. imparipinnate, leaflets alternate, entire, 5–8 in. long. Fl. bisexual, small, white, in short mostly axillary panicles, petals twice the length of sepals, glabrous except the villous base, filaments hairy. Ovary slightly pubescent at the base, 3-edged, 3-celled. Fr. indehiscent, coriaceous, with 2 or 3 broad striated wings, 2 in. long. Cotyledons folded.

FIG. 85.—Filicium decipiens, Thw. ½.

7. FILICIUM, Thwaites; Fl. Brit. Ind. 539.

(Species 3, Asia and Africa.)

F. decipiens, Thw.; Bedd. Fl. Sylv. t. 129.—*Rhus decipiens*, Wight Ill. t. 75. Vern. *Ningal*, Tam.; *Niroli*, Mal.

A middle-sized tree, leaf scars large and prominent. L. pinnate, leaflets 6–8 pair, glabrous, shining, opposite or some alternate, sessile, linear oblong, 4–6 in. long, midrib prominent, sec. n. numerous, parallel. Rachis with a leafy wing on either side between the leaflets, broad at top, narrowing

downwards. Fl. small, numerous, unisexual, pentamerous, in erect narrow axillary panicles, 6–8 in. long. Sepals narrowly imbricate, glabrous, persistent, petals in ♂ as long as calyx, in ♀ small. Disk very hairy. Ovary globose, 2-celled, 1 ovule in each cell, style short, curved. Drupe ovoid, ½ in. diam., apiculate, purple, shining, seed 1, cotyledons much crumpled.

Western Ghats from Malabar southwards. Fl. January, February. Ceylon, eastern tropical Africa. This genus has been transferred by Radlkofer from *Burseraceæ* to *Sapindaceæ*.

8. LEPISANTHES, Bl.; Fl. Brit. Ind. i. 679, including *Hemigyrosa*, ib. 670.

Trees or shrubs. L. alternate, pinnate, stipules 0, leaflets entire, nearly opposite, reticulate venation prominent. Fl. polygamous, 4–5-merous, in racemes or cylindric racemiform panicles, the branches of which are bracteate, short, and of nearly equal length, bearing one or numerous flowers, sepals large, concave, widely imbricate. Petals usually equal, each with 1 or 2 hairy scales at the base. Ovary entire, 3-celled, ovules solitary in each cell. Fr. 3-celled. Cotyledons thick, fleshy, obliquely superposed, albumen 0. Species 16, Indo-Malayan region.

A. Western species.

1. **L tetraphylla,** Radlk.—Syn. *Molinaea canescens*, Roxb. Cor. Pl. t. 60; *Hemigyrosa canescens*, Thwaites; Bedd. Fl. Sylv. t. 151. Vern. *Korivi*, Tel.

A middle-sized evergreen tree, bark grey. Branchlets, petioles and inflorescence pubescent or tomentose. Leaflets nearly opposite, 2 pair, entire, blade 4–8, petiolule thick, ⅕ in. long. Fl. white, in racemes 3–5 in. long, either fascicled, often on the old wood, or arranged in terminal or axillary panicles, ♂ petals 4, ⚥ pet. generally 5, obovate, claw hairy, basal scales woolly, laciniate, disk crenulate, one-sided. Stamens 8, unilateral, filaments hairy. Fr. ¾ in., 3-gonous, greyish-velvety.

Deccan and east side of the Peninsula, also in the Konkan. Tenasserim. Fl. Febr.–May. Ceylon. 2. **L. deficiens,** Radlk. (*Hemigyrosa deficiens*, Bedd. Fl. Sylv. t. 231); Anamalais, Cochin, Tinevelli Ghats. A middle-sized or small tree, diœcious. Leaflets 4–7 pair. Fl. in narrow racemiform panicles, up to 24 in. long, with numerous short bracteate branches.

B. Eastern species.

3. **L. andamanica,** King; Andamans. Leaflets 1–2 pair. Fl. ¼ in. diam., in compound panicles, the ultimate branchlets ⅛ in. long with 1–3 flowers. 4. **L. burmanica,** Kurz; Pegu Yoma, southern and eastern slopes. Thaukyeghat near Toungoo. Hills between Sitang and Beeling rivers (D.B. February, 1862). An evergreen tree, the trunk simple and palmlike with few branches. Leaflets 4–6 pair, coriaceous, 8–12 in., petiolule thick and short, sec. n. and reticulate veins prominent beneath. Fl. in compound panicles, the ultimate branchlets ½–⅔ in. long, many-fld. Fr. 1 in. long, obtusely 3-cornered, velvety.

9. SCHLEICHERA, Willd.; Fl. Brit. Ind. i. 681.

S. trijuga, Willd. (the only species); Bedd. Fl. Sylv. t. 119; Brandis F. Fl. t. 20. Vern. *Gausam, Kosam, Kusam*, Hind.; *Baru*, Kol; *Sagādi*, Kan.

A large deciduous tree, heartwood red or reddish-brown, very heavy, close-grained, hard, tough and strong, youngest shoots silky. L. paripinnate, leaflets opposite, sessile, those of the lowest pair 1–3, of the terminal pair 6–9 in. long. Fl. yellow, male and bisexual generally on different trees, fascicled on interrupted often slender racemes. Calyx small, 4–6-cleft, petals 0.

Stamens 6–8, longer than calyx, filaments more or less hairy, disk flat undulate. Ovary 3–4-celled, style rigid, stigma sometimes capitate, 3–4-cleft, one erect ovule in each cell. Fr. 1 in. long, usually echinate, seeds 1 or 2, testa brown, enclosed in a succulent arillus of pleasantly acid taste, cotyledons full of oil.

Subhimalayan tract, from the Sutlej eastward, ascending to 3,000 ft., Central Provinces, Western Peninsula. Burma, on the Shan plateau to 5,000 ft. (Collett). Not gregarious, singly or a few together, mixed with the other trees of the deciduous forest. The old leaves are shed January, February, the young foliage comes out towards the end of March or early in April, while the other trees of the dry forest are still leafless, the young shoots deep red. Fl. with the young leaves. Malay Archipelago.

Xerospermum muricatum, Radlk. (*X. noronhianum*, Kurz; F. Fl. i. 295, not of Bl.) Tenasserim. A small evergreen tree. Leaflets 1 or 2 pair, reticulate veins conspicuous. Fl. small, in slender axillary often fasciculate racemes, sepals 4, imbricate, the outer smaller, petals 4, scales 0. Ovary 2-celled, style 1, short, fruiting carpels densely muricate.

FIG. 86.—Sapindus laurifolius, Vahl. ½.

10. SAPINDUS, Linn.; Fl. Brit. Ind. i. 682., excluding *Aphania*, but including *Dittelasma*, l.c. 671.

Trees. L. alternate, paripinnate, occasionally unifoliolate, stipules 0. Fl. ♂ and ☿. Sepals 5, unequal, petals 4 or 5, nearly equal, disk fleshy, circular or one-sided. Stamens usually 8, filaments hairy, anthers versatile. Ovary 3-lobed, 1 ovule in each cell, style 1. Fr. coriaceous or fleshy, consisting of 1–3 distinct indehiscent carpels, pericarp contains saponine, which makes lather with water. Seeds globose, testa black, osseous, embryo curved, cells filled with oil. Species 11, tropics of Asia and America.

A. Leaflets 2–3 pair, pubescent beneath. Ovary hairy.

1. **S. laurifolius,** Vahl; Trimen Handb. Ceylon p. 306.—Syn. *S. trifoliatus*, Linn. Fl. Brit. Ind. i. 682. *S. emarginatus*, Vahl; Wight Ill. t. 51; Bedd. Fl. Sylv. t. 154. *The Soapnut.* Vern. *Ritha*, Hind.; *Aratala, Antawala*, Kan.; *Kunkudu*, Tel.

A large tree. Leaflets elliptic, generally obtuse and somewhat emarginate, at times acute, those of the terminal pair longest, 3–7 in., inflorescence and calyx rusty-pubescent, petals 4 or 5, oblong or lanceolate, without scales or with two tufts of white hair, disk concave, edge fleshy, hirsute, anthers oblong, apiculate. Ovary densely rusty-tomentose. Drupes 2 or 3, fleshy, slightly united.

Common on the Aravalli hills, and in the Western Peninsula, on the coast (Sriharikota) and inland, cultivated in Bengal and in North India. Fl. Oct.–Dec.

B. Leaflets numerous, glabrous. Ovary glabrous.

2. **S. Mukorossi,** Gaertn.—Syn. *S. detergens*, Roxb. Brandis F. Fl. 107. Vern. *Ritha, Thali*, North-West Himalaya.

A handsome tree, attaining 60 ft. Leaflets generally alternate, lanceolate, 4–6 in. long, the terminal pair smaller, sec. n. numerous, close together, with shorter intermediate nerves. Fl. $\frac{1}{10}$ in. diam., mostly bisexual, in numerous small generally 3-fld. cymes arranged in a terminal compound pyramidal thyrsus, ramifications pubescent. Sepals 5, petals mostly 4, purple, nearly glabrous outside, with ciliate edges, with two scales at the top of claw, bearded with long white woolly hairs. Stamens 8, long exserted, anthers short, elliptic, not apiculate. Disk complete, glabrous. Drupes fleshy, $\frac{3}{4}$ in. long, solitary or in pairs.

North-West Himalaya from the Sutlej eastward, 2–4,000 ft. Assam, Silhet. Cultivated in North-West India and Bengal. Fl. May, June. China, cultivated in Japan. The saponaceous pulp of the fruit is an article of trade. Similar in appearance but different in the structure of flower is 3. **S. Rarak,** Blume, Rumphia, vol. iii. t. 167 (*Dittelasma Rarak*, Hook. f.) in alluvial evergreen forests on the Mu river, 700 ft., Upper Burma (*Sinpadi*, Burm.), Malay Peninsula and Archipelago, attains 50 ft. Fl. $\frac{1}{8}$ in. diam. Sepals (5) as well as petals (4) densely silky at back, petals with a densely villous basal scale parallel to and nearly as long as blade. Disk semicircular, glabrous, sulcate. Stamens 8, as long as petals, anthers short, elliptic, not apiculate. Ripe carpels usually solitary, $\frac{3}{4}$–1 in. diam., with 2 small undeveloped carpels at the base.

11. **APHANIA,** Blume; King in Journ. As. Soc. Beng. vol. 65 (1897), 425.

Trees or shrubs. L. alternate, paripinnate, sometimes unifoliolate, leaflets entire, nearly opposite. Fl. 4–5-merous, racemose or paniculate. Sepals large, petaloid, widely imbricate, petals 4–6, small. Disk complete, slightly lobed. Fr. fleshy, deeply divided into divergent lobes, united only at the base. Species 12, one African, the others in the Indo-Malayan region.

1. **A. Danura,** Radlk.—Syn. *Sapindus Danura*, Voigt; Kurz F. Fl. i. 298. *Nuncha*, Beng.

Evergreen, a shrub or small tree. L. unifoliolate, often crowded so as to appear verticillate, glabrous, shining on both surfaces, entire, 6–12 in. long, petiole thick, very short. Fl. numerous, white and pink, pentamerous, in terminal pedunculate puberulous panicles. Sepals unequal, petals with a hairy scale at their base, disk annular. Stamens 6–8. Ovary 2-celled, style bifid. Ripe carpels fleshy, $\frac{1}{3}$–$\frac{1}{2}$ in. long, generally 1 only.

Assam, Khasi hills, Silhet, Barisal, Chittagong, Andamans. Lower Burma, on the coast but also inland, Thaungyeen valley, evergreen forest. Fl. Febr.–April. 2. **A. bifoliolata,** Radlk. (*Sapindus bifoliatus*, Hiern; *Nephelium bifoliolatum*, Bedd. Ic. t. 289). Kolay malai hills, Trichinopoli district, Ceylon, dry region. A middle-sized tree. Leaflets 2 at the end of a common petiole. Fl. 5-merous, petals slightly exceeding sepals, with a short ciliate scale at base, large masses of white blossom. 3. **A. montana,** Blume. Andamans and Nicobars. A shrub, leaflets 1–2 pair. Fl. tetramerous, in axillary panicles, petals fimbriate all round, with a short fimbriate scale at base.

4. **A. rubra,** Radlk.—Syn. *Sapindus attenuatus,* Wall.; *Nephelium rubrum*, G. Don; Wight Ic. t. 24, 25.

A shrub or small tree. L. sometimes unifoliolate, usually paripinnate, leaflets chartaceous, usually 4–5 pair, mostly opposite, glabrous, 4–18 in. long. Fl. dark red, 4–5-merous, nearly glabrous, in large terminal or axillary panicles, petals about as long as sepals. Fr. red, 1-lobed, ellipsoid, 1 in. long.

Sikkim, Terai and outer hills to 3,000 ft. Assam, Silhet, Cachar. Fl. Febr., March.

Thraulococcus erectus, Radlk. (*Sapindus erectus*, Hiern; *Nephelium erectum*, Bedd. Fl. Sylv. Manual 74). A large erect shrub, common on the western Ghats from the Wainád southwards. Leaflets chartaceous, pale, 3–5 pair, glabrous. Fl. pentamerous, in terminal panicles, petals distinctly clawed with a bifid or entire shaggy scale, fruiting carpels glabrous, yellow, 1 in. long, arillus fleshy.

12. ERIOGLOSSUM, Blume; Fl. Brit. Ind. i. 672.

(Species 2, one in New Guinea.)

E. rubiginosum, Bl.; Brandis F. Fl. 108.—Syn. *E. edule*, Blume; *Sapindus rubiginosa*, Roxb., Cor. Pl. t. 62. Vern. *Aukchinsa*, Upper Burma.

A large shrub or middle-sized tree. Branchlets, young leaves and inflorescence clothed with dense rusty-golden tomentum. L. paripinnate, leaflets opposite or alternate, 4–6 pair, 3–7 in. long, often tomentose beneath. Fl. greenish-white, in a pyramidal thyrsus composed of long racemes, bearing numerous small 3–5-fld. cymes with linear densely silky bracts, which are much longer than the buds. Sepals 5, petals 4, unilateral, longer than sepals, each with a bifid woolly scale at the base. Disk one-sided. Stamens 8. Carpels glabrous, purplish-black, $\frac{1}{2}$ in. long, sweet, edible.

Oudh forests. Sikkim Terai, Assam, Dacca. Chittagong hills. Northern Circars, North Kanara (indigenous ?). Andamans, Nicobars. Upper and Lower Burma. Fl. Febr.–April. Malay Peninsula and Archipelago, Australia.

13. NEPHELIUM, Linn.; Fl. Brit. Ind. i. 686.

Trees or shrubs. L. paripinnate. Fl. regular, ♂ and ⚥ in large terminal and axillary panicles. Calyx cup-shaped, almost truncate or deeply 4–8-cleft, petals small, without scales, often 0. Disk fleshy, complete. Stamens 5–10, filaments usually pubescent. Ovary pubescent, usually verrucose, lobes 1-celled, 1-ovuled, style erect, 2–3-lobed. Fr. indehiscent, consisting of 1–3 globose or oblong carpels, generally echinate or tubercled. Seeds globose, included in a pulpy aril, cotyledons thick, fleshy, usually obliquely superposed. Species 30, Indo-Malayan regions and South China.

1. **N. Longana,** Camb.—Syn. *Euphoria Longana*, Bedd.; Fl. Sylv. t. 156. Vern. *Wumb*, Mar.; *Kanakindali*, Kan.; *Kyetmauk* lower, *Tawthayet* upper Burma.

A middle-sized tree, attaining 50 ft. Leaflets coriaceous, 2–5 pair, shining above, glaucous and often slightly pubescent beneath, panicles ample, rusty pubescent. Fl. monoecious, $\frac{1}{8}$ in. across. Calyx tomentose, segments 5–6, narrowly imbricate, petals pubescent, spathulate, as long as calyx. Stamens 6–10, in ♂ long exserted, in ⚥ as long as calyx, filaments hairy near base, anthers glabrous. Ovary 2–3-lobed, hairy. Carpel usually one, ovoid or globose, nearly smooth, yellowish-red, ¾ in. diam. Seed entirely enclosed by the succulent sweet edible arillus.

West side of the Peninsula, in evergreen forest, from the Konkan southwards, Khasi hills, Burma. Cultivated in Northern India. Fl. H. S. Ceylon, Malay Peninsula, South China. A variety with leaves tomentose beneath and panicles 15 in. long, has been sent by Smales from Upper Burma, under the name *Kyobo*, usually the name of *Walsura piscidia*. *N. hypoleucum*, Kurz, Eastern slopes of the Pegu Yoma and Martaban hills, with ovoid carpels, probably is only a variety. 2. **N. stipulaceum**, Bedd. Fl. Sylv. t. 155. (*Otonephelium stipulaceum*, Radlk.) Moist forests in Malabar and on the Anamalais. A middle-sized tree. Leaflets 3–4 pair, the lowest pair small, obliquely curved or reniform, close to the base of petiole, resembling stipules. Calyx segments 4–6, large, valvate, petals 0, fruit carpels ovoid, densely covered with weak prickles, ¾ in. long, seed half covered with the succulent arillus. 3. **N. lappaceum**, Linn.; Pierre Fl. For. Cochinch. t. 319. Indigenous in the Malay Peninsula and Archipelago. Cultivated for its fruit (*Ramboutan*). Fl. $\frac{1}{12}$ in. diam. Sepals 4–6, subvalvate, petals 0, fruiting carpels ellipsoid, densely covered with long recurved soft puberulous broad-based bristles, 1 in. long without the bristles, orange to dark-purple when ripe, aril completely enveloping the seed, pale, edible. 4. **N. Litchi**, Camb.; Wight Ic. t. 43 (*Litchi chinensis*, Sonn.; *Kyetmauk*, Burm.). Indigenous in China (*Lichi*). Cultivated in tropical and subtropical countries on account of its delicious fruit, entirely glabrous. Leaflets 2–6 pair, glossy, pale beneath, reticulate veins indistinct. Fl. minute. Calyx cup-shaped, indistinctly toothed, petals 0, fruiting carpels red, sharply tuberculate, 1 in. diam., seed completely covered with the white succulent arillus.

The above species are classed under 4 Genera by Radlkofer.
1. **Litchi.** Calyx nearly truncate.
2. **Nephelium.** Calyx segments valvate, radicle superior.
3. **Euphoria.** Calyx segments imbricate, radicle inferior.
4. **Otonephelium.** Calyx segments imbricate, arillus covering half the seed.

ORDER XL. SABIACEÆ. Gen. Pl. i. 413.

Trees or shrubs, often climbing. L. alternate, stipules 0. Fl. small, sepals 4–5, petals as many as sepals. Stamens hypogynous, opposite to petals, anther-cells distinct, usually adnate to a large connective. Ovary 2–3-celled, styles distinct or connate, ovules 1 or 2 in each cell. Fr. drupaceous. Seed without albumen or with very thin albumen.

Climbing shrubs, petals equal, all stamens fertile . . . 1. SABIA.
Erect shrubs or trees, petals unequal, 2 stamens fertile, 3 sterile . . . . 2. MELIOSMA.

1. SABIA, Colebrooke; Fl. Brit. Ind. ii. 1.

Climbing or sarmentose shrubs, wood normal as far as known, medullary rays broad. L. simple, quite entire, the bud-scales frequently persistent at the base of branchlets. Fl. bisexual, sepals 4–5, equal, petals opposite to sepals, imbricate. Stamens all fertile, inserted on the annular 5-lobed disk, filaments thick. Ovary of two more or less distinct carpels, 2 ovules in each. Fruiting carpels 1 or 2, endocarp hard, rugose, exocarp dry or fleshy. Embryo curved. Species 17, Indo-Malayan region to China and Japan.

A. Peduncles axillary, 1- or few-fld.

1. **S. campanulata**, Wall. Himalaya, Kashmir to Sikkim 5–10,000 ft. Manipur. L. membranous, oblong-lanceolate, pale beneath, blade 2–4 in., glabrous, narrowed into petiole ¼–½ in. long, which is often minutely hairy. Peduncles 1-fld., 1–2 in. long; fl. green, brown, or pale purplish-yellow; petals ⅛–⅜ in., obtuse, parallel-veined; filaments shorter than petals. Fruiting carpels usually 2, flat, rugose, blue, ¼ in. diam. 2. **S. leptandra**, Hook. f. & Th. Sikkim 4–7,000 ft. Peduncles 1-fld., petals ⅛ in. Stamens much exceeding petals. 3. **S. purpurea**, Hook. f. & Th. Khasi and Naga hills. Peduncles 1-fld.; fl. purple, petals ⅛ in., 5-nerved. Fruiting carpels usually 2.

4. **S. malabarica,** Bedd. Anamalai hills, 3–4,000 ft. Peduncles 2–6-fld.; fl. minute. Fruiting carpels solitary, reniform, reticulate.

B. Fl. in axillary or terminal panicles.

5. **S. parviflora,** Wall. Nepal. Sikkim, 3–6,000ft. Silhet. Fl. minute, in 7- many-fld. corymbs, peduncles long, filiform. Fruiting carpel solitary, generally obovoid, $\frac{1}{3}$–$\frac{1}{2}$ in. long. 6. **S. lanceolata,** Colebrooke. Assam, Khasi hills, Manipur. L. lanceolate, blade 6–8, petiole $\frac{1}{4}$–$\frac{3}{4}$ in., sec. n. almost at right angles to midrib. Panicles axillary, many-fld., petals ovate-lanceolate $\frac{1}{8}$ in. long. Stamens shorter than petals. Fruiting carpels 1 or 2, dark blue, $\frac{3}{8}$ in. long, exocarp pulpy. 7. **S. limoniacea,** Wall. Sikkim, Assam, Khasi hills, Chittagong, hills east of Toungoo 3,000 ft. (D. B. February, 1880), Malay Peninsula. Leaves thickly coriaceous, oblong-lanceolate, blade 4–7, petiole $\frac{1}{2}$–$\frac{3}{4}$ in., veins prominently reticulate. Panicles narrow racemiform, glabrous, as long as leaves or longer. Petals obovate $\frac{1}{10}$ in. Stamens short, included. 8. **S. paniculata,** Edgew. Subhimalayan tract and outer valleys, from the Jumna eastwards, ascending to 3,000 ft. Upper Burma (*Kywè-hin-byin*, Smales, Febr. 1902). Leaves coriaceous, oblong-lanceolate, blade 5–9, petiole 1 in. long, sec. n. and reticulate veins prominent beneath. Panicles axillary and terminal, pubescent, fl. greenish-yellow, petals oblong, $\frac{1}{8}$ in. long, stamens included. 9. **S. tomentosa,** Hook. f. Upper Assam or Upper Burma (Griff.), branchlets and petioles clothed with soft spreading hairs. Fruiting carpels in pairs, obovate, $\frac{1}{3}$ in long.

2. MELIOSMA, Blume; Fl. Brit. Ind. ii. 3.

Trees or shrubs. L. simple or pinnate. Fl. in large terminal panicles, usually bisexual, supported by bracteoles, which are similar to sepals. Sepals generally 5, somewhat unequal, imbricate, usually ciliate. Petals 5, unequal, the 3 outer concave, orbicular, the 2 inner small, bifid. Stamens: two fertile, adnate to the smaller petals, three sterile, opposite to the larger petals, anther-cells of the fertile stamens globose, attached to a large flat connective. Ovary 2-celled, base surrounded by the cup-shaped membranous toothed disk, ovules 2 in each cell, style one subulate. Fr. a drupe, generally oblique, endocarp hard, as a rule 1-celled, 1-seeded, cotyledons folded, radicle long, twisted. Species over 40, Indo-Malayan region, China, Japan, a smaller number in America.

A. Leaves simple.

1. **M. simplicifolia,** Roxb., Cor. Pl. t. 254 (*Millingtonia*). Vern. *Churri*, Nep.; *Toloa*, Ass.; *Kokoh*, Mechi; *Pet-taung-gyaing*, Burm. (Upper B.); *Lalay*, Karen.

A middle-sized tree, wood reddish-brown, medullary rays broad, branchlets, petioles and panicles more or less tawny pubescent. L. entire, rarely obtusely toothed while young, oblanceolate, blade 6–16, narrowed into petiole 1–2 in. long, sec. n. arching, prominent, tertiary parallel. Fl. yellowish-white, minute, nearly sessile, bracteoles similar to sepals, teeth of inner petals long, subulate, almost filiform.

Subhimalayan tract, from Nepal eastwards, in Sikkim to 4,000 ft. Khasi hills, Chittagong, Tenasserim, Upper Burma. Western Peninsula on the Ghats from Coorg to Courtallum. Fl. December–April. Ceylon.

2. **M. Wightii,** Planchon.—Syn. *M. pungens*, Bedd. Man. 77; *Millingtonia pungens*, Wight Ic. t. 964.

A small tree, branchlets, petioles and panicle rusty tomentose. L. coriaceous, entire, elliptic-lanceolate, blade 3–5, petiole $\frac{1}{2}$–1 in. Fl. larger, sessile, $\frac{1}{10}$ in. across, bracteoles numerous, imbricate, teeth of inner petals short.

Western Ghats, from the Konkan southwards, Nilgiris. Fl. May–September. Ceylon, upper montane zone, common. 3. **M. pungens,** Walpers Rep. i. 423 (1842).—Syn. *M. rigida*, Sieb. and Zucc. (1843). North-West Himalaya (2,500–8,000 ft.). Vern. *Kapper*, *Bekesh*, *Bushkua*. Nepal. China, Japan. A small tree, similar to 2, but leaves caudate-acuminate, with large distant mucronate serratures, tapering gradually into petiole $\frac{1}{2}$–$\frac{3}{4}$ in long. Fl. in the axils of lanceolate deciduous bracts longer than buds. Calyx supported by 1–2 bracteoles, similar to sepals.

4. **M. dilleniæfolia,** Blume; Brandis F. Fl. 115; Collett Simla Fl. fig. 33. Vern. *Kann, Kanna, Karkōn, Goi*, N: W. Him.; *Shapra, Bakarshang*, Bash.

A small deciduous tree, branchlets, petioles and inflorescence clothed with ferruginous pubescence. L. membranous, pale beneath, obovate, sharply serrate, with minute hairs on both sides and rusty pubescence on midrib and nerves, blade 6–12, petiole ⅓–1 in. long, sec. n. 15–20 pair, straight, parallel. Fl. white, pedicels nearly as long as flower, in the axils of caducous bracts, no bracteoles.

Himalaya, from the Bias eastwards, 4–11,000 ft. Fl. May–July. *M. myriantha*, Sieb. & Zucc. China, Japan, is similar if not identical, the bracts are more persistent. 5. **M. Thomsoni**, King MSS. in Hb. Kew. Sikkim (Gamble no. 9704), a large tree, branchlets, petioles and underside of leaves densely and softly rusty-tomentose, upperside glabrous, except the tomentose nerves and midrib. L. coriaceous, teeth short, distant, blade 7–12, petiole ⅜–1½ in. long, panicle longer than leaves, softly tomentose. This doubtless is *M. ferruginea*, Kurz MSS., described by King in Journ. As. Soc. Beng. 65 (1897), 116. *M. ferruginea*, Sieb. et. Zucc., is Chinese, and *M. ferruginea*, Blume, a Javan and Bornean species.

B. Leaves imparipinnate.

6. **M. Arnottiana,** Wight Ill. t. 53 (*Millingtonia*); Bedd. Fl. Sylv. 160. Vern. *Huli makay*, Tam.; *Kallavi*, Mal.

A large tree with a spreading head, branchlets, common petiole, underside of leaflets and panicle rusty-pubescent. Leaflets 4–7 pair, blade 2–5, petiolule ¼–½ in. long. Fl. crowded, cream-coloured, on very short pedicels, sepals unequal, bracteoles 0.

Western Ghats from Coorg southwards. Nilgiris. Fl. April–June. Ceylon, montane zone. 7. **M. pinnata**, Roxb. (*Millingtonia*), Sikkim to 3,000 ft., Assam, Khasi hills, Cachar. Nearly glabrous, leaflets 5–10 pair, more or less serrate. Fl. white, minute, in large puberulous panicles. 8. **M. Wallichii**, Planch. Nepal, Sikkim, 5–8,000 ft., Khasi hills. Branchlets, common petiole, underside of leaflets and panicle rusty-hairy, leaflets 3–6 pair, spinulose-toothed. Fl. minute, greenish-white, on short stout pedicels. 9. **M. Colletiana**, King in Journ. As. Soc. Beng. 65 (1897), 116. Maymyo hill, Upper Burma. A middle-sized tree, leaflets 3 pair, remotely and sharply serrate, upperside glabrous except the hairy midrib, underside with scattered hairs. Fl. minute, whitish.

ORDER XLI. **ANACARDIACEÆ.** Gen. Pl. i. 415.

Trees or shrubs. L. alternate (opposite in *Bouea, Dobinea*, and occasionally in *Nothopegia*), simple, trifoliolate or imparipinnate, stipules 0. Fl. regular, unisexual or bisexual, sometimes polygamous. Calyx 3–5-cleft (spathaceous in *Gluta*), petals 3–5, free, alternate with sepals, rarely 0. Stamens usually as many as petals and alternating with them, inserted under, rarely on the disk. Ovary superior (inferior in *Holigarna* and *Drimycarpus*), 1- or 2–6-celled, ovules solitary. Fr. a drupe, seed without albumen.

Resin canals in the bark, as a rule in the bast (phloëm).

A. Leaves pinnate, trifoliolate, in *Rhus Cotinus* simple.
- Petals 4–6, stamens 4–10 . . . . 1. RHUS.
- Petals 0, stamens 3–5 . . . . 2. PISTACIA.

B. Leaves imparipinnate.
- I. Ovary 1-celled.
  - Climbers. Fl. polygamous, stamens 10 . . TAPIRIA (p. 200).
  - Trees, leaflets crenulate, fl. bisexual . . . SOLENOCARPUS (p. 200).
  - Trees, leaflets entire, fl. unisexual.
    - Deciduous, stamens 8–10 . . . . . . 3. ODINA.
    - Evergreen, stamens 4. . . . . . . 4. PARISHIA.
- II. Ovary 4–5-celled.
  - Fl. polygamous, styles 4 or 5, free above . . 5. SPONDIAS.
  - Fl. bisexual, styles connate . . . . . . 6. DRACONTOMELUM.

C. Leaves simple.

I. Petals enlarged in fruit.
- Fruit stalked . . . . 7. MELANORRHŒA.
- Fruit sessile . . . . 8. SWINTONIA.

II. Petals not enlarged in fruit, ovary inferior.
- Spurs on petioles . . . . 9. HOLIGARNA.
- Leaves undulate . . . . 10. DRIMYCARPUS.

III. Petals not enlarged in fruit, ovary superior.
- Leaves opposite, entire . . . . . . 11. BOUEA.
- Leaves opposite, serrate . . . . . . DOBINEA (p. 205).
- Leaves alternate (see *Nothopegia*).
  - Stamens twice the number of petals.
    - Drupe on a fleshy hypocarp . . . . . ANACARDIUM (p. 205).
    - Drupe on the persistent, not enlarged calyx 12. BUCHANANIA.
  - Stamens as many as petals, one only fertile . 13. MANGIFERA.
  - Stamens as many as petals, all fertile.
    - Fl. bisexual, stamens 4–6 . . . . . 14. GLUTA.
    - Fl. polygamous, stamens 4, leaves sometimes opposite . . . . . 15. NOTHOPEGIA.
    - Fl. polygamous or diœcious, stamens 5–6, drupe on a fleshy hypocarp . . 16. SEMECARPUS.

1. RHUS, Linn.; Fl. Brit. Ind. ii. 9.

Trees or shrubs, resin ducts filled with a viscous milky, often caustic juice. L. simple, trifoliolate or imparipinnate. Fl. small, generally diœcious, white or greenish, in axillary or terminal panicles. Calyx small, 4–6-cleft, persistent, segments imbricate, petals deciduous, equal, imbricate. Disk fleshy, adhering to base of calyx, often 5-lobed, the lobes alternating with stamens and opposite the petals. Ovary 1-celled, styles 3, ovules suspended from a long filiform basal funicle. Fr. a small dry compressed drupe, endocarp coriaceous, crustaceous or bony, the mesocarp often full of resin. Testa thin, membranous, radicle superior, incurved along the edges of the cotyledons (accumbent). Species 120, a few tropical, most in the warmer temperate regions of both hemispheres.

A. Leaves simple.

1. **R. Cotinus,** Linn.; Brandis F. Fl. 118; Collett Simla Fl. fig. 34.—Syn. *R. velutina*, Wall.; *Cotinus Coggygria*, Scop.; Engler u. Prantl iii. 5, 164. Vern. *Tung*, *Tunga*, *Tungla*, North-West Himalaya.

A deciduous shrub or small tree, heartwood dark yellow, mottled. Branchlets, petioles and underside of leaves with short soft pubescence. L. strongly aromatic, entire, obtuse, elliptic or obovate, petiole often longer than leaf. Fl. on slender pedicels in a large hairy panicle, fertile flowers few, the pedicels of the numerous sterile flowers elongate after flowering, they are densely covered with long silky hairs and form a spreading panicle of slender feathery branches. Drupe 1-seeded, obliquely obovate, ¼ in. long, with prominent veins when ripe.

Eastern slopes of Suleiman range. North-West Himalaya to the Sarda river. 3–6,000 ft. Fl. April–June, the red young leaves in April. South Europe, Western Asia, China.

B. Leaves trifoliolate.

2. **R. parviflora,** Roxb.; Brandis F. Fl. 119. Vern. *Tumra*, *Dungla*, *Ninas*, Jauns; *Tunga*, Kumaon.

An unarmed often gregarious shrub, sometimes a small tree. Branchlets, petioles, underside of leaves and inflorescence clothed with dense brown tomentum. Leaflets obovate, the lower portion entire, the upper irregularly crenate. Terminal leaflet 2–3 in. long, narrowed into a short marginate petiole, the lateral sessile, smaller. Panicle large, terminal, the lower branches from the axils of leaves, bracts linear, minute, pedicels shorter than flower. Sepals ovate, two narrower than the others, petals oblong, more than twice the length of sepals, disk distinctly 5-lobed. Drupe glabrous, brown, shining, $\frac{1}{8}$ in. diam.

North-West Himalaya, Sutlej to Nepal, 2–5,000 ft. Pachmarhi hills, Centr. Prov. 2,500–4,000 ft. Rampa hills, Godaveri district. Fl. May–June. 3. **R. paniculata**, Wall., Bhutan. Upper Burma, on the Shan hills and in the dry region of the Irawadi valley, often in Eng forests. A small tree, unarmed, glabrous, leaflets entire or slightly sinuate-lobed, the terminal 3–5 in. long, the lateral smaller, sec. n. prominent beneath.

4. **R. mysorensis**, Heyne. Vern. *Dasni*, *Danonia*, Rajputana; *Amboni*, Poona.

A small, aromatic, often gregarious shrub (a small tree or large shrub, Talbot List 61). Branches stiff, spinescent, leaflets deeply dentate or lobed, the terminal 1–1½ in. long, the lateral smaller, all sessile or nearly so. Disk indistinctly 5-lobed.

Sind, eastern flank of the Suleiman range. Rajputana. Dry districts of the Punjab and the Deccan. Fl. February–June. Bark used for tanning.

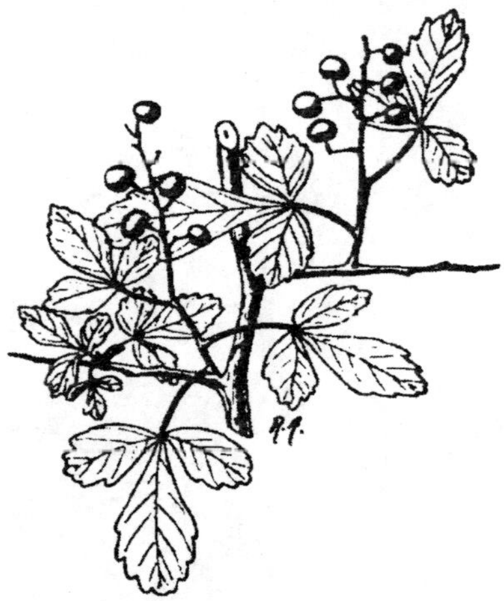

Fig. 87.—Rhus mysorensis, Heyne. $\frac{1}{2}$.

C. Leaves imparipinnate, panicles terminal.

5. **R. semialata**, Murray; Brandis F. Fl. 119.—Syn. *R. Bucki-amelæ*, Roxb.; Wight Ic. t. 561; *R. javanica*, Kurz F. Fl. i. 319. Vern. *Tekri*, *Titri*, *Titrai*, *Arkhol*, N.W. Him.

A middle-sized or small deciduous tree, resin-canals in the bark filled with white milk, which is sticky, but does not turn black. Branchlets, petioles, underside of leaves and inflorescence clothed with short, soft, brownish-grey pubescence. L. not aromatic, leaflets 4–6 pair, opposite, dentate, teeth large, triangular, often sharp, lateral leaflets sessile, the terminal on a marginate petiolule, upper part of common petiole generally marginate or winged. Panicle large, nearly as long as the upper leaves, branches spreading. Fl. white or pale yellow-green, drupe tomentose, edible.

Outer Himalayan ranges, 3–6,000 ft. Assam, Khasi and Naga hills. Shan hills, Upper Burma. Martaban. Fl. April–September. The leaves turn red before they fall. Galls of various shapes frequent on the branches. China, Japan.

6. **R. punjabensis**, J. L. Stewart; Brandis F. Fl. 120. Vern. *Titri*, *Titrai*, N.W. Him.; *Rashta*, Bash.

A small or middle-sized tree, deciduous, heartwood greenish-yellow, the annual rings marked by a narrow belt of vessels, old bark brownish, with rectangular plates, milk watery, not sticky, does not turn black. Branchlets, petioles and inflorescence clothed with minute soft pubescence. Leaflets 5–6 pair, opposite or nearly opposite, entire or with a few teeth near the apex, common petiole not marginate. Panicles compact, broad, shorter than leaves, in fruit generally bent down, ramifications rusty tomentose, drupe $\frac{1}{6}$ in. diam., clothed with dark red velvet, pulp acid, made into sherbet.

North-West Himalaya, Kashmir to Kumaon 3–8,500 ft., more frequent towards the interior. Fl. May–July. A species very similar and possibly identical with 6 is not uncommon in China.

A species with terminal panicles, possibly new, has been found by E. M. Buchanan at 5–5,500 ft. in the Ruby Mines district, Upper Burma. Leaflets 3–4 pair, ovate-lanceolate, pubescent beneath, blade 3–6, petiolule $\frac{1}{4}$ in., fl. pedicellate, in general appearance similar to *R. Griffithii*, Hook. f. Fr. unknown, hence not named.

D. Leaves imparipinnate, panicles axillary.

7. **R. Wallichii**, Hook. f.—Syn. *R. vernicifera*, Brandis F. Fl. 120. Vern. *Arkhar*, *Arkol*, *Arkhoi*, North-West Himalaya; *Hurku*, Bash.

A deciduous tree, attaining 50 ft., bark smooth, grey, resin-canals in bark filled with white milk which turns black and raises blisters on skin. Branch-

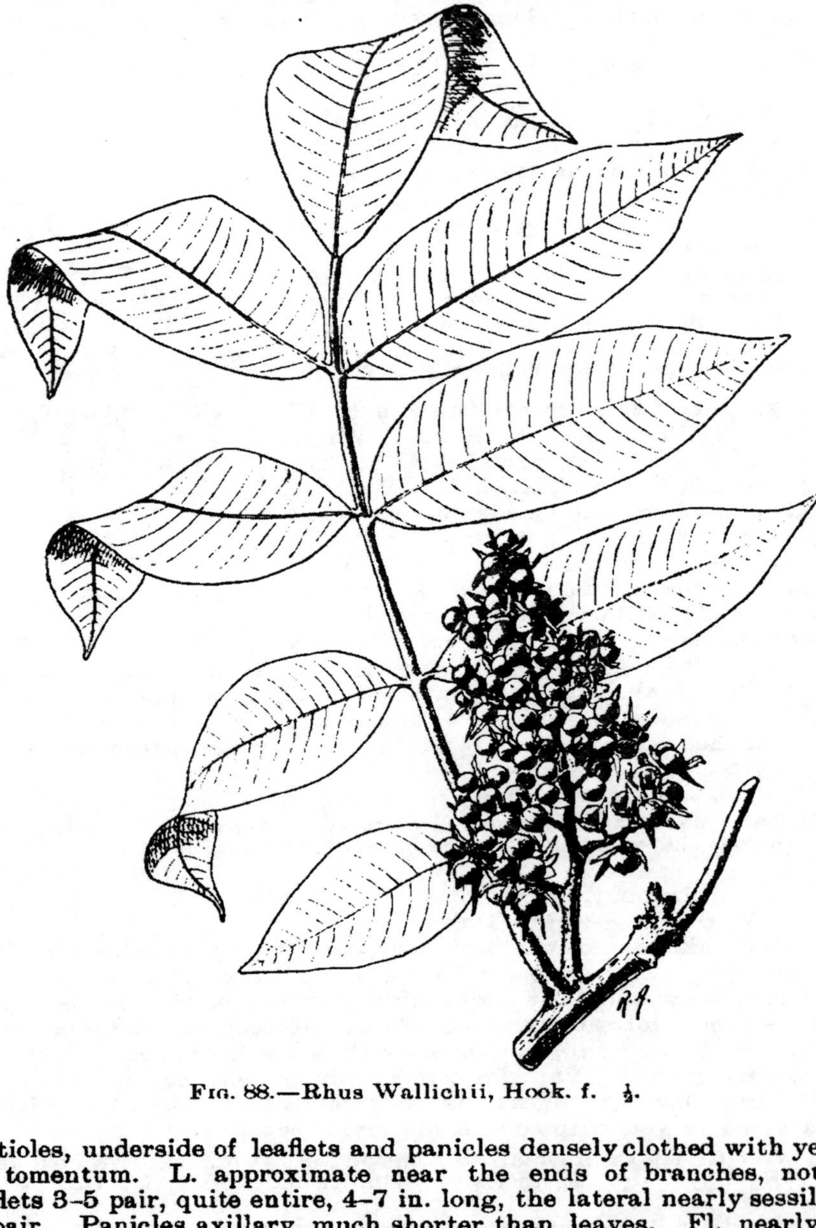

FIG. 88.—Rhus Wallichii, Hook. f. ½.

lets, petioles, underside of leaflets and panicles densely clothed with yellowish-brown tomentum. L. approximate near the ends of branches, not aromatic, leaflets 3–5 pair, quite entire, 4–7 in. long, the lateral nearly sessile, sec. n. 18–24 pair. Panicles axillary, much shorter than leaves. Fl. nearly sessile, petals much larger than sepals, obovate, greenish-white with dark veins. Drupes ⅓ in. diam., in compact pyramidal panicles, pilose when young, nearly glabrous when ripe, exocarp dry, chartaceous, splitting irregularly, endocarp hard, smooth, in a mass of vegetable wax.

North West Himalaya, Kashmir to Nepal 2–7,000 ft, Fl. May–June. *R. vernicifera*, DC., the Varnish tree of China and Japan, differs by petiolulate nearly glabrous leaflets, fl. pedicellate and panicles more lax. 8. **R. insignis**, Hook. f. Sikkim, 6–8,000 ft., Khasi hills. Deciduous, attains 50 ft., differs by glabrous petioles, panicles larger, more lax and nearly glabrous, leaflets on thick petiolules, drupes smaller.

9. **R. succedanea**, Linn.; Wight Ic. t. 560; Brandis F. Fl. 121. Vern. *Shash*, Kunawar; *Arkhol*, N.W. Him.

A middle-sized or small deciduous tree, entirely glabrous, except pedicels and ramifications of panicle, which at times are minutely hairy. Leaflets opposite, 3–6 pair, entire, ovate-lanceolate, long-acuminate, blade 3–6, petiolule slender, $\frac{1}{3}$ in., sec. n. 8–15 pair, alternating with shorter intermediate nerves. Panicles lax, drooping, ramifications slender. Fl. pedicelled. Drupes $\frac{1}{4}$ in. diam., on pedicels $\frac{1}{8}$ in. long, glabrous, yellow or light brown, endocarp hard, enclosed in a fibrous mesocarp, vegetable wax mixed with the fibres.

Himalaya, from the Jhelam eastwards, 2–8,000 ft. Not mentioned in Kanjilal's excellent F. Flora of the School Circle, but found by me in the Rupin valley in October 1874. Khasi hills. Fl. June–September. China, Japan. The milky juice of this species, like that of *R. Wallichii*, causes blisters on the skin, and makes black stains on paper. In Japan, wax is obtained from the fruit of this species and of *R. vernicifera*. A remarkable variety, possibly a distinct species, with almost coriaceous leaflets, the sec. n. more conspicuous and nearly at right angles to midrib, fruiting panicles more dense, in Sikkim and on the Khasi hills, is *R. acuminata*, DC.; Gamble List 24. 10. **R. Griffithii**, Hook. f. Sikkim, Mongpo 2,000 ft. (C. B. Clarke, October 1884). Upper Assam, Khasi hills, common at Shillong. A middle-sized or small tree, glabrous, panicles only pubescent. Leaves large, common petiole 24 in. long and longer, leaflets ovate-oblong from an unequal-sided base, caudate-acuminate, sec. n. conspicuous beneath, 16–24 pair, panicles pedunculate, 8–30 in. long.

2. PISTACIA, Linn.; Fl. Brit. Ind. ii. 13.

Trees or shrubs. L. pinnate or trifoliolate, leaflets entire, stipules none. Fl. small diœcious, in axillary racemes or panicles, supported by bracteoles, petals 0. ♂ sepals 1–2, stamens 3–5 on a small disk. ♀ sepals 2–5, disk 0, ovary 1-celled. Drupe oblique, endocarp bony, cotyledons filled with fat oil. Species 9, Mediterranean region, China, one in Mexico.

1. **P. integerrima**, Stewart; Brandis F. Fl. t. 22. Vern. *Kakra*, *Kakkar*, *Kakring*, *Kakroi*, *Kanrai*, N.W. Him.

A middle-sized deciduous tree, young shoots red, heartwood very hard, durable, close- and even-grained, brown, mottled with yellow and dark streaks. L. aromatic, impari- or pari-pinnate, finely pubescent while young, leaflets 4–5 pair, usually opposite, lanceolate from an oblique base, blade 3–6 in. long, petiolule very short. Drupe broader than long, $\frac{1}{4}$ in. diam.

Hills of Trans-Indus territory. Salt range, Punjab. Outer ranges of North-West Himalaya, 1,500 to 8,000 ft. Fl. March–May. Irregularly shaped galls (*Kakri-singi*), often 6–7 in. long, form on the leaves. 2. **P. coccinea**, Coll. et Hemsl. Shan hills, Upper Burma, 4,000 ft. A small tree. Leaves paripinnate, leaflets 5–6 pair, coriaceous, 1–1$\frac{1}{2}$ in. long, usually alternate.

3. **P. mutica**, Fisch. et Mey.; Engler in DC. Monogr. Phan. iv. 287; Lace in Journ. Linn. Soc. xxviii. 308.—Syn. *P. cabulica*, Stocks. Vern. *Gwan*, Baluch.; *Khanjak*, Peshin; *Badwar*, Hurnai district.

A small tree, often gregarious, attains 20–25 ft. and 6–10 ft. in girth, bark dark brown with longitudinal fissures, heartwood small, dark brown, very hard. L. imparipinnate, common petiole minutely hairy, marginate or narrowly winged, leaflets 2–3 pair, ovate-oblong, obtuse.

Baluchistan, 4–9,000 ft., at lower elevations associated with *Acacia modesta*, higher up occasionally with the Juniper. Afghanistan, Kuram valley, Gilgit. Fl. March–April.

Also in Persia, Asia Minor and Trans-caucasia. This and 4 yield a resin similar to Mastix, the produce of *P. Lentiscus*, Linn. 4. **P. Khinjak**, Stocks; Lace in Journ. Linn. Soc. xxviii. 308. (*Ushgai*, *Buzgai*, Baluch.) Baluchistan. A shrub, often in clefts of rocks, or a small tree, bark light grey, smooth and exfoliating. Suleiman range, Kuram valley. Afghanistan, Gilgit, Chitral. Persia. Petiole not winged, leaflets 1–2 pair, elliptic or almost orbicular, acuminate, 1–3 in. long.

Tapiria hirsuta, Hook. f. (*Phlebochiton extensum*, Wall., Engler in DC. Monogr. Phan. iv. 263; *Pegia nitida*, Colebr., Engler in Engler u. Prantl iii. 5. 152) is a large climbing shrub in Nepal, Sikkim (to 3,000 ft.). Assam, Bhutan. Khasi hills, Manipur. China. Branchlets, leaves and inflorescence softly tomentose. Leaves imparipinnate, leaflets 5–7 pair, nearly opposite, entire or more or less serrate. Fl. small, polygamous, scented, in axillary panicles. Drupes black, pericarp fleshy, resinous.

Solenocarpus indica, W. et A.; Bedd. Fl. Sylv. t. 233, is a small or middle-sized tree in the evergreen forests of the Western Ghats from North Kanara southwards, in the Anamalai hills at 2,600 ft. Leaves imparipinnate, leaflets opposite, glabrous, crenulate. Fl. small, bisexual, pure white, panicles numerous, fascicled at the ends of branchlets (the tree when in blossom a perfect mass of white). Calyx small, 5-toothed, deciduous, petals 5, ovate, valvate. Stamens 10, ovary 1-celled. Drupe obliquely-oblong, ½ in. long, pericarp full of oil, stone hard.

3. ODINA, Roxb.; Fl. Brit. Ind. ii. 29.

(Species 13, mostly African.)

O. Wodier, Roxb.; Wight Ic. t. 60; Bedd. Fl. Sylv. t. 123; Royle Ill. t. 31.—Syn. *Lannea grandis*, Engler in Engl. u. Prantl. Nachtr. 213. Vern, *Kamlai*, *Kaimal*, Punjab; *Jhingan*, *Ginjan*, Hind.; *Mohi*, *Mowai*, H. M.; *Gunj*, Bundelkhand; *Gol*, Ajmere; *Gumpan*, Tel.; *Godda*, Kan.; *Udi*, *Uthi*. Tam.; *Nabè*, Burm.

A large deciduous tree, sapwood white, heartwood scanty. L. imparipinnate, leaflets 3–4 pair, opposite, entire. Fl. appearing when the tree is leafless, small, greenish, unisexual, 4–5-merous, on short pedicels in compact fascicles, the female fl. in simple, the male in compound racemes. Racemes numerous from leafscars at the ends of branches, male and female usually on different branches, often on different trees. Calyx 4–5-cleft, persistent, lobes obtuse, ciliate, imbricate in bud. Petals oblong, longer than sepals, pink and greenish-yellow. ♂: Stamens 8–10, inserted beneath and outside the annular 8-lobed disk, rudimentary ovary 4–5-cleft; ♀: stamens small, sterile, ovary sessile, 1-celled, styles 3–4, short, stout. Drupe reniform-oblong, ½ in. long, stone hard.

Common in deciduous forests throughout India and Burma, in the subhimalayan tract extending to the Indus, and ascending to 4,000 ft. in the outer hills. Leafless as a rule from January to June, but on the east side of the Peninsula (Sriharikot, Madras, Javadies) in leaf almost throughout the year. Ugly when leafless, but a handsome tree when in full foliage. Fl. February–April. Fr. from June onwards, often remains long on the tree. Easily grown from cuttings.

4. PARISHIA, Hook. f.; Fl. Brit. Ind. ii. 29.

(Species 5, Indo-Malayan.)

P. insignis, Hook. f., Trans. Linn. Soc. xxiii. t. 26; Kurz F. Fl. i. 318.

A tall evergreen tree full of white milk. L. imparipinnate, leaflets 6–8 pair, quite entire, opposite, oblique, 6–8 in. long. Fl. ¼ in. diam., yellow, diœcious, tetramerous, in long hairy panicles. ♂: Calyx 4-lobed, lobes valvate, petals 4, stamens 4, inserted below the edge of the disk, rudimentary ovary columnar. ♀: Calyx-lobes greatly enlarged in fruit, ovary sessile, 1-celled, style unequally 3-fid. Drupe globose, pointed, ½ in. diam., supported by the pubescent enlarged calyx-lobes, 3–4 in. long.

Mergui, Andamans. Fl. February–May.—Penang.

5. SPONDIAS, Linn.; Fl. Brit. Ind. ii. 42.

L. imparipinnate, leaflets nearly opposite. Fl. small, polygamous, in terminal panicles. Calyx small, deciduous, 4–5-lobed. Petals 4–5, spreading. Stamens 8–10, inserted outside beneath the broad crenate disk. Ovary sessile, 4–5-celled. Drupe fleshy, stone 1–5-celled, hard, thick, with a tuberculate, fibrous surface. Species 8, tropics of the old and new world.

1. **S. mangifera**, Willd.; Wight Ill. t. 76; Bedd. Fl. Sylv. t. 169; Kurz F. Fl. i. 322; Kanjilal Forest Flora 102. The *Hog-plum*. Vern. *Amra*, *Ambāra*, *Amarat*, H.; *Ambāda*, M.; *Ambota*, Uriya; *Ambe*, *Amate*, Kan.; *Ambalam*, Tam.; *Gwè*, Burm.

A glabrous, deciduous tree, large in tropical, small in Northern India, wood grey, soft, light. Bark smooth, whitish or brownish-grey, aromatic. Leaflets 3–5 pair, quite entire, elliptic-oblong, acuminate, 3–6 in. long, sec. n. nearly straight, 10–20 pair, joined at the ends by a prominent nerve running along and close to the edge of leaf. Fl. pentamerous, white, nearly sessile, clustered on stout ramifications of a sparingly branched panicle, petals $\frac{1}{10}$ in. long. Drupe yellow when ripe, $1\frac{1}{2}$ in. long, is eaten, but has an astringent acid and turpentine taste.

Subhimalayan tract and outer valleys to 3,000 ft., from the Chenab eastwards. Salt-range in the Punjab. Deciduous forests of Burma and the Western Peninsula. Fl. February-May. One of the first trees to shed its leaves and one of the last to renew them, often not until the rains have set in. In Ceylon, where it is common in the moist low country it is bare of leaves for a short time at the end of the dry weather, young foliage in April beautiful orange-pink, Trimen Handb. Ceylon i., 327. Deer eat the fruit greedily and heaps of the stones are frequently found in the forests where this tree grows. Indian Archipelago, Hongkong. 2. **S. acuminata**, Roxb. Konkan Hills, North Kanara, Malabar. A middle-sized fast-growing tree, leaflets 5–8 pair, remotely crenulate, long-acuminate, stone believed to be smooth.

3. **S. axillaris**, Roxb.; Ann. Bot. Gard. Calc. ix. t. 25. Vern. *Labshi*, Nep.

A tall evergreen tree. Bark brown or reddish, peeling off in long flakes, wood dark pink, red on exposure, soft but durable. Leaflets 6–8 pair, opposite or nearly so, ovate-lanceolate, acuminate, in old trees entire, in young trees serrate, 3–5 in., petiolule $\frac{1}{4}$ in. long. Fl. polygamous, pentamerous, the male in axillary panicles, stamens 10, disk annular 10-lobed, the fertile (bisexual) solitary or 2 (sometimes 3) on axillary peduncles, $\frac{1}{4}$ in. across, ovary 5-celled, styles 5, short, erect. Drupes ovoid, $1–1\frac{1}{4}$ in. long, yellow when ripe, edible, stone 5-celled.

Sikkim, Bhutan 1–4,500 ft. Kachin hills. This is *Cedrela* sp. Gamble List 17, and is probably identical with *Poupartia Fordii*, Hemsley, Hook. Ic. Pl. t. 2,557, a tree in the Happy Valley of Hongkong.

6. DRACONTOMELUM, Blume; Fl. Brit. Ind. ii. 43.

(Species 5, tropical Asia, extending to the Pacific.)

D. mangiferum, Blume; Kurz F. Fl. 322.

A large evergreen tree, the youngest shoots tawny-pubescent. L. imparipinnate, common petiole minutely puberulous, leaflets 6–9 pair, opposite or alternate, 5–7 in. long, glabrous above, slightly hairy beneath. Fl. bisexual, pentamerous, campanulate, $\frac{1}{4}–\frac{1}{3}$ in. across, greenish-white, in large mostly axillary pubescent panicles. Stamens 10, inserted at the base of the cup-shaped crenulate disk. Ovary 5-celled. Drupe 1 in. diam., depressed, stone flat, rugulose, 2–5-celled.

Andamans and Nicobars Fl. R. S. Malay Peninsula and Archipelago.

7. MELANORRHŒA, Wall.; Fl. Brit. Ind. ii. 25.

L. coriaceous, simple, quite entire. Fl. large, bisexual, in axillary panicles. Sepals 5, cohering in the species here described into a pointed deciduous

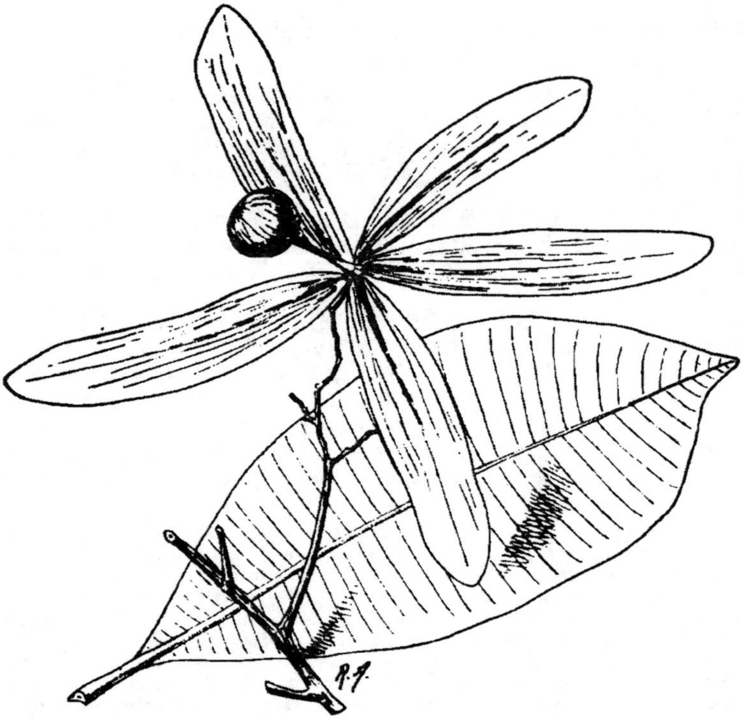

Fig. 89.—Melanorrhœa usitata, Wall. ½.

cap. Petals 5–8, imbricate, linear-oblong, persistent and, as a rule, much enlarged in fruit. Stamens 5 or numerous, inserted on a thick hemispheric or columnar disk. Ovary stalked, oblique, 1-celled. Fr. a dry drupe, more or less stalked. Species 6, Indo-Malayan.

1. **M. usitata,** Wall. Pl. As. Rar. t. 11, 12; Brandis in Ind. Forester, i. (1876), 362. Vern. *Thitsi*, Burm.

A large deciduous tree, yields the black Burmese lacquer or varnish from incisions made into the bark, while the tree is in leaf. Branchlets, petioles, underside of leaves and panicles softly tomentose. L. obovate or oblanceolate, blade 9–12, narrowed into a thick almost winged petiole ½–1 in. long. Fl. white, petals pubescent, stamens many. Drupes red, ⅓–½ in. diam., stalk thick, ⅓ in. long, supported by the oblong stellately spreading, enlarged petals, 2–4 in. long.

Burma, Upper and Lower, chiefly in Eng forests. Fl. January–March. Siam to the Mekong river. *M. laccifera*, Pierre Fl. For. Cochinch. t. 367, Cambodia, Cochinchina, yields a most valuable varnish, grows very rapidly, and can be tapped when two years old. Might be cultivated in Burma. 2. **M. glabra,** Wall. Pl. As. Rar. t. 283, Tavoy, Mergui. L. glabrous. Drupes on slender stalks 1–1¼ in. long. Fruiting petals linear or spathulate, 2–2½ in. long.

8. SWINTONIA, Griff.; Fl. Brit. Ind. ii. 26.

Evergreen trees. Leaves simple, quite entire, petioles long. Fl. bisexual or unisexual, in large terminal and axillary panicles. Calyx small, deeply 5–6-cleft, lobes rounded. Petals 5–6, persistent and much enlarged in fruit. Stamens 4–5, inserted on the thick fleshy disk. Drupe ovoid, coriaceous, not stalked, subtended by the enlarged petals. Species 7, Indo-Malayan.

1. **S. floribunda,** Griff. Proc. Linn. Soc. i. (1846), 283.—Syn. *S. Griffithii*, Kurz (1870), comprises probably *S. Schwenckii*, Kurz F. Fl. i. 316. Vern. *Thayet san*, Burm.

A lofty tree, entirely glabrous. L. lanceolate, blade 4–6, petiole very slender, 1–1½ in. long, sec. n. 16–20 pair. Fl. pale-yellow, in dense masses. Drupe sessile, supported by the enlarged reflexed linear-lanceolate purple petals, which are 2 in. long.

Chittagong hills. Pegu Yoma, rare. Martaban and Tenasserim, common near the coast, but also inland, common on the hill east of Toungoo at 2,000 ft. Fl. December–March. 2. **S. Helferi,** on rocky islands of the Mergui Archipelago. L. narrow-lanceolate, blade 6–10, petiole 1–2 in. long, sec. n. 24–30 pair.

9. HOLIGARNA, Ham.: Fl. Brit. Ind. ii. 36.

Lofty trees. L. more or less coriaceous, petiolate, simple, quite entire, crowded at the ends of branches, petioles mostly with 2 or 4 spur-like deciduous appendages. Fl. small, usually sessile, diœcious, pentamerous, in axillary or terminal racemes or panicles. Calyx superior, tube cup-shaped, petals densely villous. Stamens 5, inserted on the edge of the disk, which in the ♂ flower lines the calyx-tube, filam. glabrous, subulate, anthers small, nearly globose. Ovary inferior 1-celled, styles 3–5, terminal. Drupe oblong or ovoid, on stalks elongating after flowering, resinous, acrid, endocarp coriaceous.

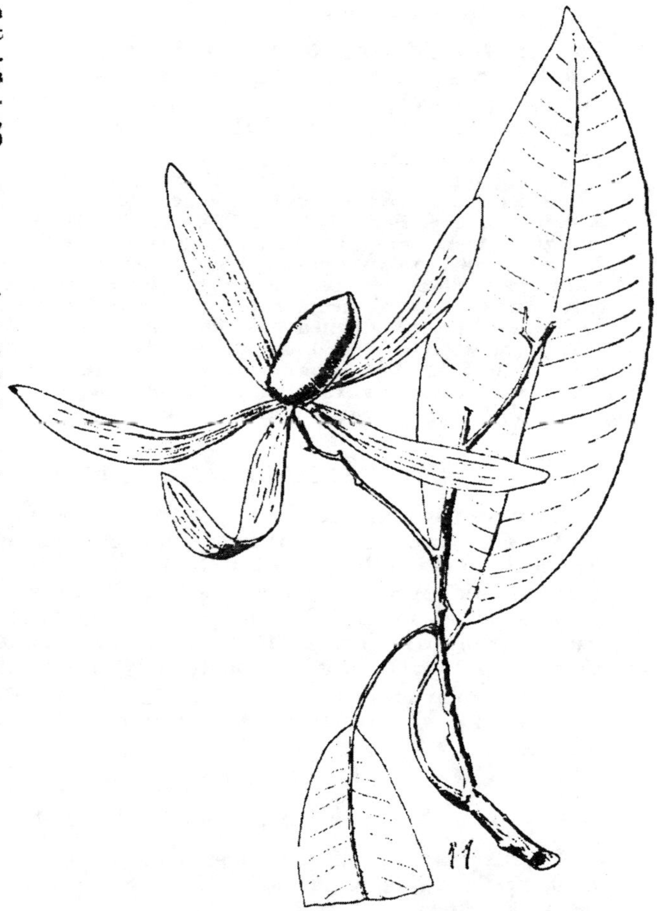

FIG. 90.—Swintonia floribunda, Griff. ½.

A. Western species.

1. **H. Arnottiana,** Hook. f. (1876).—Syn. *H. longifolia,* W. et A.; Bedd. Fl. Sylv. t. 167. Vern. *Holigar, Hulgeri, Katugeri,* Kan.; *Kattu cheru,* Tam.; *Cheru,* Mal.

A large evergreen tree, with black acrid resinous juice, young shoots rusty-tomentose. L. cuneate, obtuse or acute, blade 6-10, narrowed into petiole ¼–1 in. long, sec. n. 10–20 pair. Fl. ⅙ in. long, rusty tomentose within and without, fasciculate, in axillary sparingly branched racemiform panicles, anthers red. Drupe glabrous, obliquely oblong, stalk 1 in. long.

Evergreen forests of the western coasts and the Western Ghats, from the Konkan southwards. Coorg, Nilgiris. Common in the low country of Travancore. Fl. January–March. *H. ferruginea,* Marchand (1869), is supposed to differ by racemes shorter, more robust and less branched, clothed with red tomentum, and larger flowers. Mr. Bourdillon reports a new species from the evergreen forests of Travancore, at 2,000 ft. and higher, with smaller leaves, not exceeding 6 in., sec. n. 6–9 pair, panicles slender, up to 12 in. long. Fl. smaller, black, hairy outside, while inside they are quite white, clothed with white hairs, anthers black.

2. **H. Grahamii,** Hook. f. (*Semecarpus Grahamii,* Wight Ic. t. 235). Evergreen forests of the Western Ghats, from the Konkan southwards. *Howlagerri,* Kaans of Sorub, Mysore (D.B. April 1868). A middle-sized or large tree. L. softly pubescent beneath, oblanceolate, long-acuminate, often abruptly narrowed from the middle, blade 12–16 in., petiole thick, ½ in. long. Panicles terminal, much branched. Drupe ⅜ in. long, three-fourths enclosed in the calyx. 3. **H. Beddomei,** Hook. f. Anamalai hills. A very large tree. Young shoots and underside of leaves densely tomentose with long rufous hairs, blade 10–22 inches, narrowed into petiole ½–1 in., spurs tomentose, soft, not rigid.

B. Eastern species.

4. **H. longifolia**, Roxb. Cor. Pl. t. 282.

A tall tree, bark smooth, ash-coloured. L. glabrous and glaucous beneath, thinly coriaceous, narrowly oblanceolate, blade 12–24, petiole ½–1 in. Panicle large and spreading. Fl. dull white, rusty-tomentose. Drupe entirely enclosed by calyx-tube.

Chittagong hill tract. Lower Burma, in Eng and other Forests. Fl. C. S.

The following two species may possibly only be forms of *H. longifolia*, cf. King in Journ. As. Soc. Bengal, 65 (1897), 512. 5. **H. Helferi**, Hook. f.; Kurz F. Fl. i. 315, an evergreen tree, Lower Burma, young shoots and underside of young leaves pubescent. L. coriaceous, oblanceolate, shortly acuminate, blade 12–30, petiole ½–1 in. long. Panicles axillary, densely rusty-tomentose. Drupe almost entirely covered by the calyx-tube. 6. **H. albicans**, Hook. f. Lower Burma. L. coriaceous, oblanceolate, white and almost glabrous beneath, blade 6–8, petiole ½–¾ in., without spurs.

7. **H. Kurzii**, King in Journ. As. Soc. Beng. 65 (1897), 512 (*Semecarpus albescens*, Kurz; Engler in DC., Mon. Phan. iv. 488). Pegu, Tenasserim, Andamans. L. coriaceous, white and nearly glabrous beneath, oblanceolate, blade 10–15, petiole ½–¾ in. long, sec. n. distant, 12–18 pair, panicle large, compound, terminal.

10. DRIMYCARPUS, Hook. f.; Fl. Brit. Ind. ii. 36.

D. racemosus, Hook. f. (the only species). Vern. *Brong-Kúng*, Lepoha.

An evergreen tree, entirely glabrous except the inflorescence, wood close-grained, takes a beautiful polish. L. shining coriaceous, lanceolate, entire, margin thickened and usually strongly waved, blade 4–12, petiole stout, deeply grooved, ½ in. long. Fl. small, greenish-white, pentamerous, in fascicled short racemiform panicles, axillary or below the leaf on the old wood, stamens 5. Ovary inferior, 1-celled, style 1, very short. Drupe red, 1 in. diam.

Sikkim, common in the outer hills, 3–6,000 ft. Bhutan, Assam, Khasi hills. Cachar Chittagong. Fl. January–April.—China.

11. BOUEA. Meissn.; Fl. Brit. Ind. ii. 20.

(Species 3–4, Indo-Malay region.)

B. burmanica, Griff. (1841); Pierre, Fl. For. Cochinch. t. 366.—Syn. *B. oppositifolia*, Meissn. (1842), Kurz. F. Fl. i. 306. Vern. *Miriām*, *Uriām*, Sund.; *Mayan*, Burm.

An evergreen middle-sized tree. L. lanceolate, quite entire, blade 4–10, petiole ⅓ in. long. Fl. small, polygamous, in axillary and terminal panicles. Sepals 3–5, deciduous, petals 3–5, imbricate. Stamens 3–5, inserted within the small disk, all fertile. Drupe fleshy, yellow, 1–2 in. long, edible, taste pleasant, sweet and acid, endocarp thin woody, 1-seeded.

Sundriban. Andamans, Tenasserim. Cultivated throughout Burma. Fl. January–March. Fr. April–May. Cochinchina, Malay Peninsula and Archipelago.

Dobinea vulgaris, Hamilton, Fl. Brit. Ind. i. 696, under *Sapindaceæ*, is a shrub in Nepal, Sikkim (4–6,000 ft.), Mishmi hills. L. opposite, membranous, serrate, ovate-lanceolate. Fl. small, unisexual, in terminal panicles. ♂: Calyx cup-shaped, 4-dentate, petals 4, exceeding calyx, disk 0, stamens 8, alternately shorter. ♀: A 1-celled lenticular ovary on an annular disk, adnate to a lanceolate bract, calyx 0, petals 0, style filiform, spirally involute. Fr. indehiscent, adnate to a round or obovate emarginate penninerved thinly membranous bract, ½ in. diam.

Anacardium occidentale, Linn.; Bedd. Fl. Sylv. t. 163. *The Cashew-nut.* Vern. *Kaju*, Mar.; *Godambe*, Kan.; *Kolla-mavu*, Tam.; *Paringi mavu*, Mal.; *Thi hon Thayet*, Burm. A small or middle-sized evergreen tree, indigenous in South America, but cultivated and naturalized in many tropical countries, often found near the coast. L. glabrous, thickly coriaceous, obovate, entire, blade 5–7, petiole ¼–½ in., sec. n. 8–12 pair, conspicuous. Fl. polygamous, in large terminal bracteate panicles, pentamerous, petals linear, ⅓–½ in. long, pale yellow streaked with pink, stamens 10, one longer always fertile, the rest often sterile. Drupe kidney-shaped, 1 in. long, seated on a fleshy thick hypocarp, which is 2–3 in. long, orange or crimson, edible, formed of the enlarged torus and calyx-base.

In pericarp are sacs filled with acrid oil, which raises blisters on the skin. Seed kidney-shaped, oily, roasted and eaten.

12. BUCHANANIA, Roxb.; Fl. Brit. Ind. ii. 22.

Trees or shrubs. L. simple, quite entire. Fl. small, bisexual, panicles numerous, terminal and in the axils of the uppermost leaves at the ends of branches. Calyx 3–5-cleft, persistent, petals 4–5, oblong, imbricate in bud. Stamens 8–10, free, inserted outside and under the annular disk, which surrounds the 5–6 free carpels, 1 fertile, the others imperfect. Drupe small, flesh scanty, splitting into 2 valves at the time of germination. Species 20, Indo-Malayan region, extending to Australia and the Pacific.

A. Panicles tomentose or pubescent.

1. **B. latifolia**, Roxb.; Bedd. Fl. Sylv. t. 165; Brandis F. Fl. 127. Syn. *B. Lanzan*, Spreng.; Cooke, Bombay Flora i. 275. Vern. *Chiroli*, Pb.; *Piyal*, *Pial*, *Paira*, *Char*, *Achar*, Hind.; *Char*, *Chirauli*, *Chironji*, Mar.; *Morli*, *Sara*, Tel.; *Nurkal*, *Murkala*, Kan.; *Morala*, *Sarai*, Tam.; *Munga*, *perlu*, Mal.

A middle-sized tree, attaining 50 ft., bark dark grey, rough, with small quadrangular plates, divided by deep narrow cracks. L. coriaceous, hard, oblong, obtuse, as a rule softly hairy beneath, blade 6–10, petiole $\frac{1}{4}$–$\frac{1}{3}$ in. Sec. n. 15–20 pair, prominent. Panicles tomentose, bracts small, caducous. Fl. sessile, greenish-white. Drupe black, $\frac{1}{2}$ in. diam., edible, stone hard, bony.

Common in the deciduous forests of India and Burma, except the arid region of North-West India. In the subhimalayan tract the Sutlej is its north-western limit. Fl. January–March. Nearly leafless for a short time during the dry season. Bark used for tanning. 2. **B. lanceolata,** Wight Ic. t. 287, Quilon. L. glabrous and shining on both sides, elliptic-lanceolate, blade 4–5, petiole $\frac{1}{2}$–$\frac{3}{4}$ in., sec. n. 16–20 pair, distinct reticulate veins between them. Panicles shorter than leaves, their branches short, stout. Fr. unknown.

3. **B. platyneura,** Kurz; King in Journ. As. Soc. Bengal, 65 (1897) 462. Andamans and Nicobars, very common. A middle-sized or large tree, youngest shoots minutely pubescent. L. coriaceous, glabrous and shining on both surfaces, elliptic-lanceolate, blade 4–9, petiole $\frac{1}{2}$–1 in. Panicles puberulous, pedicels longer than flower, anthers narrow, not sagittate. 4. **B. glabra,** Wall. Maulmein. L. thickly coriaceous, broadly elliptic, panicles shorter than leaves, rusty-puberulous. Fl. nearly sessile. 5. **B. acuminata,** Turcz. (*B. sessilifolia*, Schauer; King in Journ. As. Soc. Bengal, 65 [1897] 463, the older name but misleading.) Maulmein. A shrub or small tree. L. thinly coriaceous, oblanceolate, abruptly acuminate, gradually narrowed into petiole $\frac{1}{4}$–1 in. long, panicles pedunculate, longer than the leaves, minutely pubescent, pedicels shorter than flower. Petals oblong, the apex narrower and recurved, anthers sagittate. 6. **B. lancifolia,** Roxb.; Kurz F. Fl. i. 309. Chittagong hill tracts, Arakan, Andamans. A large evergreen tree, youngest shoots rusty-tomentose. L. elliptic- or oblong-lanceolate, thinly coriaceous, blade 7–9, petiole 1–1$\frac{1}{2}$ in. long, sec. n. 15–20 pair, prominent beneath. Panicles slightly pubescent with scattered hairs, nearly sessile, shorter than leaves, pedicels shorter than flower. Petals oblong, anthers slightly sagittate.

B. Panicles perfectly glabrous.

6. **B. angustifolia,** Roxb. Cor. Pl. t. 262; Wight Ic. t. 101. Vern. *Morli*, *Sara*, Tel.; *Mudamah*, *Kolamāvu*, Tam.; *Malamāvu*, Mal.

A middle-sized tree, youngest shoots slightly pubescent. L. elliptic- or linear-oblong, obtuse, glabrous on both sides, blade 4–7, petiole $\frac{3}{4}$–1$\frac{1}{4}$ in. Panicles glabrous, as long as or longer than leaves, peduncles and branches slender. Fl. nearly sessile. Fr. oblique, $\frac{1}{2}$ in. diam.

On Sandstone in the Chanda district and in Sirpur (Nizam's territory). Western Peninsula, chiefly in the drier districts on hilly ground. Fl. R. S. 7. **B. florida,** Schauer; King in Journ. As. Soc. Bengal, 65 (1897), 463. (*B. lucida*, Bl.; Fl. Brit. Ind. ii. 23; *B. arborescens*, Bl.; Kurz F. Fl. i. 308), Andamans, Tenasserim, Malay Peninsula and Archipelago, Philippines. A small evergreen tree, entirely glabrous. L. thinly coriaceous, obovate, obtuse, narrowed into petiole $\frac{1}{2}$–$\frac{3}{4}$ in. long. Panicles lax, longer than leaves, pedicels longer than flower. Calyx minute, petals 4 or 5, elliptic, obtuse, anthers sagittate, ovary pilose. To this is referred *B. intermedia*, Wight Ic. t. 81, "Naggari hills near Madras," of which I have not seen specimens.

B. laxiflora, Kurz F. Fl. i. 307 (*Gehoilay*, Karen), Martaban, Beeling river on limestone (D.B., February 1862), is not a *Buchanania*, possibly a new genus. L. broadly ovate, pubescent, blade 6, petiole thick, ½ in. long, Panicle tomentose, terminal, ample, 12 in. long. Fl. unisexual, ♂ only known, minute. Sepals 5, triangular, petals 5, valvate. Stamens 10, filaments broad, glabrous, disk 10-lobed.

13. MANGIFERA, Linn.; Fl. Brit. Ind. ii. 13.

Evergreen trees. L. petiolate, simple, entire, coriaceous. Fl. small, polygamous, in terminal panicles. Calyx 4–5-parted, deciduous, petals equal in number, with thick prominent longitudinal nerves. Stamens 4–5, usually inserted on the fleshy lobes of the disk, one stamen only perfect, much larger than the others. Ovary sessile, 1-celled, oblique, ovule 1 attached to the side of the cavity above its base, style lateral simple. Fr. a large fleshy drupe, endocarp fibrous, cotyledons fleshy, plano-convex, often unequal and lobed. Species about 30, Indo-Malayan region.

A. Panicle pubescent or tomentose.

1. **M. indica,** Linn.; Bedd. Fl. Sylv. t. 162; Brandis F. Fl. 125. *The Mango tree.* Vern. *Am, amba, amri,* Hind.; *Uli,* Kol; *Ul,* Sonth.; *Ambi,* Mar.; *Mavu,* Kan.; *Mamidi,* Tel.; *Mad,* Tam.

A large tree. L. dark green, coriaceous, oblong-lanceolate, blade 5–12, petiole ¾–1½ in., sec. n. slightly arching, numerous, alternating with shorter intermediate nerves. Panicles large, erect, pubescent. Fl. nearly sessile, petals twice the length of calyx lobes, anther 1, oval, purple, sterile stamens minute, 2–4. Drupe 2–6 in. long, yellow when ripe.

Indigenous in Burma, Sikkim, the Nambar forest Assam, the Khasi hills, in ravines on the higher hills of the Satpura range in Khandeish and along the Western Ghats. Cultivated all over India and Burma, excepting the northern part of the Punjab. Fl. February–April. Fr. May–July. In North and Central India the fruit of ungrafted trees is stringy with a strong turpentine flavour, while the fruit of good grafts is excellent. In Burma the tree is not generally grafted, the seeds of a good kind as a rule producing good fruit of the same description. This is believed to be the case in some other parts of tropical India. 2. **M. caloneura,** Kurz F. Fl. i. 305; *Taw thayet, Sinnin thayet,* Burm. Eastern and southern slopes of the Pegu Yoma. L. oblong, acuminate, blade 4–6, petiole 1 in. long, sec. n. slender, 16–20 pair, venation between them conspicuously reticulate, intermediate nerves very slender or none. Fl. nearly sessile on a tomentose panicle, calyx pubescent. Fr. not compressed, 2 in. long, endocarp large, thin-walled.

B. Panicle glabrous.

3. **M. sylvatica,** Roxb.; Kurz F. Fl. i. 304. Vern. *Sinnin thayet,* Burm.

A large tree. L. lanceolate, chartaceous, blade 5–12, petiole 1–3 in. long, sec. n. 16–24 pair, strongly curved. Panicle glabrous, with slender branches, pedicels ¼–½ in. long, petals linear, 3–4 times the length of calyx-lobes. Drupe nearly as large as the Mango, yellow when ripe, much compressed, stone fibrous, large.

Nepal, Sikkim (to 3,000 ft.), Khasi hills. Andamans. Pegu Yoma. Hills east of Toungoo, 2,000 ft., near streams, common. Fl. February–May. 4. **M. andamanica,** King in Journ. As. Soc. Beng. 65 (1897), 470. Andamans. L. coriaceous, obovate, obtuse, blade 3–5 in., narrowed into petiole ½–¾ in. long, sec. n. 10–12 pair, reticulation prominent. Fl. tetramerous, pedicels as long as flower, petals twice the length of calyx-segments. Drupe 1–1½ in. long, pulp thin.

14. GLUTA, Linn.; Fl. Brit. Ind. ii. 21.

Evergreen trees, with acrid resinous juice. L. coriaceous, simple, quite entire, crowded at the ends of branchlets. Fl. small, bisexual, in axillary or terminal panicles. Calyx gamosepalous, opening irregularly, deciduous. Petals 4–6, on the elongated torus, contorted in bud. Stamens 4–6, filaments capillary. Ovary 1-celled, style lateral, filiform. Species 6–8, Indo-Malayan, 1 in Madagascar.

1. **G. travancorica,** Bedd. Fl. Sylv. t. 60. Vern. *Shen Kurani*, Tinnevelli.

A very large tree. L. elliptic or oblanceolate, 4–6 in. long, narrowed into a very short petiole, panicle hoary-pubescent, drupe broader than long, with a rough brownish rind, 1¼–1½ in. diam.

Evergreen forests, Tinnevelli and Travancore Ghats. 2. **G. tavoyana,** Hook. f. (*Thayetthitsi*, Burm.) Tavoy, Mergui, on the coast. A small tree, young shoots minutely pubescent, petioles thick, ¼–⅜ in. long. Fl. ⅛ in. long, in short axillary panicles, calyx pubescent. 3. **G. elegans,** Kurz, var. *Helferi*, Hook. f. Sea coast in South Tenasserim. A small tree, entirely glabrous, petioles slender, 1–2 in. long. Fl. ½–⅝ in. long, perfectly glabrous.

15. NOTHOPEGIA, Blume; Fl. Brit. Ind. ii. 39.

Small trees. L. alternate or opposite, petioled, entire. Fl. small, white, polygamous, in short axillary racemes. Calyx small, persistent, 4-lobed, petals 4, spreading, imbricate in bud. Stamens 4, inserted on the margin of the annular 4-lobed disk, filaments free, hairy. Ovary 1-celled, style very short. Species 3.

1. **N. Colebrookiana,** Blume; Bedd. Fl. Sylv. t. 164.—Syn. *Pegia* (?) *Colebrookiana*, Wight Ic. t. 236.

A small tree with milky acrid juice, glabrous excepting inflorescence. L. coriaceous, elliptic-oblong or elliptic-lanceolate, blade 2–8, petiole ½–¾ in., sec. n. 15–20 pair. Drupe red, pyriform, ¼–½ in. diam., edible, a sweet purple juice between skin and stone.

Evergreen forests of the Western Ghats, from the Konkan southwards. Fl. Jan.–March. Ceylon moist region to 3,000 ft. 2. **N. travancorica,** Bedd. Travancore. A shrub. Branchlets, petioles and midrib clothed beneath with short spreading hairs. L. chartaceous, elliptic-lanceolate, sec. n. 30–35 pair. 3. **N. aureo-fulva,** Bedd. Tinnevelli. A shrub. Branchlets, petiole and midrib densely rufous-villous beneath.

16. SEMECARPUS, Linn.; Fl. Brit. Ind. ii. 30.

Trees. L. petiolate, simple, quite entire. Fl. polygamous or diœcious, usually pentamerous, sometimes 6-, rarely 3-merous, in lateral or terminal panicles. Calyx segments deciduous, petals imbricate. Stamens 5–6, inserted at the base and outside of a broad annular disk, imperfect in the ♀ flower. Ovary 1-celled, styles 3. Drupe oblique, fleshy, seated on a fleshy hypocarp, formed of the thickened pedicel and calyx-base, pericarp filled with an acrid resinous juice. Embryo thick, cotyledons plano-convex. Species 40, Indo-Malayan region (a large number in Ceylon), extending to Australia.

A. Western species, and species common to both regions.

1. **S. Anacardium,** Linn. f.; Roxb. Cor. Pl. t. 12; Wight Ic. t. 558; Bedd. Fl. Sylv. t. 166. *The Marking Nut tree.* Vern. *Bhilawa*, *Bhilun*, Hind.; *Bela*, Beng.; *Biba*, *Bibha*, Mar.; *Gēr*, Kan.; *Shenkotta*, Tam.

A middle-sized tree, wood soft, no distinct heartwood. Branchlets, petioles, underside of leaves and inflorescence clothed with short, somewhat harsh tomentum. L. coriaceous, clustered near the ends of branches, oblong-obovate, tip rounded, blade 9–24 in., petiole thick, half round, ½–1 in. long. Fl. ¼–⅓ in. diam., nearly sessile, fascicled in erect compressed terminal panicles, bracts lanceolate, the lower branches of the panicle in the axils of leaves. Petals

oblong, greenish-yellow, ovary hairy. Drupe 1 in. long, shining, purplish-black, pericarp full of acrid resinous juice, hypocarp orange, edible.

. Subhimalayan tract from the Bias eastwards, ascending in the outer hills to 3,500 ft. Assam, Khasi hills, Chittagong. Central India and the Western Peninsula. Not in Ceylon and not yet reported from Burma. Leafless February to April. Fl. May–August. 2. **S. pandurata,** Kurz F. Fl. i. 312, *Che*, *Chi*, Burm. Common in Pegu and Martaban. L. almost membranous, suddenly narrowed below the middle, nut very oblique, is

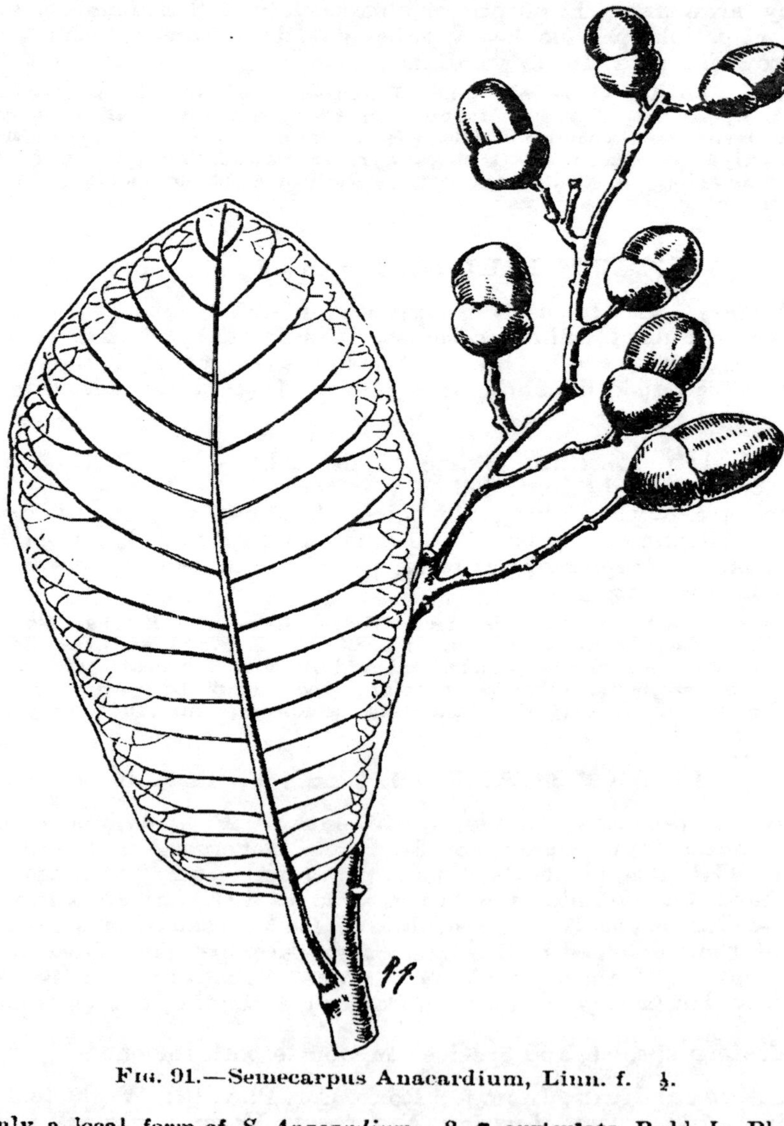

FIG. 91.—Semecarpus Anacardium, Linn. f. ½.

possibly only a local form of *S. Anacardium*. 3. **S. auriculata,** Bedd. Ic. Pl. Ind. Or. t. 187. A large diœcious tree, with black resinous juice, in the evergreen forests of the Tinnevelli and Travancore Ghats. L. glabrous, nearly sessile, oblanceolate, auriculate at base, 5–10 in. long. Male flower, small, 3–4-merous, very numerous, in long compound panicles (the tree a perfect mass of yellowish-white blossoms), the female 4–5-merous, more than twice the size of the ♂, greenish, on short few-fld. panicles. Drupe obliquely obovoid, ½ in. long, on a short broad cup-like hypocarp. 4. **S. travancorica,** Bedd. Fl. Sylv. t. 232. A large diœcious tree, common on the Tinnevelli and Travancore Ghats, 1–3,000 ft., with black resinous juice. L. thickly coriaceous, shining above, pale beneath, glabrous, oblong-obovate, blade 10–24, petiole 2 in. long, panicles as long as leaves or longer. Fl. 5–6-merous. Drupe 1 in. long, obliquely-oblong, hypocarp broad and short.

B. Eastern species.

5. **S. subpanduriformis,** Wall.; Kurz F. Fl. i. 313.—Syn. *S. acuminata*, Kurz; Fl. Brit. Ind. ii. 35.

A deciduous tree, entirely glabrous, except the minutely hairy inflorescence and youngest shoots. L. oblanceolate, acuminate, blade 5–12 in., gradually narrowed from the middle into a petiole ½–¾ in. long, sec. n. 18–22 pair. Panicle terminal, pedicel longer than flower and articulate below it. Fl. 4–5-merous, disk hispid, ovary glabrous, styles 3, elongate. Drupe shining, broader than long, ¾ in. diam., on a small cup-shaped hypocarp.

Chittagong hill tracts, Arakan. Engler, Mon. Phan. iv. 488, unites this with *S. Cassuvium*, Sprengel, Malay Archipelago, which has elliptic-oblong leaves, nearly sessile flowers and a hairy ovary. 6. **S. Kurzii,** Engler; King in Journ. As. Soc. Beng. 65 (1897), 510, (*S. heterophyllus*, Kurz F. Fl. i. 312). Andamans, Nicobars, Bati Malv island, Moung forests, Martaban (D.B., January 1859), (*Chayben*, Burm.). A small tree. Branchlets stout, clothed with deciduous rusty tomentum. L. coriaceous, oblanceolate-oblong, upper surface glabrous, lower pale-brown with short stiff deciduous hairs, blade 12–24 in., gradually narrowed into a stout broad-channelled petiole, ½–1 in. long, sec. n. 20–26 pair. Panicle terminal, longer than leaves. Fl. sessile. Drupe 1 in. long, hypocarp ½ in. long, 1 in. diam. 7. **S. Prainii,** King in Journ. As. Soc. Beng. 65 (1897), 511 (*S. heterophyllus*, Hook. fil.; Fl. Brit. Ind. ii. 35). Andamans, Coco islands, Perak. A middle-sized tree. L. oblong-oblanceolate, glabrous on both sides, underside pale-brown, blade 5–10, petiole ½–⅝ in. Panicle pedunculate, terminal, longer than leaves. Fl. nearly sessile. Drupe ½ in. long, broader than long, hypocarp obconic, ⅓ in. long.

ORDER XLII.—**Coriariaceæ.** *Coriaria nepalensis*, Wall.; Pl. As. Rar. t. 289; Collett Simla Fl. fig. 35. Vern. *Masúri*, Mussoorie; *Mesroi*, Jauns.; *Gangeru*, Tons valley; *Makola*, Kumaon. Himalaya, 3–7,000 ft., Manipur. Shan hills, Upper Burma, at 4,000 ft. A large shrub with long spreading branches, bark reddish-brown. Branchlets quadrangular. L. opposite, ovate, basal nerves 3–5. Fl. pentamerous, greenish-yellow, ⅓ in. diam., in clustered lateral racemes. Stamens 10, free, anthers red, conspicuous. Fruiting carpels 5, distinct, 1-seeded, enclosed by the much enlarged purple succulent petals, which are keeled between the carpels on the inner face.

A remarkable herbaceous shrub is **C. terminalis,** Hemsl. Ic. Pl. t. 2220. Fl. in long terminal racemes, anthers linear. Inner Sikkim, 9–12,000 ft., Tibet, China.

ORDER XLIII. MORINGACEÆ; Gen. Pl. i. 429 (*Moringeæ*).

Soft-wooded deciduous trees. L. alternate, impari- bi- or tripinnate, pinnæ and leaflets opposite, leaflets entire, caducous, glands at the base of petioles and pinnæ. Fl. large, bisexual, irregular, in axillary panicles. Calyx cup-shaped, segments petaloid, deciduous, somewhat unequal. Petals 5, upper smaller. Disk lining the calyx-tube. Stamens inserted on the free edge of disk, 5 perfect, opposite to petals, alternating with 5, sometimes 7, filaments without anthers, anthers dorsifixed, oblong, 1-celled. Ovary stipitate, 1-celled, ovules numerous, biseriate, on 3 parietal placentas. Capsule long, 3–6-angled, beaked. Seeds numerous, albumen 0, embryo straight, cotyledons plano-convex.

MORINGA, Lam.; Fl. Brit. Ind. ii. 45.

Species 3, one in Arabia and the North African desert.

1. **M. pterygosperma,** Gaertn.; Wight. Ill. t. 77; Bedd. Fl. Sylv. t. 80.—Syn. *M. oleifera*, Lam.; Engler u. Prantl iii. 2, 243, fig. 146. The *Horse-*

radish tree. Vern. *Sainjna*, *Saonjna*, *Mungna*, Hind.; *Shevaga*, Mar.; *Nugge*, Kan.; *Moringa*, *Monaga*, Tam.; *Danthalun*, Burm.

A small tree. Trunk straight, attaining a girth of 4–5 ft., bark thick, corky. L. 12–30 in. long, usually tripinnate, leaflets on short slender petiolules, ovate or obovate, pale beneath, sec. n. indistinct. Fl. strongly honey-scented, 1 in. across, bracts linear, shorter than pedicels. Petals linear-spathulate, with yellow dots at base. Ovary and base of filaments hairy. Pod 9–18 in. long, pendulous, 9-ribbed. Seeds rounded-trigonous with broad wings at the angles.

Indigenous in the Subhimalayan tract from the Chenab to the Sarda, also in the Oudh Forests. Cultivated throughout India and Burma. Fl. January–April, with or before the fresh leaves. Easily propagated by cuttings. Leaves, flowers and fruit eaten as a vegetable. The root has a strong pungent taste, is used as a vesicant. The seeds yield oil (Ben oil). 2. **M. concanensis,** Nimmo; Brandis F. Fl. 130; Hook. Ic. Pl. t. 2596, hills of Sind (*Mhūa*), Rajputana (*Sainjna*, *Segora*, *Hegu*). On dry hills in the Konkan and in Berar (Gavilgarh Fort, D. B. 1878). A small tree. L. generally bipinnate, leaflets broadly-ovate or obovate, petiolules ¼–½ in. long, sec. n. 4–6 pair, more prominent than in 1. Fl. reddish-yellow, smaller than in 1. Pod sharply 3-angled, long pointed, seeds with thin membranous wings at both ends.

ORDER XLIV. CONNARACEÆ; Gen. Pl. i. 430.

Trees or shrubs, erect or climbing. L. alternate, imparipinnate or 1–3-foliolate, leaflets quite entire, stipules 0. Fl. usually bisexual and regular, pentamerous, in racemes or panicles, calyx usually persistent. Stamens 10, free, or lower portion of filaments connate into a short tube, the epipetalous stamens generally shorter and often sterile. Carpels 5, each usually with 2 collateral ovules. Fruiting carpel in most genera one only, 2-valved. Seed one, radicle superior.

A. L. imparipinnate.
- Capsule solitary, sessile, sepals orbicular, imbricate . . . 1. ROUREA.
- Capsule solitary, stipitate, sepals imbricate . . . 2. CONNARUS.
- Capsules 1–3 from each flower, sessile, calyx valvate.
  - Fl. polygamous, capsule hairy within . . . CNESTIS (p. 213).
  - Fl. bisexual, capsule glabrous within . . . TÆNIOCHLÆNA (p. 213).

B. L. unifoliolate . . . . 3. ELLIPANTHUS.

1. ROUREA, Aubl.; Fl. Brit. Ind. ii. 47.

L. imparipinnate. Fl. small, in axillary panicles. Sepals 5, orbicular, imbricate in bud, much enlarged in fruit, filaments connate at base. Capsule sessile, curved, seed more or less enclosed in a split arillus, albumen 0. Species 40–50, tropics of both hemispheres.

A. Leaflets few, 1–5 pair, petiolulate.

1. **R. santaloides,** W. et A. (1834); Bedd. Fl. Sylv. Man. t. xi.

A large scrambling glabrous evergreen shrub. Leaflets often alternate, 1–3 pair, coriaceous, shining, elliptic- or ovate-lanceolate, acuminate, blade 2–5, petiole ⅕–⅓ in. long, sec. n. arching, conspicuous, as well as the reticulate veins between them. Fl. white, pedicels jointed, with a minute bracteole at the joint. Sepals strongly imbricate, margin more or less ciliate, petals much longer than sepals. Ovary glabrous. Capsule ¾–1 in. long, base surrounded by a leathery cup formed of the enlarged sepals, dehiscing along the inner suture and bending outwards, exposing the seed enveloped in the orange-coloured arillus.

Evergreen forests of the Western Ghats from the Konkan southwards. Fl. May–October. In Ceylon the stems are twisted into strong ropes. Nearly allied are: 2. **R. commutata,** Planch.; Kurz F. Fl. i. 324, Assam, Khasi hills, Chittagong, Lower Burma,

Malay Peninsula. A large scandent evergreen shrub, leaflets often sub-opposite, 3–8 in. long, 2–4 pair. Instead of the terminal leaflet, rachis often prolonged. The lowest bracts of axillary buds often rigid, subulate, simulating stipules. Sepals ciliate, ovary hairy on the inner side. 3. **R. pulchella,** Planch., Tenasserim. 4. **R. humilis,** Blume, Nicobars. 5. **R. caudata,** Planch. Assam, Khasi hills. Leaflets 3–5 pair, lanceolate, caudate-acuminate, 2–3 in. long, petals not much exceeding sepals, capsule slightly curved, broader upwards.

B. Leaflets numerous, sessile, small, 1–2 in. long.

6. **R. Wallichiana,** Planch., Tenasserim, from Maulmein southwards. Petioles and panicles pubescent. Leaflets glabrous, 15–30 pair, linear-oblong, $\frac{2}{3}$–1 in. long. Panicles narrow, racemiform, capsule curved, $\frac{1}{2}$–$\frac{3}{4}$ in. long. 7. **R. stenopetala,** Hook. f. Mergui. Branchlets and petiole pubescent, midrib of leaflets pubescent beneath. Leaflets 6–10 pair, oblique, emarginate at tip. Racemes short, sepals spreading, petals linear, more than twice the length of sepals. 8. **R. villosa,** Planch. Mergui. Sumatra. Branches, petioles and inflorescence softly pubescent. Leaflets hairy beneath, 12–20 pair, $\frac{3}{4}$ in. long, panicles narrow, racemiform, shorter than the leaves. Petals more than twice the length of sepals. Capsule $\frac{1}{2}$ in., curved.

Fig. 92.—Rourea santaloides, W. et A. $\frac{1}{2}$.

2. CONNARUS, Linn.; Fl. Brit. Ind. ii. 50.

L. imparipinnate, leaflets mostly 5. Fl. small, in axillary and terminal panicles. Sepals 5, imbricate, deciduous or persistent, not accrescent, petals linear or ligulate and slightly dilated upwards. Ovaries densely pubescent, usually one only fertile. Ripe carpels stipitate, inflated, albumen 0. Species 50–55, tropics of both hemispheres.

A. Western species. Leaflets quite glabrous beneath, valves of the capsule quite glabrous within.

1. **C. monocarpus,** Linn.—Syn. *C. pinnatus,* Lamk.; Bedd. Fl. Sylv. Man. t. xi. Vern. *Sundar,* Mar.

An erect shrub. Leaflets 3–4 in. long, elliptic or elliptic-lanceolate, glabrous on both sides, shining, sec. n. 3–5 pair. Panicles rusty-pubescent, sepals ovate-oblong, tomentose, petals $\frac{1}{4}$ in. long, slightly pubescent outside. Capsule $1\frac{1}{2}$–2 in., contracted into the stalk, not shining, not ribbed.

Western Ghats from the Konkan southwards. Fl. February–June. Ceylon, dry region. 2. **C. Ritchiei,** Hook. f. Ghats of the Konkan and North Kanara, probably also further south. A shrub, possibly also climbing. Fl. crowded, petals $\frac{1}{8}$–$\frac{1}{4}$ in., capsule oblong, rounded at the top, base cordate. 3. **C. Wightii,** Hook. f. A lofty climber, common in the evergreen Ghat forests of North Kanara and Belgáum. Leaflets 4–5 in., sec. n. 5–7 pair, petals $\frac{1}{8}$ in., capsules compressed, almost semicircular, shining, strongly striate.

FIG. 93.—Connarus monocarpus, Linn. $\frac{1}{2}$.

B. Eastern species. Leaflets quite glabrous beneath, valves of the capsule pubescent or sericeous within.

4. **C. paniculatus,** Roxb. Fl. Ind. iii. 139. Vern. *Nwèni*, Upper Burma.
An evergreen climbing shrub (in Chittagong a large tree, Roxb.), glabrous except inflorescence. Leaflets 3–7, coriaceous, glossy above, 3–5 in. long. Panicle pubescent, spreading. Sepals pubescent, petals $\frac{1}{4}$–$\frac{1}{3}$ in. long, linear, slightly narrowed towards the base, filaments hairy, ovary tomentose. Capsule at first softly tomentose, when mature glabrous and shining, $1\frac{1}{4}$–$1\frac{1}{2}$ in. long.

Assam, Khasi hills, Chittagong. Large rapids (Hatgyi) on the Salween (D.B., May, 1859), Amherst (D.B., April, 1880). Fl. March–June. Evergreen forests, Upper Burma, Hmangin at 2,500 ft. (Smales, Dec., 1901) To this I refer specimens collected by Dr. Henry in Yunnan. 5. **C. gibbosus,** Wall.; Kurz F. Fl. i. 327. Pegu, Tenasserim and Andamans. Leaflets 4–6 in. long, petals oblanceolate, glabrous, capsule compressed, rusty tomentose when young, glabrous when mature, obliquely striate, compressed, obovate, $1\frac{1}{4}$ in. long. 4 and 5 may possibly turn out to be the same species. 6. **C. nicobaricus,** King in Journ. As. Soc. Beng. 66 (1898), 6. Nicobar islands. Scandent. Leaflets broadly ovate, shortly acuminate, $2\frac{1}{2}$–$4\frac{1}{2}$ in. long, petals linear, pubescent on both surfaces. Capsule sessile, broad, obtuse, $1\frac{1}{3}$ in. long. 7. **C. latifolius,** Wall. Tenasserim. Capsule cylindrical, obtuse, $\frac{3}{4}$ in. long, suddenly narrowed into a stalk $\frac{1}{4}$ in. long. 8. **C. grandis,** Jack; King l.c. 7. Tenasserim, Malay Peninsula. Leaflets elliptic-oblong, 4–12 in. long. Capsule obliquely ovoid, $1\frac{1}{2}$–$1\frac{3}{4}$ in. long, woody.

C. Eastern species. L. pubescent beneath.

9. **C. semidecandrus,** Jack; King l.c. 4. Mergui, Malay Peninsula, Sumatra. A climbing or scrambling shrub. Branchlets deciduously puberulous. Leaflets 5–7, common petiole, petiolules and underside of leaflets puberulous. Capsule falcate, obovoid, at first rusty pubescent, afterwards glabrous, narrowed into a short stalk, valves sparsely sericeous inside. 10. **C. Griffithii,** Hook. f. Mergui. Imperfectly known. Leaflets ovate-lanceolate, 3–5 in. long, rusty pubescent beneath.

Cnestis ramiflora, Griff., including *C. platantha*, Griff.; Kurz F. Fl. i. 328 (*Connarus igneus*, Wall.), Lower Burma and Andamans, *Kyetmaukni*, Burm., is a shrub or small tree, often scandent. Branchlets, common petiole, underside of leaflets and inflorescence more or less softly tomentose. L. imparipinnate, leaflets usually opposite, 9–15 pair, nearly sessile, narrowly oblong, base rounded or cordate, 1–3 in. long. Fl. polygamous or diœcious, in short fascicled (often branched) racemes, axillary or from the old wood. Sepals valvate, slightly overlapping at the tip, spreading in fruit. Ripe carpels 1–3 from one flower, sessile, bright red, compressed, falcate, curved, widest in the middle, rusty pubescent, pericarp densely lined inside with long stiff hairs.

Tæniochlæna birmanica, Prain in Ann. Bot. Gard. Calc. ix. t. 26. Kachin hills, Upper Burma. A shrub. L. imparipinnate, leaflets 2–3 pair, 3–4 in. long. Fl. bisexual, in short axillary panicles, sepals $\frac{1}{8}$ in. long, valvate, reflexed in fruit. Ripe carpels 1–3 from each flower, sessile, ovoid, $1\frac{1}{2}$ in. long, glabrous inside and outside.

3. ELLIPANTHUS, Hook. f.; Fl. Brit. Ind. ii. 55.

Trees or shrubs. L. unifoliolate, quite entire. Fl. pentamerous, bisexual or polygamous, in short axillary racemes. Sepals valvate, not enlarged in fruit, petals longer than sepals, oblong-lanceolate, densely pubescent. Stamens 10, the five shorter without anthers, filaments short, connate at base. Ovary 1, pubescent, style short. Capsule stalked, oblique, velvety (glabrous in *E. sterculiæfolius*), valves glabrous within. Seed arillate, albumen 0. Species 12, Burma, Malay Peninsula and Archipelago.

A. L. pubescent beneath.

1. **E. Thwaitesii,** Hook. f.—Syn. *E. unifoliolatus*, Bedd. Fl. Sylv. t. 170; *E. monophyllus*, var. *neglectus*, O. Kuntze. Vern. *Padappan*, Mal.

A small tree. Branchlets, petioles and underside of leaves slightly pubescent. L. elliptic-lanceolate, acuminate, blade 4–5, petiole $\frac{1}{2}$ in. long, sec. n. 4–5 pair, joined by conspicuous reticulate veins and strong intramarginal nerves at a distance from margin. Fl. pale-green, in short axillary panicles, sometimes tetramerous, petals $\frac{1}{6}$ in. long. Capsule $1–1\frac{1}{2}$ in. long, pointed, base tapering into a stalk supported by the persistent calyx, densely covered with rusty hairs.

Evergreen forests, Travancore and Tinnevelli. Fl. Febr.–March. Ceylon, moist region.

2. **E. tomentosus,** Kurz F. Fl. i. 330.

A small evergreen tree. Branchlets, petioles and infloresence tawny-tomentose. L. elliptic or elliptic-oblong, glabrous above, more or less pubescent beneath, blade 4–5, petiole $\frac{3}{4}$ in. long, articulate at the insertion of blade. Fl. in small compact axillary panicles. Capsule $1\frac{1}{2}$ in. long, densely velvety.

Southern slopes of the Pegu Yoma, Tenasserim. Fl. C. S.

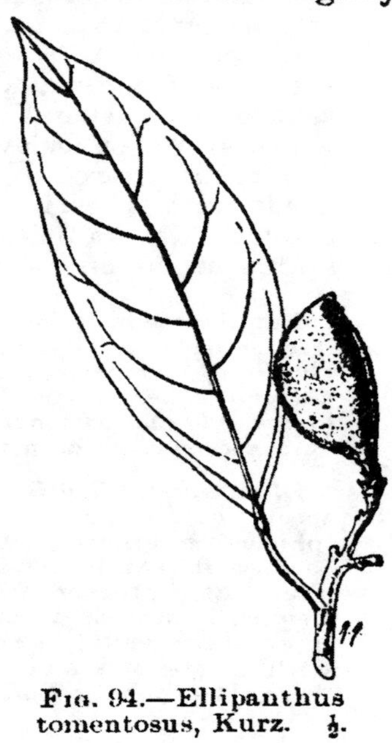

FIG. 94.—Ellipanthus tomentosus, Kurz. $\frac{1}{2}$.

B. L. glabrous on both sides.

3. **E. calophyllus,** Kurz. Andamans. L. elliptic-lanceolate, blade 4–7, petioles $1–1\frac{1}{2}$ in. long, glabrous. Petals $\frac{1}{4}$ in. long. Capsule obovoid, 1 in. long. 4. **E. Helferi,** Hook.

f. Tenasserim. Imperfectly known. Branchlets and petioles slightly puberulous, petioles ½ in. long. 5. **E. sterculiæfolius,** Prain in Journ. As. Soc. Beng. 59 (1890) tab. 8. A small tree on Diamond island. L. membranous, pale beneath, ovate, acuminate, blade 3–4, petiole slender, 2–3 in. long, capsule glabrous, ribbed, long-acuminate, 1 in., stalk ½ in. long.

ORDER XLV. **LEGUMINOSÆ.** Gen. Pl. i. 434.

Leaves generally alternate, compound and stipulate. Flowers as a rule bisexual, in panicles, racemes, spikes or heads. Calyx more or less deeply divided into 5 segments. Petals 5, rarely less, in the majority of genera unequal and zygomorphic. Stamens 10, rarely less by abortion, or numerous; anthers 2-celled, cells parallel. Pistil generally consisting of 1 carpel, ovules numerous, rarely few, attached to the inner suture. Pod generally dry, indehiscent, or separating into two valves along one or both sutures.

As far as is known, the wood fibres of *Leguminosæ* always have simple, not bordered pits. Bands of wood parenchyma, more or less concentric, often interrupted. are a common feature in this order.

Calyx gamosepalous; petals free, unequal, imbricate, the posterior outside; stamens generally diadelphous . . 1. PAPILIONACEÆ.
Calyx divided nearly to the base; petals free, mostly unequal, imbricate, the posterior inside; stamens free . . . 2. CÆSALPINIEÆ.
Calyx gamosepalous; petals more or less connate, equal, valvate; stamens free or monadelphous . . . . 3. MIMOSEÆ.

FIRST SUB-ORDER, **PAPILIONACEÆ.**

Calyx gamosepalous, often 2-lipped, the upper (posterior) lip consisting of 2, the lower (anterior) of 3 segments. Petals 5, clawed, unequal, imbricate in bud, the posterior and outside petal (standard, vexillum) broad, often reflexed, the 2 anterior and inside petals (keel, carina) often firmly cohering, the 2 lateral and intermediate petals (wings) enclosing the keel. (The standard is sometimes called the upper petal; as regards its insertion, however, it is the lowest of the 5 petals.) Stamens 10 as a rule, inserted with the petals on the edge of a disk, which lines the lower part of the calyx-tube, filaments seldom free, generally connate into a tube or sheath, open at the top, sometimes also open below, so as to form two half-sheaths of 5 stamens each, the tenth stamen opposite the standard being often free from the rest. Seeds with a coriaceous testa, without albumen, cotyledons thick, plano-convex, the radicle accumbent upon the cotyledons, reserve substances starch or fat oil.

Papilionaceous trees show great variety in the structure of their wood. Distinct heartwood, generally hard and dark coloured, occurs among others in *Millettia pendula*, *Ougeinia*, *Pterocarpus*, and most *Dalbergias*, such as *D. Sissoo. latifolia, cultrata, Kurzii, Oliveri*. There is no heartwood in *Sesbania*, *Erythrina*, *Butea frondosa*, *Dalbergia lanceolaria* and *Pongamia glabra*. Extremely soft and light is the pith-like wood of *Æschynomene*, which mainly consists of thin-walled wood parenchyma.

Of climbers *Millettia auriculata*, *Derris scandens*, *Spatholobus Roxburghii*, and some species of *Mucuna* have the usual anomalous structure, concentric strata of bast (phloëm) alternating with broader strata of wood, which is light, soft and porous, because it mainly consists of very wide vessels. The stems of these climbers being often flat, fluted or otherwise irregular, the alternating strata of bast and wood frequently do not form complete rings. *Dalbergia paniculata*, though a tree, has structure resembling that of climbing stems, viz., bands of bast (phloëm) alternating with broader strata of wood. On the other hand, some climbing *Papilionaceæ*, among them the climbing *Dalbergias*, have stems of normal structure.

Tribe I. *Podalyrieæ.*—Leaves digitate; stamens free; pod dehiscent.

Shrub with connate stipules . . . . . . 1. PIPTANTHUS.

Tribe II. *Genisteæ.*—L. simple or digitately 3-foliolate; stamens monadelphous; pod dehiscent, not jointed.

Keel beaked; pod turgid . . . . 2. CROTALARIA.
Keel beaked; pod flat . . . . PRIOTROPIS (p. 216).

Tribe III. *Galegeæ.*—L. impari—rarely pari—pinnate; stamens usually diadelphous pod dehiscent, not jointed.

Shrubs, common petiole spinescent . . . . 3. CARAGANA.
Shrubs, unarmed or branchlets spinescent.
Fl. yellow, anthers obtuse, pods inflated . . 4. COLUTEA.
Fl. pink, purple or white, anthers apiculate, pods not inflated . . . . 5. INDIGOFERA.
Soft-wooded trees, leaflets numerous, fl. large . 6. SESBANIA.
Trees or climbers.
Alternate filaments dilated . . . . . 7. MUNDULEA.
All filaments filiform . . . . . . 8. MILLETTIA.

Tribe IV. *Hedysareæ.*—L. imparipinnate, rarely simple, pod jointed or 1-seeded.

Leaflets stipellate.
Shrubs or herbs, fl. on this year's branchlets . 9. DESMODIUM.
A tree, fl. fasciculate on the old wood . . 10. OUGEINIA.
Leaves without stipels.
A tall water plant, leaflets numerous, pod of 4–8 joints . . . . ÆSCHYNOMENE (p. 224)
Spinescent shrubs, leaves simple, pod of several joints . . . . ALHAGI (p. 225).
Unarmed handsome undershrubs, leaves 3-foliolate, pod 1-seeded . . . . . . LESPEDEZA (p. 225).

Tribe V. *Vicieæ.*—Leaves paripinnate, petiole ending in a tendril or bristle.

Climbers, with polished bright coloured seeds . 11. ABRUS.

Tribe VI. *Phaseoleæ.*—Climbers, rarely erect shrubs or herbs, with trifoliolate or simple, rarely imparipinnate leaves.

Leaves pinnately 3-foliolate, not gland-dotted beneath, leaflets stipellate.
Keel and wings larger than standard, anthers dimorphic . . . . 12. MUCUNA.
Standard larger than keel and wings, anthers uniform . . . . 13. ERYTHRINA.
Petals equal, or nearly so.
Pod oblong, turgid, 1–2-seeded . . . . DIOCLEA (p. 228).
Pod linear, flat, many seeded . . . . 14. PUERARIA.
Seed one, at the end of pod.
Fl. small, in ample terminal panicles. 15. SPATHOLOBUS.
Fl. large yellow or orange, racemose . 16. BUTEA.
Leaves imparipinnate, leaflets 5 . . . . . CRUDDASIA (p. 231).
Leaves digitately 3-foliolate or simple, gland dotted beneath, no stipels . . . . 17. FLEMINGIA.

Tribe VII. *Dalbergieæ.*—Trees or shrubs, leaves imparipinnate, pod not jointed, indehiscent.

Leaflets alternate.
Fl. white, lilac or purple; pod longer than broad . . . . 18. DALBERGIA.
Fl. yellow; pod short, nearly circular . . . 19. PTEROCARPUS.
Leaflets opposite.
Pod flat, thin, winged . . . . . . 20. DERRIS.
Pod thick, almost woody, not winged . . . 21. PONGAMIA.

Tribe VIII. *Sophoreæ.*—Trees or shrubs; leaves imparipinnate, rarely simple; stamens free.

Leaflets opposite, mostly coriaceous; pod fleshy or woody . . . . 22. ORMOSIA.
Leaflets often alternate; pod moniliform . . . 23. SOPHORA.
Leaflets nearly opposite: pod flat, membranous . CALPURNIA (p. 244).

1. PIPTANTHUS, D. Don; Fl. Brit. Ind. ii. 62.

P. nepalensis, D. Don; Brand. F. Fl. 132. Vern. *Chamba*, Jaunsar.

A shrub, attaining 10 ft., with alternate, digitately trifoliolate leaves, often crowded at the ends of branchlets; leaflets lanceolate, entire, sessile, common petiole less than half the length of leaflets. Stipules connate, so as to appear opposite to the petiole, deciduous. Flowers large, bright yellow, in short hairy racemes, with broad-ovate, tomentose deciduous bracts. Pod linear-lanceolate, 2–5 in. long, ½ in. broad, 3–10-seeded, dehiscent.

Himalaya, Sutlej to Bhutan. Khasi hills, Manipur. Chin hills Upper Burma. Mostly in shady woods, 7,000 to 10,000 ft. Fl. May, June. Also in Tibet and South-Western China. A second species, *P. tomentosus*, Franchet in Yunan.

2. CROTALARIA, Linn.; Fl. Brit. Ind. ii. 65.

Herbs, rarely shrubs, with simple or digitately 3-foliolate, in a few species 5–7-foliolate leaves. Flowers mostly yellow, sometimes blue or purple, in terminal or leaf-opposed racemes, keel beaked. Stamens monadelphous in an open sheath; anthers alternately long and basifixed, short and versatile. Style bearded, stigma minute. Pod turgid. Species about 250; tropical and sub-tropical regions of both hemispheres. 77 species in India.

1. **C. Burhia,** Ham.; Brand. F. Fl. 144.

An erect or procumbent shrub; branches numerous, slender, flexible and rush-like when young, stiff and rigid when old. Leaves simple, small and scanty, linear or oblong. Fl. yellow, far apart on long racemes, forming terminal divaricate rigid panicles. Calyx clothed with long silky hairs, teeth lanceolate, as long as corolla.

Common in the plains of Sind, the Punjab, Western Rajputana, and Gujarat. Fl. C. S. Also in Afghanistan. This genus comprises numerous tall herbs or soft-wooded shrubs, with large yellow fl., in forests and on waste land. *Crotalaria juncea* Linn.; Roxb. Cor. Pl. t. 193. Sunn or Indian hemp is cultivated in most parts of India.

Priotropis cytisoides, W. et A.; Kurz, F. Fl. i. 363, is an erect much-branched shrub, 4–6 ft. high, in the Eastern Himalaya, the Khasi and Naga hills, and the hills of Burma, 3,000–6,000 ft. Leaves trifoliolate; flowers yellow racemose; pods flat, 1–1½ in. long, ⅓–½ in. broad, narrowed to both ends, on a slender stalk ¼ in.

3. CARAGANA, Lam.; Fl. Brit. Ind. ii. 115.

Spinescent shrubs with paripinnate leaves. Common petiole produced beyond the end pair and often spinescent. Stipules also frequently spinescent. Claws of petals as long, or nearly as long as calyx. Standard broad, with reflexed edges, keel obtuse, as long as wings and standard. Stamens diadelphous, anthers uniform. Style glabrous, stigma terminal minute. Pod linear, valves convex. 20 species; 7 Indian, the rest in Central Asia and China.

1. **C. brevispina,** Royle: Brand. F. Fl. 133. Vern. *Ari*, Jauns.

Leaves generally fasciculate, on short tuberculate branchlets in the axils of rigid spinescent petioles, 1–3 in. long, with or without leaflets. Stipules scarious, the outer frequently spinescent. Leaflets 5–7 pair, with soft adpressed hairs. Common petiole often not spinescent. Flowers 3–5, in pedunculate umbels, peduncles 1–3 in. long. Calyx campanulate, teeth shorter than tube. Pod turgid, woolly inside.

North-West Himalaya 5,000–9,000 ft. Indus to Ganges, also Kuram valley. Fl. April–June. Nearly allied are: 2. **C. decorticans,** Hemsley, Hook. Ic. Pl. t. 1725. Kuram valley, Hazara, Chitral. A tall shrub or small tree, with very short calyx teeth, rings of the bark placed on the leather sheath of the long Afghan knives. 3. **C. arborescens,** Lam.; Prain, Journ. As. Soc. Beng. 66, 372. Kuram valley.

4. **C. Gerardiana,** Royle Ill. t. 34, fig. 1, dry valleys of the inner N.W. Himalaya, also in Baluchistan, near Quetta, in the Juniper forests, has all petioles spinescent and

persistent at the base of the short leaf- and flower-bearing branchlets. Flowers single, on short peduncles, calyx cylindric. Besides these there is a number of low thorny shrubs.

4. COLUTEA, Linn.; Fl. Brit. Ind. ii. 103.

Shrubs with imparipinnate leaves. Fl. large, yellow or reddish, in few-flowered axillary racemes. Standard broad, biplicate or bicallose at the base, claw short. Keel broad, much incurved, not beaked. Stamens diadelphous; anthers uniform. Ovary stipitate, ovules ∞, style much incurved, bearded along the inside. Pod large, membranous inflated, indehiscent or incompletely dehiscent. Species 4–5, South Europe, Western Asia, N.W. Himalaya.

1. **C. arborescens,** Linn., var. *nepalensis*.—Syn. *C. nepalensis*, Sims; Brand. F. Fl. 136; Collett Simla Flora, 123.

Unarmed, leaflets 4–8 pair, glabrous, oval or obovate. Corolla bright yellow. Pod 2 in. long, hairy when young, splitting at the tip when ripe.

Arid valleys of the inner Himalaya 8,000–11,500 ft., Ladak to Kumaun, Kuram valley. Southern Europe and Western Asia. 2. **Colutea armata,** Hemsley and Lace Journ. Linn. Soc. xxviii. tab. 39, is a small spiny shrub of the Baluchistan hills (7,500–9,000 ft.), with grey, fibrous bark, spinescent branchlets, small flowers and pods 1 in. long.

5. INDIGOFERA, Linn.; Fl. Brit. Ind. ii. 92.

Herbs or shrubs, hairs adpressed, generally attached by the middle. Leaves simple, trifoliolate or imparipinnate, leaflets mostly opposite. Fl. in axillary racemes, calyx oblique. Stamens diadelphous, anthers uniform, apiculate. Ovary sessile, style short, stigma capitate. Pod linear, seeds numerous. Species 250, tropical and sub-tropical regions.

A. Leaflets mostly opposite, 1–15 pair. Fl. large, over ⅓ in. long.

1. **I. pulchella,** Roxb.; Wight Ic. t. 367—Syn. *I. arborea*, Roxb.; Wight Ic. t. 368. Vern. *Sakena*, Kumaon; *Baroli*, Mar.; *Taw-mè-yaing* (wild forest Indigo, Burm.)

A large handsome shrub, sometimes with a short thick trunk, branches and leaves thinly pubescent, leaflets 8–12 pair, elliptic to obovate, obtuse, often mucronate, 1⅓ in. long. Fl. pink; bracts canescent, longer than buds, early deciduous. Calyx canescent, teeth triangular, acuminate. Pod straight, turgid, sutures thick.

Subhimalayan tract and outer valleys, ascending to 3,000 ft., from Kalka eastward. Common in Sal forests. Both Peninsulas, in Burma chiefly in Eng forest. Fl. Dec. to March. Fl. eaten.

Kurz, F. Fl. I. 361, distinguishes *I. elliptica*, Roxb., Pegu and Martaban, as a separate species, leaflets 4–8 pair, pod terete, with pale prominent sutures, seeds 6–10, black, cylindric.

2. **I. atropurpurea,** Ham.; Wight Ic. t. 369. Vern. *Khenti*, Kāghān; *Kathi*, Kashmir; *Kāla Sakena*, Kumaon.

A large shrub, nearly glabrous, leaflets 5–6 pair, ovate-oblong, 1½ in. long. Fl. dark purple, in pedunculate racemes, as long as leaves or longer, compact while in bud, the long acuminate bracts longer than the buds. Calyx teeth short, triangular. Pod straight, slightly compressed, marginate, reflexed when ripe.

Outer Himalaya, from Hazara to Nepal, generally between 2,000 and 9,000 ft. Salt range. Khasi and Naga hills. Upper Burma, Yunan. Fl. R.S. 3. **I. Hamiltonii,** Grah. an undershrub, burnt down by the annual fires, like *Erythrina resupinata*, leaflets usually 1 pair, fl. purple ⅓ in. long, distant in long slender racemes.

4. **I. hebepetala,** Benth. Himalaya 6,000–10,000 ft., from Kashmir to Sikkim; a tall

shrub, bracts broad concave, long-acuminate, exceeding the buds, pods straight with a long slender point.

5. **I. Gerardiana,** Wall.; Collett Simla Flora, fig. 36.—Syn. *I. heterantha*, Wall.; Brand. F. Fl. 135. Vern. *Kathi*, Jauns.

Strigose with grey hairs. Leaflets less than ½ in. long, elliptic-oblong, obtuse, stipels setaceous, persistent. Calyx teeth lanceolate, as long as tube. Pods reflexed when ripe, straight, cylindric, marginate, with a few scattered hairs.

Outer North-West Himalaya, ascending to 8,000 ft.; eastern outskirts of the Suleiman range. Fl. May, June.

6. **I. Dosua,** Ham.; Fl. Brit. Ind. ii. 102.

A large shrub, attaining 15 ft., at times only an undershrub. Densely pubescent or tomentose, leaflets 10-20 pair, elliptic- or linear-oblong, mucronate, ¼–1 in. long. Fl. bright red, calyx densely silky, teeth very unequal.

Himalaya 6,000–8,000 ft., from Simla eastwards. Shan hills, Upper Burma. Fl. R. S. A remarkable variety is *I. stachyodes*, Lindl. Kumaon, Sikkim, Khasi hills and Shan hills in upper Burma, shoots rusty tomentose, leaflets linear.

In this section, or near it: 7. **I. galegoides,** DC., Khasi hills, Dacca, Travancore, Ceylon, Burma, Malay peninsula and Archipelago, Borneo, the Philippine islands, a tall shrub; leaflets large, pods erect, long-acuminate, 2–3 in. long. 8. **I. bella,** Prain, Ann. Bot. Gard. Cal. ix. t. 28. Upper Burma, leaflets 3–4 pair, 3 in. long, glaucous beneath. Fl. white, over ½ in.

B. Leaflets mostly opposite, 4–10 pair. Fl. small, under ⅓ in. long.

9. **I. tinctoria,** Linn.; Wight Ic. t. 365. *The Indigo plant.* Vern. *Nīl*, Hind.; *Mè*, Burm.

Branches twiggy, silvery, leaflets 4–6 pair. Fl. reddish yellow, in lax racemes, calyx teeth lanceolate, as long as tube. Pods deflexed, straight or slightly curved.

Cultivated as an annual, the plant being cut when the fl. appear, or as a biennial or triennial, a second or even a third year's crop being obtained from the same plant. Original home of this species doubtful. 10. **I. Anil,** Linn. (*I. suffruticosa*, Mill.; Prain and E. Baker in Journal of Botany, 1902, 138), possibly only a variety with falcate reflexed pods, the tip being curved upwards, is also cultivated for Indigo, and has run wild in Burma. 11. **I. argentea,** Linn., pods reflexed, torulose, 3–4 seeded, is indigenous in Sind, Western Rajputana, and the dry districts of the Deccan, also in Abyssinia and the Sudan, cultivated for Indigo in Arabia and Egypt.

To the same group belong: 12. **I. Wightii,** Grah., western peninsula from Bombay southwards, also Tenasserim, pods straight, erect, terete, 1–1½ in. long. 13. **I. constricta,** Trim. Handb. Ceylon, ii. 27; Talbot List 67, moist forests of North Kanara. Ceylon. Leaflets 4–5 pair, pods recurved, 3–7 seeded, constricted between seeds, 1½ in. long. 14. **I. nigrescens,** Kurz; Prain in Journ. As. Soc. Beng. vol. lxvii. 286. Khasi, Kachin and Shan hills. Yunnan, leaflets 8–10, fl. ⅙ in. long.

C. Leaflets not opposite, few, 1, 3 or 5.

15. **I. paucifolia,** Delile; Wight Ic. t. 331.

A small shrub, with numerous stout woody, ascending branches, the whole plant grey with fine silvery hairs, leaflets 3–5 linear-lanceolate, the terminal largest. Fl. small, brick-red, pods ½–¾ in. long, torulose.

Sind, Gujarat, North-West India as far as Benares, dry districts of Central and South India. Fl. Sept. to Jan. Ceylon, dry region. Arabia, Egypt.

Two Burma shrubs, with simple, sometimes 3-foliolate leaves: 16. **I. Brunoniana,** Kurz F. Fl. i. 359, grey with short hairs, leaves 2–5 in. long, chiefly in Eng forest. 17. **I. caloneura,** Kurz, l.c., 360, rusty tomentose, leaves 2–3 in. long.

6. SESBANIA, Pers.; Fl. Brit. Ind. ii. 114.

Herbs or short-lived trees. Wood white, soft. Leaves paripinnate, with numerous opposite deciduous leaflets. Stipules setaceous, caducous, stipels minute or wanting. Calyx broad-campanulate, with short, nearly equal teeth. Pod long, linear, dehiscent, seeds numerous, separated by distinct transverse bars. Species 20, in the tropical and sub-tropical regions of both hemispheres.

1. **S. ægyptiaca,** Pers.; Fl. Brit. Ind. ii. 114; Wight Ic. t. 32. Vern. *Jaint*, Hind.; *Jayanti*, Beng.; *Shewri*, Mar.; *Ye-tha-gyi*, Burm.

A small soft-wooded tree, 8–12 ft. high. Common petiole 4–6 in. long, leaflets 10–20 pair, linear-oblong. Fl. ½ in. long, in lax 6–12 flowered racemes, nearly as long as leaves. Petals yellow or orange and purple. Pod 6–8 in. long, valves convex, torulose.

Commonly planted and naturalized. In the Panjab as far as Peshawar, ascending to 4,000 ft. in the N.-W. Himalaya. Cultivated throughout the tropics, wild in tropical Africa. The wood makes good charcoal for gunpowder.

2. **S. grandiflora,** Pers.; Fl. Brit. Ind. ii. 115. Vern. *Basna*, Hind.; *Baka*, Beng.; *Agashi*, Mar.; *Agāti*, Tam.

Attains 20–30 ft. Common petiole 6–9 in. long, leaflets 10–30 pair, oblong, glaucous, 1–1⅓ in. long. Racemes short, fl. 2–4, 3 in. long, red or white. Pod 10–12 in. long, ⅓ in. broad, compressed, tetragonous.

Cultivated in tropical India as a support for the Betel vine, for firewood and house-posts; in the Ganges Doab chiefly for ornament.

7. MUNDULEA, DC.; Fl. Brit. Ind. ii. 110.

(12 species, of which 11 in Madagascar.)

M. suberosa, Benth.—Syn. *Tephrosia suberosa*, DC.; Wight Ill. t. 82 (79).

A small tree, with pale corky bark, branchlets and underside of leaves clothed with short silky hairs. Leaves imparipinnate, leaflets nearly opposite, without stipels, lanceolate, 6–11 pair. Fl. large, 1 in. long, pink or white, in short terminal racemes, on pedicels 2–3 times the broadly campanulate calyx, teeth unequal. Stamens monadelphous, the 10th free at the base, alternate filaments dilated above. Pod linear 3–4 in. long, straight, rostrate, thickened at the sutures, densely velvety, 2–8 seeded, irregularly contracted between seeds.

Hills of Western Peninsula, covered with blossoms May–Aug. Ceylon, Madagascar, tropical Africa.

8. MILLETTIA, Wight et Arn.; Fl. Brit. Ind. ii. 104.

Trees or climbers, leaves imparipinnate, single or fasciculate, on nodes, which are sometimes produced, leaflets opposite, often stipellate. Fl. white, pink, purple, rarely blue, in racemes or panicles. Calyx truncate or shortly toothed. Standard in most species glabrous outside. Vexillary stamen wholly free, or the middle of filament connate with the sheath, anthers uniform. Pod coriaceous or woody, dehiscent, not winged as a rule. The root of several species and the fruit of *M. pachycarpa* used to intoxicate fish. 50–60 species in the tropical and subtropical regions of the old world, of which more than one half in the Eastern Peninsula. None in Ceylon. The boundaries between *Millettia* and *Derris* are uncertain.

In the case of this genus, as well as in the case of *Dalbergia* and *Derris*, I classify the species as trees (or shrubs) and climbers, because these biological features are convenient for practical purposes. This distinction, however, is not in all cases absolute. In the deep shade of the forest *Millettia auriculata*, *Derris scandens* and other climbers remain stunted shrubs, but when light is given overhead, the internodes lengthen out; the shoots seek the light, and begin to climb, attaching themselves to other shrubs and trees. Again, in the open, exposed to the sun, climbing species may remain shrubby for want of supports to lean upon. Hence the same species is sometimes described by botanists as an erect shrub or as a climber. Foresters in India will eventually be able to clear up this interesting subject by experiment and by systematic observations.

A. Trees (all in the eastern region).

1. **M. pendula,** Benth.—Syn. *M. leucantha*, Kurz, F. Fl. i. 356. Vern. *Thinwin*, Burm.

A deciduous tree, heartwood dark purple. Youngest shoots silky, leaflets 3 pair, 3–4 in. long, pale beneath, glabrous when full grown, stipels subulate, persistent. Fl. pure white, on long pedicels, fasciculate, in compact terminal racemes, 4–6 in. long. Pod woody, flat, pointed at the ends, 2–5 in. long, 1–2 in. wide, 1–3 seeded.

Deciduous forests, Upper and Lower Burma, mostly near streams. Fl. H. S.

2. **M. glaucescens,** Kurz F. Fl. i. 357 (*Derris microptera*, Gamble List 30). Vern. *Taungka*, Burm.

A large deciduous tree, nearly glabrous, leaflets 2–5 pair, without stipels, 3–5 in. long, pale beneath, scattered hairs on the underside while young, with a very minute regular but not raised network of reticulate veins between the tertiary nerves. Fl. $\frac{1}{5}$–$\frac{1}{4}$ in. long, blue, red or purple, on capillary pedicels in axillary racemes, shorter than leaves. Standard glabrous, ovary hairy. Pod flat woody, 4–5 in. long, 1 in. wide, both sutures thickened and expanded into narrow wings.

Sikkim, common up to 3,000 ft. ("young leaves golden brown with long racemes of lilac fl.," Gamble). Lower Burma, common near streams. Fl. H. S. Also Mala y Peninsula. 3. **M. Wrightiana,** Prain in Journ. As. Soc. Beng. vol. 66 (1898), p. 359. Sha n hills, Upper Burma, nearly allied, but with thin pods, not winged along sutures.

4. **M. atropurpurea,** Benth.—Syn. *Pongamia atropurpurea*, Wall. Pl. As. Rar. t. 78. Vern. *Kwè tanyin*, Burm.

A large evergreen tree, glabrous except inflorescence. Leaflets more or less oblique at base, rigidly coriaceous, glossy, 3–4 pair, 3–6 in. long, no stipels. Fl. dark bluish purple, on the stout branches of large pubescent erect terminal panicles, pedicels short hairy, 2 bracteoles at base of calyx. Pod turgid, thickly coriaceous, 2–3 in. long, 2 in. broad.

Evergreen forest, south-eastern part of the Pegu Yoma, hills between the Thaungyin and Hlaingbwe rivers, and elsewhere in Martaban and Tenasserim. "Thickly covered with dense panicles of deep purple fl." Wall.

The other trees of this genus may be classified as follows :—

a. Leaflets 1–5 pair.

5. **M. multiflora,** Coll. and Hemsl. in Journ. Linn. Soc. xxviii. 41. Meiktila, Upper Burma, leaflets coriaceous, elliptic, 4–5 pair, 1 in. long. Fl. $\frac{3}{4}$ in., standard silky outside. 6. **M. tetraptera,** Kurz F. Fl. i. 358. Dry region of Irawaddi valley, Prome to Mandalay, leaflets elliptic or obovate, 1–3 pair, 1–3 in. long, silky-pubescent. Pod woody, 1–2 seeded, 3–4 in. long, $\frac{3}{4}$ in. wide, each suture with two narrow wings. 7. **M. pubinervis,** Kurz, l.c., 357. Upper Burma, deciduous forest on the edge of streams. Hills east of Toungoo. Deciduous, leaflets 3–4 pair, thinly chartaceous, long-acuminate, pubescent along midrib, no stipels, fl. $\frac{1}{3}$ in. long, pinkish or yellowish white. 8. **M. ovalifolia,** Kurz, l.c., 356, Prome district, leaflets elliptic, 3 pair, 1 in. long, petiolules slender. 9. **M. macrostachya,** Coll. and Hemsl. in Journ. Linn. Soc. xxviii. 41, southern Shan hills, 2,000–4,000 ft., leaflets 4–5 pair, 2–6 in. long, softly tomentose beneath. Fl. pink 1 in. long, standard silky outside.

b. Leaflets 6–10 pair, stipellate.

10. **M. Brandisiana,** Kurz, l.c., 355. Vern. *Thitpayan*, Burm. Pegu, Yamethin, deciduous, entirely glabrous, attains 60 ft., leaflets 7–10 pair, thinly coriaceous, lanceolate, 1–2 in. long. Fl. blue, standard silky. 11. **M. pulchra,** Benth.; Fl. Brit. Ind. ii. 104. Vern. *Thitpayan*, Burm. Assam, Khasi hills, Manipur, Upper Burma, leaflets membranous, young shoots tawny pubescent, sometimes densely tomentose (*M. tomentosa*, Watt MSS., Manipur), fl. purple, standard glabrous.

B. Woody climbers.

12. **M. auriculata,** Baker.—Syn. *M. macrophylla*, Kurz, F. Fl. i. 351. Vern. *Gauj*, Hind.; *Maudh*, Oudh; *Gurar*, Gond; *Wunu*, Burm.

Young shoots soft silky-tomentose, leaflets 3–4 pair, 3–6 in. long, obovate-oblong, shortly acuminate, stipels minute, secondary nerves 8–10 pair, prominent beneath. Racemes 4–9 in. long, rusty tomentose, axillary, several at the ends of short stout branchlets, fl. whitish. Pod flat, woody, rusty-tomentose, 4–6 in. long, ¾ in. broad, sutures thickened.

Subhimalayan tract, from the Sutlej eastward, Behar, Central India south to the Godavery. Common in Sal forests. Fl. April–June. A remarkable local variety, formerly regarded as a species, is *M. extensa*, Benth., Kurz, F. Fl. i. 352. Vern. *Damangè*, Burm., common in the deciduous forests of Upper and Lower Burma. Tonkin, fl. reddish-lilac, in shorter racemes, pods glabrous when ripe.

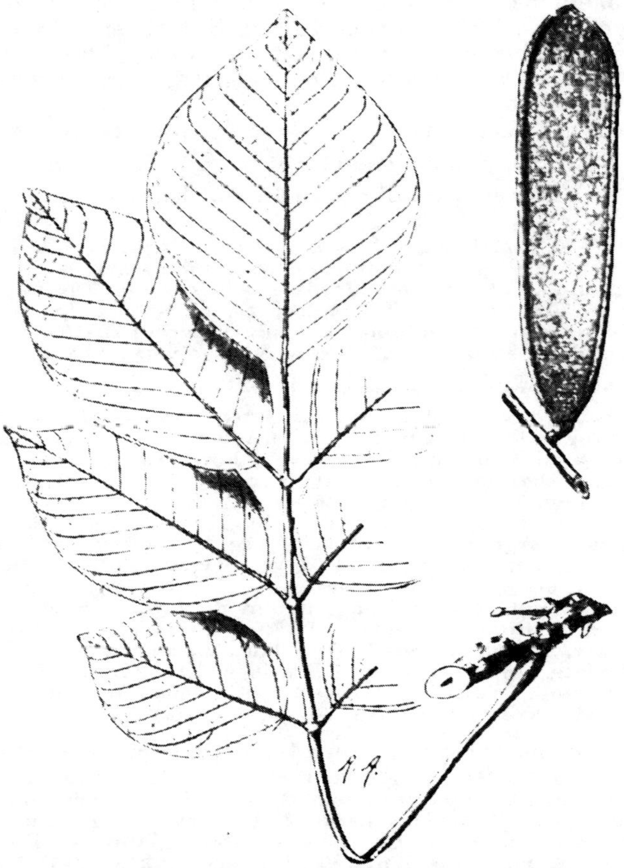

FIG. 95.—Millettia auriculata, Baker. ½.

13. **M. cinerea**, Benth.; Kurz, F. Fl. 353.

Glabrous except inflorescence, leaflets 1–3 pair, thin, membranous, 3–9 in. long, elliptic or elliptic-obovate, acuminate, perfectly glabrous beneath, secondary nerves 6–8 pair, prominent on the underside, with a conspicuous network of raised reticulate veins. Fl. white (tip of keel and wings purple), in terminal panicles, mostly single, not fasciculate, calyx tomentose, supported by 2 setaceous bracteoles, three teeth triangular, the two upper minute connate, corolla densely silky outside. Pod thick, turgid, flat between seeds, tawny-velvety, 2–4 by 1 in., seeds 1–5.

Sikkim, ascending to 4,000 ft. Dwars. Assam to Chittagong and Burma. Fl. Feb.–April. Nearly allied: 14. **M. Dorwardi**, Coll. and Hemsl. in Linn. Soc. Journ. xxviii. 40, described as a tree in one, as a climber in another place, Shan hills, Upper Burma, leaflets 2 pair, 2–3 in. long, fl. in dense terminal panicles.

15. **M. pachycarpa**, Benth.; Kurz, F. Fl. i. 353. Vern. *Kharīna*, Khasi hills.

A large spreading and scandent shrub, young parts and inflorescence rusty-brown tomentose, leaflets 5–6 pair, 3–7 in. long, pubescent beneath, secondary nerves 8–12 pair. Fl. pale pink, 1 in. long, on axillary racemes 9–10 in. long, standard glabrous. Pod thickly coriaceous, rugose, indented between seeds, 2–6 in. long, 1¼ in. broad, seeds 1–3.

Sikkim to 4,000 ft. Dwars. Assam, Khasi hills; pod used to poison fish, Manipur Upper Burma.

16. **M. racemosa**, Benth.; Fl. Brit. Ind. ii. 105.—Syn. *M. leiogyna*, Kurz, F. Fl. i. 351.

A large woody climber, deciduous, youngest parts and inflorescence rusty-tomentose. Leaflets 5–7 pair, 2 in. long, stipules subulate, ¾ in. long, stipels setaceous. Fl. whitish, in compact racemes, which are paniculate at the ends of branches, often appearing before the leaves, bracts much longer than buds. Standard and ovary glabrous. Pod dark brown, glossy, linear, 4–6 in. long, 3–5 seeded.

Deciduous forests of the Western Peninsula, and Burma. Fl. April, May.

The other climbing species of this genus may be classified as follows:—

a. Underside of full-grown leaves densely clothed with silky, lustrous tomentum (Western species).

17. **M. rubiginosa,** Wight and Arn.; Wight Ic. t. 207. Hills near Courtallum; leaflets 2–3 pair, elliptic, 4–6 in. long; secondary nerves 8–10 pair, petiolules ⅓–½ in., stipels small, fl. ½ in. long, standard densely silky on the back. Pod woody, velvety, 3–4 in. long, 1 in. broad. 18. **M. splendens,** W. & A. Nilgiris, Anamallays. Leaflets 3–4 pair, oblanceolate, 4–6 in. long, secondary nerves 12–15 pair, stipules conspicuous, standard densely silky on back. Pod woody, velvety, 3 in. long, ⅝ in. wide.

b. Underside of full-grown leaves pubescent (Eastern species).

19. **M. puerarioides,** Prain in Journ. As. Soc. Beng. vol. 66 (1898), p. 358. Tenasserim, Sitang valley, Upper Burma; leaflets 2–3 pair, 4–10 in. long, long-caudate, acuminate, finely but densely silky beneath, lower free portion of common petiole as long as, or longer than leaflet, secondary nerves 6-9 pair, prominent beneath. Racemes slender, 12 in. long, fl. ¼ in. long, standard densely silky on back; pod ultimately glabrous. This is the species described by Kurz, F. Fl. i. 353, as *Millettia sericea*, Wight and Arn., a large woody climber of the Malay peninsula and Java, leaflets lustrous silky beneath; fl. ½ in. long. Pod velvety, turgid. 20. **M. fruticosa,** Benth. Nepal in Sal forest, Assam, Silhet, Pegu; a low scrambling shrub, leaflets 4–5 pair, oblong or oblanceolate, 2–6 in. long, underside brown, finely pubescent, secondary nerves 6–8 pair, prominent beneath. Fl. in erect racemes. Pod flat, linear velvety, 3–4 in. long. *Wunu*, Burm., collected by Smales, Daungyu forest, Upper Burma, is similar, leaflets obovate obtuse, densely silky beneath. 21. **M. cana,** Benth. Yenangyaung, on the Irawaddi, Wallich, leaflets 3 pair, coriaceous, broadly elliptic, 2–3 in. long, 2 in. broad, secondary nerves 6–8 pair, prominent. Pod woody, flat, lanceolate.

c. Underside of full-grown leaves glabrous or nearly so.

22. **M. Piscidia,** Wight Ic. t. 86, Khasi Hills, Assam, Upper Burma (Thinwin, Burm.), Tonkin, glabrous, leaflets 2–3 pair, thinly coriaceous, elliptic-lanceolate, 3-4 in. long, no stipels. Secondary nerves indistinct. Fl. ¾–1 in. long, white, on capillary pedicels. Calyx membranous glabrous, standard glabrous. Pod thin, hard, glabrous, 3 in. long. 23. **M. monticola,** Kurz F. Fl. i. 354, Sikkim 6,000–7,000 ft., Assam, Nattaung, Burma (6,500–7,200 ft., in stunted hill and pine forests); leaflets 4–5 pair, membranous, pale beneath, from cuneate base oblong, shortly acuminate, 3–4 in. long, secondary nerves 6–8 pair not prominent, a minute network of reticulate veins between. Racemes compact, erect or spreading, unilateral before fl. open, generally several at the ends of branches. Fl. (blue, Nattaung, Kurz), pale lilac or purple in Sikkim. Prain, l.c., 361, 463, states the pods are indehiscent and winged along both sutures, hence the species would be *Derris monticola*. It is not *D. secunda*, Baker, Fl. Brit. Ind. ii. 247. 24. **M. caudata,** Baker, Khasi hills, Silhet, glabrous, leaflets lanceolate, caudate-acuminate 3–4 pair, 4–5 in. long. Pod linear, rigidly coriaceous, 3–4 in. long, ½ in. broad. 25. **M. cærulea,** Baker, Fl. Brit. Ind. ii. 107, found by Wallich at "Phanoc" on the Salween is doubtful.

9. DESMODIUM, Desv.; Fl. Brit. Ind. ii. 161.

Shrubs or herbs, leaves unifoliolate or pinnately trifoliolate, leaflets penninerved, stipellate. Fl. red or white, stamens diadelphous, or the 10th free at base, adhering to the sheath higher up. Pods flat, consisting of several 1-seeded, usually indehiscent joints. 150 species in the tropical and subtropical countries of both hemispheres.

A. Leaves 3-foliolate, fl. in umbels or heads.

1. **D. Cephalotes,** Wall.; Wight Ic. t. 373.—Syn. *D. congestum*, Wall.: Wight Ic. t. 209.

A large shrub, in Burma at times a small tree; branches angular, young shoots grey silky. Leaflets elliptic-lanceolate, 2-4 in. long; secondary nerves prominent, 6–10 pair. Pods in large shortly pedunculate axillary umbels, ½–⅜ in. long, brown, reticulately veined, pubescent, slightly curved, joints 3–6, pedicels slender, calyx persistent.

Subhimalayan tract, from Dehra Dun eastward. Common in both peninsulas, frequently as underwood in forests, Fl. R.S. 2. **D. olivaceum**, Prain in Journ. As. Soc. Beng. vol. 66 (1898), p. 389, Upper Burma; leaflets to 8 in. long, densely velvety beneath, fl. in dense globose axillary heads. Pods of 2 joints, ⅓ in. long.

3. **D. umbellatum,** DC.; Kurz, F. Fl. i. 385.

A large shrub, sometimes a small tree, young shoots grey-pubescent. Leaflets thinly coriaceous, broadly elliptic, glabrous above, pale grey or brownish-pubescent beneath. Fl. white, 6–12 in a pedunculate axillary umbel. Pod of 1–4 pubescent joints, 1½–2 in. long. Calyx deciduous.

Littoral, sea-coast of the Eastern Peninsula. From the Western Peninsula reported from near Surat and Belgaum. Fl.R.S. Ceylon, Malay Archipelago. Widely distributed from the Mascarene islands to Polynesia.

4. **D. Wallichii.** Prain, l.c., 388, Upper Burma, has leaflets densely fulvous-tomentose beneath. Pods 1–1½ in., strigose.

B. Leaves 3-foliolate, fl. in long racemes, bracts subulate, linear or lanceolate.

5. **D. tiliæfolium,** G. Don; Fl. Brit. Ind. ii. 168.—Syn. *D. argenteum*, Wall.

A large diffuse shrub, attains 2 in. diam. Wood hard with light brown heartwood, inner bark (bast) tough. Leaflets from a rounded or cuneate base, ovate or obovate, generally cuspidate, slightly sinuate, secondary nerves 4–6 pair. Fl. red, on slender pedicels, ⅓–½ in. long, in ample panicles, branches slender, often drooping. Pod nearly straight, 2–3 in. long, joints 6–10.

Kuram valley, trans Indus. Outer N.W. Himalaya, Indus to Nepal, 3,000–9,000 ft.; rare in Sikkim. Fl.R.S. *D. nutans*, Wall. Bashahr 6000–8000 ft., with broad, obtuse, distinctly sinuate leaflets, and long slender drooping paniculate racemes, probably is a distinct species.

6. **D. sambuense,** DC.; Prain, l.c., 394.—Syn. *D. floribundum*, G. Don; Fl. Brit. Ind. ii. 167; Collett, Simla Flora, 132.

A large shrub, with angular, densely pubescent branches. Leaflets with adpressed silky hairs, veins prominently reticulate on the underside. Fl. in erect paniculate racemes, buds shorter than the lanceolate, ribbed, deciduous bracts. Pods hairy, ¾–1 in. long.

Outer Himalaya from Dalhousie eastward, ascending to 7,000 feet. Hills of Upper and Lower Burma, 4,000–6,000 ft. Fl. R.S. To this group belong the following shrubs: 7. **D. confertum,** DC. Subhimalayan tract, often in Sal forests. Pod 1–1½ in., joints 2–5, longer than broad, clothed with long silky hairs. 8. **D. oxyphyllum,** DC.; Prain, l.c., 392, Outer Himalaya, ascending to 7,300 ft., Khasi hills. 9. **D. laxiflorum,** DC.—Syn. *D. recurvatum*, Grah.; Wight Ic. t. 374. A widely spread species. Subhimalayan tract from the Ganges eastwards, Assam, Khasi hills, Western Penins. from Bombay southwards, Java, Borneo, Philippines. 10. **D. concinnum,** DC.—Syn. *D. pendulum*, Wall. Pl. As. Rar. t. 94, Himalaya, Punjab to Assam, to 7,000 ft. Hills east of Toungoo in pine woods, 4,000–6,000 ft. 11. **D. polycarpum,** DC.; Wight Ic. t. 406.—Syn. *D. patens*, Wight Ic. t. 407; *D. heterocarpum*, DC.; Kurz F. Fl. i. 389. Widely spread over India and Burma, and from East Africa to Polynesia.

C. Leaves 3-foliolate, fl. in small fascicles, concealed by a pair of persistent orbicular bracts.

12. **D. pulchellum,** Benth.—Syn. *Dicerma pulchellum*, DC.; Wight Ic. t. 418. Vern *Taung tamin*, Burm.

Attains 4–5 ft., terminal leaflet larger than the lateral ones. Fl. in long terminal or lateral bracteate racemes, yellow, several in the axil of a 2-foliolate bract, the common petiole terminating in a shorter or longer bristle. Fl. completely concealed by the bracts. Pods small, minutely veined, joints usually 2, often emerging from between the bracts.

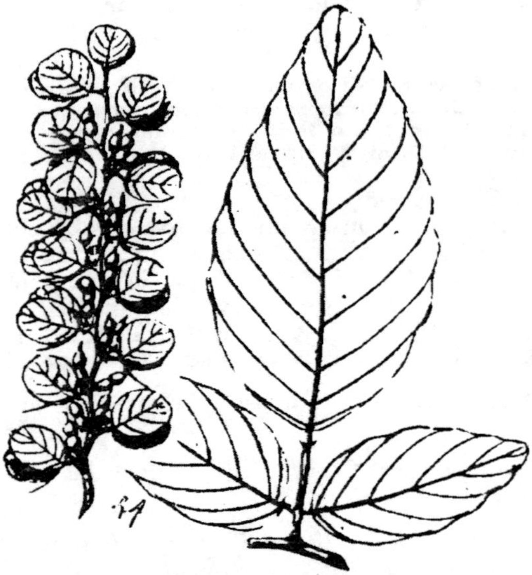

Fig. 96.—Desmodium pulchellum, Benth. $\frac{1}{2}$.

Common in both peninsulas, often as underwood in deciduous forests. Its northern limit in the Sal forests of Oudh and Gorakhpur. Fl. R.S. Also Sumatra, Java, Borneo, Philippines.

D. Leaves 1-foliolate.

13. **D. latifolium,** DC.; Wight Ic. t. 270.—Syn. *D. lasiocarpum*, DC. Vern. *Kyopan*, Burm.

A large shrub, often with a short woody stem, branchlets, petioles and underside of leaves softly tomentose. Leaves scabrous above, ovate, 3–5 in. long, slightly repand, secondary nerves 5–8 pair, stipules from a broad base cuspidate. Fl. bright purple, in dense, villous, axillary racemes. Pods $\frac{1}{3}$–$\frac{3}{4}$ in. long, clothed with hooked hairs, joints 3–6.

Sal forests of the subhimalayan tract, from Dehra Dun eastward. Both peninsulas. Eng forest of Upper Burma. Fl. July–Sept. Ceylon. From tropical Africa to New Guinea.

14. **D. gangeticum,** DC.; Wight Ic. t. 271, Subhimalayan tract from the Jumna eastward, both peninsulas, Ceylon, Java, Sumatra, Borneo, Philippines. A slender under-shrub, leaves ovate-lanceolate, acuminate, glabrous above, more or less pubescent beneath, secondary nerves 8–10 pair, fl. white in long, slender, terminal and axillary racemes. Pod falcate, $\frac{1}{2}$–$\frac{3}{4}$ in. long.

15. **D. triquetrum,** DC. Vern. *Mökso lanma* Burm., a small shrub. Dehra Dun, Oudh, Sikkim, Assam, Khasi hills, both Peninsulas and Ceylon, also Indian Archipelago; has 3- or 4-cornered branches, leaves oblong-lanceolate on a broadly-winged obovate or oblanceolate petiole. Pods sessile, straight, 1–2 in. long, joints square, $\frac{1}{4}$ in., more or less strigose with adpressed hairs.

Closely allied are the following species established by De Candolle, Prodr. ii. 326: *D. auriculatum*, DC. Silhet and coasts of Tenasserim and Andamans, attaining 10 ft. and more. Pods glabrous, firmly cartilaginous. *D. alatum*, DC. Assam, Khasi hills, Cachar, Chittagong, erect. Pods glabrous, thin. *D. pseudotriquetrum*, DC. Subhimalayan tract, Assam, Khasi and Naga hills, Bengal, a low trailing plant, branches terete. Pod ciliate along the edges, glabrous on the face. Prain in Journ. As. Soc. Beng. vol. 66 (1898), 390, classes these forms as sub-species of *D. triquetrum*.

10. OUGEINIA, Benth.; Fl. Brit. Ind. ii. 160.

O. dalbergioides, Benth. The only species. Bedd. Fl. Sylv. t. 36; Brand. F. Fl. t. 23.—Syn. *Dalbergia ougeinensis*, Roxb.; Wight Ic. t. 391. Vern. *Sannan*, *Sāndan*, *Tinnus*, Hind.; *Pānan*, Oudh; *Ruta*, Kol; *Tiwas*, Mar.

A middle-sized deciduous tree, with a short and often irregularly-shaped trunk. Heartwood hard, tough, light brown to reddish brown. Leaves pinnately trifoliolate, stipellate. Leaflets coriaceous, unequal, the terminal largest, broad-oval, the two lateral opposite, oblique, edges undulate or slightly crenate. Fl. white or pale pink, on long slender pedicels, in dense fascicles, or on short racemes, forming loose heads on the old wood, 1–2 in. across. Stamens diadelphous, anthers uniform. Pod linear-oblong, flat, veined, slightly contracted between the seeds, scarcely dehiscent. Seeds 2–5, flat.

Subhimalayan tract, from the Sutlej to Sikkim, ascending in the valleys to 4,000 ft. Central India, south to the Godavery on the east, and North Kanara on the west side of the peninsula. Often gregarious. Fl. from Feb. to May, generally before the old leaves have fallen or the young foliage has come fully out.

To this tribe also belong: **Æschynomene aspera,** Linn.; Wight Ic. t. 299, Bengal. Rare in the Western Peninsula. Ceylon. A tall, erect water-plant, attaining 12 ft.

and 3 in. diam., the well-known Sola, the soft white wood, generally called pith, is made into toys, floats, and Sola hats, invaluable as a protection against the sun.

Alhagi Camelorum, Fischer; Prain in Journ. As. Soc. Beng. vol. 66 (1898), 377. The camel thorn, a thorny shrub, sending its roots deep into the ground, with small oblong obtuse leaves and numerous axillary stout spinescent branchlets, often bearing leaves and flowers, glabrous ovaries, and turgid pods. Widely spread from Greece and Egypt, through Western Asia, Afghanistan and Baluchistan, extending over the arid and dry regions of India, in moister districts found on dry barren ground. Often gregarious. *A. Maurorum*, Tournef.; Prain, l.c., 378, has silky ovaries.

Lespedeza, Michaux; Fl. Brit. Ind. ii. 142, with trifoliolate l. and short 1-seeded pods, comprises numerous undershrubs and a few shrubs. **L. Prainii,** Coll. et Hemsl. in Linn. Soc. Journ. xxviii. 46, is a shrub 10 ft. high, common on the Shan table-land, 4,000-5,000 ft., leaflets obovate, ½–1 in., fl. purple in dense axillary racemes, longer than leaves, pod glabrous.

11. ABRUS, Linn.; Fl. Brit. Ind. ii. 175.

(6 species, in the tropics of both hemispheres.)

1. **A. precatorius,** Linn.—Vern. *Gūnchi*, *Kūnch*, Hind. Mar.; *Chūntli*, Dūn; *Ywe-gnè*, Burm.

A climber, with woody stem and slender branches, twining round supports. Leaves paripinnate, the common petiole terminating in a slender short bristle. Leaflets opposite, nearly sessile, 10–15 pair, oblong, obtuse, often mucronate. Fl. white or pink, in axillary pedunculate racemes. Pod oblong, turgid, the fruiting peduncles persistent and irregularly thickened. Seeds 3–5, ellipsoid or nearly globose, polished, generally red, with a black eye on the hilum, sometimes black with a white eye, more rarely quite white, stonyhard, used as weights by jewellers. An acrid poison in the seed.

Common in forest tracts of India and Burma, ascending in the outer Himalaya to 3,500 ft. Found in Merwara, but not known from the arid region of Sind and the southern Punjab. Fl. Sept., Oct. A sea-shore species in the Indian Archipelago (Schimper). Cosmopolitan within the tropics.

2. **A. pulchellus,** Wall.; also widely distributed, is similar, but has flat slightly curved pods with 8–12 seeds.

12. MUCUNA, Adans.; Fl. Brit. Ind. ii. 185.

Woody or herbaceous twiners, leaves pinnately trifoliolate. Fl. large, dark purple or greenish white, in pendulous racemes or corymbs, often from the old wood. Calyx campanulate, 2 upper teeth connate, the lowermost longest. Keel and wings longer than standard. Stamens diadelphous, anthers alternately longer basifixed and shorter versatile. Pod usually covered with brittle irritating bristles. Species 30, in the tropics of both hemispheres.

The structure of the woody species merits further study. Some South American *Mucunas* have soft spongy wood, irregular, more or less concentric masses of xylem, alternating with bands of phloëm. The xylem consists of thin-walled parenchyma, traversed by longitudinal strands of vessels, sieve tubes and wood fibres.

A. Face of pod covered with oblique plaits or lamellæ.

1. **M. imbricata,** DC.; Fl. Brit. Ind. ii. 185. Leaves nearly glabrous. Fl. dull purple, or white with purple spots, in short racemes, while in bud covered by large concave imbricating bracts. Pod 4–6 in. long, 2–3 in. broad, winged along both sutures; seeds 2–3.

Subhimalayan tract, Kumaon to Assam, Upper and Lower Burma, Andamans. Fl. Aug.–Dec.

2. **M. monosperma,** DC.; Wight Ic. t. 35.—Syn. *M. anguina*, Wall. Pl. As. Rar. t. 236.

Young shoots clothed with rusty tomentum. Fl. dark purple in a short nodding pubescent corymb. Pod thick, broadly elliptic, 2 in. long, with a narrow double wing all round, and with numerous oblique lamellæ on its face, the whole covered with orange-red deciduous wool mixed with red irritant bristles. Seed one, nearly circular.

Western Ghats from the Konkan southwards, Assam, Khasi hills, Chittagong, Burma, Andamans. Fl. C.S. Also Malay Archipelago.

3. **M. atropurpurea,** DC. Western Peninsula and Ceylon. Branchlets glabrous. Fl. on pedunculate, often branching racemes. Pods elliptic-oblong, 2–3 in. long, ¾–1 in. broad, winged and plaited, 2-seeded.

B. Face of pod not plaited.

4. **M. gigantea,** DC. ; Fl. Brit. Ind. ii. 186.

A glabrous climber, stems thin, but sometimes 250 ft. long. Fl. yellow or white, in corymbs, pendulous on slender peduncles. Calyx with yellow deciduous bristles. Pod 4–6 in. long, 1–2 in. broad, winged along both sutures; seeds 2–4.

A littoral species, common in the Sundriban and on the Andamans. A striking feature of the Indian mangrove-swamps. Here and there on the coast of the Western Peninsula. Malay Peninsula and Malay Archipelago to Polynesia.

5. **M. macrocarpa,** Wall. ; Kurz, F. Fl. i. 379. Vern. *Baldengra*, Nys.

A powerful woody climber, the stems to 15 in. diam. Wood soft spongy. Fl. large, 2–3 in. long, greenish purple or greenish white, in long pendulous racemes, axillary or from the old wood. Pods 1–3 ft. long, torulose, up to 1½ in. thick, narrowed between the 8–12 seeds, velvety when young, glabrous afterwards.

Nepal, Sikkim (ascending to 7,000 ft.). Hills east of Toungoo, often in pine woods (4,000–6,000 ft.). Shan plateau, Upper Burma, 4,000 ft. Fl. H.S. Also in Tonkin and Yunnan.

6. **Mucuna pruriens,** DC.—Syn. *M. utilis*, Wall. ; Wight Ic. t. 280, *Kawānch*, *Goncha*, Hind.; *Kwele*, Burm., is short-lived (biennial ?), but climbs over big trees and is common among the tall grasses of the Savannahs. The dark purple fl. appear during the rains or in autumn, the pods ripen in the cold season, are 2–3 in. long, 5–6-seeded, and densely clothed with brown irritating hairs. Subhimalayan tract from the Punjab eastwards, Assam, Khasi hills, Western Peninsula, Burma, Siam, Tonkin, Yunnan. Also Malay Peninsula, Java, and Borneo.

13. ERYTHRINA, Linn. ; Fl. Brit. Ind. ii. 188.

Trees or shrubs (a few herbaceous undershrubs), the Indian species nearly all leafless during the hot season, and in flower at that time, branches often prickly. Wood white, soft and light, medullary rays broad, pores (vessels) large, broad concentric bands of thin-walled wood parenchyma. Leaves pinnately trifoliolate, the lateral leaflets opposite, stipules small, stipels glandlike. Fl. large, generally red, fasciculate in peduncled racemes, standard, much larger than wings or keel. Stamens connate to the middle, the 10th free or connate with the rest at the base, anthers equal. Pod stipitate, dehiscent. 30 species in the tropical and sub-tropical regions of both hemispheres.

A. Calyx spathaceous, split to the base.

1. **E. indica,** Lam. ; Wight Ic. t. 58. *The Indian Coral tree.* Vern. *Pangra*, *Pangāra*, Hind. Mar. ; *Pālte Mādār*, Beng. ; *Halivara*, Kan. ; *Modugu*, Tel. ; *Kathit*, Burm.

A moderate-sized tree, of rapid growth. Bark yellowish or greenish grey. Young shoots and inflorescence clothed with stellate pubescence, black prickles on branches, which fall when a few years old, petioles unarmed. Leaflets entire, glabrous, the terminal 4–5 in. long, generally broader than long. Fl. bright scarlet in dense racemes, with peduncle to 15 in. long. Calyx 1 in., at the apex contracted, with 5 minute teeth. Wings and keel equal, one-fourth the length of standard. Pod torulose, 6–12 in. long, seeds 1–8.

Common on the coast, from the Sundriban to the Malay Peninsula. Andamans, Nicobars. Fl. Feb., March. A littoral species, widely spread from the Mascarenes to Polynesia. Reported to be indigenous inland in deciduous forests of Thana, the Konkan, and North Kanara. Cultivated and self-sown all over India, in hedge-rows in Bengal. In the Peninsula grown to support the betel- and pepper-vine.

2. **E stricta,** Roxb.; Bedd. Fl. Sylv. t. 175. Vern. *Taung Kathit*, Burm.
Trunk and branches armed with sharp conical prickles. Leaflets entire, nearly glabrous. Fl. scarlet, in dense unilateral racemes, 4–5 in. with peduncle, several racemes at the ends of stout branchlets. Calyx $\frac{1}{4}$–$\frac{1}{2}$ in., keel half the length of standard, wings much smaller. Pod lanceolate, glabrous, 1–3-seeded, 2–4 in. long.

Assam, Manipur, Chittagong. Burma (common). West side of the Peninsula. Fl. Feb.–May.

B. Calyx campanulate or turbinate, limb truncate or split into 2 or more divisions.

3. **E. suberosa,** Roxb.; Fl. Brit. Ind. ii. 189.—Syn. *E. sublobata*, Roxb.; Bedd. Manual 87. Vern. *Pangra*, Hind. Mar.; *Dhaul-dhak*, Hind.
A middle-sized tree, with a corky, deeply cracked bark. Branchlets sparingly armed with sharp stout conical whitish or light brown prickles, sometimes a few scattered prickles on petioles. Branchlets, underside of leaves and inflorescence clothed with long soft bi- or tri-furcate hairs. Leaflets rhomboid, entire or sinuate-lobed. Racemes 4–6 in. long. Calyx turbinate, 2-lipped, keel half the length of standard, wings minute. Pod narrow, 3–4 in. long, 2–4-seeded.

Subhimalayan tract, from the Ravi to the Sarda, ascending to 3,000 ft. Oudh forests, Merwara, Burma. Fl. March, April. A variety with full-grown leaves glabrous, in Kumaun, Sikkim, Upper and Lower Burma.

4. **E. ovalifolia,** Roxb.; Wight Ic. t. 247. Vern. *Kôn Kathit*, Burm.
Trunk and branches armed with dark brown prickles, arising from pyramidal corky tubercles. Leaflets elliptic or elliptic-oblong, obtuse, glabrous, whitish beneath. Racemes lax, 5–10 in. long, several at the ends of branchlets. Calyx campanulate, splitting irregularly into 2 or more unequal divisions. Corolla deep blood-red, standard obovate, emarginate, 1$\frac{1}{2}$ in. Keel 1 in., wings $\frac{3}{4}$ in. long. Pod torulose, 6–8 in. long, finely downy, constricted between the 6–8 seeds.

Silhet, Lower Bengal. Plains of Lower Burma. Fl. Feb., March. Ceylon, Malay Archipelago, Polynesia.

5. **E. arborescens,** Roxb. Cor. Pl. t. 219; Fl. Brit. Ind. ii. 190.
Few prickles on branches and petioles. Leaflets, when full grown, nearly glabrous, 5–7 in. long and equally broad. Fl. vivid scarlet, racemes (with peduncle) up to 15 in. long. Calyx turbinate, silky pubescent, limb truncate or unequally lobed. Standard ovate, acuminate, concave, more than twice the length of keel, wings shorter than keel. Pod lanceolate curved, brown-pubescent; seeds 2–10.

Outer Himalaya, from Kumaun eastward, 4,000–7,000 ft., Khasi hills. Melghat, Berar (March 1877, D.B.). Fl. Aug.–Oct.

A remarkable undershrub is 6. **E. resupinata,** Roxb. Cor. Pl. t. 220, in the Savannahs of the subhimalayan tract from Oudh eastward, also on Parasnath. From a perennial rootstock, after the fires of the hot season, spring short racemes of large bright scarlet fl., calyx 2-lipped, standard bent downwards. After the fl. comes up a short herbaceous leafy stem.

7. **E. lithosperma,** Miq.; Kurz, F. Fl. i. 367. Vern. *Ye-Kathit*, Burm.
A large tree, leafless in H.S., bark white, trunk and branches armed with straight sharp prickles, foliage dark green, young shoots mealy-puber-

ulous. Leaflets ovate, acuminate, glabrous, 4–5 in. long, stipellary glands large, oblong. Fl. appear while the tree is in leaf, in dense short racemes on stout peduncles. Calyx 2-lipped, wings and keel equal, one-third the length of standard, which is 1½ in. long. Lower portion of pod 3 in. long, flat, seedless, indehiscent, upper portion shorter and narrower, dehiscent, with 1–4 large dark purple seeds.

Burma, in moist valleys near streams to 3,000 ft. Often grown to support the betel-vine. Fl. Jan.–Feb. Malay Archipelago.

E. holosericea, Kurz, is, as pointed out by Prain, in Journ. As. Soc. Beng. 66, 72, a mistake, based upon the leavesof *E. lithosperma* and the fl. of *E. ovalifolia*.

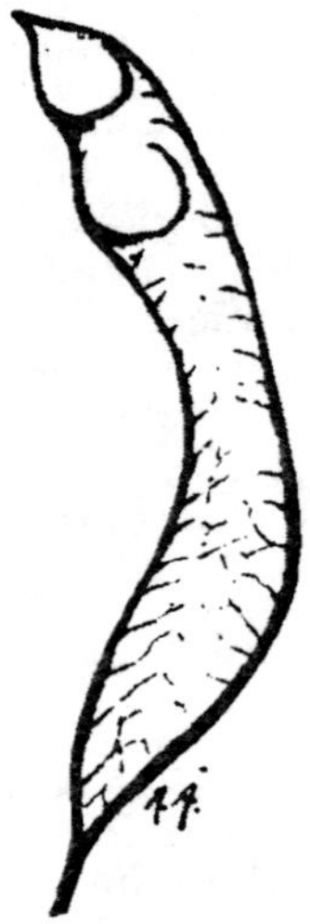

FIG. 97.
Erythrina lithosperma,
Bl. ½.

Dioclea reflexa, H.f.; Kurz, F. Fl. i. 379; Ann. Bot. Gard. Calc. ix. t. 40. Assam, Silhet, Tenasserim, Andamans, Malay Peninsula and Archipelago, tropical Africa and America, is a strong woody climber with rusty tomentose branches, and pinnately trifoliolate stipellate leaves. Fl. pale pink, in dense racemes on rusty tomentose peduncles 8–12 in. long, bracts linear, much longer than buds, subpersistent. Petals about equal in length, standard orbicular, emarginate. Vexillary stamen free below, connate with the others in the middle, with a perfect anther, the stamens in the sheath alternately with perfect and empty anthers. Pod turgid, 1–2-seeded, 3–4 in. long.

14. PUERARIA, DC.; Fl. Brit. Ind. ii. 197.

Twining shrubs or herbs with large pinnately trifoliolate stipellate leaves, which in some species are lobed. Fl. in long, mostly paniculate racemes, blue or purple. Calyx campanulate, teeth unequal. Wings and keel nearly equal to standard. Vexillary stamen entirely free or cohering with the rest. Ovary sessile or nearly so. Pod linear, flat, many-seeded. 12 species, India, Malay Archipelago, Japan, and New Guinea.

1. **P. tuberosa**, DC.; Wight Ic. t. 412. Vern. *Surāl*, *Surūr*, Hind.; *Ghora bel*, Merwara.

A large deciduous pubescent climber, with woody tubercled stem. Leaflets broadly ovate, acuminate, pubescent, 4–6 in. long, 3–5 in. broad, the two lateral unequal-sided. Bracts shorter than buds, fl. pale blue, fasciculate, in long panicled racemes, appearing when the plant is leafless. Pod flat, clothed with long rusty hairs, 2–3 in. long, 2–6-seeded, much contracted between seeds.

Subhimalayan tract from the Indus to Sikkim, ascending to 4,000 ft. Western Peninsula. Fl. March, April. The large tuberous roots are eaten.

2. **P. Wallichii**, DC.; Prain in Journ. As. Soc. Beng. vol. 66 (1898), 419.

A large glabrous climber, leaflets obovate. Bracts longer than buds, hairy, fl. appearing while the plant is in leaf, white, yellow or reddish, in racemes 3–12 in. long, fascicled and paniculate. Pod glabrous, coriaceous, 4–5 in. long.

Subhimalayan tract, Nepal and Sikkim, chiefly in the Sal forests, Khasia, Silhet, Upper Burma. Fl. Oct., Nov.

Other shrubs and climbers: 3. **P. Thunbergiana**, Benth.—Syn. *P. Thomsoni*, Benth.; Fl. Brit. Ind. ii. 198, Sikkim, Khasia, China and Japan. A vigorous climber, leaflets often lobed. Fl. large, blue or violet, ¾–1 in., calyx teeth much longer than tube. Pod 4–5 in., densely clothed with long silky hairs. 4. **P. Candollei**, Grah., Chittagong, Burma, Andamans. Calyx glabrous, edges scarious and ciliate. 5. **P. Collettii**, Prain in Journ. As. Soc. Beng. vol. 66 (1898), 420, Upper Burma. A shrub, sometimes climbing, branches and leaves clothed with soft grey velvet. Racemes axillary, longer than leaf. Pod thin, 2 in. long, ⅓ in. wide.

15. SPATHOLOBUS, Hassk.; Fl. Brit. Ind. ii. 193.

Woody climbers, with pinnately trifoliolate leaves, leaflets stipellate, the two lateral opposite. Fl. small, in ample terminal panicles. Stamens diadelphous, anthers uniform, obtuse. Pod coriaceous, one seed at the end, lower portion indehiscent. 16 species; 9 Indian, 1 in tropical Africa, the rest in the Malayan region.

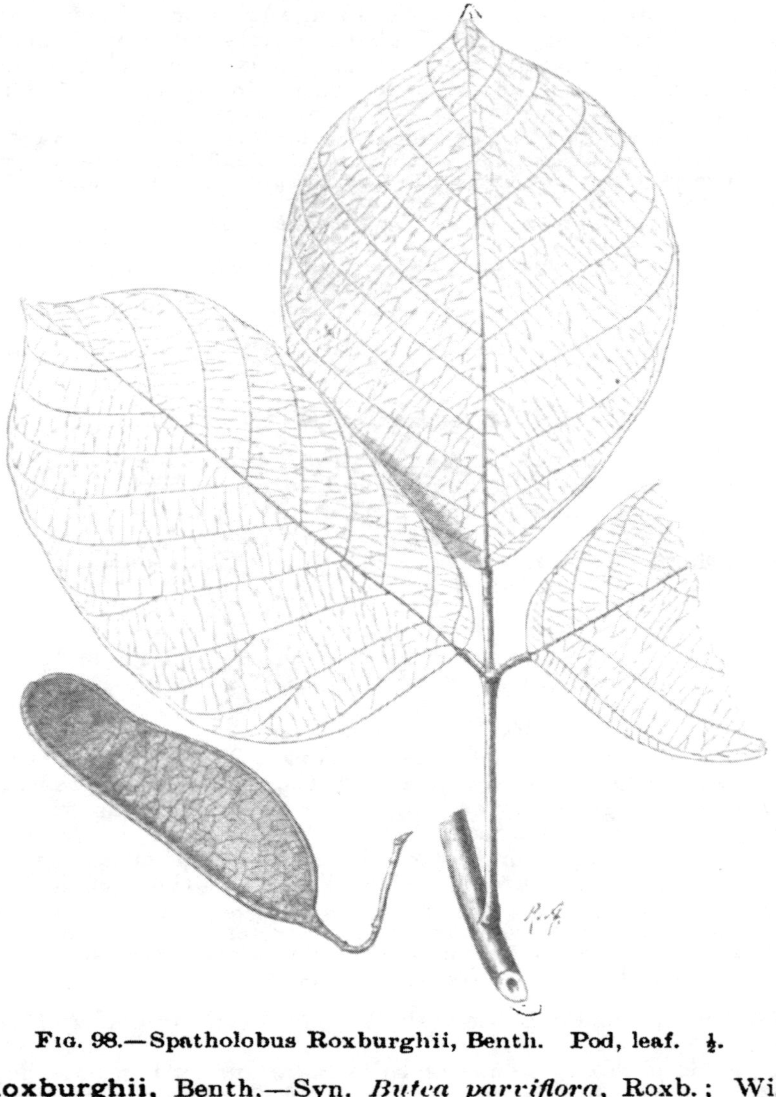

FIG. 98.—Spatholobus Roxburghii, Benth. Pod, leaf. ½.

1. **S. Roxburghii,** Benth.—Syn. *Butea parviflora*, Roxb.; Wight Ic. t. 210; Kurz F. Fl. i. 365. Vern. *Maula*, *Mula*, Hind.; *Phalsan*, Mar.; *Athambu*, Mal.; *Pauk-nwè*, Burm.

A huge climber, the stem fluted, often attaining 12–16 in. diam. The layers of bast, which separate the masses of xylem, exude a red gum when cut. Young shoots, inflorescence and underside of leaflets grey velvety. Leaflets 6–8 in. long, longer than broad, secondary nerves prominent beneath, 6–8 pair, arcuate, anastomosing by intra-marginal veins. Fl. fascicled in cylindrical panicled racemes, white, ⅓–½ in. long, calyx teeth triangular acute, nearly as

long as tube, standard twice the length of calyx, emarginate. Pod ferrugineous-tomentose, stalked, 3–5 in. long.

Subhimalayan tract from the Jumna eastward, Central and South India. Burma. Common in deciduous forests, where it does much damage. Fl. C.S. A distinct variety, canescent, not velvety, is *S. denudatus.*

2. **S. acuminatus,** Benth.; Fl. Brit. Ind. ii. 194.—Syn. *Butea acuminata,* Wall.; Kurz, F. Fl. i. 365.

A woody climber, stem as thick as a man's arm, leaflets elliptic-oblong, acuminate, 2–4 in. long, shining above, nearly glabrous beneath. Fl. ¼ in. long, in ample panicles with slender ramifications, calyx teeth obtuse, half the length of tube. Pod sessile, silky pubescent, lustrous, 2–3 in. long.

Lower Burma, Andamans. Fl. H.S. Also Malay Peninsula.

Other Indian species. 3. **S. purpureus,** Benth.; Prain in Journ. As. Soc. Beng. vol. 66 (1898), 414. Evergreen forests of North Kanara. Leaflets coriaceous, glabrous, shining on both surfaces, elliptic-oblong. Fl. dark purple. Pod 4 in. long, glabrous, seedless portion curved, shining. 4. **S. crassifolius,** Benth., Khasi hills, Silhet, and Penang. Youngest shoots and inflorescence ferrugineous-pubescent, leaves thickly coriaceous, numerous shorter intermediate nerves between the secondary nerves, which are not very prominent. The following species are described by Dr. Prain in Journ. As. Soc. Beng. vol. 66 (1898), 414–416. 5. **S. squamiger,** Prain, Pegu. 6. **S. roseus,** Prain, Martaban and Upper Burma. 7. **S. Listeri,** Prain, Chittagong. 8. **S. merguensis,** Prain, Mergui Archipelago. 9. **S. riparius,** Prain, Thaukyegat, near Toungoo, Tenasserim. 10. **S. Pottingeri,** Prain in Journ. As. Soc. Beng. vol. 67, 286. Kachin hills.

16. BUTEA, Roxb.; Fl. Brit. Ind. ii. 194.

Trees, shrubs, or large climbers, with trifoliolate leaves. Leaflets stipellate the 2 lateral opposite. Secondary and tertiary nerves very prominent. Fl. large, bright orange, scarlet or red, fascicled, in axillary or terminal racemes Standard acute, recurved. Upper stamen free, the others connate beyond the middle, anthers uniform, obtuse. Pod coriaceous, oblong, lower portion flat indehiscent, upper 1-seeded, dehiscent. 3 Indian species.

1. **B. frondosa,** Roxb. Cor. Pl. t. 21; Bedd. Fl. Sylv. t. 176.—Syn. *B. monosperma* (Lam.) Taubert, in Engler und Prantl, iii. 3, 366. Vern. *Dhāk,* Hind.; *Palās,* Hind. Mar.; *Khākdā,* Guj.; *Muttuga,* Kan.; *Moduga,* Tel.; *Pauk,* Burm.

A moderate-sized deciduous tree, trunk crooked and irregular; a red astringent gum issues from incisions in the bark. Young shoots tawny-tomentose. Leaflets coriaceous, hard, the terminal from a cuneate base obovate obtuse, often emarginate, generally as long as broad, 4–6 in. long. the lateral smaller, oblique-ovate. Flowers appear before the leaves, 2 in. long, pedicels 1 in. long, twice the length of calyx. Petals clothed outside with grey silky pubescence, keel much curved, acute, 5–6 times the length of calyx.

Common throughout India and Burma, often gregarious. In the N.W. Himalaya ascends to 3,000 ft. In Travancore not common, and confined to the drier districts. The old leaves are shed in February, the tree is covered with bright orange red fl. in March and April, before the fresh leaves appear.

2. **B. superba,** Roxb. Cor. Pl. t. 22. Vern. *Palāsvēl,* Mar.; *Pauknwè,* Burm.

A gigantic climber, stems as thick as a man's leg. Leaflets acuminate, chartaceous. Flowers larger than those of *B. frondosa,* of a gorgeous orange colour, on pedicels three times the length of calyx.

Central and South India, Burma. Fl. March, April.

3. **B. minor,** Ham.; Fl. Brit. Ind. ii. 195.

A large shrub, at times climbing, leaflets 6–15 in. long, scabrous above, silky-tomentose beneath, the terminal largest. Fl. 1 in. long, dull red, petals and calyx densely silky outside, keel obtuse, little curved, three times the length of calyx.

Kumaun, Nepal. Sikkim (rare). Assam, Khasi hills. Fl. R.S.

Cruddasia insignis, Prain in Ann. Bot. Gard. Calc. ix. t. 34, Kachin hills, Upper Burma. A slender climber, tawny pubescent; leaflets 5, stipellate, 3–6 in. long; fl. purplish, fasciculate on long axillary racemes; stamens monadelphous, anthers uniform, pod flat, linear 3 in. long.

17. **FLEMINGIA**, Roxb.; Fl. Brit. Ind. ii. 226. (*Moghania*, St. Hil.; Taubert in Engler und Prantl, iii. 3, 375).

Ercet shrubs, leaves digitately 3-foliolate or simple, gland dotted below. Lowest pair of secondary nerves basal. Stipules lanceolate, prominently ribbed, deciduous. Calyx tube short, teeth narrow acuminate, the lowest often the longest. Corolla barely exserted, petals equal in length. Stamens diadelphous, anthers uniform. Pod oblong turgid, small, 1- or 2-seeded. species 25; 3 in tropical Africa, the rest Asiatic. The more common species only are mentioned here.

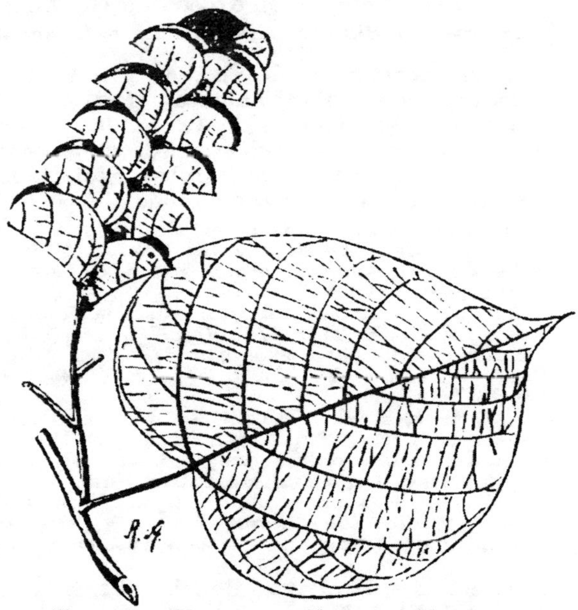

Fig. 99.—Flemingia Chappar, Ham. ½.

A. Leaves simple, bracts large, membranous, broadly ovate, folded, each enclosing a short raceme, frequently with sterile flowers.

1. **F. strobilifera**, R. Br.; Wight Ic. t. 267; Fl. Brit. Ind. ii. 227. Vern. *Kasraut*, Oudh; *Se luppya*, Upper Burma.

Leaves ovate-lanceolate, 2–4 in. long, secondary nerves 4–10 pair, petiole ¼ in. to 1 in.

This widely-spread and variable species, Prain in Journ. As. Soc. Beng. vol. 66 (1898), 486, divides into 4, with the following characters.

Erect shrubs 5–10 *ft. high, bracts* ¾–1 *in. long.*

(*a*) *F. strobilifera*, R. Br. Secondary nerves 8–10 pairs, nearly equal, bracts 1 in., finely puberulous. Subhimalayan tract from Kumaun eastwards, Assam, Khasi, and Naga hills, Chittagong, Western Peninsula and Burma, Malay Peninsula and Malay Archipelago. Fl. C. S.

(*b*) *F. bracteata*, Wight Ic. t. 268; Kurz F. Fl. ii. 372. Second. nerves 4–6 pair, the basal pair longest, bracts ¾ in., softly hirsute with long hairs. Subhimalayan tract from Garhwal eastward, Behar, Western Peninsula, and Burma. Fl. C. S.

Low shrubs 1–3 *ft. high.*

(*c*) *F. fruticulosa*, Wall.; Collett, Simla Flora, fig. 41. Leaves ovate, with subcordate base, bracts ⅝ in. long, sparsely hirsute on nerves. N.W. Himalaya from Simla to Kumaun, 5,000–7,000 ft. Fl. Aug.–Oct.

(*d*) *F. fluminalis*, C. B. Clarke. Leaves narrowly lanceolate, base cuneate. Chittagong hills, rocky river beds. Burma.

The last-named appears to be a distinct species, and *F. fruticulosa* is a well-marked local form; stunted in the climate of the N.W. Himalaya.

2. **F. Chappar**, Ham.; Fl. Brit. Ind. ii. 227. Vern. *Sālpan*, Hind. Beng.; *Kasraut*, Oudh.

Leaves broad-cordate, acuminate, 2–4 in. long and as broad as long, petiole 1½ in. long.

Underwood in forests of *Shorea robusta*, Oudh, Behar, and Ganjam, in those of *Dipterocarpus tuberculatus* in Burma. Fl. C. S.

B. Leaves trifoliolate, leaflets ovate-lanceolate, bracts lanceolate, not folded.

3. **F. stricta,** Roxb. Cor. Pl. t. 248; Wight Ic. t. 329. Vern. *Bebar*, Garhw.

Attains 6–10 ft. Stems and branches triquetrous, petiole 3–6 in. long, angular, deeply sulcate, sometimes narrowly winged (var. *pteropus*). Leaflets 6–12 in., secondary nerves 12–20 pair. Racemes cylindrical, 2–4 in. long, often fascicled, supported at their base by numerous large silky hairy bracts, 1–3 in. long, which are densely imbricate, enclosing the racemes while in bud, and are more or less persistent. At the ends of racemes are numerous imbricating lanceolate bracts, much exceeding the buds, which fall after the fl. have opened.

Dehra-Dūn, Sikkim, Assam, Burma, Coromandel coast. Fl. C. S.

4. **F. congesta,** Roxb.; Wight Ic. t. 390; Vern. *Banch hūi*, Dūn.

Branches angular, sulcate. Petiole 2–4 in. long, angular, sometimes narrowly winged, leaflets 3–12 in. long, secondary nerves 4–6 pair, the lowest pair very prominent, with conspicuous tertiary nerves on the outside. Racemes dense, oblong, often fasciculate, bracts lanceolate, $\frac{1}{4}$–$\frac{1}{3}$ in. long. Pod $\frac{1}{2}$ in. long, brown, pubescent; seeds 2, black.

Subhimalayan tract from the Jumna eastward, Khasi hills, Chittagong, Behar, Central India, both Peninsulas, Ceylon, Malay Archipelago, China.

This most variable species Prain, l.c., 439, divides into several, some of which had been recognized by Kurz.

Racemes condensed, shorter than petioles: (*a*) *F. congesta*, Roxb. (*b*) *F. prostrata*, Roxb.; Kurz, F. Fl. i. 374. (*c*) *F. ferruginea*, Graham; Kurz, F. Fl. i. 373.

Racemes elongate, exceeding petioles: (*d*) *F. Wightiana*, Graham. (*e*) *F. latifolia*, Benth.; Kurz, F. Fl. i. 375. (*f*) *F. semialata*, Roxb. Cor. Pl. t. 249; Kurz, l.c., 374; Wight Ic. t. 326.

5. **F. nana,** Roxb.; Wight Ic. t. 389. Ganges near Hardwar, Kheri Forests Oudh, Behar, Sangor, C.P. North Kanara. Pubescent, calyx and pod covered with red resinous glands, pedicel longer than calyx, and 6. **F. sericans,** Kurz, F. Fl. i. 373. Eng forests of Pegu and Martaban, Shan hills. Inflorescence densely clothed with long hairs, pedicels shorter than calyx. Two undershrubs, analogous to *Grewia sapida*, *Ochna pumila*, *Olax nana*, *Erythrna resupinata*, and others, which, from an underground stem, bring forth flowers and leaves after the fires of the hot season.

7. **F. involucrata,** Benth.; Fl. Brit. Ind. ii. 229.—Syn. *F. capitata*, Zoll.; Kurz, F. Fl. i. 376.

Attains 3–5 ft., branches nearly terete. Petiole $\frac{1}{2}$ in. long, rarely longer, leaflets 2–4 in., secondary nerves 8–12 pair, basal pair not prominent. Fl. blue, in dense softly hairy round axillary heads (short racemes) supported by persistent lanceolate bracts clothed with long silky hairs, the outer ovate-lanceolate, up to 1 in. long. Pods enclosed in the calyx, usually 1-seeded.

Subhimalayan tract from Kumaun to Assam, Central and South India, Burma. Often gregarious on open grassy glades and in moist places. Fl. C. S.

8. **F. paniculata,** Wall.; Kurz, F. Fl. i. 372; Subhimalayan tract, from Kumaun eastward, Behar, Central Prov. Bengal, Upper and Lower Burma. Fl. in lax panicles, leaves unifoliolate, 3–7 in. long. 9. **F. lineata,** Roxb.; Kurz, F. Fl. i. 372; Subhimalayan tract from Kumaun eastward, Silhet, Bengal, Centr. Prov., Western and Eastern Peninsula, Ceylon. Leaves trifoliolate, leaflets 1–3 in. long, plicate along nerves while young, basal nerves extending far beyond the middle, with numerous prominent tertiary nerves on the outside. Fl. in the axils of minute bracts, in lax axillary panicles.

18. DALBERGIA, Linn. fil.; Fl. Brit. Ind. ii. 230.

Trees, shrubs or climbers, with alternate imparipinnate leaves, leaflets alternate, without stipels. Flowers small, paniculate, white lilac or purple, bracts and bracteoles usually small. Calyx 5-dentate, the anterior tooth generally longest. Wings oblong, as long as standard, keel obtuse, shorter than standard. Stamens either diadelphous, the 10th stamen free, or monadelphous, with 9 or 10 stamens, or equally diadelphous, with two bundles of 5 stamens each. Ovary stipitate with few ovules, style short incurved, stigma small terminal. Pod flat, indehiscent, with one or few seeds. 80 species, tropical and sub-tropical regions of Old and New World.

A. Trees or erect shrubs. Stamens 9 or 10, united in a sheath split above.

1. **D. Sissoo**, Roxb.; Bedd. Fl. Sylv. t. 25; Brand. F. Fl. t. 24. The *Sissoo tree*. Vern. *Tali*, Pb.; *Sissu*, *Shisham*, Hind.

A large deciduous tree, bark grey, heartwood brown with darker veins. Leaflets 3–5, broadly-elliptic or ovate, acuminate, pubescent when young, glabrous when full grown, 1–3 in. long. Fl. yellowish white, nearly sessile, in short axillary panicles. Stamens 9, ovary pubescent, style much shorter than ovary. Pod linear-lanceolate, 1–3-seeded.

Subhimalayan tract and in the outer valleys, from the Indus to Assam, ascending generally to 3,000, and in places to 5,000 ft. Extending far into the plains along river banks. Baluchistan, Suleiman range. Planted and often self-sown throughout India. Fl. March–May.

2. **D. latifolia**, Roxb. Cor. Pl. t. 113; Wight Ic. t. 1156; Bedd. Fl. Sylv. t. 24. *Blackwood*, *Rosewood*. Vern. *Sitsal*, Bengal; *Kiri*, Kol; *Shisham*, Mar.; *Biti*, Kan.; *Jitengi*, Tel.; *Itti*, Tam.

A large deciduous tree, bark grey, heartwood dark purple with black streaks. Leaflets 3–7, broadly elliptic, orbicular or elliptic-obovate, obtuse, sometimes emarginate, $\frac{1}{2}$–3 in. long. Fl. whitish, $\frac{1}{4}$ in. long, on pedicels nearly as long as calyx tube, in short axillary much-branched panicles. Stamens 9, ovary glabrous, style slender, nearly as long as ovary. Pod oblong-lanceolate, 1–4-seeded.

Subhimalayan tract, from Oudh to Sikkim. Central and South India, extending north to Bandelkhand and to Todgarh in Merwara. Generally in deciduous forests, often associated with Teak. On the west side of the peninsula, also in evergreen forests. Fl. at Calcutta, in Sikkim and North Kanara in August, in Singbhum Sept.–Oct., elsewhere with the fresh foliage in April. Coppices well, and throws up root suckers. *D. sissoides*, Grah.; Bedd. Fl. Sylv. under tab. 24 (*Iruputu*), Wainād, Palghat, Anamallays, Madura, and Tinnevelli, is a remarkable tree, smaller in size, with smaller and more numerous leaflets, fl. $\frac{1}{3}$ in. long, which requires further study. It generally flowers in July, but has also been found to flower in March. *D. emarginata*, Roxb., Fl. Ind. iii. 224, a large tree on the Andamans (probably on North Island) resembling Sissoo in habit, with obovate emarginate leaflets, fl. $\frac{1}{4}$ in. long, pure white, fragrant, in axillary panicles generally congregated at the ends of branches, identified with *D. latifolia* in Fl. Brit. Ind. will probably prove a distinct species. Prain, Journ. As. Soc. Beng. 70, 41 unites *D. sissoides* with *D. emarginata*. To this I cannot agree.

3. **D. rimosa**, Roxb.; Wight Ic. t. 262.

A small bright green tree or large, straggling sometimes climbing, shrub. Leaflets 5–9, 2–3 in. long, elliptic, acute at both ends, glabrous above, slightly pubescent beneath, secondary nerves numerous (15–20 pair), with shorter parallel intermediate ones. Fl. white, small, in short corymbose panicles, ramifications slender. Stamens 10. Pod 2–3 in. long, 1–2-seeded.

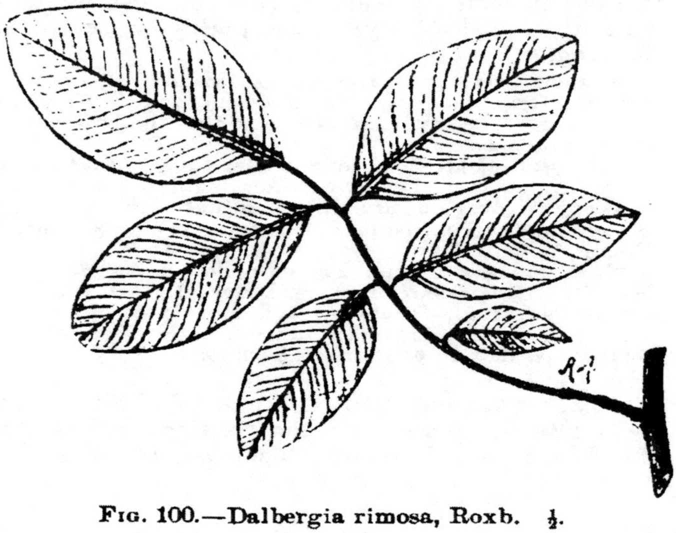

FIG. 100.—Dalbergia rimosa, Roxb. $\frac{1}{2}$.

Subhimalayan tract in Sikkim (*D. foliacea*, Gamble list 29), the Dwars, Assam, Khasi hills and Silhet. Fl. March, April. Also Tonkin, Celebes.

4. **D. foliacea,** Wall., is a large straggling or climbing shrub of Burma, similar to *D. rimosa*, but leaflets 9–13, oblong, obtuse or emarginate, quite glabrous. Fl. in ample terminal panicles.

5. **D. ovata,** Grah. Vern. *Madamā*, Burm.

A moderate-sized deciduous tree, quite glabrous, except inflorescence, which is rusty-tomentose when quite young. Leaflets 5–9, elliptic, acuminate, common petiole 3–5 in. long. Fl. white, ¼–⅓ in. long, calyx supported by an obtuse bracteole. Stamens 9. Panicles large, terminal, common peduncle flexuose, branches black divaricating. Pods oblong-lanceolate, 1–3-seeded

Lower and Upper Burma. Fl. C.S. Cochinchina. Kurz F. Fl. i. 343 separates from this *D glauca*, by obtuse mucronate leaflets. This is *D. obtusifolia*, Prain in Journ. As. Soc. Beng. vol. 70, 42.

6. **D. cultrata,** Grah.; Kurz., F. Fl. i. 342; Vern. *Yindaik*, Burm.

A deciduous tree, attaining 70 ft., with purplish black heartwood, often with lighter and darker streaks. Young shoots adpressed silky-pubescent. Leaflets 7–13, obovate-oblong, obtuse, glabrous. Fl. appearing with the fresh leaves, ⅓ in. long, white or pale pink (white, scented, Upper Burma), on pedicels as long as calyx, in unilateral paniculate racemes. Stamens 9. Pod oblong, 1–4 in. long, with 1–3 seeds.

Common in deciduous and evergreen forest of the plains and hills, Lower and Upper Burma. Dry country of the Irawaddi valley. Fl. H.S. Fr. C.S.

7. **D. Collettii,** Prain in Journ. As. Soc. Beng., vol. 66 (1898) 445. Shan hills, Upper Burma, has the branches grey-downy, leaflets 9–15, 1–2 in. long, grey-puberulous above, pubescent beneath. Fl. minute (⅙ in. long) in ample terminal panicles, pod 1–2-seeded, lanceolate on a long stalk, tapering to both ends. In Journ. As. Soc. Beng. vol. 70, 56, Prain states this is a large climber.

8. **D. burmanica,** Prain, l.c., 448. Ruby Mines district, Upper Burma, is a middle-sized tree, youngest shoots finely puberulous, leaflets 7–9, glabrous, 1½–2 in. long. Fl. purple, in short sessile brown-pubescent panicles.

B. Climbers. Stamens 9 or 10, united into a sheath split above.

9. **D. rubiginosa,** Roxb. Cor. Pl. t. 115.

A woody climber, running over the largest trees, branches stiff, divaricating, often bent and twisted, branchlets finely pubescent or softly tomentose. Common petiole rigid, 1–2½ in. long, leaflets 5–11, elliptic-oblong, obtuse, sometimes mucronate or emarginate, 1–2 in. long, upper side glabrous or finely pubescent, under side densely tomentose or silky, rarely quite glabrous. Secondary nerves not conspicuous, numerous, parallel. Fl. white, ¼ in. long, crowded in short axillary panicles, calyx brown, silky or tomentose. Pod thin, glabrous, 1½–2 in. long.

Western Ghats from Kanara to Malabar. Fl. February to May. In this I include *D. congesta*, Graham, which is pubescent, and *D. Gardneriana*, Benth., which is densely tomentose. The last form is common on the Nilgiris. Prain, l.c. 444, regards all three as separate species.

Nearly allied are 2 eastern species: 10. **D. confertiflora**, Benth. Silhet, Chittagong, Pegu, Andamans. Leaflets 11–15, 1–1½ in. long, obtuse, glabrous, fl. crowded at the ends of ramifications of ample terminal panicles. 11. **D. velutina**, Benth. Khasi hills, Burma, Malay Peninsula. Densely rusty-pubescent, leaflets glabrous at last, 13–17, oblong, 1½–2 in. long.

12. **D. rostrata**, Grah.; Prain in Journ. As. Soc. Beng. vol. 70, 45 (*D. pseudo-Sissoo*, Miq. *D. Championii*, Thw.; Fl. Brit. Ind. ii. 231). Tinnevelli, foot of Ghats, Ceylon, Malay Peninsula. Leaflets 1–5, 2–4 in. long; fl. creamy-white, pod 3–4 in., seed 1.

13. **D. Kingiana**, Prain in Journ. As. Soc. Beng. 67, 289, Kachin hills. Leaflets 5–7, coriaceous, shortly acuminate, 3 in. long.

14. **D. tamarindifolia,** Roxb.; Wight Ic. t. 242.

Deciduous, branches often twisted, branchlets and inflorescence pubescent. Leaflets 25–41, obliquely oblong ½–¾ in. long. Fl. white, in sessile compact

axillary panicles with corymbose branches. Pod thin, shining, strap-shaped, 1½–3 in. long, 1–3-seeded.

Subhimalayan tract, from Nepal eastward, ascending in Sikkim to 3,000 ft., Assam, Khasi hills, Andamans, Burma. Western Ghats from Kanara southwards. Fl. March–June. Also in the Malay Peninsula, Sumatra, Java, Borneo. Prain in Journ. As. Soc. vol. 70, 48, restricts *D. tamarindifolia* to the Eastern region. In the Western Peninsula he recognizes two species, *D. acaciæfolia*, Dalz., leaflets subcoriaceous, very oblique, glabrous above, glaucous beneath ; and *D. malabarica*, Prain, leaflets densely tomentose beneath, pod 1½ in., on a slender stalk ⅛ in. long.

15. **D. mimosoides**, Franchet ; Prain in Journ. As. Soc. Beng., vol. 70, 56. (*D. Milletti*

Fig. 101.—Dalbergia lanceolaria, Linn., leaf, pod, standard. ½.

Prain l.c. vol. 66, pt. ii. 446). Khasi hills. Yunnan, Szechuen. Leaflets not oblique, pods 1–2-seeded, thick and rugose opposite the seed. The pod figured in Wight Ic. t. 242 is supposed to belong to this species. 16. **D. multiflora**, Heyne ; Prain in Journ. As. Soc. Beng., vol. 70, 59. (*D. sympathetica* Nimmo ; Fl. Brit. Ind. ii. 234.) Deciduous forests of the Western Coast, from the Konkan southwards. Stem armed with large curved spines, branches often twisted. Leaflets 11–15 ovate or obovate-oblong, obtuse or emarginate, thinly grey silky. Pod thin, 2–3 in. long, 1–2-seeded, on a short stalk. 17. **D. coromandeliana**, Prain in Journ. As. Soc. Beng., vol. 70, 60, Shevagerry hills. A shrub ; branchlets spinous, often curved ; leaflets 7–9, glabrous, ¼–½ in. long. Pod elliptic-oblong, thin 1¼ × ½ in.

18. **D. Melanoxylon**, Guill. and Perr. (*D. Stocksii*, Benth.) of Senegambia, a small tree

with black heartwood, similar to Rosewood. Planted and run wild in Kanara. Leaflets 11–15, thin, obovate, obtuse or emarginate, ½–1 in. long. Pod thin, glabrous, mostly 1-seeded on a long slender stalk.

C. Trees. Stamens 10, in 2 bundles of 5 each.

19. **D. lanceolaria**, Linn.—Syn. *D. frondosa*, Roxb.; Wight Ic. t. 266. Vern *Tantosi*, Guj.; *Dandoshi*, Mar.

A large deciduous tree, wood white or yellowish white, without heartwood. Leaflets 11–17, 1–2 in. long, glabrous, not black when dry, ovate or obovate, obtuse, secondary nerves more distinct than the reticulate veins joining them. The 2 upper calyx teeth obtuse, the 3 lower acute. Fl. in short unilateral slightly silky racemes, these arranged in large terminal and axillary panicles, with spreading branches. Calyx brownish purple, corolla pale-pink, standard broadly-obovate. Pod 1–3-seeded.

Western Peninsula, north as far as Ajmere on the west, and Behar on the east side. Also in the Sikkim Terai. Ceylon, dry region. Fl. H.S. (August in Ceylon and the southern portion of the peninsula). A beautiful tree, when covered with fl. and young leaves.

20. **D. assamica**, Benth.; Fl. Brit. Ind. ii. 235. Vern. *Medeloa*, Assam. Fl. Nov. A tree (S.E. Peal, Prain in Journ. As. Soc. Beng., vol. 66, ii. 449). Differs from the last by finely silky pubescent leaves and short axillary flower panicles. This species (Prain) represents *D. lanceolaria* in Assam.

FIG. 102.—Dalbergia paniculata, Roxb., leaf, pod, standard. ½.

21. **D. paniculata**, Roxb. Cor. Pl. t. 114; Fl. Brit. Ind. ii. 236.—Syn. *D. nigrescens*, Kurz. Vern. *Dobin*, C.P.; *Padri*, *Pāsi*, Hind.; *Thitsanwin*, Burm. A large deciduous tree, trunk irregularly fluted, bark light grey. Wood greyish white, no heartwood, its structure most remarkable, entirely different from that of other arborescent Dalbergias. Narrow, more or less concentric bands of bast (phloëm) darker coloured, alternate with broad strata of wood; planks cut from trees fall to pieces. These bands of bast are irregularly concentric, sometimes exhibiting a spiral on a transverse section. When the stem is not circular, they are developed well on the longer and wanting on the shorter radius. Leaflets 9–13, turn black in drying, 1 in. long, pubescent along midrib, from a rounded base oblong, obtuse, often emarginate, secondary nerves not prominent, venation reticulate. Fl. blueish white, nearly sessile, crowded in short densely brown silky racemes, these arranged in compact terminal panicles. All calyx teeth acute. Disk lining the calyx tube extending to the middle of it, where petals and stamens are inserted. Standard from a narrow cordate base oblong, broader above. Pod narrowed at both ends, 1–2-seeded.

Oudh forests. Central India. Western Peninsula and Burma. Fl. April, May, with the fresh leaves.

22. **D. Kurzii**, Prain in Journ. As. Soc. Beng., vol. 66, ii. 450.—Syn. *D. purpurea*, Kurz, F. Fl. i. 344 (not of Wallich). Vern. *Thitpök*, Burm.

A large deciduous tree, with stout branchlets, perfectly glabrous, heartwood black. Leaflets 13–15, coriaceous, shortly acuminate, often nearly opposite, 2–6 in. long, common petiole to 12 in. long. Fl. appearing before the leaves, in pedunculate corymbose panicles, which are crowded at the ends of branchlets. Calyx purple, corolla white. Pod brown, distinctly veined, 1- rarely 2-seeded, 4–5 in. long, 1 in. broad.

Lower and Upper Burma, ascending to 4,000 ft. Often in Eng forest. Fl. Feb.–April.

23. **D. cana,** Grah.; Kurz, F. Fl. i. 344. Lower Burma, chiefly near streams in the hills, is distinguished by smaller more numerous, oblong-lanceolate leaflets and thin, narrow, tawny-velvety pods.

24. **D. glomeriflora,** Kurz; Fl. Brit. Ind. ii. 236. Hills of the Pegu Yoma. Young shoots tawny tomentose, leaflets 5–9, elliptic or obovate, 2–3 in. long. Fl. crowded in compact, shortly pedunculate head-like panicles, appearing before the leaves.

Fig. 108.
D. Kurzii, Prain. ½.

25. **D. sericea,** G. Don.; Prain in Journ. As. Soc. Beng., vol. 70, 51.—Syn. *D. hircina*, Benth.; Fl. Brit. Ind. ii. 236.

A small tree, with soft wood. Branchlets, petioles and inflorescence clothed with silky, grey or ferruginous tomentum. Leaflets 13–19, elliptic, obtuse, adpressed hairs on both sides. Fl. pale lilac, nearly white, in compact short axillary panicles. Pods numerous, in short panicles, small, glabrous, linear, 1–2 in. long, ¼ in. broad, 1–4-seeded.

Subhimalayan tract, from the Jumna to Sikkim. Fl. April, May.

26. **D. Oliveri,** Gamble, Prain in Journ. As. Soc. Beng., vol. 66 (1898), 451. —Syn. *D. paniculata*, Kurz, F. Fl. i. 345 (not of Roxb.). Prain l.c. vol. 70, 53. Vern. *Tamalan*, *Tabauk*, Burm.

A large tree, heartwood very tough, hard and heavy, dark red. Leaflets 10–20, glabrous, 1–1½ in. long. Fl. white, appearing with the young leaves, ¼ in. long, in large spreading terminal panicles. Calyx pubescent, edges ciliate, 4 teeth short, obtuse, that opposite the keel long linear. Pod 1–2-seeded, 3–4 by ½–1 in.

Pegu, mixed dry forest. Eng forests of Upper Burma. Fl. March, April. Smales has sent specimens from the banks of the Mu river, Upper Burma, intermediate between this and *D. assamica*. Leaflets silky pubescent, fl. white, large, in small lateral panicles. Species 20 and 26 are closely allied.

Two trees of this section in Upper Burma are: 27. **D. Hemsleyi,** Prain, and 28. **D. Fraseri,** Prain in Journ. As. Soc. Beng., vol. 66 (1898), 450, 452.

In Manipur a remarkable species of this section has been found: 29. **D. Wattii,** Clarke; Prain, l. c., 451. Leaflets nearly opposite, 4–5 pair, narrow-lanceolate, very acute, slightly pilose beneath.

D. Climbers. Stamens 10, in 2 bundles of 5 each. Pod thin.

30. **D. volubilis,** Roxb. Cor. Pl. t. 191; Fl. Brit. Ind. ii. 235. Vern. *Dauk talaung*, Burm.

A large scrambling or climbing shrub with tough wood, the branches often bent and twisted into spiral hooks. Glabrous, except inflorescence. Leaflets 9–13, elliptic or obovate, often minutely mucronate at apex, 1–2 in. long. Fl. small, crowded, pale blue, in compact, pubescent panicles. Pod 2–3 in. long, ¾ in. broad, 1- rarely 2-seeded.

Subhimalayan tract, from Kumaon eastward. Oudh forests. Central and South India. Andamans. Burma. Fl. Jan.–March.

31. **D. stipulacea,** Roxb.; Wight Ic. t. 243; Gamble list 29. Vern. *Dauktalaung,* Lower, *Thitmagyi,* Upper Burma.

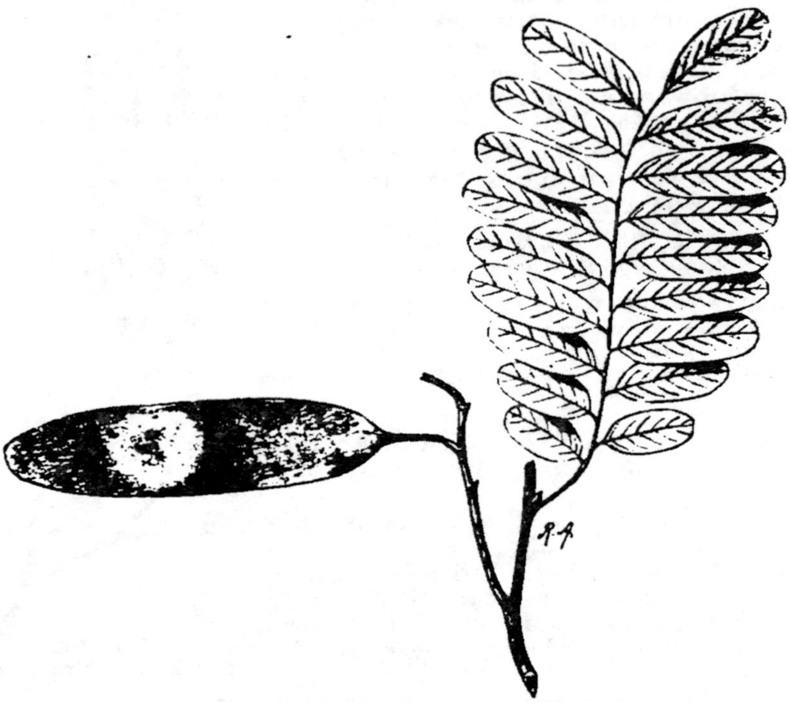

FIG. 104.—Dalbergia stipulacea, Roxb. ½.

A large climbing tree (Gamble), in open land or along streams a shrub or small bushy tree, in the interior of forests a fairly strong climber (Prain, l.c., 451), wood hard, close-grained. Leaflets 17–21, oblong, obtuse, 1–2 in. long. Fl. dull purple (pale blue, Kurz) ¼–⅓ in. long, on slender pedicels, longer than calyx, in more or less unilateral panicled racemes, bracts and bracteoles large, oblanceolate, persistent. Pod oblong, obtuse, 2–4 in. long, 1¼ in. broad, 1-seeded, thickened and more or less prominently veined opposite the seed.

Sikkim, ascending to 3,000 ft., Assam. Manipur. Chittagong. Burma. Fl. Jan.–April (August in Sikkim, Gamble). To this section belongs: 32. **D. Thomsoni,** Benth. Assam. Khasi hills. Leaflets 9–11, fl. very small.

E. Trees, shrubs or climbers. Pods broadly falcate or reniform, thick, coriaceous or almost fleshy.

33. **D. spinosa,** Roxb.; Fl. Brit. Ind. ii. 238.—Syn. *Drepanocarpus spinosus,* Kurz. Vern. *Ye-chin-ya,* Burm.

A rigid wiry scrambling shrub, with soft, silvery white wood, armed with stout divaricating branchlets, ending in pungent spines. Entirely glabrous, leaflets 7–11, often nearly opposite, obovate-oblong, ¼ to ½ in. long. Fl. yellowish white. Stamens 10, in a single sheath, sometimes in 2 separate sheaths of 5 each. Pod 1 in. long, reniform, coriaceous, 1-seeded.

Tidal forests along the coasts from Chittagong to Tenasserim, also on the coast of the Western Peninsula. Fl. May–June.

34. **D. monosperma,** Dalz.—Syn. *D. torta,* Graham; Cooke, Bombay Flora i. 397; *Drepanocarpus monospermus,* Kurz, F. Fl. i. 337.

A climbing shrub, branchlets often hooked and twisted, leaflets 5–7, obovate, obtuse, often emarginate, 1–1½ in. long. Fl. white in axillary, mostly unilateral racemes, which are often arranged in short panicles. Stamens monadelphous, pod falcate, 1-seeded.

Near the sea coast of both peninsulas; on hills as well as in mangrove-swamps and other salt marshes. Fl. June. Widely distributed over the Indian Archipelago, China and Australia. Prain in Journ. As. Soc. Beng., vol. 66 (1898), 452, prefers the older name, *D. torta*, which, however, is not based upon any description, but merely upon a number and specimens in Wallich's catalogue. In Journ. As. Soc. Beng., vol. 70, 49, it is called *D. candenatensis*, Prain.

35. **D. parviflora,** Roxb.; Prain, l.c., 452.—Syn. *Drepanocarpus Cumingii*, Kurz, F. Fl. i. 336, is a large glabrous, often spiny climber. Tenasserim, the Andamans, the Malay Peninsula and Malay Archipelago. Leaflets 5–9, 2–3 in. long, stamens monadelphous. This and allied species furnish a fragrant wood, the *Kayu-lakka* of commerce.

36. **D. reniformis,** Roxb.; Wight Ic. t. 261.—Syn. *Drepanocarpus reniformis*, Kurz, F. Fl. i. 336. Vern. *Taukma*, Burm.

A deciduous tree, branchlets rusty tomentose. Leaflets 7–11, coriaceous, ovate, acute, 1½–2 in. long. Fl. white in rusty tomentose, mostly axillary panicles. Stamens generally in 2 separate sheaths. Pod consisting of 1 or 2 reniform joints, thick, torulose, fleshy when ripe.

Assam. Silhet. Cachar. Burma. Fl. Feb. March.

19. PTEROCARPUS, Linn.; Fl. Brit. Ind. ii. 238.

Large trees, with dark-coloured heartwood. Leaflets alternate, more or less coriaceous, without stipels. Fl. yellow, in paniculate racemes, bracts and bracteoles minute, caducous. Calyx turbinate, often curved, teeth somewhat unequal. Petals exserted, with long claws, standard and wings curled. Stamens united in a single or in 2 distinct sheaths, the 10th stamen frequently free. Ovary with 2–6 ovules. Pod flat, indehiscent, more or less oblique, orbicular, ovate or falcate. Seeds 1, rarely 2 or 3. 15 species, tropics of the Old and New World.

1. **P. indicus,** Willd.; Prain in Journ. As. Soc. Bengal, vol. 66 (1898), pp. 123, 453. Vern. *Padauk*, Burm.

A large tree, generally evergreen, with reddish brown heartwood. Leaflets 5–9, glabrous, elliptic, abruptly acuminate, with a broad obtuse point, 2–3 in. long. Secondary nerves not much more prominent than the reticulate veins between them. Flowers numerous, golden-yellow, fragrant, on slender pedicels longer than calyx, in panicles at the end of branchlets, a striking contrast with the dark green shining foliage. Pod orbicular, 1–2 in. diam., silky-pubescent while young.

Often planted in Burma, believed to be indigenous in the Malay Peninsula and Archipelago. Fl. May–Aug.

2. **P. dalbergioides,** Roxb.; Wight Ic. t. 246; Prain, l.c., p. 124.—Syn. *P. indicus*, Bedd. Fl. Sylv. t. 23. *The Andaman redwood.*

A large evergreen tree, with ascending branches spreading at the ends. Differs from *P. indicus* by more numerous leaflets, which are ovate-lanceolate, acuminate, principal secondary nerves 5–8 pair, conspicuous. Pod nearly glabrous, 2 in. diam., often 2-seeded.

Common on the Andamans, where it attains a very large size. Fl. R.S. Roxburgh (Fl. Ind. iii. 236) and Prain regard these 2 species as distinct; Baker (Fl. Brit. Ind. ii. 238) and Kurz (F. Fl. i. 349) unite them. The colour of the heartwood varies from light grey to deep reddish-brown and bright red; these differences in colour, however, are not accompanied by any visible characters in leaves or flowers.

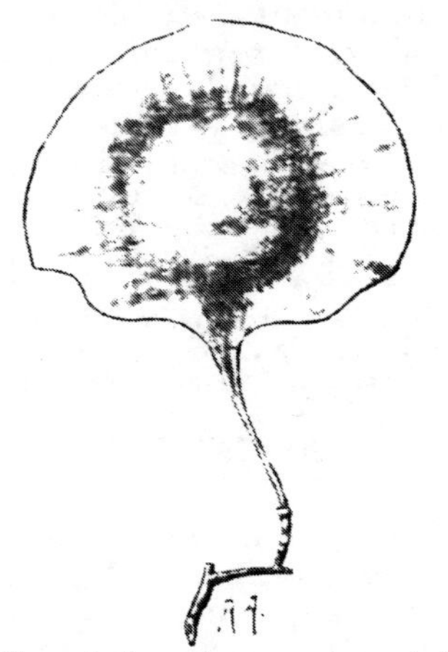

Fig. 105.—Pterocarpus dalbergioides, Roxb. ½.

3. **P. macrocarpus,** Kurz; F. Fl. i. 349. Vern. *Padauk*, Burm.

A deciduous tree, young shoots tawny-pubescent; leaflets 7–9, ovate-oblong,

mucronate, silky-pubescent beneath, as well as petiolule. Fl. yellow, in simple tawny-pubescent axillary racemes. Pod 2½–3 in. diam., velvety-pubescent.

Deciduous, evergreen and Eng forests of Upper Burma, Pegu and Tenasserim. East of the Sitang river, frequently associated with Teak (Brandis, Report on the Attaran Forests, 1860, par. 11). Fl. April, May. Species 1–3 are closely allied, and are probably only local forms.

4. **P. santalinus,** Linn. fil.; Bedd. Fl. Sylv. t. 22. *The red Sanders tree.* Vern. *Lal Chandan.*

A small tree, attaining 25 ft., with extremely hard, dark-purple heartwood. Leaflets 3, rarely 4 or 5, broad-elliptic, obtuse, 1½–3 in. long, under side pale and clothed with fine adpressed hairs. Fl. few, in short axillary or terminal racemes. Pod 1½ in. diam., oblique, gradually narrowed into a short stalk.

Dry hills of the Eastern Deccan, from the Godavery to the Palar river. Fl. July.

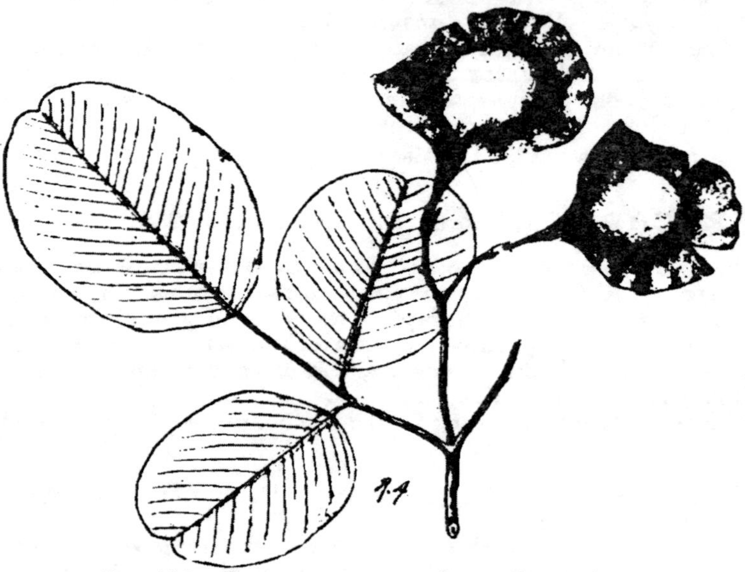

FIG. 106.—Pterocarpus santalinus, Linn. f. ½.

5. **P. Marsupium,** Roxb. Cor. Pl. t. 116; Bedd. Fl. Sylv. t. 21. Vern. *Bija Sal*, Hind.; *Hid*, Kol; *Bio*, Gujer.; *Bibla*, Mar.; *Honne*, Kan.; *Pedegu*, Tel.; *Vengai*, Tam.

A large deciduous tree, heartwood brown, with darker streaks. Leaves with soft adpressed hairs while young, dark green, shining. Leaflets 5–7, coriaceous, elliptic, obtuse, emarginate, sometimes shortly acuminate, glabrous when full grown. Secondary nerves 15–20 pair, with intermediate ones joined by prominent reticulate veins. Fl. yellow or white, pedicels much shorter than calyx, in terminal panicles. Calyx, peduncles, and pedicels clothed with dark brown hairs. Stamens monadelphous, the sheath deeply 2-fid. Pod nearly orbicular, 1½–2 in. across, often 2-seeded.

Extreme south-east corner of Kumaon. Oudh forests. Gorakhpur. Central and South India, Mount Aboo the northernmost point on the west side. Fl. July–Oct., sometimes earlier or later. Ceylon. In the bark of this and other species of this genus are sacs, filled with a red astringent oily gum, which is obtained by incisions in the bark and sold as East Indian Kino. Varies in the shape of leaflets. Prain, in Appendix to Ind. For. xxvi. 14, distinguishes two varieties: *α*, with elliptic obtuse slightly notched leaflets in the W. Peninsula and Ceylon; *β*, with acuminate l. in Central and Northern India, sometimes on the west coast of the Peninsula.

20. DERRIS, Lour.; Fl. Brit. Ind. ii. 240. (*Deguelia*, Taubert in Engler und Prantl, iii. 3, 345.)

Mostly climbers, leaves imparipinnate, leaflets opposite, without, rarely with minute stipels. Fl. white or purple, fasciculate on tumid nodes, which often are lengthened so as to form small racemes or corymbs arranged in racemiform panicles. Calyx truncate, or teeth minute. Standard generally glabrous, vexillary stamen in some instances free, filament as a rule adnate to the sheath in the middle. Pod indehiscent, narrowly winged on the upper

or on both sides. Species 40, in the tropical and subtropical regions of both hemispheres, one half in the Transgangetic peninsula. Differs from *Millettia* by the indehiscent winged pods and, in the case of some species, by the inflorescence.

A. Trees.

1. **D. robusta**, Benth.—Syn. *Dalbergia robusta*, Roxb.; Wight Ic. t. 244. Vern. *Korai*, Assam; *Thitpagan*, Burm.

A middle-sized deciduous tree, leaflets 6–13 pair, chartaceous, elliptic-oblong, 1–1½ in. long, underside pale with minute adpressed hairs. Fl. white, in slender axillary, slightly pubescent racemes, pedicels filiform, three times the length of calyx. Pod linear, minutely pubescent, 1½–3 by ½–⅓ in., upper suture winged, seeds 1–5.

Assam, Chittagong hills. Burma. Fl. H.S. A profusion of white blossoms before the leaves appear.

2. **D. dalbergioides**, Baker. Tenasserim. Upper Burma (Mu forests, Vern. *Ngayamin*, Burm., Smales). In April May covered with brilliant purple fl. Malay Penins. Leaflets 10–15 pair, 1 in. long, pale beneath, with fine adpressed hairs on both sides. Pod lanceolate, glabrous, 2–4 in. long, 1–4-seeded, a broad sharp wing on the upper suture.

B. Climbing shrubs.

3. **D. scandens**. Benth.—Syn. *Dalbergia scandens*, Roxb. Cor. Pl. t. 192; Wight Ic. t. 275. Vern. *Gonj*, Hind.; *Migyaung-nwè*, Burm.

A very large evergreen climber, often 100 ft. long; stems 3 in. diam.: leaflets coriaceous, 3–6 pair, elliptic-lanceolate, 1–2 in. long. Fl. pale rose-coloured (white in Ceylon) on slender pedicels, fasciculate on thickened nodes in slender axillary slightly pubescent racemes, much longer than leaves. Pods linear-lanceolate, 1–3 in. long, ⅓–½ in. wide, with fine silky scattered hairs, upper suture winged, seeds 1–4.

Subhimalayan tract from Oudh eastward. Assam, Chittagong, Burma, Andamans. Western Peninsula. Fl. R.S. Also in Ceylon, Malay Peninsula, China.

4. **D. uliginosa**, Benth.; Kurz, F. Fl. i. 339.

A large glabrous evergreen climber, stem 2–3 in. diam. Leaflets 1–2 pair, thinly coriaceous, broadly ovate, acuminate, 3–5 in. long, quite glabrous, polished above, no stipels. Fl. pink, ⅜ in. long, on short 3–5 fld. racemes arranged in long, slender, glabrous, raceme-like panicles. Pod glabrous, obliquely oval or almost orbicular, 1–1½ in. long, narrowly winged on the seminiferous suture, 1-seeded.

Sea-coast and tidal river

FIG. 107.—Derris scandens, Benth. ½.

banks of both peninsulas and the Andamans. Fl. C.S. Also on the coasts of Ceylon, and from Eastern Africa to Western Polynesia. The twisted stems used for cattle ropes. Nearly allied: 5. **D. elegans**, Benth. Andamans, Burma, Siam, Malay Peninsula, and Sumatra. Branchlets, underside of leaves and inflorescence clothed with long thin ferrugineous hairs, leaflets 2 pair, coriaceous, 3–8 in. long, stipels small, subulate, hairy. Fl. nearly ½ in. long, petals white with pink tips. Pod broad, generally 1-seeded.

The other climbers of this genus may be classified as follows:—

A. Pod winged on the upper suture only.

6. **D. sinuata**, Thwaites; Kurz, F. Fl. i. 340. Vern. *Myauk-gŏn-nyin*, Burm. Sea-coast of Bengal, Burma, Ceylon, Malay Peninsula and Archipelago. Leaflets 2–3 pair, glabrous, rigidly coriaceous, broad-ovate, 4–5 in. long, 2–3 in. wide. Fl. ⅜ in., in ample thyrsoid panicles. Pod coriaceous, turgid, 2–3 in. long, 1–5-seeded, contracted between seeds. 7. **D. elliptica**, Benth.—Syn. *Pongamia elliptica*, Wall. Pl. As. Rar. t. 237; Wight Ic. t. 420, Chittagong to Tenasserim, Malay Peninsula, Sumatra, Java. Young shoots, petioles, and inflorescence rusty-tomentose, leaflets 4–6 pair, 3–6 in. long. Fl. ¾ in. on few fld. pedunculate corymbs in axillary racemes, standard densely silky on back. Pod flat, thin, 2–3 in. long, sutures raised, the upper with a narrow wing. Similar in appearance to *Milletia pachycarpa*, Benth., differs by the pod and the silky standard. 8. **D. oblonga**, Benth.; Trimen Handb. p. 93, tab. 29. West coast, from the Konkan southwards, Ceylon. Glabrous, leaflets 4–6 pair, chartaceous, oblong-lanceolate or oblanceolate, 2–3 in. long, "a very ornamental climber, the white or pink fl. on short racemose panicles appearing with the young leaves, which are of the same coppery pink colour as the calyx" Trimen. 9. **D. cuneifolia**, Benth.—Syn. *D. discolor*, Benth. Outer Himalaya from Nepal eastward, ascending to 6,000 ft., Madhupur jungle, Maimansingh. Chittagong, Burma. Nearly glabrous, leaflets 3–5 pair, 3–5 in. long, pale beneath while young, with minute silky hairs chiefly beneath, chartaceous, elliptic lanceolate or oblanceolate, acute. Fl. bright red ⅓ in. long, in 2–6 fld. pedunculate umbels, on short corymbiform or racemiform axillary panicles. Pods coriaceous, 1–2-seeded, 1–2 in. long, 1 in. broad, often a narrow wing on the lower suture. From this Prain, l.c., 459 separates *D. malaccensis*, Prain, Moulmein, Malay Peninsula, with fewer but larger subcoriaceous leaflets, which are abruptly long acuminate. 10. **D. microptera**, Benth., is nearly allied to No. 9, but leaflets 2–4 pair, perfectly glabrous from the beginning, caudate-acuminate, a network of minute, very regular but not raised reticulate veins between tertiary nerves. Fl. ½ in. long, fasciculate on tumid not much produced nodes in lax drooping slender racemes 12 in. long. Pod thin, with a narrow wing on the seminal suture. (Prain, l.c. 460, describes the pod as dehiscent, consequently it should be placed under *Millettia*.)

B. Pod winged on both sutures, leaves glabrous, Western species.

11. **D. eualata**, Bedd. Ic. Pl. Ind. Or. t. 186, common in the plains of South Kanara and Malabar. Coorg, Nilgiris, Anamalais. Leaflets 3–4 pair, 2–3 in. long, fl. white, ½ in. long, in ample rusty tomentose panicles. Pod glabrous, 4–5 in. long. 12. **D. brevipes**, Baker, Western Ghats from the Konkan to the Nilgiris. Leaflets coriaceous, 3 pair, 2–3 in., fl. ⅓ in. long, in ample rusty-tomentose panicles, which generally are fasciculate at the ends of branches. Pod brown-silky, 1–2-seeded, 1–2 in. long. *D. Wightii*, Baker, and *D. ovalifolia*, Benth., probably belong to this species. 13. **D. Heyneana**, Benth. Western Ghats from North Kanara southwards. Leaflets coriaceous broadly elliptic, 2 pair, 2–3 in. long. Fl. on capillary pedicels in ample drooping panicles, with slender branches. Pod glossy, veined, 1–3-seeded, 2–4 in. long, wings broad. 14. **D. platyptera**, Baker. Plains and Ghats on the west coast, from North Kanara southwards. Leaflets 2–3 pair, rigidly coriaceous, brown when dry, shining above, pale beneath. Fl. on short racemes, in long, drooping, rusty-tomentose, racemiform panicles. Pod flat, glossy, veined, 3–5 in. long, wings broad. Stamens diadelphous (Cooke) and otherwise similar to 16, with which it may have to be united.

C. Pod winged on both sutures, Eastern species.

15. **D. ferruginea**, Benth. Dwars, Assam, Silhet, Cachar. Burma. Branchlets, inflorescence and under side of leaves rusty-tomentose, fl. white, fasciculate on slender pedicels, longer than calyx, in long drooping panicled racemes. Pod velvety while young, 2–3 in. long. 16. **D. thyrsiflora**, Benth. Assam, Khasi hills, Cachar, Andamans, Tenasserim. Also Malay Peninsula, Sumatra, Java, Borneo. Leaflets 2–4 pair, coriaceous, glabrous, as in all the following species. Fl. white on short pedicels, single, not fascicled, in ample erect thyrsoid rusty pubescent panicles; vexillary stamen free. Pod thin, glabrous, veined, 2–4 in. long, wings broad. Prain, in Journ. As. Soc. Beng., vol. 66 (1898), 99, 462, restricts this to the Malay Peninsula and Archipelago, while he includes the northern specimens from Assam to the Andamans under a new species, *D. Wallichii*, fl.

distinctly pedicelled, bracts shorter than buds. With this view I am unable to agree. This widely spread species as a rule is a big climber, but from some places it is described as a tree with spreading branches. In Journ. As. Soc. Beng., vol. 67, 288, Prain describes *D. latifolia*, Prain, a tall tree of the Kachin hills, closely allied to *D. Wallichii*, but with larger leaflets and flowers. 17. **D. marginata**, Benth.—Syn. *Dalbergia marginata*, Roxb.; Wight Ic. t. 87. Nepal, Sikkim, Khasi hills, Pegu. Leaflets 2–3 pair, pale, thinly coriaceous, 3–6 in. long, secondary nerves 6–8 pair, not prominent, joined by distinct intra-marginal veins. Network of minute but prominent raised veins between tertiary nerves. Fl. ½ in. on long capillary bracteolate pedicels, in lax drooping panicles, with slender, almost filiform ramifications. Pod straw-coloured, shining, thin, 1- rarely 2-seeded. 18. **D. polystachya**, Benth.; Prain, l.c., p. 463. Sikkim to 3,000 ft., Khasi hills. Leaflets 3 pair, elliptic, acuminate, 2–4 in. long. Fl. ⅓ in. long on 1–10 fld. short racemes, in long racemiform nodding panicles arranged in large compound terminal panicles, standard glabrous, pod thin glabrous, veined, 2-seeded. *D. secunda*, Baker, is nearly allied to this, and perhaps the same. 19. **D. andamanica**, Prain, l.c., p. 104. Andamans, Nicobars. Branchlets pale brown silky, leaflets coriaceous, 3–4 pair, 5–6 in. long. Fl. crowded on short corymbs, panicles rusty-tomentose, racemiform, several at the ends of branchlets. Pod silky. 20. **D. amœna**, Benth.—Syn. *D. Maingayana*, Baker. Tenasserim, Malay Peninsula. Glabrous, leaflets coriaceous, 3 pair, 2–4 in. long. Fl. pink or purple, ½ in. long, fasciculate on filiform pedicels longer than calyx, in long drooping racemes, forming terminal panicles.

21. PONGAMIA, Vent.; Fl. Brit. Ind. ii. 239. (*Gadelupa*, Lam.;[1] Taubert in Engler und Prantl, iii. 3, 344.)

P. glabra, Vent. The only species. Wight Ic. t. 59; Bedd. Fl. Sylv. t. 177. Vern. *Pāpar*, *Kanji*, Oudh; *Karanj*, Mar.; *Honge*, Kan.; *Kanuga*, Tel.; *Ponga*, Tam.; *Thinwin*, Burm.

A moderate-sized tree, bark soft, wood yellowish white, no heartwood. Leaves imparipinnate, glabrous, bright green, leaflets opposite, without stipels, 2–3 pair, ovate, shortly acuminate, 2–5 in. long. Fl. on slender pubescent pedicels, white and purple in axillary racemes, shorter than leaf. Stamens 10, the 10th filament free at the base, in the middle connate with the rest. Pod indehiscent, turgid, almost woody, more or less falcate, 1-seeded, 1½–2 in. long. Seed oily.

Common near banks of streams and watercourses in both Peninsulas. In Travancore ascends to 3,000 ft. Oudh forests. Here and there in the Sub-himalayan tract ascending to 2,000 ft. An oil seed of commerce. Common also in tidal and beach forests of India, Ceylon, the Malay Archipelago, extending to the coasts of South China, the Fiji islands, and tropical Australia. Prain, As. Soc. Journ. Bengal, vol. 66 (1898), 456 states that inland it only occurs planted. This does not agree with my experience.

22. ORMOSIA, Jackson; Fl. Brit. Ind. ii. 252.

Trees rarely climbers, leaves imparipinnate, leaflets opposite, mostly coriaceous. Calyx campanulate, deeply 5-cleft. Stamens free. Ovary subsessile, style filiform, incurved or circinate at the end, stigma oblique. Pod fleshy or woody, 2-valved. Species 25–30, in the tropics of both hemispheres.

1. **O. robusta**, Wight Ic. t. 245.—Syn. *Arillaria robusta*, Kurz, F. Fl. i. 334. Vern. *Kywe-tanyin*, Burm.

An evergreen tree attaining 90–100 ft., bark dark, rough, branchlets ribbed, shortly tawny-tomentose. Leaflets 4–5 pair, elliptic-oblong, acute, 3–7 in. long. Fl. dull white, in terminal rusty- or tawny-tomentose panicles. Pod nearly glabrous, bright yellow, somewhat fleshy, seeds 1, rarely 2. Seed enveloped in a red fleshy arillus.

Assam, Silhet, Chittagong. Burma. Fl. C. S. 2. **O. glauca**, Wall. Pl. As. Rar. t. 125. Nepal. Sikkim, ascending to 2,500 feet. Fl. white, in peduncled racemes shorter than the leaves. 3. **O. travancorica**. Bedd. Fl. Sylv. t. 45, Western Ghats, Kanara, Tinnevelli, and Travancore. A lofty tree, leaflets 2–3 in. long, on petiolules ¼–½ in. long. Pod thick, woody, 3 in. long, 2 in. broad. 4. **O. inopinata**, Prain in Journ. As. Soc. Beng., vol. 69, 181; and 5, **O. laxa**, Prain, l.c. 182, are trees on the Kachin hills.

[1] Eleven years later Lamarck called the tree *Pungamia*.

23. SOPHORA, Linn.; Fl. Brit. Ind. ii. 248.

Trees or shrubs with imparipinnate leaves, leaflets often alternate. Calyx oblique, stamens free or filaments connate at base, anthers versatile. Ovary shortly stipitate, ovules ∞, stigma terminal, minute. Pod moniliform, indehiscent or tardily dehiscent. Species 25, tropical and sub-tropical regions.

A. Pod without wings or ridges.

1. **S. tomentosa,** Linn.; Fl. Brit. Ind. ii. 249. Vern. *Thinbaw-magyi*, Burm.

An evergreen shrub or small tree, branches, leaves and inflorescence shortly grey-tomentose. Leaflets 11–17, thick, obliquely elliptic, obtuse. Fl. sulphur-yellow, in terminal racemes, calyx nearly truncate, teeth minute. Pod 4–6 in. long, hoary, 6–10-seeded, the seed-bearing joints often separated by long seedless stalks.

Sea coast of Burma, the Andamans, Ceylon. Fl. R. S. A littoral species, cosmopolitan within the tropics.

2. **S. glauca,** Leschen.; Wight Ic. t. 979; Spicil. Neilgh. t. 51.

A handsome shrub, branches, leaves and inflorescence clothed with persistent grey or brown tomentum. Leaflets 21–25, acute, 1–2 in. long. Fl. purple, in dense terminal racemes, calyx longer than pedicels, teeth triangular. Pod velvety, 5–6-seeded, 3–4 in. long.

Common on the Nilgiris above 6,000 ft., and on other hills of the Peninsula. Fl. throughout the year. *S. madraspatana*, described by Beddome (Manual, p. 89), from the north Arcot and Cuddapah hills, is doubtful, "leaflets 25, ½–⅜ in. long, obtuse, mucronate or retuse," would agree with *S. interrupta*, while the "villous pod" would point to *S. glauca*. Wight Ic. t. 1054, quoted by Beddome, represents the fl. of *S. glauca* and the pod of *S. interrupta*.

Other shrubs of this section are: 3. **S. Wightii,** Baker.—Syn. *S. heptaphylla*, Wight Ic. t. 1155. Belgaum, Mysore. Leaflets alternate, 11–15, lanceolate, 2–3 in. long, racemes longer than leaf, pedicels longer than calyx, corolla white or yellow, seeds red. A Ceylon species, *S. zeylanica*, Trimen Handb. Ceyl. ii. 96, t. 30 (*S. heptaphylla*, Fl. Brit. Ind. ii. 250), has smaller fl., but may prove to be the same.

4. **S. acuminata,** Benth. Nepal, Assam, Khasi hills, Burma. Leaflets nearly opposite 15–19, lanceolate, 3–4 in. long, racemes shorter than leaf, pedicels shorter than calyx. 5. **S. Bakeri,** Clarke; Prain in Journ. As. Soc. Beng., vol. 66 (1898), 466, Parasnath, Manbhum, pubescent, leaflets 11–15, tomentose beneath, corolla dark red, pod silky. 6. **S. Moorcroftiana,** Benth., a low much-branched thorny shrub of the inner arid North-West Himalaya. Branchlets and stipules spinescent, leaflets pale green, finely grey silky, ¼–⅓ in. long. Two shrubs from Upper Burma: 7. **S. Dunii,** Prain; and 8. **S. Prazeri,** Prain, l.c., p. 466.

B. Pod with 4 wings or with 4 distinct raised lines or ridges.

9. **S. mollis,** Graham.—Syn. *Edwardsia mollis*, Royle Ill. t. 32.

Leaflets 20–30, alternate or opposite, elliptic, ½–1 in. long. Fl. bright yellow in axillary racemes, generally appearing before or with the leaves. Pod glabrous, 3–4 in. long, 5–6-seeded, the joints with 4 crustaceous undulated wings.

Trans-Indus. Salt range. N.-W. Himalaya as far as Kumaun, ascending to 6,000 ft. Fl. March, April.

Other shrubs of this section are: 10. **S. interrupta,** Bedd. Ic. Pl. Ind. Or. t. 165. Pachmarhi, Central Prov., hills of the Deccan. Leaflets 18–28, ¾–1½ in. long, obtuse or emarginate. Pod nearly glabrous, with 4 membranous wings. 11. **S. Griffithii,** Stocks. Beluchistan, Quetta valley, and Juniper tracts of Ziarat, 7,000–10,000 ft. Afghanistan, Persia. Often gregarious, the large bright yellow flowers appearing shortly before or with the leaves; branches, leaves, and inflorescence clothed with soft silvery grey velvet. Leaflets 20–24, ½–¾ in. long. Pods silky, the joints with 4 narrow crenated ridges.

Calpurnia aurea, Baker.—Syn. *Virgilia aurea*, Lam.; Wight Ill. t. 81 (78), is a large shrub. Nilgiris, hills of Salem and Tinnevelli. Leaves imparipinnate, leaflets membranous, nearly opposite, 6–10 pair. Fl. large, yellow. Pod flat, membranous, indehiscent, 3–4 in. long, 5–6-seeded.

SECOND SUB-ORDER, **CÆSALPINIEÆ.**

Trees, shrubs, climbers, rarely herbs. L. pinnate, pari-bipinnate, rarely unifoliolate. Fl. bisexual, often zygomorphic. Calyx of 5 more or less connate sepals, often lined in their lower portion by a disk, which bears petals and stamens. Petals 5 or less, imbricate in bud, the posterior (upper) petal inside. Stamens 10 or fewer, rarely numerous, free or more or less connate. Seeds with or without albumen, radicle straight.

Most trees of this Sub-Order have a distinct dark-coloured heart wood, the chief exception being the arborescent *Bauhinias*. Some genera (*Hardwickia, Copaifera, Trachylobium* and *Hymenæa*) have cavities in the wood filled with gum-resin, the walls lined by a stratum of thin walled secreting cells. The climbing *Bauhinias* have an anomalous structure.

A. L. bipinnate.
- I. Calyx 5-cleft to base or nearly so, segments imbricate, stamens 10.
  - Pod not winged . . . . 1. CÆSALPINIA.
  - Pod winged on both sutures . . . . . 2. PELTOPHORUM.
  - Pod winged on one suture only . . . . . 3. MEZONEURUM.
  - Pod with a large terminal wing, 1-seeded, indehiscent . . . . 4. PTEROLOBIUM.
- II. Calyx 5-cleft to base, segments narrow, valvate or slightly overlapping.
  - Common petiole long; petals orbicular, nearly equal; pod flat . . . . 5. POINCIANA.
  - Common petiole long; petals very unequal; pod turgid . . . . COLVILLEA (p. 249).
  - Common petiole short, leaflets sinuate; pod turgid . . . . PARKINSONIA (p. 249).
- III. Calyx campanulate. Fl. in dense spikes.
  - A prickly climber. Stamens 10 . . . . . 6. WAGATEA.
  - A large tree. Stamens 5 . . . . . . 7. ACROCARPUS.

B. L. pinnate, usually paripinnate.
- I. Petals none.
  - Perfect stamens 10 . . . . 8. HARDWICKIA.
  - Perfect stamens 2–8, long exserted. Leaflets opposite . . . . 9. SARACA.
  - Perfect stamens 2. Leaflets alternate . . . DIALIUM (p. 251).
- II. Petal 1.
  - Stamens 3–8. L. papery. Pod flat, subindehiscent . . . . 10. AFZELIA.
  - Stamens 7. L. papery. Pod dehiscent, valves woody . . . . 11. PAHUDIA.
  - Stamens 10. L. coriaceous. Pod dehiscent, valves thick coriaceous, echinate . . . . SINDORA (p. 252).
- III. Petals 3 or 5, nearly equal. Perfect stamens 5 . 12. HUMBOLDTIA.
- IV. Petals 3, unequal.
  - Stamens 10 . . . . AMHERSTIA (p. 252).
  - Stamens 3 . . . . 13. TAMARINDUS.
- V. Petals 5.
  - Stamens unequal and partly imperfect . . . 14. CASSIA.
  - Stamens perfect, equal, usually 10 . . . 15. CYNOMETRA.

C. Leaflets 2, as a rule connate . . . . 16. BAUHINIA.

1. **CÆSALPINIA,** Linn.; Fl. Brit. Ind. ii. 254.

Trees, shrubs or woody prickly climbers. Fl. white, yellow or red. Calyx lobes 5, imbricate, the lowest outside and often larger. Petals 5, nearly equal, Stamens 10, free; anthers uniform, dehiscing longitudinally. Pod compressed. coriaceous.

A. Face of pods armed with sharp prickles.

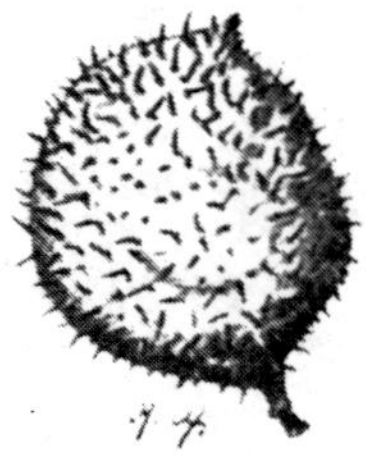

Fig. 108. Cæsalpinia Bonducella, Fleming. Fr. ½.

1. **C. Bonducella,** Fleming; Prain in Journ. As. Soc. Beng. 66, 226.—Syn. *C. Bonduca*, Kurz F. Fl. i. 406. *The Fever nut.* Vern. *Kanja*, *Karanju*, *Kath Karanj*, Hind.; *Nata*, Sundrib.; *Bagni*, Sonth.; *Sagargota*, Mar.; *Gatsakai*, Tel.; *Gazzaja*, Kan.; *Gajji*, Tam.; *Kalein*, Burm.

A large prickly scandent or straggling shrub. L. pubescent, pinnæ 6–8 pair, leaflets opposite, mucronate, 6–10 pair. Stipules cut into large segments. Fl. yellow, in axillary many-fld. racemes, bracts linear-lanceolate, spreading, longer than buds; filaments rusty-tomentose. Pod coriaceous, obliquely elliptic, 2–3 by 1½–2 in. Seeds 2–3, lead-coloured, shining.

Naturalized throughout India, to 2,500 ft. in Kumaon. Indigenous in the Sundriban, in Burma and on the Andamans. Fl. R. S. A good hedge plant.—Ceylon. On the sea coast in the Malay Archipelago and other tropical countries. 2. Closely allied, united with it by Wight & Arn. **C. Bonduc,** Roxb., naturalized in the Western Peninsula. L. nearly glabrous, no stipules, bracts erect. 3. **C. Minax,** Hance, *var. burmanica*, Prain, Fort Stedman and Saga, South Shan States, Upper Burma. (*C. Minax* is a Chinese species.) A diffuse shrub. Branches at first downy, afterwards glabrous; pinnæ 10–12. Leaflets 6–10 pair. Stipules subulate, rigid, 2–3-fid. Fl. white, in long peduncled racemes, which are sparingly branched near base; bracts very large, enveloping the young fl. Pod 4 by 2 in., with pubescent bristles.

B. Pods unarmed, dry, finally dehiscent.

4. **C. Sappan,** Linn.; Bedd. Manual t. 13. Vern. *Bakam*, Hind.; *Bakapu*, Tel.; *Pattanga*, Kan.; *Patunga*, *Sappangu*, Tam.; *Teinnyet*, Burm.

A small or middle-sized thorny tree, heart-wood red, yields a valuable dye. L. nearly glabrous; pinnæ 10–13 pair. Leaflets obtuse, very oblique, 10–20 pair. Fl. yellow, filaments woolly at base. Pods thick, polished, obovate, obliquely truncate, cuspidate. Seeds 3–4.

Chittagong. Pegu, Tenasserim. Shan Plateau. Hills east of Bhamo. Planted in the Western Peninsula, common in hedges and run wild. Fl. R. S.—Malay Peninsula and Archipelago.

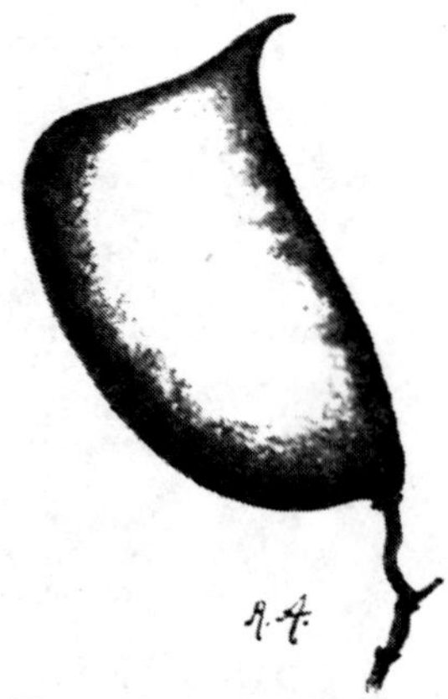

Fig. 109.—Cæsalpinia Sappan, Linn. Fr. ½.

5. **C. Nuga,** Ait.—Syn. *C. paniculata*, Roxb. Vern. *Sugauk*, Burm.; *Netu*, *Shingri-lota*, Sundrib.

A large scandent prickly shrub, glabrous, filaments densely woolly in the lower half. Pinnæ 2–5 pair. Leaflets 2–3 pair, 1–2 in. long, coriaceous, glossy above, pale beneath. Pod coriaceous, elliptic, pointed at both ends, 2 in. long, 1-seeded.

Silhet, Sundriban, Chittagong, Lower Burma, Andamans, Western Peninsula, chiefly along the coast, but also inland. Fl. May–October.—Ceylon, Malay Peninsula and Archipelago, Queensland.

6. **C. sepiaria,** Roxb. *The Mysore thorn.* Vern. *Relan*, *Karūr*, Pb.; *Aila*, Hind.; *Gilo*, Uriya; *Chillari*, Mar.; *Kurutu-gajjika*, Kan.; *Sukyanbo*, Burm.

A scrambling pubescent shrub, forming dense hedges. Pinnæ 6–10, leaflets 6–9 pair, oblong, obtuse. Stipules semi-sagittate, deciduous. Fl. bright yellow, on long pedicels. Stamens slightly longer than petals, filaments densely woolly in the lower half. Pod glabrous, obliquely oblong, cuspidate, 2–3 in. long. Seeds 4–8.

Indigenous and naturalized throughout India and Burma, ascending to 5,000 ft. in Jaunsar. Fl. February-June. An excellent hedge plant. Ceylon, Malay Archipelago. 7. **C. mimosoides**, Lam. Western Peninsula, Burma. Densely clothed with prickles, bristles and glandular hairs, pinnæ 10-30, leaflets 10-20 pair. Pod falcate, turgid, 1-2 in. long.

8. **C. pulcherrima**, Sw.—Syn. *Poinciana pulcherrima*, Linn.

A large, glabrous shrub, armed with a few scattered prickles. Fl. large, orange or bright yellow, pedicels more than twice the length of fl. Filaments nearly glabrous, twice the length of petals. Pods nearly straight, linear oblong, flat.

Commonly planted in gardens and villages throughout India and Burma. Fl. nearly at all seasons. Home unknown, has been found, apparently wild, by T. H. Aplin, in December 1887, in the Tapel Choung valley, Shan States, 1,700-5,000 ft.

FIG. 110.—Cæsalpinia sepiaria, Roxb. Fr. $\frac{1}{2}$.

C. Pods unarmed, rather fleshy, indehiscent, the sutures much thickened.

9. **C. digyna**, Rottler; Kurz F. Fl. i. 407. Vern. *Su-let-thi*, Burm.

A large scandent, sparingly prickly shrub. Branches glabrous or slightly downy, pinnæ 5-9 pair. Leaflets obtuse, pale beneath, 8-10 pair, $\frac{1}{4}$-$\frac{1}{2}$ in. long. Fl. in simple axillary racemes, 8-12 in. long; pedicels slender, 1 in. long; petals orbicular yellow, the upper streaked with red; filaments densely woolly in the lower half. Pod oblong, turgid, $1\frac{1}{4}$-2 in. long. Seeds 2-4.

Assam, Bengal, Chittagong, Burma, Upper and Lower. Sambalpur, C. P. (Griffith), Western Peninsula. Fl. July-October.—Ceylon, Malay Peninsula and Archipelago. The pods are supposed to be as valuable for tanning as those of *C. coriaria*, Willdenow, an unarmed tree of the West Indies and Central America, the Divi-divi of commerce. 10. **C. microphylla**, Ham.; Prain in Journ. As. Soc. Beng., vol. 66 (1898), 471. (*C. cinclidocarpa*, Fl. Brit. Ind. ii. 471.) Sikkim, Western Bhutan, Assam, Silhet. Pinnæ 10-12 pair. Leaflets 14-18 pair, rigid, glossy above, obliquely linear, $\frac{1}{2}$-$\frac{3}{4}$ in. long. Fl. in large compound panicles. Calyx glabrous. Pod 2-3 by 1 in. 11. **C. tortuosa**, Roxb. Tenasserim, Malay Peninsula. Differs chiefly by smaller leaflets and flowers in simple racemes.

2. PELTOPHORUM, Vogel; Fl. Brit. Ind. ii. 257.

Species 7, tropics of both hemispheres.

P. ferrugineum, Benth.; Trimen Handb. Ceylon, t. 32.

A large unarmed evergreen tree, branchlets rachis and midrib beneath ferruginous-pubescent. Leaflets opposite, obliquely-oblong, obtuse, $\frac{1}{2}$-$\frac{3}{4}$ in. long. Fl. large, yellow, on erect rusty-tomentose panicles. Petals with long ferruginous hairs on back, filaments with tufts of silky hair at base, stigma peltate. Pod flat indehiscent, 2-4 in. long, a firm broad wing along each suture.

Andamans. Fl. May. Ceylon, Malay Peninsula and Archipelago, North Australia.

3. MEZONEURUM, Desf.; Fl. Brit. Ind. ii. 257.

Large prickly climbers. Fl. yellow, zygomorphic. Calyx oblique, segments strongly imbricate, the lowest much larger than the others and hooded in bud. Stamens 10, free, anthers uniform. Pod quite flat, with a broad papery wing along the dorsal suture. Seeds few. Species 11, tropics of the old world.

A. Pods 1-seeded. Leaflets and calyx glabrous.

1. **M. cucullatum**, W. et A. Vern. *Biskoprah*, Oudh.

A large straggling climber, stem covered with strong hooked prickles on corky tubercles. Pinnæ 2–4 pair. Leaflets thinly coriaceous, shining, 2–5 in. long, nearly opposite, 3–4 pair. Racemes glabrous, simple or branched, often arranged in a terminal panicle. Pods 2–5 in. long.

Oudh forests. Nepal. Sikkim, ascending to 5,000 ft. Khasi hills, Chittagong. Andamans. Burma. Plains of Bengal. Behar. Moist evergreen forests of the Konkan and North Kanara. Fl. Sept.–Febr. Yunnan. Malay Archipelago.

B. Pods several-seeded. Leaflets and calyx glabrous.

2. **M. enneaphyllum**, W. et A.; Prain in Journ. As. Soc. Bengal, 66 (1898), 472.

FIG. 111.—Mezoneurum enneaphyllum, W. et A. Fr. $\frac{1}{2}$.

A large climbing shrub, prickles sharp curved. Pinnæ 6–11 pair. Leaflets opposite, 9–11 pair, membranous oblong, $\frac{1}{2}$ in. long. Pods red while young, 4–8 by $1\frac{1}{4}$–2 in.

Cachar, Chittagong, Andamans, Pegu. Fl. R. S.—Java. This probably is *M. glabrum*, Kurz F. Fl. i. 409. 3. **M. furfuraceum**, Prain l.c. 471, Pegu. Attaran forests (Tenasserim), is supposed to differ by less numerous alternate leaflets. 4. **M. andamanicum**, Prain l.c. 234. Andamans, common. Pinnæ 2–5 pair. Leaflets alternate, $\frac{1}{2}$–$1\frac{1}{2}$ in. long, sometimes obovate and narrowed into a short petiole, 4–5 pair. Panicle large terminal, composed of long unbranched racemes, the lower in the leaf axils. Calyx leathery. Petals yellow with red blotches and veins. Pod 5 by 1–$1\frac{1}{2}$ in.

C. Pods several-seeded. Leaflets and calyx pubescent.

5, **M. hymenocarpum**, W. et A.; Prain l.c. 233 (*M. pubescens*, Baker in Fl. Brit. Ind. ii. 259). Upper Burma as far south as Prome. Andamans, very common. Ceylon. Leaflets alternate or nearly opposite, 5–7 pair, obovate, $\frac{1}{2}$–1 in. long. Calyx leathery, pubescent. Pods thin, 4 by 1 in.

4. PTEROLOBIUM, R. Brown; Fl. Brit. Ind. ii. 259.

Large woody prickly climbers. Calyx deeply cleft, lobes imbricated, the lowest longer and more hooded than the others. Stamens 10, free, anthers uniform. Pod indehiscent with a terminal wing and one seed at the base. Species 7, of which 3 in the Indo-Malayan region, 2 in China and one each in Africa and Australia.

1. **P. indicum**, A. Rich.—Syn. *P. lacerans*, Wall.; Wight Ic. t. 196. Vern. *Korinda*, Tel.; *Karindu*, Tam.

FIG. 112. Pterolobium indicum, A. Rich. Fr. $\frac{1}{2}$.

Branchlets, common petioles of leaves and pinnæ finely pubescent, prickles numerous, sharp, curved. Pinnæ 4–8 pair. Leaflets thinly membranous, sensitive, 6–8 pair, $\frac{1}{3}$–$\frac{1}{2}$ in. long. Fl. white or yellow, $\frac{1}{3}$ in. across, in lax axillary racemes, collected near the ends of branches, pedicels slender, longer than (but less than twice as long as) calyx. Pod $1\frac{1}{2}$ in. long.

Western Peninsula, extending north to the Godavery river. Reported from Dehra Dun (Prain in Journ. As. Soc. Bengal, 66 [1898], 473), but not given in Kanjilal's Forest Flora. Fl. R. S. The following, which are closely allied to 1, are regarded by Prain as separate species: 2. **P. macropterum**, Kurz F. Fl. i. 410. Burma, Andamans. A large climber with few prickles. Pinnæ 7–10 pair. Leaflets papery, 7–10 pair. Fl. white in lax racemes, pedicels filiform, more than twice the length of calyx. Pod 2–2½ in. long. 3. **P. densiflorum**, Prain. Tenasserim (?), Malay Peninsula. Very strongly armed. Leaflets thinly coriaceous, ½ in. long. Fl. yellow, in compact racemes. Pedicels as long as or shorter than calyx. Pod 2 in. long.

5. POINCIANA, Linn.; Fl. Brit. Ind. ii. 260.

Unarmed trees. Fl. large, in corymbose racemes. Calyx segments nearly equal, oblanceolate, valvate. Petals clawed, spreading. Stamens 10, free, long exserted. Pod flat, thin. Seeds numerous.

1. **P. elata,** Linn.; Bedd. Fl. Sylv. t. 178. Vern. *Nirangi*, Kan.; *Sunkeswar*, Tel.; *Padenarayan*, Tam.

Attains 20–30 ft. Pinnæ 2–8 pair. Leaflets linear, ⅓ in. long, 10–20 pair. Corymbs few-fld. Petals four white, one greenish-yellow, all turning orange when fading. Stamens and style more than twice the length of petals. Pod 6–8 in. long, supported by persistent calyx.

Doubtfully indigenous in the Western Peninsula, cultivated throughout India. Fl. Aug.–March. Arabia, Abyssinia. 2. **P. regia,** Bojer, a native of Madagascar, is commonly grown in gardens (north-west as far as the Jumna) on account of its splendid scarlet fl. in large erect panicles.

Colvillea racemosa, Bojer, also a native of Madagascar, is a great ornament of Indian gardens, with its bright scarlet flowers in long compact cylindrical racemes.

Parkinsonia aculeata, Linn.; Bedd. Manual t. xiii. (*Vilayati Kikar*, Pb.) A large shrub or small tree, indigenous in tropical America, cultivated in most tropical countries, naturalized in India, where it is grown chiefly as a hedge plant in the drier districts. L. bipinnate, common petiole short, thick, ending in a stout sharp spine, often with a pair of stipulary thorns at its base. Pinnæ 2–4 pair, flat, coriaceous, 6–12 in. long. Leaflets pinnate, sometimes none. Fl. yellow, in lax axillary racemes. Calyx segments nearly equal, distinct almost to the base. Petals equal. Stamens free, filaments pilose at base. Pod linear, 3–6 in. long, contracted between the albuminous seeds.

6. WAGATEA, Dalz.; Fl. Brit. Ind. ii. 260.

W. spicata, Dalz. (the only species). Wight Ic. t. 1895. Vern. *Wagati*, Mar.

A woody climber, with long trailing, prickly branches. Pinnæ 8–12 pair. Leaflets glabrous, elliptic-oblong, 1–2 in. long. Fl. nearly sessile, in long dense spikes, bright scarlet on a thick, furrowed brown-velvety rachis. Calyx scarlet, campanulate, segments 5, the lowest much longer than the others. Petals 5, equal, oblanceolate, inserted with the stamens on the edge of the disk lining the calyx-tube. Pod indehiscent, 4–5-seeded, more or less constricted between seeds.

West side of the Peninsula, common in dry and moist forests. Fl. C. S. Fr. H. S.

7. ACROCARPUS, W. et A.; Fl. Brit. Ind. ii. 292.

Species 2, one in the Malay Archipelago.

A. fraxinifolius, Wight Ic. t. 254; Bedd. Fl. Sylv. t. 44. Vern. *Mandania*, Nep.; *Handige*, *Havalige*, Kan.; *Malaikonnai*, Tam.; *Karingodi*, Mal.; *Yetama*, Burm.

A lofty deciduous tree, stem tall, often with large buttresses, heart-wood dark red, moderately hard, not heavy. Young shoots bright yellow tomentose. Pinnæ 3–4 pair. Leaflets 5–6 pair, elliptic-lanceolate, 3–4 in. long. Fl. dull red or orange, nodding, on short pedicels, in dense erect racemes. Calyx campanulate, teeth 5, equal. Petals equal, slightly imbricate in bud. Stamens 5, long exserted, anthers uniform versatile. Pod stalked, thin, flat, with numerous seeds. (On account of the petals being only slightly imbricate, nearly valvate, sometimes placed under *Mimoseæ*.)

Sikkim, ascending to 4,000 ft., Western Dwars, Assam, Chittagong. Pegu Yoma, Upper Burma. Western Ghats from South Kanara southwards, ascending to 4,000 ft. Nilgiri, Anamalai and Palni hills. Fl. Dec.–Febr., with or before the young foliage, which is red. A supposed second species of the Ind. Archip. possibly is a *Mezoneurum*.

8. HARDWICKIA, Roxb.; Fl. Brit. Ind. ii. 270.

Erect unarmed trees. Leaflets few, coriaceous. Fl. small, bisexual, in panicled racemes. Sepals petaloid, usually 5 rarely 4. Petals none. Stamens twice the number of sepals, anthers short, versatile. Ovary with 1 or 2 ovules. Pod dry. Seed 1, exalbuminous. Species 3, one in Africa.

1. **H. binata**, Roxb. Cor. Pl. t. 209; Bedd. Fl. Sylv. t. 26. Vern. *Anjan*, Hind. Mar.; *Yepi, Naryepi*, Tel.; *Acha*, Tam.; *Kamara, Karachi*, Kan.

FIG. 118.—Hardwickia binata, Roxb. L. Fr. ½.

A large gregarious tree. Branchlets slender, drooping, heart-wood dark red, extremely hard. Leaflets 2, obtuse, obliquely ovate to trapezoid with 4–5 arcuate longitudinal nerves. Fl. greenish-yellow. Racemes lax, in ample axillary and terminal panicles. Pod flat, coriaceous, oblong-lanceolate, with parallel longitudinal veins, the seed near the end.

Gregarious but local in patches, in the drier districts of the Western Peninsula, south of the Soane river. Fl. R. S. Fr. C. S. Seedlings make a tap root up to 8 ft. long, and probably longer, to reach a moist underground stratum.

2. **H. pinnata**, Roxb. Fl. Ind. ii. 423; Bedd. Fl. Sylv. t. 255. Vern. *Madayan Sampirani*, Tam.; *Koda pala*, Mal.

A large tree, heart-wood brown. Leaflets 4–6, alternate, coriaceous, ovate to ovate-lanceolate, 2–4 in. long. Sec. n. numerous. Fl. minute, in dense cylindric, panicled racemes. Pod turgid, indehiscent, almost woody, 1–1½ in. long, the seed in the upper part.

Evergreen forests of the Western Ghats from South Kanara to Travancore. Fl. C. S. A balsam exudes when the heart-wood is tapped. Several species of *Copaifera*, an allied genus of South America, yield the Copaiva Balsam in a similar manner. A wedge is cut out of the trunk near the base nearly to the heart, when the balsam flows in abundance. Copal also collects in the ground near the roots of several allied trees; among others of *Hymenæa Courbaril* in Guiana, which yields the Locust Gum, and *Trachylobium Hornemannianum*, one of the species which yield the African Copal.

9. SARACA, Linn.; Fl. Brit. Ind. ii. 271.

Erect unarmed trees. Stipules intrapetiolar, more or less united. Fl. in panicles with coloured bracts and bracteoles. Calyx-tube long, funnel-shaped, limb 4-cleft, petaloid. Petals none. Stamens 2–8, exserted, oblong, versatile, anthers on long slender filaments. Pod flat, dehiscent, coriaceous. Seeds exalbuminous. Species 16, India and Malay Archipelago.

A. Bracteoles persistent.

1. **S. indica**, Linn.; Bedd. Fl. Sylv. t. 57.—Syn. *Jonesia Asoca*, Roxb.;

Wight Ic. t. 206. Vern. *Ashok*, Hind.; *Jasunda*, Mar.; *Asoka*, Tam.; *Thawka*, Burm.

Evergreen. Young shoots drooping and coloured. Leaflets 3–6 pair. Fl. in dense corymbs, 3–4 in. diam., orange on expanding, gradually changing to scarlet. Peduncles and pedicels glabrous, coloured, bracteoles persistent, $\frac{1}{8}$ in. Calyx-tube $\frac{1}{2}$ in. long, twice the length of lobes. Perfect stamens 7–8. Pod 6–10 by 2 in., valves hard, reticulate.

Khasi hills, Arakan, Tenasserim. Western Peninsula, Northern Circars and in evergreen forests of the Konkan and Kanara. Frequently planted, chiefly near temples, in India and Burma. Fl. H. S.—Ceylon. 2. **S. zollingeriana,** Miq. Martaban, Java. Leaflets 3 pair, less rigid than in 1, corymbs dense 2–3 in. broad, pedicels glabrous, very slender. Calyx-lobes less than $\frac{1}{8}$ length of tube. Perfect stamens 7. 3. **S. Griffithiana,** Prain in Journ. As. Soc. Beng., 66 (1898), 491. Upper Burma. Leaflets 4–6 pair, corymbs dense 3–4 in. broad, peduncles and pedicels pubescent. Sepals half the length of calyx-tube. Perfect stamens usually 4. Species 2 and 3 not seen, closely allied to 1. 4. **S. triandra,** Baker. Mergui, Malay Peninsula, Sumatra. A small tree, with long slender, often scandent branches. Leaflets 5–12 in. long, 2–3 pair. Fl. rich orange-yellow, in lax fascicled pubescent corymbs 5–8 in. long, axillary or above the scars of fallen leaves. Bracteoles $\frac{1}{4}$ in. long, spreading. Calyx-tube slender, about as long as lobes.

B. Bracteoles caducous.

5. **S. Lobbiana,** Baker. Tenasserim, attains 40 ft. Leaflets membranous, 6–12 in. long, 5–6 pair. Fl. yellow, changing to red, in glabrous panicles on the old wood, bracteoles oblong-spathulate, $\frac{1}{2}$ in. long, falling before the fl. expand. Calyx-lobes half the length of tube. Pod 12 by $2\frac{1}{4}$ in.

Dialium, sp. nova, is a splendid tree of the evergreen forests of South Travancore 1,000–2,000 ft., timber very hard (Bourdillon, July 1899, in fl.). L. imparipinnate, leaflets 11 alternate, thinly coriaceous, glabrous, ovate, caudate-acuminate. Fl. in axillary fulvous-pubescent panicles. Sepals 5, widely imbricate, fulvous-pubescent outside. Petals 0. Stamens 2, anthers large, extrorse, on short filaments. Ovary oblique, densely hairy, ovules 2. Fr. unknown, hence cannot be named. Nearly allied to *D. ovoideum*, Thw., Bedd. Fl. Sylv. t. 181, of Ceylon (cf. Prain in Journ. As. Soc. Beng., 66 [1898], 483).

10. AFZELIA, Smith; Fl. Brit. Ind. ii. 274 (*Intsia*, Thouars; Taubert in Engler u. Prantl iii. 3. 140).

Erect unarmed trees. L. glabrous, paripinnate. Fl. numerous, in terminal corymbose panicles. Calyx-tube cylindrical, lobes 4, much imbricated, slightly unequal. Petal one, orbicular, with a distinct claw, the others rudimentary or wanting. Perfect stamens 3, filaments nearly free, long, pilose, anthers small, oblong. Pod hard, thick, compressed. Seeds separated by transverse spongy dissepiments, generally with a cup-shaped arillus. Albumen 0. Species 10–12, tropical Asia and Africa.

1. **A. bijuga,** A. Gray. Andamans, common near the coast. Littoral from the Mascarene Islands to Polynesia. Attains 50 ft. Heart-wood reddish-brown, close grained. Leaflets 2 pair. Panicles and calyx pubescent. Petals $\frac{1}{4}$ in. long, white or pink, filaments pink. Pod 6–8 by 2–3 in., thickly coriaceous. Seeds orbicular. *A. retusa*, Kurz. Sundriban (*Bhiala, Shundal*), Andamans, Malay Peninsula. Fl. in glabrous racemes, probably is not specifically distinct.

2. **A. palembanica,** Baker (*A. bijuga*, Kurz F. Fl. i. 412). Andamans, Malay Peninsula, Siam. *Mirbow*, Malay, timber much prized. A tall tree. Leaflets bright green, very glossy, 4 pair. Panicles and calyx pubescent. Fl. green. Stamens dark claret-coloured. Pod almost woody, 10–12 by 2–3 in. Seeds broadly oblong, $1\frac{1}{4}$ by 1 in.

11. PAHUDIA, Miq.; Prain in Ann. Bot. Gard. Calc. ix. 34.

Unarmed trees. L. paripinnate. Fl. racemose, racemes frequently panicled. Calyx-lobes 4, coriaceous. Petal one, the others rudimentary. Stamens 7, filaments declinate, free in the upper part, united below in a sheath split above.

Pod 2-valved, valves woody, septate between the seeds, which are partially enclosed by a large basal arillus, albumen 0. Species 3, one in the Malay Archipelago.

1. **P. xylocarpa,** Kurz F. Fl. i. 413; Prain l.c. t. 45A. Shan hills, Upper Burma, Siam. A tall tree. Branchlets pruinose. Leaflets 2–4 pair. Pod 4–5 by 2–2½ in. Seeds 2–3, much compressed laterally, 1½ by 1 in.

2. **P. martabanica** Prain in Ind. Forester, xxvi. 312. Tenasserim, *Pyin Padauk*, Burm. A tall tree, in habit like *Pterocarpus.* Branchlets glabrous. Leaflets 4 pair. Pod 8 by 3½ in. Seeds nearly cylindric, 1½ by ½ in.

Sindora siamensis, Teysm.; Kurz F. Fl. i. 413. Siam. An evergreen tree. L. paripinnate, leaflets opposite, 3 or 4 pair, obovate, 3–4 in. long. Pod broadly elliptic, strongly echinate, resembling a hedgehog, the tips of the spines glandular, exuding a sticky, rather fragrant resin.

12. HUMBOLDTIA, Vahl; Fl. Brit. Ind. ii. 273 (*Batschia*, Vahl, Taubert in Engl. u. Prantl iii. 3. 143.

Erect unarmed trees. L. paripinnate. Stipules persistent, usually peltate, consisting of 2 separate unequal parts. Fl. in axillary racemes, each fl. subtended by a pair of persistent coloured bracteoles. Calyx-tube turbinate, lobes 4 or 5, equal, petaloid. Petals 3 or 5, nearly equal. Stamens 5, exserted, alternating with 5 minute staminodes, anthers versatile. Pod flat, coriaceous, dehiscent. Albumen 0. Species 1 in tropical Africa, 5 in the Western Peninsula and Ceylon.

A. Leaflets 4 pair or more.

1. **H. laurifolia,** Vahl; Wight Ic. t. 1605.

A shrub or small tree, the internodes of the younger branchlets frequently swollen, hollow, the cavities inhabited by small black ants. Leaflets 4–5 pair, rigid, acuminate, 2–4 in. long, upper portion of stipule erect, 1½ in. long, ovate-lanceolate, lower portion narrow, acute, much smaller, spreading horizontally. Racemes erect, 3–5 in. long. Fl. scented. Calyx pink. Petals white.

Malabar. Fl. June.—Ceylon. 2. **H. Vahliana,** Wight Ic. t. 1607–8. Malabar, Nilgiris, Tinnevelli. Travancore, common at low elevations near rivers. (*Atta Vanti*, Tam.; *Koratthi*, Mal.). Leaflets rigidly coriaceous, lanceolate, 4–6 in. long. Racemes short, softly tomentose. 3. **H. decurrens,** Bedd.; Hook. Ic. Pl. t. 2368. Tinnevelli and Travancore Ghats in evergreen forests (*Kunthani*, Mal.). A middle-sized or large tree. Leaflets 4–6 pair, 6–12 in. long, tomentose while young, rachis broadly winged. Racemes short, softly pubescent.

B. Leaflets 1–2 pair.

4. **H. Brunonis,** Wall. Pl. As. Rar. t. 233; Wight Ic. t. 1606. Western Ghats, from Coorg and South Kanara southwards. Leaflets 2 pair, elliptic-oblong, 4–6 in. long. Racemes peduncled, equalling or exceeding the leaves. Petals 3 orange. 5. **H. unijuga,** Bedd. Fl. Sylv. t. 183. Travancore Ghats. Leaflets 1 pair, 5–7 in. long, rigidly coriaceous. Racemes short, on the old wood or clustered at the ends of short woody branchlets. Fl. crimson.

Amherstia nobilis, Wall. Pl. As. Rar. t. 1. 2.; *Thawka*, Burm. Planted near Pungyi-kyaungs in Burma, believed to be wild near the Yunzalin river below Papoon. Young shoots drooping, glaucous purple. L. paripinnate; leaflets 6–8 pair. Fl. crimson, in long pendulous racemes, each fl. supported by 2 large lanceolate coloured bracteoles. Calyx segments 4, petaloid. Petals 3 large but unequal, 2 minute. Stamens 10, diadelphous, alternately shorter. Pod flat dehiscent, 5–7 in. long, broader at top.

13. TAMARINDUS, Linn.; Fl. Brit. Ind. ii. 273.

T. indica, Linn. (the only species). Bedd. Fl. Sylv. t. 184. Vern. *Amli, Imli*, Hind.; *Chinch, Chitz*, Mar.; *Koya, Tentuli*, Uriya; *Chita, Hitta*, Gond.; *Chinta*, Tel.; *Puli*, Tam.; *Magyi*, Burm.

A large unarmed tree. Leaflets 10–15 pair. Racemes lax, with 10–15 fl. Calyx-tube turbinate, segments 4. Petals 3, unequal, variegated with red and yellow, the 2 lower reduced to scales. Perfect stamens 3, filaments united to the middle, anthers oblong, versatile. Ovary stipitate, the stalk adnate to calyx-tube. Pod thick, filled with dark brown acid pulp, traversed by fibres. Seeds brown, shining, without albumen.

Culivated throughout India and Burma. Trees are found as far as the Jhelam, but the fruit does not ripen west of Amballa. Self-sown in waste and forest lands, but not originally indigenous in India or Burma. Great Coco Island, introduced by the sea, not planted (Prain in Journ. As. Soc. Bengal, 66 [1898], 201). Cultivated and run wild in the tropics of both the New and Old World, believed to be indigenous in tropical Africa. Never leafless, foliage changes in March and April. Fl. May, June. Fr. Febr.–March.

14. CASSIA, Linn.; Fl. Brit. Ind. ii. 261.

Herbs, erect shrubs or trees. L. paripinnate. Calyx-tube very short or 0. Sepals imbricate. Petals usually broad, nearly equal. Pods flat or terete, as a rule with transverse partition walls. Seeds numerous, albuminous. Species 380, in both hemispheres, mostly tropical, a few extra-tropical.

A. The three lower stamens have long curved filaments and anthers, which open by longitudinal slits, four stamens have short filaments and anthers opening by basal pores; the rest have minute anthers without pollen. Pod cylindric, indehiscent, hard.

1. **C. Fistula,** Linn.; Brandis F. Fl. 164. *The Indian Laburnum.* Vern. *Kaniar*, *Karangal*, Pb.; *Amaltās*, Hind.; *Bahawa*, Mar.; *Sonaru*, Assam.; *Hari*, Kol; *Sonari*, Uriya; *Kakke*, *Kakkai*, Kan.; *Rela*, Tel.; *Konnai*, Tam.; *Ngu*, Burm.

A middle-sized, at times a large tree, bark greenish-grey, smooth up to middle age, sapwood large, heart-wood brick-red when fresh cut, darkening on exposure, very hard, youngest shoots silky. Leaflets glabrous when full grown, 4–8 pair, ovate, acute or shortly acuminate, blade 2–5, pet. $\frac{1}{8}$–$\frac{1}{4}$ in. long, sec. n. numerous, stipules minute. Fl. large, bright yellow, in lax long pendulous racemes, bracts minute, caducous, pedicels slender, 1$\frac{1}{2}$–2 in. long, the longer filaments not thickened in the middle. Pods cylindric, 2–3 ft. long, black, seeds in black sweet pulp.

Common in deciduous forests in most parts of India and Burma. Trans-Indus on the hills near Peshawar. Ascends to 4,000 ft. in the Outer Himalaya. Scarcely ever wholly leafless; the young leaves and fl. appear in April and May. The pulp of the ripe fr. is a strong purgative.

2. **C. nodosa,** Hamilton; Kurz F. Fl. i. 392; Wight Ic. t. 410. Vern. *Gnuthein*, Burm.

A middle-sized or large evergreen tree, the youngest shoots silky. Leaflets 6–12 pair, thinly coriaceous, glabrous and glossy above, opaque beneath, elliptic-oblong, acuminate, blade 3–4, pet. $\frac{1}{4}$ in. long, stipules narrow falcate, early deciduous. Fl. showy, pink, in erect pedunculate racemes from the scars of fallen leaves, bracts narrow-lanceolate, pubescent, persistent. Petals $\frac{3}{4}$–1 in. long, the three longer filaments with a globose thickening in the middle. Pod cylindrical, 12–18 in. long.

Silhet, Chittagong hill tract, Andamans, evergreen forests of Martaban and Upper Tenasserim. Fl. H. S. Malay Peninsula, Cochinchina, Borneo.

3. **C. marginata,** Roxb.—Syn. *C. Roxburghii*, DC.; Wight Ill. t. 83; Bedd. Fl. Sylv. t. 180.

A small or middle-sized tree. Branchlets and young leaves silky. Leaflets 10–15 pair, membranous, glabrous above, oblong, emarginate and apiculate at apex, stipules hastate or falcate, early deciduous. Racemes axillary or from the old wood, bracts large, ovate or obovate, caducous, pedicels ½–1 in. Petals ½ in. long, longer filaments not thickened in the middle. Pod cylindric, 8–12 in. long.

Hills of the Karnatik, Courtallum, Tinnevelli. Deciduous forest, low country of Travancore.

4. **C. renigera,** Wall.; Kurz F. Fl. i. 392. Vern. *Ngushwe*, Lower, *Pwabet*, Upper Burma.

A small or middle-sized deciduous tree, softly tomentose. Leaflets 8–20 pair, oblong, obtuse, 1–2 in. long, membranous, softly pubescent on both sides, stipules large, reniform, early deciduous, tips shortly cuspidate. Racemes short, erect, from the old wood, often leaf-bearing at the base, bracts large, persistent, ovate, long acuminate, pedicels 1½–2 in. Fl. scented, pink or yellow. Sepals and petals silky, with long hairs on both sides. Petals elliptic-oblong, ⅔–1 in. long, the three longer filaments with a more or less cylindric thickening in the middle, the larger anthers more or less hairy on the back. Pod cylindric, 15–18 in. long.

Irawaddi valley from Prome upwards. Shan hills at 3,000 ft. Fl. April, May.

B. Seven stamens perfect, anthers nearly equal. Pod flat.

5. **C. siamea,** Lam.—Syn. *C. florida*, Vahl; Bedd. Fl. Sylv. t. 179. Vern. *Mézali*, Burm.

A middle-sized, sometimes a large tree, bark grey, nearly smooth. Leaflets 6–10 pair, chartaceous, elliptic-oblong, tipped with a minute sharp mucro, glabrous on both sides, 1½–2½ in. long, stipules caducous. Racemes often corymbose, arranged in a large pyramidal terminal panicle, often 2 ft. long, pedicels ½–1 in. long, bracts stiff, linear, much shorter than pedicels. Fl. yellow, petals ½ in. long. Pod flat, thickened at sutures, minutely velvety, 4–10 in. long.

Probably indigenous in Burma and in the southernmost part of the Western Peninsula. Cultivated throughout India and Burma. Fl. H. S.—Ceylon low country, chiefly in the moist region, Siam, Malay Peninsula and Archipelago.

6. **C. montana,** Heyne. A large shrub. Western Peninsula from Belgaum southwards. Leaflets 10–15 pair, glabrous, glaucous, elliptic-oblong, mucronate, stipules minute, caducous. Fl. yellow, in corymbose racemes, forming a large terminal panicle, pod thin, sutures not thickened, 3–5 in. long. 7. **C. timoriensis,** DC. (*Taung mézali*, Burm.). Burma, Ceylon, Malay Archipelago. A large shrub or small tree. Branchlets pubescent. Leaflets 10–15 pair, pubescent on both sides. Stipules foliaceous, often dentate, more or less persistent. Fl. yellow, in large terminal panicles, pod 4–6 by ½ in., sutures not thickened. According to Beddome, Talbot and Prain (Journ. As. Soc. Beng., 66. 477) also in the Western Peninsula. I have not seen specimens, and Trimen Handb. Ceylon ii. 109, says: "Not in Peninsular India."

8. **C. tomentosa,** Linn., is a tropical American shrub, naturalized in the Western Peninsula and Ceylon. Branchlets, petioles and inflorescence grey-velvety. Leaflets 6–8 pair, grey tomentose beneath. Stipules small, deciduous. Fl. bright yellow, in peduncled corymbose racemes. 9. **C. goensis,** Dalz.; Hook. Kew Journ. iv. 112. Described as a small tree at the foot of the Goa Ghats, fulvous tomentose, pod flat, 2–3 by ½ in.; may possibly be *C. timoriensis*.

10. **C. auriculata,** Linn.; Brandis F. Fl. 165. Vern. *Taroda, Tarwad*, Mar.; *Tangĕra, Tangedu*, Tel.; *Tangadi*, Kan.; *Avaram*, Tam.; *Peikthingat*, Burm.

A gregarious pubescent shrub. Leaflets 8–12 pair, elliptic-oblong, obtuse, mucronate, ½–1 in. long, with a filiform gland at the base of each pair, stipules large, foliaceous, persistent. Fl. yellow, in terminal corymbose bracteate panicles, the lowest branches in the axils of leaves, the upper supported by pairs of stipules. Sepals concave, unequal. Petals clawed, crisped on margin, ¾–1 in. long. Pod 3–4 by ⅔ in., thin, hairy.

Western Peninsula, extending north to Ajmere and the Jumna river, covering large areas in the Deccan. Dry region of the Irawaddi valley. Fl. Oct.–May. The bark is extensively used for tanning and dyeing. 11. **C. alata,** Linn.: Wight Ic. t. 253. Naturalized in India, possibly indigenous on the Andamans, found in the tropics of both hemispheres. A large shrub. Branches thick, finely downy. Leaflets 8–12 pair, oblong from an oblique base, obtuse, 2–6 in. long, sec. n. 15 pair, prominent beneath, stipules rigid, persistent, auriculate, ¼ in. long. Fl. on short pedicels in spiciform pedunculate racemes, the buds enveloped in large yellow caducous bracts. Petals bright yellow with darker veins, broad-ovate, 1¼ in. long. Pods dehiscent, rigid, 6 by ⅜ in., a crenulated longitudinal wing on each valve.

C. All stamens perfect, anthers nearly equal. Pod flat.

12. **C. glauca,** Lam.; Kurz F. Fl. i. 394.

A large shrub or small tree, nearly glabrous. Branchlets ribbed. Leaflets 4–10 pair, 1–3 in. long, erect, clavate glands at the base of the 2–3 lowest pairs. Fl. yellow, in axillary corymbose racemes. Pod thin, dehiscent, glabrous, 4–8 in. long.

Western Peninsula, extending north to Merwara, Burma. Often planted. Fl. throughout the year. Malay Peninsula and Archipelago.

15. **CYNOMETRA,** Linn.; Fl. Brit. Ind. ii. 267.

Erect unarmed trees or shrubs. Leaflets opposite, few, more or less coriaceous. Fl. small, numerous, fasciculate or in bracteate racemes, inflorescence in bud enclosed by imbricate deciduous scales. Calyx-tube very short, segments 4 or 5, oblong. Petals 5, equal. Stamens 10, rarely indefinite, anthers versatile. Ovary with 2 ovules. Pod turgid, indehiscent, with thick valves. Seed generally 1, exalbuminous, filling the cavity of the pod.

A. Stamens 10.

1. **C. ramiflora,** Linn.; Bedd. Fl. Sylv. t. 315. Vern. *Shingra, Shingar,* Sundrib.; *Myin-ka-ben,* Burm.

An evergreen tree. Leaflets 1 or 2 pair, 1–3 in. long. Fl. white, on slender finely puberulous pedicels, in small sessile corymbs, or short racemes, axillary or above the axils of fallen leaves. Ovary hairy. Pod fleshy, wrinkled, ½ in. long.

Tidal and coast forests from the Sundriban to Chittagong and Tenasserim. Andamans, Coast of Konkan and Kanara. Fl. C. S., H. S.—Ceylon, Malay Archipelago.

2. **C. Beddomei,** Prain in Journ. As. Soc. Beng., 66 (1898) 478. Western Ghats, South Kanara and Wainād. Leaflets chartaceous, 2–3 pair. Fl. in axillary fascicles, pedicels pubescent. Ovary pubescent, excepting a narrow strip below the insertion of the style. 3. **C. travancorica,** Bedd. Fl. Sylv. t. 316. Tinnevelli and Travancore ghats. A tall tree, young shoots creamy pink. Leaflets 1 pair, unequal-sided, almost falcate. Fl. in compact short axillary racemes, bud-scales straw-coloured, scarious, pedicels and ovary glabrous. 4. **C. cauliflora,** Linn.; Bedd. Fl. Sylv. t. 315 (in corner). Cultivated in gardens. Leaflets 1 pair. Fl. pink, numerous, on short racemes which are crowded on the old wood. Fr. thick, fleshy, edible, 1–2 in. long.

B. Stamens 40–60.

5. **C. polyandra,** Roxb. Cor. Pl. t. 286. Vern. *Ping,* Cachar.

A large tree. Leaf-buds enveloped in large imbricating scarious and membranous bracts. Leaflets 3 pair, 3 in. long. Fl. white, tinged with pink, ½ in. across. Petals reflexed, in axillary sessile corymbose racemes, enveloped in bud by hard striate scales, pedicels pubescent, ½–1 in. long. Pod woody, 2–3 in. long.

Khasi hills, Cachar. Fl. H. S.—Malay Peninsula.

16. **BAUHINIA,** Linn.; Fl. Brit. Ind. ii. 275.

Trees or woody climbers. Leaflets 2, united into one entire or 2-lobed palmately nerved blade, rarely distinct. Fl. more or less zygomorphic. Calyx

entirely closed in bud, tube cylindric or turbinate, lined by the disk, limb of 5 valvate segments or spathaceous, splitting on the upper side, or irregularly cleft. Petals 5, spreading, slightly unequal. Stamens 10, all or some only perfect, anthers versatile. Ovary stipitate, stalk free or adnate to the calyx-tube. Seeds numerous, compressed, with usually thin albumen. Species 150, tropics of both hemispheres.

The stem of the arborescent species has a normal structure, as far as known. That of the climbing species is irregular, but demands further study. The pith of all *Bauhinias* is believed to be cross-shaped.

A. Fertile stamens 10. Calyx spathaceous. **Erect trees or shrubs.**

1. **B. tomentosa,** Linn. Vern. *Vana Sampage*, Kan.; *Tiruvatti*, Tam.

A large shrub. L. 1–3 in. long, pubescent beneath, divided one-third down into two-rounded lobes. Fl. in pairs, on short, usually leaf-opposed peduncles, bracteoles linear. Calyx 1 in. long, shortly bifid at top, pubescent. Petals sulphur-yellow, the uppermost with a dark purple blotch at base, 1¾ in. long, not spreading, but forming a bell-shaped corolla. Pod dehiscent, finely pubescent. Seeds 8–12, small.

Western Peninsula, more common on the east side. Often cultivated near Hindu temples. Fl. Aug.–April. Ceylon dry region. Tropical Africa.

2. **B. acuminata,** Linn.—Syn. *B. candida*, Aiton. Vern. *Kachnar*, Hind.; *Mahahlega byu*, Burm.

An erect shrub. L. 3–6 in. long, longer than broad, divided one-third down into two ovate, obtuse, or triangular acute lobes, tertiary nerves conspicuous beneath. Fl. large, white, in short generally leaf-opposed racemes. Calyx spathaceous, 1–2 in. long, acuminate with 5 setaceous teeth. Petals elliptic, 1–1¾ in. long. Pod glabrous, at length dehiscent, 4–5 in. long, ½ in. broad.

Chittagong hill tracts. Andamans, Burma, Upper and Lower, common in Eng forest. (Probably not indigenous in Western India.) Often grown in gardens. Fl. Sept.–May. Malay Peninsula and Archipelago, China. 3. **B. polycarpa,** Wall.; Kurz F. Fl. i. 396. Burma, Upper and Lower. A small shrub. L. glabrous, blade 3–5, petiole slender, 1–1½ in. Fl. small, in slender leaf-opposed racemes. Petals white, ⅓ in. long. Specimens from the Pegu Yoma in high Teak forest, with larger leaves, 6 by 8 in., Prain (Journ. As. Soc. Beng. 66 [1898] 495) is disposed to regard as belonging to a distinct species.

4. **B. racemosa,** Lam.; Bedd. Fl. Sylv. t. 182. Vern. *Papri, Jhinjeri, Jhanjhora*, Hind.; *Makuna*, Oudh; *Jinja*, Rajputana; *Apta, Shiara*, Mar.; *Ari*, Tel.; *Atthi*, Tam.; *Hpalan*, Burm.

A small deciduous tree. L. 1–3 in. long, broader than long, lobes rounded. Fl. white, small, in long loose pubescent racemes. Petals ⅓–½ in. long, linear-lanceolate, unequal, filaments and anthers with long hairs. Pods thick, generally curved, 4–12 in. long, 1 in. broad.

Dry forests of both Peninsulas, in the subhimalayan tract as far north as the Ravi, ascending to 5,000 ft. in Kumaon. Old leaves shed C. S. New l. and fl. H. S. Ceylon dry region.

B. Fertile stamens 10. Calyx 5-dentate or limb of 5 segments.

5. **B. malabarica,** Roxb.; Brandis F. Fl. 159. Vern. *Amli, Imli*, Hind.; *Laba*, Kol; *Vatta Atthi*, Tam.; *Aràm Puli*, Mal.; *Bwègyin*, Burm.

A middle-sized, in moist districts a large tree, evergreen, with dark-green foliage. L. emarginate, hardly lobed, at times quite entire, 2–3 in. long, broader than long, glaucous beneath. Fl. white, small, often unisexual, ♂ and ♀ fl. on different trees in North Kanara (Talbot), pedicels long, slender, panicles corymbose. Calyx with 5 equal triangular teeth. Petals spathulate, equal. Pod 12–15 in. long, ⅔ in. broad, marked with raised wavy lines, descending from the middle to the edges of the valves.

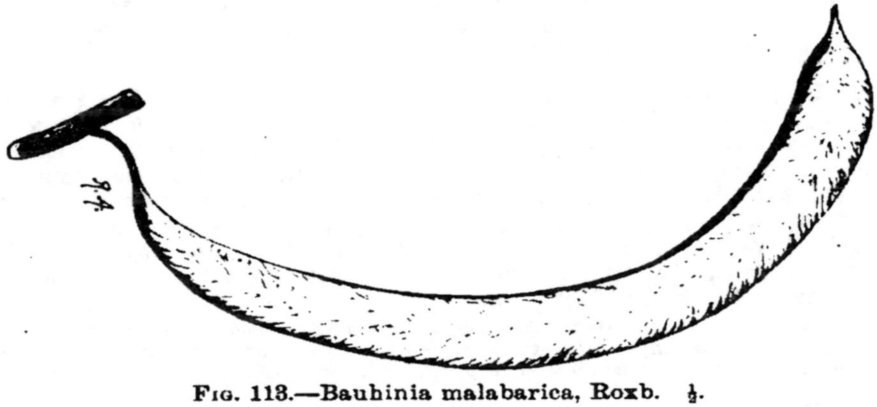

FIG. 113.—Bauhinia malabarica, Roxb. ½.

Subhimalayan tract from the Jumna eastwards, ascending to 2,000 ft. Central India, Behar, Western Peninsula, Lower Burma. Fl. Sept.–Jan. L. acid, eaten.

6. **B. tortuosa,** Coll. et Hemsl. in Journ. Linn. Soc. xxviii. (1891) t. 8. Southern Shan hills at 5,000 ft. A small tree, more or less climbing. Branchlets, petioles and underside of l. tawny-tomentose. L. shortly 2-lobed, broader than long, 1–2 in. across. Fl. in small dense racemes, on pedicels ⅛ in. long. Calyx-segments 5, spreading, obtuse. Petals spathulate, white. Stamens 10, all perfect. Ovary densely villous. Pod dehiscent, 2 by ⅓ in., obliquely acute, gradually tapering to the base. 7. **B. enigmatica,** Prain in Journ. As. Soc. Beng., 66 (1898) 496. Maymyo and Fort Stedman, Shan hills. Similar, but leaves 4 in. across. Fl. larger on slender pedicels, ½ in. long.

8. **B. foveolata, Dalzell**; Prain in Journ. As. Soc. Beng., 66 (1898) 496.—Syn. *B. Lawii*, Benth.

A tall diœcious tree. L. orbicular, shortly 2-lobed or entire, base deeply cordate, blade 5–9 in. diam., pet. 2 in. long, basal nerves 13–19, very prominent, minute pits between the closely reticulate veins on the underside. Fl. white, scented, almost sessile, in broad panicles with divaricating branches. Calyx clothed outside with a dense rust-brown felt of very minute hairs. Petals obovate. ♂ : stamens 10, all fertile, the shorter filaments epipetalous, ♀ : 10 minute staminodes. Ovary cylindric, densely clothed with long hairs, stigma broad, fleshy. Pod twisted, red-tomentose, 12 in. long.

Common in moist forests of the Konkan and North Kanara. Fl. Sept.–Oct.

9. **B. diphylla, Ham.**; Kurz F. Fl. i. 399.

A large glabrous climber. Stems 2–300 ft. long, tendrils axillary, circinnate, often forked. Leaflets quite free, 3 by 2 in. Fl. large, in loose terminal racemes, 8–12 in. long. Calyx-tube ⅔–1 in. long, segments 5, coriaceous, linear-lanceolate, 1½ in. Petals white, lanceolate, erect, as long as calyx-lobes. Stamens 10, fertile, equal. Pod flat, thin, 10–16 by 3 in., on stalk 2 in. long.

Dry region of the Irawaddi valley from Prome upwards. Fl. R. S. Specimens at Kew, collected by Stocks in the Konkan.

C. Fertile stamens 3, sometimes 4 or 5. Erect trees.

10. **B. retusa, Ham.**; Brandis F. Fl. 161. Vern. *Semla*, *Kandla*, *Kandālu*, Hind.; *Laba*, Kol; *Thaur*, Gond.; *Gondi*, Tel.

A small tree, bark grey. Branchlets long, slender, pendulous. L. entire or slightly emarginate, coriaceous, broader than long, 3–8 in. across. Fl. numerous, in pedunculate corymbose racemes, forming large terminal panicles, pedicels long, slender. Calyx-limb splitting into 2 or 3 segments. Petals clawed, hairy outside, blade orbicular, pale-yellow, marked with dark-purple veins, perfect stamens 3. Pod late dehiscing, 4–6 by 1 in., generally broader at top, seeds 6–8.

Subhimalayan tract from the Bias to Nepal, ascending to 4,500 ft., chiefly near water. Chota Nagpore, common. Central India, south to the Godavery. Fl. Sept. Oct. A gum exudes from the bark.

11. **B. purpurea**, Linn.; Brandis F. Fl. 160. Vern. *Kolār*, Pb.; *Khairwal*, *Gairāl*, *Kwillar*, *Koinar*, Hind.; *Kanchan*, Tel.; *Sarul*, *Kanchivala*, Kan.

A middle-sized tree, heart-wood brown, hard, durable. L. coriaceous, cleft about half-way down, lobes often overlapping along the inner margins. Racemes short, in terminal panicles. Fl. deep pink, sometimes white (*B. triandra*, Roxb.); pedicels bracteolate, $\frac{1}{3}$–$\frac{2}{3}$ in. Calyx-tube obconical, $\frac{1}{4}$ in. long, limb twice the length of tube, cleft to the base into two reflexed segments, one emarginate, the other 3-toothed. Petals oblanceolate. Fertile stamens 3, occasionally 4. Pod 6–12 in. long.

Subhimalayan tract, from the Indus eastwards, ascending to 5,000 ft. Assam, Khasi hills, Chittagong, Western Peninsula, in deciduous forests. Not indigenous in Burma or in Ceylon. Cultivated largely. Fl. Sept.–Nov.

12. **B. variegata**, Linn.; Kanjilal F. Fl. 139. Vern. *Kachnār*, Hind.; *Kanchan*, Mar.; *Bodantham*, *Mandari*, Tel.

A deciduous middle-sized tree, with irregular masses of dark-coloured wood near the centre. L. as long as broad, 11–15-nerved, leaflets connate beyond the middle. Fl. large, almost sessile, in short few-fld. racemes, 2 varieties, one with purple flowers (4 petals light purple, the 5th and larger deep purple), the other with white flowers (*B. candida*, Roxb.), the 5th petal variegated with yellowish-green or dark purple. Calyx-tube cylindric, as long as the ovate spathaceous 5-toothed limb. Petals obovate or oblanceolate, 2 in. long. Pod 6–10 in. long. Perfect stamens 5, rarely less.

Subhimalayan tract from the Indus eastwards. Assam, Burma, Western Peninsula. Cultivated largely. Fl. Febr.–May, generally while the tree is leafless. 13. **B. velutina**, Wall. Imperfectly known, Tavoy and Mergui. Branchlets, petioles, underside of l. and inflorescence clothed with minute, generally grey pubescence. Racemes axillary, few-fld., corymbose. Calyx-tube cylindric, 1 in. long, segments 5 linear, as long as or a little longer than tube. Petals as long as sepals, blade obovate on a long narrow claw. *B. monandra*, Kurz, is not a native of British India (Prain in Journ. As. Soc. Beng. 66 [1898] 505).

D. Fertile stamens 3, sometimes 4 or 5. Climbers.

(*a*) Fl. in dense corymbs or corymbose panicles.

14. **B. Vahlii**, Wight et Arn.; Kanjilal F. Fl. 138. Vern. *Taur*, Pb.; *Malo*, *Maljhan*, *Maurain*, *Maulein*, *Mahul*, Hind.; *Rung*, Kol; *Maljan*, *Chambal*, Mar.; *Shiali*, Uriya; *Thaur*, Gond.; *Madapu*, Tel.; *Ani padu*, *Hepparige*, Kan.

A gigantic climber, stem irregularly ridged and furrowed, often 100 ft. long and 2 ft. diam. A cross section shows numerous irregularly shaped masses of xylem, consisting mainly of large vessels, arranged in more or less concentric bands and separated by red juicy bark-like tissue, the structure of which is not yet sufficiently known. Branchlets, tendrils, petioles, underside of leaves and inflorescence clothed with dense ferruginous, rarely grey tomentum. L. deeply cordate, variable in size, often up to 18 in. diam., cleft to about one-third of their length, lobes obtuse, basal nerves 11–15, petiole stout. Tendrils axillary, often fl.-bearing, forked, bifurcations circinnate. Fl. creamy-white on long slender pedicels, in terminal corymbose racemes. Calyx-tube shorter than the 2-lobed limb. Petals densely hairy, 1–1$\frac{1}{2}$ in. long. Stamens 3. Ovary hairy. Pod flat, woody, clothed with dense brown felt, 9–18 by 2–3 in., bursting open with a loud report.

Subhimalayan tract and outer valleys ascending to 3,000 ft., from the Chenab eastwards, chiefly in Sal forests. Assam, Behar, Western Peninsula, chiefly on the west side. Fl. April–June. The most destructive climber to Sal and other trees, hence effectually exterminated in many forest tracts. Growth of climbing shoots extremely rapid. Gleadow (Ind. For. xxvi. 170) records a growth of 31 ft. in one season. Rope is made of the stem; the leaves are used as plates and made into umbrellas; the seeds are roasted and eaten. 15. **B. rufa,** Grah. (*B. Vahlii*, Kurz F. Fl. i. 401). Khasi hills, hills east of Toungoo, 2,000 ft. Tenasserim, similar to *B. Vahlii*, but calyx-tube cylindric, as long as segments of the limb.

16. **B. ornata,** Kurz (*Myaukhlega*, Burm.) A gigantic creeper. Pegu Yoma and Tenasserim. Youngest shoots rusty-tomentose, mature leaves glabrous. Fl. in dense terminal, almost globose corymbs. Calyx thinly silky, tube turbinate, segments 5, longer than tube. Stamens 3. Ovary densely rusty silky. 17. **B. glabrifolia,** Baker. Pegu, Tenasserim, Malay Peninsula, Borneo. A climber, 60–80 ft. long. L. glossy, bright green, those near the ends of branches entire, lower down cleft to one-fourth their length. Fl. small, silvery-grey, in dense corymbose bracteate panicles, bracts at the base of main branches in pairs (stipules), at the base of pedicels solitary, linear-lanceolate. Calyx grey with appressed hairs, tube shorter than the 3 segments of limb. Petals hairy, ⅛ in long, anthers 3. Ovary hairy. 18. **B. piperifolia,** Roxb. Assam, Silhet, similar, but no bracts on panicles. Fl. larger. Petals ⅓ in. long. 19. **B. Khasiana,** Baker. Assam, Khasi hills. Youngest shoots bright rusty-pubescent. L. thin, glabrous. Fl. ochreous, turning red, in large terminal corymbose panicles, and like the calyx densely clothed with bright rusty pubescence. Calyx-tube equal to the segments of limb. Petals silky, ½ in. long, claw as long as blade, anthers 3. Ovary densely silky.

(*b*) Fl. in more or less corymbose racemes.

20. **B. phœnicea,** Heyne.—Syn. *B. Benthami*, Bedd. Ic. Pl. Ind. Or. t. 107.

A gigantic climber. L. glabrous above, minutely hairy beneath. Fl. bright crimson. Calyx-tube as long as the 5 linear-lanceolate segments. Petals 1½ in. long, claw linear, as long as the ovate-lanceolate blade. Stamens 5. Pod downy, 6 by 1 in.

Common on the Ghats of South Kanara and Wainad. Coorg. Travancore in evergreen forests. Fl. Oct.–Dec. 21. **B. glauca,** Wall. Tenasserim, Malay Peninsula and Archipelago, China. Branchlets glabrous, tendrils numerous. Fl. in dense leaf-opposed and terminal corymbs. Calyx glabrous, tube nearly twice the length of the 5 lobes. Petals cream-coloured, ¾ in. long, sparsely pubescent outside, anthers 3. Ovary glabrous. Pod thin, 6–9 by 2 in. 22. **B. tenuiflora,** Watt; C. B. Clarke in Journ. Linn. Soc. xxv. t. 6. Khasi and Naga hills, Manipur. Similar to 21, but calyx-tube linear, 3–4 times the length of segments. Petals ½–⅝ in. long. 23. **B. nervosa,** Wall. Assam, Khasi hills. Youngest shoots and inflorescence thinly rusty-pubescent, tendrils numerous. Fl. in large corymbose racemes, bracts lanceolate. Calyx-tube cylindric, ¾ in. long, segments of limb 5, as long as tube. Petals 1½ in. long, densely hairy, claw as long as blade. Pod 6 by 2 in., valves thick, strongly veined. 24. **B. albo-lutea,** Prain in Journ. As. Soc. Beng., 66 (1898) 181. Pegu, Tenasserim, Nicobars. Similar to 23, but petals nearly glabrous. Prain identifies this with *B. ferruginea*, Kurz F. Fl. i. 402 (not Roxb.); but Kurz states: petals rusty appressed-villous outside. I have not seen specimens.

25. **B. mollissima,** Wall. (*B. elongata*, Korth. Nat. Verh. Bot. t. 24). Tenasserim, Malay Peninsula and Archipelago. Branchlets, petioles and underside of leaves rusty-pubescent. Fl. in short leaf-opposed racemes. Calyx-tube 1–1¼ in. long, lobes 5 of equal length. Petals 2–2¼ in. long. Pod pubescent, 4 by 1 in. 26. **B. Kurzii,** Prain (*B. rosea*, Kurz F. Fl. i. 402). Kaymapyu choung, Salween in Eng forest (D.B., May, 1859), Taepo at 5,000 ft., Gallatly (Prain in Journ. As. Soc. Beng., 66 [1898] 499). Fl. rose-coloured, on long slender pedicels in terminal corymbose tawny puberulous racemes, bracts linear-lanceolate, ⅓ in. long. Calyx-tube short, segments of limb 5 reflexed, ⅓ in. long. Petals ⅝ in. long, slightly pubescent on both sides. Ovary villous. Style thick, short. 27. **B. Pottingeri,** Prain in Journ. As. Soc. Beng., vol. 67, 289. Kachin hills. A strong climber nearly allied to *B. nervosa*, Wall.

(*c*) Fl. in elongate racemes.

28. **B. anguina,** Roxb. Cor. Pl. t. 285. Vern. *Naiwilli-lara*, Nep.

A large evergreen climber, the branches flat, 4–6 in. broad, ½ in. thick, twisted in alternate directions, stems more cylindrical, with a raised spiral ridge. Branchlets and leaves entirely glabrous, youngest shoots rusty-tomentose, tendrils slender, bifid, branches circinnate. L. thin, on the older branches entire or nearly so, on young plants and on luxuriant shoots more or

less bifid, the lobes narrow and tapering. Fl. small, white, in long slender racemes, arranged in terminal panicles. Calyx-tube campanulate, very short, lobes 5, ovate, spreading. Petals $\frac{1}{8}$ in. long. Stamens 3. Ovary glabrous. Pod thin, obliquely elliptic, 2 by 1 in., 1–2-seeded.

Sikkim Terai, ascending to 2,000 ft., Khasi hills, Chittagong, Martaban. The Burma plant (var. *Horsfieldii*) has smaller pods. Fl. R. S. *B. macrostachya*, Kurz F. Fl. 401, may possibly be this species. See Prain in Journ. As. Soc. Beng., 66 (1898) 500.

29. **B. Championii**, Benth. Tista valley, Sikkim, common. Assam. China. Similar to 27, but l. minutely pubescent beneath. Ovary pubescent. 30. **B. macrostachya**, Wall. Assam, Silhet. Branchlets and l. glabrous. Fl. in forked or simple narrow racemes, 4–6 in. long, pedicels $\frac{1}{2}$–1 in., in the axils of small triangular bracts. Calyx-tube as long as the 5-cleft limb. Petals densely silky, $\frac{1}{2}$ in. long. Pod tomentose, 4–6 by 2 in. Seeds 2-4.

THIRD SUB-ORDER, **MIMOSEÆ.**

Trees, shrubs, climbers, rarely herbs, with abruptly bipinnate, rarely pinnate leaves and small flowers in heads, spikes, racemes, or small umbels. Fl. regular, occasionally polygamous. Sepals valvate, generally connate, rarely free, usually 5. Petals valvate, as many as sepals, hypogynous, usually connate. Stamens hypogynous, definite or indefinite. Seeds without albumen, embryo straight, radicle short.

Most trees of this Sub-order have a distinct dark-coloured heart-wood. Of the climbing species, *Entada scandens* has an anomalous structure, while the climbing *Acacias* have a hard normally built wood.

A. Stamens 10, anthers with deciduous apical glands.
  Thorny trees or shrubs; fl. in cylindrical spikes.
    Pinnæ 2 pair; leaflets small, 7–10 pair . . . 1. PROSOPIS.
    Pinnæ 2 pair; leaflets 2–4 in. long, 1 pair . . . 2. PIPTADENIA.
    Pinnæ 6–10 pair; leaflets small, 12–15 pair . . . 3. DICHROSTACHYS.
  Unarmed climbers; fl. in cylindrical spikes . . . 4. ENTADA.
  Unarmed trees.
    Leaflets evenly alternate, 1 in. long; fl. racemose . 5. ADENANTHERA.
    Leaflets opposite, 8–9 in. long; fl. in globose heads 6. XYLIA.

B. Stamens 8 or 10, anthers without glands.
  Stamens 10, monadelphous . . . . 7. PARKIA.
  Stamens 8 or 10, free.
    Pod continuous . . . . LEUCÆNA (p. 262).
    Pod jointed . . . . 8. MIMOSA.
  Stamens indefinite, free. Thorny trees or climbers 9. ACACIA.
  Stamens indefinite, monadelphous.
    Pod thin, straight, sutures not thickened . . 10. ALBIZZIA.
    Pod falcate, sutures much thickened . . . 11. CALLIANDRA.
    Pod circinate or twisted . . . . . . 12. PITHECOLOBIUM.

1. PROSOPIS, Linn.; Fl. Brit. Ind. ii. 287.

(Species 25, two in Western Asia and India, two in tropical Africa, the rest in the drier regions of America, from Colorado and Utah to Patagonia.)

1. **P. spicigera**, Linn.; Roxb. Cor. Pl. t. 63; Bedd. Fl. Sylv. t. 56; Brandis F. Fl. t. 25. Vern. *Jand*, Punjab; *Kandi*, Sind; *Khejra*, Rajputana; *Semru*, *Sumri*, Guzerat; *Saunder*, Mar.; *Banni*, Kan.; *Jambi*, Tel.; *Jambu*, Tam.

A middle-sized glabrous thorny tree with a very long tap-root. Bark grey, rough, with deep fissures and cracks. Sap-wood large, irregular masses of dark-brown heart-wood in the centre of old trees. Branches and branchlets armed with scattered broad-based conical prickles. L. bipinnate, pinnæ and leaflets opposite, pinnæ 2, leaflets 7–10 pair. Spikes slender, in short axillary

When forestry has made more progress in India, when successful systems of regenerating the oak and coniferous forests of the North-Western, the magnolias, oaks, laurels, and maples of the Eastern Himalaya have been established, when the effect of fire protection upon Teak and other trees has been determined by series of comparative valuation surveys in different districts, when yield tables, showing the amount of timber production per acre per annum of the principal kinds under different circumstances, have been prepared, and when the chief enemies, insects and fungi, of these species are more fully known, then it will be time to publish complete and practically useful books, dealing with the most important trees in each province.

One branch of the subject has already been dealt with in a satisfactory manner: I mean the identification of the different timbers of India by their appearance, weight, hardness and other qualities, as well as by their structure, as far as this can be seen with the aid of a good pocket lens. The necessity of readily recognizing the more important Indian timbers had from the commencement of my Indian career in 1856 compelled me to pay attention to this subject. When in 1877 I was ordered by the Government of India to send to the Paris International Exhibition of 1878 a collection of timbers from all provinces of the British Indian Empire, I determined that all specimens should be correctly named, and this could only be accomplished by a methodical examination of their structure and other qualities. For this purpose I asked for and obtained the assistance of two young Indian foresters, Mr. J. S. Gamble and Mr. A. Smythies. The work commenced at Simla in August 1877, and early in November it was transferred to Calcutta, where a house with a large compound was hired, and where the logs and specimens sent from all provinces were collected and worked up. There we worked hard until February, the descriptions of the structure of each kind being usually dictated by me to my assistants. The result was the large collection of Indian timbers, correctly named, which was sent to Paris by the Government of India and a large number of duplicate collections deposited at the Déhra Dùn Forest School, at the Offices of Conservators in the different provinces, at the Museum, Royal Botanic Gardens, Kew, at the Nancy Forest School and at other public Institutions in Europe, America and India.

After despatching these collections I considered how to utilize the result of our labours for the benefit of Indian foresters, and I proposed to the Government of India, that Mr. Gamble should be entrusted with the publication on Government account of a *Manual of Indian Timbers*. The result has been the excellent handbook, which appeared in 1881, describing the structure and properties of the timber of 906 species, with notes regarding the distribution of the trees, their rate of growth and other matters. Since then Mr. Gamble has been indefatigable in collecting specimens of timbers not included in his *Manual*, examining them on the system established in 1877–8 and revising the descriptions previously made. The second edition of *Indian Timbers*, published by him on his own account in 1902, contains descriptions of 1,450 species, illustrated by excellent photographs, which greatly enhance the value of the work. This second edition is an entirely new book; it is based upon the intimate knowledge of the species constituting the Indian forests, which the author had acquired during his long service in the forests of Burma, Bengal, Madras and North-West India. He has greatly enlarged the notes on the geographical distribution and on the economic uses of the different species and has added notes on their mode of growth, their sylvicultural requirements and their treatment in the forest. The suggestion made on p. xix. of his Introduction, that keys of the distinguishing characters of timbers, as far as they can be seen with the aid of a good pocket lens, be prepared for the trees found on limited areas, should be borne in mind by the authors of local Forest Floras.

It appears to me doubtful whether the local Forest Floras, the preparation of

which will I trust be facilitated by the present book, can be enlarged so as to deal with those questions which are of real importance to the forester, viz., the internal structure of the different species, their mode of life, sylvicultural requirements aud treatment, as well as their protection against enemies in the shape of insects and fungi. The number of species is too large in India; it is essential that these local handbooks should be small and easily portable. The authors of future local forest floras must try to facilitate the identification of their principal timbers by means of keys to their structure and be content with the humble task which I have set before me in the present book, to make the work of determining the names of the species constituting their forests easier than it is at present. This, it is true, is not forestry, but it is the first step towards the systematic treatment of forests. This first step is singularly difficult in India, owing to the enormous number of species.

It may possibly be said that the present work as well as the local Forest Floras of the future should be limited to the more important trees. When I commenced the present work at Bonn about eight years ago, I had this intention, I proposed to limit myself to the more important kinds, and Mr. Gamble, with whom at that time I discussed the subject in the hope that we might perhaps undertake the work together, kindly drew up for me a list of what he regarded as the more important species. As the work progressed, I found the selection of the species that might be omitted exceedingly difficult, and I came to the conclusion that the usefulness of the book would be greatly impaired by such limitation. I pictured to myself one of my young colleagues in Burma who had come across a large tree, which from the wings on the fruit he recognized as a *Dipterocarp.* If this book only contained a description of the more important species, such as *Dipterocarpus alatus*, *D. tuberculatus*, *Hopea odorata*, *Pentacme suavis*, and *Shorea robusta*, it would not help him, for there are upwards of 20 similar species in Burma, and he would have to study Kurz's *Forest Flora of Burma*, the *Flora of British India* and the numerous subsequent publications. He would meet the same difficulty with species of other orders and genera. A book on this plan would be no real help to him.

My ambition has been to publish a path-finder through the bewildering variety of trees, shrubs, climbers, bamboos and palms, which constitute the forests in the different provinces of India. I do not maintain that foresters ought to know them all, but they ought to have the means of making themselves acquainted with them without undue loss of time. If my book accomplishes this, I shall be much gratified. Quite unexpectedly a shrub, a climber, a bamboo or a tree may be found to be of considerable importance from a forester's point of view, and he should then have easy means of identifying the species in question.

Though I have not limited myself to a selected number of species, I have given fuller descriptions in larger type of all common species and of those which at present are recognized as important. With the others I have dealt in small type * in a very summary manner. From the point of view of the botanist all species are of equal importance and ought to be treated alike. This book however is not intended for botanists, it is written for the use of foresters and of practical men, and for these classes of readers species which are common or valuable, obviously are at present infinitely more important than the others. Species which are doubtful or which are imperfectly known I have as a rule omitted altogether.

Many genera and species, in which some readers of this book are likely to take a special interest, I have to my great regret been compelled to leave out. I have not been able to deal with the species of *Dioscorea*, though the roots are most valuable in times of famine, nor have I seen my way to include the

* All species are numbered, though in some cases I have refrained from giving a name. It must not be thought that the species in small type are regarded as sub-species.

tall grasses, which form the Savannahs of Burma and the Subhimalayan tract. I have not been able to mention that most remarkable *Marantaceous* soft-wooded shrub of the Andamans, *Clinogyne grandis*, Benth., the stems tufted, 16 ft. high, with broad elliptic leaves and conspicuous scented white flowers. Very few of the numerous important exotic species cultivated in India have been mentioned. Several of my younger friends have urged me to describe a much larger number of introduced and cultivated kinds. This has been impossible. As it is, in spite of my efforts at shortening and condensing, the book has become inconveniently bulky.

In a few cases I have found it necessary to establish new species; as a rule I have left the task of naming new species to professional systematic botanists, and have contented myself with briefly indicating the character by which a species believed by me to be new differs from others; adding a reliable vernacular name whenever possible.

Regarding the limitation of species there will always be different opinions. My idea is, and always has been, that as long as the matter has not been fully studied in the field, it is better to leave old-established species alone and not to split them up. When writing my old *Forest Flora* I had to decide whether I should separate the Himalayan and softly tomentose *Rhus velutina*, Wall., from the glabrous *R. Cotinus*, of the Mediterranean region. I decided to leave both under *Rhus Cotinus*, and my decision in this and in other similar cases has been accepted by the authors of the *Flora of British India* and by other botanists. For similar reasons I am unable to agree with Lt.-Colonel Prain in his excellent paper on *Leguminosæ* (*Journ. As. Soc. Bengal*, LXVI. 514) in separating the Himalayan *Albizzia mollis* from *A. Julibrissin*, which I regard as a widely spread species, extending from the mountains of Abyssinia to Japan; or with the same author in dividing *Flemingia strobilifera* into 4 species. Mez in his valuable monograph of *Myrsinaceæ* classifies the Indian forms of the very variable *Mæsa indica* under 7 species. I think it quite possible that other botanists may partially adopt his views, but may be content with a smaller number separated by characters not exactly the same as those selected by Mez, the result of which will be numerous synonyms and possible confusion. Hence in this book *Mæsa indica* appears as one species.

For foresters this multiplication of species goes too far, but I trust I may not be misunderstood. *Quercus sessiliflora* and *Q. pedunculata* are two clearly distinct species, differing not only by their leaves and other characters, but what is of much greater importance, by their mode of growth and by their requirements in regard to soil and companionship of other trees. Forests of these two species require different treatment, and yet they are united under *Quercus Robur* by Parlatore (D. C. *Prodromus*, XVI. 2. 4) by Sir Joseph Hooker in his *Students' Flora*, ed. IV. 367, and by Professor Marshall Ward in his *Handbook of Forest Botany*, II. 213.

It is not possible to arrive at a final decision whether a form should be classed as a species or a variety. The fact that it comes true from seed does not settle the matter. In Burma good varieties of the Mango come true from seed, in India seedlings have to be grafted or inarched in order to produce good edible Mangoes. Sir Joseph Hooker regards the three Cedars as varieties only of *C. Libani*, though they come true from seed. To a great extent it is a matter of convenience whether we speak of species or of varieties, and the question ought not to be invested with undue importance. Guided by this consideration, that the question is not one of real importance, I have followed the *Flora of British India* in calling the Indian Oleander *Nerium odorum*, though, as explained on p. 462, I hold that *N. Oleander*, *N. muscatense* and *N. odorum* are local forms of one species, which extends from the Mediterranean region to China. In any case the forester will do well to take species in a wide sense, until it has been proved that they differ in regard to their mode of growth, their requirements and the treatment which they demand.

The necessity of condensing to the utmost has made it impossible to quote synonyms and literature more than was absolutely necessary. Under each order Bentham and Hooker's *Genera Plantarum*, and under each genus Hooker's *Flora of British India* have always been quoted, otherwise as a rule no literature has been given, with the exception of such illustrations as I thought might be accessible to those who may use the book in India.

With regard to the names of genera and species, I have with very few exceptions, unless later authors had proved to my satisfaction the necessity for a change, followed the *Flora of British India*. In this matter I have proceeded with great caution, for the change of a name always causes inconvenience, loss of time, and often creates confusion. The arguments brought forward in favour of a change may at first sight appear to be decisive, and yet it often happens that some points have been overlooked. I have not been able to follow Dr. Cooke, who, in his excellent *Flora of Bombay*, calls the well-known *Zizyphus nummularia*, W. et A., *Z. rotundifolia*, Lam., nor do I feel justified in substituting *Mitragyna*, Korthals, for *Stephegyne* of the same author.

Bentham and Hooker's *Genera Plantarum* has been my guide in regard to the sequence of orders, with this sole exception, that Gymnosperms have been placed at the end. In the following cases I have found it necessary, following generally the arrangement in Engler u. Prantl, *Natürliche Pflanzenfamilien*, to adopt a different limitation of orders: (1) *Ancistrocladaceæ* have been taken out of *Dipterocarpeæ*. (2) *Olacineæ* have been divided into the two natural and well defined orders of *Olacaceæ* and *Icacinaceæ*. (3) *Sapindaceæ* here appear as three orders: *Staphyleaceæ*, *Aceraceæ* and *Sapindaceæ* proper. (4) *Ericaceæ* here comprise two orders of Bentham and Hooker's *Genera Plantarum*, *Ericaceæ* and *Vacciniaceæ*. (5) *Hernandiaceæ* consists of *Hernandia* and 2 genera, placed under *Combretaceæ* in the *Genera Plantarum*. (6) *Urticaceæ* have been divided into *Ulmaceæ*, *Moraceæ* and *Urticaceæ* proper, and (7) *Cupuliferæ* into *Betulaceæ* and *Fagaceæ*. *Filicium* has been transferred from *Burseraceæ* to *Sapindaceæ*, *Helwingia* from *Araliaceæ* to *Cornaceæ*, and *Reptonia* from *Myrsinaceæ* to *Sapotaceæ*. The practical advantages of these alterations are very great, and will I trust eventually be recognized by those who may use this book. In the case of *Myrtaceæ* and in one or two other instances I have adhered to the classification of the *Genera Plantarum*, and have merely indicated the arrangement, which in my opinion would be more natural. Wherever feasible I have followed other Botanists in adopting the termination *-aceæ* for all natural orders.

The descriptions of orders and genera as a rule relate only to the genera and species included in this work. As regards botanical terms, I desire to remind the reader that a leaf is *oblong*, if its two sides are nearly parallel. This term is often used erroneously for leaves with curved sides, narrowing gradually towards the two ends. In such cases I employ the term *elongate-elliptic* or *ovate-lanceolate* as the case may be. *Secondary* nerves are those which branch off from the midrib, and *tertiary* those which branch off from the *secondary* nerves. In accordance with some leading systematic handbooks the term *albumen* has been used. It would have been more correct to speak of *perisperm* in the case of *Piperaceæ* and of *endosperm* in the case of the other orders. I have only done so in the case of bamboos and palms, as well as in the Synopsis of Orders. In the *Records of the Botanical Survey of India*, I noticed lately that the metrical system has been used for the dimensions of leaves and other organs. Most probably the metrical system will eventually be adopted in India and Great Britain, but until this is accomplished, foresters must continue to deal with acres, feet and inches. In a few cases, when stating the diameter of vessels or other elements which can only be seen through a microscope, I had for obvious reasons to make an exception. The few abbreviations used: l. for leaves, n. for nerves, fl. for

flowers, fr. for fruit, Haz. for Hazara, Bash. for Bashahr, Kun. for Kunawar, C.P. for Central Provinces, Kar. for Karen, will be readily understood.

Vernacular names of species, if sifted with care, are valuable whatever may be said to the contrary, and I have endeavoured to select those which seemed to me most likely to be useful. Apart from the names recorded in my old *Forest Flora*, and those collected by myself after 1874, those recorded in Kurz's *Forest Flora of Burma*, in Beddome's *Flora Sylvatica*, in Gamble's second edition of *Indian Timbers* and in his other publications, in Talbot's *List of Trees and Shrubs of the Bombay Presidency*, in the excellent lists of Burmese names by the late Mr. Corbett, I have received much help in this respect through the kindness of local forest officers and others. From Madras I have received a printed list, giving the names of trees and shrubs in the 5 principal languages of that Presidency. Similar lists, some in manuscript, others in print, I have received from many districts or forest circles in other parts of India. I hope that the selection which these abundant materials have enabled me to make will prove useful, but I know that the spelling of these names will be found to be the weakest point of the whole book. In the case of *Eng, Dipterocarpus tuberculatus*, I have adhered to the old spelling, as the name has, through the publications of Kurz and others, become familiar to Botanists outside India. When the local Forest Floras of the future come to be prepared for the different forest circles or provinces, the spelling of the vernacular names in the different languages will doubtless receive due attention. In the case of languages spoken in limited areas, or otherwise less important for the forester, such as Lepcha, Sontal, Kol, Gond, Bhil, Shan, Chin, Karen, I have only given the names of a few common and important trees.

The materials, upon the examination of which the description of genera and species in this book are based, have been as follows. *First:* The magnificent and well-arranged collections in the Herbarium and Museums, with the library and the living specimens cultivated in the houses or the grounds, of the Royal Botanic Gardens, Kew. I value highly the privilege of having been permitted the free use of these matchless treasures. I have also consulted, whenever it seemed necessary, the specimens of Wallich's Herbarium at the Linnean Society, as well as the collections preserved in the Natural History Museum at South Kensington. I cannot sufficiently express my gratitude for the assistance I have received in this work from the Director of the Royal Botanic Gardens, from all members of his staff, as well as from the officers of the Natural History Museum and the Linnean Society.

Second: The collections made by me in the different provinces of India from 1856 to 1883. These collections might have been exceedingly valuable, for there are few important forest districts in British territory which I have not visited, often repeatedly at different seasons of the year. Collecting, however, was not my business. The object of my being appointed in January 1856 by Lord Dalhousie to the charge of the Pegu forests was purely practical. My duty in Burma was to place the management of the Teak forests upon a safe footing, so as to ensure the maintenance and gradual improvement of the valuable growing stock, while utilizing timber not exceeding the amount annually produced in the forests. The difficulties with which I had to contend were great, and the opposition against methodical forest management was powerful. This is not the place to give an account of my work in India; it must suffice to say that, unless I had had in Burma the steady support of the late Sir Arthur Phayre, and at a later date, after I had been summoned to Calcutta to assist the Government of India in organizing forest business in the other provinces, the protection and guidance of Colonel (now Sir Richard) Strachey, there would perhaps be no Forest Administration in India, and there would be no need for the present book. My work during the 28 years of my Indian service has never left me leisure for collecting systematically, or for working out scientific problems.

Whenever possible I took about with me Endlicher's *Genera Plantarum*, Roxburgh's *Flora Indica*, Wight and Arnott's *Prodromus*, and in later years Kurz's *Forest Flora of Burma* and other books as they appeared. Whenever I could snatch an hour or two I examined the trees and shrubs which I had found. Unfortunately for myself I never was a keen sportsman; this, however, gave me time during my life in Burma, from 1856 to 1862, to record descriptions with rough sketches of the plants examined. Many specimens of my old Burma collections are, in accordance with my wish, at the Herbarium of the Royal Gardens, Calcutta, but a portion I have kept, and Lt.-Colonel Prain has most kindly lent me some of my old specimens for examination. Thus I have been able to utilize for the present book a considerable portion of my old Burma notes, and this will I trust increase its value. It must not be supposed that in those days I knew the systematic names of the trees and shrubs of Burma. In January 1860, I was able to spend a few weeks with the late Dr. Thomas Thomson at the Calcutta gardens, and while there obtained the names of some of the more important trees and shrubs. Until then, and in most cases afterwards, I called them by their Burmese names. In 1859 I drew up a descriptive account of eighteen kinds of bamboos, all well known to me by their dimensions, their mode of growth, their culm-sheaths and other characters, but until Munro's *Monograph of Bamboos* appeared in 1866, I only knew them by their Burmese names. After I left Burma and commenced work in the other provinces of the Empire, I had even less time for botanical studies. The result has been that to the end of my Indian career I remained ignorant of many trees and shrubs, to which my attention had not been specially drawn. Intelligent readers will discover in the Addenda appended to this book several species which I had omitted because I did not know them.

Third : The specimens and notes sent to me by my younger friends and by my former colleagues. Before speaking of foresters I desire to state that the Superintendent of the Royal Gardens, Calcutta, has for several years past most kindly sent me duplicates, which it was thought might help me in my present work. Mr. John F. Duthie, the late Superintendent of the Saharanpur Botanic Gardens, has sent me specimens, and has enabled me to examine others collected by him in Northern India. Colonel A. A. Barrett has at different times sent me most valuable material, with full notes, from Abbotabad and from the Chitral valley, and Dr. T. Cooke has most kindly, in the case of difficult genera, permitted me to examine the specimens of the rich collections made by him in the Bombay Presidency.

The first collection from forest officers came from Mr. A. E. Lowrie, at that time in charge of the forests of Ajmer-Merwara. It consisted of an almost complete set of well dried specimens of the trees and shrubs of that district, with copious and instructive notes, accompanied in many cases by pieces of wood, which enabled me to understand difficult genera, such as *Cordia*, better than before.

From Mr. J. S. Gamble, C.I.E. and F.R.S., I have received repeated consignments of splendid specimens collected by him in Bengal and in the Madras Presidency, which have been a great help to me in this work. Moreover, when I had nearly finished bamboos, Mr. Gamble at my request most generously sent for my inspection and examination the specimens which he had received from India since the publication of his great work on the Indian bamboos, including several new species named by him.

Mr. J. W. Oliver, when Conservator in Upper Burma, sent me several important collections, made, partly by him, partly by Mr. E. M. Buchanan, on the hills in the Ruby Mines district, and in that remarkable region of dry country on both sides of the Irawadi river between Thayetmyo and Mandalay. Upper Burma was annexed three years after I had left India, and these collections, with Mr. Oliver's notes, as well as a number of specimens sent me by Mr. A. Smythies, gave me some idea of the forest vegetation of that country. I had

never visited the Andamans, but it has been my good fortune that Mr. Gilbert Rogers, who for several years has had charge of the forests in these islands, has lately been able on several occasions to come to Kew and to give me excellent information, chiefly regarding the palms and bamboos, which he had studied with special care. The more important of his collections were not available, but fortunately he was able to obtain for me materials for the study of several important species. Nor had I been in Baluchistan, and hence the specimens and information which Mr. J. H. Lace has given me in regard to the forest vegetation of that country have been of the greatest value.

As soon as I had determined to undertake this work, I made my intention known to my young friends and former colleagues in India, asking them to furnish me with material for this work. This request has been responded to from nearly all provinces in the most liberal manner. From Travancore Mr. T. F. Bourdillon has from the commencement supplied me with specimens and ample notes regarding new and difficult species. Mr. A. W. Lushington has furnished me with valuable notes and specimens from the Madras Presidency, Mr. Talbot has sent me notes with specimens of various species, Mr. G. M. Ryan has been indefatigable in supplying me with material from the Thana district in Bombay, and in sending replies to my inquiries. Mr. R. S. Hole has sent me notes and specimens from Jabalpur; Mr. R. L. Heinig notes and specimens of a bamboo from Chittagong; and to Mr. H. H. Haines I am indebted for splendid collections and most valuable notes from Singbhum and Sikkim. The forest officers in Assam have favoured me with specimens and lists of bamboos in their districts. From Rai Sahib Upendranath Kanjilal I have received numerous contributions, and Mr. J. H. Lace has most kindly lent me specimens illustrating difficult genera from the North-West Himalaya.

The collections received from Burma I can only mention briefly, although for my work they have been by far the most important. To Mr. F. B. Manson I am indebted for a large collection of specimens from Tavoy, Mergui, and other districts of Tenasserim, and to Mr. E. M. Buchanan for a consignment from Tharawadi. The late H. Slade and J. Messer, who have both died prematurely—a great loss for the progress of forestry in Burma—sent me notes and specimens, chiefly of bamboos; from Mr. Montague Hill I have received several large and most valuable consignments, with lists and notes, chiefly from the hills east of Bhamo, and Mr. R. S. Troup has furnished me with excellent specimens and notes, chiefly of bamboos and palms. By far the richest and most important collections have come from Mr. C. B. Smales. He commenced sending in 1898, and continued steadily until he came home on furlough in 1903. His specimens and notes are excellent, and they have enabled me almost to feel at home in the forest vegetation of Upper Burma. His is an instance of a keen sportsman turning his attention to the study of trees, shrubs and bamboos with excellent effect.

In spite of this wealth of material, which has been at my disposal, I feel strongly that, to do full justice to the task I had undertaken, I ought to have gone to the Royal Gardens, Calcutta, to consult the untold treasures which must have accumulated at that long-established splendid institution, the result of the labours of skilful collectors, some of them foresters. For this undertaking, however, I had neither the strength nor the means, and I feel that in many respects my work is incomplete.

The publications bearing upon the woody plants of India since the appearance of the *Forest Flora* of N.W. and Central India have been very numerous and very important. In 1872 and 1873, the years devoted to that work, the *Genera Plantarum*, by Bentham and Hooker, was only available to the end of *Rubiaceæ*, and Hooker's *Flora of British India* only to page 306 of the first volume. Of Boissier's *Flora Orientalis* the first 2 volumes had appeared. These three standard works are now complete, and in addition to these the whole of Engler u. Prantl's *Natürliche Pflanzenfamilien* and a number of

monographs of important orders in Engler's *Pflanzenreich*, which will be found quoted in their proper place. Kurz's *Forest Flora of Burma* appeared in 1877, and it has been a real pleasure to witness how thoroughly this modest but most important work is appreciated and how eagerly it has been used by foresters in Burma. A most important help has been the magnificent volumes of the *Annals of the Royal Botanic Gardens, Calcutta*, chiefly I. *Ficus* (1888), II. *Artocarpus, Quercus, Castanopsis* (1889), III. 2. *Magnoliaceæ* (1891), III. 3. *Myristica* (1891), IV. 1. *Anonaceæ* (1893), all by Sir George King, VII. *Bambuseæ* by J. S. Gamble (1896), and X. *Dalbergia* by Lt.-Col. D. Prain (1904). The *Journal and Transactions of the Linnean Society* since 1873 contain numerous papers which have been utilized by me, and which are quoted in their proper place. The *Records of the Botanical Survey of India* brought a number of most important papers by Mr Pottinger, Mr. G. A. Gammie, and C. Marshall Woodrow, Lt.-Col. Wood, Signore Odoardo Beccari, Mr. Duthie, Lt.-Col. Prain and Capt. Gage. Among the numerous publications in other languages which have been useful to me in this work, apart from the two general works edited by Professor Engler, I desire specially to mention Pierre, *Flore Forestière de la Cochinchine*, an important work for the study of Burmese trees, tab. 1–400, the last published in 1899, and Koorders en Valeton, *Boomsorten op Java*, vol. I.–X., the last in 1904.

The excellent *List of trees, climbers and woody shrubs of the Bombay Presidency*, by W. A. Talbot, ed. II. 1902, has been of the greatest use, and Mr. Gamble's *Indian Timbers*, particularly the second edition (1902), which I have been able to use from *Caprifoliaceæ* onwards, has been invaluable, as well as his *List of Trees of the Darjeeling District*, ed. II. 1896. The *Flora of Simla*, by the late Sir Henry Collett, 1902, with Miss Smith's excellent illustrations in that valuable book, will be found quoted under the species illustrated. Lt.-Col. David Prain's *Bengal Plants* (2 vols., 1903) I have been able to use for the last Orders only, and the large number of additional localities quoted from that book under "addenda" will show how far from complete the specimens before me have been with regard to Chittagong and other portions of Bengal. The first volume of Mr. Duthie's *Flora of the Upper Gangetic Plain* and Dr. Cooke's *Flora of Bombay*, vol. I. and vol. II. to p. 432, have been most useful to me.

The *Journal of the Bombay Natural History Society* contains valuable papers by Bourdillon, Talbot, Marshall Woodrow and Th. Cooke. A series of most important papers has been published in the *Journal of the Asiatic Society of Bengal*, the most prominent of which are the *Materials for a Flora of the Malay Peninsula*, by Sir George King, now continued by Mr. J. S. Gamble, which commenced to appear in 1890.

It may perhaps be expected that I should say a few words regarding the geographical distribution of the species dealt with in this volume. These remarks must be brief, and as a matter of course they must be limited to species described in this volume, trees, shrubs, etc. In the introductory essay to the *Flora Indica* by J. D. Hooker and T. Thomson of 1855, p. 115, four primary divisions were recognized, viz.: I. Hindustan, including the Western Peninsula from the base of the Himalaya to Cape Comorin; II. The Himalaya; III. Eastern India, or India east of the mouth of the Ganges; IV. Afghanistan and Baluchistan; and it was clearly set forth in that admirable essay that the vegetation of the Western Himalaya had great affinity to that of Western Asia and Europe, and that genera and species of China and Japan prevailed in the Eastern Himalaya.

Since then a number of excellent papers have been published, in which these great primary divisions have been subdivided, and a larger number of botanical regions established. The most important of these papers are: C. B. Clarke, the *Botanical Subsubareas of British India, illustrated by the Distribution of Cyperaceæ, Journal Linnean Society*, XXXIV. p. 1

(1898), Lt.-Colonel Prain, *Introduction to Bengal Plants*, p. 2 (1903), Sir Joseph Dalton Hooker, *A Sketch of the Flora of British India* (1904).* In this admirable paper Hooker divides British India primarily into three Botanical areas, a Himalayan, an Eastern and a Western, the two last-named being roughly separated by a line drawn meridionally from the Himalaya to the Bay of Bengal. These areas he divides into 9 provinces, 7 of which are included in the present work, viz.: (1) The Eastern Himalaya, (2) The Western Himalaya, (3) The Indus plain, (4) The Gangetic plain, (5) Malabar in a very extended sense, (6) The Deccan in a very broad sense, (7) Ceylon, (8) Burma, (9) the Malay Peninsula. 7 and 9 are not included here. In stating the distribution of the species described in this book it was obviously in most cases necessary to go into detail, and wherever feasible, the names of the 64 subdivisions were used which had already been indicated in the introduction to the *Flora Indica* of 1855, and which in his last sketch Hooker has arranged under the 9 provinces now adopted by him. In many cases, however, the distribution of species had to be further defined, and here to a great extent the administrative division of the Empire into districts and subdivisions has been used. It is assumed that those who may use this book are familiar with the geography of India. In the case of a few of the less common, but important species, I have added the locality and the dates on which they were found by me. It will I trust be understood that I had to indicate the geographical distribution of a species in as few words as possible, so that when a species is found in Chutia Nagpur and the Western Peninsula it may be assumed also to occur in Orissa, though this is not specifically stated. Again, when a species is found on the Khasi hills and in Chittagong, it may be expected to occur also on the Lushai hills. The term Central India is sometimes used in a wide sense, comprising the Central Provinces.

The principal factors which influence the geographical distribution of trees in India are latitude, elevation, moisture and the nature of the soil. In addition to these, it must be borne in mind that there is a marked difference in the vegetation of the Western and Eastern divisions of the country. The influence of latitude and elevation above sea-level is obvious and is generally recognized; regarding the influence of soil, moisture and the difference between West and East it may be useful to say a few words. Regarding the influence of soil upon forest growth in India, only a few isolated facts are known at present. *Sal* forests are found on sandstone, conglomerate and on the sandy gravelly and shingly soil of the Subhimalayan tract; *Eng* (*Dipterocarpus tuberculatus*) chiefly affects laterite; *Hardwickia binata* most commonly grows on sandstone, and if found on trap, as in South Berar, the rock is rich in veins of quartz. *Mimusops hexandra*, as far as known, behaves in the same manner. *Cupressus torulosa* as a rule is only found on limestone. On the other hand *Teak* thrives well on the sandstone and calcareous shales of the Pegu Yoma, on gneiss, granite and other crystalline rocks east of the Sitang river above Toungoo and in North Kanara, on trap in the Satpura range, and in the Khandeish Dangs, on limestone in the Thaungyin forests of Tenasserim, and it also grows on deep alluvial soil. The same may be said of many important forest trees. *Terminalia tomentosa*, it is true, and *Diospyros Melanoxylon* thrive best on heavy clay soil, but we find them on different geological formations.

In Europe forest trees behave in a similar way. The *Beech* and the *Silver fir* thrive best on calcareous soils, but they will grow on soils differing greatly in regard to their physical and chemical constitution. The *Larch* in Switzerland and the Tyrol prefers crystalline rocks, which are poor in lime, while in Bavaria and Salzburg this tree is commonly found on calcareous and not on silicious soils.

The trees and shrubs, which grow near the sea coast and on the banks of

* A chapter in the forthcoming *Imperial Gazetteer of India* (advance copy).

tidal streams, including the Mangrove formation, are quite peculiar, the extent of these littoral forests is considerable, the habits and structure of the principal species have been thoroughly studied; * this, however, is not the place to say more regarding them.

The reader will I trust not misunderstand me. The nature of the soil, and consequently the nature of the rock, by the disintegration of which the soil has been formed, is a most important factor in forestry. It will gradually be more fully understood that Teak forests on trap require a different treatment from those on gneiss, on limestone, on sandstone and calcareous shales or on alluvial soil; and doubtless Indian foresters will eventually find that many trees thrive better on certain classes of soil than on others. The large area covered with basaltic rocks in Western India affords opportunities for promising studies in this respect. The *Sal* tree on the Satpura range has its western limit on the sandstone of the Pachmarhis. It does not thrive on trap, and hence it is not found further west in that region. A carefully prepared list of species found in the trap country of the Peninsula and of those which are wanting, though they are found on other formations in the same region, may prove instructive in many respects.

At the British Association assembled at Brighton in 1872, I had the honour to explain before the geographical section my views regarding the distribution of forests in India. My paper was published in *Ocean Highways*, 1872, p. 200, and in the *Transactions of the Royal Scottish Arboricultural Society*, VII. 88 (1873). It was illustrated by a map, on which I had, on the ground of the imperfect meteorological data then available, entered the regions of greater or less moisture, as indicated by the annual rainfall. I laid stress upon a subject which is now universally recognized, the intimate relation between moisture and forest growth in India. Since then the Indian Meteorological Department has been established, and the maps published by that Department are more accurate and much more detailed than the map which I ventured to compile in 1872. Still the great regions then established remain, and with the addition of the dry region in the Irawadi valley, not known to me in 1872, they are:

First: I. The arid region with a scanty and irregular rainfall, never exceeding 15 inches annually, and an atmosphere dry nearly throughout the year, comprising Sind, the southern Punjab and western Rajputana.

Second, the three dry regions, annual rainfall between 15 and 30 inches,† viz.: II. The northern dry region, adjoining the arid region on its north and east sides, comprising the greater portion of the plains of the Punjab to within a short distance from the foot of the Himalaya, Eastern Rajputana and a large part of what are now called the United Provinces, extending eastwards along the Ganges beyond Cawnpore. III. The Peninsular dry region, comprising the greater part of the Deccan and Mysore. IV. The Eastern dry region in the Irawadi valley, comprising the following districts. West of the river: the southern portion of Shwebo, the eastern half of the Lower Chindwin, Sagaing, Pakokku and Minbu. East of the river: the western portion of Mandalay and Kyaukse, Myingyan, Meiktila and Magwe.

Third, the two moist regions, rainfall 75 inches and upwards, viz: V. The Western moist region, extending from the Gulf of Cambay to Travancore and comprising the country from the coast to some distance east of the crest of the Ghats. VI. The Eastern moist region, comprising the eastern Himalaya with a narrow strip along the outer ranges, extending north-west as far as the Ravi, the greater part of Assam, Eastern Bengal, the northern part of Upper and nearly the whole of Lower Burma.

* Schimper, Indo-Malayische Strand Flora (1891), *Plant-Geography*, p. 90, 287 (1903). Prain, Flora of the Sundriban in Records Bot. Survey India II. 240. Hooker, Sketch of the Flora of British India, 26.

† In the excellent large *Rainfall Map of India*, published by the late Henry Blanford in 1883, and in later maps published by the Meteorological Department, the regions are limited by lines of 10–20, 20–30, etc., inches of the annual rainfall.

Fourth : VII. The intermediate region, comprising the remainder with a rainfall between 30 and 75 inches, heavier in the belts adjoining the two moist regions, in hilly districts and in places along the sea-coast.

In the paper quoted I also mentioned the large extent of arid valleys in the inner Himalaya, and described the gradual but most remarkable changes in the forest vegetation experienced when ascending the valley of the Sutlej river, from the moist ranges of the Outer Himalaya into the dry and, higher up, the arid region beyond Wangtu. Changes similar to these but much more striking, are noticed when ascending from the evergreen forest at the foot and on the slopes of the Western Ghats to the crest of the ghats and beyond into the dry country of the Deccan or Mysore. The evergreen forest disappears, its place is taken first by moist, further east by dry deciduous forest, until at last the thorny scrub of the Deccan takes the place of forest.

Excluding the Himalaya, the forester distinguishes two great classes of forests in India: the deciduous forest, which, unless specially protected, is burnt over every year, and the evergreen forest, into which as a rule fires do not enter. The deciduous forests, as is well known, are the most valuable, as they contain most of the really important species. Extensive areas of evergreen forest are only found in the two great moist regions, the western and eastern, and not everywhere in these, for there are large areas in the moist regions stocked with deciduous forest. As a rule the existence of evergreen forest indicates heavier rainfall and moister air, but there are cases where the nature of the soil seems to be an important factor in this respect. Thus in the lower portion of the Thaungyin valley on the British side there is a large stretch of evergreen forest on deep alluvial soil. Marching through this region on my way up the valley in March 1859, I found the mean height of this forest to be 200 ft., with a few specimens of *Antiaris toxicaria* towering above it. The ground was stocked with trees of all ages, from seedlings to tall poles,* brushwood and creepers, forming a dense mass of vegetation 200 ft. high. Higher up the valley on undulating ground deciduous forest with a considerable amount of Teak prevails. Something similar I have seen on the head waters of the Attaran river, where stretches of alluvial soil are stocked with evergreen, and hills or undulating ground with deciduous forest. Aspect also has something to do with the distribution of these two classes of forest. In Burma I have often seen one side of a valley clothed with evergreen, and the other with deciduous forest. The conditions which in the moist regions of India govern this matter will doubtless eventually be more fully examined. The Kans of the Sorub Taluka of Mysore, isolated patches of evergreen forest, in which the Pepper vine is cultivated, are specially recommended for study.

Stretches of evergreen forest are also found on hills in the intermediate and dry regions, for instance on the Shevaroy and Javadi hills, and in the Cuddapah and Karnūl districts of Madras, where the moisture is greater than in the country surrounding these hills. They are sometimes designated as dry evergreen forest, some of the more prominent trees being: *Ochna Gamblei, Terminalia pallida, Eugenia alternifolia, Strychnos potatorum.*

On the east side of the Peninsula, near the coast, under the influence of the North-east Monsoon, extensive tracts of waste lands and low hills are stocked with a kind of nearly evergreen forest growth, which I have designated as semi-evergreen scrub,† some of the prominent species of which are: *Flacourtia Ramontchi, Pterospermum suberifolium, Hugonia Mystax, Erythroxylon monogynum, Zizyphus Xylopyrus, Eugenia bracteata, Webera corymbosa, Canthium parviflorum, Maba buxifolia, Carissa spinarum, Ehretia buxifolia.*

* The species of the evergreen forest, even more than Beech and Silver Fir in Europe, spring up and are able to live in deep shade.

† Brandis, *Suggestions on Forest Administration*, Madras, p. 110 (1883).

Every forester and all those who are likely to use this book are familiar with the paramount influence of latitude, elevation and moisture upon forest growth in India, but it is perhaps less generally known that there are numerous species, genera, and even natural orders, which are found in the east and are wanting in the west and vice versâ. As already stated, it is generally recognized that the vegetation of the Western Himalaya has great affinity to that of Western Asia and Europe, while types of China and Japan prevail in the Eastern Himalaya. Putting aside the Himalaya for the present, the affinity of the vegetation in the Western Peninsula* with that of Africa has long been recognized; it was Hooker who first drew prominent attention to it, and, as already mentioned, in his recent sketch, divides India into three great Botanical areas or regions, a Himalayan, an Eastern and a Western. The following remarks relate to the Western and Eastern Peninsulas of India and the provinces and districts north of the two peninsulas to the foot of the Himalaya. A line drawn from Calcutta northwards to near the foot of the Himalaya will be found convenient to separate these two great divisions, the western and eastern division of India outside the Himalaya.

The Western Peninsula has no *Cupuliferæ* (*Betulaceæ* and *Fagaceæ*), no *Coniferæ* with the exception of *Podocarpus latifolia*, and no *Hamamelidaceæ* or *Saxifragaceæ*, orders which are well represented in eastern India. *Acer* is absent from the Western Peninsula and so are *Thymelæaceæ*, with the sole exception of *Lasiosiphon*. Five of the 7 Magnoliaceous genera (*Magnolia*, *Manglietia*, *Talauma*, *Illicium*, *Schizandra*) are not represented in the west. On the other hand, of *Capparidaceæ* : *Niebuhria*, *Mærua* and *Cadaba* are Western, while *Boscia* and *Roydsia* are Eastern, the principal genus, *Capparis*, having species in both peninsulas. Of the 12 genera of *Ternstræmiaceæ* 5 (*Pyrenaria*, *Schima*, *Camellia*, *Actinidia* and *Saurauja*) belong exclusively to the Eastern Flora. Two genera of *Burseraceæ* (*Boswellia* and *Balsamodendron*) belong to Africa, Arabia and the Western Peninsula, but are wanting in the East. Of the 68 species of *Meliaceæ* the majority are eastern or common to both sides, but *Turræa*, *Beddomea* and *Chloroxylon* are exclusively western. *Soymida* may possibly yet be found in the dry region of Upper Burma. Of *Sapindaceæ*, *Guioa* and *Mischocarpus* are eastern, while *Dodonæa* and *Filicium* are exclusively western genera. Among *Anacardiaceæ*, *Nothopegia* is western, while *Parishia*, *Melanorhœa*, *Swintonia*, *Dracontomelum*, *Drimycarpus* and *Bouea* are exclusively eastern genera. Of *Leguminosæ*, *Mundulea*, *Ougeinia*, *Hardwickia* and *Prosopis* are western, while *Afzelia*, *Crudia*, *Pahudia*, *Amherstia*, *Parkia* and others belong to the Eastern Division. Among *Rosaceæ*, *Pyrus*, *Docynia*, *Pourthiæa* and *Eriobotrya* are found in the Eastern but not in the Western Peninsula. Of *Myrtaceæ*, *Rhodomyrtus* belongs to the Western Peninsula, while *Decaspermum*, *Rhodamnia*, *Leptospermum*, *Tristania*, *Melaleuca* and *Planchonia* are Eastern genera. Of *Araliaceæ*, *Cornaceæ*, *Rubiaceæ* and *Palmæ*, numerous genera belong exclusively to the Eastern Flora. In *Sapotaceæ*, *Isonandra* is western, while *Sarcosperma* is eastern. *Salvadora* is western, but no *Agapetes*, *Pentapterygium*, *Styrax*, *Osmanthus*, *Congea*, *Lindera*, and *Morus* are found in the Western Region. Of Bamboos, *Ochlandra* is western with one species in the Malay Peninsula; one section of *Oxytenanthera* is Western, while the other section belongs to the eastern peninsula. Most of the other genera have species in the eastern division only, while the 4 large genera *Arundinaria*, *Bambusa*, *Dendrocalamus* and *Teinostachyum* have species both in the western and eastern divisions.

Many genera besides *Oxytenanthera* have distinct sections of Eastern and Western species: for instance *Pterospermum*, *Holigarna* and *Connarus*. Further, a number of western and eastern species are so closely allied that

* The terms Western and Eastern Peninsula are used in Hooker's great *Flora of British India*.

they may be regarded as vicarious species, unless it is preferred not to recognize any difference between them. As instances I may mention *Dipterocarpus indicus* and *D. turbinatus*, *Elæocarpus tuberculatus* and *E. aristatus*. These cases are analogous to the vicarious species on both sides of the Atlantic, such as *Cercis Siliquastrum* and *C. canadensis*, *Ostrya carpinifolia* and *O. virginiana*.

There are one or two instances of genera, which are found in Eastern India and tropical Africa, but which have not yet been discovered in the Western Peninsula. The most remarkable instance is *Dalhousiea bracteata* and *africana*, two species so closely allied, that they have been united in the Flora of British India and of Tropical Africa.

The forester will naturally wish to know to what extent these remarks relate to the more important forest trees. Omitting the trees of the Himalaya, we may single out 60 as being by far the most important among the large number of species here described. Of these sixty, 20 are Western, such as: *Shorea robusta*, *Chloroxylon Swietenia*, *Dalbergia latifolia*, *Pterocarpus Marsupium*, 17 are Eastern, such as: *Hopea odorata*, *Pterocarpus dalbergioides*, *Pinus Khasia* and *Dendrocalamus giganteus*, while 23 belong to both divisions, among them *Xylia dolabriformis*, *Acacia Catechu*, *Terminalia Chebula*, *Lagerstrœmia flos-reginæ*, *Tectona grandis* and *Bambusa arundinacea*.

The preceding remarks must not be misunderstood. Many genera and species are common to both the Western and Eastern divisions of India. A comparison of localities similar as regards moisture and elevation will show this abundantly. A very remarkable instance of this is mentioned by Hooker on p. 33 of his late *Sketch of the Flora of British India*. He compares the Nilgiri flora with that of the cool regions of the far distant Khasi, Manipur, Naga hills and the hills in Northern Burma. Moisture, elevation and soil are similar, but these localities are separated by 14 degrees of latitude and 17 degrees of longitude. The following are the most remarkable instances mentioned by him: *Rubus*, of which 2 species are common to the Nilgiris and to the hills of Eastern India, is a large cosmopolitan genus. *Hypericum* and *Rhamnus* belong to the Northern temperate zone, but have representatives in mountainous regions within the tropics, of which *Hypericum Hookerianum*, *H. mysorense* and *nepaulense*, *Rhamnus virgatus* and *R. Wightii* are found on the Nilgiris. Of *Viburnum*, a genus of the temperate and subtropical regions of the Northern Hemisphere, 15 species are found in India, and 4 of these: *V. punctatum*, *V. coriaceum*, *V. odoratissimum* and *V. erubescens*, are common to the Western and Eastern region (see p. 361). This most interesting comparison of the Nilgiris and the hills of Eastern India does not invalidate what has been said regarding Eastern and Western genera and species. The Nilgiris have no oaks, no pines, no *Pyrus*, no *Hamamelidaceæ*, no *Saxifragaceæ*, no *Agapetes* or *Pentapterygium*, and many other genera common on the hills of Eastern India, are wanting on the Nilgiris.

A most interesting and valuable account has lately been published by Capt. A. T. Gage, I.M.S., of the vegetation in the Minbu district, which forms part of the dry region of the Irawadi valley in Upper Burma. (*Records of the Botanical Survey of India*, vol. III. 17.) This district the author divides into three regions :—I. The mountainous zone comprising the eastern slopes of the Arakan Yoma and a lower range of hills running parallel to the Yoma. II. A narrow flat alluvial belt 4–5 miles wide fringing the western bank of the Irawadi river. III. The desert zone 20–30 miles wide, comprising the greater portion of the district. In this zone only 60 of the 700 species collected by him were found. The most striking feature in the vegetation of this zone, Capt. Gage states (p. 17), is the preponderance of Deccan and Indo-African species. At first sight this would seem to upset much that has been said regarding Western and Eastern species. On page 130 the author gives a list of the species found in the desert zone according to their geographical

distribution, and from this list it appears, that out of the 60 species 11 are found in the Deccan and 8 are distributed from Africa to India, while the rest are endemic in Burma, are distributed over other parts of India, over Malaya, China and Australia, or are found in a large portion of the tropical zone. Of the 19 Deccan and African species most are found in other parts of India besides the Deccan, and the remark made by Capt. Gage, interesting as it is, does not affect what has here been said regarding the difference in the vegetation of Western and Eastern India outside the Himalaya.

The effect of the climatic factors which have influenced the character of forest growth in India, the chief being elevation, latitude and moisture, is readily intelligible, while the difference in the vegetation of the Western and Eastern divisions is not so easily explained. It might be supposed that the soil in these two great divisions of India was different, and that this would account for the remarkable facts here mentioned. This view may be supported by the extensive area covered with basaltic rocks in the Western peninsula, a formation which, as far as known, is not found in the Eastern division of India. In spite of this fact, however, it cannot in any way be said that the character of the soils is essentially different in these two great divisions of the country. The difference between western and eastern species rather points to changes which in remote ages must have taken place in the configuration and climate of the country, a most interesting subject, which however cannot be discussed here.

One of the most important steps taken by Dr. Schlich, when organizing the Indian Forest School in connexion with the Cooper's Hill Engineering College, was to arrange, not only for the teaching of systematic botany, but to insist upon the students becoming familiar with the anatomy and physiology of trees, so that they should thoroughly understand the development, nutrition, and propagation of plants. Further, that their attention should be directed to important biological features, which are not generally dealt with in books on systematic botany. Professor Marshall Ward, whom Dr. Schlich fortunately secured to carry out this plan, managed to instil some of his own enthusiasm into his students, and it has often given me intense pleasure to witness the keen interest in general botanical questions on the part of young Indian foresters at home on leave, who had the privilege of his teaching. I feel assured that at the Dehra Dun Forest School also, the necessity of studying the general branches of botany is fully understood.

Under these circumstances I thought myself justified in introducing here and there a few very brief remarks on such points in regard to the anatomical structure, chiefly of the timber, and on important biological features, which I thought might be useful to foresters. Our knowledge of the structure of the stem, chiefly of climbing shrubs in India, is as yet very incomplete. What I have incidentally mentioned in this book may perhaps induce some, foresters or others, to pay more attention to this subject. Equally important is the study of anomalous wood structure in the case of trees, such as *Cocculus laurifolius*, most *Combretaceæ*, *Dalbergia paniculata*, *Strychnos*, the woody species of *Plumbaginaceæ*, *Nyctaginaceæ*, *Amarantaceæ* and *Chenopodiaceæ*.

The bright colouring of the young shoots of evergreen trees, which delights the eye in *Mesua ferrea*, *Acer oblongum*, *Amherstia nobilis*, *Quercus incana*, is well known, but has been fully described in the case of a few species only. The autumn colouring of deciduous species, which is so marked a feature in the temperate zone and which is not uncommon in the Himalaya (*Vitis semicordata*, formerly known as *V. himalayana*, *Acer Campbellii*) is rare in the rest of India, yet there are noteworthy exceptions, such as *Terminalia Catappa*, *Anogeissus latifolia*, *A. pendula* and *Antidesma diandrum*. Doubtless there are others besides. The study of gregarious species and of such as have the tendency to form pure forests naturally interests foresters. The factors, however, which enable *Shorea robusta*, *Dipterocarpus tuber-*

culatus, *Hardwickia binata* to get and retain the upper hand over other species and to form pure forests, are by no means fully understood. In connexion with this subject the coincidence in some cases of periodical flowering and gregarious habit should be mentioned (*Bamboos*, *Strobilanthes*, cf. Brandis in *Ind. For.* XXV. 1). The nature of the reserve materials which nourish the germinating seedling, starch in *bamboos*, oil in the cotyledons of *Bassia* and the endosperm of the *Coco nut*, the horny substance (cellulose) of the endosperm in *Coffea* and other *Rubiaceæ* and in *Phœnix*, is by no means known of all Indian trees. Many woody climbers, but not all to the same extent, yield, when cut like the vine in Europe in spring, large quantities of watery fluid, and the joints of many bamboos at a certain age are full of water. An accurate record on the spot of observations on these and other important biological matters will prove to be of real value. What is required in the first instance is an accurate record of facts, on the ground of which general conclusions can be framed hereafter.

A thorough study of the life, the habits and the requirements of trees will be found to be of great assistance in devising measures for guarding against diseases and other calamities, and for gradually increasing the annual yield of timber and other forest produce per acre. It is chiefly when an unexpected and unexplained calamity arises, such as the Spike disease in sandal wood, that the forester feels the need of a more intimate acquaintance with the life of trees.

There is a class of shrubs which I am disposed to call plants of mountain torrents, and which merit the attention of those who are likely to use this book. The following may here be mentioned as instances: *Camellia caduca*, *Rhazya stricta*, *Rhabdia lycioides*, *Litsæa angustifolia*, *Homonoia riparia*, *Ficus sæmocarpa*, *Ficus lanceolata*. These and other shrubs grow in masses in rocky or shingly stream-beds, dry during half the year and entirely submerged several times, often for a week or longer, during the rains. Their organization must be peculiar, and merits special study.

I have thought it right in this book to mention a number of species which are only undershrubs, because I consider that their study may be useful to foresters and others in India. They belong to genera comprising large or middle-sized trees. After the fires of the hot season have passed through the grasslands of the Subhimalayan tract and of other parts of India, in the midst of the black desolation, which is the result of these fires, we often come across a large blossom coming out of the ground, looking at a distance like a beautiful rose with numerous long delicate filaments. This is *Careya herbacea*, closely allied to *Careya arborea*, a large tree of India and Burma. Soon after the flowers a tuft of leaves appears, and during the rains the fruit ripens, looking like a large green apple. Through the action of the leaves the woody rootstock underground steadily increases in size and, though the fires of the following season destroy all shoots above ground, the rootstock remains uninjured and annually brings forth flowers, leaves and fruit. The undershrubs which behave in a similar fashion are very numerous, belonging to many orders. *Grewia sapida* with edible fruit, *Ochna pumila* with large golden yellow flowers, *Erythrina resupinata* with an upright raceme of scarlet flowers may be mentioned as instances.* They must not be confounded with temporary undershrubs, such as are formed through the action of the annual fires, by all trees that coppice readily. Seedlings of *Sal*, *Teak*, *Zizyphus jujuba*, *Terminalia* and many other trees which spring up in grasslands or in the forest, are cut back to the ground by the annual fires, and here also, through the action of the leaves, a large woody irregularly-shaped rootstock is formed, which throws up coppice shoots that are destroyed by the fires of the hot season. But when the area is protected against fire these coppice shoots grow

* The more prominent species of this class, besides those mentioned, are: *Olax nana*, *Flemingia nana*, *Combretum nanum*, *Mussænda incana*, *M. uniflora*, *Indigofera Hamiltonii*, *Jasminum Smalianum*, *Premna nana*.

panicles. Stamens 10, free, exserted, anthers gland-tipped. Pod coriaceous, indehiscent, pendulous, linear, 5–10 in. long, filled with a dry sweetish pulp, contracted between seeds.

Sind, the Punjab, Rajputana, the Deccan, as far south as Tuticorin. Baluchistan and Persia. Leafless for a short time. Fl. after the leaves have come out, from Febr. to April. Gregarious, coppices well, the base of the stem often surrounded by a mass of stiff thorny branches and suckers. 2. **P. Stephaniana**, Kunth. Peshawar, Afghanistan, Western Asia, a thorny shrub; pinnæ 2–5 pair; pods short, thick, 1–1½ in. long.

2. PIPTADENIA, Benth.; Fl. Brit. Ind. ii. 289.

(Species 40, tropics of both hemispheres, chiefly America.)

P. oudhensis, Brandis; Ann. Bot. Gard. Calc. ix. t. 43. Vern. *Genti*, *Gainti*, Oudh.

A middle-sized tree, glabrous, except inflorescence, branches armed with large conical prickles. L. bipinnate, pinnæ opposite, 2 pair, flat glands at the base of each. Leaflets 1 pair, reniform, subcoriaceous, 2–4 in. long. Fl. greenish-yellow, in dense cylindrical spikes, arranged in short panicles. Calyx cup-shaped, nearly truncate; petals 5, lanceolate, three times the length of calyx. Stamens longer than petals, terminal glands of anthers globose. Pod stalked, linear, flat, 9–12 in. long, ½ in. broad. Seeds 15–20.

Hills of the Gonda district and adjacent hills of Nepal. Oudh, discovered by R. Thompson 1871. Hills above Barmdeo, eastern Kumaon. (D. B. 1875.) Fl. April.

3. DICHROSTACHYS, DC.; Fl. Brit. Ind. ii. 288.

(Species 7, most in tropical Africa, one in tropical Australia.)

D. cinerea, W. et A.; Bedd. Fl. Sylv. t. 185.—Syn. *Mimosa cinerea*, Roxb. Cor. Pl. t. 174. Vern. *Kunlai*, Merwara; *Sigamkati*, Mar.; *Wadu*, Kan.; *Velturu*, Tel.; *Vadataram*, Tam.; *Sitbyu*, Burm.

A rigid thorny pubescent shrub or small tree, with light grey bark, heartwood dark purple, spines axillary, straight, strong and sharp, often prolonged into leaf-bearing branches. L. bipinnate; pinnæ 6–10 pair, opposite, small stipitate glands at the base of each pair; leaflets 12–15 pair, $\frac{1}{10}$ in. long, ciliate. Fl. in dense cylindrical spikes, the upper flowers of each spike bisexual, yellow, the lower sterile, purple, sometimes white, with long filiform staminodes. Pods linear, 2–3 in. long, irregularly twisted, indehiscent or opening irregularly.

Dry stony hills in Central India, Rajputana and the Deccan. Meiktila and Pakokku district in the dry region of the middle Irawaddi valley. Fl. according to the locality, at different times, in Rajputana, the northern Deccan and Burma in the H.S., Coimbatore in June, Veligondas, Nellore district in November.

4. ENTADA, Adans.; Fl. Brit. Ind. ii. 286.

(*Pusætha*, Linn.; Engler u. Prantl iii. 3. 122.)

(Species 11, tropics of both hemispheres.)

E. scandens, Benth.; Brandis F. Fl. 167. Vern. *Pangra*, Beng.; *Gila*, Sundrib.; *Garambi*, Mar.; *Gôn-nyin*, Burm.

A very large woody climber, stems angled and much twisted. The wood to a great extent consists of thin-walled parenchyma, in which are embedded longitudinal strands of vessels, sieve-tubes and wood-fibres. L. bipinnate, common petioles ending in long woody bifid tendrils; pinnæ opposite, 2 pair; leaflets 3–4 pair, 1–3 in. long, glabrous, shining. Fl. pale yellow, crowded in long slender spikes, from the axils of the upper leaves, or arranged in a terminal panicle. Calyx shortly 5-toothed; petals 5. Stamens 10, free, exserted,

anthers tipped with globose deciduous glands. Pod woody, of immense size, 2–4 ft. long, 3–4 in. broad, consisting of 10–30 one-seeded, flat, square or nearly orbicular joints, the valves thick, separating from the thick rim. Seeds flat, nearly orbicular, brown, shining, testa very hard.

Subhimalayan tract from Nepal eastwards, ascending to 2,000 ft. Silhet, Manipur, Burma, Andamans, Nicobars, Western Ghats. Fl. March–May.—Ceylon, Malay Peninsula and Archipelago. China. Sea coast of the tropics in both hemispheres.

5. ADENANTHERA, Linn.; Fl. Brit. Ind. ii. 287.

(Species 4, one in Queensland, the others in tropical Asia.)

A. pavonina, Linn.; Wight Ill. t. 84; Bedd. Fl. Sylv. t. 46. Vern. *Manjadi*, Kan.; *Ani Kundamani*, Tam.; *Ywetgyi*, Burm.

A deciduous, unarmed tree; heart-wood red, hard. L. bipinnate, pinnæ opposite, 4–6 pair; leaflets evenly alternate, 12–20, elliptic-oblong obtuse, 1 in. long. Fl. yellow, fragrant, on slender pedicels, in long panicled racemes. Calyx small, campanulate, teeth short; petals 5, connate at the base. Stamens 10, free, anthers tipped with a deciduous gland. Pods linear, curved and twisted when opening, 4–9 in. long. Seeds bright scarlet, shining, lenticular, compressed.

Subhimalayan tract from Gorakhpur eastwards. Silhet, Andamans, Burma. Western Ghats from Khandeish southwards, not common. Fl. H. S.—Malay Peninsula and Archipelago, China.

6. XYLIA, Benth.; Fl. Brit. Ind. ii. 286.

X. dolabriformis, Benth. The only species.—Syn. *Mimosa xylocarpa*, Roxb. Cor. Pl. t. 100; *Xylia xylocarpa*, Taub. in Engler u. Prantl iii. 3. 122. *The Ironwood of Burma.* Vern. *Suria*, Chanda; *Jamba*, Mar.; *Tangedu*, Tel.; *Irul*, Tam.; *Pyin*, *Pyinkado*, Burm.

A lofty tree, leafless during part of the hot season. Bark grey; heart-wood dark red, very hard. One pair of pinnæ at the end of a common petiole 1–5 in. long; leaflets 2–6 pair, oblong acuminate, 3–9 in. long. Fl. pale yellow, in globose long-pedunculate heads. Calyx-tubular, wider at mouth, teeth short; petals linear, cohering at the base; anthers with small stipitate deciduous glands. Pod flat, thick, woody, 4–6 in. long, 2–2½ in. wide at the broadest part, 2-valved, opening suddenly. Seeds 6–10, compressed, testa brown, shining.

Common in the moister districts of the Western Peninsula, on the east side in Orissa and the forests north of the Godavery; the Moharli forests in the Chanda district being its northern limit in Central India. Often gregarious. Burma, in the deciduous forests, ascending to 3,000 ft. Fl. while leafless in March and April; fr. in the ensuing cold season.

7. PARKIA, R. Brown; Fl. Brit. Ind. ii. 289.

Unarmed trees. L. bipinnate; leaflets very numerous. Fl. in globose or clavate heads, each head supported by a coriaceous bract, the upper fl. bisexual, the lower male or sterile. Stamens 10, filaments connate at base and adnate to calyx-tube. Pod flat, coriaceous, tardily dehiscent. Species 19, tropics of both hemispheres.

1. **P. Roxburghii**, G. Don. Vern. *Supota*, Beng.

Attains 60 ft., and 2 ft. diam. Pinnæ 20–30 pair; leaflets 40–80 pairs, ⅓ in. long; pod 15–20 in. long, 1½ in. broad, smooth, dark brown.

Assam, Silhet, Cachar, Chittagong. Fl. Dec. 2. **P. insignis**, Kurz. Vern. *Myank tanyet*, Burma, forests east of Toungoo. Pinnæ 4 pair; leaflets 20–25 pair, 1 in. long. 3. **P. leiophylla**, Kurz, Pegu Yoma. Pinnæ 10 pair; leaflets 15–20 pair, ½ in. long; pod 12–18 in. long, black, torulose.

Leucæna glauca, Benth.; Fl. Brit. Ind. ii. 290, naturalized, common in hedges,

originally American, is a large unarmed shrub or low tree; pinnæ 4–8 pair; leaflets 10–15 pair, ½ in. long. Fl. white, in dense globose heads, bisexual, mixed with slender bracteoles, broader at the top. Peduncle thick, woody in fruit, bearing numerous pods, which are flat, stipitate, early dehiscent, linear, 5–7 in. long; seeds numerous, shining, lenticular, made into ornaments.

8. MIMOSA, Linn.; Fl. Brit. Ind. ii. 291.

Herbs or shrubs, rarely trees; l. in many species sensitive. Pinnæ stipellate. Fl. in dense globose heads. Petals 4 or 5, rarely 3 or 6. Stamens generally twice the number of petals and more than twice their length. Pod linear or oblong, the valves separating (entire or in transverse joints) from the persistent sutures. Species 300, mostly American, a few in Asia and Africa.

1. **M. rubicaulis**, Lam.—Syn. *M. octandra*, Roxb. Cor. Pl. t. 200. Vern. *Hajero*, Sind; *Agla, Eil, Aila, Āl Rāl*, Hind.; *Vundra*, Tel.

A straggling prickly shrub, pubescent, branches, petioles and peduncles armed with short curved sharp prickles; stem attaining 5 in. diam. Pinnæ 3–12 pair, the lowest often not exactly opposite; leaflets 6–15 pair, obliquely oblong, the midrib lateral. Fl. tetramerous, pink, in fasciculate pedunculate heads. Pod stipitate, glabrous, curved, 3–4 in. long, separating in square joints from the sutural frame, sutures generally without prickles. Seeds 6–10.

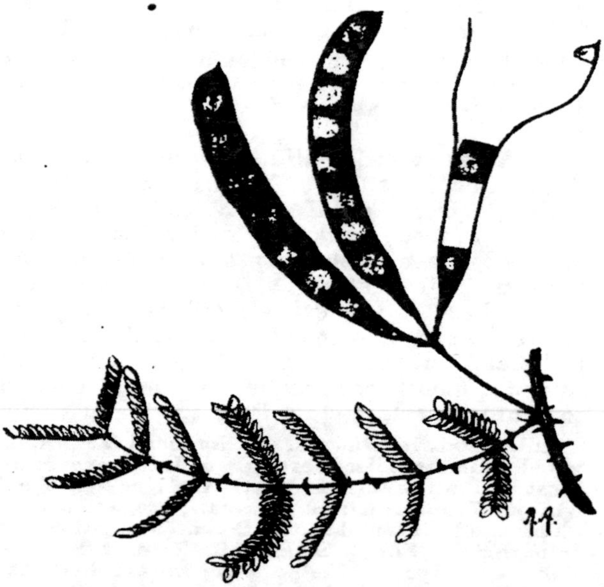

FIG. 114.—Mimosa rubicaulis, Lam. ½.

Common in most parts of India, except the arid region; in the outer Himalaya ascending to 4,000 ft. Fl. R. S. Wood used for gunpowder charcoal. 2. **M. hamata**, Willd.; Surat, Deccan and east side of the Western Peninsula; pinnæ 3–4 pair; leaflets 6–10 pair, midrib near the middle of leaflet. Sutures armed with numerous hooked prickles. Specimens of this, from Bombay, have been identified with *M. polyancistra*, Benth., an American species. 3. **M. pudica**, Linn., the Sensitive Plant, naturalized, introduced from America, clothed with long bristly hairs; pinnæ 3–4, digitate; pod ½ in. long, with abundant straw-coloured prickles. Seeds 3–4.

9. ACACIA, Willd.; Fl. Brit. Ind. ii. 292.

(The following characters relate only to the Indian species.)

Trees, shrubs and climbers, armed with stipular, infra-stipular or scattered spines. L. bipinnate, pinnæ and leaflets opposite. Fl. yellow or white, in globose heads or cylindrical spikes; numerous scaly bracteoles between the flowers. Calyx and corolla 4–5-merous. Stamens free, generally very numerous. Pod dehiscent or indehiscent. Species 450, tropical and subtropical regions of both hemispheres, chiefly Australia.

A. Trees or shrubs; stipules spinescent; fl. in globose heads.

1. **A. Farnesiana**, Willd.; Bedd. Fl. Sylv. t. 52. –Syn. *Vachellia Farnesiana*, W. et A.; Wight Ic. t. 300. Vern. *Waldyti Kikar*, Hind.

A thorny shrub; spines straight, stipular. Common petiole 1½–2 in.; pinnæ 4–8 pair; cup-shaped glands below the lowest and often at the base of the uppermost pair; leaflets 10–20 pair. Fl. bright yellow, sweet-scented, in globose fasciculate heads. Pod nearly cylindric, pointed at the ends, scarcely dehiscent, glabrous, valves with raised parallel lines; seeds embedded in dry spongy tissue.

Indigenous in America, but naturalized throughout India and Burma. Fl. Jan.–March.

2. **A. planifrons,** W. et A.; Trimen Handbook Ceylon t. 35, *The Umbrella Thorn*. Vern. *Godugu Thumma*, Tel.; *Kodaivelam, Jali Salei*, Tam.

A middle-sized tree, crown flat, spreading, umbrella-like. Spines of two kinds on the same branch: (*a*) long (1–2 in.), cylindric, ivory white, (*b*) short, slightly curved, brown. L. small, fasciculate, with the fl. on arrested branchlets; pinnæ ¼ in. long, 3–5 pair; leaflets 6–10 pair, minute, obtuse. Fl. heads yellow in bud, white when open; peduncles slender, ½–¾ in. long. Pod 2–3 in. long, glabrous, nearly cylindrical, curved nearly into a ring.

Southern Deccan: Salem, Madura, Tinnevelli, often gregarious. Fl. March. Prain in Journ. As. Soc. Bengal 66, (1898), 506, mentions a species from Southern India different from 2, possibly *A. Roxburghii*, W. et A. This is not known to me.

3. **A. arabica,** Willd.; Bedd. Fl. Sylv. t. 47.—Syn. *Mimosa arabica*, Lam.; Roxb. Cor. Pl. t. 149. Vern. *Babul*, Hind.; *Kikar*, Pb.; *Bamura*, Jabalp.; *Babar*, Sind; *Jali*, Kan.; *Nellatuma*, Tel.; *Karu Vélam*, Tam.

A large tree; bark rough with deep narrow longitudinal fissures; heart-wood pale red, when fresh cut nearly colourless, on exposure turning reddish-brown. Stipular spines straight, ½–2 in. long. Pinnæ 3–6 pair, cup-shaped glands at the base of the lowest, and generally also of the uppermost pair; leaflets small, linear, 10–20 pair. Fl. golden-yellow, in globose heads, ½ in. diam.; peduncles slender, fasciculate; a pair of scaly bracts in the middle. Pod solitary, moniliform, much contracted between seeds at both sutures, whitish-tomentose, stalk ½–¾ in. long.

Indigenous in Sind and the Northern Deccan, including Berar and Khandeish. Cultivated and naturalized throughout India, except in the most humid regions on the western coast and in the extreme North-West beyond the Jhelam, where the frost is too severe in winter. Tropical Africa, Arabia. Gregarious. Babul forests are extensive in lower Sind along the Indus, and in the Deccan along the Purna, Bhima and Kistna rivers and their tributaries. Fl. R. S. and C. S; never leafless, the young foliage comes out in Febr. and April. The pods are an excellent cattle-fodder. Gum exudes largely from wounds in the bark.

A remarkable variety is the *Kaulia* or *Kowri Babul* in Berar and Khandeish, called *Vedi Babul* in Poona, Sholapur and Satara. The spines are white, very stout, up to 2½ in. long, the pod is flat, on short stalks, ⅜ in. broad and very little constricted between the seeds. In these districts the ordinary form with moniliform pods is called *Telia* or *Godi Babul*, its wood is prized, while that of the *Kaulia* is considered only fit for firewood. The bark of the *Kaulia* is more deeply cracked and exfoliating and the crown is formed of twisted interlacing branches. In Africa and Arabia also *arabica* varies greatly.

4. **A. eburnea,** Willd.; Trimen Handbook Ceylon ii. 124.—Syn. *Mimosa eburnea*, Roxb. Cor. Pl. t. 199. Vern. *Marmat*, Mar.; *Odai*, Tam.

A large shrub or small tree. Branches armed with straight stipular spines, mostly stout, ivory-white and 1–2 in. long. L. small, clothed with long hairs; pinnæ 4–8; leaflets 8–12 pair, acute. Fl. yellow, with an unpleasant smell; heads under ½ in. diam., fasciculate, reddish-brown while in bud; membranous bracts below the middle of the peduncle. Pods linear, slender, flat, veined, generally 2–4 from one fl. head, 2–5 in. long, edges undulate.

Trans-Indus, Baluchistan. Salt range, Subhimalayan tract and outer valleys, ascending to 3,000 ft., east as far as Oudh. Sind. The Deccan. Fl. Nov.–March. Dry region of Ceylon.

5. **A. Jacquemonti**, Benth.; Brandis F. Fl. 183. Vern. *Ratabauli*, Guz.

A bushy shrub; perfectly glabrous; branches flexuose, brown, shining. Stipular spines straight, white, 1–2 in. long. Pinnæ 2–4 pair; leaflets obtuse, fleshy, 5–10 pair. Fl. heads yellow, sweet-scented; peduncles 5–10, fasciculate; a pair of small scaly bracts about the middle. Pod stalked, thin, flat, glabrous, 2–3 by ½ in.

Trans-Indus. Punjab plains and Outer Himalaya ascending to 3,000 ft. Sind, Rajputana, Guzerat (the dwarf *Babul* of Rajputana and Guzerat). Fl. Febr.–May. 6. **A. tomentosa**, Willd.; Trimen Handbook Ceylon ii. 124. Lower Bengal. Western Peninsula, doubtful. Ceylon, dry region; a small bushy tree; branches and l. tomentose; thorns from a stout base, up to 8½ in. long; pinnæ 6–10, leaflets 8–16 pair. Pod falcate, pubescent while young, somewhat torulose, 4–5 by ½ in.

7. **A leucophlœa**, Willd.; Bedd. Fl. Sylv. t. 48; Brandis F. Fl. t. 27.—Syn. *Mimosa leucophlœa*, Roxb. Cor. Pl. t. 150. Vern. *Rinj*, *arinj*, Hind.; *Raeru*, Pb.; *Hewar*, Mar.; *Tella tuma*, Tel.; *Velvaylam*, Tam.; *Tanaung*, Burm.

A deciduous, thorny tree; trunk often crooked and gnarled. Bark grey or light brown, when old almost black and very rough. Heart-wood reddish-brown, extremely hard. Spines straight, strong. Pinnæ 5–10 pair; leaflets 12–25 pair, grey, linear, ⅛–¼ in. long, glabrous or pubescent. Fl. heads pale yellow, nearly white, in large terminal, leafless densely tomentose panicles; peduncles short. Pods linear, 4–6 by ⅓ in., clothed with dense brown velvet.

Siwalik hills, Jumna to Ravi. Plains of the Punjab. Rajputana, Bundelkhand, the Satpura range, Northern Circars and the Deccan. Dry region of the Irawaddi valley from Prome to Mandalay. Fl. Aug.–Nov.

Most, but not all, Burma specimens have large leaflets, ¼–⅓ in. long, rachis and leaflets glabrous, pods glabrous, ½ in. wide. These Prain (l c. 507) prefers to consider as a distinct species, *A. microcephala*, Graham.

8. **A. Kingii**, Prain in Journ. As. Soc. Bengal (1898), 66, 506. Shan hills, Upper Burma. A tree 30–40 ft.; stipular spines weak, minute; common petiole pubescent, 2–3 in. long; pinnæ 9–10 pair, 1 in. long. Leaflets minute, 11–14 pair. Peduncles ¾ in. long, hairy, a ring of bracteoles above the middle; filaments united at the base. 9. **A.** (?) **inopinata**, Prain l.c. 507. Shan hills. Unarmed; common petiole glabrous, 8–10 in. long; pinnæ 6–7 pair, 2–3 in. long; leaflets ⅛ in. long, 10–11 pair. Fl. heads in terminal panicles; stamens monadelphous, filaments united in a tube beyond the middle. 8 and 9 possibly not *Acacia*.

B. Trees or shrubs; stipules spinescent; fl. in spikes.

10. **A. Latronum**, Willd.; Wight Ic. t. 1157. Vern. *Jala*, Tel.; *Odai*, Tam.

A gregarious shrub, sometimes a small tree; thorns of two kinds, thin solid short and stout, hollow, ivory-white, 2 in. long and ⅓–½ in. diam. at base. L. fasciculate on arrested branchlets; pinnæ 3–5 pair, ¾–1 in. long, leaflets 12–18 pair, minute. Fl. fragrant, white at first, turning yellow afterwards, in lax spikes 1½–2 in. long. Pods thin, dehiscent, broadly falcate, obtuse at the ends, dark brown, shining, 1½–2 in. by ½–¾ in.

Dry hills of the Deccan, covering large tracts with a formidable thorny scrub. Fl. R. S., C. S.

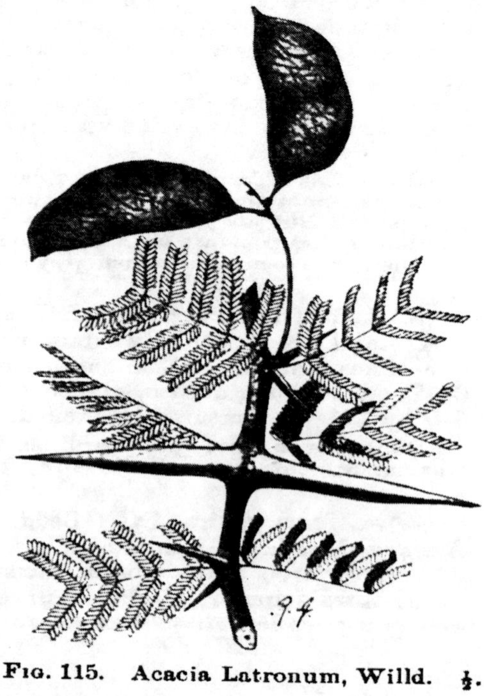

FIG. 115. Acacia Latronum, Willd. ½.

C. Trees or shrubs; stipules not spinescent; spines infra-stipular; fl. in spikes.

11. **A. Senegal**, Willd.; Fl. Brit. Ind. ii. 295.—Syn. *A. rupestris*, Stocks; Brandis F. Fl. 184. Vern. *Khor*, Sind.; *Kumta*, Rajputana.

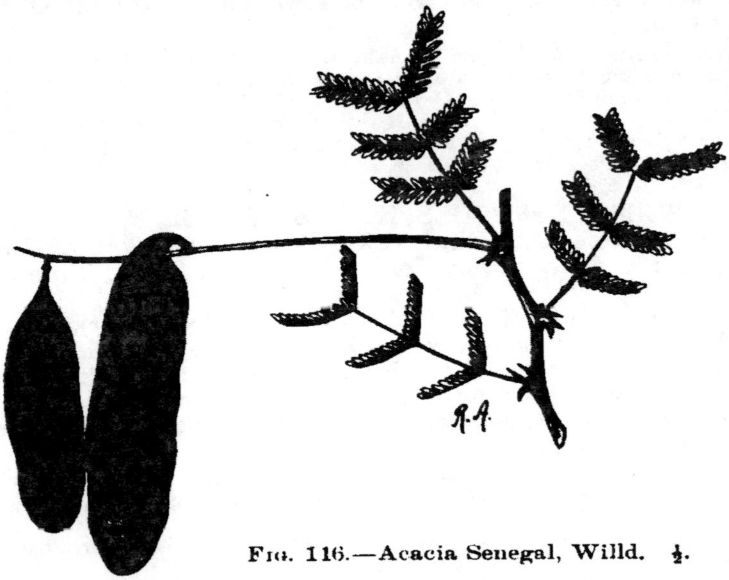

FIG. 116.—Acacia Senegal, Willd. ½.

A small thorny tree; bark smooth, shining; infra-stipular spines three, stout, conical, very sharp, dark brown, shining, the two lateral straight, the third recurved. Pinnæ 3–5 pair; common petiole often armed with minute prickles; leaflets 8–12 pair, grey, ciliate. Fl. fragrant, white, in lax pedunculate spikes; anthers lemon-yellow. Pod thin, straight, pubescent when young, tardily dehiscent, 3 in. long, ¾ in. broad.

Dry hills in Sind, Aravalli range. Fl. Aug.–Dec.—Tropical Africa.

12. **A. modesta**, Wall. Pl. As. Rar. t. 130.—Syn. *Mimosa dumosa*, Roxb. Vern. *Paloz*, Baluch.; *Phulāi*, Pb.

A middle-sized gregarious tree, thorny, rarely unarmed. Bark rough, with a multitude of irregular narrow cracks. Heart-wood dark brown with black streaks. Prickles twin, infra-stipular, dark brown, shining, conical. L. pale grey; common petiole 1–2 in. long; pinnæ 3 pair; leaflets 3–5 pair, broad ovate, or obovate, oblique. Stipules minute, deciduous. Fl. white or pale yellow, sweet-scented, in lax cylindrical drooping spikes. Pod stalked, flat, indehiscent, 2–3 in. by ½ in.

Baluchistan. Trans-Indus, east flank of the Suleiman range up to 4,000 ft. Subhimalayan tract and outer hills, between Indus and Sutlej. Salt range and northern part of the Punjab plains, as far as Saharanpur and Delhi. Fl. March–May. The white-fl. spikes contrast with the delicate green of the young foliage, but the fl. fade and the leaves soon turn an ash-grey colour.

13. **A. lenticularis**, Ham.; Brandis F. Fl. 186. Vern. *Khour*, Nep.

A small tree, perfectly glabrous. Prickles twin, infra-stipular, recurved, sometimes wanting. Common petiole 3–6 in. long. Pinnæ 2–6 pair, leaflets 6–12 pair, oblong, obtuse, glaucous, 1 in. long. Spikes 3–5 in. long. Pod flat, 6–9 by 1–1½ in., sutures thickened.

Subhimalayan tract and outer hills, Kumaon to Sikkim. Rajmahel hills in Bengal. Khamapur, Centr. Prov. This is *A. ferruginea* in Gamble List, 2nd ed. 82.

14. **A. ferruginea**, DC.; Bedd. Fl. Sylv. t. 51. Vern. *Khaiger*, Guzerat; *Khogra*, Mandevi; *Pandhra Khair*, Mar.

A large tree, with rough, dark-coloured bark, nearly glabrous. Prickles twin, infra-stipular, slightly curved. Common petiole 3–6 in. long; pinnæ 4–6 pair; leaflets 15–30 pair, grey, linear, ¼–½ in. long. Fl. pale yellow in

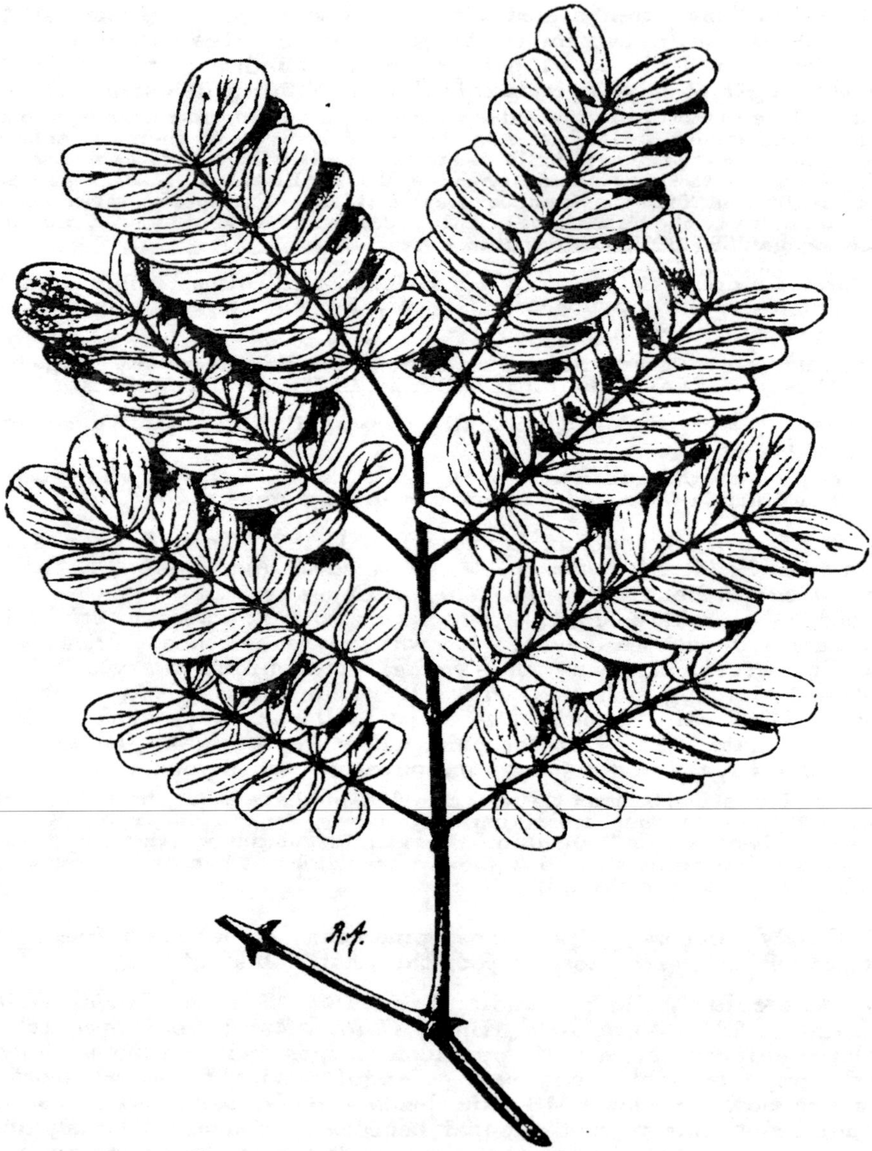

FIG. 117.—Acacia lenticularis, Ham. ½.

numerous lax axillary spikes, which are often panicled at the ends of branches. Pod glabrous, 3–7 in. by ¾ in., finally dehiscent.

Western Peninsula. Northern limit: Gujarāt, on the west and Ganjam on the east side. Fl. R. S.—Ceylon.

15. **A. Catechu,** Willd.—Syn. *A. Sandra* Bedd. Fl. Sylv. t. 50; *Mimosa Catechu,* Linn.; Roxb. Cor. Pl. t. 175; *M. Sundra,* Roxb. Cor. Pl. t. 225. Vern. *Khair,* Hind., Mar.; *Kugli,* Kan.; *Tella Tumma, Sundra,* Tel.; *Karangalli,* Tam.; *Sha,* Burm.

A middle-sized tree; trunk with dark-coloured bark peeling off in long strips, which remain hanging; branchlets slender, thorny, glabrous, brown or purple, shining. Prickles twin, infra-stipular, compressed, brown, shining. Common

petiole 3–4 in. long, often armed with scattered prickles. Pinnæ 10–20 pair, leaflets 30–50 pair, linear, imbricate, glabrous or pubescent, under $\frac{1}{4}$ in. long, turning brown in drying. Fl. pale yellow, in cylindrical spikes; petals three times the length of calyx. Pods thin, brown, shining, dehiscent.

Subhimalayan tract, from the Indus eastwards, ascending in the valleys to 3,000 ft., generally gregarious on islands and on the banks of rivers at their entrance into the plains. Common on the Aravalli hills and in the Western Peninsula, as well as in Burma. Fl. May–Oct. With this I unite *A. Sundra*, DC. Fl. Brit. Ind. ii. 295, kept separate by Talbot List 85, and Trimen Handbook Ceylon ii. 125. The species varies exceedingly, chiefly in regard to the pubescence of calyx, petals and spike-rachis. Prain in Journ. As. Soc. Bengal, 66 (1898), 508, recognizes 3 varieties:

(*a*) **Catechu** proper. Calyx, petals and rachis covered with spreading hairs. Chiefly in the Punjab, Garhwal and Kumaon, Behar, Ganjam and in the Irawaddi valley of Pegu and Upper Burma.

(*b*) **Catechuoides.** Calyx and petals glabrous, rachis puberulous. Chiefly in the Sikkim Terai and Assam, also in Upper Burma, in Mysore and on the Nilgiris.

(*c*) **Sundra.** Calyx, petals and rachis all glabrous. Chiefly in the Western Peninsula and Upper Burma.

To some extent the pubescence varies, and it is for further inquiry, whether these three forms differ in their mode of growth or in other respects.

16. **A. Suma,** Buchanan; Brandis F. Fl. 187; Kurz F. Fl. i. 421.—Syn. *A. Catechu*, Bedd. Fl. Sylv. t. 49; *Mimosa Suma*, Roxb. Fl. Ind. ii. 563. Vern. *Saikanta*, Beng.; *Dhaula Khejra*, Bauswara.

A large or middle-sized tree; bark white; branches stiff, flexuose; branchlets and petioles downy, with soft grey pubescence. Prickles in pairs, infra-stipular, conical, downy while young, brown shining afterwards. Common petiole 4–10 in. long, unarmed, with a large cup-shaped gland above the base. Pinnæ 10–20 pair, leaflets 20–50 pair, linear, approximate, imbricate, generally ciliate. Fl. white or pale yellow; spikes lax. Petals not much longer than calyx. Pod 3–5 by $\frac{3}{4}$ in., pubescent when young.

Western Peninsula, both on the west as well as on the east side, extending north to the Pertabgarh State in Southern Rajputana. Lower Bengal, Sundriban (Kurz gives it from Ava). Bentham in Trans. Linn. Soc. xxx. 519, doubts whether the proportion of calyx and corolla is constant. But *A. Suma* has a different habit and Foresters will find no difficulty in distinguishing it.

D. Woody climbers; stipules not spinescent; spines not infra-stipular but scattered; fl. in globose heads; pods thin, flat, dehiscent.

17. **A. cæsia,** Willd.; Brandis F. Fl. 189.—Syn. *A. Intsia*, Willd.; Fl. Brit. Ind. ii. 297. Vern. *Aila*, Hind.; *Chilār*, Mar.; *Korindam*, Tel.

A large climber; stem with prominent ridges twisting like a screw; bark smooth, grey; branchlets and petioles angular, with numerous short conical sharp prickles. Pinnæ 6–16 pair, leaflets 10–30 pair, coriaceous, more or less pubescent, pale or rust-coloured beneath, $\frac{1}{4}$ in. long, obliquely linear or oblong, obtuse or acute, nerves distinct, midrib nearer the middle than the upper edge. Fl. heads pale yellow, in terminal tomentose panicles; bracts minute, caducous. Pods thin, 4–6 in. long, 1 in. broad, tomentose when young, glabrous afterwards.

Subhimalayan tract from the Chenab eastwards, ascending to 3,000 ft. in Sikkim, Assam, Cachar, Chittagong. Not known from Burma, Behar, Rajputana, Western Peninsula. Fl. April–August. Ceylon, Malay Archipelago.

Prain in Journ. As. Soc. Beng. 66 (1898) 510 maintains *A. cæsia* and *A. Intsia* as distinct species, stating "that the crowded leaflets, always hairy beneath, make it very easy to recognize *A. cæsia*, even in the herbarium, and that no one dreams of confounding the two as they grow." Bentham (Mimoseæ, Trans. Linn. Soc. xxx. 530) following, as he says, my old Forest Flora, only recognizes one species: *A. cæsia*, Willd. A form collected by me on the Pachmarhi hills in April, 1869, with branchlets, petioles, underside of l. and inflorescence densely tawny-tomentose is remarkable, but the

specimens from the Kumaon Bhabar, Behar and the Konkan, which are more than usually pubescent, cannot in my opinion be regarded as a separate species.

Nearly allied are: 18. **A. pruinescens**, Kurz F. Fl. i. 424, Assam, Manipur, Upper Burma. Pegu Yoma, branchlets pruinose; leaflets narrow linear, $\frac{1}{8}$–$\frac{1}{2}$ in. long, the midrib close to the upper edge, gland on petiole $\frac{1}{2}$–1 in. above base. 19. **A. pseudo-Intsia**, Miq.; Prain in Journ. As. Soc. Beng. 66 (1898) 249, 511. Andamans, Malay Peninsula and Archip., branchlets blackish; leaflets linear-oblong, $\frac{1}{8}$–$\frac{1}{2}$ in. long, midrib close to the upper edge, gland oblong, near base of petiole, $\frac{1}{8}$ in. long. Fl. heads in bud concealed by large ovate acuminate bracts.

20. **A. pennata**, Willd.; Kurz F. Fl. i. 424. Vern. *Aila*, Hind.; *Shembi*, Mar.

A large climber, climbing over the tallest trees, bark reddish-brown; prickles on branchlets petioles and inflorescence; branchlets and petioles pubescent. Pinnæ 20–40 pair; leaflets $\frac{1}{8}$–$\frac{1}{5}$ in. long, 30–60 pair, narrow-linear, mucronate, midrib near the upper edge, closely packed, overlapping, making each pinna like the feather of a bird. Fl. heads white or pale yellow, 4–8 together in the axils of leaves or bracts, forming long racemiform panicles, bracts linear, minute. Pod shining, very thin.

Subhimalayan tract, from Kumaon eastwards, ascending in Sikkim to 3,000 ft. Behar. Khasi hills, Manipur, Cachar, Chittagong. Burma, Upper and Lower in deciduous forests. Andamans. Western Peninsula. Fl. April–August. Ceylon, Malay Peninsula and Archipelago.

E. Woody climbers; spines scattered; fl. in globose heads; pods thick, fleshy, indehiscent.

21. **A. concinna**, DC.; Fl. Brit. Ind. ii. 296. Vern. *Ban-ritha*, Beng.; *Shekakai*, Mar.; *Chikayi*, Tel.; *Subók*, Burm.

Branchlets, petioles and peduncles tomentose or pubescent, armed with numerous sharp recurved prickles. Pinnæ 4–6 pair, leaflets 12–20 pair, $\frac{1}{4}$–$\frac{1}{2}$ in. long, linear from an unequal-sided base. Stipules large, semicordate. Flower-buds purple; fl. yellow, heads in dense panicles at the ends of branches.

Subhimalayan tract, from Oudh eastwards. Assam, Behar. Western Peninsula and Burma, chiefly in evergreen forests. Fl. March–July. Malay Peninsula, Java.

Several Australian *Acacias* are cultivated on the Nilgiris and elsewhere. The most important are: **A. dealbata**, Link, *the Silver Wattle*. A tree spreading rapidly by root-suckers, with bipinnate grey hoary leaves, small linear leaflets and small yellow fl. heads in axillary and terminal panicles. **A. Melanoxylon**, R. Brown, *the Australian Blackwood*. A large tree with coriaceous, oblanceolate phyllodia (vertically dilated leaf-stalks) instead of leaves, except on young trees, which have bipinnate leaves at the end of phyllodia.

10. ALBIZZIA, Durazzini; Fl. Brit. Ind. ii. 298.

Unarmed trees, with bipinnate leaves and large (in the Indian species) globose fl. heads. Fl. white, yellow or pink. Calyx and corolla usually pentamerous. Stamens indefinite, long exserted, filaments united high up or at the base only. Pod flat, straight, usually thin, indehiscent or 2-valved.

A. Pinnæ 1 or 2 pair; leaflets distinctly penni-nerved, 1–6 pair, 2–5 in. long.

1. **A. lucida**, Benth. Vern. *Thanthat*, Burm.

A large glabrous tree, bark grey, heartwood hard, brown with dark streaks. Pinnæ 1, rarely 2 pair; leaflets 2 rarely 3 pair, a gland on petiole and at the base of the terminal pair of leaflets, none at the base of pinnæ. Leaflets elliptic, acuminate, shining. Heads of 6–10 sessile pubescent flowers, in terminal panicles. Corolla four times the length of calyx; ovary sessile, glabrous. Pod straight, shining, dehiscent, 4–8 by $1\frac{1}{2}$ in.

Subhimalayan tract, from Nepal eastwards, ascending in Sikkim to 2,000 ft. Assam, Khasi hills, Chittagong, Burma, Upper and Lower, chiefly by the banks of rivers or

FIG. 118.—Albizzia lucida, Benth. ½.

on moist ground. Fl. March–May. Leafless a short time during the hot season or nearly so.

B. Pinnæ 2–8 pair; leaflets ¾–2 in. long; fl. sessile or nearly so.

2. **A. Gamblei,** Prain in Ann. Bot. Gard. Calc. ix. 31, tab. 41.

A deciduous tree, attaining 50 ft.; pinnæ 2–3 pair. A large gland above the base of the common petiole, and glands at the base of the last pair of leaflets; leaflets 5–7 pair on the upper, 3–4 on the lowest pinna, in all cases decreasing slightly downwards, pale green above, glaucescent beneath, sparsely appressed puberulous on both surfaces. Heads many-fld., panicled; calyx campanulate, puberulous outside, half the length of corolla; corolla ⅛ in. long; pedicels much shorter than calyx. Pod 6–8 in. long.

Kangra (Prain). Sikkim. Naga hills. Fl. R. S. Yunnan.

A similar tree was found by Smales (April 1901) in Upper Burma on the edge of streams; pinnæ 2 pair; leaflets oblique, glabrous, upperside bright green, underside pale, in the upper pinnæ 6, in the lower 3 pair, those of the terminal pair the largest, in the upper pinnæ 5–6 in. long; the leaflets of the lower pair only ½–1 in. long, sec. n. prominent; glands several in a line on the common petiole below the lowest pair of pinnæ, and one at the base of each pair of leaflets, except the lowest. Fl. heads yellow, in large terminal

INTRODUCTION

THE object of this work is restricted and is entirely practical. It is intended for Foresters and others, who may wish to make themselves acquainted with the immense variety of trees, shrubs, climbers, bamboos and palms in the British Indian Empire. Ceylon and the Malay Peninsula are not included, and the book is limited to flowering plants; tree-ferns I have not been able to deal with. In this study the first step necessarily is to determine the name of a plant met with, and my principal aim has been to facilitate this difficult operation. To some extent I am told this has been accomplished for a portion of the Empire by the *Forest Flora of North-West and Central India*, which was commenced by the late Dr. Lindsay Stewart and completed by me in 1874.

Since I commenced the work about eight years ago, my hope has been that this book might facilitate the preparation of local Forest Floras, small portable handbooks, giving an account of the arborescent vegetation of limited areas, provinces or districts of the British Indian Empire. This hope has been strengthened by the publication in 1901 by Rai Sahib Upendranath Kanjilal of that excellent handbook, the *Forest Flora of the School Circle*, in what are now called the United Provinces of Agra and Oudh. The author was a pupil of Mr. J. F. Duthie, who taught systematic botany at the Dehra Dun Forest School from 1881 to 1902. Kanjilal has told me that his work has been greatly facilitated by the Forest Flora of North-West and Central India, but his book is full of original observations, made by him during his many years' work in the forests attached to the Imperial Forest School. Following the example set by him, I trust that the local Forest Floras of the future will be based mainly upon the study of the trees and shrubs as they grow in the forest, and hence as a matter of course they must be written in India.

The attainment of my principal object, to facilitate the identification of trees and shrubs, will I hope be furthered by the illustrations which I have been able to give of 201 species. I had hoped to induce Miss M. Smith, the accomplished Botanical Artist at Kew, to undertake this work. Unfortunately she had not sufficient leisure, and was only able to give me two figures in *Anonaceæ*. For the greater part of the remainder I have had the good fortune to secure the services of Dr. Roland Anheisser of Cologne, and I feel sure that those who may use this book will be grateful to him for the help which his illustrations will give them. They increase the bulk of the book, but I have gladly given up over 60 pages to them. It will be noticed that no illustrations are given of trees which may be supposed to be generally known, such as Teak, Sal, Sissoo, Deodar.

The present book does not claim to be a Forest Flora, such as we have in Europe, giving all that is known regarding the internal structure, the marketable products, the mode and rate of growth, the biological features, the sylvicultural requirements, the treatment in the forest, and the insect and fungoid enemies of the different species. Such a work for the whole of the British Indian Empire would fill several volumes and could not be written at present. France has an exceedingly rich and varied flora, and yet Mathieu's admirable *Flore Forestière de la France* (the last edition by Fliche), only deals with 397 species, while in the present volume over 4,400 species are described.

panicles, pedicels as long as calyx; calyx campanulate, minutely silky, corolla 5-fid to the middle. Ovary stalked, cylindric, pilose. Pod unknown, hence cannot be named, it might turn out to be a *Pithecolobium*.

3. **A. procera**, Benth.; Brandis F. Fl. t. 26.—Syn. *Mimosa elata*, Roxb. Cor. Pl. t. 121. Vern. *Karhar, Gurār, Safed Siris*, Hind.; *Sirsi*, Uriya; *Kinni Gurār*, Mar.; *Chigara*, Tel.; *Vagai*, Tam.; *Sit*, Burm.

A large tree, bark light brownish-grey, heartwood hard, brown, shining, with streaks of darker colour. Young shoots white-silky-pubescent. Pinnæ 3–5 pair, leaflets 6–10 pair, with scattered appressed hairs, obliquely oblong-ovate, $\frac{3}{4}$–2 in. long, midrib nearer the lower edge, pale beneath. Fl. heads in large terminal and axillary panicles; fl. sessile, $\frac{1}{3}$–$\frac{1}{2}$ in. long to extremity of stamens; calyx tubular, glabrous, more than half the length of corolla; corolla funnel-shaped, lobes bearded at the end with long white hairs. Ovary glabrous, nearly sessile.

Subhimalayan tract from the Jumna eastwards. Western Peninsula. Andamans and Burma. Chiefly on river banks and in moist places. Fl. May–August. Rarely quite leafless, the foliage renewed H. S. China, Malay Archipelago. A remarkable variety sent by E. M. Buchanan from the Tharawadi forests has pinnæ 5–6 pair, leaflets 10 pair $\frac{3}{4}$–1 in. long, panicles mostly axillary, pod not known.

4. **A. odoratissima**, Benth.; Bedd. Fl. Sylv. t. 54.—Syn. *Mimosa odoratissima*, Roxb. Cor. Pl. t. 120. Vern. *Karmaru*, Pb.; *Kalia Siris*, Hind.; *Bansa*, Jabalp.; *Siris, Chichunda*, Mar.; *Chichola*, Gondi; *Chichwa*, Chanda; *Chinduga*, Tel.; *Bilwāra*, Kan.; *Karu Vagei*, Tam.; *Thitmagyi*, Lower, *Thitpyu*, Upper Burma.

A large tree, with dark green foliage. Bark light or dark grey, marked with numerous narrow horizontal wrinkles, nearly encircling the trunk. Heartwood dark brown. Branchlets, petioles and inflorescence pubescent. Pinnæ 3–8 pair. Leaflets 10–25 pair, $\frac{3}{4}$–1 in. long, oblong, obtuse, unequal-sided, somewhat falcate, pale, glabrous or pubescent beneath. Fl. heads pale yellow, fragrant, in compact corymbs arranged in large terminal panicles. Corolla and calyx densely strigose with short hairs, the former campanulate, 5 times longer than calyx. Anthers yellow. Pods 6–8 in. long, 1 in. broad, dehiscent, tomentose when young, nearly glabrous when ripe.

Subhimalayan tract ascending to 3,000 ft. Western Peninsula and Burma. Never quite leafless, foliage renewed in spring. Fl. April–June. 5. **A. lebbekoides**, Benth.; Prain in Journ. As. Soc. Beng. 66 (1898) 513, Upper Burma, common. A tall tree, attaining 120 ft., differs from 4 by smaller linear, more numerous leaflets (25–30 pair) and a tubular corolla.

C. Pinnæ 3–12 pair; leaflets $\frac{1}{2}$–2 in. long; fl. pedicellate.

6. **A. Thompsoni**, Brandis, Ind. For. xxv. (1899) 284. Vern. *Silari*, Chanda.

A large deciduous tree, attaining 7 ft. in girth; branches spreading. Branchlets, young leaves and inflorescence tawny-tomentose. Pinnæ 8–12, leaflets 15–20 pair, pale beneath, very unequal-sided, nearly falcate, acute or mucronate, $\frac{1}{2}$–$\frac{2}{3}$ in. long. Fl. pale yellow, not scented; anthers pink; pedicels as long as or longer than calyx; corolla twice the length of calyx, both pubescent. Ovary glabrous, stipitate. Heads in dense corymbs; peduncles 1$\frac{1}{2}$–2 in. long. Pod glabrous from the beginning, shining, of a rich brown colour; dehiscent, 6–8 by 1–1$\frac{1}{2}$ in.

Mohurli and other forests in the Chanda district, often associated with *Chichwa* (*A. odoratissima*) Ganjam. Leafless January and February. Fl. with the young leaves by the end of February or beginning of March.

7. **A. Lebbek**, Benth.; Bedd. Fl. Sylv. t. 53. *Siris*. Vern. *Siris, Sirsa*, Hind.; *Chichola*, Mar.; *Bage*. Kan.; *Dirasanam*, Tel.; *Vagai*, Tam.; *Kokoh*, Burm.

A large deciduous tree, with dark grey or brownish bark, sapwood large, white, heartwood dark brown, shining, mottled. Nearly glabrous; pinnæ 2–3, leaflets 6–8 pair, 1–1½ in. long, obliquely oblong, obtuse. Midrib prominent, reticulate veins nearly as prominent as sec. n. Fl. heads large, white, fragrant, on peduncles 2–4 in. long, in fascicles of 2–4 from the upper axils, forming short corymbose racemes. Fl. 1⅓ in. long to the extremity of stamens; pedicels nearly as long as calyx; calyx half the length of corolla. Pod thin, straw-coloured, dehiscent, 8–12 by 1–2 in.

Subhimalayan tract, ascending to 5,000 ft. Both Peninsulas. Fl. April–May; pods ripen in September and remain on the tree for a considerable time. Planted largely in Egypt and throughout the tropics.

Nearly allied are: 8. **A. littoralis**, Teysm. et Binnend; Prain in Journ. As. Soc. Beng. 66 (1898) 257, Nicobars. Malay Penins. and Archipelago. A middle-sized tree; pinnæ 2–4, leaflets obovate-oblong, 3–6 pair; fl. heads white with pink stamens, under ½ in. diam. 9. **A. Kalkora**, Prain l.c. 511, Khasi and Naga hills. South China. Differs from *A. Lebbek* chiefly by the dark brown pod on a stalk ⅓ in. long. 10. **A. elegans**, Kurz F. Fl. i. 427; Prain l.c. 512, eastern slopes of the Pegu Yoma. A tall evergreen tree; pinnæ 7–14, leaflets small, 20–25 pair, linear-oblong, ⅜ in. long, midrib almost in the middle. Fl. heads in fascicles of 2–4, not panicled; pedicels a little longer than calyx; corolla twice the calyx, pubescent outside.

D. Pinnæ 6–20 pair; leaflets linear, ¼ in. long or less, midrib near middle of leaflet.

11. **A. amara**, Boivin; Bedd. Fl. Sylv. t. 61.—Syn. *Mimosa amara*, Roxb. Cor. Pl. t. 122. Vern. *Tugli*, Kan.; *Chikreni*, Tel.; *Womjai*, *Thuringi*, Tam.

A middle-sized tree, bark smooth, heartwood purplish-brown, mottled, extremely hard. Branchlets, petioles and inflorescence soft yellow-tomentose. Pinnæ 6–15, leaflets linear, 15–24 pair. Fl. yellow, fragrant, ⅓ in. long to the end of stamens; peduncles fasciculate in the axils of the uppermost leaves. Pod 5–8 by 1 in., edges undulate.

Western Peninsula on dry hills, north as far as Khandeish and Vizagapatam. Fl. April–June. 12. **A. myriophylla**, Benth. Sikkim, Assam, Khasi hills, Manipur. Tenasserim. Malay Peninsula. An evergreen shrub or strong climber; base of common petiole prolonged at the back into a recurved woody hook. Pinnæ 10–20, leaflets small, 30–50 pair. Heads small, white or pale yellow, in large terminal leafy panicles.

E. Pinnæ 6–15 pair; leaflets linear, falcate, midrib close to upper edge.

13. **A. stipulata**, Boivin; Bedd. Fl. Sylv. t. 55. Vern. *Ohi*, Kangra; *Siran*, *Sirsha*, Hind.; *Kal Vaghi*, Kan.; *Konda chigara*, Tel.; *Bonmèzá*, Burm.

A large fast-growing tree, crown broad, flat, bark dark grey, sapwood large, white, heartwood soft, brown. Young shoots and inflorescence tomentose. Stipules large, semicordate, membranous, more or less pubescent, deciduous. Pinnæ 6–18, leaflets 20–40 pair, ¼–⅓ in. long. Fl. yellowish, inodorous, to the end of stamens ⅔–1 in. long; stamens slightly tinged with red. Fl. heads fasciculate, panicled. Pod 6 in. long, ¾ in. broad.

Subhimalayan tract ascending to 4,000 ft. Western Peninsula, Burma, Nicobars. Fl. April–June. Ceylon, Malay Peninsula. A distinct variety with small stipules is mentioned by Prain l.c. 256 and Kanjilal Forest Flora of School Circle 150.

14. **A. Julibrissin**, Durazzini; Brandis F. Fl. 177; Benth. Mimoseæ in Trans. Linn. Soc. xxx. 568.—Syn. *A. mollis*, Boivin; Kanjilal Forest Flora School Circle 149; Collett Fl. Simla fig. 43; *Acacia mollis*, Wallich Pl. As. Rar. t. 177. Vern. *Sirsang*, *Shirin*, Bashahr; *Kurmura*, *Karmaru*, Hind.; *Baran*, N.W.P.; *Lakkey*, Nep. The specific name is a corruption of *Guláb-resham*, the silken rose.

A large shrub or middle-sized tree, deciduous. Young shoots, inflorescence and common petiole tomentose or pubescent. Pinnæ 6–12, leaflets 10–30 pair, from linear to obliquely oblong, ½ in. long. Fl. rose-coloured, 1–1¾ in. to extremity of stamens; calyx less than half the length of corolla, both hairy outside. Pod softly pubescent while young, glabrous when mature, 3–5 by ½–¾ in.

Outer Himalaya, Hazara to Sikkim, ascending to 5,000 and at times to 6,000 ft., in the Sutlej valley as far as Wangtu. Assam, Manipur. Fl. April–June. Mountains of Abyssinia at 6,000 ft. Forests around the southern part of the Caspian Sea. North Persia. China (Yunnan, Hupeh, Ichang, Peking). Japan. Cultivated in gardens of the Mediterranean region and in warm countries of both hemispheres. This widely spread species varies considerably, chiefly in regard to the degree of hairiness. Prain in Journ. As. Soc. Beng. 66 (1898) 514 regards *A. mollis* (Himalaya, Assam, Manipur) as a distinct species, but does not state its distinguishing characters. The specimens from this area have as a rule inflorescence and underside of leaflets softly tomentose, the leaflets are broader, and the base of the pod is rounded. The specimens from Abyssinia, Western Asia, China and Japan are slightly pubescent, they agree in all respects and cannot be separated. There are moreover intermediate forms; some Himalayan specimens have leaflets and inflorescence very slightly pubescent, and a specimen collected by Henry in Yunnan has the pods rounded at base, exactly like the Himalayan form. The specimens cultivated in India, in North and South America agree with the West Asiatic and Chino-Japanese form.

11. CALLIANDRA, Benth.; Fl. Brit. Ind. ii. 302.

Trees or shrubs; l. bipinnate; leaflets few, large, glabrous (in the Indian species). Stipules usually persistent, often spinescent. Fl. often unisexual, in globose heads. Stamens ∞, filaments connate high up or at base only. Pod flat, rigidly coriaceous, the valves bordered by much thickened sutures, and dehiscing elastically, being rolled backwards from top to bottom.

1. **C. umbrosa**, Benth.—Syn. *Jnga umbrosa*, Wall. Pl. As. Rar. t. 124. Vern. *Kyagyi*, Burm.

A small tree; stipules generally spinescent. Pinnæ 1 pair, rachis of pinnæ 1–2 in. long bearing at the end a pair of more or less oblique leaflets 3–8 in. long and a single much smaller leaflet on the outside, sec. n. prominent. Fl. white, scented, sessile in dense globose heads supported by a ring of minute bracteoles; peduncles slender, ½–1 in. long, generally clustered on the old wood, rarely axillary. Pod 6–9 in. long, seeds 4–8.

Khasi hills, Silhet, Chittagong. Upper Burma. Fl. R. S. 2. **C. Griffithii**, Benth. Khasi hills. Spinescent stipules minute. Leaflets arranged as in 1 but much smaller, the terminal 2–2½ in. long. Fl. supported by linear-lanceolate bracts. 3. **C. cynometroides**, Bedd. Fl. Sylv. t. 317, Tinnevelli and Travancore Ghats. A middle-sized tree; l. pinnate; leaflets 1 pair, 3–4 in. long; stipular spines short, straight. Fl. sessile, 6–12 in one head; peduncles axillary, solitary, 1–1½ in. long. Pod 4–5 in. long.

12. PITHECOLOBIUM, Martius; Fl. Brit. Ind. ii. 302.

Trees or shrubs; l. bipinnate. Fl. in globose heads, rarely in small loose spikes or corymbs, usually bisexual. Petals connate half way up, or further; stamens monadelphous, much exserted. Pod coriaceous, curved or twisted, usually dehiscent along the lower suture. Species 110, tropics of both hemispheres, chiefly America.

A. Armed, stipules or branchlets spinescent.

1. **P. dulce**, Benth.; Bedd. Fl. Sylv. t. 188.—Syn. *Mimosa dulcis*, Roxb. Cor. Pl. t. 99; *Jnga dulcis*, Willd.; Wight Ic. t. 198.

A middle-sized, glabrous, evergreen tree, armed with straight stipulary thorns. Pinnæ 2, each with 1 pair of pale green, coriaceous, unequal-sided usually obtuse leaflets, 1–2 in. long, common and partial rachis slender, termi-

nating in short bristles. Fl. white in small globose sessile or short-pedunculate heads, arranged in long panicled racemes. Pod linear, turgid, twisted, 4–5 in. long.

Indigenous in America, naturalized in the Western Peninsula as an excellent hedge plant Coppices readily. Fl. January–March. 2. **P. geminatum,** Benth. A small bushy tree of Ceylon, stated by Beddome, Manual 96, to occur in the southern part of the Peninsula. Stipules spinescent; pinnæ 1, leaflets 1–5 pair, the uppermost largest, the lowest wanting on the inside. Fl. to extremity of stamens ¾–1 in. long. Pods 2–4 by ⅜ in. much constricted between seeds. 3. **P. umbellatum,** Benth. East side of the Western Peninsula, common. Ceylon, dry country, rare. A small tree; branchlets and stipules often spinescent; pinnæ 2, leaflets oblong, 5–8 pair. Fl. creamy white, ¾ in. to extremity of stamens, on pedicels longer than stamens, in lax heads or umbels; peduncles 1 in. long. Pod thick, curved, much constricted between seeds, ultimately breaking up into 7–10 1-seeded indehiscent joints.

A prickly species, probably of this genus. *P. semicordatum*, C. B. Clarke MSS. Khasi hills, 1,000 ft., has 1 pair of pinnæ, leaflets 1 pair and a solitary one below outside the terminal, leaflets very unequal-sided, semicordate, 3–5 in. long, the lateral ones smaller. Fl. white; peduncles slender, fasciculate, from the old wood.

B. Unarmed; pinnæ 1–3, leaflets 2–4 pair; branchlets and rachis of panicle not prominently angled or furrowed.

4. P. glomeriflorum, Kurz F. Fl. i. 430.

A shrub or small tree; pinnæ 1, leaflets 3 pair, elliptic-lanceolate, 1–2 in. long. Fl. sessile, ¼–⅓ in. to extremity of stamens, in lax axillary and terminal rusty-pubescent panicles.

Shillong by the Bishop's falls (fl. larger, perhaps distinct). Dry forests on the hills east of Toungoo 4–7,000 ft. Fl. March–April.

5. P. lobatum, Benth.; Kurz F. Fl. i. 429. Vern. *Tanyin*, Burm.

An evergreen tree, heartwood brown, close-grained. Pinnæ 1, leaflets 2–3 pair, shining on both sides, elliptic-lanceolate, 3–8 in. long, glands usually at the base of leaflets. Fl. white, ¼ in. long to extremity of stamens, sessile, or on short pedicels; panicles axillary or on the old wood. Pod horseshoe-shaped or loosely spirally twisted, deeply lobed along the lower suture, the lobes thick, distinct, dehiscent, 1–2 in. diam., some seedless. Seeds 3–10, dark brown, orbicular, ¾ in. diam.

Pegu Yoma, Martaban, Tenasserim, chiefly near streams. Often cultivated. Fl. C. S. Seeds eaten and sold. Malay Peninsula and Archipelago. Closely allied is 6. **P. nicobaricum,** Prain, Nicobars; pinnæ 1, leaflets 2 pair, no glands at the base of leaflets. Pod purplish-red, ¾ in. wide, sinuate between seeds. 7. **P. affine,** Baker, Malay Peninsula. Prain in Journ. As. Soc. Beng. 66. 515, states: collected by D. B. in Burma (specimens probably at Calcutta). A small tree; branchlets rusty-puberulous or pubescent; pinnæ 1–2, leaflets 4 pair, glands at the base of leaflets; fl. white, in dense heads. 8. **P. ellipticum,** Hassk. (*P. fasciculatum*, Benth.) Nicobars, Malay Peninsula and Archipelago. A small tree; pinnæ 2, leaflets 3–4 pair, glands only at the base of the terminal pair; fl. yellow, in very small 2–5-fld. heads.

9. P. bigeminum, Martius; Benth. in Trans. Linn. Soc. xxx. 575.

A middle-sized tree; branchlets, common petioles and inflorescence rusty-puberulous. Pinnæ 2–3 pair, leaflets of the lowest pinnæ 1–3, of the terminal 3 sometimes 4 pair, elliptic, acuminate, glabrous, dark green. Fl. cream-coloured, ⅓ in. long to extremity of stamens, sessile or shortly pedicelled in 2–5-fld. heads. Heads in slender, terminal or supra-axillary panicles. Pod flat, not indented between seeds, 3–5 by ¾ in., bright red within, curved into a ring or spiral.

Subhimalayan tract, from Nepal eastwards, ascending in Sikkim to 4,000 ft. Assam, Cachar. Evergreen forests of the Western Ghats to 4,000 ft. Fl. February–May. Ceylon, moist region. A slender shrub (Wainad), leaflets thin, caudate-acuminate, reticulate venation prominent on the underside is *P. gracile*, Bedd. MSS. in hb. Kew.

C. Unarmed; pinnæ and leaflets numerous; branchlets and rachis of panicle furrowed and angular.

10. **P. angulatum**, Benth.; Kurz F. Fl. i. 430.

A shrub or small evergreen tree; branchlets sharply angular, young shoots rusty-pubescent. Pinnæ 2–5 pair, leaflets of the lowest pinnæ 2–3, of the upper pinnæ 4–8 pair, rhomboid-ovate, acuminate, the terminal leaflets 3–5, the lowest ¾–1 in. long. Fl. white (purple, Ruby Mines district), on slender

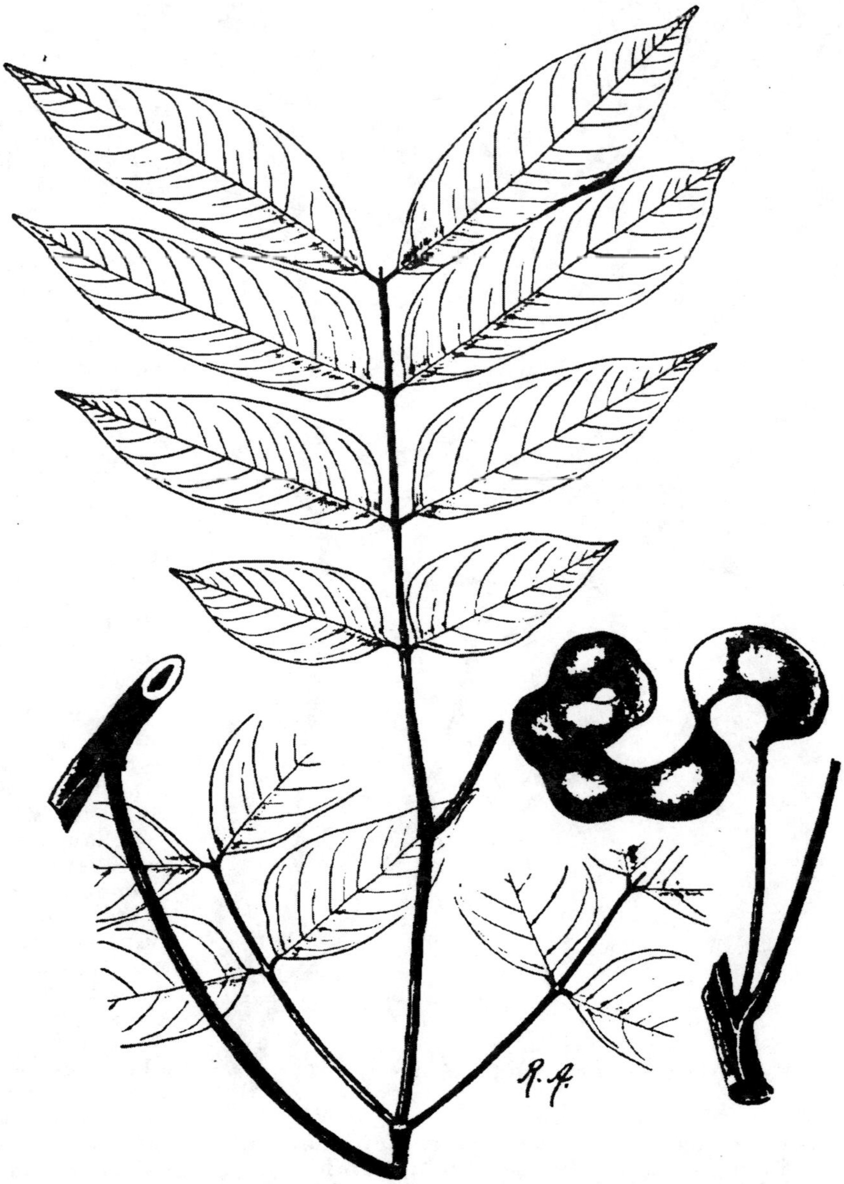

FIG. 119.—Pithecolobium angulatum, Benth. ½.

pubescent pedicels as long as, or longer than calyx, on large rusty-pubescent panicles. Pod spirally twisted, 7–8 in. long, distinctly sinuate between seeds, velvety while young.

Sikkim, Assam, Cachar, Chittagong. Hills of Upper and Lower Burma, 3–6,000 ft. Very common on the Andamans. Fl. March–April. Malay Peninsula.

11. **P. montanum**, Benth. in Trans. Linn. Soc. xxx. 580.

An evergreen tree; branchlets brown-pubescent, sharply angular. Pinnæ 6–10, leaflets 6–12 pair, very oblique, trapeziform, all nearly of the same size, ½–1 in. long, pubescent beneath; glands orbicular or linear at the base of each pair of pinnæ, except the lowest. Fl. heads white, in terminal and axillary panicles; pedicels as long as calyx. Pod glabrous, spirally twisted, 4–5 in. long, seed-bearing lobes thick, distinct.

Upper Assam, Khasi hills. Hills east of Toungoo at 2,000 ft. (D.B., February, 1880), Mooleyit, 4,500 ft. (Beddome), Mergui (Griffith, 1843). Fl. February–March. China.

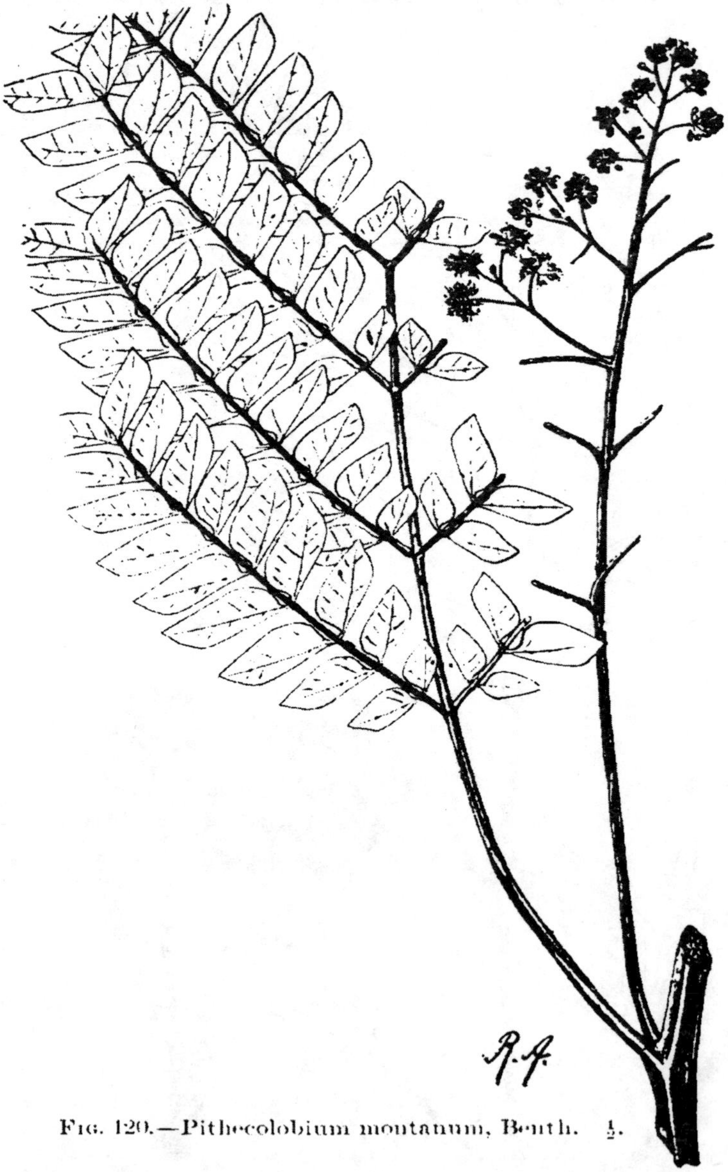

FIG. 120.—Pithecolobium montanum, Benth. ½.

12. **P. subcoriaceum**, Thwaites.—Syn. *P. anamallayanum*, Bedd. Fl. Sylv. t. 189.

A large tree with spreading branches; branchlets clothed with fine brown pubescence. Pinnæ 4–12 pair, leaflets 10–12 pair, rigidly coriaceous, oblique, ¼–⅓ in. long, glossy above, densely pubescent beneath. Several (1–3) glands on the petiole below the lowest pair of pinnæ and one gland between each pair of pinnæ. Fl. heads many-fld., forming a terminal leafy panicle, fl. nearly sessile, ½ in. long to extremity of stamens; calyx one-third the length of corolla. Pod 3–4 in. long, coriaceous, twisted.

Anamalai hills (5–8,000 ft.), Travancore Ghats (very abundant) above 4,500 ft. Fl. C. S. Ceylon. The Ceylon specimens have a smaller number of pinnæ (3–5) and the leaflets are mostly glabrous beneath.

ORDER XLVI. ROSACEÆ. Gen. Pl. i. 600.

Herbs, shrubs or trees, l. stipulate, alternate, rarely opposite, simple or compound. Fl. as a rule regular and bisexual; calyx gamosepalous, free or adnate to ovary, lobes 5, imbricate in bud. Disk annular or lining the calyx-tube; petals 5, perigynous, rarely wanting, often orbicular and concave, deciduous, claws short or none, imbricate, rarely contorted in bud. Stamens as a rule numerous, inserted with the petals or on the disk, incurved in bud. Carpels usually distinct, one or more, often adnate to calyx-tube, styles free or connate, ovules in each carpel 1 or 2, rarely more. Fruit often fleshy. Albumen none or scanty, cotyledons plano-convex, cells filled with oil, radicle short.

Apart from medullary rays, parenchyma does not form an important part in the wood of Rosaceæ. *Chrysobalaneæ* (*Parinarium, Parastemon*) are exceptional, they have narrow tangential bands of parenchyma in the wood. In this respect, as well as in the more or less zygomorphic fl., this tribe approaches *Leguminosæ*. Wood fibres in *Rosaceæ* as a rule have not bordered pits. As far as known, the wood of the climbing species has a normal structure.

A. Ripe carpels not enclosed within the calyx-tube.
(See *Neillia* and *Spiræa canescens*.)

- I. Leaves simple, quite entire. Carpel one. Fl. usually zygomorphic (tribe *Chrysobalaneæ*).
  - Calyx-tube elongate, stamens 6–30, usually unilateral . . . . . 1. PARINARIUM.
  - Calyx-tube short, stamens 2 . . . . . PARASTEMON (p. 278).
- II. Leaves simple, serrate. Carpel 1, rarely 2.
  - Calyx 5-lobed, petals large.
    - Style terminal, stone hard, bony . . . 2. PRUNUS.
    - Style basal, endocarp coriaceous . . . 3. PRINSEPIA.
  - Calyx 5–10-toothed, petals minute or 0.
    - Carpels 1 or 2, stone hard, bony . . . MADDENIA (p. 281).
    - Carpels 1, endocarp coriaceous . . . . 4. PYGEUM.
- III. Leaves simple or compound. Calyx without bracts.
  - Carpels 1–8, ovules 2 or more, fr. dry.
    - Seeds linear, testa membranous, albumen 0 or scanty . . . . . 5. SPIRÆA.
    - Seeds globose, testa crustaceous, albumen copious . . . . . NEILLIA (p. 283).
  - Carpels ∞, ovules 2, fr. usually fleshy . . . 6. RUBUS.
- IV. Leaves usually compound, calyx bracteolate, fr. dry POTENTILLA (p. 287).

B. Ripe carpels enclosed within the calyx-tube.

- I. Carpels ∞ free, when ripe enclosed in the fleshy calyx-tube . . . . . 7. ROSA.
- II. Carpels connate, forming a 1–5-celled ovary, more or less adnate to calyx-tube, which in fruit is fleshy, enclosing them.
  - Ovary 5-celled, 3 or more ovules in each cell.
    - 3 ovules in each cell . . . . . 8. DOCYNIA.
    - Many ovules in each cell . . . . . 9. CYDONIA.
  - Ovary 2–5-celled, 2 ovules in each cell.
    - Ovary 5-celled, fl. panicled . . . . . 10. ERIOBOTRYA.
    - Ovary 2–5-celled, fl. corymbose or fascicled.
      - Fr. 2–5-celled. . . . . . 11. PYRUS.
      - Drupe with 5 dehiscent stones . . . . 12. STRANVÆSIA.
    - Ovary 2–3-celled, endocarp thin.
      - Testa coriaceous or membranous . . . . 13. PHOTINIA.
      - Testa thick, reticulately lacunose . . . 14. POURTHIÆA.
    - Ovary 2–5-celled, drupe with 1–5 bony stones (pyrenes).
      - Leaves cut, toothed or serrate . . . . 15. CRATÆGUS.
      - Leaves quite entire . . . . . 16. COTONEASTER.
      - Leaves imparipinnate . . . . . OSTEOMELES (p. 295.)

1. PARINARIUM, Juss.; Fl. Brit. Ind. ii. 308.

Evergreen trees; l. simple, entire, alternate. Fl. white or pink, bisexual, slightly zygomorphic, in panicles or corymbose racemes, 2 or 3 bracts at the base of each fl. Calyx deciduous, tube tomentose, generally hairy inside, segments 5, thick, often unequal. Stamens 6–30, mostly unilateral, filaments as as a rule connate at base. Carpel one, 2-celled, hairy, more or less adnate to one side of calyx-tube, one erect ovule in each cell. Species 50, tropics of both hemispheres.

A. Western species.

1. **P. indicum,** Bedd. Ic. Pl. Ind. Or. t. 109; Fl. Sylv. t. 191.

A middle-sized tree; l. glabrous 5–9 × 2–3 in., petiole $\frac{1}{4}$–$\frac{1}{2}$ in., racemes compound, tomentose, axillary and terminal. Fl. white, pedicels very short, calyx-tube $\frac{1}{4}$ in. long, a ring of minute teeth inside at the mouth, fertile stamens 12–15, style basal, longer than stamens.

Carcoor ghat, Malabar 2,000–3,000 ft. 2. **P. travancoricum,** Bedd. Ic. Pl. Ind. Or. t. 189. Evergreen forests in the Travancore hills. Shoots and racemes silky, l. lanceolate, long silky hairs along midrib beneath, 4–5 × 1–1$\frac{1}{2}$ in.

B. Eastern species.

3. **P. Griffithianum,** Benth., Tenasserim or Andamans, Malay Peninsula. A large tree, l. coriaceous, glabrous, shining, glands at the base of midrib on the upper surface. Fl. in large corymbose or pyramidal panicles. Fr. narrowly ellipsoid, not speckled, lined inside with rufous hairs. 4. **P. costatum,** Blume, Malay Peninsula, possibly in Tenasserim, l. thinly coriaceous shortly and obtusely acuminate, without glands, thin tawny pubescence beneath. Fl. in large, lax, tawny tomentose, terminal and axillary panicles, calyx-tube tubular-campanulate, a ring of long deflexed hairs inside in the mouth. Fr. oblong with scaly patches, lined inside with rufous wool. 5. **P. Helferi,** Hook. f., on banks of Tenasserim river, a tall tree, young shoots clothed with soft bright brown tomentum, l. membranous white and downy beneath, fl. minute, in small softly tomentose panicles.

Parastemon urophyllum, A. DC. Nicobars, Tenasserim, Malay Peninsula, Borneo, a tall tree, branches slender pendulous, l. glabrous, acuminate, 2–4 in., underside with numerous minute scales. Fl. minute, polygamous, in slender axillary racemes, stamens 2, unilateral, on a raised ring at the mouth of calyx. Fr. oblong-ellipsoid, $\frac{1}{3}$ in. long. seed one, erect.

2. PRUNUS, Linn.; Fl. Brit. Ind. ii. 312.

Shrubs or trees with alternate simple glandular-serrate l., petioles with 2 glands. Calyx free, deciduous, petals 5, stamens 15–40, inserted in the mouth of calyx-tube, filaments free. Carpel 1, ovules 2 collateral, pendulous. Fr. fleshy, endocarp an indehiscent or 2 valved, 1 seeded, smooth or rugged stone.

A. Fl. solitary, fasciculate or umbellate, appearing before or with the leaves, with or after the l. in 2.

1. **P. Amygdalus,** Baillon; Brandis F. Fl. 190.—Syn. *Amygdalus communis,* Linn. *The Almond-tree.* Vern. *Badām.*

A middle-sized tree, l. greyish when full grown, oblong-lanceolate, serrulate, petiole equal to or longer than the greatest width of leaf, stipules fimbriate. Fl. white, tinged with red, appearing before the leaves from scaly buds on last year's wood, peduncles much shorter than the campanulate calyx. Drupe velvety, pericarp dry, when ripe separating into 2 valves, stone compressed with shallow wrinkles and minute holes.

Indigenous in Western Asia, also in the Kuram valley where Aitchison found it as a small tree in gregarious patches (Journ. Linn. Soc. xviii. 50). Cultivated in the Mediterranean region, also in Persia and Afghanistan, in Kashmir and the Punjab. Fl. Feb.–March. 2. **(Amygdalus) Stocksiana,** Boiss. Fl. Or. ii. 644, frequent in Baluchistan, well described by Lace (Journ. Linn. Soc. xxviii. 297), petioles slender, half the length of leaf or longer, fl. red, 1½ in. across, appearing with or after the leaves, drupe velvety, pericarp dry. Lopped by the shepherds for feeding their herds, when long pollard shoots spring up with a few narrow linear leaves.

3. **P. brahuica,** Aitch. et Hemsl. (*Amygdalus brahuica*, Boiss.) *Zarg, Zargah*, Baluch. Hills of Baluchistan and Afghanistan, 4–9,000 ft., a stiff scraggy thorny gregarious shrub; branchlets spinescent, young branches and leaves silvery-white, l. ¼–⅓ in. long, pubescent while young. Covered with a profusion of pink fl. before the leaves appear, calyx-tube cylindric glabrous, fr. velvety, yellow when ripe, the pericarp bursting open longitudinally. The kernel is eaten. *P. eburnea*, Aitch. et Hemsl., which has been stated to grow in Baluchistan and Afghanistan, l. glabrous, calyx hairy, is, I believe, limited to Persia and Western Afghanistan, but probably is not specifically distinct from 3.

4. **P. persica,** Benth. et Hook. f.: Brandis F. Fl. 191.—Syn. *Amygdalus persica*, Linn. The *Peach* with velvety and *Nectarine* with smooth fruit. Vern. *Shaftdlu*, Baluch.; *Rek, Beim*, Sutlej; *Aru*, Hind.

A middle-sized tree, foliage dark green. L. lanceolate, sharply serrate, petiole shorter than greatest width of leaf, stipules subulate, fimbriate. Fl. sessile, pink, generally appearing before the leaves, mostly solitary, from scaly buds on last year's wood. Calyx campanulate, segments woolly. Drupe downy or glabrous, pericarp tender succulent, stone deeply and irregularly furrowed.

Indigenous probably in China, commonly cultivated in Western Asia, Europe and China. Also in Baluchistan, in the Himalaya, Kunawar to 10,000 ft., in the plains of Northern India, in Manipur and Upper Burma. Fl. according to elevation, between January and May, the fr. ripening between May and October.

5. **P. armeniaca,** Linn.; Brandis F. Fl. 191. *The Apricot.* Vern. *Hari*, Hazara; *Chilu, Chuli, Shari*, N.-W. Himalaya; *Jaldāru, Zardālu*, Hind.

A middle-sized tree, l. broadly ovate, nearly as broad as long, acuminate, crenate, petiole half the length of leaf, stipules lanceolate. Fl. pinkish-white, solitary or fasciculate, from scaly buds on the previous year's wood, appearing before or with the leaves, peduncles short. Drupe downy or glabrous, pericarp tender succulent, stone smooth with a thickened sulcate margin.

Believed to be indigenous in the Caucasian region, commonly cultivated in Western and Centrial Asia and Europe, in Baluchistan to 8,000 ft., in the N. W. Himalaya, in Western Tibet to 12,000 ft. and in the plains of the Punjab. Fl. Jan.–May, the fr. ripens between June and Sept.

6. **P. communis,** Hudson; Brandis F. Fl. 192. *The Plum, Prune, Sloe, Damson.* Vern. *Alūcha*, N.W. Himal.

A shrub or middle-sized tree, unarmed or spinescent, young shoots pubescent. L. ovate or ovate-lanceolate, serrate, more or less pubescent beneath along the nerves, petioles shorter than greatest breadth of leaf, stipules linear fimbriate. Pedicels slender, 3 or 4 times the length of calyx, solitary or fasciculate from lateral often leaf-bearing buds, calyx-tube campanulate. Drupe globose or oblong, pericarp fleshy.

Indigenous in Europe and Western Asia, where the different kinds have been cultivated from time immemorial. The plum is cultivated in Kashmir and in the Punjab plains. The plum cultivated in Baluchistan, Afghanistan and the N. W. Himalaya, called *Alu Bokhara*, has been referred to **P. divaricata,** Ledebour, which may be regarded as a distinct species, or as a sub-species of **P. communis.**

7. **P. Puddum,** Roxb.; Kurz F. Fl. i. 434.—*Cerasus Puddum*, Wall. Pl. As. Rar. t. 143. Vern. *Phaja, Pajia, Padam*, Hind. *Panni*, Burm.

A middle-sized or large tree, bark peeling off in horizontal strips, wood pale red. Nearly glabrous, l. glossy, ovate, long-acuminate, sharply serrate, blade 3–5, petiole ½ in. long, 1 or more conspicuous glands on petiole, stipules pinnately or palmately divided, the divisions linear, glandular-fimbriate. Fl. white, pink or crimson, appearing before the leaves, in umbellate fascicles, approximate near the ends of branchlets, pedicels slender, as long as or longer

Fig. 121.—Prunus Puddum, Roxb. $\frac{1}{2}$.

than calyx. Calyx turbinate, lobes ovate, acute. Fr. yellow and red, ovoid or globose, $\frac{1}{2}$–$\frac{2}{3}$ in. long, acid, somewhat astringent, stone ovoid, rugose and furrowed, supported by the calyx-base, from which the tube separates after flowering.

Outer Himalaya from the Sutlej to Sikkim, mostly between 2.500 and 7,000 ft. Khasi hills, Manipur. Upper Burma 4-6.000 ft. Often cultivated. Fl. early in winter (Nov. Dec.) and in Spring (April–May). Gamble (List 34) mentions two varieties, *α*. a very big tree, fl. crimson, March, *β*. smaller, fl. pink or white, Nov.

A tree 3 ft. girth, found by Montagu Hill, Feb., 1902, on the hills east of Bhamo, fl. red, pedicels glabrous, shorter than calyx, calyx glabrous, campanulate, lobes obtuse, shorter than half the tube, ovary and style glabrous, is similar to *P. hirtipes*, Hemsl., of China, which however has calyx and pedicels hairy. Not named because l. unknown.

B. Fl. solitary or umbellate, appearing after the leaves.

8. **P. Cerasus**, Linn.; Brandis F. Fl. 193.—*The Cherry.*

A middle-sized tree, the bark of this and of several allied species peeling off in horizontal strips. L. elliptic or obovate, abruptly acuminate, irregularly crenate-serrate, petiole less than breadth of leaf, 2 glands on petiole or on the base of blade, stipules fimbriate. Fl. white on long slender pedicels, in fascicles of 2–5, from lateral generally leaf-bearing buds. Calyx turbinate, lobes obtuse. Drupe glabrous, with a polished round stone.

This includes *P. Avium*, Linn., *the sweet Cherry*, indigenous in Europe, and *P. Cerasus*, Linn., *the acid Cherry*, believed to be indigenous in Western Asia. Cultivated in N. W. Himalaya. These two may be regarded as distinct species. *P. Cerasus* produces abundant root suckers, while *P. Avium* has none. Fl. April, May.

9. **P. microcarpa**, C. A. Meyer, Baluchistan, Western Asia. A shrub with elongate branches, l. glabrous, sharply serrate, 1 in. long, petiole shorter than blade, fl. $\frac{1}{2}$ in. across, calyx-tube cylindric, slightly wider at the base, drupe fleshy, ovoid $\frac{1}{4}$ in. long. 10. **P. Jacquemontii**, Hook. f., Baluchistan, Kuram valley, dry regions of inner N.W. Himalaya, a small shrub, l. deeply and sharply serrate, blade 1–2, petiole $\frac{1}{4}$–$\frac{1}{3}$ in. Fl. solitary, pink, pedicels very short, calyx-tube funnel-shaped. Fr. bright red. 11. **P. prostrata**, Labill.; Brandis F. Fl. 193. Vern. *Talhi*, Pangi, Lahaul. Afghanistan, arid regions of the inner N.W. Himalaya 5–12,000 ft., western Asia, Greece, Crete, Sardinia, Spain, Algeria, a small scraggy shrub, branchlets hoary, L. ovate or elliptic, sharp-serrate, glabrous above, usually densely clothed beneath with white woolly tomentum, blade $\frac{1}{2}$–1 in., petiole short, without glands. Fl. red on short peduncles, on lateral buds, solitary, or in pairs. Calyx-tube glabrous or slightly hairy, cylindrical, teeth short, obtuse, hairy inside. Fr. $\frac{1}{3}$ in. long, reddish-purple, pulp scanty. The European and West Asiatic shrub has smaller fl. 12. **P. tomentosa**, Thunb., Kashmir, 5–6000 ft., North China and Japan, a shrub, l. ovate, acuminate, softly tomentose beneath, fl. on short pedicels, calyx-tube cylindric, fr. hairy, nearly sessile, scarlet. 13. **P. rufa**, Wall., Nepal, Sikkim, 9–12,000 ft. Tibet. A small tree, young shoots hairy, l. elliptic-lanceolate sharply serrate, glabrous except petiole and nerves beneath, blade 2–4, petiole $\frac{1}{4}$–$\frac{1}{2}$ in. Fl. pink, solitary or fascicled, pedicels $\frac{1}{2}$–$1\frac{1}{2}$ in., calyx glabrous. Fr. red, fleshy.

C. Fl. in axillary or terminal many-flowered racemes, l. deciduous.

14. **P. Padus**, Linn.—Syn. *Cerasus cornuta*, Wall.; Royle Ill. t. 38, f. 2.

Bird Cherry. Vern. *Kālakāt*, Hazara; *Jamun, Jamoi, Jāmu*, N.-West Himal.

A tree, attaining 50–60 ft., wood handsome, polishes well, young shoots, inflorescence and underside of leaves along nerves pubescent. L. from a slightly cordate base, obovate-oblong, acuminate, serrate, stipules thin, linear-lanceolate, early caducous. Fl. white, appearing after the leaves, racemes 3–8 in. long, at the ends of short lateral (often leaf-bearing) branchlets, bracts thin, caducous, longer than buds. Drupe globose, $\frac{1}{3}$ in. diam., first red, then dark purple or nearly black, stone rugose.

Kuram valley, Trans Indus. Himalaya, Hazara to Sikkim, 4–10,000 ft. L. turn red before they fall. Fl. April–June. Widely spread, from North and Central Europe through Western Asia and Siberia to Amur land and Kamtchatka. The ovary of this and of *P. Puddum* is often punctured by an insect and then becomes elongate curved and fusiform, 2 in. long and more, hence the name "*cornuta*." 15. **P. nepalensis,** Hook. f., Kumaon, Nepal. Sikkim 6–10,000 ft., Bhutan, Tibet. Khasi hills. Upper Burma, evergreen forest Ruby Mines district, 6,000 ft. Yunnan. A large tree, similar to 14, but l. with an acute or rounded, not cordate base, glaucous beneath, bracts small shorter than, or equal to pedicel, fr. $\frac{3}{4}$ in. long, stone smooth. 16. **P. undulata,** Ham. Kumaon 6–8,000 ft., Nepal. Sikkim 8–12,000 ft., Bhutan, Khasi hills, a small tree with slender lax racemes, small fl. and drupes.

17. **P. acuminata,** Wall. Pl. As. Rar. t. 181. Vern. *Lali*, Pah.

A small tree, entirely glabrous, l. quite entire or remotely serrate, pale beneath, racemes axillary, lax. Fl. yellowish-white, on slender pedicels, longer than calyx. Calyx open, cup-shaped, segments linear, petals oblong, stamens 15. Drupe ovoid, $\frac{1}{2}$ in. long, stone thin, quite smooth.

Nepal, Sikkim, 5–7000 ft., Assam, Khasi hills. Fl. Oct. to March.

D. Fl. in axillary or terminal many-flowered racemes, l. persistent.

18. **P. martabanica,** Kurz F. Fl. i. 434, Tenasserim, Andamans, Malay Peninsula. A large evergreen tree, l. glabrous entire, blade 4–6, pet. $\frac{1}{4}$–$\frac{3}{8}$ in., racemes solitary, or in pairs, pubescent 2–6 in. long, calyx broad-campanulate, tomentose outside, petals caducous, orbicular 1 in. diam., stamens 60–80. Fr. cylindric, pointed, 1 in. long, pericarp thin, quite dry. 19. **P. punctata,** Hook. f. & Th., Assam, Khasi hills, Manipur, China. A shrub or small tree, l. long caudate-acuminate, dotted beneath with minute dark-coloured glands, racemes axillary, compound pedicels very slender Stamens 30. 20. **P. Jenkinsii,** Hook. f. & Th., Assam (*Tarraju*), Khasi and Naga hills, a small tree with shining undulate and more or less serrate l., racemes $1\frac{1}{2}$–$2\frac{1}{2}$ in., straight erect, usually densely furnished with fl. to the base, which bears numerous concave orbicular scales, stamens about 50. Drupe $\frac{3}{4}$ in. long, broadly ovoid, stone rugose, with a thick ridge on one side, walls thick and hard.

3. PRINSEPIA, Royle; Fl. Brit. Ind. ii. 322

(Species 3, two in Mongolia and North China.)

P. utilis, Royle Ill. t. 38 fig. 1; Brandis F. Fl. 196. Vern. *Phulwāri*, Haz.; *Bekhar, Bhekal*, N.W. Himal.

A spinescent deciduous shrub, glabrous, youngest shoots only pubescent, pith large, separating when dry into horizontal layers; stout, green axillary often leaf-bearing spines, l. lanceolate, serrate. Fl. white, in short racemes, generally at the base of spines. Calyx-tube cup-shaped, lobes 5 unequal, imbricate in bud, petals rounded, claw short. Stamens numerous, inserted below the petals in several rows, anther-cells separated by a broad connective. Carpel 1, sessile, ovules 2, collateral. Fr. an oblique, oblong-cylindrical, fleshy purple drupe, scar of style basal, endocarp coriaceous, seed one only.

Outer Himalaya from **Hazara** to Bhutan, 2–9,000 ft., common on dry slopes. Khasi hills. Fl. in autumn and winter up to February, fr. in spring. In Jaunsar fl. in spring, fr. R. S. (Kanjilal F. Fl. p. 154.)—Yunnan. A common hedge plant in parts of **Hazara.** Oil expressed from the seeds.

Maddenia himalaica, Hook. f. & Thoms. Sikkim, Bhutan, Mishmi, Tibet, Szechuen, a deciduous middle-sized tree, young shoots and underside of l. clothed with dense soft brown tomentum, l. ovate- or obovate-lanceolate, acuminate, sharply serrate, the serratures in young leaves often terminating in glandular hairs, especially near the base of leaf, stipules linear-falcate, longer than petiole, deciduous. Fl. white, in terminal dense racemes 1–2 in. long. Calyx-tube turbinate, lobes 5, petals minute. Carpels solitary or in pairs, one-celled, terminating into long or short styles, two collateral ovules in each carpel. Fr. a drupe, dark purple, pericarp nearly dry, endocarp thickly crustaceous, quite smooth. 2. **M. pedicellata**, Hook f., Mishmi hills, fl. on long pedicels in lateral corymbs.

4. PYGEUM, Gærtn.; Fl. Brit. Ind. ii. 318.

Evergreen trees or shrubs, leaves usually coriaceous and quite entire, in most species large glands on blade near the base, stipules minute, fugacious. Fl. small, mostly racemose, sometimes unisexual. Calyx free, deciduous, limb 5–6-toothed, petals small, tomentose, often similar to calyx-segments. Stamens 10–50, inserted on the rim of the calyx-tube, filaments slender, incurved. Carpel 1 at the base of the calyx-tube, often oblique, ovules 2, collateral, pendulous. Fruit as a rule 2-seeded, transversely oblong, slightly didymous, pericarp thin, dry or juicy. Fr. and l., if crushed, emit a strong smell of bitter almonds. Species about 30, one African, the others of tropical Asia.

A. Western species.

1. **P. Wightianum**, Blume; Bedd. Manual 97.—Syn. *P. ceylanicum*, Bedd. Fl. Sylv. t. 59; *Polyodontia zeylanica*, Wight Ic. t. 256. Vern. *Mutta Kongu*, *Neikambagam*, Mal.

A large tree, l. glabrous, brown beneath, elliptic or elliptic-lanceolate, blade 4–7, petiole ½ in. long, 2 or more large glands on the underside. Racemes axillary, finely pubescent, 2–4 in. long, pedicels longer than calyx. Calyx pubescent outside, turbinate, teeth 5, rarely 4–6, petals villous, stamens 30, ovary glabrous, with a ring of hairs at the base.

Anamalai, Palni, Shevaroy and Tinnevelli hills (Bedd.). Fl. Nov.–June.—Ceylon. *P. zeylanicum*, Gærtner, with villous ovary, is endemic in Ceylon. 2. **P. Andersoni**, Hook. f., summit of Parasnath, a rigid shrub, quite glabrous except edge of petals, l. lanceolate shallow-serrate, racemes axillary, dense, 1 in. long, petals much longer than calyx-segments, ovary glabrous. 3. **P. Gardneri**, Hook. f. (*Pygeum acuminatum*, Wight Ic. t. 993), Western Ghats from Mahableshwar southwards, a small or middle-sized tree, l. glabrous, very coriaceous, racemes compact, 2–3 in. long, pubescent, calyx-teeth obtuse, tomentose, petals exactly like calyx-teeth. Fr. broader than long, 1–1½ in. across, 2-lobed.

B. Eastern species, l. quite glabrous.

4. **P. glaberrimum**, Hook. f., Sikkim, Khasi hills, Chittagong, racemes perfectly glabrous, petals acute triangular, ovary oblique, hairy. 5. **P. acuminatum**, Colebr., a large tree, l. coriaceous, midrib and sec. n. prominent beneath, racemes slender, tawny-pubescent, calyx-teeth 6, narrowly lanceolate, petals oblanceolate, stamens 30, long exserted, style as long as stamens, ovary glabrous, a ring of hairs around its base.

C. Eastern species, l. pubescent beneath, ovary hirsute or villous.

6. **P. montanum**, Hook. f., Sikkim, Khasi hills, a small tree, l. oblong-lanceolate, midrib and sec. n. impressed above, racemes 1–2 in. long in fl., much longer in fr., drupe obliquely ovoid, one-seeded. 7. **P. capitellatum**, Hook. f., Tenasserim and Andamans, l. broadly elliptic, fl. in globose densely tomentose axillary heads. Besides these Kurz, F. Fl. i. 435, 436, mentions: 8. **P. arboreum**, Endl., Martaban and Tenasserim hills, and 9. **P. persimile**, from Tenasserim, which according to King, Journ. As. Soc. Bengal, vol. 66 (1898), 291, is *P. Lampongum*, Miq. *P. persimile*, Kurz is a Malayan species.

5. SPIRÆA, Linn.; Fl. Brit. Ind. ii. 323.

Shrubs or perennial herbs, l. alternate, simple or compound. Fl. white or red, in axillary or terminal cymes. Calyx free, persistent in fruit, segments as well as petals 4–5. Stamens 20–60, on a fleshy often hairy disk, which is generally adnate to calyx-tube. Carpels usually 5, free or connate below, ovules 2 or more. Seeds thin, minute. Species 40, in the northern temperate zone. Of the Indian shrubs the following may be mentioned:

A. Leaves simple, toothed.

1. **S. canescens,** Don; Collett Simla Flora, fig. 44. North West Himalaya 6–9,000 ft. (*Chakis*, N. West Himal.) Sikkim, 10–12,000 ft. Softly tomentose, stem attains 2 in. diam. and more, l. nearly sessile, ⅓–½ in., entire or 3–5-toothed at the tip. Fl. white, bisexual. Ripe carpels villous, half immersed in calyx-tube. 2. **S. bella,** Sims, Himalaya, from Hazara eastwards, 7–12,000 ft. *Kŭrkan*, Haz. Nearly glabrous, l. ½–2 in. long serrate, fl. pink, unisexual. Ripe carpels glabrous. 3. **S. vaccinifolia,** Don, N. W. Himalaya 5–7,000 ft., near Simla on limestone (Naldera, Shali.) A small gregarious shrub, l. glabrous, glaucous beneath, blade ½–1½, petiole ¼–½ in. Fl. white, bisexual.

B. Leaves pinnate.

4. **S. sorbifolia,** Linn. N. W. Himalaya 5–10,000 ft. (*Kŭrkan*, Haz.; *Kukis*, Kunawar.) Leaflets 6–10 pair, narrowly lanceolate, sharply toothed, 2–4 in. long, fl. white in large terminal panicles. Small boxes made of the wood.

Neillia thyrsiflora, Don, and **N. rubiflora,** Don, are common shrubs in Sikkim and the Khasi hills, l. more or less lobed, fl. white in panicled racemes, calyx campanulate hairy persistent, ripe carpels solitary, oblique, dehiscent, half enclosed in the hairy calyx-tube, seeds 4–6, globose.

6. RUBUS, Linn.; Fl. Brit. Ind. ii. 326.

Trailing shrubs, a few low undershrubs, as a rule prickly. Leaves alternate, simple or compound, stipules more or less adnate to petiole. Fl. white or red, in terminal or axillary corymbose panicles. Calyx free, broadly cup-shaped, deeply cleft into 5 lobes, persistent in fruit, petals 5, stamens ∞. Ripe carpels numerous, usually fleshy, one-seeded, on a conical dry or spongy receptacle. Species 180–200, cosmopolitan.

A. Leaves entire, not deeply lobed, usually longer than broad.

1. **R. acuminatus,** Sm.; Gamble List 35.

Branches long arching cylindric, glabrous, prickles very few, leaves glabrous, green on both sides, ovate caudate-acuminate, petiole ⅓–1in., stipules slender, setaceous. Petals white, carpels 8. Drupes large, globose, scarlet, enclosed by the calyx.

Himalaya from Kumaon to Sikkim 4–7,000 ft. Khasi hills. Fl. July. 2. **R. hexagynus,** Roxb. (*R. pyrifolius*, Kurz F. Fl. ii. 436.) Assam, Khasi hills, Silhet. Kakhyen hills, Upper Burma. Yunnan. A large, scrambling or climbing shrub, prickles short recurved, leaves ovate-oblong, petiole ¼ in., carpels 6. 3. **R. assamensis,** Focke, Mishmi and Khasi hills. Manipur. Erect, branchlets, underside of l. and inflorescence whitish-villous with soft spreading hairs, prickles very few, short, l. ovate-oblong, stipules and bracts pectinate. Panicles terminal and in the axils of the upper leaves, petals white, carpels 10–12, glabrous.

4. **R paniculatus,** Smith; Brandis F. Fl. 196. Vern. *Kala Anchu*, Jauns.

A straggling shrub, branches, petioles, underside of leaves and inflorescence densely clothed with white or grey cottony tomentum, prickles few, minute, hooked. Leaves from a cordate base broad-ovate, serrate and sinuate, basal nerves 3–5, prominent, stipules and bracts cleft into linear segments. Fl. in lax spreading terminal panicles. Petals white, shorter than the long acuminate calyx-segments. Fr. black.

Himalaya, outer ranges 3–8,000 ft., from Hazara to Sikkim, Khasi hills. Fl. April-July. Yunnan. 5. **R. insignis,** Hook. f., Bhutan, Khasi hills. All parts except upper side of leaves densely clothed with buff tomentum, numerous prickles on petiole and midrib, leaves hastate, petals white, almost orbicular, equalling the silky calyx-lobes, stamens purple. 6. **R. ferox,** Wall. Nepal, Khasi hills. Upper Burma. Roughly tomentose, not white or buff coloured, prickles stout, numerous on branchlets, petioles and nerves, l. more or less lobed. Panicles lax, ramifications slender, calyx-lobes pectinately toothed, teeth linear.

B. Leaves deeply lobed, as broad as long, or broader than long.

7. **R. moluccanus,** Linn.; Kurz F. Fl. i. 437.—Syn. *R. rugosus,* Smith; Wight Ic. t. 225. *R. Hamiltonianus,* Wall. Pl. As. Rar. t. 234. (*R. rugosus* in text.)

A large straggling shrub, branches, petioles and underside of leaves densely clothed with soft woolly rust-coloured tomentum, branches and petioles armed with numerous small prickles, leaves deeply cordate, 3–5-lobed, upperside more or less wrinkled, stipules laciniate or pinnatifid. Fl. white, in dense axillary

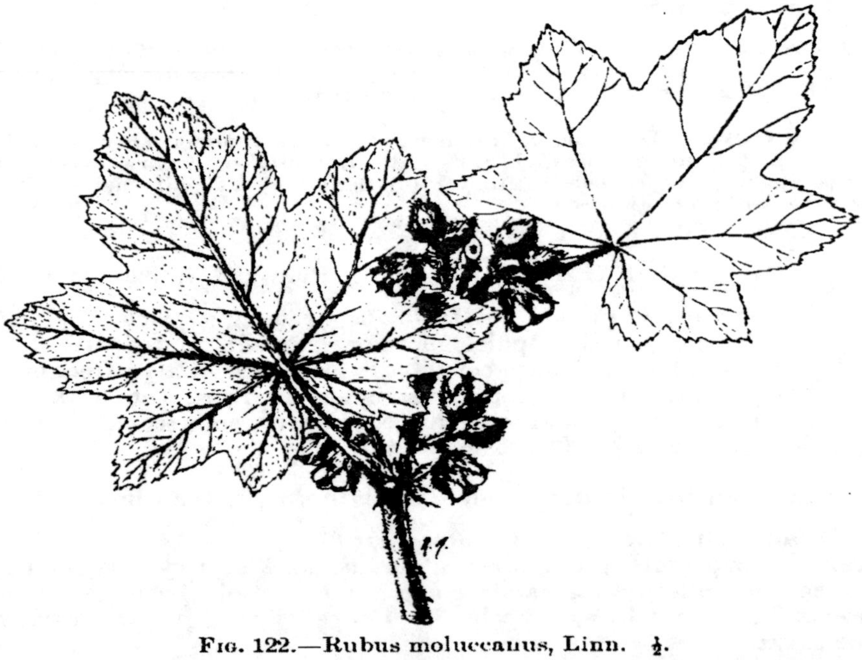

FIG. 122.—Rubus moluccanus, Linn. ½.

racemes or clusters, the upper ones usually forming a terminal silky-tomentose panicle, calyx entire or pectinate-dentate. Fr. bright red, glabrous, slightly acid.

Himalaya from Nepal eastwards, ascending to 7,000 ft., Khasi hills. Hills of Burma above 3,000 ft. Western Ghats from Mahableshwar southwards. Fl. Feb.–Aug.—Ceylon, moist country, above 1,000 ft. Malay Peninsula and Archipelago. 8. **R. reticulatus,** Wall., Himalaya, Kumaon to Sikkim, 7–10,000 ft., closely allied to 7 and perhaps not specifically distinct, branchlets and l. grey tomentose beneath, fr. very large. 9. **R. lanatus,** Wall. Kumaon, Nepal, 5–8,000 ft., inflorescence with glandular hairs, branches and underside of leaves white-cottony. 10. **R. birmanicus,** Hook. f., Patkai range. Manipur. Branchlets, petioles and underside of l. densely clothed with long soft hairs and numerous stout recurved prickles, l. greyish-brown beneath, stipules and bracts ½–¾ in. long, deeply pinnatifid, segments long, filiform. 11. **R. Treutleri,** Hook. f., Sikkim 7–10,000 ft., branchlets, petioles and l. on both sides densely clothed with long soft hairs, mixed here and there with glandular bristles, prickles slender, passing into bristles, fl. ¾–1 in. across, calyx-lobes large, laciniate or pinnatifid. Carpels numerous, dry.

C. Leaves digitately 3–5-foliolate.

12. **R. lineatus,** Reinw.; Vern. *Gempé Aselu*, Nep.

A large nearly unarmed shrub, bark peeling off in flakes, leaflets 3 or 5, elliptic-lanceolate, usually clothed beneath with dense silky silvery tomentum, sec. n. numerous, straight, parallel, terminating in sharp serratures. Stipules ovate or lanceolate, entire, semipersistent. Fl. white, in short axillary clusters. Drupes red, edible.

Sikkim 6–8,000 ft., coming up gregariously in clearances. Fl. Aug.–Sept. 13. **R. Andersoni,** Hook. f., Sikkim, 7–10,000 ft., similar, but leaflets broader. Numerous spreading gland-tipped hairs on branchlets, petioles and underside of leaflets. Fl. in axillary short spreading panicles. 14. **R. alpestris,** Blume, Himalaya, Garhwal to Sikkim 7–10,000 ft. Prickles straight, scattered, leaflets 3–5, deeply serrate, slightly pubescent while young, sec. n. 7–10 pair, stipules linear. Fl. terminal, 1–3 together, on slender pedicels.

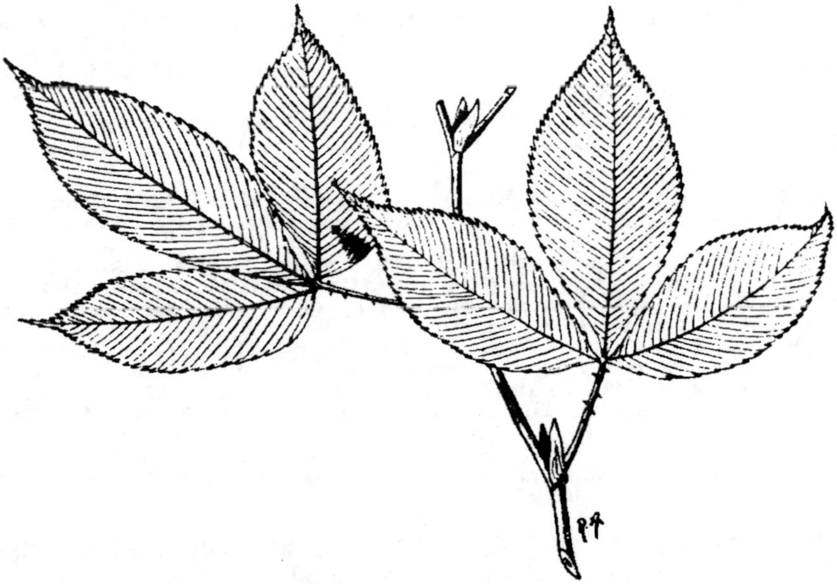

FIG. 123.—Rubus lineatus, Reinw. ½.

D. Leaves impari-pinnate, leaflets usually one pair only.

15. **R. niveus,** Wall.; Brandis F. Fl. 199. (*R. gracilis*, Roxb. is the older name, but Hooker, in Fl. Brit. Ind. ii. 336, has justly retained the well understood and more expressive name of *R. niveus*.) Vern. *Bhera*, Jauns.

A large straggling exceedingly variable, often gregarious shrub, branches dull brown or greyish-brown, often trailing over rocks; silky mostly grey pubescence on branchlets, leaves and inflorescence, numerous small conical prickles on branches and petioles, no bristles or gland-tipped hairs. Leaflets, one or two pair, membranous, deeply incised-serrate, often slightly lobed, variable in size and shape, but generally ovate, acuminate, silky pale green or white beneath, stipules linear-subulate, often 1 in. long. Corymbs lax, few-flowered, petals pink, shorter than calyx-lobes, connivent over ovaries.

Kuram valley, trans Indus. Outer Himalaya, from Kashmir to Bhutan, 6–10,000 ft. in the west, ascending to 12,000 ft. in the east. Manipur. Fl. May–July in the N. W., Oct. in Sikkim (Gamble.) 16. **R. purpureus,** Bunge, Kuram valley 9–10,000 ft. Kashmir. Lahaul, Kunawar. West Tibet, branches yellowish-red, eglandular bristles numerous on branchlets and calyx, fl. few on long slender pedicels, in lax axillary cymes. 17. **R. Hookeri,** Focke, Sikkim 7–10,000 ft., softly pubescent, prickles few, straight, glandular bristles numerous, leaflets 3, rhomboid-ovate, stipules broad pectinate. Fl large, calyx densely hispid, lobes 1 in. long with filiform points, fr. often over one in. diam.

18. **R. macilentus,** Camb.; Brandis F. Fl. 199.

A spreading shrub, nearly glabrous, prickles numerous on branches and petioles, flat, stout, sharp, often yellow and shining, no glandular hairs and bristles. Leaflets pale-green, not shining, ovate-lanceolate, 3, sometimes 1 only. Petals white, orbicular or obovate, longer than calyx-segments, fruit red or yellow, edible.

Himalaya, Kashmir to Bhutan 6–9,000 ft. Fl. Apr.–May.

19. **R. ellipticus,** Smith.—Syn. *R. Gowreephul*, Roxb.; Wight Ic. t. 230; *R. flavus*, Ham.; Brandis F. Fl. 197. Vern. *Gurācha*, Haz.; *Akhe*, Punjab; *Hishala*, *Lal Anchu*, Hind.; *Subwè*, *Sumwe*, Upper Burma.

A large shrub with long trailing angular branches, which as well as petioles are clothed with a dense soft down and long soft brown bristles without glands; stout hooked prickles on branches, petioles and midrib. Leaflets 3, sometimes only one, almost coriaceous, broadly-elliptic or obovate, obtuse or shortly acuminate, densely clothed beneath with soft grey pubescence, stipules subulate. Panicles axillary and terminal, petals white, larger than calyx-segments, fr. yellow, edible.

Outer Himalaya, Hazara to Bhutan 2–7,000 ft. Khasi hills, Manipur. Hills of Lower Burma above 3,000 ft. Upper Burma down to 700 ft. Western Ghats above 4,000 ft., from Mahableshwar southwards. Shevaroy hills. Fl. March–May.—Hills of Ceylon, common. 20. **R. fasciculatus,** Duthie in Ann. Bot. Gard. Calc. ix. t. 48. Damp shady ravines, Tons valley, Tehri-Garhwal, Chakrata, Mussoorie, nearly allied to 19: leaflets 3, thin papery, glabrous except bristles on midrib and nerves beneath, fl. in dense terminal and axillary clusters.

21. **R. fruticosus,** Linn., the European Blackberry. Afghanistan, Hazara (*Kūranchi*). Kashmir. Salt range. Europe, Northern and Western Asia. Leaves on sterile branches often 5-foliolate, stipules linear, no bristles. Fl. pink, in compact cylindrical panicles. Fr. black edible. This is *R. discolor*, Weihe et Nees. 22. **R. lucens,** Focke, Assam, Khasi hills, Manipur. Climbing over tall trees, almost entirely glabrous, branches angled and grooved, white with glaucous bloom. Leaflets shining, acuminate. Fl. small, in narrow racemiform panicles, calyx divided nearly to the base, segments oblong, densely hoary outside, erect in fr.

23. **R. biflorus,** Buch.; Brandis F. Fl. 198; Collett Simla Flora fig. 45. Vern. *Bassandur*, *Hissar*, Theog and Narkanda.

Stems and branches covered with a thick white pruinose coating, branches, petioles and peduncles armed with sharp shining prickles, subulate from a broad base, no glandular hairs or bristles. Leaflets often 2 pair, softly white-tomentose beneath, elliptic or ovate-elliptic, acute, deeply incised-serrate, the terminal often lobed, stipules lanceolate. Fl. white, ½–¾ in. diam. on slender pedicels more than twice the length of calyx, solitary or 2–6 together. Fr. yellow, globose ¾in. diam.

N. W. Himalaya 4–10,000 ft. Sikkim. Bhutan. Fl. Apr.–May.

E. Leaves imparipinnate, leaflets usually 2 pair or more.

24. **R. lasiocarpus,** Smith; Wight Ic. 232; Brand. F. Fl. 198. Vern. *Bhokaran*, Haz.; *Kala Anchu*, Simla; *Kala Hinsalu*, Jauns.; *Gariphal*, Mar.

A spreading shrub with long glabrous purple stems often overhanging and rooting at the extremities. Branches and petioles armed with stout conical prickles, no bristles or glandular hairs, branches often pruinose. Leaflets white-tomentose beneath, 2–5 pair, ovate-lanceolate, with large serratures, the terminal leaflet often lobed. Fl. in lax short, grey-tomentose panicles. Petals pink, shorter than calyx-lobes. Unripe fr. white tomentose, when ripe black, eaten.

Kuram valley. Himalaya, 2–8,000, in Sikkim to 10,000 ft. Khasi hills. Mountains of Burma. Western Ghats from Mahableshwar southwards, Bábabudan hills, Mysore. Lower Palnis, 4,000 ft. Javadi hills, 3,000 ft. Fl. March–May in the North, Jan.–Feb. in the South.—Ceylon 3–6,000 ft., Java. *R. foliosus*, Don, Fl. Brit. Ind. ii. 340, is a prostrate form of 24, with smaller leaflets.

25. **R. racemosus**, Roxb. Nilgiris, Palnis. Closely allied to 24, with copious glandular hairs and short bristles, leaflets broadly ovate, calyx prickly, petals red, large. 26. **R. opulifolius**, Bertol. Khasi hills. Branchlets, petioles and inflorescence densely woolly-tomentose, l. coriaceous, densely clothed beneath with white wool, fl. in short compact woolly and glandular hairy racemes, petals small, red. 27. **R. pungens**, Camb. Kashmir. Branchlets trailing, with numerous straight prickles, leaflets bright green on both sides. Fl. nearly 1 in. across, on long slender pedicels, solitary or 2–3 together, calyx densely prickly.

28. **R. rosæfolius,** Smith; Brandis F. Fl. 198. Vern. *Yeshul*, Kumaon.

A spreading shrub, glabrous or glandular-hairy, prickles on branches and petioles. Leaflets 1–3 pair, green on both surfaces, lanceolate, deeply serrate or lobed, stipules subulate. Fl. ¾–1 in. across, in lax panicles, petals white, exceeding the calyx, fr. cylindric, of innumerable minute orange-red drupes, edible.

Himalaya, Kumaon to Sikkim, 4–7,000 ft. Khasi hills, Manipur. Burma hills above 3,000 ft. Fl. April.—Java. Often cultivated with double flowers.

Potentilla fruticosa, Linn. Himalaya, Kashmir to Sikkim, from 8,000 ft. to the Snow limit, Caucasus, Armenia, Northern Asia. Mountains of Europe and polar regions of North America. A small stiff branched shrub, l. pinnate, leaflets 3–7, ⅓–½ in. long, silky, stipules large, membranous, adnate to petiole. Fl. yellow, solitary, nearly 1 in. across, bracteoles entire or bifid, alternating with calyx-segments. A low spreading shrub in Hayara 8,000 ft. with white fl. is perhaps *P. fruticosa* var. *ochreata*.

7. ROSA, Linn.; Fl. Brit. Ind. ii. 363.

Erect or climbing shrubs, as a rule prickly. Leaves imparipinnate, stipules more or less adnate to petiole. Fl. in terminal corymbs or panicles, rarely solitary. Calyx-tube persistent in fruit, mouth contracted, limb divided into 5 rarely 4 leafy segments. Ovaries ∞, rarely few, free, enclosed in the calyx-tube, the styles protruding and in some species united. Fr. a pulpy or dry red or black berry, enclosing numerous dry 1-seeded very hairy carpels. Species 100, temperate regions of the northern hemisphere, a few species within the tropics.

A. Styles distinct, calyx-segments deciduous.

R. damascena, Mill. (Golab) is the rose chiefly cultivated for Attar and Rose water.

1. **R. involucrata**, Roxb.; Wight Ic. t. 234; Kurz F. Fl. i. 440.—Syn. *R. Lyellii*, Lindl.; Brandis F. Fl. 199.

A large shrub, branches arching, branchlets and inflorescence densely grey-tomentose, prickles straight, frequently in pairs at the nodes. Leaflets 3–4 pair, elliptic-oblong, finely serrate, 1–1½ in. long, upper surface shining, stipules small, laciniate. Fl. white, fragrant, 2–3 in. across, bracts broad, serrate. Fr. ½ in. long, densely tomentose.

Nepal, Gorakhpur, Gangetic plain in swamps and on banks of rivers and lakes. Silhet. Assam. Manipur, banks of rivers. Mount Abū. Upper Burma. Fl. Feb.–March. 2. **R. anserinæfolia**, Boiss., Afghanistan, Baluchistan (*Surai*), Waziristan, Kuram valley, prickles curved, leaflets elliptic, sharply serrate, ½–¾ in. long, pubescent on both sides, fl. 1 in. across. In Journ. Linn. Soc. xix. 161 and xxviii. 315 this is called *R. Beggeriana*, Schrenk.

3. **R. gigantea**, Collett; Journ. Linn. Soc. xxviii. t. 9. Manipur 6,000 ft. Shan hills, 4–5,000 ft. Yunnan. A powerful climber, stems thick, branches with stout flat prickles, made into walking sticks. Fl. mostly solitary, white 3–5 in. across, fr. globose. 4. **R. Collettii**, Crépin; Journ. Linn. Soc. xxviii. t. 10. Shan hills 3–4,000 ft., on banks of streams, leaflets 3 pair, fl. corymbose, 1 in. across.

B. Styles distinct, calyx-segments persistent in fr.

5. **R. macrophylla**, Lindl.; Wall. Pl. As. Rar. t. 117; Brandis F. Fl. 203. Vern. *Ban gūlāb*, *Ban Kuja*, *Ban Kor*, Simla.

A large erect shrub, occasionally unarmed, but generally with straight prickles ¼–½ in. long, often in pairs below the nodes, no bristles, glandular hairs on stipules, bracts, pedicels and calyx. Leaves 2–8 in. long, glabrous or slightly pubescent, leaflets 3–6 pair. Fl. red, 1½–3 in. across, in large corymbs, bracts large entire. Calyx-lobes often longer than petals, apex dilated, lanceolate, toothed. Fr. elongate ovoid, soft, 1–1½ in., calyx-segments often 1 in. long.

Kuram valley. Himalaya, extending into the inner dry region, Kagan to Sikkim 6–10,000 ft. Fl. April–June, fr. Oct.—Yunnan. 6. **R. Webbiana**, Wall. Baluchistan, Kuram valley. Inner and N. W. Himalaya, ascending to 13,500 ft. *Kantai*, Pangi; *Rangyal*, Bash. Leaves ½–3 in. long, leaflets 2–4 pair, obovate or rotundate, entire near base, with deep sharp teeth in the upper half. Fl. pink, solitary, calyx-lobes caudate-acuminate. Fr. sub-globose ½ in. long. 7. **R. Eglanteria**, Linn. (*R. lutea*, Mill., Brandis F. Fl. 201). Baluchistan, Afghanistan, Kuram valley. Inner arid N. W. Himalaya, l. 1½–3 in., leaflets 2–4 pair, stipules broad, leafy, toothed. Fl. yellow 2–2½ in. across, solitary or few together, calyx-lobes caudate-acuminate, glandular. 8. **R. xanthina**, Lindl. (*R. Ecæ*, Aitchison in Journ. Linn. Soc. xix. t. 8.) Kuram valley, forming with *Prunus brahuica* the scrub on stony ridges of the Harial district. Chitral, Turkestan, Mongolia. North China. Prickles straight from a very broad base, fl. yellow, barely 1 in. across.

9. **R. sericea**, Lindl.; Royle Ill. t. 42. f. 1. Vern. *Bhibri*, Chamba.

A large shrub, in Sikkim at times a small tree with hard close grained wood, prickles on sterile branches of 2 kinds, short slender, and broad flat, shining, up to ½ in. long and 1 in. broad; on flowering branches the broad flat kind only. Leaves 1–3 in., leaflets 3–4 pair cuneate oblong, entire in the lower part, with deep sharp teeth in the upper, more or less silky beneath. Fl. white or pink, 2–2½ in. across, usually tetramerous, solitary on nodding peduncles without bracts, calyx-lobes silky-pubescent, fr. fleshy, scarlet.

Himalaya from the Sutlej to Bhutan, 7,500–14,000 ft., often gregarious. Fl. May, June. Tibet, China. This and *R. macrophylla*, when growing in shade are often without prickles, while on open dry hillsides prickles are numerous and the leaves smaller (Collett, Simla Fl. 168).

C. Styles united into a column exserted beyond the calyx-tube, calyx-segments deciduous.

10. **R. moschata**, Mill.; Brandis F. Fl. 201. Vern. *Jhal*, Haz. *Kuja*, *Kanjei*, *Kiu*, *Kunjo*, *Karer*, N. W. Himal.

A thorny shrub, climbing to the top of lofty trees, the flowering branches hanging down in rich festoons, prickles few, stout, recurved. Med. rays of two kinds, narrow and very broad, vessels large. Leaflets pubescent, membranous, 3 pair, 1–3 in. long, evenly serrate. Fl. white, 1–1½ in. across, in large compound terminal corymbs, ramifications and calyx hoary pubescent, but without bristles or prickles. Calyx-lobes twice or three times the length of tube, glandular serrate and (as well as bracts) often pinnatifid. Styles united into a hairy clavate column. Fr. dark brown, globose or ovoid, ¼–⅓ in. diam., crowned by the base of the deciduous calyx-lobes.

Kuram valley, N. W. Himalaya, east as far as Nepal 2–11,000 ft. Fl. May, June. Afghanistan. China. 11. **R. Leschenaultiana**, Wight & Arn.; Wight Ic. t. 38. Nilgiri and Palni hills, similar to 10, differs by evergreen leaves, petioles, inflorescence and calyx densely clothed with glandular bristles, and petals slightly pubescent outside. 12. **R. longicuspis**, Bertol., Khasi and Mishmi hills. Ruby Mines district, Upper Burma. L. thinly coriaceous, shining, petals outside velvety-tomentose, fr. globose ⅓–½ in. diam., nearly allied to 11 and to *R. sempervirens*, Linn., of the Mediterranean region.

8. DOCYNIA, Decaisne; Fl. Brit. Ind. ii. 369.

Small or middle-sized deciduous trees, l. simple, stipules small. Fl. white solitary, or in few-fld. umbels. Calyx-tube clavate, petals 5, with long woolly claws. Ovary 5 celled, styles 5, connate and woolly below the middle, ovules 3 in each cell. Species 2.

1. **D. indica**, Dne.—Syn. *Pyrus indica*, Wall. Pl. As. Rar. t. 173; Kurz F. Fl. i. 441.

Young shoots and underside of leaves densely white-woolly, leaves ovate-lanceolate, indistinctly toothed, blade 2–3, petiole ½–¾ in. long; on young shoots glabrous, larger and lobed, often pinnatifid. Fl. white, calyx densely white-woolly. Fr. yellow, ovoid, 1½–2 in. long, crowned by the persistent calyx-limb, edible.

Sikkim 3–6,000 ft., Bhutan, Khasi hills, Manipur. Hills of Upper Burma. Fl. Feb.–March.—China. 2. **D. Hookeriana**, Dne., Khasi hills, l. glabrous, 4–5 in. long, oblong-lanceolate, fr. between fusiform and ellipsoid.

FIG. 124.—Docynia indica, Dne. ½.

9. CYDONIA, Tourn.; Fl. Brit. Ind. ii. 368.

Deciduous shrubs or trees, l. simple, stipules large, oblique. Fl. solitary or in few-fld. umbels. Ovary 5-celled, styles 5, in the lower part connate and woolly, ovules numerous in each cell. Species 4, Mediterranean region and China.

1. **C. vulgaris**, Pers.—Syn. *Pyrus Cydonia*, Linn.; Brandis F. Fl. 205. *Quince*. Vern. *Bihi*, Hind.

A large shrub, branchlets, underside of leaves, peduncles and calyx white-tomentose. Leaves ovate from an obtuse base, entire, petioles short, stipules oblong, obtuse, glandular-serrate. Fl. white, 2 in. across. Calyx-lobes leafy, glandular-serrate, longer than tube. Fr. large, clothed with grey woolly tomentum, 5-celled, endocarp cartilaginous. Seeds many, testa mucilaginous.

Probably wild in Western Asia, cultivated in N. W. India. Fl. March–April.

2. **C. Cathayensis**, Hemsl. in Hook. Ic. Plant. tt. 2657, 2658. *Kyinzanga*, Burm., hills east of Bhamo, cultivated in Kachin villages on account of its fruit. China. A large squat tree, armed with stout woody spines ¾ in. long. Leaves glabrous when mature, lanceolate, serrate, blade 2–4, narrowed into petiole ¼–½ in. long, stipules leafy, semi-cordate, serrate, serration of l. and stipules cuspidate. Calyx-tube glabrous outside, continued beyond ovary into a campanulate cup, lobes short, obtuse, hairy within. Fr. cylindric ovoid or nearly cylindric, 2 in. long, edible, seeds numerous.

10. ERIOBOTRYA, Lindl.; Fl. Brit. Ind. ii. 370.

Small or large trees, leaves simple very coriaceous, usually serrate. Fl. white, pentamerous, in terminal mostly densely tomentose panicles, calyx-lobes small, persistent. Ovary 2–5-celled, adnate to calyx-tube, ovules 2 in each cell, styles woolly below. Fr. a dry or succulent berry, generally one-seeded, endocarp membranous. Seed large, angular, cotyledons thick, fleshy. Species 10, South-Eastern Asia.

A. Styles 2 or 3.

1. **E. bengalensis**, Hook. f.—Syn. *E. dubia*, Kurz F. Fl. i. 443. Vern. *Petsut*, Burm.

A large evergreen tree, l. elliptic-lanceolate, coarsely serrate, quite glabrous, shining above, sec. n. 8–12 pair, blade 4–8, petiole ¾–1¾ in. Panicle softly tomentose, fl. smelling of hawthorn, ⅓ in. diam., petals oblique, emarginate, styles 2, crown of ovary as well as lower part of styles very woolly. Fr. ellipsoid 1–2-seeded, ¾ in. long.

Khasi hills, Manipur. Chittagong. Mergui. Upper Burma (Smales). Fl. Feb. Malay Peninsula. 2. **E. dubia,** Dcne., Nepal. Sikkim, 5–7,000 ft. Taunggyi, Shan hills 6,000 ft. Leaves glabrous, shining above, sharply serrate, blade 3–5, pet. ¼ in. long. 3. **E. petiolata,** Hook. f., Sikkim, 5–9,000 ft., Bhutan. Leaves glabrous, firmly coriaceous, entire or coarsely serrate towards the apex, sec. n. arching. 4. **E. Hookeriana,** Dcne., Sikkim. Bhutan, 4–8,000 ft. A middle-sized tree, leaves nearly sessile, rusty tomentose when young, glabrous when full grown, oblong-lanceolate, sharply serrate, sec. n. 25–35 pair, stipules large coriaceous, semilunate. Panicles pyramidal, 4–6 in. broad, styles 2. Fr. ellipsoid, yellow, ¾ in. long. 5. **E. angustissima,** Hook. f., Khasi hills, a small gregarious rigid shrub on river banks, l. perfectly glabrous, linear-lanceolate, fl. few, ⅓ in. across, on a small almost glabrous panicle, styles 3.

B. Styles 5.

6. **E. japonica**, Lindl.; Wight Ic. t. 226. *The Loquat.*

A middle-sized tree, leaves nearly sessile, oblanceolate, acuminate, remotely serrate, as well as petiole, densely woolly beneath, nerves 10–15 pair, prominent beneath. Panicles softly woolly, with stout branches. Fl. ½ in. across, crowded, white, fragrant, petals broadly ovate. Fr. ovoid, intruded at the top, 1–1½ long, yellow, seeds 2–5.

Indigenous in China and Japan, largely cultivated in northern India. Fl. Aug.–Nov. 7. **E. elliptica,** Lindl. Nepal, Manipur. L. perfectly glabrous when full grown, entire or coarsely serrate, blade 5–11, petiole 1–3 in. long, sec. n. 15–20 pair very prominent beneath, tertiary nerves parallel.

11. PYRUS, Linn.; Fl. Brit. Ind. ii. 372.

Deciduous trees or shrubs. L. simple or pinnate, stipules deciduous. Fl. white, red or pink, in terminal corymbs, bracts subulate or linear. Ovary 2–5-celled, enclosed within and adnate to calyx-tube, ovules 2 in each cell. Fr. fleshy 2–5-celled, cells lined with a cartilaginous or bony endocarp, often 2-valved, 1–2-seeded. Species 50–60, temperate and cold regions of the northern hemisphere.

A. Leaves simple, sometimes lobed. Ovary 3–5-celled, styles 3–5, free or united. Calyx-lobes persistent or deciduous.

1. **P. Malus**, Linn.; Brandis F. Fl. 205. *The Apple tree.* Vern. *Chur*, Paugi; *Pálu*, Kunáwar; *Seo, seb*, Hind.

Young shoots, underside of leaves and inflorescence clothed with thin white silky tomentum. L. ovate, acuminate, obtusely serrate, petiole usually half the length of leaf or shorter. Fl. white, tinged with red. Styles 5, connate, ovary 3–5-celled. Fr. on a short pedicel, large, globose, intruded at both ends, crowned by the persistent calyx-lobes.

Indigenous in Europe and western Asia, supposed also to be wild in the N. W. Himalaya. Largely cultivated. Fl. March–May, fr. July–Sept.

2. **P. baccata**, Linn.; Brandis F. Fl. 205. Vern. *Patól*, *Buiról*, *Gwdlam*, N. W. Himal.; *Katsbal*, Bash.

Trunk short, bearing a rounded crown of dark green foliage. L. elliptic,

acuminate, serrulate, petiole usually longer than half the length of leaf. Fl. white, on long slender pedicels, in sessile umbelliform corymbs. Calyx-tube urceolate, glabrous or slightly pubescent, limb spreading, lobes lanceolate, deciduous, equal to or longer than tube, white cottony inside. Petals with dark veins. Styles 3–5 nearly free, woolly at base. Fr. small, red or scarlet, globose, sometimes pyriform, ½–1 in. diam., on pedicels 2 in. long.

N. W. Himalaya, Kashmir to Nepal 6–11,000 ft. Bhutan and Khasi hills. Bernardmyo, Upper Burma. Fl. spring, Fr. autumn.—Northern Asia. 3. **P. sikkimensis**, Hook. f., Sikkim 7–10,000 ft., Bhutan, is believed to differ by a woolly calyx, l. tomentose beneath and pyriform speckled fruit, but is probably not specifically distinct.

4. **P. communis,** Linn.; Brandis F. Fl. 203. *The Pear tree.* Vern. *Nāshpāti*, Hind.

Usually glabrous, branchlets on young trees often spinescent. L. broadly ovate, entire or obtusely serrate, petiole slender, nearly as long as leaf. Fl. white, styles 5, free. Fr. more or less turbinate, not intruded at base, crowned with the persistent calyx.

Indigenous in Eastern and Central Europe and in Western Asia. Largely cultivated in the N.W. Himalaya. Fl. March–April (at times in autumn). Fr. Aug.–Oct.

5. **P. Pashia,** Ham.; Collett Simla Flora t. 47.—Syn. *P. variolosa*, Wall.; Brandis F. Fl. 204. Vern *Patangi*, Hazara; *Keint*, *Mehāl*, *Mōl*, N. W. Himalaya.

A middle-sized tree, young shoots, peduncles and calyx clothed with whitish floccose tomentum. Barren branchlets often spinescent. Leaves ovate-lanceolate, from a rounded or slightly cordate base, acuminate, crenate, on coppice shoots and suckers often lobed or pinnatifid, petioles slender, half the length of leaf or longer. Petals obovate, with dark radiating veins. Fr. nearly globose when ripe, ¾–1½ in. diam., crowned with the base of calyx, rough and scurfy with numerous elevated white round spots.

Afghanistan. Trans Indus. Himalaya, Hazara to Bhutan, 2,500–8,000 ft. Khasi hills, Manipur. Upper Burma. Fl. Feb.–April, occasionally in autumn. Fr. eaten, like a medlar when it is half rotten. Closely allied, if specifically distinct, are: 6. **P. Kumaoni**, Dcne., Himalaya, Kashmir to Kumaon, leaves corymbs outside of calyx-tube glabrous, calyx-lobes broad, rounded, woolly on the margin. 7. **P. Jacquemontiana**, Dcne., Punjab Himalaya, l. glabrous, corymbs lax tomentose, young fr. smooth.

8. **P. lanata,** Don.—Syn. *P. Aria*, Brandis F. Fl. 206. Vern. *Amlok*, Kuram valley; *Doda*, Hazara; *Mohl*, *Banshara*, *Banphalta*, *Marphal*, *Pahi*, N. W. Himal.

A middle-sized or large tree, young shoots, inflorescence and outside of calyx-tube clothed with white woolly tomentum. Leaves ovate or obovate, sec. n. prominent beneath, 8–14 pair, each terminating as a rule in a small acute lobe, lobes serrate, blade 3–6, petiole ½–1 in. long; full grown leaves glabrous above, generally greyish white floccose, rarely glabrous, beneath. Fl. white, scented, ½ in. across, in compound terminal corymbs, petals unguiculate, nearly glabrous, often with a few scattered hairs, veined, styles 2–5, free, the lower half densely woolly. Fr. narrowed to the base, red, ½–1½ in., edible, crowned with the persistent calyx-lobes.

Kuram valley. Himalaya, Hazara to Kumaon. Sikkim, Rhododendron Forest, 8–10,000 ft. Fl. March–May. Fr. Aug.–Oct. 9. **P. vestita**, Wall., Himalaya, Jumna to Sikkim 6–8,000 ft. Khasi hills, Yunnan, a large tree, l. very woolly white-tomentose beneath, not lobed, calyx tomentose, petals woolly within, styles 3–5, woolly at base, fr. nearly globose. United with 8 under *P. Aria* in Brandis F. Fl. N. W. & C. India.

B. Leaves simple, ovary 2–3-celled, styles 2–3, free or united, calyx-lobes deciduous, leaving a raised ring at the top of the fruit.

10. **P. Griffithii**, Dcne., Sikkim 6–9,000 ft., Bhutan, Naga hills, a tree, sometimes epiphytic, somewhat resembles *P. vestita*, l. densely grey-tomentose beneath when young, glabrous and shining when full grown, petals glabrous, styles 2, distinct, glabrous,

stigma large, fr. ¼ in. diam. 11. **P. kohimensis,** Watt MSS., Kohima, Naga hills at 6,000 ft., is similar, but the petals have a tuft of hairs inside, the fr. is ovoid, ridged, ⅜ in. long. 12. **P. rhamnoides,** Dcne.. Sikkim 6–9,000 ft., often epiphytic. Nearly allied to *P. Griffithii*, but l. acuminate, with a few hairs beneath while young, entirely glabrous afterwards, sec. n. prominent beneath, very oblique, 10–16 pair.

13. **P. granulosa,** Bertol.; Kurz F. Fl. i. 442.

A middle-sized at times a large tree, l. entirely glabrous, elliptic, from a cuneate, often unequal-sided base, acuminate, sharp-serrate in the upper part, the base being entire, sec. n. 8–12 pair, oblique, blade 3–5, petiole 1 in. Fr. ¾ in. diam., spotted, on short stout pedicels in small terminal corymbs.

Khasi and Naga hills, near streams. Higher hills of upper and lower Burma (reported as epiphytic from the Ruby Mines hills). Fl. C. S. Fr. H.S. Malay Peninsula, Sumatra. Closely allied and probably not specifically distinct: 14. **P. Khasiana,** Dcne., Khasi hills, sec. n. more numerous, nearly straight.

15. **P. polycarpa,** Hook. f., Khasi hills, perfectly glabrous, also inflorescence, l. serrate to the base, otherwise similar to those of *P. granulosa*, petals glabrous, stamens 20, alternately longer, styles 3, fr. ¼–⅓ in. diam., rim of calyx large, the top of fr. depressed with a conical centre. 16. **P. Thomsoni,** King, Sikkim 8–10,000 ft., a large tree, entirely glabrous, also inflorescence, only claw of petals woolly, l. elliptic-lanceolate or oblanceolate, serrate above the middle, blade 2–3, petiole ¼–⅓ in. Fl. ⅓ in. across. Fr. ¾ in. diam., with a few white spots. 17. **P. cuspidata,** Bertol., Khasi hills. Tenasserim, Muleyit 6,400 ft. (Bedd.), a large tree, branches with numerous oblong lenticels, young shoots and leaves clothed with flocculent cotton, that falls away in white flakes. L. thinly membranous, pale green, not shining, ovate, long-acuminate, blade 2–4, petiole 1 in. Corymb dense, rounded, tomentose while young, fl. ½ in. across, petals obovate, claw pubescent. Fr. pyriform, ⅓ in. diam. The Muleyit specimens have the petals hairy on the upper side. 18. **P. ferruginea,** Hook. f., Bhutan, shoots, underside of l. and inflorescence clothed with ferrugineous tomentum, l. ovate, suddenly acuminate, blade 2–3, petiole ¼–⅓ in. long. Corymbs few-fld., petals woolly above, styles 3, glabrous.

C. Leaves impari-pinnate. Corymbs more or less pedunculate. Ovary 2–5-celled, styles 2–5, free. Calyx-lobes persistent.

19. **P. foliolosa,** Wall. Pl. As. Rar. t. 189.—Syn. *P. ursina*, Wall.; Brandis F. Fl. 206. Vern. *Rangrek*, Kunawar.

A large shrub or small tree, in Sikkim often epiphytic on other trees, bark peeling off in horizontal papery strips. Buds, petioles, underside of leaves along nerves and inflorescence with long soft generally rusty hairs. Leaflets 9–15 pair, 1–2 in. linear-oblong, apiculate, sharply serrate, when dry pale brown beneath. Fl. white or greenish-white, smell unpleasant, in dense, many-fld. corymbs, bracts linear, rusty-pilose, deciduous. Fr. small red or bluish red.

Himalaya, from Kashmir to Sikkim, extending into the inner arid region, 6–12,000 ft. Fl. May–July. 20. **P. microphylla,** Wall., Kashmir to Sikkim 10–14,000 ft. East Tibet. Nearly glabrous, slender, scandent or epiphytic, leaflets 12–18 pair, ½–¾ in. long, deeply serrate. Fl. deep red, corymbs lax and few-fld., on slender peduncles 1–2 in. long, fr. large bluish-white.

21. **P. Aucuparia,** Gærtn., the Mountain Ash of Europe, western and northern Asia. Afghanistan, Kuram valley. N. W. Himalaya, 9–13,000 ft., often associated with Juniper at the limit of tree vegetation. Leaflets 6–12 pair, oblong-lanceolate, green beneath when dry, fr. scarlet, in Lahaul white, ⅓–½ in. diam. 22. **P. Wallichii,** Hook. f., Sikkim 6,500–9,000 ft., Naga hills. Young shoots densely woolly, leaflets 5–8 pair, glabrous, glaucous beneath, oblong, entire or obscurely serrulate towards the tip, fl. white. 23. **P. insignis,** Hook. f., Sikkim 8–11,000 ft., Manipur, a small tree, branchlets thick, bud-scales large, brown, shining. Young shoots densely brown silky-tomentose, leaflets 4–6 pair, coriaceous, glabrous when full grown, linear-oblong, entire or obscurely serrulate, 4 by ¾ in. Corymbs dense, glabrous in fruit, ramifications lenticelled.

12. STRANVÆSIA, Lindl.; Fl. Brit. Ind. ii. 382.

Species 5, China, Tibet and Himalaya.

1. **S. glaucescens,** Lindl.; Brandis F. Fl. 210.

A small evergreen tree, leaves coriaceous, lanceolate, serrulate, glabrous above, pale and pubescent beneath along the midrib. Fl. white, pentamerous, ½ in. across, in silky corymbs. Calyx white-tomentose, segments short, erect, persistent. Ovary villous, adnate to base of calyx-tube, 5-celled, cells 2-ovuled, styles 5, glabrous, connate half-way up. Fr. fleshy, including a 5-celled capsule, dehiscing loculicidally, the dissepiments remaining attached to the inner face of the valves.

Outer ranges of the Himalaya in Garhwal and Kumaon, 3–8,000 ft. Nepal. Khasi hills. Ruby Mines district and Shan hills, upper Burma. Fl. Apr.–June. Yunnan. A species not yet described, leaves, corymbs and calyx perfectly glabrous is known from Mogok, Ruby Mines district, and from Yunnan.

13. PHOTINIA, Lindl.; Fl. Brit. Ind. ii. 380.

Evergreen shrubs or small trees, leaves coriaceous, entire or serrulate, stipules subulate, deciduous. Fl. corymbose, white. Calyx-lobes short, persistent. Ovary more or less adnate to calyx-tube, 2- (rarely 3-) celled, ovules 2 collateral in each cell, apex of ovary free, pubescent or woolly, styles short, free or united in the lower part. Fr. 1–2-seeded, endocarp crustaceous or membranous.

1. **P. Lindleyana,** Wight & Arn.; Wight Ic. t. 228. Vern. *Kodai Bikki*, Kan.

A small tree, as a rule quite glabrous. Leaves elliptic, acute at both ends, serrulate, rarely entire, blade 3–6, petiole 1–2 in. long. Fl. ¼ in. diam., calyx-tube hemispherical, fr. turbinate.

Nilgiris, common in Sholas on the plateau. Fl. March–May.

2. **P. Notoniana,** Wight & Arn.; Wight Ic. t. 991; Ill. t. 86. Bedd. Fl. Sylv. t. 192.—Syn. *Eriobotrya integrifolia*, Kurz F. Fl. i. 442. Vern. *Bikki*, Kan.

A large tree, inflorescence finely pubescent, otherwise glabrous. Leaves elliptic-oblong, acuminate, quite entire, blade 6–9, petiole ½–1½ in. long. Fl. ⅛ in. diam., fr. globose.

Nilgiri, Palni and Anamalai hills. Travancore. Khasi and Naga hills. Burma, hills east of Toungoo at 7,000 ft. Fl. May–Oct. Hills of Ceylon.

3. **P. integrifolia,** Lindl. Nepal, Sikkim, 5–7,000 ft. Bhutan. Khasi hills. Ruby Mines district, Upper Burma. Quite glabrous, l. oblanceolate, quite entire, blade 2–4, narrowed into petiole ¼–½ in. long. Fl. white, ⅛ in. across, fr. globose. Closely allied to 2. 4. **P. mollis,** Hook. f. Sikkim Terai. Branchlets, petioles and young l. silky, leaves chartaceous, ovate, acuminate, midrib silky beneath, sec. n. 8–10 pair, arching, slender but conspicuous, blade 3–4, petiole ⅛–¼ in. Fl. in white-woolly corymbs, bracts linear, almost filiform, deciduous. Calyx-tube campanulate, teeth triangular, petals ⅛ in. long. Styles 2 or 3, free or united below. 5. **P. Griffithii,** Dcne., Bhutan, branchlets, petiole and underside of midrib tawny tomentose, l. oblong, acuminate, serrulate near the tip only, blade 5–7, pet. 1½ in. long.

14. POURTHIÆA, Dcne.; Fl. Brit. Ind. ii. 382.

L. serrate, stipules minute. Ovary 2–3-celled, nearly free, base adnate to calyx-tube, often on one side only. Fr. small, globose, 1–2-seeded, endocarp crustaceous, testa thickly coriaceous with irregular often reticulate grooves. Species 5, eastern Asia.

1. **P. arguta,** Dcne. Khasi hills (abundant). Hookhoom valley, Upper Burma. An evergreen shrub, youngest shoots woolly. L. elliptic-lanceolate sharply serrate, glabrous when full grown, sec. n. impressed above, prominent beneath, blade 2–5 in., petiole ¼–½ in. Fl. white in few-fld. corymbs. A variable sp., one of the 6 forms described by Hooker in Fl. Brit. Ind., is distinct; 2. **P. salicifolia,** Dcne. Khasi hills. Upper Burma, on river banks (*Ye petsut*, Smales, Feb. 1902). A deciduous shrub, branchlets white woolly, l. lanceolate, tomentose beneath, blade 4–5, petiole ¼ in. long. Fl. creamy white in many-fld. corymbs, petals ⅛ in. long, claw hairy. Styles 2–3, free, glabrous. The specimens from Burma have larger petals.

15. CRATÆGUS, Linn.; Fl. Brit. Ind. ii. 383.

Shrubs or small trees, often spiny, leaves entire, lobed or pinnatifid, stipules deciduous. Fl. pentamerous, white or red, in terminal corymbose cymes, bracts caducous. Stamens ∞. Ovary either enclosed within and adnate to calyx-tube, cells 1–5, 2 ovules in each, styles free; or carpels distinct, the back adnate to calyx-tube, styles central or basal. Fr. dry or fleshy, enclosing one bony 1-5-celled stone, or 5 bony 1- rarely 2-seeded stones, the apex of the stones being free.

A. Leaves entire.

1. **C. crenulata,** Roxb.—Syn. *C. Pyracantha*, Brandis F. Fl. 208. Vern. *Gingāru*, N. W. Himal.

A large stiff-branched shrub or small tree, evergreen, branchlets spinescent, scattered hairs on youngest shoots and peduncles, otherwise glabrous. L. shining, coriaceous, crowded on short lateral branchlets, linear-oblong, 1–2 in. long, obtuse, narrowed into a short marginate petiole, crenate. Fl. white, carpels 5 free, back adnate to calyx-tube, fr. less than ¼ in. diam., orange or vermilion.

Himalaya, Sutlej to Nepal, 5–8,000 ft., Bhutan. Fl. Apr.–May, fr. Aug.–Sept. *C. Pyracantha*, Persoon, of Western Asia and South Europe is supposed to differ by acute leaves, larger flowers and fruit.

B. Leaves lobed or pinnatifid.

2. **C. Oxyacantha,** Linn.; Brandis F. Fl. 207. *Hawthorn*. Vern. *Ghunza*, Baluchistan; *Ban sinjli*, Haz.; *Pīngyat*, *phindāk*, Punjab Himalaya.

A small tree, branchlets spinescent, young shoots with long soft scattered hairs. Leaves from a cuneate base pinnatifid, segments 2–3 pair, oblong, lobed or dentate, stipules large, leafy, falcate or semicordate. Fl. white or pink, carpels 2–3, or 1 (*C. monogyna*, Jacq.), entirely adnate to calyx-tube. Fr. red (sometimes yellow), enclosing 1 or 2 (sometimes 3) hard 1-seeded nuts.

Baluchistan. Kuram valley. N.W. Himalaya, Indus to Ravi, 5–9,000 ft. Fl. Apr.–July. Fr. Sept.–Oct. Afghanistan, Western Asia, Siberia and Europe. 3. **C. Clarkei**, Hook. f. Kashmir, 7–8,000 ft. A small tree, branchlets leaves and inflorescence softly tomentose, l. ovate, deeply pinnatifid. Fr. 5-seeded, with 5 obtuse ridges. 4. **C. Wattiana**, Hemsley & Lace, Journ. Linn. Soc. vol. xxviii. (1891) 323, tab. 40, Zarghan range near Quetta, 7,000 ft., a small unarmed glabrous tree, l. ovate with 7–9 acute dentate lobes, blade 2–3, the slender petiole ¾–1 in. long, stipules broad, oblique, ½ in. long, deciduous. Fl. white, ovary 5-celled, fr. with 5 obtuse ribs.

16. COTONEASTER, Linn.: Fl. Brit. Ind. ii. 384.

Shrubs or small trees, unarmed, l. coriaceous, generally entire, often hairy, stipules deciduous. Fl. small, white or pink, solitary or in corymbose cymes. Calyx-segments 5, short, persistent, petals 5, ovaries 2–5, adnate by their backs to calyx-tube, 2 ovules in each. Fr. small, with 2–5 bony 1-seeded stones. Species 15–20, of the northern hemisphere.

A. Leaves deciduous, cymes with numerous flowers.

1. **C. bacillaris,** Wall.; Brandis F. Fl. 208; Collett Simla Flora fig. 48. Vern. *Lūni*, Haz.; *Rēs*, *Rēosh*, *Reūs*, Punjab Himal.; *Benang*, Kunawar; *Riūsh*, *Ruinsh*, Jaunsar.

A large shrub or small tree attaining 9 ft. girth, wood white, strong, elastic, used for spear-shafts and walking-sticks. L. ovate- or obovate-oblong, obtuse, 1–3 in. long, soft-pubescent or tomentose beneath, stipules subulate, caducous. Fl. white, ⅓ in. across, in pedunculate spreading compound many-

fld. cymes, at the ends of short leaf-bearing branchlets. Fr. numerous, dark purplish-brown, on slender pedicels, in large spreading bunches.

Kuram valley. N.W. Himalaya, Indus to Sarda 5–10,000 ft., extending into the inner dry valleys. Salt range 1,500–2,500 ft. Fl. May–June. 2. **C. rosea,** Edgew., Tehri Garhwal 8–9,000 ft. Bajamara, Jaunsar. Paternalla. Chenab valley. Branches slender, drooping, leaves less hairy, fl. pink, smaller than 1, calyx nearly glabrous, except woolly margin, said to fl. later than 1. 3. **C. frigida,** Wall., Kumaon to Bhutan. 7–9,000 ft., l. oblanceolate-oblong, 3–5 in. long, cyme and calyx woolly, fr. scarlet.

B. Leaves generally deciduous, cymes with few flowers.

4. **C. acuminata,** Lindley ; Brandis F. Fl. 209. Vern. *Der reüsh*, Bagi ; *Zam riüsh*, Kidarkanta.

A shrub, shoots and young l. pubescent with soft silky hairs, stipules subulate, ciliate, l. ovate-lanceolate, 1–2 in. long. Fl. white or pink, ¼ in. across, in small 2–6-fld. cymes at the ends of short leaf-bearing branchlets. Fr. red, turbinate or oblong, ⅓ in. long.

FIG. 125.—Cotoneaster acuminata, Lindley. ½.

Himalaya, Bias to Sikkim, 4,500–12,000 ft., often as underwood in Oak forests. Fl. May–July. 5. **C. vulgaris,** Lindl. Kashmir. Head of Rupin valley, Garhwal (D. B. 1874). Western Tibet and Waziristan. Europe, Western Asia, Siberia, l. ¾–1½, rarely 2 in., broadly oblong or ovate, softly grey-tomentose beneath, cymes 2–4-fld., bent down, nearly glabrous, as well as calyx. 6. **C. nummularia,** Fisch. et Mey. Baluchistan (*Sheru, Sherugi*). Kashmir and Western Tibet. Afghanistan, Western Asia. L. ⅓–⅝ in. orbicular or obovate, white-woolly beneath, cymes erect, white-woolly as well as calyx, 2–5-fld. 7. **C. Simondsii,** Hort., Khasi hills, erect, l. ¾ in. long, shortly acuminate, sec. n. 2–3 pair, distinct beneath, fl. solitary or twin, fr. turbinate, scarlet. 8. **C. rotundifolia,** Wall., Garhwal, Kumaon, Sikkim, a low rigid distichously branching shrub, l. ⅓–½ in., orbicular-obovate, fl. solitary, fr. turbinate, scarlet.

C. Leaves generally evergreen, fl. solitary or in pairs.

9. **C. microphylla,** Wall. ; Brandis F. Fl. 209.

A rigid, intricately branched, usually prostrate shrub, leaves ⅓–¾ in. long, obovate or ovate-lanceolate, glossy above, pubescent beneath, margins recurved, fl. white, generally solitary, or two or three together, ½ in. diam., fr. globose, scarlet.

Himalaya, 4–11,000 ft., Kashmir to Bhutan. Fl. May–June. Closely allied and probably not specifically distinct is 10. **C. thymifolia,** Hort., l. smaller than 9, obovate, tip rounded or retuse, glossy above, pubescent or tomentose beneath, fl. solitary, ⅓ in. across. 11. **C. buxifolia,** Wall.; Wight Ic. t. 992, Nilgiri, Palni hills, an exceedingly rigid shrub or small tree, forming large dense masses of stiff branches, l. ¼–½ in., elliptic, acute at both ends, densely tomentose beneath, margins recurved, cymes (as well as calyx) tomentose, 2–6-fld., fr. globose scarlet.

Osteomeles anthyllifolia, Lindl.; Shan hills upper Burma, 4,000 ft. China (common in Yunnan). Pacific islands. A shrub, branchlets, petioles and inflorescence silky, conspicuous in spring from the profusion of small white fl., l. imparipinnate, leaflets 10–15 pair, oblanceolate, quite entire, mucronate, grey-silky beneath, ⅓–½ in. long, ovary inferior 5-celled, one ovule in each cell. Fr. ¼ in. diam. crowned with the triangular lanceolate persistent calyx-lobes, enclosing 5 distinct bony pyrenes.

ORDER XLVII. SAXIFRAGACEÆ. Gen. Pl. i. 629.

Trees, shrubs or herbs, fl. regular, generally bisexual. Calyx free or adnate to ovary. Stamens free, as many as petals or double their number, rarely more. Carpels 2 or more, usually connate into a 1- or 2-celled ovary, ovules numerous, placentæ on the edge of carpels, parietal or on the dissepiment. Seeds small, embryo minute, in copious fleshy or horny albumen.

A. Leaves opposite.
- Filaments winged, stamens 10 . . . . . . 1. DEUTZIA.
- Filaments linear or subulate.
  - Stamens 2–40 . . . . PHILADELPHUS (p. 296).
  - Stamens 8–12.
    - Petals falling off as a cap, style one, short . PILEOSTEGIA (p. 296).
    - Petals sometimes falling off as a cap, styles 2–4, calyx-segments of sterile fl. enlarged in fr. . 2. HYDRANGEA.
    - Petals free, berry inferior, blue. . . . . 3. DICHROA
  - Stamens 4, fr. fleshy 1-seeded . . . . . 4. POLYOSMA

B. Leaves alternate.
- Ovary nearly free, of 2 carpels, capsule 2-valved . 5. ITEA.
- Ovary nearly free, of 3 carpels, capsule 3-valved . POTTINGERIA (p. 299).
- Ovary inferior, fr. a berry . . . . . . 6. RIBES.

1. DEUTZIA, Thunb.; Fl. Brit. Ind. ii. 406.

Shrubs, l. and branches opposite, hairs stellate. Leaves serrate, stipules 0. Fl. white, corymbose, pentamerous, stamens 10, filaments broadly winged. Ovary inferior, 3–5-celled, ovules ∞ on 3–5 axile placentas in the inner angle of the cells, styles 3–5, filiform. Capsule septicidally dehiscent, separating into 3–5 distinct cocci. Species 10. Himalaya, China, Japan, North- and hills of Central-America.

1. **D. corymbosa**, Rob. Brown; Royle Ill. t. 46 (*Bhujlu*, *Philru*, Bash.). Himalaya 6–10,000 ft., Kashmir to Bhutan. Tibet. A shrub attaining 8 ft., bark peeling off in long thin shining rolls, leaves green beneath. Calyx-teeth ovate, shorter, when in fl., than tube, petals broad, obovate, nearly glabrous, imbricate, ¼ in. long. 2. **D. staminea**, Rob. Brown in Wall. Pl. As. Rar. t. 191; Collett Simla Flora, fig. 52 (*Deosu*, Bash.). Himalaya 4–9,000 ft., Hazara to Bhutan. Naga hills and Manipur (*D. intermedia*, Watt MSS.). Usually smaller than 1, bark dark grey, peeling off in thin longitudinal strips, branchlets, inflorescence and leaves rough with harsh stellate hairs. Calyx-teeth triangular, oblong or linear, when in fl. as long as tube, petals oblong, induplicate-valvate, ⅓ in. long. 3. **D. macrantha**, Hook. f. & Thoms. Below Binsar in Kumaon, 5,500 ft., l. distantly serrate, calyx-teeth linear, longer than tube while in fl., petals lanceolate, ¾ in. long, induplicate-valvate in bud.

Philadelphus coronarius, Linn. Himalaya, Kashmir to Bhutan, 5–9,000 ft. (*Daspa*, Bash.). A shrub, bark light grey, fl. white, fragrant, usually tetramerous, axillary or in small cymes at the ends of branchlets. Petals convolute in bud, ½ in. long, stamens 20–40, filaments subulate, ovary 4-celled, ovules ∞ on 4 placentas protruding into the cell from the inner angle. Capsule dehiscing loculicidally.

Pileostegia viburnoides, Hook. f. & Thoms.; Khasi hills. China. A glabrous shrub, branches decussate, l. coriaceous evergreen, entire. Fl. small, white, in large terminal panicles, petals 4 or 5, falling off as a cap, ovary inferior, 4–6-celled, ovules ∞. Styles short, surmounted by a thicker pyramid, the 4–6 angles of which are stigmatic. Capsule 4–5-celled.

2. HYDRANGEA, Linn.; Fl. Brit. Ind. ii. 403.

Shrubs or trees, often climbing, l. opposite, stipules 0. Fl. in terminal corymbs, bracts deciduous, the outer fl. often sterile and larger than the fertile inner fl. Calyx-tube adnate to ovary, limb 4–5-dentate, petals valvate, stamens

8 or 10. Two T shaped parietal placentas, ovary incompletely 4-celled. Sterile fl. with large petaloid calyx-lobes. Capsule crowned by calyx-limb and the persistent styles, seeds ∞, testa membranous or hyaline, projecting beyond the ends of the seed. Species 30–40. Himalaya, mountains of Burma and Java. China, Japan, America.

A. Capsule truncate, base of styles not thickened.

1. **H. altissima,** Wall.; *Logora*, Jauns.; *Kathmora*, Garhwal. Himalaya from the Ravi eastward 4–8,000 feet. Often climbing or epiphytic, outer bark brown, shining, peeling off in thin papery rolls which are used as paper. Leaves ovate, acuminate, dentate, blade 3–7, petiole 1–3 in. long. Fl. cream-coloured, petals falling off in a cap. The four calyx-segments of sterile fl. entire, ⅓–⅔ in. long. 2. **H. robusta,** Hook. f. Sikkim, Bhutan, 5–8,000 ft., common as undergrowth in forests. Hills east of Bhamo, 5,500 ft. (Montague Hill, Feb. 1902). A middle-sized or large tree, branchlets quadrangular, hairy. L. ovate or elliptic, sometimes with a cordate base, serrate, serratures long cuspidate, fine appressed hairs scattered on both sides, blade 8–11, petiole (often winged) 2–5 in. Bracts enclosing the buds, large, tomentose, caducous. Fertile fl. bright blue, calyx-segments of sterile fl. in fruit 1–1⅓ in. long, on slender pedicels 1–2 in. long, cream-coloured, conspicuously veined, sharply serrate. 3. **H. aspera,** Don. Kumaon to Sikkim 4–7,000 ft. L. lanceolate, softly tomentose beneath, blade 6–10, petiole ½–2 in. Calyx-segments of sterile fl. entire or serrulate.

B. Capsule crowned by the thickened base of styles.

4. **H. vestita,** Wall. Kumaon to Bhutan, 8–11,000 ft. Khasi hills. Tibet. A small tree, l. elliptic-lanceolate cuspidate-serrate, densely and softly tomentose beneath, blade 6–10, petiole 2–4 in. Sepals of sterile fl. entire, 1 in. long. 5. **H. stylosa,** Hook. f. & Thoms. Sikkim, 8,000 ft. Styles subulate, as long as capsule, sepals of sterile fl. coarsely crenate-dentate. 6. **H. Pottingeri,** Prain in Journ. As. Soc. Beng. vol. 67. 290. Kachin hills. Capsule with enlarged base of styles globose, only half enclosed by calyx.

3. DICHROA, Lour.; Fl. Brit. Ind. ii. 406.

D. febrifuga, Lour. (the only species).—Syn. *Adamia cyanea*, Wall. Pl. As. Rar. t. 213.

A shrub, often forming undergrowth in forests, young shoots and inflorescence pubescent with short hairs. L. opposite, lanceolate, blade 4–8, taper-

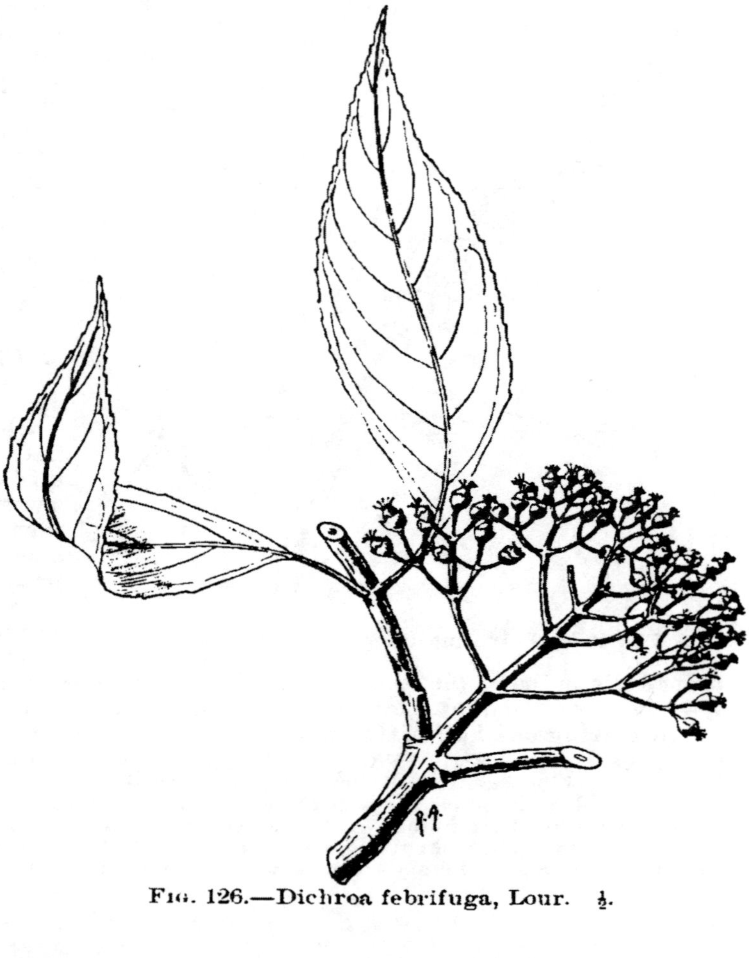

FIG. 126.—Dichroa febrifuga, Lour. ½.

ing into petiole ½–1 in. Fl. pale blue, sometimes violet, in terminal cymose panicles, petals 5 or 6, thick, valvate. Ovary ¾ inferior, ovules ∞ on 3–5 parietal placentas. Berries bright dark blue.

Himalaya, Nepal to Bhutan 4–8,000 ft. Khasi hills. Shan hills. Upper Burma. China. Mountains of the Malay Peninsula and Archipelago. Fl. R. S.

4. POLYOSMA, Blume; Fl. Brit. Ind. ii. 408.

Species 8, from the Khasi hills through the Indo-Malayan region to Australia.

P. integrifolia, Blume.—Syn. *P. Wallichi*, Benn.; Kurz F. Fl. i. 444. A middle-sized evergreen tree, the youngest shoots tawny-pubescent, l. nearly opposite, oblanceolate, entire or distantly toothed, blade 4–8, petiole ½–1 in. Fl. greenish-white, tetramerous, in terminal pubescent racemes, buds pubescent, cylindrical, ⅓–½ in. long, petals valvate often cohering, stamens 4, anthers linear, basifixed, filaments thick, hairy. Ovary inferior 1-celled, ovules ∞, in two rows attached to two parietal placentas, which protrude into the cell. Fr. an ovoid 1-seeded berry ½ in. long, crowned by the persistent calyx-tube, embryo small, at the apex of a fleshy albumen.

Assam, Khasi hills. Andamans. Malay Peninsula. Fl. R. S.

FIG. 127.—Polyosma integrifolia, Blume. ½.

5. ITEA, Linn.; Fl. Brit. Ind. ii. 407.

Shrubs or trees, l. alternate, glabrous, dentate, stipules 0. Fl. pentamerous, small, white, in many-fld. terminal and axillary racemes. Calyx-tube short, adnate to base of ovary, petals valvate. Ovary nearly free, 2-celled, ovules ∞ in 2 rows along the middle of the dissepiment (on the edges of the inflexed carpels). Capsule nearly free, base only adnate to the persistent calyx, septicidally 2-valved, each valve bearing one-half of the styles, the stigmas often cohering.

1. **I. macrophylla**, Wall. Valleys of Sikkim, ascending to 4,000 ft. Bhutan, Khasi hills. A middle-sized tree, l. coriaceous broadly elliptic, acuminate, blade 4–8, petiole ½–1 in., petals reflexed on the pedicel between the calyx-teeth. Capsule with style ¼ in. long, calyx-tube turbinate in fr. 2. **I. chinensis**, Hook. & Arn. Khasi and Naga hills. China. Formosa. A shrub or small tree, l. elliptic-oblong, acuminate, blade 3–5, petiole ¼–½ in. long. Petals erect, persistent. Capsule ⅓ in. long, almost entirely free.

3. **I. riparia,** Collett et Hemsley in Journ. Linn. Soc. xxviii. 57. Common on river banks in the Southern Shan States, 2–4,000 ft. Branchlets channelled, l. lanceolate denticulate, 3–4 in. long. Racemes terminal erect, petals lanceolate, erect, ⅛ in. long. 4. **I. nutans,** Royle; Kanjilal F. Fl. 168, Duns and valleys of the N. W. Himalaya, Hazara to Kumaon, ascending to 6,000 ft. A small tree, l. ovate, acuminate, serrate, blade 4–7, petiole 1 in. Racemes long, drooping, petals erect, capsule with styles ⅓ in. long.

Pottingeria acuminata, Prain; Ann. Bot. Gard. Calc. ix. t. 49. Kachin hills, Upper Burma, 3,700 ft., l. glabrous, rigidly coriaceous, ovate-lanceolate, 5 longitudinal nerves from the base, 3 prominent, the 2 marginal ones very slender, fl. in lateral cymes, capsule septicidally 3-valved, the 3 placentas remaining attached to the style when the capsule opens.

6. RIBES, Linn.; Fl. Brit. Ind. ii. 409.

Shrubs, prickly or unarmed, l. alternate, palmately lobed, frequently clustered on arrested branchlets. Calyx superior, tube often produced beyond the ovary, petals 4–5, stamens as many. Ovary inferior, 1-celled, ovules on 2 slender parietal placentas. Berry ovoid or globose, crowned by the persistent calyx.

A. Armed, peduncles 1–2-fld.

1. **R. Grossularia,** Linn. *Gooseberry.* Vern. *Tara, Amlu,* Pangi; *Yanghai,* Kun.

Pubescent, stout spines generally in threes under the petiole, and often numerous smaller scattered prickles in addition. L. as broad as long, 3–5-lobed, ½–1½ in. diam., petiole as long as leaf. Berry oblong hairy.

Kuram valley. Inner drier districts of the N. W. Himalaya, Kashmir to Kumaon 8–12,000 ft. Armenia, Caucasus, Mountains of Greece. Northern Europe.

B. Unarmed, fl. unisexual, calyx limb beyond the ovary short, flat.

2. **R. orientale,** Poir. Baluchistan, in the Juniper tracts. Kuram valley. Afghanistan. Kashmir. Inner arid Himalaya, 8–12,000 ft., Lahaul, Kunawar, Kumaon. West Tibet. Mountains of Greece and Western Asia. Sticky-glandular and minutely hairy. L. as broad as or broader than long, ¾–1½ in. across, more or less lobed, lobes rounded. Berries glandular-pubescent, ⅓ in. diam., reddish-yellow. 3. **R. glaciale,** Wall. Himalaya, Kashmir to Bhutan, chiefly in the inner ranges, 7–12,000 ft. In the N. W. Himalaya often at the limit of tree vegetation, associated with *Rhododendron campanulatum,* the *alpine Birch* and *Abies Webbiana,* Often epiphytic or climbing. Glabrous, a few scattered hairs occasionally on the leaves. L. longer than broad, 3–5-lobed, 1–4 in. long. Fl. reddish-brown (greenish, Kanjilal). Fl. in pubescent racemes 1–3 in. long, which are erect in fl. but drooping in fr. Berries globose, nearly glabrous, ¼ in. diam. 4. **R. desmocarpum,** Hook. fil. & Thoms. Sikkim, Bhutan 8–10,000 ft. Tibet. Closely allied to 3, but berries glandular-pubescent. 5. **R. lucidum,** Hook. f. & Thoms. Leaves glabrous, as broad as or broader than long, berries small, glabrous.

C. Unarmed, fl. bisexual, calyx tubular or campanulate beyond ovary.

6. **R. rubrum,** Linn.; Kanjilal F. Fl. 169.—Syn. *R. Himalense,* Dcne. *Red Currant.* Vern. *Ban Tilla,* Bagi.

Attains 10 ft., outer bark peeling off in long thin strips. Leaves as broad as or broader than long, 3–5-lobed, blade 1–4, petiole red, 2–3 in. long, with a few scattered grey hairs along the edge near the base. Racemes pubescent, many-fld., drooping, no l. at base, fl. greenish-yellow, pedicels equal, bracts ovate, shorter than pedicels, free part of calyx-tube and the obtuse segments prominently veined.

Kuram valley, N. W. Himalaya, Kashmir to Kumaon, 7–12,000 ft., also in the inner dry districts. Fl. Apr.–May. Northern Europe and mountains of Central Europe. Caucasus. Altai. A remarkable variety with black fr., but not aromatic, no resinous glands on calyx and leaves, in Kashmir, Lahaul, at the head of the Rupin valley, Tehri Garhwal, and elsewhere. (Brandis F. Fl. 215.)

7. **R. nigrum,** Linn. *Black Currant.* Scarce in Kunawar and the inner dry valleys of Kashmir. Aromatic, round yellow glands on calyx and underside of leaves. Racemes few-fld., pubescent, a tuft of l. at the base, bracts minute, much shorter than

pedicel, lower pedicels longer than upper. Berries black, ⅓ in. diam., very aromatic. 8. **R. Griffithii,** Hook. f. & Thoms. Sikkim 10–13,000 ft. Bhutan. L. sharply serrrate, pubescent on the nerves beneath, racemes lax, 3–6 in. long, pendent, bracts ¼–⅓ in., linear, longer than pedicels, berries red.

ORDER XLVIII. **HAMAMELIDACEÆ.** Gen. Pl. i. 664.
(*Hamamelideæ.*)

Trees or shrubs, l. alternate, stipules usually deciduous, hairs mostly fasciculate or stellate. Fl. in compact heads or spikes, usually bracteate. Calyx-tube more or less adnate to ovary, petals 4–∞, occasionally none. Ovary 2-celled, styles 2, usually persistent, ultimately divaricate. Capsule woody, loculicidally dehiscent, often also imperfectly dehiscing septicidally. Seeds 1 in each cell, or numerous, in which case the lowest only is fertile. Testa shining, embryo straight, cotyledons flat, albumen usually thin. (No species in the Western Peninsula.)

In 1836 Griffith discovered that the Indian Geneva of this Order are distinguished by bordered pits on the walls of wood-fibres, resembling the bordered pits of Conifers (Asiatic Researches xix. 95, 99, 102), and this is now recognized as an important character of *Hamamelidaceæ.* These wood-fibres have thick walls and a small lumen. The medullary rays are narrow (1 or 2 cells wide) the vessels small, and the wood parenchyma is of no importance.

A. Ovules solitary in each cell.
- Petals 0.
  - Leaves deciduous, crenate, fl. bisexual in involucrate heads . . . . 1. PARROTIA.
  - Leaves persistent, entire, fl. polygamous or unisexual.
    - Ovary superior . . . . DISTYLIUM (p. 301).
    - Ovary half-inferior . . . . SYCOPSIS (p. 301).
- Petals 4 or 5.
  - Leaves deciduous, serrate . . . . 2. CORYLOPSIS.
  - Leaves persistent, entire . . . . LOROPETALUM (p. 301).

B. Ovules several in each cell.
- Leaves entire, sometimes 3-cuspidate at the apex, stipules large, coriaceous . . . . . . 3. BUCKLANDIA.
- Leaves serrate, stipules usually deciduous . . . 4. ALTINGIA.

FIG. 128.
Parrotia Jacquemontiana, Dcne. ½.

1. PARROTIA, C. A. Meyer; Fl. Brit. Ind. ii. 426.

(Species 2, one on the south coast of the Caspian Sea.)

P. Jacquemontiana, Dcne.; Brandis F. Fl. t. 28. Vern. *Killar*, Chamba; *Shtăr*, Kan.

A large gregarious deciduous shrub or small tree, stellate hairs on branchlets, petioles, stipules, calyx and the underside of leaves. L. orbicular or obovate, obtuse, crenate, the lowest pair of sec. n. direct from the base, stipules deciduous, oblong, as long as petioles or longer. Fl. bisexual, greenish-yellow, sessile, about 20 in an ovoid head, which is supported by 4 large round membranous bracts, white or pale yellow. Calyx campanulate, adhering to base of ovary, limb thick, woolly, truncate, or with a few linear lobes, petals 0, stamens usually 15, free. Capsule ½ in. long, woolly, with stellate tomentum, girt by the adhering calyx-tube, 2-celled, the cells separating when ripe, each cell with one seed in a hard horny endocarp, which opens at the top by two rostrate valves. Embryo oblique in copious albumen.

Kuram valley (abundant, used for the wicker work, of which the walls of houses consist). Kashmir and Chamba, 3,800–8,500 ft. Fl. March–May, the leaves turn yellow before falling. The twigs are used for binding and basket work, they are the best material for making the twig bridges to cross the rivers of the Punjab Himalaya.

Distylium indicum, Benth. Khasi hills. A small tree, l. coriaceous, 3–5 in., acuminate, stipules lanceolate, deciduous. Fl. polygamous, in short upright axillary racemes. Fruit (unripe) lanceolate, ¾ in. long, densely stellate-tomentose.

Sycopsis Griffithiana, Oliv. in Trans. Linn. Soc. xxiii. t 8. Khasi hills. Leaves coriaceous, 2–4 in., acuminate, stipules minute, caducous. Fl. unisexual, in small axillary heads, ♂ and ♀ in the same head, ovary, lower half adnate to, upper half closely surrounded by calyx-tube. Capsule nearly globose, ½ in. diam., stellately tomentose.

2. CORYLOPSIS, Sieb. & Zucc.; Fl. Brit. Ind. ii. 427.

(Species 4–6, all except the following in China and Japan.)

C. himalayana, Griff. in Journ. As. Soc. xxiii. 641.; Ic. Pl. As. t. 633.

A large shrub or small tree, branchlets, petioles and underside of leaves softly stellate - tomentose, l. broad-ovate, often nearly orbicular, serrate, base more or less cordate, sec. n. oblique, nearly straight, parallel, the outer branching on the outside, stipules lanceolate, almost glabrous, deciduous. Fl. bisexual, pentamerous, yellow, scented, in drooping densely silky catkin-like spikes, each fl. in the axil of a large concave bract. Calyx-tube adnate to ovary, petals spathulate, stamens 5, with a number of scales (sterile stamens). Ovary half inferior, capsule woody, ¼ in. diam.

Bhutan, 5–8,000 ft. Khasi hills. Manipur. Fl. Dec.–March.

FIG. 129.—Corylopsis himalayana, Griff. ½.

Loropetalum chinense, Oliver, Assam, Khasi hills, China. An evergreen shrub, l. entire, branchlets, young leaves and inflorescence stellately pubescent, leaves 1–3 in. long. Fl. greenish-white, bisexual, tetramerous, 6–8 in small heads at the ends of leafy branchlets. Petals linear, ⅜ in. long. Ovary half-inferior, capsule ovoid, woody, ¼ in. long.

3. BUCKLANDIA, Rob. Brown; Fl. Brit. Ind. ii. 429.

B. populnea, R. Br. (the only species); Kurz. F. Fl. i. 445. Vern. *Pipli*, Darjeeling.

A tall tree, leaves thickly coriaceous, glabrous, rarely pubescent beneath along nerves, broadly ovate, nearly orbicular, apex acuminate, sometimes with 3 cuspidate lobes, basal nerves 5–7, blade 3–9, petiole 1–3 in. long. Stipules large, enveloping the buds, oblong, coriaceous, deciduous. Fl. polygamous, in peduncled heads of 8–20, more or less connate by their calyces. Calyx-tube adnate to ovary, limb 5-lobed. Petals in the bisexual fl. variable in number, linear-spathulate, in the female fl. rudimentary. Stamens 10–14, filaments long. Ovary half-inferior, ovules 6 in each cell, in 2 rows. Capsule subglobose, the lowest seed winged and fertile, the upper seeds sterile.

Sikkim (3–8,000 ft.). Bhutan. Assam, Khasi hills, Manipúr. Hills of Martaban. Fl. at all seasons (Gamble List 38) Malay Peninsula, Sumatra, Java.

4. ALTINGIA, Noronha: Fl. Brit. Ind. ii. 429.

(Species 2, one in China.)

A. excelsa, Noronha; Kurz F. Fl. i. 445. Vern. *Jutili*, Ass.

A very tall aromatic deciduous tree, trunk often 100 ft. to the first branch, wood hard, brown, aromatic. Almost entirely glabrous, the terminal buds ovoid acuminate, silky with minute simple hairs. Leaves lanceolate, serrate, penninerved, blade 3–5, petiole slender 1 in. long. Fl. unisexual, in dense heads, ♂ heads cylindrical, supported by large silky bracts arranged in short spikes or racemes, each head consisting of a fleshy axis having numerous closely packed almost sessile anthers, ♀ heads pedunculate, solitary, axillary, calyces confluent, petals 0. Fruit heads rough, globose, woody, ½ in. diam., capsules velvety with simple hairs, almost immersed in the confluent calyces. Seeds numerous, all but one sterile. Fertile seed at the bottom of capsule surrounded by a membranous wing.

Assam, Bhutan. Kachin hills, Upper Burma. Tenasserim, gregarious along the banks of rivers in Mergui. Fl. R. S. Fr. Feb.–May. Yunnan. Java. This like the closely allied *Liquidambar orientalis*, Mill., of Asia Minor, yields a resin (Storax) contained in canals, which accompany the vascular bundles to the last ramifications of the leaf-nerves, and which in the stem run along the circumference of the pith in close proximity to the oldest wood (protoxylem).

ORDER XLIX. RHIZOPHORACEÆ. Gen. Pl. i. 677.

(*Rhizophoreæ.*)

(Schimper in Engler u. Prantl iii. 7. 42.)

Trees and shrubs, generally glabrous, leaves opposite, usually coriaceous and entire, scars of petioles in most genera prominent on branchlets. Stipules interpetiolar deciduous. Fl. regular, generally bisexual. Calyx more or less adnate to ovary, rarely free, limb 4–14-lobed, lobes valvate, as a rule coriaceous and persistent, petals as many as sepals often 2-fid or laciniate, stamens usually twice the number of petals. Ovary 2–5- (rarely 1-) celled, ovules mostly 2 in each cell, pendulous from the apex. Style one. Fr. coriaceous, usually 1-celled 1-seeded.

The litoral species of this, together with trees and shrubs of other orders, form the Mangrove forests, which have a strikingly peculiar character. In the soft mud in which they grow, these species are firmly anchored by means of widely spreading and much branching roots, and in many cases by aërial roots descending from the branches. Thus they are protected against being uprooted by storms and by the waves during high water. The leaves have a very thick cuticle and other arrangements for diminishing transpiration, and they are full of water-storing tissue. Their structure resembles that of plants growing in deserts and in very dry localities, and the probable explanation is, that transpiration is checked, in order to prevent an injurious excess of the sea-water salts in the sap which fills their tissue. Mangrove trees and shrubs have other peculiar features, such as knees and other excrescences projecting upwards from the roots, believed to facilitate the access of air to the roots, which are immersed in mud and water; as well as the fact that their seeds often germinate on the tree, making considerable growth before they fall into the mud of the tidal swamp.

A. Ovary inferior or half-inferior, l. coriaceous.
  Litoral species, albumen 0, the seed germinates on the tree, sending down a long radicle.
    Petals 4, entire, ovary 2-celled, half-inferior . . . 1. RHIZOPHORA.
    Petals 5 or 6, emarginate, ovary 3-celled, half-inferior . . . 2. CERIOPS.
    Petals 5 or 6, bifid, lobes laciniate, ovary 1-celled, half-inferior . . . 3. KANDELIA.
    Petals 8–14, bifid or emarginate, ovary 2-4-celled, inferior . . . 4. BRUGUIERA.
  Inland species, seeds albuminous, do not germinate on the tree . . . 5. CARALLIA.

B. Ovary free, inland species.
  L. coriaceous, strongly net-veined, seeds albuminous. GYNOTROCHES (p. 306).
  L. almost membranous, perfectly glabrous, fl. ¾ in long WEIHEA (p. 306).
  L. membranous, young shoots and inflorescence pubescent, fl. ½ in. long . . . BLEPHARISTEMMA (p. 306).

1. RHIZOPHORA, Linn.; Fl. Brit. Ind. ii. 435.

Evergreen glabrous shrubs or middle-sized trees sending down numerous aërial roots into the mud of the Mangrove swamp. The lower part of the trunk dies early and the tree is then supported by a number of branching aërial roots, standing as it were on stilts. Leaves thick, stipules large, deciduous, enclosing the buds. Fl. on few-fld. cymes, calyx divided into 4 segments, persistent and enlarged in fr., anthers 8–12, nearly sessile, with numerous cells. Ovary half-inferior, 2-celled, 2 ovules in each cell. Fr. leathery, conical, indehiscent, 1-celled, 1-seeded, the seed germinating on the tree, the large cylindrical radicle perforating the apex of the fr. Species 3, one (*R. Mangle* Linn.) American.

1. **R. mucronata**, Lamarck; Wight Ic. t. 238; Bedd. Manual t. 13. Vern. *Kamo*, Sind; *Kandal*, Mar.; *Uppu Poma*, Tel.; *Bhara*, Sundr.; *Pyu*, Burm.

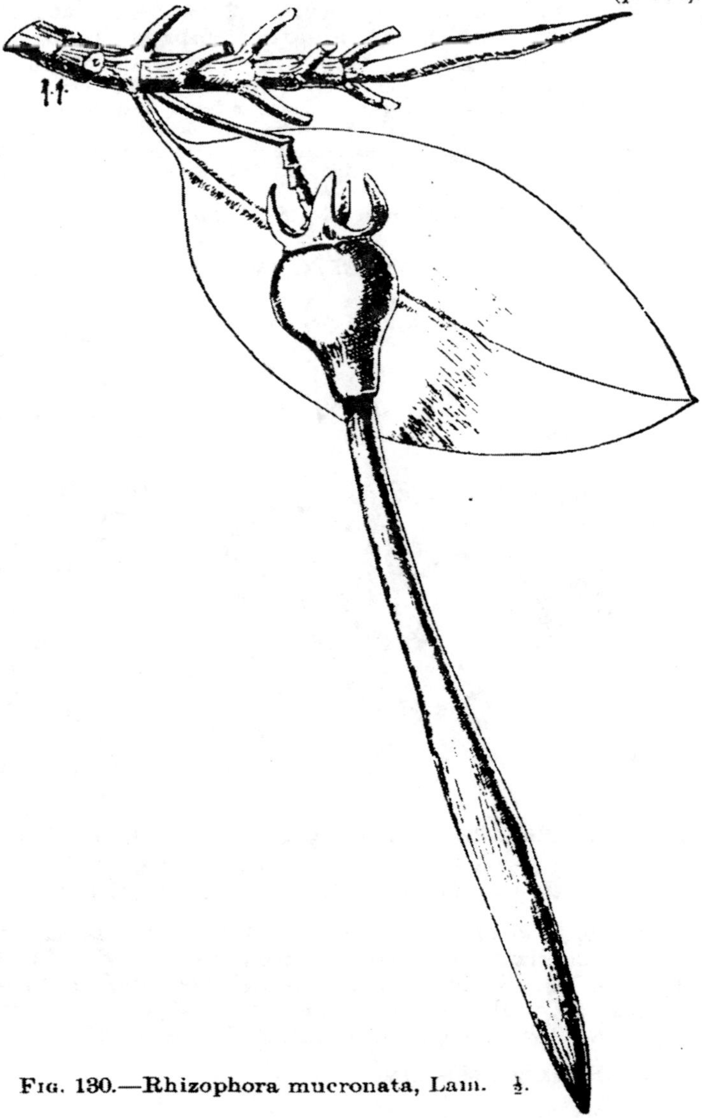

FIG. 130.—Rhizophora mucronata, Lam. ½.

Leaves elliptic, mucronate by the excurrent midrib, blade 4–7, petiole 1–1¾ in. Cymes 3-5-fld., from the axils of this year's leaves, peduncles 1–1½ in. long, pedicels short thick, calyx-segments ½ in. long, oblong-lanceolate, keeled within, petals hairy within, anthers 8. Fr. 1½–2 in. long, dark brown, embryo often attaining 30 in. before falling from the tree.

Tidal marshes in Sind, the Western Peninsula, the Sundriban and Burma. Fl. H. S., R. S. Bark used in tanning. Sea coast in the tropics of the Old World and Australia. 2. **R. conjugata**, Linn. (*R. Candelaria*, DC. Trimen Handb. Ceylon ii. 151.) Generally associated with 1. Leaves lanceolate, cymes nearly sessile, usually 2-fld., above the scars of fallen l., fl. sessile.

2. CERIOPS, Arnott.; Fl. Brit. Ind. ii. 436.

Simple stemmed shrubs or small trees, sending down aërial roots from the branches. Fl. in compact many-fld. cymes, calyx deeply divided into 5 segments, petals 5, emarginate, stam. 10, inserted between the lobes of an annular disk, ovary half-inferior, 3-celled, 2 ovules in each cell. Fr. as in *Rhizophora*, but the radicle of the germinating embryo ribbed. Species 2.

1. **C. Candolleana**, Arn.; Wight Ic. t. 240; Bedd. Manual t. 13. (*Chauri*, Sind; *Goran*. *Guttia*, Sundr.) Tidal Forests of Sind, the Western Peninsula, Bengal and the Andamans. Sea coast of tropical Asia, Africa and Australia. L. obovate, obtuse, cymes peduncled, branching, pedicels short, petals with 3 short clavate appendages at the apex, filaments much longer than anthers. Bark and fruit used in tanning. 2. **C. Roxburghiana**, Arn. (*Goran*, Sundr.; *Kabaing*, Burm.) Sundriban. Coast of Burma. Malay Peninsula and Archipelago. Cymes densely capitate on short peduncles, petals concave, apex ciliate, filaments much shorter than anthers.

3. KANDELIA, Wight & Arn.; Fl. Brit. Ind. ii. 437.

FIG. 131.—Kandelia Rheedii, W. & A. ½.

K. Rheedei, W. & A. (the only species): Wight Ill. t. 89; Bedd. Manual t. 13. Vern. *Goria*, Sundr.

A simple stemmed shrub, l. elliptic-oblong, blade 3–5, narrowed into petiole ½–1 in. long. Fl. white, in dichotomously branched cymes, peduncle 1–2 in. Calyx surrounded at the base by bracteoles connate into a cup, lobes 5 or 6, linear, ½–⅔ in. long. Petals bifid, the lobes divided into numerous capillary segments. Stamens ∞, anthers small, filaments slender. Ovary half-inferior, prolonged beyond the calyx into a fleshy cone, one-celled, ovules 6, style slender, stigma 3-lobed. Fr. ovoid, girt at the base by the reflexed calyx-lobes.

Tidal swamps of the Western Peninsula, Bengal, Andamans and Burma. Fl. May–Sept. Bark used in dyeing. China, Borneo, Formosa.

4. BRUGUIERA, Lam.; Fl. Brit. Ind. ii. 437.

Trees, base of trunk supported by short aërial roots, knees from the lower roots abundant. Calyx-tube produced considerably beyond the inferior ovary, lobes 8–14, petals 2-fid or emarginate, stamens 16–28. Ovary 2–4-celled, 2 ovules in each cell. Fr. fleshy, seed one, germination as in *Rhizophora*. Species 4 or 5, from East Africa to Australia.

A. Fl. large, solitary.

1. **B. gymnorhiza,** Lam.—Syn. *B. Rheedii,* Wight Ic. t. 239; Bedd. Man. t. xiv. Vern. *Kankra,* Sundrib.

A tree, attaining 80 ft., l. thickly coriaceous, shining, elliptic-lanceolate, not mucronate, pale beneath, blade 4–7, petiole 1–1½ in. long. Fl. solitary, axillary, deflexed, pedicel ⅓ in. long. Calyx-lobes 10–14, linear, very acute, erect, ½–¾ in. long, petals deeply bifid, glabrous except at the hairy base, ovary 3-celled, style long. Fr. crowned by the slightly enlarged calyx-segments, which are as long as fruit.

Tidal marshes of the Western Peninsula, Bengal, the Andamans and Burma. Fl. Apr.–Oct.—Bark used in tanning. Africa to Australia and the islands of the Pacific. 2. **B. eriopetala,** Wight & Arn.; Wight Ic. t. 239 B. Malabar and Travancore, Malay Peninsula and Archipelago. Cochinchina. Calyx-lobes 10, 1 in. long, exceeding the ribbed fr. Petals densely hirsute along the edges, from base to apex with silvery hairs.

B. Fl. small, peduncles 3- or more-fld.

3. **B. caryophylloides,** Blume (including *B. malabarica,* Arnott) Quilon. Ceylon. Tenasserim. Malay Peninsula and Archipelago. Leaves thinly coriaceous. Cymes axillary, pedunculate, 2–3-fld., calyx-lobes ¼ in. long, reflexed in fr. and about half its length, petals with scanty hairs outside. 4. **B. parviflora,** W. & A. Tidal forests of the Andamans and Tenasserim. Malay Peninsula and Archipelago. Cymes axillary, erect, pedunculate, 2–5-fld., calyx-tube cylindric, ½, teeth $\frac{1}{10}$ in. long. Ovary 3-celled, fruit cylindric, ribbed, 1 in., radicle 4–5 in. long before falling.

5. CARALLIA, Roxb.; Fl. Brit. Ind. ii. 439.

Trees and shrubs, not litoral. Fl. small, sessile, in short trichotomous axillary cymes. Calyx produced into a short tube beyond the ovary, teeth 5–8, petals inserted with the stamens on the edge of a crenulated disk lining the calyx-tube, unguiculate, blade deeply serrate and lobed. Ovary inferior, usually 4-celled, ovules 2 in each cell. Fruit small, globose, coriaceous, seed 1, testa fibrous, embryo curved in copious albumen. Species 7, from Madagascar to Australia.

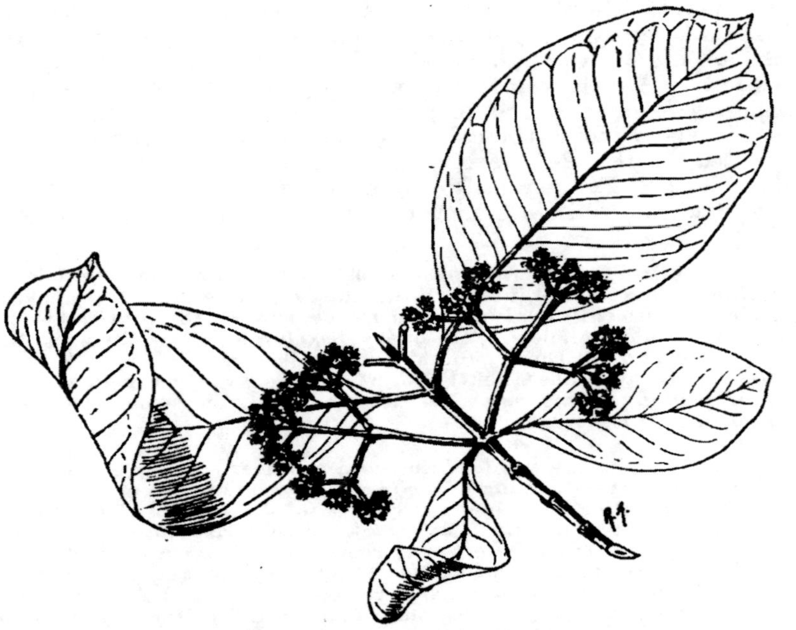

Fig. 132.—Carallia lucida, Roxb. ½.

1. **C. lucida,** Roxb. Cor. Pl. t. 211; Kurz F. Fl. i. 451; King in Journ. As. Soc. Beng. 66. 318.—Syn. *C. integerrima,* DC.; Fl. Brit. Ind. ii. 439; Bedd. Fl. Sylv. t. 193.; *C. ceylanica,* Wight Ill. t. 90. Vern. *Shengali, Panasi,* Mar.; *Andamuria,* Kan.; *Karalli,* Tel.; *Varanga,* Mal.; *Maniawga,* Lower, *Awga,* Upper Burma.

A large tree, trunk erect, wood reddish - brown, medull. rays very broad. Leaves thickly coriaceous, glossy, elliptic, sometimes obovate, entire (serrulate in Cor. Pl.), blade 3–6, petiole ¼ in. long, sec. n. numerous arching. Fl. creamy-white, sessile, in axillary short peduncled cymes.

Subhimal. tract, Nepal, Sikkim, ascending to 4,000 ft. Assam, Khasi hills, Chittagong. Singhbhum. Burma, Upper and Lower. Western Peninsula, Northern Circars. On the west side from the Konkan southwards. Fl. Oct.–April. Aerial roots (Gamble, Ind. Timb. Ed. II. 335).—Ceylon. China. Malay Penins. and Archip. to Australia.
2. **C. lanceæfolia,** Roxb ; Wight Ic. t. 604. Kurz F. Fl. i. 451. Upper Tenasserim. L. thinly coriaceous, serrate, blade of petals broad, crenulate, embracing the stamens. Fr. 2–3-seeded.

Gynotroches axillaris, Blume. Tenasserim (Kurz). A small evergreen glabrous tree, l. coriaceous, glossy, strongly net-veined. Fl. polygamous, small, yellowish-green, in axillary fascicles. Calyx free, 4–5-lobed nearly to the base, petals clawed, fimbriate, stamens 8 or 10. Ovary free, base only adnate to calyx, 3–6-celled, ovules 4 in each cell. Fr. a small globose, many-seeded berry.

Weihea zeylanica, Baill. ; Bedd. Fl. Sylv. t. 194. Ghats of South Tinnevelli and South Travancore. Ceylon. A small tree, l. thin, almost membranous, elliptic-lanceolate, 2–3 in. long, stipules oblong, ciliate. Fl. white, axillary, solitary, or 2–3 together, buds enclosed in 2 thick rounded ciliate bracts. Calyx free, cut nearly to the base into 5 lanceolate densely silky segments, ⅓ in. long. Petals cuneate, apex deeply laciniate, stamens 30, hypogynous, ovary free, 3-celled, 2 ovules in each cell. Capsule fleshy, septicidally dehiscent, seeds 4–6, embryo straight in the axis of endosperm.

Blepharistemma corymbosum, Wall. ; Bedd. Manual t. xiv. Western Peninsula, from South Kanara southwards. A tree attaining 100 ft. in Travancore, young shoots, petioles and inflorescence pubescent. L. membranous, crenate, blade 3–6, petiole ⅓ in. long. Fl. polygamous, ¼ in. long, calyx hairy, free, campanulate, lobes 4, triangular, petals twice the length of calyx, hairy, tips laciniate, stamens 8. Ovary free, 3-celled.

ORDER L. COMBRETACEÆ. Gen. Pl. i. 683.

(Brandis in Engler u. Prantl. iii. 7. 106.)

Trees or shrubs, leaves simple, entire, without stipules. Fl. bracteate, usually sessile, bisexual, rarely polygamous, regular with a zygomorphic tendency. Calyx-tube adnate to ovary and produced beyond it, free portion 4–5-cleft, segments valvate. Petals wanting, or small, inserted on the edge of calyx-tube between its segments. Stamens as many as calyx-segments or twice their number, inserted inside the calyx, anthers dehiscing longitudinally. Ovary inferior, 1-celled, ovules 2–5, rarely more, on large funicles, pendulous from the apex of the cell. Fr. generally angled or winged, seed 1, without albumen. Embryo straight, radicle superior, cotyledons oily, generally convolute.

In this, as well as in the allied Orders, *Rhizophoraceæ*, *Myrtaceæ* and *Rosaceæ*, I follow the practice of most English text-books in describing the calyx as adnate to the ovary. In reality, however, what is here called calyx should be regarded as the continuation of the axis (pedicel), which is hollow, enclosing the ovary, bearing sepals at the apex, here called calyx-segments. What in these orders usually is described as the calyx, bears bracteoles in some cases, and consequently ought to be regarded as an axial organ. (*Lumnitzera* and other genera.) This was the view taken by me, when describing *Combretaceæ* for Engler u. Prantl's work.

Combretaceæ have phloëm on the inner side of the wood-cylinder, at the circumference of the pith, either forming a continuous ring (*Terminalia*, several species of *Combretum*) or in distinct masses. This interior phloëm either consists of thin-walled elements only (*Terminalia*, *Anogeissus*), or is accompanied by thick-walled bast-fibres (species of *Combretum*). The medullary rays as a rule are narrow, *Combretum decandrum*, however, has two classes of rays, broad rays, consisting of many layers of cells, and narrow rays, consisting of one layer only. Apart from vessels and rays the wood mainly consists of wood fibres; but a few species (*Terminalia bialata* and *belerica*) have broad tangential bands of wood parenchyma. Several species, climbers as well as trees, have strands of phloëm in the wood. As far as known, the structure of the climbing species is normal, but they demand further study.

A. Fl. in spikes, calyx-limb deciduous.
- Petals 0. Large trees, l. alternate or subopposite . 1. TERMINALIA.
- Petals 4 or 5, except in *Combretum apetalum.*
  - Climbing shrubs or undershrubs, l. opposite, sometimes whorled . . . . 2. COMBRETUM.
  - Climbers, l. opposite, calyx-tube slender, long . 3. QUISQUALIS.

B. Fl. in spikes, calyx-limb persistent.
- A rambling shrub, rusty pubescent, l. opposite . 4. CALYCOPTERIS.
- Trees or shrubs, wholly glabrous, l. alternate, thick, fleshy . . . . 5. LUMNITZERA.

C. Fl. in globose heads, fr. small, flat, imbricated . . 6. ANOGEISSUS.

Two genera, *Illigera* and *Gyrocarpus*, in Gen. Pl. i. 689 included under *Combretaceæ* (Sub-order *Gyrocarpeæ*) with winged fruit, but entirely different in other respects, will be included under *Hernandiaceæ.*

1. TERMINALIA, Linn.; Fl. Brit. Ind. ii. 443.

Large trees, l. alternate or nearly opposite. Fl. sessile, small, greenish or white, generally in long spikes. Calyx-tube campanulate, constricted above the ovary, as a rule densely woolly within, deciduous, limb 5-toothed, petals 0. Stamens 10, in two rows. Seed included in a coriaceous or osseous endocarp, cotyledons convolute. Species 105, tropics of both hemispheres.

A. Fr. more or less fleshy, often angled, not winged.

(*a*) Spikes simple (see also *T. pallida*).

1. **T. Catappa,** Linn.; Wight Ic. t. 172; Bedd. Fl. Sylv. t. 18; King in Journ. As. Soc. Bengal 66 (1898), 331.—Syn. *T. procera*, Roxb. Cor. Pl. t. 224; Kurz F. Fl. i. 454. The *Indian Almond tree.*

A tall tree, branches whorled, stem often buttressed. L. clustered at the ends of branchlets, glabrous, petiole and midrib more or less hairy, obovate, from a narrow cordate base, 6–10 in. long, petiole short, stout and channelled. Fl. white, in slender axillary spikes, shorter than l., ♂ at the top, ⚥ below. Drupe glabrous, ellipsoid, somewhat compressed, keeled all round, 2 in. long, pericarp fibrous and fleshy, endocarp hard, oil expressed from the seeds.

Beach forests of the Andamans and the Malay Peninsula. Fl. Feb.–May. A widely spread litoral species within the tropics. Cultivated throughout tropical India. The l. turn deep red in autumn before falling. The seeds are eaten.

2. **T. belerica,*** Roxb. Cor. Pl. t. 198; Wight Ill. t. 91; Bedd. Fl. Sylv. t. 19; Brandis F. Fl. 222. Vern. *Bahera, Bhaira*, Hind.; *Balra, Beheda*, Mar.; *Tāre*, Kan.; *Tandi, Thandra*, Tel.; *Tani, Thani*, Tam.; *Thitsein*, Burm.

A large deciduous tree, bark bluish-grey, wood hard, yellowish-grey, no heartwood. Branchlets, ovary and outside of calyx with soft rust-coloured pubescence. L. clustered at the ends of branchlets, minutely puberulous when young, glabrous when full grown, elliptic or obovate-elliptic from an acute base, blade 4–9, petiole 1½–3 in. long. Fl. greenish-yellow, with strong offensive smell, ♂ and ⚥ mixed. Spikes simple, on the current year's shoots, in the axils of l. or of fallen l., bracts linear, early caducous. Inside of calyx woolly with long brown hairs. Fruit ovoid, grey, velvety, 1 in. long, pericarp dry.

Subhimalayan tract from near the Indus eastwards. Common throughout India and

---

* In Cor. Plants Roxburgh writes *bellerica*, in Fl. Ind. ii. 431, *belerica*. Roxb. describes and figures two glands on top of petiole, which do not exist on the specimens examined by me, nor have they been found by others.

Burma excepting the arid region of Sind, western Rajputana and the southern Punjab. L. shed Feb.–March, fresh foliage copper or tan-coloured, in April. Fl. March–May. Fr. used for dyeing and tanning. 3. **T. fœtidissima,** Griff.: Mergui, Malacca. L. shining, coriaceous, obovate, blade 5–7, tapering into petiole ⅜ in. long, drupe compressed obovate-ellipsoid.

(*b*) Spikes panicled excepting *T. pallida*, panicles often terminal.

4. **T. Chebula,** Retz.; Roxb. Cor. Pl. t. 197; Bedd. Fl. Sylv. t. 27; Brandis F. Fl. t. 29. Vern. *Har*, *Harra*, Hind.; *Hirda*, *Habra*, Mar.; *Nella* (black) *Karaka*, Tel.; *Kadukai*, Tam.; *Pangā*, Burm.

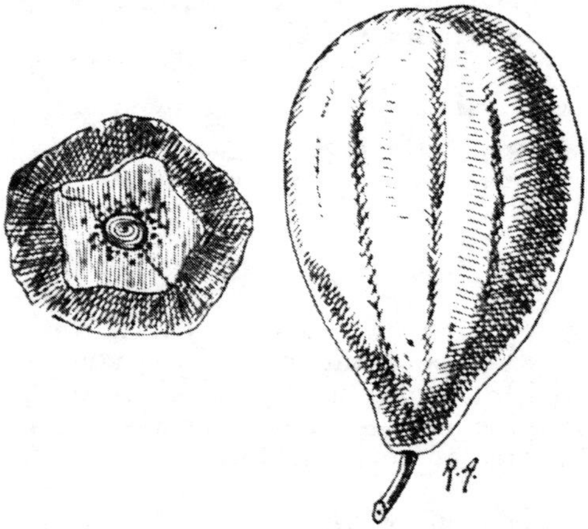

Fig. 133.—Terminalia Chebula, Retz. Fr. and transverse section enlarged.

A large deciduous tree, leaf-buds, branchlets and youngest l. with soft shining, generally rust-coloured hairs. Leaves distant, often subopposite, elliptic or ovate, sec. n. 6–8 pair, arching, prominent, blade 3–8, petiole ½–1 in. long. Two glands or swellings on petiole near the top. Fl. bisexual ⅛ in. across, sessile, dull white or yellow, with an offensive smell. Spikes sometimes simple, usually in short panicles, terminal and in the axils of the uppermost leaves. Bracts subulate or lanceolate, longer than buds, deciduous. Limb of calyx cup-shaped, cleft half-way into 5 acute triangular segments, woolly inside. Fruit more or less distinctly 5-angled, obovoid from a cuneate base, sometimes ovoid or nearly globose, 1–1½ in. long. Shape and size of fr. varies exceedingly.

Subhimalayan tract from the Sutlej eastwards, ascending to 5,000 ft, Common in the deciduous forests of both peninsulas. Sheds its l. Feb.–March, new foliage in April, fl. April–Aug. fr. ripens Oct.–January. In the Centr. Prov. two distinct flowering periods: April–May and July–August. The fl. often attacked by a gall insect. This species varies considerably. Apart from two very marked forms, known only from restricted areas, which are here accepted as species, I recognize two principal varieties (*a*) The ordinary widely spread form, young shoots silky-tomentose, l. glabrous when full grown, ovary and calyx outside glabrous or hairy, described by Kurz F. Fl. i. 456, as *T. Chebula* and *T. tomentella*, Kurz. (*b*) The tomentose form, branchlets, leaves, panicle, ovary and calyx densely and softly clothed with long silky hairs. Pachmarhi, Mahableshwar, Western Deccan and Mysore. Nilgiris. This may possibly be *T. gangetica*, Roxb. The dry fruit of *T. Chebula*, the *Chebulic Myrobalans* of commerce, is one of the best tanning materials known, export considerable, chiefly from Bombay.

The two local forms which may be regarded as species are: 5. **T. travancorensis,**, W. & Arn. Prodr. 314 (*T. angustifolia*, Roxb.; Bourdillon in Journ. Bombay Nat. Hist. Soc. vol. 12, 351, t. 4.) A lofty tree of the evergreen forests, Travancore at 500 ft., bark smooth, pale brown, sapwood yellowish white, heartwood small, brown, l. glabrous, elliptic-lanceolate. Fl. small. Fr. ¾ in. long, stone 5-angled. *T. Chebula* is also found in Travancore, but in deciduous grass forests (Bourd.). *T. angustifolia*, Jacq., is a Malayan species. 6. **T. pallida,** n. sp. (*Thella* (white) *Karaka*, Tel.) Kambakum hill (Chingleput), Veligondas. Sechachellam hills (Cuddapah). Occurs with *T. Chebula*, but is nearly evergreen, and is readily distinguished by smaller coriaceous leaves, obtuse or emarginate, petiole orange-coloured, spikes usually simple, ovary and calyx outside perfectly glabrous, shining; fr. obovoid from a narrow base. (D. B. Madras Forest Report, 1883, par. 357.)

7. **T. citrina,** Fleming; King in Journ. As. Soc. Beng. 66. 328, Assam, Maimansingh, Dacca, Tenasserim, Nicobars, Malay Peninsula. L. thickly coriaceous, elliptic-lanceolate, blade 3–7, petiole ½ in., veins minutely reticulate, the areoles between the veins on the underside very minutely velvety, fr. narrow, lanceolate, 2 in. long. 8. **T. Manii,** King in Ann. Bot. Gard. Calc. ix. t. 51, Andamans and Nicobars. L. ovate, acuminate, blade 4–5, petiole 1 in., fr. ovoid ⅝–¾ in. long. 9. **T. argyrophylla,** King & Prain in Journ. As. Soc. Beng. 67. 291, Kachin hills, Upper Burma. Branchlets slender, as well

as leaves on both sides densely and softly grey-, almost silvery-tomentose. L. ovate-oblong, blade 4–5, petiole ¾ in. long. Fl. small, yellowish, calyx densely silvery-woolly inside.

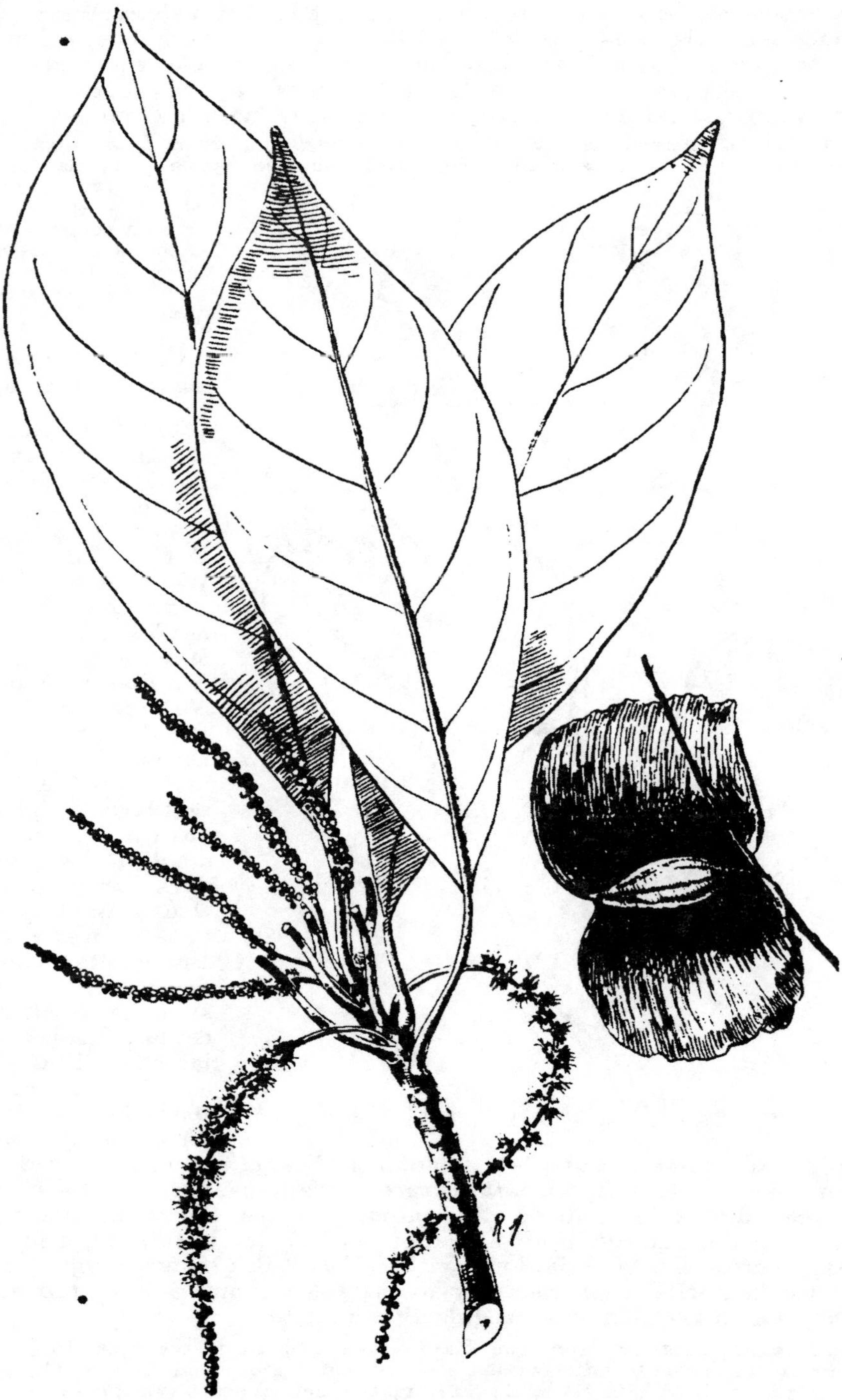

Fig. 134.—Terminalia bialata, Steudel. ½. Fl., fr.

B. Fr. dry, winged, fl. regular, wings two equal.

10. **T. bialata,** Steudel; Kurz F. Fl. i. 456. Vern. *Lein*, Burm.

A large tree, l. alternate, crowded at the ends of branchlets, perfectly glabrous, oblanceolate, blade 6–9, petiole 3–4 in. long. Spikes simple, axillary, pubescent, as long as leaves, bracts caducous, not longer than the buds, apex often inflexed, the upper fl. ♂, the lower ⚥, ovary and calyx densely pubescent Wings broad, striate and softly pubescent, fruit with the wings 3–4 in. broad.

Tenasserim. Andamans. Fl. R. S. 11. **T. pyrifolia,** Kurz. *Lein*, Burm. Pegu and Tenasserim. Often stunted, differs from 10 by shorter petioles, very slender spikes and smaller fruit, which, with the wings, is 1–2 in. broad, the seed portion being keeled on one side. Merits careful study in the Forest, as to whether it really is a distinct species.

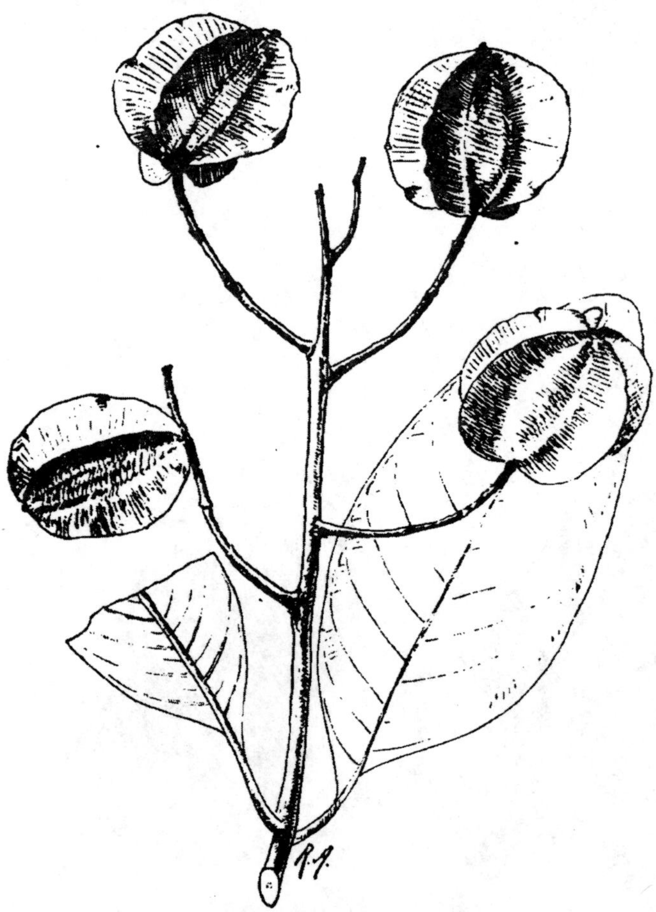

FIG. 185.—Terminalia tomentosa, Wight & Arn. $\frac{1}{2}$.

C. Fr. dry, winged, fl. regular, wings 5, equal.

12. **T. tomentosa,** W. et Arn.; Wight Ic. t. 195; Bedd. Fl. Sylv. t. 17; Brandis F. Fl. 225.—Syn. *T. crenulata*, Roth; Kurz F. Fl. i. 458; *T. coriacea*, W. et Arn. Vern. *Sain, Asaina, Saj*, Hind.; *Sadri, Hadri*, Guzerat; *Ain*, Mar.; *Maru*, Gond; *Matti, Kari matti*, Kan.; *Maddi, Nalla maddi*, Tel.: *Karra marda*, Tam.; *Taukkyan*, Burm.

A large tree, trunk tall, regularly shaped, bark rough, black, deeply cracked, heartwood hard, dark purplish-brown, mottled with darker streaks, often nearly black. Branchlets, inflorescence and young l. clothed with short, rust-coloured pubescence. Leaves hard, coriaceous, elliptic- or ovate-, sometimes obovate-oblong, blade 5–9, petiole $\frac{1}{4}$–$\frac{1}{2}$ in. long, nearly opposite, the uppermost often alternate, 1–2 glands near base of midrib, underside when full grown as a rule soft tomentose, rarely glabrous, sec. n. 10–20 pair. Fl. bisexual, dull yellow, in erect terminal panicles, the lower branches in the axils of leaves. Calyx-limb a shallow cup, hairy within, segments 5, broad, ovate, acute. Fr. 1$\frac{1}{2}$–2 in. long with 5 coriaceous brown wings $\frac{3}{4}$–1 in. broad and marked with numerous horizontal lines running from the axis to the edges, which are thin and irregularly crenulate.

Subhimalayan tract from the Ravi eastwards, in places ascending to 4,000 ft. Common throughout India (except in the arid region) and Burma, thrives best in heavy clay-soil. Fl. H. S., R. S., fruit ripens Feb.–April of the ensuing year. Sheds

its l. Feb.–April and is one of the latest trees to come out in fresh leaf. T. macrocarpa, is a variety in the Eng forests of Burma with large fr., up to $2\frac{1}{2}$ in. across.

13. **T. Arjuna**, Bedd. Fl. Sylv. t. 28; Brandis F. Fl. 224.—Syn. *T. glabra*, W. et Arn., Trimen Handb. Ceylon ii. 160; *Pentaptera Arjuna*, Roxb. Vern. *Arjūna, Kawa, Koha*, Hind.; *Dhaula Sadr*, Guzerat; *Holematti*, Kan. *Thella maddi*, Tel.

A large tree, with huge often buttressed trunk, bark smooth grey, flaking off in large thin layers, branches drooping, heartwood dark brown, very hard. Glabrous, only inflorescence slightly pubescent. Leaves generally sub-opposite, hard, coriaceous, oblong, sometimes spathulate-oblong, often crenulate, blade 3–6, petiole $\frac{1}{4}$ in. long. Fl. like 12, fr. 1 in. long with 5–7 thick narrow wings, $\frac{1}{4}$ in. broad, irregularly marked with ascending lines.

FIG. 136.—Terminalia Arjuna, Bedd. $\frac{1}{2}$.

Common on the banks of rivers, streams and dry watercourses in Central India and South Behar, in the Peninsula and Ceylon. Here and there in the Subhimalayan tract (Kangra, D.B. 1868). Not in east and central Bengal nor in Burma. Foresters readily distinguish these two species by their bark, their mode of growth and by their habitat. Botanists (Fl. Brit. Ind. ii. 448, Trimen Handb. Ceylon ii. 161) are doubtful regarding them.

14. **T. Oliveri**, Brandis in Hook. Ic. t. 2202. Vern. *Than*, Burm.

A moderate-sized glabrous tree, l. sub-opposite broadly-ovate, blade $1\frac{1}{2}$–3, petiole $\frac{1}{4}$ in., sec. n. 5–6 pair. Fl. small, nearly glabrous, in slender terminal panicles. Wings narrow, membranous, $\frac{3}{4}$ in. long, $\frac{1}{2}$ in. broad.

Dry region of the Irawaddi valley between 19 and 22 N. lat., chiefly in the Pakokku district, associated with *Acacia Catechu*. Bark thick, filled with starch, an extract of the bark used to adulterate Cutch.

C. Fr. dry, winged, fl. zygomorphic, wings unequal.

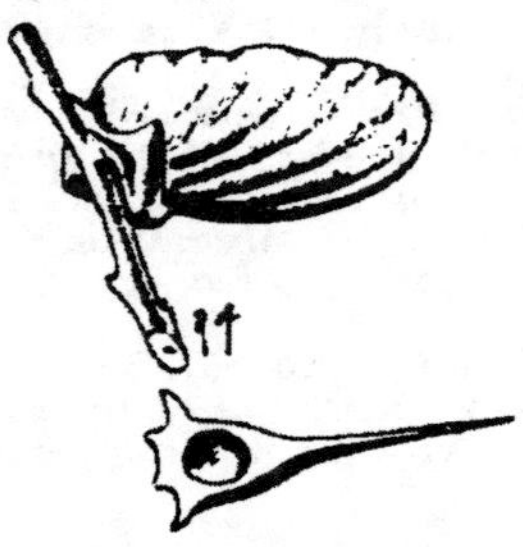

FIG. 137.—Terminalia paniculata, Roth. $\frac{1}{1}$. Fr. and transverse section.

15. **T. paniculata**, Roth; Bedd. Fl. Sylv. t. 20; Brandis F. Fl. 226. Vern. *Kinjal, Kindal*, Mar.; *Honal, Hulucc*, Kan.; *Puli maddi*, Tel.; *Pulucai*, Tam.

A large tree, l. glabrous, oblong, from a rounded, often unequal base; pale-brown beneath, blade 4–7, petiole $\frac{1}{4}$–$\frac{1}{2}$ in. long, the upper l. always alternate, the lower often opposite, sec. n. 10–15 pair. Fl. in ample rusty-pubescent panicles, bracts pubescent, acuminate, free portion of calyx glabrous reddish-brown, cup-shaped, the inside clothed with long brown hairs, ovary with 5 rounded ridges. Fr. $\frac{1}{4}$–$\frac{1}{2}$ in. long, rusty-pubescent, sessile, close set in large spreading panicles, the front ridge of ovary growing out into a wing, which is $\frac{3}{4}$–1 in. broad.

Forests on the west coast and the Ghats, on the Nilgiris,

Anamalais, Javadis and other hill ranges in the southern portion of the Peninsula. Fl. Aug.–Dec., fr. H. S. Hardly ever quite leafless.

16. **T. myriocarpa,** Heurck & Muell. Arg.; Kurz F. Fl. i. 457.

A very large evergreen tree, heartwood brown, mottled with dark streaks, takes a beautiful polish, young shoots and inflorescence rusty-pubescent. L. from a rounded base elliptic-oblong, blade 4–12, petiole thick, ¼–½ in. long, with one or two prominent cylindric glands at the top, sec. n. numerous, parallel. Fl. small, in long slender spikes, arranged in ample terminal panicles, bracts very short, calyx nearly glabrous within, fr. ⅙ in. long, 3-cornered, the two lateral angles expanded into wings. A very handsome tree when in fl. or fr., its pendent boughs loaded with pink panicles or yellow seeds (Gamble List 39).

Sikkim, ascending to 5,000 ft. Fl. Oct.–Nov. Bhutan, Assam, Khasi hills, Manipur. Upper Burma, Kurz.

2. COMBRETUM, Linn.; Fl. Brit. Ind. ii. 452.

Shrubs, sometimes trees, generally climbing, l. petiolate, opposite in some species, whorled, rarely alternate. Fl. bisexual or polygamous. Calyx-tube more or less constricted above the ovary, limb campanulate or funnel-shaped, 4–5-cleft, deciduous. Petals small, inserted between the calyx-lobes. Stamens 8 or 10, generally biseriate, those of the lower series episepalous, filaments slender, usually long exserted, anthers didymous. Ovary 1-celled, style subulate, ovules 2–6, pendulous. Fr. coriaceous, 4–6-ridged or winged, seed one. Embryo straight, radicle small, superior. Species 260, in the tropical and subtropical regions of the old and new world, the majority in Africa. Not in Australia, nor in Polynesia.

A. Fl. pentamerous, fr. with 5 membranous wings or prominent ridges.

1. **C. decandrum,** Roxb. Cor. Pl. t. 59.; Brandis F. Fl. 221. Vern. *Boddu*, Tel.; *Thamaka-nwè* Burm.

A large climbing shrub, stem cylindric, bark greyish-white, corky, branchlets, young l. and inflorescence clothed with soft silky hairs. L. opposite, nearly glabrous when full grown, elliptic-oblong, blade 3–6, petiole ⅓ in. Fl. in large terminal leafy panicles, the floral leaves (bracts) large and conspicuous, turning creamy white. Fr. 1 in. long, 5 broad equal wings.

Subhimalayan tract, from the Jumna eastwards, Sikkim to 2,000 ft. Assam, Chittagong. Burma. Behar, Central Provinces, Northern Circars and the northern Deccan. Fl. Dec.–March. 2. **C. pyrifolium,** Kurz, Pegu. Imperfectly known.

3. **C. pilosum,** Roxb. (probably including *C. ovale*, Kurz F. Fl. 462.) *Kyet tet nwè*, Burm. Silhet, Chittagong. Burma, Upper and Lower. A large climber, branchlets, petioles and inflorescence densely rusty-villous, the persistent base of petioles often more or less spinescent, l. hairy beneath, fl. in short racemes, massed together in dense cylindrical panicles, calyx rusty-villous outside, ⅛–½ in. long, slightly constricted above the ovary, free portion infundibuliform, more than twice the length of ovary. Fr. 1–1¼ in. long, winged. 4. **C. kachinense,** King & Prain. Kachin hills near Sima. A large scandent shrub, not spinescent, branchlets, petioles, underside of leaves and inflorescence rusty-pubescent, fl. in axillary, simple or sparingly branched lax racemes, pedicels very short, calyx ⅓ in. long, not constricted above ovary.

5. **C. apetalum,** Wall. Dry country of the Irawaddi valley, from Prome upwards. A straggling deciduous shrub or small tree, scrambling on to other trees. Fl. in long slender spikes, arranged in axillary panicles, bracts lanceolate, as long as ovary, rachis of spikes as well as bracts, ovary and calyx densely clothed with white-silvery hairs. Free part of calyx-tube campanulate, segments triangular, acuminate, reflexed. Fr. winged ¾ in. long.

6. **C. trifoliatum,** Vent. Burma, Upper and Lower, common on moist ground, l. often in whorls of three, coriaceous, glabrous, elliptic-oblong. Spikes axillary, compact, cylindric, densely pubescent, free part of calyx campanulate. Fr. 1–1½ in. long, not winged, with 5 very acute ridges.

B. Fl. tetramerous, fr. with 4 prominent ridges.

7. **C. acuminatum,** Roxb.—Syn. *C. costatum*, Roxb.; Kurz F. Fl. i. 465.

A large climber, l. elliptic- or ovate-lanceolate, underside often slightly hairy, blade 4–8, petiole ¼ in., sec. n. 10–15 pair. Fl. yellow, in slender axillary spikes, often forming leafy panicles at the ends of branches, free part of calyx campanulate, petals small, narrow, stamens long exserted. Fr. 1–2 in. long, narrowly ellipsoid, with four thick rounded ridges.

Assam, Khasi hills. Pegu, Tenasserim. Fl. R. S. Ceylon low country, rare. 8. **C. tetragonocarpum,** Kurz, Pegu, imperfectly known.

C. Fl. tetramerous, fr. with 4 papery wings.

9. **C. flagrocarpum,** Herb. Calc.—Syn. *C. Wallichii*, Kurz F. Fl. i. 465. A large scandent shrub, young shoots and inflorescence densely clothed with rusty peltate scales, l. broad-elliptic with numerous minute resinous dots on both sides, chiefly beneath, pubescent along the nerves, blade 5–9, petiole stout ½ in. long. Spikes axillary and in terminal panicles, bracts linear, persistent. Petals white, spathulate, exceeding the triangular calyx-segments. Fr. 1–1½ in. long and equally broad, red or red-brown, surface of seed portion densely covered between the wings with lanceolate-linear scales.

Sikkim, ascending to 5,000 ft., Assam, Khasi and Naga hills, Manipur, Chittagong. Upper Burma. Fl. May, June. Closely allied: 10. **C. Wallichii,** DC. Nepal, Sikkim, common, ascending to 5,000 ft. A straggling shrub, differs from 9 by smaller and thinner leaves with tufts of yellow hair in the axils of the sec. n. on the underside, minute fugacious bracts, and small petals.

11. **C. dasystachyum,** Kurz F. Fl. i. 464. Vern. *Semakan nwè*, Burm. A woody climber (deciduous, Smales), branchlets, petioles, underside of younger leaves (chiefly along nerves), and inflorescence pubescent. L. membranous, lanceolate from a narrowly cordate base, sec. n. 8–10 pair, arching, blade 3–9, petiole ¼–⅓ in. Fl. in axillary (sometimes compound) spikes, free portion of calyx funnel-shaped, claw of petals nearly as long as the obovate blade. Fr. shining, 1½ by 1 in.

Assam. Khasi hills. Cachar. Chittagong. Burma, Lower and Upper. Fl. H. S. Fr. C. S. Closely allied are: 12. **C. chinense,** Roxb. Assam. Khasi hills. Chittagong. Andamans. Eastern slopes of the Pegu Yoma. Hills east of Toungoo, 2,000 ft. Mergui. Malay Peninsula. A large woody climber (evergreen, Kurz), l. glabrous, thinly coriaceous, frequently in whorls of three, elliptic or obovate-elliptic, young shoots and inflorescence sparsely covered with minute scales and resinous dots, fr. 1–1½ in. long, nearly as broad as long, wings retuse at both ends. 13. **C. squamosum,** Roxb. Sikkim Terai on the banks of streams. Bhutan, Assam, Khasi hills, Cachar. Pegu, Tenasserim. Andamans. Malay Peninsula. A large climber, branchlets, leaves and inflorescence covered with round peltate scales with pale edges, l. thinly coriaceous, from a rounded base, broadly elliptic, abruptly acuminate, blade 3–5, petiole ¼–½ in. long, fr. 1–1½ in. long and equally broad. 14. **C. quadrangulare,** Kurz, Tenasserim, clothed with circular scales, branchlets sharply quadrangular, l. oblanceolate or lanceolate, gradually narrowed into the short petiole, fl. small.

15. **C. ovalifolium,** Roxb.; Trimen Handb. Ceylon ii. 163. Vern. *Dimarbola*, Jabalpúr.

A large straggling or climbing almost entirely glabrous shrub, branchlets stiff, divaricate, nearly at right angles to stem or branches, l. opposite, from an acute base elliptic, acuminate, blade 3–5, petiole ½ in. long. Fl. white, in axillary and terminal panicled spikes, with a few broadly-ovate, coloured floral leaves (bracts) at the base of ramifications, fl. outside with minute hairs and thin peltate scales, bracts minute. Fr. ¾ in. long, nearly glabrous.

Deciduous forests in the Central Provinces, Berar, and the Western Peninsula. Fl. Jan.–Mar., l. turn dark red before falling, climbs over tall trees and often carpets the ground on the banks of streams, like ivy.—Ceylon, dry country. 16. **C. nanum,** Ham.; Brandis F. Fl. 221, is a small undershrub, with a thick woody prostrate or underground stem, common in grass lands of the Subhimalayan tract, from the Jumna to Sikkim, in the Oudh forests, Behar and the Central Provinces. Also on the Shan hills of Upper Burma. The leaf- and fl.-bearing stems are burnt down to the ground annually by the fires of the hot season. L. obovate, fr. 1½ in. long, in dense clusters.

17. **C. extensum**, Roxb.; Kurz F. Fl. i. 463.—Syn. *C. Wightianum*, Wall.; Wight Ic. t. 227. Vern. *Maung-maka-nwè*, Burm.

A large woody climber, l. glabrous, broadly-elliptic or ovate, 4–10, petiole ½–1 in. long. Fl. in axillary cylindrical, often compound spikes, bracts minute, rhachis, as well as ovary and calyx, generally clothed with minute glandular hairs. Free part of calyx infundibuliform, ⅙ in. long, limb 4-fid, segments triangular, reflexed. Fr. 1¼ in. long.

Both Peninsulas and Ceylon. Fl. C. S.

3. QUISQUALIS, Linn.; Fl. Brit. Ind. ii. 459.

Rambling, almost climbing. Fl. in short spikes, pentamerous, free part of calyx a long slender tube, to the side of which the style is more or less adnate, stamens 10, short. Fr. dry, coriaceous, 5-angled, cotyledons fleshy, plano-convex. Species 4, Asia and Africa.

1. **Q. indica**, Linn. Vern. *Dawèh maing*, Burm.

A large evergreen woody climber, young shoots pubescent or villous. L. elliptic or ovate-oblong, acuminate, those on leafy rambling shoots alternate, those on flowering branches opposite, petioles articulate, the portion below the articulation persistent, becoming hard and woody, hooking the branches on to supports. Fl. showy, first white, then red or orange, bracts leafy, ovate-lanceolate, free part of calyx filiform, 2–3 in. long, hairy within and on the outside. Fr. 1 in. long, glossy, with 5 deep furrows between the angles.

Wild in Burma and Yunnan, cultivated throughout India. Fl. March–April. 2. **Q. densiflora**, Wall. Maulmein, Malay Archip. Fl. in dense rusty-pubescent spikes, calyx-tube above the ovary ¼–½ in. long, mouth funnel-shaped, teeth lanceolate-subulate, petals ⅛ in. long, scarlet. 3. **Q. malabarica**, Bedd. Ic. Pl. Ind. Or. t. 155. Wainād, Travancore. Fl. in lax slightly pubescent spikes, calyx-tube above the ovary ½ in., petals pink, ½ in. long.

4. CALYCOPTERIS, Lamk.; Fl. Brit. Ind. ii. 449.

1. **C. floribunda**, Lamk. (the only species).—Syn. *C. nutans*, Kurz F. Fl. i. 468. *Getonia floribunda*, Roxb. Cor. Pl. t. 87. Vern. *Ukshi*, Mar.; *Kyut-nwway*, Burm.

A large scandent shrub, branches drooping, young shoots rusty villous, l. opposite, ovate, shortly acuminate, entire. Fl. bisexual, in tomentose terminal and axillary panicles. Free portion of calyx infundibuliform, petals 0, stamens 10, inserted in two lines on the inside of the calyx-tube, the 5 upper alternating with the calyx-teeth. Fr. 5-ribbed, villous, ¼ in. long, surmounted by the enlarged calyx, the segments of which are ½–1 in. long.

Western Peninsula, in deciduous forests. Assam. Chittagong. Upper and Lower Burma. Fl. Jan.–May. A remarkable form in Upper Burma (Smales, March 1899, *Nabu nwè*) with obtuse l. and very short bracts.

5. LUMNITZERA, Willd.; Fl. Brit. Ind. ii. 451.

Glabrous evergreen shrubs or small trees, l. alternate, clustered towards the ends of branches, fleshy, spathulate or narrowly obovate, sec. n. not visible. Fl. bisexual, pentamerous, shortly pedicellate, 2 bracteoles on the calyx-tube. Fr. crowned by the persistent calyx-limb, ½–1 in. long. Two litoral species, both in the tropics of the old world and of Australia. (Engler u. Prantl iii. 7. 129 fig. 65.)

1. **L. racemosa**, Willd.; Bedd. Manual t. xxi. fig. 2; Brandis F. Fl. 221. Vern. *Kirpa*, Sundriban; *Yinyè*, Burm.

A shrub or tree, attaining 40 ft., l. 2 in. long, cuneate, slightly emarginate and crenate, fl. white, sessile, in axillary spikes, stamens 10, as long as petals. Endocarp hard, exocarp spongy.

Coasts of India and Burma, in Mangrove swamps and other tidal forests. Fl. March, April. 2. **L. coccinea,** W. et A. (*L. littorea*, Voigt; Kurz F. Fl. i. 469) Mergui, Nicobars, has fl. in terminal corymbose racemes, petals and stamens scarlet, stamens twice the length of petals. Pericarp spongy.

6. ANOGEISSUS, Wall.; Fl. Brit. Ind. ii. 450.

L. alternate, fl. small, bisexual, in globose heads. Calyx-tube compressed at the base, prolonged beyond the ovary into a slender tube, which expands at the top into a campanulate deciduous 5-cleft limb. Petals 0. Stamens 10, biseriate, filaments filiform, exserted. Fr. small, coriaceous, broadly 2-winged, terminating in a beak, formed by the persistent calyx-tube. Species 5, one in tropical Africa, the others in India.

A. Persistent calyx-tube shorter than fruit.

1. **A. pendula,** Edgew.; Brandis F. Fl. 229. Vern. *Dhao*, *Dhaukra*, Meywar.

A small gregarious tree, branches drooping, leaves turning red before falling. Branchlets and l. densely clothed with short soft appressed hairs. L. broadly lanceolate or oblanceolate, blade $\frac{3}{4}$-1, petiole $\frac{1}{8}$–$\frac{1}{6}$ in. long, sec. n. not prominent, 5–7 pair. Fl. heads under $\frac{1}{4}$ in. diam., on slender axillary peduncles $\frac{1}{2}$–1 in. long. Ripe fr. (here and in the other species including the wings) nearly orbicular, upper portion and short beak hairy, lower portion glabrous.

Rajputana and Bundelkhand, extending south to the Panch Mahals (Gujarat) and to Nimar on the Nerbudda river. The principal forest tree of Merwara and Meywar. Fl. R. S. Leaves shed in January.

B. Persistent calyx-tube as long as or longer than fruit.

2. **A. latifolia,** Wall.; Bedd. Fl. Sylv. t. 15; Brandis F. Fl. 227.—Syn. *Conocarpus latifolia*, DC.; Royle Ill. t. 45; Wight Ic. t. 694. Vern. *Dhaura*, *Dhawa*, *Bakli*, Hind.; *Arma*, Gond; *Dindaga*, *Dindal*, Kan.; *Chirimanu Yellam ma*, Tel.; *Vellay naga*, Tam.

A large tree, l. broadly elliptic, pubescent when young, glabrous when full grown, blade 1$\frac{1}{2}$–3$\frac{1}{2}$, petiole $\frac{1}{4}$–$\frac{3}{4}$ in. long, sec. n. 8-14 pair, tertiary n. prominent beneath. Fl. heads $\frac{1}{4}$–$\frac{1}{3}$ in. diam., on short peduncles, often in axillary racemes, ripe fr. almost glabrous, nearly orbicular.

Subhimalayan tract from the Ravi to Nepal, ascending to 3,000 ft. Central India. Western Peninsula, ascending to 4,000 ft. on the Nilgiris. Not in Assam, eastern Bengal nor Burma. Bare during the greater part of the dry season. In Nov. the foliage begins to have a fine copper tint, is shed in Feb. and the young l. come out in May. Fl. May–Aug., sometimes Nov.–Feb.—Ceylon, dry country.

3. **A. sericea,** Brandis, Ind. Forester. vol. xxv. 287. Vern. *Kardahi*, Jabalpur.

A middle-sized, on good soil a large tree, young shoots silvery, branchlets and underside of l. clothed with long silky hair. L. elliptic, shortly acuminate, blade 1–2, petiole $\frac{1}{8}$ in., sec. n. 4-6 pair. Fl. heads $\frac{3}{4}$ in. diam., on long peduncles, frequently bearing leafy bracts, and sometimes two or more flower-heads. Fr. tomentose, broader than long, wings jagged. Calyx-limb sometimes persistent at the end of the long tube.

Common on the Pachmarhi hills. Jabalpur district near the Nerbudda river. Garhakota, Saugor district. Panch Mahals (Gujarat). Fl. Feb. to April. A variety with smaller greyish-pubescent l. and smaller fl. heads, $\frac{1}{2}$ in. across, in Merwara.

4. **A. acuminata,** Wall.; Bedd. Fl. Sylv. t. 16; Brandis F. Fl. 228. Vern. *Pasi*, Tel.; *Yôn*, Burm.

A large tree with hanging branches, branchlets and underside of full grown l. softly pubescent. L. lanceolate, acuminate, blade 1–3, petiole $\frac{1}{4}$ in., sec. n. 6–8 pair. Fl. heads $\frac{1}{2}$–$\frac{3}{5}$ in. diam., on peduncles, which as a rule are as long as or shorter than the diameter of the flower-head. Fr. generally broader than long.

Chanda district C.P. Northern Circars. Chittagong hill tracts. Burma, Upper and Lower. Fl. Feb.–March. *A. phillyreæfolia*, Heurck & Muell., Fl. Brit. Ind. ii. 451, is a variety with narrower more glabrous l. and smaller fl.-heads, in the dry region of the Irawaddi valley between Prome and Mandalay, analogous to the variety of *A. sericea* on the dry hills of Merwara.

ORDER LI. **MYRTACEÆ.** Gen. Pl. i. 690.

Trees or shrubs, l. simple, generally quite entire, either opposite (rarely alternate) with translucent glands (*Myrtaceæ* proper) or alternate without glands (*Lecythidaceæ*). Stipules 0. Fl. regular, generally bisexual. Ovary 2- or more celled, enclosed in and generally entirely adnate to the calyx-tube. Petals 4 or 5, imbricate in bud. Stamens numerous inserted with the petals in the mouth of the calyx-tube or on the disk lining it. Fruit usually fleshy, in some genera a capsule.

Myrtaceæ comprise two distinct groups, correctly treated in Engler u. Prantl iii. 7. 26, 57, as separate orders. *Myrtaceæ* proper have cavities, containing ethereal oil, lined with small thin-walled cells, in leaves, branchlets and generally in all green parts, as a rule immediately under the epidermis. In leaves these oil cavities may often be seen as translucent points. Further there are strands of phloëm in the circumference of the pith, usually without thick-walled bast fibres. Apart from the med. rays, which are always narrow, parenchyma does not form an important element in the wood. *Lecythidaceæ* have no oil cavities and there is no phloëm in the pith, transverse bars of wood parenchyma between the rays are not uncommon. The chief character, however, of the last-named order is that the leaf traces (vascular bundles) which enter the petiole separate from the central cylinder some distance below the insertion of the leaf. Hence the transverse section of a branchlet shows, as is the case in *Dipterocarps*, a number of vascular bundles in the bark. In the petiole and midrib these vascular bundles do not coalesce, but remain distinct.

A. *Myrtaceæ* proper. Leaves opposite, rarely alternate, gland-dotted.

- I. Leaves as a rule opposite, penninerved.
  - Calyx 4-lobed, ovary 2-celled, seeds one or few . . . 1. EUGENIA.
  - Calyx 4-5-lobed, ovary 4- or 5-celled, seeds several
    - Peduncles 1-flowered . . . . MYRTUS (p. 326).
    - Fl. paniculate . . . . DECASPERMUM (p. 326).
  - Calyx closed in bud, splitting irregularly, seeds numerous . . . . PSIDIUM (p. 326).
- II. Leaves opposite, 3 longitudinal nerves.
  - Ovary 1-celled, ovules numerous on parietal placentas . . . . RHODAMNIA (p. 326).
  - Ovary 3–6-celled, l. tomentose beneath . . . . RHODOMYRTUS (p. 326).
- III. Leaves (of older plants) alternate.
  - Calyx truncate, the orifice closed in bud by a cap (operculum) formed of the concrete petals . 2. EUCALYPTUS.
  - Calyx 5-lobed.
    - Stamens free . . . . LEPTOSPERMUM (p. 328).
    - Stamens in 5 bundles, opposite the petals.
      - Leaves penninerved . . . . . . 3. TRISTANIA.
      - 3–7 longitudinal nerves . . . . . . MELALEUCA (p. 329).

B. *Lecythidaceæ*. Leaves alternate, not gland-dotted.

- All stamens fertile, fl. in spikes or racemes . . . . 4. BARRINGTONIA.
- The stamens of the exterior and interior circle without anthers . . . . 5. CAREYA.
- The stamens of the inner circle only without anthers. PLANCHONIA (p. 332).

1. EUGENIA, Linn.; Fl. Brit. Ind. ii. 470.

Trees or shrubs, nearly always evergreen; leaves gland-dotted, with rare exceptions opposite. Fl. usually tetramerous; inflorescence terminal or lateral, usually cymose but in some species centripetal, racemose. Calyx-tube frequently with resin cavities below the surface, articulate with pedicel, two bracteoles frequently at its base, enclosing the two-celled ovary and in most species produced beyond it as a more or less campanulate cup. Calyx segments persistent or deciduous. Petals gland-dotted, either free, expanding, or united into a cap (calyptra). Stamens numerous in several series, inserted on a more or less conspicuous disk at the mouth of calyx-tube, anthers small versatile. Ovules several or many in each cell, placenta in the middle of the dissepiment. Fr. a berry, 1- or few-seeded, embryo thick and fleshy with a very short radicle, the cotyledons fleshy, either separate or united in a homogeneous mass. Species 650 tropical and subtropical, in Asia and tropical America, a few in tropical Africa and Australia.

The species here enumerated are frequently classed under 3 genera: *Jambosa*, *Eugenia* and *Syzygium*. Engler u. Prantl. iii. 7. 78.

Sect. I. *Jambosa*, II. *Syzygium*. Calyx-tube produced beyond ovary, free portion cup-shaped or campanulate.

A. Fl. large, calyx-tube (from articulation to rim) ⅓ in. or longer. (Species 1–27).

(a.) Flowers pedicelled.

a. Base of leaves rounded or cordate.

1. **E. aquea**, Burm.; Wight Ic. t. 216, 550; Kurz F. Fl. i. 494.
A middle-sized tree, glabrous, bark smooth grey, l. coriaceous, shining, elliptic-oblong, obtuse, narrowed to the rounded or slightly cordate base, blade 4–12 in., petiole stout, generally very short. Fl. white or purplish-pink, in 3–9-fld. pedunculate cymes, at the ends of branchlets or from the upper axils, pedicels shorter than the 1 in. long calyx-tube with 2 bracteoles at its base. Fr. turbinate, ¾–1 in. diam. crowned by the persistent calyx-limb and segments.

Sikkim 1,000 ft., Khasi hills (to 4,000 ft.). Cultivated in Burma. Fl. H. S.—Ceylon. 2. **E. macrocarpa**, Roxb. Cachar, Chittagong. Burma, Upper and Lower, to 3,000 ft. A middle-sized tree, l. coriaceous, oblong-lanceolate from a rounded or cordate base, blade 8–15, petiole stout ¼ in. long, sec. n. distant, joined by marginal veins at a distance from the edge. Fl. scented, white, calyx pink, in a terminal 5–9-fld. inflorescence, calyx-tube clavate, free portion a very shallow cup, 1–1¼ in. long, ribbed when dry, pedicels short, stout. Fr. globose, the size of an orange, crowned by the spreading calyx-lobes, seeds up to 5.

3. **E. formosa**, Wall. Pl. As. Rar. t. 108; Kurz F. Fl. i. 492. Vern. *Thabye pinbwa*, *Wabaw*, Burm. (Upper Burma).
A middle-sized or large tree, entirely glabrous, branchlets almost terete, bark pale grey. L. chartaceous, oblong-lanceolate tapering towards the acute apex, rounded or cordate at the base (the upper ones usually in threes), blade 8–18, petiole stout, ⅛ in. or shorter. Sec. n. distant, 10–12 pair, a few shorter intermediate nerves between. Fl. on the old wood, large, sometimes solitary, generally in sessile or shortly pedunculate few-fld. cymes, the terminal fl. generally opening first, pedicels bracteolate below flower, ⅓–⅔ in., calyx and petals purple, calyx-tube broadly turbinate, ⅔ in. long. Fr. white, globose 2 in. diam., contracted towards the base, crowned by the spreading calyx-lobes. Seeds 2.

Sikkim, Terai and outer valleys. Assam. Chittagong. Burma, Upper and Lower, in evergreen forests along streams. Fl. March–May. **4. E. amplexicaulis**, Roxb.; Wight Ic. t. 608. Chittagong, a large tree, l. nearly sessile, obtuse, 6–8 by 3–4 in. Fl.

large, white, 3–9 in a shortly peduncled inflorescence. Fr. 2 in. diam., greenish-yellow when ripe, crowned with the inflexed calyx-lobes. Closely allied to this is a large tree (Dacca, C. B. Clarke, April, 1872) with 9–27-fld. lax panicles from the axils of fallen l., petals yellow, anthers yellow, stigma yellow-green.

5. **E. Munronii,** Wight, Ic. t. 546; Bedd. Manual 109.

A middle-sized very beautiful tree, glabrous, l. coriaceous, from a cordate base lanceolate, blade 6–9, petiole stout channelled, $\frac{1}{8}$ in., sec. n. 18–24 pair, slender but prominent beneath, joined by conspicuous intramarginal veins. Fl. white, 1–1½ in. across in terminal many-fld. trichotomous compound cymes, calyx-tube obconic, $\frac{1}{3}$ in. long, tapering into the pedicel which is as long as the calyx-tube.

Western Ghats from South Kanara to Cape Comorin, Nilgiris. Fl. Dec.–Feb. A variety with broader leaves found by Bourdillon on the lower hills of Travancore. 6. **E. diospyrifolia,** Wall. Khasi and Garo hills. Upper Burma, near streams. A small or middle-sized tree, branchlets sharply quadrangular, l. from a narrow cordate base oblong-lanceolate, fl. solitary or in terminal 3–5-fld. cymes, calyx-tube turbinate, $\frac{1}{2}$–$\frac{3}{4}$ in. long, free portion above the ovary shallow-cupshaped, fr. globose 1–2 in. diam., red.

7. **E. Rama Varma,** Bourdillon MSS.

A middle-sized or large tree, l. from a cordate base gradually narrowed into a long acumen, blade 5–7 in. long, petiole stout, very short, midrib impressed on the upper surface, very prominent beneath, as well as the 15–20 pair of sec. n. which are joined by straight intramarginal veins. Fl. white, on the old wood, solitary or in few-fld. racemes, pedicels longer than calyx. Calyx-tube $\frac{1}{3}$ in. long and as wide at the mouth, segments semicircular, petals orbicular $\frac{1}{2}$ in. diam. Fr. greenish-pink, globose, 1½ in. diam.

Travancore, evergreen forests at high elevations 4–4,500 ft. Fl. March. Called after His Highness the Maharajah of Travancore, who wisely insists on a good management of his forests in the interest of future generations.

β. Leaves more or less elliptic, narrowed towards both ends.

8. **E. Jambos,** Linn.; Kurz F. Fl. i. 495.—Syn. *Jambosa vulgaris* DC; Wight Ic. t. 435. *The Rose Apple.* Vern. *Gulāb Jāman*, Hind.; *Thabye*, Burm.

A middle-sized tree, l. thinly coriaceous, oblong- or elliptic-lanceolate, tapering to both ends, blade 4–7, petiole $\frac{1}{4}$ in., sec. n. and intramarginal veins slender but distinct. Fl. greenish-white, 2–3 in. across, in short terminal corymbs, composed of 2–4 pair of opposite fl., those of the uppermost pair often opening first. Calyx-tube obconical, $\frac{1}{2}$ in. long, stamens 1¾ in. long, pedicel often as long as calyx-tube. Fr. globose or pear-shaped, 1½–2 in. long, yellow or pink, edible.

Indigenous in the Malay Archipelago and Upper Burma (Shwebo district, 1,000 ft. on stream banks). Cultivated throughout India and Burma, run wild in places. Fl. Feb.–April, but also at other times. 9. **E. læta,** Ham. (*E. pauciflora*, Wight Ic. t. 526.) Western Ghats from Bombay southwards. L. chartaceous, elliptic-lanceolate, acuminate, blade 4–5, petiole $\frac{1}{4}$–$\frac{1}{3}$ in., sec. n. slender, distant. Fl. large, crimson, sometimes white, solitary or in 3–5-fld. cymes, calyx-tube $\frac{3}{4}$ in. almost cylindrical, slightly widening upwards, free portion shallow-campanulate, pedicel often longer than tube, ovary-cells in the middle of tube, petals $\frac{1}{3}$ in. diam., stamens 1 in. long. Fr. ovoid 1 in. long, crowned by the calyx-segments. 10. **E. javanica,** Lamk. (*E. alba*, Roxb.; Wight Ic. t. 548.) Andamans and Nicobars, Sundriban (C. B. Clarke). A middle-sized tree, l. thinly coriaceous, fl. large white pedicellate, in many-fld. terminal and lateral compound cymes, some fl. occasionally sessile, calyx-tube turbinate, $\frac{1}{3}$ in. long, cylindrical below. Fr. white, shining, depressed-turbinate, almost flat, 2 in. diameter, crowned by the fleshy incurved calyx-lobes.

11. **E. hemisphærica,** Wight Ic. t. 525.; Bedd. Fl. Sylv. t. 203. Vern. *Ven nyāra*, Mal.

A large tree, l. elliptic-lanceolate, blade 3–6, narrowed into petiole $\frac{1}{2}$ in. long, sec. n. faint, distant, 8–10 pair. Fl. white, in ample compound terminal and axillary, usually three-fld. cymes at the ends of ramifications, the central fl. nearly sessile, the 2 lateral pedicelled. Calyx-tube ½ in. long, almost hemispherical on a short cylindrical base, free portion a very shallow cup. Petals free, orbicular, glandular-dotted. Stamens ⅓–½ in. long. Fr. globose, 1 in. diam., crowned by the persistent calyx-lobes.

Western Ghats in evergreen forests from the Konkan southwards. Fl. March, April. 12. **E. Kurzii**, Duthie; Kurz F. Fl. i. 491. Sikkim 3–6,000 ft., common, chiefly in moist places. Assam, Cachar. Andamans. Hills east of Toungoo. A large tree, l. chartaceous, blade 4–8, petiole ¼–⅓ in., sec. n. distinct, 8–10 pair. Fl. in compound trichotomous, terminal and axillary cymes, pedicels slender, as long as calyx-tube. Calyx-tube ⅓ in. long, cylindrical below, widening in the upper part, free portion shallow-campanulate, segments broad, continuous with tube. Petals white, free. Fr. globose, ½ in. diam. 13. **E. bifaria**, Wall. Pl. As. Rar. t. 161 (*E. laurifolia*, Roxb.: Wight Ic. t. 609). Khasi hills. L. chartaceous, bifarious, elliptic, blade 3–5, petiole ⅛ in. Fl. white, in trichotomous few-fld. pedunculate cymes, peduncles and pedicels slender, Calyx-tube punctate with raised dots, funnel-shaped, the free portion above the ovary campanulate, segments obtuse, continuous with tube, with a smooth membranous edge, petals orbicular. Fr. yellow, oblong, 1 in. long, crowned with the incurved calyx-lobes. 14. **E. ramosissima**, Wall. Sikkim Terai, ascending to 3,000 ft. Khasi hills. Probably Tenasserim. A middle-sized tree, l. elliptic lanceolate, acuminate, blade 4–5, narrowed into petiole ⅓ in. long. Fl. in compound, pedunculate, usually terminal cymes, pedicels generally as long as calyx-tube. Calyx-tube obconical, ⅛ in., petals free, orbicular, glandulose-punctate, stam. ⅜ in. 15. **E. Helferi**, Duthie. Tenasserim, Malay Peninsula, very similar, fl. often sessile or shortly pedicellate. Calyx-tube ⅛ in., lobes very short, much shorter than petals. Stam. ⅛ in. long.

γ. Leaves linear-lanceolate or obovate.

16. **E. polypetala**, Wight Ic. t. 610. Vern. *Yesaya*, Burm.

A large shrub or small tree, l. usually ternate, linear-lanceolate, blade 4–6, petiole stout, ⅛ in., sec. n. distinct. Fl. white, scented, 1–2 in. across, solitary or in few-fld. cymes, axillary or from above the scars of fallen leaves, calyx-tube at its base supported by small deciduous bracteoles, obconical, ½ in. long, free portion campanulate, lobes 4 or 6, petals 4–16, pedicel as long as calyx-tube.

Khasi hills, Chittagong. Upper Burma, on edges of rivers. Fl. March–April. Yunnan. 17. **E. occidentalis**, Bourdillon MSS. A small tree in the evergreen forests of Travancore, l. opposite, thinly coriaceous, linear-lanceolate, fl. 2–2½ in. across, in terminal opposite-fld. racemes, pedicels as long as or longer than calyx, calyx-tube from a cylindrical base funnel-shaped, 1 in. long, lobes 4, ovate-oblong, petals 4, on a broad claw, stamens 1½–2 in. long.

(b.) Flowers sessile.

18. **E. claviflora**, Roxb.; Wight Ic. t. 606.; Kurz F. Fl. i. 480.—Syn. *E. leptantha*, Wight Ic. t. 528.

A large shrub or small tree, l. thinly coriaceous elliptic-lanceolate, shortly acuminate, blade 4–6, petiole ⅛ in. long, sec. n. slender, numerous, with reticulate intermediate nerves between. Fl. sessile, in compact axillary sessile or shortly pedunculate clusters. Calyx-tube ½–¾ in. long, cylindrical below, gradually widening upwards. Petals 4 or 5, white, free, stamens ⅓ in. long. Fr. ovoid-oblong ¾ in. long, crowned by the short inflexed calyx-segments.

Sikkim, to 4,000 ft. Khasi hills. Chittagong. Andamans. Lower Burma. Fl. Feb.–April. Malay Peninsula. 19. **E. Wightiana**, Wight Ic. t. 529 (*E. lanceolata*, Lam.: Wight Ic. t. 530). Western Ghats from the Konkan southwards. Ceylon. Similar, petals more numerous, up to 12. 20. **E. andamanica**, King, Andamans. A small tree, l. coriaceous, broadly elliptic, blade 2–3, petiole ⅛ in. Fl. in fasciculate compound cymes, terminal and from the axils of the uppermost leaves, calyx-tube ⅓–½ in. long, petals calyptrate.

21. **E. malaccensis**, Linn. *The Malay Apple.* Indigenous in the Malay Archip., cultivated in India. A beautiful tree with deep green glossy foliage. L. thinly coriaceous, elliptic-lanceolate or oblanceolate, blade 6–11, petiole thick, ⅓–½ in., sec. n. 10–12 pair, arching. Fl sessile, crimson, 1–1½ in. across, in fasciculate, sessile or shortly pedunculate usually 3-fld. cymes from the old wood. Calyx-tube funnel-shaped, ¾,

segments ¼ in. long. Petals free, with a broad claw ⅓ in. long. Fr. turbinate or ovoid, 2 in. long, crowned by the inflexed calyx-lobes, glossy, from white to rose-coloured and dark purple.

22. **E. grandis,** Wight Ic. t. 614; Kurz F. Fl. i. 489.

A middle-sized or large tree, branchlets terete. L. thickly coriaceous, shining on both surfaces, broadly elliptic, blade 4–7, narrowed into petiole ⅓–1 in., sec. n. numerous, parallel, joined by distinct intramarginal veins. Inflorescence of several (up to 8) stout panicles, terminal or in the axils of the uppermost pair of leaves. Fl. sessile, calyx-tube ⅓–½ in. long, lower solid portion cylindric, upper free portion hemispherical, segments unequal, petals large. Fruit oblong-ovoid, 1½ in. long, crowned by the cup-shaped calyx-limb. Seed 1.

Assam, Silhet, Chittagong, Lower Burma. Fl. Feb.–April. Malay Peninsula. A tree similar to this, perhaps the same species, in Queensland (Benth. Fl. Austr. iii. 285). *Thabu thabye* Shwebo district, Upper Burma (Smales), is probably this sp., sec. and intramarginal nerves less distinct. 23. **E. Beddomei,** Duthie. South Tinnevelli, 4,500 ft. A large tree, l. thickly coriaceous, shining, broadly elliptic, blade 4–5, petiole thick, ½ in. long, sec. n. numerous prominent, ramifications of inflorescence stout, calyx-tube broadly turbinate ⅓ in. long, sessile or shortly pedicellate. 24. **E. lepidocarpa,** Wall. (*E. grandis* var. *lepidocarpa*, Kurz F. Fl. i. 490.) Tenasserim. Malay Peninsula, similar to 22, but l. smaller, petiole shorter, and sec. n. less numerous, ovary raised above the bottom of calyx-tube so as to be almost half superior. Calyx-tube ⅓ in. long. Fr. globose ½ in. diam.

25. **E. mangifolia,** Wall. (*E. reticulata*, Wight Ic. t. 541.) Khasi hills. L. coriaceous, shining, blade 4–5, petiole ⅓ in. Sec. n. numerous, alternating with reticulate intermediate nerves. Fl. usually sessile, some very shortly pedunculate, in compound trichotomous cymes, calyx-tube broadly obconical, free portion campanulate, as long as or longer than the lower solid portion, segments very short, filaments ½ in. long. To this I refer a tree found by me on the hills east of Toungoo, Feb. 1880. 26. **E. pachyphylla,** Kurz, Bithoko range Martaban 3,000 ft. Malay Peninsula, branchlets white, l. thickly coriaceous, obovate, blade 3–5 in., narrowed into petiole ⅓ in. long. Panicles erect, terminal or axillary, common peduncle 1–1½ in. long, often several at the ends of branches, fl. sessile, calyx-tube ⅓ in. long, broadly funnel-shaped, cylindrical below. 27. **E. tristis,** Kurz, Eng forests of Pegu, l. coriaceous, elliptic, blade 4–6, narrowed into petiole ½–⅜ in. long.

B. Fl. middle-sized, calyx-tube ⅙–⅓ in. long, broad, width at mouth half its length or more, fl. sessile, except *E. albiflora*. (Species 28–37.)

(a) Sec. n. 10–25 pair, more prominent than the shorter intermediate nerves.

28. **E. præcox,** Roxb.; Wight Ic. t. 619; Kurz F. Fl. i. 483.—Syn. *E. Wallichii*, Wight Ic. t. 536; Fl. Brit. Ind. ii. 475; *E. lanceæfolia*, Roxb.; Wight Ic. t. 621.

A middle-sized or large tree, branchlets quadrangular, l. oblong-lanceolate, thinly coriaceous, shining above, blade 2–6, petiole ½–¾ in. Fl. white, sessile, in fasciculate, lax, many-fld. often drooping panicles, axillary and from the axils of fallen leaves, the terminal fl. often opening last, calyx-tube turbinate, ⅕–¼ in. long, the lower half cylindric, pedicel-like, petals usually free. Fr. ovoid, ½ in. long, crowned with the cup-shaped calyx-limb.

Subhimalayan tract and outer valleys, Sikkim, Western Dwars, and Bhutan. Assam, Khasi hills, Chittagong, Mergui. Fl. Nov.–January.

29. **E. Smaliana,** nova sp. Vern. *Tawgyi-gangaw*, Burm.

A middle-sized tree, branchlets terete, l. coriaceous, shining, elliptic-lanceolate, blade 4–6, pet. ⅓ in., sec. n. 18–22 pair, as well as intramarginal veins prominent beneath, with intermediate reticulate veins between. Fl. greenish, sessile, in short erect, 3–11-fld. cymes, terminal and in the axils of the uppermost l. Calyx-tube ¼–⅓ in., stamens ¾ in. long.

Evergreen forests, Hmangin, Shwebo district, 2,500 ft. Fl. Dec.–Jan. 30. **E. albiflora,** Duthie. Pegu. Upper Burma (*Thabye-ka*). A tree, branchlets grey, l. elliptic, acuminate, blade 4–5, narrowed into petiole ⅓ in. long. Fl. white, scented, in fasciculate compound trichotomous cymes, terminal and in the axils of the uppermost leaves, buds white, globose, pedicels slender, equal to or longer than calyx. Calyx-tube funnel-shaped, $\frac{1}{8}$ in. long, free portion shallow-campanulate, petals free, orbicular.

31. **E. Thumra**, Roxb.; Wight Ic. t. 617; Kurz F. Fl. i. 488.

A middle-sized or large tree, branchlets light grey, l. firmly coriaceous, when dry dark above, copper coloured beneath, elliptic-oblong, blade 4–8, petiole stout, $\frac{1}{4}$–$\frac{1}{2}$ in. long, sec. n. 15–20 pair. Panicles many-fld., terminal and from the uppermost axils, fl. sessile, small, white, in umbelliform heads of 3 or more fl. Calyx-tube $\frac{1}{8}$ in. long, funnel-shaped, free portion campanulate, about as long as the lower solid portion, segments finally deciduous. Ovary near the apex of the solid portion, petals small, free. Fr. nearly globose, $\frac{1}{3}$ in. long, crowned by the calyx-rim.

Pegu and Tenasserim. Fl. H. S. Malay Peninsula. *E. ferruginea*, Wight Ic. t. 554. Mergui, petals 8, is referred to this in Fl. Brit. Ind. ii. 482. The figure shows the ovary-cells not near the apex, but in the middle of calyx-tube. 32. **E. rubens**, Roxb. Chittagong. Tenasserim, is similar, but fl. larger, greenish-white, calyx-tube $\frac{1}{4}$ in., filaments $\frac{1}{2}$ in. long. Specimens of two different species with the ovary almost free in the calyx-tube, one from Malacca, the other grown in the Bot. Garden Calcutta are preserved under this name in Herb. Kew.

(b.) Sec. n. very numerous, slender, closely parallel.

33. **E. cymosa**, Lamk.; Wight Ic. t. 555; Kurz F. Fl. i. 486.

A shrub or small tree, l. thinly coriaceous, ovate- or elliptic-lanceolate, caudate-acuminate, sec. n. numerous, close, very slender, blade 3–4, petiole $\frac{1}{4}$ in. long. Fl. white, sessile, supported by small bracts, in 3–5-fld. heads, these arranged in terminal and axillary trichotomous panicles with slender ramifications. Calyx-tube funnel-shaped $\frac{1}{8}$ in. long, free portion campanulate, as long as the inferior solid part. Petals free, stamens $\frac{1}{5}$ in. long. Fr. nearly globose, $\frac{1}{4}$ in. diam. crowned by the persistent calyx-rim.

Khasi hills, Cachar. Andamans and Nicobars. Tenasserim. Fl. Autumn. Malay Peninsula. Java. *E. rubricaulis*, Duthie. Tenasserim, l. broader, sec. n. very numerous, closely parallel, is a doubtful species. 34. **E. Gardneri**, Thw. (*E. kanarensis*, Talbot, Journ. Bomb. Nat. Hist. Soc. xi. 236. t. 4.) Gairsoppa ghat, Kanara. Anamalais. Evergreen forests of Travancore, to 4,000 ft. (*Shen nyāra*, Mal.) A very large tree, l. thinly coriaceous, elliptic-lanceolate, blade 2–4, petiole $\frac{1}{2}$ in. long, fl. sessile, in terminal and axillary compound trichotomous cymes. Calyx-tube $\frac{1}{8}$ in. broadly funnel-shaped from a cylindrical base, petals orbicular, free or slightly cohering, stamens $\frac{1}{4}$–$\frac{1}{3}$ in. long. Fr. purple, nearly globose $\frac{1}{3}$ in. diam. without a trace of calyx-segments on the small calyx-rim. 35. **E. lineata**, Duthie. Banks of Tenasserim river (Helfer). Similar. Fl. often shortly pedicellate, larger, without bracts, calyx-tube $\frac{1}{6}$–$\frac{1}{4}$, stamens $\frac{1}{3}$ in. long. 36. **E. toddaloides**, Wight Ic. t. 542. Assam, Khasi hills, l. caudate acuminate, blade 3–5, petiole $\frac{1}{4}$ in., sec. n. very close, slender, numerous. Fl. sessile in few-fld. axillary compound cymes, calyx-tube funnel-shaped $\frac{1}{4}$ in. long, $\frac{1}{8}$ in. wide at mouth, segments small, petals free, stamens $\frac{1}{3}$ in.

37. **E. Arnottiana**, Wight Ic. t. 999. Vern. *Nāval*, Tam.

A very large tree, usually with a short bole and widely spreading branches, l. rigidly coriaceous, elliptic-lanceolate, blade 2–3, petiole $\frac{1}{2}$–$\frac{3}{4}$ in. long, sec. n. very numerous, closely parallel. Fl. showy, cream-coloured, sessile, crowded in dense clusters, forming a compact terminal compound trichotomous cyme, buds crimson. Calyx-tube broadly funnel-shaped, $\frac{1}{6}$ in. long, $\frac{1}{5}$ in. wide at mouth, free portion shallow cup-shaped. Petals free or calyptrate, stamens $\frac{1}{3}$ in. long. Berries oblong, dark purple, succulent, eaten, but astringent.

Nilgiris, Palnis, Anamalais, Travancore. Fl. Jan.–April. Fr. May–June.

C. Fl. middle-sized and small, calyx-tube $\frac{1}{8}$–$\frac{1}{4}$ in. long, narrow, width at mouth less than half its length. (Species 38–41.)

38. **E. zeylanica**, Wight; Bedd. Fl. Sylv. t. 202.—Syn. *E. spicata*, Lam.; Trimen Handb. Ceyl. ii. 171. *Syzygium zeylanicum*, DC.; Wight Ic. t. 73. Vern. *Nyāra*, Mal.

A small or middle-sized tree, l. coriaceous, minutely glandular-punctate, both surfaces shining, lanceolate- or ovate-lanceolate, blade 1½–3, petiole ⅛ in. long. Fl. numerous, white, sessile or shortly pedicellate, in pedunculate clusters, these arranged in large terminal and axillary panicles, bracteoles 0. Calyx-tube tubercled, very resinous, ¼ in. long, from a cylindrical base narrow funnel-shaped, segments persistent, petals 4 or 5, usually free, early deciduous. Fr. nearly globose, white, ⅓ in. diam.

Western Ghats, from the Konkan southwards. Nepal and Silhet (Wallich), Andamans, Tenasserim. Fl. April–June. Ceylon, very common in the dry and intermediate region. Malay Peninsula. Java. Borneo. Varies greatly in regard to size and shape of leaves. Forms with narrowly linear l. are known from the Western Peninsula (*E. linearis*, Wall.) and from Tenasserim; a remarkable form with broadly ovate l. from Coorg. 39. **E. grata,** Wight. Tenasserim, Andamans, Malay Peninsula. Similar but fr. black, ovoid ¼ in. long. 40. **E. microphylla,** Bedd., abundant on the banks of a river in the Asambu hills, Travancore, 4,500 ft., a small tree with dense foliage, branchlets angled and narrowly winged, l. elliptic-oblong, obtuse, ⅓–½ in. long. Fl. in clusters of 5–10 at the ends of branches, calyx-tube ⅛ in., more or less covered with resinous scales, free portion as long as solid portion, petals small, free, stamens ¼ in. long. Erroneously placed under *Eueugenia* in Fl. Brit. Ind. ii. 505. 41. **E. pellucida,** Duthie (*E. contracta*, Wall.; Kurz F. Fl. i. 481). Martaban and Tenasserim, frequent in stony or rocky stream beds. A small shrub, l. linear-lanceolate, 3–5 in. long, sec. n. distant, calyx-tube ½ in. slender.

D. Fl. small, calyx-tube less than ⅛ in. long, inflorescence lateral, petals free. (Species 42–44.)

42. **E. polyantha,** Wight Ic. t. 543. Mergui. Malay Peninsula and Archip. A tall slender tree, l. chartaceous, elliptic-lanceolate, blade 3–5, petiole ¼ in., sec. n. slender, 8–10 pair, with shorter intermediate nerves between. Fl. small, sessile, in many-fld. short compound cymes on the old wood, rarely axillary, calyx-tube broadly turbinate, $\frac{1}{10}$ in. long, wider at mouth, segments broadly triangular, acute, petals free, white, stamens shorter than petals. Fr. irregularly globose, crowned by the rim and the more or less persistent segments of the calyx, when 2-seeded much broader than long, up to ½ in. broad. 43. **E. Manii,** King in Journ. As. Soc. Beng. v. 70, 104. Andamans. A middle-sized tree, very similar to 42, sec. n. 6–8 pair, arching, prominent beneath, fl. larger, very numerous, crowded in compound cymes 3–4 in. long, calyx-tube ⅟ in. Fr. depressed globose, ⅓ in. diam., crowned by the small circular remains of calyx. 44. **E. malabarica,** Bedd. Fl. Sylv. t. 199. Wainad 2–4,500 ft., common in swampy places, a middle-sized tree, l. spathulate, obovate or obcordate, blade 2–5, petiole ⅛–½ in. Fl. sessile, minute, in short compound cymes from last year's branchlets, small lanceolate bracts at the base of ramifications and flowers. Petals free, fr. globose ¼ in. diam.

E. Fl. middle sized and small, calyx-tube ¼ in. long and under, inflorescence lateral, petals calyptrate. (Species 45–53.)

(a.) Sec. n. 8–18 pair, distant.

45. **E. alternifolia,** Wight Ic. t. 537; Bedd. Fl. Sylv. t. 198. *Manchi Movi, Mogi, Movi*, Tel.

A large tree, l. alternate, thickly coriaceous, from broad-ovate to nearly orbicular, blade 5–9, petiole 1–1½ in. long, sec. n. 12–18 pair, branching, with shorter intermediate nerves between. Fl. sessile, yellowish-white, sweet-scented, supported by lanceolate bracteoles, in compound trichotomous cymes on the old wood. Calyx-tube ¼ in., funnel-shaped, petals calyptrate, stamens twice the length of calyx-tube. Fr. nearly globose ½ in. diam., edible.

Nallamalai hills, Karnul district. Palkondas and Veligondas. Hills of Cuddapah and North Arcot. Kambakum hill, Chengalpat district.

46. **E. tetragona,** Wight; Kurz F. Fl. i. 484. Sikkim ascending to 6,000 ft. Khasi hills. Upper Burma, Kurz. A large tree, branchlets quadrangular, angles often winged, l. opposite, lanceolate to elliptic-oblong, blade 4–11, narrowed into petiole ½–1 in., sec. n. 12–18 pair, prominent beneath as well as intramarginal veins. Fl. sessile, small, in short compound cymes from the previous year's wood, rarely from the leaf-axils, calyx-tube ⅛ in. Fr. red and black, nearly globose, ¼ in. long, edible.

47. **E. operculata,** Roxb.; Wight Ic. t. 552; Brandis F. Fl. 234.—Syn.

E. cerasoides, Roxb.; Wight Ic. t. 615. Vern. *Piāman, Rai Jāman*, Hind. *Kōn thabye*, Upper Burma.

A small or middle-sized, sometimes a large tree, l. thinly coriaceous, turning red before falling, broadly-ovate or elliptic, sometimes obovate, blade 3–8, petiole ½–1 in. long, sec. n. 8–12 pair. Fl. sessile, greenish, in broad compound trichotomous cymes, ramifications divaricate, from the previous year's wood. Calyx-tube turbinate ⅓, stamens ⅛ in. long. Berry dark purple, juicy, edible, ⅓–½ in. diam. crowned by the broad and large calyx-rim. Seed 1.

Subhimalayan tract from the Jumna eastwards. Common in Savannahs in Sal forests. Behar. Orissa. Assam, Silhet, Cachar, Chittagong. Burma, Upper and Lower. Fl. April, May. 48. **E. balsamea,** Wight. Sikkim Terai, in swampy places and along rivers. Assam. Khasi hills. Chittagong. Upper Burma on stream banks (*Ye thabye thein*). A shrub attaining 15 ft., l. membranous, lanceolate to elliptic-lanceolate, blade 3–5, narrowed into petiole ¼–½ in. long, sec. n. 8–12 pair, prominent beneath, as well as intramarginal veins. Fl. very small, in short fasciculate compound trichotomous cymes with slender ramifications, calyx-tube from a short cylindrical base turbinate, $\frac{1}{12}$ in. long, mouth truncate, fr. nearly globose, ¼ in. long, crowned by the broad calyx-rim. 49. **E. Stockesii,** Duthie, Konkan and Wainad. Similar to 48, but branchlets acutely quadrangular, inflorescence and fl. larger, calyx-tube ⅛ in. long. fr. not known. 50. **E. nicobarica,** King in Journ. As. Soc. Beng. 70, 130 (*E. occlusa*, Kurz not Miq.; Fl. Brit. Ind. ii. 498) l. thinly coriaceous lanceolate or elliptic, blade 2½–4½, petiole ⅜ in. long, fl. sessile or on short 4-angled pedicels, calyx $\frac{1}{10}$ in. long.

(b.) Sec. n. numerous, slender, closely parallel.

51. **E. Jambolana,** Lam.; Wight Ic. t. 535; Bedd. Fl. Sylv. t. 197, Brandis F. Fl. t. 30. Vern. *Jaman, Jamun*, Hind. *Phalinda*, Garhwal; *Kāla jam*, Nep.; *Kuda*, Kol; *Jambul*, Mar.; *Neredu*, Tel.; *Nerale*, Kan.; *Naval*, Tam.; *Nāga*, Mal.; *Thabye*, Burm.

A large tree, bark light grey. L. coriaceous, elliptic or elliptic-lanceolate, blade 3–6, petiole ½–1 in. long, sec. n. numerous, very fine, closely parallel. Fl. whitish, scented, sessile, in compound trichotomous cymes on the previous year's wood, rarely axillary, calyx-tube turbinate, $\frac{1}{9}$–¼ in. long, base short cylindrical, limb almost truncate, segments very short. Petals united in a calyptra, stamens as long as calyx-tube. Fr. ½–1½ in. long, pink while ripening, black when fully ripe, juicy, edible.

Subhimalayan tract from Hazara eastwards, ascending to 3,000 ft. Common throughout India and Burma, excepting the arid region of Sind and the southern Punjab. Fl. March–May. Fr. June–July. The l. are renewed in April, the old l. turning red before being shed. This species varies in the shape of its leaves and the size of fl. and fr. A very striking form has large fl., calyx-tube ⅓–¼ in. long, it is the most common form in the Western Peninsula, but has also been found in N.-Western India, Bengal, Assam and the Andamans. It occurs both with elliptic and elliptic-lanceolate l. In Kumaon and Gurhwal I have found the large fruited form with both elliptic and lanceolate l. In the evergreen forests of Travancore occurs a middle-sized tree, perhaps a distinct species (Bourdillon, No. 105) with small fl. and inflorescence often axillary. A similar form I found in the Yoonzaleen in March 1880. *E. caryophyllifolia*, Lam. Wight Ic. t. 553 is supposed to be distinguished by lanceolate l. 52. **E. fruticosa,** Roxb. Maimansingh, Dacca, Chittagong. Sundriban (*Ban-jam*). Burma, Upper and Lower, often in Eng forest (*Thabye-gale, Yethabye*). A shrub similar to 51, but inflorescence larger, its ramifications sharply quadrangular, fl. white, calyx $\frac{1}{12}$–⅛ in., turbinate without a cylindrical basis, petals often free, fr. globose, ¼ in. diam.

53. **E. Heyneana,** Wall. (*E. salicifolia*, Wight Ic. t. 539.) *Jamnera*, Hind.; *Par Jambul*, Mar. Gregarious in the beds of watercourses in Behar and the Central provinces. Also in the Konkan, North Kanara, Travancore and elsewhere on the west side of the Peninsula. A shrub, l. coriaceous, lanceolate, blade 4, petiole ¼–½ in. long, sec. n. numerous, slender, with reticulate intermediate n. between. Fl. sessile, white, in compound trichotomous cymes from the old wood, calyx-tube turbinate ⅙–⅛ in. long. Fr. oblong, ½–⅜ in. long, not edible.

F. Fl. middle sized and small, calyx-tube ¼ in. and under, rarely larger, petals calyptrate, inflorescence terminal and axillary. (Species 54–67.)

(a) Leaves large, blade over 3 in.

54. **E. oblata,** Roxb.; Wight Ic. t. 622; Kurz F. Fl. i. 488.

A middle-sized tree, l. coriaceous, elliptic or elliptic-oblong, shortly acuminate, blade 3–5, petiole $\frac{1}{4}$–$\frac{1}{3}$ in. long, sec. n. numerous, anastomosing close to the margin. Fl. white, sessile, or very shortly pedicellate, in many-fld. compound trichotomous terminal and axillary cymes. Calyx-tube $\frac{1}{4}$ in. long and as wide at mouth, lower portion cylindrical, shorter than the upper free hemispherical portion. Petals united in a large calyptra, stamens $\frac{1}{2}$ in. long. Fr. globose, $\frac{1}{2}$ in. diam. Seed one.

Khasi hills, Chittagong. Forests east of Toungoo. Tenasserim. Fl. Feb.–May. Nearly allied, probably a distinct species, is a tree of the evergreen forests of North Travancore (Bourdillon 899). L. elliptic, shortly acuminate, blade 3–6, petiole $\frac{1}{3}$–$\frac{2}{3}$ in. long. Fl. sessile in axillary and terminal compound cymes, shorter than l. Calyx-tube turbinate, truncate, $\frac{1}{4}$–$\frac{1}{3}$ in. long and as wide in the mouth, petals calyptrate, stamens longer than tube.

55. **E. montana,** Wight Ic. t. 1060. Nilgiris. A large tree, branchlets stout, acutely quadrangular, often narrowly winged. L. occasionally alternate, thickly coriaceous, broadly elliptic or obovate, 3–6 in. long, narrowed into a short thick channelled petiole, sec. n. 12–18 pair, alternating with shorter intermediate nerves, joined by intramarginal veins at a distance from margin. Fl. sessile in 3-fld. cymes terminating the ramifications of broad compound trichotomous cymes, calyx-tube funnel-shaped $\frac{1}{3}$ in. long, petals calyptrate, stamens shorter than tube. Fr. nearly globose, $\frac{1}{3}$ in. diam. A remarkable tree, common in swampy places in the low country, Travancore (Bourdillon, 450), has branchlets 4-angled but more slender and differs further from *E. montana* by thinner leaves, intramarginal veins indistinct, petioles $\frac{1}{3}$ in. long, compound cymes, axillary on peduncles 2–4 in. long. Possibly a new sp.

56. **E. rubicunda** Wight Ic. t. 538 (*E. lissophylla*, Thwaites) Western Ghats from the Konkan southwards. A middle-sized tree, branchlets obtusely quadrangular, l. elliptic or elliptic-lanceolate, 2–4 in. long, narrowed into a short petiole, sec. n. fine, numerous, closely parallel. Calyx-tube $\frac{1}{8}$ in., stamens longer than calyx-tube. Fr. nearly globose $\frac{1}{4}$ in. diam. 57. **E. frondosa,** Wall. Nepal, probably also Kumaon. L. coriaceous, elliptic-lanceolate, blade 3–5, petiole $\frac{1}{3}$ in., sec. n. numerous, joined by intramarginal veins at some distance from the leaf edge. Fl. usually sessile, sometimes shortly pedicellate, in compound trichotomous cymes, terminal and from the axils of the uppermost l. Calyx-tube nearly truncate, broadly turbinate, $\frac{1}{7}$ in. long and broader at the mouth than long, petals united, stamens $\frac{1}{4}$ in. long. *E. areolata*, DC. Nepal, probably is the same species. 58. **E. Khasiana,** Duthie. Maimensingh, Assam, Khasi hills. Tenasserim. A middle-sized spreading tree, l. lanceolate, blade 3–4, petiole $\frac{1}{4}$ in. long, sec. n. numerous slender, more distinct above than beneath, ramifications of panicle angular, calyx-tube $\frac{1}{8}$ in., stamens longer than tube. Fr. cylindric, $\frac{1}{4}$ in. long, crowned by the cup-shaped calyx-limb.

59. **E. corymbosa,** Lam.; Trimen Handb. Ceylon ii. 174. (*E. caryophyllæa*, Wight Ic. t. 540). Western Peninsula on the west side, from the Konkan southwards, near river banks, also near the coast. Ceylon. A large shrub or small tree, l. obovate or elliptic, 2–4 in., narrowed into a short petiole, sec. n. numerous, joined by reticulate veins. Fl. sessile, in terminal compound trichotomous cymes, calyx-tube broadly turbinate, $\frac{1}{8}$ in. long, limb nearly truncate, petals calyptrate, fr. depressed globose, $\frac{3}{8}$ in. diam., nearly black, shining, edible. 60. **E. utilis,** Talbot in Journ. Bomb. Nat. Hist. Soc. xi. 235, t. 3. *Hennerl*, Kan. A large tree, with a straight cylindrical trunk and grey scaly bark, evergreen forest in the southern parts of N. Kanara. L. coriaceous, elliptic, acuminate, blade 2–3, petiole $\frac{1}{3}$ in. long, sec. n. slender, very numerous and close. Fl. sessile, small, supported by small bracteoles, in compound cymes, terminal and axillary, calyx-tube $\frac{1}{10}$ in. long, almost truncate. Fr. small, black, succulent.

61. **E. bracteolata,** Wight Ic. t. 531. Tenasserim, Malay Peninsula. A middle-sized tree, l. from a cuneate base elliptic or elliptic-lanceolate, blade 3–6, petiole $\frac{1}{3}$–$\frac{1}{2}$ in. long. Fl. in 3-fld. cymes at the ends of the ramifications of terminal trichotomous broadly corymbiform compound cymes, ovate bracts at the base of ramifications, and similar bracteoles supporting the flowers. Calyx-tube $\frac{1}{10}$ in., almost truncate, teeth obscure, pedicels nearly as long, stamens longer than tube. 62. **E. pseudosubtilis,** King (*E. cinerea*, Kurz F. Fl. i. 483; *E. brachiata*, Duthie, Fl. Brit. Ind. ii. 496 in part). Southern portion of Pegu Yoma. Martaban, Tenasserim. A middle-sized tree, branches pale, almost white, l. thinly coriaceous, elliptic-oblong, blade 4–6, narrowed into petiole $\frac{1}{2}$ in. long, sec. n. slender, 5–7 pair. Fl. very small, sessile in compound trichotomous terminal and axillary cymes, ramifications slender, at right angles to rachis, calyx-tube $\frac{1}{15}$ in. Fr. $\frac{1}{3}$ in. diam.

63. **E. calophyllifolia,** Wight Ic. t. 1000. Nilgiris. A large tree with spreading branches, l. thickly coriaceous, obovate or broadly-elliptic $\frac{1}{2}$–$1\frac{1}{2}$ in., petiole very short, prominent reticulate veins between the numerous sec. n. Fl. sessile in dense clusters

of 3-fld. cymes in a terminal corymbiform inflorescence, calyx-tube $\frac{1}{8}$ in., segments broadly triangular, petals calyptrate, sometimes free. Fr. ovoid-oblong, $\frac{1}{2}$ in. long, dark purple. 64. **E. revoluta,** Wight, l. thickly coriaceous, $1\frac{1}{2}$–3 in., obovate, obtuse, often emarginate, petals small, usually distinct, fr. globose $\frac{1}{2}$ in. diam., is a Ceylon tree. I have seen no specimens from the Nilgiris. 65. **E. Myhendræ,** Bedd. MSS. A large tree on the Tinnevelli and Travancore ghats, branchlets and ramifications of inflorescence sharply quadrangular, l. oblanceolate, $1–1\frac{1}{4}$ in. long, sec. n. slender, very numerous, closely parallel, fl. sessile in terminal compound trichotomous cymes, calyx-tube $\frac{1}{6}$ in. long, segments broad, rounded, fr. unknown. 66. **E. cuneata,** Wall. Assam. Khasi hills. Upper Burma in stream beds (*Ye-thabye*, Burm. Smales). A shrub, branchlets and ramifications of inflorescence quadrangular, l. lanceolate, blade $1\frac{1}{2}$–$2\frac{1}{2}$ in., petiole $\frac{1}{8}$ in. long. Fl. sessile, in small terminal compound cymes, calyx-tube $\frac{1}{8}$ in., petals calyptrate, stamens $\frac{1}{4}$ in., fr. red, nearly globose, $\frac{1}{3}$ in. diam. 67. **E. myrtifolia,** Roxb. Tenasserim (Kurz). Malay Peninsula, branchlets quadrangular, l. elliptic-lanceolate 2–3 in. long, petiole very short. Fl. sessile or shortly pedicellate, in trichotomous compound cymes. Calyx-tube broadly funnel-shaped, $\frac{1}{6}$ in. long and at mouth $\frac{1}{8}$ in. wide, the free portion a shallow cup. Petals 4 calyptrate, stamens $\frac{1}{4}$ in. long.

Sect. III. *Eu-eugenia.* Calyx-tube not produced beyond ovary, petals distinct, fl. solitary or fasciculate; 2 bracteoles at the base of calyx-tube. Nearly all Western species. (Species 68–79.)

A. Young shoots and inflorescence pubescent, pedicels longer than calyx-tube.

68. **E. bracteata,** Roxb.—Syn. *E. Willdenowii*, Wight Ic. t. 545.

A shrub or small tree, young shoots and inflorescence rusty-pubescent, l. coriaceous, elliptic, blade 1–3, petiole $\frac{1}{4}$ in. Fl. white, showy, on slender axillary, usually 1-fld. peduncles, these frequently in pairs. Calyx-tube hairy, bemispherical, segments large, obtuse, reflexed after flowering. Petals hairy at back, ciliate at margin, twice the length of calyx-segments. Berry orange or red, globose, $\frac{1}{2}$ in. diam., 1–2-seeded, crowned by the persistent calyx-segments.

Western Peninsula, on the east side in semi-evergreen scrub as far north as Orissa. On the west side in evergreen forests, ascending to 5,000 ft. Assam and the Khasi hills. Fl. Nov.–May. Ceylon dry region. 69. **E. Rottleriana,** W. et A.; Wight Ic. t. 100. Tinnevelli and Travancore ghats. A small or middle-sized tree, l. narrowly lanceolate, $2 \times \frac{1}{3}$ in., fl. fasciculate on short peduncles, top of ovary and base of style hairy. 70. **E. argentea,** Bedd. Wainád, a small tree, branchlets and underside of l. with dense silky silvery hairs, l. lanceolate from a rounded base, blade 3–5, petiole $\frac{1}{6}$ in., sec. n. slender, nearly at right angles from midrib, bracteoles linear persistent, fr. globose $\frac{3}{4}$ in. diam. 71. **E. Jossinia,** Duthie (*Jossinia indica*, Wight Ill. t. 97* Ic. t. 523). Tinnevelli hills. A shrub or small tree, l. coriaceous oblanceolate, blade 1–2, narrowed into petiole $\frac{1}{8}$ in. long, fr. velvety. 72. **E. calcadensis,** Bedd. Ic. Pl. Ind. Or. t. 162. Calcad hills, Tinnevelli. A small tree, peduncles axillary, solitary, mostly 2-fld., petals white, $\frac{3}{4}$ in. long.

73. **E.** (?) **Wynadensis,** Bedd. Ic. Pl. Ind. Or. t. 161. Wainád (2–3,000 ft.). A large shrub or small tree, young shoots and inflorescence densely fulvo-tomentose, peduncles fasciculate, axillary or supra-axillary, each fl. supported by a pair of lanceolate bracteoles larger than calyx, calyx lobes lanceolate, as long as petals, disk on top of ovary glabrous, ovules pendulous from the top of the two cells, 4 in each. Probably a new genus.

B Young shoots and inflorescence pubescent, fl. sessile or nearly so.

74. **E. floccosa,** Bedd. Fl. Sylv. t. 200, Tinnevelli ghats above Calcad. A beautiful large tree, l. thickly coriaceous, blade elliptic, 3–5 by 2–3 in., petiole $\frac{1}{2}$ in. long. Fl. rusty tomentose on short pedicels in terminal compact cymes, disk on the top of the ovary densely woolly, petals white. 75. **E. macrosepala,** Duthie, ghats of North Kanara on the edge of evergreen forests, locally common, a bushy spreading shrub, branchlets pubescent, l. elliptic or elliptic-lanceolate, blade 3–4, petiole $\frac{1}{4}$ in., fl. clustered, sessile, clusters axillary or above the scars of fallen l., calyx-tube shorter than bracteoles, lobes lanceolate, longer than petals. 76. **E. codyensis,** Munro, Coorg and Nilgiris. A shrub, l. elliptic, blade 2–3, petiole $\frac{1}{8}$ in., fl. sessile, clustered, axillary and above the scars of fallen l., calyx-lobes broad, half the length of petals.

C. Young shoots glabrous.

77. **E. Mooniana,** Wight Ic. t. 551. Evergreen forests of the Western ghats, from the

Konkan southwards. A shrub or small tree, wholly glabrous, l. elliptic or elliptic-lanceolate, acuminate, blade 2–3, petiole ⅛ in. long. Fl. white fasciculate, pedicels slender, ½–1 in. long, calyx-segments lanceolate, fr. ovoid, pendulous, scarlet or crimson, ½–¾ in. long. 78. **E. memecylifolia,** Talb. Journ. Bomb. Nat. Hist. Soc. xi. 236 t. 5. Gregarious in the Sholas of the higher ghats of North Kanara, 3,400 ft. Fl. sessile, large, calyx tomentose, segments ovate, obtuse. Fr. white, pulpy, irregularly globose, ¾–1 in. diam., seeds 1 or 2. Perhaps a form of 76. 79. **E. singampattiana,** Bedd. Ic. Pl. Ind. Or. t. 273. Tinnevelli ghats in evergreen forest. A small tree, l. ovate from a broad base, 3 in. long. Fl. white, shortly pedicelled, in terminal clusters, bracteoles and calyx slightly pubescent.

Myrtus communis, Linn. *Myrtle, Mûrad,* Hind. A glabrous evergreen shrub, indigenous in the Mediterranean region, in Persia and some parts of Afghanistan, planted in North West India. Leaves ovate-lanceolate, 1–1½ in. long, fl. white, usually solitary, on long slender peduncles, free part of calyx-tube short, 4–5-cleft, berries black.

Decaspermum paniculatum, Kurz (*Nelitris paniculata,* Lindl.; Wight Ill. t. 97*, fig. 10. Ic. t. 521). Khasi hills. Hills between Sitang and Salween, 3–4,000 ft., common on deserted toungyas. Tenasserim. An evergreen shrub or tree, youngest shoots silky, l. opposite, lanceolate, petiole and midrib silky, blade 1–3, petiole ⅛–¼ in. long. Fl. in axillary and terminal panicles, ⅛ in. diam., often polygamous. Calyx-tube silky outside, enclosing and adnate to the 4- or 5-celled ovary, with 2 or few ovules in each cell. Berry globose, $\frac{1}{10}$ in. diam.

Psidium Guayava, Linn. *The Guava tree.* Indigenous in tropical America, cultivated in most tropical countries, naturalized in India. A small tree or large shrub, l. elliptic-oblong, nearly glabrous above, pubescent beneath, blade 4–6, petiole ⅛–⅓ in. long, sec. n. 15–20 pair, prominent beneath. Fl. white, 1½ in. across, peduncles axillary, 1–1½ in. long, 1–3-fld. Fr. edible, seeds numerous.

Rhodamnia trinervia, Blume. Tenasserim, Maulmein to Mergui. Malay Peninsula and Archipelago to Australia. A shrub, young shoots and inflorescence silky, l. elliptic or elliptic-lanceolate, often silky beneath, with 3 longitudinal nerves, blade 2–4, petiole ⅛–⅓ in. long. Fl. small, supported by a pair of small bracteoles axillary, generally fasciculate, pedicels much shorter than leaves. Berries globose, red, ⅛–⅓ diam.

Rhodomyrtus tomentosa, Wight Ill. t. 97,* fig. 3. Ic. t. 522. Nilgiris, Palnis, Ceylon, Malay Peninsula and Archipelago. China (*The Hill Gooseberry. Koratta,* Mal.). A shrub, branchlets and inflorescence tomentose. L. opposite, the lower often ternate, glabrous above, softly tomentose beneath, with 3 strong longitudinal nerves. Peduncles axillary, 1–3-fld. Fl. ½–¾ in., supported by a pair of linear bracteoles, calyx densely tomentose, adnate to ovary, not produced beyond it, petals tomentose on back. Fr. purple, nearly globose, crowned by the persistent calyx-segments, pulpy, edible, 3-celled, a double row of seeds in each cell.

2. EUCALYPTUS, L'Héritier; Brandis F. Fl. 230.

Evergreen, glabrous trees, many attaining a gigantic size, often flowering when quite young, usually secreting aromatic resinous gum. Leaves of saplings generally opposite, sessile, cordate and horizontal, those of the adult tree (here described) as a rule alternate, petiolate and vertical. Fl. in umbels or heads, usually pedunculate. Calyx-tube enclosing the ovary, adnate to it and as a rule produced beyond it, not articulate at the base, but continued without a break into the pedicel, truncate, the orifice closed in bud by the petals being united into a cap (operculum), which falls off entire, when the stamens expand. Stamens ∞. Ovary inferior, the summit glabrous, flat, convex or conical, 3–6-celled, ovules numerous, on an axile placenta. Fruit consisting of the more or less enlarged calyx-tube, usually hard and woody, full of resin-sacs. Seeds numerous but a large proportion abortive, these usually larger than the fertile seeds. Species about 140, all Australian, excepting a few in New Guinea and the Indian Archipelago. Many species cultivated in India, chiefly on account of their wonderfully rapid growth, producing an extraordinary quantity of hard heavy wood per acre per annum. Of these I mention the following, which, as far as known at present, are likely to be of some importance in India.

A. Anthers globose or broader than long, opening by pores or slits.

1. **E. Leucoxylon**, F. Muell. *Iron Bark* (*White Gum*, South Australia); Benth. Fl. Austral. iii. 209.

L. falcate-lanceolate, rarely ovate-lanceolate. Umbels mostly 3-fld., pedicels longer than calyx, tube at mouth ⅓ in. wide. Filaments yellow, rarely pink, outer stamens long, sterile, anthers minute, truncate, opening by terminal pores or short slits, stigma broad, operculum conical equal to calyx. Fr. nearly hemispherical, ¼ in. diam.

South Queensland, New South Wales, Victoria, South Australia. Cult. Abbottabad, Changa Manga, Lucknow. 2. **E. obliqua**, L'Her.; Brandis F. Fl. 231. *Stringy Bark* (*Messmate tree*, Victoria). Constitutes vast forests in Victoria, South Australia and Tasmania, ascending to 4,000 ft. Cult. Nilgiris. A lofty tree, attaining 300 ft., l. very oblique, falcate, sec. n. slender but distinct, oblique. Umbels 5–9-fld., calyx turbinate, narrowed into short pedicel, ¼ in. wide at mouth, operculum hemispherical, at times pointed. Anthers reniform, opening by terminal confluent slits. 3. **E. pilularis**, Sm. *Black butt*. South Queensland to Victoria. Cult. Nilgiris. Attains 300 ft., branchlets angular, l. lanceolate, sec. n. very slender. Umbels 6–20-fld., peduncles angular or compressed, calyx narrowed into a short pedicel, ⅛ in. wide at mouth, anthers reniform. Fr. almost hemispherical, ⅓ in. diam. *E. acmenoides*, Schauer, Queensland and New South Wales, very similar, possibly not distinct.

4. **E. marginata**, Smith. *Jarrah*. West Australia. A large tree, attaining 150 ft., timber very durable, l. lanceolate, usually falcate, sec. n. slender, but distinct, umbels 4–12-fld., calyx turbinate, narrowed into pedicel, mouth ⅓ in. wide, operculum elongate conical, twice the length of calyx, anthers reniform. Fr. ovoid, ½ in. diam., contracted at the mouth.

5. **E. amygdalina**, Labill. *Giant Eucalypt.* (*Wangara*, Gippsland). Benth. Fl. Austral. iii. 202.

A gigantic tree, attaining 420 ft., l. now and then opposite, lanceolate or linear-lanceolate, sec. n. generally inconspicuous. Umbels 4–8-fld. Calyx ⅛–⅙ in. wide at mouth, operculum hemispherical, shorter than calyx, anthers small, round. Fr. nearly hemispherical, ⅛–¼ in. diam.

New South Wales, Victoria and Tasmania. Cult. Nilgiris, with narrow linear alternate and (under the name of *Red Gum*) with lanceolate opposite l.

B. Anthers oblong or ovate, longer than broad, opening by longitudinal slits.

(a) Calyx-tube not produced beyond ovary, upper portion of ovary conical, free.

6. **E. rostrata**. Schlecht.; Benth. Fl. Austr. iii. 240. *Red Gum*.

A large tree, heartwood dark red, exceedingly hard and durable. Leaves lanceolate, falcate, sec. n. faint. Umbels 4–14-fld. Calyx at mouth ⅕–⅙ in. wide, operculum hemispherical with a shorter or longer point. Stamens not inflected, upper part of ovary with large resin cavities. Fr. nearly globose, ¼ in. diam., valves 4 rarely 5, long exserted.

Along river banks and in alluvial valleys in many parts of the Australian continent, not in Tasmania. Cult. Poona, Calcutta, Oudh. 7. **E. tereticornis**, Sm. Queensland, New South Wales, Victoria. Cult. Abbottabad, Lucknow, Khasi hills. A tree, not generally exceeding 100 ft. L. falcate, lanceolate, or ovate-lanceolate, sec. n. and intramarginal veins slender but distinct, calyx at mouth ⅛–¼ in. diam. Operculum much longer than calyx, elongate-conical. Ovary and fr. like 6.

(b) Calyx-tube produced beyond ovary.

a. Fl. large or middle-sized, ⅓ in. or more across mouth of calyx.

8. **E. globulus**, Labill.; Brandis F. Fl. 231. *Blue Gum*.

A lofty tree, attaining 300 ft., highly aromatic, young shoots and foliage glaucous-grey, l. on older trees linear-lanceolate, falcate, blade 6–9, petiole 1–2 in. long. Fl. large, calyx covered with a bluish-white bloom, broadly turbinate, warty and ribbed, mouth ¾–1 in. diam. Operculum shorter than calyx-

tube. Capsule angular, $\frac{3}{4}$–1 in. diam., the sterile seeds much narrower than the fertile seeds.

Victoria, Tasmania. Planted extensively in the countries round the Mediterranean and on the Nilgiris. Annual timber production per acre to the age of 20 years on the Nilgiris 470 cub. ft. solid wood per acre per annum, while Spruce in Europe up to that age under the most favourable circumstances only produces 70 cub. ft. per acre annually. Also grown at Abbottabad and in Kulu.

9. **E. calophylla**, R. Br. South West Australia, often associated with Jarrah. Cult. Nilgiris, Lahore. L. rigid, equilateral, ovate or ovate-lanceolate, blade 4–6, petiole 1–1$\frac{1}{2}$ long, sec. n. ∞, closely parallel. Umbels 4–6-fld., in ample terminal corymbs, rachis and peduncles angular. Free portion of calyx longer and wider than the solid portion, mouth nearly $\frac{1}{2}$ in. across, stamens pale-yellow, rarely pink. Fr. urn-shaped, 2 by 1 in., capsule deeply sunk. Seeds large. 10. **E. corymbosa**, Sm. *Bloodwood.* Queensland. New South Wales. Cult. Nilgiris. Leaves and inflorescence similar, fl. smaller, capsule $\frac{3}{4}$ by $\frac{1}{3}$ in.

11. **E. longifolia**, Link and Otto. *Woolly Butt.* New South Wales. Cult. Nilgiris. L. falcate, lanceolate, sec. n. slender but distinct. Umbels axillary 2–4-fld., peduncles often curved. Calyx $\frac{5}{12}$ in. at mouth. Operculum conical as long as or longer than calyx-tube. Fr. campanulate, narowed into stalk, $\frac{3}{8}$ in. wide at mouth. 12. **E. robusta**, Sm. *Swamp Mahogany*, New South Wales. Cult. Nilgiris. L. oblong-lanceolate, slightly unequal-sided, blade 5–7, petiole 1 in. long, sec. n. numerous, slender but distinct. Umbels axillary 4–12-fld., peduncles stout, angular and compressed, calyx at mouth $\frac{1}{3}$ in. wide, operculum as long as calyx, at base conical and wider than calyx-tube, suddenly narrowed towards the tip. Fr. ovoid-oblong $\frac{1}{2}$ in. long.

β. Fl. small, $\frac{1}{4}$ in. or less at mouth of calyx.

13. **E. resinifera**, Sm. Queensland and New South Wales, but not far inland. Bark rough, branchlets angular, sec. n. slender but distinct. Umbels 6–12-fld., calyx-mouth $\frac{1}{4}$ in. across, operculum conical, equal to or longer than calyx, upper portion of ovary free, conical. A form cultivated at Lucknow with the sec. n. more prominent and the intramarginal veins at a distance from the edge has been called *E. Kirtoniana.* 14. **E. saligna**, Sm. New South Wales, cult. Kulu, differs from 13 chiefly by the smooth bark of the stem. 15. **E. botryoides**, Sm. *Bastard Mahogany*, New South Wales, Victoria. Cult. Nilgiris. A tall tree with a dense shady crown, branchlets angular, l. horizontal, dark green and shining on the upper, pale on the lower surface, broad-lanceolate, more or less falcate, sec. n. slender, distinct, numerous. Fl. sessile, 4–10 in one umbel, peduncle short, thick, angular. Operculum hemispherical, shorter than calyx. Fr. campanulate-oblong $\frac{1}{3}$–$\frac{1}{2}$ in. long.

16. **E. Stuartiana**, F. Muell. *But-But* or *Apple-scented Eucalypt.* New South Wales, Victoria, South Australia, Tasmania. Cult. Abbottabad. L. lanceolate, more or less falcate. Umbels 3–8-fld., axillary or on the old wood below the leaves. Calyx $\frac{1}{8}$–$\frac{1}{4}$ in. at mouth. Operculum hemispherical, slightly pointed. Capsule turbinate, $\frac{1}{4}$ in. long, valves broad-triangular, usually three. 17. **E. pulverulenta**, Sims. New South Wales. Cult. Nilgiris. A middle-sized tree, branchlets, leaves and calyx glaucous or nearly white. Leaves all sessile and opposite, orbicular or broadly ovate from a cordate base. Umbels axillary, 3-fld., peduncles very short, fl. sessile, calyx-mouth $\frac{1}{4}$ in. across. Capsule nearly hemispherical, $\frac{1}{3}$ in. diam.

Leptospermum flavescens, Sm. Var. *javanica* (*L. javanicum*, Blume; Fl. Brit. Ind. ii. 464). Tenasserim, 5,000 ft., a small shrub, branchlets quadrangular, l. alternate, coriaceous, oblanceolate, obtuse, nearly sessile, 1 in. long. Fl. pentamerous, axillary, nearly sessile, solitary or clustered, $\frac{1}{2}$ in. across, stamens numerous, free, shorter than petals, ovary semi-inferior, enclosed in the calyx-tube, 5-celled. Capsule loculicidally 5-valved, seeds numerous.

3. TRISTANIA, R. Br.; Fl. Brit. Ind. ii. 465.

Evergreen trees or shrubs, l. coriaceous, glabrous, generally alternate. Fl. pentamerous, small, yellow or white, in pedunculate axillary cymes. Calyx-tube campanulate, lobes persistent, petals imbricate. Stamens numerous, united in 5 bundles, which stand opposite to the petals. Ovary hairy, enclosed within the calyx-tube but only adnate to its base, 3-celled, ovules numerous. Capsule loculicidally 3-valved, seeds few, embryo straight, cotyledons broad, longer than radicle. Species 22, Malay Peninsula and Archipelago, New Caledonia and Australia.

1. **T. burmanica,** Griff. ; Kurz F. Fl. i. 474. Vern. *Taungyo-pyizin*, Lower, *Taung-thabye* Upper Burma.

A middle-sized tree, young shoots silky pubescent, l. 2–3 in. long, oblanceolate, petiole short, hairy. Calyx ⅛ in. across, capsule ¼ in. diam., protruding far beyond the calyx-tube.

Pegu, Martaban. Tenasserim, ascending to 3,500 ft. Upper Burma. Fl. March, April. ' 2. **T. merguensis,** Griff. Tenasserim. Malay Peninsula, Borneo. L. glabrous, rigidly coriaceous, oblanceolate, obtuse or obtusely acuminate, blade 3–5 in., narrowed into a very short petiole. Cymes pubescent, calyx ⅕ in. across, pubescent on both surfaces, capsule ⅓ in. diam.

FIG. 138.—Tristania burmanica, Griff. ½.

Melaleuca Leucadendron, Linn. Mergui, Malay Peninsula and Archipelago. Australia. A middle-sized tree, bark pale, peeling off in papery layers, branches slender, pendulous. L. alternate, coriaceous, lanceolate, more or less oblique, 2–5 in. long, tapering into a short petiole, with 3–7 distinct longitudinal nerves. Fl. yellowish-white sessile in erect axillary spikes 2–6 in. long, the rachis generally prolonged and leaf-bearing. Stamens numerous, the filaments united at their base into 5 bundles inserted opposite to the petals. Ovary half-inferior enclosed in the calyx-tube. Capsule loculicidally 3-valved, Yields the Cajuput oil of commerce.

4. BARRINGTONIA, Forst. ; Fl. Brit. Ind. ii. 506.

Trees as a rule evergreen, l. alternate, not gland-dotted. Fl. in spikes or racemes, bracts usually deciduous. Calyx-tube enclosing the 2- or 4-celled ovary, not produced beyond it. Petals 4, rarely 5, more or less adnate at the base to the staminal tube. Stamens ∞, connate at the base into a short tube, all fertile. Ovules pendulous, 2–8 in each cell. Fr. fibrous-succulent, more or less angular and crowned by the persistent calyx-segments, pericarp fibrous, endocarp sometimes bony. Seed one, embryo large fleshy, consisting of two concentric homogeneous masses of cellular tissue, separated by a thin layer of delicate vessels and fibres. Albumen 0. Species 30, tropics of Africa, Asia, Australia and Polynesia.

A. Calyx quite closed in bud, splitting irregularly into 2 or 3 segments.

1. **B. racemosa**, Blume; Wight Ic. t. 152; Kurz F. Fl. i. 496. Vern. *Kumia*, Beng.; *Nivar*, Mar.; *Samudra*, Tam.

A middle-sized tree, branches with numerous large leaf-scars. L. obovate or oblanceolate, blade 6–12 in. long, narrowed into a very short petiole. Fl. $2\frac{1}{2}$ in. across, in slender pendulous racemes, cream-coloured, filaments often crimson. Fr. 2–$2\frac{1}{2}$ in. long, ovoid.

West coast, from the Konkan southwards near rivers and backwaters, but also inland. Sundriban (Heinig). Andamans, Nicobars. Fl. H. S. Ceylon, moist low country. Coasts of the Malay Peninsula and Polynesia. 2. **B. speciosa**, Forst.; Wight Ic. t. 547. Andamans. Seashore of the Malay Peninsula and Archipelago, Australia and Polynesia. A middle-sized tree, l. sessile, obovate, 6–14 in. long, reticulate veins prominent. Fl. 5–7 in. across, in erect terminal racemes, pedicels 3–4, petals $2\frac{1}{2}$, filaments 3–4 in. long. Fr. 3–4 in. diam., depressed turbinate, 4–5-angled and more or less lobed. 3. **B. conoidea**, Griff. Mergui, Malay Peninsula. A shrub or small tree, l. slightly crenulate, from a rounded or cordate base oblanceolate, blade 5–10 in. long, petiole short stout. Fl. 1 in. across, in short erect few-fld. racemes, pedicels slender $\frac{1}{2}$ in. long, petals fleshy, ovate-lanceolate. Fr. conical, at the base produced into 8 wing-like fleshy processes.

B. Calyx not closed in bud, segments 4, slightly imbricate.

(a) Petiole short, less than 1 in.

4. **B. acutangula**, Gaertn.; Bedd. Fl. Sylv. t. 204; Brandis F. Fl. 235. Vern. *Neora*, *Jujar*, Hind.; *Kumia*, Beng.; *Tivar*, *Jugli*, Mar.; *Kanapa*, Tel.; *Kyi*, Burm.

A middle-sized tree, l. obovate or oblanceolate, minutely denticulate, blade 2–5, narrowed into petiole $\frac{1}{6}$–$\frac{1}{3}$ in. long. Fl. red, $\frac{1}{3}$ in. across, in long slender pendulous racemes 6–15 in. long. Calyx-segments rounded, ciliate, ovary 2-celled. Fr. oblong, glabrous, bluntly quadrangular 1 in. long.

Subhimalayan tract from the Ganges eastwards. Bengal, Central India, the Peninsula and Burma, chiefly on banks of streams and in moist places. L. shed and renewed in March, April. Fl. Dec.–May.—Ceylon, dry region. Malay Archipelago and Northern Australia. 5. **B. augusta**, Kurz, Tenasserim (*Kyaigyee* Burm.). A middle-sized tree, not flowering every year, leaves large, crowded at the ends of branches, obovate or oblanceolate, blade 6–18 in., narrowed into a very short petiole, sec. n. 8–12 pair, prominent, arching. Fl. conspicuous, sessile, in pairs, one above the other, in terminal pendulous spikes, rachis stout, calyx-segments $\frac{1}{8}$ in. long, petals greenish, filaments white. Fr. oblong, crowned by the persistent calyx-segments, 4-winged. 6. **B. pterocarpa**, Kurz, Pegu and Martaban, petiole $\frac{1}{2}$ in. Fl. white or rose-coloured, sessile in very long pendulous spikes, calyx velvety, segments more than $\frac{1}{4}$ in. long. Fr. 2 in. long with 4 thick narrow wings. 7. **B. Helferi**, C. B. Clarke, Tenasserim, l. narrowly oblanceolate, 12–20 in. long, sec. n. 20–30 pair, prominent, fl. in pendulous racemes, rachis slender, pedicels $\frac{1}{2}$ in.

(b) Petiole long.

8. **B. macrostachya**, Kurz. South Tenasserim. Malay Peninsula. Borneo. A shrub or small tree, l. elliptic-oblong, blade 6–12, petiole 1–3 in. long, sec. n. prominent, 15-20 pair. Fl. sessile, purple, in pendulous spikes, calyx-tube 4-angled, $\frac{1}{4}$ in. long, lobes broad, obtuse, petals 1, filaments 2 in. long. Fr. ovoid, obtusely angled, $1\frac{1}{2}$–2 in. long, on a thick rachis. 9. **B. pendula**, Kurz. South Tenasserim. *Kyaithe*, Burm., l. narrowly lanceolate, blade 10–15, petiole 1–4 in. long, reticulate veins nearly as prominent as the sec. n. Fl. sessile, in spikes up to $2\frac{1}{2}$ ft. long, calyx-tube clavate, 4-angled, $\frac{1}{3}$ in. long, segments acute, filaments 1 in. long. Fr. boldly 4-angled, more than 2 in. long.

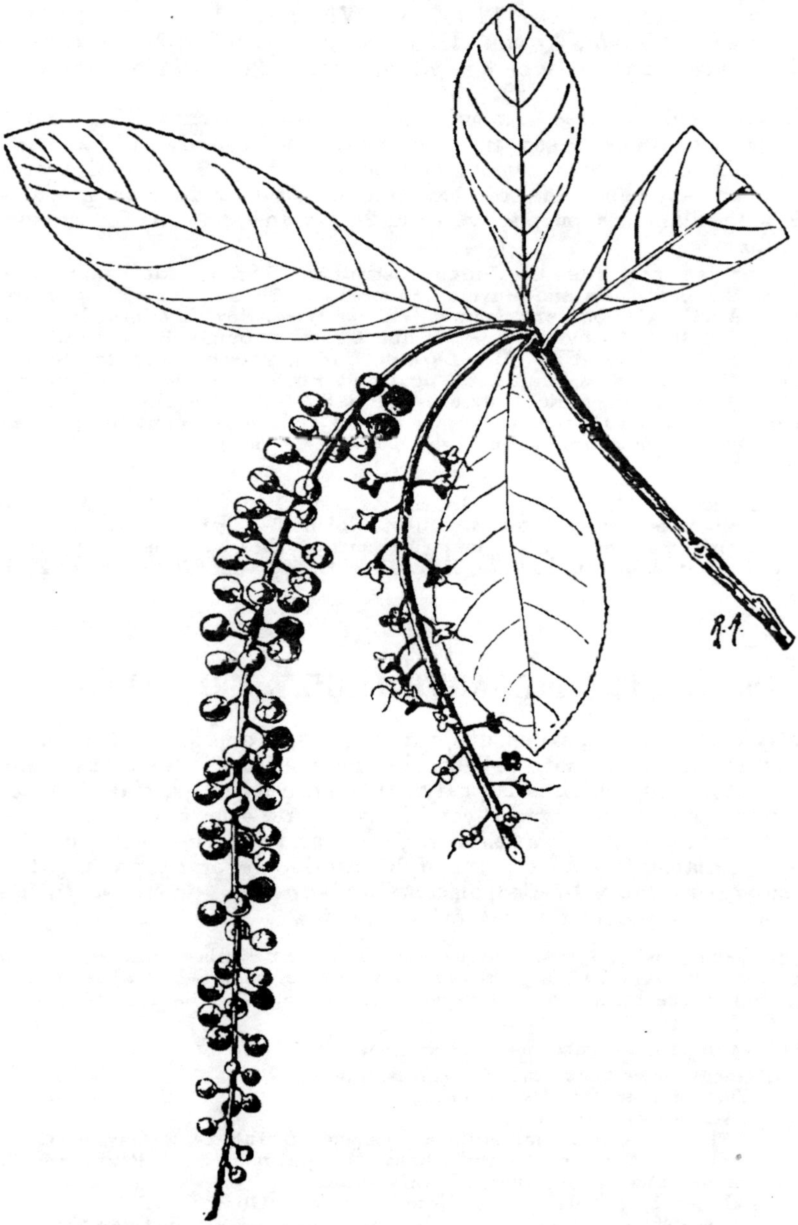

FIG. 139.—Barringtonia acutangula, Gaertn. ½.

5. CAREYA, Roxb.; Fl. Brit. Ind. ii. 510.

Leaves alternate, not gland-dotted. Fl. large, showy, tetramerous. Calyx-tube adnate to ovary and not produced beyond it. Stamens ∞, in several circles, united at the base into a thick fleshy ring, the stamens of the exterior and interior circle generally without anthers. Ovary 4-celled, ovules numerous, attached to axile placentas. Fr. globose, rind thick, seeds numerous, embedded in a fleshy pulp. Embryo large, structure similar to that of *Barringtonia*, albumen 0. Species 3, one in North Australia and Queensland.

1. **C. arborea**, Roxb. Cor. Pl. t. 218; Wight Ill. tt. 99, 100; Bedd. Fl. Sylv. t. 205. *Kumb*, *Kumbi*, *Kumhi*, Hind. Beng.; *Kumbia*, Mar.; *Gadava*, Tel.; *Kaval*, *Kaulu*, Kan.; *Ayama*, *Ayima*, Tam.; *Pera*, *Pela*, Mal.; *Bambwe*, Burm.

A large deciduous tree, l. membranous, obovate, narrowed into a short marginate petiole, crenate, sec. n. prominent, 10–12 pair. Fl. 2–4 in. across, sessile, with an unpleasant smell, each supported by 3 unequal bracts, a few fl. clustered at the ends of branchlets, petals white or greenish-white, 1–2 in. long, filaments purple, ovules in 2 rows in each cell. Fr. green, fleshy, 2–3 in. diam.

Subhimalayan tract, from the Jumna eastwards. Throughout Bengal, the Central Provinces, the Peninsula and Burma. Common in Savannahs. Fl. with young l. in March and April. Ceylon, very common. *C. sphærica*, Roxb.; Wight Ic. t. 147, Chittagong, supposed to differ by acute petals and 6 rows of ovules in each cell, is doubtful. 2. **C. herbacea**, Roxb. Cor. Pl. t. 217 (*Lapkan*, Oudh), grasslands in the Subhimalayan tract from the Jumna eastwards. Bengal and Burma. A small undershrub, with a thick woody rootstock, which produces annually (after the fires of the hot season) herbaceous shoots with cuneate dentate leaves and large beautiful purple fl., each supported by 2 oblong bracts, on a short bracteate raceme, pedicels 1–2 in. long, fr. 1–1½ in. diam.

Planchonia andamanica, King in Journ. As. Soc. Beng. 70. 142. Andamans. An evergreen tree, wood heavy, l. broadly elliptic, blade 3–4, petiole ¾ in. long, fl. 2 in. long, in short racemes, pedicels 1–2 in. long, stamens ∞, those of the inner series without anthers. This probably is *P. valida*, Kurz F. Fl. I. 500 and *P. littoralis* of Fl. Brit. Ind. ii. 511.

ORDER LII. MELASTOMACEÆ. Gen. Pl. i. 725.

Mostly herbaceous, some shrubs, rarely trees, l. opposite, entire or nearly so, the majority of genera with 3–7 basal nerves, stip. 0. No translucent glands in the l. Fl. regular, bisexual, calyx-tube entirely or partially adnate to the ovary, more or less prolonged beyond it, segments 4 or 5, deciduous. Stamens twice the number of calyx-segments, inserted with the petals on the edge of calyx-tube, filaments inflexed in bud, connective generally prolonged and often much enlarged. Ovary 4-celled, placentas axile, ovules numerous. In *Memecylon* ovary 1-celled, placenta free central, ovules few.

Except *Memecylon*, the genera here described have vascular bundles, sometimes consisting of phloëm only, in the pith, and several (*Melastoma*, *Osbeckia*) have such bundles (leaf-traces) in the bark also. *Memecylon* and *Pternandra* have strands of Phloëm in the wood.

A. Seeds numerous. Basal nerves prominent, 3–7.
    Stamens twice the number of petals, unequal.
        Apex of ovary bristly, fr. pulpy . . . . . 1. MELASTOMA.
        Apex of ovary glabrous.
            Fl. in long terminal panicles. Capsule 8-ribbed. 2. OXYSPORA.
            Fl. in axillary compound cymes. Fr. pulpy . PTERNANDRA (p. 333).
    Stamens twice the number of petals, equal.
        Calyx-tube clothed with stellate hairs or pectinate scales . . . . 3. OSBECKIA.
        Calyx-tube glabrous. Usually epiphytic.
            Capsule 4–6-valved . . . . KENDRICKIA (p. 334).
            Fruit a berry . . . . 4. MEDINILLA.
    Stamens as many as petals, fl. small . . . . BLASTUS (p. 335).
B. Seed one, rarely two, l. penninerved . . . . . 5. MEMECYLON.

1. MELASTOMA, Linn.; Fl. Brit. Ind. ii. 523.

Shrubs, leaves petioled, 3–7-nerved. Fl. terminal, solitary or in compact cymes, rose or purple, usually pentamerous, calyx-tube clothed with simple hairs or scales, lobes deciduous. Stamens usually 10, inserted with petals on the calyx-rim, very unequal, 5 longer, with purple anthers, connective long, produced at the base, and terminating in two lobes, alternating with 5 shorter stamens, with yellow anthers, connective not produced. Ovary adnate to the base of calyx-tube, usually 5-celled, apex clothed with bristles, ovules on large axile placentas, which become pulpy in fruit. Seeds minute. Species 40, tropical Asia and Australia. Polynesia.

1. **M. malabathricum,** Linn.; Wight Ill. t. 95, includes *M. normale*, Don; Kurz F. Fl. i. 504. Vern. *Futki*, Ass.; *Myetpyè*, Lower, *Shamè*, Upper Burma.

An evergreen shrub or small tree, branchlets, petioles and peduncles densely clothed with acute or acuminate, often serrulate scales. L. 3–5-nerved, strigose and often tomentose on the underside, blade 2–6, petiole ¼–½ in. long. Fl. purple, 2–3 in. across, calyx densely clothed with pale linear acuminate entire or serrate scales. Fr. ¼ in. diam.

Subhimalayan tract and outer hills from Nepal eastwards, ascending in Sikkim to 6,000 ft. Assam, Khasi hills. Chittagong, Andamans, Burma. Western Peninsula. Fl. throughout the year, chiefly March–July. Ceylon moist country to 3,000 ft. Seychelles. Malay Peninsula and Archipelago. China, Australia, New Caledonia. Nearly allied are: 2. **M. decemfidum,** Roxb. (*M. sanguineum*, Sims). Tenasserim, Malay Peninsula, Tonkin, China. Branchlets, petioles and peduncles clothed with long spreading bristles, l. scattered, appressed hairs above, glabrous beneath. Fl. bright purple, 2–3 in. diam., calyx-tube clothed with long shining bristly hairs. 3. **M. imbricatum,** Wall. Assam, Khasi hills, Andamans. Burma. Branchlets, petioles, peduncles and calyx clothed with closely appressed serrulate scales. L. strigose on both sides, appressed scales on nerves beneath, blade 4–9, petiole ½–1½ in. Fl. 1½ in. across, petals oblong. 4. **M. Clarkeanum,** Cogniaux in DC. Monogr. Phan. vii. 346 (*M. Houtteanum*, Kurz, not Naudin), Pegu Yoma. Tenasserim, calyx-tube clothed with ciliate pale coloured scales about ⅛ in. long.

2. OXYSPORA, DC.; Fl. Brit. Ind. ii. 525.

Large shrubs with spreading and drooping branches. L. long-petioled, ovate, acuminate, 5–7-nerved, sec. n. numerous, at right angles to main nerves. Fl. in long terminal panicles. Calyx-tube cylindric-turbinate, teeth 4, short, triangular. Stamens 8, the anthers of 4 on long filaments, purple, the others yellow. Ovary inferior, 4-celled. Capsule fusiform, dry, 8-ribbed. Seeds ∞, falcate. Species 7. India, Malay Peninsula and Archipelago.

1. **O. paniculata,** DC.; Wall. Pl. As. Rar. t. 88.

Branchlets, petioles and nerves beneath with scanty fugacious stellate tomentum and long soft bristles. Panicle ample, calyx, petals and pedicels purple or lilac, base of larger anthers deeply 2-lobed.

Outer Himalaya, from Nepal eastwards, 4-6000 ft. in Sikkim. Assam. Khasi hills. Fl. Aug.-March.—Yunnan. 2. **O. vagans,** Wall. Assam, Khasi hills. Manipur. Branchlets, petioles and nerves beneath with long, thin soft hairs, base of larger anthers shortly 2-lobed, connective spurred at base. 3. **O. cernua,** Triana. Upper Assam. Chittagong. Scandent, glabrous, leaves pale or brown beneath, blade 4–12, petiole ½–1½ in. long. Fl. rose-coloured, in long narrow drooping panicles, rachis sharply quadrangular at the base. Anther-cells of longer stamens slightly diverging at base, connective not spurred.

Pternandra caerulescens, Jack, including *P. capitellata*, Jack. Tenasserim, Malay Peninsula and Archipelago. An evergreen large shrub or small tree; l. elliptic, shortly acuminate, 3 prominent basal nerves. Fl. blue in axillary compound cymes, calyx adnate to ovary and prolonged beyond it, truncate, tesselate outside, petals 4 thick, ovate, reflexed, stamens 8, filaments short, perfect anthers 4 or 5, ovate, blunt, the others narrow. Fr. pulpy, turbinate, truncate, ⅓–¼ in. diam.

3. OSBECKIA, Linn.; Fl. Brit. Ind. ii. 513.

Hairy herbs or shrubs. Fl. large, 4- or 5-merous, in small, mostly bracteate terminal cymes. Calyx-tube campanulate, adnate to lower half of ovary and prolonged beyond it, outside usually clothed with hairs or scales, segments deciduous. Stamens 8 or 10, equal, anthers large, connective not produced at base. Ovary half-inferior, 4- or 5-celled, bristly at the apex, ovules ∞ on placentas radiating from the axis. Capsule enclosed in calyx-tube and partially adnate to it, the free apex 4–5 valved, seeds numerous, kidney-shaped. Species 30–40, nearly all Indian. Only a few of the larger and more common kinds are mentioned here.

1. **O. rostrata**, Don. Subhimalayan tract, from Nepal eastwards. Assam, Khasi hills, East Bengal. Burma. Tonkin. A tall shrub, stem erect, undivided, quadrangular, l. often in whorls of 3, blade 3–8, pet. ⅓–½ in. Cymes compound, spreading, calyx densely stellate-hairy, petals 1½ in. long, free portion of fruiting calyx as long as and narrower than fruit. 2. **O. crinita**, Benth. Sikkim, 4–8,000 ft. Khasi hills. Muleyit, Tenasserim 7,000 ft. A much branched shrub, clothed with long spreading hairs, fl. purple or pure white, calyx densely clothed with stellate hairs, petals ¾ in. long, free portion of fruiting calyx as long as and narrower than fr. 3. **O. stellata**, Wall.; Collett Simla Fl. 190, fig. 56. Outer Himalaya, from the Sutlej eastwards, in Sikkim to 6,000 ft. Naga hills at 5,000 ft. Clothed with appressed rigid hairs, fl. purple in compact terminal clusters, calyx densely covered with stellate hairs, petals 1 in. long, free portion of fruiting calyx much shorter than fr. 4. **O. nepalensis**, Hook. Subhimalayan tract and outer hills, ascending to 5,000 ft., from Nepal eastwards. Assam, Khasi hills. Hills east of Bhamo at 4,000 ft. Yunnan. Branches sharply quadrangular, often narrowly winged, young shoots with stiff appressed hairs, l. nearly sessile, oblong lanceolate, softly hairy on both surfaces, fl. purple or white, in ample corymbiform compound cymes, supported by large concave bracts, hairy on back, calyx-tube with broad flat persistent scales, fringed with bristles, 5 of them on the limb, alternating with the deciduous segments. Fr. ovoid, free portion of calyx-tube very short.

Kendrickia Walkeri, Hook f.; Bedd. Ic. t. 271. Anamalai hills, Ceylon. An epiphytic climbing glabrous shrub, l. fleshy, ovate, elliptic or ovate-lanceolate, three basal nerves and higher up on the midrib two sec. n., petioles short, stems and branches creeping up trees, the leaves on these small, distichous, those on the fl. shoots larger, 2–3 in. long, all round the branch. Fl. large, in few-fld. terminal umbels, calyx red, produced slightly beyond ovary, petals 4, fleshy, 1–1¼ in. long, bright rose cold., stamens 8, nearly equal, anthers opening by pores, connective produced at base into a short horn-like process.

FIG. 140.
Medinilla rubicunda, Blume, ½.

4. MEDINILLA, Gaud.; Fl. Brit. Ind. ii. 546.

Shrubs, often epiphytic, l. mostly glabrous. Fl. 4- or 5-merous, white or rose, in terminal or axillary cymes. Calyx-limb truncate or obscurely toothed. Stamens 8 or 10, equal or nearly so, anthers opening by pores, connective with 2 tubercles and a short spur at the base of anthers. Ovary usually adnate to the calyx by 8 or 10 plates, between which in bud the anthers are included, the filaments being bent down, ovules on an axile placenta. Berry crowned by the calyx-limb. Species 100, Eastern Peninsula, Ceylon, Malay Archipelago, Mascarene and Fiji Islands.

A. Fl. in axillary cymes.

1. **M. rubicunda**, Blume. Sikkim 3–6,000 ft. Khasi hills. Assam (Makúm Forest D. B. Apr. 1879). A shrub, frequently epiphytic, branches thick, almost fleshy. L.

elliptic, 3-nerved, often a second pair higher up, blade 3–6 in., petiole short. Fl. pink, anthers dark blue, fr. ovoid, red or black when ripe, edible. 2. **M. Beddomei,** C. B. Clarke (*M. radicans,* Bedd. Ic. t. 184). Evergreen forests of the Western Ghats from Coorg southwards. A fleshy epiphyte, l. thick-fleshy, obtuse, nearly orbicular, 1½ in. Fl. 1½ in. long, solitary, on axillary peduncles, petals 4, pure white, spathulate. 3. **M. malabarica,** Bedd. Ic. t. 157. Nilgiris, western slopes. Anamalais. Epiphytic, l. very fleshy, elliptic, prominently 3- occasionally 5-nerved. Peduncles axillary, sometimes several together, 3–5-fld. Fl., peduncles and pedicels of a brilliant crimson.

B. Fl. in terminal cymes.

4. **M. himalayana,** Hook f. Sikkim 2,500–6,000 ft. Khasi hills. L. nearly sessile, broadly elliptic, ramifications of cymes slender, pedicels divaricate in fruit. Fl. ¾ in. across, rose coloured. 5. **M. pauciflora,** Hook. f. Darjiling. Branchlets obtusely quadrangular, l. sessile, cymes few-fld.

Blastus cochinchinensis, Lour. Assam (Nambar Forest, March 1879 D.B.). China, Tonkin, Cochin China, Formosa. A shrub, young shoots and young l. clothed with round resinous scales, l. elliptic-lanceolate, blade 3–6, petiole ½–1 in. long, 3 basal nerves joined by distant sec. n. Fl. small, tetramerous, white, on minutely tubercled pedicels in sessile umbels sometimes axillary, more often from the axils of fallen leaves, stamens 4, equal. Capsule tightly enclosed by the calyx, loculicidally 4-valved. Seeds minute, numerous, on a central 4-winged placentiferous axis, at both ends long acuminate, falcate.

5. MEMECYLON, Linn.; Fl. Brit. Ind. ii. 553.

Evergreen glabrous shrubs or trees. L. coriaceous, penninerved, sec. n. often obscure, rarely apparently 3-nerved. Fl. blue or white, tetramerous, in lateral compound, often umbelliform cymes, or sessile in compact fascicles. Free portion of calyx produced far beyond and generally much wider than the ovary. Stamens 8, equal, anthers small opening by slits, connective generally large, fleshy, prolonged considerably below the anthers. Ovary inferior 1-celled, apex glabrous, surmounted by a disk, frequently with 8 radiating grooves, style long, filiform. Fr. more or less fleshy, surmounted by the calyx-limb, 1-, rarely 2-seeded, cotyledons convolute. Species about 130, most in India, the Malay Peninsula and Archipelago, several in tropical Africa, a few in Polynesia and Australia.

A. Leaves petiolate, acute at both ends, elliptic or elliptic-lanceolate, fl. pedicelled, in pedunculate cymes.

1. **M. edule,** Roxb. Cor. Pl. t. 82 (1795).—Syn. *M. umbellatum,* Burm. f. Fl. Ind. 87 (1768) (which may have to take precedence of the well-known name *M. edule*); *M. tinctorium,* Koenig; Wight Ill. t. 93; *M. ramiflorum,* Lam. Vern. *Nirasu,* Uriya; *Anjun, Anjani, Kurpa,* Mar.; *Udatalli,* Kan.; *Alli,* Tel.; *Kassan, Kayan,* Tam.

FIG. 141.—Memecylon edule, Roxb. fr. fl. ½.

A shrub or small tree, l. 2–4 in. long, sec. n. more or less obscure. Cymes pedunculate, rarely axillary, generally above the scars of fallen l. Fl. brilliant blue, calyx sometimes pink. Fr. fleshy, edible, black when ripe, ¼ in. diam.

Western Peninsula, mostly on the coast. Inland mostly in evergreen and semi-evergreen scrub. Orissa, Assam, Silhet, Tenasserim. Fl. C. S. Fr. H. S. Combs made of the wood. Ceylon, Malay Peninsula and Archipelago. Includes *M. ovatum, punctatum* and *scutellatum*, Kurz F. Fl. i. 512, 518. 2. **M. angustifolium**, Wight Ic. t. 276. Banks of streams, Tinnevelli ghats. Ceylon, low country to 2,000 ft. A small shrub, branchlets obtusely quadrangular, l. linear-lanceolate, blade 2–3 in., narrowed into petiole ⅛–¼ in. long, sec. n. invisible. Umbels many-fld., on short peduncles, fl. bright purplish-blue, pedicels slender, fr. ⅓ in. diam. black-purple. 3. **M. Helferi**, Cogn. (*M. angustifolium*, var. *Helferi*, C. B. Clarke). Tenasserim and Andamans, similar but branchlets sharply quadrangular.

4. **M. andamanicum**, King in Journ. As. Soc. Beng. 69. 85, Andamans, Nicobars. A shrub, l. pale beneath, ovate-lanceolate, long acuminate, blade 2–3, petiole ¼ in. Peduncles slender, ¼–½ in. long, in pairs from the axils of l. or of fallen l., bearing bracteate corymbiform compound cymes. Fr. ½ in. diam. 5. **M. plebejum**, Kurz, Khasi hills. Pegu, Tenasserim. A small tree, l. long acuminate, blade 3–4, petiole ⅛ in. long, sec. n. slender but usually distinct. 6. **M. grande**, Retz. Khasi hills, Mergui, sec. n. distinct, blade 3–7, narrowed into petiole, ¼ in. long, probably the same as *M. celastrinum*, Kurz.

7. **M. elegans**, Kurz. Andamans, very common. A shrub, bark pale, branchlets sharply 4-angled, sometimes winged, sec. n. almost invisible. Cymes lax, often in pairs, peduncle longer than petiole, free portion of calyx much wider than ovary, petals blue. Fr. globose, ½ in. diam. 8. **M. pauciflorum**, Blume, Chittagong, Andamans, Tenasserim, Malay Peninsula. A small tree, branchlets quadrangular, l. elliptic-rhomboid 1–1½ in. long, petiole very short, sec. n. barely visible. Cymes often in pairs, 7–10-fld., pedicels slender, free part of calyx shallow-cup-shaped, more than twice the width of ovary, segments triangular, acute. Fr. ⅜ in. diam. 9. **M. gracile**, Bedd. Ic. Pl. Ind. Or. t. 164, Travancore and Tinnevelli ghats. A large shrub or small tree, l. ovate-lanceolate, long acuminate, 1–2 in. long. Peduncles slender, drooping, 2–3-fld., bracts at the base of and bracteoles on pedicels, calyx white, petals pale blue.

B. Leaves petiolate, acute at both ends, fl. sessile or nearly so, in compact, usually sessile heads. Western species.

10. **M. Heyneanum**, Benth. (*M. jambosioides*, Wight Ic. t. 277). Common on the Tinnevelli and Travancore ghats to 2,000 ft. A shrub, branchlets terete, l. coriaceous, lanceolate, pale beneath, blade 5–8, pet. ⅓–½ in. Fl. in compact rounded axillary clusters, on bracteate tubercles, pedicels barely as long as calyx, petals blue. Fr. ⅜ in. diam. *M. discolor*, Cogniaux (*M. Heyneanum*, var. *angustifolia*, Clarke in Fl. Brit. Ind. ii. 560). Bolampatti valley, doubtless is the same species.

11. **M. Talbotianum**, sp. nova, Mahabaleshwar (D.B. Oct. 1881) Konkan (Stocks) Kanara (Ritchie, May 1853) North Kanara (Talbot, 3568, 3658, March 1896) Nilgiri and Coorg (T. Thomson). A large shrub or small tree, branchlets terete, slightly quadrangular below the nodes, l. thickly coriaceous, ovate or elliptic, shortly and obtusely acuminate, blade 3–4, narrowed into petiole ¼ in. long, sec. n. invisible. Fl. small, sessile in compact clusters on bracteate nearly sessile tubercles, connective shorter than anthers, fr. yellow, ¼ in. diam., pericarp thickly coriaceous. Somewhat resembles *M. urceolatum*, but fl. entirely different.

12. **M. capitellatum**, Linn. Trimen Handb. Ceylon t. 41; Bedd. Fl. Sylv. t. 206 A. Tinnevelli and Travancore ghats to 2,000 ft. Ceylon, low country to 1,000 ft., in both moist and dry regions, common. A shrub or small tree, branchlets terete, l. 2–5 in., narrowed into very short petiole, sec. n. slender but distinct, intramarginal veins having the appearance of basal nerves. Fl. violet-blue, sessile, in small heads at the ends of stiff peduncles ¼–1½ in. long, from the axils of present or fallen l. Free part of calyx shallow, mouth ⅛ in. wide, segments conspicuous, disk rays winged. Fr. black-purple, ⅓–½ in. diam. crowned with the persistent calyx-segments.

C. Leaves acute at both ends, sometimes rounded at base, fl. in compound cymes, sessile or nearly so. Eastern species.

13. **M. Griffithianum**, Naud., Mergui, branchlets winged, l. lanceolate, base acute or rounded, pale beneath, 5–7 in. long, petiole very short, sec. n. indistinct. 14. **M. cerasiforme**, Kurz, Chittagong, l. coriaceous, acuminate, blade 2–4, narrowed into pet. ¼ in. long. Fr. ½–⅜ in. diam. bluish-black.

D. Leaves sessile or nearly so, base cordate or rounded.

15. **M. malabaricum**, Cogniaux.—Syn. *M. amplexicaule*, Roxb. var. *malabarica*, Fl. Brit. Ind. ii. 559; *M. amplexicaule*, Wight Ic. t. 279; *M. umbellatum*, Bedd. Fl. Sylv. t. 206.

A shrub or small tree, branchlets round, l. coriaceous, sessile or nearly so, oblong-lanceolate from a cordate, often amplexicaul base, 2–6 in. long, sec. n. generally obscure. Fl. on slender pedicels, in 10- to many-fld. umbels, peduncles very short, thickened at the end, numerous small bracts at the base of pedicels. Free part of calyx wide-campanulate $\frac{1}{9}$–$\frac{1}{10}$ in. at mouth, anthers much shorter than connective. Fr. black $\frac{1}{12}$ in. diam.

Western ghats down to the coast, from North Kanara to Travancore, mostly in evergreen forests. Fl. Feb.–June. **M. amplexicaule**, Roxb. is an eastern species from Penang, sec. n. and intramarginal veins prominent beneath, calyx $\frac{1}{8}$ in. wide at mouth, anther cells nearly as long as connective. 16. **M. deccanense**, C. B. Clarke, Western Peninsula, imperfectly known, possibly only a form of 15, l. membranous, narrower than 15. 17. **M. Wightii**, Thwaites, Kanara, Ceylon, differs from 15 by branchlets acutely quadrangular and winged.

18. **M. amabile**, Bedd. Ic. Pl. Ind. Or. t. 168. South Kanara ghats, to 2,000 ft. A large shrub or small tree, branchlets acutely quadrangular, l. 2–3 in. long, sec. n. obscure, fl. small, deep blue, pedicels slender, in many-fld. often compound axillary umbels, peduncle $\frac{3}{4}$ in. long. 19. **M. terminale**, Dalz., evergreen forests of North Kanara, a large shrub, very similar to 18 and possibly not specifically distinct. Peduncles often in the axils of the uppermost l., hence appearing terminal. Fr. globose $\frac{1}{3}$ in. diam.

20. **M. caeruleum**, Jack. Andamans, Tenasserim, Malay Peninsula and Archipelago. A shrub, branches terete, often quadrangular below the nodes. L. sessile, coriaceous, ovate or ovate-lanceolate, 3–6 in. long. Fl. deep steel-blue, in shortly pedunculate axillary bracteate compound cymes. Fr. elongate-ellipsoid, crowned by the deep-cup-shaped calyx-limb, $\frac{3}{8}$ in. long. 21. **M. Kurzii**, King in Journ. As. Soc. Beng. 69. 77. Nicobar islands. A shrub, l. nearly sessile, thinly coriaceous, 8–10 in. long, sec. n. straight, 15–20 pair, joined by an intramarginal vein at a distance from edge. Cymes 3–4-fld., from the axils of fallen leaves, calyx mouth $\frac{1}{6}$ in. wide, wavy, with 4 broad teeth. Fr. ellipsoid, $\frac{3}{4}$ in. long.

ORDER LIII. LYTHRACEÆ. Gen. Pl. i. 773 (*Lythrarieæ*).

Herbs, shrubs or trees, l. simple, entire, generally opposite, stipules 0, or minute. Calyx cup-shaped, persistent, segments often with intermediate teeth, valvate, petals imbricate and crumpled in bud, sometimes wanting, filaments inflexed in the bud. Ovary superior, sometimes adnate to the bottom of calyx, inferior in *Punica*. Ovules numerous. Seeds many, without albumen.

In Engler u. Prantl iii. 7. p. 1, 16, 22, the genera here described are classed under three separate Orders, *Lythraceæ*, *Sonneratiaceæ* (*Sonneratia*, *Duabanga*, *Crypteronia*) and (with inferior ovary) *Punicaceæ* (*Punica*).

A. Ovary superior, fl. bisexual, symmetric.
  Inland trees or shrubs, fr. a dry capsule.
    Calyx-segments 6, capsule 3–6-valved . . . 1. LAGERSTRŒMIA.
    Calyx-segments 6, capsule circumsciss. . . . PEMPHIS (p. 339).
    Calyx-segments usually 7, capsule 4–8-valved. . 2. DUABANGA.
    Calyx-segments 4, capsule bursting irregularly . LAWSONIA (p. 340).
  Litoral trees, fr. fleshy, indehiscent . . . . 3. SONNERATIA.
B. Ovary superior, fl. bisexual, zygomorphic . . . WOODFORDIA (p. 341).
C. Ovary superior, fl. male and bisexual, petals 0 . . 4. CRYPTERONIA.
D. Ovary inferior . . . . PUNICA (p. 341).

1. LAGERSTRŒMIA, Linn.; Fl. Brit. Ind. ii. 575.

Trees or shrubs; l. nearly opposite, or the uppermost alternate, entire. Fl. in axillary or terminal panicles, calyx-tube broadly turbinate or hemispherical, cleft into 6 ovate lobes, petals unguiculate, edge undulate. Stamens numerous, inserted at or above the bottom of calyx-tube, 6 often stouter and longer than the others, anthers versatile. Ovary free, 3–6-celled, style filiform, ovules numerous, attached to axile placentas. Capsule coriaceous, 3–6-celled, girt at base by the persistent calyx, dehiscing loculicidally into 3–6 valves. Seeds winged.

A. Calyx-tube smooth, neither ribbed nor grooved.

1. **L. parviflora**, Roxb. Cor. Pl. t. 66; Wight Ic. t. 69; Bedd. Fl. Sylv. t. 31. Vern. *Dhaura*, *Asidh*, *Lendia*, *Seja*, Hind.; *Bonda*, *Bhondara*, Mar.; *Chennangi*, Tel.; *Channangi*, Kan.; *Ventek*, Tam.; *Zaung balè*, Upper Burma.

A large tree, youngest shoots and leaves, as well as inflorescence, pubescent with very short simple hairs. L. opposite, sessile or very shortly petiolate, 2–4 in. long. Fl. white, fragrant, $\frac{1}{4}$ in. across, in axillary and terminal panicles, pedicels slender. Calyx not ribbed, hoary, from the base to the end of segments $\frac{1}{5}$–$\frac{1}{4}$ in. long. A raised line inside at the base of segments. Segments erect, ultimately appressed to the capsule, which is $\frac{3}{4}$–1 in. long.

Subhimalayan tract from the Jumna eastwards, ascending to 3,000 ft. Assam, Lower Bengal, Central India and the Western Peninsula in deciduous forests. Upper Burma. The l. are shed March–April, young foliage in May. Fl. H. S. Fr. R. S., remains long on the tree. A form with larger greenish-white fl. on few-fld. axillary peduncles, in Bamboo forest, Shwebo district, Upper Burma, *Tawkyetsa*, Burm. (Smales, May 1901).

2. **L. lanceolata**, Wall.—Syn. *L. microcarpa*, Wight Ic. t. 109; Bedd. Fl. Sylv. t. 30. Vern. *Nana*, Mar.; *Nandi*, Kan.; *Ventek*, Tam.

A large tree, l. sometimes alternate, glabrous, bluish-white beneath, blade 2–4, petiole $\frac{1}{4}$–$\frac{1}{2}$ in., sec. n. prominent, arching, 6–10 pair. Fl. in large terminal panicles. Calyx hoary; segments reflexed in fl., not appressed to capsule, no raised line at the base of segments. Capsule $\frac{1}{3}$–$\frac{1}{2}$ in. long.

West side of the Peninsula, extending east as far as Bellary. Fl. H. S. 3. **L. Thomsoni**, Koehne MSS., Mysore and Karnatik, similar but l. larger and softly tomentose beneath. 4. **L. indica**, Linn.; Wight Ic. t. 86, indigenous in China and possibly on the Shan hills in Upper Burma; cultivated in gardens throughout India on account of

FIG. 142.—Lagerstrœmia lanceolata, Wall. Fr. fl. $\frac{1}{2}$.

its fl., 1½–2 in. across, rose-coloured, white or lilac, l. generally alternate, petals long clawed, much curled.

The following imperfectly known species have the calyx densely clothed with ferrugineous or fulvous stellate tomentum: 5. **L. Rottleri**, C. B. Clarke, Deccan, l. stellately tomentose beneath. 6. **L. calyculata**, Kurz (*Pyinmabyu*, Burm.). Forests east of Taungoo, evergreen, l. puberulous and strongly net-veined beneath.

B. Calyx-tube with as many ribs as segments.

7. **L. villosa**, Wall.; Kurz F. Fl. i. 524. Vern. *Zaung gale*, Lower, *Zaung bale*, *Zinbye*, Upper Burma.

A small or middle-sized tree, branchlets, petioles and underside of l. softly pubescent, hairs simple, l. broadly lanceolate, blade 2–3, petiole $\frac{1}{6}$–$\frac{1}{5}$ in., stipules small but distinct. Fl. white, slightly scented, in compact head-like softly pubescent panicles at the ends of branches, pedicels shorter than calyx-tube. Calyx turbinate with 6 winged ribs, petals minute. Capsule ovoid-oblong, ½ in. long, base supported by the 6-ribbed calyx. Seed angular, with the broad triangular wing ⅓ in. long.

Pegu and Upper Burma, often in Eng forest. Fl. H. S.

Specimens, in bud only, collected by the late Sir Henry Collett in Upper Burma, l. glabrous, broadly lanceolate, blade 5, petiole ¼ in. ridges on calyx 5–6, almost winged, allied to the Philippine species *L. pirifolia*, Koehne.

C. Ribs or grooves on calyx-tube twice the number of segments.

8. **L. Flos Reginæ**, Retz.; Roxb. Cor. Pl. t. 65 (*L. Reginæ*); Wight Ic. t. 413; Bedd. Fl. Sylv. t. 29.—Syn. *L. speciosa*, Pers.; Koehne in Engler Jahrb. iv. 28. Vern. *Jarul*, Beng.; *Ajhar*, Ass.; *Taman*, Mar.; *Challa*, Kan.; *Pumarathu*, Tam.; *Manimarathu*, Mal.; *Pyinma*, Lower, *Eikmwe*, Upper Burma.

A large tree, l. glabrous, blade 6–10, petiole stout, ¼–½ in. long, fl. purplish-lilac, 2–3 in. across, in ample terminal panicles, calyx strongly 12-ribbed, ribs rounded, broader than the furrows between, segments long-triangular, stamens of equal length. Capsule broadly ovoid, ¾–1 in. long, the lower third enclosed in the persistent calyx, seed with wing ½–¾ in. long, pale brown.

Assam, Chittagong. Lower Burma, chiefly near river banks. Foot of the Western ghats ascending to 2,000 ft. Leafless during the hot season, fl. May–June. Ceylon, moist low country, Malay Peninsula. 9. **L. macrocarpa**, Kurz (*Kônpyinma*). Upper Burma, Pegu, Maulmein, Thaungyin (D. B. March 1862). Chiefly in Eng forests. A small tree, nearly allied to 8, but l. larger, petiole ½–¾ in., fl. in short terminal panicles, calyx furrowed but not ribbed.

10. **L. hypoleuca**, Kurz, Andamans, common. A large tree, l. glabrous, whitish-glaucous beneath, elliptic-oblong, blade 6–8, petiole ¼–⅓ in. long. Fl. lilac, 1–1½ in. across, in elongate terminal panicles, calyx tube turbinate, with 12 prominent ribs. Fr. ovoid, ⅞–1 in. long, base supported by calyx, the segments of which are reflexed. 11. **L. floribunda**, Jack (*Pyimma byu*). Country between Sitang and Salween rivers. Attaran, Thaungyin. Mergui. Malay Peninsula, Siam, China. A large tree, l. almost sessile, elliptic-oblong 5–7 in. long, when young stellate-tomentose beneath, sec. n. prominent, terminating in arching, intramarginal veins. Fl. rose-coloured, turning white, in ample terminal panicles, clothed (as well as calyx) with dense stellate ferrugineous tomentum. Calyx turbinate with 12 prominent ridges, segments short. Capsule ovoid, ¾ in. long, the lower fourth enclosed in the calyx.

12. **L. tomentosa**, Presl. Vern. *Lèzah*, Burm.

A large tree, branchlets, petioles, underside of l., inflorescence and calyx densely clothed with stellate tomentum, l. lanceolate, blade 3–6, petiole ¼ in. long, sec. and tertiary nerves prominent. Fl. white, 1 in. across, in terminal pyramidal panicles, calyx campanulate-turbinate, ribs 10–12, segments short, triangular. Capsule ovoid, ⅔ in. long, lower third enclosed in the persistent calyx.

Pegu, Tenasserim, Upper Burma. Fl. H. S.

Pemphis acidula, Forst.; Bedd. Man. t. 14 f. 5.—Syn. *Maclelandia Griffithiana*, Wight

Ic. t. 1996. Sea coast and tidal backwaters on the West Coast, from Malabar southwards, also in Tinnevelli. Coast of Tenasserim and the Andamans.—Ceylon. Tropical coasts of East Africa to Australia and Polynesia. A grey silky-hairy shrub or small tree, l. thick, fleshy, numerous, ½–1½ in. long, readily disarticulating, fl. pink, solitary, axillary, hexamerous, calyx campanulate, 12-ribbed, segments short, with minute teeth between, stamens 12, ovary free, imperfectly 3-celled. Capsule enclosed for ¾ of its length in the persistent calyx-tube, opening by the top coming off like a cap, seeds numerous.

2. DUABANGA, Ham.; Fl. Brit. Ind. ii. 578.

Species 2, one in the Indian Archipelago.

D. sonneratioides, Ham.; Kurz F. Fl. i. 525. Vern. *Lampatia*, Nep.; *Myaukngo*, Lower, *Maū*, Upper Burma.

A tall handsome tree, wood greyish-brown, branchlets drooping with the weight of the flowers. L. opposite, distichous, from a cordate base oblong, tapering to the end, blade 7–15, petiole stout, ⅛–¼ in., sec., tertiary and intramarginal nerves prominent. Fl. 2–3 in. across, in terminal corymbs, buds large globose. Calyx cup-shaped, segments 6–8, usually 7, thick triangular. Petals white, crumpled, falling off early with the stamens. Stamens ∞, in a single row, filaments as well as style inflexed in bud. Ovary adnate to the calyx at its base, 4–8-celled, ovules ∞, stigma 4–8-lobed. Capsule coriaceous, opening loculicidally into 4–8 valves, supported by the thick spreading calyx. Seeds ∞, minute, testa produced at both ends into long pointed tails.

Subhimalayan tract from Nepal eastwards, ascending to 3,000 ft. Assam, Khasi hills, Manipur, Chittagong. Andamans and Nicobars. Burma, common near streams. Fl. Jan.–April.—Perak. Tonkin. Yunnan.

Lawsonia alba, Lam.; Wight Ill. t. 87; Bedd. Manual t. 14 fig. 6. *The Henna Plant.* Vern. *Mendi*, *Mehudi*, Hind.; *Manidi*, Sind; *Goranti*, Kan.; *Gorinta*, Tel.; *Dan*, Burm. Indigenous in Arabia and Persia, probably also indigenous in the drier parts of the Peninsula and Ceylon (sand dunes near Tuticorin. D. B. Feb. 1882). Cultivated and naturalized throughout India. A glabrous shrub, branchlets often spinescent, l. opposite 1–1½ in. long. Fl. greenish-yellow, very fragrant, tetramerous, ¼ in. across, on short slender pedicels, in large terminal panicled cymes. Stamens usually 8, in pairs between the petals. Ovary free, 2–4-celled. Capsule globose, base supported by the persistent calyx, pericarp brittle, bursting irregularly. Seeds numerous, angular, truncate, testa thick, cotyledons flat, orbicular. Leaves powdered and made into a paste, used to stain finger-nails, teeth and beard.

3. SONNERATIA, Linn. f.; Fl. Brit. Ind. ii. 579.

Litoral evergreen trees, entirely glabrous. L. opposite, entire. Calyx thickly coriaceous, usually 4- or 6- (rarely 7- or 8-) lobed. Petals none or as many as calyx-segments. Stamens ∞, inserted at the mouth of calyx-tube, inflexed in bud. Ovary nearly free, many-celled, placentas thick, axile, ovules ∞. Fr. fleshy, indehiscent, supported by the persistent calyx, base adnate to calyx. Seeds numerous, angular. Species 4–6, tropics of the old world.

A. Petals as many as calyx-segments.

1. S. acida, Linn. f.; Wight Ic. t. 340; Bedd. Fl. Sylv. Manual t. 15, fig. 1, Vern. *Ora*, *Orcha*, Sundr.; *Tiwar*, Mar.; *Blatti*, *Thirala*, Mal.; *Tabu*, *Tamu*. Burm.

A small tree, attaining 30 ft., l. obovate, gradually tapering into a broad short petiole, 2–4 in. long. Fl. 2 in. across, solitary at the ends of branchlets, calyx-tube shallow, not ribbed, segments 6–8, usually 6, acute, longer than tube, petals dark purple, linear, acuminate, 1½ in. long. Fr. depressed-globular, 2–2½ in. diam., edible.

Sundriban. Coast from Chittagong to Tenasserim, ascending the rivers as far as the tides. Delta of the Indus. Coast and tidal waters of the Peninsula. Fl. R. S.

Ceylon, Malay Peninsula and Archipelago. This and other species of *Sonneratia*, as well as a few other Mangrove trees, send up from their widely spreading horizontal roots vertical branches with soft pith-like wood, which serve to facilitate the interchange of gas between the atmosphere and the roots buried in the mud of the tidal swamp.

B. Petals none.

2. **S. apetala,** Ham. Vern. *Keora*, Sundr.; *Tivar*, Mar.; *Kanbala*, Burma.
A gregarious tree, attaining 50 ft., wood reddish-brown, hard, branches pendulous, foliage light glaucous-green. L. lanceolate, blade 3–5, petiole $\frac{1}{3}$–$\frac{1}{2}$ in. long. Fl. whitish, 1 in. across, in 3–5-fld. terminal corymbs, calyx not ribbed, segments 4, longer than tube, stigma large peltate, top convex. Capsule depressed-globose, $\frac{3}{4}$ in. diam.

Sundriban, banks of tidal rivers. Pegu and Tenasserim, tidal forests. Coasts of the Konkan. Fl. April–June. Ceylon. 3. **S. alba,** Smith, Andamans, Mergui, Konkan, Ceylon (rare). Coasts of tropical Africa, Asia and Australia. A shrub or small tree, l. broadly ovate, fl. 1½–2 in. across, usually 2 or 3 at the ends of branchlets, calyx-segments 6, rarely 7 or 8, fruiting calyx ribbed, ribs as many as segments. 4. **S. Griffithii,** Kurz. Coasts of Pegu and Tenasserim, ascending the rivers as far as the tide. Similar to *S. acida* but without petals. Regarded by King in Journ. As. Soc. Beng. vol. 67, 11, as an apetalous form of *S. acida*.

Woodfordia floribunda, Salisb.; Collett Simla Fl. 193, fig. 57.—Syn. *W. tomentosa*, Bedd. Man. t. 14, f. 4; *W. fruticosa*, Kurz F. Fl. i. 518; *Grislea tomentosa*, Roxb. Cor. Pl. t. 31. Vern. *Dha, Dhawi, Dhewtie, Dhau, Dhawla*, Hind.; *Icha*, Kol; *Dhaiti*, Mar.; *Jaji, Velakkai*, Tel.; *Yet kyi, Pattagyi*, Upper Burma. Widely spread, from tropical Africa, Arabia to India, ascending to 5,000 ft. in the Himalaya, and to both Peninsulas. China and the Indian Archipelago. A large ornamental shrub, more or less pubescent, l. opposite, sometimes in whorls of 3, sessile, from a broad base lanceolate, 2–4 in. long, underside white with black dots. Fl. numerous, hexamerous, slightly zygomorphic, bright brick-red, in round lateral clusters, generally from the axils of fallen leaves, pedicels dilated above. Calyx tubular curved, coloured, mouth oblique, segments short, alternating with minute teeth, petals 6, short, linear-lanceolate. Stamens 12, inserted near the bottom of calyx, filaments long-exserted, ovary 2-celled. Capsule $\frac{1}{3}$–$\frac{1}{2}$ in. long, enclosed by calyx-tube, splitting irregularly. Fl. used for dyeing silk.

4. CRYPTERONIA, Blume; Fl. Brit. Ind. ii. 573.

Evergreen trees, l. opposite. Fl. polygamous, male and bisexual on different branches, possibly on different trees. Fl. minute, in elongate panicled racemes. Calyx cup-shaped, adnate to base of ovary, segments 5, rarely 4, petals 0. ♂: Stamens long exserted, alternating with calyx-segments, surrounding a rudimentary ovary, anther cells on the edges of a broad connective. ⚥: Stamens short, ovary 2-celled, style cylindric. Capsule 2-celled, 2-valved, crowned by the two halves of the persistent style. Seeds numerous, testa produced at each end. Species 5, India and Indian Archipelago.

C. paniculata, Blume; Kurz F. Fl. i. 519; King in Journ. As. Soc. Beng. vol. 67. 5.—Syn. *C. pubescens*, Blume.—*Henslovia pubescens*, Wall. Pl. As. Rar. t. 221; *C. glabra*, Blume. Vern. *Ananbo*, Burm.
A large tree, bark silvery grey. L. elliptic, acute at both ends, glabrous or thinly pubescent beneath, blade 3–6, pet. $\frac{1}{4}$ in. long. Fl. numerous, greenish-white, calyx-teeth triangular.

Khasi hills, Chittagong. Pegu, Martaban and Tenasserim. Fl. Nov.–Feb. Malay Peninsula.

Punica Granatum, Linn.; Wight Ill. t. 97. *The Pomegranate.* Vern. *Nargosah*, Bal.; *Darūna, Dharu*, Punj.; *Anar*, Hind.; *Dalimbe*, Kan.: *Danima*, Tel. Indigenous in Persia and Afghanistan. Common in Hazara, 4–6,000 ft., apparently wild. Cultivated and naturalized from remote antiquity in India, Syria, Palestine, North Africa, Greece and Italy. A deciduous shrub or small tree, branchlets often spin-

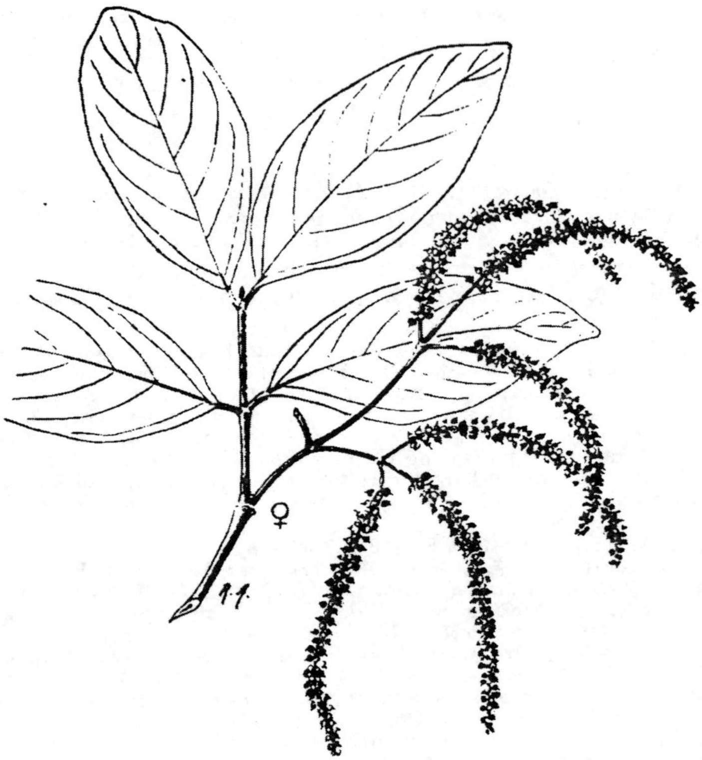

Fig. 143.—Crypteronia paniculata, Blume. ¼.

escent, l. opposite, often fascicled on arrested branchlets, oblong-lanceolate or oblanceolate, obtuse, 1–3 in. long, narrowed into a slender petiole. Ovary inferior, free part of calyx campanulate, cleft into 5–7 valvate lobes. Petals inserted in the mouth of calyx-tube, crumpled in bud. Stamens ∞, inserted at different levels below the petals, anther-cells attached to the edges of a broad connective. Carpels in several tiers on the inside of the hollow receptacle, here called calyx-tube (see remarks on p. 306 under *Combretaceæ*, and Brandis F. Flora 240), ovules numerous in each. Carpels coalesce early and form a large globose indehiscent fruit, crowned by the persistent calyx and containing under a coriaceous rind two tiers of cells, 8 in the lower, 5–9 in the upper tier. Numerous seeds in each cell, embedded in a sweet pellucid pulp. Cotyledons foliaceous, spirally convolute.

Order LIV. SAMYDACEÆ. Gen Pl. i. 794.

Trees or shrubs, l. alternate, distichous, stipules small. Fl. inconspicuous, regular, generally bisexual. Calyx persistent, tube short, segments 3–7, imbricate or valvate in bud. Petals none, or alternate with calyx-segments and similar to them in substance. Ovary free or lower portion adnate to calyx-tube, ovules numerous, attached to 2–4 parietal placentas. Capsule 2–4-valved, seeds numerous, attached to the middle of the valves. Embryo in a copious fleshy albumen.

The 2 genera here described are included under *Flacourtiaceæ* by Warburg in Engler u. Prantl iii. 6a, p. 34, 50.

Petals 0, fl. in axillary fascicles . . . . 1. Casearia.
Petals present, fl. in racemes or spikes . . . . . . 2. Homalium.

1. CASEARIA, Jacq.; Fl. Brit. Ind. ii. 591.

Trees or shrubs, l. alternate, distichous, stipules small, caducous. Fl. small, greenish-yellow, regular, usually bisexual. Calyx coriaceous, deeply 4–5-lobed, lobes imbricate, more or less persistent. Petals 0. Stamens double the number of calyx-lobes, often 8 only with a pentamerous calyx, united into a short tube with alternating staminodes. Ovary free, 1-celled, ovules numerous, attached to 3–4 parietal placentas. Capsule succulent, 3-valved. Seeds numerous, with a fleshy usually coloured aril, embryo straight, cotyledons flat. Species 120; tropical regions of both hemispheres.

Resin cavities, lined by thin-walled cells, in the leaves of most Indian species, visible as transparent dots or lines.

A. Full grown leaves glabrous.

1. **C. esculenta,** Roxb.—Syn. *C. varians*, Thw.; Bedd. Fl. Sylv. t. 208. Vern. *Mori*, Mar.; *Vella Kunnan*, Mal.

FIG. 144.—Casearia esculenta, Roxb. ½

A tree, l. thick, often coriaceous, quite entire, blade 4–6, pet. ¼–¾ in. long. Fl. glabrous, $\frac{1}{12}$ in. long, pedicel glabrous, longer than calyx. Fr. 2- or 3-valved, ellipsoid, ½–¾ in. long.

Western Ghats, from the Konkan southwards, mostly in evergreen forests. Northern Circars, Śriharikot. Tenasserim. Fl. R. S. Malay Peninsula. Ceylon, moist and dry regions, ascending to 5,000 ft. 2. **C. rubescens,** Dalz. Western Ghats, North Kanara to Coorg. A shrub, l. coriaceous, petioles and midrib of young l. red, pedicels pubescent.

3. **C. glomerata,** Roxb.—Syn. *C. graveolens*, Dalz.; Brandis F. Fl. 243; Kanjilal F. Fl. 185. Vern. *Chilla*, Hind.; *Giridi*, Uriya; *Gilchi*, Gond; *Bokhada*, Mar.

A deciduous shrub or middle-sized tree, branches long, spreading, l. more or less serrate, blade 4–8, petiole ¼–½ in. long, translucent glands (resin cavities) elongate and round. Fl. 4- or 5-merous, $\frac{1}{12}$–⅛ in. long, with an offensive smell, clustered on scaly tubercles, in the axils of leaves or of fallen l., calyx pubescent, pedicel generally longer than calyx, glabrous or pubescent. Stamens 8 or 10, alternating with hairy linear scales, half the length of stamens or more. Fr. ¾ in. long, 3-valved, glabrous. Aril orange.

Subhimalayan tract and outer ranges from the Chenab eastwards, ascending in Kumaon to 5,000, in Sikkim to 7,000 ft. Khasi hills. Burma, Upper and Lower. Singbhum, Orissa, Northern Circars, Western Ghats and country between the ghats and the coast from Surat to South Kanara. Fl. Dec.–June.—China. *C. graveolens* is supposed to differ by the pedicel being glabrous above the articulation. Specimens with hairy pedicels are known from the western, and with glabrous pedicels from the eastern region. 4. **C. andamanica,** King in Journ. As. Soc. Beng. vol. 67. 16. Andamans. A middle-sized tree, l. rigidly coriaceous, blade 6–10, petiole ¾ in. long, sec. n. very prominent beneath, fl. ⅛ in. long., glabrous, as well as pedicel.

B. Midrib and petiole of full grown l. hairy.

5. **C. tomentosa,** Roxb.; Brandis F. Fl. t. 31; Collett Simla Flora p. 197 fig. 59.—Syn *C. elliptica*, Willd.; Wight Ic. t. 1849. Vern. *Bheri*, *Chilla*, Hind.; *Tundri*, Gond; *Giridi*, Uriya; *Chilaka duddi*, Tel.

A small deciduous tree, branches spreading, all parts bitter. Branchlets and underside of leaves tomentose. L. serrate, elliptic-oblong, narrowed towards the apex, base oblique, blade 3–7, petiole ¼–½ in. long, translucent glands round or broad-elliptic. Fl. tomentose, ⅑ in. long, densely clustered on scaly axillary tubercles, calyx-segments usually 5, stamens usually 8, alternating

with short ciliate staminodes. Fr. 6-ribbed, 3-valved, seeds embedded in a red pulp, consisting of the agglomerate arils.

Subhimalayan tract from the Indus eastwards, ascending to 3,000 ft., common in deciduous forests. Salt Range, Rajputana. Central Provinces. Behar. Western Peninsula. From Burma I have not seen specimens. *C. Canziala*, Kurz F. Fl. i. 529, is doubtful. Fl. Jan.–May. The pounded fruit of this and other species is used to poison fish. Wood made into combs. *C. Lobbiana*, Turcz, very similar to 4, with more acuminate l. has been reported from Tenasserim.

6. **C. Vareca,** Roxb. Sikkim, foot of the hills. Assam (*Ban Kasseru*). Khasi hills, Cachar. A small tree, l. oblong, closely serrate, underside clothed with soft long hairs, pedicels glabrous above the articulation. Fr. ⅓ in. long, yellow, aromatic, seeds in a bright red pulp. From Burma no specimens seen.

7. **C. wynadensis,** Bedd. Ic. Pl. Ind. Or. t. 160. Common on the slopes of the Wainád. A small tree, young shoots densely aureo-villous, branches, petioles and underside of l. softly pubescent, l. membranous, elliptic-lanceolate, base entire, upper part serrate. Fl. on slender pedicels in fascicles of 6–8 in the leaf-axils. Calyx-segments hairy within, ovary and style densely hairy. 8. **C. Kurzii,** C. B. Clarke, Chittagong, Upper Burma. L. elliptic-lanceolate, more or less crenate, with long soft hairs on the underside. Fl. on slender pedicels ¼–½ in. long, in axillary 3–6 fld. fascicles.

2. HOMALIUM, Jacq.; Fl. Brit. Ind. ii. 595.

Leaves more or less crenate. Fl. small, hairy, in slender simple or panicled racemes or spikes, calyx-tube adnate to ovary, segments 4–7, narrow persistent, as well as the linear petals; round hairy glands (staminodes) opposite the sepals

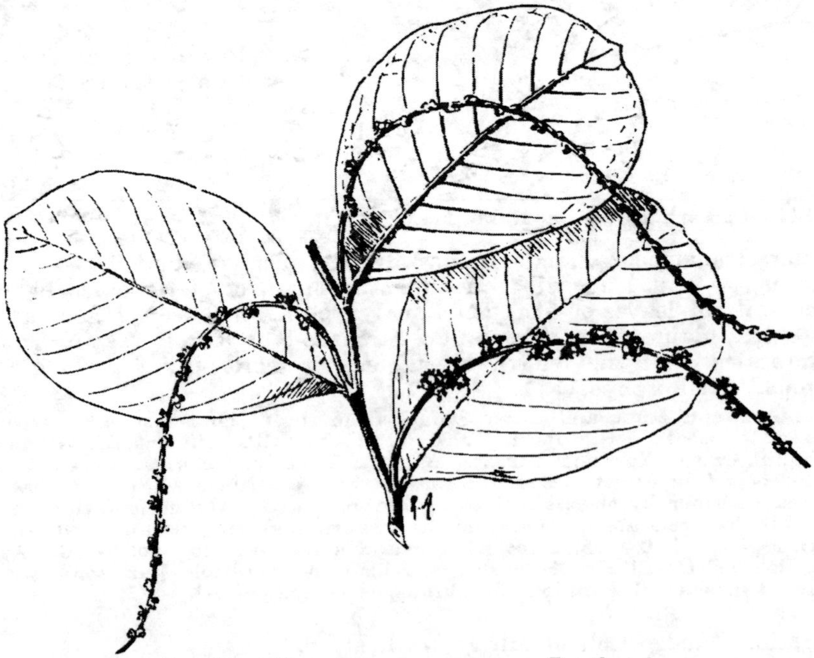

Fig. 145.—Homalium tomentosum, Benth. ½.

Stamens epipetalous, solitary or in fascicles of 2–7. Ovary half-superior, 1-celled, styles 2–6, filiform, placentas parietal, as many as styles, in the upper free portion of the ovary. Capsule 2–6-valved. Species about 70, tropics of both hemispheres.

A. Stamens solitary, opposite to petals.

1. H. tomentosum, Benth.; Kurz F. Fl. i. 531. Vern. *Myaukchaw*, Burm.

A large deciduous tree, bark thin, white, very smooth, branchlets, young leaves and inflorescence softly pubescent, l. obovate 4–6 in. long, petiole stout, very short, sec. n. 10–14 pair, straight, prominent beneath. Fl. nearly sessile, $\frac{1}{8}$ in. across, greenish, in small clusters on simple axillary spikes, longer than leaves. Calyx tomentose, segments 5 or 6, linear-oblong, petals similar to calyx-segments.

Common in deciduous forests from Chittagong to Martaban. Ganjam (Gamble). Fl. Nov.–Jan. 2. **H. minutiflorum,** Kurz, Pegu. Fl. pedicellate, minute, $\frac{1}{12}$ in. across, tetramerous, calyx-tube glabrous, turbinate, segments and petals pilose, pedicel glabrous, longer than calyx-tube. 3. **H. longifolium,** Benth. Upper Burma, Smales, April 1899 (*Pyaukseik*) Malay Peninsula. A tree, l. elliptic slightly hairy, blade 5, petiole $\frac{1}{2}$ in. long, sec. n. arching, 5–7 pair. Fl. pedicellate, tetramerous, calyx and petals hairy, tube narrowly turbinate, as long as pedicel, segments much smaller than petals. Ovules on long funicles attached to the parietal placenta at the top of the ovary. The Malayan specimens are slightly different, the above description relates to those from Upper Burma.

4. **H. zeylanicum,** Benth. Western Ghats from North Kanara southwards, in evergreen forests. A lofty, at times a small tree, l. glabrous elliptic, acuminate, base acute, blade 4–5, petiole $\frac{1}{3}$ in. long, sec. n. arching, 6–8 pair. Fl. pedicellate, hairy, $\frac{1}{3}$ in. across, petals longer than sepals, pedicels articulate. The Travancore specimens have larger fl. and the sec. n. very prominent.

5. **H. nepalense,** Benth. (*Blackwellia nepalensis*, Wall. Pl. As. Rar. t. 179). Nepal. Singhbhum-Mahendragiri and Rumpa hills. A large tree, l. glabrous, ovate, blade 4–5, narrowed into pet. $\frac{1}{3}$–$\frac{1}{2}$ in. long. Fl. fetid, nearly sessile, grey-tomentose, $\frac{1}{8}$ in. across, in axillary panicles, petals nearly equal to calyx-segments.

B. Stamens in fascicles opposite to petals.

6. **H. Griffithianum,** Kurz, Mergui, Malay Peninsula. A small tree, branchlets, petioles, midrib and inflorescence clothed with long spreading hairs. Fl. almost sessile, $\frac{1}{3}$ in. across, petals twice the length of calyx-segments, stamens in pairs before the petals. 7. **H. Schlichii, Kurz.** Chittagong,. An evergreen tree, l. glabrous, elliptic-lanceolate, blade 5, petiole $\frac{1}{3}$ in. long. Fl. slightly grey pubescent, pedicellate, $\frac{1}{4}$ in. across, stamens in threes opposite the petals, racemes in terminal hoary panicles. 8. **H. propinquum,** C. B. Clarke, is reported from Pegu.

9. **H. travancoricum,** Bedd. Fl. Sylv. t. 211. Travancore and Tinnevelli Ghats. A middle-sized tree, l. glabrous, 3–4 in. long, racemes shorter than l., fl. $\frac{1}{4}$ in. across, densely hairy, nearly sessile, petals three times the size of calyx-segments, 3 or 4 stamens opposite each petal. 10. **H. grandiflorum,** Benth., a middle-sized tree of the Malay Peninsula and Cochinchina, fl. $\frac{3}{4}$ in. across, calyx-segments enlarged after flowering, stamens 7–12 opposite each petal, has been reported from Tenasserim.

ORDER LV.—**Passifloraceæ.** 1. **Carica Papaya,** Linn.; Wight Ill. t. 106, 107. Classed in a separate order *Caricaceæ*, in Engler u. Prantl iii. 6 (*a*) 94. Vern. *Papaya*, Northern India; *Poppaya*, Tel.; *Thinbaw*, Burm. Indigenous in tropical America. Cultivated in India and in all tropical countries. A small soft-wooded fast growing tree, usually unbranched, with milky juice, l. glabrous, palmatifid, 12–24 in. across, on long hollow petioles, forming a round tuft at the top of the stem, stipules 0. Fl. pale yellow, fragrant, in axillary panicles, generally diœcious, but occasionally a few female fl. on a male plant. ♂ fl. in long drooping panicles, ♀ in short clusters. Calyx small, 5-lobed. Corolla: ♂ tubular, 5-lobed, ♀ of 5 linear deciduous petals. Stamens 10, inserted in two rows in the mouth of the corolla. Ovary free, ovules numerous, attached to 5 parietal placentas. Fr. indehiscent, fleshy, sulcate, seeds black, numerous, embedded in sweet pulp, the testa consisting of an inner hard and an outer soft layer. Embryo straight, cotyledons flat, in oily albumen. 2 **Passiflora,** Linn., is a large, chiefly American genus of shrubs, climbing with tendrils, numerous species of which are grown in gardens. Fl. bisexual, pentamerous, a corona, usually of numerous fine threads on the calyx tube inside the petals, stamens 5, filaments flat, enclosing and partly adnate to the gynophore, which bears a 1-celled ovary with ∞ ovules on 3 parietal placentas. Two species in India: 1. *P. Leschenaultii*, DC. Khasi hills, Manipur, Nilgiri and Palni hills, l. semicircular, truncate, 3-dentate, fl. 2 in. across, petals white, fr. ovoid $1\frac{1}{2}$ in. long. 2. *P. nepalensis*, Wall, Nepal, Sikkim, Khasi hills, l. entire, ovate or ovate-lanceolate, fl. $\frac{1}{3}$–$\frac{1}{2}$ in. across, fr. nearly globose $\frac{1}{4}$ in. diam.

ORDER LVI. DATISCACEÆ. Gen. Pl. i. 884. (Datisceæ.)

TETRAMELES, R. Br.; Fl. Brit. Ind. ii. 657.

T. nudiflora, R. Br. (the only species); Bedd. Fl. Sylv. t. 212.—Syn. *T. Grahamiana*, Wight Ic. t. 1956. Vern. *Yermal*, Kan.; *Chini*, Tam.; *Chini Vella Pasa*, Mal.; *Thitpôk*, Lower, *Baing*, Upper Burma.

FIG. 146.—Tetrameles nudiflora, R. Br. ½.

A very tall, fast growing deciduous tree, wood soft, trunk straight, often much buttressed at the base, bark smooth, grey, leaf-scars prominent on branchlets; petioles and young l. hairy. L. broadly ovate, base cordate, 5 basal nerves, blade 5–7, petiole 2–4 in. long, stipules 0. Fl. diœcious, tetramerous, apetalous, ♂ in panicles fasciculate at the ends of branchlets, calyx deeply cut into 5 segments, stamens 4, round a depressed disk, opposite to calyx-segments. ♀ in numerous terminal pendulous racemes, pedicels very short, ovary inferior, 8-ribbed, 1-celled, ovules ∞ on 4 parietal placentas. Capsule crowned by the persistent calyx-segments, opening at the summit, the valves terminating in the persistent styles. Seeds minute, embryo cylindrical, in scanty albumen.

Terai and outer hills, Darjeeling district ascending to 3,000 ft. Andamans. Burma, Upper and Lower. Western Ghats and Nilgiris, in Sholas and evergreen forest. L. shed early in January. Fl. Feb.–Apr. while leafless.—Ceylon. Ind. Archip.

ORDER LVII.—**Cactaceæ. Opuntia Dillenii**, Haw.; Wight Ill. t. 114. *Prickly Pear*. Vern. *Nagphana*, Hind.; *Nagajemmadu*, Tel.; *Mullugalli*, *Papaskalli*, Kan. Indigenous in South America, naturalized in India, extending North as far as the Jhelum, and ascending to 2,000 ft. in the N.-West Himalaya. Branches flat, succulent, jointed, the joints more or less obovate, bearing dense woolly hairs with tufts of numerous bristles and long sharp spines. Fl. bisexual, regular, yellow, tinged with red, open during the day only, arising from the tufts on the upper edge of the joints. Calyx-tube adnate to the ovary, not prolonged beyond it, lobes numerous, on the upper edge and on the surface of the calyx-tube (more correctly called a hollow receptacle, see p.

306, under *Combretaceæ*). Petals numerous, spreading, stamens ∞, about half the length of petals. Fruit fleshy, pear-shaped, umbilicate at the top, with spine-bearing tubercles near the apex. The joints strike root, but it is chiefly spread by birds, which eat the fruit and drop the seed.

ORDER LVIII. **ARALIACEÆ.** Gen. Pl. i. 931.

Trees or shrubs, rarely herbs, erect or climbing, sometimes epiphytic, l. alternate, simple or compound. Fl. regular, usually pentamerous, umbellate, rarely racemose or capitate. Calyx adnate to ovary, limb short, usually entire, rarely toothed or lobed, petals mostly triangular, caducous. Stamens as many as petals, rarely numerous, filaments inflexed in bud, anthers didymous, versatile, disk epigynous. Ovary 2- or more celled, 1 ovule in each cell. Fr. a drupe or berry, seeds pendulous, embryo minute in dense fleshy albumen.

All *Araliaceæ* have canals in the bark and pith, filled with resin or gum. In many species vascular bundles are found in the pith. The wood is generally light and soft, and many species have a large pith, among others, *Fatsia papyrifera*, Benth., the rice-paper plant of Japan and Formosa.

A. Cells of ovary 5, rarely 4 or 6.	
L. digitate, petals 5 or 6, valvate	1. HEPTAPLEURUM.
L. pinnate, petals imbricate	2. PENTAPANAX.
L. pinnate, petals valvate, thick	POLYSCIAS (p. 349).
L. simple, umbels numerous, panicled	3. HEDERA.
L. simple, umbels solitary or few	4. DENDROPANAX.
B. Cells of ovary 2–5.	
Albumen ruminated, petals valvate, edge of leaves bristly-ciliate	5. GAMBLEA.
Albumen uniform, petals slightly imbricate	6. ARALIA.
C. Cells of ovary 2, petals valvate.	
Pedicels continuous, styles distinct.	
L. digitate	ACANTHOPANAX (p. 351).
L. tripinnate	7. HETEROPANAX.
Pedicels continuous, styles united	8. BRASSAIOPSIS.
Pedicels articulate, styles united, l. digitate	9. MACROPANAX.
D. Ovary one-celled, l. simple, pinnate and bi- or tri-pinnate	ARTHROPHYLLUM (p. 353).
E. Cells of ovary 6–12.	
L. digitate, fl. in heads	BRASSAIA (p. 353).
L. palmate, fl. umbellate	10. TREVESIA.
F. Cells of ovary very numerous, stamens ∞	TUPIDANTHUS (p. 354).

Helwingia belongs more properly to *Cornaceæ*, in which order it has been entered.

1. **HEPTAPLEURUM,** Gaertn; Fl. Brit. Ind. ii. 727.

(Included in *Schefflera* by Harms in Engler u. Prantl iii. 8. 35.)

Unarmed trees or large shrubs, often epiphytic. Leaves digitate, leaflets of old trees entire or remotely toothed, of coppice shoots and young trees often lobed. Umbels generally in panicled racemes, bracts woolly, pedicels not articulate. Fl. often polygamous, male and bisexual, petals valvate, generally 5 or 6, often cohering in a cap which is raised by the stamens. Ovary with as many cells as there are petals. Fr. often fleshy, generally ridged when dry, enclosing 3–6 pergamentaceous or membranous pyrenes in which the seeds lie loose. Albumen often more or less ruminate. Species 55, tropics of the old world.

A. Fr. crowned by the long connate styles, seeds convex, albumen often ruminate.

1. **H. impressum,** C. B. Clarke. Vern. *Balu chinia*, Nep.

A large tree, leaflets 8, lanceolate, entire, those on young trees often distantly serrate, upperside shining, the nerves impressed, underside softly stellate-tomentose, blade 6–10, pet. 1 in., common petiole 5–15 in. long. Umbels many-fld., in large pyramidal panicles. Fr. obtusely and indistinctly 5-ridged when dry.

Garhwal, 10,000 ft. Nepal. Sikkim, 6–10,000 ft. Bhutan. Fl. May–Aug. 2. **H. Lawranceanum,** Prain in Journ. As. Soc. Beng. vol. 67. 298. Kachin hills, Upper Burma. Leaflets thickly coriaceous, broadly elliptic, glabrous on both sides. Fr. 7-ridged.

3. **H. hypoleucum,** Kurz F. Fl. i. 539.

A small tree, branchlets, inflorescence and underside of l. clothed with floccose deciduous wool. Leaflets 6 or 7, on old trees entire or sharply serrulate, on young trees deeply lobed, nerves not impressed above, sec. n. prominent beneath, blade 6–12, pet. 1–5 in. long. Umbels solitary or a few on long peduncles, these arranged in racemes or corymbs on a stout rachis 10–15 in. long, thick triangular bracts at the base of peduncles, petals clothed with dense stellate wool. Fr. globose, ¼ in. diam., 5-celled, 5-seeded, obtusely 5 ribbed, crowned by the lobed disk and the short column of connate styles. Albumen ruminate.

Assam, Khasi hills, Manipur. Fl. Nov.–January. 4. **H. elatum,** C. B. Clarke.—Syn. *H. glaucum*, Kurz. Nepal. Sikkim 5–7,000 ft. Bhutan. Hills of Martaban and Tenasserim, Muleyit, Nattoung (Parish). An evergreen tree or large shrub. Leaflets glabrous, elliptic-lanceolate, almost entire, pale beneath, blade 4–7, pet. 1–2 in. Fl. polygamous, umbels bracteate, in racemes, these panicled, bracts and bracteoles, peduncles, pedicels and petals on the outside clothed with deciduous rust-coloured wool, often of stellate hairs. Petals 4–5, thick at apex and keeled inside. Fr. obtusely 5-ridged. 5. **H. glaucum,** C. B. Clarke, Assam, Khasi hills. A small tree similar to 4, differs by oblanceolate leaflets, broader in the upper portion. *H. birmanicum*, Watt MSS., Manipur 8,000 ft., probably belongs to this.

6. **H. racemosum,** Bedd. Fl. Sylv. t. 214.—Syn. *Hedera racemosa*, Wight Ic. t. 1015. Common on the Nilgiri and Anamalai hills. Ceylon 3–6,000 ft. A large tree, branchlets stout, marked with the scars of fallen l. Leaflets acuminate, glabrous, entire, margin undulate, blade 3–5, pet. 1–2 in. long. Fl. as a rule not umbellate, except those at the ends of the panicle ramifications, but in elongate racemes, united in large lateral panicles. 7. **H. rostratum,** Bedd.—Syn. *Hedera rostrata*, Wight Ic. t. 1013. Nilgiri and Anamalai hills, 5–6,000 ft., Travancore 4,000 ft. Similar to 6 except the umbellate inflorescence, the branches of the panicle bear one or a few umbels near the end.

B. Fr. crowned by the conical disk, bearing 5–9 round stigmas. Seeds flat, albumen not ruminate.

8. **H. venulosum,** Seem.—Syn. *Paratropia venulosa*, W. & A. Vern. *Kath Semal*, Hind.; *Myauk letwa, Tauktè letwa, Balu letwa*, Burm.

A soft-wooded scandent shrub, attaching itself to supports by rootlets from branches. Leaflets 5–7, glabrous, entire, elliptic or elliptic-lanceolate, blade 4–8, pet. 1–2 in. long, stipules connate between branch and petiole. Common petiole 6–9 in. long. Fl. yellowish-green or cream-coloured, polygamous, generally glabrous, 5–6-merous, umbels in racemes, these on a short rachis, forming an ample panicle, umbels in early bud enveloped by large woolly caducous bracts. ♂: petals sometimes cohering in a cap, which is uplifted by the stamens. ♀: styles short, connate at the base into a fleshy conical mass. Fruit 5-ridged.

Subhimalayan tract and outer ranges, from the Jumna eastwards, ascending to 5,000 ft. Assam. Khasi hills. Chittagong. Andamans. Burma, Upper and Lower. Central Prov., Behar and throughout the Peninsula. Fl. Jan.–June.—Yunnan. Malay Penins. and Archip. Australia. *H. eugenifolium*, Watt MSS., Manipur, 5,000 ft., probably belongs to this. 9. **H. stellatum,** Gaertn.—Syn. *Hedera obovata*, Wight Ic. t. 1011. Southern portion of the Western Peninsula, in the Deccan as well as on the West side. Ceylon common in the moist low country. A large scandent epiphytic shrub, branchlets stout, marked with leaf-scars. Leaflets 4–7, elliptic, obtuse or acute, not acuminate, at times orbicular, blade 2–3, pet. ½–3 in., common petiole 3–7 in. sheathing at base. Petals glabrous. 10. **H. Wallichianum,** C. B. Clarke. Coorg. Nilgiris. Leaflets thickly coriaceous, glabrous, umbels numerous on elongate racemes, arranged in a panicle on a short stout rachis. Fl. ¼ in. across, pedicels, calyx and petals glabrous. Fr. 6-ribbed. 11. **H. khasianum**, C. B. Clarke. Assam. Khasi hills. A small tree, branched from near the base. Leaflets thickly coriaceous, glabrous. Racemes of umbels elongate, often compound below, forming ample panicles on a rachis 6–8 in. long. Pedicels, calyx and petals generally with white stellate tomentum. Fr. 8-ridged. 12. **H. ellipticum**, Seem. Andamans and Nicobars. Scandent. Panicles shorter than l., often composed of compound umbels. Peduncles slender, pedicels filiform. Fr. 5-ridged.

2. PENTAPANAX, Seem.; Fl. Brit. Ind. ii. 723.

Trees or shrubs, often scandent. L. pinnate, leaflets 3–9. Fl. bisexual or polygamous, pentamerous, in umbels or compound racemes, pedicels articulate close under the fl. Petals imbricate in bud, ovary 4- or 5-celled. Fr. angled, albumen uniform. Species 5–6.

A. Fl. in panicled or compound umbels.

1. P. Leschenaultii, Seem.; Bedd. Manual t. 15, fig. 3.—Syn. *Hedera trifoliata*, W. & A.; Wight Ic. t. 307.

An unarmed, frequently epiphytic and climbing shrub or small tree, often trailing on rocks. Leaflets 3 or 5, ovate, bristly-serrate, blade 4–7, pet. (of lateral leaflets) ¼–½ in. long. Umbels many-fld., arranged in panicles or in compound umbels (var. *umbellatum*), styles united nearly to the apex. Fr. more or less distinctly ribbed.

Kumaon 8,500–10,000 ft. Nepal. Sikkim 5–10,000 ft. Tibet. Bhutan. Mishmee. Khasi hills. Upper Burma. Nilgiris and other mountains on the West side of the Peninsula. Fl. May–June, sometimes August. Yunnan. 2. **P. parasiticum**, Seem.: Kanjilal F. Fl. 187. Mussoorie hills, scarce. Kumaon, Nepal. Khasi hills. Yunnan. A climbing soft-wooded shrub, attaching itself to supports by rootlets on branches, leaflets 5, entire, glaucous beneath, lanceolate, 2–2½ in. long. Panicles consisting of 2–8 umbels, styles united nearly to the apex. 3. **P. stellatum**, King in Journ. As. Soc. Beng. vol. 67. 298. Shan hills near Fort Stedman. Scandent, leaflets 5, entire, glabrous above, densely clothed with stellate tomentum beneath. Umbels numerous in long erect terminal panicles. Styles united half way up.

B. Fl. in panicled racemes.

4. **P. racemosum**, Seem. Sikkim 6–8,000 ft. Khasi hills. A large climber, leaflets 5-7, ovate or elliptic, acuminate, remotely denticulate, blade 4–9, pet. ¼–½ in. long. Panicles unisexual, 8–10 clustered at the ends of branches, rachis 10–14 in., racemes 2–3 in. long, at right angles to rachis. Styles in ♀ fl. 3–5, free, recurved. 5. **P. subcordatum**, Seem. Khasi hills. A small tree, leaflets 3–5, acuminate, sinuate-crenate, blade 3–5, pet. of the lateral ¼–1 in. long. Racemes 6–12 in., ascending, longer than rachis. Styles connate to near the apex, short, cylindric.

Polyscias acuminata, Seem.; Bedd. Fl. Sylv. t 213.—Syn. *Hedera acuminata*, Wight Ic. t. 1062. Nilgiri and Anamalai hills, Tinnevelli ghats. Ceylon rare. A middle-sized or small unarmed tree, quite glabrous, l. pinnate, rachis 8–9 in. long, stout, with a broad almost sheathing base, leaflets acuminate, 3–6 in. long. Umbels 10–15-fld. in elongate racemes, sometimes in corymbs, these arranged in panicles or compound umbels. Pedicels articulate under the fl. Calyx distinctly 5-dentate, petals thick valvate, ovary 4- or 5-celled, styles 4 or 5, distinct.

3. HEDERA, Linn.; Fl. Brit. Ind. ii. 739.

(Species 2, one in Australia.)

H. Helix, Linn. Ivy. Vern. *Arbambal*, Haz.; *Kaneri*, Sutlej; *Mithiári* Jauns.

A large woody climber, adhering to trees, rocks or walls by numerous fine rootlets. L. coriaceous, glabrous, shining, simple, exceedingly variable in shape and size, those of flowering branches ovate or lanceolate with a tapering base, the others more or less triangular in outline, lobed, with a rounded or cordate base, blade 2–5, petiole ½–3 in. long. Fl. yellowish-green, polygamous, pentamerous, in globose umbels. Petals valvate, ovary 5-celled, styles connate. Berry bright yellow, seeds 3-4, albumen ruminate.

Afghanistan. Punjab Salt range. Himalaya, Hazara to Bhutan 2-9,000 ft. Khasi hills. Manipur. Fl. Oct.-April. Europe, North Africa, Western Asia. China. Japan. The berries of the European Ivy are usually black.

4. DENDROPANAX, Dcne. & Planch.; Fl. Brit. Ind. ii. 733.

Gilibertia, Ruiz et Pavon; Harms in Engler u. Prantl iii. 8. 40.

Unarmed, glabrous trees or shrubs. L. simple entire, on coppice shoots and young plants palmately 3-5-lobed. Fl. umbellate, pedicels not articulate.

FIG. 147.—Gamblea ciliata, C. B. Clarke. ½.

Petals 5, thick, valvate in bud. Ovary 5-celled, styles united at the base into a column, their summits spreading. Fr. ribbed, seeds compressed, albumen uniform. Species 12, mostly American.

1. **D. japonicum**, Seem. Khasi hills. China, Japan. A tree with strong smell of Asafœtida. L. on young plants and coppice shoots deeply palmatifid with long petioles, on older plants elliptic-lanceolate, penninerved, blade 3-6, petiole 1-3 in. long. Umbels manyfld., solitary or few in a short terminal panicle. Fr. ellipsoid nearly ½ in. long. 2.

D. Listeri, King in Ann. Bot. Gard. Calc. ix. t. 55. Daphla hills, Assam. A small tree, l. with 3 basal nerves, the lateral half as long as the blade of leaf. Fr. globose, ⅓ in. diam.

5. GAMBLEA, C. B. Clarke; Fl. Brit. Ind. ii. 739.

G. ciliata, C. B. Clarke, the only species.

A handsome unarmed tree, l. digitate, leaflets 3–5, sometimes 1 only, edge bristly-ciliate, on the upper side with short harsh hairs on nerves and veins, blade 3–7, pet. ¼, common petiole 3–8 in. long. Fl. polygamous, pentamerous, umbels in short panicles. Petals valvate, ovary 3–5-celled, styles connate nearly half their length. Seeds not compressed, albumen ruminated.

Sikkim, 9–12,000 ft., on the ridge dividing Nepal from Sikkim in the region of *Rhododendrum Falconeri*. Jakpho, Naga hills, 9,900 ft. Fl. July.

6. ARALIA, Linn.; Fl. Brit. Ind. ii. 721.

Leaflets digitate, pinnate or bipinnate, a pair of leaflets often at the base of pinnæ, leaflets membranous, serrulate. Fl. umbellate, petals 5, ovate, not unguiculate, slightly imbricate in bud. Ovary 2–5-celled. Drupe more or less ribbed, with 2–5 crustaceous or hard pyrenes. Albumen not ruminated. Species 25–30, India, Malay, Japan to North America.

1. **A. cachemirica,** Dcne.; Collett Simla Fl. 217, fig. 66. Vern. *Akhola*, Jauns.

A large herbaceous, roughly pubescent unarmed shrub, l. large, bipinnate, leaflets serrate, ovate-lanceolate, base generally unequal sided, blade 3–6, pet. ⅛–¼ in. long. Fl. white, umbels many-fld. in large terminal panicles. Fr. black with 5 pyrenes.

Kuram valley, in Birch forests 9–10,000 ft. Himalaya, Kashmir to Sikkim, 5–9,000 in the North West, 4–14,000 ft. in Sikkim, extending into the inner arid valleys. Fl. June–Oct. 2. **A. malabarica,** Bedd. Manual, t. 15 fig. 2. Western Ghats from Malabar southwards. A large prickly shrub or small tree, nearly glabrous, with scattered weak prickles and bristles. L. bipinnate, leaflets caudate acuminate, sharply serrate, panicles bracteate.

3. **A. armata,** Seem.; Kurz F. Fl. i. 536.

A small evergreen tree, youngest shoots puberulous. L. large triangular, bipinnate, at the base four pinnæ from one point, and a leaflet at the base of each pinna, main and secondary rachis with sharp prickles. Leaflets numerous, 3–5 in. long, with short stiff hairs, chiefly along nerves, the lateral shortly petiolulate. Umbels many-fld. in large panicles, pedicels slender, ⅓ in. long, as well as the last ramifications roughly hispid. Fr. with 5 broad ridges.

Sikkim 2–5,000 ft. Khasi hills. Tenasserim. Fl. June–Sept. Malay Peninsula. 4. **A. foliolosa,** Seem. Sikkim 3–5,000 ft. A small graceful, evergreen tree, stem covered with prickles. Leaves bi- or tripinnate, rachis with sharp prickles, up to ⅓ in. long, frequently at the base of pinnæ. Leaflets 2–3 in. long, slightly or deeply serrate, bristles or slender prickles along nerves, panicles and umbels bracteate, petals slender ¼–⅓ in., slightly hispid.

5. **A. Thomsoni,** Seem.; King in Journ. As. Soc. Beng. vol. 67. 44.

A large prickly, softly tomentose shrub. Leaves large 2–3-pinnate, leaflets entire or minutely serrulate, the lateral nearly sessile. Umbels bracteate, many-fld., panicles with lanceolate bracts at the ramifications.

Assam, Khasi hills, Fl. R. S. Malay Peninsula. 6. **A. cissifolia,** Griff. Upper Ganges valley, Tibri Garhwal, 9–10,000, Kumaon 9,000, Sikkim 9–13,000 ft. A large bush or small straggling tree. Leaves tufted at the ends of arrested branchlets, digitate, petiole 3–6 in. long, leaflets 3–5. Peduncles axillary, solitary, each bearing a many-fld. umbel. The western specimens are unarmed (*A. scandens*, Edgew.), those from Sikkim and Bhutan are prickly.

Acanthopanax aculeatum, Seem. Assam, Khasi, Jaintia and Naga hills.—China,

Japan. A prickly shrub or small tree, l. digitate, leaflets 3–5, sinuate-dentate, blade 1–3, pet. ¼–½ in. long. Umbels many-fld or in short racemose panicles, pedicels numerous, ¾–1 in. long, not articulate. Petals 4–5, valvate, ovary 2-celled, styles 2. Albumen uniform.

7. HETEROPANAX, Seem.; Fl. Brit. Ind. ii. 734.

H. fragrans, Seem. (the only species), Vern. *Tarlā*, *Dinha*, N.-W. Prov.; *Tachanza*, Burm.

A small glabrous soft-wooded deciduous tree, attaining 60 ft. in Burma. L. tripinnate, 2–4 ft. long, leaflets ovate, elliptic or elliptic-lanceolate, 3–7 in. long. Fl. yellow, fragrant, polygamous, tomentose, in elongate panicled racemes, the ♂ fl. sessile or nearly so, in globose heads, the bisexual fl. in umbels usually at the ends of racemes. Pedicels not articulate, petals 5, valvate, ovary 2-celled, styles 2, distinct, filiform. Fr. laterally compressed, ⅓ in. diam., endocarp crustaceous, albumen ruminate.

Subhimalayan tract from the Jumna eastwards. Assam, Khasi hills, Chittagong. Andamans, Burma. Fl. Dec.–Feb. China, Tonkin, Java. The l. resemble those of *Oroxylum indicum*.

8. BRASSAIOPSIS, Dcne. & Planch.; Fl. Brit. Ind. ii. 735.

Trees or large shrubs, usually prickly, l. simple, palmate or digitate. Inflorescence and calyx stellately hairy while young, pedicels not articulate, bracteate at base. Bracts on ramifications of inflorescence persistent. Fl. pentamerous, often polygamous, pedicels not articulate, petals valvate. Ovary 2-celled, styles united. Fr. often 1-seeded, albumen in some species ruminated. Species 11. India, Malay Archipelago.

A. Leaves undivided.

1. **B. simplicifolia**, C. B. Clarke. Mishmi hills. Branchlets prickly, leaves ovate-lanceolate, serrate, glabrous, penninerved, the lowest pair basal, blade 8, pet. 1½ in. long. 2. **B. Hainla**, Seem. Sikkim 1–5,000 ft. Bhutan. Naga hills, Manipur. Yunnan. A small evergreen much branched and sometimes scandent tree, branches prickly, young shoots stellate-tomentose. L. divided less than half-way down into triangular cuspidate segments, blade 5–8, pet. 5–10 in. long, basal nerves 5–7. Fr. generally 2-seeded, ⅓ in. diam. 3. **B. alpina**, C. B. Clarke. Sikkim, 10–11,000 ft. Branchlets, leaves and inflorescence densely villous with tawny tomentum. L. cordate, serrate, often slightly tricuspidate, blade 3–5, pet. 5–9 in. long, basal nerves 3–5. C. B. Clarke thinks that this may possibly be a high level form of 2.

B. Leaves palmatifid, divided half-way down or more.

4. **B. palmata**, Kurz F. Fl. i. 537. Sikkim 2–4,000 ft. Chittagong. Andamans, Malay Penins. A small sparingly branched tree, young shoots with rusty scurfy tomentum. l. cordate, deeply 5–7-fid, blade 5–10, petiole 5–11 in. long. Closely allied to 2, and possibly not specifically distinct. In *Brassaiopsis* as well as in other *Araliaceæ* the leaves vary considerably, and the 3 sections here accepted may on further study prove to be untenable. 5. **B. mitis**, C. B. Clarke, *Moqchini*, Nep. Sikkim 6–8,000 ft., common about Darjeeling. A small upright deciduous tree, branches once or twice forked, leaves only near the tops of branches. L. deeply 9–13-fid, blade 6–18, pet. 6–24 in. long, basal n. 9–13. L. slightly hairy beneath, petiole with soft bristles near the end. Umbels many-fld. in long panicles below the tuft of leaves. 6. **B. hispida**, Seem. Sikkim 5–7,000 ft. Mishmi hills. Yunnan. A small prickly tree, l. deeply 7–9-fid, segments oblong, spinulose-serrate, blade 6–18 in. long, pet. sheathing at base, as long as blade. Calyx-tube and pedicels densely stellate-tomentose. 7. **B. Griffithii**, C. B. Clarke. Assam. Imperfectly known, apparently unarmed, l. very large, almost glabrous, thickly membranous. Calyx distinctly toothed, petals reflexed after flowering, disk conical.

C. Leaves digitate.

8. **B. speciosa**, Dcne. & Planch. Ver. *Baw*, Burm.

A small simple-stemmed tree, prickles on the stem and often also on the panicle. Leaflets almost entire, elliptic-oblong, when young often with scattered stellate hairs, sec. n. arching, prominent beneath, blade 4–8, pet. 1–3, common petiole 12–24 in. long. Umbels many-fld., peduncles 1–4 in. long, in drooping panicled racemes. Fr. more or less globose, hardly ribbed, $\frac{1}{3}$ in. diam. crowned by the flat circular disk and the connate styles. Seeds usually 1, sometimes 2, surface irregularly grooved. Albumen not or very slightly ruminate.

Sikkim, to 5,000 ft. Assam. Khasi hills. Cachar. Chittagong. Hills east of Bhamo, Upper Burma, at 5,500 ft. Fl. R. S. Yunnan. 9. **B. Hookeri,** C. B. Clarke. Sikkim 2–7,000 ft. Khasi hills. A prickly tree, young shoots, inflorescence, petioles and leaves beneath with stellate woolly tomentum, leaflets coarsely serrate, blade 4–18, pet. $\frac{1}{2}$–3 in. long. 10. **B. aculeata,** Seem. Kumaon 2,000 ft. Nepal. Khasi hills. A small tree, armed with stout conical prickles, young shoots densely rusty tomentose, leaflets serrate, thinly membranous, blade 6–9, pet. $\frac{1}{4}$–$\frac{3}{4}$ in. long, sometimes one leaflet only, full grown leaflets with minute scattered stellate hairs on both surfaces.

9. MACROPANAX, Miq.; Fl. Brit. Ind. ii. 738.

Small unarmed trees. L. digitate, leaflets 3–5, glabrous. Panicles large, bracts small deciduous, fl. umbelled, polygamous, pentamerous, pedicels articulate under the fl. Petals valvate, ovary 2-celled, styles united. Fr. ribbed, seed dorsally compressed. Species 2.

1. M. oreophilum, Miq.; Kurz F. Fl. i. 541.

A middle-sized evergreen tree. Leaflets glabrous, lanceolate, denticulate, serrate or crenulate, blade 4–6, pet. $\frac{1}{4}$–3, common petiole 4–10 in. long. Umbels in long compound panicles, the ramifications of which, as well as pedicels, are clothed with rusty stellate pubescence. Fr. elongate-ovoid, $\frac{1}{4}$–$\frac{1}{3}$ in., disk conical, style $\frac{1}{6}$ in. long.

Kumaon, outer hills, ascending to 5,000 ft., Nepal, Sikkim, Bhutan. Assam. Khasi hills. Chittagong. Hills east of Toungoo. Yunzalin. Upper Burma (Kurz). Fl. July–Sept. Yunnan. 2. **M. undulatum,** Seem. Sikkim, outer hills to 5,000 ft. (*Chinia*, Nep.) Assam. Khasi hills. Silhet. Yunnan. A small tree, leaflets entire, panicle glabrous.

Arthrophyllum diversifolium, Blume.—Syn. *A. javanicum*, Blume; Kurz F. Fl. i. 540. Andamans, Malay Peninsula. A shrub or small tree. Leaves glabrous or nearly so, the lower bi- or tripinnate, the intermediate pinnate, the uppermost opposite, simple or trifoliolate. Inflorescence a compound umbel, peduncles and pedicels clothed with rusty-brown deciduous stellate tomentum, pedicels not articulate. Calyx-teeth 5, small, petals valvate, ovary 1-celled, 1-ovuled, style simple. Seed nearly globose, not ridged, albumen ruminate.

Brassaia capitata, C. B. Clarke. Nilgiris. L. digitate, leaflets entire, rigidly coriaceous elliptic, blade 4–7, pet. 2 in. long. Fl. in compact globose pedunculate heads, each fl. surrounded by 4 bracteoles, as long as ovary and united below into a tube. Peduncles 1–1$\frac{1}{2}$ in. long, in the axils of ovate persistent membranous bracts, in racemes 12–16 in. long, on a stout rachis. Petals 6–10, thick, valvate, stamens and ovary cells as many as petals. Fr. obconic, ribbed below.

10. TREVESIA, Visiani; Fl. Brit. Ind. ii. 731.

(Species 4, Malay Archip.)

T. palmata, Vis.; Kurz F. Fl. i. 539. Vern. *Baw*, Burm.

A small evergreen generally unbranched tree, armed with short very sharp prickles, young shoots rusty pubescent and very prickly. Leaves orbicular in general outline, 12–24 in. diam., deeply palmatifid, lobes acuminate, serrate, sometimes lobed, often cut away in one or several places, so as to leave the midrib of the lobe free, petiole often prickly. Fl. large, umbels panicled, pedicels not articulate. Young panicles clothed with rusty tomentum, bracts 1 in. long. Calyx-limb free, undulate or repand-toothed, petals 8–12, valvate,

often cohering and coming off as a cap. Stamens and ovary-cells as many as petals. Fr. fleshy, ovoid, ½ in. diam., crowned by the stout style.

Nepal. Sikkim Terai, banks of streams, ascending to 3,000 ft. Khasi hills. Chittagong. Burma, Upper and Lower. Fl. Feb.–April, Yunnan. Malay Peninsula.

Tupidanthus calyptratus, Hook. fil. & Thoms. Khasi hills. Burma, eastern slopes of the Arakan Yoma, Terai of Shan hills. A large glabrous shrub, often developing into a huge climber, wood hard. L. digitate, leaflets 7–9, coriaceous, entire, blade 4–7, pet. 1–2 in., common petiole 8–12 in. long, stipules connate within the petiole. Umbels 3–7-fld., in a short panicle with stout branches, pedicels thick, not articulate. Fl. large, resembling mallets, calyx-tube thickly coriaceous, petals connate, falling off in a cap, stamens 50–70, crowded, ovary-cells numerous, narrow, up to 90, arranged on both sides of a line which usually bifurcates at the ends. Stigmas linear, sessile, as many as ovary cells. Fr. succulent, depressed, 1–1½ in. diam.

ORDER LIX. CORNACEÆ. Gen. Pl. i. 947.

Shrubs or trees, l. petiolate, entire, stipules 0. Fl. regular, calyx-tube adnate to ovary, limb persistent, the segments small, open or valvate in bud. Petals 4 or 5 inserted round an epigynous disk, stamens usually as many as petals, ovary inferior 1–4-celled, one, rarely two pendulous ovules in each cell. Fruit generally drupaceous with a 1–4-celled putamen or with 2 distinct stones. Embryo in a copious fleshy albumen, cotyledons generally thin, foliaceous.

A. Flowers bisexual, petals long, linear.
  Stamens more numerous than petals . . . . . 1. ALANGIUM.
  Stamens as many as petals . . . . 2. MARLEA.
B. Flowers bisexual, petals short.
  Ovary 2-celled . . . . 3. CORNUS.
  Ovary 1-celled . . . . 4. MASTIXIA.
C. Flowers unisexual, l. opposite . . . . AUCUBA (p. 356).
D. Flowers unisexual, l. alternate.
  Fl. in dense heads, ovary 1-celled. . . . . . 5. NYSSA.
  Fl. in large pendulous panicles, ov. 3–5-celled . . TORRICELLIA (p. 357).
  Fl. on the mid-rib of leaf, ov. 2–3-celled . . . HELWINGIA (p. 357).

1. ALANGIUM, Lam.; Fl. Brit. Ind. ii. 741.

Shrubs or small trees, l. alternate, entire, penninerved, the lowest pair of nerves from the base. Fl. white, bisexual, in axillary fascicles or cymes. Calyx-tube turbinate, free portion short, truncate or 5–10-dentate. Petals 5–10, strap-shaped, valvate, afterwards reflexed. Stamens over 20, filaments short, hairy, anthers linear, cells adnate to the connective and dehiscing laterally. Ovary 1-celled, style filiform. Fr. crowned with the persistent calyx-limb. Species 16, Tropical and Subtropical Asia and Africa. Australia. Polynesia.

1. **A. Lamarckii**, Thwaites; Bedd. Fl. Sylv. t. 215.—Syn. *A. hexapetalum*, Roxb.; Wight Ill. t. 96.; *A. decapetalum*, Lamk.; Wight Ic. t. 194. Vern. *Akola, Akhaul, Kweli*, Hind.; *Ankol*, Mar.; *Ankola*, Kan.; *Uru, Udaga*, Tel.: *Alangi*, Tam.

A shrub or small tree, bark grey, wood fine-grained, tough and strong, branchlets generally spinescent. L. membranous, varying exceedingly in shape, from oblong to elliptic and obovate, from obtuse to acuminate, blade 3–6, pet. ¼–⅓ in. long, pubescent while young, glabrous or pubescent on the underside when full grown. Fl. fragrant, solitary or fasciculate, pedicels and calyx hairy, petals 1 in. long, 5–10, usually 6, hairy outside. Fr. ⅔ in. long, black when ripe, seed enclosed in red pulp. Cotyledons large flat, with 3 basal

nerves, in copious albumen, which is not ruminated. (If collected unripe, the seeds, when dry, have a central cavity and the cotyledons in drying become crumpled.)

Subhimalayan tract, from the Saharunpore Sewaliks to Oudh. Gangetic Plain, Rajputana, Central Provinces and the Western Peninsula. Never quite leafless, foliage renewed April, May. Fl. Feb.–April. A variety with broadly elliptic, acuminate l. tertiary nerves prominent, in the Peninsula. Coppices well. Fr. eaten, oil extracted from the seeds. Ceylon, Malay Archip. South China. 2. **A. Kingianum**, Prain in Journ. As. Soc. Beng. vol. 67. 294. Kachin hills, Upper Burma. A scandent unarmed shrub. Fl. $\frac{1}{4}$–$\frac{1}{3}$ in. long, in lax pedunculate axillary cymes, much shorter than l.

2. MARLEA, Roxb.; Fl. Brit. Ind. ii. 742.

(Included under *Alangium* by Harms in Engler u. Prantl iii. 8. 261.)

Trees or shrubs, l. alternate. Fl. bisexual in axillary cymes. Petals 6–10, linear, valvate in bud. Stamens as many as petals, filaments short, adhering to base of petals, anthers linear. Ovary 1 or 2-celled, one ovule in each cell. Style filiform, stigma 4-lobed. Drupe with thin pericarp, putamen grooved. Species 10, India to Australia and Polynesia.

1. **M. begoniæfolia**, Roxb. Cor. Pl. t. 283. Vern. *Kakshu*, *Khagshi*, *Ban kimu*, *Garh kimu*, Hind.; *Timil*, Nep.; *Tawposa*, Upper Burma.

A small tree, bark smooth, grey, branches horizontal, young shoots pubescent. Leaves pubescent or glabrous, varying from broad ovate, acuminate, to cordate, often with an oblique base and angularly lobed, blade 4–10, pet. $\frac{3}{4}$–$1\frac{1}{2}$ in. long, basal nerves 3–5. Fl. white, in axillary dichotomous cymes, petals 6–8, $\frac{2}{3}$ in. long, slightly hairy on back, ovary 2-celled. Fr. ovoid, $\frac{1}{3}$ in. long, pulp scanty, putamen bony, 2-celled.

Subhimalayan tract and outer ranges, ascending to 6,000 ft. Assam. Khasi hills. Chittagong. Burma. Fl. March–June.—China. Japan. *M. tomentosa*, Endl.; Kurz F. Fl. i. 545, petals nearly an inch long, probably belongs to this species. 2. **M. alpina**, Gamble MSS. Sikkim 6–9,000 ft., l. usually not angled or lobed, fr. $\frac{3}{4}$ in. long, putamen crustaceous, one-seeded, one cell abortive. 3. **M. barbata**, R. Br. Assam, Bhutan, Cachar, Tenasserim. Shaggy with much soft spreading hair, l. ovate-oblong, acuminate, cymes many-fld., ovary 1-celled.

3. CORNUS, Linn.; Fl. Brit. Ind. ii. 744.

Shrubs and trees, l. opposite, rarely alternate. Fl. bisexual, tetramerous, white or yellow, in heads or dichotomous cymes. Calyx-teeth minute, petals valvate in bud, stamens alternating with petals, anthers oblong. Ovary 2-celled, one ovule in each cell. Fruit drupaceous, putamen hard, crustaceous or osseous, 2-celled, 2-seeded. Cotyledons foliaceous in a fleshy albumen.

A. Fl. in compound cymes.

1. **C. macrophylla**, Wall.; Brandis F. Fl. t. 32. Vern. *Kandar*, Haz. *Shka*, *Kanchhinu*, Bash.; *Kayshi*, Jauns.

A middle-sized tree, l. broad-ovate acuminate, pale glaucous beneath, blade 4–6, pet. $\frac{1}{2}$–1 in. long, sec. n. 5–8 pair. Fl. white, in ample terminal dichotomous cymes, on short peduncles, buds $\frac{1}{4}$–$\frac{1}{3}$ in. long, calyx urceolate. Pedicels, calyx and outside of petals clothed with white appressed hairs. Drupe globose, $\frac{1}{5}$ in. diam.

Himalaya, Hazara.—Nepal, 4–8,000 ft., frequent in shady valleys. Fl. April–June. The wood of this and other species of *Cornus* is close- and even-grained, similar to that of *C. florida*, L., largely used in turnery in North America. A species with alternate l. and campanulate calyx, Sikkim 3–6,000 ft. Bhutan, Manipur (*C. macrophylla*, Gamble List 45) is nearly allied to *C. alternifolia*, Linn. f., of Western North America. 2. **C. oblonga**, Wall.; *Korhoi*, Jauns.; *Baunri*, Kum. Himalaya, outer hills, 3–7,000 ft. Kashmir-Bhutan. Khasi hills, Yunnan. A small tree, l. narrowly oblong, petiole

$\frac{1}{4}$–$\frac{3}{4}$ in. long, sec. n. 3–5 pair, impressed above. Calyx and petals very slightly hairy. Drupe ovoid, $\frac{1}{3}$ in. long. 3. **C. sanguinea,** Linn. On a high mountain range south of the Kashmir valley at 7,000 ft., found once only by Dr. J. L. Stewart. Europe and Siberia. L. elliptic. Sec. n. 3–4 pair, the lowest pair basal, peduncles longer than cymes.

FIG. 148.—Cornus oblonga, Wall. $\frac{1}{2}$.

B. Fl. in globose bracteate heads.

4. **C. capitata,** Wall. Pl. As. Rar. t. 214; Collett Simla Fl. 219, fig. 67. Vern. *Thama*, *Tharmal*, Pb., *Bamora*, *Bamaur*, N.-W. P.; *Tumbuk*; Lepcha.

A small deciduous tree, branchlets and l. rough with short stiff appressed hairs. L. coriaceous, pale beneath, approximate at the ends of branchlets, blade 2–4, narrowed into petiole $\frac{1}{2}$ in. long. Fl. closely packed in terminal heads with a conspicuous involucre of 4 large yellow petaloid bracts. Drupes uniting into a fleshy strawberry-like head, 1 in. diam., each drupe with a hard 1-seeded stone.

Outer Himalaya from Kulu to Bhutan. Khasi and Naga hills. Fl. April–Oct.

4. MASTIXIA, Blume; Fl. Brit. Ind. ii. 745.

Trees, resin-canals in the pith. L. alternate or opposite, entire. Fl. small, bisexual, 4–5-merous, 2-bracteolate, in terminal many-fld. panicles. Calyx-tube as well as the valvate petals pubescent; disk large, fleshy. Ovary inferior, 1-celled, ovule 1, pendulous. Drupe with a hard fleshy pericarp and a bony endocarp, which is deeply intruded down one side, dividing the seed into 2 lobes, embryo in copious fleshy albumen, radicle long. Species 18, India and Malaya.

1. **M. arborea,** C. B. Clarke; Bedd. Fl. Sylv. t. 216.—Syn. *Byrsinopetalum arboreum*, Wight Ic. t. 956. Cachar. Evergreen forests of the Western ghats and adjoining hill ranges 2–7,000 ft., from the Konkan southwards. Ceylon. A very large evergreen tree, l. coriaceous, blade 2–9, petiole $\frac{1}{2}$–2 in. long. Fl. green, disk yellow, the lowest branches of panicle often in the axils of small l. or large bracts, fr. ellipsoid $1\frac{1}{2}$ in. long, purplish-green. Possibly identical with *M. pentandra*, Blume, of Java. If proved, this name will take precedence. No specific difference between *M. arborea* and *pentandra* of Fl. Brit. India. 2. **M. euonymoides,** Prain in Journ. As. Soc. Bengal, vol. 67. 295. Kachin hills. L. opposite, blade 4, pet. $\frac{3}{4}$ in. long, fr. almost cylindrical, $\frac{5}{8}$ in. long. Perhaps the same as a very large tree 200 ft. high, bole 100 ft. to first branch found by Watt at Kupra, Manipur, 6,000 ft.

Aucuba himalaica, Hook f. Sikkim 5–9,000 ft. Bhutan. Manipur 8,000 ft. A large shrub or small tree, evergreen, young shoots clothed with long silky hairs. L. opposite, lanceolate, denticulate or serrate, blade 3–8, pet. 1 in. long. Fl. diœcious, tetramerous, lurid-purple, in small axillary and terminal, often fasciculate hairy panicles. Calyx-tube hairy, petals lanceolate, valvate, ♂: stamens 4, around a quadrangular fleshy disk. ♀: ovary 1-celled. Berry scarlet or orange, $\frac{1}{3}$ in. long. This may possibly be only a form of the Japanese *A. japonica*, Thunb., cultivated in all temperate countries, often with variegated leaves.

5. NYSSA, Linn.; Fl. Brit. Ind. ii. 747.

Species 5, one in China, 3 in eastern North America.

N. sessiliflora, Hook. fil.—Syn. *Daphniphyllopsis capitata,* Kurz F. Fl. i. 240. Vern. *Pani kadam,* Ass.

A large evergreen tree, l. membranous, glaucous beneath, numberless raised dots on both surfaces, blade 5–8, pet. 1–1½ in. long. Fl. sessile, usually pentamerous, sometimes 6–7-merous, green, many ♂ and one or a few ♀ fl., with numerous bracts, in a dense globose pedunculate head, these in short axillary pubescent panicles, often solitary near the ends of branches. ♂: calyx short cup-shaped, petals imbricate, hairy, stamens usually 10, inserted round a large circular disk. Fr. ovoid, endocarp long, exceedingly hard.

Sikkim 5–7,000 ft. Assam (Makúm Forest D. B. April 1879). Khasi hills. Cachar, hills east of Toungoo, 4–6,000 ft. Fl. April, May. Perak, Sumatra, Java.

FIG. 149.—Nyssa sessiliflora, Hook. fil. ½.

Torricellia tiliæfolia, DC. Nepal. Sikkim 6–10,000 ft. A small deciduous tree, branchlets thick, with large pith. L. alternate, when full grown glabrous or slightly pubescent beneath, cordate, sharply serrate, blade 5–7, petiole 3–4 in. long, sheathing. Fl. small, white, diœcious, usually pentamerous, numerous in pendulous panicles. ♂: calyx-tube short, petals acuminate, induplicate-valvate, stamens usually 5, inserted around a flat disk. ♀: petals 0, ovary inferior 3–5-celled, stigmas 3–5, sessile, cylindric. Drupe small purple, seed linear, curved, embryo minute in a fleshy albumen.

Helwingia himalaica, Hook. f. & Thoms. Sikkim 7–9,000 ft. Khasi hills. Manipur China. A small shrub, l. alternate, lanceolate, sharply serrate, blade 3–5, pet. 1 in. long. Fl. unisexual, in small few-fld. umbels, sessile on the midrib of leaf or of large bracts. Calyx truncate, petals and stamens 3–5, ovary 3–4-celled, styles short combined at base. Fruit sessile, 1–3 on the leaf, ellipsoid, ⅓ in. long, 2–3-celled, with furrows between the carpels. Embryo minute, in copious albumen.

ORDER LX. CAPRIFOLIACEÆ. Gen. Pl. ii. 1.

Shrubs or small trees, rarely herbs. L. opposite, usually without stipules. Calyx-tube adnate to ovary, limb 3–5-toothed. Corolla gamopetalous, often zygomorphic, lobes 5, imbricate in bud. Stamens usually as many as corolla lobes, inserted in the corolla tube, often unequal, anthers versatile. Ovary 1–8-celled. Fr. a berry or drupe, rarely capsular, 1- or many-seeded. Embryo minute, in copious fleshy albumen.

In most genera the wood fibres have bordered pits. As far as known the wood of the climbing species (*Lonicera*) has a normal structure with numerous and in some species large vessels.

A. Corolla tubular or campanulate. Ovary cells 1- or many-ovuled, style filiform.
Stamens 5, calyx 5-dentate, ovary 2–3-celled . . . 1. LONICERA.
Stamens 5, calyx lobes 5, linear, ovary 5–8-celled . . 2. LEYCESTERIA.
Stamens 4, calyx lobes 5, linear, ovary 3-celled . . 3. ABELIA.

B. Corolla rotate or broadly campanulate. One ovule in each cell, style short or stigma sessile.

Leaves simple . . . . 4. VIBURNUM.
Leaves pinnate . . . . 5. SAMBUCUS.

1. LONICERA, Linn.; Fl. Brit. Ind. iii. 9.

Erect, prostrate or climbing shrubs, l. entire, bark as a rule peeling off in long thin shreds or in papery flakes. Fl. pentamerous, sessile, in pairs, these on axillary peduncles, or forming terminal corymbs or panicles. Each pair of fl. subtended by pairs of bracts and bracteoles, ovaries often confluent. Corolla tubular, funnel- or bell-shaped, often gibbous at base, oblique, or two-lipped. Stamens 5. Ovary 2–3-celled, style filiform, stigma capitate, ovules many in the inner angle of each cell. Berry fleshy, few-seeded. Species over 100, temperate regions of the Northern Hemisphere.

A. Climbers, corolla bilabiate, and (excepting *L. ovata*) more than 1 in. long, ovaries free.

(*a*) Corolla glabrous outside.

1. **L. Hildebrandiana,** Coll. et Hemsl. in Journ. Linn. Soc. xxviii. 64, t. 11. Shan hills, Upper Burma 3-5,000 ft. Yunnan. Entirely glabrous, l. elliptic or ovate, blade 4, pet. $\frac{1}{2}$–$\frac{3}{4}$ in., sec. n. arching, 3–5 pair. Fl. up to 7 in., lower lip 1–2 in. long, pale yellow on opening, changing into reddish-orange. Fr. 1 in. long. 2. **L. Braceana,** Hemsl. l. c. 64. Khasi hills. Similar to 1, l. almost fleshy, elliptic-lanceolate, sec. n. obscure, blade 4–6, petiole $\frac{3}{4}$–1 in. long, fl. up to 4 in., lobes of upper lip short, lower lip 1–1$\frac{1}{4}$ in. long.

3. **L. glabrata,** Wall. Himalaya from Nepal eastwards 4–8,000 ft., branchlets and petioles thinly pubescent, l. ovate from a rounded or cordate base, glabrous and shining above, hairy along nerves beneath, blade 2–4, petiole $\frac{1}{4}$ in. long, sec. n. prominent beneath, 3–5 pair. Fl. often arranged in short panicles, corolla $\frac{3}{4}$ in. long, nearly white, glabrous without, with deflexed hairs within, lower lip $\frac{1}{3}$–$\frac{1}{2}$ in. 4. **L. obscura,** Coll. & Hemsl. in Journ. Linn. Soc. xxviii. 63. Shan hills at 3–4,000 ft. Hills between Sitang and Salween rivers at 3,000 feet. Foliage like 3. Corolla white, glabrous, very slender, 1–2 in., lower lip $\frac{1}{4}$ in. long.

(*b*) Corolla hairy outside.

5. **L. Leschenaultii,** Wall. Baba Budan hills, Mysore. Coorg. Nilgiris. Palnis. Branchlets, petioles, underside of l. and inflorescence softly grey-tomentose. L. ovate, base rounded or cordate, blade 2–3, pet. $\frac{1}{4}$–$\frac{1}{2}$ in. long. Fl. generally in compact corymbs at the ends of branches; corolla white, slender, 1–1$\frac{1}{2}$ in., lower lip $\frac{3}{4}$ in. long.

6. **L. macrantha,** DC. Nepal. Sikkim 4–10,000 ft. Assam, Khasi hills, Manipur. Shan hills Upper Burma, 4–5,000 ft. China. Branchlets, l. and inflorescence densely clothed with long soft hairs. L. from a broad often cordate base, gradually narrowed to a sharp point, upperside more or less rugose, underside and edges with long soft hairs, blade 2–5, pet. $\frac{1}{8}$–$\frac{1}{4}$ in. long. Fl. often massed in short compact terminal panicles, calyx-teeth with long hairs, corolla 1–2 in. lower lip $\frac{1}{3}$ in. long. *L. japonica*, L., closely allied to 6, has been reported from Myitkyina, Upper Burma. 7. **L. acuminata,** Wall. Nepal. Sikkim 7–10,000 ft. Branchlets and petioles clothed with long soft hairs, l. ovate-lanceolate, more or less hairy on both sides, blade 2–4, pet. $\frac{1}{8}$–$\frac{1}{4}$ in. long. Fl. sometimes in compact terminal heads, as a rule in long pedunculate pairs, supported by long linear bracts, corolla funnel-shaped, $\frac{1}{2}$ in., lower lip $\frac{1}{3}$ in. long. Fl. globose, $\frac{1}{3}$ in. diam. 8. **L. ovata,** Ham. Assam, Upper Burma. China. A slender climber, branchlets and l. slightly hairy. L. ovate, thinly membranous, blade 2–3, pet. $\frac{1}{2}$–$\frac{3}{4}$ in. long. Fl. yellowish-white, slightly scented, in pairs on slender pubescent peduncles. Corolla $\frac{1}{2}$ in. long, the upper lip cut barely to the half into 4 lobes, the lower linear $\frac{1}{3}$ in. long.

B. Erect, mostly large shrubs, corolla bilabiate half in. long or less, bracteoles small or 0.

9. **L. alpigena,** Linn. Kuram valley 10–11,000 ft. N. W. Himalaya 8–12,000 ft. Mountains of Europe. A large shrub, glandular-pubescent, bark peels off in papery flakes, l. ovate-lanceolate, blade 3–4, pet. $\frac{1}{4}$–$\frac{1}{3}$ in. long. Peduncles single, 1–2 in. long, bracts linear, bracteoles small. Calyx pubescent, corolla hairy, very gibbous at the

base, berries separate in the Indian, connate in the European specimens, hence the Indian form often regarded as distinct and called *L. Webbiana*, Wall. 10. **L. heterophylla**, Dcne. Inner arid N.W. Himalaya. Similar to 9, glabrous, l. often irregularly sinuate.

11. **L. orientalis**, Lam. Kuram valley, 12,000 ft. N.W. Himalaya above 6,000 ft., east as far as Garhwal. Western Asia, China. A large shrub, nearly glabrous, bark peeling off in thin shreds. L. elliptic, blade 1–3, pet. $\frac{1}{8}$–$\frac{1}{4}$ in. long. Fl. pink, on peduncles $\frac{1}{2}$–$\frac{3}{4}$ in., corolla $\frac{1}{2}$ in. long, nearly glabrous outside, deeply 2-lipped, ovaries connate, bracteoles minute, rounded, sometimes wanting, bracts subulate. Berries black when ripe. 12. **L. cærulea**, Linn. Baltistan 11,000 ft. (Duthie July 1892). Europe and Northern Asia. Similar to 11, but hairy, l. oblong or elliptic-oblong, peduncles $\frac{1}{8}$ in., corolla hairy outside, lobes nearly equal, bracteoles 0, berries confluent, blueish-black when ripe. 13. **L. microphylla**, Willd. Kuram valley. Inner arid N.W. Himalaya 9–14,000 ft. Western Tibet and Western Siberia. Nearly glabrous, l. grey $\frac{1}{2}$–$\frac{3}{4}$ in. long. Fl. whitish-yellow, corolla bilabiate, bracteoles 0, berries partially confluent, bright red.

C. Erect, mostly large shrubs, corolla bilabiate, $\frac{3}{4}$ in. long or less, bracteoles connate.

14. **L. hypoleuca**, Dcne. Baluchistan, Juniper tracts. Arid tracts of the inner N.W. Himalaya 8–10,000 ft. Branchlets hairy, l. nearly sessile, broad-ovate, or nearly orbicular, obtuse, white- or grey-tomentose beneath, $\frac{3}{4}$–$1\frac{1}{4}$ in. long. Fl. orange-red, $\frac{1}{2}$ in. long, in pairs, on peduncles $\frac{1}{4}$–$\frac{1}{2}$ in. long. Glandular hairs on calyx and fruit. 15. **L. decipiens**, Hook. f. & Thoms. Sikkim 10–12,000 ft. A shrub 8–12 ft., branchlets minutely hairy, l. membranous, ovate-lanceolate, blade 2–5, pet. $\frac{1}{8}$ in. Fl. red-purple, $\frac{1}{3}$ in., on axillary peduncles, $\frac{1}{4}$–$\frac{1}{2}$ in. long.

16. **L. quinquelocularis**, Hardw.; Collett, Simla Flora 225 fig. 69. Vern. *Gurazah*, Bal.; *Bakhru*, Chenab; *Sbang*, Kunawar; *Taknoi*, Jauns. Baluchistan. Kuram valley. N.W. Himalaya 8–9,000 ft, Bhutan. China. A large deciduous shrub or small tree, softly pubescent, bark grey, peeling off in long fibrous strips, l. ovate, blade 1–3, pet. $\frac{1}{8}$–$\frac{1}{4}$ in. long. Fl. white, yellow afterwards, in axillary nearly sessile clusters of 2–4, bracts linear, hairy, bracteoles ovate, obtuse, connate at base, corolla $\frac{1}{2}$–$\frac{3}{4}$ in. long, hairy outside. Berries free $\frac{1}{4}$ in. diam.

D. Erect shrubs, corolla 5-lobed 1 in. long or less, bracts large, ovate, bracteoles small or 0.

17. **L. hispida**, Pall. (*L. bracteata*, Royle Ill. t. 53.) Inner dry Himalayan districts 10–13,000 ft. from Baltistan to Sikkim and East Tibet. Siberia, China. L. thinly membranous, hairy or glabrous, ovate-oblong, base rounded or cordate, blade 1–3 in. long, pet. very short. Fl. in pairs, buds and fruit enveloped in large bracts, peduncles $\frac{1}{2}$ in., corolla broadly funnel-shaped $\frac{1}{2}$ in. long, fr. red $\frac{1}{3}$ in. long, confluent or entirely separate. 18. **L. asperifolia**, Hook. f. & Thoms. Inner arid N.W. Himalaya and adjoining districts of Tibet, Baltistan to Kumaon 11–14,000 ft. A low much branched shrub, branchlets more or less hispid. L. ovate, blade $\frac{1}{2}$–$1\frac{1}{2}$, petiole $\frac{1}{4}$–$\frac{1}{3}$ in. long. Fl. $\frac{1}{2}$–1 in. long, in pairs on short peduncles. Fr. separate, crowned by the persistent calyx-limb. 19. **L. glauca**, Hook. f. & Thoms. Kuram valley above 12,000 ft. Lahaul. Inner arid Himalaya 12–16,000 ft. Lahaul-Kumaon. A small shrub growing in fissures of rocks. L. elliptic-oblong, $\frac{1}{2}$–$\frac{3}{4}$ in. long, fl. lemon-yellow, $\frac{1}{2}$ in. long.

E. Erect, mostly large shrubs, l. $\frac{3}{4}$–2 in. long, corolla 5-lobed, bracts linear, bracteoles usually connate.

20. **L. ligustrina**, Wall., Wight Ic. t. 1025; Bedd. Manual t. xv. f. 5. Nepal, Khasi hills, Nilgiris. A shrub or small bushy tree, stem twisted, branchlets and petioles pubescent, l. firm, shining, lanceolate, blade 1–$2\frac{1}{2}$ in., pet. $\frac{1}{8}$ in. long, midrib beneath more or less hairy. Fl. nearly sessile, corolla hairy in- and out-side, $\frac{1}{4}$ in. long, gibbous at base. Berries usually confluent, bracteoles enlarged in fruit, forming an involucre, enclosing the 2 (or 3) ovaries.

21. **L. angustifolia**, Wall. Vern. *Geang*, *Chilu*, *Pirlu*, Jaunsar. N.W. Himalaya 6–10,000 ft. Sikkim 10–12,000 ft. A shrub, attaining 12 ft., bark exfoliates in long papery flakes, l. lanceolate, pale and nearly glabrous beneath, blade 1–2, pet. slender $\frac{1}{8}$ in. or less. Peduncles single, axillary, slender, $\frac{1}{2}$–1 in. long, calyx-teeth lanceolate. Corolla scented, white or pale rose-coloured, ovaries connate enclosed in the campanulate tube, formed of the connate bracteoles. Berry red, edible. 22. **L. purpurascens**, Hook. f. & Thoms. Kuram valley. Himalaya 9–13,000 ft. Kashmir to Sikkim.

Branchlets hairy, l. oblong or obovate-oblong, more or less hairy on both sides, blade ⅔–2, petiole slender ⅛–¼ in. Peduncles single, axillary, ⅓–1 in. Corolla hairy, purple, funnel-shaped. Berries more or less confluent, black. 23. **L. tomentella,** Hook. f. & Thoms. Sikkim 8–12,000 ft. Attains 10 ft., pubescent, l. gradually narrowed from a broad base ⅔–1⅓ in. long, pet. short. Peduncles under ¼ in. Fl. white, bracts foliaceous, lanceolate. Berries black, more or less confluent.

F. Rigid, prostrate or straggling shrubs, l. as a rule less than ½ in. long. Corolla 5-lobed.

24. **L. parvifolia,** Edgew. Kuram valley, Himalaya 8–14,000 ft., Kashmir to Sikkim. A prostrate shrub, l. elliptic-oblong, pale beneath, ⅓–½ in., petiole short. Fl. white, peduncles shorter than fl., bracts lanceolate longer than calyx, corolla-tube cylindric, style included. Berries orange-red, not confluent. *L. Myrtillus*, Hook. f. & Thoms. is supposed to differ by narrower bracts. 25. **L. obovata,** Royle. Kuram valley. Himalaya 8–14,000 ft. Kashmir to Sikkim, extending into the inner arid districts. A glabrous straggling or prostrate shrub, up to 6 ft. high, l. ⅓–½ in. obovate. Fl. pale-yellow, peduncle shorter than fl., bracts linear, ciliate, longer than calyx, corolla-tube wider upwards, style exserted. Berries confluent, dark blueish-purple. 26. **L. rupicola,** Hook. f. & Thoms. Districts of Tibet adjoining Kumaon and Sikkim 12–14,000 ft., branchlets pubescent, rigid, nearly spinescent, l. linear or oblong ¼–⅜ in. tomentose beneath. Fl. nearly sessile, bracts linear-obovate ¼ in. long, tomentose beneath, berries not confluent, crowned by the long linear calyx-teeth. 27. **L. spinosa,** Jacquemont. Inner arid N.W. Himalaya and adjoining tracts of Tibet 11-15,000 ft. A small glabrous, rigid shrub, branchlets often leafless and spinescent. L. small narrow-oblong, peduncles short, style exserted, berries not confluent.

2. LEYCESTERIA, Wall.; Fl. Brit. Ind. iii. 16.

Includes *Pentapyxis*, Hook. f.; Fl. Brit. Ind. iii. 17.

Shrubs, branches herbaceeous. L. distichous, sometimes stipulate. Fl. pentamerous, more or less zygomorphic, in axillary spikes. Calyx-lobes persistent, often unequal, corolla funnel-shaped, stamens 5, inserted on the throat of the corolla. Ovary 5-8-celled, style slender, stigma capitate, ovules ∞, biseriate in each cell. Berry many-seeded, seeds minute, testa crustaceous, shining. Species 3.

A. Leaves glabrous, as a rule no stipules, but petioles connate at the base.

1. **L. formosa,** Wall. Pl. As. Rar. t. 120; Wight, Ill. t. 121. D. Himalaya in shady forests 5–10,000 ft. from the Sutlej eastwards. Stem and branches hollow, young shoots pubescent. L. ovate-lanceolate, margin undulate, blade 3–5, pet. ⅓–½ in. long. Spikes axillary, consisting of bracteate whorls, corolla ½–1 in. long, red or white with a purple tinge, bracts sessile, large, ovate or ovate-lanceolate, greenish purple. Berry dark-purple, glandular-hairy. 2. **L. glaucophylla,** C. B. Clarke. Sikkim 5–6,000 ft., not common. Bhutan. Yunnan. Branches slender, hollow, l. lanceolate, sinuate-dentate. Fl. in pairs on lax axillary spikes, bracts shorter than ovary.

B. Leaves densely tomentose beneath with broad interpetiolar stipules.

3. **L. stipulata,** Fritsch (*Pentapyxis stipulata*, Hook. f.). Sikkim 6–10,000 ft., common round Darjeeling. A large straggling shrub, densely grey tomentose. L. sinuate-toothed 4–8 in. long, pet. short, stipules round, ¼–⅜ in. diam. Fl. in short axillary bracteate spikes, corolla white, hairy outside, ⅜ in. long. Berry hairy ⅜ in. long.

3. ABELIA, Rob. Brown; Fl. Brit. Ind. iii. 9.

Included under *Linnæa*, Gronov. in Engler u. Prantl. iv. 4, 166.

(Species 11, 3 in Mexico, the others in Asia.)

A. triflora, R. Brown; Wall. Pl. As. Rar. t. 15. A large shrub, l. ovate-lanceolate, pale beneath, hairy all over or along the edge and midrib, blade 1–3, pet. ⅛–¼ in. Fl. white, tinged with pink, scented, in 3-fld. shortly pedunculate cymes, supported by linear-lanceolate bracts, massed in terminal bracteate heads. Calyx hairy, 5-ribbed, lobes linear long-ciliate, persistent, ⅓–1 in. long at the time the seed ripens. Ovary 3-celled, fruit coriaceous indehiscent 1-seeded.

N.-W. Himalaya, Kashmir to Kumaon 4–10,000ft., chiefly on limestone; also Trans-Indus. Fl. May–Aug.

FIG. 150.—Abelia triflora. ½.

4. VIBURNUM, Linn.; Fl. Brit. Ind. iii. 3.

Shrubs or trees, wood close-grained, leaves simple, when bruised smell often disagreeable. Fl. white or pink, pentamerous, regular, in a compound umbel, thyrsus or corymb, the outer fl. sometimes sterile, larger and zygomorphic (*V. Opulus*, L., The Guelder Rose of Europe, Siberia and North America). Stamens 5, ovary 1–3-celled, one pendulous ovule in each cell. Drupe dry or fleshy, endocarp crustaceous, 1-seeded, seed flat, or concave by the endocarp projecting into the cavity. Species about 100, a few in Europe and the Mediterranean region, the majority in the temperate and subtropical regions of Eastern Asia and North America. Of the 15 species here described, 4 are found both in the Western and Eastern region. Two of these, *V. coriaceum* and *erubescens*, extend from Ceylon to China, *V. odoratissimum* is found in China, while *V. punctatum* is limited to India.

A. Seed flat, often with shallow grooves. Fl. in compound umbels.

(*a*) Corolla short, rotate, funnel-shaped, or campanulate, l. deciduous, generally membranous.

1. **V. cotinifolium**, Don; Wight Ill. t. 121; Collett Simla Fl. 221. fig. 68. Vern. *Banguch*, Haz.; *Bhutnoi*, Jauns.; *Battonda*, *Gwia*, Garhwal, Kumaon.

A large deciduous shrub, young shoots and underside of l. woolly, with grey stellate tomentum. L. rugose, ovate, elliptic or orbicular, obtuse, crenulate or nearly entire, base rounded or nearly cordate, blade 2–5, pet. stout, ¼–½ in. long. Corolla white, tinged with pink, tube ⅕ in. long, turbinate, fr. red, ⅓–½ in. long, edible.

Baluchistan, in the Juniper tracts. Kuram valley, common, 7–9,000 ft. N. W. Himalaya above 4,000 ft., chiefly on sunny slopes. Bhutan 8,500–10,000 ft. Fl. April–June. 2. **V. corylifolium**, Hook. f. & Thoms. Khasi hills. A thin and straggling shrub, branchlets, petioles and underside of l. densely clothed with long soft hairs. Corolla white, almost rotate. Drupe bright red, ¼ in. long.

3. **V. stellulatum**, Wall. Pl. As. Rar. t. 169.—Syn. *V. involucratum*, Wall. Vern. *Richi*, *Richhoi*, *Ensi*, N. W. Him.

A shrub, branches long, bark dark grey. Branchlets, petioles and inflorescence with brown stellate pubescence. L. glabrous above, sparingly stellate-pubescent beneath, ovate or ovate-lanceolate, long-acuminate, with large distant teeth, blade 3–5, pet. slender, ½–1 in. long. Fl. small, very numerous, compound umbels large, sessile or shortly pedunculate, calyx hirsute, corolla white, pubescent, rotate. Drupe bright red, ¼ in. long.

Himalaya, Kashmir to Sikkim, above 6,000 ft. Fl. April–July. 4. **V. Griffithianum**, C. B. Clarke. Upper Burma (Griffith). Branchlets, petioles and inflorescence densely clothed with soft stellate hairs, leaves on both sides stellate-hairy, elliptic to obovate, sharply serrate, compound umbels pedunculate, peduncles 1–2 in. long, calyx glabrous. 5. **V. cordifolium**, Wall. Himalaya, Kumaon to Bhutan 8–12,000 ft. A deciduous tree, young shoots, inflorescence and l. beneath stellately pubescent, l. membranous, ovate, acuminate, base rounded or cordate, sharply serrate, blade 3–5, pet. ⅓–⅔ in. long, sec. n. 6–8 pair, oblique, 3–4 pair basal, prominent beneath, as well as the obliquely transverse veins. Fl. white, appearing with or before the leaves, crowded in terminal sessile compound umbels, corolla rotate. Drupes ¾ in. long, in lax spreading umbels, peduncles and pedicels having lengthened out. Seed flat with incurved edges. Album. ruminate, the intruded testa full of red resinous glands. 6. **V. Colebrookianum,** Wall. Sikkim Terai and outer hills, ascending to 4,000 ft. Assam (*Mala*). Khasi hills. Manipur. Amber mines, Upper Burma. L. elliptic-oblong, crenate-serrate, nearly glabrous, blade 6–8, pet. ½–1 in. long. Compound umbels pedunculate, axillary, fl. white, calyx glabrous, drupe ⅓ in. red.

(*b*) Corolla short, l. coriaceous.

7. **V. punctatum,** Ham.; Bedd. Fl. Sylv. t. 217.—Syn. *V. acuminatum*, Wall.; Wight Ic. t. 1021.

An evergreen shrub, wholly glabrous, branches stout. L. shining, elliptic, almost entire, acuminate, narrowed into petiole ½ in. long, on the underside clothed with minute orbicular multicellular, peltate scales. Compound umbels terminal. Drupe ⅓ in. long, seed grooved, 2 grooves on the dorsal, 3 on the ventral face.

Outer Himalaya from Kumaon to Sikkim, ascending to 5,000 ft. Western Ghats from Kanara southwards. Nilgiris, Anamalai, Palni and Shevaroy hills. Fl. Aug.–Oct. 8. **V. fœtidum,** Wall. Pl. As. Rar. t. 61.; Kurz F. Fl. ii. 2. Khasi hills. Assam. Manipur. Hills of Upper Burma. Yunnan. Branchlets, petioles and inflorescence clothed with stellate hairs, l. rhomboid-lanceolate, glabrous above, pubescent on nerves beneath, repand-toothed, blade 1–4, petiole ⅛–½ in. long. sec. n. 3–4 pair, prominent, the lowest pair basal. Fl. small, white, in compound pedunculate umbels, bracts numerous, hairy, calyx-tube glabrous.

(*c*) Corolla tubular, lobes short, erect.

9. **V. coriaceum,** Blume.—Syn. *V. capitellatum*, W. & A.; Wight Ic. t. 1022.

A shrub or small tree, wood white, hard, close-grained, youngest shoots and nodes slightly hairy. L. coriaceous, glabrous, usually quite entire, blade 5–9, petiole 1 in. long. Inflorescence pedunculate, calyx glabrous, corolla white, tubular, glabrous or pubescent, anthers red. Fr. ⅕ in. long, black, succulent.

Himalaya 4–8,000 ft., from the Sutlej eastwards. Khasi hills. Lower Burma: hills between Sitang and Salween 3–4,000 ft. Upper: hills east of Bhamo 6–7,000 ft. Nilgiris, Palnis. Fl. March–Aug. Oil extracted from the seeds in Nepal and Sikkim. —Ceylon, China. *V. hebanthum*, Wight & Arn.; Gamble Ind. Timb. ed. ii. 395, Nilgiris and other hills on the west side of the Peninsula, differs by the densely tomentose corolla, while in the Himalayan and eastern specimens the corolla is glabrous. All specimens from the Western Peninsula have larger fruit, up to ⅓ in. long. Until further characters are discovered to separate the Western from the Eastern species, it will be convenient to class both under *V. coriaceum*. Beddome, Manual 124, says the corolla of *V. hebanthum* is pubescent or glabrous.

B. Seed concave, endocarp deeply intruded, transverse section half moon-shaped.

(*a*) Fl. appearing with or after the l., generally in 3-fid. cymes, arranged in a terminal thyrsus.

10. **V. odoratissimum,** Ker in Botanical Register, t. 456.

A shrub or small tree, l. coriaceous, glabrous, entire or distantly and slightly dentate, obtuse or shortly acuminate, blade 3–7, narrowed into petiole ⅓ in. long, sec. n. distant, 6–8 pair. Fl. white, scented, yellow when fading, nearly sessile in 3-fid cymes, arranged in a pedunculate pyramidal glabrous thyrsus. Calyx not constricted beyond ovary, free part short with 5 triangular teeth, corolla glabrous, campanulate. Fr. ¼–⅓ in. long, seed concave, section half moon-shaped, albumen uniform.

Assam, Khasi hills. Upper Burma, near Serpentine Mines. Mahabaleshwar (D.B. Oct. 1881). Fl., North-East in April and May, at Mahabl. in Oct. China, Japan.

11. **V. atrocyaneum,** C. B. Clarke. Mishmi hills. Manipur 6–8,000 ft. An evergreen shrub, l. shining, almost entire, blade 3–4, pet. ½–1 in. long. Fl. in small terminal compound umbels, drupe dry, hard, blue, seed concave, albumen ruminate, red resinous glands as in *V. cordifolium*. Nearly allied to *V. Tinus*, L., of the Mediterranean region.

12. **V. erubescens,** Wall. Pl. As. Rar. t. 134.—Syn. *V. Wightianum*, Wall.; Wight Ic. t. 1024.

A small deciduous tree. Youngest shoots, inflorescence and l. on the nerves beneath slightly pubescent. L. ovate or elliptic, upper part serrate, blade 2–4, pet. ½–1 in. long. Fl. white or pale rose-coloured, in a pedunculate drooping thyrsus at the ends of short branchlets, the last ramifications having usually 3-fid. cymes, bracts linear. Calyx-teeth ovate, corolla tubular ¼–½ in. long. Drupe red, ¼ in. long. Seed deeply grooved.

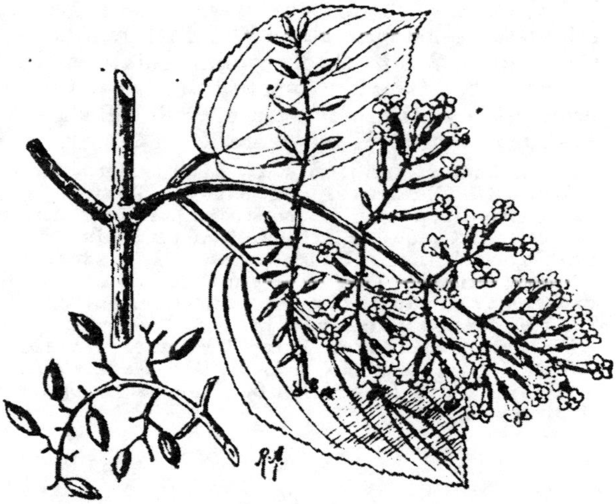

FIG. 151.—Viburnum erubescens, Wall. Fl., Fr. ½.

Himalaya from Kumaon eastwards, in Sikkim common in second growth at 6–10,000 ft. Nilgiris. Fl. March–May. Ceylon. China 13. **V. Simonsii,** Hook. f. & Th. Khasi hills. A shrub or small tree, l. coriaceous, elliptic, glabrous, blade 3–4½, pet. ½–¾ in. long, sec. n. oblique, 6–8 pair. Fl. white in an erect terminal thyrsus, corolla short, campanulate. Drupe ¼ in. long, dull red.

FIG. 152.—Viburnum nervosum, Don. ½.

(*b*) Fl. appearing before the l. in compact terminal corymbs, seed deeply concave, endocarp T-shaped.

14. **V. nervosum,** Don. Vern. *Gūch*, Haz.; *Kalin*, Bash.; *Tilni*, *Tirnoi*, Jaunsar.

A shrub or small tree, young shoots and inflorescence softly tomentose, l. membranous, elliptic, serrate, hairy on nerves beneath, blade 3–4, pet. ¾–1 in. long, sec. n. 8–10 pair, closely parallel. Fl. white or rose-coloured, fragrant, in terminal short dense sessile corymbs, corolla ¾ in. long, funnel-shaped with a spreading limb. Drupe ½–¾ in. long, edible.

Himalaya, Kulu to Sikkim, 7–12,000 ft. Fl. May–July.

Closely allied, 15. **V. fœtens,** Dcne. Himalaya 5–11,000 ft. Kashmir–Garhwal. Glabrous, l. elliptic, serrate, blade 4–6, pet. $\frac{3}{4}$–1 in. long, sec. n. distant 6–8 pair. Fl. scented, branches fetid when bruised. Drupe $\frac{1}{2}$–$\frac{3}{4}$ in., edible.

5. SAMBUCUS, Linn.; Fl. Brit. Ind. iii. 2.

Tall herbs, shrubs or trees, pith large. L. large, imparipinnate, often stipulate, leaflets serrate. Fl. small, regular, in compound bracteate corymbs. Calyx-limb 3–5-toothed, corolla rotate or broadly campanulate, 3–5-cleft, stamens 5. Ovary 3–5-celled, one pendulous ovule in each cell. Drupe crowned by the calyx-teeth, 3–5-celled, endocarp cartilaginous. Species 15–20, Northern Hemisphere, 2 in Australia and 1 in South America.

1. **S. Ebulus,** Linn. Dwarf Elder. Vern. *Gandal*, *Gandala*, Chenab. Kashmir 6–10,000 ft. Europe. North Africa. Western Asia. Gregarious, large herbaceous stems, from a perennial rootstock, l. fetid when bruised, leaflets 3–5 pair, oblong lanceolate, stipules foliaceous often pinnatilobed. Inflorescence glabrous, fl. white, pink or dark lilac. Drupe purple. 2. **S. adnata,** Wall. Nepal. Sikkim 5–10,000 ft. China. A shrub, l. often bipinnate, stipules small or 0, leaflets nearly sessile, often decurrent and adnate to rachis, inflorescence hairy. Drupe red. 3. **S. javanica,** Blume. Sikkim 4–8,000 ft., common in second growth. Assam. Khasi hills. Maimansingh (*S. Thunbergiana*, Blume, Kurz F. Fl. ii. 3. Kachin hills, Upper Burma, is this species). China, Japan. A shrub or small tree, leaflets oblong or oblong-lanceolate, blade 4–8, pet. $\frac{1}{3}$–$\frac{1}{2}$ in., stipules small or 0. Inflorescence puberulous or almost villous. Fl. white, drupe black.

Order LXI. RUBIACEÆ. Gen. Pl. ii. 7.

Trees, shrubs or herbs, rarely climbers, l. opposite or whorled, stipules interpetiolar, sometimes intrapetiolar. Corolla gamopetalous inserted round the epigynous disk, lobes usually 4–5. Stamens inserted in the corolla-tube, alternating with its lobes, anthers dorsifixed, cells 2 parallel, dehiscing longitudinally. Ovary wholly inferior, usually 2-celled, ovules 1 or more in each cell. Embryo in a copious, rarely thin, fleshy or horny albumen.

In most genera the wood fibres have bordered pits; exceptions are: *Guettarda, Hamiltonia, Leptodermis, Pæderia, Morinda, Damnacanthus, Psychotria, Chasalia.*

I. *Naucleæ.*—Fl. collected into dense globose heads. Corolla funnel-shaped, stigma simple. Fruit 2-celled, pericarp thin, more or less fleshy, endocarp cartilaginous.
  Erect trees or shrubs.
    Ovaries confluent; fruits forming a globose fleshy mass . . . . 1. Sarcocephalus.
    Ovaries free, common receptacle often fleshy in fruit.
      Ovary 2-celled, ovules solitary in each cell . 2. Cephalanthus.
      Ovary 4-celled in the upper part, ovules numerous . . . . 3. Anthocephalus.
    Ovaries free, common receptacle usually dry in fruit.
      Stigma clavate, fl. mixed with numerous filiform bracteoles . . . . 4. Adina.
      Stigma globose or ovoid, corolla lobes imbricate 5. Nauclea.
      Stigma mitræform, corolla-lobes valvate . . 6. Stephegyne.
  Climbers with hooked peduncles, bracteoles 0 . . 7. Uncaria.

II. *Cinchoneæ.*—Ovules numerous, capsule 2-celled, seeds winged.
  Corolla-lobes valvate, large foliaceous reticulate persistent bracts.
    Style entire, trees or large shrubs . . . . . 8. Hymenodictyon.
    Style bifid, small epiphytic shrubs . . . . Hymenopogon (p. 372).
  Corolla-lobes valvate, lobes fringed . . . . . 9. Cinchona.
  Corolla-lobes imbricate, style 2-fid . . . . . 10. Luculia.

III. *Rondeletieæ.*—Ovules numerous, capsule 2-celled, seeds angular, not winged, corolla-lobes imbricate or twisted.
  Fl. in trichotomous panicles . . . . . . 11. Wendlandia.
  Fl. in scorpoid cymes . . . . 12. Greenea.

IV. *Hedyotideæ.*—Ovules numerous, capsule 2- or 4-celled, or cocci 2–4, corolla-lobes valvate.

Leaves entire, stamens 4 . . . . 13. HEDYOTIS.
Leaves dentate, stamens 2 . . . . SILVIANTHUS (p. 375).

V. *Mussændeæ.*—Ovules numerous, fr. a berry or drupe, seeds minute, corolla valvate.

Inflorescence terminal, one of the calyx-lobes usually enlarged . . . . 14. MUSSÆNDA.
Inflorescence axillary, l. coriaceous.
Calyx-limb truncate . . . . AULACODISCUS (p. 376).
Calyx-teeth lanceolate, tertiary nerves prominent MYRIONEURON (p. 376).
Inflorescence axillary, l. membranous.
Calyx-limb cup-shaped, truncate, tertiary nerves conspicuous . . . . UROPHYLLUM (p. 376).
Calyx-teeth as long as ovary . . . . . . ADENOSACME (p. 377).

VI. *Gardenieæ.*—Ovules few or numerous in each cell, one in species of *Webera*. Fr. a berry, seeds large, corolla-lobes twisted.

Inflorescence terminal.
Fl. 5-merous, in terminal corymbiform compound cymes, anthers exserted . . . . . . 15. WEBERA.
Fl. 4-merous, fertile fl. solitary, male in few-fld. corymbs, anthers included . . . . . BYRSOPHYLLUM (p. 378).
Inflorescence axillary, supra-axillary or leaf-opposed.
Stigma fusiform, buds resinous, corolla-lobes 5 or more, ovary 1-celled . . . . 16. GARDENIA.
Stigma fusiform, corolla-lobes 5, ovary 2-celled . 17. RANDIA.
Stigma 2-lobed or style bifid, ovules numerous
Fl. in axillary or leaf-opposed cymes . . . BRACHYTOME (p. 383).
Fl. ♂ in supra-axillary pedunculate heads, ♀ often solitary . . . . . . MORINDOPSIS (p. 384).
Style bifid, ovules 2–10 in each cell.
Fl. sessile, in opposite axillary fascicles . . HYPTIANTHERA (p. 384).
Fl. nearly sessile, in axillary bracteate spikes . PETUNGA (p. 384).
Style bifid, ovules 2 or 3 in each cell.
Inland trees or shrubs, berry 2- or 3-celled . 18. DIPLOSPORA.
Litoral, drupe cylindric, ribbed . . . . SCYPHIPHORA (p. 384).

VII. *Vanguerieæ, Guettardieæ, Alberteæ.*—Ovules solitary in each cell, radicle superior.

Corolla-lobes valvate.
Ovary 2-celled, stigma large, usually ribbed . . 19. CANTHIUM.
Ovary 5-celled, stigma 4–5-lobed , . . . VANGUERIA (p. 386).
Ovary 8–12-celled, style 4–12-branched . . . TIMONIUS (p. 386).
Corolla-lobes imbricate, ovary 4–9-celled . . . GUETTARDA (p. 386).
Corolla-lobes twisted, ovary 1- or 2-celled . . . 20. OCTOTROPIS.

VIII. *Ixoreæ.*—Ovules solitary, radicle inferior, corolla-lobes twisted.

Inflorescence terminal, corolla-tube long, slender.
L. membranous, bracts at the lower cyme branches membranous, more or less sheathing, style twice the length of corolla-tube . . . . . . 21. PAVETTA.
L. and bracts coriaceous, style less than twice the length of corolla-tube . . . . 22. IXORA.
Inflorescence axillary, corolla-tube cylindrical . . 23. COFFEA.

IX. *Pæderieæ.*—Ovules solitary, radicle inferior, corolla-lobes valvate.

Fruit capsular, l. fetid when bruised.
Capsule 5-valved at the top . . . . . HAMILTONIA (p. 390).
Capsule 5-valved to the base . . . . . 24. LEPTODERMIS.
Fruit of 2 cocci or pyrenes, separating when ripe.
Pyrenes flat, orbicular or elliptic . . . . 25. PÆDERIA.
Two cylindrical cocci . . . . . . AITCHISONIA (p. 391).

X. *Morindeæ.*—Ovules solitary, radicle inferior, corolla-lobes valvate, fr. a drupe or berry.

Fl. in dense heads, the calyx-tubes cohering.
Heads many-fld., fl. white, calyx-limb truncate . 26. MORINDA.
Heads few-fld., fl. violet, calyx-limb 4-toothed . RENNELLIA (p. 392).
Flowers free, ovary 2- or 4-celled.
Fl. axillary, solitary or in pairs on short pedicels, calyx-limb 4- or 5-fid . . . . DAMNACANTHUS (p. 393).
Fl. in axillary compact cymes or heads, calyx-limb annular . . . . GYNOCHTHODES (p. 393).

Fl. in axillary and terminal fascicles or umbels calyx-limb truncate	PRISMATOMERIS (p. 393).
Fl. in a terminal thyrsus, calyx-limb truncate .	CŒLOSPERMUM (p. 393).

XI. *Psychotrieæ.*—Ovules solitary, radicle inferior, corolla-lobes valvate, ovules basal erect, fr. a drupe or berry.

Ovary 2-celled, fl. in terminal trichotomous cymes.	
Corolla-tube short, straight, seeds plano-convex .	27. PSYCHOTRIA.
Corolla-tube slender, curved, seeds concave, cup-shaped	CHASALIA (p. 395).
Corolla-tube short. A small epiphytic shrub .	HYDNOPHYTUM (p. 395).
Corolla bell- or funnel-shaped, cymes often few-fld., ramifications and peduncles slender	28. SAPROSMA.
Ovary 4–9-celled, fl. in axillary clusters or short cymes, l. distichous, tertiary n. parallel . . .	29. LASIANTHUS.

1. SARCOCEPHALUS, Afzel.; Fl. Brit. Ind. iii. 22.

Shrubs or trees. Fl. heads single, on bracteate, mostly terminal peduncles, bracteoles 0. Ovaries confluent. Fl. 4- or 5-merous without bracteoles, corolla narrow-tubular, lobes imbricate in bud. Stamens inserted in the mouth of the corolla-tube, style long-exserted, stigma fusiform, ovary 2-celled, ovules numerous. Fr. a globose, fleshy syncarpium, seeds not winged. Species 13, from tropical Africa to New Guinea.

1. **S. Missionis**, Haviland, in Journ. Linn. Soc. xxxiii. 32.—Syn. *Nauclea Missionis*, Wall.; Fl. Brit. Ind. iii. 27.

A small tree, l. glabrous, shining, elliptic-lanceolate, blade 3–6, narrowed

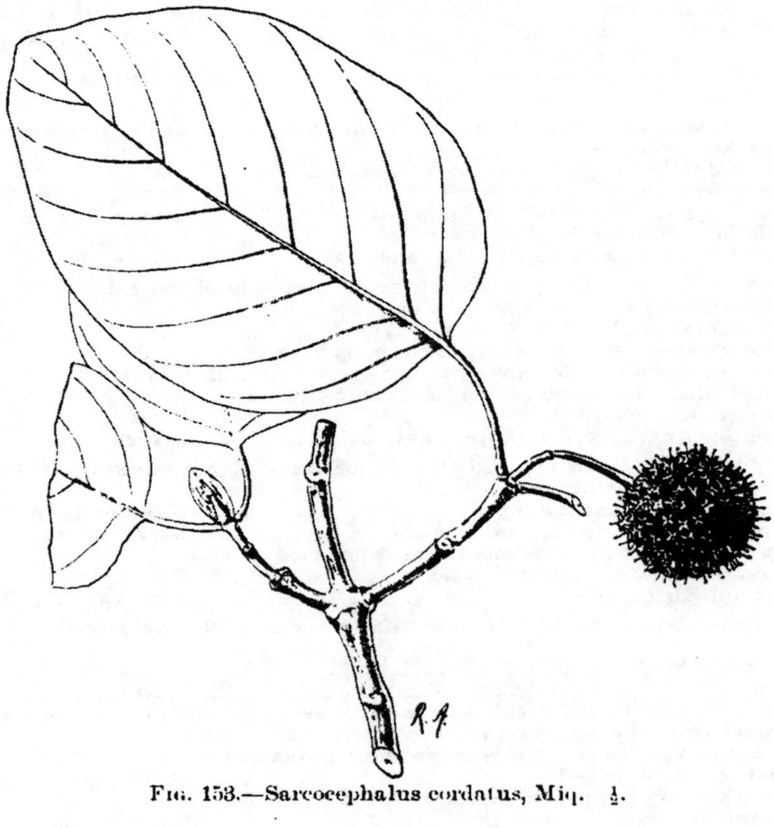

FIG. 153.—Sarcocephalus cordatus, Miq. ½.

into petiole ¼ in. long, stipules large concave almost persistent. Peduncle ½–¾ in., with numerous bracts near base, calyx-lobes densely hairy, oblong, obtuse, less than half the length of corolla-tube, corolla-lobes hairy on both sides.

West side of the Peninsula, from the Konkan southwards, common along rivers and watercourses. Fl. H. S.

2. **S. cordatus,** Miq.; Bedd. Fl. Sylv. t. 318. Vern. *Ma-u lèlan*, Upper; *Ma-u lettanshè*, Lower Burma.

A large or middle-sized deciduous tree, branchlets grey, l. broadly ovate, from a broad, often cordate base, often hairy beneath, blade 3–7, petiole 1 in., stipules obtuse, ½–¾ in. long. Peduncle 1–1½ in., heads yellow or orange, calyx-lobes clavate, minutely hairy, corolla ¼ in. long, quite glabrous, lobes obtuse.

Burma, Upper and Lower. Fl. H. S. Ceylon. Malay Archip. Cochin China. Queensland. A specimen sent by Duthie from Harnapur, Gonda district, Oudh, has the leaves similar, but differs by linear calyx-lobes, more than half the length of corolla-tube, corolla ½ in. long, and apiculate anthers.

2. CEPHALANTHUS, Linn.; Fl. Brit. Ind. iii. 23.

Species 8, 1 in India, China and North America, 1 in South Africa, the rest mostly in South America.

C. occidentalis, Linn.—Syn. *C. naucleoides*, DC.; Kurz F. Fl. ii. 68. Vern. *Momaka gale*, *Sein ban*, Burm.

A shrub or small tree, glabrous pubescent or tomentose. L. opposite or in whorls of 3 or 4, ovate or ovate-lanceolate, blade 3–6, petiole ½–¾ in. long. Fl. heads white, scented, in terminal trichotomous leafy panicles. On a large globose hairy, more or less fleshy receptacle, numerous tetramerous fl., closely packed, free portion of calyx-tube more or less cleft into obtuse segments, corolla ¼–⅓ in. long, tube 2–5 times the length of calyx, lobes usually woolly inside and with small black glands near the sinus of the lobes. Ovaries glabrous or hairy, not confluent, one ovule in each cell. Seeds 2, upper portion enveloped in a snow-white spongy arillus.

Subhimalayan tract, Oudh (in swamps) and Sikkim. Assam (in swamps, gregarious), Khasi hills, Cachar, Upper Burma. Fl. March–May. China. North America, extending across the whole continent, along the banks of slow streams, in extensive thickets, rising from stout contorted roots and from large, prostrate, root-like trunks, sometimes forming stems 40–50 ft. high. I follow Hemsley (Journ. Linn. Soc. xxiii. 369) and Haviland (Journ. Linn. Soc. xxxiii. 38) in regarding the American and Asiatic tree as one species. The American specimens have a short calyx and a long slender corolla, but so have specimens from Assam.

3. ANTHOCEPHALUS, A. Rich.; Fl. Brit. Ind. iii. 23.

Species 3, India and Malay Archipelago.

A. Cadamba, Miq.—Syn. *A. indicus*, A. Rich.; Haviland in Journ. Linn. Soc. xxxiii. 22. t. iv. fig. 38–43; *Nauclea Cadamba*, Roxb.; Bedd. Fl. Sylv. t. 35. *Sarcocephalus Cadamba*, Kurz. Vern. *Kadam*, Hind.; *Roghu*, Ass.; *Kadambe*, Tel.; *Ma-u*, Burm.

A large deciduous tree of rapid growth, wood soft, branches horizontal, l. coriaceous, shining and glabrous above, pubescent beneath, ovate, acuminate, stipules linear, early caducous. Fl. heads single, terminal, yellow, 1½–2 in. diam., peduncles 1–1½ in. long, corolla glabrous, lobes erect, calyx-lobes oblong persistent. Ovaries not confluent, 4-celled in the upper, 2-celled in the lower portion, bracteoles 0. Fr. a fleshy receptacle, on which are inserted numerous closely packed few-seeded capsules. Seeds not winged.

Terai and outer hills of Sikkim to 3,000 ft. Evergreen forests of North Kanara. Northern Circars. Cuddapah and Karnul. Eastern slopes of the Pegu Yoma. Commonly planted. Fl. Dec.–July. The fr. is eaten.—Malay Archip. New Guinea.

4. ADINA, Salisb.; Fl. Brit. Ind. iii. 24.

Fl. pentamerous, mixed with numerous filiform bracteoles. Corolla-lobes valvate or slightly imbricate, stigma clavate. Species 9, from tropical Africa to Japan and the Malay Archipelago.

1. **A. cordifolia**, Hook. f.; Bedd. Manual t. xxix.; Brand. F. Fl. t. 33.—Syn. *Nauclea cordifolia*, Willd.; Roxb. Cor. Pl. t. 53; Bedd. Fl. Sylv. t. 33. Vern, *Haldu*, Hind.; *Heddi*, Mar.; *Rudrakadapa*, Tel.; *Hettiga*, *Yuethagada*, Kan.; *Hnaw*, Burm.

A tall deciduous tree, bark rough, wood yellow when fresh cut, afterwards reddish-brown, even-grained, no heartwood. L. cordate-orbicular, abruptly acuminate, pubescent beneath, blade 4–9 in. diam., pet. pubescent, 3–4 in., stipules pubescent, ½–¾ in. long, concealing the uppermost pair of leafbuds. Peduncles 2–4 in. long, single or 2–3 from one leaf-axil, fl. heads yellow, ⅔–1 in. diam., receptacle and bracteoles hairy, calyx and corolla densely pubescent, calyx-tube 5-angled, lobes linear deciduous.

Subhimalayan tract from the Jumna eastwards, ascending to 3,000 ft. Behar, Centr. Prov. Common in deciduous forests of both Peninsulas. Combs made of the wood. Fl. June–Sept., leafless for a short time in the H. S.—Ceylon, Cambodia. 2. **A. polycephala**, Benth.; Haviland in Journ. Linn. Soc. xxxiii. t. iv. fig. 25–31. Khasi hills, Chittagong. Tenasserim. Cambodia. Sumatra, Java. A small evergreen tree, l. glabrous, glossy, lanceolate or elliptic-lanceolate, blade 4–8, pet. ½–1 in. long. Fl. heads ⅓–⅔ in. diam. to end of style, in trichotomous terminal panicles, ramifications slender. Calyx-lobes oblong, obtuse. 3. **A. oligocephala**, Haviland l. c. 46, Khasi hills, similar, but differs by the calyx limb being entire.

5. NAUCLEA, Linn.; Fl. Brit. Ind. iii. 26.

Peduncles undivided, terminal, single or 3 together. Fl. pentamerous, calyx-lobes narrow, deciduous, corolla-lobes imbricate in bud, ovaries not confluent. Stigma globose or broadly conical, seeds winged, the wing bifid at one end. Species about 30, from India to the Islands of the Pacific.

A. Bracteoles mixed with the fl.

1. **N. purpurea**, Roxb. Cor. Pl. t. 54.—Syn. *N. elliptica*, Dalz. & Gibs. Bombay Fl. 118; Bedd. Manual t. xxix.; Ic. Pl. Ind. Or. t. 19. Vern. *Phuga*, Mar.

A middle-sized or small tree, l. glabrous, elliptic, blade 4–7, pet. ½ in. long, stipules deciduous. Peduncles single, 1–2½ in. long, in the middle with 2 caducous bracts. Fl. mixed with numerous hairy bracteoles, calyx-lobes purple, subulate, hairy, stigma globose. Fr. crowned with the persistent base of calyx-lobes.

Western Ghats from the Konkan southwards. Rumpa hills, Northern Circars. Fl. Feb.–March. 2. **N. Griffithii**, Haviland (*Adina Griffithii*, Hook. f.). Khasi hills, similar to 1. 3. **N. Gageana**, King MSS., Andamans. L. broadly elliptic, glabrous, petiole flattened and winged in its upper part. Corolla-lobes densely hirsute with long hairs, bracteoles villous, stigma ovoid.

4. **N. sessilifolia**, Roxb.; Kurz F. Fl. ii. 65.—Syn. *Adina sessilifolia*, Hook. f. Vern. *Teinkala*, Burm.

A large deciduous tree, l. glabrous, coriaceous, nearly sessile, from a cordate base elliptic, 5–9 in. long, sec. n. distant, 6–8 pair. Peduncles stout, mostly single, corolla-lobes appressed grey-pubescent.

Cachar, Chittagong. Burma. Fl. R. S.—Cochinchina. Formosa.

5. **N. excelsa,** Blume. Myodwin, Pegu (D. B. Oct. 1862). *Thitpayaung*, Burm. A large tree, l. glabrous, shining on both sides, elliptic-oblong, blade 6–10, narrowed into petiole $\frac{3}{4}$ in. long, sec. n. 8–12 pair. Fl. heads $1\frac{1}{3}$ in. diam. to extremity of stigma. peduncles in threes, 2–3 in. long, bracts immediately below the heads, caducous, Receptacle densely hairy, calyx-lobes nearly as long as corolla, narrow linear with a thick clavate end, corolla glabrous. Stigma broadly ovoid. May possibly not be *N. excelsa* of Java. 6. **N. nicobarica,** Haviland. Nicobars, l. glabrous, from a slightly unequal-sided base ovate or obovate-elliptic, blade 4–6, petiole $\frac{3}{4}$ in, long. Peduncles solitary or in threes, 1–3 in. long, bracts close under the heads, caducous.

6. STEPHEGYNE, Korth.; Fl. Brit. Ind. iii. 25.

Mitragyna, Korth.; Haviland in Journ. Linn. Soc. xxxiii. 68.

Fl. heads solitary or panicled. Fl. pentamerous, intermixed with linear bracteoles, corolla-lobes valvate, ovaries free, stigma concave at base. Seeds winged.

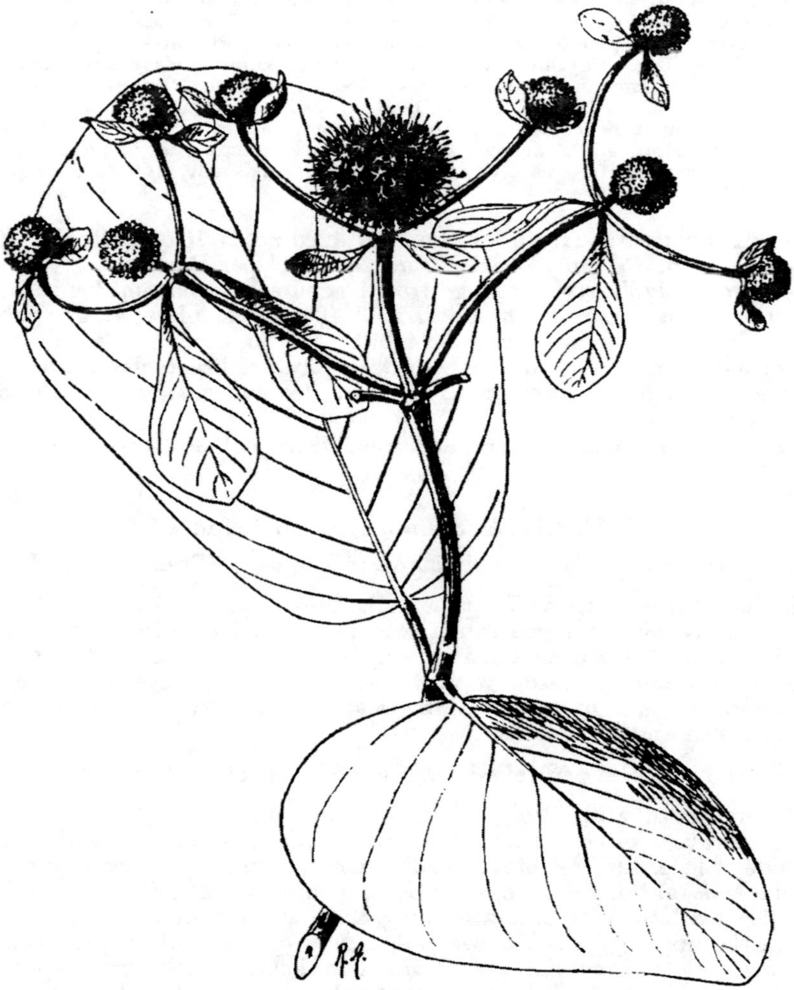

FIG. 154.—Stephegyne diversifolia, Hook. f. $\frac{1}{2}$.

Species 8, from tropical Africa to New Guinea.

1. **S. parvifolia,** Korth.—Syn. *Nauclea parvifolia*, Willd.; Roxb. Cor.

Pl. t. 52; Wight Ill. t. 123; Bedd. Fl. Sylv. t. 34. Vern. *Kaim*, *Kalamb*, *Karma*, Hind.; *Kalamb*, Mar.; *Mundi*, Gond; *Rattaganapa*, Tel.; *Kadaba*, Kan.; *Tein*, *Teinthe*, Burm.

A large deciduous tree, trunk short, often irregularly shaped and buttressed, bark smooth, dark patches of old exfoliating scales leaving exposed the inner light-coloured bark. Leaves glabrous or pubescent, very variable in shape and size, ovate or obovate, often nearly orbicular or oblong, blade 2–7, pet. ½–1½ in. long, stipules obovate, early deciduous. Fl. heads white or pale yellow, 1 in. diam. to the end of stigma, single or in cymes of three heads, the terminal head sessile or on a short peduncle, the 2 lateral on peduncles 1–2 in. long, supported by foliaceous bracts narrowed into a slender pet. ¼ in. long. Bracteoles numerous, linear, hairy at apex. Free part of calyx-tube short, truncate or indistinctly 5-toothed, concave portion of stigma often 2-fid. Seeds with a thin hyaline wing at both ends, generally bifid at the lower end.

Foot and outer hills of the North-West Himalaya, from the Bias eastwards, ascending to 4,000 ft. Behar, Centr. Prov. Common in both Peninsulas, often gregarious, particularly in moist places, combs made of the wood. Fl. Jan.–Aug., leafless for a short time in spring.—Ceylon dry region. A remarkable variety with small oblong obtuse l. in Upper Burma. 2. **S. tubulosa**, Hook. f.; Bedd. Manual t. xxix.; Ic. Pl. Ind. t. 18. Cochin, Kambakum Hill D. B. Nov. 1881. Ceylon. A small tree, l. membranous, pubescent beneath, elliptic-obovate, shortly acuminate, base rounded, blade 4–6, pet. ¼–1 in., stipules 7–11-nerved, ½–⅔ in. long. Fl. heads pink or purple, bracteoles shorter than capsules, free part of calyx tubular, persistent, half the length of the ribbed capsule.

3. **S. diversifolia**, Hook. f.—Syn. *Nauclea rotundifolia*, Roxb.; Kurz F. Fl. ii. 67. Vern. *Bingah*, Lower, *Hnawthein*, Upper Burma.

A deciduous middle-sized or large tree, l. generally pubescent beneath, broad-ovate, often from a cordate base, blade 3–10, petiole often stout, pubescent, ½–1½ in. long. Fl. heads greenish-white, ¾–1 in. diam., in ample terminal trichotomous cymes, with or without leafy bracts, bracteoles glabrous, apex thick and blunt, free portion of calyx short, deciduous, capsules ribbed, seeds winged at both ends.

Chittagong. Andamans. Upper and Lower Burma. Fl. Sept.–Jan. Java. Philippine islands.

7. UNCARIA, Schreb.; Fl. Brit. Ind. iii. 28.

Ourouparia, Aubl.; Schumann in Engler u. Prantl iv. 4. 57.

Climbing shrubs with axillary tendrils (sterile peduncles), stipules usually bifid, peduncles not enlarged into a receptacle, axillary, often hard and woody after flowering. Pedicels usually lengthen out in fruit. Fr. a capsule, dehiscent septicidally, seeds with two long narrow wings at the ends, one bifid. Species 36, 2 in tropical America, 1 in tropical Africa, the rest from India to Japan and Queensland.

A. Fl. and capsules pedicelled, bracteoles 0, petiole ½–1 in. long.

1. **U. sclerophylla**, Roxb.—Syn. *U. ferruginea*, DC.; Kurz F. Fl. ii. 69. A large evergreen climber, branchlets stout, quadrangular as well as petioles, underside of l., peduncles, bracts, pedicels, calyx and capsules rusty-pubescent. L. coriaceous, shining above, elliptic or ovate, blade 4–6, pet. ½–1 in. long. Peduncles axillary, single, 2–4 in. long, with a whorl of 6 acute bracts ⅓ in. long, in the upper part. Fl. pedicelled, free part of calyx ½ in., constricted above ovary, lobes lanceolate. Corolla 1 in. long, densely grey silky outside. Capsule 1 in., crowned by the persistent calyx, pedicel 1½ in. long. Seed with wings ⅕ in. long.

Eastern slopes of the Pegu Yoma. Tenasserim. Fl. R. S. Malay Penins. and Archip. 2. **U. pedicellata**, Roxb. Tenasserim. Andamans. Malay Peninsula and Archip. to New Guinea. Differs by smaller fl., free portion of calyx ¼, corolla ¾–1, capsule ½–⅔ in., seeds with wings ⅛ in. long. Haviland in Journ. Linn. Soc. xxxiii. 78 transposes 1 and 2, calling the large-fld. sp. *U. pedicellata*. 3. **U. ovalifolia**, Roxb.—Syn. *U. acida*, Roxb. Mergui. Malay Penins. and Archip. Branchlets and l. nearly glabrous, l. ovate or elliptic, blade 2–3, pet. ⅓ in. long. Peduncle gradually narrowed from a broad often woody base, upper part or the whole slender. Pedicels generally shorter than calyx, calyx-lobes broad, nearly orbicular, corolla pubescent. Capsule slender.

B. Fl. sessile or subsessile, bracteoles 0, petiole short, under ¼ in.

4. **U. macrophylla**, Wall.—Syn. *U. sessilifolia*, Roxb.; Kurz F. Fl. ii. 69. Bhutan, Assam, Khasi hills, Manipúr, Cachar. Lower Burma, Kurz. A large climber, branchlets, petioles, underside of l. and peduncles rusty pubescent, l. 4–6 in. long, sec. n. 6–8 pair. Peduncles slender, 1–1½ in. long, calyx lobes linear, as long as tube, corolla hirsute outside. Capsule ⅝ in. long, pedicel as long as or longer than capsule. 5. **U. ferrea**, DC. Mergui. Malay Peninsula. L. 3–4 in., sec. n. 6–9 pair, calyx-lobes filiform, densely hairy, corolla glabrous. 6. **U. Gambir**, Roxb. Malay Penins. Cultivated in India. Branchlets and l. glabrous, l. coriaceous, shining, stipules entire. Fl. pubescent, corolla-lobes white, silky. Capsule glabrous, fusiform, ⅜ in. long, pedicels shorter than capsule. Yields the Gambier of commerce, used in tanning and dyeing.

C. Fl. and capsules sessile or nearly so, bracteoles usually present, filiform.

7. **U. pilosa**, Roxb.; Kurz F. Fl. ii. 70. Vern. *Baisi kara*, Nep.

A large evergreen straggling and climbing shrub, branchlets, petioles, underside of l. and peduncles tawny hairy, l. ovate, acuminate, blade 4–5 in. long, petiole very short. Peduncles gradually narrowed from a stout base. Calyx hirsute, lobes linear, longer than tube, corolla yellow, ⅜ in. long, slightly hairy. Capsule ¼–⅓ in. long, nearly sessile, slightly hairy, ribbed, crowned by the linear calyx-lobes.

Outer hills and valleys from Kumaon eastwards, ascending in Sikkim to 5,000 ft. Assam, Garo and Khasi hills. Chittagong. Burma, Upper and Lower. Fl. April–June. 8. **U. sessilifructus**, Roxb. Nepal, Sikkim, to 5,000 ft. Bhutan. Assam. Khasi and Naga hills. Cachar, Chittagong. Lower Burma. A large climber, l. glabrous, shining above, pale beneath, blade 3–5, petiole ¼–½ in. long. Peduncles slender, 1–1½ in. long, often forming terminal panicles, calyx-lobes short, obtuse, corolla pale yellow. Similar and closely allied is 9. **U. laevigata**, Wall. Khasi and Naga hills. Tenasserim.

8. HYMENODICTYON, Wall.; Fl. Brit. Ind. iii. 35.

Trees or shrubs, bark bitter, wood soft. Stipules glandular-serrate, deciduous. Fl. pentamerous, in spikes or panicles with a few large foliaceous reticulate persistent bracts, corolla-lobes short, valvate, anthers linear or oblong, filaments short, attached to the back of a broad connective. Ovary 2-celled, style filiform, long exserted, stigma spindle-shaped. Capsule 2-valved, dehiscing loculicidally, seeds numerous, imbricate, winged at both ends, the lower wing bifid. Species 4–5, tropical Asia and Africa.

1. **H. excelsum**, Wall.; Wight Ic. t. 79.—Syn. *H. thyrsiflorum*, Wall.; Kurz F. Fl. ii. 72; *H. utile*, Wight; Bedd. Fl. Sylv. t. 219 fig. A.; *Cinchona excelsa*, Roxb. Cor. Pl. t. 106. Vern. *Barthua*, Kangra; *Bhaulan*, *Bhurkul*, *Kukurkat*, Hind.; *Dondro*, Guz.; *Bhorsal*, Mar.; *Pottaka*, Tel.; *Kusan*, Burm.

A large deciduous tree, l. elliptic, blade 4–10, narrowed into petiole 2–4 in. long. Fl. pedicellate, white, fragrant, in dense cylindrical compound racemes in terminal drooping panicles, with linear or lanceolate bracts as long as or longer than fl., corolla tube slender, more than three times the length of calyx-lobes. Capsules ¾–1 in., on recurved pedicels ¼–½ in. long.

Subhimalayan tract, frequent in the Sāl forest, also in Savannahs, from the Ravi eastwards. Behar, Central Provinces. Deciduous forests of the Peninsula and Burma, Upper and Lower. Fl. June–Aug.—Cochinchina, Tonkin. Java. 2. **H. flaccidum**, Wall. Pl. As. Rar. t. 188. Subhimalayan tract and outer valleys, ascending to 5,000 ft., from Garhwal eastwards. Khasi hills. Yunnan. Fl. nearly sessile, fasciculate in simple drooping axillary spikes, bracteoles minute, shorter than calyx, each spike with one long-pedunculate floral leaf on the peduncle. Corolla glabrous, tube short, less than twice the length of calyx-lobes. Capsules ½ in., reflexed, on pedicels ⅛ in. long. 3. **H. obovatum,** Wall.; Wight Ic. t. 1159; Bedd. Fl. Sylv. t. 219. *Karwai*, Mar.; *Yella Mala Kai*, Tam. Western Ghats, from Bombay southwards. L. elliptic or obovate, fl. nearly sessile in slender spikes which are arranged in terminal erect panicles. Calyx hirsute, teeth nearly as long as the short corolla-tube. Capsules erect.

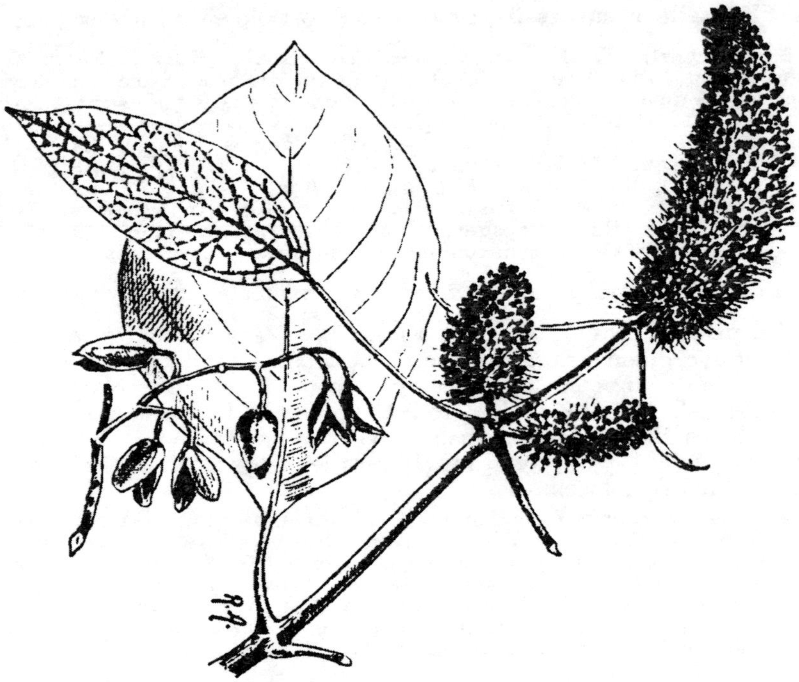

FIG. 155.—Hymenodictyon excelsum, Wall. Fr. Fl. ½.

Hymenopogon parasiticus, Wall. Pl. As. Rar. t. 227. Outer Himalaya from Garhwal eastwards 5–8,000 ft. Khasi hills. Pegu Yoma at 3,000 ft. (Kurz). Yunnan. A small epiphytic shrub, l. oblanceolate, blade narrowed into pet. ¼–1 in. long, sec. n. 15–18 pair. Fl. corymbose with large leafy reticulated white bracts, corolla white, 1½–2 in. long, capsule crowned with the linear calyx-lobes. 2. **H. assamicus,** Hook. f. Assam, sec. n. 30–40 pair, corolla ¾ in.

9. CINCHONA, Linn.; Brandis F. Fl. 264.

Evergreen shrubs or trees, bark bitter, coppicing freely, stipules deciduous. Fl. pentamerous, scented, in terminal panicles, calyx pubescent, limb 5-dentate, persistent. Corolla tubular, pubescent outside, lobes valvate in bud, edge fringed with soft hairs. Ovary 2-celled, style slender with 2 short obtuse branches, papillose inside. Capsule 2-celled 2-valved, dehiscing septicidally from the base, seeds numerous peltate, the broad wings with irregularly lacerated edge, albumen fleshy. Species 30–40; Andes of South America from Venezuela (10° N.L.) to Bolivia (19° S.L.). Of the numerous species and varieties cultivated in India it must suffice to mention the following :—

1. **C. officinalis,** Linn. (*C. Condaminea*, Humb. et Bonpl.). Ecuador on the east side of the Andes 6–9,000 ft. Cultivated chiefly on the Nilgiris, does not thrive in Sikkim L. glabrous, lanceolate or ovate-lanceolate, acute or shortly acuminate, blade 3–6, pet. 1–1½ in. long, sec. n. 8–10 pair, hairy pits in their axils. Fl. red, in short corymbiform compound cymes, terminal and axillary, corolla-tube densely silky with white appressed hairs, slightly pentagonal, ½–⅝ in. long, capsules ovoid-oblong, ⅝–¾ in. long. The bark of stems contains from 1·75 to 10·6 % of Quinine. (M. N. Reimers, Les Quinquinas de

Culture, Paris, 1900.) 2. **C. Calisaya,** Weddell. Peru and Bolivia (13°–16°30 S. L.) 4,800–6,000 ft. L. glabrous, shining above, obtuse, oblong-lanceolate or -obovate, blade 3–6, pet. ½–⅜ in. long, axillary pits indistinct. Fl. pale flesh-coloured, cymes few-fld., arranged in a terminal pyramidal panicle, the lower branches in the axils of leaves. Corolla ⅓–⅜ in. long, lobes lanceolate, rose-coloured, fringe of hairs pure white. Capsule ovoid-oblong ⅓–⅜ in. long. The bark of stems contains up to 4 % of Quinine. 3. **C. Ledgeriana,** Moens, De Kina cultuur in Azie, 1882, 73, tab. 12, 13, 23. North Bolivia. L. glabrous, lanceolate or elliptic-oblong, acute, blade 3–6, pet. ¼–⅓ in. long, those of coppice shoots much larger. Fl. strongly scented, yellowish white on pedicels ⅛ in. long, inflorescence like 2. Corolla ⅓–½ in. long, tube pentagonous, lobes same colour as tube, fringed with very long white hairs. Capsule ovoid-lanceolate ⅓–½ in. long on pedicels ¼–⅓ in. long. The bark of stems contains from 4 to 13 % of Quinine. 4. **C. micrantha,** Ruiz et Pavon. Peru and Bolivia. L. glabrous, broadly elliptic or obovate, acute, blade 3–7 in., narrowed into a marginate petiole ½–1 in. long, those of coppice shoots much larger. Fl. sweetly scented, yellowish-white, corolla ⅓ in. long, tube enlarged at base, not pentagonous. Capsule ovoid-lanceolate ½–⅜ in. long. Bark only contains traces of Quinine. 5. **C. succirubra,** Pavon. Ecuador: a large tree, attaining 80 ft., l. soft pubescent or tomentose, and often red beneath, elliptic, acute at both ends, blade 6–12, pet. 1–1½ in. long, no pits in the axils of sec. n. Fl. rose-coloured, cymes compact in a large pyramidal thyrsus, corolla ½–⅜ in. Capsule oblong, narrowed towards the apex, 1–1¼ in. long. The bark of stems contains from 0·82 to 1·37 % of Quinine and from 3·20 to 5·13 % of Cinchonidine.

10. LUCULIA, Sweet; Fl. Brit. Ind. iii. 36.

Species 2.

1. **L. gratissima,** Sweet. *Dowari*, Nep. Himalaya 4–6,000 ft., from Nepal eastwards. Shan hills and hills east of Bhamo 4–6,000 ft. Yunnan. A tall shrub, branches lenticellate. L. lanceolate, blade 5–7, narrowed into pet. ½–⅜ in. long, sec. n. 9–12 pair. Fl. pink, scented, ⅜–1 in. across, in many-fld. generally pubescent corymbs, calyx-lobes deciduous, corolla tube 1–1½ in. long, style slender, included, stigmas 2, linear. Capsule septicidally 2-valved. Seeds ∞, imbricate upwards, with a long wing at each end. 2. **L. Pinceana,** Hook. Khasi and Mishmi hills. Yunnan. Very similar, sec. n. more numerous, inflorescence perfectly glabrous, fl. larger, 1½–2 in. across, with a pair of raised tubercles in the sinus between the lobes.

11. WENDLANDIA, Bartl.; Fl. Brit. Ind. iii. 37.

Shrubs or small trees, l. entire, opposite or in whorls of 3. Fl. 4- or 5-merous, small, white or pink, in the axils of linear bracts, in large terminal compound trichotomous cymes. Calyx-lobes persistent, nearly equal. Corolla funnel-shaped or tubular, lobes imbricate in bud. Stamens alternating with the corolla-lobes, anthers exserted. Ovary 2-celled, style filiform, stigma entire or 2-fid. Ovules ∞ on small globose placentas adnate to the dissepiment. Capsule 2-valved, many-seeded. Seeds minute, testa obscurely winged.

A. L. opposite, corolla-tube short, less than twice the length of lobes.

1. **W. exserta,** DC. Vern. *Chaulai, Chila, Chilkiya, Tilki*, Hind.; *Til, Tila*, Mar.

A small tree, grey tomentose. L. lanceolate or ovate lanceolate, entire, pubescent above, clothed with short soft grey tomentum beneath, blade 4–9, petiole ½–1 in. long, sec. n. 12–16 pair, stipules recurved. Fl. sessile, white, fragrant, in large pyramidal terminal panicles, calyx grey-hairy, corolla-lobes equal to tube, anthers exserted.

Subhimalayan tract and Sinalik hills from the Chenab to Sikkim. Gregarious in places. Central Provinces, Orissa, Northern Konkan and Deccan. Fl. March–April. Usually deciduous. Will probably be found useful in afforesting waste lands. 2. **W. puberula,** DC. Dehra Dún. Jaunsar. Garhwal. Kumaon. Nepal. L. glabrous above except along midrib and nerves, brown-pubescent beneath with long hairs, stipules erect, persistent. Fl. small, blueish white, corolla-lobes shorter than tube, anthers linear exserted. 3. **W. Wallichii,** W. et A. Sikkim Terai and lower hill forests. Khasi and Naga hills. Manipur. A small tree, stipules caducous, calyx glabrous, corolla-lobes a little shorter than tube, anthers linear exserted.

B. L. usually opposite, corolla-tube twice the length of lobes or longer, usually slender.

4. **W. paniculata,** DC. Vern. *Tagyin, Sagyin*, Upper Burma.

A small tree, l. usually rough above through the raised roots of fallen hairs, softly pubescent beneath with long hairs, stipules broad-orbicular or reniform or oblong-obtuse, the upper part usually reflexed. Fl. sessile, white or greenish-white, scentless, in large hairy terminal panicles, calyx supported by one or two linear hairy bracts as long as itself. Calyx hairy, lobes as long as or shorter than tube, corolla funnel-shaped, lobes half the length of tube or less. Anthers exserted.

Assam, Khasi hills. Manipur. Tenasserim. Upper Burma (often on low ground). Yunnan. Perak. Fl. March–April.

5. **W. tinctoria,** DC.; Brandis F. Fl. 269. Vern. *Padhera*, Kum.; *Tulalodh*, Oudh; *Taung Sagyin*, Upper Burma.

A small tree, l. smooth and glabrous above, more or less minutely pubescent beneath, stipules erect, stiff, terminating in a subulate point or laterally compressed appendage. Fl. yellowish-white, sessile, often supported by numerous short bracts in dense fascicles, forming compact terminal panicles, ramifications and calyx more or less hairy, calyx and corolla like 4, calyx often hirsute with long hairs. Varies in regard to hairiness, shape and size of leaves.

Subhimalayan tract and outer hills from Kumaon and Oudh eastwards, ascending in Sikkim to 5,000 ft. Assam, Khasi hills. Chittagong. Behar. Burma, Upper and Lower (on hilly ground and in Eng forest). Fl. Jan.-March. Yunnan. 6. **W. nitens,** Wall. Tenasserim, l. coriaceous, nearly glabrous, elongate-elliptic, obtuse, stipules short erect, apiculate, calyx hairy, corolla slender, lobes short.

7. **W. glabrata,** DC.; Kurz F. Fl. ii. 74. Vern. *Thitpyu*, Burm.

A small evergreen tree, entirely glabrous, l. opposite, sometimes in whorls of 3, elliptic-lanceolate, blade 4–6, narrowed into pet. ¼–1 in. long, stipules small, erect, triangular. Fl. white, calyx glabrous, teeth minute, triangular.

Nepal 4,000 ft. (*Pater Hieronymus*). Mahendragiri, Ganjam 4,500 ft. Rumpa hills, Godavari 2,000 ft. (Gamble). Naga hills and Manipur 3–6,000 ft. Chittagong hills. Shan hills, Upper Burma. Hills east of Toungoo 2–4,000 ft., often in evergreen forests. Tenasserim. Fl. Feb.–April.—Yunnan, Java, Tonkin, Formosa. 8. **W. coriacea,** DC. Nepal, Sikkim Terai and lower hills. Evergreen, quite glabrous, l. coriaceous, sec. n. very slender, stipules erect, triangular, calyx glabrous, teeth nearly as long as tube. 9. **W. ligustrina,** Wall. Upper Burma. L. glabrous or puberulous on the nerves beneath, stipules appressed, broadly triangular, cuspidate, calyx glabrous, teeth filiform, longer than tube. 10. **W. glomerulata,** Kurz. Mergui. L. membranous, glabrous, narrow-lanceolate, narrowed into a very short petiole, stipules large, orbicular, recurved. Fl. large, ½ in. long, calyx hirsute, teeth much longer than tube.

C. L. usually in whorls of 3.

11. **W. Notoniana,** Wall.; Wight Ic. 1033; Bedd. Fl. Sylv. t. 224. Vern. *Thovara*, Mal.

A small tree, branchlets, petioles, underside of l. and inflorescence hairy, l. usually in whorls of 3, elliptic-lanceolate, blade 3–6, narrowed into petiole ⅓–½ in. long, stipules usually recurved, often 2-fid. Calyx hirsute, teeth as long as tube, corolla-tube hairy within.

West side of the Peninsula, from the Konkan southwards. Fl. Feb.–June. Ceylon, moist region. 12. **W. Lawii,** Hook. f. Ramandrug, Bellary. Bababudan hills. Branchlets slender, minutely pubescent, l. glabrous above, minutely pubescent beneath, stipules erect. Fl. generally pedicelled, in lax, softly hairy large pyramidal panicles. Calyx hairy, lobes filiform, longer than tube. 13. **W. angustifolia,** Wight. Courtallum. Entirely glabrous, l. linear-lanceolate, midrib prominent, sec. n. slender, calyx-teeth short, subulate. 14. **W. pendula,** DC. Nepal, Manipur, Yunnan. Branchlets glabrous, l. often opposite, ovate or ovate-lanceolate, nearly sessile, slightly pubescent on the nerves beneath. Calyx glabrous, teeth lanceolate, as long as tube. Corolla ½ in. long.

12. GREENEA, Wight et Arn.; Fl. Brit. Ind. iii. 41.

Evergreen shrubs, l. opposite or whorled in threes. Fl. 4–5-merous, small, white, sessile in terminal panicles consisting of scorpioid cymes. Calyx-tube globose, lobes persistent slightly unequal, ovary 2-celled, style filiform, stigmas 2, linear, involute. Capsule septicidally 2-valved, seeds 8, narrowly winged. Species 5–6, Eastern Penins. and Malay Archip.

1. **G. Wightiana**, W. et A. Wight Ic. 1161.—Syn. *Wendlandia secunda*, Griff. Tenasserim. An evergreen shrub, l. membranous, oblanceolate, glabrous above, sometimes slightly hairy on midrib beneath, blade 6–10, pet. 1 in. long, stipules contracted into a long point. Fl. numerous, close set, hairy, corolla ½ in. long, tube 3 times the length of lobes. 2. **G. Jackii**, Wight et Arn.—Syn. *Wendlandia corymbosa*, DC. Mergui. Malay Peninsula. Branchlets, petioles, underside of l. and inflorescence softly tomentose, corolla-tube twice the length of lobes.

13. HEDYOTIS, Linn.; Fl. Brit. Ind. iii. 49.

Herbs or small shrubs, sometimes climbing. L. usually opposite. Fl. tetramerous, small, white or lilac, in compound cymes, mostly terminal, corolla campanulate or funnel-shaped, lobes valvate in bud. Ovary 2-celled, style filiform, stigma 2-fid. Species 80, chiefly in tropical Asia. A few only of the more striking species can be mentioned here.

A. Scandent, stipules connate into a short truncate 2-cuspidate cup.

1. **H. scandens**, Roxb. Nepal. Sikkim Terai to 6,000 ft. Assam, Khasi hills, Manipur. Chittagong. A soft-wooded glabrous climber, branches terete, l. lanceolate 3–5 in. long, fl. greenish-white, capsule splitting septicidally into 2 many-seeded cocci, the top raised and protruding between the calyx-teeth.

B. Erect, stipules connate, pectinate.

2. **H. stylosa**, Rob. Brown; Wight Ic. 1027. Nilgiris, Palni and Travancore hills. A large shrub, stem deeply grooved, the furrows often nearly reaching the centre, l. glabrous lanceolate, blade 1–2, pet. ⅛ in., stipules hairy. Corolla white, lobes lanceolate, hairy within. 3. **H. articularis**, Rob. Brown; Wight Ic. t. 1028. Nilgiris. A small rigid shrub, l. glabrous, sessile, rigid, stipules glabrous, calyx-tube produced beyond the ovary, lobes short.

Silvianthus bracteatus, Hook. f. Silhet, Cachar. Khasi and Naga hills, Manipur. A glabrous unarmed shrub, l. membranous, elliptic or elliptic-lanceolate, irregularly toothed, blade 5–8, pet. 1–2 in. long. Fl. large, in dense, nearly sessile axillary bracteate cymes, calyx purplish-green, lobes 5, oblong, foliaceous, persistent and enlarged after flowering. Corolla white, funnel-shaped, tube ½ in. long, hairy within, lobes 5, short, orbicular. Stamens 2, inserted half way down the corolla-tube, ovary 2-celled, ovules numerous. Fr. red, a fleshy 5-valved capsule. Seeds large imbricate, testa spongy.

14. MUSSÆNDA, Linn.; Fl. Brit. Ind. iii. 86.

Shrubs or undershrubs, fl. pentamerous, in terminal compound cymes, rarely solitary. Some of the outer fl. of each cyme usually with one calyx-lobe enlarged, forming a large petioled white or coloured leaf. Corolla tubular, widening upwards, usually silky outside, throat villous, lobes valvate in bud. Ovary 2-celled, stigmas 2 linear, ovules ∞. Berry many-seeded. Species 30–40, tropics of the Old World and Polynesia.

A. Calyx-teeth deciduous.

1. **M. frondosa**, Linn.; Wight Ill. t. 124; Bedd. Manual t. xvi. f. 3. Vern. *Yweth la*, Burm.

A large shrub, tomentose or nearly glabrous, l. acuminate, cymes softly silky-tomentose, calyx-lobes lanceolate twice the length of ovary or longer, corolla orange, pubescent or hirsute, lobes acute or acuminate. Berries obovoid, glabrous.

Subhimalayan tract and outer hills from Nepal eastwards, in Sikkim to 4,000 ft. West side of the Peninsula, Nilgiris. Upper Burma. Fl. May–Aug.—China. Malay Archip. 2. **M. macrophylla,** Wall. Pl. As. Rar. t. 180. Nepal. Sikkim 4-6,000 ft. Khasi and Naga hills. Yunnan. A large shrub or small tree, branchlets, petioles underside of l. and inflorescence hirsute or villous, l. elliptic acute, blade 4–5, pet. ¼–⅜ in. long. Bracts and calyx-lobes foliaceous, oblanceolate obtuse, corolla orange, tube hirsute, lobes orbicular, apiculate. Berry hairy. To this in Fl. Brit. Ind. iii. 89, is referred *M. calycina*, Wall., Kurz F. Fl. ii. 58 of Burma. 3. **M. glabra,** Vahl. Sikkim from the Terai to 5,000 ft. Assam. Khasi hills, Cachar, Chittagong; Martaban and Tenasserim hills. Malay Peninsula. China. A rambling, almost climbing shrub, glabrous, excepting the appressed hairy inflorescence, calyx-teeth varying in length, less than twice the length of ovary. Corolla-tube slender, usually with appressed hairs, lobes short, acute, berry globose glabrous. Species 1–3 vary exceedingly and are often difficult to distinguish. 4. **M. variolosa,** Wall. Arakan. Pegu Yoma, southern slopes. Tenasserim, common at Amherst. Hispid, with spreading rufous hairs, l. hairy beneath and often above, lanceolate, usually sessile, the lower sometimes petiolate.

B. Calyx-teeth persistent.

5. **M. Roxburghii,** Hook. f. Sikkim Terai to 4,000 ft. Assam. Khasi hills, Manipur, Cachar, Chittagong. Perak. A shrub, l. membranous, glabrous above, lanceolate, or elliptic-lanceolate, blade 6–12, pet. ¼–1 in. long. Cymes very dense, many-fld., calyx-teeth long filiform hairy, petioles of the enlarged lobes long and slender, corolla slender, silky, lobes orange, small with filiform tips, berries glabrous, crowded in large rounded heads. On the Khasi hills a variety, the branches hirsute with long hairs. 6. **M. tomentosa,** Wight. Gingee hills, Karnatik, branchlets, leaves and inflorescence densely clothed with soft grey velvety tomentum, l. ovate, blade 3–4, pet. ½–⅜ in. long. Cymes without leafy coloured calyx-lobes. 7. **M. Wallichii,** G. Don (united by Kurz with *M. glabra*, Vahl). Lower Burma. L. ovate-lanceolate, appressed hairs on nerves beneath, blade 4–6, petiole ⅜, stipules ⅜ in. long, subulate, entire or 2-fid. Inflorescence and corolla-tube entirely glabrous, bracts and calyx-teeth long, subulate. 8. **M. incana,** Wall. An undershrub, chiefly in grass lands of the Sikkim Terai and the Khasi hills. Chutia Nagpur. Shan hills. Yunnan. Softly grey tomentose, fl. and enlarged calyx-lobes lemon-yellow. The stems above ground probably burnt down by the annual fires of the hot season. Analogous is perhaps 9. **M. uniflora,** Wall. Tenasserim. Cochinchina, stems 6 in. high, from a stout rootstock, fl. solitary, terminal, all calyx-segments linear, tube hirsute, berry ellipsoid, hairy with a few teeth remaining.

Aulacodiscus premnoides, Hook. f. Tenasserim. Malay Peninsula. A small tree, branchlets stout, obtusely 4-angled. L. coriaceous, glabrous, shining, elliptic-oblong, blade 6–9, pet. ¼–⅓ in. long, sec. n. 12–15 pair, arching, stipules from a triangular base long-acuminate. Fl. polygamous, 8–16-merous, in axillary trichotomous pubescent cymes, bracts foliaceous at the lowest pair of ramifications, none higher up. Calyx truncate, corolla broadly campanulate, disk large prominently lobed, lobes opposite the corolla-lobes. Ovary 6–16-celled, stigma large peltate. Berry ¼ in. diam., seeds numerous, minute, albumen oily.

Myrioneuron nutans, Wall. Bhutan, Assam, Khasi and Naga hills. Chittagong. Upper Burma. Tonkin. A small shrub sometimes climbing, branches stout, bark thick, pale, spongy. L. coriaceous, obovate-elliptic, minutely pubescent beneath along the nerves, blade 6–9, narrowed into petiole ⅛–½ in. long, sec. n. 18–20 pair, prominent beneath, as well as the parallel tertiary nerves, stipules ½–⅜ in. long. Fl. yellow, in dense shortly pedunculate bracteate heads, in the axils of the uppermost l., bracts rigid, lanceolate. Calyx-teeth lanceolate, persistent, much exceeding corolla. Corolla tubular, lobes short erect, pubescent on the back. Berries fleshy, white, crowned by the long scarious calyx-lobes, seeds numerous, angular, black.

Urophyllum longifolium, Wight Ic. t. 1165 (Axanthes). (*U. strigosum*, Kurz F. Fl. ii. 58). Mergui. Malay Penins. A large evergreen shrub, young shoots, stipules, petioles and underside of l. pubescent. L. membranous, elliptic-lanceolate, blade 5–11, pet. ⅓ in. long, sec. n. 12–15 pair, tert. n. slender, but conspicuous, stipules linear ½ in. long. Fl. small 5–7-merous, white, glabrous, in small axillary pubescent cymes, bracts villous. Free portion of calyx cup-shaped, truncate, corolla villous in the throat, lobes valvate. Ovules numerous. 2. **U. glabrum**, Wall. South Tenasserim. Malay Penins. and Archip., glabrous; only leafbuds and cymes pubescent, fl. dioicous.

Adenosacme longifolia, Wall. Outer Himalaya, ascending to 6,000 ft. from Kumaon eastwards. Assam, Khasi and Naga hills. Cachar, Chittagong. Lower Burma. China. A small shrub, l. membranous, lanceolate or oblanceolate, more or less pubescent, chiefly on the underside, blade 4–11, pet. ½–2in. long, stipules membranous, lanceolate-oblong. Fl. in compound trichotomous cymes, dimorphic, (*a*) with short style, anthers inserted at the base of the short corolla-tube, (*b*) with long style and anthers inserted at the mouth of the campanulate corolla-tube. Calyx-tube not produced beyond the 2-celled ovary, lobes 4–6, as long as ovary, persistent. Corolla fleshy, lobes 4–6, valvate in bud. Berries snow-white, ¼ in. diam. 2. **A. stipulata**, Hook. f. East Nepal, Sikkim 2–5,000 ft., stipules orbicular ¾–1 in. diam., berries glassy white. 3. **A. Lawii**, Hook. f. Nilgiris and Western Ghats, similar to 1 but ovary 5–6-celled.

15. **WEBERA**, Schreb.; Fl. Brit. Ind. iii. 101. (*Tarenna*, Gærtn.; Hiern in Fl. Trop. Afr. iii. 88; *Chomelia*, Linn.; Schumann in Engler u. Prantl iv. 4. 74.)

Unarmed shrubs or trees, usually drying black. Calyx-limb produced beyond ovary. Fl. usually pentamerous, in terminal corymbiform compound cymes. Corolla-lobes twisted in bud, anthers exserted. Ovary 2-celled, style short, usually pubescent, stigma spindle-shaped, ovules 1–2, rarely numerous in each cell. Drupe 1- or 2-celled, seeds few or one only, plano-convex with a deep groove or concave. Species 30–40, tropical Asia and Africa.

Fig. 156. Webera corymbosa, Willd. ½.

A. *Stylocoryna*, Cav. Ovules 2 or more in each cell. These species should probably form a distinct genus.

(*a*) Corolla glabrous outside.

1. **W. corymbosa**, Willd.—Syn. *W. asiatica*, Bedd. Manual t. xvi. 2; *W. glomeriflora*, Kurz; *Tarenna zeylanica*, Gærtn.; *Stylocoryna Webera*, A. Rich.; Wight Ic. t. 309, 584. Vern. *Karè*, Mar.; *Kommi*, Tel.; *Tereni*, *Papatan*, Tam.

A large evergreen shrub or small tree, usually quite glabrous, bark dark-coloured, smooth. L. coriaceous, hard, shining above, blade 3–6, pet. ¼–½ in. long, stipules coriaceous. Fl. white, fragrant, in terminal trichotomous compound cymes which frequently are pubescent. Corolla-lobes as long as tube, puberulous within. Berry glabrous, dull green, finally black, calyx-teeth persistent or deciduous, seeds 4–10, albumen horny, cells of embryo filled with oil.

Chanda district, Centr. Prov. Peninsula both on the West and East side, common. Pegu Yoma, rare. Fl. March–July.—Ceylon, very common from the coast to 7,000 ft. Java. 2. **W. pallida,** Franchet MSS. *Mandaw byu*, Burm. Upper Burma in evergreen forest 2–3,000 ft. (Smales). Yunnan 2,500–5,000 ft. (Henry, Abbé Delavay). An evergreen tree, attaining 60 ft., l. coriaceous glabrous, oblong-lanceolate, blade 6–9, pet. ¾–1½ in. long, sec. n. 10–14 prominent, arching. Fl. 4- or 5-merous, yellow, cymes compressed terminal and from the axils of the uppermost l., pubescent, trichotomous, but ramifications frequently alternate. Free portion of calyx-tube campanulate, teeth short. Fr. a yellow drupe, seeds 4–6, albumen horny. 3. **W. monosperma,** Wight et Arn.; Wight Ic. t. 317 (*Stylocoryne*). Courtallum. Cymes glabrous, corolla-tube glabrous outside, lobes ⅛ in. Berry white, 1-seeded.

(*b*) Corolla hairy outside.

4. **W. odorata,** Roxb. Assam, Khasi hills. Manipur. L. membranous, cymes large, corymbiform, bracts linear, corolla-tube ⅓–¼ in. long, shorter than the linear lobes. 5. **W. disperma,** Hook. f. Khasi hills. Berry 2-seeded. 6. **W. pumila,** Hook. f. Khasi hills. A dwarf shrub, branches crooked, l. rigid, lanceolate 1–1½ in. long, fl. white, in small compact hirsute cymes.

B. *Webera* proper. One ovule in each cell.

7. **W. Kurzii,** Hook. f.—Syn. *Ixora weberifolia*, Kurz F. Fl. ii. 18. Andamans. Nicobars, common. A small evergreen glabrous tree, l. elliptic-lanceolate, blade 5–7, pet. ⅛ in. long, cymes sessile, or nearly so, terminal, trichotomous, fl. ebracteolate, pedicelled, white, corolla glabrous outside, throat woolly, seeds deeply excavate centrally, testa coriaceous. 8. **W. lucens,** Hook. f.—Syn. *Coffea alpestris*, Wight Ic. t. 1040 and *C. grumelioides*, Wight Ic. t. 1041. West side of the Peninsula from Mangalore southwards. Quite glabrous, l. lanceolate or oblanceolate 2–4 in. long, narrowed into a very short petiole, corolla-tube ¼ in. long, shorter than the linear lobes, glabrous outside, pubescent inside. Berry 2-seeded. 9. **W. canarica,** Hook. f. Ghats of South Kanara, Nilgiris, Cochin, Travancore, evergreen forests 2,000 ft., l. lanceolate or oblanceolate, blade 5–7, pet. ½ in. long, cyme terminal, with stout minutely puberulous branches, 1–2 pair of minute bracteoles on calyx below fl., calyx-lobes triangular acute, corolla 1–1¼ in. long glabrous outside, tube inside hairy, anthers ½ in. long linear, style hairy. 10. **W. nilagirica,** Hook. f. Similar to 8, but l. membranous pubescent beneath, corolla ⅜–⅝ in. long, style glabrous. 11. **W. campaniflora,** Hook. f. Chittagong, l. elliptic-lanceolate, glabrous above, rough beneath with minute stiff hairs, blade 4–12, pet. ⅓–⅔ in. long. Cymes nearly sessile, hirsute, bracts lanceolate, persistent, calyx hirsute, teeth longer than ovary, corolla ⅝ in. long, from a short tubular base widened into a large campanulate limb. 12. **W. Helferi,** Hook. f. Tenasserim. Cymes pedunculate, branches slender, calyx-teeth subulate shorter than ovary. Corolla-tube slender ⅝ in. long, lobes broad, much shorter than tube.

13. **W. compactiflora,** Brandis (*Ixora compactiflora*, Kurz F. Fl. ii. 17). Donat pass 2,000 ft. on the Thaungyin side (D.B. April 1859), l. glabrous, elliptic acuminate, blade 4–5, tapering into a strong pet. ¼–½ in. long, cymes forming a dense head 1 in. diam. at the end of branchlets, calyx-teeth broad oblong obtuse with a wide membranous edge, corolla-tube ¼ in., the lobes as long as tube, style glabrous. This, like 10, is anomalous, on account of the glabrous style.

Byrsophyllum tetrandrum, Hook. f. Bedd. Fl. Sylv. t. 326. *Gardenia tetrandra*, Bedd. Pl. Ind. Or. t. 20. Travancore Ghats. A small glabrous tree, l. very coriaceous, elliptic, obtuse, blade 2–5, narrowed into pet. ½–1 in. long, stipules large, deciduous. Fl. polygamous, tetramerous, terminal, white, tinged with rose, corolla-tube 1 in., lobes ½ in. long, twisted in bud, anthers included. Berry ¾ in. diam., seeds numerous, flat, imbricate, immersed in pulp.

16. GARDENIA, Linn.; Fl. Brit. Ind. iii. 115.

Shrubs or trees, generally resinous, wood whitish, close-grained. Stipules more or less connate round the stem within the petioles, often early deciduous. Calyx-limb produced beyond the ovary. Corolla-tube cylindrical or slightly wider upwards, lobes 5 or more, contorted in bud. Ovary 1-celled, incompletely divided by 2, 3 or more projecting parietal placentas. Fr. fleshy, indehiscent, usually crowned with the persistent calyx-limb, endocarp hard. Seeds numerous, embedded in the fleshy or pulpy placenta. Species 60, Old World, tropical and subtropical.

A. Unarmed. Fl. large, bisexual, usually solitary, corolla-tube more than 1 in. long.

1. **G. lucida,** Roxb.; Wight Ic. t. 575, Bedd. Manual t. xv. fig. 6.—Syn. *G. resinifera*, Roth; Kurz F. Fl. ii. 42. Vern. *Dikamali*, Mar.; *Yerra bikki*, Tel.

A small tree, l. elliptic-oblong, 4–10 in. long, narrowed into the short marginate petiole, sec. n. 20–25 pair, stipules sheathing. Calyx-lobes 5, linear-subulate. Corolla large, pure white, fragrant, tube 1–2 in., lobes 5, obovate-oblong. Fr. ovoid, crowned with the persistent calyx-limb, endocarp thick, woody, nearly 2-celled with the prominent placentas.

Chanda district. Western Peninsula in the drier as well as in the moist districts. Chittagong. Not known from Burma. Fl. March–June, November in Nellore (D.B. 1881). Wood made into combs. The Dikamali resin exudes from wounds made in the bark of 1 and 2. 2. **G. gummifera,** Linn.; Wight Ic. t. 576. Centr. Prov. Purulia, Ch. Nagpore. Western Peninsula. *Dikamali*, Hind.; *Kurmuri*, Satpura; *Manchi bikki*, Tel. A large shrub, l. cuneate or obovate, sessile, often with a narrow cordate base. Calyx-limb short, lobes 5–6, ovate or triangular. Fr. 1–1½ in. oblong, endocarp thin crustaceous, nearly 4- or 5-celled.

3. **G. latifolia,** Aiton; Wight Ic. t. 759. Vern. *Papra*, Hind.; *Banpindalu*, Oudh; *Ghogar*, Mar.; *Pedda bikki*, Tel.

A small tree, bark grey, peeling off in flakes, young shoots pubescent, mature l. dark green and glossy. L. opposite or in threes, broadly-elliptic or obovate, 6–8 in. long, narrowed into a short broad petiole, sec. n. prominent, 15–20 pair, small hairy glands in their axils on the underside. Free portion of calyx campanulate, deeply cleft into 5–9 lanceolate unequal segments. Corolla white or pale lemon-yellow, orange when fading, tube 2–3 in. long, hirsute on the outside, lobes 5–9, obliquely obovate. Fr. 1¼–2¼ in. long, hairy when young, grey or speckled greenish-yellow when ripe, endocarp thin hard, brittle, with 4–5 parietal placentas.

Subhimalayan tract, Ganges to Sarda, not common. Behar. Western Peninsula. Fl. April–May. Combs made of the wood.—Ceylon, moist low country. It is doubtful whether the tree figured under this name in Roxb. Cor. Pl. t. 134, and described as *G. enneandra*, Koenig, in Wight et Arn. Prodr. 394 is this species or not.

4. **G. obtusifolia,** Roxb. *Yingat-gale*, Burm. Pegu, Tenasserim, common in Eng forest. Upper Burma. Cambodia. A small deciduous tree, buds resinous, sticky, l. obovate-oblong, nearly sessile, 3–7 in. long. Calyx-limb shortly 5-toothed, corolla white, turning yellow, tube slender 1½–2 in. long, lobes 5, rarely 4. 5. **G. florida,** Linn. China, Japan, cultivated on account of its very fragrant fl., l. coriaceous 2-4 in., calyx-lobes linear, ¾ in. long.

6. **G. coronaria,** Ham. Vern. *Yingat-gyi*, Burm.

A small deciduous tree, buds very resinous, l. shining, obovate, 4–10 in. long narrowed into a short petiole, stipules connate into a somewhat persistent sheath, branchlets marked by the scars of l. and stipules. Calyx-tube ¾–1 in. long, often split on one side, corolla white fragrant, tube 2–3 in. long, lobes 5. Fr. elongate-ellipsoid, 1 in. long.

Chittagong. Burma, Upper and Lower, often in Engdaing. Fl. March, April.

B. Usually armed. Fl. small, usually of two kinds, fertile and sterile, the former usually sessile, solitary, the latter shortly pedicellate, fasciculate. The sterile fl. with anthers, style and stigma, but ovary imperfect. In some cases

(*G. erythroclada*, Kurz), one kind of fl. bears smaller fr. than the others. Cf. Kurz F. Fl. ii. 40, 41 and C. B. Clarke in Journ. Linn. Soc. xvii. 161, 310.

FIG. 157. Gardenia coronaria, Ham. $\frac{1}{2}$.

7. **G. turgida**, Roxb.; Wight Ic. t. 579. — Syn. *G. montana*, Roxb.; Wight Ic. t. 577. Vern. *Thanela, Karamba, Ghurgia*, Hind.; *Phetra, Pendra*, Mar.; *Yerra bikki*, Tel.; *Thaminzani*, Burm.

A small deciduous tree, armed with strong axillary often leaf-bearing spines, bark smooth, blueish-grey, mealy on branches. L. often crowded at the ends of branchlets, 1–4 in. long, obovate, narrowed into a short marginate petiole, tomentose or pubescent beneath, glabrous or pubescent above when mature. Fl. white, fragrant, corolla-tube $\frac{1}{3}$–$\frac{1}{2}$ in. long. Fertile solitary sessile, calyx-lobes oblong. Sterile clustered on short pedicels, calyx-teeth minute, sometimes unequal. Fr. grey, obovoid or globose, 2–3 in. long, endocarp woody, placentas 2–6.

Submontane tract of the North West Himalaya, Jumna to Sarda, ascending to 4,000 ft. Rajputana. Central Prov. Behar. Western Peninsula. Pegu, chiefly in Eng forest. Shan hills at 4,000 ft. Fl. H. S. 8. **G. campanulata**, Roxb.; Wight Ic. t. 578. Sikkim, foot of hills. Assam. Lower Bengal. Chittagong. Pegu (Kurz). A large shrub or small tree, deciduous, armed with long straight sharp spines, often leaf-bearing. L. membranous, glabrous, lanceolate, blade 2–4, narrowed into a slender petiole $\frac{1}{4}$–$\frac{1}{2}$ in. long. Fl. greenish-white, corolla-tube $\frac{1}{3}$ in. long, upper portion campanulate. Fertile solitary sessile, calyx-teeth oblong or spathulate, foliaceous. Sterile fasciculate, shortly pedicellate. Fr. $\frac{3}{4}$–$1\frac{1}{4}$in. long, endocarp woody, placentas 5. 9. **G. sessiliflora**, Wall. *Thaminzabyu*, Burm. Pegu, in deciduous and Eng forests. A deciduous shrub or small tree, branchlets short stout, nearly at right angles to the main branch, terminating in sharp woody spines, bearing fl. and tufts of l. below the spine. L. pubescent, obovate, blade 3–4 in., narrowed into a slender petiole $\frac{1}{3}$–$\frac{1}{2}$ in. long. Sterile fl. fasciculate on short pedicels, calyx-tube villous, with 5 obtuse foliaceous teeth. Corolla pubescent, tube $\frac{1}{4}$ in. long, lobes almost orbicular. 10. **G. erythroclada**, Kurz. *Hmanni*, Burm. Pegu, Martaban, Shan hills at 3,000 ft. Cambodia. A small deciduous tree, stem and branches brick-red, branchlets usually spinescent. L. broadly elliptic or obovate, blade 4–10, pet. 1–2 in. long. Fl. greenish, sterile and fertile fl. on different trees. *G. cuneata*, Kurz, Ava, is imperfectly known.

17. RANDIA, Linn.; Fl. Brit. Ind. iii. 109.

Shrubs or trees, stipules short, often connate. Fl. pentamerous, axillary, in cymes, fascicles or solitary. Calyx-tube produced beyond ovary, corolla-lobes twisted in bud, anthers subsessile, narrow. Ovary 2-celled, ovules numerous on thick placentas attached to the septum. Berries 2-celled, seeds 4 or more in each cell. Seeds angled, testa thin, albumen horny, cotyledons orbicular. Species about 100, tropical and subtropical regions of both hemispheres.

A. Armed, l. glabrous.

1. **R. tetrasperma**, Roxb. (*Gardenia*). *Kikra*, Haz.; *Bhadra*, Jaunsar. Baluchistan. Mt. Tilla, Salt range. Himalaya ascending to 6,000 ft. Assam. A small shrub, branches rigid, grey, decussate, branchlets short, often spinescent. L. glabrous, approximate near ends of branchlets, obovate or oblanceolate, ½–2 in. long, narrowed into short petiole. Fl. pentamerous, greenish-white, scented, sessile. Corolla-tube glabrous, ⅓ in. long, lobes oblong, apex subulate. Fr. a globose berry, ¼ in. diam. crowned with the persistent calyx.

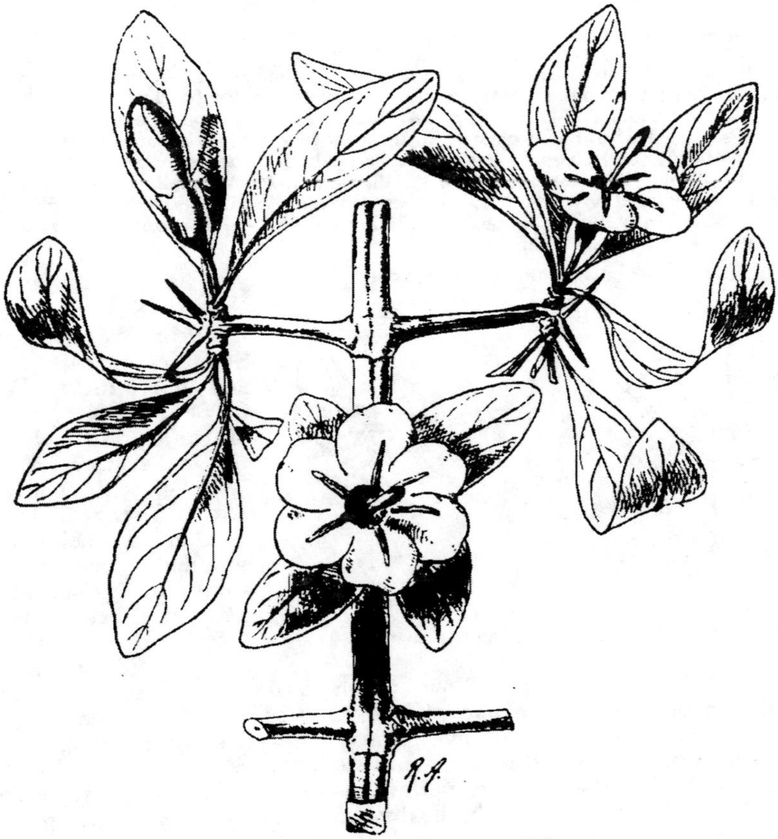

FIG. 158. Randia uliginosa, DC. ½.

2. **R. uliginosa**, DC.; Wight Ic. t. 397.—Syn. *Gardenia uliginosa*, Retz.; Roxb. Cor. Pl. t. 135. Vern. *Pindara*, *Panar*, *Pirar*, Hind.; *Pindra*, *Pendroy*, Mar.; *Konda manga*, Tel.; *Kāre*, Kan.; *Hmanbyu*, Burm.

A small rigid tree, bark reddish-brown. Branches quadrangular, usually bearing short, terete, decussate branchlets, with several pairs of approximate leaves, and above them 2–4 strong sharp decussate thorns. L. glabrous and shining above, often pubescent beneath, obovate from a cuneate base, blade 3–6, pet. ½ in. long. Fl. solitary, axillary, white, scented, dimorphic, either large and sessile or small and pedicelled. The former have 2 separate stigmas, the corolla is 2 in. across, while its tube is longer than the free portion of calyx. The pedicellate fl. have a short corolla-tube and a clavate stigma marked with spiral lines. Calyx-lobes very short, corolla-tube glabrous outside. Fr. yellow, edible, with a hard pulp, those produced by the large fl. are 2 in. long, while those of the others only attain half that size.

Subhimalayan tract from the Jumna eastwards, chiefly in Savannahs and on low ground, ascending to 2,500 ft. Bundelkhand, Central Provinces, Behar. Burma, Upper and Lower. Western Peninsula. Gregarious in places. Fl. April–June. L. renewed March, April. 3. **R. longiflora,** Lamk.—Syn. *Webera longiflora, bispinosa,* and *siamensis,* Kurz F. Fl. ii. 48, 49. Assam. Khasi hills. Chittagong. Pegu. Martaban and Tenasserim. Malay Peninsula. Tonkin. A large evergreen rambling shrub, entirely glabrous, usually armed with stout recurved spines. L. coriaceous, shining, elliptic-oblong, blade 4–6, pet. ½ in. long. Fl. white, turning yellow, in compound, sessile or shortly pedunculate cymes. Corolla-tube ½–1½ in. much longer than the oblong lobes. Berry ovoid or globose, ⅓–½ in. long.

4. **R. malabarica,** Lamk.—Syn. *Griffithia fragrans,* W. et A.; Wight Ic. t. 310. *Pedda Malli,* Tel.; *Todi Matti,* Tam. Deccan. Mysore, Karnatik. Also on the West side of the Peninsula. Often planted in hedges. Ceylon. A rigid glabrous shrub, thorns short, sharp, sometimes absent, when grown in rich soil. L. coriaceous, obovate to oblanceolate, 2–3 in. long, narrowed into short petiole. Fl. white fragrant, in nearly sessile leaf-opposed cymes, bracts ovate, cuspidate, connate in pairs. Calyx glabrous or hairy, teeth short, triangular, corolla ¾ in. across, tube shorter than lobes. Berry ¼ in. diam., first orange, finally black. 5. **R. Griffithii,** Hook. f. Khasi and Naga hills. Bernardmyo 7,000 ft. Upper Burma. Spines short, straight, sometimes wanting. L. membranous, lanceolate, blade 2–5, pet. ⅛–¼ in. long. Berries soft black, ⅓ in. diam., seeds 4 in each cell.

B. Armed, l. pubescent or tomentose.

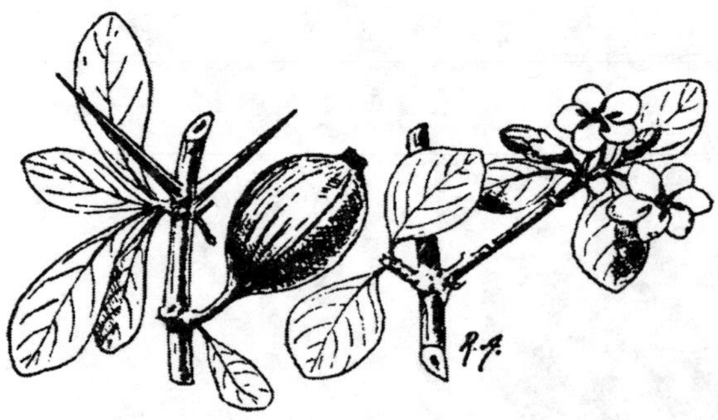

Fig. 159.—Randia dumetorum, Lamk. ½.

6. **R. dumetorum,** Lamk.; Wight Ic. t. 580.—Syn. *R. nutans, longispina* and *floribunda,* Wight Ic. t. 581, 582, 583. Vern. *Maindal, Mainphal,* Hind.; *Ghela, Mindhal,* Mar.; *Mangu,* Tel.; *Mangari,* Kan.; *Madu Karray,* Tam.

A large deciduous shrub or small tree, armed with stout axillary spines, 1–1½ in. long, bark grey. L. obovate, 1–2 in. long, glabrous or hairy. Fl. greenish-yellow or nearly white, turning yellow when fading, fragrant, on short pedicels, solitary or a few together at the ends of short leaf-bearing branchlets, sometimes on the axillary spines. Calyx strigose with stiff hairs, lobes large, broad-ovate, often with minute intermediate lobes. Corolla ½–¾ in. across, tube hairy outside. Fr. yellow, 1–1½ in. long, frequently crowned by the semi-persistent calyx-teeth, fleshy under a leathery pericarp, seeds embedded in a gelatinous pulp.

Subhimalayan tract and outer hills from the Bias eastwards, ascending to 4,000 ft., chiefly in Sal and mixed forests. Rajputana. Central Provinces. Both Peninsulas. Fl. March–June. Fruit eaten when ripe, unripe used to poison fish. Ceylon. Malay Archipelago. South China. Eastern tropical Africa. A remarkable form, possibly a distinct species, with l. densely velvety beneath, hairy above, sec. n. prominent, 10–12 pair, fr. ribbed and crowned with the semipersistent calyx-lobes. Sattara Ghats and Mahabaleshwar (May 1870 and Oct. 1881, D.B.; *Ghera*, *Ghela*, Mar.) Sigùr Ghats, (Nilgiris, Gamble), is similar to 7. **R. tomentosa,** Blume (*Gardenia dasycarpa*, Kurz F. Fl. ii. 42), Pegu, Tenasserim and Shan hills, U. Burma, a small deciduous tree, spines straight 1–2 in. long, l. coriaceous, fr. velvety. 8. **R. fasciculata,** DC.—Syn. *R. rigida*, DC.; *Webera fasciculata*, Kurz. Subhimalayan tract and outer valleys from Nepal eastwards. Assam. Khasi hills, Tenasserim. A large straggling shrub armed with straight axillary spines, ¼–½ in. long, branchlets, petioles and underside of leaves slightly pubescent, l. glabrous above, ovate or ovate-lanceolate, blade 1–4, pet. ⅛–¼ in. long. Fl. white, fragrant, nearly sessile, in few-fld. axillary fascicles, calyx-lobes deciduous, corolla-tube ¾–1¼ in. long, lobes oblong. Berry purple, ¼ in. diam.

C. Unarmed, calyx-teeth minute. Corolla-tube less than 1 inch long.

9. **R. densiflora,** Benth.—Syn. *Webera oppositifolia*, Roxb.; Kurz F. Fl. ii. 47.

A middle-sized or large evergreen tree, unarmed, wood heavy, very hard. L. lanceolate or elliptic-oblong, glabrous, coriaceous, blade 4–8, pet. ½ in. long. Fl. white, fragrant, cymes leaf-opposed, or from leafless nodes, sessile or shortly pedunculate, glabrous or pubescent, bracts persistent, small. Calyx usually minutely hairy, teeth minute or 0. Corolla ½–¾ in. diam., lobes oblong, as long as or longer than tube, edges generally ciliate, throat villous. Berry ovoid or globose, ⅓ in. long, seeds numerous.

Assam, Manipur, Cachar. Andamans. Pegu Yoma, eastern slopes. Martaban. Tenasserim. Cochin and Travancore in evergreen forest.—Malay Peninsula and Archipelago. North Australia. Hongkong. *R. Gardneri*, Hook. f., moist region of Ceylon, with lanceolate l. and leaf-opposed cymes agrees with the Travancore specimens of *R. densiflora*. 10. **R. Wallichii,** Hook. f. Sikkim to 4,000 ft. Khasi hills. Chittagong. Andamans. Pegu, Tenasserim and Upper Burma. A small tree or large rambling shrub, similar to 9 but cymes axillary sessile, bracts caducous, fl. yellow (Gamble) ¼ in. diam. Berry ½ in. diam., seeds peltate, smooth.

11. **R. Candolleana,** W. et A.—Syn. *R. deccanensis*, Bedd. Ic. Pl. Ind. Or. t. 237. *Karu Maram*, Tam. Deccan, Karnul, Anantapúr. Mysore. Karnatik. Javadi hills (D. B. Jan. 1882). A small tree, young shoots pubescent, l. broadly elliptic, obovate or orbicular, glabrous above, pubescent beneath, blade 2–6, pet. ¾–1¼ in. long. Cymes sessile, bracts deciduous, calyx glabrous, free portion much wider than ovary, teeth short, triangular, corolla ⅓ in. across, tube silky outside. 12. **R. rugulosa,** Hook. fil.—Syn. *R. speciosa*, Bedd. Ic. Pl. Ind. Or. t. 37. Western Ghats, mostly in evergreen forest, from Matheran southwards. Ceylon, moist low country. A large evergreen climbing shrub, with long drooping branches, entirely unarmed. L. glabrous, elongate-elliptic, blade 6–10, pet. ½–1 in. long. Fl. white, fragrant, in leaf-opposed cymes with ovate cuspidate bracts. Calyx appressed-pilose, teeth minute, corolla glabrous, ½–⅜ in. across, tube shorter than lobes. Seeds rugose.

D. Unarmed. Corolla-tube 1 in. or longer.

13. **R. exaltata,** Griff.; Kurz F. Fl. ii. 46.—Syn. *Gardenia pulcherrima*, Kurz F. Fl. ii. 43. Mergui, Andamans, in Mangrove swamps but also inland. Penang. A middle-sized evergreen tree, l. glabrous, coriaceous, elliptic, acuminate, blade 5–7, petiole ⅓ in. long. Cymes subsessile, few-fld. Calyx tomentose, teeth triangular. Corolla white, scented, 3 in. long. Berry 1–1½ in. diam., pericarp woody, seeds embedded in pulp. 14. **R. sikkimensis,** Hook. f. Sikkim, outer hills, to 4,000 ft. A shrub, l. in unequal pairs, upperside rough, underside pubescent, calyx-teeth subulate. Corolla 1 in. long, silky outside. 15. **R. hygrophila,** Kurz F. Fl. 44 (*Gardenia*). Pegu, Swamp forests and low ground in Savannahs. A small evergreen glabrous shrub, l. membranous, very shining above. Fl. solitary, white, turning black in drying, calyx-lobes linear-lanceolate, more than half the length of tube, corolla-tube 1 in. long, ⅓ in. wide at mouth.

Brachytome Wallichii, Hook. f. Khasi hills. Upper Burma. A glabrous shrub or small tree, nearly allied to some species in Sect. D of *Randia*, l. membranous, lanceolate or oblanceolate, blade 6–9, narrowed into petiole ¼ in. long, stipules persistent. Fl. white, polygamous, pentamerous, in axillary, or by abortion of one of the pairs of l., leaf-opposed cymes, calyx-limb 5-toothed persistent, corolla funnel-shaped, tube ⅓ in. long, as well as the short lobes glabrous within, stigma of 2 short oblong lobes. Berry ellipsoid, ⅓ in. long, seeds crowded, cuneate, compressed, testa reticulate.

Morindopsis capillaris, Kurz. Upper Burma. Pegu. Tenasserim, on river banks and in damp places. Cambodia. An evergreen shrub or small tree, l. glossy, rigidly but thinly coriaceous, lanceolate or elliptic, almost sessile, stipules ovate, persistent. Fl. small, white, sessile, diœcious, tetramerous. ♂ in small, usually few-fld. heads, supported by stiff linear subulate bracts on supra-axillary, often opposite, slender or capillary peduncles, usually 1–2 in. long. ♀ solitary or in subsessile few-fld. heads. Ovary 2-celled, ovules numerous on peltate placentas. Berry cylindric, 1 in. long, crowned by the persistent calyx-teeth.

Hyptianthera stricta, W. et A. Subhimalayan tract from Kumaon eastwards. Nindhaur Valley (D. B. 1880). Oudh forests. Sikkim to 3,000 ft. Khasi hills. Chittagong. Yunnan. An aromatic evergreen shrub or small tree, wholly glabrous, l. shining, lanceolate, blade 3–6, pet. ⅓ in. long. Fl. small, white, 4–5-merous, bracteolate, sessile in opposite axillary fascicles, corolla-tube short, hairy within, style short, bifid, branches erect hispid, ovules pendulous, 6–10 in each cell. Seeds imbricate, angular, testa thick fibrous and plaited, embryo small.

Petunga Roxburghii, DC. (*Hypobathrum racemosum*, Kurz). Chittagong. Lower Burma near streams and in swamp forests. An evergreen shrub, l. lanceolate, blade 2–5, pet. ¼ in. long, stipules broad, caducous. Fl. 4-merous, white, almost sessile, in 4 rows, on axillary sessile or shortly pedunculate spikes, corolla funnel-shaped, throat villous, berry stalked, orange-yellow.

18. DIPLOSPORA, DC.; Fl. Brit. Ind. iii. 122.

(Included under *Tricalysia*, A. Rich., in Engler und Prantl iv. 4. 81.)

Evergreen shrubs or trees, petioles short, stipules triangular, acuminate or with a long setaceous point. Fl. small, polygamous, bracteolate, in axillary fascicles or short cymes. Corolla-tube short, lobes 4 or 5, twisted in bud. Ovary 2-, rarely 3-celled, style bifid, ovules 2–3 in each cell. Berry 2-celled, seeds flat, imbricate. Species 10. India and the Malay Archip.

A. Stipules acuminate.

1. **D. singularis**, Korth. Khasi hills. Cachar. Pegu Yoma, eastern slopes. Tenasserim. Indian Archip. A middle-sized tree, resinous and entirely glabrous, the stem fluted, L. coriaceous, shining, elliptic, blade 3–7, petiole ¼–½ in. long. Fl. 4-merous, greenish-white, in dense axillary clusters, pedicels with several pairs of bracts, connate at base and sheathing. Calyx deeply lobed, corolla-tube ⅛ in., lobes linear. Fr. ⅜ in. diamt. crowned by the persistent calyx-limb. Seeds 8–10. 2. **D. apiocarpa**, Hook. f.; Bedd. Fl. Sylv. t. 223.—Syn. *Discospermum apiocarpum*, Dalz.; Ic. Pl. Ind. Or. t. 40. Western Ghats from the Konkan southwards, above 2,500 ft. A middle-sized or large resinous tree, petioles ½–⅔ in., fl. 4-merous, cream coloured, scented, male and bisexual on different trees, bracts not sheathing, calyx-teeth minute, fr. ellipsoid, sessile. 3. **D. sphærocarpa**, Hook. f. Western Ghats. Similar to 2, but calyx-teeth longer, obtuse, ciliolate, fr. globose, ⅜ in. diam., on bracteolate pedicels ¼ in. long.

B. Stipules with long setaceous points.

4. **D. confusa**, Hook. f. Tenasserim. Glabrous, fl. minute, in small axillary heads, calyx truncate. 5. **D. pubescens**, Hook. f., Mergui. Similar, but pubescent. 6. **D. Griffithii**, Hook f., Upper Burma, a small shrub, l. oblanceolate, cymes spiciform ⅓–⅜ in. long. 7. **D. Kurzii**, Hook. f. *Urophyllum biloculare*, Kurz. Hills east of Toungoo at 2,000 ft. A small evergreen tree, l. membranous, elliptic-lanceolate, sec. n. arching 4–6 pair, tertiary nerves numerous, slender, horizontal. Fl. minute, sessile, in axillary clusters, fr. orange, ¼ in. diam., 3–4 black seeds in each cell.

Scyphiphora hydrophyllacea, Gærtn.; Bedd. Manual 134–3 t. xxix. fig. 5. Mangrove swamps of the Andamans, of the Karnatik coast (rare), Ceylon, the Malay Peninsula and New Caledonia. A small evergreen glabrous tree or shrub, much like *Lumnitzera*. L. coriaceous, obovate, blade 2–3, narrowed into petiole ⅓–1 in. long. Fl. white, 4- or 5-merous, corolla-tube cylindric ⅙ in. long, throat hairy, anthers exserted, ovary 2-celled, 2 superposed ovules in each cell, style bifid, branches linear, obtuse. Drupe nearly cylindric, with 8–10 prominent ribs, pyrenes crustaceous 4–5-ribbed. *Lumnitzera* has alternate l. and a 1-celled ovary.

19. CANTHIUM, Lam.; Fl. Brit. Ind. iii. 131.

(*Plectronia*, Sec. II. *Canthium*, Schumann in Engler u. Prantl iv. 4. 92.)

Shrubs, erect or climbing, stipules connate. Fl. small, in axillary fascicles or peduncled compound cymes, calyx-tube shortly produced beyond ovary, corolla-tube shorter than, as long as, or rarely longer than lobes, throat villous, lobes valvate in bud, at length reflexed. Ovary 2-celled, stigma large, usually ribbed, ovule one, attached to the upper part of the cell. Drupe with thin pericarp, endocarp 2-celled more or less woody. Seeds oblong, testa membranous, albumen fleshy, embryo nearly as long as seed. Species about 70, tropics of the Old World.

A. Unarmed, fl. 5-merous.

1. **C. didymum**, Roxb.; Bedd. F. Sylv. t. 221.—Syn. *C. umbellatum*, Wight Ic. t. 1034. Vern. *Nalla balsu*, *Naikinna*, *Nakkareni*, Tel.; *Myauk-laung*, Upper Burma.

A small or middle-sized evergreen tree with deep-green foliage, branchlets often angular, wood hard, even grained. L. coriaceous, glabrous, glossy, elliptic, blade 4–6, narrowed into a stout petiole $\frac{1}{4}$ in. long. Fl. white, fragrant, in compact axillary many-fld. often umbelliform cymes, sessile on a short stout peduncle. Corolla-tube cylindric, $\frac{1}{8}$–$\frac{1}{4}$ in. long, a little longer than the reflexed lobes, anthers slightly, style usually long exserted. Drupes more or less didymous, on long slender pedicels, purple, $\frac{1}{4}$–$\frac{1}{2}$ in. long.

Western Ghats from Kandala southwards, chiefly in evergreen forests. Nilgiris. Common on the hills of the Salem and adjoining districts. Northern Circars, Orissa. Upper Burma, in Engdaing (fl. umbellate, stigma very little exserted). Mergui. Fl. Nov.–May.—Ceylon, low country to 4,000 ft., common; large beaked leaf galls frequent on the young branches. Malay Peninsula and Archip. China. Very variable, the structure of endocarp not uniform, should be studied. 2. **C. Kingii**, Hook. f. (var.). Sikkim 1,500 ft. L. elliptic-lanceolate, caudate-acuminate, fl. in pedunculate umbels, corolla-tube $\frac{1}{4}$ in. long much widened upwards, lobes barely half the length of tube. 3. **C. pergracile**, Bourdillon in Journ. Bombay Nat. Hist. Soc. xii. 352, t. 5, a tall graceful tree, in evergreen forest Travancore at low elevations, l. very glossy, lanceolate caudate-acuminate, fl. yellowish-green, in shortly peduncled umbelliform cymes, corolla-tube $\frac{1}{8}$ in. long, as long as lobes, fr. $\frac{3}{4}$–1 in. diam., endocarp thick, woody, ribbed. 4. **C. neilgherrense**, Wight Ic. t. 1064 bis. Nilgiri and Palni hills. L. elliptic, or ovate, often hairy beneath, fl. few in small axillary nearly sessile umbels. Fr. cream-coloured, obovate, succulent. 5. **C. ficiforme**, Hook. f. Shevagherry hills, l. thickly coriaceous, drying black, fr. 1–1$\frac{1}{4}$ in. long, compressed, narrowed into pedicel $\frac{1}{2}$ in. long, enclosing 2 hard bony irregularly furrowed nuts.

6. **C. glabrum**, Blume (*Plectronia glabra*, Kurz F. Fl. ii. 35). Southern spurs of the Pegu Yoma. Tenasserim. Malay Peninsula. Java. A small evergreen tree, l. glabrous, ovate-oblong, blade 5–7, pet. $\frac{1}{2}$ in. long. Fl. in shortly peduncled, often lax axillary cymes, corolla-tube equal to lobes, $\frac{1}{12}$ in. long, fr. $\frac{3}{4}$–1 in. long, enclosing two smooth trigonous stones.

B. Unarmed, fl. 4-merous.

7. **C. travancoricum**, Bedd. Ic. Pl. Ind. Or. t. 239 (*Plectronia*). Tinnevelli and Travancore Ghats, a middle-sized tree, l. membranous, glabrous, ovate, acuminate, blade 2, pet. $\frac{1}{2}$ in. long, stipules from a broad base narrowed into a long subulate point. Fl. very small, in lax pedunculate cymes with slender ramifications, corolla $\frac{1}{10}$ in., lobes as long as tube. 8. **C. gracilipes**, Kurz F. Fl. ii. 36 (*Plectronia*). Andamans, frequent. A shrub, branchlets thinly pubescent, l. membranous, elliptic to oblong-lanceolate, stipules, petioles and nerves finely hairy. Fl. very small, on long slender fascicled pedicels, fr. $\frac{1}{2}$ in. across.

C. Armed, fl. mostly 5-merous.

9. **C. parviflorum**, Lamk.; Roxb. Cor. Pl. t. 51. Vern. *Kirna*, *Kadbar*, Mar.; *Balasu*, Tel.

A rigid shrub, branches stiff spreading, spines numerous, axillary or supra-axillary, straight, stout and sharp, wood hard, close-grained. L. glabrous, elliptic, obovate or orbicular ½–2 in. long, stipules small with long cuspidate points. Fl. 4-merous, yellowish, in many-fld. peduncled cymes, calyx-teeth minute, corolla-tube broad-campanulate, $\frac{1}{10}$ in. long, a little longer than lobes, stigma globose, tuberculate. Fr. yellow, edible, enclosing two hard stones.

Wardha valley, Nizam's territory and southwards throughout the drier districts of the Western Peninsula. Common in the semi-evergreen scrub near the Coromandel coast. Fl. chiefly R. S. but also at other times. Ceylon, dry region. 10. **C. angustifolium,** Roxb.—Syn. *C. Leschenaultii*, Wight et Arn.; Wight Ic. t. 826. Silhet, Sundriban, Chittagong. Peninsula, chiefly on the west side. A scandent shrub with slender spinescent stems. L. chartaceous, shining, ovate, acuminate or ovate-lanceolate, blade 1–3, pet. ⅛–¼ in. long, spines axillary, straight or curved. Calyx-teeth minute, corolla-tube short, lobes lanceolate, acuminate, forming a long point in bud. Style hairy. 11. **C. Rheedii,** DC. Peninsula, Ceylon, may possibly only be a pubescent variety. 12. **C. parvifolium,** Roxb. Khasi hills, Chittagong, Pegu. A rigid spreading shrub, spines straight, sharp, branchlets and leaves softly hairy, fr. ⅓ in. diam. 13. **C. horridum,** Blume, differs from 12 by short compressed hooked spines and much larger fr.

Vangueria spinosa, Roxb., including *V. pubescens*, Kurz. Sikkim Terai, along roadsides (Gamble). Jowai, Khasi hills (D. B. May, 1879). Lower Bengal. Burma, Upper and Lower. Deciduous forests of the Peninsula. Java. A small thorny tree, l. membranous ovate or ovate-lanceolate, glabrous or tomentose, blade 2–4, pet. ¼–1 in. long, stipules early deciduous. Fl. pentamerous, greenish, calyx-segments from a triangular base linear, nearly as long as the 5-celled ovary, corolla-lobes acuminate. Drupe yellow, ½–1 in. diam., fleshy, edible, with 4–5 smooth hard 1-seeded stones. 2. **V. edulis,** Vahl, a native of Madagascar, cultivated in India on account of its fruit, unarmed, l. elliptic 4–8 in. long.

Timonius Jambosella, Thw.; Bedd. Ic. Pl. Ind. Or. t. 190.—Syn. *Polyphragmon flavescens*, Kurz. Andamans, Nicobars. Ceylon. Malay Penins. and Archip. A small evergreen tree, l. thinly coriaceous, pale and silky beneath, blade 3–5, pet. ⅓ in. long. Fl. supported by 2 small bractlets, polygamous, sterile in pedunculate cymes, fertile solitary or 3 together on long slender peduncles, tetramerous, corolla tubular, pubescent outside, longer (½ in.) in the sterile fl., lobes valvate, ovary 8–12-celled, one pendulous ovule in each cell, style with 4 or more branches. Drupe globose, ⅓–½ in. diam., lobed or ribbed, enclosing 8–12 compressed pyrenes, seed with scanty albumen, embryo long.

Guettarda speciosa, Linn.; Bedd. Manual t. xvii. Litoral and tidal forests of the Andamans. Scarce on the coast of the Western Peninsula, often cultiv. in gardens. Ceylon (rare on the coast). Sea coast within the tropics. A small tree, branchlets stout, pubescent, marked with leaf-scars. L. crowded at the ends of branchlets, obovate, pubescent, chiefly beneath, blade 6–10, pet. ¾–1½ in. long, stipules ovate deciduous. Fl. polygamous, 5–9-merous, white, sweet scented, nearly sessile, crowded on the short arms of a pubescent cyme, peduncles 1½–3 in., from the scars of fallen l. Calyx velvety, limb tubular, indistinctly toothed, corolla velvety outside, glabrous within, tube 1–1½ in. long, anthers included. Ovary 4–9-celled, one pendulous ovule in each cell. Drupe depressed globose, ¾ in. diam., stone woody with 5–9 angles and as many cells.

20. OCTOTROPIS, Bedd.; Fl. Brit. Ind. iii. 131.

Shrubs, fl. 4- or 5-merous, in pedunculate cymes. Corolla-tube cylindric, widened upwards, lobes longer than half the tube. Anthers and style exserted, style ribbed, stigma bifid at top. Ovary 2-celled, dissepiment very thin disappearing early, ovules 2 pendulous from the top of the cell. Species 2.

1. **O. travancorica,** Bedd. Fl. Sylv. t. 327; Manual 134/12. Wainād (4,500–5,500 ft.). Shevagherri hills. Tinnevelli and Travancore Ghats, evergreen forest, 1–5,000 ft. A large shrub or small tree, l. chartaceous, glabrous, ovate-lanceolate, blade 4–6, pet. ⅓ in. long. Fl. white, each supported by 2 appressed bracteoles, cymes bracteate on long filiform peduncles, corolla-tube ⅛ in., anthers apiculate. Fr. ellipsoid, ⅜ in. long, seeds 1 or 2, albumen horny. 2. **O. terminalis,** C. B. Clarke, Journ. Linn. Soc. xxv. 33, t. 17. Nambar forest, Assam. Cymes fasciculate in the axils of the uppermost l., corolla-tube ⅜ in. long, anthers included (doubtfully referred to this genus).

21. PAVETTA, Linn.; Fl. Brit. Ind. iii. 149.

Differs from *Ixora* by membranous leaves, the bracts at the lower cyme branches membranous, more or less sheathing, and the style as a rule twice the length of the corolla-tube, with a slender, entire, rarely notched stigma. Species about 70, tropics of the Old World.

1. **P. indica**, Linn.—Syn. *P. Brunonis*, Wight Ic. t. 1065; *Ixora tomentosa*, Roxb.; Wight Ic. t. 186. Vern. *Angari, Puldu*, N. W. India; *Tapra, Papidi*, Tel.; *Pávate*, Kan.; *Pavettai*, Tam.; *Hmit naban, Hmitgyin, Sebaung-gyan*, Burm.

A large shrub, glabrous or tomentose, branchlets obtusely quadrangular, l. elliptic-lanceolate, sometimes lanceolate or obovate, blade 4–9 narrowed into petiole ½–1 in. long. Fl. white, scented, pedicelled in ample trichotomous, sessile, usually pubescent cymes, often globose, up to 6 in. diam., terminal, or at the ends of short branchlets. Calyx as a rule pubescent, truncate or with short triangular teeth, corolla-tube ½–¾ in. long, hairy inside, outside usually glabrous.

Fl. March–July. Three well marked varieties, two of which were described in my old Forest Flora as distinct species: (a) *indica* proper, branchlets, l., cymes and calyx glabrous or nearly so. Sikkim, to 2,000 ft. Bhutan. Lower Bengal. Andamans. Burma, Upper and Lower. Western Peninsula. Ceylon. Malay Peninsula and Archipelago. China. New Guinea. (b) *minor*, glabrous, l. small, lanceolate, calyx-teeth acute, Tinnevelli and Travancore. (c) *tomentosa*, branchlets, leaves and cymes tomentose, sec. n. distinct. Subhimalayan tract from the Jumna eastwards. Behar. Lower Bengal. Khasi hills, Manipur. Burma, Upper and Lower. Malay Peninsula. Tonkin.

The following 5 species are nearly allied to *P. indica*. A. Western species: 2. **P. hispidula**, W. et A. (*P. siphonantha*, Dalz.). Western Ghats of the Peninsula, generally in evergreen forest. A slender shrub, l. lanceolate or oblanceolate, glabrous or pubescent beneath, turn black when dry, calyx-teeth triangular, acute, fl. yellow, corolla-tube 1–1¼ in. 3. **P. Wightii**, Hook. f. Nilgiris. Almost wholly glabrous, l. shining oblanceolate, cymes at the end of slender axillary branches, naked below, but with a few l. at the base of cyme, calyx-teeth lanceolate, longer than ovary, corolla-tube slender, ⅝ in. long. 4. **P. Brunonis**, Wall. Nilgiris. L. softly hirsute with long hairs, obovate or oblanceolate, cymes densely tomentose at the end of short naked branches, with a few l. supporting the cyme, bracts large, calyx-teeth lanceolate, often recurved, corolla-tube ½ in. long. B. Eastern: 5. **P. subcapitata**, Hook. f. Assam, Khasi hills. L. caudate-acuminate, pubescent beneath, cymes sessile, compact, capitate, calyx-teeth distant, very short, corolla-tube ⅜ in. long. 6. **P. naucleiflora**, Wall. (*Ixora naucleiflora*, Kurz). Bhutan, Assam, Khasi hills. Tenasserim. Malay Peninsula. Branchlets, l., cymes and calyx densely pubescent, cymes at the ends of long axillary naked branches with a pair of l. at the base of cyme, calyx-teeth subulate.

7. **P. breviflora**, DC.; Wight Ic. t. 1035. Travancore at 4,000 ft. in evergreen forest. Nilgiris, on the higher ranges, common. A large glabrous shrub or small tree, l. black when dry, lanceolate, oblanceolate or elliptic-lanceolate, blade 3–4, gradually narrowed into petiole ⅓–⅔ in. long. Fl. white, cymes small, sessile or nearly so, at the ends of short branchlets, naked below, often with a few l. at the base of the cyme, corolla-tube ⅛–⅓ in. long, style glabrous, less than twice the length of corolla-tube. Somewhat resembles *Webera lucens*, which has 5-merous fl. and a pubescent style.

22. IXORA, Linn.; Fl. Br. Ind. iii. 137.

Shrubs or small trees, as a rule evergreen, wood hard, branchlets usually round, not angled, l. mostly coriaceous. Fl. tetramerous, bi-bracteolate, in terminal trichotomous compound cymes, the l. at the base of cyme often sessile, corolla-tube long, very slender, as a rule glabrous outside, lobes twisted in bud. Ovary 2-celled, style filiform, exserted less than twice the length of corolla-tube, stigma slender, branches 2, rarely persistently connate. Drupe more or less didymous, pericarp coriaceous or fleshy, endocarp coriaceous, 2-celled. Seeds two, peltate or concave, sometimes by abortion one only.

Testa membranous, radicle inferior, albumen usually fleshy. Species about 100, tropics of Asia and Africa, a few in America.

A. Cal.-teeth longer than ovary. Cymes compact, corymbiform, usually sessile.

1. **I. acuminata**, Roxb.; Wight Ic. t. 706. Sikkim, outer hills and valleys. Assam, Bhutan. Khasi hills. Cachar. A large shrub, l. large, almost membranous, blade 5–18, pet. ¼–¾ in. long. Fl. crowded, occasionally 5-merous, white, fragrant, bracts and calyx red, corolla-tube 1–1¼ in., very slender, mouth ⅜ in. across. Drupe ⅓–⅜ in. long, crowned with the slender calyx-teeth. 2. **I. subsessilis**, Wall. Assam. Khasi and Naga hills. Manipúr. Yunnan. A shrub, l. thinly coriaceous, lanceolate, blade 5–8, pet. ¼ in. long. Fl. pink or white, corolla-tube very slender, ½–1½ in. long, mouth ¼–½ in. across. 3. **I. Brunonis**, Wall. Khabaung forests, Pegu Yoma. Tavoy. Malay Peninsula. A small shrub, branchlets, l. and cymes pubescent. L. sessile or nearly so, oblanceolate, 6–10 in. long. Fl. pale rose-coloured, corolla-tube ½ in. long, hairy. 4. **I. merguensis**, Hook. f. Mergui. Glabrous, l. oblanceolate, blade 7–12, narrowed into a stout pet. ¼–¾ in. long. Fl. flesh coloured, corolla-tube ½–¾ in. long. 5. **I. polyantha**, Wight Ic. t. 1066. West side of the Peninsula, from the Konkan southwards. A large, very ornamental shrub. L. elongate-elliptic, glabrous, blade 8–16 in. long, pet. short. Cymes woolly, with dense spreading hairs, bracts, bracteoles and calyx-lobes ovate-lanceolate, calyx hairy. Corolla glabrous, tube ½–1½ in. long, mouth ⅜ in. across. Fr. ovoid, ½ in. long, sparsely hairy, crowned with the calyx-lobes. 6. **I. Johnsoni**, Hook. f. Cochin. Similar, but entirely glabrous, l. coriaceous, calyx-teeth linear.

B. Cal.-teeth longer than ovary, cymes pedunculate, lower branches spreading.

7. **I. lanceolaria**, Colebr.; Wight Ic. t. 827. West side of the Peninsula, in evergreen forests, from North Kanara southwards. A small shrub, l. glabrous, lanceolate, blade 4–7, pet. ¼ in. long. Fl. white, corolla-tube ½–¾ in. long, mouth ⅜ in. across, lobes linear. 8. **I. notoniana**, Wall. Nilgiri and Palni hills. L. thickly coriaceous, glabrous, elongate-elliptic, blade 6–8, pet. stout, ½–¾ in. long, stipules with long cuspidate points. Cymes ample, up to 10 in. across, peduncle up to 5 in. long, fl. red, corolla-tube glabrous, ⅓ in. long, lobes oblong.

C. Cal.-teeth as long as or shorter than ovary, cymes long-pedunculate.

9. **I. spectabilis**, Wall. Burma. Arakan to Tenasserim. A small evergreen tree, l. pale beneath, elongate-elliptic, blade 5–8, pet. up to ¾ in. long, the uppermost pairs often sessile, with rounded or cordate base. Cymes pubescent, with long spreading branches, peduncles 6–10 in. long with one or two pairs of large sessile foliaceous bracts in the lower half. Fl. white, sessile, corolla ½–⅝ in. long, lobes linear. 10. **I. diversifolia**, Wall. Martaban and Tenasserim, similar but l. not pale beneath, cymes glabrous and fl. pedicelled. 11. **I. Brandisiana**, Kurz. Tenasserim. L. oblong-lanceolate, finely acuminate, peduncles 4–5 in. long, deflexed, cymes pubescent, compact, 2 in. diam., branches short. 12. **I. elongata**, Heyne. Western Ghats from the Konkan to Coorg, similar to 9, but corolla-tube shorter, ½ in. long, lobes short, oblong. 13. **I. villosa**, Roxb.; Wight Ic. t. 150. Sikkim, foot of hills. Assam. Garo and Khasi hills. Cachar. Khabaung forests (Kurz). A shrub, branchlets, petioles, underside of l., stipules and cymes pubescent, l. thinly coriaceous, variable in shape, blade 6–10, petiole ⅓–½ in., stipules ½–1 in. long, with long filiform points. Fl. white, fragrant, in peduncled cymes with long brachiate branches, corolla-tube 1 in. long.

D. Cal.-teeth as long as or shorter than ovary, cymes on short peduncles, less than 2 in. long, branches spreading.

14. **I. parviflora**, Vahl; Wight Ic. t. 711; Bedd. Fl. Sylv. t. 222. Vern. *Kura*, *Undi*, *Lokandi*, Mar.; *Korī*, *Gorivi*, Tel.; *Goravi*, Kan.; *Korivi*, Tam.

A small glabrous tree, cymes sometimes slightly pubescent. L. coriaceous, hard, shining, sessile or shortly petiolate, oblong or obovate-oblong, with a rounded or slightly cordate base, 4–5 in. long, the reticulate veins nearly as prominent as the second. nerves. Fl. white or pink, scented, in ample, nearly sessile, compound trichotomous cymes. Corolla glabrous, tube ⅓–½ in., lobes oblong, style pubescent, tip of corolla ellipsoid in bud.

Western Peninsula, extending north to the Satpura range, common in deciduous forest. Behar. Chutia Nagpur, Orissa. Rare further east. Sundriban. Chittagong. Nicobars. Prome district. Thaungyin at 5,000 ft. (Lobb). Fl. Feb.–April.—Ceylon dry region. Branches of the green wood make excellent torches. 15. **I. brachiata,** Roxb. Peninsula in evergreen forest, on the West side and in Ganjam. Similar to 14, but l. narrowed into petiole $\frac{1}{4}$–$\frac{1}{3}$ in. long, lower cyme branches long, tip of corolla globose in bud, tube $\frac{1}{6}$–$\frac{1}{3}$ in.

16. **I. grandifolia,** Zoll. and Morr. (*I. rosella*, Kurz and *I. macrosiphon*, Kurz). Andamans and Nicobars. Malay Peninsula and Archipelago. A shrub or small tree, l. elongate-elliptic or elliptic-lanceolate, blade 6–12, petiole $\frac{1}{2}$–1 in. long, stipules large with a long, often bifid cusp, fl. white or pale rose, pedicels usually longer than calyx, corolla glabrous, tube $\frac{1}{3}$–$1\frac{1}{2}$ in. long. 17. **I. brunnescens,** Kurz. Andamans and Nicobars. A small tree, nearly allied to 16, l. obovate, 5–7 in. long, sessile or on a very short stout petiole, base rounded or cordate. 18. **I. cuneifolia,** Roxb. Wight Ic. t. 709. Silhet. Pegu, Martaban, Tenasserim. A shrub, young shoots, petioles and underside of l. minutely puberulous, sometimes almost glabrous. L. elongate-elliptic or elliptic-lanceolate, blade 6–9, pet. $\frac{1}{4}$ in. long, sec. n. 10–12 pair, arching, terminating in distinct intramarginal veins, numerous shorter intermediate nerves, stipules with short filiform cusps. Fl. white, sessile or shortly pedicelled, corolla-tube $\frac{1}{2}$–$\frac{2}{3}$ in. long, fr. red.

19. **I. nigricans,** Br.; Wight Ic. t. 318. Vern. *Sawkan*, Burm.

A small tree, entirely glabrous, turning black in drying. L. chartaceous, lanceolate, oblanceolate or elliptic-lanceolate, blade 5–7, pet. $\frac{1}{4}$–$\frac{1}{2}$ in. Cymes shortly pedunculate or nearly sessile, rounded, broader than long, bracts subulate. Fl. white, pedicels usually as long as or longer than calyx, with 2 lanceolate bracteoles. Corolla-tube glabrous within and without, $\frac{1}{2}$–$\frac{2}{3}$ in. long, lobes linear $\frac{1}{8}$–$\frac{1}{4}$ in. long, forming a narrow bud, not much broader than tube, filaments nearly as long as anthers. Fr. black $\frac{1}{4}$–$\frac{1}{3}$ in. diam.

Assam, Manipúr, Cachar. Burma, Upper and Lower, in evergreen and deciduous forest. Western Peninsula, chiefly on the west side, common in evergreen forest. Fl. Jan.–May. Malay Peninsula. Java. 20. **I. erubescens,** Wall. (*I. memecylifolia*, Kurz). Pegu, Tenasserim. Similar, l. thinly coriaceous, nearly sessile, base rounded or cordate.

21. **I. undulata,** Roxb.; Wight Ic. t. 708. Sikkim Terai and lower hills. Bhutan, Assam, Khasi hills. Upper Burma (*Daukyat po*). A large shrub or small tree, l. chartaceous, glabrous, lanceolate, edges undulate, blade 5–9, pet. $\frac{1}{2}$ in. long. Cymes often pubescent, shortly pedunculate, spreading, pyramidal or top rounded, ramifications slender. Fl. greenish-white, supported by several linear bracteoles, calyx-teeth lanceolate, usually equal to ovary in length. 22. **I. barbata,** Roxb. Andamans and Nicobars. Cultivated at Calcutta and elsewhere. A large shrub, l. elliptic, blade 6–8, pet. $\frac{1}{4}$–$\frac{1}{2}$ in. long, the uppermost pair at the base of peduncle smaller, sessile cordate. Cymes sometimes compact, 4–12 in. broad, broader than high, calyx-teeth short, triangular, acute, corolla white, tube 1–$1\frac{1}{2}$ in., mouth woolly. 23. **I. oblonga,** Br. Tenasserim, similar, but corolla-tube shorter.

E. Cal.-teeth as long as or shorter than ovary. Cymes compact, corymbiform, usually sessile.

24. **I. coccinea,** Linn.; Wight Ic. t. 153.—Syn. *I. Bandhuca*, Roxb.; Wight Ic. t. 149. Vern. *Rangan*, Beng.; *Bakora, Pendkul*, Mar.

A large shrub, entirely glabrous. L. coriaceous, sessile or nearly so, elliptic-, sometimes obovate-oblong, cymes sessile, dense-fld. Fl. brilliant scarlet, sometimes yellow, corolla-tube 1–$1\frac{3}{4}$ in. long, lobes ovate, acute, mouth naked, anthers short, yellow, exserted.

Western Peninsula, common near the Western coast, also along the Ghats on river banks. Chittagong (indigenous?). In Burma only cultivated. An ornament of Indian gardens. Fl. throughout the year.—Ceylon low country to 2,000 ft. common.

25. **I. stricta,** Roxb. Tenasserim (Kurz), similar to 24, fl. from scarlet to pale rose and white, corolla-tube $\frac{3}{4}$–1 in., lobes small, rounded. 26. **I. amœna,** Wall. Tenasserim. Malay Penins. and Archipel., l. petioled, lanceolate. 27. **I. fulgens,** Roxb.; Wight Ic. t. 151. (*Pavetta Lobbii*, Teysm. and Binnend.). Tenasserim, Malay Penins. and Archip., l. shining, petioled, lanceolate, sec. n. 20–30 pair, fl. orange, then scarlet. 28. **I. congesta,** Roxb. Attaran, Mergui, Malay Penins., l. rigidly coriaceous, lanceolate, blade 8–12, pet. $\frac{1}{4}$–$\frac{1}{2}$ in. long, fl. orange and scarlet, calyx-teeth broad, very short. 29.

29. **I. rugosula**, Wall. (*I. sessiliflora*, Kurz). Martaban and Tenasserim, fl. white or pale rose-coloured, corolla-tube $\frac{1}{2}$–$\frac{5}{8}$ in. 30. **I. opaca**, Br. Tenasserim, fl. pink, corolla-tube 1 in. long.

23. COFFEA, Linn.; Fl. Brit. Ind. iii. 153.

Shrubs, stipules free. Fl. usually white, axillary, solitary, in pairs or in dense axillary fascicles. Free portion of calyx short. Corolla-lobes 4–9, twisted in bud. Anthers 4–7, linear, attached in the middle of the back to the short filaments. Ovary surmounted by an annular more or less fleshy disk. Drupe with two coriaceous or cartilaginous pyrenes. Seed plano-convex, as a rule with a deep inwardly curved groove on the flat vertical face. Embryo short, near the base of seed, radicle inferior, cotyledons thin, cordate, albumen horny. Species 25, tropics of the Old World.

A. Fl. in axillary many-fld. fascicles, corolla-tube less than $\frac{1}{2}$ in.

1. **C. arabica**, Linn.; Wight Ic. t. 53; Bedd. Man. t. xvii.; Brandis F. Fl. 276. *Coffee.*

A glabrous evergreen shrub or small tree, l. elliptic-oblong 5–7 in. long, narrowed into short petiole. Calyx-limb truncate, corolla funnel-shaped, tube $\frac{1}{4}$–$\frac{1}{3}$ in. long, lobes oblong, as long as tube, filaments shorter than anthers. Berry fleshy, purple when ripe.

Indigenous in Abyssinia and the Sudan. Cultivated in Arabia since the 15th, on the mountains of the Peninsula since the 17th century. Fl. March–June. 2. **C. liberica**, Hiern. *Liberian Coffee*, indigenous in tropical Western Africa, thrives at lower elevations within the tropics, and is less exposed to the ravages of the fungus *Hemileia vastatrix* than 1, has larger l., the corolla 6–9-lobed, fr. black 1 in. long. 3. **C. Khasiana**, Hook. f. Khasi and Naga hills, Manipur. A large rambling almost climbing shrub, branchlets pubescent with short hairs, l. elliptic-lanceolate, caudate-acuminate, blade 5–8, pet. $\frac{1}{4}$–$\frac{1}{2}$ in. long. Fl. yellowish-green on very short pedicels bracteate at the base, which lengthen out as the fr. ripens. Calyx with 4 triangular acute teeth, corolla-tube $\frac{1}{10}$–$\frac{1}{8}$ in., lobes 4, short, hairs in throat white, anthers yellow. Fr. $\frac{1}{4}$ in. diam., calyx-teeth persistent. 4. **C. Jenkinsii**, Hook. f. Khasi hills. Similar, but glabrous, l. narrower, corolla-tube $\frac{1}{8}$ in., fr. $\frac{1}{3}$ in. long, seeds plano-convex without a central furrow.

B. Fl. solitary or 3–4 together, corolla-tube $\frac{1}{2}$ in. or longer.

5. **C. bengalensis**, Roxb.; Kanjilal F. Fl. 207. Vern. *Zalat-pyu*, Burm.

A deciduous shrub, youngest shoots slightly pubescent. L. membranous, not shining, 2–5 in., suddenly contracted into the short petiole, stipules subulate from a broad basis. Fl. pure white, fragrant, solitary or in pairs, calyx with 5 broad often indistinct teeth, divided into numerous linear segments, corolla 1–1$\frac{1}{2}$ in. across, tube $\frac{1}{2}$–1 in. Fr. $\frac{1}{2}$ in. long, black.

Subhimalayan tract and outer hills from the Jumna eastwards. Sikkim Terai. Assam, Silhet. Chittagong. Tenasserim. Upper Burma. Fl. Feb.–April. 6. **C. fragrans**, Wall. Silhet, Tenasserim, l. lanceolate, fl. usually solitary, calyx with numerous teeth, corolla-tube slender, $\frac{5}{8}$–1 in. long.

7. **C. Wightiana**, Wall.; Wight Ic. t. 1598. Western Peninsula from Coorg to Travancore. Ceylon, dry region. A small shrub, bark white, branches rigid almost spinescent, divaricate, l. $\frac{1}{2}$–1$\frac{1}{2}$ in., nearly sessile, stipules short rigid with a sharp point. Fl. solitary, sessile, calyx with 5 broad deeply laciniate teeth, corolla-tube $\frac{1}{2}$ in., lobes shorter than tube, fr. didymous, much broader than long. 8. **C. travancorensis**, W. et A.; Trimen Handb. Ceylon t. 53. Western Peninsula from Coorg to Travancore.—Ceylon, moist and intermediate region, ascending to 3,000 ft. A small shrub, branchlets slender, l. lanceolate 2–4 in. long, petiole short, stipules caducous. Fl. solitary or in threes, calyx pubescent, limb truncate, corolla-tube $\frac{3}{8}$ in., glabrous within. Fr. broader than long, $\frac{3}{8}$ in. broad.

Hamiltonia suaveolens, Roxb.; Bedd. Man. t. xvii. fig. 3; Collett Simla Flora, 231 fig. 71 (includes *H. mysorensis*, W. et A.)—Syn. *Spermadictyon suaveolens*, Roxb. Cor. Pl. t. 236.

Vern. *Ghetra*, Haz. *Padēra*, Hind. Subhimalayan tract and outer hills, from the Punjab to Bhutan ascending to 5,000 ft., mostly on dry stony hillsides, often gregarious. Salt range, Punjab. Merwara and Mt. Aboo. Behar. Western Peninsula, on the Ghats of the Konkan and North Kanara, on the hills of the Northern Circars, Karnúl and Mysore. A small or large shrub, sometimes a small tree, more or less pubescent, branches divaricate, almost herbaceous. L. rigid, elliptic-lanceolate, blade 6–12, pet. ½–1 in. long, sec. n. 10–16 pair, stipules persistent. Fl. 4–5-merous, blue-lilac or white, fragrant (but, like the leaves, fœtid when crushed), in a large terminal thyrsus, consisting of trichotomous compact cymes, bracts, the lower foliaceous, the upper subulate. Calyx hairy, teeth linear, persistent, longer than ovary. Corolla pubescent, funnel-shaped, lobes short, spreading. Ovary 5-celled, style slender, 5-branched at top. Capsule 1-celled, opening at the apex into 5 valves. Seeds 5 or less, triquetrous, testa reticulate on the surface.

24. LEPTODERMIS, Wall.; Fl. Brit. Ind. iii. 198.

Shrubs fœtid when bruised, l. opposite, several pairs often approximate on arrested branchlets, stipules small, persistent. Fl. usually 5-merous, often unisexual, white or purple, nearly sessile, in compact few-fld. cymes, 2 bracteoles under each fl., connate into a scarious, 2-cuspidate tube. Corolla-tube slender, hairy within, throat glabrous, lobes valvate with inflexed edges. Ovary 5-celled, style filiform, arms 5, linear, ovules erect, basal. Capsule 5-valved to the base, seeds 5, each enveloped in a loose fibrous netted covering. Species 8, Himalaya, China and Japan.

1. **L. lanceolata**, Wall. Outer Himalaya, 3–9,000 ft. Kashmir-Bhutan. A small shrub, l. lanceolate, blade ½–3, pet. ⅛–¼ in. long. Fl. white, corolla ⅜ in. long, capsule cylindric ¼–⅜ in. 2. **L. virgata**, Edgew. Salt range. N. W. Himalaya, Hazara to Kulu. North China. A rigid, much branched shrub, l. linear ¼–½ in. long. 3. **L. Griffithii**, Khasi hills, Manipur. L. lanceolate, ½–1½ in. long, stipules with long pungent points. 4. **L. crassifolia**, Coll. et Hemsl. Journ. Linn. Soc. xxviii. 67. Shan hills, Upper Burma 4–5,000 ft. common on grassy slopes. Young shoots more or less hairy, l. ovate or orbicular, ½ in. long, fl. sessile, white, corolla ⅛ in. long.

25. PÆDERIA, Linn.; Fl. Brit. Ind. iii. 195.

Slender twining shrubs, fœtid when bruised, stipules deciduous. Fl. 4–5-merous, in axillary and terminal compound trichotomous cymes, calyx-limb persistent, corolla tubular or funnel-shaped, pubescent, lobes valvate with inflexed crisped edges. Ovary 2-celled, stigmas 2, capillary, twisted, ovules basal, erect. Fr. (in the species here mentioned) flat, a thin shining fragile pericarp, separating from two flat orbicular or elliptic membranous or coriaceous pyrenes. Species 9 or 10, most in tropical Asia.

1. **P. fœtida**, Linn. *Gundali*, Hind. Nepal. Sikkim, from Siligori to 8,000 ft. Assam, Khasi hills. Calcutta, Chittagong. Tenasserim. Yunnan. Malay Peninsula and Archip. Nearly glabrous, l. ovate-acuminate or ovate-lanceolate, blade 2–5, pet. ½–2 in. long. Cymes pedunculate, 2–6 in. long, branches long, in distant pairs, bracts often foliaceous, corolla ½–⅝ in. long. Pyrenes black, with a broad pale wing. 2. **P. lanuginosa**, Wall. Pl. As. Rar. t. 165. Martaban, Tenasserim, often in deserted Taungyas. Foot of Shan hills, Upper Burma. Yunnan. A large twining shrub, stem as thick as a man's arm, branchlets, petioles, underside of l. and cymes densely tomentose, upperside of l. rough when young with short stiff hairs; when mature with the raised roots of fallen hairs, l. cordate acuminate, blade 3–6, pet. 1–3 in. Fl. dull purple, crimson within, corolla ½–⅝ in. long.

Aitchisonia rosea, Hemsley, Journ. Linn. Soc. xix. t. 14. Kuram valley, at 6,000 ft. Baluchistan (var. *Elliottii*, Stapf.) A gregarious undershrub, growing in dense clumps 1–2 ft. high and 6–8 ft. across, kept as dense cushions by the continuous browsing of sheep and goats, l. opposite, petiolate, stipules interpetiolar, persistent. Fl. pink, in congested head-like involucrate cymes. Fr. didymous, separating into 2 cylindrical 1-seeded cocci.

26. MORINDA, Linn.; Fl. Brit. Ind. iii. 155.

Erect or climbing shrubs or trees, stipules connate, sheathing. Fl. white, sessile on a globose receptacle, the calyces more or less connate, forming dense peduncled fl. heads, which are solitary or arranged in panicles or umbels. Calyx-limb short, truncate. Corolla-lobes 4–7, coriaceous, valvate in bud. Stamens 4–7. Ovary 2- or by the prolongation of the placentas spuriously 4-celled, style slender, with 2 stigmatic lobes. Fr. as a rule formed of the succulent coalescing drupes, enclosing many cartilaginous or bony 1-seeded pyrenes, which sometimes cohere, drupes rarely free. Species 40, tropics of both hemispheres.

A. Corolla 5–7-merous, tube ¼ in. or longer.

1. **M. citrifolia**, Linn.; Fl. Brit. Ind. iii. 155. Vern *Al*, *Ach*, Hind.

A large shrub or small tree, glabrous, l. shining, elliptic, blade 6–10, narrowed into pet. ½–¾ in. long, stipules large, broadly oblong or semilunar, often 2–3-fid. Peduncles ½–1½ in., usually solitary, leaf-opposed, the supporting leaf not developed, fl. 5-merous, corolla-tube ⅓–½, fr. of many drupes coalescent into a fleshy head, pale greenish-white, 1 in. diam.

Indigenous in the Darjeeling, Terai and outer hills (Gamble, List 49) and (var. *bracteata*) on the Andamans (Kurz) as well as along the coast of the Konkan, quite near the sea (Talbot). Cultivated largely in India and Burma on account of the roots, which yield a dye. Fl. H. S., R. S. China, Formosa. *M. bracteata*, Roxb., Wight Ill. t. 126, is a variety, the calyx-limb with a lanceolate or spathulate foliaceous lobe. In Indian Timbers Ed. II. 423 Gamble restricts *M. citrifolia*, Linn. to the form growing on the sea coast. The matter demands further research.

2. **M. tinctoria**, Roxb.—Syn. *M. citrifolia*, Bedd. Fl. Sylv. t. 220; *M. exserta*, Roxb.; Brandis F. Fl. 277; *M. leiantha*, Kurz; Vern. *Al*, *Ach*, Hindi; *Maddi*, *Togaru*, Tel.; *Nibasè*, Burm.

A small or middle-sized tree, usually pubescent or tomentose, bark spongy, deeply cracked, greyish-yellow. L. not shining, elliptic-obovate or lanceolate, blade 4–8, narrowed into petiole ⅓–1 in. long. Peduncles solitary, axillary or leaf-opposed, frequently in short trichotomous panicles at the ends of branchlets. Fl. scented, 5-merous, corolla usually tomentose outside, tube ½–¾ in. long, anthers exserted or included. Syncarpium ¾ in. diam.

Behar, Central Provinces, Peninsula. Burma, Upper and Lower, often in Engdain. Frequently cultivated (Berar D. B. March 1877). Fl. March–June. *M. tomentosa*, Heyne, is the softly tomentose form. 3. **M. angustifolia**, Roxb. Cor. Pl. t. 237. Vern. *Assu*, Assam; *Nipasè-gyi*, Burm. Sikkim Terai and lower hills. Assam. Khasi hills, Upper Burma. Pegu (wild and cultivated by Karens). Tenasserim. Malay Penins. A large glabrous shrub, l. thinly membranous, lanceolate, blade 4–12, narrowed into petiole ¼–1 in. long, fl. numerous, fragrant, peduncles axillary or leaf-opposed, corolla glabrous, drupes free. 4. **M. persicæfolia**, Ham. Pegu, Tenasserim, Malay Penins. A low shrub or undershrub, l. oblanceolate or linear, stipules subulate, peduncles short, leaf-opposed, drupes coalescent.

B. Corolla 4-, rarely 5-merous, tube less than ¼ in. long.

5. **M. umbellata**, Linn. West side of the Peninsula in evergreen forests from Coorg southwards. Khasi hills, Tenasserim. Malay Peninsula. Ceylon moist region to 4,000 ft., common. China. A large shrub, climbing by long slender branches, internodes long, l. usually glabrous and lanceolate, blade 2–5, pet. slender ¼ in. long, fl. heads in terminal sessile umbels, peduncles 5–10, glabrous or tomentose, ½–1 in. long, corolla almost rotate, throat bearded. Syncarpium ¼ in. diam. irregularly lobed. 6. **M. villosa**, Hook. f. Khasi hills. A climbing shrub, branchlets, underside of l. and peduncles tomentose, l. obovate-elliptic, acuminate, 4–5 in. long, sec. n. 10–15 pair, prominent beneath. Fl. heads in terminal umbels, drupes confluent.

Rennellia speciosa, Hook. f.—*Morinda speciosa*, Kurz. Tenasserim. Malay Penins. and Archip. An evergreen climbing shrub, quite glabrous. L. thinly coriaceous, lanceolate or elliptic-lanceolate, blade 6–9, pet. ½–1 in. long. Fl. violet, sweet-scented, 3–6 in one head, heads shortly pedicelled, arranged in compact terminal pedunculate panicles, calyx-limb shortly 4-toothed.

Damnacanthus indicus, Gærtn. Assam (Mishmi hills). China. Japan. A small rigid much branched spinous shrub, branchlets pubescent, l. nearly sessile, ovate, cuspidate ½ in. long, spines ½–1 in., straight, slender, interpetiolar (possibly standing in the axils of the minute stipules). Fl. 4–5-merous, white, axillary, solitary or in pairs on short bracteolate pedicels, corolla-tube ½ in. long, funnel-shaped, throat villous, lobes triangular-ovate, valvate in bud. Ovary 2–4-celled, ovules 1 in each cell. Possibly a second species in Manipur (Watt), l. lanceolate 1½ in. long, spines shorter than l.

Gynochthodes macrophylla, Kurz. Sea coast of South Andaman. Malacca. An evergreen climbing shrub, entirely glabrous, l. coriaceous, elliptic, blade 4–6, narrowed into pet. ⅓ in. long. Fl. 4–5-merous, unisexual, in short axillary compact cymes or heads, bracts deciduous. Corolla-tube short, throat hairy, lobes valvate, ovary 4-celled. Fr. sea green, fleshy, ⅓ in. diam., pyrenes 2–4, papery, 1-seeded.

Prismatomeris albidiflora, Thw.; Bedd Ic. Pl. Or. t. 93; Manual t. 29, fig. 4. Assam, Khasi hills, Chittagong, Andamans. Tenasserim. Cochinchina. Malay Penins. and Archip. Ceylon, moist region. A large evergreen shrub, wholly glabrous, branches divaricating, branchlets slender 4-gonous, L. coriaceous, shining, elliptic-lanceolate, blade 3–5, pet. ½–1 in. long. Fl. yellowish-white, scented, unisexual, 4–5-merous, fasciculate, rarely in pedunculate umbels, pedicels long, filiform. Corolla-tube cylindric, ¾–1 in. long, lobes valvate in bud, linear ⅓ in. long, ovary 2-celled. Drupe purple, didymous, ⅜ in. diam., 2-celled, seeds concave.

Cœlospermum scandens, Blume. Andamans. Malay Peninsula and Archip. A climbing shrub, glabrous, except the puberulous inflorescence and calyx. L. coriaceous, dark green, elliptic, acuminate, blade 3–5, pet. ¾–1 in. long. Fl. strongly scented, in dense umbelliform pedunculate cymes, forming a terminal thyrsus. Calyx truncate, corolla coriaceous, tube white, ¼ in. long, glabrous outside, hairy within, segments yellow, narrow, valvate, as long as tube. Ovary 4-celled with 1 ovule, or 2-celled with 2 ovules in each cell.

27. PSYCHOTRIA, Linn.; Fl. Brit. Ind. iii. 161.

Shrubs or small trees, usually glabrous and evergreen, sometimes climbing, rarely herbaceous. Fl. in terminal, rarely axillary, corymbose or paniculate cymes. Corolla-tube straight, short, lobes 5, rarely 4 or 6, valvate in bud. Ovary 2-celled, style bifid, ovules basal, erect, one in each cell. Drupe with 2 one-seeded plano-convex pyrenes, endocarp thin. Seeds plano-convex, ventrally flat or grooved, embryo small basal. Species about 500, tropics of both Hemispheres.

A. Pyrenes plano-convex, no dorsal ridges, no ventral groove, albumen strongly ruminated.

a. Western species.

1. **P. Thwaitesii,** Hook. f.; Trim. Handb. Ceylon ii. 358.

A large gregarious shrub, l. lanceolate or oblanceolate, blade 4–8, petiole ¼–1 in. long, sec. n. 12–16 pair. Fl. greenish, capitate, mixed with rufous hairs, heads sometimes solitary pedunculate, generally in sessile or pedunculate cymes, the lower branches of which are whorled. Fr. ⅓–½ in. long.

West side of the Peninsula, in evergreen forests, from the Konkan southwards. Fl. March–April. Ceylon moist region, very common to 6,000 ft. 2. **P. congesta,** Wight et Arn.; Wight Ic. t. 1037 (*Grumilea*); possibly *P. elongata*, Bedd. Manual t. xvii. Nilgiris, Palnis. Similar, but l. smaller, sec. n. 8–10 pair, fl. shortly pedicelled, crowded, cymes often trichotomous, no hairs among the fl., fr. always crowned by the persistent calyx-limb. 3. **P. macrocarpa,** Hook. f. Tinnevelli Ghats, fr. ellipsoid ⅜ in. long. 4. **P. subintegra,** W. et A. Shevagherry and Dindigal hills. Cymes trichotomous, the lower pair of branches long spreading, rachis arrested. 5. **P. truncata,** Wall. West side of the Peninsula in evergreen forests from the Konkan southwards. L. broadly obovate, blade 6–8, narrowed into pet. ½–1½ in. long, sec. n. 14–16 pair, prominent, stipules large. Lower branches of cyme whorled, fr. not crowned by calyx. 6. **P. Dalzellii,** Hook. f. West side of the Peninsula in evergreen forests from North Kanara southwards, often gregarious, branchlets stout green, l. obovate or oblanceolate, 5–10 in. long, petiole short stout, lower cyme branches whorled. Fr. black, succulent, edible, ⅓ in. diam., crowned with the enlarged calyx, seeds with 1 dorsal ridge. 7. **P. elongata,** Wight Ic. t. 1036 (*Grumilea*). Nilgiris and Shevagerry hills. Ceylon hills to

7,000 ft., l. oblanceolate, blade 4–5, pet. stout ¼ in. long. Fl. white in narrow elongate cymes, branches short opposite. 8. **P. nudiflora**, W. et A. (*P. flavida*, Talbot List (1894) 118). West side of the Peninsula from the Konkan southwards, abundant in evergreen forests of North Kanara. A small shrub, l. lanceolate or oblanceolate, blade 4–5, narrowed into petiole ½ in. long. Cymes trichotomous pedunculate, sometimes compact, calyx truncate, corolla ⅛–¼ in. long. Fruiting cymes bright yellow (Talbot)

b. Eastern species.

9. **P. adenophylla**, Wall., including *P. connata*, Kurz.

An evergreen perfectly glabrous shrub, l. thinly coriaceous, elliptic-lanceolate, blade 4–6, narrowed into petiole ½ in. long, sec. n. arching, 16–18 pair, stipules connate, sheathing, those sheathing the peduncle at the uppermost pair of leaves truncate. Fl. white, in small short-peduncled or almost sessile cymes, arranged in an elongate narrow thyrsus. Fr. purplish-black, ¼ in. diam.

Khasi hills, Chittagong, Andamans. Bhamo, in low evergreen forest (M. Hill.). Pegu Yoma and Tenasserim. Fl. H. S. 10. **P. tylophora**, Kurz. Nicobars. Similar, but fr. ellipsoid, nearly ½ in. long. 11. **P. pendula**, Hook. f. Andamans. Thyrsus in fr. very long, pendulous, fr. ⅓ in. broad, broader than long crowned by the 5-toothed calyx-limb. 12. **P. platyneura**, Kurz. Andamans. L. elliptic-lanceolate, 6–7 in. long, sec. n. 18–22 pair, cymes trichotomous, branches spreading, fr. slightly obovoid, ⅓ in. long.

B. Pyrenes plano-convex, dorsal ridges none or very slight, frequently a T-shaped ventral groove, albumen uniform.[1] Eastern species.

13. **P. calocarpa**, Kurz (including *P. viridiflora*, Kurz F. Fl. ii. 12, not Reinw.) Nepal. Sikkim, to 3,000 ft. Assam, Khasi hills, Cachar, Chittagong. Pegu and Tenasserim. Perak. A shrub, almost herbaceous, youngest shoots minutely puberulous. L. membranous, lanceolate or elliptic-lanceolate, margins often crenate or undulate, blade 5–7, pet. ½–2 in. long, stipules ⅓ in. diam. Cymes small axillary and terminal, calyx-teeth linear, ciliate. Fr. ⅓ in. long, succulent, orange or red, pyrenes with 3 or 4 slight dorsal ridges. 14. **P. Thomsoni**, Hook. f. Khasi hills, l. similar, cymes terminal, trichotomous, elongate, pedunculate, calyx-teeth short triangular. 15. **P. denticulata**, Wall. Nepal. Sikkim 2–6,000 ft. Assam, Bhutan. Khasi hills, Manipur. Tenasserim. L. elliptic or obovate, blade 5–8, pet. ⅓–⅜ in., stipules ⅜ in. long. Cymes terminal and axillary, peduncles 2–4 in. long, branches whorled or opposite. 16. **P. silhetensis**, Hook. f. Assam, Khasi hills, Cachar. L. elongate-elliptic, underside as well as cymes often minutely puberulous, blade 8–14, pet. stout, ½–1 in. long, sec. n. 15–20 pair, prominent, stipules 1 in. diam. Cymes terminal and axillary, peduncles 1–2 in. long, bracts minute caducous. Fr. ⅓–½ in. diam., pyrenes smooth on back, with a deep T-shaped ventral groove. Resembles in appearance *P. fulva*. 17. **P. montana**, Blume (*P. viridissima*, Kurz). Assam, Silhet. Thaukyeghat forests, Tenasserim. Java. A small glabrous shrub, l. membranous, elliptic-lanceolate, blade 3–7, pet. slender, 1–2 in. long, sec. n. 8–10 pair, slender. Cymes terminal and axillary, branches slender, often whorled, corolla $\frac{1}{10}$ in. long. Fr. red ¼ in. long.

C. Pyrenes with sharp ridges on the back, albumen usually uniform.

a. Western species and species of both peninsulas.

18. **P. sarmentosa**, Blume; Wight Ic. t. 1038; Trimen Handb. Ceylon ii. 359.

A large evergreen glabrous shrub, climbing by adventitious rootlets, stems sarmentose with long internodes, l. lanceolate, or elliptic-lanceolate, blade 2–3, pet. ¼–½ in. long, sec. n. faint, stipules sheathing. Cymes trichotomous lax, branches divaricate. Fl. green, calyx hairy, corolla-tube with a dense belt of yellow hairs in mouth, fr. pure white, nearly ½ in. diam., pyrenes with 5 obtuse ribs on the back.

West side of the Peninsula from Coorg southwards. Tenasserim. Fl. Feb.–April. Malay Peninsula and Archipelago. Ceylon, common in the low country. 19. **P.**

---

[1] The albumen ruminated by the intrusion of the testa is nevertheless uniform or homogeneous. I use the term "uniform" in contradistinction to "ruminated," because it is generally understood, though it is not logical.

octosulcata, Talbot, Journ. Bombay Nat. Hist. Soc. xi. 237. Falls of Gairsoppa, North Kanara. An erect shrub with green branches, cymes short sessile, trichotomous, branches slender. Fr. black and succulent when ripe, pyrenes ½ in. long, 4-ridged on back. 20. **P. canarensis,** Talbot Journ. Bomb. Nat. Hist. Soc. xi. 691 t. xii. Falls of Gairsoppa, North Kanara. A small erect shrub, fr. ovoid, curved, ½ in. long, pyrenes with 2 furrows down the back. 21. **P. bisulcata,** W. et A. Nilgiris, fr. ⅓ in. ovoid, pyrenes with 2 shallow furrows on the back. 22. **P. connata,** Wall. (*P. lævigata*, W. et A.; Wight Ic. t. 828). Courtallum. L. coriaceous, shining above, nearly sessile, 4–7 in. long, stipules ovate or lanceolate, simple or bifid. Cymes pedunculate, lower branches whorled, bracts coriaceous, connate, persistent, pyrenes with 2 broad shallow furrows. 23. **P. anamallayana,** Bedd. Ic. Pl. Or. t. 236. Anamalais, 3–4,500 ft. on banks of rivers. A large shrub or small tree, l. chartaceous, oblanceolate, blade 8–10, narrowed into petiole 1½–3 in. long. Cyme short, on a stout peduncle, lower branches whorled, bracts deciduous.

b. Eastern species, pyrenes with 4 dorsal ridges.

24. **P. erratica,** Hook. f. Nepal. Sikkim, ascending to 6,000 ft. Khasi and Naga hills. Siam. An evergreen shrub, l. thinly membranous, lanceolate, blade 5–7, pet. slender ¼–¾ in. long, stipules often with 2 recurved lobes. Cymes trichotomous, 1 in. diam., bracts lanceolate. Calyx-teeth longer than tube. Fr. succulent, red and yellow. 25. **P. sulcata,** Wall. Pegu and Tenasserim, l. lanceolate, blade 3–9, narrowed into pet. ½–1½ in. long, stipules large, almost persistent. 26. **P. andamanica,** Kurz. Andamans and Nicobars, possibly only a form of 25 with broader l. 27. **P. fulva,** Ham. (including *P. monticola*, Kurz). Assam. Khasi hills. Cachar. Pegu. L. elliptic-lanceolate, blade 5–12, pet. ½–1 in. long, sec. n. 15–18 pair, stipules ½–1 in., bifid. Cymes axillary or terminal, compact, usually pedunculate, fr. ¼–½ in. long.

c. Eastern species, pyrenes with 1, rarely 3 dorsal ridges.

28. **P. angulata,** Korth. Tenasserim. Malay Penins. and Archip., l. coriaceous, shining, oblanceolate, blade 4–8, pet. ½ in. long. Cymes pedunculate, branches stout, whorled. 29. **P. symplocifolia,** Kurz. Khasi and Naga hills. Hills east of Toungoo. L. oblanceolate, caudate-acuminate, blade 3–5, pet. ⅓ in. long. Cymes pedunculate trichotomous, branches slender. 30. **P. Helferiana,** Kurz. Pegu. Tenasserim. Malay Penins. Yunnan. Branchlets, underside of l. hirsute, l. elliptic, blade 5–10, pet. ½–2 in. long. Cymes pubescent axillary or terminal, peduncled, fl. minute, greenish-white in dense heads, mixed with hirsute persistent bracteoles, fr. often hirsute ovoid, crowned by the prominent calyx-segments.

Chasalia curviflora, Thw.—Syn. *Psychotria ambigua*, W. et A.; Wight Ill. t. 127. Sikkim 2–6,000 ft. Assam, Khasi hills. Tenasserim. Western Peninsula on the west side, from the Konkan southwards, mostly in evergreen forests. Malay Penins. Ceylon, moist region to 6,000 ft. A slender shrub, l. membranous, elliptic-lanceolate or oblanceolate, blade 4–8, pet. ½–3 in. long. Cymes terminal trichotomous, peduncles 1–2 in. long. Fl. 4–5-merous, dimorphic, anthers exserted, stigmas included or the reverse, calyx-teeth triangular. Corolla ¼–½ in. long, waxy white, throat yellow, disk prominent, conical. Fr. ½ in. diam., inky purple, pyrenes cup-shaped, very concave ventrally.

Hydnophytum formicarium, Jack; Kurz F. Fl. ii. 8. Mangrove swamps of South Andamans. Malay Penins. and Archip. A small evergreen epiphytic perfectly glabrous shrub, with a thick tuber-like trunk, often hollow, in which ants make their nests, branches few, stout. L. coriaceous, elliptic or obovate, obtuse, 2–4 in. long, sessile or narrowed into a short stout petiole. Fl. white, sessile, solitary or in few-fld. fascicles, corolla-tube $\frac{1}{12}$ in. long, glabrous without, hirsute within, lobes 4, valvate in bud. Ovary 2-celled, stigma 2-lobed. Drupe oblong 2–3 in. long (Kurz), orange-crimson.

28. SAPROSMA, Blume; Fl. Brit. Ind. iii. 192.

Shrubs, fetid when bruised, l. opposite or whorled, membranous, stipules deciduous. Fl. usually white, 4–5-merous, axillary or terminal, solitary or cymose, bracts and bracteoles minute. Calyx-tube obconic, limb dilated, persistent. Corolla bell- or funnel-shaped, throat villous, lobes broad, obtuse, valvate with inflexed edges. Ovary 2-celled, stigmas 2, ovules basal, erect. Drupe small with 1 or 2 pyrenes, endocarp crustaceous, embryo nearly as long as seed. Species 8 or 9. India. Tonkin and South China. Malay Archip.

1. **S. ternatum**, Hook. f. Assam. Bhutan. Khasi hills, Manipur. Upper Burma (*Thwebok*). Andamans. Yunnan. Tonkin. A shrub or thin small straggling tree almost entirely glabrous, l. ternately whorled, elliptic-lanceolate, acuminate, blade 6–9, pet. stout, ¼–⅓ in. long, tertiary n. parallel, conspicuous, stipules lanceolate with needle-like points, sometimes pubescent. Fl. in trichotomous, often fasciculate cymes, branches long, slender. Calyx-teeth 4–6, triangular. Fr. black when ripe, succulent, ellipsoid, crowned by the conical disk, girt by the toothed calyx-limb. 2. **S. corymbosum**, Bedd. Ic. Pl. Ind. Or. t. 17. (*Serissa.*) Tinnevelli and Travancore Ghats, above 2,500 ft. in evergreen forest. Similar, but tertiary n. more reticulate, cymes often pedunculate.

3. **S. ceylanicum**, Bedd. Manual 134/12; *Serissa Wightii*; Ic. Pl. Ind. Or. t. 15. Gardn. Nilgiris and Shevagherry hills, glabrous, branchlets flattened and dilated below the nodes, l. shining above, lanceolate, blade 2–4, pet. ¼ in. long, tertiary n. inconspicuous. Fl. pale sulphur yellow, fetid, solitary, on slender peduncles ½–¾ in. long, with 2 small linear bracts below the middle, corolla ⅜ in. long. Fr. ⅔–1 long, bright blue.

4. **S. fragrans**, Bedd.—Syn. *Serissa fragrans*, Bedd. Ic. Pl. Ind. Or. t. 14. Western slopes of the Nilgiris. Tinnevelli hills. Fl. very fragrant, but branchlets and l. very fetid when crushed. L. elliptic-lanceolate, blade 3–4 in. long, pet. very short. Fl. in sessile cymes or clusters. 5. **S. indicum**, Dalz.—Syn. *Serissa glomerata*, Gardn.; Bedd. Ic. Pl. Ind. Or. t. 16. Western Ghats from Bombay southwards, in evergreen forests. Ceylon, rare. A large shrub, l. sessile elliptic-oblong 3–5 in. long. Fl. on short pedicels in few-fld. terminal clusters. Fr. ellipsoid ¼–⅓ in. long, bright blue, fetid, seed one. 6. **S. consimile**, Kurz. Khasi hills. Martaban and Tenasserim, 3–5,000 ft., glabrous, l. lanceolate, blade 2–4, pet. ⅛–¼ in. long, stipules stiffly fimbriate. Fl. terminal, solitary or few together, sessile or nearly so.

29. LASIANTHUS, Jack; Fl. Brit. Ind. iii. 178.

Shrubs, usually evergreen, often hairy, some species fetid, l. distichous, as a rule caudate-acuminate, tertiary nerves numerous, parallel. Fl. in axillary clusters or short cymes. Calyx-limb persistent. Corolla funnel- or salver-shaped, throat villous, lobes 3–7, valvate in bud, anthers included. Ovary 4–9-celled, stigmas 3–9, short, obtuse, ovules erect. Drupe small with 3–9 triquetrous, 1-seeded pyrenes. Species 80, mostly in India and the Indian Archip., extending to China, Japan and North Australia.

A. Fl. sessile or nearly so, in axillary clusters, bracts conspicuous.

a. Outer bracts longer than fl.

1. **L. stipularis**, Blume. Tenasserim or Andamans. Singapore. Malay Archip. Cymes embraced by the large coriaceous stipules. 2. **L. cyanocarpus**, Jack. Naga hills, Chittagong. Andamans, Nicobars. Malay Peninsula. Hongkong. A small evergreen shrub, softly hirsute all over, l. elliptic-lanceolate, blade 6–10, pet. ½ in., outer bracts ovate, ½–2 in. long. Drupe dry, bright blue, pyrenes 4–5. 3. **L. Jackianus**, Wight; Bedd. Ic. Pl. Ind. Or. t. 12. Nilgiris. Similar, softly hirsute all over, l. nearly sessile 4–6 in. long. 4. **L. sikkimensis**, Hook. f. Sikkim 2–3,000 ft. Khasi hills. Branches, petioles and underside of l. finely tomentose, l. lanceolate, blade 6–8, pet. ¼–½ in. long, bracts subulate. 5. **L. Wallichii**, Wight. Assam, Khasi hills, Manipur, Cachar. Andamans. Martaban, Tenasserim (Kurz). Malay Penins. China. Formosa. Branches and underside of l. densely hirsute with long hairs, l. nearly sessile, from a rounded or cordate, often unequal base, oblong or oblong-lanceolate, 2–6 in. long, bracts subulate. Drupe blue-black. 6. **L. tentaculatus**, Hook. fil. Silhet. Branches glabrous, l. oblanceolate from an unequal-sided base, long scattered hairs on midrib and nerves beneath, bracts subulate or filiform, hispid.

b. Outer bracts shorter than fl.

7. **L. tubiferus**, Hook. f. Khasi and Jaintia hills. L. lanceolate, rough beneath with minute hairs, blade 5–7, narrowed into pet. ¼–⅓ in. long, tertiary n. conspicuous. Fl. sessile, clustered, calyx ⅛ in. long, limb shortly 5-toothed, tubular after flowering, bracts orbicular, coriaceous. Drupe ⅓ in. long, crowned by the calyx-limb. 8. **L. oblongifolius**, Bedd. Ic. Pl. Ind. Or. t. 11. Tinnevelli Ghats. Branches glabrous, petioles, stipules and nerves beneath strigose, l. elliptic-oblong, blade 6–7, pet. ½ in. long, tertiary n. prominent beneath. Calyx hairy, limb cleft to the base. 9. **L. obscurus**, Blume; Tenasserim, Andamans. Sumatra, Java. Branches, petioles and stipules tomentose, l. lanceolate, blade 4–7, pet. ¼ in. long, nerves on the underside hairy. Bracts strigose, outer ovate, inner subulate or filiform. Drupe snow-white.

10. **L. Kurzii**, Hook. f. (*L. stercorarius*, Kurz). Tenasserim. Andamans. Branches, petioles and nerves beneath pubescent with minute hairs, l. lanceolate, blade 5–6, pet. ¼ in. long. Calyx strigose, limb cleft to the base. 11. **L. sessilis**, Talbot List (1894) 114. Evergreen forests Yellapur to Gairsoppah, North Kanara. A stout gregarious shrub, branchlets appressed hairy, petiole and stipules hairy, l. glabrous above, hairy on nerves beneath, elliptic, blade 2–5, pet. ¼ in. long. Fl. small, tetramerous, white, sessile, bracts hairy, triangular. Calyx-teeth triangular, hairy outside. Drupe fleshy, black, pyrenes 4, triquetrous, tubercled on back.

B. Fl. sessile or nearly so, in axillary clusters, bracts minute or 0.

a. Calyx toothed, Western species.

12. **L. Blumianus**, Wight; Bedd. Ic. Pl. Ind. Or. t. 22. Tinnevelli and Travancore hills. A large shrub or small tree, almost glabrous, l. lanceolate, blade 3–6, pet. stout, ¼ in. long. Calyx-teeth much longer than tube. 13. **L. ciliatus**, Wight. Nilgiris. Branches, petioles and underside of l. densely brown-tomentose, l. oblong-lanceolate, blade 6–8, pet. stout, ⅛–½ in. long, sec. n. 6–8 pair, prominent beneath, as well as tertiary nerves. Fl. hairy, surrounded by stiff bristly hairs, calyx-teeth oblong, obtuse, hispid. 14. **L. strigillosus**, Hook. f. Courtallum. Branchlets, petioles and nerves beneath clothed with appressed soft hairs, l. lanceolate, blade 4–6, pet. ¼–⅓ in. long. Calyx hispid, teeth minute, triangular, corolla hirsute. 15. **L. acuminatus**, Wight. Nilgiris, Palni and Shevagherry hills. Nearly glabrous, l. lanceolate, blade 4–5, pet. ¼ in. long, sec. n. 4–5, oblique, the 2 lowest pairs reaching beyond the middle of leaf. Calyx hairy, teeth triangular, corolla glabrous outside. 16. **L. parvifolius**, Wight. Courtallum. Quite glabrous, l. coriaceous shining, lanceolate or oblanceolate, almost obtuse at apex, blade 1½–2, pet. ¼ in. long. Calyx-teeth small, obtuse, corolla glabrous outside. 17. **L. obovatus**, Bedd. Ic. Pl. Ind. Or. t. 10. Travancore Ghats 5,000 ft. A rigid much branched shrub, l. glabrous, coriaceous, obovate obtuse, margins recurved, blade 1 in. long, narrowed into a short petiole. Calyx-teeth ovate or triangular, corolla-tube short, glabrous outside.

b. Calyx toothed, Eastern species.

18. **L. lucidus**, Blume. Khasi hills. Upper Tenasserim (Kurz). Java. Branchlets usually minutely hairy, l. lanceolate, blade 3–5, pet. ¼ in. long, petioles and nerves beneath minutely hairy. Calyx-teeth lanceolate, corolla white, ⅓ in. long, hairy outside. 19. **L. Hookeri**, C. B. Clarke. Khasi hills. Minutely strigose, l. rigid lanceolate, blade 6–9, pet. ⅓ in. long. Calyx-teeth lanceolate. 20. **L. inconspicuus**, Hook. f. Khasi and Jaintia hills. Almost glabrous, l. lanceolate, blade 3–4, pet. slender puberulous, ¼ in. long. Calyx glabrous, limb cup-shaped, broader than tube, teeth 5, triangular, acute. 21. **L. lancifolius**, Hook. f. Khasi hills. Branchlets, petiole and midrib hoary-puberulous, l. membranous, narrow-lanceolate, blade 7–9, pet. ⅛–½ in. long. Corolla ⅓ in. long, slender, puberulous outside. Drupes blue, pyrenes 5. 22. **L. constrictus**, Wight. Tenasserim and Andamans, common (Kurz). Branchlets, petioles, stipules and nerves beneath more or less appressed pubescent. Calyx-limb constricted above the ovary, dilated above, 4-lobed (sinuate-toothed, almost truncate, Kurz). 23. **L. pauciflorus**, Wight, Calc. Journal of Natural History vi. 515, Mergui, branchlets, petioles, stipules and l. beneath softly pubescent with long spreading hairs, l. thin, lanceolate, nearly sessile, 3–4 in. long, calyx with 4 triangular teeth.

c. Calyx-limb tubular, truncate or nearly so.

24. **L. truncatus**, Bedd. Ic. Pl. Ind. Or. t. 9. Myhendra hill, Ganjam 4,500 ft. Branches, petioles and nerves beneath appressed pubescent, l. narrow-lanceolate, 4–6 in. long, petiole short, tertiary nerves distinct. Fl. solitary or in few-fld. clusters. Calyx-limb ovoid, truncate, or nearly so. Corolla ⅜ in. long, pubescent outside, lobes 5. 25. **L. andamanicus**, Hook. f. Amherst. Andamans. Branches, petioles, stipules and l. beneath strigose with long hairs, l. oblong-lanceolate, blade 6–8, pet. ¼ in. long, tertiary nerves prominent. Calyx-limb shortly tubular, truncate. 26. **L. Helferi**, Tenasserim or Andamans. Branchlets and petioles glabrous, nerves minutely hairy beneath. L. oblong-lanceolate, blade 4–6, pet. ¼ in. long, sec. nerves 10–12 pair, tertiary obscure. Calyx-limb shortly tubular, truncate or obscurely lobed.

C. Fl. in peduncled cymes.

a. Western species.

27. **L. venulosus**, Wight, Nilgiris 6–8,000 ft., common. Sattarah Ghats, very rare (Dalzell). A very branching, glabrous shrub, l. coriaceous, elliptic, blade 2–4 in. long, pet. short, tertiary nerves prominent. Fl. pale yellow, on short pedicels, in few-fld. short-peduncled cymes, sometimes solitary. Calyx hirsute, lobes 4–5, subulate, as long as the corolla-tube, which is glabrous outside, corolla ⅓ in. long. Drupes blue, crowned by the calyx-teeth. 28. **L. capitulatus**, Wight. Nilgiris, nearly allied to 27, almost glabrous or minutely strigose, l. larger, petioles longer. Fl. nearly sessile, in few-fld. compact short-peduncled cymes, corolla hairy outside. 29. **L. dichotomus**, Wight. Tinnevelli Ghats, Shevagherry hills, nearly glabrous, petiole and cymes sometimes strigose. L. elliptic-lanceolate, blade 2–4, pet. ⅛–¼ in. long. Fl. tetramerous, in narrow dichotomous cymes, with the slender peduncle 1–1½ in. long, bracts subulate, calyx-teeth long lanceolate.

b. Eastern species.

30. **L. Biermanni**, King. Sikkim 5–9,000 ft. Khasi hills. Manipur. Branches, petioles, cymes and nerves beneath minutely strigose. L. elliptic-lanceolate, blade 5–7, pet. ¼–½ in. long. Fl. pale lilac or blueish, in short few-fld. cymes, calyx-teeth broad, foliaceous, corolla ¼–½ in., tube glabrous outside. Drupe bright blue, crowned by the conniving calyx-teeth. 31. **L. longicauda**, Hook. f. Khasi hills. Glabrous, l. lanceolate, long caudate-acuminate, the linear tip 1–1½ in. long, blade 4–5, pet. ⅓ in. long, sec. n. numerous, with shorter intermediate ones between. Cymes few-fld., calyx-teeth triangular. 32. **L. micranthus**, Hook. f. Mishmi hills. Young shoots, petioles and nerves beneath minutely strigose, l. lanceolate from a rounded base, blade 4–6, petiole ⅓ in. long, tertiary n. conspicuous, fl. minute.

ORDER LXII. **COMPOSITÆ.** Gen. Pl. ii. 163.

Herbs, rarely shrubs or trees. L. with few exceptions alternate, stipules 0. Inflorescence a head of many small fl. sessile on the receptacle (dilated top of the peduncle), enclosed in an involucre of whorled or imbricate bracts, the outer fl. opening first. Fl. all tubular (corolla lobes 4–5, valvate in bud) all ligulate, or the marginal ray fl. ligulate (or filiform) and the inner (disk) fl. tubular. Fl. all bisexual, or some unisexual or sterile. Calyx superior, usually a pappus of hairs on the top of the ovary. Stamens 4–5, inserted on the corolla, anthers basifixed, usually connate, connective produced upwards. Ovary 1-celled, ovule solitary. Fr. indehiscent, seed 1, albumen 0.

A. Invol. bracts imbricate.
- All fl. tubular.
  - L. usually dentate, anther base obtuse or minutely sagittate . . . . 1. VERNONIA.
  - L. quite entire, anther-cells tailed . . . . . 2. LEUCOMERIS.
- Marginal fl. ligulate.
  - Erect herbs or shrubs, anther-cells tailed . . 3. INULA.
  - Straggling or climbing. Anther base obtuse . MICROGLOSSA (p. 401).
- Marginal fl. filiform.
  - Pappus of denticulate hairs.
    - L. penninerved.
      - Invol. bracts narrow, linear . . . . . 4. BLUMEA.
      - Invol. bracts broad rigid . . . . . 5. PLUCHEA.
    - L. with 3–9 longitudinal nerves . . . . . HELICHRYSUM (p. 402).
  - Pappus 0 . . . . ARTEMISIA (p. 402).

B. Only one row of invol. bracts, sometimes a minute outer row . . . . 6. SENECIO.

1. **VERNONIA**, Schreb.; Fl. Brit. Ind. iii. 229.

Herbs, shrubs sometimes climbing, rarely trees, l. alternate. Heads homogamous, involucre of many imbricate bracts, the inner longest. Corollas all equal, tubular or funnel-shaped, usually outside with minute stipitate glands, lobes 5, narrow, one-third or one-half the length of tube, anther base obtuse or minutely sagittate. Achenes ribbed or angled, pappus of numerous denticulate hairs, often girt with an outer row of short hairs or flat bristles. Species 450, mostly tropical, more than one half in America.

A. Western species and species of both regions.

a. Trees.

1. **V. arborea**, Ham.—Syn. *Monosis Wightiana*, DC.; Wight Ic. t. 1085; Bedd. Fl. Sylv. t. 226.

A middle-sized tree, branchlets and inflorescence pubescent, l. coriaceous, elliptic, almost entire, glabrous or pubescent beneath, blade 5–8, pet. $\frac{1}{2}$–1 in. long. Fl. heads 1–6-fld., invol. bracts oblong, obtuse, the outer much shorter than the inner. Pappus white, hairs all equal and in one row, $\frac{1}{4}$ in. long.

Western Ghats and adjoining mountain ranges, from the Bababudan hills southwards. Assam, Khasi hills. Andamans. Burma. Fl. Febr.–May. Ceylon, moist region to 5,000 ft. Malay Penins. and Archip. 2. **V. travancorica**, Hook. f.—Syn. *V. volkamerifolia*, Bedd. Fl. Sylv. t. 225. Tinnevelli and Travancore Ghats, standards over the dense masses of *Ochlandra*. A middle-sized tree, branchlets, inflorescence and sometimes underside of l. minutely pubescent, l. obovate, obtuse, sinuate-dentate, blade 2–6, narrowed into pet. $\frac{1}{4}$–$\frac{1}{2}$ in. long. Invol. bracts silky, pappus snow-white, deciduous.

b. Shrubs or undershrubs.

3. **V. divergens**, Benth.—Syn. *V. nilgherryensis*, DC.; Wight Ic. t. 1078; *Decaneuron divergens*, DC. Wight Ic. t. 1084. Assam, Manipur. Burma, Upper and Lower. Parasnath. Bundelkhand. Centr. Prov. Western Peninsula. L. elliptic-lanceolate, serrate, blade 2–5, narrowed into pet. $\frac{1}{2}$–$\frac{3}{4}$ in. long, heads 8–12-fld., outer invol. bracts short ovate. Pappus dirty white or pale reddish-brown. Var. *Lawii*, C. B. Clarke. Khandala, Konkan (*Kadechi*, *Buradi*, Mar.), invol. bracts densely white-woolly, often with an excurrent green point, fl. lilac. 4. **V. pectiniformis**, DC.; Wight Ic. t. 1077, Nilgiris and Palni hills, l. rigid, more or less rough, chiefly beneath, elliptic-lanceolate, serrate, blade 3–6, pet. $\frac{1}{2}$–$\frac{3}{4}$ in. long. Heads 10–25-fld., outer invol. bracts small, ovate, pappus reddish. 5. **V. indica**, Clarke. West side of the Peninsula from the Konkan southwards. Branchlets and underside of l. densely white tomentose, l. coriaceous, broadly elliptic, pet. very short, invol. scales densely tomentose, the outer short.

6. **V. Roxburghii**, Less. Subhimalayan tract, Jumna to Sarda. Behar. Chutia Nagpore. Konkan (doubtful). Upper Burma. Branchlets and l. rough with stiff minute hairs, l. rigid, cuspidate-serrate, elliptic-lanceolate, nearly sessile, 3–5 in. long, head 30-fld., large, invol. bracts apiculate or pungent, pappus dirty white.

7. **V. cinerascens**, Schultz-Bip. Baluchistan, Sind. Peshawar. Ajmere and Merwara (*Laha*). A low shrub, clothed with greyish-white pubescence, l. spathulate $\frac{1}{2}$–$1\frac{1}{2}$ in. long, heads $\frac{1}{4}$ in. diam. on slender peduncles, pappus white.

B. Eastern species, corolla-tube cylindric.

a. Erect, heads large, fl. numerous, more than 10 in one head.

8. **V. volkamerifolia**, DC.—Syn. *V. acuminata*, DC.; Kurz F. Fl. ii. 79. Sikkim, outer hills, to 4,000 ft. Bhutan, Assam. Khasi hills, Manipur. Myit Kyina, Upper Burma. L. oblanceolate, entire or coarsely serrate, glabrous above, more or less pubescent beneath, 6–12 in. long, narrowed into a very short petiole, fl. lilac, invol. bracts obtuse, more or less hairy, pappus dirty white. Specimens from the following localities differ by a white pappus, and densely silky invol. scales, the achenes ribbed and more or less clothed with long thin hairs. Dry hill forest, east of Bhamo 5,000 ft. (Mont. Hill.); Schwebo district in deciduous forests with Teak (*Segyi*, Smales); Katha district (J. W. Oliver).

9. **V. talaumifolia**, Hook. f. Sikkim, lower hills. Assam. A middle-sized tree, l. rigidly coriaceous, glabrous and shining above, obovate or oblanceolate, blade 10–20, narrowed into stout amplexicaul petiole $\frac{1}{2}$ in. long, sec. and reticulate tertiary nerves prominent beneath, invol. bracts almost glabrous, broad-ovate or -elliptic, obtuse, often toothed at tip, pappus red.

10. **V. solanifolia**, Benth. Pegu. Hills east of Toungoo. Yunnan. China. Similar to *V. arborea*, differs by the l. hirsute on the upper, softly tomentose on the underside. L. with a rounded or cordate base, sinuate dentate, fl. heads smaller.

b. Erect, heads small, fl. less than 10 in one head.

11. **V. Aplinii**, Coll. et Hemsl. Shan hills, Upper Burma 1,700–5,000 ft. A middle-sized tree, underside of l. and ramifications of inflorescence greyish-white-tomentose. Heads sessile, numerous, in ample terminal panicles 12 in. broad and 18 in. long, the inner 6–8 invol. scales linear, acute, $\frac{1}{4}$–$\frac{1}{3}$ in. long, outer ovate shorter, numerous, imbricate, all silky on back, fl. 8–9 in each head, achenes glabrous, slightly papillose. 12. **V. Parishii**, Hook. f. Between Lomatee and Kolodo, headwaters of Yunzalin river 3,000 ft. (D. B. March, 1880). Attaran district (Parish). Branchlets, underside of l. and inflorescence velvety, l. oblanceolate, distantly dentate. Heads purple, sessile or pedunculate, in ample terminal panicles, inner invol. scales linear, acute, $\frac{1}{3}$–$\frac{1}{2}$ in. long, outer numerous imbricate, ovate, much shorter, all densely silky outside, fl. 6–8. Pappus white.

c. Climbing.

13. **V. scandens**, DC. Sikkim, outer hills. Assam, Khasi hills, Manipur. Pegu. Kachin hills. Branchlets and inflorescence slightly pubescent, l. elliptic-lanceolate, blade 2–4, narrowed into slender petiole $\frac{1}{3}$ in. long. Heads 5–10-fld. pedicelled, in long terminal leafy panicles, pappus red. 14. **V. blanda**, DC. Lower Burma. Yunnan. Similar to 13; but l. larger and achenes pubescent. 15. **V. elæagnifolia**, DC. Pegu, Tenasserim, Siam. Branchlets, petioles, underside of l. and inflorescence softly grey-pubescent, l. variable, from elliptic to linear-lanceolate, blade 2–3, pet. slender $\frac{1}{3}$ in. long. Heads $\frac{1}{4}$ in. diam., few at the ends of the rigid divaricate branches of a leafy terminal panicle.

C. Eastern species, corolla funnel-shaped widened from a slender cylindrical base.

16. **V. cylindriceps**, C. B. Clarke in Journ. Linn. Soc. xxv. 35. Naga and Manipur hills, 4,500–5,800 ft. Yunnan 4,500–5,500 ft. A large shrub or small tree, l. membranous, rough on both sides with minute stiff hairs, oblanceolate, blade 5–7, narrowed into pet. $\frac{1}{4}$–$\frac{1}{2}$ in. long. Heads purple, cylindric when in bud, arranged in broad terminal corymbs, fl. 4–6. Invol. scales obtuse, nearly glabrous, imbricate, the outer shorter, the 4–6 inner $\frac{1}{3}$ in. long. Achenes obscurely ribbed, pappus red. A small tree with dirty white pappus found by Montague Hill (143) in dry hill forest east of Bhamo at 5,000 ft., in other respects is exactly like *V. cylindriceps*. 17. **V. peguensis**, Clarke, Pegu Yoma, similar to 16, but invol. scales sharply cuspidate with an excurrent nerve, the outermost subulate, heads with 12 fl.

2. LEUCOMERIS, Don; Fl. Brit. Ind. iii. 386.

Shrubs or small trees, l. quite entire. Heads white, 4–8-fld. in terminal corymbs. Invol. bracts imbricate, coriaceous, peduncles bracteolate. Fl. all ☿, fertile, tubular, segments 5, narrow, revolute. Anther-base sagittate, tails ciliate. Species 2.

1. **L. spectabilis**, Don; Wall. Pl. As. Rar. t. 111. Outer North-West Himalaya, Jaunsar to Nepal, 2–6,000 ft. A large shrub or small tree, bark white corky, branches stout, grooved. L. coriaceous, white-felted beneath, oblong-lanceolate, blade 4–14, narrowed into marginate petiole $\frac{1}{2}$–1 in. long. Heads 1 in. long, invol. scales glabrous. 2. **L. decora**, Kurz. Manipur. Pegu, in the Eng forest of the Prome district. Shan hills, ascending to 5,000 ft. Yunnan. A small deciduous tree, l. nearly glabrous when mature, pet. 1–2 in. long. Heads fragrant, crowded at the ends of the leafless branchlets, invol. scales woolly at the base.

3. INULA, Linn.; Fl. Brit. Ind. iii. 291.

Herbs, rarely shrubs. Heterogamous, radiate, invol. bracts ∞-seriate, inner rigid and narrow. Ray fl. ligulate ♀ fertile, in one or several rows, ligule 3-toothed, disk fl. ☿ fertile, tubular, yellow, limb elongate with 5 short teeth. Anther-base sagittate, tails long usually branched. Species 90. Europe, Asia and Africa.

1. **I. Cappa**, DC. Outer hills from Simla eastwards 3–6,000 ft., often gregarious on clearances. Khasi hills, Manipur. Burma. Attains 10 ft., branches, l. beneath and

corymbs densely silky or woolly, l. sessile or nearly so, oblong-lanceolate, toothed, heads numerous in terminal corymbs ⅓ in. diam., invol. bracts all linear, rigid, hairy ligulate fl. very small, few or wanting, achenes silky, pappus dirty white, hairs thickened at the end. 2. **I. eupatorioides,** DC. Subhimalayan tract, Sikkim, Bhutan, often in Sāl forest Khasi hills. Branches and underside of l. pubescent, l. rigid, lanceolate, blade 4–7, pet. stout ¼ in., ligules narrow. 3. **I. cuspidata,** C. B. Clarke; Collett, Simla Flora, 258, fig. 78. North-West Himalaya 4–7,000 ft. Nearly glabrous, l. elliptic-lanceolate, blade 3–5, pet. ⅓ in. long. Ligulate fl. numerous, ligule short, broad.

Microglossa volubilis, DC. Khasi and Naga hills. Burma, Upper and Lower, up to 3,500 ft. Malay Penins. and Archip. China. A large evergreen, straggling or climbing shrub, branches grooved, branchlets and l. slightly pubescent, l. ovate-lanceolate, obscurely toothed, blade 2–3, pet. slender ¼ in. long. Heads yellow, clustered on the branches of a rounded corymb, invol. bracts lanceolate, imbricate, ligule of marginal fl. minute, anther-base obtuse, achenes minute, 4-angular, pappus red much longer than the achenes.

4. BLUMEA, DC.; Fl. Brit. Ind. iii. 260.

Annual or perennial, a few shrubs, glandular-pubescent or woolly. Invol. bracts imbricate, many-seriate, the outer smaller. Marginal fl. ♀, numerous, filiform, minutely dentate at the apex. Disk fl. bisexual, corolla tubular, limb with 5 short teeth, anther-base sagittate, tails small, slender. Species 60, Asia, Africa, Australia.

1. **B. chinensis,** DC. Nepal. Sikkim 2–4,000 ft. Bhutan. Khasi hills, Manipur. Upper Burma, dry hill forest 5,000 ft., east of Bhamo. China. A shrub, scrambling or scandent, glabrous, only inflorescence pubescent. L. coriaceous, shining, lanceolate, slightly serrate. Heads yellowish, clustered on the distant branches of a long terminal panicle, receptacle densely clothed with long thin multicellular hairs.

2. **B. balsamifera,** DC.; Kurz F. Fl. ii. 82 (*Conyza balsamifera*, Linn.). *Pôn-mathein*, Burm. Sikkim, ascending to 4,000 ft. Assam, Khasi hills. Chittagong. Burma, Upper and Lower. China, Formosa. Malay Peninsula and Archipelago. A large short-lived very aromatic shrub with herbaceous branches, sometimes a small tree, coming up gregariously on deserted Taungyas, branches, l. and inflorescence densely clothed with silky tomentum, l. lanceolate or elliptic-lanceolate, blade 4–10, petiole ⅓–1 in. long, with several lanceolate lobes resembling pinnæ. Heads yellow, ¼–⅓ in. diam., densely clustered on the branches of a large terminal leafy panicle, pappus red. Yields camphor, which is an article of trade in China. 3. **B. aromatica,** DC. Subhimal. tract and outer hills, from Kumaon eastwards. Khasi hills. Tenasserim. China. Attains 6–10 ft. Glabrous or with thin cottony, sometimes glandular hairs, l. membranous, narrowed into a short petiole rarely bearing lateral lobes.

5. PLUCHEA, Cass.; Fl. Brit. Ind. iii. 271.

Shrubs, tomentose or glutinous, l. alternate. Heads campanulate, heterogamous, disciform, outer fl. ♀ fertile filiform, disc. fl. few, sterile tubular, limb 5-fid, invol. bracts imbricate, dry, rigid, the outer smaller. Anther-base sagittate. Achenes 4- or 5-angled, pappus hairs 1-seriate, slender, rigid. Species 30, warmer regions of both hemispheres.

A. L. broad, obovate or elliptic.

1. **P. indica,** Lam.; Wight Ill. t. 131. Beach and tidal forests on the coast from Bengal to the Malay Peninsula. Andamans. Also inland in stream beds, Upper Burma. Malay Archip. China. Nearly glabrous, l. obovate obtuse more or less dentate, 1–2 in., narrowed into a short slender petiole. 2. **P. tomentosa,** DC. Sind. Gangetic plain from Dehra Dûn to Lower Bengal. Western Peninsula. Attains 10 ft., branchlets and l. pubescent or tomentose, l. sessile, elliptic or broadly obovate, obtuse, coarsely toothed, base auricled, pappus reddish.

B. L. narrow, lanceolate or oblanceolate.

3. **P. Wallichiana,** DC. Sind, Baluchistan, Gujarat, Punjab. Glandular-pubescent and scabrid, l. rigid, 1–2 in. long, oblanceolate or oblong, sessile, faintly toothed. 4. **P. lanceolata,** Oliv. Sind. Punjab. Gangetic plain as far as Cawnpore. Afghanistan,

North Africa. L. coriaceous, sessile, linear-lanceolate or oblanceolate, cuspidate, sec. n. oblique, conspicuous, invol. bracts short, rounded, obtuse, fl. pink. 5. **P. arguta,** Boiss. Baluchistan, Sind, Punjab. Glandular-pubescent, l. succulent, when growing on the coast, thin inland, sessile, 1–2 in. long, varying much in breadth from oblanceolate or nearly obovate to linear, when broad deeply cut. Heads pedunculate, solitary or few together, invol. bracts rigid, subulate-lanceolate.

Helichrysum buddleioides, DC. Hills on the West side of the Peninsula from Kanara southwards. A shrub attaining 6 ft., often gregarious, underside of l. and corymbs densely cottony. L. sessile, lanceolate, quite entire, 4–6 in. long, 8–9 longitudinal nerves. Heads yellow, in globose clusters, forming terminal corymbs, inner invol. bracts broad, scarious, outer hairy. Marginal fl. ♀, filiform, disk fl. ☿ tubular.

Artemisia vulgaris, Linn. Subhimalayan tract and Himalaya ascending to 12,000 ft., often gregarious in clearances. Khasi hills. Hills of the Western Peninsula. Siam. Java. Temperate Europe and Asia. A shrub, very aromatic, pubescent or tomentose, l. ovate, lobed, or pinnatipartite, white pubescent or tomentose beneath, lobes acute irregularly serrate, uppermost linear-lanceolate entire. Heads $\frac{1}{8}$–$\frac{1}{6}$ in. long, in more or less one-sided panicled racemes, invol. bracts more or less woolly, the inner scarious, the outer smaller herbaceous. Ray fl. ♀ slender, 2–3-toothed, disk fl. tubular, all fertile. Pappus 0.

6. SENECIO, Linn.; Fl. Brit. Ind. iii. 338.

Mostly herbaceous, a few small trees, shrubs and woody climbers, l. alternate, in the herbaceous species often radical. Heads yellow, rarely white, invol. bracts one-seriate or with an outer row of small bracts. Ray fl. ♀ ligulate, sometimes wanting, disk fl. bisexual, tubular, anther-base obtuse or minutely tailed. Species 1,000–1,200 chiefly in temperate climates and mountains of the tropics.

A. Fl. few, 12 or less in one head, all tubular.

1. **S. araneosus,** DC.—Syn. *S. Walkeri*, Arn.; Wight Ic. t. 1131. Sikkim 5–8,000 ft. Assam, Khasi hills. Nilgiris. Ceylon. Java. A woody climber, l. ovate from a cordate base, dentate or sinuate, sometimes slightly lobed, often grey cottony beneath, blade 4–7, pet. 1–3 in. long, basal nerves 5–7. Fl. heads bracteolate, in open terminal and axillary bracteate corymbs, invol. bracts 8. 2. **S. corymbosus,** Wall.; Wight Ic. t. 1130. Nilgiris, Ceylon. Similar, l. coriaceous smaller almost orbicular, tawny tomentose beneath.

B. Fl. few (6–10) in one head, ligulate fl. 2–5.

3. **S. triligulatus,** Ham. Nepal. Sikkim, 6–10,000 ft. Mishmi and Naga hills. Manipur. Dry hill forest east of Bhamo (Montague Hill). Yunnan (Henry). A woody climber, glabrous, except corymbs which are often puberulous, l. elliptic- or oblong-lanceolate, caudate-acuminate, blade 4–5, pet. $\frac{1}{2}$ in. long. Fl. white (Hill), yellow (Henry), invol. bracts 5–8, $\frac{1}{6}$ in. long. Fl. 2–3 ligulate and 3 tubular in each involucre, ligules very short 2-nerved, lobes of tubular fl. revolute. Pappus dirty white. From the same locality, 4,500 ft., Mont. Hill (141) has sent specimens of a small tree, very similar, but peduncles and ramifications of corymbs capillary, fl. smaller, invol. bracts $\frac{1}{8}$ in. long, pappus pure white. 4. **S. vagans,** Wall. Nepal, has capillary peduncles but larger fl. heads, ligulate fl. conspicuous.

5. **S. rufinervis,** DC. Kunawar. Simla. Garhwal and Kumaon, 6–8,000 ft. L. ovate to ovate-lanceolate, sharply toothed, lower surface white-tomentose, except the red-brown nerves. Heads 6–10-fld., invol. bracts 5–8, much shorter than fl.

C. Fl. numerous. Climbers.

6. **S. scandens,** Don.—Syn. *S. Wightianus*, DC.; Wight Ic. t. 1136; *S. intermedius*, Wight Ic. t. 1135. Kumaon. Sikkim, 6–10,000 ft. Mishmi and Khasi hills. Manipur Hills of Upper Burma. Yunnan. Tonkin. Nilgiris. Palnis. Ceylon. Climbing, branches zig-zag, grooved or ribbed, nearly glabrous, l. lanceolate or hastate, blade 3–4, pet. $\frac{1}{2}$–1 in. long, often with foliaceous lobes and auricles at base. Heads yellow, on the divaricate branches of lax terminal corymbs, invol. bracts 10–15. 7. **S. candicans,** DC.; Wight Ic. t. 1134. Nilgiris. Climbing, branches angular. Similar to 6, but branches and l. beneath densely white-tomentose, petiole always auricled. 8. **S. Buimalia,** Ham. Nepal. Sikkim 5–6,000 ft., branches, underside of l. and inflor-

escence cottony, l. ovate-acuminate from a cordate base, blade 3–5, pet. 1–2 in. long, heads large few in axillary pedunculate corymbs, invol. bracts 8, white-tomentose, with thin glabrous edges.

D. Fl. numerous. Erect.

9. **S. densiflorus**, Wall. Nepal. Sikkim, 5–7,000 ft. Bhutan. Khasi and Naga hills. Tenasserim. Branches stout, as well as underside of l. and corymbs clothed with white cottony wool, l. lanceolate, sharply serrate, blade 5–9, pet. ½–1 in. long, heads numerous, corymbs usually arranged in a large terminal panicle. 10. **S. Nagensium**, C. B. Clarke in Journ. Linn. Soc. xxv. 39, and 11. **S. Rhabdos**, C. B. Clarke l.c. 40, t. 19, both Naga hills and Manipur, similar to 9.

ORDER LXIII.—**Goodeniaceæ.** *Scævola*, Linn.; Fl. Brit. Ind. iii. 421. Shrubs with large pith, l. alternate, stipules 0. Fl. in short axillary cymes, calyx adnate to ovary, lobes 5. Corolla oblique, split to the base on the back, stamens 5, inserted at the base of corolla. Ovary 2-celled, ovules basal, 1 in each cell. Style simple, a cup-shaped indusium, including the stigma. Fr. a drupe, crowned by the enlarged calyx-segments. 1. **S. Kœnigii**, Vahl (*S. Taccada*, Roxb.; Wight Ill. t. 137); *Bhadrak*, Mar.; *Pinlè-tan*, Burm. Sand hills near the sea, Sind, both Peninsulas, Andamans, Malay Peninsula, Tonkin. Ind. Archip. New Guinea. Australia and Polynesia. L. glabrous or silky, obovate, obtuse, 3–8 in., narrowed into a short petiole. Fl. white or pale lilac, soon turning brown, calyx-lobes oblong-lanceolate, corolla funnel-shaped, hairy within, tube curved, ¾ in. long, lobes spreading. Drupe white, ⅓–½ in. diam., very succulent, stone rough, bony. 2. **S. Plumieri**, Vahl; Trimen Handbook Ceylon iii. 55 (*S. Lobelia*, Linn.; Fl. Brit. Ind. iii. 421; *S. uvifera*, Stocks; Wight Ic. t. 1613). Sea coast of Sind, the Western Peninsula and Ceylon. Littoral in the tropics of both hemispheres. L. smaller, calyx-lobes very short, obtuse, drupe purple, resembling a grape berry.

ORDER LXIV. ERICACEÆ (including *Vacciniaceæ*, Gen. Pl. ii. 564 and *Ericaceæ* 577).

Shrubs, small trees or wiry herbs, l. simple, alternate, stipules 0. Fl. bisexual, 4- or 5-merous, corolla gamopetalous, stamens as a rule twice the number of corolla-lobes, anthers 2-celled, opening at the top by 2 pores or short slits. Ovary inferior or superior, 4-, 5- or many-celled, ovules on an axile placenta, numerous in each cell. Style slender, stigma entire or minutely lobed. Seeds small, a straight embryo in fleshy albumen.

Tribe I. *Vacciniaceæ*.—Ovary inferior.
  Corolla long and tubular, or campanulate with long segments, fl. corymbose or fascicled.
    Calyx-limb 5-lobed, tube terete . . . . . 1. AGAPETES.
    Calyx-limb 5-lobed, tube 5-ribbed . . . . . 2. PENTAPTERYGIUM.
    Calyx-limb entire . . . . DESMOGYNE (p. 406).
  Corolla campanulate or ovoid, teeth short.
    Fl. in axillary racemes . . . . . . 3. VACCINIUM.
    Fl. in corymbs from the old wood . . . . CORALLOBOTRYS (p. 408).

Tribe II. *Ericaceæ*.—Ovary free.
  Capsule loculicidally 5-valved.
    Calyx succulent in fr., enclosing the capsule.
      Anthers with 2 horns on back . . . . . 4. GAULTHERIA.
      Anthers without horns . . . . . . 5. DIPLYCOSIA.
    Calyx not altered in fr., fl. solitary or fascicled.
      L. small, sessile, appressed to stem, imbricate CASSIOPE (p. 408).
      L. petioled, approximate at the ends of branches ENKIANTHUS (p. 408).
    Calyx not altered in fr., fl. in racemes.
      Seeds linear-oblong, not fringed . . . 6. PIERIS.
      Seeds nearly orbicular, fringed . . . . LEUCOTHOE (p. 409).
  Capsule septicidally 5–20-valved, fl. showy . . . . 7. RHODODENDRON.

In taking this Order in the wider sense, I follow my Flora of North-west and Central India 279, and Drude in Engler u. Prantl iv. 1. 15. *Diplycosia* stands intermediate between the genera with superior and those with inferior ovary.

1. AGAPETES, D. Don; Fl. Brit. Ind. iii. 443.

Evergreen shrubs, usually epiphytic. L. coriaceous, in most species entire. Fl. in corymbs or fascicles, rarely in racemes or solitary. Calyx-tube globose, adnate to ovary, limb deeply 5-lobed. Anthers elliptic, produced upwards in 2 long beaks opening by apical pores or slits, often spurred behind. Seeds very numerous, outer coat usually very lax. Species 30, eastern Himalaya, hills of the Eastern Peninsula and the Indian Archipelago. Fiji.

A. Corolla long, tubular, lobes short, bracts short, l. large.

(*a*) Calyx not supported by an epicalyx.

α. L. sessile or nearly so, not gradually narrowed into petiole.

1. **A. setigera**, D. Don (*Vaccinium verticillatum*, Wight Ic. t. 1181; Kurz F. Fl. ii. 87. var. 1; *V. hirsutum*, Wight Ic. t. 1182). Nepal, Khasi hills, Cachar. Shan hills 6,000 ft. (Collett). Bithoko range between Yunzalin and Salween 2,000 ft. (D. B. March 1880). L. glabrous, generally crowded with short internodes, so as to appear whorled, lanceolate or elliptic-lanceolate, 3–5 in. long, narrowed suddenly into the very short petiole. Fl. scarlet or crimson, in pedunculate corymbs, axillary from the whorls of l., or above the scars of fallen l., peduncles, pedicels and calyx often hirsute with long hairs, bracts minute. Corolla $\frac{3}{4}$–1 in., slightly curved, outside pubescent or hirsute, anther beaks not spurred. Fr. $\frac{1}{3}$ in. diam., calyx-teeth half the length of fr. 2. **A. macrostemon**, Clarke (*Vaccinium macrostemon*, Kurz). Hills east of Toungoo, 4–6,000 ft. L. 4–6 in. long, almost sessile with a rounded base, fl. scarlet, in 3 in. long pedunculate glabrous racemes, bracts linear $\frac{1}{4}$ in. long, corolla glabrous, distinctly curved, $1\frac{1}{4}$ in. long.

3. **A. loranthiflora**, D. Don (*Vaccinium verticillatum β elegans*, Kurz). Pegu Yoma, higher ridges. Headwaters of Yunzalin 4,000 ft. (D. B. March 1880). Tenasserim. L. often falsely whorled, almost sessile, lanceolate or oblanceolate, 3–5 in. long. Fl. axillary, solitary, fasciculate or in short corymbs, corolla 2–$2\frac{1}{2}$ in. long, anthers spurred, pedicels and calyx more or less hispid with long hairs. 4. **A. miniata**, Hook. f. Khasi hills. Patkoi range. L. elliptic-lanceolate, remotely serrate, nearly sessile, falsely whorled, sec. n. prominent. Corymbs with numerous short bracts. 5. **A. grandiflora**, Hook. f. Mishmi and Naga hills. Lakhimpur district, Assam. L. nearly sessile, oblong-lanceolate. Fl. on the old wood, fasciculate, calyx-teeth triangular $\frac{1}{8}$ in., corolla 2–$2\frac{1}{2}$ in., lobes lanceolate $\frac{1}{3}$–$\frac{1}{2}$ in. long, anthers spurred on beak.

6. **A. Hillii**, n. sp. Hills east of Bhamo 4,500 ft. (Mont. Hill, Oct. 1901). Epiphytic on tall trees, stem swollen. L. sessile oblong-lanceolate 4–6 in. long, fl. in pedunculate corymbose racemes, pedicels 1–$1\frac{1}{2}$ in. long, thickened at apex and conspicuously articulate with calyx. Calyx divided nearly to the base, lobes linear $\frac{1}{3}$ in. long. Corolla tubular, widened upwards, 2 in. long, purple with darker V-shaped markings. Filaments flat, hairy, not geniculate, anthers not spurred.

β. L. petiolate, or narrowed towards base. Anthers not spurred.

7. **A. saligna**, Hook, f. (*Vaccinium salignum*, Hook. f. Ill. Him. Pl. t. 15A). Sikkim 1–5,000 ft. Thaungyin 5,000 ft., Tenasserim. Stems often greatly thickened at the base, l. scattered, lanceolate, acuminate, blade 3–4, narrowed into petiole $\frac{1}{4}$ in. long, sec. n. conspicuous. Fl. dark red, in short glabrous corymbs, calyx-teeth lanceolate, $\frac{1}{16}$–$\frac{1}{8}$ in. long, corolla 1 in. widened upwards, lobes long-acuminate, $\frac{1}{4}$–$\frac{1}{3}$ in. long, anthers not spurred on back. 8. **A. Parishii**, Clarke. Tenasserim. Nearly allied, l. larger, sec. n. slender, intramarginal vein continuous, calyx-teeth triangular. 9. **A. salicifolia**, Clarke. Mishmi hills. L. linear-lanceolate, petiole very short, corolla $\frac{3}{4}$ in. long, lobes short, triangular.

10. **A. macrantha**, Hook. f. (*Vaccinium variegatum*, Kurz, var *macranthum*) Khasi and Chittagong hills. Tenasserim. Fl. fascicled. corolla pale purple, with darker transverse bands, $1\frac{1}{2}$–2 by 1 in. 11. **A. macrophylla**, Clarke. Khasi hills. L. broad-lanceolate, blade 9–11, pet. stout, $\frac{1}{3}$ in. long, sec. n. prominent. Fl. in pedunculate corymbs, calyx-teeth narrow-lanceolate, $\frac{1}{3}$ in., corolla $1\frac{1}{4}$ in. long.

γ. L. petiolate, anthers spurred.

12. **A. variegata**, D. Don (*Vaccinium odontocerum*, Wight Ic. t. 1187; *V. variegatum*, Kurz). Khasi hills. Cachar. Chittagong and Martaban hills. L. lanceolate, blade 5–8, narrowed into a thick pet. $\frac{1}{4}$ in. long. Fl. on the old wood, densely fascicled on slender glabrous pedicels, much longer than calyx, calyx-teeth triangular-lanceolate.

Corolla rose-purple, with darker V-shaped transverse bands $\frac{3}{4}$–1 in. Seeds with a firm, shining minutely foveolate testa. The seeds of the sp. of *Agapetes* require further study. 13. **A. angulata,** Hook. f. (*Vaccinium odontocerum*, Kurz). Patkoi hills. Branches sharply angular. Similar to 12, but calyx-teeth shortly triangular. 14. **A. campanulata,** Clarke (*Vaccinium campanulatum*, Kurz). Nattoung, Martaban 7,000 ft. L. elliptic, narrowed into a very short petiole. Corolla campanulate, deep scarlet, lobes broadly triangular.

(*b*) Calyx supported by an epicalyx (enlarged pedicel or connate bracteoles).

15. **A. auriculata,** Hook. f. (*Vaccinium auriculatum*, Kurz). Sikkim, 3–4,000 ft. Bhutan. Khasi hills. L. often falsely whorled, sessile 6–8 in. long, oblong-lanceolate from a rounded base, intramarginal nerves distinct. Corymbs from the old wood or from the whorls of l., peduncles stout, pedicels much dilated and cup-shaped at the apex, corolla $\frac{3}{4}$ in., tube narrowing upwards, fr. $\frac{1}{4}$ in., bright red, calyx-teeth $\frac{1}{4}$ in. long, broadly lanceolate, striate. Very similar, but possibly a new species, is a shrub growing on granite boulders on the hills east of Bhamo at 6,500 ft. (Mont. Hill). Corolla widening upwards, calyx supported by a double epicalyx, the outer spreading, the inner adnate to calyx-tube with a free margin.

16. **A. glabra,** Clarke. Bhutan, Khasi hills. Similar to 12, but corymbs and corolla-tube densely pubescent, corolla green and white, often with rose-cold. V-shaped transverse bars. 17. **A. Nuttallii,** Clarke. Bhutan. L. elliptic, acuminate, blade 5–7, narrowed into stout pet. $\frac{1}{4}$ in., corymb lax, corolla 1 in. long.

B. Corolla-lobes short, bracts short, l. under 2 in.

18. **A. obovata,** Hook. f. Khasi hills, common. A small dense shrub, branches rigid, l. obovate, less than $\frac{1}{2}$ in., margins recurved. Fl. solitary on long slender pedicels, cal.-teeth triangular acuminate, corolla $\frac{1}{4}$ in. long, acutely conical in bud. 19. **A. Mannii,** Hemsl. in Gard. Chron. 1892, xii. 364. Khasi hills. Similar, but pedicels shorter, barely as long as fl., corolla $\frac{1}{3}$ in. long, reddish-brown, fr. fleshy globose, $\frac{1}{2}$ in. diam. 20. **A. manipurensis,** Watt MSS. Manipur 6,000 ft., l. similar, fl. in few-fld. corymbs, corolla $\frac{1}{3}$ in. long.

21. **A. buxifolia,** Nutt. Duphla hills. L. lanceolate or oblanceolate, 1–1$\frac{1}{4}$.in., crenate, peduncles solitary, hairy, $\frac{1}{3}$ in., corolla bright red, $\frac{3}{4}$ in. long. 22. **A. mitrarioides,** Hook. f. Mishmi hills. Branches slender, l. elliptic, serrate $\frac{1}{2}$–$\frac{3}{4}$ in., peduncles slender solitary, 1$\frac{1}{2}$ in. long, bifurcating and bearing 2 fl., corolla 1 in. long.

C. Corolla campanulate, divided to $\frac{1}{3}$ its length or further down, bracts small.

23. **A. nana,** Hook. f. Naga hills. A small epiphyte with thick tuber-like stems, l. lanceolate, narrowed into a very short petiole. epicalyx deeply 10–fid, segments linear, corymbs axillary or from the old wood, corolla $\frac{1}{4}$–$\frac{1}{3}$ in. lobed nearly to the base. 24. **A. discolor,** Clarke. Sikkim 3,500 ft. Bhutan. Patkoi range. L. white beneath, scattered, elliptic-lanceolate, 1–2 in. long, narrowed into short petiole, corolla $\frac{1}{3}$-$\frac{1}{2}$ in. long, divided nearly to the base. 25. **A. pilifera,** Hook. f. Khasi and Mishmi hills. L. scattered, elliptic, caudate-acuminate, base rounded, blade 2–3, petiole $\frac{1}{8}$ in. Fl. fascicled on slender hairy pedicels, 1 in., corolla $\frac{1}{4}$ in. long.

26. **A. Lobbii,** Clarke. Jaintia and Naga hills. Thaungyin, 5,000 ft. L. lanceolate, caudate-acuminate, 3–4 in., petiole very short. Corymbs peduncled, lax, glabrous, corolla crimson with a white tip, narrow-tubular, $\frac{3}{4}$–1, lobes $\frac{1}{3}$ in. long.

D. Bracts longer than half the pedicel, glandular hairs on inflorescence, anthers spurred.

27. **A. bracteata,** Hook. f. Tenasserim hills 5,000 ft. A small shrub on rocks, l. elliptic, caudate-acuminate, blade 2–2$\frac{1}{2}$, pet. $\frac{1}{8}$ in. Fl. in axillary bracteate racemes, bracts nearly as long as pedicel. Corolla campanulate, tube $\frac{3}{8}$ in., lobes narrow, recurved, nearly as long as tube. 28. **A. Pottingeri,** Prain, Ann. Gard. Calc. ix. 45, t. 58. Kachin hills 4,100 ft. An epiphytic shrub, branchlets hairy, l. ovate acuminate, 4–5 in. long, petiole short. Calyx-limb large, campanulate, reticulate, teeth triangular, corolla tubular $\frac{1}{2}$–$\frac{5}{8}$ in. long, lobes short, blunt.

2. PENTAPTERYGIUM, Klotzsch ; Fl. Brit. Ind. iii. 449.

Epiphytic evergreen shrubs, differing from *Agapetes* by the 5-angled or -winged calyx-tube and the 5-winged or distinctly-ribbed berry. Species 5.

A. L. small, pedicels solitary or in pairs, anthers not spurred.

1. **P. serpens**, Klotzsch; Wight Ic. t. 1188; Hook. f. Ill. Him. Pl. t. 15 B. Sikkim, 8–8,000 ft. Bhutan. Base of stem large, tuberous, branches pendulous, hispid, densely leafy, l. glabrous, bifarious, margins recurved, corolla ⅝ in. long, tubular, bright red with V-shaped marks.

B. L. large 2–5 in., pedicels fascicled or corymbose, beaks of anthers spurred.

2. **P. rugosum**, Hook. f. Khasi hills, Bhutan. L. serrate rugose, sec. n. very prominent, corolla ⅝ in. white or rose. 3. **P. Listeri**, King. Bhutan 7,000 ft. L. nearly entire, not rugose, corolla ½ in., rose. 4. **P. flavum**, Hook. f. Bhutan. L. rugose, slightly crenate, corolla ⅜ in., yellow. 5. **P. Hookeri**, Clarke. Sikkim 5–8,000 ft. Bhutan. L. serrate, corolla ⅜ in., yellow.

Desmogyne neriifolia, King et Prain; Ann. Gard. Calc. ix. 46, t. 59. China. Kachin hills, Upper Burma. An epiphytic shrub, l. lanceolate, blade 4–5, pet. ⅛ in. long. Fl. in axillary corymbs, bracts small, pedicels enlarged below the calyx into a cup, partially enclosing calyx-tube (connate bracteoles?) Calyx-limb inflated, wide campanulate, reticulate, margin entire, corolla 1½ in. long, lobes short, fr. crowned by the persistent calyx-limb. The authors of this genus (Journ. As. Soc. Bengal vol. 67. 298) justly observe that *Agapetes*, *Pentapterygium* and *Desmogyne* might be united. In that case the present species would belong to the section of *Agapetes*, represented by *A. auriculata* (p. 405).

3. VACCINIUM, Linn.; Fl. Brit. Ind. iii. 451.

Shrubs or small trees, a few species epiphytic, l. coriaceous. Fl. usually small, generally in racemes, rarely solitary. Racemes in bud often covered by the imbricating bracts. Corolla campanulate cylindric or ovoid, lobes short, anthers oblong, often spurred at the top, produced into 2 cylindric tubes opening by terminal slits. Seeds ellipsoid, testa firm, shining, minutely foveolate. Species 100, Northern Hemisphere and mountains in the Tropics.

A. L. large, racemes solitary.

a. L. lanceolate, serrate, mostly falsely whorled.

1. **V. serratum**, Wight Ic. t. 1184; (*Gaylussacia serrata*, Lindl.; Royle Ill. t. 79, fig. 2.) Sikkim 4–9,000 ft. Khasi hills. A shrub, often epiphytic, stem often thick, tuberiform, l. often approximate near the ends of branchlets (falsely whorled), lanceolate 3–4 in. long, gradually narrowed into a very short petiole. Fl. greenish-white, racemes several at the ends of branchlets, bracts small, linear. Corolla ¼ in. long, glabrous outside, hairy inside, filaments hairy, anthers not spurred. Berry globose, white or yellowish, ⅛ in. diam. 2. **V. venosum**, Wight Ic. t. 1185. Sikkim 4–7000 ft. (the hispid form). Bhutan, Khasi hills. Branchlets sometimes hispid, l. sessile with a rounded base or suddenly narrowed into a very short petiole, sec. n. prominent. Racemes several near the ends of branches, peduncles with numerous persistent elliptic bracts at their base. Filaments glabrous, anthers not spurred.

b. L. elliptic, minutely serrulate, scattered.

3. **V. gualtheriæfolium**, Hook. f. Bhutan. Attains 8 ft. Berry blue-black ¼–⅓ in. diam. 4. **V. glauco-album**, Hook. f. Sikkim 9–10,000 ft. Bhutan. Bracts ¼–⅜ in. long, often persistent until the fr. ripens.

c. L. entire.

5. **V. Dunalianum**, Wight Ic. t. 1194. Sikkim 5–8,000 ft. Bhutan, Khasi hills, Manipur. Yunnan. A shrub, often epiphytic. L. alternate almost distichous, lanceolate, long caudate-acuminate, blade 3–5, pet. ⅛ in. long. Racemes in bud enclosed by the broad imbricating, subsequently deciduous bracts at the base of peduncle. Fl. pink, corolla ovoid-conic, ⅓ in. long, anthers spurred. 6. **V. ardisioides**, Hook. f. Ruby Mines, Upper Burma. Hills east of Toungoo. Thaungyin, Tenasserim. L. sessile, falsely whorled at the ends of branchlets, elliptic-lanceolate, racemes umbellate in the axils of the uppermost l. 7. **V. arbutoides**, Clarke. Patkoi range. L. scattered, ovate, acuminate, blade 4–5, pet. stout, ⅛ in., sec. n. oblique, several pairs from near the base, racemes hairy.

8. **V. Kachinense**, sp. nova. *Panka-pun*, Kachin. Hills east of Bhamo in evergreen

forest 7,500 ft. (Montague Hill, Febr. 1902). A large tree, l. approximate near the ends of branches, rigid, oblanceolate, blade 3–4 in. long, suddenly narrowed into a short stout petiole, sec. n. prominent. Racemes on the old wood below the l., glabrous, bracts red, ¼ in. long, lanceolate, with prominent, very oblique nerves, edge fimbriate, imbricate and covering the buds, bracts at the base of peduncle numerous, similar. Fl. 4- and 5-merous, red, on slender pedicels, calyx-lobes triangular-lanceolate half the length of corolla. Corolla urceolate, ⅛ in. long, glabrous outside, minutely hairy inside, lobes short, recurved, anthers spurred, filaments clothed with long soft spreading hairs.

B. L. large, racemes more or less panicled.

a. Western Species.

9. **V. Leschenaultii**, Wight Ic. t. 1188; Bedd. Fl. Sylv. t. 227.—Syn. *V. rotundifolium*, Wight Ill. t. 139. Vern. *Kilavu*, Tam.; *Anduvan*, Bad.

A small or middle-sized tree, youngest shoots and inflorescence minutely pubescent, l. ovate or nearly orbicular, 1½–3 in., pet. short. Bracts caducous, calyx-teeth triangular, edges ciliate, corolla pink, ⅓–½ in. long, filaments hairy, anthers spurred.

Nilgiris, abundant. Anamalai and Palni hills. Fl. January–June. Fr. edible.—Ceylon, common about 4,000 ft. 10. **V. nilgherrense**, Wight Ic. t. 1189. Western Ghats and adjoining hill ranges from Wainad southwards. A shrub or small tree, l. lanceolate, bracts large, less caducous than in 9, fl. white, calyx and corolla pubescent without.

b. Eastern species.

11. **V. Donianum**, Wight Ic. t. 1191.—Syn. *V. affine*, Wight Ic. t. 1190.

A shrub or small tree, youngest shoots and inflorescence glabrous, l. lanceolate, entire or minutely serrate, blade 2–3, pet. ⅛–¼ in. Fl. pink or white, bracts lanceolate, early deciduous, calyx-teeth often irregularly denticulate, corolla glabrous outside, filaments with long thin hairs, anthers spurred at apex.

Khasi hills, Manipur. Shan hills, Upper Burma. Hills between Sitang and Salween, Lower Burma. Fl. March–May. Similar to some forms of *V. Leschenaultii*. 12. **V. bancanum**, Miq. (*V. exaristatum*, Kurz). Shan hills. Hills east of Toungoo, 5–6,000 ft. Malay Penins. Bangka. A shrub or small tree, l. elliptic, entire, racemes and calyx usually (corolla often) pubescent, spurs of anthers very short. 13. **V. malaccense**, Wight Ic. t. 1186. Thaungyin 5,8000 ft. Malay Peninsula and Archip. L. elliptic-lanceolate, minutely crenate-serrate, racemes and corolla pubescent, anther spurs almost 0. It is not impossible that the Burma specimens of 12 and 13 may eventually all be referred to *V. Donianum*.

FIG. 160.—Vaccinium Donianum, Wight. ½.

C. L. small, 2 in. and under.

14. **V. Griffithianum**, Wight Ic. 1192. Khasi hills, China. A shrub, attaining 6 ft. youngest shoots and racemes pubescent, l. elliptic-lanceolate, serrulate, 1–2 in. long, pet. short. Racemes often panicled, pedicels shorter than fl., bracts large, leaflike, as well as the linear bracteoles, persistent, calyx minutely hairy, corolla ovoid, white, ¼ in. long, spurs on the beak of anthers prominent. 15. **V. Nummularia**, Hook. f. & Thoms. Sikkim 8–10,000 ft. Bhutan. Epiphytic, branches long, pendent, densely clothed with long bristles. L. ½–⅔ in., broadly elliptic, obtuse, margins recurved, fl. pink.

16. **V. retusum**, Hook. fil. Sikkim 7–9,000 ft. Bhutan, Naga hills. A large shrub, often epiphytic, branches pendent, pubescent, l. obovate 1–1¼ in. long, obtuse. Racemes at the ends of branchlets, bracts pure white, membranous, ½–⅓ in. long, enclosing the buds, persistent until the fl. open, corolla pink with 5 red stripes, filaments with long

hairs, spurs at the ends of anthers large. 17. **V. sikkimense,** Clarke. Singalelah range, Sikkim 12–18,000 ft. A small procumbent bush, l. elliptic or obovate, acute, serrulate, calyx-teeth very short, obtuse. 18. **V. pumilum,** Kurz. Hills east of Toungoo 4–6,000 ft. A small epiphyte, branches and racemes hairy, l. elliptic ¾–1 in. Calyx pilose, teeth lanceolate, as long as tube.

Corallobotrys acuminata, Hook. f. Khasi hills, Bhutan. A small shrub, l. coriaceous, more or less serrate, blade 6–9, pet. ⅛ in. long. Fl. in corymbs on the old wood below the leaves, corolla, calyx, pedicels and peduncles coral red, bracts minute. Corolla globose-campanulate, ⅓ in. long, anthers oblong, produced into short tubes, opening by terminal slits.

4. GAULTHERIA, Linn.; Fl. Brit. Ind. iii. 456.

Shrubs, mostly small procumbent, a few large, erect, l. persistent, serrulate. Fl. pentamerous, supported by 2 bracteoles, sometimes dimorphic, usually in bracteate racemes. Calyx enlarged, succulent and coloured in fruit, enclosing the capsule. Corolla ovoid, teeth small, recurved. Filaments pilose, anther-cells opening by short terminal slits, with 1 or 2 horns at the back. Capsule 5-celled, loculicidally 5-valved from the apex. Species 90–100, mostly mountainous, chiefly American.

1. **G. fragrantissima,** Wall.; Wight Ic. t. 1196 (*G. Leschenaultii*, DC.; Wight Ill. t. 141 c and Ic. t. 1195; *G. punctata*, Bl.). Nepal. Sikkim 6–8,000 ft. Bhutan, Khasi hills. Hills east of Toungoo 6–7,000 ft. Nilgiris, here gregarious. Palnis, Travancore hills. Ceylon, upper montane zone. Yunnan. Mtns. of Java and Sumatra. A large shrub, bark thin, shining. L. faintly aromatic when bruised, coriaceous. elliptic, or elliptic-oblong, sometimes lanceolate, blade 1⅓–4, pet. ⅛–¼ in., sec. n. 3–7 pair, the 2nd and 3rd pair from the base reaching beyond half the length of leaf. Racemes axillary, shorter than l. Fl. white, pedicels short, (dimorphic fl. with short stamens and sterile anthers not horned). Fr. ⅓ in. diam., hairy, enclosed by the bright turquoise blue enlarged calyx, edible. Closely allied and perhaps only an alpine form is 2. **G. Hookeri,** Clarke. Sikkim 8–11,000 ft., branches hispid, l. smaller, bracts large elliptic ¼ in. long, fl. pink and white. 3. **G. Griffithiana,** Wight Ic. t. 1197. Nepal. Sikkim 6–9,000 ft. Bhutan, Khasi hills. Manipur. A stout shrub, l. coriaceous, elliptic-oblong, caudate-acuminate, blade 3–6, pet. ¼ in. long, sec. n. 3–4 pair, obliquely arching, excurrent into an intramarginal vein. Fl. green, anthers brick red, pedicels ¼ in. long, corolla campanulate, open, fr. black. From the l. of a small creeping North American species (*Gaultheria procumbens*) a volatile oil known as Oil of Wintergreen is distilled.

5. DIPLYCOSIA, Blume; Fl. Brit. Ind. iii. 458.

Small shrubs, differing from *Gaultheria* by anther-cells without horns at the back and calyx partly adnate to ovary in some species. Species 20, Malay Penins. and Archip., more than half in Borneo.

1. **D. discolor,** Clarke. Bhutan. Hills east of Toungoo. Branchlets pilose, l. coriaceous, glabrous, elliptic, 1–2 in. long, sec. n. 2–3 pair, the lowest from near the base, the upper reaching to the apex, underside glandular-dotted, racemes pubescent, 1 in. long. 2. **D. semi-infera,** Clarke. Bhutan 7–9,000 ft. Similar, l. elliptic-lanceolate, 2–3 in. long, sec. n. 3–4 pair, ovary half-inferior.

Cassiope fastigiata, D. Don (*Andromeda fastigiata*, Wall. Pl. As. Rar. t. 284; Royle Ill. t. 68). Higher Himalayan ranges 10–14,000 ft. Kashmir–Bhutan. A small heather-like shrub covering large areas, l. small, rigid, ciliate, densely and more or less 4-fariously imbricate. Fl. pentamerous, axillary, sometimes 2–4 together, on slender woolly pedicels up to ⅓ in. long, calyx of 5 free sepals thickened at the base, edge scarious, corolla white, widely campanulate, anthers truncate, each cell 1-horned. 2. **C. selaginoides,** Sikkim 10–13,000 ft. Tibet, China, stems more slender and pedicels longer.

Enkianthus himalaicus, Hook. f. & Thoms. Sikkim and Bhutan 8–11,000 ft. China, A small tree, l. membranous, approximate at the ends of branches, elliptic when young pubescent beneath, blade 1–2, pet. slender, ⅓ in. Fl. red-orange, on slender axillary often fasciculate pedicels, ¾–1½ in. long. Corolla broad campanulate, at mouth ⅓ in. across, anthers oblong, each cell with a long hairy awn at the back. Capsules ¼ in. diam. loculicidally 5-valved. Perfect seeds few, angular, testa very lax, membranous.

6. PIERIS, D. Don; Fl. Brit. Ind. iii. 460.

(Included under *Lyonia*, Nutt. by Drude in Engler u. Prantl iv. 1. 44.)

Trees or shrubs. Fl. pentamerous, in bracteate racemes, pedicels bracteolate. Ovary 5-celled, capsule loculicidally 5-valved, seeds ∝ linear-oblong, not winged or fringed, testa loose. Species 12, from the Himalaya to Japan. Mexico and N.-E. America.

1. **P. ovalifolia,** D. Don; Collett Simla Fl., 293, Fig. 89.—Syn. *Andromeda ovalifolia*, Wall.; Wight Ic. t. 1199; Brandis F. Fl. 280. Vern. *Ailan*, Pb.; *Erau, Yerta, Ladrang,* Bash.; *Ayar*, *Anyar*, Hind.

A small deciduous tree, l. ovate- or elliptic-oblong, entire, acute or shortly acuminate, often pubescent when young, base rounded, blade 3–8, pet. ¼–¾ in. long. Racemes axillary more or less pubescent, 4–10 in. long, fl. white, sometimes pink or blueish, calyx-teeth triangular, corolla ¼–½ in. long, filaments hairy, with 2 horns near the apex.

Outer Himalaya, in the North West 4–8,000 ft. often associated with *Quercus incana* and *Rhododendron arboreum*, in Sikkim associated with Sāl in the Tista valley at 2,000 and with the Rhododendrons of Tonglo at 10,000 ft. (Gamble). Khasi hills. The Sikkim and Khasi hills specimens have a longer corolla. Burma; Kachin hills, Bernard myo and headwaters of Yunzalin 5–7,000 ft.—China, Japan. Fl. April–June. 2. **P. villosa,** Hook. f. Himalaya higher ranges 10–13,000 ft. Garhwal to Sikkim (probably in Jaunsar at 7,500 ft., Gamble Ind. Timb. ii. ed. 481). A small tree, similar to 1, but l. smaller, villous beneath, calyx-tube linear-lanceolate, corolla broadly campanulate, no horns at the top of filaments. 3. **P. formosa,** D. Don (*Andromeda formosa*, Wall.; Wight Ic. t. 1200). Himalaya 6–10,000 ft. from Nepal eastwards. Khasi hills. Manipur. A small, evergreen, glabrous tree, l. coriaceous, lanceolate, serrate, blade 3–5, pet. ¼ in. Racemes in large terminal panicles, corolla white, filaments with 2 horns at the end.

Leucothoe Griffithiana, Clarke. Bhutan. 6,800 ft. Branchlets flexuose, l. long acuminate, entire or minutely serrulate upwards, blade 4–6, pet. ⅛ in. long. Racemes axillary, 3–5 in. long. Capsule depressed-globose ¼ in. diam. Seeds flat nearly orbicular, edge with a dense fringe of short blunt unicellular hairs.

7. RHODODENDRON, Linn.; Fl. Brit. Ind. iii. 462.

Small trees or shrubs, often epiphytic (the species here described evergreen, the deciduous species commonly known as *Azalea*). L. entire, usually coriaceous and crowded at the ends of branches. Fl. showy, as a rule large, mostly in terminal clusters or umbelliform corymbs, bracts at the base of peduncle numerous, large, coriaceous, deciduous, enclosing the buds. Calyx 5-lobed, entire or obsolete. Corolla widely funnel-shaped, campanulate or cylindric, lobes 5–10, anthers oblong, opening by terminal pores. Ovary 5–20-celled, ovules ∝. Capsule septicidally 5–20-valved from the apex, the valves breaking away from the placentas. Seeds ∝, testa often produced at the ends, one end frequently ciliate. Species 200, chiefly in Eastern Asia, a smaller number in temperate North America, a few in Europe and Western Asia, 1 in tropical Australia.

I. Capsule cylindric, valves woody or coriaceous, the placentas remaining attached to the central axis.

A. Underside of l. without glandular scales, calyx-lobes short or obsolete not enlarged in fr.

(*a.*) Corolla-lobes 5, stamens 10.

a. Corolla purple, rose or white, underside of l. hairy.

1. **R. arboreum,** Sm.; Wall. Pl. As. Rar. t. 123; Wight Ill. t. 140 and Ic. t. 1201; Bedd. Fl. Sylv. t. 228. Syn. *R. nilagiricum*, Zenker; *R. Camp-*

belliæ, Hook. f. Rhod. Sikk. t. 6. Vern. *Chahān*, Haz.; *Cheū*, Chamba; *Brās*, *Sprāk*, Bash.; *Burāns*, *Brons*, N. W. Him.; *Billi*, Tam.; *Zalatni*, Burm.

A small tree, often attaining a great girth, bark thick, rough. L. elliptic-oblong, acute at both ends, glabrous above, rusty tomentose or with a dense silvery film of minute hairs and scales beneath, sec. n. impressed above, conspicuous beneath, blade 4–6, pet. ¼–¾ in. Corymbs dense many-fld. Fl. commonly deep crimson, rarely pink or nearly white, pedicels short, corolla-lobes emarginate. Ovary densely silky. Capsule cylindric, curved, 1 in. long, longitudinally ribbed.

Outer Himalaya 5–11,000 ft. in the North-West chiefly associated with *Quercus incana*. Khasi hills, Manipur. Hills east of Toungoo. Bernard myo, Ruby Mines district. Nilgiris and Palni hills. Never leafless, the foliage is renewed gradually. Fl. March–May, if checked by hail or otherwise it often flowers in June or July (Simla 1849, 67, 1902). Ceylon above 5,000 ft., gregarious. A remarkable form, found by Sir George Watt in Manipur 9,000 ft. is var. *Kingianum*, Hooker f. in Bot. Mag. t. 7696, l. dark almost glossy, calyx with 5 short lobes, divisions of the corolla deeply lobed. 2. **R. niveum**, Hook. f. Sikkim 10–12,000 ft. Similar to 1, but l. mealy tomentose beneath and not impressed above, fl. lilac.

3. **R. campanulatum**, Don.—Syn. *R. æruginosum*, Hook. f. Rhod. Sikk. t. 22. Vern. *Shargar*, Kulu; *Sim-rang*, Bash.; *Simris*, Garhwal.

A gregarious evergreen shrub, bark thin smooth, peeling off in thin papery flakes, l. glabrous above, with a dense cinnamon-coloured tomentum beneath, concealing the nerves, midrib prominent. Fl. in lax terminal corymbs, purple or lilac, pedicels as long as corolla-tube. Ovary glabrous.

Inner Himalaya, at the upper limit of tree vegetation (9–14,000 ft.), often forming a dense belt. Also at high elevations in the outer ranges. Fl. May–July. 4. **R. fulgens**, Hook. f. Nepal. Sikkim 10–14,000 ft. Similar to 3, l. elliptic with a rounded base, fl. heads dense, corolla scarlet.

β. Corolla red or purple, underside of l. glabrous.

5. **R. Elliotti**, Watt MSS. in herb. Kew. Naga hills 8,500–10,000 ft. L. elliptic-oblong, acute, on the underside minutely and elegantly reticulate, blade 4–6, pet. 1–1½ in. Heads terminal, many-fld., pedicels ⅓ in. as well as calyx ovary and style with minute glandular hairs, calyx small, almost flat, indistinctly lobed, corolla 2 in. long and 1½ in. wide at mouth, lobes obtuse. Capsule ⅜ in. long, finally glabrous. 6. **R. Kendrickii**, Nutt. Bhutan. Yunnan. L. lanceolate, on the underside with raised minutely reticulate veins, blade 5–7, pet. ⅓ in., corolla bright red, ovary strigose. 7. **R. Shepherdi**, Nutt. Bhutan. Calyx shortly 5-lobed, ovary glabrous.

γ. Corolla yellow.

8. **R. Wightii**, Hook f. Rhod. Sikk. t. 27. East Nepal and Sikkim, 11–14,000 ft. A small shrubby tree, bark thin, peeling off in papery flakes; l. mucronate, closely cinnamomeous tomentose beneath, pedicels hairy, corolla yellow with crimson spots, ovary ferrugineous-woolly. 9. **R. lanatum**, Hook. f. Rhod. Sikk. t. 16. Sikkim 12–13,000 ft. Similar to 8, branchlets and l. beneath densely woolly, fl. 5–7 in a head, nodding. 10. **R. campylocarpum**, Hook. f. Rhod. Sikkim t. 30. East Nepal and Sikkim, 11–14,000 ft. A shrub with a resinous scent, l. glabrous on both surfaces, fl. scented, corolla pale sulphur, pedicels and ovary with stalked glands.

(*b*) Corolla-lobes 6–10, stamens 10–18.

11. **R. grande**, Wight Ic. t. 1202. (*R. argenteum*, Hook. f. Rhod. Sikkim t. 9.) Sikkim, 6–9,000 ft. Bhutan. A middle-sized tree, l. glabrous, silvery beneath, blade 8–15, pet. ¾–1½ in. Heads many-fld., dense, fl. pure white. Capsule stout, curved, more or less tomentose, 1–2 in. long. 12. **R. Hodgsoni**, Hook. f. Nepal to Bhutan, 10–12,000 ft., common. A large shrub, similar to 11, l. cinnamomeous or whitish beneath, fl. pink-lilac, capsules narrowly-cylindric 2 in. long. 13. **R. Falconeri**, Hook. f. Rhod. Sikkim t. 10. Nepal to Bhutan 9–13,000 ft. Naga and Manipur hills 7–10,000 ft. Yunnan. A large gregarious shrub or middle-sized tree with a straight bole, l. rigidly coriaceous, broad-elliptic, obtuse, rugose above by impressed nerves, densely rusty tomentose beneath, blade 6–15, petiole 1–2 in. long. Fl. white or cream-coloured, with purple spots at the base within.

B. Underside of l. without glandular scales, calyx deeply lobed or enlarged in fr.

(*a*) Branches not woolly.

14. **R. barbatum,** Wall.; Hook. f. Rhod. Sikkim t. 3. Himalaya, from Kumaon eastwards, 8–12,000 ft. Naga hills 9,000 ft. A small or middle-sized tree, l. glabrous, green on both sides, acute, petioles, branchlets and midrib beneath with long coarse bristles. Heads dense, corolla deep red, ovary hairy, capsule $\frac{3}{4}$ in. long, hirsute. 15. **R. Thomsoni,** Hook. f. Rhod. Sikkim t. 12 (*R. Candelabrum*, Hook. f. l. c. t. 29). East Nepal and Sikkim 11–13,000 ft. A large shrub attaining 15 ft., l. broadly elliptic, obtuse at both ends, base often cordate, glaucous beneath, blade 3–4, pet. $\frac{1}{2}$–1 in. Calyx cup-shaped unequally lobed, enlarged in fr., partly enclosing the glaucous purple $\frac{3}{4}$ in. long capsule. Corolla deep crimson. 16. **R. Hookeri,** Nutt. Bhutan, similar and possibly only a variety of 15. L. oblong, underside with minute raised reticulate veins. Calyx cup-shaped, unequally lobed. 17. **R. Griffithianum,** Wight Ic. t. 1203 (*R. Aucklandii*, Hook. f. Rhod. Sikk. t. 11). Sikkim and Bhutan 7–9,000 ft. A shrub, at times a middle-sized tree, l. glabrous, oblong, base rounded, blade 4–9, pet. 1–1$\frac{1}{2}$ in. Fl. large white with a pink tinge, calyx saucer-shaped, margin nearly entire, in fr. often unequally enlarged. Capsule 10 in. long, very woody.

(*b*) Branches woolly. Usually epiphytic.

18. **R. Edgeworthii,** Hook. f. Rhod. Sikk. t. 21. Sikkim 7–9,000 ft. Bhutan. Branchlets, petioles, underside of l., pedicels, calyx and capsule, while young, densely clothed with rusty wool. L. mostly scattered, upperside glabrous but strongly rugose with the deeply impressed nerves and veins. Fl. white, sweet scented, calyx divided nearly to the base, lobes obtuse, somewhat unequal, $\frac{1}{3}$ in. long, corolla 2–3 in. across. 19. **R. pendulum,** Hook. f. Rhod. Sikk. t. 13, branches pendulous, 2-4 ft. long, l. mostly approximate at the ends of branches, rusty-woolly beneath, blade 1–2, pet. $\frac{1}{4}$ in. long. Calyx-lobes obtuse, $\frac{1}{3}$ in. long, rose-coloured, corolla white, 1 in. across, glandular outside.

C. Underside of l. with round appressed glandular scales.

(*a*) Calyx-lobes short or obsolete, not enlarged in fr.

20. **R. cinnabarinum,** Hook. f. Rhod. Sikkim t. 8; Gamble Ind. Timb. ed. ii. 436 (*R. Roylii*, Hook. f. Rhod. Sikkim t. 7) Sikkim 10–12,000 ft. and higher. Bhutan. A large shrub, l. glabrous and shining above, densely clothed beneath with glandular scales, blade 3–4, pet. $\frac{1}{3}$–$\frac{3}{8}$ in. long, midrib excurrent, sec. n. visible on the upper side. Heads with 5–8 fl., pedicels $\frac{1}{4}$–$\frac{1}{2}$ in. long, calyx-lobes obtuse, usually short, sometimes the upper longer, corolla orange or brick red, long narrow-campanulate, almost tubular, lobes ovate, acute, equal (Hooker's figure of *R. cinnabarinum* possibly represents a different species with dense fl. heads and the uppermost calyx-tooth linear, almost subulate. If so, the species described above should be called *R. Roylii*). 21. **R. triflorum,** Hook. f. Rhod. Sikkim t. 19. Sikkim, Manipur 7–10,000 ft. Attains 8 ft., l. closely scaly beneath. Fl. few, sometimes solitary, corolla yellow, broad-campanulate, 1$\frac{1}{2}$-2 in. across at mouth.

22. **R. Keysii,** Nutt. Bhutan 8–10,000 ft. L. lanceolate, fl. on short axillary spurs, corolla-tube cylindric, pale brick-red. 23. **R. virgatum,** Hook. f. Rhod. Sikkim t. 26. Sikkim 7–9,000 ft. Bhutan. A shrub attaining 4 ft. with slender branches and scattered oblong-lanceolate l. Fl. axillary, solitary or in pairs, pedicels sheathed at the base by imbricate coriaceous deciduous bracts, corolla purple, 1 in. across at mouth.

24. **R. formosum,** Wall. Pl. As. Rar. t. 207. *Panlaung pun*, Kachin.

A shrub, l. lanceolate, usually broadest above the middle, acute, glabrous above, glandular scales beneath numerous, but epidermis distinctly visible between them. Corymbs 2-5-fld., corolla white, widely funnel-shaped, 2 in. across at mouth.

Bhutan, Khasi hills, often near streams. Kachin hills 7,500 ft. and Ruby Mines district, Upper Burma. Hills east of Toungoo 4–7,000 ft. Moolejit 6–6,500. Yunnan 4–8,000 ft. Very variable, two varieties may be noted: *R. salicifolium*, Khasi hills, with linear-lanceolate l. *R. Johnstonianum*, Watt MSS., Naga and Manipur hills, 6–9,000 ft., with elliptic l., the glandular scales approximating beneath, corolla with pink streaks and dots. 25. **R. Veitchianum,** Hook. Tenasserim hills 4–7,000 ft. Sometimes epiphytic, is supposed to differ by a larger corolla with a crisped crenulate margin.

(*b*) Calyx deeply lobed.

a. L. large, more than 2 in. long.

26. **R. Dalhousiæ**, Hook. f. Sikk. Rhod, tt. 1, 2. Sikkim 6–9,000 ft. Manipur, 9,000 ft. Yunnan. An epiphytic shrub, 6–10 ft. high, l. approximate near the ends of branches, blade 4–5, pet. ½ in. long. Heads of 2–5 large, scented fl., 3½ in. long, 3 in. across at mouth, corolla white, pink when fading. 27. **R. Nuttallii**, Booth. Bhutan, 4–5,000 ft. Similar, l. larger, rugose above, sec. and tertiary n. prominent beneath, calyx-lobes ¾ in. long. 28. **R. Maddeni**, Hook. f. Sikk. Rhod. t. 18. Sikkim 6,000 ft. Bhutan. Naga and Manipur hills 8–10,000 ft. A shrub 6–8 ft. high, l. densely scaly beneath, blade 4–6, pet. ½–1 in. long. Corymbs 4–12-fld., calyx-lobes oblong, often unequal, corolla white, 3–4 in. across.

29. **R. Boothii**, Nutt. Bhutan. Epiphytic, branchlets and petioles villous with long hairs, young l. sprinkled with long lax hairs, adult l. hairy on the margin, blade 4–5, pet. ¼ in. Corymbs dense, many-fld., corolla yellow. 30. **R. ciliatum**, Hook. f. Sikk. Rhod. t. 24. Sikkim 9–10,000 ft. A small rigid shrub, branchlets, petioles, edge of l. and pedicels with long soft bristles, l. acute, blade 2½–3 in., pet. ¼ in. Corymbs of 2–6 fl., corolla white, rosy on fading. 31. **R. camelliæflorum**, Hook. f. Sikk. Rhod. t. 28. East Nepal to Bhutan 9–13,000 ft. Corolla white, shortly campanulate, lobes widely spreading, 1½ in. across, capsule ½ in. long, densely clothed with glandular scales. 32. **R. glaucum**, Hook. f. Sikk. Rhod. t. 17. Sikkim and Bhutan 10–12,000 ft. A small shrub, with strong resinous smell, l. glaucous, almost white beneath, blade 2–3, pet. ¼ in. long. Corymbs 4–10-fld., pedicels and calyx densely covered with glandular scales, corolla pale pinkish-purple, 1 in. across. 33. **R. leptocarpum**, Nutt. Bhutan, imperfectly known.

β. L. small, under 2 in.

34. **R. lepidotum**, Wall.; Royle Ill. t. 64 (*R. salignum* and *elæagnoides*, Hook. f. Rhod. Sikk. t. 23). Higher ranges of the Himalaya from Kashmir eastwards 9–15,000 ft. A small aromatic shrub, l. ¾–1 in. long, sessile or nearly so. Fl. yellow or purple, solitary or 2–3 together, pedicels ½–1½ in. long, scabrous, calyx-lobes not ciliate. 35. **R. pumilum**, Hook. f. Rhod. Sikk. t. 14. Sikkim 12–14,000 ft. Stems slender, creeping among moss, l. ½ in. long, fl. 1–3 together, pedicels 1–2½ in. long, corolla campanulate, rose-coloured. 36. **R. setosum**, D. Don; Hook. f. Rhod. Sikk. t. 20. Sikkim 13–16,000 ft. Small, attains 12 in., with strong resinous smell, branchlets, petioles, edge of l. with long soft bristles. Fl. 3–8, pedicels short, corolla red, 1½ in. across at mouth, lobes narrow. 37. **R. nivale**, Hook. f. Sikk. Rhod. t. 26. Sikkim 13–16,000 ft., prostrate, fl. solitary rose-col'd., nearly sessile.

38. **R. Anthopogon**, D. Don; Royle Ill. t. 64. *Talts*, Pb.; *Talishang*, Kun. Himalaya, from Kashmir eastwards, 11–16,000 ft. Yunnan. Eastern Siberia (*R. fragrans*, Maxim). A small gregarious shrub, strongly aromatic, l. 1–1½ in. long, upperside shining, underside brown tomentose and scaly. Fl. yellow, in dense terminal corymbs, corolla delicate, translucent.

II. Capsule linear, valves membranous, placentas separating from a slender central axis as 5 filiform ribs, attached to the apex.

39. **R. moulmainense**, Hook. Hills of Martaban, Tenasserim and Upper Burma. *Zalat pyu*, Burm. A large shrub or small tree, l. glabrous on both sides, blade 4–5, pet. ¼ in. Heads terminal 2–10-fld., calyx-lobes minute, corolla white, tube ½ in. long, shorter than the 5 erect-patent lobes.

40. **R. vaccinioides**, Hook. f. Sikkim 7–9,000 ft. A small shrub often epiphytic, branches scabrous, l. scattered, spathulate, ½–1 in. long, glandular scaly beneath, fl. solitary, corolla white or pinkish.

ORDER LXV.—**Epacridaceæ**. *Leucopogon malayanus*, Jack (*Styphelia malayica*, Drude in Engler u. Prantl iv. i. 78) Tenasserim. Malay Peninsula and Archipel. A small rigid evergreen shrub, entirely glabrous, branches densely leafy, l. rigidly coriaceous, sessile, linear-lanceolate, mucronate, glaucous beneath, with numerous parallel slender longitudinal nerves. Fl. 5-merous, white, sessile, in few-fld. axillary spikes, each supported by a pair of bracteoles. Corolla funnel-shaped, lobes bearded within, valvate in bud. Anthers 1-celled, opening by a single longitudinal slit, ovary 5-celled, one ovule in each cell, at the base surrounded by a disk of 5 hypogynous scales. *Epacrideæ* belong almost entirely to the southern hemisphere, nearly all species being natives of Australia.

ORDER LXVI. PLUMBAGINACEÆ. Gen. Pl. ii. 623 (*Plumbagineæ*).

Mostly herbs, a few shrubs, fl. regular bisexual, bracts usually scarious on the edge, sheathing the fl. Calyx tubular, 5-ribbed, mouth frequently scarious. Petals 5, free or connate at base, stamens 5, epipetalous. Ovary 1-celled, ovule 1, pendulous from a basal funicle.

The stems of the two genera here described have an entirely anomalous structure. *Vogelia* on a transverse section shows concentric bands of bast (phloëm), alternating with broader strata of wood, similar to *Dalbergia paniculata*, *Cocculus laurifolius* and to many climbing shrubs. A transverse section of *Aegialitis* shows numerous distinct vascular bundles consisting of thick-walled wood fibres and a radial line of vessels (Gamble, Indian Timbers, ed. ii. 436).

1. **Aegialitis rotundifolia,** Roxb. (*A. annulata*, Kurz F. Fl. ii. 96), Mangrove swamps and tidal forests of Bengal and Burma. Andamans, Malay Peninsula. A simple stemmed, glabrous evergreen shrub, with a thick conical trunk, branchlets marked by the scars of the amplexicaul petiole. L. alternate, thickly coriaceous, nearly orbicular, blade 2–3 in. long, petiole sheathing, longer than blade. Fl. in panicled racemes. Calyx tubular 5-ribbed, the ribs ending in short teeth, petals white, linear, the upper portion deciduous, the lower united with the filaments into a persistent tube. Capsule linear, 3 in. long, pentagonal, dehiscing finally along the angles. *A. annulata*, R. Br., is a widely spread littoral species of tropical Asia and Australia.

2. **Vogelia indica,** Gibson; Wight Ic. t. 1075. Sind, Rajputana, dry districts of the Northern Deccan. A shrub with long branches, l. alternate, entire, amplexicaul or perfoliate. Fl. in spikes arranged in terminal panicles. Calyx deeply 5-fid, broad transversely undulate wings between the ribs, style filiform, with 5 stigmatose branches. Capsule included in the calyx, circumsciss at the base.

ORDER LXVII. MYRSINACEÆ. Gen. Pl. ii. 639 (*Myrsineæ*).

(Mez, *Myrsinaceæ*, in Engler's Pflanzenreich, 1902.)

Shrubs or small trees. L. alternate, undivided, generally gland-dotted, stipules 0. Fl. bisexual or polygamous, usually 5-merous, calyx persistent, often enlarged in fr. Corolla-tube short or none, segments (petals) contorted or imbricate. Stamens opposite the corolla-lobes, and frequently adnate to them, anthers usually dehiscing by longitudinal slits. Ovary 1-celled, narrowed into the style, ovules inserted on a free central placenta. Embryo transverse in copious albumen.

Resin cavities and resin ducts are found in the leaves, pith, wood and bark. The account given in Gamble's Indian Timbers ed. ii. 438–440 of *Myrsine africana*, *capitellata* and *Embelia robusta*, makes it probable that these species have resin cavities or special cells filled with resin in the medullary rays, analogous to the wood oil in the rays of *Dipterocarpus alatus* (p. 64, 66).

I. Ovary inferior or half superior, berry many-seeded . 1. MÆSA.
II. Ovary inferior, fr. one-seeded.
  A. Filaments 0 or shorter than anthers.
    Fl. in dense axillary clusters, corolla-segments imbricate or valvate in bud . . . 2. MYRSINE.
    Fl. in simple or compound, often panicled, racemes, corolla-segments imbricate or contorted in bud . . . . . . 3. EMBELIA.
    Fl. usually umbellate, corolla-segments twisted, the right hand edge overlapping
      Anthers free, calyx glabrous. . . . . 4. ARDISIA.
      Anthers free, calyx hairy . . . . . PIMELANDRA (p. 420).
      Anthers connate.
        Corolla middle-sized, segments acute . HYMENANDRA (p. 420).
        Corolla minute, segments emarginate . AMBLYANTHUS (p. 420).

Fl. in sessile umbels, corolla-segments twisted, the left hand edge overlapping . . 5. ANTISTROPHE.

B. Filaments as long as anthers. Fr. a globose berry . . . . AMBLYANTHOPSIS (p. 421).

C. Filaments long, exserted. Fr. dry cylindric, curved . . . . 6. AEGICERAS.

Reptonia, A. DC., is classed under *Sapotaceæ*.

1. MÆSA, Forsk.; Fl. Brit. Ind. iii. 507.

Evergreen shrubs or small trees, leaf-blade opaque in a few species, as a rule with a system of anastomosing resin ducts, transparent when the dry leaf is wetted, often enlarged near the edge; in some cases without such a system of resin ducts, but with minute translucent dots. Fl. white, pentamerous, often unisexual, in simple or compound racemes, bracts small, two bracteoles under each fl. Inflorescence often monstrous, the fl. replaced by densely imbricating bracteoles. Calyx-tube adnate to ovary, corolla rotate or campanulate, stamens inserted on the corolla, at or above the base, filaments usually short. Ovary inferior or half superior, ovules numerous. Berry many-seeded, crowned by the persistent calyx-lobes. Species 35 (Clarke), 102 (Mez), tropics of the Old World, Australia and Polynesia.

A. Corolla almost rotate, lobes as long as or longer than tube.

(*a*) Leaves glabrous, distinctly toothed.

6. **M. indica**, Wall.; Wight Ic. t. 1206. Vern. *Nanapadhera*, Kumaon; *Atki*, Mar.; *Kirithi*, Travancore.

A large shrub or small tree, often gregarious, branches long, straggling. L. elliptic, elliptic-oblong or elliptic-lanceolate, blade 3–7, pet. ½–1 in. long. Racemes axillary, shorter than l., often compound, generally glabrous. Calyx-segments ciliate along the edge (Northern India) or naked (Peninsula), more or less veined, corolla almost rotate, ⅛ in. across at mouth. Berries small, pinkish-white, edible.

Outer Himalaya, ascending to 6,000 ft., from the Jumna eastwards. Assam. Khasi hills, Manipur. Chittagong, Burma, Upper and Lower. Western Peninsula, chiefly on the West side, but also in the Northern Circars and on the hills of the Deccan and the Karnatic. Fl. almost throughout the year, chiefly Dec.–May. Yunnan. Malay Archip. Mez classes the Indian forms of this variable plant under 7 species, as follows:

Calyx-segments ciliate, veined.
- Inflorescence short, resin ducts in leaves conspicuous . . a. *M. indica*, Wall.
- Inflorescence short, resin ducts not visible . . . . b. *M. montana*, A. DC.
- Inflorescence 4 times length of petiole . . . . . c. *M. Martiana*, Mez.

Calyx-segments ciliate, not veined . . . . . . d. *M. elongata*, Mez.

Calyx-segments not ciliate.
- Stamens inserted at the base of corolla . . . . e. *M. coriacea*, Mez.
- Stamens inserted higher up, calyx-segments veined.
  - Resin ducts in leaves distinct . . . . . . f. *M. Perrottetiana*, A. DC
  - Resin ducts not visible . . . . g. *M. maxima*, Mez.

Besides these Mez describes *M. bengalensis* and *M. manipurensis*, which also are nearly allied to *M. indica*, Wall. Before these can be accepted as distinct species, they must be further studied in the forest.

2. **M. Chisia**, Don. Nepal, Sikkim 2–7,000 ft. Bhutan, Khasi hills. A gregarious shrub, l. thinly membranous, lanceolate, veins very slender, closely reticulate, blade 4–5, pet. ⅛ in. long. Racemes glabrous, lax, generally branched, about half the length of l., pedicels as long as fl., calyx-segments not ciliate, distinctly veined, as well as corolla, stamens in ♂ fl. exserted. 3. **M. paniculata**, A. DC. Khasi hills. Tenasserim. L. ovate, acuminate, base rounded, blade 4–8, pet. ½–1. long. Racemes panicled, longer than leaf, often forming a large terminal panicle, calyx-segments not ciliate.

(*b*) Leaves glabrous, entire or minutely denticulate.

4. **M. ramentacea**, A. DC. Bhutan, Khasi hills, Cachar. Chittagong. Andamans. Manipur. Burma, Upper and Lower, common in the second growth on deserted Taungyas. Yunnan. Malay Penins. and Archip. A shrub or small tree, gregarious,

branches long, scrambling, l. thinly coriaceous, ovate-lanceolate, quite entire, blade 4–8, pet. ½ in. long, sec. n. distant, 6–8 pair. Racemes glabrous, compound, axillary, as long as l. sometimes longer or shorter. 5. **M. andamanica,** Kurz F. Fl. ii. 575. South Andaman, rare, very similar to 4, but l. minutely denticulate.

6. **M. rugosa,** Clarke. Sikkim 5–7,000 ft. Bhutan. A stout shrub, l. coriaceous, lanceolate, caudate-acuminate, remotely and minutely denticulate, sec. n. 12–18 pair, prominent beneath, as well as the tertiary and shorter intermediate nerves, blade 6–8, pet. ½–1 in. Racemes compound, 1–2 in. long, berries yellowish-white. Near this are possibly *M. grandiflora*, Mez, Assam, and *M. populifolia*, Mez, Kohima, Naga hills.

(*c*) Leaves hairy.

7. **M. dubia,** Wall. (*M. indica*, Bedd. Manual t. xviii. fig. 4.) Evergreen forests of the Western Ghats, Konkan to Malabar. Branchlets and l. rusty-tomentose, l. ovate-lanceolate, blade 4–7, pet. ½–1 in. long. Racemes compressed, less than half the length of l. Near this probably *M. velutina*, Mez, Bombay. 8. **M. argentea,** Wall. Garhwal, Kumaon, Nepal. Sikkim 3–7,000 ft. A large shrub, branchlets softly pubescent, l. often whitish beneath, ovate, acuminate, base acute, blade 6–10, pet. ½–1 in. long. Racemes 1–2 in. long, fr. ⅛ in. diam. 9. **M. macrophylla,** Wall. Nepal. Sikkim, 3–5,000 ft. Bhutan. A large shrub, branches velvety, l. elliptic or orbicular, evenly serrate, base more or less cordate, blade 6–8, pet. 1–1½ in. long, sec. n. 10–14 pair, prominent beneath, bifurcating near edge of l. Racemes compound, pubescent, 5–10 in. long, sometimes forming a terminal panicle.

10. To this group belongs a shrub or small tree sent by Montague Hill from the hills east of Bhamo, l. minutely pellucid-punctate, branchlets, nerves on the underside of l. with long slender hairs, racemes covered with a profusion of white fl., 1–3 in. long, with long branches above the base, often fasciculate in the axils, and forming a terminal panicle. Pedicels as long as fl., calyx-segments ciliate, not veined, corolla with prominent brown veins.

B. Corolla campanulate, lobes shorter than tube.

11. **M. permollis,** Kurz.—Syn. *M. mollissima*, Kurz F. Fl. ii. 100; *M. mollis*, Clarke (*M. mollis*. A. DC. is a Javan species). Hills of Upper and Lower Burma, ascending to 4,000 ft. Yunnan. A slender shrub, branchlets, petioles and underside of l. hairy, l. elliptic, acuminate, dentate, blade 5–7, pet. ⅜–1 in. long. Inflorescence compact, densely hirsute, shorter than petiole, bracts minute.

12. **M. Kurzii,** Mez.—Syn. *M. muscosa*, Kurz F. Fl. ii. 100 (*Mœsa muscosa*, A. DC. is a species of the Malay Archip.). Upper Burma. Branchlets and l. glabrous, except for a few scattered hairs, l. elliptic or obovate, acuminate, dentate, blade 5–10, pet. ⅜–1 in. Racemes usually hirsute, compound, twice the length of petioles or longer, bracts lanceolate, persistent, as long as fl. or nearly so. Specimens collected by Smales in the Shwebo district, 1,000 ft. *Natcho sein*, Burm., have l. entire glabrous and racemes slightly hairy.

2. MYRSINE, Linn.; Fl. Brit. Ind. iii. 511.

Evergreen trees or shrubs, l. coriaceous. Fl. polygamous or dioicous, subsessile or on short pedicels, in dense clusters, usually axillary. Calyx small, persistent, 4–5-fid, corolla white, 4–5-partite, segments in bud imbricate or valvate, both with resinous dots. Ovary free, globose, stigmas 2–5, erect or spreading, sessile or on a short style. Fr. red or purple, seed 1. Species 80 (Clarke), 140 (Mez) chiefly tropical. Mez (*Myrsinaceæ* 342) includes under *Rapanea* the species with sessile stigmas.

1. **M. capitellata,** Wall.; Wight Ic. 1211; Bedd. Fl. Sylv. t. 234. A small tree, l. entire, pellucid-punctate. lanceolate or elliptic-lanceolate, blade 3–7, narrowed into a marginate petiole ½ in. long. Fl. 5-merous, sessile or shortly pedicellate, in dense fascicles on short woody protuberances in the axils of fallen l., stigmas sessile, erect, more or less combined. Berry ⅙–⅓ in. diam., purple. Calyx-segments ciliate, corolla-lobes spreading or reflexed. Anthers nearly sessile in the ☿, on short filaments in the ♂ fl.

Outer Himalaya, ascending to 4,000 ft., from Nepal eastwards. Assam, Khasi hills, Burma, Upper and Lower. West side of the Peninsula, chiefly in evergreen forests, from North Kanara southwards. Common in the Nilgiri sholas. Fl. Oct.–June. Ceylon, moist region. Malay Peninsula and Archip. China, Japan. An exceedingly variable tree. Mez restricts his *Rapanea capitellata* to the forms with sessile or nearly sessile fl. and classes those with pedicellate fl. (including some new species established by him) as follows: Western Peninsula: *R. Wightiana*, *striata* and *daphnoides*, Burma: *R. lucida* and *Griffithiana*.

2. **M. semiserrata,** Wall. Outer Himalaya from the Beas eastwards 3–9,000 ft. (*Bains*, *Gaunta*, Garhw.). Khasi hills, Manipur. Hills east of Toungoo 6–7,200 ft. Upper Burma. Yunnan. A shrub or small, sometimes a middle-sized tree, quite glabrous, l. thinly coriaceous, elliptic-lanceolate, entire or in the upper half with sharp spinulose serratures, blade 3–5, petiole ¼ in. long. Fl. white, with a slight pink tinge, fr. red, ⅛–⅕ in. diam. on pedicels ¼ in. long.

3. **M. africana,** Linn.; Collett Simla Fl. 304, fig. 94. Afghanistan, Baluchistan. Trans Indus. Salt range. Outer N. W. Himalaya from Nepal westwards 3–9,000 ft. Azores, Mountains of East and South Africa. Western Asia. China. Vern. *Kukal*, Haz.; *Gugil*, Kashm.; *Chitring*, Bash.; *Banwan*, Jauns. A small shrub, branches hairy. L. ½–1 in. long, minutely cuspidate-serrate, fl. dioicous in axillary clusters of 4–6, stigma large capitate, fimbriate. Berries usually solitary, red or black, $\frac{1}{10}$ in. diam., often densely covered with cylindrical capitate protuberances (*M. scabra*, Gærtner).

3. EMBELIA, Burm.; Fl. Brit. Ind. iii. 512.

Shrubs or small trees, as a rule evergreen, most species climbing, l. usually entire. Fl. small, polygamous, often dioicous, in simple or compound, often panicled racemes. Calyx free, persistent, petals free or slightly coherent at base, filaments more or less adnate to petals, style cylindric, stigma capitellate, ovules few. Calyx, petals, anthers and ovary usually with glandular dots. Seed one, albumen more or less ruminate. Species 60–90, tropics of the Old World.

A. Petals imbricate in bud, fl. 5-merous.

(*a*) Inflorescence terminal.

1. **E. Ribes,** Burm.—Syn. *E. glandulifera*, Wight Ic. t. 1207. Vern. *Waiwarang*, Mar.; *Silgilla*, Ass.

A large climbing shrub, l. glabrous, coriaceous, elliptic-oblong, acuminate, blade 3–4 in., narrowed into a more or less marginate or glandular petiole ⅓ in. long; sec. n. slender, numerous, glands sometimes along midrib. Fl. greenish-yellow, more or less pubescent, on pedicels as long as fl., longer than bracts, in large terminal more or less pubescent panicles. Berry black, succulent, wrinkled when dry, $\frac{1}{6}$ in. diam.

Sikkim, foot of hills, ascending to 4,000 ft. Assam. Manipur 3–5,000 ft. Chittagong. Burma, Upper and Lower, 3,000 to 6,500 ft. Hills of the Western Peninsula, in evergreen forest. Fl. Nov.–Febr. Ceylon, moist region to 4,000 ft. Malay Penins. and Archip. Tonkin. China. 2. **E. sessiliflora,** Kurz, Burma, Upper and Lower, rare. An evergreen scandent shrub, l. ovate, entire, glabrous. Fl. sessile, otherwise similar to *E. Ribes*.

3. **E. adnata,** Bedd. Palghat hills. A very large climber, branchlets stout, angular, warty, young foliage red, l. coriaceous, blade 4–6, pet. stout ¼ in. long, terminal panicle large, ramification stout. 4. **E. microcalyx,** Kurz. Nicobars. Scandent, branchlets and underside of l. and panicles brown villous, l. elliptic, obtuse at both ends.

(*b*) Inflorescence axillary.

5. **E. robusta,** Roxb.; Bedd. Manual t. xix. fig. 2.—Syn. *E. Tsjeriam Cottam*, A. DC; Wight Ic. t. 1209. Vern. *Gaia*, Dún; *Nununta*, Uriya; *Eikmwenwè*, Burm.; *Baibrang*, *Bebrang*, *Bhingi*, Hind.; *Waiwarang*, *Ambuti*, Mar.

A large shrub or small tree with long spreading and scrambling branches, branchlets, petioles and underside of l. more or less rusty-pubescent, sometimes glabrous. L. membranous, entire or slightly denticulate, elliptic, blade 2–5, petiole slender, ¼–½ in. long, sec. n. slender but conspicuous beneath. Racemes 1–2 in. long, sometimes 2 or 3 from one leaf axil. Fr. red, nearly dry, longitudinally ribbed, $\frac{1}{9}$–$\frac{1}{6}$ in. diam.

Subhimalayan tract and outer valleys from the Jumna eastwards. Assam. Khasi hills. Bengal, Behar, Central Provinces. Western Peninsula. Lower Burma. Fl. R. S.—Ceylon, Java. A most variable species. Mez, l.c. 320, regards as separate species the forms with pubescent l. viz.: *E. ferruginea*, Wall. and *reticulata*, Wall. Burma, *villosa*, Wall. Bengal. Most of the glabrous forms he calls *E. Tsjeriam Cottam*, A. DC. and restricts *E. robusta*, Roxb. to the specimens with short racemes and rounded, not acuminate anthers.

6. **E. furfuracea**, Coll. et Hemsl. in Journ. Linn. Soc. xxviii. 82. Shan hills, Upper Burma 5,000 ft. Branchlets, petioles and underside of l. softly rusty-tomentose. Racemes dense, undivided, axillary, 1–1½ in. long, fl. almost sessile. 7. **E. parviflora**, Wall. Khasi and Naga hills. Branchlets, petioles and midrib beneath rusty-pubescent, l. ½–1½ in. long, nearly sessile. Fl. few in short nearly sessile umbelliform corymbs. 8. **E. Clarkei**, Bedd.; Mez l.c. 323. Mooleyit, Tenasserim 4,000 ft. A large shrub, l. ovate, acuminate, the upper portion serrate, blade 2–2½, pet. slender ¼ in. long. Fl. minutely glandular hairy, in short umbelliform corymbs.

B. Petals imbricate in bud, fl. 4-merous.

9. **E. viridiflora**, Scheff.—Syn. *Choripetalum aurantiacum*, A. DC.; Wight Ic. 1210; *Samara Rheedii*, Wight Ic. t. 1591; *E. Basaal*, Roem. et Schult; Mez l. c. 328, fig. 54. Hills of the Peninsula. Nilgiris, Palnis, javadies, etc. Ceylon. Yunnan. A large climber, entirely glabrous, l. coriaceous, elliptic or obovate, blade 3–6, pet. ½–1 in. long. Racemes simple, compact, 1 in. long, from the previous year's or from the older wood. ♂ yellowish-purple, stamens long exserted. Fr. crimson ovoid-globose ¼–⅓ in. long. Mez call this species *E. Basaal*, separating it from the Javan *R. viridiflora*, which he distinguishes by large resinous dots on the back of anthers. 10. **E. Nagushia**, Don. Sikkim 3–6,000 ft. Khasi hills. A large shrub with divaricating often climbing branches, at times a tree, similar to 9, differs by l. usually membranous, shorter petioles and fr. depressed globose, ¼–⅓ in. diam. Mez calls this *E. undulata*, as he identifies *E. Nagushia*, Don, with *E. vestita*, Roxb. He separates from it *E. subcoriacea* with subcoriaceous l.

11. **E. Gamblei**, Kurz. Sikkim 6–8,000 ft. A powerful evergreen climber with thick spongy bark, youngest shoots rusty-tomentose, l. coriaceous glabrous, elliptic-oblong, blade 5–6, pet. ¾–1 in. long, sec. n. 15–18 pair, joined by finely reticulate veins. Racemes numerous, 1–2 in. long in the axils of deciduous scales on the current year's branchlets, often below a tuft of leaves. The l. of this and allied species are eaten.

C. Petals twisted in bud, fl. 5-merous.

12. **E. floribunda**, Wall. Nepal. Sikkim 4–7,000 ft. Khasi hills. A climbing shrub, branchlets flexuose, l. glabrous coriaceous, shining, lanceolate, long acuminate, blade 5–8, pet. ¼–⅓ in. long. Racemes in large axillary panicles, petals slightly overlapping. 13. **E. vestita**, Roxb. Nepal. Bhutan. Khasi hills. Branchlets glabrous, l. elliptic-lanceolate, serrate, glabrous, blade 2–4, pet. ¼ in. long, racemes simple, axillary, rusty-pubescent, 1–2 in. long. 14. **E. nutans**, Wall. Assam, Khasi hills. Similar to 13, youngest shoots, petioles and midrib rusty pilose, racemes ½–1 in. long. Ovary beaked. 15. **E. Gardneriana**, Wight Ic. t. 1208. Nilgiris. A large climber, branchlets flexuose, rusty-hairy, l. coriaceous, ovate-lanceolate, crenate-serrate, sec. n. and the finely reticulate veins prominent on both surfaces, blade 2–9, pet. ¼ in. long. Corymbs axillary, rusty-hairy, almost umbelliform, petals pale yellow, ovary pink, beaked.

4. ARDISIA, Swartz; Fl. Brit. Ind. iii. 518.

Shrubs, small trees or undershrubs, l. as a rule entire. Fl. bisexual, usually pentamerous, in axillary or terminal, simple or compound umbels or corymbs, the lateral peduncles frequently in the axils of bracts instead of leaves. Fl. not supported by bracteoles, calyx of 5 sepals connate at base, persistent. Corolla red, white or spotted, segments (petals) twisted, the right hand edge overlapping, stamens 5, filaments shorter than anthers, style cylindric, stigma punctiform, ovules in several tiers on the globose placenta. Fr. fleshy, globose, 1-seeded, pedicels lengthening in fr., embryo horizontal in an oily albumen. Species 230, tropics of both hemispheres.

I. L. entire, excepting *A. Icara*.

A Sepals broad, in bud overlapping with the right hand edge. Style in bud shorter than the petals. Inflorescence lateral, usually simple corymbs or racemes and in the axils of bracts.

(*a*) Leaves glabrous.

1. **A. humilis,** Vahl; Wight Ic. t. 1212.—Syn. *A. solanacea*, Roxb. Cor. Pl. t. 27; *A. polycephala*, Wight Ill. t. 145; *A. littoralis*, Andr.; Kurz F. Fl. ii. 110; *A. arborescens*, Wall. Vern. *Jalkaima*, *Kantena*, Hind.; *Kyetmaôk*, Burm.

A large shrub or small tree, attaining 30 ft. L. glabrous, entire, obovate-oblong, 4–8 in. long, narrowed into a short petiole. Fl. light pink in pedunculate, mostly axillary corymbs, pedicels ¼–½ in. long, sepals slightly connate at base or almost distinct, more or less ciliate, sepals and petals with round black dots, often confluent into longitudinal lines, anther-cells more or less transversely rugose.

Subhimalayan tract from the Jumna eastwards, ascending to 3,000 ft. Assam. Khasi hills, Manipur. Cachar. Lower Bengal. Chutia Nagpore. Orissa. Northern Circars. Deccan and West side of the Peninsula, chiefly on the banks of streams. Burma, Upper and Lower, on the sea coast and inland.—Fl. at all seasons, chiefly March–June. Ceylon, on the South-Western Coast. Malay Peninsula. China. Mez *Myrsinaceæ* 132 and 128, fig. 20 separates *A. solanacea* by free, not ciliate sepals and restricts *A. humilis*, to the littoral plant. He also recognises *A. arborescens* as a separate species. 2. **A. Wallichii**, A. DC. (*A. sanguinolenta*, Wall.; Mez, l. c. 129) Rangoon, Prome, Upper Burma, with l. minutely denticulate in the upper part, is probably not specifically distinct from 1. 3. **A. polycephala**, Wall. Manipur. Upper Burma, common (*Kyetmaok*). L. oblanceolate, blade 6–10, narrowed into petiole ¾–1 in. long, midrib prominent beneath, sec. n. numerous, slender but distinct, fl. large, pink, waxy, in elongate bracteate racemes, peduncles 2–4 in., petals ⅓ in. long. Closely allied and possibly not distinct is 4. **A. oxyphylla,** Wall. Tenasserim, Malay Peninsula, from which Mez separates *A. attenuata*, Wall., and *A. oblonga*, A. DC.

Of 5. **A. parviflora**, Talbot, List 2nd ed. 204, with distantly crenate and pellucid punctate l. and small white fl., evergreen scrub jungle near the coast of North Kanara. I have seen no specimens. *A. parviflora*, Blume, is a Javan species.

6. **A. rhynchophylla**, Clarke. Khasi hills. A small shrub, branchlets and petioles glabrous, l. lanceolate, long-acuminate, blade 3–5, pet. ¼–⅓ in. long, sec. n. arching, slender but distinct beneath, as well as the reticulate veins. Fl. large, white, in few-fld. axillary racemes, pedicels 1 in., petals ½ in. long. 7. **A. Khasiana**, Clarke, from which Mez separates *A. Thomsonii*, Mez, Khasi hills, Manipur, Chittagong, is a small shrub, branchlets and petioles fulvous hairy, l. glabrous, linear-lanceolate or oblanceolate, 4–6 in. long, narrowed into a very short petiole. Fl. in 2–5-fld. pedunculate axillary umbels, peduncles 1 in., pedicels equally long, petals ¼–⅓ in. long. berry red, fleshy ¼–⅓ in. diam.

8. **A. involucrata**, Kurz. Mixed plain forests; Terai and banks of streams in the outer hills, ascending to 5,000 ft. Fl. in lateral involucrate umbels, peduncles stout, 1–3 in., pedicels 2–5, bracts as many as pedicels, persistent, ½ in. long, fl. large, sepals waxy corolloid, pink, petals ⅓–½ in. long, both with copious black round or elongate dots, sepals enlarged in fr., connivent over the berry.

(*b*) Leaves hairy beneath.

9. **A. Helferiana**, Kurz. Manipur, Tenasserim. Branches, l. and inflorescence densely rusty tomentose, l. elliptic-lanceolate, blade 4–6, pet. ¼ in., peduncles axillary, 3–4 in. long, bearing short umbelliform racemes. Other species with l. hairy beneath, Burma: 10. **A. reflexa**, Wall., 11. **A. grandifolia**, A. DC. Cachar and Manipur: 12. **A. Keenani**, Clarke.—Mez l. c. 129 separates specimens of *A. reflexa* with nearly glabrous l. as *A. Amherstiana*, A. DC.

B. Sepals narrow, open in bud. Style in bud longer than petals, usually exserted. Inflorescence usually (exc. *A. rhomboidea*) of compound corymbs or racemes, axillary or forming terminal panicles.

(*a*) Sepals and petals not punctate.

13. **A. floribunda**, Wall. in Roxb. Fl. Ind. ed. Carey & Wall. ii. 272; Brandis F. Fl. 287; Mez *Myrsinaceæ*, p. 107.—Syn. *A. neriifolia*, Wall.; Fl. Brit. Ind. iii. 522.

A large shrub or small tree, l. lanceolate, entire, upperside glabrous, underside with exceedingly minute thin rounded scales, blade 4–6, pet. ½ in. long.

Fl. pink in a large terminal panicle, its ramifications (as well as the short pedicels) minutely lepidote. Calyx open in bud, segments ovate, anthers shortly mucronate, style filiform ¼ in. long.

Outer Himalaya from Garhwal eastwards, ascending to 5,000 ft., often along streams. Assam. Khasi hills, Manipur, Chittagong. Fl. April, May. 14. **A. Icara,** Ham. (*A. serrulata*, Kurz). Assam, North-East Bengal. Burma. Similar to 13, but l. slightly serrulate, calyx-segments linear-lanceolate and anthers with a long terminal awn.

15. **A. depressa,** Clarke. Sikkim 4–6,000 ft. Khasi hills. Singbhum. Upper Burma. L. lanceolate or elliptic-lanceolate, blade 3–4, pet. ¼ in. long. Fl. small, in axillary long pedunculate compound umbels, shorter than l. 16. **A. rhomboidea,** Wight Ic. t. 1213. Anamalai hills. Travancore and Tinevelli Ghats 2–4,000 ft. A small tree, l. elongate-rhomboid, acuminate, 2–3 in. long, gradually narrowed into short petiole, peduncles axillary 1–5-fld., shorter than l.

(*b*) Sepals and petals distinctly punctate.

17. **A. pauciflora.** Heyne; Wight Ic. t. 1214. A large shrub or small tree, common on the Nilgiris and other hills on the West side of the Peninsula. L. lanceolate, blade 5–8, pet. ⅙ in. Racemes short, axillary, 1–5-fld., petals acuminate, berries red. 18. **A. pedunculosa,** Wall. Assam. Khasi hills. L. lanceolate, 4–6 in. long, narrowed into a short petiole. Fl. rose-red, in many-fld. axillary pedunculate compound corymbs, often forming a large drooping panicle at the ends of branches, buds very acute, pedicels slender, ⅓ in., petals ¼–⅓ in. long.

19. **A. quinquangularis,** A. DC. Bengal. L. similar to 13. Fl. in a large terminal panicle, petals ⅙ in. long, drupes obtusely 5-ribbed. 20. **A. Griffithii,** Clarke. Khasi hills. Similar to 13, but l. larger, elliptic-oblanceolate, 8–12 in. long, sec. n. numerous, parallel, slender but distinct, sepals oblong, drupes vertically striated.

C. Fl. small, in axillary and terminal panicles, petals less than ⅙ in. long.

21. **A. colorata,** Roxb. (*A. anceps*, Wall.; Kurz F. Fl. ii. 107), Assam, Khasi hills, Cachar, Chittagong, Martaban and Tenasserim. A small tree, branchlets and underside of l. covered with minute often shining scales. L. lanceolate-oblong, blade 8–12, pet. ½ in. long, sec. n. numerous, slender, almost at right angles to midrib. Fl. small, in axillary panicles, usually forming large terminal panicles, peduncles often flattened, fl. small, petals ⅛ in., style much longer than petals. 22. **A. andamanica,** Kurz. Andamans. Mergui. A small shrub, perfectly glabrous, branches slender. L. thin, lanceolate, blade 3–7, pet. ⅙ in. long. Fl. minute, in axillary lax panicles, pedicels slender, divaricating, ¼–½ in. long, petals $\frac{1}{12}$ in., with copious black, more or less elongate dots, style a little longer than petals.

23. **A. amplexicaulis,** Bedd. Ic. Pl. Ind. Or. t. 170; Manual t. xviii. Wainad, Travancore. L. thin, sessile, with an unequal-sided (almost amplexicaul) base, 5–6 in. long, with a belt of numerous raised dots along the margin. Fl. small, in a lax terminal panicle, petals ⅐ in. long.

D. Fl. in terminal panicles, supported by a false whorl of leaves.

24. **A. paniculata,** Roxb. Assam. Khasi hills. Dacca, frequent. Chittagong hills. A large shrub, l. oblanceolate, glabrous, 8–20 in. long, narrowed into a short stout petiole, midrib and sec. n. prominent beneath. Fl. middle-sized, rose-coloured, in ample pyramidal terminal panicles 8–12 in. long, supported at base by a false whorl of large l., rachis and ramifications angular, glabrous, petals ⅙ in., style longer than petals, pedicels in fl. ⅙–⅓ in. long, sepals and petals not punctate. 25. **A. missionis,** Wall. (*A. courtallensis*, Wight Ic. t. 1215). Hills on the West side of the Peninsula from Coimbatore southwards. Ceylon, moist region, common. Similar to 24. Pedicels in fl. ½–1 in. long, sepals and petals black-punctate, petals ⅙–¼ in. long, style as long as petals.

26. **A. rigida,** Kurz. Tenasserim, on the coast. Siam. L. elongate-elliptic, 5–7 in. long, narrowed into a very short petiole, sec. n. arching, prominent beneath, panicle contracted, 4–5 in. long, sepals and petals punctate, anthers with a long point. 27. **A. Kurzii,** Clarke (*A. polycephala*, var. *acuminata*, Kurz F. Fl. ii. 110). Pegu Yoma, eastern slopes. Hills east of Toungoo (D. B. Febr. 1880). A large shrub, l. coriaceous, glabrous, lanceolate, blade 6–9, narrowed into pet. ⅓–⅜ in., sec. n. arching running out below the margin into distinct intra-marginal veins. Fl. in pedunculate umbelliform corymbs, 3–4 at the ends of branches, supported by a false whorl of large l.

II. Leaves crenate or serrate.

A. Branchlets and petioles glabrous.

28. **A. macrocarpa,** Wall. *Chumlani*, Nep. Nepal. Sikkim 4–8,000 ft. Bhutan. A small single-stemmed shrub, forming undergrowth in forests. L. membranous, lanceolate, crenate, 5–6 in. long, narrowed into a very short petiole, a row of large raised dots on the margin. Fl. large waxy, pale pink, in axillary pedunculate umbels near the ends of branches, often forming a terminal panicle, sepals oblong, after flowering ¼ in., petals ¼–⅓ in. long. Berries bright red ⅓–½ in. diam. dotted. 29. **A. crenata,** Roxb., including *A. undulata*, Clarke (*A. crispa*, A. DC., Mez Myrsin. 144). Khasi hills. China. Japan, Malay Archip. Similar to 28, but l. often with large raised dots all over, without a row of marginal dots, fl. smaller, petals ⅙ in. long. berries smaller. 30. **A. bhotanica,** Clarke (*Amblyanthopsis bhotanica*, Mez) fl. small, umbels in short lateral panicles.

31. **A. virens,** Kurz F. Fl. ii. 575. Assam. Khasi and Naga hills, Manipur. Cachar. Upper Burma. Yunnan. A single-stemmed shrub with horizontal branches. L. chartaceous, elliptic-oblong, blade crenate, 6–7 in. narrowed into petiole ¼ in. long, Umbels arranged in a terminal glabrous corymb, sepals elliptic obtuse, petals ⅓ in. long, both prominently black-dotted. Berries ¼–⅓ in. diam., yellow, spotted. 32. **A. Kachinensis,** Mez. Khasi hills, sepals ovate-triangular, as well as petals with black oblong dots. 33. **A. Brandisiana,** Kurz. Thaungyin and Upper Salween forests. L. coriaceous, slightly crenate, elliptic, obtuse or acute, blade 6–7, pet. 1–1½ in. long, sec. n. slender, arching, joined by prominent reticulate veins. Fl. large in axillary umbels on peduncles 3–5 in., sepals ⅕, petals ⅓ in. long, not dotted.

B. Branchlets and petioles hairy.

34. **A. villosa,** Roxb. (*A. vestita*, Wall.; Mez Myrsin. 141). Martaban and Tenasserim. A small shrub, branchlets, petioles, young l. and inflorescence rusty villous, l. membranous slightly crenate, elliptic-lanceolate, blade 6–7, pet. ½ in. long. Fl. in pedunculate axillary bracteate umbels, sepals linear-lanceolate, ¼ in., petals hardly as long as sepals. 35. **A. sonchifolia,** Mez (*A. villosa*, var. *obtusa*). Shevagherry hills. Western Peninsula, l. spathulate, fl. in broad axillary panicles, rusty pubescent, like the elongate-triangular sepals.

36. **A. odontophylla,** Wall. Khasi hills, Patkoi range, Cachar. Malay Penins. A small shrub, branchlets, petiole, midrib and sec. n. beneath rusty pubescent or villous. L. membranous, finely and sharply serrate, elongate-elliptic, blade 6–8, pet. 1–2 in. long. Fl. in simple or compound lax few-fld. racemes, pedicels slender, ¼–½ in. long with minute hairs, petals ⅙ in. long. Berry scarlet, ¼ in. diam.

1. **Pimelandra eugeniæfolia,** Hook. f. (*Sadiria eugeniifolia*, Mez). Khasi hills, common. A shrub with spreading horizontal branches, l. nearly glabrous, caudate-acuminate, crenate, blade 6–10, pet. ¼ in. long, sec. n. very prominent beneath. Fl. ⅙ in. long, in short axillary branched racemes, calyx and pedicel hairy, corolla campanulate, lobes shorter than tube, ovules few in one horizontal line on the conical placenta, berries bright red. Three other species in Assam and on the Khasi hills: 2. **P. Griffithii,** Clarke, 3. **erecta,** Clarke, and 4. **Sadiria solanifolia,** Mez.

Hymenandra Wallichii, A. DC. (*Ardisia Hymenandra*, Wall. Pl. As. Rar. t. 175). Upper Assam. Khasi hills. Cachar. A low, stout, usually simple-stemmed shrub, l. glabrous, membranous, crenate, nearly sessile, 8–16 in. long, from a narrow base gradually widening upwards, sec. n. numerous, parallel, joined by distinct intramarginal veins. Fl. pink, in many-fld. umbels, several at the ends of short branchlets, supported by 2–4 floral l., umbels 2–3 in., peduncles 1, pedicels ½ in. long. Sepals and petals punctate, sep. short, pet. lanceolate, ⅓–½ in. long, the right edge overlapping in bud. Anthers connate into a tube by broad membranous edges, which terminate in a long thin membranous appendix.

Amblyanthus glandulosus, A. DC. Khasi hills. A small glabrous shrub, l. glabrous, membranous, narrow-lanceolate, slightly dentate, teeth often glandular-thickened, raised dots on the underside, often a belt of such dots along the edge, blade 5–7, narrowed into slender pet. ¼–½ in. long. Fl. minute, a cluster of small pedunculate umbels supported by 2–4 l. at the ends of long otherwise naked branchlets, peduncles slender 1–2 in. long, pedicels short. Buds obtuse, calyx and corolla punctate, corolla $\frac{1}{12}$ in. long, segments obovate, emarginate, anthers connate by their edges into a tube, ovules 3–4, in one line on the globose placenta. Mez (Myrsin. 210) adds 2 species: *A. prætervisus*, Mez, Khasi hills and *A. multiflorus*, Mez, Assam.

5. ANTISTROPHE, A. DC.; Fl. Brit. Ind. iii. 531.

Fl. bisexual, in sessile lateral umbels, pedicels slender. Calyx-lobes lanceolate, persistent. Corolla-lobes twisted in bud, the left edge overlapping. Anthers rostrate-acuminate. Ovules 3–4, in one line around the globose placenta. Species 2.

1. **A. oxyantha,** Wall. Khasi hills. Malay Peninsula. A single-stemmed shrub, with horizontal branches and very dark foliage. L. membranous, glabrous, lanceolate, blade 5–7, pet. slender $\frac{1}{4}$–$\frac{1}{3}$, petals $\frac{1}{3}$ in. long. Buds long acuminate, sepals, petals and ovary glandular-dotted. 2. **A. serratifolia,** Hook. f. (*Ardisia serratifolia*, Bedd. Ic. Ind. Or. t. 113). Young shoots and l. beneath along the nerves rusty tomentose, l. sharply serrate, petals $\frac{1}{8}$ in. long.

Amblyanthopsis membranacea, Mez (*Ardisia membranacea*, Wall.). Khasi hills. Cachar. A small almost herbaceous shrub, l. thinly membranous, glabrous, lanceolate, crenate, underside with numerous black glandular dots. Fl. small, in pedunculate axillary umbels, corolla-lobes round, emarginate, anthers free, basifixed, filaments as long as anthers, ovary obovoid.

6. AEGICERAS, Gærtn.; Fl. Brit. Ind. iii. 533.

A. majus, Gærtn. (probably the only species); Wight Ill. t. 146; Bedd. Man. t. xix.—Syn. *A. corniculata*, Blanco. Vern. *Kulsi*, *Khalshi*, *Koilsha*, Beng.; *Kanjala*, Mar.; *Butalet*, Burm.

A large evergreen glabrous shrub or small tree, gregarious, coppices well, bark grey. L. scattered, coriaceous, obovate, blade 2–3, narrowed into pet. $\frac{1}{4}$ in. long. Umbels many-fld. at the ends of branches usually naked below, with a few l. below the umbel, pedicels slender. Fl. white, fragrant, sepals and corolla-lobes twisted in bud, the right hand edge overlapping, corolla $\frac{1}{3}$–$\frac{1}{2}$ in. long, lobes reflexed. Anther-cells transversely septate. Ovules numerous, in several tiers on the globose placenta. Fr. cylindric, curved, acuminate, 1–2 in. long, seed one, same shape as fr., albumen none. The seed germinates within the pericarp on the tree, sending down a long radicle.

Sea coast and banks of tidal rivers, Sind, Western Peninsula on both sides, Sundriban, Andamans, Burma. Fl. Dec.–May. Sea coasts of tropical Asia, Australia and the South Pacific Islands. Mez (Myrsin. 57) describes a second species (*A. floridum*, Roem. et Schult.) from islands in the Pacific.

FIG. 161.—Aegiceras majus, Gærtn. $\frac{1}{2}$.

ORDER LXVIII. SAPOTACEÆ. Gen. Pl. ii. 650.

Trees, sometimes shrubs, l. entire, usually alternate and coriaceous, stipules early caducous or none. Fl. bisexual, as a rule in axillary clusters, bracts and bracteoles minute or 0. Calyx persistent, segments 4–8, almost distinct, corolla-tube short, lobes 4–24. Stamens inserted on the tube, as many as corolla-lobes and opposite them, or 2–3 times as many; filaments usually shorter than anthers. Ovary free, 1–12-celled, style filiform or cylindric, stigma punctiform, ovules solitary in each cell. Fr. a 1–8-seeded berry, seeds with a crustaceous shining testa, oily, exalbuminous with large fleshy cotyledons or albuminous with flat cotyledons.

Young shoots and young l. of most *Sapotaceæ* are clothed with fine, often minute unicellular hairs, which, as a rule, are attached in the middle and hence are two-armed. Another feature are strings of cells filled with a milky substance, which in some species yields the Gutta Percha of commerce, accompanying the vascular bundles in the bark and leaves. The wood is readily recognized by numerous narrow, often very fine, more or less concentric bands of wood parenchyma, and frequently by radial irregular belts of parenchyma surrounding the vessels. The pits in the walls of wood fibres are simple, not bordered. The heartwood is generally red.

A. Ovary 4–12-celled.
  I. Calyx-segments, corolla-lobes and stamens isomerous.
    Calyx-segments 5, similar.
      Staminodes alternating with stamens . . . 1. SIDEROXYLON.
      No staminodes . . . . 2. CHRYSOPHYLLUM.
    Calyx-segments 6, three larger, forming an outer circle . . . . ACHRAS (p. 424).
  II. Stamens twice, sometimes three times the number of calyx-segments and corolla-lobes.
    Calyx-segments 4 . . . . 3. ISONANDRA.
    Calyx-segments 6 . . . . 4. PALAQUIUM.
  III. Corolla-lobes twice or thrice the number of calyx-segments.
    Calyx-segments in 2 series, staminodes alternating with stamens . . . . . . 5. MIMUSOPS.
    Calyx-segments imbricate, no staminodes.
      Fl. many usually near the ends of branches, albumen 0. . . . . 6. BASSIA.
      Fl. few, in axillary clusters, seeds albuminous . . . . PAYENA (p. 427).
B. Ovary 1–2-celled, fl. in axillary panicles . . . . 7. SARCOSPERMA.
C. Ovary 1-celled, fl. in axillary clusters, filaments long.
    A spinescent shrub or tree . . . . . . REPTONIA (p. 427).

1. SIDEROXYLON, Linn.; Fl. Brit. Ind. iii. 536

Evergreen trees, stipules 0. Calyx-segments 5, strongly imbricated. Staminodes broad-ovate or lanceolate. Ovary villous, as a rule 5-celled. Berry usually 4–5-seeded. Seeds albuminous, testa hard. Species 60–80, tropics of the Old World, a few beyond the tropics.

A. Fl. large, corolla $\frac{1}{4}$ in. and longer, filaments short.

(*a*) Branchlets and underside of l. pubescent.

1. **S. tomentosum**, Roxb. Cor. Pl. t. 28.—Syn. *Sapota elengoides*, Wight Ic. t. 1218; *Achras elengoides*, Bedd. Fl. Sylv. t. 235; *Kumbul*, *Kanta Kumla*, Mar.; *Kùmpoli*, Kan.; *Pala*, Tam.; *Holay*, Badaga; *Thitcho*, Burm.

A small, occasionally a large tree, branchlets often spinescent. Young shoots, petioles, underside of l., pedicels and calyx grey- or tawny-tomentose. L. thinly coriaceous, from a cuneate base, elliptic or obovate, blade 2–3, pet. $\frac{1}{4}$–$\frac{1}{3}$ in. Pedicels $\frac{1}{4}$–$\frac{1}{3}$ in., corolla white, $\frac{1}{3}$ in. long, style twice the length of corolla. Berry tomentose when young, yellow when ripe, $\frac{3}{4}$–1 in. long.

Western Peninsula, on the east and west side. Common in the Sholas of the Nilgiris and in the evergreen forests of the Bombay Ghats. Upper Burma. Fl. Jan.–March (on the Nilgiris throughout the year). A variable species, Burma specimens (Smales, dry deciduous Forest Shwebo district) have the l. obtusely obovate, membranous in fl. thickly coriaceous in fr.

2. **S. assamicum**, C. B. Clarke. Assam, Cachar. Branchlets, petioles and (usually) underside of l. rusty-pubescent. L. elongate-elliptic, blade 3–6, pet. $\frac{1}{4}$–$\frac{1}{3}$ in. long, sec. n. conspicuous beneath.

(*b*) Branchlets and underside of l. glabrous or nearly so.

3. **S. Hookeri**, C. B. Clarke; Sikkim 5–6,000 ft. Bhutan. L. elliptic-lanceolate, blade 5–7, pet. $\frac{1}{3}$ in., sometimes with long thin scattered hairs along the midrib, sec. n. prominent, pedicels as long as fl., silky as well as calyx, corolla $\frac{1}{3}$ in. long, staminodes linear-lanceolate, densely hairy. To this I refer a small tree, 20 ft. (*Thitcho*, Burm.), fl. white, near villages 800 ft. Schwebo district, Upper Burma (Smales, March 1900), l. smaller, sec. n. less conspicuous. 4. **S. burmanicum**, Coll. et Hemsl. in Journ. Linn. Soc. xxviii.

32. *Thitcho*, Burm. Upper Burma (a large, tree, Smales). Shan hills 4,000 ft., Collett. Similar to 3, but l. broader, pet. 1 in. long, staminodes slightly hairy. Species 1–4 are closely allied.

B. Fl. small, corolla less than $\frac{1}{8}$ in. long, filaments as long as or longer than anthers.

5. **S. longepetiolatum**, King & Prain, Ann. Gard. Calc. ix. 50 t. 63 (*Gluta longipetiolata*,

FIG. 162. Sideroxylon tomentosum, Roxb. $\frac{1}{2}$.

Kurz F. Fl. i. 310). Andamans, Narkondam. Attaran forests. A considerable tree, blade 6–24, pet. $1\frac{1}{2}$–3 in. long, sec. n. prominent beneath. Fl. fascicles on axillary racemes 1–2 in., pedicels slender, pubescent, $\frac{1}{8}$ in. long.

6. **S. ferrugineum**, Hook. & Arn.—Syn. *S. attenuatum*, A. DC.; Wight Ic. t. 1590. Mergui, Malay Penins. and Archip. South China. Young shoots, young l. and pedicels rusty pubescent, l. coriaceous shining, from a cuneate base elliptic or obovate, blade 3–6, pet. $\frac{1}{2}$ in. Pedicels $\frac{1}{8}$, corolla $\frac{1}{12}$ in. long. 7. **S. grandifolium**, Wall. Khasi hills. Martaban, hills between Beeling and Sitang rivers. A large tree (Kurz), l. crowded at the extremities of the thick branchlets, glabrous, chartaceous, from oblanceolate to obovate, blade 6–10, pet. $\frac{1}{2}$ in. Fl. greenish, almost sessile, usually on the old wood below the l. in dense clusters on wartlike tubercles above the leaf-scars, corolla $\frac{1}{12}$ in. long.

8. **S. (?) Gamblei**, C. B. Clarke, Sikkim up to 4,000 ft. A large tree, l. elliptic, blade 5–7, pet. 1 in. long, sec. n. very prominent beneath, fr. ellipsoid, $1\frac{1}{2}$ in. long. Fl. unknown, genus uncertain.

2. CHRYSOPHYLLUM, Linn.; Fl. Brit. Ind. iii. 535.

Species 60, chiefly in tropical America.

C. Roxburghii, G. Don; Bedd. Fl. Sylv. t. 236. *The Star Apple.* Vern. *Tarsi*, *Dongrima*, Mar.; *Hali*, Kan.; *Kát Iluppa*, Tam.; *Pala*, Mal.

A middle-sized, at times a large evergreen tree, branchlets and often nerves beneath clothed with fine rusty hairs. L. coriaceous, shining, elliptic-oblong, abruptly acuminate, blade 3–7 in. long, narrowed into a short petiole, sec. n. ∞, parallel, resembling *Calophyllum*. Fl. small, greenish-white, in dense axillary clusters, pedicels slender, $\frac{1}{5}$ in. long, glabrous or rusty-pubescent, calyx-segments 5, obtuse, corolla broadly campanulate, lobes short, rounded, ciliate, ovary 5–6-celled, villous. Berry rusty-tomentose when young, yellow when ripe, edible, 5–6-ridged, obscurely when fresh, sharply when dry. Seeds 5–6, compressed, testa coriaceous.

Assam, Khasi hills, Pegu. Western Ghats from the Konkan southwards. Fl. March-May. Ceylon moist region. Malay Penins. and Archip.

Achras Sapota, Linn.; the *Sapodilla* Plum. A native of tropical America, cultivated in India on account of its excellent fr. L. crowded near the ends of the thick branchlets, shining, elliptic-lanceolate, blade 3–6, pet. slender, ½–1 in. long, fl. 6-merous, whitish, stamens 6, alternating with lanceolate staminodes resembling the corolla-lobes, ovary 12-celled. Fr. as large as an orange, rind rough, brown, thin, seeds 5 or more.

3. ISONANDRA, Wight; Fl. Brit. Ind. iii. 538.

L. alternate, coriaceous, glabrous. Fl. small, shortly pedicelled or nearly sessile, in more or less dense clusters, axillary or over the scars of fallen l. Sepals 4, nearly equal, corolla-tube short. Stamens 8, all perfect, no staminodes. Ovary villous, 4-celled, style linear. Fr. ellipsoid, 1-seeded, embryo large, cotyledons flat, in fleshy albumen. Species 4, one in the Sandwich Islands.

1. **I. lanceolata,** Wight Ic. t. 359 (1843); Trimen, Handb. Ceylon iii., 77.—Syn. *I. Wightiana*, A. DC. Prodr. viii. 187 (1844); *I. villosa*, Wight Ic. t. 360; *I. Candolliana*, Wight Ic. t. 1220; *I. Perottetiana*, Wight Ic. t. 1219.

A small or middle-sized tree, young shoots rusty-pubescent, l. very variable, from lanceolate to broadly and obtusely elliptic, blade 2–6, pet. ¼ in. long sec. n. 6–10 pair, arching, prominent beneath, tertiary n. slender, numerous, transverse, finely reticulate. Calyx rusty-silky, corolla ⅛ in. long, lobes obtuse, often emarginate, stamens included, anther-tips often hairy, style exserted. Fr. ¾–1 in. long, scarlet, seed hard, polished.

Western Ghats above 4,000 ft., from Coorg southwards, common on the Nilgiris. Fl. March–Aug. Ceylon moist region. Five species of Fl. Brit. India are here classed as one. Gamble, Indian Timbers Ed. ii. 445, describes two species from the Nilgiris, structure and weight of wood different, which however in the forest he was unable satisfactorily to recognize. The subject demands further study. 2. **I. Stocksii,** C. B. Clarke. Concan, Stocks, not found by Talbot, List Ed. ii. 206. L. obovate obtuse, tertiary n. laxly reticulate, not transverse. Fl. sessile on short thick lateral spurs.

3. **I. diplostemon,** C. B. Clarke (*Diospyros obovata*, Wight Ic. t. 1226), an entirely anomalous, imperfectly known species, probably from the Western Ghats, l. obovate obtuse, glabrous, sepals 4, petals 5–6, stamens 15–18 1-seriate.

4. PALAQUIUM, Blanco; Trimen Handb. Ceylon iii. 81.

(*Dichopsis*, Thwaites; Fl. Brit. Ind. iii. 540.)

Trees, fl. 6-merous, cal.-segments in 2 series, the outer 3 valvate, the inner imbricate. Corolla-lobes as a rule contorted in bud, stam. 12–18, in one or two rows on the corolla-tube, anthers extrorse or lateral, connective produced beyond anthers, sometimes bifid. Ovary villous, 6-celled, style simple. Fr. fleshy, seed 1, cotyledons large, oily, albumen 0.

A. Western species.

1. **P. ellipticum,** Benth. (*Dichopsis*).—Syn. *Bassia elliptica*, Dalz.; Bedd. Fl. Sylv. t. 43. Vern. *Panchonta*, Kan.; *Kat Illupei*, Tam.

A very tall tree, wood reddish-brown, durable, young shoots, pedicels and calyx minutely rusty-pubescent. L. approximate near the ends of branches, elliptic or obovate-elliptic, blade 3–5, gradually narrowed into petiole ½ in. long. Fl. in axillary fascicles of 2–8, pedicels 1–1½ in., calyx ⅓, corolla ½–⅔ in. long, filaments hairy. Fr. ellipsoid, pulpy, 1½ in. long.

Western Ghats from North Kanara southwards, common in Wainad. Fl. C. S. Yields an inferior kind of Gutta Percha. 2. **P. Bourdilloni,** sp. nova. Travancore evergreen forests up to 4,000 ft. A small tree, l. rigidly coriaceous, pale, glabrous, lanceolate or oblanceolate, blade 5–7, narrowed into petiole ⅓ in. long, sec. n. prominent beneath, joined by intra-marginal veins, tertiary n. finely reticulate. Fl. in axillary few-fld. fascicles, pedicels ⅓ in., sepals ¼ in. long, obtuse, the outer tawny-tomentose, the inner rusty-pubescent. Corolla glabrous outside, tube less than ¼ the length of the oblong lobes, filaments rusty-hairy, connective obtuse.

B. Eastern species.

(*a*) L. velvety beneath.

3. **P. polyanthum,** Benth. (*Dichopsis*) (*Isonandra polyantha*, Kurz). Silhet, Cachar, Chittagong. Arakan, Pegu, Tavoy. A middle-sized tree, l. clothed beneath with very short brown or silvery velvet, glabrescent when mature, obovate-oblong, blade 6–12, petiole stout, 1 in. long. Fl. fragrant, cream-coloured, in axillary fascicles, pedicels 1½ in., sepals ⅛ in., corolla a little longer than sepals. Fr. obovoid 1½ in. long.

4. **P. Gutta,** Burck, in Ann. Jardin Buitenzorg v. 24 t. 4 (*Dichopsis Gutta*, Benth.; *Isonandra Gutta*, Hooker.) The *Gutta Percha* tree. Malay Peninsula, extirpated in many places. A tall tree, branchlets rusty-pubescent, l. obovate-oblong, shortly acuminate, underside clothed with a shining golden-orange velvet, blade 4–5, pet. ¾ in., pedicels ⅓, corolla twice the length of calyx, ⅓ in. long. 5. **P. oblongifolium,** Burck l.c. t. 5. Malay Peninsula, Sumatra, Borneo. Believed to be the chief species yielding Gutta Percha at present. Similar to 4, l. oblong-lanceolate, long-acuminate, blade 8, pet. ¾ in. long. Species 4 and 5 are here mentioned, as it may not be impossible to grow them on a large scale in the Mergui district.

(*b*.) L. entirely glabrous.

6. **P. obovatum,** C. B. Clarke (*Dichopsis*). Tenasserim, Malay Peninsula. L. crowded near the ends of the thick branchlets, which are marked by the scars of petioles, obovate from a cuneate base, blade 6–8, pet. ¾ in., sec. n. 10–12 pair, straight, parallel, prominent beneath, tertiary n. obscure. Fl. fascicles as a rule from above the scars of fallen l., pedicels ⅓–⅔ in., corolla ⅓ in. long, glabrous outside, more than twice the length of calyx, lobes lanceolate, stamens exserted, style twice the length of corolla. Fr. globose ¾ in. diam. Yields an inferior kind of Gutta Percha. 7. **P. Helferi,** C. B. Clarke (*Dichopsis*). Tavoy, Mergui. A middle-sized tree, similar to 6. Young shoots minutely rusty-tomentose, sec. n. distant, 6–9 pair, arching, tert. n. parallel, slender but distinct. This may possibly be *Isonandra obovata*, Kurz, F. Fl. ii. 120.

5. MIMUSOPS, Linn.; Fl. Brit. Ind. iii. 548.

Evergreen trees, rarely shrubs. Midrib prominent, sec. n. numerous, fine, parallel. Fl. axillary, mostly fasciculate, calyx-segments 6–10, in two series. Corolla rotate, lobes 18–24 in 2 or 3 series. Stamens usually 6–8, inserted opposite the inner corolla-lobes, alternating with staminodes, anthers lanceolate, extrorse. Ovary hairy, 6–8-celled. Fr. fleshy, seeds compressed, testa hard, shining, cotyledons broad, flat, in fleshy albumen. Species 30, tropics of both hemispheres.

1. **M. Elengi,** Roxb. Cor. Pl. t. 14; Wight Ic. t. 1586; Bedd. Fl. Sylv. t. 40. Vern. *Mulsari*, *Maulsari*, Hind.; *Bukal*, Beng.; *Owli*, *Wovali*, Mar.; *Pogada*, Tel.; *Bakul*, *Pagade*, Kan.; *Magadam*, Tam.; *Elenji*, Mal.; *Khaya*, Burm.

A large tree, youngest shoots, pedicel and outside of calyx with short rusty pubescence. L. scattered, wholly glabrous when full grown, shining, elliptic, shortly acuminate, blade 3–4, pet. ¾ in. long. Fl. white, fragrant, nearly 1 in. across, pedicels ½–¾ in. long, calyx-segments 8, corolla-lobes in 2 series, stamens usually 8, staminodes short, densely hairy on the back. Fr. yellow, ovoid, 1 in. long, seed one.

Western Peninsula, southwards from the Kandala Ghat on the west and the Northern Circars on the east side. Andamans, Martaban and Tenasserim. Commonly planted, north as far as Lahore. Fl. Jan.–April.—Ceylon. Malay Penins. and Archip. 2. **M. Roxburghiana,** Wight Ic. t. 1588. Common at the foot of the Nilgiris and Anamalais and elsewhere on the West side of the Peninsula. Similar to 1 but l. obtuse at both ends, calyx-segments 6, staminodes glabrous, irregularly jagged, as long as filaments.

3. **M. hexandra,** Roxb. Cor. Pl. t. 15.—Syn. *M. indica*, A. DC.; Wight Ic. t. 1587; Brandis F. Fl. 291. Vern. *Khirni*, Hind.; *Ranjana*, *Raini*, Mar.; *Pala*, Tel.; *Palla*, Tam.

A large tree, sometimes a shrub only, often gregarious, l. wholly glabrous, shining, generally crowded at the ends of branchlets, obovate-oblong, obtuse or emarginate, blade 2–4, pet. ¼–¾ in. Fl. ¼ in. across, pale yellow, pedicels ¼–⅓ in., calyx-segments 6, stamens 6–8, staminodes glabrous, frequently bifid. Berry ½ in. long, 1- (sometimes 2-) seeded.

Banda district (Edgew.). Sandstone of Pachmarhi and adjoining hill ranges. Chanda district. Gujarat. Khandesh. Deccan. Sriharikota (D. B. Nov. 1881). Fl. Nov.–Feb. Fr. eaten. Ceylon, dry region. 4. **M. Kauki**, Linn. Amherst (Wall.). Malay Penins. and Archip. L. obovate, densely silky-white beneath, blade 3–5, pet. 1½–2 in. long. Berry globose, ¾–1 in. diam., seeds 3–4.

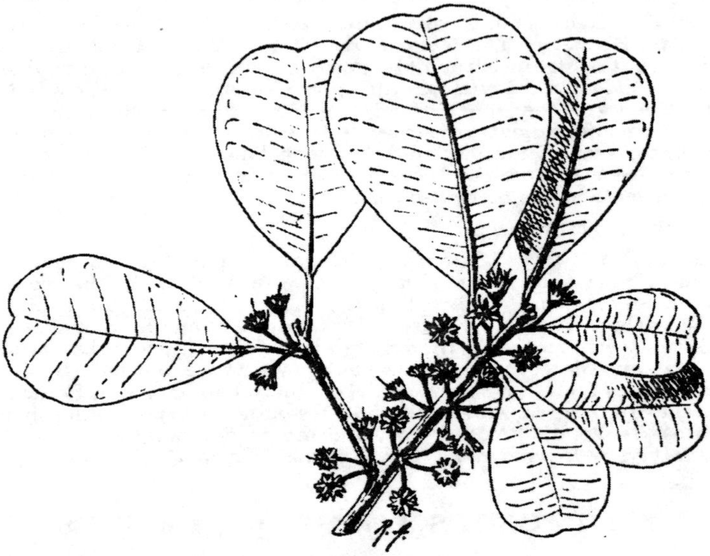

FIG. 163.—Mimusops hexandra, Roxb. ½.

5. **M. littoralis**, Kurz F. Fl. ii. 123. *Andaman Bullet wood*. Vern. *Katpali*, Burm.

A tall tree, quite glabrous, l. approximate at the ends of thick branchlets, obovate-oblong, blade 5–8, pet. ½–1 in. long. Fl. small, solitary, pedicels ½–¾ in., fr. 1–2 in. long, calyx-lobes usually 6, corolla-lobes 18, stamens twice the number of calyx-lobes, alternating with small scale-like staminodes. Berry depressed-globose, 1–1½ in. diam., seeds 5–6.

Andamans, Cocos and Nicobar islands, forming nearly pure forests. Upper Tenasserim (Kurz). Fl. June, July.

6. BASSIA, Linn.; Fl. Brit. Ind. iii. 543.

(*Illipe*, Kœnig, Engler in Engler u. Prantl iv. 1. 133.)

Leaves silky or tomentose beneath when young, stipules caducous. Calyx-segments 4 or 5, imbricate, corolla-tube ovoid or campanulate, lobes 6–12, contorted in bud, stamens usually twice the number of corolla-lobes, anthers lanceolate acute. Ovary villous, 4–12-celled, style long exserted. Fr. a berry, seeds 1–4. Albumen 0, cotyledons large, fleshy, radicle very small. Species 30, India, Malaya, Polynesia.

1. **B. latifolia**, Roxb. Cor. Pl. t. 19; Bedd. Fl. Sylv. t. 41. Includes *B. villosa*, Wall.; Kurz F. Fl. ii. 122. Vern. *Mohwa*, *Mahua*, Hind.; *Madkum*, Kol; *Ippi*, *Sanna Ippa*, Tel.; *Kat Illipi*, Tam.

A large tree, usually with a short trunk and a rounded crown, young shoots, young l., stipules and pedicels tawny tomentose. L. firm, clustered near ends of branches, elliptic or oblong-elliptic, blade 5–8, pet. 1–1½ in. long. Fl. in dense clusters at the ends of branches, pedicels 1–2 in. long, calyx coriaceous, segments 4 or 5, densely tomentose outside. Corolla ⅔ in. long, cream-

coloured, fleshy, sweet, early caducous, lobes short erect, usually 8 or 9, stamens 24–26, anthers subsessile, hairy at the back. Fr. green, fleshy 1–2, seeds ½–1 in. long.

Planted in most parts of India, propagating itself by self-sown seed. Indigenous in the Subhimalayan tract from the Ravi to the Great Gandak, in the Satpura range, and the Peninsula. Upper Burma (?). The old l. are shed gradually from Feb. to April, fl. March–April, the fresh l. open out after the corolla has fallen.

2. **B. longifolia**, Linn.; Wight Ill. t. 147; Bedd. Fl. Sylv. t. 42. Vern. *Pedda Ippa*, Tel.; *Ippe*, Kan.; *Nat Illupai*, Tam.; *Mèzè*, Burm. Commonly cultivated in the Peninsula, an excellent avenue tree. Indigenous chiefly in the moist forests on the West side, from the Konkan southwards, but also in the Deccan. Common in Mysore. Cult. in Upper Burma. Ceylon dry region. A large tree, young shoots silky, l. elliptic-lanceolate, glabrous when full grown, blade 4–6, pet. slender, 1–1½ in. long. Fl. similar to 1, pedicels slender 2–2½ in., outer calyx-segments nearly glabrous, inner finely tomentose, anthers apiculate, 3-toothed at apex. Fr. velvety when young, obliquely ovoid 2, seed 1½ in. long. The sweet fleshy fl. of both species, 1 and 2, are dried and eaten, spirit is distilled from them, oil is expressed from the seeds. 3. **B. malabarica**, Bedd. West side of the Peninsula, from North Kanara southwards, ascending to 4,000 ft., chiefly along the banks of rivers. A small or middle-sized tree, branchlets glabrous, l. scattered, oblong-lanceolate, often obtuse, blade 8–10, petiole ½ in. long. Anthers long apiculate, fr. glabrous when young.

4. **B. butyracea**, Roxb.; Brandis F. Fl. t. 35. Vern. *Phalwara*, *Phulel*, *Phulwa*, *Chiùra*, Hind.

A large deciduous tree, branchlets, petioles, underside of l. and pedicels with fine silky hairs, l. clustered near ends of branches, coriaceous, obovate or obovate-oblong, blade 6–12, pet. 1–1½ in. long, sec. n. 15–20 pair, prominent, stipules minute, caducous. Calyx-segments 5, corolla not fleshy, lobes 8–10, spreading. Stamens 30–40, filaments glabrous, as long as anthers. Fr. fleshy, 1, seeds ¾ in. long.

Subhimalayan tract from the Eastern Dún eastwards, ascending to 5,000 ft. Fl. Nov.–Jan. The seeds yield a white vegetable butter, of the consistence of fine lard.

Two imperfectly known species: 5. **B. caloneura**, Kurz, Andaman Report 41. (*Isonandra caloneura*, Kurz F. Fl. ii. 119.) South Andaman, common. A large evergreen tree, young shoots and young l. densely appressed, rusty-pubescent, l. scattered, chartaceous, elliptic-oblong, blade 6–8, pet. ½ in. long. 6. **B. Lobbii**, C. B. Clarke, Attaran forests. L. membranous, elliptic, blade 2½, pet. ½ in. long.

Payena paralleloneura, Kurz. Martaban and Tenasserim. A large evergreen tree, l. scattered, chartaceous, glabrous, elliptic-lanceolate, blade 3–4, pet. ½–¾ in. long, sec. n. numerous, slender, parallel. Fl. white, in axillary few-fld. clusters, pedicels ½ in., calyx-segments 4, corolla deeply lobed, stamens 12–24. Seed one, rarely two. *P. lucida*, A. DC.; Gamble Ind. Timb. Ed. II. 449 is a tree of Cachar and the Malay Peninsula. Yields a kind of Gutta Percha.

7. SARCOSPERMA, Hook. f.; Fl. Brit. Ind. iii. 535.

Evergreen trees, l. coriaceous, nearly opposite, stipules caducous. Fl. small, 5-merous, fascicled on the branches of axillary panicles. Minute staminodes alternating with stamens, ovary 1–2-celled. Berry ellipsoid, 1- or 2-seeded. Testa crustaceous, albumen 0, embryo fleshy. Species 5, 2 in China, 1 in Perak.

1. **S. arboreum**, Benth. Subhimalayan tract and outer hills, ascending to 4,000 ft. from Sikkim eastwards, Assam. Khasi hills, Manipur. Hills east of Toungoo 3,000 ft. (D. B. Feb. 1880). Upper Burma 1–5,000 ft. (*Tawgyi Kyitya*) Yunnan. A tall tree, l. elliptic-oblong, blade 6–12, pet. ½–1½ in., sec. n. arching, 8–10 pair, pits in the axils, tert. n. transverse, parallel. Fl. greenish-yellow, scented, panicles pubescent, calyx hairy outside, staminodes obscure. Fr. ellipsoid, 1 in. long, 1- or 2-seeded. 2. **S. Griffithii**, Benth. Assam, Khasi hills. Similar to 1, l. smaller, tertiary nerves obscure, panicle and calyx glabrous.

Reptonia buxifolia, A. DC.; Brandis F. Fl. t. 34. *Garar*, Pushtu; *Gurgūra*, Punjab. Common in the western part of the Punjab Salt range and on the hills trans-Indus from Dera Ishmael Khan northwards, ascending to 4,500 ft. Afghanistan, Arabia. A large evergreen shrub or small tree, bark dark grey, tesselated into small irregularly quadrangular pieces, branchlets terminating in spines, besides leafless axillary spines, young shoots and young leaves clothed with delicate pubescence. L. thickly coriaceous, 1–1½ in. long, entire, obovate, narrowed into a short petiole. Fl. small, greenish-yellow or whitish, almost sessile in compact axillary clusters. Corolla-tube short, lobes round, spreading, stamens inserted on the edge of the tube, filaments long exserted, anthers dehiscing outwardly. Ovary clothed with 2-armed hairs, 1-celled, with rudimentary dissepiments at the base, ovules 5–7, basal. Fr. fleshy, usually one-seeded. This genus, as shown by Radlkofer, belongs to *Sapotaceæ*.

Order LXIX. **EBENACEÆ.** Gen. Pl. ii. 662.

Trees or shrubs. L. alternate, rarely subopposite, entire, stipules 0. Fl. usually diœcious, calyx gamosepalous, persistent and usually enlarged in fr. Stamens 2–16 times the number of corolla-lobes, filaments often paired or in bundles, styles 2–8, cells as many or twice as many as the styles. Seeds pendulous, a small axile embryo in a horny often ruminated albumen.

Fl. 4–5-merous, ovary 4–5- or 8–10-celled . . . . . 1. Diospyros.
Fl. mostly 3-merous, ovary 3- or 6-celled . . . . . 2. Maba.

Like *Sapotaceæ*, the Ebonies have concentric bands of wood parenchyma, appearing like transverse bars across the medullary rays, but they are often extremely fine and difficult to see. The wood-fibres have minute bordered pits. The wood of many species is dark grey, and in the stems of some species when old, irregular masses of jet-black wood are formed, sometimes alternating with strata of lighter coloured wood. In this jet-black wood (Ebony) the vessels and wood fibres are filled with a black substance, the nature and origin of which is not yet fully understood.

1. **DIOSPYROS,** Linn.; Fl. Brit. Ind. iii. 553.

Trees, rarely shrubs. L. alternate, entire, subopposite in a few species. Fl. in most species white, mostly 4-, in some species 5-, rarely 6-merous, corolla-lobes usually overlapping to the right. ♂ and ♀ usually on separate trees, often polygamous, the ♀ fl. larger, with the calyx usually divided nearly to the base. Stamens ordinarily 8–32, often in pairs or otherwise connate, anthers basifixed, in most species linear, staminodes in ♀ fl., ovary 4–10-celled. Fr. generally supported by the enlarged calyx, rind coriaceous, seeds embedded in soft or viscid pulp. Embryo small in horny albumen, which often is ruminated by the intrusion of the dark coloured testa. Species 180, tropics of the whole world, a few species beyond the tropics.

I. Female fl. solitary, sometimes in pairs.

A. Calyx of ♂ and ♀ fl. similar, stamens usually in pairs.

(*a*) Corolla of ♂ fl. hairy or tomentose, l. glabrous.

a. ♂ fl. in short cymes or fascicles.

1. **D. nilagirica** Bedd. Ic. Pl. Ind. Or. t. 136.

A middle-sized tree, young shoots and young l. rusty-tomentose, l. thickly coriaceous, glabrous when full grown, blade 4–5, narrowed into pet. ¼ in. long, sec. n. oblique, more or less distinct. Fl. densely rusty-tomentose, ♂ in small compact fascicles, ⅜ in. long, calyx large, teeth broad as long as tube, edges reflexed; ♀ solitary, broad, ⅓–½ in. long, ovary densely rufous-tomentose, style cylindric, stigmas 4. Fr. globose 1 in. diam., calyx not enlarged nor foliaceous.

Sispara, Nilgiris. Travancore, common in evergreen forests at 3,500 ft. 2. **D. insignis,** Thwaites; Bedd. Ic. t. 130. Anamalais, Travancore, Ceylon. A large tree, youngest shoots appressed-pubescent. L. glabrous, blade 4–12, pet. stout ¼ in. long. Fl. nearly sessile, 4-merous, ♂ in crowded clusters, ♀ solitary or in pairs, ovary 8-celled. fr. 1¼ in. diam. supported by the woody calyx, forming a shallow cup.

3. **D. oocarpa,** Thwaites; Trimen Handb. Ceylon iii. 97.

A middle-sized tree, young shoots minutely puberulous, l. chartaceous,

FIG. 164. Diospyros nilagirica, Bedd. $\frac{1}{2}$.

glabrous, shining, ovate, blade 3–6, pet. $\frac{1}{3}$ in. Fl.: ♂ in small rusty tomentose cymes with large long-ciliate bracts, cal. cylindrical, nearly truncate, corolla tubular, tomentose outside; ♀ solitary, calyx cupshaped, truncate, fr. ovoid-cylindric, 1 by $\frac{1}{2}$ in., supported by the cup-shaped slightly enlarged calyx, albumen uniform.

Evergreen forests of the Western Ghats from the Konkan southwards. Fl. Jan.–March. Ceylon. Heartwood regularly streaked with black bands, somewhat like *Calamander* wood, the produce of *D. quæsita*, Thw., a large tree of the moist low country of Ceylon.

β. ♂ fl. in pedunculate panicles.

4. **D. paniculata**, Dalz.; Bedd. Ic. t. 125.

A middle-sized, at times a tall tree, glabrous, except inflorescence. L. chartaceous or coriaceous, elliptic-oblong, blade 4–7, pet. broad $\frac{1}{3}$ in. long, closely reticulate raised veins between the sec. nerves, conspicuous on both surfaces. Fl. large, pentamerous, calyx of both sexes large with reflexed edges, corolla hairy. ♂ in long drooping bracteate pubescent panicled cymes, bracts large, foliaceous, peduncle $1\frac{1}{2}$ in. long, stamens 20, glabrous in pairs. ♀ solitary, sometimes in pairs, on bracteate pedicels $\frac{2}{3}$ in. long. Fr. hairy while young, ovoid $1\frac{1}{2}$ in. long, supported by the enlarged foliaceous calyx.

Evergreen forests along the Western Ghats, from the Konkan southwards. Common in Travancore. Fl. Dec.–March. Wood streaked with black.

(*b*) Corolla of ♂ fl. hairy, l. hairy.

5. **D. pruriens**, Dalz.; Bedd. Ic. t. 129. Western Ghats from North Kanara southwards, in evergreen forests, very common throughout the Wainad. Ceylon. A small or middle-sized tree, branchlets villous with long yellowish hairs, l. chartaceous, elliptic-oblong, 2–4 in. long when full grown, softly tomentose beneath, chiefly along midrib and sec. n., pet. short. Fl. 4- or 5-merous, calyx hairy on both sides, corolla

FIG. 165. Diospyros paniculata, Dalz. ½.

½–¾ in. long, densely silky outside, segments longer than tube. ♂ in the axils of the upper l., 1 or 2 together, stamens 14, glabrous, filaments on a fleshy torus, which surrounds the hairy ovary rudiment, unequal in length, the 5–6 longer ones (often variously connate) forming an inner circle. ♀ solitary, pedicels up to ¼ in. long, ovary hairy. Fr. ovoid, ⅜–1 in. long, densely clothed with stinging hairs, calyx scarcely enlarged.

6. **D. stricta,** Roxb. Silhet. Tipperah. A tall tree, trunk straight to the top, branchlets and petioles softly tomentose, leaves more or less hairy, membranous, ovate-lanceolate, long-acuminate, blade 8–4, pet. ⅓ in. Fl. 4-merous, white, ♂ sessile, in axillary hirsute bracteate cymes, calyx and corolla hirsute, stamens 14–16, glabrous, single, filaments as long as anthers. Fr. glabrous, ovoid, 1¼ in., on a stout stalk ¼ in. long, supported by the small hairy 4-lobed calyx, albumen uniform.

(*c*) Corolla of ♂ fl. with lines of hairs along midrib of lobes, otherwise glabrous.

7. **D. Chloroxylon,** Roxb. Cor. Pl. t. 49.—Syn. *D. capitulata*, Wight Ic. t. 1224 ♂, 1588 (bis) ♀. Vern. *Nensi*, *Ninai*, Mar.; *Ullingi*, *Ullinda*, *Valinda*, Tel.

A shrub or small tree, axillary spines and spinescent branches frequent, branchlets densely rusty-tomentose. L. thinly coriaceous, upperside pubescent, underside rusty-tomentose, elliptic or obovate, blade 1–2, pet. ⅕–⅓ in. long. Fl. very small, white, 4-merous, sessile or nearly so, calyx cleft nearly to the base, strigose outside with stiff hairs, ♂ in small axillary clusters of 6–10 fl., corolla ⅛–⅙ in. long, glabrous outside, except 4 longitudinal lines of stiff hairs, segments erect, stamens 16, in 2 rows, slightly connate at the base in pairs, anthers ovate-lanceolate, as long as filaments, ♀ solitary, corolla and ovary glabrous. Fr. $\frac{1}{3}$ in. diam., edible, albumen uniform.

Western Peninsula, extending north to the Nasik and Chanda districts and to Orissa. Fl. R. S.

8. **D. microphylla**, Bedd. Ic. t. 133. Western Ghats, from North Kanara southwards, in evergreen forests. Malay Peninsula and Archip. A large tree, attaining 100 ft., stem straight, buttressed at base, branchlets hirsute with long yellowish hairs, l. membranous, almost sessile, 1–2 in. long, with long soft hairs along midrib and margin, hairy all over when young. Fl. small, nearly sessile, ♂ in short 3- or 4-fld. axillary cymes, corolla hairy along midrib and edge of segments, otherwise glabrous, stamens glabrous, 16, in pairs, filaments longer than the ovate anthers. ♀ solitary, upper portion of ovary pubescent. Fr. ovoid, 1-seeded, $\frac{1}{3}$–$\frac{1}{2}$ in. long, albumen uniform.

(*d*) Corolla of ♂ fl. glabrous or slightly pubescent, stamens in pairs, l. glabrous or pubescent.

9. **D. montana**, Roxb. Cor. Pl. t. 48.; Wight Ic. t. 1225. — Syn. *D. cordifolia*, Roxb. Cor. Pl. t. 50; Wight Ill. t. 148. Vern. *Bistendu*, Hind.; *Tembhurni*, Mar.; *Pudu Maddi*, *Mulla Tumiki*, Tel.; *Vakkanai*, Tam.; *Tawbut*, *Chôk*, Burm.

Fig. 166. Diospyros Chloroxylon, Roxb. $\frac{1}{2}$.

A large shrub or small tree, branches sometimes spinescent. Branchlets and young l. softly tomentose. L. bitter (Kanjilal), thinly chartaceous, ovate-oblong, base rounded or cordate, blade 2–4, pet. slender, $\frac{1}{5}$–$\frac{1}{3}$ in. long, sec. n. 6–8 pair slender. Fl. white, as a rule 4-merous, ♂ in velvety, shortly pedunculate or nearly sessile, usually 2–8-fld. cymes, with small bracts and bracteoles, pedicels shorter than calyx, buds conical, calyx deeply 4-fid, segments obtuse, velvety on both sides. Corolla $\frac{1}{4}$ in. long, campanulate, outside glabrous or pubescent, lobes short, spreading. Anthers 16, slightly hairy, in 8 pairs. ♀ solitary, drooping on short pedicels, calyx-segments ovate $\frac{1}{4}$ in. long, corolla nearly glabrous outside, ovary glabrous. Fr. bitter, not edible, $\frac{1}{2}$–1 in. diam., yellow when ripe, supported by the enlarged foliaceous calyx-lobes, albumen uniform.

Subhimalayan tract from the Ravi eastwards. Rajputana and the Southern Punjab. Not in the arid region of Sind. Fl. March–May. Malay Archip. Tropical Australia. Varies exceedingly in shape and hairiness. A common form with cordate-based, usually more tomentose l. is by some botanists regarded as a distinct species (*D. cordifolia*). Another sp. allied to *montana*, probably new, was found by Collett at Meiktila, Upper Burma, l. rigidly chartaceous, sec. n. 8–12 pair, reticulate veins conspicuous on both surfaces, fl. (♂ only) dull orange, in compact cymes, corolla elongate-campanulate $\frac{1}{3}$–$\frac{1}{2}$ in. long. A second allied species with orange col'd scented fl. is a large shrub or small tree (Môn, Burm.) sent by Smales from Upper Burma, the ♂ cymes often producing a profusion of small hairy l. in the place of fl.

10. **D. sylvatica**, Roxb. Cor. Pl. t. 47; Bedd. Ic. Pl. Ind. Or. t. 121. Vern. *Thella Gada*, Tel.; *Kaka suroli*, Kan.

A middle-sized, at times a large tree, branchlets nearly glabrous. L. chartaceous or thinly coriaceous, glabrous or slightly puberulous, elliptic, acuminate, blade 2–4, narrowed into petiole $\frac{1}{4}$ in. long (in coppice shoots much larger), sec. n. slender but distinct. ♂ buds nearly globose, cymes pedunculate, many-fld., corolla white, nearly glabrous, urceolate, ♀ solitary, calyx similar to but larger than in ♂. Fr. globose, $\frac{1}{2}$–$\frac{3}{4}$ in. diam., supported by the enlarged spreading foliaceous often striate calyx-lobes, albumen ruminate.

Western Peninsula, extending north as far as Bombay and Orissa. Fl. C. S. Ceylon, moist low country. 11. A tree with glabrous branchlets, l. glabrous, chartaceous, elongate-elliptic, blade 4–6, pet. ¼ in. long, sec. n. slender but prominent beneath, fr. 1–1½ in. diam., supported by the spreading foliaceous calyx-segments, albumen not ruminate, has been collected in Dehra Dún (Kanjilal 1070, the species mentioned under *D. montana* on p. 221 of his F. Flora) and in (in fr. only) the Ganjam district (Gamble 13675).

(*e*) Corolla of ♂ fl. glabrous.

α. L. membranous.

12. **D. Lotus,** Linn.; Brandis F. Fl. t. 36. Vern. *Amlōk*, Punj.

A middle-sized deciduous tree, branchlets and underside of young l. with scattered hairs. L. membranous, elliptic-oblong, acuminate, blade 3–6, pet. slender, ½ in. long, sec. n. slender, 6–8 pair, tertiary not raised on the underside of l., closely and elegantly reticulate. Fl. nearly sessile, ♂ in small clusters. Calyx similar in ♂ and ♀, lobed half-way down, slightly pubescent. Corolla glabrous outside, stamens 16, anthers lanceolate, cuspidate, connective hispid on both faces. ♀ solitary, staminodes hairy. Ovary glabrous, only hairy at apex. Fr. sweet, edible, globose or ovoid, ½–¾ in. diam., dark purple when ripe, with a blueish bloom, supported by the enlarged flat calyx.

Western Asia, extending as far as Hazara and Kashmir in the North West Himalaya. Fl. April, May. China. Cultivated on account of its fruit in the Punjab and in the Mediterranean Region. 13. **D. Kaki,** Linn. f.; Wight Ic. t. 415. *Tayōk Tè*, Burm. Khasi hills. Upper Burma. China and Japan, where numerous varieties are cultivated. Similar to 12, branchlets and l. softly pubescent or tomentose, fl. pedicellate, calyx deeply 4-fid, densely silky, corolla tomentose outside near apex, ♂ in clusters of 1–3, often solitary, stamens 16–24, filaments and connective hairy. Fr. red or yellow, edible. The (unripe ?) fr. used in China to make hats and umbrellas watertight.

β. L. chartaceous or coriaceous.

14. **D. ehretioides,** Wall. *Aukchinza* Burm. Pegu. Tenasserim. A large tree, wood grey with darker streaks. Branchlets and l. glabrous, l. thickly chartaceous, brown beneath when dry, elliptic, base rounded, blade 6–13, petiole stout ⅜ in. long, sec. n. 10–12 pair, distinctly anastomosing under the edge. Fl. 4-merous, ovary 8-celled, fr. globose, 1 in. diam. 15. **D. orixensis,** Wight (*D. humilis*, Bourdillon in Journ. Bombay Nat. Hist. Soc. xii. 352 t. 6). Courtallum. Travancore, evergreen forest 2,000 ft. (Bourdillon 593, 595, 893). A small tree, branchlets softly tomentose, l. chartaceous, ovate-lanceolate, blade 2–4, pet. ⅛ in., glabrous except the hairy petiole and midrib on the underside. Fl. white, 4- or 5-merous, calyx divided nearly to the base, segments obtuse, glabrous or sparsely hairy outside, edges ciliate, corolla glabrous. ♂ in few-fld. hairy cymes, corolla narrowly tubular, ¼–⅓ in. long, stamens 12–20, glabrous, anthers small, ovate, shorter than filaments, these connate in pairs, and more or less connate at base into a short tube. ♀ on short bracteolate pedicels, corolla ovoid, ⅓ in. long, ovary glabrous, 4–5-celled. Fr. globose, ½–⅔ in. diam., calyx-segments appressed, not enlarged in fr., slightly hairy outside. 16. **D. Toposia,** Ham.; Bedd. Ic. t. 122.—Syn. *D. racemosa*, Roxb.; Wight Ic. t. 416. Khasi hills. Cachar. Chittagong. Tinnevelli hills (Bedd.). Ceylon moist region. An evergreen middle-sized tree, branchlets glabrous, l. coriaceous, glabrous, elliptic-lanceolate, blade 4–8, pet. ⅓–½ in., closely reticulate raised veins conspicuous on both surfaces. Fl. white, tetramerous, buds globose, glabrous, minutely tuberculate, the calyx completely closed in bud and rupturing irregularly. ♂ in lax pedunculate cymes; corolla glabrous, coriaceous, ovoid-urceolate, teeth short, stamens 32, in pairs, anthers linear, glabrous. ♀ sometimes in pairs, ovary hairy. Fr. 1–1½ in. diam., seeds 4, albumen uniform.

B. Calyx of ♂ and ♀ dissimilar.

(*a*) Corolla of ♂ fl. tomentose, stamens single.

17. **D. melanoxylon,** Roxb. Cor. Pl. t. 46.—Syn. *D. Wightiana*, Wall.; Bedd. Fl. Sylv. t. 67; *D. dubia*, Wall.; Wight Ic. t. 1223; *D. exsculpta*, Bedd. Fl. Sylv. t. 66 (probably). *The Ebony of Northern India.* Vern. *Tendu Abnūs* (the wood), Hind.; *Tumri*, Gond.; *Timburui*, Mar.; *Tumiki*, Tel.

A middle-sized deciduous tree attaining 50 ft., and 6 ft. in girth, bark dark grey or black, exfoliating in rectangular scales, branchlets and inflorescence clothed with soft grey or ferrugineous tomentum. L. mostly opposite, thickly coriaceous, tomentose on both sides while young, hairy or glabrous on the underside when full grown, elliptic or ovate, blade 3–12, pet. ⅓ in., sec. n. 6–10 pair, as well as the reticulate tertiary n. raised on the upper side. Fl. 4–6-merous, ♂ in short cymes, calyx woolly, campanulate or cup-shaped, corolla tubular, ferrugineous woolly outside, stamens 12–16. Female fl. solitary, calyx broad, edges recurved, ovary densely hairy. Fr. globose or ovoid, 1–1¼ in. diam., yellow when ripe, supported by the thickly coriaceous calyx, the segments with more or less recurved edges. Seeds 4–8, compressed, oblong, testa rugose, shining, albumen ruminate.

Common in deciduous forests of the Central provinces, Chutia Nagpore, Behar and the Western Peninsula. Fl. April–June.—Ceylon, rare. C. B. Clarke in Fl. Brit. Ind. iii. 563, separates *D. Tupru*, Ham. (Peninsula, *Tapa rada*, Kan.) by smaller l., obtuse at both ends, densely fulvous woolly while young. 18. **D. tomentosa,** Roxb.; Wight Ic. tt. 182, 183. Kanjilal F. Fl. 222. Vern. *Tendu*, Hind. Subhimalayan tract, Ravi to Nepal. Eastern Rajputana, Central provinces. Chutia Nagpore, Behar. Orissa, Northern Circars, Poona. Sec. and tertiary n. impressed as deep furrows on the upper surface of full grown l. According to Gamble, Indian Timbers Ed. ii. 462, the wood is less heavy than that of *D. Melanoxylon*. In my old F. Fl. I united 17 and 18, and I doubt whether they are really distinct. Both species coppice well and throw up root-suckers in large numbers, they often occupy patches of considerable extent to the exclusion of other trees. In the centre of old stems are found (but not always) irregularly shaped masses of jet-black ebony, often with purple streaks.

19. **D. burmanica,** Kurz. Vern. *Tè*, Burm.

A small or middle-sized deciduous tree, branches stiff and hard, almost spinescent, branchlets, petioles, underside of l. and inflorescence densely clothed with fine tawny tomentum, hairs frequently affixed in the middle. L. chartaceous, elliptic-oblong, when full grown shining and almost glabrous on the upper side, blade 3–5, pet. ⅙ in., sec. n. slender, joined by closely reticulate veins, both more conspicuous on the upper than on the underside. Fl. greyish-green, buds conical, calyx and corolla densely tomentose outside. Calyx of ♂ cup-shaped, lobes 4, triangular, of ♀ much broader, lobes 4–6, edges reflexed, ovary woolly. Fr. 1–1½ in. diam., globose, 2–4-seeded, albumen ruminate.

Burma, Upper and Lower. Common in the open country with grass or scrub, as well as in the Eng forest. Fl. March–May. Throws up abundant root-suckers, the seeds yield oil.

20. **D. affinis,** Thwaites; Bedd. Ic. t. 127. Tinnevelli Ghats. Ceylon. A middle-sized tree, youngest shoots slightly pilose, l. thinly coriaceous, glabrous, shining, elongate-elliptic, blade 2–3½, pet. ⅛ in. long. Fl. hairy, 4-merous, ♂ pedicellate, in small lax axillary cymes, calyx campanulate, segments short acute, stamens 9, single, glabrous. ♀ on pedicels ⅓ in. long, calyx 4-fid nearly to the base, segments long acuminate, edges reflexed. Fr. 1 in. diam., albumen ruminate. 21. **D. crumenata,** Thwaites; Bedd. Ic. t. 126; Talbot in Journ. Bombay Nat. Hist. Soc. vol. xi. 692 t. 14. Evergreen forests of North Kanara. *Kan tumri*, Kan. A large tree attaining 150 ft., differs from 20 chiefly by more numerous stamens, 12–16, the ♀ calyx-segments apiculate, and fr. 2–2½ in. diam. It seems not improbable that 20 and 21 may eventually be united.

(*b*) Corolla of ♂ fl. tomentose, stamens in pairs.

22. **D. lanceæfolia,** Roxb. Upper Assam. Khasi hills. Cachar. Manipur. Upper Tenasserim (Kurz). A middle-sized tree, youngest shoots pubescent. L. coriaceous, glabrous, lanceolate, blade 4–6, pet. ⅓ in., midrib deeply impressed on the upper surface. Fl. 4- or 5-merous, sessile, calyx and corolla tomentose, ♂ in few-fld. axillary clusters, calyx cup-shaped, segments triangular, corolla ⅓–½ in. long, anthers in pairs, filam. and connective slightly hairy, ♀ solitary, calyx-segments broad, margin reflexed, fr. ovoid, 1 in. long, rusty-tomentose, supported by the enlarged spreading calyx. 23. **D. undulata,** Wall. Tenasserim, Andamans. A large evergreen tree, l. glabrous, coriaceous, ovate-oblong, blade 8–14, pet. ½ in. long. Fl. 4-merous, tomentose, ♂ pedicelled in short bracteate tomentose cymes, calyx cup-shaped, segments triangular, hairy on both sides. Corolla ⅓–½ in. long, anthers in pairs, 10–14, rudiment of ovary with long hairs. ♀ solitary, fr. hairy, 1–1¼ in. long, supported by the thick woody fruiting calyx.

(c) Corolla of ♂ glabrous, stamens in pairs or in bundles.

24. **D. Ebenum,** Koenig; Wight Ic. t. 188; Bedd. Fl. Sylv. t. 65. *Ebony.*

A large tree, bark dark grey, youngest shoots with fine soft hairs. L. thinly coriaceous, glabrous, elliptic-oblong, blade 2–4, pet. ⅕ in., minutely reticulate raised veins conspicuous on both surfaces. Fl. 4-merous, ♂ sessile 5–6 in shortly stalked clusters, calyx cup-shaped, segments short, obtuse, ciliate, corolla glabrous, anthers about 16, glabrous, connate in pairs, sometimes in threes, ♀ solitary, calyx-segments long, acute, in fr. much enlarged and deflexed. Fr. ½–¾ in. diam., the enlarged calyx forming a shallow woody cup, from the back of which project the thick acute segments, albumen uniform.

Hills of the Deccan, extending north to the Cuddapah and Karnūl districts, not common. Ceylon, chiefly in the dry region, common and often gregarious. Heartwood jet black without streaks. 25. **D. assimilis,** Bedd. in Madras For. Rep. 1866–7. 20 t. 1. *Kara mara*, Kan. Evergreen forests of the Western Ghats from the Konkan southwards. A moderate sized tree, heartwood jet black, l. chartaceous, anthers 20–30 connate in 8 bundles. Yields ebony in Kanara and Travancore.

26. **D. Embryopteris,** Pers.; Bedd. Fl. Sylv. t. 69.—Syn. *Embryopteris glutinifera*, Roxb. Cor. Pl. t. 70; Wight Ic. t. 843, 844. Vern. *Gāb, Kala Tendu*, Hind.; *Timbūri*, Mar.; *Niti tumiki*, Tel.; *Panicha*, Mal.

An evergreen middle-sized tree, buds silky with appressed hairs. L. distichous, coriaceous, glabrous, shining, oblong, blade 5–8, pet. wrinkled when dry, ⅓–½ in. long, closely reticulate veins conspicuous on both sides. Fl. as a rule 4-merous, white or cream-coloured, scented, calyx hairy, corolla glabrous, ♂ in axillary pedunculate cymes of 3–6 fl., calyx cup-shaped, stamens 32–64, in pairs, anthers linear hairy, much longer than filaments. ♀ larger, usually solitary, sometimes in pairs, sepals cordate, dilated at the base, ovary hairy. Fr. yellow when ripe, 1½–2 in. diam., seeds 5–8, embedded in a viscid pulp, sweet when ripe.

Subhimalayan tract from the Jumna to the Tista, chiefly in ravines and moist shady places. Central India. Western Peninsula, common in the Northern Circars. On the west side in the evergreen forest of the Ghats and near creeks and backwaters on the coast. Martaban and Tenasserim. Fl. March–Aug. The pulp of the unripe fr. is used as gum and in the place of tar for paying the seams of boats.—Ceylon, low country, common in the dry region. Siam. Malay Archip. Var. *atrata*, Travancore, evergreen forest above 4,000 ft. Tenasserim, Ceylon. Inflorescence, chiefly ♂, densely clothed with black sooty hair. 27. **D. foliolosa,** Wall.—Syn. *D. calycina*, Bedd. Fl. Sylv. t. 68 and Ic. t. 123. Hills of Madura and Tinnevelli districts. A middle-sized tree, branchlets and l. glabrous. L. thinly coriaceous, lanceolate, blade 4, pet. ⅙–¼ in., closely reticulate raised veins conspicuous on both surfaces. Fl. ♂ in peduculate lax 8–9-fld. cymes, half as long as leaf, calyx small 4-toothed, corolla bright yellow, anthers 12–16, in pairs, rudiment, ovary 5-lobed, long acuminate. ♀ solitary, calyx of 4 sometimes 3 large cordate sepals, ovary hairy 4-celled. Fr. ⅜ in. diam. calyx often longer than fr.

II. Female fl. in short, 2–10-fld. cymes in the axils of l. or fallen l.

28. **D. Candolleana,** Wight Ic. t. 1221–2.—Syn. *D. canarica*, Bedd. Ic. Pl. Ind. Or. t. 134.

A small tree, young shoots and midrib of l. underneath with fine hairs, as a rule affixed in the middle. L. coriaceous, nearly glabrous, elliptic-oblong, blade 4–7, pet. ¼ in. long, sec. n. faint, numerous, more visible on the upper than on the underside of l. Fl. 5-merous, densely tomentose, ♂ ⅓ in. long, numerous, in dense, often globose axillary fascicles, calyx-teeth short, edges not reflexed, corolla tubular, yellow tomentose without, stamens 10–12, filaments connate in pairs, connective long-cuspidate, ♀ in short axillary 2–10-fld. cymes, fr. globose 1 in. diam., segments of fruiting calyx triangular, hairy outside, edges reflexed, albumen ruminate.

Scrub and evergreen forests along the Western Coast and foot of Ghats from the Konkan southwards, ascending to 1,000 ft. Fl. March–May. Also on Mahendragiri,

Ganjam district (Gamble No. 13916). 29. **D. ovalifolia,** Wight Ic. t. 1227. Hills of the Peninsula, chiefly on the West side, common in places. A middle-sized tree, heartwood streaked with black, branchlets glabrous. L. coriaceous, glabrous, elongate-elliptic, blade 4–5, pet. $\frac{1}{4}$ in., sec. n. prominent beneath. Fl. cream-coloured, 4- or 5-merous, sessile, in clusters of 2–6 in the axils of fallen l. ♀ sometimes solitary, calyx pubescent, edges of segments ciliate, corolla entirely glabrous. ♂ cal. cup-shaped, segments obtuse, glabrous inside, stamens 14–20, free, glabrous, anthers linear, much longer than filaments. ♀ cal. lobed to the base, densely tomentose within, ovary tomentose 4-celled. Fr. glabrous, $\frac{3}{4}$ in. diam., segments of enlarged calyx thick, reflexed, densely tomentose on both sides, seed usually 1, albumen uniform.

30. **D. Kurzii,** Hiern ; *Andaman Marble or Zebra wood.*

A large evergreen tree, bark grey, smooth, thin, heartwood streaked black and grey, branchlets, petioles and midrib beneath minutely pubescent. L. chartaceous, drying black, elliptic-oblong, acuminate, blade 2–3, pet. slender, $\frac{1}{4}$ in. long, sec. n. slender, numerous, close together. Fl. (♀ only known) 4-merous, in 2–3-fld. short-peduncled cymes, calyx nearly glabrous, corolla $\frac{1}{8}$ in. long, velvety outside. Fr. $\frac{1}{2}$ in. diam., albumen uniform.

Andamans, frequent. Nicobars. Coco islands. Fl. May, June. 31. **D. Helferi,** C. B. Clarke. Tenasserim (or Andamans). Cambodia. Branchlets pubescent, l. nearly glabrous, coriaceous, oblong, blade 4–6, pet. $\frac{1}{4}$–$\frac{1}{3}$ in. long, fl. (♀ only known) sessile, 2 or 3 together, on short pubescent protuberances, calyx divided to the base into 5 ovate-oblong lobes, velvety at back, cor. hairy outside $\frac{1}{2}$ in. long.

III. Female fl. in many-fld. compound cymes usually on the old wood.

32. **D. Brandisiana,** Kurz. Evergreen forest on the hills between Yunzalin and Salwin rivers 3,000 ft., also in the Domdamee district. Upper Burma. A middle-sized evergreen tree, l. thinly chartaceous, slightly pubescent beneath. Fl. white, fragrant, 4- or 5-merous, in pedunculate cymes from irregular woody protuberances on the trunk or branches, pedicels longer than calyx. Calyx cleft to the base, segments lanceolate, corolla $\frac{1}{3}$–$\frac{1}{2}$ in. long, narrowly tubular, pubescent outside, lobes oblong nearly as long as tube. 33. **D. ramiflora,** Roxb. *Uri-gāb, Gulal.* Beng. Wight Ic. t. 189. Khasi hills, Tipperah. A large tree, l. thinly coriaceous, glabrous, shining, blade 4–8, pet. $\frac{1}{3}$ in., sec. n. arching, slender, but distinct. Fl. cream-coloured, 5- or 6-merous, in dense compact cymes on the old branches, pedicels bracteolate, not longer than calyx. ♀ calyx campanulate, thickly coriaceous, like pedicels clothed with dark olive-coloured tomentum, teeth triangular, shorter than tube. Corolla thick fleshy in the upper part, $\frac{1}{3}$–$\frac{1}{2}$ in. long, tomentose outside, ovary densely hairy. Fr. as large as an orange, on the thick orbicular calyx, seeds 10–12, in a yellow edible pulp. 34. **D. Bourdilloni,** sp. nova. Travancore evergreen forests below 1,000 ft., common. A large tree, no black heartwood, youngest shoots strigose with delicate hairs, mostly affixed in the middle. L. glabrous, coriaceous, elliptic-oblong, short-acuminate, blade 2–3½, pet. $\frac{1}{4}$ in. long, nerves almost invisible. Fl. 5-merous, ♂ shortly pedicellate in short rusty-tomentose axillary cymes, calyx divided beyond the middle, segments acute, tomentose outside, and inside along the edges, corolla ovoid-campanulate, tomentose outside, glabrous inside, tube ovoid-campanulate, $\frac{1}{3}$–$\frac{1}{2}$ in. long, lobes spreading, $\frac{1}{3}$ the length of tube, velvety on both surfaces. ♀ on pedicels much longer than calyx in compound cymes on the old wood, calyx and corolla similar to ♂, but slightly larger. Fr. upwards of 3 in. diam., supported by the hard woody pentagonal calyx 1½–2 in. across, cells 9–10. This is the species mentioned in Beddome's Manual 146 from the Anamalais and Tinnevelli Ghats.

35. **D. Horsfieldii,** Hiern. Tenasserim (Kurz) Malay Penins. Java. L. rigidly coriaceous, glabrous, shining above, elongate-elliptic, blade 8–10, pet. $\frac{1}{4}$ in., midrib, sec. and tertiary n. very prominent beneath, impressed on the upper surface. Fl. both ♂ and ♀ in compound cymes, the ♀ cymes large, up to 4 in. long. 36. **D. densiflora,** Wall. Lower Burma, rare (Kurz), similar, l. smaller, nerves elevated on the upper surface.

IV. Not sufficiently known to be classified.

A. branchlets and l. glabrous.

37. **D. flavicans,** Hiern. Mergui. Malay Peninsula. A shrub or small tree, branchlets nearly glabrous, l. chartaceous, glabrous, copper-coloured beneath when dry, elongate-elliptic, acuminate, blade 3–4, pet. $\frac{1}{8}$ in. Male fl. white, 4- or 5-merous, calyx and corolla pubescent outside, bracts large foliaceous, calyx-lobes ovate, auriculate, corolla slender, $\frac{1}{2}$ in. long. 38. **D. sapotoides,** Kurz. Eastern slopes of Pegu Yoma. A middle-sized evergreen tree, leaflets hairy, branchlets glabrous, l. thinly coriaceous, glabrous, elongate-elliptic, blade 6–10, pet. $\frac{1}{4}$ in., sec. n. joined by distinct intra-

marginal veins. Male fl. 4-merous, nearly sessile, densely clustered, supported by small ovate bracts, calyx-segments ovate-lanceolate, edges reflexed, corolla ⅓–½ in. long, densely silky on the 4 angles. 39. **D. variegata**, Kurz. Assam. Pegu and Martaban. A large tree, shedding l. in H. S. (Kurz), branchlets glabrous. L. thinly coriaceous, glabrous, oblong, blade 5–8, pet. stout, ⅓–½ in. long, sec. n. prominent beneath. Male fl. yellow, 2–4 together on short bracteolate pedicels, calyx deeply 4-cleft, corolla ⅓ in. long, lobes as long as tube. 40. **D. oleifolia**, Wall. (*Chôk*, Burm.) Martaban and Tenasserim. A large evergreen tree, branchlets glabrous, l. coriaceous glabrous, polished, elliptic-lanceolate, blade 4–6, pet. ¼ in., sec. n. obscure. Male fl. white, 4-merous, shortly pedicelled in short 3-fld. axillary cymes. Young fr. densely tomentose. 41. Bourdillon's No. 615, Travancore 2,000 ft., probably new, a middle-sized black stemmed tree, l. glabrous, coriaceous, elliptic-oblong, acuminate, blade 4–5, pet. ¼ in. ♂ fl. only known, in compact almost globose hairy cymes, 5-merous, buds globose, calyx deeply 5-lobed, corolla short, hairy outside, stamens glabrous.

B. Branchlets and underside of young l. hairy, mature l. glabrous, at least on the upper surface.

(*a*) Leaves less than 4 inches long.

42. **D. Packmanni**, C. B. Clarke. Tavoy. Branchlets, young l., petioles and inflorescence clothed with dense ferrugineous wool, which gradually disappears from the upper side, but remains on midrib and nerves beneath. ♂ fl. pentamerous in threes on short peduncles, calyx and corolla densely ferrugineous woolly, stamens 16, in pairs. 43. **D. nigricans**, Wall. Khasi hills. Branchlets and petiole grey-pubescent. L. chartaceous, nearly glabrous, elliptic-lanceolate, blade 3–4, pet. ⅛ in. ♂ corolla tubular, nearly glabrous. Fr. nearly sessile, ellipsoid, ⅜ in. long, calyx-lobes ovate, foliaceous, nearly glabrous, black when dry. 44. **D. pilosula**, Wall. (*Gunisanthus pilosulus*, DC.). Khasi hills. Andamans. Pegu Yomah (*Gjut*, Burm.) A small tree, branchlets, petiole and midrib on the underside hairy, l. chartaceous, lanceolate or oblanceolate, 2–4 in. long, pet. short. Fl. ♂ and ♀ solitary, dull orange or yellow, calyx-segments lanceolate, ¼ in. long, young fr. densely rufous-hirsute.

(*b*) Leaves more than 4 in. long.

45. **D. martabanica**, C. B. Clarke (*Gunisanthus mollis*, Kurz). Thaukyeghat forests east of Toungoo. Donat range, Tenasserim. A small tree, branchlets densely villous, l. oblong-lanceolate, 4–6 in. long, pet. very short. Fl. (♂ only known) ochre-yellow, densely pubescent outside, solitary near the ends of branchlets, having the appearance (after the l. have fallen) of racemes, bracts ovate, deciduous, pedicels ⅓–⅜ in., calyx-lobes linear-lanceolate, corolla-tube slender, ⅓–½ in., lobes narrow, as long as tube. 46. **D. dasyphylla**, Kurz. Hills east of Toungoo 4,000 ft. Branchlets and petioles tawny-tomentose, l. glabrous above, chartaceous, pubescent beneath, from a cordate base elliptic-oblong, blade 5–6, pet. ¼ in. long. Male fl. sessile, 2–4 together, calyx deeply 4-lobed, rusty-tomentose, as well as the corolla, which is ¾ in. long, lobes as long as tube.

47. A tree or climber, (*Neyarum*), evergreen forests on the Periyar river, Travancore (Bourdillon 1268, ♂ fl. only). Fl. white, very fragrant, 4-merous, in short axillary racemes with obtuse imbricating bracts, calyx segments divided to near the base, obtuse, like the bracts ciliate on the edges and pubescent outside, corolla ¼ in. long, hairy, stamens 12-14, filaments unequal, connate in 2 or 3 bundles.

(*c*) Mature l. hairy on both surfaces.

48. **D. mollis**, Griff., Journ. Agri. and Hort. Soc. of India iii. 145. Kurz F. Fl. ii. 130 Martaban hills 2–4,000 ft. Upper Burma. Siam. A shrub or middle-sized tree, heartwood jet black, branchlets and l. on both sides softly pubescent,. L. membranous, ovate or ovate-lanceolate, blade 2–5, narrowed into pet. ¼ in. long. Fl. small, pale yellow, ♂ tetramerous, in short densely pubescent 3- or more fld. cymes. Fr. globose, ¾ in. diam., supported by the deflexed coriaceous calyx, lobes rounded, concave underneath. The fr. yields the black dye of the Shans.

2. MABA, J. R. et G. Forster; Fl. Brit. Ind. iii. 550.

Differs from *Diospyros* by the flowers 3- rarely 4-merous, ovary 3- or imimperfectly 6-celled, ovules 6. Species 60, tropics of both Hemispheres.

A. Ovary densely hairy.

1. **M. buxifolia**, Persoon; Wight Ic. t. 763; Bedd. Manual t. 19.—Syn. *M. neilgherrensis*, Wight Ill. t. 148, bis; *M. Ebenus*, Wight Ic. t. 1228–9; *Ferreola buxifolia*, Roxb. Cor. Pl. t. 45. *Uti*, Tel.; *Irambali*, Tam. Western Peninsula, extending to Orissa on the east side, common in the semi-evergreen scrub of the Coromandel coast. Martaban, Tenasserim. Ceylon, Malay Penins. and Archip. A much branched shrub or small tree, branchlets nearly glabrous, l. coriaceous, very variable in size and shape, ¼–1 in. long, petiole very short. Fl. small, white, pinkish or yellowish, 3-merous, calyx hairy, segments triangular, acute, corolla twice as long as calyx, campanulate, hairy outside. Fr. ovoid, red, ⅜ in. diam. 2. **M. nigrescens**, Dalz. Western Ghats from the Konkan to South Kanara, in evergreen forests. A large shrub or small tree, branchlets, petiole and midrib beneath with long fulvous hairs, l. lanceolate, blade 2–3, pet. ⅛ in. long, reticulate veins distinctly visible on both sides. Fl. ♂ 3–4-merous, corolla ⅛ in. long, stamens 4–9, ♀ solitary or in pairs, ovary 3-celled. Fr. ovoid ⅜ in. long. 3. **M. andamanica**, Kurz, Andamans, Nicobars. A small shrub, branchlets, petiole and midrib beneath softly tomentose, l. chartaceous, elliptic-oblong, blade 4–8, pet. ⅛ in., sec. n. 6–9 pair, prominent beneath, fr. ellipsoid, more than 1 in. long.

B. Ovary glabrous.

4. **M. micrantha**, Hiern. Western Ghats of the Konkan. A small tree, branchlets glabrous, l. coriaceous, ovate-lanceolate, glabrous, except the minutely puberulous petiole, blade 3–4, pet. ⅛ in. long. 5. **M. merguensis**, Hiern. Mergui. Malay Penins. and Archip. Branchlets nearly glabrous, l. chartaceous, glabrous, ovate-lanceolate, blade 4–6, pet. ⅛ in. Fl. 4- rarely 3-merous, ♂ in dense compound minutely pubescent cymes, ♀ in small cymes, fr. ½ in. long, supported by the thick calyx ½–⅝ in. across, lobed half-way down into 3 or 4 segments.

ORDER LXX. STYRACEÆ. Gen. Pl. ii. 666.

Symplocaceæ and *Styracaceæ*, Gürke in Engler u. Prantl iv. i. pp. 165, 172.

Trees or shrubs, l. alternate, stipules 0. Fl. bisexual, regular, 4–5-merous, calyx campanulate, superior or inferior, limb persistent, petals free or connate. Stamens 10 or numerous, adnate to petals, ovary 2–5-celled, style filiform, ovules 1 or few on the inner angle. Seeds few, albuminous, radicle as long as or longer than cotyledons.

Stellate hairs and flat round peltate scales are frequent. The wood fibres have bordered pits.

Stamens numerous in several series, ovary inferior 3-celled . . . 1. SYMPLOCOS.
Stamens 10 in one series, ovary free, dissepiments reaching only to the middle . . . . 2. STYRAX.

1. SYMPLOCOS, Linn.; Fl. Brit. Ind. iii. 572.

(Brand in Engler, Pflanzenreich iv. 242. 13.)

Leaves often drying yellow. Fl. white or pale yellow, rarely pink, supported by 1–3 bracteoles, and one bract at the base of pedicel. Petals imbricate in bud, in a few species connate into a tube. Stamens numerous, adnate to corolla-tube, often more or less distinctly pentadelphous, anthers short. Ovary inferior, usually 3-celled, ovules 2, pendulous from the inner angle. Drupe with a woody 1–3-seeded endocarp, embryo often curved. Species 282, according to Brand, tropical and subtropical regions of America, Australia and Asia. A few of the Indian species have a wide distribution, the majority have only been found within a restricted area. Not less than 17 sp. endemic in Ceylon.

I. Petals free or nearly so, fl. buds subglobose.

A. Fl. solitary, axillary.

1. **S. villosa**, Brand l.c. 63. Travancore 3–4,000 ft., in moist forests, common (Bourdillon 21, 901). A small tree, branchlets, young shoots, petioles and midrib beneath clothed with long soft spreading hairs, l. lanceolate, blade 2–3, pet. ⅛ in. long. Fl.

white, sessile or nearly so, each fl. supported by 6 lanceolate villous bracts. Fr. ⅜ in. long, narrow-cylindric, crowned by the hairy calyx-lobes. 2. **S. monantha,** Wight Ic. t. 1236. Tinnevelli hills. A much branched shrub, branchlets glabrous, l. glabrous, acuminate, 1–1½ in. long. Fl. sessile or nearly so. 3. **S. anamallayana,** Bedd. Anamalais 5–6,000 ft. A small tree, wholly glabrous, l. 1–2 in. long, fl. white, supported by a pair of bracteoles, on slender pedicels 1 in. long, solitary or 2 in one leaf-axil. Fr. narrow-cylindric ½–⅔ in. long.

B. Fl. in axillary fascicles on short spikes or racemes not over ½ in. long.

(*a*) L. coriaceous.

4. **S. phyllocalyx,** Clarke. *Lal Chandan,* Nep. Sikkim 8–12,000 ft. Bhutan. Yunnan. A small tree, l. glabrous, coriaceous, serrulate, blade 3–4, pet. ⅓–½ in. Fl. in compact bracteate spikes, bracts ovate, persistent. Stamens 40–50, twice the length of corolla. Fr. ½ in. long, crowned by the broad obtuse calyx-teeth. 5. **S. glomerata,** King. Sikkim from the Terai to 9,000 ft. Bhutan. Khasi and Naga hills. Manipur. Yunnan. Tonkin. A small tree, l. glabrous, lanceolate, glandular-serrate, blade 4–5, pet. ½ in. Fl. in dense axillary fascicles, corolla ⅛ in. long, fr. cylindric ¼ in. long, calyx-rim nearly as wide as fr., seed one.

6. **S. microphylla,** Wight Ic. t. 1232. Nilgiris. A densely branched shrub, branchlets glabrous, l. rigidly coriaceous, serrate, elliptic, acute or obtuse, blade 1–2, pet. ¼–⅛ in., sec. and tertiary n. prominent beneath. Fl. white, in compact axillary clusters (short spikes), bracts villous or conspicuously ciliate, calyx glabrous, petals ⅛–¼ in. long. Specimens of this or a new closely allied sp. coll. by me at Mahabaleshwar have l. less rigidly coriaceous, shortly acuminate, nerves not prominent, fl. in sessile axillary fascicles, bracts glabrous, disk glabrous, top of ovary and style hairy, fr. ½ in. long, endocarp thin chartaceous, embryo slightly curved. 7. **S. oligandra,** Bedd. Ic. t. 272. Travancore Ghats. A small or middle-sized tree, l. 2 in. long, fl. small in very short axillary racemes, stamens 12–14, as long as corolla.

(*b*) L. membranous or nearly so.

8. **S. leucantha,** Kurz. Swampy places, Irawadi valley. *Thalè,* Burm. A small tree, l. glabrous, elliptic, acuminate, base slightly unequal, blade 4–5, pet. slender ¼ in. Fl. white, fragrant, in compact tomentose racemes ½ in. long, bracts ovate, pubescent, stamens in 5 bundles opposite to petals. 9. **S. viridissima,** Brand l. c. 41 (included under *S. lancifolia,* in Fl. Brit. Ind. iii. 577). Patkoi range. Yunnan. Japan. A small tree, branchlets glabrous, l. caudate-acuminate, blade 3–4, pet. ¼ in., sec. n. slender, at a distance from edge joined by intramarginal veins. Racemes hairy up to ½ in. long, bracts and calyx hirsute, petals ⅛ in. long, stamens 80–100.

C. Racemes or spikes undivided, over ½ in. long.

(*a*) Fl. white or yellow, l. coriaceous.

α. Fr. ovoid or cylindric, less than 1 in. long.

([1]) Fr. glabrous, l. more than 3 in. long.

10. **S. racemosa,** Roxb.; Vern. *Lodh,* Hind.; *Daukyat,* Burm.

A small evergreen tree, bark thick, spongy. L. glabrous, coriaceous, elliptic-lanceolate, obscurely crenate, blade 4–6, pet. ⅓–⅔ in. Fl. yellow, fragrant in simple hairy axillary more or less lax racemes, pedicels as long as calyx-tube, stamens about 100. Fr. cylindric, nearly ½ in. long.

Subhimalayan tract, Dūns and outer valleys, chiefly in Sāl forest, from the Ganges eastwards, ascending to 3,000 ft. and higher. Oudh forests. Chutia Nagpore. Khasi hills, Manipúr. Lower and Upper Burma, chiefly in Eng forest. L. and bark used in dyeing. Fl. Nov.–Feb. China. 11. **S. subglabra,** Brand l. c. 59. Nilgiris (?), reported to differ by fewer stamens (not seen). 12. **S. Beddomei,** Clarke (*reticulata,*[1] Grah.; Brand l. c. 59). Western Ghats from Mahabaleshwar to Coorg. Similar to 10, l. serrulate, perhaps not specifically distinct. 13. **S. Stocksii,** Brand l. c. 59, Konkan, said to differ by hirsute branchlets. 14. **S. obtusa,** Wall.; Wight Ic. t. 1233. Nilgiris, Anamalais 4–8,000 ft. Ceylon, common in the upper montane zone. A middle-sized tree, glabrous, excepting the ciliate rounded calyx-lobes, l. coriaceous, obovate, sometimes elliptic, obtuse, almost entire, blade 2–4, narrowed into pet. ¼–½ in. Racemes 1–4 in., petals white, ¼ in. long, fr. ovoid-cylindric, ribbed when dry, ⅓ in. long.

---

[1] *S. reticulata,* Grah. does not exist.

15. **S. Huegeliana,** Brand l. c. 57. Nilgiris (probably), reported to differ by 5–7 petals and smaller fr.

16. **S. Sumuntia,** Ham. Nepal. Sikkim, 3–7,000 ft. Bhutan. Assam. Khasi hills, Manipur. Yunnan. A small tree, branchlets glabrous, coriaceous, elliptic-lanceolate, blade 3–5, pet. ¼–⅓ in. Racemes 1½–4 in. long, more or less hirsute, bracts densely villous with long hairs, enveloping the buds, caducous, calyx-teeth much shorter than ovary, both nearly glabrous, petals veined, ⅛–⅙ in. long, stamens 30–40. Fr. ovoid, ⅓ in. long. 17. **S. pyrifolia,** Wall. Nepal, Sikkim, Bhutan, Khasi hills, similar, l. rigid, petioles longer, calyx-teeth nearly as long as ovary, back densely strigose, fr. more cylindric. 18. **S. macrophylla,** Wall. Khasi hills. Branchlets stout; rusty-hirsute, l. thickly coriaceous 8 in. long, rugose from the deeply impressed nerves, fr. unknown, possibly belongs to this subsection.

FIG. 167. Symplocos racemosa, Roxb. ½.

(²) Fr. glabrous, l. under 3 in.

19. **S. foliosa,** Wight Ic. t. 1234 (*S. nervosa*, Wight Ic. t. 1235). Nilgiris, common. A middle-sized tree, l. serrate, hairy beneath, chiefly along nerves, blade 1½–3, pet. ⅛ in. long, sec. n. prominent, 8–10 pair. Spikes axillary, hairy, rigid 1–1½ in. long, developing from large globose buds enveloped in hairy bracts, petals ⅙ in. Fr. cylindric, ½ in. long, embryo straight.

(³) Fr. cylindric, densely villous.

20. **S. Gardneriana,** Wight Ic. t. 1231, Bedd. Fl. Sylv. t. 237. Nilgiris, Anamalais. Travancore hills. A large tree, branchlets, petioles and spikes thick, villous, l. elliptic, hairy beneath, blade 4–5, pet. stout, ½–1 in. long, sec. n. prominent beneath. Fl. white in axillary spikes, 1–2½ in. long, congregating near the ends of branches, growing out from large globose buds enveloped by villous bracts. Calyx densely hirsute, petals ¼ in. long. Fr. cylindric, densely villous ⅓ in. long, crowned by persistent calyx, as broad as fr. 21. **S. Hohenackeri,** Clarke. Coorg. Similar and perhaps not specifically distinct, calyx-tube glabrous, teeth densely silky, fr. unknown.

β. Fr. cylindric, over 1 in. long.

22. **S. macrocarpa,** Wight. Courtallum. Travancore 2,500 ft., in evergreen forest. A middle-sized tree, branchlets and racemes rusty-tomentose. L. elliptic-lanceolate, slightly crenulate, blade 5–8, pet. ½ in., sec. n. 8–12 pair. Racemes axillary, stout, 1–2 in. long, fr. 1¼ by ½ in., 3-celled, endocarp crustaceous. 23. **S. kanarana,** Talbot List Ed. ii. 214; Journ. Nat. Hist. Bombay, vol. 11. 238, t. 9. Evergreen forest, North Kanara. A small tree, branchlets and l. glabrous. L. chartaceous, ovate, coarsely dentate, blade 3–6, pet. ½ in. Fr. ovoid, smooth, yellow, 1¼ by $\frac{9}{10}$ in., in a copious pulp an exceedingly hard, thick walled 1–3-celled stone with 5 or 6 deep longitudinal furrows and sharp narrow ridges between.

γ. Fr. nearly globose.

24. **S. dryophila,** Clarke. East Nepal and Sikkim, 8–10,000 ft. A tree, branchlets glabrous, youngest shoots slightly hairy, l. glabrous, entire, oblanceolate, shortly acuminate, blade 4–6, pet. ½–¾ in. Racemes axillary, lax, 3–4 in. long, pedicels as long as or longer than calyx. Fr. 2-celled, embryo slightly curved. Similar to *S. Sumuntia*, both species have globose axillary buds ¼ in. diam., enveloped in hairy scales, which develop into racemes.

(*b*) Fl. white or yellow, l. chartaceous.

a. Racemes many-fld., fr. ellipsoid or conical.

25. **S. caudata,** Wall.—Syn. *S. prunifolia*, Sieb. & Zucc. Khasi hills. Chittagong. Upper Tenasserim (Kurz). China, Japan. A shrub or small tree, l. glabrous, broadly lanceolate, caudate-acuminate, more or less serrulate, blade 2–3, pet. ¼ in. Racemes hairy, shorter than l., calyx glabrous, petals white, ⅛ in. long. Fr. conical. Chinese specimens have coriaceous l. and dense racemes 1–1½ in. long.

26. **S. ramosissima,** Wall. Himalaya, 5–9,000 ft., Garhwal to Bhutan, Khasi hills. *Lodh*. Hind. A small tree, l. chartaceous, lanceolate, serrulate, blade 4–6, pet. ¼ in. Racemes lax, ½–1 in. long, 4–8-fld., pedicels as long as calyx-tube. Fr. ellipsoid ¼–⅜ in. long, calyx-rim narrow. 27. **S. nicobarica,** Clarke. Nicobars (included in *S. leiostachya*, Kurz). Young shoots hairy, l. thickly chartaceous, elliptic-oblong, blade 4–6, pet. ½–¾ in. Racemes (in fr.) half the length of l., fr. ovoid-conic, ½ in. long, calyx-rim wide.

β. Racemes many-fld., fr. cylindric.

28. **S. grandiflora,** Wall. Assam, Khasi hills. Branchlets glabrous, l. lanceolate nearly entire, glabrous, blade 5–7, pet. ¼ in. Racemes lax, 3–4 in. long, bracts lanceolate, longer than buds, deciduous, corolla ⅓, fr. nearly cylindric, ½ in. long. 29. **S. Hookeri,** Clarke, Khasi hills. Yunnan. Branchlets thick, glabrous. L. elongate-elliptic, often broader in the upper half, glabrous, minutely toothed, blade 8–12, pet. 1–1½ in., sec. n. 10–12 pair, prominent beneath, tertiary parallel. Racemes (in fr.) 2–3, pedicels ¼, fr. cylindric, ¾ in. long. 30. **S. sulcata,** Kurz. Hills between Sitang and Salween rivers. Tenasserim. A shrub or small tree, young shoots rusty-tomentose. L. lanceolate or elliptic-lanceolate, blade 4–6, pet. ¼ in. Racemes lax, 1–1½ in. long, fr. cylindric-ovoid, sulcate, ⅜ in. long. 31. **S. leiostachya,** Kurz. Tenasserim. L. lanceolate, racemes lax, numerous at the ends of branches, rachis slender, fr. unknown.

γ. Spikes many-fld., fr. globose.

32. **S. lancifolia,** Sieb. & Zucc. Assam. Khasi hills. China, Japan. A shrub or small tree, branchlets more or less hairy, l. chartaceous, glabrous, lanceolate, blade 2–4, pet. ⅛ in. Spikes axillary, slender, ½–1½ in. long, more or less hairy, calyx strigose, lobes obtuse, petals ⅛–⅙ in. long, stamens 18–25. Fr. ⅛ in. diam., calyx-rim narrow, embryo curved.

δ. Racemes 2–8-fld.

33. **S. pulchra,** Wight Ic. t. 1230. Nilgiris, 3–4,000 ft. A shrub, branchlets and petioles densely clothed with long spreading fulvous hairs, l. membranous, oblong-lanceolate, hairy on both surfaces and along the edge, blade 5–7, pet. ⅛ in., nerves oblique. Racemes usually axillary, sometimes terminating branchlets, peduncles slender, 1–2 in. long, sometimes branching, hairy at the ends, 2–4 large pure white fl. supported by linear bracts ⅓–½, petals ¼–⅜ in. long. 34. **S. acuminata,** Bedd. Ic. t. 117. Syn. *S. tenella*, Brand l. c. 54. Wainad, 5000 ft., very common. Tinnevelli ghats. Travancore evergreen forest 4,000 ft. A shrub, branchlets and l. glabrous. L. membranous, lanceolate, blade 2–3, pet. ⅛ in. Racemes axillary, slender, 5–8-fld., bracts linear, hairy, petals ⅛ in. long.

(c) Fl. rose coloured.

35. **S. rosea,** Bedd. Ic. Pl. Ind. Or. t. 115. Anamalais. Courtallum. Cochin. Travancore, common in all evergreen forests up to 2,000 ft. Branchlets hairy, l. membranous or chartaceous, oblanceolate, acuminate, a few hairs on midrib and nerves beneath, blade 5–6, pet. ⅛ in. long. Racemes hairy, 1–1½ in. long, pedicels shorter than calyx, calyx-lobes oblong, acute, as long as or longer than tube, fr. cylindric, ½–⅝ in. 36. **S. complanata,** Brand l. c. Nilgiris (probably), reported to differ by coriaceous elliptic l. (not seen).

D. Racemes or spikes compound.

(*a*) Fr. globose or nearly so.

37. **S. cratægoides,** Ham.; Brandis F. Fl. 299.; Collett Simla Fl. 305. fig. 95. Vern. *Ludh*, Hind.; *Lojh*, Bash.; *Daukyat*, Upper Burma.

Deciduous, a large shrub or middle-sized tree, branchlets and l. hairy. L. membranous, broad-elliptic or ovate, shortly acuminate, sharply serrate, blade 2–4, pet. ⅛–¼ in. Fl. snow-white, fragrant, in terminal panicles, filaments connate in 5 bundles, ovary 2-celled. Fr. glabrous, ovoid or nearly globose, ¼ in. long, calyx-rim small, much narrower than fr., embryo curved.

Himalaya, Kashmir to Assam 3–8,000 ft. Khasi and Naga hills. Hills between Sitang and Salween. Upper Burma. Fl. March–June. Yellow dye from l. and bark. China. Japan.

38. **S. spicata**, Roxb.; Wight Ill. t. 150; Kurz F. Fl. ii. 146; Brandis F. Fl. 300. Vern. *Lodh*, Hind.; *Dhaka*, Mar.

A middle-sized tree, l. coriaceous, glabrous, acuminate, serrulate, blade 4–7, petiole ⅓–½ in. Fl. cream-coloured, sessile, in paniculate axillary pubescent or glabrous spikes, each fl. supported by 3 ovate bracts, ovary 3-celled, glabrous, as well as calyx-segments. Drupes sessile, nearly globose, ribbed, ⅓ in. diam.

Assam, Khasi hills, Cachar. Chittagong hill tracts. Tenasserim. Western Ghats, Nilgiris, Shevaroy hills. Fl. Sept.-Dec.—Malay Penins. China. Japan. A remarkable form (Thaungyin, D. B. 1859) with entire, thickly coriaceous l., sec. n. indistinct, probably a new species. Brand l. c. 39 separates *S. attenuata*, Wall., Assam and Khasi hills, by smaller l. and more strictly globose fr., and *S. Candolleana*, Coorg and Anamalais, by more pubescent inflorescence, larger bracts and a straight embryo. 39. **S. ferruginea**, Roxb. (including *S. polystachya*, Wall. and *javanica*, Kurz). Garhwal, Kumaon, Sikkim (4–6,000 ft.). China. A small tree, branchlets rusty-villous. L. hairy on the nerves beneath, blade 6–8, pet. ¼–½ in., sec. n. 10–12 pair, prominent on the underside, fl. sessile in large compound axillary rusty-villous panicles, bracts longer than the short calyx-tube. Fr. globose, ribbed, ⅛ in. diam., crowned by the enlarged calyx-segments.

(*b*) Fr. cylindric, ellipsoid or conical.

40. **S. theæfolia**, Ham. Kumaon. Nepal. Sikkim, 5–10,000 ft. Assam. Khasi hills. A middle-sized tree, l. glabrous, blade 3–6, pet. ⅓ in., midrib raised, not impressed on the upper side. Fl. white, sessile, in short dense compound spikes, 1 in. long, stamens 10–20, a little longer than corolla, disk densely clothed with long white hairs. Fr. ellipsoid-cylindric, ⅓ in. long, embryo straight, calyx in fr. inconspicuous. Specimens with larger l., blade 8, pet. ¾ in. Hills east of Toungoo 2,000 ft. (D. B. Feb. 1880). 41. **S. Kurgensis**, Clarke. Coorg. Similar, young shoots rusty-tomentose, l. hairy beneath, midrib impressed, spikes compound, 2–3 in. long. 42. **S. Warburgii**, Brand l. c. 66. Nilgiris, stamens 25, twice the corolla otherwise like 40 (not seen). 43. **S. oxyphylla**, Wall. (*S. pedicellata*, Kurz.) Assam. Khasi hills. Forests east of Toungoo. A large evergreen tree, l. elliptic-lanceolate, blade 4–6, pet. ⅓ in., sec. n. slender 5–7 pair, joined by intramarginal veins. Fl. shortly pedicellate, in racemes, simple or branching from near the base, fr. conical, ¼–⅓ in. long.

II. Cal.-tube produced beyond ovary, petals connate into a tube, on which are inserted the stamens. L. glabrous.

44. **S. sessilis**, Clarke. Travancore, evergreen forests 4–5,000 ft. A middle-sized tree, l. spathulate 1½–2½ in. Fl. sessile, solitary, corolla ⅓ in. long, fr. cylindric ⅜ in. long. 45. **S. pendula**, Wight Ic. t. 1237. Anamalai and Palni hills. Ceylon upper montane zone common (*S. pauciflora*, Wight). A shrub or small tree, l. coriaceous, elliptic, 1½–2½ in. long, pale beneath. Fl. pendulous, often from the axils of fallen l. on 1–5-fld. peduncles with numerous minute persistent bracts, corolla ⅓–½ in. long.

2. STYRAX, Linn.; Fl. Brit. Ind. iii. 588.

Hairs often stellate, fl. white. Calyx campanulate, free or slightly adnate to base of ovary, truncate or 5-toothed. Corolla-tube short. Stamens 10, inserted in the corolla-tube, filaments short, anthers linear. Ovary incompletely 3-celled, the dissepiments reaching to the middle. Fr. dry, supported by the persistent calyx-tube, breaking up irregularly. Seed 1, rarely 2, embryo straight, cotyledons flat. Species 60, America, China, Japan, India.

1. **S. serrulatum**, Roxb.; Kurz F. Fl. ii. 142. Vern. *Shigriti*, Assam.

A shrub or small tree, l. serrulate, young shoots and underside of leaves minutely pubescent, inflorescence, calyx and outside of petals densely white stellately tomentose. Fl. mostly in short racemes, corolla ⅓ in. long. Calyx nearly truncate, with minute teeth.

Khasi hills. Manipur. Cachar. Chittagong. Tenasserim. Nepal, Sikkim, Assam, Upper Burma. Fl. March–May. Leaf-and flower-buds often grow out into galls, up to 10 in. long. China, Japan. *S. virgatum*, Wall., is a form with long acuminate leaves, usually widest below the middle, and larger fl. *S. Benzoin*, Dryander, is a tree of the Malay Peninsula and Archipelago, which yields from incisions in the bark a balsamic resin, called Benzoin, used medicinally and in the preparation of incense. 2. **S. Hookeri**, Clarke. Sikkim, Bhutan, 6–7,000 ft. closely allied to 1, fl. 1 in. long. 3. **S. rugosum**, Kurz. Hills east of Toungoo. Shan hills. Mogok valley, Ruby Mines district. A shrub or small tree, branchlets, underside of l. and inflorescence densely white tomentose, l. sharply and often deeply dentate, fl. in terminal bracteate and leafy racemes, bracts with long linear teeth, calyx-lobes triangular.

4 **S. Polysperma**, Clarke. Khasi hills, branchlets and l. glabrous, inflorescence compound dichotomous, fr. 5–6-seeded, possibly does not belong to this genus.

ORDER LXXI. OLEACEÆ. Gen. Pl. ii. 672.

Unarmed shrubs or trees, sometimes climbing. Leaves opposite (alternate in a few species of *Jasminum*), stipules 0. Inflorescence mostly racemose, rarely cymose, in trichotomous panicles. Fl. regular, as a rule bisexual, often dimorphic. Calyx small, truncate or 4-lobed, lobes sometimes 4–9. Corolla-lobes usually 4, sometimes 4–12, in some cases petals distinct or none. Stamens 2, filaments usually short, ovary free, 2-celled, ovules 1–2 in each cell, attached to the inner angle.

The climbing species of *Jasminum* have, as far as known, wood of a normal structure, but the stems are often spirally twisted and in some cases wedges of bast intrude into the wood.

Usually trees or shrubs, l. or leaflets penniveined.
  Fr. flat dry, separating when ripe into 2 flat 1-seeded cells, l. simple . . . . 1. NYCTANTHES.
  Fr. an indehiscent samara, l. imparipinnate . . . . 2. FRAXINUS.
  Fr. a capsule, dehiscing loculicidally, the valves septiferous.
    L. imparipinnate, capsule woody, albumen 0 . . . 3. SCHREBERA.
    L. simple or pinnatifid; capsule coriaceous, albumen fleshy . . . . 4. SYRINGA.
  Fr. a drupe, endocarp bony or crustaceous.
    Corolla-lobes imbricate . . . . 5. OSMANTHUS.
    Corolla-lobes valvate.
      Corolla tubular or 0, inflorescence usually axillary . . . . 6. OLEA.
      Corolla funnel-shaped, panicles or racemes terminal . . . . 7. LIGUSTRUM.
    Petals distinct or connate in pairs . . . . . 8. LINOCIERA.
  Fr. a 2-lobed berry, one lobe sometimes wanting, corolla-tube cylindrical, albumen 0 . . . . . . 9. JASMINUM.
A large climber, l. prominently 3-nerved . . . . MYXOPYRUM (p. 452).

1. NYCTANTHES, Linn.; Fl. Brit. Ind. iii. 603.

1. **N. Arbortristis**, Linn. (the only species), Bedd. Fl. Sylv. t. 240. Vern. *Har*, *Siharu*, *Saihari*, *Harsinghar*, *Kuri*, Hind.; *Kharasli*, Mar.; *Hursing*, *Parijata*, Kan.; *Krishti*, Tell.; *Seikpalu*, Burm.

A large deciduous shrub or small tree, branches quadrangular, rough all over with an uneven epidermis and stiff white hairs. L. ovate, acuminate, entire or with a few large distant teeth. Fl. sessile, in pedunculate bracteate fascicles of 3–5, arranged in short trichotomous cymes. Calyx campanulate, indistinctly dentate, corolla-lobes 5–8, white, crenate or emarginate, contorted in bud. Anthers sessile in the orange-coloured corolla-tube. Capsule chartaceous, flat, splitting into two 1-seeded cells, cotyledons flat, radicle inferior, albumen 0.

Subhimalayan tract, from the Chenab southwards. Oudh Forests. Singbhum Central

India, Jumna to the Godavery. Cultivated throughout India on account of its fragrant fl. which open in the evening and drop at sunrise. Fl. more or less throughout the year, generally during the rains. Often gregarious in dry places, coppices vigorously. One of the species to be employed when the necessity for utilizing the waste lands in the plains of Northern India comes to be recognized.

2. FRAXINUS, Linn.; Fl. Brit. Ind. iii. 605.

Trees, rarely shrubs, l. opposite, imparipinnate, leaflets opposite. Fl. polygamous or dioicous, in racemes or compact rounded panicles. Calyx cup-shaped or wanting, petals 4 or 0, stigma bifid. Fr. indehiscent, winged at the end, 1-seeded. Albumen fleshy or somewhat horny, embryo cylindric, radicle superior. Species 40, northern temperate regions of both hemispheres.

A. Petals 4, fl. appearing after the leaves.

1. **F. floribunda,** Wall. Pl. As. Rar. t. 277; Brandis F. Fl. t. 37. Vern. *Sum*, *Angu*, *Ango*, N.W. Himal.

A middle-sized or large deciduous tree, leaflets 2–4 pair, membranous, hairy beneath while young, ovate-oblong, acuminate, serrate, blade 3–6, pet. $\frac{1}{4}$–$\frac{1}{2}$ in., sec. n. 10–14 pair, prominent beneath. Fl. white, in large compound terminal panicles. Petals linear-oblong, narrowed at both ends, 2–3 times the length of calyx. Fr. oblanceolate, 1–1$\frac{1}{2}$ in. long, supported by the enlarged calyx.

Afghanistan. Trans Indus territory. Himalaya, 5–9,000 ft., locally on rich soil chiefly on or near limestone. Khasi hills. Shan Hills at 4,000 ft. Fl. April, May.
2. **F. Griffithii,** Clarke. Mishmee hills, leaflets coriaceous, entire.

B. Petals 0, fl. appearing before the leaves.

3. **F. excelsior,** Linn. N.W. Himalaya, basin of the Jhelam, Chenab and Ravi rivers,

Fig. 168. Fraxinus xanthoxyloides, Wall. $\frac{1}{2}$

4–9,000 ft. Europe and Mountains of Western Asia. A tall tree, leaflets sessile, or nearly so, 2–4 pair, base entire, upper part slightly serrate. Fl. appearing before the l. in short often fascicled racemes from above the scars of the previous year's l., ♂ and ☿, often in the same inflorescence, calyx usually 0. Samara 1–1½ in. long, without a trace of calyx. Differs from the European Ash by fewer slightly serrate leaflets and by longer more slender racemes. Described as *F. Hookeri*, Wenzig in Engler Jahrb. iv. 179. 4. **F. oxyphylla**, M. Bieb. Baluchistan, Afghanistan. Similar to 3, leaflets 1–4 pair, coarsely serrate, samara narrowed to both ends.

5. **F. xanthoxyloides**, Wall.—Syn. *F. Moorcroftiana*, Brandis, F. Fl. 304. Vern. *Sanjal*, Punj.; *Hanūz*, Haz.; *Thūm*, Kunawar.

A shrub or small tree. L. approximate at the ends of branchlets, very variable in size, leaflets 3–5 pair, 1–2 in. long, sessile or nearly so, common petiole marginate. Fl. in compact sessile lateral many-fld. fascicles, supported by a number of undeveloped woolly l., calyx cup-shaped, 4–6-dentate. Samara linear-spathulate, 1–1½ in. long, seed part thick, ribbed and furrowed, supported by the persistent but not enlarged calyx.

Afghanistan, Baluchistan, Trans Indus territory. N. W. Himalaya, 3–9,000 ft., chiefly in the inner dry valleys. Often gregarious. Fl. March, April.

3. SCHREBERA, Roxb.; Fl. Brit. Ind. iii. 604.

Species 4, of which 3 in Africa.

S. swietenioides, Roxb. Cor. Pl. t. 101; Wight Ill. t. 162; Bedd. Fl. Sylv. t. 248. Vern. *Mokha*, *ghaut*, Hind.; *Mokkalapa*, Tel.; *Kalgante*, Kan.; *Mogalinga*, Tam.; *Thitswelwè*, Burm.

Fig. 169. Schrebera swietenioides, Roxb. ½.

A middle-sized deciduous tree, branches grey. L. imparipinnate, leaflets opposite 3–4 pair entire, ovate, base often unequal-sided, blade 3–5, pet. ¼–½ in., branchlets thickened at nodes and common petioles thickened at the insertion of leaflets. Fl. yellowish-brown, fragrant at night, in terminal trichotomous corymbose compound cymes, calyx campanulate, teeth 5, unequal. Corolla $\frac{1}{3}$–$\frac{1}{2}$ in. long, lobes 5–7, on the upper side with brown glandular raised dots. Capsule pendulous, pear-shaped, 2–3 in. long, 2-valved, seeds 8, ending in long wings, albumen 0, radicle short, superior, cotyledons fleshy, longitudinally plaited.

Subhimalayan tract from Kumaon eastwards. Central India, Rajputana. Western Peninsula. Burma Upper and Lower. Fl. Feb.–April.

4. SYRINGA, Linn.; Fl. Brit. Ind. iii. 604.

L. entire or pinnatifid, usually deciduous. Fl. numerous, in a terminal erect thyrsus. Calyx campanulate, 4-toothed, more or less persistent. Corolla-lobes 4, valvate in bud. Fr. a coriaceous more or less cylindrical capsule, 2-valved, the valves septiferous. Seeds pendulous in pairs from the top of each cell, with a narrow wing all round. Embryo straight in a fleshy albumen, radicle superior. Species 10, Europe, Western Asia, Himalaya, China and Japan.

1. **S. Emodi,** Wall.; Royle Ill. t. 65. Vern. *Shapa*, Bash.; *Chara*, Pangi; *Shaphroi*, Jauns.

A large shrub, youngest shoots and inflorescence pubescent. L. entire, pale beneath, blade 3–5, pet. 1 in. long. Fl. white or purplish, strongly scented, crowded in short compact cymes. Capsule cylindrical, $\frac{3}{4}$ in. long, often curved.

Trans Indus 9,000 ft. N. W. Himalaya, Indus to Sarda, in the outer moister as well as in the inner more arid tracts. Fl. May–July. 2. **S. persica,** Linn., indigenous in Persia, Afghanistan and Waziristan, cultivated in Kashmir and at Lahore, l. lanceolate, entire or pinnatifid, capsule $\frac{1}{2}$ in. long. 3. **S. vulgaris,** S.-Eastern Europe, l. broadly ovate or cordate on long petioles.

5. OSMANTHUS, Lour.; Fl. Brit. Ind. iii. 606.

Evergreen shrubs or trees, glabrous, l. coriaceous, fl. tetramerous, usually polygamous, in axillary fascicles. Corolla-lobes obtuse, imbricated in bud. Drupe usually one-seeded, albumen fleshy or horny, embryo cylindric, radicle superior. Species 10–15, Eastern Himalaya. China, Japan, New Caledonia, the Sandwich Islands, Eastern North America.

1. **O. fragrans,** Lour. (*O. fragrans*, Thunb.; Brandis F. Fl. 309). Himalaya from Garhwal eastwards, 4–7,000 ft., in Garhwal and Kumaon possibly not indigenous, though frequent. China, Japan. A shrub or small tree, l. coriaceous, lanceolate, entire or serrate, mid-rib, sec. n. and the minutely reticulate veins impressed on the upper side, blade 4–6, narrowed into pet. $\frac{1}{2}$–$\frac{3}{4}$ in. long. Fl. white or light yellow, exquisitely fragrant, dioicous, on long slender pedicels, in axillary fascicles. Drupe glaucous-blue, $\frac{3}{4}$ in. long, endocarp hard, woody. 2. **O. suavis,** King. Eastern Nepal, Sikkim 9–10,000 ft. Manipur. A small tree, l. coriaceous, lanceolate, minutely crenate-serrate, blade 1–3, pet. $\frac{1}{8}$ in. Calyx membranous, segments obtuse, ciliate. Corolla-tube $\frac{1}{4}$–$\frac{1}{3}$ in., lobes $\frac{1}{8}$ in. long. Drupe ellipsoid, $\frac{1}{3}$–$\frac{1}{2}$ in. long, endocarp crustaceous.

6. OLEA, Linn.; Fl. Brit. Ind. iii. 611.

Trees or shrubs, l. entire or toothed. Fl. small, often unisexual, tetramerous, in axillary or terminal panicles. Calyx short, truncate or dentate. Corolla-tube short, lobes spreading, valvate in bud, stamens exserted, style short, stigma capitate or bifid. Fruit a fleshy drupe, endocarp usually hard. Seed usually one, albumen fleshy, oily. Embryo straight, cotyledons foliaceous, radicle superior. Species 30–35, South Africa, India, Australia and Polynesia.

A. All fl. with corolla.

1. **O. cuspidata,** Wall.; Brandis F. Fl. t. 38.—Syn. *O. ferruginea*, Royle Ill. t. 65. Vern. *Zaitūn*, Pushtu; *Kaho*, *Kān*, N.W. Him.; *Wī*, Kunawar.

A middle-sized tree, heartwood olive-brown to nearly black, often beautifully mottled, extremely hard. L. lanceolate, cuspidate, entire, the upper side deep glossy green, the under side, as well as branchlets and petioles clothed with a dense ferrugineous or red, sometimes grey film of minute orbicular more or less lobed scales, midrib prominent, sec. n. obscure, blade 2–4, pet. ⅓–½ in. long. Fl. whitish, bisexual, in axillary panicles, about half the length of l. Corolla rotate, lobes ovate, acute. Drupe ovoid, ¼–⅓ in. long, black when ripe, supported by the remains of calyx, pulp scanty, oily, stone thick, hard, bony.

Baluchistan. Afghanistan. Suliman range, Trans Indus. North West Himalaya, ascending to 6,000 ft.; also in the dry inner valleys. Fl. April–June. Combs made of the wood. Closely allied to *Olea europæa*, Linn., the *European Olive*, which (the ungrafted tree) has spinescent branchlets, leaves grey above, white beneath, a more dense inflorescence and larger fruit.

2. **O. glandulifera**, Wall.; Wight Ic. t. 1238; Bedd. Fl. Sylv. t. 238. Vern. *Gair*, *Gaild*, Jaunsar, Garhwal.

A small or middle-sized wholly glabrous tree, trunk short, with a broad

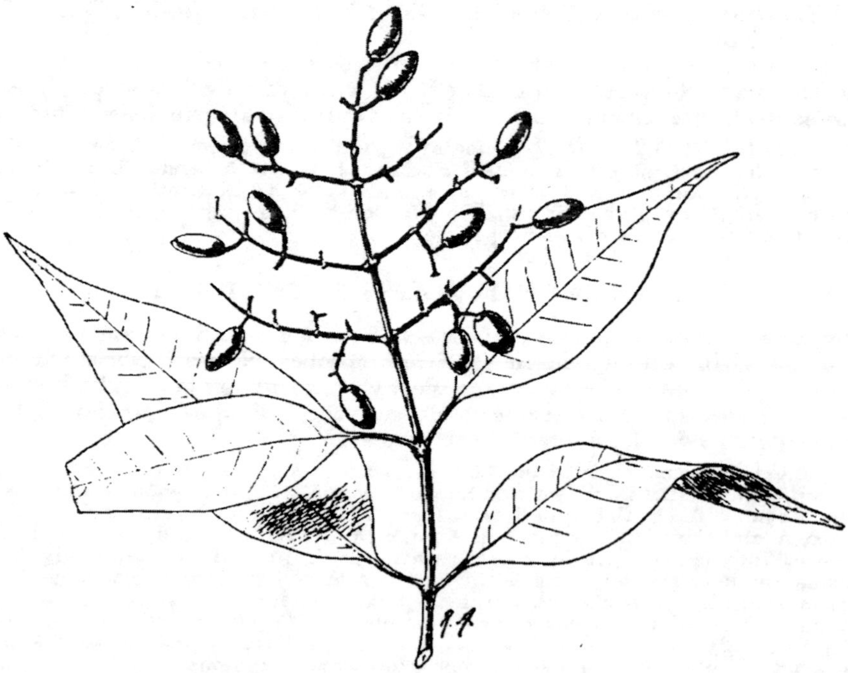

Fig. 170. Olea glandulifera, Wall. ½.

umbrageous crown, wood reddish, close-grained, hard. L. elliptic or ovate, long acuminate, sec. n. 6–8 pair, in their axils on the underside small oval cavities, blade 4–5, petiole 1–1½ in. long. Fl. white, bisexual, in terminal and lateral compound pyramidal trichotomous panicles, corolla rotate. Fr. ovoid, ½ in. long, endocarp crustaceous.

Outer Himalayan ranges, Kashmir to Nepal 1,900–6,000 ft., scattered in mixed woods, often associated with *Acer oblongum*. Bababudan hills. Coorg. Nilgiris, Anamalais. Fl. March–May. 3. **O. dentata**, Wall. Mishmee and Khasi hills. Hills of Lower and Upper Burma. Branchlets and panicles more or less pubescent, l. coriaceous, toothed or entire, lanceolate, blade 5–7, pet. ½ in. long. Fl. dioicous, in panicles as long as or longer than l., calyx hairy, corolla ⅛ in. long. 4. A large climber (Clarke 42047. Manipur 6,500 ft., Nov. 1885). L. coriaceous, lanceolate, caudate-acuminate, blade 5–6 narrowed into pet. ½–¾ in. long, midrib, sec. and intramarginal n. deeply impressed on the upper surface. Fl. ♂ in lateral pedunculate glabrous trichotomous panicles, pedicels nearly as long as fl. Calyx glabrous, segments triangular, acute, corolla campanulate ⅓ in. long, filaments shorter than anthers.

5. **O. polygama,** Wight Ic. tt. 1239, 1240. Hills on the east side of the Peninsula, Palkonda hills (Gamble 14055). Veligonda hills (D. B. Dec. 1881). Nilgiris. Ceylon. Glabrous, l. rigidly coriaceous, entire, elliptic, blade 2–3, narrowed into pet. ¼ in. long. Fl. ♂ and ☿ on different trees, in panicles 1–2 in. long, corolla campanulate, 1/12 in. Drupe ovoid ⅜ in. long, endocarp thin, crustaceous.

B. Female or all fl. without petals.

6. **O. dioica,** Roxb.; Wight Ill. t. 151. Vern. *Karamba*, Mar.; *Parrjamb*, *Mudla*, Kan.; *Koli*, *Payar*, Tam.

A middle-sized, sometimes a large tree, glabrous. L. elliptic-lanceolate, entire or toothed, blade 3–6, petiole ¼–½ in. Fl. small, white, dioicous, in axillary and extra-axillary panicles, ramifications slender. Corolla 1/9–1/12 in. long, wanting or caducous in ♀ fl. Drupe ellipsoid, ½–⅔ in.

Lower hills of Sikkim. Western Duars. Assam. Khasi hills, Cachar. Chittagong hills. Western Ghats in evergreen forests, from the Konkan southwards. Upper Burma (Griffith). Fl. March, April. 7. **O. Gamblei,** Clarke. Sikkim, lower and outer hills, 2–3,000 ft. *Jamu*, Nep. A small tree, l. coriaceous, elliptic-oblong, acuminate, blade 4–5, pet. ⅓ in. Fl. dioicous, all without corolla, calyx minute, nearly truncate, ciliate, anthers nearly sessile, ovary glabrous. Drupe ¾–1 in. long, endocarp bony.

7. LIGUSTRUM, Linn.; Fl. Brit. Ind. iii. 614.

Trees or shrubs, l. entire. Fl. bisexual, tetramerous, in terminal panicles. Calyx usually truncate, corolla funnel-shaped, lobes induplicate-valvate in bud. Fr. a berry, 2-celled and 2–4-seeded, endocarp membranous or crustaceous. Species 30, one in Europe (*L. vulgare*, Privet), one in Australia, the rest in Asia, of which 14 in China. The 11 species here mentioned will probably eventually be reduced to 5.

A. Drupe longer than broad.

(*a*) Corolla-tube shorter than or as long as calyx, rarely slightly longer. Eastern and Himalayan species.

1. **L. robustum,** Blume.—Syn. *Olea robusta*, Wall. Silhet, Dacca, Chittagong, in the plains and at the foot of the hills. Pegu Yoma. Upper Burma, 4–6,000 ft. Malay Archip. China. A large shrub or middle-sized tree, l. glabrous, elliptic-lanceolate, blade 3–4, pet. ¼ in. Panicles 6–12 in. long, pyramidal, pubescent or villous, corolla ⅛ in. Drupe ⅓ in. long, cylindric, often curved. 2. **L. compactum,** Hook. f. & Th.; Kanjilal F. Fl. 230. Outer ranges of the N. W. Himalaya, 4–9,000 ft. A large shrub or small tree, closely allied to 1, branches less lenticellate, panicle glabrous or pubescent, fl. nearly sessile, densely clustered, corolla ⅛ in. long, tube sometimes slightly longer than calyx, fr. ⅓ in. long.

(*b*) Corolla-tube as long as calyx, or slightly longer. Western species.

3. **L. Roxburghii,** Clarke (*Visiania robusta*, Wight Ic. t. 1242). Nilgiris, Shevagherry hills. A small tree, branches lenticellate, l. coriaceous, ovate-lanceolate, blade 3–4, pet. ⅓ in. Panicle stout pubescent, lanceolate bracts often present, corolla ⅛ in., sometimes longer than calyx. 4. **L. Walkeri,** Dcne. Nilgiris. Travancore, at 3,500 ft. Ceylon. Fl. scented, corolla ⅛ in. Drupe ¼ in. long. 5. **L. Decaisnei,** Clarke. Nilgiris. Courtallum, Shevagerry hills. Similar to 4, but l. smaller.

(*c*) Corolla-tube twice the length of calyx.

6. **L. neilgherrense,** Wight Ic. t. 1243. Western Ghats from Bombay southwards. Nilgiris, frequent. Branches lenticellate, l. thinly coriaceous, elliptic or ovate, blade 2–3, pet. ⅓ in., sec. n. 6–8, slender but distinct. Panicle glabrous, calyx with 4 shallow teeth, corolla ½ in. long, anthers exserted. 7. **L. Perrottetii,** A. DC., Wight Ic. t. 1244. *Kholi*, Tam. Nilgiris, Palnis. Closely allied to 6 with which Beddome unites it. Supposed to

differ by the branches rarely lenticellate, l. smaller and panicles minutely pubescent. Further study in the forest of species 3–7 will probably lead to their being united.

8. **L. Massalongianum,** Visiani. Khasi hills. A small shrub, branches lenticellate, densely leafy, l. lanceolate and linear-lanceolate, 1–3 in., petiole short. Panicles small, densely hairy, corolla ⅙ in. long, tube slender.

B. Drupe globose. Eastern and Himalayan species.

9. **L. confusum** Dcne. Sikkim 4–8,000 ft. Bhutan. Khasi hills. Yunnan. A middle-sized tree, branches lenticellate, l. lanceolate or ovate-lanceolate, blade 1–5, pet. ⅙–½ in. long. Panicles pubescent, bracts 0. Corolla ⅙ in. long, tube as long as calyx. Drupe ⅙ in. diam. 10. **L. nepalense,** Wall. Garhwal, Kumaon, Nepal. Similar to 9 and probably not specifically distinct, the lower branches of panicles in the axils of large leaf-like bracts up to 2 in. long. 11. **L. Myrsinites,** Dcne. Khasi hills. A small much branched shrub, branchlets densely hairy, l. ½–⅜ in. long. Fl. usually sessile, in terminal 8-12-fld. racemes, corolla ⅛–¼ in. long, tube longer than calyx. Drupe ⅙ in. diam.

8. LINOCIERA, Swartz; Fl. Brit. Ind. iii. 607.

Trees or shrubs, rarely climbing, as a rule evergreen, l. entire. Fl. tetramerous, ☿ and ♂ in lateral fascicles or opposite-branched racemes and panicles, often from the axils of the uppermost leaves and from the middle of internodes. Petals free or cohering in pairs, rarely connate to the middle, in bud induplicate-valvate, anthers dehiscing laterally, sessile or on short filaments, ovules 2 in each cell, pendulous from the apex. Seed usually solitary, radicle superior. Species 40, tropics of both hemispheres.

A. Petioles more than half inch long.

1. **L. intermedia,** Wight Ic. t 1245.—Syn. *Chionanthus intermedia,* Bedd. Fl. Sylv. t. 239. *Taw Petsut,* Burm.

A middle-sized tree. L. chartaceous or thinly coriaceous, elongate-elliptic, acuminate, blade 4–8, narrowed into petiole ½–1¼ in. long, sec. n. 10–14 pair, slender but conspicuous. Fl. ☿ and ♂, white, in large glabrous trichotomous compound often fascicled panicles, 3–5 in. long, axillary, or from the middle of the internode, bracts lanceolate, often foliaceous. Calyx glabrous, petals oblong, at base only slightly connate in pairs, ⅛–¼ in. long, anthers sessile or nearly so, ovary glabrous. Fr. ½–¾ in. long.

Hills on both sides of the Western Peninsula, on the east side extending to Orissa, Sambulpur and Chutia Nagpur. Hills east of Toungoo 3,000 ft. (D. B. Feb. 1880). Upper Burma (Smales). Fl. Feb.–May. 2. **L. macrophylla,** Wall. (*Chionanthus macrophyllus,* Kurz). Duars, Assam, Khasi hills. Andamans. Burma, Upper and Lower. Similar to 1 but l. larger. Fl. yellowish, in dense panicles, less than one-third the length of l. petals $\frac{1}{10}$–⅛ in. long. Fr. ¾ in. long. 3. **L. insignis,** Clarke (*Chionanthus montanus,* Kurz, not of Blume). Hills east of Toungoo. Tenasserim. A small tree, young shoots minutely grey-pubescent, l. glabrous, shining, oblanceolate, blade 7–9, pet. 1 in. long, sec. n. 10–12 pair, conspicuous beneath. Fl. in pedunculate pubescent panicles, 3–4 in. long, calyx pubescent, petals ⅙–⅛ in. long, ovary minutely pilose. Fr. black, 1 in. long

B. Petioles short, less than half inch long.

4. **L. malabarica,** Wall.; Wight Ic. t. 1246.—Syn. *Chionanthus malabarica,* Bedd. Fl. Sylv. t. 239, fig. in corner. Vern. *Punisi,* Tel. Evergreen forests of the Western Ghats from the Konkan southwards. A small tree, l. glabrous, chartaceous or coriaceous, elongate-elliptic, blade 4–5, narrowed into petiole ¼–⅜ in. long. Fl. white, on 1-5-fld. pedunculate hairy cymes, in lateral fascicles, generally on short hairy protuberances, axillary or from the middle of the internode, pedicels and calyx grey pilose, petals linear-lanceolate, ¼ in. long, ovary hairy. 5. **L. Wightii,** Clarke (*Olea linocieroides,* Wight Ic. t. 1241). Javadis, 3,000 ft., Gingee hills, South Arcot (D. B. Jan. 1882). Courtallum. Travancore. L. coriaceous, elliptic, more or less acuminate, blade 3–4, narrowed into petiole ¼ in. long, fl. sessile or shortly pedicellate, in short axillary panicles, often from the axils of the l. near the ends of branchlets, calyx glabrous, edge of segments ciliate, petals ¼–⅜ in. long, linear-lanceolate, often connate to one-third of their length, ovary glabrous. 6. **L. courtallensis,** Bedd. (*L. leprocarpa,* var. *courtallensis,* Clarke). Courtallum. South Travancore. L. coriaceous, elliptic-lanceolate, blade 4–6, narrowed into pet. ⅓ in., sec. n. visible on the underside. Fl. in axillary glabrous

short and stiff racemes, sometimes compound, pedicels shorter than calyx. Calyx glabrous, petals thick, distinct, the edges curved inwards, anthers minutely apiculate, filaments broad, shorter than anthers, ovary glabrous.

7. **L. caudata,** Coll. et Hemsl. in Journ. Linn. Soc. xxviii. 84. Terai of Shan hills 3,000 ft. Shwebo district, 750 ft. associated with Oaks and Chestnuts. A middle-sized evergreen tree, l. glabrous, chartaceous, elongate-elliptic, acuminate, blade 4–5, narrowed into pet. $\frac{1}{4}$–$\frac{1}{2}$ in. long, midrib and sec. n. impressed on the upper side. Fl. ☿, greenish-yellow, sessile, in pedunculate panicles, about half the length of l., axillary or from the middle of internode. Calyx glabrous, edges of segments ciliate. Petals $\frac{1}{4}$ in. long, connate in pairs to one-third or one-half of their length, anthers sessile, ovary compound, hirsute. 8. **L. terniflora,** Wall. (*Olea terniflora*, Kurz). Chittagong. Lower Burma. A middle-sized evergreen tree, wholly glabrous. Fl. small, sessile, in 3-fld. pedunculate heads, forming short stiff narrow pubescent racemes or panicles, axillary or from the middle of internodes, calyx-segments ciliate, petals shortly connate in pairs $\frac{1}{12}$–$\frac{1}{8}$ in. long. 9. **L. minutiflora,** Clarke (*Chionanthus minutiflorus*, Kurz). Koonong forests, N. E. of Toungoo (D. B. March 1861). Fl. minute, in ample pedunculate panicles 3–4 in. long, petals free, $\frac{1}{8}$ in. long, ovary glabrous.

9. JASMINUM, Linn.; Fl. Brit. Ind. iii. 591.

Shrubs, mostly climbing, l. opposite or alternate, simple, trifoliolate or imparipinnate, petioles frequently articulate in the middle, the persistent lower portion becoming woody. Calyx-teeth 4–9, corolla salver-shaped, white, pink or yellow, lobes 4–7, imbricate in bud, patent in fl. Style cylindric (species frequently dimorphic, some fl. having a long, others a short style), stigmas 2, linear, ovules 2 in each cell. Berry of two more or less distinct 1-seeded carpels, one carpel often abortive. Albumen 0, radicle inferior. Species 140–160, tropical and subtropical regions, one species in America and one in South Europe.

A. L. opposite, simple, calyx pubescent.

(*a*) Calyx-teeth (in fl.) twice the length of tube or longer.

1. **J. Sambac,** Aiton; Wight Ic. t. 704. Vern. *Bēl*, *Mugra*, *Chamba*, Hind; *Mallige*, Kan.; *Sabè*, Burm.

A shrub, often more or less climbing, branchlets and petioles pubescent, l. ovate nearly glabrous. Fl. white, fragrant, in terminal cymes, sometimes solitary, calyx-teeth hairy, $\frac{1}{4}$ in. long, corolla-lobes as long as tube. Ripe carpels 1 or 2 nearly globose.

Believed to be indigenous in the Western Peninsula. Cultivated throughout India and in most tropical countries on account of its delightfully fragrant fl. in numerous varieties, erect and climbing, with large and small, double and single fl. Fl. H. S. 2. **J. undulatum,** Ker, Sikkim 2–5,000 ft. Bhutan, Assam, Khasi hills. Upper Burma, China. Climbing, l. ovate-lanceolate, calyx-teeth subulate, $\frac{1}{3}$–$\frac{1}{2}$ in. long, corolla-lobes shorter than tube.

3. **J. pubescens,** Willd.—Syn. *J. hirsutum*, Willd.; Wight Ic. t. 702. Brandis F. Fl. 312; *J. bracteatum*, Wight Ic. t. 1248. Vern. *Kunda*, *Chameli*, Hind.; *Sabè*, Burm.

A large shrub, more or less scandent, branchlets and as a rule leaves also grey-tomentose, l. ovate, from a rounded or cordate base, blade 1–3, petiole $\frac{1}{4}$–$\frac{1}{3}$ in. Fl. white, fragrant, sessile or on very short pedicels, crowded in softly tomentose compact terminal nearly sessile corymbiform cymes, bracts small, ovate, calyx-lobes very hairy, reaching nearly to the apex of corolla-tube. Corolla-lobes oblong-lanceolate, cuspidate, shorter than tube.

Subhimalayan tract from the Jumna eastwards, ascending to 3,000 ft. Central provinces. Western Peninsula. Burma. Fl. Jan.–April, also in the rains. 4. **J. Rottlerianum**, Wall.; Wight Ic. t. 1249. Western Ghats and adjoining mountain ranges, 2–5,000 ft., from the Konkan southwards. A climbing shrub, branchlets, petioles and inflorescence villous, l. elliptic, pubescent or nearly glabrous (*J. glabriusculum*, Blume; Trimen Handb. Ceylon iii. 118.), blade 3–4, pet. jointed, $\frac{1}{4}$ in. Fl. in compact terminal, often panicled heads, bracts conspicuous, white, up to $\frac{3}{4}$ in. long, calyx-teeth ¼ in., corolla-tube slender, ¾–1¼ in. long. 5. **J. coarctatum**, Roxb. Assam. Khasi hills. Cachar. Lower Burma. Similar to 4 and possibly not distinct. L. almost glabrous, bracts petaloid, ovate-lanceolate ½–1 in. long.

6. **J. malabaricum**, Wight Ic. t. 1250. Western Ghats and adjoining hill ranges from the Konkan southwards. Scandent, branchlets and l. almost glabrous. L. membranous, ovate from a broad almost flat base, blade 3–5 in. long and often nearly as broad, petiole ¾–1 in. long. Fl. in large compound terminal cymes, pedicels longer than calyx-tube, calyx-teeth ⅓, corolla-tube ½–⅝ in. long, lobes linear, very acute, shorter than tube.

(*b*) Calyx-teeth shorter than twice the length of tube.

7. **J. scandens**. Vahl (*Tawsabè, Thingwè*, Burm.). Western Duars. Assam, Khasi hills. Cachar. Ganges delta. Chittagong. Lower Burma. A large climber, stems as thick as a man's arm, and up to 50 ft. long, branchlets, petioles and nerves beneath minutely pubescent, l. ovate-lanceolate, blade 3–4, pet. ¼–½ in. Fl. white, in dense pedunculate minutely pubescent cymes, axillary and at the ends of short branchlets, pedicels as long as calyx-tube or shorter, corolla-tube ⅓–½ in. long, lobes 5–8. 8. **J. syringæfolium**, Wall. Assam, Tenasserim. Closely allied to 7. Pet. ½ in., Cymes lax, trichotomous, corolla-tube ½–⅝ in. long, lobes 5–7. 9. **J. brevipetiolatum**, Duthie Mss. Pilibhit, Kheri, Oudh. L. glabrous, linear-lanceolate, blade 3–4½, pet. ¼ in. long, cymes glabrous terminal, calyx-teeth minutely hairy, longer than tube, but less than twice its length, corolla-tube ⅜ in. long, lobes 5. 10. **J. decussatum**, Wall. Martaban and Tenasserim. Branchlets, petioles and inflorescence villous. L. softly pubescent beneath, blade 3–5, pet. ⅓–½ in. Fl. in large trichotomous compound cymes, corolla-tube ⅓–¼ in., lobes longer than tube.

11. **J. arborescens**, Roxb.; Wight. Ic. t. 699.—Syn. *J. latifolium*, Wight Ic. t. 703. Vern. *Chameli*, Hind.; *Kusar*, Mar.

Erect or climbing, branches smooth, grey, branchlets pubescent, l. ovate, soft tomentose when young, glabrous when full grown, blade 3–5, pet. ½–¾ in. Fl. white, fragrant, in lax terminal trichotomous compound cymes, calyx-lobes 5 or 6, short, as long as or slightly longer than tube. Corolla-lobes 10 or 12, linear, as long as tube. Berries one or two, ovoid, often oblique, ⅓–½ in. long.

Subhimalayan tract from the Jumna to Nepal and Oudh. Throughout the Central Provinces and the Western Peninsula. Fl. H. S. 12. **J. Roxburghianum**, Wall. Eastern Satpuras. Chutia Nagpur. Belgaum, Bellary, Mysore. Upper Burma, 4,000 ft. Softly tomentose, calyx-teeth much shorter than tube, otherwise like 11.

B. L. opposite, simple, calyx glabrous.

(*a*) Calyx-teeth (in fl.) twice the length of tube or longer.

α. Western species and species of both regions.

13. **J. cordifolium**, Wall. (*J. erectiflorum*, DC.; Wight Ic. t. 1251). Nilgiris. A large glabrous climbing shrub, l. ovate, long-acuminate, blade 4–5, pet. ¾ in. Cymes terminal, many-fld., crowded, calyx-teeth ⅓, corolla-tube ⅞–1 in. long, lobes lanceolate, acute, shorter than tube. 14. **J. rigidum**, Zenker; Wight Ic. t. 1247. Nilgiris, Palnis and hills of the Deccan. Shan Hills 4,000 ft., Upper Burma. Glabrous, l. thinly coriaceous, shining, ovate to ovate-lanceolate, blade 1–2, pet. ⅛ in. Cymes 1–5-fld., sessile, pedicels short, calyx-teeth rigid, corolla-tube ⅜ in. long, lobes shorter than tube. 15. **J. sessiliflorum**, Vahl. Hills of the Deccan and Mysore. Branchlets minutely pubescent, l. glabrous, blade ½–¾ in., pet. short, slender. Cymes 1–3-fld., sessile, pedicels shorter than calyx-tube, corolla-tube ⅓–½ in. long, lobes as long as tube.

β. Eastern species.

16. **J. laurifolium**, Roxb. Khasi hills. Martaban and Tenasserim. Yunnan. Glabrous, scandent, l. lanceolate or linear-lanceolate, thinly coriaceous, blade 3–4, pet. ¼ in. long. Cymes pedunculate, trichotomous, 3–5-fld., lax, axillary or at the ends of short branchlets, pedicels 1 in. long. Calyx-teeth 5 or 6, slender, spreading or recurved, corolla-tube ⅝ in., lobes linear, 10–15, as long as tube. 17. **J. subtriplinerve**, Blume. Sikkim. Assam. Khasi hills. Manipur. Cachar. China. Glabrous, l. ovate or ovate-lanceolate, blade 2–5, pet. ⅓–⅜ in., a pair of nerves from the base or above the base extending beyond half the length of l. Cymes sessile, axillary, pedicels short, calyx-teeth sometimes minutely hairy. Corolla-tube ½–¾ in., lobes 5–8, shorter than tube. 18. **J. anastomosans**, Wall. Bhutan, Khasi hills, Cachar. Burma, Lower and Upper. Glabrous, l. ovate-lanceolate, blade 3–5, pet. ¼ in., a pair of basal nerves extending to the apex of leaf and anastomosing with the sec. n. Cymes axillary, 1–5-fld., corolla-tube ¾ in., lobes 7–10, linear, as long as or longer than tube. 19. **J. nobile**, Clarke.

Hills between Thaungyin and Haundrow rivers, 4–5,000 ft. An extensive climber. Fl. scentless, in 3–5-fld. cymes, pedicel longer than calyx-tube. Corolla-tube 1–1¼ in., lobes 7–9, lanceolate, equal to tube.

20. **J. Smalianum,** sp. nova. (*Taw sabè*, Burm.) Gaungbyu, Shwebo district in Eng forest (Smales April 1900). An undershrub, with a thick woody rhizome, the stems above ground killed annually by the fires of the hot season, l. membranous, lanceolate, blade 1; pet. slender ⅛ in. long, sec. n. faint, the lowest pair from the base. Fl. white, scented, solitary, pedicels thick, compressed, longer than calyx-tube. Calyx-teeth 7, corolla-tube cylindric, ½–⅝ in. long, lobes 11, linear, longer than tube.

(*b*) Calyx-teeth as long as or shorter than tube.

a. Western species.

21. **J. angustifolium,** Vahl; Wight Ic. t. 698. Deccan. Ceylon, common in the dry region. Branchlets pubescent, l. glabrous, from broad-ovate, almost orbicular to lanceolate, ⅓–2 in. long, pet. very short. Cymes 1–3-fld., pedicels ⅛ in. long. Calyx-segments usually as long as tube. Corolla-tube ½–⅝ in. long, lobes linear-lanceolate, as long as tube. Carpels obliquely ellipsoid. 22. **J. Ritchiei,** Clarke. Western Ghats from the Konkan southwards, in evergreen forests. Scandent, branchlets and l. nearly glabrous, l. ovate-lanceolate, blade 2–4, pet. slender, ⅛ in. Cymes pedunculate, lax, trichotomous, terminal, pedicels slender, ½–¾ in. long. Calyx-teeth equal to tube. Corolla-tube ½ in., lobes equal to tube. Carpels spherical. 23. **J. Wightii,** Clarke. Bolampatti hills, Coimbatore. Glabrous, l. lanceolate, blade 2–3, pet. slender, ½ in. long. Calyx-teeth triangular, shorter than tube.

24. **J. trichotomum,** Heyne. Nilgiris. Branchlets glabrous, l. minutely puberulous beneath, ovate-lanceolate, blade 1–3, pet. slender ¼–½ in. Cymes compound trichotomous, many-fld. Calyx-teeth minute, triangular. Corolla-tube conical, ⅓–½ in. lobes erect, longer than tube.

β. Eastern species.

25 **J. glandulosum,** Wall. Outer Himalaya from Kumaon eastwards, ascending to 6,000 ft. Khasi hills, frequent. A climbing shrub, glabrous. L. ovate-lanceolate, blade 3–4, pet. ¼ in. Fl. white, sweet-scented, in lax few-fld. cymes, often solitary, pedicels long, slender. Calyx-teeth shorter than tube, corolla-tube slender 1–1¼ in. long, lobes linear nearly as long as tube. 26. **J. attenuatum,** Roxb. Assam, Khasi hills, Manipur. Hills between Sitang and Salween river, 4–7,000 ft. An evergreen, climbing shrub, perfectly glabrous. L. elliptic-oblong to lanceolate, blade 5–7, pet. ½–¾ in. Cymes pedunculate, lax, usually several from one leaf-axil, pedicels ½–¾ in. long. Calyx-teeth minute, corolla red or white, tube wider upwards, ½–⅝ in. long, lobes 5, shorter than tube. The Manipur specimens, Clarke 41952, Watt 6145, 6842, have narrower l., shorter petioles and short triangular calyx-teeth. 27. **J. subglandulosum,** Kurz, Andamans, Pegu Yoma and Tenasserim, is supposed to differ by nerves more prominent, and a larger number (8) of corolla-lobes. 28. **J. latipetalum,** Clarke. Thaungyin hills, 5,000 ft. Glabrous, l. coriaceous, lanceolate from a broad base, blade 4–5, pet. ⅛ in., sec. n. nearly at right angles to midrib, invisible beneath. Fl. scented. 29. **J. extensum,** Wall. Upper Burma, imperfectly known, glabrous, l. membranous, calyx 5-ribbed, almost truncate.

C. L. opposite, unifoliolate and trifoliolate, lateral leaflets very small.

30. **J. auriculatum,** Vahl; Wight Ic. t. 700.—Syn. *J. affine* and *ovalifolium*, Wight Ic. tt. 1255, 1256. Vern. *Malla tiga*, Tel. Deccan in dry forests. Nilgiris. Ceylon, dry region, common. Generally scandent, more or less pubescent, l. unifoliolate, or trifoliolate, lateral leaflets small, often minute, terminal 1–2 in. long. Cymes panicled, terminal pedicels generally very short, calyx-lobes 5, obtuse, short, corolla-tube ½ in. long, lobes elliptic, shorter than tube. Ripe carpels globose, ¼ in. diam. 31. **J. brevilobum,** A. DC. Nilgiris. Palnis, common in sholas. A large climber, similar to 30, but more pubescent or tomentose, l. cordate, mostly unifoliolate, cymes dense, sessile, corolla-tube 1 in. long. 32. Watt No. 7386, Manipur, is a new sp. allied to the above, softly tomentose, terminal leaflet 2–3 in., calyx hairy, teeth linear, obtuse, as long as or longer than tube.

D. L. opposite, as a rule trifoliolate.

33. **J. flexile,** Vahl; Wight Ic. t. 1253. Evergreen forests of the Western Ghats, from North Kanara southwards. Ceylon. A large climber, stems very long, glabrous, l. 3-foliolate, leaflets thinly coriaceous, ovate, ovate-lanceolate, sometimes elliptic, terminal 3–4, the lateral 2–3 in. long. Fl. white, scented, in lax pedunculate axillary and terminal cymes, calyx-teeth minute, corolla-tube ⅞–1 in. 34. **J. caudatum,** Wall. Khasi hills, Mishmee. Closely allied, leaflets membranous, ovate-lanceolate, caudate-acuminate, fl. scentless, corolla-tube ¾–1¼ in. long. *J. flexile*, var. *Hookeriana* is intermediate between 33 and 34. 35. **J. lanceolaria,** Roxb. Khasi hills, Manipur. China.

Glabrous, l. trifoliolate, leaflets thickly coriaceous, elliptic, shortly acuminate, the terminal 3–4½ in. long, the lateral a little shorter, nerves obscure. Fl. white, in terminal compound trichotomous cymes, calyx-teeth triangular, shorter than tube, corolla-tube 1 in., lobes ½–⅝ in. long. Carpels on thickened pedicels, ⅓–½ in. diam.

E. L. opposite, imparipinnate.

36. **J. dispermum,** Wall. Pl. As. Rar. t. 274. Dúns and outer hills from the Jumna eastwards, in Sikkim at 6–7,000 ft. Khasi hills. Manipur. A glabrous climber, l. imparipinnate, leaflets 1-2 pair, the upper l. often unifoliolate, the terminal leaflet 3–4 in., the lateral smaller, shortly stalked. Fl. white or lilac, fragrant, usually in an elongated terminal thyrsus, pedicels twice the length of calyx or less, calyx-teeth minute. Berries dark purple, ½ in. long.

37. **J. officinale,** Linn.; Brandis F. Fl. 313. Vern. *Sonu*, Sutlej; *Suni*, Muttiana.

A large twining shrub, youngest shoots slightly pubescent, leaflets 2–3 pair, the terminal largest, lanceolate, 2–3 in. long. Fl. white, fragrant, in few-fld. terminal cymes, pedicels longer than calyx. Calyx-teeth 5, subulate, 3 or 4 times longer than tube. Corolla-tube ⅔ in. long, lobes acute.

Afghanistan. Mount Tillah, Salt range at 3,000 ft. N. W. Himalaya, 3–9,000 ft., extending into the inner dry valleys. Fl. May–June. Persia, Caucasus. Commonly cultivated. 38. **J. excellens,** King & Prain in Journ. As. Soc. Bengal, 69. 169. Kachin Hills 5,000 ft. Similar, cymes axillary, calyx-teeth as long as tube.

39. **J. grandiflorum,** Linn.; Wight Ic. t. 1257; Kanjilal 227. Vern. *Chameli*. Hind. *Joi*, Garhw. Indigenous in Bashahr, Jaunsar, Garhwal, Kumaon, Nepal and on Mt. Abu in Rajputana. Commonly cultivated in India and Burma (*Myatle*, Burm.). A large glabrous shrub, erect while young, usually climbing or scrambling when older, branches ribbed, leaflets ¾–1 in. long, 2–4 pair, common petiole marginate. Fl. white with a purple tinge, delightfully fragrant. Calyx-teeth twice the length of tube, corolla-tube ¾ in. long.

F. L. alternate, rarely opposite.

40. **J. heterophyllum,** Roxb.; Wall. Pl. As. Rar. t. 275. Nepal. Mishmi, Khasi and Naga hills. Manipur. L. glabrous, uni- and trifoliolate, leaflets ovate or ovate-lanceolate, 3–4 in. long, nearly equal, the lateral shortly stalked. Fl. yellow, in large terminal compound corymbiform minutely pilose cymes, calyx-teeth minute, corolla-tube ¼–⅓ in. long. 41. **J. calophyllum,** Wall. (*J. courtallense*, Wight Ic. t. 1252). Nilgiris, Courtallum. Nearly allied, leaflets broadly ovate, 2 in., the lateral on slender stalks 1 in. long, corolla-tube ⅝ in. long.

42. **J. humile,** Linn.—Syn. *J. revolutum*, Sims; Wight Ic. t. 1258; Brandis F. Fl. 313. Vern. *Chamba*, Haz.; *Suni*, Pangi; *Kurang*, Kun.; *Shanjoi*, *Shunjai*, Jauns.

An erect, rigid, entirely glabrous shrub, occasionally a small tree, branches angled. L. alternate, imparipinnate, leaflets opposite, 1–5 pair, ½–2 in. long. Fl. yellow, fragrant, in short terminal corymbose panicles, pedicels longer than calyx, calyx-teeth 5, shorter than tube, corolla-lobes, 5, broad-ovate, obtuse, shorter than tube. Fruit didymous, berries globose.

Baluchistan, Afghanistan. Salt range. Himalaya, 2-10,000 ft., extending to the inner dry valleys. Nilgiris. Travancore on the higher ranges at 7,000 ft. Fl. April–June. Ceylon, rare. 43. **J. pubigerum,** Don, Baluchistan. Naldera near Simla and elsewhere in the N. W. Himalaya, similar, but softly tomentose.

Myxopyrum smilacifolium, Blume (*Chondrospermum smilacifolium*, Wall.; Wight Ill. t. 151*b*). Sikkim Terai. Assam, Cachar, Chittagong. Pegu, Tenasserim. Anamalai hills. Travancore. Malay Archip. Admiralty islds. A large twining glabrous evergreen shrub, branches green, more or less quadrangular. L. coriaceous, elliptic, entire or serrate, blade 6–9, pet. stout ⅛ in. long, 3 prominent basal nerves. Fl. small, yellowish, numerous in axillary and terminal trichotomous panicles, calyx deeply 4-cleft, corolla-tube longer than calyx. Fr. ⅓ in. diam., dark purple, in large hanging bunches, pericarp crustaceous.

ORDER LXXII. SALVADORACEÆ. Gen. Pl. ii. 680.

Glabrous shrubs or trees, l. opposite, entire, stipules minute. Fl. small, tetramerous, in panicled spikes or racemes. Calyx small, corolla membranous, deeply 4-cleft or petals distinct, imbricate in bud. Stamens 4, filaments short, inserted at the base of corolla-tube, alternating with its lobes, disk hypogynous, 4-lobed. Ovary free, 1-2-celled, stigma subsessile, 2-lobed, ovules 1 or 2 in each cell, ascending. Seeds 1–4, cotyledons fleshy, plano-convex, albumen 0.

Islands of phloëm in the wood of most species.

Unarmed, corolla gamopetalous, ovary 1-celled . . 1. SALVADORA.
Unarmed, petals free, ovary 1-celled . . . . . DOBERA (p. 453).
Armed, petals free, ovary 2-celled . . . . . . 2. AZIMA.

1. SALVADORA, Linn.; Fl. Brit. Ind. iii. 619.

Evergreen, leaves between coriaceous and fleshy. Fl. in the axils of deciduous bracts. Ovary 1-celled, fr. a small 1-seeded berry, supported by the persistent calyx, endocarp crustaceous. Species 2.

1. **S. persica**, Linn.; Roxb. Cor. Pl. t. 26; Wight Ic. t. 1621.—Syn. *S. indica*, Wight Ill. t. 181; *S. Wightiana*, Planch.; Bedd. Fl. Sylv. t. 247. Vern. *Kabbar*, *Pilu*, Sind; *Jhāl*, *Jāl*, Rajputana; *Khakhin*, *Kickni*, Mar.; *Ghunia*, Tel.; *Goni*, Kan.; *Opa*, Tam.

A large evergreen shrub or small tree, the trunk often attaining a considerable size, wood soft, whitish-yellow. Bark of old stems irregularly rugose, that of branches shining, often almost white. Branches spreading, extremities drooping, l. glaucous-green, obtuse, rarely acute, varying from ovate to lanceolate, blade 2–3, pet. ½–¾ in. Fl. greenish-white, pedicellate, in lax axillary and terminal panicles, which often are nodding and longer than leaves, branches racemose, divaricate. Corolla-lobes twice the length of calyx and generally reflexed. Berries red when ripe.

Baluchistan, Sind. Trans Indus. Punjab. Aravalli hills. Guzerat, the Konkan and North Kanara near the coast. Along tidal creeks Thana district with *Ægiceras* and *Avicennia* (Ryan). Babul Koruns and elsewhere in the Deccan. Frequent on saline soils. Fl. Nov.–May, also at other times.—Ceylon, dry country, chiefly near the coast. Dry regions of Western Asia. Egypt. Abyssinia.

2. **S. oleoides**, Dcne.; Brandis F. Fl. t. 39. Vern. *Kabbar*, *Diar*, *Jhar*, Sind; *Jāl*, *Van*, *Pilu*, Punjab.

A gregarious shrub or small tree, branches stiff, divergent, l. dull grey, linear or lanceolate. Fl. greenish-white, sessile, in erect compact axillary panicled spikes, shorter than l. Corolla as long as or a little longer than calyx. Fr. yellow when ripe, reddish-brown when dry.

Central and Northern Sind. Common in the driest part of the Punjab on both sides of the Indus, ascending to 3,000 ft. Trans Indus and to 2,400 ft. in the Salt range. Merwara, less common than 1. Fl. Feb.–April. Aden, Arabia.

Dobera Roxburghii, Planch. Sind. Arabia. Abyssinia. Kordofan. Eastern tropical Africa. A glabrous tree, l. coriaceous, elliptic or obovate, blade 2–3, pet. ⅛–¼ in. long. Fl. dioicous, sessile, on short axillary panicles. Calyx ovoid, irregularly 3–5-toothed, petals 4, narrowly oblong, imbricate, stamens 4, filaments connate, ovary 1-celled, ovule 1, basal. Fr. globose ¾ in. diam., seed erect.

2. AZIMA, Lam.; Fl. Brit. Ind. iii. 620.

Shrubs, spines axillary, single or 2–7. Fl. dioicous, tetramerous, calyx campanulate, 4-fid or irregularly 2–4-lobed, petals 4, oblong, imbricate in bud. Berry globose 1–2-seeded, endocarp membranous. Species 2.

1. **A. tetracantha**, Lamk.; Wight Ill. t. 152. Common in the drier districts of the Western Peninsula, often gregarious. Sundriban. Fl. throughout the year. Ceylon, dry region. Arabia. Madagascar. Tropical Africa. A rigid shrub, branches green

herbaceous, quadrangular, young shoots pubescent, spines ¼–1 in. long. L. stiff, shining, sharply mucronate, ½–2 in. long, narrowed into a short petiole. Fl. greenish-white, sessile, ♀ solitary or in two-fld. clusters, ♂ in dense globose fascicles, the supporting l. of the upper fascicles reduced to bracts or obsolete, so that the fl. branches end in naked interrupted spikes. Pet. linear-lanceolate, acute, spreading. Berry ¼ in. diam., white. **2. A. sarmentosa,** Benth. Dry region of the Irawaddi valley. Malay Archipelago. Rambling, spines ¼ in. long, fl. in narrow axillary panicles, berries ¼ in. diam. on slender pedicels up to ⅓ in. long.

ORDER LXXIII. **APOCYNACEÆ.** Gen. Pl. ii. 681.

Trees, shrubs, often twining, rarely perennial herbs, juice frequently milky. L. entire, opposite or whorled, rarely alternate, stipules 0 or small gland-like, intra- or inter-petiolar. Fl. regular, bisexual, usually pentamerous. Calyx free, divided nearly or quite to the base into 5 segments or sepals, generally imbricate in bud. Corolla hypogynous, gamopetalous, lobes 5, spreading, in bud contorted, rarely valvate, throat often hairy or closed with a corona of scales Stamens 5, alternating with corolla-lobes inserted in the tube, filaments usually short. Ovary of 2 carpels, 2-celled with axile, or 1-celled with parietal placentas. Seeds often with a tuft of hairs, usually with scanty albumen, embryo straight.

The vascular bundles of both *Apocynaceæ* and *Asclepiadaceæ* are bicollateral, consequently phloëm is found on the outer edge of the pith. Most species of these two orders have milky juice, which is contained in nonarticulated laticiferous tubes in pith and bark, and accompanying the nerves in the leaves. The milk of several species yields Caoutchouc. In both orders the vessels in the wood are usually arranged in longer or shorter radial lines. Many of the climbing species have wood of normal structure with large vessels, some however, are abnormal, the wood having furrows filled up with phloëm, while in other species the stem consists of numerous more or less radial edges of wood, separated by phloëm.

I. Anther-cells rounded at the base. Carpels connate, forming one 1- or 2-celled ovary. Seeds without wing or hairs.

A. Ovary 2-celled, placentas on the septum.
Armed, erect or climbing . . . . . . 1. CARISSA.
Unarmed, climbing.
L. chartaceous or membranous, sec. n. 15–20 pair . . . . 2. MELODINUS.
L. thinly coriaceous, sec. n. ∞. . . . . WINCHIA (p. 456).

B. Ovary 1-celled, placentas parietal.
Erect shrub, corolla yellow, more than 2 in. long. ALLAMANDA (p. 456)
Woody climber, corolla white ⅝ in. . . . WILLUGHBEIA (p. 456).
Woody climber, corolla yellow, ½ in.. . . . CHILOCARPUS (p. 456).

II. Anther-cells rounded at the base. Carpels more or less distinct, united by the style.

A. Calyx without glands.
L. usually whorled, disk cup-shaped . . . 3. RAUWOLFIA.
L. often whorled, disk 0 . . . . 4. ALYXIA.
L. opposite . . . . HUNTERIA (p. 457).
L. alternate
Second. and intramarginal n. inconspicuous . 5. CERBERA.
Second. and intramarginal n. prominent . PLUMERIA (p. 458).

B. Calyx glandular within.
L. alternate, fr. broad, obtriangular, seeds 2–4. THEVETIA (p. 458).
L. alternate, fr. of 2 many-seeded follicles . RHAZYA (p. 458).
L. alternate or whorled, bright yellow drupes usually in pairs . . . . . OCHROSIA (p. 458).
L. opposite or whorled . . . . . .
Corolla-lobes overlapping to the right . . KOPSIA (p. 458).
Corolla-lobes overlapping to the left.
A twining shrub . . . . ELLERTONIA (p. 458).
Trees or erect shrubs.
L. whorled . . . . 6. ALSTONIA.
L. opposite, seeds with a tuft of hairs . 7. HOLARRHENA.
L. opposite, seeds in an orange col'd arillus . . . . 8. TABERNÆMONTANA.

III. Anthers conniving in a cone around the stigma and adhering to it, each cell produced downwards into a subulate empty spur. Ovary of 2 distinct carpels, united by the style. Fr. of two follicles, seeds hairy at one or both ends.

A. Corolla-lobes valvate in bud.
- Corolla $\frac{1}{3}$ in. long, filaments spirally twisted . PARSONSIA (p. 460).
- Corolla $\frac{1}{10}$ in. long, filaments short . . . URCEOLA (p. 460).

B. Corolla-lobes overlapping to the left.
- Corolla $\frac{1}{3}$–$\frac{3}{8}$ in. long. Trees or erect shrubs . 9. WRIGHTIA.
- Corolla $\frac{1}{3}$ in. long. Climbing . . . . PARAMERIA (p. 461).

C. Corolla-lobes overlapping to the right.
- Anthers exserted (see also *Trachelospermum*).
  - Corolla rotate, limb $\frac{3}{4}$ in. across . . . 10. VALLARIS.
  - Corolla salver-shaped . . . . . POTTSIA (p. 462).
- Anthers included, corolla-throat with 5–10 scales
  - L. whorled, follicles erect . . , . NERIUM (p. 462).
  - L. opposite, follicles divaricate . . . 11. STROPHANTHUS.
- Anthers included, corolla-throat naked.
  - Corolla large, $1\frac{1}{2}$–4 in. long.
    - Cor. bell- or funnel-shaped . . . . BEAUMONTIA (p. 463).
    - Cor. salver-shaped, upper part of tube campanulate . . . . 12. CHONEMORPHA.
  - Corolla middle-sized $\frac{1}{3}$–$1\frac{1}{2}$ in. long.
    - Cor.-lobes twisted to the left, overlapping to the right.
      - Cor.-lobes large, longer than tube, seed long-beaked . . . . . . RHYNCHODIA (p. 463).
      - Cor.-lobes small, shorter than tube.
        - Cor.-tube tomentose outside . . . EPIGYNUM (p. 463).
        - Cor-tube glabrous or nearly so.
          - Ovary hidden in disk, seeds beaked . ANODENDRON (p. 463).
          - Ovary exserted from disk, seeds not beaked . . . . . . 13. TRACHELOSPERMUM.
    - Cor.-lobes straight, overlapping to the right. 14. AGANOSMA.
  - Corolla small, $\frac{1}{4}$ in. and shorter.
    - Cor.-lobes long, narrow, upper half deflexed in bud.
      - Sec. n. few, distant . . . . . 15. ICHNOCARPUS.
      - Sec. n. numerous . . . . . . MICROCHITES (p. 465).
    - Cor.-lobes short, tip not deflexed in bud . ECDYSANTHERA (p. 465).

1. CARISSA, Linn.; Fl. Brit. Ind. iii. 630.

Shrubs or trees, sometimes climbing, armed with opposite axillary spikes. Corolla-tube cylindric, slightly swollen round the anthers, lobes spreading, throat without scales, anthers included. Ovary 2-celled, ovules 1–4 in each cell, style filiform, stigma thickened. Fr. a berry, supported by the persistent calyx, seeds 1–4, without hairs. Species 18, Africa, Asia, Australia.

A. Spines straight.

1. **C. spinarum**, A. DC.—Syn. *C. diffusa*, Roxb.; Wight. Ic. t. 427; Brandis F. Fl. 321. Vern. *Garna*, *Garaunda*, Pb.; *Karaunda*, Hind.; *Karwand*, *Karanda*, Mar.; *Kavali*, *Garji*, Kan.; *Kalivi*, *Kalli*, Tel.

A gregarious evergreen thorny shrub, branches spreading, sometimes climbing over tall trees. Young shoots more or less, inflorescence always pubescent, spines often forked or trifid. L. coriaceous, ovate or elliptic, glabrous or pubescent beneath, blade 1–2, pet. $\frac{1}{6}$–$\frac{1}{4}$ in. long. Fl. white, sometimes with a pink tinge, scented, in few-fld. corymbiform cymes at the ends of branches, sepals lanceolate, ciliate, corolla-tube cylindric $\frac{1}{3}$ in. long. Berry dark purple, edible, $\frac{1}{6}$–$\frac{1}{4}$ in. long, seeds 2.

Trans-Indus. Subhimalayan tract and outer valleys, ascending to 3,000 ft. Plains of Northern India. Bengal. Central provinces. Western Peninsula. Forms underwood under Bamboos, Sal, Teak, and under *Pinus longifolia* in Kangra. Springs up abundantly in clearances. Dry region of the Irawadi valley from Prome upwards. Fl. Jan.–May. L. generally renewed in March. A softly pubescent form is *C. hirsuta*, Roth (*C. villosa*, Roxb.; Wight Ic. t. 437). Belgaum district. Pakokku, Upper Burma and elsewhere. 2. **C. Carandas**, Linn.; Roxb. Cor. Pl. t. 77; Wight Ic. t. 426; Bedd. Manual t. 19, f. 6. Cultivated for its fruit in most parts of India. A taller shrub, l.

larger, fr. ½–1 in. long, 4- or more-seeded, black when ripe. Probably the cultivated form of 1.

3. **C. paucinervia**, A. DC.; Wight Ic. 1290. Nilgiris. A small shrub, l. glabrous, lanceolate, 1–1½ in., sepals linear-lanceolate, corolla white, tinged with pink, fr. ovoid ⅓ in. long.

B. Spines decurved.

4. **C. macrophylla**, Wall. (*C. Dalzellii*, Bedd.). Western Ghats from North Kanara to Tinnevelli, a large shrub, spines 1–1½ in. long, flowering branches unarmed, l. shining, drying dark brown, 2–4 in. long, ending in a fine, sharp point, corolla-tube 1, lobes ½ in., berry ellipsoid, 1 in. long. 5. **C. suavissima**, Bedd. Madura Hills. North Kanara and Konkan Ghats (Talbot). A lofty climber, entirely glabrous, spines small, corolla-tube ⅜ in. long, fr. ovoid nearly 2 in. long very milky, most delicious.

2. MELODINUS, Forst.; Fl. Brit. Ind. iii. 628.

Evergreen, erect or climbing shrubs. Corolla salver-shaped, mouth with thick more or less lobed scales, left hand edge of lobes overlapping. Anthers included, on very short filaments, cells obtuse at the base. Ovary 2-celled, ovules ∞ on a thick placenta. Fr. globose, pericarp coriaceous, seeds numerous imbedded in pulp, cotyledons thin flat, in fleshy albumen.

1. **M. monogynus**, Roxb.; Wight Ic. t. 394. Assam, Khasi hills, Manipur. China. Malay Peninsula. A tall climber, l. glabrous, chartaceous, elliptic-oblong, acuminate, blade 5–6, pet. ⅓ in., sec. n. slender, 15–20 pair with numerous shorter intermediate nerves between. Fl. white large, in terminal compound trichotomous slightly puberulous cymes, corolla-tube villous within, ½–⅝ in. long, lobes as long as tube. Fr. size and colour of an orange. 2. **M. khasianus**, Hook f., Khasi hills. Shwebo district, Upper Burma (*Nyansein nwè*) in evergreen forest at 3,000 ft. Climbing, l. membranous, fl. yellow or white, corolla-tube ¼ in., lobes short, fr. white 1½ in. diam.

Winchia calophylla, A. DC. Martaban. A climbing glabrous evergreen shrub, l. often in whorls of 3, thinly coriaceous, elliptic-lanceolate, obtusely caudate, blade 3–4, pet. 1 in. long, sec. n. ∞, close together, at right angles to midrib. Corolla-tube ⅓–½ in., mouth without scales, lobes short, white, velvety.

Allamanda cathartica, Linn. Indigenous in Central America, the West Indies and Brazil, largely cultivated and sometimes run wild in India and Burma. A large evergreen glabrous shrub, l. often whorled, lanceolate to oblanceolate, blade 2–4 in. long, narrowed into the short petiole, fl. yellow, corolla large, tube 1 in. long, limb campanulate, longer than tube. Capsule compound, echinate, 2-valved, cotyledons leafy, in scanty albumen.

Willughbeia edulis, Roxb. Cor. Pl. t. 280.—Syn. *W. martabanica*, Wall. Pl. As. Rar. t. 272. Vern. *Thitchauk nwè*, *Talaing no*, Burm. Assam, Silhet, Cachar, Chittagong, Lower Burma. Malay Penins. and Archip. An immense glabrous climber, with long branched tendrils, l. thinly coriaceous, elongate-elliptic, blade 4–10, pet. ½ in. long, sec. n. prominent, nearly straight, 15–20 pair. Fl. white, in small few-fld. shortly peduncled axillary cymes, calyx-lobes short, rounded, ciliate, corolla-tube ⅓, lobes ½ in. long, Fr. yellow, edible, 3–4 in. long, seeds large, numerous, embedded in soft fibrous pulp, albumen 0, cotyledons plano-convex. Yields an inferior kind of Caoutchouc. *W. firma*, Blume, of Sumatra and Borneo, yields the Borneo Caoutchouc. H. Jumelle, Les plantes à Caoutchouc et à Gutta. Paris 1903. p. 395.

Chilocarpus atroviridis, Blume (*C. malabaricus*, Bedd. Ic. t. 175; *Winchia atroviridis* Kurz). South Kanara, Malabar and Travancore in evergreen forests. Tavoy and Mergui. A large woody climber, l. thinly coriaceous, elliptic-oblong, acuminate, blade 4–5, pet. ⅓ in., sec. n. numerous, slender, joined by a distinct intra-marginal vein. Fl. yellow in axillary trichotomous cymes, shorter than l., corolla ⅓ in., lobes short obtuse, the left hand edge overlapping.

3. RAUWOLFIA, Linn.; Fl. Brit. Ind. iii. 632.

Glabrous shrubs, l. usually 3–4-nately whorled. Peduncles in the axils of the uppermost l. Calyx 5-fid., corolla salver-shaped, tube hairy within, inflated over the anthers, the cells of which are rounded at the base. Disk large, cup-shaped or annular, entire or lobed. Carpels 2, distinct or connate, ovules 2-collateral in each carpel. Fr. of 2 connate or distinct 1-seeded drupes, cotyledons flat in a fleshy albumen. Species 50, tropics of both hemispheres, extending beyond the tropics in South Africa.

A. Corolla-tube slender, inflated slightly above the middle.

1. **R. serpentina**, Benth. (*Ophioxylon serpentinum*, Wight Ic. t. 849). Subhimalayan tract from Sirhind eastwards, ascending to 2,000 ft. Andamans. Lower Burma, common. Western Peninsula. Ceylon, moist region, common. A small shrub, in a rich soil climbing (Roxburgh). L. lanceolate, blade 4–7, pet. ⅓ in. long, sec. n. 8–10 pair. Peduncle 2–5 in., pedicels and calyx bright red, fl. white, 1 in. long, disk lobed. Drupes in pairs or single, black, ¼ in. diam. 2. **R. peguana**, Hook. f. Pegu. Tenasserim. (Donat pass at 5,000 ft. D. B. April 1859, named by Kurz *Tabernæmontana ophiorrhizoides*.) Upper Burma (Collett 645). L. often opposite, whorled in the Upper Burma specimens, from elliptic-lanceolate to obovate, acuminate, blade 3–6, narrowed into pet. ½ in. long. Fl. ½ in. long, in axillary sessile or shortly pedunculate compound cymes, disk cup-shaped entire.

B. Corolla-tube wide, inflated below the mouth.

3. **R. densiflora**, Benth. (*Ophioxylon neilgherrense* and *O. ceylanicum*, Wight Ic. t. 1292, 1291; *O. densiflorum*, Thwaites; Bedd. Manual t. 20). Khasi hills. Western Ghats and adjoining hill ranges from the Konkan southwards. Ceylon, ascending to 6,000 ft. A large shrub, branches densely lenticellate, l. oblanceolate, blade 6–9, pet. ½ in., sec. n. arching, 10–15 pair. Fl. pink or white, ⅓ in. long. Drupes free, in pairs or single, scarlet, ellipsoid, ⅛–⅙ in. long. *R. decurva*, Hook. f. Poona, Konkan, North Kanara, with short recurved peduncles is regarded by Talbot as a variety. 4. **R. micrantha**, Hook. f. Malabar. Fl. ⅙ in., drupes short, connate to the middle, ⅓ in. broad. 5. **R. Beddomei**, Hook. f. (*Tabernæmontana verticellata*, Bedd. Man. t. 20). Tinnevelli and Travancore Ghats. Peduncles very slender, dichotomous, bearing racemes of small white fl.

4. ALYXIA, Rob. Brown; Fl. Brit. Ind. iii. 634.

Shrubs, often climbing, l. often 3–4-nately whorled, sec. n. numerous, faint, straight, nearly at right angles to midrib. Corolla small, salver-shaped, tube cylindric, anthers lanceolate, base of cells rounded. Carpels of ovary distinct, style filiform. Drupes 1-seeded or consisting of 1–4, 1-seeded joints. Species 20, extending to Australia and Polynesia.

1. **A. fascicularis**, Benth. Khasi hills. Yunzalin, 3,000 ft., Martaban (D. B. March 1880). A large, woody, almost entirely glabrous climber, l. coriaceous, elongate-elliptic, shortly acuminate, blade 4–5, pet. ⅙ in. long, upper side shining. Cymes axillary, shortly peduncled, glabrous or puberulous, corolla-tube ⅙ in. long. Drupes ellipsoid-cylindric ¾ in., on stalks ⅛–¼ in. long, supported at the base of the stalk by the persistent calyx. *Gynopogon stellatum*, Labill.; Kurz F. Fl. ii. 176, a climber on the rocky shores of Tenasserim and the Andamans, corolla-tube ½ in. long, is an *Alyxia*, but imperfectly known.

2. **A. gracilis**, Benth. Sikkim Terai. Khasi hills. Twining, panicles spreading, axillary, 3–4 in. long, peduncles and branches very slender, corolla ⅛–⅙ in. long.

Hunteria corymbosa, Roxb.; Wight Ic. t. 428 (*H. zeylanica*, Gard.; Bedd. Fl. Sylv. t. 265 ' *H. Roxburghiana*, Wight Ic. t. 1294; *Gynopogon lanceolatum*, Kurz). Courtallum Tinnevelli Ghats. Tavoy. Malay Penins. Ceylon. A small tree, wood hard, close-grained, l. opposite, thinly coriaceous, shining, from lanceolate to elongate-elliptic blade 4–6, pet. ⅙ in., sec. n. numerous, slender. Fl. yellow, in axillary or terminal pedunculate umbelliform cymes, corolla-tube ⅙ in. lobes shorter than tube. Carpels distinct, 2–4 ovules in each, style filiform, top thickened. Ripe carpels orange-coloured, globose, stipitate, 2-seeded, ½–¾ in. diam.

5. CERBERA, Linn.; Fl. Brit. Ind. iii. 637.

Species 4, sea coast of Madagascar, tropical Asia and the Pacific islands.

C. Odollam, Gærtn.; Wight Ic. t. 441. Vern. *Dakur*, *Dabur*, Sundr. *Sukanu*, Mar.; *Othalam*, Mal.; *Kalwa*, Burm.

A shrub or middle-sized evergreen tree, wholly glabrous, wood very soft. Branchlets stout, marked with leaf scars. L. alternate, crowded at the ends of branches, lanceolate or oblanceolate, blade 6–12, narrowed into petiole 1–1½ in. long. Fl. large, white, scented, in ample terminal, pedunculate cymes, bracts coloured, ½–1 in. long, caducous. Calyx-segments recurved, deciduous, corolla-tube ½ in., lobes longer than tube, contorted in bud. Ovary of 2 distinct carpels, united by a single style. Fruit (from the abortion of one carpel) a drupe 2–4 in. long, flattened on one side, with a fibrous endocarp, seed usually one, oily, albumen 0.

Tidal Forests: Western Peninsula, Sundriban, Chittagong, the Andamans and Burma. Fl. throughout the year.—Near the coast in Ceylon, the Malay Archipelago, China, Formosa and New Guinea.

Thevetia neriifolia, Juss. Tropical America, cultivated in gardens. A large glabrous poisonous shrub or small tree, l. alternate, linear, sessile, 4–6 in. long, with a strong mid-rib, fl. yellow, corolla funnel-shaped, 2–3 in. long, fr. obtriangular. 1–1½ in. broad, seeds 2–4, cotyledons orbicular. oily, albumen 0.

Plumeria acutifolia, Poiret (*P. acuminata*, Roxb.; Wight Ic. t. 471). Vern. *Guláchin*, Hind.; *Goalanchi*, Ass.; *Khair Champa, Son Champa*, Mar.; *Ganagala*, Kan. A native of Mexico and Guatemala, cultivated in India from time immemorial. The other species of this large genus are all indigenous in South America and the West Indies. A small tree, wholly glabrous, with thick branches, full of tenacious white milk. L. alternate, lanceolate or oblanceolate, spirally arranged at the ends of branches, sec. n. numerous, straight, transverse, joined by straight intramarginal veins, blade 6–15, pet. 1–2 in. long. Fl. usually when the tree is leafless, large, fragrant, white with a pale yellow centre, in compound pedunculate cymes. Rarely produces seed in India.

Rhazya stricta, Dcne. Vern. *Gandera*, Trans Indus; *Vena*, Salt range; *Sewar, Sainwar*, Sind. Baluchistan to 4,000 ft., in all dry stony water courses, covers large areas in the Bolan pass. Trans-Indus, Punjab between Indus and Jhelam. Afghanistan. Arabia. A small gregarious glabrous shrub, l. alternate, lanceolate or oblanceolate, 2–4 in. Fl. in short axillary cymes, bracts subulate, persistent. Corolla white, tube ½ in. long, lobes short. Ovary of two distinct carpels, ovules numerous, 2-seriate in each carpel. Fr. of 2 erect slender follicles, seeds numerous, flat, with short membranous wings at the two ends. Embryo straight, in a fleshy albumen.

Ochrosia borbonica, Gmel.; Trimen Handb. Ceylon t. 60 (*O. salubris*, Blume). Tidal forests of the Andamans. Ceylon. Malay Peninsula and Archip. A small littoral wholly glabrous tree, branchlets stout, marked with large l. scars, usually in whorls. L. whorled or alternate, crowded near the ends of branches, obovate, blade 4–9, tapering into pet. ½–1½ in. long, sec. n. numerous, nearly at right angles to midrib. Fl. white, small, on the short thick branches of small pedunculate dichotomous panicles, corolla-tube ⅓–¼ in. long, lobes overlapping to the right. Drupes bright yellow, usually in pairs, free or connate at the base, more or less diverging, 2–2½ in. long, pericarp thick spongy-fibrous.

Kopsia fruticosa, A. DC. (*Calpicarpium Roxburghii*, G. Don; Wight Ic. t. 431.) *Salat*. Burm. Pegu, Martaban and Tenasserim. Malay Penins. and Archip. Often planted. A large evergreen shrub, entirely glabrous, l. chartaceous, glossy, elliptic 3–7 in. long, pet. very short. Fl. large, pink or white, in a dense, bracteate, terminal, sessile or shortly pedunculate corymb. Corolla-tube slender, 1–1½ in. long, throat hairy, lobes overlapping to the right. Ovaries 2, alternating with 2 hypogynous subulate scales. Follicles 1-seeded, coriaceous, usually solitary by abortion, obliquely truncate. Seeds oblong, albumen 0.

Ellertonia Rheedii, Wight Ic. t. 1295. Western coast and ghats from the Konkan southwards. A glabrous, twining shrub, l. thinly coriaceous, of a peculiar dark grey colour when dry, opposite or in whorls of 3, elliptic, blade 4–5, pet. slender ¼ in. long. Cymes terminal, fascicled, corolla slender, ½ in. long, stamens in the middle of the tube, filaments ciliate, carpels 2 distinct, ovules many, style filiform, ovoid at top, stigma linear, 2-fid. Fr. of 2 linear divaricating follicles, seeds numerous, flat, winged at both ends, with the wings over 1 in. long.

6. ALSTONIA, R. Brown; Fl. Brit. Ind. iii. 641.

Trees, rarely shrubs, l. mostly whorled, sec. n. numerous, close, nearly at right angles to midrib. Corolla-tube cylindrical, lobes spreading, shorter than tube, overlapping to the left in bud. Stamens included. Ovary of 2 distinct carpels, united by the style, ovules numerous. Fr. of 2 distinct long linear follicles. Seed flat, peltate, a dense fringe of hairs all round on the edge. Cotyledons oblong, flat, in scanty albumen. Species 30, Indo-Malayan region, extending to Australia and Polynesia.

A. L. coriaceous, obtuse or acute, in whorls of 5–10, follicles 12–24 in. long.

1. **A. scholaris,** R. Brown; Wight Ic. t. 422; Bedd. Fl. Sylv. t. 242. Vern. *Satni, Chatiun*, Hind.; *Satiana*, Ass.; *Satuin*, Mar.; *Mudhol*. Kan.; *Eda Kula*, Tel.; *Palai*, Tam.; *Lettôk, Taungmèôk*, Burm.

A large tree with bitter milky juice, stem tall, base often fluted or buttressed, branches spreading in tiers of whorls. L. glabrous, coriaceous, in whorls of 5–10, shining above, opaque and pale underneath, oblong or obovate-oblong, blade 4–8, narrowed into petiole $\frac{1}{4}$–$\frac{1}{2}$ in. long. Fl. greenish-white, in compact many-fld. pedunculate pubescent cymes, peduncles whorled, 1–2 in. long, corolla-tube $\frac{1}{6}$–$\frac{1}{3}$ in. long. Follicles slender, numerous, pendulous.

Subhimalayan tract, ascending to 3,000 ft., from the Jumna eastwards. Western Peninsula and Burma, mostly in deciduous forests. Fl. Dec.—Ceylon, Malay Peninsula and Archipelago. China. *A. Kurzii*, Hook. f. (*A. spectabilis*, Kurz not R. Br.) Andamans, probably belongs to this species.

B. L. membranous, acuminate, opposite or in whorls of 3–6, follicles 4–7 in. long.

2. **A. venenata,** Br.; Wight Ic. t. 436. Western Ghats, from North Kanara southwards, in evergreen forests. Nilgiris, Palnis. Surada, Ganjam (Gamble 13973). A shrub, sometimes a small tree, corolla-tube slender, $\frac{3}{4}$–1 in. long, follicles narrowed into a stalk $\frac{1}{2}$–1 in. and into a straight beak equally long. Seeds with a wing-like margin all round or at both ends, hairs shorter than seed. 3. **A. neriifolia,** Don. East Nepal. Sivoke, Sikkim (D. B. Dec. 1879). Bhutan. Corolla-tube cylindric, widened upwards, $\frac{1}{3}$–$\frac{1}{2}$ in. long, follicles sessile, 5–7 in., beak short, seeds not marginate, hairs as long as seeds. It seems doubtful whether 2 and 3 are distinct species, the l. vary from glabrous to pubescent, shape and length of corolla also varies. The subject is well worth further study.

7. HOLARRHENA, R. Br.; Fl. Brit. Ind. iii. 644.

Species 7, tropical Africa and Asia.

H. antidysenterica, Wall.; Brandis F. Fl. t. 40.—Syn. *H. Codaga*, G. Don; Wight Ic. t. 1297; *Chonemorpha antidysenterica*, G. Don; Wight Ic. t. 439. Vern. *Kewar*, Pb.; *Dudhi, Kura, Koira, Kachri.* Seeds: *Indarjau*, Hind.; *Kudla*, Mar.; *Kodaga*, Tel.; *Lettôkgyi*, Burm.

A small or middle-sized deciduous tree, glabrous or pubescent, young shoots sometimes tomentose, wood white soft. L. nearly sessile, 6–12 in. long, elliptic- or ovate-oblong, sec. n. 10–16 pair. Fl. white, 1–1$\frac{1}{2}$ in. across, on slender pedicels in terminal sessile cymose corymbs, corolla-tube slender, $\frac{1}{3}$–$\frac{2}{3}$ in., follicles distinct, smooth, 8–14 in. long, $\frac{1}{5}$ in. diam. Seeds linear, $\frac{1}{2}$ in. long, numerous, pendulous, a tuft of long silky hairs (twice the length of seed) at the upper end, radicle superior, shorter than the plaited and involute cotyledons, albumen thin.

Subhimalayan tract, ascending to 3,500 ft., from the Chenab eastwards, common in Sal forest. Aravali hills south of the Dewair pass. Behar, Central Provinces. Western Peninsula, common in deciduous forests, often gregarious. Upper and Lower Burma, often in Eng forest. Fl. April–July. Root suckers abundant. One of the trees to be employed in reclaiming waste lands. The pubescent form is known to me from Rajputana, Gauhati, Bellary and the dry country of Upper Burma. Bedd. (Manual 161) states that it is more common on the Western side of the Peninsula.

8. TABERNÆMONTANA, Linn.; Fl. Brit. Ind. iii. 645.

Trees or shrubs, l. opposite, stipules axillary. Fl. usually white in pedunculate cymes from the axils of the uppermost leaves, often apparently terminal. Calyx frequently persistent, usually divided to the base into segments (sepals) bearing on the inside above the base 2–5 minute glands. Corolla salver-shaped, tube inflated over the acuminate anthers, lobes usually overlapping to the left. Carpels distinct, ovules numerous. Fr. of 2 dry or fleshy follicles, usually many-seeded.

I. *Ervatamia*, DC. (Stapf in Fl. Trop. Afr. iv. 126, genus). L. chartaceous or membranous, sec. n. arching. Style filiform when the fl. opens. No resinous exudations.

A. Corolla-lobes overlapping to the left.

(*a*) Calyx-segments ovate.

1. **T. coronaria**, Willd.; Wight Ic. t. 477.—Syn. *T. divaricata*, Bl.; Kurz F. Fl. ii. 174; *Ervatamia coronaria*, Stapf in Fl. Trop. Afr. iv. 127. Vern. *Chāndni, Taggar*, Hind.; *Zalat*, Burm.

An evergreen glabrous shrub, dichotomously branched, bark grey, often with copious lenticels. L. membranous, elliptic-oblong, acuminate, blade 4–6, narrowed into petiole $\frac{1}{4}$–$\frac{1}{3}$ in. Fl. pure white, fragrant at night, often double, corolla-tube $\frac{1}{2}$–1 in., follicles ribbed, recurved, red inside, 1–2 in. long, seeds 3–6.

Subhimalayan tract, from the Jumna eastwards, ascending to 2,000 ft. Upper Burma. Common in gardens of India and Burma. Fl. May–Dec. Grown in gardens throughout the tropics. The specimens from the Peninsula have the anthers in the middle of the corolla-tube and a long style, while the subhimalayan specimens have a short style, and the corolla-tube inflated at $\frac{1}{3}$ from the base (Stapf, l. c. 127). 2. **T. graciliflora,** Wall. Tenasserim. Peduncles 3–4 in. long, corolla-tube very slender, 1 in., follicles turgid, $\frac{1}{3}$ in long, 1-2-seeded. 3. **T. subcapitata,** Wall. Pegu, Tenasserim. Upper Burma (*Zulat thein*). Peduncles 1–2 in. Corolla-tube $\frac{1}{3}$–$\frac{1}{2}$ in. long, follicles 1–2-seeded. 4. **T. crispa,** Roxb.; Wight Ic. t. 470 (*T. alternifolia*, Roxb. not L., Kurz F. Fl. ii. 174) Diamond Island. Andamans, frequent on the coast. A large evergreen shrub, cymes many-fld., peduncles 1–4 in. long, sepals almost foliaceous, ovate, $\frac{1}{4}$–$\frac{1}{3}$ in. long, deciduous.

(*b*) Calyx-segments lanceolate.

5. **T. recurva,** Roxb. Chittagong, Pegu and Tenasserim. *Taw Zalat*, Burm. Sepals unequal, ciliolate, follicles broad, 1 in. long, many-seeded. 6. **T. membranifolia,** Kurz. Forests east of Toungoo. 7. **T. calycina,** Wall. Tenasserim. Sepals one-third of the corolla-tube, which is $\frac{3}{4}$ in. long, and swollen at the top.

B. Corolla-lobes overlapping to the right.

8. **T. Heyneana,** Wall. Western Ghats in evergreen forests from the Konkan southwards. A small glabrous tree, bark grey, rough, with much milky juice. L. elliptic-oblong, acuminate, blade 6–8, pet. $\frac{1}{2}$–1 in. long. Cymes many-fld., peduncles 1–2 in. Corolla-tube 1 in. long, swollen at the top, limb 1 in across. 9. **T. rostrata,** Wall. Upper Burma, banks of the Irawadi. Imperfectly known. Follicles beaked.

II. *Rejoua*, Gaudichaud (genus). L. coriaceous, sec. n. prominent, straight, nearly at right angles to midrib. Corolla fleshy, style short. Resinous exudations at the base of l., in the bifurcations of the cyme and on the fl. buds.

10. **T. dichotoma,** Roxb.; Wight Ic. t. 433. Common at the foot of the Western Ghats, Bedd. Ceylon, moist low country, common. A small dichotomously branched tree, bark pale grey, smooth, branchlets marked with scars of fallen l., young parts covered with a shining resinous coat. L. elliptic-oblong, blade 4–10, pet. $\frac{1}{2}$–1 in. long. sec. n. 20–24 pair. Cymes lax, peduncle stout 2–6 in. long. Fl. sweet-scented, corolla-tube yellow, $\frac{3}{4}$–1 in., lobes white, longer than tube. Follicles orange, 2 in. long, more or less fleshy. Called *Eve's Apple* or *Forbidden Fruit* in Ceylon.

Parsonsia spiralis, Wall. (*Heligme Rheedii*, Wight Ic. t. 1303). Assam. Lower Bengal. Lower Burma. Western Ghats from the Konkan southwards, in evergreen forest. Ceylon, low country, very common. Malay Penins. and Archip. China. A twining shrub, l. glabrous, ovate to ovate-lanceolate, blade 3–6, pet. $\frac{1}{2}$–1 in., sec. n. 6–8 arching. Fl. 5-merous, yellow or purplish-green, in axillary pedunculate minutely pubescent compound cymes, bracts small ovate. Corolla-tube cylindric, short, barely longer than sepals, lobes valvate, sometimes slightly overlapping to the right. Filaments spirally twisted, longer than anthers, slightly hairy. Ovary glabrous, surrounded by 10 fleshy scales, alternately smaller and more or less adnate to calyx-tube. Fr. cylindrical, 6 in. long, at last septicidally 2-valved, seeds ∞, beaked, $\frac{1}{2}$ in. long, on the beak a dense tuft of silky hairs more than twice the length of seed.

Urceola esculenta, Benth. (*Chavannesia esculenta*, A. DC. Strettell, Note on Caoutchouc. Rangoon, 1874.) *Kyetpaung*, Burm. Pegu and Tenasserim. A large woody creeper, youngest shoots and young l. pubescent, mature l. glabrous, coriaceous, elliptic, caudate-acuminate, blade 4–7, pet. ⅓–⅜ in. long, sec. n. 9–11 pair, prominent. Fl. small, white, in large pubescent trichotomous terminal panicles, the lower bracts leaf-like, the upper membranous, lanceolate, 1-nerved. Sepals hairy, elliptic-oblong, glandular. Corolla $\frac{1}{10}$ in. long, hairy, lobes short, valvate, stamens inserted at the base of the corolla, disc cupular, ovaries truncate, hirsute. Follicles 3–5 in., acuminate, narrowed into a stalk ½ in. long. Seeds villous, tip bearded with persistent brown hairs and crowned with a long white deciduous coma. Yields Caoutchouc of a good quality. The Rangoon specimens, called *U. lucida*, Benth, probably belong to this sp.

9. WRIGHTIA, R. Br.; Fl. Brit. Ind. iii. 652.

Trees or shrubs, wood moderately hard, close-grained. Fl. in terminal compound corymbiform cymes, 5–10 scales on the inside of the calyx at its base. Corolla-tube cylindrical, very short, usually a number of fleshy scales in the throat, lobes long, in bud overlapping to the left. Stamens in the mouth of the tube, filaments short broad, prolonged into a broad connective, hairy on the back, anthers exserted, conniving around and adhering to stigma, cells with solid spurs at the base. Follicles linear, connate or distinct. Seeds linear, a deciduous tuft of hairs at the lower end, cotyledons convolute, radicle short, superior. Species about 10, tropical Asia and Australia, one in Natal.

A. Corolla-tube (when the fl. opens) as long as or longer than sepals.

1. **W. tinctoria,** R. Br.; Wight Ic. t. 444; Bedd. Fl. Sylv. t. 241. Vern. *Khirni, Dudhi*, Hind.; *Kala Kuda*, Mar.; *Repala, Jedda Pala*, Tel.; *Vepala, Hale*, Kan.; *Nila Palei*, Tam.

A small deciduous tree, glabrous or pubescent, l. membranous, elliptic-oblong, shortly acuminate, blade 3–4, petiole ⅛–¼ in. long. Fl. ½–¾ in. across, white or pale yellow, in lax spreading corymbs, ramifications slender. Corona of numerous linear scales, varying in length, anthers prominent. Follicles slender, 10–25 in. long, as a rule two, cohering at the tip.

Deciduous forests of Rajputana, Central Provinces and the Western Peninsula. Fl. March–July. The l. yield indigo. 2. **W. religiosa,** Benth. Tenasserim (Kurz), Siam. A small glabrous shrub, l. lanceolate 1–3 in. long, fl. white ½ in. across, in few-fld. cymes on long filiform pedicels, corolla-tube ⅓ in., much longer than sepals, filaments distinct, no scales in the mouth of corolla.

3. **W. tomentosa,** Roem. & Schultes; Wight Ic. t. 443, Ill. t. 154.—Syn. *W. mollissima*, Wall. Pl. Rar. t. 146.; *W. Wallichii*, A. DC.; Wight Ic. t. 1296, Vern. *Dudhi*, Seeds: *Indarjau*, Hind.; *Thella pala*, Tel.; *Pala*, Tam.; *Lettŏkthein*, Burm.

A small deciduous tree, branchlets and leaves softly tomentose. L. elliptic or obovate, acuminate, blade 3–5, petiole ¼–⅓ in. Fl. with an unpleasant smell, 1 in. across, pale yellow or yellowish-brown, turning into a dull purple, in shortly pedunculate, stiff, erect, tomentose corymbs, corona orange of 5–10 oblong often laciniate scales. Fr. cylindric, 6–12 in. long, ½ in. diam., rough, with numerous white elevated specks, two shallow furrows at the junction of carpels.

Subhimalayan tract, ascending to 4,000 ft., rare west of the Bias. Rajputana. Behar. Assam. Chittagong. Burma, Upper and Lower. Western Peninsula. Fl. January-June. Ceylon.

B. Corolla rotate, tube shorter than sepals.

4. **W. coccinea,** Sims, Sikkim, outer hills to 4,000 ft. W. Duars. Khasi hills. A small tree, l. with a few scattered minute hairs, otherwise glabrous. Fl. bright scarlet, in few-fld. nearly sessile terminal cymes, sepals round, ⅛ in. diam. Corolla 1½ in. across, tube ¼ in. long, scales in the throat 5, round, entire, ¼ in. diam.

Parameria glandulifera, Benth. Borders of tidal forests, Andamans, Tenasserim. Malay Penins. and Archip. A large glabrous evergreen scandent shrub, l. sometimes ternate, coriaceous, shining, 2–3 in. long. Fl. small, in pyramidal terminal and axillary panicles. Corolla ⅛ in. long, ¼–⅓ in. across, lobes overlapping to the left, stamens inserted at the base of tube. Follicles 6–12 in. long, torulose, the slender seedless intervals 1–2 in. long. Caoutchouc, supposed to be the produce of this species, is exported from Tonkin.

10. VALLARIS, Burm.; Fl. Brit. Ind. iii. 650.

Species 5–6, Indo-Malayan region.

V. Heynei, Sprengel.—Syn. *V. dichotoma*, Wall.; Wight Ic. t. 438 Brandis F. Fl. 327. Vern. *Dudhi Bel*, Hind.; *Kinbot gyi*, Burm.

A woody twining shrub, bark ash-coloured, young shoots and inflorescence pubescent, otherwise glabrous. L. elliptic-oblong, blade 3–5, petioles ⅓–1 in. long, above their insertion a circle of small cylindric glands. Fl. white, fragrant, on slender pedicels, in lateral 7–15-fld. corymbs, corolla-tube short, cylindric, limb spreading, ¾ in. across. Anthers exserted, conniving in a cone adhering to the stigma, cells with long basal spurs, connective with a large dorsal gland. Fr. 6 by 2 in. straight, tapering from a rounded base, the two carpels separating when ripe, seeds ⅓–½ in. long, ovate, ending in a short beak, which bears a tuft of long silky hairs.

Subhimalayan tract, from the Jumna eastwards, ascending to 5,000 ft. Assam, Lower Bengal. Central Provinces. Western Peninsula. Burma, dry region of the Irawadi valley from Prome upwards. Fl. Dec.–May. Often grown in gardens.

Pottsia cantonensis, Hook. & Arn. (*P. Hookeriana*, Wight Ic. t. 1306 bis; *P. ovata*, A. DC.). Assam, Khasi hills, Cachar. Tenasserim. Malay Penins. and Archip. Tonkin. China. An evergreen climbing shrub, young shoots minutely puberulous. l. ovate, blade 3–4, pet. slender 1 in. long. Fl. pink, in lax axillary and terminal panicles, pedicels slender, ½ in. long, corolla-tube cylindric, ⅛ in. long, lobes nearly as long. Anthers exserted, cells with basal empty spurs, filaments hairy, carpels distinct, hairy, enclosed in a deeply 5-fid disk. Follicles slender, flexuous, 12 in. long, seeds linear with a deciduous coma.

Nerium odorum, Solander (*Ganēra*, Pb.; *Kanēr*, Hind.). A poisonous but beautiful shrub, common in rocky stream beds or in ravines and river beds which are dry in winter. Afghanistan. Baluchistan (to 6,000 ft.). Outer N. W. Himalaya, to 5,500 ft. Central India. China. Grown in gardens with single and double white or pink sweet scented fl. L. in whorls of 3, linear-lanceolate, 4–6 in. long. Fr. linear 6–9 in. long. *N. Oleander*, Linn., with broader l. and larger scentless fl. is a common shrub in the Mediterranean region, and Western Asia, as far as Syria and Kurdistan. A third species, *N. muscatense*, A. DC., with scented fl. grows in Muscat and Southern Persia in dry water courses like the two others. These species are supposed to be distinguished by the segments of the corona-lobes. These, however, vary exceedingly, in *N. odorum* from 3 to 7 and in *N. Oleander* from 3 short triangular to numerous linear or irregular segments. They may be regarded as local forms of one species which extends from the Mediterranean region to China. A number of Indian trees or shrubs of wide distribution bear different names in different countries, such as: *Rhus Cotinus* (*velutina*), *Cratœgus crenulata* (*Pyracantha*), *Albizzia Julibrissin* (*mollis*), *Cephalanthus occidentalis*. *naucleoides*), *Cedrus Deodara* (*Libani, atlantica*).

11. STROPHANTHUS, DC.; Fl. Brit. Ind. iii. 655.

Glabrous shrubs, usually climbing, l. opposite. Fl. in terminal corymbs Sepals glandular within. Corolla-tube cylindric, often short, widening into a funnel-shaped or campanulate mouth, lobes acuminate or produced into long narrow tails, scales 10, paired, free or connate. Stamens inserted at the upper end of the cylindric tube, anthers lanceolate, acuminate or produced into a long bristle. Follicles large, hard, divaricate, seeds spindle-shaped. Species about 40, Africa and tropical Asia.

A. Corolla-lobes long, 2 in. and upwards.

1. **S. Wallichii**, A. DC. (*S. dichotomus*, Wall. Wight Ic. t. 599; *S. caudatus*, Kurz) Assam. Khasi hills. Tenasserim (Kurz). Singhbum. Northern Circars. Corymbs lax spreading, many-fld., sepals and bracts linear-lanceolate ⅓ in. long. Corolla yellow and pink, lobes 1–3 in. long. 2. **S. dichotomus**, DC. (*D. longicaudatus* and *Griffithii*,

Wight Ic. t. 1299, 1300). Tenasserim (Kurz). Malay Penins. and Archip. L. thinly coriaceous, sec. n. 8–10 pair, joined by distinct intra-marginal veins. Corolla-lobes 4–6 in. long.

B. Corolla-lobes $\frac{1}{3}$ in. and less.

3. **S. Wightianus,** Wall.; Wight Ic. t. 1301. Western Coast from Mangalore southwards. L. thinly coriaceous, elliptic, blade 2–3, pet. $\frac{1}{8}$–$\frac{1}{4}$ in. long. Corymbs pedunculate, bracts small ovate, acuminate, cylindrical portion of corolla-tube $\frac{1}{4}$, lobes $\frac{1}{3}$ in. long, narrowed into a linear tail. Seeds with a long slender beak and a large feathery coma. 4. **S. brevicaudatus,** Wight Ic. t. 1302. Mergui (Kurz), Malay Penins. and Archip. Edge of l. undulate, cor.-tube $\frac{1}{4}$, lobes ovate, acuminate, $\frac{1}{4}$ in. long.

Beaumontia grandiflora, Wall. Nepal. Sikkim, from the Terai to 5,000 ft. Silhet, Cachar, Chittagong. China. A large evergreen climber, bark thick, corky, shoots rusty-pubescent. L. opposite, chartaceous, elliptic-obovate, blade 7–12, pet. $\frac{1}{2}$–1 in. long, sec. n. 8–15 pair, arching. Fl. very large, pure white, in terminal corymbiform cymes, pedicels and calyx velvety. Sepals oblong-lanceolate or oblanceolate, 1–2 in., corolla between funnel-shaped and campanulate, 3–4 in. long, lobes short. Fr. 5–10 by 2 in., hard, at length dividing into 2 follicles, seeds $\frac{3}{4}$ in., coma twice as long. 2. **B. Jerdoniana,** Wight Ic. t. 1314–15, evergreen forests of the Konkan and Kanara Ghats is the western representative of 1, with smaller fl. and cylindric fr. 3. **B. Khasiana,** Hook. f., Khasi hills, corolla broadly campanulate, lobes equalling the tube.

12. CHONEMORPHA, G. Don; Fl. Brit. Ind. iii. 661.

Climbing shrubs, fl. large, in lax terminal cymes. Corolla-tube narrow below, upper part wider, lobes broad, oblique, overlapping to the right, filaments short villous. Disk thick, annular or cupular. Follicles long, straight, hard. Seeds shortly beaked, coma long. Species 2.

1. **C. macrophylla,** G. Don; Wight Ic. t. 432. Vern. *Phaldu*, Hind. Outer Himalaya from Kumaon eastwards, 2–6,000 ft. Assam, Khasi hills. Andamans. Tenasserim. Evergreen forests of the Western Ghats from the Konkan southwards.—Ceylon. Malay Penins. and Archip. Yields caoutchouc. 2. **C. Griffithii,** Hook. f. Sikkim, Khasi hills. L. smaller, calyx of 5 distinct sepals, $\frac{1}{8}$–$\frac{1}{2}$ in. long. A large evergreen scandent shrub, branches stout, young shoots, inflorescence and underside of l. pubescent or tomentose. L. ovate, obovate or nearly orbicular, base rounded or cordate, blade 6–18, petiole $\frac{1}{2}$–2 in. long, sec. n. 10–15 pair, prominent beneath. Fl. 2–3 in. across, white, rarely pale pink, in terminal trichotomous corymbose cymes, bracts large ovate, acute. Follicles hard, angled, 12–18 in. long.

Rhynchodia Wallichii, Benth. (*Echites rhynchosperma*, Wall. Pl. As. Rar. t. 49; *Cercocoma Wallichii*, Miq.). Sikkim, 2–3,000 ft. Assam. Silhet, Cachar. Pegu Yoma, eastern slopes. Martaban, Tenasserim. A large climber, branches tubercled, l. membranous, ovate or elliptic, acuminate, blade 5–9, pet. slender 1 in. long. Fl. showy, fragrant, white, tube and throat red, in loose, pedunculate axillary cymes, peduncles and pedicels slender. Calyx divided nearly to base, segments oblong or lanceolate, shorter than corolla-tube. Corolla-tube $\frac{1}{3}$ in. long, 5-angled, limb 1 in. diam., lobes twisted, narrowly obovate. Follicles 12–18 in., seeds 1 in., beak slender, as long as seed.

Epigynum Griffithianum, Wight Ic. t. 1308, South Tenasserim. A shrub, l. glabrous shining, membranous, elliptic-lanceolate, blade 3, pet. $\frac{1}{3}$ in. Fl. in terminal dense rusty-tomentose cymes, pedicels shorter than calyx. Carpels enclosed in the calyx-tube and adhering to it. Calyx segments acute, many times shorter than corolla-tube. Corolla salver-shaped, tube swollen at the base, $\frac{1}{8}$–$\frac{1}{2}$ in. long, tomentose outside, hairy within, lobes obovate, shorter than tube.

Anodendron paniculatum, A. DC. (*Echites paniculata*, Roxb.; Wight Ic. t. 396). Khasi hills. Chittagong. Chutia Nagpur. Lower Burma (*Twin net*, Burm.) Evergreen forests of the Western Ghats from the Konkan southwards. Ceylon, very common in the moist low country. Malay Penins. and Archip. A very large glabrous climber with a thick fluted stem. L. elliptic-oblong, blade 4–7, pet. $\frac{1}{3}$ in. long, sec. n. 12–15 pair, prominent. Fl. small, numerous, white or yellow, on slender pedicels in large axillary and terminal trichotomous cymes, corolla $\frac{1}{4}$ in. long. Follicles straight, woody, 5–6 in. long, narrowed from a thick base, seeds flat $1\frac{1}{4}$ in., beak slender, coma white, 2 in. long.

13. TRACHELOSPERMUM, Lemaire; Fl. Brit. Ind. iii. 667.

Climbing shrubs, l. opposite. Fl. in compound usually axillary cymes, calyx small, corolla salver-shaped, lobes oblique, overlapping to the right, stamens sometimes slightly exserted, filaments broad, disk annular or of oblong glands. Seeds linear not beaked. coma long, cotyledons linear in copious albumen. Species 8, Himalaya to Japan.

A. Corolla-tube much wider near mouth, stamens inserted in the upper portion.

1. **T. fragrans**, Hook. f. (*Ichnocarpus fragrans*, Wall.: Brandis F. Fl. 327. Himalaya, from Hazara eastwards, 3–7,000 ft. Assam, Cachar. Upper Burma, 4–5,000 ft. Fl. April–June. A tall climber, young shoots often hairy. L. glabrous, elliptic-lanceolate, blade 3–4, narrowed into petiole ¼ in. long. Fl. white, scented, in lax compound trichotomous axillary pedunculate cymes, corolla ½ in. long, lobes slightly pubescent at base, very unequal sided, disk of 2–5 obtuse, obovate glands, ovary and style glabrous. Follicles slender, 5–12 in. long, while young cohering with the tips like a horse collar. 2. **T. gracilipes**, Hook. f. Assam. Khasi hills. Cymes lax, peduncles and pedicels capillary, corolla-tube ¼ in. long, lower portion very slender.

B. Corolla-tube cylindric, not much wider near mouth, stamens in the lower portion.

3. **T. axillare**, Hook. f. Sikkim 4–6,000 ft. A stout climber, entirely glabrous, l. coriaceous, abruptly caudate-acuminate, cymes short, axillary, nearly sessile. Corolla dull purple, tube ⅛ in. long, ovary pubescent. Follicles cylindric, tomentose, 6–8 in. long.

14. AGANOSMA, G. Don; Fl. Brit. Ind. iii. 663.

Stout evergreen climbers. Sepals usually lanceolate or linear-lanceolate. Corolla salver-shaped, lower portion of tube short, cylindric, wider or narrower than the upper campanulate or cylindrical portion, stamens included, inserted at the base of the upper portion, a bearded longitudinal band behind each anther. Lobes linear or lanceolate, as long as or longer than corolla-tube, overlapping to the right. Disk cup-shaped. Species 6, India and Malaya.

A. Sepals ⅓ in. long, shorter than corolla-tube.

1. **A. marginata**, G. Don; Wight Ic. t. 425 (*A. acuminata*, G. Don; Wight Ic. t. 424). Silhet. Chittagong. Burma, Upper and Lower. *Khaung nwè*, Burm. Malay Penins. and Archip. Siam, Cochinchina. Stems stout, twisted, young shoots and inflorescence minutely pubescent. L. coriaceous, elliptic oblong, blade 3–4, pet. ¼ in. long, sec. n. straight, joined by intramarginal veins. Fl. white, lower portion of tube wider than the upper, ovary glabrous.

B. Sepals ⅔ in. long and more, longer than corolla-tube.

2. **A. caryophyllata**, G. Don (*A. Blumei*, Wight Ic. t. 1305). Oudh. Behar. Deccan, frequent in the Cuddapah district. *Gura pala Tiga*, Tel. Frequently grown in gardens. Young shoots and inflorescence tomentose. L. coriaceous, ovate or elliptic, blade 4–5, pet. ½ in. long, sec. n. oblique, arching. Sepals red, ¾ in. long, corolla white, tube 5-ribbed, ½ in. long. 3. **A. gracilis**, Hook. f. Sikkim from the foot of hills to 4,000 ft. Khasi hills. L. membranous, fl. on slender pedicels up to 1½ in. long, sepals hoary, linear, 1½ in., corolla-tube slender ¾, lobes obliquely oblanceolate 1½ in. long. 4. **A. calycina**, A. DC. Similar to 3, branches pubescent, l. coriaceous, inflorescence tomentose, corolla-tube ½ in. long.

5. **A. cymosa**, G. Don (*A. elegans*, G. Don; *A. Doniana*, Wight Ic. t. 1306; *Echites cymosa*, Roxb.; Wight Ic. t. 395). Silhet. Shan hills, Upper Burma 2–4,000 ft. Evergreen forests of the Western Ghats from the Konkan southwards. China. Glabrous or young shoots and l. beneath thinly silky. Fl. in compound rounded, densely tomentose cymes, sepals linear ¼–½ in., corolla-tube ⅙–⅓, lobes ovate acuminate, ¼–¾ in. long, ovary hirsute.

15. ICHNOCARPUS, R. Br.; Fl. Brit. Ind. iii. 669.

Evergreen, twining shrubs, fl. small or minute, corolla salver-shaped, lobes overlapping to the right in bud, longer than tube, narowed to a linear appendix, which is deflexed in bud. Disk 5-lobed, carpels hairy. Follicles slender, divaricate. Species 5–6, Indo-Malayan region to China and Queensland.

1. **I. frutescens**, R. Br.; Wight Ic. t. 430. Vern. *Dudhi*, Hind; *Koram pala*, Tel.

Taw-sa-pè, Burm. Subhimalayan tract ascending to 2,000 ft., from the Sutlej eastwards. Gangetic plain. Chutia Nagpur. Assam. Khasi hills. Sundriban. Chittagong. Burma Upper and Lower. Western Peninsula. The twisted stems made into cattle ropes. Fl. Aug.–Dec. China. Branchlets, underside of leaves and inflorescence with ferrugineous pubescence. L. elliptic-oblong, blade 2–4, pet. $\frac{1}{4}$–$\frac{1}{3}$ in. Fl. greenish-white, more or less scented, in small compact axillary cymes, forming an elongated thyrsus at the ends of branches, corolla $\frac{1}{3}$ in. long, lobes falcate, acuminate, woolly on the upper side. Disk of 5 linear lobes. Follicles spreading 2–5 in. long, seeds not rostrate, with a tuft of hairs at the upper end. 2. **I. ovalifolius**, A. DC. Khasi hills, Manipur. China. Tavoy. Malay Penins. and Archip. Often nearly glabrous, l. broadly ovate or elliptic, corolla-tube pubescent outside. 3. **I. pubiflorus**, Hook. f. Khasi hills. Branchlets and l. glabrous, fl. in rusty tomentose dense axillary cymes, corolla $\frac{1}{4}$ in., sepals nearly as long.

Microchites elliptica, Hook. f. Sikkim 4–6,000 ft. A large climber, branches often rooting, l. elliptic-lanceolate, blade 4–6, pet. $\frac{1}{2}$ in. long, sec. n. numerous, slender, nearly straight. Fl. small, in an elongate axillary, sometimes terminal thyrsus, shorter than l. Corolla salver-shaped, tube $\frac{1}{8}$ in. long, lobes narrow overlapping to the right, upper half deflexed in bud, stamens inserted near the bottom of tube. Seeds oblong compressed not beaked, coma caducous.

Ecdysanthera micrantha, A. DC. (*E. brachiata*, A. DC.) Sikkim from the Terai to 5,000 ft. Assam. Khasi hills. Cachar. Ava hills (Kurz). Hongkong. A tall glabrous climber, l. opposite, elliptic-oblong, blade 3–6, pet. $\frac{1}{8}$–$\frac{3}{8}$ in. long. Fl. minute, white, in large trichotomous axillary and terminal compound cymes, often leaf-opposed through the abortion of a leaf. Corolla urceolate $\frac{1}{12}$ in. long or less, lobes falcate, spreading, follicles divaricate 3–6 in. long. Caoutchouc obtained from this species is exported from Laos. Jumelle, Les plantes à caoutchouc et à Gutta, Paris, 1903, p. 425.

ORDER LXXIV. ASCLEPIADACEÆ. Gen. Pl. ii. 728 (*Asclepiadeæ*).

Perennial herbs or shrubs, frequently climbing, l. entire, with rare exceptions opposite, sometimes wanting, stipules 0. Fl. regular, bisexual, pentamerous, usually middle-sized or small, inflorescence axillary or interpetiolar, usually cymose. Calyx inferior, as a rule divided to the base, sepals imbricate in bud. Corolla-lobes valvate or contorted in bud, usually overlapping to the right. Stamens 5, inserted on the base of the corolla, anthers cohering or connate, enclosing the stigma, usually with inflexed membranous tips, filaments in most genera connate into a staminal-tube, the end of the style being as a rule a broad pentagonal disk (style-table) with the stigmatic surface underneath. Pollen-grains rarely free, in most genera united into waxy masses, one or two in each anther-cell. The pollen-masses of the adjoining cells of two contiguous anthers are attached in pairs or in fours to solid dark coloured bodies, the pollen-carriers (corpuscles), which lie on the edge of the style-table. Corona either *coralline*, inserted inside the corolla-tube between its lobes, or *staminal*, consisting of variously shaped appendages, attached to the back of the anthers. Ovary of 2 distinct carpels, ovules usually numerous, 2-seriate in each carpel. Fr. of 2 follicles (or one by abortion), seeds compressed, usually winged and surmounted by a dense brush of hairs (coma). Embryo large, cotyledons flat, in copious albumen, radicle short, inferior.

I. Filaments usually free, pollen-masses granular. Climbing shrubs, excepting *Utleria*.
  A. Corolla-lobes contorted, overlapping to the right.
    Leaves opposite, fl. large . . . . CRYPTOSTEGIA (p. 466).
    Leaves opposite, fl. middle-sized.
      Inland species, l. middle-sized, coriaceous or chartaceous.
        Corolla-lobes long, linear . . . . . . 1. CRYPTOLEPIS.
        Corolla-lobes oblong or elongate elliptic.
          Corona-scales connate into a lobed ring . 2. PERIPLOCA.
          Corona-scales 0. . . . . PENTANURA (p. 467).
      Inland species, l. large, membranous . . . MYRIOPTERON (p. 467).
      Littoral species, l. thickly coriaceous . . . FINLAYSONIA (p. 467).
    Leaves opposite, fl. small.

Corona-scales long, filiform . . . . . . Streptocaulon (p. 467).
Corona-scales short, broad . . . . . . Brachylepis (p. 468).
Leaves alternate. A small tree . . . . . Utleria (p. 468).
B. Corolla-lobes valvate.
Corolla-lobes glabrous, purple within . . . Hemidesmus (p. 468).
Corolla-lobes densely white-bearded . . . Decalepis (p. 468).

II. Filaments connate into a staminal-tube, pollen-masses waxy, solitary in each cell (in pairs on the pollen-carriers) or, in a few genera (*Secamone*, *Toxocarpus*, *Genianthus*), in pairs in each cell (in fours on the pollen-carriers).
A. Corolla-lobes contorted, overlapping usually to the right.
(*a*) Corolla rotate, large, 1 in. across and more.
Base of l. deeply cordate . . . . . Holostemma (p. 468).
Base of l. rounded or cuneate . . . . . Treutlera (p. 468).
(*b*) Corolla rotate, middle-sized.
Trailing leafless shrubs . . . . . . Sarcostemma (p. 468).
Climbers, l. ovate, often with a cordate base.
Fl. bright green, in umbelliform cymes . Dregea (p. 468).
Fl. greenish-yellow and red, in corymbose racemes . . . . Cosmostigma (p. 468).
Climbers, l. lanceolate . . . . . . Secamone (p. 468).
(*c*) Corolla campanulate, funnel- or salver-shaped.
Pollen-masses 2 in each cell (20 in all), corolla-lobes overlapping to the left . 3. Toxocarpus.
Pollen-masses 1 in each cell (10 in all).
Pollen-masses pendulous.
Fl. greenish-yellow, follicles densely clothed with long soft spines . . Dæmia (p. 469).
Fl. pure white, follicles smooth . . Raphistemma (p. 469).
Pollen masses erect.
No staminal corona.
Corona corolline, of double raised villous ridges on the inside of the corolla-tube . . . . . . 4. Gymnema.
No corolline corona, follicles solitary, globose or ellipsoid, seeds without coma. Littoral climbers . . Sarcolobus (p. 470).
Corona scales adnate to staminal column.
Corolla-tube ½ in. long . . . . . Pergularia (p. 470).
Corolla-tube under ½ in.
Corona-scales large . . . . . 5. Marsdenia.
Corona scales small or 0 . . . . Gongronema (p. 471).
B. Corolla-lobes valvate in bud.
Fl. large, corolla ½ in. across or more.
Erect shrubs, wood soft, or branches almost herbaceous . . . . 6. Calotropis.
A climbing shrub, bark corky . . . . . Dittoceras (p. 472).
Fl. middle-sized or small.
Scales in the corolla-mouth between the lobes, and an undulate ring at the base of staminal-tube. Anthers without a membranous tip.
Calyx half the length of corolla, or shorter . 7. Leptadenia.
Calyx longer than half the corolla . . Orthanthera (p. 472).
No scales in the corolla-mouth. Anthers with a membranous inflexed tip.
Staminal-corona of 5 horizontally spreading lobes . . . . 8. Heterostemma.
Staminal-corona of 5 erect lobes . . . . Genianthus (p. 473).

Cryptostegia grandiflora, Br.; Wight Ic. 832 and Ill. t. 182, f. 9.—Syn. *Nerium grandiflorum*, Roxb. Commonly cultivated in gardens, probably a native of Madagascar. A large climbing shrub, l. glossy, fl. pale purple, funnel-shaped, limb 1½–2 in. across. Corona-scales corolline, cleft to the base into 2 long filiform segments. Follicles thick, straight, divaricate, 4–5 in. long. Said to yield a good kind of Caoutchouc.

1. CRYPTOLEPIS, R. Br.; Fl. Brit. Ind. iv. 5.

Twining glabrous shrubs. Fl. in lax slender dichotomous terminal or axillary cymes, corolla-tube short, lobes long linear, twisted. Corona-scales 5, in or above the middle of the tube, linear or spathulate. Filaments slightly connate by their broad base, anthers short, adhering to the broadly conical stigma. Species about 20, tropical Asia and Africa.

1. **C. Buchanani**, Roem. & Sch.; Wight Ic. t. 494, Ill. t. 182, f. 8. Vern. *Dudhi, Karanta*, Hind.

L. elliptic-oblong, shining above, white beneath, sec. n. numerous, slender, nearly at right angles to midrib, blade 3–6, pet. ¼ in. Cymes axillary, many-fld., corolla greenish- or yellowish-white, ¼–½ in. long. Follicles 2–4 in. long, straight, rigid, divaricate, ½–¾ in. diam.

Subhimalayan tract and outer hills, from Kashmir eastwards, ascending to 4,900 ft. Oudh. Behar. Central Provinces. Singbhum. Western Peninsula, common in hedges. Prome. Upper Burma. Fl. April–Aug. Ropes and fishing nets made of the fibre.—Ceylon. China. 2. **C. grandiflora,** Wight. Nilgiris, Anamalais, Gingee hills. A very large climber, l. elliptic, blade 3–4, pet. ½ in. long, nerves impressed above, dark and prominent beneath, corolla ⅜ in. long. 3. **C. elegans,** Wall. (*C. pauciflora*, Wight Ic. t. 493). Sikkim Terai, ascending to 3,000 ft. Assam, Khasi hills. Lower Bengal. Orissa. Java. China. Corolla ⅜ in. long. Follicles 5–8 in., slender, nearly straight.

2. PERIPLOCA, Linn.; Fl. Brit. Ind. iv. 11.

Glabrous shrubs, erect or twining, sometimes leafless. Fl. in lax terminal or axillary cymes. Corolla rotate, lobes generally hairy above. Corona a 10-lobed ring, the lobes often produced behind the stamens into filiform or branched appendages. Filaments free, broad, short, anthers bearded on the back, pollen-grains cohering in fours. Species 12, South Europe, Asia, Africa.

1. **P. aphylla**, Decaisne; Brandis F. Fl. 330. Vern. *Shabbi, Batah, Barrar*, Bal.; *Bāta*, Pb.

An erect shrub, stems green, surface covered with gum, usually leafless, at times with a few minute thick ovate leaves. Fl. ½–⅜ in. across, scented, dark purple, in short lateral rounded cymes. Follicles on short thick peduncles, divaricate, rigid, 3 in. long.

Baluchistan to 3,500 ft. Sind. Trans-Indus. Salt range. Outer Himalaya, eastwards to the Chenab. Merwara. Fl. March, April.—Afghanistan, Persia, Arabia, Egypt. Fodder for camels and goats, the flowers are sweet and are eaten. 2. **P. hydaspidis,** Falc. Kuram valley. Punjab Himalaya. A large more or less twining shrub, branches often fascicled, leafless or nearly so, fl. ¼ in. across, bright yellow.

3. **P. calophylla,** Falconer. *Parh*, Jauns. Outer Himalaya from the Jumna eastwards, ascending to 7,000 ft. Khasi hills. China. A small shrub, l. shining, lanceolate, 1½–4 in. Fl. red, ¼ in. across, corolla-segments ciliate, appendages of corona hairy. Follicles erect, 3–8 in. long.

Pentanura khasiana, Kurz. Khasi hills. Yunnan. L. elongate-elliptic, blade 3–4, pet. ½–¾ in., sec. n. arching, prominent beneath, as well as the finely reticulate veins. Fl. in short axillary bracteate cymes, corolla between campanulate and rotate, fleshy, pink, ⅓ in. across, lobes papillose or hairy above. Follicles short, elongate-ovoid.

Myriopteron paniculatum, Griff. (*Streptocaulon extensum*, Wight Ill. t. 182 f. 3). Assam. Chittagong. Burma, Upper and Lower. Yunnan. A woody twiner, l. membranous, broadly elliptic or ovate, blade 4–8, pet ½–1½ in. long. Fl. whitish ⅓–½ in. across on slender pedicels in large bracteate panicles with slender ramifications, axillary and at the ends of branches. Follicles elongate-ovoid 3 in. long with many longitudinal membranous wings.

Finlaysonia obovata, Wall. Pl. As. Rar. t. 162; Wight Ill. t. 182 f. 5. Tidal forests of Bengal and Burma. A large glabrous woody climber, l. thickly coriaceous, blade 3–4, pet. 1 in. long. Fl. pale brownish-yellow, fetid, in trichotomous axillary cymes, corolla rotate, ⅓ in. across, corona-lobes filiform. Follicles turgid, 3 by 2 in. ribbed and with 1–3 longitudinal wings.

Streptocaulon tomentosum, Wight & Arn.; Wight Ill. t. 182 f. 2. Irawadi valley, often in Eng forest. Tenasserim. Yunnan. A woody climber, branchlets, underside of l. and inflorescence softly tomentose, l. from obovate to broadly elliptic, blade 4–6, pet. ¼–⅜ in. long, sec. n. 15–18 pair. Cymes many-fld., branches divaricate, bracts persistent, corolla glabrous, rotate, $\frac{1}{10}$ in. across, corona-scales long, filiform. 2. **S. Griffithii,** Hook. f. Tenasserim, densely rusty-tomentose. 3. **S. Kleinii,** Wight & Arn.

Western Peninsula. L. densely white-tomentose beneath, corolla ⅓ in. across, hairy outside.

Brachylepis nervosa, Wight & Arn.; Wight Ic. t. 1284. Nilgiris. A twining shrub, pubescent or tomentose. L. coriaceous, elliptic or ovate, acuminate, blade 2–3, pet. ½ in. long, sec. n. 8–10 pair, reticulate veins prominent. Cymes villous, bracts persistent, corolla ⅓ in. across, green outside, purple within, corona-scales short, broad.

Utleria salicifolia, Bedd. Anamalais 3–4,000 ft. A small tree, l. more or less crowded near the ends of branches, lanceolate to linear-lanceolate, margin thickened, waved or crenulate, blade 5–7, narrowed into pet. 1–1½ in. long. Fl. minute, at the ends of long bracteate branches of axillary dichotomous panicles. Follicles divaricate, 2 in. long, gradually narrowed from a thick base.

Hemidesmus indicus, R. Br.; Wight Ic. t. 594. *Indian Sarsaparilla.* Oudh. Behar. Bundelkhand. Central Provinces. Peninsula, common in hedges. Ceylon, low country very common. A semiherbaceous twiner, l. glabrous or densely pubescent beneath, very variable, from broad-elliptic to linear, 2–4 in. long, petioles short. Fl. small, in short sessile compact axillary clusters, supported by numerous ovate acute bracts. Corolla rotate, ⅓ in. across, green without, purple within, lobes thick, valvate. Follicles slender, divaricate, 4–8 in. long.

Decalepis Hamiltonii, Wight & Arn.; Wight Ic. t. 1285, Ill. t. 182 fig. 6. Anamalais and hills on the east side of the Peninsula. A glabrous twining shrub, l. thinly coriaceous, broad-elliptic, finely reticulate. Cymes axillary, peduncles ½ in. long, branches few spreading, bracts persistent, corolla rotate, lobes valvate, with a dense white beard within.

Holostemma Rheedei, Wall.; Wight Ic. t. 597 (*H. Brunonianum*, Royle Ill. t. 66). Subhimalayan tract and outer hills from Kumaon eastwards, ascending to 6,000 ft. Moist forests of the Western Ghats and hills of the Deccan and Mysore. A glabrous climbing shrub, l. membranous, ovate, acuminate from a deeply cordate base, blade 3–6, pet. 1–3 in. long. Fl. purple, on pedicels 1–2 in. long, corolla rotate, 1–1½ in. across, lobes thick, ovate, overlapping to the right. Corona a fleshy ring, adnate to the staminal-tube.

Treutlera insignis, Hook. f. Sikkim 3–8,000 ft. A glabrous climbing shrub, l. coriaceous, elliptic or elongate-elliptic, blade 3–5, pet. ½–1½ in. Fl. large, in axillary simple pedunculate umbels, peduncle 1–2, pedicels 1–1½ in. Corolla rotate, coriaceous, glabrous, purple, 1–1½ in. across.

Sarcostemma brevistigma, W. & A. Deccan, in dry stony places. A trailing jointed leafless shrub with thick rough bark and green pendulous branches. Fl. pale greenish, in corymbiform cymes at the nodes or at the ends of branches, pedicels ½ in. long. Corolla rotate, ⅓ in. diam., lobes broad, overlapping to the right. Follicles thinly coriaceous, 4–5 in., seeds ovate, ¼–⅓ in. long. 2. **S. Brunonianum,** W. & A.; Wight Ic. t. 1282. Deccan, Ceylon, dry region of the Irawadi valley, fl. bright yellow. 3. **S. intermedium,** Dcne.; Wight Ic. t. 1281. Singbhum. Deccan, fl. white. 4. **S. Stocksii,** Hook. f. Sind. Deccan, follicles thickly coriaceous, 2½–3½ in., seeds linear ⅓ in. long.

Dregea volubilis, Benth.—Syn. *Hoya viridiflora*, R. Br.; Wight Ic. t. 586; Kanjilal F. Fl. 244. Subhimalayan tract and outer valleys, ascending to 5,000 ft. from the Sutlej eastwards. Gangetic Plain, Lower Bengal. Todgarh, Merwara (*Mora Bel*, D. B. Dec. 1869). Central Provinces. Western Peninsula, common in hedges. Ceylon, low country. Java. China. A twining shrub, stem woody, branchlets and l. minutely pubescent, sometimes almost glabrous, l. thick, ovate, pale beneath, blade 3–6, pet. 1–3 in. long. Fl. bright green in many-fld. usually interpetiolar umbelliform cymes, peduncle 1–3, pedicels slender, ½–1 in. long. Corolla almost rotate, ½ in. across, lobes triangular. Corona of 5 fleshy radiating scales, inner angle cuspidate, adnate to the base of the short staminal column, pollen-masses erect. Follicles turgid, 3–4 in. long, seeds shining, broad-elliptic ¼ in., coma fine white silky 1½ in. long. *D. angustifolia* is a narrow leaved variety, annual stems from a woody perennial rootstock. West side of the Peninsula. N. E. Brown in Fl. Trop. Africa iv. 417, unites *Dregea* with *Marsdenia*.

Cosmostigma racemosum, Wight Ic. t. 591.—Syn. *C. acuminatum*, Wight Ic. t. 1270. Silhet, Chittagong. Western Ghats, often in hedges. Ceylon low country. A stout climber, nearly glabrous. L. chartaceous, ovate, blade 3–5, pet. 1–1½ in. long. Fl. greenish-yellow, speckled with red dots, in pedunculate corymbose racemes, corolla fleshy, rotate, ⅓ in. across, lobes overlapping to the right, corona-lobes short, membranous, truncate or bifid.

Secamone emetica, R. Br.; Wight Ic. t. 1283, hills of the southern Deccan. Ceylon. A twining shrub with slender branches, the stems with corky excrescences, l. glabrous, lanceolate, or linear-lanceolate, 1–2 in. long, fl. light yellow, in small axillary cymes, corolla ⅙–⅓ in. across, lobes oblong, obtuse, bracts and calyx pubescent, follicles tapering, 3 in. long.

3. TOXOCARPUS, Wight & Arn.; Fl. Brit. Ind. iv. 13.
(Included under *Secamone* in Engler u. Prantl iv. 2. 261.)

Twining shrubs. Fl. small, in axillary dichotomous cymes. Corolla salver-shaped, tube short, lobes narrow, spreading, overlapping to the left. Stigma cylindrical or filiform, produced far beyond the staminal column. Species about 15, tropical Asia and Africa.

A. Corolla-lobes hairy at the base on the inside.

1. **T. himalensis**, Falc. MSS. Garhwal (doubtful), Assam. Khasi hills. L. pubescent when young, from broad-elliptic, almost orbicular to lanceolate, blade 4–6, pet. ½ in. long. Inflorescence, bracts and calyx rusty hirsute, corolla glabrous outside, tube ⅛, lobes linear, ⅛ in. long. 2. **T. villosus**, Dcne. Tenasserim. Java. 3. **T. Griffithii**, Tenasserim. Malay Penins.

B. Corolla-lobes entirely glabrous.

4. **T. Kleinii**, Wight & Arn.; Wight Ic. t. 886. Western Peninsula. Ceylon low country, chiefly in the dry region. L. thinly coriaceous, elliptic, blade 2–4, pet. ⅛ in. Cymes, bracts and calyx hairy. Corolla ¼ in. long, tube extremely short, lobes lanceolate. 5. **T. Roxburghii**, W. & A. Northern Circars. 6. **T. concanensis**, Hook. f. Bababudan hills, Mysore. 7. **T. Kurzii**, Hook. f. Andamans. 8. **T. acuminatus**, Benth. Silhet.

Dæmia extensa, R. Br.; Wight Ic. t. 596. Kuram valley. Northern India. Bengal. Western Peninsula. Ceylon. A slender climber, fetid when bruised, branchlets hispid, l. membranous, cordate, pubescent beneath, blade 1–3, pet. 2–4 in. long. Fl. greenish-yellow on slender pedicels ½–2 in. long, in pedunculate axillary generally corymbiform cymes. Corolla-tube short, limb spreading, lobes ciliate, overlapping to the right. Follicles ½–2 in. long, densely clothed with long soft spines.

Raphistemma pulchellum, Wall. Pl. As. Rar. t. 163. Sikkim, hot valleys at 2,000 ft. Assam. Cachar. Singbhūm. Pegu. Tenasserim. Yunnan. A glabrous twining shrub, l. membranous, ovate from a cordate base, blade 5–7, pet. 2–5 in. Fl. white, on slender pedicels 1½–2 in. long, corolla campanulate, lobes spreading, in bud overlapping to the right. Corona-scales membranous, produced into long linear ligules.

4. GYMNEMA, R. Br.; Fl. Brit. Ind. iv. 28.

Twining shrubs and undershrubs. Fl. in axillary or interpetiolar umbelliform cymes. Corolla usually campanulate, lobes thick, more or less overlapping to the right, corona of 5 fleshy villous double ridges on the inside of tube, alternating with the lobes. Seeds comose. Species about 20, Africa, Asia and Australia.

A. The ridges of the corona more or less protruding from the mouth of the corolla.

1. **G. sylvestre**, R. Br.; Wight Ic. t. 349. Banda district. Western Peninsula, common in hedges, also in forests covering high trees.—Ceylon. A stout woody climber, branchlets, petioles and inflorescence softly pubescent, l. ovate, shortly acuminate, hairy along the nerves, chiefly beneath, blade 1–2½, pet. ¼–⅓ in. Fl. pale yellow, corolla $\frac{1}{10}$ in. across, follicles 2–3 in. long. 2. **G. hirsutum**, Wight et Arn. Wight Ic. t. 1272.—Syn. *G. Decaisneanum*, Wight Ic. t. 1271. Behar. Nilgiris. Similar to 1, but more densely pubescent, cymes sessile, corolla ¼ in. across. 3. **G. molle**, Wall. Meiktila, Upper Burma. Similar to 2, corolla ⅛ in. across, follicles broad, turgid, woody, seeds ovate, ⅜ in. long. 4. **G. acuminatum**, Wall. Silhet. Eastern Bengal. Shan hills, 4,000 ft. Tenasserim. Malay Penins. A large climbing shrub, bark spongy, deeply cracked. Branchlets, petioles, underside of l. and inflorescence densely tomentose, l. ovate acuminate, blade 3–6, pet. ½–¾ in. long, fl. white, in shortly peduncled compact cymes, corolla ⅛ in. across, lobes not ciliate, follicles ovoid beaked, woody, seeds broadly winged ⅜ in. long. 5. **G. lactiferum**, R. Br. Khasi hills. Mergui. Ceylon. Malay Penins. and Archip. Branchlets slightly pubescent, l. nearly glabrous, elongate-elliptic, blade 2–4, pet. slender ½–¾ in.

B. The ridges of the corona in the tube not extending to the mouth of corolla.

6. **G. tingens**, Wight et Arn.; Wight Ic. t. 593. Subhimalayan tract from the Jumna eastwards. Assam. Tenasserim. Anamalai hills and possibly elsewhere in

the Western Peninsula. China. Philippine islands. Nearly glabrous, l. membranous, ovate, acuminate, blade 4–6, pet. 1–1½ in. long. Fl. yellowish-white, corolla ⅛ in. long, follicles mostly single, 4 by 1 in. 7. **G. montanum,** Hook. f.—Syn. *G. tingens*, var. *ovalifolia*, Wight Ic. t. 592. Western Ghats from the Konkan southwards. Similar to 6, l. thinly coriaceous, ovate-oblong, corolla ¼ in. long.

Sarcolobus globosus, Wall. Tidal waters of Bengal (*Baoli-lota*) and the Burma coast. Malay Penins. A glabrous twining shrub, l. membranous, elliptic, blade 3–5, pet. ½–1 in. Fl. in axillary or interpetiolar corymbiform cymes, corolla rotate, ⅓–½ in. across, white outside, hairy and pale purple within, staminal-column orange, corona O. Follicle globose, one follicle only by abortion, 4 in. diam., seeds ∞ imbricate broadly ovate, ⅝–1 in. long, flat with a thick raised border, without a coma. 2. **S. carinatus,** Wall. Tidal rivers in Bengal and Burma. Coast of the Andamans. L. elliptic-lanceolate, corolla glabrous inside, follicle one, ellipsoid, 3 in. long, curved, beaked.

Pergularia pallida, Wight et Arn.; Wight Ic. t. 585. Subhimalayan tract and outer hills, from the Punjab eastwards, ascending to 4,000 ft. Plains of Northern India and Bengal. Dry region of the Irawadi valley. Deccan, in scrub jungle and on stony hills. A large twining shrub, bark of old stems corky, branchlets and l. while young pubescent with slightly curved hairs. L. membranous, ovate, base often cordate, blade 2–4, pet. 1–1½ in. long. Fl. yellowish-white, nearly scentless, corolla salver-shaped, ½ in. across, tube ¼ in. long, as long as sepals, lobes linear, as long as or longer than tube. Corona-scales erect, membranous, connivent over the apex of the style. Follicles 3–4 in. long. Two kinds with very fragrant fl. cultivated in gardens under the name of Cowslip- or West Coast-Creeper. 2. **P. odoratissima,** Smith, and 3. **P. minor,** Andrews; Wight Ic. t. 414, corolla-lobes broad, shorter than the tube, which is pubescent within, are closely allied to *P. pallida*, and possibly not specifically distinct.

5. MARSDENIA, R. Br.; Fl. Brit. Ind. iv. 34.

Twining, rarely erect shrubs. Fl. middle-sized, in some species small. Corona-scales adnate to the back of the staminal-tube. Pollen-masses 20, erect. Species 60–70, tropical and subtropical.

A. Corona-scales longer than, as long as or a little shorter than staminal-tube.

(*a*) Corolla ¼ in. or more long.

a. Style-table short, conical, l. pubescent or tomentose.

1. **M. tenacissima,** Wight & Arn.: Wight Ic. t. 590.—Syn. *Asclepias tenacissima*, Roxb. Cor. Pl. t. 240. Vern. *Jiti*, *Marua Bel*, Hind.

A large twining shrub, bark grey, corky, deeply furrowed on old stems, branchlets, l. and inflorescence softly tomentose. L. cordate, acuminate, blade 4–6, pet. 2–4 in. long, basal nerves 3–5. Fl. greenish-yellow, on slender pedicels somewhat longer than fl., in dense interpetiolar drooping pedunculate compound cymes. Calyx and corolla hairy outside; corolla ¼ in. long, lobes as long as or longer than tube, glabrous within. Corona-scales lanceolate, as long as stamens. Follicles downy, ovate-lanceolate, 3–6 in. long, seeds flat ½ in. long.

North-west Himalaya, foot of hills and outer valleys, ascending to 4,500 ft. Oudh Forests. Behar, Chittagong. Upper Burma. Fl. April, May. Ceylon. The bast of vigorous shoots yields a very strong beautiful fine silky fibre. 2. **M. Roylei,** Wight; Collett Simla Fl. 318, fig. 99. Salt range. Himalaya from the foot to 7,000 ft., Bashahr to Sikkim. Fl. pale orange, in compact shortly peduncled axillary cymes, corolla-lobes as long as tube, hirsute in and outside, corona-scales subulate, much longer than staminal-column, follicles turgid, deeply wrinkled, beaked, 3 in. long. 3. **M. Hamiltonii,** Wight. Foot of North-west Himalaya. A twining undershrub, bringing forth, after the annual fires, l.- and fl.-bearing shoots from a thick woody rootstock.

β. Style-table short, conical, l. glabrous or nearly so.

4. **M. Brunoniana,** Wight et Arn.; Wight Ic. t. 356. Coromandel coast. L. membranous, ovate, base often cordate, blade 4–5, pet. 2 in. long. Corolla glabrous within and without, ⅓ in. long, tube broadly cylindric, lobes equal to tube, corona-lobes obtuse, as long as staminal-tube. 5. **M. Jenkinsii,** Hook f. Assam. Branches stout, l. coriaceous, broadly elliptic, cuspidate, blade 7–10, pet. 2–3 in., sec. n. 6–8 pair, prominent.

Corolla ⅜ in. diam., tube globose, lobes villous within, corona-lobes acute, much longer than staminal-column.

γ. Style longer than staminal-column, apex bifid.

6. **M. lucida**, Edgew. Vern. *Dudhi*, Hind. Kumaon, in shady valleys. Oudh Forests. A large evergreen climber, branchlets, petioles, l. beneath and inflorescence finely pubescent. L. thinly coriaceous, elliptic or ovate, pale beneath, blade 3–5, pet. ½–1½ in. Fl. purple, scented, sepals densely hirsute, less than half the length of corolla. Corolla ⅓ in. long, lobes hairy within, shorter than tube. Follicles 5 in. long, stout, pericarp thickly coriaceous. 7. **M. Griffithii**, Hook. f. Khasi hills. Glabrous, except the slightly puberulous cymes, fl. greenish-yellow, sepals ciliate, half the l. of corolla.

(*b*) Corolla much less than ¼ in. long.

8. **M. tinctoria**, R. Br.; Wight Ic. t. 589. Sikkim 2–3,000 ft. Assam. Khasi hills. Prome district (Kurz). Tonkin. China. Malay Penins. and Archip. A tall climber, nearly glabrous. L. membranous, turning dark blue when dry, ovate from a more or less cordate base. blade 4–9, pet. 1–3 in. Fl. small, in a dense elongate axillary thyrsus, sepals one third the length of corolla-tube which is $\frac{1}{10}$ in. long, clothed inside with deflexed hairs, lobes shorter than tube. Staminal-column minute, corona-lobes subulate as long as or a little longer than anthers. Follicles slightly pubescent. The l. yield a kind of Indigo. 9. **M. eriocarpa**, Hook. f. Silhet. Follicles broad at base, villous with long spreading hairs. 10. **M. leiocarpa**, King & Prain in Journ. As. Soc. Bengal 69. 170. Kachin Hills, Upper Burma. A large climber, nearly glabrous, l. ovate-lanceolate, blade 3–6, pet. ¾–1½ in. long, follicles, only one of a pair developed, 1–2 in. long, quite glabrous.

B. Corona-scales very short, like spurs or teeth at the base of anthers.

11. **M. Calesiana**, Wight. Subhimalayan tract of Nepal and Sikkim, ascending to 2,500 ft. Branchlets, petioles, l. beneath and cymes pubescent, l. membranous, cordate, blade 3–6, pet. 1–3 in. long. Cymes large, much branched. Sepals small, obtuse, less than ¼ the length of corolla, hairy on both sides, corolla ¼–⅓ in. long, hirsute outside, glabrous within, lobes shorter than tube. Staminal-tube cylindric, pentagonous, 5 teeth at the base, prolonged upwards as narrow ridges alternating with the anthers each terminating at the top in a sharp tooth. Follicles stout, woody 6 by 2 in. 12. **M. thyrsiflora**, Hook. f. Assam, Khasi hills, Jessore, Dacca. A powerful climber, fl. small, in cymose clusters arranged in slender racemes on a flexuose rachis 4–5 in. long, the upper clusters in bud, while the fl. in those below are open, corolla ⅛ in. long, green and yellow, the lobes erect, follicles coriaceous, 2 in. long, base turgid.

13. **M. barbata**, Collett & Hemsl. in Journ. Linn. Soc. xxviii. 87. Meiktila, Upper Burma. A twining shrub, softly pubescent, l. rhomboid-ovate, blade 2–3, pet. ½–1 in. long. Cymes axillary on short peduncles, 10–12-fld., sepals nearly orbicular, margin hyaline ciliolate, corolla purple, globose, ⅛ in. diam., glabrous outside, hairy within, dense tufts of hair between the lobes. Staminal-column pentagonal.

Gongronema nepalense, Dcne. Himalaya 2–4,000 ft., from Kumaon to Sikkim. Assam. Khasi hills. Chittagong. An extensive twiner, l. glabrous, slightly rough beneath with numerous minute raised dots, membranous, from ovate to oblong-lanceolate, blade 3–7, pet. 1–2 in. long. Peduncles axillary 2–6 in. long, branching into 3 long divaricate arms, each bearing 3 many-fld. pedunculate umbels. Corolla yellow, campanulate deeply 5-lobed, ¼ in. across. Follicles slender 2–3 in. long.

6. CALOTROPIS, R. Br.; Fl. Brit. Ind. iv. 17.

Large shrubs, wood very soft or branches herbaceous, l. large. Fl. large in umbelliform pedunculate cymes, sepals glandular within, corolla broad-campanulate, lobes valvate. Corona of 5 compressed fleshy appendages, adnate to and radiating from the staminal column, the lower end free and incurved. Anthers with a broad membranous tip, inflexed on the stigma, pollen-masses 10, in pairs, stipitate, stigma large, flat, pentagonous. Follicles broad, short, oblique, seeds flat ovate with a long silky coma.

A. L. sessile or nearly so.

1. **C. gigantea**, R. Br.; Wight Ill. t. 155, 155–6. Vern. *Ak*, *Madār*, Hind.; *Muda*, *Rui*, Mar.; *Yekkada gida*, Kan.; *Nalla Jelledu*, Tel.; *Yerriku*, Mal. Common in the plains of Northern India and in the Peninsula. Singbhum, often gregarious. Lower Burma (Kurz). Ceylon. Malay Penins. and Archip. Young shoots, inflorescence and underside of l. clothed with soft white appressed woolly tomentum. L. 4–8 in. long, obovate or obovate-oblong, gradually narrowed into a cordate often amplexicaul base.

Fl. purplish-lilac or white, inodorous, corolla ½–1 in. across, lobes spreading or reflexed, buds ovoid. Appendages of corona hairy, much longer than broad. Fibre silky, made into rope, paper and cloth. 2. **C. procera**, R. Br. Vern. *Spalmai*, Bal., *Ak*, *Madar*, Hind, *Jelledu*, Tel. Common in Sind, the Punjab and in the subhimalayan tract east to the Sarda river. Drier districts of the Deccan. Dry region of the Irawadi valley. Afghanistan, Persia, Arabia, Syria, Egypt and tropical Africa. L. slightly larger and somewhat less tomentose than 1, fl. with a strong (not unpleasant) smell, purplish-red, corolla campanulate, lobes erect, buds hemispherical. Appendages of corona glabrous, rarely pubescent, nearly as broad as long.

B. L. narrowed into petiole.

3. **C. Acia**, Hamilton, Subhimalayan tract from Dehra Dún eastwards. Maimansingh. A small shrub or stout herb, l. glabrous when mature, blade 6–10, pet. 1 in.

Dittoceras Andersoni, Hook. f. Sikkim outer hills, 2–4,000 ft. A large climbing shrub, bark corky, branchlets, l. beneath, petioles and pedicels rusty-pubescent. L. ovate, blade 4–5, pet. 1½–2 in. long. Fl. large in sessile umbelliform few-fld. cymes, sepals minute, corolla dark purple, rotate 1½ in. across, hairy outside, lobes triangular, corona deeply 5-lobed, lobes oblong, lying flat on the corolla, staminal column minute. Follicles recurved, 4–5 by ⅜ in., seeds black 1¼ in. long.

7. LEPTADENIA, R. Br.; Fl. Brit. Ind. iv. 63.

Fl. small, in crowded umbelliform cymes, calyx shortly turbinate, lobes much shorter than corolla. Corolla rotate, lobes pubescent or bearded, margins recurved. Staminal column short, girt at the base by a raised undulate ring. Follicles rigid, acuminate, seeds flat, winged, comose. Species about 10, tropical Asia and Africa.

1. **L. Spartium**, Wight. Baluchistan. Sind (*Kip*). Punjab, extending eastwards as far as Agra. Kattiawar. Arabia. Tropical Africa. A small glabrous erect, almost leafless shrub, branches green, l. few, 3–4 in. long, linear. Corolla ⅛ in. across. Follicles 3–5 in. long, beak straight long slender. The fibre used in Sind for ropes to draw water from wells.

2. **L. reticulata**, Wight et Arn.; Wight Ic. t. 350, Kanjilal F. Fl. 244. Northern India near the foot of the hills, from Ambala eastwards. Central India and Western Peninsula chiefly in the dry districts of the Deccan but also on the coast. Ceylon, dry country. A twining shrub, bark of old stems corky, branchlets more or less minutely pubescent. L. ovate or ovate-lanceolate, blade 2–3, pet. ½–¾ in. long. Fl. dirty- or brownish-white, in many-fld. umbelliform cymes, peduncles ¼–½ in. long, pedicels shorter, varying in length. Calyx silky outside, corolla pubescent outside. ⅛–¼ in. long, tube very short, widening into a cup divided into 5 narrow lobes, the edges reflexed, the tip hairy often inflexed. Follicles generally solitary, hard, straight 2–3 in. long, with a short incurved beak.

Orthanthera viminea, Wight et Arn.; Royle Ill. t. 66. Subhimalayan tract, eastwards as far as the Gonda district of Oudh, common in dry watercourses on sand and shingle. Delhi and elsewhere in the plains of North-West India. Merwara. A small erect glabrous leafless shrub, branches green. Fl. dirty-brown, in compact woolly cymes, peduncles ½–1 in. long, pedicels very short. Sepals linear-lanceolate nearly as long as corolla, corolla ⅛ in. long, tube ovoid, lobes erect, as long as tube. Minute scales between the corolla-lobes and the staminal-tube girt at the base by an undulate ring. Follicles solitary, 4–6 in. long, compressed, linear, pericarp thin, brown within, seeds ⅛, coma ½ in. long. Ropes made of the fibre.

8. HETEROSTEMMA, Wight et Arn.; Fl. Brit. Ind. iv. 47.

Twining shrubs or undershrubs, l. thin, usually with 3–5 basal nerves. Cymes umbelliform or racemiform, sessile or shortly peduncled, pedicels slender. Calyx small, corolla rotate, lobes veined, broad-triangular, valvate in bud. Corona on the base of the minute depressed staminal column, consisting of 5 large horizontally spreading lobes. Follicles slender, terete, pericarp thin. Species 10–12, Indian and Malayan.

A. Western species.

1. **H. tanjorense**, W. et A.; Wight Ic. t. 348. East side of the Peninsula. Ceylon. Glabrous, l. ovate or ovate-lanceolate, blade 2–4, pet. 1–1½ in. long. Corolla ½ in. across,

corona-lobes orbicular-obovate with a large erect fleshy appendix on the surface. 2. **H. Dalzellii,** Hook. f. The Konkan. Poona. Similar to 1, corona-lobes spathulate without appendage.

B. Eastern species.

3. **H. alatum,** Wight. Outer Himalaya from Jaunsar to Sikkim (2–6,000 ft.). Khasi hills. Yunnan. A twining shrub, branches with two lines of grey hairs down the internodes, l. ovate to ovate-lanceolate, blade 3–6, pet. 1–2½ in. long, sec. n. 3-5 pair, the lowest basal, nerves and midrib on the underside with longitudinal wings. Fl. yellow in umbelliform or racemiform cymes, peduncles short stout, pedicels ¼–½ in. long. Sepals minute. Corolla ½ in. across, lobes veined, longer than tube, glabrous inside. Corona-lobes spreading, acuminate, with a large concave acute appendage on the surface. Follicles cylindric, 3–8 in. long, divaricate and reflexed upon the common peduncle. 4. **H. Wallichii,** Wight. Nepal, Assam, Khasi hills. Branchlets hairy, chiefly along two lines, corolla ⅓–½ in. across, corona-lobes orbicular. 5. **H. stellatum,** Hook. f., hairy lines on branchlets obscure, l. lanceolate, corolla ⅓ in. across. Corona stellately 5-lobed, lobes triangular, acute.

Genianthus laurifolius, Hook. f.—Syn. *Toxocarpus laurifolius,* Wight Ic. t. 598. Sikkim up to 5,000 ft. Chittagong. Pegu. Evergreen forests of the Konkan and N. Kanara Ghats. A large evergreen climber, l. coriaceous, glabrous, elliptic, blade 3–5, pet. 1 in., sec. n. 6–8 pair slender, but distinct. Cymes compound trichotomous, rusty pubescent, corolla rotate ⅙ in. across, lobes triangular, villous above, valvate in bud.

ORDER LXXV. LOGANIACEÆ. Gen. Pl. ii. 786.

Trees, shrubs, often climbing, or herbs. L. opposite, undivided, generally connected by interpetiolar stipules or by a raised line. Fl. regular, usually bisexual, 4- or 5-merous, inflorescence usually cymose. Corolla hypogynous, stamens inserted on the corolla-tube, alternating with its lobes. Ovary free, 2-celled, ovules one or more in each cell. Embryo straight, in copious albumen.

In regard to the anatomical structure two groups may be distinguished. *Buddleia* and allied (not Indian) genera have collateral vascular bundles and the structure of the wood is normal. The other genera have bicollateral bundles and consequently phloëm is found on the outside of the pith and (in most species of *Strychnos*) in the wood, on a transverse section as islands of softer texture. See Scott and Brebner, Anatomy and Histogeny of *Strychnos*, Ann. Botany vol. iii. (1889) 275.

A. Ovules in each cell numerous.
  Corolla valvate, fr. indehiscent . . . . . . 1. STRYCHNOS.
  Corolla imbricate, capsule 2-valved.
    Style clavate . . . . 2. BUDDLEIA.
    Style 4-fid at apex . . . . GELSEMIUM (p. 476).
  Corolla contorted, fr. indehiscent . . . . . 3. FAGRÆA.
B. Ovule 1, rarely 2 in each cell, corolla-tube short, anthers large, exserted . . . . 4. GARDNERIA.

1. STRYCHNOS, Linn.; Fl. Brit. Ind. iv. 86.

Trees or scandent shrubs with short axillary tendrils, evergreen, or leafless for a short time before the young foliage comes out, l. usually coriaceous, entire, with 3–5 basal nerves. Fl. pentamerous, calyx generally hairy, corolla-lobes valvate in bud, stamens 5, filaments usually short and anthers oblong. Ovary 2-celled throughout, or 1-celled in the upper portion. Berry usually with a hard rind, seeds large, compressed, embedded in a fleshy pulp, embryo small, albumen horny. Species 60–65, tropics of both hemispheres.

A. Erect trees, anthers and ovary glabrous.

1. **S. Nux-vomica,** Linn.; Roxb. Cor. Pl. t. 4; Bedd. Fl. Sylv. t. 243. Vern. *Kuchla, Kajra,* Hind.; *Kachila,* Orissa; *Kar,* Mar.; *Nanjīna, Kasa Kana,* Kan.; *Mushti,* Tel.; *Yetti,* Tam.; *Kanjiram,* Mal.; *Kabaung,* Burm.

A middle-sized often a large tree, bark smooth, whitish, l. broadly elliptic, shining, blade 3–6, petiole ¼–½ in. long. Fl. greenish-white, in terminal pubescent pedunculate compound cymes. Calyx-lobes acute, corolla-tube cylindric, ⅓ in. long, about three times the length of lobes, slightly puberulous outside, throat glabrous. Style filiform, glabrous, stigma undivided. Berry as large as an orange and of the same colour. Seeds flat, grey, shining, nearly circular.

Gorakhpur forests (D. B.). Near Pundua (Wall.). Orissa. Western Peninsula. Burma, Upper and Lower. Fl. Febr.–April. Ceylon. Changes its l. during the hot season, occasionally for a short time leafless. The seeds contain strychnine, an extremely bitter and most poisonous alkaloid, which also is found in bark and root of other species. A tree found by Kurz on the eastern slopes of the Pegu Yoma, and described by him (F. Fl. ii. 167) as *S. Wallichiana*, Steudel, is similar, but has the corolla-throat villous between the anthers, and a hairy style. It demands further study on the spot.

2. **S. potatorum**, Linn. f.; Roxb. Cor. Pl. t. 5.; Wight Ill. t. 156. The *clearing nut tree.* Vern. *Nirmali*, Hind.; *Kotako*, Uriya; *Chilla*, Tel.; *Tettan Kottai*, Tam.

A middle-sized tree, wholly glabrous, trunk often fluted, bark dark coloured, deeply furrowed. L. ovate or elliptic, coriaceous, blade 2–3 in., petiole very short. Fl. white, fragrant, in short lateral sessile glabrous cymes. Corolla ⅛–¼ in., tube campanulate, 2–4 times the length of lobes, tufts of white hair at the mouth between the stamens. Style glabrous, cylindric, from a conical base, stigma indistinctly 2-lobed. Berry black when ripe, ¾ in. diam. Seeds 1 or 2.

Central provinces, Behar, Western Peninsula. Fl. H. S. Ceylon. Seeds used to clear muddy water.

B. Scandent shrubs with tendrils, which often are stout and woody.

(*a*) Corolla-tube very short, shorter than calyx.

a. Western species.

3. **S. colubrina**, Linn. *Kanal*, Mar.; *Naga mushti*, Tel. Western Ghats from the Konkan southwards. Ceylon. A lofty climber, tendrils generally simple, l. elliptic-lanceolate, blade 2–4, pet. ¼ in. Cymes axillary, compound trichotomous, puberulous, anthers glabrous, ovary hairy in the upper portion. 4. **S. Bourdilloni**, sp. nova. South Kanara. Travancore, common in evergreen forest at 2,000 ft. Fl. Feb.–Apr., fr. Oct. (Bourdillon No. 75). A gigantic climber, l. (young) elongate-elliptic, blade 2, pet. ⅛ in., tendrils simple, thick, woody. Fl. in terminal compact trichotomous pubescent cymes at the ends of branchlets, pedicels very short, calyx-segments pubescent, obtuse, corolla glabrous, tube almost 0, lobes thickened and cucullate at apex. Anthers glabrous, oblong apiculate, cells slightly diverging at base, filaments very short, ovary glabrous. 5. **S. Dalzellii**, Clarke. Belgaum and North Kanara Ghats. Bababudān Hills, Mysore. L. ovate, or ovate-lanceolate, blade 3–5, pet. ¼ in. Fl. in dense, shortly pedunculate, axillary cymes. Corolla-tube one-third the length of lobes, long hairs in throat, anthers bearded at base, ovary glabrous. Fr. 1 in. diam.

6. **S. Rheedii**, Clarke. Malabar. Travancore, evergreen forest at 2,500–3,700 ft. L. ovate-lanceolate, blade 3–5, pet. ⅛ in., tendrils forked. Inflorescence glabrous axillary 5–15-fld., the lower fl. often opening first, pedicels longer than fl., calyx glabrous, segments triangular, edge minutely ciliate. Corolla-tube almost none, segments usually 5, at times 4 or 6, oblong-lanceolate, edges minutely ciliolate. the lower half with long thin hairs on the upper surface. Anthers small, ovate, glabrous on long, slender filaments, ovary glabrous.

β. Eastern species.

7. **S. acuminata**, Wall. Pegu, Tenasserim. Nicobars, Rocky sea shores of South Andaman. Borneo. A large evergreen scandent shrub, l. ovate, blade 4–6, pet. ¼ in., 5 basal nerves, the 2 outer marginal. Fl. small, in axillary minutely hairy compound cymes, petals shortly connate, slightly hairy at base, anthers glabrous, ovary slightly hairy, fr. ¾ in. diam. 8. **S. hypogyna**, Clarke. Mergui. Similar to 7, if distinct. Basal nerves 3.

(*b*) Corolla campanulate, tube not much longer than lobes, but longer than calyx.

9. **S. Beddomei**, Clarke. Travancore, foot of Ghats. Ceylon. Cymes pubescent,

axillary, nearly sessile, fl. fragrant, calyx very small, segments short, obtuse, corolla campanulate $\frac{1}{4}$ in. across, lobes acute, villous within. 10. **S. laurina,** Wall. Cachar. Tenasserim. Malay Penins. and Archip. L. ovate, blade 4–6, pet. $\frac{1}{8}$ in. long, tendrils usually forked. Fl. in a large axillary (sometimes terminal) fulvous-pubescent thyrsus, corolla campanulate, villous within, anther-cells slightly hairy, ovary hairy. 11. **S. axillaris,** Colebr. Khasi hills. L. ovate-lanceolate, long acuminate, blade 2–3, pet. $\frac{1}{8}$ in., tendrils simple. Fl. white, in small, axillary, almost sessile cymes, corolla hairy within, anther-cells bearded at base. 12. **S. malaccensis,** Benth. Tenasserim (?). Malay Penins. L. 5-nerved, anthers densely hairy, ovary glabrous.

(c) Corolla-tube cylindric, 5–10 times the length of calyx.

13. **S. cinnamomifolia,** Thwaites: Wight Ic. t. 434. Travancore, low country. Ceylon. A very large woody climber, l. elliptic or elliptic-lanceolate, blade 3–4, pet. $\frac{1}{8}$ in. Fl. white, in compact corymbiform cymes at the ends of short branchlets, corolla $\frac{1}{2}$ in. long, anthers and ovary glabrous, style long filiform, exserted, stigma capitate. Fr. orange cold. 2–5 in. diam., seeds 7–14. 14. **S. Wallichiana,** Benth. Khasi hills. Assam. Mikir hills. L. elliptic-oblong, suddenly caudate-acuminate, blade 4–6, pet. $\frac{1}{4}$ in. Corolla $\frac{1}{3}$–$\frac{1}{2}$ in. long, throat villous, anthers glabrous, style hairy, ovary glabrous.

2. BUDDLEIA, Linn.; Fl. Brit. Ind. iv. 81.

Shrubs, usually clothed with stellate or glandular hairs or scales, petioles united by a stipulary line. Fl. 4-merous in 3–5-fld. cymes arranged in panicled spikes and racemes, calyx persistent, corolla-lobes imbricate, stamens 4, anthers nearly sessile. Capsule opening septicidally, leaving the dissepiments free in the centre, valves 2 entire or bifid. Seeds small, numerous, testa loose, often expanded into a wing all round. Species 70, South Africa, tropical and subtropical countries of Asia and America.

A. Fl. small or middle-sized.

1. **B. asiatica,** Lour.; Bedd. Man. t. 21.—Syn. *B. discolor*, Roth; Wight Ic. t. 894; *B. Neemda*, Roxb. Vern. *Banna*, Pb.; *Dhaula*, Kumaon; *Kyaung migu*, Lower, *Kyauk miku*, Upper Burma.

A large shrub, branches, underside of leaves inflorescence and calyx clothed with a dense grey felt of stellate hairs, l. lanceolate, entire or minutely serrulate, 3–6 in. long, usually glabrous above, narrowed into a short petiole. Fl. white, scented, sessile or nearly so, in dense terminal and axillary panicled spikes, bracts deciduous. Calyx 4-cleft to near the middle, lobes acute, corolla tubular, hairy outside, tube $\frac{1}{8}$ in., twice the length of calyx, lobes round obtuse. Capsule nodding, $\frac{1}{8}$ in., seeds with a finely reticulate wing all round.

Outer Himalaya, ascending to 5,000 ft. Behar. Singbhum. Central Prov. Assam, Khasi hills, Manipur, Chittagong. Burma, in Savannas; in the hills chiefly on deserted Toungyas. Western Peninsula. Fl. Feb. to July. Malay Peninsula and Archipelago. Anam. China. Not in Ceylon.

2. **B. paniculata,** Wall.; Collett Simla Fl. 322 fig. 100.—Syn. *B. crispa*, Benth. Vern. *Chiti boi*, Punj.; *Prind*, Kun.; *Sendroi*, *Ghuttia*, N. West.

A shrub or small tree, stem gnarled and crooked, bark peeling off in long shreds, branchlets, leaves, inflorescence, bracts and calyx densely clothed with soft white or tawny tomentum. Leaves extremely variable, those at the ends of flowering branches oblong-lanceolate, entire, those lower down hastate, deeply sinuate-dentate, blade 2–6, petiole $\frac{1}{4}$–$1\frac{1}{2}$ in. long, on the interpetiolar line sometimes a round or lobed leafy stipule, petiole sometimes winged. Fl. nearly sessile, fragrant, pale mauve, pink or white, in short dense spikes arranged in large terminal leafy panicles, bracts lanceolate, tomentose, calyx and corolla densely tomentose outside, calyx-lobes short, obtuse, corolla-tube $\frac{1}{3}$ in. long.

Baluchistan. Common Trans Indus and in the N.-West Himalaya, up to 7,500 ft. Nepal. Rare in Sikkim and Bhutan. Manipur at 5,000 ft. Fl. Feb.–June. Afghanistan. 3. **B. macrostachya,** Benth. Sikkim. Bhutan, Mishmi. Khasi hills, Manipur. Branches stout, quadrangular, often narrowly winged, branchlets, leaves and inflorescence rusty-woolly, l. serrulate, 5–10 in. long, narrowed into a very short petiole. Fl. middle-sized, white, tinged with pink and orange, in dense terminal and axillary elongate spikes. Corolla-tube $\frac{1}{3}$ in. long, woolly outside. Capsule villous, $\frac{1}{4}$ in. long, reflexed wing-like testa of seeds 3–6 times as long as nucleus.

B. Fl. large.

4. **B. Colvillei,** Hook. f. Sikkim 9–12,000 ft. A large shrub or small tree, l. elliptic-lanceolate acuminate serrate, glabrous above, stellate-rusty-tomentose or nearly glabrous beneath, blade 6–7 in., narrowed into a short petiole. Masses of crimson fl. in terminal drooping racemes, pedicels $\frac{1}{4}$ in. long with a few small setaceous bracteoles. Calyx broad-campanulate, $\frac{1}{4}$ in. long, lobes hairy, corolla funnel-shaped, 1 in. long, anthers on short filaments. Capsule lanceolate, tomentose, $\frac{1}{2}$–$\frac{3}{4}$ in. long.

Gelsemium elegans, Benth. Manipur. Hookhoom valley (Griffith). Hills east of Bhamo 4,000 ft. Mogok, Ruby Mines district 4,000 ft, Katha district, in Taungya ponzo, 3,200 ft. Southern Shan States.—China. Vern. *Palaung se*, Burm.; *Lashi*, Kachin. A climbing glabrous evergreen shrub, bark corky, wood porous, vessels numerous, uniformly distributed. L. ovate to ovate-lanceolate, blade 3–4, pet. $\frac{1}{3}$ in. long. Fl. bright yellow in terminal compound trichotomous cymes. Sepals ovate, $\frac{1}{8}$ in., margin minutely ciliate, corolla funnel-shaped $\frac{1}{2}$ in. long, lobes imbricate in bud. Ovules numerous in each cell, style filiform, at the apex with 4 short stigmatic branches. Capsule inflated, $\frac{1}{2}$ in. long, seeds numerous, surrounded by a broad lacerate wing. Roots and leaves very poisonous, a decoction of the root or leaves kills instantly. *G. sempervirens*, Hook. f. (*G. nitidum*, Michaux), of the Southern States of North America and of Mexico contains two poisonous alkaloids, Gelsemine and Gelseminine, which, in small doses, are used medicinally.

3. FAGRÆA, Thunb.; Fl. Brit. Ind. iv. 82.

Trees or shrubs, glabrous, evergreen, sometimes scandent, often epiphytic, branchlets with prominent leaf-scars. L. usually entire, petioles dilated at base, auriculate or united by a short stipulary sheath. Fl. supported by a pair of bracteoles, in bracteate cymes, rarely solitary, calyx deeply 5-fid, lobes thick, broad, much imbricate, persistent in fr. Corolla funnel-shaped, lobes 5, twisted in bud, the right hand edge overlapping. Stamens 5, filaments filiform. Ovary 2-celled throughout, or 1-celled in the upper portion, style filiform, stigma capitate, ovules ∞. Seeds numerous, immersed in pulp, testa crustaceous, embryo straight, small, in horny albumen. Species 30, Indo-Malayan region, China, Japan, Australia, Pacific Islands

A. Fl. large, more than 1 in. long.

1. **F. obovata,** Wall.; Kurz, F. Fl. ii. 205.—Syn. *F. malabarica*, Blume; Wight Ic. t. 1317; *F. coromandeliana*, Wight Ic. t. 1316, Bedd. Fl. Sylv. t. 244. Vern. *Yerrimushti*, Tel.; *Thagyalet wa*, Burm.

A shrub or small tree, often epiphytic on Teak, Terminalia and other trees, germinating on the branches, and then clasping the stem with its interlacing aerial roots, l. obovate, sometimes elongate-elliptic, blade 3–7, narrowed into petiole $\frac{1}{4}$–$\frac{1}{2}$ in. long, stipules thick, more or less adnate to petiole, sec. n. oblique, scarcely visible. Fl. white or cream coloured, scented, in terminal cymes, calyx-lobes blunt, as long as tube, corolla-tube 1–1$\frac{1}{2}$ in. long, upper half campanulate, lobes obtuse, 1–1$\frac{1}{2}$ in. long. Berry glossy green, black when ripe, 1–1$\frac{1}{2}$ in. long.

West side of the Peninsula, from the coast to 6,000 ft. Nilgiris. Western Duars. Khasi hills, Cachar, Manipur, Chittagong, Upper and Lower Burma. Fl. March–Oct. —Ceylon. Malay Peninsula. 2. **F. carnosa,** Jack, Tenasserim. An epiphytic shrub, l. thickly coriaceous, obovate, mucronate, blade 3–4, narrowed into pet. $\frac{1}{2}$ in. long. Fl. solitary, terminal, yellowish-white, corolla-tube cylindric, 4–5 in. long. 3. **F. zeylanica,** Thunb. Western Peninsula, Ceylon. Similar, corolla white, yellowish-green outside, tube 2–3 in. long. 4. **F. auriculata,** Jack (*F. auricularia*, Benth.). Tenasserim, Malay Penins. A large shrub, l. coriaceous, obovate and oblanceolate, blade 6–11, narrowed into pet. $\frac{1}{2}$ in., stipules adnate to petiole, broad, reflexed. Fl. white, turning yellow, terminal, solitary or in few-fld. cymes, calyx 1$\frac{1}{2}$–2 in., cor. funnel-shaped, tube 2–3 in. long, 2 in. wide at the mouth, lobes 2–3 in. long, anthers elliptic, $\frac{1}{4}$–$\frac{1}{2}$ in. long. 5. **F. Khasiana,** Benth., Khasi hills, Assam, a middle-sized tree, l. elongate-elliptic, acuminate, blade 5–6, pet. 1 in. long, stipules adnate. Fl. in compound terminal cymes, calyx $\frac{1}{4}$–$\frac{1}{3}$ in., cleft $\frac{1}{3}$ way down, corolla funnel-shaped, tube $\frac{3}{4}$ in. long, width at top $\frac{1}{2}$ in., lobes $\frac{1}{2}$ in. long.

FIG. 171. Fagræa obovata, Wall. $\frac{1}{2}$.

B. Fl. 1 in. long or less.

6. **F. morindæfolia**, Blume, Andamans, Malaya. A rambling shrub, l. broadly elliptic, very shortly acuminate, blade 6–12, petiole $\frac{1}{2}$ in., sec. n. prominent beneath. Fl. in trichotomous cymes, arranged in a terminal pedunculate thyrsus 6–9 in., pedicels $\frac{1}{3}$–$\frac{1}{2}$ in. long. Calyx $\frac{1}{4}$ in., corolla funnel-shaped, tube $\frac{1}{3}$ in., lobes $\frac{1}{2}$ in. long. Kurz, *F. racemosa*, F. Fl. ii. 205, probably is this species. 7. **F. fragrans**, Roxb. (*Anan*, Burm.) Tenasserim, common in Eng forests. Andamans, Malay Peninsula and Archipelago. A middle-sized tree, wood light brown, close-grained, moderately hard, l. elliptic-lanceolate, blade 4–6 in. decurrent into slender petiole $\frac{3}{4}$ in. long, sec. n. almost at right angles to midrib, slender but visible. Fl. white, cymes arranged in terminal and axillary corymbs, peduncles 2–3, pedicels $\frac{1}{4}$–$\frac{1}{3}$ in., calyx $\frac{1}{7}$ in. long, corolla funnel-shaped, tube $\frac{1}{4}$, lobes $\frac{1}{4}$ in. long, stamens much exserted.

4. GARDNERIA, Wall. ; Fl. Brit. Ind. iv. 93.

Large scandent glabrous shrubs, l. quite entire. Fl. solitary or in pedunculate cymes, calyx small, persistent, lobes fringed with a few short hairs, corolla-tube very short, lobes thick, valvate in bud. Anthers nearly sessile, connivent into a cone, cells adnate on the inside of a broad coriaceous connective. Ovary 2-celled, glabrous, 1 rarely 2 ovules in each cell, style cylindric, stigma shortly 2-lobed. Berry globose, seeds usually 2, rarely 3, embryo small. Species 3, India, China Japan.

1. **G. ovata**, Wall. Pl. As. Rar. t. 231.—Syn. *G. Wallichii*, Wight Ic. t. 1313; Wall. Pl. As. Rar. t. 281.

L. ovate-lanceolate, blade 2–5, pet. $\frac{1}{3}$ in. long. Fl. in axillary cymes, peduncles $\frac{1}{2}$–1 in., pedicels bracteolate $\frac{1}{4}$–$\frac{1}{2}$ in. Calyx-lobes broad, obtuse, corolla-lobes $\frac{1}{5}$ in. long, anthers connate in the lower portion. Berry $\frac{1}{3}$ in. diam., scarlet.

Khasi hills. Nilgiris, Shevaroy hills. Fl. Jan.–June.—China. 2. **G. angustifolia**, Wall. Himalaya 5–7,000 ft., from Kumaon eastwards, Khasi hills. Yunnan. L. lanceolate, blade 2–4, pet. $\frac{1}{4}$–$\frac{1}{3}$ in. Fl. solitary in opposite leaf-axils, peduncles $\frac{1}{2}$–$\frac{3}{4}$ in., calyx-lobes triangular, corolla-lobes $\frac{1}{3}$ in. long, upperside usually densely hairy, berry $\frac{1}{3}$–$\frac{1}{2}$ in. diam., scarlet.

ORDER LXXVI. BORAGINACEÆ. Gen. Pl. ii. 832 (*Boragineæ*).

As a rule herbs; trees and shrubs in a few genera only. L. alternate, rarely opposite, usually undivided, stipules 0. Fl. bisexual, as a rule regular, mostly pentamerous, in unilateral spikes or racemes, the ends rolled back when young, and often dichotomous. Calyx free, persistent, lobes valvate in bud. Corolla hygogynous, gamopetalous, stamens inserted in the tube, alternating with lobes. Ovary free, of 2 carpels, entire or 4- rarely 2-lobed, style simple or 2–4-fid, terminal or inserted between the lobes. Embryo straight, radicle short, superior, albumen none or scanty.

Remarkable anatomical characters.—Stiff one-celled hairs, erect or slanting, walls often thick and granular, base often large and rounded, are common in plants of this order. *Cordia* and allied genera have also stellate and branched, sometimes glandular hairs. In many cases the rough surface of the leaves is caused by cells of the epidermis containing cystoliths, concretions mainly consisting of Calcium Carbonate. Cystoliths often are found in the enlarged base of hairs and not rarely (species of *Cordia*) in groups of epidermis cells, which appear as white disks, mostly on the upper surface of leaves.

Style twice forked, drupe with one stone . . . . . 1. CORDIA.
Style bifid to the middle or lower down, drupe with 2–4 pyrenes . . . . 2. EHRETIA.
Style filiform, stigma 2-lobed, cymes few-flowered . . RHABDIA (p. 482).
Style short, undivided, cymes many-fld. . . . . . 3. TOURNEFORTIA.

1. CORDIA, Linn.; Fl. Brit. Ind. iv. 136.

Trees or shrubs, usually deciduous, gum issues from wounds in the bark. Medullary rays broad, 3–5 cells wide, prominent on a radial section, vessels large, up to 0·2 mm. diam.; transverse, often broad bands of wood parenchyma at right angles to med. rays. L. as a rule alternate. Fl. polygamous, usually ♂ and ☿ in dichotomous cymose panicles or corymbs. Calyx obconical, campanulate or tubular, enclosing the fl. until they open, teeth short, 4–5, often irregular. Corolla funnel-shaped, lobes 4–8. Stamens 4–8, filaments often hairy at the base, anthers shortly exserted. Ovary glabrous, 4-celled, 1 ovule in each cell, style terminal, twice forked. Fr. a drupe partly enclosed in the enlarged and hardened calyx, endocarp hard, often perforated at the apex, seed usually one, albumen 0, cotyledons plaited lengthwise. Species over 200, tropical countries of both hemispheres, chiefly America. Species 4, 7, 9, 10, 12 deserve attention on account of their beautiful timber.

I. Fl. small or middle-sized, white, corolla-tube as long as or shorter than calyx.

A. L. alternate, basal nerves 3–5.

(*a*) Cystolith cells not conspicuous on upper surface of leaves.

1. **C. Myxa**, Linn.; Wight Ill. t. 169; Bedd. Fl. Sylv. t. 245A.—Syn. *C. obliqua*, Willd. Vern. *Lessora*, *Bhairala*, *Rasalla*, Hind.; *Buhal*, Beng.; *Shelu*, *Bhokar*, Mar.; *Iriki*, *Nakkeri*, Tel.; *Challe*, Kan.; *Vidi*, Tam.; *Virasham*, Mal.; *Thanat*, Burm.

A middle-sized tree, branchlets glabrous, wood soft, light grey, no heartwood. L. entire or slightly dentate, glabrous, but more or less rough when full grown, variable in shape, from elliptic-lanceolate to broad ovate, often with a rounded or cordate base, basal n. 3, rarely 5, blade 3–6, pet. 1–2 in. long. Fl. small, in large lax terminal and axillary pedunculate almost glabrous cymes, peduncles 1–2 in., buds nearly globose. Drupe ½–1 in. long, when ripe yellowish-brown, pink or nearly black, shining, but minutely rugose, endocarp rugose, very hard, in a sweetish viscid, almost transparent pulp.

Subhimalayan tract and outer ranges, ascending to 5,000 ft. Punjab Salt range. Rajputana. Central India and Centr. Prov. Western Peninsula. Khasi hills. Burma. Largely cultivated in gardens and avenues. Fl. March–May. Fr. and kernel eaten, the unripe fr. as a vegetable and pickled.—Ceylon chiefly in the dry region. Malay Penins. and Archip. China. Formosa. Cultivated and possibly indigenous in Western Asia. 2. A species mentioned by Kurz F. Fl. ii. 208 (*Hmaikya*, Burm.). Pegu. A small tree, l. elliptic, acuminate, a few large teeth in the upper half, blade 5–10, pet. 1–2½ in. long, short hairs on the underside, chiefly along nerves, upperside rough with minute cystolith cells, fl. unknown. L. greatly prized as covering leaf of the Burmese cheroots.

3. **C. Wallichii,** G. Don; Bedd. Fl. Sylv. t. 245; Brandis F. Fl. 337; Talbot List ed. ii. 243; probably *C. obliqua* of Wight's Ic. t. 1378.—Syn. *C. obliqua*, Willd., var. *Wallichii*, C. B. Clarke in. Fl. Brit. Ind. iv. 137; *Sepistan*, *Pistan*. Guz. Western Peninsula in deciduous forest. A middle-sized tree, l. entire or nearly so, densely and softly tomentose beneath with stellate hairs, otherwise similar to 1, of which it may possibly be a tomentose variety. 4. **C. Lowriana,** sp. nova. Merwara (*Gundi*) (D. B. Dec. 1878; A. F. Lowrie Oct. 1884; Duthie No. 4754. Jan. 1886). A shrub or small tree, heartwood brown, beautifully mottled on a radial section, foliage bright green. Wholly glabrous, excepting the minutely hairy inflorescence, l. elliptic or elliptic-lanceolate, acute at both ends, base more or less unequal sided, deeply dentate in the upper half, blade 2–3, pet. ½ in. long, sec. n. faint, 4–6 pair, the lowest pair from near the base. Fl. (nearly throughout the year) in small compact pedunculate cymes from the axils of the uppermost l., calyx-tube in fl. more cylindrical than of *Myxa*. Very similar to *C. crenata*, Delile, cultivated in Egypt.

(*b*) Cystolith cells conspicuous as raised, generally white disks on upper surface of l.[1]

a. Calyx not distinctly ribbed.

5. **C. monoica,** Roxb. Cor. Pl. t. 58.—Syn. *C. polygama*, Roxb. Western Peninsula, from the Centr. Prov. southwards. L. ovate or elliptic with a cuneate base, slightly pubescent beneath, rough above with numerous raised disks, blade 1–3, pet. ½–1 in. Cymes small, calyx obconical, ¼ in. long, ♂ and fertile fl. on separate branches. 6. **C. grandis,** Roxb. Assam. Chittagong. Burma (Kurz). L. ovate, underside generally glabrous with scanty hairs along nerves, upperside rough with numerous white raised disks, blade 5–8, pet. 1–2½ in. Fl. in compact cymes, arranged in large pedunculate panicles.

7. **C. fragrantissima,** Kurz. *Kalamet*, *Taung kalamet*, Burm.; *Kawoh*, Kar. Pegu and Martaban. Paunglin forests (D. B. Jan. 1862). Hills east of Taungoo (D. B. May 1859). Heartwood brown, beautifully mottled, in structure resembling *C. Macleodii*, but fragrant. L. ovate, upperside when young with fugacious hairs, when mature rough with innumerable white disks, underside clothed with a soft dense but fugacious tomentum of stellate hairs, blade 5–10, pet. 1-2 in. long. Fl. almost sessile in unilateral racemes, arranged in dichotomous panicles. 8. A shrub, Khasi hills (C. B. Clarke, 8088, 48264A), Chittagong (C. B. Clarke, 19760), Western Penins. (Herb. Rottler), China (Henry, 414), similar to 7, but l. broadly elliptic, fl. pedicellate, and racemes not markedly unilateral.

β. Calyx distinctly ribbed and furrowed.

9. **C. Macleodii,** Hook. f. & Thoms.; Brandis F. Fl. t. 41. Vern. *Dhaiman*, *Dhagan*, *Dengan*, Hind.; *Dhaiwan*, Mar.; *Godela*, Ajmere; *Pedda Battava*, Tel.

A middle-sized tree, bands of wood parenchyma narrow, heartwood reddish-brown, beautifully mottled. Branchlets, underside of l., inflorescence and calyx clothed with dense grey or tawny tomentum of stellate hairs. L. sometimes subopposite, cordate, firm and hard when full grown, rough with raised groups of cystolith cells, blade 5–7, pet. 2–3 in. long, the basal as well as secondary and transverse tertiary nerves prominent on the underside of mature l.

[1] I have adopted this as a distinguishing character of species 5–11 with some hesitation, for it is not impossible that the appearance of the cystolith cells on the upper surface of leaves may vary. The species of this difficult but important genus require further study in the forest.

Fl. middle-sized, nearly sessile, in lateral compact, shortly pedunculate or nearly sessile cymes, calyx turbinate, $\frac{1}{3}$ in. long, corolla-lobes spathulate, spreading or reflexed. Drupe $\frac{1}{2}$–$\frac{3}{4}$ in. long, ovoid, acute, not edible.

Rajputana. Central Provinces. Ch. Nagpur, Orissa. Western Peninsula, in deciduous forests. Fl. March–May. 10. **C. vestita,** Hook. f. & Thoms. Vern. *Kumb,* Pb.; *Rarola, Bairola, Ajanta,* Hind. Subhimalayan tract, Jhelam to Sarda. Oudh Forests. Similar to 9, but less densely tomentose, sometimes quite glabrous, l. with a cuneate or rounded not cordate base, fl. pedicelled in unilateral racemes, arranged in pedunculate panicles, calyx clavate $\frac{1}{3}$ in. Drupe $\frac{1}{2}$–$\frac{5}{8}$ in. long, edible. 11. **C. fulvosa,** Wight Ic. t. 1380. Deccan, Karnatik. Similar to 10, but l. smaller, inflorescence of 9.

B. Leaves often nearly opposite, no distinct basal nerves.

12. **C. Rothii,** Roem. &. Schult.; Wight Ic. t. 1379. Vern. *Liar,* Sind; *Gondi, Gundi,* Rajputana.

A small or middle-sized tree, bands of wood parenchyma broad, heartwood dark brown, not scented. L. nearly opposite, cuneate-oblong, obtuse, entire, stellate pubescent beneath, rough above, blade 3–4, narrowed into petiole $\frac{1}{2}$ in. long, sec. n. faint, 4–6 pair. Fl. white, generally tetrandrous. Drupe ovoid, mucronate, $\frac{1}{2}$ in. long, glabrous, longitudinally striate, yellow or reddish-brown when ripe, with gelatinous pellucid edible pulp.

FIG. 172. Cordia Rothii, Roem. et Schult. $\frac{1}{2}$.

Sind, Punjab, Rajputana, Guzerat and the Deccan. Fl. April–Sept. Coppices well.—Ceylon. Arabia, Abyssinia. 13. **C. Perrottetii,** Wight Ic. t. 1381, Deccan. Closely allied to 12 and probably not specifically distinct, l. clustered, often alternate, elliptic-oblong.

II. Fl. large, white, yellow or red, corolla-tube longer than calyx.

14. **C. octandra,** A. DC. *C. serrata,* Roxb.; Wight Ic. t. 469. Travancore, open forest at 1,000 ft. A small or middle-sized tree, almost glabrous, l. ovate, acuminate, more or less serrate, blade 3–6, pet. 1–2 in. Fl. white, calyx cylindric-campanulate, corolla-tube slightly longer than calyx, lobes 7–9, stamens usually 8. 15. **C. subcordata,** Lamk. Sea coast of the Andamans and South Tenasserim. A littoral species. Malay Peninsula and Archipelago, Australia and islands of the Pacific. Often cultivated in gardens. A large evergreen shrub or small tree, l. nearly glabrous, ovate, very shortly acuminate, blade 3–6, pet. 1–1$\frac{1}{2}$ in. Fl. showy, brick-red or orange, calyx cylindric, corolla-tube twice the length of calyx, limb 6-lobed, nearly 1 in. across, stamens 6, style 6-cleft, drupe 1 in. long, entirely enclosed in the calyx.

2. EHRETIA, Linn.; Fl. Brit. Ind. iv. 141.

Shrubs or trees, l. alternate. Fl. small, white, bisexual, pentamerous, in axillary or terminal corymbs or panicles. Calyx small, in bud not enclosing the corolla, in fr. persistent, but not as a rule accrescent. Ovary 2-celled, cells 2-ovuled, style terminal, bifid. Cotyledons ovate, not plaited, in scanty albumen. Species 40–50, tropics of the Old World, a few in America.

A. Leaves serrate or with a few teeth at the apex, corolla rotate.

1. **E. acuminata**, Rob. Br.—Syn. *E. serrata*, Roxb.; Wight Ill. t. 170; Brandis F. Fl. 339. Vern. *Shawahi*, Pushtu; *Ponravi*, Haz.; *Pania*, *Puna*, Hind.; *Bual*, As.

A middle-sized evergreen tree, bark grey with longitudinal fissures, wood brown, even grained, easily worked. Nearly glabrous, young l. and inflorescence with scattered short appressed hairs. L. elliptic-oblong, acuminate, sharp-serrate, blade 4–8, pet. ¾–1½ in. long. Fl. numerous, white, fragrant, nearly sessile in large terminal and axillary pyramidal panicles, corolla rotate, drupe orange, red or nearly black when ripe, pyrenes 2, 1- or 2-seeded.

Subhimalayan tract and outer hills, ascending to 5,000 ft. West Duars, Assam. Khasi and Chittagong hills. Upper Burma (*Petthin*, Smales). Fl. Feb.–April.—China, Formosa, Japan, Australia. 2. **E. macrophylla**, Wall. Nepal, China, l. ovate, serratures unequal, upper side rough with short stiff hairs on a conical base, blade 4–6, pet. ⅜–⅝ in. Fl. in short rounded terminal panicles, corolla-tube more than twice the length of calyx. Fr. globose, mucronate ½ in. diam.

3. **E. buxifolia**, Roxb. Cor. Pl. t. 57. Vern. *Pichika bira*, Tel. Western Peninsula, chiefly on the east side, common in the semi-evergreen scrub. Fl. Nov.–June. Ceylon, Malay Archipelago, China, Formosa. A shrub with stiff branches, l. ½–1 in., fasciculate on arrested branchlets, oblanceolate, apex with a few obtuse teeth, pale beneath, upperside rough with short stiff hairs, standing generally on white disks (cystolith cells). Fl. solitary or a few together, on slender hairy peduncles. Calyx hairy, segments spathulate, longer than tube, corolla ¼–⅓ in. across, style 2-fid to near the base, or two distinct styles. Drupe globose, ¼–⅓ in. diam., yellow or scarlet when ripe, stone one, 4-celled.

B. Leaves quite entire, corolla rotate or broadly campanulate.

4. **E. lævis**, Roxb. Cor. Pl. t. 56; Wight Ic. t. 1382; Bedd. Fl. Sylv. t. 246; Brandis F. Fl. t. 42.—Syn. *E. floribunda*, Benth.; *E. aspera*, Roxb. Cor. Pl. t. 55. Vern. *Chamror*, *Koda*, Hind.; *Tambolia*, Rajputana; *Datrang*, Mar.; *Pogadi*, Tel.; *Kappura*, Kan.; *Chavandi*, Mal.; *Gyaung byu*, Upper Burma.

A middle-sized tree, pubescent or glabrous, branches whitish-grey. L. elliptic, sometimes obovate, blade 3–8, petiole ⅓–1 in. Fl. in loose terminal or axillary cymes, composed of unilateral racemes, calyx hairy, lobes ovate, corolla rotate or broadly campanulate, lobes as long as or twice the length of tube. Drupe nearly 2-lobed, somewhat broader than long, ⅕ in. broad, red, afterwards black, a sweet pulp enclosing 3–4 one-seeded pyrenes.

Sind. Trans Indus, ascending on the Suliman range to 2,500 ft. Sub-himalayan tract to 2,500 ft. Gangetic plain. Rajputana. Central Provinces. Singbhum, Western Peninsula. Burma, Upper and Lower. The old leaves are shed January, Febr., new foliage Febr.–April. Fl. before or with the young l., sometimes before the l. are shed—Persia. Ceylon. Ind. Archip. China. Australia, Polynesia. A very variable species, 2 remarkable varieties in the Western Peninsula are: *a. aspera*, l. small, hairy beneath when mature, *β. canarensis*, glabrous, l. elongate-elliptic evenly narrowed at both ends. The following four species are closely allied to 4: 5. **E. ovalifolia**, Wight Ic. t. 1383. Hills of the Southern Deccan. Inflorescence hairy, l. glabrous, elliptic, nearly obtuse. 6. **E. Wightiana**, Wall.; Wight Ic. t. 1384. Mysore, Karnatik, Courtallam. L. glabrous, lanceolate, corolla campanulate. 7. **E. retusa**, Wall. 8. **E. parallela**, Clarke, both from Upper Burma, imperfectly known.

9. **E. obtusifolia**, Hochst.; Brandis F. Fl. 340. Vern. *Manak*, Bal.; *Tambolia*, Merwara, Afghanistan, Baluchistan. Sind. Salt range, Punjab. Ajpore and Merwara. A small shrub, branches grey. L. rough and hairy, obovate or spathulate, blade 1–2 in., narrowed into pet. ¼ in. long. Fl. white or blue in lax hairy cymes, corolla-tube twice the length of calyx, lobes as long as tube.

C. L. quite entire, corolla tubular.

10. **E. Wallichiana**, Hook. f. & Thoms. Vern. *Boeri*, *Dowari*, Nep.; *Kalet*, Lepcha; *Kyet maók*, Burm. Sikkim, 2–7,000 ft., often gregarious, forming the second growth on clearances. Bhutan. Khasi hills, Upper Burma, Shan hills and Irawadi valley. Fl. March–June. A middle-sized deciduous tree, nearly glabrous, l. elliptic-lanceolate, acuminate, blade 3–6, sometimes longer, petiole ⅓–1 in. long. Fl. before the leaves, in minutely pubescent compact cymes, mostly at the ends of lateral branchlets, corolla-

tube 3 times the length of calyx. Drupe subglobose, ¼–⅓ in. diam., longitudinally ribbed, pyrenes 4, 1-seeded, compressed.

Rhabdia lycioides, Mart.—Syn. *R. viminea*, Dalz.; *Ehretia cuneata*, Wight Ic. t. 1385. In rocky and shingly stream beds, submerged during the rains. Outer Himalaya from Kumaon eastwards, ascending to 6,000 ft. Assam, Khasi hills. Burma. Singbhum. Central Provinces and Peninsula.—Ceylon. Tropics of both Hemispheres. A gregarious prostrate creeping or ascending shrub, branches rooting, branchlets and young l. silky-pubescent, rarely glabrous. L. often fasciculate on arrested branchlets, ½–1 in. long, spathulate, entire, narrowed into a short petiole. Fl. 5- rarely 6-merous, reddish-lilac, in 2-3-fid. shortly pedunculate cymes at the ends of branchlets, calyx pubescent, lobes lanceolate, corolla glabrous, tube very short, lobes large, obtuse, stigma minutely 2-lobed. Fr. crimson, glossy, fleshy, with four one-seeded pyrenes.

3. TOURNEFORTIA, Linn.; Fl. Brit. Ind. iv. 145.

Shrubs, rarely small trees, mostly rambling, l. alternate, entire. Fl. white or greenish-yellow, numerous, sessile or shortly pedicelled, 4- or 5-merous, in terminal dichotomous cymes, consisting of dense unilateral scorpioid spikes or racemes. Sepals hairy, corolla-tube cylindric, hairy outside, naked in the throat, lobes short, spreading. Stamens included, inserted near the base of the tube, ovary 4-celled, style short, 1 ovule in each cell. Fr. a dry drupe, with 2 two-seeded pyrenes. Species 100–120, tropical and subtropical regions of both hemispheres.

A. L. sparsely hairy, more so on the underside.

(*a*) Corolla pentamerous, Western species.

1. **T. Heyneana,** Wall., Nilgiris. L. lanceolate, blade 4–5, petiole ¼–½ in. Sepals lanceolate $\frac{1}{10}$ in., cor. ⅛ in. long. 2. **T. Wightii,** Clarke, Western Penins. L. ovate-lanceolate, blade 3, pet. ⅓ in. Sepals one-fourth the length of corolla, corolla ⅓ in. long. 3. **T. reticosa,** Wight Ic. t. 1386, Coorg, Nilgiris. L. lanceolate, blade 5, pet. ½ in. Fl. pedicellate, sepals $\frac{1}{12}$ in., corolla ½ in. long.

(*b*) Corolla pentamerous, Eastern species.

4. **T. viridiflora,** Wall. Assam, Khasi hills. L. ovate-lanceolate, blade 2–5, pet. ½ in. Sepals half the length of corolla, corolla ⅓ in. 5. **T. Hookeri,** Clarke, Sikkim to 5,000 ft. L. ovate, acuminate, sec. n. arching, prominent beneath, blade 3–5, pet. ½ in. Cymes long-pedunculate, spreading, sepals lanceolate, ⅛ in., corolla ¼–⅓ in. long. 6. **T. Candollei,** Clarke, Assam, Khasi hills, Manipur, Chittagong. L. ovate-lanceolate, blade 2-5, pet. ½ in. Fl. sessile, in large spreading cymes, corolla ¼–⅓ in. long. 7. **T. Roxburghii,** Clarke, Chittagong. Upper Burma (*Sin lamaung*). L. ovate-lanceolate, blade 3–4, pet. ¼–½ in. Sepals ⅛, corolla ⅓–½ in. long. 8. **T. Khasiana,** Clarke. Assam, Khasi hills. l. ovate-lanceolate, blade 3–4, pet. ⅓ in. Fl. green, sessile, sepals lanceolate $\frac{1}{12}$ in., corolla ⅓ in. long. 9. **T. ovata,** Wall. Pegu, Andamans, China. L. elliptic-lanceolate, acuminate, blade 3–6, pet. ¼–½ in. Fl. short, pedicellate, calyx minute, corolla ⅓–½ in. long.

(*c*) Corolla tetramerous.

10. **T. Wallichii,** DC. Nicobars, Malay Peninsula. L. ovate, acuminate, blade 2–4, pet. ¼–½ in. Sepals half the length of corolla, corolla ¼ in. long.

B. Branchlets and leaves densely silky.

11. **T. argentea,** Linn. f. Sea coast of the Andamans, Nicobars, Madagascar, Ceylon, Malay Peninsula and Archipelago. Australia, islands of the Pacific. An erect shrub or small tree, branchlets stout, leaf-scars conspicuous. L. crowded at the ends of branchlets, 3–5 in. long, obovate, gradually narrowed into very short petioles. Panicles large, densely silky, terminal or from the upper axils. Fl. sessile, calyx-segments ovate, ciliate, corolla-tube very short.

ORDER LXXVII. CONVOLVULACEÆ. Gen. Pl. ii. 865.

Herbs, rarely shrubs, often twining. L. alternate, stipules 0. Fl. bisexual, regular, pentamerous, generally large and showy. Calyx of 5 distinct sepals, much imbricate in bud, persistent, often enlarged in fruit. Corolla campanulate or funnel-shaped, limb 5-angled or 5-lobed, usually folded in bud, stamens 5, often of unequal length. Seeds with scanty mucilaginous albumen.

The vascular bundles of *Convolvulaceæ* are bicollateral and the wood-fibres have bordered pits. The stem of the climbing species has a most varied anomalous structure. Cf. Gamble Ind. Timbers, ed. ii. 505, Schenck, Anatomie der Lianen 206 and Solereder, Anatomie d. Dicotyl. 645.

A. Fr. indehiscent (in *Rivea* irregularly breaking up).
- Stigma sessile . . . . 1. ERYCIBE.
- Style filiform, stigmas 2, linear-oblong . . . . 2. RIVEA.
- Style filiform, stigmas 2, globose.
  - L. small, $\frac{1}{2}$–1 in. long, lanceolate . . . . BLINKWORTHIA (p. 484).
  - L. large, usually cordate.
    - Ovary 4-celled . . . . 3. ARGYREIA.
    - Ovary 2-celled . . . . 4. LETTSOMIA.

B. Fr. indehiscent or 2-valved, sepals much enlarged in fr. 5. PORANA.

C. Capsule 2- or more valved.
- Style undivided, stigma usually 2-lobed . . . . 6. IPOMŒA.
- Styles 2, distinct from the base, or united half their length, stamens included . . . . . . 7. BREWERIA.
- Styles 2, distinct, fr. supported by a greatly enlarged bract . . . . NEUROPELTIS (p. 488).

1. ERYCIBE, Roxb.; Fl. Brit. Ind. iv. 180.

(Hans Hallier in Bulletin de l'Herbier Boissier, v. 736.)

Large evergreen climbing shrubs, l. coriaceous, entire. Sepals broad, coriaceous, persistent, appressed to the base of fruit, corolla-tube short, coriaceous, hairy outside, lobes bifid, segments folded in bud. Filaments short, inserted at the base of tube, anthers ovate-lanceolate. Ovary 1-celled, ovules 4, erect, stigma sessile, lobed. Fr. an indehiscent 1-seeded berry, cotyledons folded. Species 10–20, from India to Australia and the Pacific.

A. Branchlets densely rusty-tomentose, inflorescence terminal and axillary.

1. **E. paniculata,** Roxb. Cor. Pl. t. 159; Wight Ill. t. 180. Vern. *Ankole*, Kan.; *Unankodi*, Tam.

Young shoots and inflorescence densely clothed with rust-coloured tomentum. L. elliptic-oblong, abruptly acuminate, blade 3–5, petiole $\frac{1}{3}$ in. long. Fl. yellowish-white, in elongate narrow terminal panicles, petals crisped. Berry $\frac{1}{2}$ in. diam., black when ripe.

Subhimalayan tract from Nepal eastwards, ascending to 4,000 ft. Oudh forests. Singbhum, Western Peninsula. Fl. May-Nov.—Malay Archipel., Australia. 2. **E. Wightiana,** Grah. Western Ghats from Bombay southwards, fl. white, fragrant. 3. **E. peguensis,** Prain, Journ. As. Soc. Bengal, vol. 63 (1894), p. 83. Chittagong, Burma, Andamans, Nicobars, l. cuneately acuminate at both ends, panicles large pyramidal, fl. white, fr. much larger than 1. 4. **E. subspicata,** Wall. Khasi hills. Upper Burma. Yunnan. L. elliptic-lanceolate, gradually acuminate, inflorescence rusty-tomentose, narrow, spiciform, fl. large. 5. **E. expansa,** Wall. Tenasserim, Malay Penins. L. elliptic, shortly acuminate, base rounded or cordate, blade 2–3, pet. $\frac{1}{3}$–$\frac{1}{2}$ in., inflorescence broad, bracts often prominent.

B. Branchlets glabrous or nearly so, inflorescence mostly axillary.

(*a*) Tertiary nerves distinct, parallel and reticulate.

6. **E. lævigata,** Wall. Sikkim 3–5,000 ft. Khasi hills. A large straggling or climbing shrub, branchlets slightly pubescent, l. elongate-elliptic, blade 3–7, pet. $\frac{1}{4}$–1 in. long. Panicles short, mostly axillary, fl. yellowish-white, fr. globose, $\frac{3}{4}$ in. diam. 7. **E. Wallichii,**

Prain et Hallier in Bull. Herb. Boiss. v. 382, 738.—Syn. *E. glomerata*, Wall.; Fl. Brit. Ind. iv. 183. Maulmein. A small tree, with strong straggling shoots, l. rigidly coriaceous, blade 4–6, pet. stout, channeled, ¼ in. long, sec. n. conspicuous below. Fl. in sessile axillary clusters, creamy yellow with a strong smell. 8. **E. Stapfiana**, Prain in Journ. As. Soc. Beng. 63. 87. Tenasserim, Malay Peninsula. A slender climber, l. elliptic-lanceolate, blade 4–7, pet. ¼ in., sec. n. arching, 4–6 pair, the lower 2–3 pair extending beyond half the length of l. Fr. ovoid, ⅝ in. long, densely dark-brown velvety. 9. **E. Griffithii**, Clarke. Mergui. Malay Peninsula. Fr. ellipsoid, 1 in. long.

(*b*) Tertiary nerves indistinct, underside of l. minutely granular.

10. **E. coriacea**, Wall.—Syn. *E. fragrans*, Wall.; Prain in Journ. As. Soc. Beng. 65. 536. Chittagong. Tenasserim. Branchlets nearly glabrous, l. thickly coriaceous, midrib prominent beneath. Panicles short, compact, minutely puberulous. 11. **E. glaucescens**, Wall. Silhet, Cachar. Tenasserim. Glabrous, except inflorescence. Fl. white, fragrant, petals with a firm rusty-silky back.

2. RIVEA, Choisy; Fl. Brit. Ind. iv. 183.

Twining shrubs, l. ovate-cordate, silky or hirsute beneath. Peduncles axillary 1–3-fld., bracts 2–3, narrow. Sepals ovate or oblong, nearly equal. Corolla large, tube long cylindric, limb wide, funnel-shaped, plaited, anthers included, not twisted. Ovary 4-celled, ovules 4, disk annular, style filiform, stigmas linear-oblong. Fr. subglobose, shining, nearly dry, indehiscent or irregularly breaking up. Seeds 1–4, glabrous, in mealy pulp. Species 3.

1. **R. ornata**, Choisy; Wight Ill. t. 168 b. fig. 1; Ic. t. 1356. Western Penins. in dry forests. Ceylon. A woody climber, branchlets and underside of l. white-tomentose. Blade 3–5 in. diameter, petiole 1–2 in. long. Peduncles ½ in., usually 3-fld., fl. cream-coloured, sweet-scented, opening at night, sepals ½–¾ in. long, corolla silky outside. 2. **R. Roxburghii**, Prain in Journ. As. Soc. Beng. 63. 89.—Syn. *R. ornata*, var. *Griffithii*, Fl. Brit. Ind. iv. 183; *Argyreia ornata*, Sweet; Brandis F. Fl. 343. Subhimalayan tract from the Jumna eastwards, common in the Sal forests of Jalpaiguri and the Western Duars. Singbhum. Southern Shan States. A stout erect shrub, branches often twining, l. reniform, sparsely grey hirsute beneath, peduncles long, mostly 7-fld. 3. **R. hypocrateriformis**, Choisy.—Syn. *Lettsomia bona-nox*, Roxb.; *Argyreia uniflora*, Sweet. *The Midnapore Creeper.* Sind. Plains of Northern India. Rajputana. Chutia Nagpur. Central Provinces. Western Peninsula. Common in hedges and dry forests. L. silky beneath, fl. fragrant, pure white, opening at sunset, solitary or in pairs, sepals ¼–⅓ in. long, corolla glabrous outside.

Blinkworthia lycioides, Choisy; Journ. Linn. Soc. xxviii. 94, tab. 15. Dry region of Irawadi valley from Prome upwards, often in Eng forest. A shrub, 6–10 ft. high, branchlets, l., pedicels and bracteoles strigose with long hairs, l. lanceolate ½–1 in. long, pet. short. Fl. solitary, axillary, supported by an involucre of 4 bracteoles, pedicels ¼ in. long, corolla white, waxy, ½–¾ in. long, limb entire, disk cylindric, including the 2-celled ovary. Prain in Journ. As. Soc. Beng. 63, 91 distinguishes *B. convolvuloides*, Prain, Kendat, Myingnan, Upper Burma, by its climbing habit and larger l.

3. ARGYREIA, Lour.; Fl. Brit. Ind. iv. 184.

Twining, rarely erect shrubs. Fl. showy, as a rule purple or rose, sepals often unequal, corolla funnel-shaped, limb shortly lobed, stamens included, anthers oblong, not twisting, base of filaments usually hairy. Ovary 4-celled, disk annular, usually prominent, style filiform, stigmas 2, globose. Fr. indehiscent, often fleshy. Species 30–40, one African, the rest in India, Malaya and South China.

A. Bracts persistent, l. broad, usually cordate.

1. **A. sericea**, Dalz. & Gibs. Konkan. Kanara. Coorg. L. hairy above, densely white-silky beneath, fl. in bracteate heads, peduncles 1–4 in., cor. pink. 2. **A. bracteata**, Choisy. Deccan. L. glabrous above, shining silky beneath, fl. pedicellate, in bracteate heads, peduncles ½–2 in. long. 3. **A. involucrata**, Clarke. Konkan and North Kanara, near the coast. Bababudan hills. L. sparingly hairy, ovate, sometimes longer than twice their breadth. 4. **A. populifolia**, Choisy. Travancore. Ceylon. L. nearly glabrous, peduncles 3–5 in. long. 5. **A. Leschenaultii**, Choisy and **A. nellygherya**, Choisy, Nilgiris, **A. malabarica**, Choisy, Malabar, probably one species. L. softly hairy on both sides. 6. **A. cymosa**, Sweet; Wight Ic. t. 839. Western Peninsula, frequent. Grey

pubescent, l. cordate, shortly acuminate. Fl. heads dense, single or arranged in large pedunculate panicles or corymbs, bracts orbicular, corolla lilac, hairy outside. 7. **A. hirsuta,** Arn.; Wight Ic. t. 891. Nilgiris. Clothed with long soft hairs, peduncles 4–8 in., bracts lanceolate, the outer often petiolate, leaf-like. Corolla hairy outside.

8. **A. Wallichii,** Choisy. Sikkim, Terai to 4,000 ft. Assam. Khasi and Naga hills. Yunnan. L. densely grey tomentose beneath, fl. sessile or nearly so, in dense heads, peduncles short, corolla narrow, 1½ in. long, white, tinged with pink.

B. Bracts persistent, l. ovate or oblong, breadth three-fourths of length or less.

9. **A. pilosa,** Arn. Konkan. Belgaum. Kanara. Bababudān hills. Often procumbent, running along the ground, peduncles stout, varying in length, bracts linear, very hairy, sepals lanceolate, acute, ⅓–½ in. long. 10. **A. Lawii,** Clarke. Konkan. Bababudān hills. L. acuminate, grey silky beneath, peduncles slender, sepals ovate, obtuse, ¼ in. long. 11. **A. Choisyana,** Wight. Karnatik. L. ovate-lanceolate, hairy on both surfaces, peduncles 1–3-fld., 1–2 in. long, hirsute.

12. **A. Daltoni,** Clarke. Singbhum. L. ovate-lanceolate, nearly glabrous above, fulvous-strigose beneath, blade 6–9, pet. 1–3 in. long. Fl. in lax corymbs, peduncles rigid, silky, 2–4 in. long, bracts narrowly oblong.

C. Bracts deciduous, l. broad, usually cordate.

13. **A. speciosa,** Sweet; Wight Ic. t. 851. *The Elephant Creeper.* Assam, Plains of Bengal. Sundriban. Western Peninsula, common on the sea coast in the Konkan. A large woody climber, branches, underside of l. and inflorescence persistently white-tomentose. L. glabrous above, blade 3–12 in. diam., pet. 1–9 in. long. Corymbs many-fld., peduncles 3–12 in. long, bracts large foliaceous deciduous, corolla 2 in. across, white woolly outside, bright purple within.

14. **A. argentea,** Choisy; Sikkim Terai, Assam, Khasi hills. Plains of Bengal. L. hairy above, densely white silky beneath, blade 3–6 in. diam., pet. 2–5 in. long. 15. **A. Roxburghii,** Choisy. Nepal. Sikkim Terai. Assam. L. softly hairy on both sides, peduncles 2–3 in. long, bracts semi-persistent, corolla red. 16. **A. venusta,** Choisy; Prain in Journ. As. Soc. Bengal 63, 89.—Syn. *A. argentea*, var. *venusta*, Clarke; *A. argentea*, var. *hirsuta*, Kurz. Burma, Upper and Lower. L. glabrous above, grey-silky beneath. 14, 15 and 16 are closely allied.

17. **A. Hookeri,** Clarke.—Syn. *Lettsomia* (?) *Kurzii*, Clarke; *Argyreia zeylanica*, Kurz, var. *populifolia*. Nepal. Sikkim, Terai and Lower hills, to 4,000 ft. Andamans, Cocos island. Pegu. Chin hills, Upper Burma. Young shoots silky, l. cordate, 4–9 in. diam., pet. 3–6 in. long. Corymbs few-fld., dichotomous, peduncles 6–10 in., bracts caducous, sepals ⅓ in. long.

18. **A. tiliæfolia,** Wight Ic. t. 1358. Sundriban. Lower Burma. Western Peninsula. Ceylon. Philippines. Formosa. A large climber, stems long, twisted and ridged, l. cordate, glabrous above, slightly hairy beneath, blade 3–6 in. diam., pet. as long as diam. of l. Peduncles 3-fld. shorter than petiole, fr. globose, 1–1½ in. diam., dry, enclosed in the much enlarged and hardened calyx.

D. Bracts deciduous, l. ovate, oblong, lanceolate or spathulate, width ¾ of length or less.

(*a*) Western species.

19. **A. pomacea,** Choisy; Wight Ill. t. 168 (bis), fig. 2; Wight Ic. t. 888. Coimbatore, Nilgiris. Branchlets, underside of l. and inflorescence softly grey silky, upperside of l. hairy. Corymbs few-fld., peduncles short, fr. pulpy, yellow-brown. 20. **A. fulgens,** Choisy; Wight Ic. t. 1357. Courtallum. Branchlets, underside of l. and inflorescence white silky. Corymbs 3–7-fld., peduncles 1 in. long. 21. **A. cuneata,** Ker; Wight Ic. t. 890. Deccan. Mysore. Nilgiris, Palnis. Javadis (D. B. Jan. 1882). An erect shrub, often gregarious, sometimes twining, when it meets with supports. L. obovate-spathulate, densely hairy beneath, blade 2–4, pet. ¼ in. Peduncles usually 3-fld., slender ½–1 in., corolla deep crimson, 1½–2 in. long.

(*b*) Eastern species.

22. **A. splendens,** Sweet. Khasi and Naga hills. Yunnan. L. coriaceous, elliptic, acuminate, glabrous above, silky-white beneath, blade 5–7, pet. 2–4 in. long. Corymbs few- or many-fld., peduncles 1–4 in. long. 23. **A. Championi,** Benth.; Prain in Journ. As. Soc. Beng. 63, 89.—Syn. *A. obtecta*, Clarke. Andamans, very common. Burma, Upper and Lower. Malay Penins. China. L. elongate-elliptic or obovate, densely grey silky below, blade 4–5, pet. ½–1½ in., peduncle ½–1 in. long. 24. **A. lanceolata,** Choisy. Tenasserim. L. narrowly lanceolate, shining silky beneath, corymbs 3-fld., almost sessile, sepals ⅜ in. long.

4. LETTSOMIA, Roxb.; Fl. Brit. Ind. iv. 191.

Differs from *Argyreia* mainly by a 2-celled ovary. Species 32, tropical Africa and Asia.

A. Stamens exserted, corolla less than 1 in. long, limb lobed.

1. **L. aggregata,** Roxb.; Wight Ic. t. 1359. Deccan, common in hedges. Burma, Upper and Lower. Ceylon dry region, very common. A large woody climber, stems fluted, structure see Talbot 249. Branches long, as well as underside of l. and inflorescence densely white tomentose, l. ovate from a cordate base, blade 3–5, pet. 1–2 in. long. Fl. heads bracteate, arranged in long terminal panicles, peduncles grooved, corolla ½ in. long, very hairy outside. 2. **L. mysorensis,** Clarke. Mysore. Similar to 1, fl. in pedunculate axillary corymbs, bracts deciduous. 3. **L. laxiflora,** Prain in Journ. As. Soc. Beng. 63. 92. Upper Burma. Fl. in lax axillary and terminal corymbs or panicles. 4. **L. bella,** Clarke. Nepal. Chutia Nagpur, common. Ganjam. Yunnan. L. cordate, 4 in. diam., pet. 2–3 in. long. Fl. in axillary heads, peduncles terete 1–2 in. long.

B. Stamens included, corolla 1 in. long and longer.

(*a*) Bracts persistent, broad, 1 in. long or less.

5. **L. strigosa,** Roxb. Sikkim Terai. Assam, valleys of the Khasi hills. Plains of Bengal. Chittagong. Andamans. Burma, Upper and Lower. Branchlets, l. and inflorescence strigose with long soft hairs, l. ovate with a cordate or rounded base, blade 3–4, pet. 2–4 in. long, fl. in dense axillary bracteate heads, peduncles 2–5 in., bracts elliptic-oblong 1 in. long. Nearly allied and perhaps not specifically distinct are: 6. **L. peguensis,** Clarke, and 7. **L. barbigera,** Clarke.

(*b*) Bracts persistent, lanceolate or linear, longer than 1 in.

8. **L. atropurpurea,** Clarke. *Convolvulus atropurpureus,* Wall. Pl. As. Rar. t. 43. Nepal. Sikkim Terai. L. more or less hairy, ovate-lanceolate, blade 4–6, pet. 1–2 in. Fl. in bracteate heads, peduncles ½ in., corolla dark purple, sometimes white, 1½ in. long. 9. **L. barbata,** Clarke. *Convolvulus barbatus,* Wall. Pl. As. Rar. t. 155. Pegu. Tenasserim. Branchlets, petioles, underside of l. and inflorescence with long fulvous hairs, l. lanceolate, gradually narrowed from a broad base, blade 5–8, pet. ½ in. Heads few-fld., nearly sessile, bracts linear 1 in. long, forming an involucre converging over the flowers, corolla pale yellow and rose-coloured. 10. **L. Mastersii,** Prain in Journ. As. Soc. Beng. 63, 98. Garo and Naga hills. Chin hills. L. hairy beneath, ovate, blade 4–6, pet. 1–6 in. long, bracts linear, hairy, 1–1½ in. long. 11. **L. longifolia,** Coll. et Hemsley in Journ. Linn. Soc. xxviii. 95. Shan hills Terai. Slightly strigose, l. linear-lanceolate, blade 6–8, pet. ½–¾ in., bracts lanceolate.

(*c*) Bracts deciduous, sepals densely clothed with long stiff hairs.

12. **L. setosa,** Roxb.; Wight Ic. t. 1360. Mount Abu. Central Provinces. Oudh forests. Chutia Nagpur. Centr. Prov. Western Peninsula. Burma, Upper and Lower. L. more or less strigose, cordate, blade 3–5, pet. 1–3 in. long. Fl. rose-coloured, in large corymbs, peduncles strigose, 2–8 in. long, bracts falling when the fl. open. Corolla 1½–2 in. long, densely strigose outside. 13. **L. hirsutissima,** Clarke. Upper Burma. L. ovate or ovate-lanceolate, on both sides softly strigose, corymbs axillary, peduncles 1–2 in. long. 14. **L. Thomsoni,** Clarke. Siwalik hills and Outer Himalaya, from Kasauli to Sikkim. L. sparsely strigose, fl. rose-purple in few-fld. heads, peduncles 1–3 in. long, bracts spathulate, sometimes persistent. I5. **L. confusa,** Prain in Journ. As. Soc. Beng. 63, 96. Burma, Upper and Lower. L. sparingly hirsute to nearly glabrous on both surfaces.

(*d*) Bracts deciduous, sepals glabrous or nearly so.

16. **L. elliptica,** Wight. Peninsula, chiefly on the West side. Ceylon. L. thin, elliptic, sparsely strigose, blade 3–5, pet. slender ½–2 in. long, sec. n. oblique, 8–10 pair. Fl. in loose corymbs, peduncles 2–5 in., corolla 1¼ in. long, nearly glabrous outside. 17. **L. sikkimensis,** Clarke. Sikkim 3,000 ft. Assam. Khasi and Naga hills. Cachar. Upper Burma. Similar to 16 and possibly not specifically distinct. Fl. and fr. larger. 18. **L. pallida,** Prain, *Argyreia pallida,* Choisy. Middle Irawadi valley and foot of Shan hills. L. thin, nearly glabrous, almost orbicular, blade 3–4 in. diam., pet. 1–3 in. long. Corymbs lax, slightly grey-hairy, corolla 1 in. long.

5. PORANA, Linn.; Fl. Brit. Ind. iv. 221.

Twining shrubs or herbs, leaves petiolate, ovate, usually entire. Fl. purple, white or steel blue, in racemes or large panicles, bracts persistent. Sepals all or 3 much enlarged, scarious and prominently nerved in fruit. Ovary 2-celled, capsule membranous, indehiscent or 2-valved, 1-seeded. Seed glabrous, cotyledons plaited. Species 12. Tropical Africa, India, Malay Archipelago, China, Australia.

A. Fl. small, ¼–½ in. long.

1. **P. paniculata,** Roxb. Cor. Pl. t. 235; Brandis F. Fl. 342. *Bel Kanu, Safed Bel*, Hind.

Branches, underside of l., panicle and bracts softly grey- or brown-pubescent. L. cordate, acuminate, blade 2–5, petiole ⅓–1 in. long. Fl. white, numerous, in large axillary and terminal drooping panicles. Three sepals greatly enlarged in fruit, ¾-1 in. long, pubescent, reticulate.

Subhimalayan tract from the Jumna eastwards, ascending to 4,500 ft. Assam. Khasi and Naga hills. Behar. Central Provinces. Upper Burma. Fl. Oct.–Feb., covering the crowns of tall trees with a mass of white blossoms.—Malay Archipelago. 2. **P. volubilis,** Burm.; Wight Ill. t. 168 (bis), fig. 8; Ic. t. 347. Lower Burma (doubtful). Malay Penins. and Archip. Branchlets and l. glabrous, fl. white, panicles large terminal, minutely pubescent, all sepals enlarged in fr., spathulate, ⅓ in. long.

The following 3 herbaceous climbers, with all sepals enlarged in fr., may be mentioned: 3. **P. malabarica,** Clarke. Higher Ghats of Sattara. Bababudān hills. Fruiting sepals elliptic, ¾–1 in. long. 4. **B. racemosa,** Roxb.; Wight Ic. t. 1376. Outer Himalaya ascending to 4,500 ft., from Kumaon eastwards. Khasi hills. Manipur. Burma, Upper and Lower. Fr. sepals oblong-spathulate, ⅓ in. long. 5. **P. truncata,** Kurz. Khasi hills. Fr. sepals narrowed to both ends ⅜ in. long.

B. Fl. large.

6. **P. grandiflora,** Wall. Nepal. Sikkim 4–7,000 ft. L. when young villous beneath, cordate, blade 3–5, pet. 2–4 in. long. Racemes 4–12-fld., peduncles 3–6 in. long, corolla mauve, tube narrow cylindrical, limb funnel-shaped, nearly entire, 1¾ in. across. Sepals in fr. oblong 5-nerved, the 3 larger 1¾, the smaller 1 in. long. 7. **P. spectabilis,** Kurz. Naga and Lushai hills. Upper Burma. Evergreen forests east of the Sitang river. Andamans. China. A large climbing shrub, tawny tomentose, l. ovate from a cordate base, velvety on both sides, petiole short. Fl. white in long axillary racemes, corolla funnel-shaped, 1½ in. long. Three sepals enlarged in fr. tomentose, prominently veined, 2–3 in. long, the others minute. 8. **P. stenoloba,** Kurz, Sikkim 5–6,000 ft. Herbaceous, all sepals enlarged in fr., linear, three 1 in. long, the others smaller.

6. IPOMŒA, Linn.; Fl. Brit. Ind. iv. 196.

Herbs, rarely twining shrubs, l. usually entire. Fl. in some species opening at night, purple, white or yellow, in axillary racemes, corymbs or panicles. Corolla campanulate or funnel-shaped, limb plaited, very shortly lobed. Stamens unequal, filaments as a rule hairy at base, anthers oblong often twisted. Ovary usually 2-celled 4-ovuled, disk annular, style filiform, stigma entire or 2-globose. Capsule 3–4-valved. Species 300, warmer regions of both hemispheres. Of the 64 species known from British India, a few only of the more common kinds can here be mentioned.

I. L. entire or nearly so.

A. Corolla large, salver-shaped, tube slender (*Calonyction*, Choisy).

1. **I. glaberrima,** Bojer; Prain in Journ. As. Soc. Beng. 63. 102.—Syn. *I. grandiflora*, Clarke (not Lam. *fide* Prain), Fl. Brit. Ind. iv. 198. Seashores of India and Burma. A large twining shrub, stems muricate, l. cordate, blade 3–6 in. diam., pet. 2–5 in. long. Fl. white, 1–3 on peduncles 1–4 in., sepals elliptic, obtuse, ¾–1 in. long, corolla-tube slender, straight, 2–3 in. long, limb 3 in. across, anthers included, seeds villous with shaggy margins. 2. **I. bona-nox,** Linn. *The Moon-flower.* Probably American, cultivated and run wild in India. Similar to 1. Fl. pure white, fragrant, opening after dark and fading early next morning, sepals long-cuspidate, anthers exserted, seeds glabrous.

B. Corolla large, campanulate or funnel-shaped, 1½ in. and longer.

(*a*) Pedicels not thickened below the fl.

3. **I. campanulata,** Linn.; Wight Ic. t. 1375. Western Peninsula. Burma, Upper and Lower. Malay Peninsula and Archip. Ceylon. A large twiner, resembling

Argyreia tiliæfolia. Young parts hoary, l. glabrous or nearly so, cordate-ovate, blade 3–5, pet. 2–3 in. long. Corymbs many-fld., peduncles stout, 1–3 in. long, sepals obtuse, corolla campanulate, purple, 1½–4 in. long, seeds with long hairs. Var. *illustris*, chiefly on the seashore of Bengal and Burma, corymbs often few-fld, corolla large. 4. **I. Turpethum,** R. Brown. Throughout India and Burma, in the open country as well as in deciduous forests and Savannahs. Stems climbing, stout, angular, winged, l. ovate or ovate-lanceolate, base rounded or slightly cordate, blade 2–4, pet. 1–5 in. Peduncles few-fld.,1–8 in. long, bracts 1 in., oblong, often reddish, deciduous, sepals in fr. orbicular, concave, 1 in. diam., corolla white, tubular-campanulate, 1½ in. long, seeds smooth.

(*b*) Pedicels thickened below the fl.

5. **I. Kingii,** Prain in Journ. As. Soc. Beng. 63, 110.—Syn. *I. cymosa*, var. *macra*, Clarke. Sikkim 2,500–5,000 ft., common. Bhutan, Assam. Khasi and Naga hills, Karen and Shan hills 3,000 ft., Burma. L. pubescent beneath and slightly hairy along midrib above, ovate, base cordate with large rounded lobes, peduncles 1–12-fld., longer than petioles. Corolla glabrous, white, 2½ in. long, mouth 2 in. across. 6. **I. petaloidea,** Choisy.—Syn. *I. xanthantha*, Kurz. Kumaon. Oudh and Gorakhpur forests. Andamans. Burma, Upper and Lower. L. ovate, the upper generally lanceolate or linear. Fl. in axillary racemes, peduncles ½–1 in. long, often solitary. Corolla yellow, 1¾ in. long, shaggy outside.

C. Corolla middle-sized, 1 to 1½ in. long.

7. **I. staphylina,** Roem. et Schult. Deccan, common in hedges. A twining and spreading shrub, glabrous, l. ovate, base usually cordate, blade 2–4, pet. 1–2 in. long. Panicles axillary, many-fld., sepals obtuse, corolla 1 in. long, funnel-shaped, tube purplish, limb nearly white. 8. **I. cymosa,** Roem. et Schult. Nepal. Sikkim. Assam, Silhet. Andamans. Burma, Upper and Lower. Western Peninsula. Ceylon, very common. Malaya, Australia. Glabrous or softly hairy. L. ovate-oblong, blade 1–4, pet. slender, ½–1½ in. long. Corymbs axillary, sepals usually glabrous, corolla white, often with a yellow tinge, 1–1½ in. long, in bud hairy at the tip.

II. L. lobed, bifid or emarginate.

9. **I. vitifolia,** Sweet. Sikkim, foot of hills. Assam. Bengal. Centr. Prov. W. Peninsula. Burma, Upper and Lower. Ceylon. Malay Penins. and Archip. An extensive climber, scarcely woody, hairy, l. cordate, palmately 5-lobed, blade 2–6 in., pet. ½–3 in. long. Peduncles 1–7-fld., sepals clothed with long spreading hairs, corolla yellow, campanulate, 1½ in. long, seeds glabrous. 10. **I. biloba,** Forsk. *The Goat's foot creeper.* Sands on the coasts of both Peninsulas, also on sandy river-banks. Seashores within the tropics of both hemispheres. A widely spreading glabrous creeper, branches herbaceous, often 10 ft. long, numerous adventitious roots at the nodes from the creeping stems, useful in binding the sand. L. orbicular, deeply 2-lobed, or only emarginate. Peduncles 1–3-fld., corolla purple, 2 in. long, seeds villous.

7. BREWERIA, R. Br.; Fl. Brit. Ind. iv. 223.

Twiners or small rigid erect shrubs. Sepals not enlarged in fr., corolla campanulate or funnel-shaped, limb plaited, stamens included, styles 2 distinct from the base or united half their length, stigmas capitate. Species 25, warmer regions of both hemispheres.

1. **B. cordata,** Blume.—Syn. *B. Roxburghii*, Choisy; Wight Ic. t. 1370. West side of the Peninsula. Silhet, Chittagong, Lower Burma. Ceylon. Malaya. A large twining shrub, rusty tomentose, l. ovate-cordate, blade 2–3, pet. ½–2 in. long. Corolla pure white, wide funnel-shaped, hairy without, 1½ in. long. 2. **B. latifolia,** Benth. Sind. Salt range, Punjab. Aden. A small much branched rigid shrub, l. elliptic, densely silky, ¼–⅜ in. long, fl. small, white or pinkish, axillary, sessile, styles distinct. 3. **B. evolvuloides,** Choisy.—Syn. *Seddera evolvuloides*, Wight Ic. t. 1369. Tuticorin. Similar to 2, l. nearly glabrous, fl. often in twos or threes, on slender bracteolate pedicels ⅛–¼ in. long.

Neuropeltis racemosa, Wall.; Bedd. Ic. t. 291. North Kanara and Malabar, in evergreen forest. Eastern slopes of Pegu Yoma. Tenasserim, Malay Penins. Borneo. A lofty climber, stem tubercled, branchlets and young l. rusty-tomentose. Fl. small white, in axillary rusty-villous racemes 1–6 in. long, corolla wide-campanulate, rufous-tomentose without, lobed nearly to the base, stamens exserted, styles 2. Each fl supported by a bract, which in fr. is orbicular, scariose, nerved, 1–1¾ in. diam.

ORDER LXXVIII. SOLANACEÆ. Gen. Pl. ii. 882.

Mostly herbaceous, some genera comprise shrubs and soft-wooded trees. Leaves as a rule alternate, stipules 0. Fl. usually bisexual, regular, pentamerous. Calyx free, usually gamosepalous, corolla-lobes induplicate, imbricate or valvate in bud. Stamens alternating with corolla-lobes. Ovary free, generally 2-celled, ovules numerous. Fruit an indehiscent berry, rarely a capsule. Embryo curved or spiral, albumen fleshy.

On the circumference of the pith *Solanaceæ* have a continuous or interrupted ring of phloëm, often with bast fibres.

Corolla limb plaited in bud, anthers opening by pores at the apex . . . . 1. SOLANUM.
Corolla lobes valvate in bud, calyx enlarged and enclosing the fr. . . . . 2. WITHANIA.
Corolla lobes imbricate in bud, calyx not enlarged in fr. . 3. LYCIUM.

1. SOLANUM, Linn.; Fl. Brit. Ind. iv. 229.

Herbs, shrubs or small trees, spinous or unarmed, hairs usually stellate, l. alternate, often in pairs. Inflorescence often supra-axillary, calyx 5–10- (rarely 4-) lobed or entire, corolla rotate, sometimes broadly campanulate, limb 5- (rarely 4- or 6-) lobed. Stamens in the throat of the corolla, filaments short, anthers oblong, narrowed upwards, opening by terminal pores or short slits, ovary 2-celled. Berry with numerous seeds. Species about 800, cosmopolitan, the largest number in South America.

A. Unarmed.

1. **S. verbascifolium,** Linn.; Wight Ic. t. 1898. Subhimalayan tract and outer hills, from the Jumna eastwards. Chutia Nagpur. Western Peninsula in deciduous forests. Hills of Lower and Upper Burma, abundant on deserted Taungyas.—Ceylon, Malay Archipelago, China, Australia, Tropical America. A large shrub or small tree, densely woolly, l. elliptic or elliptic-lanceolate, acuminate, entire, blade 4–8, petiole 1–2 in. long. Fl. white or pale blue, ¾ in. across, in compact dichotomous pedunculate corymbs, calyx-teeth triangular, corolla woolly without. Berry yellow, hairy at first, ⅓ in. diam., calyx enlarged in fruit, lobes shorter than berry.

2. **S. pubescens,** Willd.; Wight Ic. t. 1402. Southern part of Deccan, common in low jungle at the foot of the hills. Ceylon. A small tree, l. ovate, sinuate, with thin stellate pubescence, fl. in lax lateral and terminal densely woolly racemes, pedicels ½–1½ in. long, calyx-teeth lanceolate, corolla 1 in. across, blue or purple. 3. **S. Kurzii,** Brace in Journ. As. Soc. Beng. 65, 541. Sikkim, 4,000 ft. Khasi hills. A small tree, branchlets, petioles, l. beneath and inflorescence densely clothed with stellate wool, l. deeply lobed, fl. in short lateral racemes, corolla purple.

B. Prickly, l. entire.

4. **S. giganteum,** Jacq.; Wight Ic. t. 893. Mountains of the Western Peninsula from the Konkan southwards.—Ceylon, South Africa. A large shrub or small tree, branchlets, underside of l. and inflorescence clothed with soft white tomentum. L. elliptic-lanceolate, blade 5–8, petiole ½–2 in. long. Fl. blue or purple, ½ in. diam., in compact dichotomous corymbs on short peduncles. Berry ⅓ in. diam., glabrous, shining, scarlet, calyx-lobes acute, less than half the diam. of berry.

C. Prickly, l. more or less lobed or sinuate.

(*a*) Fr. ¼–⅓ in. diam., calyx-lobes shorter than fr.

a. L. large.

5. **S. torvum,** Swartz; Wight Ic. t. 346. *Kayangyin,* Burm. Western Duars. Lower Bengal, common. Manipur. Chittagong. Chutia Nagpur. Burma, Upper and Lower, common in deserted Taungyas. Ceylon, moist region, very common. China, Malay Peninsula and Archipelago. A shrub with herbaceous branches, hirsute, prickles few on branches and petioles, none on l. L. tomentose beneath, broad, deeply lobed, sinuate, rarely almost entire. Fl. in dense dichotomous cymes, corolla white, 1 in. across, lobes triangular, tomentose outside. 6. **S. indicum,** Linn.; Wight Ic. t. 346. *Begaun,* Beng. Subhimalayan tract and outer hills, ascending to 5,000 ft. Assam. Khasi hills. Lower Bengal. Chutia Nagpur. Burma, Upper and Lower, on river banks, in Savannahs and on deserted Taungyas. China. Malay Penins. and Archip. A much-branched shrub, branchlets, petioles and l. above pubescent or tomen-

tose, underside of l. always densely woolly, prickles numerous, also on l., stout, up to ½ in. long. L. from sinuate to pinnatifid, blade 1–5, pet. ½–1 in. long. Racemes lateral, corolla blue, ¾–1 in. across.

β. L. small.

7. **S. trilobatum**, Linn.; Wight Ic. t. 854. Common on the sea coast of the Western Peninsula, in the Sundriban and in the tidal forests of Burma and the Malay Peninsula. Ceylon. A small straggling and climbing evergreen shrub, nearly glabrous, prickles numerous, short stout recurved also on l. Peduncles short, 2–8-fld., pedicels ½–1½ in. long, corolla blue, sometimes white, 1–1½ in. across. 8. **S. gracilipes**, Dene. Sind. Baluchistan. Kuram valley. Punjab. A small shrub, pubescent with minute stellate hairs, prickles few, none on l. L. 1½ in. diam., sinuate, base usually cordate, blade 1½ in. diam., pet. slender, ½–1 in. long. Peduncles very short, 1–3-fld., pedicels slender ½–1½ in., corolla ¾ in. across.

(*b*) Fr. ½ in. diam. overtopped by the enlarged sepals.

9. **S. Wightii**, Nees; Wight Ic. t. 841. Nilgiris. Softly velvety, l. and sepals without prickles, peduncles short, 1–3-fld., pedicels slender, in fl. ½–1½ in. long, corolla blue, 2 in. across. Calyx-segments in fr. ovate-lanceolate ¾ in. long. 10. **S. barbisetum**, Nees. Sikkim, 1–6,000 ft. Assam. Tenasserim. Hirsute. Prickles straw-cold., up to ½ in. long, abundant on petioles and l. Racemes lateral, many-fld., 2–3 in. long, pedicels ¼ in. long, corolla blue. Berry enclosed by the enlarged densely prickly calyx.

(*c*) Fr. large, 1 in. long and more.

11. **S. ferox**, Linn.; Wight Ic. t. 1399. Vern. *Sinkadi*, *Sinkayan*, Burm. Assam, Khasi hills, Chittagong. Burma. Western Peninsula. Ceylon. Malay Penins. China. A shrub or small tree, branchlets, petioles and l. densely clothed with soft stellate wool, prickles flat, shining, abundant on l., the longest ½ in. L. with broad triangular lobes, blade 6–12, pet. 1–2½ in. long. Fl. in short dense lateral woolly racemes, corolla white, 1–1½ in. across, berry globose, 1–1½ in. diam., densely clothed with needle-like hairs. 12. **S. Khasianum**, Clarke. Khasi hills. Maymyo, Upper Burma. Yunnan. Hirsute with long soft hairs, prickles straw-coloured, the largest ¾ in., base broad flat. Lobes of l. ovate, corolla white or pink, ¾ in. across, berry 1 in. diam. glabrous. 13. **S. Melongena**, Linn. *Brinjal*. Vern. *Banbhata*, Centr. Prov.; *Kayan*, Burm. Cultivated and run wild throughout India and Burma. Herbaceous, sometimes unarmed, fl. blue, in few-fld. cymes, corolla 1–1½ in. across, lobes broadly triangular, hairy outside. Fr. white or dark purple, 1–9 in. long.

2. WITHANIA, Pauquy; Fl. Brit. Ind. iv. 239.

Unarmed shrubs, l. entire. Fl. 5–6-merous, axillary, solitary or fascicled, calyx enlarged and enclosing the fr., corolla campanulate, lobes short, valvate in bud, anthers oblong, dehiscing longitudinally. Berry many-seeded, embryo curved. Species 5. Canaries. Mediterranean region. South Africa. India.

1. **W. somnifera**, Dunal.—Syn. *Physalis somnifera*, Link; Wight Ic. t. 853. Sind. Kuram valley. Punjab. Merwara (*Asind*). Gangetic plain, also at the foot of the Himalaya, to 1,000 ft. Central Provinces. Western Peninsula, Ceylon. Mediterranean region. Tropical and South Africa. Attains 5 ft., thinly velvety, l. ovate, blade 3–5, pet. 1–1½ in. long, fr. calyx inflated, papery. 2. **W. coagulans**, Dunal.—Syn. *Puneeria coagulans*, Stocks; Wight Ic. t. 1616. Sind. Baluchistan (*Khamdzar*). Trans Indus, to 3,000 ft. Kuram valley. Salt range. Sutlej valley at 3,000 ft. (*Panir*). Southern Punjab. Afghanistan. A small shrub, l. densely clothed with minute grey stellate tomentum. L. ovate-lanceolate or oblanceolate, blade 1–2, narrowed into pet. ⅓ in. long. Fl. polygamous, fr. calyx leathery closely surrounding the berry.

3. LYCIUM, Linn.; Fl. Brit. Ind. iv. 240.

Shrubs, branchlets often spinescent. L. entire, mostly fasciculate on arrested branchlets. Fl. solitary or few together, 4- or 5-merous, corolla funnel-shaped, lobes imbricate in bud. Stamens usually unequal, ovary 2-celled. Fr. a small berry, seeds compressed, embryo curved, cotyledons linear. Species 50–60, temperate and subtropical regions of both hemispheres, most numerous in South Africa and South America.

1. **L. europaeum**, Linn.—Syn. *L. indicum*, Wight Ic. t. 1403. Sind. Punjab. Merwara. Guzerat. Fl. Oct.–March. Western Asia and South Europe (fl. mostly light purple). Vern. *Gangro*, Sind; *Ganger*, Punj.; *Chirchitta*, Delhi; *Erk Mehndi*, Merwara; *Gangro*,

Mar. A thorny shrub, branches grey, l. lanceolate or oblanceolate, ½–1 in. long. Fl. white, ½ in. long, solitary, pedicels shorter than fl., calyx-teeth 5, equal. Corolla-tube cylindrical, widening upwards, more than twice the length of lobes. Berry globose, edible, yellow or red. ⅛ in. diam. 2. **L. barbarum**, Linn., Baluchistan (***Karghanna***), Peshin valley, Sind, Punjab, Rajputana (*Moraili*, Kishengarh), pedicels as long as fl., corolla-lobes nearly as long as tube, stamens exserted. 3. **L. ruthenicum**, Murray. North Kashmir, Ladak and Baltistan, 10–13,500 ft., l. linear, calyx-lobes 3–4, unequal, corolla funnel-shaped, tube somewhat longer than lobes, but not twice their length, anthers long exserted, berry globose, ¼ in. diam.

ORDER LXXIX. SCROPHULARIACEÆ. Gen. Pl. ii. 913.

(*Scrophularineæ.*)

Herbs, rarely shrubs or trees, l. usually opposite, stip. 0. Fl. usually bisexual, pentamerous and zygomorphic. Calyx inferior, corolla hypogynous, stamens usually 4, didynamous, with a rudimentary 5th. Ovary as a rule 2-celled, style simple. Fr. usually a capsule, seeds as a rule numerous, albumen as a rule fleshy.

Calyx 3–4 lobed. Anthers glabrous . . . . . . WIGHTIA.
Calyx 5-toothed. Anthers bearded. . . . . . . BRANDISIA.

Wightia gigantea, Wall. Pl. As. Rar. t. 81. Nepal. Sikkim 3–7,000 ft. Manipur. Shan Hills, 4,000 ft. Bithoko range, Salween river 3,000 ft. (D. B. March 1880). A huge evergreen epiphytic tree, with horizontal aërial roots, clasping the stem of the tree on which it grows, wood light and soft. L. glabrous coriaceous, elliptic, blade 6–12, pet. stout 1–1½ in. Fl. pink, numerous in an erect narrow axillary thyrsus 4–8 in. long. Corolla 1 in. long, mealy, upper lip erect 2-lobed, stamens far exserted. Capsule 1½ by ¾ in., the valves separating from the placentiferous axis.

Brandisia discolor, Hook. f. & Thoms. Hills between Sitang and Salween rivers 3–6,000 ft. (several other species of this genus in Yunnan). An evergreen scrambling shrub, branchlets, petioles, underside of l., pedicels and calyx with grey stellate pubescence. L. ovate-lanceolate, blade 2–3, pet. ¼ in. Fl. dull purplish-brown, axillary, solitary or in pairs, pedicels ⅓ in. long. Corolla curved, tomentose, ¾ in. long.

ORDER LXXX. BIGNONIACEÆ. Gen. Pl. ii. 1026.

Trees, shrubs or woody climbers. L. usually opposite, compound, leaflets opposite, rarely simple, stipules 0. Fl. bisexual, generally zygomorphic, calyx free, gamosepalous, truncate, split or toothed. Corolla tubular or campanulate, lobes 5, imbricate, rarely valvate in bud. Stamens 2 or 4, rarely 5, often a short staminode in place of the 5th stamen. Ovary free, supported by an annular disk, 2-celled, ovules ∞ on two distinct placentas in each cell, attached to the dissepiment, style filiform, with 2 short stigmatic lobes. Fr. often elongated, generally dehiscent, the two valves separating from the dissepiment, to which the seeds are attached, seeds winged, albumen 0.

As far as known, the wood of the Indian arborescent *Bignoniaceæ* has a normal structure. Numerous climbers of this family are found in America with a varied and anomalous structure, cf. Schenck, Anatomie der Lianen, 212.

A. L. simple, linear-oblong, fl. orange . . . . . 1. TECOMA UNDULATA.
  L. alternate, pinnate, fr. large, gourd-like . . . KIGELIA (p. 492).
  L. opposite, trifoliolate, a climber . . . . . NYCTOCALOS (p. 492).
B. L. opposite, imparipinnate.
  Capsule not winged.
    Caylx spathaceous . . . . 2. DOLICHANDRONE.
    Calyx irregularly 3–5-cleft . . . . . . 3. HETEROPHRAGMA.
  Capsule winged . . . . 4. PAJANELIA.
C. L. pinnate and bipinnate, dissepiment cylindric, corky 5. STEREOSPERMUM.
D. L. bi- or tripinnate.
  Fl. white, corolla-tube 3–4 in. long . . . . MILLINGTONIA (p. 496).
  Fl. orange, from the old wood . . . . . MAYODENDRON (p. 496).
  Fl. red and white, corolla campanulate . . . OROXYLUM (p. 496).
  A spreading shrub, rachis of l. narrowly winged . 1. TECOMA (?) BIPINNATA.

1. TECOMA, Juss.; Fl. Brit. Ind. iv. 378.

Species 80, mostly American.

1. **T. undulata,** G. Don; Brandis F. Fl. 352.—Syn. *Tecomella undulata*, Seemann; Engler u. Prantl iv. 3B. 239. Vern. *Rori*, Bal.; *Lohĕro*, Sind; *Lahūra*, Punjab; *Roira*, *Rohera*, Merwara.

A shrub or small tree, youngest shoots and inflorescence often minutely pubescent. L. grey, glabrous but somewhat rough, linear-oblong, entire, blade 2–4, petiole 1 in. long. Fl. large, from pale yellow to deep orange, in short 5–10-fld. corymbs at the ends of branchlets, calyx campanulate, teeth 5, obtuse, corolla campanulate, limb oblique, 2 in. across. Capsule curved 6–8 in. long.

Baluchistan, Sind. Suliman range, Trans-Indus, ascending to 4,000 ft. Punjab, Salt range and Sivalik tract, extending eastwards to the Jumna. Guzerat. L. renewed in Jan. and Feb. Fl. January to April, coppices well, easily raised from seed and cuttings.—Arabia.

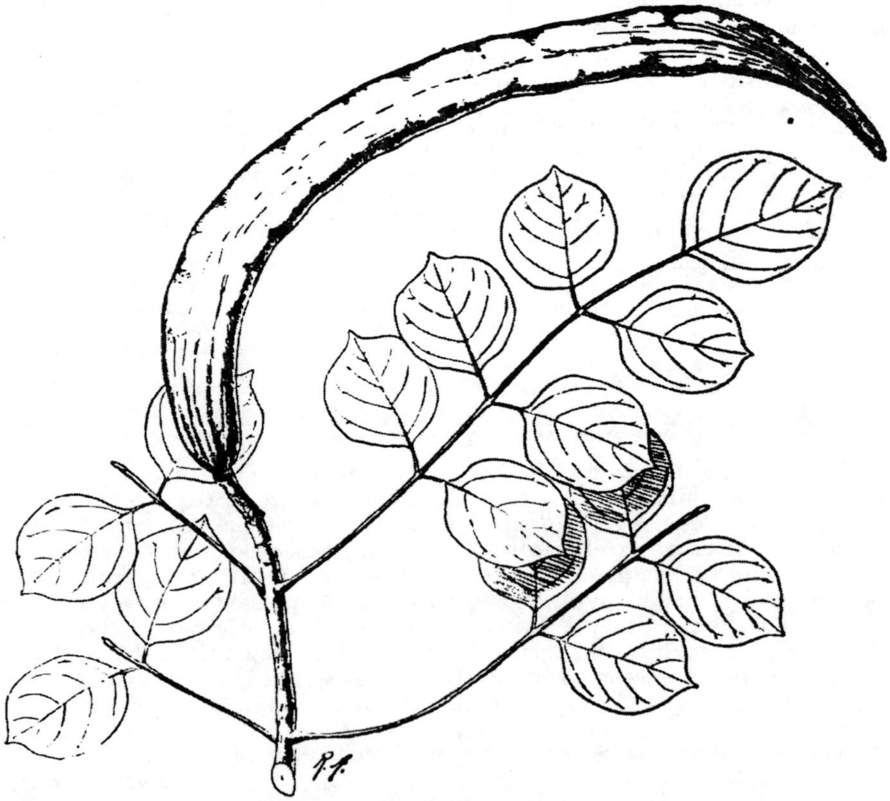

FIG. 173. Dolichandrone falcata, Seem. $\frac{1}{2}$.

2. **T. (?) bipinnata,** Collett & Hemsl. Journ. Linn. Soc. vol. xxviii. 102. Shan hills 4,000 ft. (Collett) Ruby Mines district (Oliver). A spreading shrub, l. bipinnate, rachis narrowly winged, leaflets ovate-lanceolate, $\frac{1}{2}$–$1\frac{1}{2}$ in., fl. $2\frac{1}{2}$ in. long in terminal pedunculate racemes, corolla tubular, mouth wide, oblique. Capsule unknown, hence genus doubtful.

Kigelia pinnata, DC. Tropical Africa, planted largely in India. A large tree, l. alternate, imparipinnate, crowded at the ends of branches. Fl. large dark maroon, in pendulous panicles. Fr. gourd-like, 2–3 ft. long.

Nyctocalos Thomsoni, Hook. f. Assam. A large glabrous climber, l. trifoliolate, leaflets broadly elliptic, caudate-acuminate, blade 5–6, pet.[1] $\frac{3}{4}$ in. long. Fl. white, in terminal few-fld. drooping racemes, calyx-teeth $\frac{1}{10}$ in., cuspidate, corolla-tube 6 in. long, limb $2\frac{1}{2}$ in. across. Capsule 6 by 2 in., valves almost woody.

2. DOLICHANDRONE, Seem.; Fl. Brit. Ind. iv. 378.

Trees, as a rule deciduous, l. imparipinnate. Fl. in terminal few-fld. racemes or corymbs. Calyx in bud enclosing the corolla, in fl. spathaceous, cleft on one side to the base. Corolla-tube: lower portion cylindric, upper campanulate or funnel-shaped, lobes 5, nearly equal, round, crisped or crenate. Capsule more or less compressed, seeds with a broad wing at each end. Species 6–10, Africa, Asia, Australia.

1. **D. falcata**, Seem.—Syn. *Bignonia spathacea*, Roxb. Cor. Pl. t. 144; *Spathodea falcata*, Wall.; Bedd. Fl. Sylv. t. 71; Brandis F. Fl. 350. Vern. *Dudga*, Centr. Prov.; *Medshing*, *Mersinghi*, *Bhersing*, Mar.; *Chitti woddi*, Tel.

A middle-sized tree, more or less pubescent, wood close- and even-grained. Leaflets 5–7, broadly elliptic, obovate or almost orbicular, blade $\frac{1}{2}$–$1\frac{1}{2}$, pet. $\frac{1}{8}$ in. long (too long in fig.). Fl. white, in few-fld. corymbs, calyx $\frac{1}{2}$–$\frac{3}{4}$ in., corolla-tube slender 1–$1\frac{1}{2}$ in. long, capsule flat, much curved, 10–18 by $\frac{3}{4}$ in.

Bundelkhand, Central Provinces, Berar. Western Peninsula, scattered in deciduous forests. Fl. May–June. 2. **D. Lawii**, Seem. Rajputana. Centr. Prov. Thana district. Deccan. Probably a var. of 1. Nearly glabrous, capsule less curved. 3. **D. arcuata**, Clarke (*Spathodea arcuata*, Wight Ic. t. 1340), Coimbatore. Palghat. Karnūl hills. Leaflets 9–11, velvety, blade 2–3 in., corolla white, tube 2 in. long, limb 2 in. across.

4. **D. stipulata**, Benth. —Syn. *Spathodea stipulata*, Wall. Pl. As. Rar. t. 238. Vern.

FIG. 174. Dolichandrone crispa, Seem. $\frac{1}{2}$.

[1] Pet. in this and the subsequent genera means the petiolule of the lateral leaflets.

Mahlwa, *Petthan*, Burm. Pegu and Martaban. Upper Burma, in deciduous forest. A middle-sized tree, wood close-grained, orange-red, beautifully mottled. Branchlets and inflorescence clothed with dense but deciduous wool, leaflets 7–11, sometimes serrulate, blade 5–8, pet. $\frac{1}{8}$ in. or less, a pair of small leaflets sometimes at the base of the common petiole, simulating stipules. Calyx $\frac{3}{4}$–$1\frac{1}{4}$ in. long, leathery, densely woolly, tip curved in bud, corolla yellow, fœtid but eaten, opening in the morning, early caducous, lower portion wide, 1 in. long, slightly narrowed above, upper half campanulate, lobes large, crisped and crenate. Capsule velvety, 18–24 by 1 in.

5. **D. crispa**, Seem.—Syn. *Spathodea crispa*, Wall. Vern. *Pumbadri*, *Nirruddi*, Tel. Common in the deciduous forests of the Deccan and Karnatik. Fl. March–Dec. A middle-sized tree, nearly glabrous, leaflets 3–7, acuminate, blade 2–4, pet. $\frac{1}{4}$–1 in. long. Corolla white, tube cylindric, 1–2 in. long, capsule slightly compressed, 12 by $\frac{3}{8}$ in., valves coriaceous, speckled.

6. **D. Rheedii**, Seem.—Syn. *Spathodea Rheedii*, Wall.; Wight Ic. t. 1339. Common in the plains of Malabar (Bedd.). Sundriban. Pegu. Tenasserim. Andamans. Ceylon. Malay Penins. and Archip. New Guinea. A middle-sized tree, almost glabrous, leaflets 7–9, ovate-lanceolate, acuminate, blade 3–4, pet. $\frac{1}{4}$–$\frac{3}{8}$ in. long. Corolla white, narrow portion of tube 3–5 in. long. Capsule 18 by 1 in. nearly straight, seeds rectangular, wings corky, not transparent, with the wings $\frac{3}{4}$ in. long. 7. A species coll. by me in 1857 near Prome, a large tree (*Thakoppo*), by J. W. Oliver at Thabet Kyin, and by Smales in the Shwebo district, Upper Burma (*Thakut*) has small dentate, very unequal-sided leaflets (2–3 in. long), narrow part of corolla-tube 2–4 in., gradually widened into the upper funnel-shaped portion, capsule 32 × $\frac{3}{8}$ in., seeds with the thin transparent wings 1–$1\frac{1}{2}$ in. long.

3. HETEROPHRAGMA, DC.; Fl. Brit. Ind. iv. 380.

Differs from *Dolichandrone* chiefly by the calyx which also is closed in bud, but in fl. irregularly 3–5-lobed. Species 3.

1. **H. Roxburghii**, DC.—Syn. *Bignonia quadrilocularis*, Roxb. Cor. Pl. t. 145; *Spathodea Roxburghii*, Sprengel; Brandis F. Fl. 350. Vern. *Waras*, *Warsi*, Mar.

A large tree, bark grey, l. tomentose while young, glabrous afterwards, generally approximate near the ends of branches, leaflets 3–4 pair, often serrulate, nearly glabrous when full grown, 3–$4\frac{1}{2}$ in. long. Fl. in large terminal erect densely tawny-tomentose panicles. Calyx obtusely bilabiate, corolla campanulate, $1\frac{1}{2}$ in. long, white, tinged with pink. Capsule straight, $\frac{1}{2}$ in. thick, 8–12 by 2 in., velvety while young, dissepiment 4-winged, horizontal section cross-shaped.

Chanda district, C. P., Godavery forests. Western Coast and Western Ghats, Khandeish and Thana to Kanara. Fl. January–April.

2. **H. adenophyllum**, Seem.; Kurz F. Fl. ii. 236.—Syn. *Spathodea adenophylla*, A. DC.; Wight Ill. t. 160. Vern. *Petthan*, Burm.

A large deciduous tree, young shoots and inflorescence brown-tomentose, leaflets 2–3 pair, elliptic, entire, softly pubescent beneath, nearly sessile, 6–12 in. long, often on the petiole at its base a pair of small auricle-like leaflets. Fl. large, yellow-brown, in many-fld. terminal erect brown-tomentose panicles, calyx campanulate, $\frac{1}{2}$–1 in. long, irregularly 3–5-lobed, corolla densely brown-tomentose outside, mouth 2 in. across. Capsule 1–3 ft. long, cylindric, ribbed.

Assam, Chittagong. Coco island, common. Andamans. Burma, Lower and Upper. Fl. April–May, also Sept. (Upper Burma, Smales). 3. **H. sulfureum**, Kurz. Vern. *Thitlinda*. Irawadi valley in Engdain. Pegu Yoma. Terai of Shan hills. A middle-sized deciduous tree, leaflets 3–4 pair, slightly pubescent beneath while young, fl. pale yellow, in short densely tomentose panicles, calyx cylindrical, 1–$1\frac{1}{2}$ in. long, corolla glabrous, or with scattered stellate hairs, mouth $2\frac{1}{2}$ in. across, capsule 2 ft. long, compressed, densely tawny tomentose.

4. PAJANELIA, DC.; Fl. Brit. Ind. iv. 384.

P. Rheedii, DC. (the only species): Wight Ic. t. 1343–44.—Syn. *P. multijuga*, Kurz F. Fl. ii. 237; *Bignonia multijuga*, Wall. Pl. As. Rar. t. 95, 96. Vern. *Kyaungdauk*, Burm.

A large tree, entirely glabrous, l. imparipinnate 1½–3 ft. long, rachis angular, leaflets 10–12 pair, from an unequal base ovate to ovate-lanceolate, entire, 3–7 in. long. Fl. in ample robust erect panicles, corolla 2½ in. long, dull purple, lobes round 1 in. long. Capsule straight, compressed, winged, 12–20 by 2½–3½ in.

Assam. Andamans. Lower Burma. Fl. Nov.–Feb. North Kanara, in moist forest, fl. C. S. (Talbot 259). Between Coimbatore and Palghāt, Malabar common up to 2,000 ft. Wainād. The Malabar species, which Beddome, Manual 169, calls a small weak tree, regarding which Wight stated: fl. July, August, and which he considered different from the Eastern tree, may possibly turn out to be distinct.

5. STEREOSPERMUM, Cham.; Fl. Brit. Ind. iv. 382.

Differs from *Dolichandrone* and *Heterophragma* by the calyx, which is truncate or shortly and unequally lobed, and the thick corky, nearly cylindric dissepiment. Fl. in large large lax terminal panicles. L. in 2 species bipinnate, in the others imparipinnate. Species 12, tropical Africa and Asia.

A. L. imparipinnate.

1. **S. chelonoides**, DC.; Wight Ic. t. 1341; Bedd. Fl. Sylv. t. 72. Vern. *Pader*, *Para*, Hind.; *Padal*, Mar.; *Kandior*, Kol; *Kal udi*, *Malaili*, Kan.; *Pumpadri*, Tam.; *Karing Kura*, Mal.; *Thakut po*, Burm.

A large tree, leaflets glabrous, 3–5 pair, elliptic, caudate acuminate, blade 4–6, pet. ⅓–½ in. long. Panicle branches slender, glabrous, fl. fragrant, corolla yellow, tinged and marked pale red, ¾ in. long, thinly hairy within and without. Capsule slender, curved, 12–30 by ⅓ in., valves coriaceous, midrib raised, seeds wedge-shaped inserted in deep notches of the dissepiment.

Oudh forests. Sikkim, ascending to 2,000 ft. Western Duars. Singbhum, rare. Silhet, Cachar, Chittagong. Burma, Upper and Lower, ascending to 4,000 ft. in the Southern Shan States. Western Peninsula, chiefly on the West side, from the Konkan southwards. L. shed Feb.–March, renewed April, Fl. appear after the l., April–June. Specimens from Khasi hills 2,000 ft. (D. B. April 1879) have unifoliolate l., petiole articulate at base. 2. **S. neuranthum**, Kurz (*Thandè*, Burm.). Lower Burma, young shoots softly pubescent, leaflets 2–3 pair, shortly acuminate, grey-tomentose while young, rough when mature, panicle short, corymbose, viscous-hairy, corolla 1¼ in., pale lilac, with dark purple veins, capsule linear, 12–18 in.

3. **S. suaveolens**, DC.; Wight Ic. t. 1342. Vern. *Pādal*, Hind.; *Patalo*, Mar.; *Hussi*, Kol; *Padri*, Kan.; *Kyoè magyo lein*, Upper Burma.

A middle-sized tree, young shoots covered with viscid pubescence, leaflets 3–5 pair, elliptic, shortly acuminate, often serrulate, blade 3–6 in. long, rough on the upper, pubescent on the under side, petiolule very short. Fl. exquisitely fragrant, in large lax trichotomous viscid panicles, corolla dull crimson, 1–1½ in. long, pubescent, funnel-shaped, limb oblique, the 3 inferior lobes longer and the edges of all much curled. Capsule straight, cylindric, 12–24 by ⅔ in., dark grey or purple, slightly ribbed, rough with elevated specks, valves thick, hard.

Subhimalayan tract and outer hills, ascending to 4,000 ft., from the Jumna eastwards, rare between Jumna and Jhelam. Rajputana. Singbhum. Central India. Western Peninsula. Burma, Upper and Lower. Often in Sal and Eng forest. The old l. are shed in April, the young foliage with the fl. appears April–June. 4. **S. fimbriatum**, DC. (*Thanthat*, Burm.), hills between Sitang and Salween. Tenasserim. Malay Peninsula. Viscid-pubescent, leaflets elliptic-oblong, caudate-acuminate, blade 5–8, pet. ⅓ in., corolla 2 in. long, pale lilac, the lobes nearly equal, cut into linear segments ¼ in. long. 5. **S. glandulosum**, Miq. Tenasserim. Malay Peninsula. Glabrous or nearly so, leaflets 1–3 pair, elliptic, blade 4–7, pet. ⅓ in. long. Panicles narrow, racemiform, corolla 1½ in., capsule narrow, 6–9 in. long.

B. L. bipinnate.

6. **S. xylocarpum**, Benth. & Hook. f.—Syn. *Bignonia xylocarpa*, Roxb.; Wight Ic. t. 1335–6; Bedd. Fl. Sylv. t. 70; *Spathodea xylocarpa*, T. And.;

Brandis F. Fl. tab. 43. Vern. *Paral*, Centr. Prov.; *Khar sing*, Mar.; *Udi*, Kan.; *Pathiri*, Tam.; *Edang Korna*, Mal.

A middle-sized tree, bark grey, heartwood brown, very hard. L. bi- or tripinnate, 1–4 ft. long, leaflets glabrous, hard and slightly rough when full grown, 2–3 in. long, nearly sessile. Fl. fragrant, white with a tinge of yellow, in dense compound pubescent panicles. Corolla campanulate from near the base, 1½–2 in. long. Capsule 12–30 in. long, a little curved, rough with numerous large irregular hard tubercles, valves 1–1½ in. broad, woody, dissepiment cylindric, shining, seeds including the wings 1¼ by ¼ in.

Satpura range. Chanda district. Khandeish Dangs. Western Peninsula. Fl. April, May, when nearly leafless, the fresh foliage about the commencement of the rains. 7. **S. hypostictum**, Miq. (*Spathodea amœna*, A. DC.; Brandis F. Fl. 349: *Bignonia amœna*, Wall. Pl. As. Rar. t. 183; *Radermachera amœna*, Seem. Tavoy. Malay Peninsula and Archipelago. Grown in gardens, glabrous, corolla 2 in. long, white, orange inside, lobes equal crenulate, capsule rust-coloured, pendulous, slender, 12–18 in. long, valves thin.

Millingtonia hortensis, Linn. f.; Bedd. Fl. Sylv. t. 249.—Syn. *Bignonia suberosa*, Roxb. Cor. Pl. t. 214. Believed to be indigenous in Burma (Kurz). Cultivated largely in most parts of India and in other tropical countries. A large tree, youngest shoots and inflorescence slightly pubescent. L. bipinnate, 1–2 ft. long, leaflets ovate, blade 1–2, pet. slender, ¼ in. long. Fl. numerous, white, fragrant, corolla-tube 3–4 in. long, slender, cylindrical, widened into a short funnel-shaped mouth, at the base of which the 4 stamens are inserted, lobes 5, nearly equal. Capsule linear, 12 in. long, seeds surrounded on 3 sides by fine transparent wings.

Mayodendron igneum, Kurz, Prelim. Report Pegu 1875, App. D. with fig. Vern. *Egayit*, Upper Burma. Hills between Sitang and Salween, 2–3,000 ft. Myit Kyina, Bhamo, Upper Burma. A middle-sized tree, bark grey, longitudinally wrinkled, young shoots minutely puberulous, l. ample, bi-tripinnate, leaflets entire, obliquely ovate-lanceolate, 3–4 in. long, glabrous, glossy. Fl. orange, in short corymbs, mostly from the old wood, appearing together with the young leaves, which come soon after the old l. fall. Calyx spathaceous, corolla glabrous outside, tubular, widening upwards, lobes equal, very short. Capsule slender, 18–22 by ¼ in., seeds, including the thin transparent wings ⅜ by ⅛ in.

Oroxylum indicum, Vent.—Syn. *Calosanthes indica*, Blume; Wight Ic. t. 1337, Vern. *Pharri*, Hind.; *Sanna*, Oudh; *Totilla*, Nep.; *Taitu*, Mar.; *Tetu*, Kan.; *Kyaung ya*, Burm. Subhimalayan tract, from the Jumna eastwards, rare west of the Jumna. Singbhum. Both Peninsulas.—Ceylon, Malay Peninsula and Archipelago. China. A small soft-wooded, deciduous, glabrous tree, l. bipinnate, 3–5 ft. long, leaflets ovate, acuminate, blade 3–8, pet. ¼–½ in. long. Fl. large, fleshy, purplish, with an unpleasant smell, in erect, terminal racemes, peduncles long, stout, rough, pedicels 1 in. long. Calyx coriaceous, persistent, indistinctly toothed, corolla campanulate, 2–3 in. long and nearly as wide at the mouth, stamens 5, all fertile and nearly equal. Capsule flat, 15–30 by 2–3½ in., dehiscing at the edges, the dissepiments parallel to the valves, seeds imbricate with a broad transparent wing on three sides, 2–3 in. long, including the wing.

ORDER LXXXI. ACANTHACEÆ. Gen. Pl. ii. 1060.

Mostly herbs, rarely shrubs or trees, l. opposite, rarely lobed, stipules 0. Fl. usually in the axils of bracts, each fl. supported by 2 bracteoles, calyx usually 5-lobed or of 5 sepals, corolla as a rule 2-lipped or 5-lobed, lobes imbricate or contorted in bud. Stamens 4 or 2, inserted in the corolla-tube. Ovary free, 2-celled, style filiform, bifid, one branch often obsolete. Capsule loculicidal, seeds often clothed with white elastic hairs (best seen when wetted), seated on hard upcurved acute supports, albumen 0.

The l. of most genera here mentioned have in the epidermis of the upper surface numerous conspicuous cystolith cells, usually single and elongated, readily visible as raised lines (in *Barleria* in pairs). Exceptions are *Thunbergia* and *Acanthus*. *Adhatoda vasica* has cystolith cells in the tissue of the leaf, not in the epidermis.

I. Calyx reduced to an entire or indistinctly crenulated ring. Capsule beaked . . . . . . 1. THUNBERGIA.
II. Calyx of 4 sepals, the outer pair larger.
  Corolla 1-lipped, stamens 4 . . . . . . 2. ACANTHUS.
  Corolla 5-lobed, stamens 2 . . . . . . 3. BARLERIA.

III. Calyx of 5 lobes or sepals, ovules two in each cell.
  One anther-cell higher than the other.
    Anther-cells spurred, bracts linear, short . . JUSTICIA (p. 498).
    Anther-cells acute, bracts ovate, large . . ADHATODA (p. 498).
  Both anther-cells on the same level.
    Stamens 2, corolla-tube long linear . . . 4. DÆDALACANTHUS.
    Stamens 4, corolla-tube ventricose . . . PETALIDIUM (p. 499).
    Stamens usually 4, corolla tubular-ventricose, calyx persistent. . . . . 5. STROBILANTHES.
IV. Calyx of 5 lobes, ovules 3 or more in each cell.
  Bracts small, often caducous, stamens 2.
    Corolla 2-lipped, lobes spreading . . . . 6. PHLOGACANTHUS.
    Corolla-lobes equal, erect . . . . . CYSTACANTHUS (p. 501).
  Bracts as long as or longer than calyx, stamens 4.
    Bracts linear, branchlets densely woolly . . ÆCHMANTHERA (p. 501).
    Bracts lanceolate, imbricating, branchlets and l. rough . . . . HEMIGRAPHIS (p. 501).

1. THUNBERGIA, Linn. f. ; Fl. Brit. Ind. iv. 390.

Herbaceous or shrubby climbers, fl. (of the sp. mentioned) in bracteate racemes, each fl. enclosed in bud by two large bracteoles, more or less cohering at the margin. Calyx an entire or indistinctly crenulated ring. Corolla conspicuous, tube ventricose, curved, limb oblique, lobes rounded. Stamens 4, disk annular or cushion-shaped, ovules 2 in each cell. Capsule globose, narrowed suddenly into a flat beak. Species 70–80, Africa to Australia.

A. Corolla blue.

1. **T. grandiflora**, Roxb.; Wight Ic. t. 872, Sikkim Terai and outer valleys. Assam, Khasi hills, Manipur, Cachar, China. L. ovate, base cordate, often angularly lobed, basal nerves 5–7, blade 4–7, pet. 1–6 in. Racemes short, bracteoles 1 in., falcate-elliptic. 2. **T. laurifolia**, Lindl. Burma, Upper and Lower, Andamans.—Malay Peninsula. L. from an acute or rounded base ovate-lanceolate, dentate, basal nerves usually 3.

3. **T. Wightiana**, T. And. (*Schmidia bicolor*, Wight Ic. t. 1848). Nilgiris, l. ovate, acuminate, toothed, racemes pendulous 6–12 in. long, bracteoles conspicuous, purple and cream-coloured, orbicular, 1 in. diam., with 7 longitudinal nerves.

B. Corolla red or yellow.

4. **T. coccinea**. Wall. Outer Himalaya 2–7,000 ft., from Kumaon eastwards. Khasi hills, Tenasserim, l. ovate, acuminate, toothed, racemes lax, pendulous, 6–18 in. long, bracteoles broadly ovate, purple or dark orange. 5. **T. mysorensis**, T. And. (*Hexacentris mysorensis*, Wight Ic. t. 871). Nilgiris, Mysore. L. lanceolate or ovate-lanceolate, toothed, strongly veined, racemes elongate pendulous, bracteoles falcate-elliptic, 1 in. long, corolla yellow.

2. ACANTHUS, Linn. ; Fl. Brit. Ind. iv. 480.

Herbs or shrubs, sometimes twining, l. often spinescent. Sepals 4, the outer pair larger, corolla-tube short, horny, limb expanded into a large entire or 3-lobed lip, the upper lip wanting. Stamens 4, anthers 1-celled adnate, bearded and fringed, ovules 2 in each cell. Capsule compressed shining, 4-seeded. Species 20, warm and hot regions of the Old World and Australia, some species littoral, others inhabiting dry and arid regions. As usual, the littoral species have the structure of xerophilous plants.

A. Armed erect shrubs.

1. **A. ilicifolius**, Linn. (*Dilivaria ilicifolia*, Nees ; Wight Ic. t. 459). Vern. *Moranna*, *Mendli*, Mar. ; *Hargoza*, *Kentki*, Beng. ; *Khaya*, Burm. Tidal forests of the Peninsula, Bengal and Burma, often forming the underwood under mangrove trees. Malay Penins. and Archip. extending to Australia. An evergreen spinescent shrub, according to Schimper (Indo-Mal. Strandflora 35), often standing on stilts like *Rhizophora*. L. glossy, rigidly coriaceous, lobed or toothed, the lobes or teeth terminating in sharp prickles, blade 4–8 in., petiole short or none. Fl. supported by two pairs of bracteoles $\frac{1}{4}$–$\frac{1}{3}$ in. long, in terminal, sometimes axillary, bracteate spikes 1–12 in. long, corolla $1\frac{1}{4}$ in. long, bright blue, capsule shining, blunt, $\frac{1}{2}$–1 in. long. 2. **A. ebracteatus**, Vahl.

Sundriban. Andamans. Tenasserim. Malay Penins. and Archip. L. oblong, lobes triangular. Bracts caducous, bracteoles minute, corolla white, ¾ in. long.

B. Unarmed climber.

3. **A. volubilis**, Wall. Pl. As. Rar. t. 172. Sundriban. Coasts of Burma and the Malay Peninsula. L. elliptic-obovate, narrowed into pet. ½ in. long, spikes terminal, bracteoles 0, corolla white, 1 in. long.

3. BARLERIA, Linn.; Fl. Brit. Ind. iv. 482.

Herbs or undershrubs, a few shrubs. Fl. large, sessile, mostly in dense spikes. Sepals 4, in 2 opposite pairs, those of the outer pair large, conspicuous. One of the large sepals consists of 2, connate nearly to the tip. Corolla-lobes 5, nearly equal, tube elongate. Stamens 2, ovules 2 in each cell. Species over 100, tropics of the Old World, a few in America. Of the 22 species described from British India the following only can be mentioned.

A. Armed, capsule 2-seeded with a solid beak.

1. **B. Prionitis**, Linn. Vern. *Kanta-jati*, Beng.; *Mullugunta*, Tel.; *Leit-thay-we*, Burm. Throughout India and Burma, perhaps not indigenous in all districts. Ceylon. Malay Penins. and Archip. Tropical Africa. Useful as a hedge plant. Nearly glabrous, sharp trifid axillary spines, ½–1 in. long Outer sepals ovate-lanceolate, bracteoles linear. Corolla bright yellow, 1¼–1½ in. long. Very variable.

B. Unarmed, capsule usually 4-seeded.

(*a*) Bracteoles linear, not conform to outer sepals.

2. **B. longiflora**, Linn. f. Central Provinces. Coromandel coast. Deccan. Pubescent all over, l. ovate, ¾–1¼ in. Fl. white, solitary, or in few-fld. spikes, bracteoles linear, ½–1 in. long, patent or recurved, outer sepals ovate, nervose, ¾–1 in., corolla-tube linear 2–4 in. long. 3. **B. cristata**, Linn.; Wight Ic. t. 453. Throughout India and Burma, excepting the arid region. A diffuse, hairy undershrub, outer sepals prominently veined, ovate or ovate-lanceolate, often spinulous-toothed. Corolla blue, purple or white.

(*b*) Bracteoles lanceolate or elliptic, more or less similar to outer sepals.

4. **B. strigosa**, Willd. Subhimalayan tract from the Jumna eastwards, ascending to 4,000 ft. Behar. Chutia Nagpur. Western Peninsula. L. strigose with scattered hairs, elliptic, acuminate, blade 4–8, decurrent into pet. 1 in. long, spikes dense, many-fld., outer sepals 1 in., corolla blue, 1½–2 in. long. 5. **B. polytricha**, Wall. Pl. As. Rar. t. 82. Chittagong, Lower Burma. Similar to 4, branches and l. hirsute, pet. short, corolla 2 in. long.

Justicia Gendarussa, Linn. f.—Syn. *Gendarussa vulgaris*, Nees; Wight Ic. t. 468. Vern. *Kala-adulsa*, *Bakas*, *Tao*, Mar.; *Aduthoda gida*, Kan.; *Bawanet*, Burm. Sikkim Terai. Burma, in the rocky bed of hill streams. West side of the Peninsula (indigenous?). Grown in gardens and naturalized throughout India. China, Formosa, Philippines Nearly glabrous, l. lanceolate, blade 4–5, narrowed into pet. ¼–⅓ in. long, cystolith cells minute, visible on upper side. Spikes 2–5 in. long, often panicled, bracts linear, shorter than calyx, cor. ½ in., white, sparingly stained with purple, capsule ½ in. long, 4-seeded.

Adhatoda Vasica, Nees. (*Justicia Adhatoda*, Linn.) Vern. *Bhekar*, Pb.; *Bansa*, *Rusa*, *Bashing*, Hind.; *Adulsa*, *Vasuka*, Mar.; *Addasaram*, Tel.; *Adhatoday*, Tam. Kuram valley. Punjab Salt range. Subhimalayan tract as far as Kumaon, on dry slopes, ascending to 5,000 ft., common in Hazara. Plains of Northern India. Assam, Khasi hills, Manipur. Behar. Western Peninsula. Upper Burma. Mergui. Ceylon. Malay Penins. and Archip. China. Roots large, going deep. One of the shrubs to be employed in reclaiming waste lands. A large gregarious shrub, with a strong smell, not browsed by cattle, nearly glabrous. L. ovate-lanceolate, entire, blade 5–8, pet. ½–1 in. long, cystoliths in the tissue below the epidermis, not in the epidermis cells. Fl. white, with red spots and streaks, in pedunculate mostly axillary compact spikes, bracts ovate, ⅝–¾ in. long, bracteoles half as long, lanceolate, corolla 2-lipped. Capsule ¾ in. long, clavate, pubescent, 4–seeded.

4. DÆDALACANTHUS, T. And.; Fl. Brit. Ind. iv. 417.

(*Eranthemum*, L., Lindau in Engler u. Prantl iv. 3. b. 311.)

Perennial herbs or large herbaceous shrubs, l. narrowed into petiole, entire or indistinctly dentate. Fl. in bracteate spikes, bracts large, imbricating, bracteoles linear-lanceolate not longer than calyx. Corolla-tube long, linear, lobes obovate, twisted in bud. Stamens 2, anthers not spurred. Seeds 4 finely hairy. Species 17, Indo-Malayan region.

A. Lower half of corolla-tube cylindric, upper half ventricose.

1. **D. splendens**, T. And. Sikkim, Sāl and lower Hill forests, ascending to 2,000 ft. Upper Burma. L. entire or nearly so, spikes 3–12 in. long, bracts obovate, nerves dark green. Corolla 1½ in., purple or brick red.

B. Corolla-tube slender, narrowly cylindric.

2. **D. nervosus**, T. And. Subhimalayan tract and outer valleys from the Sutlej eastwards, often as underwood under Sāl. Assam. Silhet, Barisāl. Chutia Nagpur. L. crenulate, spikes 1–8 in. long, in dense terminal panicles, bracts elliptic, shortly acuminate, not ciliate, pale, almost white, nerves green, corolla bright blue. 3. **D. purpurascens**, T. And.—Syn. *Justicia pulchella*, Roxb. Cor. Pl. t. 177. Assam. Behar. Singbhūm Sambalpúr. Chanda. Belgaum. North Kanara. Similar to 2, spikes few, long pedunculate, bracts ovate-lanceolate, long acuminate, ciliate, corolla lilac or pale blue. 4. **D. tetragonus**, T. And. Upper and Lower Burma. L. lanceolate, nearly entire, spikes hairy, dense, oblong, bracts oblanceolate, green, clothed with long hairs, corolla purplish-blue, tube 1–1½ in. long.

Petalidium barlerioides, Nees. Subhimalayan tract from the Jumna to the Great Gandak. Behar. Singbhūm in Sāl forests. Central Provinces (dense underwood in the Teak forests of Ahiri). Ganjam and the Northern Deccan. A gregarious shrub, bark exfoliating in long papery strips (Hole), fl. yellowish-white, solitary or on short leafy racemes, each fl. supported by a pair of large scarious, elliptic acuminate, strongly veined bracteoles ¾ in. long.

5. STROBILANTHES, Blume; Fl. Brit. Ind. iv. 429.

Herbs or shrubs, often gregarious. The l. of the same pair often unequal, cystolith cells linear, broader at one end, conspicuous on the upper surface. Fl. mostly capitate or in strobiliform spikes. Calyx persistent, more or less accrescent in fr., one segment often larger than the others. Corolla tubular-ventricose, lobes nearly equal, contorted in bud. Anthers muticous, ovules 4, style linear, stigma of one long lanceolate branch, the other minute. Species 180, mostly Asiatic. Many species of this and allied genera are eminently gregarious, either covering open hill sides or forming a dense underwood under the forest, covering the ground so completely as to impede regeneration by self-sown seed. Some of these gregarious species flower annually, but the majority flower periodically at intervals of 5 years or longer. After ripening their seed, the stems die, giving a chance for the seeds of the forest trees to come up.

A. Stamens 2. Fl. in dense heads, calyx-segments equal.

1. **S. Kunthianus**, T. And. (*Phlebophyllum Kunthianum*, Nees; Wight Ic. t. 448). Nilgiris, Palnis, Shevaroys. A small gregarious shrub with rigid branches, covering extensive bare slopes, fl. once in 5 or 6 years. L. rigid, underside white-tomentose between the prominent sec. n., blade 1–2, pet. ¼ in. Corolla ventricose from near the base, bright blue, seeds densely hairy when wetted. 2. **S. foliosus**, T. And. (*Endopogon foliosus* and *capitatus*, Wight Ic. t. 1501, 1499). Nilgiris, common in sholas above 6,000 ft. A small shrub, l. glabrous, serrulate, bright green, blade 1–3, pet. ½–1½ in. long, fl. annual, blue, corolla-tube: lower half linear, upper campanulate, staminodes 2, sometimes 3, seeds glabrous. 3. **S. jeyporensis**, Bedd. Ic. t. 214. Hills of the Northern Circars, common in sholas. A large shrub, l. nearly glabrous, broad-ovate, acuminate, blade 6–7, narrowed into pet. 3 in. long, sec. n. 10–12 pair, arching. Fl. white, in axillary viscous hairy spikes 2 in., bracts lanceolate, ⅜ in. long, recurved, bracteoles linear, as long as calyx, corolla ½ in.

B. Stamens 4. Fl. in heads or short spikes, calyx-segments nearly equal.

4. **S. heteromallus**, T. And. Nilgiris. A large hairy shrub, attaining 20 ft., gregarious, forming the underwood in sholas, fl. at long intervals. L. hispid above (hairs stiff on a tubercular basis) villous beneath, blade 3–5, decurrent into petiole 1–2 in. Bracts narrow, oblong, corolla 1 in. long, lilac. 5. **S. Perrottetianus**, Nees; Wight Ic. t. 1513. Nilgiris, in the deep shade of sholas. A large, softly rufous-hairy shrub, fl. annually, l. 2–4, petiole 1–2 in., fl. heads 1–2 in. long, pedunculate, corolla light blue, lilac or pink. 6. **S. Wightianus**, Nees; Wight Ic. t. 1514. Nilgiris, on grass lands or in sholas. A small shrub, fl. annually, clothed with long spreading hairs, l. ovate, thick rugose, blade 1–2, pet. ½ in. Fl. heads ovoid, hairy, in dense cylindrical panicles, corolla ¾–1 in., blue.

7. **S. barbatus**, Nees; Bedd. Ic. t. 212. Western Ghats from the Konkan southwards in evergreen forest, fl. once in 7 years. A large gregarious shrub, branches winged, l. glabrous shining, elliptic, 6–8 in. long, tapering into a winged pet. Fl. heads axillary, pedunculate, peduncles with 1–3 pair of small l., bracts long acuminate, 1 in., spreading, corolla white, ¾–1 in. long, cylindrical portion as long as the upper campanulate.

8. **S. pectinatus**, T. And. Sikkim 6–8,000 ft., common (*Kibu*). Bhutan. Khasi, Jaintia and Naga hills. A large gregarious shrub, fl. once in 4 or 5 years. L. thinly hairy above, more or less villous beneath, elongate elliptic, acuminate, blade 3–6, pet. ½–1½ in. long. Heads pedunculate, peduncles often with 1 or 2 pairs of l., bracts ovate, ¾–1 in., corolla pale purple, 1½–2½ in. long.

C. Stamens 4. Fl. in cylindrical or strobiliform spikes, bracts imbricating.

(*a*) Bracts coriaceous or chartaceous.

9. **S. luridus**, Wight Ic. t. 1515–6. Nilgiris, Anamalais. A large gregarious shrub, attaining 18 ft., forming underwood in sholas, fl. annually. L. hairy on both surfaces, blade 3–8, petiole 1–2 in. Fl. dark purple, sometimes white, spikes 3–11 in. long, pendulous from the old wood, often near the ground, bracts large orbicular, entire. 10. **S. callosus**, Nees.—Syn. *S. Grahamianus*, Wight Ic. t. 1520. Vern. *Karvi*, Mar.: *Marua Dana*, Pachmarhi.—Mount Abu. Thana district. Melghat. Satpura range. Hills of the Northern Deccan and Western Ghats, southwards as far as Kanara. A large shrub, forming underwood in forests and attaining 30 ft., fl. in periods of 7–9 years, branchlets warted and tubercled. L. crenate rough, cystolith cells very numerous, often stellate at the base of hairs, blade 5–10, pet. 1–3 in. Spikes strobiliform, 1–4 in., bracts ½–1 in. long, elliptic or orbicular, sepals equal, corolla large, purplish-blue or pink. 11. **S. gregalis**, Collett & Hemsl. Journ. Linn. Soc. xxviii. 104. Shan Hills, Upper Burma 4,000 ft. Gregarious, l. nearly sessile, 2 in. long, bracts rigid, coriaceous, edge white-woolly.

(*b*) Bracts soft, membranous.

12. **S. auriculatus**, Nees; Wall. Pl. As. Rar. t, 295. Subhimalayan tract and outer valleys from the Jumna eastwards, ascending to 4,000 ft. Behar. Chutia Nagpur (*Hutid*, Kol). A common underwood in Sâl and other forests 4–6 ft. high. Pachmarhi, Khasi hills, Manipur. Burma Upper and Lower, Shan hills to 5,000 ft., Mu valley in great profusion, (varies with a white and purple style, A. Smythies). Branches quadrangular, usually zigzag, l. elliptic-lanceolate, those of the same pair often very unequal, crenate, sessile, with a narrow, cordate or auriculate base, scattered white soft hairs on both sides, short cystolith cells numerous on the upper side. Fl. once in 6 years, blue or pale purple in narrow hairy spikes 3–5 in. long, bracts imbricating, obovate or obcordate. Lower cylindric portion of corolla-tube very short, upper campanulate portion ⅜ in. long. Closely allied, 13. **S. Maclellandi**, Clarke. Pegu. L. acuminate to both ends, often petiolate, spikes linear, bracts spathulate, with long white hairs.

14. **S. rufescens**, T. And.; Ind. For. xxi. 47. Manipur. Chittagong. Upper Chindwin (*Moyan* Shan), Pegu (on dry rocks, D. B.), Tenasserim. A gregarious shrub, with a pungent disagreeable smell, flowering once in 6 years, branches densely clothed with soft long ferruginous hairs. Spikes axillary, cylindric, clothed with long soft hairs 1–2 in. long. Calyx divided to the base into two lips, the upper with 2, the lower with 3 teeth, corolla blue, 1 in. long.

D. Spikes lax, often short, bracts linear, not imbricating.

15. **S. perfoliatus**, T. And.—Syn. *Leptacanthus alatus*, Wight Ic. t. 1527. Vern. *Gurgi*, Kan. Western Ghats and near the coast, from Bassein to South Kanara. A gregarious shrub, fl. once in 7–9 years. l. glabrous, 6–15 in. long, tapering into a marginate petiole with a cordate base, cystolith cells on both surfaces, very plentiful on the upper, few on the underside, which is pale or steel grey. Spikes lax viscid with glandular and eglandular hairs, 2–5 in., bracts, linear, recurved ¾ in., corolla 1¼ in. long, blue or bluish-purple. 16. **S. glutinosus**, Nees. *Bekar*, Haz. Outer Himalaya, ascending to 6,000 ft., from Hazara to Nepal. A straggling shrub with a woody stem, often forming underwood in forests, aromatic, inflorescence and calyx viscid with glandular hairs, l. softly hairy on both sides, spikes short, often reduced to 1 or 2 pairs of fl. Corolla 2 in., glabrous, pale mauve, the narrow cylindric nearly as long as the upper campanulate portion.

E. Stamens 4. Fl. paniculate, bracts mostly deciduous, one calyx-segment longer than the others.

17. **S. Wallichii**, Nees, *Jânu*, *Zânu*, Jauns. Himalaya, Jaunsar to Sikkim, 7–12,000 ft., a small gregarious shrub, a common underwood in forests of *Quercus semecarpifolia*. A perennial stout, low, branching stem, sending up annually herbaceous branches, which die down in autumn, the perennial stem continuing growing slowly. At intervals of probably 12 years the herbaceous branches bear fl. and seed, when the

plants die (Kanjilal F. Fl. 260). Branches quadrangular, slightly winged, l. elliptic-acuminate, blade 2–5 in., narrowed into petiole 1 in. long, upper l. sessile. Fl. opposite, in pairs, but both turned to one side, forming leafy unilateral interrupted spikes, corolla bluish-purple, 1¼ in. long. 18. **S. atropurpureus,** Nees. Kashmir to Nepal, 6–10,000 ft. Closely allied to 17 and perhaps not different.

Two annually flowering shrubs of the North West Himalaya are: 19. **S. Dalhousianus,** Clarke; Collett Simla Flora 378 fig. 118.—Syn. *Goldfussia Dalhousiana,* Nees, corolla-tube yellow, limb purple. 20. **S. alatus,** Nees, corolla purple.

21. **S. flaccidifolius,** Nees (*S. flaccidus,* Kurz F. Fl. ii. 239). Assam (*Room*), Manipur (*Khumna*), Bhamo (*Mègyi,* Burm.). A perennial herb, cultivated in North-Eastern India and China, to make Indigo. L. thin, glabrous, elliptic, blade 4–6, narrowed into pet. 1 in. long. Pairs of fl. in lax spikes, bracts petiolate, deciduous, calyx-segments linear-spathulate, corolla 2 in. long, purple, nearly glabrous.

6. PHLOGACANTHUS, Nees.; Fl. Brit. Ind. iv. 510.

Tall herbs or shrubs, l. entire or nearly so. Fl. orange-red or pink, bracts small, often caducous, bracteoles 0. Corolla tubular, curved, limb oblique, 2-lipped. Stamens 2, more or less exserted, anthers 2-celled. Capsule elongate, more or less tetragonous, many-seeded. Species 11, all Indian.

A. Fl. in a dense cylindric terminal thyrsus.

1. **P. thyrsiflorus,** Nees. Outer Himalaya, from the Jumna eastwards, ascending to 4,000 ft. Ravines in Chutia Nagpur. Khasi hills. Burma, Upper and Lower. An evergreen glabrous shrub, attaining 10 ft., wood white, branches 4-sided. L. oblanceolate, blade 6–10, narrowed into pet. ¾–1½ in. long. Fl. brick-red in a cylindrical compact thyrsus, 4–12 in. long, bracts ¼–½ in., conspicuous in bud, calyx-teeth ¼–⅓ in., corolla, velvety, ⅞–1 in. long. 2. **P. curviflorus,** Nees.—Syn. *Justicia curviflora,* Wall. Pl. As. Rar. t. 112. Khasi hills, Manipur. Pegu and Tenasserim. L. elongate-elliptic, petiole 2–4, calyx-teeth, ⅓, corolla 1½–2 in. long. 3. **P. tubiflorus,** Nees. Assam, Khasi hills, Manipur. Upper Burma, Shwebo district, undergrowth with *Strobilanthes* in damp evergreen forests (*Mauk salu*). Attains 5 ft., l. broad-elliptic, blade 8–12, pet. 2–3 in. long. Calyx-teeth ⅛, corolla ⅞ in., tubular, curved, crimson (Burma).

B. Fl. in numerous lax axillary and terminal cymes.

4. **P. pubinervius,** T. And. Sikkim 5–7,000 ft. Bhutan, Assam, Khasi hills, Manipur. Upper Burma, hills east of Bhamo 4,000 ft. (*Mauk salon*). A shrub or small tree, l. elliptic or elliptic-lanceolate, blade 4–6, pet. ½–1 in. long. Inflorescence glandular-pubescent, bracts 0 or early caducous, pedicels slender as long as calyx, calyx ¼–⅓ in. long, segments free nearly to the base, 3-nerved, corolla ½–⅝ in. long, stamens long exserted.

Cystacanthus insignis, Clarke.—Syn. *Phlogacanthus insignis,* Kurz. Shan hills 2,000 ft. Pakokku district, Upper Burma. Higher ridges of the Pegu Yoma, 2–3,000 ft. A tall strict erect glabrous shrub, stem white, terete, with 4 elevated lines, fl. purple in a terminal narrow panicle, corolla ventricose, 1¼ in. long, villous in the throat, lobes equal, nearly erect, capsule 1⅓ in. long.

Aechmanthera tomentosa, Nees.—Syn. *Ruellia gossypina,* Wall. Pl. As. Rar. t. 42. Outer Himalaya, 3–5,000 ft., Kashmir to Sikkim. Chittagong. A small gregarious shrub, which flowers at intervals of 4–5 years. Young shoots and underside of young l. densely clothed with white wool, tomentum of young shoots purple. Fl. in clusters of 4–8, in terminal panicles, corolla 1 in. long, seeds 6–8, when wetted seem to be clothed with long slender hairs. Somewhat resembles *Strobilanthes glutinosa.*

Hemigraphis flava, Kurz.—Syn. *Strobilanthes flava,* Kurz F. Fl. ii. 243. Vern. *Myet-hnapan, Tamasè kyau,* Lower; *Kyipasit,* Upper Burma. Upper and Lower Burma, frequent, ascending to 2,500 ft. A large very bushy shrub, attaining 12 ft., fl. annually. L. harsh and brittle, rough on both sides, elliptic or obovate, crenulate, upper side wrinkled and rough with numerous large cystoliths, blade 7–9, tapering into pet. ½–1 in. long. Fl. conspicuous, yellow, in short obtuse glandular-hairy spikes, arranged in short terminal panicles, bracts lanceolate, long acuminate, bracteoles linear, similar to calyx-segments, corolla 1–1½ in. long. Seeds 6–8.

ORDER LXXXII. VERBENACEÆ. Gen. Pl. ii. 1131.

Herbs, shrubs or trees, l. opposite, whorled, rarely alternate, stipules 0. Fl. zygomorphic, rarely regular, 4- or 5-merous. Calyx usually gamosepalous, persistent, often enlarged in fr. Corolla gamopetalous, hypogynous, lobes imbricate in bud. Stamens usually 4, nearly equal or one pair longer, ovary 2- or 4-celled, 1 ovule in each cell, style terminal, as a rule filiform, shortly bifid. Embryo straight, cotyledons thick, radicle inferior, albumen, in the Indian species, 0 or very thin.

As far as known, the Indian climbing species (excepting *Congea*) have normally built wood with large vessels. The stem of *Avicennia* has an entirely abnormal structure.

A. Fl. in centripetal spikes.
  Fr. a drupe with 2 bony pyrenes . . . . . 1. LANTANA.
  Fr. dry, separating into two 1-seeded pyrenes . LIPPIA (p. 502).
B. Inflorescence in compound corymbiform pyramidal or thyrsoid cymes.
  Leaves digitate rarely unifoliolate. . . . . 2. VITEX.
  Leaves simple.
    Calyx much enlarged in fr.
      Calyx enclosing the fr.
        A climbing shrub . . . . HYMENOPYRAMIS (p. 505).
        Trees . . . . 3. TECTONA.
      Calyx-limb flat, orbicular . . . . . HOLMSKIOLDIA (p. 506).
      Calyx campanulate or deeply divided . . 4. CLERODENDRON.
    Calyx not or slightly enlarged in fr.
      Corolla large, 1 in. and longer . . . . . 5. GMELINA.
      Corolla under 1 in. long.
        Calyx small shortly 2–5-toothed
          Fr. a drupe.
            Corolla 2-lipped, endocarp 1–4-celled . 6. PREMNA.
            Corolla 4- rarely 5-lobed, pyrenes 4, 1-seeded . . . . 7. CALLICARPA.
          Fr. a 4-valved capsule . . . . . GLOSSOCARYA (p. 512).
        Calyx deeply 4–6-lobed . . . . . . 8. CARYOPTERIS.
C. Cymes simple, capitate, fl. few sessile.
  Bracts forming an involucre, calyx 4–6-dentate.
    Bracts 3–4, corolla 2-lipped . . . . . . 9. CONGEA.
    Bracts 6.
      Corolla 5–6-lobed, l. entire . . . . . 10. SPHENODESME.
      Corolla 5–16-lobed, l. usually dentate . . 11. SYMPHOREMA.
  No regular involucre, calyx of 5 sepals . . . 12. AVICENNIA.

1. LANTANA, Linn.; Fl. Brit. Ind. iv. 562.

Rambling shrubs, pubescent or scabrous, branches 4-sided, l. simple, crenate. Fl. in peduncled ovoid or cylindric spikes, bracts conspicuous, exceeding the calyx, bracteoles 0, corolla-tube slender, cylindric, lobes 4–5, spreading. Ovary 2-celled, one ovule in each cell, style short. Drupe with 2 bony 1-seeded pyrenes. Species 50, tropical or subtropical, mostly American.

L. indica, Roxb.; Wight Ill. t. 173b fig. 3. Ic. t. 1464.—Syn. *L. dubia*, Wall.; Royle Ill. t. 73 fig. 2; *L. alba*, Brandis F. Fl. 369. Vern. *Ghaneri*, Mar. Throughout India also in Baluchistan, Sind, Kuram valley, ascending in the Himalaya to 3,000 ft. Upper Burma. Fl. April–June. Pubescent, fl. light-purple, yellow or white, almost scentless, corolla ⅓ in. long, hairy, limb oblique, lobes 4, unequal. Drupe purple, enclosed by the thin transparent calyx. 2. **L. aculeata**, Linn.; Trimen Handb. Ceylon iii. 346 (*L. Camara*, Linn.; Talbot Ed. ii. 267). A tropical American shrub with recurved prickles on the branches, fl. sweet-scented, corolla ⅓ in. long, tube pink, lobes orange, drupe purple. Birds eat the fr. and spread the seed widely. It is known in India as *The Lantana* and has spread with extraordinary vigour in Ceylon and the Peninsula. In clearances made in evergreen forests it sometimes is useful in giving shelter to young forest growth, but in deciduous forests it is a most troublesome weed, though it might perhaps in many cases be made useful. The *Lantana* is considered by some to be the cause of the Spike disease of Sandalwood in Coorg.

Of the allied genus **Lippia**, Linn., which has a dry fruit, separating into 2 one-seeded pyrenes, should be mentioned: 1. **L. nodiflora,** Rich. (*Wakem*, Sind), common in moist places throughout India, a spreading annual often rooting from the nodes, l. spathulate, sharply serrate. 2. **L. geminata,** Humb. Bonpl. Kunth. Indigenous in tropical America, common in Lower Bengal and elsewhere. Very similar to *Lantana indica.*

2. VITEX, Linn.; Fl. Brit. Ind. iv. 583.

Trees or shrubs, l. opposite, digitately 3–5-foliolate. Hairs thin pluricellular, not stellate, in some species round thin-walled trichomes (glands) on the underside of l. Calyx campanulate, truncate or shortly 5-toothed, corolla small, tubular, limb 2-lipped, usually hairy outside and the lower lip bearded. Stamens 4, didynamous, anther-cells at first parallel, afterwards divaricate. Ovary 2–4-celled, ovules 4, style filiform, shortly bifid. Drupe supported by

FIG. 175.—Vitex altissima, Linn. f. ½.

the more or less enlarged calyx, endocarp bony, 1–4-celled. Species 60, tropical and subtropical, in both hemispheres.

A. Inflorescence usually a terminal thyrsus.

1. **V. Negundo,** Linn.; Wight Ic. t. 519. Vern. *Marwan, Wana*, Pb.; *Shiwali, Ningori, Nisinda*, Hind.; *Nirguda, Lingur*, Mar.; *Vavili*, Tel.; *Lakki, Nukki*, Kan.; *Nochi*, Tam.

A large shrub or small tree, strongly scented, branchlets, underside of l. and inflorescence clothed with short grey or white pubescence. Leaflets 3 or 5, lanceolate, entire, toothed or pinnatifid, the central 3–4 in. long, on pet. ½–1 in., the lateral smaller, on petiolules up to ½ in. long. Fl. small, bluish-purple, in opposite cymes, forming an elongated terminal thyrsus, often compound at the base, calyx-teeth triangular or oblong, half or one-third the length of tube, corolla ¼–⅓ in. long, very hairy in the throat, distinctly 2-lipped.

Common, often gregarious, nearly everywhere in the plains and lower hills of India, ascending to 5,000 ft. in the N. West Himalaya, extending west to Peshawar and Sind. Common near streams. Fl. May–Dec. Ceylon, low country. China.

2. **V. trifolia**, Linn. f. (*Indrani*, Mar.; *Kyaung ban*, Burm.). Western Peninsula. Burma, Upper and Lower. L. 3- often 1-foliolate, leaflets sessile, pleasantly aromatic. 3. **V. Agnus castus**, Linn. Gregarious in dry stony watercourses in Baluchistan to 4,000 ft. (*Mehrwan*). Afghanistan, Western Asia and the Mediterranean region. Calyx-teeth very short, corolla ⅓–½ in. long, pale purple, throat glabrous, tufts of hairs only at the insertion of stamens, lobes nearly equal.

4. **V. altissima**, Linn. f.; Wight Ic. t. 1466; Bedd. Fl. Sylv. t. 252. Vern. *Nevali Adugu*, Tel.; *Mairole, Nauladi*, Kan.; *Maila*, Tam.; *Maiyella*, Mal.

A very large tree, young shoots villous with soft hairs. Leaves 3- rarely 5-foliolate, leaflets lanceolate, nearly sessile, nearly entire, when full grown upperside glabrous, (excepting midrib), underside pubescent, petiole 1–3 in. long, often with a narrow wing, widening upwards, inflorescence 3–8 in. diam., branches spiciform, interrupted. Fl. white with a tinge of blue, calyx-teeth short, triangular, corolla woolly and ciliate at edges. Ovary and young fr. fulvous-villous at apex. Drupe ¼ in. diam.

Western Peninsula, common in the evergreen forests of the Western Ghats, also in the Deccan. Fl. R. S. 5. **V. alata**, Heyne, Western Peninsula, wing of petiole ⅛ in. wide, generally wider below, is probably not specifically distinct. 6. **V. limonifolia**, Wall. *Kyetyo*, Burm. Khasi hills (D. B. April, 1879). Chittagong (C. B. Clarke. Feb. 1878). Burma, Upper and Lower. Common petiole more or less winged, leaflets sessile, usually 3, from lanceolate to broad-elliptic, 3–10 in. long, sometimes serrate, underside with shining resinous glands, sparsely hairy or softly tomentose. Branches of thyrsus spiciform.

7. **V. pubescens**, Vahl.—Syn. *V. arborea*, Roxb.; Wight Ic. t. 1465. Vern. *Nemali adugu*, Tel.; *Myladi*, Tam.; *Kyetyo*, Burm.

A large evergreen tree, wood brown, very hard, branches quadrangular, branchlets, petioles, underside of l. and inflorescence densely clothed with soft minute tawny pubescence, leaflets usually 3, the lateral sessile or nearly so, elliptic, 4–8 in. long. Inflorescence dense, pyramidal, 3–5 in. across, top rounded, bracts persistent, ¼–½, corolla ⅓–½ in. long.

Western Peninsula, on the east side from Orissa, on the west side from the Nilgiris southwards. Silhet. Lower Burma. Andamans. Fl. Jan.–Mar.. Malay Penins. 8. **V. diversifolia**, Kurz. Andamans. L. simple and 3-foliolate, glabrous, only midrib pubescent beneath, closely reticulate veins conspicuous on both surfaces, bracts ovate, conspicuous. 9. **V. canescens**, Kurz. *Harmala*, Ass.; *Tauksha*, Burm. Assam, Khasi hills. Pegu. Upper Burma. Yunnan. A middle-sized tree, branches quadrangular, branchlets, petioles, underside of l. and inflorescence softly pubescent or tomentose, leaflets 3 or 5, blade 3–6, lateral petiolules up to ½ in. long. Fl. white, with a faint pink tinge, pedicels as long as calyx, in half whorls, rarely in short cymes, on the branches of the terminal, rarely axillary thyrsus, bracts caducous, calyx campanulate. 10. **V. heterophylla**, Roxb.; Wall. Pl. As. Rar. t. 226. Assam. Tipperah. Pegu. Tenasserim. China. Formosa. Ind. Archip. A large tree, leaflets membranous, as a rule 5, nearly glabrous, blade 3–7, pet. of the lateral ¼–1 in. long. Branches of thyrsus elongate, narrow, fr. ⅛ in. diam. 11. **V. coriacea**, Clarke. Mergui (*Kyet-ho hpo*). Malay Penins. Similar to 10, leaflets as a rule 3, coriaceous, shining fr. ¼–½ in. long, supported by the enlarged cup-shaped calyx.

B. Inflorescence always axillary.

12. **V. Leucoxylon**, Linn. f.—Syn. *Wallrothia Leucoxylon*, Roxb.; Wight Ic. t. 1467. Vern. *Lokki, Kondavavili*, Tel.; *Sengeni, Lakki*, Kan.

A large deciduous tree, bark white, young shoots slightly puberulous. L. 3- or 5-foliolate, leaflets lanceolate, almost coriaceous, glabrous, only midrib hairy on underside, blade 4–6, petiolule of the lateral up to ¾ in. long. Cymes trichotomous corymbiform, lax, branches divaricate, fl. fragrant, whitish, corolla hairy outside, 4 lobes equal, the 5th much larger, on the upper side bearded with purple hairs. Drupe oblong ovoid ¾ in. long, dark purple, stone 4-celled.

Western Peninsula, chiefly on banks of streams, from the Chanda district, southwards. Fl. Feb.–April.—Ceylon, dry country.

13. **V. peduncularis,** Wall.—Syn. *Vitex alata*, Roxb.; Kurz F. Fl. ii. 272. Vern. *Boruna*, Beng.; *Osai*, Ass.; *Kyetyo*, *Pazin-nyo*, Burm.

A middle-sized or large deciduous tree, wood hard, close-grained. Youngest shoots minutely grey pubescent, branchlets, petioles and l. glabrous. Leaflets 3, membranous, lanceolate, 5–7, in., the lateral on petiolules up to ¾ in. long, common petiole channelled and narrowly marginate, in young plants and coppice shoots often broadly winged. Shining resinous glands usually on the underside of l., on calyx and corolla. Cymes in a lax pedunculate thyrsus, up to 10 in. long, ramifications slender, pedicels as long as calyx. Fl. yellowish- or greenish-white, corolla ⅓ in. long, lower lip longer than tube.

Subhimalayan tract from Nepal eastwards. Assam, Khasi hills. Cachar, Chittagong. From the Rajmahal hills through Chutia Nagpur to Orissa and the Circars. Burma, Upper and Lower, common. Fl. March–June.

14. **V. glabrata,** R. Brown.—Syn. *V. Leucoxylon*, Kurz F. Fl. 273. Vern. *Goda*, Beng.; *Tauksha*, Burm.

A large deciduous tree, wood grey, handsome. Youngest shoots slightly pubescent, l. almost glabrous, leaflets 5, blade 5–7 in., petiolules of the lateral up to 1 in. long, underside without resinous glands. Cymes pedunculate, dichotomous, lax corymbiform, calyx usually glabrous in the lower, hairy in the upper part, corolla ⅓–½ in. long, white and purple. Fr. succulent ½ in. long.

Assam. Garo hills, Cachar, Eastern Bengal and Chittagong. Andamans. Burma, Upper and Lower. Fl. April, May. Malay Penins. and Archip. New Guinea. North Australia. 15. **V. vestita,** Wall. Assam, Khasi hills. Upper Burma. Yunnan. Malay Peninsula and Archip. A shrub or small tree, branchlets, petioles, underside of leaflets and inflorescence pubescent or woolly with long soft hairs. Leaflets 3, acuminate, 4–6 in., the lateral on petiolules up to ¼ in. long. Cymes shorter than petioles, peduncles up to ¾ in. long, shining resinous glands on calyx, corolla and underside of l., corolla ⅓–½ in., tube 2–3 times longer than calyx, fr. ¼ in. diam. Specimens coll. in bud on the hills between Yunzalin and Salween 3,000 ft. (D. B. March 1880) have leaflets 8–9 in. long, densely grey tomentose beneath, no resinous glands but black dots on the underside.

Hymenopyramis, brachiata, Wall. Dry districts of the Irawadi valley, Upper Burma. An extensively scandent shrub, branches and underside of l. grey-tomentose. Fl. white in compact cymes arranged in a large pyramidal thyrsus. Capsule small, 4-valved in the greatly enlarged acutely 4-winged membranous almost entirely closed calyx.

3. TECTONA, Linn. fil.; Fl. Brit. Ind. iv. 570.

Deciduous trees with angular branchlets, young shoots, inflorescence and leaves clothed with stellate tomentum. L. large, opposite or ternate, entire. Fl. small, in large terminal erect trichotomous panicles, bracts small, narrow, calyx campanulate, shortly 5- or 6-lobed, enlarged in fruit, corolla-tube short, limb spreading, equally 5- or 6-lobed, anthers exserted. Ovary 4-celled, style shortly 2–4-fid. Fr. 4-celled, endocarp bony, enclosed in the calyx. Embryo enclosed in a thin layer of endosperm. Species 3, one in the Philippines.

1. **T. grandis,** Linn. fil.; Roxb. Cor. Pl. t. 6; Bedd. Fl. Sylv. t. 250; Brandis F. Fl. t. 44. *The Teak tree*. Sans. *Sāka*; Pers. *Sāj*, *Sal*. Vern. *Sagun*, *Sagon*, Hind.; *Saguan*, Rajp.; *Sāg*, *Sāgwan*, Mar.; *Teka*, Gond; *Téku*, Tel.; *Tegu*, Kan.; *Thékku*, Tam.; *Kyūn*, Burm.

A large tree, heartwood golden yellow when fresh cut, turning brown, oily to the touch, with a strong scent, moderately hard, does not warp or split, extremely durable, weight 45 lb. per cub. ft., annual rings marked by a narrow belt of vessels. Branchlets quadrangular and channelled, with large quadrangular pith. L. elliptic or obovate, upperside rough, underside clothed with dense stellate, grey or tawny tomentum, blade 12–24 in., narrowed into petiole 1–1½ in., of seedlings and coppice shoots the l. often 2–3 ft. long. Fl. white, panicles erect, 1–3 ft. long. Fr. a hard bony nut, enclosed in a thick spongy covering, consisting of a dense felt of branched hairs, seeds 1–3, rarely 4, a central cavity having the appearance of a 5th cell. When the seed germinates, the outer wall of each cell comes off bodily like a round concave cap. The inflated calyx, which encloses the fr. like a bladder, is generally ovoid, 1–1½ in. diam., reticulate and more or less corrugated.

The Teak tree is indigenous in both Peninsulas of India, in the north-eastern drier part of Java and in other islands of the Indian Archipelago. In Western India it attains its northern limit in the Western Aravallis at 24° 42′ N. Lat. (A. E. Lowrie). In Central India its northernmost point is the Jhansi district at 25° 33′ and from that point the line of northern limit continues in a south-easterly direction to the Mahanadi river in the Central Provinces. In Upper Burma it extends to lat. 25° 30′, and ascends to 3,000 ft. Teak, however, is not uniformly distributed over this large area, for there are many districts where it is entirely absent. It is cultivated in Bengal and Assam, and in Northern India as far as Debra Dùn.

Teak grows on a great variety of soils, but requires perfect drainage. It thrives equally well on the sandstone of the Pegu Yoma, on the granite of the eastern Sitang and the North Kanara Forests, on limestone in the Thaungyeen forests of Tenasserim, and on basaltic rocks in the Khandeish Daugs, and the Satpura range. On alluvial soil the stems generally are fluted and irregularly shaped.

It is not gregarious, though on deep alluvial soil small patches of nearly pure Teak forest are occasionally found (Beeling, Domdamee in Martaban. Banks of the Godavari [Gamble]). A large area of pure Teak is in the Katu forest (Katha district) of Upper Burma. Woods in which Teak, mostly stunted, preponderates, also occur here and there on dry rocky ground. Its associates are, besides Bamboos, the trees of the deciduous forest.

In dry and hot situations Teak loses its leaves in November, December or early in January. Where the ground is moist, the tree often remains green until March. The new foliage comes out in May. It flowers during the rains in July and August, and ripens its seed between November and January. In summer it is readily recognized at a considerable distance by the flower panicles, which overtop the green foliage, and in winter the feathery erect fruit panicles distinguish it from all other trees.

On good soil and in a suitable climate Teak has an exceedingly rapid growth while young. It coppices well. It demands much light and in this respect its requirements are similar to those of *Quercus sessiliflora* and *Pinus sylvestris* in Europe. Its strong point is the vigorous terminal shoot, which enables it, like *Fraxinus excelsior*, to pierce through dense brushwood, provided there is sufficient light overhead, to stimulate its growth. The white mineral deposit found in cavities in the wood, as far as known, mainly consists of Calcium Phosphates.

2. **T. Hamiltoniana,** Wall. Pl. As. Rar. t. 294; Kurz F. Fl. ii. 259. Vern. *Dahat*, Burm.

A middle-sized tree, branchlets 6–8-angular. Leaves mostly in whorls of 3, sometimes opposite or in whorls of 4, ovate, blade 4–8, petiole ⅔ in. long. Fl. greenish-white, corolla very hairy in the throat. Fr. tightly enclosed in the flask shaped calyx.

Dry country of the Irawadi valley, from Prome upwards. Fl. March–May, with the young foliage.

Holmskioldia sanguinea, Retz. Subhimalayan tract, ascending to 4,000 ft., from the Sutlej eastwards, ascending to 4,000 ft. Irawadi valley from Prome upwards. A large straggling and scandent shrub, l. ovate, entire or crenate, blade 2–4, petiole ½–1 in. long. Cymes red, scarlet in fr. Calyx widely obconic, limb ¾–1 in. across, almost entire, corolla brick-red or orange, tube cylindric, curved, limb oblique, anther-cells parallel. Drupe obovoid, 4-lobed, supported by the enlarged calyx.

4. CLERODENDRON, Linn.; Fl. Brit. Ind. iv. 589.

Trees or shrubs, sometimes herbs. L. simple, opposite or whorled in threes or fours. Fl. pentamerous, calyx persistent and enlarged in fruit, often coloured. Corolla-tube slender, usually long, filiform, limb spreading, oblique, lobes equal, anthers long exserted, cells parallel. Ovary imperfectly 4-celled, ovules 4, style filiform, shortly bifid. Drupe succulent or almost dry, the endocarp or the entire fr. separating into four 1-celled or two 2-celled pyrenes. Species about 100, in the warmer regions of the Old World, a few in America.

I. Corolla-tube under 1½ in. long.

A. Cymes axillary.

1. **C. inerme,** Gærtn. Vern. *Batraj*, Beng.

A straggling almost scandent evergreen shrub, young shoots minutely grey-pubescent. L. dark green, as a rule opposite, entire, elliptic or obovate, nearly coriaceous, blade 1–2, petiole ⅛–⅓ in. long. Fl. white, in axillary, pedunculate, 3–9-fld. cymes. Calyx-teeth short, corolla-tube 1 in., lobes oblong. Drupe dry ½ in. long, pear-shaped, separating into 4 woody pyrenes.

Tidal jungles and sea coast of Bengal and both Peninsulas. Fl. throughout the year, chiefly July–Nov.—Ceylon, Malay Archipelago, China, New Guinea, North Australia, Formosa, Polynesia. Closely allied, classed by Kurz as a variety, 2. **C. neriifolium,** Wall. Sea coast of Chittagong, Aracan and Tenasserim, l. frequently ternate, linear or lanceolate, 2–4 in. long, drupe larger.

3. **C. phlomoides,** Linn. fil.; Wight, Ic. t. 1473. Vern. *Urni*, Hind. *Irun*, *Arni*, Guzerat.

A tall pubescent shrub, branches cinereous. L. ovate or rhomboid, more or less sinuate-crenate, blade 1–2, petiole ¼–¾ in. Fl. white or pink, fragrant, in axillary 3–9-fld. pubescent cymes, forming a terminal rounded leafy thyrsus. Calyx cleft half-way down, corolla-tube 1 in., lobes elliptic, drupe dry, ⅓–½ in. long, separating into 4 pyrenes.

Baluchistan, Punjab, Upper Gangetic plain, Oudh, Rajputana, Behar, Chutia Nagpùr, Orissa, the Deccan, common in hedges and in Babul Koruns. Fl. Nov. Dec., also at other times.—Ceylon dry region.

B. Inflorescence terminal.

(*a*) Inflorescence corymbiform or capitate.

α. Corolla-tube under ¾ in. long.

4. **C. infortunatum,** Gærtn.: Wight Ic. t. 1471; Kurz F. Fl. ii. 267. Vern. *Karu*, *Kari*, *Bhânt*, Hind.; *Ghentu*, Beng.; *Bokkudu*, Tel.; *Ka-aung gyi*, Burm.

A tall gregarious shrub, branches, petioles, underside of l. and inflorescence softly pubescent. L. ovate, often from a cordate base, entire or dentate, blade 5–9, petiole 1–6 in. long. Fl. white, tinged with pink, in an ample terminal trichotomous corymbiform thyrsus. Calyx cleft to near the base, segments lanceolate, corolla-tube longer than calyx-segments. Drupe fleshy, slightly 4-lobed, ⅓ in. diam., black, shining, enclosed in the enlarged red leathery calyx.

Subhimalayan tract from the Jumna eastwards, often as underwood in Sāl forest, attaining 12 ft. Gangetic Plain in Mango groves. Singbhum. Centr. Prov. Both Peninsulas. Fl. Nov.–April.—Ceylon, moist region. Malay Penins. and Archip. The roots go deep; a species to be employed when reclaiming waste lands in the plains. 5. **C. villosum, Blume.** Kohima, Naga hills 4,500 ft. Martaban hills east of the Sitang river, 2–4,000 ft., common on deserted Toungyas. Tenasserim. Malay Penins. Densely and softly tomentose, l. cordate, nearly entire, corolla-tube not longer than the glandular calyx-segments.

β. Corolla-tube slender 1 in. long.

6. **C. Griffithianum,** C. B. Clarke. Assam. Upper Burma. Yunnan. A small tree, branchlets, petioles and underside of l. along midrib and nerves clothed with long soft hairs l. lanceolate, blade 3–7, pet. ½–1 in. long. Fl. white in lax cymes, teminal and from the axils of the uppermost l., forming a corymbiform thyrsus, calyx pubescent, lobes lanceolate, longer than the campanulate tube, corolla glabrous, tube 1 in. long. 7. **C. Colebrookianum,** Walpers. Sikkim from the foot of the hills to 6,000 ft., common in second growth forest. Assam, Khasi hills. Burma. A small evergreen tree, with a strong disagreeable smell, bark silvery-grey, l. nearly glabrous, broad-ovate often 9 in. diam., pet. 4–8 in. Fl. white, on short pedicels, densely clustered in broad corymbiform compound cymes, calyx-teeth short, corolla-tube slender, 1 in. long. Drupe bright turquoise-blue. 8. **C. lasiocephalum,** Clarke. Mishmi and Dufla hills. Khasi hills. Shan hills, Upper Burma. Branchlets and l. pubescent or tomentose.

L. ovate dentate, base cuneate or rounded, blade 6–10 pet. 2–6 in. long. Cymes compact, corymbiform almost capitate, calyx-segments $\frac{1}{2}$–$\frac{3}{4}$ in. long, lanceolate, tip filiform, corolla-tube slender 1 in. long. 9. **C. bracteatum**, Wall. Sikkim 2–4,000 ft., chiefly in clearings. Assam, Khasi hills. Manipur. Cachar. A shrub or small tree, branchlets and underside of l. fulvous-villous. L. ovate, entire, blade 5–8, pet. 1–4 in. long. Fl. in bracteate pedunculate heads, forming a leafy corymbiform thyrsus, bracts $\frac{3}{4}$ in. long, tomentose, calyx $\frac{1}{2}$ in. long, deeply divided, segments ovate-lanceolate, corolla white, pubescent, tube 1 in. long. Drupe purple.

(*b*) Thyrsus erect, elongate, bracts conspicuous, calyx-teeth very short.

10. **C. serratum**, Sprengel; Wight Ic. t. 1472; Brandis F. Fl. 364; Kurz F. Fl. ii. 267. Vern. *Bèyyo*, Burm. Subhimalayan tract and outer ranges, ascending to 5,000 ft. Assam, Bengal. Singbhum valleys and shady slopes, not common. Central Prov. Both Peninsulas. Tall annual stems from a thick woody rootstock, youngest shoots and inflorescence pubescent. L. glabrous, opposite or in whorls of three, lanceolate or elliptic-lanceolate, as a rule deeply serrate, 4–8 in. long, narrowed into a very short petiole. Fl. blue, cymes trichotomous, forming a terminal more or less cylindrical thyrsus, bracts ovate, often coloured, bracteoles lanceolate. Calyx campanulate, corolla-tube not more than twice the length of calyx, mouth oblique. Drupe succulent, lobed, shining black, $\frac{1}{4}$ in. diam. A specimen from the Winyo Forest, Attaran (D. B. July 1858), has l. entire, almost sessile, with a broad base, bracts prominent, calyx truncate, possibly a new species. 11. **C. venosum**, Wall. Assam, Khasi hills. Upper Burma. A tree, glabrous, only thyrsus and calyx with minute grey pubescence. L. elliptic-lanceolate serrate, blade 6–8, narrowed into pet. 1–2 in. long. Fl. blue with a greenish-white tinge, thyrsus pyramidal, bracts leaf-like, 1–2 in. long.

(*c*) Thyrsus erect, lax, pyramidal, calyx divided to near the base, petioles connected by a ring of hairs, underside of l. with numerous round raised glands.

12. **C. paniculatum**, Linn. Pegu, Tenasserim. Malay Peninsula. Siam, Cochinchina, China, Formosa. A shrub with herbaceous branches, l. nearly glabrous, ovate, serrate, often lobed, base usually deeply cordate, blade 6–9, pet 1–3 in. long, thyrsus 4–12 in., calyx in fl. $\frac{1}{8}$–$\frac{1}{4}$ in. long. 13. **C. squamatum**, Vahl. Sikkim to 3,000 ft. Assam, Silhet. Singapore. China. Often cultivated. Similar to 12, l. not lobed, calyx in fl. $\frac{1}{4}$–$\frac{1}{3}$ in. long.

(*d*) Thyrsus long, lax, drooping.

14. **C. nutans**, Wall. Sikkim, ascending to 5,000 ft., Assam, Khasi hills. Chittagong. Upper Burma (*Kinmauk kayyi*). Malay Peninsula. A glabrous shrub, l. lanceolate or oblanceolate, remotely repand-toothed, 4–7 in. long, narrowed into a short petiole. Fl. white on slender pedicels, in lax cymes, forming an elongated racemiform drooping terminal glabrous thyrsus, bracts subulate, minute. Calyx ample, deeply cleft, segments triangular, corolla glabrous, tube longer than calyx-segments, lobes obovate $\frac{1}{2}$ in. long. Drupe succulent, dark purple, $\frac{1}{2}$ in. diam., supported by the stellately spreading crimson calyx. 15. **C. penduliflorum**, Wall. Lower Burma. Malay Penins. L. lanceolate or elongate-elliptic, blade 5–7, pet. 1–2 in. long. Fl. white, on filiform pedicels in few-fld. cymes, forming an elongated pendulous slender thyrsus, 8–12 in. long, calyx-segments linear or elongate-triangular, corolla-lobes oblanceolate. 16. **C. macrostachyum**, Turcz. On limestone above Chela, Khasi hills. Tenasserim on limestone rocks. Herbaceous, l. cordate, toothed, almost lobed, blade 4–7, pet. 1–6 in. long. Fl. pale blue or purple, in several long slender thyrsi in the axils of the uppermost l., forming a large terminal panicle, pedicels filiform, calyx truncate, small.

II. Corolla-tube more than 3 in. long.

17. **C. Siphonanthus**, R. Br.; Wight Ill. t. 173. Vern. *Barangi*, Hind.; *Chingári*, Dehra Dún. Common in many parts of India and Burma. Savannahs in the Duars. Sundriban. Often as an escape from cultivation. A tall, straight-stemmed glabrous shrub, branches herbaceous, hollow, channelled. L. opposite or whorled, linear-lanceolate, almost sessile, pale beneath, 6–9 in. long. Fl. white when opening, changing gradually into cream-colour, in lax pedunculate axillary cymes, forming a large terminal thyrsus. Calyx campanulate, cleft more than half-way, segments ovate, corolla-tube slender, 2–4 in. long, curved. Drupes 1–4, blue, ovoid, joined at the base and supported by the enlarged red spreading calyx. 18. **C. hastatum**, Lindley. Silhet, Khasi hills. Pubescent, l. hastate, often lobed, cymes dense, forming a broad corymbiform terminal inflorescence. Corolla white, tube 4 in. long, drupe succulent, black-purple, supported by the enlarged dark red calyx.

5. GMELINA, Linn.; Fl. Brit. Ind. iv. 581.

Trees or shrubs, leaves usually entire. Fl. large, corolla-tube slender below, wider upwards, limb oblique, anther-cells oblong, diverging. Ovary 4-celled, style slender, shortly bifid, rarely 4-fid. Drupe succulent, stone bony, 1–4-celled. Seeds oblong, albumen 0. Species 8, Indo-Malayan region, tropical Australia.

A. Unarmed trees.

1. **G. arborea,** Linn.; Roxb. Cor. Pl. t. 246; Wight Ic. t. 1470; Bedd. Fl. Sylv. t. 253. Vern. *Gamhār,' Gambhar, Khamara,* Hind.; *Sewan,* Rajputana; *Gomari,* Ass.; *Kasmar,* Kol; *Shivan,* Mar.; *Gummadi,* Tel.; *Kuli,* Kan.; *Kumbili,* Mal.; *Yamane, Yemane,* Burm.

A large deciduous tree, bark pale, wood greyish-white, light and strong, bark smooth, young shoots, petioles, underside of l. and inflorescence softly tawny-tomentose. Leaves broad-ovate acuminate, often with a cordate base, basal nerves 3–5, blade 4–9, petiole 3–5 in., with shining glands at the insertion of leaf. Fl. yellow, tinged with brown, in a narrow terminal racemiform thyrsus, calyx 5-toothed, as well as corolla softly tomentose, bracts, linear-lanceolate, corolla 1–1½ in. long, ventricose. Drupe yellow when ripe, 1 in. long.

Subhimalayan tract from the Chenab eastwards, ascending to 3,000 ft. Aravalli hills. Central India. Singbhum. Western Peninsula. Burma. Leaves are shed Feb.–April, the new foliage appears April–May. Fl. Feb.–April, generally before the l. are out. Coppices well. 2. **G. oblongifolia,** Roxb. East Bengal. A tall tree. l. ovate or oblong, corolla rosy, drupe bright crimson when ripe.

B. Branchlets frequently spinescent.

3. **G. asiatica,** Linn.; Wight Ill. t. 174; Brandis F. Fl. 365. Vern. *Gumudu, Karu gummadi,* Tel.; *Adivi Gumadi,* Sriharikota and Madras. A common bush on the Coromandel coast, south as far as Tuticorin, also inland in the Deccan and Karnatik. An excellent hedge plant.—Ceylon. A large shrub, l. ovate or obovate, frequently lobed, pubescent when young, blade ½–1½ in., petiole ¼ in. Fl., yellow, in narrow racemiform panicles at the ends of branches, calyx 4-toothed, corolla 1½ in. long, bracts small caducous. Drupe ¾ in. long, ovoid or obovoid, 1–2-seeded. 4. **G. villosa,** Roxb. (*G. asiatica,* Kurz F. Fl. ii. 265). Pegu, Martaban, Nicobars, Malay Peninsula and Archipelago. Young shoots and inflorescence densely tawny villous, l. elliptic, entire, hairy above, densely villous beneath, blade 2–4, pet. ½–1 in., bracts broadly lanceolate, corolla 1½ in., almost tubular, calyx tomentose, minutely 4-toothed, with several large glabrous glands. 5. **G. Hystrix,** Kurz. Tenasserim. Siam. Philippines. A large scandent shrub, l. nearly glabrous, sometimes with a few large teeth, blade 2–4, pet. ½–⅝ in., fl. protected by the large ovate coloured bracts, 1 in., corolla yellow, 2 in. long.

6. PREMNA, Linn.; Fl. Brit. Ind. iv. 571.

Trees or shrubs, frequently climbing or epiphytic, l. undivided. Fl. greenish– or yellowish-white, in bracteate, trichotomous compound cymes. Calyx small, corolla short, tubular, throat hairy, limb 2-lipped or subequally 4– or 5–lobed. Stamens 4, ovary 2–or 4-celled, ovules 4. Fr. a fleshy drupe, stone hard, rugose or tubercled, 2–4-celled. Seeds oblong, albumen 0, radicle inferior. Species 40–50, Indo-Malayan region, 17 in Africa.

I. Shrubs, trees or climbers.

A. Inflorescence elongate, narrow, spiciform or thyrsoid.

1. **P. interrupta,** Wall.; Outer Himalaya 5–8,000 ft. from Kumaon to Sikkim. Khasi hills. A shrub or small tree, usually climbing, youngest shoots and inflorescence pubescent. L. obovate, 4–8 in. long, narrowed into a very short petiole. Fl. sessile, in compact nearly sessile cymose clusters supported by foliaceous lanceolate bracts, forming a simple cylindrical terminal spike, often interrupted near the base. 2. **P. racemosa,** Wall. Assam, Khasi hills, Yunnan. L. and spikes smaller, blade 2–3 in., petiole ¼–½ in., corolla ⅛ in. long, tube longer than calyx. 3. **P. bracteata,** Wall.

Sikkim, 2–5,000 . ft. Bhutan, Khasi hills. Ta Oo table land, Tenasserim (D. B. March 1862). Climbing, l. glabrous, pet. ½–¾ in., fine reticulate veins conspicuous on the underside, spikes panicled. 4. **P. punduana**, Wall. Khasi hills. Cymes pedunculate, forming a large compound terminal thyrsus, which like the 5-toothed calyx is stellately tomentose.

B. Inflorescence corymbiform, l. entire or undulate.

(*a*) Calyx distinctly 2-lipped or truncate. L. as a rule glabrous or nearly so.

α. Petiole longer than 1 in.

5. **P. coriacea**, Clarke. *Chambari, Rawan*, Mar. Evergreen forests of the Western Ghats, from North Kanara southwards. Siligori. Khasi hills, Silhet (var. *oblonga* and *cuneata*). Shan hills 4,000 ft. A large tree (Collett). A large ornamental shrub, generally climbing, often epiphytic, l. coriaceous, ovate or elliptic, blade 3–8, pet. 1–1½ in. long, tertiary nerves parallel. Corymbs large, red or purple, petals white, calyx truncate. 6. **P. khasiana**, Clarke. Khasi hills. Similar to 5, but calyx 2-lipped. 7. **P. villosa**, Clarke. Coorg. Wainād. Nilgiris. Similar to 5, but l. softly tomentose beneath.

8. **P. scandens**, Roxb. Subhimalayan tract, Sikkim, West Duars, mixed forest, chiefly on banks of streams. Assam, Khasi hills. Hills east of Toungoo. A large climbing shrub, l. elliptic-oblong, long-acuminate, membranous, glabrous, blade 5–10, pet. slender, 1–1½ in. long. Fl. small, in large compound trichotomous cymes 4–10 in. diam., calyx cup-shaped, nearly entire. 9. **P. cordifolia**, Roxb. Assam. Naga Hills. Malay Peninsula. L. glabrous, ovate or elongate-elliptic, acuminate, blade 4–6, pet. 1 in., corymbs dense, corolla-tube twice the length of calyx. 10. **P. longifolia**, Roxb. Assam. Bengal. A tree, l. ovate, blade 6–8, pet. 1–2½ in. long.

β. Petiole 1 in. or less.

11 **P. integrifolia**, Linn.; Wight Ic. t. 1469.—Syn. *P. serratifolia*, Linn.; *P. sambucina*, Wall. Vern. *Arni*, Guz.; *Khara-Narvel, Aran*, Mar.; *Taungtangyi*, Burm. Western Penins., Bengal, Burma, near the sea coast, but also inland. Andamans. Nicobars. Ceylon, dry region. Malay Penins. and Archip. Sea shore of China and Tropical Africa. A small evergreen tree, wood scented, trunk and large branches often thorny, l. ovate or elliptic, sometimes coarsely serrate, blade 2–4, pet. ¼–¾ in. Fl. small, greenish-yellow, as well as l. with a peculiar scent, corymbs and calyx minutely hairy, calyx 3-toothed. 12. **P. parasitica**, Blume. Tenasserim. Malay Penins. A large climber, l. elliptic or obovate, inflorescence nearly glabrous, calyx glabrous. 13. **P. divaricata**, Wall.—Syn. *P. lucidula*, Kurz F. Fl. ii. 268. Mergui. Andamans. A climber, l. ovate, acuminate, calyx nearly truncate with 2 minute teeth. 14. **P. corymbosa**, Rottl. & Willd.—Syn. *P. cordifolia*, Wight Ic. t. 1483. Karnatik. Cuddapah. L. ovate, blade 2–4, pet. 1 in., tert. nerves strongly reticulate, corymbs small, corolla-tube longer than calyx.

(*b*) Calyx equally 4–5-toothed. L. hairy or tomentose.

α. Hairs stellate.

15. **P. tomentosa**, Willd.; Wight Ic. 1468; Bedd. Fl. Sylv. t. 251. Vern. *Narvu, Narva, Narāva*, Tel.; *Ijé, Iti*, Kan.; *Podanganari*, Tam.

A middle-sized deciduous tree, branchlets, leaves and inflorescence densely clothed with soft tawny tomentum of stellate hairs. Leaves ovate, acuminate, entire, base often cordate, blade 5–8, petiole 1–2 in. long. Fl. yellow, calyx-segments short, corolla more or less bilabiate, very hairy in the throat. Ovary very hairy, style minutely 2-fid.

Rajmahal Hills. Chutia Nagpur, Orissa. Deccan and Karnatik. Fl. March, April with the young l. Ceylon. 16. **P. pyramidata**, Wall. (*P. tomentosa*, Kurz F. Fl. ii. 260). Vern. *Kyun-nalin, Kyunbo*, Burma, Lower and Upper. A moderate-sized deciduous tree, wood hard, close grained. Branchlets, petioles, underside of l. and inflorescence softly and densely stellate-pubescent. L. ovate, base rounded or slightly cordate, entire or slightly sinuate, blade 6–12, pet. 1–3 in., sec. n. 6–9 pair, prominent beneath, as well as tertiary n. Cymes compound, 6 in. across, bracts linear, fl. yellowish-white. Drupe ovoid, glabrous ⅛ in. long 17. **P. bengalensis**, Clarke. Subhimalayan tract from Nepal eastwards, chiefly on river banks. Silhet, Cachar. Assam (*Gohora*). Tavoy, on low land (*Kyun-nalin*). A moderate-sized tree, evergreen, stem irregularly indented (Gamble). Similar to 16, petiole shorter, l. stellately-pubescent beneath, on the upper side often with shining glandular dots and with dense stellate hairs on midrib. Bracts linear, ¼–½ in. long, fl. white. These two closely allied species require further study on the spot. They may eventually prove not to be specifically distinct.

β. Hairs as a rule not stellate.

18. **P. latifolia,** Roxb.; Wight Ic. t. 869.—Syn. *H. viburnoides*, Kurz. Vern. *Bakar*, Hind.; *Pedda Nellakura*, Tel.; *Kyetyo*, Burm. Subhimalayan tract, from the Chenab eastwards, ascending to 2,000 ft. Oudh forests. Bengal plain. Western Peninsula, chiefly on the east side. Burma, Upper and Lower. A small or middle-sized deciduous tree, branchlets and young l. pubescent or velvety, l. membranous, with a strong unpleasant smell, generally drying black, blade 3–5, pet. ⅓–⅔ in. long. Corymbs hairy, frequently at the ends of short leafy branchlets, fl. greenish-white, calyx hairy on both sides, densely outside, teeth 5, corolla ⅛ in. long, very hairy within. A most variable species, *P. mucronata*, Roxb. (Brandis F. Fl, 366) with acuminate l. with a cuneate base, may be a distinct species. 19. **P. milleflora,** Clarke. Assam. Manipur. L. hairy along nerves, pet. 2–3 in. long, fl. ∞ in large corymbs, up to 12 in. diam. 20. **P. flavescens,** Ham. Sikkim Terai. Dacca. Chutia Nagpur. L. more or less villous beneath, upper side with scattered stiff hairs, blade 5–7, pet. 1 in. long. 21. **P. micrantha,** Schauer. Silhet. Similar to 20, l. smaller, fl. minute.

(c) Calyx equally 4–5-toothed, l. glabrous or nearly so.

22. **P. glaberrima,** Wight Ic. t. 1484; Bedd. Man. 172.—Syn. *P. integerrima*, C. B. Clarke. Tinnevelly hills. A shrub, l. elongate-elliptic, acuminate, blade 6–8, pet. ½ in. Corymb broad, minutely pubescent. 23. **P. Wightiana,** Schauer. Southern portion of Western Peninsula. L. with few minute hairs, blade 1–3, pet. slender, ½ in. long, inflorescence narrow, pyramidal.

C. Inflorescence corymbiform or pyramidal, l. usually dentate.

24. **P. barbata,** Wall. Vern. *Ganhila*, Pb.; *Bakar*, *Lammar*, Hind. Subhimalayan tract and outer Himalayan ranges, from the Punjab eastwards, ascending to 6,000 ft. Western Duars in Sal forest (H. H. Haines). Assam, Khasi hills. Singbhum. Centr. Prov. Upper Burma. A shrub or small tree, l. serrate, sometimes entire with only a few teeth towards the tip, ovate, base rounded or cordate, underside minutely pubescent, blade 3–6, pet. slender, 1–2 in. long, the fine reticulate veins dark, conspicuous. Cymes trichotomous, compound, dense, clothed with minute simple hairs, calyx-lobes 4, enlarged and ribbed in fr., corolla ⅛ in. long. 25. **P. esculenta,** Roxb. Assam. Chittagong. A short-stemmed shrub, entirely glabrous. L. sharply, usually deeply serrate, 5–7 in. long, pet. very short, corymbs dense, globose on short peduncles. 26. **P. thyrsoidea,** Wight Ic. t. 1485. Palni, Tinnevelli and Travancore hills. A large shrub or small tree, trichotomous cymes arranged in a terminal woolly thyrsus, calyx hairy, 5-toothed, corolla-tube twice the length of calyx.

II. Low undershrubs, from a woody rootstock, annual stems with l. and fl. which are burnt down by the jungle fires of the hot season.

27. **P. pinguis,** Clarke. Assam, Khasi hills, Upper Burma. Similar to *P. barbata*, Wall. 28. **P. amplectens,** Wall. Pegu, and 29. **P. macrophylla,** Wall. Manipur, Pegu and Martaban. Similar to *P. esculenta*, Roxb. 30. **P. herbacea,** Roxb. Subhimalayan tract in grasslands from Kashmir eastwards. Singbhum. Manipur. Southern part of Western Peninsula (Bedd.). Annual stems very short, with flat rosettes of 2 or 3 pairs of sessile cuneate pubescent l., 1–5 in. long, falsely whorled, internodes not developed. Fl. white, drupe black, globose. 31. **P. nana,** Collett et Hemsl. in Journ. Linn. Soc. xxviii. 109. Shan hills 3,000 ft. Pegu (D. B. 1858). Internodes developed, annual stems up to 6 in. high with 3–4 pairs of softly tomentose oblanceolate l., drupe ovoid.

9. CALLICARPA, Linn.; Fl. Brit. Ind. iv. 566.

Shrubs, generally clothed with soft stellate tomentum. L. simple. Fl. purple or red, in axillary dichotomous cymes, branches divaricate, bracts small, tomentose. Calyx small, campanulate, minutely 4-, rarely 5-dentate, corolla-tube short, limb spreading, lobes 4, rarely 5, nearly equal, stamens exserted. Fr. a small succulent drupe, the endocarp of 4 distinct 1-seeded pyrenes. Species 30–40. Indo-Malayan region, China, Japan, Australia, Islands of the Pacific, North- and Central-America.

A. Petiole long, l. entire, sinuate or slightly dentate.

1. **C. arborea,** Roxb. Vern. *Ghiwāla*, Kumaon; *Gochlo*, Nep.; *Daung satpya*, Lower, *Sigye*, Upper Burma.

A tree, attaining 40 ft., branches, petioles, underside of l. and inflorescence densely grey tomentose, with short soft stellate hairs. L. ovate or elongate-elliptic, acuminate, glabrous above, blade 6–12, pet. 1–2½ in. long, sec. n. 8–12 pair. Fl. lilac or pale purple, with an unpleasant smell, cymes large, spreading, peduncle 1–2 in. long, calyx stellately pubescent.

Kumaon, Oudh forests. Nepal. Singbhum in valleys, not common. Sikkim, foot of the hills and ascending to 3,000 ft. (common in clearings). Western Duars. Khasi hills, Manipur. Burma, Upper and Lower to 4,500 ft., common on deserted Taungyas. Fl. April–June. 2. **C. vestita,** Wall. Nepal. Sikkim 1–6,000 ft. Khasi hills. Similar to 1., underside of l. white, densely matted with long silky hairs, peduncles 2 in. long, calyx in fl. nearly glabrous. 3. **C. lanata,** Linn.—Syn. *C. Wallichiana*, Walp.; Bedd. Manual t. 21 fig. 6.; Wight Ill. t. 178b, fig. 5, Ic. t. 1480. Vern. *Khanphulia*, Mar.; *Yettalai patta*, Tam.; *Thin perivellum*, Mal. West side of the Peninsula from Bombay southwards, common on grass lands on the Tinnevelli ghats.—Ceylon. A large shrub or middle-sized tree, branches, petioles, underside of l. and inflorescence densely tomentose. L. ovate or ovate-lanceolate, base often rounded, blade 6–15, pet. 1–3 in., peduncle ½–1 in. long, bracts and corolla pale purple or red, calyx stellate-tomentose.

B. Petiole long, l. broad, cordate, lobed.

4. **C. lobata,** Clarke. Sikkim 10–11,000 ft. L. 12–15 in. diam., palmately 5–7-nerved.

C. Petiole short, under 1 in., l. sharply serrate.

5. **C. macrophylla,** Vahl. *Daya*, Hind. Subhimalayan tract, from Hazara eastwards, ascending to 6,000 ft. Assam. Abundant in the plains of Bengal. Singbhum, Upper and Lower Burma. A tall shrub, branches, petioles, underside of leaves and inflorescence clothed with tawny or grey stellate tomentum. L. from an acute base elliptic-lanceolate, blade 6–10, pet. ½–1 in. long, sec. n. 12–16 pair. Cymes much branched, globose, 1–3 in. diam., peduncles ½–1 in. long, fl. numerous, pink, berry white. 6. **C. rubella,** Lindley. Sikkim 2–3,000 ft., Khasi hills, Manipur. Hills between Sitang and Salween. L. oblong or oblanceolate 5 by 1¼ in., base cordate, pet. very short, peduncle slender. ¼–½ in.

7. **C. longifolia,** Lam. Assam (Nambar Forest, D. B. March 1879). Khasi hills. Chittagong. Nicobars. Tenasserim (Attaran, D. B. Aug. 1858). Malay Penins. and Archip. North Australia. L. thinly membranous, lanceolate, blade 5–7, narrowed into pet. ½–1 in. long, upperside glabrous, underside thinly stellate pubescent, calyx white stellate-tomentose, fr. white. 8. **C. psilocalyx,** Clarke. Khasi hills. Manipur. A small tree, branchlets stellate tomentose, l. thinly membranous, elliptic-lanceolate, blade 4–8, pet. ⅓ in. long, calyx glandular, not hairy, fr. white.

Glossocarya mollis, Wall. Tenasserim. A climbing shrub, branchlets and underside of l. softly pubescent, fl. in ample terminal corymbiform compound softly grey villous cymes, capsule cylindric, 4-valved, ⅓ in. long, clothed with long patent hairs, nearly twice the length of the campanulate 5-toothed calyx.

8. CARYOPTERIS, Bunge: Fl. Brit. Ind. iv. 597.

Shrubs, l. opposite, more or less toothed, on both surfaces with minute yellow glistening glands (globose trichomes, consisting of several cells filled with essential oil). Calyx deeply 5- sometimes 6- or 7-fid, slightly enlarged in fruit, corolla-tube short, cylindric, limb spreading, lobes 5, imbricate in bud, 4 equal, the 5th interior larger. Stamens exserted, anther-cells divergent at base. Ovary imperfectly 4-celled, 4-ovuled, style filiform, shortly 2-fid. Capsule dividing into 4 valves with incurved margins, holding the 4 one-seeded slightly winged pyrenes. Species 10, India, Mongolia, China, Japan.

A. Corolla ½ in. long.

1. **C. Wallichiana,** Schauer; Collett Simla Fl. 381, fig. 121. Vern. *Chingari*, *Karui*. Dehra Dún. Subhimalayan tract and outer ranges, ascending to 7,000 ft. Punjab Salt range. Oudh forests. A shrub with 4-sided glabrous branches, young shoots pubescent. L. lanceolate, serrate, blade 2–4, pet. ½ in. long. Fl. sweet-scented, blue and purple, in compact bracteate cymes, forming cylindrical axillary and terminal thyrsi, 3–5 in. long. Calyx-segments lanceolate with a distinct midrib, erect in fruit.

B. Corolla ⅙ in. long and less.

2. **C. grata,** Benth. Outer Himalaya, Jaunsar to Nepal, to 6,000 ft. Branches and l. pubescent, cymes lax, axillary, segments of fruiting calyx triangular patent. 3. **C.**

paniculata, Clarke. Outer eastern Himalaya to 6,000 ft. Assam, Manipur, Lushai hills. Shan hills 5,000 ft. Hills east of Bhamo 4,000 ft. Yunnan 5–6,000 ft. Branches terete, slender, pubescent, l. glabrous when full grown, fl. violet or lilac, in small axillary thyrsus, shorter than l., calyx hardly enlarged in fr., segments 5–7, long-acuminate.

9. CONGEA, Roxb. ; Fl. Brit. Ind. iv. 602.

Scandent shrubs, l. opposite, quite entire. Fl. sessile in pedunculate involucrate 3–9-fld. heads, involucre of 3 or 4 bracts connate at base, much enlarged and generally coloured in fr. Calyx funnel-shaped, teeth 5, shorter than tube, corolla-tube slender, limb 2-lipped, upper lip erect, of 2 linear-oblong lobes, lower of 3 much shorter obovate lobes. Stamens 4, anthers exserted ovate, cells parallel. Ovary imperfectly 2-celled, ovules 4, pendulous from the top of the axile placenta. Species 4.

A. Calyx lobed ⅓ the way down, densely clothed with long soft hairs.

1. **C. tomentosa,** Roxb. Cor. Pl. t. 293 ; Wight Ic. t. 1479/2. Vern. *Thamaka-nwè*, Burm. Manipur. Chittagong. Burma, Upper and Lower, common. Siam. A large deciduous scandent shrub, stems fluted, an irregular central cylinder of wood, surrounded by a layer of phloëm, and outside of these rounded masses of wood tissue enclosed by phloëm. Branchlets, underside of l. and inflorescence densely clothed with soft tomentum of simple and fasciculate hairs, l. ovate, blade 4–6, pet. ⅓–½ in. long. Involucral bracts violet or pale lilac, sometimes white, elliptic-oblong, 1 in. long, calyx-teeth elongate triangular. *C. azurea*, Wall. ; Wight Ic. t. 1479. A, is a variety commonly cultivated in gardens. 2. **C. vestita,** Griff. Tenasserim. Branchlets fulvous hirsute with long hairs, l. villous beneath, involucral bracts broad-elliptic densely white-silky, conspicuously veined.

B. Calyx tomentose, teeth very short.

3. **C. velutina,** Wight Ic. t. 1479, 3. Tenasserim. L. glabrous when mature, bracts distinctly nervose. 4. **C. villosa,** Wight Ic. t. 1479, fig. B. Pegu. Tenasserim. L. villous beneath.

10. SPHENODESME, Jack ; Fl. Brit. Ind. iv. 600.

Scandent shrubs, l. quite entire, hairs simple or stellate. Fl. sessile in involucrate pedunculate 3- or 7-fld heads usually arranged in terminal panicles, involucre of 6 bracts, much enlarged in fr. Calyx cup-shaped, campanulate or tubular, teeth 5, rarely 4 or 6. Corolla-tube short, cylindric, limb more or less zygomorphic, lobes 5, rarely 6. Stamens 5, as a rule included. Ovary imperfectly 2-celled, ovules 4, pendulous from the apex of the axile placenta. Drupe 1- rarely 2-seeded. Species 10, Indo-Malayan.

A. Stigma sessile or nearly so.

1. **S. unguiculata,** Schauer.—Syn. *Symphorema unguiculatum*, Kurz. Vern. *Nwèzat*, *Kanwè*, Burm. Khasi and Naga hills. Cachar. Chittagong. Lower Burma. A large deciduous climbing shrub, stems twisted, as thick as a man's arm, branchlets and inflorescence pubescent or tomentose, hairs stellate. L. thinly coriaceous, glabrous above, blade 4–6, pet. ¼ in. long. Involucral bracts in fruit 1–1⅕ in. long, obtuse, lanceolate or oblanceolate, pubescent, membranous, prominently reticulate, fl. cream-coloured, corolla-lobes obovate, ovary glabrous, stigma sessile, bifid. 2. **S. microstylis,** Clarke. Tenasserim, Siam. L. softly pubescent or villous beneath, corolla ½ in. long, lobes 5–6, linear, involucral bracts pubescent, in fr. 1 in. long.

3. **S. paniculata,** Clarke, Western Ghats from Coorg southwards, common in evergreen forests. L. pubescent beneath, fl. sweet-scented, corolla ⅓ in. long, lobes 5–6, obovate, obtuse, involucral bracts rusty tomentose.

B, Style filiform, bifid at the apex.

(*a*) Involucral bracts longer than calyx, heads in ample terminal panicles.

4. **S. pentandra,** Jack; Wight Ic. t. 1475.—Syn. *S. acuminata*, Wight Ic. t. 1476 ; *Symphorema Jackianum*, Kurz. Assam, Khasi hills. Manipur, Burma, Upper and Lower. Malay Peninsula. Nearly glabrous, ovary hairy, involucral bracts linear-

oblong, in fr. 1 in. long, calyx glabrous, mouth inflated in fruit, with 5 linear accessory teeth alternating with the others. 5. **S. Griffithiana**, Wight Ic. t. 1477 (under the plate *S. Jackiana*).—Syn. *Symphorema pentandrum*, Kurz, Tenasserim. Similar to 4, but calyx clothed with long hairs, a reflexed tooth in each sinus of the 5 lobes.

(*b.*) Involucral bracts shorter than calyx, heads sessile or nearly so, in axillary sometimes branched spikes.

6. **S. eryciboides**, Kurz.—Syn. *Symphorema grossum*, Kurz. Vern. *Nwèzat*, Burm. Lower Burma, common on the banks of streams and in damp places. A large evergreen shrub, or a small tree, often climbing, l. pubescent or tomentose beneath, fl. heads fulvous tomentose.

11. SYMPHOREMA, Roxb.; Fl. Brit. Ind. iv. 599.

Large woody climbers, hairs stellate. Fl. sessile, in involucrate pedunculate 7-fld. heads, involucre of 6 bracts, much enlarged in fr. The 7-fld. head is a dichotomous cyme with 3 central and 4 lateral fl., one pair of bracts supports the primary, while 2 pairs support the two secondary bifurcations. Calyx turbinate, teeth 4–8, short, corolla small, white, tube cylindric, lobes 6–16, narrowly oblong, equal. Stamens as many as corolla-lobes, anthers exserted, ovate, cells parallel. Ovary imperfectly 4-celled, ovules one in each cell, suspended from the top of a central placenta, style filiform, shortly bifid. Fruit nearly dry, included in the calyx, 1-seeded. Species 3, one in the Philippines.

1. **S. involucratum**, Roxb. Cor. Pl. t. 186; Wight Ic. t. 362. *Nwèzat*, Lower. *Sigyi*, Upper Burma. Behar. Western Peninsula. Burma, Upper and Lower. Branchlets, petioles and underside of l. pubescent. L. ovate, usually toothed, blade 2–3, pet. ½ in. Corolla ½ in., bracts of involucre in fr. slightly pubescent, thinly membranous, prominently reticulate. 2. **S. polyandrum**, Wight Ic. t. 363, Ill. t. 173 b. fig. 7. Mohurli forest, Chanda district. Singbhum. Deccan. Stems twisting from left to right, l. ovate, tomentose, blade 4–9, pet. ½–½ in.; corolla ½ in. long, bracts of involucre densely grey-tomentose.

14. AVICENNIA, Linn.; Fl. Brit. Ind. iv. 604.

Species 3 on the sea coast within the tropics of both hemispheres.

A. officinalis, Linn.; Bedd. Man. t. 22. fig. 2.—Syn. *A. tomentosa*, Wall. Pl. As. Rar. t. 271 (not Jacq.); Wight Ic. t. 1481; Kurz F. Fl. ii. 276. Vern. *Tiwar*, Mar.; *Ipati*, Kan.; *Baen*, *Bani*, *Bini*, Sundrib.; *Thamè net* and *Thamì pyu*, Burm. The true *A. tomentosa*, Jacq., is limited to South America, and has white fl. (Schimper, Indo-Mal. Strandflora 98).

A large evergreen shrub or tree, in the Sundriban attaining 60 ft. and a great girth. Branchlets, petioles, underside of leaves and inflorescence clothed with a dense white or silvery tomentum of very minute hairs. Fl. yellow, sessile, in bracteate heads (contracted cymes) which are arranged in trichotomous corymbs. Calyx divided to the base into 5 imbricate sepals, corolla-tube short, limb 4–5-lobed. Stamens 4, in the throat of the tube, anther-cells parallel. Ovary hairy, imperfectly 4-celled, ovules 4, suspended from a central 4-winged placenta. Capsule compressed, dehiscing into two thick valves. Seed one, cotyledons large, folded lengthwise, hypocotyl (radicle) villous.

Often gregarious, in tidal forests or on tidal sandy flats along the coasts of the Peninsula, the Sundriban, the Andamans and Burma. Fl. R. S.—Ceylon, East Africa, the Malay Archipelago, New Guinea, Australia, Polynesia, New Zealand. The long cable-like roots, which run horizontally through the mud, send up numerous erect blind suckers, the ends of which stand above the surface of the water. They facilitate the access of air to the roots, but sometimes they produce leaves and grow up into bushes. The seed often germinates before it falls. The hairs of the hypocotyl are stiff and recurved, they aid the seedling to fix itself in the mud.

Avicennia coppices freely. On a transverse section the wood shows alternating narrow concentric rings of xylem and phloëm (wood and bast), which often anastomose. A.W. Lushington reports (Ind. Forester xxiv. 59) that coppice shoots 25 and 35 months old showed an apparent relation between the number of phloëm rings and the age of the shoots in months. Prain (Flora of the Sundriban 331) separates *A. alba*, Blume (*Dudhi Báen*) by lanceolate acute l. and a narrow conical capsule, In the same place see his remarks regarding the slanting run of the fibres in *Avicennia* wood.

ORDER LXXXIII. **LABIATÆ.** Gen. Pl. ii. 1160.

Herbs, rarely shrubs, usually aromatic. Essential oil is secreted in hairs with glandular heads or in sessile glands. Branches usually four-sided, l. opposite or whorled, stipules 0. Fl. zygomorphic, calyx persistent, 4- or 5-toothed or cleft or 2-lipped. Corolla hypogynous, gamopetalous, 2-lipped, sometimes regularly 4-5-lobed, lobes imbricate in bud. Stamens inserted in the corolla-tube, 4, didynamous, or the 2 upper imperfect. Ovary free, usually 4-lobed, supported by the annular disk, style inserted between the lobes. Ovules 4, erect, anatropous. Fr. of 4 one-seeded nutlets.

A. Calyx two-lipped, stamens 2 . . . . . . MERIANDRA (p. 515).
B. Calyx 10-toothed, upper lip of corolla densely white-woolly . . . . LEUCAS (p. 515).
C. Calyx 5-cleft nearly to the base, the segments much elongated and feathery in fruit . . . . COLEBROOKIA (p. 515).
D. Calyx 5-toothed, enlarged in fr.
  Unarmed.
    Fruiting calyx with 5 spathulate reticulate teeth ROYLEA (p. 515).
    Fr. cal. enlarged, but not altered in shape.
      Corolla 4- or 5-lobed, fl. in narrow cylindrical spikes . . . . ELSHOLTZIA (p. 516).
      Cor. deeply 2-lipped, lower lip boat-shaped . 1. PLECTRANTHUS.
  Armed, calyx-limb expanding in fr. into a long reticulated 5-angled cup . . . . . OTOSTEGIA (p. 516).
E. Calyx 5-toothed, not enlarged in fr.
  Stamens long exserted ¾–1 in. long . . . . LEUCOSCEPTRUM (p. 516).
  Stamens not much exserted.
    Filaments hairy, corolla ¼ in. long . . . . POGOSTEMON (p. 516).
    Filaments glabrous, corolla ¾–1 in. long, nutlets winged at apex . . . . . . 2. COLQUHOUNIA.

Meriandra strobilifera, Benth.; Collett Simla Fl. 398, fig. 125. N. W. Himalaya, Sutlej to Sarda, 4–7,000 ft. A small aromatic shrub, branchlets and underside of l. white-woolly. L. thick, crenulate, gradually narrowed from a broad hastate base, upperside prominently rugose, blade 2–4, pet. ¼ in. long. Fl. small, white, in tomentose dense cylindrical spikes, bracts imbricating, hard, almost woody in fr. Fertile stamens 2, anther-cells separate, pendulous from a long connective.

Leucas lanceæfolia, Desf.; Wight Ic. t. 1452. Nilgiris. A large often gregarious shrub, branches and underside of l. soft-tomentose, l. lanceolate, entire, blade 3–5, narrowed into pet. ⅛ in. long. Fl. white in distant whorls, bracts linear, hairy, nearly as long as calyx. Calyx ¼ in. long, teeth 10, minute, spinulose. Corolla 2-labiate, upper lip concave, densely white-woolly outside.

Colebrookia oppositifolia, Smith.—Syn. *C. ternifolia*, Roxb. Cor. Pl. t. 245. Vern. *Dashane*, Pb.; *Binda, Bindu*, Hind.; *Chota Bhandara*, Melghat. Subhimalayan tract and valleys, ascending to 4,500 ft. Punjab Salt range. Singbhum. Central provinces. Berar. Western Peninsula. Tenasserim. Shan hills, Upper Burma, Hills east of Bhamo, 4,000 ft. China. A large shrub or small tree, stem deeply channelled, branches, petioles, underside of leaves and inflorescence densely clothed with soft whitish tomentum. L. opposite or in threes, elliptic-lanceolate, crenulate, blade 5–12, pet. ¾–1¾ in. long, sec. n. 12–18 pair, prominent beneath. Fl. often polygamous, in sessile 4–6-fld. heads, each head supported by numerous hirsute bracts, the heads arranged in long paniculate spikes. Calyx divided nearly to the base into 5 linear teeth, lengthening out in fr. and then capillary and feathery. Corolla white, minute, tube short, lobes 4. Nut, usually one only, hairy.

Roylea elegans, Wall. Pl. As. Rar. t. 74. Vern. *Kaur*, Pb.; *Karanoi*, Jauns.; *Tilpati*, Garhw. Outer North West Himalaya, Kashmir to Kumaon 2–6,000 ft. A small shrub, branchlets and underside of l. softly tomentose. L. ovate, deep-crenate, sometimes lobed, blade 1–2, pet. ¼ in. long. Whorls 6–10-fld., axillary, calyx 10-ribbed, lobes much enlarged in fr., spathulate, rigid, reticulate.

Elsholtzia polystachya, Benth.; Collett Simla Fl. 388, fig. 123.—Syn. *Aphanochilus polystachyus*, Benth. in Wall. Pl. As. Rar. t. 33. Vern. *Pathoi, Potha*, Jauns. Himalaya, also in the inner arid valleys. 7–9,500 ft. Khasi hills. China. A shrub, attaining 8 ft., bark peels off in long strips, branches, l. and inflorescence pubescent. L. sessile or nearly so, elliptic-lanceolate, serrate, 3–6 in. long. Fl. shortly pedicelled or sessile, in long usually fascicled or panicled spikes, bracts minute, corolla white, pubescent. Fruiting calyx pedicellate, tubular, teeth erect.

1. PLECTRANTHUS, L'Herit.; Fl. Brit. Ind. iv. 616.

Mostly herbs, a few shrubs. Fl. small, cymes arranged in a terminal usually compound thyrsus. Calyx enlarged in fr., corolla 2-lipped, upper lip short, broad, recurved, lower much longer, boat-shaped, narrowed at base. Stamens 4, included in the lower lip. Species 90, tropical and subtropical Asia and Africa. Australia, Polynesia.

1. **P. ternifolius,** Don. Subhimalayan tract and outer hills, ascending to 5,000 ft., from Kashmir eastwards. Bengal. Khasi hills. Manipur. Upper Burma. Tonkin. A strict, tomentose shrub, attaining 6 ft. L. in whorls of 3, nearly sessile, lanceolate, 2–4 in. long. Fl. white, thyrsus long dense spiciform, panicled, fruiting calyx tubular, equally 5-toothed. 2. **P. rugosus,** Wall. Vern. *Boi, Bui*, Haz. Baluchistan, Kuram valley. Western Himalaya, on dry slopes, 3–9,000 ft., also in the inner arid valleys. Mt. Abu. A small shrub, stellately pubescent, l. ovate, rugose above, white-tomentose beneath, blade ½–1, pet. ⅓ in. Fl. bluish- or purplish-white, in lax pedunculate axillary cymes, fruiting calyx 5-toothed, somewhat 2-lipped.

Otostegia limbata, Benth. Punjab, Salt range, Hazara (*Chiti boi*), common in very dry places. Kashmir, Chamba, ascending to 6,000 ft. A small grey-pubescent spiny shrub, l. nearly sessile, lanceolate or oblanceolate, ½–1 in. long; sharp pubescent often trifid spines between petioles (transformed bracts). Fl. in distant axillary whorls, calyx with a broad membranous 5-toothed limb, in fr. expanding into a reticulated 5-angled cup, ⅜ in. diam.

Leucosceptrum canum, Smith. Outer Himalaya, Kumaon to Bhutan 2–8,000 ft., common in clearings and on deserted fields. Khasi and Manipur hills. Shan hills and hills east of Bhamo, 4-000 ft., Upper Burma. Yunnan. A shrub or small tree, attaining 30 ft., branches, petioles, underside of l. and inflorescence densely clothed with short usually white sometimes buff or brown wool, branches stout, nearly terete. L. elliptic-lanceolate, entire or crenate, glabrous above, blade 6–12, pet. 1 in. Fl. in dense cylindrical erect spikes 4-6 in. long, 1 in. diam. with the stamens, bracts large transversely oblong, early caducous, imbricating and covering the very young buds. Corolla white, filaments involute in bud, stout, yellow, ⅜ in. long, anthers reniform. Drops of viscid sweet liquid in each fl.

Pogostemon plectranthoides, Desf. Subhimalayan tract and outer hills, ascending to 5,000 ft., Simla to Nepal. Central provinces. Behar. Chutia Nagpore, Western Peninsula. Upper Burma. *Phangli*, Mar. A large gregarious, very aromatic shrub, stem dark purple, pith large. Fl. in dense bracteate whorls, crowded in cylindric spikes, forming large terminal panicles, bracts numerous, large, clothed with long soft hairs. Calyx-teeth 5, equal, corolla ¼ in. long, white, tinged with pink. Stems used for rāb (wood-ash manure) in paddy nursery beds. A species with small glabrous bracts, near *P. glabrum*, Benth., Bhamo 4,000 ft. reported by Montague Hill to be a shrub or small tree with white fl. *P. Patchouli*, Pelletier, believed to be a native of the Indian Archip., yields the well-known perfume.

2. COLQUHOUNIA, Wall.; Fl. Brit. Ind. ii. 674.

Prain in Journ. As. Soc. Bengal 62. 30.

Tall, rambling or climbing shrubs, branches terete. Whorls axillary or forming lax-fld. spikes, fl. pink, orange, scarlet or brown. Calyx 10-nerved equally 5-toothed, throat naked. Corolla 2-labiate, tube narrowed, longer than calyx, throat inflated. Stamens 4, anther-cells divergent. Nutlets compressed, tip produced into a wing. Species 2.

1. **C. coccinea,** Wall. *Bhilmora*, Kum. Himalaya, 5–9,000 ft., from Kumaon east-

wards. Khasi hills, Manipur. Upper Burma. Branchlets and l. clothed with stellate hairs, in some forms (*C. vestita*) white tomentose, calyx-teeth triangular, hairs on corolla often glandular at the tip, wing of nutlets more or less laciniate, shorter than seed. 2. **C. elegans,** Wall. Manipur. Martaban hills 4–5,000 ft. Upper Burma. Yunnan. Branchlets and l. slightly pubescent with simple hairs, calyx-teeth acuminate, hairs on corolla of 2–3 cells, not glandular at tip, wing of nutlets entire, as long as seed.

ORDER LXXXIV. NYCTAGINACEÆ. Gen. Pl. iii. 1.

(*Nyctagineæ.*)

Mostly herbs, a few genera of shrubs and trees. L. usually opposite, stip. 0. Fl. often involucrate, perianth gamopetalous, the lower portion persistent, enclosing the fr. Stamens hypogynous, filaments as a rule connate at base, usually unequal. Ovary free, more or less oblique, 1-celled, ovule one, basal. Fr. dry, indehiscent, radicle inferior, albumen soft or mealy.

The woody species of the three Orders: *Nyctaginaceæ*, *Amarantaceæ* and *Chenopodiaceæ* have an anomalous structure. The vascular bundles remain distinct and are arranged in more or less interrupted concentric belts, separated by interfascicular prosenchymatic (rarely parenchymatic) tissue. A number of vascular bundles are frequently found in the pith. In some cases, as in *Haloxylon*, the interfascicular tissue consists of sclerotic fibres, giving the appearance on a transverse section of concentric hard horny layers, alternating with interrupted bands of softer tissue with groups of vessels.

Bougainvillæa spectabilis, Willd. Commonly grown in gardens. A large scrambling, more or less thorny shrub of South America, l. alternate, fl. in threes, perianth cylindric each fl. adnate to a large purple bract.

PISONIA, Linn.; Fl. Brit. Ind. iv. 710.

Trees or shrubs, l. usually entire and opposite. Fl. in corymbose cymes with minute bracteoles, usually dioicous. Perianth 5–10-toothed, stamens 6–10, exserted. Fr. more or less 5-angled, cotyledons convolute, enclosing the scanty soft albumen. Species 40, tropics of both hemispheres.

A. Armed.

1. **P. aculeata,** Linn.; Wight Ic. t. 1763–4; Bedd. Manual t. 22. Western Peninsula, often forming impenetrable thickets. Andamans and Tenasserim, near the coast. Ceylon. Sea coast, tropics of both hemispheres. A large straggling or climbing shrub, young shoots and inflorescence pubescent, armed with sharp axillary more or less curved thorns. L. glabrous, blade 2–3, petiole $\frac{1}{4}$–$\frac{1}{2}$ in. long. Fl. greenish-white in compact sometimes paniculate axillary cymes. Fr. on long slender pedicels, oblong, blunt, pubescent, $\frac{1}{2}$–$\frac{2}{3}$ in. long, faintly 5-angled, with 5 double lines of viscid protuberances.

B. Unarmed.

2. **P. alba,** Spanoghe.—Syn. *T. morindæfolia*, R. Br.; Wight Ic. t. 1765. Beach forests of the Andamans. Malay Archip. Often grown in gardens (*the Lettuce Tree*). A middle-sized evergreen tree, glabrous except youngest shoots and inflorescence. L. elliptic, blade 6–10, pet. $\frac{1}{2}$–$1\frac{1}{2}$ in. Fr. on long slender pedicels, club-shaped, $\frac{1}{2}$–$\frac{3}{4}$ in. long, with 5 single lines of protuberances. 3. **P. excelsa,** Blume.—Syn. *P. umbellifera*, Seem. Andamans. Malay Archip. L. alternate, opposite or whorled, blade 12, pet. 1 in. long, fr. 1–$1\frac{1}{2}$ in. long on short stout pedicels, angles without glands or protuberances.

ORDER LXXXV. AMARANTACEÆ. Gen. Pl. iii. 20.

Mostly herbs. L. opposite or alternate, stipules 0. Fl. supported by bracts and bracteoles, in terminal simple or panicled spikes. Perianth of 5 sepals, usually scarious or rigid, persistent, imbricate in bud. Stamens 1–5, opposite the sepals, filaments often connate. Ovary 1-celled, ovules basal, 1 or more. Seed one, erect, compressed, testa crustaceous, embryo horseshoe-shaped or annular, surrounding a mealy albumen.

Leaves alternate, ovules numerous . . . . . . 1. DEERINGIA.
Leaves alternate, ovule 1 . . . . BOSIA (p. 518).
Leaves opposite . . . . STILBANTHUS (p. 518).

1. DEERINGIA, Rob. Brown; Fl. Brit. Ind. iv. 714.

Species 5–6, from Madagascar to Queensland.

D. celosioides, Rob. Brown; Wight Ic. t. 728. Vern. *Latman*, Hind. *Chŭndri*, Dehra Dún.

A large scrambling shrub, l. alternate, quite entire, blade 2–4, petiole ¼–1 in. Fl. greenish-white, sepals herbaceous, pedicels short, in racemes 4–10 in. long, forming terminal panicles. Berries scarlet, ⅛–¼ in. diam., supported by the spreading sepals.

Subhimalayan tract and outer Himalaya, from the Sutlej eastwards, ascending to 5,000 ft. Assam, Khasi hills. Behar, Chittagong. Upper Burma. Malay Archip. China. Australia.

Bosia Amherstiana, Hook. f. *Bhengoi*, Jauns. N. W. Himalaya 4–7,000 ft. A stout glabrous rambling shrub, l. alternate, ovate, blade 2–4, pet. ¼–½ in. Fl. small greenish, in terminal and axillary panicles, supported by numerous closely imbricated rounded bracts with white margin, perianth herbaceous. Berries bright crimson.

Stilbanthus scandens, Hook. f. Sikkim Himalaya 5–7,000 ft. Naga Hills. A large climber, trunk as thick as a man's thigh, covering tall trees with its masses of white flowers and whitish foliage. Branches obtusely 4-angled, branchlets silky. L. pubescent, opposite, elliptic, blade 4–6, petiole ½–1 in. Fl. in cylindric spikes, 2–3 in. long, arranged in terminal trichotomously branched panicles. Sepals scarious, striate, shining, ½ in. long, tip bearded, bracts oval villous. Stamens 5, alternating and at the base connate with long fimbriate staminodes. Ovule 1, pendulous from a long basal funicle.

ORDER LXXXVI. CHENOPODIACEÆ. Gen. Pl. iii. 43.

Mostly herbs, l. simple, usually alternate, stipules 0. Fl. small, usually regular, perianth of 3–5 sepals, stamens opposite the sepals. Stigmas 2–4. Fr. a utricle, enclosed in the often enlarged perianth.

Nearly all plants of this order are Halophytes, living near the sea shore and inland in saline tracts. As far as known, their roots largely take up salts of Sodium, while most other trees and shrubs mainly take up Potassium salts, though Sodium salts are always present in the soil. Their ashes are rich in Sodium Chloride, and many species were formerly and are still here and there employed to make an impure Carbonate of Soda (*Barilla, Sajji*).

L. usually alternate, branchlets not articulate.
  Fruiting sepals with a large dorsal wing . . . . 1. SALSOLA.
  Fruiting sepals not winged . . . . 2. SUÆDA.
L. usually opposite, branchlets articulate, fruiting sepals
    with a large dorsal wing . . . . 3. HALOXYLON.

1. SALSOLA, Linn.; Fl. Brit. Ind. v. 17.

Saline herbs or shrubs, branchlets not articulate, l. mostly alternate, often small. Fl. small, usually bisexual, solitary or fasciculate, axillary, each fl. supported by a pair of bracteoles. Sepals 4–5, concave, in fr. enlarged, with a broad dorsal wing, stamens 5, rarely 4, disk usually inconspicuous, stigmas

2–3, subulate or linear. Embryo spiral, albumen 0. Species 40. Europe, Temperate Asia, North and South Africa, a few also in America and Australia.

1. **S. fœtida,** Delile. Syn. *S. spinescens,* Wight Ic. t. 1795. Baluchistan. Sind. Trans Indus. Punjab plains.—Afghanistan, Persia, Arabia, North Africa. A spreading bush, much branched, l. minute, wings of fruiting perianth $\frac{1}{16}$–$\frac{1}{20}$ in. diam., silvery white. 2. **S. verrucosa,** M. Bieb. Baluchistan. Trans Indus. North Western Punjab.—Persia, Armenia, Caucasus, Turkestan, Arabia. Similar to 1, but wings of fruiting perianth larger, dark brown, $\frac{1}{8}$–$\frac{1}{6}$ in. diam. 3. **S. Arbuscula,** Pallas. Northern Baluchistan (Aitchison). Afghanistan, Persia, Turkestan, Songaria, Mongolia. A squarrose shrub, branchlets stiff, almost spinescent, l. linear subulate, up to 2½ in. long, wings of perianth $\frac{1}{3}$ in. diam.

2. SUÆDA, Forskål; Fl. Brit. Ind. v. 13.

Saline herbs, rarely shrubs, l. fleshy. Fl. minute, axillary, supported by bracts and bracteoles. Perianth 5-lobed, stamens short. Seed erect, albumen scanty, embryo plano-spiral. Species 40. Sea coasts and saline deserts of both hemispheres.

1. **S. fruticosa,** Forsk. Baluchistan (*S. vermiculata,* Forsk. *Shorag*). Plains of Sibi, covering large areas of land impregnated with salt. Sind. Trans Indus (*Zamai*). Punjab plains (*Lunak*). Merwara.—Mediterranean region. Western Asia. A gregarious bush, l. $\frac{1}{8}$–$\frac{1}{2}$ in. long, fl. bisexual, solitary or in clusters of 2–3, forming slender leafy spikes. 2. **S. monoica,** Forsk.; Wight Ic. t. 1792. Tidal flats on the coast of South India and Ceylon. Fl. polygamous, clustered, bracts scarious, entire. 3. **S. nudiflora,** Moquin.—Syn. *S. indica,* Moq.; Wight Ic. t. 1796. Associated with 2, fl. polygamous, in dense globose clusters, bracts hyaline, toothed.

3. HALOXYLON, Bunge; Fl. Brit. Ind. v. 15.

Saline perennial herbs, a few shrubs or small trees, branchlets articulate, l. opposite, often connate at base. Fl. small, solitary in the axils of opposite l. or bracts, bisexual, supported by a pair of bracteoles. Sepals 5, concave, enlarged in fr. with a large dorsal wing. Stamens 5 or less, inserted on an annular or cupular often lobed disk, stigma 2–4-lobed. Utricle globose or depressed, enclosed in the winged perianth, seed horizontal, embryo spiral, albumen 0. Species 8–10. Mediterranean region. West Africa.

A. Disk shorter than ovary.

1. **H. recurvum,** Bunge. Baluchistan. Sind. Trans Indus. Punjab plains. Salt range, to 2,500 ft. Coimbatore. Dry region of Upper Burma. A straggling gregarious shrub, branches dark brown, stout, often recurved, branchlets terminating in strict spikes, 2–6 in. L. thick, $\frac{1}{8}$–$\frac{1}{3}$ in. long. Wings of fruiting calyx orbicular, scarious, $\frac{1}{4}$ in. diam. 2. **H. Griffithii,** Boissier Fl. Or. iv. 950. Baluchistan, Afghanistan. A small shrub with numerous rigid branches, bark whitish, l. small, $\frac{1}{8}$ in. and less. Style short, stigma 2–4-lobed. Wings of fruiting calyx obovate, elegantly striate, edge denticulate.

B. Disk longer than ovary.

3. **H. Ammodendron,** Boiss.; Engler u. Prantl iii. 1. a, p. 88, fig. 89. *Saxaul.* Vern. *Tar-gaz,* Bal. Baluchistan (Stocks, Aitchison).—Arid districts of Afghanistan, Persia and Turkestan, extending north to the Altai. A shrub or gnarled tree, up to 14 ft. high and 12 ft. in girth, branchlets bright green, l. minute triquetrous. Spikes $\frac{1}{4}$–$\frac{1}{2}$ in. long, wings of fruiting calyx $\frac{1}{3}$ in. diam.

ORDER LXXXVII. POLYGONACEÆ. Gen. Pl. iii. 88.

Herbs, rarely shrubs or trees, l. alternate, simple, stipulate, stipules usually sheathing. Fl. small, usually bisexual, jointed on the pedicel. Perianth of 3–6 free or connate persistent sepals, imbricate in bud, stamens 5–8, sometimes more. Ovary free, usually 3-gonous, styles 1–3, ovule 1, basal, orthotropous. Nut hard, usually enclosed in the calyx, seed erect, radicle superior, albumen mealy or horny.

Perianth of 4 or 5 sepals or segments.
- Nut trigonous or biconvex, included in the more or less equally enlarged perianth-segments . . . . . 1. POLYGONUM.
- Nut flat, enclosed by 2 large reticulate wings (the inner sepals) . . . . ATRAPHAXIS (p. 520).
- Nut oblong, densely covered with long branching bristles placed in vertical lines . . . . 2. CALLIGONUM.
- Nut with 6 broad wings in 2 tiers . . . . PTEROPYRUM (p. 521).

Perianth of 6 sepals, nut trigonous, included in the 3 inner much enlarged membranous sepals . . . . RUMEX (p. 521).

1. POLYGONUM, Linn.; Fl. Brit. Ind. v. 23.

Stipules tubular, membranous. Fl. small, clustered, bracts and bracteoles membranous, ochreate. Segments of a glandular disk often alternating with stamens. Ovary usually trigonous, styles 2 or 3. Nut included in the more or less enlarged perianth. Species 150, in both hemispheres.

A. Perianth $\frac{1}{12}$ in. across. Hairy.

1. **P. molle,** Don. Bashahr (?). Nepal. Sikkim, 4-8,000 ft. Bhutan. Naga hills. A large gregarious trailing shrub, branches stout, softly tomentose with erect or spreading hairs. L. elliptic-lanceolate, softly tomentose beneath. 2. **P. rude,** Meissner. Khasi hills and hills of Upper Burma. Similar to 1, strigose, hairs on branches reflexed.

B. Perianth $\frac{1}{12}$ in. across. Quite glabrous.

3. **P. paniculatum,** Blume. Garhwal. Nepal. Sikkim, 5–10,000 ft. Naga hills.—Java. L. elliptic-lanceolate, panicle lax, nut entirely included in the perianth. 4. **P. frondosum,** Meissn. Garwhal and Kumaon 7–9,000 ft. L. ovate, acuminate, panicle compact, nut larger than perianth.

C. Perianth $\frac{1}{4}$ in. across.

5. **P. polystachyum,** Wall.; Collett Simla Fl. 425 fig. 135. Himalaya from Hazara eastwards, 5–15,000 ft. also in the inner arid region,—Afghanistan. Attains 6ft., stems angled, l. hairy beneath, oblong-lanceolate, base cordate or rounded, stipules ample.

Atraphaxis spinosa, Linn.; Boiss. Fl. Or. iv. 1020. Baluchistan.—Afghanistan, Persia, Turkestan, Arabia, Egypt, Songaria. A rigid shrub, branchlets spinescent, l. thick, glabrous, from obovate to elliptic and almost orbicular, blade $\frac{1}{4}$–$\frac{1}{2}$ in. long, penniveined, narrowed into a short petiole. Perianth 4-cleft to the base, the outer sepals smaller, in fr. unchanged and reflexed, the 2 inner enlarged into broad-ovate reticulate wings, $\frac{1}{4}$ in. diam., closely appressed to, but much larger than the flat nut enclosed by them. *A. sinaica*, is a variety with smaller l.

2. CALLIGONUM, Linn.; Fl. Brit. Ind. v. 22.

Species 20, desert regions of Africa, Western and Central Asia.

C. polygonoides, Linn.; Brandis F. Fl. 372.—Syn. *C. comosum*, L'Her. Vern. *Phōk*, *phōg*, Pb.

A rigid glabrous, almost leafless shrub, sometimes a small tree, trunk 2–3 ft. girth, heartwood dark brown, very hard, branches grey or reddish-grey, numerous and twisted, branchlets green, mostly fascicled, slender, with a few thin linear-subulate leaves. Fl. small, pink, in fascicles of 2–5 from the axils of the sheathing thin transparent stipules. Perianth deciduous, deeply cleft into 5 thin obtuse membranous segments, red with broad white edges. Stamens 10, filaments dilated and pubescent at base. Nuts oblong, $\frac{1}{3}$ in. long, densely clothed with long filiform branching bristles placed in 8–16 vertical lines, bases thickened and confluent along these lines, so as to form irregularly shaped crests.

Baluchistan. Dry and arid districts of North Western India on both sides of the Indus, north as far as Lahore, and east to Bikanir. Abundant and often gregarious. The young shoots come out Febr.–March, soon afterwards the shrub is covered with pinkish fl., filling the air with a strong pleasant odour. Fr. June. The fl. are swept up and eaten, cooked. I adhere to the view of my old Forest Flora, p. 372, that *C. comosum* is not distinct. Accordingly this species has a wide distribution outside India from Algeria to Afghanistan.

Pteropyrum Olivieri, Jaub. et Spach. Sind, Baluchistan, Persia. A rigid much branched shrub, l. fascicled, thick, glaucous, from spathulate to linear, nerveless, $\frac{1}{4}$–$\frac{3}{4}$ in. long. Fl. small, in many-fld. clusters, sepals 5, in fruit not much enlarged, the inner erect and appressed to the nut, alternating with its wings, the 2 outer reflexed. Nut with 6 broad wings in two tiers, those of the lower tier larger. *P. Aucheri*, Jaub. et Spach, Northern Baluchistan (Aitchison) Western Asia, supposed to be distinguished by narrow linear l., probably is not distinct.

Rumex hastatus, Don ; Collett Simla Fl. 428 fig. 136. Vern. *Khatimbal*, Haz. Outer ranges of the North West Himalaya, mostly on dry slopes ascending to 8,000 ft. Afghanistan. An undershrub with a stout woody rootstalk, sometimes a shrub, branches numerous, slender. L. triangular or hastately 3-lobed, the lobes narrow, almost linear, blade $\frac{3}{4}$–$1\frac{1}{2}$ in. long, pet. as long as or longer than blade. Fruiting sepals orbicular, pink, prominently net-veined.

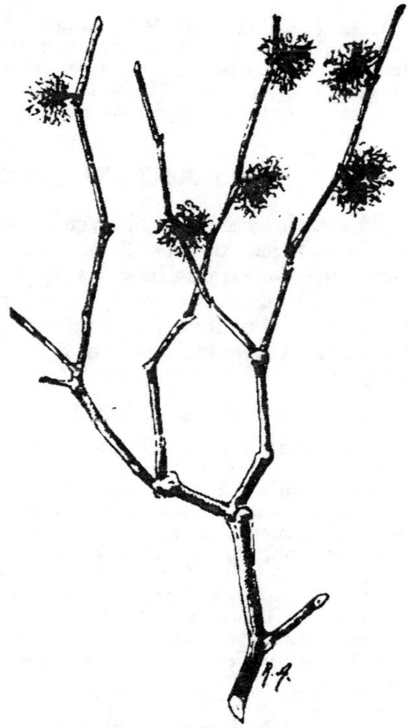

FIG. 176. Calligonum polygonoides, Linn. $\frac{1}{2}$.

ORDER LXXXVIII. ARISTOLOCHIACEÆ. Gen. Pl. iii. 121.

Herbs or shrubs, often climbing, l. alternate, entire or 3–5-lobed, stipules 0. Fl. bisexual, often large. Perianth superior, regular or zygomorphic, 3-lobed or tubular. Stamens 6 or more, free, or anthers sessile in a ring on the stylar column, cells parallel, opening by dorsal slits. Ovary inferior, 4–6-celled, placentas parietal, ovules numerous, style columnar. Fr. capsular or baccate, seeds numerous, embryo minute in a copious, fleshy albumen.

Oil cells in the parenchyma of leaves and outer bark are common in most species. The wood is very porous, the structure is usually normal with broad medullary rays and large vessels, the wood fibres have bordered pits. The radial wedge-shaped masses of wood often appear bifurcated by the formation of broad second. med. rays. The wood of *Bragantia* is peculiar, cf. Gamble Ind. Timbers, ed. ii. 558 ; Masters in Journ. Linn. Soc. xiv. 487.

Perianth campanulate, 3-lobed . . . . 1. BRAGANTIA.
Perianth tubular, base inflated, limb zygomorphic . . . 2. ARISTOLOCHIA.

1. BRAGANTIA, Lour. ; Fl. Brit. Ind. v. 72 (*Apama*, Lamk. ; Solereder in Engler u. Prantl iii. 1. 272).

Shrubs or undershrubs, l. entire, 3 or 5 basal nerves, tertiary nerves and reticulate veins conspicuous beneath. Perianth shortly campanulate, 3-lobed. Stamens 6–12, 1-seriate, filaments short, connective thick. Ovary elongate, 4-celled, ovules 2-seriate. Fr. a four-sided, 4-valved pod, valves separating from a central placentiferous column. Species 4–5, Indo-Malayan.

1. **B. Wallichii**, Rob. Br.; Wight Ic. t. 520. *Chakrani*, Mar. Western Ghats from the Konkan southwards, in evergreen forest. Ceylon, moist region, common. A large erect shrub, l. distichous 5–8 in., slightly aromatic, fl. purple or greenish, pods 3–8 in. long. 2. **B. Dalzellii**, Hook f. The Konkan (only found once). L. 12 by 3 in. Pod 5–8 in., trigonous, rugose and deeply pitted.

2. ARISTOLOCHIA, Linn.; Fl. Brit. Ind. v. 74.

Perennial herbs or shrubs, often twining. L. entire or lobed, base generally cordate, basal nerves 3–5. The lowest leaf of a more or less developed axillary bud sometimes has the appearance of an intrapetiolar stipule. Perianth tube inflated at the base, then contracted, hairy within, limb dilated, obliquely 2-lipped. Anthers 6, adnate to the stylar column, the apex of which is 3- or 6-lobed. Capsule septicidally 6-valved. Species 180, cosmopolitan, chiefly tropical.

A. Stylar column 6-lobed.

1. **A. Roxburghiana**, Klotzsch.—Syn. *A. acuminata*, Roxb.; Wight Ic. t. 771. Sikkim, 1–4,000 ft. Assam. Khasi hills. Maimensingh. Chittagong. Burma. Western Ghats. Malay Penins. and Archip. A twining shrub, stem attaining 1 in. diam. L. deeply cordate, ovate or ovate-lanceolate, basal n. produced far beyond the middle. Fl. pale green, in lax pedunculate axillary corymbs, lip of perianth villous, capsule stipitate, oblong or subglobose, 1–2½ in. long. 2. **A. indica**, Linn.—Syn. *A. lanceolata*, Wight Ic. t. 1858. Vern. *Isharmal*, Sund.; *Sapshi*, *Kadula*, Kan. Sundriban. Chittagong. Western Ghats. Sriharikot, Coromandel coast (D. B. Nov. 1881).—Ceylon, low country to 3,000 ft. Prostrate or climbing, stems slightly woody at base, l. variable, linear, ovate or obovate-oblong, base cuneate or rounded, basal nerves short. Corymbs short, pedunculate. Perianth greenish-white, lip glabrous, purple and brown.

B. Stylar column 3-lobed.

(*a*) L. lobed and pinnatifid.

3. **A. platanifolia**, Ducharte. East Nepal. Sikkim to 6,000 ft. Assam. Khasi hills. A large climber, l. up to 12 in. long, and often as broad. Fl. generally fasciculate on the old wood, perianth yellowish-purple, mouth 1 in. diam. Capsule 4–6 in. long.

(*b*) L. entire.

4. **A. saccata**, Wall. Pl. As. Rar. t. 103. Kumaon. Nepal. Sikkim, from the Terai to 6,000 ft. Assam. Khasi hills. Stems up to 1 in. diam. from a thick rootstock. L. ovate-lanceolate, acuminate, base deeply cordate, tomentose, rarely glabrous beneath, blade 12–16, pet. 1–2 in. long. Fl. mostly from the old wood, perianth purple, mouth nearly circular, capsule cylindric. 5. **A. Cathcartii**, Hook. f. Sikkim to 3,000 ft. Khasi hills. Manipur. Similar to 4, branches, petioles and l. beneath softly silky, inflorescence clothed with long spreading hairs, mouth of perianth square, edge broad, recurved, fringed with long purple hairs. 6. **A. Griffithii**, Hook. f. Sikkim 7–10,000 ft. Bhutan. L. broadly ovate or orbicular, densely tomentose beneath. Fl. mostly solitary, axillary, capsule 7 in. long.

ORDER LXXXIX. PIPERACEÆ. Gen. Pl. iii. 125.

L. entire, fl. minute, subtended by bracts, which often are peltate, in catkin-like spikes. Perianth 0, stamens hypogynous. Embryo minute, in a copious mealy albumen.

The wood is separated by broad medullary rays into wedge-shaped masses. Pith large, with numerous vascular bundles and a hard undulating belt, mostly consisting of sclerotic fibres, on the outside.

PIPER, Linn.; Fl. Brit. Ind. v. 78.

Perennial herbs or shrubs, often climbing by adventitious roots at the nodes, usually aromatic, nodes swollen, l. alternate, basal n. 3 or more, supra-basal n. one (rarely several) pair, alternate or opposite, stipules membranous, enclosing the buds. Spikes commonly leaf-opposed, fl. dioicous or polygamous, rarely 2-sexual, stamens 1–4, filaments short. Ovary 1-celled, stigmas 2–5. Berry 1-seeded, seed globose. Species 500, tropical or subtropical, a few only can be mentioned here.

A. Spikes simple.

(*a*) Fruiting spikes compact, dense.

1. **P. Betle,** Linn.—Syn. *Chavica Betle*, Miq.; Wight Ic. t. 1926. Vern. *Pān*, Hind.; *Kun*, Burm. The *Betel vine*, cultivated for its leaf throughout tropical and subtropical India, in Burma planted near forest trees, in the Peninsula with *Erythina*, *Sesbania* and other fast growing trees, in Bengal under the shade of matting. Home uncertain. L. ovate, base usually cordate and unequal-sided, blade 3–8, pet. ½–1 in., supra-basal n. alternate. Fruiting spike cylindric, pendulous, 1–5 in. long. Propagated by cuttings, most plants ♀. 2. **P. longum,** Linn.—Syn. *Chavica Roxburghii*, Miq.; Wight Ic. t. 1928. Wild and cultivated in Sikkim, Assam, Lower Bengal, the west side of the Peninsula, in Malacca and the Malay Archipelago. Cultivated in Ceylon and elsewhere in the tropics. Rootstock erect, thick, jointed, branched, stems herbaceous, numerous. L. membranous, deeply cordate, upper sessile, blade 2–5, pet. (of the lower) 1–3 in. long. Fruiting spike (the *long pepper* of commerce) solid, fleshy, 1–1½ in. long, blackish green, shining. 3. **P. brachystachyum,** Wall.—Syn. *Chavica sphærostachya*, Miq.; Wight Ic. t. 1931. Subhimalayan tract and outer hills from Simla eastwards, ascending to 5,000 ft. Assam. Khasi hills. Nilgiri, Anamalai and Shevagherri hills. L. elliptic-lanceolate, blade 2–6, narrowed into pet. ¼–¾ in. long. Fruiting spike nearly globose, shortly stalked.

(*b*) Fruiting spikes loose, glabrous.

α. Supra-basal n. usually opposite.

4. **P. Hamiltonii,** Cas. D.C. Sikkim Terai. Khasi hills. Chittagong. A stout climber, quite glabrous, l. coriaceous, fruiting spikes slender, 4–6 in. long. 5. **P. Hookeri,** Miq. Western Ghats from Bombay to Kanara. Bababudan hills in Mysore. A climbing shrub, branchlets, petioles and l. beneath hairy, l. scarcely coriaceous, fruiting spikes slender, 3–6 in. long.

β. Supra-basal n. usually alternate.

6. **P. nigrum,** Linn.; Wight Ic. t. 1934.—Syn. *P. trioicum*, Roxb.; Wight Ic. t. 1935. *The Black Pepper*. Vern. *Kali mirch*, Hind.; *Milaku*, Tam.; *Nga-yok-kaung*, Burm. Cultivated in the Kāns of Mysore and other evergreen forests of tropical India and Burma, doubtfully indigenous on the Western Ghats. A stout climber, perfectly glabrous, l. more or less coriaceous, base cuneate or rounded, blade 4–6, pet. ½–1 in. long, basal n. 3 or 5. Fruiting spike slightly interrupted, drooping, 4–6 in. long, red when ripe. 7. **P. argyrophyllum,** Miq. Western Ghats. Ceylon, moist country 1–4,000 ft. Grows up the trunks of trees, rooting like ivy, stems up to 2½ in. diam. L. ovate-lanceolate, base cuneate, not unequal, blade 3–5, pet. ½ in. long.

(*c*) Fruiting spikes loose, hairy.

8. **P. trichostachyon,** Cas. DC.—Syn. *Muldera trichostachya*, Miq.; Wight Ic. t. 1944. Western Ghats from Bombay to Kanara. Nilgiri and Shevagherry hills. A stout climber, l. coriaceous, tert. n. distinct, fr. spikes 3–4 inches long, interrupted, fr. yellow, globose, ⅛ in. diam.

B. Spikes umbellate, fl. 2-sexual.

9. **P. subpeltatum,** Willd.—Syn. *Pothomorphe subpeltata*, Miq.; Wight Ic. t. 1925. Western Ghats from North Kanara southwards. Ceylon, moist region. An erect shrub, branches thick soft, l. orbicular, deeply cordate, blade 8–12 in. diam., pet. 4–8 in., spikes 3–5 in. long.

ORDER XC. MYRISTICACEÆ. Gen. Pl. iii. 135 (*Myristiceæ*).

(Warburg, Monographie der *Myristicaceen*, Halle, 1897.)

Evergreen and aromatic trees or large shrubs, l. often distichous, usually glabrous beneath, entire, penninerved, often pellucid-punctate. Fl. 1-sexual, with rare exceptions dioicous, perianth as a rule 3-lobed, valvate in bud. ♂, anthers usually sessile 6–30, on a sessile or stipitate column or disk. ♀, ovary one, free, style short or none, ovule 1, erect. Seed enclosed in a thin or fleshy entire or lacerate mostly red arillus. Embryo basal, surrounded by a large oily ruminate albumen.

Hairs peculiar, mostly consisting of one row of superposed, generally branching, and often horizontal cells. The branches or ends of the cells spread out in two or several directions, often giving the appearance of stellate hairs. Med. rays numerous, very fine. The bark of most species contains long sacs filled with brown or red juice.

Warburg divides this Order into 15 genera, 6 of which belong to tropical Africa, 5 to tropical America, while 4 are Asiatic. Here these genera are entered as sections of *Myristica*.

MYRISTICA, Linn.; Fl. Brit. Ind. v. 102.

(George King, the species of *Myristica* of British India, Ann. Bot. Gard. Calc., iii. 3. 1891.)

I. *Myristica*, Linn. (in part); Warburg 374. Fl. urceolate or campanulate, anthers 12–30, linear, adnate to a column, which is often stipitate and frequently prolonged beyond the anthers, stigmas sessile. Bracteoles appressed to the perianth. Arillus laciniate to the base. Species 81, from India to tropical Australia.

A. ♂ fl. numerous, on a thick woody tubercle.

1. **M. magnifica**, Bedd. Fl. Sylv. t. 268; King, Ann. Bot. Gard. Calc. iii. t. 119. Vern. *Chura pânu*, Tam.; *Kottha panu*, Mal. Evergreen forest on the Gairsoppah Ghat (Talbot) and at the foot of the Travancore Ghats. A very tall tree, when young the trunk furnished in its lower portion with large aërial roots, which later on support the tree. Young shoots, underside of l. and inflorescence densely clothed with reddish or golden tomentum of stellate hairs. L. coriaceous, elliptic-oblong, blade 12–24, pet. stout, deeply channelled, ½–1 in. long. ♂ fl. sessile, or nearly so, 8–20 crowded on a thick woody often forked tubercle, very short or up to ⅜ in. long. Fr. solitary or in pairs on thick short pedicels, oblong, 3–4 by 2 in., arillus deeply cleft into a few broad divisions, these subdivided into numerous linear branches attaining to the apex of the seed. 2. **M. laurifolia**, Hook. f. & Thoms.; Bedd. Fl. Sylv. t. 267. Wild Nutmeg. Vern. *Jaiphal*, Mar.; *Jathika*, Tam. Western Ghats from the Satara district southwards, ascending from the foot to 5,000 ft. Nilgiris, Anamalais. A middle-sized or large tree, youngest shoots and inflorescence rusty tomentose, branchlets wrinkled. L. coriaceous, glabrous beneath, blade 6–10, pet. ⅝–1¼ in. long. Sec. n. impressed above. ♂ fl. 6–15 together, each supported by a broad ovate bract at the base of the cylindrical perianth. Fr. ellipsoid or globose, 2–3 in. long. Aril deeply cut into 10–14 lobes, which are divided into filiform segments. Warburg l.c. 504, 507 distinguishes 2 species: *M. Beddomei*, King, Ann. t. 118 figs. 2–8, fr. globose and *M. contorta*, Warb., fr. ellipsoid. *M. laurifolia*, King, Ann. t. 112 he restricts to the Ceylon tree.

B. ♂ fl. in panicled cymes, peduncles slender.

3. **M. fragrans**, Houttuyn: Ann. Bot. Gard. Calc. iii. t. 108.—Syn. *M. aromatica*, Lamk.; Roxb. Cor. Pl. t. 274. *The Nutmeg*. Vern. *Jaiphal*, Hind.; *Jathikai*, Tam. Originally indigenous in the southern Moluccas. Cultivated on a large scale in places in the Malay Peninsula and the Archip., also on Grenada and a few other West Indian islands. In gardens throughout the tropics. Attains 30–60 ft., l. glaucous beneath, blade 3–5, pet. ½ in. long. ♂ peduncles 3–20-, sometimes only 1–2-fld., perianth urceolate, ¼ in. long. Fruit yellow, solitary, shortly stalked, 1½–2½ in. long, aril (*mace*) red, fleshy, fenestrate from the base, enclosing the seed. 4. **M. malabarica**, Lam.; Bedd. Fl. Sylv. t. 269; King, Ann. iii. t. 109. *False Nutmeg*. Vern. *Kat Jathikai*, Tam.; *Ponnam panu*, Mal. Evergreen forest at the foot of the Western Ghats, from the Konkan southwards. A moderate-sized tree, branchlets nearly smooth, slightly ribbed, l. chartaceous, glaucous or dull brown beneath, blade 5–7, pet. slender ¾–1 in. long, tert. n. very faint. ♂ fl. numerous, in trichotomous panicles, perianth nearly globose, ⅛ in. diam., peduncles often extra-axillary. Fr. rusty brown-pubescent, hard, oblong, 2 × ½ in., aril yellow, completely enclosing the seed. 5. **M. andamanica**, Hook. f. (*M. elliptica*, Kurz F. Fl. ii. 282). King, Ann. iii. t. 115. Andamans, on the hills. A middle-sized tree, young shoots glabrous, l. rigidly coriaceous when full grown, blade 9–15 by 4–6 in., sec. n. prominent, 12–15 pair. ♂ fl. 8–12 in supra-axillary pedunculate cymes, perianth subglobose ¼ in. diam. Fr. ovoid, glabrous, 2–2½ in. long.

II. *Horsfieldia*, Willd.; Warburg l.c. 262. Fl. small, globose, anthers 12–30, stigma minute, sessile, ♂ fl. in large compound panicles, bracteoles 0. Aril frequently not laciniate. Species 51 from India to New Guinea.

A. Perianth usually 3-valved, anthers connate, entirely enclosing the globose column.

(*a*) Staminal-column sessile.

6. **M. amygdalina,** Wall. Pl. As. Rar. t. 90; King, Ann. iii. t. 128. Assam. Khasi hills. Cachar. Andamans. Southern spurs of the Pegu Yoma, Martaban, Tenasserim.—Malay Penins. A moderate-sized glabrous tree, l. membranous, blade 4–7, pet. ½–¾ in. ♂ panicles spreading, 3–4 in. long, perianth $\frac{1}{12}$–$\frac{1}{16}$ in. diam. Fr. narrowly ovoid, 1½ in. long, aril laciniate at the apex. King, Ann. iii. 310, refers the Andaman and part of the Burma specimens to *M. glabra*, Bl. 7. **M. Kingii,** Hook. f.; King, Ann. iii. t. 127. Sikkim 1–2,000 ft. Assam. Cachar. Young shoots scurfy pubescent, l. thinly coriaceous, blade 6–10, pet. ½–1 in. long. ♂ panicles 3 in. long, branches short, perianth ⅐ in. diam. Fr. 1½ by 1 in., supported by the persistent perianth. Aril entire.

(*b*) Staminal-column shortly stipitate.

8. **M. Prainii,** King, Ann. iii. t. 126. Andamans. A large tree, glabrous, only inflorescence rusty-pubescent. L. thinly coriaceous, blade 6–10, pet. stout, ½–¾ in. ♂ panicles lax, broader than long, 5–7 in. wide. Fr. ovoid, 1½ in., peduncle stout, ½ in. long, aril deeply laciniate.

B. Perianth 2-valved, anthers free.

9. **M. Irya,** Gærtn.; King, Ann. iii. t. 141, 141 (b). Tenasserim. Andamans. Ceylon. Malay Penins. and Archip. A middle-sized tree, youngest shoots slightly pubescent, branchlets glabrous, more or less angular. L. chartaceous, oblong to oblong-lanceolate, blade 5–8, pet. ⅓ in. ♂ panicles axillary, 3–5 in. long, fl. $\frac{1}{20}$ in. diam., fascicled on short pedicels. Anthers 6–18, free, on the edge of a flat topped obovate column. Fr. globose, ¾ in. diam., aril red, undivided, completely enclosing the seed.

III. *Gymnacranthera*, Warb. l.c. 354. Anthers 6–12, linear, lower portion adnate to an ovoid column, upper portion free, stigma sessile, more or less 2-lobed. Aril laciniate nearly to the base. Fl. in axillary panicles, bracteoles 0.

10. **M. canarica,** Bedd. MSS.; King, Ann. iii. t. 138.—Syn. *M. Farquhariana*, Hook. f. & Thoms.; Bedd. Fl. Sylv. t. 270. Vern. *Undgi pânu*, Mal. Western Ghats in evergreen forests. Konkan (?). Plains of South Kanara. Coorg. Wainâd. Tinnevelli and Travancore. A moderately-sized tree, immense in Travancore, youngest shoots minutely pubescent, l. coriaceous, glaucous beneath, ♂ panicles rufous pubescent, perianth obovoid, ⅐ in. long. Fr. globose, 1 in. diam.

IV. *Knema*, Loureiro; Warburg l.c. 543. Fl. obconical or subglobose, anthers 8–20, sessile or nearly so on the edge of a circular stipitate and peltate disk, style short thick. Bracteoles on the pedicel, in the middle, above or below it. Pericarp tomentose, aril laciniate at the apex only. Species 38, from India to New Guinea.

A. ♂ fl. more than ⅛ in. diam.

11. **M. attenuata,** Wall.; King, Ann. iii. t. 152.—Syn. *M. corticosa*, Bedd. Fl. Sylv. t. 271. Vern. *Chôra panu*, Mal. Evergreen forests of the Western Ghats from the Konkan southwards ascending to 3,000 ft. A middle-sized or large tree, young branchlets and inflorescence densely rusty-tomentose, l. glaucous beneath, lanceolate or oblong-lanceolate, blade 6–8, pet. ¼–½ in. long. Sec. n. prominent beneath, tert. n. slender, parallel. ♂ fl. nearly globose, ⅛–⅙ in. diam. Fr. ovoid, 1½ in. long, densely tomentose.

12. **M. linifolia,** Roxb.; Warb. l.c. 558.—Syn. *M. longifolia*, Wall.; Fl. Brit. Ind. v. 110 (partly); King, Ann. iii. t. 164, 166. Assam. Khasi hills. Chittagong. Arakan. Upper Burma. Young shoots and inflorescence densely dark-brown tomentose, l. coriaceous, blade 12–30, pet. ½–¾ in. long, base usually rounded or cordate, sec. n. conspicuous, 25–35 pair, distinctly anastomosing under the margin, tert. n. parallel. ♂ fl. obconical, ¼ in. long, bracteole small at or below the middle of pedicel. Fr. on thick woody tubercles, often solitary, ellipsoid, velvety, 1½ in. long. *M. Clarkeana*, King, Ann. t. 165, Chittagong, is a form with narrower l., the fr. more pointed at both ends. 13. **M. angustifolia,** Roxb.; Warb. l.c. 561.—Syn. *M. longifolia*, Wall., var. *erratica*, Fl. Brit. Ind. v. 110; *M. erratica*, Hook. f. & Thoms.; King, Ann. iii. t. 162.

Sikkim, Khasi hills. Cachar. Chittagong. Burma, Upper (*Nyaungma Kunthwe*) and Lower. A middle-sized tree, young shoots slightly hairy, l. coriaceous, pale beneath, oblong-lanceolate, blade 6–12, pet. $\frac{1}{2}$–$\frac{5}{8}$ in. long, base cuneate, sec. n. 18–25 pair. ♂ fl. obovoid or globose, $\frac{1}{8}$–$\frac{1}{4}$ in. diam., pedicel usually longer than fl., bracteole above the middle. Fr. 2–3 on axillary woody tubercles $\frac{3}{4}$ in. long, pedicels slender, $\frac{1}{8}$–$\frac{1}{4}$ in., aril membranous. Smales describes the Upper Burma tree with a regular pyramidal crown, ♂ fl. outside greenish, andrœcium crimson. *M. gibbosa*, Hook. fil. & Thoms.; King, Ann. iii. t. 159 probably is only a variety with the fr. gibbous at base.

B. ♂ fl. less than $\frac{1}{8}$ in. diam.

14. **M. glaucescens**, Hook. f. in Fl. Brit. Ind. v. 111, including *M. glauca*, Blume; King, Ann. iii. t. 157 and *M. missionis*, Wall.; King, Ann. iii. t. 158. Andamans, Nicobars, Tenasserim.—Malay Peninsula. L. chartaceous, lanceolate or linear-lanceolate, glaucous beneath, blade 5–8, pet. $\frac{1}{2}$–$\frac{5}{8}$ in. long. ♂ fl. nearly globose, $\frac{1}{10}$–$\frac{1}{8}$ in. diam., pedicels twice the length of fl. Fr. ovoid or (*M. missionis*) globose up to 1 in. long. 15. **M. malayana**, Warburg (Knema).—Syn. *M. glaucescens*, King, Ann. iii. t. 161. Malay Peninsula. Burma (?). Differs by longer pedicels of ♂ fl. and of fr.

ORDER XCI. LAURACEÆ. Gen. Pl. iii. 146 (*Laurineæ*).

Aromatic trees or erect shrubs with alternate, sometimes whorled, rarely opposite leaves, as a rule entire and mostly evergreen. No stipules. Flowers solitary or in involucrate heads, often dioicous. Perianth regular, deeply 6- (sometimes 4-) cleft, segments in 2 circles, the tube often enlarged in fruit. Stamens perigynous, normally 12 in 4 circles, the 3 stamens of the innermost circle generally reduced to more or less fleshy staminodes or wanting, the filaments of the next circle biglandular at base, the stamens of the two outer circles opposite to the perianth-segments. Filaments flat, anthers adnate, cells 2 or 4, opening by valves. Ovary free, 1-celled, usually one pendulous ovule, style simple. Fruit a berry or drupe, often supported by the persistent perianth. Seed one, without albumen, cotyledons thick, oily, enclosing the plumule and short superior radicle.

Laurels, as far as known, have no heart-wood, the timber is not heavy, not hard, that of many species is handsome and of some very durable. From a forest point of view the Order deserves more attention in India than it has hitherto received. And it should be borne in mind that their aromatic essential oil may give to some species not yet known commercially, considerable importance for perfumery and in other ways. Medullary rays fine, uniform and equidistant. Vessels small or moderate sized, uniformly distributed. In the parenchyma of young shoots, of leaves, bracts and perianth, as well as in the bark and often also in the wood, large cells filled with essential oil, and frequently also cells filled with mucilage. In the bracts and perianth the oil cells are readily seen as transparent dots. Hairs always unicellular. As far as known, Laurels coppice well.

A. Flowers solitary, bisexual, generally paniculate.
  a. Anthers 2-celled, perfect stamens 9.
    Perianth-tube accrescent, enclosing the fruit . . . 1. CRYPTOCARYA.
    Fruit supported at its base by the 6-cleft perianth . . . . APOLLONIAS (p. 528).
    Perianth deciduous, pedicel thickened, coloured in fruit . . . . DEHAASIA (p. 528).
    Perianth deciduous, pedicel not thickened in fruit . 2. BEILSCHMIEDIA.
  b. Anthers 2- or 1-celled, perfect stamens 3 or 4.
    Perianth-segments 6, perfect stamens 3 . . ENDIANDRA (p. 529).
    Perianth-segments 4, perfect stamens 4 . . SYNDICLIS (p. 529).
  c. Anthers 4-celled, perfect stamens 9 or more,
    Perfect stamens 9, sepals 6, persistent, spreading or reflexed in fruit . . . . . . 3. MACHILUS.
    Perfect stamens 9, fruit on the thickened pedicel, perianth-segments deciduous . . . . . 4. ALSEODAPHNE.
    Perfect stamens 10–15, fr. on the flat thick perianth-tube . . . . 5. DODECADENIA.
B. Flowers solitary, polygamous or bisexual, paniculate, anthers 4-celled.
  Segments of perianth erect, hard, clasping base of fruit 6. PHŒBE.
  Fruit on enlarged perianth-tube, segments mostly deciduous . . . . 7. CINNAMOMUM.

C. Flowers in bracteate heads, dioicous.
Anthers 4-celled, bracts imbricating, not whorled . 8. ACTINODAPHNE.
Anthers 4-celled, heads supported by 4–6 whorled bracts . . . . 9. LITSÆA.
Anthers as a rule 2-celled, bracts mostly whorled . 10. LINDERA.

1. CRYPTOCARYA, Rob. Br.; Fl. Brit. Ind. v. 117.

Evergreen, l. mostly penniveined. Fl. paniculate, bisexual. Anthers 2-celled. Perianth-tube constricted at apex after fl., accrescent, enclosing the fr. Sp. 40, tropical and subtropical.

A. Western species.

1. **C. Wightiana,** Thwaites; Bedd. Fl. Sylv. t. 299.—Syn. *C. floribunda*, Wight Ic. t. 1829. Vern. *Gulmur*, Kan.

A large tree, branchlets and inflorescence rusty pubescent. L. coriaceous, whitish and nearly glabrous beneath, elliptic or elliptic-oblong, shortly acuminate, blade 4–10, pet. ½–1 in. long, sec. n. 6–10 pair. Panicles spreading, fr. purplish-black, obtusely ovoid, ½–⅔ in. long.

Evergreen forests along the Western Ghats from Matheran southwards. Fl. Nov.–Jan. Ceylon. 2. **C. Stocksii,** Meissn. Western Ghats from Kanara southwards. Branchlets, panicle, and as a rule the underside of l. rusty-pubescent. L. rigidly coriaceous, more or less rounded at both ends, blade 2–4, pet. stout, ¼ in. long. Panicles contracted, shorter than l.

B. Eastern species.

(*a*) Branchlets, inflorescence and l. beneath densely rusty-tomentose.

3. **C. Griffithiana,** Wight Ic. t. 1830, South Tenasserim, Malay Peninsula. L. rigidly coriaceous, shining above, glaucous beneath, elliptic-oblong, caudate-acuminate, blade 9–12, pet. stout ⅓ in. long, sec. n. 8–10 pair, arching, impressed above, very prominent beneath, as well as midrib and tertiary n. Panicles compact, 1–2 in. long, bracts conspicuous. Fr. 1 in. long, globose or ovoid, narrowed into a thick neck. 4. **C. andamanica,** Hook. f. Andamans. L. elliptic-oblong, blade 3–5, pet. ¼ in. long, sec. n. 10–14 pair, strong beneath, not impressed above. Fr. narrow-ellipsoid 1 in. long.

FIG. 177. Cryptocarya Wightiana, Thwaites. ⅓.

(*b*) Full grown l. glabrous or thinly pubescent beneath.

5. **C. amygdalina,** Nees.—Syn. *C. floribunda*, Wall. in part. *Patmero*, Nep. Foot of Eastern Himalaya from Sikkim eastwards. Khasi hills. Andamans. Chittagong. Attains 40 ft., branchlets and inflorescence minutely dark grey pubescent. L. glabrous, coriaceous, shining above, opaque beneath, oblong-lanceolate, blade 3–12, pet. ¼–½ in.

long, sec. n. 6–12 pair, oblique, nearly straight. Panicles large, up to 12 in. diam., peduncle long. Fr. black, ⅝ in. long, ellipsoid, pointed at the ends. 6. **C. Ferrarsi,** King. Andamans. A shrub, l. thinly coriaceous, minutely rusty-pubescent beneath, oblong, base cuneate, sec. n. prominent, arching, tert. n. conspicuous. Fr. ½ in. long. 7. **C. cæsia,** Blume. Andamans. Branchlets, petioles and panicle rusty pubescent. L. glabrous, glaucous above, white beneath, ovate-lanceolate, blade 5–7, pet. ¼–⅜ in. long, sec. n. 6–8 pair, arching, strong beneath, reticulate venation very fine and regular, prominent on both sides. Fr. globose ⅜ in. diam.

8. **C. Kurzii,** Hook. f.—Syn. *C. ferrea*, Kurz F. Fl. ii. 295. Mergui. Branchlets black, glabrous, as well as l. L. glaucous beneath, blade 4–8, pet. ¼ in., sec. n. 6–8 pair, conspicuous beneath.

Apollonias Arnotti, Nees; Wight Ic. t. 1819. *Chenthanam*, Mal. Western Ghats from Malabar southwards. An evergreen tree, l. thinly coriaceous, glabrous when full grown, lanceolate, 3–5 in. long, fl. bisexual, fr. supported by the 6-cleft hardened perianth. Somewhat resembles *Phœbe lanceolata*, differs by 2-celled anthers. The only other species, *A. canariensis*, Nees, is a tree of the Canaries.

1. **Dehaasia cuneata,** Blume (*Alseodaphne grandis*, Kurz F. Fl. ii. 293). Arakan. Pegu Yoma, southern and eastern slopes. Thaukyeghat forest. Martaban and Tenasserim. Andamans. Java. A large evergreen tree, branchlets white. L. congregated at the ends of branchlets, almost whorled, glabrous, cuneate, obovate, blade 5–9, pet. ½–1 in. long. Fl. bisexual, in axillary lax panicles, peduncles and branches very slender. Perfect stamens 9, anthers 2-celled. Fr. pruinose, bluish-black, ellipsoid, 1–1½ in. long, seated on the much swollen pedicel which is as long as fr., perianth-segments finally deciduous. Similar and possibly not specifically distinct: 2. **D. Kurzii,** King. Chittagong (Prain). Pegu. Martaban. Tenasserim, 3. **D. elongata,** Blume. Andamans.

No. 550 Haines, Lower hills of British Bhutan, *Malagiri*, Nep. (fl. unknown), may possibly be a species of *Dehaasia*. "A valuable timber tree, yielding excellent planks." Young shoots and underside of l., chiefly along nerves, clothed with fine hairs. L. membranous, elliptic, acuminate, blade 4–6, pet. slender ½–1 in. long, sec. n. arching 3–6 pair. Fr. globose-reniform, purple, ⅜ in. diam., seated on a much swollen furrowed pedicel ⅜ in. long, bearing the undulating coriaceous perianth.

2. BEILSCHMIEDIA, Nees; Fl. Brit. Ind. v. 121.

Trees or shrubs, as a rule evergreen, l. penninerved, often opposite. Fl. small, bisexual, in racemes or panicles, often fasciculate. Perianth deeply divided into 6 nearly equal segments. Perfect stamens 9, the 3 inner biglandular with extrose anthers. None or only slight remains of perianth in fr. Species 20, tropical.

A. L. usually alternate.

1. **B. Roxburghiana,** Nees; Wight Ic. t. 1828; Brandis F. Fl. 378.—Syn. *B. fagifolia*, Nees; Bedd. Fl. Sylv. t. 263. Vern. *Kamatti*, Kan.

A tree, greatly varying in size. Terminal buds and inflorescence pubescent. L. coriaceous, glabrous, shining and finely reticulate on both sides, elongate-elliptic or elliptic-lanceolate, blade 6–9, pet. ½–1 in. long. Racemes short, often branched at base, peduncles and pedicels hirsute, pedicels often fasciculate. Perianth divided to near the base, segments ⅛ in. long, hairy on both sides, oblong, spreading or reflexed, filaments hairy. Ovary glabrous (Dacca), hairy (Kanara). Fr. ½–1½ in. long, from short ovoid, almost globose to cylindric-obovoid (Singbhum).

A widely distributed species. Durga Deo Forest, Kumaon (D. B. 1863). Oudh Forests (R. Thompson). Assam. Khasi hills. Dacca. Tipperah. Manipur. Burma, Upper and Lower. Singbhum. Western Ghats from Matheran to South Kanara. Yunnan. Fl. March, April, when the old l. fall, so that a tree in fl. may occasionally be leafless. The specimens from Singbhum and the Western Ghats are usually called *B. fagifolia*, but, as far as the specimens examined go, there is no real difference, shape of l. and fr. vary greatly. Foliage very similar to that of *Cryptocarya amygdalina*, the difference is in the inflorescence and fruit. 2. **B. Bourdilloni,** sp. nova. Travancore, evergreen forest, 300–1,500 ft. (Bourdillon 87). Shevaroy hills (D. B. 1882). A large evergreen tree, l. coriaceous, elliptic, blade 5–7, pet. ½–1 in. long. Inflorescence compact, grey velvety, axillary and terminal, consisting of short fascicled racemes, at the base branching and bearing numerous broad round concave bracts, fl. fascicled in the axils of similar bracts, before opening ovoid-globose ⅛ in. diam., perianth-segments ovate. Filaments and ovary hairy, fr. unknown. 3. **B. Brandisii,** Hook. f. Nambar forest, Assam. A moderate-sized tree, l. glabrous, thinly coriaceous, blade 6–10, pet. 1 in. long, sec. n. 6-8 pair. Panicles or racemes axillary 1-2 in. long, pedicels solitary, a little longer than fl. Perianth-segments obtuse $\frac{1}{12}$ in. long, filaments hairy, ovary glabrous. Fr. on stout peduncles, 2-2½ in. long. 4. **B. macrophylla,** Meissn. Mergui. Terminal buds, branchlets and petioles rusty pubescent. L. thickly coriaceous, blade 9–12, pet. ½ in. long, sec. n. 10–12 pair, prominent beneath, distinctly anastomosing under the edge. Similar to *B. malaccensis*, Hook. f. Malay Penins.

B. L. usually opposite.

(*a*) Terminal buds enclosed in large glabrous coriaceous scales, inflorescence glabrous.

5. **B. Wightii,** Benth.—Syn. *Haasia Wightii*, Nees; Bedd. Fl. Sylv. t. 298. Anamalais, Tinnevelli and Travancore Ghats. Quite glabrous, l. elliptic, acuminate, blade 3-4, narrowed into slender pet. ¾ in. long. Panicles slender on long peduncles, fl. minute.

6. **B. assamica,** Meissn. Assam, Manipur, Upper Burma. Yunnan. Buds lanceolate, fr. elongate-elliptic, 1½ in. long. 7. **B. Gammieana,** King. East Nepal. Sikkim, common 5–7,000 ft. (*Thulo Tarsing*). Closely allied to 6, buds ovoid, fr. glabrous or obovoid, ¾–1 in. long. 8. **B. globularia,** Kurz. Hills east of Toungoo, 3-4,000 ft. Buds ovoid, fr. globose, fleshy, 1–1½ in. diam.

FIG. 178. Beilschmiedia Roxburghiana, Nees. ½.

(*b*) Terminal buds and inflorescence pubescent.

9. **B. sikkimensis,** King; Gamble, Ind. Timb. Ed. ii. 559. Vern. *Tarsing*, Nep. Sikkim and Bhutan, ascending to 6,500 ft. L. elongate-elliptic, obtuse at both ends, blade 3, pet. ¼ in. Fr. ellipsoid 1 in. long. 10. **B. Clarkei,** Hook. f. Sikkim: Reinak 4,500 ft. (C. B. Clarke), Lopchu 5,200 ft. (*Sanu Tarsing*) (B. B. Osmaston). A large tree, l. membranous, acuminate, blade 5–7, pet. ½ in. Panicles hairy, 3–4 in. long, fasciculate at the ends of branchlets from the uppermost leaf-axils, fl. mostly solitary, pedicels as long as or a little shorter than fl., perianth divided to the base, segments hairy on both sides, ovary glabrous.

Endiandra firma, Nees. Silhet. Cachar. Terminal buds and inflorescence slightly puberulous, l. glabrous, concolorous, elongate-elliptic, blade 5–8, pet. ⅓ in. long, sec. n. 6–8 pair, arching, veins minutely and regularly reticulate, prominently raised on both surfaces. Panicles axillary 1–2 in. long, branches slender, perianth glabrous outside, tomentose within. Anthers 3, sessile, tomentose, 2-celled, valves oblong. Fr. ovoid 1 in. long.

Syndiclis paradoxa, Hook. f. in Ic. Pl. t. 1515. Bhutan. L. glabrous chartaceous, elongate-obovate, blade 3–5, pet. ½ in. long. Fl. minute, panicles axillary, branches filiform. Perianth-segments 4, broad, glandular-punctate, anthers 4, sessile, 1-celled. Ovary glabrous.

3. MACHILUS, Nees; Fl. Brit. Ind. v. 136.

Evergreen trees, leaves alternate, often clustered at the ends of branchlets, penninerved. Fl. bisexual, in axillary and pseudo-terminal panicles. Perianth

of 6 nearly always (cf. *M. edulis*) persistent sepals, spreading or reflexed in fruit. Anthers 4-celled. Berry oblong or globose, as far as known, the cotyledons remain underground. Species 15–20 from India to Japan.

The beautiful and very durable dark olive brown *Nanmu* wood, used for coffins in China, is the produce of *Machilus Nanmu*, Hemsley (*Persea Nanmu*, Oliv.), and other species of this genus.

A. Sepals glabrous, fr. oblong or ellipsoid.

1. **M. odoratissima**, Nees. *Kaula, Kaunla, Kawala*, Hind. Outer Himalayan ranges and valleys from the Sutlej eastwards, 2–7,000 ft. Khasi hills. Ruby Mines district, Upper Burma. A moderate sized tree, l. glabrous, dark green and shining above, pale beneath, blade 4–6, pet. ½–1 in. long, sec. n. slender, minute raised reticulate veins prominent on both sides. Panicles shortly pedunculate, about 3 in., perianth-segments ⅓, fr. purple, ½ in. long, supported by the reflexed sepals. 2. **M. parviflora**, Meissn. Assam, Khasi hills. L. glaucous beneath, sepals ⅛ in. long.

B. Sepals tomentose or silky, fr. globose.

Fig. 179. Machilus bombycina, King. ½.

(*a*) The young and as a rule the mature l. densely pubescent beneath.

3. **M. villosa**, Hook. f.—Syn. *Phœbe villosa*, Wight Ic. t. 1822. Subhimalayan tract and outer hills from Nepal eastwards, ascending to 6,000 ft. Assam. Silhet. Cachar. Chittagong. Patkoi range. Upper Burma. Hills between Sitang and Salwin 3,000 ft. (D. B. 1880). A large or middle-sized tree, young shoots panicles and fl. softly tomentose, sec. n. prominent beneath, 6–8 pair, panicles large, fasciculate at the ends of branchlets, in the axils of bracts or of the uppermost l., sepals ⅙–⅛ in. long, fr. 1 in. diam., seated on the reflexed perianth. 4. **M. edulis**, King. Vern. *Lepcha phal*, Nep., Sikkim and Bhutan, 4–8,000 ft. A large tree, branchlets stout with prominent leaf-scars, l. thickly coriaceous, oblanceolate, blade 5–12, pet. ½ in., sec. n. straight, oblique. Fr. edible, 1½ in. diam. on a stout woody peduncle, perianth almost deciduous.

(*b*) L. glabrous or finely silky beneath.

a. Filaments villous. Western species.

5. **M. macrantha**, Nees; Wight Ic. t. 1824: Bedd. Fl. Sylv. t. 264. Vern. *Gulum*, Mar.; *Kurma, Kroma, Gulmavu*, Kan.; *Kollamavu*, Tam.; *Uravu*, Mal. Western Ghats and adjoining hill ranges, from Matheran southwards. Ceylon. A large tree, l. glabrous, elliptic-oblong or elongate-elliptic, blade 4–10, pet ¾–1¾ in. long, panicles much branched, hoary, fl. yellow tomentose, ¼ in. long, fr. black, ¼–⅜ in. diam. *M. glaucescens*, Wight Ic. t. 1825, is supposed to differ by larger fr.

β. Filaments hairy at the base only (cf. *Gammieana*).

6. **M. bombycina**, King. *The Soom* tree (*Machilus odoratissima*, Nees; Brandis, The Muga silk industry, Ind. For. v. 35).

A middle-sized tree, young shoots and inflorescence silky, l. elliptic-lanceolate, clothed beneath with minute silky hairs, blade 4–5, pet. ½ in. long, sec. n. arching, slender, 6–8 pair. Perianth silky, segments ¼ in. long, fr. ¼ in. diam.

Forms extensive forests in the Sibsagar district, Assam, this being the principal species on which the Muga silkworm is raised. Western Duars, Chittagong (Prain). Yunnan (?). Nearly allied and possibly not specifically distinct are the 2 following: 7. **M. Kurzii**, King. Sikkim 6–9,000 ft. Upper Burma. Yunzalin, Martaban 2.500 ft. (D. B. March 1880). Young shoots and l. beneath almost glabrous, sec. n. slender. 8. **M. Gamblei**, King. Subhimalayan tract and outer hills from the Jumna eastwards, ascending to 7,000 ft., shoots and young l. beneath finely silky, adult l. quite glabrous. L. from elliptic-lanceolate to obovate, sec. n. 8–12 pair, fr. ¼–½ in. diam.

9. **M. Duthiei**, King, Ann. Bot. Gard. Calc. ix. t. 83; Collett Fl. Simla 431, fig. 138. Vern. *Chān*, Haz.; *Khawala*, *Bhojo*, Jauns.; *Bhadrao*, Garhw.; *Kaula*, Kumaon. N. W. Himalaya, Hazara to Kumaon 4–8,000 ft., on northern slopes and in shady ravines. A large or moderate-sized, sometimes gregarious tree, l. glabrous, glaucous beneath, lanceolate, blade 6–10, pet. ½–1 in. long, sec. n. arching, 12–18 pair. Panicles pedunculate, about 6 in. long, perianth silky-tomentose outside, segments ¼ in. long, filaments glabrous, fr. ½ in. diam.

10. **M. Gammieana**, King.—Syn. *M. Clarkeana*, King. Sikkim, common, 5–8,000 ft. A large tree, leaf-buds covered with large obtuse silky scales, l. glabrous, lanceolate, blade 6–10, pet. ⅓–½ in. long. Panicles glabrous, shorter than l., in the axils of broad silky bracts and of the uppermost l. Perianth-segments ¼–⅜ in. long, 5-nerved, finely silky on both surfaces, rarely glabrous, filaments hairy at base, with a few long deciduous hairs in the upper part. Fr. ⅞–1½ in. diam.

11. **M. fruticosa**, Kurz. Martaban and Tenasserim. A shrub, l. glabrous, rigidly coriaceous, the reticulate veins almost as distinct as the sec. n. Panicles axillary, hoary, 3–8, perianth-segments silky, $\frac{1}{10}$ in. long.—Some of the species here described will probably disappear when more thoroughly studied in the forests. Imperfectly known are: *M. Listeri*, King; *M. bootanica*, Meissn.; *M. Kingii*, Hook. f. and others.

4. ALSEODAPHNE, Nees; Fl. Brit. Ind. v. 143.

Section II. of *Persea* in Engl. u. Prantl, iii. 2. 115.

Evergreen trees, l. penninerved. Fl. bisexual, in axillary panicles, anthers 4-celled. Fr. ellipsoid, seated on the club-shaped end of the thick fleshy peduncle. Species about 15, tropical Asia.

1. **A. semecarpifolia**, Nees; Wight Ic. t. 1826, 1827; Bedd. Fl. Sylv. t. 297. *Phudgus*, Mar.; *Nelthare*, Kan. Western Ghats from the Konkan southwards. Ceylon, dry region. A large tree, l. coriaceous, glaucous beneath, glabrous or on the underside minutely tomentose, usually obovate, in var. *angustifolia* elongate-elliptic, blade 4–7, pet. ⅓–⅜ in. Panicles pedunculate, longer than l., perianth in fl. ⅛ in. long, pedicels slender, longer than fl. 2. **A. petiolaris**, Hook. f. Assam. Cachar. Upper Burma (Griff.). A tall tree, l. rigidly coriaceous, blade 8–12, pet. stout, 1½–2 in., sec. n. very strong beneath, tert. n. parallel. Fr. 1½ in. long. Imperfectly known: 3. **A. grandis**, Nees. 4. **A. costalis**, Nees.

5. DODECADENIA, Nees; Fl. Brit. Ind. v. 180.

Evergreen trees with perulate buds and scattered coriaceous penninerved leaves. Flowers bisexual. Perianth-tube short, funnel- or cup-shaped, segments 6–9, spreading. Perfect stamens 10–18, anthers 4-celled. Fruit seated on the dilated thick flat perianth-tube.

1. **D. grandiflora**, Nees. Kumaon 8,000 ft. Nepal, Upper Burma (Kurz). Branchlets, petioles and midrib on the upperside tomentose, leaves thinly coriaceous, lanceolate, the finely reticulate veins prominent. Fl. ½ in. across, solitary, on very short pedicels, marked with the scars of deciduous bracts, stamens exserted, villous. Fr. ½ in. long, seated on the flat perianth-tube. 2. **D. Griffithii**, Hook. f. Bhutan. Similar, but branchlets quite glabrous, bracts 7 to each fl., perianth-segments 6. 3. **D. paniculata**, Hook. f. Sikkim 3,000 ft. Bhutan. Khasi hills. Manipur. A small tree, glabrous except inflorescence, l. coriaceous, shining above, opaque beneath, ovate-lanceolate, blade 6–8, pet. ½ in., sec. n. arching, 10–12 pair. Fl. in axillary panicles, pedicels rusty-

pubescent, $\frac{1}{4}$–$\frac{1}{3}$ in. long. Peduncles ridged, minutely hairy, as well as outside of perianth. Fl. $\frac{1}{3}$ in. across, no bracts, stamens 18, anthers and the short filaments minutely hairy. Fr. obovoid or clavate, 1–$1\frac{1}{2}$ in. long, pedicel thickened into the obconic calyx-tube.

6. PHŒBE, Nees; Fl. Brit. Ind. v. 141.

Evergreen trees or shrubs, leaves alternate, often clustered at ends of branchlets, penninerved. Fl. bisexual or polygamous, paniculate. Segments of perianth-tube erect, hard, clasping the base of fruit. Anthers 4-celled. Species about 50, those of section I. Indian and Malayan, those of section II. with two exceptions American. Of the Indian species 2 are common to the two Peninsulas, the rest belong to the Eastern region.

I. Lobes of fruiting perianth appressed, rigid, almost horny.

A. Perianth glabrous.

1. **P. lanceolata,** Nees; Wight Ic. t. 1821. Vern. *Bhadroi*, Jaunsar; *Tūmri*, Dehra Dūn; *Katkaula*, Kumaon. Subhimalayan tract and outer ranges, from the Bias eastwards, ascending to 6,500 ft. Oudh forests. Khasi hills. Chittagong. Upper Burma. Wainād, Anamalais, Tinnevelli and Travancore. A small or middle-sized tree, l. glabrous, chartaceous, lanceolate, caudate-acuminate, blade 5–8, pet. $\frac{1}{2}$–$\frac{3}{4}$ in., sec. n. slender, 6–10 pair. Panicles axillary, pedunculate, perianth-segments $\frac{1}{10}$–$\frac{1}{8}$ in., fr. narrowly ellipsoid, $\frac{1}{2}$ in. long. 2. **P. angustifolia,** Meissn. Khasi hills. Upper Burma, stream banks and swamps. Yunnan. A shrub or small tree, l. very aromatic, linear-lanceolate, blade 6–10, narrowed into pet. $\frac{1}{4}$–1 in. long, sec. n. slender, arching. Panicles axillary, on slender peduncles 8–5 in. long, fl. greenish, umbellate at the ends of panicle branches, perianth-segments $\frac{1}{8}$ in. long.

B. Perianth silky or pubescent, $\frac{1}{8}$ in. long and under.

3. **P. pallida,** Nees. Subhimalayan tract and outer ranges, from Kumaon eastwards, ascending to 6,000 ft. Assam (*Seling*). Khasi hills. Upper Burma. A moderate-sized tree, similar to 1, shoots, inflorescence and underside of young leaves pubescent, l. lanceolate or oblanceolate, sec. n. 6–10 pair, prominent beneath. 4. **P. paniculata,** Nees; Wight Ic. t. 1820.—Syn. *P. Wightii*, Meissn.; Bedd. Fl. Sylv. t. 292; *P. pubescens*, Nees; Kurz F. Fl. II. 290. Nilgiris (*Kamara*). Anamalais. Nepal. Chittagong. Burma, Upper and Lower. A moderate-sized tree, young shoots rusty-tomentose, l. pubescent beneath and often also on the midrib above, elliptic or obovate-elliptic, blade 4–8, narrowed into petiole $\frac{1}{3}$–$\frac{3}{4}$ in. long, sec. n. 6–12 pair prominent beneath. Panicles and fl. pubescent, on long slender peduncles, fr. $\frac{1}{3}$–$\frac{1}{2}$ in. long partly enclosed by the persistent perianth. 5. **P. attenuata,** Nees. *Angaria*, Nep. Sikkim and Bhutan outer hills, ascending to 8,000 ft. Assam. Mogok, Ruby Mines district 4–5,000 ft. (*Hlega* or *Thityawa*). A large tree, branchlets stout, shoots, petioles, underside of l. and inflorescence rusty-tomentose with long soft hairs, l. oblanceolate, blade 5–10, narrowed into pet. $\frac{1}{2}$ in. long, sec. n. 15–20 pair, tert. n. parallel. Panicles spreading, peduncles stout, 3–6 in. long, fr. narrowly ellipsoid, $\frac{1}{2}$ in., fruiting calyx $\frac{1}{4}$ in. long. 6. **P. tavoyana,** Hook. f.—Syn. *Machilus tavoyana*, Meissn. Binedah forest, Pegu (D. B. Feb. 62). Thaungyin (D. B. Apr. 62). Tavoy, Mergui. L. membranous, oblanceolate, finely acuminate, with scattered often minute hairs beneath, blade 6–10, narrowed into pet. $\frac{1}{2}$–2 in. long, sec. n. arching, 6–8 pair, with shorter intermediate n. Flowering panicles slender.

II. Lobes of fruiting perianth coriaceous, not appressed. Perianth in fl. softly tomentose, $\frac{1}{6}$ in. long.

7 **P. Hainesiana,** Brandis in Hook. Ic. Pl. t. 2803. Outer hills, Sikkim, Bhutan, 3–5,500 ft. (H. H. Haines No. 303). *Angaria*, Nep. A large timber tree, attaining 150 ft. and 20 ft. girth, bark thick, dark grey, wood yellow, makes excellent planking. L. glabrous, pale beneath, clustered at the ends of branches, oblanceolate to obovate, blade 5–9, pet. 1–$1\frac{1}{2}$ in. long, sec. n. straight, 12–16 pair, prominent beneath. Peduncles stout, in fl. 3–4, in fr. 5–9 in. long, perianth in fl. on both sides grey tomentose. Fr. black, fleshy, $1\frac{1}{4}$ in. long, base enclosed by the campanulate 6-lobed perianth, which is $\frac{1}{2}$ in. long. This remarkable species is nearly allied to *Phœbe indica*, Pax, of the Azores, Madeira and Teneriffe, which yields a beautiful furniture wood.

7 CINNAMOMUM, Blume; Fl. Brit. Ind. v. 128.

Evergreen trees or shrubs, l. opposite or alternate, in most species tripli-nerved. Fl. in large axillary panicles, often from the axils of the uppermost l., appearing terminal. Fl. bisexual or polygamous, stamens 9, the 3 inner 2-glandular at base, anthers 4-celled, staminodes 3, cordate or hastate. Fr. seated on the more or less enlarged perianth, the lobes of which are wholly or partly deciduous, rarely persistent. Species about 130, tropical and subtropical Eastern Asia, Australia and the Pacific.

Section I. *Malabathrum*. Buds with small scales, l. mostly opposite, triplinerved.

A. L. as a rule opposite. Eastern species.

(*a*) Buds and young shoots more or less silky. L. glabrous.

1. **C. Tamala**, Fr. Nees.—Syn. *C. albiflorum*, Nees, Wight Ic. t. 140. Vern. *Dalchini*, *Tezpat* (the leaves), Hind.; *Thitchabo*, Burm. Subhimalayan tract and outer ranges, ascending to 7,000 ft., from the Jumna eastwards, chiefly in damp ravines. Khasi hills. Silhet. Tipperah. Upper Burma. A moderate-sized tree, very aromatic, l. glabrous, opposite or nearly so, often alternate on the same branch, blade 3–6, pet. $\frac{1}{2}$ in. long, the young foliage pink. Fl. $\frac{1}{4}$ in. diam., perianth silky, lobes in fr. breaking off transversely about the middle. Fr. black when ripe, succulent, $\frac{1}{2}$ in. long, supported by the thickened pedicel and the base of perianth, with short truncate teeth. *Kyeik-tapo*, Burm.; *Thabihay*, Kar., a tree (leaves only), found by me on the headwaters of the Yunzalin, March 1880, bark very thick and extremely aromatic, l. minutely hairy beneath, may be *C. Cassia*, Blume, China, which yields the true Cassia lignea or Cassia bark. 2. **C. obtusifolium**, Nees; Wight Ic. t. 139. Vern. *Nalingyaw*, *Lulingyaw*, *Thitkyabo*, Burm. Outer Eastern Himalaya, ascending to 7,000 ft. Khasi hills. Chittagong. Andamans. Burma, Upper and Lower. Differs from 1 by larger more thickly coriaceous l., blade 9–13, pet. stout $\frac{1}{2}$–$\frac{3}{4}$ in. and the perianth-segments persistent in fruit. 3. **C. impressinervium**, Meissn. Sikkim, 4–6,000 ft. L. glabrous, upper side shining, lower pale, blade 3–4, pet. $\frac{3}{8}$ in., in mature l. the nerves deeply impressed on the upper side. Panicles shorter than l. silkily tomentose, fl. $\frac{1}{8}$ in. across, perianth-lobes quite deciduous in fr. 4. **C. iners**, Reinw.; Wight Ic. t. 122. Mergui, Malay Penins. L. elliptic-lanceolate, panicles lax, slender, long pedunculate, often longer than l., fl. $\frac{1}{8}$ in. across, segments of perianth persistent in fr. 5. **C. nitidum**, Blume (*C. Culitlaban*, Wight Ic. t. 137), similar to 4, but fl. larger.

(*b*) Buds, branchlets, petioles, underside of l. and inflorescence velvety.

6. **C. tavoyanum**, Meissn. (*C. sulphuratum*, Kurz. F. Fl. ii. 288). Vern. *Hmanthin-po*, Burm. Tenasserim. L. lanceolate, blade 6–8, pet. $\frac{1}{2}$–$\frac{3}{4}$ in. long. Peduncles long slender, fl. $\frac{1}{6}$ in. across, pedicels as long as or longer than fl. Fr. on slender 4–5 in. long peduncles more than half immersed in the campanulate acutely 6-toothed perianth.

(*c*) Buds, young shoots and l. quite glabrous.

7. **C. pauciflorum**, Nees (*C. recurvatum*, Wight Ic. t. 133). Assam. Khasi hills, near streams. Shan States, 3,000 ft. (*C. vimineum*, Nees). A large shrub or small tree, wood very aromatic. L. firmly coriaceous, ovate or ovate-lanceolate, blade 3–4, pet. $\frac{1}{3}$ in. long. Panicles nearly glabrous, few-fld., on slender peduncles, fl. $\frac{1}{5}$ in. across, segments of perianth deciduous in fr. 8. **C. pedunculatum**, Nees, var. *angustifolium*, Hemsl. Khasi hills, 4,500 ft. China, Japan. A shrub or small tree, upper l. opposite or nearly so, the lower often alternate, l. lanceolate, blade 2–6, pet. $\frac{1}{4}$–$\frac{1}{2}$ in. Fl. in umbels terminating the slender panicle branches, pedicels slender, often twice the length of fl., perianth-segments silky within, $\frac{1}{5}$–$\frac{1}{6}$ in. long. Fr. oblong $\frac{1}{3}$ in. long, fruiting perianth entire or with the short truncate base of 6 teeth.

B. L. as a rule opposite, Western species and sp. of both regions.

9. **C. zeylanicum**, Breyn; Wight Ic. t. 123, 129, 134; Bedd. Fl. Sylv. t. 262. The Cinnamon tree. Vern. *Dalchini*, Kan.; *Karuva*, Tam.; *Varana*, *Lavangu*, Mal.; *Hmanthin*, Burm.

A large tree, all parts very aromatic, l. thick coriaceous, glabrous, upperside shining, underside dull, 3–5 basal nerves, young foliage pink. Panicles as long as or not much longer than l., sometimes terminal, fl. grey-silky, $\frac{1}{6}$–$\frac{1}{5}$ in. diam., fr. dark purple, elongate ellipsoid $\frac{2}{3}$–1 in. long, supported by the much enlarged perianth.

Western Ghats and adjoining hill ranges, from the Konkan southwards. Tenasserim. Fl. Nov.–June. An exceedingly variable species, differs from *C. Tamala* chiefly by the more thickly coriaceous l. and the more acute lobes of the much enlarged fruiting calyx. Grown in Ceylon for its bark in irregular coppice woods. 10. **C. Wightii**, Meissn. Nilgiris. Branchlets and petioles stout, buds globose, silky, l. rigidly coriaceous, panicles fulvous tomentose. 11. **C. macrocarpum**, Hook. f.

North Kanara, evergreen forest. Peduncles 3–4 in. long, fruiting perianth ⅜ in. diam., fr. 1 in. long. 12. **C. sulphuratum**, Nees. Coorg, Wainād. Nilgiris. Branchlets, young l. and panicles densely fulvous-tomentose, peduncles 2–3 in., fr. ½–⅝ in. long, ellipsoid, fleshy, base included in the 6-lobed perianth, lobes obtuse. 13. **C. gracile**, Hook. f. Tinnevelli hills. L. thinly coriaceous, blade 2–3, pet. ⅓–⅔ in., tertiary n. and reticulate veins distinct on both surfaces, panicles few-fld., shorter than l., fl. minute, pedicels long, slender.

C. L. as a rule alternate.

14. **C. caudatum**, Nees. Subhimalayan tract and outer ranges, from Nepal eastwards, ascending to 4,000 ft. Upper Burma. L. chartaceous, orbicular or elliptic, obtusely caudate-acuminate, fl. minute, in short axillary few-fld. contracted pubescent panicles. Fruiting perianth clavate, fleshy, lobes persistent. 15. **C. Perrottetii**, Meissn. Nilgiris. Densely fulvous tomentose, petiole 1–1½ in. Beddome, Manual 184, regards *C. Wightii*, *sulphuratum*, and *Perrottetii* as forms of *C. zeylanicum*.

Section II. *Camphora*. Leaf-buds enclosed in large silky orbicular concave imbricating caducous scales, l. alternate, penninerved.

16. **C. Cecicodaphne**, Meissn. Subhimalayan tract and outer hills, from Sikkim eastwards, ascending to 4,000 ft. Khasi hills, Manipur. Vern. *Malligiri*, Nep. L. elliptic, blade 3–4, pet. ½–1 in., sec. n. 4–8 pair. Panicles crowded, densely tomentose, fr. oblong, 1¼ in. long. 17. **C. glanduliferum**, Meissn. Kumaon (?). Nepal. Assam. Khasi hills. Similar to 16, panicles long-peduncled, few-fld., nearly glabrous. 18. **C. Camphora**, F. Nees.—Syn. *Camphora officinarum*, Bauh.; Wight Ic. t. 1818. *The Japan Camphor tree.* China, Japan, grown in gardens in India. L. long-acuminate, blade 2–4, pet. 1–1½ in., sec. n. 2–3 pair, the lowest pair proceeding from near the base of l.

19. **C. Parthenoxylon**, Meissn.—Syn. *Sassafras Parthenoxylon*, Nees; Wight Ic. t. 1832. Mergui. Malay Penins. and Archip. China. A large tree, l. glaucous beneath, blade 3–8, pet. slender, 1–1½ in. long. 20. **C. inunctum**, Meissn. Vern. *Karawe*, Burm. South Tenasserim, Malay Peninsula. Fl. diœcious, small, sepals $\frac{1}{12}$ in. long. Fruiting perianth infundibuliform, narrowed into a stout peduncle.

8. ACTINODAPHNE, Nees; Fl. Brit. Ind. v. 147.

Evergreen shrubs or trees. Leaves more or less whorled, rarely opposite or scattered. Flowers dioicous, in bracteate umbels, clusters or racemes, bracts imbricating, caducous, not whorled. ♂ Stamens 9, anthers 4-celled, all introrse, no staminodes. ♀ Staminodes 9, ovary usually glabrous. Fruit seated on the enlarged flat or concave perianth-tube. Species 50, Eastern Asia and Malaya.

A. Leaves penninerved, more or less whorled. Western species.

(*a*) Perianth-tube entire in fr.

1. **A. Hookeri**, Meissn. Vern. *Pissa*, *Pisha*, *Pichli*, Mar.; *Thāli*, Tam.; *Malavirimji*, Mal. Western Ghats in evergreen forest, from Matheran southwards. Branchlets and young leaves usually rusty-tomentose, leaves coriaceous, elliptic- or ovate-lanceolate, finely acuminate, glabrous and shining above, but often tomentose beneath when full grown, blade 5–7, pet. ⅛–⅜ in., sec. n. 6–8 pair, the lowest pair often extending almost to the middle of the leaf. Clusters of ♀ fl. sessile, fr. ellipsoid, seated on the campanulate entire perianth-tube. 2. **A. madaraspatana**, Bedd.—Syn. *A. Hookeri*, Bedd. Fl. Sylv. t. 296. Hills on the east side of the Penins., also on the Nilgiris and in Travancore. A middle-sized tree, branchlets and young l. pubescent, coriaceous, upperside shining, underside glaucous, quite glabrous when full grown, lanceolate, blade 6–11, pet. ½ in. long, sec. n. 8–10 pair, prominent beneath. Clusters of ♀ fl. pedunculate.

3. **A. hirsuta**, Hook. f. Quilon. Branchlets, pet. and l. beneath densely brown-tomentose, l. elongate-elliptic, shortly acuminate, blade 4–6, pet. ½ in. long. Fr. seated on the cup-shaped, entire perianth-tube. 4. **A. stenophylla**, Thwaites, Travancore, evergreen forest, 4,000 ft. (Bourdillon 543). Ceylon. A small tree, young shoots and bud-scales minutely pubescent, l. glabrous, glaucous or white beneath, linear-lanceolate, obtuse, blade 2–5, pet. ¼–⅓ in. long. Fr. in sessile clusters, globose, ⅜ in. diam., seated on the entire shallowly cup-shaped perianth-tube, pedicels as long as or longer than fr. 5. **A. campanulata**, Hook. f.—Syn. *A. salicina*, Bedd. Fl. Sylv. t. 295. Tinnevelli. Closely allied to 4, if distinct.

(*b*) Perianth-tube 6-lobed in fr.

6. **A. lanata**, Meissn. Nilgiris. Branchlets and young l. densely rusty-tomentose, l. coriaceous, glaucous beneath, glabrous when mature, lanceolate, blade 3–4, pet. ⅜ in.

long. Clusters of ♀ fl. sessile, fr. globose ½ in. diam., seated on the enlarged 6-lobed perianth-tube. 7. **A. salicina,** Meissn. Nilgiris. L. linear-lanceolate, probably a narrow leaved form of 6.

B. L. penninerved, more or less whorled. Eastern species.

8. **A. angustifolia,** Nees; Wight Ic. t. 1841.—Syn. *Litsæa angustifolia*, Kurz. Vern. *Nalingyo*, Burm.

A large or moderate-sized tree, branchlets stout, as well as young l. softly tomentose. L. coriaceous, glaucous beneath, shining above, lanceolate, blade 8–12, pet. ½–¾ in. long, sec. n. 6–8 pair, prominent beneath, midrib and underside of the sec. n. usually hairy. Clusters of ♀ fl. very shortly peduncled, fr. ⅓ in. diam., seated on the small cup-shaped entire perianth-tube.

West Duars in partially evergreen forest. Assam, Garo and Khasi hills. Chittagong. Singbhum rare, in valleys. Common in the evergreen forest patches of the Pegu Yoma. Martaban and Tenasserim. Fl. R. S. 9. **A. sesquipedalis,** Hook. f. & Thoms. —Syn. *Litsæa macrophylla*, Kurz. Mergui. Penang. Branchlets very stout, tomentose, l. rigidly coriaceous, glossy above, lanceolate, blade 12–24, narrowed into a stout pet. 1 in. long. Fl. in large clusters, fr. globose, ¾–1 in. diam., seated on the broad flat entire or crenate perianth. 10. **A. reticulata,** Meissn. Khasi hills. Sikkim, 6,500 ft. (B. B. Osmaston). Buds silky, branchlets and young l. minutely pubescent, sometimes glabrous. L. lanceolate, blade 4–6, pet. ⅓ in., sec. n. faint, very fine raised reticulate veins conspicuous on both surfaces. Fr. broadly ellipsoid, ½ in. long, seated on the cupular quite entire perianth-tube, pedicels longer than fr.

11. **A. sikkimensis,** Meissn. Vern. *Phirphiri*, Nep. Sikkim, 3–6,000 ft. Bhutan. Manipur. Branchlets slender, l. membranous, lanceolate, caudate-acuminate, blade 3–5, pet. ¼–½ in. long, sec. n. slender. Fr. in sessile clusters, oblong, seated on the very small quite entire base of perianth. 12. **A. concolor,** Nees. Tenasserim. Imperfectly known.

C. Leaves, some whorled, others opposite or alternate, almost triplinerved, the lowest pair of the sec. n. reaching to the middle of the leaf.

13. **A. obovata,** Blume. Vern. *Muslindi*, Nep.; *Pattikuta*, Ass. Evergreen forest and damper portions of Sal forest in the subhimalayan tract from Sikkim eastwards, ascending to 2,000 ft. Assam. Khasi hills. Manipur. A large very handsome tree, branchlets, leaf buds and leaves rusty-pubescent or tomentose. L. elliptic, bluish-white beneath, blade 10–18, pet. 1–2 in. long, sec. n. 4–6 pair, prominent beneath; tert. n. parallel, slender. Flowers on short compound, compact lateral racemes, while in bud covered by rounded coriaceous scales. Fr. ⅜–1 in. long, seated on the entire cup-shaped perianth-tube. 14. **A. confertiflora,** Meissn. Bhutan. Glabrous, l. alternate, broadly ovate or elliptic, blade 4-7, pet. 1 in. long. Fl. numerous in dense axillary compound clusters, pedicels long, 15. **A. leiantha,** Hook. f.—Syn. *Litsæa leiophylla*, Kurz. Tenasserim (or Andamans). Glabrous, except the rusty pubescent inflorescence. L. scattered, lanceolate, blade 5–9, pet. 1 in. Fl. in lateral racemes covered while in bud by imbricate rounded caducous bracts.

9. LITSÆA, Lamk.; Fl. Brit. Ind. v. 155.

Trees, rarely shrubs, l. as a rule alternate, mostly penninerved. Fl. dioicous in 4–6-fld. heads, which in bud are enclosed by 4–6 large concave whorled bracts, fl. sometimes supported by bracteoles. Anthers 4-celled, generally all introrse. The pedicels of ♀ fl. lengthen out in fr. hence when several fruits of one head come to maturity they are umbellate. Species 140, tropical, rare in Africa and America.

I. Leaves deciduous, penninerved. Perianth-segments 6, tube not enlarged in fruit.

(*a*) Leaf-buds naked.

1. **L. citrata,** Blume.—Syn. *Tetranthera polyantha*, Wall. Vern. *Siltimber*, Nep.; *Adakori*, *Edenkuri*, Ass.

A small tree, with a delightful fragrance of oranges, youngest shoots silky, otherwise entirely glabrous. Branches and leaves black when dry. Leaves membranous, 4–7 in. long, lanceolate, fresh bright green above, dull glaucous beneath, blade 4–7, pet. slender ⅓–¾ in. long, sec. n. slender. Fl. with the l., heads ⅛ in. diam., enclosed by 4 membranous glabrous bracts, ciliate at the

edges, 4–6 flowers in each head. Heads on very slender peduncles in sessile or shortly stalked corymbs. Fr. ¼–⅓ in. diam.

Subhimalayan tract and outer ranges from Nepal eastwards, ascending to 9,000 ft. Common in the West Duars. Assam valley, here chiefly in the Dibrugarh district, used to feed the silk worm which yields the valued Mezenkuri silk. Khasi hills. Cachar. Upper Burma (Kurz). Java. Fl. C. S., at high elevations later. 2. L. Kingii. Hook. f. Sikkim 6–8,000 ft. Khasi hills. An aromatic shrub, l. elliptic-lanceolate, fl. before the l., heads on stout peduncles.

(*b*) **Leaf-buds perulate.**

3. **L. sericea,** Wall. (*Tetranthera*). Nepal. Sikkim, 9–11,000 ft. Manipur. A middle-sized very aromatic tree, branchlets, petioles, underside of l. and peduncles with long silky hairs, fl. before the l. 4. **L. oreophila,** Hook. f. Inner Sikkim 10–11,000 ft. L. ovate-lanceolate, blade 2–3, pet. slender ⅛ in. long.

II. Leaves persistent, penninerved.

A. Perianth-segments incomplete or wanting, tube hardly enlarged in fruit. Stamens numerous, more than 9.

5. **L. tomentosa,** Heyne.—Syn. *Tetranthera tomentosa*, Roxb.; Wight Ic. t. 1834. Vern. *Chikna*, Mar.; *Peru Panjetti, Peram Pandali*, Tam. Western Ghats from Mahabaleshwar to the Nilgiris. Hills of the Cuddapah, South Arcot, Salem and other districts in the Southern Deccan. Ceylon. Fl. Aug.–Jan. A middle-sized tree, densely and softly tomentose, except the upperside of leaves. Leaves crowded at the ends of branches, elliptic-lanceolate, blade 4–6, pet. ½–1 in. long, sec. n. 10–15 pair, prominent beneath. Flower-heads solitary, ⅓ in. diam. before opening, pale yellow, on peduncles ½ in. long. ♂: Stamens 18–20, filaments long slender, villous. ♀: staminodes long, strap-shaped, numerous. Fr. ⅓–½ in. diam.

6. **L. sebifera,** Pers.—Syn. *L. chinensis*, Lam.; Trimen Handb. Ceylon ii. 449; *Tetranthera laurifolia*, Roxb.; Brandis F. Fl. 379; *T. apetala*, Roxb. Cor. Pl. t. 147. Vern. *Maida*, Hind., Mar.; *Ondôn*, Burm.; *Singhor, Banborla*, Kumaon.

A middle-sized tree, very variable, inner bark viscid. Branchlets, inflorescence and underside of leaves more or less pubescent, sometimes almost glabrous. L. ovate or elliptic-lanceolate, pale beneath, blade 5–10, pet. ½–2 in. long, sec. n. 8–12 pair, joined by finely reticulate veins. Flower-heads white or yellowish, ¼ in. diam. before opening, in pedunculate umbels, filaments clothed with long soft hairs. Fr. ¼ in. diam.

Subhimalayan tract extending into the plains, from the Ravi eastwards, often in Sāl Forests ascending to 4,500 ft. Punjab Salt range. Assam. Khasi hills. Bengal. Burma. Central and South India. Fl. May–July. 7. **L. ligustrina,** Nees; Fl. Brit. Ind. v. 158.—Syn. *Tetranthera ligustrina*, Nees; Wight Ic. t. 1885. Western Ghats, from the Nilgiris southwards. Glabrous, l. coriaceous, blade 3–4, pet. ⅓–⅔ in. long, obovate, sec. n. 6–8 pair, veins on both sides finely and very prominently reticulate. Fl.-heads solitary or clustered, ¼ in. diam. before opening. Perianth persistent in fr. but not enlarged. 8. **L. membranifolia,** Hook. f. Upper Assam. A middle-sized tree, l. thin, membranous, pubescent beneath, obovate, blade 8–12, pet. ½–1 in. long, sec. n. 10–14 pair, tert. n. parallel.

B. Perianth-segments 6, tube hardly enlarged in fr.

(*a*) L. alternate, pubescent or tomentose beneath.

9. **L. polyantha,** Juss.—Syn. *Tetranthera monopetala*, Roxb. Cor. Pl. t. 148; Brandis F. Fl. t. 45. Vern. *Katmarra, Singran*, Hind.; *Karkawa*, Dehra Dūn; *Leja*, Gond; *Sualu*, Ass.; *Ondôn*, Burma.

A middle-sized tree, branchlets, underside of l. and inflorescence with soft brown or rust-coloured pubescence. L. elliptic-oblong, blade 4–8, pet. ¼–½ in., sometimes longer, sec. n. 8–10 pair, joined by the parallel transverse veins. ♂ fl.-heads ⅙–⅕ in. diam. before opening, in sessile or nearly sessile clusters, fl. 5–6 in each head, sessile or on short hairy pedicels, involucre of 5 rounded membranous bracts. Fr. ⅓ in. long, seated on the persistent base of perianth.

Subhimalayan tract from the Ravi eastwards, ascending to 3,000 ft. Punjab Salt range. Assam (associated with Soom and also used for rearing the Muga silk-worm). Khasi and Naga hills. Cachar. Bengal plains. Chittagong. Satpura range. Northern Circars. Burma (everywhere in the plains and in the valleys of the principal rivers). Fl. March–May. 10. **L. amara,** Bl.—Syn. *Tetranthera amara*, Nees. Pegu

Yoma, eastern slopes (Kurz), Tenasserim. Malay Penins. and Archip. Branchlets, petioles, underside of l. and inflorescence minutely brown-tomentose. L. thinly coriaceous, elliptic or lanceolate, blade 4–6, pet. ¼ in., sec. n. 10–15. ♂ fl.-heads $\frac{1}{10}$ in. diam. on short slender peduncles in axillary sessile clusters, ♀ fl.-heads nearly sessile. Fr. ovoid, ¼–⅓ in. long. 11. **L. rangoonensis**, Meissn. (*Tetranthera*). Similar to 10, l. more acuminate, sec. n. 8–12. ♀ fl.-heads pedicellate. 12. **L. Kurzii**, King. Andamans. Branchlets, petioles, underside of l. and inflor. harshly brown-tomentose. L. coriaceous, elliptic-oblong, blade 6–9, pet. stout, ⅓ in., sec. n. 10–15 pair, tertiary parallel, prominent. ♂ heads ⅓ in. diam. before opening. 13. **L. grandis**, Wall. (*Tetranthera*). Not unfrequent in Pegu, Martaban and Upper Tenasserim (Kurz). Malay Peninsula. Branchlets stout, marked with the scars of fallen l. L. rigidly coriaceous, upperside shining, underside densely and softly brown-tomentose, broadly elliptic or obovate, blade 9–11, pet. stout, 1 in. long, sec. n. 10–15 pair, very prominent beneath as well as the parallel tertiary n. ♂ heads ¼ in. diam. before opening, on stout peduncles, ¼–½ in. long. Specimens from Burma not seen. Specimens (in leaf only) coll. by me in the Meplay evergreen forest (March 1862) (*Momoh*, Karen), a large tree, wood yellow, fl. said in my notes to be bisexual, marked by Kurz as *Tetranthera grandis*, Wall., var. ?, are quite different.

(*b*) L. glabrous beneath or nearly so, sometimes opposite.

14. **L. lancifolia**, Roxb. Sikkim, foot of hills. Bhutan. Assam. Khasi hills. Cachar. Chittagong. Tenasserim. A shrub or small tree, branchlets, petioles and midrib finely tomentose, l. thinly chartaceous, glaucous beneath, usually opposite or nearly so, elliptic-lanceolate, blade 4–6, pet. ¼ in. long, sec. n. 6–8 pair. Fl. white, fr. globose, on the small flat perianth-tube. The Sikkim specimens have lanceolate alternate l. 15. **L. mishmiensis**, Hook. f. Mishmi hills, Assam. A large glabrous tree, l. thinly coriaceous, blade 4–6, pet. ⅜ in., sec. n. faint. 16. **L. assamica**, Hook. f. Assam. L. thinly coriaceous, blade 4–6, pet. ⅓ in., sec. n. slender. 17. **L. Wallichii**, Hook. f.—Syn. *Lindera nervosa*, Kurz. Bhutan. Tenasserim. A glabrous tree, l. coriaceous, elongate-elliptic, blade 6–8, pet. ⅓–½ in. long, sec. n. 6–8 pair, arching, impressed above, veins on both surfaces raised, minutely and regularly reticulate. Filaments glabrous, fr. nearly globose, ⅛ in. long, seated on the persistent but not enlarged 6-lobed perianth.

18. **L. venulosa**, Meissn. Tinnevelli hills. An evergreen straggling shrub, quite glabrous, l. thinly coriaceous, glaucous beneath, elliptic-oblong, obtusely caudate-acuminate, blade 3–5, pet. ¼ in. long.

C. Perianth-segments usually 6, tube much enlarged in fr.

(*a*) Fl.-heads solitary or fascicled.

a. L. more or less pubescent or tomentose beneath.

19. **L. Khasyana**, Meissn. Subhimalayan tract from Sikkim eastwards, ascending to 3,000 ft. Upper Burma. Ruby Mines district 5,000 ft. (*Ondôn*). Branchlets, l. beneath and inflorescence finely pubescent, l. usually glaucous beneath, varying in shape, blade 6–12, pet. ½–¾ in., sec. n. 10-15 pair, nearly straight, prominent beneath. Heads before opening ¼ in. diam., fascicled on stout peduncles. Fr. 1 in. diam., seated on the enlarged fleshy turbinate perianth-tube. 20. **L. martabanica**, Kurz (*Tetranthera*). Martaban, hills south of Taëpo, 4,000 ft. Salween 2,000 ft. (D. B. 1859 and 1880). A shrub or small tree, branchlets, pet., underside of l. and inflorescence finely tawny-tomentose. L. coriaceous, elliptic-lanceolate, blade 3–8, pet. ½–1 in. long, sec. n. arching, 6–8 pair, tertiary n. and finely reticulate veins prominent beneath. Fl.-heads ¼ in. diam. before opening, 2–4 in axillary pedunculate umbels. Involucral bracts 4, fl. 4, perianth thin. Fr. ellipsoid, ½ in. long, base enclosed in the salver-shaped perianth-tube. 21. **L. semecarpifolia**, Wall. (*Tetranthera*). *Patmoro*, Nep. Western Duars, common in Sāl and mixed forest. Manipur. Pegu Yoma, eastern slopes. Martaban. A moderate-sized tree, branchlets, petioles, underside of l. and inflorescence velvety, l. coriaceous, obovate or elongate-elliptic, blade 6–8, pet. ½–¾ in. long. Fl.-heads ¼ in. diam. before opening, in compact axillary clusters, stamens long exserted. Fr. globose, ¾ in. diam. seated on the broad cup-shaped perianth-tube. 22. **L. elongata**, Wall. Outer Himalayan ranges from the Jumna eastwards, common in Sikkim 6–9,000 ft., rare further west. Assam. Khasi hills. A moderate-sized or small tree, branchlets stout, densely rusty-tomentose as well as petioles, underside of l. and inflorescence. L. elliptic-lanceolate, blade 4–11, pet. ⅓–½ in. long, tert. n. parallel. ♂ heads often solitary, ⅓ in. diam. before opening, peduncles ¼–¾ in. Fr. elongate-ellipsoid, ½ in. long, usually 2 or 3 from one head, seated on the spreading more or less lobed soft-tomentose pedicelled perianth. 23. **L. nuculanea**, Kurz. Tenasserim. Siam. Branchlets, petioles and underside of l. finely tomentose, l. coriaceous, obovate-elliptic, blade 5–7, pet ¼ in. Fr. ¾ in. long, the lower half included in the thickly coriaceous cup-shaped perianth.

24. **L. coriacea**, Heyne. Courtallum. Travancore, common in secondary forest, ascending to 3,000 ft. A small tree, branchlets, petioles and underside of l. more or less harshly pubescent, l. coriaceous, blade 5–7, pet. ⅓ in. loug. ♂ fl.-heads subsessile,

⅛ in. diam. before opening, crowded in compact axillary clusters, lower part of fr. enclosed in the cup-shaped perianth.

β. L. glabrous beneath or nearly so.

25. **L. salicifolia,** Roxb.—Syn. *Tetranthera lancifolia,* Kurz, and *T. glauca,* Wall. Subhimalayan tract (often associated with Sal on damp ground) and outer ranges from Nepal eastwards ascending to 6,000 ft. Oudh forests. Assam. Garo, Khasi and Naga hills. Bengal plains, Sundriban, Chittagong. Burma, Lower and Upper. A small tree, branchlets minutely hairy, l. chartaceous, usually glaucous beneath, very variable in shape, from elliptic- to linear-lanceolate, blade 3–10, pet. ¼–1 in. long, sec. n. 10–15 pair prominent beneath. ♂ heads 4–6-fld., on short peduncles, in axillary clusters. Fr. dark purple, narrowly elliptic, ⅜ in. long, seated on the funnel- or club-shaped perianth, which is narrower than the fr. Resembles *L. lancifolia,* differs by alternate l. and the almost cylindrical fr. Closely allied: 26. **L. oblonga,** Wall. Nepal. Sikkim. Assam. Khasi hills. Quite glabrous, heads of ♂ fl. in pedunculate corymbs, fr. ⅜ in. long.

27. **L. læta,** Wall. Subhimalayan tract from Sikkim eastwards, ascending to 2,000 ft. Assam. Khasi hills. A shrub or middle-sized tree, youngest shoots, petioles and midrib sometimes hairy, l. usually entirely glabrous. L. coriaceous, glaucous beneath, blade 6–14, pet. ½–1 in., sec. n. 6–9 pair, veins finely reticulate beneath. ♂ heads ¼ in. diam. before opening, fascicled on a short thick peduncle, partial peduncles slender, up to 1 in. long. Fr. black 1 in. diam., seated on the large fleshy salver-shaped perianth. 28. **L. Thomsonii,** Meissn. Silhet. A large tree, l. firmly coriaceous, elliptic-oblong, blade 6–8, pet. stout ½–1 in. long, tertiary n. and veins obscure. Unripe fr. globose, in lateral corymbs, lower half included in the cup-shaped perianth, on thick spreading pedicels. 29. **L. chartacea,** Wall. (*Tetranthera*). Nepal. Sikkim, 5–6,000 ft. L. thinly coriaceous, blade 3–6, pet. slender, ½ in. long, sec. n. slender, 6–10 pair, reticulate veins raised and prominent beneath. Fr. ⅜ in. long, ellipsoid, obtuse, base immersed in the cup-shaped perianth. 30. **L. Meissneri,** Hook. f. Khasi and Naga hills. L. thinly coriaceous, lanceolate, obtusely caudate-acuminate, blade 4–6, pet. ¼–½ in. long, sec. n. slender, 10–15 pair. ♂ heads solitary, subsessile or on short stout peduncles, bracts fringed with long brown silky hairs.

31. **L. myristicæfolia,** Wall. (*Tetranthera*).—Syn. *Lepidadenia Griffithii,* Wight Ic. t. 1846. Pegu, above Rangoon (Kurz), Meplay Forest, Thaungyin (D. B. March 1862). Malay Peninsula. A small tree, perfectly glabrous, l. coriaceous, pale beneath, lanceolate or oblanceolate, blade 4–8, narrowed into pet. ⅓–1 in. long, sec. n. slender, reticulate veins obscure. ♂ fl. heads ⅛ in. diam. before opening, glabrous, numerous, on peduncles up to ⅜ in. long, in dense axillary fascicles, stamens 12, in pairs, opposite to the perianth-segments, the 6 inner biglandular at base, filaments glabrous. Fr. globose ⅓ in. diam., half immersed in the cupular fleshy perianth, pedicels up to ⅓ in. long. 32. **L. longipes,** Meissn. (*Cylicodaphne*). Mergui. Closely allied to 31, of which Kurz makes it a variety. Fruiting perianth larger, pedicel 1½ in. long. 33. **L. leiantha,** Kurz (*Tetranthera*). Andamans. A middle-sized entirely glabrous tree, l. coriaceous, broadly elliptic, blade 5–7, pet. 1–1½ in. ♂ fl. heads before opening ⅛ in. diam. on slender peduncles ⅓ in. long. 34. **L. Helferi,** Hook. f. Tenasserim (or Andamans). L. glabrous, coriaceous, ovate-lanceolate, finely acuminate, blade 3–4, pet. slender ⅙–⅓ in. long. 35. **L. albicans,** Kurz (*Tetranthera*). Eastern slopes of the Pegu Yoma, along streams (Kurz). Upper Thaungyin, east side of the Doyukyi pass in evergreen forest (D. B. March 1862). A shrub or small tree, l. glabrous, thinly coriaceous, lanceolate- or oblanceolate-oblong, blade 6–10, narrowed into pet. ½ in. long, sec. n. slender, 6–8 pair, veins raised, conspicuously reticulate on both surfaces. ♂ heads grey-pubescent, ⅛ in. diam. before opening, in fascicles, sessile or on short stout peduncles, partial peduncles up to ⅓ in. long. Fr. fleshy, aromatic, seated on the large fleshy rugose cup-shaped perianth.

36. **L. angustifolia,** Wall. (*Tetranthera*). Assam (Sibsagar, D. B. March 1879), Silhet. Cachar. Chittagong, in rocky streambeds. Young shoots and underside of young l. finely pubescent, l. narrowly linear-lanceolate, blade 4–8, pet. ¼ in., sec. n. slender, numerous. ♂ fl. heads ⅛ in. diam. on slender peduncles ¼ in. long, in axillary fascicles.

(*b*) Fl. heads in axillary racemes.

a. Eastern species.

37. **L. nitida,** Roxb. (*Tetranthera*). Bhutan. Silhet. Assam, Nambar forest (D. B. March 1879). Pegu, Hlaing forests. Singbhum, in deep valleys, not common. A middle-sized, sometimes a large tree, branchlets stout, shining, angular. L. dark green, shining, rigidly coriaceous, oblanceolate, mostly obtuse, blade 8–12, narrowed into stout pet. ⅜–1 in. long, sec. n. faint. Fl.-heads in axillary racemes, ♂ 2–4, ♀ 1–2 in. long, ♂ heads ⅙–⅕ in. diam. before opening, partial peduncles slender, ⅛ in. long. Fr. purple when ripe, ellipsoid, ½ in. long, while unripe entirely enclosed in the indistinctly lobed perianth. 38. **L. Panamonja,** Ham. (*Tetranthera*). Assam. Chittagong. Tenas-

serim. Malay Penins. A large tree, young shoots minutely puberulous. L. glabrous, thinly coriaceous, elliptic-oblong, blade 6–8, pet. ⅛–1 in. ♂ racemes slender, drooping, 5–7 in. long.

β. Western species.

39. **L. Wightiana,** Hook. f.—Syn. *Cylicodaphne Wightiana*, Nees; Wight Ic. t. 1833; *Tetranthera Wightiana*, Wall.; Bedd. Fl. Sylv. t. 293. Vern. *Kenju*, Nilg.; *Hammadi*, Kan.

FIG. 180. Litsæa Wightiana. Hook. f.

A large tree, branchlets, petioles, underside of l. and inflorescence clothed with dense rusty-tomentum. L. coriaceous, elliptic or elliptic-lanceolate, blade 3–9, pet. ¼–½ in., sec. n. 8–15 pair impressed above, prominent beneath. ♂ heads ¼ in. diam. before opening, racemes 1–4 in. long, perianth tomentose, stamens 12, filaments hairy. Fr. ⅔ in. long, base enclosed in the cup-shaped, more or less lobed, perianth.

Western Ghats in evergreen forest, from North Kanara southwards. Fl. July–Nov. 40. **L. Beddomei,** Hook. f. Tinnevelli hills. L. silvery glaucous beneath, narrow lanceolate, blade 2–3, pet. ¼ in. 41. **L. Stocksii,** Hook. f. Western Ghats from Mahabaleshwar southwards. A moderate-sized tree, glabrous, except the brown velvety inflorescence, and very minute hairs occasionally on the underside of l. L. coriaceous, glaucous beneath, elliptic-oblong or oblanceolate, blade 4–7, pet. ½–1 in. ♂ heads ¼–⅓ in. diam. before opening, racemes stout 1–3 in. long, perianth grey silky. Nearly allied to 39. 42. **L. glabrata,** Wall. (*Tetranthera*). Dindigal. Travancore. A small or middle-sized tree, youngest shoots minutely silky. L. glabrous, elongate-elliptic, blade 5–7, pet. ½ in., sec. n. faint. ♂ racemes 3–5 in. long.

43. **L. oleoides,** Meissn. Nilgiris. Youngest shoots and racemes finely grey-silky, otherwise quite glabrous, branchlets stout. L. usually opposite or nearly so, rigidly coriaceous, elongate-elliptic, blade 3–5, pet. stout, ½ in., sec. n. faint, midrib prominent beneath. ♂ heads ⅛ in. diam., racemes erect, 2 in. long. Fr. globose, seated on the broad turbinate perianth-tube.

III. L. persistent, more or less triplinerved. Fl.-heads in sessile clusters. Perianth turbinate, segments usually 4, deciduous. Stamens usually 6, the 2 inner biglandular. Perianth-tube not enlarged in fr. In Engler u. Prantl, iii. 2. 119, the species of this section are classed under a separate genus: *Tetradenia*, Nees.

44. **L. zeylanica**, C. & Fr. Nees; Wight Ic. t. 1844; Bedd. Fl. Sylv. t. 294.—Syn. *L. oblonga*, Nees; Wight Ic. t. 1845; *L. foliosa*, Nees; *Laurus involucrata*, Vahl; Roxb. Cor. Pl. t. 187. Vern. *Kanvel*, *Chirchira*, Mar.; *Shembaga*, *Palai*, Tam.

A large tree, leaf-buds ovoid or ovoid-lanceolate, minutely silky. L. coriaceous, glabrous, elliptic or elliptic-lanceolate, acuminate, blade 3–5, pet. ½–1 in. long. Two distinct basal nerves extending to the middle of leaf, above these 2–3 pair of sec. n. Heads 4–5-fld. in sessile axillary fascicles, perianth silky 4–5-lobed, pedicels of ♀ fl. generally glabrous lengthening out in fr. to ½ in. Fr. ovoid or globose ½ in. long.

Bhutan. Khasi hills. Manipur. Chittagong. Martaban hills east of Toungoo (Kurz). Western Ghats from Mahabaleshwar southwards. Nilgiris. Anamalais. Rumpa hills, Northern Circars. Javadies and other hills in the Peninsula. Fl. Oct.–Jan. Malay Penins. and Archip. 45. **L. lanuginosa**, Nees. Outer Himalaya from the Jumna eastwards, usually 3–6,000 ft. In the Dehra Dūn at 1,900 ft. Khasi hills. A small tree, young shoots and young l. underneath clothed with long soft silky hairs, buds often 1 in. long. L. (when full grown) glabrous and glaucous underneath, blade 6–12, pet. ½–1 in. Heads in dense silky clusters 1 in. across, fr. oblong ½ in. long, 46. **L. Clarkei**, Prain, Bengal Plants 903. Chittagong. A small tree, buds finely silky, branchlets and l. glabrous, l. rigidly coriaceous, elliptic, caudate-acuminate, triplinerved, the 2 suprabasal n. extending to near the apex of l., raised finely reticulate veins prominent on both surfaces, ♂ heads in short axillary racemes, common peduncle with small imbricating bracts. Fl. silky, 6 in each head. 47. **L. umbrosa**, Nees.—Syn. *L. consimilis*, Nees; Collett Simla Fl. 434 Fig. 139. Vern. *Sharūr*, Jauns.; *Narik*, Rupin; *Puteli*, Nep. Himalaya, from the Chenab eastwards, 4–9,000 ft. also in some of the inner valleys (Nogli and Rupin. Serahn in the Sutlej valley). Assam. Khasi hills. A moderate-sized tree, bark dark brown, young shoots minutely silky. L. glabrous, thinly coriaceous, underside with a white bloom, lanceolate, long acuminate, blade 3–6, pet. ½ in., sec. n. 3–5 pair, the lowest pair from near the base often extending to the middle of l., so that the l. appear triplinerved. Fl.-heads yellowish-white, pedicels silky, those of the ♀ lengthen out to ⅜ in. Fr. nearly globose ⅓ in. diam. 44 and 47 are united in my old F. Fl. The N. West Himalayan tree is different from that of the eastern districts and the Peninsula, but there are intermediate forms, and it is not impossible that further study of the tree on the spot (not from Herbarium specimens) may lead to the union of the 2 species. 48. **L. Mannii**, King. Khasi hills. L. triplinerved, minutely impressed punctate on both surfaces, lanceolate, blade 2–3, pet. slender, ¼ in., sec. n. obscure.

10. LINDERA, Thunb.; Fl. Brit. Ind. v. 182.

Characters of *Litsæa* but fl. in each head usually numerous (1 in *L. caudata*), pedicels of ♂ fl. longer and anthers usually 2-celled.

A. Leaves persistent, penninerved, ♂ flower-heads on peduncles ¼ in. long and longer.

1. **L. assamica**, Kurz F. Fl. ii. 308.

A large tree, branchlets and l. beneath rusty pubescent. Leaves lanceolate, blade 4–7, pet. ½ in. long, midrib and 6–10 pairs of sec. n. prominent beneath, as well as intermediate and transverse veins. Fl.-heads on peduncles ⅓ in. long, solitary, fascicled or in short racemes, involucral bracts 4, veined, glabrous outside. Fl. 10–15 in each head, on silky pedicels ⅙–⅛ in. long, perianth-segments hyaline, ciliate, filaments silky. Fr. nearly globose, ⅓–¼ in. long, up to 6 from each fl.-head on peduncles ½–1 in. long, hence forming pedunculate umbels.

Sikkim 6–8,000 ft. Bhutan. Assam. Nattaung, Martaban (Kurz). A tree found by Montague Hill in dry hill forests east of Bhamo at 5,000 ft., has youngest shoots silky but branchlets and l. entirely glabrous, l. thinly coriaceous, shining above, opaque beneath, sec. n. 5–7 pair. otherwise same as 1. 2. **L. Meissneri**, King. Mikir hills, Assam. L. chartaceous, quite glabrous, fl. 9 in each head, may possibly prove to be the tree found by Mont. Hill mentioned under 1.

3. **L. (?) aromatica**, Brandis in Hook. Ic. Pl. t. 2784. *Karawe*, Burm.; *Le-u*, Karen. Hills between Thaungyin and Haundraw above 4,000 ft. (D. B. April 1859). Mountains east of Toungoo, 2,000 ft. (D. B. Febr. 1880). A glabrous

shrub, l. scattered, thinly coriaceous, blade 2–5, pet. slender, ⅜ in. long, sec. n. arching, slender 6–8 pair, anastomosing under the margin. ♂ fl.-heads white, ⅛ in. diam. before opening, on slender glabrous peduncles ½ in. long, solitary or in short axillary racemes. Involucre of 4 bracts, 3–5-nerved, minutely hairy at the base, otherwise glabrous, fl. ⅛ in. long, 4–5 in each head, shortly pedicelled, pernaith-segments 6, hairy, hyaline, obovate, stamens 9, the 3 inner biglandular, filaments hairy, anthers mostly 4-, sometimes 2-celled. Fr. globose, seated on the thick pedicel ⅙ in. long, pericarp fleshy, very aromatic, edible. The fr. is sold. Closely allied to this remarkable shrub are specimens collected in Yunnan, ♂ by Hancock 244, 5,000 ft., fl. yellowish-green, by Henry 10439, 6,000 ft., 11395, 11395A, 5,000 ft., fl. white, single fl. ⅛ in. long, per.-segments and filaments glabrous, anthers all 4-celled, and in Tonkin ♀ by Balansa, "a shrub wild and cultivated for its aromatic fruit." Species 1–3 ought to be placed in a separate genus, together with *Lindera citriodora*, Hemsley, an exceedingly fragrant deciduous shrub of Japan, Formosa and China, with 4-celled anthers.

4. **L. latifolia,** Hook. f. Khasi hills. A small tree, branchlets, petioles and underside of l. along nerves rusty- or tawny-tomentose. L. membranous, elliptic, blade 5–9, pet. ⅜ in. long, sec. n. 6–10 pair, impressed above, prominent beneath. ♂ heads tomentose, ⅜ in. diam. before opening, in axillary fascicles, peduncles ¼ in., fl. 10–12. Fr. globose, ¼ in. diam., up to 8 from one fl. on pedicels ⅓ in. long, in pedunculate umbels.

B. Leaves persistent, penninerved, ♂ flower-heads sessile or nearly sessile.

5. **L. bifaria,** Benth.—Syn. *Daphnidium bifarium*, Nees; Brandis F. Fl. 383. Himalaya, from Kumaon eastwards. Assam. Khasi hills, Manipur, China. A shrub or small tree, branchlets, underside of l. and inflorescence brown-tomentose. L. coriaceous, blade 1½–5 in., pet. ¼ in. long. Fl.-heads sessile in compact axillary clusters, fl. in each head 6–10, hairy, on hairy pedicels up to ¼ in. long. Fr. globose, ¼ in. diam., seated on the small shallow cup-shaped perianth-tube. 6. **L. Laureola,** Coll. et Hemsl. in Journ. Linn. Soc. xxviii. 119. Shan hills, Upper Burma, at 4,000 ft. Similar to 5, but glabrous, excepting the silky pedicels. 7. **L. reticulata,** Benth. Assam. Silhet. Rusty-tomentose, l. obovate to broadly oblanceolate, blade 6–9, pet. ⅜ in. long. Heads 4–9-fld., fr. ellipsoid, ½ in. long. 8. **L. venosa,** Benth. Bhutan A moderate-sized tree, nearly leafless in winter. Glabrous, branchlets stout, l. approximate towards the ends of branches, chartaceous, elliptic-lanceolate, blade 6–10, narrowed into slender pet. ⅜–1 in. long. Heads on short peduncles, ⅓ in. diam. before opening, 6–10 fl. in each head.

C. L. persistent with 3 (sometimes 5) basal nerves.

9. **L. caudata,** Benth.—Syn. *Daphnidium caudatum*, Nees. Khasi and Naga hills. Hills south-east of Toungoo at 4,000 ft. (D. B. 1859 and 1880). A small tree, wood reported to be very durable. Young shoots silky, branchlets and young l. thinly rusty pubescent, l. chartaceous, ovate-lanceolate, caudate-acuminate, 3 basal nerves extending to the apex of l. Fl.-heads $\frac{1}{12}$ in. diam. before opening, sessile on dense very short axillary spikes. Involucral bracts 2, one fl. in each head, perianth and filaments pilose. Fr. globose ⅛ in. diam. seated on the 6-cleft perianth. 10. **L. pulcherrima,** Benth.—Syn. *Daphnidium pulcherrimum*, Nees; Brandis F. Fl. 383. Himalaya from Kumaon eastwards, 4-9,000 ft. Khasi hills. Manipur. Hills east of Toungoo (Kurz). A large tree, terminal buds silky, branchlets with a few minute hairs. L. glabrous, chartaceous, pale or glaucous beneath, ovate-lanceolate, long caudate-acuminate, blade 2–5, pet. slender, ¼–½ in. Heads sessile, solitary or few together, 5–6-fld., involucral bracts 4–6, deciduous, pedicels hairy, ⅛–¼ in. long. Fr. ellipsoid, ⅓ in. long, perianth almost entirely deciduous. 11. **L. melastomacea,** Benth. Khasi hills. Bhutan. A shrub or small tree similar to 10, but perfectly glabrous, l. coriaceous, acute or shortly acuminate.

D. L. deciduous, basal nerves 3–7, fl. appearing before the l.

12. **L. heterophylla** Meissn. Sikkim, 8–11,000 ft. Bhutan. A small tree, branchlets, petioles and underside of l. rusty-tomentose. L. coriaceous when full grown, broadly ovate, base rounded or cordate, blade 3–5, pet. ½ in. long, basal nerves 5–7, tert. n. parallel. Fl. when leafless, heads solitary, nearly sessile, involucral bracts 3–5, very coriaceous, each fl. in the axil of a hairy bracteole, pedicels short villous. Fruiting pedicels villous, ½–⅜ in. long. 13. **L. Neesiana,** Benth. Nepal. Sikkim, 6–9,000 ft. Mishmi hills. Martaban and Upper Tenasserim, 4–5,000 ft. (Kurz). A middle-sized very aromatic tree, quite glabrous, excepting the hairy pedicels. L. membranous, ovate or lanceolate, blade 2–5, pet. slender ¼–1 in. long, basal nerves 3, the lateral short, not reaching the middle of l. Fl.-heads ⅛ in. diam. before opening, on peduncles ⅛–½ in. long, solitary or fascicled, 5–7-fl. in each head. Fr. globose ⅙ in. diam. seated on the 6-lobed unaltered perianth.

Imperfectly known: 14. **L. bootanica,** Meissn. Bhutan. 15. **L. Griffithii,** Meissn. Bhutan. 16. **L. (?) sikkimensis,** Meissn. Sikkim 11–12,000 ft. 17. **Daphniphyllum argenteum,** Kurz. Thaukyeghat forest, Martaban.

ORDER XCII. HERNANDIACEÆ. Engler u. Prantl, iii. 2. 126.

In Gen. Plant. i. 689 *Illigera* and *Gyrocarpus* are included under *Combretaceæ*, while *Hernandia* stands under *Laurineæ*.

Climbing shrubs or large trees, l. alternate, stipules 0, fl. bisexual or monœcious. Ovary inferior, ovule 1 pendulous. Perianth of 4 to 10 segments, stamens 3–5, anther-cells 2, opening by valves. Fr. often winged, seed exalbuminous.

A. L. trifoliolate, fr. with 2 broad lateral wings. . . . 1. ILLIGERA.
B. L. peltate, fr. ovoid, not winged . . . . HERNANDIA (p. 542).
C. L. broadly ovate, often lobed, fr. with 2 long wings at the apex . . . . 2. GYROCARPUS.

1. ILLIGERA, Blume ; Fl. Brit. Ind. ii. 460.

Climbers, l. of 3 (in the African sp. 5) petiolulate leaflets. Fl. bisexual, in lax pedunculate compound cymes, each fl. supported by 1–3 bracteoles, inflorescence and perianth outside clothed with 2-celled glandular hairs. Perianth-segments in two circles of 5 each, stamens 5, opposite to those of the outer circle, filaments with 2 oblong hooded scales at the base, stigma orbicular, broad, undulate. Fr. broadly 2-winged, sometimes with 1 or 2 additional narrower wings. Cotyledons plano-convex. Species 1 in tropical Africa, 7 in India and the Malay Archip.

1. **I. appendiculata**, Blume; Kurz F. Fl. i. 479; King in Journ. As. Soc. Beng. vol. 66, ii. 1898. 343.—Syn. *I. Coryzadenia*, Meissn.; Fl. Brit. Ind. ii. 460. Assam. Khasi hills. Lower Burma. Andamans. Malay Archipelago. A powerful climber, young branches tawny-pubescent soon becoming glabrous, petioles and peduncles often twisted round supports. L. alternate, trifoliolate, leaflets elliptic or elliptic-lanceolate, pubescent beneath along nerves, blade 3–5, common petiole 3–4 in. long, sec. n. 3–4 pair. Fl. white, sepals ⅛ in. long. Fr. 2-winged, including the wings up to 3 in. broad. *I. Kurzii*, C. B. Clarke, Fl. Brit. Ind. ii. 460 (species) is a variety with glabrous more coriaceous l. 2. **I. Khasiana**, C. B. Clarke, Khasi hills, l. glabrous, with tufts of yellowish hairs in the nerve axils beneath, sepals ¼ in. long, the outer dull lurid purple, the inner whitish, staminodes deeply emarginate. 3. **I. villosa**, Clarke in Journ. Linn. Soc. xxv. 22, tab. ix. Kohima, 5,000 ft. Branchlets fulvous-villous, fr. 2–4-winged.

Hernandia peltata, Meissn.; Bedd. Fl. Sylv. t. 300.—Syn. *H. Sonora*, Linn.; Wight Ic. t. 1855. Beach forests on the coast of the Andamans. Coast of Ceylon, the Malay Penins. and Archip., the Pacific Islands, North Australia, Madagascar and East Africa. A large evergreen tree, wood light, soft, grey. L. glabrous, ovate, peltate, blade 4–8, pet. as long as blade, 5–7 basal nerves. Fl. white, in involucrate heads of 3 fl., at the ends of the ramifications of large axillary finely tomentose panicles; the central fl. ♀ supported at the base by a cupular involucel, which becomes greatly enlarged and thickened in fr., perianth-segments 8; the 2 lateral fl. ♂, perianth-segments 6, stamens 3, biglandular, opposite to the segments of the outer circle. Fr. ovoid, nearly 1 in. long, cotyledons fleshy, much lobed.

2. GYROCARPUS, Jacq. ; Fl. Brit. Ind. ii. 461.

G. americanus, Jacq. (the only species); King in Journ. As. Soc. Beng. 66. 344.—Syn. *G. Jacquini*, Roxb. Cor. Pl. t. 1; Bedd. Fl. Sylv. t. 196. Vern. *Zaitūn*, Hind.; *Poliki*, *Thanaku*, Tel.; *Pinlè-thitkauk*, Burm.

A deciduous tree, bark whitish, wood light, soft, greyish-white, young shoots and often the underside of l. pubescent. L. crowded at the ends of thick branchlets marked with the scars of fallen l. L. of adult trees entire, broadly ovate, acuminate, blade 4–5, pet. 1–4 in. long, those of young plants larger, pubescent and often deeply lobed. Fl. small, cream coloured or yellow, in large terminal dense compound hairy cymes without bracts, a few bisexual, scattered among a mass of male fl. ♂ Perianth of 4–7 sepals, stamens generally 4, alternating with fleshy club-shaped staminodes, anthers opening by 2 lateral valves. ☿ Perianth of 4 unequal segments, stigma sessile. Fr. ovoid, velvety, ⅓ in. long, terminated by two wing-like oblanceolate coriaceous perianth-segments 2–3 in. long. Cotyledons convolute, stalked in the seed.

Sea coast and on the hills some distance inland in both Peninsulas; wood used for making catamarans, toys and boxes. Fl. R. S. Throughout the tropics.

ORDER XCIII. PROTEACEÆ. Gen. Pl. iii. 165.

Trees or shrubs, rarely herbs, l. hard, mostly alternate, stipules 0. Fl. bisexual, perianth inferior, consisting of 4 segments, in bud valvately cohering into a cylindrical tube, gibbous at the base, with free recurved tips. Stamens 4, filaments short, inserted on the perianth-segments, anthers erect, 2-celled, introrse. Ovary 1-celled, often oblique. Seeds few, cotyledons often unequal, albumen 0.

The medull. rays as a rule are very broad and prominent, both on the transverse and on the radial section; the vessels are scattered in narrow bands of parenchymatic tissue which run at right angles to the rays, alternating with bands of hard tissue consisting of wood-fibres.

Fr. a hard indehiscent nut . . . . 1. HELICIA.
Fr. a dehiscent follicle . . . . GREVILLEA (p. 544).

1. HELICIA, Lour.; Fl. Brit. Ind. v. 189.

Trees or shrubs, l. entire or toothed, in some species pinnatifid. Fl. bracteolate, in pairs on short peduncles, arranged in axillary racemes. Perianth regular, segments at length revolute. Anthers oblong, 4 hypogynous scales, free or confluent into a cup-shaped or annular disk. Ovary sessile, ovules 2, style slender, stigma terminal. Fr. a hard globose nut, seed one. Species 26, tropical Asia, Japan, Australia.

A. Racemes glabrous.

(*a*) L. petiolate.

1. **H. erratica,** Hook f.—Syn. *H. cochinchinensis*, Kurz F. Fl. ii. 189. Vern. *Daukyat kyi*, Burm. Sikkim, 2–6,000 ft. Khasi hills. Hills of Upper Burma often associated with Oaks and Chestnuts. Tenasserim. A small or middle-sized evergreen tree, quite glabrous, l. elliptic-lanceolate or oblanceolate, entire or coarsely serrate, blade 4–9, narrowed into petiole ½–1 in. long. Fl. slender ¾ in. in racemes 6–9 in. long, filaments yellow, style whitish. Fr. obliquely globose, 1–1½ in. diam. 2. **H. nilagirica,** Bedd. Nilgiris. Similar to 1. 3. **H. terminalis,** Kurz. Kachin hills, Upper Burma. Tenasserim, 4,000 ft. Yunnan. L. entire, racemes narrow, fl. ¼ in. long.

(*b*) L. sessile or nearly so.

4. **H. robusta,** Wall.—Syn. *Rhopala robusta*, Roxb.; Wight Ic. t. 191. Assam. Khasi hills. Martaban and Tenasserim 2–4,000 ft. Vern. *Daukyat*, Burm. Malay Peninsula and Archip. A small tree, perfectly glabrous, branchlets stout, l. on very short stout petioles or sessile, oblong-lanceolate, coarsely serrate, 8–12 in. long, sec. n. 8–12 pair, prominent beneath. Racemes up to 12 in. long, fr. apiculate, 1 in. diam. 5. **H. travancorica,** Bedd. Fl. Sylv. t. 301 (called *H. robusta*). Tinnevelli and Travancore hills 4,000 ft., l. coriaceous sessile, 6 in., racemes 3 in. long, fr. ¾ in. diam.

B. Rachis of the racemes rusty-tomentose.

6. **H. excelsa,** Blume.—Syn. *Rhopala excelsa*, Roxb.; Wight Ic. t. 190. Vern. *Daukyat*, Burm. Khasi hills. Chittagong. Andamans. Martaban. Tenasserim. Upper Burma, hills east of Bhamo 6,500 ft. Malay Penins. Cambodia. A moderate-sized tree, l. coriaceous, glabrous, usually oblanceolate, entire or deeply serrate, blade 4–10, narrowed into pet. ½–1½ in. long. Racemes about as long as l., clothed with deciduous rusty-tomentum, fl. ¼–⅓ in. long, fr. smooth, nearly globose, ½–¾ in. diam. 7. **H. pyrrhobotrya,** Kurz. Hills between Sitang and Salween rivers, 4,000 ft. Branchlets stout, l. oblanceolate, sharply serrate, blade 10–12, narrowed into pet. 1 in. long, racemes densely rusty villous 12 in. long, rachis stout, fl. 1–1¼ in. long.

8. A species with entire and pinnatifid l. 10–30 in. long, segments linear-lanceolate, the larger ones 12 by 2 in. from a pollard 10 ft. high, in Ponzo and Wabo forest Thabyetha, Shwebo district, Upper Burma (leaves only. Smales Feb. 1902) somewhat resembles *H. incisa*, Koorders et Valeton, of Java, but is quite different.

Grevillea robusta, A Cunningham. *Silky Oak.* Indigenous in Queensland and New South Wales, cultivated in Dehra Dūn, the Nilgiris and elsewhere. A large tree, young shoots rusty-tomentose. L. pinnate, pinnæ 4–12 in. long, deeply pinnatifid, so that the l. are almost bipinnate, sometimes tripinnate. Fl. orange coloured, in one-sided racemes 3–4 in. long fascicled on short leafless branchlets, pedicels slender, ½ in. long. Perianth-segments recurved to one side. Fr. an oblique coriaceous follicle, ⅝–¾ in. long, dehiscing on 1 side, seeds 1 or 2.

ORDER XCIV. THYMELÆACEÆ. Gen. Pl. iii. 186.

Shrubs or trees, rarely herbs, bast tough. L. alternate or opposite, simple, quite entire. Fl. usually bisexual, perianth tubular or campanulate, lobes 4 or 5, imbricate in bud. A few genera have scales alternating with the lobes, regarded as petals by some Botanists, while the lower portion of the perianth is regarded as a hollow receptacle or torus, on the edge of which are inserted sepals and, in some cases, petals (Gilg in Engler u. Prantl, iii. 6A 216 and Engler's Jahrbücher xviii, 1894 pp. 491, 492). Stamens inserted on the inside of the perianth, usually twice as many as lobes, those of the outer (upper) series opposite to the lobes. Disk annular, cupular or of distinct scales, sometimes wanting. Ovary superior, usually 1-celled, ovules 1 in each cell, pendulous from near the apex. Fr. usually indehiscent, seed one, radicle superior.

Bast fibres are abundant in the bark, and the wood-fibres have bordered pits. An interior phloëm, often accompanied by thick-walled bast-fibres, is found on the outside of the pith.

A. Lobes of Perianth 4, stamens 8.

- L. alternate, stigma nearly sessile . . . . 1. DAPHNE.
- L. alternate, style long, stigma linear . . . EDGEWORTHIA (p. 545).
- L. as a rule opposite, style short, stigma large globose . . . . 2. WIKSTRŒMIA

B. Lobes of Perianth 5.

- L. mostly opposite, fl. in dense globose heads . LASIOSIPHON (p. 545).
- L. opposite or nearly so, fl. in compound cymes . 3. LINOSTOMA.
- L. alternate, fl. umbellate . . . . . . 4. AQUILARIA.

1. DAPHNE, Linn.; Fl. Brit. Ind. v. 193.

Shrubs, usually evergreen, l. alternate, mostly coriaceous. Fl. generally in terminal heads, perianth coloured, segments 4 nearly equal, spreading. Anthers 8 on short filaments. Stigma capitate, subsessile. Fr. coriaceous or fleshy, mostly enclosed until near maturity in the inflated perianth-tube (receptacle). Testa thick, crustaceous. Species 80, Europe, N. Africa, temperate Asia, Himalaya.

A. Fl. heads sessile, bracts 0 or early deciduous.

1. **D. oleoides**, Schreber.—Syn. *D. mucronata*, Royle Ill. t. 81, f. 2.; *Pipal*, Bal.; *Jiko*, *Agru*, Bash. Baluchistan. Kuram valley to 11,000 ft. Himalaya as far east as the Junína, 3–9,000 ft., also in the inner arid valleys. Mediterranean region. Western Asia. Afghanistan. A tall shrub, young shoots pubescent. L. subsessile, lanceolate or linear-lanceolate, midrib prominent, terminating in a short sharp mucro. Fl. white with a pink tinge, slightly scented, in terminal heads of 3–9 fl. Perianth-tube ⅓ in. long, outside densely grey-tomentose, inside glabrous. Fr. orange or scarlet, ¼–⅓ in. long.

2. **D. cannabina**, Wall.; Collett Simla Flora 435, fig. 140.—Syn. *D. papyracea*, Wall. Vern. *Satbaru*, Bash.; *Satpura*, N. W. Him.; *Kaghuti*, Nep.

A tall shrub, branches often bi- and tri-furcate, youngest shoots slightly pubescent. L. glabrous, lanceolate, blade 3–5, narrowed into marginate petiole ¼ in. long. Fl. sweet-scented, white or lilac, in terminal heads of 6–12, surrounded by numerous oblong or lanceolate bracts. Perianth-tube ½ in. long, pubescent outside. Fr. ovoid, succulent, acrid, ¼–½ in. long, orange or red.

Himalaya, from Chamba eastwards, 5–10,000 ft. Khasi hills. Manipùr. Hills east of Bhamo 7,000 ft. A large tree (Montague Hill). Fl. Oct.–Feb. Paper is made of the inner fibrous bark. *D. cannabina* is possibly a local variety of *D. odora*, Thunb., of China and Japan.

B. Fl. heads pedunculate, in bud enclosed in concave bracts.

3. **D. involucrata,** Wall. Sikkim, outer hills to 6,000 ft. Khasi hills. Patkoi range. Hills of Martaban and Tenasserim 4–6,000 ft. A tall shrub, attaining 20 ft., fl. heads on peduncles up to 1 in. long, before opening enclosed in 2 coloured concave bracts, fl. densely silky ⅓–⅝ in. long, white, limb pink, fr. black. 4. **D. pendula,** Smith. Java, Sumatra. Closely allied to 3, peduncles longer, slender, fl. smaller.

Edgeworthia Gardneri, Meissn. Nepal (common, *Aryili*, paper made of the inner bark). Sikkim, 3–7,000 ft. Assam. Manipúr. China. Japan. A large shrub, branches long, scrambling, l. lanceolate, pubescent beneath, blade 3-5, narrowed into pet. ⅓ in. long. Fl. golden-yellow, sweet-scented, densely crowded in pedunculate heads, perianth densely silky, ovary villous.

2. WIKSTRŒMIA, Endl.; Fl. Brit. Ind. v. 195.

Deciduous trees or shrubs, l. usually opposite. Perianth tubular, lobes 4, anthers 8, ovary villous, style short, stigma large, globose. Disk of 1–4 scales. Fr. dry or fleshy. Species 20, Eastern Asia, Australia, Pacific islands.

1. **W. canescens,** Meissn.—Syn. *W. virgata*, Meissn.; Bedd. Manual t. 25, f. 4.; Brandis F. Fl. 386. Vern. *Chamboi*, Jauns.; *Chamlia*, N.W. Him. Kuram valley, common. N. W. Himalaya, 5–9,000 ft. Khasi hills. Upper Burma. In Kumaon ropes and paper are made of the inner bark.—Ceylon, China. A small shrub, branches slender, branchlets, petioles, underside of l. and inflorescence silky, l. membranous, alternate and opposite, oblong-lanceolate, blade 1–3, pet. ⅛ in. Fl. yellow, in axillary and terminal peduncled few-fld. racemes or panicles. Perianth ¼–⅓ in. long, silky outside, disk scales linear. Fr. black, ¼ in. long, silky, pericarp thin. 2. **W. indica,** C. A. Mey. —Syn. *W. viridiflora*, Meissn. Chittagong. Shan hills, Upper Burma. Tenasserim. China, l. opposite, glabrous, thinly coriaceous, obovate-oblong 1-1½ in. long, sec. n. numerous slender, oblique. Fl. greenish-yellow, perianth glabrous. Fr. ¼ in. long, scarlet.

Lasiosiphon eriocephalus, Dcne.: Bedd. Man. t. 25, f. 2.—Syn. *Gnidia eriocephala*, Meissn.; Wight Ic. t. 1859; *G. sisparensis*, Gardn.; Wight Ic. t. 1860. Vern. *Ramita*, Mar. West side of the Peninsula and Western Ghats, from Mahabaleshwar southwards. Ceylon, paper made of the bark. A large shrub or small tree, l. subsessile, lanceolate-oblong, opposite or scattered, 2–3 in. long. Fl. thickly clothed with white or buff long silky villous hairs, in dense globose heads 1-2 in. diam., supported by silky involucral bracts shorter than fl. Perianth yellow ⅓–⅝ in. long, scales in its mouth, alternating with the lobes, variable in shape, oblong, obcordate or bifid. Fr. dry, included in the lower persistent half of the perianth (hollow receptacle).

3. LINOSTOMA, Wall.; Fl. Brit. Ind. v. 197.

Shrubs, erect or climbing, l. opposite or nearly so. Fl. bisexual, in compound cymes. Perianth-tube cylindric, lobes 5, spreading, 10 scales in the mouth above the stamens, free or connate in pairs. Stamens 10 in one row at the mouth of perianth, exserted, filaments much longer than anthers. Ovary 1-celled, style filiform. Albumen 0 or scanty. Species 3 Indian, 3 (*Lophostoma*, Meissn.) in Northern Brazil.

A. Erect shrubs, glabrous, sec. n. ∞, closely parallel.

1. **L. decandrum,** Wall.; Engler u. Prantl iii. 6A 232, fig. 82. Silhet. Chittagong, Tenasserim (Kurz). Evergreen, branches numerous dichotomous, l. ovate- or elliptic-lanceolate, long acuminate, blade 2–3, pet. ⅛ in. long. Fl. greenish-white, fragrant, fr. ½ in. long, at the base usually with the remains of the perianth which splits lengthwise. 2. **S. pauciflorum,** Griff. Hills east of Toungoo 3–4,000 ft., common in the forests of *Pinus Kasya*. Malay Penins. and Archip. L. elliptic to obovate, 1–1¼ in. long. Fr. enclosed in the persistent thin perianth-tube.

B. Climbing; branchlets, underside of l. and inflorescence rusty tomentose.

8. **L. scandens**, Kurz (including *L. siamense*, Kurz). Eng forests, Prome (Kurz). Shan hills 2,000 ft. Malay Peninsula. L. elliptic, blade 8–4, pet. ¼ in. long, sec. n. 15–25 pair, tertiary n. parallel. Fl. in large compound cymes, bracts conspicuous. Fr. ⅓–½ in. long, at the base with the remains of the split perianth.

4. AQUILARIA, Lamk.; Fl. Brit. Ind. v. 199.

Trees, l. alternate, Fl. in axillary or terminal umbels, bracts 0. Perianth campanulate, 10 densely woolly scales in the mouth, lobes 5, triangular. Stamens 10, disk 0. Ovary villous 2-celled. Capsule compressed, loculicidally 2-valved. Seeds ovoid, with a long tail-like appendage, albumen 0. Species 4, 1 in China, 1 in Cambodia.

1. **A. Agallocha**, Roxb. in Trans. Linn. Soc. xxi. 199, t. 21; Royle Ill. t. 86, f. 1. Vern. *Aggar*, Beng.; *Sasi*, Ass.; *Akyaw*, Burm. Assam. Silhet. Cachar. Hills east of Toungoo (Kurz). Mergui. A tall evergreen tree, young shoots silky. L. thinly coriaceous, shining, caudate-acuminate, sec. n. slender, with ∞ parallel intermediate nerves. Fl. white, in many-fld. sessile or shortly peduncled silky umbels, pedicels slender ¼ in. long. Perianth ¼ in. long, silky without, densely villous within. Fr. thinly velvety 1½–2 in. long, obovoid, thinly coriaceous. In the wood of the stem and larger branches are frequently found irregular masses of harder and dark coloured, highly scented wood (the Eagle wood of commerce) used as incense, commanding a high price. The bast, when prepared, resembles parchment and was used by the old kings of Assam to write upon. 2. **A. malaccensis**, Lamk. Tenasserim (?). Malay Peninsula and Archip. Similar to 1 but fl. smaller, lobes of perianth reflexed, $\frac{1}{10}$ in. long. Capsule glabrous obovate, 1¼ in. long, valves thick, woody. This also yields scented wood (*Garu*, Malay).

ORDER XCV. ELÆAGNACEÆ. Gen. Pl. iii. 203.

Shrubs or trees, often spinescent, with copious silvery or brown stellate scales, sometimes with stellate hairs. L. (in the Indian genera) alternate, quite entire, stipules 0. Fl. bisexual or polygamous. Ovary 1-celled, ovule 1. Fr. indehiscent, entirely enclosed within the lower part of the perianth, which is fleshy when the seed ripens. Embryo straight, axile, radicle inferior, albumen scanty or 0.

Fl. solitary or fascicled, perianth-limb campanulate, usually 4-fid. 1. ELÆAGNUS.
Fl. in bracteate spikes, perianth ♂ of 2 sepals, ♀ 2-fid. . . . 2. HIPPOPHAË.

1. ELÆAGNUS, Linn.; Fl. Brit. Ind. v. 201.

Fl. ♂ and bisexual, pedicellate, solitary or in axillary fascicles. Base of perianth (hollow receptacle) closely enveloping the ovary, limb 4- sometimes 6-lobed, deciduous. Stamens alternating with the perianth-lobes. Fr. a fleshy drupe. Species 12, northern hemisphere.

A. Endocarp hard, bony.

1. **E. hortensis**, M. Bieb.—Syn. *E. angustifolia*, Linn.; *E. orientalis*, Linn. (in part). Vern. *Sanzi*, Bal.; *Sinjit*, *Sanjit*, Pushtu; *Sirsing*, Tibet.

A middle-sized deciduous tree, the annual rings in the wood marked by a broad band of vessels, branchlets and l. silvery-grey, branches glabrous, shining, reddish-brown. L. lanceolate, often ovate on young trees and vigorous shoots, blade 1–3, pet. ¼ in. long, underside covered entirely by circular scales composed of radiating cells, upperside dull greyish-green, scales scattered. Fl. fragrant, usually bisexual, 1–3 together, often appearing before the l., the flowering branchlets having the appearance of racemes. Perianth silvery outside, glabrous and yellow within, the upper free portion campanulate. Fr. ovoid-oblong, ¾ in. long, sometimes smaller and globose, red, sweet and mealy when ripe.

Indigenous in Macedonia and Greece, Western Central Asia and China. Cultivated in Baluchistan, Afghanistan and North West Himalaya, 7–10,000 ft., possibly wild in Chitral. Fl. April–July.

B. Endocarp ribbed, coriaceous, clothed inside with a dense felt of white hairs.

2. **E. latifolia**, Linn.; Wight Ic. t. 1856; Brandis F. Fl. t. 46; Bedd. Fl. Sylv. Manual t. xxv. fig. 1.—Syn. *E. arborea*, Roxb.; *E. conferta*, Roxb. Vern. *Ghiwāi*, *Nigali*, N. W. Him.; *Jarila*, Nep.; *Nurgi*, *Ambgul*, Mar.; *Mingu*, Burm.

An evergreen tall straggling or scandent shrub, or a small tree, branchlets, petioles and underside of l. densely clothed with ferrugineous or silvery circular, dentate and lobed scales. L. elliptic, acuminate, blade 3–5, pet. ¼–½ in. long. Fl. ♂ and ☿, scented, pedicellate in few- or many-fld. often pedunculate fascicles, perianth clothed outside with silvery or ferrugineous scales, in the fertile fl. much constricted above the ovary. Fr. 1–1⅓ in. ovoid-oblong, succulent, red or yellow when ripe, edible.

Subhimalayan tract and outer ranges, from the Jumna eastwards ascending to 8,000 ft. Khasi hills. Manipùr. Chittagong. Burma, Upper and Lower. Along the western Ghats from Mahabaleshwar southwards. Hills of the Deccan. Fl. at various times, chiefly March–Oct.—Ceylon, Malay Archip. China. A variety with larger l. 4–6 in. and fruit 1–2 in. long, cultivated by the Karens on the hills east of Toungoo and by the Shans at Fakial vill. beyond Makūm, Assam.—(*Mingu*, Burm.; *Maloh*, Shan), should be studied.

3. **E. umbellata**, Thunb.; Collett Simla Fl. 437, fig. 141.—Syn. *E. parvifolia*, Wall.; Royle Ill. t. 81. f. 1. Vern. *Chindar*, Pangi; *Ginroi*, *Gehain*, Jauns.; *Ril*, Bash. Kuram valley, wild and cultivated. Himalaya 3–10,000 ft, Manipùr.—China, Japan. A deciduous shrub, annual rings distinct, branchlets and underside of l. densely clothed with shining silvery scales, upperside bright green with scattered stellate hairs. L. elliptic-lanceolate, blade 1–3, pet. ¼ in. long. Fl. white, exquisitely scented, axillary often fasciculate, on the current year's branchlets, appearing with or after the leaves. Upper free portion of perianth slender, tubular. Fr. ovoid or globose, ¼ in. long, succulent.

C. Endocarp crustaceous, not ribbed, glabrous within.

4. **E. pyriformis**, Hook. f. Mishmi hills. Fr. shortly pedicelled, in lateral clusters, pyriform, narrowed at both ends, ½–⅓ in. long.

2. HIPPOPHAË, Linn.; Fl. Brit. Ind. v. 202.

Deciduous, diœcious shrubs or small trees, usually spinescent. Fl. before the leaves, ♂ in the axils of deciduous bracts, perianth of two opposite sepals, stamens 4; ♀ in the axils of young leaves, perianth tightly enclosing the ovary, minutely bifid at mouth, fleshy in the mature fruit. Species 2.

1. **H. rhamnoides**, Linn. Vern. *Suak*, Pangi. Inner arid tract of the N. W. Himalaya, chiefly in moist gravelly streambeds, gregarious, forming dense thickets, continuous for miles. Lahoul, Ladak, Piti, Upper Kunawar, Inner Kumaon. Tibet, 7–15,000 ft.—Afghanistan, Central Asia, Siberia, Caucasus. In Europe on the Carpathians, Alps and Apennines in shingly and gravelly valleys, descending along the rivers into the plains. Also on the sea coast of the Mediterranean, the Atlantic, the German Ocean and the Baltic. A large thorny shrub, sometimes a small tree, branchlets and underside of l. densely clothed with silvery or rust-coloured circular or irregularly indented scales. L. thinly coriaceous, ½–2 in. long, linear-lanceolate or oblanceolate, narrowed into short petiole, upper side glabrous and dull green, with a few scales while young. Fr. scarlet or orange. Seed dark brown, shining. 2. **H. salicifolia**, Don. Vern. *Sutz*, Kun.; *Chug*, Lahaul. Outer and Middle Himalaya, 5–10,000 ft. Branchlets, petiole and midrib beneath clothed with circular irregularly indented rust-coloured scales, l. membranous 2–3 in. long, linear-lanceolate, white velvety beneath with dense soft tomentum of short stellate hairs.

ORDER XCVI. LORANTHACEÆ. Gen. Pl. iii. 205.

Evergreen parasitic shrubs, living mostly on stems and branches of other shrubs or trees. L. entire, usually opposite, often coriaceous, sometimes wanting. Fl. regular 1- or 2-sexual, perianth simple or double. Stamens equal to and opposite the petals or perianth-lobes, usually inserted on them. Ovary inferior, 1-celled, ovule 1, adnate all round to the walls of the ovary, which thus on a section presents a homogeneous appearance. Fruit a berry or drupe, usually viscid, seed adnate to pericarp, albumen fleshy, embryo straight, radicle superior.

The species here described in reality are half parasites, taking up carbon dioxide through their green leaves and branchlets, but relying upon the foster plant, on which they grow, for mineral and nitrogenous substances. When the seeds of a *Loranthus* or *Viscum* germinate on the bark of a tree, the roots penetrate through the bark to the wood, where they spread and are gradually enclosed by the new layers of wood. The roots of the parasites thus embedded decay readily, and hence the wood of the foster tree becomes riddled and worthless. Some species of *Loranthus* also send out aerial roots, which twist round the branches of the foster plant.

Flowers bisexual, showy, petals 4–6, linear, usually more or less connate . . . . 1. LORANTHUS.
Flowers unisexual, inconspicuous.
  Anthers with many cells, dehiscing by numerous pores . 2. VISCUM.
  Anthers dehiscing by longitudinal slits, leaves flat . . GINALLOA (p. 552).
  Anthers globose, bursting transversly, l. reduced to minute scales . . . . 3. ARCEUTHOBIUM.

1. LORANTHUS, Linn.; Fl. Brit. Ind. v. 203.

L. opposite, in some sp. both alternate and opposite, in some alternate. Fl. as a rule supported by a small concave bract, appressed to calyx, bisexual, usually large, showy. Calyx adnate to ovary, and often produced beyond it, regarded by some Botanists as the enlarged end of the axis (Engler u. Prantl iii. i. 169), petals 4–6, free or more or less connate into a tubular corolla, tips often reflexed, stamens inserted on the petals. Species about 300, Tropical Asia, Africa and Australia.

Vern. names used indiscriminately for several species: *Bana*, *Banda*, *Pand*, Hind.; *Manda*, Beng.; *Vanda*, Mar.; *Banje*, *Banduka*, Kan.; *Bajinike*, Tel.; *Kyibaung*, Burm.

I. No bracteoles, no involucral bracts.

A. Entirely glabrous, petals free mostly 6.

1. **L. odoratus**, Wall. Nepal. Darjeeling (7,000 ft.). Chumbi valley. Khasi hills. Cachar. Manipùr. Shan hills, Upper Burma, 5,000 ft.—Syn. *L. Hemsleyanus*, King Journ. Linn. Soc. xxviii. 120. L. fleshy, mostly opposite, elliptic-lanceolate, blade 3–5, pet. $\frac{1}{3}$–$\frac{1}{2}$ in. long. Fl. $\frac{1}{3}$–$\frac{1}{2}$ in., sessile, on spikes 1–2 in. long, calyx produced beyond the ovary, truncate, petals 6, free, spathulate. 2. **L. heteranthus**, Wall.—Syn. *L. eleutheropetalus*, Kurz. Southern slopes of the Pegu Yoma.—Java, Borneo. L. opposite or nearly so, thickly coriaceous and veinless, blade 3–5, tapering into pet. $\frac{1}{3}$–$\frac{1}{2}$ in. long. Fl. $1\frac{1}{2}$ in. long, in racemes 3–4 in., pedicels $\frac{1}{3}$ in., calyx tubular $\frac{1}{4}$ in. long, limb truncate.

B. Petals more or less connate into a 4- or 5-lobed corolla. Fl. small, under 1 in., in racemes or spikes.

(*a*) Racemes or spikes many-fld., glabrous.

3. **L. Wallichianus**, Schultes. Wight Ic. t. 143. Western Ghats from the Konkan southwards. Entirely glabrous, l. elliptic, blade 3–4, pet. $\frac{1}{3}$ in. long. Fl. $\frac{1}{4}$ in., pale red, racemes 1–3 in. long. Calyx hardly produced beyond ovary, corolla deeply 4-cleft, buds cylindric. 4. **L. intermedius**, Wight. Nilgiris and other hills of the Peninsula. Similar to 3 but fl. larger, $\frac{1}{2}$–$\frac{5}{8}$ in. long. 5. **L. obtusatus**, Wall. Western Ghats from Mahabaleshwar southwards. Pet. $\frac{1}{2}$–$\frac{3}{4}$ in., fl. $\frac{1}{2}$–1 in. long, buds clavate, 4-angled. Calyx not produced beyond ovary.

6. **L. pentapetalus**, Roxb.; Wall. Pl. As. Rar. t. 225. Nepal. Sikkim 4–8,000 ft. common. Assam. Cachar. Burma, Upper and Lower. Yunnan. Siam. Malay Peninsula and Archipelago. Quite glabrous. L. usually opposite, coriaceous, blade 2–4, pet. $\frac{1}{2}$–$\frac{5}{8}$ in. Spikes crimson, solitary or in pairs, axillary, erect, 3–6 in. long, fl. $\frac{3}{4}$ in. 4–5-merous, calyx-limb obscurely toothed, base of corolla much inflated, almost globose. Style jointed in the middle, lower part angular and verrucose, fr. ellipsoid, $\frac{1}{4}$ in. long. 7. **L. Parishii**, Hook. f. Donat range, Tenasserim 2,000 ft. Branches stout, l. very coriaceous, narrow-lanceolate, blade 6–7, pet. stout, $\frac{1}{2}$ in. long, sec n. obscure, spikes strict erect, rachis stout, fl. bright scarlet $\frac{3}{4}$ in. long.

(*b*) Spikes many-fld., pubescent.

8. **L. coccineus**, Jack. Cachar. Pegu. Tenasserim. Siam. Malay Penins. and Archip. Similar to 6, but l. usually alternate, racemes and fl. rusty-tomentose, fl. 4-merous, fr. ovoid, prolonged into a narrow neck, crowned by the 4-toothed calyx. 9. **L. Hookerianus**, Wight & Arn. Southern hills of the Peninsula.—Ceylon. Similar to 8, fl. ⅓ in long, fr. small globose, crowned with the cupular calyx. 10. **L. Wightii** Hook. f. Courtallum. L. 1–1½ in., fl. ⅓ in. long.

(*c*) One or two pairs of fl. on short axillary racemes.

11. **L. ligustrinus**, Wall. Subhimalayan tract from the Jumna eastwards, ascending to 4,000 ft. Assam. Chittagong. Young shoots and inflorescence rusty pubescent, L. opposite, the uppermost sometimes alternate, blade 1–3, narrowed into pet. ⅛ in. Fl. ⅓ in. long, pale pink outside, deep red within, on axillary racemes much shorter than the subtending l., pedicels opposite, 2 pairs of fl. often with a terminal. 12. **L. terrestris**, Hook. f. Similar to 11. Probably a root parasite, quite glabrous, racemes larger, often compound.

C. Petals connate into a usually 4-lobed corolla, deeply cleft behind. Fl. between ⅓ and 1¾ in., in axillary fascicles, rarely racemose, calyx scarcely produced beyond ovary, anthers narrow, cells indistinct.

(*a*) L. glabrous or nearly so, fr. turbinate.

13. **L. elatus**, Edgew. (*L. umbellifer*, Brandis F. Fl. 397). Vern. *Naratha*, Jumna. Himalaya 5–8,000 ft. from the Sutlej eastwards. L. glabrous, coriaceous, ovate, acuminate, base rounded or cordate, blade 4–6, pet. ½ in. Fl. 1–1⅓ in. long, on short axillary racemes. 14. **S. umbellifer**, Schultes. Himalaya from Nepal eastwards, 2–5,000 ft. Khasi hills, common. Similar to 13. Youngest shoots rusty pubescent. L. elongate-elliptic, base acute, blade 2–5, pet, ½ in. Fl. red.

(*b*) L. mealy or scurfy, usually strictly opposite, fr. pyriform or clavate.

15. **L. Scurrula**, Linn.; Roxb. Cor. Pl. t. 140. Vern. *Bindukli*, *Betungli*, Thana. Common throughout India and Burma, not in the Punjab and Sind. In the Subhimalayan tract, ascending to 2,000, in the Burma hills to 4,000 ft.—Found on many different species, in Bombay common on *Pterocarpus Marsupium*, in Singhbum abundant on *Woodfordia floribunda*.—Ceylon. Malay Penins. and Archip. Young shoots, underside of young l. and inflorescence densely clothed with grey or brown scurfy tomentum, l. usually elliptic, base rounded, blade 1–5, pet. ⅙–⅜ in. Fl. ½–1 in. long, in dense axillary fascicles or short racemes, corolla slender, curved, greenish-yellow, lobes 4, linear, short, filaments purple, fr. pear-shaped ⅓ in. long. Exceedingly variable. 16. **L. cordifolius**, Wall. North West Himalaya, ascending to 5,000 ft. Hazaribagh. Nilgiris. Ceylon. Hardly specifically distinct from 15. Branchlets and leaves white-tomentose, l. ovate, base cordate. 17. **L. rhopalocarpus**, Kurz. Arakan. Pegu. Tenasserim. Small, densely branched. L. sometimes alternate, obovate or cuneate, 1–2 in., fr. linear-club-shaped, ½–¾ in. long, apex truncate. 18. **L. pulverulentus**, Wall. Subhimalayan tract and outer ranges ascending to 3,000 ft., from Chamba eastwards, Manipûr. Upper Burma. Branches stout, shoots and young l. densely clothed with soft fugacious tomentum. L. ovate, blade 2–8, pet. ½–1 in., sec. n. distinct. Racemes axillary, often fasciculate, as well as fl. and fr. shortly white-tomentose, fl. slender, curved, 1–1¾ in. long, lobes 4, short. Fr. clavate, ⅓–½ in. long. 19. **L. thelocarpus**, Hook. f. Chittagong. Shoots and underside of l. with fine tawny tomentum, l. ovate, blade 2–3, pet. ⅓ in. Fr. club-shaped, top rounded, tuberculate.

(*c*) L. tomentose, opposite, fr. ellipsoid.

20. **L. vestitus**, Wall. Pl. As. Rar. t. 230; Collett, Simla Fl. 439, fig. 142. North West Himalaya, from the Ravi to the Sarda river, common on *Quercus incana*. Oudh forests. Nepal. Khasi hills. Branches stout, branchlets, petioles, underside of l. and inflorescence clothed with soft brown or tawny tomentum. L. ovate- or elliptic-lanceolate, blade 2–4, pet. ½ in. long. Fl. ½–¾ in., pedicellate, in sessile or pedunculate fascicles, fr. ⅓–½ in. long.

D. Petals connate into a usually 5-lobed corolla. Fl. between ¾ and 2½ in. long in axillary clusters or racemes (solitary in *L. Stocksii*). Calyx toothed, produced beyond ovary.

(*a*) Fl. glabrous, corolla-lobes shorter than tube.

21. **L. longiflorus**, Desrousseaux; Wight Ic. t. 302.—Syn. *L. bicolor*, Rŏxb. Cor. Pl. t. 139. Vern. *Rana*, Kashm.; *Parand*, Kangra; *Ajeru*, Nep.; *Pagacha*, Hazaribagh; *Kaurak*, Bhil; *Kainguli*, Mar.; *Bindukli*, Thana; *Badanike*, Kan.

A large parasite, as a rule wholly glabrous, branches numerous, bark grey. L. thick-coriaceous, usually opposite, extremely variable in shape, generally broad-ovate, sec. n. obscure. Fl. 1–2½ in. long, in unilateral racemes, calyx-tube produced beyond the glabrous ovary, truncate or with short sharp teeth. Corolla curved, tube scarlet or orange, sometimes pink or white, lobes 5, linear, green or yellow. Anther linear, equal in length to the free portion of filament. Berry ⅓–½ in., oblong, pulpy, crowned by the cup-shaped calyx.

The most common of the Indian species. Subhimalayan tract from the Jhelum eastwards, ascending to 7,500 ft. in Kumaon. Bengal. Central India. Singbhum, chiefly on Sal. Both Peninsulas. Fl. Nov.–July. On many kinds of trees, commonly on the Mango, the branches on which it grows swell, get sickly and eventually die. Three very marked varieties: (a) *amplexifolia*. Western Peninsula and Ceylon. L. large, sessile almost amplexicaul, inflorescence often terminal. (b) *falcata*. Anantapùr. Mysore. Nellore. Sea coast from Sriharikotu to Tinnevelli. Often on *Albizzia amara*. Ceylon. L. narrow linear, fl. 1 in. long. (c) *pubescens*. Chanda district. Western Peninsula. L. oblong or elliptic-oblong, corolla in bud, peduncle and pedicels minutely pubescent. Closely allied and possibly not specifically distinct: 22. **L. sarcophyllus**, Wall. Nilgiris. 23. **L. elegans**, Wall. Irawadi near Yenangyaung.

24. **L. cuneatus**, Heyne. Western Ghats and Western Penins. Ceylon low country, common. Youngest shoots silky, otherwise glabrous. L. alternate cuneate or obovate, ½–1½ in. long, narrowed into a short petiole. Fl. ¾–1¼ in. long, pedicelled, in axillary fascicles. Fr. elongate-ovoid, ⅓–½ long, crimson.

(*b*) Fl. finely pubescent, corolla-lobes twice the length of tube.

25. **L. pentandrus**, Linn. Silhet. Chittagong. Upper Burma. Pegu. Tenasserim. Malay Penins. and Archip. L. usually alternate, glabrous, coriaceous, elliptic, blade 3–6, narrowed into pet. ¼–½ in. long. Fl. ⅝–1 in. long, in short axillary often fascicled racemes, corolla green without, yellow within, tube campanulate, lobes 4 or 5, linear, the upper half reflexed. Fr. ⅓ in. long, crowned by the cupular 5-toothed calyx-limb.

(*c*) Fl. glabrous, corolla-lobes as long as or longer than tube. Western species.

26. **L. neelgherrensis**, W. & A.—Syn. *L. pyranthus*, Wight Ic. t. 1020. Nilgiris.—Ceylon moist region. Branches stout, nodes much thickened, l. thickly coriaceous, opposite and alternate, usually ovate or ovate-lanceolate, obtuse, blade 3–6 in., narrowed into stout pet. ¼ in. long, sec. n. distinct, the lowest pairs frequently from near the base. Fl. scarlet, 1 in. long, in short, often fascicled corymbs, calyx-limb short, truncate, corolla straight, not split, lobes as long as tube, at first cohering at the top, afterwards the upper half reflexed. 27. **L. memecylifolius**, Wight & Arn. Nilgiris. Mysore. L. opposite and alternate, glabrous, lanceolate, 1–4 in. long, narrowed into a short petiole. Fl. 1–1½ in. long, in shortly pedunculate fascicles, corolla slender, lobes as long as or longer than tube. 28. **L. elasticus**, Desrouss.; Wight Ic. t. 343.—Syn. *L. Euphorbiæ*, Wight Ic. t. 1063. West coast and Ghats from the Konkan southwards. Quite glabrous, l. opposite, branches dichotomous. L. thickly coriaceous, elliptic, sessile, 2–4 in. long, basal n. 3–5. Fl. 1 in. long, sessile, in axillary fascicles. Corolla-lobes 5, linear, much longer than tube, twisted spirally, as also the long filaments. Fr. ovoid red, ½ in. long.

(*d*) Fl. tomentose, l. alternate, not exceeding 3 in. in length. Western species.

29. **L. tomentosus**, Heyne. Nilgiris and other hills of the Western Peninsula.—Ceylon. Branches and underside of l. rusty-tomentose. L. elliptic or obovate, blade 1–3, pet. ¼ in. Fl. ⅝ in. long, in axillary fascicles, densely rusty villous with hispid hairs. 30. **L. gibbosus**, Talbot Bombay List, ed. ii. 289. *Dade*, Kan. Konkan and North Kanara Ghat Forests. Similar to 29, branches scaly-tomentose, long, pendent. Corolla inflated and gibbous near the base, without hispid hairs, fr. pink, ovoid ⅓ in. long. 31. **L. bracteatus**, Heyne.—Syn. *L. tomentosus*, Wight Ic. t. 378. Western Peninsula, from Karnùl southwards. Branchlets, underside of young l. and inflorescence clothed with thin grey or buff tomentum, l. orbicular or broad-elliptic, blade ½–1½, pet. ⅛–¼ in. long. 32. **L. Stocksii**, Hook. f. Konkan, rare. Similar to 31, but l. sessile, fl. solitary or in few-fld. fascicles, fr. pyriform. 33. **L. recurvus**, Wall.—Syn. *L. Candolleanus*, Wight Ic. t. 305. Nilgiris. L. elliptic or obovate, blade 1–2, narrowed into pet. ¼ in. Fl. numerous, ⅝ in. long, in dense axillary fascicles, corolla curved, lobes linear-oblong.

II. No bracteoles, fl. in involucrate heads.

34. **L. lageniferus**, Wight Ic. t. 306. Vern. *Bandyali*, *Bindukli*, Mar. Hills of the Konkan, rare in the Thana district. North Kanara, common in deciduous forest.

Malabar. Glabrous, l. broad elliptic, 2–3 in. long, sessile or on short petioles. Bracts connate into a coloured bell-shaped involucre, 1–1½ in. long, fl. green and red, 1½–2 in. long, 5 in one involucre. 35. **L. involucratus,** Roxb. Sikkim Terai, ascending to 2,000 ft. Assam. Khasi hills. L. minutely pubescent, l. ovate or ovate-lanceolate, blade 4–6, pet. ¼–½ in. Fl. villous, white, 4 in one involucre, ¾ in. long, bracts free, as long as fl.

III. Each fl. supported by 1 bract and 2 bracteoles. L. glabrous, opposite or nearly so, corolla-segments 6, sometimes 5.

A. Fl. in short fascicled racemes, corolla-segments as long as tube.

36. **L. trigonus,** Wight & Arn. Ghats of the South Konkan and North Kanara, common. Along backwaters in Travancore. Branchlets robust, triquetrous, l. thickly coriaceous, opposite or in whorls of 3, broadly elliptic, obtuse, blade 4–6, pet. stout, ¼–½ in. Fl. ¾–1 in. long, racemes often from the old wood. Bracteoles connate into a small cup, corolla-lobes thick spathulate, stigma globose.

37. **L. ampullaceus,** Roxb. Vern. *Brigmara,* Ass. Subhimal. tract from Nepal eastwards, ascending to 2,000 ft. Assam. Khasi hills. Cachar. Chittagong. Burma, Upper and Lower.—Malay Peninsula. China. L. opposite, elliptic, blade 3–5, pet. ¼ in., sec. n. slender. Fl. purple and yellow (Upper Burma, Smales), white (Roxb. MSS. drawing 2229), ½–¾ in. long, pedicels often very short, corolla-tube 6-angled, stigma clavate, fr. ellipsoid or nearly globose. 38. **L. globosus,** Roxb., from the same localities as 37 and probably the same species, is supposed to differ by narrower l., sec. n. obscure, fr. globose. 39. **L. Brandisianus,** Kurz. Hills east of Toungoo 3,000 ft. L. rigidly coriaceous, lanceolate, blade 4–6, narrowed into pet. ⅛ in. long, midrib prominent, sec. n. obscure. Fl. 1¼ in. long, corolla sharply 6-gonous, stigma clavate. 40. **L. hypoglaucus,** Kurz. Hills east of Toungoo, 5–6,000 ft. L. elliptic-lanceolate, glaucous beneath, sec. n. obscure, blade 3 in. long, narrowed into short petiole, fl. bright crimson, 1¼–1¾ in. long. Possibly identical with *L. evenius,* Bl., of Java.

B. Fl. sessile, decussate on short 2–6-fld. spikes, rachis stout.

(*a*) Bracts and bracteoles shorter than calyx, free portion of calyx tubular, longer than ovary.

41. **L. loniceroides,** Linn.; Wight Ic. t. 303. *Batungli,* Thana. Western Coast and Western Ghats, from the Thana district southwards. Ceylon. L. coriaceous, ovate-lanceolate to lanceolate, blade 3–4, pet. ¼–½ in. Fl. red, 1–2 in. long, anthers exserted, yellow, filaments green. 42. **L. capitellatus,** Wight & Arn.; Wight Ic. t. 304. Western Ghats from Mahabaleshwar southwards. Ceylon. Fl. ½–1 in. long. Possibly a var. of 41. 43. **L. psilanthus,** Hook. f. Sikkim, 4–6,000 ft. Assam. Khasi hills. Manipur. Similar to 41, l. larger, pet. longer, spikes often from the old wood, corolla very slender, red and yellow.

(*b*) Bracts and bracteoles longer than calyx, free portion of calyx shorter than ovary.

44. **L. albidus,** Blume. Mergui. Malay Penins. and Archip. L. thinly coriaceous, blade 4–5, pet. ½–1 in. Spikes with 1–3 pairs of fl., the rachis thick, fl. immersed in shallow decussate cavities of the rachis, which terminates in a hard pyramidal point. Bracts and bracteoles coriaceous, ¼–⅓ in. long. Corolla 1–1½ in. long, tubular, curved, lobes half the length of tube. 45. **L. Collettii,** King. Shan hills plateau 5,000 ft. (Collett). Hills east of Bhamo. 4,500 ft. (Mont. Hill). L. ovate-lanceolate, blade 6, pet. 1 in. One pair of large blood-red fl. 2–2½ in. long on stout peduncles ⅛ in. long, rachis prolonged between the fl. into a broad conical tip, bracteoles coriaceous, broad, truncate, enclosing the ovary, corolla-tube wide at base, then constricted, afterwards gradually widening.

2. VISCUM, Linn.; Fl. Brit. Ind. v. 223.

Glabrous parasites, branches dichotomous or trichotomous. L. opposite, often reduced to scales. Fl. unisexual, small or minute, solitary or fascicled at the nodes or in the leaf-axils. ♂: perianth 3–4-fid., anthers broad, adnate to perianth-lobes, cells numerous, opening by many pores. ♀ perianth-tube adnate to ovary, stigma sessile or nearly so, large, pulvinate. Fr. succulent, pulp viscid. Embryos sometimes 2–3 in each seed, terete, in fleshy albumen. Species 30, Europe, Asia, Africa, Australia.

Vern. names used indiscriminately for several species: *Bana, Banda, Pand,* Hind.; *Ottu,* Tam.

A. Leaves conspicuous, perianth-segments deciduous.

(*a*) Fl. fascicled, terminal in the forks of branches.

1. **V. album,** Linn. *Mistletoe.* Vern. *Perbikh*, Rawalpindi; *Rini*, Kulu: *Runath*, Sutlej; *Hurchu*, Nep. Kuram valley, common on *Olive* and *Quercus Ilex*. Drosh, Chitral. Himalaya, Kashmir to Nepal 3–9,000 ft., also in the inner arid valleys. Martaban hills, 5–6,000 ft. (Kurz). Fl. March–May. Afghanistan.—Europe, Western and Northern Asia, Japan. A large green rounded bush, branches dichotomous, sometimes whorled, jointed, terete. L. flat, cuneate-oblong or oblanceolate, apex rounded, 1-2 in. long. Fl. diœcious, sessile in clusters of 3–5, in the bifurcations of branches, each cluster supported by a pair of fleshy, slightly ciliate, concave bracts. Perianth-segments triangular, thick, deciduous. Berry white, $\frac{1}{4}$–$\frac{1}{3}$ in. diam., almost transparent.

(*b*) Fl. in axillary sessile or peduncled fascicles.

2. **V. orientale,** Willd. Behar. Chutia Nagpur. Sambalpur. Western Peninsula. Chittagong. Meiktila, U. Burma. Mergui.—Ceylon. Malay Penins. and Archip. China, New Guinea, Australia. A large parasite, branchlets usually angular and grooved, often whorled. L. obtuse, elliptic or elliptic-lanceolate, blade 1–2 in. narrowed into short petiole, basal nerves 3–5. Fr. ovoid or nearly globose, $\frac{1}{4}$ in. long. 3. **V. verruculosum,** Wight & Arn. Dindigal hills, 8,500 ft. Closely allied to 2, fr. linear-oblong, warty. 4. **V. orbiculatum,** Wight Ic. t. 1016. Nilgiris. Similar to 2, main branches strongly angular and grooved, l. 1–1$\frac{1}{2}$ in. long, much waved. 5. **V. monoicum,** Roxb. Vern. *Banda*, *Pargatcha*, Beng. Oudh, north of Bahraich. Gorakhpur. Sikkim, lower hills. Khasi hills. Western Peninsula. L. thin, falcate, acute or acuminate, blade 1–5 in. long, narrowed into short petiole, basal nerves 3–5, prominent. Fr. oblong, narrowed at both ends, $\frac{1}{4}$–$\frac{1}{3}$ in. long. A remarkable variety or distinct species is *V. Edgeworthii*, Banda district on *Zizyphus*, branchlets more robust, l. broader, thickly coriaceous.

6. **V. ovalifolium,** Wall. Taongdong, Ava. Tenasserim. Andamans. Malay Penins. China. Branches stout, terete, l. coriaceous, obtuse, elliptic or elongate-elliptic, 2-4 in., narrowed into a short petiole, basal n. 3–5. Fl. crowded in axillary frequently spicate clusters. 7. **V. capitellatum,** Sm. Western Peninsula, chiefly on the west side, often parasitic on *Loranthus*. Ceylon. A dwarf, tufted shrub, tufts 6–10 in. diam. L. spathulate or orbicular, $\frac{1}{4}$–1 in. long, fr. ovoid.

B. Leaves as a rule wanting.

(*a*) Branches terete, angular or not.

8. **V. ramosissimum,** Wall. Western Peninsula. Ceylon. Branches not angular, long, slender, occasionally with a few l. at the base of the main branches, fr. minute, subglobose. 9. **V. angulatum,** Heyne. Syn. *V. ramosissimum*, Wight Ic. t 1017. Western Ghats and adjoining hill ranges, from the Konkan southwards. Branches angular.

(*b*) Branchlets flat.

10. **V. articulatum,** Burm.; Collett Simla Fl. 440, Fig. 143.—Syn. *V. attenuatum*, DC. Brandis F. Fl. 394. Vern. *Budu*, Hind.; *Hurchu*, Nep. Outer Himalaya, from Chamba eastwards, ascending to 6,000 ft. Assam. Khasi hills. Manipur. Burma, Upper and Lower. Centr. Prov. Western Peninsula. Ceylon. Malay Penins. and Archip. Internodes linear, 1–2 in. long, $\frac{1}{8}$–$\frac{1}{3}$ in. broad, striate and furrowed. Fr. $\frac{1}{8}$ in. diam., sessile, in clusters of 4–6 at the nodes, each fr. supported by a shallow cup-shaped bract, perianth deciduous. 11. **V. japonicum,** Thunb.—Syn. *V. moniliforme*, Wight Ic. t. 1018; *V. articulatum*, Brandis F. Fl. 393. Kuram valley. Himalaya 5–8,000 ft., also in the inner dry valleys, commonly on Oaks. Nilgiris. Ceylon, above 6,000 ft. Mount Ophir, Malacca; Mauritius. China. Japan. Australia. Internodes cuneate, much narrowed above the node $\frac{1}{4}$–$\frac{3}{4}$ in. long, $\frac{1}{10}$–$\frac{1}{6}$ in. broad, not furrowed. Fr. nearly globose, in dense clusters of 10–20 at the nodes, each cluster subtended by a pair of connate bracts, perianth-segments 3–4, minute, persistent.

Ginalloa Helferi, Kurz. Tenasserim. L. cuneate 3 in. long, tapering into the very short pet., 5-nerved, tip obtuse or emarginate. Fl. minute, in slender spikes 1–2 in. long, perianth-segments 3, anthers large sessile.

3. ARCEUTHOBIUM, M. Bieberstein; Fl. Brit. Ind. v. 227.

Small shrubs with fleshy articulate branches, parasitic on Conifers, each joint terminating in a minute cup-shaped entire or bidentate sheath, which encloses the base of the next joint. Fl. diœcious minute, at the ends of branchlets; ♂ perianth 2–5-partite, anthers sessile on the inner face of the segments, 1-celled, dehiscing by a transverse slit. ♀ perianth-tube adnate to ovary, minutely 2-dentate. Species 9–12, Northern Hemisphere.

1. **A. Oxycedri**, M. Bieb. Lahaul on the Upper Chenab 9–11,000 ft., on *Juniperus macropoda.* Mountains of Western Asia and South Europe, on species of Juniper. Stems 2–5 in. long, dividing dichotomously into numerous branches and forming close tufts, the lowest joints $\frac{1}{4}$ in. long, sheaths truncate. Long spreading roots between bark and wood of the foster tree, which is often killed by the parasite. Fr. short stalked, ovoid, $\frac{1}{12}$ in. long, seed cylindric, embedded in viscous pulp and thrown out with great force when the fr. is ripe. 2. **A. minutissimum**, Hook. f. On *Pinus excelsa.* N. W. Himalaya, Kashmir to Nepal 8–11,000 ft. Stems $\frac{1}{4}$ in. long, often much shorter, the fl. just emerging from the bark, joint sheaths bidentate, usually imbricating, the joints being minute.

ORDER XCVII. SANTALACEÆ. Gen. Pl. iii. 217.

Trees, shrubs or herbs, mostly parasitic on the roots, some genera on stems and branches, of the foster plant. L. entire, alternate or opposite, stipules 0. Fl. usually bracteate and bracteolate, regular, 1- or 2-sexual. Perianth mostly superior, 3–8-lobed, stamens inserted on the perianth and opposite the lobes. Ovary 1-celled, ovules 2–3, rarely solitary. Embryo in a copious fleshy albumen.

I. Perianth superior, tube adnate to the ovary, not produced above it.
- A. Leaves opposite . . . . 1. SANTALUM.
- B. Leaves alternate.
  - (*a*) Parasites on stems and branches, endocarp of drupe with hard or membranous plates projecting into fissures of the stellately lobed seed . . . . . 2. HENSLOWIA.
  - (*b*) Independent trees and shrubs, or root parasites.
    - Unarmed, branchlets sharply 3-sided, 1–2 in. long, ♂ in axillary pedunculate clusters . . . . OSYRIS (p. 554).
    - Sometimes spinescent, deciduous, buds covered with densely white silky scales. ♂ fl. in tomentose panicles . PYRULARIA (p. 554).
    - A thorny tree, l. coriaceous, ♂ fl. in catkin-like spikes . . . . . . SCLEROPYRUM (p. 554).
- C. Leafless parasitic shrubs . . . . . . 3. PHACELLARIA.

II. Perianth inferior, 3–4-partite, ovary half immersed in the disk . . . . CHAMPEREIA (p. 555).

1. SANTALUM, Linn.; Fl. Brit. Ind. v. 231.

Species about 8, Indo-Malayan region, Australia, Pacific islands.

S. album, Linn.; Bedd. Fl. Sylv. t. 256.—Syn. *Sirium myrtifolium*, Roxb. Cor. Pl. t. 2. *Sandalwood.* Sans. *Chandana.* Vern. *Chandan, Chandal, Sandal*, Hind.; *Suket*, Guz.; *Gandha, Gandada*, Kan.; *Chandaṇam*, Tel.; *Srigandam*, Tam.; *Santagu*, Burm.

A small, evergreen, glabrous tree, with slender drooping branchlets, sapwood white and scentless, heart-wood yellowish-brown, strongly scented. Medullary rays short, one or two cells wide, vessels 0·05 mm. diam., less than the distance between medull. rays, solitary, rarely two together. The great mass of the wood consists of wood-fibres, interrupted by narrow bands (1 cell wide) of wood parenchyma, joining the med. rays in a slanting direction. L. opposite, ovate or ovate-lanceolate, blade $1\frac{1}{2}$–$2\frac{1}{2}$, pet. $\frac{1}{2}$ in. long. Fl. brownish-purple, in axillary or terminal panicled cymes. Perianth campanulate, limb of 4 valvate triangular segments. Stamens 4 exserted, alternating with 4 rounded obtuse scales, which may be regarded either as petals or as lobes of the disk. Drupe globose, $\frac{1}{2}$ in. diam., black, endocarp hard.

Indigenous in the Western Peninsula from Nasik and the Northern Circars southwards. Grown in gardens north as far as Saharanpur. Fl. Feb.–July. As far as known, the Sandal seedling for a time lives independently, the roots being furnished with minute root hairs, which disappear when it has attached itself to the roots of a foster plant (Brandis in Ind. For. xxxix, 3, and M. Rama Rao same vol. 386).

2. HENSLOWIA, Blume; Fl. Brit. Ind. v. 232.

Parasitic glabrous shrubs, sometimes probably root parasites, l. alternate, fl. minute, supported by small bracts, unisexual or ♂ and ☿. Males: stamens 5 or 6, inserted on the perianth-lobes, anthers didymous. Fertile; perianth-tube adnate to ovary, segments 5 or 6, stamens 0 or short. Species about 12, India, China and Ind. Archip.

1. **H. heterantha**, Hook. f. & Thoms. Kumaon 4,000 ft. Nepal. Sikkim 2–7,000 ft. Khasi hills. Manipùr. Hills east of Toungoo 4–7,000 ft. L. variable, from obovate to orbicular, 1–3 in. long, narrowed into a short pet., basal nerves 5–9. ♂ fl. sessile, in pedunculate heads, fr. fascicled on pedicels ⅛ in. long with bracts at base and below the fr. 2. **H. granulata**, Hook. f. & Thoms. Sikkim. Bhutan. Khasi hills. Similar to 1, branchlets densely pustulate, l. obovate to spathulate, basal nerves usually more numerous, less distinct, fruiting pedicels covered the whole length with broad imbricating bracts. A specimen from the Southern Shan hills, 5,000 ft. (Collett, May 1888), has branchlets not pustulate and pedicels with bracts only at base and at apex. 3. **H. varians**, Blume. Mergui. Malay Penins. L. 3-nerved, elliptic-lanceolate. ♂ fl. pedicellate, in short racemes, fr. up to ¼ in. long.

Osyris arborea, Wall.; Collett Simla Fl. 442, Fig. 144.—Syn. *O. Wightiana*, Wall.; Wight Ic. t. 1853. Vern. *Dalmi*, *Dalima*, N. W. Himal.; *Popoli*, *Lotal*, Mar.; *Jhuri*, Nep. Outer Himalaya, ascending to 7,000 ft., from Kulu eastwards (not found in Sikkim). Manipùr. Upper Burma (*Zaung gyan*) often in Eng forest. Central Provinces. Western Peninsula. Ceylon. Tonkin. Yunnan. A twiggy shrub or small tree, as a rule glabrous, branchlets 3-sided, with prominent sharp angles. L. coriaceous, elliptic or obovate, 1–2 in. long, mucronate, nearly sessile. Fl. minute, 3-sometimes 4-merous. ♂ ⅛ in. across, in axillary pedunculate 5–10-fld. clusters, perianth-lobes triangular, stamens opposite the lobes, disk fleshy 3-lobed, the lobes alternating with the stamens. ☿: solitary sometimes 2–3 together, axillary, on long, slender peduncles. Perianth superior, obconical. Drupe yellow, ¼–⅓ in. diam., seed one. A remarkable variety, branchlets, leaves and inflorescence densely pubescent, ♂ fl. ⅛ in. across in small sessile cymes, on the Satpura range. Sandstone hills north of Bori 2,500 (D. B. Dec. 1876).

Pyrularia edulis, A. DC.—Syn. *Sphærocarya edulis*, Wall.; Wight Ic. t. 255. Vern. *Amphi*, Nep. Nepal. Sikkim, 4–5,000 ft. Mishmi hills. Khasi and Naga hills. A small or middle-sized thorny deciduous tree, leaf-buds covered with broad densely white silky scales. L. elongate-elliptic, blade 5–7, narrowed into pet. 1 in. long, sec. n. 4–6 pair, oblique, arching. Fl. ♂ in tomentose racemiform panicles, ♂ solitary. Fr. a large edible pyriform drupe, seed globose.

Scleropyrum Wallichianum, Arn.; Wight Ic. t. 241.—Syn. *Pyrularia Wallichiana*, Bedd. Fl. Sylv. t. 304. Vern. *Bodlige*, *Benduga*, Kan. Western Ghats from the Konkan southwards, common in North Kanara, Coorg and the Wainād. Southern Shan hills 4,000 ft. Ceylon 4–6,000 ft. A small or moderate-sized tree, armed with sharp woody often fascicled spines. L. coriaceous, elongate-elliptic, blade 3–7, pet ⅓ in. long, sec. n. 3–5 pair. Fl. yellowish-red, polygamous, male in catkin-like spikes, axillary, or above the scars of fallen leaves, perianth-tube solid, segments 5, slightly imbricate in bud, filaments inserted at the base of lobes, 2-fid, anthers 10. Fertile in compact cylindric racemes, perianth-tube adnate to ovary, stigma large peltate. Drupe brown, pyriform, stalked 1½–2 in. long. Seed 1, nearly globose.

3. PHACELLARIA, Benth.; Fl. Brit. Ind. v. 235.

Small leafless parasitic shrubs, usually growing on *Loranthus*. Fl. minute, monœcious, sessile or sunk in the branch. Perianth-tube of ♂ solid, of ♀ adnate to the ovary, lobes 4 or 5 short, valvate, anther-cells diverging. Species 4.

A. Stems under 5 in. long.

1. **P. compressa**, Benth. Shan hills 5,000 ft. Moulmein. Stems simple, not branching, more or less flattened. 2. **P. rigidula**, Benth. Mergui. Stems branched, terete.

B. Stems over 6 in. long, branched.

3. **P. caulescens**, Hemsl. South Shan hills 4,000 ft. Glabrous, fl. scattered, fr. sessile,

elongate-ovoid ⅛–¼ in. long. 4. **P. Wattii**, Hook. f. Manipùr 7,500 ft. Hoary, fl. in compact clusters.

Champereia Griffithiana, Planchon. Tenasserim. Andamans. Malay Penins. and Archip. Formosa. Philippines. A small glabrous tree, branchlets pale, flexuose. L. alternate, elliptic or elliptic-lanceolate, blade 3–8, pet. ⅛–¼ in. long. Fl. minute, bisexual, in axillary panicles 2–4 in. long, peduncles and pedicels slender. Perianth inferior, segments 5, valvate. Stamens 5, filaments longer than perianth. Drupe bright red, ellipsoid, obtuse, seed 1.

ORDER XCVIII. EUPHORBIACEÆ. Gen. Pl. iii. 239.

Herbs, shrubs or trees, milky sap in some genera. L. alternate (exceptions: *Buxus, Mischodon, Trewia, Cælodiscus*, species of *Mallotus* and *Excæcaria*), undivided (exceptions: *Bischofia, Dalechampia*), usually stipulate. Fl. mostly small, nearly always unisexual. Perianth usually simple and calycine, petals present in several genera, connective often thick and large. Ovary superior, as a rule of 3 carpels, more or less united, styles as many as cells or carpels, free or united, ovules 1–2 in each cell, pendulous from the inner angle. In many genera the micropyle is covered by an excrescence of the placenta (caruncle). Fruit either a capsule of 2-valved 1–2-seeded cocci, usually separating from a persistent axis, or a drupe. Embryo straight, radicle generally superior, cotyledons in most cases broad, flat in a fleshy oily albumen, in a few genera cotyledons fleshy without or with scanty albumen.

Baillon and others separate *Buxus* and *Sarcococca* (raphe dorsal, micropyle towards the axis) from *Euphorbiaceæ*. In Engler u. Prantl iii. 5. 130, they and a few other genera form a separate order: *Buxaceæ*. All genera here described belong to the Division of *Platylobeæ*, the genera with narrow cotyledons (*Stenolobeæ*) are limited to Australia and South America.

In species of *Croton, Hymenocardia, Macaranga, Mallotus, Coccoceras*, and *Homonoia* the underside of l. is densely clothed with minute orbicular often shining scales, consisting of radially arranged cells or rows of cells. In these cases as well as in *Elæagnus, Heritiera* and other trees, the close covering of these minute scales doubtless affects the transpiration of the leaves as well as the interchange of air. Their action probably is analogous to that of a dense felt of stellate or other hairs. No sharp limit exists between these scales and the flat stellate hairs which clothe the underside of l. in some of the genera mentioned and in other genera of this Order.

I. Flower-heads resembling single fl., consisting of a calyx-like involucre, enclosing several fl. without perianth, viz., one central ♀ fl. (a pedicellate pistil) and several ♂ fl., each a single pedicellate stamen.

One ovule in each cell . . . . 1. EUPHORBIA.

II. Flowers not united in heads, each fl. with a perianth, 2 ovules in each cell, as a rule collateral, in a few cases superposed, one pendulous from the apex the other from half-way up the axis. Inflorescence mostly axillary or lateral, petals none or minute.

(1) L. trifoliolate, fl. panicled . . . . . 2. BISCHOFIA.
(2) L. undivided, opposite . . . . . . 3. BUXUS.
(3) L. undivided, whorled . . . . . . MISCHODON (p. 559).
(4) L. undivided, alternate.
  A. ♂ calyx-lobes valvate, petals scale-like.
    Ovary 2-celled, fr. a drupe, fl. in axillary clusters . . . . . . 4. BRIDELIA.
    Ovary 2-celled, capsule flat obcordate, ♂ fl. in catkins . . . . . . HYMENOCARDIA (p. 561).
    Ovary 3-celled, fr. a dehiscent capsule, fl. in axillary clusters. . . . 5. CLEISTANTHUS.
  B. ♂ sepals or calyx-lobes imbricate.
    (*a*) Petals scale-like.
      ♂ disk 5-lobed . . . . . 6. ACTEPHILA.
      ♂ disk of 5 bifid glands . . . ANDRACHNE (p. 562).
    (*b*) Petals 0, ♂ fl. in axillary, rarely terminal, spikes, racemes or panicles.

Fr. globose, in bunches, mostly from the old wood, seeds embedded in a fleshy aril . . . 7. **Baccaurea.**
Fr. a capsule bursting irregularly, pericarp sometimes fleshy, ♂ fl. in catkins . . . . . . 8. **Aporosa.**
Fr. a 4-valved 1-seeded capsule, fl. in lax panicles . . . . . **Scortechinia** (p. 564).
Fr. indehiscent, 1–2-seeded, fl. diœcious in spikes or racemes.
Petiole short, under 1 in.
Ovary 1-celled, raphe ventral. 9. **Antidesma.**
Ovary 2–3-celled, raphe dorsal **Sarcococca** (p. 565).
Petiole long, over 1 in. . . . 10. **Daphniphyllum.**

(c) Petals 0, ♂ fl. solitary, in clusters or fascicles.
α. Style-arms much dilated, fr. an indehiscent drupe, l. often serrulate.
Stamens 2–4 central, drupe 1-seeded . . . . . . 11. **Putranjiva.**
Stamens few or ∞, inserted round an orbicular disk.
Ovary usually 1-celled . 12. **Hemicyclia.**
Ovary 2–4-celled . . . . 13. **Cyclostemon.**
β. Styles and style-arms slender.
Disk 0 in either sex, stamens 3, filaments united into a column.
Anthers adnate to the whole length of the column . 14. **Breynia.**
Column short, trigonous, anthers sessile on the angles . . . . . 15. **Sauropus.**
Disk present in ♀ and often in ♂ fl.
Filaments free round a large 2–3-fid pistillode . . 16. **Fluggea.**
Filaments free or united, pistillode 0 or minute . 17. **Phyllanthus.**
γ. Styles as a rule connate into a fleshy mass, conical, columnar or spherical, disk 0, anthers 3–8 adnate to a central column 18. **Glochidion.**

III. Flowers not united in heads (exception; *Dalechampia*), each fl. with a perianth, one ovule in each cell.
A. Petals present, inflorescence terminal.
Fl. in androgynous compound cymes.
L. penninerved, stamens 8 . . . . . **Tritaxis** (p. 576).
Basal nerves 3–7.
Sepals 5, imbricate, stamens 8–12 . . 19. **Jatropha.**
Calyx-lobes 2–3, valvate, stamens 8–20 . **Aleurites** (p. 576).
Fl. in androgynous spikes or racemes, stamens 10–30, filaments inflexed in bud . . . 20. **Croton.**
Fl. in unisexual racemes, stamens 10 . . . 21. **Galearia.**
B. Petals present, inflorescence as a rule axillary.
(a) ♂ sepals imbricate, petals united, fr. a drupe . 22. **Givotia.**
(b) ♂ sepals imbricate, petals free, fr. capsular.
♀ sepals not enlarged in fr.
Stigma broad, sessile, stam. 4–5 . . **Platystigma** (p. 579).
Styles short 2-fid.
Fl. in axillary clusters, stam. 10 . . **Microdesmis** (p. 579).
Fl. in racemes or panicles.
Anthers 3, sessile on a cylindric column . . . . 23. **Trigonostemon.**
Stames 8–35. . . . . 24. **Ostodes.**
Styles slender, entire, recurved . . **Codiæum** (p. 580).
♀ sepals as a rule enlarged in fr. . . 25. **Blachia.**
(c) ♂ calyx open in bud, 5-toothed, ♀ sepals enlarged in fr., petals in ♂ and ♀ . . . 26. **Dimorphocalyx.**
(d) ♂ sepals valvate.
Glabrous, anther-cells distinct, pendulous. 27. **Agrostistachys.**
Stellately tomentose, anther-cells contiguous, parallel . . . . **Sumbavia** (p. 582).

C. Petals 0. Calyx campanulate.
Stamens 10, filaments free . . . . . MANIHOT (p. 582).
Anthers 5–10, adnate to a central column. . HEVEA (p. 582).

D. Petals 0. ♂ sepals imbricate.
♂ fl. fascicled.
Fr. smooth tardily dehiscent. Resinous trees, stipules sheathing . . . . . . 28. GELONIUM.
Capsule echinate . . . . CHÆTOCARPUS (p. 582).
♂ fl. in panicles or racemes . . . . . 29. BALIOSPERMUM.

E. Petals. 0. ♂ sepals or calyx-segments valvate.
(a) Twining shrubs.
L. undivided, base cordate.
♂ calyx 3-lobed, anthers 3, cocci not winged, sepals not enlarged in fr. . CNESMONE (p. 583).
♂ sepals 4–5, stamens 8–30, cocci winged, sepals enlarged in fr. . . . . PLUKENETIA (p. 583).
L. deeply lobed or trifoliolate, fl. in involucrate heads . . . . . . 30. DALECHAMPIA.
(b) Trees or erect shrubs.
α. Filaments free, stamens 2 or 3, fl. in androgynous or unisexual spikes.
♂ calyx 2–3-lobed . . . . . . 31. SAPIUM.
♂ sepals 3, small . . . . . . 32. EXCŒCARIA.
β. Filaments free, stamens 4, anthers 2-celled.
Filaments slender, anther-cells parallel, adnate to a thick connective 33. ADENOCHLÆNA.
Filaments short, flat, anther-cells divaricate . . . . CŒLODEPAS (p. 586).
γ. Filaments free or only united at base, stamens 6–∞, anthers 2-celled.
L. alternate, anther-cells divaricate.
Styles short, entire, densely plumose 34. CLAOXYLON.
Styles filiform, with numerous slender branches . . . . . . 35. ACALYPHA.
L. alternate, anther-cells contiguous, parallel.
Back of cocci rounded . . . . 36. ALCHORNEA.
Back of cocci sharply keeled . . COCCOCERAS (p. 587).
L. alternate or opposite, anther-cells globose or shortly oblong, widely separated by the thick connective 37. MALLOTUS.
L. opposite, anther-cells contiguous, parallel.
L. entire, fr. a drupe . . . . . 38. TREWIA.
L. dentate or sinuately lobed, fr. a capsule . . . . 39. CŒLODISCUS.
δ. Filaments free, stamens 1–∞, anthers 3–4-celled.
Styles entire . . . . 40. MACARANGA.
Styles with 2–3 long filiform arms . . CLEIDION (p. 592).
ε. Filaments connate in bundles, stamens ∞.
Fl. in terminal androgynous panicles . RICINUS (p. 593).
Fl. usually diœcious, in axillary spikes . 41. HOMONOIA.
Fl. monœcious, ♂ in axillary spikes, ♀ solitary . . . . LASIOCOCCA (p. 593).

Position uncertain . . . . . SPHYRANTHERA (p. 593).

1. EUPHORBIA, Linn.; Fl. Brit. Ind. v. 244.

Mostly herbs, a few shrubs or soft-wooded trees with fleshy branches, abounding in milky juice, contained in continuous laticiferous tubes. L. of the stem alternate, without stipules, or with stipular spines, those on the flowering branches opposite. Fl. heads resembling single fl., consisting of a calyx-like cup-shaped involucre, lobes 4–5, alternating with broad fleshy glands, enclosing 10–15 male and one central female fl. ♂: one 2-celled, often didymous anther on an articulated filament. ♀: a solitary stipitate 3-celled ovary, styles 3, free or combined, simple or 2-fid. Capsule separating into three 2-valved cocci. Species over 600, absent only in the arctic zone.

The species here described all belong to the Section *Euphorbium* with fleshy green stems and branches. L. (excepting floral l.) often wanting. Lobes of involucre membranous, numerous fimbriate bracts among the male fl.

A. Unarmed, branches terete or flat.

1. **E. Tirucalli**, Linn.; Brandis F. Fl. 439.—*Milk-bush*. Vern. *Sehnd*, Hind.; *Nevli*, Mar.; *Nandu-kalli*, Kan.; *Sanna-Jamudu*, Tel.; *Tiru kalli*, Mal.; *Tazaung lethnyo*, Burm. A native of Africa, naturalized in Bengal and the Western Peninsula, chiefly as a hedge plant. Cultivated in Burma and in North-West India as far north as Hushiarpur. A shrub or small tree, bark of stem cracked, dark olive-brown, branches terete, smooth, green, jointed, l. fleshy, linear or linear-cuneate, sessile, up to ½ in. long. Involucres crowded at the ends and in the forks of the branches. Capsules deeply 3-lobed, villous, dark-brown, ¼ in. long. 2. **E. epiphylloides**, Kurz. South Andaman on the rocky coast. Great Nicobar. Attains 15 ft., branches flat with thick crenate wings, capsule glabrous.

B. Armed usually at the nodes with pairs of sharp spines.

(*a*) Styles simple, stigma capitate.

3. **E. Nivulia**, Ham.; Wight Ic. t. 1862. Vern. *Thor*, *Thuhar*, *Thura*, *Senhūr*, Hind.; *Sij*, Beng.; *Etki*, Kol; *Newrang*, Mar.; *Bontha-Jamudu*, Tel.; *Yella-kalli*, Kan.; *Shasaung*, Burm.

A bushy tree, attaining 30 ft., trunk with thick corky bark when old, stems and branches round without ribs or angles, branchlets generally whorled. L. fleshy, sessile, obtuse, cuneate or obovate, 4–12 in. long. Involucres usually 3 in a short cyme at or just above the nodes, the lateral peduncled, bisexual, the central sessile, male, common and partial peduncles up to ¼ in. long, cymes often fascicled.

Garhwal, on dry rocky slopes. Oudh. Rajputana. Behar. Singbhum, Satpura range, Centr. Prov. Western Peninsula. Chittagong. West side of the Pegu Yoma, common on dry ridges in the Prome and Tharawadi districts. Leafless C.S., fl. and fresh l. H.S. 4. **E. neriifolia**, Linn. On waste land and near villages: Singbhum. Centr. Prov. Western Peninsula. Burma, Upper and Lower. Vern. *Zizaung*, Burm. A small tree, attaining 20 ft., stems cylindric, branches round, but the nodes arranged in 5 more or less spirally twisted ribs, branchlets 5-angled. L. few, cuneate or oblanceolate, usually acute or mucronate, 6–12 in. long. Involucres in small compact shortly pedunculate dichotomous cymes from the sinus between the nodes, styles connate high up.

5. **E. Royleana**, Boissier.—Syn. *E. pentagona*, Royle Ill. t. 82, f. 1. Vern. *Thor*, Hind. Common on dry slopes with a south aspect in the outer ranges of the North-West Himalaya, ascending to 7,000 ft. Attains 15–16 ft. and a girth up to 6 ft., branches with 5, sometimes 7, broad flat faces, separated by sharp undulating angles, spines in pairs at the nodes, l. few or wanting. Involucres yellow, in compact sessile 3-fld. cymes from the sinus between the nodes, styles free nearly to the base. Grows readily from cuttings, even in the driest soil. Cultivated in places at the foot of the hills, but does not thrive far out in the plains. 6. **E. trigona**, Haworth; Wight Ic. t. 1868—Syn. *E. Cattimandoo*, W. Elliot in Wight Ic. t. 1993. Vern. *Kattimandu*, Tel. Branches twisted, with 3 or 5 sharp ridges, which are deeply sinuate between the nodes.

(*b*) Styles bifid at the apex.

7. **E. antiquorum**, Linn.; Wight Ic. t. 897. Vern. *Tidhara-Sehnd*, Hind.; *Tandhari-Send*, Guz.; *Bonta Kalli*, Kan.; *Pedda Jamadu*, Tel.; *Sadura-Kalli*, Tam.; *Chethura-Kalli*, Mal.; *Tazaung*, *Pyathat*, Burm. Bengal. Both Peninsulas. Cultivated by Meehis and Garos in Assam. Often grown as a hedge plant.—Ceylon. A small tree, attaining 25 ft., branches stout, jointed, sharply 3- sometimes 5-angled, the ridges undulating, l. small, caducous, involucres in lax cymes, common and partial peduncles ¼ in. long. Wild on the higher ridges of the Arakan Yoma. 8. **E. tortilis**, Rottler; Wight Ic. t. 898. Western Peninsula.—Ceylon (?). Branches jointed, sharply 3- or 4-angled, as a rule spirally twisted.

2. BISCHOFIA, Blume; Fl. Brit. Ind. v. 344.

B. javanica, Blume (the only species); Bedd. Fl. Sylv. t. 259—Syn. *Micrœlus Rœperianus*, Wight & Arn.; Wight Ic. t. 1880. Vern. *Kain*, *Pankain*, Hind.; *Uriana*, Assam; *Gobra-nerul*, *Nilimara*, Kan.; *Mila-chittyan*, Tam.; *Pogaung za*, Burm.

A large glabrous deciduous tree, l. alternate trifoliolate, common petiole 3–8 in., leaflets elliptic, crenate, acuminate, 3–8 in. long. Fl. greenish-yellow, diœcious, apetalous, disk 0, racemose, bracts lanceolate, early caducous, in ample pedunculate panicles, axillary or above scars of fallen l. ♂: sepals 5, obtuse, concave, concealing the anthers, stamens 5 opposite to sepals, filaments short, round an obtuse pistillode. ♀: Sepals ovate caducous, ovary 3–4-celled, styles linear, entire. Fr. globose, fleshy, $\frac{1}{4}$–$\frac{1}{3}$ in. diam., seeds 3 or 4 smooth, shining.

Subhimalayan forests and outer hills, from the Jumna eastwards, ascending to 4,000 ft. Chutia Nagpur. Western Peninsula. Assam. Chittagong. Burma, Upper and Lower. Chiefly in shady ravines and on the banks of streams. Fl. March, April, foliage turns red before falling. In Burma the ♂ panicles are often pubescent. A beautiful wood, does not warp, deserves attention.—Malay Penins. and Archip. Polynesia.

3. BUXUS, Linn.; Fl. Brit. Ind. v. 267.

Species 20, Northern Hemisphere.

B. sempervirens, Linn. *Box.* Vern. *Shamshad, Sansadu, Chikri, Papri, Poppar,* N. W. Him.

An evergreen shrub or small tree, wood yellowish-white, hard, very close- and even-grained, consisting chiefly of thick-walled wood-fibres; med. rays 1, rarely 2 or 3 cells wide. Vessels small, uniformly distributed, wood parenchyma scanty. Branchlets and young l. pubescent, l. coriaceous, opposite, varying from lanceolate to ovate, quite entire, 1–3 in. long, narrowed into a short petiole. Fl. yellowish, monœcious, smell unpleasant, in dense short axillary spikes, the terminal fl. being usually female. ♂: Sepals 4 biseriate, imbricate, stamens 4 free, opposite to sepals, inserted round a 4-sided rudimentary ovary. ♀: Sepals 6, in two circles of 3 each, ovary 3-celled, 3-cornered, top flat, the corners terminating in thick short styles. Capsule coriaceous, 3-valved, each valve ending in 2 horns, being the halves of two styles, dissepiments attached to the valves. Seeds black.

Suliman range, trans-Indus. Salt range. Here and there, chiefly in shady ravines, forming small nearly pure woods, in the N. W. Himalaya 4–8,000 ft. Not in Sikkim, but in Bhutan. Fl. March–May. Canary Islands. North Africa. Southern and Western Europe. Western Asia. China and Japan. Formosa.

Mischodon zeylanicus, Thwaites; Bedd. Fl. Sylv. t. 290. Tinnevelli hills.—Ceylon. A large evergreen tree, branchlets angular, minutely hairy. L. whorled, rigidly coriaceous, oblong, blade 6–14, pet. $\frac{1}{2}$–2 in., the young foliage of a fine rich lake colour. ♂ fl. numerous, in short axillary bracteate pubescent panicles, sepals 5–8, often unequal, stamens opposite the sepals, filaments free, hairy, exserted, pistillode 3-lobed. Capsules $\frac{3}{4}$ in. diam., on long panicled pedicels, trigonous, of 3 two-valved cocci.

4. BRIDELIA, Willd.; Fl. Brit. Ind. v. 267.

Trees, shrubs or climbers, l. alternate, short petiolate, generally distichous, sec. n. prominent, parallel. Fl. small, monœcious or diœcious, sessile or nearly so, in axillary or spicate clusters, bracteoles numerous between the flowers. Calyx-tube short and flat, segments 5, valvate in bud, petals 5 smaller than calyx-segments. Disk broad, ♂ lining the calyx-tube, ♀ conical or tubular, often enclosing the ovary. ♂: Stamens 5, inserted in a whorl on a central tube, enclosing the rudimentary ovary, anther-cells parallel. ♀: Ovary glabrous 2- rarely 3-celled, the base enclosed in the calyx-tube, styles 2, bifid, in *B. minutiflora* 1 only. Drupe with 1 or 2, 1-seeded pyrenes. Cotyledons thin in fleshy albumen or fleshy with membranous albumen. Species 30, tropical Africa, Madagascar, Indo-Malayan region, South China, tropical Australia, New Caledonia.

A. Sec. n. numerous, usually 12–30 pair.

1. **B. retusa**, Spreng.; Bedd. Fl. Sylv. t. 260; Brandis F. Fl. t. 55.—Syn. *Cluytia spinosa*, Willd.; Roxb. Cor. Pl. t. 172. Vern. *Kaj, Khaja, Kajja*, Hind.; *Kassi, Kassei, Karka*, C. P.; *Kaka*, Kol; *Lamkana*, Ajmere; *Angnēra*, Banswara; *Monj*, Guzerat; *Haklo*, Mandevi; *Kohir*, Ass.; *Asana kutgi*, Mar.; *Goje*, Kan.; *Koramadi*, Tel.; *Mullu-maruthu*, Tam.; *Mullu-venga, Mullu-Kayani*, Mal.; *Seikchi*, Burm.

A large or moderate-sized deciduous tree, bark dark coloured, heart-wood grey to olive-brown. Young stems spinescent, branchlets and underside of leaves usually shortly tomentose. L. rigidly coriaceous, elongate-elliptic, sec. n. straight, prominent, 15–25 pair, blade 5–10, pet. $\frac{1}{4}$–$\frac{1}{2}$ in., stipules subulate, deciduous. Fl. diœcious, yellow, crowded in lateral sessile clusters, these commonly arranged in axillary or terminal often paniculate spikes. Disk of female fl. double, the outer lining the calyx-tube, the inner 5-lobed. Drupe fleshy purplish-black, edible, $\frac{1}{3}$ in. diam., supported by the slightly enlarged calyx.

Subhimalayan tract from the Chenab eastwards, ascending to 3,500 ft. Common in the Oudh Forests and the Terai of Sikkim. Rajputana. Central Provinces. Chutia Nagpur and Behar. Western Peninsula and Burma. Fl. May–July. Fr. eaten and the seeds widely distributed by the green pigeon. The l. before falling take a pinkish-brown autumn tint. Coppices well. Ceylon. 2. **B. assamica**, Hook. f. Assam, Silhet. Branches sparsely pubescent, l. membranous, minutely puberulous beneath, blade 6–12, pet. $\frac{1}{3}$ in., sec. n. slightly arching 15–20 pair, fl. sessile, in minute axillary clusters, fr. nearly 1 in. long ovoid, on the unaltered calyx. 3. **B. montana**, Willd. (*Cluytia montana*, Roxb. Cor. Pl. t. 171). *Gondni*, Hind. Subhimalayan tract from Jhelum eastwards, ascending to 3,500 ft. Khasi hills. Central Provinces. Behar, Orissa. Upper Burma. A middle-sized tree, glabrous, branchlets tuberculate, l. usually obovate, shining above, pale beneath, margin undulate, blade 3–7, pet. $\frac{1}{8}$–$\frac{1}{4}$ in., fl. in small dense axillary clusters. Fr. elongate-ovoid narrowed at both ends, seated on the unaltered calyx. 4. **B. burmanica**, Hook. f. (*B. amœna*, Kurz F. Fl. ii. 368). Cult. in Hort. Bot. Calc. believed to have been brought from Upper Burma. Quite glabrous, l. membranous, obtuse, margin undulate, blade 4–7, pet. $\frac{1}{8}$ in. long, sec. n. 12–20 pair, slender, reticulate veins anastomosing between the tertiary n. prominent, fl. in small axillary clusters, green and red.

B. Sec. n. few, usually 5–12 pair.

(*a*) L. pubescent or tomentose beneath.

5. **B. stipularis**, Blume.—Syn. *Cluytia scandens*, Roxb. Cor. Pl. t. 173. Vern. *Harinhara*, Beng.; *Dunki-bura*, Tel. Subhimalayan tract from the Ganges eastwards, ascending to 2,000 ft. Abundant in the Sal forests of Oudh, Jalpaiguri, and the Western Duars. Behar. Bengal. Both Peninsulas. Fl. May–Oct.—Ceylon, rare. Ind. Arch. A large scrambling or climbing shrub, branchlets, petioles and underside of l. with soft tawny tomentum. L. elliptic or obovate, blade 2–6, pet. $\frac{1}{4}$–$\frac{1}{3}$ in. long, sec. n. arching, 8–12 pair, transverse veins at right angles, parallel. Fl. greenish-yellow, in compound clusters in the axils of leaves or bracts, often supported by broad-lanceolate stipular bracts, and frequently forming long panicled spikes at the ends of branches, calyx nearly glabrous, petals orbicular, similar in both sexes, disk of ♀ fl. fimbriate. Fr. oblong $\frac{1}{2}$ in. long, seated on the slightly enlarged calyx. 6. **B. dasycalyx**, Kurz. Pegu forests. Similar, calyx densely hairy outside. 7. **B. pubescens**, Kurz. Eastern Nepal and Sikkim, hot valleys ascending to 5,000 ft. Khasi hills. Singbhum. Eastern slopes of the Pegu Yoma. Martaban hills, common. A large or middle-sized tree, branchlets and l. beneath tawny pubescent, l. membranous, elliptic or obovate, shortly acuminate, blade 4–6, pet. $\frac{1}{2}$ in., sec. n. 9–12 pair, arching. Fl. pubescent in compact axillary clusters, fr. $\frac{1}{3}$ in. long, ovoid, almost cylindric. 8. **B. tomentosa**, Blume. Sikkim Terai. Assam. Khasi hills. Cachar. Eastern Bengal. Lower Burma. Malay Penins. and Archip. China. Australia. A shrub or small tree, branchlets and l. beneath minutely pubescent, l. undulate, lanceolate, glaucous beneath, blade 1–3, pet. slender $\frac{1}{8}$ in. long. Fr. globose $\frac{1}{8}$–$\frac{1}{6}$ in. diam.

(*b*) L. glabrous, or nearly so.

9. **B. Hamiltoniana**, Wall. Behar. Chanda district. Konkan. A straggling shrub, branchlets glabrous, l. glabrous or minutely hairy beneath, elongate- or obovate-elliptic, often rhomboid, sec. n. 6–9 pair, nearly straight, branched, blade 1–4, narrowed into pet. $\frac{1}{8}$–$\frac{1}{4}$ in. long, stipules linear-lanceolate. Fr. globose $\frac{1}{4}$ in. diam. Prain, Bengal Plants 927 unites this with *B. montana*, Willd. 10. **B. Kurzii**, Hook. f. Andamans. Nicobars. Malay Penins. Glabrous, l. elliptic-oblong, obtuse, base rounded, blade 2–4, pet. $\frac{1}{8}$ in. long, reticulate veins distinct on both sides. Fl. minute, fr.

globose ¼–⅓ in. diam. 11. **B. Griffithii**, Hook. f. South Andaman. Malacca. Scandent, glabrous, l. thinly coriaceous, elongate-elliptic, acuminate, blade 2–4, pet. ¼ in., sec. n. 5–7 pair, arching. 12. **B. minutiflora**, Hook. f. Mergui. Malay Archip. Nearly glabrous, branches pustulate, l. membranous, elongate elliptic, acuminate, base acute, blade 2–3, pet. ¼ in. Style solitary, bifid half-way down.

Hymenocardia punctata, Wall.—Syn. *H. Wallichii*, Tulasne. Banks of streams and moist places, Pegu and Tenasserim, possibly also in Upper Burma. Siam. Cambodia. Sumatra. A shrub or small tree, deciduous, branchlets and petioles pubescent, young shoots, underside of l. and ♂ spikes densely clothed with minute shining orange-coloured scales. L. elliptic, blade 1–3, pet. slender, ⅓ in. long. ♂ catkins ½ in. long, 2-3 together, fl. minute, single in the axils of peltate pedicelled bracts, calyx membranous, irregularly 4–6-lobed, stamens 4–6, filaments nearly free. ♀ in few-fld. racemes, sepals narrow, caducous. Capsule flat, obcordate, ¾ in. broad, reticulately veined, consisting of 2 broad flat wing-like cocci, separating from a central axis, seeds flat.

5. CLEISTANTHUS, Hook. f. Fl. Brit. Ind. v. 274.

Trees or shrubs, l. alternate, quite entire. Petals minute, ovary 3-celled, styles 3, bifid, capsule sessile or shortly pedicellate, of 3 two-valved, 1-seeded cocci, separating from a central axis, cotyledons often folded. Species about 30, Tropical Africa. Indo-Malayan region. Trop. Australia. New Caledonia.

A. Ovary quite glabrous.

1. **C. collinus**, Benth.—Syn. *Lebidieropsis orbicularis*, Muell. Arg.; Bedd. Man. t. 23, fig. 5; *Cluytia collina*, Roxb. Cor. Pl. t. 169. Vern. *Garar*, *Garari*, C. P.; *Korshe*, Tel.; *Wodan*, *Wodishi*, Tam.

A large shrub or small tree, wood red, heart-wood darker, small, foliage bright green. L. broadly ovate or obovate, obtuse, often orbicular, blade 2–4, pet. ¼ in., sec. n. 4–8 pair, slender. Fl. yellowish-green, in small axillary silky clusters, calyx-lobes lanceolate. Capsule woody, sessile, globose 3- rarely 4-lobed, ⅜–¾ in. diam., dark brown, shining. Seeds 3, albumen scanty.

Behar. Chutia Nagpur. Satpura range. Chanda district (abundant). Western Peninsula. Not known north of the Ganges, nor from Rajputana. Fl. R. S. Coppices readily. 2. **C. chartaceus**, Muell. Arg. Silhet. Branchlets and inflorescence rusty-tomentose, l. glabrous when mature, elliptic-lanceolate, acuminate, blade 5–8, narrowed into pet. ½ in. long, sec. n. arching, 6–8 pair. Capsule stipitate, ½ in. long, woody, 3-lobed. 3. **C. myrianthus**, Kurz. Lower Burma. Andamans. Malay Penins. A middle-sized evergreen tree, branchlets and l. finely fulvous-tomentose, l. coriaceous, lanceolate, acuminate, blade 6–10, pet. ¼ in., sec. n. 10–15 pair, arching. Capsule stipitate, woody, obtusely 3-lobed, ½ in. diam.

B. Ovary villous or hirsute.

4. **C. malabaricus**, Muell. Arg. Evergreen forests of the Konkan and North Kanara. A large shrub or small tree, branchlets and petioles densely rufous-villous. L. oblanceolate, acuminate, glaucous and thinly hairy beneath, blade 4–6 in. narrowed into a very short petiole, stipules long, setaceous. Capsule sparsely hairy, ⅓ in. diam., deeply 3-lobed. 5. **C. lancifolius**, Hook. f. Tenasserim. Glabrous, l. lanceolate, caudate-acuminate, blade 4–5, pet. ¼ in. long, sec. n. slender.

6. **C. patulus**, Muell. Arg.; Bedd. Man. t. xxiii. fig. 4.—Syn. *Amanoa indica*, Wight Ic. t. 1911. Western Peninsula. Ceylon. Glabrous, l. ovate or ovate-lanceolate, acuminate, blade 1–3, pet. ⅓ in. long, sec. n. very slender. Capsule ⅓ in. diam., deeply 3-lobed.

6. ACTEPHILA, Bl.; Fl. Brit. Ind. v. 282.

L. quite entire, stipules deciduous. Fl. monœcious, sometimes diœcious, ♂ in axillary clusters, ♀ solitary or a few on a long peduncle. Sepals 5–6, petals small, sometimes wanting, disk broad, usually 5-lobed. ♂ Stamens 3–6, filaments free or connate at the base round a 3-cleft pistillode. Fr. a hard capsule of 3 two-valved cocci. Cotyledons fleshy, albumen scanty or 0. Species about 10, Malayan and Australian.

1. **A. excelsa**, Muell. Arg.; Bedd. Man. t. 23.—Syn. *A. neilgherrensis*, Wight Ic. t. 1910. Vern. *Tawzalat pyu*, Burm. Western Ghats from Mahabaleshwar southwards.

Assam. Khasi hills. Cachar. Chittagong. Upper Burma. Andamans. A shrub or small tree, young shoots minutely hairy, l. obovate or oblanceolate, base acute, blade 2–7, pet. ¼–½ in., rarely longer. Fr. depressed, orbicular, 3-lobed, 1 in. diam. on pedicels 1–3 in. or several on a common peduncle. *A. Thomsoni*, Muell. Arg., and *A. javanica*, Miq., probably belong to this species. 2. **A. puberula,** Kurz. Andamans. Nicobars. A shrub, base of l. rounded or slightly cordate, pet. ½–1½ in.

Andrachne cordifolia, Muell. Arg.; Collett Simla Flora 449 fig. 147. N. W. Himalaya, Hazara to Kumaon, 5–8,000 ft. China. A small shrub with slender branches, young shoots, petioles and underside of l. hairy. L. tapering from a broad rounded base, obtuse, blade 1–2, petiole slender ¼–⅔ in. Fl. monœcious, axillary, on long filiform pedicels, calyx-segments obovate, petals keeled, disk of 5 flat bifid glands. Capsule ¼ in. diam., supported by the enlarged calyx.

7. BACCAUREA, Lour.; Fl. Brit. Ind. v. 367.

Evergreen trees, l. alternate usually entire. Fl. generally diœcious, apetalous, hoary or tomentose, in long spiciform racemes or racemiform panicles, often on the old wood. Disk 0 or obscure. ♂: sepals 4–5, imbricate, stamens 4–8, filaments free, round a pubescent pistillode. ♀ sepals 4–6 linear or oblong, ovary 2–5-celled, stigmas 2–5 small sessile, ovules 2 in each cell. Fruit globose, pericarp coriaceous, seeds enclosed in a fleshy arillus. Species 40–50, mostly Indo-Malayan, a few in tropical Africa and Polynesia.

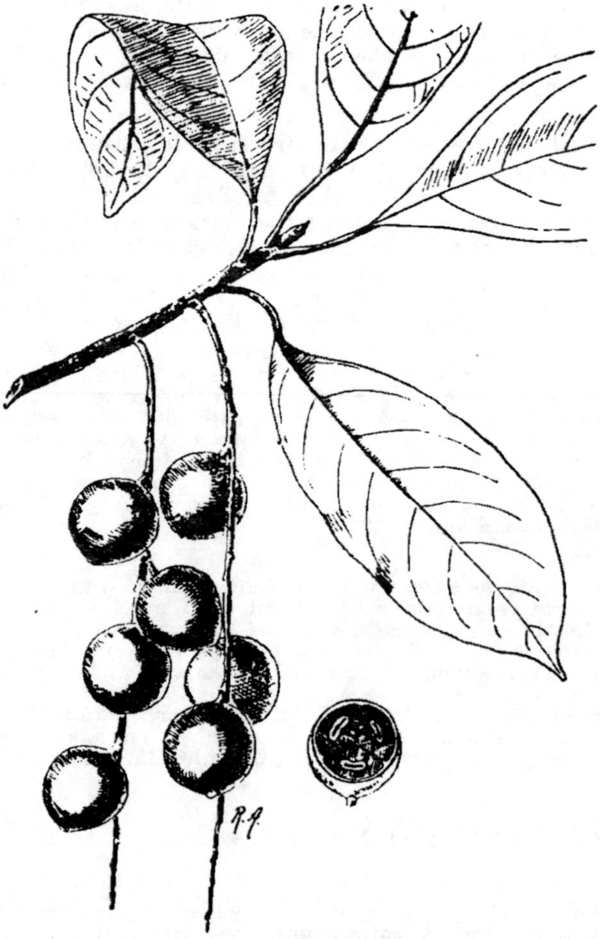

FIG. 181.—Baccaurea sapida, Muell. Arg. ½.

1. **B. sapida,** Muell. Arg. Vern. *Latqua*, Beng.; *Leteku*, Ass.; *Kala Bogati*, Nep.; *Kanazo*, Burm.

A middle-sized tree, young shoots hairy, l. glabrous, membranous, elongate-elliptic, often obovate, blade 4–10, narrowed into the thickened, geniculate and 1–2 in. long petiole. Fl. tomentose on short pedicels in simple bracteate spiciform densely fascicled racemes, from below the l. or from the old wood. ♂ bracts $\frac{1}{10}$–⅕ in., longer than the sessile fl. clusters, sepals minute. ♀, bracts minute, sepals oblong, ¼ in., ovary densely tomentose. Fr. yellow, velvety, ⅔–1 in. diam., in long bunches, hanging down usually from the trunk and branches, pericarp leathery, seeds 3, embedded in pale rose-coloured delicious pulp, the arillus of the seeds.

Subhimalayan tract and outer valleys from Sikkim eastwards. Assam. Silhet. East Bengal. Tippera. Burma, Upper and Lower. Specimens from Martaban (D.B. 1880) have sinuately dentate l. Fl. March, Fr. May. 2. **B. flaccida,** Muell. Arg. Tenasserim. Similar to 1, bracts of ♂ fl. short, very deciduous. 3. **B. parviflora,** Muell. Arg.—Tenasserim, Malay Penins. and Archip. L. thin oblanceolate or obovate, bracts minute, ♂ racemes very slender, ♀ sepals linear. Fr. narrow-ellipsoid.

4. **B. courtallensis,** Muell. Arg.—Syn. *Baccaurea sapida*, Bedd. Fl. Sylv. t. 280; *Pierardia macrostachys*, Wight Ic. t. 1912 ♂, t. 1913 ♀. *Mutta thuri, Mutta keipu*, Mal. Western Ghats from North Kanara southwards, common in evergreen forest. A large or middle-sized tree, l. glabrous, elliptic, shortly acuminate, sometimes opposite, blade 3–8, pet. ½–1½ in. Fl. hairy, bracts minute, ♂ reddish in long narrow racemiform panicles densely crowded on the trunk, branches of panicles short, 3–5-fld. ♀ on short pedicels in slender racemes, 8–12 in., sepals ⅛–⅓ in. long. Fr. bright crimson, 1 in. diam., subglobose with 3 ridges, hanging in great profusion all round the trunk, which appears as a mass of crimson. Hooker, in Fl. Brit. Ind. v. 371 refers Wight Ic. t. 1913 to *B. sapida*.

8. APOROSA, Blume; Fl. Brit. Ind. v. 345.

Trees, usually evergreen, l. alternate. Fl. small, usually diœcious, apetalous, disk 0. ♂: in axillary catkin-like often clustered spikes, 1–3 fl. in the axils of large imbricating bracts. Sepals 3–6, usually 4, stamens 1–5, central filaments slender. ♀: in short spikes or racemes, peduncles clothed with numerous imbricating bracts, sepals 3–6, small. Ovary 2- (rarely 1- or 3-) celled, stigmas plumose, spreading or recurved, simple or 2–4-cleft, ovules 2 in each cell. Fr. bursting irregularly from the base upwards. Cotyledons flat broad, in fleshy albumen. Species 30–40, Indo-Malayan region.

Kokra, Beng. and *Yemein*, Burm. are used indiscriminately for several species.

A. Ovary pubescent or tomentose.

(*a*) ♀ fl. sessile, l. glabrous beneath.

a. Fr. ovoid.

1. **A. Roxburghii,** Baill. Vern. *Yemein*, Burm. Subhimal. tract from Sikkim eastwards in Sāl and mixed forest. Orissa. Assam. Khasi hills. Cachar. Comillah. Chittagong—Burma, Upper and Lower, common in Engdain. A small or middle-sized tree, glabrous except inflorescence. L. elliptic or elliptic-lanceolate, acuminate, entire or obscurely sinuate-toothed, blade 4–6, pet. ⅓–½ in. ♂ spikes clustered, 1–1½ in. long, bracts broad, ciliate, sepals pubescent. Fr. ovoid-oblong, ⅓–½ in. long. 2. **A. oblonga,** Muell. Arg. Amherst, Tenasserim. Glabrous, l. elliptic-oblong, blade 3–5, pet. ½–⅝ in. 3. **A. Clellandii,** Hook. f. Rangoon. Glabrous, l. lanceolate, thinly coriaceous, blade 5–6, pet. ¼–⅓ in., sec. n. very slender. Fr. ¼–½ in. long, pericarp very thin, fragile. 4. **A. glabrifolia,** Kurz. Nicobars. Branchlets robust, shoots tomentose, l. broad-elliptic, sparsely hairy beneath, blade 3–5, pet. ½ in., fr. ⅜ in. finely pubescent. 5. **A. acuminata,** Thwaites. Vern. *Nir Vittil*, Mal. Tinnevelli and Travancore ghats 3–3,500 ft. Ceylon. A shrub or small tree, youngest shoots silky, l. thin, glabrous, lanceolate, caudate-acuminate, blade 3–4, narrowed into pet. ¼–⅓ in. ♂ catkins ¼–¾ in., fr. ⅜ in. long, red, hairy, pericarp fleshy.

β. Fr. globose or nearly so.

6. **A. macrophylla,** Muell. Arg. *Ingyin*, Burm. Eng forest of Upper and Lower Burma. A small tree (deciduous, Kurz), perfectly glabrous, save inflorescence, branchlets stout, l. coriaceous, ovate, base deeply cordate, blade 9–24, pet. 2–3 in. long. Fr. sessile, yellow, velvety, ¾ in. diam. 7. **A. villosula,** Kurz. Vern. *Thitsat*, Burm. Andamans. Lower Burma. A small tree, youngest shoots hairy, l. elliptic-oblong, acuminate, blade 5–7, pet ¼–1 in. long. Fr. apiculate, ⅓ in. diam.

(*b*) ♀ fl. sessile, l. tomentose beneath.

8. **A. villosa,** Baill. Vern. *Ingyin*, Burm. Burma, Lower and Upper, in Eng forest. —Cochin China. A middle-sized deciduous tree, bark thick, grey, deeply cracked, branchlets, petioles and leaves beneath softly hairy. L. rigidly coriaceous, broadly elliptic-oblong, quite entire, blade 4–9, pet. ½–1 in. long. ♂ spikes ½–2 in. long, bracts hairy. ♀ spikes few-fld., sessile, often on the old wood, ovary densely rusty-villous. Fr. ovoid, densely tawny tomentose, ⅓ in. long, usually 1-seeded.

(*c*) ♀ fl. pedicelled.

9. **A. Lindleyana**, Baill.; Bedd. Fl. Sylv. t. 286.—Syn. *Scepa Lindleyana*, Wight Ic. t. 361. Vern. *Sulla*, Kan.; *Vittil*, Tam. Evergreen forests of the Konkan and the Western Ghats, common in places. A small or middle-sized tree, youngest shoots more or less silky. L. glabrous, elliptic-oblong, acuminate, blade 5–7, pet. $\frac{1}{8}$–$\frac{3}{8}$ in., stipules large, hairy, caducous. ♂ catkins 1–1$\frac{1}{2}$ in. long, bracts glabrous, ciliate. ♀ fl. in short hairy often clustered racemes. Fr. globose, $\frac{1}{3}$–$\frac{1}{2}$ in. diam. 10. **A. Bourdilloni**, Stapf in Hook. Ic. Pl. t. 2204. Travancore low country, moist forest. A small tree, branchlets, petioles and underside of l. along n. shortly pubescent, l. elliptic-oblong, acuminate, blade 5–7, pet. $\frac{1}{2}$ in. ♂ catkins $\frac{1}{4}$ in. long, bracts ovate puberulous. ♀ fl. solitary, on bracteate axillary peduncles, $\frac{1}{4}$ in. long, ovary densely covered with long bristles.

B. Ovary glabrous, fr. sessile.

11. **A. Wallichii**, Hook. f. Assam. Khasi hills. Chittagong. Tenasserim. A large tree, glabrous excepting ♂ bracts, l. lanceolate or oblong-lanceolate, bracts of ♂ fl. tomentose, fr. ellipsoid $\frac{1}{2}$ in. long. 12. **A. aurea**, Hook. f.—Syn. *A. microstachya*, Muell. Arg. Chittagong. Burma (Kurz). A small tree, entirely glabrous, l. yellowish-green when dry, elliptic-oblong, blade 6–9, pet. $\frac{1}{2}$–1 in., bracts of ♂ fl. glabrous, fr. globose $\frac{1}{2}$ in. diam. 13. **A. Planchoniana**, Baill.—Syn. *A. lanceolata*, Kurz Fl. ii. 363. Tenasserim. Perak. Entirely glabrous, l. lanceolate, blade 2–4, pet. $\frac{1}{8}$ in. long, sec. n. obscure. ♂ catkins $\frac{1}{2}$–1 in., bracts glabrous. fr. ellipsoid, beaked, $\frac{1}{2}$ in. long.

Scortechinia nicobarica, Hook. f. Nicobars. L. elliptic, sinuate-serrate, blade 6, pet. 1$\frac{1}{2}$ in. long, sec. n. 8 pair. Fl. minute, diœcious, sepals 4–5, imbricate, petals 0. ♂: Stamens 4–5, filaments stout, free, pistillode 3-lobed, hairy. ♀: Capsule hoary, crustaceous, 1 in. long, 1-celled, 4-valved. Seed 1, albumen scanty.

9. ANTIDESMA, Linn.; Fl. Brit. Ind. v. 354.

Trees or shrubs, l. alternate, entire, stipules as a rule not early deciduous. Fl. diœcious, small, numerous, apetalous, in slender often terminal simple or panicled spikes or racemes. Calyx-lobes or -teeth 3–5, rarely 6–8. ♂: Disk entire or lobed, stamens 2–5, filaments free, often inserted between the lobes of the disk, anther-cells globose, didymous, or inserted at the ends of a thick connective, pistillode glabrous or hairy, sometimes minute or none. ♀: Disk annular or pulvinate, ovary 1-celled, ovules 2, stigmas 2–4, bifid. Fr. a small drupe, crowned with the persistent stigmas. Species 60–70, tropical Africa, Asia, Australia and Polynesia.

A. Ovary tomentose.

1. **A. Ghæsembilla**, Gærtn.—Syn. *A. paniculatum*, Roxb.; Wight Ic. t. 820; *A. pubescens*, Roxb. Cor. Pl. t. 167, Wight Ic. t. 821. Vern. *Umtoa*, Hind.; *Bān masūri*, Oudh; *Khudi jamb*, Beng.; *Matasura*, Kol; *Jondhri*, Mar.; *Pullam-Purasi*, Kan.; *Pollai*, Tel.; *Kinbalin*, *Pyisin*, Burm. Subhimalayan tract from the Sarda eastwards. In the Oudh forests common. Assam. Bengal. Both peninsulas. In Burma in tidal, Savannah and Eng forests. A small deciduous tree, branchlets, petioles, young leaves and inflorescence usually soft-tomentose, rarely glabrous. L. broad-elliptic, sometimes obovate, mostly obtuse, blade 2–4, pet. $\frac{1}{8}$–$\frac{3}{8}$ in., stipules early deciduous. Fl. sessile in slender panicled spikes, stamens 4–7, anthers horse-shoe shaped, disk 5-lobed, pubescent. Ovary pubescent, fr. red to black, $\frac{1}{8}$–$\frac{1}{4}$ in. diam. edible. 2. **A. Roxburghii**, Wall. (*Stilago tomentosa*, Roxb.; Wight Ic. t. 767, 768.) Assam. Silhet. Branches, l. and inflorescence densely rusty-villous, l. acuminate, 4–8 in., pet. short, stipules persistent, spikes simple, stout, erect, 4–6 in. long. 3. **A. velutinosum**, Blume. Tenasserim. Malay Penins. and Archip. A small tree, branchlets, petioles and l. beneath along midrib and nerves softly tomentose, l. 5–8 in., pet. short, spikes stout, solitary. 4. **A. Helferi**, Hook. f. Tenasserim (or Andamans). Branches and l. glabrous, l. coriaceous, spike terminal, stout.

B. Ovary glabrous.

(*a*) ♂ fl. sessile, calyx not deeply lobed.

5. **A. Bunius**, Spreng.; Wight Ic. t. 819; Bedd. Man. t. 24. Vern. *Amati*, Mar.; *Naikuti*, Kan.; *Anepu*, Tel.; *Kywè pyisin*, Burm. Subhimalayan tract from Nepal eastwards, ascending to 3,000 ft. Assam. Khasi Hills. Manipùr. Chutia Nagpur. Western Ghats. Upper Burma. Arakan Yoma 3–4,000 ft. Ceylon. China. Malay Archip. A small evergreen tree, youngest shoots hairy, l. glabrous, elongate-elliptic or elliptic-lanceolate, acuminate. Fl. spikes pubescent, ♀ simple, ♂ often compound, calyx of ♂ usually hairy, sometimes glabrous, ciliate on margin. Anthers 3. ♂ fl.

shortly pedicelled, fr. ⅛ in. diam., very juicy, red, turning black when ripe. 6. **A. zeylanicum,** Lam.; Trimen Handb. Ceylon iv. 44.—Syn. *A. Alexiteria*, Linn. (comprises 5 and 6). Western Penins. in the south. Ceylon. A small much branched tree, young shoots glabrous. L. glabrous, shining, blade 1–3, pet. ⅛ in. Fr. ovoid ⅛ in. long.

b. ♂ fl. sessile, calyx deeply 4-lobed.

7. **A. velutinum,** Tulasne. Burma, Upper and Lower. A small evergreen tree, branchlets, petioles, underside of l. and inflorescence tomentose, l. elongate-elliptic, acuminate, blade 4–6, pet. ⅛ in. long. ♂ sepals 3–4, orbicular, villous, stamens 3–4. 8. **A. fruticulosum,** Kurz. Tidal forests of Pegu. A small shrub, l. 1–2⅓ in. long, harshly tomentose. 9. **A. cuspidatum,** Muell. Arg. Shan hills, 5,000 ft. Malay Peninsula. Branchlets, petioles and inflorescence finely pubescent, l. elongate-elliptic, acuminate, blade 5–8, pet. ⅛–⅜ in., sec. n. 8-10 pair, arching, prominent beneath. ♂ spikes panicled, bracts larger than fl., ♀ disk villous. 10. **A. nigricans,** Tulasne. Assam. Silhet. Branches, pet. and spikes densely tomentose, l. elliptic-lanceolate, blade 4–7, pet. ⅛–⅛ in., sec. n. 6–10 pair, arching, joined by intramarginal veins. ♂ cal. 4-partite, stamens 4.

(*c*) ♂ fl. pedicelled.

11. **A. diandrum,** Roth.—Syn. *Stilago diandra*, Roxb. Cor. Pl. t. 166. Vern. *Amli, Imli, Amari*, Hind.; *Dakhi*, Oudh; *Multa*, Beng.; *Sana Kulipa*, Kan.; *Manchi pulleri*, Tel.; *Kinbalin*, Burm. Subhimalayan tract from the Jumna eastwards, common in Sāl forests. Behar. Chutia Nagpur. Central Provinces. Western Peninsula. Assam. Khasi hills. Manipùr. Bengal. Burma, Upper and Lower.—Ceylon. A large shrub or small tree, deciduous, glabrous or branchlets rusty-pubescent. L. thin, lanceolate or elliptic-lanceolate, base acute, blade 1½–5, pet. ⅛ in., stipules deciduous. Racemes lax, slender, often simple, quite glabrous, fl. all pedicelled, calyx 4-lobed. Stamens 2, rarely 3, at the base of the small glabrous disk. Fr. ⅛ in. diam., purplish-red, edible. The leaves turn brick-red before falling, leaves acid made into preserve. 12. **A. Khasianum,** Hook. f. Assam. Khasi hills. Cachar. Young shoots and inflorescence hairy, otherwise glabrous, l. from elliptic-lanceolate to linear-lanceolate, blade 2–7, pet. ⅛ in. ♂ racemes hairy, lax, 1–1⅓ in. long, calyx glabrous, cupular, shortly 3-4-lobed, stamens 2–4. Fr. ¼ in. long, tipped by the 2–3 rigid bases of the stigmas. 13. **A. acuminatum,** Wall.; Wight Ic. t. 1991. Sikkim, foot of hills, ascending to 3,000 ft. Assam. Khasi hills. Chutia Nagpur. A large shrub, branchlets, petioles, stipules and midrib of l. tomentose, l. shining above, elliptic-lanceolate, blade 4–12, pet. ⅛–⅛ in. long. ♂ racemes 2–6 in. long, mostly panicled, rachis and bracts densely hairy, pedicels longer than bracts, calyx of 4 broadly ovate sepals, glabrous or hairy, stamens 3–4. ♀ fl. sometimes with short stamens. Fr. ⅛ in. long, acuminate. 14. **A. Moritzii,** Muell. Arg. Tenasserim.—Malay Penins. and Archip. A small tree, branchlets, petioles, stipules, midrib and racemes finely tomentose, l. elongate-elliptic 5–10 in. long, ♂ racemes slender 2–3 in., paniculate, fl. minute, stamens 4–5. Fr. sub-globose, acute, ⅛–¼ in. diam. 15. **A. martabanicum,** Presl. Tenasserim. Similar to 14, stipules large, calyx 3–4-partite, stamens 3–4. Fr. ellipsoid or subglobose ⅛–⅛ in. long.

16. **A. Menasu,** Miquel. Western Ghats from the Konkan southwards, near streams and in evergreen forest. Common near Coonoor. A small or middle-sized tree, branchlets, petioles, stipules and inflorescence velvety, l. glabrous, underside shining, elliptic-oblong, acuminate, blade 4–7, pet. ⅛–¼ in. ♂ fl. pedicellate, calyx 3–4-partite, stamens 3–4, inserted between the lobes of the disk. Fr. ovoid, acute, ⅛–¼ in. long.

Sarcococca pruniformis, Lindl.; Collett Simla Fl. 448, Fig. 146.—Syn. *S. saligna*, Muell. Arg. *S. trinervia*, Wight Ic. t. 1877. Vern. *Shangal*, Sutlej; *Tiliari*, Jaunsar; *Chilikat*, Nep.; *Kwe-i-pok*, Burm. Afghanistan. Himalaya 5,9000 ft., often gregarious in shady places. Khasi hills and Manipùr. Upper Burma. Western Ghats from South Kanara southwards.—Ceylon. Ind. Archip. China. A glabrous evergreen shrub, bark green, l. coriaceous, alternate, lanceolate or elliptic-lanceolate, triplinerved or penninerved, the lowest pair extending below the middle of l., blade 2–5, pet. ¼–⅜ in. Fl. yellowish-white, monœcious, in short compact axillary spikes, sepals 4, biseriate, supported by decussate bracts similar to sepals, more numerous in the female fl., which generally are at the base of the spikes. ♂: Stamens 4, free, opposite to sepals. ♀: Ovary 2-3-celled, styles as many as cells, at length recurved, ovules 2 in each cell. Berries purple, ovoid ¼–½ in. long. Very variable, var. *Hookeriana* has narrower, usually penninerved l., fr, globose.

10. DAPHNIPHYLLUM, Blume; Fl. Brit. Ind. v. 353.

Glabrous evergreen trees, l. alternate, long petioled, quite entire, usually glaucous beneath, approximate near the ends of branches. Fl. in axillary

racemes, diœcious, apetalous, sepals small, 3–8, more or less connate. ♂: Stamens 5–18, anthers large, basifixed, often apiculate, pistillode 0. ♀: Disk 0 or of 4–6 scales or glands, ovary imperfectly 2-celled, stigmas short, distinct, thick, recurved, entire, ovules 2 in each cell. Drupe oblong, usually 1-seeded. Embryo small, in thick fleshy albumen. Species 12, chiefly Indo-Malayan, a few in China and tropical Africa.

1. **D. glaucescens,** Blume; Bedd. Fl. Sylv. t. 288.—Syn. *Goughia neilgherrensis*, Wight Ic. t. 1878–9. Vern. *Soluvan*, Tam. Common on the Nilgiris, Anamalais, Palnis, and on the Travancore Ghats from 4,000 ft. upwards.—Ceylon, 4–7,000 ft., China, Corea, Java. A large shrub or middle-sized tree, l. elliptic, base acute, tip often obtuse, blade 3–5, pet. ¾–2 in. Drupe black, ellipsoid ⅓ in., pedicel nearly as long. 2. **D. himalayense,** Muell. Arg. Vern. *Ratendu*, Jauns. Himalaya from the Jumna eastwards, 4–9,000 ft. Khasi hills. Tenasserim, on Mooleyit 6,800 ft. (Beddome). A small tree, wood greyish-brown, with streaks of bright crimson, l. oblong-lanceolate or oblanceolate, blade 4–10, pet. 1–2 in. Fr. ellipsoid ½–¾ in. long.

11. PUTRANJIVA, Wall.; Fl. Brit. Ind. v. 336.

Species 2, India and Ceylon.

P. Roxburghii, Wall.; Royle Ill. t. 83 (bis); Wight Ic. t. 1876; Bedd. Fl. Sylv. t. 275; Brandis F. Fl. t. 53. Vern. *Jiaputa*, *Putranjiva*, Hind.; *Putrajiva*, Kan.; *Kuduru*, Tel.; *Karupale*, Tam.; *Daukyat*, Pegu; *Badibyu*, Chindwin.

A middle-sized evergreen tree with hanging branches, foliage dark green, branchlets and petioles minutely pubescent. Leaves coriaceous, shining, elliptic-oblong, distantly serrulate, base unequal-sided, blade 2–4, pet. ¼ in. Fl. generally diœcious, apetalous, disk 0. ♂: in dense axillary clusters, calyx 3–5-partite, stamens 3, filaments free or connate at the base. ♀: pedicellate, solitary or a few together, calyx 5–6-cleft, segments small. Ovary pubescent, 3-celled, styles 3 short, dilated into broad fleshy stigmas. Fr. ellipsoid, white-tomentose, on pedicels ½–1 in. long, stone pointed, rugose, very hard, seed one.

Subhimalayan tract, from the Chenab eastwards, ascending to 2,500 ft. Both Peninsulas, in damp evergreen forests and on banks of streams, but not common. Often planted. Fl. March–May, fr. takes 12 months to ripen. The nuts are strung up in rosaries.—Ceylon. The sepals generally are semipersistent, traces remaining until the fr. ripens, in some cases (specimens from Upper Burma) they fall immediately after flowering.

12. HEMICYCLIA, Wight & Arn.; Fl. Brit. Ind. v. 337.

Evergreen trees or shrubs, l. alternate, base often unequal-sided. Fl. small, diœcious, sepals 4–5, imbricate. ♂: Stamens 4–23 inserted round an orbicular disk, filaments free, anther-cells parallel. ♀: Disk flat annular, ovary 1- rarely 2-celled, stigma sesile or nearly so. Fruit with a hard endocarp, seeds grooved on one face. Species 9, Indo-Malayan region, Australia.

A. Western species.

1. **H. sepiaria,** Wight & Arn.; Wight Ic. t. 1872. Vern. *Virai*, Tam.; *Bira*, Tel.; *Hira*, Kan.; *Vellelambu*, Tam.; *Vella Kasavu*, Mal. Common in the semi-evergreen scrub and forests of the Karnatik and Deccan.—Ceylon dry region. A rigid much-branched shrub, young shoots minutely pubescent, wood very hard, close- and even-grained, l. glabrous, rigidly coriaceous, elliptic-oblong, obtuse, base rounded or cordate, blade 1½–3 in., pet. ⅛–¼ in. long. Fr. crimson, globose ¼–⅓ in. diam. 2. **H. venusta,** Thwaites.—Syn. *Astylis venusta*, Wight Ic. t. 1992. Western Ghats from Kanara southwards, common in evergreen forests. Northern Circars (Gamble). A middle-sized tree, branchlets nearly glabrous, l. glabrous, coriaceous, blade 3–5, pet. ⅛ in. long. Fl. ♂, pedicels and both surfaces of sepals velvety, sepals 4 obtuse, ⅛ in. long, 2 outer 2 inner, stamens usually 8, filaments and anthers hairy. Fr. obovoid ¾, pedicel ½–1½ in long. Nearly allied are the following: 3. **H. elata,** Bedd. Fl. Sylv. t. 279. Wainād, Anamalais, Tinnevelli. A large tree, l. thinly coriaceous, fl. larger and on longer pedicels than 2. 4. **H. Porteri,** Gamble in Hook. Ic. t. 2701. Varsanad valley, Madura district, near streams, 2,000 ft. A small gregarious tree, ♂ fl. large, ½ in. across, stamens

24–25, glabrous, inserted round a broad orbicular crenate disk. 5. **H. Wightii**, Hook. f. Nilgiris. Nearly glabrous, l. narrow, elliptic or oblong-lanceolate, entire or obscurely crenate, fr. ⅜ in. long, pedicel shorter than fr. (not seen). 6. **H.** sp. nova. Bourdillon 227, 534. Travancore, evergreen forest, 1,000 ft. (*H. lanceolata*, Thwaites, Gamble Ind. Timb. ed. ii. 605). A middle-sized or large tree, branchlets and petioles minutely pubescent, l. coriaceous, dentate, blade 2–8, pet. ¼ in. Fl. ♂ (in bud) sessile, sepals glabrous, edge fimbriate and minutely ciliate, stamens 8, glabrous. Fr. ⅓–½ in. long, 1-celled, 1-seeded, pericarp succulent, endocarp crustaceous, cotyledons large in a fleshy albumen, pedicels shorter than fr. **H. lanceolata**, a Ceylon species, has l. entire, long acuminate.

B. Eastern species, imperfectly known.

7. **H. sumatrana**, Muell. Arg. Plains of Pegu and Martaban, not unfrequent in marshy places (Kurz). A middle-sized entirely glabrous tree, l. dentate, fr. obtuse at both ends, ⅓, pedicel ⅛ in. long. 8. **H. andamanica**, Kurz. Coast forests of the Andamans, frequent in low places (Kurz). A middle-sized glabrous tree, l. nearly entire, fr. ⅜, pedicel ⅙–¼ in. long.

13. CYCLOSTEMON, Blume; Fl. Brit. Ind. v. 339.

Evergreen trees, l. alternate usually coriaceous. Fl. diœcious, apetalous, axillary or on the old wood, sepals 3–6, broad, imbricate, often supported by a number of small imbricate bracts. ♂ : Stamens 6–8 or ∞, inserted round a flat or depressed disk. ♀ : disk usually annular, ovary hairy 2–4-celled, stigmas in most species sessile, broad fleshy, two collateral ovules from the apex of each cell under a fleshy excrescence of the placenta (caruncle). Fr. indehiscent, 2-celled, often supported by the persistent calyx or the remains of it, seeds solitary in each cell, or one only by abortion, cotyledons broad in a fleshy albumen. Species 20, Africa, India, Malay Archipelago.

I. *Eucyclostemon*. Stamens numerous, stigmas 2, large sessile.

A. Fl. axillary.

1. **C. assamicus**, Hook. f. Vern. *Chipla*, Dún; *Kat behula*, Kum.; *Ban-bokal*, Beng. Subhimalayan tract from the Dehra Dún eastwards. Assam. Singhbúm. Sundriban. Chittagong. Andamans. Coco island. A small tree, branchlets slender, glabrous, l. quite entire, shining, elongate-elliptic, blade 4–8, pet. ¼ in. Fr. scarlet, nearly sessile, velvety, laterally compressed with 2 furrows, almost 2-lobed, ½–⅝ in. long. 2. **C. eglandulosus**, Kurz. Tippera. Chittagong. Arakan, rare (Kurz) A middle-sized tree, branchlets glabrous, l. elliptic, caudate-acuminate, blade 2–4, pet. ¼–⅓ in. Fl. ♀ in axillary few-fld. panicles, pedicels velvety, ⅜ in. long, sepals 4, velvety on both surfaces, unequal, the larger ¼ in. long. Two imperfectly known sp. coll. by Dr. Helfer 1837, either in Tenasserim or on the Andamans. 3. **C. Helferi**, Hook. f. L. glabrous, elliptic-lanceolate, repand denticulate, blade 4–6, pet. ⅓ in., veins prominently reticulate, fr. velvety, crowned by a large fleshy stigma, pedicel ½ in. long. 4. **C. ellipticus**, Hook. f. L. glabrous, thinly coriaceous, elliptic, acuminate, blade 4–5, pet. ¼ in. ♂ fl. pubescent, on short pedicels, axillary and on the old wood, sepals ⅛ in. long.

5. **C. Jaintensis**, C. B. Clarke MSS. in herb. Kew. Jowai, Jaintia hills, 3,500 ft. A tree, stem with strong prickles, youngest shoots finely silky, l. membranous, denticulate, fr. sessile, solitary, always axillary, ellipsoid, velvety, ⅜ in. long, 2-celled, but 1-seeded, supported by the 8 round persistent sepals and crowned by the stigma, consisting of 2 sessile circular plates (fl. unknown, hence position in the genus uncertain).

B. Fl. all on the old wood.

6. **C. macrophyllus**, Blume (including *C. zeylanicus*, Baill.); Bedd. Fl. Sylv. t. 278. Evergreen forests of the Western Ghats from Coorg southwards. Common on the Anamalais. Western Duars (D. B. Feb. 1879). Andamans.—Malay Peninsula. Ceylon. Java. A middle-sized tree, stem often attaining a large diameter, branches spreading. Youngest shoots with deciduous brown hairs, l. glabrous, elliptic-oblong, usually entire, blade 6–12, pet. stout, ¼–⅓ in. Fl. sessile (Coorg, Western Duars), pedicellate (Travancore, Andamans, Ceylon, Malay Penins.). Pedicels and sepals hairy, sepals 4 or 5. Placenta enlarged, fleshy, resembling a hood on the 2 collateral ovules. Fr. pubescent, yellow when ripe, nearly globose, ¾–1 in. diam. 7. **C. malabaricus**, Bedd. Tinnevelli ghats. Branchlets, young l. and fl. golden-tomentose, sepals 4, fr. tomentose, pedicel ½ in. long. 8. **C. confertiflorus**, Hook. f, Vern. *Augai mara*, Kan. North Kanara, evergreen forests. A large tree, quite glabrous, l. elliptic-oblong, blade 6–8, pet. stout, ¼ in. ♂ fl. sessile in dense clusters, disk depressed, funnel-shaped, glabrous, radiately ribbed, with a membranous lobed border.

II. *Stenogynium*. Stamens 6–8. Ovary 2-celled, styles as a rule 2, slender, stigma peltate. Fl. axillary.

9. **C. Griffithii,** Hook. f. Vern. *Thitègyin*, Burm. Mishmi hills, Assam. Upper Burma, evergreen hill forests 3–7,000 ft. A large tree, wood hard, light brown. L. membranous or thinly coriaceous, lanceolate or elliptic-lanceolate, acuminate, blade 4–7, pet. ¼–⅓ in. Fr. ellipsoid, clothed when young with deciduous velvet, 1 in. long, yellow when ripe, crowned with the remains of the styles, pedicel slender up to 2 in. long, 10. **C. lancifolius,** Hook. f. Sikkim, ascending to 5,000 ft. Khasi hills. A tree with long slender branches. Young shoots glabrous, l. lanceolate, margins thickened, blade 4–6, pet. ⅓–½ in. long, large glabrous lanceolate buds ⅓–⅝ in. long in the leaf-axils. Fl. ♂ and ♀ in pubescent axillary racemes. Fr. 2-celled, 1 in. pedicel 1 in. long, thickened at apex. 11. **C. indicus,** Muell. Arg. Khasi hills. L. glabrous, obliquely ovate-lanceolate, caudate-acuminate, blade 3–5, pet. ⅛ in. long. ♂ fl. minute, solitary or 2–3 together, pedicels capillary up to ¼ in. long. 12. **C. subsessilis,** Kurz. Arakan. Thaukyeghat forest, frequent (Kurz). A small tree, l. glabrous, oblong-lanceolate, blade 6–9, pet. ¼–½ in. Fl. ♂ minute nearly sessile; clusters axillary or above the scars of fallen l. Fr. orange coloured, minutely velvety, ⅜–⅝ in., pedicels $\frac{1}{10}$ in. long.

14. BREYNIA, Forst.; Fl. Brit. Ind. v. 329.

Shrubs or small trees, l. small, alternate, quite entire. Fl. small, monœcious, petals and disk 0. ♂: Calyx turbinate or hemispheric, rim of tube thickened, lobes 6, small, sometimes with an inner series, opposite to the outer segments. Anthers 3, linear, adnate for their entire length to the central column, cells parallel. ♀: Calyx coriaceous, hemispheric or rotate, persistent and often enlarged in fruit, lobes 6, broad. Ovary 3-celled, styles 3, bifid, or 3 minute stigmas in the cavity at the top of the ovary. Fr. more or less succulent, globose or depressed, indehiscent or 6-valved, cocci 3–6 triquetrous. Species 15, tropical Asia, Australia and Pacific islands.

1. **B. patens,** Benth.—Syn. *Melanthesopsis patens*, Muell. Arg.; *M. obliqua*, Wight Ic. t. 1898; *M. truncata*, Wight Ic. t. 1897. Vern. *Kangli*, Mar. Subhimalayan tract, ascending to 3,000 ft., from Nepal eastwards. Assam. Khasi hills, Manipùr. Cachar. Chittagong, Burma, Upper and Lower. Western Peninsula. Fl. March–May.—Ceylon. A deciduous entirely glabrous shrub, branchlets quadrangular, l. elliptic, usually obtuse, turning black in drying, ½–1 in., pet. very short. Fl. greenish-yellow, ♂ on short filiform pedicels, staminal-column produced beyond anthers, acute. ♀: Style stout with 3 forked arms. Fr. seated on the greatly enlarged coloured calyx, depressed, ½–⅝ in. diam., orange-red, fleshy but dehiscent. 2. **B. angustifolia,** Hook. f. Pegu. Tenasserim. Malay Penins. Branchlets terete, l. oblong or linear-oblong ¾–1 in. long, fr. ¼ in. diam. 3. **B. rhamnoides,** Muell. Arg.—Syn. *Melanthesa rhamnoides*, Wight Ic. t. 1898. Vern. *Yellari*, Tel. Oudh Forests. Gangetic plain. Bengal. Western Peninsula. Andamans. Arakan, chiefly near the sea (Kurz).—Ceylon. common in the moist region. Malay Peninsula and Archipelago, China. A large shrub or small tree, wholly glabrous. L. ovate, or elliptic 1–1½ long, pet. very short. Fl. solitary on short pedicels. ♂: Staminal-column truncate. Fr. purple, globose, ¼ in. diam., calyx hardly enlarged.

15. SAUROPUS, Blume; Fl. Brit. Ind. v. 332.

Shrubs or undershrubs, l. alternate, distichous, membranous, quite entire. Fl. monœcious, apetalous. ♂: calyx 6-lobed, lobes thickened at base, and often concave with an appendix vaulting over stamens. Stamens united into a short fleshy truncate 3-armed column, the anthers attached to the ends of the arms and opening downwards, cells parallel. ♀: calyx 6-cleft, persistent, accrescent, ovary 3-celled, styles bifid. Species 20, Indo-Malayan region. A few only of the more common species can here be noticed.

A. *Eusauropus*. L. 1½–4 in. long, styles on the apex of an ovoid ovary.

1. **S. albicans,** Blume.—Syn. *S. indicus*, Wight; *S. zeylanicus*. Wight Ic. t. 1952; *S. Gardnerianus*, Wight Ic. t. 1951. Sikkim and Bhutan, foot of Himalaya and outer hills, ascending to 5,000 ft. Khasi hills. Cachar. Burma. Anamalai hills. Travancore.—Ceylon, moist region. Malay Penins. and Archip. China. A small shrub with a simple stem and numerous elongated branches, quite glabrous, l. ovate-oblong or

ovate-lanceolate, blade 2–4, pet. $\frac{1}{8}$ in. Fl. reddish-green, fr. globose, $\frac{3}{4}$ in. diam., fleshy, white, tinged with rose, on a nodding pedicel $\frac{1}{2}$–1 in. long, supported by the reddish-brown calyx. 2. **S. trinervius,** Muell. Arg. Teesta valley, Sikkim. Assam. Khasi hills. Cachar. L. 3–5 in. long, triplinerved, fr. 1 in. diam.

B. *Ceratogynum.* L. $\frac{1}{2}$–1 in., distichous on branchlets which are often deciduous and have the appearance of pinnate leaves, at the base of these branchlets 3 stipuliform bracts. Ovary broad, depressed, styles 3 on the edge of its broad concave top.

3. **S. quadrangularis,** Muell. Arg.—Syn. *Ceratogynum rhamnoides*, Wight Ic. t. 1900. Vern. *Chikli*, Mar. Behar, Chutia Nagpur. Western Peninsula on the west side, from Vingorla southwards. Anamalai hills. A low shrub, branchlets angled, the 2 lateral stipuliform bracts lanceolate, l. elliptic acute. Fl. $\frac{1}{8}$ in. diam. ♂ : on filiform pedicels $\frac{1}{4}$–$\frac{1}{3}$ in., calyx-segments lanceolate acute, curved upwards, basal appendices blunt, vaulting over the minute staminal-column. 4. **S. compressus,** Muell. Arg.; (probably also *S. quadrangularis*, Kurz F. Fl. ii. 350. Vern. *Taung tama*, Lower, *Hmansi*, Upper Burma. Sikkim, Bhutan, foot of hills, ascending to 2,000 ft. Burma, often in Engdaing. Fl. H. S. A shrub or small tree, often an undershrub if kept down by the action of the annual jungle fires. Branchlets angled and compressed, l. elliptic, often broad, nearly orbicular, $\frac{1}{2}$–1 in. long, on a short slender petiole, the 2 lateral stipuliform bracts broad, ovate or triangular, often oblique. Fl. ♂ minute, dark crimson, pedicels $\frac{1}{8}$ in., calyx-segments 5–6, obovate, emarginate, base slightly concave.

16. FLUGGEA, Willd.; Fl. Brit. Ind. v. 328.

L. small, alternate, quite entire. Fl. minute, diœcious, apetalous, on short slender pedicels, sepals 5, imbricate in bud. ♂ in dense clusters, stamens 5, alternating with small round disk glands, filaments free, exserted, pistillode large trifid. ♀ : in lax fascicles, ovary usually 3-celled, disk annular, toothed, styles connate at base, bifid or notched, sometimes entire. Fr. dry or fleshy, supported by the persistent calyx, seeds triquetrous, the ventral edge concave, embryo curved, in scanty albumen. Species 6, tropics of the Old World.

1. **F. microcarpa,** Blume.—Syn. *Securinega obovata*, Muell. Arg.; Brandis F. Fl. t. 54 (the ♀ and ♂ branches on the right); *Cicca obovata*, Kurz. Vern. *Halepan*, *Salepan*, Merwara; *Rithoul*, Dehra Dún; *Kodarsi*, Mar.; *Konchinya*, Burm. Thoughout India and Burma, ascending in the outer Himalaya to 5,000 ft.—Tropical Africa. Malay Penins. and Archip. Australia. China. A large unarmed shrub or small tree, wholly glabrous, branches angular, l. elliptic or obovate, blade 1–4, pet. $\frac{1}{8}$–$\frac{1}{4}$ in. Fr. generally large, white, fleshy $\frac{1}{3}$ in. diam. In Dehra Dún most fr. remain small and dry (Kanjilal). 2. **F. Leucopyrus,** Willd.; Wight Ic. t. 1875.—Syn. *Securinega Leucopyrus*, Muell. Arg.; Brandis F. Fl. t. 54 (partly, see 1). Vern. *Kamo*, Sind; *Salepan*, Rajput.; *Posheri*, Mar.; *Tella pulu kudu*, Tel. Sind. Salt range. Southern Punjab. Rajputana (common). The Deccan and the Coromandel coast. A rigid thorny shrub, the l. and fl. bearing branches terminating in sharp spines, l. obovate $\frac{1}{2}$–$1\frac{1}{2}$ in. long. Fr. fleshy, white, globose, $\frac{1}{4}$ in. diam. Somewhat resembles *Flacourtia sepiaria*, Roxb. (crenate l.).

17. PHYLLANTHUS, Linn.; Fl. Brit. Ind. v. 285.

Herbs, trees or shrubs, usually deciduous, l. alternate, distichous, quite entire, often on deciduous branchlets, petioles very short. Fl. small, unisexual, usually monœcious, apetalous. Sepals 4–6, in two series, imbricate in bud, disk of distinct glands, alternating with sepals, sometimes wanting. ♂: Stamens central, 2–5, filaments free or connate. Ovary 3–15-celled, styles free or connate, usually 2-fid, ovules 2 in each cell. Fruit usually 3-celled, and supported by the persistent sometimes enlarged sepals, seeds trigonous, 2 in each cell, testa crustaceous, albumen fleshy. Species 350–400, in all tropical and subtropical countries.

I. Pericarp succulent.

A. Stamens 5–6, sepals 4–6.

1. **P. reticulatus**, Poiret.—Syn. *Anisonema multiflorum*, Wight Ic. t. 1899; *Cicca reticulata*, Kurz F. Fl. ii. 354; *C. microcarpa*, Benth.; Kurz F. Fl. ii. 355. Vern. *Kamu*, Sind; *Kabonan*, Merwara; *Sikat*, Gorakhpur; *Panjuli*, Hind.; *Amluki*, Ass.; *Pavan*, Mar.; *Pandi barrankae*, Tel.; *Pullan*, Tam.

A large straggling or climbing shrub, glabrous or pubescent, branches numerous stout, woody, branchlets long, drooping, l. thin, oblong or elliptic, 1–2 in., stipules subulate, hard. Fl. solitary or several together on slender axillary peduncles. Calyx-segments ovate, membranous, alternating with the glands of the disk. ♂: Stamens 5, the filaments of the 3 inner longer, connate. ♀: Ovary 5–10-celled, styles short, ovules 2 in each cell, superposed. Fr. a purple berry, $\frac{1}{8}$ in. diam., often racemose on leafless branches. Seeds 8–16, triquetrous, finely granulate.

Common on low moist ground in the drier regions of India and Burma. Sind, in the forests along the Indus, climbing over the largest trees. Fl. nearly throughout the year.—Ceylon, common in the dry region. Tropical Africa. Malay Penins. and Archip. China. 2. **P. glaucus**, Wall. Nepal. Sikkim. Khasi hills. Similar to 1, quite glabrous, l. smaller, stamens free, ♀ pedicel clavate, styles slender, long exserted, quite entire, hairy $\frac{1}{4}$–$\frac{1}{3}$ in. diam.

B. Stamens 4, sepals 4.

3. **P. distichus**, Muell. Arg.—Syn. *Cicca disticha*, Linn. Vern. *Chalmeri*, Hind.; *Hariphal*, Beng.; *Kirunelli*, Kan.; *Ratsavusiriki*, Tel.; *Thimbaw Zibyu*, Burm. Malay Archip. In gardens throughout India, in Burma near Pungyi-Kyaungs. A small deciduous tree, entirely glabrous, branches robust, leafy branchlets slender, mostly deciduous, l. ovate, acute or acuminate, blade 2–3, pet. $\frac{1}{6}$ in. long. Fl. minute, brownish-red, ♂ and ♀ and sometimes ☿ together densely crowded on fascicled racemes, 2–4 in. long, generally from the old wood, sometimes in axillary clusters, pedicels slender, as long as fl. Sepals 4, stamens 4, filaments free, styles 3–4, bifid. Fr. globose, often crowded, 6–8-lobed, pericarp fleshy, acid, endocarp 3–4-celled.

C. Stamens 3, filaments united into a column, sepals 5–6.

4. **P. Emblica**, Linn.; Bedd. Fl. Sylv. t. 258; Brandis F. Fl. t. 52.—Syn. *Emblica officinalis*, Gærtn.; Wight Ic. t. 1896. *Cicca Emblica*, Kurz. Vern. *Amla, Aonla, Amlika* Hind.; *Avala*, Mar.; *Miral*, Kol; *Nalli*, Gond.; *Nelli, Usiriki*, Tel.; *Nelli*, Tam.; *Tasha*, Lower, *Zibyu*, Upper Burma.

A deciduous small or middle-sized tree, bark greenish-grey, peeling off in conchoid scales, wood red, hard, med. rays broad, conspicuous on a vertical section. Foliage feathery, light green, branchlets mostly deciduous, hairy, 4–8 in. long, closely set with distichous narrowly-linear glabrous l. $\frac{1}{2}$ in. long, imbricate when young, having the appearance of pinnate leaves, stipules ovate, fimbriate. Fl. greenish-yellow, fascicled in the axils of fimbriate bracts on the leaf-bearing branchlets, usually on the naked portion below the leaves, ♂ numerous on short slender pedicels, ♀ few subsessile, both on the same branchlet. Calyx segments 6, oblong, obtuse. ♂: Disk of 6 minute glands, often wanting, anthers 3, on a short central column. ♀: Disk cup-shaped, edge toothed, ovary 3-celled, styles connate at base irregularly twice bifid, segments acute. Fr. fleshy globose, $\frac{1}{2}$–$\frac{3}{4}$ in. diam., with 6 vertical furrows, pale yellow, sometimes reddish when ripe, acid, astringent and bitter, 3-celled, 6 seeded.

Common in deciduous forests in most parts of India and Burma, except in the arid region and the extreme N.W., ascending to 4,500 ft. in the Himalaya. Fl. March–May. The l. and fl. bearing deciduous branchlets, which have the appearance of pinnate leaves, often come out on old woody branches, from irregular tubercular protuberances, which have given rise to a succession of three deciduous branchlets. When branchlets are on the current year's shoots, 3 bracts will be found at their base, one dorsal, in the axil of which the branchlet has developed, and two lateral, which are the stipules of the dorsal bract. These branchlets, which arise from the current year's shoot, probably are not always deciduous, but serve to form permanent branches. The fr. is the *Emblic Myrobalan*, is pickled and eaten, and used for dyeing and tanning.—Ceylon. Malay Penins. and Archip. China. 5. **P. pomiferus**, Hook. f.—Syn. *Cicca macrocarpa*, Kurz. Vern. *Zibyu*, Burm. Burma, Upper and Lower, chiefly in Engdain. Similar to 4, but bark longitudinally and irregularly fissured, disk in ♂ fl. of distinct glands, alternating with sepals, styles connate high up, simply bifurcate, occasionally 3-furcate. Fr. 1 in. diam., juicy, acid, not bitter. 6. **P. Prainianus,** Coll. et Hemsl. Southern Shan Hills, 5,000 ft. Branchlets pubescent, l. nearly glabrous, pale beneath, from broadly elliptic to orbicular, ½ in. long. Fl. on short capillary pedicels, fasciculate, supported by small reddish fimbriate bracts. 7. **P. albizzoides,** Hook. f.—Syn. *Cicca albizzoides*, Kurz. *Shama*, Burm. Pegu Yoma, west side. A small deciduous tree, branchlets minutely hairy, bark grey, peeling off in irregular conchoid flakes, l. glabrous, glaucescent beneath, nearly sessile, oblong, obtuse, 1–1½ by ½ in. Fr. globose 1 in. diam., pericarp hard fleshy, acid, edible, endocarp woody, 3-celled.

II. Pericarp dry, crustaceous or coriaceous.

A. Stamens 4 or 6, filaments free.

8. **P. indicus,** Muell. Arg. Vern. *Pan Nana*, Kan. Western Ghats, from the Konkan southwards. A middle-sized tree, bark smooth, white, perfectly glabrous. L. membranous elliptic, blade 3–5, pet. ¼ in. Fl. on short pedicels, in dense fascicles, usually at the base of the current year's shoots. Stamens 4, filaments exserted. Capsule smooth, green, with 3 vertical furrows, ⅓–½ in. diam., seeds blue. 9. **P. Chorizandra,** Barber in Ind. For. xxvii. 288.—Syn. *Chorizandra pinnata*, Wight Ic. t. 1994, included under *Fluggea microcarpa*, in Fl. Brit. Ind. v. 328. Western Penins. on the east side, from the Northern Circars to Chingleput. A gregarious glabrous shrub, 3–5 ft. high, l. distant, elliptic. Fl. usually diœcious, fascicled, often appearing before the l., stamens 6, long exserted, sepals 6 reflexed. Capsule 3-celled, ⅓ in. diam. Gamble first drew attention to this species in Ind. For. xxvii. 131.

B. Stamens 3, ♂ sepals 5–6.

(*a*) L. linear, less than ⅔ in. long.

10. **P. Lawii,** Grah. Behar. West Bengal. Chutia Nagpur. Central Provinces. Western Peninsula, often forming dense thickets along the banks of rivers, also in Babul Koruns, Poona district. A gregarious shrub, quite glabrous, l. ¼ in. long, pet. very short, sec. n. obscure. Capsule globose, 3-celled, ⅛–⅙ in. diam. 11. **P. polyphyllus,** Willd. Deccan and Karnatik.—Ceylon, dry country, common. A shrub or small tree, quite glabrous, l. sessile, ½–⅜ in. long, sec. n. 6–8 pair, fl. on slender pedicels up to ¼ in. long. Capsule ⅛ in. diam.

(*b*) L. lanceolate, elliptic or obovate, less than 1¼ in. long. Fl. axillary, generally clustered, on leaf-bearing branchlets.

12. **P. parvifolius,** Ham. Himalaya 2–8,000 ft., from the Ravi eastwards, often in the crevices of rocks. Khasi hills. A small shrub, stems prostrate or erect, in the Khasi hills attaining 8 ft., branchlets sometimes minutely hairy, l. glabrous, glaucous beneath, oblong, elliptic or elliptic-oblong, sessile ¼–⅓ in. long, stipules hastate. Fl. pedicelled, capsule globose ¼ in. diam. 13. **P. brevipes,** Hook. f. Mishmi hills, Assam. Quite glabrous, l. elliptic-obovate, ½–⅜ in. long, fl. nearly sessile from tufts of fimbriate bracts. 14. **P. missionis,** Hook. f. Deccan. Quite glabrous. l. thinly membranous, obovate, blade ¼–½, pet. slender 1/12 in. long. Fl. on capillary pedicels up to ⅛ in. long. 15. **P. Rœperianus,** Wall. Khasi hills. Manipùr. A small glabrous shrub, branches rigid, densely fascicled, branchlets slender, ribbed. L. coriaceous, linear-lanceolate, blade ¼–⅜, pet. 1/10 in. Fl. from tufts of minute fimbriate bracts, pedicels slender up to ¼ in. long. Capsule 1/10 in. diam. 16. **P. Griffithii,** Muell. Arg. Khasi hills, Manipùr. Quite glabrous, branches and branchlets ribbed. L. elliptic-lanceolate, subsessile, ½–¾ in. long, stipules peltate, lacerate. Fl. axillary, on capillary pedicels up to 1 in. long. Capsule ⅙ in. diam. 17. **P. Clarkei,** Hook. f. Sikkim, 6,000 ft. Assam. Khasi hills. Glabrous, branchlets grooved, stiff. L. obovate, blade ½–¾, pet. 1/10 in. Fl. on capillary pedicels up to ⅓ in. long. 18. **P. Leschenaultii,** Muell. Arg. Nilgiris. Khasi hills. Quite glabrous, branches slender, l. very thin, glaucous beneath, elliptic, blade ¾–1¼, pet. very slender, 1/10 in, long. Fl. on capillary pedicels, ♀ ¼ in. long.

(*c*) L. 1–5 in. long. Fl. often on leafless racemes.

19. **P. bæobotryoides,** Wall. Silhet. Tenasserim. Malay Peninsula. A shrub, entirely glabrous, branchlets slender, prominently angled. L. thinly coriaceous, nearly sessile, ovate-lanceolate, 2–5 in. long. Fl. on short pedicels, in slender axillary racemes shorter than l. 20. **P. columnaris,** Muell. Arg. Vern. *Kalôn letthe*, Lower, *Yechin-ya*, Upper Burma. Andamans. Along the edge of streams, Burma, Upper and Lower. A small deciduous tree, branchlets and underside of l. pubescent. L. thin, glaucous beneath, elliptic-oblong, acute at both ends, blade 1–2, pet. ⅙ in. Fl. on short pedicels, in compound clusters on branchlets which sometimes are leafless or with a few l., often with several pairs of stipules below the fl. bearing portion. Anthers minute, on a long exserted slender staminal-column. Capsule ⅓ in. diam., 3-celled, valves separating from a central column, pericarp thin, endocarp hard.

C. Anthers 2–4, sessile on the top of a column, around a minute pistillode.

♂ : Sepals 4 often toothed or lacerate (*Reidia*).

(*a*) L. less than 1½ in. long.

21. **P. longiflorus,** Heyne.—Syn. *Reidia ovalifolia*, Wight Ic. t. 1904 fig. 2 (on the plate the names of figs. 2 and 3 have been transposed). Courtallum. L. obliquely oblong, ½–¾ in. long, fl. mostly solitary, pedicels slender up to ¾ in., sepals entire, of ♂ ⅛ in., staminal-column slender $\frac{1}{12}$ in. long. 22. **P. Wightianus,** Muell. Arg.—Syn. *Reidia floribunda*, Wight Ic. t. 1903. Nilgiris and Palnis. L. membranous, obliquely oblong, ½–1 in. long. Fl. ♀: pedicels 1 in., sepals hairy, triangular ⅛ in. long. Capsule ⅛ in. diam., hirsute with rust-coloured bristles. 23. **P. Hamiltonianus,** Muell. Arg. Subhimalayan tract from Sikkim eastwards. Assam. L. membranous, glaucous beneath, elliptic or ovate, ¾–1½ in. long. Fl. ♀ on capillary pedicels up to 1 in. long.

(*b*) L. 2–5 in. long.

24. **P. fimbriatus,** Muell. Arg.—Syn. *Reidia fimbriata*, Wight Ic. t. 1904 fig. 1. Nilgiris, Sispara Ghat. Quite glabrous, l. ovate 2–3 in. long, sec. and tertiary n. elegantly reticulate. Fl. ♂ and ♀ pedicelled, sepals lacerately toothed, ⅛ in. long. 25. **P. Roxburghii,** Muell. Arg. Silhet. Branchlets terete, rusty-pubescent, l. glabrous, lanceolate, 2–3½ in. long. Fl. red, densely fascicled, pedicels up to ½ in. long, of ♂ capillary, of ♀ slender, sepals of ♂ pectinately fimbriate, of ♀ serrate. 26. **P. elegans,** Wall. Tenasserim. Quite glabrous, l. ovate-lanceolate, acuminate, 3–4 in. long. Fl. bracteate, ♂ densely clustered on the branchlets below the l., pedicels short, ♀ solitary, on slender pedicels 1 in. long, in the axils of leaves or bracts, sepals of both lacerate. Capsule ½ in. diam. 27. **P. macrocalyx,** Muell. Arg.—Syn. *Reidia latifolia*, Wight Ic. t. 1904 fig. 3 (see 21). Bababudan and Shevagerry hills. Quite glabrous, l. ovate- or elliptic-lanceolate, acute, fl. solitary, ♂ in the lower axils, pedicels ½, sepals ⅛ in. long, ♀ pedicels ¾ in., thickened upwards, sepals ¼ in., in fr. much enlarged, ¾ in. long.

18. GLOCHIDION, Forst.; Fl. Brit. Ind. v. 305.

Trees or shrubs, as a rule evergreen, l. alternate, bifarious, entire, pet. short, stipules often rigid. Fl. unisexual in axillary fascicles or clusters, perianth simple, disk 0. ♂ as a rule on long slender pedicels, sepals 6, biseriate, anthers sessile more or less connate, cells linear, connectives produced. ♀ calyx persistent, carpels connate into a 3–15-celled ovary, ovules 2 in each cell, styles usually lengthening after flowering, and connate into a globose conic cylindric or clavate column, lobed or notched at the tip. Fr. a loculicidal 3–15-celled capsule, usually lobed, lobes often double the number of cells. Seeds red, testa often with a succulent coat.

Tamasôk, Lower, and *Thitmaleinma*, Upper Burma, are used indiscriminately for several species.

I. Styles connate into a more or less fleshy cylindric, conical, clavate or globose column.

A. Anthers 4 or more, usually 5–7. ♀ sepals 5–6, distinct, or only connate at the base.

a. Ovary 8–12-celled, style short globose or conical.

1. **G. multiloculare,** Muell. Arg. Oudh forests. Sikkim Terai, Duars. Behar. Chutia Nagpur. Sambalpur. Chittagong. Burma, Upper and Lower, on river banks. Branchlets angular, pubescent, sometimes glabrous, l. elongate-elliptic, elliptic-oblong or lanceolate, purplish grey when dry. Fl. ♂, sepals $\frac{1}{10}$ in., pedicels stout, ¼ in. long, anthers 4–12, connective very short. ♀, pedicels stout, sepals 6–12, ⅛ in. long, spreading, style broad, convex with a hollowed top, capsules on short stout pedicels, orbicular depressed, ¾–1 in. diam., 10–15-celled, apex orbicular, concave. 2. **G. littorale,** Blume. Malabar, near the coast. Quite glabrous, l. broadly elliptic, nearly orbicular, anthers 5–6, connective long, acute. 3. **G. coccineum,** Muell. Arg. Pegu, Martaban, Tenasserim, common in deciduous forests. A shrub or small tree, branchlets angular, pubescent, L. glabrous when mature, elliptic-oblong, blade 3–7, pet. ⅛ in. Fl. ♂ glabrous or slightly hairy, pedicels capillary ¼–½, sepals ⅛ in. long, connective short. ♀ sessile clustered, hairy, style conical, truncate, ovary more or less hairy. Capsule sessile, much depressed, 16–20-lobed. 4. A species somewhat resembling **G. hongkongense**, Muell. Arg., of China, Shwebo district, Upper Burma, common in swamps (pubescent, *Thitmaleinma*) on edges of marshes in the Engdain (glabrous, *Sauk*), Smales in 1900 and 1902. A shrub or small tree, l. firmly chartaceous, brown beneath, obliquely ovate-oblong, blade 4–5, pet. ⅛–¼

in. Fl. ♂ and ♀ fascicled on short woody axillary and supra-axillary peduncles, anthers 6–7. Ovary narrowed into the short conical 6-toothed style. Capsule nearly globose, hardly lobed, $\frac{1}{4}$ in. diam.

β. Ovary 3–8-celled, style exserted in fl.

5. **G. lanceolarium**, Muell. Arg. (not Dalzell).—Syn. *Bradleia lanceolaria*, Roxb.; *Phyllanthus lanceolarius*, Muell. Arg.; *Glochisandra acuminata*, Wight Ic. t. 1905. Vern. *Anguti*, Beng. Subhimalayan tract and outer valleys, from the Jumna eastwards. Behar. Chutia Nagpur. Sambulpur. Orissa and the Circars (Gamble). Western Ghats (Bedd. Man. 192, Talbot List 301.) Assam. Silhet. Chittagong. Pegu Yoma, eastern slopes (Kurz). Upper Burma on banks of streams and in deep valleys. A middle-sized evergreen tree, branchlets angular, glabrous, l. coriaceous, glossy, elliptic or elliptic-lanceolate, base acute, blade 4–6, pet. $\frac{1}{4}$–$\frac{1}{2}$ in. long. Fl. in axillary fascicles, ♂ numerous, perfectly glabrous, on pedicels $\frac{1}{2}$–$\frac{3}{4}$ in., sepals $\frac{1}{5}$ in. long, anthers 4–6, connective $\frac{1}{4}$ the length of anthers, ♀ sessile, mostly in the upper axils, a few mixed with the ♂, sepals glabrous, rigidly coriaceous, cuspidate. Ovary hairy usually 6-, sometimes 7- or 8-celled, hairy, narrowed gradually into the conic-cylindric style, which is quite glabrous near the 6-toothed apex, and in fl. is a little longer than the sepals. Capsule orbicular, depressed, usually 6-celled and 12-lobed, $\frac{3}{4}$ in. diam. 6. **G. tomentosum**, Dalzell. Kanara, along streams and watercourses. Malabar. Bababudan hills, Mysore. A shrub or small tree, branchlets fl. and l. beneath pubescent, l. ovate or oblong-elliptic, base rounded or cordate, blade 3–6, pet $\frac{1}{8}$–$\frac{1}{5}$ in. long. Capsule pubescent, obscurely lobed. 7. **G. calocarpum**, Kurz. Andamans and Nicobars. Quite glabrous, l. obliquely ovate, blade 4–7, pet. $\frac{1}{8}$–$\frac{1}{4}$ in. long. Ovary glabrous, 4–5-celled, narrowed into the conical style, capsule $\frac{1}{3}$–$\frac{1}{2}$ in. diam., 8–10-lobed.

8. **G. Gamblei**, Hook. f. Vern. *Paili*, Nep. Sikkim, Terai and lower hills. A small tree, glabrous excepting ovary, l. lanceolate, blade 4–5, pet. $\frac{1}{8}$ in. long, ♂ and ♀ fl. usually in separate clusters, style twice the length of sepals, clavate, contracted above the tomentose ovary, apex truncate but 4–5-lobed. Fr. sessile, $\frac{1}{2}$–$\frac{5}{8}$ in. diam., depressed, 8–10-lobed. 9. **G. Desmogyne**, Hook. f. Tenasserim. Branchlets, l. beneath and inflorescence pubescent or tomentose, l. lanceolate, ovary with style villous, twice the length of sepals, ovary 6-celled. Capsule villous, sessile, or shortly stalked, $\frac{1}{3}$ in. diam., deeply 6-lobed crowned with the glabrous cylindric 3-toothed style. 10. **G. Helferi**, Hook. f. Tenasserim. Nearly glabrous, l. thin, lanceolate, blade 4–5, pet. $\frac{1}{5}$ in. long. Ovary with style glabrous, twice the length of sepals. Capsule globose, obscurely ribbed, $\frac{1}{4}$ in. diam. 11. **G. zeylanicum**, A. Juss. Tent. Euphorb. 107, t. 3., including *G. nitidum*, Dalz. et Gibs. and *G. canarum*, Bedd. Man. 192. Chanda district (Duthie, Dec. 1889). West side of the Peninsula from the Konkan southwards. Hills of the Northern Circars.—Ceylon, moist low country. A small or middle-sized tree, almost entirely glabrous, l. shining, oblong or ovate-oblong, base rounded, sometimes cordate, usually oblique, blade 5–7, pet. $\frac{1}{8}$ in. Fl. ♂ and ♀ usually in axillary more or less pedunculate clusters, ♀ fl. numerous, pedicelled. Sepals, ovary and style glabrous. style long exserted, often curved, apex 5-dentate. Capsule stalked, nearly globose, $\frac{1}{3}$–$\frac{3}{8}$ in. diam., usually 5-celled, obscurely 10-lobed.

γ. Ovary 3–8-celled, style not exserted in fl.

12. **G. hirsutum**, Muell. Arg.—Syn. *Bradleia hirsuta*, Roxb. Subhimalayan tract from Sikkim eastwards. Assam. Khasi hills. Cachar. Chittagong. Andamans.—Malay Penins. A small or middle-sized tree, branchlets, petioles and l. beneath softly tomentose, l. elliptic-oblong, base rounded or cordate, blade 5–7, pet. $\frac{1}{8}$ in. Fl. ♂ and ♀ usually in the same axillary or supra-axillary clusters, which often are on short stout peduncles. ♂ on slender pedicels $\frac{1}{4}$–$\frac{1}{2}$ in. long, sepals 6, hirsute outside, glabrous within, the 3 outer larger $\frac{1}{8}$–$\frac{1}{10}$ in. long, anthers 6, connective very short. ♀ hirsute, shortly pedicelled, sepals 6, the outer slightly broader, ovary globose, glabrous or hairy, narrowed into the short conical style, which is shorter than the sepals and often entire. Capsule 4–6-celled, globose obscurely lobed. *G. hirsutum*, as here defined, includes the Assam and Silhet specimens of *G. zeylanicum*, Fl. Brit. Ind. v. 310. Assam specimens C. B. Clarke 38,045 (possibly a different species) have 2 larger outer and 4 smaller inner sepals, the ovary glabrous, the style slightly exserted with 4 distinct teeth. 13. **G. oblatum**, Hook. f. Subhimalayan tract from Sikkim eastwards. Khasi hills. Cachar. A small tree, branchlets finely tomentose, l. lanceolate, glaucous and often thinly pubescent beneath, blade 2–4, pet. $\frac{1}{8}$ in. long, sec. n. very slender, stipules filiform. Fl. ♂ pubescent, sepals spathulate, ♀ minute, nearly sessile, densely tomentose, style not exserted. Capsules on short stout pedicels, orbicular very depressed, obscurely lobed, pubescent, crown not intruded.

B. Anthers 3, sepals 5–6, distinct or only connate at the base.

(a) Style exserted in fl.

a. ♀ fl. pedicelled, branchlets glabrous.

14. **G. Thomsoni**, Hook. f. Khasi hills. Entirely glabrous, l. elongate-elliptic, very glaucous beneath 2–4 in. long, fl. ♂ few minute, ♀ numerous fascicled, pedicels long, slender, sepals minute, style a fleshy, 3-grooved cone. Capsule ⅓ in. diam., on slender pedicels up to ¾ in. long. 15. **G. rigidum**, Muell. Arg.—Syn. *Gynoon triandrum*, Wight Ic. t. 1908. Travancore, evergreen forest, 4,000 ft. (Bourdillon 560). Ceylon, common. A small tree, perfectly glabrous, l. elliptic-lanceolate, acute at both ends, 2–4½ in. long, ♂ pedicels capillary ⅓ in., sepals oblong, ⅛ in. long, connective acute ⅓ length of anther. ♀ pedicels shorter, style stout cylindric. Capsule ¼–⅓ in. diam., depressed.

β. ♀ fl. pedicelled, branchlets pubescent.

16. **G. velutinum**, Wight Ic. t. 1907.—Syn. *G. nepalense*, Kurz F. Fl. ii. 344; *Phyllanthus nepalensis*, Muell. Arg. Vern. *Kambal*, Kulu; *Kat-mohwa*, Kumaon. Subhimalayan tract and outer valleys, from Kashmir eastwards, occasionally ascending to 5,000 ft. Khasi hills. Upper Burma. Hills east of Toungoo, 3,000 ft. Chutia Nagpur. Cent. Prov. Berar. Western Ghats. Nilgiris. Anamalais. A small tree, branchlets, l. and fl. softly tomentose. L. ovate or elliptic, blade 2–6, narrowed into the short petiole. Fl., both sexes pedicelled often together in axillary clusters. ♂: anthers 3 slightly cohering, connective acute, shorter than anther. ♀ style a thick fleshy 4–8-toothed column, hairy at base, ovary hairy 4–7-celled. Capsules pubescent, depressed-globose, 4–8-lobed, ⅓–⅝ in. diam., often fasciculate, pedicels short, under ¼ in. 17. **G. Heyneanum**, Wight Ic. v. 29 and t. 1908 (right hand figure). Subhimalayan tract from Sikkim eastwards. Makeim Forest, Assam (D. B. April 1879). East Bengal. Chittagong. Northern Circars. A large tree, branchlets, underside of l. and inflorescence finely pubescent. Pedicels of ♂ ⅛–¼, of ♀ ⅛–⅙ in. long. Style cylindric slender, twice the length of sepals or longer, capsule ⅓ in. diam., 4–5-celled, pedicel ¼–½ in. long. 18. **G. acuminatum**, Muell. Arg. Subhimalayan tract from Nepal eastwards, ascending in the outer hills to 4,000 ft. Khasi hills. A middle-sized tree with drooping branches. Branchlets and underside of l. minutely pubescent. L. thin, very glaucous beneath, lanceolate, blade 4–5, pet. ⅛ in. long. Pedicels ♂, ⅛ in. long, ♀ shorter. Style twice the length of sepals. Capsules often clustered along the branches, deeply 4–6-lobed, ¼–⅓ in. diam., pedicels up to ¼ in. long.

γ. ♀ fl. sessile or nearly so, branchlets glabrous.

19. **G. Daltoni**, Kurz. Sikkim, outer hills ascending to 2,500 ft. Poona district. Tenasserim. Upper Burma.—Yunnan. A deciduous shrub or tree, attaining to 40 ft., branchlets and l. glabrous, l. shining, lanceolate, 3–5 in. long. Fl. ♂ and ♀ usually in the same fascicles, ♂ glabrous, pedicels ¼–½ in. long, sepals obtusely oblanceolate, ♀ nearly sessile, sepals 1/12 in. long, glabrous without, near the base minutely hairy within, ovary tomentose, style clavate, glabrous, less than twice the length of sepals, 4–6-toothed, teeth obtuse. Capsule nearly sessile, 8–10-lobed, while young crowned by the stout deciduous style. In foliage this resembles *G. Gamblei* (4–5 anthers) and *G. Khasicum* (style slender acutely 2–3-toothed). 20. **G. Khasicum**, Hook. f. Sikkim 4,500 ft. Khasi hills. A small or middle-sized tree, entirely glabrous. L. rigid, elliptic, acuminate, 3–6 in. long. Fl. ♀ nearly sessile, sepals very unequal, style slender cylindric, 2 or 3 times the length of sepals. Capsule 3–6-lobed, ⅓ in. diam., while immature crowned by the long deciduous style. 21. **G. glaucifolium**, Muell. Arg. Tenasserim. A small evergreen tree, branchlets and l. glabrous. L. obliquely elliptic, acuminate, 3–4 in. long, fl. ♀ nearly sessile, sepals hispid, style nearly cylindric, tapering upwards.

22. **G. malabaricum**, Bedd. Western Ghats from the Konkan to Nilgiris. A small tree, branchlets and l. glabrous. L. elongate-elliptic or elliptic-lanceolate, acuminate. 4–5 in. long, sec. n. 6–8 pair, arching, stip. subulate. ♂ sepals 1/10 in. long, style and ovary hairy, style conical, 4–7-toothed. Capsule nearly sessile ⅓–½ in. diam. 23. **G. ellipticum**, Wight Ic. t. 1906.—Syn. *G. diversifolium*, Bedd. Western Ghats from North Kanara southwards. Closely allied to 22, stipules broader, style scarcely exserted.

δ. ♀ fl. sessile or nearly so, branchlets pubescent.

24. **G. coronatum**, Hook. f. Tenasserim.—Malay Peninsula. A shrub, branchlets hirsute, l. membranous, elliptic-oblong, acuminate, sparsely hirsute beneath, 2–5 in. long, ♀ fl. sessile, ovary villous, style long, slender cylindric 2–3 times the length of sepals. Capsule hairy, nearly sessile, ⅓ in. diam., 3–6-lobed. 25. **G. villicaule**, Hook. f. Upper Burma. Tenasserim. Malay Penins. Branchlets rusty-hirsute with spreading hairs, l. 3–5 in. long, hairy beneath, tert. n. strongly reticulate. ♀ fl. minute sessile, style nearly cylindric, hispid, 2 or 3 times the length of sepals. Capsule nearly sessile, densely hirsute, ½ in. diam. 26. **G. leiostylum**, Kurz. Pegu Yoma, eastern slopes, Tenasserim. Malay Penins. A shrub or small tree, branchlets minutely hairy, l. elliptic, acuminate, 1–3 in. long. Style long exserted, slender, acutely 3-cleft. Capsule shortly stipitate ¼ in. diam., crowned while young by the long slender style.

(*b*) Style not or slightly exserted in fl.

27. **G. lævigatum,** Hook. f. Mergui. Malay Peninsula. A middle-sized tree, entirely glabrous, branchlets angled, l. obliquely ovate or elliptic, acuminate, 1–3 in. long, sec. n. very faint. Fl. ♂, pedicels fasciculate, capillary, $\frac{1}{3}$, sepals oblong $\frac{1}{12}$ in. long. ♀ pedicels shorter rigid, sepals $\frac{1}{24}$ in. long, style minute. 28. **G. assamicum,** Hook. f. Subhimalayan tract and outer valleys, from Sikkim eastwards. Imperfect specimens from Oudh and Vizagapatam. Assam. Khasi and Garo hills. Cachar. East Bengal. Chittagong. Upper Burma. A shrub, or small or middle-sized tree, branchlets glabrous, sharply angled. L. glabrous, elliptic or elliptic-oblong, 4–8 in. ♂ fl. as well as the capillary pedicels glabrous, sepals $\frac{1}{8}$–$\frac{1}{5}$ in., anthers in rare instances 4. ♀ sessile, sepals glabrous, acute, ovary as a rule glabrous, in some specimens hairy, style glabrous, usually columnar, conical (Upper Burma). Capsule $\frac{1}{3}$ in. diam., sessile or on short pedicels, often densely clustered along the branchlets. A variable species which should be studied on the spot, chiefly in regard to ovary, style and size of ♂ fl. What has here been united may prove to be several species. 29. **G. andamanicum,** Kurz. Andamans. A small tree, branchlets and l. glabrous. L. thin, glaucous beneath, broad-elliptic, 2–4 in. long. ♀ fl. minute, sessile, sepals hairy outside, ovary with the fleshy style ovoid, glabrous. Capsule sessile, hairy, strongly 8–12-lobed, $\frac{1}{2}$–$\frac{3}{4}$ in. diam. 30. **G. sphærogynum,** Kurz. Sikkim. Bhutan. Khasi hills. Manipur. Chittagong. Pegu Yoma, eastern slopes. Martaban. Tenasserim. A small or middle-sized evergreen tree, entirely glabrous, l. lanceolate, base acute, 4–14 in. long. ♀ subsessile, ovary glabrous, crowned by the subglobose entire style. Capsule $\frac{1}{2}$ in. diam. nearly sessile, deeply 6–8-lobed, with the large globose style in the depressed apex.

C. Anthers 3, calyx 4–6-toothed.

(*a*) Branchlets glabrous.

31. **G. Hohenackeri,** Beddome.—Syn. *G. lanceolarium*, Dalzell, Bombay Flora 235 (probably). Vern. *Bhoma*, Mar.; *Nirchalli*, Kan. Western Dún, fairly common in moist places. Western Ghats from Mahabaleshwar to Travancore, common in places. A small tree, entirely glabrous, l. elliptic-lanceolate, blade 3–6, pet. $\frac{1}{8}$ in., stipules broad, oblique acute. Fl. ♂ on capillary pedicels up to $\frac{3}{8}$ in., sepals $\frac{1}{8}$–$\frac{1}{5}$ in. long, oblong, broader near apex; anthers 3, connective $\frac{1}{3}$–$\frac{1}{2}$ the length of anthers. ♀ sessile, calyx irregularly 4–5-fid, glabrous, style subglobose, apex notched, a little longer than calyx, much broader than the ovary. Capsule nearly sessile, $\frac{1}{4}$–$\frac{1}{2}$ in. diam., 6–8-lobed, crowned by the globose style in the sunk top. Dalzell does not mention that his species is triandrous, but speaks of the small capsule, which would not apply to *G. lanceolarium*, Hook. f. Of *G. lanceolarium* with numerous anthers I have only seen one specimen said to have come from Bombay. 32. **G. Ralphii,** Hook. f. Ghats of the Konkan and North Kanara. Closely allied to 31, l. lanceolate, blade 2–3, pet. $\frac{1}{8}$ in. long, ovary villous, capsule $\frac{1}{3}$ in. diam., faintly 3–6-lobed. 33. **G. fagifolium,** Miquel. Nilgiris. Tenasserim (*G. fagifolium*, Kurz. Pegu, Martaban is doubtful). Entirely glabrous, branchlets angular, l. lanceolate, 3–4 in. long, sec. n. thin but prominent, anthers 3 or 4, ♀ fl. nearly sessile, style subglobose larger than the ovary. 34. **G. neilgherrense,** Wight.—Syn. *G. Perottetianum*, Bedd. Nilgiris, 6–7,000 ft. A small tree, as a rule glabrous except the ♀ fl., young shoots sometimes minutely pubescent, l. olive-green above, reddish-brown beneath, unequal sided, often falcate, blade 3–5, narrowed into pet. $\frac{1}{8}$ in. Fl. ♂ on pedicels as long as or shorter than fl., sepals $\frac{1}{8}$ in. long, connective half the length of anthers or longer, ♀ subsessile, calyx thickly coriaceous, hairy outside, teeth unequal, style stout, exserted, with 4–6 large lobes, ovary minute, 4–6-celled. Capsule sessile, $\frac{1}{3}$–$\frac{1}{2}$ in. diam., distinctly lobed, much depressed, crowned with the stout short 4–6-lobed style.

(*b*) Branchlets hairy.

35. **G. arboreum,** Wight Ic. t. 1907. Nilgiris and Shevagherri hills. Similar to 34, but branchlets finely pubescent, l. larger, tert. n. prominently reticulate, capsule obscurely lobed, crowned with the 4–6 spreading lobes of the style. 36. **G. Johnstonei,** Hook. f. Western Ghats, North Kanara and Cochin. A middle-sized tree, branchlets tomentose, l. thin, glabrous or sparsely pubescent beneath, elliptic-lanceolate, 4–5 in. long. Capsules deeply 6-lobed, crowned by the 3-lobed stigma. 37. **G. nubigenum,** Hook. f. Sikkim 2–7,000 ft. Shan hills, Upper Burma 4,000 ft. (Collett 709). Attains 60 ft. Branchlets pubescent, l. thin, minutely hairy beneath, ovate or elliptic, acuminate, blade 4–6, pet. $\frac{1}{8}$–$\frac{1}{4}$ in. Ovary 10-12-celled, at the base of the glabrous short 4–6-angled style.

II. Styles 3 distinct, short, filiform.

38. **G. dasystylum,** Kurz. Hills east of Toungoo, ascending to 3,500 ft. A small tree, branchlets and l. beneath softly tomentose, l. ovate, acuminate, 3-4 in. long, fl. unknown, capsule $\frac{1}{4}$–$\frac{1}{3}$ in. diam., 3–4-celled, 6–8-lobed, clothed with long hairs, topped by 3 short filiform hairy styles, united at the base, pedicels hairy, $\frac{1}{3}$ in. long.

Tritaxis (?) Beddomei, Benth. Tinnevelli, foot of ghats. Quite glabrous, l. alternate, entire or with very shallow teeth, penninerved, pale beneath, ovate-oblong, blade 3–4, pet. ¼–½ in. ♂ fl. ⅛ in. across, in lax pedunculate terminal compound cymes, calyx 4-lobed, petals oblong much longer than calyx-segments, stamens 8, the 2 or 3 inner combined into a slender column, filaments of the outer free, anthers broadly oblong, cells contiguous, parallel. ♀ fl. and fr. unknown.

19. JATROPHA, Linn.; Fl. Brit. Ind. v. 382.

Perennial herbs, shrubs or trees, often prickly. L. alternate, often digitately lobed, stipules mostly ciliate. Fl. monœcious, in terminal cymes, the central fl. usually ♀. Sepals 5, imbricate, often petaloid, petals 5, contorted, free or connate. ♂: Stamens 8–12, all or the inner only connate, disk entire or of 5 glands. ♀: Ovary 2–4-celled, styles connate below, 2-fid. Capsule of 2–4 two-valved cocci. Species 70, chiefly American.

A. Petals free or nearly so.

1. **J. glandulifera**, Roxb. Vern. *Jangli Arandi*, Mar.; *Nela Amidam*, Tel. Western Peninsula.—Ceylon. Tropical Africa. A small evergreen tree, edges of leaves, inflorescence, bracts and calyx with long stipitate glands, petioles naked. L. palmately 3–5-lobed, stipules divided into long capillary gland-tipped segments. Petals oblong, yellow, stamens 8, monadelphous, capsule ½ in. long. 2. **J. gossypifolia**, Linn. *Lal Bharenda*, Beng. Native of Brazil, cultivated and run wild in many parts of India and Burma. Similar to 1, petioles with numerous fascicled and branched glandular bristles, sepals lanceolate, densely glandular-ciliate, petals red, obovate. 3. **J. multifida**, Linn. Native of South America, cultivated and run wild in Bengal and the Peninsula. Glabrous, l. orbicular, palmately cut into numerous narrow entire or subdivided segments, blade 3–9 in. diam., petiole as long. Peduncle and fl. scarlet.

4. **J. nana**, Dalz. and Gibs. Dry stony places near Poona. A glabrous undershrub, no glandular bristles, l. entire or 3-lobed, lobes entire, petiole short, stout.

B. Petals cohering to the middle or beyond it.

5. **J. Curcas**, Linn. Vern. *Safed Arand*, Hind.; *Bag Verendi*, Beng.; *Kadu-haralu*, Kan.; *Adivi Amidam*, Tel.; *Thinbaw-Kyetsu*, Burm. Indigenous in tropical America, cultivated in most tropical countries, naturalized in India. Makes excellent hedges, cut branches sprout readily. A soft-wooded shrub or small tree, young shoots and cymes often pubescent, otherwise glabrous. L. angular or 3–5-lobed, blade 4–6 in., pet. as long as blade. Fl. yellowish-green, stamens 10, the 5 inner connate into a central column. Capsule 1–1½ in. long.

6. **J. Wightiana**, Muell. Arg.—Syn. *J. peltata*, Wight Ic. t. 1169. Stony plains at the foot of the hills near Coimbatore. A low shrub, shoots rusty-villous, eglandular. L. peltate, tomentose beneath, entire or with 5–7 obtuse entire lobes, blade 4–6 in. diam., pet. as long as blade. Fl. pale yellow.

Aleurites moluccana, Willd.; Bedd. Fl. Sylv. t. 276.—Syn. *A. triloba*, Forst. *Indian Walnut*. Indigenous probably in the Malay Archipelago, cultivated in most tropical and subtropical countries, and here and there naturalized. A large evergreen tree, shoots, young l., petioles and inflorescence densely clothed with brownish or grey stellate tomentum, l. ovate to ovate-triangular, often lobed, blade 4–12, pet. 2–5 in. Fl. monœcious, white, in large cymose terminal panicles, calyx velvety, bursting into 2 valvate lobes, petals five, ¼ in. long. ♂: Stamens 15–20, on a hairy receptacle. Ovary 2-celled, hairy, styles bifid to the base. Drupe 2–2½ in. diam., seeds large oily. 2. **A. cordata**, Steudel. A tree of China and Japan. Cultivated in North-West India. L. glabrous, broadly ovate-cordate, often deeply lobed, petals ½ in. long. Yields the wood oil of China, sometimes called Ningpo Varnish.

20. CROTON, Linn.; Fl. Brit. Ind. v. 385.

Trees or shrubs, rarely herbs, usually with stellate hairs or orbicular scales, consisting of radiating cells, often separate at the ends, intermediate between scales and stellate hairs. L. alternate, rarely opposite or whorled. Fl. as a rule monœcious, in terminal spiciform racemes, ♀ at the base. Calyx 5-parted, petals in the ♂ alternating with calyx-segments, in the ♀ often wanting, disk glands opposite to sepals. ♂: Stamens 10–30, inserted on a central hairy receptacle, filaments free, inflexed in bud. Ovary 2–4-, generally 3-

celled. Capsule 6-valved or of 3 deciduous 2-valved cocci. Species 5–600, in all hot countries.

A. Ovary lepidote or tomentose.

(*a*) Inflorescence lepidote.

a. L. densely lepidote beneath.

(1) L. crenate.

1. **C. scabiosus,** Bedd. Fl. Sylv. t. 283. Vern. *Chilla*, Tel. Hills of Karnul and Caddepah. A small tree, branchlets, leaves on both surfaces and inflorescence clothed with minute orbicular scales, l. ovate, base cordate, blade 2–4, pet. 1–2 in., 3–5 basal nerves. Raceme erect, 1–4 in. long, stamens 10–12, glabrous. Capsule nearly globose, ½ in. long.

(2) L. entire.

2. **C. reticulatus,** Heyne; Bedd. Ic. t. 233. Western Ghats from the Konkan southwards, common and gregarious in places.—Ceylon. A shrub, underside of l. and inflorescence densely clothed with white silvery scales. L. elliptic-lanceolate, blade 3–7, pet. ½–1 in. Racemes erect, lax, 2–3 in., pedicels of ♂ longer than fl. Capsule ½ in. long, broadly oblong. 3. **C. malabaricus,** Bedd. Ic. t. 181. Ghats of Malabar, ascending to 4,000 ft. A small tree, branchlets, underside of l. and inflorescence densely clothed with white silvery scales. L. ovate, acuminate, blade 2–6, pet. 1–2 in. Racemes solitary or clustered 1–2 in. long. 4. **C. argyratus,** Blume. Martaban and Tenasserim (Kurz). Andamans. Nicobars. Malay Penins. and Archip. A small evergreen tree, wood with scanty but very wide vessels, branchlets, petioles, underside of l. and inflorescence densely clothed with silvery or rufous scales. L. ovate- or elliptic-lanceolate, blade 4–8, pet. 1–2 in. Racemes 4–8 in. long; capsule globose, ⅓ in. diam.

β. L. glabrous when full grown.

5. **C. oblongifolius,** Roxb. Vern. *Akh*, Nep.; *Gunsur*, Mar.; *Bhutan Kusam*, Tel.; *Thityingyi*, Burm. Gonda district Oudh, in belts through miles of forest. Sikkim, ascending to 2,000 ft. Silhet. Bengal. Chutia Nagpur. Central Provinces. Western Peninsula. Burma, Upper and Lower.—Ceylon. A middle-sized tree, shoots and branchlets, inflorescence, calyx and ovary densely clothed with minute orbicular silvery scales. Leaves pale green, glabrous when full grown, oblong-lanceolate, penninerved, more or less serrate, blade 5–10, pet. 1–2 in. long. Fl. pale yellowish-green, on short pedicels, solitary or fascicled, in the axils of minute bracts, on long erect often fascicled racemes. Petals villous inside, stamens 12, filaments sparingly pubescent, ovary lepidote. Capsule globose, indistinctly 3-lobed, ¼–½ in. diam. 6. **C. Joufra,** Roxb. Assam. Khasi hills. Burma, Upper and Lower. Similar to 5, petioles shorter, l. often entire, fr. ovoid 1–1½ in. long. 7. **C. robustus,** Kurz. Pegu and Tenasserim, low country. A small evergreen tree, branchlets robust, rusty-scaly, l. coriaceous, entire, glabrous, a few minute scales on the underside, lanceolate, obtuse, blade 4–8, pet. ½–¾ in.

(*b*) Inflorescence stellately tomentose or glabrous.

a. Basal n. 3–5, l. pubescent on both surfaces.

8. **C. caudatus,** Geisel; *Nan bhantur*, Beng. Sikkim, ascending to 4,000 ft. Assam. Khasi hills. Bengal. Chittagong. Burma, Upper and Lower.—Malay Peninsula and Archipelago. A large shrub, more or less scandent, stem often attaining 1–1½ ft. girth, branchlets, petioles, young l. and inflorescence rough with stellate hairs. L. ovate, acuminate, base cordate, irregularly toothed, basal n. 3–5, blade 2–7, pet. 1–2 in., stipules laciniate, glandulose. Racemes slender, 4–10 in. ♂: Petals as long as sepals, woolly, stamens 18–30, filaments silky below. ♀: sepals oblong, petals minute, ovary densely woolly, styles bifid, arms long slender. Capsule ⅜–1 in. long, hairy. 9. **C. aromaticus,** Linn. Western Peninsula. Ceylon. An erect shrub or small tree, closely allied to 8, with which Beddome identifies it. Petioles ½–1½ in. long, styles short, fr. nearly globose ⅓–½ in. diam. 10. **C. calococcus,** Kurz. Rangoon. A shrub, branchlets, l. and inflorescence densely clothed with stiff stellate hairs. L. entire or denticulate, elliptic, blade 2–3, pet. ¼–½ in. long, basal n. extending beyond the middle. Capsule deeply 3-lobed and stellately hispid. 11. **C. birmanicus,** Muell. Arg. Burma. Imperfectly known, l. ovate-cordate, finely gland-toothed.

12. **C. tomentosus,** Muell. Arg. Pegu. An undershrub with a woody rhizome, thickly clothed with stellate tomentum, l. ovate-oblong, entire or denticulate, blade 2–3, pet. 1 in., basal n. not extending beyond the middle of blade.

β. Basal n. 3–5, l. glabrous when full grown.

13. **C. Tiglium,** Linn. Vern. *Jayapala*, Hind.; *Neppalam*, Tel.; *Kanakho*, Burm. Cultivated and naturalized throughout tropical India and Burma. A native of the

Malay Archip. A small evergreen tree, the youngest shoots sparsely stellately hairy. L. membranous, glabrous, ovate-acuminate, more or less serrate, 3–5 basal nerves, blade 2–4, pet. 1–2 in. Racemes 2–8 in., rachis glabrous. ♂: sepals and pedicels nearly glabrous, petals woolly, stamens 15–25, glabrous. ♀: pedicels and ovary stellately hispid, petals 0. Capsule ¾–1 in. long, white, obovoid, obtusely trigonous. 14. **C. flocculosus,** Kurz. Irawaddi valley. A small tree, young shoots with deciduous stellate tomentum, l. broad-ovate, crenate, base rounded or cordate, blade 3–4, pet. ¾ in. Capsule ½ in. diam., densely stellate-tomentose.

γ. L. penninerved.

(1) Inflorescence tomentose.

15. **C. Wallichii,** Muell. Arg. Pegu. Tenasserim. A middle-sized deciduous tree, youngest shoots and inflorescence stellately tomentose, l. nearly glabrous, more or less serrate, elongate-elliptic or oblanceolate, blade 6–8, narrowed into pet. ½–1½ in., sec. n. slender. Racemes fascicled, slender, 4–8 in. long. 16. **C. sublyratus,** Kurz. Tenasserim. Andamans. A deciduous shrub, young shoots rusty scurfy, l. from a narrow cordate base gradually widening upwards, blade 3–8, pet. ½ in. 17. **C. rhodostachyus,** Muell. Arg. Upper Burma, imperfectly known.

(2) Inflorescence glabrous.

18. **C. Klotzschianus,** Wight. Ic. t. 1914 (*Tiglium*). Hills of the Deccan. Nilgiris. Travancore. A shrub or small tree, young shoots stellately pubescent, and on young l. a few tufts of stellate hairs. L. membranous, elliptic-oblong, blade 2–3, pet. slender ⅓–⅔ in. Racemes slender, 1–3 in. long. 19. **C. Gibsonianus,** Nimmo. Ghats of the Konkan and North Kanara. A tall shrub, nearly glabrous, l. membranous, elliptic-oblong, acuminate, base rounded, blade 5–7, pet. 1 in., at the base of blade usually 2 minute stipitate glands. Racemes slender, 5–10 in. long, capsule 3-lobed, stellately hairy, ½ in. diam. 20. **C. laevifolius,** Blume. Khasi hills.—Java, Sumatra. A small tree, young shoots with scattered scales or dense tufts of stellate hairs. L. membranous, glabrous, elongate-elliptic, blade 2–5, pet. ½–1½ in. Racemes 2–4 in., capsule shining, ¼ in. diam.

B. Ovary glabrous, sepals much enlarged in fr.

21. **C. Lawianus,** Nimmo. Bababudan hills, Mysore. A small tree, branchlets and young l. softly stellate-tomentose, l. quite entire, ovate, acuminate, blade 3–5, pet. ⅛ in., basal n. 3, sometimes 5. ♂ fl. large, in few-fld. pedunculate racemes, pedicels longer than fl. Capsule ⅜ in. diam., glabrous, rugose, shorter than the enlarged leafy sepals. 22. **C. chlorocalyx,** Wall. Silhet. Quite glabrous, l. lanceolate, caudate-acuminate, penninerved, slightly serrulate, blade 6–9, narrowed into pet. ½–¾ in. long.

21. GALEARIA, Zollinger & Moritzi; Fl. Brit. Ind. v. 377.

Shrubs or small trees, l. alternate, quite entire, penninerved, sec. n. joined by distinct intra-marginal nerves, veins prominently reticulate, pet. short. Fl. minute, diœcious, in long slender terminal racemes, bracts minute or 0. Calyx 5-toothed, or -partite, petals 5, concave, induplicate-valvate, keeled down the middle within. Fl. ♂ fascicled, stamens 10, filaments very short, anthers didymous. ♀ styles short, slender, 2-partite. Fr. small, broad, endocarp hard, 1–2-celled. Species 12–15, Indo-Malayan region.

1. **G. Helferi,** Hook. f.—Syn. *G. Wallichii*, Kurz. Tenasserim. Branchlets, petioles and racemes minutely pubescent, l. membranous, elliptic-oblong, 8–12 in. long, ♂ racemes as long as l. 2. **G. Wallichii,** Hook. f. Tenasserim. Malay Penins. Quite glabrous, l. thinly coriaceous, oblong-lanceolate, acuminate, 5–7 in. long, racemes longer than l.

22. GIVOTIA, Griff.; Fl. Brit. Ind. v. 395.

G. rottleriformis, Griff. (the only species); Wight Ic. t. 1889; Bedd. Fl. Sylv. t. 285. Vern. *Polki*, Mar.; *Puliki*, Tel.; *Vendule*, Tam.

A middle-sized tree, wood white, very light and soft, but even-grained, branchlets, petioles, underside of leaves and sepals densely clothed with white stellate tomentum. L. alternate, cordate, sinuate-toothed, blade 5–10, pet. 4–6 in. long. Fl. diœcious, in axillary panicled cymes 4–8 in. long, near the ends of branches, bracts narrow-linear. Sepals 5, imbricate, petals 5, longer than sepals, more or less cohering. ♂: Disk of 5 orbicular glands.

Stamens 13–25 on a woolly receptacle, filaments connate at base, hairy below, pistillode 0. ♀: Disk cupular, ovary stellately hairy, 2–3-celled, ovule 1 in each cell. Fruit a subglobose drupe, ¾–1 in. diam. Seed 1, cotyledons flat, broad, in a fleshy albumen.

Fig. 182.—Givotia rottleriformis, Griff. ½.

Dry forests on the Western Ghats and on the hills of the Deccan. Mysore and Karnatik. Fl. H. S.—Ceylon, dry region.

Platystigma myristiceum, Rob. Brown; Hook. Ic. Pl. t. 1707. Silhet. Branches woody, branchlets minutely rusty-pubescent, l. alternate, coriaceous quite entire, blade 5–7, pet. ¾–1 in. Fl. diœcious, sessile or shortly pedicelled, in short axillary bracteate panicles. ♂: sep. 4–5, imbricate, pet. 4–5 ovate, valvate, stamens 4–5, opposite to petals, filaments very short, anthers parallel. ♀: on stout pedicels, sepals 5 broadly ovate, imbricate, pet. 0, ovary rusty-tomentose, 1-celled, ovule 1, stigma sessile thick, broader than ovary.

Microdesmis caseariæfolia, Planchon. Tenasserim.—Malay Penins. and Archip. China. A small evergreen tree, branchlets and young l. minutely pubescent, l. alternate, distichous, broadly lanceolate, blade 4–5, pet. ½ in. Fl. diœcious, minute, in axillary clusters, sepals 5 small, pet. 5, twisted and imbricate. ♂: stamens 10, alternately shorter, connective apiculate, pistillode columnar. ♀: ovary glabrous, 2-celled, fr. bright red, globose ⅓–½ in. diam.

23. TRIGONOSTEMON, Blume; Fl. Brit. Ind. v. 395.

Evergreen shrubs or small trees, l. alternate, penninerved. Fl. monœcious, in racemes or panicles, as a rule lateral or axillary. Sepals 5, imbricate, petals 5, sometimes more in ♀, disk of 5 glands, often united in a lobed cup.

Stamens 3, anthers sessile or on a cylindrical column, pistillode 0. Ovary 3-celled, styles bifid or twice bifid.

A. Anthers sessile on a subglobose receptacle.

1. **T. nemoralis**, Thwaites; Bedd. Ic. Plant. t. 182. Tinnevelli hills, 2-3,000 ft. Ceylon. Young shoots strigose, l. crowded at the ends of branchlets, thin-coriaceous, irregularly and shallowly crenate-serrate, lanceolate or oblanceolate, blade 4-8, narrowed into thick channelled pet. ¼ in. long. Fl. red, in terminal erect stiff spiciform racemes 2-6 in. long, ♂ on short slender pedicels, clustered, ♀ solitary on stout pedicels. Capsule ½ in. diam., 3-lobed, roughly pubescent.

B. Anthers at the end of a cylindric column.

2. **T. heteranthus**, Wight Ic. t. 1890. Tenasserim. Young shoots tawny pubescent, l. glabrous, membranous, sometimes serrate, blade 8-12, pet. 1-4 in. long. Fl. ♂ and ♀ together, in a lax axillary racemiform panicle or thyrsus 6-8 in. long, consisting of numerous 3-7-fid. cymes along a long slender rachis, pedicels filiform. ♂ fl. ½ in. across, sepals entire ciliate, petals twice the length of sepals, anthers 3 on a staminal-column with 6 branches at the top, each branch having one anther-cell. ♀: sepals glandular dentate, as long as petals, ovary glabrous. 3. **T. lætus**, Baillon. Tenasserim. L. thick-chartaceous, broadly lanceolate, blade 4-6, pet. 1-2 in. long, ♀ sepals entire, minutely ciliate, ovary greyish, silky pubescent. 4. **T. longifolius**, Baillon. Tenasserim. Malay Penins. Shoots and young l. clothed with long brown silky hairs, l. membranous, oblanceolate, blade 9-15 in. long, gradually narrowed into a short marginate petiole. Fl. clustered on the long narrow pubescent racemes, rachis angled, bracts subulate. Capsule ½ in. diam., densely clothed with short stiff hairs. 5. **T. semperflorens**, Muell. Arg. Assam. Khasi hills. Silhet. Cachar. Branchlets hispid, l. often spuriously whorled at the ends of branches, 4-10 in. long, sessile or nearly so, from a narrow cordate base gradually widening, acuminate. Racemes very short, pedicels short stout, ovary hispid. Capsule 3-lobed, ⅓-½ in. diam.

24. OSTODES, Blume; Fl. Brit. Ind. v. 400.

Trees, l. alternate, penniveined. Fl. diœcious or monœcious, fascicled on long racemes, usually arranged in terminal or axillary panicles. Sepals 3-6, imbricate, petals usually 5. ♂: stamens 8-35, filaments short, inserted on a receptacle, hairy at base, which often lengthens out into a column, anther-cells parallel, connective broad. ♀: ovary 3-celled, styles short, 2-cleft. Species 6-8, Indo-Malayan region.

A. L. coriaceous.

1. **O. zeylanica**, Muell. Arg.; Bedd. Fl. Sylv. t. 274. Western Ghats, common in evergreen forest from the Wainad southwards.—Ceylon. A large evergreen tree, bark smooth, purple, branchlets angular, young shoots and inflorescence clothed with minute stellate hairs. L. elliptic-lanceolate, serrate, blade 8-18, pet. 2-3 in. Bracts lanceolate, deciduous. Fl. scented, ♂: petals white, ¼-⅓ in. long, more or less cohering in a tube, stamens 8-15, filaments glabrous, receptacle elongating into a long column. ♀: petals free, ovary densely clothed with long hairs. Capsule 6-ribbed, 1¼ in. diam. 2. **O. Helferi**, Muell. Arg. Tenasserim. Blade 10-12, pet. ½ in. long.

B. L. membranous or chartaceous.

3. **O. paniculata**, Blume. Sikkim 2-6,000 ft. Bhutan. Khasi hills. Ruby Mines district, U. Burma, 6-7,000 ft. in evergreen forest (*Yebadon galè*). Hills east of Toungoo, 2-3,000 ft. L. ovate, acuminate, serrate, blade 8-12, pet. 2-10 in. Inflorescence clothed with simple hairs. ♂: Sepals 3, petals 4-5, free. Stamens 20-35, filaments free, minutely hairy at base, on a hemispherical receptacle.

Codiæum variegatum, Blume. Native of the Moluccas, often cultivated in gardens on account of its leaves, which are variable in shape, mottled and variegated with red, yellow and green. Fl. in unisexual racemes, ovary 3-celled, styles long, slender, recurved, entire.

25. BLACHIA, Baill.; Fl. Brit. Ind. v. 402.

Glabrous shrubs or small trees, l. entire, eglandular, penninerved. Fl. usually monœcious, ♂ in terminal pedunculate racemes or corymbs, peduncles and pedicels slender, sepals 4-5, concave, membranous, imbricate, petals alternating with sepals, small, round, hyaline. Stamens 10–24, on a convex receptacle, anther-cells on the edges of the connective, ultimately confluent at the apex, disk consisting of scales, alternating with petals. ♀ fl. solitary or fascicled, pedicels thickened above, sepals 4–6, more or less enlarged, in 1 sp. deciduous in fr., petals 0. Ovary 3–4-celled, styles 3–4, filiform, 2-partite, recurved or revolute. Cotyledons broad, flat in a fleshy albumen. Species 5 or 6, one in China.

1. **B. calycina**, Benth.—Syn. *Croton umbellatum*, Wight Ic. t. 1874; *Codiæum umbellatum*, Bedd. Man. t. 23. Western Ghats from Coorg southwards, in evergreen forests. A shrub or small tree, l. elliptic-lanceolate, blade 3–4, pet. ⅛ in. ♂ fl. corymbose, peduncles 2–3 in., sepals ⅛ in., petals $\frac{1}{24}$ in. diam., anthers 20–24. Fruiting sepals ½–⅝ in. long. 2. **B. umbellata**, Baill. Ceylon; also reported from Travancore, is very near to 1 and possibly not specifically distinct. ♂ fl. umbellate, fruiting sepals smaller. 3. **B. reflexa**, Benth. Nilgiris. Travancore. A shrub. ♂ fl. umbellate, sepals in fr. slightly enlarged, spreading or reflexed. 4. **B. denudata**, Benth. Evergreen forests of the Western Ghats, from the Konkan to the Bababudan hills. A large shrub or small tree, l. lanceolate, blade 3–7, pet. ⅙ in. long, ♂ fl. racemose, calyx deciduous in fr. 5. **B. andamanica**, Hook. f.—Syn. *Codiæum andamanicum*, Kurz. Andamans. Narcondam. Coco island. A large evergreen shrub, l. elongate-elliptic, blade 4–6, pet. ½–⅝ in. Ovary hirsute.

26. DIMORPHOCALYX, Thw.; Fl. Brit. Ind. v. 403.

Glabrous trees, l. alternate quite entire, penninerved. Fl. large, racemose usually diœcious, the ♀ often solitary. ♂: Calyx cup-shaped 5-lobed, petals 5, longer than calyx, stamens 10–20, filaments stout, free or the inner connate inside a fleshy 5-lobed disk. Pistillode 0. ♀: Sepals 5, imbricate, greatly enlarged in fr., petals 5. Ovary 3-celled, styles 2-fid., ovule 1 in each cell. Capsule of 3 two-valved crustaceous cocci. Cotyledons flat broad, in fleshy albumen. Species 3–4, Indo-Malayan.

1. **D. Lawianus**, Hook. f.—Syn. *Trigonostemon Lawianus*, Bedd. Fl. Sylv. t. 273. Vern. *Yenega*, *Nara gonji*, Tel. (Veligondas). Western Ghats from the Konkan southwards, in evergreen forest. Anamalais. Veligonda hills (D. B. Dec. 1881). A small or middle-sized tree, l. elliptic-lanceolate, blade 4–8, pet. ½–⅜ in., stam. 15, ovary tomentose, segments of fruiting perianth ¾–1 in. long, capsule ½ in. diam. Closely allied: 2. **D. glabellus**, Thwaites; Trimen Handbook Ceylon t. 84. Western Ghats from Matheran southwards.—Ceylon very common in the dry region. Differs by smaller leaves, shorter petioles, 10 stamens and a smaller fruiting perianth.

27. AGROSTISTACHYS, Dalz.; Fl. Brit. Ind. v. 405.

Glabrous shrubs or small trees, l. alternate, coriaceous, pet. short. Fl. diœcious, in bracteate short compact or elongate racemes. ♂: cal. globose, splitting into 2–5 valvate lobes. Petals usually 5, glands of the disk alternating with petals. Stamens 8–13, on a convex receptacle, anther-cells pendulous from a thick connective, pistillode 0 or 2–3-fid. ♀: sepals 2–4, petals usually 5, larger than sepals, caducous, ovary 3-celled, styles short, thick, spreading, entire or bifid. Capsule tricoccous, cotyledons broad in fleshy albumen.

1. **A. indica**, Dalz.; Bedd. Ic. t. 241. Western Ghats from the Konkan southwards in evergreen forests on the banks of streams. L. lanceolate, serrate, teeth sharp, incurved, blade 6–11, narrowed into pet. ¼–1½ in. long. Fl. in short axillary and supra-axillary densely bracteate flat racemes, bracts imbricating, fl. solitary in the bract axils. 2. **A. Gaudichaudi**, Muell. Arg. (*A. longifolia*, Kurz). Tenasserim (or Andamans), Penang. L. oblanceolate, obtusely sinuate-dentate, blade 12–16 in. long, narrowed into pet. ½–1½ long., fl. in short densely bracteate racemes. 3. **A. longifolia**, Benth. —Syn. *Sarcoclinium longifolium*, Wight Ic. t. 1887-8; Bedd. Man. t. 23. Vern *Mancharei*, Tam.; *Mulimpalei*, Mal. Western Ghats from North Kanara southwards. Branches stout, marked with the scars of petioles and stipules, young shoots very

resinous, l. crowded at the ends of branches, oblanceolate, nearly sessile, quite entire, 6–20 in. long, racemes stiff, shorter than l., bracts distant, ♂ fl. clustered, ♀ solitary in the axils of bracts.

Sumbavia macrophylla, Muell. Arg. Darrang district, Assam (D. B. March 1879). Upper Burma (Griffith, March, 1837). Eastern slopes of the Pegu Yoma. Martaban and Tenasserim, frequent along streams (Kurz). A small evergreen tree, branchlets, petioles and underside of l. with a dense white or grey tomentum of stellate hairs, buds and racemes rusty tomentose. L. narrowly peltate, edge undulate, ovate or elliptic, acuminate, blade 8–12, pet. 2–4 in. long, sec. n. 8–10 pair, prominent beneath, the lowest pair from the insertion of the pet., transverse veins parallel. Fl. in androgynous axillary bracteate racemes, ♂ clustered, nearly sessile, ♀ pedicelled. ♂: globose, splitting into 5 valvate sepals, petals conspicuous, stamens 8, on a central convex hairy receptacle. Capsule tricoccous.

Manihot Glaziovii, Muell. Arg. *Ceara Rubber.* Indigenous in the Province Ceara of Brazil 4° S. L. Cultivated in Ceylon, Pegu and other tropical countries. A middle-sized tree, l. nearly glabrous, narrowly peltate, blade 6–10 in. diam., palmately deeply cut into 3–7 elliptic- or obovate-oblong acute segments, pet. 2–6 in. long. Fl. large, on terminal panicles in the forks of branches, the ♂ above, the ♀ below, calyx campanulate, outside greyish-white with a purplish tinge, internally pale dull purple, stamens 10, 5 longer, 5 shorter, between the lobes of a large bright yellow disk. Capsule pendulous about 1 in. diam. with 6 shallow grooves, seeds polished, greyish-brown, mottled with purplish-black, testa very hard and thick. 2. **M. utilissima,** Pohl, a native of South America, cultivated in India and Burma, the root yields Cassava starch and Tapioca meal.

Hevea brasiliensis, Muell. Arg. Province of Para on the Amazon river, cultivated at Mergui. A large evergreen tree, l. glabrous, trifoliolate on long petioles, leaflets entire, acuminate. Fl. monœcious, in large whitish pubescent lateral panicles. Calyx campanulate, 5–6-lobed, petals 0, anthers adnate to a central column. Fr. a large 3-lobed, 6-valved capsule having the appearance of 3 connate cylinders, rounded at the ends. Seeds shining, spotted. This and other closely allied species yield the Para rubber, the finest and most durable caoutchouc known.

28. GELONIUM, Roxb.; Fl. Brit. Ind. v. 458.

Evergreen, glabrous resinous shrubs or small trees. L. usually alternate, stipules sheathing, caducous, bearing a raised line at the nodes. Fl. diœcious, apetalous, in leaf-opposed corymbs or clusters, sepals 5 or 6, imbricate. ♂: stamens 10–60, crowded on a convex receptacle, filaments free, anther-cells parallel, pistillode 0. ♀: disk cupular, sometimes bearing staminodes, ovary 2–4-celled, styles minute, bifid or semi-lunate, 1 ovule in each cell. Fr. tardily dehiscent, pericarp often fleshy, the valves separating from a persistent axis. Seeds arillate. Species 15, tropical Asia and Africa.

1. **G. lanceolatum,** Willd.; Wight Ic. t. 1867. Vern. *Velidaba, Yelladabba,* Tel. Hills and dry evergreen forests on the east side of the Peninsula. Anamalais, Cochin, Travancore. A small or middle-sized tree, l. coriaceous, often spinulose-serrate, elliptic or elliptic-lanceolate, blade 3–5, narrowed into pet. $\frac{1}{3}$–$\frac{1}{2}$ in. Fl. ♂ $\frac{1}{6}$–$\frac{1}{4}$ in. across, mostly on short racemes with a woody rachis, marked by the scars of the bracts. Capsule tricoccous, $\frac{1}{3}$–$\frac{1}{2}$ in. diam., cocci keeled. 2. **G. multiflorum,** A. Juss.—Syn. *G. fasciculatum,* Roxb.; Bot. Mag. t. 3231. *Ban Naringa,* Hind.; *Sethanbaya,* Burm. Bengal, to the foot of the hills. Chutia Nagpur. Orissa. Northern Circars. Chittagong. Lower Burma. Andamans.—Malay Penins. and Archip. A middle-sized tree, l. coriaceous, entire, elongate-elliptic, blade 6–9, narrowed into pet. $\frac{1}{4}$–$\frac{1}{2}$ in. Fl. ♂ yellow, very fragrant, $\frac{1}{2}$ in. across, in pedunculate corymbs, pedicels $\frac{1}{6}$–$\frac{1}{4}$ in. Stamens 40–60. Fr. globose, obscurely 3-lobed, $\frac{1}{2}$–$\frac{3}{4}$ in. diam., pericarp thick fleshy, rough when dry. 3. **G. bifarium,** Roxb. Andamans (Kurz). Pegu (D. B. 1858).—Malay Penins. and Archip. Fl. ♂ $\frac{1}{6}$–$\frac{1}{3}$ in. across, in sessile fascicles, capsule $\frac{1}{2}$ in. diam. deeply 2- (rarely 3-) lobed.

Chætocarpus castanocarpus, Thwaites; Bedd. Fl. Sylv. t. 284. Vern. *Bulkokra,* Beng. Silhet. Chittagong. Andamans. Lower Burma. Malay Penins. Ceylon. An evergreen middle-sized tree, l. coriaceous, alternate, quite entire, penninerved, ovate or elongate-elliptic, blade 4–8, pet. $\frac{1}{4}$–$\frac{1}{3}$ in. long. Fl. $\frac{1}{6}$ in. diam., diœcious, apetalous, in axillary clusters, sepals 4 imbricate in pairs, hairy outside, disk lobed. ♂: stamens 8 lower portion of filaments combined into a slender column. Capsule $\frac{3}{4}$–1 in. long, densely clothed with tawny, stiff bristles.

29. **BALIOSPERMUM,** Blume; Fl. Brit. Ind. v. 461.

Shrubs, l. alternate toothed or lobed. Fl. small, usually diœcious, apetalous. ♂: Sepals 4–6 concave, imbricate, disk lobed, stamens 10–30 central, filaments mostly free, anther-cells diverging, adnate to the broad connective, which is continuous with the filament, pistillode 0. ♀: Sepals 5–6, lanceolate, disk nearly entire, ovary 3-celled, styles stout 2-fid, stigmatic surfaces smooth (not fimbriate). Capsule of 3 two-valved crustaceous cocci, separating from the persistent axis. Seeds ovoid, glabrous. Species 6, Indo-Malayan region.

A. Usually monœcious. Lower different from the upper l.

1. **B. axillare,** Blume.—Syn. *B. polyandrum*, Wight Ic. t. 1885; *B. montanum*, Muell. Arg.; Kurz F. Fl. ii. 410. Vern. *Danti, Hakún*, Beng.; *Natcho*, Burm. Subhimalayan tract from Kashmir eastwards. Assam. Khasi hills. Chittagong. Upper and Lower Burma (common as underwood in forests on low ground). Chutia Nagpur. Western Peninsula. Malay Penins. and Arch. A shrub with herbaceous branches, young shoots and often underside of l. hairy. Leaves sinuate toothed, upper small, lanceolate, penninerved, lower large, ovate, often palmately 3–5-lobed, basal nerves 3–5, blade of larger l. 6–12, pet. 2–6 in., stipules of two glands. Fl. monœcious, in contracted panicles, green, styles dull red. Calyx of ♂ glabrous, of ♀ hairy, as well as the ovary. Fruiting calyx not accrescent, capsule ⅓–½ in., 3-lobed, pedicel recurved, ¼–½ in. long. A remarkable variety with strongly marked parallel tert. n. and diœcious fl. in Singbhum (Haines).

B. Diœcious. L. uniform.

2. **B. corymbiferum,** Hook. f. Eastern Nepal and Sikkim, 4–5,000 ft. Stem slender, naked or sparingly branched, branches finely pubescent. ♂ panicles much longer than l., on long slender peduncles. 3. **B. calycinum,** Muell. Arg. Mishmi hills, Upper Assam. Pubescent, ♂ panicles ample, much longer than l., on long peduncles. ♀ sepals ½ in. long. 4. **B. sinuatum,** Muell. Arg. Mishmi and Patkoi hills. Almost entirely glabrous. L. from obovate-oblong to linear, often above the middle with 3 or 5 large triangular acuminate lobes, blade 6–8, pet. ½–1½ in. long. ♂ fl. in long narrow racemes, ovary glabrous, fruiting calyx accrescent.

Cnesmone javanica, Blume. Assam. Khasi hills. Cachar. East Bengal. Lower Burma. A large evergreen twining shrub, all parts densely clothed with soft tomentum of long stinging hairs. L. ovate-oblong, base deeply cordate, acuminate, serrate, blade 4–6, pet. 1–2 in., basal n. 3 or 5, stipules ovate, persistent. Fl. in androgynous bracteate racemes, a few ♀ fl. at the base. ♂: calyx-lobes 3 broad valvate, anthers 3, connective produced into a long linear reflexed appendix. Capsule ½–⅝ in. diam. of 3 hispid cocci, supported by the enlarged velvety calyx-lobes.

Plukenetia corniculata, Smith. Sikkim 2,000 ft. Assam. Mergui. Malay Penins. and Archip. A twining shrub, nearly glabrous, l. membranous, gradually tapering from a broad cordate base, acuminate, dentate, blade 4–6, pet. 1–2 in. Capsule on pedicels 1–2 in. long, consisting of 4 stellately spreading granulate cocci, each produced into a linear obtuse wing, ¼ in. long, seeds keeled, pale, with irregular brown patches.

30. **DALECHAMPIA,** Linn.; Fl. Brit. Ind. v. 467.

Twining shrubs or undershrubs, l. alternate, deeply lobed or trifoliolate, petioles long. Fl. in androgynous involucrate heads, often mixed with sterile deformed fl., involucre of 2 large 3-lobed serrulate bracts, with a whorl of smaller ones outside. ♂: sepals 4–6, valvate, stamens 20–30, on a convex receptacle, anther-cells contiguous, parallel. ♀: sepals 5–12, pinnatifid, hirsute. Species 60, tropical, chiefly American.

1. **D. indica,** Wight Ic. t. 1882. East side of the Western Peninsula.—Ceylon. L. 3-foliolate, involucral bracts yellow, segments of ♀ sepals subulate, tips glandular. 2. **D. velutina,** Wight Ic. t. 1881. Nilgiris. L. deeply 3-lobed, tomentose beneath, segments of ♀ sepals hirsute, eglandular.

3. **D. Kurzii,** Hook. f.—Syn. *D. scandens*, Kurz, F. Fl. ii. 400. Southern parts of Pegu Yoma. L. deeply 3-lobed, lobes lanceolate, blade 2–5, pet. 1 in. long, segments of ♀ sepals linear, $\frac{1}{10}$ in. long.

31. SAPIUM, Patrick Browne; Fl. Brit. Ind. v. 469.

Trees and shrubs, l. alternate, penninerved, often 2 glands on petiole below insertion of blade. Fl. monœcious, apetalous in terminal simple or panicled spikes or racemes, ♂ several or many, ♀ solitary in the axil of the bract, a pair of large glands at the base of each bract, disk 0. ♂: Calyx 2–3-toothed or -lobed, stamens 2–3, filaments free, anther-cells contiguous, parallel, pistillode 0. ♀: Calyx 3-fid, ovary 2–3-celled, styles free or connate below, undivided, 1 ovule in each cell. Capsule loculicidally 3-valved.

Fig. 183.—Sapium insigne, Benth. ½.

A. Spikes androgynous, the ♀ fl. usually in the lower portion.

1. **S. baccatum,** Roxb.; Wight Ic. t. 1950, called *S. populifolium* on plate; *Excœcaria baccata*, Muell. Arg.; *Carumbium baccatum*, Kurz F. Fl. ii. 412. Vern. *Billa*, Silhet; *Awlè*, Upper, *Lèlun*, Lower Burma. Sikkim, foot of the hills and outer valleys. Assam. Khasi hills. Chittagong. Burma, usually in evergreen forest. The young shoots, which come out in April, are orange-red. A middle-sized, at times a large glabrous evergreen tree, l. ovate, or ovate-lanceolate, acuminate, quite entire, glaucous beneath, blade 3–7, pet. 1–3 in. Racemes spiciform, usually arranged in large terminal panicles, bracts, broadly-ovate, acute, with a large gland at each side, 3 ♂ fl. usually in one bract. Fl. minute, yellowish-white, stamens 2, anthers red, usually didymous. Drupe red or purple, ⅓–½ in. diam., edible. 2. **S. sebiferum,** Roxb. (*Excœcaria sebifera*, Muell. Arg.), the *Chinese tallow tree*, a native of China, cultivated in North-West India. Glabrous, l. rhomboid, entire, on long slender petioles, fl. in terminal spiciform racemes, ovary glabrous, narrowed into a style with 3 long, spreading stigmas. Seeds 3, attached to a central column which splits into 3 slender divisions, enclosed in a thick layer of white fatty substance (*vegetable tallow*). 3. **S. indicum,** Willd.; Wight Ic. t. 1950.

—Syn. *Excœcaria indica*, Muell. Arg. Vern. *Huru*, *Batul*, Beng. Tidal forests, Sundriban, Tenasserim. Travancore on the banks of rivers.—Ceylon. Malay Penins. A small glabrous evergreen milky tree, wood soft, l. elliptic-lanceolate, serrate, not glaucous beneath, blade 3–5, pet. ¼–½ in. Racemes spiciform, solitary, ♂ fl. clustered, nearly sessile, ♀ larger, pedicellate. Fr. 1 in. diam., young succulent, old woody, obscurely 3-lobed.

4. **S. eugeniæfolium**, Ham. Himalaya, from Kumaon eastwards, 2–4,000 ft. Khasi hills. Glabrous, l. elliptic, blade 3–5, pet. 1–4 in. Racemes dense, simple, solitary, capsule globose, ⅓–½ in. diam., valves thick, woody, separating from the persistent broadly 3-winged axis.

B. Spikes unisexual.

5. **S. insigne**, Benth.—Syn. *Excœcaria insignis*, Muell. Arg.; *Falconeria insignis* and *F. Wallichiana*, Royle Ill. t. 84A; *F. malabarica*, Wight Ic. t. 1866; *Carumbium insigne*, Kurz, F. Fl. ii. 412. Vern. *Boddar*, N. W. Himal.; *Khindra*, *Khinna*, *Lendua*, Hind.; *Ura*, *Hure*, *Dudla*, Mar.

A middle-sized glabrous, deciduous tree, usually small but in places attaining 50 ft., abounding in thick milky sap, branches thick, foliage bright green. L. elongate-elliptic, acuminate, dentate, blade 6–15, pet. 1–2 in. long. Fl. in unisexual robust spikes, 3–10 in. long, ♂ fl. sessile in round clusters, the central fl. opening first, stamens 2. ♀ fl. shortly pedicelled, sepals ovate, acuminate, styles very short. Fr. a spike of numerous ovoid capsules on a thick rachis, the capsules 2–3-celled, fleshy at first, dry and irregularly dehiscent when ripe.

Subhimalayan tract and outer valleys, from the Bias eastwards, ascending to 5,500 ft. Assam. Chittagong. Pegu Yoma. Western Peninsula, on the West side from the Konkan southwards, on dry rocky soil near the coast and in evergreen forest on the ghats. Also on the hills of Karnúl and Cuddapah. Kambakum hill (D. B. Nov. 1881). Fl. Jan.–March, while the tree is leafless.

32. EXCŒCARIA, Linn.; Fl. Brit. Ind. v. 472.

Glabrous trees or shrubs with acrid milk, l. in some species opposite, racemes or spikes bracteate, unisexual or androgynous, generally lateral. Fl. ♂ 1–3 on each bract, sepals 3 small, stamens 3, anther-cells contiguous, parallel. ♀: Calyx 3-fid or -partite, styles stout, shortly connate, spreading or recurved, entire. Capsule of 3 cocci separating from the persistent axis.

A. L. alternate.

1. **E. Agallocha**, Linn.; Wight Ic. t. 1865, fig. 1–5 left-hand corner. Vern. *Gengwa Geogheria*, Beng.; *Geva*, *Suran*, *Surund*, Mar.; *Komatti*, Mal.; *Kayaw*, *Tayaw*, Burm. Tidal forests, Sundriban, Andamans and on the coast of Burma. On the coast and along brackish backwaters of the Western Peninsula. Fl. H. S., R. S. Sea coast Ceylon, Indian Archipelago, North Australia, New Caledonia. A small evergreen bushy tree, sap extremely acrid, causing blisters on the skin, l. bright green, elliptic, acuminate, usually shallow sinuate-crenate, blade 2–4, pet. slender ½–1¼ in. Fl. minute, fragrant, yellowish-green, ♂ in catkin-like spikes, each fl. on a broad bract, imbricating in bud with several minute bracteoles, anthers long exserted, ♀ pedicelled, in short racemes, the upper fl. usually imperfect, sepals broadly ovate, serrulate. Capsule varying much in size, ½–1 in. diam., coriaceous, deeply 3-lobed.

2. **E. acerifolia**, F. Didrichs.—Syn. *Stillingia himalayensis*, Klotzch in Bot. Prinz Waldemar t. 21. Central Himalaya, Kumaon and Nepal, 3-5,000 ft. Khasi hills. A large glabrous shrub, foliage deep green. L. membranous, elliptic-lanceolate, serrate, blade 4–6, pet. ⅓–½ in. Spikes androgynous, ♂ fl. sessile, 2–3 in the axil of a broadly-ovate bract, ♀ at the base of spikes. Capsule ⅜ in. diam., 2–3-lobed. 3. **E. holophylla**, Kurz. Martaban and Tenasserim, evergreen forest. L. lanceolate or oblanceolate, quite entire, spikes slender, terminal androgynous, the ♀ fl. at the base. 4. **E. rectinervis**, Kurz. Nicobars. Branchlets stout, l. coriaceous, obovate-oblong, blade 6–9, pet. 1 in. long.

B. L. opposite, spikes unisexual.

5. **E. crenulata**, Wight Ic. t. 1865.—Syn. *E. cochinchinensis*, Muell. Arg.; Bedd. Manual t. xxii. f. 5; *E. oppositifolia*, Thw. (non Jack). Western Ghats from Coorg southwards, Nilgiris, Anamalais. A small evergreen usually diœcious tree or shrub branchlets slender. L. thinly coriaceous, elliptic-lanceolate, acuminate, crenulate

blade 2–6 in. narrowed into pet. ¼–½ in. Spikes often at the ends of branches, ♂ 2–6 in. long, slender, bracts 1-fld., broadly ovate, acute, erose, a pair of round glands at the base, bracteoles obliquely lanceolate, sepals lanceolate, toothed. ♀ few- often only 1-fld., sepals broadly ovate, erose. Capsule ½–⅝ in. diam., deeply 3-lobed. 6. **E. robusta,** Hook. f. Western Ghats from the Konkan southwards. Branchlets robust, ♂ spikes axillary, rachis stout, bracts 1-fld., broadly ovate, biglandular at base, bracteoles broadly falcate, serrate, sepals unequal, the 2 lateral falcate, the third broad, lobed and serrate. 7. **E. oppositifolia,** Griffith. Silhet. L. thinly coriaceous, lanceolate, entire or serrulate, blade 8–12, pet. ⅜ in., sec. n. 15–20 pair, prominent beneath. ♂ spikes terminal, very slender, bracts entire 1-fld., bracteoles 0, sepals toothed.

33. ADENOCHLÆNA, Baill.; Fl. Brit. Ind. v. 417.

Trees or shrubs. Fl. monœcious, in spiciform racemes, ♂ clustered, ♀ few at the base of spike, disk 0. ♂: Buds globose, sepals 4–6, valvate, stamens 4–6, filaments free exserted round a columnar pistillode, anthers dorsifixed, versatile, cells parallel, adnate to thick connective. ♀: Sepals 5–8, narrow, unequal, ovary 3-celled, styles long, connate below, spreading, bifid with recurved plumose multifid arms. Capsule of 3 two-valved cocci.

1. **A. indica,** Bedd.—Syn. *Cephalocroton indicum*, Bedd. Fl. Sylv. t. 261. North Kanara, Coorg, Anamalais and Travancore in evergreen forest, 1,500–4,000 ft. A shrub or moderate-sized tree, young shoots and inflorescence puberulous, l. elliptic, blade 3–7, pet. ½–4 in., thickened at the top, sec. n. 4–8 pair prominent beneath. Spikes interrupted, 2–6 in., ovary and style tomentose. Capsule scabrous, ⅜ in. diam. 2. **A. silhetiana,** Benth. Khasi hills. Branchlets, petioles and rachis of racemes finely stellate tomentose, l. crowded at the ends of branches, thinly coriaceous, sessile or nearly so, lanceolate gradually narrowed into a cordate base.

Cœlodepas calycinum, Bedd. Fl. Sylv. t. 320. Vern. *Kātpira*, Tam. Foot of the Tinnevelli hills. A small tree, wood very hard, young shoots with deciduous stellate hairs. L. alternate, thinly coriaceous, crenate-serrate, elongate-elliptic, acuminate, blade 3–7 in., pet. very short, stipules subulate, lacerate. ♂ spikes 4–5 in. long, slender, sep. 4, stamens 4–5, filaments thick flat, adnate to the pistillode, anther-cells 2, divaricate. ♀ racemes short few-fld., sepals 5, concave, tomentose, ovary hairy. Capsule 3-lobed, ⅓ in. diam., stellately hairy, sepals in fr. enlarged, broadly ovate.

34. CLAOXYLON, A. Juss.; Fl. Brit. Ind. v. 410.

Trees or shrubs, rarely herbs, l. alternate usually long-petioled. Fl. small or minute, usually diœcious, in axillary or lateral spikes or racemes, buds globose, sepals valvate. ♂: Stamens few or many, inserted on or around a central receptacle, often intermixed with glands or long linear ciliate scales, filaments free, anthers erect, cells distinct, connate at the base only. Ovary 3-celled, styles short entire, densely plumose. Testa crustaceous, cotyledons broad flat in fleshy albumen.

A. ♀ fl. without hypogynous scales.

1. **C. indicum,** Hassk. Tenasserim. Malay Penins. and Archip. China. A shrub or small tree, branchlets pubescent, l. elliptic, blade 6–10, pet. 2–5 in. ♂ racemes 4–6 in. long, fl. minute, clustered, pedicels very short, filaments mixed with filiform scales. ♀ racemes shorter, pedicels longer. Capsule tomentose ¼ in. diam., cocci keeled. This is possibly *C. longifolium*, Kurz F. Fl. ii. 396. 2. **C. Khasianum,** Hook. f. Assam. Khasi hills. Cachar. Similar to 1, filaments mixed with minute scales; fr. of 1–3 globose membranous hoary carpels. 3. **C. anomalum,** Hook. f. Courtallum. Branchlets glabrous, l. lanceolate, blade 4–6, pet. 1–2 in., anthers sessile, imbricating around the edge of a flat naked receptacle.

B. ♀ fl. with 3 oblong hypogynous scales, alternating with the carpels.

Three little known shrubs of the Travancore and Tinnevelli hills: 4. **C. Wightii,** Hook. f., sparsely softly hispid, l. lanceolate, blade 2–3, pet. ⅓–1 in., racemes very slender, anthers 6–9 nearly sessile, capsule hispid ⅛ in. diam. 5. **C. Beddomei,** Hook. f. Similar to 4, anthers 15–20, nearly sessile, capsule glabrous, ⅓ in. diam. 6. **C. hirsutum,** Hook. f. Softly tawny-tomentose, stamens 8, filaments longer than anthers.

35. ACALYPHA, Linn.; Fl. Brit. Ind. v. 414.

Herbs, a few shrubs or trees. L. alternate, toothed or crenate. Fl. usually monœcious, minute, ♂ in axillary spikes, calyx splitting into 4 valvate sepals. Stamens usually 8, on a convex receptacle, anther-cells divaricate, ♀ at the base of the ♂ raceme or in separate racemes or heads, sometimes solitary. Sepals minute 3–4, ovary 3-celled, styles filiform, generally long, branched or fimbriate, often bright-coloured. Capsule of 3 small crustaceous cocci. Species 220, tropical and subtropical.

1. **A. fruticosa,** Forsk. Western Peninsula. Pegu and Martaban (Kurz).—Ceylon. A shrub, young shoots finely hairy, l. ovate, underside with numerous shining orbicular glands, blade 1–3, pet. $\frac{1}{2}$–1 in. Spikes hairy, $\frac{1}{2}$–1 in. long, the upper portion occupied by densely crowded minute ♂, while the lower portion bears isolated ♀ fl., in the axils of broad foliaceous crenate and radially ribbed bracts, sepals 4 hyaline, ciliate, ovary densely hairy, styles with numerous lateral branches. Capsules tomentose $\frac{1}{6}$ in. diam. 2. **A. acmophylla,** Hemsley in Journ. Linn. Soc. xxvi. 436. Upper Burma.—Hupeh. Similar to 1, young shoots and young l. clothed with long fascicled hairs, l. eglandular, long-acuminate, blade 2-4, pet. slender, 1–2 in., spikes usually ♂, 1–2 in. long, ♀ fl. solitary. 3. **A. alnifolia,** Klein. Western Peninsula. Branches and petioles softly pubescent. L. tomentose while young, more or less hairy when full grown, eglandular, ovate, blade $\frac{1}{2}$–2, pet. $\frac{1}{4}$–$\frac{3}{4}$ in., spikes ♂ , 2-3 in. long, ♀ fl. in terminal heads or short spikes, bracts 1-fid., styles pink, plumose with capillary branches, capsule hispid. 4. **A. Dalzellii,** Hook. f. Bombay. Glabrous, eglandular, l. thinly membranous, ovate-lanceolate, obscurely crenate, blade 2–3, pet. capillary, $\frac{3}{4}$–1$\frac{1}{4}$ in. long. ♀ fl. in pairs on long filiform peduncles in the axil of one large reniform quite entire bract $\frac{1}{4}$–$\frac{1}{2}$ in. diam. Ovary glabrous. 5. **A. hispida,** Burm. New Guinea. Cultivated in India and the Malay Archip. A shrub, l. broad-ovate, ♀ racemes drooping, scarlet, 12-18 in. long, styles deeply pinnatifid, segments linear subulate.

36. ALCHORNEA, Swartz; Fl. Brit. Ind. v. 420.

Trees or shrubs, l. alternate, fl. diœcious or monœcious, small, apetalous, in clusters on simple or panicled terminal spikes or racemes, bracts minute, disk 0. ♂: calyx globose, splitting into 2–4 valvate segments. ♀: sepals 3–6, imbricate. Capsule of 2–3 two-valved crustaceous cocci. Species about 30, tropical.

1. **A. mollis,** Muell. Arg. Outer valleys of Nepal and Sikkim, ascending to 2,000 ft. Assam. Northern Circars. A small tree, branchlets, petioles, underside of l. and racemes finely tomentose. L. broad ovate, dentate, acuminate, base rounded or slightly cordate, blade 4–6 in. long and nearly as broad, pet. 3–5 in., basal n. 3. Capsule $\frac{1}{2}$ in. diam., faintly 3-lobed, smooth, densely pubescent, styles short spreading. 2. **A. tiliæfolia,** Muell. Arg. Sikkim foot of hills, ascending to 4,000 ft. Assam. Khasi hills. Tenasserim or Andamans (Kurz). Similar to 1 but l. hairy along nerves only, serrate, base often cuneate, capsules oblong, tubercled, finely pubescent, $\frac{1}{3}$ in. long, crowned by the long filiform styles. 3. **A. rugosa,** Muell. Arg. Tenasserim.—Malay Penins. China. L. penninerved, l. elliptic-lanceolate or oblanceolate, blade 4–8, pet. 1 in. long, capsules glabrous tridymous, $\frac{1}{4}$–$\frac{1}{3}$ in. diam.

Coccoceras plicatum, Muell. Arg.—Syn. *Hymenocardia plicata*, Kurz. Pegu, Martaban and Tenasserim in swamp forests and on low ground in the Savannah forests (*Yegyin*, Burm.). A middle-sized deciduous tree, branchlets and petioles with rusty pubescence. L. elongate-elliptic, abruptly acuminate, repand-crenate, blade 4–6, pet. $\frac{1}{2}$–1 in. long, underside densely covered with minute orbicular scales. ♂ fl. minute in distant clusters on long slender axillary racemes. ♀ solitary on short pedicels in racemes 2–3 in. long, ovary trigonous.

37. MALLOTUS, Lour.; Fl. Brit. Ind. v. 427.

Shrubs or trees, l. mostly evergreen and alternate, in some species opposite, petiole usually long. Fl. monœcious or diœcious, apetalous, disk usually 0. ♂: Calyx globose or ovoid, valvately 3–5-partite, stamens 20–30, crowded on a central receptacle, anther-cells adnate to and often widely separated by the thick connective. Pistillode 0 or minute. ♀: Calyx usually valvately 3–6-lobed. Ovary 2–4-celled, styles spreading or recurved. Capsule 2–3-celled, dehiscing loculicidally, 2–3-valved. Species 70–80, chiefly Indo-Malayan.

I. Disk 0, or if present annular or cupular. Seeds without a fleshy coat.

A. Capsule echinate or tubercled.

(*a*) L. orbicular or broadly ovate, usually alternate.

α. L. peltate.

1. **M. albus,** Muell Arg.—Syn. *M. tetracoccus*, Kurz F. Fl. ii. 382; *Rottlera peltata*, Wight Ic. t. 1873. Vern. *Marleya*, Beng.; *Kukoti*, Kan.; *Mulla-polavu*, Tam.; *Pattha*, *Paral*, Mal.; *Petwaing*, Upper Burma. Western Ghats, from the Konkan southwards. Outer ranges and valleys of the Sikkim Himalaya, ascending to 3,000 ft., common in second growth forest. Assam. East Bengal. Chittagong. Upper Burma.—Ceylon, moist low country, very common. A middle-sized tree, branchlets, petioles, underside of l. and inflorescence densely clothed with grey or tawny stellate tomentum. L. mostly alternate, broad-ovate, acuminate, entire or sinuate-toothed, base narrowly peltate, rounded or truncate, basal n. 3–5. Fl. diœcious, in axillary and terminal pyramidal panicles, ♂: Buds globose $\frac{1}{8}$ in. diam., anther-cells parallel. ♀: calyx 4–5-lobed, ovary densely clothed with stellate hairs, styles 4–5, densely papillose. Capsule loculicidally 4-valved, white tomentose, with soft conical tomentose protuberances. Seeds black, tuberculate. 2. **M. barbatus,** Muell. Arg. Tenasserim. Malay Penins. Konkan (doubtful). Branchlets, petioles, underside of l. and inflorescence softly white flocculently woolly. L. alternate, peltate, orbicular, shortly 3-lobed, blade 8–14 in. diam., pet. 2–6 in. long. Fl. in narrow racemes, 6–10 in. long. Capsules $\frac{3}{4}$ in. diam., densely clothed with masses of stellate hairs. 3. **M. Roxburghianus,** Muell. Arg. Subhimalayan tract and outer hills from Sikkim eastwards. Assam. Khasi hills, Chittagong. Forests east of Toungoo (Kurz). A small evergreen tree, branchlets, petioles and underside of l. stellately pubescent, l. alternate, peltate, orbicular or ovate, acuminate, not lobed, more or less toothed, upperside pubescent with simple hairs, blade 4–7 in. diam., pet. 2–4 in. long. Racemes stout, 6–12 in. long, capsules deeply 3-lobed, $\frac{1}{2}$ in. diam., hairy and prickly.

β. L. not or very narrowly peltate.

4. **M. nepalensis,** Muell. Arg. Himalaya from Nepal eastwards, 5–8,000 ft., common in second growth forests. Branchlets, petioles, underside of l. and inflorescence shortly rusty-tomentose, l. sometimes opposite, quite entire, ovate or orbicular, blade 5–10, pet. 3–8 in. long. Racemes stout, 6–12 in. long, capsules $\frac{1}{2}$ in. diam., tomentose and clothed with long soft tomentose bristles, crowded, forming dense cylindrical masses. 5. **M. cochinchinensis,** Lour.—Syn. *M. paniculatus*, Muell. Arg. Pegu Yoma, eastern slopes. Martaban and Tenasserim. Malay Penins. and Archip. China. A middle-sized tree, branchlets, petioles, underside of l. and inflorescence shortly white- or rusty-tomentose, l. alternate, rhomboid or orbicular, entire or acutely 3-lobed, blade 3–7, pet. 2–6 in. long. Fl. in ample panicles, branches slender. Capsule 3-coccous, densely clothed with soft white-tomentose bristles. 6. **M. ricinoides,** Muell. Arg. Upper Tenasserim (Kurz).—China. Philippines. A shrub, branchlets, young l. and inflorescence densely clothed with floccose fugacious tomentum of stellate hairs. L. broadly ovate, acuminate, blade 5–8, pet. 2–5 in. Capsules crowded in short cylindric spikes, $\frac{1}{2}$–$\frac{3}{4}$ in. diam., densely clothed with long soft stellately tomentose bristles.

(*b*) L. elliptic, oblong or obovate (excepting *M. floribundus*).

α. Calyx spathaceous.

7. **M. acuminatus,** Muell. Arg. Andamans. Tenasserim. Malay Penins. and Archip. A large shrub, young shoots minutely hairy, branchlets usually glabrous. L. membranous, sometimes opposite, elongate-elliptic, base peltate or cordate, blade 4–8, pet. 1–3 in. long, racemes ♂ 3–6 in. long, fl. in crowded clusters, buds $\frac{1}{12}$ in. diam., ♀ stout, shorter. Capsule tridymous. 8. **M. floribundus,** Muell. Arg. Mergui. Malay Penins. and Archip. Branchlets nearly glabrous, l. membranous, glaucous beneath, orbicular or broadly-ovate, base peltate, blade 4–5, pet. 2–3 in. Male spikes 2–3 in. long, fl. crowded, in bud concealed by large imbricating bracts. Capsule tridymous $\frac{3}{4}$ in. diam., with scattered soft prickles. 9. **M. Helferi,** Muell. Arg. Pegu (Kurz). Yunzalin (D.B. March 1880). Thoungyin (D.B. 1859). Malay Penins. A shrub, branchlets, petioles and sometimes midrib minutely hairy, l. sinuate-dentate, elliptic or elliptic-lanceolate, acuminate, base rounded or nearly cordate, not peltate. Male racemes slender, 3–5 in. long, fl. glabrous, green, on short pedicels, clustered, sepals 3, anther-cells at the ends of a cylindrical connective. The Burma specimens have only ♂ fl.

β. Calyx 3–6-partite. L. usually opposite.

(1) Western species. Minute shining orbicular scales on the underside of l.

10. **M. Lawii,** Muell. Arg. Western Ghats from the Konkan southwards, chiefly in evergreen forest. A small shrub, branchlets, petioles and inflorescence pubescent, l. nearly glabrous, lanceolate, repand-toothed, blade 4–8, pet. $\frac{1}{4}$–$\frac{1}{2}$ in. long. Racemes

slender, shorter than l., capsule 3–4-dymous, ¾ in. diam., tomentose, densely covered with long villous filaments. 11. **M. Beddomei**, Hook. f. Anamalais and Tinnevelli Ghats. Very similar to 10, if specifically distinct, petioles longer, ½–2 in. long, capsule stellately pubescent and clothed with long soft spines. 12. **M. stenanthus**, Muell. Arg. Western Ghats from North Kanara southwards. A small shrub, branchlets and inflorescence more or less pubescent, l. lanceolate, entire or sinuate-toothed, blade 4–8, pet. ⅛–¼ in. long, capsule with scattered short conical tubercles. 13. **M. muricatus**, Bedd.—Syn. *Claoxylon muricatum*, Wight Ic. t. 1886. Similar, but quite glabrous, each coccus with two rows of tubercles.

(2) Eastern species, branchlets hairy.

14. **M. Clellandii**, Hook. f. Vern. *Indaing thidin*, Burm. Rangoon. Mu valley, Upper Burma. A shrub, branchlets, petioles and inflorescence more or less clothed with stellate hairs, l. eglandular beneath, from elliptic-oblong to lanceolate, base rounded or cordate, blade 4–5, pet. ½–2 in. long, stipules subulate, hairy, basal n. 3–5, tert. n. parallel, prominent, as well as the reticulate veins. Fl. diœcious, ♂ racemes ½–1½ in. long, bracts subulate. ♀ racemes or corymbs pedunculate, few-fld., sepals 3 or 4, coriaceous, linear, longer than ovary, afterwards reflexed, ovary with cylindrical tubercles, densely clothed with long hairs. Capsules densely woolly, ¾ in. diam., with long hairy soft prickles. The Rangoon specimens, ♂, are in very young bud, and the sepals are coriaceous, while in the ♂ sp. from Upper Burma the sepals are membranous.

Of the following 3 species from Tenasserim the ♂ fl. only are known: 15. **M. Wallichianus**, Muell. Arg., also known from Rangoon. Branchlets and infl. with deciduous stellate hairs, l. alternate and opposite, elongate-elliptic, dentate, blade 4–6, pet. 1–1½ in., 3 basal nerves, underside closely covered with minute orbicular glands. ♂ spikes slender, longer than l. 16. **M. filiformis**, Hook. f. and 17. **M. leptostachyus**, Hook. f. Branchlets, petioles, underside of l. and spikes softly tomentose, l. alternate or uppermost pair opposite, entire, elongate-elliptic, blade 5–10, pet. 1–2 in., sec. n. 4–6 pair, the lowest pair basal, minute shining glands scattered on the underside. ♂ spikes 6–12 in. long.

18. **M. decipiens**, Muell. Arg.—Syn. *Cœlodiscus eriocarpoides*, Kurz. Tenasserim. A shrub, branchlets, petioles, underside of l., chiefly along n., as well as racemes softly tomentose. L. often in unequal pairs, elliptic, acuminate, repand-toothed, sec. n. 6–8 pair, the lowest pair basal, tert. n. parallel, blade 5–10, pet. ½–1 in. long. ♂ racemes slender, fl. small, nearly sessile, stamens surrounding a minute pistillode. Capsule ½ in. diam.

(3) Eastern species, branchlets glabrous.

19. **M. Khasianus**, Hook. f. Khasi hills. Mu valley, Upper Burma. A small tree, glabrous except inflorescence. L. thinly coriaceous, elliptic-lanceolate, base usually acute, more or less sinuate-toothed, eglandular beneath, blade 5–10, pet. ¾–1½ in., ♂ racemes 4–6 in. long, stellately tomentose, buds globose $\frac{1}{16}$ in. diam. before opening, pedicels as long as fl., bracts short, broad-ovate. Capsule ¾ in. diam., clothed with slender prickles, pedicels ½ in. long, seeds brown, shining. 20. **M. polyneurus**, Hook. f. Tenasserim. L. alternate, membranous, sinuate-dentate, elliptic, acuminate, blade 6–8, pet. 1–1½ in., sec. n. 10–12 pair, ♀ racemes few-fld., peduncle long, slender. 21. **M. andamanicus**, Hook. f.—Syn. *M. muricatus*, Kurz (not Muell. Arg.). Andamans. A large shrub, almost entirely glabrous, young shoots, ovary and capsule densely covered with minute orbicular golden glands, branchlets strongly compressed, almost flat. L. elongate-elliptic, slightly sinuate-dentate, base acute, blade 3–7, pet. ¼ in. ♂ spikes sessile, dense-fld., catkin-like, bracts broadly ovate. Capsules tridymous, ¾ in. diam., with stiff scattered prickles.

B. Capsule smooth, basal nerves 3.

(*a*) Petiole less than ⅓ the length of blade. Western species.

22. **M. distans**, Muell. Arg. Tinnevelli ghats. A straggling shrub, branchlets, petioles, underside of l. and inflorescence softly stellate tomentose. L. opposite, ovate- or elliptic-oblong, blade 5–10, pet. 1–2 in. long, basal n. 3 and 3–4 pair of sec. n., tert. n. parallel. ♂ racemes short, fl. ¼ in. diam. Capsule ⅓ in. diam., tridymous, densely stellate tomentose, pedicels ½–1 in., peduncles 4–5 in. long. 23. **M. rhamnifolius**, Muell. Arg. Southern districts of the Western Peninsula.—Ceylon low country, common. Branchlets, petioles and inflorescence pubescent, l. opposite and alternate, lanceolate or elliptic-lanceolate, blade 3–5, pet. ¼–1 in., 3 basal n., tert. n. parallel. ♂ fl. clustered, on erect spikes 3–5 in. long. Cocci almost distinct, globose, finely stellate-pubescent. 24. **M. atrovirens**, Muell. Arg. Cochin, Travancore, low country. Quite glabrous, but underside of l., inflorescence, sepals and ovary densely clothed with minute orbicular scales. L. alternate, oblanceolate or obovate, scattered minute scales on the upper surface, blade 2–5, narrowed into pet. ¼–¾ in. long.

(*b*) Petiole ⅓ the length of blade or longer.

25. **M. philippinensis,** Muell. Arg.; Bedd. Fl. Sylv. t. 289.—Syn. *Rottlera tinctoria,* Roxb. Cor. Pl. t. 168. Vern. *Raini, Rohni, Roli, Rora,* Hind.; *Kapila, Hulichellu,* Kan.; *Kapila,* Tam.; *Manjana,* Mal.; *Taw thidin,* Burma.

A large shrub or small tree, branchlets, young l. and inflorescence tawny- or rusty-pubescent, l. alternate, ovate or ovate-lanceolate, entire, glabrous above, underside pubescent and with numerous minute red orbicular glands, blade 4–9, pet. 2–3 in. long, basal n. 3, midrib penninerved. Fl. diœcious, in terminal often panicled brown or brick-red spikes. Ovary tomentose, 3-celled, styles ¼ in. long, thickly papillose. Capsule 3-lobed, loculicidally 3-valved, densely covered with a bright red powder consisting of resin mixed with minute stellate hairs.

Subhimalayan tract, from the Punjab eastwards, ascending to 4,500 ft. Bengal. Central India. Both Peninsulas. Fl. July–January. Never quite leafless. The powder which covers the capsules (*Kamela, Kamala*) is used for dyeing silk.—Ceylon. Malay Penins. and Archip. Australia. China. 26. **M. repandus,** Muell. Arg. Assam. Silhet. Bengal. Chittagong. Burma, Upper and Lower. Western Peninsula.—Ceylon. Malay Penins. and Archip. China. New Caledonia. A large straggling or climbing diœcious shrub, stem often fluted with very rough bark, and (Talbot) large often fascicled spines 1–3 in. long. Branchlets, petioles, underside of l. and inflorescence with tawny stellate tomentum. L. broadly triangular-ovate, blade 2–4, pet. slender 1–1½ in. long, 3 basal n., underside with minute shining orbicular scales. ♂ racemes panicled, anther-cells of the inner stamens often quite separate, attached at different levels of the connective, Capsule didymous, clothed with dense stellate tomentum.

II. Disk glandular in both sexes. Seeds with a thick fleshy coat.

27. **M. Kurzii,** Hook. f.—Syn. *Blumeodendron Tokbrai,* Kurz. Andamans. Perak. A large evergreen tree, perfectly glabrous. L. opposite or in whorls of 3, rigidly coriaceous, entire, elliptic, blade 6–9, pet. 1–2 in., sec. n. prominent beneath, 4–6 pair, the lowest pair basal, tert. n. obscure. ♂ fl. in short racemes, hypogynous glands (disk) minute, thick.

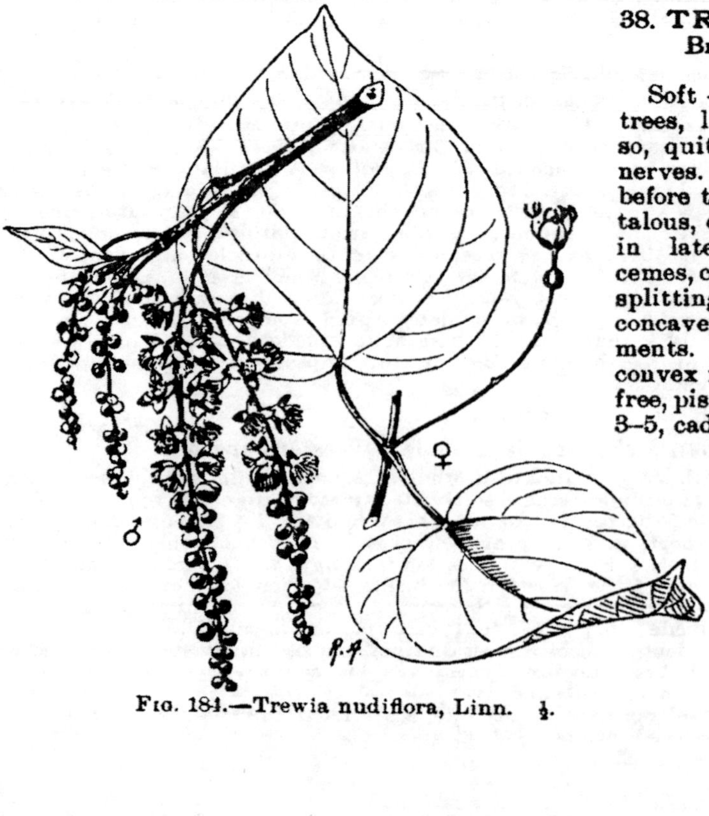

FIG. 184.—Trewia nudiflora, Linn. ½.

38. **TREWIA,** Linn.; Fl. Brit. Ind. v. 423.

Soft-wooded deciduous trees, l. opposite or nearly so, quite entire, 3–5 basal nerves. Fl. often appearing before the l., diœcious, apetalous, disk 0. ♂: fascicled in lateral pendulous racemes, calyx globose in bud, splitting into 3–4 broad concave, often reflexed segments. Stamens ∞ on a convex receptacle, filaments free, pistillode 0. ♀: sepals 3–5, caducous, ovary hairy, 2–4-celled, styles connate below, long, entire, papillose all over. Fr. fleshy, endocarp crustaceous. Species 2.

1. **T. nudiflora,** Linn.; Wight Ic. t. 1870. Vern. *Tumri,*

Gamhar, *Khamara*, Hind.; *Pitali*, Beng.; *Petari*, Mar.; *Pambara-Kumbil*, Mal.; *Set-Kadon*, Upper, *Yehhmyot*, Lower Burma.

A middle-sized or large tree, young shoots, inflorescence and sometimes full grown l. beneath clothed with flocculent cottony wool. L. ovate from a cordate or rounded base, acuminate, blade 4–6, pet. 1–3 in. long. Female fl. on long peduncles, solitary or 2–3 together, styles yellow, $\frac{1}{2}$–$\frac{3}{4}$ in. long. Fr. globose 1–1$\frac{1}{2}$ in. diam., pericarp thick, almost woody.

Subhimalayan tract, from the Jumna eastwards, ascending to 3,000 ft. Assam. Khasi hills. Bengal. Behar. Singbhum. Central India. Both Peninsulas. Chiefly in moist places and on river banks, reproduces abundantly from root suckers. Fl. Feb.–Apr.—Ceylon. Malay Peninsula and Archipelago. Closely allied and perhaps not specifically distinct: 2. **T. polycarpa**, Benth. in Gen. Pl. iii. 318 (*T. nudiflora*, Bedd. Fl. Sylv. t. 281, Wight t. 1871), Western Peninsula, ♀ in many-fld. short racemes, fr. $\frac{1}{2}$ in. diam., pericarp crustaceous, thin.

39. CŒLODISCUS, Baill.; Fl. Brit. Ind. v. 425.

Shrubs or small trees with stellate hairs, l. opposite, dentate or sinuately lobed, basal n. 3–7. Fl. diœcious, small, in axillary bracteate spikes or racemes, ♂ clustered in the bracts, ♀ solitary, disk 0. ♂: sepals 3, valvate, stamens 20–∞ surrounding a naked central receptacle, filaments free, pistillode 0. Capsule of 3 two-valved cocci, tomentose or clothed with soft prickles and separating from a central axis. Species 5 or 6, Indo-Malayan region.

1. **C. lappaceus**, Kurz. Upper Burma. Yunnan. Branchlets, petioles, underside of l. and inflorescence densely clothed with soft stellate tomentum, l. ovate, often lobed, upperside rough with raised dots and distant stellate hairs, blade 4–6, pet. 1–2$\frac{1}{2}$ in. long, stipules subulate. Racemes short, bracts linear. Capsules crowded $\frac{3}{4}$ in. diam., densely clothed with long soft hairy bristles. 2. **C. longipes**, Kurz. Eng and dry forests of Pegu and Martaban. A small deciduous undershrub, the annual (l. and fl. bearing) stems on a thick woody rootstock, mature l. nearly glabrous, orbicular, 3–5 in. diam., pet. $\frac{1}{2}$–3 in. long. ♀ racemes numerous, 5–7 in. long, arising mostly from the head of the rootstock, capsules muricate, pedicel 2–4 in. long. Two deciduous small shrubs or undershrubs, of which ♂ fl. only are known. 3. **C. hirsutulus**, Kurz. Pegu. Pet. 4–12 in. and 4. **C. glabriusculus**, Kurz. Pegu Yoma and Martaban, near streams, pet. 1–3 in. long.

40. MACARANGA, Thouars; Fl. Brit. Ind. v. 445.

Trees or shrubs of rapid growth but not long lived, wood soft spongy, l. alternate, often large and peltate, underside with numerous orbicular scales. Fl. apetalous, usually diœcious, in axillary panicles, rarely racemose, bracts often large, ♂ fl. numerous, clustered, minute, sepals 2–4, valvate, stamens 1–15, central, anthers almost peltate, 3–4-celled, the connective shorter than the anther-cells, pistillode 0. ♀: Calyx 2–4-lobed or toothed, ovary 1–3-celled, styles entire, 1 ovule in each cell. Capsule mostly didymous, often globose, of one coccus only. Embryo small, cotyledons flat, in fleshy albumen. Species 80–90. Tropics of the Old World.

I. ♂ and ♀ fl. in much-branched panicles, styles short, recurved.

A. Bracts of ♂ panicles not enclosing the fl. clusters.

(*a*) L. peltate.

1. **M. denticulata**, Muell. Arg.; Kurz F. Fl. ii. 387. Vern. *Burna*, Beng.; *Taung petwun*, Lower; *Petwaing*, Upper Burma.

A middle-sized or large evergreen tree. Young shoots and l. rusty-tomentose with long slender thin-walled hairs, branchlets and petioles glabrescent, glaucous. L. broadly ovate, acuminate, denticulate while young, blade 6–10, pet. 4–8 in. long, underside pale, densely covered with minute orbicular scales, often pubescent, basal n. numerous, midrib with 10–12 pair sec. n., prominent beneath, stipules small, fugacious. ♂ fl.: clusters pubescent, approximate, almost continuous on the ramifications of panicle, bracts minute. Sepals 2–3, stamens 6–30. ♀ panicles short, fl. on short thick pedicels, bracts minute. Sepals 3–4, ovary 2-celled, styles short. Capsule didymous, ¼ in. diam., black, glabrous with minute orbicular glands.

Subhimalayan tract from Sikkim eastwards, ascending occasionally to 5,000 ft., in mixed forest and on grass lands. Assam. Khasi hills. Chittagong. Burma, Upper and Lower. Fl. March, April, in the hills later. Exudes a clear red gum resin. 2. **M. indica,** Wight Ic. t. 1883 and 1949 f. 2; Bedd. Fl. Sylv. t. 287A. Vern. *Papri*, Dehra Dún. Malkot hills, Dehra Dún 4–5,000 ft. Bahraich forests, on the Nepal frontier. Sikkim, outer hills. Singbhúm, in damp valleys, rare. Assam. Khasi hills. Andamans. Nilgiris and other hills in the southern portion of the Peninsula.—Ceylon. A small evergreen tree, often gregarious, branchlets stout, glaucous, young shoots and young l. tawny-tomentose. L. orbicular-ovate, acuminate, usually entire, broadly peltate, glabrous above, minutely hairy or softly tomentose beneath, with numerous orbicular shining scales, blade 5–12 in. diam., pet. 3–8 in. long, basal n. numerous, sec. n. from midrib 6–8 pair. ♂ panicle branches zigzag, fl. clusters sessile, distant, usually pubescent, in the axils of a thick fleshy bract, which terminates in a quadrangular or elliptic shining glandular blade, sepals 2–3, stamens 6–10. ♀ panicle hairy, bracts small, sepals usually 4, ovary mostly 1-celled, densely covered with round resinous yellow glands, capsule as a rule globose, ⅛ in. diam.

(*b*) L. not peltate.

3. **M. pustulata,** King. Vern. *Mallata*, Nepal. Himalaya from Kumaon eastwards, 3–6,000 ft., chiefly on old clearings. A small often gregarious tree, youngest shoots rusty tomentose. L. entire, broad-ovate, base truncate, blade 4–7 in. long and often broader than long, pet. as long as blade, underside pale, with numerous minute orbicular glands. ♂ panicles glandular. Capsule didymous, ¼ in. diam., densely tomentose, each coccus with a large glabrous glandular patch on the back. 4. A sp. nearly allied to 3, collected at Bernardmyo, Upper Burma 5–6,000 ft., by J. W. Oliver, ♂ only, has branchlets, underside of l. and inflorescence softly tomentose, l. ovate, slightly lobed, base truncate or broadly cuneate, blade 4–8, pet. 2–4 in. long, fl. in dense clusters on long interrupted racemes, pedicels short, sepals 5, ⅛ in. long, hairy on both sides, stamens ∞, glabrous. 5. **M. gmelinaefolia,** King. Kurseong 4–5,000 ft. Similar to 3, base of l. broadly cuneate, ♂ panicles with minute deciduous stellate hairs. 6. **M. Gamblei,** Hook. f. Dulkajhar forest, Darjeeling terai. A small tree, l. lanceolate, blade 3–5, pet. ½–¾ in., orbicular glands on underside of l. few, scattered, ♂ panicles pubescent.

B. Bracts of ♂ fl. large, concealing the fl. clusters.

(*a*) L. peltate, entire.

7. **M. Roxburghii,** Wight Ic. t. 1949 fig. 4.—Syn. *M. tomentosa*, Wight Ic. t. 1949 fig. 1; Bedd. Fl. Sylv. t. 287; *M. peltata*, Muell. Arg.; Prain Bengal Plants 951. Vern. *Chanda*, Mar.; *Upaligi*, Kan.; *Vatta*, Tam. Western Ghats from the Konkan southwards, common in evergreen forest. Hills of Orissa and the Circars.—Ceylon, moist region, very common. A small or middle-sized tree, branchlets stout, youngest shoots stellate-tomentose, l. deltoid or orbicular, broadly peltate, entire or minutely toothed, basal n. numerous, blade 5–10, pet. 3–8 in. long. Panicles rusty tomentose, bracts tomentose, large, dentate, veined, bracteoles concave. ♂ clusters enveloped in bracts and bracteoles, sepals 3, stamens 2–3. ♀ ovary 1-celled, style lateral. Capsule ⅙–⅓ in. diam., covered with hairs and glands. 8. **M. Tanarius,** Muell. Arg.—Syn. *M. moluccana*, Wight Ic. t. 816. Andamans. Nicobars. Malay Peninsula and Archipelago. China. Branchlets stout, young shoots and young l. softly pubescent, bracts ⅓–½ in. long, tomentose, acute, toothed or pectinate, capsules 2–3-lobed ⅓–½ in. diam., densely covered with orbicular scales, with 6–12 subulate soft bristles ¼ in. long.

(*b*) L. not peltate.

9. **M. minutiflora,** Muell. Arg. Tenasserim. Branchlets, underside of l. and inflorescence softly tomentose, l. ovate, caudate-acuminate, denticulate, blade 4–6, pet. 1–2 in. long, basal n. 3. Male panicles sessile, flaccid, shorter than petiole, bracts villous, ovate, pectinately toothed, ⅓–½ in. long, stamens 2.

II. ♀ fl. in few-fld. racemes, styles long and slender, l. not peltate.

10. **M. Brandisii,** King. Muleyit, Tenasserim, 2–5,000 ft. Quite glabrous, l. lanceolate, penninerved, blade 4–5, pet. ½–1 in. long. Capsules didymous, with a few soft bristles, in long-pedunculate 1–3-fld. racemes, in the axils of large ovate-lanceolate leafy bracts.

Cleidion javanicum, Blume; Bedd. Fl. Sylv. t. 272. Vern. *Vellarei*, Tam. Western Ghats from the Konkan southwards in evergreen forests. Outer hills of the eastern Himalaya from Sikkim eastwards. Chittagong. Manipur. Burma, Upper and Lower. Ceylon.

Java. A glabrous evergreen middle-sized tree, l. alternate, coriaceous, usually sinuate-toothed, blade 4–10, pet. 1–4 in. Fl. ♂ in long axillary racemes, cal. globose, splitting into 3-4 valvate segments, stamens ∞, on a conical receptacle, filaments free, anthers 4-celled, pistillode 0, ♀ one or two on a long axillary peduncle, sepals 3-5 usually deciduous, styles 2 or 3 united below, each with 2 or 3 long filiform arms. Capsule didymous 1–1⅓ in. diam., peduncle 2–4 in. long. 2. **C. nitidum,** Thwaites. Andamans (Kurz). Ceylon. Petiole under ¼ in.

Ricinus communis, Linn. *The Castor Oil plant.* Vern. *Arend, Erandi,* Hind.; *Bherenda,* Beng.; *Bindi,* Kol; *Haralu,* Kan.; *Amidam,* Tel.; *Kyetsu,* Burm. Probably indigenous in Africa, cultivated and run wild in India. A soft-wooded tree, often cultivated as an annual. L. peltate, palmately lobed, fl. monœcious, the ♀ as a rule in the upper, the ♂ in the lower portion of erect racemiform panicles. Capsule as a rule prickly, consisting of 3 nearly cylindrical lobes, rounded at the ends.

41. HOMONOIA, Lour.; Fl. Brit. Ind. v. 455.

Rigid shrubs, l. alternate. Fl. apetalous, usually diœcious, in axillary spikes, disk 0. ♂: Calyx globose splitting into 3 valvate segments, stamens 8, filaments connate, branched, anther-cells nearly distinct, connective minute. Pistillode 0. ♀: Sepals 5–8, imbricate, narrow, unequal, caducous. Ovary 3-celled, styles entire papillose, spreading, cells 1-ovuled. Capsule loculicidally 3-valved. Species 3 or 4, Indo-Malayan.

1. **H. riparia,** Lour.; Bedd. Manual t. xxiv. f. 1.—Syn. *Adelia neriifolia,* Roth; Wight Ic. t. 1868. Vern. *Sheran, Sherni,* Mar.; *Taniki,* Tel.; *Kullur, Vangi,* Mal.; *Momaka, Yetagyi,* Lower, *Yenè,* Upper Burma. Rocky and stony river beds. Sikkim (Ranjit and Tista). Assam, Khasi hills. Upper and Lower Burma. Behar. Singbhúm. Bundelkhand. Central Provinces. Western Peninsula.—Ceylon. Malay Penins. and Archip. China. An evergreen gregarious shrub, resembling a willow, branchlets, young leaves and inflorescence hairy. L. usually entire, linear-lanceolate, underside with scattered hairs and minute orbicular scales, blade 4–10, pet. ¼–½ in. Fl. in axillary bracteate spikes, shorter than l. Ovary pubescent, styles red. 2. **H. retusa,** Muell. Arg. (*Adelia retusa,* Wight Ic. 1869). River beds, Western Peninsula, from the Chanda district southwards. Glabrous, l. obovate or oblanceolate, dentate, rarely entire, 1–2 in., narrowed into very short petiole, underside with a few scattered shining scales, spikes short, bracts subulate.

Lasiococca symphylliæfolia, Hook. f. in Ic. Plant. t. 1587. Damp forests of the lower Darjeeling hills. A middle-sized evergreen tree, stem fluted, wood close-grained. L. glabrous, alternate, quite entire, sometimes in false whorls of 3, lanceolate, narrowed into a broad cordate base, blade 3–6, pet. ⅓–¼ in. Fl. apetalous, monœcious, ♂ in axillary spikes, stamens ∞, in a dense globose head of branched filaments, anther-cells divaricate, connective arching over top and sides of the cells. ♀ solitary, peduncled, in the upper leaf-axils, sepals 5–7, unequal, imbricate, persistent and enlarged in fruit, styles 3 filiform, combined into a column below. Capsule densely clothed with rigid multifid paleæ.

Sphyranthera capitellata, Hook. f. Ic. t. 1702.—Syn. *Codiæum lutescens,* Kurz. Middle Andaman in Bamboo forest. A large evergreen shrub, probably diœcious, branchlets minutely pubescent. ♂ fl. minute, crowded in small umbels on a slender axillary peduncle, supported by numerous minute pubescent imbricate bracts, sepals 4 valvate, pubescent without, petals much smaller than sepals. Stamens about 20, central, filaments filiform, free, anther-cells globose, distinct, one at each end of the broad connective. ♀ fl. and fr. unknown.

ORDER XCIX. ULMACEÆ. Engl. in Engl. u. Prantl iii. 1. 59.

(*Urticaceæ,* tribes I. *Ulmeæ,* II. *Celtideæ.* Gen. Pl. III. 343.)

Trees or shrubs, sap watery, l. undivided, distichous, stipulate. Fl. bisexual or unisexual. Perianth alike in all fl., 4–9-lobed, stamens opposite to perianth-lobes, rarely twice their number, anther-cells contiguous, parallel. Ovary of 2 carpels, usually 1-celled, ovule 1, pendulous. Seeds without albumen.

Cystolith cells often conspicuous in the epidermis. No laticiferous tubes.

A. Fruit a winged samara.
- L. serrate, cotyledons flat . . . . 1. ULMUS.
- L. entire, cotyledons folded . . . . 2. HOLOPTELEA.

B. Fruit a drupe.
- ♂ sepals imbricate.
  - Stipules free, mostly chartaceous . . . . . 3. CELTIS.
  - Stipules connate, convolute, l. coriaceous . . . 4. GIRONNIERA.
- ♂ sepals induplicate-valvate . . . . 5. TREMA.

1. ULMUS, Linn.; Fl. Brit. Ind. v. 480.

Trees, mostly deciduous, stipules caducous, fl. in most Indian sp. before the leaves, usually bisexual, in lateral racemes or fascicles, supported by deciduous coriaceous bracts, pedicel articulate, the lower portion (peduncle) hairy, the upper (pedicel proper), usually glabrous. Perianth campanulate, generally persistent, 4–9-lobed, segments imbricate in bud, stamens adnate to perianth-tube. Ovary 1–2-celled, styles 2, papillose on the inner face. A few only of the fl. as a rule produce seed. Fr. indehiscent (a flat samara) surrounded by a broad membranous wing. Species 16, temperate regions of the Northern Hemisphere.

A. Pedicels longer than perianth.

(*a*) Articulation near the base of pedicel, the lower hairy portion shorter than the upper glabrous one.

1. **U. Wallichiana,** Planchon; Brandis F. Fl. tab. 51. Vern. *Kain*, Haz.; *Maral*, *Naray*, *Imbri*, *Emvoi*, N.-W. Himal.

A tall tree, often attaining a large diameter, bark rough, grey, exfoliating in diamond-shaped scales, branchlets and underside of l. usually softly pubescent, l. elliptic or obovate, long-acuminate, upperside rough, blade 4–8, pet. $\frac{1}{6}$–$\frac{1}{4}$ in., sec. n. straight, parallel, 15–20 pair, each terminating in a large serrature, the outer edge of which is serrulate, veins minutely reticulate. Fl. numerous, densely fascicled on short racemes, forming globose heads in the axils of the fallen l., peduncle supported at the base by coriaceous caducous bracts. Perianth $\frac{1}{8}$ in. long, narrowed into a glabrous pedicel as long as itself, which is articulated with a hairy peduncle $\frac{1}{12}$ in. long, lobes 5 obtuse, ciliate along the edge, ovary slightly hairy. Samara thinly membranous, elliptic, $\frac{3}{4}$ in. long, seed in the centre of the samara.

North-West Himalaya, Indus to Nepal, 3,500–10,000 ft. Fl. March, April. Branches often erect. Often planted and lopped for cattle fodder every other year.

(*b*) Articulation of pedicel near the perianth, the lower hairy portion much longer than the upper glabrous one.

2. **U. lancifolia,** Roxb.; Wall. Pl. As. Rar. t. 200. Vern. *Thalè*, Lower, *Thitkauk-hnyin*, Upper Burma. Sikkim, foot of hills, ascending to 6,000 ft. Bhutan. Assam. Khasi hills. Chittagong. Burma, Upper and Lower. A large tree, branchlets and petioles minutely hairy, l. coriaceous, lanceolate, serrate, blade 1–5, pet. slender $\frac{1}{8}$ in. long, tert. n. reticulate, nearly as prominent as sec. n. Perianth 5-lobed, pedicel in fl. $\frac{1}{8}$–$\frac{1}{4}$ in. Samara 1 in. long, very oblique. Generally leafless during part of the H. S. when the tree is in fl.

B. Fl. nearly sessile, pedicel in fl. shorter than, rarely as long as perianth.

3. **U. villosa,** Brandis in Ind. For. xxv. 229. Vern. *Mannu*, Hazara; *Marn*, Kulu, Sutlej and the Pabar valley; *Maldang*, Kunawar.

A large tree, branches drooping, branchlets and l. glabrous. L. ovate-oblong, blade 1½–4 in., pet. slender, $\frac{1}{6}$–$\frac{1}{3}$ in. long, sec. n. 14–18 pair, each nerve terminating in a large serrature, the outer edge of which is serrulate, the meshes of the reticulate veins larger than in 1. Fl. 10–15, in dense sessile fascicles. Perianth $\frac{1}{8}$ in. long, sessile and articulate on a short hairy peduncle, the perianth-tube lengthening out after flowering into a short glabrous pedicel, lobes 5 obtuse not ciliate, ovary and styles densely woolly with long hairs. Samara (unripe) densely villous, lanceolate, ½ in. long.

North-West Himalaya 4-7,000 ft. Fl. Febr., March. Ripe seed not seen. Colonel Barrett reports that in Hazara the seed falls before ripening. 4. **U. campestris,** Spach. Baluchistan. Kuram valley, 7-9,000 ft. Indigenous in Central and South Europe and Western Asia (planted and naturalized, not indigenous in England). A large tree, bark often corky, l. rough, 2-3 in. long, seed above the middle of the samara.

5. **U. parvifolia,** Jacquin. — Syn. *U. virgata*, Roxb.; Wall. Pl. As. Rar. t. 290. Introduced from China into the Bot. Garden Calcutta, possibly wild in Nubra (North Kashmir). An evergreen shrub, l. glabrous rigid, 1-2 in. long, ♂ and fertile fl. mixed, perianth 4-lobed. Samara with prominently reticulate veins.

Fig. 185.—Ulmus villosa, Brandis. ½.

2. HOLOPTELEA, Planch.; Fl. Brit. Ind. v. 481.

H. integrifolia, Planch. (the only species); Wight Ic. t. 1968.—Syn. *Ulmus integrifolia*, Roxb. Cor. Pl. t. 78; Bedd. Fl. Sylv. t. 310. Vern. *Papri, Kanju*, Hind.; *Kunj, Bisenda*, Oudh; *Karanji, Karinga*, C. P.; *Wavuli, Papara*, Mar.; *Tapassi*, Tel. Kan.; *Avali*, Tam.; *Myaukseik, Pyaukseik*, Burm.

A large deciduous tree, young shoots and inflorescence pubescent, otherwise mostly glabrous. L. elliptic, entire, those of seedlings and coppice shoots usually serrate, blade 3–5, pet. ⅓–½ in. long, sec. n. 5–7 pair. Fl. in short lateral often compound corymbs, ♂ and ☿ fl. mixed, perianth cleft nearly to the base, segments 5, hairy. ♂: Stamens 8, anthers hairy, no rudiment of ovary. ☿: Stamens 5, ovary compressed, 1-celled, stalked, the stalk lengthening as the seed ripens, sometimes with the remains of calyx at its base. Samara nearly orbicular, 1 in. diam. on a long slender stalk.

Subhimalayan tract, Kashmir to Nepal, ascending to 2,000 ft. Ajmere, Bundelkhand and Behar. Central Provinces, Berar and the Peninsula. Upper and Lower Burma. Leaves shed between Sept. and January, fresh l. soon after the fl., which come out Febr., March.—Ceylon, Cochinchina.

3. CELTIS, Linn.; Fl. Brit. Ind. v. 481.

Trees or shrubs, l. triple-nerved. Fl. small, polygamous, solitary or cymose. Sepals 4–5, imbricate, stamens 4–5, short, erect in bud. Ovary on a hairy disk, stigmas 2, sessile, deciduous. Drupe ovoid or globose, endocarp hard. Albumen 0 or scanty, cotyledons oily, broad, surrounding the upcurved radicle. Species 50–60, temperate and tropical.

A. Leaves serrate or crenate, base unequal-sided, ♂ fl. fascicled in compact dichotomous panicles.

(*a*) Fertile fl. on long axillary peduncles, solitary or in pairs.

1. **C. australis,** Linn.; Brandis F. Fl. tab. 50.—Syn. *C. caucasica*, Willd. Vern. *Taghar*, Pushtu; *Batkar*, Haz.; *Kharik, Kharak, Khirk,* N.-W. Himal.; *Kū*, Kun.

A middle-sized deciduous tree, bark smooth, bluish-grey, often with horizontal wrinkles, branchlets, petioles and young l. glabrous or hairy. L. ovate to ovate-lanceolate, acuminate, base very oblique, sharply serrate, sometimes entire, blade 3–5, pet. ½ in. long, the lateral basal n. extending beyond the middle but not to the tip of the leaf. Fl. with or before the l. Drupe ¼–½ in. long. Two distinct varieties, *a*. fr. large purplish-black nearly ½ in. long (*Kū*, Nachar), *β*. fr. yellow or red ¼–⅓ in. long (*Tiku*, *pjaku*, Nachar).

Baluchistan. Suleiman range. Salt range. North-West Himalaya, from the foot to 8,500 ft. Often planted, also in the plains of the Punjab. Fl. March–May. Pollarded for cattle fodder.—Western Asia. Mediterranean region. *C. eriocarpa*, Dcne. has pubescent drupes. 2. **C. tetrandra**, Roxb.—Syn. *C. serotina*, Planch.; Wight Ic. t. 1970; *C. trinervia*, Roxb.; Bedd. Fl. Sylv. t. 312; *C. Hamiltonii*, Planch. Oudh. Nepal. Sikkim from foot of hills to 5,000 ft. Behar. Central Prov. (*Majni*). Orissa. Northern Circars and hills of the Eastern Deccan. Western Ghats. Garo and Khasi hills. Chittagong. Manipur. Burma, Upper (*Thitpôk*) and Lower. Nearly allied to 1, l. often entire in the lower half, sepals usually 4. *C. mollis*, Wall., a softly pubescent form in Upper Burma.

(*b*) Fertile fl. in axillary dichotomous panicles.

3. **C. cinnamomea**, Lindl. Sikkim, lower hills to 3,000 ft. Chittagong. Pegu. Martaban, Konkan. Ceylon, moist region, common, the wood when fresh cut smells badly. Branchlets usually tawny-pubescent, l. long-acuminate, remotely and often indistinctly crenate, tert. n. and veins obscure, sepals usually 5.

B. Leaves almost entire, base equal-sided. ♂ and fertile fl. in axillary dichotomous panicles.

4. **C. Wightii**, Planch.; Wight Ic. t. 1969.—Syn. *Solenostigma Wightii*, Miq. Hills of the Northern Circars, the Deccan and Mysore. Nilgiris. Tinnevelli. Andamans (Kurz).—Ceylon. *Thella-Kaka-Mushti*, Tel.; *Hadawa*, Nilg. A small or middle-sized evergreen tree, l. rigidly coriaceous, entire or very sparsely crenate-serrate, blade 2–6, pet. ½–⅔ in. long, young foliage pink, panicles usually twice the length of petiole, fr. scarlet, ¼–⅓ in. long.

4. GIRONNIERA, Gaud.; Fl. Brit. Ind. v. 485.

Evergreen trees or shrubs, l. coriaceous, penninerved, entire or serrulate at the tip, sec. n. impressed on the upper and very prominent on the underside. Fl. diœcious. ♂: Sepals 5, broad, obtuse, imbricate, stamens 5, erect in bud, pistillode woolly. ♀: Sepals narrow, acute, ovary sessile, style central, arms 2, filiform, ovule pendulous. Drupe usually 2-keeled, endocarp hard, embryo contorted. Species 8–10, Indo-Malayan region, China.

1. **G. subæqualis**, Planch.—Syn. *G. nervosa*, Planch., var. *subæqualis*, Kurz F. Fl. ii. 470. Andamans, Tenasserim.—Ceylon. Malay Penins. and Archip. China. A middle-sized tree, branchlets, stipules, petioles, underside of l. and cymes strigose with long hairs, l. elliptic, acuminate, rough beneath, blade 5–8, pet. ¼–½ in., tert. n. often prominent, veins strongly reticulate. ♂ cymes 1–3 in. long. ♀ fl. solitary or a few together. Drupe ellipsoid, ⅓–½ in. long, compressed, minutely hispid. 2. **G. reticulata**, Thw.; Bedd. Fl. Sylv. t. 318.—Syn. *G. cuspidata*, Kurz F. Fl. ii. 470, Sikkim, outer hills to 4,000 ft. Khasi and Naga hills. Upper Burma. Eastern slopes of the Pegu Yoma (Kurz). Evergreen forests of the Western Ghats from North Kanara southwards. Kāns of Sorub, Mysore (D.B. 1868).—Ceylon. Java. A tall tree, stems buttressed. Youngest shoots minutely strigose, otherwise glabrous. L. elliptic- or ovate-lanceolate, acuminate, veins minutely and elegantly reticulate. Drupes glabrous, ¼–⅜ in. long. 3. **G. lucida**, Kurz. Andamans. A middle-sized tree, quite glabrous. L. shining on both surfaces, rigidly coriaceous, entire, sec. n. arching, tert. n. and veins obscure.

5. TREMA, Lour.; Fl. Brit. Ind. v. 483.

Shrubs or trees, l. serrate, basal nerves 3–7, stipules lateral, free, deciduous. Fl. unisexual and bisexual, in small axillary cymes, sepals 4–5 induplicate-valvate. ♂: Stamens 4–5, erect in bud, pistillode small glabrous. Drupe supported by the persistent sepals, endocarp hard. Albumen fleshy, embryo curved cotyledons narrow. Species 20–30 tropical and subtropical.

1. **T. orientalis,** Blume.—Syn. *Sponia orientalis*, Planch.; *S. Wightii*, Planch.; Wight Ic. t. 1971; Bedd. Fl. Sylv. t. 311. *The Charcoal tree.* Vern. *Jiban*, *Chikan*, Beng.; *Kagol*, *Gol*, Mar.; *Oman*, *Mini*, Tam.; *Gada nelli*, Tel.

A small rapidly growing, short-lived tree, branches straight, spreading, branchlets pubescent. L. ovate, acuminate, blade 2–6, pet. ¼–⅓ in., the lateral basal nerves reaching to half the length of leaf, base unequal-sided cordate, upperside more or less rough, underside white or grey-pubescent or tomentose. Cymes longer than petiole, ♂ compact, ♀ lax.

Subhimalayan tract from the Jumna eastwards. Bengal. Behar. Singbhum. Central Provinces. Western Peninsula. Springs up abundantly on clearances in the forest. Fl. nearly throughout the year.—Ceylon, very common. Malaya. China. Australia. 2. **T. amboinensis,** Blume.—Syn. *Sponia velutina*, Planchon; Wight Ic. t. 1990. Sikkim, foot of hills. Assam. Khasi and Naga hills. Chutia Nagpur (Prain). Chittagong, Andamans and Nicobars. Burma, Upper (*Kywèsa*) and Lower (*Satsha*), abundant in the secondary growth on deserted Taungyas.—Malay Penins. China. Australia. Nearly allied to 1, of which Kurz regards it as a variety; perhaps not specifically distinct, supposed to differ by the branchlets pubescent with spreading hairs, l. beneath softly tomentose, shining, cymes more dense and compact. Some specimens of the Central Provinces and the Western Peninsula cannot be distinguished from the Eastern specimens. G. M. Ryan considers that both species grow in the Thana district. 3. **T. politoria,** Planch.—Syn. *Sponia politoria*, Planch. Vern. *Rabna*, Merwara; *Khagshi*, *Khardal*, *Kuri*, Hind. Subhimalayan tract and outer valleys ascending to 3,000 ft. Salt range. Rajputana and Central Provinces, common on clearings, landslips, road cuttings or embankments. Singbhúm. Upper Burma (*Petsat*) on sandbanks and islands in streams. L. hard, rigid, very rough on both surfaces, used to polish wood and horn, oblong-lanceolate, base equal-sided, blade 2–3, pet. ¼ in. long. Cymes unisexual, ♂ compact, usually shorter than petiole. 4. **T. timorensis,** Blume. Tenasserim. Malay Penins. China. A small evergreen tree, branchlets slender, drooping, l. nearly glabrous, membranous, lanceolate or ovate-lanceolate, long-acuminate, cymes few-fld., glabrous.

ORDER C. MORACEÆ. Engl. in Engl. u. Prantl iii. 1. 66.

(*Urticaceæ*, tribes IV. *Moreæ*, V. *Artocarpeæ*, VI. *Conocephaleæ*, Gen. Pl. iii. 344.)

Trees or shrubs, rarely herbs, sap milky. L. usually alternate, undivided in old, often lobed in young trees, stipules large, often amplexicaul. Fl. unisexual, frequently crowded on unisexual receptacles, which are globose, cylindric or hollow (*Ficus*). ♂ perianth of 2–6 segments or sepals, to which the stamens are opposite, (1 stamen in *Artocarpus*.) ♀ perianth of 4 sepals or segments, often persistent and fleshy in fr. Ovary 1-celled, ovule 1, pendulous, rarely erect and basal. Seed with or without albumen, cotyledons often unequal.

Bast-fibres strongly developed in the bark, often very long, useful for the manufacture of paper, cloth and ropes. Cystolith cells conspicuous in the epidermis. Continuous (not articulated) laticiferous tubes in bark and leaves.

A. Fl. minute, unisexual, in a hollow receptacle, which is fleshy in fr. . . . . 1. FICUS.

B. Fl. diœcious, in open funnel-shaped receptacles, the ♀ fleshy in fr. . . . . HULLETTIA (p. 610).

C. Fruit a syncarpium, consisting of the fleshy perianths, on a globose or cylindrical receptacle.
- (*a*) Unarmed (see also *Plecospermum*).
  - L. penninerved, the lowest pair sometimes basal. Climbing shrubs.
    - ♂ and ♀ fl. in globose heads, arranged in dichotomous cymes . . . . CONOCEPHALUS (p. 610).
    - ♂ fl. in fascicled spikes, ♀ in globose heads . . . . 2. ALLÆANTHUS
  - Trees . . . . 3. ARTOCARPUS.

L. palminerved, basal n. 3–7 prominent.
Ripe carpels (achenes) enclosed in the syncarpium . . . . 4. MORUS.
Ripe carpels pendulous on long fleshy stalks . . . . 5. BROUSSONETIA.
(*b*) Armed (excepting *Plecospermum andamanicum*).
Stamens included, syncarpium many-seeded 6. CUDRANIA.
Stamens exserted, syncarpium few-seeded . 7. PLECOSPERMUM.

D. Fruit the result of one flower.
(*a*) Unarmed trees or shrubs.
Glabrous, l. quite entire, fr. enclosed by 4 orbicular concave accrescent coriaceous sepals . . . . PSEUDOSTREBLUS (p. 614).
Hairy, l. entire or serrulate.
A tall tree, young shoots velvety, l. 3–6 in. ♀ perianth 0, fr. velvety, enclosed in a fleshy involucre of connate bracts . . . . . . 8. ANTIARIS.
A rigid shrub or small tree, l. 2–4 in., very rough. ♀ perianth of 4 sepals, fleshy in fr. . . . . 9. STREBLUS.
(*b*) More or less armed.
L. rigidly coriaceous, spinulose-dentate, fl. ♂ in catkin-like spikes, ♀ in racemes . BALANOSTREBLUS (p. 615).
L. membranous, serrate.
Fl. ♂ in clustered involucrate heads. ♀ solitary, berry enclosed in the enlarged lanceolate sepals . . . . PHYLLOCHLAMYS (p. 615).
Fl. ♂ minute, in short axillary compact racemes, ♀ in lax few-fld. axillary and terminal racemes, fr. obliquely subglobose . . . . . . TAXOTROPHIS (p. 616).

1. FICUS, Linn.; Fl. Brit. Ind. v. 494.

Tree or shrubs, often epiphytic, sending out aërial roots, many species creeping and climbing by means of adventitious roots on stems, on the ground and over rocks, at times subsequently developing an erect stem with a spreading crown. Juice milky. Narrow undulating concentric bands of parenchyma in the wood. L. usually alternate, stipules deciduous in most species, leaving annular scars. Fl. minute, together with numerous thin bracteoles covering the inner surface of a hollow globose or pear-shaped receptacle (*fig*) which sometimes lengthens out into a stalk, supported by 3 or 4 basal bracts, the mouth of the receptacle closed by numerous scales in several rows, the inner scales turned downwards, those of the outer row being erect or spreading. Fl. of 5 kinds: ♂ with 1–3 anthers (*a*) without, (*b*) with a rudimentary pistil. (*c*) ♀ fl. (*d*) gall fl., ♀ with a short style, (*e*) neuter fl. consisting of a pedicellate perianth without stamens or pistil. Perianth of 2–6 sepals, or gamosepalous, 2–6-partite. In the species of one section (*Urostigma*) ♂, ♀ and gall fl. are in the same receptacle, in the other species ♂ and gall fl. as a rule are in one set and ♀ fl. in another set of receptacles. In some species of *Urostigma* the ♂ fl. are mixed with the others, as a rule they are only found near the mouth of the receptacle, in some species few, in others numerous, covering half the inner surface. The gall fl. do not usually develop an embryo, but are visited by Hymenopterous insects (*Blastophaga*) which lay their eggs in them. The perfect insect, on leaving the receptacle, takes away the pollen of the ♂ fl. and thus fertilizes the ♀ fl. in another receptacle. The ♀ receptacles generally require several months to ripen; the fr. as a rule becomes fleshy and encloses numerous minute achenes. Embryo curved, in a scanty albumen.

The following key to the species of this large genus may be found useful:

I. Receptacles axillary or above the scars of fallen l., solitary or in pairs, rarely on the old wood: I. *Palæomorphe*, III. *Synœcia*, IV. *Sycidium*, VI. *Eusyce*.
  A. L. lanceolate or oblong, width as a rule less than one third the length.
    (*a*) L. entire: 2. *subulata*, 39. *sikkimensis*, 62. *silhetensis*, 64. *pyriformis*, 65. *nemoralis*.
    (*b*) L. serrate or lobed: 45. *quercifolia*, 59. *chrysocarpa*.
  B. L. elliptic-ovate or obovate, width as a rule more than one third the length.
    (*a*) L. entire or nearly so: 37. *callicarpa*, 60. *lepidosa*, 61. *erecta*, 63. *glandulifera*, 66. *chartacea*, 68. *ramentacea*, 69. *crininervia*, 70. *scandens*, 71. *lævis*.
    (*b*) L. denticulate, dentate or lobed: 4. *brevicuspis*, 42. *asperrima*, 46. *nigrescens*, 55. *palmata*, 56. *fulva*, 57. *Carica*.
  C. L. variable, from lanceolate to broadly ovate: 47. *heterophylla*, 58. *hirta*.
  D. L. lyrate, deeply lobed: 50. *bhotanica*.
  E. L. very unequal-sided: 41. *obscura*.
  F. L. as a rule caudate-acuminate, tertiary nerves very prominent: 1. *gibbosa* 3. *urophylla*, 38. *clavata*, 44. *rostrata*, 67. *foveolata*, 70. *scandens*.
II. Receptacles in axillary pairs, mostly sessile. Large trees, epiphytic while young, often stem-clasping, l. alternate: II. *Urostigma* (sp. 4–36).
III. Receptacles in dense clusters on tubercles or on leafless racemose or panicled branches, from the trunk or larger branches. L. sometimes opposite: V. *Covellia* (sp. 48–54), VII. *Neomorphe* (sp. 72–79).

Sect. I. *Palæomorphe*. ♂ fl. monandrous, containing a rudimentary pistil, in the same receptacles with gall fl. ♀ fl. in separate receptacles.

1. **F. gibbosa**, Blume; King, Ann. Bot. Gard. Calc. I. t. 2.—Syn. *F. Allimeeraloo*, Roxb.; Wight Ic. t. 650; *F. Ampelos*, Roxb.; Wight Ic. t. 652; *F. tuberculata*, Roxb.; Wight Ic. t. 651; *F. parasitica*, Koenig; Brandis F. Fl. 420; *F. excelsa*, Vahl; Kurz F. Fl. ii. 451. Vern. *Chanchri*. Garhwal; *Majni*, Jabalpur; *Chirwal*, Satpura range; *Datiri*, *Datri*, Mar.; *Itthi*, Tam.; *Nyaung thabye*, Burm.

A small, at times a large tree, often epiphytic or climbing, enclosing the trunks of trees in a perfect network of branches, or creeping along walls and on the sides of wells. L. thinly coriaceous, smooth above, rough beneath, elliptic, more or less acuminate, often very unequal-sided, angular and with a few large teeth, blade 3–6, pet. ½ in., sec. n. 4–6 pair, joined by arching intra-marginal veins, the lowest pair from the base usually running near the edge, intermediate and tertiary n. distinct. Receptacles minutely hairy, ¼–⅓ in. diam., peduncle up to ⅓ in. long, bracts at base of peduncle. Ovary in fertile fl. sessile. Fr. yellow when ripe. A variable species, two varieties: α. *cuspidifera*, l. elongate, acuminate, nerves pellucid, β. *parasitica*, l. broad rhomboid, nerves opaque.

Subhimalayan tract from the Jumna eastwards. Assam. Chittagong. Andamans. Lower Burma. Behar. Chutia Nagpur. Centr. Prov. Western Peninsula. Fr. Jan.–May.—Ceylon, low country, common. Malay Penins. and Archip. China. 2. **F. subulata**, Blume; King, Ann. i. t. 6. Chittagong. Pegu Yoma, eastern slopes. Martaban.—Malay Penins. and Archip. China. A large diœcious shrub, the ♂ erect, the ♀ climbing, young shoots minutely pubescent. L. membranous, glabrous, entire, margin undulate, elliptic-lanceolate or oblanceolate, blade 4–10, pet. ¼–⅓ in. long, sec. n. 10–20 pair, stipules subulate ½–1 in. Fl.: ♂ (containing a rudimentary pistil) and gall fl. in ovoid, the ♀ in globose receptacles on different plants, perianth gamophyllous, hairy, with 4 oblong lobes. Fr. orange-yellow with white dots. 3. **F. urophylla**, Wall.: King, Ann. i. t. 9. Assam. Khasi hills. Chittagong. Burma.—Malay Penins. An erect shrub or small tree, l. subcoriaceous, ovate or elliptic, the apex with an abrupt narrow tail, blade 2½–4, pet. ½ in., stipules minute. Receptacles shortly pedunculate, scabrid-hispid, reddish-yellow when ripe. Very similar to *F. rostrata*, Lamk., which is climbing, has larger l. and ♂ fl. without a pistillode.

Sect. II. *Urostigma*. ♂ fl. as a rule monandrous, in the same receptacle with ♀ and gall fl., stigma elongate, usually acute and feathery. Large trees, the majority of species evergreen, as a rule epiphytic when young, frequently producing aërial roots, which either descend straight into the ground, developing into secondary stems, or form a network, enclosing the trunk of the tree on which the fig has germinated, often coalescing into a more or less complete hollow cylinder. Eventually the support is often killed by the more powerful foliage of the *Ficus*. L. mostly alternate, entire, coriaceous, glabrous or hairy, never rough, stipules broad, as a rule minutely hairy, stipular scars annular. Receptacles mostly sessile, in pairs, axillary or above the scars of fallen l., each supported by 3 basal bracts.

A. Sec. n. prominent, distant, not more than 16 pair.

(*a*) petioles short, less than one-third the length of blade.

a. Mature l. glabrous.

4. **F. bengalensis**, Linn.; King, Ann. i. t. 13.—Syn. *F. indica*, Roxb.; *Urostigma bengalense*, Gasp.; Wight Ic. t. 1989; *Banyan*. Sans. *Vata*, Vern. *Bor, Bar, Bargat*, Hind.; *Wad*, Mar.; *Marri*, Tel.; *Ala*, Tam.; *Alada*, Kan.; *Pyi nyaung*, Burm.

A large tree, branches spreading, sending down to the ground numerous aërial roots, which afterwards become trunks. Young shoots pubescent, l. glabrous when mature, approximate near the ends of branches, ovate, mostly obtuse, base cordate or rounded, basal n. 3–5, the midrib with 4–6 pair of sec. n.; blade 4–8, pet. 1–2 in. Fr. globose, pubescent, ½–¾ in. diam., sessile, scarlet when ripe, supported by 2–4 broad obtuse bracts.

Indigenous in the subhimalayan tract and the Western Peninsula. Commonly planted by Hindoos throughout India as far north as Peshawar and in the Outer Himalaya as high as 4,000 ft. Banyan trees often have a crown 3–500 ft. in diam., supported by numerous often more than 100 root-drops. Fr. Apr.–June. 5. **F. altissima**, Blume; King, Ann. i. t. 30, 31.—Syn. *F. laccifera*, Roxb.; Wight Ic. t. 656. Outer Himalaya, from Nepal eastwards, ascending to 3,000 ft. Assam. Khasi hills. Chittagong. Andamans. Lower Burma.—Ceylon. Malay Penins. and Archip. China. A tall tree, aërial roots few, young shoots and outside of stipules minutely hairy, otherwise quite glabrous. L. elliptic, sometimes ovate, base rounded, blade 4–7, pet. stout, channelled, 1–2 in., stipules 1–2 in. long. Fr. sessile, ovoid, ¾–1 in. long, red or yellowish when ripe.

6. **F. Beddomei**, King, Ann. i. t. 24.—Syn. *F. Rama Varmæ*, Bourdillon in Journal Bombay Natural History Society xiii. 155. Tinnevelli and Travancore hills, in evergreen forests, 1–4,000 ft. A large tree, wholly glabrous, trunk irregularly shaped, branches wide spreading. L. shining, dark green when old, pale when young, broad-ovate, shortly acuminate, blade 6–12, pet. 1–4 in., sec. n. 12–16 pair, the lowest pair basal, stipules golden yellow, often several in. long. Anthers sessile. Fr. ovoid or subglobose, 1 in. long, with several more or less distinct vertical ridges, green with yellow spots when ripe, basal bracts 3, small, peduncles up to 1 in. long. 7. **F. travancorica**, King, Ann. i. t. 26. North Travancore hills, 3,500 ft. A straggling shrub, l. lanceolate, base cuneate, blade 5–6, pet. ½–⅔ in. Fr. globose ½ in. diam., peduncle shorter than fr.

8. **F. globosa**, Blume; King, Ann. i. t. 25.—Syn. *F. onusta*, Wall. Tenasserim, Kurz. A large climber, l. elliptic-oblong, shortly cuspidate, blade 3–7, pet. ½–1½ in., sec. n. 7–10 pair, the lowest basal, stipules up to 2½ in. long. Fr. almost turbinate, ½–1 in. diam., peduncle short.

9. **F. glaberrima**, Blume; King, Ann. i. t. 43.—Syn. *F. Thomsoni*, Miq. Vern. *Kakhri, Durla*, Hind. Subhimalayan tract, ascending to 2,000 ft., from the Jumna eastwards. Khasi hills. Chittagong. Meplay forest, Tenasserim (D.B. March 1862). Andamans. —Malay Archip. A large tree, at times a large epiphytic shrub (D.B. Kotri Dún, Garhwal, March 1881). As a rule quite glabrous, minute hairs sometimes on young shoots, l. and peduncles, L. oblong-lanceolate, acuminate, base usually acute, blade 5–7, pet. 1–1½ in. long, sec. n. 8–10 pair, at an angle of 80° to the midrib, the lowest pair basal, running near the edge of l. Fr. ¼ in. diam., orange-coloured when ripe, basal bracts deciduous, peduncle slender, as long as fr. 10. **F. Hookeri**, Miq.; King, Ann. i. t. 42. Sikkim, lower hills. Khasi hills. Glabrous, l. broad-elliptic, blade 6–12, pet. 2–3 in., sec. n. 8–10 pair, the lowest pair from the base, stipules up to 4 in. long, caducous. Fr. sessile, ½–1 in. diam., the lower third in an entire cartilaginous cup, consisting of the connate basal bracts.

11. **F. nervosa**, Roth; King, Ann. i. t. 65. Vern. *Icha*, Mal.; *Nyaung peinnè*, Burm. Assam. Cachar. Chittagong. Lower Burma. Chutia Nagpur. Rampa hills, Godavari. Evergreen forests of the Western coast, ascending to 3,000 ft., from North Kanara southwards.—Malay Penins. and Archip. China. A very large umbrageous tree, in a dry climate smaller, trunk cylindric, no aërial roots, young

shoots velvety. L. dark green, shining above, ovate, elliptic or elliptic-oblong, short-acuminate, blade 4–8, pet. ½–1 in. long, sec. n. 8–12 pair, arching, prominent beneath, joined by strong intra-marginal nerves, intermediate n. few, tertiary n. reticulate. Fr. globose, ¼–⅜ in. diam., peduncles slender up to ½ in. long. Specimens in l. only (Garhwal, D.B. Febr. 1875) very similar. 12. **F. callosa,** Willd.; King, Ann. i. t. 85.—Syn. *F. cinerascens*, Thw. Vern. *Nireti mara*, Kan.; *Koli-al*, Tam. Evergreen forest of the Western Coast and Ghats, from the Konkan southwards, in the Kāns of Sorub and on the Bababudan hills, Mysore. In Travancore common up to 3,000 ft. Andamans. Lower Burma.—Ceylon. Java. A large smooth-barked tree, aërial roots 0, fruiting at an early age (Kurz). L. elliptic, obtuse or shortly and obtusely acuminate, blade 6–11, pet. 1–2 in. long, sec. n. 10–12 pair, distinct on the upper side, prominent below, the lowest pair basal, tert. n. distinct. Stamens 1 or 2. Fr. usually solitary, sometimes in pairs, pubescent, yellow when ripe, 1 in. diam., narrowed into the peduncle which is hairy and ¾–1 in. long, basal bracts 3, small, rounded. 13. **F. vasculosa,** Wall.; King, Ann. i. t. 86. Tenasserim.—Malay Penins. and Archip. China. A moderate-sized evergreen tree, l. elliptic-lanceolate, blade 3–5, narrowed into slender angular pet. ½–⅜ in. long, sec. n. slender, 8–10 pair, confluent under the margin, intermediate joined to transverse n. by reticulate veins. Stamens 2. Fr. in axillary pairs, pale yellow, ¼–⅓ in. diam., glabrous, bracts 3, minute.

β. Mature l. velvety or tomentose beneath.

14. **F. Dalhousiæ,** Miq.; King, Ann. i. t. 11. Nilgiris, 2–3,000 ft. A moderate-sized umbrageous tree, branchlets at first softly pubescent, afterwards glabrous. L. thinly coriaceous, as well as petioles velvety beneath, upperside glabrous or puberulous, broadly ovate, acute or shortly acuminate, base cordate, blade 4–9, pet. 1–2½ in., sec. n. 12–15 pair, prominent, the lowest pair basal, stipules ovate-lanceolate, much acuminate, ½–1 in. long. Fr. obovoid, ½ in. long, shortly pedunculate. 15. **F. tomentosa,** Roxb.; Wight Ic. t. 647; King, Ann. i. t. 18. Bundelkhand. Banda. Behar. Chutia Nagpur. Central Provinces. Western Peninsula. A large shady tree, thin aërial roots from the branches, young shoots, petioles and underside of young l. clothed with grey usually short tomentum. L. glabrous above, ovate, ovate- sometimes obovate-oblong, acute, base often cordate, blade 3–7, pet. ½–2 in., sec. n. 5–7 pair, the lowest pair from the base, often extending nearly to the middle of blade. Fr. globose, ¼–⅓ in. diam., tomentose, with glabrous darker coloured scales closing the mouth.

16. **F. mysorensis,** Heyne; King, Ann. i. tt. 14, 15. *Bhurvar*, Mar.; *Goni*, Kan. Subhimalayan tract and lower hills, from Sikkim eastwards, ascending to 3,000 ft. Assam. Khasi hills. Chittagong. Eng forests east of Toungoo. Western Peninsula.—Ceylon. A large tree, trunk usually short, aërial roots few, young shoots, petioles and underside of young l. densely clothed with soft grey or tawny, sometimes rust-coloured omentum. L. glabrous above, and often also on the underside when old, elliptic or ovate, usually shortly acuminate, base often cordate, sec. n. 10–15 pair, joined by intramarginal n., the lowest pair basal, tert. n. parallel, those proceeding from two adjoining sec. n. often meeting half-way at an angle. Fr. ovoid or oblong, sessile, pubescent, 1 in. long. 17. **F. pilosa,** Reinw. Upper Tenasserim (Kurz). Chindwin 1,500 ft. (Muriel, Febr. 1889).—Malay Penins. and Archip. Closely allied to 16 and probably not specifically distinct. L. inclined to be obovate.

(*b*) Petioles long, one-third to one-half the length of blade.

18. **F. religiosa,** Linn.; Wight Ic. t. 1967; Bedd. Fl. Sylv. t. 314; King, Ann. i. t. 67. *The Peepul tree.* Sans. *Pippala.* Vern. *Pipal*, Hind.; *Asvattha*, Beng.; *Borbur*, Cach.; *Ashvatha*, Mar.; *Hissa*, Kol; *Ali*, Gond.; *Arāsu*, Mal.; *Arasi*, Tam.; *Arali*, Kan.; *Ravi*, *Ragi*, Tel.; *Nyaung bawdi*, Burm.

A large entirely glabrous tree, trunk irregularly shaped, branches widespreading, often epiphytic. L. broad-ovate, margin undulate, tail 1–3 in. long, ⅓ the length of the whole blade, pet. 3–4 in. Male fl. few, near the mouth, in many receptacles none. Fr. sessile, ½ in. diam., dark purple, basal bracts broad, coriaceous.

Indigenous in the subhimalayan tract and the Pegu Yoma (Kurz). Cultivated throughout India, in the outer Himalaya as high as 5,000 ft. Rare in the arid region of North-West India. Common on and destructive to buildings in Bengal. Leafless during a short time during the H. S. Fr. April, May, sometimes (in the Centr. Prov.) a second crop Oct., Nov. Sacred to Hindus and Buddhists. 19. **F. Rumphii,** Blume; King, Ann. i. t. 67.—Syn. *F. cordifolia*, Roxb.; Wight Ic. t. 640; Brandis F. Fl. t. 48. Vern. *Pilkhan*, *Khabar*, Hind.; *Galasvattha*, Beng.; *Satbur*, Cach.; *Payar*, *Asht*, Mar.; *Nyaung byu*, Burm. Subhimalayan tract and outer hills, ascending to 5,000 ft., from the Chenab eastwards. Merwara. Assam. Lower Bengal. Singbhūm. Both Peninsulas.

A large deciduous tree, often stem-clasping, entirely glabrous. L. broad-ovate, base rounded or truncate and narrowed into the petiole, tail ½–1 in., pet. 2–3 in. long, basal n. 3–5 pair. Fr. sessile, ½ in. diam., black when ripe, basal bracts small. 20. **F. Arnottiana**, Miq.; King, Ann. i. t. 68. Vern. *Pipar*, *Paras Pipal*, Hind. Tons valley, Jaunsar, 4,000 ft. Garhwal. Ajmere. Central Provinces. Behar. Chutia Nagpur. Western Peninsula, in the Deccan and near the coast. A large shrub or small tree, often epiphytic, also creeping over rocks, l. broad-ovate, base cordate, pet. 1–5, tail ⅓–1 in. long, basal n. 5–7 pair, stipules large. Fr. often peduncled, ¼–⅓ in. diam., often densely clustered, basal bracts membranous.

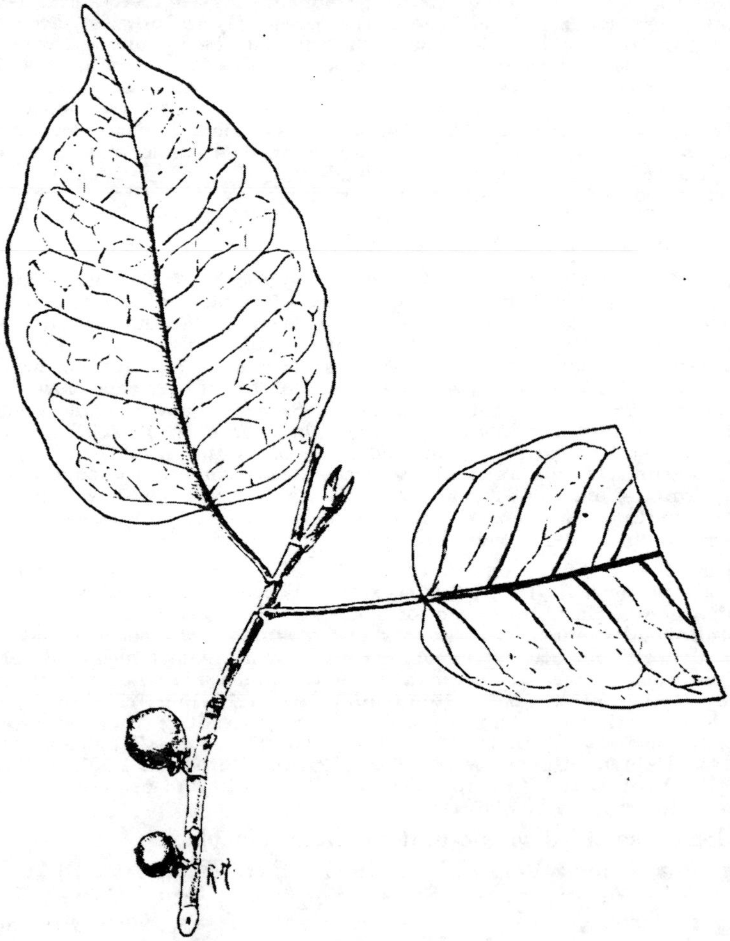

FIG. 186.—Ficus infectoria, Roxb. ½.

21. **F. infectoria**, Roxb.; Wight Ic. t. 665; King, Ann. i. tt. 75–79. Vern. *Palakh*, *Pilkhan*, Punjab; *Khabar*, *Pakhar*, Hind.; *Kel*, Thana.; *Juvvi*, Tel.; *Bassari*, Kan.; *Jovi*, Tam.; *Chela*, Mal.

A large widely spreading deciduous fast-growing tree, young shoots and stipules minutely hairy. L. thinly coriaceous, glabrous, shining, ovate or ovate-oblong, shortly acuminate, margin undulate, base acute, rounded or cordate, blade 3–6, pet. 1–3 in. long, sec. n. 8–10 pair, the lowest pair from the base. Fr. sessile or shortly peduncled, ¼–⅓ in. diam., basal bracts minute.

Suleiman range, TransIndus. Mount Tilla, Salt range, common in crevices of rocks. Subhimalayan tract and outer hills, ascending to 5,000 ft. Common in Northern India, the Central Provinces, Berar and the Western Peninsula. Forests east of Toungoo (Kurz). Fr. Febr.–June.—Ceylon, Malaya. China. Var. *Lambertiana* has broader l. and larger fr. on pubescent pedicels. 22. **F. geniculata**, Kurz; King, Ann. i. t. 80. Vern. *Nyaung thabye*, Burm. Sikkim, hot valleys. Bhutan. Khasi hills. Chittagong. Lower Burma.—Malay Penins. and Archip. A large deciduous usually epiphytic tree, branchlets stout, prominently marked with the scars of fallen l., extremities and stipules minutely silky. L. coriaceous, glabrous, shining, elliptic or ovate, blade 4–7, pet. 3–5 in., long. Fr. sessile or nearly so, ¼–⅓ in. diam., yellowish-red, dotted when ripe, basal bracts broadly ovate. 23. **F. insignis**, Kurz. Dry forests of the Prome district. A middle-sized tree, probably evergreen, similar to 22, branchlets, stipules and receptacles grey- or tawny-tomentose, fr. ½ in. diam., greyish-white with pink dots on short thick tomentose peduncles.

24. **F. Tsiela,** Roxb.; Wight Ic. t. 668; King, Ann. i. tt. 73, 74. Vern. *Bili basri*, Kan.; *Jadi, Juvvi*, Tel.; *Sela-Kallichi*, Tam. Ajmere. Chanda district. Western Peninsula, a common avenue tree in the drier districts.—Ceylon. A large glabrous tree, bark smooth, greenish-white. L. more or less coriaceous, ovate, acuminate, base acute, blade 2–6, pet. 1–2 in., sec. n. 8–12 pair, the lowest pair basal; intermediate n. few, very slender, tert. n. obscure, edge thickened, upper surface covered with minute raised dots. Receptacles sessile, in pairs $\frac{1}{4}$–$\frac{3}{8}$ in. diam., basal bracts minute. Fr. purple. At the ends of branches may often be seen tufts of small l. with very long petioles. 25. **F. Tjakela,** Burm.; King, Ann. i. t. 70. Vern. *Kel*, Mar.; *Kāral*, Mal. Western Peninsula.—Ceylon. Often planted. A large tree, leafless for a short time during the dry season, outer bark rough, dark coloured. L. similar to 24, but base rounded, sometimes cordate, tert. n. distinct, the young l. enveloped in large thin caducous bud-scales. Fr. $\frac{1}{3}$ in. diam., usually in clusters of 2–6 on short woody tubercles above the scars of fallen l., basal bracts bifid.

B. Sec. n. slender, numerous less distinct intermediate n. between them, joined by reticulate veins.

26. **F. retusa,** Linn.; King, Ann. i. tt. 61, 62.—Syn. *F. nitida*, Thunb.; Wight Ic. t. 642. Vern. *Barri. Ajān*, Kum.; *Jamu*, Nep.; *Nandruk*, Mar.; *Yerra-Juvvi*, Tel.; *Pilala*, Kan.; *Ichi*, Tam.; *Kal atthi*, Mal.; *Nyaung ók*. Burm. Subhimalayan tract from Kumaon eastwards. Assam. Chittagong. Andamans. Lower Burma. Behar. Chutia Nagpúr. Bundelkhand. Central Provinces. Western Peninsula. Frequently planted. Fr. H. S.—Ceylon, common. Malay Penins. and Archip. China. New Caledonia. A large evergreen umbrageous tree, often epiphytic, aërial roots slender, quite glabrous, l. elliptic, ovate or obovate, apex rounded, or shortly and bluntly acuminate, blade 2–4, narrowed into pet. $\frac{1}{4}$–$\frac{1}{2}$ in. Receptacles finely pubescent while young, fr. sessile, yellow or reddish, $\frac{1}{3}$ in. diam., basal bracts broadly ovate, obtuse, spreading. Var. *nitida*, has elliptic, *retusa* proper more rounded l. 27. **F. glabella,** Blume; King, Ann. i. t. 60.—Syn. *F. affinis*, Wall. Bhutan. Khasi hills. Andamans. Burma, Upper and Lower.—Malay Penins. A tree with a large dense crown, young shoots sometimes minutely hairy, otherwise perfectly glabrous, l. elliptic or elliptic-lanceolate, sometimes broader at apex, acuminate, blade 2–4, pet. $\frac{1}{2}$–1 in. Fr. $\frac{1}{6}$–$\frac{1}{3}$ in. diam., sessile or on peduncles up to $\frac{1}{3}$ in. long, basal bracts minute. 28. **F. Talboti,** King, Ann. i. t. 63. Common in evergreen forest of Belgaum and on the southern Ghats of North Kanara. A large smooth-barked epiphytic tree, quite glabrous, fr. greenish-yellow $\frac{1}{4}$ in. diam., basal bracts ovate, acute.

29. **F. indica,** Linn.; King, Ann. i. t. 45. Vern. *Nyaung thabye*, Burma, Paunglin forest, Pegu Yoma (D.B. Jan. 1862). Martaban, Tenasserim. Andamans. Malay Penins. and Archip. A large spreading tree, stipules and sometimes young shoots and bracts pubescent, otherwise glabrous, l. elongate-elliptic, shortly and usually abruptly acuminate, blade 4–6, pet. $\frac{1}{3}$–1 in., sec. n. slender, 6–8 pair, the lowest pair basal, numerous intermediate nerves between, joined by reticulate veins. Fr. sessile, yellow, often cylindric, $\frac{1}{2}$ in. long, basal bracts 3, ovate, acute, spreading. 30. **F. obtusifolia,** Roxb.; Wight Ic. t. 662; King, Ann. i. t. 49. Vern *Nyaung gyat*, Burm. Sikkim, foot of hills. Khasi hills. Manipúr. Chittagong. Burma, Upper and Lower. Malay Penins. A large tree, often epiphytic, perfectly glabrous, l. thickly coriaceous, shining, elongate-elliptic or obovate, blade 4–7, pet. stout $\frac{1}{2}$–1 in., midrib prominent, sec. n. slender, 15–18 pair with numerous intermediate ones. Fr. sessile, often crowded above the scars of fallen l. (the internodes being short), globose, somewhat trigonous, $\frac{1}{2}$ in. diam., basal bracts 3, large, coriaceous, rounded.

31. **F. rhododendrifolia,** Miq.; King, Ann. i. t. 58. Western Duars (D.B. Jan. 1879) Assam (Makum forest, D.B. Apr. 1879). Khasi hills. Chittagong. Pegu Yoma. A moderate-sized or large tree, sometimes epiphytic, glabrous, save stipules. L. elongate-elliptic or elliptic-oblong, acuminate, blade 3–7, pet. $\frac{1}{2}$–1 in. Fr. sessile, red, $\frac{1}{3}$–$\frac{3}{8}$ in. diam., basal bracts 3, triangular or ovate. This is probably var. 1 of *F. nuda*, Kurz, F. Fl. ii. 445. not Miq. 32. **F. Kurzii,** King Ann. i. t. 57.—Syn. *F. nuda*, Miq. var. *macrocarpa*, Kurz; *F. euphylla*, Kurz (doubtful). Pegu and Tenasserim.—Java. Similar to 31. Sec. n. 10–12 pair, joined by intramarginal veins, the lowest pair basal, parallel intermediate n. joined by reticulate veins, on the underside almost as distinct as sec. n. Fr. dark purple, $\frac{1}{2}$ in. diam. on slender peduncles $\frac{1}{4}$ in. long, 3 minute caducous bracts at base of peduncle, basal bracts 0. 33. **F. Maclellandi,** King, Ann. i. t. 64. Pegu. Branchlets grey-silky, l. coriaceous, elliptic-oblong, blade 5, pet. $\frac{1}{2}$ in. long. Receptacles sessile, grey-tomentose, $\frac{1}{3}$ in. diam., basal bracts small, silky.

C. Sec. n. ∞, nearly at a right angle to midrib, reticulate veins few.

34. **F. elastica,** Roxb.; Wight Ic. t. 663; King, Ann. i. t. 54. *Indian Caoutchouc tree.* Vern. *Bor Attah*, Ass. *Nyaung Kyetpaung*, Burm.

A gigantic tree, perfectly glabrous, sending down numerous aërial roots from the branches, trunk supported by high, branching buttresses. L. shining, elliptic, abruptly and shortly acuminate, blade 5–10, pet. $\frac{1}{2}$–2$\frac{1}{2}$ in., stipules pink, up to 6 in. long. Receptacles enclosed, while young, by hooded involucres which fall off, leaving a saucer-shaped base under the fr. Fr. sessile, greenish-yellow when ripe, ovoid-oblong, $\frac{1}{2}$ in. long.

Outer Himalaya from Nepal eastwards, ascending to 5,000 ft. Assam. Khasi hills. Upper Burma south to 24° N. Fr. H. S. The tree as a rule germinates on the branches of tall forest trees, grows very slowly at first, but soon sends down aërial root-drops, and when these have taken root begins to make rapid progress. Eventually the tree stands on its own legs, and attains a height of 100–200 ft., with a diam. of the crown of 150–200 ft. Cultivated on a large scale for the yield of India Rubber since 1872 in Java and since 1874 in Assam. 35. **F. Benjamina,** Linn. (*a*) Var. *comosa*, Kurz; King, Ann. i. t. 52.—Syn. *F. comosa*, Roxb. Cor. Pl. t. 125; Wight Ic. t. 658. Vern. *Kabra*, Nep.; *Chilu Bòr*, Assam; *Vel âl*, Mal.; *Nyaung thabye*, Burm. Foot of the Eastern Himalaya. Assam. Chittagong. Andamans. Pegu. Martaban. Tenasserim. Chutia Nagpur. Northern Circars. Travancore, 1,000–3,000 ft. common (Bourdillon).—Malay Archip. China. A large tree with a spreading crown and drooping branches, perfectly glabrous. L. thinly coriaceous, shining, elliptic, abruptly acuminate, blade 3–5, pet. $\frac{1}{2}$–$\frac{3}{4}$ in. Fr. sessile, yellow or red when ripe., $\frac{3}{4}$ in. diam. ($\frac{1}{3}$–$\frac{1}{2}$ in. Singbhùm, Haines), basal bracts small. (*b*) *F. Benjamina* proper, fr. small, red, $\frac{1}{3}$ in. diam. Andamans (Kurz). Malay Peninsula (cultivated), Archipelago (wild). The size of the ripe fr. however varies greatly. 36. **F. Trimeni,** King. Kanara. Dharwar, Bellary.—Ceylon. A very large tree, entirely glabrous, l. coriaceous, elliptic, blade 3–4, pet. $\frac{3}{4}$ in. Fr. sessile, globose, orange-yellow or red, not dotted, $\frac{1}{2}$–$\frac{3}{4}$ in. diam., basal bracts small, ovate-cordate.

Sect. III. *Synœcia*. ♂ fl. monandrous, in the same receptacle with gall fl.; ♀ and neuter fl. in separate receptacles. Neuter fl. consist of 3 linear sepals on a long pedicel without any trace of either anther or pistil.

37. **F. callicarpa,** Miq.; King, Ann. i. t. 90.—Syn. *F. pomifera*, Kurz. Tenasserim (Kurz).—Malay Penins. and Archip. Climbing, stems often flat, 40–100 ft. long, clinging to the bark of trees by innumerable slender branching rootlets. L. glabrous, rigidly coriaceous, entire, obovate, blade 3–4, narrowed into pet. $\frac{1}{4}$–$\frac{1}{2}$ in., sec. n. slender, 3–4 pair, on the underside of the l. the surface raised between the tesselate veins. Fr. on the old wood, solitary, pale yellow or orange when ripe, 1–1$\frac{1}{2}$ in., peduncle 1–2 in. long.

Sect. IV. *Sycidium*. ♂ fl. monandrous with gall fl. in one set of receptacles, ♀ in another set. L. in most species small and rough.

A. Erect shrubs or trees.

(*a*) L. entire or nearly so, caudate-acuminate.

38. **F. clavata,** Wall.; King, Ann. i. t. 111.—Syn. *F. trachycarpa*, Miq. Vern. *Khanoi*, Jauns.; *Ka-aung gale*, Burm.

An erect shrub or small tree, sometimes attaining a large size, branchlets rough. L. rigidly membranous, lanceolate, sometimes oblanceolate or obovate, upper part dentate, caudate-acuminate, tail tapering, $\frac{1}{2}$–1 in., blade 4–8, pet. $\frac{1}{8}$–$\frac{1}{4}$ in., sec. n. 5–10 pair, the lowest pair from the base and running as intramarginal nerves to the apex, tert. n. and reticulate veins prominent beneath, stipules $\frac{1}{3}$ in., lanceolate, caducous. Receptacles solitary and axillary, of two kinds, globose, $\frac{1}{3}$ in. diam. and obovoid, up to $\frac{3}{4}$ in. long, smooth or warted, the ♀ receptacles smaller than those with ♂ and gall fl., peduncles $\frac{1}{10}$–$\frac{1}{4}$ in., basal bracts small, fr. yellow.

Himalaya, outer hills, ascending to 6,000 ft., from the Sutlej eastwards. Nepal frontier north of Bahraich (Duthie). Khasi hills. Manipùr. Upper Burma. Fr. April–June.—Malacca. China. 39. **F. sikkimensis,** Miq. Sikkim 2–4,000 ft. Khasi hills. A small tree, sometimes epiphytic, l. membranous, nearly glabrous, entire, lanceolate or oblanceolate, tail $\frac{1}{4}$–$\frac{1}{2}$ in., blade 3–7, pet. $\frac{1}{8}$–$\frac{1}{4}$ in. Recept. solitary or clustered, nearly sessile, $\frac{1}{3}$ in. diam.

(*b*) L. denticulate, crenate, serrate or deeply lobed, not caudate-acuminate.

40. **F. brevicuspis,** Miq.; King, Ann. i. t. 106. Andamans.—Johore. Java. A shrub, branchlets sparsely hispid. L. elongate-elliptic or obovate, slightly denticulate, blade 5–10, pet. $\frac{1}{2}$–2 in. Receptacles globose, $\frac{1}{2}$ in. diam., pedunculate, solitary, axillary or from the scars of fallen l. 41. **F. obscura,** Blume; King, Ann. i. tt. 102, 103. Sikkim, outer hills and valleys, ascending to 5,000 ft. Khasi hills. Burma (King).—Malay

Archip. Formosa. A shrub or small tree, branchlets rough with short stiff hairs and scales. L. thinly membranous, very unequal-sided, unequally serrate, rough with raised dots and minute stiff hairs, chiefly along the nerves, blade 4–10, pet. $\frac{1}{4}$–$\frac{3}{4}$ in. Fr. $\frac{1}{3}$–$\frac{3}{4}$ in.

FIG. 187.—Ficus clavata, Wall. $\frac{1}{3}$.
(The form with globose receptacles.)

diam. with 1 or 2 wart-like bracts on the outer surface, no basal bracts, reddish or orange when ripe, peduncle $\frac{1}{10}$–$\frac{1}{2}$ in. 42. **F. asperrima,** Roxb.: Wight Ic. t. 633: King, Ann. i. t. 100. Rocky bed of Pranhita river, Chanda district. Hills of the Western Peninsula.—Ceylon, moist region, common. A shrub or small tree, aërial roots 0, branchlets rough with short stiff hairs. L. rough on both sides with raised dots, more or less densely pubescent beneath, elliptic, crenate in the upper part, blade 3–5, pet. $\frac{1}{4}$–$\frac{1}{2}$ in., sec. n. 4–5 pair, the lowest pair basal, often extending beyond the half of leaf. Fr. globose, hispid, $\frac{1}{2}$–1 in. diam., yellow when ripe, peduncles $\frac{1}{8}$ in. long. 43. **F. bhotanica,** King, Ann. i. t. 205 B. Eastern Duars. Assam. A shrub, branchlets and underside of l. pubescent, l. membranous deeply lobed. Fr. in axillary pairs $\frac{3}{4}$ in., peduncle $\frac{1}{8}$ in. long.

B. Creeping, straggling or decumbent shrubs.

44. **F. rostrata,** Lamk.: King, Ann. t. 110.—Syn. *F. radicans*, Roxb.; Wight Ic. t. 671; *F. uniglandulosa*, Wall. Bhutan. Assam. Khasi hills. Cachar. Chittagong. Lower Burma.—Malay Penins. Climbing or creeping, rooting at the nodes, growing on trees and walls. L. thinly coriaceous, elliptic or elongate-elliptic, apex abruptly caudate-acuminate, often with a few coarse irregular teeth in the upper part, tail linear, $\frac{3}{4}$–$1\frac{1}{2}$ in. long, blade 4–10, pet. $\frac{1}{4}$–$\frac{3}{4}$ in., sec. n. 4–6 pair, prominent beneath, terminating in arching intramarginal nerves, which extend from the base to the tip of the leaf, intermediate and tertiary n. as well as reticulate veins conspicuous beneath, stipules minute. Receptacles hispid, $\frac{1}{4}$ in. diam., pedunculate or nearly sessile, in fascicles of 2–6, axillary or above the scars of fallen l. Ovary stalked, stigma cylindric blunt. 45. **F. quercifolia,** Roxb.; Wight t. 646; King, Ann i. t. 95.—Syn. *F. humilis*, Roxb.; Wight Ic. t. 635; *F. anastomosans*, Wall. Tenasserim.—Malay Penins. and Archip. A creeping or decumbent shrub. Branchlets hispid with short hairs, l. thickly membranous, lanceolate, coarsely crenate or lobed, blade 2–3, pet. $\frac{1}{8}$–$\frac{1}{3}$ in. Fr. crimson, depressed, $\frac{1}{4}$–$\frac{1}{2}$ in. diam., ped. $\frac{1}{4}$–$\frac{1}{2}$ in. 46. **F. nigrescens,** King, Ann. i. t. 95A. Manipur and Naga hills. A small creeping shrub, rooting at the nodes, l. pubescent beneath, minutely hairy above, ovate, toothed, blade 1–2, pet. pubescent, $\frac{1}{3}$–$\frac{3}{4}$ in., stipules

lanceolate, ⅓ in. long. Fr. black, hairy, ⅛ in. diam., peduncle short. 47. **F. heterophylla**, Linn. fil.; King, Ann. i. t. 94; Wight Ic. t. 659.—Syn. *F. scabrella*, Roxb.; Wight Ic. t. 661; *F. repens*, Willd.; Wight Ic. t. 686. Vern. *Datir*, Mar. Subhimalayan tract from the Jumna eastwards, and thence through the greater part of India and Burma, generally near water.—Malay, China. A creeping or straggling shrub, harshly pubescent, l. alternate, extremely variable in size and shape and length of petiole, blade 1–5, pet. 0–8 in. long, stipules small, linear, glabrous. Fr. axillary solitary, yellow when ripe, ½–1 in. long, generally narrowed into a stalk up to ⅓ in. long, at the base of which are 3 minute bracts, peduncle ½–1 in. long. Two varieties: *a. F. scabrella*, l. shortly petioled, usually not lobed, peduncle short. *β. F. repens*, l. long petioled, broad, usually lobed, ped. long.

Sect. V. *Covellia.* ♂ fl. monandrous, in the same receptacle with gall fl. ♀ fl. in separate receptacles, perianth none or small, or very thin and transparent. Receptacles on leafless racemose or panicled branches from the old wood, generally on the trunk.

A. Leaves mostly opposite.

48. **F. hispida**, Linn. f.; King, Ann. i. tt. 154, 155.—Syn. *F. oppositifolia*, Roxb. Cor Pl. t. 124; Wight Ic. t. 638; *F. dæmonum*, Koenig; Wight Ic. t. 641. Vern. *Dadūri*, Punj.; *Gobla, Kat Gular*, Hind.; *Katumar*, Gond; *Dher-Umbar*, Mar.; *Sosokera*, Kol; *Bamari*, Tel.; *Chona Atthi*, Tam.; *Eruma-nakku*, Mal.; *Kadut, Kaaung*, Burm. Subhimalayan tract and outer hills, ascending to 3,500 ft. from the Chenab eastwards. Throughout India and Burma, excepting the arid regions of the North West. Hong Kong. North Australia. A small or moderate-sized tree, throwing up abundant root-suckers, branchlets stout, often hollow, marked by the scars of petioles and stipules, branchlets, petioles and underside of l. clothed with short stiff hairs, upperside rough with minute scattered hairs. L. membranous, opposite, at times alternate, elongate-elliptic or obovate, entire or dentate, base rounded, blade 8–16, pet. ½–2 in., sec. n. 8–10 pair, tert. n. parallel and reticulate. Style hairy. Fr. obovoid, 1 in. long, supported by 3 persistent basal bracts, usually clustered on long leafless panicles hanging from the old wood of trunk and branches; on young plants, coppice shoots and sometimes also on old trees, often in axillary pairs. 49. **F. conglobata**, King, Ann. t. i. 123. Sikkim, outer hills to 3,000 ft. Bhutan. Manipur. Chittagong. A small tree, young shoots and leaves harsh-silky with long ferruginous hairs, branchlets, petioles and nerves on the underside of l. clothed with stiff rusty hairs, l. opposite or alternate, regularly serrate, base often cordate, pet. 1–5 in. long. Receptacles in the axils of scarious bracts, from the base of the stem, in densely crowded corymbs on stout branches creeping along or under the ground. Sterile recept. small, numerous, with a few fertile ones ½ in. diam. on slender peduncles, up to 5 in. long, usually narrowed into a stalk, at the base of which are 3 large united bracts. Ovary and style without hairs.

50. **F. semocarpa**, Miq.; King, Ann. i. t. 152.—Syn. *F. pyrrhocarpa*, Kurz; *F. tuberculata*, Wall. *Yethapan*, Burm. On the shingly or rocky beds of mountain streams. Subhimalayan tract and outer valleys, from the Jumna eastwards. Assam. Khasi hills. Lower Burma. A gregarious shrub, almost cæspitose, 1–4 ft. high, young shoots hirsute with stiff hairs, sometimes branchlets and l. hairy. L. lanceolate, opposite, usually crowded at the ends of branches, blade 4–8, narrowed into pet. ¼–¾ in. long, stipules broad-lanceolate ½ in. long. Receptacles ½–1 in. diam., ribbed, hispid, with scattered bracts on the outside, solitary axillary, or in short leafless bracteate panicles from the old wood, often underground. Ovary and style with long thin hairs. King, Ann. i. 116, thinks it may be a form of *F. hispida*, modified by the peculiar conditions of the localities where it occurs.

B. Leaves mostly alternate.

51. **F. Cunia**, Ham.; Wight Ic. t. 648; King, Ann. i. tt. 126, 127.—Syn. *F. conglomerata*, Roxb.; Wight Ic. t. 669. Vern. *Khini, Khunia, Khain*, Hind.; *Kanhya*, Nep.; *Ye ka ôn*, Lower, *Thadut*, Upper Burma.

A small or moderate-sized tree, usually evergreen, branchlets, young shoots and midrib pubescent. L. alternate, entire or serrate, rough above, more or less pubescent beneath, semicordate, the lower half of the base large, rounded, shape and size very variable, blade 8–16, pet. ⅕–¾ in., stipules ¾–1 in. long, base broad, scar annular. Receptacles ½ in. diam. in pairs or clusters on long leafless scaly branches from the trunk near the base, often ripening underground.

Subhimalayan tract, and outer hills from the Chenab eastwards, ascending to 4,000 ft. Chutia Nagpur. Eastern Satpura hills. Khasi hills. Manipur. Chittagong. Burma,

Upper and Lower. Fr. edible, ripe May–Sept.—Perak. 52. **F. prostrata,** Wall.; King, Ann i. t. 135. Sikkim, outer ranges, ascending to 5,000 ft. Khasi hills. Cachar. A glabrous shrub or small tree, often creeping. L. lanceolate, entire, long acuminate, blade 6–10, pet. ½ in., stipules as long as pet. Receptacles ⅓ in. diam., in the axils of scarious bracts, solitary or in short racemes, on long prostrate branches. 53. **F. Ribes,** Reinwdt.; King, Ann. i. t. 144. South Tenasserim (Kurz). Malay Penins. and Archip. New Guinea. Similar to 52, shoots strigose with minute hairs, l. 3–5 in., receptacles ¼ in. diam. This and some allied species are diœcious (Solms-Laubach in Bot. Zeit. 1885, 534). 54. **F. fistulosa,** Reinwdt.; King, Ann. i. tt. 150, 151. Khasi hills. Chittagong. Lower Burma (Kurz). Malay Penins. and Archip. Formosa. (Kurz's *F. fistulosa* probably also includes *F. Miquelii*, King, a Malayan species.)—A shrub or small tree, branches stout, often hollow, nodes of young shoots most minutely hairy, l. sometimes opposite, glabrous, granulate beneath, entire or slightly serrate, elongate-elliptic, blade 4–10, pet. ½–1½ in. long, stipules scarious. Receptacles ½–1 in. diam., axillary, or on the old wood, often clustered, peduncles up to 1½ in. long.

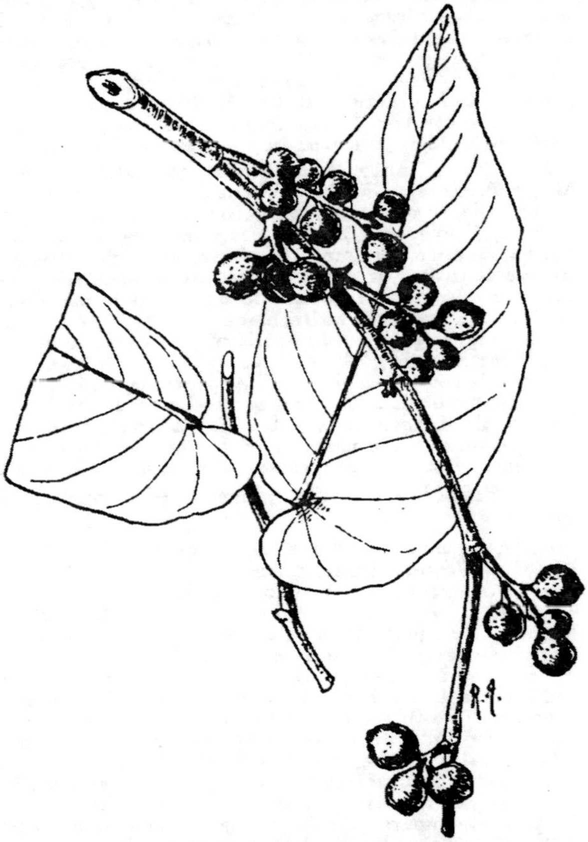

Fig. 188.—Ficus Cunia. Ham. ½.

Sec. VI. *Eusyce.* ♂ fl. as a rule diandrous (*lepidosa* 1, *hirta* 1–3, *nemoralis* and *laevis* 2 or 3, *Carica* generally 3 stamens) in the same receptacle with gall fl. ♀ fl. in distinct receptacles. L. alternate, receptacles axillary.

A. Erect shrubs or trees.

(*a*) Branchlets and underside of l. densely hairy; l. dentate, serrate or lobed.

55. **F. palmata,** Forsk.; Collett Simla Fl. 460, fig. 148; King, Ann. i. t. 185.—Syn. *F. caricoides*, Roxb.; *F. virgata*, Roxb.; Wight Ic. t. 649. Vern. *Bedu*, *Khemri*, Hind.; *Phagwara*, Haz.; *Pheru*, Jauns.; *Kembri*, Merw. Baluchistan. Eastern slopes of the Suleiman range. Salt range and plains of the Punjab. Mt. Abu. Merwara. North-West Himalaya from the foot to 5,000, on the Sutlej to 9,000 ft., eastwards as far as Nepal. Cultivated in North India. A small or middle-sized tree, bark smooth, grey, branches solid with a large pith, branchlets, petioles, young shoots and underside of l. soft-tomentose. L. rough above, broad-ovate, dentate, at times deeply lobed, base truncate or cordate, sometimes abruptly narrowed to the petiole, blade 3–5, pet. 1–2 in. long, 3–5 basal nerves, sec. n. on midrib 3–6 pair. Perianth ciliate with long hairs. Receptacles axillary, more or less pear-shaped, ½–1 in. diam., usually pubescent, yellow, edible when ripe, basal bracts deciduous, at the base of the stalk, which often lengthens out to ½ in., as the fr. ripens, peduncle ½–1 in. 56. **F. fulva,** Reinwdt.; King, Ann. i. t. 187. Andamans and Nicobars.—Malay Penins. and Archip. L. ovate, denticulate, often deeply lobed. Receptacles sessile, ½ in. diam., densely hairy, perianth glabrous. 57. **F. Carica,** Linn.; Hemsley in Trans. Linn. Soc. iii. (1888) t. 46; Solms-Laubach in Bot. Zeit. 1885. 562. *The Fig tree.* Vern. *Anjir*, Hind. Indigenous in Baluchistan, Afghanistan, Western Asia and the eastern Mediterranean region. Cultivated in N. W. India and the Deccan. A shrub or small deciduous tree, branchlets and under-

side of l. pubescent or tomentose. L. cordate, more or less deeply lobed, lobes obtuse, blade 4–8, pet. 2–3 in. long, upperside rough. The tree is diœcious, that is, some trees have elongated receptacles with ♂ and gall fl. while others have shortly pyriform, nearly globose receptacles, containing only ♀ fl. The leaves in both sexes are the same, but the difference in the shape of receptacles and fl. is so great, that at one time they were regarded as distinct genera or species, the ♂ tree being called *Caprificus*. The receptacles of both sexes lengthen out into a stalk, at the base of which are the membranous bracts. In the Mediterranean region twigs with receptacles of the *Caprificus* are tied to the female tree, in order to facilitate fertilization. A few seeds are occasionally produced in the receptacles of the *Caprificus*.

58. **F. hirta,** Vahl; King, Ann. i. tt. 188, 189.; Wight Ic. t. 672.—Syn. *F. Roxburghii*, Miq.; *F. hirsuta*, Roxb.; Wight Ic. t. 670; *F. triloba*, Ham. Subhimalayan tract and outer hills, from Nepal eastwards, ascending to 5,000 ft. Assam. Khasi hills. Cachar. Burma, Upper and Lower, often in deserted Taungyas.—Malay Penins. and Archip. China. A shrub or small tree, branchlets, petioles, underside of l. and receptacles clothed with soft tawny or rusty tomentum of long silky hairs. L. serrate, variable in shape and size, from broad-ovate to oblong-lanceolate, entire or deeply 3–5-lobed, upperside harsh with scattered hairs, blade 8–16, pet. 1–7 in. long, basal n. 3–7. Receptacles clothed with long stiff hairs, in axillary pairs, sessile or nearly so, ½–¾ in. diam., dimorphous, those with ♀ fl. globose, those with ♂ and gall fl. ovoid, almost conical, the fertile receptacle red when ripe. The species is diœcious, ♀ and ♂ receptacles as a rule are on different bushes (Graf zu Solms-Laubach in Bot. Zeit. 1885, 516). 59. **F. chrysocarpa,** Reinwdt.; King, Ann. t. 191. Martaban (Kurz).—Malay Penins. and Archip. Branchlets, petioles and underside of l. more or less tawny or brown-tomentose, l. lanceolate or oblanceolate, serrate, recept. ½ in. diam., densely golden-hairy.

(*b*) Branchlets and underside of l. minutely or sparsely hairy; l. entire or nearly so.

60. **F. lepidosa,** Wall.; King, Ann. i. t. 207.—Syn. *F. Lamponga*, var. 1., Kurz F. Fl. ii. 451. Western Duars. Assam. Khasi hills. Cachar. Chittagong. Pegu Yoma, southern spurs. Tenasserim.—Perak. An erect shrub or small tree, young shoots silky with long hairs, branchlets pubescent, stout, marked with scars of petioles, pith large. L. membranous, glabrous above, pale and minutely hairy beneath, entire, elongate-elliptic, blade 4–8, pet. 1–3 in. long, sec. n. 6–8 pair, prominent beneath, the lowest pair basal, stipules amplexicaul. Fr. in axillary pairs, orange-red, ½ in. diam., peduncle ⅓–½ in., basal bracts 3, acute. Under *Sycidium* in Fl. Brit. Ind. v. 522. 61. **F. erecta,** Thunb.; King, Ann. i. t. 178. Sikkim. Khasi hills.—China. Japan. A small tree, buds minutely hairy, otherwise quite glabrous. L. ovate, obovate or lanceolate, usually entire, blade 3–8, pet. ½–2 in. long. Receptacles ½ in. diam. in axillary pairs, peduncles up to 1 in. long. 62. **F. silhetensis,** Miq.; King, Ann. i. t. 194. Sikkim, hot valleys. Assam. Khasi hills. Cachar. A shrub, branchlets softly pubescent. L. pale and sparsely hairy beneath, entire, lanceolate, oblanceolate or oblong, blade 4–8, pet. ⅓–⅔ in. long. Receptacles axillary, solitary or in pairs, sparsely hairy, ¼ in. diam. 63. **F. glandulifera,** Wall.; King, Ann. i. t. 180. Tenasserim (Falconer).—Malay Penins. and Archip. Branchlets and pet. rusty pubescent. L. nearly glabrous, entire, underside pale, and minutely hairy along midrib and n., elliptic, acuminate, blade 3–5, pet. 1–2 in. long. Receptacles ovoid, ⅓ in. diam., yellow when ripe, peduncle ¼ in. 64. **F. pyriformis,** Hook. & Arn.; King, Ann. i. tt. 200. 201.—Syn. *F. subpyriformis*, Miq.; *F. ichnopoda*, Miq. In rocky stream beds. Khasi hills. Burma, Upper and Lower.—Malaya. China. A small shrub, young shoots pubescent, l. minutely hairy beneath, entire, lanceolate, or linear-lanceolate, blade 4–6, pet. ¼ in. Receptacles pyriform, narrowed into a short stalk, solitary, axillary, ⅗ in., peduncle up to 1 in. long. In similar localities: *F. lanceolata*, Ham., with larger and globose fr. and *F. sæmocarpa*, Miq., with opposite l.

(c) Branchlets and underside of l. glabrous; l. entire.

65. **F. nemoralis,** Wall.; King, Ann. i. t. 203.—Syn. *F. gemella*, Wall.; *F. Fieldingii*, Miq.; *F. trilepis*, Miq. Vern. *Dudhla*, Hind.; *Dudila*, Nep. Himalaya, 3–8,000 ft. from Hazara eastwards, often planted near villages for cattle fodder. Assam. Khasi hills. A small glabrous tree, not epiphytic, l. membranous, entire, ovate or elongate-elliptic to lanceolate, long acuminate, base acute, blade 4–6, pet. ¾–1 in. long. Receptacles varying in shape from clavate to globose, sessile or on short peduncles, ⅓–½ in. diam., glabrous, when ripe reddish, edible; ♂ fl. in all receptacles, few in those with ♀, numerous in those with gall fl. 66. **F. chartacea,** Wall.—Syn. *F. Lamponga*, var. *chartacea*. Kurz F. Fl. II. 451. Tenasserim.—Malay Penins. A shrub, young shoots minutely strigose, l. glabrous, entire, pet. slender, receptacles globose, ¼ in. diam., yellow when ripe.

B. Epiphytic or creeping.

67. **F. foveolata,** Wall.; King, Ann. i. tt. 166–168.—Syn. *F. pubigera*, Wall.

Himalaya from Hazara eastwards 2–7,000 ft. Assam. Khasi hills. Behar. Chittagong. Martaban (?).—China. Japan. Creeping or climbing, rooting at the nodes, sometimes erect. Branchlets, petioles, underside of l. as a rule pubescent. L. rigidly membranous to thinly coriaceous, entire, ovate or elliptic to lanceolate, blade 3–8, pet. ¼–¾ in., sec. n. 8–10 pair, the lowest pair basal, tertiary n. joined by closely and elegantly reticulate veins. Receptacles hairy, solitary, globose or ovoid, ⅓–⅔ in. diam., usually pedunculate, basal bracts ovate. The barren creeping stems have small l., and send out fl.-bearing branches with much larger l., in the same manner as *F. pumila*, Linn., of the same section from China and Japan, commonly cultivated on walls in India. 68. **F. ramentacea**, Roxb.; King, Ann. i. t. 169. Sikkim, hot valleys. Assam. Silhet. Chittagong. Pegu Yoma.—Malay Penins. and Archip. China. A large epiphytic climber, stems 50–60 ft. long, at times a tree, l. glossy, bright green, nearly glabrous, entire, ovate or elliptic, blade 4–10, pet. ¾–1½ in. long, sec. n. 4–8 pair, prominent beneath, the lowest pair basal. Recept. ⅓–½ in. diam., axillary, solitary or clustered, sessile or on short peduncles. 69. **F. crininervia**, Miq.; King, Ann. i. t. 173. Assam. Chittagong. Malay Archip. Creeping, stems and branches rooting. Young shoots, branchlets, petioles and underside of l. (chiefly along midrib and nerves) densely silky with long tawny hairs, l. coriaceous, entire, ovate-oblong, base cordate, finely reticulate. Recept. ⅓–½ in. diam. 70. **F. scandens**, Roxb.; Wight Ic. t. 643; King, Ann. i. t. 162. Subhimalayan tract and outer ranges, ascending to 4,000 ft., from Kumaon eastwards. Behar. Khasi hills. Lower Burma. A large scandent shrub, rooting at the nodes, trailing on rocks and ascending tall trees, branchlets and l. slightly rough. L. chartaceous, entire, ovate, blade 3–5, pet. ¼–1 in., sec. n. prominent, 4–6 pair, the lowest pair basal. Receptacles globose, solitary or in pairs, ⅓ in. diam., peduncles ¼ in. 71. **F. laevis**, Blume; King, Ann. i. t. 161. Himalaya outer hills, ascending to 5000 ft., from Nepal eastwards. Assam. Khasi hills. Cachar. Often epiphytic, l. broadly ovate, entire or nearly so, base often cordate, blade 6–9, pet. 1½–3 in. long, upperside glabrous excepting the nerves, underside more or less pubescent. Recept. ½–1 in. diam., axillary, usually solitary.

Sect. VII. *Neomorphe.* ♂ fl. as a rule diandrous (*F. Clarkei* often has 3 stamens) in the same receptacle with gall fl. ♀ in distinct receptacles. *F. glomerata*, has all 3 kinds of fl. in the same receptacle. Trees, never epiphytic, some species climbing, l. alternate. Receptacles in dense clusters from tubercles on the trunk and larger branches, often very large.

A. Erect trees.

(*a*) L. serrate or denticulate, base often cordate, petiole long.

72. **F. Roxburghii**, Wall.; King, Ann. i. frontispiece and t. 211.—Syn. *F. macrophylla*, Roxb.; Wight Ic. t. 673. Vern. *Hurmal*, Haz.; *Timla*, *Tirmal*, Hind.; *Sinthapan*, Burm. Subhimalayan tract and outer Himalaya, ascending to 6,000 ft. Chutia Nagpur. Orissa. Khasi hills. Manipùr. Chittagong. Burma.—Hainan. Formosa. A small or middle-sized tree, branchlets hollow, young shoots and stipules minutely velvety, petioles and underside of l. softly pubescent. L. broadly ovate, entire or dentate, base deeply cordate, sometimes rounded, basal n. 5–7, blade 8–18, pet. 1–6 in. Receptacles sometimes narrowed into a stalk, up to ⅓ in. long, at the base of which are 3 broad bracts, peduncle ¾–2 in. long. Fr. depressed-turbinate, 2–3 in. diam., longitudinally ribbed, russet-brown or purple when ripe, edible, in large often immense clusters upon short thick leafless branches from the trunk, often near the ground, and from the larger branches. For the development of fl. and their fertilization see D. D. Cunningham's paper in the appendix to Ann. Gard. Calc. i. 73. **F. pomifera**, Wall.; King, Ann. i. t. 215.—Syn. *F. regia*, Miq. (in part). Subhimalayan tract from Sikkim eastwards, ascending to 3,000 ft. Khasi hills. Chittagong. Martaban and Tenasserim.—Malay Penins. and Archip. A tall tree, nearly glabrous, l. coarsely serrate, ovate or ovate-lanceolate, blade 5–10, pet. 2–5 in. Fr. globose or pyriform, 1 in. diam. on peduncles up to 2½ in., on short leafless branches. 74. **F. variegata**, Blume; King, Ann. i. tt. 212, 213.—Syn. *F. racemifera*, Roxb.; Wight Ic. t. 639. Chittagong. Andamans. Malay Penins. and Archip. A tall spreading tree, glabrous, only stipules minutely pùbescent. L. ovate, repand or denticulate, base cordate or rounded, blade 4–7, pet. 1–2 in. Fr. red, globose 1 in. diam., peduncles ¼–2 in. long, fascicled on woody tubercles on the old wood.

(*b*) L. entire, base acute or rounded, petiole generally short.

75. **F. glomerata**, Roxb. Cor. Pl. t. 123; Wight Ic. t. 667; Brandis F. Fl. t. 49; King, Ann. i. tt. 218, 219.—Syn, *F. Chittagonga*, Miq. Vern. *Umar*, *Gular*, Hind.; *Trimbal*, Chamba; *Umbri*, Merw.; *Umbar*, *Umra*, Mar.; *Atti*, Tel.; *Thapan*, *Ye thapan*, Burm. Salt range. Subhimalayan tract and outer valleys, in ravines, on the banks of rivers, and in damp places. Ajmere and Merwara, Mount Aboo. Behar. Chutia Nagpur Bengal plains. Khasi hills. Chittagong. Lower Burma. Dry region of the Irawadd

valley. Western Peninsula. A middle-sized or large tree, young shoots minutely hairy, mature l. glabrous. L. entire, elongate-elliptic, ovate- or elliptic-lanceolate, base acute or rounded, blade 3–8, pet. ¾–2 in., sec. n. 6–8 pair, the lowest pair basal. ♂ ♀ and gall fl. together in one receptacle (Solms-Laubach in Bot. Zeit. 1885, 548 and King, Ann. i. 173). Fr. nearly globose, 1–1½ in. diam., clustered on leafless branches, from trunk and larger branches; rarely axillary. L. renewed between Jan. and April, when the tree is sometimes bare for a short time.

(c) L. as a rule entire, lanceolate or oblong, pet. short.

76. **F. lanceolata**, Ham.; Wight Ic. t. 645; King, Ann. i. t. 224. Khasi hills. Beds of streams in Chittagong and Singbhum. A much-branched, nearly glabrous shrub, usually prostrate, l. lanceolate, entire base mostly rounded, blade 4–8, pet. ¼–¾ in., stipules as long as petiole, base broad, scar annular. Receptacles glabrous, pear-shaped, depressed, 1–2 in. diam., purple when ripe, in clusters of 5–6, on short lateral branchlets on the old wood, often near the ground. Ovary and style glabrous, fr. edible. 77. **F. Clarkei**, King in Ann. i. t. 221. Khasi hills. A tall tree, nearly glabrous. L. oblong, acuminate, base acute, entire or with a few large teeth near the apex, unequal-sided, blade 9, pet. ½ in., sec. n. 8–10 pair, the lowest pair basal, running close under the edge of l. Stamens 2–3. Fr. pyriform, red, edible, 1 in. diam., contracted into a long stalk, at the base of which are 3 ovate-lanceolate bracts.

B. Climbing shrubs, leaves entire, broadly-ovate, 3–5-nerved.

78. **F. guttata**, Wight Ic. t. 1966 (*Covellia*), King, Ann. i. t. 209. Nilgiris. Palnis. Branchlets, pet. and underside of l. rusty-pubescent, l. sparsely and minutely hairy above, blade 5–6, pet. ½–¾ in. long. Fr. 1–1¼ in. diam., on short peduncles in dense clusters on the old wood. 79. **F. macrocarpa**, Wight MSS.; King, Ann. i. t. 208.—Syn. *Pogonotrophe macrocarpa*, Miq. in Wight Ic. t. 1965. Nilgiris. Branchlets, petioles and underside of l. minutely hairy. L. glabrous above, blade 6–8, pet. 1–2½ in. Fr. 1–2½ in. diam., in large clusters on the old wood.

Hullettia Griffithiana, King.—Syn. *Dorstenia Griffithiana*, Kurz. Tenasserim. An evergreen shrub, branches stout, branchlets pubescent, l. rigidly chartaceous, upperside glabrous and glossy, underside rough with very minute stiff hairs, oblanceolate, base rounded or cordate, sec. n. joined by prominent intramarginal veins. Fl. diœcious, 10–12, sunk in cavities of axillary peduncled open funnel-shaped 3–4-lobed receptacles. ♂ perianth tubular 2-lobed, stamens 2, filaments connate into a column. ♀ perianth tubular, clavate, mouth minute. Ovary free, ovule erect. Fruiting receptacles velvety, 1–2 in. diam.

Conocephalus suaveolens, Blume.—Syn. *Urtica naucleiflora*, Roxb.; Wight Ic. t. 684. Subhimalayan tract and outer hills from Sikkim eastwards. Assam. Khasi hills. Chittagong. Burma, Upper and Lower.—Malay Peninsula. A large evergreen climber, l. glabrous, broadly ovate or elliptic, cystolith cells prominent, usually as raised whitish dots on the upper and as raised whitish lines on the lower surface, blade 6–10, pet. 1–6 in., sec. n. 8–12 pair, the lowest pair basal, stipules large, deciduous. Fl. fragrant, diœcious, in dense globose heads, ♂ heads ¼ in. diam. in broad shortly peduncled dichotomous cymes, fl. sessile, stamens 3–4, ♀ heads usually 4–6, in short cymes, fl. shortly peduncled, perianth tubular, including the free ovary, styles short, undivided. Bracts at the bifurcation of both ♂ and ♀ cymes opposite, broad, concave, deciduous.

2. ALLÆANTHUS, Thwaites; Fl. Brit. Ind. v. 490.

Species 3, Indo-Malayan region.

A. Kurzii, Hook. f.—Syn. *Malaisia tortuosa*, Kurz F. Fl. ii. 466. Vern. *Malaing*, Burm.: *Yeyun*, Shan.

A large deciduous climber, stem attaining 2 ft. in girth, glabrous or young shoots minutely pubescent, l. ovate-oblong, acuminate, dentate, penninerved, blade 3–5, pet. ¼–⅓ in. long, stipules broad, deciduous, Fl. diœcious, ♂ in short pedunculate-fascicled spikes, 1–2 in. long, sepals 4, thin, each fl. supported by 3–4 hyaline bracteoles. ♀ in globose heads, ⅛ in. diam. on lateral minutely pubescent racemes, sometimes solitary, bracteoles and perianth confluent into a fleshy mass, in which the ovaries are embedded, style one, long, slender, stigmatose from the base. Syncarpium fleshy, ⅓ in. diam., seeds 2–3, ellipsoid, ⅛ in. long, albumen 0, embryo curved, cotyledons folded, radicle incumbent, as long as cotyledons.

Assam. Burma, Upper and Lower. Fl. Feb.–April. Paper and cardboard are made from the inner bark. Cultivated in the Bhamo district.

3. **ARTOCARPUS,** Forst.; Fl. Brit. Ind. v. 539; King, Annals Royal Bot. Garden Calcutta, vol. ii. 1.

Trees with milky sap, l. alternate, in the majority of species entire when mature, but l. of seedlings and coppice shoots often deeply lobed or pinnatifid. Fl. monœcious, ♂ and ♀ closely packed, as a rule together with scales, which are often thickened or peltate at the apex, in unisexual globose or cylindrical heads. ♂: perianth usually 2-fid., segments concave, obtuse, stamen 1. ♀: perianth tubular, confluent with each other and the receptacle, mouth minute. Fr. fleshy more or less globose or cylindric, consisting of the receptacle and the fleshy perianths, most of which are sterile, enclosing a small number of seeds. The tips of the perianths are hard and often free, appearing as spines or tubercles. Species about 40, from India to the islands of the Pacific Ocean.

A. Fr. spinous, stipules amplexicaul, leaving annular scars on branchlets.

1. **A. hirsuta,** Lamk.; Wight Ic. t. 1957; Bedd. Fl. Sylv. t. 308; Ann. Cal. ii. t. 5. Vern. *Ran-* or *Pat-phannas*, Mar.: *Heb halasu*, Kan.; *Anjili*. Tam.; *Ayani*, Mal.

A tall evergreen tree, attaining 200 ft., young shoots, petioles and peduncles hirsute with long tawny hairs, l. broadly elliptic or ovate, blade 6–10, pet. stout, $\frac{1}{2}$–$\frac{3}{4}$ in. long. ♂ receptacle cylindric, slender, pendulous, 4–6 in. long. Fr. ovoid, 2–3 in., spines hispid, $\frac{1}{4}$ in. long.

Western Ghats from the coast to 4,000 ft., from the Konkan southwards. Fl. Jan., Feb. 2. **A. rigida,** Blume; Ann. Calc. ii. t. 3.—Syn. *A. echinata*, Roxb.; Wight Ic. t. 680; Tenasserim. L. elliptic or obovate, blade 4–9, pet. $\frac{1}{2}$–$\frac{3}{4}$ in. long, underside with short hairs, upperside glabrous, excepting midrib. ♂ fl. heads globose. 3. **A. calophylla,** Kurz; Ann. Calc. ii. t. 2. Tenasserim. L. broadly ovate, upperside rough with short white bristles on minute tubercles, underside softly tomentose.

B. Fr. tubercled, stipules amplexicaul, annular scars on branchlets.

4. **A. integrifolia,** Linn.; Roxb. Cor. Pl. t. 250; Wight Ic. t. 678. *The Jack tree.* Vern. *Kanthal*, *Kathar*, Hind.; *Phannas* Mar.; *Panasa*, Tel.; *Halasu*, Kan.; *Pilla*. Tam; *Peinnè*, Burm.

A large evergreen tree, glabrous, youngest shoots and midrib with soft stiff hairs. L. thickly coriaceous, shining above, elliptic or obovate, midrib prominent beneath, blade 4–8, narrowed into pet. $\frac{1}{2}$–1 in. long, stipules large, early caducous. Fl.-heads in bud enveloped in large stipular deciduous sheaths, ♂ stout cylindric, 2–6 in. long. Fr. 12–30 by 6–12 in. hanging on short stalks from the trunk and larger branches, the rind with conical protuberances, seeds reniform, oily.

In dense forests along the Western Ghats up to 4,000 ft., wild (Beddome, Gamble). In Burma I have often found it in large and dense forests, but only in the vicinity of deserted settlements. Cultivated throughout Burma and India, north as far as Lahore. Fl. C. S. 5. **A. peduncularis,** Kurz; Ann. Calc. ii. t. 6. Nicobars.—Perak. L. with a rounded base, fl.-heads ♂ and ♀ cylindric, erect, on peduncles $2\frac{1}{2}$–$4\frac{1}{2}$ in. long. Fr. much smaller than 1.

6. **A. Chaplasha,** Roxb.; Wight Ic. t. 682; Ann. Calc. ii. t. 12. Vern. *Lutta*, Nep.; *Chaplash*, *Chaplis*, Beng.; *Taung peinnè*, Burm.

A large deciduous tree, young shoots and stipules densely clothed with long stiff hairs, branchlets, petioles and underside of l. rough with minute stiff hairs, on old trees thinly coriaceous, broadly ovate or elliptic, entire, blade 6–10, pet. $\frac{1}{4}$–$\frac{1}{2}$ in. long, those on young trees and coppice shoots almost membranous, oblong, serrate, lobed or pinnatifid, blade up to 1 in. long, stipules large, amplexicaul. Fl.-heads ♂ and ♀ globose, peduncles $1\frac{1}{2}$–2 in. long. Fr. globose, pubescent, tuberculate, 3–4 in. diam., seeds few.

Subhimalayan tract and outer ranges from Nepal eastwards. Khasi hills. Cachar. Chittagong. Andamans. Lower Burma. Fl. March, April. 7. **A. incisa,** Linn. f. The *Breadfruit tree.* Native of the South Sea islands, introduced into most tropical countries. Cultivated on the western coast and in Burma. L. deeply pinnatifid, 1–3 ft. long, ♂ in club-shaped spikes.

C. Fr. smooth, tips of anthocarps flat. Stipules not amplexicaul.

8. **A. Lakoocha,** Roxb.; Wight Ic. t. 681; Ann. Calc. ii. t. 13.—Syn. *A. mollis*, Wall. Vern. *Dheu*, *Dhao*, *Lakuch*, Hind.; *Dehua*, Beng.; *Dewa*, Ass.; *Naka-renu*, Tel.; *Myauk lôk*, Lower, *Myauk laung*, Upper Burma.

A middle-sized, at times a large deciduous tree, young shoots, petioles and l. beneath densely clothed with soft grey, tawny or rusty tomentum. L. coriaceous, entire, elliptic or ovate, blade 6–10, pet. 1 in. Fl.-heads axillary, globose, ♂ nearly sessile, perianth of 2–4 sepals. ♀ pedunculate. Fr. velvety, yellow when ripe, 2–4 in. diam, irregularly lobed, seeds oblong.

Subhimalayan tract and outer hills, from Kumaon eastwards, ascending to 4,000 ft. Khasi hills. Burma, Upper and Lower. Malay Penins. Evergreen forests of the Western Ghats from the Konkan southwards. Fl. H. S.—Ceylon. 9. **A. Gomeziana,** Wall.; Ann. Calc. ii. t. 14. Andamans. Tenasserim.—Malay Penins. L. shining, entirely glabrous, oblong cuspidate, fr. globose or ovoid, ¾–1¼ in. diam.

4. MORUS, Linn.; Fl. Brit. Ind. v. 491.

Trees or shrubs, l. with 3–5 basal nerves, stipules deciduous. Fl. unisexual, monœcious or diœcious, ♂ in deciduous spikes, sepals 4 imbricate, stamens 4, inflexed in bud, pistillode minute. ♀ in spikes or heads, sepals 4, accrescent and succulent in fruit. Styles 2, more or less connate. Fr. a compound berry, consisting of the succulent perianths, each enclosing a one-seeded carpel, pericarp afterwards gelatinous. Embryo curved in a fleshy albumen. Species 6–8, tropical and temperate.

A. Spikes short, under 2 inches.

(*a*) Perianth of ♀ fl. of 4 sepals, the 2 inner flat, the outer more or less keeled.

1. **M. alba,** Linn.; Brandis F. Fl. t. 47. *Mulberry*. Vern. *Tūt*, *Tutri*, Hind.

A middle-sized deciduous tree, young shoots, petioles and underside of l. along n. slightly pubescent. L. ovate, dentate, frequently lobed, base often cordate, blade 2–3, sometimes larger, pet. ½–1 in. long, basal nerves 3–5. Fl. monœcious, the sexes often on distinct branches; ♂ sepals elliptic, ♀ spikes ovoid, pedunculate, styles free. Fruit white or red, sweet.

Commonly cultivated in Baluchistan, Afghanistan and the northern part of the Trans-Indus territory. Also in the Punjab plains, Kashmir and the North-West Himalaya. Fl. March, April. Fr. April–June. Cultiv. in Europe, Western and Central Asia and in China. The following species are closely allied if specifically distinct: 2. **M. nigra,** Linn. Cultivated in Baluchistan (*Shah tūt*). L. broader, firm, thick, 5-nerved, sepals and styles densely hairy, fr. purple. 3. **M. atropurpurea,** Roxb., Fl. Ind. iii. 595. China, cultivated in India, fr. cylindric, 2 in. long, dark purple.

4. **M. indica,** Linn.; Wight Ic. t. 674. Vern. *Tūt*, Pb.; *Siah tūt*, Hind.; *Tūt*, Beng.; *Posa*, Burm.

A deciduous tree, for silkworms grown as a shrub, l. ovate, caudate-acuminate, coarsely and unevenly serrate, blade 2–5, pet. ½–1 in., ♂ spikes lax, on short slender peduncles, ♀ spikes short ovoid, styles connate high up, very hairy. Fr. dark purple.

Wild in the subhimalayan tract in dry forest from the Sutlej eastwards, ascending to 5,000 ft. Fl. Febr., March. Extensively cultivated to feed the silkworm in Bengal and Burma. In the Punjab plains the Mulberry comes up readily from seed sown by birds. In December 1870 I first noticed an underwood of Mulberry in Sissoo plantations on islands of the Jhelum river. Since then the Mulberry has come up in all Sissoo plantations in the Punjab plains. Gamble (Ind. Timbers, ed. ii. 635) thinks it is *M. indica*. Specimens collected by me in Changa Manga, with white and red fr. are *M. alba*.

(*b*) Sepals thin, hyaline, equal, oblong, 3 or 4.

5. **M. serrata,** Roxb. Vern. *Karūn*, *Krūn*, *Chimu*, *Kimu*, N.-West Himal.

A large deciduous tree, up to 9 ft. diam., buds scaly, young shoots and underside of l. velvety tomentose. L. from a cordate base ovate, shortly acuminate, coarsely toothed, often deeply lobed, blade 3–8, pet. 1–2 in. long, stipules broadly lanceolate. ♂ spikes very hairy, 1–2 in. ♀ ½–1 in. long, cylindric, sepals densely ciliate, styles very hairy, connate below. Fr. purple.

Himalaya from Kashmir eastwards, 4–9,000 ft. Fl. Apr., May. Fr. June–Aug. Frequently lopped for cattle fodder and cultivated for that purpose.

B. Spikes 2–5 in. long.

6. **M. lævigata,** Wall. Vern. *Kimbu*, Nep.; *Tawpwèsa*, Burm. Outer Himalaya from Kumaon eastwards. Assam. Khasi Hills. Upper Burma. Martaban and Tenasserim (evergreen forests Thaungyin, March, 1859, D. B.). Cultivated as far north as Lahore. A large tree, young shoots, stipules and bud-scales with long soft hairs. L. ovate acuminate, finely serrate, blade 3–7, pet. 1–1½ in. Spikes drooping, ♂ very hairy, ♀ nearly glabrous, sepals thin, the 2 inner flat, the 2 outer keeled, ovary compound, oblique, styles nearly free, glabrous, papillose from the base, fr. long-cylindric, yellowish-white, insipid.

5. BROUSSONETIA, Vent.; Fl. Brit. Ind. v. 490.

Species 2–3, Indo-Malayan region, China, Japan, Pacific Islands.

B. papyrifera, Vent. *The Paper Mulberry.* Vern. *Malaing*, Burm.

A middle-sized deciduous tree, l. ovate, dentate, often lobed, upperside rough,

Fig. 189—Broussonetia papyrifera, Vent. ½.

underside softly tomentose, basal nerves 3, blade 4–8, pet. 1–2 in. long. Fl. diœcious, ♂ in cylindrical catkins, perianth 4-fid, segments valvate, stamens 4, long, inflexed in bud. ♀ in globose pedunculate heads, mixed with persistent bracts, perianth tubular, 2–4-toothed, persistent, including the stipitate ovary, style pink, filiform. Achenes hanging down on long fleshy stalks. Cotyledons oblong, albumen scanty.

Valley of the Maytharauk, Solo and other tributaries of the Salween river south of the Karennee country (D. B. Febr. 1859 and March 1880). Paper and the thick card-boards (Palabaik) used like slates in schools, are made of the inner bark in Siam and Burma. In Japan paper, and in the South Sea islands Tapa cloth is made of it. The tree is cultivated at Dehra Dún, it is hardy in Europe and is a most remarkable instance of a tree which thrives in temperate and tropical climates. Coppices well and throws up abundant root-suckers.

6. CUDRANIA, Trécul; Fl. Brit. Ind. v. 538.

Straggling or climbing shrubs, armed with stout axillary spines, l. alternate, quite entire, penninerved. Fl. in naked globose heads, diœcious, sessile, with bracteoles inserted on a globose receptacle. Sepals free, not connate, stamens included, anthers oblong, filaments short, ovary straight, style terminal, often appearing simple, through the abortion of one of its branches. Fr. a compound irregularly shaped many-sided berry formed of the enlarged fleshy bracteoles and perianths, each perianth enclosing a one-seeded nut. Species 7, from India to China, Japan, New Caledonia and Australia.

1. **C. javanensis**, Trécul.—Syn. *C. amboinensis*, Kurz F. Fl. ii. 434; *Cudranus Rumphii*, Thwaites; Bedd. Manual t. 27. Vern. *Manda*, Hind.; *Peinnè nwè*, Burm. Sub-himalayan tract from the Jumna eastwards. Assam. Chittagong. Upper Burma. Orissa (Prain). Ceylon. East Africa. Malay Penins. and Archip. Australia. China. Formosa. A straggling or scandent shrub, armed with straight or recurved axillary spines, bark very milky, branchlets pubescent. L. elongate-elliptic or oblanceolate, blade 1–4, pet. ¼–⅓ in. Fl.-heads yellow, pubescent, axillary, solitary or in pairs, ♂ ½ in. diam., ♀ smaller. Fr. velvety, green with a silvery tinge, 1–3 in. diam., seeds numerous. 2. **C. fruticosa**, Wight; Kurz F. Fl. ii. 434. Khasi hills. Chittagong. Burma, Upper and Lower. Branchlets glabrous, l. glabrous, elongate-elliptic, abruptly and thinly acuminate, blade 4–6, pet. ¼ in. long, sec. n. 3–4 pair prominent beneath. 3. **C. pubescens**, Trécul. Pegu Yoma, eastern slopes. Martaban (Kurz). Branchlets and underside of l. softly pubescent, no specimens seen.

7. PLECOSPERMUM, Trécul; Fl. Brit. Ind. v. 491.

Trees or shrubs, l. alternate, quite entire, penninerved. Fl. diœcious, perianth gamophyllous, ♂ closely packed, ♀ connate in dense globose heads. Stamens long-exserted, anthers globose, styles 1 or 2. Fr. an irregularly shaped fleshy syncarpium, 1- or few-seeded. Albumen 0, cotyledons thick, very unequal, the larger enclosing the smaller, which is folded lengthwise. Species 2.

1. **P. spinosum**, Trécul; Wight Ic. t. 1963. Vern. *Koriti*, Tel. Salt range. Sub-himalayan tract from the Punjab eastwards. Western Peninsula.—Ceylon, low country. A large thorny shrub, bark peeling off in thin flakes, branchlets minutely pubescent, spines stout, axillary, straight. L. glabrous, obovate or elliptic, blade 2–3, narrowed into pet. ¼–½ in. long. ♂ heads ¼ in. diam., peduncles ¼ in. long, often fascicled. Fr. pubescent, lobed, ½ in. diam. Resembles *Cudrania javanensis*, differs by the long exserted stamens and the few-seeded fr. 2. **P. andamanicum**, King. Andamans. Tenasserim. Unarmed, young shoots rusty tomentose, l. glabrous, coriaceous, elliptic-oblong, blade 4–6, pet. 1–1½ in. long. Fr. ⅝ in. diam., seeds 1 or 2.

Pseudostreblus indica, Hook. f. Khasi hills. A glabrous tree, sap milky, l. alternate, coriaceous, quite entire, elliptic-oblong, blade 4–6, pet. ¼ in., sec. n. slender, numerous, straight, joined by a distinct intramarginal nerve. Fl. monœcious, axillary, ♂ in short cymes, ♀ solitary or mixed with the ♂, sepals 4, orbicular concave, accrescent, enclosing the fr.

8. ANTIARIS, Leschen.; Fl. Brit. Ind. v. 537.

Species 5–6 Indo-Malayan region.

A. toxicaria, Leschen.—Syn. *A. saccidora*, Wight Ic. t. 1958; *A. innoxia*, Blume; Bedd. Fl. Sylv. t. 307. *The Upas tree.* Vern. *Karwat*, *Chandkura* Mar.; *Alli*, Tam.; *Aranji*, Kan.; *Hmyaseik*, Burm.

A very tall tree, attaining 250 ft. trunk often buttressed, young shoots, petioles, and midrib velvety. L. glabrous or hairy beneath, elliptic-oblong, acuminate, entire or serrulate, blade 3–6, pet. ¼ in. Fl. monœcious, ♂ crowded on the surface of flat pedunculate and usually fascicled receptacles, which are supported by imbricating bracts, sepals 3–4, stamens 3–8, ♀ solitary, enclosed in a pear-shaped involucre of numerous confluent bracts, perianth 0, ovary adnate to the involucre. Fr. red, velvety, fleshy, ¾ in. diam.

Evergreen forests of the Western Ghats from Khandala southwards. Wuntho, Upper Burma. Eastern slopes of the Pegu Yoma (Kurz). Fl. Sept., Oct. Tenasserim. In the lower Thaungyin this tree towers over the trees of the dense evergreen forest, which have a mean height of 200 ft. (Brandis, Attaran Report, 1860, p. 55). Bast very tough, made into ropes and sacks, the bottom of these being a section of the branch.—Ceylon, low country. Malay Penins. and Archip.

FIG. 190.—Antiaris toxicaria, Leschen ½.

9. STREBLUS, Lour.; Fl. Brit. Ind. v. 489.

S. asper, Lour. (probably the only species); Bedd. Man. t. 26.—Syn. *Epicarpurus orientalis*, Blume; Wight Ic. t. 1961. Vern. *Siora*, *Sahora*, *Dahia*, Hind.; *Poi*, *Kharota*, *Paraya*, Mar.; *Pakki*, Tel.; *Mitli*, Kan.; *Parayan*, *Pira*, Tam.; *Okhnè*. Burm.

A rigid shrub or small scraggy tree, all parts full of milky juice, branchlets hairy. L. elliptic or obovate, penninerved, irregularly dentate, rough on both sides with minute raised round dots, blade 2–4 in., pet. very short, stipules obliquely lanceolate. Fl. diœcious, ♂ in globose heads, perianth campanulate, deeply 4-fid, pubescent outside, segments imbricate, stamens long, inflexed in bud. ♀ solitary, on axillary usually fascicled peduncles, ¼ in. long, perianth of 4 decussate, closely imbricating sepals, styles 2, filiform, connate at base. Fr. a yellow, 1-seeded berry, enclosed in the enlarged fleshy sepals.

Subhimalayan tract from the Beas eastwards. Oudh forests. Bengal. Behar. Both Peninsulas, often near the coast. Fl. Jan.–March, leaves renewed in March. The l. used to polish wood and ivory, paper made of the bast.—Ceylon. Malay Penins. and Archip. *S. mitis*, Kurz F. Fl. ii. 464, is doubtful.

Balanostreblus ilicifolia, Kurz. Chittagong. Bhamo. Malay Penins. A small, nearly glabrous evergreen tree, branchlets often spinescent, l. rigidly coriaceous, shining, spinulose-dentate, broad-elliptic to elliptic-lanceolate, blade 1–5, pet. ⅛–¼ in. Fl. monœcious, ♂ in cylindric, catkin-like spikes, ♀ racemose, base of perianth connate with ovary, free above, mouth minute. Fr. a globose drupe, enclosed in the fleshy perianth.

Phyllochlamys spinosa, Bureau.—Syn. *Epicarpurus spinosus*, Wight Ic. t. 1962 (upper and right-hand figures); *Taxotrophis Roxburghii*, Blume; Bedd. Man. t. 26 fig. 3 (1–9); *Streblus taxoides*, Kurz. Vern. *Sukali*, Tel. Orissa. Hills of the Northern Circars, the Deccan and the Karnatik. Andamans. Swamp forests of the Irawadi alluvium.—

Ceylon, dry region. Malay Penins. and Archip. A small gnarled glabrous evergreen tree, armed with spinescent branchlets and straight sharp, woody spines, l. membranous, lanceolate or rhomboid-oblanceolate irregularly serrate, 1–4 in. long, pet. very short. Fl. diœcious, ♂ in clustered nearly sessile involucrate heads, ♀ solitary, perianth of 4 lanceolate sepals, much enlarged in fr., longer than the yellow cup-shaped pericarp, from which the seed, enclosed in a thin endocarp, protrudes in a way similar to the seed of *Taxus*.

Taxotrophis zeylanica, Thwaites; Bedd. Man. t. 26, fig. 3 (10–16).—Syn. *Epicarpurus zeylanica*, Thw.; Wight Ic. t. 1962 (the lower left-hand figure); *Streblus zeylanica*, Kurz. Western Duars, in places forming thickets at the foot of the hills. Upper Burma.—Ceylon. A large rigid shrub, sometimes armed with axillary spines, l. alternate, penninerved, membranous, serrate. Fl. diœcious, fr. obliquely subglobose, subtended by sepals, crowned by the lateral 2-partite style.

ORDER CI. URTICACEÆ. Engler in Engl. u. Prantl iii. 1. 98.

(*Urticaceæ*, tribe VII. *Urticeæ*. Gen. Pl. iii. 348.)

Mostly herbs, in a few genera shrubs and trees, sap watery L. as a rule dentate, alternate stipulate, with 3 basal nerves. Fl. unisexual, sessile, as a rule in compact heads or clusters, stamens 4–5, opposite to sepals or perianth-segments, filaments inflexed in bud; ♀ perianth campanulate, ovoid or tubular, free not confluent, often succulent in fr., rarely 0. Ovule erect, orthotropous.

Bast-fibres strongly developed in the bark, often very long. Cystolith cells conspicuous in the epidermis. No laticiferous tubes. Stinging hairs in some genera.

I. Branchlets, petioles and inflorescence armed with stinging hairs . . . . LAPORTEA (p. 616).

II. No stinging hairs.

- A. ♀ perianth tubular, ovoid or campanulate.
  - Fruiting heads dry.
    - Stigma filiform, persistent . . . 1. BŒHMERIA.
    - Stigma filiform, deciduous . . . POUZOLZIA (p. 617).
  - Fruiting heads succulent.
    - Style long-exserted, curved . . . PIPTURUS (p. 617).
    - Stigma sessile, ciliate or pedunculate.
      - Perianth obliquely campanulate . . SARCOCHLAMYS (p. 618).
      - Perianth ovoid, mouth minute.
        - L. white or grey beneath, tertiary n. parallel, prominent . . . . 2. DEBREGEASIA.
        - L. green beneath, tertiary n. not prominent . . . . . . 3. VILLEBRUNEA.
- B. ♀ perianth 0 . . . . MAOUTIA (p. 619).

Laportea crenulata, Gaud.; Bedd. Fl. Sylv. t. 306.—Syn. *Urtica crenulata*, Roxb.; Wight Ic. t. 686. Vern. *Chorpatta*, Beng.; *Otta-pilavu*, Tam.; *Ana-choriya*, Mal.; *Pet-ya-gyi*, Burm. Subhimalayan tract from Nepal eastwards. Assam. Silhet. Cachar. Maimansingh. Lower Burma. Rumpa hills, Northern Circars. Western coast, ascending to 5,000 ft. on the Ghats.—Ceylon. A shrub or small tree, branchlets, petioles, and inflorescence clothed with hairs of two kinds (minute and long stinging), l. ovate or elliptic, crenulate in the upper part or nearly entire, blade 6–14, pet. 1–4 in. long, with a few long hairs, otherwise glabrous, round raised cystolith cells prominent on both surfaces. Fl. minute, green, diœcious, in axillary panicled cymes, longer than petioles, ♂: perianth deeply 4-fid. Achenes oblique, ⅛ in. diam., seated on the cup-shaped perianth and crowned by the style. The sting of this Nettle is very bad and the effects last for many days.

1. BŒHMERIA, Jacq.; Fl. Brit. Ind. v. 575.

Shrubs or small trees, a few herbs, l. opposite and alternate, 3-nerved, toothed, stipules usually free. Fl. in unisexual sessile clusters. ♂: perianth 3–5-partite, valvate, pistillode clavate or globose. ♀: perianth tubular, 2–4-toothed, including the ovary, stigma filiform, long-exserted, persistent.

A. Fl. clusters axillary or from the axils of fallen l.

1. **B. malabarica,** Wedd.—Syn. *B. travancorica*, Bedd. Man. 225, t. 27 fig. 2. Subhimalayan tract from Sikkim eastwards, ascending to 5,000 ft. Assam. Khasi hills. Chittagong. Burma. Western Ghats from the Konkan southwards.—Ceylon. Java. A shrub or small tree, l. alternate, glabrous above, usually pubescent beneath, crenate, blade 4–8, pet. 1–4 in. long. Clusters ⅛–¼ in. diam. 2. **B. sidæfolia,** Wedd.—Syn. *B. diffusa*, Wedd. Subhimalayan tract and outer hills, from Nepal eastwards, ascending to 6 ,000 ft. Khasi hills. Burma. Branchlets, l. on both sides and fl. clusters usually hispid with long hairs, l. sometimes opposite, fl. clusters often on naked branchlets with a tuft of l. at the end. Two sp. mentioned by Kurz are more or less herbaceous; 3. **B. Helferi,** Blume. Tenasserim. 4. **B. Didymogyne,** Wedd. Moulmein.

B. Fl. clusters in usually long and simple spikes.

(*a*) L. alternate.

5. **B. rugulosa,** Wedd. Vern. *Genti*, *Genthi*, Hind.; *Dar*, Nep. Subhimalayan tract and outer hills, ascending to 4,000 ft., from the Sutlej eastwards. A small or middle-sized tree, l. thinly coriaceous, upperside dark green, glabrous but rough, underside velvety, pale, often white, obtusely but distinctly crenulate, elliptic-lanceolate, blade 2–5, pet. ½–1½ in., stipules connate, basal n. prominent, extending to the tip of leaf, tert. n. elegantly reticulate and joined by intramarginal veins. Spikes simple, clusters supported by cordate bracts. Wood reddish-brown, even-grained, seasons well and is easy to work. 6. **B. nivea,** Hook. et Arn.—Syn. *Urtica tenacissima*, Roxb.; Wight Ic. t. 688. *The Rhea plant. China grass.* Indigeneous and cultivated in China and Japan. Cultivated in Assam and elsewhere. A shrub with herbaceous branches, tomentose with long hairs, l. broad-ovate, acuminate, dentate, upperside rough, underside usually white, densely matted with appressed hairs. Fl. greenish, monœcious, in axillary unisexual panicles, shorter than leaves, which generally are in pairs, ♂ panicles in the lower, ♀ in the upper axils, style much exserted, hairy. A variety with the leaves green on both surfaces ("*Ramie*") is distinguished as *B. tenacissima*, Gaud.

(*b*) L. as a rule opposite, petioles in one pair unequal.

7. **B. macrophylla,** Don. Vern. *Bara Siáru*, Dehra Dún; *Kamli*, Nep. Subhimalayan tract and outer valleys, ascending to 4,000 ft. from the Jumna eastwards. Singbhum. —Yunnan. A large shrub or small tree, branchlets, petioles and underside of l. strigose with short stiff hairs, l. lanceolate gradually tapering into a narrow point, evenly serrulate, rugulose and pustular above, blade 6–12, pet. ½–1 in. long. Fl. monœcious, spikes drooping, as long as or longer than l., clusters ⅛–¼ in. diam. 8. **B. Kurzii,** Hook. f. Pegu. Glabrous, excepting the pubescent spikes. L. elliptic-lanceolate, entire, blade 3–7, pet. 1–1½ in. long. Spikes slender, longer than l. 9. **B. Hamiltoniana,** Wedd. Vern. *Satcha*, Burm. Subhimalayan tract and outer hills, ascending to 5,000 ft., from Nepal eastwards. Assam. Khasi hills. Pegu and Martaban. Glabrous, except the pubescent spikes, l. membranous, crenulate, lanceolate, blade 4–7, pet. 1–3 in. long. Spikes slender. 10. **B. polystachya,** Wedd. Outer Himalaya, 2–7,000 ft., from Kumaon eastwards. Assam. Khasi hills. Salween hills, Martaban 3,000 ft. (D. B. March 1880).—Yunnan. Glabrous, branches stout, l. broadly ovate, deeply dentate, broad-ovate, blade 4–10, pet. ½–2 in., spikes panicled, shorter than the l.

11. **B. platyphylla,** Don.—Syn. *B. caudata*, Poiret. Vern. *Siár*, Dehra Dún; *Khaksha*, Garhwal; *Kamli*, Nepal. Outer Himalaya, ascending to 7,500 ft. Assam. Khasi hills. Chittagong. Burma. Chutia Nagpúr. Orissa. Central Provinces, Western Peninsula.—Ceylon, moist region, common.—Malay Archip. China Japan. Africa. A large shrub, l. sometimes alternate, broadly ovate, elliptic or orbicular, acuminate, coarsely toothed, more or less rough, spikes often sparingly branched. An exceedingly variable plant, of which 9 principal varieties are recognized in Fl. Brit. Ind. v. 578. Prain, Bengal Plants 964, regards *B. scabrella*, Gaud., with short stout erect fruiting spikes as a distinct species.

Pouzolzia viminea, Wedd.—Syn. *P. borbonica*, Wight Ic. t. 2100 fig. 44. Vern. *Chipali*, Nep. Outer Himalaya from Kashmir eastwards, ascending to 6,000 ft. Assam. Khasi hills. Chittagong. Upper Burma. Malay Penins. A large shrub with long slender branches, stunted in dry localities, branchlets, and petioles more or less strigose, l. usually white on the underside. L. ovate-lanceolate, acuminate, dentate, blade 1–6, pet. ¼–1 in. long, basal n. 3, the lateral extending to ⅔ the length of l. or further, sec. n. usually prominent. Fl. monœcious or diœcious, in sessile axillary clusters, ♀ perianth tubular, mouth narrow, 3–5-toothed, stigma filiform, deciduous.

Pipturus velutinus, Wedd.—Syn. *Morus paniculata*, Roxb.; Wight Ic. t. 676. Nicobars Malay Penins. and Archip. New Guinea. A small tree, branchlets, petioles and underside of l. grey or silvery pubescent, l. broadly ovate, base often cordate, crenate, blade 4–8, pet. 2–4 in. long. Fl. diœcious, in globose heads on simple or branched spikes. ♀ perianth ovoid, narrowed to a minute mouth. Syncarpium white, pellucid, formed by the succulent perianth, ¼ in. diam., enclosing numerous achenes.

Sarcochlamys pulcherrima, Gaud. Vern. *Satcha*, Burm. Assam. Khasi hills. East Bengal. Chittagong. Lower Burma, abundant on deserted Taungyas.—Sumatra. A large shrub or small tree, evergreen, branchlets pubescent, l. alternate, lanceolate, serrate, upperside rough but shining, underside white and grey-pubescent or velvety, basal n. 3, strong, the lateral extending to the tip, sec. n. and tert. n. elegantly reticulate, the meshes quadranglar, blade 4–7, pet. 1–2 in. long. Spikes sessile, branching, 1–3 in. long, clusters confluent. ♀ perianth campanulate, accrescent and fleshy in fr.

2. DEBREGEASIA, Gaud.; Fl. Brit. Ind. v. 590.

Shrubs or trees, l. alternate, 3-nerved, midrib and lateral n. on the outside penninerved, tert. n. parallel, stipules bifid. Fl. sessile, not connate, in round compact heads, which are sessile on the branches or arranged in dichotomous panicles. ♀ receptacle fleshy, perianth ovoid or obovoid, mouth minute, succulent in fr. Stigma penicillate, sessile or nearly so. Species 5, from Abyssinia to Japan.

A. L. narrow, petiole short.

1, **D. velutina,** Gaud.—Syn. *Conocephalus niveus*, Wight Ic. t. 1959; *Morocarpus longifolius*, Blume; Bedd. Man. t. 26 fig. 5. Vern. *Tashiari, Sansaru, Siaru*, Hind.; *Put chaw*, Lower, *Kyet Kyidauk*, Upper Burma. Outer Himalaya, 2–7,000 ft., from the Jumna eastwards. Assam. Khasi hills. Burma, Upper and Lower, often in deserted Taungyas. Western Ghats from the Konkan southwards.—Ceylon, moist region up to 3,000 ft., common, Java. A shrub or small tree, young shoots silky with long hairs, branchlets, pet. and underside of l. grey-pubescent or tomentose, l. lanceolate, serrulate, upperside rough and uneven, blade 3–6, pet. ½ in. Heads in small lateral dichotomous panicles, fr. bright orange-yellow, edible. 2. **D. hypoleuca,** Wedd.—Syn. *D. bicolor*, Wedd. Vern. *Chinjli*, Haz.; *Siaru, Seharu*, Hind. North-West Himalaya, Indus to Sarda, 2–6,500 ft.—Afghanistan, Abyssinia, common in ravines and on the edge of rice terraces. A large shrub, sometimes a small tree, branchlets and underside of l. clothed with snow-white wool, l. serrulate, lanceolate, upperside rough, blade 3–6, pet. ¼–1 in. long. Fl.-heads sessile or nearly so. ♂ ⅕ in. diam., stamens exserted, ♀ smaller, fr. amber-coloured, edible.

B. L. broad-ovate, pet. long.

3. **D. Wallichiana,** Wedd.—Syn. *Morocarpus Wallichianus*, Kurz. Sikkim 4–7,000 ft. Assam. Khasi hills. Pegu Yoma, rare in the upper mixed forests. Tenasserim. A small tree, sometimes epiphytic, l. sinuate-dentate, sometimes entire, white beneath with closely appressed tomentum, glabrous above, blade 5–12, pet. 3–10 in. long. Fl.-heads in dichotomous cymes, peduncles 2–3 in. long, fruiting heads ¼ in. diam., very succulent, glassy white, tips of perianth pink. 4. **D. dentata,** Hook. f. Chittagong. A large shrub, l. membranous, serrate, upperside rough, underside ashy-grey with minute hairs, blade 4–8, pet. 2–6 in. long, fl.-heads in shortly peduncled cymes, peduncles and ramifications slender.

3. VILLEBRUNEA, Gaud.; Fl. Brit. Ind. v. 589.

Trees or shrubs, l. alternate. Fl. usually diœcious, sessile in compact heads, but not connate. ♂ stamens exserted. ♀: perianth tubular-ventricose, adnate to the ovary and enclosing it, stigma sessile, discoid, long papillose-ciliate. Fl. supported by connate bracteoles, which in fr. become succulent, enclosing the lower portion of the achene. Species 8, eastern Asia.

1. **V. integrifolia,** Gaud.—Syn. *Oreocnide acuminata*, Kurz; *O. sylvatica*, Miq.: Bedd. Man. t. 26 fig. 4. Outer Himalaya, 2–5,000 ft., from Nepal eastwards. Assam. Cachar. Manipúr. Chittagong. Andamans. Burma, Upper and Lower.—Tonkin. Ceylon. On deserted Taungyas in the Yunzalin district. A small evergreen tree, branchlets, petioles, l. beneath and inflorescence pubescent or tomentose, l. elongate-elliptic, penninerved, entire or obscurely crenate, blade 8–16, pet. 1–6 in., stipules ½–1 in. long, deciduous, clothed with long silky hairs. Fl.-heads in lateral dichotomous fascicled panicles 1 in. long. 2. **V. frutescens,** Blume. Vern. *Gar-tushiara*, Kum. Subhimalayan tract and outer Himalaya, from the Sutlej eastwards, ascending to 5,000 ft. Khasi hills. China. Japan. A shrub with slender pubescent branches, l. serrate, with 3 basal n. Fl.-heads sessile or shortly pedunculate.

Maoutia Puya, Wedd. Subhimalayan tract from the Jumna eastwards, ascending to 4,000 ft. Khasi hills. Shan hills. Martaban hills, 2,500–5,000 ft. Vern. *Poi, Pua* Hind.; *Puya*, Nep. A shrub, young shoots silky with long hairs, branchlets, petiole, and upperside of l. hairy, underside densely clothed with a white felt, l. alternate, elliptic, acuminate, coarsely dentate, basal n. 3, blade 3–8, pet. 1–4 in. long. Fl.-heads small, often androgynous, in lateral dichotomous panicles. ♀ perianth 0, achenes with a thick fleshy pericarp.

ORDER CII. **Platanaceæ.**—*Platanus orientalis*, Linn. B. Clarke on *Plataneæ* in Annals and Mag. of Nat. Hist. 3rd Series i. 102 (1858); Schoenland in Engler's Jahrbuch iv. 308 (1883). *Oriental Plane.* Vern. *Chinār*, Persian; *Buna, Boin, Bhunj*, Kashmir. Indigenous in the eastern Mediterranean region. Cultivated in Afghanistan and the N.W. Himalaya, particularly in Kashmir, eastwards to the Sutlej, in Ladak ascending to 8,300 ft. It grows well at Peshawar and at the foot of the North-Western Himalaya. A large deciduous tree, bark of young trees always, of old trees frequently, peeling off in large thin flakes, buds densely clothed with long hairs, branchlets and young l. with soft deciduous tawny or ferrugineous tomentum. L. alternate, palminerved, glabrous when mature, deeply 3–5-lobed, blade 5–8, pet. 1–3 in., stipules large, deciduous. Fl. monœcious, in unisexual usually sessile globose heads, 2–5 on long axillary peduncles, ♂ and ♀ heads sometimes on the same peduncle, sepals 3–6, petals as many, all extremely minute scale-like, often more or less confluent, formerly regarded as bracteoles. ♂: Stamens as many as sepals, each consisting of a long almost sessile anther, the 2 cells parallel, adnate to a cuneate connective with a truncate top. ♀: Ovaries hairy at base, as many as sepals, surrounded by staminodes, narrowed into a long subulate style, ovule 1 pendulous. Fruiting head 1–1½ in. diam., consisting of numerous 1-seeded achenes, densely clothed at base with long fine hairs, the broad apex narrowed gradually into the persistent long style. Seedlings slender, cotyledons raised above the ground. *P. occidentalis*, Linn.; Sargent Silva vii. 102, of the Eastern and Central U.S. of North America, differs by fewer fl.-heads (1–3) on the peduncle, achene truncate, style early deciduous. *P. acerifolia*, Willd., the London Plane, is generally regarded as a variety of *P. orientalis*.

ORDER CIII. JUGLANDACEÆ. Gen. Pl. iii. 397 (*Juglandeæ*).

Trees, rarely shrubs, l. alternate, pinnate, often aromatic, stipules 0. Axillary buds often several superposed in a vertical series. Fl. monœcious, ♂ in lateral pendulous catkins, anthers 2 or more, nearly sessile, inserted on the upper surface of a bract, which bears on its edge 2–6 membranous perianth-lobes. ♀ in few-fld. erect terminal or in many-fld. lateral spikes, perianth adnate to the 1-celled ovary, ovule 1, erect. Fr. a 2-valved nut or drupe, seed exalbuminous, cotyledons oily, lobed, radicle superior.

Peltate scales with an orbicular blade of radiating cells. No resin canals.

♀ fl. terminal, solitary or 2–3. Bracts not enlarged in fr.
Drupe with leathery pericarp and woody endocarp . . 1. JUGLANS.

♀ fl. in lateral pendulous spikes. Nut coriaceous, adnate to the much enlarged 3-lobed bracts . . . . 2. ENGELHARDTIA.

1. JUGLANS, Linn.; Fl. Brit. Ind. v. 595.

Species 10, of which 3 in the Old World.

J. regia, Linn. *The Walnut.* Vern. *Dūn*, Kashm.; *Thān*, Pangi; *Khol, Kā*, Kunawar; *Khor, Akhor*, Hind. (fruit: *Akhrot*); *Thitcha*, Burm.

A large deciduous aromatic tree, young shoots tomentose. L. imparipinnate, leaflets 5–13, subsessile, opposite or nearly so, usually entire, those of seedlings serrate. ♂ catkins on the previous year's wood above the leaf-scars, often two superposed, green, 2–5 in. long, bracts stalked, ¼ in. long, perianth-lobes 5–6, anthers 10–20, oblong apiculate. ♀ fl. sessile, terminal, solitary or 2–3, limb of calyx minute, indistinctly 4-toothed, petals linear-lanceolate, green, usually minute. Fr. 2 in. long, green, pericarp leathery, very aromatic, enclosing an irregularly furrowed more or less thick-shelled nut, which is divided by two thin coriaceous dissepiments into four incomplete cells, one

dissepiment separating the 2 cotyledons, the other dividing them into 2 lobes. The cotyledons remain underground when germinating.

Indigenous trans-Indus in the Kuram valley, the North-West Himalaya, Sikkim and the hills of Upper Burma. Cultivated in the North-West Himalaya from 3,500 to nearly 11,000 ft., also in the inner arid valleys. Fl. Feb.–April. Mountains of Greece and Western Asia. Cultivated in China.

2. ENGELHARDTIA, Leschen.; Fl. Brit. Ind. v. 595.

Species 6, India, Malaya, China.

1. **E. spicata**, Blume, including *E. Roxburghiana*, Lindley, *E. aceriflora*, Blume, *E. Colebrookiana*, Lindl. in Wall. Pl. As. Rar. t. 208 and *E. villosa*, Kurz. Vern. *Mowa, Gadmawa*, Hind.; *Petsut, Thitsawbwa*, Upper, *Taungtamasôk*, Lower Burma; *Pyinsit*, Mergui.

A large, in places a small, deciduous monœcious tree, often gregarious, wood pink-grey with a satiny lustre on the radial section. Branchlets, petioles and underside of l. from glabrous or slightly hairy to densely tomentose, usually with numerous shining orbicular glands. L. as a rule paripinnate (by abortion of the terminal leaflet), leaflets 6–14, sessile or shortly petiolulate, nearly opposite, 3–10 in. long, usually entire, in young plants serrate. ♂ fl. in slender often panicled catkins, 3–7 in. long, from the previous year's wood. Perianth of 4–5 variously shaped scales, adnate to a generally 3-lobed bract. Anthers 4–12, hispid, mucronate, nearly sessile, inserted on the upper surface of the bract. ♀ fl. in bracteate pendulous spikes 6–12 in. long, often in the same panicle with the ♂ catkins. Bracts cup-shaped, with 3 large unequal lobes enclosing the base of the glabrous or hairy calyx, which is adnate to the ovary, limb 4-dentate, petals 0, style divided into 2–4 densely papillose branches. Fr. a small globose, coriaceous, 1-seeded nut, adnate to the greatly enlarged scarious reticulate 3-lobed bract, the base of which is densely tomentose with long hairs, lobes spathulate-oblong, obtuse, with a conspicuous midrib, the middle one 1–1¼ in. long, the 2 lateral half that length. Cotyledons foliaceous, much folded and twisted.

Subhimalayan tract and outer hills, ascending to 6,000 ft., from the Chenab eastwards. Assam. Khasi hills. Manipúr. Chittagong. Burma, Upper and Lower, ascending to 6,000 ft. Leafless only a very short time, fl. at different times from Sept. to May. Coppices well and reproduces readily from self-sown seed.—Malay Penins. and Archip. China. Three different species are doubtfully recognized in Fl. Brit. Ind. v. 595. (*a*) *E. spicata*, Blume. Nepal to Burma. Java. Cochinchina. Leaflets petiolulate, pubescent beneath, at length glabrous. (*b*) *E. aceriflora*, Blume; Prain Bengal Plants 984. From Sikkim to Burma. Yunnan. Ind. Archip. Leaflets sessile. (*c*) *E. Colebrookiana*, Lindley; Gamble Ind. Timbers Ed. ii. 664. From the Punjab to Burma.—China. Leaflets petiolulate, tomentose beneath, branchlets and petioles tomentose. 2. **E. polystachya**, Radlk. in Sitzungsberichte d. Königl. Bayer. Akademie d. Wissensch. Mathem. Physikal. Classe, 1878, 385. East Bengal (Griffith No. 1020/3) imperfectly known, glabrous but clothed with golden peltate glands.

ORDER CIV. **Myricaceæ.**—*Myrica Nagi*, Thunb.; Collett Simla Fl. 470, Fig. 151.—Syn. *M. sapida*, Wall.; *M. integrifolia*, Roxb.; Wight Ic. t. 764, 765. Outer Himalaya from the Ravi eastwards, 3–6,000 ft., not known from Sikkim. Khasi hills. Martaban and Tenasserim.—Malay Penins. and Archip. China. Japan. Vern. *Kaiphal*, Hind. A moderate-sized evergreen aromatic monœcious or diœcious tree, branchlets pubescent. L. alternate, coriaceous, lanceolate or oblanceolate, entire, on young plants membranous, with large and sharp serratures, underside pale or rust-coloured, with resinous dots, stipules 0. ♂ fl. in cylindric catkins, usually racemose on a common peduncle, occasionally with ♀ fl. at the top, stamens 3–6 with several small scales in the axils of broad bracts, filaments short. ♀ fl. in solitary slender axillary catkins; 1–3 one-celled ovaries, surrounded by glandular bracteoles, in the axil of each bract, styles 2, stout, recurved, ovule 1 erect, orthotropous. Fr. edible, red or brown, sessile, few on axillary peduncles, globose or ovoid, tubercled, ½–¾ in. long, endocarp long, pericarp fleshy. Albumen 0, cotyledons plano-convex, radicle superior.

ORDER CV. **Casuarinaceæ.**—*Casuarina equisetifolia*, Forst. Vern. *Chowku*, Tel.; *Tinyu, Pinlè-Kabwè*, Burm. Sand hills on the coast of Chittagong, Tenasserim and the Andamans. Largely cultivated for the production of fuel on the Coromandel Coast, on the coast of North Kanara and in places inland in the Peninsula. Planted in gardens and as a roadside tree in Central and Northern India, North as far as Ambala.—Malay Penins. and Archip. Australia. Pacific islands.

A tall, straight-stemmed tree, the ends of branches thickly set with numerous long slender branchlets, which are mostly deciduous and fulfil the function of leaves. Branchlets jointed, the internodes ⅙–¼ in. long, 6–8-ribbed, with fine hairs at the bottom of the furrows between the ribs and stomata in the furrows only. The ribs of each joint terminate upwards in the teeth of a membranous sheath, alternating with the ribs of the next joint above. Opposite these teeth are axillary vegetative buds, of which as a rule only one or a few grow out into branchlets. These axillary buds mostly develop at the ends of branchlets, where the joints have not yet lengthened out. Here the teeth of the annular sheaths are much longer (up to ⅛ in.) than on the lower and older joints, and they are densely clothed with fine hairs.

The leaftraces or vascular bundles, which enter the teeth of the sheath, giving off branches to the axillary buds, leave the central cylinder at the base of the internode and run in the bark through its entire length; hence a transverse section of a branchlet shows, outside the central cylinder, a detached vascular bundle under each rib and between two furrows. The wood-fibres have bordered pits, and on a transverse section of the wood numerous wavy concentric bands of soft wood parenchyma are conspicuous.

Fl. unisexual, ♂ monandrous, axillary under the teeth of the annular sheaths of terminal short-jointed cylindric spikes 1 in. long. Perianth of 2 large scales enclosing the anthers, and 2 smaller ones at right angles to the first, anthers oblong, 4-celled, filament short. ♀ in small ovoid spikes at the ends of lateral branchlets, consisting of very short joints, one fl. under each tooth of the annular sheath, Perianth of 2 large scales enclosing the ovary, which, as the seed ripens, grow out into 2 large woody valves, more or less hairy, supported before maturity by the tooth of the sheath. Ovary 1-celled, with 2 pendulous ovules, only one of which develops into a seed. Style short, dividing into 2 long filiform, garnet-coloured branches. Fr. a woody globose cone, ⅗ in. diam., testa adnate to the walls of the achene, which terminates in a long membranous wing, albumen 0, embryo straight, radicle superior, cotyledons flat. The cotyledons rise above the ground, followed by a pair of leaves, and afterwards by several whorls of four. The tree is monœcious, ♂ and ♀ fl. are sometimes found on the same branch, but (as often happens with monœcious trees) some trees habitually bear male, others female fl. only.

In Indian Timbers ed. ii. 665, Mr. Gamble justly states that the importance of the *Casuarina* for reclaiming the stretches of sand on the Coromandel coast cannot be overestimated. The production of wood is rapid, 250 cub. ft. of wood (15,000 lb.) per acre per annum; moreover, other trees and shrubs come up under its shelter, and it thus prepares the ground for a more varied forest growth. The wood is very hard, cracks and splits, but makes excellent fuel.

ORDER CVI. **BETULACEÆ.** Prantl in Engler u. Prantl iii. 1. 38.

(*Cupuliferæ*, tribes I. *Betuleæ*, II. *Coryleæ*, Gen. Pl. iii. 403.)

Trees, sometimes shrubs, monœcious, with few exceptions deciduous. L. alternate, usually penninerved, undivided, as a rule serrate, stipules deciduous. Fl. buds ready formed in autumn, open early in spring, with or before the l. ♂ fl. in drooping catkins, anther-cells as a rule distinct. ♀ fl. in long or short spikes, 2 or 3 fl. in the axil of one or several bracts. Each fl. consists of a 2-celled ovary, one pendulous ovule in each cell, and 2 long filiform styles, perianth 0 or adnate to ovary. Fr. indehiscent, seed one, cotyledons usually oily, radicle superior, albumen 0. The cotyledons of *Corylus* remain underground, those of the other genera here described are raised above ground when germinating.

Most species of *Alnus*, *Carpinus* and *Corylus* have, besides the fine med. rays, others which may be called compound rays, consisting of a number of fine sometimes broader rays alternating with elongated parenchymatic cells and wood-fibres. These compound rays run through the ordinary tissue which is traversed by vessels The wood fibres as a rule have bordered pits.

A. Stamens 4–12 on each bract, more or less distinctly arranged in 3 fl., each with a perianth of 2–4 leaves, anther-cells without tufts of hairs. Ovary without perianth.
- Anther-cells distinct, scales of ♀ spikes thin, deciduous . . . 1. BETULA.
- Anther-cells distinct or connate, scales of ♀ spikes persistent, woody in fr. . . . . 2. ALNUS.

B. One 3–6-androus fl. on each bract without perianth, anther-cells with a tuft of hairs. A thin perianth adnate to ovary.
- Fr. small in drooping spikes, in the axil of large membranous reticulate bracts . . . . 3. CARPINUS.
- Fr. a large nut enclosed in a thick, cut and lobed, sometimes spinescent involucre . . . . 4. CORYLUS.

1. BETULA, Tourn.; Fl. Brit. Ind. v. 599.

Pith oblong, often lobed, med. rays all narrow, of 1–4 rows of cells. Stamens 4–6, inserted on the stalk or on the inside of the bract and more or less distinctly arranged into diandrous fl., each with 2 or 4 perianth leaves, one of which is much larger than the others. Anthers on very short filaments, the 2 cells distinct to the base. ♀ fl. in dense cylindric spikes, 3 ovaries in the axil of a deciduous bract, which usually is 3-fid. Nuts winged. Species 24, Northern hemisphere.

FIG. 191.—Betula utilis, Don. ½.

1. **B. utilis**, Don.—Syn. *B. Bhojpattra*, Wall.; *B. Jacquemontii*, Spach in Jacquemont Voy. Bot. t. 158. Vern. *Bhuj*, *Burj*, *Bhuj pattra*, N.-West Himal.; *Shāk*, *pad*, Kunawar; *Bhuja pat*, Nep.

A moderate-sized tree, attaining at times 60 ft., a shrub near its upper limit, bark smooth, with white horizontal lenticels, the outer bark consisting of numerous thin papery layers, exfoliating in broad horizontal rolls, youngest shoots pubescent. L. ovate, acuminate, unequally serrate, slightly hairy along midrib and nerves, blade 2–3, pet. ½ in. long. Bracts of ♂ fl. nearly glabrous, anther-cells with a few hairs at the tip. ♀ spikes solitary, bracts pubescent, 3-lobed down to the base. Nuts with a narrow wing, bracts in fr. coriaceous, deeply 3-lobed, broader than the wings of the nut.

Kuram valley, 10–11,000 ft. Himalaya, 10–14,000, in the Punjab as low as 7,000 ft., also in the inner arid region. Often gregarious at the upper limit of tree vegetation, associated with *Rhododendron campanulatum*, and with an underwood of *Rhododendron Anthopogon*,—Mountains of China and Japan. The outer bark is used as paper for writing and packing, for umbrella covers and for the roofing of houses. 2. **B. alnoides**, Ham.—Syn. *B. acuminata*, Wall. Pl. As. Rar. t. 109; Brandis F. Fl. t. 56; *B. nitida*, Don; *B. cylindrostachys*, Wall. Vern. *Sheori*, Bash.; *Kath bhuj*, Jauns.; *Sauer*, Garhw., Nepal. Himalaya from the Sutlej eastwards, 5–10,000 ft. Khasi hills. Manipúr. Hills of Upper and Lower Burma above 5,000 ft. At times gregarious in patches.—China. A moderate-sized tree, wood grey, the outer bark peels off in thick rolls, the lenticels shorter than in 1, branchlets and underside of young l. softly pubescent, root-suckers and luxuriant shoots densely tomentose. L. ovate to ovate-lanceolate, serrate, teeth cuspidate, often aristate. Bracts of ♂ catkins pubescent, with 3 diandrous fl. on the midrib, perianth of 4 hairy linear l. ♀ spikes panicled, nuts with a wing much broader than nut, bracts in fr. membranous, narrower than the wings of the nut, with 2 obtuse or acute teeth or short lobes.

Gamble, List ed. ii. 79 and Indian Timbers ed. ii. 669, mentions *B. cylindrostachys*, Gamble, as a distinct low level species: Darjeeling hills from the Terai to 6,000 ft. A large tree, 80 to 100 ft. high, bark peeling off in large vertical flakes, wood red, hard, seasons well, heavier than *B. alnoides*. This species merits careful study.

2. ALNUS, Gærtn.; Fl. Brit. Ind. v. 600.

Pith similar to *Betula*, med. rays in most species of two classes, a few compound with numerous narrow rays. L. on the underside often with tufts of hairs in the axils of the sec. n. ♂ catkins pendulous, usually 12 stamens in the axil of a membranous bract, more or less distinctly arranged in 3 tetrandrous fl., the stamens opposite to the 4 l. of the perianth, filaments usually short, anther-cells distinct or more or less connate, ♀ spikes short erect, 2 ovaries in the axil of the bract, each ovary with 2 bracteoles. Fruit a small cone, bracts and bracteoles coalescing and becoming woody, covering the small crustaceous 1-seeded nuts. Species 15, Northern temperate zone.

1. **A. nepalensis,** Don; Wall. Pl. As. Rar. t. 131. Vern. *Piak*, Chamba; *Kuntz*, *Ni*, *Neun*, Bash.; *Kunis*, Garhw.; *Utis*, Kumaon, Nepal. Himalaya 3–9,000 ft., from the Ravi eastwards. Khasi hills. Upper Burma 6,000 ft. Yunnan. A large tree, bark smooth, silvery-grey, branchlets glabrous. L. elliptic, entire or slightly denticulate, blade 3–8, pet. ½–¾ in., sec. n. 10–18 pair. Anther-cells connate. Cones nearly cylindric, ½–1 in. long, in lateral panicles. Nut with a narrow somewhat irregular membranous wing. 2. **A. nitida,** Endl.; Brandis F. Fl. t. 57. Vern. *Sharól*, Haz.; *Koish*, Kulu; *Kunsh*, Bash.; *Utis*, *Kunis*, Hind. North-West Himalaya, extending eastwards to the Jumna, usually at low elevations, fringing the banks of rivers, not uncommonly descending with them some distance into the plains, in places, however, ascending to 9,000 ft. On the Sutlej common in the dry region of Kunawar as far as Spui on the right and Namgia on the left bank. A large tree, bark blackish, with thin quadrangular scales, branchlets and petioles pubescent. L. glabrous, thinly coriaceous, elliptic-ovate, entire or obscurely crenate, blade 4–6, pet. 1 in. Anther-cells nearly distinct. Cones ¾–1½ in. long, three to five in erect lateral racemes, nut with a narrow thickened edge.

3. CARPINUS, Tourn.; Fl. Brit. Ind. v. 625.

Pith oblong, usually 6-sided, leaf-buds elongated, protected by imbricating scales, l. membranous, serrate. ♂ catkins lateral, sessile, drooping. In the axil of a broad-ovate scale 3–6 stamens on short filaments, anther-cells distinct, shortly stipitate. ♀ spikes terminal, pairs of fl. in the axils of deciduous bracts, each fl. supported by a persistent often 3-lobed inner bract or involucre, which in fr. is much enlarged, prominently veined and reticulate. Perianth adnate to ovary, limb dentate. Species 12, Northern hemisphere.

1. **C. viminea,** Wall. Pl. As. Rar. t. 106. Vern. *Lolti*, *Kosh*, Bash.; *Kangei*, *Shinroi*, *Shangri*, Jaunsar; *Phamnai*, Kumaon. Himalaya, 5–7,000 ft., from the Chenab eastwards. Khasi hills. Mogok, Upper Burma, 4,000 ft. Hills between Sitang and Salween rivers, 3,500–6,000 ft., common near streams on the Upper Yunzalin (D. B. March 1880). Yunnan. A moderate-sized tree, stems fluted, bark of young trees whitish, smooth, of old trees grey with darker streaks, branches verrucose. L. glabrous, ovate-lanceolate, caudate-acuminate, the serratures serrulate on the outside, blade 3–5, pet. slender, often hairy, ¼–½ in., sec. n. 10–12 pair. ♂ bracts ribbed, shining, but ciliate along the edge, anther-cells with a tuft of long hairs at the tip. Fruiting bracts lanceolate, unequal-sided, more or less serrate, often with a lobe near base. 2. **C. faginea,** Lindl.; Brandis F. Fl. t. 66. On the Bias, 4–5,500 ft. in the Sutlej, Upper Tons and Rupin valleys, 6–7,000 ft. Kumaon. Bhutan.—China. A moderate-sized tree, branchlets, young l. and petioles clothed with soft silky hairs, l. thinly membranous elongate-elliptic, acuminate, serratures cuspidate, blade 3–5, pet. ⅛–¼ in., sec. n. 12–16 pair. Fruiting bracts thinly membranous, serrate, very unequal-sided, almost falcate, basal nerves 5–9.

4. CORYLUS, Linn.; Fl. Brit. Ind. v. 625.

Pith more or less circular, buds with imbricate scales, branchlets and petioles often with glandular hairs, l. serrate, basal n. 3–5. ♂ catkins hairy, drooping, fascicled or 2–3 on a common peduncle, stamens 4 attached on the inside of a broad bract, supported by 2 bracteoles, which are half or more than half adnate to the bract, filaments either with 2 contiguous but distinct anther-cells, or more or less irregularly bifurcating, each arm bearing an anther-cell, tufts of hairs at the apex of anther-cells. ♀ spikes small, lateral, sessile, ovoid, bud-like, consisting of numerous imbricate bracts, the fl. in pairs in the axils of a few of the uppermost bracts. Perianth adnate to the ovary, minutely toothed, soon obliterated. Each fl. surrounded by 2 or more minute scales (involucre), which enlarge in fr. and form a leafy usually lobed sheath, the lobes sometimes spinescent. Nut hard, woody or bony. The thick oily cotyledons remain underground in the fr. when germinating. Species 7, Northern hemisphere.

1. **C. Colurna**, Linn.—Syn. *C. Jacquemontii*, Dcne. in Jacq. Voy. Bot. t. 160; *C. lacera*, Wall. Vern. *Thangi*, *Thangoli*, Pangi; *Shurli*, *Sharoli*, *Bandilla*, Bash.; *Kapasi*, Jauns. North-West Himalaya, 5–10,000 ft., in places gregarious and sometimes associated with *Parrotia*. On the Sutlej as far as Pangi on the right and Poari on the left bank.—South-East Europe and Asia Minor. China. A moderate-sized tree, the scales of the bark often detaching themselves at the base and exfoliating upwards, buds short, nearly hemispherical. L. glabrous when mature, obovate, shortly acuminate, base cordate, unequally serrate, and often slightly lobed, blade 5–6, pet. 1-1½ in. ♂ bracts obovate, acute, bearing along the midrib 8 one-celled anthers on short more or less connate filaments. Fr. usually in clusters, involucre coriaceous, cleft into linear-lanceolate lobes with glandular hairs, much longer than nuts, supported by large laciniate bracts.

2. **C. ferox**, Wall. Pl. As. Rar, t. 87. Nepal. Sikkim 8–10,000 ft.—China (var. *thibetica*), A small tree, buds silky, elongated. L. ovate-lanceolate, serratures cuspidate, unequal, blade 4–5, pet. ½ in. long, hairy. ♂ scales bearing at their base 4 subsessile stamens, each with 2 distinct contiguous anther-cells. Fr. in clusters of 3–6, involucre villous, thick, almost fleshy, lobes pinnatifid, the segments terminating in slender spines ½ in. long.

ORDER CVII. FAGACEÆ. Prantl in Engler u. Prantl iii. 1. 47.

(*Cupuliferæ*, tribe iii. *Quercineæ*, Gen. Pl. iii. 403.)

Monœcious trees, rarely shrubs, l. alternate, simple, but often deeply lobed, penninerved, stipules deciduous. ♂ fl. in drooping catkins or in erect spikes, anther-cells not separate. ♀ fl. in spikes, each fl. or group of 2–3 fl. enclosed in an involucre of numerous bracts, coalescing in fr. Perianth adnate to the ovary, limb minutely toothed. Ovary more or less completely 3–6-celled, ovules 2 in each cell, pendulous. Nuts indehiscent, one or several supported by or enclosed in the enlarged coriaceous, crustaceous or woody involucre, the rudiments of the abortive ovules at the base or at the apex of the seed. Pericarp coriaceous or woody, cotyledons thick fleshy, albumen 0.

Ovary 3-celled.
- One ♀ fl. in each involucre, nuts supported by a cup or enclosed in an involucre not clothed with hard spines . 1. QUERCUS.
- Usually 2–3 ♀ fl. in each involucre, nuts enclosed in the enlarged involucre, which usually is spinous . . . 2. CASTANOPSIS.

Ovary 6-celled.
- Usually 3 ♀ fl. in each involucre, nuts enclosed in the enlarged 2–4-valved spinous involucre . . . . CASTANEA (p. 635).

1. QUERCUS, Linn.; Fl. Brit. Ind. v. 600.

(*Pasania* and *Quercus*, Prantl in Engler u. Prantl iii. 1. 55.)

Trees, rarely shrubs, pith in most species pentagonal, the angles often projecting. Med. rays of two classes, broad or very broad and narrow.

Several species of Sect. *Pasania: lappacea, acuminata, pachyphylla* and *fenestrata* have uniform very fine rays, numerous and equidistant. Wavy soft, more or less concentric bands of wood-parenchyma (often very narrow) in most species. Wood-fibres with bordered pits. ♂ fl. in drooping catkins or erect spikes, perianth of 3–8 segments, more or less connate at the base, stamens as many as or twice the number of segments, a rudimentary ovary in some species. ♀ fl. on erect axillary, often very short spikes, each fl., or in a few species a pair of fl., in an involucre of numerous bracts or scales, which in fr. coalesce and form a cup or a bag entirely enclosing the nut and are often connate into concentric belts. Ovary 3-celled, styles 3, stigmatose on the inner surface or at the apex only, often red. Cotyledons thick fleshy, remain underground when germinating, starch as a rule the reserve substance. Species about 300, Europe, Mediterranean region, Asia, North America. *Thitcha*, Burm. and in Upper Burma *Zagat* and *Metlein* are used indiscriminately for several species.

Sect. i. *Lepidobalanus*. Spikes unisexual, ♂ simple, lax, mostly pendulous, deciduous, usually fascicled. Fruiting spikes short, often with 1 or 2 acorns only, rachis softly hairy, not ribbed. Cup hemispherical, bracts imbricate, tips free. L. usually serrate or lobed.

A. Mature l. hairy or tomentose beneath.

1. **Q. semecarpifolia**, Smith; Wall. Pl. As. Rar. t. 174; Brandis F. Fl. t. 64; King in Ann. Gard. Calc. ii. t. 15A; Collett Simla Fl. 474, fig. 152. Vern. *Banjar*, Haz.; *Kharshu*, Hind.; *Maru*, *Kreo*, Chamba; *Khor*, Bash.

A large gregarious tree, sometimes leafless for a few weeks in spring, bark dark grey, cut by shallow cracks into small more or less 4-sided scales, shoots and young l. softly rusty-tomentose. L. rigidly coriaceous, glabrous and dark green above, generally hairy on the underside, entire or (on young trees always) dentate with long spinescent teeth, elliptic or elliptic-oblong, blade 2–5 in., pet. very short, sec. n. generally bifurcating and branching. ♂ catkins fascicled, 2–6 in. long, perianth-segments obtuse, ciliate. ♀ spikes short, few-fld., styles 3–5 linear, recurved. Fr. usually solitary, on the previous year's wood, glabrous, 1 in. diam., black when ripe, base enclosed by the thin concave cup.

Kuram valley 9–11,000 ft. Himalaya, 8–10,000 ft., occasionally descending to 6,500 and ascending to 12,000 ft. East Manipúr on the Burma frontier, 8–10,000 ft.—China. New l. and fl. April–June. The fr. ripens Aug.–Sept. of the next year, 15 months after flowering. Seeds profusely every second year, but a few trees here and there bear acorns every year. Trees that bear acorns do not shed l. that year, whereas those which produce ♂ fl. are generally leafless by the middle of May (Kanjilal 838). 2. **Q. Ilex**, Linn.; King Ann. ii. t. 17.—Syn. *Q. Baloot*, Griff. Vern. *Balat*, Afg.; *Breh*, Kun. Kuram valley 6,500–9,000 ft., common. Hills north of the Peshawar valley at 3,500 ft. Chitral, 6–8,000 ft. Arid valleys of the inner Himalaya, on the upper Jhelam, Chenab, Ravi and Sutlej, 3–8,500 ft. In the Sutlej valley the lower limit: Chergaon and Panwi, the upper: Teling and Purbni.—Mediterranean region. Afghanistan. A middle-sized evergreen tree, often only a shrub, branchlets, petioles and underside of l. densely grey-pubescent with stellate hairs. L. coriaceous, elliptic or elliptic-oblong, entire or with large spinescent teeth, blade 2–3 in. long, pet. short, sec. n. not prominent. Anthers hairy. Acorns 2–3 on a peduncle 1–2 in. long, nuts at first nearly enclosed in the cup, scales hoary, closely appressed. Gamble, p. 672, mentions a tree from the Chumbi valley which, he thinks, may possibly be this species.

3. **Q. Griffithii**, Hook. f. & Thoms.; King Ann. ii. t. 18. *Thitcha*, Lower, *Metlein*, Upper Burma.

A large deciduous gregarious tree, bark silvery grey, branchlets and young l. pale-, often rusty-tomentose. L. coriaceous, underside usually pubescent, obovate or oblanceolate, blade 6–9, pet. $\frac{1}{8}$–$\frac{1}{2}$ in., stout, sec. n. 14–18 pair, prominent, nearly straight, terminating in large triangular serratures. Fr. solitary or in short spikes, cup hemispherical, $\frac{1}{2}$ in. diam., scales closely appressed, nut $\frac{1}{2}$–$\frac{2}{3}$ in. long, nearly cylindric.

Bhutan. Khasi and Naga hills. Manipúr. Hills of Upper Burma, east of the Irawadi. Hills between the Sitang and the Salween, south as far as Lomatee, common on the upper Yunzalin at about 8,000 ft. Fl. Oct.-March. Wood similar to that of *Quercus sessiliflora*. Remarkable galls on the branches, consisting of densely packed subulate scales, up to 1½ in. long. Var. *oblonga*, Khasi and Naga hills, has nearly entire l. *Q. aliena*, Blume, of Japan and several other sp. of Japan and China will probably eventually be united with this sp.

4. **Q. incana,** Roxb.; King Ann. ii. t. 20; Collett Simla Fl. 475, fig. 154. Vern. *Rhin*, Haz.; *Shiddar*, Kashm.; *Ban*, *Banj*, Hind.

A middle-sized or large evergreen gregarious tree, foliage grey, branchlets, petioles and underside of l. white-tomentose. L. coriaceous, elliptic-lanceolate, serrate, teeth sharp, mucronate, base acute, blade 3–6, pet. ⅓ in., stipules linear, scarious, ⅓ in. long, early caducous. Catkins hairy, bracts obtuse, scarious, perianth of 4–5 short unequal segments, anthers glabrous. Fr. mostly solitary, ripe nuts ovoid-conical, 1 in. long, half enclosed in the rough woody cup.

Outer North-West Himalaya, eastwards as far as Nepal, 4–8,000 ft., occasionally lower (Mothronwala swamp, in the Dún 1,900 ft.). Generally associated with *Rhododendron arboreum* and *Andromeda*. The Deodar, often self-sown, readily comes up under its shade. Leaves renewed in March and April, the young foliage coming out with a lilac and purple tinge. Fl. about the same time, but occasionally irregularities occur; thus at Simla the Bān flowered abundantly in July 1902. Fr. in autumn, 15–17 months after fl. Coppices freely. Wood splits and warps, but makes excellent fuel, bark rich in tannin. 5. **Q. lanuginosa,** Don; King Ann. ii. t. 19. Kumaon, 4–8,000 ft., gregarious in patches, often associated with *Q. incana*. Nepal. Bhutan. Vern. *Ranj*, *Rianj*, *Rai banj*, Kumaon; *Banga*, Nep. A large evergreen tree, branchlets and underside of l. densely clothed with rufous or tawny wool. L. coriaceous, upper surface rugose, midrib often hairy, serratures distant, blade 4–8, pet. ½–1 in. long. Fr. solitary or in short spikes, cup ½ in. across, scales thin, appressed, nut woolly with a short cylindric umbo.

B. Leaves glabrous when mature.

6. **Q. serrata,** Thunb.; King Ann. ii. t. 16. A middle-sized straight-stemmed deciduous tree, annual rings conspicuous by numerous very large pores in the spring wood, concentric bands of wood - parenchyma obscure. Youngest shoots and young l. clothed with soft hairs, l. thinly coriaceous, glabrous when mature, shining, lanceolate or elliptic - lanceolate, blade 5–7, pet. 1–1¼

FIG. 192.—Quercus serrata, Thunb. ½.

in. long, slender, sec. n. straight 10–20 pair, each nerve terminating in a sharp serrature, up to $\frac{1}{4}$ in. long. Fr. on the previous year's wood, nearly sessile, cup $1\frac{1}{2}$ in. diam., scales spreading, hoary, up to $\frac{1}{3}$ in. long, nut shining, globose to cylindric, $\frac{3}{4}$–1 in. diam.

Himalaya, from Kumaon eastwards, 3–8,000 ft. Khasi hills. Manipúr. Shan hills, Upper Burma. Fl. March–May.—China. Japan. Korea. One of the species of Oak on which the Yamamâi silkworm in Japan is raised. 7. **Q. dilatata,** Lindley; Royle Ill. t. 84 fig. 2; King Ann. ii. t. 15; Collett Simla Fl. 474 fig. 153. Vern. *Barungi*, Haz.; *Moru*, Punj. Hind.; *Tilonj*, Garhw. Kuram valley, 7–8,500 ft. N.W. Himalaya, 5–9,000 ft., in the zone below that of *Q. semecarpifolia*, often associated with the Himalayan Spruce and Silver fir. In Kunawar as far as Jani.—Afghanistan. A large tree, nearly evergreen, bark dark, peeling off in longitudinal scales. Compound med. rays, similar to *Corylus*. Youngest shoots nearly glabrous. L. glabrous, shining, coriaceous, entire or with sharp spinescent teeth, blade 2–3, pet. $\frac{1}{4}$ in. ♂ catkins fascicled, ♀ spikes short. Fr. mostly solitary, nearly sessile, the lower half enclosed in the cup $\frac{1}{2}$ in. across, scales closely appressed. Fl. April, May, fr. C. S., 16–18 months after fl. 8. **Q. calathiformis,** Skan in Journ. Linn. Soc. xxvi. 508. Vern. *Naba*, Burm. Ruby Mines district, Upper Burma, 4–5,000 ft.—Yunnan 4–6,000 ft. A shrub or small tree, branchlets ridged and furrowed with a few minute stellate hairs. L. thinly coriaceous, obtusely serrate or crenate, elongate-elliptic, blade 4–8, pet. $\frac{1}{3}$ in., upperside shining, underside pale, sec. n. slightly arching, 15–20 pair. ♂ spikes from the axils of the uppermost l., often branching, 2–9 in. long, rachis ribbed, glabrous, with a few very minute stellate hairs, 6–8 fl. in compact oblong clusters, in the axils of small bracts. Stamens glabrous, surrounding a hairy pistillode. Acorns sessile, solitary on spikes 4–6 in. long, cup pubescent hemispheric, $\frac{1}{3}$ in. across, nut ovoid-cylindric $\frac{3}{4}$ in. long. Differs from the other species of *Lepidobalanus* by the rachis of the ♂ spikes being ribbed, nearly glabrous, not softly hairy, and by the rudimentary ovary.

Sect. ii. *Cyclobalanopsis*. Male spikes as in i. Cup hemispheric or campanulate, bracts connate into concentric belts (lamellæ). L. more or less serrate.

A. Mature nut exserted, less than half enclosed in the cup.

9. **Q. semiserrata,** Roxb.; Wight Ic. t. 211; King Ann. ii. t. 22. *Thitcha*, Lower; *Zagat*, Upper Burma.

A middle-sized evergreen tree, youngest shoots and l. clothed with soft deciduous tomentum. L. coriaceous, glabrous when mature, elliptic-lanceolate, upper portion serrate, lower entire, blade 5–10, pet. 1 in. long, sec. n. straight, faintly anastomosing close under the edge. Fr. on short thick stalks, solitary or in pairs, cup $1\frac{1}{4}$ in. across, belts 5–8, thick, velvety, enclosing one-third of the nut, which is cylindric-ovoid, $1\frac{1}{2}$ in. long.

Assam. Garo and Khasi hills. Cachar. Manipúr. Burma, Upper and Lower, often in Eng forest. Fl. H. S. Var. *Mannii*. Assam. Khasi hills. L. with a long cuneate base, cup with the edge densely velvety and turned over.

10. **Q. glauca,** Thunb. (1784); King Ann. ii. t. 23; Collett Simla Fl. 475 fig. 155.—Syn. *Q. annulata*, Smith (1819); Brandis F. Fl. t. 65. Vern. *Barin*, Haz.; *Banni*, Hind.; *Phanât*, Kum.; *Phalat*, Nep.

A large evergreen tree, leaf-buds usually 4-sided, youngest shoots silky. L. thinly coriaceous, on the underside glaucous and often minutely pubescent with appressed hairs, upperside and petiole glabrous, blade 3–6 in., upper half sharply serrate, base entire, sec. n. 12–18 pair, straight, excurrent into the serratures, tert. n. slender, parallel, pet. slender, $\frac{1}{2}$–$\frac{3}{4}$ in. long. Bracts of ♂ catkins long, early deciduous. Fr. sessile, on axillary, short, often only 1-fruited spikes, cups hemispheric, belts thin, thinly silky, crenate, often divided into broad truncate teeth, nut ovoid, apiculate, shining, $\frac{1}{2}$–$\frac{2}{3}$ in. long.

Valleys of the outer Himalaya, ascending to 6,000 ft. Coppice woods of this and of *Q. incana*, with standards of *Albizzia stipulata* in the Kangra valley. Khasi hills. Fl. March–June. Fr. 15–17 months after fl.—China. Closely allied: 11. **Q. lineata,** Bl. (1825); King Ann. ii. tt. 26, 27. Eastern Himalaya from Nepal eastwards 6–9,000 ft., common near Darjeeling. Khasi and Naga hills. Arakan. Hills of Upper Burma.—Mal. Archip. China. L. often tomentose beneath, sec. n. 15–20 pair. Nut hemispheric, often broader than long. The foll. Indian varieties of *Q. lineata* are described by King in Ann. ii. 33: *Oxyodon, Lobbi, Griffithii, Thomsoniana, Hilldebrandi*.

B. Half the mature nut enclosed in the cup.

12. **Q. Brandisiana**, Kurz; King Ann. II. t. 25 A. Shan hills, Upper Burma. Hills east of Toungoo, in hill Eng forest. Donat range 2–5,000 ft., Tenasserim. A

FIG. 198.—Quercus semiserrata, Roxb. ½.

middle-sized evergreen tree, young shoots thinly pubescent, l. rigidly coriaceous, glabrous when mature, from elliptic to obovate, undulate, or with a few shallow serratures, blade 4–7, pet. 1–1½ in. long, sec. n. straight, 10–12 pair, midrib, sec. n. and often tert. n. prominent on the under and impressed on the upperside. Fr. on spikes 2–3 in. long, cup softly velvety within and without, shallow, ½–⅝ in. across, nut nearly globose, apiculate. 13. **Q. velutina**, Lindl. Chittagong hill tracts. Pegu, frequent in Eng forest. A large tree, young shoots rusty-tomentose, l. serrulate near apex, nearly glabrous, thin, lanceolate, blade 5–8, pet. ½ in., sec. n. slender curved, 10–14 pair. Cup densely tomentose, 1¼ in. across, lamellæ crenate, nut depressed, velvety. 14. **Q. xanthoclada**, Drake in Journal de Botanique 1890, 149, t. iii. fig. 1. Wuntho district, Upper Burma, 1,500 ft. (*Dowaing*, Burm.).—Tonkin. A large tree, branchlets, petioles and axillary buds tawny-tomentose. L. coriaceous, minutely serrate near the apex, elliptic, blade 4–6, pet. slender 1 in. long, upperside glabrous, underside glaucous with scattered thin hairs, sec. n. 10–12 pair. Cup densely fulvous-velvety, 1–1¼ in. across. 15. **Q. Helferiana**, A. DC.—King Ann. II. t. 25 B. Manipur. Ruby Mines and other hills of Upper Burma east of the Irawadi, also hills east of Toungoo and on headwaters of Yunzalin 3–5,000 ft. A large tree, stunted in exposed situations, branchlets and underside of leaves densely tawny-tomentose, l. coriaceous, glabrous above, except midrib, sec. n. 10–14 pair, impressed above, prominent beneath. Fr. on spikes 2 in. long, peduncle stout, cup almost flat, the edge incurved, 1 in. across, lamellæ 8, very regular, denticulate, nut velvety, depressed, hemispheric. This might perhaps be included under A.

C. More than half the nut enclosed in the cup.

16. **Q. lamellosa,** Smith; Wall. Pl. As. Rar. t. 149; Hook. f. Ill. Himal. Pl. t. 20; King Ann. ii. t. 30. Vern. *Shalshi, Budgrat,* Nep.; *Būk,* Lepcha.

A very large evergreen tree, wood very hard and heavy. Buds silky, young shoots with tawny deciduous pubescence. L. elongate-elliptic, acute at both ends, sharply serrate to near the base, upperside glabrous, underside glaucous, with deciduous pubescence while young, blade 8–18, pet. 1–2 in. long, sec. n. 18–25 pair, straight, impressed on the upper, very prominent on the underside. Fr. sessile on short spikes, peduncles thick, cup very large, up to 3 in. across, woody, with 10 thin broad loose lamellæ, enclosing the greater part of the nut.

Nepal. Sikkim, 6–9,000 ft. Bhutan. Manipúr, 7–9,000 ft. Fl. April, May. 17. **Q. mespilifolia,** Wall.; King Ann. ii. t. 28. Manipúr. Hills of Upper Burma. Pegu. Martaban. Young shoots tawny-tomentose, l. elongate-elliptic, obtusely serrate to near the base, deciduously velvety, upperside glabrous when mature, blade 4–8, pet. ½–1 in. Cup deep, enclosing more than half the nut, lamellæ numerous, more or less denticulate, nut depressed globose. 18. **Q. oidocarpa,** Korth.; King Ann. II. t. 21 A. Tenasserim (?). Malay Penins. A tall tree, l. glabrous, elliptic-lanceolate, the upper fourth serrate, blade 3–7, pet. slender ½–1 in., sec. n. 10 pair, arching. Cup deep, covering ½–⅔ of the nut, lamellæ pubescent, appressed, more or less crenate, nut ovoid, 1¼ in. long.

Sect. iii. *Pasania.* Male spikes stout, erect, usually in terminal panicles, rachis more or less persistent. Female involucres mostly in clusters of three, often at the base of male spikes. Fruiting spikes usually long. Cups hemispheric or ovoid, bracts imbricate. L. entire, edge undulate in *Q. Lindleyana.*

A. Of the mature nut half or less enclosed in the cup.

19. **Q. spicata,** Smith; Wall. Pl. As. Rar. t. 46.—Syn. *Q. squamata,* Roxb.; Wight Ic. t. 213. Vern. *Arkaula,* Nep.; *Bara chakma,* Beng.

A large or middle-sized evergreen tree, glabrous excepting the hairy ♂ spikes. L. shining, variable in shape. ♂ spikes hairy, stout, 2–8 in. long, usually in dense terminal panicles, fl. closely packed in oblong woolly clusters in the axils of acuminate bracts. Fr. more or less confluent in clusters of 3–6, on stout divergent spikes, 3–9 in. long, cup ½–1 in. across, embracing one-third part of the shining nut, scales more or less confluent, tips usually free. Nut adnate to the cup with the circular base only.

Eastern Himalaya, from Nepal eastwards, 2–5,000 ft. Assam. Khasi and Naga hills. Manipúr. Fl. at different times, Sept. to May. Fr. ripens in autumn of the following year.—China. Malay Peninsula, Sumatra, Java, Bangka.

Two principal forms may be distinguished: (a) *spicata* proper. King Ann. II. t. 41 l. coriaceous, from elliptic to obovate, lower part usually narrowed towards the rounded or cordate base, blade 5–12, pet. 0–½ in., sec. n. prominent, nut globose, often depressed. (b) *Collettii* (*Chittagonga*). Ann. II. t. 42. l. thinly coriaceous, lanceolate or elliptic-lanceolate, narrowed to both ends, blade 3–8, pet. ⅛–⅜ in., sec. n. mostly slender, nut ovoid. Regarding the distribution of these 2 forms in Chittagong and Burma, the following may be mentioned: (a) ***spicata***: Upper Burma, hills east of the Irawadi, 2–5,000 ft. (*Ywetchan,* Burm.). Martaban and Tenasserim, sometimes in Eng forest. (b) ***Collettii***: Chittagong. Upper Burma, hills west of the Irawadi, 1-2,000 ft. (*Zagat, Zagat pyaung,* Burm.). Hills east of the Irawadi, 3–7,500 ft. (*Thit-è,* Burm.; *Wadun-pun,* Kachin). Tenasserim. These two forms merit careful study in the forest, chiefly in regard to their biological characters. They may prove to be distinct species, analogous to the European *Quercus sessiliflora* and *pedunculata.*

20. **Q. Lindleyana,** Wall.; King Ann. ii. t. 55. Hills of Upper Burma, east of the Irawadi river. A middle-sized tree, branchlets, petioles, underside of l., upperside of midrib, and sometimes the entire upper surface, softly grey- or tawny-tomentose, l. thickly coriaceous, obovate, edge undulate, blade 6–9, pet. stout ¼ in., sec. n. 10–15 pair, as also tertiary n. impressed on the upper surface. Male spikes softly tomentose, axillary and in large terminal panicles. Fr. connate in clusters of 3–6, on spikes 8–12 in. long, peduncle stout and woody, cup enclosing one-fourth of the nut, which is cylindric-conic, indistinctly angular. 21. **Q. lappacea,** Roxb.; Wight Ic. t. 220; King Ann. ii. t. 33. Assam. Khasi hills. Tenasserim, near the great falls of the Salween, in evergreen forest (D. B. April 1859).—Malay Penins. A middle-sized tree, branchlets rusty-tomentose. L. hairy along midrib and nerves, elongate-elliptic, acuminate, sec. n. 12–18 pair, anastomosing under the margin, blade 5–9, pet. ¼ in.

♂ spikes softly tomentose as long as l., filaments long. Fr. 2–6 on spikes 2–5 in. long, cup enclosing the base of the nut, bracts hairy, long-acuminate, appressed and spreading, nut ovoid-conic, velvety. 22. **Q. acuminata,** Roxb. Chittagong Hill tracts. Dōnat

FIG. 194. Quercus spicata, Smith. ½.

pass, Tenasserim (D. B. April 1859). Similar to 21, but entirely glabrous, l. on both sides shining, cup hemispheric, velvety, bracts confluent, tips free. Nut broad-ovoid with a flat base.

23. **Q. polystachya,** Wall.; King Ann. ii. t. 44. Manipur. Hills of Upper Burma, 1,500–5,000 ft. Martaban hills near Lomatee. A middle-sized tree, l. glabrous, glaucous beneath, elongate elliptic, narrowed to both ends, blade 4–7, pet. ½–1 in. ♂ spikes in large terminal panicles. Fr. 2–3 together, often with small abortive acorns, in shortly stalked clusters, cups shallow, ⅓ in. across, nuts ovoid, shining. 24. **Q. Amherstiana,** Wall.; King Ann. ii. t. 32a. Pegu Yoma, near streams or in evergreen forest. Bithoko range, near Hatgyi 2,000 ft., Martaban (D. B. 1859). Amherst. A large evergreen tree, entirely glabrous, l. thinly coriaceous, lanceolate or oblong-lanceolate, acuminate, blade 6–12, narrowed into pet. ¼–⅜ in., sec. n. slender. Spikes 6–9 in. long, fr. solitary or in groups, cup embracing lower half of nut, edge thick, reflexed, bracts indistinct, nut ellipsoid with rounded ends, 1¼ in. long. 25. **Q. Falconeri,** Kurz; King Ann. ii. t. 34. Tenasserim. Similar to 24, l. shining, coriaceous, oblong-lanceolate, blade 12–18, pet. stout, ½ in., sec. n. arching, impressed above, prominent

beneath anastomosing near the edge. Cup shallow, edge thin, undulating, much wider than nut, bracts distinct. Nut nearly globose, ⅜ in. diam.

B. More than half the mature nut enclosed in the cup.

26. **Q. pachyphylla,** Kurz; King Ann. ii. t. 38. Vern. *Sungre Katūs*, Nep.

A large tree, l. elliptic-lanceolate, long-acuminate, glabrous above, underside pale, with minute stellate hairs, midrib and nerves glabrous, blade 5–8, pet. ⅓ in., sec. n. 8–10 pair, impressed above, arching and anastomosing under the margin. Spikes sometimes androgynous. Cups 1½–2 in. across, always con-

Fig. 195.—Quercus pachyphylla, Kurz. ½.

fluent, forming large irregularly shaped masses, nuts glabrous shining, nearly globose, almost entirely included. Var. *fruticosa*, Manipúr, a shrub or small tree, l. smaller, upper portion of nuts free.

Sikkim, 6–10,000 ft. common on the Singalila range. Manipúr 8,000–9,500 ft. 27. **Q. magnifica,** sp. nova. Kachin hills east of Bhamo. Southern Shan States 5,200 ft., in evergreen forest (*Maiman pau-wau*, Shan. Montague Hill, Oct. 1903). A large tree, l. entire, glabrous, rigidly coriaceous, elongate-elliptic, blade 6–9, pet. 1 in. long, upperside shining, underside dull, sec. n. 10–12 pair, prominent. Fr. on stout woody spikes 3–7 in. long, clustered, but cups hardly confluent, cups enclosing ⅞ of the nut, leaving a circular mouth open, walls woody, ⅛ in. thick, bracts thick, hard, triangular, acuminate. Nut globose, lower half rough, upper half polished, pericarp woody, in the upper half ¼, in the lower half ⅛ in. thick. Cotyledons thick fleshy, plano-convex. Several other species have an unusually thick pericarp: *Q. Rex* and *Fordiana*, Hemsl., of China, and *Q. cornea*, Lour., of China and Tonkin. These 3 species have lobed cotyledons, like the Walnut. The acorns mentioned under *Q. Jenkinsiana*, Benth., in Fl. Brit. Ind. v. 618 also have a very thick-walled nut. They however belong to Sect. v., the nut is entirely included in an ovoid involucre 2 in. long, tips of bracts large, pyramidal. *Q. pulchra*, King Ann. ii. t. 81, Borneo, differs from 27 by the flat, not shining top of the nut; *Q. spicata*, Smith, by smaller confluent cups, and the nut adhering to the cup with its circular base only, pericarp $\frac{1}{15}$ in. thick; *Q. pachyphylla*, Kurz, has acorns as large but they are confluent, the base only of the nut is rough, while the greater part is polished, the pericarp in this portion being ⅛ in. thick.

28. **Q. fenestrata**, Roxb.; Wight Ic. t. 219; King Ann. ii. t. 39. Vern. *Patlè Katûs*, Nep. Sikkim, 5–8,000 ft. Khasi hills. Manipúr. Upper Burma, east of the Irawadi, ascending to 5,000 ft. Martaban and Tenasserim, not known from Pegu. A middle-sized or large tree, young shoots often with deciduous hairs. L. coriaceous, lanceolate, blade 6–9, narrowed into pet. ¼–½ in. long, upperside glabrous, underside often clothed with a dense felt of very minute stellate hairs, sec. n. 10–16 pair. ♂ spikes grey-pubescent, in dense terminal panicles, bracts long acuminate, deciduous. ♀ spikes long, generally branching. Fr. crowded, but not confluent, cup ⅝ in. diam., crustaceous, usually thin, enclosing ⅓ or more of the mature nut, scales connate, apex free, triangular, acuminate, nut globose, polished, pericarp $\frac{1}{16}$ in. thick. This somewhat variable species merits careful study in the forests. One form with l. up to 12 in. long at 4,000 ft. in the southern Shan States (*Mailon*, Shan, Mont. Hill, Oct. 1908). Another with l. thinly coriaceous, 5–6 in. long, grey beneath, tert. n. conspicuous, cup almost closed, very thin, as well as pericarp, in the hills east of Bhamo 3,000 ft. (*Let shap pun*, Kachin, Mont. Hill, Feb. 1902), also in the Ruby Mines district. 29. **Q. dealbata**, Hook. fil. & Thoms.; King Ann. ii. t. 40. Bhutan. Khasi hills (*Kasning*). Manipúr. A shrub or small tree, similar to 28, branchlets and underside of l. minutely tomentose, l. smaller, sec. n. 8–12 pair, cup and nut hoary.

Sect. iv. *Cyclobalanus*. Male spikes stiff, erect. Bracts of cup connate into concentric ridges or belts. L. entire.

30. **Q. Thomsoni**, Miquel; King Ann. ii. t. 69a.—Syn. *Q. turbinata*. Roxb.; Wight Ic. t. 221. Khasi hills. Chittagong (Roxb.). Hills east of Bhamo, 6,000 ft., in evergreen forest (*Wami pun*, Kachin). Hmangin, west of the Irawadi 1,500–2,000 ft. (*Zagat Wunbyu*, Burm.). Bithoko range near Hatgyi, 3,000 ft. A large tree, l. thinly coriaceous, upperside glabrous, underside grey or silvery with very fine stellate hairs, lanceolate, blade 5–8, narrowed into pet. ¼–½ in. long. Fr. tightly packed in clusters of 3–12, cup thin, shallow, ⅜–1 in. across, nuts depressed, grey, velvety. 31. **Q. eumorpha**, Kurz; King Ann. ii. t. 54b. Martaban and Tenasserim hills: Nattaung, 6–7,000 ft., in stunted hill forest. Mooleyit 6,500 ft. A small evergreen glabrous tree, l. elliptic-lanceolate, margin undulate, blade 3–4, pet. ½–⅜ in., sec. n. slender. Cup velvety, ¾ in. across, concentric belts more or less distinct. ♂ fl. unknown.

Sect. v. *Chlamydobalanus* and vi. *Lithocarpus*. Male spikes erect, stiff. Involucre ovoid or globose, enclosing the whole nut, marked on the outside with concentric belts or densely clothed with acuminate scales, tip sometimes free. L. quite entire.

A. Involucre with concentric belts and a few scales or tubercles.

32. **Q. lancesfolia**, Roxb.; Wight Ic. t. 212; King Ann. ii. t. 74. Vern. *Patlè Katûs* Nep. Subhimalayan tract from Sikkim eastwards, ascends to 5,000 ft. Assam. Khasi hills. Chittagong. Shan hills 5,000 ft. A small evergreen tree, fine med. rays numerous and equidistant, broad rays very few. Branchlets and l. glabrous, l. pale beneath, lanceolate, blade 5–8, pet. ½–¾ in. Female spikes hairy, involucres mostly solitary. Acorns 5–10, distant on spikes 4–7 in. long, on short thick stalks, involucre thin, enveloping the whole nut, marked outside with 4–6 wavy rings (tuberculate in var. *semicristata*). Nut silky, obliquely-ovoid. 33. **Q. truncata**, King Ann. ii. t. 80. Naga hills. Manipúr. Upper Burma, hills east of the Irawadi river 4–6,000 ft. (*Maicheng*, Shan.) A middle-sized (at times a large) tree, branchlets ribbed, glabrous. L. glabrous, thinly coriaceous, pale beneath, lanceolate or elliptic-lanceolate, blade 6–12, narrowed into pet. ¼–¾ in. long, sec. n. 10–12 pair, arching. Acorns on spikes up to 6 in. long, in sessile clusters of three, cups confluent. Cups hoary or pubescent, urceolate, almost turbinate, marked in the lower portion with uneven more or less concentric belts, and on the flat truncate top with triangular scales. Nuts entirely included or tips free, ovoid or obovoid, ¾–1 in. long, the lower three-fourths adhering to involucre, rough, the upper fourth depressed, hoary, not polished, pericarp thin, cotyledons plano-convex. Some acorns from Upper Burma, possibly a new species, have the involucre clothed with flat appressed scales, more or less arranged in concentric belts. 34. **Q. Olla**, Kurz in Journ. As. Soc. Bengal 44. 107 tab. 14, fig. 9. Assam (acorns only known). Fruit spikes stout, 4 in. long, acorns distinct with 1 or 2 abortive ones adnate to the base, cup very thick-walled, woody, campanulate, but narrowed at the mouth, scales broad, appressed, abruptly acuminate, arranged in regular vertical rows. Nut depressed globose, polished, the apex only free. In Fl. Brit. Ind. v. 619 this is supposed to be near *Q. truncata*. Kurz thought it to be near *Q. spicata*.

B. Involucre densely covered with acuminate scales ⅛–⅓ in. long.

35. **Q. xylocarpa**, King Ann. ii. t. 79. Naga hills. Manipúr 6–7,000 ft. A large evergreen tree, youngest shoots thinly hairy. L. pale beneath, lanceolate finely

acuminate, blade 4–6, pet. $\frac{1}{3}$ in., sec. n. 10–12 pair, arching, prominent beneath. Acorns confluent in sessile clusters of three, involucre $\frac{3}{4}$–$1\frac{1}{4}$ in. diam., completely enclosing the nut, scales tapering from a pyramidal base into a long acumen, walls woody, $\frac{1}{8}$ in. thick, adhering tightly to the nut. Nut depressed-globose, diam. $\frac{3}{4}$ in., the upper fourth polished, the lower three-fourths rough, pericarp $\frac{1}{8}$ in. thick, intruded into the cavity, cotyledons probably lobed. *Q. xylocarpus*, Kurz in Journ. As. Soc. Bengal 44, 196, tab. 14, figs. 5–8, Arakan hills east of Akyab, 5–6,000 ft., is probably this species, but the scales are blunt and the apex of the nut is stated to be free. 86. Acorns only, similar to 85, from the hills east of Bhamo 7,500 ft. (*Sakè pun*, Kachin, Mont. Hill, Feb. 1902), nut almost hemispherical, polished, except the flat circular base, pericarp thin. 87. **Q. Wrayi**, King Ann. ii. t. 104. Mergui (Manson).—Perak. Branchlets, petioles, underside of l. and nerves on the upperside tawny-tomentose. L. lanceolate, blade 6–8, pet. $\frac{1}{4}$ in., sec. n. slender, 15–20 pair, near the edge curving and anastomosing. Cups sessile, on spikes 4 in. long, $\frac{2}{3}$–$1\frac{1}{3}$ in. diam., scales soft, densely tomentose, up to $\frac{1}{4}$ in. long.

2. CASTANOPSIS, Spach; Fl. Brit. Ind. v. 619 (included in *Castanea* by Prantl in Engler u. Prantl iii. 1. 54).

Evergreen trees, pith usually quadrangular, med. rays of most species uniform, very fine and equidistant. ♂ catkins erect, mostly in terminal panicles. ♀ fl. 1–3 in one involucre, nuts wholly enclosed in the involucre, which is covered with spines or tubercles or marked with more or less concentric tubercled lines. Species 28, one in Pacific North America, the rest in Eastern Asia. *Kyanza*, Burm. and *Thit-è* in Upper Burma, are used indiscriminately for several species.

I. Involucre ovoid or globose, dehiscent, spinous.

A. Leaves sharply serrate.

Fig. 196.—Castanopsis indica, A. DC. $\frac{1}{2}$.

1. **C. indica**, A. DC.; King Ann. ii. t. 83.—Syn. *Castanea indica*, Roxb.; Wight Ic. t. 417. Vern. *Dalne katûs*, Nep.; *Thit-è*, Burm.

A middle-sized or large tree, bark silvery-grey. Vessels in irregular radial bands of wood parenchyma. Narrow tangential lines of wood parenchyma. Branchlets, petioles, underside of l. and inflorescence rusty-tomentose. L. coriaceous, elliptic-oblong, sharply serrate, blade 5–8, pet. ¼–½ in., sec. n. 15–20 pair, prominent beneath. ♀ involucre mostly solitary. Fruiting spikes 4–6 in. long, often branching, involucres thin-walled, 1–1½ in. diam., spines crowded, concealing the surface of the involucre, slender, simple, straight, hairy, unequal, the longest ½ in.

Valleys and outer Himalayan ranges, from Nepal eastwards, 1–6,000 ft. Assam. Khasi hills. Cachar. Chittagong. Hills of Upper Burma east of the Irawadi river, 2–6,500 ft. Fl. Nov.–Dec., Sikkim. Feb., March, Burma. Coppices well, the wood splits easily, used for shingles.—Tonkin. 2. **C. Clarkei**, King Ann. ii. t. 88 bis. Kalimpung, Bhutan 5,000 ft. Hills of Upper Burma east of Irawadi. A large tree, nearly allied to 1, l. pale beneath, thinly pubescent, chiefly along nerves, pet. ½–1 in. long. Spikes slender pubescent, ♀ solitary, axillary. Ripe involucres ¾–1 in. diam., spines slender, in tufts, leaving the velvety surface of the involucre exposed. Specimens from the Ruby Mines district, 4,000 ft., have petioles ¼ in. long and fr. ⅝ in. diam.

B. Leaves usually entire.

(*a*) Surface of involucre more or less concealed by the crowded spines.

α. Branchlets, petioles and underside of l. pubescent or tomentose.

3. **C. Hystrix**, A. DC.; King Ann. ii. t. 84.—Syn. *C. rufescens*, Hook. f. & Th. Vern. *Bara Katûs*, Nep.; *Hingori*, Ass. Sikkim, 6–8,000 ft. Bhutan. Assam. Khasi Hills. Ruby Mines hills, Upper Burma. Upper Yunzalin 3,500 ft., Martaban.—Malay Peninsula. Yunnan. A tall tree, young shoots and inflorescence pubescent. L. lanceolate, underside clothed with minute ferruginous tomentum, blade 3–6, pet. ¼–½ in. Spines of involucre stellately branched. Seed edible. 4. **C. diversifolia**, King Ann. ii. t. 85a.—*Castanea diversifolia*, Kurz. Vern. *Kyanza*, Burm. Hills east of Toungoo 3–6,000 ft., common. Branchlets tawny-tomentose, l. rigidly coriaceous, entire, broadly ovate or elliptic, greatly varying in shape and size on the same branch, blade 5–9, pet. thick ¼–½ in., petioles, midrib and sec. n. thinly pubescent. Sec. n. 10–12 pair, as well as the parallel tert. n. prominent beneath and impressed above. Spines simple, stout, radiating, ¼ in. long. 5. **C. javanica**, A. DC.; King Ann. ii. t. 88.—Syn. *Castanea javanica*, Blume.—Malay Peninsula, Tonkin and Archip. Branchlets, petioles and underside of l. from rusty-pubescent to tomentose. According to Kurz frequent in Pegu, Martaban and Tenasserim, but Kurz describes it as glabrous, the leaves beneath with minute indistinct tomentum. This has to be cleared up by studying the tree in the forest.

β. Branchlets, petioles and l. glabrous or nearly so.

6. **C. argentea**, A. DC.; King Ann. ii. t. 89.—Syn. *Castanea argentea*, Blume; *Castanea martabanica*, Wall. Pl. As. t. 107. Hills east of Bhamo, 7,000 ft., Upper Burma, wood used for building (*Kyiran*, Kachin, Mont. Hill, Feb. 1902). Hills of Pegu, Martaban and Tenasserim.—Malay Penins. and Archip. A large tree, bark smooth, light grey, branchlets and l. glabrous. L. thinly coriaceous, pale beneath, oblong-lanceolate, acuminate, blade 6–10, pet. ¼ in. Spikes pubescent, ♀ fl. solitary. Spines of involucre pubescent, ½ in. long, in dense tufts on short woody stalks. 7. **C. castanicarpa**, Spach; King Ann. ii. t. 91.—Syn. *Castanea Roxburghii*, Lindl.; *Quercus castanicarpa*, Roxb. Pl. Corom. t. 296. Chittagong. A large evergreen tree, young shoots minutely silky. L. thin, glabrous, oblong-lanceolate, acuminate, blade 6–12, pet. ¼ in., sec. n. 8–10 pair. Female involucres solitary on axillary spikes, 6–8 in. long. Fr. ovoid, pubescent, 1¼ in., spines ¼ in. long united by their base into tufts.

(*b*.) Spines in tufts or belts, not completely concealing the surface of involucre.

8. **C. argyrophylla**, King Ann. ii. t. 85b.—Syn. *Castanea tribuloides*, var. *ferox*, Kurz F. Fl. ii. 481. Vern. *Thit-è*, *Thit-tat*, Burm.; *Maikaw*, Shan. Upper Burma, Ruby Mines hills 5–6,000 ft. Shan hills, 4–5,000 ft. Arakan, Pegu, Martaban and Tenasserim. A middle-sized tree, branchlets minutely pubescent. L. thinly coriaceous, glabrous, pale beneath, blade 5–9, pet. ½–⅝ in., sec. n. 10–12 pair. Fr. nearly globose, 1–1¼ in. diam., with stout short simple spines in tufts or on short ridges, nut adnate high up to the inside of the involucre, tomentose where free.

9. **C. tribuloides**, A. DC.; King Ann. ii. tt. 94, 95, 96.—Syn. *Castanea tribuloides*, Wall.; *Quercus ferox*, Roxb.; Wight Ic. t. 218. Vern. *Tumari*,

Katonj, Kumaon; *Musre katūs*, Nep.; *Kyanza*, Lower, *Thitè ni*, *Thitègyin*, Upper Burma.

A middle-sized (rarely large) evergreen tree, young shoots pubescent. L. coriaceous or thinly coriaceous, entire, sometimes serrate near the apex, lanceolate, long acuminate, blade 4–8, pet. ⅓ in., upperside glabrous, underside pale or reddish, sometimes pubescent. Involucres distant, solitary or in pairs, styles long, linear. Fr. ¾–1 in. diam., on spikes up to 10 in. long. Involucres not confluent, tomentose, spines up to ⅓ in. long, usually on short ridges, often stellate or branched, as a rule leaving portions of the involucre uncovered, nuts 1–3, glabrous when mature, cotyledons ruminated.

Outer Himalaya from the Ganges eastwards, ascending to 6,000 ft. Assam. Khasi hills. Manipúr. Cachar. Chittagong. Hills of Upper Burma and Martaban.—Formosa. Fl. March–May, sometimes later. More or less gregarious (Gamble). King l. c. 102 recognizes the following varieties: (a) *typica*. L. entire, pubescence cinereous, spines numerous, long, slender, covering the walls of involucre, nuts usually solitary. (b) *ferox*. Involucres larger than in (a), spines stouter but fewer. (c) *longispina*. L. large, spines stout curving, often ½ in. long. (d) *echidnocarpa*. Pubescence ferruginous, involucre smaller than in (a), less covered by the spines, which are fewer and shorter, nut one. (e) *Wattii*. Manipúr, also Khasi hills and Sikkim. Involucre small, almost woody, densely clothed with short often rufous spines, nuts 2–3.

FIG. 197.
Castanopsis tribuloides, A. DC. ½.

10. **C. armata**, Spach; King Ann. ii. t. 98.—Syn. *Quercus armata*, Roxb. Cor. Pl. t. 296: Wight Ic. t. 770; *Castanea tribuloides, var. armata*, Kurz F. Fl. ii. 481. Vern. *Nekari*, Beng.; *Kanta Singar*, Assam; *Singhara*, Tipperah; *Kanta-lal batana*, Chittagong. Assam. Khasi hills. Tipperah. Chittagong, Maymyo, Upper Burma, 4,000 ft. A large tree, branchlets thinly pubescent, l. entire, lanceolate, blade 6–9, pet. ¼–½ in., sec. n. arching, 6–9 pair. Involucres solitary. Fr. 1–1½ in. diam., grey pubescent, spines pubescent, conical, very sharp, in stellate stalked clusters, arranged in imperfectly concentric ridges. Nuts single, pubescent.

II. Involucre irregularly ovoid, usually indehiscent, tuberculate or with short conical spines.

11. **C. rhamnifolia**, A. DC.; King Ann. ii. t. 100b.—Syn. *Castanea rhamnifolia*, Kurz. Southern Pegu Yoma, Paunglin, one of the most common trees in the evergreen forest (*Kyanza*, D. B. Jan. 1862). Mergui (*Wet thitta*, Manson, March 1902).—Malay Penins. and Archip. A tall tree, bark greenish-grey, youngest shoots minutely puberulous, branchlets and l. glabrous, l. thinly coriaceous, ovate or elliptic-lanceolate, acuminate, blade 3–6, pet. ¼–⅜ in. Spikes pubescent, in terminal panicles, ♀ involucres frequently at the base of spike. Fr. obliquely ovoid or obovoid, ¾–1½ in. long, grey-velvety, the side towards the rachis flat, uneven, the rest densely covered with short conical or pyramidal spines with sharp tips, nut one. 12. **C. Sumatrana**, A. DC.; King Ann. ii. t. 97.—Syn. *Castanea inermis*, Lindl. Hills east of Toungoo (Kurz).—Malay Penins. and Archip. L. glabrous, thinly coriaceous, lanceolate, blade 4–7, pet. ¾–1 in., spikes pubescent. Fr. irregularly ovoid, 1–1¼ in. long, with 3 or 4 irregularly concentric tuberculate lines.

Castanea sativa, Miller (1768).—Syn. *C. vulgaris*, Lamarck (1783); *C. vesca*, Gærtner (1788). *Sweet Chesnut*. Mediterranean region. China. Japan. Cultivated with some success in the Dún and elsewhere. A long-lived deciduous tree, growth rapid while young, coppices readily, med. rays uniform, very fine. L. sharply serrate, spikes erect, axillary, the lower ♂, the upper androgynous, the ♀ fl. at base. ♂ fl. 3 or more in the axil of one bract, stamens numerous. ♀ fl. usually 3 in one involucre, ovary 6-celled, styles 6. Ripe involucre 1–2 in. diam., densely spinous, dehiscing into 2–4 valves. A variety in China with l. densely tomentose beneath. Chesnuts are imported from China into Upper Burma.

ORDER CVIII. SALICACEÆ. Gen. Pl. iii. 411 (*Salicineæ*).

Deciduous, fast growing, as a rule not very long-lived trees or shrubs, with scaly buds. L. alternate, simple, stipulate. Fl. diœcious in catkins, which are similar in both sexes, each bract bearing one fl. in its axil. Perianth 0, a more or less developed disk at the base of stamens and ovary. ♂: stamens 2 or more, filaments usually free, no rudimentary ovary in normal fl. ♀: ovary 1-celled, ovules ∞ on 2–4 parietal placentas, style short, 2–4-fid. Capsule usually 2-valved, the valves spreading or rolling back. Seeds ∞, minute, enclosed by a mass of long silky deciduous hairs attached to the funicle, embryo straight, radicle minute, inferior, albumen 0.

Wood soft, medullary rays narrow, vessels small, uniformly distributed, wood-parenchyma not much developed, wood fibres wide, walls not thick, pits simple.

Petioles short, disk of 1 or 2 separate glands, stamens 2–12, in most species 2, long-exserted. . . . . 1. SALIX.
Petioles long, disk flat or cup-shaped, stamens 4–30 . . . . . 2. POPULUS.

1. SALIX, Linn.; Fl. Brit. Ind. v. 626.

Leaves lanceolate, ovate or elliptic, petioles short, as a rule less than one-fourth the length of leaf. Bracts of catkins entire, disk of 1 or 2, rarely more, glands or scales. Stamens 2–12, in most species 2, filaments long, filiform. Valves of capsule generally rolled back, placentas near the base of valves. Species about 160, nearly all in the Northern Hemisphere.

Sect. i. *Pleiandræ.* Stamens 3–12, filaments free, villous at the base.

1. **S. tetrasperma,** Roxb. Cor. Pl. t. 97; Wight Ic. t. 1954; Bedd. Fl. Sylv. t. 302; Brandis F. Fl. t. 58. Vern. *Bins*, Haz.; *Bed*, *Bains*, Hind.; *Bilsa*, *Birsa*, Oudh; *Bhè*, Ass.; *Bitasa*, *Walunj*, Mar.; *Niranji*, Kan,; *Vanti*, Mal.; *Momaka*, Lower, *Yenè*, Upper Burma. Subhimalayan tract and outer ranges, ascending to 6,000 ft. Common and in places gregarious, on river banks and in moist places throughout India, in the Himalaya ascending to 6,000, in the Nilgiris to 7,000 ft. On the Aravali hills, but not known from the arid region of Sind and the southern Punjab. Burma, Upper and Lower. China. Malay Penins. and Archip. Not in Ceylon. A middle-sized tree, sometimes a shrub, wood reddish, bark rough with deep vertical furrows, the lower 2–3 ft. of stem, if subject to inundation, often covered with numerous small rootlets. Young shoots and young l. silky, branchlets and underside of l. sometimes pubescent. L. glaucous beneath, lanceolate, rarely ovate-lanceolate, as a rule minutely and regularly serrulate, blade 2–6, pet. ⅛–1 in. long. Fl. after the l., catkins ♂ 2–4, ♀ 3–5 in. long, bracts pale. Stamens 5–10, capsules glabrous or puberulous, often in groups of 3–4, pedicel as long as capsule, or nearly so, style short, stigmas 2 spreading, generally entire, seeds 4–6. In Burma often leafless during the rains. Remarkable varieties: (a) *pyrina.* Kumaon, Nepal. Branchlets, petioles, underside of l. and rachis of catkins pubescent, l. nearly entire, (b) *calophylla.* Pegu, Tenasserim. Glabrous, l. broadly lanceolate, pet. long. 2. **S. ichnostachya,** Lindl.; Wight Ic. t. 1953. North Kanara and the Konkan, along river banks. Mysore. Shevaroy hills. L. lanceolate, pet. ½–1½ in. Capsule broadly ovoid, densely woolly, nearly sessile. 3. **S. acmophylla,** Boiss. Vern. *Bed*, *Bada*, Hind., Punj.; *Jalmdla*, Dún. Baluchistan, wild and cultivated. Kuram valley. Kashmir. Subhimalayan tract east to the Ganges. Northern Punjab, often cultivated.—Western Asia. A middle-sized tree, young shoots and young l. silky. L. linear-lanceolate, as a rule entire, blade 1–5, pet. ¼ in. Fl. after the l., catkins on leafy peduncles. ♂ compact 1–2 in. ♀ lax 1 in. long, bracts pale. Stamens 4–6, capsule glabrous, ovoid-conical, pedicellate, style short.

Sect. ii. *Diandræ.* Stamens 2, filaments free (see 4. *elegans*).

A. Trees or large shrubs.

(*a*) Fl. with or after the l., catkins as a rule on leafy peduncles.

4. **S. elegans**, Wall.; Collett Simla Fl. 479, fig. 156. Vern. *Bushal*, *Kalishan*, Sutlej. North-West Himalaya 6–11,000 ft., very common, extending to the inner arid valleys. —Turkestan. China. A gregarious shrub, young shoots very minutely pubescent, branchlets glabrous. L. glabrous, often drying black, elongate-elliptic or obovate, entire or minutely serrate, blade 1–2½, pet. ⅛–⅜ in. long. ♂ catkins slender, 1–1½ in. long, bracts obovate, at times emarginate, filaments hairy in the lower portion, sometimes more or less cohering, glands 2. ♀ fl. frequently occupying the upper portion of ♂ catkins. ♀ catkins 2–4 in. long, leafy peduncles longer than half the catkin, capsule glabrous, style short. 5. **S. alba**, Linn. Cultivated in the North-West Himalaya, indigenous in Europe, Western and Northern Asia. A large tree with grey foliage. L. white beneath with appressed silky hairs, narrow-lanceolate, denticulate, stipules lanceolate, deciduous. Capsule pubescent, subsessile, style short bifid, each branch bearing a 2-lobed stigma. 6. **S. fragilis**, Linn. Cultivated at Alikhel in the Kuram valley, in Gilgit, Ladak and Lahaul, indigenous in Europe and Western Asia. A fast growing middle-sized tree, foliage green, branches divergent, easily breaking off at the junction. L. glabrous or nearly so, lanceolate or oblanceolate, crenate or serrate. Catkins 1½–2½ in. long. Capsules glabrous, narrowed into a short bifid style. Specimens coll. by Lace, Peshin 5,200, Quetta 5,600 ft., named *S. triandra, var.?* in Journ. Linn. Soc. xxviii. 319, belong to this species. 7. **S. babylonica**, Linn.; Brandis F. Fl. t. 59. Weeping Willow. *Majnūn*, Punj. Cultivated in Baluchistan, Northern India, the Punjab and (less commonly) in the plains further east, also in the Himalaya. Indigenous in Northern China, also reported from Northern Persia and Kurdistan. The female tree was introduced into Europe about the 16th century, and has since that time been propagated by cuttings. In Northern India the ♂ is more common than the ♀ tree. A large tree, usually with drooping branches, branchlets glabrous, shining, buds thin, acute. L. glabrous, linear-lanceolate, 3–6 in. long, finely serrulate, stipules falcate, serrate. ♂ catkins short, cylindric, ½–1 in. long. Capsules sessile, conical, glabrous or slightly hairy at the base, stigmas 2, sessile.

8. **S. hastata**, Linn. North-West Himalaya, chiefly in the inner dry and arid valleys, 9–15,000 ft. Also here and there on the outer ranges, Kashmir, Hattu. Sikkim, high up the Lachen river, 11,500 ft.—Alps and mountains of Central Europe, also in Scandinavia. Northern and Western Asia. A small shrub, branchlets glabrous, dark coloured, l. elliptic or elliptic-oblong, glabrous or midrib and sec. n. hairy beneath, blade 2–4, pet. ⅛–⅜ in., stipules broadly ovate or semicordate. Fl. with the l., catkins ♂ 1–1½, ♀ 2–6 in. long. Capsules stipitate, glabrous, style filiform.

9. **S. Daltoniana**, And. Lachen and other inner valleys of Sikkim, 9–14,000 ft. Bhutan. A small tree, shrubby at high elevations, branchlets black, glabrous. L. lanceolate, 1–3 in. long, underside silky and coppery. Catkins slender, ♂ 1, ♀ 4–6 in. long, filaments hairy below. Capsule sessile, $\frac{1}{12}$ in. long. 10. **S. longiflora**, And. Inner Sikkim Himalaya, 9–10,000 ft. A small tree, branchlets and petioles thinly silky, l. glabrous when mature, lanceolate, entire, blade 1–2, pet. ⅛ in. ♀ catkins very slender, nearly glabrous, 2–5 in. long, on leafy peduncles, bracts minute. 11. **S. eriostachya**, Wall. Nepal. L. oblanceolate, entire, sparsely silky on both sides. ♀ catkins pubescent, 1½–2 in. long, bracts hairy, broadly ovate. Capsules sessile, style 2-cleft, stigmas long filiform, quite entire. The Bhutan specimens doubtfully referred to this in Fl. Brit. Ind. v. 683 fl. before the l.

(*b*) Fl. before the l., catkins sessile or nearly so.

12. **S. Wallichiana**, And.; Brandis F. Fl. t. 61.—Syn. *S. grisea*, Wall. Vern. *Bhainshra*, Jauns. Kuram valley 10–12,000 ft., common. Himalaya, common 7–8,000 ft., descending to 2,000 and ascending to 9,000 ft.—Afghanistan. China. A large shrub or small tree, young shoots grey-silky, branchlets, petioles and underside of l. silvery pubescent. L. lanceolate, quite entire, blade 2–5, pet. ⅛–¼ in. Catkins densely silky, on very short peduncles, supported by a few rudimentary l., ♂ 1, ♀ 2–4 in., ♂ bracts black. Capsules downy, slender, ¼ in. long, shortly stalked, stigmas subsessile. Regarding projections of the wood into the bark see Gamble Ind. Timbers ed. ii. 687. 13. **S. daphnoides**, Vill.; Brandis F. Fl. t, 62. Vern. *Bhashli*, *Shān*, Bash.; *Bāshroi*, Jauns. North-West Himalaya, 2,500–15,000 ft., common in the inner arid tract.—Alps and mountains of Central Europe, descending into the plains along river valleys. Russia. Siberia. China. A tall shrub or small tree, wood reddish, branches usually covered with glaucous bloom, youngest shoots silky, branchlets glabrous or hoary. L. lanceolate or linear-lanceolate, glabrous, glaucous beneath, serrate. Fl. before the l., catkins densely silky, ♂ 1–1½, ♀ 3–4 in., bracts black at apex, fringed with long silky hairs. Capsules glabrous or minutely silky, subsessile, style long, slender. 14. **S. insignis**, And. Kashmir, 6-8,000 ft. Pangi, 12,000 ft. (Lace, Aug. 1899). Piti 11,000 ft. (T. Thomson, Sept. 1847). A large shrub, branchlets tomentose, stipules semi-cordate, ♀

bracts black, obtuse, capsules hairy. 15. **S. Caprea**, Linn.; Brandis F. Fl. t. 60. *Sallow*. Cultivated in the Punjab (*Bed mushk*). Wild in Europe, Northern and Western Asia. A shrub or small tree. L. crenate, broadly elliptic or obovate, glabrous and more or less rugose above, grey-tomentose beneath, stipules large, reniform. Catkins densely silky, nearly sessile, ♂ sweet-scented, erect, 1-1½ in long, bracts tipped with black. Capsules downy, stigmas subsessile.

16. **S. viminalis**, Linn. Kashmir, Chamba, Lahaul, 5-9,000 ft. Baspa valley, Kunawar 9,000 ft. (D. B. Sept. 1864).—Europe (one of the principal kinds in Osier beds). Northern Asia. China. A shrub, branchlets and underside of l. densely matted with grey silky hairs. L. linear-lanceolate, margin revolute, blade 4–5 in., narrowed into a short pet., stipules lanceolate. ♂ catkins 1, ♀ 2–4 in. long, bracts brown or black at the apex, fringed with long silky hairs. Capsule grey tomentose, narrowed into a long slender style. 17. **S. obscura**, And. Lachen, Sikkim 9–14,500 ft. —China. A diffuse shrub, young shoots silky, l. lanceolate, 2½ in. long, glabrous or slightly silky beneath, midrib pubescent above. ♀ catkins sessile, bracts minute. 18. **S. eriophylla**, And. Khasi hills, probably also Sikkim.—China. A spreading shrub, branchlets and underside of l. with dense silvery tomentum. L. lanceolate, 2–4 in. long, sec. n. conspicuous. Catkins supported by a few small l., ♂ slender 1 in., ♀ 1½-2 in., capsule $\frac{1}{12}$ in. long, sessile, woolly.

19. **S. Sikkimensis**, And. Inner Sikkim, 9–14,000 ft. A tree, shrubby at high elevations, common in stream-beds.—China. Branchlets stout, angled, shining. L. lanceolate, underside densely silky and coppery. ♂ catkins supported by a few small deciduous l., stout, 1-2 in. long. Capsules sessile, densely silky, nearly hidden by the villous bracts. 20. **S. sclerophylla**, And. Inner arid valleys of the North-West Himalaya, 10–15,000 ft. A stout much-branched shrub, branches glaucous. L. rigid, glabrous or underside silky, pale beneath, elliptic or elliptic-oblong, 1-1½ in., veins finely reticulate, catkins ½ in. long.

B. Small, usually prostrate shrubs, the creeping stem often half buried in the ground. L. small, usually coriaceous and strongly nerved. Catkins after the l., terminating leafy branches.

(*a*) L. narrow, width less than one-third the length.

21. **S. Lindleyana**, Wall. Himalaya, Kashmir to Sikkim, 10–15,000 ft.—Yunnan. L. glabrous denticulate, elliptic-lanceolate ¼-⅜ in. ♂ catkins ¼-½ in. long, rachis, bracts and filaments glabrous. 22. **S. furcata**, And. in DC. Prodr. 16, ii. 291 (*S. fruticulosa*, And. in Journ, Linn. Soc. iv. 58 is older, but is described: foliis integris, capsulis dense cinereo-villosis). Bashahr, Garhwal, Kumaon 10–12,000 ft. Young shoots, rachis of catkins and filaments with long thin hairs, l. glabrous, glaucous beneath, serrate, elliptic-lanceolate or oblanceolate, ¼-½ in. long. Catkins: ♂ ½-1 in. long, bracts purple, glands of disk 3–4, red. ♀ ½ in., two long styles, ending in clavate stigmas, early deciduous. Capsules glabrous. 23. **S. Serpyllum**, And. Sikkim 10-14,000 ft. Branchlets hairy, l. glabrous, oblanceolate, ¼-½ in. long. Bracts of catkins black, obtuse, with long white hairs. 24. **S. Thomsoniana**, And. Inner Sikkim, 8–10,000 ft. A dwarf shrub, l. ¾-1 in., lanceolate, white-silky beneath, sec. n. oblique, prominent. ♂ catkins villous, 2-3 in. long.

(*b*) L. comparatively broad, width one-third the length of blade or more.

25. **S. flabellaris**, And. Himalaya, chiefly in the inner arid valleys, 11-15,000 ft., but also in the outer ranges, Hazara, Kashmir. Branchlets angled, glabrous, l. glabrous, crenulate, elongate-elliptic or obovate, blade ½-1½, pet. ¼-⅜ in. 26. **S. calyculata**, Hook. f. Lachen valley, Sikkim, 12–15,000 ft. Young shoots and young l. silky, with long hairs, l. obovate, blade ⅓-⅜, pet. ⅛ in. 27. **S. oreophila**, Hook. f. Sikkim, 14-16,000 ft. —China. L. $\frac{1}{12}$-¼ long, deeply serrulate at the apex, catkins minute, hidden among the foliage.

Sect. iii. *Synandræ*. Stamens 2, filaments connate entirely or to about the middle.

28. **S. pycnostachya**, And. Inner dry valleys of the North-West Himalaya, 12-15,000 ft., growing in clumps in dry stream-beds, cultivated in Ladak. Generally a shrub, at times a small tree, 16 ft. high with a trunk 2 ft. girth and divaricate branches. Young shoots silky, branchlets smooth, shining. L. lanceolate or linear-lanceolate, entire or serrulate, 1-3 in. long, sometimes slightly hairy beneath. Fl. after the l., ♂ catkins on leafy peduncle 1 in., ♀ 2 in. long, bracts yellow or brown. The l. turn red before falling. 29. **S. oxycarpa**, And. Outer and middle ranges of the North-West Himalaya 6-11,000 ft. A shrub or small tree. Similar to 28, l. larger, lanceolate, serrate, fl. with or a little before the l., bracts of ♂ catkins black, of ♀ brown. ♀ catkins 2-3 in. long. 30. **S. angustifolia**, Willd. Inner dry valleys of the North-West Himalaya 7-15,000 ft.—Western Tibet. Yarkand, Kashgar. Songaria. North

Persia and the Caucasus. A shrub or small tree, branchlets glabrous. L. very narrowly linear, rigid 1-3 in. long. Fl. after the l. ♂ catkins $\frac{1}{2}$, ♀ $\frac{3}{4}$–1 in. long, bracts glabrous, capsule sessile, silky. 31. **S. divergens,** And. Kishtwar. Baltistan. Zanskar, 12-15,000 ft. A small, much-branched shrub, l. oblong or obovate-oblong, $\frac{1}{2}$–$\frac{3}{4}$ in. long. Catkins, ♂ $\frac{1}{3}$–$\frac{1}{2}$ in. long, ♀ longer, capsules densely silky.

2. POPULUS, Linn.; Fl. Brit. Ind. v. 637.

Leaves as a rule broad, petioles generally exceeding one-fourth the length of blade. Bracts of catkins caducous, crenate or lobed. Stamens 4–30, inserted on the cup-shaped oblique disk, filaments generally less than twice the length of anthers. Capsule usually supported by the flat membranous circular or lobed disk, 2–4-valved, the valves spreading, a placenta along the median line of each valve. Species 18, northern temperate regions.

A. Leaves more or less lobed, buds pubescent, not viscid.

1. **P. euphratica,** Olivier, Brandis F. Fl. t. 63. Vern. *Padar*, Bal.; *Bahan*, Sind; *Bhan*, *Safedar*, Punj.

A middle-sized, usually gregarious tree, extremities sometimes hoary, buds

Fig. 198. Populus euphratica, Olivier. $\frac{1}{2}$.

slightly pubescent, not viscid. L. most variable in shape, those of seedlings, young trees, pollard- and coppice-shoots linear, short petiolate, 3–6 in. long, those of older trees on branches with short internodes, as a rule broad-ovate, rhomboid or cordate, blade 2–3, pet. 1–2 in. The broader l. are dentate, cut or lobed, while the narrow l. are generally entire. Intermediate forms frequent on the same tree and on the same branch. ♂ bracts oblanceolate, disk flat, 8-cleft, on a long slender stalk, stamens 8–12. Capsule lanceolate, 3-valved, $\frac{1}{4}$–$\frac{1}{2}$ in., on a long slender pedicel.

Common in the forest belt of Sind along the Indus, particularly in upper and middle Sind, where it forms standards over the underwood of Tamarisk. Not uncommon in the valleys of Baluchistan and the Suliman range on small feeders of the Indus, up to 3,000 ft., also here and there on the main river below Attock. On the lower course of the Sutlej river. Nubra along the Shayok river 10,000–13,500 ft., forming pure woods, often of considerable extent. Fl. Febr., nearly leafless Jan. to March. Coppices vigorously and throws up abundant root-suckers. Where subject to inundation the lower part of the trunk often gets covered with short horn-like roots, and short, hard, spine-like processes are found projecting from the wood into the bark.—On the banks of rivers in Afghanistan, Turkestan, Persia, Kurdistan and Central Arabia. Along the Euphrates and Tigris as well as along the Jordan in Palestine. Northern China. Algeria, on the hills of Oran. Witu, tropical East Africa. 2. **P. alba**, Linn. Vern. *Speddr*, Bal., Afg.; *Safeda*, Haz.; *Mal.* Bash. North-West Himalaya, 4–10,000 ft., wild and cultivated. Planted in Baluchistan, Sind, Trans Indus and the Punjab.—Europe, North Africa, Northern and Western Asia. China. In India a middle-sized, in Europe a tall tree. Buds, branchlets, petioles and underside of l. densely clothed with white tomentum. L. deeply lobed, blade 2–4, pet. 1–2 in., basal n. 5, midrib penninerved. Catkins hairy, stamens 4–10.

B. Leaves not lobed, buds viscid.

3. **P. ciliata**, Wall.; Royle Ill. t. 84.—Syn. *P. rotundifolia*, Griff. Ic. Pl. As. t. 546. Vern. *Palăch*, Haz.; *Chăm*, *Krammal*, Bash.; *Chelaun*, Simla; *Pahari Pipal*, Hind. North-West Himalaya 4–10,000 ft., not known from the inner arid valleys, though not uncommon near Chini and Pangi in Kunawar. Sikkim 3,500–9,000 ft. Bhutan. A lofty tree, buds lanceolate, viscid, the yellow resinous gum sometimes secreted in large masses. L. as a rule finely ciliate along the edge, pale and often minutely pubescent beneath, denticulate, usually cordate, blade 3–7, pet. 2–4, basal n. 3–5, midrib penninerved. ♀ catkins 6–12 in. long, pedicels as long as fl. Capsule glabrous or nearly so, ovoid, ¼–⅓ in. long, 3–4-valved, supported by the lobed disk. Gamble, Ind. Timbers ed. ii. 690, mentions a species evidently distinct in woods about Kalimpung and Dumsong, 3–4000 ft. l. quite glabrous, base not cordate, but rounded or truncate, bracts of ♂ fl. long, not early deciduous, capsule 2-valved, valves bifid at the apex. Haines sends specimens (826 Tonglu, Pankasari, 7,500–10,000 ft.) of a large tree with thick fluted bark, branchlets cottony, young l. densely tomentose, mature glabrous, base straight or cordate, sec. n. bright red above, petioles compressed, red. Capsules 2–3-valved, valves densely tomentose. This as well as the tree mentioned by Gamble merit careful study in the forest. *P. ciliata*, it must be remembered, is a very variable species. 4. **P. microcarpa**, Hook. f. & Thoms. Bhutan 7,000 ft. Quite glabrous, l. orbicular, sinuate, base rounded or subcordate, capsule ⅛ in. long, nearly sessile. 5. **P. nigra**, Linn. The pyramidal (rather cupressiform) variety (Lombardy Poplar) is frequently planted in the North-West Himalaya, particularly in Kashmir, in Ladak as high as 12,500 ft. Also occasionally in the plains of the Punjab, and of late years in Baluchistan. The variety with spreading branches is indigenous in Europe, in Northern and Western Asia and Northern China. A large tree, buds viscid, branchlets and l. glabrous. L. almost triangular, acuminate, crenate, blade 2–4, pet. 1–2½ in. long, basal n. 3, midrib penninerved. Catkins glabrous, ♂ pink, stamens 15–30, ♀ lax, drooping, disk shallow, pedicel short. Fruiting catkins 4–6 in. long. *P. canadensis*, Moench (*P. deltoidea*, Sargent Silva t. 494), the cotton wood of North America, differs chiefly by ribbed branchlets, more deeply toothed l. and more numerous stamens. 6. **P. balsamifera**, Linn. Indigenous on the Shayok river in West Tibet and in arid valleys of the inner N.-W. Himalaya 8–14,000 ft. Afghanistan.—Northern Asia. China. A large tree, buds viscid, resinous, branchlets angular. L. glabrous, pale beneath, ovate or ovate-lanceolate, dentate, blade 2–5, pet. 1–3 in. Fr. spikes 5 in. long, capsules nearly sessile, valves 2–4, usually 3, thick, almost woody, rachis pubescent. The North American *P. balsamifera* (the *Balsam Poplar* or *Tacamahac*), usually united with this, is considered by Sargent, Silva tt. 490, 491 as a distinct species.

ORDER CIX. LILIACEÆ. Gen. Pl. iii. 748.

Perennial herbs, with a creeping rootstock, bulbs or fibrous roots. Shrubs or trees in a few genera. Fl. as a rule bisexual. Perianth usually 6-merous in 2 series, imbricate in bud. Stamens 6 in most genera, ovary 3-celled, style 1, ovules 2 or more, rarely one, in the inner angle of the cells. Embryo small, surrounded by the horny or fleshy albumen.

The stems of *Dracæna* and *Cordyline* have a regular bark, and as they grow older they increase in diameter by means of a concentric layer of cambium cells, in which additional parenchyma and fibro-vascular bundles are formed.

Stem simple or slightly branched, erect or procumbent, l. lanceolate or linear, with numerous longitudinal nerves, basal or at an acute angle from the midrib.

Ovule 1 in each cell . . . . 1. DRACÆNA.
Ovules numerous in each cell . . . . . CORDYLINE (p. 641).

Mostly climbing, stems much branched.
L. broad, 3–7 basal n. joined by reticulate veins . . . . 2. SMILAX.
Narrow linear cladodia in the place of leaves . 3. ASPARAGUS.

1. DRACÆNA, Linn.; Fl. Brit. Ind. vi. 327.

Stem erect or procumbent, usually annulate, simple or forked, sometimes with a large branching head (*Dracæna Draco*, L., of Teneriffe), L. usually crowded, forming a terminal crown, lanceolate or linear, with a midrib often faint, and ∞ longit. n., transverse veinlets oblique. Fl. in terminal panicles. Perianth tubular or campanulate, 6-cleft, lobes narrow. Stamens 6, inserted at the mouth of the perianth-tube, anthers versatile. Ovary 3-celled, style filiform, 1 ovule in each cell. Berry 1–3-seeded, albumen horny, embryo small. Species 35, tropical and sub-tropical regions of Africa, Asia, and Australia. Besides the two following, a number of smaller species in India.

1. **D. angustifolia,** Roxb.—Syn. *D. ensifolia*, Wall. Vern. *Kunlinnet*, Burm. Khasi hills. Andamans. Tenasserim—Malay Archip. New Guinea. Australia. China. Stem 8–30 ft. high, l. linear, sessile with a broad base, 12–24 by 1–1½ in. Fl. white or with purplish tips, ¾–1 in. long, in large spreading panicles. 2. **D. spicata,** Roxb. Assam. Khasi hills. Cachar. Chittagong. Andamans. Western Ghats and Nilgiris. Stem 10–15 ft. high, l. elliptic-lanceolate, narrowed into a broad-based petiole, 12–15 by 1½–2 in., the midrib evanescent towards the apex. Fl. greenish-yellow, scented, slender, in a long, contracted, racemiform panicle. Berry crimson.

Cordyline terminalis, Kunth. Cultivated in gardens, and run wild in India and Burma, original home probably Malaya. Attains 8–10 ft., stem slender, l. lanceolate or elliptic-lanceolate, narrowed into a broad-based petiole, nerves branching off from the midrib at a very acute angle, blade (often variegated purple and black, var. *ferrea*) 12–24, pet. 3–6 in. long. Fl. white or purple, in an ample terminal panicle. Ovary 3-celled, ovules several in each cell, biseriate.

2. SMILAX, Linn.; Fl. Brit. Ind. vi. 302.

Climbing shrubs, stems slender, from a creeping rootstock, a few herbs. L. persistent, basal n. 3–7, joining at the apex, with a system of reticulate veins, petiole usually with 2 tendrils at the base. Fl. umbellate, diœcious. Perianth-segments 6, free. Ovary trigonous, 3-celled, 1 or 2 pendulous ovules in each cell. Berry globose, seeds usually 2, hemispheric. Species 180, cosmopolitan in the tropics and temperate regions. Of the Indian species only three, large and widely distributed, can be mentioned.

A. Umbels sessile.

1. **S. aspera,** Linn.; Collett Simla Fl., 522, fig. 175.—Syn. *S. maculata*, Roxb.; Wight Ic. t. 2059. Outer Himalaya from Kashmir eastwards, ascending to 6,000 ft. Khasi Hills. Upper Burma. Nilgiris, Palnis.—Ceylon, montane zone up to 7,000 ft. Mediterranean region. An extensive climber, branches armed or unarmed, l. often blotched, triangular or ovate, base more or less cordate, blade 2–5, pet. 1 in., basal n. usually 7. Inflorescence spiciform, umbels numerous sessile. Berry ¼ in. diam. in large pendulous bunches, red, finally blue-black.

B. Umbels pedunculate.

2. **S. prolifera,** Roxb. Vern. *Rām-dataun*, Dehra Dún; *Seinnabaw*, Burm. Subhimalayan tract and outer hills, from the Jumna eastwards, ascending to 4,000 ft., common in Sál forest. Deciduous forests in the moister parts of India and Burma. Ceylon moist region to 3,000 ft. A stout climber, stem prickly, up to 1 in. diam. L. rigidly coriaceous, ovate to orbicular, the 2 inner nerves separating from the midrib some distance above the base, blade 4–8, pet. 1 in., usually auricled. Umbels in large axillary panicles, fl. pale-green. Berry ¼ in. diam., red when ripe.

3. **S. macrophylla,** Roxb. Vern. *Ramdatūn*, Hind. Subhimalayan tract from Kumaon eastwards. Behar. Chutia Nagpur. Central Provinces, common. The Konkan. Assam. Chittagong. Pegu. Coco islands. A large prickly climber, l. ovate to orbicular, blade 6–18 in. diam., basal n. 5–7, pet. narrowly sheathing, not auricled. Umbels 2–3, alternate on a common peduncle. Berries large.

3. ASPARAGUS, Linn.; Fl. Brit. Ind. vi. 314.

Stems straggling or climbing. Minute scales, often spinescent, in the place of leaves, bearing in their axils tufts of needle-like branchlets, "cladodes," which have the function of l. Fl. rarely unisexual, pedicels jointed. Perianth deeply 6-fid, ovary 3-gonous, cells 2- or more ovuled. Berry globose, seeds 2–6. Species 100, temperate and tropical regions of Europe, Africa and Asia. Only two of the larger and more common species can here be named.

1. **A. racemosus**, Willd.; Wight Ic. t. 2056. Vern. *Satrāwal*, Dehra Dūn; *Sat-muli*, *Sada-bori*; Hind. Subhimalayan tract and outer hills, ascending to 5,000 ft. Common in most parts of India, not reported from Burma.—Ceylon, mostly in the dry region. Tropical Africa. Java. Australia. A tall, much branched, rambling and climbing spinous undershrub on a tuberous rootstock, prickles $\frac{1}{4}$ in., cladodes $\frac{1}{3}$–1 in. long, in tufts of 2–6. Fl. white, fragrant, in racemes 1–4 in. long. 2. **A. filicinus**, Ham. Outer North-West Himalaya, Kashmir to Kumaon, 4–9,000 ft. Bhutan. Assam. Khasi hills. Manipur. Upper Burma.—China. Erect unarmed, cladodes flat, $\frac{1}{3}$–$\frac{1}{2}$ in. long, in tufts of 2–5. Fl. white, single or in pairs, on long slender pedicels.

ORDER CX. PALMÆ. Gen. Pl. iii. 870.

Stem solid, either an underground perennial rhizome, producing flower-stalks and tufts of leaves, or more commonly above ground, erect or climbing. The stem above ground is in a few instances forked or sparingly branched; as a rule it is cylindric, simple and without leaf-bearing side branches. As regards the surface of the trunk two great classes may be distinguished. The stem of the first class is smooth and shining, annulate with raised rings (the scars of the leaf-stalks), and according to the length of the internodes these rings are at greater or less distance from each other. Many species of this class have the l. close together at the top of the trunk (*Areca*, *Cocos*), while in others (*Calamus*) the internodes are longer, the l. stand at some distance, often occupying a considerable length of the stem. The species of the second class (*Borassus*, most sp. of *Phœnix*) always have short internodes, and the surface of the stem is covered with the persistent base of petioles or their scars, which are arranged around the stem in a series of close spirals.

The l. of seedlings, as a rule, are undivided, while the l. of mature plants are either pinnately or palmately divided, the pinnæ or segments being mostly folded longitudinally, provided with numerous longitudinal nerves and transverse veins, which in the dry leaf are conspicuous in many genera. The petiole is always broad-based and generally amplexicaul or sheathing. The l. here designated as pinnate are in reality pinnatifid, the segments not appearing as distinct protuberances in the young bud, but being united in the youngest stage (Eichler, Palmenblätter, in Abhandlungen d. Königl. Preuss. Akademie d. Wissensch. Berlin, 1885). The pinnate l. of *Phœnix* and other genera have a more or less pronounced spiral twist.

The inflorescence is terminal in a few species, but as a rule lateral, in the axils of existing or fallen leaves. It generally is a panicle enclosed in bud by large sheathing bracts (spathes), the common peduncle (spadix) being often thick and sometimes woody. The species of several genera are monocarpic, not only those with terminal (*Corypha*) but also some with axillary inflorescence (*Caryota*, *Arenga*) the stem of which dies after the last spadix has ripened its seed. The fl. are usually sessile on the last ramifications (spikelets) of the spadix, and they are supported by one or several bracts (spathels), which are often cup-shaped or tubular. They are diœcious, monœcious, or polygamous, rarely bisexual. Calyx and corolla, as a rule, consist of 3 segments or leaves each, the perianth of the fertile fl. being commonly persistent in fr. Stamens 6, rarely 3, 9 or numerous, anthers 2-celled. Ovary 3-celled, one ovule in each cell, sometimes 3 distinct 1-celled carpels. Seed with a small embryo and a large endosperm, the cells of which are either filled with oil or have their walls much thickened, forming a hard, horny substance, which, when the seeds germinate, is converted into sugar.

The base of petioles as a rule occupies the entire circumference of the trunk, and consequently the leaf-traces (fibro-vascular bundles) of each leaf enter the stem from all sides. If we follow their course downwards we find that in their upper portion they bend towards the centre of the stem, while lower down they gradually bend outwards, and (frequently uniting with the traces of earlier leaves) run down near the circumference of the trunk. In their upper portion each leaf-trace consists of a few vessels which in *Calamus* and other scandent palms (as in *Vitis* and other climbers) are very large, over 0·5 mm. diam., with thin-walled phloëm, tracheides, and parenchyma, as well as a large mass of thick-walled wood-fibres, whereas the lower portion almost entirely consists of thick-walled wood-fibres. The space between the fibro-vascular bundles is occupied by parenchymatous tissue, which as a rule predominates in the centre of the trunk. Hence it follows that the hardest portion is near the outside of the trunk, consisting mainly of closely packed bundles of wood-fibres. Near the centre the tissue is softer, and hence in some species old stems are often hollow.

Preparatory to the production of flowers and seed the parenchyma in the trunk of *Phœnix* and other genera (analogous to what we find in the Beech before a seed year) is full of starch, which at the time of flowering is transformed into sugar. The starch of many species is utilized as Sago, while the sugary sap is obtained either from the cut spadix or (in the case of *Phœnix*) from the trunk below the crown of leaves.

I. Leaves pinnate or pinnatisect.

A. L. simply pinnate, leaflets induplicate, no midrib, fl. diœcious . . . . . . 1. PHŒNIX.

B. L. simply pinnate, leaflets, in the species here described, linear or lanceolate with midrib and reduplicate sides, the terminal leaflets often confluent as a plaited limb.

(*a*) Spadix androgynous, on the stem below the leaves.

a. Tips of spikes with ♂ only.

♂ fl. minute, stamens 3 or 6, anthers basifixed . . . 2. ARECA.

♂ fl. in the axils of broad bracts, stamens 6, anthers versatile . PTYCHORAPHIS (p. 647).

β. ♂ fl. in upper portion of spikes, both sexes in lower portion, fl. sunk in cavities of the spike . 3. BENTINCKIA.

γ. Clusters of 3 fl. (1 ♀ between 2 ♂) all along the spike, stamens numerous . . . . . . 4. PINANGA.

(*b*) Spadix among the leaves.

a. Erect, unarmed, spadix usually unisexual, fr. sessile, epicarp smooth, naked.

(1) Stems tall, stout.

Leaflets præmorse, auricled, stamens ∞ . . . . . 5. ARENGA.

Leaflets acute, stamens 6 . 6. COCOS.

(2) Tufts of large l. from a creeping rhizome . . . . . NIPA (p. 648).

β. Mostly climbing, armed, epicarp clothed with scales, usually shining.

(1) Stem short or none . . . . 7. ZALACCA.

(2) Stem elongate.

Spikelets concealed under large spathels . . . . . 8. PLECTOCOMIA.

Spikelets in the axils of large cymbiform or open deciduous spathels . . . . 9. DÆMONOROPS.

Spikelets in the axils of tubular or infundibuliform spathels.
Upper leaves reduced to a flagellum without leaflets . PLECTOCOMIOPSIS (p. 650).
All l. with leaflets, rachis mostly without flagellum . 10. CALAMUS.

C. Leaves pinnate or decompound, leaflets rhomboid or cuneate, præmorse.
(*a*) L. decompound . . . . . 11. CARYOTA.
(*b*) L. simply pinnate.
(1) Fl. bisexual, fr. covered with scales KORTHALSIA (p. 654).
(2) Fl. unisexual, fr. naked.
♂ calyx tubular or of 3 concave sepals, stamens 6 or more . . 12. WALLICHIA.
♂ calyx cup-shaped, stamens 10–30 13. DIDYMOSPERMA.

II. Leaves flabelliform.
A. Spadix axillary, among the leaves.
(*a*) Petiole unarmed . . . . . . NANNORHOPS (p. 655).
(*b*) Petiole spinous.
α. Fl. bisexual, carpels 3, distinct.
Leaf-segments connate to the middle 14. LIVISTONA.
Leaf-segments free . . . . . 15. LICUALA.
β. Fl. polygamo-monœcious, drupes 1–3 16. TRACHYCARPUS.
γ. Fl. diœcious, drupe large, with 1–3 fibrous pyrenes . . . . . 17. BORASSUS.
B. Spadix terminal, tree monocarpic . . . . 18. CORYPHA.

1. PHŒNIX, Linn.; Fl. Brit. Ind. v. 424.

Tall trees or low shrubs, the entire stem or the upper portion only closely covered by the more or less rhomboid bases of the petioles, stems occasionally branched. The first l. of seedlings, and sometimes the first l. of root-suckers are lanceolate, entire. Leaves pinnate, leaflets entire, linear, folded longitudinally and attached obliquely with their folded base to the woody common petiole, the lowest pinnæ usually transformed into spines. No midrib, a slender nerve on either side of the fold, nerves longitudinal, parallel, stout and slender, the slender n. often obscure. Transverse veinlets present, but as a rule only visible under the microscope in thin sections, cut parallel with the surface of leaf. In the majority of species the leaflets in the lower portion of the petiole stand in fascicles of 4 or 6, two or three on each side of the petiole, while the upper leaflets are usually alternate or opposite. Common petiole semiterete or flat, often widening at the base into a sheath, which frequently expands into a mass of tough reticulate fibres. Fl. diœcious, sessile on the bends of long glabrous undulating spikelets, usually supported by one or two minute subulate or triangular bracts, the ♀ fl. often approximate in pairs. The spikelets are inserted in horizontal or oblique lines on both sides of a flat woody peduncle. Calyx cup-shaped, 3-toothed and often 3-keeled, petals 3, in ♂ oblong, valvate, and much longer than calyx, in ♀ rounded, much imbricate and usually less than twice the length of calyx. Anthers as a rule 6, almost sessile, carpels 3, distinct. Peduncle often lengthening after flowering, fr. a single oblong 1-seeded berry, seeds with a deep longitudinal groove dilated inwards. Endosperm horny, embryo small, usually dorsal. Species 11, Africa and Asia. *Thinbaung* applies to all species indigenous in Burma.

A. Leaflets in the lower portion of the leaf markedly fascicled and often quadrifarious.

1. **P. sylvestris,** Roxb.; Griffith Palms t. 228. *The wild Date Palm.* Vern. *Khajūri, Khaji, Salma, Thakil,* Hind.

An erect tree, attaining 40 ft., trunk densely covered with the bases of leaf-stalks, and near the ground often with a dense mass of rootlets, no root-suckers. L. greyish-green, 7–12 ft., spines up to 4 in. long, leaflets 6–18 by $\frac{3}{4}$–1 in. Common petiole at base $\frac{3}{4}$–1 in. broad, the fascicles of leaflets up to 3 in. apart. Male inflorescence white, scented, compact, on a short peduncle. Fruiting peduncle 2–$2\frac{1}{2}$ ft. long, 1–$1\frac{1}{3}$ in. wide, terminating in large bunches of spikes, spathe thick, almost woody. Fr. 1–$1\frac{1}{3}$ in., from yellow to reddish-brown when ripe. Seed $\frac{3}{4}$ in. long.

Indigenous and gregarious in many parts of India, not in Burma. On the low ground along the Ramganga river in Rohilkhand, in the subhimalayan tract, and along river banks and on stretches of low ground in the Deccan and Mysore. Planted largely. Fl. H. S., Fr. Sept. Oct. Mats and baskets made of the l. The sugary juice is extracted in the cold season by removing in one place the lower sheaths, and by cutting a notch into the trunk, a thin slice being taken off daily from the surface of the cut.

2. **P. dactylifera,** Linn. *The Date Palm.* Vern. *Khajūr, Khaji,* Hind (Fr. *Khūrma*); *Sunbalun,* Burm. Cultivated and self-sown in Sind and the southern Punjab, also Trans-Indus. Attempts to grow it have been made in other parts of India. Believed to be indigenous in the Euphrates and Tigris Doab, and in the oases of the great African Sahara. A tall tree, attaining 100–120 ft., the foot often surrounded by a dense mass of root-suckers. L. grey, longer than those of 1, leaflets making a very acute angle with the common petiole. Fr. 1–3 in. long, pulp sweet. Many varieties are cultivated.

3. **P. humilis,** Royle; Kanjilal F. Fl. 360.—Syn. *P. pedunculata,* Griff. Palms 139; *P. Ouseleyana,* Griff. Vern. *Khajur,* Hind.; *Thakal,* Kumaon; *Konda Ita,* Tel.

Stem $\frac{1}{2}$–12 ft. long, diam. up to 9 in., densely covered with the stumps of leaf-stalks, more or less spirally arranged. Root-suckers develop frequently, when the primary stem has been burnt or injured. L. 4–8 ft., leaflets pliable, 10–20 in. long, $\frac{1}{3}$–$\frac{1}{2}$ in. wide, fascicled, more or less quadrifarious, the uppermost sometimes confluent, base not thickened and not decurrent on the common petiole, which is 1 in. broad at the base, spines up to 3 in. long. Fruiting peduncle 2–4 ft. long, $\frac{1}{2}$ in. broad, fr. $\frac{1}{2}$ in. long, orange, then black, edible.

Subhimalayan tract, Siwaliks and outer valleys from the Jumna eastwards. Assam and Khasi Hills (stems short). Upper Burma. Central Provinces. (Stems short in the Jabalpùr district, long on the Pachmarhis), Singbhūm, North Kanara, Nilgiris, Shevaroys, and other hills in the Peninsula (stems long slender on the Bababudān hills). Grasshills of Travancore, up to 6 ft. high. Fl. C. S. Dehra Dún. Nilgiris H. S. —China. Closely allied, and probably not specifically distinct, are the two following, with tall and robust stems:—4. **P. robusta,** Hook. f. Parasnath 4,000 ft. Stem 15–20 ft., diam. 12–15 in., tessellated with short persistent rhomboidal leaf-bases. 5. A species found by G. Marshall Woodrow on the western Ghats, near Nandgaon, gregarious on the flat top of trap hills (*Shaela,* Mar.), and described by him in "Notes of a Journey from Poona to Nagotna; Records of the Bot. Survey of India," i. 94. Stem 25–30 ft. high, diam. 15 in., marked with very closely and spirally-arranged leaf-bases. Leaflets broader than *P. humilis.* Spathe fringed with brown wool on the keel. A *Phœnix* with tall stems is reported by Gamble on the western side of Mahendragiri, Northern Circars. (Indian Timbers, Ed. ii. 731.)

6. **P. farinifera,** Roxb. Cor. Pl. t. 74. Vern. *Sanna ita, Chittu ita,* Tel. Coromandel coast, south as far as Madras. Trunk short, not over 4 ft., diam. 6–8 in., gregarious, forming dense masses, very difficult to pass through. L. shining dark green, 3–5 ft. long, leaflets quadrifarious, the upper sometimes opposite, 9 in. long, stiff and very pungent, with a hard yellow cushion at the base. Inflorescence 1–2 ft., fr. $\frac{1}{2}$–$\frac{3}{4}$ in. long, black when ripe, edible. In this as in other species of *Phœnix* the soft tissue in the centre of the stem is full of starch.

7. **P. acaulis,** Buch. Ham. Vern. *Thakal, Khajur, Khajeria,* Hind.; *Chindi,* Gond; *Chinnita, Konda ita,* Tel.; *Thinbaung,* Burm.

Stem thick ovoid, like a bulb, densely covered with the persistent bases of petioles, the ends of which are often bristly with the protruding hard fibro-vascular bundles. L. 2–6 ft. long, leaflets stiff, fascicled, the base thickened and decurrent, 10–20 in. long, ⅓–⅔ in. wide, spines 2–6 in. long. Fruiting peduncle short, generally concealed among the l. Fr. ½–⅔ in. long, edible, blackish when ripe.

Subhimalayan tract from the Jumna eastwards, common in grasslands and in forests of Sāl and *Pinus longifolia*. Chutia Nagpur, Behar. Sāl forests of the Satpura hills. Common in the Eng. forests and grasslands of Upper and Lower Burma. Fl. C. S. Dehra Dùn, H. S. Burma.

B. Leaflets nearly bifarious, not distinctly fascicled.

8. **P. rupicola,** T. And. Sikkim, on steep cliffs near the Tista and Mahanadi rivers. (*Schiap*, Lepcha). Trunk 12–20 ft. high, 8–10 in. diam. L. up to 10 ft. long, spiral twist very marked, leaflets 18 by ½–1 in., not stiff, bifarious, alternate or nearly opposite, transverse veinlets faintly visible in the green leaf. Fruiting peduncle 3–4 ft., fr. shining, yellow, astringent but eaten. Seed ½–⅝ in. long. 9. **P. paludosa,** Roxb.; Griff. Palms t. 229B. Common in the tidal forests of Bengal, the Andamans, and Burma.—Malay Penins. Siam and Cochin China. Gregarious, stem tufted, slender, 2–3 in. diam., 6–20 ft. long, upper portion densely covered with the long pointed leaf-bases, lower portion clear and annulate. L. 4–10 ft., leaflets 12–18 in. long, glaucous beneath, flexible, bifarious, fine nerves very distinct, ♀ fl. with 6 staminodes. Fruiting peduncle long, spathe scurfy outside. Fr. ½ in. long, black when ripe, embryo at the base of the albumen.

10. **P. Rœbelenii,** O'Brien. Siam, abundant on the rocky banks of the river Mekong, may possibly be found in Upper Burma. Stem tufted, 4 ft. high, slender, almost annulate, leaf-bases deciduous. L. 2–3 ft. long, rachis thin, leaflets bifarious, in the lower portion irregularly grouped, thin, 8 by ¼–⅓ in.

11. Mr. Gilbert Rogers informs me that a species similar to 8 forms forests on Cinque Island, Andamans, and is also found on the north-east corner of Rutland island. Stem single, not annulate, l. bifarious, base of petiole with much dark brown fibre. Spadix and fr. orange. He thinks that this may possibly be the *Phœnix* mentioned by Kurz in "Report on the Andaman Islands, 1870," 50.

2. ARECA, Linn.; Fl. Brit. Ind. vi. 405.

Stem erect, smooth, green in the upper portion, annulate, l. pinnate, base of petiole expanding into a smooth green amplexicaul sheath, leaflets thin, often confluent, with several midribs, attached to the rachis in a vertical line. Spadix androgynous, below the l., branched, bearing numerous close-set spikes, spathes several. ♂ fl. many, minute, occupying the upper portion of the spikes, petals much longer than calyx, stamens 3 or 6, filaments short. ♀ fl. larger, few at the base of spikes, sepals and petals broad, imbricate. Carpels connate into a one-celled ovary, stigmas 3 sessile, ovule 1 basal, erect. Fr. ovoid or oblong, supported by the persistent perianth, mesocarp fibrous. Seed with a truncate base, endosperm deeply ruminate, embryo basal. Species 24, tropical Asia and Australia.

1. **A. Catechu,** Linn.; Roxb. Cor. Pl. t. 75. The *Areca Palm*. Sans. *Guvaka*. Vern. *Supari*, Hind.; *Gua*, Beng.; *Poka*, Tel.; *Adike*, Kan.; *Kun*, Burm.

Cultivated in the tropical and subtropical regions of India and Burma, in gardens and orchards on the West Coast and in North Bengal; in extensive woods, usually irrigated, in the Martaban hills between the Sitang and Salween. A graceful, single-stemmed palm, attains 100 ft., diam. 6–9 in., l. 4–6 ft. long. Leaflets quite glabrous, with one or several midribs, upper confluent. Lowest spathe large, glabrous, pale straw-coloured, parallel veined. Stamens 6. Fr. 1½–2 in. long, fleshy-fibrous, supported by the persistent perianth, orange or scarlet, seed in the upper half of fr. The seeds (Betel nuts) are an important article of trade, the spathes are used to write upon, to wrap up parcels, and as covering leaf of cheroots in Burma.

2. **A. triandra,** Roxb. Vern. *Bangūa*, Beng.; *Tawkun*, Burm. Khasi hills. Cachar. Chittagong. Andamans. Martaban. Tenasserim.—Malay Penins. and Archip. Stems usually in tufts of 4–8, 12–25 ft. high, 1–3 in. diam. Stamens 3. Fruiting spadix large, much branched, spreading or erect, spikes terminating in long deciduous fringes, the seat of the fallen ♂ fl., fr. few at the base of the spikes, ellipsoid, ¾ in. long. 3. **A. nagensis,** Griff. Naga hills. Vern. *Tatpat*, Naga. Similar to 2, but larger, attaining 40 ft., fr. elongated, 1 in. long, used by the Nagas instead of Betel nut.

Ptychoraphis augusta, Becc. Syn. *Areca augusta*, Kurz in "Journ. of Botany," 1875, tab. 170. Nicobars, frequent. A tall slender palm, stem 80-100 ft. high, 1 ft. diam. L. 8-12 ft., leaflets narrow-linear, 2-3 ft. long, the lowest pair much longer. Spadix deflexed, bearing numerous long spikes, ♂ fl. at the ends, supported by broad bracts. Fr. 1 in. long, scarlet.

3. BENTINCKIA, Berry; Fl. Brit. Ind. vi. 418.

Tall unarmed slender palms, stem annulate, l. pinnate, pet. short, base amplexicaul, leaflets linear, not confluent, midrib distinct. Spadix androgynous, on the stem below the l., much branched, the spikes bearing in their upper portion ♂ fl., while the lower portion is occupied by groups of one ♀ with one or several ♂ fl., spathes numerous. All fl. are sunk in cavities of the spike and supported by several bracts. Fr. exserted, oblique, trace of stigma near the base. Seed spherical, grooved, pendulous, embryo basal, endosperm uniform. Species 2.

1. **B. Coddapanna**, Berry. Vern. *Văru Kamăvu* (*Rock Areca*), Mal. South Travancore, 2,500-6,000 ft., on precipitous cliffs, local, but very common within its restricted areas. Stem annulate, 20-30 ft. high, 6 in. diam. L. 3-5 ft., leaflets 30-40 pair, 24-30 by 1-1½ in. Spathe enclosing the young inflorescence, 12 by 2 in., pale brown, stands out horizontally from the stem. Spadix, after emerging from the sheathing spathe, much ramified, bears numerous short spikes, 9-15 by ¼ in., the entire inflorescence red, 2 ft. long and 3 ft. broad, ♂ fl. ⅛, ♀ ⅛ in. diam. Fr. bright chocolate coloured when ripe, ½-⅝ in. diam.

2. **B. nicobarica**, Becc.—Syn. *Orania nicobarica*, Kurz in Journ. Bot. xiii. (1875) t. 171. Kamorta, Nicobars. Common, associated with *Areca Catechu*, *Pinanga Manii* and *Ptychoraphis augusta*. Stem 50-60 ft. high, 9 in. diam. L. 5-8 ft., leaflets 6-24 in. long. Inflorescence 1½-2 ft. Fr. 1 in. long, scarlet.

4. PINANGA, Blume; Fl. Brit. Ind. vi. 406.

Similar to *Areca*, but spathe usually one, spadix sometimes simple, fl. along the spike as a rule in clusters of 3, one ♀ between 2 ♂ fl., ♀ fl. smaller than ♂. Stamens more than 6. Fr. ellipsoid, pointed at the ends. Species 24, India and Malaya.

A. Fruits in 3-6 rows on the spikes.

1. **P. gracilis**, Bl.; Syn. *Areca gracilis*, Griff. Palms t. 232 A. C. Vern. *Ram gua*, Beng.; *Tawkun*, Burm. Sikkim, subhimalayan tract and valleys up to 2,000 ft., common. Assam. Khasi hills. Cachar. Chittagong. Arakan Yoma. Pegu. Martaban, Tenasserim, in damp evergreen forest, ascending to 3,500 ft. A graceful palm, stems usually in tufts of 4-8, 6-20 ft. high, 1-1½ in. diam. L. 3-4 ft. long, the upper leaflets confluent. Fruiting spadix stout, 6-12 in. long, pendulous, often simple, fruits in 3 rows, ½-¾ in. long, scarlet or orange. 2. **P. Griffithii**, Becc. Khasi hills. Fr. in 4 rows on the spike. 3. **P. hexasticha**, Scheff. Southern end of the Pegu Yoma. Stem 25-30 ft. high, 4-5 in. diam. Spadix simple, reflexed, fl. spirally arranged in 4-6 rows, rachis thick fleshy.

B. Fruits in 2 rows on the spikes.

4. **P. Dicksonii**, Blume. Syn. *Areca Dicksonii*, Roxb. Western Ghats in evergreen forest up to 3,000 ft., from North Kanara southwards. Slender, soboliferous, often gregarious, stem smooth, 16-25 ft. high, 1-3 in. diam. Leaflets confluent. Spikes distichous on a short stout spadix, enclosed in bud by a thick rigid compressed spathe. ♂ sepals nearly as long as petals, stamens 20-30. Fr. ½-¾ in. long. 5. **P. Hookeriana**, Becc. Khasi hills. Stem slender, 3-4 ft. high, internodes clavate, scurfy while young, as also petioles and leaflets. Leaflets thin, opposite, 12 by 1 in., obliquely acuminate, the uppermost pair connate at base. Spikes distichous, 4-8 in. long, on a short spadix. Fr. ½ in. long, edible.

6. **P. Kuhlii**, Blume. Syn. *P. costata*, Bl.; Kurz F. Fl. ii. 538. Andamans.—Sumatra, Java. Stems tufted slender, 20-30 ft., 1½-2 in. diam. L. 3-4 ft. long. Spikes numerous, 6-15 in., on a stout spadix 8-10 in., fr. ½ in. long. 7. **P. Manii**, Becc. Andamans and Nicobars. Stem solitary, 50 ft. high, 5½ in. diam. L. 15-20 ft., leaflets 3ft. by 3in., leaf sheaths 4ft. long, clasping the stem. Spikes numerous, slender pendulous. Fr. broadly ovoid. 8. **P. hymenospatha**, Hook, f. Tenasserim. Stem slender ½ in. diam., petiole and leaf-rachis scurfy. L. 12-15 in. long, leaflets numerous, alternate, not confluent, 3-4 by ¼-½ in., finely acuminate, slender n. obscure, no stout n. besides the prominent midrib. Spike simple, stamens 9, spathe membranous, 1½ in. long.

5. ARENGA, Labill.; Fl. Brit. Ind. vi. 421.

Tall, stout palms, upper portion of trunk densely clothed with the black fibrous remains of the leaf-sheaths. Leaflets long, linear, usually præmorse, with a midrib and numerous longitudinal nerves, and one or two auricles at base. Spadix large, much branched, peduncle clothed with numerous imbricating spathes, branches pendulous, slender, fl. sometimes in groups, one ♀ between 2 ♂. Male: sepals 3, orbicular, petals oblong; stamens ∞, filaments short, anthers apiculate. Female: subglobose, petals triangular, ovary 3-celled. Seeds 2–3, compressed or plano-convex, endosperm uniform, embryo dorsal. Species 10, tropical Asia and Australia.

1. **A. saccharifera**, Labill.; Griff. Palms t. 235 A. *Malay Sago Palm.* Vern. *Taungôn*, Burm. Assam. Martaban and Tenasserim, occasionally on the Pegu Yoma. Commonly cultivated in India.—Malay Penins. and Archip. Trunk 20–40 ft. high. L. 20–28 ft. long, forming a dense crown, leaflets very numerous, white beneath, 2–3 ft. long, denticulate, towards the tip præmorse and slightly lobed. Spadices several, axillary, 6–10 ft. long, those of the uppermost axils flowering first, and having often mature fr. when the lowest come into fl. ♂ and ♀ fl. together on most branches, one sex generally preponderating, ♂ oblong-clubshaped, up to 1 in. long, petals three times the length of sepals, smell unpleasant. ♀: one in. diam., petals coriaceous. Fr. 2–2½ in. long, turbinate, supported by the somewhat accrescent calyx and petals, and crowned by the persistent stigmas, pericarp coriaceous, endocarp gelatinous, adhering to the seeds, acrid, and abounding in raphides. After all spadices have matured their seed, the tree dies. The black fibre of the petioles makes excellent cordage, the sap which runs from the cut fl. stalk yields sugar, and the heart of the stem yields large quantities of sago. The trunks of trees which have died after seeding are almost hollow, and are used as water-pipes. 2. **A. Wightii**, Griff. Palms t. 235 E. Vern. *Dhudasal*, Kan.; *Alam panei*, Tam. North Kanara, evergreen forest of the Ghats, very common near the falls of Gairsoppah. Nilgiris. Travancore 500–3,000 ft. Locally gregarious, with numerous root-suckers, trunk stout, 8–30 ft. high, covered with the bases of the leaf-sheaths, l. 18–28 ft. long, leaflets alternate, linear, auricles large unequal, the lower 1–2 in. long. Spadix 4, common peduncle 2 ft. long, quite concealed by the sheathing lacerate spathes. The cut fl. stalks yield toddy.

6. COCOS, Linn.; Fl. Brit. Ind. vi. 482.

Species 30. American.

C. nucifera, Linn. Roxb. Cor. Pl. t. 73. *The Cocoa-nut tree.* Sans. *Narikera.* Vern. *Narel*, *Nariyal*, Hind.; *Narikel*, Beng.; *Tenkaya*, *Kobbari*, Tel.; *Tengina*, Kan.; *Tennai*, *Tenkai*, Tam.; *On*, Burm. Trunk annulate, often curved, rarely branching, base thickened with a mass of rootlets. L. 6–12 ft. long, leaflets equidistant, linear lanceolate. 2–3 ft. long, petiole stout. Spadix stout, androgynous, divided into numerous drooping spikes bearing at their base ♀ with a few ♂ fl., the upper portion being densely covered with ♂ fl. Male fl.: sepals small, valvate, petals ½ in. long, stamens 6. Female fl.: ovoid, supported by several broad bracteoles, perianth accrescent, sepals 1 in. diam., round, concave, petals similar to sepals, but smaller. Fr. 3-cornered, 10–15 in. long, pericarp thick, fibrous, endocarp bony with 3 basal pores, indicating the 3 cells of the ovary. Cavity of endosperm before maturity large, filled with the cocoa-nut milk. The cut fl. stalks yield toddy.

Cultivated throughout the tropics, chiefly in the vicinity of the sea, but also inland. Original home uncertain. Abundant on the Coco and other uninhabited islands in the Bay of Bengal (on the Andamans locally), but possibly not originally wild. Prain in Journ. As. Soc. Beng. 60, 332. In India fl. in the dry season, the nuts require 9–10 months to ripen.

Nipa fruticans, Wurmb; Griff. Ic. Pl. As. Rar. t. 244–247. Vern. *Gulga*, *Gabua*, Beng.; *Dani*, Burm. Estuaries of rivers and tidal swamps, Sundriban, Andamans, Chittagong and the Burma coast. Ceylon. Malay Penins. and Archip., Australia. From a stout branching rhizome, creeping, either underground or along the surface, and rooting on the underside, spring tufts of huge pinnate l., 15–30 ft. long, leaflets numerous, coriaceous, 2–4 ft. long, many longitudinal n. on both sides of midrib. Fl. monœcious, densely crowded, the ♂ in cylindric spikes, the ♀ on a globose head, the spadix of both sexes with sheaths and bracts on the peduncle. **Male:** sepals and petals uniform, linear, valvate, anthers 3, adnate in their entire length to a cylindric staminal-column. **Female:** 3 distinct 1-celled carpels, surrounded by a few scales. Fruit a large nodding head, 1 ft. diam., consisting of numerous densely crowded angular one-seeded drupes, the exocarp fibrous-fleshy, the mesocarp hard, fibrous, and the endocarp spongy. Seed erect, the size of a hen's egg, grooved on one side, endosperm horny, with a central cavity, embryo basal, obconic. L. used extensively for thatching.

7. ZALACCA, Reinw.; Fl. Brit. Ind. vi. 472.

Stemless, soboliferous, armed. L. pinnate, leaflets linear-lanceolate, longitud. n. numerous, transverse veinlets conspicuous. Spadix usually unisexual, having cylindric, pendulous, catkin-like spikelets, in the axils of, and at first enveloped by, persistent spathes, fl. densely crowded. ♂: calyx 3-fid. stamens 6, inserted on the tubular rigidly coriaceous corolla, at the base of the 3 segments. ♀: sepals 3, more or less cohering, membranous, petals cohering, rigidly coriaceous, ovary densely clothed with stiff hairs, which (as the fr. ripens) develop into scales, the tip of which is brittle and often breaks off. Seeds 1–3, outer coat fleshy. Species 9 or 10. India and Malaya.

1. **Z. Wallichiana,** Mart.—Syn. *Z. edulis*, Reinw.; Wall. Pl. As. Rar. t. 222–224 (*Rumphii*); Griff. Palms t. 175; *Z. macrostachya*, Griff. Palms t. 178 A. B. C. Vern. *Yingan*, Burm. Pegu, Martaban, Tenasserim, common in evergreen forests.—Malay Penins. and Archip. L. 15–20 ft. petiole half the l. or longer, leaflets lanceolate, margin distantly spinulose ciliate, approximate in groups of 2–4, 12–20 by 1½–2½ in., the upper confluent, 4–6 stouter n. on either side of midrib. Sheaths and petiole densely armed with flat sharp spines in oblique half whorls, on the rachis gradually becoming solitary. Spadix nearly as long as petiole, spreading and often touching the ground, bearing distant cylindric, villous, pale rose-coloured, all but the lowest sessile, spikelets 2–3 in. long, enclosed by long spathes, which, as the fl. develop, split up into long shreds, rachis deciduously rusty-woolly. Fr. obliquely obovoid, 1–3 in. long, densely clothed with retrorse scales, terminating in a reflexed brittle bristle. 2. **Z. Beccarii,** Hook. f. Pegu. Leaflets strict, 18–24 by 1½ in., shining on both surfaces, margins with numerous strong sharp bristles, stouter n. 2–4 on either side of midrib. 3. **Z. secunda,** Griff. Palms t. 186. Upper Assam. Naga hills. Spikelets peduncled, much longer than spathes, fr. clothed with spreading lanceolate scales.

8. PLECTOCOMIA, Mart.; Fl. Brit. Ind. vi. 477.

Lofty climbers, stem up to 100 ft. long, l. pinnate, leaflets linear-lanceolate, petiole spiny, rachis prolonged into a thorny flagellum. Inflorescence terminal in *P. himalayana*, in the other species as far as known axillary. According to Hooker Fl. Brit. Ind. vi. 405, *Plectocomia* and *Plectocomiopsis* are monocarpic. Fl. diœcious on short spikelets, each spikelet in the axil of and concealed by large, usually imbricating distichous bracts (spathels). ♂: calyx cup-shaped, 3-toothed or -lobed, petals lanceolate, valvate, stamens 6–12, filaments connate below. ♀: ovary 3-celled, surrounded by 3 staminodes, perianth accrescent. Fr. globose, usually 1-seeded, protruding beyond the spathels, pericarp thin, clothed with tightly appressed scales, which terminate in pointed, soft or stiff, spreading or recurved appendages.

1. **P. himalayana,** Griff. Palms t. 219. Vern. *Takri Bet*, Nep.; *Ranûl*, Lepcha. Sikkim 4–7,000 ft., common. Leaflets alternate, green on both sides, linear-lanceolate, narrowed into filiform tips 2–3 in. long, 2 stout longitud. n. on either side of midrib, rachis armed with stout hooked prickles, confluent at the base. Inflorescence a terminal panicle, clothed with rust-coloured tomentum, branches drooping, the lower supported by perfect l., the upper in the axils of sheaths and flagella, without leaflets, bracts (spathels) distant, not markedly imbricating, 1–2 in. long, cuneate, with a triangular apex, ♂ fl. ¼ in. long, supported by 3 narrow bristle-pointed bracteoles, spikelets half the length of spathels. Fr. ½ in. diam., scales shining, fimbriate.

2. **P. khasyana,** Griff. Palms t. 218.—Syn. *P. assamica*, Hook. Bot. Mag. t. 5105.

Khasi hills. Stems 60–80 ft. long, as thick as the arm. L., including the flagellum, 30 ft. long, leaflets pale beneath, 8–16 by 2–3 in., stouter n. 3–5 on either side of midrib, the underside of rachis armed with short digitate spines. Male spadix branched from the base, branches 2–3 ft. long, drooping, bearing numerous spikelets, enveloped by the oblong imbricating distichous spathels, 1½–2½ in. long, which are white with a green tip and a brown band across. Fr. 1 in. diam., scales smooth or with ciliate margins. 3. **P. macrostachya,** Kurz in Journ. As. Soc. Beng. 43, tt. 16, 17. Vern. *Kyeinban*, Burm. Bithoko range, between the Yunzalin and the Salween at Great Rapids. (D. B. April 1859.) Probably not uncommon elsewhere in Lower Burma. A lofty climber, internodes short, l. 10, flagellum 2 ft. long, leaflets approximate in pairs or in threes, white farinose beneath, lanceolate, 8–24 by 1½–3 in., midrib and two longitudinal nerves close under the edge very stout, sheath and rachis with straight slender spines up to ½ in. long, in groups of 2 or 3 or in half whorls, appendage of scales stiff linear. Branches of male spadix 4–5 ft. long, pendulous, closely covered with broadly obovate distichous imbricating spathels, brown with black border, in the axils of which are the spikelets, shorter than bracts with alternate distichous fl. Calyx very shortly 3-toothed, limb woolly or ciliate, petals rigid, lanceolate mucronate, stamens 6. Fr. ¾–1 in. diam.

4. **P. assamica,** Griff. Assam. Leaflets white-furfuraceous beneath, 9–20 by 1½–2 in., margins thickened, stouter longitud. n. numerous on either side of midrib, but not very conspicuous, pet. stout, 1½ in. broad, armed with clusters and oblique lines of straight slender spines on a thick conical base. Branches of fruiting spadix 4–5 ft. long, rachis rusty-tomentose, spathels 2½ in. long. Fr. globose, 1 in. diam., bright rusty-red, villous from the long-ciliate recurved points of the scales.

9. DÆMONOROPS, Blume ; Fl. Brit. Ind. vi. 462.

Included under *Calamus* by Drude in Engler u. Prantl ii. 3, 52.

Leaf rachis produced into a long flagellum. Spathes large, at first concave and completely enclosing the branches of spadix, the outer largest, deciduous, ♀ fl. pedicelled. A red resin (Dragon's blood) exudes from the fruit of several species. Species 80, India, Malay Penins. and Archip.

1. **D. Jenkinsianus,** Mart.—Syn. *Calamus nutantiflorus*, Griff. Palms t. 208. Vern. *Gola bent*, Ass. Sikkim Terai, locally common. Assam. Khasi hills. Cachar Tippera. Chittagong. Climbing, stem stout, l. large, leaflets linear, equidistant, 20–30 by ⅝–⅞ in., the midrib and the 2 stouter n. sparsely setose with long bristles. Sheath armed with long, petiole rachis and flagellum with short spines. Fl. densely crowded on the branches of the much ramified unisexual spadix, spathes flat, lanceolate, coriaceous, the outer 1–2 ft., densely armed with spines ½–⅜ in. long, the inner unarmed. Fl. single, on the bends of a flexuose rachis, ♂ ¼ in. long, sessile, calyx campanulate, elegantly ribbed, ciliate along the edge, chiefly near the teeth, base of filaments connate with the 3-toothed pistillode into a fleshy mass, ♀ pedicelled, supported by an acuminate bract, pedicel enclosed in 3 tubular, overlapping sheaths, calyx campanulate nearly truncate, petals narrow. Fr. ⅞ in. diam., brown, scales trapezoid, deeply channelled. 2. **D. Manii,** Becc. Andamans. L. light yellow-green, 12, flagellum 3 ft. long, leaflets narrow. Fr. pedicel ¼ in. long, scales slightly channelled. 3. **D. Kurzianus,** Hook. f.—Syn. *Calamus grandis*, Kurz (non Griff.). Andamans. A lofty climber, the sheathed stems as thick as the arm, the canes up to 1 in. diam., "sheaths and (outer) spathe fearfully armed with whorls of broad sharp spines about an inch long" (Kurz). L. 4–6, leaflets 1–2 ft. long, linear, equidistant, rachis stout, angular, 1½ in. broad. Fr. ⅞ in. diam., pale brown, scales slightly channelled, calyx and petals explanate.

Plectocomiopsis paradoxus, Becc.—Syn. *Calamus paradoxus*, Kurz in Journ. As. Soc. Beng. 43. tt. 29, 30. Thaukyeghat forests, Toungoo. An extensive glabrous climber, the sheathed stems 1–2 in. diam. L. 5–7 ft. long, terminating in a flagellum with hooked thorns, the sheaths armed with sharp flat spines in half whorls, petiole and rachis with stout recurved thorns, often connate in claws. The upper l. reduced to sheaths with long flagella and no leaflets. Leaflets thin, inequidistant, 12–18 by 1–1½ in., stouter longitudinal n. 4–6 on either side of midrib. Male spadix decompound, ample, drooping, spathes and spathels tubular, limb truncate, shortly acuminate, spikelets ⅓–½ in. long, few-fld. Calyx striate, deeply 3-cleft, petals rigid, ⅛ in. long, stamens 6.

10. CALAMUS, Linn.; Fl. Brit. Ind. vi. 436.

Armed, rarely erect, usually climbing by whip-like thorny prolongations (flagella) of the rachis, of the spadix, or of the leaf-sheath, stem simple, in some species attaining 3–400 ft., annulate, the upper internodes clothed with spinous leaf-sheaths. L. pinnate, leaflets linear or lanceolate, with a midrib and numerous longitudinal nerves, some of which are stouter and prominent. Transverse veinlets conspicuous. Fl. usually unisexual, diœcious, monœcious or polygamous, spadix often unisexual, peduncle and branches sheathed by more or less tubular spathes, often with a lanceolate blade, the fl. in the axils of one or several, more or less concave or sheathing bracts (spathels). ♂ spikelets often varying in length in the same species, calyx campanulate or tubular, 3-toothed, usually membranous, petals rigidly coriaceous, valvate, stamens 6, anthers dorsifixed, filaments dilated and frequently connate at base, pistillode 3-toothed. ♀ perianth often more or less accrescent, staminodes connate into a cup. Fr. globose or ellipsoid, beaked, pericarp clothed with appressed closely imbricate deflexed polished scales, seed one, endosperm hard, bony, uniform, or ruminate. Species 160–170. India. Malay Archip. South China. North Australia. A few in tropical Africa.

I. Leaf rachis without flagellum.

A. Leaflets few, 20 or less.

1. **C. erectus**, Roxb.; Kurz in Journ. As. Soc. Bengal 43, t. 23, 24. Syn. *C. schizospathus*, Griff. Palms t. 187; *C. collinus*, Griff. Palms t. 186; *C. macrocarpus*, Griff. Palms t. 186 A, fig. 1, 2. Vern. *Kadam bet*, Beng. *Thaing*, Burm. Himalaya from Nepal eastwards, ascending to 3,000 ft. Assam. Khasi hills. Manipùr. Chittagong. Pegu, in evergreen forests. Stems erect, annulate, densely tufted, 12–18 ft. high, 1–2 in. diam., internodes short. L. 12–18 ft., leaflets 18–24 in. long, leaf-sheaths petiole and rachis armed with flat sharp pale spines, up to 1 in. long, semi-verticillate below, single above, leaflets green beneath, 18–24 in. long. ♂ spikelets 4–8, in. long, ⅓ in. broad across the imbricating spathels, fl. ⅓ in. long. Fr. ovoid, 1¼ in. long. dark brown, scales trapezoid, endosperm ruminate. 2. **C. platyspathus**, Mart. Tavoy. Leaflets alternate, rigid 10–12 by 1–1¼ in. ♂ spadix long, very slender, sparsely armed, spikelets ¼–⅓, fl. $\frac{1}{10}$ in long, spathes with long, flat, lanceolate blades. 3. **C. acanthospathus**, Griff. Palms t. 190 AB. Vern. *Gouri bet*, Nep.; *Rue*, Lepcha. East Nepal. Sikkim 3–6,000 ft. Khasi hills. Forms dense thickets mixed with *Plectocomia*. Leaflets few, inequidistant, lanceolate, 8–15 by 1½–2 in., sheath stout, densely armed with long and short spines, pet. long, very stout, armed with short spines on a conical base. Flagella on sheath and spadix. Fr. stipitate, shining, chestnut-brown, ⅜ in. diam., scales slightly channelled, fruiting calyx cupular, ⅓ in. diam., seed deeply pitted. 4. **C. Feanus**, Becc. Tenasserim. Similar to 3, but fr. opaque, scales not channelled. 5. **C. floribundus**, Griff. Palms t. 197. Upper Assam. Khasi hills. Silhet. Climbing, sheaths densely armed with bristles and long spines, rachis with long spines and short curved prickles. Leaflets bright green, linear-lanceolate, few, the uppermost crowded and often connate. Spadix long, decompound, spikes distichous, short, spreading and recurved, flagellum on the spadix long, armed with simple or compound recurved spines. Spikelets numerous, short, recurved. Fr. globose, ½ in. diam., shortly beaked, scales pale yellow, channelled down the back.

6. **C. Brandisii**, Becc. Courtallum. Stem slender, leaflets few, fascicled, sheath with solitary or aggregate slender flat straight spines, mouth with long needle-shaped spinules, pet. slender with few very long straight slender spines. ♂ spadix elongate, shortly flagelliferous, spathes narrow, tubular.

B. Leaflets numerous, equidistant.

(*a*) Fruiting calyx not pedicelliform.

7. **C. arborescens**, Griff. Palms t. 188A, B; Kurz in Journ. As. Soc. Bengal, 43 t. 22. Vern. *Zanôn*, *Danôn*, Burm. Pegu Yoma, southern part, common and gregarious in evergreen forest. Stems erect 15–20 ft. high, annulate, green and glossy, stoloniferous, internodes 7 in., leaves 6–8 ft. long, no flagellum on sheath or spadix. Sheaths and pet. armed with more or less oblique whorls or half whorls of brown or black broad sharp spines, up to 1⅓ in. long, the spines on the rachis smaller and less numerous. Leaflets white beneath, nearly opposite, 1–2 ft. long, black bristles along the edges and here and there on the stouter nerves. Spadix 5 ft. long, pendulous, spathes tubular, the lower armed with scattered spreading black spines, ♂ spathels short, closely imbricate, truncate, fl. nearly ½ in. long. 8. **C. Flagellum**, Griff. Palms 48. Syn. *C. Jenkinsianus*, Griff. Palms t. 186 A, fig. iii. Sikkim, ascending to 3,000 ft. Assam. Khasi hills. Cachar. East Bengal. Somewhat resembles 1, but scandent and l. smaller, 6–7 ft., leaflets numerous, equidistant, 24–30 in. long. Petiole deeply channelled, armed along the back with a solitary row of large hooked, along the edges with fascicled spines,

leaf-rachis armed with solitary and fascicled prickles, leaf-sheaths bearing a whip-like tendril armed with spines and bristles. Spadix long, peduncle long, armed with stout claw-shaped prickles. Fr. 1 by ¾ in., scales deeply furrowed, pale with a dark band down the middle. 9. **C. Guruba**, Ham.—Syn. *C. Mastersianus*, Griff. Palms t. 206. Vern. *Sundi bet*, Ass.; *Kyeinni*, Burm. Assam. Khasi hills. Cachar. Mouth of Megna. Chittagong. Burma, in evergreen forest. Slender, climbing, l. 3–4 ft. long, petiole and rachis rusty pubescent while young, armed with reddish-brown spines, leaflets equidistant, linear, 6–13 by ½–¾ in., usually 3-nerved. Thorny flagella on sheath and spadix. Spadix long slender, spathes tubular, terminating in long flat brown or green blades, the lower spathes armed, the upper often unarmed. Male and female fl. on separate spadices, spikelets distichously alternate on the slender ramifications of the spadix. Fr. ½ in. diam., scales pale, margin brown. My old notes of April, 1859, say: Sheath, rachis and flagella purple. 10. **C. nitidus**, Mart. Tenasserim. Similar to 9, spathes also terminating in long leafy blades. Possibly not distinct. 11. **C. leptospadix**, Griff. Palms t. 194, C. Sikkim, in damp places along rivers, ascending to 2,000 ft. Khasi hills. Manipùr. Scandent, forming tangled thickets, stems slender, foliage feathery. L. 3–4 ft. long, leaflets very numerous, thin, 8–10 in. long, narrow, acuminate, 2 stout n. as prominent as the midrib, rachis armed with single recurved spines. Spadix long, slender, pendulous, flagellum very long, armed with recurved claws, spikelets numerous, recurved, ½–1 in. long, spathels acute, membranous, fr. globose, ½ in. diam.

12. **C. pseudotenuis**, Becc. Western Ghats and adjoining hill ranges from North Kanara southwards.—Ceylon, low country. Extensive climber, stems slender. Leaflets finely acuminate, 10–15 by ¾–1 in., stouter nerves on either side of midrib 3–5. Pet. and lower part of rachis with straight spines up to 1 in. long, upper part of rachis with single stout recurved spines. Spadix with long flagella, armed with short stout recurved spines, usually several connate into a claw. ♂ fl. ⅛ in. long, closely packed on short recurved spikelets up to ½ in. long with 10–16 fl., sometimes short and only with 2–3 fl. Fr. nearly globose, with beak ⅓ in. long, scales pale, edge and basal appendix dark brown. 13. **C. Thwaitesii**, Becc. Ghats of North Kanara in evergreen forests, and near the sea coast at Marmagoa.—Ceylon, moist low country below 2,000 ft. A large climber, stems stout, 300 ft. long, forming impenetrable cane brakes. Leaflets sharply acuminate, 12–18 by 1–1¾ in., stouter nerves on either side of midrib 3–5, edges with long sharp bristles. Pet. and lower part of rachis with straight flat (often fascicled) spines, upper portion of rachis with claws of short recurved spines. Spadix with flagella, 15–20 ft, long, armed with claws of 3–7 spines. Fl. ♂: ¼ in. long, closely packed and strictly distichous, on spikelets 3–6 in. long. Fr. ellipsoid, including beak, ¾ in. long, scales furrowed, pale brown with dark border, endosperm uniform.

(*b*) Fruiting calyx pedicelliform.

14. **C. tenuis**, Roxb.; Griff. Palms t. 193 A. B. C.—Syn. *C. Royleanus*, Griff. t. 191. Vern. *Bet*, *Bent*, Hind. Damp places in the subhimalayan tract locally abundant from the Dehra Dùn eastwards. Assam. East Bengal. Sundriban. Chittagong. Pegu. A slender climber, forming extensive canebrakes, stem without the leaf-sheaths not thicker than a common quill. L. 1½–2 ft., pet. 5–9 in. long, leaflets usually 3-nerved, 6–12 by ⅓–½ in., pet. and rachis with single thorns. Thorny flagella from leaf-sheaths and spadix. Fl. ♂ ⅛ in., distichous, usually on separate spikelets, 1½–2 in. long, often on the same spadix with ♀ spikelets, sometimes ♂ and ♀ fl. on the same spikelet. Fr. straw-coloured, nearly globose, with stalk and beak ½ in. long, endosperm uniform. Called *C. Rotang*, Linn., in Brandis F. Fl. 559. 15. **C. melanacanthus**, Mart. Tenasserim. Rachis with a single row of short recurved black spines, fr. ¾ in. long, ellipsoid, scales pale, channelled, endosperm ruminate, embryo lateral. 16. **C. Rotang**, Linn.—Syn. *C. Roxburghii*, Griff. Palms t. 192. Vern. *Bethama*, Tel.; *Pirambu*, Tam. Coromandel coast. Pulicat. Courtallam.—Ceylon, dry region, common. Closely allied to *C. tenuis*, differs by shorter petioles, ♂ spikelets ½–1 in. fl. 1/12–⅛ in. long. Fr. subglobose, ½ in. diam., pale yellow with a shallow median channel.

17. **C. Huegelianus**, Mart.—Syn. *C. Wightii*, Griff. Palms t. 216 C. Nilgiris. Leaflets equidistant, pale beneath, linear, long acuminate, 12–16 by ¾–1 in., pet. and rachis armed with very stout short recurved spines. Spadix erect, spathes tubular, truncate. Fruiting spikes recurved, fr. globose, black, shining, ⅜–¾ in. diam., seated on the pedicelliform calyx with spreading lobes. 18. **C. Gamblei**, Becc. Nilgiris. Leaflets 20–30 in. long, fr. pale brown, scales deeply channelled, pedicel, including the campanulate calyx, ¼–⅓ in. long.

C. Leaflets numerous, more or less fascicled.

(*a*) Fruiting calyx not pedicelliform (fr. unknown in 21 and 22).

19. **C. viminalis**, Willd.—Syn. *C. fasciculatus*, Roxb.; Griff. Palms t. 195 A. B. Vern. *Bara bet*, Beng.; *Pepa*, Tel.; *Kyein ka*, Burm. Lower Bengal, common in the village

Bamboo jungles. Orissa. Ganjam. Chittagong. Andamans. Lower Burma.—Malay Penins. Cochinchina. Tufted, erect while young and in the open, usually climbing, stems long, without the sheaths ½–⅔ in. diam., the younger parts and sheaths covered with white powder. L. 3–5 ft. long, leaflets fascicled, linear-lanceolate, stouter longitudinal nerves 2–3 on either side of midrib, nerves, midrib and edge of leaf with sharp bristles, pet. and rachis armed with straight sharp spines ½–1½ in. long, sheaths with flat whorled or single spines. Spadix 15 ft. long, much branched, drooping, terminating in a long flagellum. Fr. globose, mucronate, ¼–⅓ in. diam., endosperm uniform. 20. **C. concinnus**, Mart. Mergui (Dr. Helfer, Jan. 1839). Climbing, leaflets glossy, nearly equidistant, 12–20 by 1–1½ in., 4–6 stout n. on either side of midrib. 21. **C. hypoleucus**, Kurz in Journ. As. Soc. Beng. 43, t. 18.—Syn. *Dæmonorops hypoleucus*, Kurz. Thaungyin. L. 2–3 ft. long, leaflets fascicled, lanceolate, white beneath, 6–9 by 1½ in., stouter n. numerous, sheaths densely spiny, rachis with short sharp recurved spines. ♀ spadix short slender, spathes large, oblong-lanceolate. 22. **C. myrianthus**, Becc. Tenasserim. Leaflets 30 by 2 in., white beneath, stouter n. numerous. ♂ spadix long, slender, much ramified, spikelets ⅛ in. long.

(*b*) Fruiting calyx pedicelliform.

23. **C. longisetus**, Griff. Palms t. 189 AB.—Syn. *C. tigrinus*, Kurz in Journ. As. Soc. Beng. 43 t. 25, 26. Andamans. Coco islands (*C. tigrinus*, Kurz; Prain in Journ. As. Soc. Beng. 60, p. 332). Pegu Yoma, eastern slopes in evergreen forest. Martaban. Tenasserim. Stems scandent (erect, stemless, Griffith), surrounded by tufts of leaves. Pet. and rachis armed with black broad sharp spines up to 1½ in. long, in oblique whorls or half whorls, in the upper portion less numerous and often single, leaflets green beneath, thorny whip-like tendrils from the leaf-sheath. Spadix decompound, nodding, terminating in a long flagellum. Fr. ovoid, beaked and stipitate, 1 in. long, with yellow and brown horizontal bands, scales produced downwards into a large membranous lacerate appendage, endosperm uniform. 24. **C. gracilis**, Roxb.; Griff. Palms t. 196. Vern. *Mapuri bent*, Beng. Upper Assam. Khasi hills. Cachar. Chittagong. Climbing, slender. L. 2–3 ft. long, leaflets lanceolate, in opposite groups of 3–5 on either side of the rachis, sheath, the short petiole and rachis armed with short hooked spines. Flagella on sheath and spadix. Spadix slender, drooping, spathes tubular, sparingly spinous, spathels not imbricate. Fr. oblong, ⅝ in. long, seated on the campanulate calyx, scales straw-coloured. 25. **C. Helferianus**, Kurz. Tenasserim. Slender, climbing, sparingly armed, rachis slender, trigonous, leaflets 8–12 by ½–⅝ in., in series of 2–6 on one side. Spadix very slender, spathes narrow, tubular, ♂ fl. ⅛ in. long, corolla smooth, not striate.

26. **C. travancoricus**, Bedd. Vern. *Tsjeru tsjurel*, Mal. Malabar. Travancore. Climbing, stem very slender. L. 18–24 in. long, leaflets in distant opposite groups of 3–5, 4–6 by ½–⅝ in., the greatest width at or above the middle, thence tapering to a capillary point, stouter n. not very prominent. Spadix long, slender, spathes with a long lanceolate blade, ♂ spikelets ¼–½ in. long. 27. **C. Rheedei**, Griff. Vern. *Katu tsjurel*, Mal. Malabar. Leaflets in very distant groups of 3, linear-lanceolate, longer than in 26. Fr. ellipsoid or oblong, endosperm ruminate.

II. Leaf rachis produced into a long flagellum.

A. Fruiting calyx pedicelliform.

28. **C. latifolius**, Roxb.; Griff. Palms t. 198.—Syn. *C. macracanthus et C. inermis*, T. And. Vern. *Korak bent*, Beng. *Yamata*, Burm. Subhimalayan tract from Sikkim eastwards, ascending to 2,000 ft. Assam. Khasi hills. Cachar. Chittagong. Lower Burma. A powerful climber, stem more than 100 ft. long, without the sheaths, up to 1 in. diam., l. 8–12 ft. long, leaflets usually in pairs on the same side of the rachis, lanceolate, 10–20 by 1–4 in., stouter n. 2–5 on either side of midrib, margins spinose-ciliate, n. naked. Sheaths densely armed with short spines and large broadly triquetrous ones up to 1 in. long, rachis and flagellum armed with claws of stout recurved thorns. Spadix very large, fr. nearly 1 in. long, pale, seated on the broadly campanulate rigid calyx-tube, endosperm ruminate. On the Salween in Tenasserim, in 1859, this species was esteemed most for rafting, and the ropes at the Kyodan were mostly made of it. Other Rattans considered useful in those days were: *C. Garuba*, Ham. (*Kyeinni*), and *Korthalsia laciniosa*, Mart. (*Wapo Kyein*). *Plectocomia macrostachya*, Kurz (*Kyeinbau*) was pronounced to be useless. 29. **C. Dorisi**, Becc. Burma. Fr. oblong, ¾–1 in. long.

B. Fruiting calyx not pedicelliform.

30. **C. andamanicus**, Kurz. Andamans. Nicobars. Coco islands. A lofty climber, not tufted, the sheathed stems as thick as the arm, the canes up to 1 in. diam. L. 6–8 ft. long, leaflets equidistant, alternate, linear, 24–30 by 1 in., margin and n. on the underside with scattered long spinescent bristles, sheaths reddish-brown armed with oblique

half whorls of slender black spines, which break off readily, rachis stout (as well as flagellum), armed with stout recurved spines connate in groups (claws). Spadix large, nodding, fruiting spikelets on naked peduncles partly enclosed by the spathes. Fr. numerous, distichous, ovoid, ½ in. long, pale brown, scales convex, not furrowed, appendix fimbriate. The best large cane of the Andamans. 31. **C. palustris**, Griff. Palms t. 199. Andamans. Tenasserim.—Malay Penins., Cochinchina. Foliage similar to *C. latifolius*, with which Kurz unites it. Fr. smaller, calyx-tube not pedicelliform.

Imperfectly known:—

32. **C. quinquenervius**, Roxb. Silhet. 33. **C. dilaceratus**, Becc. Nicobars. 34. **C. nicobaricus**, Becc. Nicobars.

11. CARYOTA, Linn.; Fl. Brit. Ind. vi. 422.

Tall Palms, l. few, broad, bipinnate, leaflets (pinnules) green beneath, very obliquely cuneate, tip præmorse or rounded. Spadices large, axillary, much branched, the branches pendulous, spathes 3–5, tubular. Fl. usually in groups of three, the central and lowest being ♀, the two others ♂. Male: sepals rounded, imbricate, petals coriaceous, oblong, valvate, stamens numerous. Female: fl. subglobose, sepals imbricate, petals triangular, valvate, ovary 3-celled. Fr. globose, seeds 1–2, endosperm ruminate, embryo dorsal. Species 10, from India to Australia.

1. **C. urens**, Linn. The *Mhar palm* of Western India. Vern. *Mari*, Hind; *Birli*, Mar.; *Baini*, Kan.; *Jiluga*, Tel.; *Konda panni*, *Thippali*, Tam.; *Chunda pana*, Mal.; *Minbaw*, Burm. Trunk annulate, attaining nearly 50 ft. and a diam. of 2 ft., no root-suckers. L. 18–20 by 10–12 ft., outer margin of leaflets produced into a narrow triangular point, terminal leaflets 2- or 3-lobed. Spadix 10–12 ft. long, the uppermost flowering first, and so on, until that next the ground has flowered and seeded, when the tree dies. Peduncle stout, curved, entirely covered with large coriaceous spathes, branches long pendulous, resembling a huge horse-tail. ♂ fl. half in. long or more, stamens 40–45, tip of anthers bifid or emarginate. Fr. reddish, ⅔–¾ in. diam.

Subhimalayan tract from Nepal eastwards, ascending to 5,000 ft. Assam. Khasi hills. Manipùr. Chittagong. Upper Burma. Pegu. Western Ghats, in evergreen forest. Orissa. The Circars. Shady valleys of the hills on the east side of the Peninsula.—Ceylon. Malaya. Fl. H. and R.S. The *Kitul* fibre from the leaves, sago from the interior of the stem, sugar and toddy from the cut spadix.

2. **C. obtusa**, Griff. Palms t. 236 A, B (*obtusidentata*). Mishmi hills 8,400 ft. Similar to 1, but leaflets obtuse, outer margin not tailed, ♂ fl. smaller. 3. **C. mitis**, Lour.—Syn. *C. sobolifera*, Wall.; Griff. Palms t. 236 C. Arakan Yoma. Martaban. Andamans.—Malay Penins. and Archip. Tufted, trunk 8–40 ft. high, 4–5 in. diam., with numerous root-suckers. L. 8–9 ft. long, leaflets (pinnules) obliquely præmorse, the outer margin acuminate. Fl. not regularly arranged in groups of 3, ♂ ½ in. long, flesh-coloured, stamens 17.

Korthalsia laciniosa, Mart.—Syn. *K. scaphigera*, Kurz (non Mart.) Journ. As. Soc. Beng. 43 t. 20, 21.; *Calamosagus laciniosus*, Griff. Palms t. 188. Vern. *Wapokyein*, Burm. Andamans. Tenasserim. Climbing, often forked, the cane (without sheaths) up to ¾ in. diam. L. pinnate, 2–4, flabellum stout, 2 ft. long, leaflets narrowed into a short petiolule, equidistant, alternate, ovate- or cuneate-rhomboid, præmorse, n. flabellate, stouter 8–12, transverse veinlets numerous, sheath produced into a tubular ochrea 4–5 in. long, splitting up into fibres. Spadix stout, piercing through the back of the leaf sheath, branched, fl. bisexual, densely crowded on catkin-like cylindric tawny tomentose spikelets, in the axils of tubular persistent spathes. Ovary imperfectly 3-celled. Fr. ⅕–⅓ in. long, 1-seeded, clothed with retrorsely imbricate trapezoid scales. *K. scaphigera*, as well as a few other Malayan species, have an inflated ligule on the leaf-sheath, inhabited by ants. In the Mergui district may probably be found *K. polystachya*, Mart., with slender spikelets 5–7 in. long.

12. WALLICHIA, Roxb.; Fl. Brit. Ind. vi. 418.

L. pinnate, leaflets white or pale beneath, with numerous longitudinal n. separating at acute angles from the prominent midrib, the terminal leaflets confluent, pet. angular, the edges separating into dark brown or black fibres. Fl. monœcious, ♂ and ♀ either on a distinct spadix, or the ♂ at the ends of branches with ♀ fl. Spathes numerous, sheathing, enclosing the peduncle of the much branched drooping spadix. ♂ fl.: calyx tubular or of 3 concave sepals, petals 3, stamens 6 or more, anthers linear. ♀ fl. not sunk in the substance of the spadix; calyx shallow cup-shaped or flat, 3-toothed or of 3 sepals, petals 3. Ovary 2- or 3-celled. Seed plano-convex, endosperm uniform, embryo dorsal.

A. Stemless, ♂ calyx tubular, stamens always 6.

1. **W. densiflora**, Martius; Bot. Mag. t. 4584.—Syn. *Harina oblongifolia*, Griff. Palms t. 237, A, B, C. Vern. *Kala aunsa*, *Goraunsa*, Kum.; *Takoru*, Nep. Subhimalayan tract, ascending to 4,000 ft., from Garhwal (Patlidun) eastwards, in shady and moist valleys, often gregarious, forming extensive thickets. Khasi hills. Chittagong. Stemless, thick tufts of large l., 10 ft. long or more, arising from the rhizome. Pet. nearly as long as the leaf-bearing rachis, leaflets lanceolate, slightly lobed, lobes præmorse, the nerves terminating in sharp points. ♂ calyx truncate, ribbed, ¼ in. long, petals linear, twice the length of calyx. ♀: sepals 3, petals concave, not ribbed.
5. **W. caryotoides**, Roxb. Cor. Pl. t. 295. Vern. *Saingpa*, Burm. Chittagong. Upper Burma, hills west of Katha, 2–3,000 ft., in evergreen forest. Martaban and Tenasserim. Stemless, tufts of l. from the rhizome 4 ft. long, leaflets fascicled in the lower part of the petiole, cuneate, lobed, the lobes large, præmorse. ♂: calyx tubular, striate, ⅛ in. long, petals linear, twice the length of calyx. ♀: sepals spreading, striate, petals ribbed. Ovary 2–3-celled.

B. Trunk 5–10 ft., ♂ calyx of 3 concave sepals, stamens numerous.

3. **W. disticha**, F. And.—Syn. *W. Yomae*, Kurz. Vern. *Minbaw*, Upper, *Zanaung*. *Letmè*, Lower Burma. Gonda hills, Oudh (D. B., March, 1875). Valleys of Sikkim Himalaya to 2,000 ft. Makùm forest, Assam (D. B., April, 1879). Upper Burma, ascending to 4,000 ft. in the hills east of Bhamo. Pegu Yoma, chiefly on the eastern slopes. Trunk 15–20 ft. high, 6–12 in. diam., in the upper portion covered with the fibrous leaf-bases, l. 6–8 ft. long, leaflets fascicled, linear-cuneate, præmorsely lobed. Spadix stout, drooping, 3–4 ft. long, ♂ fl. mostly at the ends of branches, calyx small, fleshy, consisting of 3 concave sepals, petals ovate acute, $\frac{1}{12}$ in. long, with 4–5 longitudinal n., more than twice the length of calyx. ♀: pet. broad-ovate, prominently ribbed. Ovary usually 3- sometimes 2-lobed.

13. DIDYMOSPERMA, H. Wendl. and Drude; Fl. Brit. Ind. vi. 420.

Small, leaflets few, similar to those of *Wallichia*. Spadix erect, simple or branched, spathes numerous, fl. larger than in *Wallichia*, monœcious or diœcious. ♂: calyx cup-shaped, 3-fid, petals coriaceous, valvate, longer than calyx, stamens 10–30, anthers linear. ♀: subglobose, sepals rounded, coriaceous, petals thick, triangular. Ovary 2–3-celled. Species 6. India and Malaya.

1. **D. nana**, H. Wendl. & Drude; Bot. Mag. t. 6836.—Syn. *Harina nana*, Griff. Palms t. 238 A. B. Assam and Khasi hills. Stem 2–5 ft., clothed with the rusty-hairy leaf-sheaths, leaflets about 5, trapezoid or cuneate, the lateral 7–10 in. long. Spadix stout, simple or sparingly branched, rustily scurfy, dense-fld. Fr. white, oblong, ½ in. long.
2. **D. gracilis**, Hook. f. Daphla hills, Assam. Stem 2 ft., slender, leaflets 6–8, broadly cuneate, fruiting spadix 8 in. long, sparingly branched.

Nannorhops Ritchieana, H. Wendl.—Syn. *Chamærops Ritchieana*, Griff.; Vern. *Pfis Fease*, *Pfarra*, Sind; *Mazri*, Trans Indus; *Kilu*, *Kaliân*, Salt range. Sind on arid hills. Trans Indus. Salt range. Gregarious, usually tufts of l. from an underground much-branched rhizome, at times an erect branching stem up to 20 ft. high. Petioles unarmed, concave, shortly produced into the blade, base with a mass of rust-coloured wool, blade cuneately flabellate, greyish-green, consisting of 8–15 linear rigid segments, 12–15 in. long, folded, bipartite. Fl. polygamous, male and bisexual in a large erect pyramidal much-ramified panicle, the branches in the axils of coriaceous sheaths, narrowed into a lanceolate blade, pairs of fl. in the axils of hyaline bracts in pairs, distinct or connate and bicuspidate. Calyx and petals thinly membranous, calyx flat, 3-toothed, petals connate at base, stamens 6 (sometimes 9 in the male fl.), anthers sagittate, dorsifixed, filaments dilated below and adnate to petals, ovary 3-celled, narrowed into the filiform style. Fr. 1-seeded, globose, ¾ in. diam.

14. LIVISTONA, Rob. Brown; Fl. Brit. Ind. vi. 434.

Trunks tall, annulate, l. nearly orbicular, segments linear, connate to the middle, each with a midrib, pet. spinous. Fl. bisexual, spadix axillary, sheathed by numerous tubular spathes. Sepals rounded, imbricate. Corolla coriaceous, 3-lobed. Stamens 6, filaments short, their dilated base united into a ring, anthers versatile. Carpels 3, globose, free, styles free or cohering. Drupes 1–3, seed one, ventral face hollowed, endosperm uniform, embryo dorsal. Species 13, tropical Asia and Australia.

1. **L. speciosa,** Kurz in Journ. As. Soc. Bengal 43 t. 13, 14. Vern. *Taung tan*, *Taw tan*, Burm. Evergreen forests in Pegu and Upper Tenasserim. Trunk 40–70 ft., pet. armed with dark-coloured, curved sharp spines, up to $\frac{1}{2}$ in. long and $\frac{1}{3}$ in. broad at base, blade 6–7 ft. diam., segments sharply 2–cleft at apex, transverse veins prominent. Spadix panicled, 2–4 ft. long, drupe dark blue, $\frac{3}{4}$–1 in. long, 1-seeded. 2. **L. Jenkinsiana,** Griff. Palms t. 226 A. B. Sikkim, lower hills and outer valleys. Assam. Naga hills. Vern. *Toko Pat*, Ass. Trunk 20–30 ft. high, 6–7 in. diam. Leaf-blade 5–6 ft. across, segments 70–80 obtusely 2-loded at the apex, transverse veins prominent. Spadix 2–3 ft. long, the peduncle entirely covered with chestnut-red coriaceous spathes. Drupe leaden-blue, $\frac{3}{4}$–1 in. diam. 3. **L. chinensis,** Rob. Brown. China and Japan. cultivated in gardens, trunk 25 ft., l. reniform, segments deeply 2-fid., long acuminate, drooping.

15. LICUALA, Rumph.; Fl. Brit. Ind. vi. 430.

L. nearly orbicular, divided to the petiole into numerous mostly cuneate segments, each with several main longitudinal nerves, pet. spinous. Fl. bisexual, spadix axillary, branches adnate to or beyond mouth of the coriaceous tubular persistent spathes, calyx tubular, 3-fid, corolla-lobes coriaceous, valvate. Stamens 6, anthers with a caudate base, filaments dilated below, adnate to the corolla-tube. Carpels 3, triquetrous, free or nearly so, styles filiform, cohering. Drupe one, by the abortion of 2 carpels, supported by the persistent calyx-tube, 1-seeded, endosperm horny, uniform, embryo dorsal, oblique. Species 45, trop. Asia, Australia and Pacific islands.

A. Fl. large $\frac{1}{2}$–$\frac{2}{3}$ in. long.

1. **L. peltata,** Roxb.; Griff. Palms t. 222. Vern. *Kurud*, Beng.; *Patti*, Ass.; *Salu*. Burm. Sikkim, deep hot valleys near the Teesta river. Assam. Khasi hills. Cachar. Chittagong. Andamans. Burma, Upper and Lower, common in damp ravines of the Pegu Yoma. Trunk 3–10 ft. high, sometimes thicker in the upper portion, due to the persistent petiole bases. Pet. up to 6 ft. long, blade peltate, orbicular, horizontal. segments cuneate, 16–20, plaited and 6–10-dentate at the apex. Spadix erect, longer than l., simply branched, with 3–5 drooping spikes, densely covered with greenish-white fl., rachis and fl. tomentose. Fr. red, $\frac{1}{2}$ in. long.

B. Fl. small.

2. **L. longipes,** Griff. Palms t. 224 A. B. Mergui. Malay Penins. Nearly stemless. pet. stout, 4–5 ft. long, blade 2 by 3 ft., peltate, segments 20–22, the lateral 3–4-lobed. the terminal broader, cuneate. Spadix erect, shorter than l., much branched, the branches in the axils of large sheathing spathes, lacerate at mouth, spikes and fl. pubescent. 3. **L. spinosa,** Wurmb.—Syn. *L. paludosa*, Kurz. Andamans, tidal forests. Nicobars. Malay Penins. Tufted, trunk 8–15 ft. high, 2–4 in. diam., pet. up to 4 ft. long, blade reniform in outline, 4 ft. across, segments 18–22, linear-cuneate. Spadix a little longer than l. Fr. red, $\frac{1}{4}$ in. long.

16. TRACHYCARPUS, H. Wendl.; Fl. Brit. Ind. vi. 435.

Trunk tall, l. reniform or suborbicular, segments linear, connate to the middle or nearly so, each with a midrib, pet. semi-cylindric, upper surface flat, edges spinous, separating near the base into a network of stiff fibres. Fl. polygamo-monœcious. Spadix axillary or from the axils of fallen leaves, stout, much branched, spathes numerous, coriaceous, tomentose, sheathing. Sepals 3, ovate, petals broadly ovate, valvate, stamens 6, filaments free, anthers dorsifixed. Carpels 3, distinct, stigmas recurved. Drupes 1–3, seeds erect,

ventrally grooved, endosperm uniform, embryo dorsal. Species 2 or 3, Himalaya, China, and Japan.

1. **T. Martiana**, H. Wendl.—Syn. *T. khasiana*, H. Wendl.; Bot. Mag. t. 7128; *Chamærops Martiana*, Wall. Pl. As. Rar. t. 211; *Ch. Khasyana*, Griff. Palms t. 227 A. B. Vern. *Jhangra, Jhaggar, Tal, Takil*, Kumaon; *Pakha*, Ass. Central Himalaya, Kumaon and Nepal, 5–8,000 ft. Khasi hills. Manipur, 6,000 ft. Kachin hills, Upper Burma. Forests of *Pinus Khasya*, Martaban hills, 4–6,500 ft. (Kurz). Trunk slender, attaining 50 ft., but often stunted, obscurely annulate. Pet. 3 ft. long, the lower sheathing portion separates into brown tough fibres, forming a close network of rhomboid meshes, the upper portion half round, the edges slightly denticulate. Blade orbicular, segments 30–40, linear, 15–20 in. long, connate to one-third or one-half their length. Spadix stout, drooping, clothed with dark rust-coloured down, branches stout, in the axils of large coriaceous sheathing bracts. Petals ovate, concave, whitish, filaments longer than anthers. Ovary and the rudiment of ovary in ♂ fl. hairy. Drupe one, oblong, yellow at first, dark glossy blue when ripe. Beccari regards the Kumaon tree as distinct and describes it as *T. Takil* in Webbia 52, fr. reniform, similar to *T. excelsa*. 2. **T. excelsa**, H. Wendl.—Syn. *Chamærops Fortunei*, Hook. in Bot. Mag. t. 5221. Upper Burma.—China, Japan. Trunk mostly clothed with old leaf-sheaths, fl. 2–4 clustered on tubercles. Fr. reniform, hollowed on one side.

17. BORASSUS, Linn.; Fl. Brit. Ind. vi. 481.

B. flabellifer, Linn. (the only species). *The Palmyra.*—Syn. *B. flabelliformis*, Roxb. Cor. Pl. t. 71, 72. Sans. *Trinarāja.* Vern. *Tāl, Tār*, Hind.; *Tād, Tamar*, Mar. *Potu Tādi*, the male; *Penti tādi*, the female tree, Telugu; *Tan*, Burm. Trunk attains 100 ft. and 2 ft. diam. near the ground, with a dense mass of long rootlets; while young covered with dry l. or the base of petioles, old stems marked with the black narrow scars of the petioles. L. 3–5 ft. diam., segments 60–80, shining, folded along the midrib, linear-lanceolate, pet. 2–4 ft. long, semiterete, edges with hard horny spinescent serratures. Fl. diœcious, spadix simply branched, sheathed with numerous open spathes, ♂ spikes 1–3 at the ends of branches, cylindric, densely clothed with thick closely imbricating bracts, numerous minute unilateral spikelets concealed by these bracts, so as to appear immersed in the spike, the fl. coming to the surface one by one, as they successively open, stamens 6, filaments connate with the corolla into a stalk. ♀ spikes terminating the branches of spadix, fl. globose, 1 in. diam., sepals imbricate, petals convolute, ovary 3–4-celled. Fr. subglobose, 6 in. diam., enclosed by the enlarged and partly fleshy perianth. Pyrenes 1–3, obcordate, fibrous outside, endosperm horny, hollow.

A native of tropical Africa. Cultivated and self-sown throughout India and Burma, as far north as Lat. 30°. The leaves are used for writing upon, the cut fl. stalks yield sugar and toddy, the fr. is roasted and eaten. Fl. March, April.

18. CORYPHA, Linn.; Fl. Brit. Ind. vi. 428.

Tall, monocarpic, dying after ripening their seed, at the age between 17 and 40 years. L. very large, orbicular or lunate, flabellately multifid, segments folded lengthwise, pet. stout concave, spinous at the edges. Spadix terminal, erect, paniculate. Fl. bisexual, small, calyx 3-fid, petals 3, connate at base, stamens 6, filaments subulate, anthers dorsifixed, ovary 3-lobed. Fr usually one globose drupe $\frac{3}{4}$–$1\frac{1}{2}$ in. diam., with 2 abortive carpels at the base. Seed erect, embryo at the summit of the uniform hard horny endosperm. Species 6, tropical Asia.

1. **C. umbraculifera**, Linn. *The Talipot palm.* Sans. *Tali.* Vern. *Tara, Tarit*, Beng.; *Tali, Shri-tali*, Kan. Indigenous on the Andamans and in the moist forests of the Kumta and Honāvar talukas of North Kanara, covering extensive areas near Gairsoppa and Yena, Talbot List, ed. ii. 343. Not wild in Travancore. Cultivated in tropical India, Ceylon and Burma. Trunk annulate, attains 80 ft. and $2\frac{1}{2}$ ft. diam., pet. stout, 5–10 ft. long, shortly bifid at the base, blade 8–16 ft. diam., cleft to about the middle into 80–100 linear segments up to 6 in. broad. Spadix pyramidal, 10–20 ft.

high, the broad sheathing bracts often pierced by the primary branches, drupes large. The broad leaf-segments of this and the following are highly prized for writing upon. Umbrellas made of the l. are largely exported from Kanara.

2. **C. Taliera**, Roxb. Cor. Pl. t. 255, 256. (*Talliera*, Roxb. Fl. Ind. ii. 174; Fl. Brit. Ind. vi. 428). United with 1 by Prain in Bengal Plants 1091 (1903). but kept distinct by the same author in Records of Bot. Survey of India iii. 293 (1905). Cultivated in Bengal, home uncertain. Trunk 30 ft., rough from the scars of the fallen petioles, pet. entire at base, segments united beyond the middle. Spadix 20 ft. high or more, primary branches in the axils of the broad sheathing bracts, drupes large.

3. **C. elata**, Roxb.; Griff. Palms t. 220 D. Vern. *Bajar*, Beng. Cultivated in Bengal. Trunk 60–70 ft., strongly marked with spiral ridges, the scars of the spirally-arranged petioles. Pet. slender, 6–12 ft. long, segments united to the middle, narrow. Panicle small, compact, drupes small. To this species Prain in Journ. As. Soc. Beng. 60, 331, had referred *C. macropoda*, Kurz F. Fl. ii. 525 and *C. Gebanga*, Kurz ibid. (non Blume), which is very common in Little Coco, and is also found on Great Coco. Later information however has induced him to refer the Coco as well as the Andaman tree to *C. umbraculifera*, L.

ORDER CXI. PANDANACEÆ. Gen. Pl. iii. 949.

Warburg in Engler's Pflanzenreich, iv. 9.

Diœcious trees or shrubs, some scandent with aërial roots, the stem often forked and supported, as if standing on stilts, by numerous adventitious roots. Leaves coriaceous, linear or lanceolate, sessile with a sheathing base, in tristichous spirals, edges and midrib usually spinous, the spines on the edges erect, those on the midrib usually retrorse, transverse n. prominent. Spadix axillary or terminal, simple or branched, clothed with leafy spathes, fl. small, crowded, perianth 0, no bracts or bracteoles. Stamens numerous, filaments either free, on the axis of the catkin, or connate below into a staminal-column, anthers basifixed. Ovary consisting of 1 or numerous carpels, free or connate. Syncarpium consisting of numerous more or less obconical fruits, the apex of each fruit or carpel distinct, pyramidal conical or convex, crowned by the hardened style or stigma, either drupaceous, or a many-seeded berry. Endosperm oily, abundant, embryo minute, basal.

A transverse section through the stem shows numerous fibro-vascular bundles, each consisting of a great hard horny mass of wood-fibres with one or several groups of vessels and sieve-tubes. The leaf-traces bend inwards from the leaf-basis and join on to other fibro-vascular bundles, but they do not show a regular bend outwards as is the case in Palms.

Erect or procumbent, syncarpium drupaceous, pyrenes as many as fertile ovaries . . . . 1. PANDANUS.
Climbing, carpels connate, forming a 1-celled ovary. Syncarpium a berry, seeds numerous, small . . . . 2. FREYCINETIA.

1. PANDANUS, Linn. f.; Fl. Brit. Ind. vi. 483.

Erect or procumbent. Ovary of 1 or several one-celled carpels, 1 ovule in each. Carpels free or connate, no staminodia. In fr. the upper half of each carpel hollow or filled with spongy, pith-like tissue, seeds large, testa membranous. Syncarpia as a rule solitary. Species 156, tropical Africa, Asia, Australia, and Polynesia.

A. Carpels distinct.

(*a*) Filaments free, on the axis of the catkin.

1. **P. fœtidus**, Roxb.; Kurz in Seemann's Journal of Botany v. (1867) 101, t. 62, fig. 4–6. Vern. *Keor kanta*, Hind.; *Kotki kanta*, Beng.; *Thagyet*, *Tawthagyet*, Burm. Khasi hills. Cachar. Central and East Bengal. Chittagong and coast of Burma in tidal forests. Prostrate, soboliferous, 3-5 ft. high, l. glaucous-green, linear, 4-6 ft. long. Spathes yellow, glossy, short sharp spines along the edges. Fl. fœtid, stamens free, on a fleshy axis, filaments short, connective long, mucronate. Syncarpium solitary, 2–5 in. long, drupes 5–6-gonous, apex pyramidal, terminating in a long spinescent

style. 2. A sp. mentioned by Talbot (List 846) as an "evergreen prostrate thin-stemmed soboliferous gregarious shrub, found in some of the North Kanara evergreen forests of the Siddapûr subdivision, which may be *P. fœtidus*, Roxb.," will perhaps be found to be identical with Hohenacker's No. 586 from Bantwalla, South Kanara, ♂ only. This seems to be the same as specimens from Ceylon which have been described as *P. Thwaitesii* by Ugolino Martelli, in Webbia 369. The ♂ spadix is very flexuose, the spikes 2–3 and the anthers ½ in. long.

(*b*) Filaments connate into a column, bearing a number of umbellate anthers at the top.

a Style forked.

3. **P. furcatus,** Roxb. Vern. *Jarika*, Nep.; *Satthwa*, Burm. Sikkim, outer hills up to 3,000 ft., Khasi and Manipùr hills. Chittagong. Lower Burma, frequent. Malay Penins. and Archip. Erect, branched, aërial roots from the lower portion of trunk, stem 10–40 ft. high, up to 6 in. diam. L. dark green, 8–15 ft. by 4–8 in., short stout and sharp spines on edge and midrib. Spathes inodorous, the lowest of the ♂ spadix up to 3 ft. long. Staminal-column ½ in. long, with 3–5 anthers at the apex. Syncarpium usually solitary, orange-red when fully ripe, up to 18 in. long (occasionally racemose and smaller, Kurz), drupes connate, nearly cylindric, apex convex, styles spiny, shining, deeply 2–3-forked. Talbot, List ed. ii. 345, states that this sp. is common in the Ghat forests of Belgaum and North Kanara, a low gregarious tree, forming dense almost impenetrable thickets in marshy places near watercourses. 4. **P. canaranus,** Warb. Mangalore, S. Kanara, in marshy places. The lower spathes of the ♂ spadix produced into a long spinulose flagellum, staminal column ⅛ in., anthers $\frac{1}{12}$ in. long. Drupes clavate, slightly forked.

β Style not, or only slightly forked.

5. **P. minor,** Ham.—Syn. *P. unguifer*, Hook. f. in Bot. Mag. t. 6347. Subhimalayan tract of Sikkim, ascending to 3,000 ft. Khasi hills. Chittagong. A dwarf shrub 2–3 ft. high, with long prostrate densely-matted stems and roots. L. lanceolate 1½–2 ft., terminating in a narrow tail, 1–3 in. long, stout sharp spines up to ⅕ in. long along the edges. Syncarpium solitary, 5 in. long, drupes smooth, clavate, apex convex, style sharp, entire or slightly forked. 6. **P. Scopula,** Warburg l.c. 76. Burma, *Satthwa*, Burm., fr. only known. Syncarpium ovoid, 5 in., carpels 1½ in. long, the outer surface of each pyrene splitting up into numerous fibres giving the fr. the appearance of a hard brush. 7. **P. graminifolius,** Kurz. Tenasserim. L. narrow linear, 12–18 by ¼ in., glaucous beneath, edges and midrib finely spinulose.

B. Ovary of 4–12 connate carpels.

8. **P. tectorius,** Solander; Warburg l.c. 46.—Syn. *P. fascicularis*, Lam.; Prain Bengal Plants 1101; *P. odoratissimus*, Roxb. Cor. Pl. t. 94–96. Includes *P. lævis*, Kurz F. Fl. ii. 508. Vern. *Keura*, *Keora*, Hind.; *Kea*, Beng.; *Kaide*, Kan.; *Mogali*, Tel.; *Talai*, Tam.; *Satthapu*, Burm. Sundriban. Sea coast of the Peninsula on both sides. On sand along the coast of Burma. Andamans. Coco islands, common on the sea shore. —Ceylon on the coast, "usually forming a belt above high water mark, very common." Mascarenes and Seychelles. Malay Penins. and Archip. China. Polynesia. Much cultivated. Gregarious, much branched, stem bent, sometimes up to 25 ft. high, but more often shrubby, resting on strong aërial roots. L. glaucous-green, 3–5 ft. long, caudate-acuminate, usually with strong spines on edges and midrib (var. *lævis* unarmed or nearly so), ♂ spadix with numerous sessile cylindric spikes 2–3 in. long, enclosed by long white fragrant caudate-acuminate spathes, staminal-column ¼–½ in. long, anthers cuspidate, inserted along the whole length of the upper portion. Syncarpium solitary, drooping, scarlet, drupes numerous (50–60), each consisting of 5–12 carpels, the apex of each carpel distinct, more or less convex with a small, variously-lobulate stigma.

9. **P. Leram,** Jones in Asiat. Researches iii. 163, with 2 plates. Nicobars, (*Larum.*) Stem branched, 30–50 ft. high, supported by long strong aërial roots. l. dark green. Syncarpium solitary, yellow when ripe, 20–30 in. long, weighing 30–40 lb., drupes 4–12-celled, lower portion fleshy, edible. 10. **P. andamanensium,** Kurz. Andamans. Stem simple or shortly forked, 40–50 ft. high, 8–14 in. diam., l. 8–15 ft. by 4–5 in. Syncarpium solitary, drooping, the size of a man's head, scarlet when ripe.

2. FREYCINETIA, Gaudichaud; Fl. Brit. Ind. vi. 487.

Slender climbers, stems annulate, attached to supports by adventitious rootlets. Ovary 1-celled, of 1–10 carpels, often surrounded by minute staminodia, ovules numerous on parietal placentas as many as carpels.

Syncarpium a globose or cylindric berry, seeds small, numerous, **testa** crustaceous. Species 62, Ceylon, Andamans, Malay Penins. and **Archip.**, Australia, Polynesia, New Zealand.

1. **F. angustifolia**, Blume. Tavoy. Malay Penins. and Archip. Scandent, stem slender annulate, attaching itself to supports by adventitious rootlets, l. linear, 12–18 by ¼–⅓ in., terminating in a trigonous spinulose serrate tail, base sheathing. Inflorescence a short terminal raceme bearing 3–5 spikes in the axils of large cymbiform yellowish bracts, the outer narrowed into a spinulose serrate tail. ♂ spikes pedunculate, 8–12 in. long, filaments short thick. ♀ 9–12 in. long, ovary surrounded by minute staminodes, stigmata 3–4. 2. **F. insignis**, Blume. Andamans. Java. L. 18–36 by ¾–1 in., spinulose-serrate on the margin and on the midrib beneath. Inflorescence terminal, consisting of 2–3 peduncled spikes, bracts concave, the inner pink, the outer green, stigmata 2–3. Syncarpium cylindric, 2½ in. long.

Order CXII. GRAMINEÆ.

Tribe XIII. BAMBUSEÆ. Gen. Pl. iii. 1094.

With the assistance of C. B. Smales, Indian Forest Dept.

(Munro, A Monograph of the *Bambusaceæ* in Trans. Linn. Soc. xxvi. 1, 1868.—Gamble, The *Bambuseæ* of British India in Annals Royal Bot. Gard. Calcutta vii. 1896.—Brandis, Biological Notes on Indian Bamboos in Indian For. xxv. 1, 1899.)

Perennial grasses, as a rule of extremely gregarious habit. A woody rootstock or rhizome, consisting, in the case of tufted species, of short twisted and entangled branches, producing a large number of more or less closely-packed woody stems (culms), or, in the case of single-stemmed species, with long creeping branches, producing a number of culms standing 1–3 ft. apart. The culms are jointed, hollow between joints, rarely climbing, usually erect, the outer culms of the clumps often overhanging, in some species the culms almost lying on the ground. The young shoots which come up in the rainy season, either in the midst of dense clumps or, in the single-stemmed species, separately from the ground, have the full diameter of the culm, but are quite soft. They are enclosed in large, generally coriaceous sheaths, often hairy outside, which arise from the joints or nodes, and as a rule terminate in a more or less imperfect blade. These sheaths, like those which bear the ordinary green l. of the Bamboos, are strictly alternate, there is an angle or interval of 180° between the axillary buds of two successive sheaths. The shoots grow with great rapidity, usually attaining their full length in less than a month. As the internodes lengthen out telescopically and the nodes separate, the green surface of the internodes appears between the sheaths, which usually are yellow or brown, often producing a remarkable contrast. The general appearance, length, texture and shape of these sheaths and their blade afford good characters for distinguishing the different species. In many species the internodes, while young, are covered with minute silky hairs. After the culms have attained their full length, the buds, which are in the axils of the sheaths, develop, in the upper portion of the culm, into leaf-bearing, jointed, woody branches, which generally stand in half-whorls. In many species the buds in the lower portion of the stem develop not at all or only very sparingly, while in others they grow into half-whorls of branches, one or a few of which often are much stouter and larger than the others, or they grow out into short stiff, sometimes spinescent branches, leafless or with a few leaves. At the nodes two rings may generally be distinguished, the lower is the scar of the culm-sheath, while the upper ring, which is not always clearly marked, corresponds to the node itself. Above the lower ring is the axillary bud, and in the lower portion of the culm not unfrequently a ring of rootlets. The rootlets, as well as the branches, when they develop before the culm-sheaths have fallen, pierce through the sheath at its base. These rootlets rarely reach the ground, and often become hard and spinescent.

The leaves are distichous, and consist of a tubular sheath, split to the base, and a linear-oblong or lanceolate blade with a midrib and numerous longitudinal veins (fibro-vascular bundles), usually of two classes, stout or coarse and thin, generally 5–9 thin between two stout nerves. The blade is joined to the sheath by a short petiole. Half-way between two longitudinal nerves and parallel to them is a transparent band, due to several lines of large cells, belonging to the upper epidermis, which are frequently, but not in all cases, filled with bright colourless masses of Silica (Silicon dioxide). All Bamboo leaves have transverse veins, consisting of wood-fibres, which run across from one longitudinal nerve to the next, straight, oblique, or with a bend in the middle. In many species these transverse veins are conspicuous, particularly on dry leaves, but they can usually be distinguished, under the lens or microscope, as bright translucent dots at the point where they cross the band of Silica cells. (Translucent glands, Gamble.) Pieces of dry l. boiled in water, and examined in glycerine, often show the transverse veins; they can be made more conspicuous by bleaching reagents or by scraping off part of the tissue filled with chlorophyll. On the under side of the leaf the epidermis has numerous solid protuberances or hairs, which usually are short and thick-walled, in some species long and soft. The leaves being distichous, an inner and an outer edge may be distinguished; on the inner edge (in many species on both edges) we find as a rule a colourless band, fringed with longer or shorter thick-walled sharply-pointed hairs, while the outer edge is often rough on the upper side, with lines of short rigid hairs along the outermost veins.

The identification of many species, when leaves only are available, may be facilitated by counting the number of longitudinal nerves on $\frac{1}{4}$ in. In most genera the number varies between 20 and 50. *Dendrocalamus* and *Melocalamus* have 20–30, and the following species have less than 24: *Arundinaria Walkeriana* (leaf 1–1$\frac{2}{3}$ in. wide), *A. Hookeriana* ($\frac{1}{2}$–1$\frac{1}{2}$ in.), *Bambusa khasiana* (1–1$\frac{1}{2}$ in.), *B. Griffithiana* (3 in.), *Pseudostachyum polymorphum* (1–2 in.), *Dinochloa McClellandi* (2–4 in.), *D. andamanica* (1–2 in.), *Teinostachyum Helferi* (1$\frac{1}{2}$–3$\frac{1}{2}$ in.), *T. Wightii* (1–3 in.), *Cephalostachyum capitatum* (1–2 in.), *C. latifolium* (2–4 in.), *C. Fuchsianum* (2–4 in.), *Meocanna bambusoides* (1–4 in.). As may be expected, many broad-leaved species have the longitudinal n. far apart, but there also are broad-leaved species with the longitudinal nerves close together. For most species the number of n. on $\frac{1}{4}$ in. has here been stated. Conspicuous transverse veins are found in *Phyllostachys*, in the majority of *Arundinaria*, in *Pseudostachyum polymorphum*, and a few other species. When close together they form squares or short rectangles with the longitudinal nerves (*Phyllostachys*, *Arundinaria densifolia*, *racemosa*, *elegans*, *jaunsarensis*, *hirsuta*). In counting the number of nerves on $\frac{1}{4}$ in., only full-grown l. should be selected, and the nerves must be counted in the middle, half-way between base and tip. If this is done the results will be found to be fairly uniform, whether the leaf selected is broad or narrow. Leaves grown under exceptional conditions, for instance, in a hothouse, are apt to be irregular, and should be avoided. The nerves are often closer together near the edge of the leaf, hence an average should be struck between the countings near the edge and the midrib. Care must be taken to count the *nerves* only, not the translucent lines of silica cells, a strong lens or a small microscope should be used; and in the case of dry leaves it is advisable to boil a small piece in water and place it in glycerine.

Fl. mostly bisexual, in distichous spikelets, usually arranged in large panicles. The spikelet consists of a number of distichous bracts (or glumes), the lower and sometimes the upper being empty. Each flowering glume bears in its axil the palea, a membranous, usually transparent bract, which has its back appressed to the axis of the spikelet and which, except when terminal, is 2-keeled as a rule and strongly ciliate along the keels. Enclosed by palea and flowering glume is a one-celled ovary with a terminal style, with 2 or 3 linear plumose stigmas, surrounded by 3 or 6, rarely more stamens, and in most genera by 2 or 3 membranous, often ciliate scales (lodicules). Anthers 2-celled, cells parallel, contiguous, opening longitudinally. Fr. in some genera with a thick, more or less fleshy, but more usually thin crustaceous or membranous pericarp (caryopsis). Seed as a rule with a large mealy endosperm, embryo small, basal on the outside. Embryo with a broad fleshy cotyledonary body (scutellum) contiguous to the endosperm. Some genera (*Dinochloa*, *Melocalamus*, *Melocanna* and *Ochlandra*) have no endosperm in the ripe seed, and the germinating embryo derives its nourishment through a very large scutellum from the pericarp.

In regard to their habit of flowering, Bamboos may be divided into three great classes. *First*, those which flower annually or nearly so, the flower panicle terminating leaf-bearing culms. Instances: *Arundinaria Wightii*, *Bambusa lineata*, *Ochlandra stridula*. In these cases the plant does not die after flowering. *Second*, those which flower gregariously and periodically, all culms of one clump and all clumps in one district flowering simultaneously. The leaves fall, and the whole culm is one huge flowering panicle. In these cases the culms die after ripening their seed, and usually the underground rhizome also dies. Instances: *Bambusa polymorpha*, *arundinacea*, *Melocanna bambusoides*. The area over which these species flower simultaneously is circumscribed. In different districts they flower at different times. (Ind. For. xxv. 10.) *Third*, irregularly flowering species. One or a few culms in one clump, or a few clumps in one locality, are in flower at any one time, while at other times all culms of one clump and all clumps in one district are simultaneously covered with flowers. Instances: *Oxytenanthera albociliata*, *Dendrocalamus strictus*, *D. Hamiltonii*, *Cephalostachyum pergracile*. The majority of species belongs to the third class. Some species may be considered to hold an intermediate place, but as a rule it will be found convenient to maintain the three classes here indicated. It should here be mentioned that offsets taken from a clump some time before it flowers come into flower at the same time as the parent clump. There are indications, that in dry stony places and in exceptionally dry seasons Bamboos flower earlier and more abundantly.

In districts where clearings are made for purposes of temporary cultivation (Taungya, Dhya, Kumri) in Bamboo Forest, it will be found that in the secondary growth, which springs up after the crop has been reaped and the fields have been deserted, different species of Bamboo show a different behaviour. In a forest consisting of tufted species a mass of tall grasses and large herbs, together with the coppice shoots of trees and some seedlings will usually form the second growth, in which the slender shoots coming up from the burnt Bamboo clumps, only gradually assert themselves. The huge and intricate mass of rhizomes of a tufted species is close to and often partially above the surface, and hence suffers more damage from the Taungya fire than the long branches of the rhizome of single-stemmed species, which as a rule are at some depth underground. As a matter of fact, when Taungyas are cut in forests of single-stemmed species, the second growth frequently consists entirely of a dense mass of Bamboos. There are however exceptions; thus in the Shan States east of the Salween river the second growth over large areas is reported to consist entirely of *Oxytenanthera albo-ciliata*, a densely-tufted species (H. N. Thompson, in Forest Report Southern Circle Upper Burma, 1900–1901, p. 50).

When after the flowering of Bamboos in a certain district the fires of the hot season have swept away the tangled mass of dry stems, the next rainy season produces millions of seedling Bamboos, which soon grow up into slender plants, 2–3 ft. high, forming dense waving green masses on the ground. Among these millions of plants the stronger gradually get the upper hand, and these in course of time develop into those remarkable rhizomes, consisting in tufted species of innumerable stout twisting and interlaced branches, which produce the leaf-bearing culms. The development of Bamboo seedlings into a clump is a most remarkable process, which has not yet been sufficiently studied (cf. Brandis, in Ind. For., xxv. 4). Nor has it yet been ascertained how many years a seedling requires to form a clump consisting of full-sized stems. In the case of *Bambusa polymorpha* and *arundinacea* the period is probably between 8 and 12 years. Offsets from mature clumps produce full-sized culms in 2 or 3 years.

The mature culms of Bamboos as a rule are hollow, with transverse dissepiments at the nodes. The tissue of the culm is very firm, consisting of closed fibro-vascular bundles and, chiefly near the surface, large masses of sclerenchymatous cells and fibres. The branches of the rhizome are solid. As mentioned above, the young shoots of Bamboos are solid, consisting of exceedingly soft tissue. They grow with extreme rapidity up to their full height in the first part of the rainy season. During this period the young culm would not be able to stand without the support of the culm-sheaths which at first entirely enclose it. At a later period the tissue of the culm hardens, the internodes become hollow, and branches with leaves are formed in the upper part. The ashes of Bamboos are rich in silica. In culms a few years old some internodes are full of a watery fluid, which doubtless contains Potassium silicate in solution. This probably is the origin of the Silica (Tabasheer), which is often found in the internodes of old Bamboo culms (Brandis on Tabasheer, Ind. For. xiii. 107. Also Sir Wm. Thiselton-Dyer's note on Tabasheer, p. 185 of the same volume). It has been found in *Dendrocalamus strictus*, *Bambusa arundinacea* and *Oxytenanthera nigrociliata*, and is doubtless found in many other species.

I. Culms as a rule not over 20 ft. Stamens usually 3, pericarp thin, membranous, adnate to seed.

A. Branches terete, transverse veins conspicuous in most species, dividing the leaf into rectangles or squares. Spikelets often pedicelled, 1- to many-fld., empty glumes 1–2 . . . . 1. ARUNDINARIA.

B. Branches flattened on the inside, transverse veins always conspicuous, close together, usually dividing the leaf into minute squares. Spikelets sessile, supported by prominent sheathing bracts, often with a leafy blade. Fl. 1–4, empty glumes 2–3 . . . . 2. PHYLLOSTACHYS.

II. Culms tall, as a rule erect. Stamens 6, pericarp thin, membranous, adnate to seed.

A. Filaments free.

(*a*) Paleæ entire or slightly 2-dentate, all prominently 2-keeled . . . . . . 3. BAMBUSA.

(*b*) Paleæ deeply 2-dentate, the teeth awned, the uppermost nearly entire, indistinctly keeled . . . . 4. THYRSOSTACHYS.

B. Filaments connate.

(*a*) Spikelets many-fld., paleæ all prominently keeled . . . . 5. GIGANTOCHLOA.

(*b*) Spikelets few-fld., paleæ of upper fl. indistinctly or not at all keeled . . . . 6. OXYTENANTHERA.

III. Culms tall, sometimes climbing. Stamens 6, in *Ochlandra* numerous.

A. Fruit small, pericarp crustaceous, endosperm large.

(*a*) Single-stemmed, culms overhanging, transverse veins conspicuous . . . . . 7. PSEUDOSTACHYUM.

(*b*) Tufted, transverse veins as a rule not conspicuous.

α. Lodicules none, spikelets 2–6-fld., in large globose heads . . . . . 8. DENDROCALAMUS.

β. Lodicules 3, conspicuous.

(1) Spikelets in long, narrow spikes.

* Spikelets 2–5-flowered . 9. TEINOSTACHYUM.

** Spikelets 1-flowered . . SCHIZOSTACHYUM (p. 679).

(2) Spikelets crowded, in globose or obconical heads . . . . 10. CEPHALOSTACHYUM.

B. Fruit large, pericarp fleshy or ultimately coriaceous, no endosperm in the ripe seed.

(*a*) Stamens 6, sometimes 4 or 5.

α. Lodicules none. Climbing, culms zigzag, geniculate. Spikelets 1-fld., minute . . . . 11. DINOCHLOA.

β. Lodicules 2 or 3.
(1) Loosely tufted, culms spreading, often climbing over large trees. Spikelets small, in distant compact globose heads . . 12. MELOCALAMUS.
(2) Usually single-stemmed. Spikelets in large panicles . . 13. MELOCANNA.
(*b*) Stamens 6–120. Tufted, stems often overhanging . . . . 14. OCHLANDRA.

1. ARUNDINARIA, Michaux; Fl. Brit. Ind. vii. 376.

Usually tufted and erect, rarely single-stemmed or climbing, culms slender, terete, branches in half whorls. L. small, n. as a rule 21–36 on ¼ in., noteworthy exceptions: *A. falcata* 36–48, *microphylla* 48, *jaunsarensis* 33–42: transverse veins in most species conspicuous, in the Indian species usually forming long rectangles with nerves. Spikelets often pedicelled, in racemes or panicles, 1- to many-fld., empty glumes 2, palea two-keeled, lodicules 3, ciliate. Stamens as a rule 3 (6 in *A. Prainii* and *Clarkei*), style short, stigmas 2 or 3, plumose. Species 50, 15 in America, 1 in South Africa, the rest Asiatic.

I. Erect, unarmed, bracts of inflorescence small.
A. Inflorescence usually at the end of leafy culms, mostly flowering annually, transverse veins conspicuous as a rule.
(*a*) Western species.

1. **A. Wightiana**, Nees; Gamble, Bambuseæ t. 2. Bedd. Man. t. 28. Nilgiris above 6,000 ft., common as underwood in Sholas, but also in the open. Palghat. Tinnevelli. Tufted, fl. annually, culms slender 6–10 ft., internodes 10-14 in. long, culm-sheaths papery, straw-coloured, in the lower part with stiff golden hairs, ribs prominent, blade subulate, 1–1½ in. L. thin, 5–7 by ½–1 in., n. 27–33 on ¼ in., transverse veins oblique, distance between them more than twice the interval between 2 nerves, a few bristles at the mouth of leaf-sheath. Panicles leafy, branchlets capillary, as well as the long pedicels, spikelets purple, ⅓–½ in. long, fertile fl. 2–4. 2. **A. Walkeriana**, Munro; Gamble t. 1. Palnis.—Ceylon. L. thick, elliptic-lanceolate, 5–11 by 1–1⅜ in., n. 18–24 on ¼ in., margins cartilaginous, thickened and recurved, serrulate.

3. **A. densifolia**, Munro; Gamble t. 7. Anamalais 8,500 ft.—Ceylon. A small gregarious shrub, ½–3 ft. high: stiff densely-leafy culms arising from a thick rhizome, internodes 1½–3 by ⅛ in. L. densely imbricate, 1–1½ by ⅛–¼ in., transverse veins close together, making horizontal narrow rectangles with the n. Panicle dense, leafy, consisting of spikes bearing 5–6 1-fld. spikelets. Style short, soon branching into 2 feathery stigmas.

(*b*) Eastern species

4. **A. racemosa**, Munro; Gamble t. 8. Vern. *Maling*, Nep. *Phiung*, Bhutia. East Nepal and Sikkim 6–9,000 ft. Gregarious, single-stemmed, culms 10–30 ft. high, internodes rough in the upper portion, 12–15 in. long, ⅜–1½ in. diam., culm-sheaths 7–10 in., prominently ribbed, blade subulate 2–3 in. long, ligule fimbriate. L. 5–7 by ½–⅝ in., n. 27–36 on ¼ in., transv. veins forming rectangles with nerves. This low-level species, which is common about Darjeeling, and is largely used for mat-making, for the roofs of houses, for fences and as fodder for cattle and ponies, apparently flowers at long intervals. According to the Bengal Forest Report for 1903–4, p. 9, a small patch of it flowered that year in the Darjeeling division, but I have not seen fl. Gamble unites it with a small high-level bamboo ascending to 12,000 ft. in Sikkim and the adjoining districts of Nepal, stems 3 ft. high, reddish, l. 3 by ¼–½ in., n. 33–39 on ¼ in., transverse veins close, forming with n. squares and short rectangles, which has a leafy panicle, the branches of which are supported by persistent sheaths, spikelets 1–1½ in. long, 4-8-fld., anthers purple, bifid at top, style short, stigmas 2 or 3, papillose. 5. **A. elegans**, Kurz; Gamble t. 4. Naga hills, 5,500 ft. (*Jilli*). Hills east of Toungoo (Nattaung), 5–7,500 ft. Tufted, fl. annually, culms slender, 12–20 ft. high. L. 4–5 in. long, n. 27–33 on ¼ in. transverse veins close, forming squares or short rectangles. Spikelets 1 in. or longer, 7–8-fld., anthers purple, stigmas white, plumose, separate, sessile each on a thick bulbous base. 6. **A. polystachya**, Kurz MSS.; Gamble. t. 5. Sikkim 3–5,000 ft. Khasi hills. L. soft, 6–8 by ½–1 in., transv. veins none or few, ligule long, striate, blunt, fimbriate. Inflorescence a large leafy racemose panicle, spikelets 4–6-fld., stigmas sessile, plumose (not seen).

B. Flowering culms leafless, transverse veins not conspicuous.

7. **A. falcata**, Nees; Brandis in Ind. For. xii. 206; Gamble t. 11, 12; Collett Simla Fl. 634, fig. 199. Vern. *Ringál*, Hind.; *Go Ningál*, Jauns. Erect, densely tufted, more or less gregarious, flowers irregularly, at times gregariously over large areas, while a few clumps may be found in flower almost every year, fl. stems leafless. Culms slender, 6–10 ft. high, often glaucous with a waxy covering, rims of sheath-nodes swollen, pubescent or velvety, internodes 6–12 in. long, walls thin. Culm-sheaths thinly membranous, as long as or longer than internodes, gradually narrowed from the middle to a narrow truncate tip, blade subulate, ½–2 in. long. L. thin, 3–5 by ¼–⅓ in., n. 36–45 on ¼ in., transv. veins obscure. Spikelets ½–¾ in. long, some sessile, others on long slender pedicels, in long densely-whorled racemiform panicles, each with 1–3 fertile and one terminal sterile fl., style short, stigmas 2, long, plumose. Caryopsis ½ in. long.

North-West Himalaya. Chamba to Nepal, 4–7,500 ft., often as underwood in forests of *Quercus incana*. Fl. May–Oct. 8. **A. Khasiana**, Munro; Gamble t. 13. Khasi hills, 5–6,000 ft. (*Namlang*). Similar to 7, but stems stronger and harder, l. broader, transverse veinlets often faintly visible, n. 27–42 on ¼ in., inflorescence more dense. 9. **A. intermedia**, Munro; Gamble, t. 14. Vern. *Titi Nigala*, Nep.; *Parmiok*, Lepcha. Sikkim lower hills to 7,000 ft. Erect, tufted, gregarious, culms 8–12 ft. high, internodes 5–10 in. long, culm-sheaths as long as internodes, l. 3–5 by ⅓–⅝ in., n. 27–36 on ¼ in. (24 in specimens cult. at Kew, l. $\frac{7}{16}$ in. wide), transverse veins faintly visible, leaf-sheaths prominently striate, terminating in falcate auricles with numerous long cilia. Fl. stems leafless, spikelets ½–1 in. long in racemes varying in length and often compound, crowded in compact half-whorls, each spikelet with 3–4 fertile fl. 10. **A. Hookeriana**, Munro; Gamble, t. 15. Vern. *Singhani*, Nep.; *Prong*, *Praong*, Lepcha. Sikkim and West Bhutan 4–7,000 ft. Culms 12 30 ft., glaucous, with whitish scurf when young, internodes 8–12 in. long, ¾–1½ in. diam., culm-sheaths 12–24, blade 3-6 in. long. L. 6–12 by ½–1⅓ in., n. 21–24 on ¼ in., transv. veins just visible. Fl. stems leafless, spikelets ¼ in. long with 1 fertile fl. Caryopsis $\frac{1}{16}$ in. long. Fl. in Sikkim and British Bhutan 1848, 1885, 1892, and 1908.

II. Erect, a ring of thorns at the nodes, bracts of inflorescence small, transverse veins prominent.

11. **A. Griffithiana**, Munro; Gamble t. 9. British Bhutan. Khasi and Jaintia hills (*Khnap*), Chin hills, Upper Burma. Tufted, gregarious, culms 10-30 ft., internodes 6–9 in. long, 1–1½ in. diam., thorns short, stout, conical. Culm-sheaths as long as internodes, coriaceous, hairy outside, a thick belt of long soft tawny hairs at the base. L. 4–5 by ⅓–⅝ in., n. 21–27 on ¼ in. Panicle large, terminal, leafy, branches in the axils of sheathing bracts, spikelets 1–1⅓ in. long on slender peduncles, fl. 4–6, rather distant, glumes mucronate. Found in fl. at Moflong 1835 (Griffith). 12. **A. callosa**, Munro; Gamble t. 10. Daphla and Khasi hills (*Uskong*, *Uspar*, Khasi). Similar to 11, culm-sheaths thin, striate, glabrous. L. 8–9 by ⅝–1¼ in., n. 21–24 on ¼ in. Panicles axillary, spikelets 2–3 in. long. Found in fl. at Shillong 1885 (C. B. Clarke). To this I am disposed to refer a thorny Bamboo sent from the Kala Naga hills, Manipúr, above 4,000 ft., by Mr. Inanada Charan Sen. Culms in thin clumps 15–20 ft., internodes 7–9 in., diam. 1 in., thorns ¼–1 in. long. Culm-sheaths as long as internodes, very thin, almost hyaline, ribbed, transverse veins prominent, also on blade, blade narrow, 2 in. long. L. 8–12 by 1–1⅓ in., n. 18 on ¼ in. 13. **A. armata**, Gamble t. 119. Bernardmyo, Upper Burma, 5,500 ft. (*Maitut*, Shan, J. W. Oliver, Feb. 1894). Single stemmed, 20 ft. high, internodes 8 in., diam., 1–1⅜ in., walls thin, culm-sheaths thinly coriaceous, straw-coloured, 4-8 in. long, base 2–4 in. wide, tapering to a very narrow tip. L. 6–9 by ¾–1¼ in., n. 24 on ¼ in. Fl. unknown. Possibly of this group: 14. **A. Pantlingii**, Gamble t. 118. British Bhutan 11,000 ft. (in fl. 1895). Similar to 11, but doubtfully spinescent. L. 5–7 by ½–¾ in., n. 27–36 on ¼ in. Spikelets 6–10-fld., 1–2 in. long, on long slender peduncles.

III. Erect, unarmed, bracts of inflorescence large, sheathing.

15. **A. spathiflora**, Trinius; Brandis in Ind. For. xii. 206; Gamble, t. 16. Syn. *Thamnocalamus spathiflorus*, Munro; Brandis F. Fl. 563. Vern. *Ringal*, *Nagal*, Hind.; *Deo Ningal*, Jauns.

Erect, densely tufted, gregarious, fl. periodically, probably in intervals of 10 years (Nepal 1821, Wallich; Jaunsar 1881 and 1882, Brandis, Fisher; Deoban 1892 and Kedarkanta 1893, Gamble). Culms 20–30, sometimes

40 ft. high, internodes 6–15 in. long, ½–1 in. diam., culm-sheaths glabrous, thin, straw-coloured, very smooth and shining within, 6–8 in. long, sides parallel to near the apex, where they are narrowed to a truncately-rounded apex ½ in. broad, blade caducous, 2–4 in. long. L. 3–5 by ⅓–½ in., narrowed into a short petiole, which is articulate with the sheath, n. 24–30 in ¼ in., transverse veins conspicuous, dividing the area of the leaf into long rectangles, leaf-sheaths coriaceous, straw-coloured, ribbed, fimbriate at the apex, persistent after the l. fall, forming an acute angle with the branch. Flowering distinct from the leaf-bearing stems, but the former always with a few l. Spikelets 1–2½ in. long, with 4–8 fertile fl. often 2–3 together in the axil of a large membranous ribbed sheath 2–3 in. long, fimbriate at the apex like a leaf-sheath; sometimes bearing a green, but usually terminating in a short dry early deciduous membranous blade. Fl. glumes long—acuminate. Stigmas 3, long, plumose, sessile.

North-West Himalaya, Sutlej to Nepal 7-10,000 ft., often forming underwood under Deodar, Cypress, the Himalayan Spruce, Silver Fir, and *Quercus semecarpifolia*, but also forming forests of its own with a few scattered trees among the Bamboo. The clumps generally stand close together, forming extensive thickets, so that adjoining clusters cannot often readily be separated. The culms die after ripening their seed. The stems are exported largely to the plains for hookah tubes, fishing rods and other purposes. 16. **A. aristata**, Gamble, t. 17. Vern. *Rato-nigalo*, Nep.; *Babain*, Lepcha; *Bhebham*, Bhutia. Sikkim and British Bhutan 9–11,000 ft. Culms 8-12 ft. high, shining yellow when mature, internodes 8–12 in. long, ½ in. diam., walls thick, nodes prominent through the persistent cup- or ring-like base of the fallen sheath, culm-sheaths prominently ribbed. Branchlets purple, l. approximate at the ends, n. 24–33 on ¼ in., transverse veins like 15, leaf-sheaths loose, strongly ribbed. Inflorescence with numerous large spathaceous bracts, often with a leafy blade, enclosing clusters of 3–5 spikelets on short pedicels. Spikelets 1–2 in. long, with 4–8 fertile fl., fl. glume long acuminate. Caryopsis linear-oblong, acute. Flowered on the Singalila range in 1868, 1869, 1890, and (over a small area) in 1900. 17. **A. Falconeri**, Benth. and Hook. f.; Gamble, t. 18; O. Stapf in Bot. Magazine t. 7947, and in Gard. Chron. xxxv. (1904) 305; Gilbert Rogers in Ind. For. xxvii. 785. Syn. *A. nobilis*, Mitford. Himalaya from Jaunsar eastwards, 6–10,000 ft. Chakrata 6,000 ft. (D.B., in fl. April 1881). Loosely tufted, attains 20 ft., culms ½–¾ in. diam., not glaucous, sometimes striped, yellow and green, node rim glabrous, internodes 8–15 in. long. Culm-sheaths oblong, shortly narrowed towards the apex with convex margins. L. 3–6 by ¼–¾ in., thin, transverse veinlets obscure, but often visible on the underside of dry l., n. 21–27 on ¼ in. Spikelets 1-fld. with an elongate slender sterile rachilla, fl. glumes shortly mucronate. Racemes of 5–7 spikelets in the axils of sheathing bracts, ¾–1½ in. long, usually truncate. Fl. gregariously. Madden found it in seed near the Pindari glacier, Sept. 1846, and in 1847 sent quantities of the seed to England, which was the origin of the plants that flowered all over Europe and in Algeria in 1875 and 1876. In Sikkim it fld. in 1876 and at Darjeeling in 1900. Readily distinguished from *A. falcata* by the distant longitud. nerves, l. resembling those of *A. Hookeriana*.

IV. Mostly climbing, transverse veins not conspicuous.

18. **A. Prainii**, Gamble, t. 19. Syn. *Microcalamus Prainii*, Gamble in Journ. As. Soc. Beng. 59, 207. Vern. *Sampit*, Naga. Naga and Jaintia hills 3,500–8,000 ft. A small wiry climber, culms up to 30 ft. long, internodes usually 8–9 in. long, walls thick, often quite solid, l. thin, 2–4 in. long, n. 33–39 on ¼ in., transverse veins faintly visible. Spikelets 3–6-fld., 1–1¼ in. long, rachis flexuose, on lax slender racemes in leafy panicles, fl. glume broad-ovate acute, stamens 6. In fl. Naga hills 1886 (Prain). 19. **A. Mannii**, Gamble, t. 26. Khasi hills (*Beneng*). Slender tufted wiry climbing culms up to 30 ft., internodes 3 ft. long, ½ in. diam., quite solid, culm-sheaths 12–18 in. long, thin and slender, blade continuous with sheath, linear, 9–10 in. long. L. thin 6–9 by ½–¾ in. n. 24 on ¼ in., transverse veins few, bent, not prominent, fl. unknown. 20. **A. Clarkei**, Gamble MSS. Manipùr. A slight shrub 10 ft. high, l. 4–7 by ½–¾ in., n. 28-33 on ¼ in. Stamens 6, hence placed here.

V. Fl. unknown.

A. Transverse veins conspicuous.

(*a*) Single stemmed.

21. **A. Jaunsarensis**, Gamble, t. 22; Kanjilal F. Fl. 366. Tutuagadh, Mundali, Jaunsar 7–8,000 ft. Ramni and Duduloli, Garhwal, 8,500–9,000 ft, Strachey and Winterbottom. Culms single, 10–15 ft. high, arising from a long creeping rhizome, internodes 9–11 in. long, ½ in. diam. L. 4–6 by ½–⅔ in., n. 33–42 on ¼ in., transv.

veins close together, forming squares or short rectangles with the n., fl. unknown. L. similar to *A. spathiflora*, but the venation quite different. 22. **A. Rolloana,** Gamble, t. 23. Naga hills 5–7,000 ft. Culms 8 ft. high, distant from creeping rhizomes, internodes 8–12 in. long, ⅓ in. diam. L. 6–8 by 1–1½ in., n. 21–24 on ¼ in. 23. **Lading wa,** Burm. Hills east of Bhamo, 6,500 ft. (Montague Hill 188). Single-stemmed, erect, culms 21 ft. high, ¾–1½ in. diam., nearly solid. L. 4–5 by ½ in., fine hairs on the underside, n. 27–42 in. on ¼ in., transv. veins mostly close, forming short rectangles and squares with longitudinal nerves. Similar to *A. elegans*, Kurz, but reported to be single-stemmed.

(*b*) Tufted.

24. **A. hirsuta,** Munro; Gamble, t. 20. Vern. *Ustoh*, Khasi. Khasi and Naga hills, 5–9,500 ft. Tufted, 3–8 ft. high (humilis, culmis spinosis, in tufts, Hook. f. in herb. Kew, stems solitary from the rhizome, Gamble). l. 2–7 by ⅜–1¼ in., n. 21–33 on ¼ in., transv. veinlets forming with the n. squares or horizontal rectangles, leaf-sheaths clothed with long stiff hairs, auricles at the mouth bearing long stiff bristles. 25. **A. microphylla,** Munro. Bhutan 6–10,000 ft. Gregarious. 2–4 ft. high, forming large patches in wet places, l. ½–1 by ⅒–⅙ in., the inner edge with very long pointed hairs, appressed to the edge, n. 48 on ¼ in., transverse veins forming squares and rectangles with the n. 26. **A. Gallatlyi,** Gamble, t. 21. Muleyit 6,000 ft., Tenasserim. Gregarious, stems thin, l. 3–4 by ½–¾ in., whitish beneath, sheath with about 3 long stiff bristles at the mouth (not seen).

B. Transverse veins not conspicuous.

27. **A. suberecta,** Munro; Gamble, t. 24. Khasi and Jaintia hills, 3–5,000 ft., gregarious by the river, stems densely tufted, erect, thin, 10–20 ft., internodes 6–10 in. long, ⅒ in. diam., cavity very small. L. 2–4 by ⅓–½ in., n. 33–42 on ¼ in. Specimens coll. by Gustav Mann in 1889 on the banks of the Mahtedu river below Jowai 3,500 ft. (*Lombnang*) referred to this sp. by Gamble have l. 3 by ¼ in., n. 48–51 on ¼ in. 28. **A. Kurzii,** Gamble, t. 25. Coasts of Tenasserim, the only low-level sp. known from India. L. very thin, 2–4 by ⅓–⅒ in., on numerous long wiry filiform branchlets (not seen).

2. PHYLLOSTACHYS, Sieb. et Zucc.: Fl. Brit. Ind. vii. 386.

Usually tufted, but the rhizome often with long creeping branches which send up tufts of culms at a distance from the parent clump. Principal branches flattened above the axillary bud, hence angular, branches few (2–3) from each node. L. tesselated with numerous prominent transverse veins, forming squares with the n., sheath loose. The Indian species frequently have the uppermost l. apparently in pairs, the internodes between these l. being very short. Panicle terminal, leafy, spikelets sessile 1–4-fld., in the axils of large imbricating bracts, the bracts often with a small leafy blade. Empty glumes 2–3, palea 2-keeled, many-nerved, often bimucronate, stamens 3, style long with 3 long feathery stigmas. Species about 30, Eastern Asia.

1. **P. assamica,** Gamble MSS. Mishmi hills, forming extensive patches covering the hillside, 10–11 ft. high, makes excellent walking sticks (Griffith MSS. Notes and Journals, p. 38). Namdáng, Lakhimpúr district, Sadiya. Also cultivated near Sibsagar. Culm-sheaths straw-colour, at the base of the narrow blade with narrow oblong auricles, covered with long bristles, transverse veins prominent on the inside of culm-sheaths. L. thin, linear-lanceolate, 4–6 by ½–¾ in., pet. slender ⅛ in. long. n. 36–42 on ¼ in., leaf-sheaths long bristly-ciliate at mouth. Fl. unknown. Following Munro, Gamble in Bambuseæ united this with *Phyllostachys bambusoides*, Sieb. et Zucc.; Gamble t. 27, but he has since informed me that in his opinion the Indian plant is distinct.

2 **P. Mannii,** Gamble t. 28. Cult. at Shillong, said to have been brought from the Naga hills. Cult. at Bernardmyo, Upper Burma, brought from China. *Mai paung pûk* (imported Bamboo), Shan. Culm 15–20 ft. internodes up to 10 in. long and 1¼ in. diam. Culm-sheaths thin, without auricles at the apex, transverse veins not prominent, ligule long-fimbriate. L. similar to 1, but thicker, and pet. longer (¼ in. long), leaf-sheaths with few or no bristles at mouth. 3. Similar to 2, and possibly identical are specimens in leaf only (Montague Hill 196). Hills east of Bhamo, 6,500 ft., *Sêdan*, Burm. A small Bamboo, internodes 8 in. long, ½ in. diam., used for pipe stems: the stems are flat on one side, and some of the l. are in pairs, pet. slender, ¼ in. long, n. 39–42 on ¼ in. To this I also am inclined to refer a specimen mentioned by Gamble under *Arundinaria elegans*, collected by J. Anderson on the Yunnan expedition at Poneshee in 1868, l. ⅝ in. wide, n. 46 on ¼ in. A specimen mentioned by Gamble in the same place, collected by G. Gallatly (746), Tenasserim 5,000 ft., I have not seen.

3. BAMBUSA, Schreber; Fl. Brit. Ind. vii. 386.

Tufted, a few species (*nutans, Khasiana*) nearly single-stemmed, culms tall, erect, rarely overhanging or climbing. Transverse veins of l. not conspicuous, n. 21–40 on ¼ in. Exceptions: *nana* (45–54), *polymorpha* (40–45), *Binghami* (42–45), *Khasiana, Griffithiana* (18–21). Spikelets sessile, palea 2-keeled, not cleft or only slightly. Stamens 6, ovary oblong or obovate, tip hairy. Caryopsis on one side grooved, pericarp thin, adherent to the seed. Species about 50. Eastern Asia, 1 in Australia.

I. Unarmed.

A. Fertile fl. numerous, spikelets terete, not flat.

(*a*) Culm-sheaths with large auricles.

1. **B. Tulda,** Roxb. Gamble t. 29. Vern. *Peka, Chau,* Hind.; *Tulda,* Beng.; *Deo-bans, Jati, Jao,* Ass.; *Mitenga,* Chittagong; *Thaik-wa,* Burm.

Gregarious, densely tufted, culms 20–70 ft. high, lower branches stiff, horizontal, often leafy, internodes 1–2 ft., 2–4 in. diam., walls thick. Culm-sheaths 6–9 in. long, and as broad at the base, polished within, blade triangular, cuspidate, slightly hairy within, base decurrent into large rounded long-fringed auricles or into a wavy band along the upper edge of sheath. L. 6–10 by 1 in., glaucescent and usually softly hairy beneath, n. 30–43 on ¼ in., leaf-sheath glabrous, ligule narrow, inconspicuous. Flowering culms usually quite leafless, each stem being converted into an immense oblong waving panicle, composed of innumerable supra-decompound ramifications (Roxb.). Spikelets glossy, sessile, in length between 1 and 3 in., in distant clusters or half-whorls on the glabrous branches of the panicle. At the base of each spikelet 1 or 2 bracts, then 2–4 empty glumes, then 4–6 fertile, and at the end 1 or 2 imperfect fl. Fl. glume distinctly many-nerved, ½–1 in. long, palea shorter, with long white cilia on the keels, penicillate at the tip, 3–5 n. between the keels. Anthers long-exserted, purple, blunt at the tip or emarginate. Caryopsis cylindric, ⅓ in. long, apex obtuse and hirsute.

Bengal, Assam, Chittagong. Burma, common on flats and along streams. Northern Circars. Cultivated around villages in Bengal and further north as far as Oudh. At times flowers gregariously, while at other times single clumps will be found in flower. The specimens from Upper Burma (Bhamo and Ruby Mines district) have the l. always hairy beneath. 2. **B. longispiculata,** Gamble MSS. Vern. *Mitenga,* Chitt.; *Thaikwa,* Burm. Chittagong hill tracts. Ruby Mines district, 3,500 ft. Tufted, culms 40 ft. high, 3 in. diam. Differs from 1 chiefly by the very long slightly compressed spikelets, up to 6 in. long. L. 7–12 by 1–2½ in., n. 24–31 on ¼ in. Spikelets polished, in the axils of long coriaceous sheaths without a blade, in half whorls on erect often branching spikes 11–15 in. long. Glumes empty 2, fertile 6–12, 1 in. long.

3. **B. nutans,** Wall.; Gamble, t., 30. Vern. *Mahlu,* Sikkim. Subhimalayan tract from Kangra eastwards (probably cultivated west of the Sarda), ascending to 5,000 ft. Assam. Tufts loose, the culms not crowded, otherwise similar to 1, n. 30–39 on ¼ in., leaf-sheaths hairy when young, auricles falcate with a few long bristles, ligule elongated, obtuse, hairy. Spikelets ½–1 in. long, glumes with prominent longitudinal and often with transverse nerves, anthers apiculate or slightly penicillate at apex. As far as known flowers periodically at long intervals. 4. **B. teres,** Ham.; Gamble, t. 31. Assam. Densely-tufted, culms attaining 60 ft., internodes 20 in. long, 3 in. diam. L. 12–14 in., n. 33–40 on ¼ in. Spikelets up to 2 in. long, fl. glume ovate-lanceolate from a broad base, many-nerved, sometimes with a foliaceous blade. 5. **B. burmanica,** Gamble, t. 33. *Thaikwa, Thaikwa gyi,* Burm. Katha district, Upper Burma, on dry hill slopes. Culms dull green, nearly solid, nodes marked by a white ring of hairs below them. L. of mature culms 8–10 by 1–1½ in., whitish and pubescent beneath, pet. very short, n. 24–27 on ¼ in., l.-sheaths of young plants very hairy, of full-grown nearly glabrous. Spikelets up to 1 in. long, narrow, 5–6-fld., in distant clusters supported by long truncate bracts (sheaths without a blade). Palea obtuse white-ciliate along keels, rachilla short, stout, glabrous, anthers ⅕–¼ in. long, apiculate. Caryopsis cylindric, ¼ in. long, hairy at top, very short.

6. **B. Khasiana,** Munro; Gamble, t. 37. Vern. *Serim, Tyrah,* Khasi; *Tirriah,* Naga. Khasi, Jaintia, and Naga hills. Manipur. Culms single, from a creeping root-stock, 30–40 ft. high, internodes clothed with appressed golden hairs when young, 5–15 in.

long, 1–1½ in. diam., walls thin. Culm-sheaths 5–6 in. long, top but little narrower than the base, blade from a broadly cordate auriculate and almost amplexicaul base narrowed into a subulate point, middle portion thick, ribbed, lanceolate, outer membranous, wing-like. L. pale, 4–9 by 1–1½ in., ending in a subulate hairy point, n. 18–21 on ¼ in. Spikelets partly short, sterile, partly long fertile, in distant often nearly globose heads, on long spikes, arranged in leafy panicles. Two to three fertile fl. in the middle with 1–4 empty glumes at base and 1–2 imperfect fl. at the apex. Keels of palea with minute cilia, ovary attenuated into a short style. L. resemble *Melocanna bambusoides*, but culm-sheaths quite different. Has been found in fl. 1850 and 1885.

7. **B. polymorpha**, Munro; Gamble, t. 34. Vern. *Kyathaung-wa*, Burm. Pegu Yoma abundant above 500 ft. Rare in Martaban. Tufted, gregarious, culms 60–80 ft. high, erect, lower part naked, upper part gracefully bent, the leaf-bearing branches in half-whorls, internodes 12–30 in. long, 3–5 in. diam., walls thin, rings of rootlets at the lower nodes. Culm-sheaths about ⅓ the length of joint, blade concave, mucronate, extending below into elongate falcate auricles, fringed by strong pale-brown bristles. L. 4–6 by ⅓–½ in., n. 40–45 on ¼ in. Spikelets sessile, clustered, ½ in. long, empty glumes several, acuminate, often with a distinct blade separated from the sheath by a hairy callus, fertile fl. 3, with a terminal imperfect fl. on a long slender rachilla, palea not or very slightly ciliate along the keels, anthers emarginate, style short. Flowers at long intervals. Coll. in fl. by Dr. M'Clelland in Pegu in 1854. In 1856, '57, '58 I found it in leaf in the Pegu Yoma. In 1859 it fld. on the west side of the Pegu Yoma in its southern and 1860 in its northern portion. Gamble in Ann. Calc. Gard. vii. 37 states that flowering specimens were collected by me in the Zamayee forests in 1862 and by Kurz in the Thaukyeghat forests in 1871, and (in Nature, vol. 70, p. 423) that since then flowers have been once reported from Bassein. To this Gamble, Bambuseæ, 37, refers *Betua*, Beng., and doubtfully *Jai*, Beng., both from Sylhet. *Betua* was coll. in fl. Dec., 1889, in Silhet. 8. Specimens (fl. and seedlings) sent by Troup from the Bawben forests, Pegu (*Kyathaungtu-Thaiktu*, Burm., similar to *B. polymorpha* and *Tulda*), come near to 7. Tufted, 50–60 ft., internodes 1½–2 ft. long, densely clothed with white silky hairs, walls ⅜ in. thick, often nearly solid, nodes with a ring of rootlets like *B. Tulda*. Spikelets polished 3–4-fld. purple at the apex, palea not or very slightly ciliate at the keels, lodicules broad, base fleshy, anthers purple, emarginate, ovary obovoid, hairy, stigmas 3, long, plumose, sessile or nearly so. The seedlings resemble those of *B. Tulda*, but the n. are closer together, 39–45 on ¼ in.

(*b*) Culm-sheaths with small auricles or without auricles.

9. **B. affinis**, Munro. Vern. *Thishe*, Burm.; *Wabuè*, Kar. In an old Taungya between Wimpa and the Bithoko range, Yunzalin (D.B. May, 1859). Tufted and somewhat scrambling, internodes under 2 in. diam. L. 4–8 by ⅜–1 in., n. 33 on ¼ in., sheaths ribbed, perfectly glabrous, loose, baggy, not tightly enclosing the internode. Spikelets sessile, coriaceous, polished, 1 in. long, supported by large bracts, in distant clusters on long spikes, forming terminal leafy panicles. Empty glumes 4–8, not ciliate, the lowest ⅜ in. long, often consisting of a distinct sheath and blade. Some male and a few fertile fl., palea much smaller than flowering glume, with very long cilia in the upper half of keel, 7 nerves between keels. Ovary obovoid, glumes in the lower portion. Kurz F. Fl. ii. 551 states that *B. affinis*, Munro grows in the Eng forest of Martaban, east of the Sitang river. Gamble, Bambuseæ, 39, t. 36, identifies with this a low bush growing in the Calcutta Botanic Garden on the edge of the muddy river bank. The specimens of this in Herb. Kew, however, have entirely different l., 1½ in. wide, n. 18–21 on ¼ in., with a different structure. The l.-sheaths are sharply keeled and tightly appressed to the internode, and the ligule is large. 10. **B. pallida**, Munro: Gamble t. 35. Vern. *Pshi*, Lepcha; *Bijli*, *Walkthai*, *Makal*, Ass.; *Usken*, *Seskien*, *skhen*, Khasi; *Gyawa*, Burm.; *Maipyu*, Kachin. Indigenous in Sikkim, Bhutan, up to 6,000 ft., the Khasi, Jaintia, and Naga hills. Bhamo district, in evergreen forest. Cultivated in Assam, the Khasi hills, and in the plains of Eastern Bengal. Tufted, culms 40–60 ft. high, olive-green, the young shoots covered with white powder, internodes 18–30 in. long, 2–3 in. diam. Culm-sheaths 7–12 in. long, blade as broad as, and usually longer than sheath. L. 4–8 in. long, n. 33–42 on ¼ in. Spikelets pale, 1–1½ in. long, fertile fl. 3–8, at the end 3–5 imperfect fl. gradually decreasing in size. Ovary gradually narrowed into a short hairy style. Gamble, Bambuseæ 38, identifies with this *Dendrocalamus criticus*, Kurz, Kambalu Taung, Pegu Yoma, 3,000 ft. *Gyawa*, Burm., is also applied to *Teinostachyum Dullooa*, Gamble. 11. **B. nana**, Roxb.; Gamble t. 38. A native of Japan, cultivated in India and Burma, often as a hedge plant. *Pulopinang wa*, Burm. Densely tufted, culms 6–10 ft. high, internodes 8–15 in. long, ½–1 in. diam., culm-sheaths glabrous, 4–6 in. long, green first, afterwards yellow, blade 2–3 in. long, hairy beneath. L. 2–4 by ⅓ in., n. 45–54 on ¼ in. Spikelets sessile, distichous, ½–1½ in. long, many-fld., in a poor

diffuse leafy panicle, palea minutely ciliate at the tip only, anthers exserted, yellow, ovary obovate, pubescent above, stigmas almost sessile.

B. Fertile fl. numerous, spikelets flat, more or less distichous.

12. **B. Balcooa**, Roxb.; Gamble, t. 39. Vern. *Bhalkua*, Beng.; *Baluka*, *Deobans*, Ass.; *Wamna*, Garo.

Densely tufted, culms 50–80 ft., lower branches stiff, leafless, internodes 8–18 in., 3–6 in. diam., walls thick. Culm-sheaths with ciliate edges, auricles narrow, not falcate, the upper 10–14 in. long, blade 6–8 in., lower culm-sheaths smaller. L. 6–12 by 1–2 in., pet. very short, sheath with long white hairs, ligule membranous, broadly triangular, n. 21–30 on $\frac{1}{4}$ in. Spikelets ovate, $\frac{1}{3}$–$\frac{1}{2}$ in. long, conspicuous by the protruding fimbriate keels of paleæ, 4–6-fld., in compact half-whorled heads, on long spikes in large compound, sometimes leaf-bearing panicles. Anthers apiculate, yellow. Ovary ovoid, narrowed into a long hairy style.

Assam. Lower Bengal. Behar. Gorakhpur. Flowers at long intervals. Highly esteemed in Bengal for scaffolding and building. Commonly cultivated near villages. (Upendranath Kanjilal, the Bhalkua Bans of Bengal, Ind. For. xvii. 53.) 13
B. vulgaris, Schrader; Gamble, t. 40. Syn. *B. Thouarsii*, Kunth. Vern. *Bariala*, Chittagong. *Vansa Kullaka*, Bombay. Home uncertain. Cultivated in tropical India. Tufted, but clumps not dense, culms polished, often striped green and yellow, 20–50 ft. high, internodes 10–18 in. long, diam. 3–5 in., culm-sheaths clothed outside with brown hairs, when young often streaked with green and yellow, 6–10 in. long, top concavely truncate, blade triangular with falcate ciliate auricles at the base. L. 16–12 by 1–2 in., hairy beneath when young, n. 21–39 on $\frac{1}{4}$ in., transverse veins visible on the lower surface, leaf-sheath appressed white hairy. Spikelets compressed, $\frac{1}{2}$–$\frac{5}{8}$ by $\frac{1}{3}$ in., 6–10-fld., palea thin, nerves between the keels indistinct, style long hairy, stigmas 3, plumose. 14. **B. Kingiana**, Gamble, t. 42. *Thaik-wabo*, Burm. Katha district, Upper Burma. Culms 60–70 ft. long, up to 4 in. diam. L. 10–12 by 1–2$\frac{1}{3}$ in., n. 27–36 on $\frac{1}{4}$ in., transv. veins indistinctly visible. Spikelets purple, $\frac{1}{2}$ in. long, in clusters of 1–6, fertile fl. 4–6, empty and fl. glumes ciliate along the edges, anthers with a tuft of penicillate hairs. 15. **B. lineata**, Munro; Gamble, t. 43. Syn. *B. Rumphiana*, Kurz in Ind. For. i. 341. Rutland Island, Andamans.—Marshy coast forests of Amboina and other islands of the Malay Archip. Tufted, internodes 16–24 in. long, $\frac{1}{2}$–1 in. diam., walls thin, branches single, not whorled, culm-sheaths about 6 in. long, clothed when young with golden-brown hairs, blade as long as sheath, ovate cuspidate. L. 10–15 by 1–3 in., pale beneath, n. on $\frac{1}{4}$ in. 24–27, pet. broad. very short, leaf-sheaths ribbed, keeled, fringed at the mouth with long stiff bristles, ligule stiffly fimbriate. Fl. annually, panicle leafy, branches as well as spikelets in the axils of truncate sheaths. Spikelets sessile, $\frac{1}{2}$ in. long, fertile fl. about 10, glumes —empty and flowering—long-mucronate, edges ciliate. Lodicules 0. 16. **B. Binghami**, Gamble, t. 41. *Nyachat-wa*, Burm. Nyaungdaungle forest, Tenasserim. L. 3–6 by $\frac{1}{3}$–$\frac{1}{2}$ in., a few white stiff cilia at the mouth of sheath, n. 42–45 on $\frac{1}{4}$ in. Spikelets often in the axils of truncate sheaths, $\frac{1}{2}$ in. long, fertile fl. 5–6, glumes mucronate. keel cilia of palea conspicuous.

C. Fertile fl. 1–4.

17. **B. Oliveriana**, Gamble, t. 116. Vern. *Wapyusan*, Burm. Upper Burma, hills east of the Irawaddi north of Mandalay, 1–2,000 ft., in moist deciduous forest in patches. Tufted, culms 40–45 ft., branched from the base upwards, internodes about 14 in. long. 1–2 in. diam. Culm-sheaths thin, nearly glabrous, striate, 8–10 in., top convex, blade triangular, 4–8 in. long. L. thin, glabrous, 4–7 by $\frac{1}{3}$–$\frac{5}{8}$ in., n. 33–39 on $\frac{1}{4}$ in., leaf-sheaths striate, glabrous. Spikelets $\frac{1}{2}$ in. long, 1–3 together in bracteate clusters on drooping one-sided spikes. Fertile fl. 2–4, with an imperfect fl. on a long glabrous rachilla, lodicules 3, obovate, long fimbriate, anthers obtuse, long-exserted, striped red and yellow, afterwards dull purple. Ovary hairy, style short, stigmas 2, plumose. 18. **B. schizostachyoides**, Kurz; Gamble, t. 44. Syn. *Cephalostachyum schizostachyoides*, Kurz F. Fl. ii. 565. South Andaman. Tufted, culms 20–30 ft., internodes 18–24 in. long, 3–4 in. diam., walls very thin. L. 4–7 by $\frac{1}{2}$–1 in., n. 30–38 on $\frac{1}{4}$ in. Spikelets $\frac{1}{2}$ in. long, sessile in lateral clusters supported by truncate bracts (sheaths without a blade), fertile fl. 2–3, palea narrow, membranous, acuminate, anthers apiculate, base unequal. 19. **B. Griffithiana**, Munro; Gamble t. 45. Syn. *Dendrocalamus Griffithianus*, Kurz, F. Fl. ii. 562. Manipúr. Near Mogaung, Upper Burma. Subscandent, culms slender, l. 15–18 by 3 in., pale beneath, n. 18–20 on $\frac{1}{4}$ in., leaf-sheath at the mouth with large auricles, fringed with long bristles. Branches of panicle thick, hollow, wal-

thin, bearing lateral heads of spikelets at intervals of 3–4 in. Spikelets cylindric acute, fertile fl. 1, anthers bifid at the apex, stigmas long, plumose, sessile.

II. Branchlets spinescent.

20 **B. arundinacea**, Willd.; Roxb. Cor. Pl. t. 79; Bedd. Fl. Sylv. t. 321. Gamble t. 48. Syn. *B. spinosa*, Roxb. Vern. *Kanta Bans*, *Kattang*, Hind.; *Kata*, *Koto*, Assam; *Kalak*, *Padhai*, Konkan; *Kates Tokar*, Thana; *Bidru*, *Hebbidru*, *Bidungulu*, Kan.; *Bongu*, *Mundla Veduru*, *Mungil*, Tam.; *Mula*, *Illi*, Mal.; *Kyakat-wa*, Burm.

Gregarious, densely tufted, culms 50–120 ft., internodes 12–18 in. long, 4–6 in. diam., walls 1–2 in. thick, the nodes in the lower part of the culm bearing dense half-whorls of stiff almost leafless branches, the upper part of the culm bending over, with large distichous leafy branches, alternating at even distances, resembling Prince of Wales' feathers. Culm-sheaths coriaceous, 9–12 in. long, shorter than the full-grown internodes, outside hairy and orange-yellow while young, shining and prominently-ribbed on the inside, blade triangular, shorter than sheath, upper side clothed with a dense brown felt of bristly hairs. Branchlets with short sharp spines at the nodes. L. small, thin, not exceeding 8 by $\frac{3}{4}$ in., often hairy beneath, leaf-sheaths usually hairy, n. 30–45, usually 33–39, on $\frac{1}{4}$ in. Spikelets sessile, $\frac{1}{2}$–1 in. long, glabrous, shining, glumes as a rule not ciliate, palea slightly longer than fl. glume, the ciliate keels prominently protruding, anthers yellow. Ovary almost cylindric, style glabrous, with 3 long plumose stigmas. Grain $\frac{1}{5}$–$\frac{1}{3}$ in. enclosed in the persistent glume and palea.

Indigenous in both Peninsulas in the plains and lower hills, ascending to 3,000 ft. In Burma chiefly along the banks of rivers and in valleys on alluvial soil. Cultivated largely in Northern India. Cultivated in many parts of China. Flowers periodically and simultaneously in one district, when all buds on each culm develop into flowers, exceptionally with a few leaves. At that time as a rule all clumps in the district come into fl., a few clumps flowering in the preceding and others in the following year. The following data seem to justify the assumption that a general flowering takes place in periods of 30–32 years in one district. Malabar, South Kanara, the Wainad and Coorg 1804, 1836, and 1866. On the Nerbudda river near Jabalpur 1839, at Jabalpur 1870. (See list of the flowerings of this species in Ind. (For. xxv. 11.) Rheede, Hortus Malabaricus i. 26 t. 16 (1678), however, states that this Bamboo flowers when 60 years old. A remarkable Bamboo found on the Javadi hills, Salem district, *Jru vare* (D.B. Jan. 1882), the culms not crowded in the clumps, branches single, thorns few, culm-sheaths short, leaves like *B. arundinacea.*

21. **B. Copelandi**, Gamble MSS. Vern. *Wagyi*, Burm. Largely cultivated in the Northern Shan States. A large species of uncertain position in the genus, resembling *Dendrocalamus latiflorus* in general appearance. Culm-sheaths thick, scanty black hairs outside, polished inside, 15 in. long, top rounded towards the short and narrow blade. L. ovate-lanceolate, 12–15 by 1$\frac{3}{4}$–2$\frac{3}{4}$ in., n. 21–26 on $\frac{1}{4}$ in. Spikelets glabrous, 1-1$\frac{1}{2}$ in. long, empty glumes 2–4, with conspicuous transverse veins, flowering 2–8, longitudinal, n. 26, transverse veins obscure. Palea keeled and shortly bidentate at apex, lodicules lanceolate, hyaline. Anthers $\frac{1}{4}$ in. long, mucronate at tip. Ovary and style hirsute. Caryopsis $\frac{1}{2}$–$\frac{3}{4}$ in. long, contracted towards the apex.

4. THYRSOSTACHYS, Gamble; Fl. Brit. Ind. vii. 397.

Panicles consisting of numerous compound pedunculate spikes, in the axils of sheathing bracts, peduncles bearing coriaceous sheaths, usually without a blade. Branches of compound spikes short, in the axils of sheathing bracts, bearing perfect and imperfect spikelets in the axils of membranous sheaths. Paleæ hyaline, keeled, ciliate along the keels, those of the lower fl. in each spikelet deeply bifid, that of the uppermost fl. entire, or nearly so. Species 2.

1. **T. Oliveri**, Gamble, t. 50. Vern. *Thanawa*, Burm.; *Maitong*, Kachin. Upper Burma, on low hills, not in the northern moister districts. Flowered in 1891, and, sporadically, in the Ruby Mines district in 1902, Bruce in Ind. For. xxx. 270. Tufted, culms erect, 50–80 ft., lower half naked, internodes 14–24 in. long, 2–3 in. diam., bright green with white bloom on young stems, afterwards dull green. Culm-sheaths green

on young shoots, thin, persistent, tightly appressed to stem, half to three-fourths the length of internode, blade caducous, 3–9 in. long. L. 7–10 by ½–1¼ in., n. 27–36 on ¼ in., sheaths keeled, minutely ciliate along the edges. Compound spikes 6–10 in. long, branches with a few perfect and numerous imperfect spikelets in the axils of sheaths, which frequently bear well-developed green triangular blades up to ¼ in. long, perfect spikelets ½–1 in. long, fl. 2–3, ♂ and ☿. Fl. glume with transverse nerves, minutely hairy on the back, anthers yellow, connective produced into a blunt point, filaments purple, long-exserted. Grain ⅜ in. long, cylindric, beaked. At the base of culms frequently large tufts of thin filiform much-ramified branches resembling fine grass, clothed with membranous sheaths, with or without blades. 2. **T. siamensis,** Gamble, t. 51. Syn. *Bambusa regia*, Thoms. Vern. *Tiwa*, *Ti-yo-wa*, Burm. Indigenous in small side valleys of the Salween river between the Solo and Kèmapyu Chaungs (D. B. May 1859). Also in Siam. In Upper Burma cultivated largely in monastery gardens. Tufted, culms 25–40 ft., straight, naked below, with dense half-whorls of branches near the top. Internodes 8–13 in. long, of uniform length in the same culm, diam. 1½–3 in., nodes straight and elegant, walls thick. Culm-sheaths deciduous, as long as internodes, blade narrowly triangular. L. 3–6 by ⅓–½ in., n. 33–48 on ¼ in. Branches of panicle slender, drooping, glumes clothed on the back near the base with long soft hairs. Fl. periodically, cult. at Royal Gardens, Calcutta, where it flowered in 1892. In 1893 tufts of thin wiry branchlets appeared with small l. and a few fl. The handles of the best class of Burmese umbrellas made of the culms.

5. GIGANTOCHLOA, Kurz; Fl. Brit. Ind. vii. 398.

Erect or scandent, stems branchless in the lower portion. Fertile fl. 2–4, glumes ciliate along the edge, palea of all fl. 2-keeled, keels ciliate. Filaments connate into a tube, ovary hairy. Species about 11, Eastern Peninsula and Malay Archip.

1. **G. macrostachya,** Kurz; Gamble, t. 54. Vern. *Wapyugyi*, Burm. Hills east of Shwegyin between the Sitang and Beeling rivers (D.B. March 1862). Also further east on the feeders of the Salween river. Clumps lax, not compact, culms with white longitudinal stripes, 20–30 ft. high, 4 in. diam., walls ⅜ in. thick. When Taungya clearings have been made in the forest of this species, the Bamboo shoots spring up immediately after the harvest, instead of the usual mass of tall grasses and herbaceous plants. L. pale beneath, 4–6 by ½–⅔ in., n. 30–35 on ¼ in., mouth of sheath with long bristles. Long fertile and short sterile spikelets in heads 1½–3 in. apart, up to 3 in. diam. Fertile spikelets linear, sharply subulate, 1–2 in. long, glumes with a conspicuous black fringe on the edge and a few black stiff hairs on the back. Caryopsis narrowly cylindric, tipped with the persistent style. I adopt the above name, as it is supported by Gamble's t. 54, the main portion of which is taken from the specimens at Herb. Calc. collected by me in 1862.

Here may be mentioned the following chiefly Burmese Bamboos, which have some resemblance to *Gigantochloa macrostochya*, though the flowers being unknown, it is quite uncertain whether they belong to this genus:—

A. Single stemmed.

(*a*) *Tabindaing*, Burm. Karen hills south-east of Toungoo (D. B. Feb. 1880, see Brandis, Suggestions regarding Forest Administration in British Burma, 1881, p. 141). Culm-sheaths 6 in. long, gradually narrowed from a base 8 in. wide to an apex 4 in. wide, a broad undulated band on both sides of the 2 in. broad base of the triangular blade. L. 8 by 1 in., glaucous and hairy beneath, n. 30–36 on ¼ in. The Taungya clearings made in forests of this species mostly grow up in Bamboo, and the period which in 1880 was allowed for the Bamboo forest to grow up, before it was cut again, varied from 7 to 15 years. To this probably belongs Kurz's No. 156, from Burma, without locality.

(*b*) *Tabindaing*, Burm.; *Wabgai*, *Wamè*, Karen. Hills on the headwaters of the Maitharauk river, ascending to the crest of the Bithoko range, also in the Sinzway forest of the Yunzalin valley. (D.B. March, 1880, see Brandis, Suggestions, etc. pp. 151, 153, 156, 157.) Culms 2–3 ft. apart, bright green, often with yellow stripes, lower half naked, culm-sheaths thick, clothed outside with black irritating hairs. L. 8–12 by ⅔–1½ in., n. 30–40 on ¼ in. It is possible that Kurz may have based his *B.* (?) *villosula* upon specimens collected by me of this Bamboo at an earlier date.

(*c*) *Tabindaing*, Burm. Mogaung Forests, Upper Burma (J. W. Oliver, Feb. 1895). Culms single, long-spaced on the rhizome. Culm-sheaths and l. similar to (*b*), n. 29–3 on ¼ in.

(*d*) *Tabindaing*, Wuntho, Upper Burma, in cool evergreen forest, 500 ft. (Smales

Jan., 1902). Culms 2 ft. apart, naked below on ¾ of their length, 50 ft. high, internodes 18 in. long, diam. 3–4 in., walls ⅛ in., nodes not prominent, hence the culm smooth, cylindric. Culm-sheaths 6–8 in. long, from stone- to orange-colour, contrasting with the light green colour of the culms, blade 2–4 in. L. glabrous, glaucous beneath, 8–12 by 1–2 in., n. 25–33 on ¼ in. Accidental branches on the lower portion of the culm, and partially suppressed branchlets have leaf-sheaths with long bristles at the mouth, while the normal l. on the upper portion of the stem are without such bristles, and have keeled naked sheaths.

(c) ***Tabindaing.*** Hills west of Katha, 2,000 ft., in cool evergreen forest (Joseph Messer, March 1904). Culms 1–2 ft. apart, naked more than half-way up, 75 ft. high, a few conspicuous rings of arrested rootlets on the lowest 3 or 4 nodes. Culm-sheath very broad at base, 6, blade 2–3 in. long. Internodes 1–2 ft., 4 in. diam., nodes thick with a conspicuous arrested bud (***myelsan***) at every node, ½–1 in. diam. L. bluish-white underneath, 10 by 1½ in., n. 29–37 on ¼ in., leaf-sheaths keeled, ligule large, triangular.

B. Tufted or probably so.

(*f*) ***Wanet.*** Shwegu, Upper Burma (Pocock, 1902). Culms tufted, stems branched in the lower half, culm-sheaths thick, not much narrowed towards the truncate mouth, with broad, wavy fimbriate auricles. L. pale beneath and slightly velvety, 12 by 1½–1¾ in., ligule conspicuous, n. 30–40 on ¼ in., pet. ⅛ in. long.

(*g*) ***Wanet.*** Kachin hills, Bhamo district, in moist forest, 1,500 ft. (Oliver, April 1893). Culm-sheaths woody, 8 in. long, blade triangular, as long as sheath, tip spinescent, l. 9–12 by 1¼–2 in., glaucous and finely-pubescent beneath, n. 28–33 on ¼ in., ligule very small.

(*h*) ***Tekserah***, Garo hills (G. Mann, 1889). Culm-sheath broad, 6, blade 8 in. long, blade membranous, glabrous, conspicuously ribbed, continued into a broad fimbriate band on the top of sheath. L. hairy beneath, 9 by 1⅜ in., narrowed into pet. ⅕–¼ in., apex running out into a long hairy point, n. 40–45 on ¼ in., ligule minute.

Of the Bamboos here mentioned, *a*, *b*, *g*, and *h* are included by Gamble under *G. macrostachya*. He also includes ***Mādi*** or ***Maday-wa*** from Chittagong, of which I have seen no specimens.

2. **G. Kurzii**, Gamble, t. 56. South Tenasserim. Malay Penins. L. 8–13 by ½–1½ in., n. 36–39 on ¼ in. Panicle leafy, half whorls of 2–6 lanceolate spikelets ½ in. long, marked by the dense fringe of long brown hairs along the edge of the glumes, style long, ending in a single plumose stigma. 3. **G. verticillata**, Munro; Gamble, t. 52. Syn. *G. maxima*, Kurz, Ind. For. i. 343. Cultivated and wild in the Malay Peninsula and Archipelago, forming large forests in Java. China. Probably also in Tenasserim. Tufted, culms 80–120 ft., light coloured, with yellow stripes when young, internodes 18 in., 4–6 in. diam., culm-sheaths 12 in. long, densely clothed outside with golden-brown stiff hairs, rounded to a top 1–1½ in. broad, blade small reflexed. L. 10–15 by 1–2 in., pet. ⅛–¼ in. long, n. 21–30 on ¼ in. Panicle leafy, compound, branches long, slender, bearing distant half-whorls of ovate spikelets ⅓ in. long, stamens exserted, tube long, membranous, anthers yellow.

6. OXYTENANTHERA, Munro; Fl. Brit. Ind. vii. 400.

Spikelets narrow-cylindric, acuminate, fl. 1–3. Palea of the lower fl. 2-keeled, that of the uppermost slightly or not at all keeled. Stamens 6, filaments united into a thin membranous tube. Caryopsis grooved, terminated by a beak. As far as known the species fl. frequently, some probably annually, inflorescence often leafy. Species the following, one in New Guinea, and one or two in tropical Africa.

A. Panicle large, branches long, with distant half-whorls of spikelets. Eastern species:—

1. **O. albo-ciliata**, Munro; Gamble, t. 61. Syn. *Gigantochloa albo-ciliata*, Kurz. Vern. ***Wapyugale***, ***Wanwè***, ***Wagök***, ***Wagauk***, Burm.

Very gregarious, tufted, generally deciduous, culms 20–30 ft., not erect, but bending over in all directions, forming dense low masses of nearly horizontal stems, branches in the lower part single, stout, often erect, higher up smaller, leafy, half-whorled. Internodes of culms and larger branches 24 in. long, 1–1¼ in. diam., nodes oblique. Culm-sheaths thick, hard, one-third the length of internode, clothed with dark appressed hairs, blade often as long as sheath, ligule large, $\frac{1}{2}$–1 in. long. Lower internodes of leaf-bearing branchlets 5–7 in. long, l. 6–10 by 1 in., n. 27–34 on $\frac{1}{4}$ in., pet. very short. Fl. irregularly, at times in single clumps, at others gregariously over large areas. Branches of panicle long, slender, fistulose, spikelets $\frac{1}{2}$–$\frac{3}{4}$ in. long, slender, curved, in compact half-whorls, glumes conspicuously white-ciliate. Grain cylindric, glabrous, beaked.

Upper Burma. Shan States east of the Salween river. Martaban and Tenasserim, abundant, less common in Pegu. A bad companion for Teak, as the tangled masses of low arching stems tend to smother and break down the saplings, while those which survive are not drawn up by the Bamboo and not forced to form tall and clean stems. Tree growth does not generally flourish where the species is abundant (cf. H. N. Thompson in Forest Report Southern Circle, Upper Burma, 1900–1901).

2. **O. nigrociliata**, Munro; Gamble, t. 60. Syn. *O. auriculata*, Prain, Bengal Plants 1234; *Gigantochloa andamanica*, Kurz, and *auriculata*, Kurz; *Bambusa auriculata*, Kurz; Gamble, t. 49. Vern. *Kalia*, Beng.; *Talagu wa*, Burm. (Kurz). Garo hills (*Washut*). Silhet. Chittagong. Lower Pegu (Kurz). Tenasserim. Andamans, in the semi-deciduous forest, often associated with Padouk, also on banks of streams forming the lower fringe of the evergreen forest. Nicobars.—Singapore. Densely tufted, evergreen, gregarious, culms erect, straight, 30–50 ft., internodes 18–30 in., diam. 2–4 in. Culm-sheaths 6-16 in., densely covered with black hairs, which readily come off on the middle line, leaving two longitudinal hairy belts, apex 1$\frac{1}{2}$–3 in. wide, convexly truncate, blade triangular or lanceolate, shorter than sheath, with two small round auricles. L. 8–16 by 1–2$\frac{1}{2}$ in., thin hairs up to $\frac{1}{10}$ in. long on the underside, chiefly on young l., n. 24–30 on $\frac{1}{4}$ in., transverse veins distinctly visible, leaf-sheaths terminating in 2 small thick glossy auricles. Panicles large, leafy, branches pubescent, fertile spikelets narrow, cylindric-lanceolate, $\frac{1}{2}$–1$\frac{1}{2}$ in. long, with numerous smaller sterile ones, in distant half-whorls, supported by broad sometimes elongate coriaceous bracts. Fl. 1–3, glumes conspicuously fringed along the edge with stiff black or brown hairs, longitud. n. 15–27, transv. veins few or none. Empty glumes usually 4, ovate, mucronate, palea bristly bidentate at apex, lodicules 0. Staminal-tube in the young fl. as long as ovary, thick, 6 fibro-vascular bundles leading to the teeth which bear the anthers, growing out rapidly into a thin hyaline tube up to 1 in. long, elegantly marked by 6 lines of torn spiral vessels, the remains of the fibro-vascular bundles. Anthers $\frac{1}{4}$–$\frac{3}{8}$ in. long, purple, exserted, terminating in a sharp hispid apiculus. Ovary and style densely clothed with stiff hairs. Caryopsis cylindric. Easily propagated by cut pieces of culms with the sheaths on, which, if pegged down upon the ground, root at the nodes. Fl. frequently. To this Mr. Gamble refers *Bolangi Bans* of Khorda, Orissa. Specimens (l. culms and culm-sheaths) received from Southern Pegu as *Talagu-wa* may possibly belong to this. They differ in the following points: Internodes softly velvety while young, walls thick, ring at the nodes slanting, l.-sheaths keeled, elegantly ribbed, apex rounded not auriculate. 3. **O. parvifolia**, Brandis; Gamble, t. 63. Yunzalin. *Thaiktu-myintu*, Burm.; *Wamō*, Kar. (D. B. March, 1880). Culm-sheaths coriaceous, 8–10 in. long. L. 3–5 by $\frac{1}{2}$–$\frac{3}{4}$ in., pet. slender, $\frac{1}{12}$ in. long, n. 33 on $\frac{1}{4}$ in. Spikelets $\frac{3}{4}$ in. long, 3–10 in one half-whorl, lower glumes minutely ciliate along the edges, the upper glumes not ciliate, empty glumes 3–4, fertile 2–3, palea in the upper part minutely ciliate along the keels, staminal-tube long, base of ovary glabrous.

B. Spikelets in dense globose heads on erect usually panicled spikes. Western species.

4. **O. monostigma**, Bedd. Ic. Pl. t. 234; Gamble t. 65. Vern. *Chiwa*, *Choua*, *Chawa*, Kan.

Gregarious, culms single, erect, when young clothed with deciduous tawny or whitish velvet, grey when old, 10–30 ft. high, internodes 15–18 in. long, 1 in. diam., cavity small, culm-sheaths nearly as long as internodes. L. 5–12 by $\frac{1}{2}$–1$\frac{3}{4}$ in., n. 18–36 on $\frac{1}{4}$ in., ligule long, leaf-sheaths striate. Heads of spikelets usually approximate on short leafy spikes, spikelets glabrous, long spinescent-acuminate, fertile $\frac{3}{4}$–1 in. long, sterile shorter, style glabrous, stigma usually undivided.

Western Ghats and adjoining hill ranges, from the Poona district to the Anamalais, often forming underwood in Teak—and other deciduous forests. A soft Bamboo, not much used. 5. **O. Stocksii**, Munro; Gamble, t. 66. *Konda*, Kan. Commonly cultivated along the coast of North Kanara, rare on the ghats. A strong Bamboo, culms almost solid, used for punt-poles. L. 4–8 by $\frac{1}{2}$–$\frac{3}{4}$ in., n. 33–39 on $\frac{1}{4}$ in. Fertile spikelets 2-fld., $\frac{1}{2}$ in. long, style hairy. 6. **O. Thwaitesii**, Munro; Bedd. Fl. Sylv. t. 322; Gamble, t. 64. Western Ghats and adjoining hill ranges from the Bababudān hills southwards. Karnūl hills. Gregarious, straggling or climbing, culms 10–15 ft. long, branched from the base, branchlets whorled, ending in pliant whips with whorls of small branchlets and very small l., internodes 12–18 in. long, diam. 1 in., walls thin. Culm-sheaths $\frac{1}{2}$ or $\frac{1}{3}$ the length of internode, at the apex with large falcate auricles, which are thickly set with long stiff curved bristles, l. 4–12 by $\frac{1}{2}$–$1\frac{1}{2}$ in., n. 18–36 on $\frac{1}{4}$ in., leaf-sheaths with bristles at the mouth while young. Panicle huge, often leafy, spikelets $\frac{1}{3}$–$\frac{1}{2}$ in. long, usually 1-fld., anthers long-apiculate, style hairy, stigmas 3, short, plumose. 7. **O. Bourdilloni**, Gamble, t. 67. Vern. *Kāmbu*, Tam.; *Arambu*, Mal. Travancore ghats, 3–4,000 ft., rare, found only on rocky cliffs. Tufts loose, not compact, culms 20–30 ft. high, internodes 3 ft. long, walls thin, culm-sheaths 6-12 in., blade triangular, sharply mucronate. L. thin, 6–9 by 1–$1\frac{1}{2}$ in., n. 18 on $\frac{1}{4}$ in., ligule long, serrate. Heads $1\frac{1}{2}$ in. diam. in long spikes, spikelets polished, $\frac{3}{8}$ in. long, mucronate, 3-fld., ovary hairy, style hairy, stigmas 3. Fl. at long intervals, Travancore in 1887.

7. PSEUDOSTACHYUM, Munro; Fl. Brit. Ind. vii. 409.

P. polymorphum, Munro, the only species; Gamble, t. 85. Vern. *Filing*. Nep.; *Bajāl*, *Basāl*, *Nal*, *Tolli*, Ass.; *Wachall*, Garo; *Bawa*, *Baukwa*, Burm.; *Wana*, Kachin.

Single-stemmed, culms 25–50 ft., overhanging, often supported by neighbouring trees, lower part branchless, internodes 8–15 in. long, 1–2 in. diam., walls thin. Culm-sheaths loose, much shorter than internodes, blade early deciduous, ribbed and often with transverse veins, lanceolate or triangular, often longer than sheath. L. thin, 6–15 by 1–2 in. usually glabrous, sometimes fine hairs on the underside, pet. varying in length up to $\frac{1}{3}$ in., n. 18–22 on $\frac{1}{4}$ in., transverse veins conspicuous, often bent, where they cross the band of silica cells. Flowers frequently, in most cases fl. deformed and sterile, usually appearing as large round masses of hairy glumes. Spikelets solitary, $\frac{1}{6}$ in. long, in the axils of narrow bracts on the slender branches of a large leafy panicle. One fertile fl., palea convolute 2-keeled, keels not ciliate, lodicules large, ciliate, anthers apiculate. Caryopsis depressed-globose, surmounted by the base of style and supported by the persistent glumes, palea and lodicules.

Sikkim and Bhutan, from the foot of the hills to 5,000 ft. Garo hills. Assam. Manipúr. Moister districts of Upper Burma.

8. DENDROCALAMUS, Nees; Fl. Brit. Ind. vii. 403.

Tall unarmed Bamboos, in dense clumps. Culm-sheaths often very large. L. mostly large, n. 20–30 on $\frac{1}{4}$ in., usually 24 or 25 (*membranaceus* 30–40), transverse veins, if not obscured by hairs, more or less visible in dry leaves on the underside. Spikelets ovate, fl. few, rarely more than 6, usually bisexual. Glumes many-nerved, empty 2–3. Paleæ of lower fl. 2-keeled, ciliate, only those of the terminal fl. rounded on the back and not keeled. Lodicules as a rule none, sometimes 1–2 in *D. patellaris*, *Brandisii*, and *flagellifer*. Stamens 6, filaments free. Ovary hairy in the upper part, style long hairy, undivided, in a few species 2–3-fid. at the apex. Seed enclosed in a hard crustaceous pericarp. Species 16, South-Eastern Asia.

A. Spikelets numerous, spinescent, in dense, usually globose heads, rachis of spike solid or nearly so.

1. **D. strictus**, Nees; Bedd. Fl. Sylv. t. 325; Brandis F. Fl. t. 70, Gamble, t. 68, 69. *Male Bamboo.* Vern. *Bāns*, Hind.; *Karail*, Beng.; *Halpa*, *Wadūr*, Gond.; *Indo*, Kurku; *Manwel*, *Bundi*, Thana; *Sanna Veduru*, *Kanka Veduru*, Tel.; *Kib-Bidaru*, Kan.; *Kal-Mungil*, Tam.; *Myinwa*, Burm.

Middle-sized, deciduous, culms greyish-green, often blotched, closely packed in dense clumps, the lower portion with short stiff spreading generally leafless branches, one of which is much larger than the others, those on the upper portion slender, and leafy. Internodes 10–15 in. long, 2–3 in. diam., in dry

districts almost solid, in a moist climate hollow with thick walls. Culm-sheaths a little shorter than internodes, glabrous or with yellowish-brown hairs, narrowed into the elongate-triangular blade which is hairy, especially within. Leaves densely clothed on both sides with deciduous hairs, linear, 4–10 in. long, n. 27–33 on $\frac{1}{4}$ in. Spikelets hairy, $\frac{1}{3}$–$\frac{1}{2}$ in. long, ∞ in dense globose heads, 1–1$\frac{1}{2}$ in. diam. Glumes spinescent, empty numerous, fertile 2–3. Caryopsis shining, hairy only at the apex, $\frac{1}{4}$–$\frac{1}{3}$ in. long, ovoid, beaked, a large portion of the style persistent, embryo distinctly visible on the outside.

Widely spread and very common throughout India and Burma, up to the borders of the arid tract of North-Western India. Salt range. Subhimalayan tract from the Indus eastwards, ascending to 3,500 ft. Aravalli hills. In lower Burma common on dry ridges and in Engdaing, in Upper Burma, not beyond 24° N., the climate further north being probably too moist. Flowers irregularly, that is, a few culms in a clump here and there or a few clumps in one locality come into flower, while at times it flowers gregariously over large areas. Bruce, Ind. For. xxx. 269 reports, that in the Ruby Mines district, 1902, this Bamboo had flowered on the most exposed situations, and in the hottest localities, while the clumps growing in sheltered and cooler areas had remained green. An abnormal case of seedlings 18 months' old coming into fl. is recorded in Ind. For. xxv. 22. Muriel, Ind. For. xxix. 507, describes (Pyinmana district) longitudinal partitions in the hollows of this species, which thicken in the higher internodes, until the upper portion of the bamboo becomes quite solid. *D. sericeus*, Munro; Gamble, t. 79, Parasnath, spikelets densely silky, has in Gamble. Ind. Timb. ed. ii. 751, been reduced to a variety of 1, but is maintained as a distinct species by Prain, Beng. Plants, 1235.

2. **D. membranaceus**, Munro; Gamble, t. 71. Vern. *Wapyu*, Burm.; *Meshang, Maisang, Mai-lai-law*, Shan. Upper Burma: Martaban (Kurz). A most useful Bamboo, gregarious, clumps very loose, of about 6–12 stems, culms 60–70 ft., white-powdery when young, smooth, bright green when older, branches in the lower part numerous, short, stiff, internodes 9–20 in., 1–5 in. diam., walls thick, nodes prominent, culm-sheaths early deciduous, longer than internodes, narrowed into dark brown, waved and fringed auricles, blade narrow, ligule $\frac{3}{8}$ in. long, hairy and roughly serrate. L. glaucous below with a few hairs near base, 5–10 by $\frac{1}{2}$–$\frac{3}{4}$ in., n. 30–40 on $\frac{1}{4}$ in., transverse veins often faintly visible. Spikelets nearly glabrous, $\frac{1}{3}$–$\frac{1}{2}$ in. long, empty glumes 2, fertile 2–3. Grain $\frac{1}{4}$–$\frac{1}{3}$ in. long, broadly ovoid, ending in a sharp point, the persistent base of style. Groups of 5–12 or more shorter internodes, 2–6 in. long, not uncommon, caused by the attack of an insect. The name *Wapyu* (white Bamboo) is applied to other species besides this in Burma. A Bamboo similar in mode of growth and other characters sent (l. only) by the late Mr. Messer as *Wanet*, Burm. Cool Hill forests, Kachin hills, Katha, 5,000 ft. L. 5–7 by $\frac{1}{2}$ in., n. 40–50 on $\frac{1}{4}$ in.

B. Spikelets numerous, in large soft dense usually globose heads, rachis of spike hollow, usually green.

(*a*) Spikelets blunt, culm-sheaths glabrous or nearly so.

3. **D. Hamiltonii**, Nees et Arn.; Brandis F. Fl. 570; Gamble, t. 74. Vern. *Kaghsi bans*, Hind.; *Tama*, Nep.; *Pao*, Lepcha; *Kotoha, Kokwa*, Ass.; *Wah*, Mechi; *Wabo myetsangyè*, Burm.; *Maik-hôk*, Shan; *Uga Kawa*, Kachin.

Culms attaining 80 ft., white-pubescent when young, mostly overhanging and often horizontal, branching, the branches often single and as long as the main stem. This species forms impenetrable thickets, the inner stems of a clump are often upright and clear of branches, somewhat resembling *Dendrocalamus giganteus*. Internodes 12–20 in. long, 4–5 in. diam., walls $\frac{1}{3}$–$\frac{1}{2}$ in. thick. Culm-sheaths stiff, persistent, often as long as internode, convexly truncate at top, blade ovate-lanceolate, up to 12 in. long. The branches on the nodes in the lower portion of the stem are usually seated on woody knobs as large as a fist, and at these nodes when the branches have not, or have only imperfectly developed, are large very conspicuous swellings (arrested or half-developed buds), covered with brown shining undeveloped sheaths. These buds are above the lower oblique node ring (scar of the fallen culm-sheath) and below the upper ring, on which often abortive rootlets appear, their shape is lenticular and they often extend over half the circumference of

the culm. The Burmese name indicates the resemblance of this swelling to an eye. L. glabrous, but rough beneath, on vigorous shoots up to 18 by 5 in., on ordinary branches smaller, n. 18–28 on ¼ in., transverse veins faintly visible, leaf-sheaths with stiff appressed hairs, ligule long, oblique. Like *D. strictus*, this species flowers sporadically and at times gregariously. Fl. heads semiglobose, ½–1½ in. diam., supported by broad leathery shining bracts, on a stout very hollow rachis 1–3 in. apart. Spikelets glabrous, purple, ovate, ⅓ in. long, glumes broad, apiculate, long-ciliate along the edges, empty 2–3, fertile 2–4, anthers purple on long glabrous filaments, ovary and style hairy. Caryopsis broadly ovoid, ¼ in. long, beaked, hairy at apex.

Garwhal 4,000 ft. (indigenous ?). East Himalaya, lower hills and valleys, ascending to 3,000 ft. Assam. Garo, Khasi and Naga hills. Burma, Upper and Lower, chiefly near streams and in hollows, ascending to 3,000 ft. Cultivated in the Duns and outer hills of the North-West Himalaya, north as far as Kangru. *Bambusa Falconeri*, Munro, was based upon the l. of this and fl. of *Bambusa nutans*. 4. Allied to 3, but quite different is *Wabo è*, a valuable large Bamboo, found in cool valleys and on the high evergreen Kachin hills in the Katha district, fl., l., and notes sent by the late Joseph Messer, after whom it should be named, when more perfectly known. Tufted, culms 85–100 ft. high, internodes 12–21 in. long, 5 in. diam., walls ¾–1 in. thick, branches all the way up, near the base thickly set and sometimes 20 ft. long, conspicuous rings of arrested rootlets for 8–10 ft. from the ground, buds of undeveloped branches smaller and less prominent than in 3. Culm-sheaths 18 in. long, ligule serrate, ½ in. broad, blade as long as sheath, blade and ligule hairy. L. 8–9 by 1 in., n. 36 on ¼ in. Spikelets ⅜ in. long, numerous in dense nearly globose heads, branches of inflorescence very hollow, up to ⅜ in. diam. Glumes glabrous, edges minutely ciliate, the 2 lowest empty, fl. 8–10, of which the lowest are usually ♂. Ovary broad, entirely hairy. 5. **D. patellaris**, Gamble, t. 75. Vern. *Pagjiok*, Lepcha; *Futung*, Mikir Hills. Sikkim and British Bhutan 2–5,000 ft. Mikir and Naga Hills. Tufted, culms 20–30 ft. high, internodes 12–18 in. long, 1–1⅓ in. diam., walls thin, a broad softly hairy ring below the nodes. Culm-sheaths persistent, 10–12 in. long, upper part narrowed and furnished with a pale long-fimbriate fringe, ligule conspicuous, fringed like the sheath. L. 8–16 in. long, n. 20–30 on ¼ in. Fl. similar to 3, but sometimes 1 or 2 lodicules.

(*b*) Spikelets acute, culm-sheaths usually very hairy.

6. **D. Hookeri**, Munro; Gamble, t. 73. Sikkim (*Tili bans*, Nep.; *Patu*, Lepcha). Daphla Hills 2–3,000 ft. Khasi and Jaintia hills (*Sieijong*), Bhamo. Cultivated near Naini Tal, Kumaon (E. E. Fernandez 1881). Tufted, branches overhanging. Culms 50–60 ft., naked below, internodes 18–20 in. long, diam. 4–6 in., walls 1 in. thick. Culm-sheaths gradually narrowed from a broad base to a truncate top, 8–12, blade 3–7 in. long. L. 12–15 by 2–3 in., pet. short, n. 18–26 on ¼ in. Spikelets often minutely pubescent, ⅓ in. long, in dense globose heads ½–1 in. diam., rachis ⅓ in. diam., hollow, but walls firm. *D. Parishii*, Munro; Gamble, t. 82, probably belongs to this species, but spikelets glabrous. 7. **D. sikkimensis**, Gamble, t. 72. Vern. *Pugriang*, Lepcha; *Wadah*, Garo. Sikkim and Bhutan, 4–6,000 ft. Tura peak, Garo hills. Tufted, but culms few, 50–70 ft. high, naked below, internodes 18 in. long, 5–7 in. diam., walls thick. Culm-sheaths 12 in. long, densely clothed with a dark golden-brown felt of matted hairs, blade decurrent on each side into a large long-fringed auricle. L. 6–12 by 1½–3 in., strigose beneath with long appressed hairs, n. 20–24 on ¼ in., in specimens cult. at Kew as low as 12, leaf-sheaths glabrous, shining, keeled, ligule short hairy. Spikelets ⅓–⅜ in. long in dense red-brown globose heads 1⅓ in. diam. Grain obovoid, with a few hairs at apex.

C. Spikelets usually few (exceptions: *D. Brandisii*, *Collettianus*, and 16), in small heads, rachis of spike usually solid.

(*a*) Spikelets short, ½ in. long and less.

8. **D. longispathus**, Kurz; Gamble, t. 78. Vern. *Ora*, Chittagong; *Khang*, Beng.; *Waya*, sometimes *Talagu-wa*, *Wanet*, Burm.

Tufted, culms 60 ft., glaucous or nearly white when young, lower half naked, often with a ring of rootlets at the nodes, internodes 18–30 in. long, 3–5 in. diam., walls ⅓ in. thick, node line horizontal, undulate, hardly thickened. Culm-sheaths densely clothed on the outside with dark (almost black) stinging hairs, thin, fragile, but long persistent, 14–36 in. long, overlapping the internodes, blade recurved, narrow, early deciduous, a little shorter than sheath, ligule a broad band of closely-packed long hairs. L. 6–9 by 1 in., underside soft to the touch, with extremely minute hairs, base cuneate, narrowed into a very short petiole, n. 25–30 on ¼ in., l. sheaths keeled, striate and with minute deciduous appressed hairs. Spikelets glabrous, blunt, ¼ in. long, 2–3, sometimes more, in distant heads, ⅜ in. across or less, supported by broad, polished coriaceous bracts. Glumes conspicuously nerved, minutely ciliate at edges, paleæ minutely pubescent. Caryopsis broadly ovoid.

Silhet. Chittagong. Arakan. Pegu, common near streams in the upper mixed forests. Martaban. Tenasserim. Flowers frequently, known to have flowered in Pegu: 1862 (D. B. Zamayi), 1871 (Kurz), 1875 (D. B. Tharawadi), 1891 (Carter). The name *Wanet* (black Bamboo) is applied to other species besides this in Burma.

9. **D. Brandisii**, Kurz; Gamble, t. 79. Vern. *Kyello-wa, Wabo*, Burm.; *Waklü*, Kar.

Tufted, evergreen, culms erect, 80 to 120 ft., near the ground often with a tuft of branches, otherwise naked in the lower portion, but with rootlets at the nodes. Internodes 20–27 in. long, 5–7 in. diam., walls thick. Culm-sheaths thick, coriaceous, 15–24 in. long, blade linear-lanceolate, contracted at base, often green, longer than sheath. L. 9–15 by 2–3 in., very minutely hairy beneath, n. 20–28, usually 24 on ¼ in., ligule conspicuous. Spikelets broad-ovate, nearly ¼ in. long, in dense heads, fertile spikelets few, sterile numerous, heads ⅓–½ in. diam., on long flagelliform spikes, rachis solid, distance between heads ½–1½ in. Sometimes 1 or 2 lodicules. Caryopsis ovoid-cylindric. $\frac{1}{10}$–⅛ in. long.

Upper Burma: Katha (*Thaikwabo*). Bhamo. Ruby Mines district, 2,400 ft. Lower Burma: Eastern slopes of the Pegu Yoma, Salwin, Yunzalin, Thaungyin, common on limestone. Attaran. South Andaman.—Singapore. Fl. frequently. 10 **D. flagellifer**, Munro; Gamble, t. 80. Mooleyit, Tenasserim 2,000 ft.—Malay Peninsula. L. 10–14 by 1–2⅜ in., n. 21–30 on ¼ in. Spikelets few, heads small on long whip-like spikes, the uppermost nodes bearing leaf-sheaths only, with a small blade. Sometimes 1 or 2 lodicules. 11. **D. longifimbriatus**, Gamble, t. 81. Kyaukshat and Maliwón forest, Mergui district. (*Wapyaw*, Burm.). Leaf-sheaths hairy, with long falcate and amplexicaul auricles, thickly set with stiff curved bristles, transverse veins distinctly visible.

(*b*) Spikelets ⅓ in. and longer, ovate, acute.

12. **D. giganteus**, Munro; Gamble, t. 76. Vern. *Wabo*, Burm.

Densely tufted, evergreen, culms erect, 80–100 ft. high, usually naked in the lower portion, internodes 15–20 in. long, diam. 6–8 in., walls ½ in. thick. Culm-sheaths hard, shining within, thinly hairy outside, 15–20 in. long, blade shorter than sheath, ligule stiff, dark brown, ¼–⅓ in. broad. L. 9–20 by 2–4 in., glaucous and minutely hairy beneath while young, n. 20–28 on ¼ in. Spikelets ovate, ½ in. long, 2–5 in a head, on long spikes, which are often leafy at top, distance between heads ¼–¾ in., rachis solid, glumes mucronate, 1–2 empty, 3–6 fertile, the top fl. consisting of a long, involute glume. Caryopsis oblong, $\frac{3}{10}$ in. long.

Probably indigenous in the hills of Martaban. Cultivated largely in Burma, in India (north as far as Makúm, Assam, D.B. Apr., 1879), and in most tropical countries. The plantations of *Wabo* near Myanoung (Ind. For. ii. 311) probably are of this species. Used for building and for carrying water. Does not split well (M. Hill). 13. **D. latiflorus**, Munro; Gamble, t. 117. Southern Shan States (*Wani*, Burm.), possibly introduced from China.—Tonkin. China. Formosa. Tufted, internodes short, 5 in. diam., walls thin. L. 7–10 by 1½–3 in., n. 24–30 on ¼ in. (Burma specimens). Spikelets broadly ovate, ½–⅝ in. long, 3–6 in reddish-purple heads, on long spikes, often leafy at top, rachis often hollow. Glumes pubescent on the back, ciliate along the edge, empty 2, fl. glumes 6–8, the lowest and uppermost sometimes sterile. 14. **D. calostachyus**, Kurz; Gamble, t. 77. Bhamo and lower Kachin hills. Culm-sheaths clothed with appressed tawny hairs, ligule narrow. Spikes long flagellate. Not seen. 15. **D. Collettianus**, Gamble, t 83. Fort Stedman, Southern Shan States. Fl. only known. Spikes often compound, heads ½–1 in. diam. with 6–12 fertile and a few sterile spikelets. Spikelets ½–⅜ in. long, softly pubescent. Not seen. 16. **Wabo,** Burm. Cultivated in villages, Southern Shan States, 1,500–2,000 ft. (Montague Hill). Culm-sheaths 18 in. long, thick, hard, shining within, thinly hairy outside, l. thin, grey, 6–9 by 1–1¼ in., scabrid on both surfaces, n. 20–24 on ¼ in., petiole very short, sheath glabrous, edges ciliate. Heads of 10–20 spikelets, approximate, nearly confluent, spikelets ½–¾ in. long, nearly glabrous, tip hard, pungent, fl. 2–3, ♂, ♀, and bisexual. Palea long-ciliate at keels, between keels 2–5 n., ovary and style densely hairy.

9. TEINOSTACHYUM, Munro; Fl. Brit. Ind. vii. 410.

Culms thin, overhanging, sometimes climbing. Spikelets up to 3 in. long, slender, many-fld., sometimes pedunculate, in bracteate whorls on the spiciform branches of a leafy panicle, upper and lower fl. imperfect, rachilla elongate between the fl., glumes mucronate, palea convolute, keeled, keels ciliate near the apex. Lodicules 3, 3–9-nerved. Style enclosed in and partly adnate to a cylindric sheath. Caryopsis ovoid, beaked, pericarp crustaceous. Species 5, of which one in Ceylon.

1. **T. Wightii,** Bedd. Fl. Sylv. t. 323; Gamble, t. 87. Vern. *Nanyura*, Tam. Western Ghats from North Kanara southwards, 3–5,000 ft. Nilgiris, Anamalais, in the undergrowth of high tree forest. Culms 10–20 ft. long, supported by the neighbouring trees, branches flexuose, internodes 14–18 in. long, diam. 1–1½, walls thin. Culm-sheaths thin, nearly as long as internodes, brownish-black hairs on the back, blade narrow, half the length of sheath or more. L. 6–15 by 1–3 in., pet. ¼–⅓ in. long, n. 16–20 on ¼ in. Panicle large, contracted, drooping, consisting of long slender spikes. Fl. at long intervals, Travancore in 1887. 2. **T. Griffithii,** Munro in Trans. Linn. Soc. xxvi. t. 3; Gamble, t. 86. Syn. *Cephalostachyum Griffithii*, Kurz. Assam (*Beti*, *Behti*). Chittagong. Burma (Kurz). Straggling or subscandent, culms 25–50 ft., internodes 12–24 in. long, diam. ¾ in. L. 6–10 by ½–1½ in., glaucous beneath, pet. short, n. 20–36 on ¼ in. Spikelets pubescent, 2–3 in. long. 3. **T. Dullooa,** Gamble, t. 89. British Bhutan 2,000 ft. (*Tokré bans*, Nep.). Garo hills (*Wadru*). Assam (*Dalu*, *Dolo*, *Dollu*, *Dallu*). Silhet. Cachar (*Bajail*). Chittagong (*Dolu*). Upper Burma: Katha (*Thaikwabo*), Mogaung (*Wamyet*). Tufted, more or less scandent, culms 20–60 ft., internodes 15–30 in long, diam. 2–3 in. Culm-sheaths 6–12 in. long, blade very narrow, recurved, often as long as sheath, edges convolute. L. 8–12 by 1–1½ in., pet. ¼ in., n. 21–30 on ¼ in. Spikelets softly hairy. *Gyawa* (Bhamo), which may possibly belong to this, is described by Montague Hill as a tall straight-growing graceful Bamboo, growing in clumps, but each stem very distinct, internodes 30–44 in. long, diam. 2–4 in. 4. **T. Helferi,** Gamble, t. 90. Syn. *Pseudostachyum Helferi*, Kurz. Assam. Garo (*Wali*), Khasi (*Tumoh*), and Jaintia hills. Pegu Yoma, chiefly on the east side (*Wathabut*). Hills east of Toungoo, 4,000 ft. Salween hills, 2,000 ft. (*Thochi*, Karen). Evergreen, eminently gregarious, forming impenetrable thickets of large extent, culms 20–40 ft. long, bending over in all directions and more or less climbing, internodes greyish-green, while young with appressed whitish bristles, 20–50 in. long, 1–1½ in. diam., walls very thin. Culm-sheaths thick, persistent, 8–10 in. long, blade narrow, recurved, nearly as long as sheath. L. 6–18 by 1½–3½ in., pet. broad, ¼–⅓ in long, n. 12–21 on ¼ in.

Schizostachyum Rogersii, sp. nova. Andamans (G. Rogers). Tufted, culms weak, up to 30 ft. long, to ¾ in. diam., overhanging or supported by trees, walls thin. Culm-sheaths much shorter than internodes, thin, 3–4 in. long, hairs very fugacious, base 2–2½ in. broad, tapering to ¾ in., with two small auricles at the apex, blade narrow, reflexed, as long as sheath. L. 7–9 by 1–1½ in., long fine hairs on the underside, n. 21 on ¼ in., transverse veins prominent, oblique and bent. Inflorescence a long spike, terminating leafy branchlets, with distant half-whorls (supported by bracts, which are often furnished with a blade) of 1–fld. glabrous spikelets, the fertile ½ in. long, the sterile shorter. Empty glumes 2–4, palea convolute, minutely 2-dentate, keels indistinct. Lodicules 3, unequal, anthers yellow, obtuse, ⅛ in. long. Ovary glabrous, continued into a thick cylindric hollow style, terminated by 3 long plumose stigmas. Caryopsis ellipsoid-cylindric, crowned by the long, persistent style, endosperm farinaceous. Somewhat resembles *S. chilianthum*, Kurz; Gamble, t. 101 of the Malay Peninsula, Sumatra and Java.

10. CEPHALOSTACHYUM, Munro; Fl. Brit. Ind. vii. 411.

Tufted, in most species the stouter nerves very broad, transverse veins often visible, but not conspicuous. Fl. heads dense, broadly obconical or nearly globose, consisting of numerous short spikes, each spike with several spikelets, the lowest spikelets usually sterile with numerous empty glumes, the uppermost with one fertile and several empty glumes. Palea thin, convolute, many-nerved, the two keels close together. Caryopsis glabrous, beaked, supported by the persistent glumes and lodicules and imbedded in a densely-packed mass of dry sterile spikelets. Species 7.

A. Heads along elongated spikes, forming a large panicle.

1. **C. pergracile,** Munro; Gamble, t. 95. Vern. *Tinwa*, Burm.; *Wablō*, Kar.; *Maikpang*, Shan.

Tufted, but not densely, culms erect, 30–40 ft. high, nodes in the lower part with dense half-whorls of rigid, simple green, usually leafless branches, spinescent at the ends. Internodes near the base 6, higher up 12–18 in. long, diam. 2–3 in., walls $\frac{1}{4}$ in., nodes horizontal. Culm-sheaths thick, one-third the length of internode, polished orange-brown, the lower part densely clothed with black stiff deciduous hairs, on young shoots forming a marked contrast with the green internodes, as they, while gradually lengthening out, emerge from the sheaths, blade triangular, cuspidate, on both sides with a fimbriate fringe, bordering the top of sheath. L. green beneath, 6–14 by $\frac{3}{4}$–2 in., n. 27–30 on $\frac{1}{4}$ in.; prominent but deciduous cilia at the mouth of sheath. Fl. frequently, at times gregariously over large areas. Heads globose, to broadly obconical, clothed with long soft hairs, supported by sheathing bracts 1–1$\frac{1}{2}$ in. long, on long slender, but wiry pendulous branches of a large leafless panicle, distance between heads 2–3 in. Caryopsis cylindric, grooved, $\frac{1}{3}$–$\frac{1}{2}$ in. long, beak hairy, straight, as long as caryopsis, pericarp coriaceous, embryo visible on the outside.

Burma, Upper and Lower, common, chiefly in the lower hills, in deciduous forest near streams. One of the most useful Bamboos, made into houseposts, walling, mats shingles and baskets. Rice is cooked in the joints, the outer green layer of the stem may be split very fine. Gamble refers to *C. pergracile* a Bamboo cultivated in the Sibsagar district of Assam (*Latang*, Naga; *Khawlam*, Singhpo), said to be wild on the lower Naga hills, as well as specimens coll. by himself in 1881 in the Singbhum district. F. Dalton communicates *Tinka*, Burm., from Myitkyina, Upper Burma, which has the same culm-sheaths and l. as *C. pergracile*, but is stated to have isolated stems and a few leaf-bearing branches in the lower part of the culm. 2. **C. flavescens,** Kurz; Gamble, t. 96. Introduced from Pegu into the Royal Botanic Gardens, Calcutta (Kurz). Culms 10–20 ft. high, internodes long, 1–1$\frac{1}{2}$ in. diam., culm-sheaths grey- or golden-hairy, 4–5 in., blade triangular, 1–2 in. long, base decurrent into a broad wavy fringe, bordering the top of sheath and extending beyond it into auricles fringed with long bristles. L. linear, 3–6 by $\frac{1}{2}$ in., n. 48 on $\frac{1}{4}$ in., leaf-sheaths produced into long narrow auricles. Panicle leafy, heads smaller than in 1, hairy, on rigid spikes. 3. **C. virgatum,** Kurz; Gamble, t. 97. Upper Burma, Mogaung, Griffith (July 1837), and Indawgyee lake, in evergreen forest (J. W. Oliver, March 1895). (*Waba*, Burm.; *Lakra*, Kach.). Middle-sized, culm-sheath thick, hard, 6–8 in., blade triangular, cuspidate, 3–5 in. long, decurrent along the top of sheath into a narrow band, bordered with stiff bristles. L. softly hairy beneath, 6–12 by 1–2 in., n. 21–24 on $\frac{1}{4}$ in., sheaths ciliate, ligule hairy. Panicle large, leafless, heads obconical, often approximate, and nearly confluent.

B. Heads usually single, terminal.

4. **C. capitatum,** Munro; Gamble, t. 91. Sikkim and British Bhutan 2–8,000 ft., forming dense thickets on the hillsides (*Gobia*, *Gope*, Nep.) Khasi hills (*Sillea*, *sullea*), Hills east of Bhamo 5,500–6,000 ft. (Mont. Hill). Gregarious, densely-branching. more or less scandent, culms 12–30 ft., yellow, internodes 2–3 ft. long, diam. 1–1$\frac{1}{2}$ in. Culm-sheaths thin, 6–12 in., blade long. L. pale green, ovate-lanceolate, blade 6–8 by 1–2 in., pet. $\frac{1}{8}$ in., n. on $\frac{1}{4}$ in. 18–21. Leaf-sheaths glabrous, shining. Fl.-heads not hairy, usually single, at the ends of leaf-bearing branches, which often stand in dense half-whorls, sometimes axillary and then forming large panicles (var. *decomposita*). Empty and flowering glumes convolute, concave below, ending in a long scabrous awn, palea convolute with more or less conspicuous transverse veins, lodicules veined, lanceolate $\frac{1}{8}$–$\frac{1}{4}$ in. long. 5. **C. pallidum,** Munro; Gamble, t. 92. Bhutan, Mishmi hills. Khasi hills, Manipúr and Patkoi range. Small, shrubby, culms 5 ft. high, l. 3–6 by $\frac{1}{2}$–1$\frac{1}{2}$ in., n. 24–27 on $\frac{1}{4}$ in. Fl.-heads single at the ends of leafy densely-

whorled branchlets, palea bifid at apex. 6. **C. latifolium,** Munro; Gamble, t. 98. Bhutan. Manipur. Shrubby, culms 6–10 ft. high, culm-sheaths thin papery. L. 10–16 by 2–4 in., n. 15–21 on ½ in. Fl.-heads globose, up to 2 in. diam. Caryopsis large, chestnut-brown, shining, ovoid, not grooved, ⅓–⅔ in. long, pericarp crustaceous, not adhering to the testa, embryo not visible on the outside. 7. **C. Fuchsianum,** Gamble, t. 94. British Bhutan, 6–8,000 ft., in dense thickets with *Plectocomia*. Daphla hills. Semiscandent, culms small, soft, thin-walled, culm-sheaths thin, top concave, sinus fringed, 12, blade 6–8 in. long., subulate, reflexed. L. ovate-lanceolate, 8–14 by 2–4 in., n. 15–21 on ½ in., the leaves immediately below the fl.-head shorter. Long white bristles on top and margin of leaf-sheath. Fl. in globose terminal heads, 2½ in. diam., or in a short densely-packed spike of superposed heads.

11. DINOCHLOA, Büse; Fl. Brit. India vii. 414.

Evergreen, climbing, culms zigzag, geniculate. Transverse veins often visible on the underside of the dry leaf. Spikelets minute 1-fld., with 1–4 empty glumes, palea convolute, not keeled, lodicules 0. Fr. ovoid, mucronate. Dr. Stapf has kindly informed me that the mature seed of *D. Tjankorreh*, which is enclosed in a leathery pericarp (fleshy while immature) has no endosperm, but consists mainly of a large and hard scutellum, traversed by fibro-vascular strands, its cells having much thickened walls. Species 3, possibly 5.

1. **D. andamanica,** Kurz.—Syn. *D. Tjankorreh*, Büse, *var. andamanica*, Gamble, t. 98. Andamans (the most generally distributed Bamboo in the islands). Nicobars. Culms single, green, glossy, up to 300 ft. long, creeping along the ground (rooting at the nodes) or climbing over the tallest trees. Branches geniculate, single, as long and as stout as the culm, from which they spring, branchlets slender, numerous, in whorls, hanging down with their dense foliage. New main branches develop annually, at first leafless, curved, tendril-like, later in the season covering themselves with a dense mass of foliage, which hangs down from the supporting trees and eventually smothers them. Where no large trees exist, this Bamboo forms an impenetrable tangled mass, spreading over shrubs and saplings. Internodes 9–18 in. long, 1 in. diam., walls thin, culm-sheaths green, less than one-fourth the length of internodes, as well as culms covered, while young, with a fugacious white bloom, blade leafy, deciduous, nearly as broad as sheath. L. 9–12 by 2–3 in., n. 18–24 on ½ in., upper side polished, ligule short, entire. Panicle terminal, narrow, often leafy, spikelets minute, glossy, straw-coloured. The Malayan *D. Tjankorreh*, Büse, Munro, Bambusaceæ, t. 5, has smaller leaves and the nerves closer together, 27–36 on ½ in., ligule often long, fimbriate. The fr. is described as fleshy, ½ in. diam. or more. The fr. of the Andaman species is unknown. 2. **D. M'Clellandi,** Kurz, F. Fl. ii. 571; Gamble, t. 99. Vern. *Wanwè*, Burm., Chittagong. Pegu Yoma, common on slopes with northerly aspect, chiefly where the heads of the strata crop out. Martaban. Tenasserim. Evergreen, climbing over tall trees and forming extensive thickets, culms greyish-green, while young silvery from minute appressed fugacious bristles, internodes 3–4 ft. long, up to 1 in. diam., walls thin, branches often single. Culm-sheaths more or less persistent, shorter than internodes, rounded at the mouth and bordered by a thickened, polished green margin, blade leafy, often longer than sheath. L. 12–15 by 2–4 in., n. 12–21 on ½ in. Fl. not known. The l. are very similar to those of *Teinostachyum Helferi*, Gamble. Two species, of which the fl. are unknown, placed by Munro under *Bambusa*, may possibly, when more perfectly studied, find their place in *Dinochloa*, as suggested by Gamble for one of them. 1. **B. Mastersii,** Munro. Vern. *Bentibans*, Assam. Dibrugarh, Assam. An extensive climber, like *Calamus Rotang*, l. 10–13 by 1½ in., n. 21–27 on ½ in. 2. **B. Marginata,** Munro. Vern. *Wamè*, Karen. Donat range between Thaungyin and Haundrow, 5,000 ft. D.B. April 1859. A climber, interlacing stems and branches of oak and chestnut trees, culms dark coloured, branches almost solitary. L. 6–7 by 1–1½ in., the edges in the upper part densely shaggy, with long silky hairs, n. 24–27 on ½ in.

12. MELOCALAMUS, Benth.; Fl. Brit. Ind. vii. 409.

M. compactiflorus, Benth. The only species. Gamble, t. 24. Syn. *Pseudostachyum compactiflorum*, Kurz, Ind. For. i. t. ii. fig. 13; F. Fl. ii. 567. Vern. *Daral*, Beng.; *Latha*, Cachar; *Lota*, Chitt.; *Wanwè*, Burm.; *Nachinwa*, Kachin.

Loosely tufted, spreading and climbing over tall trees, culms 50–90 ft. long, nearly solid, internodes 12–24 in. long, diam. ½–1½ in. Culm-sheaths thick coriaceous, shorter than internodes, blade linear-lanceolate, recurved. L. 9–12 by 1–2 in., pet. $\frac{1}{8}$ in., n. 20–30 on $\frac{1}{4}$ in. Fl. frequently, panicle large, often leafy, branches fistulose, bearing half-whorls of long hairy spikes, with globose compact fl. heads $\frac{1}{3}$ in. diam., like the beads of a rosary, $\frac{1}{2}$–2 in. apart. Spikelets small, $\frac{1}{8}$ in. long and as broad, fertile fl. 2, lodicules large, ciliate, ovary glabrous, style short, stigmas 2 or 3. Fr. 1–1$\frac{1}{2}$ in. diam., the pericarp fleshy while immature, ultimately coriaceous, the embryo has a large scutellum without endosperm. The seed often germinates while attached to the branch, putting forth a shoot and tuft of roots before falling to the ground.

Silhet, Cachar, Chittagong. Upper Burma: hills N.E. of Bhamo 6,000 ft. Ruby Mines district 4,000 ft. Lower Burma: Arakan Yoma, Thayetmyo district and hills east of Toungoo 4–6,000 ft. A flowering on a large scale on the hills n. east of Bhamo reported in Ind. For. xxviii. 482. In Yunnan sandals are made of the outer green fibrous layers of the internodes.

13. **MELOCANNA,** Trinius; Fl. Brit. Ind. vii. 417. Dr. Otto Stapf, On the fruit of *Melocanna* in Trans. Linn. Society, ser. 2, Botany, vol. vi. 401, 1904.

Spikelets usually 2–5 on an arrested axis, so as to appear fascicled, in the axils of large bracts, each spikelet with numerous empty glumes and one fl., rarely bisexual, usually ♂ with a rudimentary pistil or ♀ with sterile anthers. In the axils of the lower empty glumes, or rather bracts, are frequently buds which develop into short branchlets with a spikelet at the end. The fascicles of spikelets are on unilateral spikes, which are 1–6 in. long and are arranged in long narrow pedunculate more or less unilateral panicles. The peduncle of these panicles consists of several often elongated internodes, at the nodes with sheathing bracts, rarely with well-developed l. The panicles are of unequal length (the longest up to 3 ft.) and stand in dense lateral fascicles at the nodes of the culm. Most of these panicles are androdynamous, that is predominantly or exclusively male, while others, chiefly the shorter panicles, are gynodynamous, that is, predominantly or exclusively female, bisexual fl. occurring occasionally in either. In some cases the spikelet is 2-fld., and the palea of the lower fl. has one or two pairs of nerves. Fr. large, pyriform, beaked, the cells of the thick fleshy pericarp filled with starch. Seed when ripe, without endosperm, the embryo with a large scutellum, which is separated from the pericarp by a thin layer of thin-walled more or less crushed cells. When the seed germinates the embryo derives its first nourishment from the starch of the pericarp. (This description relates to *M. bambusoides*, fl. and fr. of the other species not being known.)

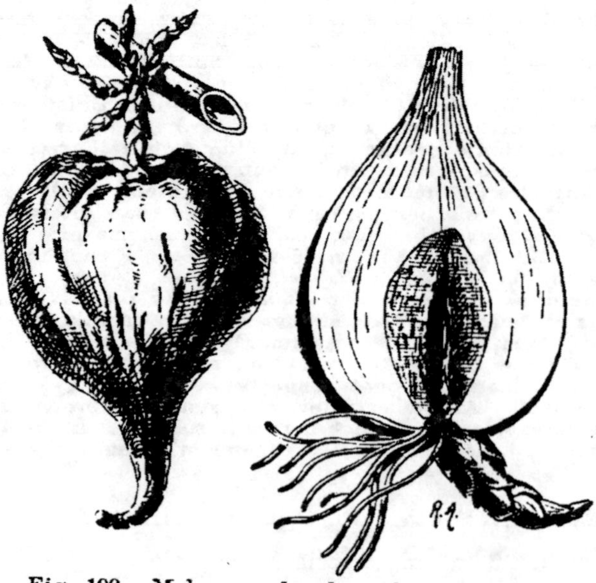

Fig. 199. Melocanna bambusoides, Trin.; the right-hand figure represents the germinating fruit. $\frac{1}{2}$.

1. **M. bambusoides,** Trin.; Kurz F. Fl. ii. 569, Gamble t. 105.—Syn. *Bam-*

busa baccifera, Roxb. Cor. Pl. t. 243. Vern. *Muli*, Beng.; *Tarai*, Ass.; *Watarai*, Garo; *Wati*, Cachar; *Kayaung*, Arakan; *Kayinwa, Tabindaingwa*, Burm.

Rhizome with long creeping scaly branches, which turn upwards at the end to form new culms. Culms distant, erect, 40–70 ft. long, the lower two-thirds bare of branches, sometimes with a few short branchlets at the lowest nodes, internodes 10–22 in. long, 1–3 in. diam., smooth, walls thin. Buds (myetsan) small, flat. Culm-sheaths firmly coriaceous, persistent, brown, contrasting with the bright green of the young internodes, 5–7 in. long, upper third wavy, not appressed to the culm, sparsely hairy outside, top concavely truncate with rounded auricles, blade recurved, narrow ($\frac{1}{3}$ the top of sheath), longer than sheath, evenly narrowed into a long convolute apex, glabrous and striate on both sides. L. 6–14 by 1–4 in., underside glaucous, glabrous or with a few scattered hairs near the base, n. 18–24 on $\frac{1}{4}$ in., inner edge closely set with fine hairs on a broad colourless band. Transverse n. visible as evenly-distributed pellucid dots, tip long acuminate with a flat brush of rigid hairs below the scabrid point, pet. $\frac{1}{3}$ in. long. Sheaths keeled, glabrous with ciliate edges, white soft deciduous bristles $\frac{1}{2}$–$\frac{3}{4}$ in. long at mouth, ligule short.

Garo, Khasi, and Lushai hills. Chittagong forests. Forms extensive forests in Arakan and the Upper Chindwin. Fl. at long intervals; Kurz (Ind. For. i. 257) states that in Arakan it flowers every 30 to 35 years. The data at present available are as follows; they are not sufficient to justify any definite conclusions: Garo and Khasi hills, 1889, 1900, 1902. Chittagong, 1801, 1902. Arakan, 1864–1865, 1902. Bot. Garden, Calcutta, 1863, 1866. The fruit is 3–4 in. long, it hangs on a short peduncle clothed with sheathing bracts, and frequently germinates on the tree. 2. **M. humilis**, Kurz; Gamble t. 106. Arakan. Pegu, Paunglin valley near Wanet village (Kurz). Tufted 8–15 ft. high, l. 4–6 by $\frac{3}{8}$–1 in., subulate-acuminate, glaucescent and minutely roughish pubescent beneath (not seen). 3. A species found by C. B. Clarke in 1885 on the high road from Manipur town to Silchar, near the Irang river. There was a large pure forest of this Bamboo, and he was in that forest for two days' march. The culms were solitary, distant, 20 ft. high, unbranched below, but on the lower nodes with sharp thorns 1–3 in. long, which rendered the forest very difficult to penetrate. L. similar to those of 1, 10 by 1–1$\frac{1}{4}$ in., narrowed into a long tip with long stiff hairs, n. 24–30 on $\frac{1}{4}$ in., inner edge closely set with fine hairs on a colourless band. This species has not been found again, since 1885 the forest along that road has been jhumed twice by the Nagas. A thorny Bamboo brought from that locality in 1905 is *Arundinaria callosa* or near it.

4. Tabindaing. Attaran (Manson, Dec. 1908). Branches of rhizome 4 in. diam., bending upwards and terminating in a culm nearly naked in the lower part, internodes striped 25–30 in. long, diam. 2$\frac{1}{2}$ in., nodes hardly swollen, walls $\frac{1}{4}$ in. Culm-sheaths sometimes green, very thick, persistent, 8–10 in. long, truncate, blade reflexed, long, striate, 3 in. broad at base, decurrent on both sides into a wavy fringed band $\frac{1}{2}$–$\frac{3}{4}$ in. broad. L. 15–20 by 2–2$\frac{3}{4}$ in., pale beneath and sometimes minutely velvety, transverse veins visible, n. 20–25 on $\frac{1}{4}$ in., ligule prominent. This probably is the single-stemmed Bamboo mentioned on p. 50 of my Attaran Report. (Selections from the Records of the Govt. of India, Foreign Dept. xxxii. Calcutta, 1861). "Abundant in the Attaran, frequent near limestone rocks." From *M. bambusoides* this species is distinguished by the longer culm-sheaths, tightly appressed to the internodes, blade broad not convolute, decurrent into a broad wavy band, tip of leaf without a brush, sheath quite glabrous, ligule large. From the single-stemmed Bamboos enumerated under *Gigantochloa macrostachya*, it differs by larger leaves and the distant longitudinal nerves. It has been mentioned under *Melocanna*, because an entry in Herb. Kew. shows that a flowering specimen ticketed "Falconer, Moulmein," was sorted out because it was identical with a flowering specimen of *Melocanna bambusoides* from Hort. Bot. Calc., and this possibly was the single-stemmed Attaran Bamboo. It is not mentioned in Falconer's Report on the Attaran Forests. Kurz (F. Fl. ii. 570) and Gamble mention Tenasserim as a locality of *Melocanna bambusoides*.

Here may be mentioned a single-stemmed Bamboo (Tabindaing) found by me in March 1859, in the upper Salween forests, of which I have no specimens, but a description with sketch in my Notes.—Culms very tall, branches from the lower nodes simple, stiff, leafless, in dense half-whorls, the upper part of the culm with leaf-bearing branches. Internodes 12–16 in. long, 3–4$\frac{1}{2}$ in. diam., node-rings horizontal. Sheaths glabrous outside, ciliate on the edges, deciduous, 20 in. long, top truncate. L. 5 by $\frac{1}{2}$ in., glaucous beneath.

14. OCHLANDRA, Thwaites; * Fl. Brit. Ind. vii. 418.

Tufted, gregarious, culm-sheaths thin, persistent. Spikelets mostly arrested in their growth, remaining small, with a few large fertile ones, the latter consisting of 2–6 empty and one flowering glume, the glumes as a rule with conspicuous transverse veins. Palea thinly membranous, convolute, often emarginate, longitudinal nerves numerous, two often stronger than the rest. Lodicules 2–12, stamens 6–120, filaments free or more or less connate, anthers long exserted, linear, usually mucronate. Style elongated, stigmas 4–8, linear, plumose, usually closely twisted before expanding. Fr. beaked, large, supported by the persistent glumes, pericarp thick, fleshy, filled with starch, endosperm in the immature fr. soft, fleshy, probably crushed by the expansion of the scutellum, as the seed ripens. Some species flower annually, others at long periods, as far as known the inflorescence always bears leaves.

A. Filaments free.

1. **O. Rheedii,** Benth.; Gamble, t. 107. Vern. *Beesha, Amma,* Mal. Malabar, Cochin and Travancore, low country near rivers. Culms 10–15 ft. generally mottled dark and light green, internodes about 17 in. long, 1 in. diam., walls $\frac{1}{5}$ in. thick. Culm-sheaths 4–6 in. long, purplish green, hairy while young. L. 4–10 by $\frac{1}{3}$–1 in., ending in a long setaceous point, n. 39–45 on $\frac{1}{4}$ in. Spikelets in distant whorls on long fascicled pedunculate spikes, the peduncles consisting of several long internodes, the fertile spikelets 1–$1\frac{1}{3}$ in. long. Lodicules 2, lanceolate, $\frac{1}{2}$ in. long. Stamens 14–17, anthers $\frac{1}{5}$ in. Fr. oblong, $2\frac{1}{4}$ in. long, $\frac{3}{8}$ in. diam., crowned by the persistent indurated style. Flowers annually and does not die down after flowering.

2. **O. stridula,** Thwaites; Gamble, t. 109. Ceylon, low country, very common in the south of the island. May possibly be found in the Peninsula. Gregarious, culms erect, 6–18 ft. high, internodes 12–14 in. long, $\frac{1}{2}$–$\frac{3}{4}$ in. diam. L. 8–12 by $1\frac{1}{2}$–$2\frac{1}{4}$ in., n. 19–22 on $\frac{1}{4}$ in. Spikelets 1 in. long, lodicules lanceolate, 6–12, persistent round the fr. Stamens numerous, up to 30. Fr. 1 in. long, beak as long. Flowers annually.

3. **O. Talboti,** sp. nova. Vern. *Hūda,* Mar.; *Wontenulgi,* Kan. North Kanara. Culms numerous, in dense clumps, slender, $\frac{1}{4}$–$\frac{3}{4}$ in. diam., hollow, sometimes scandent, nodes thickened, shining, glabrous. L. glabrous, pale, lanceolate, long-acuminate, 8–12 by $1\frac{1}{2}$–$2\frac{1}{2}$, pet. $\frac{1}{4}$ in., sheath glabrous, bristles at mouth early deciduous, n. 30–36 on $\frac{1}{4}$ in. Spikelets in half-whorls on a terminal erect spike, 4–8 in. long, glabrous or nearly so, a few soft hairs at the tips of glumes, fertile spikelets few, $1\frac{1}{4}$ in. long. Empty glumes 3–6, lodicules 6, linear, veined. Stamens 25–40, anthers $\frac{1}{2}$ in. long, connective minutely apiculate, filaments long, slender. Fr. ovoid, 2–3 by $\frac{1}{3}$ in., narrowed into a long beak, supported by 4 persistent glumes. Fl. 1896 throughout North Kanara, had not been seen in fl. for many years in that district. (This species had been identified with *O. Rheedi, var. sivagiriana* and with *O. stridula*, but Talbot. List 348, justly states that it differs from both.) 4. **O. Beddomei,** Gamble, t. 110. Wainād. Western slopes of the Nilgiris below Sispara, 3–4,500 ft. Gregarious. l. ovate-lanceolate, long acuminate into a twisted scabrous, setaceous point, 8–12 by 1–$2\frac{1}{4}$ in., n. 15–24 on $\frac{1}{4}$ in., leaf-sheaths minutely pubescent, with numerous erect stiff bristles at the mouth and decurrent bristly auricles at the sides. Spikelets in few approximate half-whorls in erect terminal spikes 1–3 in. long, clothed with long brown hairs, fertile spikelets $1\frac{1}{2}$ in. long. Empty glumes 2–4, lodicules 5, $\frac{1}{2}$–$\frac{3}{4}$ in. long lanceolate, 3–7-veined. Stamens 20–35, anthers $\frac{1}{2}$–$\frac{3}{4}$ in. long, tip tricuspidate, the anther-cells and connective being apiculate. Fl. on the Sispara ghat in 1875 and 1876, died down after flowering; had not been known to flower for 20 years previously.

5. **O. Brandisii,** Gamble, t. 113. Vern. *Ira-Kalli.* Tinnevelli ghats above 3,500 ft., with *O. travancorica*, which it greatly resembles. Leaves smaller on short pet.. n. 24–27 on $\frac{1}{4}$ in., ligule long, membranous. Lodicules 3, lanceolate, $\frac{1}{4}$ in. long. Stamens about 100, filaments free, anthers $\frac{3}{4}$ in. long, apiculate. In fl. Feb. 1882 D.B.

---

* In this genus I have had the kind assistance of Dr. Otto Stapf, who will I hope at an early date publish the result of his researches regarding flowers and seeds of *Ochlandra*, *Melocalamus*, and *Dinochloa*, in continuation of his paper on *Melocanna bambusoides*.

B. Filaments monadelphous.

6. **O. travancorica**, Benth.; Gamble, t. 111. Syn. *Beesha travancorica*, Bedd. Fl. Sylv. 324. *The Elephant Grass.* Vern. *Iral*, *Ita Kalli*, Tam. Ghats between Travancore and Tinnevelli above 2,000 ft., covering immense areas, often to the exclusion of almost all other vegetation, with impenetrable thickets up to 15 ft. high, from which stand out a few scattered trees of *Vernonia*, *Eugenia*, and other kinds. Culms erect or straggling, internodes 2–5 ft. long, 1–2 in. diam., walls thin. Culm-sheaths thin, 6–8, blade narrow, subulate, 1½–3 in. long. L. 6–24 by 2–6 in., pet. thick, ¼–⅓ in. long, n. 18–21 on ¼ in. Fl. panicles leafy, fertile spikelets few, 2 in. long, with numerous sterile ones in distant heads on fascicled spikes, which are arranged in large leafy panicles. Lodicules usually 3, lanceolate, more or less unequal, one dentate, sometimes bifid. Stamens up to 120, anthers ½–¾ in. long, with a long point, filaments monadelphous, free at apex. Fr. ovoid, 3–4 in. long, 1¼ in. diam., fleshy, surrounded by the persistent glumes and palea. Beddome collected it in fl. about 1868. I found it in fl. on the Tinnevelli ghats in Feb. 1882, and in Travancore the species was expected to flower in 1905. Believed to die down after flowering. Var. *hirsuta*, Gamble, t. 112, spikelets thickly clothed with light brown velvety pubescence.

Fl. unknown.

7. **O. setigera**, Gamble, t. 115. Ravines above Gudalur, Nilgiris 3,000 ft. Culms 20 ft., internodes 10–12, diam. ½–⅝ in. Culm-sheaths persistent, 6–7 in. long, thin, gradually narrowed to a subulate hair-like blade. L. 6–9 by ¾–1 in., n. 30–33 on ¼ in., sheath at mouth with long bristles.

Bamboos from Upper Burma, the flowers of which are unknown:—

1. **Wakha**, Burm. On Hmangin daung, 2,500 ft., gregarious in Taungya ponzo (C. B. Smales, March 1902). Tufted, stems 35 ft. long, weak, widely overhanging, often breaking when without support, internodes 9 in. long, slightly swelling in the middle, diam. 1–1¼ in., walls very thin, $\frac{1}{16}$ in. Culm-sheaths light buff-coloured, thin, closely clasping the stem, brown hairs outside in the lower portion, blade early deciduous glabrous, finely ribbed, 3–3½ in. long. Young shoots olive-brown just above and olive-grey just below the nodes. L. glabrous, light green, 10 by 1½ in., n. 19–21 on ¼ in., transverse veins conspicuous, distant, mostly oblique, sheaths green with a few scattered brown hairs on the margin. Similar to *Pseudostachyum polymorphum*, Munro, but reported to be tufted. 2. **Sinthana**, Burm. Pyinyaung forests, Meiktila district, along banks of streams and on low, moist ground (Troup, June 1902). Culms erect, clothed with light brown silky hairs, which are matted together like felt near the nodes, 50 ft. high, internodes 15–24 in. long, diam. 3½–4 in., walls ½ in. thick, rootlets at the lowest 3 or 4 nodes. Culm-sheaths 7–10 in. long, brown-hairy outside, blade persistent, ribbed on the outside. L. densely clothed with fine hairs beneath, 6–8 by ½–¾ in., n. 21 on ¼ in., transverse veins distant. 3. **Thalaw-wa**, Burm. Cultivated in the Northern Shan States, 2–4,000 ft. (Troup, June 1902). Tufted, culms light green, with minute white silky hairs, erect, 40–50 ft., internodes 1½–2½ ft., 3–4 in. diam., walls ⅓ in. thick, small branchlets at most of the nodes. Culm-sheaths thick, nearly glabrous, 5–6 in. long, 12 in. wide at base, the sides curving to a slightly concave top, 4 in. broad, with a brown fringe, blade triangular, on the inside densely clothed with brown hairs, sharply cuspidate, base 1½ in. L. 7–9 by 1 in., n. 25 on ¼ in., transv. veins visible, oblique, distant. 4. **Wamin**, Burm. Cultivated in gardens in the Northern Shan States, said by some to have been brought from China, by others from Chengmai, in Siam (Troup, May 1902). Culms loosely tufted, erect or bending stiffly up to 40 ft., usually smaller, dark green, shining and perfectly glabrous. Internodes 4–6 in. long, rarely longer, much swollen in the lower half, the swollen part 4–5 in. diam. Rootlets on the lowest 3 or 4 nodes. Culm-sheaths resembling those of *Bambusa vulgaris*, brown hairy outside, 5 in., blade 2–3 in. long with two rounded ciliate auricles at the base. L. 7–9 by ¾ in., n. 30–33 on ¼ in., sheaths keeled, edges minutely ciliate. The short swollen internodes may be a deformity analogous to that described by Kurz in Ind. For. i. 252, t. 1.

ORDER CXIII. **GNETACEÆ.** Gen. Pl. iii. 417.

(E. Strasburger, Die Coniferen und die Gnetaceen, 1872.)

Stem and branches jointed at the nodes. L. opposite, whorled, or reduced to a short, sometimes 2–4-dentate sheath. Fl. unisexual, ♂ with 2–8 anthers. ♀: one erect ovule with one integument, prolonged into a tube, which

has the functions of a style, and enclosed by a single or double perianth. Perianth or bracts supporting the ♀ inflorescence become fleshy in fr.

The general structure of the wood resembles that of normally built Dicotyledons, it consists of vessels, wood-fibres, wood-parenchyma and medullary rays. No resin canals. *Gnetum scandens*, like many dicotyledonous climbers, shows on the transverse section concentric bands of wedge-shaped masses of xylem and phloem, separated by medullary rays.

Membranous sheaths at the base of internodes . . . . . 1. EPHEDRA.
Leaves evergreen, opposite . . . . 2. GNETUM.

1. EPHEDRA, Linn.; Fl. Brit. Ind. v. 640.

(Dr. Otto Stapf, Die Arten der Gattung *Ephedra*, Wien, 1889. Dr. Paul Jaccard, Recherches sur l'*Ephedra helvetica*, Lausanne, 1894.)

Rigid shrubs or undershrubs, a few species climbing, old stems often ribbed, branches terete, striate, opposite or whorled, with membranous sheaths at the nodes, which often bear 2–4 narrow leafy blades. Fl. usually diœcious, ♂ in short bracteate spikelets, which are whorled or in pairs, perianth of two opposite, compressed membranous sepals, anthers 2–8, on a central column, cells 2, opening by a short slit at the apex. ♀ fl. usually in pairs, sometimes 3 or solitary, each fl. consisting of one ovule with a single integument, prolonged into a tube, which has the functions of a style (tubillus) and enclosed in a bag, which may be regarded as a perianth. Each ♀ inflorescence (spikelet) supported by several pairs of decussate bracts. Fr. in the species here described fleshy, consisting of the succulent bracts, enclosing 1 or 2 seeds. Species 31, dry regions of Europe, North Africa, Asia and America.

A. Tall, scandent, with slender branchlets.

1. **E. foliata,** Boiss.—Syn. *E. Alte*, Brandis F. Fl. t. 69 (non C. A. Meyer), *E. peduncularis*, Boiss. Baluchistan. Sind. Kuram valley. Punjab plains, excepting the North-East, ascending in the Salt range to 3,000 ft. Probably in Rajputana.—Southern Arabia. Persia. Afghanistan. Vern. *Kuchan*, Punj. A tall scandent shrub, often gregarious, forming dense thickets, stem 3 in. diam., bark exfoliating in fibrous shreds, branches slender, flaccid, generally whorled, branchlets often filiform, internodes 1–4 in. long, leaf-sheath short, bearing at the upper nodes 2–4 small linear leafy blades. Fl. often monœcious, male fl. in strictly decussate pairs, 4–12 pairs in one spikelet, bracts rounded, obtuse, edge thinly fimbriate, anthers 3 or 4. Female spikelets pedunculate, often in small terminal cymes, tubillus short, straight. Fr. globose, 1/4 in. diam., semitransparent, red or milky-white, showing two dark-coloured seeds.

B. Rigid erect shrubs, generally numerous stems from a woody rootstock.

2. **E. Gerardiana,** Wall.; Collett Simla Flora 481.—Syn. *E. vulgaris*, Brandis F. Fl. 501; Kanjilal F. Fl. 346. Vern. *Tutgantha*, Jauns. Hariab district, Kuram valley 11,000 ft., common. Himalaya 8–14,000 ft., also in the inner arid tracts, ascending in Sikkim to 16,500 ft.—Pamirs. Yarkand. Tibet. A rigid, nearly erect shrub, up to 1–2 ft. high. Tufts of short branches with opposite or whorled branchlets from a woody much-branched usually creeping rootstock, internodes about 1 in. long, under 1/12 in. diam. Male spikelets ovate, 1/8–1/6 in. long, solitary or in pairs, rarely in whorls of 3, fl. 2–4 pairs, anthers 5–8. Female spikelets 1/4 in. long, usually solitary, bracts 2–3 pairs, tubillus straight. Fr. sweet, edible, red when ripe. 3. **E. nebrodensis,** Tineo. Baluchistan, Juniper tracts, 7–10,000 ft. (*Omah*, *Umah*). Balti. Lahaul.—Mediterranean region, Western Asia and Caucasus. Internodes smooth, slender, 1/2–1 in. long, 1/24–1/18 in. diam. Male spikelets few-fld., solitary or 2–3 together, female solitary short-pedunculate, tubillus straight. Fr. globose, 1/4 in. diam. 4. **E. intermedia,** Schrenk u. Meyer.—North-West Himalaya, chiefly in the inner arid valleys. Chitral 4–5,000 ft. on dry rocky slopes (*Sumani*), Gilgit, Zanskar, Upper Chenab., Kunawar (*Khanna*).—Persia, Turkestan, Bokhara. Western China. A small erect shrub, often glaucous, internodes rough, 1½–2½ in. long, 1/12–1/8 in. diam. Fl. sometimes monœcious, male spikelets 1/5–1/4 in. long, numerous, in dense whorls at the nodes. Female spikelets shortly pedunculate, whorled at the nodes, tubillus twisted. Fr. 1/4 in. long, fleshy, red when ripe. 5. **E. pachyclada,** Boiss. Baluchistan, Kákar Lora valley, 5,500–6,000 ft.—Southern Persia. Afghanistan. A small gregarious shrub, internodes 1–2½ in. long, 1/10–1/8 in. diam., anthers 6–8, sessile, crowded, large.

2. GNETUM, Linn.; Fl. Brit. Ind. v. 641.

(Lotsy, Life history of Gnetum in Annales du Jardin Botanique de Buitenzorg, xvi. 46, 1899.)

Climbing, one species erect, branches jointed and thickened at the nodes. L. opposite, quite entire, penninerved. Fl. unisexual, usually diœcious, whorled in the axils of a cup-shaped bract, usually surrounded with multicellular hairs (a belt of (always ?) imperfect ♀ fl. frequently above the ring of ♂ fl.), on spikes, which are solitary or in dichotomous panicles, axillary or terminal. Male fl.: perianth fleshy, clavate, more or less 2-fid.; anther-cells 2, opening by terminal slits. Female fl.: one ovule with a single integument, prolonged into a tube, which has the functions of a style, with a lacerate mouth, enclosed in two bags, which may be regarded as an inner and outer perianth, the inner perianth wanting in flowers that remain sterile. Fruit resembling a drupe, consisting of the fleshy perianths, enclosing a hard seed. Species 15, tropical Asia, Africa, America and Pacific islands.

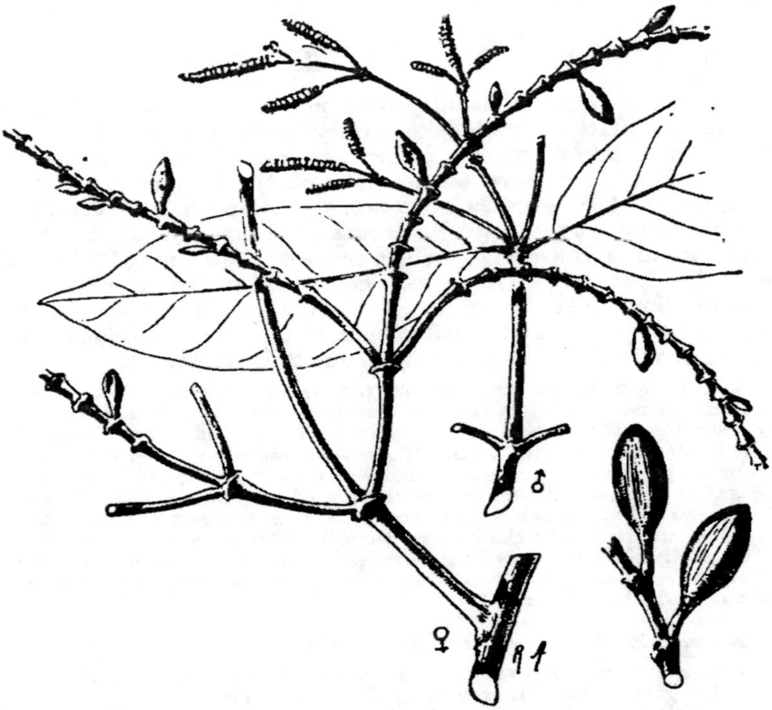

Fig. 200.—Gnetum scandens, Roxb. ½.

A. Ovary and fruit sessile.

1. **G. Gnemon**, Linn.—Syn. *G. Brunonianum*, Griff. Cachar. Manipùr. Mogaung, Upper Burma. Tenasserim. Nicobars.—Malay Penins. and Archip. A small or middle-sized evergreen tree, l. elongate-elliptic or elliptic-oblong, acuminate, blade 4–8, pet. ½ in. long. Fl. diœcious, female and pseudo-androgynous spikes on different trees, the imperfect female fl. of the latter without an inner perianth. Fr. oblong, apiculate, ½ in. long, glossy, orange-coloured or red when ripe. The tree cultivated in the village groves of Java is diœcious. According to Karsten and Lotsy the ♀ fl. in the pseudo-androgynous spikes, though often attaining a considerable size, are not fertilized, and do not produce mature seed. It is, however, for inquiry whether the Burma and Indian tree is not, as stated by Kurz, monœcious. 2. **G. neglectum**, Blume. Mergui.—Malay Penins. and Archip. A climber, l. rigidly coriaceous, blade 4–5, pet. ¼–⅓ in. long.

B. Ovary and fruit stalked. Climbers.

3. **G. scandens,** Roxb.—Syn. *G. edule,* Blume; *G. funiculare,* Wight Ic. t. 1955. Vern. *Kumbal, Umbli,* Bombay; *Milgandi,* Kol; *Gyut-nwè,* Burm.

An immense diœcious evergreen climber, trunk often flattened, 9–12 in. broad, branches dichotomous. L. elliptic, blade 3–9, pet. $\frac{1}{3}$–$\frac{2}{3}$ in. long, reticulate veins lax, thin. Spikes in stiff panicles, often on the old wood. A single whorl of (imperfect ?) ♀ above a double whorl of ♂ fl., surrounded by a mass of transparent hairs. Fr. covered with silvery scales when young, orange-coloured, edible when ripe, 1$\frac{1}{2}$ in., stalk thick, $\frac{1}{4}$ in. long.

Western Ghats in evergreen forest, from the Konkan southwards, ascending to 7,000 ft. Hills of the Northern Circars. Sikkim, ascending to 3,000 ft. Assam. Khasi hills. Chittagong. Burma, Upper and Lower. Andamans, common.—Not in Ceylon. Malay Penins. and Archip. China. 4. **G. macropodum,** Kurz. Nicobars. Closely allied to 3, differs by fruit-stalk $\frac{3}{4}$–1$\frac{1}{2}$ in. long. 5. **G. funiculare,** Blume. Chittagong. Lower Burma. A large climber, stem as thick as the arm. L. elliptic, rigidly coriaceous, reticulate veins close, prominent. Fr. glabrous, stalk slender, $\frac{1}{4}$–$\frac{1}{2}$ in. long.

ORDER CXIV. CONIFERÆ. Gen. Pl. iii. 420.

Trees, sometimes shrubs, usually resinous, monœcious or diœcious. Leaves rigid, linear, subulate or scale-like, rarely with a broad blade. Fl. without perianth, ♂ (catkins) consisting of more or less numerous antheriferous scales (stamens) bearing 2 or more anther-cells on the back (underside). ♀ (cones) consisting of ovuliferous scales (open carpels, often with a second or supporting scale), either numerous, spirally or decussately arranged around the axis and at maturity concealing the seeds (perfect cones), or few (up to 20 in *Cephalotaxus*) not concealing the seeds (imperfect cones). In the case of most species a considerable time (sometimes more than a year) intervenes between the shedding of the pollen and fertilization of the ovule. Endosperm fleshy and oily (in *Araucaria* farinaceous), cotyledons 2 or numerous.

The trunk of Coniferous trees shows the same general arrangement of tissues which we find in normal Dicotyledons, but the wood is without vessels, hence on a transverse section without pores. It consists of medullary rays and of long thick-walled tracheides, arranged in radial lines, with large bordered pits, usually on their radial walls only. In the earliest formed wood, contiguous to the pith, the tracheides have a spiral or annular thickening of their walls. The annual rings are distinctly marked by belts of very thick-walled tracheides in the outer (autumn) wood and of thinner-walled tracheides in the spring wood of the succeeding year. Resin canals, lined by small thin-walled secreting cells (as in *Dipterocarps*) are found in the leaves, the bark and the wood, in the wood they are vertical among the tracheides, and horizontal in the medullary rays.

I. Seeds concealed by the scales of a perfect cone.

A. Ovules reversed, scales of cone numerous, spirally arranged round the axis. Pollen-grains winged, excepting *Larix* and *Tsuga*.

(*a*) L. persistent, in clusters of 2, 3, or 5, scales of cone more or less thickened at the apex . . 1. PINUS.

(*b*) L. persistent, in large tufts at the ends of arrested branchlets, scales of cone broad with a thin edge, deciduous . . . . . . 2. CEDRUS.

(*c*) L. persistent, single.

α. Cones cylindric, erect, scales deciduous, l. flat, more or less distichous . . . 3. ABIES.

β. Cones cylindric, pendulous, scales persistent, l. 4-sided, all round the branchlets . 4. PICEA.

γ. Cones ovoid, small, scales persistent. l. flat, distichous . . . . TSUGA (p. 698).

(*d*) L. deciduous in large tufts at the ends of arrested branchlets . . . . LARIX (p. 698).

B. Ovules erect, scales of cone few. Pollen grains not winged (*Cupressineæ*).

(*a*) Scales of cone opposite, in several tiers.

α. Scales of cone woody, seeds with an orbicular wing . . . . 5. CUPRESSUS.

β. Scales of cone succulent, forming a berry-like fruit, seeds not winged . . . . 6. JUNIPERUS.

(*b*) Scales of cone spirally arranged on the axis, pectinate at apex, supporting scales adnate to them CRYPTOMERIA (p. 695).

II. Cones imperfect, seeds 1 or few, not concealed by the scales (*Taxaceæ*).

A. Ovules reflexed, pollen-grains winged . . . 7. PODOCARPUS.

B. Ovules bent down, seeds erect. Two anther-cells at the base of the male catkin scales. Pollen-grains winged . . . . DACRYDIUM (p. 696).

C. Ovules erect, solitary, seed enclosed in a red fleshy cup. 3–8 anther-cells on the underside of a peltate male catkin scale. Pollen-grains not winged . . . . 8. TAXUS.

D. Ovules erect, in pairs at the base of scales. Male fl. in involucrate heads (compound catkins). Pollen-grains not winged . . . . . . 9. CEPHALOTAXUS.

TAXACEÆ are treated as a separate order by Pilger in Engler's Pflanzenreich iv. 5.

1. PINUS, Linn.; Fl. Brit. Ind. v. 651.

Monœcious trees, the branches generally in whorls. Leaves dimorphous, those of seedlings and elongating shoots single, those of ordinary branches in clusters of 2, 3, or 5, on arrested branchlets, consisting of a short tubercular axis with a number of membranous sheathing scales surrounding the leaves. Axillary buds as a rule develop into branches only at the end of each year's terminal shoot, one whorl of side branches being formed annually, so that the age of a tree may be determined, not only by counting the annual rings in the wood, but in the case of young trees also by the number of whorls on the stem. There are however exceptions: *Pinus excelsa* sometimes forms 2 whorls in one season, and *P. Gerardiana* is apt to throw out scattered side branches, not in regular whorls. The male fl. (catkins) are in crowded whorls in the axils of membranous bracts at the base of the current year's shoot, hence on those branches, which habitually bear ♂ fl., there are breaks in the foliage, which indicate the position of previous year's catkins. Antheriferous scales numerous, imbricate, each scale with 2 anther-cells on its under-surface, prolonged beyond them into a membranous crest. Female fl. (cones) on separate branches, solitary or in whorls, often pedunculate, peduncles with scaly bracts. Ovules reversed, in pairs at the base of the carpellary scales, each carpellary with a supporting scale, which disappears before the cone ripens. Cones formed of the enlarged woody carpellary scales, which are spirally arranged around the axis and are more or less thickened at the apex. Seeds in shallow excavations at the base of the scales, oily with a hard woody testa, usually winged.

A. Leaves in clusters of five, cones cylindric, scales not much thickened at the apex.

1. **P. excelsa,** Wall. Pl. As. Rar. t. 201; Griff. Ic. Pl. As. t. 366, also t. 365 (*P. Griffithii*, MacClell.); Collett Simla Fl. 485 fig. 157. *The Blue Pine.* Vern. *Chīwīch*, Chitral. *Biār*, Haz.; *Kail*, Hind.; *Chīl*, Jumna; *Lim*, Kunawar.

A tall tree, attaining 150 ft., bark smooth, slate-coloured on young, rough with shallow fissures on mature trees, foliage bluish-green, at high elevations greyish-green. L. slender, 6–8 in. long, sheaths deciduous. Male catkins ovoid, $\frac{1}{3}$ in. long. Cones generally 2 or 3 together, 6–12 in. on peduncles 1–3 in. long, erect while young, pendulous afterwards, scales spathulate,

2–2½ in., seed ⅓ in. long, wing obliquely truncate, about 3 times the length of seed, cotyledons usually 9.

Kuram valley 8–11,000 ft. Safed Koh. Kafiristan. Himalaya, also in some of the more arid valleys, such as Lahaul, Kunawar. Eastwards as far as Nepal, not in Central and North-West Kumaon nor (indigenous) in Sikkim, but (in alpibus altissimis, Wallich) in Bhutan.—Afghanistan. The original home of this tree is at high elevations up to 12,500 ft., where it forms extensive forests with the Himalayan Spruce and Silver Fir. As the seed comes up in open grass-lands without shelter and as it is readily carried about by the wind, there is abundant second growth of it at lower elevations down to 5,000 ft. Wherever the trees grow at lower elevations the shoots are very luxuriant, often bent and irregular. The leaves remain 3–4 years on the branches. Fl. April–June, the cones ripen in the autumn of the second year. *P. Peuce*, Griseb., mountains of Montenegro and Macedonia is closely allied.

B. Leaves in clusters of three; cones ovoid or ovoid-conical, scales much thickened at the apex.

2. **P. longifolia,** Roxb.; Royle Ill. t. 85; Griff. Ic. Pl. Asiat. t. 369, 370; Collett, Simla Flora 486 fig. 158. Vern. *Chil, Chir*, Hind.; *Shti*, Bash; *Sarol, Sirli*, Jaunsar; *Dhup*, Nep.; *Nyit*, Lepcha.

A tall eminently gregarious tree, branches symmetrically whorled, high up the trunk, forming a rounded head of light foliage. Bark 1–2 in. thick, cut by deep fissures into large plates. Leaves 9–15 in. long, slender, nearly triquetrous, sheath ½–1 in. long, greyish-brown, fimbriate, persistent. Male catkins ½ in. long, cones on short stiff stalks, spreading or recurved, solitary or in whorls of 2–5, 4–8 in. long, diam. 3–5 in., scales 1–2 by ¾ in., beak thick, pyramidal, pointed and somewhat recurved. Seeds ⅓ in. long, wing thin membranous, rather longer than seed. Cotyledons about 12.

Subhimalayan tract and outer Himalaya. Abundant as far east as Nepal, forming extensive pine forests 1,500 to 6,500, occasionally to 7,500 ft. Not in the inner arid valleys, on the Sutlej its upper limit is at Wangtu. Further eastwards less common. in Sikkim usually on dry southern slopes between 1,000 and 3,000 ft. on the north side of the Great Ranjit and Tista rivers, often mixed with Sāl. It is supposed (see Gamble, Darjeeling List ed. ii. 83) that the rainfall in the subhimalayan tract here is too heavy for this species. Fl. Febr.–April, there is some uncertainty whether the cones require 15 or 29 months to ripen. The leaves remain 2–3 years on the branches.

3. **P. Khasya,** Royle*; Griff. Ic. Pl. As. tt. 367, 368. Vern. *Dingsa*, Khasia; *Tinyu*, Burm.; *Shja*, Kar.

A tall tree, 100–150 ft., branches more or less whorled, bark thick, deeply cracked, resin-ducts numerous in the outer and middle belt of each annual ring. L. 6–10 in. long, slender, back convex, sheath persistent, grey, lacerated at apex. Cones solitary or in pairs, sometimes in threes, ovoid, 2–3 in. long, greatest diam. 2 in., beak of scales depressed-pyramidal, with a blunt knob at the end, wings four times the length of seed.

Khasi and Naga hills. Manipúr. Hills on the Upper Chindwin. Shan hills. Mountains on the head waters of the Yunzalin and further north on the watershed between Sitang and Salween, 2,500–7,000 ft. Fl. Febr.–March, the cones require 2 years to ripen. Cones of several years, also empty cones, remain long on the tree. The l. persist 1–2 years on the branches. *P. insularis*, Endl., of the Philippines and *P. Yunnanensis*, Franchet, of China, are very similar and possibly not specifically distinct.

4. **P. Gerardiana,** Wall.; Royle Ill. t. 85, fig. 2; Brandis F. Fl. t. 67. Vern. *Chūjin*, Chitral (*Jalghōza*, seed); *Miri*, Pangi; *Rhi*, Kunawar.—The seed: *Neoza*.

A middle-sized tree, branches not whorled, bark grey, smooth, thin, peeling off in large flakes, on old trees rough and cracked, foliage dark green. Leaves stiff, 2–4 in. long, back rounded, sheath deciduous. Male catkins ⅓–½ in. long. Cones ovoid-oblong, glaucous when mature, 6–9 in. long, diam. 4–5 in.

* The name given by Royle to this Pine was *Kesiya* (Gordon in Gardener's Magazine xvi. 8, 1840). Parlatore (DC. Prod. xvi. 2) called it *P. Khasya*, Royle. The above name is that adopted in the Fl. of Brit. Ind., and should be: *P. Khasya*, Hook. f.

Scales broad, beak stout, recurved, obtusely triangular. Seeds irregularly cylindric, 1 in. long, edible, wing short caducous.

Kafiristan. Hariab district in the Kuram valley, 7–11,000 ft. North-West Himalaya, in the inner valleys with a dry climate, 5–10,000 ft. Chitral. Gilgit. Indus, between Astor and Iskardo. Upper Chenab. A few trees on the Upper Ravi. Kunawar, occupying the lower slopes of the mountain sides near the river above Chergaon and Jani. British Garhwal, below the Niti pass. Fl. June and July, the cones ripen in the autumn of the second year. The l. remain 3–4 years on the branches. The cones of the Hariab tree have not the stout recurved beak of the scales.

C. Leaves in clusters of two.

5. **P. Merkusii**, Jungh. Vern. *Tinyuben*, Burm. Thaungyin valley above Mirawadi on stretches of high ground, 500–1,500 ft., associated with *Dipterocarpus tuberculatus* (first reported by Capt. Latter in 1848, Selections from the Records of the Bengal Government, ix., Calcutta 1852, p. 154). Shan States of Burma, in forests of *Pentacme, Shorea obtusa, Melanorrhœa*, and occasionally *Dipterocarpus tuberculatus.*—Sumatra. Cochinchina. Philippines. Attains 100 ft., the trunk 5 ft. diam., branches forming a flat umbrella-like crown, somewhat resembling *P. Pinea*, wood very resinous. L. green, 6–10 in. long, back convex, sheaths grey with white fimbriate edge. The new l. appear (in the Thaungyin) Feb. March, and the old l. fall early in their second year. Cones usually in pairs, 2–3 in. long, cylindric-conical, peduncle ½ in. long, scales with a thick but flat pyramidal beak, the faces of which are sulcate. Seeds small, many times shorter than the unequal-sided wing.

2. CEDRUS, Link; Fl. Brit. Ind. v. 653.

Three local forms, which come true from seed, here classed as species, viz., 1. C. atlantica, Manetti. Atlas mountains, forming extensive forests at 4–7,000 ft. Leading shoot stiff erect, l. short. 2. C. Libani, Barr. Taurus and Anti-Taurus in Asia Minor 4–6,400 ft., forming forests with *P. Laricio*. Mountains of Cyprus. Lebanon chain. Extremities of branches stiff.

3. **C. Deodara**, Loudon; Brandis F. Fl. 516.—Syn. *C. Libani*, var. *Deodara*, Hook. f.; Collett, Simla Flora 486, fig. 159. *Pinus Deodara*, Griff. Ic. Pl. As. t. 364. *The Himalayan Cedar*. Sans. *Devadaru*. Vern. *Rōgh*, Chitral; *Diār, Kelu*, N.W. Himal.; *Kelmang*, Kunawar.

A tall tree, attaining 250 ft. under favourable circumstances, the leading shoots and extremities of branchlets drooping, heart-wood yellowish-brown, strongly scented, very durable. Foliage (in its native home) usually dark green, sometimes bluish-green. L. 1–1½ in. long, triquetrous, single on elongated shoots and on seedlings, otherwise in dense fascicles on arrested branchlets. Catkins cylindric, single, at the ends of arrested branchlets. Cones erect, 4–5 in. long, 3–4 in. diam., obtuse, scales closely imbricate, broadly cuneate, upper edge thin and rounded, broader than long, deciduous, leaving the axis of the cone standing erect on the branches. Seeds ⅓–⅔ in., wing triangular, ⅔ in. long. Cotyledons usually 10.

Afghanistan. Kuram valley 7,500–10,000 ft. Chitral. N.W. Himalaya 4–10,000, ascending in places to 12,000 ft. in the basin of the principal tributaries of the Indus, of the Tous, Jumna and Bhagirati rivers. On two feeders of the Alaknanda. Cultivated in Kumaon and in Nepal. Fl. Sept. Oct., the cones ripen in the autumn of the following year, about 13 months after flowering. ♂ and ♀ fl. generally are on different trees, sometimes on different branches of the same tree. Young Deodar requires shelter and stands a great deal of shade, self-sown seedlings readily come up under Oak and other trees, and in spite of the soft and drooping terminal shoots they pierce with great vigour through thickets of other trees. At Kew the Deodar is the first of the 3 Cedars to come out with a flush of young leaves, the Lebanon Cedar usually follows a fortnight later, and the Atlas cedar comes last, after an interval of a few days. Old trees of all three kinds, when growing isolated, particularly in exposed situations, are apt to form tabulated tops.

3. ABIES, Juss.; Fl. Brit. Ind. v. 654.

Tall trees, leaves more or less bifarious, linear, 1-nerved. Cone erect,

cylindric, scales thin, deciduous, leaving a woody axis, supporting scale free under the ovuliferous scale and sometimes produced beyond it. Species about 20, Northern temperate and Arctic zone.

1. **A. Pindrow,** Spach; Royle Ill. t. 86; Collett, Simla Flora 488, Fig. 161; Gamble, Ind. Timb. ed. ii. 719; Nicholson, Dictionary of Gardening, i. 2. *The Himalayan low level Silver fir.* Vern. *Paludar*, Haz; *Rēwar*, Kagan; *Kachal*, Kunch valley; *Rai*, Chamba; *Tōs*, Kulu; *Span*, *Krok*, Kunawar; *Pindrau*, Hattu; *Morinda*, Jaunsar.

A tall tree, attaining 250 ft. under favourable conditions, with a dense cylindric crown of dark-green foliage, bark smooth on young stems, greyish-brown, deeply cleft in vertical fissures, when old. L. distichous, 2–3 in. long, apex with two sharp teeth, underside with two faint lines on either side of the raised midrib, upper side dark green shining. Male catkins axillary, numerous, $\frac{1}{2}$–$\frac{3}{4}$ in. long. Cones cylindric, 4–7 in. long, $1\frac{1}{2}$–3 in. diam., dark purple when ripe, scales obovate, edge rounded, thin. Seeds $\frac{1}{6}$–$\frac{1}{5}$ in., wing twice as long.

Kuram valley 8–11,000 ft. Chitral. Outer Himalaya, 8–10,000 ft., eastwards as far as Nepal. Fl. April, May. Fr. autumn of the same year. As shade-enduring as *Abies pectinata*, the Silver Fir of Europe.

2. **A. Webbiana,** Lindl.; Gamble, Ind. Timb. ed. ii. 718; Nicholson, Dict. of Gard. i. 2. The high level Silver fir. North-West Himalaya 10–14,000 ft., often with the Birch and *Rhododendron campanulatum*. Usually stunted and gnarled, l. all round the branchlets, $\frac{3}{4}$–1 in. long on raised rough, prominent leaf-cushions, emarginate, cones shorter and thicker than 1.

3. The East Himalayan Silver Fir. Vern. *Gobre Salla*, Nep.; *Dunshing*, Bhutia. Sikkim 10–13,000 ft. on the Singalila range, in the Chumbi valley and in Bhutan 8,000–12,500 ft. (*Abies densa*, Griff., Notulæ iv. 19). A tall gregarious tree, forming dense forests, l. crowded, more or less distichous, 1–2 in. long, retuse or emarginate, underside silvery-glaucous on either side of the raised midrib, catkins purple before opening (G. Rogers), cones cylindric, bracts long-acuminate in a young state, protruding beyond the scales, scales broader than in *A. Pindrow*. This form might be called by the name given by Griffith to the Bhutan tree, if further study on the spot should show it to deserve specific rank.

I doubt whether the three Himalayan Silver firs here enumerated should be regarded as distinct species. The eastern form I have kept separate at the suggestion of Professor Heinrich Mayr of Munich, who visited the North-West Himalaya and Sikkim in 1887. As regards the 2 western forms my own experience is to the effect that, as you ascend to the higher ranges, the low level long-leaved form, with a tall trunk and a dense cylindric crown, gradually changes into the stunted tree with spreading branches and short leaves of the high level form. I have never seen the two growing together. The high level spruce of the Alps is analogous, it is a stunted tree with stiff branches and shorter leaves than the low level spruce, yet both are justly regarded as one species.

There is, however, this remarkable fact, that hitherto the seed of the two Silver firs of the Western Himalaya has come true, whenever cultivated in England and Ireland, and hence gardeners and arboriculturists in this country regard them as distinct species, in the same way as the three Cedars, *C. Deodara*, *Libani* and *atlantica* are regarded as distinct species. In his Flora of British India v. 653, Sir Joseph Hooker calls the Himalayan Cedar: *C. Libani*, var *Deodara*. In this case I venture to think that it is more consistent to abide by the old-established practice and to regard the 3 Cedars as distinct species. They most probably are local forms of a tree, which in remote ages, when the climate of the Mediterranean region and Western Asia was moist and cool, extended from the Atlas to the Himalaya, but they have been separated so long that they have acquired distinct though not very important characters. In deference to Mr. Gamble and to English arboriculturists, I have in this Book separated the 2 West Himalayan Silver firs, but I wish it to be distinctly understood that their case is quite different from that of the 3 Cedars. Seeds of the high level *A. Webbiana* should be cultivated in Jaunsar to see whether there also the tree comes true from seed.

4. PICEA, Link; Fl. Brit. Ind. v. 653.

Species 12, Northern temperate and arctic zone.

P. Morinda, Link; Collett, Simla Fl. 487, fig. 160.—Syn. *Abies Smithiana*, Forbes; Brandis, F. Fl. 525; *Pinus Smithiana*, Wall. Pl. As.

Rar. t. 246; *P. Khutrow*, Royle Ill. t. 84; *Abies spinulosa*, Griff. Ic. Pl. As. t. 363. *The Himalayan Spruce.* Vern. *Achara*, Chitral; *Kachal*, Haz.; *Rai*, Kulu to Jaunsar; *Rau*, *Raiang*, Sutlej; *Tos*, Kangra, Chamba.

A tall tree, usually 100–120, sometimes over 200 ft. high, branches horizontal, branchlets hanging tassel like, foliage dark green, bark greyish-brown, divided by shallow cracks into small rounded or 4-sided scales. L. spirally arranged all round the branches, stiff, pungent, 4-sided, 1–1½ in. long, readily deciduous when dry, articulate on a persistent ultimately woody base or cushion, the young shoots often capped by the old bud-scales. Male catkin usually single, cylindric, 1 in. long, sessile, antheriferous scale with a broad rounded denticulate apex, anthers linear. Cones cylindric, obtuse, 4–6 in. long, pendulous, dark brown, scales with a thin edge, seeds ⅕ in. long, wing broad, obliquely spathulate, ½ in. long.

Kuram valley 8–12,000 ft., associated with *Pinus excelsa*. Kafiristan. Chitral. Gilgit. Himalaya, common from Kashmir to Garhwal, 7–11,000 ft., often associated with *Quercus dilatata* and *semicarpifolia* and other broad-leaved trees, as well as with *Deodar*, *Pinus excelsa* and the Himalayan Silver fir. Does not extend far into the arid region; in Kunawar, Pangi is its limit on the right and Rispa on the left side of the valley. In Sikkim and Bhutan it grows in the inner valleys 8–15,000 ft. Fl. April–May, the cones ripen in the autumn of the same year. Specimens from the Chumbi valley have harder wood, but do not seem otherwise to differ from *Picea Morinda*. (See Addenda.)

Tsuga Brunoniana, Carr.—Syn. *Pinus Brunoniana*, Wall. Pl. As. Rar. t. 247; *Abies dumosa*, Loudon. Vern. *Tengre Salla*, Nep.; *Tangshing*, Bhutia. North-East Kumaon, forming forests at 9–10,000 ft. Nepal. In the Sirikola valley, tributary of the little Ranjit and elsewhere in the middle and inner ranges of Sikkim, forming extensive forests below the Silver fir at 6–10,000 ft. Bhutan. A tall tree, attaining 120 ft., branches spreading, branchlets pendulous. L. distichous, ½–1 in. long, white-mealy beneath. Cones ovoid, ½–¾ in. long, scales broadly elliptic, obtuse, supporting scales not projecting in the mature cone. Fl. May, June, cones ripen the same year.

Larix Griffithii, Hook. f. & Thoms.; Hook. Him. Plants t. 21. Vern. *Sah*, *Saar*, Sikkim. Inner ranges of East Nepal, Sikkim and Bhutan, 8–12,000 ft. Tibet, 9–13,500 ft. A moderate-sized tree, heart-wood red, branches long, pendulous, foliage pale green. L. deciduous, slender, 1 in. long, single on elongated shoots and seedlings, otherwise in dense fascicles on arrested branchlets. Cones cylindric, 2–3 in. long, erect (reversed) on the pendulous branchlets, scales persistent, supporting longer than ovuliferous scales, tips reflexed cuspidate.

5. CUPRESSUS, Linn.; Fl. Brit. Ind. v. 645.

Leaves small, scale-like, closely appressed, opposite, mostly imbricate, those of seedlings (juvenile form) needle-like, spreading, in whorls of 3 or 4. Fl. monœcious at the ends of short branchlets, male catkins cylindric, numerous, stamens stipitate, peltate, bearing on their lower edge 2–4 subglobose anther-cells. Scales of ♀ cones few, decussate, those at the base and at the apex sterile, the others bearing above their base 4–8 erect ovules, supporting scales none. As the cones mature the scales become woody peltate and angular, each with 4 or more small compressed winged seeds, cotyledons 2–3.

1. **C. torulosa**, Don. The Himalayan Cypress. Vern. *Devi diar*, Ravi; *Galla*, Sutlej; *Leauri*, Jauns.; *Surai*, *Raisal*, Garhwal, Kumaon.

A large tree, branches horizontal, whorled, with drooping branchlets, forming a broad pyramidal crown, bark peeling off in long thin strips, heartwood light brown, fragrant. L. closely imbricate, triangular. Cones clustered, ½ in. diam.

Outer range of the Himalaya from Chamba to Nepal, 6–9,000 ft., chiefly on limestone, in places abundant, but more local and less common than most other Himalayan Conifers. Fl. Feb.–Apr., fr. ripens in the autumn of the second year, and is often long persistent on the tree. 2. **C. sempervirens**, Linn. Planted in gardens in Afghanistan and North-West India, as well as throughout the Mediterranean region. A tall tree, stem fluted, branches erect, forming a narrow dense cylindric crown of dark green foliage. Cones few, 1 in. diam., scales rough, with a projecting, convex or keeled, point or boss. 3. **C. glauca**, Lamk. (*C. lusitanica*, Mill.), commonly cultivated in Western India above Ghat, foliage and cones bluish, may belong either to 1 or to 2.

4. **C. funebris**, Endl. The *weeping Cypress*, *Chandang*, Bhutia. Indigenous on the hills about Ichang, China. Cultivated, chiefly near Buddhist temples and monasteries, in Nepal, Sikkim, and Bhutan. A large handsome tree, branches pendulous, branchlets distichous, cones $\frac{1}{2}$–$\frac{3}{4}$ in. diam., seeds small, broadly winged.

6. JUNIPERUS, Linn.; Fl. Brit. Ind. v. 646.

Shrubs or trees, with distinct, generally red and fragrant heart-wood. Leaves either all linear or subulate, in whorls of 3, or dimorphous, viz. (*a*) scale-like, imbricate, usually opposite and decussate, (*b*) subulate and spreading. Fl. monœcious or diœcious, axillary or at the ends of short branchlets, ♂ small cylindric or ovoid catkins, stamens broad-ovate, whorled, imbricate, each with 3–6 anther-cells at its base. Cone ripening the second year, fleshy, nearly globose, consisting of 3–6 connate carpellary scales (the lower sterile), the tips of which are often visible on the surface of the ripe fruit. Seeds 1–3, testa coriaceous.

A. All l. linear, pungent.

1. **J. communis**, Linn. Vern. *Betar*, *Bithal*, Chamba; *Pama*, *Tailu*, Kunawar.—Almost throughout the temperate and subarctic regions of the Northern Hemisphere. Kuram valley, 11–13,000 ft. North-West Himalaya, 5,400–14,000 ft., as far as Garhwal and Kumaon, east of the Sutlej restricted to high elevations. Werang pass, Kunawar. A dense diffuse shrub, sometimes a small tree, procumbent at high elevations. L. in whorls of 3, spreading, $\frac{1}{4}$–$\frac{1}{2}$ in. long, pungent, whitish above, convex or obtusely keeled beneath, with a more or less prominent cushion on the branchlets, persistent 3–4 years. Fl. axillary, supported by small imbricating bracts, the male catkins ovoid, yellow, antheriferous scales broad-ovate, acuminate, the ♀ small, resembling leaf-buds. Berries blue-black, $\frac{1}{4}$–$\frac{1}{3}$ in. diam., the tips of the carpellary scales visible at the apex, pulp sweet, resinous, seeds generally 3. A dwarfed variety at high elevations with broader l. and very pronounced leaf-cushions may perhaps be identified with *J. nana*, Willd., the dwarf Juniper of Europe. *Bhiterrik*, Chitral (prostrate, Barrett).

2. **J. recurva**, Ham. *The weeping blue Juniper*, Hook. Him. Journ. ii. 28. Vern. *Bettar*, Punj.; *Bhéntra*, Kaghan; *Guggal*, N.W. Himal. Kuram valley, 10–12,000 ft. Himalaya, Kashmir to Bhutan, 7,500–12,000 ft. Occasionally planted near temples.—Tibet. A gregarious shrub, often covering large areas, either pure or mixed with *J. communis*, the stems decumbent, at times 6 in. diam., very long, running underground or along the surface. From these creeping stems rise numerous short erect branches, which make these thickets almost impenetrable. In Sikkim and Bhutan, a graceful tree, attaining 30 ft., with drooping branchlets, foliage glaucous blue, heart-wood reddish-brown. L. more or less appressed, in whorls of 3, $\frac{1}{8}$ in. long, lanceolate, pungent, back convex, often approximate and imbricated, when the branchlets are more or less 6-sided. Male catkins and berries at the end of short lateral leafy branchlets. Berries ovoid, pointed, $\frac{1}{3}$–$\frac{1}{2}$ in. long, dark brown or blackish-purple when ripe, seed 1, oblong. *J. squamata* is the procumbent variety with broader often incurved leaves.

B L. dimorphous, on most branches scale-like, decussate, appressed, imbricate, on some subulate, pungent, erect or spreading.

3. **J. macropoda**, Boiss.—Syn. *J. excelsa*, Brand. F. Fl. t. 68. *Himalayan Pencil Cedar*. Vern. *Appurz*, *Ghushki*, Baluch.; *Obusht*, Pushtu; *Sārūs*, Chitral; *Shūr*, Lahaul and Kunawar; *Shūr*, Upper Chenab and Sutlej; *Dhup*, Garhwal and Kumaon.

A small or middle-sized tree, rarely attaining 50 ft., trunk short but of great girth, bark exfoliating in long fibrous strips. Foliage light and open, the scale-like l. usually opposite, rhomboid, convex, obtuse, closely appressed up to the apex, with a large resinous gland on the back, the subulate l. opposite or in whorls of 3, pungent, $\frac{1}{3}$ in. long. Male catkins at the ends of branchlets $\frac{1}{8}$–$\frac{1}{6}$ in. long, closely set with imbricate scales. Berries nearly globose, bluish-black when ripe, very resinous, the tips of the scales forming transverse ridges, seeds 2–5.

Baluchistan, 7-10,000 ft., forming open forests of considerable extent, often pure sometimes mixed with *Pistacia* and *Fraxinus*. Kuram valley, forming fully half the forests at 9,000 ft. in the Hariāb district. Chitral, in forests above 8,000 ft.

Inner arid ranges and valleys of the North-West Himalaya, as far as Nepal, 5–14,000 ft. Fl. in summer, the fr. ripens in Sept. of the second year.—Afghanistan. Persia. Mascat. Nearly allied to and probably not different from *J. excelsa*, M. Bieb., a tree of the mountains of Asia Minor and Syria, with which it was identified in my old Forest Flora. 4. **J. Wallichiana,** Hook. f. & Thoms.—Syn. *J. pseudo-sabina*, Fisch. & Mey.; Hook. f. in Fl. Brit. Ind. v. 646. Himalaya 9–15,000 ft., extending into the dry region of Western Tibet and Kunawar. In the North-West a large gregarious shrub, covering extensive areas at the limit of tree vegetation, associated with the alpine Birch and *Rhododendron campanulatum*. In the inner ranges of Sikkim, a tree with spreading branches, attaining 60 ft. (*the black Juniper*, Hook. Him. Journ. ii. 55). Foliage bushy, the scale-like l. opposite, decussate, ovate, in 4 rows, so as to make the branchlets 4-sided, more or less keeled at the back, apex not closely appressed. Berries ovoid, acute, $\frac{1}{4}$–$\frac{1}{3}$ in. long, blue when ripe, seed 1.

Cryptomeria japonica, Don. China and Japan. A stately fast-growing tree with dark green foliage, heart-wood fragrant, dark reddish-brown. L. sharply quadrangular, the lower edge decurrent upon the branch. Fl. monœcious, male catkins $\frac{1}{8}$–$\frac{1}{4}$ in. long, clustered at the ends of branchlets, anther-cells 3–5 at the base of scales, pollen globose. Cones globose at the ends of branchlets, the axis often growing out into a leafy shoot. Supporting scales acuminate, half adnate to the ovuliferous scales, ovules erect, 2 at the base of each scale. Mature cones $\frac{3}{4}$ in. diam., scales woody pectinate, and persistent after the seeds have fallen. Seeds $\frac{1}{8}$–$\frac{1}{4}$ in. long, compressed angular, with a narrow sharp edge. This valuable tree has been planted with other species on a very large scale in Japan, more than 200 years ago, a proof of the wonderful foresight of the great Japanese nation.

7. PODOCARPUS, L'Herit.; Fl. Brit. Ind. v. 649.

Shrubs or large trees, l. linear, lanceolate or elliptic-lanceolate, sometimes small, appressed. Fl. usually diœcious, ♂ axillary, solitary or fascicled, often cylindric, antheriferous scales numerous, imbricate, with two cells on the under side, pollen-grains with two large round wings. ♀ usually solitary and pedunculate. Ovules reflexed on a stalk, consisting of connate bract and scale. Seed globose or ovoid, seated on the enlarged fleshy stalk, testa often fleshy outside, cotyledons 2.

1. **P. neriifolia,** Don.—Syn. *Nageia bracteata*, Kurz. Vern. *Gūnsi*, Nep.; *Thitminpo*, Burm.

A tall tree, branches whorled, bark thin, fibrous, wood light yellow, even-grained, moderately hard. L. scattered, linear, thickly coriaceous, 5–10 in. long, midrib prominent on both surfaces. Fl. ♂ 1–2 in. long, sessile, clustered. Seeds solitary, globose, $\frac{1}{4}$–$\frac{1}{3}$ in. diam.

Nepal. Sikkim, evergreen forests of the outer hills, ascending to 3,000 ft. Assam. Khasi hills. Cachar. Chittagong. Andamans, at the bottom of valleys, not on the hills, often gregarious. Evergreen forests of the Bithoko range, Martaban, 2-3,000 ft. (D.B, May 1859). Tenasserim (Kurz). Wood highly prized in Burma. The leaves remain 2 years on the branches.

Fig. 201. Podocarpus latifolia, Wall. $\frac{1}{2}$.

2. **P. latifolia,** Wall. Pl. As. Rar. t. 30; Bedd. Fl. Sylv. t. 257.—Syn. *P. Wallichianus*, C. Presl; Pilger in Engler's Pflanzenreich iv. 5, 59; *Nageia latifolia*, Gordon. Vern. *Nirambali*, Tam.; *Thitmin ma*, Burm.

A large tree, wood slightly aromatic. L. opposite or nearly so, 4–7 by ½–2 in., lanceolate or elongate-elliptic, acuminate, longitudinal n. numerous. Fl. ♂ ½ in. long, in pedunculate clusters, antheriferous scales ovate acuminate. Seeds solitary, ¾ in. diam., seated on a cylindric fleshy scaly stalk.

Khasi hills. Cachar. Martaban and Tenasserim. Tinnevelli ghats 3–5,000 ft.—Malay Penins. Java. This must not be confounded with *P. latifolius*, R. Br.; Pilger in Engler's Pflanzenreich iv. 5, 90.—Syn. *P. Thunbergii*, Hook.; *Taxus latifolia*, Thunb., which is the Yellow Wood (*Geelhout*) of South Africa.

3. **P. cupressina**, Rob. Brown; Blume, Rumphia iii. 218, t. 172, fig. 2.—Syn. *P. imbricatus*, Blume; Pilger in Engler's Pflanzenreich iv. 5, 56. Upper Burma on water parting between Hukong and Mogaung valleys (N. R. Thompson, March 1896). Mogaung valley near Serpentine Mines (Griffith, April 1837).—Malay Penins. and Archip. Philippines. New Guinea. A tall tree, l. dimorphous, (*a*) on short sterile branchlets linear, flat, pungent, distichous, ⅓–½ in. long, (*b*) on longer branchlets small acute, more or less appressed, $\frac{1}{10}$ in. long. The seed-bearing branchlets frequently have small appressed l. in the lower part and longer ones, up to ⅓ in. long in the upper portion. ♀ fl. almost enclosed by the uppermost l. Seed and fleshy stalk red.

Dacrydium elatum, Wall. Tenasserim, Kurz. (doubtful).—Hills of Malay Peninsula. Ind. Archip. Cochinchina. Tonkin. A large tree with spreading branches and weeping branchlets. Leaves dimorphous, (*a*) small closely imbricate, triquetrous and (*b*) needle-shaped, 4-sided, pungent, ½–¾ in. long. Fl. ♂, small catkins at the ends of branchlets, scales flat with 2 anther-cells on the back at the base. ♀, a few ovuliferous scales in a short spike, ovule 1 at the base of scale often bent down when young. Seed erect, base enclosed in a shallow cup (epimatium, Pilger).

8. TAXUS, Linn.; Fl. Brit. Ind. v. 648.

T. baccata, Linn. (the only species). Vern. *Barma, Barmi, Thunu*, Pb.; *Arkhau*, Bash.; *Yamdal*, Kunawar; *Thuner*, Jauns.; *Dhengre Salla*, Nep.

A slow-growing and long-lived tree or shrub, bark reddish-grey, thin, smooth, peeling off in longitudinal shreds, heart-wood hard, usually reddish-brown. Foliage dark green, l. flat, linear, distichous, 1–1⅓ in. long, 1-nerved, narrowed into a very short petiole, no resin canal. Fl. diœcious, on short axillary branchlets, which are densely clothed with imbricating bracts. ♂ pedicelled, subglobose, with numerous peltate scales, each bearing on the underside 3–6 anther-cells, dehiscing longitudinally. ♀ a single erect ovule, surrounded at the base by a disc, which is membranous in fl. but enlarges into a red fleshy cup, surrounding the seed, testa hard, embryo in the upper portion of the endosperm, cotyledons 2, thick fleshy.

Throughout the Northern hemisphere in the temperate and warmer regions, on mountains in the tropics. 6 subspecies are recognized, subsp. *Wallichiana* in India. Kuram valley 7,500–9,000 ft. Himalaya 6–10,000 ft. in shady ravines. Khasi hills. Ruby Mines hills in Upper Burma above 5,000 ft. Fl. March–May. Fr. Sept.–Nov. L. persist 6–8 years.

9. CEPHALOTAXUS, Sieb. et Zucc.; Fl. Brit. Ind. v. 647.

Diœcious shrubs or trees, l. alternate, distichous, flat, linear, a large resin-canal near the underside, between epidermis and the fibro-vascular bundle of the midrib. ♂ fl. 6–11, in axillary globose heads (compound catkins) supported by a small involucre of imbricating scales, fl. in the axils of membranous bracts, stamens 7–12, each consisting of a stipitate scale, bearing on its back 2–3 anther-cells, pollen-grains globose. ♀ fl. small pedunculate cones, several in the axils of bracts at the base of terminal shoots, which lengthen out after the cones have been fertilized, bracts at the base of peduncle and sometimes also higher up. Scales 6–20 on the fleshy axis of the cone, each with 2 ovules at the base, one of which only develops. At a later stage the scales become fleshy and often confluent, so that the immature seeds appear as if enclosed in fleshy cups. Seeds large, usually one or two only in each cone, testa fleshy, resinous, with a thin inner hard woody layer. Embryo in the upper portion of the endosperm, cotyledons 2. Species 6, closely allied. Eastern Asia.

A. L. narrowed towards the base.

1. **C. Mannii**, Hook. f. Khasi, Jaintia and Naga hills 4,500–8,500 ft. A small tree, l. green beneath, 1–1⅜ in. long, gradually narrowed into a sharp point, midrib prominent on the upper, less so on the underside. Seed 1¼ in. long, striate. Gamble, Indian Timbers ed. ii. p. 700, gives this from Upper Burma. I have not seen specimens. *Taxus baccata*, which is common in the Ruby Mines hills, has sometimes been confused with this species, from which it may be distinguished by the absence of resin-canals in the leaves. 2. **C. Fortunei**, Hook. f. China. Pilger, Taxaceæ, 103, gives this from the Ruby Mines, Upper Burma. I have not seen specimens. A small tree, l. white beneath, 2½–3½ by ⅛–⅙ in., gradually narrowed into a sharp point. Peduncle of ♀ fl. surrounded at base by broad and short, higher up by lanceolate bracts ⅛ in. long, ovules 2 at the base of an ovate scale.

B. L. with a broad rounded base.

3. **C. Griffithii**, Hook. f. Mishmi hills, Assam. Manipur. Bernardmyo, Ruby Mines district, 5,500–6,500 ft. A middle-sized tree, bark brown, polished. L. falcate, whitish beneath, 1½ by ⅛ in., abruptly narrowed into a point, midrib prominent on the upperside. Pilger, Taxaceæ, 104, refers *C. Griffithii*, Oliver, Ic. Plant. t. 1933 (non Hook. f.) to *C. Oliveri*, a Chinese species with thick rigid l., the midrib not prominent above.

ORDER CXV. **CYCADACEÆ.** Gen. Pl. iii. 443.

Small trees, trunk cylindric, sometimes branched. A terminal crown of leaves, bands of short coriaceous mostly woolly scales alternating with bands of large pinnate palm-like leaves. Fl. diœcious, at the apex of the trunk among the leaves, the male usually in erect cones, sometimes two together, formed of numerous thickened, flat or variously peltate scales, bearing innumerable globose anther-cells on the under-surface. Anther-cells dehiscing by a longitudinal slit, often arranged in stellate groups of 3–5. Female: carpellary leaves (carpophylls) in cones or in crowded whorls round the apex of the stem, ovules large, sessile, orthotropous, integument one, near the micropyle free and often prolonged into a beak. Several months elapse between the growth of the pollen-tube and fertilization, which is effected through motile spermatozoids, analogous to Ferns and to *Gingko* among Conifers. Seed large, embryo enclosed in copious endosperm, the radicle attached to a long twisted filiform suspensor. Cotyledons 2.

In many species (*Cycas* particularly) the alternate bands formed by the persistent base of scales and leaves can be clearly distinguished on the outside of the trunk, the bands formed by the base of leaf-stalks being more prominent, having the appearance of thick annular cushions. The stem of Cycads is remarkable by the large size of pith and bark, both consisting of parenchymatous cells, usually filled with starch. Mucilage canals, often branched and anastomosing, lined by thin-walled secreting cells, are frequent in the bark, whence they extend to the leaves, and they are also found in the pith. Wood, cambium, bast, and medullary rays are arranged as in Conifers; the wood, apart from the medullary rays, consists entirely of long tracheides, more or less radially arranged, usually with several parallel lines of bordered pits on the radial face, the pits oblong, not circular as in Conifers. These tracheides in some cases have spirally and scalariform thickened walls, and they might, save that their ends are not perforated, be classed as vessels. The fibro-vascular bundles (leaf-traces), which enter the petiole, run for a considerable distance through the bark before joining the central cylinder; their course is not straight, they are bent in a remarkable manner, and often anastomose. In *Cycas* and *Encephalartos* the action of the cambium ceases, after the first central cylinder (wood and bast) has been formed, and then a fresh more or less concentric cambium layer appears in the bark, which forms a second ring of wood and bast outside the first, and this process is repeated several times, the result being on a transverse section a number of more or less concentric masses of wood, which sometimes anastomose, separated by softer layers of bast and parenchymatous tissue.

CYCAS, Linn.; Fl. Brit. Ind. v. 656.

(Ikeno, Befruchtung bei *Cycas revoluta*, Pringsheim, Jahrbücher, xxxiii. 557.)

Trunk annulate or clothed with the woody bases of the petioles, leaves pinnate, leaflets coriaceous, linear, quite entire, usually stiff and pungent, with a prominent midrib, involute in vernation, the lower often reduced to spines. Scales of the ♂ cone closely imbricated, cuneate, and usually prolonged in a long acuminate point. Carpophylls densely woolly, numerous in crowded whorls round the top of the trunk, at first loosely imbricate on an apparently terminal cone, then spreading, narrowed into a shorter or longer flat stalk, which bears 1–5 pairs of ovules on its edge, upper portion more or less dilated into an entire or pectinate blade. Species 12, tropical Africa to Polynesia.

A. Margin of leaflets flat.

(*a*) Blade of carpophyll dentate, longer than broad.

1. **C. circinalis,** Linn.; Rheede, Hort. Malab. iii. t. 13–21. Vern. *Oruguna*, *Orguno* Uriya; *Per ita*, Tel.; *Todda Panna*, Mal. Western Peninsula, deciduous forests of the Western Ghats to 3,500 ft., from Malabar southwards. Hills on the east side, north as far as Orissa.—Ceylon, moist region up to 1,500 ft. Eastern tropical Africa, Madagascar and Comoro islands. Malay Archip. Attains 40 ft. and grows to the age of 100 years (Rheede), trunk usually 15 ft. high, with prominent annular leaf-scars. L. 5–9 ft. long, leaflets 80–100 pairs, 8–12 by $\frac{1}{4}$–$\frac{1}{3}$ in., upperside shining, petiole with numerous short spines. Male cone 1–2 ft. Carpophylls 6–12 by 1–1$\frac{1}{2}$ in., blade ovate-triangular with sharp narrow teeth, stalk long, bearing in its upper portion 6–12 ovules. After flowering the terminal bud in this and other species often grows out into a prolongation of the trunk. Seeds ovoid, pale reddish-yellow, 1 in. long, endosperm filled with starch.

2. **C. Rumphii,** Miq. Vern. *Môndaing*, Burm. Beach Forests on the coast of the Andamans, Nicobars, Coco islands and South Tenasserim.—Malay Penins. and Archip. New Guinea. North Australia. Similar to 1. Attains 50 ft. and nearly 5 ft. in girth on the Coco islands (Prain), on the Andamans it generally is only 4–6 and not more than 15 ft. high. Trunk very rough, often branched. L. dark glossy-green, 3–6 ft. long, leaflets 50–60 pair, 9–15 by $\frac{1}{2}$–$\frac{3}{4}$ in., petiole at base 1$\frac{1}{2}$ in. broad. Carpophylls densely tawny-villous, blade from ovate to ovate-lanceolate, teeth small, ovules 6–10 on the upper portion of the stalk. Seeds compressed, ovoid-oblong, 2–3 in. long, poisonous when raw.

(*b*) Blade of carpophyll as broad as long, deeply pectinate.

3. **C. pectinata,** Griff.—Syn. *C. Jenkinsiana*, Griff. Vern. *Thakal*, Nep.; *Môndaing*, Burm. Nepal, foot of hills. Sal forests of the Sikkim Terai and outer valleys. Assam, Khasi hills. Manipúr. Chittagong. Shan States. Forests of *Dipterocarpus obtusifolius* and *Pinus Khasya* on the Martaban hills. Trunk 4–8, l. glabrous, 4–5 ft. long, leaflets 6–10 by $\frac{1}{4}$–$\frac{1}{2}$ in. Carpophylls densely tawny-silky, blade almost orbicular, 3 in. diam., cut into strong subulate spiny teeth, $\frac{1}{2}$–$\frac{3}{4}$ in. long, and terminating in a strong, subulate acumen, about 1 in. long, stalk as long as, or shorter than blade, ovules 4–6, glabrous. Seed ovoid, glabrous, 1$\frac{1}{2}$–2$\frac{1}{2}$ in. long, orange-red or yellow.

4. **C. siamensis,** Miq. Vern. *Môndaing*, Burm. Eng forests of the Prome district and of Upper Burma.—Siam, Cochinchina. Yunnan. Often almost stemless, but at times with a trunk up to 5 ft. long, 8–12 in. diam., l. 2–3 ft. long, rusty-villous while young, leaflets thin, 3–8 by $\frac{1}{3}$ in. Carpophyll blade ovate-rhomboid, long-acuminate, at first densely tawny-tomentose, ultimately nearly glabrous, one ovule on each side of the stalk at the base of blade. Seed ovoid-oblong, smooth, 1$\frac{1}{3}$ in. long. It is doubtful whether this is the species cultivated as *C. siamensis* in European gardens.

B. Margin of leaflets revolute.

5. **C. revoluta,** Thunb. China. Southern Japan. Formosa. Tonkin. Commonly cultivated in gardens. Trunk 6 ft., densely clothed with the old leaf-bases, l. 2–6 ft. long, petiole thick, quadrangular, leaflets narrow. Carpophylls 4–9 in. long, blade ovate, laciniate nearly to the midrib, stalk longer than blade with 4–6 ovules. Immature seed densely tomentose. 6. **C. Beddomei,** Dyer in Trans. Linn. Soc. Ser. 2, Bot. ii. t. 17. Cuddapah district, Madras. Trunk short, l. 3 ft. long, rachis quadrangular, leaflets 5–7 by $\frac{1}{10}$–$\frac{1}{8}$ in. Male cone 9–13 in. long, 2–3 in. diam., scales long-acuminate, the lower erect, the upper strongly recurved. Carpophyll 4–8 in., blade ovate-lanceolate, with long linear teeth, ovules 2–4. Seeds nearly globose, 1$\frac{1}{2}$ in. long.

ADDENDA

While the printing of the present work was in progress a considerable number of books and papers were published which have greatly increased our knowledge regarding the characters and geographical distribution of species mentioned in this book. Some of these publications also contain descriptions of new species, alterations of names and valuable notes which it is desirable to record here. The principal of these publications are the following :—

1. Theodore Cooke, C.I.E. Flora of the Presidency of Bombay, Vol. I. (1903), Vol. II. part I. (1904), part II. (1905).
2. David Prain. Bengal Plants (1903).
3. J. F. Duthie. Flora of the Upper Gangetic Plain, Vol. I. part I. (1903), part II. (1905).
4. Annals of the Royal Botanic Garden, Calcutta, Vol. IX. New and rare Indian Plants (1901), Vol. X. Prain, the species of *Dalbergia* of South Eastern Asia (1904).
5. Records of the Botanical Survey of India, Vol. I. (1902), Vol. II. (1903), III. 1 (1904), 2 (1905).
6. Hooker's Icones Plantarum.
7. Journal of the Asiatic Society of Bengal.
8. Journal of the Bombay Natural History Society.
9. Annals of the Royal Botanic Gardens, Peradeniya.
10. The Indian Forester, with botanical contributions by Prain, Duthie, Bourdillon, Hole, Rogers, Osmaston, A. W. Lushington and others.
11. The following parts of Engler's Pflanzenreich: Pax, *Aceraceæ* (1902); Koehne, *Lythraceæ* (1903); Winkler, *Betulaceæ* (1904).

In addition to these I owe to the kindness of my friends in India numerous specimens and notes which arrived after the orders to which they belong had been printed, and which, as far as was possible, have been noticed here. Authorities are omitted in the names quoted from the book.

P. 2. *Clematis Gouriana.* North Bengal. Chutia Nagpur.
" " *C. Wightiana.* Orissa.
" " *C. orientalis.* Punjab Salt Range.—Western Asia. Baluchistan.
" " *C. Buchananiana.* Vern. ***Kaunia-bali***, Jauns.
" " *C. acuminata.* Burma.
" " *Naravelia zeylanica.* Bengal.
" 3. Dillenia, strike out : with an arillus.
" 4. *Dillenia pentagyna.* Behar. Chutia Nagpur.
" 8. *Michelia Champaca.* Shady valleys in Singbhum (Haines).
" 11. *Saccopetalum longiflorum.* Ryang valley, Sikkim.
" 12. *Miliusa macrocarpa.* Upper Burma.
" 15. *Polyalthia fragrans.* Orissa.
" 16. *Unona dumosa.* Upper Burma.
" " *Unona præcox.* Ryang valley, Sikkim. Upper Assam.
" 17. *Uvaria ferruginea.* Tipperah.
" " *U. Narum*, Wall. Orissa.
" 20. *Goniothalamus Griffithii.* Andamans.
" " Add : 7. **G. peduncularis**, King and Prain in Ann. Gard. Calc. IX. t. 1. Kachin hills, Upper Burma. Glabrous, fl. solitary, erect, 1⅜ in. long.
P. 23. *Cissampelos Pareira.* Branches from a long creeping woody rhizome or on a short stout stem.
P. 24. *Cyclea peltata.* Great Coco. Andamans. Nicobars.

P. 24. *Tinospora cordifolia.* Punjab. Bengal, common. Minbu district, Upper Burma.
P. 25. *Anamirta paniculata.* Orissa.
„ 26. *Tiliacora racemosa.* Minbu district, Upper Burma.
„ 27. *Pycnarrhena pleniflora.* Chittagong.
„ „ *Hæmatocarpus Thomsoni.* Chittagong.
„ 28. *Holbœllia latifolia.* Vern. *Ban kakri*, Haz. Fr. purple.—From Hazara eastwards.
P. 32. *Boscia variabilis.* Vern. *Thamon*, Burm.
„ „ Add: 2. **B. prunoides,** Gage in Records Bot. Survey, India III. 23. Minbu district, Upper Burma. A shrub, branches softly pubescent, l. ovate or obovate, nearly glabrous, fr. dark brown, smooth, 1 in. diam.
P. 32. *Cratæva religiosa*, Forst. Dr. Stapf has kindly informed me that this name only applies to the Tahiti tree, and that the species of tropical Africa are different from the Indian and Polynesian species. Kurz, in Journal of Botany 1874 p. 193. describes 5 species of British India: 1. *C. Roxburghii*, which should now be the name of the common Indian tree. 2. *C. hygrophila.* 3. *C. lophosperma.* 4. *C. unilocularis*, Ham. Subhimalayan tract from Sikkim eastwards. 5. *C. Nurvala*, Ham. Along the western coasts of Hindustan.
P. 33. *Capparis zeylanica.* Midnapore. Orissa.
„ 34. *C. aphylla.* Waste lands of the Doab.
„ „ *C. grandis.* Minbu district, Upper Burma.
„ „ *C. sepiaria.* Often climbing. Bengal. Sundriban, near the coast. Coco islands. Andamans.
P. 35. *C. floribunda.* Orissa.
„ „ *C. horrida.* Vern. *Ardanda*, Sind.
„ „ *C. andamanica*, King, is *C. floribunda*, Wight; King in Ann. Gard. Calc. IX. 8.
„ „ Add: **C. Cathcarti,** Hemsl.; Ann. Gard. Calc. IX. t. 10. Sikkim, outer hills, 4–5000 ft. A large glabrous climbing shrub, nearly allied to *C. floribunda*, fl. in pedunculate umbels, 1½ in. across, stamens 28–36.
P. 36. *C. crassifolia*, Kurz, and *polymorpha*, Kurz, dry districts of the Irawadi valley, probably are forms of *C. horrida.*
P. 36. *C. sabiæfolia*, Hook. f. and Thoms. Upper Burma.
„ 39. *Flacourtia cataphracta.* From the Jumna eastwards. Chittagong.
„ 40. Fig. 16 is *F. sepiaria*, Roxb., not *F. Ramontchi.*
„ „ *Xylosma longifolium.* Singbhum. Upper Burma.
„ „ *Gynocardia odorata.* Makūm forest, common, pulp of ripe fr. powerfully fragrant.
P. 42. *Taraktogenos Kurzii.* Chittagong. Minbu district, Upper Burma.
„ „ Add: **Asteriastigma macrocarpa,** Bedd. Fl. Sylv. t. 266, Manual t. 27. Syn. *Hydnocarpus macrocarpa*, Warburg in Engler u. Prantl, III. 6a, 21. Travancore ghats 2,500 ft. A large tree, young shoots minutely aureo-pubescent, l. entire, blade 10–12 by 3½ in. Fl. whitish, 1 in. across, polygamous, ♂ and ⚥ in few-fld. fascicles on the older branches. Sepals 4, much imbricate, petals 12–16, shorter than sepals, ciliate on the edge with broad scale-like hairs, furnished inside near the base with a thick hairy 8-lobed scale. Stamens 60–70, in two or three rows, ovules ∞ on 6–7 parietal placentas, stigmas as many as placentas, large, sessile, 2-lobed. Fr. globose, 5 in. diam., pericarp woody, seeds numerous, angular, testa crustaceous. Warburg unites *Taraktogenos* and *Asteriastigma* with *Hydnocarpus.*
P. 46. *Tamarix gallica.* Bengal. Banks of the Irawadi river.
„ „ *T. Pallasii*, Desv., a glaucous form of *T. gallica.* Baluchistan. Western Tibet.—Western Asia.
P. 47. *Myricaria germanica.* Vern. *Shushar*, Pangi, Lahaul, this name does not apply to *Tamarix ericoides* (p. 46).
P. 48. *Hypericum patulum.* Upper Burma.
„ 52. *Garcinia lanceæfolia.* Kachin hills. Upper Burma.
„ „ *Garcinia Cowa.* Upper Burma. Vern. *Yekabyin*, Burm.
„ 53. *Ochrocarpus longifolius.* Orissa. Chittagong.
„ 54. *Calophyllum Inophyllum.* Vern. *Pon nyit*, Tavoy. Saline tracts, Minbu district, Upper Burma.
P. 56. Add: 4. **Kayea assamica,** King and Prain in Ind. For. XXVII. p. 62. Vern. *Sia nahor*, Ass. North Lakhimpur. A large tree, bole straight, wood hard and heavy. L. 3½–4½ in., sec. n. faint (in *K. floribunda* more conspicuous). Fr. ¾ in. diam. (in *K. florib.* 1½–1¾ in.).
P. 58. Eurya. Species 10, Eastern Asia, Pacific islands.
P. 58. *Eurya japonica.* Western Duars. Chittagong.
„ 60. *Schima khasiana.* A large tree, hills east of Bhamo 6–7,500 ft., common.
„ 62. *Saurauja napaulensis.* A glabrous variety, l. spinulose-serrate, numerous subulate scales on petiole and underside of l., in Sikkim and the Khasi hills.

P. 65. *Dipterocarpus obtusifolius.* Andamans.
„ 66. *D. tuberculatus.* Chittagong.
„ „ *D. alatus.* Andamans.
„ „ Add: 10. **D. Griffithii,** Miq. Andamans. Mergui. A tall tree, leaf-buds clothed with yellow shining hair, fruiting calyx 1½–2½, wings 5–7 in. long, wings of calyx ½ in. broad.
P. 66. Add: 11. **D. scaber,** Ham. Tipperah; Prain, Bengal Plants 252. Regarding this and allied species see Brandis in Journ. Linn. Soc. XXXI. 36.
P. 67. *Anisoptera glabra.* Mergui.
„ 68. *Pentacme suavis.* Namlao, upper Irawaddi, lat. 25° 20′.
„ 67 and 71. *Hopea parviflora* and *Wightiana*, known in Tinnevelli as *White Kongu*, may readily be distinguished as follows: *H. parviflora.* Vern. *Thambagam*, Travancore. Leaves: blade 3½ by 1½, pet. ⅛ in., fl. cream-coloured, ⅛ in. across, wings of fr. straw-coloured, under 2 in. *H. Wightiana.* Leaves: blade 5–8 by 2–3 in., pet. ½ in., fl. yellow, tinged with red, ⅓ in. across, wings of fr. red, 2–3 in. long. The two species of *Balanocarpus*, known in Tinnevelli as *Black Kongu*, differ by the following characters: *B. erosa.* Branchlets and panicles glabrous, pet. ¼ in., fruit 1¼ in. long. *B. utilis.* Branchlets and panicles hoary, petiole over ½ in. long, fr. globose, ½ in. diam. See Indian Forester, P. M. Lushington, XXIX. 429. Bourdillon, XXX. 18.
P. 72. *Vatica Scaphula.* Mergui.
„ 75. *Hibiscus tiliaceus.* Andamans. Grows as a tree on the sea coast and as a rampant climber in the dense forests of the Sundriban.
P. 75. *Thespesia populnea.* Sundriban.
„ 76. *Thespesia Lampas.* Behar. Chutia Nagpur. Seeds dark brown and slightly rugose.
P. 77. *Bombax insigne.* Style nearly undivided (in *B. malabaricum* 5-branched). The Travancore tree has large prickles on trunk, fl. salmon-pink, capsule pubescent (Bourdillon). A new sp. reported by Gage from the Minbu district, Upper Burma, in Records Bot. Survey India vol. III. 29.—Prain in Journ. As. Soc. Bengal vol. LXII. (1893). 65, unites *Eriodendron* and *Bombax* and makes *B. anceps* a sub-species of *B. insigne.*
P. 78. *Kydia calycina.* Vern. *Bhendi*, Mar. *Petshat*, Upper Burma.
„ 79. Add to *Malvaceæ*: **Dicellostyles jujubifolia,** Benth.—Syn. *Kydia jujubifolia*, Griff. Ic. Plant. As. t. 595. Sikkim and Bhutan, 1,000–3,500 ft. A large tree, attaining 6 ft. in girth, young shoots grey-stellately tomentose, l. ovate, acuminate, blade 3–6½, pet. ½–1½ in., basal n. 5. Fl. axillary, pedunculate, often in pairs. Calyx supported by a whorl of 4–5 leafy bracteoles, longer than calyx. Petals white, spathulate 1¼ in. long. Staminal-column ⅛–¼ in., divided into 15 short filaments, anthers uniform. Capsule enclosed by the calyx and supported by the persistent bracteoles, seeds 1–2.
P. 80. *Sterculia urens.* Assam.
„ 83. *S. guttata.* Chittagong.
„ „ *S. coccinea.* Vern. *Shaw-a*, Upper Burma.
„ 84. Add: 14 (*a*). **S. Kingii,** Prain in Journ. As. Soc. Bengal 73 (1904), 192. Sikkim 3–6,000 ft. A small tree, l. ovate-lanceolate, 9–12 by 4–6 in., pet. 2–2½ in. Calyx-lobes lanceolate, ½ in. long. Fr. of 4–5 red follicles, 4–5 by 1½ in.
P. 84. *S. rubiginosa.* Andamans. Nicobars.
„ „ *S. colorata.* Lushai hills. Andamans. Vern. *Kodarro*, Kattiawar.
„ 85. *S. campanulata.* Andamans.
„ 85. *Heritiera littoralis.* Strike out: Vern. *Sunder*, *Sundri*, Beng.
„ 86. *H. Fomes.* Vern. *Sunder*, *Sundri*, Beng. Forms nearly pure forests of large extent, stems buttressed, innumerable blind root-suckers under the trees.
P. 88. *Eriolæna quinquelocularis.* Chutia Nagpur.
„ 89. *Helicteres Isora.* Bengal.
„ „ *H. hirsuta.* Chittagong.
„ 90. *Buettneria aspera.* Behar.
„ 92. Add to *Sterculiaceæ*: **Mansonia Gagei,** Drummond. D. Prain in Journ. Linn. Soc. XXXVII. 250. Vern. *Kalamet*, Burm. On the hills along the Siamese frontier, 100 miles above the old town of Tenasserim, in evergreen forest. A tree with hard brown heart-wood which has an unpleasant smell when felled green, while the heart-wood of trees which have died naturally and have lain a long time in the forest gradually becomes scented, and is an article of export from Mergui. In structure the wood somewhat resembles Sandal wood, the medullary rays are narrow, but they are long, not short (as in Sandal) on a transverse section, the vessels are more numerous, smaller and often in radial groups of 2–4, the distance between med. rays is a little greater than the diameter of vessels. There are narrow oblique tangential lines of wood parenchyma between the rays, but they are less conspicuous than in Sandal. The structure is quite different from that of *Cordia fragrantissima.* See Brandis in Ind. For. XXVII. 516. L. elongate-elliptic, base

slightly cordate, blade 3–5 by 1–2 in., pet. ½ in., stipules lanceolate, deciduous. Fl. bi-sexual, in axillary pedunculate minutely stellate-pubescent compound corymbs, pedicels fascicled, ¼ in. long. Calyx spathaceous, enclosing the bud, stellately pubescent outside. Petals 5, obovate, contorted in bud, ⅓ in. long. On a slender gynophore ⅙–⅓ in. long, 10 stamens, filaments longer than the versatile one-celled anthers. Between stamens and carpels 5 oblanceolate petaloid staminodes. Carpels 5, alternating with staminodes, each carpel terminating in a filiform style, ovules 5–9 on the inner angle. Fr. a samara 1 in. long, seed 1. Placed by Prain in *Mansonieæ*, a new tribe of *Sterculiaceæ*, together with *Triplochiton*, Schumann, an African genus.

A tree, also called *Kalamet*, and reported to yield scented wood, in the Kywè-thonbaung forest, Mergui district, ♂ fl. only, l. cordate, margin sinuate, blade 3–6, pet. 1–2 in., upper side with few minute stellate hairs, underside densely clothed with round shining scales, consisting of radiating cells. Fl. unisexual, in bud enclosed in a bag of 3 valvate membranous bracteoles, stellately hairy outside. Sepals 5, lanceolate, coriaceous, ¾–1 in. long, outside densely clothed with stellate hairs. Petals 5, broadly ovate, almost reniform, base slightly cordate, shortly unguiculate, large oil cavities between the reticulate veins. Stamens 60–80, filaments glabrous, the base slightly connate in 5 bundles, anther-cells 2, parallel, attached to the thick connective, pollen-grains large, globose, aculeate. A new genus which cannot be named without the ♀ fl. and fruit.

P. 92. Add to *Sterculiaceæ*: **Paradombeya burmanica**, Stapf in Ic. Plant. t. 2743a. Upper Shan States, 3,500 ft. A shrub, branchlets and l. with simple hairs, l. lanceolate, serrate, 2–5 in. long. Fl. snow-white, crowded in axillary fascicles all along the slender branches; pedicels slender, ⅓ in. long, above the base with a whorl of 3 lanceolate bracteoles. Calyx glabrous, of 5 nearly free sepals, petals obliquely obovate. Stamens 15, five groups of 3 each, alternating with 5 linear staminodia, longer than stamens. Ovary sessile, stellate-tomentose, 2–5-celled, 2 ovules in each cell, fr. unknown.

P. 93. *Plagiopteron suaveolens*.—Syn. *P. fragrans*, Griff.; Fl. Brit. Ind. I. 399. Griffith called the plant *P. suaveolens* in the text and *P. fragrans* on the plate.

P. 96. *Grewia nagensium* is *G. denticulata*, Wall.; Prain in Ann. Gard. Calc. IX. t. 12. Peduncles sometimes fascicled.

P. 97. *G. lævigata*. Chutia Nagpur. Coco islands.

„ „ *G. salvifolia*. Vern. *Bihul*, Sind. Behar. Chutia Nagpur. Orissa.

„ 98. *G. asiatica* and *leptopetala* I regard as two parallel polymorphous species, the petals of the former with a distinct claw and a well developed gonophore, while the petals of *G. leptopetala* have no claw and no distinct gonophore. These species are parallel, because their forms exhibit the same variation in regard to hairiness and the shape of leaves. The figure of *G. elastica*, Royle Ill. t. 22 apparently belongs to *G. leptopetala*. Another possible view is, that the claw of the petals and the gonophore are variable characters. Against this stands the fact that a number of species in Asia and Africa are characterized by the absence of claw and gonophore. Foresters in India will have abundant opportunities of settling this question, not by examining isolated herbarium specimens, but by studying these difficult species in Gardens and in the Forest.

P. 98. Add under *G. asiatica*: **G. cinnamomea**, Gamble; Prain, Bengal Plants 283. Chutia Nagpur, l. densely tawny-white tomentose beneath, stipules lanceolate falcate; cymes many (not seen).

P. 98. *G. sapida*. Chutia Nagpur. East Bengal.

„ 99. *G. scabrophylla*. Fl. white. Chutia Nagpur. Chittagong.

„ „ *G. Microcos*. Vern. *Mya-ya*, Burm.

„ 100. *G. orbiculata*. Western Behar, rare.

„ 101. *G. hirsuta*. Chutia Nagpur. *Gursakri*, Jabalpúr.

„ „ *Echinocarpus sterculiaceus*. Assam.

„ 102. *Echinocarpus dasycarpus*. Hills east of Bhamo 7,000 ft. (Montague Hill, 157).

„ 103. *Elæocarpus robustus*. Kachin hills, Upper Burma.

„ „ *Elæocarpus Braceanus*. Hills east of Bhamo 6,500 ft. A low spreading tree, trunk 8 ft. girth (Mont. Hill).

P. 107. *Reinwardtia trigyna*. N. W. Himalaya to 6,000 ft.

„ 108. *Hiptage Madablota*. Vern. *Kampthi*, Jabalpur. Behar. Chutia Nagpur. Chittagong.

P. 108. *H. acuminata*. A tall climber. South Lushai hills.

„ 110. *Aspidopterys nutans*. Chittagong.

„ 112. *Glycosmis pentaphylla*. Bengal. Andamans.

„ 113. *Murraya exotica*. Fl. ½–1 in. across. Behar. Chutia Nagpur. Andamans.

„ 114. *Murraya Kœnigii*. Chutia Nagpur. Bengal.

„ „ *Micromelum pubescens*. Berry yellow. Singhbúm.

„ „ *Clausena excavata*. Vern. *Pyindawthein*, Upper Burma.

„ 116. *Acronychia laurifolia*. Upper Burma.

„ 117. *Zanthoxylum Acanthopodium*. Upper Burma.

P. 117. *Z. alatum.* Hills east of Bhamo 5,500 ft.
„ 118. *Z. ovalifolium.* Kachin hills.
„ „ *Limonia acidissima.* Jabalpur. Behar. Chutia Nagpur.
„ 119. *Toddalia aculeata.* Vern. *Makat-nwè*, Upper Burma.
„ „ *Feronia Elephantum.* Probably indigenous in Upper Burma (fl. white). Bark used as a cosmetic.
„ „ *Ægle Marmelos.* Singbhum.
„ 122. *Paramignya monophylla.* Andamans.
„ „ *P. longispina.* Sundriban. Malay Penins.
„ 123. *Citrus medica.* Western Duars.
„ „ *C. Aurantium.* Indigenous in the Mothronwala swamp Dehra Dún (Kanjilal); in secluded ravines of Singbhum, spinescent, fr. 2–2½ in. diam., oblate, not mamillate, with copious sweet, slightly acid juice (Haines).
P. 126. *Ailanthus.* Species 9 in India, Indo-china, Malaya, Australia, 1 in China.
„ 127. *A. glandulosa.* China (not Japan).
„ „ Add: 4. **A. Kurzii**, Prain in Ind. For. XXVIII. 133 t. 8. Pegu Yoma, eastern slopes. Andamans. 5. **A. grandis**, Prain in Ind. For. XXVIII. 131, 210 t. 1. Vern. *Gogul*, Nep.; *Actaluca*, Ass. Rungagora, Assam. Ryang and other tributaries of the Tista river, Sikkim. A tall tree, 120–150 ft., leaflets entire, 5–8 pair, 6–8 in. long, ripe carpels 4–6 in. long, apex rounded, obtuse.
P. 127. *Picrasma quassioides.* A tall shrub or small tree.
„ „ *Brucea mollis.* Myitkyina, Upper Burma.
„ 128. *Ochna pumila.* Behar. Chutia Nagpur.
„ 130. *Boswellia serrata.* Central India. Behar. Chutia Nagpur.
„ „ CANARIUM. Calyx persistent.
„ 132. *Garuga pinnata.* From the Sutlej eastwards. Chutia Nagpur. Chittagong, Andamans.
P. 133. *Balsamodendron Mukul.* Sind. Kattiawar, Rajputana. S. E. Punjab.
„ 136. *Walsura villosa.* Andamans.
„ 137. *W. robusta.* Chittagong.
„ 138. *Dysoxylum procerum.* Singbhum. Chittagong.
„ „ *D. reticulatum*, King Ann. Gard. Calc. IX. t. 22.
„ 139. *Chisocheton paniculatus.* Chittagong.
„ „ *C. dysoxylifolius.* Chittagong.
„ „ *Azadirachta indica.* Line 6 from below, omit the words: *afterwards purple.*
„ 140. *Melia Azedarach.* Indigenous in West Kashmir and Hazara.
„ 141. *Carapa obovata.* Fl. C. S. and R. S.
„ „ *Carapa moluccensis*, when growing in tidal mud, sends up copious vertical blind root-suckers, while the horizontal snake-like winding roots of *C. obovata* protrude through the mud and act as respiratory organs. (Schimper Indo-malayische Strandflora 36, 39; Prain in Records Bot. Survey II. 293.)
P. 141. *Amoora Rohituka.* Vern. *Pittaraj*, *Tiktaraj*, Beng. Seeds 1–2. Chittagong. Great Coco.
P. 142. *A. cucullata.* Nepal. Long blind root-suckers in the Sundriban.
„ „ *A. Wallichii.* Western Duars. Fr. obovoid, tawny-tomentose.
„ „ *Aglaia odoratissima.* Chutia Nagpur.
„ 143. *A. andamanica.* Fl. scented.
„ „ *A. perviridis.* Chittagong.
„ 144. *Lansium decandrum.* Kachin hills.
„ „ *Soymida febrifuga.* Leaflets rarely serrate.
„ 146. *Cedrela microcarpa.* Tippera. Chittagong.
„ „ *Chloroxylon Swietenia.* Chutia Nagpur.
„ 147. *Olax scandens.* Vern. *Kakundan*, Jabalpur.—Sundriban. Chittagong.
„ 148. *O. acuminata.* Tipperah. Kachin hills. Upper Burma.
„ „ *O. nana.* Arakan Yoma, Minbu district.
„ 149. *Schœpfia fragrans*, Wall. Myitkyina, Upper Burma.
„ 150. *Cansjera Rheedii.* Upper Burma.
„ „ *Lepionurus sylvestris.* Chittagong.
„ „ *Opilia amentacea.* Behar.
„ 151. Add: 6. **Gomphandra serrata**, King and Prain in Journ. As. Soc. Bengal LXIX. 169. Kachin hills, Upper Burma. A small glabrous tree, l. serrate, fr. ½ in. long.
P. 152. *Phlebocalymna Griffithiana.* Vern. *Wun-the-chi*, Burm. (Mergui).
„ 153. Add: 3. **Miquelia gibba**, Baill.; Prain, Bengal Plants 326. West Bengal. A climbing shrub.
P. 154. *Sarcostigma Wallichii.* Andamans. Tenasserim.
„ 156. *Ilex Godajam.* Hills east of Bhamo 7,000 ft., fr. red.
„ 158. *Euonymus lacerus.* Chumbi. Bhutan.
„ 159. Prain in Journ. As. Soc. Beng. LXXIII. 195, regards *E. Lawsonii* as a distinct species.

P. 159. Add: 23. **Euonymus kachinensis**, Prain in Journ. As. Soc. Beng. LXXIII. 193. Kachin hills 6,500 ft. A shrub, calyx ½ in. diam., sepals rounded, spreading, fr. deeply 4-lobed, ¾ in. long. 24. **E. subsulcatus**, Prain l.c. 194. Muleyit hill, Tenasserim 5,000 ft. A shrub, branches distinctly quadrangular, fr. deeply 4-lobed, ½ in. long. 25. **E. siluruoides**, Prain l.c. 194. Sikkim 5,500–6,500 ft. A shrub, near *E. bullatus*, fr. depressed, slightly 4-ridged, ¾ in. across.

P. 160. *Microtropis discolor*. Western Duars. Myitkyina.

„ „ *M. bivalvis*. Fl. often unisexual.

„ „ HIPPOCRATEA. Anthers often apparently one-celled.

„ „ *Hippocratea indica*. Behar. China.

„ 161. *H. obtusifolia*. Probably in the Eastern Peninsula.—China.

„ „ Add: 4 (*a*). *H. sp. nova*. Vern. *Nwè ngan bo*, Burm. Upper Burma. (C. B. Smales, March 1900). A climbing shrub, nearly allied to *H. obtusifolia*, fl. green, scented, in large terminal cymose panicles, petals $\frac{1}{10}$ in. long, linear-spathulate, imbricate in bud. Fr. unknown, hence not named.

P. 162. *Celastrus paniculata*. Behar. Chutia Nagpur. Assam. Prain in Journ. As. Soc. Beng. LXXIII. 195 separates the following from *C. paniculata*: *C. multiflora*, Roxb. Central and Eastern Himalaya. Khasi hills. Burma, l. oblong. *C. nutans*, Roxb. Western Peninsula, l. obovate.

P. 162. From *C. stylosa*, Wall., Prain separates *C. Hookeri*, Prain. Eastern Himalaya. Khasi hills. Burma. L. thin, reddish-brown when dry, petals faintly toothed, filaments glabrous.

P. 163. *C. monosperma*. South Lushai hills.—China.

„ „ Add: 5. **C. Championi**, Benth. Sikkim 2–6,000 ft. Naga hills. Silhet.—Malaya. China. A very large climber, capsules obovoid, with 3 prominent angles, ½ in. long. 6. **C. membranifolia**, Prain. Khasi hills. A shrub, l. membranous, ovate-lanceolate, serrate, pet. slender, ¾ in. long. 7. **C. Listeri**, Prain. Daphla hills. A small tree, l. ovate or obovate, entire, 8 by 3½ in. Fr. ½ in. across, 8-seeded.

P. 163. *Gymnosporia emarginata*. Orissa.

„ „ *G. pallida*. Myitkyina.

„ 164. Add: 17. **Gymnosporia sikkimensis**, Prain. Tista valley, Sikkim. A small unarmed tree, l. ovate, obtuse, very obscurely serrate.

P. 165. *Siphonodon celastrineus*. Sikkim. Andamans.

„ „ SALACIA. Species about 85, throughout the tropics, most numerous in South America.

P. 165. *S. Smaliana*. Fr. red, globose, 1½ in. diam. on pedicel ¾ in. long, fleshy, sweet, edible, seeds 2 or 3.

P. 166. *S. verrucosa*. Chittagong.

„ „ *S. prinoides*. Behar.

„ 167. VENTILAGO. Species 10, most in India and Malaya.

„ „ *V. madraspatana*. Vern. *Keoti*, Jabalpur.

„ 170. *Zizyphus Œnoplia*. Sundriban. Andamans.

„ 171. *Z. glabra*. Upper Burma.

„ „ *Z. Xylopyrus*. Vern. *Karkata*, Kol. Behar.

„ „ *Z. rugosa*. Vern. *Sagra*, Jabalpur; *Sirka*, Kol.

„ 172. *Z. rugosa*. Assam. Chittagong. Upper Burma.

„ „ *Rhamnus virgatus*. Nilgiris.

„ 175. *Gouania leptostachya*. Singbhum. Chittagong.

„ „ *G. microcarpa*. Yunnan.

„ „ *Helinus lanceolatus*. Singbhum.

„ 176. *Vitis adnata*. Chittagong.

„ „ *V. tomentosa*. Chutia Nagpur. Behar.

„ 177. *V. quadrangularis*. Sundriban. Orissa.

„ „ *V. barbata*. Chittagong.

„ 178. *V. lanceolaria*. Chutia Nagpur. Chittagong.

„ 179. *V. pedata*. Chutia Nagpur. Bengal.

„ „ The following large climbers should be added:—

A. L. simple, fl. tetramerous.

28. **Vitis assamica**, Lawson. Base of eastern Himalaya. Assam. Cachar. Chittagong. Upper Burma. L. glabrous, nearly orbicular, suddenly acuminate, cordate, fr. turbinate, seed 1. 29. **V. gigantea**, Bedd.; Cooke, Fl. Bombay I. 250. Kanara. L. 6–8 by 5–6 in., cordate with a deep sinus, long acuminate, bristle-dentate, glabrous above, slightly tomentose beneath. 30. **V. Aubertiana**, Gage in Records Bot. Survey India III. 36. Minbu district, Upper Burma. L. glabrous, blade 4½–10½ in. diam., palmately divided into 3–6 long narrow segments, pet. 2 in. long.

B. L. 3-5-foliate, fl. tetramerous.

31. **V. japonica**, Thunb.—Syn. *V. mollis*, Wall. Sikkim 1–3,000 ft. Khasi hills. Chittagong. Andamans.—Malaya. China. Pubescent, leaflets serrate, seeds 3 or 4, back convex, rugose, sides flat and pitted. 32. **V. bracteolata**, Wall. Sikkim Terai.

North Bengal. Chittagong. Fl. minute, cymes pubescent, divaricate, branches slender or filiform. Seeds 2–3, obovoid or globose. 33. **V. oxyphylla**, Wall.—Syn. *V. dubia*, Lawson. Sikkim 1–4,000 ft. Chittagong. Glabrous, leaflets deeply serrate acuminate. Fr. $\frac{1}{4}$ in. diam., seeds 2, oblong $\frac{1}{4}$ in. long. 34. **V. auriculata**, Roxb. (*Cissus*). Chutia Nagpur. Sikkim 3–5,000 ft. Leaflets glabrous above, pubescent beneath. Fr. globose $\frac{3}{8}$ in. diam., seed 1, obliquely ovoid. 35. **V. andamanica**, King in Journ. As. Soc. Beng. LXV. 393. Andamans. Leaflets 3–5, glabrous, thinly coriaceous, with remote shallow teeth. Fr. $\frac{1}{3}$ in. diam., pulp scanty, seed 1.

P. 179 *Leea alata.*—Syn. *L. rubra*, Royle.

" " *L. sambucina.* Chittagong.

" " *L. robusta.* Chittagong. North Kanara.

" 180. *L. herbacea.* Vern. *Thagyanwethan*, Burm. Himalaya from Nepal eastwards 1–5,000 ft. Khasi hills. West Bengal. Chutia Nagpur. Burma.

P. 180. *L. macrophylla*, Roxb. (not Hornemann).

" " Add: 14. **L. compactiflora**, Kurz. Arakan Yoma, Minbu district. Hills east of Toungoo 3–4,000 ft. Attains 12–15 ft., l. bipinnate, leaflets 4–6 in. long, linear to oblong-lanceolate, blunt at the base, serrate. Fl. small, greenish-white, sessile between broad short scaly bracts.

P. 181. *Acer oblongum.* China.

" " *A. lævigatum.* China.

" " Add: 2 (*a*). **A. Schwerinii**, Pax in Engler's Pflanzenreich IV. 163, p. 33. Himalaya.

P. 181. *A. niveum.* Malay Archip.

" " *A. sikkimense.* Yunnan.

" 183. Add: 11 (*a*). **A. molle**, Pax l.c. p. 15.

" " *A. caudatum*, Wall.—Syn. *A. acuminatum*, Wall.; Pax l.c. p. 15.

" " *A. pictum.* Pax l.c. 47 has now adopted the following arrangement: *A. pictum*, Thunb. Japan, China, Manchuria. *A. Lobelii*, Tenore. Southern Italy. *A. lætum*, C. A. Meyer. Western Asia. Himalaya, Yunnan and Central China.

P. 184. *A. Campbellii.* Yunnan.

" 185. *Æsculus indica.* Bark peels off upwards in long strips.

" " *Æ. punduana.* Assam.

" 186. *Allophylus Cobbe.* Bengal. Andamans.

" 187. *Dodonæa viscosa.* Great Coco and Barren Island, common. Sea coast of Burma and the Western Peninsula.

P. 187. *Harpullia cupanioides*, Roxb. See Cooke, Bombay Flora I. 269, under *H. imbricata*, Thwaites

P. 189. *Lepisanthes tetraphylla.* *Kurpa, Lakhandi*, Mar.

" " *L. andamanica.* Myitkyina.

" " *Schleichera trijuga.* *Koshimb*, Mar. Fr. usually echinate, while young, with stout blunt prickles.—Behar. Chutia Nagpur.

P. 190. Add: 2. **Xerospermum glabratum**, Radlk. in: Die Sapindaceen Holländisch Indiens (1877), 23.—Syn. *Cupania glabrata*, Kurz F. Fl. I. 284. Khasi hills. Pegu Yoma, eastern slopes. Tenasserim near the great rapids of the Salween (D. B. April 1859). A middle-sized aromatic tree, l. glabrous, leaflets 2 pair, lanceolate, 4–8 in. long, reticulate veins conspicuous on both sides. Fl. small in terminal and axillary panicles, ♂ and ⚥, sepals 4 or 5, unequal, petals linear-spathulate, densely woolly, stamens 8, filaments villous. My old notes of 1859 say: Ovary of 4 carpels. This would suggest another genus. Materials here not sufficient to decide the point. 3. **X. lævigatum**, Radlk. l.c. Mergui.—Malay Penins. Leaflets 1 pair, very shining.

P. 191. *Sapindus Mukorossi.* Wild on the Arakan Yoma, Minbu district.

" " *Aphania Danura.* Bengal.

" 192. *A. rubra.* Chittagong.

" " Nephelium, read: Ovary pubescent 2–3-lobed.

" 193. *N. stipulaceum.* Travancore. Petals minute, early caducous.

" " Add: 5. A doubtful species is **N. Griffithianum**, Kurz in Journ. As. Soc. Bengal XLIV. 187 and F. Fl. I. 294 (Sapindacea, Griff. Ic. Pl. As. t. 599. I.). Dewangiri, Bhutan 1,500 ft. Dekho valley, Assam. Hills, Upper Burma (Kurz).—Malacca, Singapore. Leaflets 3–4 pairs, oblong, 6–8 in. long, glaucous beneath, the reticulate veins very prominent on both sides. Fr. $1\frac{1}{2}$ in. long, covered with soft conical prickles $\frac{1}{2}$ in. long (fl. not seen). Identified in Fl. Brit. Ind. I. 687 with *N. mutabile*, Blume and by Radlkofer, Die Sapindaceen Holländisch-Indiens with *N. lappaceum.* Griffith in Itinerary Notes 112, no. 168 states: corolla 5-petala, petalis basi bisquamatis, stam. 8, stylus brevis. These are not the characters of *Nephelium*, hence the genus is doubtful.

P. 194. *Meliosma simplicifolia.* Singbhum. Assam. ♀ specimens sent by Smales from Upper Burma (*Paya-ama*, Burm.) are apetalous.

P. 196. *Rhus Cotinus*, lines 14 and 15 from below, read: pedicels elongate after flowering.

P. 197. *R. semialata.* Vern. *Bakia mila*, Nep.
„ 199. *R. insignis.* Sometimes epiphytic, the milky juice raises blisters on the skin.
„ „ Add: 11. **R. khasiana,** Hook. f.; Prain, Bengal Plants 355. Khasi hills. Chittagong. A large tree similar to *R. punjabensis*, differs by a glabrous slender petiole and leaflets incised-serrate.
P. 199. *Pistacia mutica.* Drosh, 4–5,500 ft.
„ 200. Add: 5. **P. cabulica,** Stocks, Baluchistan.
„ „ *Tapiria hirsuta.* Chittagong.
„ „ *Odina Wodier.* Vern. *Jhingan*, *Jigna*, Hind.; *Maredo*, Kattiawar; *Nanum*, Kol.—Andamans.
P. 201. *Spondias mangifera.* Assam. Andamans.
„ 203. The species mentioned under 1 is **Holigarna nigra,** Bourdillon, Ind. Forester XXX. 95. t. 1.
P. 204. *H. Kurzii.* Vern. *Che*, Mergui.
„ 205. *Buchanania latifolia.* Vern. *Sareka*, Gond; *Lunbo*, Burm.
„ 206. *Mangifera indica.* Indigenous in Singbhum.
„ „ *M. sylvatica.* Chittagong.
„ „ Add: 5. **M. longipes,** Griff. Chittagong; Prain, Bengal Plants 351.
„ 207, *Semecarpus Anacardium.* Vern. *Thitsi bo*, Burm.—Behar. Chutia Nagpur. Upper Burma.
P. 209. Add: **S. subspathulatus,** King in Journ. As. Soc. Beng. LXV. 117. Upper Burma. A small tree, branchlets glabrous, l. obovate-oblanceolate, narrowed from the middle into the short petiole. ♂ fl. only known.
P. 210. *Moringa pterygosperma.* Vern. *Damnishekat*, Thana. *M. concanensis.* Vern. *Ranshekat*, Thana.—Karuûl and Kistna districts.
P. 210. Rourea. Fl. small, regular.
„ „ *R. commutata.* Andamans.
„ 211. *R. santaloides.* Fig. 92 in fruit.
„ 216. *Crotalaria Burhia.* Vern. *Ghagri*, Mar.
„ 217. *Indigofera pulchella.* Central Provinces. Chutia Nagpur. Ascends to 7,500 ft. in Jaunsar.
P. 217. *I. Hamiltonii*, Grah.; Ann. Gard. Calc. IX. t. 29. Oudh. Gorakhpur.
P. 218. Add: **I. minbuensis,** Gage in Records Bot. Survey of India III. 40. Arakan Yoma, Minbu district. A shrub, l. simple subsessile, linear mucronulate, pale green, 1½ in. long.
P. 219. *Mundulea suberosa.* *Supti*, Mar.
„ 220. *Millettia glaucescens.* A species near this (*Thinwin*) Wèpon, Upper Burma, April 1902, C. B. Smales. A small tree, 25 ft. high, leaflets 8–10 pair, fl. nearly 1 in. long, lilac, standard pubescent on back, ovary pubescent, fr. unknown.
P. 220. *M. ovalifolia.* Minbu district, Upper Burma.
„ „ *M. Brandisiana.* Minbu district.
„ „ *M. pulchra.* Thayetmyo district (*Swethe*), C. B. Smales.
„ 222. *M. racemosa.* The stipules sometimes hard, spinescent, pods nearly black.—Behar.
P. 222. *M. cana.* Minbu district.
„ „ Add: **Wistaria chinensis,** Sieb. and Zucc. Wild in the Kachin hills N.E. of Myitkyina. Records Bot. Survey of India I. 237.—China. A large climber. fl. large, blue, in terminal racemes, pods thin, coriaceous, dehiscent.
P. 223. *Desmodium Cephalotes.* Chutia Nagpur. Behar. East Bengal. Minbu district, Upper Burma.
P. 223. *D. umbellatum.* Sundriban. Andamans.
„ „ *D. laxiflorum.* Chutia Nagpur. East Bengal.
„ 224. *D. triquetrum.* Andamans.
„ „ *Ougeinia dalbergioides.* Vern. *Tinsa*, Jabalpûr.
„ 225. *Abrus precatorius.* Vern. *Ywe-ngè*, Burm. Sundriban. Andamans near the coast.
P. 225. *Mucuna imbricata.* Subhim. tract, Dehra Dùn to Assam. Singbhum.
„ 226. *M. atropurpurea.* Dehra Dùn.
„ „ *M. pruriens.* Bengal.
„ 227. *Erythrina stricta.* Orissa.
„ „ *E. suberosa.* Vern. *Haruwa*, Jabalpur.
„ „ *E. arborescens.* Vern. *Phaleda*, Nep.
„ 228. *Dioclea reflexa.* Chittagong.
„ „ *Pueraria tuberosa.* Vern. *Dari*, Mar.—Chutia Nagpur.
„ „ *P. Thunbergiana.* Myitkyina, Upper Burma.
„ 230. *Butea frondosa.* Vern. *Mur*, Gond; *Morud*, Kol.
„ „ *B. superba.* Chutia Nagpur.
„ 232. *Flemingia stricta.* Singbhum.
„ „ *F. congesta.* Vern. *Ban-chhai.* Dún.

P. 232. *F. nana.* Singbhum. Minbu district, Upper Burma.
" " *F. involucrata.* East Bengal.
" " Add : **Rhynchosia pseudo-cajan**, Camb. Vern. *Ladā*, Haz. Outer North West Himalaya and Siwaliks, ascending to 7,000 ft. A shrub, softly grey-tomentose with minute yellow glands on l. and calyx. L. 3-foliolate, fl. yellow in short corymbs, pod oblong, 1 in. long, 1–2-seeded, persistently grey-woolly.
P. 233. *Dalbergia Sissoo.* Ann. Gard. Calc. X. t. 34.
" " *D. latifolia.* Ann. X t. 62.
" " **D. sissoides**, Grah.; Ann. X. t. 63; Bourdillon in Ind. For. 1905, 124, may now be regarded as a distinct species. Vern. *Vel-itti* Travancore (*D. latifolia : Kār itti*). In Travancore it grows on the outer hills, up to 2,000 ft. Young foliage bright green, leaflets 5–10, generally 7, pointed at both ends, petiolules ¼–⅓ in. long. The heartwood never has any tint of red.
P. 233. In Ann. Gard. Calc. X. 82 Colonel Prain unites *D. emarginata*, Roxb. with *D. latifolia*.
P. 233. *D. rimosa*, Ann. X. t. 11.—Myitkyina, Upper Burma.
" 234. *D. foliacea*, Ann. X. t. 31. *D. ovata*, Ann. t. 59.
" " **D. obtusifolia**, Prain, Ann. X. t. 58 may be regarded as distinct. Vern. *Moksoma*, Burm. Burma, Upper and Lower. Attains 50 ft., leaflets 5–7, 3–5 by 2–4 in. Fl. greenish white, sweet scented.
P. 234. *D. cultrata*, Ann. X. t. 32. *Collettii*, Ann. X. t. 30. *burmanica*, Ann. X. t. 51. *rubiginosa*, Ann. X. t. 40. *congesta*, Ann. X. t. 43. *Gardneriana*, Ann. X. t. 44. *confertiflora*, Ann. X. t. 28. *velutina*, Ann. X. t. 55. *rostrata*, Ann. X. t. 36. *Kingiana*, Ann. X. t. 37. *tamarindifolia*, Ann. X. 48.—Chittagong.
P. 235. *acaciæfolia*, Ann. X. t. 47. *malabarica*, Ann. X. t. 46. *mimosoides*, Ann. X. t. 25. *multiflora*, Ann. X. t. 18. *coromandeliana*, Ann. X. t. 21. *Melanoxylon*, Ann. X. t. 22. The two last species should stand under A. Trees or erect shrubs.
P. 235. *D. Melanoxylon.* Eastern Tropical Africa, possibly indigénous in the Western Peninsula.
P. 236. *D. paniculata.* Regarding the anatomy of the stem, see Thomas G. Hill in Annals of Botany. XV. 183.
P. 236. *D. lanceolaria.* Ann. X. t. 76. Subhimalayan tract from the Jumna eastwards, rare in the western portion. *D. assamica*, Ann. X. t. 71. *paniculata*, Ann. X. t. 68. *Kurzii*, Ann. X. t. 83.
P. 237. *D. cana*, Ann. X. t. 84. *D. glomeriflora*, Ann. X. t. 6b. *D. sericea*, Ann. X. t. 66. *D. Oliveri*, Ann. X. t. 75. In Ann. Gard. Calc. X. 92. *D. Prazeri* is united with this species. *D. Hemsleyi*, Ann. X. t. 77. *D. Wattii*, Ann. X. t. 78. *D. volubilis*, Ann. X. t. 85. —Behar. Chutia Nagpur. Chittagong.
P. 238. *D. stipulacea*, Ann. X. t. 87. *D. Thomsoni*, Ann. X. t. 13. *D. spinosa*, Ann. X. t. 9.—Sundriban. *D. torta*, Ann. X. t. 42.—Sundriban.
P. 239. *D. parviflora*, Ann. X. t. 8. *D. reniformis*, Ann. X. t. 91.
" " *Pterocarpus dalbergioides*, the Andaman Padauk, is leafless for one or two months between March and May. Its principal associates are: *Terminalia bialata*, *Bombax insigne*, *Sterculia alata*, *Lagerstrœmia hypoleuca*, and in places *Oxytenanthera nigrociliata*. Near creeks which run up into the Padauk bearing tracts *Licuala peltata* and *spinosa* are found. In typical Padauk forests generally a dense underwood 10–30 ft. high of shade-bearing shrubs.
P. 240. *P. Marsupium.* Santal Parganas. Singbhum.
" 242. *Derris scandens.* Bengal.
" " *D. canarensis*, Baker; Cooke, Bombay Flora I. 406 probably is *D. oblonga*, Benth.
P. 243. *D. marginata.* Chittagong.
" " Add: 21 **Derris pulchra**, Gage in Records Bot. Survey India III. 49. Arakan Yoma. Minbu district.
P. 243. *Pongamia glabra.* Andamans.
" " Add: **Ormosia tavoyana**, Prain in Journ. As. Soc. Beng. LXXIII. 46. Vern. *Talaing-zin*, Burm. Tavoy. Leaflets 4–6 in. long, ovate-lanceolate, pod brown polished, 2–3 in. long, seed scarlet.
P. 244. *Sophora Bakeri.* Singbhum.
" " Add: **Dalhousiea bracteata**, R. Grah. Assam. Silhet (*Gopuri*). Naga hills. Cachar. Chittagong. A large shrub, erect or scandent, l. rigid, ovate or elliptic, base sometimes slightly peltate, pet. 1–4, blade 4–12 in. Fl. terminating the long bracteate branches of an axillary inflorescence, bracts and bracteoles in pairs, opposite, nearly orbicular, ½ in. diam., the bracteoles enclosing the buds. Corolla white, longer than bracteoles, stamens 10, free. Pod 3 × 1¼ in., seeds 1–3. *D. paucisperma*, Griff. Notulae IV. 445; Ic. Pl. As. t. 608, Assam is similar and perhaps identical. According to Griffith *D. bracteata* has persistent stipules and a 1-seeded pod, *D. paucisperma* deciduous stipules and 1–3 seeds. A closely allied species, *D. africana*, S. Moore, grows in tropical Africa.
P. 246. *Cæsalpinia Bonducella.* Vern. *Gataran*, Jabalpur.

P. 248. *Mezoneurum cucullatum.* Singbhum.
„ 249. *Poinciana elata* reported to be wild on the hills of the Porbandar State Kathiawár (Vern. *Sidhsaro*).
P. 250. *Hardwickia binata.* Grows best on sandstone or quartzose rocks. Where it is found on Trap, this rock will be found to contain much quartz in veins and nuggets. Some seed is produced annually, but good seed-years occur only at intervals of 4–5 years. The seedlings as a rule are cut back year after year during the hot season, and in dense matting of grass roots or on hard soil, they are generally killed outright. On loose soil and under favourable circumstances, where the taproot can develop easily, so as to reach a moist underground stratum, they gradually gain strength, to live through the fierce heat of the hot season, after having been cut back to the ground during 6–7 years in succession. In such cases well protected Anjan forests have all age classes, from old trees down to young seedlings. See Fernandez in Ind. For. XXIX. 517, H. F. Arbuthnot XXX. 123, and E. D. M. Hooper XXXI. 102.
P. 251. *Dialium* sp. nova is *D. travancoricum*, Bourd. in Ind. For. XXX. 243. Fr. ovoid, $\frac{5}{8}$ in. long, seed one.
P. 251. *Afzelia retusa.* Tenasserim. The Sundriban tree is called *Intsia retusa*, O. Kuntze in Prain, Bengal Plants 445 and *Intsia bijuga*, O. Kuntze, in Prain, Flora of the Sundribans. Records Bot. Survey of India II. 303.
P. 251. Add: **Trachylobium verrucosum**, Oliver. Mergui, probably cultivated. Madagascar. Seychelles. An unarmed tree, leaflets one pair, coriaceous, shining above, very unequal-sided, 3 by $1\frac{1}{2}$ in. Fl. in axillary panicles, ramifications woody. Sepals 5, coriaceous, imbricate. Petals white, 3 or 5, unguiculate, orbicular, with numerous large oil glands, claw linear, as long as blade. Stamens 10, ovary oblique, verrucose, a ring of long hairs at the base, ovules 3–6. One of the trees yielding Gum Copal, worth cultivating.
P. 251. Add: **Crudia Mansoni**, Prain in Journ. As. Soc. Bengal LXXIII. 199. Tavoy. A tree, l. glabrous, imparipinnate, stipules connate at base, leaflets 5, alternate, 6–8 by 2–3 in. Fl. white, in long narrow racemes, calyx-tube short, lobes 4, imbricate, reflexed in fl., petals 0. Ovary shortly stipitate, densely tawny-velvety, style slender. Pod oblong, finely velvety, $2\frac{1}{2}$ by $1\frac{1}{2}$ in.
P. 252. Add: 6. **Humboldtia Bourdilloni**, Prain in Journ. As. Soc. Beng. LXXIII. 200. Travancore, 3,000 ft. A tree, attaining 50 ft. Leaflets 3 pair, sessile, 2–4 in. long, rachis and petiole winged, pod silky, bright crimson, 4 in. long.
P. 253. *Cassia Fistula.*—Syn. *C. rhombifolia*, Roxb.; Wight Ic. t. 269.
„ „ *Cassia nodosa.* Myitkyina, Upper Burma.
„ 254. *C. siamea.* Leaflets sometimes emarginate.
„ „ *C. timoriensis.* South Lushai hills.
„ 255. *Cynometra mimosoides*, Wall. Sundriban. Is separated from *C. ramiflora* by Prain in Records Bot. Survey India II. 303.
P. 255. *C. polyandra.* Assam. Chittagong.
„ 256. *Bauhinia tomentosa.* Minbu district, Upper Burma. Andamans.
„ „ *B. racemosa.* Chutia Nagpur.
„ 257. *B. malabarica.* Pod often straight. Upper Burma.
„ 258. *B. purpurea.* Singbhum. Minbu district, Upper Burma; Gage in Records Bot. Survey of India III. 53.
P. 258. *B. variegata.* Singbhum.
„ „ *B. Vahlii.* Chutia Nagpur.
„ 259. *B. rufa.* South Lushai Hills.
„ „ *B. glauca.* South Lushai Hills.
„ 260. *B. macrostachya.* Chittagong.
„ 261. *Prosopis spicigera.* Behar (Prain, Bengal Plants, 453).
„ „ *Dichrostachys cinerea.* Orissa.
„ „ *Entada scandens.*—Syn. *E. Pursætha*, DC.—Orissa. Singbhum.
„ 262. *Adenanthera pavonina.* Vern. *Thorla-ganj*, Mar.—Chittagong.
„ 263. *Mimosa pudica.* Pinnæ almost digitate.
„ 265. *Acacia Jacquemonti.* Vern. *Kandiari*, Sind.
„ „ *A. Kingii.* Minbu district, Burma.
„ 266. *A. Senegal.* Vern. *Gorad*, Kathiawár.
„ 268. *A. Catechu.* Central Provinces. Chutia Nagpur. Behar.
„ „ *A. Suma.* Vern. *Shenkhair*, Thana. Chutia Nagpur.
„ „ *A. cœsia.* Vern. *Gurdr*, Jabalpúr.—Fl. heads white or pale yellow.—Andamans. Burma (the words *not known from Burma*, should be struck out).
P. 269. *A. pennata.* Vern. *Ramna*, Jabalpúr.—Chutia Nagpur.
„ „ Add: 20 (*a*) **A. canescens**, Graham. Minbu district.
„ „ *A. concinna*, DC. Stamens white, as the buds open, afterwards turning yellow.—Chittagong.
P. 271. *Albizzia procera.* Vern. *Pandrai*, Kol; *Kinhai*, Thana.—Singbhum. Reproduces readily from root-suckers.

P. 271. *A. odoratissima.* Vern. *Taungmagyi*, Tenasserim.—Singbhúm.
„ 272. *A. Lebbek.* Andamans. Mr. J. R. Drummond has kindly informed me that in his opinion the tree indigenous in the Subhimalayan tract of the Punjab is not identical with the cultivated *Albizzia Lebbek.*
„ „ *A. amara.* Orissa. Chittagong.
„ „ *A. stipulata.* Singbhum. South Lushai hills. Chittagong.
„ 274. *Pithecolobium bigeminum.* Myitkyina, Burma.
„ 279. *Prunus brahuica.* Chitral.
„ 281. *P. undulata.* A moderate-sized tree.
„ „ *P. acuminata.* Myitkyina. Burma.
„ 282. *Pygeum Andersoni.*—Syn. *P. lucidum*, Anders. ; Prain, Bengal Plants 464.
„ „ Add : 4 (*a*) A small tree on the hills east of Bhamo 6,500 ft. in dry hill forest (Montague Hill, Febr. 1902), similar to *P. glaberrimum*, no glands on l., pet. 5, linear-oblong, stamens 10, style short. Fr. unknown.
P. 282. *P. acuminatum.* Khasi hills, East Bengal. Burma, Upper and Lower.
„ 283. *Neillia thyrsiflora.* Myitkyina, Burma.
„ „ *Rubus hexagynus.* Chittagong.
„ 287. *Rosa involucrata.* Chutia Nagpur. In Journ. As. Soc. Bengal, LXXIII. 201. Prain maintains *R. Lyellii* as a distinct species, with long peduncled fl. and entire bracts.
P. 290. *Eriobotrya petiolata.* Vern. *Mya*, Nep.
„ 292. *Pyrus Khasiana.* Naga hills. Kachin hills, Burma.
„ „ Add: **P. Kurzii**, Watt ; Prain in Journ. As. Soc. Beng. LXXIII. 203. Sandakphu, Phalut, 11–12,000 ft. A small tree, glabrous, leaflets 4–5 pair, ¾ in. long.
P. 293. *Photinia mollis.* Duars.
„ „ *Pourthiæa arguta.* Duars.
„ 297. *Hydrangea robusta.* Myitkyina, Burma. A shrub or tree.
„ 298. *Dichroa febrifuga.* Myitkyina, Burma.
„ „ *Itea macrophylla.* Kachin hills, Upper Burma.
„ 300. *Parrotia Jacquemontiana.* Vern. *Sha*, Kunawar.
„ 303. *Rhizophora mucronata.* Vern. *Khamo, Bhora*, Beng.
„ 304. *Ceriops Candolleana.* Doubtful whether in the Sundriban. (Prain in Records Bot. Surv. of India II. 306.)
P. 305. *Bruguiera gymnorhiza.* When germinating on the tree, the hypocotyl and radicle of this species as well as of *Rhizophora* break through the pericarp, but while in *Rhizophora* the embryo separates from the fruit and calyx before it falls to the ground, in *Bruguiera* the germinating seed remains longer attached to the fruit and calyx, and the top of the pericarp, crowned by the style, frequently remains attached to the tip of the radicle. The hypocotyl (and radicle) of *B. gymnorhiza* attains 6–12 inches, is green, and the cells are filled with starch. See A. W. Lushington in Ind. For. XXX. 122.
P. 305. *Carallia lucida.* Vern. *Kierpa*, Beng.—Dehra Dún, in swamps. Cooke, Flora of Bombay I. 476, regards *C. lucida*, Roxb. and *C. integerrima*, DC., as distinct species.
P. 307. Add : 1 (*a*) **Terminalia burmanica**, King in Journ. As. Soc. Beng. LXXIII. 204. Sagain, Burma. A tree, young branches densely rusty-tomentose, l. 4–5 by 2½–3 in.
P. 307. *T. belerica.* Vern. *Lupung*, Kol. Add to the footnote : Kanjilal reports glands on seedlings and coppice shoots and occasionally on l. of flowering branches.
P. 308. *T. Chebula.* Vern. *Rola*, Kol.—Chutia Nagpur.
„ „ *T. citrina.* West and North Bengal.
„ 310. *T. pyrifolia.* Upper Burma.
„ „ *T. tomentosa.* Vern. *Hatana*, Kol.
„ 311. *T. Arjuna.* Jammu, Kashmir. Chutia Nagpur.
„ „ *T. Oliveri.* J. W. Oliver informs me that the bark is rich in tannin.
„ 312. *Combretum decandrum.* Bengal. Andamans.
„ „ *C. pyrifolium.* Minbu, Upper Burma.
„ „ *C. trifoliatum*, Vent. Vern. *Sauk*, Burm.
„ 313. *C. acuminatum.* North Bengal. Chittagong.
„ „ *C. flagrocarpum.* East Bengal.
„ „ *C. chinense.* Minbu district, Upper Burma.
„ „ *C. squamosum.* East Bengal.
„ „ *C. ovalifolium.* Chutia Nagpur. Orissa.
„ „ *C. nanum.* Chutia Nagpur.
„ 314. *C. extensum.* Fr. dark red. Chutia Nagpur. Chittagong.
„ „ *Quisqualis indica.* Vern. *Dawè-hmaing*, Burm.
„ „ *Calycopteris floribunda.* The cut stem yields large quantities of watery fluid. Vern. *Kyut-ne-nwè*, Burm.—Orissa.
P. 315. *Lumnitzera racemosa.* Andamans.

P. 315. *Anogeissus pendula*. S. E. Punjab
„ „ *A. latifolia*. Vern. *Dohu*, Hind.; *Hesel*, Gond.—Chutia Nagpur. Behar. Orissa.
P. 315. *A. sericea*. Peduncles frequently bearing leaves and leafy bracts.
„ „ *A. acuminata*. Vern. *Chakwa*, Beng.—Behar. Chutia Nagpur. South Lushai hills.—Prain, Bengal Plants 480, separates *A. lanceolata*, Wall., from *A. acuminata*.—Chittagong. L. narrow lanceolate, bracteoles small, linear, very deciduous.
P. 317. *Eugenia aquea*. Chittagong.
„ „ *E. formosa*. Vern. *Phul-jamb*, Beng.
„ 318. *E. Rama Varma*, Bourdill. in Indian Forester XXX. 147 t. 2.
„ 319. *E. occidentalis*, Bourd. in Ind. For. XXX. 195.
„ „ *E. claviflora*. Myitkyina.
„ „ *E. Wightiana*.—Syn. *Syzygium Wightianum*, Wall.; Wight & Arnott, Prodromus 330.
„ „ P. 321. Add: 32 (*a*) **E. Griffithii**, Duthie, in Fl. Brit. Ind. II. 481. Myitkyina, Burma, Singapore.
P. 321. *E. toddaloides*. South Maratha country, Cooke Bombay Flora I. 490.
„ „ Add: 35 (*a*). **E. praetermissa**, Gage in Ind. For. XXXII. 6. t. 2. Assam. Khasi and Lushai hills. Kendat, Upper Burma. A tree attaining 50 ft., resembling *E. Griffithii*, Duthie, allied to the Malayan *E. chlorantha*, Duthie.
„ 322. *E. polyantha*. Vern. *Mathaka*, Burm.
P. 322. Read: E. petals *as a rule* calyptrate.
P. 323. *E. operculata*. Vern. *Boti-Jamb*. *E. obovata*, Wall., is sometimes regarded as a distinct species.
P. 323. *E. Heyneana*. Chutia Nagpur.
„ „ Add: 58 (*a*). **E. venusta**, Roxb. Vern. *Thabyega*, Burm. Tipperah. Lower Burma. Branchlets white, petals free.
P. 323. Strike out: (*a*) Leaves large, blade over 3 in.
„ 325. *E. macrosepala*. Ahmednagar, Cooke, Bombay Fl. I. 494.
„ „ *E. codyensis*. North Kanara, Cooke, Bombay Fl. I. 494.
„ 326. *Myrtus communis*. Vern. *Mañru*, Pushtu. Panjkora valley, Bajour, 3–3,500 ft. very common, truly wild, attaining 12–15 ft. Fr. eaten. (Barrett Nov. 1908.)
P. 330. *Barringtonia acutangula*. Vern. *Hidjal*, Beng.; *Pivar ingli*, Mar.
„ 333. *Melastoma malabathricum*. Vern. *Paloré*, Mar.
„ „ *Oxyspora paniculata*. Myitkyina, Burma.
„ 334. *Osbeckia stellata*. Chittagong.
„ „ *O. nepalensis*. East Bengal.
„ 336. *Memecylon edule*. Chittagong.
„ 337. *M. cæruleum*. Vern. *Thabye-ôn*, Burm.
„ 338. Add: 2 (*a*). **Lagerstrœmia venusta**. Wall. Irawadi near Thayetmyo. Calyx with 6 linear accessory teeth.
P. 339. *Lagerstrœmia Flos Reginæ*. Vern. *Eik-hmwe*, Upper Burma.—Chutia Nagpur, Prain, Bengal Plants 504.
P. 339. Add: 8 (*a*). **L. hirsuta**, Lam. A doubtful species, based upon t. 22 of Rheede, Hort. Malab. IV.—Malabar.
P. 339. *L. macrocarpa*. Chittagong.
„ 340. *Lawsonia alba*.—Syn. *L. inermis*, Linn., and *L. spinosa*, Linn. Koehne Lythraceæ in Engler, Pflanzenreich IV. 216 p. 270, and Cooke, Bombay Flora I. 511 adopt *L. inermis*.
P. 340. *Sonneratia acida*. Vern. *Lamu*, Burm.—Andamans.
„ 341. *Punica Granatum*. Vern. *Thalè*, Burm.
„ 344. *Casearia tomentosa*. Bengal.
„ „ *C. Vareca*. Tipperah. Chittagong.
„ 345. *Homalium grandiflorum*. Vern. *Taung-thit-yin-bo*, Burm. Mergui.
„ 346. *Tetrameles nudiflora*. Vern. *Ugad*, *Bondsa*, Mar.
„ 348. *Heptapleurum venulosum*. Vern. *Dain*, Hind.—Behar. Singbhum.
„ 351. *Aralia armata*. Myitkyina, Burma.
„ „ *A. foliolosa*. Chittagong.
„ 352. *Acanthopanax aculeatum*. At times climbing.
„ „ *Heteropanax fragrans*. Singbhum.
„ „ Brassaiopsis. A. Leaves undivided *or divided less than half-way down*.
„ 353. *Trevesia palmata*. Vern. *Paw*, Upper Burma.
„ 354. Add: **Woodburnia penduliflora**, Prain in Journ. As. Soc. Beng. LXXIII. 23. Kachin hills between Myitkyina and Sadon, 4,500 ft. A small tree, attaining 15 ft., trunk unbranched, prickly, with a tuft of large digitate l. at the top. Blade 30 in. diam. on a stout pet. 24 in. long, leaflets on broadly winged petiolules. Fl. densely rusty-tomentose, with the stout pedicel 2–2½ in. long, in axillary umbels on long peduncles. Calyx with 7-10 linear-lanceolate segments, petals 5 small, stamens 5, ovary 8–13-celled.

P. 356. *Mastixia arborea.* Bourdillon regards *M. pentandra* as a distinct species with larger and pubescent leaves.
P. 356. ***M. euonymoides*, Prain, Brit. Bhutan, in evergreen forest 1,000 ft. A tree 50, ft. with smooth bark, ramifications of thyrsus clothed with deciduous hairs, fl. 5-merous. Drupe 1 × ½ in., olive green or blackish when ripe.** (Haines 916, specimens received Jan. 1906.)
P. 359. Add: 16 (*a*). **Lonicera Xylosteum,** Linn. Jambatai 5–6,000 ft. (Duthie, Chitral Relief Expedition in Records Bot. Survey of India I. 156). Differs from *L. quinquelocularis* by smaller fl. in pairs on axillary peduncles.
P. 359. *L. asperifolia.* Chitral.
„ 360. Add: 28. **L. Griffithii,** Hook. f. and Thoms. Drosh, Chitral valley, 5–6,000 ft. Climbing on *Quercus Ilex*, l. broadly elliptic to orbicular, blade 2, pet. slender ½ in. long, the uppermost l. almost sessile. Fl. numerous in dense peduncled solitary heads, the bractlets of each whorl of fl. connate, corolla bilabiate, glandular-hairy outside, 1 in. long. Fr. a compound berry ⅜ in. diam. consisting of numerous confluent carpels, edible.
P. 360. *Leycesteria formosa.* From the Ravi eastwards.
„ 362. *Viburnum coriaceum.* Myitkyina.
„ 363. *V. nervosum.* Dir, Mirga, 7–8,000 ft. (Duthie, Chitral Relief Expedition, 156.)
„ 366. *Sarcocephalus Missionis.* Vern. *Atta vanji*, Mal.
„ 368. *Anthocephalus Cadamba.* Assam.
„ „ *Adina cordifolia.* Vern. *Hedu*, Thana; *Manja kadamba*, Mal. and Tam.
„ „ *Nauclea Griffithii.* Peduncles often two or three, shorter than in *N. purpurea*, with 2 pairs of bracts.
P. 369. Stephegyne. Korthals, in a dissertation, printed at Bonn in 1839, established the genus *Mitragyna.* In his great work: Kruidkunde in Verhandelingen over de Natuurlijke Geschiedenis (1839–42) he substituted the name *Stephegyne*, giving a description of the genus and of the Indian *S. parvifolia.* As synonym he gives *Mitragyne*, without however quoting the Bonn dissertation. *Stephegyne* was adopted (as a subgenus of *Nauclea*) by Miquel in his Flora of Nederlandsch Indie (1856), and as a genus in Genera Plantarum and Fl. Brit. Ind. The Index Kewensis however prefers *Mitragyna*, followed by Haviland and Cooke, Flora of Bombay I. 581. Common sense seems to demand the retention of *Stephegyne.* Miquel, Bentham and Hooker doubtless had good grounds for their decision.
P. 370. *Stephegyne parvifolia.* Vern. *Chinna kadamba*, Tam. East Bengal.
„ „ *S. diversifolia.* Fl. heads sometimes orange-coloured. There may be two species in Burma under this name.
P. 371. *Uncaria macrophylla.* North Bengal. Myitkyina.
„ „ *U. sessilifructus.* Myitkyina.
„ „ *U. lævigata.* Kachin hills, Upper Burma.
„ „ Add: 10. **U. homomalla,** Miq. Jaintia and South Lushai hills.—Sumatra.
„ „ *Hymenodictyon excelsum.* East Bengal.
„ 373. *Luculia gratissima.* Myitkyina.
„ „ *Wendlandia exserta.* Behar.
„ „ *W. puberula.* Chamba. Kangra. Tirhut.
„ 374. *W. tinctoria.* Chutia Nagpur. Maimensingh.
„ 375. *Hedyotis scandens.* Myitkyina.
„ „ *Mussænda frondosa.* Vern. *Sarvad, Bhutkes*, Mar.
„ 376. *M. macrophylla.* South Lushai hills. Kachin hills, Upper Burma. Andamans.
P. 376. *M. Roxburghii.* Myitkyina.
„ 378. *Webera corymbosa.* Andamans.
„ 379. *Gardenia latifolia.* Chutia Nagpur. Central Provinces.
„ 380. *G. turgida.* Vern. *Karhar*, Jabalpúr.—Andamans. Minbu, Upper Burma. Mr. A. E. Lowrie reports from Raipúr, Centr. Prov., that, in the hot season, by stroking the stem gently up and down, the whole tree is set vibrating in all its branches and leaves, while other trees around do not show the slightest movement.
P. 380. *G. erythroclada.* Upper Burma.
„ 382. *Randia uliginosa.* Vern. *Pendhru*, Mar.—East Bengal.
„ „ *R. dumetorum.* Vern. *Kaw*, Burm.—Bengal.
„ 383. *R. fasciculata.* Chutia Nagpur.
„ 384. *Hyptianthera stricta.* Bengal. Chutia Nagpur.
„ „ *Petunga Roxburghii.* Sundriban.
„ „ *Diplospora singularis.* Chittagong.
„ „ *D. confusa.* Minbu, Upper Burma.
„ 385. *Canthium didymum.* Behar. Chutia Nagpur.
„ „ *C. glabrum.* Duars. Andamans.
„ 387. *Pavetta indica* (c) *tomentosa*, from the Bias eastwards.
„ 388. *Ixora acuminata.* Chittagong.

P. 389. *I. subsessilis.* South Lushai hills.
„ „ Add: 4 (*a*). **I. Kingstoni,** Hook. fil. Andamans.—Malay Penins. A shrub or small tree, l. shining, glabrous, blade 5–9, pet. ½ in., sec. n. 15–18 pair. Compound cymes dense, 3–4 in. diam., peduncle stout, 1 in. long, calyx-lobes broad, blunt.
P. 388. *I. spectabilis.* Chittagong.
„ „ *I. parviflora.* Vern. *Kau,* Jabalpur.
„ 389. *I. cuneifolia.* Chittagong.
„ „ Add: 18 (*a*). **I. villosa,** Roxb. Sikkim, foot of hills. Assam. Garo, Khasi, and South Lushai hills. Khabaung forests, Pegu. A shrub, branchlets, petioles and cymes pubescent or tomentose, stipules with long filiform points. Corolla-tube 1–1¼ in. long, very slender.
P. 389. *I. undulata.* Behar. Chutia Nagpur.
„ 390. COFFEA. Stipules broad.
„ „ *C. arabica.* Berry crimson.
„ „ *C. liberica.* Berry crimson.
„ „ *C. Jenkinsii.* Kachin hills, Upper Burma.
„ „ *C. bengalensis.* Chutia Nagpúr.
„ 391. *Hamiltonia suaveolens.* Chutia Nagpur. Central Provinces.
„ „ Add: 3. **Pæderia tomentosa,** Blume. Sikkim, to 6,000 ft. Assam. Khasi hills. Upper Burma.—Malay Penins. and Archip. China. Japan. Leaves ovate-lanceolate, blade 3–5, pet. 1–2 in., fr. globose, ¼ in. diam. 4. **P. Cruddasiana,** Prain in Records Bot. Survey of India I. 248. Myitkyina. Similar to 3, fr. ovoid, crowned by acute calyx lobes.
P. 392. Prain in Bengal Plants, 578, regards *Morinda bracteata*, Roxb., as distinct from *M. citrifolia.* River banks and sea face of the Sundriban. Sea coast of the Andamans and Tenasserim.
P. 392. *M. tinctoria.* Vern. *Nipase,* Burm.
„ 394. *Psychotria flavida,* Talbot, Dr. Cooke, Bombay Flora I. 617, regards as a distinct species.
P. 394. *P. adenophylla.* Myitkyina.
„ „ *P. calocarpa.* Kachin hills, Upper Burma.
„ 395. *P. erratica.* Kachin hills, Upper Burma.
„ „ *Chasalia curviflora,* Myitkyina.
„ 396. *Lasianthus Wallichii.* Chittagong. Myitkyina.
„ „ Add: 5 (*a*). **L. pilosus,** Wight. Mergui.—Malay Penins. A shrub or small tree, branchlets, petioles, underside of l. and cymes hirsute with long dark-coloured spreading hairs, outer bracts as long as or shorter than flowers.
P. 397. *L. truncatus.* Orissa.
„ 399. *Vernonia cinerascens.* Punjab Salt range.
„ 401. *Inula cuspidata.* Punjab Salt range.
„ „ *Blumea balsamifera.* Tipperah.
„ 402. *Artemisia vulgaris.* Kachin hills, Upper Burma. Strike out the words: "uppermost linear-lanceolate, entire."
P. 402. *Senecio araneosus.* Myitkyina, Upper Burma.
„ 414. *Mæsa paniculata.* South Lushai hills.
„ 415. *M. dubia,* united with *M. indica* by Cooke in Bombay Flora II. 82.
„ 416. *Myrsine semiserrata.* South Lushai hills.
„ 417. *Embelia viridiflora.* Mahabaleshwar.
„ 418. *Ardisia humilis.* Andamans.
„ 420. *A. crenata.* Kachin hills, Upper Burma.
„ „ *Pimelandra Griffithii.* Kachin hills, Upper Burma.
„ 421. *Antistrophe oxyantha.* South Lushai hills.
„ „ *Ægiceras majus.* Vern. *Chawer,* Sind.
„ 422. *Sideroxylon tomentosum.* From Behar to Orissa.
„ 423. *S. grandifolium.* Vern. *Taw-tha-pwot,* Burm.
„ „ *Chrysophyllum Roxburghii.* Vern. *Thangya,* Burm.
„ 425. *Palaquium Gutta.* See Burn Murdoch in Ind. For. XXXI. 309.
„ 426. *Bassia latifolia.* Vern. *Mhowra,* Mar; *Iru,* Gond.
„ 427. *Reptonia buxifolia.* Drosh, 4,500 ft.
„ 428. DIOSPYROS. Herbert Wright, The Genus *Diospyros* in Ceylon. Annals Royal Gardens Peradeniya II. 1 (1904). Wright states that many species are often polygamous, among those here described: *D. insignis, nilagirica, sylvatica, affinis, Embryopteris.* He also states that the ♀ fl. of the following species are frequently in clusters of 3–6: *insignis, oocarpa, sylvatica, Toposia, Embryopteris.*
P. 430. *D. Chloroxylon.* Vern. *Anduli,* Orissa.
„ 431. *D. microphylla.* Vern. *Thora Kari,* Mal.
„ „ *D. montana.* Central Prov. Bengal. Minbu district, Burma. Travancore, common.—Ceylon. Vern. *Kenda, Kaindu,* Pb.; *Pasend,* N. E. Rajputana.
P. 432. *D. sylvatica.* Chutia Nagpur.

P. 432. 11 is **D. Kanjilali**, Duthie in Ind. For. XXXI. 307 t. 29. Dehra Dùn. Siwalik range. Chanda, Centr. Prov. Santal Parganas. Ganjam. Anantapùr. Bellary.
P. 432. *D. Lotus*, line 21, strike out *in the Punjab and.*
„ 433. According to Wright, l.c. p. 195, *D. affinis* in Ceylon has 6–9–16 stamens in the ♂ fl., while *D. crumenata*, p. 197, has 8–14; the seeds of *affinis* are ovate, wedge-shaped, ¾ in. long, while those of *crumenata* are flattened and elliptic, nearly 2 in. long.
P. 434. *D. assimilis*. Vern. *Karun thali*, Tam.
„ „ *D. Embryopteris*. Bengal.
„ 435. *D. ovalifolia*. Orissa.—Ceylon.
„ „ *D. Bourdilloni*. Vern. *Karun chatthi*, Tam. ♂ fl. read: corolla ovoid-campanulate, tube tomentose outside, glabrous inside, ⅓–½ in. long, lobes spreading.
P. 436. 47. Is a large tree.
„ „ Add: 49. *D. sp. nova*, not named, because specimens are imperfect. Travancore. Evergreen and secondary forests at low elevations (Bourdillon 1323, 1584. Vern. *Kari*). A middle-sized tree, l. glossy on both sides, coriaceous, elliptic-oblong, blade 6–9 by 2–4, pet. ⅓–⅔ in. long. ♀ fl. axillary or on the old wood, sessile, solitary, or in clusters of 2–5, supported by thick round bracts. Calyx thick-coriaceous, on both sides densely velvety, deeply divided into 5 triangular auricled lobes. Corolla tomentose, lobes 5, thick, cohering, staminodes 5. Ovary densely clothed with long hairs, styles 5, glabrous. Fr. a truncate cone with 10 deep furrows, hairy when young, 1¼ in. long, diam. at base 1, at the apex ½ in., supported by the flat thickly-coriaceous calyx with undulating margins. Seeds 10, black, flat, ¼ in. wide and nearly 1 in. long. Embryo ½ in. long, radicle longer than cotyledons. Albumen uniform.
P. 438. *Symplocos Beddomei*. A middle-sized tree, racemes 1–5 in. long, fl. white, fragrant.
P. 439. *S. macrocarpa*. Vern. *Paralei*, Tam.
„ 441. *S. theæfolia*. Haines reports that specimens collected in Sikkim have a curved embryo.
P. 442. *Styrax serrulatum*. Duars. Assam.
„ „ OLEACEÆ omit: *attached to the inner angle.*
„ „ *Nyctanthes arbor tristis*. Vern. *Khirsari*, Gond.
„ 443. *Fraxinus excelsior*. Basin of the Indus.
„ 444. *Fraxinus xanthoxyloides*. Dr. Aug. Henry informs me that *F. dimorpha*, Cosson et Durieu, of Algiers and Morocco, is very closely allied and possibly the same species.
P. 445. *Schrebera swietenioides*. Chutia Nagpur. Orissa.
P. „ *Syringa Emodi*, ascends to 12,000 ft.
„ 446. *Olea cuspidata*. Punjab Salt range.
„ 447. *Olea dioica*. Vern. *Yeddalei*, Tam. (Bourdillon).
„ 449. Add: 2 (*a*). **Jasminum Listeri**, King in Records Bot. Survey of India I. 349. South Lushai and Chittagong hills. A scandent shrub, l. nearly glabrous, lanceolate, blade 3–5 by 1¼ in., sec. n. prominent beneath, corolla white, lobes 6.
P. 449. *J. pubescens*. From the Ravi eastwards.
„ „ *J. Rottlerianum*. Behar. Chutia Nagpur.
„ 450. *J. coarctatum*. Chittagong.
„ „ *J. scandens*. Myitkyina.
„ „ *J. decussatum*. Myitkyina.
„ „ *J. arborescens*. Behar. Chutia Nagpur.
„ „ *J. laurifolium*. Chittagong.
„ „ *J. anastomosans*. South Lushai hills.
„ 452. *J. dispermum*. From the Ravi eastwards.
„ 453. *Salvadora persica*. Western Behar, Prain, Bengal Plants, 663.
„ „ *S. oleoides*. Gujarat.
„ „ *Azima tetracantha*. Orissa.
„ 455. *Carissa spinarum*. Vern. *Kau*, Burm.—Andamans.
„ 456. *C. paucinervia*. Behar. Prain, Bengal Plants, 669.
„ „ *C. macrophylla*.—Syn. *C. inermis*, Vahl; Cooke, Bombay Flora II. 125.
P. 456 **Melodinus**, Species 15–20. India to the Pacific islands.
„ „ *M. monogynus*. North Bengal.
„ 457. *Rauwolfia serpentina*. Bengal.
„ „ Add: 1 (*a*). **R. chinensis**, Hemsl. South Lushai hills.—China. Nearly allied to 1, sec. n. faint, fl. ½–⅔ in. long.
P. 457. *Gynopogon stellatum* is *Alyxia stellata*, Roem. and Schult.; Fl. Brit. Ind. III. 636.
P. 458. *Plumeria acutifolia*. Vern. *Tayok-saga*, Burm.
„ 459. *Alstonia scholaris*. Bengal. Assam. Andamans.
„ „ *Holarrhena antidysenterica*. Vern. *Kala Kura*, Mar.—Bengal.
„ 460. *Wrightia tinctoria*. Vern. *Pandra Kura*, Mar.
„ 461. *Wrightia coccinea*. Chittagong.
„ 462. *Vallaris Heynei*. From the Ravi eastwards. Myitkyina.

P. 462. *Pottsia cantonensis.* Myitkyina.
" " *Nerium odorum.* Aravali range. S. E. Punjab.
" " *Strophanthus Wallichii.* Chittagong.
" 464. *Aganosma elegans*, G. Don; Wight Ic. t. 1304.
" 465. *Ichnocarpus frutescens.* From the Jhelam eastwards. Jabalpur.
" 467. *Cryptolepis Buchanani.* Assam. Bengal.
" " *Periploca Hydaspidis.* Punjab Salt range.
" " *Periploca calophylla.* From the Jhelam eastwards.—Myitkyina.
" 468. *Hemidesmus indicus.* Sundriban.
" " *Holostemma Rheedii.* Chutia Nagpur. Minbu district, Burma.
" " *Sarcostemma brevistigma.* Chutia Nagpur.
" " *Dregea volubilis.*—Syn. *Marsdenia volubilis*, T. Cooke, Bombay Fl. II. 166.
" " *Dregea angustifolia.* North Bengal.
" 469. *Dœmia extensa.* Outer Himalaya, ascending to 4,000 ft. Jabalpur.
" " *Raphistemma pulchellum.* Upper Burma.
" " *Gymnema hirsutum.* Chutia Nagpur.
" " *G. acuminatum.* Chittagong.
" " *G. tingens.* Behar. Minbu district.
" 470. *Marsdenia tenacissima.* Jabalpur.
" " *M. Roylei.* Chamba.
" 471. *M. tinctoria.* Chittagong.
" " *Calotropis gigantea.* Vern. *Akauwa*, Jabalpur.—Sundriban, sea-face.
" 472. *Leptadenia reticulata.* Minbu district.
" 475. *Strychnos Wallichiana.* Chittagong.
" 476. *Gelsemium elegans.* Myitkyina.
" " *Fagrœa obovata.* Assam.
" 477. *F. morindæfolia.* A tree 50 ft. high, Kurz, Report on the Andamans, 43.
" 478. *Cordia Myxa.* Vern. *Gidora*, Sind.—Bengal.
" 479. *C. Wallichii.* Chutia Nagpur.
" " *C. monoica.* Orissa.
" " The species mentioned under No. 8 may possibly be **C. Clarkei**, Brace, in Prain, Bengal Plants, 714, described as a large tree. East Bengal. Chittagong. C. B. Clarke's 8088 is from Maimansingh, not from the Khasi hills.

P. 481. *Ehretia aspera*, Roxb., is regarded as a distinct species by Cooke, Bombay Flora II. 204.

P. 482. *Tournefortia viridiflora.* Chittagong.

" 483. Add: 1 (*a*). **Erycibe albiflora,** Hallier; Prain in Journ. As. Soc. Bengal LXXIII. 14. Sikkim 1–6,000 ft. Assam. Khasi hills. Silhet. A large climber, stems over 50 ft. long, branches and branchlets angled, l. glabrous on both surfaces. Fl. in narrow but lax terminal panicles, corolla white, ½ in. across.

P. 483. Cooke, Bombay Flora II. 226, regards *E. Wightiana* as a variety of *E. paniculata.*
" " *E. lævigata.* Yunnan.

" 484. Add: 10 (*a*). **E. citriniflora,** Griff.; Prain in Journ. As. Soc. Bengal LXXIII. 17. Sea-coast near Tavoy and Mergui. A small tree, branches terete, l. coriaceous, quite glabrous, obovate-lanceolate. Fl. in dense subsessile axillary rusty-pubescent cymes, corolla creamy-yellow within, ⅓ in. across.

P. 484. *Rivea ornata.* North Bengal. Duars. A large spreading shrub, Prain, Bengal Plants 739.

P. 484. *R. hypocrateriformis.* Vern. *Boddi*, Haiderabad. Leaves, after boiling, eaten in times of famine.

P. 485. *Argyreia argentea.* Chittagong.

" " Add: 15 (*a*). **A. Burneyi,** Gage in Records Bot. Survey of India III. 78. Upper Burma. A scandent shrub, branches, petioles and underside of l. clothed with dense soft silky grey tomentum, l. cordate, blade 5–6, pet. 2–2½ in. long.

P. 485. *A. tiliæfolia.*—Syn. *Stictocardia tiliæfolia*, Hallier f.; Prain, Bengal Plants, 740.
" " *A. splendens.* Chittagong.

" 486. Add: 15 (*a*). **Lettsomia campanuliflora,** Gage in Records Bot. Survey of India III. 79. Minbu district, Upper Burma. A scandent shrub.

P. 487. *Porana paniculata.* Vern. *Senga*, Jabalpur.—From the Ravi eastwards. East Bengal. South Lushai hills.

P. 487. *P. racemosa.* South Lushai hills.

" " Add: 1 (*a*). **Ipomœa longiflora,** R. Br. Sundriban. Konkan and Kanara near the coast.—Coasts of South East Asia, Australia, Polynesia. L. often lobed, corolla-tube wide-funnel-shaped. *I. glaberrima*, given by Prain in Journ. As. Soc. Bengal, LXIII. (1894) 102, from the Sundriban is referred to *I. longiflora*, R. Br. in Bengal Plants and in the Flora of the Sundriban (1908). 1 (*b*) **I. Yomæ,** Kurz. Pegu Yoma. Tenasserim. Branchlets, petioles, underside of l. and sepals in fl. appressed pilose. Corolla white, tube straight, 5–6 in. long. 1 (*a*) and 1 (*b*) are included under *Ipomœa grandiflora* and *trichosperma* in Fl. Brit. Ind. IV. 198.

P. 487. *I. bona nox.*—Syn. *Calonyction bona nox*, Boj.; Prain, Bengal Plants, 788; *C. speciosum*, Choisy; Cooke, Bombay Flora, II. 252.
P. 488. *I. illustris*, Prain, as a distinct species in Bengal Plants, 785.
„ „ *I. Turpethum*, R. Br.—Syn. *Operculina Turpethum*, Manso; Prain, Bengal Plants, 781.
P. 488. *I. biloba.*—Syn. *I. Pes Capræ*, Sweet; Prain, Bengal Plants, 786.—Andamans.
„ „ *Breweria cordata.*—Syn. *Bonamia semidigyna*, Hallier f.; Bengal Plants, 726.
„ „ *B. latifolia.* Kathiawar.
„ 489. *Solanum verbascifolium.* Vern. *Arasa*, Bengal.—From the Ravi eastwards. Assam. Bengal.
P. 489. *S. torvum.* Assam.
„ „ *S. indicum.* South Lushai hills.
„ 490. *S. gracilipes.* Salt range.
„ „ *S. ferox*, var. *inermis*, Prain. Myitkyina. No trace of prickles, needle-like hairs on fr. less numerous.
P. 490. *Withania somnifera.* Chamba, common at 5,000 ft., G. A. Gammie in Records Bot. Survey of India, I. 205. Minbu district, Upper Burma.
P. 490. *W. coagulans.* The locality: Sutlej valley at 8,000 ft. requires verification.
P. 491. *Wightia gigantea.* Assam. Khasi hills. Ruby Mines district.
„ 492. *Tecoma undulata*, S. E. Punjab. Northern Rajputana.
„ 493. *Dolichandrone Lawii.* Behar.
„ 494. *D. stipulata.* Andamans.
„ „ *D. Rheedii.* Upper Burma.
„ „ *Heterophragma sulfureum.* Minbu district, Upper Burma.
„ „ *Pajanelia Rheedii.* Vern. *Arlantha*, Mal. Travancore. Chittagong.
„ 495. *Stereospermum chelonoides.* Assam.
„ „ *S. suaveolens.* Behar.
„ „ *S. glandulosum.* South Lushai hills.
„ „ *S. xylocarpum.*—Syn. *Radermachera xylocarpa*, K. Schum.; Cooke, Bombay Flora, II. 888.
P. 496. *Oroxylum indicum.* From the Ravi eastwards. Assam. South Lushai hills. Andamans.
P. 497. *Thunbergia grandiflora.* Behar. South Lushai hills. Chittagong. Upper Burma.
P. 497. *T. coccinea.* Assam. Myitkyina, Burma.
„ „ *Acanthus ilicifolius.* Andamans.
„ 498. *Barleria longiflora.* Orissa.
„ „ *B. strigosa.* Minbu district, Burma.
„ „ *Justicia Gendarussa.* Assam. Bengal.
„ „ *Adhatoda Vasica.* Vern. *Bakās, Vasaka*, Beng.—Bengal. Centr. Prov.
„ 499. *Dædalacanthus nervosus.* From the Ravi eastwards.
„ „ *D. purpurascens.* Minbu district, Burma.
„ 500. *Strobilanthes pectinatus.* Flowers once in 12 years. Osmaston in Ind. For. XXX. 195.
P. 501. *Phlogacanthus thyrsiflorus.* From the Ravi eastwards. Assam.
„ „ *P. curviflorus.* Assam. Chittagong. Myitkyina, Burma.
„ „ *P. tubiflorus.* South Lushai hills.
„ 502. *Lantana aculeata.* Often climbing.
„ 504. *Vitex Negundo.* Sundriban.
„ „ *V. trifolia.* Bengal. Chittagong.
„ „ *V. pubescens.* East Bengal. Chittagong.
„ „ *V. Leucoxylon.* Sontal Parganas. Andamans.
„ 506. *Tectona grandis.* Regarding Teak in evergreen forest, see Bruce in Ind. For. XXIX. 20. Brandis, ibidem, 187, Burn-Murdoch. XXX. 460, and Oliver, XXXI. 417.—Coppice shoots in Jabalpúr 3 years old, 18 ft. high, Hole in Ind. For. XXX. 585.
P. 506. *Holmskioldia sanguinea.* Chutia Nagpur.
„ 507. *Clerodendron Phlomidis* (not *phlomoides*), Cooke, Bombay Flora II. 481. Vern. *Gharait*, Sind.
P. 507. *C. infortunatum.* South Lushai hills. Chittagong. Andamans. In Travancore this sp. and *C. serratum* come up in large masses in places where fires have been kept out.
P. 507. *C. serratum.* Chittagong.
„ „ *C. squamatum.* Andamans.
„ 508. *Gmelina arborea.* Assam. Central Bengal. South Lushai hills. Chittagong. Andamans.
P. 510. *Premna bengalensis.* Chittagong.
„ 511. *P. latifolia.* Jabalpur. Orissa.
„ „ *P. milleflora.* Myitkyina.

P. 511. *P. herbacea.* Behar. Myitkyina.
„ „ *Callicarpa arborea.* Vern. *Bormalla*, Beng.—Assam.
„ 512. *Caryopteris Wallichiana.* Tirhūt.
„ 513. *C. paniculata.* Myitkyina.
„ „ *Sphenodesme unguiculata.* Andamans.
„ 514. *Symphorema polyandrum.* Orissa.
„ 516. *Plectranthus ternifolius.* Assam. Maimansingh. Chutia Nagpur.
„ 516. *Pogostemon Patchouli.* Regarding the plants which yield this perfume see Prain in Journ. As. Scor. Beng. LXVI. 519.
„ 517. Add: **Perowskia atriplicifolia**, Benth. Baluchistan. Kuram valley. Afghanistan. Drosh. Iskardo. Karakorum range. Lahaul. A gregarious undershrub with a strong lavender scent, covering large areas in the Chitral valley to the exclusion of other vegetation (Barrett). Fl. purple, sometimes white, in large hairy terminal panicles, calyx tubular, densely clothed with long silky hairs, upper lip nearly entire, lower 2-dentate. Corolla bilabiate, upper lip 4-lobed. Stamens 2, anther-cells parallel, stigma with 2 broad lobes.
P. 517. *Pisonia aculeata.* Orissa.
„ „ *Pisonia excelsa.* A tree with a short thick stem, up to 3 ft. diam. and soft wood, filled with a sweet juice, which is a favourite fodder of elephants.
P. 518. *Deeringia celosioides.* From the Chenab eastwards. Central Bengal.
„ 519. *Haloxylon recurvum.* Vern. *Lanakhar.* For Punjab plains substitute S. W. Punjab.
P. 519. *Suæda nudiflora.* Orissa.
„ 520. *Polygonum molle.* Vern. *Totnai*, Nep. Large panicles of white fl.
„ 521. *Calligonum polygonoides.* East as far as Hissar and northern Jaipūr.
„ 522. *Aristolochia Roxburghiana.*—Syn. *A. Tagala*, Chamisso in Linnæa, VII. 207 (the older name); Gage in Records Bot. Survey of India III. 97.—China. Philippines.
P. 522. *A. indica.* Burma.
„ „ *A. saccata.* Chittagong.
„ 527. *Cryptocarya amygdalina*, Nees—Syn. *C. floribunda*, Nees; Prain, Bengal Plants, 897.—Assam.
P. 528. *Dehaasia* sp. (Haines 550). Haines informs me that he has obtained fl. which are similar to those of *Cinnamomum Cecicodaphne*, anthers 4-celled.
P. 528. *Beilschmiedia Bourdilloni.* Fr. ellipsoid, 1½ by ¾ in., blue, peduncle red.
„ 529. *Beilschmiedia assamica.* South Lushai hills.
„ 531. *Alseodaphne petiolaris.* South Lushai hills.
„ 532. *Phœbe attenuata.* Kachin hills, Burma, 2–5,000 ft.
„ 533. *Cinnamomum obtusifolium.* Assam.
„ 535. *Actinodaphne sikkimensis.* Myitkyina.
„ 536. *Litsæa sebifera.* Andamans.
„ 540. **LINDERA**, Species 60. Eastern Asia and North America.
„ 540. *L. assamica.* Kachin hills. Burma.
„ 544. *Daphne oleoides.* Vern. *Churing*, Chitral.
„ 545. *D. pendula.* Pegu. Myitkyina.
„ 548. Identification of *Loranthaceæ* by their leaves. A. W. Lushington in Ind. For. XXVIII. 56.
„ 548. *Loranthus heteranthus.* Chittagong.
„ „ *L. pentapetalus.* Chittagong.
„ 549. *L. terrestris.* Khasi hills.
„ „ *L. cordifolius.* Behar.
„ „ *L. longiflorus.* Vern. *Betungli.* Thana.
„ 550. *Loranthus longiflorus* is known to grow on the following genera and species: *Bombax, Shorea robusta, Melia, Mangifera indica, Buchanania, Bauhinia, Inga dulcis, Acacia Catechu, Albizzia, Heritiera, Terminalia, Anogeissus latifolia, Adina cordifolia, Stepheygyne parviflora, Bassia latifolia, Diospyros, Mallotus philippinensis, Ficus religiosa, Quercus dilatata.* A. E. Lowrie reports from Raipur, Central Provinces, that nearly all Mowah trees in that district had been badly attacked and that large numbers were being killed by *Loranthus*, this or other species.
P. 551. *L. involucratus.* Chittagong. Myitkyina.
„ 552. *Viscum monoicum.* Behar. Chutia Nagpur.
„ „ *V. articulatum.* Vern. *Harmore*, Thana.—Chutia Nagpur.
„ 553. *Santalum album.* As stated by me in Ind. For. XXIX. 3, Mr. John Scott in 1871 established the fact that *Santalum album* is a parasite on the roots of numerous species. In connection with the Spike disease, the life history of Sandal has lately been carefully studied. Mr. Barber (Ind. For. XXVIII. 340) drew special attention to its being a root parasite, M. Rama Rao (Ind. For. XXIX. 386 and XXX. 248, 397) examined its attachment to the roots of about 70 species, on which it lives. Mr. Barber (Ind. For. XXX. 545 and XXXI. 189) investigated the structure of the haustoria, by which the Sandal tree takes up water, mineral and other substances

from the roots of the foster plant, finally Dr. Butler and Mr. Barber have investigated the nature of the Spike disease (Ind. For. XXIX.).

P. 554. *Osyris arborea.* A species, which occurs Trans-Indus and in Baluchistan, may possibly be distinct.

P. 558. *Euphorbia Nivulia.* The central sessile involucre sometimes fertile (Haines).

„ 558. *E. neriifolia.* Orissa, wild, in rocky places (Prain, Bengal Plants 923).

„ „ *E. antiquorum.* Andamans.

„ 559. *Buxus sempervirens*, var. *microphylla.* A dwarf shrub in North East Kumaon and West Nepal, 11–12,000 ft. Also in China and Japan.

„ 560. *Bridelia retusa.* Assam.

„ „ *B. burmanica.* Arakan Yoma, Minbu district.

„ „ *B. stipularis.* South Lushai hills.

„ „ *B. pubescens.* Kachin hills, Burma.

„ 561. *Cleistanthus collinus.* Andamans.

„ „ *C. patulus.* Orissa.

„ 562. *Andrachne cordifolia.* Chitral.

„ 563. *Baccaurea sapida.* Andamans.

„ „ *Aporosa oblonga.* South Lushai hills. Upper Burma.

„ 564. *Antidesma Ghæsembilla.* Andamans.

„ „ *A. Bunius.* South Lushai hills.

„ 565. *A. velutinum.* Chittagong.

„ „ *Sarcococca pruniformis.* Himalaya, 5–10,000 ft.

„ 566. *Daphniphyllum himalayense.* Vern. *Lal Chandan*, Nep.—Upper Burma.

„ 568. *Breynia patens.* Chutia Nagpur. Orissa.

„ 569. *Sauropus trinervius.* Brit. Bhutan 1,000 ft. A small tree, l. 2–4 in. long, stipules subulate, conspicuous.

P. 570. *Phyllanthus reticulatus.* Vern. *Mukhru*, Jabalpúr.—Assam. Bengal. Andamans.

P. 571. *P. albizzioides.* Minbu district. Burma.

„ „ *P. Clarkei.* Brit. Bhutan 600–1,500 ft. Branchlets deciduous, leaf blade ½–1 in. long.

P. 573. *Glochidion Helferi.* Andamans.

„ „ *G. zeylanicum.* Vern. *Kambalu*, Mal.

„ 576. Croton. ♀ fl. usually at the base.

„ 577. *C. oblongifolius.* Assam. South Lushai hills.

„ „ *C. Joufra.* Chittagong.

„ „ *C. Tiglium.* Vern. *Lepcha Bis*, Nep.—Truly wild in British Bhutan above 5,000 ft., in forests remote from any cultivation (Haines).

P. 578. *Givotia rottleriformis.* Vern. *Vandarlei*, Tam.

„ 582. *Gelonium multiflorum.* Myitkyina.

„ 583. *Baliospermum axillare.* Central Provinces.

„ „ Add: **Endospermum chinense**, Benth.; Prain, Bengal Plants, 946. Chittagong.—Malay Penins. Hong Kong. A tree, l. alternate, coriaceous, entire, hoary or almost silvery beneath, broadly ovate, obtuse, blade 3–7, pet. 1½–4 in., basal n. 3–5. Fl. diœcious, in simple spikes or racemes, ♂ clustered, subsessile, ♀ solitary, pedicelled, petals 0. Ovary 2-celled, ovule 1 in each cell. Fr. tomentose, nearly ½ in. diam.

P. 585. *Excœcaria Agallocha.* Schimper, Indo-Mal. Strandflora 85, reports having seen it in Ceylon on short stilts, similar to those of *Bruguiera.*

P. 587. Alchornea, fl. on simple or panicled unisexual spikes or racemes.

„ „ *A. rugosa.* South Lushai hills.

„ 588. *Mallotus Roxburghianus.* Behar.

„ „ *M. nepalensis.* Myitkyina.

„ 589. *M. muricatus.* Courtallum.

„ „ *M. polyneurus.* Peduncle leaf-opposed.

„ 590. *M. philippinensis.* Assam. Andamans.

„ 592. *Macaranga Roxburghii.* Andamans.

„ „ *Cleidion javanicum.* Assam.

„ 593. *Homonoia riparia.* Chittagong.

„ 595. *Holoptelea integrifolia.* S. E. Punjab.

„ „ *Celtis australis.* Vern. *Binju*, Chitral. Not often planted in the plains of the Punjab.

P. 596. *C. tetrandra.* Travancore, 3–6,000 ft. Attains 50 ft, 1 ft. diam.

„ „ *C. cinnamomea.* Travancore, up to 7,000 ft.

„ 597. *Trema orientalis.* Vern. *Ami*, Mal.

„ „ *T. politoria.* Vern. *Andia*, *Majni*, Jabalpur.

„ 599. *Ficus subulata.* South Lushai hills.

„ 601. *F. Dalhousiæ.* Travancore.

„ „ *F. mysorensis.* Myitkyina.

„ „ *F. Rumphii.* Sundriban.—Usually begins as an epiphyte.

P. 602. *F. infectoria*. Chutia Nagpúr. Sundriban. Chittagong. Andamans.
„ 603. *F. retusa*. Sundriban.
„ „ *F. glabella*. Chittagong.
„ 606. *F. hispida*. Andamans.
„ „ *F. semocarpa*.—Syn. *F. laminosa*, Hardw.; Prain, Bengal Plants, 982. In January 1905 Kanjilal found in the valley of the Palain river, Garhwal, on the water-edge, in a very shady place, a remarkable specimen with lanceolate opposite l. narrowed into a very short pet. and prominent lanceolate stipules, but 12 ft. high and 15 in. girth, with the characters of *F. semocarpa*, but in habit approaching F. *hispida*.
P. 606. *F. Cunia*. Bengal.
„ 607. *F. palmata*. Chitral, common (*Kāwit*).
„ 608. *F. hirta*. South Lushai hills.
„ „ *F. pyriformis*. Chittagong.
„ 609. *F. scandens*. Jabalpur. Chutia Nagpur. Chittagong.
„ „ *F. lævis*. Chittagong.
„ „ *F. glomerata*. Central Provinces.
„ 610. *Allæanthus Kurzii*. South Lushai hills.
„ 612. *Artocarpus Lakoocha*. Vern. *Thini pilavu*, Tam.—Bengal. South Lushai hills.
„ 612. *Morus alba*. Vern. *M'răch*, Chitral.
„ 614. *Broussonetia papyrifera*. See W. H. Craddock in Ind. For. XXVI. 613.
„ 615. *Streblus asper*. Vern. *Majni*, Jabalpur.—Central Provinces. Andamans.
„ 617. *Bœhmeria macrophylla*. Assam. Kachin hills, 2–2,500 ft.
„ 618. *Sarcochlamys pulcherrima*. Minbu district. Burma.
„ „ *Debregeasia hypoleuca*. Punjab Salt range.
„ 619. *Juglans regia*. Vern. *Birbōgh*, Chitral.
„ „ *Platanus orientalis*. Not now cultivated in Kashmir, the existing trees are mostly old. (J. R. Drummond.)
P. 620. *Myrica Nagi*. Probably not indigenous in the Punjab Himalaya.
„ 621. *Casuarina equisetifolia*. From a paper by E. R. Murray on the Casuarina plantations Nellore (Ind. For. XXXI. 475) it appears that in that district the yield per acre per annum is under 2½ tons.
P. 625. *Quercus Ilex*. Vern. *Banj*, Chitral.
„ 626. *Q. incana*. Salt range, above 3,500 ft., rare.
„ 629. *Q. Lindleyana*. Arakan Yoma.
„ 632. *Q. dealbata*. Minbu district, Upper Burma.
„ 633. Add: To section V. probably belong 2 imperfectly known species: 38. **Q. Listeri**, King, Ann. II. t. 82. Syn. *Q. Jenkinsii*, Benth. in Hook. Ic. Pl. t. 12–13. Upper Assam. L. coriaceous, entire, acuminate, base acute, upper surface glabrous, shining, lower pale, minutely pubescent, blade 10–14, pet. 1½–2 in. ♂ fl. in narrow erect axillary panicles, the branches stiff, ½–¾ in. long, nearly at right angles on the rachis. ♀ fl. in clusters of 3, on stout short simple spikes. Acorns supposed to belong to this, resemble those of *Q. lanceæfolia*. 39. **Q. Jenkinsii**, Benth. in Hook. Ic. Pl. t. 1212. Upper Burma. A doubtful species, cf. King, Ann. II. 89.
P. 636. *Salix acmophylla*. Vern. *Budka*, Sind.
„ 640. *Populus ciliata*. Mirga, Chitral 7,200 ft.
„ „ Add: 3 (*a*). **P. Jacquemontiana,** Dode in Extraits d'une Monographie du Genre *Populus*, p. 60, Paris 1905. North West Himalaya. Differs from *P. ciliata* by pubescent capsules. The 2 species mentioned under *P. ciliata* have now been named as follows: 7. **P. Gamblei,** Dode, l.c. 63, the species mentioned by Gamble, Ind. Timb. ed. II. 690. British Bhutan, 1–4,000 ft. Leaves variable, those of the normal form with a straight, not cordate base, repand-serrate, teeth large, those of the large-leaved form cordate, evenly serrate, blade 8–10, pet. 2–3 in. long, 2 large glands at base of leaf. Bracts of ♂ fl. lanceolate, ⅛ in. long, nearly entire, not caducous, edges densely ciliate with long silky hairs. Capsule very narrowly ovoid, 3 times as long as broad, disk scarcely toothed. 8. **P. glauca,** Haines MSS. From Nepal to Bhutan, 7,500–10,000 ft., chiefly on the crest of ridges, but not common. Attains 50 ft. and 5½ ft. in girth, branchlets with prominent leaf-scars. L. glabrous, very glaucous beneath, nerves and petioles red. Fl. ♀ or ⚥, male not yet found, rachis and pedicels woolly. Bracts from elliptic to orbicular, ⅓–½ in. long, laciniate and fimbriate. Disk large, unequally 3–7-fid, stamens usually 1–4, sometimes more, anthers red. Capsule tomentose, 3–4-valved.
P. 641. *Dracæna angustifolia*. Lt.-Col. Prain informs me that *D. ensifolia*, Wall., is a distinct species of British Bhutan, Assam, the Khasi, Naga and Lushai hills, and the Kachin hills of Upper Burma. *D. angustifolia*, Roxb., he regards as a littoral species. See Kurz F. Fl. Burma II. 543 and Prain in Records Botanical Survey of India I. 363.
P. 641. *Smilax macrophylla*. Andamans.
„ 646. *Phœnix* sp. No. 11. Endosperm ruminate, embryo dorsal (Rogers).
„ 647. *Pinanga gracilis*. Kachin hills, Upper Burma.

P. 648. *Nipa fruticans.* The midrib of leaflets on the underside has (attached by the middle) a number of soft linear brown scales.
P. 650. *Plectocomia macrostachya.* The range of mountains mentioned in connection with this and other species in this book, and called *Bithoko* in my time, separates the Yunzalin from the Metharauk and further south the Yunzalin from the Salween river. (See Map appended to Selections from Records Govt. of India, Foreign Dept. XXIX. 1861). Mr. Manson informs me that the correct name is Bu-so-kho.
P. 650. DÆMONOROPS. Leaf-rachis mostly produced into a long flagellum.
" " *D. Manii.* Leaf-sheaths sparingly armed, spines short, recurved.
" " *D. Kurzianus,* Becc. Pegu. Tenasserim. Leaves dark green.
" " Add: **Plectocomiopsis geminiflorus,** Becc. Tenasserim.
" 651. *Calamus arborescens.* Bassein. Pegu.
" 653. *C. viminalis.* Mandalay.
" " *C. longisetus.* Vern. *Khabaung* or *Thabaung,* Burm. G. Rogers reports an erect species on the Andamans, otherwise similar to *C. longisetus.*
P. 653. *C. Doriæi.* Mandalay.
" " *C. andamanicus.* Leaflets usually alternate.
" 654. *C. palustris.* Less armed than *C. latifolius,* short scattered spines on leaf-rachis.
P. 654. Add: The following three climbing imperfectly-known kinds, the leaf-rachis without flagellum, are according to G. Rogers exported as rattans from the Andamans: 35. **C. pseudorivalis,** Becc. Vern. *China bet.* Leaflets equidistant, leaf-sheaths unarmed, saccate at the top. Stems 50–80 ft. long, canes without sheaths $\frac{1}{2}$–$\frac{3}{4}$ in. diam., split readily, used for cane furniture. 36. A cane also called *China bet,* but leaf-sheaths armed with numerous broad stiff flat spines up to $\frac{3}{4}$ in. long. 37. Vern. *Safed Kupri.* Leaflets fascicled, does not split, not used for making cane furniture.
P. 654. *Korthalsia laciniosa.* G. Rogers reports a second species from the Andamans. Ochrea (ligule) 1–2 in. long, closely clasping the stem, leaves, leaflets and spikelets smaller, fr. much larger than that of *K. laciniosa.*
P. 655. *Wallichia densiflora.* Assam.
" 655. *Nannorhops Ritchieana.* Vern. *Patha,* S. W. Punjab.
" 656. *Livistona speciosa.* Chittagong.
" " *Licuala peltata.* Fr. orange.
" " *L. spinosa.* Trunk smooth. Fr. red, nearly globose, $\frac{1}{4}$ in. diam. (Rogers).
" 659. *Pandanus Leram.* Discovered and described by Nicolas Fontana in 1778. Aërial roots 8–10 ft. long.
P. 667. Add: **Phyllostachys,** No. 4. Hills north of Papūn, generally near streams, F. B. Manson, April 1905. Vern. *Bawa,* Burm.; *Mèpwè,* Kar. Single-stemmed, but forming large dense patches. Culms 12–20, sometimes up to 30 ft. Internodes 5–9 in. long, 1 in. diam. L. often apparently in pairs, 4–5 by $\frac{1}{2}$ in., pet. slender, $\frac{1}{4}$ in. long, ligule with deciduous bristles, n. 36–40 on $\frac{1}{4}$ in., transverse veins forming squares and rectangles with the nerves. Leaves similar to *Phyllostachys* No. 3.
P. 672. *Gigantochloa macrostachya.* A further examination of the fl. specimens collected by me in 1862, which were kindly lent me by the Royal Bot. Gardens Calcutta, and a comparison with fl. specimens of *Oxytenanthera nigrociliata* from different localities has convinced me that this species is an *Oxytenanthera* and should be called *O. macrostachya.* Gamble's tab. 60 shows the palea of *O. nigrociliata* with an entire pointed apex, and the style bifid, while tab. 54 (*G. macrostachya*) has the apex of palea bidentate and the style entire. I find palea and style in both species alike; the palea is always bidentate, though in a young state the teeth may not have separated. The style is neither bifid, nor trifid (Munro, Trans. Linn. Soc. XXVI. 129), it is densely clothed with short stiff hairs in the greater portion of its length, and with long soft often branched papillæ near the apex. The character, given for *Oxytenanthera,* that the uppermost palea is only slightly or not at all keeled, cannot, according to my experience, be depended upon. Kurz, F. Fl. II. 555, placed all Burmese *Oxytenantheras* in *Gigantochloa,* and as this is the older name, it may eventually be right to follow him. From *O. nigrociliata* this species differs by the broad wavy band at the apex of culm-sheath on both sides of the blade, described by Kurz and figured on Gamble's t. 54, and the numerous long cilia at the mouth of leaf-sheath.
P. 672 (*b*). *Tabindaing,* Burm. *Wabgai,* Karen. Yunzalin valley above Papūn and on the head-waters of the Beeling river in Martaban. Specimens collected by F. B. Manson, April 1905 (received in November) have ♂ fl. only, without any trace of ovary. Spikelets polished, lanceolate, 1–1$\frac{1}{2}$ in. long, in small fascicles of 2–8 spikelets, supported by coriaceous polished sheaths, 1–2 in. long. Glumes glabrous, not ciliate on the edges empty 2, flowering 4–5; glumes $\frac{3}{8}$, palea $\frac{1}{8}$–$\frac{1}{8}$ in. long. Anthers 6, glabrous, bidentate at the tip, sagittate at base, with very short filaments, seated on a fleshy torus. Palea ciliate and obtuse at apex, with 5 longitudinal nerves between the densely ciliate keels, lodicules none. Culms 40–60 ft. high, lower half naked

with the exception of a few short branches near the ground. Internodes 22–29 in. long, 2½–3 in. diam., culm-sheaths firm, outside with black irritating hairs, apex with two broad undulating bands on both sides of the blade. Genus unknown, neither *Gigantochloa* nor *Oxytenanthera*. The distinctly keeled palea is against *Melocanna*.

P. 674. *Oxytenanthera nigrociliata*. Vern. *Wapyugyi*, Burm. *Wamay*, Karen (Papūn). Plentiful in Martaban, on the hills between the Beeling and Salween rivers. The culms of the first year bright glossy green, finely streaked with white lines, stiff black hairs $\frac{1}{12}$ in. long on the upper part of internode, below the nodes (Manson). The lowest fl. in the spikelet is the youngest, staminal-tube short, enclosing the ovary; in the middle fl. the anthers are shedding their pollen, the staminal-tube being nearly as long as the style and enclosing it. In the uppermost fl. the caryopsis is nearly mature, ½ in., crowned by the persistent style ¾–1 in. long.

P. 676. *Dendrocalamus membranaceus*. Vern. *Hmyin-byu-wa*, Burm. Papūn, Martaban. F. B. Manson.

P. 679. *Teinostachyum Helferi*, Gamble. *Thaw-khwè*, Kar. Hills east of Papūn, Martaban, F. B. Manson.

P. 681. *Dinochloa M'Clellandi*. Vern. *Sin-nin-wa*, Burm.; *Baw*, Kar. Hills on the head-waters of the Maitharauk stream.

P. 684. **Ochlandra.** Species 7 in India, 1 in the Malay Peninsula.

P. 692. *Abies Webbiana*. Dr. Augustine Henry has drawn my attention to a remarkable character observed by him in all specimens cultivated in Great Britain, viz., that the furrows between the raised leaf cushions are clothed with minute brown hairs, while the branchlets of *A. Pindrow* are perfectly glabrous. It would be interesting to ascertain the origin of the seed, from which the specimens of *A. Webbiana*, now growing in Great Britain, have been raised.

P. 698. Dr. Henry informs me that the Spruce of the Chumbi valley is **P. morindoides**, Rehder in Sargent Trees and Shrubs, I. p. 95, tab. 48, described from a specimen cultivated in France.

P. 170. *Zizyphus Jujuba*. A shrubby form, more or less gregarious, in the sub-himalayan tract, Oudh, Chutia Nagpur and elsewhere.

A. W. Lushington in Ind. For. XXX. 161 and G. M. Ryan on p. 450 have justly drawn attention to the large number of Indian trees which reproduce themselves by root-shoots, commonly known as root-suckers.* The following list is based almost entirely upon these two most useful communications. The subject will doubtless receive more attention in future, and many species will then be added to the present list:—

Polyalthia cerasoides, *Anona squamosa*, *Kydia calycina*, *Eriolæna quinquelocularis*, *Helicteres Isora*, *Grewia orbiculata*, *Ægle Marmelos*, *Balanites Roxburghii*, *Ailanthus glandulosa*, *Garuga pinnata*, *Boswellia serrata*, *Protium caudatum*, *Azadirachta indica*, *Soymida febrifuga*, *Chloroxylon Swietenia*, *Gymnosporia emarginata*, *Elæodendron glaucum*, *Zizyphus nummularia*, *Dodonæa viscosa*, *Schleichera trijuga*, *Odina Wodier*, *Buchanania latifolia*, *Ougeinia dalbergioides*, *Butea frondosa*, *Dalbergia latifolia*, *D. Sissoo*, *D. paniculata*, *Pterocarpus Marsupium*, *P. santalinus*, *Pongamia glabra*, *Hardwickia binata*, *Cassia Fistula*, *C. siamea*, *C. montana*, *C. auriculata*, *Tamarindus indica*, *Prosopis spicigera*, *Xylia dolabriformis*, *Acacia arabica* (doubtful, Ryan), *A. eburnea*, *A. leucophlœa*, *A. Catechu*, *A. dealbata*, *Albizzia procera*, *A. odoratissima*, *A. Lebbek*, *A. amara*, *Terminalia tomentosa*, *Anogeissus latifolia*, *Alangium Lamarckii*, *Randia dumetorum*, *R. uliginosa* (abundantly, Ryan), *Ixora parviflora*, *Morinda tinctoria*, *Diospyros melanoxylon*, *Chloroxylon*, *Schrebera swietenioides*, *Holarrhena antidysenterica* (abundantly, Ryan), *Wrightia tinctoria*, *Dolichandrone falcata*, *D. crispa*, *Heterophragma adenophyllum*, *Stereospermum chelonoides*, *Millingtonia hortensis*, *Lantana aculeata*, *Vitex negundo*, *V. altissima*, *Hippophaë salicifolia*, *Santalum album*, *Bridelia retusa*, *Antidesma Ghæzembilla*, *Fluggea Leucopyrus*, *Croton oblongifolius*, *Excœcaria Agallocha*, *Mallotus philippinensis*, *Trewia nudiflora* (abundantly, Ryan). *Ficus hispida*, *Artocarpus hirsuta*, *Alnus incana*, *Populus euphratica*.

FURTHER ADDENDA.

P. xvi. Mr. Talbot's excellent account of the Forest Flora of Bombay and Sind., Ind. For. XXXII. 8, 56, 126, containing on p. 60 a detailed description of the Kaus and evergreen forests, reached me after the Introduction had been printed.

* Mr. Lushington objects to the term root-sucker because roots do not as a rule produce leaf-buds. But the roots of Elms and Poplars which in Europe produce abundant root-suckers (French drageon) are real roots, not rhizomes, and this doubtless is the case with the Indian trees here mentioned.

P. XVII. The Sal forests of the Raigarh range, Balaghat Division, Central Provinces, are stated to be on trap and laterite.
P. 28. C. K. Schneider (Bulletin Herbier Boissier 1905, p. 666) considers that the North-west Himalayan shrub, hitherto referred to *Berberis vulgaris*, is *B. pachyacantha*, Koehne.
P. 29. C. K. Schneider classes the Nilgiri *Berberis* under 3 species: *B. tinctoria*, Leschen. *B. Wightiana*, C. K. Schneider, and *B. ceylanica*, C. K. Schneider. The Himalayan shrub, hitherto called *B. aristata*, he classes under *B. aristata*, DC., and *B. chitria*. Lindl. (p. 459). He also describes *B. garhwalensis*, C. K. Schneider, from Garhwal, and *B. Thomsoniana*, C. K. Schneider, from Sikkim.
P. 40. *Gynocardia odorata* is called by Prain, Bengal Plants 232, *Chaulmoogra odorata*, Roxb.
P. 42. *Taraktogenos Kurzii*, Vern. *Chaulmugra*, Chittagong. It is now certain that this tree yields the Chaulmugra oil of commerce., cf. D. Hooper in Agricultural Ledger, No. 5. of 1905.
P. 158. *Euonymus grandiflorus.* Chumbi. Bhutan.
P. 287. *Rosa Collettii.* Prain, in Journ. As. Soc. Bengal LXXIII. 203, states "styles connate."
P. 290. *Pyrus* is now generally divided into 4 genera: *Malus*, *Pyrus*, *Sorbus* and *Micromeles.*
P. 291. *Pyrus vestita* is called by C. K. Schneider (Laubholz kunde I. 683), *Sorbus cuspidata*, Hedlund.
P. 292. C. K. Schneider (l.c. p. 680) calls *Pyrus foliolosa Sorbus ursina*, Dcne, and *P. Wallichii Sorbus foliolosa*, Spach.
P. 292. The Afghan and Indian tree here called *P. Aucuparia*, is identified by C. K. Schneider (l.c. p. 668) with *Sorbus thianshanica*, Ruprecht.
P. 295. *Cotoneaster Simondsii*, Hort., and *C. thymifolia*, Hort., should be *C. Simonsii*, Baker, and *C. thymifolia*, Baker.
P. 359. Alfred Rehder, in his Synopsis of the Genus *Lonicera*, published in the 14th Annual Report of the Missouri Botanic Gardens (1903), p. 124, substitutes for *Lonicera decipiens* the older name *L. lanceolata*, Wall.
P. 359. *L. glauca* is identified by A. Rehder (l.c. 92), with the older species *L. Semenovii*, Regel, from Turkestan.
P. 360. A. Rehder (l.c. 56), identifies *L. parvifolia*, Edgew., with *L. obovata*, Royle, and on p. 44 calls the species described under no. 24 *L. Myrtillus*, Hook. fil. et Thoms.
P. 479. *Cordia Macleodii.* Vern. *Hadang.* Kan.
P. 568, line 29, 30: *Melanthesa* (not *Melanthesopsis*) *obliqua* and *M. truncata.* In the letterpress Wight calls the last-named species: *M. turbinata.*
P. 568, line 16 from below: *Breynia rhamnoides*, the female fl. are solitary.
P. 578, line 5 read: *Glochidion lanceolarium.* Voigt. Syn. *Phyllanthus lanceolarius*, Muell. Arg.
P. 575, line 35, read: *G. lanceolarium*, Voigt.
P. 580. Add: **Nepenthandra lanceolata**, Spencer le M. Moore in Journal of Botany XLIII. 149, tab. 471. Muleyit hill, Tenasserim. A shrub or small tree, branchlets and l. pubescent or tomentose, l. alternate, entire, subcoriaceous. Fl. monœcious panicled, ♂ numerous, ♀ solitary on long pedicels at the end of the ramifications of panicle. ♂: sepals 5, petals 5, anthers 8, on a slender column, at the base with a disk of 5 fleshy glands. ♀: petals 0, the sepals accrescent in fr.
P. 609. *Ficus pomifera*, Vern. *Ka-aungyyi*, Burm.
P. 667. A thorny bamboo, collected on the Hmin-Fang range, Lushai hills, Vern. *Phar*, Lushai (two culm pieces, a few twigs and detached l., no notes, recd. May 1906), may possibly be an *Arundinaria.* Internodes 3–6 in., diam. 1½–2 in., walls thick. At each node a ring of numerous sharp thorns, up to 25, slightly bent downwards, mostly ½, some ¾ in. long. Culmsheaths membranous, longer than internodes, densely clothed with dark brown hairs, the thorns piercing the sheath, blade triangular. L. 6 by ½–¾ in., 22 n. on ½ in., transverse veins conspicuous.
P. 671. *Bambusa arundinacea.* Vern. *Dongi*, Kan.
P. 683. *B. baccifera.* Chittagong 1801. Roxb. Hort. Beng. p. 25.
P. 693 and 720. The Spruce of Sikkim and Bhutan probably is *P. morindoides*, Rehder. Griffith (Journal 259, Itin. Notes 145) called this tree *Abies spinulosa* and figured it in Ic. Pl. As. t. 363, under the name of *Pinus spinulosa.* Cf. Hooker's Himalayan Journals II. 35, 45.

INDEX OF VERNACULAR NAMES

INDEX OF EUROPEAN NAMES

INDEX OF ORDERS, GENERA AND SPECIES

Authorities are only quoted in those cases where the same specific name has been used by two or more authors in a different sense. Synonyms are printed in italics.